This book is dedicated to
Robert Zonka, 1928–1985.
God love ya.

Other Books by Roger Ebert

An Illini Century
A Kiss Is Still a Kiss
Two Weeks in the Midday Sun: A Cannes Notebook
Behind the Phantom's Mask
Roger Ebert's Little Movie Glossary

With Daniel Curley
The Perfect London Walk

With John Kratz
The Computer Insectiary

With Gene Siskel
The Future of the Movies: Interviews with Martin Scorsese,
Steven Spielberg, and George Lucas

ROGER EBERT'S
VIDEO COMPANION
1996
EDITION

ANDREWS AND McMEEL
A UNIVERSAL PRESS SYNDICATE COMPANY
KANSAS CITY

Roger Ebert's Video Companion 1996 Edition
copyright © 1985, 1986, 1987, 1988, 1989,
1990, 1991, 1992, 1993, 1994, 1995
by Roger Ebert.
For information write Andrews and McMeel,
a Universal Press Syndicate Company,
4900 Main Street,
Kansas City, Missouri 64112.

ISBN 0-8362-0457-3
ISSN 1072-561X

Acknowledgments

Donna Martin, editor and friend, was instrumental in the conception of this book. The design is by Cameron Poulter, the typographical genius of Hyde Park. My thanks to Patty Donnelly and Richard Hill, who compiled the electronic manuscript, and Dorothy O'Brien, who assembled the book. I have been blessed with the expert and discriminating copy-editing of Avis Weathersbee, Kaarin Tisue, Laura Emerick, and Tim Bannon at the *Chicago Sun-Times*, Sue Roush at Universal Press Syndicate, and Matt Lombardi at Andrews and McMeel. Many thanks are also due to the production staff at "Siskel & Ebert," and to Marsha Jordan at WLS-TV. My gratitude goes to Carol Iwata, my expert office assistant, and to Marlene Gelfond, at the *Sun Times*. And special thanks and love to my wife, Chaz.

ROGER EBERT

Contents

Key to Symbols

★ ★ ★ ★   A great film
★ ★ ★   A good film
★ ★   Fair
★   Poor

G, PG, PG-13, R, NC-17: Ratings of the Motion Picture Association of America

G	indicates that the movie is suitable for general audiences
PG	suitable for general audiences but parental guidance is suggested
PG-13	recommended for viewers 13 years or above; may contain material inappropriate for younger children
R	recommended for viewers 17 or older
NC-17	intended for adults only

141 m.   Running time

1983   Year of theatrical release

NEW   Indicates a review that appears for the first time in this edition

Introduction to the 1996 Edition

As I now move, graciously, I hope, toward the door marked Exit, it occurs to me that the only thing I ever really liked to do was go to the movies. Naturally, Sex and Art always took precedence over the cinema. Unfortunately, neither ever proved to be as dependable as the filtering of present light through that moving strip of celluloid which projects past images and voices onto a screen.
—Gore Vidal, *Screening History*

Thoughts on the centennial of cinema:

We know more, much more, about Marilyn Monroe and Jack Nicholson than we know about Julius Caesar and Thomas Jefferson. We know what they looked like when they stood up and walked to a window, how they sounded when they were sad, and how they smiled when something struck them as funny. We know because we have seen them in the movies.

Oh, we have a lot of facts about Jefferson—but we don't know what he was *like*. In the everyday world we base our judgments of people on countless little clues of bearing, voice, and expression; we size them up and render a verdict, based on instinct and experience. That's why people never get hired from résumés, only after interviews, and why people can't really fall in love on the Internet.

The movies allow us to size someone up without ever meeting them. We sit in the dark, privileged voyeurs, watching actors express moments so intimate we rarely experience them in our own lives. If we go to the movies a lot, we can honestly say we've seen Gerard Depardieu or Jessica Lange through more of the critical moments of life than anyone in our own families.

It has been only one hundred years since "the cinema" became possible—a century, since the Lumiere brothers in Paris patented the first projector. The invention had been a long time coming, and "moving pictures" were available much earlier in various forms, from flip cards to the spinning Zeotrope to Edison's Kinetoscope, but the Lumieres invented the cinema as we know it by combining the three crucial elements: A projector behind, an audience in the middle, and a screen in the front. Their 1895 film of a train arriving at a Paris station caused audiences, so it is said, to dive out of the way.

If the Lumieres invented cinema, another Frenchman, George Melies, invented "the movies," by using the medium to tell stories. He was the producer of *Voyage to the Moon* (1902), with its famous image of a spaceship plunging into the eye of the Man in the Moon.

Although there are all kinds of movies for all kinds of reasons, for most people "the movies" will always mean sitting in a darkened theater with a crowd of strangers, watching imaginary stories on the screen. François Truffaut said the most moving sight he ever saw in a theater was when he walked up to the front and turned around, and saw all those eyes lifted up to the screen.

The twentieth century was the first in which men could fly, could send voices and pictures through the air, could peer into the soul of the atom and glimpse the most distant reaches of the universe. But the invention that most profoundly affected us may have been the movies. They allowed us to escape from our box of space and time, and they allowed us to see the past as it was actually happening.

The movies are still too young for the full impact to have settled in. But imagine what it would be like if movies had existed five hundred or two thousand years ago. If we could see moving, talking pictures of Jesus, how would that affect us? Would it enhance his stature in our imagination, or diminish it? If we could see Shakespeare's plays as they were originally performed, would we be moved, or only confused by strange accents and acting customs? What if we could see our great-great-great-grandmother as a little girl?

Movies are pieces of time, Peter Bogdanovich said. Bogart is dead, but he still walks across the floor of Rick's Café Americaine and stops in the middle of a sentence when he sees Ilsa sitting next to the piano player. And he still has the power to move us in that moment. *Casablanca* is an experience that for many of us was as real as anything else that has happened in our lives.

"The fact is I am quite happy in a movie, even a bad movie," Walker Percy wrote in his novel *The Moviegoer.* "Other people, so I have read, treasure memorable moments in their lives: the time one climbed the Parthenon at sunrise, the summer night one met a lonely girl in Central Park and achieved with her a sweet and natural relationship. . . . I too once met a girl in Central Park, but it is not much to remember. What I remember is the time John Wayne killed three men with a carbine as he was falling to the dusty street in *Stagecoach,* and the time the kitten found Orson Welles in the doorway in *The Third Man."*

Books and plays can provide us with stories. But the movies uniquely create the impression that we have *had* an experience. The key word is "we." I have seen a lot of movies by myself, but the experience is not the same as seeing a film with a large group of strangers. Two of the greatest moviegoing experiences of my life—the premieres of *Apocalypse Now* and *Do the Right Thing,* both at the Cannes Film Festival—were great not just because of the movies but because nowhere else do more people gather in the same theater to see them. Together, *we*—a cross-section of humanity—had an experience, and because it mirrored our shared humanity, it was somehow spiritual; we were giving witness.

That is what movies can do at their best. At their worst, they can cheapen us, and make us think less of ourselves. Here I'm not talking about subject matter, because subject matter is neutral: It is possible to make a great, uplifting film about the most tragic imaginable subject (Spielberg did it with *Schindler's List*) or a demeaning film about the most innocent (this would be true of movies that congratulate the audience on its stupidity).

The best movies are usually made because one person, or a small group, have a story they believe must be told, because it strikes a chord in their hearts. It can be a comedy, a musical, a drama, a polemic—the important thing is that they feel it.

The worst movies are made out of calculation, to reach a large audience. There is nothing wrong with a large audience, nothing wrong with making money (some of the best films have been the most profitable), but there is something wrong with the calculation. If the magical elements in a movie—story, director, actors—are assembled for magical reasons—to delight, to move, to astound—then something good often results. But when they are assembled simply as a "package," as a formula to suck in the customers, they are good only if a miracle happens.

Today movies are promoted with skillful advertising and marketing campaigns. A herd mentality encourages us to go to the "hits." This is the wrong approach. We have, after all, only so many hours in a lifetime to see movies. When we see one, it enters into our imagination and occupies space there. When we see movies that enlarge and challenge us, our imaginations are enriched. When we see dumb movies, we have left a little of our better selves behind in the theater.

A century ago "the movies" were invented, and allowed us to empathize with other people in a way never before possible. But like all inventions the cinema is neutral, and we decide whether it makes our lives better or worse. As the second century begins, our choices are about the same as they were in the beginning: We can fly to the moon, or duck to get out of the way of that train.

★　★　★

★ This is the eleventh annual edition of the *Companion,* which has tripled in size over the years. About 150,000 words are new. Perhaps it might be timely to mention that I see all of the movies myself, and write every word in the book. Not all of the many movie guides in the bookstores can make a similar claim; there is at least one new paperback guide to movie videos which was compiled by assigning freelancers to submit twenty-five reviews a day. One of them told me that when he asked how he could possibly see that many movies, it was suggested he simply rewrite the entries in other books.

★ Again this year we are including a little booklet with the big book: a pocket guide to movies and their ratings, small enough to slip into your pocket for a trip to the video store.

★ Every year we remove reviews of some movies in which interest has faded, in order to include more recent titles. Over eleven years this process has tended to skew the *Companion* toward favorable reviews; indeed, a critic in Kansas complained that I seem to like "everything." Out of curiosity I consulted all of the reviews I wrote for 1994, some 206, and found that the average star rating was 2.6, or "thumbs down." The average in this book is higher, because I have kept more favorable reviews than unfavorable ones.

★ Most of the movies reviewed were made since 1967, when I began as a film critic. But check out the "Revivals and Restorations" section, where I write new reviews of classic films as they are restored for theatrical and video release. The additions this year include *Dr. Strangelove, The Wild Bunch, Diabolique, Easy Rider, Doctor Zhivago, Stairway to Heaven, My Fair Lady, Faster, Pussycat! Kill! Kill!,* and *Woodstock.*

★ Again this year, the "Movie Answer Man" section deals with many of the queries that arrive at the movie desk every day.

★ Faithful readers may recall the "Glossary of Movie Terms," a popular section of the *Companion* for many years, until it outgrew its space. This compilation of movie clichés and stereotypes has now been greatly expanded into a book of its own. *Ebert's Little Movie Glossary* (Andrews and McMeel) can now be found in bookstores.

★ Many of the questions and *Glossary* entries came from subscribers to CompuServe, the computer on-line service, where my reviews and articles can be accessed (at the prompt, type "Go Ebert"). I hang out in a section of the ShowBiz Forum (type "Go ShowBiz"). The *Companion* is also available in the CD-ROM format, as part of "Microsoft Cinemania."

★　★　★

During the past year four books of special importance to all movie lovers were published. I recommend them highly. *For Keeps,* by Pauline Kael, brings together a generous selection from her many previous books of reviews, providing an overview of the career of the most influential of film critics. The greatly revised and expanded edition of David Thomson's *Biographical Dictionary of Film* is an opinionated, informed, concise summary of hundreds of key careers. The late Ephraim Katz's *Film Encyclopedia* is an invaluable one-volume survey of the world of film. And *Distinguishing Features,* by Stanley Kauffmann, is the latest collection of reviews by the critic whose superb writing and scholarship have distinguished *The New Republic* for decades.

The *Companion* is not intended as a comprehensive listing of every film available on video, but as a collection of essays on more than 1,300 of the best, most important, most popular, or even worst movies I have reviewed. The back-of-the-book material is changed or updated every year. For laserdisc fans, there is no better guide than the newly revised *Laser Video Disc Companion,* by Douglas Pratt. For the critics who shaped today's film criticism, I recommend the collected works of Kael, Kauffmann, Manny Farber, Andrew Sarris, Dwight Macdonald, James Agee, and Graham Greene.

Thanks to the many readers who have written with suggestions and corrections. I can be reached in care of my faithful and patient publishers, Andrews and McMeel, 4900 Main Street, Kansas City, Missouri 64112.

ROGER EBERT

A

About Last Night . . . ★ ★ ★ ★
R, 116 m., 1986

Rob Lowe (Danny), Demi Moore (Debbie), James Belushi (Bernie), Elizabeth Perkins (Joan), George DiCenzo (Mr. Favio), Michael Alldredge (Mother Malone), Robin Thomas (Steve), Joe Greco (Gus). Directed by Edward Zwick and produced by Jason Brett and Stuart Oken. Screenplay by Tim Kazurinsky and Denise DeClue.

If one of the pleasures of moviegoing is seeing strange new things on the screen, another pleasure, and probably a deeper one, is experiencing moments of recognition—times when we can say, yes, that's exactly right, that's exactly the way it would have happened. *About Last Night* . . . is a movie filled with moments like that. It has an eye and an ear for the way we live now, and it has a heart, too, and a sense of humor.

It is a love story. A young man and a young woman meet, and fall in love, and over the course of a year they try to work out what that means to them. It sounds like a simple story, and yet *About Last Night* . . . is one of the rarest of recent American movies, because it deals fearlessly with real people, instead of with special effects.

If there's anyone more afraid of a serious relationship than your average customer in a singles bar, it's a Hollywood producer. American movies will cheerfully spend millions of dollars on explosions and chases to avoid those moments when people are talking seriously and honestly to one another. After all, writing good dialogue takes some intelligence.

And intelligence is what sparkles all through *About Last Night* . . .—intelligence and a good, bawdy comic sensibility. The movie stars Rob Lowe as a salesman for a Chicago grocery wholesaler, and Demi Moore as an art director for a Michigan Avenue advertis-

ing agency. They meet at a softball game in Grant Park. Their romance blossoms in the singles bars of Rush Street, with a kindly bartender as father figure. At first they are attracted mostly by biological reasons (they belong to a generation that believes it's kind of embarrassing to sleep with someone for the first time after you know them too well). Then they get to like each other. Then it is maybe even love, although everyone tap-dances around that word. Commitment, in their world, is the moment when Lowe offers Moore the use of a drawer in his apartment. Her response to that offer is one of the movie's high points.

Meanwhile, there is counterpoint, too. Lowe's best friend is his partner at work, played by James Belushi. Moore's best friend is Elizabeth Perkins, her roommate and fellow warrior on the singles scene. While Lowe and Moore start getting really serious about each other, Belushi and Perkins grow possessive—and also develop a spontaneous dislike for one another.

The story is kind of predictable in *About Last Night* . . . , if you have ever been young and kept your eyes open. There are only a limited number of basic romantic scenarios for young people in the city, and this movie sees through all of them. What's important is the way the characters look and sound, the way they talk, the way they reveal themselves, the way they grow by taking chances. Time after time, there are shocks of recognition, as the movie shows how well it understands what's going on.

Lowe and Moore, members of Hollywood's "Brat Pack," are survivors of 1985's awful movie about yuppie singles, *St. Elmo's Fire*. This is the movie *St. Elmo's Fire* should have been. The 1985 movie made them look stupid and shallow. *About Last Night* . . . gives them the best acting opportunities

either one has ever had, and they make the most of them. Moore is especially impressive. There isn't a romantic note she isn't required to play in this movie, and she plays them all flawlessly.

Belushi and Perkins are good, too, making us realize how often the movies pretend that lovers live in a vacuum. When a big new relationship comes into your life, it requires an adjustment of all the other relationships, and a certain amount of discomfort and pain. Belushi and Perkins provide those levels for the story, and a lot of its loudest laughs, too.

The movie is based on *Sexual Perversity in Chicago*, a play by David Mamet. The screenplay by Tim Kazurinsky and Denise DeClue smooths out Mamet's more episodic structure, and adds three-dimensional realism. It's a wonderful writing job, and Edward Zwick, directing a feature for the first time, shows a sure touch. His narrative spans an entire year, and the interest never lags.

Why is it that love stories are so rare from Hollywood these days? Have we lost faith in romance? Is love possible only with robots and cute little furry things from the special-effects department? Have people stopped talking? *About Last Night* . . . is a warm-hearted and intelligent love story, and one of 1986's best movies.

Absence of Malice ★ ★ ★
PG, 116 m., 1981

Paul Newman (Michael Gallagher), Sally Field (Megan Carter), Bob Balaban (Rosen), Melinda Dillon (Teresa), Wilford Brimley (Official), John Harkins (Libel Lawyer). Directed and produced by Sydney Pollack. Screenplay by Kurt Luedtke.

There are at least two ways to approach *Absence of Malice*, and I propose to take the second. The first approach, no doubt, would be to criticize this film's portrait of an investigative newspaper reporter—to say that no respectable journalist would ever do the things that Sally Field does about, to, and with Paul Newman in this movie. She is a disgrace to her profession. What journalistic sins does she commit in this film? She allows the facts of a secret investigation to be leaked to her. She prints an unattributed story about the investigation. Then she becomes "personally involved with the subject of the investigation," as they say. In other words, she falls in love with Paul Newman. Then she prints another story she should never have printed, and as a result an innocent bystander commits suicide. Then . . .

But you get the idea. Would real investigative reporters actually commit Field's mistakes, improprieties, misjudgments, indiscretions, and ethical lapses? Generally speaking, no, they wouldn't. And if they did, they shouldn't have. And furthermore, their editors would never let them get away with it. (The unbelievable laxity of the editors in *Absence of Malice* creates the movie's greatest credibility gap.) But let's face it: Sometimes reporters *do* commit acts such as Sally Field allows herself in this movie. Sometimes news of an investigation is printed without official attribution. And so on.

One of my colleagues cornered me at the water fountain to say indignantly that, whatever else you might think about this movie, you'd have to admit that no reporter would *ever* sleep with a news source.

"Oh yeah?" asked a woman who was standing by. "Who was the news source?"

"Paul Newman," I said.

"I'd sleep with that news source in a second," she said.

And that leads us out of the first, or socially responsible, approach to *Absence of Malice*, and into the second, or romantic, approach. I not only liked this movie despite its factual and ethical problems—I'm not even so sure they matter so much to most viewers. In the newspaper business we're quick to spot the errors in movies about newspaper reporters, but where were we when the archaeologists squirmed over Harrison Ford's barbaric conduct in *Raiders of the Lost Ark*? The fact is, this movie is *really* about a woman's spunk and a common man's sneaky revenge. And on that level it's absorbing and entertaining. Sally Field's newspaper reporter is created through a quietly original performance that is *not* Norma Rae with a

pencil behind her ear, but is an earnest, nervous, likable young woman who makes mistakes when she listens too closely to her heart, her ambition, or her editor (which of us cannot admit the same?).

Paul Newman's character is a liquor distributor who is (presumably) totally innocent of the murder for which he is being investigated. But because his father was a Mafioso, he finds his name being dragged through the press, and he achieves a vengeance that is smart, wicked, appropriate, and completely satisfying to the audience. Besides these two performances, there are some other good ones, most notably one by Wilford Brimley, as a lawman who takes brusque command of an informal hearing and reduces everyone but Newman to quivering surrender, and another by John Harkins, as a newspaper libel lawyer who is able to make the restraints (and freedoms) of libel law clear not only to Sally Field but even to us.

There's a story about a legendary Chicago editor who was presented with a major scoop obtained by dubious means. First he convinced himself the story was factually sound. Then he issued the classic instruction: "Print it tonight, and call the lawyers in the morning." Now there's an editor who might have enjoyed *Absence of Malice*. He would not have approved of what Sally Field does in this movie. But he would have understood it.

The Accidental Tourist ★ ★ ★ ★
PG, 121 m., 1988

William Hurt (Macon Leary), Kathleen Turner (Sarah, His Wife), Geena Davis (Muriel Pritchett), Amy Wright (Rose Leary), David Ogden Stiers (Porter Leary), Ed Begley, Jr. (Charles Leary), Bill Pullman (Julian), Robert Gorman (Alexander), Bradley Mott (Mr. Loomis). Directed by Lawrence Kasdan and produced by Kasdan, Charles Okun, and Michael Grillo. Screenplay by Frank Galati and Kasdan.

"Yes, that is my son," the man says, identifying the body in the intensive care unit. Grief threatens to break his face into pieces, and then something closes shut inside of him. He has always had a very controlled nature, fearful of emotion and revelation, but now a true ice age begins, and after a year, his wife tells him she wants a divorce. It is because he cannot seem to feel anything.

The Accidental Tourist begins on that note of emotional sterility, and the whole movie is

a journey toward a smile at the end. The man's name is Macon Leary (William Hurt), and he writes travel books for people who detest traveling. He advises his readers on how to avoid human contact, where to find "American food" abroad, and how to convince themselves they haven't left home. His own life is the same sort of journey, and maybe it began in childhood; his sister and two brothers still live together in the house where they were born, and any life outside of their routine would be unthinkable.

Macon's wife (Kathleen Turner) moves out, leaving him with the dog, Edward, who does like to travel, and is deeply disturbed by the curious life his masters have provided for him. He barks at ghosts and snaps at strangers. It is time for Macon to make another one of his overseas research trips, so he takes the dog to be boarded at a kennel, and that's where he meets Muriel Pritchett (Geena Davis). Muriel has Macon's number from the moment she walks in through the door. She can see he's a basket case, but she thinks she can help. She also thinks her young son needs a father.

Macon isn't so sure. He doesn't use the number she gives him. But later, when the dog trips him and he breaks his leg, he takes Edward back to the kennel, and this time he submits to a little obedience training of his own. He agrees to acknowledge that Muriel exists, and before long they are sort of living together (lust still exists in his body, but it lurks so far from the center of his feelings that sex hardly seems to cheer him up).

The peculiarity about these central passages in the film is that they are quite cheerful and sometimes even very funny, even though Macon himself is mired in a deep depression. Geena Davis, as Muriel, brings an unforced wackiness to her role in scenes like the one where she belts out a song while she's doing the dishes. But she is not as simple as she sometimes seems, and when Macon gets carried away with a little sentimental generalizing about the future, she warns him, "Don't make promises to my son that you are not prepared to keep."

There is also great good humor in the characters in Macon's family: brothers Porter (David Ogden Stiers) and Charles (Ed Begley, Jr.) and sister Rose (Amy Wright), a matriarch who feeds the family, presides over their incomprehensible card games, and supervises such traditional activities as alphabetizing the groceries on the kitchen shelves. One evening Macon takes his publisher, Julian (Bill Pullman), home to dinner, and Julian is struck with a thunderbolt of love for Rose. He eventually marries her, but a few weeks later Julian tells Macon that Rose has moved back home with the boys; she was concerned that they had abandoned regular meals and were eating only gorp.

This emergency triggers the movie's emotional turning point, which is subtle but unmistakable. Nobody knows Rose as well as Macon does, and so he gives Julian some very particular advice: "Call her up and tell her your business is going to pieces. Ask if she could just come in and get things organized. Get things under control. Put it that way. Use those words. 'Get things under control,' tell her."

In context, this speech is hilarious. It is also the first time in the film that Macon has been able to extend himself to help anybody—and it starts him on the road to emotional growth. Clinging to the sterility and loneliness that has been his protection, he doesn't realize at first that he has turned the corner. He still doubts that he needs Muriel, and when she buys herself a ticket and follows him to Paris, he refuses to have anything to do with her. When his wife also turns up in Paris, there is a moment when he thinks they may be able to patch things together again, and then finally Macon arrives at the sort of moment he has been avoiding all of his life: He has to make a choice. But by then the choice is obvious; he has already made it by peeking so briefly out of his shell.

The screenplay for *The Accidental Tourist*, by Lawrence Kasdan and Frank Galati, is able to reproduce a lot of the tone and dialogue of the Anne Tyler novel without ever simply being a movie version of a book. The textures are too specific and the humor is too quirky and well-timed to be borrowed from anywhere; the filmmakers have reinvented the same story in their own terms. The movie is a reunion for Kasdan, Hurt, and Turner, who all three put their careers on the map with *Body Heat* (1981). Kasdan used Hurt again in *The Big Chill* (1983), and understands how to employ Hurt's gift for somehow being likable at the same time he seems to be withdrawn.

What Hurt achieves here seems almost impossible: He is depressed, low-key, and intensely private through most of the movie, and yet somehow he wins our sympathy. What Kasdan achieves is just as tricky; I've never seen a movie so sad in which there was so much genuine laughter. *The Accidental Tourist* was one of the best films of 1988.

The Accompanist ★ ★ ★ ½
PG, 110 m., 1994

Richard Bohringer (Charles Brice), Elena Safonova (Irene Brice), Romane Bohringer (Sophie Vasseur), Samuel Labarthe (Irene's Lover), Julien Rassam (Benoit Weizman), Nelly Borgeaud (Sophie's Mother). Directed by Claude Miller and produced by Jean-Louis Livi. Screenplay by Miller and Luc Beraud.

France in the winter of 1942–43 is in the grip of the Nazi occupation, and for most Parisians there is little food, heat, or joy. But for a few, like the opera singer Irene Brice and her husband, Charles—who will do business with anyone—life is still a giddy whirl of parties, receptions, recitals, all launched from the stage of their luxurious apartment.

For Sophie Vasseur, a young pianist who lives with her mother in desperate poverty, such a life is beyond her dreams, until she is hired to accompany Mrs. Brice and is swept into her opulent sphere. Yet all is not as it seems, even there, and the quiet, almost mousy girl finds that in the shadows of Irene's brilliance she can sit unnoticed, and see everything.

What she sees, and what she thinks about it, are what make Claude Miller's *The Accompanist* so absorbing. This is not a film about greedy French collaborationists, nor is it a remake of *All About Eve*, although for a time it seems to be heading in the direction of that mocking story about the understudy who replaces her patroness. No, it is more about how nothing is as simple as it seems; about how people will do much to assure their comfort and success, but there are some things that some people will not do.

The relationship between Sophie (Romane Bohringer) and Irene (Elena Safonova) is easily grasped. At first we think it cannot be as simple as it seems, but apparently it is: Irene is a generous, friendly woman who wants her accompanist with her at all times, and so makes her at home in a world of luxury. Sophie's visits to her mother's cold, barren flat are not frequent; at the Brices', she may be an employee but is treated like one of the family.

If she is grateful for this treatment, she also has complex feelings about Irene, who is beautiful, gracious, talented, and always seems to know the right way to handle any situation. Sophie believes, with some reason, that Irene is none of those things. Sophie is a very good pianist, but that is taken for granted. And so behind her big open eyes, thoughts

form, and we begin to guess what they are. We may, however, not be correct.

The key to the Brice household is the extraordinary energy and almost arrogant self-confidence of Charles Brice (played by Richard Bohringer, Romane's father). He likes luxury. He demands the best. It costs a lot, and he works hard to make money, which is easy in wartime Paris if you will deal with the Nazis, and more or less impossible otherwise. Yet there is a quirk in him. He will not kiss their boots. He will even insult them to their faces, and because they need him they will let him go almost too far (there is a trace of Oskar Schindler here).

Sophie, who sees everything, begins to realize that Irene is having an affair with a handsome young man who is active in the Resistance. Sophie runs errands she is not supposed to understand, but she does. She follows her employer. She begins to understand the nature of the affair. In Paris in the 1940s, it is of course not unheard of for married people to have affairs, but still—for Irene to be married to a collaborationist and to be sleeping with a member of the Resistance. . . .

Here, too, the movie surprises us. There is none of the clear-cut *Casablanca* ethic at work. In the real world, not everyone in the Resistance is perfect, and not everyone in Charles Brice's position is irredeemable. There comes a time when Charles realizes, decisively, that it is time for them all to get out of France, and he acts swiftly; like all true entrepreneurs, he is a gambler, willing to be a rich man one day and a refugee the next. After a journey on which they are nearly killed, they arrive in London, where . . .

Our attention is on Sophie during all of this. She has learned and grown. She does not make the same mistake twice. She loves Irene, resents her, and feels competitive with her in ways Irene does not suspect. And when Sophie has a shipboard romance with an almost insufferably idealistic young man, there comes a time when she must choose between her lover and her employer, and . . .

It is all so complicated. That is the joy of it. This movie offers no quick Hollywood solutions in which the good and evil characters are clearly identified. There is no parceling out of blame and praise at the end. Perhaps Miller is telling a parable, and Sophie is Vichy France, coexisting with collaborators to survive, yet remaining watchful and aloof. Perhaps he is simply telling a story, in which Sophie decides not to force a dramatic change, because it is more interesting, and certainly more comfortable, to stay on board for the ride.

The performances require our close attention. All three are very complex. A lot is going on. If Irene is more or less consistent and Sophie remains an enigma, Charles is fascinating because he acts decisively in ways we can understand. In the background, the world is at war. Charles tries to make a separate peace, not so much with the warring parties as with himself. The movie asks if this is possible. Its title perhaps means more than at first it seems.

The Accused ★ ★ ★
R, 110 m., 1988

Kelly McGillis (Kathryn Murphy), Jodie Foster (Sarah Tobias), Bernie Coulson (Kenneth Joyce), Ann Hearn (Sally Frazer), Steve Antin (Bob Joiner), Leo Rossi (Cliff Albrecht), Carmen Argenziano (District Attorney Rudolph), Terry David Mulligan (Detective Duncan), Woody Brown (Danny Rudkin), Peter Van Norden (Ted Paulson). Directed by Jonathan Kaplan and produced by Stanley R. Jaffe and Sherry Lansing. Screenplay by Tom Topor.

The Accused demonstrates that rape victims are often suspects in their own cases. Surely they must have been somehow to blame. How were they behaving at the time of the crime? How were they dressed? Had they been drinking? Is their personal life clean and tidy? Or are they sluts who were just asking for it?

I am aware of the brutal impact of the previous sentence. But the words were carefully chosen because sometimes they reflect the unspoken suspicions of officials in the largely male criminal justice system. *The Accused* is a movie about Sarah Tobias, a young woman who is not a model citizen. One night she has a fight with her live-in boyfriend, who is a drug dealer. She goes to a sleazy bar and has too much to drink, and does a provocative dance to the jukebox, and begins to flirt with a man in the bar's back room.

And then things get out of hand. The man, also drunk, picks her up and lays her down on top of a pinball machine, and begins to assault her. Two other men hold her down, helpless. The music pounds. The other guys in the back room begin to cheer and chant and egg him on, and when he is finished they push another guy forward, and then another. Finally she escapes and runs

weeping out onto the highway, crying for help.

The film shows most of this sequence only later, in a flashback. Its opening scenes deal with the immediate aftermath of the rape, as the woman (Jodie Foster) is moved through the emergency care and legal systems, where she meets professionals who are courteous and efficient, but not overly sympathetic. Then she meets Kathryn Murphy (Kelly McGillis), the assistant district attorney who will handle her case. McGillis is not impressed with some of the things she discovers, such as Tobias's previous conviction on drug possession charges, or her drinking on the night of the crime. And one of the rape suspects is a young fraternity man whose parents hire a good lawyer. In conference, the assistant D.A. agrees to reduce charges to "aggravated assault."

Sarah Tobias feels betrayed. She was raped, brutally, repeatedly, in front of many witnesses. It was not "aggravated assault." And the argument of the movie is that although a young woman may act improperly, even recklessly, she should still have the right to say "no" and be heard. This is something the McGillis character has difficulty in understanding at first; she is so comfortable within the informal compromises of the criminal justice system that she has lost some of her capacity for outrage.

In a sense, the movie is about the relationship between these two women, one an articulate lawyer, the other an inarticulate, angry alcoholic who sometimes lacks the words for the things she feels. One of the interesting choices in the screenplay by Tom Topor was to make it so hard for the Foster character to express herself, so that when she speaks we can almost feel each word being wrung out of her emotions. During the course of the film, the woman attorney comes to identify some of her client's feelings as actual experiences, not simply legal evidence. And the rape victim begins to see herself as others see her; we feel it is possible that the relationship between the two women will eventually lead the Foster character to clean up her act, stop drinking, and start taking responsibility for herself.

The other current in the film is equally interesting. This is the first film I can remember that considers the responsibility of bystanders in a rape case. The drunken fraternity boys and townies who climb on the furniture and chant and cheer are accessories to rape, although our society sometimes

has difficulty in understanding that. When the McGillis character finally decides to bring some of them to trial, she gets no support at all from the chief district attorney, and many of her colleagues feel she's lost her mind. Assistant D.A.s are supposed to try cases they can win, not go looking for lost causes. But the lesson learned in the movie's second trial may be the most important message this movie has to offer.

I wonder who will find the film more uncomfortable—men or women? Both will recoil from the brutality of the actual scenes of the assault. But for some men, the movie will reveal a truth that most women already know. It is that verbal sexual harassment, whether crudely in a saloon back room or subtly in an everyday situation, is a form of violence—one that leaves no visible marks but can make its victims feel unable to move freely and casually in society. It is a form of imprisonment.

Ace Ventura: Pet Detective ★
PG-13, 85 m., 1994

Jim Carrey (Ace Ventura), Courteney Cox (Melissa), Sean Young (Einhorn), Tone Loc (Emilio), Dan Marino (As Himself), Noble Willingham (Riddle), Troy Evans (Podacter), Raynor Scheine (Woodstock). Directed by Tom Shadyac and produced by James G. Robinson. Screenplay by Jack Bernstein, Shadyac, and Carrey.

You know that the French consider Jerry Lewis the greatest screen comedian of all time. You've looked at some Lewis comedies, but you don't get the joke. You know that a lot of critics praised Steve Martin in *The Jerk*, but you liked him better after he started acting more normal. You are not a promising candidate to see *Ace Ventura: Pet Detective*.

The movie stars Jim Carrey, best known as the all-purpose white guy on "In Living Color," as a Miami detective who specializes in animals. He'll find your missing bird or your kidnapped pedigreed dog. And as the movie opens he's hired by the Miami Dolphins football team to find their mascot, a dolphin named Snowflake which is mysteriously missing from its home in a large tank at the stadium. The plot deepens, if that is the word, when Dolphin quarterback Dan Marino also goes missing.

Carrey plays Ace as if he's being clocked on an Energy-O-Meter, and paid by the calorie expended. He's a hyper goon who likes to screw his mouth into strange shapes while playing variations on the language. He shares his house with so many animals he's like that zookeeper on the Letterman show who's always got pets crawling out of his collar. And he is simultaneously a spectacularly good and bad detective.

The story eventually involves Sean Young, who is much too talented for roles like Lieutenant Einhorn of the Miami police department; Udo Kier, once a distinguished German actor-director, now Ronald Camp, sinister millionaire; Courteney Cox, as the Dolphins' chief publicist; and Noble Willingham as the team's owner. Most of the people look as if they would rather be in other movies. Sean Young is a trouper, however, and does her best with dialogue like, "Listen, pet dick. How would you like me to make your life a living hell?"

The movie basically has one joke, which is Ace Ventura's weird, nerdy strangeness. If you laugh at this joke, chances are you laugh at Jerry Lewis, too, and I can sympathize with you even if I can't understand you. I found the movie a long, unfunny slog through an impenetrable plot. Kids might like it. Real little kids.

The Addams Family ★ ★
PG-13, 110 m., 1991

Anjelica Huston (Morticia Addams), Raul Julia (Gomez Addams), Christopher Lloyd (Fester), Christina Ricci (Wednesday Addams), Jimmy Workman (Pugsley Addams), Judith Malina (Granny). Directed by Barry Sonnenfeld and produced by Scott Rudin. Screenplay by Caroline Thompson and Larry Wilson.

There are a lot of little smiles in *The Addams Family*, and many chuckles and grins, but they don't add up to much. The movie is like a series of the Charles Addams cartoons that inspired it, in which each individual line or image is self-contained. I was mildly entertained, but I was hoping for big laughs and with one exception I didn't find them.

The movie, based on characters created by Addams in his immortal *New Yorker* cartoons and on the early 1960s TV series, looks uncannily like the original Addams drawings; the art direction must have been a rip-and-paste job. The ghoulish family lives in a many-turreted Gothic mansion, next to its own graveyard, on a blasted heath where nothing grows except for dead things. Inside the house, all the ordinary rules of human nature are reversed, as when the mother finds her daughter going after a little brother with a

kitchen knife, and sternly takes it away from her in order to hand over a meat cleaver.

Mother, named Morticia, is played by Anjelica Huston, who in makeup is a dead ringer for the original character. Her husband, Gomez, is played by Raul Julia, and despite the weirdness of their characters I did somehow feel chemistry between them. They're having fun. Many of the better moments involve the two Addams children, Wednesday (Christina Ricci) and Pugsley (Jimmy Workman), who before they go off to school are handed their lunches in brown bags with something alive inside.

Wednesday and Pugsley are responsible for the one big laugh in the movie, at a school pageant that ends with half of the audience drenched in stage blood. At least I hope it's stage blood. The plot otherwise involves a scheme by the calculating family attorney (Dan Hedaya), who convinces the son of a client to impersonate the long-lost older brother of the Addams family, Fester. The son (Christopher Lloyd, from the *Back to the Future* movies) stares out in dismay at the world through large black eye sockets, and is a miserable wretch until he begins to feel he actually belongs in the Addams household.

There are the beginnings of a lot of inspirations in the film, but somehow they're not pushed through to true comic invention. Take Thing, for example, the intelligent, disembodied hand that is a family pet. When the family is evicted from its home and forced to take real jobs, Thing gets a job as delivering Federal Express parcels—but the movie throws away the funny possibilities here by merely showing Thing in fast-motion, racing on its rounds. Wasn't there anything actually funny they could dream up involving the problems that a disembodied hand would have on the job?

I was not one of the great admirers of *Beetlejuice*, the 1988 comedy by Tim Burton, but, seeing this movie, I realize how much more creatively Burton used his special effects. Both movies are about strange, evil creatures inhabiting a tricky haunted house, and yet in *The Addams Family* the effects seem put in for their own sake, to be looked at, and are not really exploited in the story.

That leaves the individual moments. Yes, a lot of them are funny. In the months before this movie opened, there were a lot of brief trailers for it in the theaters. You've probably seen some of them—like the one where the kids ask if the Girl Scout cookies are made from real Girl Scouts. By themselves, these

lines are funny, as were the cartoon captions that inspired some of them. But they don't build. They get a laugh, and then the movie has to build up to the next one. This is the kind of film that isn't as much fun to see as it is to hear about.

Addams Family Values ★ ★ ★
PG-13, 88 m., 1993

Anjelica Huston (Morticia Addams), Raul Julia (Gomez Addams), Christopher Lloyd (Fester), Carol Kane (Granny), Christina Ricci (Wednesday Addams), Jimmy Workman (Pugsley Addams), Joan Cusack (Debbie Jelinsky), Carel Struycken (Lurch). Directed by Barry Sonnenfeld and produced by Scott Rudin. Screenplay by Paul Rudnick.

"Isn't he a lady killer!" the sexy young nanny says when she first meets Gomez, patriarch of the Addams family.

"Acquitted," Gomez explains.

And we are back again in the upside-down world of the Addamses, who find solace in sadism, cheer in gloom, pride in boasting that their little son has been given probation. They live in a one-joke universe, arrived at by embracing the mirror images of all respectable values. But the good news is, this time I found the joke funnier than in the original *Addams Family* (1991).

It's the rare sequel that is better than its original, and yet *Addams Family Values* qualifies. Nothing much seems to have changed; the stars are about the same, the director is still Barry Sonnenfeld, the Addams mansion still towers above a blasted heath, next to a graveyard. Maybe I liked it more than the original because I was in a different mood? Perhaps, knowing I was going to see wee little Macaulay Culkin in *The Nutcracker* right after seeing this film, I was in the mood for macabre bad taste?

Or perhaps the screenplay, by Paul Rudnick, contains more invention than the 1991 effort. *Addams Family Values* involves not one but three subplots, all of them funny and one of them (about the birth of a new baby boy) the source of one great sight gag after another. "I'm going to have a baby," Morticia (Anjelica Huston) announces to Gomez (Raul Julia). "Right now." In an inevitable twist on the usual movie childbirth scene, she's in agony in the delivery room—and loving every minute of it.

The little newcomer, named Pubert, sure does take after his dad. Even to the pencil mustache. "He has my father's eyes," Gomez murmurs. "Take them out of the baby's mouth!" Morticia exclaims. The preexisting Addams children, Wednesday and Pugsley, are insanely jealous, and even try to arrange the baby's decapitation on the guillotine that is conveniently in the basement.

The services of a nanny are clearly required, and the family hires Debbie Jelinsky (Joan Cusack), who arrives in a low-cut uniform, and takes charge. Nothing in the household seems to bother her, not even the unexpected arrival of Thing, a disembodied hand that leaps onto her shoulder. She's not worried: "I'm good with my hands."

Debbie is revealed to have sinister designs on poor Fester (Christopher Lloyd), the long-lost Addams brother whose reappearance provided most of the story in the 1991 film. After all, he is one of the richest men in the world, in addition to being probably the ugliest. In an attempt to get the older children out of her hair, she convinces Morticia and Gomez to send them to summer camp, where they do not, needless to say, fit right in. Then Wednesday meets her first boyfriend, and there is little doubt they were, alas, made for one another.

What is most beguiling about *Addams Family Values* is the way the relationship between Gomez and Morticia has ripened. Raul Julia and Anjelica Huston are given a lot of one-liners and payoff gags, of course, but what's funny is the stuff that comes in between—the real affection with which they embrace each other, and the way they delight in their unspeakable lifestyle. English is not language enough to contain their emotions. They venture into French and Spanish, the tongues of romance, to reflect the happiness they feel, living at the center of a nightmare.

Joan Cusack, a natural comedian, makes a good addition to the cast. "I just adore little babies," she says, looking at tiny Pubert. "I just want to grab them and squeeze them until there's not a breath left in their tiny little bodies." Her attempts to lure Fester away from the family crypt and into a more comfortable lifestyle lead to one of Huston's great lines, when she visits Fester's new digs. She doesn't mind that he is miserable and unhappy, the captive of a gold-digging bitch, but . . . "the decor, Fester! Pastel?"

Of the previous film, I said, probably unfairly, that it so closely resembled Charles Addams's original *New Yorker* cartoons that the art direction must have been a rip-and-paste job. Looking more thoughtfully at *Addams Family Values*, I no longer agree. Addams in his cartoons created one of the most easily recognizable imaginary worlds of the century, but the achievement of this film is to make it concrete, to put the family in a physical setting where their ghoulish lifestyle seems, well, almost appropriate.

The Adjuster ★ ★ ★
R, 102 m., 1992

Elias Koteas (Noah), Arsinee Khanjian (Hera), Maury Chaykin (Bubba), Gabrielle Rose (Mimi), David Hemblen (Bert), Jennifer Dale (Arianne). Directed by Atom Egoyan and produced by Camelia Frieberg. Screenplay by Egoyan.

The Adjuster is one of those movies where you back into the story. It begins with people performing mysterious actions, and then, gradually, you discover what they're doing and why. Then everything makes sense—except, in this case, the characters have obscure motivations and bizarre secrets even though they lead their lives in the most proper of occupations.

Noah, the hero, is an insurance adjuster. He walks into people's lives after they have been devastated by tragedy, and tries to decide in an almost godlike way what really happened and how it can be fixed. Hera, his wife, is a sweet-faced, almost angelic woman who works as a film censor, sitting hour after hour in a darkened room looking at pornographic images. They live in a house that is the only occupied residence in a suburban development that went broke; around them are nothing but billboards showing the other houses that may eventually be built.

Both of these people are evaluators—Noah of fire damage, Hera of film standards—and both of them abuse their positions. Noah (Elias Koteas) moves his homeless clients into a motel, where he plays far too intimate a role in their lives. Hera (Arsinee Khanjian) secretly videotapes the films she's viewing—so she can show them to her sister, since they have shared everything since childhood. Now their lives are entered by a wealthy and bizarre couple who "adjust" others in far more devious ways.

Bubba (Maury Chaykin) and Mimi (Gabrielle Rose) have a most unconventional marriage centered around his voyeurism, her exhibitionism, and their great wealth. It is nothing for him to hire a football team so that his wife can prance in front of them, acting out her cheerleader fantasies. When they stumble upon the adjuster and his wife, they realize they have hit a gold mine; the isolated house is ideal as a location for one of their more involved scenarios.

The Adjuster was directed by Atom Egoyan, a Canadian who finds strange comedy in familiar things. "I wanted to make a film," he writes in his notes, "about believable people doing believable things in an unbelievable way." Often this involves the way Egoyan photographs them. A shot of Noah with a bow and arrow, for example, seems inexplicable until the camera explains it. The first appearance of Bubba is an optical illusion. Throughout the film, the characters seem in danger of being blotted out by their backgrounds—of disappearing back into the billboards and advertising symbols that surround them.

What is interesting is how Egoyan creates this intensely personal universe while at the same time making a movie that is funny and challenging. He isn't one of those directors who delights in confusion and frustration. When he shows us something we cannot understand, and then pulls back to explain it, he takes the same delight in his revelation as a magician would—or a silent comedian like Buster Keaton. That's why the movie is so consistently entertaining. Instead of just sitting there while the plot unfolds—one, two, three, so we can see that each event does indeed follow the last—he keeps us watching and guessing as the jigsaw of his story and relationships finally becomes a complete picture.

Having never met Atom Egoyan, I am willing to guess that he is one of those people who loves puzzles and paradoxes, who sees the world in a wry, skewed way, who is vastly amused that what we take for granted might be a complete deception. He would probably be gifted at card tricks. But he would want a deck with more than fifty-two cards.

The Adventures of Baron Munchausen ★ ★ ★
PG, 126 m., 1989

John Neville (Baron Munchausen), Eric Idle (Desmond/Berthold), Sarah Polley (Sally Salt), Oliver Reed (Vulcan), Charles McKeown (Rupert/Adolphus), Winston Dennis (Bill/Albrecht), Valentina Cortese (Queen/Violet), Robin Williams (King of the Moon), Sting (Heroic Officer). Directed by Terry Gilliam and produced by Thomas Schuhly. Screenplay by Charles McKeown and Gilliam.

"I have ever confined myself to facts."
—Attributed to Baron Munchausen

There really was a Baron Munchausen. His full name was Karl Friedrich Hieronymus, Freiherr von Munchausen, and he lived from 1720 to 1797 and fought for the Russians against the Turks. He was, it is said, in the habit of embellishing his war stories, and in 1785 a jewel thief from Hanover named Rudolph Erich Raspe published a book in England that claimed to be based on the baron's life and times.

The real von Munchausen apparently did not complain about this book that made free with his reputation, even though it included such tall stories as the time the baron tethered his horse to a "small twig" in a snowstorm, and discovered when the snow melted that the twig was actually a church steeple.

I remember the illustration that appeared with that story when I read it as a child: The baron on the ground, looking up in perplexity at his horse, which was still hanging from the steeple. I remember asking my father how the horse was going to get down, and my father speculating that he would have to wait until it snowed again, which seemed like a bleak prospect for the horse. And so I asked if the baron could feed his horse in the meantime by climbing up the steeple with hay. The mind of a child is wonderfully literal. And one of the charms of seeing *The Adventures of Baron Munchausen* is to see some of the baron's other impossible adventures looking for all the world as if they had really happened, thanks to extraordinary special effects.

For adults, this is a "special effects movie," and we approach it in that spirit, also appreciating the sly wit and satire that sneaks in here and there from director Terry Gilliam and his collaborators, who were mostly forged in the mill of Monty Python. They have not made a "children's movie," but children may find it fascinating, because these adventures involve castles and sultans and horses and knights and the man in the moon—subjects that seem fresh, now that the high-tech hardware of outer space is taken for granted by most kids.

Terry Gilliam's film is, in itself, a tribute to the spirit of the good baron. Gilliam must have had to embellish a few war stories himself, to get Columbia Pictures to spend a reported $46 million on this project, which is one of the three or four most expensive films ever made. The special effects are astonishing, but so is the humor with which they are employed. It is not enough that one of the baron's friends is the fastest runner in the

world. He must run all the way to Spain and back in an hour to fetch a bottle of wine and save the baron's neck. And he must be able to outrun a speeding bullet, stop it, and redirect it back toward the man who fired it.

These adventures, and others, are told with a cheerfulness and a light touch that never betray the time and money it took to create them. It's one thing to spend $46 million; it's another to spend it insouciantly. The movie begins when the baron indignantly interrupts a play that is allegedly based on his life, and continues as he tells the "real" story of his travels which took him not merely to Turkey but also to the moon, to the heart of a volcano, and into the stomach of a sea monster so big that people actually lived there quite comfortably, once they had been swallowed.

The baron (John Neville) is accompanied on some of these adventures by his friends, including not only the world's fastest man, but also the world's strongest man, the man with the best hearing in the world, and another friend who does not have great eyesight, but owns glasses that allow him to see almost any distance. Even when he is separated from these comrades, the baron travels in good company; when a Venus appears from a seashell, she is played by Uma Thurman, the young innocent from *Dangerous Liaisons*, and when the King of the Moon appears, he is Robin Williams, with a detachable head that is able to spin off into the night on its own.

Some of the effects in this movie are actually quite wonderful, as when the baron and a friend return from the moon by climbing down two lengths of the same rope again and again, while the markings of a celestial globe apportion the sky behind them. In another scene, a giant feather falls softly onto a vast plain, while the baron tries to understand what strange new world he has found. Neville, a veteran of the Stratford, Canada, Shakespeare festival, keeps his composure in the midst of these special effects, and seems sensible and matter-of-fact, as anyone would if he had spent a lifetime growing accustomed to the incredible.

The wit and the spectacle of *Baron Munchausen* are considerable achievements. I wish only that Gilliam, who cowrote the screenplay as well as directed, had been able to edit his own inspiration more severely as he went along. The movie is slow to get off the ground (the prologue goes on forever before we discover what it's about), and some-

times the movie fails on the basic level of making itself clear. We're not always sure who is who, how they are related, or why we should care. One of the things you have to do, when you fill a movie with extravagant fantasies, is to explain the story in clear and direct terms, so it doesn't fly apart with intoxication at its own exuberance.

I was confused sometimes during *Baron Munchausen,* and bored sometimes, but this is a vast and commodious work, and even allowing for the unsuccessful passages, there is a lot here to treasure. Gilliam said it was the third part of a trilogy. His first film, *Time Bandits,* was about childhood. His second, *Brazil,* was about adulthood. *Baron Munchausen* is about old age. He may have been telling us the truth. He may also have been telling us he tethered his film to a twig in a snowstorm.

The Adventures of Huck Finn ★ ★ ★
PG, 95 m., 1993

Elijah Wood (Huck), Courtney B. Vance (Jim), Robbie Coltrane (The Duke), Jason Robards (The King), Ron Perlman (Pap Finn), Dana Ivey (Widow Douglas). Directed by Stephen Sommers and produced by Laurence Mark. Screenplay by Sommers.

Ernest Hemingway once said that all American literature began with a novel by Mark Twain named *Huckleberry Finn.* There are two obvious reasons why this might be so: It is the first great novel to be told in the American vernacular, and it is the first great novel to deal honestly and decently with the subject of race relations. The novel has regrettably been under fire in recent years from myopic advocates of Political Correctness, who do not have a bone of irony (or humor) in their bodies, and cannot tell the difference between what is said or done in the novel, and what Twain means by it.

The book is about a half-literate outcast white boy, the son of a drunk, who runs off down the Mississippi with an escaping slave named Jim. Huck subscribes to many of the racist views prevailing at that time about blacks, but he has never really thought about them, and during the long days and nights on the river Jim reeducates him. Huck finally decides that if it is a sin to help a slave escape, he must be a sinner.

The story of Huck and Jim has been told in six or seven earlier movies, and now comes *The Adventures of Huck Finn,* a graceful and entertaining version by a young director named Stephen Sommers, who doesn't dwell on the film's humane message, but doesn't avoid it, either. The transformation of Huck is there on the screen, although much more time is devoted to the story's picaresque adventures, as Huck and Jim meet a series of colorful characters—including some desperate criminals, some feuding neighbors, and the immortal con men the King and the Duke.

Huck is played by Elijah Wood, from *Radio Flyer* and *Forever Young*, who mercifully seems free of cuteness and other afflictions of child stars, and makes a resolute, convincing Huck. The real Huck (based on a childhood friend of Twain's) was probably much tougher and had rougher edges, but Huck has been sanitized for years in the movies (just as the Widow Douglas tried to "sivilize" the original). Jim, the crucial character in the story, is played by Courtney B. Vance, a New York stage actor who is able to embody the enormous tact with which Jim guides Huck out of the thickets of prejudice and sets him on the road to tolerance and decency.

The supporting cast is uniformly splendid, especially Jason Robards and Robbie Coltrane, as the King and the Duke, who impersonate visitors from England in an attempt to swindle two innocent sisters out of their inheritance. And the fetching Laura Bundy is Wood's match as Susan Wilks, the twelve-year-old who gives him his first kiss and distracts him, however momentarily, from his downstream destiny. She and others are stops along the way on Huck's journey to adulthood. It is a little eerie, halfway through the movie, to realize that Twain wrote the original American road picture, and that in some way not only all of American literature, but also *Easy Rider, Bonnie and Clyde, Five Easy Pieces,* and *Thelma and Louise* came out of his novel.

I read the book for the first time when I was seven, understanding every other word, and I have read it a dozen times since. For me, the best passages are those in which Huck and Jim are alone on the river, debating such curiosities as why the French speak a foreign language, and how many stars there are in the sky, and whether it is all right to steal fruits that are in season if you make a solemn vow not to steal fruits that are out of season. Twain punctuates these passages with lyrical descriptions of the mighty river, and of a thunderstorm that reminds him of barrels rolling down a giant staircase.

And then Huck and Jim drift onto the subjects of race and slavery, and Huck is bound to admit, after Jim explains it to him, that black people have the same feelings as everyone else, and are deserving of his respect. This process of Huck's conversion is one of the crucial events in American literature. Some cannot admire it and think it should not be taught in schools because Huck, like every boy of his time, used the word *nigger*. They are very shortsighted.

The movie, of course, doesn't use the word, nor does it really venture very far into the heart of Huck's transformation. It wants to entertain and fears to offend. But it is a good film with strong performances. Nothing in it is wrong, although some depths are lacking. I admired the performances, and Sommers's sense of time and place, and I hope the movie guides more people toward the book—which contains values that sometimes seem as rare today as when Jim was first teaching them to Huck.

The Adventures of Priscilla, Queen of the Desert ★ ★ ½ |NEW|
R, 102 m., 1994

Terence Stamp (Bernadette), Hugo Weaving (Tick/Mitzi), Guy Pearce (Adam/Felicia), Bill Hunter (Bob), Sarah Chadwick (Marion), Mark Holmes (Benji), Julia Cortez (Cynthia), Ken Radley (Frank), Alan Dargin (Aboriginal Man), Rebel Russell (Logowoman). Directed by Stephan Elliott and produced by Al Clark and Michael Hamlyn. Screenplay by Elliott.

Dr. Johnson famously remarked of a dog's ability to stand on its hind legs, that it was not done well, but he was surprised to find it done at all. I thought of that while I was watching *The Adventures of Priscilla, Queen of the Desert,* which stars Terence Stamp in drag. The macho British actor, best known for *Billy Budd* and the villain in *Superman,* plays an aging transsexual named Bernadette, and it *is* done well, yet one is nevertheless surprised to find it done at all.

The movie opens in Sydney, Australia, where Bernadette is well known in gay circles. She's part of a trio of flamboyant local drag performers, also including Tick, also known as Mitzi (Hugo Weaving), and Adam, a.k.a. Felicia (Guy Pearce). Their act involves lip-synching to recordings while performing a vaguely choreographed stage show and wearing tacky gowns, a great many feather boas, and a lot of eye shadow. Bernadette, who is clearly an intelligent person, has perhaps been amused by this scene in the past, but it is beginning to wear on her, and questions of mortality begin to surface, especially

after a friend dies (of exposure to peroxide fumes; the film likes to juxtapose pathos and black comedy).

Sydney is also getting tired of Bernadette, and so when an opportunity comes for a gig in the backwater town of Alice Springs, the three friends decide to go on tour. Mitzi's former wife, now running a gambling casino, could use an act, and that sets up the introduction of Priscilla, which is the name of the lavender school bus which doubles as their dressing room and living quarters. Off they go into the outback, with Priscilla converted into a traveling dressing room and wardrobe closet.

I happened to see *Easy Rider* (1969) again at about the same time I saw *Priscilla,* and it occurred to me that the structures were similar: The nonconformist heroes, whether hippies or drag queens, were taking a dangerous chance by making a road trip into reactionary territory. If you think Peter Fonda, Dennis Hopper, and Jack Nicholson made a juicy target in the redneck South with their choppers and long hair, imagine how warmly Bernadette, Mitzi, and Felicia are welcomed in the outback.

The film settles into the rhythms of many road pictures, with lots of drive-by scenery, soul-searching talks during camp-outs on the road, and dicey encounters with the locals. There's a drinking contest with a tough-talking woman who thinks she's more of a man than the queens. The bus attracts some nasty antigay graffiti. Bernadette looks more and more weary of this life. (It must not be easy in the best of times to live and travel in a school bus with two drag queens, and middle age takes its toll: Was this trip necessary?)

At about the time when the possibilities of life on the road have been exhausted, Priscilla arrives in Alice Springs, where Mitzi's ex-wife (Sarah Chadwick) seems fairly serene about the new life her former husband has chosen. Mitzi's son also seems cool about the gender-blender situation. The drag act is received cordially, if not ecstatically. And there's a subplot about an auto mechanic whose own wife is a stripper so loony she makes Bernadette look good, and not only by comparison.

I guess the scenes of homophobic hostility in the movie are obligatory, but the writer-director, Stephan Elliott, doesn't seem to have his heart in them, and I wonder if he would have been happy to make the whole story as lighthearted as his best scenes. It's too bad that the requirements of plotting require movies like this to crank up the event count, when actually what works is just the daily minutiae of Bernadette's life. At the beginning of the film we're distracted by the unexpected sight of Terence Stamp in drag, but Stamp is able to bring a convincing humanity to the character, and eventually we realize that the real subject of the movie is not homosexuality, not drag queens, not show-biz, but simply the life of a middle-aged person trapped in a job that has become pointless.

After Hours ★ ★ ★ ★
R, 96 m., 1985

Griffin Dunne (Paul Hackett), Rosanna Arquette (Marcy), Linda Fiorentino (Kiki), Verna Bloom (June), Thomas Chong (Pepe), Teri Garr (Julie), John Heard (Bartender), Catherine O'Hara (Gail). Directed by Martin Scorsese and produced by Amy Robinson, Griffin Dunne, and Robert F. Colesberry. Screenplay by Joseph Minion.

Martin Scorsese's *After Hours* is a comedy, according to the strict definition of that word: It ends happily, and there are indications along the way that we're not supposed to take it seriously. It is, however, the tensest comedy I can remember, building its nightmare situation step by insidious step until our laughter is hollow, or defensive. This is the work of a master filmmaker who controls his effects so skillfully that I was drained by this film—so emotionally depleted that there was a moment, two-thirds of the way through, when I wondered if maybe I should pause and gather my thoughts and come back later for the rest of the "comedy."

The movie tells the story of a night in the life of Paul Hackett (Griffin Dunne), a midtown Manhattan word processing specialist who hates his job and his lonely private life. One night in a restaurant he strikes up a conversation with a winsome young woman (Rosanna Arquette). They seem to share some of the same interests. He gets her telephone number. He calls her, she suggests he come downtown to her apartment in Soho, and that is the beginning of his Kafkaesque adventure.

The streets of Soho are dark and deserted. Clouds of steam escape from the pavement, as they did in Scorsese's *Taxi Driver*, suggesting that Hades lurks just below the field of vision. The young woman is staying for a few days in the apartment of a friend (Linda Fiorentino), who makes bizarre sculptures, has kinky sexual tastes, and talks in a strange, veiled way about being burned. In Arquette's bedroom, Dunne

makes the usual small talk of a first date, and she gushes that she's sure they'll have a great time, but then everything begins to fall apart.

At first, we think perhaps Dunne is the victim of random bad luck, as he is confronted with nightmares both tragic and trivial: Ominous strangers, escalating subway fares, a shocking suicide, sadomasochistic sexual practices, a punk nightclub where he almost has his head shaved, a street mob that thinks he is a thief. Only later, much later, on this seemingly endless night, do we find how everything is connected—and even then, it doesn't make any logical sense. For Paul Hackett, as for the Job of the Old Testament, the plague of bad luck seems generated by some unexplained divine wrath.

And yet Scorsese does not simply make a horror movie, or some kind of allegory of doom. Each of his characters is drawn sharply, given quirky dialogue, allowed to be offbeat and funny. Teri Garr has a scene as a waitress who has tried to make sense of New York for so long that it has driven her around the bend. Fiorentino has a dry, sardonic angle on things. Arquette speaks wonderingly of a lover who was so obsessed by *The Wizard of Oz* that he always called her Dorothy in bed. John Heard is a bartender who has seen everything walk in through the doors of his all-night saloon and has lost the capacity for astonishment.

After Hours is another chapter in Scorsese's continuing examination of Manhattan as a state of mind; if he hadn't already used the title *New York, New York*, he could have used it this time. The movie earns its place on the list with his great films *Mean Streets, Taxi Driver,* and *Raging Bull.* For New Yorkers, parts of the film will no doubt play as a documentary. In what other city is everyday life such an unremitting challenge?

After Hours is a brilliant film, one of the year's best. It is also a most curious film. It comes after Scorsese's *The King of Comedy,* a film I thought was fascinating but unsuccessful, and continues Scorsese's attempt to combine comedy and satire with unrelenting pressure and a sense of all-pervading paranoia. This time he succeeds. The result is a film that is so original, so particular, that we are uncertain from moment to moment exactly how to respond to it. The style of the film creates, in us, the same feeling that the events in the film create in the hero. Interesting.

After the Rehearsal ★ ★ ★ ★
R, 72 m., 1984

Erland Josephson (Henrik Vogler), Ingrid Thulin (Rakel), Lena Olin (Anna Egerman), Nadja Palmstjerna-Weiss (Anna at Twelve). Directed by Ingmar Bergman and produced by Jorn Donner. Screenplay by Bergman.

Ingmar Bergman's *After the Rehearsal* seems to be as simple and direct as a tape recording of actual conversations, and yet look at the thickets of interpretation it has inspired in its critics. After seeing it, I thought I understood the film entirely. Now I am not so sure. Like so many of Bergman's films, and especially the spare "chamber films" it joins *(Winter Light, Persona),* it consists of unadorned surfaces concealing fathomless depths.

It is safest to begin with the surfaces. All of the action takes place on a stage prepared for a production of Strindberg's *A Dream Play.* An aging director sits among the props, and every chair and table reminds him of an earlier production. The rehearsal has ended some time ago, and now the director simply sits, as if the stage were his room. A young actress returns to the stage for a missing bracelet. But of course the bracelet is an excuse, and she wants to talk to the great man, and perhaps to begin a relationship with him (as, perhaps, she has heard that many other actresses have done over the years). The old director was once the lover of the girl's mother. It is even possible that this girl is his daughter. They talk. Then an older actress enters. She has a few lines in the play, and wants to know—frankly, brutally—if her career as a leading actress is really over because she is known as a drunk. She cries, she rants, she bares her breasts to show the old man that her body is still sound, if sodden. The director is tempted: He was once this woman's lover, and perhaps her daughter is his.

The young girl stays on stage during the extraordinary display of the older actress. When the older woman leaves, the director and ingenue talk again, and this time the old man, who has been through the turmoil of love too many times, talks her through their probable future: We could make love, we could have an affair, we would call it part of our art, you would be the student, I would be the teacher, I would grow tired, you would feel trapped, all our idealism would turn into ashes. Since the relationship is foredoomed, why bother with it?

Just in terms of these spare passages of dialogue and passion, *After the Rehearsal* is an important and painful confessional, for the old director, of course, bears many points of resemblance to Bergman, whose lovers have included his actresses Harriet Andersson, Bibi Andersson, and Liv Ullmann, among others, and whose daughter by Ullmann appeared in *Face to Face*. But the film is not a scandalous revelation: It is actually more of a sacramental confession, as if Bergman, the son of a Lutheran bishop, now sees the stage as his confessional and is asking the audience to bless and forgive him. (His gravest sin, as I read the film, is not lust or adultery, but the sin of taking advantage of others—of manipulating them with his power and intellect.)

If that were the extent of *After the Rehearsal*, it would be deep enough. But Bergman has surrounded the bare bones of his story with mystifying problems of interpretation. Just as in *Persona* he included scenes in which his characters exchanged personalities and engaged in scenes that might have or might not have been fantasies and dreams, so here, too, he gives us things to puzzle over. Reading the earlier reviews of the film, I discover that one critic realized only belatedly that the younger actress, Anna, was onstage the whole time the older actress, Rakel, poured out her heart. Strange, and yet another critic thought the whole scene with Rakel was the director's own dream. Yet another suggested that Anna represents not only herself but also Rakel's absent daughter. And another theory is that Anna is the daughter of the director and Rakel, and is brought into being by the residual love between them, as a sort of theatrical Holy Spirit. The age of Anna has been variously reported as ranging from twelve to twenty, with one critic reporting that both ages of the character are represented.

Which is the correct interpretation? They are all correct. Each and every one is equally correct; otherwise what is the use of a dream play? The point is not to find the literal meaning, anyway, but to touch the soul of the director, and find out what still hurts him after all these years. After all the sex and all the promises, all the lies and truths and messy affairs, there is still one critical area where he is filled with guilt and passion. It is revealed when Anna tells him she is pregnant. He is enraged. How could she, a young actress given the role of a lifetime, jeopardize her career and his play by getting pregnant? Then she tells him she has had an abortion, for the sake of the play. And then he really is torn in two, for he does not believe, after all, that a play—not even his play—is worth the sacrifice of a life. What we are left with at the end of *After the Rehearsal*, however, is the very strong sense of an artist who has sacrificed many lives for the sake of his art, and now wonders if perhaps one of those lives was his own.

Against All Odds ★ ★ ★
R, 128 m., 1984

Rachel Ward (Jessie Wyler), Jeff Bridges (Terry Brogan), James Woods (Jake Wise), Alex Karras (Hank Sully), Jane Greer (Mrs. Wyler), Richard Widmark (Ben Caxton). Directed by Taylor Hackford and produced by Hackford and William S. Gilmore. Screenplay by Eric Hughes.

There have been too many sweet girls in thrillers. What we need are more no-good, double-dealing broads who can cross their legs and break your heart. *Against All Odds* has a woman like that, and it makes for one of the most intriguing movie relationships in a long time; in thirty-five years, to be exact, which is when they told this story for the first time. You may remember the original movie. It was called *Out of the Past*. It starred Robert Mitchum and Kirk Douglas, and it was the greatest cigarette-smoking movie of all time. Mitchum and Douglas smoked all the way through every scene, and they were always blowing sinister, aggressive clouds of smoke at each other. The movie was shot so there was always a lot of light on the place in midair where their smoke was aimed. The only drawback to the fact that smoking is no longer fashionable in movies is that we don't get any great smoking scenes anymore. Anyway, if you remember that movie, you remember that Kirk Douglas was a hoodlum and Robert Mitchum was a guy who would take a job for a buck, and Douglas hired Mitchum to track down his missing girlfriend, who was played by Jane Greer. After Mitchum found Greer, they had a big love affair—or so Mitchum thought. But Greer, that no-good, two-timing, double-crossing broad, liked security more than passion.

Against All Odds is not really a remake of *Out of the Past*. The only similarity between the two movies is in the cynical love triangle. And it was a real inspiration to tell that story again, since it makes for an intriguing, complicated, interesting romance. This time, the bad guy is a gambler, played by James Woods. His girlfriend (Rachel Ward) is the daughter of the owner of a pro-football team (played by Jane Greer, of all people). And the guy who tracks her down (Jeff Bridges), is a team player who's just been fired after a knee injury. There is a lot of plot in this movie—probably too much. The best thing to do is to accept the plot, and then disregard it, and pay attention to the scenes of passion. They really work. Bridges and Ward have an interesting sexual tension in *Against All Odds*, since their relationship is not simply sweetness and light, but depends upon suspicion, dislike, and foul betrayal. That's ever so much more interesting than just falling in love. And the situation liberates Ward from the trap she'd been in; the trap of playing attractive, sexy, strong heroines. This time, as a complicated schemer, she's fascinating.

The movie has a lot of muted social criticism in it, involving professional sports and ecology. The Jane Greer character has a plan to destroy several beautiful canyons to build houses. The Bridges character is a victim of unfair labor practices. And so on. Sometimes we get the idea we're watching a clone of *Chinatown*—but not with that jealous triangle. Woods is the villain, so he does smoke, of course. But Bridges and Ward are so consumed with passion, they don't even need to.

The Age of Innocence ★ ★ ★ ★
PG, 132 m., 1993

Daniel Day-Lewis (Newland Archer), Michelle Pfeiffer (Ellen Olenska), Winona Ryder (May Welland), Geraldine Chaplin (Mrs. Welland), Mary Beth Hurt (Regina Beaufort), Miriam Margolyes (Mrs. Mingott), Richard E. Grant (Larry Lefferts), Alec McCowen (Sillerton Jackson). Directed by Martin Scorsese and produced by Barbara De Fina. Screenplay by Jay Cocks and Scorsese.

We live in an age of brutal manners, when people crudely say exactly what they mean, comedy is based on insult, tributes are roasts, and loud public obscenity passes without notice. Martin Scorsese's film *The Age of Innocence*, which takes place in the 1870s, seems so alien it could be pure fantasy. A rigid social code governs how people talk, walk, meet, part, dine, earn their livings, fall in love, and marry. Not a word of the code is written down anywhere. But these people have been studying it since they were born.

The film is based on a novel by Edith Wharton, who died in the 1930s. The age of innocence, as she called it with fierce irony, was over long before she even wrote her book. Yet she understood that the people of her story had the same lusts as we barbaric moderns, and not acting on them made them all the stronger.

The novel and the movie take place in the

elegant milieu of the oldest and richest families in New York City. Marriages are like treaties between nations, their purpose not merely to cement romance or produce children, but to provide for the orderly transmission of wealth between the generations. Anything that threatens this sedate process is hated. It is not thought proper for men and women to place their own selfish desires above the needs of their class. People do indeed "marry for love," but the practice is frowned upon as vulgar and dangerous.

We meet a young man named Newland Archer (Daniel Day-Lewis), who is engaged to marry the pretty young May Welland (Winona Ryder). He has great affection for her, even though she seems pretty but dim, well-behaved rather than high-spirited. All agree this is a good marriage between good families, and Archer is satisfied—until one night at the opera he sees a cousin who has married and lived in Europe for years. She is Ellen, the Countess Olenska (Michelle Pfeiffer). She has, he is astonished to discover, ideas of her own. She looks on his world with the amusement and detachment of an exile. She is beautiful, yes, but that isn't what attracts Archer. His entire being is excited by the presence of a woman who boldly thinks for herself.

The countess is not quite a respectable woman. First she made the mistake of marrying outside her circle, taking a rich Polish count and living in Europe. Then she made a greater transgression, separating from her husband and returning to New York, where she stands out at social gatherings as an extra woman of undoubted fascination, whom no one knows quite what to do with. It is clear to everyone that her presence is a threat to the orderly progress of Archer's marriage with May.

This kind of story has been filmed, very well, by the Merchant-Ivory team. Their *Howards End, A Room With a View,* and *The Bostonians* know this world. It would seem to be material of no interest to Martin Scorsese, a director of great guilts and energies, whose very titles are a rebuke to the age of innocence: *Mean Streets, Taxi Driver, Raging Bull, GoodFellas.* Yet when his friend and cowriter Jay Cocks handed Scorsese the Wharton novel, he could not put it down, and now he has filmed it, and through some miracle it is all Wharton, and all Scorsese.

The story told here is brutal and bloody, the story of a man's passion crushed, his heart defeated. Yet it is also much more, and

the last scene of the film, which pulls everything together, is almost unbearably poignant because it reveals that the man was not the only one with feelings—that others sacrificed for him, that his deepest tragedy was not what he lost, but what he never realized he had.

The Age of Innocence is filmed with elegance. These rich aristocrats move in their gilded circles from opera to dinner to drawing room, with a costume for every role and every time of day. Scorsese observes the smallest of social moments, the incline of a head, the angle of a glance, the subtle inflection of a word or phrase. And gradually we understand what is happening: Archer is considering breaking his engagement to May, in order to run away with the countess, and everyone is concerned to prevent him—while at no time does anyone reveal by the slightest sign that they know what they are doing.

I have seen love scenes in which naked bodies thrash in sweaty passion, but I have rarely seen them more passionate than in this movie, where everyone is wrapped in layers of Victorian repression. The big erotic moments take place in public among fully clothed people speaking in perfectly modulated phrases, and they are so filled with libido and terror that the characters scarcely survive them.

Scorsese, that artist of headlong temperament, here exhibits enormous patience. We are provided with the voice of a narrator (Joanne Woodward), who understands all that is happening, guides us, and supplies the private thoughts of some of the characters.

We learn the rules of the society. We meet an elderly woman named Mrs. Mingott (Miriam Margolyes), who has vast sums of money and functions for her society as sort of an appeals court of what can be permitted and what cannot be.

And we see the infinite care and attention with which May Welland defends her relationship with Newland Archer. May knows or suspects everything that is happening between Newland and the countess, but she chooses to acknowledge only certain information, and works with the greatest cleverness to preserve her marriage while never quite seeming to notice anything wrong.

Each performance is modulated to preserve the delicate balance of the romantic war. Daniel Day-Lewis stands at the center, deluded for a time that he has free will. Michelle Pfeiffer, as the countess, is a woman

who sees through society without quite rejecting it, and takes an almost sensuous pleasure in seducing Archer with the power of her mind. At first it seems that little May is an unwitting bystander and victim, but Winona Ryder gradually reveals the depth of her character's intelligence, and in the last scene, as I said, all is revealed and much is finally understood.

Scorsese is known for his restless camera; he rarely allows a static shot. But here you will have the impression of grace and stateliness in his visual style, and only on a second viewing will you realize the subtlety with which his camera does, indeed, incessantly move, insinuating itself into conversations like a curious uninvited guest. At the beginning of *The Age of Innocence,* as I suggested, it seems to represent a world completely alien to us. By the end, we realize these people have all the same emotions, passions, fears, and desires that we do. It is simply that they value them more highly, and are less careless with them, and do not in the cause of self-indulgence choose a moment's pleasure over a lifetime's exquisite and romantic regret.

Airplane! ★ ★ ★
PG, 88 m., 1980

Lloyd Bridges (McCroskey), Peter Graves (Captain Oveur), Kareem Abdul-Jabbar (Murdock), Julie Hagerty (Elaine), Robert Hays (Ted Striker), Leslie Nielsen (Dr. Rumack), Howard Jarvis (Man in Taxi), Ethel Merman (Lieutenant Hurwitz). Directed and written by Jim Abrahams, David Zucker, and Jerry Zucker and produced by Howard W. Koch.

Airplane! is a comedy in the great tradition of high school skits, the Sid Caesar TV show, *Mad* magazine, and the dog-eared screenplays people's nephews write in lieu of earning their college diplomas. It is sophomoric, obvious, predictable, corny, and quite often very funny. And the reason it's funny is frequently *because* it's sophomoric, predictable, corny, etc. Example:

Airplane Captain (Peter Graves): Surely you can't be serious!

Doctor (Leslie Nielsen): Of course I am! And stop calling me Shirley!

This sort of humor went out with Milton Berle, Jerry Lewis, and knock-knock jokes. That's why it's so funny. Movie comedies these days are so hung up on being contemporary, radical, outspoken, and cynically satirical that they sometimes forget to be funny. And they've lost the nerve to be as corny as *Airplane!*—to actually invite loud groans from the audience. The flop *Wholly Moses*, for example, is no doubt an infinitely more intelligent comedy—but the problem was, we didn't laugh.

Airplane! has a couple of sources for its inspiration. One of them is obviously *Airport* (1970) and all of its sequels and rip-offs. The other might not come immediately to mind unless you're a fan of the late show. It's *Zero Hour!* (1957), which starred the quintessential 1950s B-movie cast of Dana Andrews, Linda Darnell, and Sterling Hayden. *Airplane!* comes from the same studio (Paramount) and therefore is able to cheerfully borrow the same plot (airliner is imperiled after the crew and most of the passengers are stricken with food poisoning). The *Zero Hour!* crisis situation (how to get the airplane down) was also borrowed for the terrible *Airport 1975*, in which Karen Black played a stewardess who tried to follow instructions radioed from the ground.

Airplane! has two desperate people in the cockpit: Julie Hagerty, as the stewardess, and Robert Hays, as a former Air Force pilot whose traumatic war experiences have made him terrified of flying. (The cockpit also contains a very kinky automatic pilot . . . but never mind.)

The movie exploits the previous films for all they're worth. The passenger list includes a little old lady (like Helen Hayes in *Airport*), a guitar-playing nun (like Helen Reddy in *Airport 1975*), and even a critically ill little girl who's being flown to an emergency operation (Linda Blair played the role in *Airport 1975*). Predictable results occur, as when the nun's guitar knocks loose the little girl's intravenous tubes, and she nearly dies while all the passengers sing along inspirationally.

The movie's funniest scene, however, occurs in a flashback explaining how the stewardess and the Air Force pilot first met and fell in love years ago. The scene takes place in an exotic Casablanca-style bar, which is miraculously transformed when somebody's hurled at the jukebox and it starts playing "Stayin' Alive" by the Bee Gees. The scene becomes a hilarious send-up of the disco scenes in *Saturday Night Fever*, with the young pilot defying gravity to impress the girl.

Airplane! is practically a satirical anthology of classic movie clichés. Lloyd Bridges, as the ground-control officer, seems to be satirizing half of his straight roles. The opening titles get an enormous laugh with an unexpected reference to *Jaws*. The neurotic young pilot is talked back into the cockpit in a scene from *Knute Rockne, All American*. And the romantic scenes are played as a soap opera. None of this really adds up to great comic artistry, but *Airplane!* compensates for its lack of original comic invention by its utter willingness to steal, beg, borrow, and rewrite from anywhere.

Airport ★ ★
G, 137 m., 1970

Burt Lancaster (Mel Bakersfield), Dean Martin (Vernon Demerest), Jean Seberg (Tanya), Jacqueline Bisset (Gwen Meighen), George Kennedy (Patroni), Helen Hayes (Ada Quonsett), Van Heflin (D.O. Guerrero). Directed by George Seaton and produced by Ross Hunter. Screenplay by Seaton.

On some dumb fundamental level, *Airport* kept me interested for a couple of hours. I can't quite remember why. The plot has few surprises (you know and I know that no airplane piloted by Dean Martin ever crashed). The gags are painfully simpleminded (a priest, pretending to cross himself, whacks a wise guy across the face). And the characters talk in regulation B-movie clichés like no B-movie you've seen in ten years. Example: A bomb blows a hole in the airplane and weakens the tail structure. Martin's co-pilot says: "Listen, Vern, I want you to know that if there's anything I can do. . . ." What's he talking about? Martin's girl.

The movie has a lot of expensive stars, but only two (Helen Hayes and Van Heflin) have wit enough to abandon all pretense of seriousness. Even Martin, who can be charming in a movie when he relaxes, plays a straight hero-type this time. Burt Lancaster is even straighter and more heroic, as needs be, since he has to run the airport, supervise George Kennedy in pulling out a stuck Boeing 707, and decide to divorce his wife, all at the same time.

But Miss Hayes and Heflin apparently realized early on that *Airport* was going to be a deadly dull affair, and they went about salvaging their own roles, at least. Miss Hayes milks her role of a little-old-lady stowaway for all it's conceivably worth, and I have a suspicion she wrote some of her own dialogue. It's warmer and more humorous than the stiff lines everyone else has to recite, and she won an Oscar for the role.

Heflin, as the guy with the bomb in his briefcase, is perhaps the only person in the cast to realize how metaphysically absurd *Airport* basically is. The airplane already has a priest, two nuns, three doctors, a stowaway, a customs officer's niece, a pregnant stewardess, two black GIs, a loudmouthed kid, a henpecked husband, and Dean Martin aboard, right? So obviously the bomber has to be typecast, too. Heflin sweats, shakes, peers around nervously, clutches his briefcase to his chest, refuses to talk to anybody, and swallows a lot. The customs officer sees him going on the plane and notices "something in his eyes." Also in his ears, nose, and throat. What Heflin does is undermine the structure of the whole movie with a sort of subversive overacting. Once the bomber becomes ridiculous, the movie does, too. That's good, because it never had a chance at being anything else.

Airport 1975 ★ ★ ½
PG, 106 m., 1974

Charlton Heston (Murdock), Karen Black (Nancy), George Kennedy (Patroni), Efrem Zimbalist, Jr. (Stacy), Susan Clark (Mrs. Patroni), Helen Reddy (Sister Ruth). Directed by Jack Smight and produced by William Frye. Screenplay by Don Ingalls.

The original *Airport* was never one of my favorite movies, but I had to admire the slick, competent way it worked us over for two hours. Its clichés were ancient and its typecasting was relentless, but it didn't bore us. *Airport 1975*, a reworking of the same good old ingredients happens, by some happy chance, to be better than the original.

The story is familiar to anyone. A private plane crashes into the flight deck of a 747, killing or disabling its crew. A stewardess pilots the plane by following radioed instructions, and then a rescue pilot (Charlton Heston, inevitably) is lowered from an Air Force helicopter into the gaping hole in the plane. Meanwhile, a young kidney patient grows weaker, a drunk accosts the pilot, and Gloria Swanson dictates the finishing touches on her autobiography ("I never did want the damn thing published while I was alive, anyway").

What makes this work so well is that the screenplay and direction concentrate on the action, instead of getting bogged down in so many subplots, as *Airport* did. It can't be helped, I suppose, that Heston and the brave stewardess (Karen Black) have been having an affair for six years, or that the airline vice president (George Kennedy, promoted from his operations command in *Airport*) has a wife and daughter on the crippled plane, or that we have the usual ecumenical mixture of stereotypes, racial groups, ages, sexes, and occupants on board. That's all part of the formula.

But at least *Airport 1975* introduces its characters quickly and without fuss, and then gets on with the business at hand. And after the midair collision (which has been telegraphed for at least twenty minutes), the movie's excellent special effects become really gripping. With *Airport,* you never quite felt those people were on a real plane. The exterior shots looked faked. *Airport 1975* has a much more plausible look and a lot of effective aerial photography.

It also gives us a compelling performance by Karen Black, the stewardess. She's probably too good an actress for a role like this, but she makes it real. (And who could ever quite believe Dean Martin as the pilot in *Airport?*) The only quarrel I have with the role is that it falls into the trap of assuming she's incompetent because she's a woman. Her lip quivers, her eyes well up with tears, she's indecisive at key moments. The men on the ground decide they have to get a real pilot on board. My notion is that a real stewardess, faced with such an unlikely situation, would respond professionally and coolly.

No matter. While the wind rips into the plane and the passengers bundle up with blankets and the mountains loom up ahead and the first rescue pilot falls to his death and Gloria Swanson remembers her first flight ("It was in 1917, Cecil B. DeMille was the pilot, and we flew nonstop from Los Angeles to Pasadena"). *Airport 1975* is good, exciting, corny escapism and the kind of movie you would *not* want to watch as an in-flight film.

Aladdin ★ ★ ★
G, 90 m., 1992

With the voices of: Scott Weinger (Aladdin), Robin Williams (Genie), Linda Larkin (Jasmine), Jonathan Freeman (Jafar), Frank Welker (Abu), Randy Cartwright (The Carpet). Directed and produced by John Musker and Ron Clements. Screenplay by Clements, Musker, Ted Elliott, and Terry Rossio.

Robin Williams and animation were born for one another, and in *Aladdin* they finally meet. Williams's speed of comic invention has always been too fast for flesh and blood; the way he flashes in and out of characters can be dizzying. In Disney's new animated film *Aladdin,* he's liberated at last, playing a genie who has complete freedom over his form—who can instantly be anybody or anything.

The genie is the best thing in the movie, which is good fun but not on a par with *The Little Mermaid* and *Beauty and the Beast,* the two films with which Disney essentially gave rebirth to feature-length animation. The weakness of the film is in its leads, a street urchin named Aladdin and a sultan's daughter, Jasmine. As a romantic couple, they're pale and routine, especially compared to the chemistry between the beast and the beauty. They look unformed, somehow, as if even the filmmakers didn't see them as real individuals.

All of the film's best moments come from the genie and the other supporting characters, which include a plump little sultan, his scheming vizier, an angry parrot named Iago, a chattering monkey, a friendly flying carpet, and even a magic cave that turns into a fearsome face, so that Aladdin has to venture down its throat.

Ever since Jiminy Cricket first danced onto the screen, Disney animators have created entertaining supporting casts, and the magic carpet is one of the most ingenious: With only tassels and body language to work with, it somehow possesses a complete personality, whisking Aladdin and Abu, his monkey, on terrifying swoops around the kingdom.

But it's the genie who stops the show, and I would like to know which came first, the pictures or the words, because Williams sounds like he's improvising as he careens from one character to another: from Ed Sullivan to Elvis to Arsenio Hall to a tailor to a Scottish terrier. There is genuine exhilaration in these passages.

The plot is basic fairy tale: The sultan informs his daughter that she has three days in which to get married (fathers are always providing fearsome deadlines to their daughters in these stories). Distraught, she flees from the palace and encounters Aladdin, who knows his way around the streets and alleys of the city, and enchants her with his cheerful ways.

Back at the palace, the evil adviser schemes to marry the princess and become the sultan—not difficult, since the sultan falls under his spell and doesn't seem too alert at the best of times. Meanwhile, Aladdin explores the magic cave, finds a lantern, rubs it, and unleashes the Robin Williams scenes, which are so captivating we almost forget about the rest of the movie.

One distraction during the film was its odd use of ethnic stereotypes. Most of the Arab characters have exaggerated facial char-

acteristics—hooked noses, glowering brows, thick lips—but Aladdin and the princess look like white American teen-agers. Wouldn't it be reasonable that if all the characters in this movie come from the same genetic stock, they should resemble one another?

Original music was one of the key qualities of both *The Little Mermaid* and *Beauty and the Beast,* and the composers of those films, Alan Menken and Howard Ashman, collaborated on three songs for this one before Ashman's death last year (their work includes Williams's showstopper, "Friend Like Me"). Menken then collaborated with Tim Rice on three more songs, but some ineffable quality seems missing; the music isn't as magical as in the two previous films. The bottom line is that *Aladdin* is good but not great, with the exception of the Robin Williams sequences, which have a life and energy all their own.

Alex in Wonderland ★ ★ ★
R, 109 m., 1971

Donald Sutherland (Alex), Ellen Burstyn (Beth), Meg Mazursky (Amy), Glenna Sergent (Nancy), Viola Spolin (Mother), Paul Mazursky (Hal Stern). Directed by Paul Mazursky and produced by Larry Tucker. Screenplay by Mazursky and Tucker.

"Who are you," said the Caterpillar.

This was not an encouraging opening for a conversation. Alice replied rather shyly. "I—hardly know, Sir, just at present—at least I know who I was when I got up this morning, but I think I must have changed several times since then."

That was exactly the case in Hollywood in the early seventies. Works of genius were showered on us by bright, radical, young, etc., filmmakers who announced their intention to overturn the Hollywood establishment. Occasionally one of their films did make it very big, as *Easy Rider* did. Within weeks, the Hollywood hills were jammed with other would-be geniuses, shooting nihilistic cycle flicks with pseudo-Dylan lyrics. Meanwhile, the original boy wonders . . . have got to make themselves another film. That was the situation for Paul Mazursky and Larry Tucker, who wrote, produced, and directed *Bob & Carol & Ted & Alice.* That movie was an artistic and financial success. It was chosen to open the New York Film Festival. It was argued about in all the best publications. Elliott Gould became a star. Natalie Wood made her comeback. Tucker and Mazursky got rich. The whole enchilada, baby.

Alex in Wonderland was their response to that situation; it's a movie about a director whose first movie is a success and who's at a loss for another project. In this sense, it's autobiographical; not in the details of life, but in the crises. Mazursky himself even appears, as Hal Stern, the doggedly mod movie producer who hopes to interest Donald Sutherland in *Don Quixote* as a Western? Or maybe . . . ?

If the director's dilemma sounds familiar, perhaps you're reminded of Fellini's *8½*. Mazursky and Tucker were. The blocked director's daughter even asks why he doesn't do a movie about not knowing what to do next, and he says, no, Fellini already did that. *Alex in Wonderland* is a deliberately Felliniesque movie, all the same, and all the more fun for that. Fellini himself appears briefly, to no special purpose, and Fellini trademarks like parades, circuses, and clowns keep turning up in the hero's daydreams.

If *Alex* had been left just on this level, however, it would have been of little interest. What makes it so good is the gift Mazursky, Tucker, and their actors have of fleshing out the small scenes of human contact that give the movie its almost frightening resonance.

Sutherland, as the director, has trouble handling his success. His uncertainty about what to do next spills over into aloofness, even cruelty, toward his wife (Ellen Burstyn) and mother (Viola Spolin). A short scene in a car with his mother, and a long scene in a kitchen with his wife, actually make the rest of the movie work, because they give the character a depth that sticks even through the superficial dream sequences.

And beyond these intimate scenes, there are icily observant portraits of the "new Hollywood." Of aimless "idealistic" arguments on the beach, of luncheon meetings, of idle people trying somehow to be idly committed. These scenes are the 1970 equivalent of Fitzgerald's *The Last Tycoon* or Nathanael West's *The Day of the Locust:* Unforgivingly accurate studies of the distance between America and the filmmakers who would be "relevant" about it.

The Fellini elements are laid onto the film and don't quite sink in (although buffs will enjoy them just as parody). But the human story does work, remarkably well, and if the movie doesn't hold together we're not disposed to hold that against it. Half an enchilada is better than none.

Alice ★ ★ ★
PG-13, 106 m., 1990

Joe Mantegna (Joe), Mia Farrow (Alice), William Hurt (Doug), Cybill Shepherd (Nancy Brill), Gwen Verdon (Alice's Mother), Bernadette Peters (Muse). Directed by Woody Allen and produced by Robert Greenhut. Screenplay by Allen.

Woody Allen's *Alice* snatches its heroine out of the cradle of luxury and takes her on a dizzying tour of the truths in her life, fueled by the mysterious herbal teas of an enigmatic acupuncturist. It's a strange, magical film, in which Allen uses the arts of the ancient Chinese healer as a shortcut to psychoanalysis; at the end of the film, which covers only a few days, Alice has learned truths about her husband, her parents, her marriage, her family, and herself, and has undergone a profound conversion in values. Because this is a Woody Allen film, a lot of that metaphysical process is funny.

Mia Farrow stars as Alice, who has no apparent relationship to Alice in Wonderland, but finds her own looking glass in the dingy walk-up offices of the highly recommended Dr. Yang, in New York's Chinatown. He asks her to gaze into a spinning wheel while he hypnotizes her, and then he discovers, as he suspected all along, that her pains are not in her back, as she claims, but in her heart.

She leads a comfortable life, cut off from all sources of suffering and, therefore, also of joy. She and her husband (William Hurt) live in a Manhattan apartment that has been interior-designed to within an inch of its life. Also occupying their home, in supporting roles, are a cook ("I couldn't get free-range chickens today!"), a nanny, and, of course, their small assortment of two children. It's the kind of house where support personnel are constantly ringing the doorbell: Here comes the trainer now.

Alice has been married for sixteen affluent years to Doug, a stockbroker played by Hurt as a kind of human deflecting machine, whose physical and verbal postures seem designed to avoid any kind of actual contact. He's always changing the subject, usually into silence.

One day Alice is taking the kids to school and drops a book on the stair, and the book is returned by a dark, handsome stranger (Joe Mantegna), and instantly she begins thinking about having an affair. The very notion shocks and thrills her, and after Dr. Yang (Keye Luke) discovers her secret, he

gives her various herbal potions, including one to make her invisible and another that gives her the knack of talking seductively.

What Dr. Yang has really done is to release her from all inhibitions, psychological and physical, so she's free to range widely through her current and past life. She confronts her sister. She has an imaginary conversation with her husband. She levels with her mother. She is even taken on a flight over Manhattan by the ghost of a former boyfriend. The movie uses Allen's unique style of off-center, fast-thinking dialogue, with throwaway lines and quick topical references. Everyone in the story is fairly smart, although some are in over their heads, like the Mantegna character, who cannot quite understand why this strange woman is first seducing, then abandoning him. A lot of the material in the film spins out of Alice's childhood Catholicism; perhaps she still clings to a notion that someday she might become a nun, instead of a parasitic consumer of goods.

The world of *Alice* is the rich world of Manhattan, where the homeless and the poor are seldom seen. This is a world inhabited by countless stars in supporting roles, including Blythe Danner, Judy Davis, Keye Luke, Bernadette Peters, Cybill Shepherd, and Gwen Verdon. (The old boyfriend is played by Alec Baldwin, who is transparent in every scene. It is somehow typical of Woody Allen to obtain the latest box office superstar for his cast, and then neglect to make him opaque.)

The women in this world are intimate with boutiques, hair salons, chic restaurants, and the interiors of limousines. Yet Alice can somehow not get the image of Mother Teresa out of her mind. Perhaps if she went to Calcutta, if she became a follower of Mother Teresa, then these vague stirrings of unease would stop tormenting her. In a Woody Allen picture all such developments and U-turns are, of course, eminently thinkable, and one of the best things about *Alice* is that the characters are not linear creatures, hell-bent on moving in a straight line from the beginning of the movie to the end.

Alice lacks the philosophical precision of Allen's *Crimes and Misdemeanors* and the psychological messiness of *Hannah and Her Sisters,* and it also lacks the rigorous self-discovery of his underrated *Another Woman.* It's in the tradition of his more whimsical films like *A Midsummer Night's Sex Comedy.* And yet lurking in the shadows are some seductive questions. Wouldn't it be wonderful if there *were* a man like Dr. Yang, a *deus ex machina* to drop into our lives with his herbs and paraphernalia, and lift the scales from our eyes, and free us from our petty routines and selfishness, and allow us to practice the sainthood we have always suspected lies buried deep inside?

Alice Doesn't Live Here Anymore
★ ★ ★ ★
PG, 113 m., 1974

Ellen Burstyn (Alice Hyatt), Kris Kristofferson (David), Billy Green Bush (Donald), Diane Ladd (Flo), Alfred Lutter (Tommy), Harvey Keitel (Ben). Directed by Martin Scorsese and produced by David Susskind and Audrey Maas. Screenplay by Robert Getchell.

Martin Scorsese's *Alice Doesn't Live Here Anymore* opens with a parody of the Hollywood dream world little girls were expected to carry around in their intellectual baggage a generation ago. The screen is awash with a fake sunset, and a sweet little thing comes strolling along home past sets that seem rescued from *The Wizard of Oz.* But her dreams and dialogue are decidedly not made of sugar, spice, or anything nice: This little girl is going to do things her way.

That was her defiant childhood notion, anyway. But by the time she's thirty-five, Alice Hyatt has more or less fallen into society's rhythms. She's married to an incommunicative truck driver, she has a precocious twelve-year-old son, she kills time chatting with the neighbors. And then her husband is unexpectedly killed in a traffic accident and she's left widowed and—almost worse than that—independent. After all those years of having someone there, can she cope by herself?

She can, she says. When she was a little girl, she idolized Alice Faye and determined to be a singer when she grew up. Well, she's thirty-five, and that's grown-up. She has a garage sale, sells the house, and sets off on an odyssey through the Southwest with her son and her dreams. What happens to her along the way provides one of the most perceptive, funny, occasionally painful portraits of an American woman I've seen.

The movie has been both attacked and defended on feminist grounds, but I think it belongs somewhere outside ideology, maybe in the area of contemporary myth and romance. There are scenes in which we take Alice and her journey perfectly seriously, there are scenes of harrowing reality and then there are other scenes (including some hilarious passages in a restaurant where she

waits on tables) where Scorsese edges into slight, cheerful exaggeration. There are times, indeed, when the movie seems less about Alice than it does about the speculations and daydreams of a lot of women about her age, who identify with the liberation of other women, but are unsure on the subject of themselves.

A movie like this depends as much on performances as on direction, and there's a fine performance by Ellen Burstyn (who won an Oscar for this role) as Alice. She looks more real this time than she did as Cybill Shepherd's available mother in *The Last Picture Show* or as Linda Blair's tormented mother in *The Exorcist.* It's the kind of role she can relax in, be honest with, allow to develop naturally (although those are often the hardest roles of all). She's determined to find work as a singer, to "resume" a career that was mostly dreams to begin with, and she's pretty enough (although not good enough) to almost pull it off. She meets some generally good people along the way, and they help her when they can. But she also meets some creeps, especially a deceptively nice guy named Ben (played by Harvey Keitel, the autobiographical hero of Scorsese's two films set in Little Italy). The singing jobs don't materialize much, and it's while she's waitressing that she runs into a divorced young farmer (Kris Kristofferson).

They fall warily in love, and there's an interesting relationship between Kristofferson and Alfred Lutter, who does a very good job of playing a certain kind of twelve-year-old kid. Most women in Alice's position probably wouldn't run into a convenient, understanding, and eligible young farmer, but then a lot of the things in the film don't work as pure logic. There's a little myth to them, while Scorsese sneaks up on his main theme.

The movie's filled with brilliantly done individual scenes. Alice, for example, has a run-in with a fellow waitress with an inspired vocabulary (Diane Ladd, an Oscar nominee for this role). They fall into a friendship and have a frank and honest conversation one day while sunbathing. The scene works perfectly. There's also the specific way her first employer backs into offering her a singing job, and the way Alice takes leave from her old neighbors, and the way her son persists in explaining a joke that could only be understood by a twelve-year-old. These are great moments in a film that gives us Alice Hyatt: female, thirty-five, undefeated.

Aliens ★ ★ ★ ½
R, 135 m., 1986

Sigourney Weaver (Ripley), Carrie Henn (Newt), Michael Biehn (Corporal Hicks), Paul Reiser (Burke), Lance Henriksen (Bishop), Jenette Goldstein (Private Vasquez). Directed by James Cameron and produced by Gale Anne Hurd. Screenplay by Cameron.

This movie is so intense that it creates a problem for me as a reviewer: Do I praise its craftsmanship, or do I tell you it left me feeling wrung out and unhappy? When I walked out of the theater, there were knots in my stomach from the film's roller-coaster ride of violence. This is not the kind of movie where it means anything to say you "enjoyed" it.

Aliens is a sequel to the very effective 1979 film, *Alien,* but it tells a self-contained story that begins fifty-seven years after the previous story ended. The first time around, you may recall, Sigourney Weaver and a shipload of her fellow space voyagers were exploring a newly discovered planet when they found an abandoned spaceship. Surviving in the ship was an alien life-form that seemed to consist primarily of teeth. The aliens were pure malevolence; their only function was to attack and eat anything that was warm and moved. And they incubated their young inside the bodies of their victims.

Weaver was the only survivor of that first expedition, and after saving her ship by expelling an alien through the air lock into deep space, she put herself into hibernation. She is found fifty-seven years later by a salvage ship, and when she awakes she is still tormented by nightmares. (The script does not provide her, however, with even a single line of regret after she learns that fifty-seven years have passed and everyone she knew is dead.)

A new expedition is sent back to the mystery planet. Weaver is on board. She knows what the aliens are like and thinks the only sane solution is to nuke them from outer space. But in the meantime, she learns to her horror that a human colony has been established on the planet and billions of dollars have been invested in it. Now Earth has lost contact with the colony. Has it been attacked by aliens? Are there stars in the sky?

The crew is made up of an interesting mixed bag of technicians and military personnel. My favorites were Lance Henriksen as a loyal android, Jenette Goldstein as a muscular marine private, and Michael Biehn as the uncertain Corporal Hicks. Also on board is the slimy Burke (Paul Reiser), who represents the owners of the planet's expensive colony and dreams of making millions by using the aliens as a secret weapon.

The movie gives us just enough setup to establish the characters and explain the situation. Then the action starts. The colony has, of course, been overrun by the aliens, all except for one plucky little girl (Carrie Henn) who has somehow survived by hiding in the air ducts. The marines explore the base on foot, which seems a little silly in view of the great speed with which the aliens attack. Nobody seems very interested in listening to Weaver's warnings. After all, she's only the one person who has seen an alien, so what does she know? And then the movie escalates into a nonstop war between human and alien.

It's here that my nerves started to fail. *Aliens* is absolutely, painfully, and unremittingly intense for at least its last hour. Weaver goes into battle to save her colleagues, herself, and the little girl, and the aliens drop from the ceiling, pop up out of the floor, and crawl out of the ventilation shafts. (In one of the movie's less plausible moments, one alien even seems to know how to work the elevator buttons.) I have never seen a movie that maintains such a pitch of intensity for so long; it's like being on some kind of hair-raising carnival ride that never stops.

I don't know how else to describe this: The movie made me feel bad. It filled me with feelings of unease and disquiet and anxiety. I didn't want to talk to anyone. I was drained. I'm not sure *Aliens* is what we mean by entertainment. Yet I have to be accurate about this movie: It is a superb example of filmmaking craft.

The director, James *(The Terminator)* Cameron, has been assigned to make an intense and horrifying thriller, and he has delivered. Weaver, who is onscreen almost all the time, comes through with a very strong, sympathetic performance: She's the thread that holds everything together.

The supporting players are sharply drawn. The special effects are professional. I'm giving the movie a high rating for its skill and professionalism and because it does the job it says it will do. I am also advising you not to eat before you see it.

Footnote 1992: I observed in this review that the Sigourney Weaver character utters not a line of regret when she learns that fifty-seven years have passed and everyone she knows is dead. This oversight, and others, are repaired in the expanded "Special Widescreen Collector's Edition" of *Aliens,* which James Cameron supervised for 1992 video release. He added about eighteen minutes of footage that was originally shot for the movie, then taken out to provide a shorter running time for theatrical release. The 1986 version ran 135 minutes according to its press materials and 137 minutes according to the materials supplied with the expanded video version. The new version is 154 minutes long.

The scenes restored by Cameron emphasize human family life, as contrasted to the egg-laying horror discovered in space. We learn that Ripley, the Weaver character, had a daughter, who died at age sixty-six. We meet the mother, father, and brother of little Newt, the girl who is treasured by Ripley—and we see how Newt's parents rediscovered the alien creature. Other scenes establish the remote automatic weapons, clear up details of the space station's construction, add speculation about the creatures, and flesh out relationships.

Watching this new version of *Aliens* on laser disc, I was struck again by what impressed me the first time around: How well the movie is made, and what a disquieting effect it has.

Alien³ ★ ½
R, 105 m., 1992

Sigourney Weaver (Ripley), Charles S. Dutton (Dillon), Charles Dance (Clemens), Lance Henriksen (Bishop II). Directed by David Fincher and produced by Gordon Carroll, David Giler, and Walter Hill. Screenplay by Giler, Hill, and Larry Ferguson.

Alien³ is one of the best-looking bad movies I have ever seen. It is a triumph of art direction and a disaster of screenwriting, and the eyes appreciate it more than the mind. Watching it in the moment, we are absorbed. After it's over, we are disappointed, because what actually happens in the movie is so much less interesting than where it happens and how it looks while it's happening.

The movie takes place entirely on the drab prison world of Fiorina 161, an all-male world inhabited by a handful of sex criminals. This is a world running down toward complete disintegration. Once it was a modern mining facility, but now everything leaks and nothing works and the inhabitants are like prisoners left to supervise their own punishment.

Ripley (Sigourney Weaver) arrives at this world in an interstellar lifeboat, after her spaceship is incapacitated. On board with her are characters from *Aliens* (1986), including the young girl she rescued from the creatures of the second film, and Bishop, the android. All are killed (or disabled, in Bishop's case) except for Ripley, who is nursed back to consciousness by Clemens (Charles Dance), the disgraced doctor who ministers to the ill of Fiorina 161.

Her attention is filled with a burning question: How did the others die? Are their deaths connected to the alien beings we have come to know and loathe in the first two movies in this series? Ripley herself has formed a deep and obsessive hatred for the creatures: "I've known you so long I can't remember a time when you weren't in my life."

Fiorina 161 is seen almost entirely from the inside; the humans seem to inhabit a world made of tunnels and rusting steel compartments, pipes and drains, and huge pieces of machinery of no apparent purpose. There is a lot more space than they need, and they have shut off sections of their station and withdrawn into the gloomy, dark, damp, decomposing remnants of what was once a thriving operation. Their heads are shaven because of lice, their manners are crude, their clothing filthy, and in this world they look right at home.

Ripley, the one woman on a planet of sex offenders, is played by Weaver as a character whose attention is elsewhere. She believes that the alien creatures (who have acid for blood and murder as their only response to other beings) will destroy human society if they ever escape their long wait in the outer reaches of space. She knows that the Corporation wants these creatures to further its biological warfare plans, and that if she does not destroy them, they will wipe out the Corporation along with everything else. She is on a mission, and eventually she gets the men of Fiorina to help her.

All of this is actually fairly interesting; *Alien³* is more ambitious than your average monster movie, and in the way the isolated men track the creature through the cold, forbidding spaces of their station, it owes more than a little to the masterpiece of this genre, Howard Hawks's *The Thing* (1951). But eventually the atmosphere grows monotonous, the strategies grow obvious, and good ideas are permitted to run on far too long.

Look, for example, at the first shot from the monster's point of view. The world, seen through its eyes, seems stretched out, as if it sees through anamorphic lenses. It can be upside down, because the spiderlike creature is happy to run along ceilings. One shot like this is interesting. Two make the point. The movie goes on and on, repeating the chase sequences, until we begin to realize uncomfortably that no human in the movie could ever possibly outrun this monster—all of these sequences are fudged.

The monster itself is more clearly seen here, but not half as effective as in *Aliens,* or in *Alien,* where the *idea* of the creature was actually more frightening than its appearance. There is still no explanation as to why a creature with a perfectly good head would need another one, as its tongue (and I am still curious about whether the second creature has a *third* one as *its* tongue, and so on infinitum).

By the end of *Alien³,* we are thoroughly depressed and exhausted. That's partly because the human relationships in the movie are left incomplete; Charles Dance, as the doctor, and Charles S. Dutton, as the toughest prisoner, are potentially interesting, but we don't get to know them and Ripley barely acknowledges them, aside from a brief off-camera bout of horniness. Much of the dialogue is deliberately hard to comprehend. The first-time director, David Fincher, has worked with production designer Norman Reynolds, art director James Morahan, and set decorator Belinda Edwards to make a great-looking movie. But the screenplay, by David Giler, Walter Hill, and Larry Ferguson, is so limited and simplistic that finally we just don't care.

Alive ★ ★ ½
R, 123 m., 1993

Ethan Hawke (Nando Parrado), Vincent Spano (Antonio Balbi), Josh Hamilton (Roberto Canessa), Bruce Ramsay (Carlitos Paez), John Haymes Newton (Tintin), David Kriegel (Gustavo Zerbino). Directed by Frank Marshall and produced by Robert Watts and Kathleen Kennedy. Screenplay by John Patrick Shanley.

There are some stories you simply can't tell. The story of the Andes survivors may be one of them. After their plane crashed high in the mountains on a flight to Chile, they survived for most of a winter in the shell of their wrecked aircraft, living on wine, chocolate, and the flesh of their dead comrades. Finally

three of them set out to find help, and two finally did break through to civilization.

Accounts of this adventure stress its religious, almost mystical nature. Many of the survivors were members of a sports team, devout Catholics, and after they realized they would die if they did not resort to cannibalism, they told themselves their act was a form of the Eucharist. Some of the boys made the others promise to eat their flesh if they died. *Alive* stresses this metaphysical level in scenes like one where a survivor, stranded without hope in the middle of a vast expanse of frigid ice and rock, exults that he has never felt closer to God. This is the same sort of euphoria that mountain climbers report after their harrowing climbs, and it may be absolutely true, or a case of rapture of the heights, or a little of both.

The problem is, no movie can really encompass the sheer enormity of the experience. As subtitles tick off "Day 50" and "Day 70," the actors in the movie continue to look amazingly healthy (and well fed). Although some despair, most remain hopeful. But what would it *really* be like to huddle in a wrecked aircraft for ten weeks in freezing weather, eating human flesh? I cannot imagine, and frankly, this film doesn't much help me.

I was reminded of one of the most powerful books I have ever read, *The Worst Journey in the World,* by Apsley Cherry-Gerard, a member of Scott's doomed expedition to the Antarctic. All by himself, Cherry-Gerard walked nine hundred miles across the polar ice to observe the mating habits of penguins. He walked through twenty-four-hour darkness, ate only biscuits, and lived to tell the story. The book, now back in print, is one of the great first-person accounts in English literature, but one of the things it teaches us is that we cannot quite know what that journey was like.

Alive is a movie that has taken a long time to come to the screen. The Andes plane went down in the early 1970s. Novelist Piers Paul Read wrote a book about the experience, which was optioned for the movies, but then a 1976 Mexican quickie named *Survive!* was dubbed into English and upstaged a more elaborate production.

Now the adventure has been filmed by Frank Marshall *(Arachnophobia),* a veteran associate of Spielberg, and given a first-rate cast, including Ethan Hawke and Vincent Spano. The location photography is impressive, the scenery is awesome, the reenactment of the air crash is terrifying and uses convinc-

ing special effects. We care about the characters while we watch the movie. But at the end it all seems elusive. The movie characters complete their dreadful ordeal, but somehow, walking out, we feel the real Andes survivors would not quite recognize themselves.

All Dogs Go to Heaven ★ ★ ★
G, 87 m., 1989

With the voices of: Burt Reynolds (Charlie B. Barkin), Dom De Luise (Itchy), Vic Tayback (Carface), Judith Barsi (Anne-Marie), Charles Nelson Reilly (Killer), Melba Moore (Whippet Angel), Loni Anderson (Flo). Directed by Don Bluth, codirected by Dan Kuenster and Gary Goldman, and produced by Morris F. Sullivan and George A. Walker. Screenplay by David Weiss.

The first thing I noticed about Don Bluth's *All Dogs Go to Heaven* was the colors, the rich, saturated colors I identify with the early days of animated features. When Technicolor shut down its classic color operation and led the movie world to an inferior but cheaper system, animated films suffered more than live-action movies because their bright primary colors were essential to their overall effect. Most movies made from the early 1960s to the late 1970s have suffered serious fading—but the animated movies looked a little pale even to begin with.

Now Technicolor is back with an improved color system, and in *All Dogs Go to Heaven* it permits such a voluptuous use of color that the movie is an invigorating bath for the eyes. The bright palette is used to paint animated characters who are also a treat, because in his latest animated feature Don Bluth has allowed his characters to look and behave a little more strangely. There is a lot of individualism in this movie, both in the filmmaking and in the characters themselves.

Bluth is the former Disney animator who led a group of artists away from the studio during its doldrums in 1979 and set up his own animation operation. His feature credits so far include *The Secret of NIMH,* the dinosaur adventure *The Land Before Time,* and *An American Tail*—the story of an immigrant mouse that set box-office records for an animated film. Now here he is with a fantasy about canine lowlife in New Orleans.

The movie involves the adventures of Charlie B. Barkin (who has not only the voice of Burt Reynolds but even some of the mannerisms). Barkin is a professional criminal who has teamed up in the past with a pit bull named Carface, but now Carface has Barkin rubbed out, and he finds himself in heaven, which should not be a surprise if he has read the title of his movie. Bent on revenge, Barkin returns to earth, and then the main story of the movie begins as he makes friends with a little girl who has an amazing knack for predicting winners out at the track.

The movie tells its story with several time-outs for song and dance numbers, notably one in which an alligator does an Esther Williams imitation. The plot is not particularly inventive (all but the younger viewers should be able to call most of the big surprises), but the style and tone of the movie are fresh. Although Walt Disney's very earliest movies had a lot of fun playing around with animation, most modern animated characters seem to come out of the same image bank. They look more or less like residents of the same reality level. What Bluth has done in *All Dogs Go to Heaven* is to allow the characters to be drawn in a more parodistic, even slightly bizarre way, so that their very shapes seem to change to echo their moods. It's fun.

All of Me ★ ★ ★ ½
PG, 93 m., 1984

Steve Martin (Roger Cobb), Lily Tomlin (Edwina Cutwater), Victoria Tennant (Terry Hoskins), Madolyn Smith (Peggy), Richard Libertini (Prahka Lasa), Jason Bernard (Tyrone Wattell). Directed by Carl Reiner. Screenplay by Phil Alden Robinson.

All of Me shares with a lot of great screwball comedies a very simple approach: Use absolute logic in dealing with the absurd. Begin with a nutty situation, establish the rules, and follow them. The laughs happen when ordinary human nature comes into conflict with ridiculous developments.

We can identify with almost all of the motives of the characters in *All of Me*. There is, for example, the millionaire spinster Edwina Cutwater (Lily Tomlin), who wants to live forever and thinks she has found a way to do that. There is the unhappy lawyer Roger Cobb (Steve Martin), who is desperately unhappy with his work and will do anything to get a promotion—even cater to nut-case clients like Edwina. There is the evil Terry Hoskins (Victoria Tennant), who plans to cruelly deceive Edwina, and there is the beatific Prahka Lasa (Richard Libertini), who hopes to transfer Edwina's soul into a brass pot, and then insert it in Miss Hos-

kins's body. There is, however, a terrible psychic miscalculation, and when Edwina dies, she transmigrates instead into Cobb's body. When I heard *All of Me* described, I couldn't think of any way this plot could possibly work. To begin with, why put one of my favorite comedians, Tomlin, inside Martin, a man whose movies I have not admired? And yet it does work. The moment it starts to work is the first time Martin has to deal with this alien female entity inside his brain. He retains control of the left side of his body. She controls the right. They are trying to cross the sidewalk together, each in their own way, and this sets up a manic tug-of-war that is one of the funniest scenes I've seen in a long time.

There are other great scenes, some of them probably obligatory, as when Martin has to go to the bathroom. The movie doesn't just go for obvious physical jokes, however; it scores a lot of points by speculating on the ways in which a man and a woman could learn to coexist in such close quarters. Against all the odds, a certain tenderness and sweetness develops by the end of the film. Although it is Tomlin who disappears into Martin's body, she does not disappear from the movie. For one thing, her reflection can be seen in mirrors, and there is some exquisite timing involved in the way they play scenes with each other's mirror images. For another thing (and this is really curious), there is a real sense of her presence even when Martin is alone on the screen: The film's premise, which seems so unlikely, begins to work.

The movie is filled with good supporting performances. My favorites are Richard Libertini, as the guru of transmigration, who speaks incomprehensible words in a tone of complete agreement, and Jason Bernard, as a black musician who is Martin's friend and partner during several tricky scenes of body-snatching and brain-grabbing. *All of Me* is in a class with *Ghostbusters*, and for some of the same reasons.

All the President's Men ★ ★ ★ ½
PG, 135 m., 1976

Robert Redford (Bob Woodward), Dustin Hoffman (Carl Bernstein), Jack Warden (Harry Rosenfeld), Martin Balsam (Howard Simons), Hal Holbrook (Deep Throat), Jason Robards (Ben Bradlee), Jane Alexander (Bookkeeper), Stephen Collins (Hugh Sloan), Robert Walden (Donald Segretti), Frank Wills (Frank Wills). Directed by Alan J. Pakula and produced by

Walter Coblenz. Screenplay by William Goldman.

All the President's Men is truer to the craft of journalism than to the art of storytelling, and that's its problem. The movie is as accurate about the processes used by investigative reporters as we have any right to expect, and yet process finally overwhelms narrative—we're adrift in a sea of names, dates, telephone numbers, coincidences, lucky breaks, false leads, dogged footwork, denials, evasions, and sometimes even the truth. Just such thousands of details led up to Watergate and the Nixon resignation, yes, but the movie's more about the details than about their results. That's not to say the movie isn't good at accomplishing what it sets out to do. It provides the most observant study of working journalists we're ever likely to see in a feature film (Bob Woodward and Carl Bernstein may at last, merciful God, replace Hildy Johnson and Walter Burns as career models). And it succeeds brilliantly in suggesting the mixture of exhilaration, paranoia, self-doubt, and courage that permeated the *Washington Post* as its two young reporters went after a presidency.

Newspaper movies always used to play up the excitement and ignore the boredom and the waiting. This one is all about the boredom and the waiting and the tireless digging; it depends on what we already know about Watergate to provide a level of excitement. And yet, given the fact that William Goldman's screenplay is almost all dialogue, almost exclusively a series of scenes of people talking (or not talking) to each other, director Alan J. Pakula has done a remarkable job of keeping the pace taut. Who'd have thought you could build tension with scenes where Bernstein walks over to Woodward's desk and listens in on the extension phone? But you can. And the movie's so well paced, acted, and edited that it develops the illusion of momentum even in the scenes where Woodward and Bernstein are getting doors slammed in their faces.

When Robert Redford announced that he'd bought the rights to *All the President's Men*, the joke in the newsroom was about reporters becoming movie stars. What in fact has happened is that the stars, Redford as Woodward and Dustin Hoffman as Bernstein, became reporters: They sink into their characters and become wholly credible. There's not a false or "Hollywood" note in the whole movie, and that's commendable—but how much authenticity will viewers settle for? To what secret and sneaky degree do they really want Redford and Hoffman to come on like stars?

There must have been a temptation to flesh out the Woodward and Bernstein characters, to change the pace with subplots about their private lives, but the film sticks resolutely to its subject. This is the story of a story: of two reporters starting with an apparently minor break-in and following it, almost incredulously at times, as it finally leads all the way to the White House. At times the momentum of Watergate seems to propel Woodward and Bernstein, instead of the other way around. It must have occasionally been like that at the time, and it's to the movie's credit that it doesn't force its characters into the center of every scene.

All the President's Men doesn't dwell on the private lives of its characters, but it does have a nice touch with their professional lives, and especially with their relationships with editors. The Watergate story started as a local story, not a national one, and it was a continuing thorn in the side of the *Post*'s prestigious national staff as Woodward and Bernstein kept it as their own. We meet the *Post* metro editor, Harry Rosenfeld (Jack Warden), defending and badgering "Woodstein" as the team came to be known. Martin Balsam plays Howard Simons, the managing editor, and Jason Robards is Benjamin Bradlee, the executive editor. All three are well cast; they may never have been in a newspaper office before, but they've learned the correct tone, they carry on a news conference as if they've held one before, and they even exhibit typical shadings of office fashion—the closer in time you are to having once covered a daily beat, the more you're permitted to loosen your tie and have baggy pants.

The movie has dozens of smaller character roles, for all the people who talked to Woodstein, or who refused to, and there's one cameo from real life: Frank Wills, the Watergate guard who found the fateful tape on the lock, plays himself. Some of the other roles tend to blend into one faceless Source, but Robert Walden makes a memorable Donald Segretti, playing the "dirty tricks" expert with bravado shading into despair. And two of the key informants are portrayed in interestingly different ways. Jane Alexander is a bookkeeper who gives the team some of their best leads, and is plain, honest, and scared; Hal Holbrook, as the mysterious "Deep Throat," the source inside the administration, is disturbingly detached, almost as if he's observing the events with a hollow laugh.

All of these elements in *All the President's Men* are to be praised, and yet they don't quite add up to a satisfying movie experience. Once we've seen one cycle of investigative reporting, once Woodward and Bernstein have cracked the first wall separating the break-in from the White House, we understand the movie's method. We don't need to see the reporting cycle repeated several more times just because the story grows longer and the sources more important. For all of its technical skill, the movie essentially shows us the same journalistic process several times as it leads closer and closer to an nd we already know. The film is long, and would be dull if it weren't for the wizardry of Pakula, his actors, and technicians. What saves it isn't the power of narrative but the success of technique. Still, considering the compromises that could have been made, considering the phony "newspaper movie" this could have been, maybe that's almost enough.

All the Right Moves ★ ★ ★
R, 91 m., 1983

Tom Cruise (Stef), Craig T. Nelson (Nickerson), Lea Thompson (Lisa). Directed by Michael Chapman and produced by Stephen Deutsch. Screenplay by Michael Kane.

I started on newspapers as a sportswriter, covering local high school teams. That was a long time ago, and I had almost forgotten, until I saw *All the Right Moves*, how desperately important every game seemed at the time. When the team members and the fans are all teen-agers, and when a school victory reflects in a significant way upon your own feelings of worth, when "We won!" means that we won, a football game can take on aspects of Greek tragedy.

All the Right Moves remembers the strength of those feelings, but does not sentimentalize them. The movie stars Tom Cruise (from *Risky Business*) as a high school football player in a small Pennsylvania mill town where unemployment is a way of life. His ticket out of town is a football scholarship to a good engineering school. The high school football coach (Craig T. Nelson) also is looking for a ticket, to an assistant coaching job in a college. On the night of the big game, these two people get into a position where each one seems to have destroyed the hopes of the other.

The movie plays this conflict against an interesting background. This isn't another high school movie with pompon girls and funny principals and weirdo chem teachers. The movie gets into the dynamics of the high school student body and into the tender, complicated relationship between the Cruise character and his girlfriend (Lea Thompson).

After all the junk high school movies in which kids chop each other up, seduce the French teacher, and visit whorehouses in Mexico, it is so wonderful to see a movie that remembers that most teen-agers are vulnerable, unsure, sincere, and fundamentally decent. The kid, his girlfriend, and all of their friends have feelings we can recognize as real. The plot feels real, too, because it centers around those kinds of horrible misunderstandings and mistakes that we all remember from high school. A lot of teenagers walk around all day feeling guilty, even if they're totally innocent. Get them into a situation that gives them the appearance of guilt and they're in trouble. And it is so easy to get into trouble when you are old enough to do wrong but too young to know independently to avoid it. A lot of kids who say they were only along for the ride are telling the simple truth.

The movie frames the Cruise character in a situation like that, one we can identify with. And then it does an interesting thing. Instead of solving the problem with a plot twist, it solves it through the exercise of genuine human honesty: Two people finally tell each other the truth. This is, of course, an astonishing breakthrough in movies about teen-agers, and *All the Right Moves* deserves credit for that achievement.

All the Vermeers in New York ★ ★ ★
NO MPAA RATING, 87 m., 1992

Emmanuelle Chaulet (Anna), Stephen Lack (Mark), Grace Phillips (Felicity), Gracie Mansion (Herself), Gordon Joseph Weiss (Gordon), Laurel Lee Kiefer (Ariel Ainsworth), Roger Ruffin (Max), Katherine Bean (Nicole). Directed by Jon Jost and produced by Henry S. Rosenthal. Screenplay by Jost.

The woman pauses before a painting by Vermeer, and looks closely at it—seems ready almost to disappear into it. The man observes her. He follows her from one room in the museum to another. Then back again. It is a quiet, subtle chase, something like the long opening sequence of Brian De Palma's *Dressed to Kill*, but this is not a thriller; it's a strange, introspective cat-and-mouse game by Jon Jost, whose *All the Vermeers in New York* is the kind of film you have to think and think about, and then finally you realize you admire it.

The man approaches the woman. He is very polite. He cannot help but observe that she herself looks like the subject of a painting by Vermeer. He would like to see her again. She agrees. We see something of her life. She is French, lives with two other women, shares with one roommate an annoyance that the other one rehearses opera all day long. It is impossible to think with such a noise. They gang up on her.

The man works in the trading room of a big brokerage. Some days go well. Some days go badly. He has a laconic, flat, ironic way of talking into the phone, especially as he is consulting with customers over whether they want to bail out of bad investments. He meets the girl and her roommate. They talk. He gets her alone on their next date, and begins to feel they may have a future together. She doesn't think that way. She propositions him rather boldly for "rent money," which he hands her in cash.

And then . . . but I cannot tell you what happens next, except to say that it is arbitrary and maddening, although no more so than everyday life. The film reminds us that most fiction movies have a very narrow range of action, because they permit the characters to do only what is more or less expected.

When *All the Vermeers in New York* was over, I stayed for a moment in my seat, because I didn't feel as if the film had ended. It got me involved, it got me intrigued, and my interior clock estimated that it would take another thirty minutes to conclude. And then it stopped. I thought for a time that I didn't approve of that, but now I'm over my frustration and I can see what Jost was doing. He has a conclusion, all right; just not the conventional three-point landing that Hollywood has taught us to expect.

The movie takes place in the world of Manhattan art galleries and lofts and roommates struggling to live in a rich world on no money. It also takes place in a world of ideas. The stock trader (Stephen Lack) is in love not with the woman before him, but with his idea of her; he loves her because he loves Vermeer more. The young woman (Emmanuelle Chaulet, from Rohmer's *Boyfriends and Girlfriends*) is so absorbed in her own life that she can hardly be bothered. Their relationship is so superficial and trivial that the concluding scene comes as an affront: What happens when you have to treat a relative stranger as if she were your closest—your only—friend?

Jon Jost has been making films since 1974, at first with the antiwar collective Newsreel. I've seen only a few of his films, and thought of him as an "underground" filmmaker, if that word still has any meaning. But this film, beautifully photographed and acted with calm grace, is frankly aimed at the commercial theatrical market; in approach and subject matter, he falls somewhere between Woody Allen's noncomedies and Eric Rohmer. If *All the Vermeers in New York* had been in French with subtitles, I would have known right away what to expect. It's unusual to find a film this brainy in English.

Altered States ★ ★ ★ ½
R, 103 m., 1980

William Hurt (Eddie Jessup), Blair Brown (Emily Jessup), Bob Balaban (Arthur Rosenberg), Charles Haid (Mason Parrish), Thaao Penghlis (Eccheverria), Miguel Godreau (Primal Man). Directed by Ken Russell and produced by Howard Gottfried. Screenplay by Sidney Aaron.

Altered States is one hell of a movie—literally. It hurls its characters headlong back through billions of years to the moment of creation and finds nothing there except an anguished scream of "No!" as the life force protests its moment of birth. And then, through the power of the human ego to insist on its own will even in the face of the implacable indifference of the universe, it turns "No!" into "Yes!" and ends with the basic scene in all drama, the man and the woman falling into each other's arms.

But hold on just a second here: I'm beginning to sound like the movie's characters, a band of overwrought pseudo-intellectuals who talk like a cross between Werner Erhard, Freud, and Tarzan. Some of the movie's best dialogue passages are deliberately staged with everybody talking at once: It doesn't matter what they're saying, only that they're incredibly serious about it. I can tell myself intellectually that this movie is a fiendishly constructed visual and verbal roller coaster, a movie deliberately intended to overwhelm its audiences with sensual excess. I know all that, and yet I *was* overwhelmed, I *was* caught up in its headlong energy.

Is that a worthy accomplishment for a movie? Yes, I suppose it is, if the movie earns it by working as hard as *Altered States* does. This is, at last, the movie that Ken Russell was born to direct—the same Ken Russell whose wretched excesses in the past include

The Music Lovers, The Devils, and *Lisztomania.* The formula is now clear. Take Russell's flair for visual pyrotechnics and apocalyptic sexuality, and channel it through just enough scientific mumbo jumbo to give it form. The result may be totally meaningless, but while you're watching it you are not concerned.

The movie is based on a Paddy Chayevsky novel, which was, in turn, inspired by the experiments of Dr. John Lilly, the man who placed his human subjects in total immersion tanks—floating them in total darkness so that their minds, cut off from all external reality, could play along the frontiers of sanity. In *Altered States,* William Hurt plays a Harvard scientist named Jessup who takes such an experiment one step further, by ingesting a drug made from the sacred hallucinatory mushrooms of a primitive tribe. The strange thing about these mushrooms, Hurt observes in an easily missed line of dialogue in the movie, is that they give everyone who takes them the same hallucinatory vision. Perhaps it is our cellular memory of creation: There is chaos, and then a ball of light, and then the light turns into a crack, and the crack opens onto Nothing, and that is all there was and all there will be, except for life, which has its only existence in the mind.

Got that? It hardly matters. It is a breathtaking concept, but *Altered States* hardly slows down for it. This is the damnedest movie to categorize. Just when it begins to sound like a 1960s psychedelic fantasy, a head trip—it turns into a farce. The scientist immerses himself in his tank for too long, he regresses to a simian state, physically turns into some kind of ape, attacks the campus security guards, is chased by a pack of wild dogs into the local zoo, and kills and eats a sheep for his supper before turning *back* into the kindly Professor Jessup, the Intellectual Hulk.

The movie splits up into three basic ingredients: The science, the special effects, and the love relationship between the professor and his wife. The science is handled deliciously well. We learn as much as we need to (that is, next to nothing) about total immersion, genetics, and the racial memory. Then come the special effects, in four long passages and a few short bursts. They're good. They may remind you at times of the sound-and-light extravaganza toward the end of 2001, but they are also supposed to evoke the birth of the universe in a pulsating celestial ovum. In the center of this vision is

Dr. Jessup, his body pulsing in and out of an apeshape, his mouth pulled into an anguished "O" as he protests the hell of being born. These scenes are reinforced by the music and are obviously intended to fuel the chemically altered consciousness of the next generation of movie cultists.

But then there is the matter of the love relationship between the professor and his wife (Blair Brown), and it is here that we discover how powerful the attraction of love really is. During the professor's last experiment, when he is disappearing into a violent whirlpool of light and screams on the laboratory floor, it is his wife who wades into the celestial mists, gets up to her knees in eternity, reaches in, and pulls him out. And this is despite the fact that he has filed for divorce. The last scene is a killer, with the professor turning into the protoplasm of life itself, and his wife turning into a glowing shell of rock-like flesh, with her inner fires glowing through the crevices (the effect is something like an overheated Spiderman). They're going through the unspeakable hell of reliving the First Moment, and yet as the professor, as Man, bangs on the walls and crawls toward her, and she reaches out, and the universe rocks, the Man within him bursts out of the ape-protoplasm, and the Woman within her explodes back into flesh, and they collapse into each other's arms, and all the scene really needs at that point is for him to ask, "Was it as good for you as it was for me?"

Altered States is a superbly silly movie, a magnificent entertainment, and a clever and brilliant machine for making us feel awe, fear, and humor. That is enough. It's pure movie and very little meaning. Did I like it? Yeah, I guess I did, but I wouldn't advise trying to think about it very deeply.

Always ★ ★
PG, 121 m., 1989

Richard Dreyfuss (Pete Sandich), Holly Hunter (Dorinda Durston), Brad Johnson (Ted Baker), John Goodman (Al Yackey), Audrey Hepburn (Hap), Roberts Blossom (Dave), Keith David (Powerhouse), Ed Van Nuys (Nails), Marg Helgenberger (Rachel). Directed by Steven Spielberg and produced by Spielberg, Frank Marshall, and Kathleen Kennedy. Screenplay by Jerry Belson.

Sometimes there are movies that strike you in a certain way, that haunt your memory and provide some of the terms with which you view your own life. For Steven Spielberg and Richard Dreyfuss *A Guy Named Joe* must have been a movie like that. Released in 1944, it starred Spencer Tracy as a pilot who dies in combat and is assigned by heaven to return to earth to inspire the younger pilot (Van Johnson) who will take his place. The kicker is that Tracy also has to stand by helplessly and watch while Johnson falls in love with Tracy's girlfriend (Irene Dunne).

Richard Dreyfuss says he has seen *A Guy Named Joe* at least thirty-five times. Steven Spielberg watched it again and again on the late show when he was a kid, and it was one of the films that inspired him to become a movie director. When Spielberg and Dreyfuss were making *Jaws* in 1974, they quoted individual shots from the movie to each other, and finally, in 1989, they got to make it themselves. The remake is called *Always*, and it takes place now instead of then, and the pilots are fighting forest fires instead of enemy planes, but the basic ideas are all still in place. They do not, unfortunately, add up to much; this is Spielberg's weakest film since *1941*.

Dreyfuss stars as a guy named Pete, who fights fires in the Pacific Northwest and spends his off-duty hours romancing a cute forest service air traffic controller played by Holly Hunter. Pete is a guy who likes to take chances, and there are cliff-hanging scenes early in the movie where he runs out of gas and glides to a landing and another when he nearly crashes into a blazing forest fire. His best pal is a pilot named Al (John Goodman), who also likes to take chances and crashes into some burning trees one day, setting his plane on fire. Pete the daredevil goes into a dive and puts out the fire on Goodman's plane by dumping chemicals all over it, but then Pete's own plane crashes, and he wakes up in a heavenly forest grove presided over by an angel (Audrey Hepburn).

That sets up the second act of the movie, in which poor Pete has to come back to earth and be an invisible inspiration for the youngster (Brad Johnson) who has replaced him. And he has to watch, impotently, as the kid and Pete's former girl fall in love. There is a lot of pathos to be exploited here somewhere, but I didn't feel much; my reaction to this version resembled the critic James Agee's merciless review of the 1944 film, which he admired a good deal less than Spielberg and Dreyfuss. "Joe's affability in the afterlife is enough to discredit the very idea that death in combat amounts to anything more than getting a freshly pressed uniform," he wrote, adding that Tracy "is so unconcerned as he watches Van Johnson palpitate after Irene Dunne that he hardly bothers to take the gum out of his mouth."

One of the problems with *Always* is that the cause itself seems less urgent. It's one thing to sacrifice your life for a buddy in combat and quite another to run unnecessary risks while fighting forest fires. Another problem seems to stem from Spielberg's love of spectacular special effects. The airplanes in this movie—World War II surplus bombers modified to dump chemicals on fires—seem to crash and bludgeon their way through acres of blazing treetops. You'd think a collision with just one of these trees would cause a plane to crash, but the fire fighters in *Always* mow through the woods like airborne Lawnboys. The effects are so spectacular they're not believable. All the movie's risks seem to be the same—laughable.

The best casting in the movie is Holly Hunter, as the air traffic controller, bringing some of the same urgency and hard-bitten impatience that made her right for *Broadcast News*. She has a no-nonsense approach that works better than the derring-do and unflappability of Dreyfuss and Goodman. The scenes where the angelic Dreyfuss watches while Hunter and Johnson fall in love are the most awkward in the film; the screenplay gives Dreyfuss flip lines like "That's my girl, pal!" when maybe a hurt look or a silent turn away would have been more effective.

The film's most curious quality, given the fact that it was directed by Spielberg, is a lack of urgency. Even though pilots are flying into the jaws of hell, they have an insouciance, a devil-may-care attitude, that undermines the drama. The feeling of the film is more 1940s than 1980s, which is no doubt what Spielberg was hoping for, but I'm not sure it works. Some of the dialogue seems dated, too, and a lot of it sounds "written" instead of "spoken"—as if these guys learned to talk by studying old pulp magazines. The result is a curiosity: a remake that wasn't remade enough.

Amadeus ★ ★ ★ ★
PG, 158 m., 1984

F. Murray Abraham (Salieri), Tom Hulce (Mozart), Elizabeth Berridge (Constanze), Simon Callow (Emanuel Schikaneder), Roy Dotrice (Leopold Mozart), Christine Ebersole (Katerina Cavalieri), Jeffrey Jones (Joseph II). Directed by Milos Forman and produced by Saul Zaentz. Screenplay by Peter Shaffer.

Milos Forman's *Amadeus* is one of the riskiest gambles a filmmaker has taken in a long time—a lavish movie about Mozart that dares to be anarchic and saucy, and yet still earns the importance of tragedy. This movie is nothing like the dreary educational portraits we're used to seeing about the Great Composers, who come across as cobwebbed profundities weighed down with the burden of genius. This is Mozart as an eighteenth-century Bruce Springsteen, and yet (here is the genius of the movie) there is nothing cheap or unworthy about the approach. *Amadeus* is not only about as much fun as you're likely to have with a movie, it also is disturbingly true. The truth enters in the character of Salieri, who tells the story. He is not a great composer, but he is a good enough composer to know greatness when he hears it, and that is why the music of Mozart breaks his heart. He knows how good it is, he sees how easily Mozart seems to compose it, and he knows that his own work looks pale and silly beside it.

The movie begins with the suggestion that Salieri might have murdered Mozart. The movie examines the ways in which this possibility might be true, and by the end of the film we feel a certain kinship with the weak and jealous Salieri—for few of us can identify with divine genius, but many of us probably have had dark moments of urgent self-contempt in the face of those whose effortless existence illustrates our own inadequacies. Salieri, played with burning intensity by F. Murray Abraham, sits hunched in a madhouse confessing to a priest. The movie flashes back to his memories of Wolfgang Amadeus Mozart, the child genius who composed melodies of startling originality and who grew up to become a prolific, driven artist.

One of the movie's wisest decisions is to cast Mozart not as a charismatic demigod, not as a tortured superman, but as a goofy, immature, likable kid with a ridiculous laugh. The character is played by Tom Hulce, and if you saw *Animal House,* you may remember him as the fraternity brother who tried to seduce the mayor's daughter, while an angel and a devil whispered in his ears. Hulce would seem all wrong for Mozart, but he is absolutely right, as an unaffected young man filled with delight at his own gifts, unaware of how easily he wounds Salieri and others, tortured only by the guilt of having offended his religious and domineering father.

The film is constructed in wonderfully well-written and acted scenes—scenes so carefully constructed, unfolding with such delight, that they play as perfect compositions of words. Most of them will be unfamiliar to those who have seen Peter Shaffer's brooding play, on which this film is based; Shaffer and Forman have brought light, life, and laughter to the material, and it plays with grace and ease. It's more human than the play; the characters are people, not throbbing packages of meaning. It centers on the relationships in Mozart's life: with his father, his wife, and Salieri. The father never can be pleased, and that creates an undercurrent affecting all of Mozart's success. The wife, played by delightful, buxom Elizabeth Berridge, contains in one person the qualities of a jolly wench and a loving partner: She likes to loll in bed all day, but also gives Mozart good, sound advice and is a forceful person in her own right. The patrons, especially Joseph II, the Austro-Hungarian emperor, are connoisseurs and dilettantes, slow to take to Mozart's new music but enchanted by the audacity with which he defends it. And then there is Salieri (F. Murray Abraham), the gaunt court composer whose special torture is to understand better than anybody else how inadequate he is, and how great Mozart is.

The movie was shot on location in Forman's native Czechoslovakia, and it looks exactly right; it fits its period comfortably, perhaps because Prague still contains so many streets and squares and buildings that could be directly from the Vienna of Mozart's day. Perhaps his confidence in his locations gave Forman the freedom to make Mozart slightly *out* of period. Forman directed the film version of *Hair,* and Mozart in this movie seems to share a spirit with some of the characters from *Hair.* Mozart's wigs do not look like everybody else's. They have just the slightest suggestion of punk, just the smallest shading of pink. Mozart seems more a child of the 1960s than of any other age, and this interpretation of his personality—he was an irreverent proto-hippie who trusted, if you will, his own vibes—sounds risky, but works.

I have not mentioned the music. There's probably no need to. The music provides the understructure of the film, strong, confident, above all, *clear* in a way that Salieri's simple muddles only serve to illustrate. There are times when Mozart speaks the words of a child, but then the music says the same things in the language of the gods, and all is clear.

Amadeus is a magnificent film, full and tender and funny and charming—and, at the end, sad and angry, too, because in the character of Salieri it has given us a way to understand not only greatness, but our own lack of it. This movie's fundamental question, I think, is whether we can learn to be grateful for the happiness of others, and that, of course, is a test for sainthood. How many movies ask such questions and succeed in being fun, as well?

Amarcord ★ ★ ★ ★
R, 127 m., 1974

Magali Noel (Gradisca), Bruno Zamin (Titta), Pupella Maggio (His Mother), Armando Drancia (His Father), Giuseppe Lanigro (His Grandfather), Nando Orfei (Pataca), Chiccio Ingrassia (Uncle Teo), Luigi Rossi (Lawyer). Directed by Federico Fellini and produced by Iranco Cristaldi. Screenplay by Fellini.

Federico Fellini's *Amarcord* takes us back to the small Italian town of his birth and young manhood, and gives us a joyful, bawdy, virtuoso portrait of the people he remembers there. He includes a character undoubtedly meant to be young Federico—earnest, awkward, yearning with all the poignancy of adolescent lust after the town beauties. But the movie's not an autobiography of a character. It's the story of the town itself.

We see it first when the dandelion seeds blow in from the fields, signaling the arrival of spring. The townspeople gather in the piazza to build a ceremonial bonfire and burn the witch of winter, and as they dance around the flames in one of Fellini's beloved processions, we get to know them.

They're of all sizes, sexes, and ages, but they're bound together by their transparent simplicity and a strain of cheerful vulgarity. Fellini likes their weaknesses as much as their virtues, and gives us the pompous lawyer, the egotistical theater owner (who cultivates a resemblance to Ronald Colman), the buxom beautician Gradisca flaunting her delightful derriere, and especially the lustful adolescents and their tormenting fantasies.

Fellini also gives us, in a much more subtle way, some notion of the way fascist Italy of the early 1930s helped to shape these people. In an authoritarian system, the individual has fewer choices to make, and there's a temptation to surrender the responsibilities of freedom. The townspeople are almost children in their behavior, taking delight in the simple joys of eating and making love and parading around the square and gossiping about each other and about the hypnotic Gradisca. Fellini implies that this simple behavior is nourished by a system that encourages a mindless going along—but *Amarcord* isn't a political movie. It is a memory, fond but merciless, of how it was in Italy at a certain time.

It's also absolutely breathtaking filmmaking. Fellini has ranked for a long time among the five or six greatest directors in the world, and of them all, he's the natural. Bergman achieves his greatness through thought and soul-searching, Hitchcock built with meticulous craftsmanship, and Bunuel used his fetishes and fantasies to construct barbed jokes about humanity. But Fellini . . . well, moviemaking for him seems almost effortless, like breathing, and he can orchestrate the most complicated scenes with purity and ease. He's the Willie Mays of movies.

He did hit upon hard critical times, though. After the towering success of *La Dolce Vita* and *8½*, and such 1950s landmarks as *La Strada* and *I Vitelloni*, he began to indulge himself (his critics said). *Juliet of the Spirits* was too fantastical and structureless, and *Satyricon* was an exercise in excess, and *The Clowns* was really only a TV show, and *Fellini Roma* was episodic—a great director spinning out sequences that contained brilliance, yes, but no purpose or direction.

I couldn't agree with those criticisms. I find Fellini's magic spellbinding even when he's only marking time, as he was to some extent in *Roma*. But now, with *Amarcord*, Fellini returns to the very top of his form. And he has the last laugh on the critics of his "structureless" films. Because *Amarcord* seems at first to be a series of self-contained episodes and then reveals a structure so organic and yet so effortless that at its end, we can only marvel at this triumph over ordinary movie forms.

And we can marvel, too, at how universal *Amarcord* is. This is a movie for everybody, even those who hardly ever see foreign or "art" films. Fellini's greatest achievement, in my opinion, was *8½*. But that was a difficult film that revealed its meaning only after a good deal of thought and repeated viewings. *Amarcord*, on the other hand, is a totally accessible film. It deals directly, hilariously, and sometimes poignantly with the good people of this small town (actually Fellini's birthplace, Rimini). It's no more complicated than they are, it understands them inside-out, and the audiences I've seen it with (three times) have been moved to horselaughs, stilled

by moments of beauty, and then brought back almost to tears. It's not only a great movie, it's a great joy to see.

Someone once remarked that Fellini's movies are filled with symbols, but they're all obvious symbols. At the beginning of *La Dolce Vita*, for example, he wanted to symbolize the gulf between modern, decadent Rome and its history as the center of the Church, so he gave a statue of Christ being helicoptered by pilots who wave and whistle at girls sunning themselves in bikinis. The scene says everything it needs to say, openly and with great economy.

Amarcord is obvious in that way, with a showman's flair for the right effect. There is a night, for example, when all the people of the town get into their boats and sail out to wait for the great new Italian liner to pass by. And when it comes, it towers hundreds of feet above the waves and has thousands of portholes—and is, of course, only a prop built by the special-effects men. It drifts away into invisibility like a candle dying out. The image is of Italy itself in the 1930s: all grandeur and pomp and nationalism, but with an insubstantial soul.

The movie is filled with moments like that, and they're just right. But then there are moments of inexplicable, almost mystical beauty, as when the dandelion seeds drift in on the wind, or when an old lady sweeps up the ashes of the bonfire, or when a peacock spreads its tail feathers in the snow. At moments like that we're almost blinded with delight. Hitchcock once said he wanted to play his audiences like a piano. Fellini requires the entire orchestra.

Amateur ★ ★ ½
R, 105 m., 1995 | NEW |

Isabelle Huppert (Isabelle), Martin Donovan (Thomas), Elina Lowensohn (Sofia), Damian Young (Edward), Chuck Montgomery (Jan), David Simonds (Kurt), Pamela Stewart (Officer Melville), Erica Gimpel (Irate Woman). Directed by Hal Hartley and produced by Ted Hope and Hartley. Screenplay by Hartley.

Hal Hartley makes movies that take place resolutely in the real world, insisting on their flat, realistic dialogue and deadpan characters even while the story line takes flight for the far shores of fancy. If you were to watch *Amateur*, his new film, without being able to hear the dialogue, you would think it was a slice of life about urban crime and isolation. The sights on the screen would seem reason-

able enough, and you would assume the characters existed in some kind of plausible movie universe.

You would be wrong. In a Hartley film, the plot gradually unfolds to reveal bizarre secrets and unexpected relationships, and the characters usually have two conflicting identity tags: pro baseball player and murderer, for example, or friendly garage mechanic and serial killer. In *Amateur*, there is an ex-nun who is a pornographer. It almost goes without saying that she's also a nymphomaniac . . . and a virgin.

The character, named Isabelle, is played by Isabelle Huppert. We see her first in a coffee shop, where she occupies the same booth hour after hour, writing pornography on her portable computer. Later, another character not unreasonably asks her, "How can you be a nymphomaniac and never have sex?" She looks back with those big, grave eyes and says, "I'm choosy."

The movie has started with a man lying apparently dead in the street. Later he staggers into the coffee shop and tries to spend Dutch money, although from his words we can tell he's an American. "Do you smoke?" he is asked. "I don't know," he says. He has amnesia after a nasty fall from an upper window.

He looks like an agreeable, regular kind of guy, and is played by Martin Donovan, one of Hartley's favorite actors, who is as cleancut as a dad in a 1950s sitcom. Of course he harbors nasty secrets, and later a woman named Sofia (Elina Lowensohn) will explain that he got her hooked on drugs when she was twelve, married her, made her appear in porno films, and threatened to disfigure her. That's when she pushed him out the window.

Who is this man? Huppert invites him back to her tiny flat, talks about herself, and gets involved in trying to re-create his past. Other characters turn up: an arms dealer, and the porno publisher who pays Huppert for her stories. I was going to say none of these people are quite as they seem, but actually, they are: What happens in a Hartley movie is not that people reveal surprises about themselves, but that they surprise themselves, by changing their natures.

It's as if all the characters are a little dazed—by a blow on the head, say—and have awakened to find themselves assigned names and identities, which they dutifully try to portray, until their heads clear and choices become visible. They realize that nothing in their lives is obligatory, and that they have the freedom to become someone else, completely.

Isabelle has already exercised that freedom by leaving the convent and starting to write dirty books, although we will discover that her motives for both actions are far from what we might guess. Now Thomas (the Martin Donovan character) and Sofia can both be emboldened by Isabelle into reinventing themselves.

But what is Hartley up to? Having seen four of his films, I think he wants to free himself of the lockstep tyranny of traditional plots, where characters are assigned names and personalities, choose up sides, and struggle for two hours. The audience knows who it likes and who it hates and can guess what will happen, and is essentially bored, although it may not realize it. In a Hartley film you are not bored, although you may grow disinterested when you see that his manipulations are as arbitrary, in their way, as old-fashioned plots.

Several directors seem to be experimenting with new ways of assembling the old pieces of familiar movie landscapes: Hartley joins Atom Egoyan, Milcho Manchevski, Krzysztof Kieslowski, Quentin Tarantino, and David Lynch, among others. Maybe something is happening here. I've received some e-mail about a guy who has identified a "nine-act structure" that he says is followed by every single one of the one hundred most successful films of all times. Hartley and these other guys would like to take all nine acts and shove them where the movies don't play.

In the meantime, is *Amateur*, ah . . . a good movie? Worth seeing? I found the idea of the plot more interesting than the plot itself, and am finding the movie more fun to write about than to see. I find myself applauding Hartley more than his movie. He's on an intriguing journey. The scenery may grow more interesting.

American Dream ★ ★ ★ ★
NO MPAA RATING, 100 m., 1992

A documentary directed by Barbara Kopple and produced by Kopple and Arthur Cohn. Edited by Cathy Caplan, Tom Haneke, and Lawrence Silk.

In 1984 the Hormel meat-packing company offered its Austin, Minnesota, union workers a new contract in which their wage would be cut from $10.69 to $8.25 an hour, and other benefits would be cut by 30 percent. The workers were not overjoyed. The company had just declared an annual profit of $29 million, and the cuts seemed inspired by a management desire to maximize profits at the cost of any other consideration. In the climate of the times—shortly after Reagan had fired all of the striking air controllers—a strike seemed like a dangerous risk, but the meat packers of local P-9 in Austin walked out.

Their decision and its repercussions are the subject of *American Dream*, the documentary by Barbara Kopple that won a 1991 Academy Award. This is the kind of movie you watch with horrified fascination, as families lose their incomes and homes, management plays macho hardball, and rights and wrongs grow hopelessly tangled.

Kopple is the woman who went to Kentucky to document a bitter miner's strike in *Harlan County, U.S.A.*, one of the best documentaries I have ever seen. That strike offered clear-cut choices between good and evil. The Hormel strike, which she follows as it spans long, agonizing months and years, weaves a more tangled web. The local union, which has decided to act independently from its parent international union in Washington, hires a free-lance strike consultant named Ray Rogers, who comes in with charts, graphs, and promises of national press attention. He delivers, but at the cost of denying local P-9 the experienced negotiating skills that the international could have supplied.

After P-9's campaign is under way and its position has solidified, the international sends in Lewis Anderson, an experienced negotiator who despairs at the naïveté of the locals. "They made the critical mistake of opening up the whole contract," Anderson says despairingly at one moment. "That allows the company the chance to renegotiate language it took us forty years to win."

Anderson, a chain-smoking everyman with the weary charisma of a Lech Walesa, wants to compromise with Hormel, and arrive at a new contract. The P-9 militants, fired up by Rogers and by their local president, Jim Guyette, want no compromise. They want their $10.69 an hour or else. The company locks out the striking workers and eventually begins to hire replacements, while some dissident local members break away from P-9 and side with Anderson. The international in Washington eventually declares the strike illegal, siezes control of P-9, and negotiates its own deal with Hormel. But the majority of P-9 members remain loyal to the strike, and eventually some 80 percent of them lose their jobs.

The outcome is even more complicated than that. Although Hormel negotiates a compromise wage with the union, it soon closes down half the plant and then rents it to another meat packer who pays $6.50 an hour. As *American Dream* documents these developments, we are torn two ways. We want to see the movie as a battle between right and wrong, good and evil. On the other hand, we also see it as a struggle between two strategies. Would P-9 have been luckier if it had never heard of Ray Rogers and his consulting wizardry, and allowed Lewis Anderson to negotiate a settlement? Or would Hormel have shut down half its plant anyway, in a transparent move to allow the $6.50 operation?

One of the key issues in *American Dream* is the legality of employers who hire permanent replacements for workers who are engaged in a legal strike. Some companies are so cocksure these days that they hire replacements and, if found in violation of labor laws, are happy to pay a fine. They're millions ahead in the long run. In a climate of high unemployment and White House hostility to unions, there are always a lot of workers only too glad to take someone else's job.

The people in this film are so real they make most movie characters look like inhabitants of the funny page. Families are torn apart. One brother goes back to work; another stays on the picket lines. Workers have tears in their eyes as they describe not being able to support their families. It becomes clear that no possible win by the members of P-9 could compensate them for the wages they have already lost—especially as they are striking, not for a raise, but against a pay cut. A nobility creeps onto the scene, as people make enormous financial and personal sacrifices simply for what they believe is morally right. Our hearts are torn, because on the basis of this film we are not sure they have chosen the wisest path.

Stories like the Hormel strike are too long and complicated to be told on a daily basis. Newspapers and TV newscasts are, by their nature, focused on the events of the day—or the week or month at the longest. How can they make sense of a strike that drags on forever, with conflicting loyalties and strategies? Only a documentary like this has a canvas big enough for the whole picture.

Is there a lesson at the end of *American Dream*? I think there is. I think the lesson is that the American tradition of collective bargaining will break down if companies can simply ignore a legal strike, hire replacements, and continue as before. There was a time in American history when such behavior by management would have been seen as not only illegal but immoral. The new management philosophers who won ascendency in the 1980s dismiss such views as sentimentalism. They are concerned only with the bottom line, where they see profits, not people. The White House announced that for a 1992 overseas trip, the video library on *Air Force One* was stocked with *Gone With the Wind*. Next flight, could they take along *American Dream*?

American Gigolo ★ ★ ★ ½
R, 117 m., 1980

Richard Gere (Julian), Lauren Hutton (Michelle), Hector Elizondo (Sunday), Nina Van Pallandt (Anne), Bill Duke (Leon Jaimes), Brian Davies (Stratton). Directed by Paul Schrader and produced by Jerry Bruckheimer. Screenplay by Schrader.

The bare outline of its plot makes *American Gigolo* sound like a fairly sleazy package: A Hollywood male prostitute is framed in a kinky murder case, tracks down the pimp who's responsible for the framing, watches in horror as the pimp himself is killed, and then finds himself faced with prison unless the wife of a senator provides him with an alibi. This is strong stuff—almost sensational enough for daytime soap opera.

But the film *American Gigolo* is a stylish and surprisingly poignant handling of this material. The experiences in the film may be alien to us, but the emotions of the characters are not: Julian Kay, the gigolo of the title, is played by Richard Gere as tender, vulnerable, and a little dumb. We care about him. His business—making love to rich women of a certain age—allows him to buy the baubles by which Beverly Hills measures success, and he has his Mercedes, his expensive wardrobe, his antique vases, his entrée to country clubs.

But he says he's in business for reasons other than money, and we believe him, if only because he hardly seems to value his possessions as anything other than props. He feels a sense of satisfaction when he makes a middle-aged woman happy, he says. He seems to see himself as a cross between a sexual surrogate and a therapist, and the movie does,

too: Why, he's hardly a whore at all, not even counting his heart of gold.

The movie sentimentalizes on this point, setting up the character of Julian Kay as so sympathetic that we forgive him his profession. That's a tactic that *American Gigolo's* writer and director, Paul Schrader, is borrowing from one of his own heroes, the French director Robert Bresson, whose *Pickpocket* makes a criminal into an antihero. Schrader is setting the stage for the key relationship in the film, between Julian and the senator's wife (Lauren Hutton).

He tries to pick her up in an exclusive restaurant, but breaks off their conversation when he decides she's not a likely client. But she is all *too* likely, and tracks him down to his apartment. They fall in love, at about the time he's being framed for the murder of a Palm Springs socialite, and the movie wants us to believe in the power of love to redeem both characters: Julian learns to love unselfishly, without money, and the woman learns to love honestly, without regard for her husband's position.

This business of redemption would work better if *American Gigolo* had at least a few more scenes developing the relationship between Gere and Hutton: Her character, so central to the movie's upbeat conclusion, isn't seen clearly enough. We aren't shown the steps by which she moves from sex to love with him (unless she's simply been won over by the old earth-shaking orgasm ploy). We aren't given enough detail about their feelings.

That's a weakness, but not a fatal one, because when Schrader cuts away from their relationship, it's to develop a very involving story about the murder, the framing, and the police investigation. The movie has an especially effective performance by Hector Elizondo as a cigar-chomping vice detective who cheerfully admits he thinks Gere is guilty as sin.

Gere tries to find out who's framing him by descending into the Los Angeles sexual underground. Schrader explored this same universe in his previous film, *Hardcore*, but this time he seems more restrained: The sexual netherlands seem less lurid, more commonplace and sad.

The whole movie has a winning sadness about it; take away the story's sensational aspects and what you have is a study in loneliness. Richard Gere's performance is central to that effect, and some of his scenes—reading the morning paper, rearranging some

paintings, selecting a wardrobe—underline the emptiness of his life. We leave *American Gigolo* with the curious feeling that if women weren't paying this man to sleep with them, he'd be paying them: He needs the human connection and he has a certain shyness, a loner quality, that makes it easier for him when love seems to be just another deal.

American Graffiti ★ ★ ★ ★
PG, 112 m., 1973

Ron Howard (Steve), Cindy Williams (Laurie), Richard Dreyfuss (Curt), Paul Le Mat (John), Mackenzie Phillips (Carol), Charles Martin Smith (Terry), Candy Clark (Debbie), Wolfman Jack (Disc Jockey). Directed by George Lucas and produced by Francis Ford Coppola. Screenplay by Lucas, Gloria Katz, and Willard Huyck.

My first car was a '54 Ford and I bought it for $435. It wasn't scooped, channeled, shaved, decked, pinstriped, or chopped, and it didn't have duals, but its hubcaps were a wonder to behold.

On weekends my friends and I drove around downtown Urbana—past the Princess Theater, past the courthouse—sometimes stopping for a dance at the youth center or a hamburger at the Steak 'n' Shake ("In Sight, It Must Be Right"). And always we listened to Dick Biondi on WLS. Only two years earlier, WLS had been the Prairie Farmer Station; now it was the voice of rock all over the Midwest.

When I went to see George Lucas's *American Graffiti* that whole world—a world that now seems incomparably distant and innocent—was brought back with a rush of feeling that wasn't so much nostalgia as culture shock. Remembering my high school generation, I can only wonder at how unprepared we were for the loss of innocence that took place in America with the series of hammer blows beginning with the assassination of President Kennedy.

The great divide was November 22, 1963, and nothing was ever the same again. The teen-agers in *American Graffiti* are, in a sense, like that cartoon character in the magazine ads: the one who gives the name of his insurance company, unaware that an avalanche is about to land on him. The options seemed so simple then: to go to college, or to stay home and look for a job and cruise Main Street and make the scene.

The options were simple, and so was the music that formed so much of the way we saw ourselves. *American Graffiti*'s sound track is papered from one end to the other with Wolfman Jack's nonstop disc jockey show, that's crucial and absolutely right. The radio was on every waking moment. A character in the movie only realizes his car, parked nearby, has been stolen when he hears the music stop: He didn't hear the car being driven away.

The music was as innocent as the time. Songs like "Sixteen Candles" and "Gonna Find Her" and "The Book of Love" sound touchingly naive today; nothing prepared us for the decadence and the aggression of rock only a handful of years later. The Rolling Stones of 1972 would have blown WLS off the air in 1962.

American Graffiti acts almost as a milestone to show us how far (and in many cases how tragically) we have come. Stanley Kauffmann, who liked it, complained in the *New Republic* that Lucas had made a film more fascinating to the generation now between thirty and forty than it could be for other generations, older or younger.

But it isn't the age of the characters that matters; it's the time they inhabited. Whole cultures and societies have passed since 1962. *American Graffiti* is not only a great movie but a brilliant work of historical fiction; no sociological treatise could duplicate the movie's success in remembering exactly how it was to be alive at that cultural instant.

On the surface, Lucas has made a film that seems almost artless; his teen-agers cruise Main Street and stop at Mel's Drive-In and listen to Wolfman Jack on the radio and neck and lay rubber and almost convince themselves their moment will last forever. But the film's buried structure shows an innocence in the process of being lost, and as its symbol Lucas provides the elusive blonde in the white Thunderbird—the vision of beauty always glimpsed at the next intersection, the end of the next street.

Who is she? And did she really whisper "I love you" at the last traffic signal? In *8½*, Fellini used Claudia Cardinale as his mysterious angel in white, and the image remains one of his best; but George Lucas knows that for one brief afternoon of American history angels drove Thunderbirds and could possibly be found at Mel's Drive-In tonight . . . or maybe tomorrow night, or the night after.

American Me ★ ★ ★ ½
R, 120 m., 1992

Edward James Olmos (Santana), William Forsythe (JD), Pepe Serna (Mundo), Danny De La Paz (Puppet), Evelina Fernandez (Julie). Directed by Edward James Olmos and produced by Sean Daniel, Robert M. Young, and Olmos. Screenplay by Floyd Mutrux and Desmond Nakano.

There is a scene late in *American Me* where a police squad car pulls up at a bus stop where a man and woman are standing. It is late at night. The couple have attended a wedding and are in formal clothes. A cop gets out of the car, looks at the man, and asks him if he has done time in prison. Just like that. Is there a sad aura of some kind that allows a cop to look at a man and know he has spent most of his life behind bars?

American Me tells the story of the man at that bus stop. His name is Santana. He is a Hispanic-American who grows up in East Los Angeles, joins a street gang, and is in prison while he is still of an age to be in high school. Prison is his school. By the time he is back on the streets again, he is a skillful, educated criminal. The U.S. penal system has done its work—which, in this movie, is neither the punishment nor the eradication of crime, but the training of criminals.

Edward James Olmos, who directed the movie and plays Santana, says the film is based on a true story. That doesn't mean much to me; by the time the movies finish with them, true stories are as fictional as any other. What I felt watching *American Me,* however, was that it is based on a true situation—on the reality that street gangs and prison, mixed with the drug sales that finance the process, work together to create a professional criminal class.

Santana is two men, according to the woman's voice that we hear in the first moments of the film. One of those men is shy and sweet, and doesn't know how to dance or make love. The other man is a murderer. The movie covers many years in Santana's life, as the sweet man inside gradually tries to make himself heard over the killer. The film is not optimistic about the outcome of this struggle.

Olmos, a strong actor who was nominated for an Oscar for *Stand and Deliver,* creates a Santana who keeps all of his secrets very well hidden. Chain-smoking (because to have cigarettes is a status symbol in prison), he stands hunched, his eyes on the ground, saying hard

truths. He is a natural leader. From inside the prison, he runs a drug operation on the outside—and the movie makes the surprising case that this is the norm, that the prisons control the drug ttaffic. Outside, where he falls in love with an understanding woman (Evelina Fernandez), he is already a big man because of his stature in prison.

In echoes from *The Godfather,* Santana leads his gang in a revolt against the Mafia don (Tony Giorgio) who controls all the street drugs. A war breaks out. It is the wrong war at the wrong time, and it makes enemies of the blacks—the wrong enemies. Santana struggles to hold things together as a hotheaded new generation comes along. He was a hothead himself once.

The movie was mostly shot on two difficult locations: the streets of East L.A. and inside Folsom Prison. It knows these worlds. The language, the clothes, the attitudes are all shown with the understated conviction of a director who is sure of his material. Olmos even reaches behind the natural boundaries of his story to include an opening sequence that takes place before Santana is born. He shows the zoot-suit riots in Los Angeles in 1943 and 1944, when Hispanics were beaten up by uniformed servicemen. These scenes are not included simply for atmosphere, but because they set up a crucial secret that will color Santana's whole life.

American Me is unusual in its approach to its material. Although it shows Hispanic neighborhoods in crisis and a generation being lost to drugs, guns, and crime, it does no scapegoating—the tragedy is not blamed on the dependable standby of racism, but is seen as part of the disintegration of society as a whole. In interviews, Olmos talks about the grim statistics: nearly eight hundred murders in Los Angeles in 1991; more than half of all the juvenile offenders accused of murder. He spends a lot of time working with young prisoners. He knows their streets. He sees a world in which gang killings are being replaced by murders that are committed simply for the adrenaline rush of pulling the trigger. A world in which drugs and gangs define the reality. A world without alternatives.

A character like Santana, born into an earlier version of such a world, may eventually, through hard lessons and his own underlying strength of character, find out what is wrong and what he must do. But *American Me* questions whether the society will let him. We often hear of the need for leadership in ethnic ghettos like the one Santana knows.

But what if only one kind of leadership is possible? What if the choices are crime or death?

An American Tail: Fievel Goes West
★ ★ ½
G, 75 m., 1991

With voices of: Phillip Glasser (Fievel), James Stewart (Wylie), Erica Yohn (Mama), Cathy Cavadini (Tanya), Nehemiah Persoff (Papa), Dom DeLuise (Tiger), Amy Irving (Miss Kitty). Directed by Phil Nibbelink and Simon Wells and produced by Steven Spielberg and Robert Watts. Screenplay by Flint Dille.

It is tempting to compare *An American Tail: Fievel Goes West* with *Beauty and the Beast*, because both animated features opened on the same day, but actually these are different films for different markets. *Beauty and the Beast* is a film of grand ambition, breaking new ground in the marriage of animation and musical comedy, aimed at audiences of all ages. The *American Tail* sequel is a more traditional children's film, trying to do some of the same old things and do them well.

In that uncritical way in which children accept movies as facts of existence, kids will end up liking both. The difference will be that their parents will probably love *Beauty and the Beast* but find themselves growing mighty restless during *An American Tail: Fievel Goes West*.

The movie continues the adventures of Fievel, the little mouse from Russia, who emigrated to America in the first movie and is now living with his family in a tenement in nineteenth-century New York. In the earlier film, as you may recall, Fievel's family home was burned by rampaging czarist cats, and he was lost at sea during the crossing to America, washing up as an orphan on the shores of the New Land. It was only after many harrowing adventures (in a story surprisingly depressing for the kiddie audience) that he found his family again.

Fievel Goes West is much more upbeat— more of a traditional cartoon. The little mouse dreams of going out West and becoming a cowboy, and his fantasies are populated with hero worship for the famous sheriff Wylie Burp. Wylie's voice was dubbed for the movie by James Stewart—and in his imagination, Fievel talks like John Wayne; one of the funny moments comes when the little mouse calls someone "pilgrim." Since Fievel lives before the invention of movies or the creation of the romantic cowboy image, his fantasies are a little anachronistic, but so what?

We meet some of Fievel's friends and enemies from the first film, including the tubby Tiger (voice by Dom DeLuise), who falls head over heels for the seductive Miss Kitty (the voice of Amy Irving), who trails lurid clouds of purple scent and is an alley cat with a heart of gold. Tiger is a friendly cat, but most cats dream of feasting on mouse pie, including the slick villain Cat R. Waul (voice of John Cleese).

Events conspire to realize Fievel's dreams, and he does indeed find himself out West, where there is a real Sheriff Wylie Burp. James Stewart has a lot of fun doing the voice and offering sound and sage western advice to the little mouse, who is inclined to run headlong into danger and to overestimate his cowboy skills.

There is nothing really the matter with *An American Tail: Fievel Goes West*, except that it is not inspired with an extra spark of imagination in addition to its competent entertainment qualities. No doubt it suffers in my mind by comparison with *Beauty and the Beast*, which allowed a certain psychological complexity in its characters. The mice, cats, dogs, and tarantulas in *Fievel Goes West* are all well within the tradition of "children's cartoons," and so we quickly sense we can expect few surprises from them.

An American Werewolf in London ★ ★
R, 95 m., 1981

David Naughton (David), Griffin Dunne (Jack), Jenny Agutter (Alex), John Woodvine (Dr. Hirsch). Directed by John Landis and produced by George Folsey, Jr. Screenplay by Landis.

An American Werewolf in London seems curiously unfinished, as if director John Landis spent all his energy on spectacular set pieces and then didn't want to bother with things like transitions, character development, or an ending. The movie has sequences that are spellbinding, and then long stretches when nobody seems sure what's going on. There are times when the special effects almost wipe the characters off the screen. It's weird. It's not a very good film, and it falls well below Landis's work in the anarchic *National Lampoon's Animal House* and the rambunctious *Blues Brothers*. Landis never seems very sure whether he's making a comedy or a horror film, so he winds up with genuinely funny moments acting as counterpoint to the gruesome undead. Combining horror and comedy is an old tradition (my favorite example is *The Bride of Frankenstein*), but the laughs and the blood coexist very uneasily in this film.

One of the offscreen stars of the film is Rick Baker, the young makeup genius who created the movie's wounds, gore, and werewolves. His work is impressive, yes, but unless you're single-mindedly interested in special effects, *American Werewolf* is a disappointment. And even the special effects, good as they are, come as an anticlimax if you're a *really* dedicated horror fan, because if you are, you've already seen this movie's high point before: the onscreen transformation of a man into a werewolf was anticipated in *The Howling*, in which the special effects were done by a Baker protegé named Rob Bottin.

The movie's plot involves two young American students (David Naughton and Griffin Dunne), who are backpacking across the English moors. They stumble into a country pub where everyone is ominously silent, and then one guy warns them to beware the full moon and stick to the road. They don't, and are attacked by werewolves. Dunne is killed, Naughton is severely wounded, and a few days later in the hospital Naughton is visited by the decaying cadaver of Dunne—who warns him that he'll turn into a werewolf at the full moon. Naughton ignores the warning, falls in love with his nurse (Jenny Agutter), and moves in with her when he's discharged from the hospital. Then follows a series of increasingly gruesome walk-ons by Dunne, who begs Naughton to kill himself before the full moon. Naughton doesn't, turns into a werewolf, and runs amok through London. That gives director Landis his chance to stage a spectacular multi-car traffic accident in Piccadilly Circus; crashes have been his specialty since the homecoming parade in *Animal House* and the nonstop carnage in *Blues Brothers*.

The best moments in *American Werewolf* probably belong to Dunne, who may be a decaying cadaver but keeps right on talking like a college student: "Believe me," he says at Naughton's bedside, "this isn't a whole lot of fun." The scene in which Naughton turns into a werewolf is well done, with his hands elongating and growing claws, and his face twisting into a snout and fangs. But it's as if John Landis thought the technology would be enough. We never get a real feeling for the characters, we never really believe the places (especially that awkwardly phony pub and its stagy customers), and we are particularly disappointed by the ending. I won't reveal the ending, such as it is, except to say it's so sudden, arbitrary, and anticlimactic that, although we are willing for the movie to be over, we still can't quite believe it.

An Angel at My Table ★ ★ ★ ★
R, 160 m., 1991

Kerry Fox (Janet), Alexia Keogh (Young Janet), Karen Fergusson (Teen-age Janet), Iris Churn (Mum), K.J. Wilson (Dad). Directed by Jane Campion and produced by Bridget Ikin. Screenplay by Laura Jones.

Here is the story of a curly-haired little redhead who grew up to be one of New Zealand's best authors, after enduring ordeals that would have put most people into a madhouse. The irony is that she was already in the madhouse, misdiagnosed as a schizophrenic, and subjected to more than two hundred electroshock treatments even though there was nothing really wrong with her except for shyness and depression.

Janet Frame is today the author of some twenty novels, books of poetry, plays, and autobiography. The first two books were actually written and published while she was in a mental hospital, and it is possible to wonder if the act of writing them saved her life—giving her a place to order her thoughts in the middle of chaos.

Jane Campion's *An Angel at My Table* tells her story in a way that I found strangely engrossing from beginning to end. This is not a hyped-up biopic or a soap opera, but simply the record of a life as lived, beginning in childhood with a talented, dreamy girl whose working-class parents loved her, and continuing to follow her as she was gradually shunted by society into a place that almost killed her. Janet is played in the film by three different actresses (from girlhood through her twenties into her thirties, they are Kerry Fox, Alexia Keogh, and Karen Fergusson), who have uncanny physical and personality similarities, and so we get a real sense of a life as it unfolds, as things go wrong and a strong spirit struggles to prevail.

The movie opens in prewar New Zealand, a green and comfortable land where Janet's father works for the railroad and she fits comfortably into a family including a brother and two sisters that she adores. She is a funny-looking child, with bad teeth and a mop of unruly scarlet hair, but there is something special about her. She has a poet's imagina-

tion, and when she writes a poem for grade school, she is absolutely sure what words she wishes to use, and cannot be persuaded by authority to change one word.

She grows up slowly, doesn't date, doesn't have much of a social life. In school, she socializes with the outcasts—the brains, the nonconformists, the arty set—but looks with envy on the popular girls and their boyfriends. It is a world she does not hope to understand. In college, too, she's a loner, shy, keeping to herself, confiding everything to a journal, and then, in her first job as a schoolteacher, she does not join the other teachers for tea because she cannot think of what to say to them. One day the school inspector comes to visit her class, and she freezes up and cannot say anything.

She is essentially having a panic attack, but one officious and ignorant diagnosis leads to another, and she is committed to a mental home, beginning eight years of unspeakable horror as she is given shock treatments and even threatened with a lobotomy by professionals whose complete ignorance of her condition does not inhibit their cheerful eagerness to deprive her of mind and freedom.

Her books help her keep her mind, and eventually help her win her release—her father, cowed by the professionals, vows he will never let her go back to the asylum again—and at last, in her thirties, her true life begins as she gets a grant to study abroad, and falls in with a group of bohemian writers and painters in Spain. She even finally loses her virginity, and although she will always be a little odd, a loner, wrapped in a cocoon of privacy, we can see her gradually becoming more comfortable with life.

Jane Campion, who directed from a screenplay by Laura Jones, is the author of last year's *Sweetie*, a movie about a family almost destroyed by a disruptive sister. That was a film I had to struggle with. I did not relate to it on the first viewing, but I could sense that something was there, and eventually, after two more viewings, I came to love it. *An Angel at My Table* does not require a struggle: It is told with a clarity and simplicity that is quietly but completely absorbing. Yes, it is visually beautiful, and, yes, it is well acted, but it doesn't call attention to its qualities. It tells its story calmly and with great attention to human detail, and watching it, I found myself drawn in with a rare intensity.

Angel Heart ★ ★ ★ ½
R, 113 m., 1987

Mickey Rourke (Harry Angel), Robert De Niro (Louis Cyphre), Lisa Bonet (Epiphany Proudfoot), Charlotte Rampling (Margaret Krusemark), Brownie McGhee (Toots Sweet), Stocker Fontelieu (Ethan Krusemark). Directed by Alan Parker and produced by Alan Marshall and Elliott Kastner. Screenplay by Parker.

After everything is all over and the dust has settled and the blood has dried, it is possible to unsort the plot of *Angel Heart* and see that it's really fairly simple. But it doesn't feel that way at the time. It has the unsettled logic of a nightmare, in which nothing fits and everything seems inevitable and there are a lot of arrows in the air and they are all flying straight at you.

The movie stars Mickey Rourke as Harry Angel, an unwashed private eye who works out of an office that looks like Sam Spade gave it to the Goodwill. He gets a call to visit some kind of devil-worship cult in Harlem, where a strange man wants to talk to him. The man's name is Louis Cyphre (Robert De Niro), and he wants Angel to track down a missing person for him. Angel takes the case for five grand and follows a trail that is littered with stale leads and fresh corpses.

This sounds like a million other private-eye movies, and, in a way, it is. A few things make it different: a sly sense of humor, good acting and directing, and a sudden descent into the supernatural as Harry Angel discovers the horrifying true nature of his investigation.

The movie is by Alan Parker, a director who has vowed to work in every genre before he dies. After *Angel Heart*, he can cross two off his list: private-eye movies and supernatural horror films. Parker's films are always made with great gusto, as if he were in up to his elbows and taking no hostages.

He enjoys what timid folks might call stylistic excess, and that's what got him in trouble with the MPAA ratings board over a scene involving Rourke and Lisa Bonet, who plays a young Louisiana woman who holds the secrets of the past. They meet in a leaky hotel room during a rainstorm, and while they make love the raindrops from the ceiling turn to blood. In the context of the movie, the blood makes perfect sense, although the scene had to be trimmed to qualify the movie for an R rating. It has been reinstated, however, in an unrated version of the video.

The scene is consistent with the whole

film, which is sensuous and depraved. The De Niro character sets the tone, with his sharp, pointed fingernails and his elegant black suits. De Niro must have had fun preparing for the character: He uses a neatly trimmed black beard, slicked-back hair, and tricks of lighting and makeup to make himself look uncannily like Martin Scorsese, his favorite director. Given what we eventually discover about the character, it's a wicked homage.

Rourke occupies the center of the film like a violent unmade bed. No other actor, with the possible exception of France's Gerard Depardieu, has made such a career out of being a slob. He looks unshaven, unwashed, hungover, and desperate, and that's at the beginning of the film, before things start to go wrong. By the end, he is a man whose nerves are screaming for help.

His odyssey in *Angel Heart* takes him from New York to Algiers, Louisiana, a town across from New Orleans that makes the fleshpots of Bourbon Street look like Disneyland. He is advised to go back home by a crusty old blues player (played by the fast-talking Brownie McGhee in a performance that proves Dexter Gordon wasn't the only old musician who could act). But he doesn't listen and gets drawn deeper into bayou country, where he spies on the forbidden rituals of a voodoo cult.

Bonet is the priestess of the cult and plays the role with an abandoned sexuality that you wouldn't have expected after watching her on the "Cosby Show." She was probably right to take this controversial role as her movie debut; it was such a stretch from the Cosby character that it established her as a plausible movie actress.

The movie's final revelations make a weird sense, once we figure them out. This is one of those movies where you rerun the plot in your head, re-interpreting the early scenes in terms of the final shocking revelations. *Angel Heart* is a thriller and a horror movie, but most of all it's an exuberant exercise in style, in which Parker and his actors have fun taking it to the limit.

Angels in the Outfield ★ ★
PG, 105 m., 1994

Danny Glover (George Knox), Brenda Fricker (Maggie Nelson), Tony Danza (Mel Clark), Christopher Lloyd (Al the Angel), Ben Johnson (Hank Murphy), Jay O. Sanders (Ranch Wilder), Joseph Gordon-Levitt (Roger),

Milton Davis, Jr. (J.P.). Directed by William Dear and produced by Irby Smith, Joe Roth, and Roger Birnbaum. Screenplay by Dorothy Kingsley, George Wells, and Holly Goldberg Sloan.

Angels are the celestial beings of choice. They get good press in the newsweeklies, Broadway plays are written about them, and here is a retread of the 1951 film *Angels in the Outfield*, about how they help a losing team turn around its season, all because of the faith of a little boy.

I have always had my doubts about any form of divine intervention in sports contests. The power of prayer may be remarkable in many other arenas, but why should God want my team to win instead of the other side? Isn't it insulting to request God to even take an interest in baseball?

Angels, on the other hand, seem to represent less of a problem, maybe because they have murkier theological functions. Milton saw them shaking the very heavens, but in our trivializing times they've been downgraded to starring roles in greeting cards and pop songs. This movie is a good career move.

The film opens on a sad note, with little Roger (Joseph Gordon-Levitt), a foster child, in court hoping to be reunited with his father. But the father is a motorcycle loner with no room for a kid on the bike, and so Roger is sent back to stay with the warm woman (Brenda Fricker) who runs his foster home. When will he ever be part of a "real family" again, he asks his dad, who laughs and says, "Not until the Angels win the pennant."

He is referring to the California Angels, mired in last place at this point in the film, but Roger consults with little J.P. (Milton Davis, Jr.), who also lives in the foster home, and then prays for heavenly intervention in the team's fate. And before long, amazingly, the Angels start to win. There are plays so sensational that they seem to defy the laws of physics. And only Roger, who can see angels in the outfield and elsewhere, knows why these miracles are happening.

The team is being managed by a bitter, angry veteran named George Knox (Danny Glover). Among its members is the once-great pitcher Mel Clark (Tony Danza), who has been benched for much of the season. When George's team starts to win, he is astonished, until he learns from his little fan Roger that angels are helping the team. He doubts it, but cannot argue with results. And

when Mel starts pitching again, he gets help from the angels, too, and regains his former form.

The movie then reduces itself to a formula, alternating between baseball action (angels appear, work miracles, and announcer goes into ecstasy) and human redemption (the manager becomes more of a human being). The baseball action isn't very interesting because the angels (led by Christopher Lloyd) manipulate the outcomes. And the human-interest stuff is canned and unconvincing. The only character who really rings true is the comeback pitcher played by Danza.

Angels in the Outfield closely follows another movie about kids and baseball, *Little Big League*. Both are about how small boys control the destinies of major league teams. But while *Little Big League* is a smart movie about a kid who really understands baseball, *Angels* is a dumb movie about soppy sentimentality. The choice is clear.

Angie ★ ★ ½
R, 108 m., 1994

Geena Davis (Angie), Stephen Rea (Noel), James Gandolfini (Vinnie), Aida Turturro (Tina), Philip Bosco (Frank), Jenny O'Hara (Kathy), Michael Rispoli (Jerry), Betty Miller (Joanne). Directed by Martha Coolidge and produced by Larry Brezner and Patrick McCormick. Screenplay by Todd Graff.

The ads for *Angie* promise a lighthearted comedy about a cheerful young woman who has a baby out of wedlock, and upsets her friends, although not too badly. The movie itself delivers all of that, and more—so much more that the burden finally weighs down the story, which collapses under its own gathering gloom. This is not so much a comedy as a soap opera crossbred with confessions from the daytime TV talk shows.

The movie stars Geena Davis as Angie, and let it be said that she is more than equal to all of the twists and turns that the odd screenplay subjects her to. She has a lightness, a brightness, that is always a joy to see on the screen, and she was the right choice to play the character that *Angie* at first seems to be about. Perhaps no actress could have portrayed the character the movie is finally about; the two-hour form of a movie story is exhausted by all of the things that happen.

Angie grows up with her best friend Tina (Aida Turturro, very high energy and convincing) in the kind of ethnic neighborhood where the guys hang around on street corners, making hopeful groin movements when girls walk by, and the girls are kind of flattered. She works in Manhattan. For a long time she has been engaged to the same guy, Vinnie (James Gandolfini), but somehow they've never gotten married. Then she gets pregnant, and Vinnie is eager to race to the altar, but Angie isn't so sure. For one thing, she's met another guy, an Irish lawyer named Noel (Stephen Rea), who is sweet and funny and sort of like a big puppy dog. She thinks she loves him.

This leads to predictable results around the house, which she still shares with her father (Philip Bosco) and her stepmother (Jenny O'Hara). Her own mother packed up and moved out when Angie was three years old; the neighbors vaguely remember that she liked to dance in the snow. Everyone close to Angie thinks she ought to get married, and that Vinnie is a perfectly nice guy. But Vinnie has started getting bossy and possessive, and Noel is so understanding, and . . .

It's about here that the movie seriously loses its way. The baby is born, and there are complications (at least one more complication, in my opinion, than the movie possibly needed). There are also complications with Noel (such arbitrary complications they come from a screenplay, not life). And there is a frantic cross-country bus trip in search of the long-lost mother, leading to a sequence so pointless that when it's over the movie sort of stands around wondering what to do next.

The latter half of *Angie* is essentially a series of plot inventions that do not flow convincingly out of the tone or the logic of what's gone before. It's as if *Angie* begins as a long, slow ascent to some possible goal, and then suddenly turns into a roller-coaster ride into the darkness.

The best thing in the movie is the relationship between Davis and Turturro as the two women who have been friends since childhood. Turturro has married, to a guy who is no angel, but she is fiercely loyal to the *idea* of marriage—of sticking to a commitment once you've made it. Angie is more of a free spirit, haunted by the memory of her mother, dancing in the snow. But then, as her life fills unexpectedly with one crisis after another, we lose the sense that the movie has a clear direction. It's episodic desperation. And people expecting a comedy are going to be in for some big surprises.

Annie ★ ★ ★
PG, 128 m., 1982

Aileen Quinn (Annie), Albert Finney (Daddy Warbucks), Carol Burnett (Miss Hannigan), Bernadette Peters (Lily), Ann Reinking (Grace Farrell), Tim Curry (Rooster), Geoffrey Holder (Punjab), Edward Herrmann (F.D.R.). Directed by John Huston and produced by Ray Stark. Screenplay by Carol Sobieski.

In the abstract, *Annie* is fun. It has lots of movement and color, dance and music, sound and fury. In the particular, it has all sorts of problems, and I guess the only way to really enjoy the movie is to just ignore the particulars. I will nevertheless mention a few particulars. One is the story itself, about how Little Orphan Annie is rescued from a cruel orphanage by a billionaire who wants a Rent-An-Orphan for Christmas. This is said to be a universal story. Critics have written that you just can't help cheering for Annie as she faces the cold world with pluck and courage. I didn't find myself cheering much, though, since Annie didn't seem to need the encouragement; as played by the feisty young Aileen Quinn, she is the sort of child who makes adults run for the hills.

The adventures she gets herself into are likewise questionable. I've never thought of *Oliver!* as a particularly realistic musical, but at least when its little hero said "Please, sir, more food?" there was a hint of truth. *Annie* has been plunged into pure fantasy, into the mindless sort of musical boosterism that plays big for Broadway theater parties but almost always translates to the movie screen as sheer contrivance. *Annie* is not *about* anything. It *contains* lots of subjects (such as cruel orphanages, the Great Depression, scheming conmen, heartless billionaires, and President Franklin Delano Roosevelt) but it isn't *about* them. It's not even really about whether Annie will survive her encounters with them, since the book of this musical is so rigorously machine-made, so relentlessly formula, it's one of those movies where you can amaze your friends by leaving the auditorium, standing blindfolded in the lobby and correctly predicting the outcome.

And yet I sort of enjoyed the movie. I enjoyed the energy that was visible on the screen, and the sumptuousness of the production numbers, and the good humor of several of the performances—especially those by Albert Finney, as Daddy Warbucks, and Carol Burnett, as the wicked orphanage super-

visor, Miss Hannigan. Aileen Quinn sort of grew on me, too. She cannot be said to really play a child—at least not the sort of plausible flesh-and-blood child that Henry Thomas creates in *E.T.* But Quinn is talented, can dance well and sing passably, and does not seem to be an overtrained puppet like, say, Ricky Schroeder. She seems more like the kind of kid who will get this acting out of her system and go on to be student body president.

If there is a center to the film, it belongs to Albert Finney. He has a thankless task: He must portray Daddy Warbucks as a self-centered, smug rich man who has everything in the world, except love, and who learns to love through the example of a little girl. This is the sort of role actors kill over—to avoid playing. Albert Finney has the true grit. He's gone through this personality transformation twice; he starred in *Scrooge* in 1970. This time, he even pulls it off, by underplaying. He isn't too aloof at the beginning, and he's not too softhearted at the end. He has a certain detachment. Annie may win his heart, but she'll still have to phone for an appointment.

Will kids like the movie? I honestly don't know. When I was a kid, I didn't much like movies about other kids, maybe because I was jealous (why does *that* kid get to ride a horse in the Derby?). The movie was promoted as a family entertainment, but was it really a family musical, even on the stage? I dunno. I think it was more of a product, a clever concoction of nostalgia, hard-sell sentiment, small children, and cute dogs. The movie is the same mixture as before. It's like some kind of dumb toy that doesn't do anything or go anywhere, but it is fun to watch as it spins mindlessly around and around.

Annie Hall ★ ★ ★ ½
PG, 95 m., 1977

Woody Allen (Alvy Singer), Diane Keaton (Annie Hall), Tony Roberts (Rob), Carol Kane (Allison), Paul Simon (Tony Lacey), Shelley Duvall (Pam), Janet Margolin (Robin), Colleen Dewhurst (Mom Hall). Directed by Woody Allen and produced by Charles H. Joffe. Screenplay by Allen and Marshall Brickman.

Woody Allen's *Annie Hall* explores new dimensions of the persona Allen has constructed in movies, on the stage, and even in a comic strip. We're all familiar by now with "Woody," the overanxious, underachieving intellectual with the inept social life. We've watched him develop from bits in a stand-up comedy routine to a fully developed comic character in the tradition of Chaplin's tramp or Fields's drunk. We know how "Woody" will act in so many situations that we're already laughing before the punch line. Maybe nobody since Jack Benny has been so hilariously predictable.

And yet there's always the realization that "Woody" is a projection of a real Woody Allen. That beneath the comic character is a certain amount of painful truth. That just as W.C. Fields really *was* a drunk, so Woody Allen perhaps really is insecure about his height, shy around girls, routinely incompetent in the daily joust with life.

It's not that the "real" Woody Allen is as hapless as his fictional creation, but that the character draws from life by exaggerating it. *Annie Hall* is the closest Allen has come to dealing with that real material. It's not an autobiography, but we get the notion at times that scenes in the movie have been played before, slightly differently, for real.

Allen plays Alvy Singer, stand-up comic and incurable combination of neurotic and romantic. He's self-consciously a New Yorker, a liberal, a Jew, an intellectual, a seeker after the unattainable, and an expert at *making* it unattainable. One of Alvy Singer's problems is that he understands this all so well. He's not a victim of forces beyond his control, but their author.

And one of the problems he keeps providing for himself is the problem of love. He falls in love too easily, to girls who are right for him in all the little ways and incompatible in all the big ones. His girls tend to reflect the stages he's going through. When he's an Adlai Stevenson liberal in the late 1950s, he marries another one. When he's a romantic ten or fifteen years later, he finds another one, a kookier one. His only trouble is that women are people, not stages.

The movie dares to go into this material a little more seriously and cohesively than is usually the case in an Allen film. *Annie Hall* is a comedy, yes, and there are moments in it as funny as anything Woody has done, but the movie represents a growth on Allen's part. From a filmmaker who would do anything for a laugh, whose primary mission seemed to be to get through the next five minutes, Allen has developed in *Sleeper, Love and Death,* and this film into a much more thoughtful and (is it possible?) more mature director.

Maybe that's why *Annie Hall* is called a "nervous romance": because Allen himself is

a little nervous about this frankly nostalgic, romantic, and sentimental material. He throws in a few gags (like the hilarious walk-on by Marshall McLuhan) almost to reassure his old fans that all's well at the laugh works. But he wants to do a lot more this time than just keep us laughing. By looking into some of his own relationships, some of his own patterns, he wants to examine how a personality works.

And so there are two Woody Allens here: Our old pal the original Woody, who's given to making asides directly into the camera, and a new Allen who creates Alvy Singer in his own image and then allows him to behave consistently, even sometimes at the cost of laughs. It's this new Woody who has the nervous romance, the complicated relationship with the would-be nightclub singer Annie Hall (played by Diane Keaton with an interesting mixture of maternal care, genuine love, and absolute craziness).

At the end of the affair, we've learned only two things for certain: That enduring relationships are very likely impossible in this time and place (i.e., New York City during Woody Allen's lifetime), and that life without the search for relationships is unthinkable. In the movie, Woody quotes Groucho Marx's statement that he'd never belong to any club that would accept someone like him as a member. Then Allen muses that maybe he should never get into a relationship in which one of the partners is himself. Tricky, isn't it? And in *Annie Hall* he makes it very funny, and sad, and tricky indeed.

Another 48 HRS ★ ★
R, 102 m., 1990

Eddie Murphy (Reggie Hammond), Nick Nolte (Jack Cates), Brion James (Ben Kehoe), Kevin Tighe (Blake Wilson), Ed O'Ross (Frank Cruise), David Anthony Marshall (Willy Hickok), Andrew Divoff (Cherry Ganz). Directed by Walter Hill and produced by Lawrence Gordon and Robert D. Wachs. Screenplay by John Fasano, Jeb Stuart, and Larry Gross.

You know how sometimes in a dream you'll see these familiar scenes and faces floating in and out of focus, but you're not sure how they connect? *Another 48 HRS* is a movie that feels the same way. The broad outlines are familiar from the original *48 HRS,* and the villains and cops are all basic movie stereotypes. But what exactly is happening here?

Everybody seems to be looking for the Iceman. The Iceman is the criminal master-

mind in control of all drug traffic in the San Francisco Bay area. A cop named Cates (Nick Nolte) has been on his trail for years—but every time he gets close, the Iceman slips away. Meanwhile, a convict named Hammond (Eddie Murphy) is about to be released from prison. Maybe he knows who the Iceman is. Maybe he can help Cates. On the other hand, maybe he can't. He sure doesn't want to.

Watching the movie, I was trying to remember the details of the earlier 1982 film. In that one, Nolte was on the trail of some cop killers and he sprung Murphy from prison for forty-eight hours to help him out. They turned into quite a team—the hungover cop and the confident young black man, both suspicious of each other, both learning to be friends. The movie contained the scene that made Murphy into a star, a scene where he walked into a redneck bar, impersonated a police officer, and intimidated everyone with the sheer force of his personality.

In *Another 48 HRS,* years have passed. Nolte has stopped drinking (and also apparently lost his long-suffering girlfriend). Murphy is back in prison, but Nolte is holding $500,000 for him, for when he gets out. Meanwhile, in a shoot-out during a motorcycle race, Nolte kills a man who fired at him. But the other guy's gun disappears, and with no evidence apart from Nolte's troublesome personnel record, his badge is lifted and he's charged with manslaughter.

Meanwhile, there are a bunch of longhaired, leather-jacketed, tattooed motorcycle gang members who cruise the desert blowing people away. They apparently work for a young black man who works for the Iceman. They want Murphy dead—so badly that they try to kill him by opening fire on the prison bus that's returning him to civilization. You might ask why the bus driver couldn't simply push them off the road during the high-speed chase, but that would be too logical a question for this movie, which specializes in confusing and endless action scenes.

There's one crucial difference between this movie and the original: We never get much of an idea of the friendship and camaraderie between Murphy and Nolte. Their idea of friendship boils down to hitting each other as hard as they can, "to even the score." They have no dialogue scenes together of any depth. The plot they're in is so confusing that at one point they simply go back to the prison and ask a long-timer (Bernie Casey) to identify the guy they're after. He gives them the man's name and address. How does he know all this stuff? Don't even ask.

Meanwhile, back at police headquarters, the cop plot is recycled from dozens of other movies. How often do we have to sit through that scene where the Internal Affairs guy makes the hero hand over his badge and gun? Leaving all the other movies out of it, this was the second time in a few months that Nike Nolte personally had to go through that scene (after *Q & A*). And when the big secret of the Iceman's identity is finally revealed, ask yourself this question: Would the drug kingpin of the entire Bay Area really need to keep the daytime job?

Another 48 HRS was directed by Walter Hill, who also did the previous movie, and who knows how to shoot violence so it looks convincing, although here he stages a scene which sets some kind of indoor record for the amount of glass that is broken. Hill and his writers, John Fasano, Jeb Stuart, and Larry Gross, have not exactly extended themselves to create a new and original story for this movie, and the big set piece once again involves Murphy and Nolte inside a redneck bar. It's an aimless scene with a lot of loose ends, a reminder of how well the earlier scene worked.

What holds the movie together to some extent is the simple star presence of Murphy and Nolte, who are not given great dialogue or much of a plot, but who have a certain magnetism that's interesting to watch. Murphy in particular needed this movie, I think, as a corrective after his unfortunate *Harlem Nights*—a movie that was seen by a great many people, many of whom didn't enjoy it all that much. If it does nothing else, *Another 48 HRS* reminds us that Murphy is a big, genuine talent.

Another Woman ★ ★ ★ ★
PG, 81 m., 1988

Gena Rowlands (Marion), Philip Bosco (Sam), Betty Buckley (Cathy), Martha Plimpton (Laura), Blythe Danner (Lydia), Sandy Dennis (Claire), Mia Farrow (Hope), Gene Hackman (Harry), John Houseman (Marion's Father), Ian Holm (Ben). Written and directed by Woody Allen. Produced by Robert Greenhut.

Film is the most voyeuristic medium, but rarely have I experienced this fact more sharply than while watching Woody Allen's *Another Woman*. This is a film almost entirely composed of moments that should be private. At times, privacy is violated by characters in the film. At other times, we invade the privacy of the characters. And the central character is our accomplice, standing beside us, speaking in our ear, telling us of the painful process she is going through.

This character is named Marion Post (Gena Rowlands), and she is the kind of woman who might feel qualified to advise the rest of us how to organize our lives by "balancing" the demands of home, job, spouse, and friends. She is fearsomely self-contained, well-organized, sane, efficient, and intelligent. *Another Woman* is about the emotional compromises she has had to make in order to earn that description.

She is the head of a university department of philosophy. She is married to a physician, and, childless, has a good relationship with her husband's teen-age daughter from an earlier marriage. She dresses in a fashion that is so far above criticism as to almost be above notice. She is writing a book, and to find a place free of distractions, she rents an office in a downtown building. She tells us some of these details on the sound track, describing her life with a dry detachment that seems to hide an edge of concern.

The office is in one of those older buildings with a tricky ventilation system. Sitting at her desk one day, Marion discovers that she can hear every word of a therapy session taking place in the office of the psychiatrist who has his office next door. At first she blocks out the sound by placing pillows against the ventilation outlet. Then, frankly, she begins to listen.

While he is establishing this device of the overheard conversations, Allen does an interesting thing. Not only can Marion Post (and the rest of us) easily eavesdrop on the conversations, but when the pillows are placed against the air shaft, they completely block out every word. The choice—to listen, or not to listen—is presented so clearly that it is unreal. It's too neat, comprehensive, final. Although most of the scenes in *Another Woman* are clearly realistic, I think the treatment of sound in the office is a signal from Allen that the office is intended to be read in another way—as the orderly interior of Marion Post's mind, perhaps. And the cries coming in through the grillwork on the wall are the sounds of real emotions that she has put out of her mind for years. They are her nightmares.

During the course of the next few weeks, Marion Post will find the walls of her mind tumbling down. She will discover that she intimidates people, and that they do not love her as much as she thinks, nor trust her to share their secrets. She will find that she knows little about her husband, little about her own emotions, little about why she married this cold, adulterous doctor instead of another man who truly loved her.

If this journey of discovery sounds familiar, it is because *Another Woman* has a great many elements in common with Ingmar Bergman's *Wild Strawberries*, the story of an elderly doctor whose day begins with a nightmare and continues with a voyage of discovery. The doctor finds that his loved ones have ambiguous feelings about him, that his "efficiency" is seen as sternness, and that he made a mistake when he did not accept passionate love when it was offered to him. Allen's film is not a remake of *Wild Strawberries* in any sense, but a meditation on the same theme—the story of a thoughtful person, thoughtfully discovering why she might have benefited from being a little less thoughtful.

There is a temptation to say that Gena Rowlands has never been better than in this movie, but that would not be true. She is an extraordinary actor who is usually this good, and has been this good before, especially in some of the films of her husband, John Cassavetes. What is new here is the whole emotional tone of her character.

Great actors and great directors sometimes find a common emotional ground, so that the actor becomes an instrument playing the director's song. Cassavetes is a wild, passionate spirit, emotionally disorganized, insecure, and tumultuous, and Rowlands has reflected that personality in her characters for him—white-eyed women on the edge of stampede or breakdown. Allen is introspective, considerate, apologetic, formidably intelligent, and controls people through thought and words rather than through physicality and temper. Rowlands now mirrors that personality, revealing in the process how the Cassavetes performances were indeed *acting* and not some kind of ersatz documentary reality. To see *Another Woman* is to get an insight into how good an actress Rowlands has been all along.

I have not said much about the movie's story. I had better not. More than with many thrillers, *Another Woman* depends upon the audience's gradual discovery of what happens. There are some false alarms along the way.

The patient in the psychiatrist's office (Mia Farrow), pregnant and confused, turns up in the "outside" world of the Rowlands character, and we expect more to come of that meeting than ever does. Some critics have asked why the Rowlands and Farrow characters did not interact more deeply—but the whole point is that the philosopher has suppressed everything inside of her that could connect to that weeping, pregnant other woman.

There is also an actual "other woman" in the film, as well as a dry, correct performance by Ian Holm as a man who must have a wife so he can be unfaithful to her. Gene Hackman is precisely cast as the earlier lover whose passion was rejected by Marion, and there is another of Martha Plimpton's bright, somehow sad, teen-agers. In the movie's single most effective scene, Betty Buckley plays Holm's first wife, turning up unexpectedly at a social event and behaving "inappropriately," while Holm firmly tries to make her disappear (this scene is so observant of how people handle social embarrassment that it plays like an oppn wound).

In this last performance before his death, John Houseman finally cut loose from all the appearances of robust immortality and allowed himself to be seen as old, feeble, and spotted—and with immense presence. (In a scene involving the character when he was younger, David Ogden Stiers makes an uncanny Houseman double.)

Another Woman ends a little abruptly. I expected another chapter. And yet I would not have enjoyed a tidy conclusion to this material, because the one thing we learn about Marion Post is that she has got her package so tightly wrapped that she may never live long enough to rummage through its contents. At least by the end of the film she is beginning to remember what it was that she boxed up so carefully, so many years before.

Antonia and Jane ★ ★ ★
NO MPAA RATING, 77 m., 1991

Imelda Staunton (Jane Hartman), Saskia Reeves (Antonia McGill), Bill Nighy (Howard Nash), Brenda Bruce (Therapist), Allan Corduner (Stephen Carlinsky), Lila Kaye (Jane's Mother). Directed by Beeban Kidron and produced by George Faber. Screenplay by Marcy Kahan.

I have a lot of friends who treasure their eccentricities. They see themselves as flawed—but colorfully flawed, you know, and in conversation they're likely to get into little competitions about who's more screwed up. Friends like that would like *Antonia and Jane*, which is the story of a lifelong friendship between two basket cases who love each other more than they like each other.

We meet Jane Hartman first. Played by Imelda Staunton, she wears glasses that are too big for her face—not stylishly big, too big. She wears her hair in a curly mess that she despises. She believes the people at the beauty salon hate her and that her hair is their revenge. She may be right. She has been the "best friend" of Antonia McGill since childhood. Their relationship, seen through Jane's eyes, has been based on Antonia's compulsion to make her feel bad. Why else would little Antonia have founded a secret society for the sole purpose of excluding Jane from membership?

Now Jane and Antonia (Saskia Reeves) have grown and gone their separate ways, except for a ritual dinner once a year, about which they agonize so much that both prepare for it with visits to their psychoanalyst. (They have the same analyst, but, of course, have never discovered that fact.) Jane always arrives first for the dinner, Antonia is always late, and Jane, who perhaps has a talent for dramatizing Antonia's lateness, is always reading *The Brothers Karamazov* at the table.

They talk, but say little. Their feelings run too deeply for words. Jane would be amazed, for example, to find that Antonia is also envious of Jane. Each measures her life by the progress made by the other. Meanwhile, they talk about men. They seem to have a genius for picking the wrong ones. Take Norman, for example, one of Jane's lost causes, who is impotent until he finally asks Jane to do him "a favor." What arouses him, he confides, is the prose of the English novelist Iris Murdoch. Could Jane . . . maybe . . . read to him a little? Could she . . . start with the back cover? So deep is Norman's erotic fixation that even the blurb from *The Sea, the Sea* causes instant arousal.

Some women would be delighted to find a man so dependably aroused at such a small cost to their own self-esteem. Not Jane, who hates Iris Murdoch. Antonia also has men problems. One of her dates likes to tie her up and then ask her trivia questions, such as the origin of quotations from Shakespeare. "*Macbeth*?" she asks hopefully. "*Richard III*?" Or there is Howard, who Jane meets first and who Antonia later steals away from her. Howard specializes in photographs of body parts ("I'm beginning a series on toes").

Antonia and Jane knows one thing about women's friendships that I'm sure is true: They project onto their friends just those qualities they feel lacking in themselves. Maybe they choose their friends as a way of assuming the missing qualities. Jane sees Antonia as beautiful, which she is, to a degree. Antonia sees Jane as independent and self-contained, which she is, also to a degree. Both of them see men as a mysterious other race with ways so inexplicable that love affairs are good mostly for the anecdotes they supply, after the fact.

Antonia and Jane, directed by Beeban Kidron, written by Marcy Kahan, was shot as a film for BBC-TV and embraces its small budget as a virtue. Some of the sets (the psychiatrist's room, Jane's bedroom) look like furniture arranged in the corner of an otherwise empty space, and there is a deliberate attempt to fill the frame with generic furniture, of the same kind that furnishes the worlds of Tom & Jerry or Sylvester and Tweetie Pie. Against this anonymous background, Antonia and Jane continue their struggle, neither one quite aware that the other is the stick by which she measures herself.

Apocalypse Now ★ ★ ★ ★
R, 139 m., 1979

Marlon Brando (Colonel Kurtz), Robert Duvall (Lieutenant Colonel Kilgore), Martin Sheen (Captain Willard), Frederic Forrest (Chef), Albert Hall (Chief), Sam Bottoms (Lance), Larry Fishburne (Clean), Dennis Hopper (Photographer). Directed and produced by Francis Ford Coppola. Screenplay by John Milius and Coppola.

In his book *The Films of My Life*, the French director François Truffaut makes a curious statement. He used to believe, he says, that a successful film had to simultaneously express "an idea of the world and an idea of cinema." But now, he writes: "I demand that a film express either the joy of making cinema or the agony of making cinema. I am not at all interested in anything in between; I am not interested in all those films that do not pulse."

It may seem strange to begin a review of Francis Coppola's *Apocalypse Now* with those words, but consider them for a moment and they apply perfectly to this sprawling film. The critics who rejected Coppola's film mostly did so on Truffaut's earlier grounds: They had arguments with the ideas about the world and the war in *Apocalypse Now*, or they disagreed with the very idea of a film that cost $31 million to make and was then carted all over the world by a filmmaker *still* uncertain whether he had the right ending.

That "other" film on the screen—the one we debate because of its ideas, not its images—is the one that caused so much controversy about *Apocalypse Now.* We all read that Coppola took as his inspiration the Joseph Conrad novel *Heart of Darkness,* and that he turned Conrad's journey up the Congo into a metaphor for another journey up a jungle river, into the heart of the Vietnam War. We all read Coppola's grandiose statements (the most memorable: "This isn't a film about Vietnam. This film *is* Vietnam."). We heard that Marlon Brando was paid $1 million for his closing scenes, and that Coppola gambled his personal fortune to finish the film, and, heaven help us, we even read a journal by the director's wife in which she disclosed her husband's ravings and infidelities.

But all such considerations are far from the reasons why *Apocalypse Now* is a good and important film—a masterpiece, I believe. Now, when Coppola's budget and his problems have long been forgotten, *Apocalypse* stands, I think, as a grand and grave and insanely inspired gesture of filmmaking—of moments that are operatic in their style and scope, and of other moments so silent we can almost hear the director thinking to himself.

I should at this moment make a confession: I am not particularly interested in the "ideas" in Coppola's film. Critics of *Apocalypse* have said that Coppola was foolish to translate *Heart of Darkness,* that Conrad's vision had nothing to do with Vietnam, and that Coppola was simply borrowing Conrad's cultural respectability to give a gloss to his own disorganized ideas. The same objection was made to the hiring of Brando: Coppola was hoping, according to this version, that the presence of Brando as an icon would distract us from the emptiness of what he's given to say.

Such criticisms are made by people who indeed are plumbing *Apocalypse Now* for its ideas, and who are as misguided as the veteran Vietnam correspondents who breathlessly reported that *The Deer Hunter* was not "accurate." What idea or philosophy could we expect to find in *Apocalypse Now*—and what good would it really do, at this point after the Vietnam tragedy, if Brando's closing speeches *did* have the "answers"? Like all great works of art about war, *Apocalypse Now* essentially contains only one idea or message, the not-especially-enlightening observation

that war is hell. We do not see Coppola's movie for that insight—something Coppola, but not some of his critics, knows well.

Coppola also well knows (and demonstrated in the *Godfather* films) that movies aren't especially good at dealing with abstract ideas—for those you'd be better off turning to the written word—but they *are* superb for presenting moods and feelings, the look of a battle, the expression on a face, the mood of a country. *Apocalypse Now* achieves greatness not by analyzing our "experience in Vietnam," but by re-creating, in characters and images, something of that experience.

An example: The scene in which Robert Duvall, as a crazed lieutenant colonel, leads his troops in a helicopter assault on a village is, quite simply, the best movie battle scene ever filmed. It's simultaneously numbing, depressing, and exhilarating: As the rockets jar from the helicopters and spring through the air, we're elated like kids for a half-second, until the reality of the consequences sinks in. Another wrenching scene—in which the crew of Martin Sheen's Navy patrol boat massacres the Vietnamese peasants in a small boat—happens with such sudden, fierce, senseless violence that it forces us to understand for the first time how such things could happen.

Coppola's *Apocalypse Now* is filled with moments like that, and the narrative device of the journey upriver is as convenient for him as it was for Conrad. That's really why he uses it, and not because of literary cross-references for graduate students to catalog. He takes the journey, strings episodes along it, leads us at last to Brando's awesome, stinking hideaway . . . and then finds, so we've all heard, that he doesn't have an ending. Well, Coppola *doesn't* have an ending, if we or he expected the closing scenes to pull everything together and make sense of it. Nobody should have been surprised. *Apocalypse Now* doesn't tell any kind of a conventional story, doesn't have a thought-out message for us about Vietnam, has no answers, and thus needs no ending. The way the film ends now, with Brando's fuzzy, brooding monologues and the final violence, feels much more satisfactory than any conventional ending possibly could.

What's great in the film, and what will make it live for many years and speak to many audiences, is what Coppola achieves on the levels Truffaut was discussing: the moments of agony and joy in making cinema. Some of those moments come at the

same time; remember again the helicopter assault and its unsettling juxtaposition of horror and exhilaration. Remember the weird beauty of the massed helicopters lifting over the trees in the long shot, and the insane power of Wagner's music, played loudly during the attack, and you feel what Coppola was getting at: Those moments as common in life as art, when the whole huge grand mystery of the world, so terrible, so beautiful, seems to hang in the balance.

See also Hearts of Darkness, *a documentary on the making of* Apocalypse Now.

Apollo 13 ★ ★ ★ ★
PG, 135 m., 1995

Tom Hanks (Jim Lovell), Bill Paxton (Fred Haise), Kevin Bacon (Jack Swigert), Gary Sinise (Ken Mattingly), Ed Harris (Gene Kranz), Kathleen Quinlan (Marilyn Lovell), Mary Kate Schellhardt (Barbara Lovell), Emily Ann Lloyd (Susan Lovell). Directed by Ron Howard and produced by Brian Grazer. Screenplay by William Broyles, Jr., and Al Reinert.

There is a moment early in *Apollo 13* when astronaut Jim Lovell is taking some press on a tour of the Kennedy Space Center, and he brags that they have a computer "that fits in one room and can send out millions of instructions." And I'm thinking to myself, hell, I'm writing this review on a better computer than the one that got us to the moon.

Apollo 13 inspires many reflections, and one of them is that America's space program was achieved with equipment that would look like tin cans today. Like Lindbergh, who crossed the Atlantic in the first plane he could string together that might make it, we went to the moon the moment we could, with the tools that were at hand. Today, with new alloys, engines, fuels, computers, and technology, it would be safer and cheaper—but we have lost the will.

Apollo 13 never really states its theme, except perhaps in one sentence of narration at the end, but the whole film is suffused with it: The space program was a really extraordinary thing, something to be proud of, and those who went into space were not just "heroes," which is a cliché, but brave and resourceful.

Those qualities were never demonstrated more dramatically than in the flight of the thirteenth Apollo mission, in April 1970, when an oxygen tank exploded en route to the moon. The three astronauts on board—Jim

Lovell, Fred Haise, and Jack Swigert—were faced with the possibility of becoming marooned in space. Their oxygen could run out, they could be poisoned by CO_2 accumulations, or they could freeze to death. If somehow they were able to return to the Earth's atmosphere, they had to enter at precisely the right angle. Too steep an entry, and they would be incinerated; too shallow, and they would skip off the top of the atmosphere like a stone on a pond, and fly off forever into space.

Ron Howard's film of this mission is directed with a single-mindedness and attention to detail that make it riveting. He doesn't make the mistake of adding cornball little subplots to popularize the material; he knows he has a great story, and he tells it in a docudrama that feels like it was filmed on location in outer space.

So convincing are the details, indeed, that I went back to look at *For All Mankind,* the great 1989 documentary directed by Al Reinert, who co-wrote *Apollo 13.* It was an uncanny experience, like looking at the origins of the current picture. Countless details were exactly the same: the astronauts boarding the spacecraft, the lift-off, the inside of the cabin, the view from space, the chilling sight of the oxygen venting into space, even the little tape recorder floating in free-fall, playing country music. All these images are from the documentary, all look almost exactly the same in the movie, and that is why Howard has been at pains to emphasize that every shot in *Apollo 13* is new. No documentary footage was used. The special effects—models, animation, shots where the actors were made weightless by floating inside a descending airplane—have re-created the experience exactly.

The astronauts are played by Tom Hanks (Lovell), Bill Paxton (Haise), and Kevin Bacon (Swigert). The pilot originally scheduled for the *Apollo 13* mission was Ken Mattingly (Gary Sinise), who was grounded because he had been exposed to the measles. The key figure at Houston Mission Control is Gene Kranz (Ed Harris). Clean-cut, crewcut, wearing white collars even in space, the astronauts had been built up in the public mind as supermen, but as Tom Wolfe's book and Phil Kaufman's movie *The Right Stuff* revealed, they were more likely to be hotshot test pilots than straight arrows.

The movie begins with the surprise selection of Lovell's group to crew *Apollo 13.* We meet members of their families, particularly Marilyn Lovell (Kathleen Quinlan); we follow some of the training, and then the movie follows the ill-fated mission, in space and on the ground. Kranz, the Harris character, chain-smoking Camels, masterminds the ground effort to figure out how (and if) *Apollo 13* can ever return.

A scheme is dreamed up to shut down power in the space capsule, and move the astronauts into the Lunar Landing Module, as sort of a temporary lifeboat. The lunar lander will be jettisoned at the last minute, and the main capsule's weakened batteries may have enough power left to allow the crew to return alive.

Meanwhile, the problem is to keep them from dying in space. A scrubber to clean CO_2 from the capsule's air supply is jerry-built out of materials on board (and you can see a guy holding one just like it in *For All Mankind*). And you begin to realize, as the astronauts swing around the moon and head for home, that, given the enormity of the task of returning to Earth, their craft and equipment is only a little more adequate than the rocket sled in which Evil Knievel proposed to hurtle across Snake River Canyon at about the same time.

Ron Howard has become a director who specializes in stories involving large groups of characters: *Cocoon, Parenthood, Backdraft, The Paper.* Those were all films that paid attention to the individual human stories involved; they were a triumph of construction, indeed, in keeping many stories afloat and interesting. With *Apollo 13,* he correctly decides that the story is in the mission. There is a useful counterpoint in the scenes involving Lovell's wife, waiting fearfully on the ground. (She tells their son, "Something broke on your daddy's spaceship and he's going to have to turn around before he even gets to the moon.") But Howard adds no additional side stories, no little parallel dramas, as a lesser director might have.

This is a powerful story, one of 1995's best films, told with great clarity and remarkable technical detail, and acted without pumped-up histrionics. It's about men trained to do a job, and doing a better one than anyone could have imagined. The buried message is: When we dialed down the space program, we lost something crucial to our vision. When I was a kid, they used to predict that by the year 2000, you'd be able to go to the moon. Nobody ever thought to predict that you'd be able to, but nobody would bother.

The Apprenticeship of Duddy Kravitz
★ ★ ★
PG, 121 m., 1974

Richard Dreyfuss (Duddy), Micheline Lanctot (Yvette), Jack Warden (Max), Randy Quaid (Virgil), Joseph Wiseman (Uncle Benjy), Denholm Elliott (Friar), Henry Ramar (Dingleman), Joe Silver (Farber). Directed by Ted Kotcheff and produced by John Kemeny. Screenplay by Mordecai Richler.

Duddy Kravitz has grown up hearing about the Boy Wonder. The Wonder, real name Dingleman, started out in life picking up bus transfers from the street and selling them for three cents. When he had a quarter, he got into a gin game and ran it up to ten dollars. With that as a nest egg, the Wonder parlayed a string of poker games and fly-by-night investments into a fortune, and returned home (according to legend) in a chauffeured limousine and with his own string of racehorses. And all from a handful of lousy three-cent bus transfers!

Duddy thinks he can do better than that. When we meet him, he's a sixteen-year-old Jewish kid from Montreal whose mother is dead and whose father drives a cab and does a little part-time pimping to send the older son through medical school. The Boy Wonder was a boyhood friend of Duddy's father; the story, whether true or not, has been told so many times that Duddy naturally assumes he will be a millionaire, or something, by the time he's twenty. And he's right. By the time he's twenty, he's something.

The Apprenticeship of Duddy Kravitz is a movie that somehow manages to be breakneck and curiously touching at the same time. It's a story of ambition and greed, with a hero that will stop at almost nothing (by the movie's end, Duddy has succeeded in alienating the girl who loves him, has lost all his friends, has brought his grandfather to despair, and has paralyzed his most loyal employee). And yet we like Duddy, with a kind of exasperation, because we get some notion of the hungers that drive him, and because nobody suffers at his hands more than he does himself.

The movie's a sort of Canadian *What Makes Sammy Run?* Duddy Kravitz even gets into the movie business, as Budd Schulberg's hero did. But Duddy doesn't exactly get to Hollywood. He runs across a blacklisted, alcoholic American director, in exile from Hollywood during the dark days of McCarthyism (the film is set somewhere in the late 1940s and early 1950s).

Duddy forms a movie production company (Dudley Kane Productions, inevitably), hires the director, and produces films of bar mitzvahs. Their first production, shown in its entirety, is a lunatic montage of off-the-wall images that have no perceptible relevance to the bar mitzvah itself; the director arguably got himself drunk and spliced together stock footage (after the opening temple scenes played over Beethoven's Fifth). But Duddy's client is (somewhat dazedly) pleased by the film, and Duddy is off and running.

His ambition is to own land. "A man without land is a nobody," his grandfather has told him. During a summer spent as a waiter at a resort, he finds a beautiful, half-hidden lake. He determines to buy it and develop it, and his dream is shared by a plain-pretty French Canadian girl who is a maid at the resort. They fall in love. Or, more precisely, she loves him and Duddy loves a prospect of his future life which includes her, slightly to one side of center. The ways in which he finally succeeds in driving her away, the ways in which he makes himself miserable before he is even twenty-one, are played against his own series of get-rich-fast schemes (during which he not only succeeds in meeting the real Boy Wonder but even unknowingly smuggles heroin over the border for him).

The movie is based on a Mordecai Richler novel and was the most popular film to have come out of Canada through the early seventies (that country which, in cinema as in other things, remains more foreign for many Americans than any place in Europe). It was filmed on location with a great sense of life and energy and with details seen as Duddy sees them. It's populated with an incredible gallery of character roles (I've only suggested a few of them). It's a little too sloppy, and occasionally too obvious, to qualify as a great film, but it's a good and entertaining one, and it leaves us thinking that Duddy Kravitz might amount to something after all, should he ever grow up.

Arachnophobia ★ ★ ★
PG-13, 103 m., 1990

Jeff Daniels (Ross Jennings), Harley Jane Kozak (Molly Jennings), John Goodman (Delbert McClintock), Julian Sands (Dr. James Atherton), Stuart Pankin (Sheriff Parsons), Brian McNamara (Chris Collins). Directed by Frank Marshall and produced by Kathleen Kennedy and Richard Vane. Screenplay by Don Jakoby and Wesley Strick.

Spiders are among the most elegant of God's creatures, with their delicate, spindly legs and infinite patience. Contained in their tiny memories is the geometry for a million webs, and when you see a web wet with dew in the morning sunlight, you know there is order in the universe, because the spider has found it and didn't even know what it was looking for.

Cockroaches, now, are another matter. They are fearsome, ugly little amphibious vehicles that lurk under the sink and eat anything, even Brillo pads. A horror movie based on roaches would be almost unbearable, and indeed I remember with revulsion an episode from George Romero's *Creepshow* in which a man was covered with a swarm of roaches and eaten alive.

Compared to such loathsome horrors, *Arachnophobia* is a relatively benign thriller, in which spiders kill a few people and scare a lot more, but never get really disgusting the way cockroaches would. The movie begins in the mysterious rain forests of South America, where a new species of spider is discovered. It's a formidable beast, about the size of a baseball mitt, and it has a deadly bite. It kills one of the expedition members and then hitches a ride back to California inside his coffin. Once it arrives in a bucolic rural town, it crossbreeds with a domestic spider and starts lurking in the shoes and toilet bowls of the locals.

The movie's plot includes the elements common to all titles in this genre: (a) the old fuddy doctor who refuses to accept the alarming evidence, (b) the narrow-minded local policeman who resents outsiders, (c) the bright young doctor whose warnings are ignored, (d) the loyal wife and kids, (e) the plain-spoken local woman who sticks up for the new doc, and, of course, (f) the scientist, called in at the crisis to shake his head gravely and announce that a deadly infestation seems to be at hand. There are also, of course, the usual cats and dogs, necessary for the obligatory scene in which they can sense something even when the humans can't.

The bright young doctor, hero of the movie, is played by Jeff Daniels as a man who literally has a paralyzing fear of spiders. He moves with his wife (Harley Jane Kozak) and their kids into one of those charming little Victorians you find only on the back lots of movie studios. It has a barn, suitable for spiders' nests, and a cellar filled with places you wouldn't want to stick your hand into if you thought there might be a deadly arachnoid the size of a coffee cake in there.

Soon bad things start to happen. The kindly local widow bites the dust. A young football player topples over dead. The old-fogey doctor refuses to order an autopsy, but then events conspire to prove him wrong, and soon the spider man (Julian Sands) has been called in from the university and is shaking his head in the approved manner.

You wouldn't think spiders would be good visual elements for a movie. Remember that awful horror movie *The Swarm*, in which killer bees completely failed to make an impression? But the spiders in *Arachnophobia* are wonderfully photogenic, partly because the director, Frank Marshall, is good at placing them in the foreground, shooting them in close-up, and allowing their shadows to cast alarming images when the characters aren't looking. He's also clever at establishing where the spiders are, and then allowing us to cringe as the people in the movie do exactly the wrong thing. The toilet seat scene is a splendid case in point.

And yet for all of the creepy-crawly shocks in the film, *Arachnophobia* never goes over the edge into sheer disgusting horror. It maintains a certain humorous edge—especially in the scenes involving John Goodman as the friendly local exterminator who knows a big spider when he sees one, throws away his biodegradable and ecologically sound chemicals, and gets out the dangerous stuff. This is the kind of movie where you squirm out of enjoyment, not terror, and it's probably going to be popular with younger audiences—it doesn't pound you over the head with violence. Like the spider itself, it has a certain respect for structure.

Aria ★ ★ ★
R, 90 m., 1988

Produced by Don Boyd, with segments directed by Robert Altman, Bruce Beresford, Bill Bryden, Jean-Luc Godard, Derek Jarman, Franc Roddam, Nicolas Roeg, Ken Russell, Charles Sturridge, and Julien Temple.

Aria could be described, somewhat disrespectfully, as an operatic hit parade. The film is a labor of love by a British producer named Don Boyd, who convinced ten different directors to interpret ten famous arias in any style they chose. The result is uneven, of course, but stimulating and sometimes outrageous, as such diverse talents as Robert Altman, Ken Russell, and Jean-Luc Godard go to work.

None of the directors chose to just go ahead and film his aria in a straightforward, traditional way; Bill Bryden comes closest, with a wraparound segment starring John Hurt as a has-been virtuoso remembering his happier days. His story continues between each of the other arias, and finally he stands alone on stage and sings the famous aria from *I Pagliacci*, an opera about a man who found he could smile through his sadness. (John Hurt did not learn to sing for the movie; he mimes Caruso, and indeed all the segments feature prerecorded performances.)

Of the ten segments, I particularly enjoyed Franc Roddam's interpretation of *Liebestod*, from Wagner's *Tristan und Isolde*. He uses Bridget Fonda and James Mathers as young lovers who arrive in Las Vegas, drive slowly and (given the music) sadly down Glitter Gulch, check into a cheap hotel room, make love, and kill themselves. Despite, or perhaps because of, the unlikely setting, the episode is truly poignant in its portrait of the two doomed lovers.

Among the other segments, Nicolas Roeg's vision of Verdi's *Un Ballo in Maschera*, stars his wife, Theresa Russell, made up as a man, in a story based on the attempted assassination of King Zog of Albania in 1931 (you see how fanciful the directors were allowed to become). Charles Sturridge begins with Verdi's *La Vergine Degli Angeli*, from *La Forza del Destino*, and illustrates it with the story of three teenagers who skip school and end up in a traffic accident. Godard uses Lully's *Armide* as an excuse for a segment about bodybuilders. Julien Temple, the brash young British director, shoots his illustration of Verdi's *Rigoletto* in the famous Madonna Inn in San Luis Obispo, California, and stars Buck Henry as a movie producer who sneaks away with Beverly D'Angelo to the very hotel where his wife has also repaired with her lover.

Robert Altman's segment on Rameau's *Abaris ou les Boreades* re-creates the Parisian opening night in 1734 at the Ranelagh Theater, where he imagines the audience as being filled with a raffish and perhaps diseased assortment of lowlifes and the decadent. Bruce Beresford re-creates the seemingly dead city of Bruges, Belgium, to illustrate Korngold's *Die Tote Stadt*. Ken Russell chooses Puccini's *Turandot*, and uses the British pinup model Linzi Drew as his subject. She imagines her body being adorned by jewels, then wakes up in an operating room where she is receiving emergency care after a car crash. The mixture is typical of Russell's taste for exoticism and sensation. The final segment by Derek Jarman shows a veteran opera singer

at her last performance, intercut by 8mm home movies of an early love affair.

At the end of *Aria* one must decide, I suppose, what it all means. I am not sure that any indispensable statement about opera has been made here, and purists will no doubt recoil at the irreverence of some of the images. But the film is fun almost as a satire of itself; as a project in which the tension between the directors and their material allows them to poke a little fun at their own styles and obsessions. It's the first MTV version of opera.

Ariel ★ ★ ★
NO MPAA RATING, 74 m., 1990

Turo Pajala (Taisto Kasurinen), Susanna Haavisto (Irmeli), Matti Pellonpaa (Mikkonen), Eetu Hilkamo (Riku), Erkki Pajala (Miner), Matti Jaaranen (Mugger). Directed and produced by Aki Kaurismaki. Screenplay by Kaurismaki.

Ingmar Bergman made a film at the dawn of his career named *It Rains on My Future*, and I thought of that title while I was watching *Ariel*. This is the new film by Aki Kaurismaki, the director from Finland whose work has been winning festivals and inspiring articles in the film magazines calling him the best young director from Europe. I went expecting to see the new Fassbinder or Herzog or Almodovar, and what surprised me was how traditional the film is; it's a despairing *film noir* with a "happy" ending that taunts us with its irony.

The story involves Taisto, a miner from northern Finland who loses his job when the mine closes. He sits in a café with a depressed friend who gives him his old Cadillac convertible and then walks into the men's room and blows his brains out. Taisto drives the convertible to southern Finland, where he is quickly relieved of his life savings by muggers. He gets a day-labor job, gets a bed in a skid row mission, and then strikes up an instant romance with a meter maid, who throws away her parking tickets and goes for a ride in the Cadillac.

Meeting the meter maid is a stroke of luck for Taisto, but life is not going to be kind to him, and the plot of *Ariel* involves one crushing misfortune after another. It's like one of those 1940s B movies—*Detour*, maybe—where the hero tells you on the sound track that his luck is always rotten, and the story proves that he's right.

One of the special qualities of the movie is the physical clumsiness of most of the characters. They move like real people, not like

the smoothly choreographed athletes we see on TV and in American movies. When the hero runs, he looks like he's not accustomed to running. When cops race up to nab somebody, they run flat-footed and grab him in an awkward and uncoordinated tussle.

A similar clumsiness adds conviction to the action. Events occur in a stark and naive way. A bank robbery ends with money being dropped all over the sidewalk. Conversations are blunt. Motives are simple. The movie's lack of physical and social finesse is a positive quality; it makes the characters seem touchingly real. Watching their clumsiness, I became aware of how actions sometimes don't seem spontaneous in Hollywood films. Nobody ever seems to be performing an action for the first time, and the moves all seem practiced and familiar.

The hero of *Ariel* is played by Turo Pajala, an actor who bears a passing resemblance to Bruno S., the star of Herzog's *Kaspar Hauser*. He projects the qualities of a congenital victim, a man so overwhelmed by the relentless malice of the universe that he's punch-drunk with bad luck. The movie surrounds him with people who are on the same wavelength. Misfortune is their companion. The strongest character in the movie is the meter maid's young son, who keeps his nose stuck in comic books and accepts his roller-coaster life with stoic calm.

Ariel is the first film of Kaurismaki's I've seen, and on the basis of it, I want to see more. He has a particular vision. It isn't the vision of a flashy stylist with fashionable new attitudes, but the vision of a man who has found a filmmaking rhythm that suits his own bruised sensibility. *Ariel* speaks for the dispossessed with a special conviction because it isn't even angry. It's too tired to be angry. It's resigned. The more you think about it, the last scene, the "happy" ending, may be the only really angry scene in the movie.

Arizona Dream ★ ★ ★
R, 142m., 1995

Johnny Depp (Axel), Jerry Lewis (Leo Sweetie), Faye Dunaway (Elaine), Lili Taylor (Grace), Vincent Gallo (Paul), Paulina Porizkova (Millie), Michael J. Pollard (Fabian), Candyce Mason (Blanche). Directed by Emir Kusturica and produced by Claudie Ossard. Screenplay by David Atkins.

Accordion music makes me feel happy. Heaven, if I am given a choice, will include an Italian restaurant with an outdoor patio, shaded by a grape arbor, under which large plates of spaghetti are served while an accordion plays in the twilight ("Arreviderchi Roma," please). There is a lot of accordion music in *Arizona Dream*—too much for most people, I suppose, especially since the song is usually "Besame Mucho," played over and over, sometimes to turtles. But I am forgiving, especially since the accordion player is the irreplaceable Lili Taylor, with a cigarette stuck in her mug.

Here is a movie containing wonderful sights. Ambulances to the moon. Unsuccessful suicide by bungee cord. Johnny Depp. A dog saving a man from death in the Arctic. Faye Dunaway. Turtles crawling through meatballs. Jerry Lewis. A man who counts fish. Paulina Porizkova. Airplanes that look like they were borrowed from *Those Magnificent Men in Their Flying Machines*. Michael J. Pollard. Thunderstorms.

Arizona Dream is one of those movies that slips through the cracks. Hollywood bureaucracy has been established precisely to prevent films like this from being made. And yet it *was* made, and it is goofier than hell—you can't stop watching because nobody in the audience, and possibly nobody on the screen, has any idea what's going to happen next.

The movie was directed by Emir Kusturica, a Yugoslovian (if such a place still exists), whose *Underground* won Palme d'Or at the 1995 Cannes Film Festival. In his world, strange magic happens. People want to fly, and sometimes they can. Eccentricity is prized. His *Time of the Gypsies* (1989) followed a Gypsy family as it traveled through Yugoslavia and Italy, taking its occult knowledge with it. Now Kusturica has come to Arizona, which he sees as a similar land of enchantment.

The story involves Johnny Depp as a fish-counter who works in New York harbor: "Most people think I count fish, but I don't. I listen to their dreams." He is summoned west by an uncle (Jerry Lewis), who runs a Cadillac dealership near Tucson and wants his nephew to continue the family business. Depp arrives reluctantly, uninterested in cars, fascinated by the dreams of fish, to find his uncle preparing to wed a young girl (Candyce Mason). "He's trying to teach me to stop crying," she helpfully explains to Depp, during a fitting for a wedding gown.

Depp has never much liked his uncle ("He reminded me of the smell of car dealers' cheap cologne; he always looked like a ten-year-old boy whose sleeves were too long"). But he decides to stay for a time, and one day an exotic sight appears at the car lot: Faye Dunaway, widow of a rich miner, with her stepdaughter, played by Lili Taylor. Depp and Dunaway immediately feel a deep gravitational pull, and Depp finds himself out at their ranch, engaged in torrid lust, while Taylor wanders in the yard, playing the accordion.

What happens next, involving airplanes and ambulances, turtles and yo-yo suicides, I dare not say. There is a talent show at which someone does a credible imitation of Cary Grant during the crop-dusting scene in *North by Northwest*. And strange scenes on rooftops and treetops in thunderstorms. Needless to say, Warner Bros., having somehow made this film, did not want to encourage such a lapse by releasing it, and so it was only seen on the specialized circuit.

What we are dealing with here is a filmmaker who has his own peculiar vision of the world, and it does not correspond to the weary write-by-numbers formulas of standard screenplays. If he has a guide, it might be his fellow Yugoslavian Dusan Makavejev, whose own films show a similar cheerful mix of odd people and strange inventions. The movie is completely batty, and better suited probably to a giggly 1960s audience than to today's grim seekers after cinematic value for money.

Arthur ★ ★ ★ ½
PG, 97 m., 1981

Dudley Moore (Arthur Bach), Liza Minnelli (Linda Marolla), John Gielgud (Hobson), Geraldine Fitzgerald (Martha Bach), Jill Eikenberry (Susan), Stephen Elliott (Burt), Tod Ross (Bitterman), Barney Martin (Linda's Father). Directed and written by Steve Gordon. Produced by Robert Greenhut.

Only someone with a heart of stone could fail to love a drunk like Arthur Bach, who spends his wasted days in a poignant search for someone who will love him, will care for him, will inflame his passions, and soothe his pain, and who, most of all, will laugh at his one-liners. Arthur is such a servant of humanity that he even dedicates himself to thinking up new one-liners and holding them in reserve, lest he be unprepared if someone walks into his life and needs a laugh, quick.

Arthur, played by Dudley Moore, is the alcoholic hero of *Arthur*, a comedy about a man who is worth $750 million and who would never think of trying to buy anyone's love with his money. Arthur is like the woman in the poem by Yeats, who spent her days in innocent good will, and her nights in argument, till her voice grew shrill. Arthur, God love him, is a drunk. He slips into his bath of a morning, and his butler brings him a martini. After he completes his bath, Arthur sets about the day's business, which consists of staying drunk, and being driven about Manhattan in a limousine in his endless quest for love.

Now the problems with searching for love while you are drunk are many. They include (a) no one will want to love you while you are drunk, (b) you are not at your best while you are drunk, so they won't know what they're missing, (c) you may be too drunk to notice it if someone does finally fall in love with you, and (d) if you survive all of these pitfalls, you will nevertheless wake up hung over, and scientific studies prove that hangovers dissolve love. All of these things having been said, Arthur, against all odds, does find love. He finds it in the person of Linda (Liza Minnelli), a smart cookie who doesn't care about his money but is overwhelmed by the dimensions of his needs. Arthur would like to marry Linda. But his billionaire father insists that he marry a perfectly boring WASP (Jill Eikenberry) whose idea of a good holiday is probably the January white sales.

Arthur turns for help to his loyal butler, Hobson, who is played by John Gielgud with an understated elegance and a naughty tongue. Hobson is dying. But Hobson wishes to see Arthur prevail, for once, against Arthur's father, a sadistic puppet-master. So Hobson subtly manipulates the situation so that the lovers are thrown together at the party announcing Arthur's engagement to the WASP. That inspires a rupture within the family, and a very drunken odyssey by Arthur, who wants to press $100,000 upon Linda, and visits her at home. When Linda turns him down, her father (Barney Martin) becomes a grown man who sheds tears, creating perhaps the funniest moment in the movie.

Dudley Moore became a star, of course, with *10*, playing a man who became obsessed with Bo Derek, and who could blame him? In *Arthur*, he makes his bid for world-class status as a comic character actor. He brings a wonderful intensity to scenes like the one near the beginning of the film where he has invited a hooker to dinner at the Plaza and then forgotten who she is, and what she is, or why he is with her. It is marvelous to see him try to focus his attention, which he seems to believe is all concentrated in his eyebrow muscles.

Apart from Moore, the treasure of *Arthur*

is in its many supporting performances, especially Gielgud's, although everyone in this movie has great moments. You might be tempted to think that *Arthur* would be a bore, because it is about a drunk who is always trying to tell you stories. You would be right if *Arthur* were a party and you were attending it. But *Arthur* is a movie. And so its drunk, unlike real drunks, is more entertaining, more witty, more human, and more poignant than you are. He embodies, in fact, all the wonderful human qualities that drunks fondly, mistakenly believe the booze brings out in them.

At Close Range ★ ★ ★ ½
R, 115 m., 1986

Sean Penn (Brad, Jr.), Christopher Walken (Brad, Sr.), Mary Stuart Masterson (Terry), Christopher Penn (Tommy), Millie Perkins (Julie), Eileen Ryan (Grandma). Directed by James Foley and produced by Elliott Lewitt and Don Guest. Screenplay by Nicholas Kazan.

Here is a spare, violent, unforgiving story of a boy's need for a father who does not love him and who would, if necessary, murder him. It is also a story with passages of love and adventure and cheerfulness, as a teenager grows up in the hills of rural Pennsylvania. The way that the two sides of the story grow together creates a tragedy that reminds me of myth, of the ancient stories of children betrayed by their parents, and yet *At Close Range* is based on a true story. It happened in 1978.

The movie stars Sean Penn, probably the best of the younger actors, as Bradford Whitewood, Jr. He lives with his divorced mother and grandmother and half-brother in a setting of shabby poverty, nonstop TV watching, and boredom. Once in a while, his father, Brad Senior, appears out of nowhere and throws money on the table. Then Brad Senior drives away in a fast car with a pretty girl. The kid would like a taste of his father's life. It looks a lot better than what he has.

The father is played by Christopher Walken, in one of the great hateful performances of recent years. Walken is a strange actor, hard to pin down, but when he is given the right role (as he is here, and in *Dead Zone* and *The Deer Hunter*), there is nobody to touch him for his chilling ability to move between easy charm and vile evil. In the movie, he's the leader of a gang of professional thieves who have recently been specializing in stealing

tractors. He likes to play the big shot, and in a way he enjoys the fact that his young son has started to idolize him.

Penn, as Brad Junior, isn't really criminal material, but he's a misfit and an outcast and absolutely nothing is happening for him in his own life. He drifts into the orbit of his father, looking for love but also looking for action. He's the leader of a young gang of his own, and his father assigns the kids to a couple of easy jobs—getting them ready for the big time. But when the big time turns dangerous, and it looks as if the gang might be busted, the Walken character is absolutely prepared to save his own skin, even at the cost of betraying his own child.

At Close Range is not a pleasant movie. Few recent films have painted such a bleak picture of human nature. The Walken character is pure evil, wrapped in easy charm, and most of the other characters in the film are weak, or deprived, or lacking in the ability to see beyond their own immediate situation. That's especially true of Brad Junior's mother (Millie Perkins) and grandmother (Eileen Ryan), who sit endlessly around the house, their eyes straying away from every conversation, toward the TV set. Only Brad Junior and his local girlfriend (Mary Stuart Masterson) have a chance of breaking free, and their love affair is on a collision course with Brad Senior.

Because this film is violent and cruel and very sad, why would you want to see it? For a couple of reasons, perhaps. One might be to watch two great actors, Penn and Walken, at the top of their forms, in roles that give them a lot to work with. Another might be to witness some of the dynamics of a criminal society, some of the forces that push criminals further than they intend to go. It's the same dynamic you could see in the great crime film *In Cold Blood* (1967)—seemingly ordinary people whose moral sense is missing, and who drift into actions so evil that perhaps even they are appalled.

At Play in the Fields of the Lord
★ ★ ★ ½
R, 190 m., 1991

Tom Berenger (Lewis Moon), John Lithgow (Leslie Huben), Daryl Hannah (Andy Huben), Aidan Quinn (Martin Quarrier), Tom Waits (Wolf), Kathy Bates (Hazel Quarrier). Directed by Hector Babenco and produced by Saul Zaentz. Screenplay by Jean-Claude Carrière and Babenco.

The most striking image in Peter Matthiessen's novel *At Play in the Fields of the Lord* describes an Amazonian Indian, standing in the center of a forest clearing, defiantly raising his bow and arrow against an airplane that flies between himself and the sun. The image has been used as the logo for the new film of the novel, but actually two planes cast their shadows on these Indians. One brings the drunken bush pilots Wolf and Moon, to be hired by a tinpot jungle general to bomb the Indians. The other brings earnest missionaries from North America, to preach their religion to the tribe. In Matthiessen's world, both of these aircraft are machines bearing destruction.

Matthiessen's novel was published some twenty-five years ago, but could not be more contemporary in its issues. At the same time, few great modern novels offer more problems for those who would adapt them to the screen. So much of the action in *At Play in the Fields of the Lord* takes place inside the minds and souls of the characters—inside Andy, the blond woman missionary whose dormant sexuality is awakened, and inside Martin Quarrier, who comes to question everything about his faith after his child is taken by God, and inside Lewis Moon, the American-Indian gunrunner whose identity is reawakened when he sees the Indian in the forest below, pointing his arrow at the plane. What happens in the material world of this story is not the point; it is a book about how the identities and beliefs of its characters are changed.

The film has been produced by Saul Zaentz, an independent producer who seems to seek out "unfilmable" source material (his credits include *One Flew Over the Cuckoo's Nest*, *Amadeus*, and *The Unbearable Lightness of Being*). With the Brazilian director Hector Babenco he went into the middle of the rain forest to film on location, and the mood and feel of those real places, the impenetrable, throbbing jungle on either side of the vast, indifferent Amazon, is one of the central qualities of his film.

At a desperately poor but defiantly colorful little jungle settlement—the bright colors of the paint disguise the abashed rotting buildings—the first plane arrives. It bears Lewis Moon (Tom Berenger) and Wolf (Tom Waits), compadres in a series of mercenary skirmishes in minor Latin American wars, now washed up here without funds. The district commander confiscates their worthless passports and keeps them prisoner, trying to talk them into bombing a local tribe that stands in the way of "progress," by which he means the destruction of the jungle.

On another flight, the Martin Quarrier family arrives: Aidan Quinn as a dedicated but naive missionary, Kathy Bates as his hysterical wife, and Niilo Kivirinta as Billy, their perfect child. They are welcomed by two local missionaries, Leslie and Andy Huben (John Lithgow and Daryl Hannah), who have become legendary because of Leslie's optimistic letters to the missionary magazines—letters that do not reflect their complete lack of progress in converting any Indians, aside from a mercenary straggler who has sold out for money.

In an atmosphere of dank rot and decay, headquartered in a foul hotel where the prostitutes outrank them, the Quarriers prepare to reoccupy a station where the previous missionaries were murdered by the Indians. The local Catholic priest, whose religion seems more pragmatic and adapted to the region, listens to their hymns and observes their preparations and wishes them well, no doubt convinced he will never see them again. Then the Quarriers (Quinn, Bates, and the child) go off to staff the isolated station, their canoe filled with trinkets to use as bribes.

Meanwhile, in the other great sweep of the story, Lewis Moon grows drunk and insane on local brews and drugs, and flies his airplane off over the jungle, parachuting into the green carpet below, where he is greeted by the Indians as an emissary of the gods. He learns bits of the language, is accepted as a member of the tribe, and then tries to lead them in a crusade to drive out the missionaries. But this is only the surface of the story, which reveals itself in a series of tragedies and a quiet, sad, sweeping conclusion.

In Matthiessen's novel, each of the characters has his or her day. In the film, choices have been made, and in most cases they reflect the elements that could most easily be filmed. Berenger's stay with the Indian tribe provides the most impressive scenes, and Babenco and Zaentz are patient here, providing time for us to get to know some of the tribe members and their ways. Amazonian Indians play themselves and are subtitled; these are not screenplay Indians.

In the world of the missionaries, the Aidan Quinn character becomes the most important because he changes the most, and the struggle between him and his wife (Bates) over the fate of their child becomes the movie's dramatic centerpoint. The characters played by John Lithgow and Daryl Hannah tend to recede because they provide fewer dramatic opportunities, and although I missed the novel's insights into the slow, deep changes within the Hannah character, I must admit I am not sure how they could have been visualized.

At Play in the Fields of the Lord does not build to a conventional plot climax. It is about beliefs more than actions. Watching it, we are looking at a morality play about a world in which sincere people create unwitting mischief so that evil people can have their way. The movie essentially argues that all peoples have a right to worship their own gods without interference, but it goes further to observe that if your God lives in the land and the trees, then if we destroy your land, we kill your God. These messages are buried in the very fabric of the film, in the way it was shot and in its use of locations, and we are not told them; we absorb them.

At the Max ★ ★ ★ ★
R, 89 m., 1992

A documentary featuring the Rolling Stones (Mick Jagger, Keith Richards, Charlie Watts, Ron Wood, and Bill Wyman). Directed by Julien Temple and produced by Michael Cohl and André Picard.

It was probably only a matter of time before the Rolling Stones, billed as the greatest rock 'n' roll band in the world, got together with the IMAX format, which is certainly the greatest movie format in the world. The result is *At the Max,* which in its theatrical impact is the greatest concert film ever made. That doesn't mean it's the best film about a concert; there are some better ones, including *Woodstock.* But no other musical film in my experience has so overwhelmed the eyes and ears, drawing us into the feeling and texture of a rock concert.

If you have been to any of the museums and tourist centers that include an IMAX theater, you are familiar with the format. You are confronted with a screen that is four or five stories high, and surrounded by sound from speakers so powerful that even a whisper sounds like a message from God. The image, projected from special 70mm film, is both enormous in size and dazzling in clarity, and it fills your field of vision so completely that some viewers have actually suffered from vertigo.

This format is usually employed for educational and travelogue material: good films like *Antarctica,* which took us inside icebergs, or the NASA documentaries, which took us into space, and bad films like one I saw at the Polynesian Cultural Center, which took a condescending view of Pacific Islanders. Whatever the subject matter, the visual and aural experience at an IMAX film is always startling.

And now here are the Stones, in *At the Max,* recorded and filmed in IMAX during the 1991 Rolling Stones concert tour. All of the concert is here; most IMAX films are limited to forty minutes because the reels of film are so cumbersome that the projectors can't handle more, but this one is double-length, with an intermission while the reels are changed.

In its impact on the senses, seeing this film is better than being at a Stones concert. It's like being onstage with the Stones, except that even a member of the band doesn't have an omnipresent point of view, and the cameras do, cutting from one side of the enormous stage to another, and providing close-ups so large and clear that we can count the cigarettes in Bill Wyman's pack.

The film was shot by Julien Temple *(The Great Rock and Roll Swindle),* using several of the big IMAX cameras, and it has been edited to preserve the impact of the concert, not to upstage it. Some of the most important shots are taken from far back in the arena, giving an impression of the massive nature of a modern rock concert, with its tens of thousands of spectators. Others are so close we get four-story close-ups of Mick Jagger, although for the most part, aware of the overwhelming nature of the format, Temple keeps his camera back far enough for us to see the full body lengths of the musicians.

The central impression you come away with after any Stones concert, in person or on film, is of Mick Jagger's physical and psychic energy as a performer. Here the camera follows him as he climbs scaffolding to sing a hundred feet above the stage, or when he does a strange duet with huge inflatable dolls. (Those mildly suggestive dolls, and the language, earned the movie an R rating, but most teen-agers will hear little to surprise them.) The eerie effect of IMAX is that it takes such passages and makes them both performance and documentary. They work as part of the show, but because the screen is so large and the picture so clear, we also feel like part of the experience; no other movie has communicated so well what it must feel like to be a rock star.

Do I need to write about the music? There are few surprises; this is your basic Stones concert. A lot of the Stones standards are here, and some new songs, and they sound wonderful through the big surround speakers. But the music is not really the point; it's the actual moviegoing experience that makes *At the Max* worth seeing. In the computer world, they talk about "virtual reality," a kind of cyberspace in which computers would take over what we see, hear, and feel, so that we could have the sensation of an experience without actually being there. *At the Max* is a rock concert brought to a point approaching virtual reality.

The movie is available on tape and disc, but see it in an IMAX theater if you can.

Au Revoir les Enfants ★ ★ ★ ★
PG, 103 m., 1988

Gaspard Manesse (Julien Quentin), Raphael Fejto (Jean Bonnet), Francine Racette (Madame Quentin), Stanislas Carre de Malberg (Francois Quentin), Philippe Morier-Genoud (Father Jean), Francois Berleand (Father Michel), Francois Negret (Joseph), Peter Fitz (Muller). Directed, written, and produced by Louis Malle.

Which of us cannot remember a moment when we did or said precisely the wrong thing, irretrievably, irreparably? The instant the action was completed or the words were spoken, we burned with shame and regret, but what we had done could never be repaired. Such moments are rare, and they occur most often in childhood, before we have been trained to think before we act. *Au Revoir les Enfants* is a film about such a moment, about a quick, unthinking glance that may have cost four people their lives.

The film was written and directed by Louis Malle, who based it on a childhood memory. Judging by the tears I saw streaming down his face on the night the film was shown at the Telluride Film Festival, the memory has caused him pain for many years. His story takes place in 1944, in a Catholic boarding school in Nazi-occupied France. At the start of a new semester, three new students are enrolled, and we realize immediately that they are Jews, disguised with new names and identities in an attempt to hide them from the Nazis.

To Julien Quentin (Gaspard Manesse), however, this is not at all obvious. Julien, who is intended as Malle's autobiographical double, does not quite understand all of the distinctions involving Jews and gentiles in a country run by Nazis. All he knows is that he likes one of the new boys, Jean Bonnet (Ra-

phael Fejto), and they become friends. Bonnet is not popular with the other students, who follow the age-old schoolboy practice of closing ranks against newcomers, but then Julien is not very popular either; the two boys are a little dreamy and thoughtful—absorbed in themselves and their imaginations, as bright adolescents should be. Malle's film is not filled with a lot of dramatic incidents. Unlike such roughly comparable Hollywood films as *The Lords of Discipline*, it feels no need for strong plotting and lots of dramatic incidents leading up to the big finale. Instead, we enter the daily lives of these boys. We see the classroom routine, the air-raid drills, the way each teacher has his own way of dealing with problems of discipline. More than anything else, we get a feeling for the rhythm of the school. Malle has said that when, years later, he visited the actual site of the boarding school he attended, he found that the building had disappeared and the school was forgotten. But to a student enrolled in such a school, the rules and rituals seem timeless, handed down by innumerable generations and destined to survive forever. A schoolboy cannot be expected to understand how swiftly violence and evil can strike out and change everything.

Julien and Jean play together, study together, look at dirty postcards together. One day, one of those cold early spring days when the shadows seem ominous and there is an unsettling wind in the trees, they go exploring in a nearby forest, and darkness falls. They get lost, or almost lost, and they weather this adventure and become even closer friends. One day, Julien accidentally discovers that "Jean Bonnet" is not his friend's real name. A few days later, when Julien's mother comes to visit, he invites Jean to join them at lunch in a local restaurant, and they witness an anti-Semitic incident as a longtime local customer is singled out because he is Jewish.

That is about all the input that Julien receives, and it is hard to say exactly what he knows, or suspects, about Jean. But when Nazis visit the school, Julien performs in one tragic second an action that will haunt him for the rest of his days. Malle has said that the incident in *Au Revoir les Enfants* does not exactly parallel whatever happened in real life, but the point must be the same: In an unthinking moment, action is taken that can never be retrieved.

Is the film only about guilt? Not at all. It is constructed very subtly to show that Julien only half-realized the nature of the situation,

anyway. It isn't as if Julien knew absolutely that Jean was Jewish. It's more as if Julien possessed a lot of information that he had never quite put together, and when the Nazis came looking for hidden Jews, Julien suddenly realized what his information meant. The moment in which he makes his tragic mistake is also, perhaps, the moment when he comprehends for the first time the shocking fact of racism.

Autumn Sonata ★ ★ ★ ★
PG, 97 m., 1978

Ingrid Bergman (Charlotte), Liv Ullmann (Eva), Lena Nyman (Helena), Halvor Bjork (Viktor), Georg Lokkeberg (Leonardo), Knut Wigert (The Professor). Directed by Ingmar Bergman. Screenplay by Bergman.

Ingrid Bergman was certainly one of the most beautiful women to ever appear in a film, but that is not the source of her mysterious appeal. There is something there, in that voice and those eyes and in the way her mouth thinks words before she says them, that is, quite simply, unduplicated in the movies. It took Ingmar Bergman thirty-five years to finally cast her in one of his films, and then, in her fortieth year as an actress, Ingrid Bergman called *Autumn Sonata* her last film. Sweden's two most important film artists finally worked together.

The movie is a historic event, taking us back to so many different areas of our memories. We remember Ingrid Bergman from some of the basic cinematic artifacts of all time, movies like *Casablanca* and *Notorious*. But we've never seen her really pushed, really tested, by a director whose commitment to honesty is nothing short of merciless.

Ingmar Bergman didn't cast her for reasons of nostalgia, or sentiment: He cast her because he had an idea for a role she could brilliantly contain and that would contain her, and in *Autumn Sonata* she gives nothing less than the performance of her lifetime. We can only be quietly grateful that she performs opposite Liv Ullmann, who is herself good enough to meet her on the same very high level.

They play mother and daughter. The mother is an internationally famous pianist (and we remember Ingrid Bergman's first great success, as the pianist in *Intermezzo*). She has not seen her daughter for seven years. She's too busy and always traveling and booked up almost every night of the week . . . and, not incidentally, terrified of confronting her daughter.

There are, in fact, two daughters: The one played by Ullmann, who is serious and introspective and filled with guilt and blame and love, and then the other daughter (Lena Nyman), who lives with her, and who suffers from a degenerative nerve disease. The mother's solution to this daughter's illness was to place her in a "home"; Ullmann has taken her out of the institution and brought her home to live with her.

On the morning when the mother arrives for her long-delayed visit, she has no idea that the sick daughter will be there. Her response, on learning that her other daughter is upstairs, is dismay. She's never been able to deal with the illness—but, then, she's never been able to deal at all with the fact of being a mother. She doesn't merely reject the responsibility; she flees from it.

Autumn Sonata then gives us a sort of long day's journey into night in which the pleasantries of the opening hours give way to deeper and deeper terrors and guilts, accusations and renunciations, cries and whispers. And Ingmar Bergman, standing apart from this material and regarding it with clarity and detachment, refuses to find any solutions. There are none, I suppose. A lesser filmmaker would have resolved everything at the end in some sort of neat Freudian bookkeeping, but Bergman finds in his story only two people, each demanding love from the other, each doomed by the past to fall just short of the ability to love.

This is excruciatingly difficult material. Ingrid Bergman and Liv Ullmann confront it with a courage and skill that is astonishing. We've always known that Liv Ullmann was a great actress (that is one of the givens of film in the past two decades), and we've known, too, that Ingrid Bergman was a great movie star. But how important that in her sixties, acting in her native language for the first time in four decades, working with one of the supreme film directors, Bergman was able to use not only her star qualities but also every last measure of her artistry and her humanity. It is not just that *Autumn Sonata* was Ingrid Bergman's last film. It's that she knew she had to make it before she died.

Avalon ★ ★ ★ ½
PG, 126 m., 1990

Leo Fuchs (Hymie Krichinsky), Eve Gordon (Dottie Kirk), Lou Jacobi (Gabriel Krichinsky),
Armin Mueller-Stahl (Sam Krichinsky), Elizabeth Perkins (Ann Kaye), Joan Plowright (Eva Krichinsky), Kevin Pollak (Issy Kirk), Aidan Quinn (Jules Kaye). Directed by Barry Levinson and produced by Mark Johnson and Levinson. Screenplay by Levinson.

"All happy families are alike but an unhappy family is unhappy after its own fashion."
—Tolstoy

This is one of the most familiar quotations in literature for the excellent reason that it states a truth everyone can recognize. The strength of Barry Levinson's *Avalon* is that it starts as a movie about a happy family and shows why it became unhappy after its own fashion. During the first half hour of the film, my heart sank because it seemed to be another of those potted biopics about an immigrant family's legends and eccentricities, all three times as colorful as life. Then the colors began to darken and the mood began to change, and the film deepened into the story of many American families that have grown apart over the generations.

Consider for a moment the term "nuclear family." It reflects a goal we aspire to in our society: mom and dad and all the kids gathered around the hearth with the family dog and the television set. But there is something missing from the picture: grandparents, uncles, aunts, cousins, in-laws. We call such a family nuclear because it revolves around the nucleus of a single family home. But it is also nuclear because it flies in a lonely orbit of its own.

Levinson's *Avalon* is inspired by the experiences of his own family. His grandparents came to America from Russia, part of a large Jewish family that pooled its resources and brought over one relative after another until at last the five Krichinsky brothers had all settled in Baltimore. They were musicians—violinists, available for hire—but during the week they worked as paper-hangers. They worked hard and raised large families and their extended family was the center of their social life. They lived near to one another, held family councils, and pooled their money for charitable giving and to help out family members in need. And they had glowing ambitions for their children. One parent tells his son he will never teach him how to hang wallpaper, because "it is not a job you should grow up to do." Notes like this are struck with absolute accuracy; I remember my own father refusing to teach me his trade for the same reason.

The world of Baltimore in the first half of the century is re-created by the film with an unforced, but rich detail. The clothes and cars are just right, of course, but so are the values. We understand how for some of the brothers, especially Gabriel (Lou Jacobi), family traditions are sacred. He objects when one of his brothers moves to the suburbs after the war. He complains that he cannot find the suburbs, that it is too far a drive—but his real complaint is that the family is flying apart and losing its solidarity. This process is dramatized in the film's central scene, a Thanksgiving dinner where Gabriel and his wife arrive late and the family has already cut the turkey.

It is a trivial incident, perhaps, but it symbolizes a much larger event, the cutting of the family's close ties. Each generation is a little more alienated from the sense of community that the first generation brought over from Russia. Each new family drifts a little further from the center of the family circle. This is a process that may have something to do with the nature of American society. Europeans are vertically conformist; they want to do things as their ancestors did. Americans are horizontally conformist; we want to do things as our neighbors do. This process breaks down the richness of ethnic heritage and creates a bland Middle American who, in a way, is from nowhere—who was invented in TV commercials.

Television gets a lot of the blame from Levinson for the breakdown of the family. At first the whole family gathers around the first set they've seen, staring in fascination at the test patterns. Later the big, loud family meals are replaced by smaller groups eating off of TV trays, looking at prime time.

Meanwhile, material success comes quickly to some of the Krichinskys. Issy and Jules (Kevin Pollak and Aidan Quinn), two cousins of the second generation, "Americanize" their surnames to Kirk and Kaye and open a big appliance store. They advertise on TV in hambone commercials that have the customers lined up around the block. They expand and eventually take over a big warehouse, opening the first discount department store in Baltimore. Things are going well when two of their children—including a character probably meant to be Levinson himself—do something I will not reveal here, but which is told with such empathy, with such memory for how young children do and remember things, that it becomes the other central pillar of the film.

In a way, the kids do what they do because of what they've seen on television. The result, indirectly, is that one of their fathers gets a job selling advertising time on TV. Television is a thread all through the movie. It's a socially divisive force, but it's also an entertainment, a hypnotic pastime, an occupation, an influence, a presence. Levinson seems to feel that TV is a disastrous invention that has cut our human society off from its roots. That may be true (although it will not, of course, prevent the eventual sale of this film to television).

Avalon is often a warm and funny film, but it is also a sad one, and the final sequence is heartbreaking. It shows the way in which our modern families, torn loose of their roots, have left old people alone and lonely—warehoused in retirement homes. The story of the movie is the story of how the warmth and closeness of an extended family is replaced by alienation and isolation. The title of the film comes from the name of the Baltimore neighborhood where the family first settled. In Celtic mythology, Avalon was an island of blessed souls, an earthly paradise somewhere in the western seas. Who would think, sailing for it, that they would fall off the edge of the Earth?

Awakenings ★ ★ ★ ★
PG-13, 121 m., 1990

Robert De Niro (Leonard Lowe), Robin Williams (Dr. Malcolm Sayer), Julie Kavner (Eleanor Costello), Ruth Nelson (Mrs. Lowe), John Heard (Dr. Kaufman), Anne Meara (Miriam), Lolly Esterman (Lolly), Penelope Ann Miller (Paula). Directed by Penny Marshall and produced by Walter F. Parkes and Lawrence Lasker. Screenplay by Steven Zaillian.

We do not know what we see when we look at Leonard. We think we see a human vegetable, a peculiar man who has been frozen in the same position for thirty years, who neither moves nor speaks. What goes on inside his mind? Is he thinking in there? Of course not, a neurologist says, in Penny Marshall's film *Awakenings*. Why not? "Because the implications of that would be unthinkable." Ah, but the expert is wrong, and inside the immobile shell of his body, Leonard is still there. Still waiting.

Leonard is one of the patients in the "garden," a ward of a Bronx mental hospital that is so named by the staff because the patients are there simply to be fed and watered. It ap-

pears that nothing can be done for them. They were victims of the great "sleeping sickness" epidemic of the 1920s, and after a period of apparent recovery they regressed to their current states. It is 1969. They have many different symptoms, but essentially they all share the same problem: They cannot make their bodies do what their minds desire. Sometimes that blockage is manifested through bizarre physical behavior, sometimes through apparent paralysis.

One day, a new doctor comes to work in the hospital. He has no experience in working with patients; indeed, his last project involved earthworms. Like those who have gone before him, he has no particular hope for these ghostly patients, who are there and yet not there. He talks without hope to one of the women, who looks blankly back at him, her head and body frozen. But then he turns away, and when he turns back she has changed her position—apparently trying to catch her eyeglasses as they fell. He tries an experiment. He holds her glasses in front of her, and then drops them. Her hand flashes out quickly and catches them.

Yet this woman cannot move through her own will. He tries another experiment, throwing a ball at one of the patients. She catches it. "She is borrowing the will of the ball," the doctor speculates. His colleagues will not listen to this theory, which sounds suspiciously metaphysical, but he thinks he's on to something. What if these patients are not actually "frozen" at all, but victims of a stage of Parkinson's disease so advanced that their motor impulses are canceling each other out—what if they cannot move because all of their muscles are trying to move at the same time, and they are powerless to choose one impulse over the other? Then the falling glasses or the tossed ball might be breaking the deadlock!

This is the great discovery in the opening scenes of *Awakenings*, preparing the way for sequences of enormous joy and heartbreak, as the patients are "awakened" to a personal freedom they had lost all hope of ever again experiencing—only to find that their liberation comes with its own cruel set of conditions. The film, directed with intelligence and heart by Penny Marshall, is based on a famous 1972 book by Oliver Sacks, the British-born New York neurologist whose *The Man Who Mistook His Wife for a Hat* is a classic of medical literature. These were his patients, and the doctor in the film, named Malcolm Sayer and played by Robin Williams, is based on him.

What he discovered in the summer of 1969 was that L-dopa, a new drug for the treatment of Parkinson's disease, might, in massive doses, break the deadlock that had frozen his patients into a space-time lock for endless years. The film follows some fifteen of those patients, particularly Leonard, who is played by Robert De Niro in a virtuoso performance. Because this movie is not a tearjerker but an intelligent examination of a bizarre human condition, it's up to De Niro to make Leonard not an object of sympathy, but a person who helps us wonder about our own tenuous grasp on the world around us.

The patients depicted in this film have suffered a fate more horrible than the one in Poe's famous story about premature burial. If we were locked in a coffin while still alive, at least we would soon suffocate. But to be locked inside a body that cannot move or speak—to look out mutely as even our loved ones talk about us as if we were an uncomprehending piece of furniture! It is this fate that is lifted, that summer of 1969, when the doctor gives the experimental new drug to his patients, and in a miraculous rebirth their bodies thaw and they begin to move and talk once again, some of them after thirty years of self-captivity.

The movie follows Leonard through the stages of his rebirth. He was (as we saw in a prologue) a bright, likable kid, until the disease took its toll. He has been on hold for three decades. Now, in his late forties, he is filled with wonder and gratitude to be able to move around freely and express himself. He cooperates with the doctors studying his case. And he finds himself attracted to the daughter (Penelope Ann Miller) of another patient. Love and lust stir within him for the first time.

Dr. Sayer, played by Williams, is at the center of almost every scene, and his personality becomes one of the touchstones of the movie. He is shut off, too, by shyness and inexperience, and even the way he holds his arms, close to his sides, shows a man wary of contact. He really was happier working with those earthworms. This is one of Robin Williams's best performances, pure and uncluttered, without the ebullient distractions he sometimes adds—the schtick where none is called for. He is a lovable man here, who experiences the extraordinary professional joy of seeing chronic, hopeless patients once again sing and dance and greet their loved ones.

But it is not as simple as that, not after the

first weeks. The disease is not an open-and-shut case. And as the movie unfolds, we are invited to meditate on the strangeness and wonder of the human personality. Who are we, anyway? How much of the self we treasure so much is simply a matter of good luck, of being spared in a minefield of neurological chance? If one has no hope, which is better: to remain hopeless, or to be given hope and then lose it again? Oliver Sacks's original book, which has been reissued, is as much a work of philosophy as of medicine. After seeing *Awakenings,* I read it, to know more about what happened in that Bronx hospital. What both the movie and the book convey is the immense courage of the patients and the profound experience of their doctors, as in a small way they re-experienced what it means to be born, to open your eyes, and discover to your astonishment that "you" are alive.

B

Babyfever ★ ★ ★
R, 110 m., 1994

Victoria Foyt (Gena), Matt Salinger (James), Dinah Lenney (Roz), Eric Roberts (Anthony), Frances Fisher (Rosie), Elaine Kagan (Milly), Zack Norman (Mark). Directed by Henry Jaglom and produced by Judith Wolinsky. Screenplay by Jaglom and Victoria Foyt.

Henry Jaglom's *Babyfever* is another one of his engagingly offhand fictionalized documentaries, in which the characters talk earnestly and all too comprehensively about the problem *du jour:* in this case, whether or not to have a baby. Like many of his films, it has an appeal almost despite itself. It's too long, it's too talky, it indulges itself, and yet because it is sincere and sometimes funny, we are willing to watch.

At some point there will be a retrospective of all of Jaglom's films, and what we will be watching will be the most expensive personal journal anyone has ever kept. Faithfully following Jaglom through the years, I have clocked his girlfriends, his thoughts about marriage, about careers, about movies. I have suffered along with his friends as they agonized about fidelity, about eating disorders, about "choices." Now we have a film about babies, and it comes as no surprise that the star and coauthor, Victoria Foyt, is Mrs. Henry Jaglom, and that they have recently had their second child.

Foyt plays a character named Gena, who as the movie opens is just about ready to commit to her boyfriend, James (Matt Salinger). He's sort of safe and sort of boring, but, darn it, she argues, maybe what she *needs* is someone safe and boring. Before long we meet the dangerous and exciting man (Eric Roberts) she's trying to recover from, and we see her point.

Foyt and all of her friends are of an age

when the biological clock starts ticking audibly. If they want to ever have a baby, the time is now (or *now, today!* as one woman puts it) and yet where is the father? Should they still hold out for the perfect father? Enlist a friend as a volunteer? Visit the sperm bank? Get "accidentally" pregnant? ("Only two kinds of women get accidentally pregnant," a character observes. "Idiots and liars.")

Burdened by these thoughts, and torn between her bland current boyfriend and her maddening former one, Foyt attends a baby shower for a friend. And this gives Jaglom his chance to switch into his preferred mode, the pseudo-documentary. Using the excuse that a documentary is being shot about the baby shower, he intercuts the thoughts of more than a dozen women. Some have babies. Some want babies. Some never want babies. Some do not know. Most are articulate, most notably Frances Fisher (who later said the experience of making this movie helped her decide she wanted a baby with her companion, Clint Eastwood).

Jaglom is up against a slight problem here. None of these women, intelligent as they are, has anything really new to say on the subject—because there *is* nothing really new to say. These issues have been aired for years in print and on the talk shows, and what they always boil down to is: Most people think it would be nice to fall in love with the perfect partner and have perfect babies. Some people do not. Many who wish they could cannot, or have not.

Jaglom avoids wall-to-wall interviews by using a funny subplot, involving Mark (Zack Norman), the husband of the hostess and employer of Gena. He is a realtor desperately short on funds, and is raising cash any way he can. (One shot begins with a closeup of a nail hole in a wall, and pans down to the angry wife, asking him what happened to the

painting that was there this morning.) Norman brings a comic desperation to his character, and it's welcome in the midst of all the earnestness.

Leaving the movie, I had the feeling I'd been at a party with some nice, interesting people, and it went on a little too long. I was happy to meet them, I wish them well, and now I don't want to hear anything about babies for several weeks.

Baby, It's You ★ ★ ★
R, 105 m., 1983

Rosanna Arquette (Jill), Vincent Spano (Sheik), Joanna Merlin (Mrs. Rosen), Jack Davidson (Dr. Rosen). Directed by John Sayles and produced by Griffin Dunne and Amy Robinson. Screenplay by Sayles.

Rosanna Arquette has a way about her. She's a natural actress, and by that I don't mean she was born talented (although perhaps she was), but that she is able to appear onscreen with such an unaffected natural quality that I feel as if I'm looking past the script and direction and actually experiencing the life of her character. That's the feeling I got during *Baby, It's You,* a sometimes very good, sometimes disappointingly uneven movie that she carries from beginning to end. Even when her scenes aren't working, her character is, and we're getting to know this young woman she plays, this Jill Rosen, who turns from an uncommonly engaging high school student to a scared-stiff college freshman.

The movie is by John Sayles, who has built a career for himself out of the carefully observed events that make up ordinary lives. His first film was *Return of the Secaucus Seven,* about some thirty-fiveish survivors of the 1960s. Then he made *Lianna,* about a thirty-fiveish faculty wife who discovers, with fear and some anticipation, that she is a lesbian.

Now here is Jill Rosen, a high school student from the 1960s who could, we suspect, easily grow up to be any of the women in Sayles's first two films.

Jill is smart and pretty, especially when she smiles. Her brains and her smile are only the half of it. She's also got a personal style. She has this way of letting you know she's listening, even when she seems to be ignoring you. A way of caring for you, even when she's mad at you. You get the feeling this is a woman whose love would be a very important thing for you to count on. And that's certainly the opinion of the Sheik (Vincent Spano), a semi-greaser who is consumed by his desire to be exactly like Frank Sinatra. The Sheik and (actually) a lot of this movie seem to belong more to the fifties than the sixties—but never mind. Here is a kid who's a sharp dresser, has a lot of apparent self-confidence, and doesn't mind that he stands out like a sore thumb with his brazen ways and his Sinatra wardrobe. He's a rebel with ambitions. Jill loves him, but when she leaves Trenton, New Jersey, and enters the uncertain world of Sarah Lawrence College, the Sheik doesn't fit in.

Baby, It's You does two things with this material. First, it remembers it accurately, right down to the irritating mannerisms of preppy college boys with too much unearned self-confidence. Then, it uses it as a meditation on growing up—which means learning to listen to your heart as well as to your ambitions. The movie works best in its high school segments, and the opening hour is wonderful. Then the infuriating stuff begins, when this movie that has been so surefooted loses its way in the college scenes, and allows us to wonder at times what we're supposed to be thinking. Rosanna Arquette is equally good, however, in the good parts and the disappointing ones.

Baby's Day Out ★ ½
PG, 99 m., 1994

Joe Mantegna (Eddie), Lara Flynn Boyle (Laraine), Joe Pantoliano (Norby), Brian Haley (Veeko), Cynthia Nixon (Gilbertine), Fred Dalton Thompson (FBI Agent), John Neville (Mr. Andrews), Matthew Glave (Bennington), Adam and Jacob Worton (Baby Bink). Directed by Patrick Read Johnson and produced by John Hughes and Richard Vane. Screenplay by Hughes.

Baby's Day Out looks like an attempt to make a live-action comedy out of the same kinds of

material that inspired the Baby Herman sequence at the beginning of *Who Framed Roger Rabbit*. It demonstrates that what's funny in animation does not always translate to the real world. I laughed when Baby Herman went fearlessly crawling on top of the refrigerator, but here, when Baby Bink crawled under a taxi and out into traffic, I wasn't as amused.

The movie is a curious mixture of 1930s images of crooks and society people, crossed with modern locations, mostly in Chicago. It opens as three would-be kidnappers pose as baby photographers to gain entry to the mansion of the millionaire Cotwells, where Baby Bink is about to have his portrait taken. The leader of the gang (Joe Mantegna) talks Mrs. Cotwell (Lara Flynn Boyle) and the nanny and butler out of the room, and then he and his sidekicks (Joe Pantoliano and Brian Haley) escape with the infant.

That's the setup. Most of the rest of the movie consists of cartoon-style sight gags, as Baby Bink (played by twins Adam and Jacob Worton) fecklessly crawls through the city on an odyssey inspired by his favorite storybook. While all adults (except for the kidnappers) somehow never notice him, Bink crawls on high rooftops, boards a bus, takes a cab, visits Marshall Field's, and goes to the zoo, where he is embraced by a protective great ape. Before the movie is over we've even been treated to the venerable cartoon gag of Bink crawling out on an I-beam, high in the air at a construction site. And when, a little later, one of the bad guys hits the ground, he makes a dust cloud just like Wile E. Coyote.

If the action is inspired by cartoons, the three kidnappers are inspired by the Three Stooges. They're not really evil, of course, simply stupid and incompetent, as they allow the kid to crawl out of captivity and then somehow can't recapture him even though he's usually in sight.

John Hughes, who produced and wrote the movie, and Patrick Read Johnson, who directed it, are counting on one of the basic gimmicks of animated humor: Physical pain doesn't really hurt. Characters can get slammed and flattened, but they pick themselves up, dust themselves off, and start all over again. The joy in physical pain here, inflicted mostly on the crooks, reflects the same comic taste that shaped the treatment of the burglars in Hughes's *Home Alone* movies.

A closer look at cartoons reveals, however,

that little time elapses between pain and payoff. One of the worst sequences in *Baby's Day Out* involves Mantegna hiding the kid under a coat on his lap, while two cops question him. Baby Bink finds Mantegna's lighter, snaps it on, and sets his crotch on fire. The hidden fire lasts forever, it seems, while Mantegna's face tries to mask the pain. Then the cops leave, Mantegna leaps up, his pants burst into flame, and one of his pals saves him by stamping out the fire—grinding his heel into the burning crotch, of course. The sequence was agonizing, but I didn't think it was funny.

It's a strange thing, humor. It often works best when it involves pain and humiliation. But it has to walk a finely drawn line. *Baby's Day Out* contains gags that might have worked in a Baby Herman cartoon, but in live action, with real people, real taxis, and buses and streets and a real baby, they're just not funny. The Worton twins are adorable as Baby Bink, however; the audience produced an audible coo the first time they saw Bink on the screen. The more they like him, unfortunately, the less they're likely to enjoy him crawling along a ledge.

Backbeat ★ ★
R, 100 m., 1994

Stephen Dorff (Stuart Sutcliffe), Sheryl Lee (Astrid Kirchherr), Ian Hart (John Lennon), Gary Bakewell (Paul McCartney), Chris O'Neill (George Harrison), Scot Williams (Pete Best), Kai Weisinger (Klaus Voormann), Jennifer Ehle (Cynthia Powell). Directed by Iain Softley and produced by Stephen Woolley and Finola Dwyer. Screenplay by Softley, Stephen Ward, and Michael Thomas.

There's the old story about the actor who plays the gravedigger in *Hamlet*. He's asked what the play is about. "It's about this gravedigger who meets a prince." The movie *Backbeat* illustrates the same thought process. It's about a painter who was almost a Beatle.

Stuart Sutcliffe died in April 1962 of a brain hemorrhage, just a few months before the Beatles made the first recordings that would make them famous. He played bass with the group for about two years, in Hamburg and Liverpool, but his heart was never in performing, and after he fell in love with Astrid Kirchherr, a German photographer, he drifted away from the band. He preferred painting.

There is a lot more to the story than that, of course, and *Backbeat* makes the most of it.

Sutcliffe's best friend in the band was John Lennon, and the film suggests, subtly, that Lennon was in love with him, and maybe with Astrid, too. The other Beatles (George, Paul, and Pete Best, who was then the drummer instead of Ringo Starr) weren't so thrilled with Sutcliffe. They believed he was a bad musician, and Sutcliffe agreed with them. A bigger problem was that he simply didn't much care about being in a rock 'n' roll band, and stayed as long as he did only because of Lennon's insistence.

The story of the early days of the Beatles is the stuff of folklore; how they discovered their sound in the smoky dives of Hamburg, how the producer George Martin masterminded their early great records, how they became the most famous performers in the world, almost overnight. It is a good story, but it isn't the one *Backbeat* wants to tell. It wants to make Stuart Sutcliffe the focus of the film, and it's never able to convince us there's a story there.

Sutcliffe (Stephen Dorff) somewhat resembled James Dean, and it was probably Astrid's haircut for her boyfriend—modeled on her own—that influenced the original moptop look. The other Beatles wanted to look more like Elvis. When Astrid replaced the ducktails with the Beatles cut, she created an image that was to become instantly marketable; if the Beatles had only had the Look and the early records, they still would have been big stars. That they had extraordinary talent made them enduring.

It would appear, on the basis of this film, that Sutcliffe would not have had the musical talent to keep up with the others. Nor did he have the joy of performance that is so obvious in early films like *A Hard Day's Night*. He was more introspective, and what suited him was to paint large abstract canvases in Astrid's apartment, and discuss painting and photography with her.

Many of his paintings can be seen in the film. They are not especially interesting, although perhaps he might have developed if he had not died so young. Albert Goldman's book about John Lennon contends that Lennon kicked Sutcliffe in the head during a drunken fight, and was guilt-ridden for years with the thought that the kick might have led to the hemorrhage some two years later. In the movie, the kick to the head comes in a pub brawl. Whatever caused his death, Sutcliffe died too young to be of enough interest for a biopic—*except*, of course, that he just missed becoming famous as a Beatle.

This irony does not go unremarked by the movie's dialogue, which even has Sutcliffe being told, "We're going to be big—really big—and you're gonna kick yourself for missing out." There is also an attempt to show what made the Beatles special, even from the beginning; a lot of early songs by the Beatles and others are performed by the band (dubbed by veteran rock performers). What all of this demonstrates is that hindsight is everything; if the Beatles had not become famous, neither Sutcliffe's story nor the story of the band in Hamburg would have been worth filming, unless . . .

Well, unless the filmmakers had brought their own imaginations to the material, and seen something valid and original in the story of five young men in a rock band, trying to break loose from the crowd, while one of them thinks he would rather be a painter. This in itself could make a good movie, but only if the story pulled its own weight and didn't hitch a ride on the Beatles legend.

The music in the movie is fun to listen to (the Beatles version of "Mister Postman" is drool). Ian Hart, who plays John Lennon, looks uncannily like Julian Lennon and speaks in a harsher tone than Lennon had, but he is a good actor who has played Lennon before (in *The Days and Hours*, another speculation about his bisexuality), and his dialogue has real wit. The actors playing McCartney and Harrison are used primarily as a chorus, advising Lennon to drop Sutcliffe, and Pete Best is hardly seen (not, I hope, because there is also a movie in his story).

At the end, I felt cheated. It is indeed ironic that a young man named Stuart Sutcliffe might have been a billionaire rock star, but instead dropped dead in the flower of his youth and became an answer in Trivial Pursuit. It is of some interest that his girlfriend invented the famous haircuts. It is good that his paintings survive, and "have been exhibited all over the world." But the exhilaration of the young Beatles has already been captured in one of the best musicals ever made, *A Hard Day's Night,* and this movie never convinces us Stuart Sutcliffe could have held his own in the band. What's this movie about? It's about—I don't want to sound cruel—a man digging his own grave.

Backdraft ★ ★ ★
R, 132 m., 1991

Kurt Russell (Stephen McCaffrey), William Baldwin (Brian McCaffrey), Robert De Niro (Donald Rimgale), Donald Sutherland (Ronald Bartel), Jennifer Jason Leigh (Jennifer Vaitkus), Scott Glenn (John Adcox), Rebecca De Mornay (Russell's Wife). Directed by Ron Howard and produced by Richard B. Lewis, Pen Densham, and John Watson. Screenplay by Gregory Widen.

Ron Howard's *Backdraft* is a movie half in love with fire, a film like *Fahrenheit 451* that finds something seductive in tendrils of smoke and boiling cauldrons of flame. Never before in the movies have I seen fire portrayed by such convincing, encompassing special effects. Unfortunately, they are at the service of an unworthy plot. If the story of this movie had risen to the level of the production values, it might really have amounted to something.

The movie grafts no less than three formulas onto its wonderful action scenes. We get brothers who are rivals, two broken couples trying to find love again, and a crooked politician who may be behind a series of crimes. Each of these formulas unwinds with relentless conventionality.

The movie takes place in Engine Company 17, based in Chicago's Chinatown, where Kurt Russell is the grizzled veteran and William Baldwin is his kid brother, a rookie fresh from the Fire Academy. Many years before, their father died as a hero in a fire, and Baldwin, then a small boy, made the cover of *Life* magazine as he grasped his dad's blackened helmet while tears ran down his face. The two brothers have been rivals ever since—Russell trying to prove he is the true heir to the family's tradition of heroism; Baldwin trying to prove himself as a man. These character traits have probably not been explored in the movies more than several thousand times.

Russell lives the life of an untidy bachelor in his dad's old boat, permanently aground. He and his wife, played by Rebecca De Mornay, are still really in love with one another, but have separated because she can't count on him to be there when she needs him, because fire fighting comes first in his life, and she can no longer bear the fear of what could happen to him, she loves him too much to lose him, etc. De Mornay brings more intelligence to this situation than the screenplay deserves.

Meanwhile, Baldwin's former girlfriend (Jennifer Jason Leigh) now works as the aide to a powerful alderman (J.T. Walsh), who is running for mayor, apparently on a platform of slashing the budget of the fire department. And a series of mysterious fires have broken out. The canny veteran fire inspector (Robert De Niro) has determined that they were set by an expert, to create a backdraft that would instantly kill their victims with such force that they would then blow themselves out.

If you were not born yesterday, you can probably take this information and correctly predict how everything in the movie turns out. The producers did not get their money's worth from the screenplay by Gregory Widen—unless, of course, all they wanted was a clothesline from which to hang their special effects. That's all they got. We know that the director, Ron Howard, can handle more truthful and complex plots, because he has made *Parenthood* and *Cocoon*. Maybe this time he deliberately chose to make a no-brainer.

But then you have the scenes involving fire. They're so good they make me recommend the movie anyway, despite its brain-damaged screenplay. With special effects and pyrotechnics coordinated by Allen Hall, a battalion of stunt men and visual experts allow the camera to plunge into the center of roaring fires so convincingly that there is never a moment's doubt that we are surrounded by flames.

What is particularly impressive is the way the filmmakers are able to convince us the stars are in the middle of the action. A conventional fire scene uses doubles and stand-ins, over-the-shoulder shots, and other evasive tricks, for brief scenes showing men in the middle of a fire. Then they use close-ups of the actors in front of a back-projection screen filled with flames.

Similar techniques may have been used here, but they are not detectable. It actually looks as if Russell, Baldwin, and the others are right there in the center of blazing tenements and exploding factories, hanging by their fingernails over boiling balls of flame. I personally doubt that anyone, even an expert fireman, could actually survive in such conditions for more than a moment or two. And Russell's exploits are especially dubious, since he prefers not to wear a mask and likes to run bare-faced into hell, in search of heroism. But it sure plays well.

Back to School ★ ★ ★
PG-13, 94 m., 1986

Rodney Dangerfield (Thornton Melon), Sally Kellerman (Diane), Burt Young (Lou), Keith Gordon (Jason Melon), Robert Downey, Jr. (Derek), Paxton Whitehead (Philip Barbay),

M. Emmet Walsh (Coach Turnbull), Ned Beatty (Dean Martin). Directed by Alan Metter and produced by Chuck Russell. Screenplay by Steven Kampmann, Will Porter, Peter Torokvei, and Harold Ramis.

Rodney Dangerfield has given many interviews on the subject of his loneliness. Why, he asks, should a guy like him, who is able to fill up giant concert halls and pull down millions of dollars a year, be condemned to go through life without the love of a woman? This is not the sort of thing you want to hear from a comedian. You want him to be zany and madcap, to stand astride the problems of the mundane world and laugh at them.

Yet in Dangerfield, there has always been something else in addition to the comedian. This is a man who has failed at everything, even comedy. Rodney Dangerfield is his third name in show business; he flopped under two earlier names as well as his real name. Who is really at home inside that red, sweating face and that knowing leer?

The most interesting thing about *Back to School*, which is otherwise a pleasant but routine comedy, is the puzzle of Rodney Dangerfield. Here is a man who reminds us of some of the great comedians of the early days of the talkies—of Groucho Marx and W.C. Fields—because, like them, he projects a certain mystery. Marx and Fields were never just being funny. There was the sense that they were getting even for hurts so deep that all they could do was laugh about them. It's the same with Dangerfield.

He plays Thornton Melon, a millionaire clothing manufacturer who owns a chain of Tall & Fat Shops. His father was a penniless Italian immigrant who took him into the family business as a child. He never had the opportunity to get an education. Now he is rich, his second wife is an obnoxious bauble, and all he cares about is his son, Jason, who is a college student.

Dangerfield fondly believes Jason is a fraternity member and a star of the diving team. But actually Jason is the campus wimp, the team's towel boy, and, naturally, he gets no respect. When Dangerfield discovers the truth, he decides to enroll in the university as a freshman so he can teach his son the ropes. Of course, there's resistance to this plan, but not after Dangerfield endows the Melon School of Business Administration.

The campus characters are predictable, but well-cast. Sally Kellerman is the sexy English teacher, Paxton Whitehead is the An-

glophile business teacher, and Ned Beatty is the venal administrator, always referred to as Dean Martin. Dangerfield takes the "drinks for everybody" approach, throwing his money around and hiring expensive coaches to help him pass his classes. Kurt Vonnegut, Jr., turns up as a paid expert on his own work. Meanwhile, young Jason learns how to be a big man on campus.

This is exactly the sort of plot Marx or Fields could have appeared in. Dangerfield brings it something they might also have brought along: a certain pathos. Beneath his loud manner, under his studied obnoxiousness, there is a real need. He laughs that he may not cry.

Back to the Beach ★ ★ ★ ½
PG, 94 m., 1987

Frankie Avalon (The Big Kahuna), Annette Funicello (Annette), Lori Loughlin (Sandi), Tommy Hinkley (Michael), Demian Slade (Bobby), Connie Stevens (Connie). Directed by Lyndall Hobbs and produced by Frank Mancuso, Jr. Screenplay by Peter Krikes, Steve Meerson, and Christopher Thompson.

This movie absolutely blind-sided me. I don't know what I was expecting from *Back to the Beach*, but it certainly wasn't the funniest, quirkiest musical comedy since *Little Shop of Horrors*. Who would have thought Frankie Avalon and Annette Funicello would make their best beach party movie twenty-five years after the others?

For those who have never seen them, a description is probably better than the actual experience: The beach party movies were a series of chaste comedies in which Frankie and Annette and the gang hung out on the beach, rode the big waves, necked a little, and tried to defend their lifestyle against the old fogeys who were always trying to ban rock & roll. The movies were a tie between harmless and brainless.

Back to the Beach is a wicked satire that pokes fun at Frankie, Annette, and the whole genre, but does it with a lot of good humor and with the full cooperation of the victims. Avalon and Funicello do a better job of satirizing themselves than anyone else possibly could.

The story: Frankie and Annette have gotten married and moved to Ohio, where Frankie sells cars on television, riding a phony surfboard in his sharkskin suit, while Annette prepares endless meals of peanut butter sandwiches. They have two children: a daughter who has moved to Malibu and a young teenage son who is a punk, wears leather, flicks his switchblade, and mercilessly attacks the inane banality of his parents.

The kid (Demian Slade) almost steals the opening scenes of the movie. He has spray-painted graffiti on the fireplace in the living room, he practices karate moves on the family dog, and when Frankie and Annette exchange empty-headed clichés, he's ironic: "This is the sort of conversation you'd hear at the Kissingers.'"

The three of them head to Hawaii on vacation but get sidetracked to Malibu, where Frankie is horrified to learn that his daughter has shacked up with a beach bum (in the beach party movies, the sexes always were strictly segregated at bedtime). Meanwhile, he and Annette discover that some of the old gang still is hanging out at the beach, including Connie Stevens, Miss Lip Gloss of 1962, who still looks luscious.

Frankie flirts with Connie. Annette pouts. There is a confrontation between the cleancut surfers and the punk surfers. There's a surfing competition, and Frankie comes out of retirement to win it. Annette sings a reggae song. Frankie sings a few rock songs. So does Connie Stevens. And at one point, Pee-wee Herman jets in from nowhere, does a virtuoso version of "Surfin' Bird," and disappears.

All of this sounds, I suppose, like the kind of movie you could afford to miss, because a plot summary only suggests the elements of the movie, not the style. Director Lyndall Hobbs, an Australian making her feature debut, has a good eye and a good ear, and the movie is filled with satirical angles from beginning to end. It's a quirky little gem filled with good music, a lot of laughs, and proof that Annette still knows how to make a polka-dot dress seem ageless.

Back to the Future ★ ★ ★ ½
PG, 116 m., 1985

Michael J. Fox (Marty McFly), Christopher Lloyd (Dr. Brown), Lea Thompson (Lorraine Baines), Crispin Glover (George McFly), Thomas F. Wilson (Biff Tannen), Claudia Wells (Jennifer Parker). Directed by Robert Zemeckis and produced by Bob Gale and Neil Canton. Screenplay by Zemeckis and Gale.

One of the things all teen-agers believe is that their parents were never teen-agers. Their parents were, perhaps, children once. They are undeniably adults now. But how could they have ever been teen-agers, and

yet not understand their own children? This view is actually rather optimistic, since it assumes that you can learn something about teen-agers by being one. But *Back to the Future* is even more hopeful: It argues that you can travel back in time to the years when your parents were teen-agers and straighten them out right at the moment when they need help the most.

The movie begins in the present, with a teen-ager named Marty (Michael J. Fox). His parents (let's face it) are hopeless nerds. Dad tells corny jokes and Mom guzzles vodka in the kitchen and the evening meal is like feeding time at the fun house. All that keeps Marty sane is his friendship with the nutty Dr. Brown (Christopher Lloyd), an inventor with glowing eyes and hair like a fright wig.

Brown believes he has discovered the secret of time travel, and one night in the deserted parking lot of the local shopping mall, he demonstrates his invention. In the long history of time-travel movies, there has never been a time machine quite like Brown's, which resembles nothing so much as a customized DeLorean.

The gadget works, and then, after a series of surprises, Marty finds himself transported back thirty years in time, to the days when the shopping mall was a farmer's field (there's a nice gag when the farmer thinks the DeLorean, with its gull-wing doors, is a flying saucer). Marty wanders into town, still wearing his 1985 clothing, and the townsfolk look at his goose-down jacket and ask him why he's wearing a life preserver.

One of the running gags in *Back to the Future* is the way the town has changed in thirty years (for example, the porno house of 1985 was playing a Ronald Reagan movie in 1955). But a lot of the differences run more deeply than that, as Marty discovers when he sits down at a lunch counter next to his dad—who is, of course, a teen-ager himself. Because the movie has so much fun with the paradoxes and predicaments of a kid meeting his own parents, I won't discuss the plot in any detail. I won't even get into the horrifying moment when Marty discovers his mother "has the hots" for him. The movie's surprises are one of its great pleasures.

Back to the Future was directed by Robert *(Romancing the Stone)* Zemeckis, who shows not only a fine comic touch but also some of the lighthearted humanism of a Frank Capra. The movie, in fact, resembles Capra's *It's a Wonderful Life* more than other, conventional time-travel movies. It's about a

character who begins with one view of his life and reality, and is allowed, through magical intervention, to discover another. Steven Spielberg was the executive producer, and the movie's world view (smart kid in Yuppie suburb redefines reality for his parents) is part of the basic Spielberg approach. This time it comes with charm, brains, and a lot of laughter.

Back to the Future Part II ★ ★ ★
PG, 108 m., 1989

Michael J. Fox (Marty McFly, Marty McFly, Jr., and Marlene McFly), Christopher Lloyd (Dr. Emmett Brown), Lea Thompson (Lorraine), Thomas F. Wilson (Biff Tannen and Griff), Harry Waters, Jr. (Marvin Berry), Charles Fleischer (Terry), Elisabeth Shue (Jennifer), Jeffrey Weissman (George McFly). Directed by Robert Zemeckis and produced by Bob Gale and Neil Canton. Screenplay by Gale.

Back to the Future Part II is an exercise in goofiness, an excursion into various versions of the past and future that is so baffling that even the characters are constantly trying to explain it to each other. I should have brought a big yellow legal pad to the screening, so I could take detailed notes just to keep the time lines straight. And yet the movie is fun, mostly because it's so screwy.

Any story involving travel through time involves the possibility of paradoxes, which have provided science-fiction writers with plots for years. What happens to you, for example, if you kill your grandfather? What do you say if you meet yourself? In one famous S-F story, a time traveler to the distant past steps on a single bug, and wipes out all the life forms of the future.

Back to the Future Part II is the story of how the heroes of the first movie, Marty McFly and Doc Brown, try to manipulate time without creating paradoxes, and how they accidentally create an entirely different future—one in which Marty's beloved mother is actually married to his reprehensible enemy, Biff Tannen. McFly and Brown are played again this time by Michael J. Fox and Christopher Lloyd, the stars of the 1985 box-office hit, and they not only made *Part II* but went ahead and filmed *Part III* at the same time.

The script conferences on the set of this movie must have been utterly confusing, as director Bob Zemeckis and writer Bob Gale tried to find their way through the labyrinth they had created. The movie opens in 1985. McFly has just returned from his previous adventure when Doc Brown appears once again in that souped-up DeLorean. He's breathless with urgency, and wants McFly to join him on a trip to the year 2015, where absolutely everything has gone wrong and McFly is needed to save his own son from going to jail.

The city of Hill Valley in the year 2015 looks like the cover of an old pulp magazine; the town square we remember from the previous film has been transformed with ramps heading for the skies, and jet-powered vehicles cruise through the clouds. The kids even have skateboards that operate on the same principle as hovercraft, which leads to one of the movie's best special-effects numbers when McFly tries to evade a gang of rowdies. He more or less accomplishes his mission in 2015, but makes the mistake of buying a sports almanac that has all of the scores from the years 1950 to 2000 in it.

The almanac and the DeLorean are stolen by Biff, who travels back in time to give them to himself, so that he can place lots of winning bets and become a billionaire. In the process, Hill Valley in the future turns into a hellhole lorded over by the evil billionaire who is produced by this scheme, and so McFly and Doc travel back to 1955 to try to steal the almanac away from Biff, and if you are following all of this, you are a very clever reader. I won't even begin to try to explain the ways in which the various parents and children of the main characters also get involved in the story, or what happens when McFly very nearly attends a high school dance on a double date with himself, or how Fox plays three roles including his own daughter.

What's entertaining about *Back to the Future Part II* is the way Christopher Lloyd, as Doc, breathlessly tries to figure out what's happening as he flies through time trying to patch everything together again. At one point he even finds a blackboard and delivers a lecture to the baffled McFly. The flaw in his reasoning, of course, is his assumption that he knows which is the correct time line that *should* be restored. How does he know that the "real world" of the first movie was not itself an alternate time line? It's a job for God.

One thing I'd better make clear is that *Part II*, for all its craziness, lacks the genuine power of the original film. The story of the 1985 film has real heart to it: If McFly didn't travel from 1985 to 1955 and arrange for his parents to have their first date, he might not even exist. The time travel in that film in-

volved his own emotional confrontation with his own parents as teen-agers. *Part II*, on the other hand, is mostly just zaniness and screwball jokes. But on that level, it's fun.

Back to the Future Part III ★ ★ ½
PG, 120 m., 1990

Michael J. Fox (Marty/Seamus McFly), Christopher Lloyd (Dr. Emmett Brown), Mary Steenburgen (Clara Clayton), Thomas F. Wilson (Buford "Mad Dog" Tannen, Biff Tannen), Lea Thompson (Maggie McFly, Lorraine McFly), Elisabeth Shue (Jennifer). Directed by Robert Zemeckis and produced by Bob Gale and Neil Canton. Screenplay by Gale.

One of the delights of the first two *Back to the Future* movies was the way the story moved dizzyingly through time. Paradoxes piled on top of paradoxes, until we had to abandon any attempt to follow the plot on a rational level, and go with the temporal flow. That looking-glass quality is missing, alas, from *Back to the Future Part III*, which makes a few bows in the direction of time-travel complexities, and then settles down to be a routine Western comedy.

The movie was shot back-to-back with *Back to the Future Part II*, which, you will recall, took Marty McFly (Michael J. Fox) forward to a thoroughly depressing future which he had created by meddling around in the immediate future. He had to travel back in time in order to undo his damage, so that the eventual future would be a nicer place to live.

Now comes *Back to the Future Part III*, in which Marty receives a letter from the past—a letter written by his old friend Doc Brown (Christopher Lloyd) from a century ago, explaining that he has traveled back to the Old West and is generally happy there, and asking Marty to simply leave him alone. This letter, of course, has taken a hundred years to arrive.

Doc Brown does, however, reveal where he hid the DeLorean time-travel machine, in an abandoned mine near town. McFly does some historical research and discovers to his horror that Doc Brown was killed only a week after writing the letter, so he determines to venture back in time, whatever the risk, to rescue his friend. He goes looking for the machine in the old mine and finds it still there, and it even starts after a century, which is more than you can say for most cars after a month in the garage. McFly travels back into

time, and, unfortunately, once he gets there he mostly stays there.

The Old West of *Back to the Future Part III* might have been interesting if it had been an approximation of the real Old West—the one we saw in *McCabe and Mrs. Miller*, say. But this movie's West is unfortunately a sitcom version that looks exactly as if it were built on a back lot somewhere. The movie is so filled with old Western clichés that the regulars in the bar even include Pat Buttram. Now don't get me wrong: I was delighted to see Buttram again (he was Gene Autry's sidekick in the old days) and even happier to hear that his voice is still in need of oiling. But the town in *Future III* is made up of lots of pieces from old movies, including even a shoot-out on Main Street and the usual troubles with the local sheriff.

One element of the Old West story is sweet and entertaining: The romance between the eccentric Doc Brown and a local woman named Clara (Mary Steenburgen). They fall in love at first sight, and then Doc gets to thinking about his duty to the future and mankind, and he grows depressed about the mischief he has wrought in the world by inventing time travel, and he decides it is his duty to return to the time he came from, and leave poor Clara behind.

This is easier said than done, since no gasoline exists in the past and McFly has ruptured the fuel line of the DeLorean, a development that leads Doc Brown to an ingenious scheme to get the car up to time-travel velocity (88 mph) by having it pushed by a train. All of this is sort of fun (the movie did not stint on its budget), but it's somehow too linear. It's as if Robert Zemeckis, who directed, and Bob Gale, who wrote, ran out of time-travel plot ideas and just settled into a standard Western universe.

The one thing that remains constant in all of the *Back to the Future* movies, and which I especially like, is a sort of bittersweet, elegiac quality involving romance and time. In the first movie, McFly went back in time to be certain his parents had their first date. The second involved his own romance. The third involves Doc Brown and Clara. In all of these stories, there is the realization that love depends entirely on time; lovers like to think their love is eternal, but do they ever realize it depends entirely on temporal coincidence, since if they were not alive at the same time romance would hardly be feasible?

Bad Boys ★ ★ ★ ½
R, 123 m., 1983

Sean Penn (Mick O'Brien), Reni Santoni (Ramon Herrera), Esai Morales (Paco Moreno), Jim Moody (Gene Daniels), Eric Gurry (Horowitz), Clancy Brown (Viking Lofgren). Directed by Richard Rosenthal and produced by Robert Solo. Screenplay by Richard Di Lello.

Bad Boys tells the story of some tough Chicago street-gang kids who get in a lot of trouble, get sent to a juvenile correctional institution, and get in a lot more trouble once they're inside. Following the tradition governing such movies, the story eventually comes to a moral crossroad at which a bad boy has to decide whether to become a good man—and that's too bad, because until the movie turns predictable it is very, very good. The acting, the direction, and the sense of place in *Bad Boys* is so strong that the movie deserves more than an obligatory fight scene for its conclusion.

The movie stars Sean Penn as Mick O'Brien, a teen-age Irish-American hood and Esai Morales as Paco, a Latino hood. They are both tough, mean, anti-social kids; this movie doesn't sentimentalize street gangs. Their paths cross in connection with a drug deal that Paco is doing with a black gang. There's a misunderstanding, a sudden, shocking exchange of gunfire, and Paco's kid brother is dead. Mick killed him. Mick is sent to prison, and then Paco has his revenge by raping Mick's girlfriend (Ally Sheedy). Paco is caught and sent to the same prison where Mick is being held. Mick already has learned the ropes, and Paco learns them quickly: The prison guards preside sincerely but ineffectually over a reign of terror enforced by the toughest kids in the prison. Violence and sexual crimes are commonplace. The strongest survive. This situation is complicated, of course, by the fact that everyone in the prison immediately knows that Mick and Paco will have to fight to the death over the feud of honor.

And it's at precisely that moment, when the two kids are being set up for an eventual showdown, that *Bad Boys* begins to unwind. The first hour of this movie is so good it's scary; Penn and Morales and the supporting actors are completely convincing, and *Bad Boys* is the first movie I've seen in which the street gangs are not glamorized *(West Side Story)*, stylized *(The Warriors)*, or romanticized *(The Wanderers)*. We believe, watch-

ing *Bad Boys*, that we are observing an approximation of the real thing. The direction, by Richard Rosenthal, is sure-footed, confident, and fluid; we are in the hands of a fine director, even if he *did* make *Halloween II*. Sean Penn is mean and defiant in a real star performance, and the other kids in the prison include such inimitable characters as Horowitz (Eric Gurry), a bright kid who invents things and talks casually of his arson conviction; Viking (Clancy Brown), the hard but vulnerable boss of the prisoners; and Tweety (Robert Lee Rush), who rules at Viking's side.

These performances are good. That's why it's such a disappointment when the movie allows itself to become just another prison picture. Although the second half of the movie continues its close, convincing observations of everyday life in the youth prison, the story structure begins to feel programmed: We know we're heading for a big fight, we think we know who'll win—and what is this, anyway? They've *already* made *Rocky* three times. *Bad Boys* misses its chance at greatness, but it's saying something that this movie *had* a chance. It stands as one of those benchmark movies that we'll look back at for the talent it introduced. On the basis of their work here, Penn, Morales, and Rosenthal prove they have important careers ahead of them, and some of the supporting actors do, too. This movie's not a complete success, but it's a damned good try.

Bad Boys ★ ★
R, 126 m., 1995

NEW

Martin Lawrence (Marcus Burnett), Will Smith (Mike Lowrey), Tea Leoni (Julie Mott), Tcheky Karyo (Fouchet), Theresa Randle (Theresa Burnett), Marge Helgenberger (Alison Sinclair), Nestor Serrano (Detective Sanchez), Julio Oscar Mechoso (Detective Ruiz). Directed by Michael Bay and produced by Don Simpson and Jerry Bruckheimer. Screenplay by Michael Barrie, Jim Mulholland, and Doug Richardson.

Bad Boys tries with all the energy at its command to redeem an exhausted story with sheer technique. This movie is so good-looking it deserves a decent screenplay, instead of one more lope down memory lane. The movie gives us a Miami filled with midnight glitz, shot with the flair of a fashion photographer—backlighted monochrome tilt shots and all. It has relentless editing, slick

action sequences, and blows up stuff real good.

But what is it about? Two cops. Buddies. Partners. Narcs. Whose evidence from a $100 million heroin bust is stolen. Who get in trouble with the chief, who yells at them, and with a chick from Internal Affairs, who takes them off the case. And who pick up a sexy, wise-cracking sidekick along the way. Oh, and one of the cops is a sexy bachelor and the other one is a family man. The plot is like a jigsaw puzzle with pieces supplied by *48 HRS, Internal Affairs, Beverly Hills Cop*, and *Lethal Weapon*.

The movie is a production of Don Simpson and Jerry Bruckheimer, who actually made several of the movies they've ripped off, including *Beverly Hills Cop* parts one and two, so maybe they're recycling. Or maybe they thought the chemistry of their actors would make everything seem fresh.

The movie stars Martin Lawrence and Will Smith, both comic actors, both talented, both allowed to talk way too much in the course of this film. The dialogue runs on endlessly; consider, for example, the basic scene where the commanding officer reams out the two cops. He goes on, and on, and on, screaming at them. Later he screams some more.

There are also a lot of curious interludes in which Lawrence and Smith do verbal riffs, interrupting each other, stream of consciousness, finishing each other's sentences or not bothering to complete thoughts at all, to show a kind of easy familiarity, I guess. We are glad they know each other so well. We wish we knew them well enough to figure out what the hell they think they're saying.

The plot: A criminal mastermind (Tcheky Karyo) engineers the theft of $100 million in heroin from the evidence locker at police headquarters. Lawrence and Smith are assigned to the case. Smith asks Theresa (Theresa Randle), a hooker he knows, to keep an eye open for high rollers. Sure enough, she gets a call from a guy who's sky-high on drugs and wants to spend $2,000. She asks her girlfriend Julie (Tea Leoni) to tag along. Julie isn't a hooker but, what the heck, the guy's so out of it they'll be back on the street with the dough in fifteen minutes.

Theresa gets murdered, in an ugly, unpleasant scene. Julie witnesses it all, and contacts the cops. There is an ungainly subplot in which Lawrence, the family man, has to pretend to be Smith, the bachelor, and live for a few days with Julie, and meanwhile his wife gets suspicious, etc. This stuff isn't even recycled from old action movies; it's out of those Idiot Plots where retards don't catch on to *anything*.

Like, for example, why is Lawrence's apartment filled with photographs of Smith? Is Lawrence gay? Is Smith his boyfriend? He comes up with a sitcom-style excuse, to conceal the fact that they are actually in Smith's apartment. Unasked and unanswered is why Smith would have his apartment filled only with photos of himself. The answer, of course, is that the photos are there to support the vacuum-brained dialogue. There are a lot of photos in this movie, if you get my drift.

The climax is ideal for those with an attention-span deficit. That way they won't know they've seen similar climaxes hundreds of times before. This one is shot well, with good special effects, but takes all the usual shortcuts, including the Fallacy of the Talking Killer.

Imagine. Bodies are stacking up like cordwood. Propane tanks are exploding. A bad guy appears in the doorway of a plane. He's aiming his automatic weapon at one of the heroes. All he has to do is pull the trigger. And then, what? He talks? Nope, the *good guy* talks, finding time to say, "You forgot your boarding pass" before pulling the trigger. By then, of course, he should have been dead, but the filmmakers violate credibility to give us a smartass remark that is not believable, funny, or original. Who do they make these movies for? What exercise in self-deception inspires them to go to such effort and expense for what is obviously going to be a lame exercise in retreadmanship?

Bad Company ★ ★ ★ ½
R, 108 m., 1995   NEW

Ellen Barkin (Margaret Wells), Laurence Fishburne (Nelson Crowe), Frank Langella (Vic Grimes), Michael Beach (Tod Stapp), Gia Carides (Julie Ames), David Ogden Stiers (Judge Beach), Spalding Gray (Walter Curl). Directed by Damien Harris and produced by Amedeo Ursini and Jeffrey Chernov. Screenplay by Ross Thomas.

Bad Company is a thriller of extravagant complexity, a thinking man's Grisham film. It is about smart, ruthless people who once worked for the CIA and now engage in free-lance espionage. They are greedy, relentless, and willing to kill, and of course they are expensively dressed and housed; these are the kind of people who touch themselves as if afraid of leaving prints.

As the movie opens, a man named Nelson Crowe (Laurence Fishburne) is being interviewed for a job in the Grimes Organization, which specializes in industrial dirty tricks. He is hired by Margaret Wells (Ellen Barkin), the second in command, who takes him in to her boss, Vic Grimes (Frank Langella). All of these people hold themselves with studied casualness, and talk in elegant, mannered understatement: There is the implication in many crime movies that the villains have been to finishing schools the rest of us couldn't afford.

The movie succeeds in fascinating us simply with its manner and decor before much of the plot has been revealed—and, believe me, there is a *lot* of plot to reveal. The movie was directed by Damien Harris from the first original screenplay written by Ross Thomas, the superb crime novelist, and it is a movie that *feels* written: The dialogue has a sleek cruelty, and the supporting characters have a quirkiness that you don't find in movies that were knitted in screenwriting class.

Langella and Barkin go to visit a man named Walter Curl, played by the nervous Spalding Gray, who spends much of the movie sucking on his handkerchief. He fears a $25 million fine because his corporation has poisoned some kids with toxic waste. Wells tells him that for 4 percent of that—$1 million—she can bribe a state judge and affect the outcome of the trial. Their client is uncertain. "Look at us!" Langella says. "Do we look like the kind of people who want to go to prison?" (He is always assuring people in this way; it's a running joke.) Langella is a smooth, polished actor who implies wit without revealing it, but listen to the way he says, "Before you attempt to suborn a superior court judge, you make sure he has his hand out. Way out. Way out to here."

The judge is played by David Ogden Stiers, as a man who likes to gamble and owes money to card players and horse-racing bookies. There is a nice supporting role for his mistress (Gia Carides), who watches as he is bribed, and who turns out to like him more, and be smarter, than we think. Meanwhile, the Barkin character has suggested to Fishburne that together they could knock off poor Grimes and take over the organization themselves.

But that is only one of many meanwhiles in Thomas's labyrinthine script. There are many other surprises, none of which I will reveal, because watching this movie is like seeing an onion unpeeled: Each level seems complete and whole, until you find another underneath. And the Thomas dialogue speeds it all along, with scenes like the one where the mistress learns how to arm a gun, or when Langella explains about fly fishing.

I found myself fascinated by the decor. The movie is set in Seattle and was shot largely in Vancouver, and the production notes mention the architect Tadao Ando, whose buildings and style influence the interiors. The production designer, Andrew McAlpine, makes spaces that add to the characters: The Fishburne character, for example, lives in a house of deep reds and blues, where except for the kitchen there is no place to sit down except on an exercise machine.

The photographer, Jack N. Green, has shot this world in a seductive way. It is so expensive, so closed-in, so decadent, so witty, that it encourages the actors in their cool, mannered behavior. Everybody poses. They are formal. Mannered. Barkin has sex with both men, but mostly keeps her clothes on. There are times when these characters would rather keep their cool than stay alive.

The plot moves like clockwork, surprising us, then surprising us again, but I liked *Bad Company* more for its style, look, and feel. That's what will stay. Looking carefully at this movie is like savoring the very best that craft can accomplish on a big budget in modern Hollywood. Every shot is loaded; the movie makes its statement about this world, not with what is said, but with how and where it is said, and how people look when they are saying it. The movie's an example of possessoporn, in which the audience's lust is stirred not by how the characters look but by what they possess.

Bad Girls ★ ½
R, 98 m., 1994

Madeleine Stowe (Cody Zamora), Mary Stuart Masterson (Anita Crown), Andie MacDowell (Eileen Spenser), Drew Barrymore (Lilly Laronette), James Russo (Kid Jarrett), James Le Gros (William Tucker), Robert Loggia (Frank Jarrett), Dermot Mulroney (Josh McCoy). Directed by Jonathan Kaplan and produced by Albert S. Ruddy, Andre E. Morgan, and Charles Finch. Screenplay by Ken Friedman and Yolande Finch.

What a good idea, to make a Western about four tough women. And what a sad movie.

Bad Girls is like *Young Guns* in drag, a B-minus Western in which the only novelty is supplied by the quickly exhausted surprise of finding cowgirls instead of cowboys. Nothing in the plot shows the slightest invention. After *Silverado, Unforgiven,* and *Tombstone,* here's a throwback to the assembly line.

The movie assembles a wonderful cast: Madeleine Stowe, Mary Stuart Masterson, Andie MacDowell, and Drew Barrymore. They're supported by an assortment of male actors who somehow look like they want to wipe their feet on the mat before walking into a scene. No wonder: They've never seen anything like these four before. The women are dressed and made up like models in a Calvin Klein ad. (In an early scene requiring them to be smudged with dust, each one gets a smudge just where rouge would otherwise adorn their famous cheekbones.)

At the beginning of the film the four women are, of course, prostitutes. (The four professions available to women in the Old West were marriage, schoolmarming, prostitution, and old biddyhood.) After the straight-shooting Stowe kills a drunken colonel who is molesting Masterson, a lynch mob prepares to hang her—but her three friends help her escape, and they go on the lam, pursued by a couple of Pinkerton detectives. (Stowe gallops out of town on a horse while her hands are tied behind her, a trick Buffalo Bill would have paid her to turn.)

The plot does not thicken exactly, but it jells. We get the obligatory Ol' Swimmin' Hole scene, in which all four women are modestly submerged to a depth just above their cleavage. The obligatory handsome young cowboy (Dermot Mulroney) happens along, and becomes smitten by Stowe. Later, while trying to withdraw her savings from a bank, Stowe gets inadvertently involved in a bank robbery pulled by the whiskery Kid Jarrett (James Russo), who takes her savings. The rest of the plot involves the women trying to get the money back, trade hostages, rescue the young cowboy, etc. The screenplay could have been dictated at a seance by the shade of Hopalong Cassidy.

There were, of course, women in the West. And there have even been some good movies about them. Three come to mind: *Cattle Annie and Little Britches, The Ballad of Little Jo, A Thousand Pieces of Gold.* These movies made some attempt to imagine what it might have been like to be a woman who did not fit into the narrow categories available on the ignorant, intolerant frontier. (*Little Jo* con-cludes that a woman simply would not be accepted as an independent rancher, and has its heroine disguise herself as a man.)

These difficulties do not much bother Cody, Anita, Eileen, and Lilly, the four bad girls, who, despite their positions in the entertainment industry, have all somehow learned to ride, shoot, handle explosives, and deliver a right to the jaw. The lot of the frontier prostitute was not a happy one; the girls upstairs over the saloon were treated like slaves, as the opening scenes of *Unforgiven* make clear. To develop such outdoor skills these girls must have had their weekends free. Even so, after a rattlesnake startles a team of horses (what an original idea!), you must admit it is amazing to witness Drew Barrymore gallop on horseback after a runaway wagon, jump onto it, and rein in the team.

Have these women been degraded by a life of prostituting themselves to drunken, hairy, smelly, illiterate old coots? Hardly. The dialogue makes a few bows in the direction of their relief to be free of such duty, and moves on. Nor do any of the men note that, with their supermodel looks, the girls could probably earn a lot more in Chicago or Kansas City than in the brothels of Echo City.

The failure of *Bad Girls* is all the more poignant because the actresses were at the top of their forms, and could have been inspired by a more ambitious production. Think of Stowe in *Blink,* MacDowell in *Four Weddings and a Funeral,* Masterson in *Fried Green Tomatoes,* Barrymore in *Guncrazy.* Better still, see them in those films, and reflect how lame they seem in this concoction.

Bad Influence ★ ★ ★
R, 100 m., 1990

James Spader (Michael Boll), Rob Lowe (Alex), Lisa Zane (Claire), Christian Clemenson (Pismo Boll), Kathleen Wilhoite (Leslie). Directed by Curtis Hanson and produced by Steve Tisch. Screenplay by David Koepp.

Bad Influence is like one of those old Charles Atlas ads, where the bullies on the beach kicked sand into the eyes of the ninety-nine-pound weakling, until Atlas came along and showed the wimp how to build some muscle. The primary difference between the ads and this thriller is that the role of Atlas is now filled by a sadistic sociopath. He walks into the life of a cowardly financial analyst and treats him to some assertiveness training that is more than he bargained for.

The analyst is played by James Spader, whose cool diffidence is just right for the early scenes, in which the office bully hacks into the computer system and hides three months' worth of Spader's work. In response, Spader does what any normal coward would do, and walks across the street to a bar to have a beer. It isn't his day. In the lounge, a big guy is having a fight with his girlfriend, and when Spader looks at him wrong, he gets his face mashed into the bar.

That's when Rob Lowe comes in, breaks a beer bottle off at the neck, and has a few words with the bully while waving the jagged edge at his face. The bully leaves. Spader is grateful, and over the next few days he becomes friends with this mysterious stranger, who offers to teach him how to stand up for himself. At first the lessons are innocuous, as Spader outsmarts his rival in the office. Then they get more troublesome, and finally they get deadly.

Bad Influence reminded me a little of *Strangers on a Train,* the 1951 Hitchcock movie where Robert Walker offers to trade murders with Farley Granger—his father for Granger's wife—so they can both be rid of people they hate. Granger doesn't take him seriously, but Walker is very serious indeed. In *Bad Influence,* Lowe has the smooth Walker role, but the difference is, Spader has no idea he's made a bargain until it's much too late.

The movie sneaks up on you. At first you're not even sure where it's going: Maybe this will be the story of a creepy relationship between Spader, who is a born innocent, and Lowe, who likes to change identities and accents every night while he's picking up girls in the Los Angeles underground bar scene. Lowe is slick and likable, and very attractive except for those sinister shadows that always seem to be playing over his eyes.

There's a hint of homosexuality in their relationship; Spader clearly likes Lowe, who seduces him with compliments and friendship. "Tell me what you really desire, and what you really fear," Lowe tells Spader one night when they're both looped. Spader says he fears marriage, even though he is engaged to a rich girl, the kind who pecks her future hubby on the cheek as if she were a bird and he were a mirror. Lowe is able to end the unwanted engagement with a spectacular act of social embarrassment, by infiltrating a party given by the future in-laws, and showing a home video of Spader having sex with another woman.

This scene, and another one with Lowe in bed with two girls, will no doubt stir memories of his celebrated scandal involving a videotape. Indeed, the parallels between *Bad Influence* and the Lowe videotape incident are so numerous that I would almost believe him if he claimed to have been doing research. Believers in coincidence can also savor the fact that this is Spader's first big role since *sex, lies, and videotape*—which would have made an excellent title for *Bad Influence*. The movie is strong enough and the performances so convincing, however, that echoes from real life never distracted me.

Like many thrillers that begin with an intriguing premise, *Bad Influence* is more fun in the setup than in the payoff. For at least the first hour, we are not quite sure what game Lowe is playing, and the full horror of his plan is only gradually revealed. The climax of the movie discharges a lot of the suspense by turning into a more conventional cat-and-mouse game. But I was grateful for the final shots, which played fair with the logic of the plot and didn't try to sneak in the cheap surprise I was waiting for.

Movies like this do raise a few questions, and one I kept asking was, how does Spader do it? As a broker based in Los Angeles, he has to be at work when the New York markets open, and there is indeed one scene where he's at his desk at 5:30 A.M. Since he spends night after night with Lowe, turning into a zombie in one bar after another, how does he manage to hit the deck every morning looking like a preppie fresh from business school? On one occasion, he is drunk enough to stick up some convenience stores after the clubs close, and sober enough to be horrified at his behavior only a few hours later.

Bad Influence was written by David Koepp and directed by Curtis Hanson, and is a much superior exploitation of a theme that Koepp used in his screenplay for his previous *Apartment Zero*: A passive hero falls for the spell of a virile man who enters his life under false and deadly pretenses. *Apartment Zero* was lurid and overwrought, almost a self-parody, while Hanson's direction of *Bad Influence* makes it into a somber, introspective study of the relationship. Perhaps it says something about our times that when strangers meet in movies these days, one of them is almost always operating out of some kind of secret depravity.

Badlands ★ ★ ★ ★
PG, 94 m., 1974

Martin Sheen (Kit), Sissy Spacek (Holly), Warren Oates (Holly's Father), Ramon Bieri (Cato), Ramon Vint (Deputy). Directed, produced, and written by Terence Malick.

They meet for the first time when she is in her front yard practicing baton-twirling. He has just walked off his job on a garbage truck. She thinks he is the handsomest man she's ever seen—he looks just like James Dean. He likes her because he never knew a fifteen-year-old who knew so much: "She could talk like a grown-up woman, without a lot of giggles." Within a few weeks, they will be the targets of a manhunt after he has shot down half a dozen victims.

Terence Malick's *Badlands* calls them Kit and Holly, but his characters are inspired, of course, by Charles Starkweather and Caril Ann Fugate. They went on a wild ride in 1958 that ended with eleven people shot dead. The press named him the Mad Dog Killer, and Sunday supplement psychoanalysts said he killed because the kids at school kidded him about his bowlegs. Starkweather got the electric chair on June 25, 1959. From time to time a story appears about Caril Fugate's appeals to her parole board. She was sentenced to life.

She claimed she was kidnapped and forced to go along with Starkweather. When they first were captured, he asked the deputies to leave her alone: "She didn't do nothing." Later, at his trial, he claimed she was the most trigger-happy person he ever knew, and was responsible for some of the killings. It is a case that is still not closed, although *Badlands* sees her as a child of vast simplicity who went along at first because she was flattered that he liked her: "I wasn't popular at school on account of having no personality and not being pretty."

The film is tied together with her narration, written like an account of summer vacation crossed with the breathless prose style of a movie magazine. Some of the dialogue is loosely inspired by a book written by James Reinhardt, a criminologist who interviewed Starkweather on death row. Starkweather was offended by his death sentence. He viewed his crimes with total uninvolvement and asked how it was fair for him to die before he'd even been to a big city, or eaten in a fine restaurant, or seen a major-league game. That's what the movie captures, too: The detachment with which Kit views his kill-

ings, as Holly eventually draws away from him. He gets no pleasure from killing. He sees it only as necessary. He offers explanations which satisfy her for a while: "I killed them because they was bounty hunters who wanted the reward money. If they was policemen, just being paid for doing their job, that would have been different."

The movie makes no attempt to psychoanalyze its Kit Carruthers, and there are no symbols to note or lessons to learn. What comes through more than anything is the enormous loneliness of the lives these two characters lived, together and apart. He is ten years older than she is, but they're both caught up in the same adolescent love fantasy at first, as if Nat King Cole would always be there to sing "A Blossom Fell" on the portable radio while they held their sweaty embrace. He would not. To discourage his daughter from seeing "the kind of a man who collects garbage," her father punishes her by shooting her dog. She is "greatly distressed."

Kit is played by Martin Sheen, in one of the great modern film performances. He looks like James Dean, does not have bowlegs, and plays the killer as a plain and simple soul who has somehow been terribly damaged by life (the real Starkweather, his father explained at the time, was never quite right after being hit between the eyes with a two-by-four). Holly is played by the freckle-faced redhead Sissy Spacek. She takes her schoolbooks along on the murder spree so as not to get behind. She is in love with Kit at first, but there is a stubborn logic in her makeup and she eventually realizes that Kit means trouble. "I made a resolution never again to take up with any hellbent types," she confides.

After the first murder and their flight, they never have any extended conversations about anything, nor are they seen to make love, nor is their journey given any symbolic meaning. They hope to reach refuge in the "Far North," where Kit might find employment as a mounted policeman. They follow their case in the newspapers, become aware of themselves as celebrities, and, in a brilliant scene at the end, the captured Kit hands out his comb, his lighter, and his ball-point pen as souvenirs to the National Guardsmen who had been chasing him.

The movie is very reserved in its attitude toward the characters. It observes them, most of the time, dispassionately. They are strange people, as were their real-life models; they had no rationalizations like Dillinger's regard for the poor or Bonnie and Clyde's ability to idealize themselves romantically. They were just two dumb kids who got into a thing and didn't have the sense to stop. They're something like the kids in Robert Altman's *Thieves Like Us* and the married couple in *The Sugarland Express*. They are in over their heads, incapable of understanding murder as a crime rather than a convenience, inhabitants of lives so empty that even their sins cannot fill them.

Bad Lieutenant ★ ★ ★ ★
NC-17, 96 m., 1993

Harvey Keitel (Lieutenant), Frankie Thorn (Nun), Brian McElroy (His Son), Frankie Acciarito (His Son No. 2), Peggy Gormley (His Wife), Stella Keitel (His Daughter), Victor Argo (Beat Cop). Directed by Abel Ferrara and produced by Edward R. Pressman and Mary Kane. Screenplay by Zoe Lund and Ferrara.

Bad Lieutenant tells the story of a man who is not comfortable inside his body or soul. He walks around filled with need and dread. He is in the last stages of cocaine addiction, gulping booze to level off the drug high. His life is such a loveless hell that he buys sex just for the sensation of someone touching him, and his attention drifts even then, because there are so many demons pursuing him. Harvey Keitel plays this man with such uncompromised honesty that the performance can only be called courageous; not many actors would want to be seen in this light.

The lieutenant has no illusions about himself. He is bad and knows he is bad, and he abuses the power of his position in every way he can. Interrupting a grocery store stickup, he sends the beat cop away and then steals the money from the thieves. He sells drug dealers their immunity by taking drugs from them. In the film's most harrowing scene, he stops two teen-age girls who are driving their parents' car without permission. He threatens them with arrest, and then engages in what can only be described as an act of verbal rape.

Remember the Ray Liotta character in the last sequence of Scorsese's *GoodFellas*, when he is strung out on cocaine and paranoid that the cops are following him? His life speeds up, his thinking is frantic, he can run but he can't hide. The Keitel character in *Bad Lieutenant* is like the same character, many more agonizing months down the road. Life cannot go on like this much longer.

We learn a few things about him. He still lives in a comfortable middle-class home, with a wife and three children who have long since made their adjustment to his madness. There is no longer a semblance of marriage. He comes in at dawn and collapses on the couch, to be wakened by the TV cartoons, which cut through his hangover. He stumbles out into the world again, to do more evil. When he drives the kids to school, his impatience is palpable; he cannot wait to drop them off and get a fix.

The movie does not give the lieutenant a name, because the human aspects of individual personality no longer matter at this stage; he is a bad cop, and those two words, expressing his moral state and his leverage in society, say everything that is still important about him.

A nun is raped. He visits the hospital to see her. She knows who attacked her, but will not name them, because she forgives them. The lieutenant is stunned. He cannot imagine this level of absolution. If a woman can forgive such a crime, is redemption possible even for him?

The film dips at times into madness. In a church, he hallucinates that Jesus Christ has appeared to him. He no longer knows for sure what the boundaries of reality are. His temporary remedies—drugs and hookers—have stopped working. All that remain are self-loathing, guilt, deep physical disquiet, and the hope of salvation.

Bad Lieutenant was directed by Abel Ferrara, a gritty New Yorker who has come up through the exploitation ranks *(Ms. .45, Fear City)* to low-budget but ambitious films like *China Girl, King of New York,* and *Cat Chaser.* This film lacks the polish of a more sophisticated director, but would have suffered from it. The film and the character live close to the streets. The screenplay is by Ferrara and Zoe Lund, who can be seen onscreen as a hooker, and played the victim in *Ms. .45.* They are not interested in plot in the usual sense. There is no case to solve, no crime to stop, no bad guys except for the hero.

Keitel starred in Martin Scorsese's first film and has spent the last twenty-five years taking more chances with scripts and directors than any other major actor. He has the nerve to tackle roles like this, that other actors, even those with street images, would shy away from. He bares everything here—his body, yes, but also his weaknesses, his hungers. It is a performance given without reservation.

The film has the NC-17 rating, for adults only, and that is appropriate. This is not a film for younger people. But it is not a "dirty movie," and in fact takes spirituality and morality more seriously than most films do. And in the bad lieutenant, Keitel has given us one of the great screen performances in recent years.

Bagdad Cafe ★ ★ ★ ½
PG, 91 m., 1988

Marianne Sägebrecht (Jasmine), CCH Pounder (Brenda), Jack Palance (Rudi Cox), Christine Kaufmann (Debby), Monica Calhoun (Phyllis), Darron Flagg (Sal, Jr.), George Aquilar (Cahuenga), G. Smokey Campbell (Sal), Alan S. Craig (Eric). Written, produced, and directed by Percy Adlon. Also written and produced by Eleonore Adlon.

The heavy-set German lady, her body and soul tightly corseted, her hair sprayed into rocklike permanence, is having a fight with her husband, right there in the Mohave Desert. They are in the middle of some kind of miserable vacation, touring America as a version of hell. She can take no more. She grabs her suitcase and stalks away from their Mercedes, and he drives away into the red, dusty sky, and she walks to a miserable truck stop and asks for a room.

An opening like that makes you stop and think, doesn't it, about how cut-and-dried most Hollywood movies are. There would seem to be no place in today's entertainment industry for movies about fat German ladies and homesick truck stops, and yet *Bagdad Cafe* sets us free from the production line of Hollywood's brain-damaged "high concepts," and walks its own strange and lovely path. There is poetic justice in the fact that this movie, shot in English in America by a German, was one of the biggest box-office successes in recent European history.

The German woman is named Jasmine (Marianne Sägebrecht), and she is appalled by the conditions she finds at the Bagdad Cafe. It is simply not being run along clean and efficient German lines. The proprietor is a free-thinking black woman named Brenda (CCH Pounder—yes, CCH Pounder), who shares the premises with her teen-age children, a baby, a bewildered Italian cook, a tattoo artist, and a shipwrecked former Hollywood set painter who is played by Jack Palance as if he had definitely painted his last set.

Jasmine sets to work. She gets a mop and a pail and begins to clean her room, while the motel regulars look on in amazement. Back and forth she goes, like some kind of natural force that has been set into implacable motion against dirt. Gradually her sphere extends to other rooms in the motel, and to the public areas, and she gives Brenda little lectures about cleanliness and the importance of maintaining high standards for the public.

Day by day, little by little, however, Jasmine herself is changed by this laid-back desert environment. Her too-tight hausfrau dresses give way to a blouse that billows outside her slacks. A stray wisp of hair escapes from the glistening spray, and then finally her hair comes tumbling down in windswept freedom. And she reveals that she can do magic tricks.

Yes, magic tricks. After she whips the cook into shape and the truck stop's restaurant begins to do some business, she starts entertaining some of the customers with close-up illusions, which eventually grow in scale until the Bagdad Cafe is presenting its own cabaret night after night, with all the regulars pressed into the act.

All of this sounds rather too nice, I suppose, and so I should add that Percy Adlon, the director, maintains a certain bleak undercurrent of despair, of crying babies and unpaid bills, and young people who have come to the ends of their ropes.

He is saying something in this movie about Europe and America, about the old and the new, about the edge of the desert as the edge of the American Dream. I am not sure exactly what it is, but that is comforting; if a director could assemble these strange characters and then know for sure what they were doing in the same movie together, he would be too confident to find the humor in their situation. The charm of *Bagdad Cafe* is that every character and every moment is unanticipated, obscurely motivated, of uncertain meaning, and vibrating with life.

The Ballad of Little Jo ★ ★ ★
R, 120 m., 1993

Suzy Amis (Little Jo), Bo Hopkins (Frank Badger), Ian McKellen (Percy Corcoran), David Chung (Tinman Wong), Carrie Snodgress (Ruth Badger), Rene Auberjonois (Streight Hollander), Heather Graham (Mary Addie), Sam Robards (Jasper Hill). Directed by Maggie Greenwald and produced by Fred Berner and Brenda Goodman. Screenplay by Greenwald.

The Old West must not have been a very nice place. It was violent, dirty, undernourished, disease-ridden, cursed with alcoholism and

venereal disease, and thickly populated with varmints human and otherwise. It was no place for a woman—not even the two kinds of women most familiar in Western movies: schoolmarms and hookers.

In the opening scenes of *The Ballad of Little Jo*, a young woman is discovering this for herself. Cast out by her wrathful family after giving birth out of wedlock, Little Jo has escaped to the West like so many pariahs before her. But her dress, bonnet, and parasol are like red flags to the cowboys along the trail, who can guess she ain't no schoolmarm. Abused and mistreated, she accepts a ride from a stranger and finds herself sold into bondage. Escaping, she realizes there is only one course for her. She walks into a store and buys some men's clothes, and from then on, Josephine is a man named Jo.

The movie casts Suzy Amis in this crucial role, but to tell you the truth, I never really believed that she could pass as a man. She pulls her hat brim down low, and talks in a gruff voice, and slaps chaps on the back a lot, but it's fairly clear there's a deficit in the testosterone department. Amis is a wonderful actor (see her as the addled older sister in *Rich in Love*), however, and works some kind of magic, so that we accept her as a man despite our doubts, as the story begins to take hold.

The writer and director, Maggie Greenwald, wisely avoids an old-fashioned plot, and concerns herself more with the daily texture of life in the West. Ruby City, the town where Little Jo settles, is a grim collection of saloons and whorehouses, of smelly bearded men and womenfolk who stay indoors or in church a lot. Little Jo buys herself a spread outside of town and raises sheep. Her nearest neighbor is the appropriately named Frank Badger (Bo Hopkins), who is fearsome and cruel, but by no means entirely evil, and maybe suspects more about Jo than he's prepared to admit, even to himself. Other locals include the exiled Englishman Percy Corcoran (Ian McKellen), who is a friend when he is sober and an animal when he is drunk, and whose idea of sex consists of getting drunk and beating up prostitutes.

Little Jo stays strictly to herself, outside of town, until one day when she stumbles upon the baiting of a Chinese man, Tinman Wong (David Chung). At Badger's insistence, she hires the man as a cook and laborer, and it doesn't take him long to discover her secret and for the movie to reveal its real subject, which is the role-playing that allowed women

and minorities to survive in the macho, racist West.

The Ballad of Little Jo is based, I gather, on many real stories. So ingrained was the notion that only men could do "men's work," Greenwald says, that if a woman could ride and rope and run a ranch, she was accepted as a man even in the face of other evidence. At one point in the movie, Jo is pointedly referred to as a "dude," which in the context seems to suggest she's considered a homosexual. There is even the slightest hint that Frank Badger may think Tinman Wong is a good match for her—which he is, but in ways Badger does not imagine.

When the film's ending arrives, pay it particular attention. It is rather rough and crude, but it's in the spirit of the film, in which men of poor breeding lived and worked together in desperate poverty of mind and body, and were so enclosed inside their roles that they hardly knew each other at all.

The Ballad of the Sad Café ★ ★ ★
NO MPAA RATING, 100 m., 1991

Vanessa Redgrave (Miss Amelia), Keith Carradine (Marvin Macy), Cork Hubbert (Cousin Lymon), Rod Steiger (Reverend Willin). Directed by Simon Callow and produced by Ismail Merchant. Screenplay by Michael Hirst.

The Ballad of the Sad Café comes wrapped in cultural glory; it is based on a novel by Carson McCullers and a play by Edward Albee, and yet it persists in sounding like a sketch for "Saturday Night Live." McCullers was a gifted member of the Southern Gothic school who built on Faulkner and made the South seem peopled with grotesque heroes and villains in a hothouse of sex, scandal, vice, secrecy, and unwholesome family secrets. If she were to revisit the South today, and discover that shopping malls and skyscrapers have largely replaced the folks sipping moonshine down in the incestuous rural hollow, she would no doubt be mightily disappointed.

And yet *Sad Café*, like all fictions that are twisted and warped into a shape larger than life, provides great opportunities for actors. I remember seeing the play on stage in New York in the early 1960s, with Colleen Dewhurst and Michael Dunn, and being impressed with the largeness of the roles: McCullers and Albee were not timid modernists, straining to eject small pellets of mannered prose, but old-fashioned, even Shakespearian, writers in love with the grand gesture, the flamboyant speech, the crisis in which character is revealed and secrets are unveiled.

Now comes this movie version of *The Ballad of the Sad Café*, made by a British director and an Indian producer. The director is the actor-writer Simon Callow, whose recent book about Charles Laughton reveals his own affection for grandiose performance, and the producer is Ismail Merchant, of *A Room With a View*. Their star, in the showboat role of Miss Amelia, is Vanessa Redgrave, six feet tall with hair shorn close, so that she seems part woman, part votary of some obscure Southern order.

Miss Amelia has retired for some time to the rooms upstairs over her café, and yet she still holds considerable sway over the local backwoods folk, thanks to her skill in healing, and the quality of her moonshine. She is not quite a spinster. She was married for ten days once to Marvin Macy (Keith Carradine), who has since disappeared, but not before giving Miss Amelia the only serious competition she has experienced in life.

One day, Cousin Lymon, a noisy dwarf (Cork Hubbert), arrives in town, introduces himself as Miss Amelia's kin, and starts preparing the way for the arrival of Marvin Macy, much as John the Baptist once performed similar duties in a different story. Lymon is a clown who deflects mockery by performing for folks, and he leaps onto the counter to sing and dance and bring more joy than the Sad Café has seen in many a year. Soon he has convinced Miss Amelia to reopen it, and provide the townsfolks with a gathering place.

It is clear that Lymon is half in love with Marvin, who arrives on schedule and brings the party to a halt with his laconic manner, his ironic guitar solos, and his history of emotional warfare with Miss Amelia. The townsfolk, who are astonished, baffled, cheered and depressed, always on cue, watch hungrily as Miss Amelia and Marvin Macy edge toward an inevitable showdown: A bare-knuckle fight.

All of this is about as believable as those breathless "Dateline America" reports you read in the British trash press about snake-worshipping cults in Louisiana Sunday schools. But it plays well, if you can dismiss from your mind any remote expectation that the behavior in the film will mirror life as we know it. And Vanessa Redgrave, imperious and vibrating with passion, makes a proud, sad Miss Amelia.

I suppose there was once a time when *The Ballad of the Sad Café* was thought to contain truths about life as lived. I can no longer relate to it that way. It now plays more like a prose opera, in which jealousy and passion inflame the characters, who are trapped in the sins of the past. To see the movie for its story is an exercise in futility. But it works well as gesture and flamboyance, a stage for outsize tragic figures.

Bang the Drum Slowly ★ ★ ★ ★
PG, 98 m., 1973

Michael Moriarty (Henry Wiggen), Robert De Niro (Bruce Pearson), Vincent Gardenia (Dutch Schnell), Phil Foster (Joe), Ann Wedgeworth (Katie), Patrick McVey (Mr. Pearson). Directed by John Hancock and produced by Maurice and Lois Rosenfield. Screenplay by Mark Harris.

Bang the Drum Slowly is the ultimate baseball movie—and, despite what a plot summary might suggest, I think it's more about baseball than death. It takes place during the last season on this Earth of one Bruce Pearson, an earnest but dumb catcher from Georgia who learns, in the movie's first scene, that he is suffering from an incurable disease. The movie is about that season and about his friendship with Henry Wiggen, a pitcher, who undertakes to see that Bruce at least lives his last months with some dignity, some joy, and a few good games.

On the surface, then, the movie seems a little like *Brian's Song*. But it's not: It's mostly about baseball and the daily life of a major league club on the road. The fact of Bruce's approaching death adds a poignancy to the season, but *Bang the Drum Slowly* doesn't brood about death and it isn't morbid. In its mixture of fatalism, roughness, tenderness, and bleak humor, indeed, it seems to know more about the ways we handle death than a movie like *Love Story* ever guessed. The movie begins at the Mayo Clinic, follows the team through spring training, and then carries it through a season that feels remarkably like a Chicago Cubs year: a strong start, problems during the hot weather, dissension on the team, and then a pennant drive that (in the movie, anyway) is successful. There isn't a lot of play-by-play action, only enough to establish the games and make the character points. So when the team manager and the pitcher conspire to let Bruce finish his last game, despite his illness, the action footage is relevant and moving.

Bang the Drum Slowly was adapted for the screen by Mark Harris, from his observant 1955 novel. He seems to understand baseball players, or at least he can create convincing ones; if real baseball players aren't like the ones in this movie, somehow they should be. The director, John Hancock, is good with his actors and very good at establishing a lot of supporting characters without making a point of it (in this area he reminds me of Robert Altman's shorthand typecasting in *M*A*S*H* and *McCabe and Mrs. Miller*). Some of the best scenes are in the clubhouse, an arena of hope, despair, anger, practical jokes, and impassioned speeches by the manager.

He's played by Vincent Gardenia as a crafty, tough tactician with a heart of gold he tries to conceal. ("When I die," he says during one pre-game pep talk, "in the newspapers they'll write that the sons of bitches of this world have lost their leader.") He knows Bruce and Henry are concealing something, but he doesn't know what, and his efforts to find out are hilariously frustrated. At various times, the midwinter visit to the Mayo Clinic is explained as a fishing trip, a hunting trip, a wenching trip, and a secret mission to rid Bruce of the clap.

Gardenia, as the manager, is the third angle of a triangle that includes very good acting by Michael Moriarty, as Henry, and Robert De Niro, as Bruce. Henry is the All Star with the $70,000 contract and Bruce is a mediocre catcher who is constantly being ragged by his teammates. Henry's his only friend, until somehow when the team comes together for the pennant stretch, Bruce starts playing the best ball in his life, and the club (somewhat predictably) accepts him.

Hancock and Harris avoid any temptation to structure *Bang the Drum Slowly* as a typical sports movie. Although the team does win the pennant, not much of a point is made of that. There are no telegraphed big moments on the field, when everything depends on a strikeout or a home run or something. Even Bruce's last big hit in his last time at bat is limited, tactfully, to a triple.

Instead of going for a lot of high points, the movie paints characters in their everyday personalities. We get some feeling of life on the road as Henry talks with a hotel telephone operator who's a baseball fanatic, and Bruce moons over the prostitute he's in love with. Phil Foster has a great cameo role as a first-base coach with a genius for luring suckers into card games with remarkably elastic rules. Occupying the background in a lot of shots is the team's Cuban third baseman, who has it written into his contract that he be provided with a translator. And then, as the movie's shape begins to be visible, we realize it's not so much a sports movie as a movie about those elusive subjects, male bonding and work in America. That the males play baseball and that sport is their work is what makes this the ultimate baseball movie; never before has a movie considered the game from the inside out.

Barcelona ★ ★ ★
PG-13, 101 m., 1994

Taylor Nichols (Ted Boynton), Chris Eigeman (Fred Boynton), Tushka Bergen (Montserrat), Mira Sorvino (Marta), Pep Munne (Ramon), Nuria Badia (Aurora Boval), Hellena Schmied (Greta). Directed and produced by Whit Stillman. Screenplay by Stillman.

Whit Stillman's *Barcelona* is a reminder that there is a broad strata of American society that goes all but ignored by the movies. His subjects are smart, intense, but somewhat naive white-collar workers, young men in their twenties and early thirties, who wear suits and ties to work and are very serious about themselves and still try, self-consciously, to talk in a way that might sound impressive at an undergraduate management seminar. Stillman brings great wit and wicked humor to his subjects, but he doesn't make fun of them—he likes them.

In *Metropolitan* (1990), his first film, he showed this generation in its embryo stage, as Park Avenue preppies. Now he shows them in their first jobs. The time is the early 1980s. The place is Barcelona, where Ted Boynton (Taylor Nichols) is the Spanish representative for a Chicago firm that makes electric engines.

Ted is earnest and ambitious and has room within his heart for a vast yearning which can only be filled by a girl. But not a pretty girl. He has determined, after several unhappy experiences, to have nothing more to do with beautiful women. He tries to explain this to a young woman (neither pretty nor plain) he has met at a party: Beautiful women make an observation about a man, and use it to ridicule him, "as if impertinence were cute and charming." A plainer woman, on the other hand, "would be more apt to use observation for comprehension. . . ." He talks that way a lot, as if reciting from term papers.

Ted's cousin arrives in Barcelona. Fred Boynton (Chris Eigeman) is a lieutenant junior grade in the navy, and has been assigned

as an advance man for the Sixth Fleet's upcoming shore leave. Apparently a previous shore leave did not go smoothly, and Fred's task is to scout the territory, which he does by following Ted to the clubs and bars frequented by "trade-show girls," who are the scrubbed and respectable English-speaking hostesses at various international fairs.

One of Fred's pastimes is inventing shocking stories, and he solemnly informs the beautiful Marta (Mira Sorvino) and several of Ted's friends that his cousin is a follower of the Marquis de Sade, and wears various garments of torture under his clothes. (This news spreads quickly through her set, and when Ted protests that this is an insane suggestion, one of his dates decides it means nothing that he is wearing no leather straps at present: "Maybe they're at the cleaners.")

The movie's plot is as lighthearted as a Scott Fitzgerald short story, all about young people skimming the surface of the pond of life, flitting here and there, making small talk and flirting. Ted, as a certain type of American, tends to be profound about subjects the Europeans have long since stopped taking seriously, and it is a delight to listen to him, because his talk so clearly reflects his hard-won ideals. There is a kind of touching earnestness to him; his speech is like overhearing a young exec explaining himself to a like-minded stranger during a long airplane flight.

The movie develops like a Woody Allen autobiographical picture, with a narrator who seems puzzled but sincere in trying to figure out his life, which everyone else seems to understand better than he does. He is worried about losing his job, about not being destined to work in sales, about girls. He doesn't make much progress with the friendly trade-fair crowd because he is convinced they must feel a profound commitment to a man before they will get involved in a relationship, and when he explains this theory in discos, they quickly lose interest.

Meanwhile, there's an undercurrent: The presence of these Americans in Spain—one a capitalist, the other a militarist—makes them a target for left-wing groups, and it doesn't help that Fred believes in maintaining a high profile (called a "fascist," he explains, "Young men wearing this uniform died to protect Europe from fascism").

I've seen *Barcelona* twice. It seemed deeper to me the second time. It appears at first to be about the casual lives of young men trying to launch their careers, but eventually (again, like an Allen movie) it reveals darker depths

and meanings. What it also does is give voice to a generation. If there is one part of American society that American movies are usually not interested in, it is the wage-earning, nine-to-five, ambitious, competitive, white-collar society of business and management. Watching this movie, I realized that although I'd seen a lot of amazing things on the screen before, I'd hardly ever seen young WASPs earning a living.

Barfly ★ ★ ★ ★
R, 110 m., 1987

Mickey Rourke (Henry), Faye Dunaway (Wanda Wilcox), Alice Krige (Tully), Jack Nance (Detective), J.C. Quinn (Jim), Frank Stallone (Eddie), Gloria LeRoy (Grandma Moses). Directed by Barbet Schroeder and produced by Schroeder, Fred Roos, and Tom Luddy. Screenplay by Charles Bukowski.

Louis Armstrong was trying to explain jazz one day, and he finally gave up and said, "There are some folks that, if they don't know, you can't tell 'em." The world of Charles Bukowski could be addressed in the same way. Bukowski is the poet of Skid Row, the Los Angeles drifter who spent his life, until age fifty, in an endless round of saloons and women, all of them cheap, expensive, bad, or good in various degrees. *Barfly*, based on his original screenplay, is a grimy comedy about what it might be like to spend a couple of days in his skin—a couple of the better and funnier days, although they aren't exactly a lark.

The movie takes place in a gutbucket bar down on the bad side of town, where the same regulars take up the same positions on the same bar stools every day. Your private life is nobody's business, but everybody in the joint knows all about it. To this bar, day after day, comes Henry (Mickey Rourke), a drunk who is sometimes also a poet. The day bartender hates him, probably for the same reason all bartenders in gutter saloons hate their customers: It's bad enough that they have to serve these losers, without taking a lot of lip from them, too.

Henry and the bartender head for the back alley to have a fight. Henry is beaten to a pulp. Hawking up spit and blood, he tosses down another drink and heads off for the hovel he calls his room. Another day, another adventure. One day he looks up from his drink and sees, sitting at the other end of the bar, a woman named Wanda (Faye Dunaway). She looks like she belongs in the place, and she doesn't look like she belongs in the place, you know? She looks like a drunk, all right, but she's still kind of classy. Henry and Wanda strike up a conversation, and, seeing that Henry is broke, Wanda invites him home.

The dialogue scenes between Rourke and Dunaway in this movie are never less than a pleasure, but their exchanges on that first night are poetry. She explains that if a guy comes along with a fifth, she is likely to leave with that guy, since when she drinks she always makes bad decisions. He nods. What other kinds of decisions are there when you're drunk? They drink, they talk, they flirt, they coexist. Another day, another adventure.

One day a beautiful rich girl with long hair (Alice Krige) comes to the bar looking for Henry. She publishes a literary magazine and has purchased some of Henry's stuff. He likes this development. They go to her house and drink, talk, flirt, and coexist. The next time she turns up in the bar, Wanda is already there. The rich girl and Wanda do not coexist.

That's basically what the movie is about. *Barfly* is not heavy on plot, which is correct, since in the disordered world of the drinker, one thing rarely leads to another through any visible pattern. Each day is a window that opens briefly after the hangover and before the blackout, and you can never tell what you'll see through that window.

Barfly was directed by Barbet Schroeder, who commissioned the original screenplay by Bukowski and then spent eight years trying to get it made. (At one point, he threatened to cut off his fingers if Cannon Group president Menahem Golan did not finance it; the outcome of the story can be deduced by the fact that this is a Cannon release.) Rourke and Dunaway take their characters as opportunities to stretch as actors, to take chances and do extreme things. Schroeder never tries to impose too much artificial order on the events; indeed, he committed to filming Bukowski's screenplay exactly as written, in all its rambling but romantic detail.

The result is a truly original American movie, a film like no other, a period of time spent in the company of the kinds of characters Saroyan and O'Neill would have understood, the kinds of people we try not to see, and yet might enjoy more than some of our more visible friends. *Barfly* was one of 1987's best films.

Bar Girls ★ ½
R, 95 m., 1995

NEW

Nancy Allison Wolfe (Loretta), Liza D'Agostino (Rachael), Camila Griggs (J.R.), Michael Harris (Noah), Justine Slater (Veronica), Lisa Parker (Annie), Pam Raines (Celia), Paula Sorge (Tracy). Directed by Marita Giovanni and produced by Lauran Hoffman and Giovanni. Screenplay by Hoffman.

Bar Girls is the kind of movie that likes itself just for, well, being so darn nice. It's about a small circle of lesbians in Los Angeles, who all hang out at the same bar, and who, in the course of the movie, more or less all sleep with one another. It's the kind of movie where monogamy is more honored in the breeches than in the observance. And forgive me that pun; this is the kind of movie where you find yourself writing down stuff like that.

The screenplay is by Lauran Hoffman, based on her play, and apparently on most of the soap operas she's seen. Her story construction consists of establishing each of the major characters, and providing each one with a romance, a heartbreak, a reversal, a fling, and a resolution. It's so difficult at the beginning to get all the characters actually *into* the story that she resorts to a sequence where two new friends sit on a bed and tell each other about their past lovers, and we see flashbacks to scenes involving those women. What's curious is that the women sharing these stories look at the camera as if they can see the movie, too.

Much of the film takes place in a bar. It may, for all I know, be a real bar, but it looks uncannily like a basement rec room, and almost all the customers are characters in the story. The women seem to use the bar as a stage, living their lives in front of their fellow customers, as they make new friends, break up, have romantic arguments and reconciliations, and pour their hearts out to the understanding bartender. It's all spats and sex, makeups and breakups, broken hearts and new friends. Even the filmmakers seem to sense we are spending a lot of time in the bar, since at one point they offer a Hat Night, in which the characters at least wear funny hats while furthering the plot.

The characters are a mixed bag: a triathlete, a cop, and a producer of a cable cartoon show named "Super Myrtle," for example. They rarely seem to have thoughts, or dialogue for that matter, that does not relate to lesbianism, and in the course of the film I wrote down such lines as:

"I have to be in love to do it."

"You? Friend of semen!?"

"I have to make love with that woman!"

"Tracy's very learned in the ways of lesbianism."

"She's my dream girl."

"She'll be outta here like a hot flash."

All of this does not mean *Bar Girls* doesn't have an audience. It's the kind of movie that's embraced not because it does something well, but because it does it at all. There have been relatively few films about lesbianism, and they tend to reflect the cultures in which they were made. Thus *Bar Girls*, filmed in Los Angeles, is essentially about physical attractiveness and psychobabble, while *Go Fish*, filmed in Chicago, is more serious and mature, and allows many of its characters to look exactly like real people. It would be unfair, but not uncalled-for, to speculate that the actresses in *Go Fish* might be aiming for Steppenwolf, and those in *Bar Girls* for Fox sitcoms. Somehow *Bar Girls* captures its own note perfectly in a closing credit which reads, "Thanks to the people of Los Angeles."

Barton Fink ★ ★ ★ ½
R, 117 m., 1991

John Turturro (Barton Fink), John Goodman (Charlie Meadows), John Mahoney (W.P. Mayhew), Judy Davis (Audrey Taylor), Michael Lerner (Jack Lipnick), Jon Polito (Lou Breeze). Directed by Joel Coen and produced by Ethan Coen. Screenplay by Ethan Coen and Joel Coen.

If there is a favorite image in the movies by the Coen brothers, it's of crass, venal men behind desks, who possess power the heroes envy. Maybe that's because, like all filmmakers, the Coens have spent a lot of time on the carpet, pitching projects to executives. In *Blood Simple*, the guy behind the desk was M. Emmet Walsh, as a scheming private detective. In *Raising Arizona*, it was Trey Wilson's furniture czar. In *Miller's Crossing*, it was Albert Finney as a mob boss. In *Barton Fink*, it is Michael Lerner, as the head of a Hollywood studio. All of these men are vulgar, smoke cigars, and view their supplicants with contempt.

To their desks come characters who want to make a deal with the devil. They *know* these men are evil, compromised, and corrupt. But they want what they have—a lot of money. *Barton Fink*, the latest Coen film (directed by Joel, produced by Ethan, written by both) tells the story of a man who would like to sell out to Hollywood, if only he had the talent. Barton Fink is a left-wing New York playwright, modeled on the Clifford Odets of *Waiting for Lefty*, who writes one proletarian hand-wringer in the late 1930s and then is summoned to Hollywood, where Jack Lipnick (Lerner), the vulgarian in charge of Capitol Pictures, pays him piles of money and assigns him to write a wrestling picture for Wallace Beery.

Fink, played with a likable, dim earnestness by John Turturro, checks into an eerie hotel that looks designed by Edward Hopper. There is apparently only one other tenant, the affable Charlie Meadows (John Goodman), a traveling salesman who lives next door and says he could tell Fink a lot of interesting stories. But Fink, who claims to be the poet of the working man, is not interested in a real proletarian, and spends most of his time staring at his typewriter in despair. He has writer's block.

Lou Breeze (Jon Polito), the studio czar's right-hand man, tells Fink he should look up W. P. Mayhew (John Mahoney), another great American writer on the studio payroll. Mayhew is obviously modeled on William Faulkner, and Mahoney, with a mustache, is his uncanny double. Fink arrives breathlessly at the great man's feet, only to discover that he is a raving drunk and that his "secretary" (Judy Davis) has written most of his recent work. The three go on a picnic one day, and the scene builds into a wry comic vignette—some satire, some slapstick.

Like all of the Coen productions, *Barton Fink* has a deliberate visual style. The Hollywood of the late 1930s and early 1940s is seen here as a world of Art Deco and deep shadows, long hotel corridors, and bottomless swimming pools. And there is a horror lurking underneath the affluent surface. Goodman, as the ordinary man in the next room, is revealed to have inhuman secrets, and the movie leads up to an apocalyptic vision of blood, flames, and ruin, with Barton Fink unable to influence events with either his art or his strength.

The Coens mean this aspect of the film, I think, to be read as an emblem of the rise of Nazism. They paint Fink as an ineffectual and impotent left-wing intellectual, who sells out while telling himself he is doing the right thing, who thinks he understands the "common man" but does not understand that, for many common men, fascism had a seductive appeal. Fink tries to write a wrestling picture and sleeps with the great writer's mistress, while the Holocaust approaches and the nice guy in the next room turns out to be a monster.

It would be a mistake to insist too much on this aspect of the movie, however, since *Barton Fink* is above all a black comedy in the tradition of David Lynch, Luis Buñuel, and the Coens themselves. Turturro is the right man for the role, making Fink a plodding, introspective, unsure intellectual whose lack of insight is matched only by his lack of talent. The movie is a little unfair to Odets, its inspiration (even if he did go to Hollywood in the late 1930s and write a boxing picture, *Golden Boy*, which did not drip with political commitment). But it is even more unfair, hilariously, to Faulkner, whose works were not written by a "secretary," but who was by all accounts just as much of a boozer as the Mayhew character.

Barton Fink won the Palme d'Or at the 1991 Cannes Film Festival, and an unprecedented two more prizes as well, for director and actor. Since Cannes juries traditionally limit themselves to one award per film, their ecstasy would seem to indicate *Barton Fink* is one of the greatest films ever made. It is not. But it's an assured piece of comic filmmaking, and perhaps a warning by the Coens to themselves about what can happen when brilliant young talents from the East make that trek out to the land of the guys behind the desks.

Basic Instinct ★ ★
R, 122 m., 1992

Michael Douglas (Detective Nick Curran), Sharon Stone (Catherine Tramell), George Dzundza (Gus), Jeanne Tripplehorn (Dr. Beth Garner), Denis Arndt (Lieutenant Walker), Leilani Sarelle (Roxy). Directed by Paul Verhoeven and produced by Alan Marshall. Screenplay by Joe Eszterhas.

In their protests against Paul Verhoeven's *Basic Instinct,* gay activists took to giving away the ending of the movie. With some thrillers, that would be a damaging blow. But the ending of *Basic Instinct* is so arbitrary that it hardly matters. This is not a movie where the outcome depends upon the personality or behavior of the characters. It's just a wind-up machine to jerk us around.

Consider the last shot of the movie (no, I will not reveal it). This shot allows us to discover whodunit—whether one of the characters is a murderer, or not. The screen has faded to black. Then we get the last shot, and it answers our question. But if the last shot had provided the *opposite* answer, it still would have been consistent with everything that had happened in the film. Almost every shred of evidence throughout the entire movie supports two different conclusions.

This is the kind of ending beloved by marketing experts. The audience likes the heroine? Make her innocent. They hate her? Make her the killer. Only one shot has to be changed. As a result, I left the movie feeling depressed and manipulated—because it didn't matter how hard I tried to follow the plot and figure things out, the whole movie was just toying with me. At least some of the other recent titles in this genre—like *Fatal Attraction* and *Sea of Love*—played fair.

The movie stars Michael Douglas as a troubled police detective who has been up before Internal Affairs, after shooting some tourists in a murky misunderstanding. He gets involved in the investigation of the kinky murder of a rock star. The rock star's sometime girlfriend (Sharon Stone) has written a novel in which a rock star is murdered in precisely the same way. Does this mean she is guilty? Or did a copycat killer try to frame her?

The police questioning of the woman is the best scene in the movie, as Stone flirts shamelessly and toys with their male libidos. Douglas is entranced. The woman may be a killer and is obviously twisted and manipulative, and yet he's mesmerized—attracted by the danger as much as by her sensuous magnetism. As his investigation progresses, however, he finds the woman is more complicated than he suspected. She has a lesbian lover, for one thing. And she has a past—which, in one of those coincidences much beloved by whodunits and thrillers, she shared with the very same female psychologist who is currently Douglas's police therapist.

The screenplay, by Joe Eszterhas, resembles his *Jagged Edge* (1985) in keeping the secret until the last shot. It's not really the last shot technique that I object to. What bothers me is that the whole plot has been constructed so that every relevant clue can be read two ways. That means the solution, when it is finally revealed, is not *necessarily* true. It is simply the writer's toss of the dice.

Apart from the whodunit elements, the movie exists for its sexual content. The Sharon Stone character, described as "world class" by Douglas after one night in the sack, is a kinky seductress with the kind of cold, challenging verbal style that many men take as a challenge. Her friends include a woman who once killed her entire family; she needs these people, she says, as inspiration for her novels. Her next book, she tells Douglas, staring him straight in the eye, will be about a police detective who falls in love with the wrong woman.

The sex scenes, threatened with the NC-17 rating until forty-five seconds were removed to qualify for the R, belong in that strange neverland created by the MPAA's Hollywood morality. They aren't much by the standards of really daring movies, but they do go far enough to make the R rating into a fiction. Seeing movies that walk the ratings line like this, I realize that good soft-core is more erotic than trimmed-down would-be hard-core, and that the movie would have been more of a turn-on if it hadn't tried so hard. The sex resembles a violent contact sport, with a scoring system known only to the players.

As for the allegedly offensive homosexual characters: The movie's protesters might take note of the fact that this film's heterosexuals, starting with Douglas, are equally offensive. Still, there is a point to be made about Hollywood's unremitting insistence on typecasting homosexuals—particularly lesbians—as twisted and evil. That's especially true in the same season when *Fried Green Tomatoes*, a story about two women in love, is cravenly constructed to obscure the story's obvious lesbian elements. Hollywood is fearless in portraying lesbians as killer dykes, but gets cold feet with a story that might portray them (gasp!) as warm, good-natured, and generous.

Since most people will be viewing *Basic Instinct* in less than a Politically Correct frame of mind, however, does the movie deliver? In a way, it does. It kept me interested, and guessing, right up until that final shot, which revealed that all of my efforts were pointless since the guilt or innocence of the characters was a flip of the coin, based on evidence that could be read both ways. The film is like a crossword puzzle. It keeps your interest until you solve it. Then it's just a worthless scrap with the spaces filled in.

CANNES, France, May 7, 1992—*The Cannes Film Festival is, of course, a citadel of world cinematic art, and therefore one question was on everyone's mind Thursday: What's in those missing forty-five seconds of* Basic Instinct?

The movie, which has been America's box office best-seller for weeks, was threatened with the dreaded NC-17 rating before the offending seconds were pulled out by director Paul Verhoeven. But they were reinserted for the film's European premiere on the opening night of Cannes.

The untrimmed version was on everybody's

mind as American critics gathered Wednesday night at La Pizza, down by the old yacht harbor, for their traditional pre-festival summit conference.

"Surely you aren't going to sit through it again, just to see the forty-five seconds?" asked Jack Matthews of Newsday.

"I might," I said. "My editor called me long-distance and said there's a lot of interest in it."

"But what can you say in print?" asked Kenneth Turan of the Los Angeles Times. *"I mean, to describe what goes on, you'll have to use words your editor won't like."*

Turan, who once wrote a book titled Sinema *about dirty movies, knows what he's talking about.*

"My editor has been around," I said. "He used to be the TV critic."

"These forty-five seconds, you're not gonna see on TV."

"Maybe on cable?"

"They'll use the R-rated cut."

"This is a big-budget major movie with Michael Douglas," somebody said. "How shocking are those forty-five seconds possibly gonna be?"

"That's just what David Letterman said," I said. "He asked Douglas what you could do in forty-five seconds, and Douglas said he could do plenty."

"Basically, what I hear is, it's just forty-five seconds of ____," Turan said.

"____?" I said.

"Yeah, ____."

Never having seen Michael Douglas ____ in a movie before, I was up bright and early Thursday morning, got my press credentials, and hurried into the Grand Auditorium Lumiere in the Palais des Festivals. This is the most famous movie theater in the world, with the largest screen and 4,000 seats, most of which were filled by the time the lights went down.

The first eighty to ninety minutes of the movie were exactly as before, with Catherine looking guilty and then innocent and then guilty again, and Roxy looking suspicious before she drives her car off the on-ramp, and then Beth coming out of nowhere to develop into a major suspect.

Then came the big sex scene between Michael Douglas and Sharon Stone. I leaned forward intently in my seat, determined not to blow this big story. Caress by caress, one drop of sweat and saliva after another, the scene developed exactly as it had in the American version, until suddenly Michael Douglas began to ____, ____ and ____ Sharon Stone. Sure enough, this was the footage cut out of the U.S. version!

"It didn't seem like forty-five seconds to me," I said to my wife.

"It never does," she said.

The Basketball Diaries ★ ★

NEW

R, 102 m., 1995

Leonardo DiCaprio (Jim Carroll), Bruno Kirby (Swifty), Mark Wahlberg (Mickey), Patrick McGaw (Neutron), James Madio (Pedro), Lorraine Bracco (Jim's Mother), Ernie Hudson (Reggie), Juliette Lewis (Diane Moody), Roy Cooper (Father McNulty), Michael Rapaport (Skinhead). Directed by Scott Kalvert and produced by Liz Heller and John Bard Manulis. Screenplay by Bryan Goluboff.

Jim Carroll's cult book *The Basketball Diaries*, published in 1978, describes in grungy detail how the author passed in a few short months from being a Catholic high school basketball star to being a strung-out heroin addict who turned tricks for drugs. Like many such stories, it lingers lovingly over the horrors, and ends with unseemly haste after happiness is regained.

Will there ever be a market for a movie about a character who hurries past his drug phase because he can't wait to tell you what he did after he pulled his act together? Probably not. If there's anything more boring than a juicy parable with a moral at the end, it's the moral without the parable. And so *The Basketball Diaries* informs us in great detail that if you get strung out on drugs, you are likely to find yourself living desperately on the streets, peddling a body that looks less and less like a good buy.

Of course, the Carroll book was more than this; he struck a personal note, of a kid who despite his suffering tried to turn his experience into poetry. The problem with Scott Kalvert's film is that the camera tends to make the experiences too literal: Jim, the hero of the story, is so desperately sick and unhappy that the romanticism seems unconvincing. He plays basketball at night in the rain after his best friend dies of leukemia, and it just looks wet, not touching.

As the movie opens, Jim (Leonardo DiCaprio) is on the basketball team at St. Vitus High School in New York, where a perverted priest salivates while spanking naughty students with a big paddle as the rest of the class watches. This scene owes more to Victorian pornography than to any actual parochial school in twentieth-century America, but no matter: The message, I guess, is that the teachers are such hypocrites you might as well go out and destroy yourself.

Jim and his friends are not good Catholic lads. The student manager of the basketball team steals from the lockers of the opposing team, and the favorite off-court pastime is experimenting with inhalants and pills. The coach, named Swifty and played by Bruno Kirby, is a closet homosexual who expends great effort making unlikely passes at Jim ("Do we understand each other?" he asks in the shower room, offering money). And Jim's mother, played by Lorraine Bracco, is a one-dimensional character who exists in the movie solely to exercise Tough Love by throwing him out.

Life for Jim is a downward spiral of pills, cough medicine, booze, jumping off cliffs into the Harlem River, passing out during a game, and masturbating under the stars (the movie heroically declines to score this scene with "Up on the Roof"). There are also exciting glimpses into the underworld of users, pushers, hookers, and pimps, as Jim drifts loose from his secure moorings, while writing everything down in his diary.

Jim's poetry serves as a narration for part of the film. Like most poetry written by teenagers, it is puerile romanticism, painfully sincere, viewing life as tragic because the author is not happy. Soon, however, he is happy. He tries heroin, and "any ache or pain or sadness or guilt was completely flushed out."

Amazing, how real life has a way of unfolding just like the movies. The movie depends on three durable clichés: (1) Jim helps his dying friend escape from the hospital so he can push his wheelchair down 42nd Street (the movies know that hospitals kill and the only cure is freedom); (2) Jim sees his teammate Neutron on TV, playing in an all-star game while Jim is in a skid row bar (one always happens to see on TV exactly what the story requires); (3) Jim is saved by a noble black man, who finds him unconscious in a playground, brings him home, and puts him through cold turkey (in stories like this, you can always count on a heroic black ex-junkie, scouring the streets for troubled white kids who need to get whupped into shape; there's just not the same cachet being saved by a white dude).

Leonardo DiCaprio (What's Eating Gilbert Grape?) does what he can with the part, but is miscast, I think, as the hard-boiled hero. Ernie Hudson is strong as the ex-junkie, and there is real emotion in Lorraine Bracco's underwritten mother. Oh, and Juliette Lewis, as a scuzzy hooker, once again finds an absolutely authentic note. But the movie is unconvincing. At the end, Jim is seen going in through a "stage door," and

then we hear him telling the story of his descent and recovery. We can't tell if this is supposed to be genuine testimony, or a performance. That's the problem with the whole movie.

Batman ★ ★
PG-13, 126 m., 1989

Jack Nicholson (The Joker/Jack Napier), Michael Keaton (Batman/Bruce Wayne), Kim Basinger (Vicki Vale), Robert Wuhl (Alexander Knox), Pat Hingle (Police Commissioner Gordon), Billy Dee Williams (District Attorney Harvey Dent), Michael Gough (Alfred), Jerry Hall (Alicia), Jack Palance (Carl Grissom). Directed by Tim Burton and produced by Jon Peters and Peter Guber. Screenplay by Sam Hamm and Warren Skaaren.

The Gotham City created in Batman is one of the most distinctive and atmospheric places I've seen in the movies. It's a shame something more memorable doesn't happen there. Batman is a triumph of design over story, style over substance—a great-looking movie with a plot you can't care much about. All of the big moments in the movie are pounded home with ear-shattering sound effects and a jackhammer cutting style, but that just serves to underline the movie's problem, which is a curious lack of suspense and intrinsic interest.

Batman discards the recent cultural history of the Batman character—the camp 1960s TV series, the in-joke comic books—and returns to the mood of the 1940s, the decade of film noir and fascism. The movie is set at the present moment, more or less, but looks as if little has happened in architecture or city planning since the classic DC comic books created that architectural style you could call Comic Book Moderne. The streets of Gotham City are lined with bizarre skyscrapers that climb cancerously toward the sky, held up (or apart) by sky-bridges and steel struts that look like webs against the night sky.

At street level, gray and anonymous people scurry fearfully through the shadows, and the city cancels its two-hundredth-anniversary celebration because the streets are not safe enough to hold it. Gotham is in the midst of a wave of crime and murder orchestrated by The Joker (Jack Nicholson), and civilization is defended only by Batman (Michael Keaton). The screenplay takes a bow in the direction of the origin of the Batman story (young Bruce Wayne saw his parents

murdered by a thug and vowed to use their fortune to dedicate his life to crime-fighting), and it also explains how The Joker got his fearsome grimace. Then it turns into a gloomy showdown between the two bizarre characters.

Nicholson's Joker is really the most important character in the movie—in impact and screen time—and Keaton's Batman and Bruce Wayne characters are so monosyllabic and impenetrable that we have to remind ourselves to cheer for them. Kim Basinger strides in as Vicki Vale, a famous photographer assigned to the Gotham City crime wave, but although she and Wayne carry on a courtship and Batman rescues her from certain death more than once, there's no chemistry and little eroticism. The strangest scene in the movie may be the one where Vicki is brought into the Batcave by Alfred, the faithful valet, and realizes for the first time that Bruce Wayne and Batman are the same person. How does she react? She doesn't react. The movie forgets to allow her to be astonished.

Remembering the movie, I find that the visuals remain strong in my mind, but I have trouble caring about what happened in front of them. I remember an astonishing special-effects shot that travels up, up to the penthouse of a towering, ugly skyscraper, and I remember the armor slamming shut on the Batmobile as if it were a high-tech armadillo. I remember The Joker grinning beneath a hideous giant balloon as he dispenses free cash in his own travesty of the Macy's parade, and I remember a really vile scene in which he defaces art masterpieces in the local museum, before Batman crashes in through the skylight.

But did I care about the relationship between these two caricatures? Did either one have the depth of even a comic-book character? Not really. And there was something off-putting about the anger beneath the movie's violence; this is a hostile, mean-spirited movie about ugly, evil people, and it doesn't generate the liberating euphoria of the Superman or Indiana Jones pictures. It's rated PG-13, but it's not for kids.

Should it be seen, anyway? Probably. Director Tim Burton and his special-effects team have created a visual place that has some of the same strength as Fritz Lang's Metropolis or Ridley Scott's futuristic Los Angeles in Blade Runner. The gloominess of the visuals has a haunting power. Jack Nicholson has one or two of his patented moments of inspiration—although not as many as I would have expected. And the music by Prince, intercut with classics, is effectively joined in the images. The movie's problem is that no one seemed to have any fun making it, and it's hard to have much fun watching it. It's a depressing experience. Is the opposite of comic book "tragic book"?

Batman Forever ★ ★ ½
PG-13, 121 m., 1995

NEW

Val Kilmer (Batman/Bruce Wayne), Tommy Lee Jones (Two-Face/D.A. Harvey Dent), Chris O'Donnell (Robin/Dick Grayson), Jim Carrey (Riddler/Edward Nygma), Nicole Kidman (Dr. Chase Meridian), Pat Hingle (Commissioner Gordon), Drew Barrymore (Sugar), Debi Mazar (Spice), Ed Begley, Jr. (Fred Stickley), Michael Gough (Alfred). Directed by Joel Schumacher and produced by Tim Burton and Peter MacGregor-Scott. Screenplay by Lee Batchler, Janet Scott Batchler, and Akiva Goldsman.

A question has been nagging at me ever since the first Batman movie, and *Batman Forever* makes it inescapable: Would Bruce Wayne continue his keen interest in crime-fighting if he didn't get to wear the Batman costume? The opening scene plays like a commercial for a rubberwear shop, and throughout the movie the dominant images are of fetishistic gear: the belt buckles, boots, gloves, capes, masks, and of course the cute little dimesized nipples on Batman's and Robin's chests. When Batman tries on his new prototype costume late in the movie, and there's a close-up of its gleaming buttocks, the audience chuckles knowingly.

Batman would be a sensation in any leather bar, but *Batman Forever* is at pains to show that he has heterosexual tastes. Nicole Kidman plays Dr. Chase Meridian, who sounds like a bank but is, in fact, a student of abnormal psychology. She's powerfully attracted to Batman the moment she meets him, and wonders what he's looking for in a woman: Would it help, she wonders, if she carried a whip? She's thrilled that Batman reads her books ("Not every girl makes a superhero's night table"), but less than thrilled when her date for the Gotham Charity Circus is boring old bachelor Bruce Wayne. Maybe the clothes do make the man.

This theme—the girl in love with the image but not the reality—is also standard in the Superman series, where Lois Lane chases the Man of Steel but rejects Clark Kent. What's new in *Batman Forever* is that Bat-man himself (Val Kilmer) has to do a little seduction. At the circus, young acrobat Dick Grayson (Chris O'Donnell) saves the crowd by rolling Two-Face's TNT bomb into the river. His family is killed during this process. Bruce Wayne, impressed by the orphaned young man, invites him to stay at Wayne Manor, but Dick is a rebellious motorcycle freak who wants outta there—until Wayne shows him his collection of bikes, including priceless old Harleys and Indians. The subtexts in this scene are so deep you have to wade through them.

The plot of the movie involves the embittered Two-Face (Tommy Lee Jones), a former district attorney who is deranged after half his face is scarred by acid. He's mean, but not brilliant. For brains, the movie provides Edward Nygma (Jim Carrey), who uses a computer program to name himself the Riddler, and who hooks up with Two-Face in a plot to steal lots of loot to finance his evil scheme.

The Riddler's scheme is one of the more amusing aspects of *Batman Forever*, considering that the movie's distributor is Warner Bros., which owns HBO and other cable outlets. The Riddler wants to put a copy of "The Box" on top of every TV set in Gotham. This device is not exactly an Internet provider. It works by sucking up the brainwaves of its users and transferring them to the Riddler, whose own I.Q. expands at dizzying speed.

Although the first two Batman movies were big winners at the box office, there was a feeling after *Batman Returns* (1992) that the series had grown too dark and gloomy. Batman was a reclusive neurotic, his enemies included the deformed Penguin (raised from childhood in sewers), and the movies tried for a marriage of superheroes and *film noir*. That didn't work: The message of *noir* is that there are no heroes.

Tim Burton, director of the first two brooding Batman films, steps up to producer for *Batman Forever*, and the new director, Joel Schumacher, makes a generally successful effort to lighten the material. There are more clever one-liners for Alfred the Butler (Michael Gough), lots of laughs for the Riddler (played by Jim Carrey like a riff on his character in *The Mask*), and even sitcom moments like the one when Alfred tells Bruce Wayne that the "young master" has run off with the car. "The Jaguar?" asks Wayne. "No, sir. The *other* car."

The movie looks great, of course; Gotham City is a web of towering spires, bridges, and expressways, planted in a swamp of despond. Boardrooms and laboratories look like German Expressionist sets, and the Charity Circus could come straight from Murnau's *Sunrise*. There are neat gimmicks, like the Riddler's brainwave helmet, and neat stunts, as when the Batmobile climbs straight up the side of a skyscraper. And there is a consistent visual motif: Two hands clasping in a firm grip. Dick Grayson is caught in such a grip by his acrobat father during a dangerous trick, and later the shot is repeated to show that Bruce Wayne is now his surrogate father.

But somehow Batman *still* doesn't come alive. Val Kilmer is a completely acceptable substitute for Michael Keaton in the title role, but in all three of the movies Batman remains shadowy and undefined. The movies exist for their villains, who this time both seem to be playing the same note; the Riddler and Two-Face alternate in overacting, until the pace grows wearying. There is no rhythm to the movie, no ebb and flow; it's all flat-out spectacle.

Is the movie better entertainment? Well, it's great bubble gum for the eyes. And younger children will be able to process it more easily (some kids were led bawling from *Batman Returns*, where the PG-13 rating was a joke). I liked the look of the movie and Schumacher's general irreverence toward the material.

But the great Batman movie still remains to be made. Here is the most complex and intriguing of classic comic superheroes, inhabiting the most visually interesting world, but somehow a story hasn't been found to do him justice. A *story*—with a beginning, a middle, and an end, and a Batman at its center who emerges as more than a collection of costumes and postures. More than ever, after this third movie, I found myself asking, who *was* that masked man, anyhow?

Batman Returns ★ ★
PG-13, 130 m., 1992

Michael Keaton (Batman), Danny DeVito (Penguin), Michelle Pfeiffer (Catwoman), Christopher Walken (Max Shreck), Michael Murphy (Mayor), Michael Gough (Alfred the Butler), Pat Hingle (Commissioner Gordon). Directed by Tim Burton and produced by Denise DiNovi and Burton. Screenplay by Daniel Waters.

The gloomy undertone of the Batman movies is like a tow line, holding the movie back, keeping it from springing free into the wind.

Tim Burton's *Batman Returns,* even more than the original *Batman,* is a dark, brooding film, filled with hurt and fear, childhood wounds, and festering adult resentments. It is also a most intriguing movie, great to look at, fun to talk about. There is no doubt Burton is a gifted director, but is he the right director for *Batman*?

The film opens in cruelty and shame, as the parents of a deformed baby put him into his bassinet and drop him into the river on a cold, snowy Christmas night. The frail little craft floats downstream and into the sewers of Gotham City, where the infant is rescued and raised by the penguins who luckily happen to live there. Arriving at adulthood, his hands like lobster claws, the Penguin (Danny DeVito) learns about the human world by peering out through sewer gratings. His soul burns with the need to discover who his parents were, and why they treated him so meanly.

Elsewhere in Gotham, the mayor (Michael Murphy) presides over the municipal Christmas tree lighting before cold crowds under sullen skies. He is joined by the vile tycoon Max Shreck (Christopher Walken), who has a scheme to build a power plant that will drain the city of its energy. His browbeaten secretary (Michelle Pfeiffer), killed after she discovers the scheme, is licked back to life by alley cats and vows vengeance, sewing herself a skintight, fetishistic costume and venturing out into the night as Catwoman. Meanwhile, in the Batcave beneath his gloomy mansion, Batman (Michael Keaton) ponders whatever deep needs led to his own peculiar existence.

Even back in the days when Batman lived in comic books, his world was a little darker than, say, Superman's. There was a shade of *film noir* in Gotham City, in contrast to the deco 1930s optimism of Superman's Metropolis. *The Dark Knight,* a graphic novel that inspired the Batman movies, was darker still, and now Burton takes it all of the way—into a movie set mostly at night, photographed on refrigerated sets, so that the actors sometimes look as if they would rather have a mug of hot chocolate than all the passion and wealth in the city.

The movie's plot doesn't exactly unwind like a well-coiled machine. The movie proceeds in fits and starts, from one little drama to another, as the Penguin ventures out from his subterranean haunts, and a newspaper circulation war peddles scare stories about his alleged crimes. The evil Max Shreck, meanwhile, directs his henchmen in a con-

spiracy to deliver Gotham into his own megalomaniac hands, and Murphy, as the incumbent mayor, blathers like an ineffectual nonentity while the Penguin mounts a campaign against him.

Batman meantime is summoned by the Batsignal to the side of Police Commissioner Gordon (Pat Hingle), to do battle against the Gotham crime wave. And on hii nocturnal rounds, he crosses paths with Catwoman, whose claws can draw blood, and who is as skilled as Batman in climbing high buildings, swinging through the air, and employing the martial arts. Dressed in their fetishistic costumes, they would obviously make an ideal couple—something that occurs to them more gradually than it does to us. Their few erotic moments together are, alas, so incomplete and unsatisfying they look as if they might have been trimmed for the PG-13.

Remembering the movie and contrasting it to my childhood memories of the comic books, I wonder if perhaps I cannot fully respond to this film because I was shaped in a kinder, gentler time. I always thought it would be fun to be Batman. The movie believes it is more of a curse—that Batman is not a crime-fighting superhero but a reclusive neurotic who feels he has to prove himself to a society he does not really inhabit.

All of Tim Burton's films *(Pee-wee's Big Adventure, Beetlejuice, Edward Scissorhands,* and the two *Batmans)* are about characters whose strange qualities place them outside the mainstream, and who live in worlds that owe everything to art direction and set design. Looking at these movies is a pleasure—they are not ordinary or boring. Perhaps I would have enjoyed Batman more if the movie had been about someone else, perhaps one of those Marvel superheroes who frankly concede their personal inadequacies. I can admire the movie on many levels, but I cannot accept it as Batman. And I was disappointed that the disjoined plot advanced so unsteadily, depriving us of the luxury of really caring about the outcome.

It is a common theory that when you have a hero, like James Bond, Superman, or Batman, in a continuing series, it's the villain that gives each movie its flavor. *Batman* had the Joker, played by Jack Nicholson, to lend it energy, but the Penguin is a curiously meager and depressing creature; I pitied him, but did not fear him or find him funny. The genius of Danny DeVito is all but swallowed up in the paraphernalia of the role. *Batman Returns* is odd and sad, but not exhilarating.

I give the movie a negative review, and yet I don't think it's a bad movie; it's more of a misguided one, made with great creativity, but denying us what we more or less deserve from a Batman story. Looking back over both films, I think Burton has a vision here and is trying to shape it to the material, but it just won't fit. No matter how hard you try, superheroes and *film noir* don't go together; the very essence of *noir* is that there are no more heroes. I had a feeling by the end of this film that Batman was beginning to get the idea.

Beauty and the Beast ★ ★ ★

G, 84 m., 1991

With the voices of: Paige O'Hara (Belle), Robby Benson (Beast), Richard White (Gaston), Jerry Orbach (Lumiere), David Ogden Stiers (Cogsworth), Angela Lansbury (Mrs. Potts), Jesse Corti (LeFou). Directed by Gary Trousdale and Kirk Wise and produced by Don Hahn. Animation screenplay by Linda Woolverton.

Beauty and the Beast slipped around all my roadblocks and penetrated directly into my strongest childhood memories, in which animation looked more *real* than live-action features. Watching the movie, I found myself caught up in a direct and joyous way. I wasn't reviewing an "animated film." I was being told a story, I was hearing terrific music, and I was having fun.

The film is as good as any Disney animated feature ever made—as magical as *Pinocchio, Snow White, The Little Mermaid.* And it's a reminder that animation is the ideal medium for fantasy, because all of its fears and dreams can be made literal. No Gothic castle in the history of horror films, for example, has ever approached the awesome, frightening towers of the castle where the Beast lives. And no real wolves could have fangs as sharp or eyes as glowing as the wolves that prowl in the castle woods.

The movie's story, somewhat altered from the original fable, involves a beauty named Belle, who lives in the worlds of her favorite library books and is repelled by the romantic advances of Gaston, the muscle-bound cretin in her little eighteenth-century French village. Belle's father, a dotty inventor, sets off on a journey through the forest, takes a wrong turn, and is imprisoned in the castle of the Beast. And Belle bravely sets off on a mission to rescue him.

We already know, from the film's opening

narration, that the Beast is actually a handsome young prince who was transformed into a hideous monster as a punishment for being cruel. And a beast he will be forever, unless he finds someone who will love him. When Belle arrives at the castle, that lifesaving romance is set into motion—although not, of course, without grave adventures to be overcome.

Like all of the best Disney animated films, *Beauty and the Beast* surrounds its central characters with a large peanut gallery of gossipy, chattering supporting players. The Beast's haunted castle contains his entire serving staff, transformed from humans into household objects, and so we meet Lumiere, a candlestick; Cogsworth, a clock; and Mrs. Potts, a teapot with a little son named Chip. These characters are all naturally on Belle's side, because if the Beast can end his magic spell, they, too, will become human again.

There are some wonderful musical numbers in the movie, and animation sets their choreography free from the laws of gravity. A hilarious number celebrates the monstrous ego of Gaston, who boasts about his hairy chest and the antlers he uses for interior decoration. "Be Our Guest" is a rollicking invitation to Belle from the castle staff, choreographed like Busby Berkeley running amok. And there is the haunting title song, sung by Mrs. Potts in the voice of Angela Lansbury.

The songs have lyrics by the late Howard Ashman and music by Alan Menken, the same team who collaborated on 1989's *The Little Mermaid,* and they bubble with wit and energy ("Gaston" in particular brings down the house). Lansbury is one of a gifted cast on the sound track, which also includes Paige O'Hara as the plucky Belle; Robby Benson (his voice electronically lowered and mixed with the growls of animals) as the Beast; Jerry Orbach as the candlestick who sounds uncannily like Maurice Chevalier; David Ogden Stiers as the cranky Cogsworth; and Richard White as the insufferable Gaston, who degenerates during the course of the film from a chauvinist pig to a sadistic monster.

Beauty and the Beast, like *The Little Mermaid,* reflects a new energy and creativity from the Disney animation people. They seem to have abandoned all notions that their feature-length cartoons are intended only for younger viewers, and these aren't children's movies but robust family entertainment. Perhaps it is inevitable, in an age when even younger kids see high-voltage special-effects films like *Die Hard* or *Terminator II,* that animation could no longer be content with jolly and innocuous fairy tales. What a movie like *Beauty and the Beast* does, however, is to give respect to its audience.

A lot of "children's movies" seem to expect people to buy tickets by default, because of what the movie *doesn't* contain (no sex, vulgarity, etc.). *Beauty and the Beast* reaches back to an older and healthier Hollywood tradition in which the best writers, musicians, and filmmakers are gathered for a project on the assumption that a family audience deserves great entertainment, too.

Beetlejuice ★ ★
PG, 105 m., 1988

Alec Baldwin (Adam), Geena Davis (Barbara), Michael Keaton (Betelgeuse), Jeffrey Jones (Charles), Catherine O'Hara (Delia), Winona Ryder (Lydia), Sylvia Sidney (Juno). Directed by Tim Burton and produced by Michael Bender, Larry Wilson, and Richard Hashimoto. Screenplay by Michael McDowell and Warren Skaaren.

Beetlejuice gets off to a start that's so charming it never lives it down. The movie is all anticlimax once we realize it's going to be about gimmicks, not characters. During the enchanted opening minutes of the film, we meet a young married couple who have just moved into a strange new house, and we're introduced to some of the local townspeople. All of these characters have an offhand, unforced innocence, and no wonder: The movie was directed by Tim Burton, who created a similar feeling in *Pee-wee's Big Adventure.*

It's hard to describe what makes the opening scenes so special. Alec Baldwin and Geena Davis, as the young couple, seem so giddy, so heedlessly in love, that they project an infectious good cheer. The local folks are so goshdarn down-home they must have been sired by L.L. Bean out of the *Prairie Home Companion.* The movie is bathed in a foolish charm. And, fool that I am, I expected that note to be carried all the way through the film. But it was not to be.

The young couple die in a silly accident. But they still live in the same house. The only problem is, there's nothing outside the door except for a strange science-fiction landscape that looks borrowed from Paul Schrader's *Cat People.* It takes them a while to figure out they're dead, and even longer to realize what has happened: Their fate is to remain in their former home as ghosts, while it is sold to a New York family (Jeffrey Jones and Catherine O'Hara, and Winona Ryder as their daughter) who have big plans for remodeling it.

This is all, I guess, a fairly clever idea. And the movie is well-played, especially by Davis (the girlfriend in *The Fly*) and Jones (the emperor in *Amadeus,* the principal in *Ferris Bueller's Day Off*). But the story, which seemed so original, turns into a sitcom fueled by lots of special effects and weird sets and props, and the inspiration is gone.

To be sure, there has never before been a movie afterworld quite like this one. Heaven, or whatever it is, seems a lot like a cruise ship with a cranky crew. The "newlydeads" find a manual that instructs them on how to live as ghosts, and they also find an advertisement from a character named Betelgeuse (Michael Keaton), who specializes in "exorcisms of the living." They enlist him to try to scare the New Yorkers out of the house, but he turns out to be a cantankerous demon, and a lot more trouble than he's worth.

The best thing about the movie, apart from the opening, is the set design by Bo Welch. Both he and Burton seem inspired by the spirit of "Pee-wee's Playhouse" and *Pee-wee's Big Adventure,* in which objects can have lives of their own, and architectural details have an unsettling way of rearranging themselves. The look of the film might be described as cartoon surrealistic. But the film's dramatic method isn't nearly as original.

One of the problems is Keaton, as the exorcist. Nearly unrecognizable behind pounds of makeup, he prances around playing Betelgeuse as a mischievous and vindictive prankster, but his scenes don't seem to fit with the other action, and his appearances are mostly a nuisance. It's also a shame that Baldwin and Davis, as the ghosts, have to spend most of their time playing tricks on Jones and O'Hara and winning the sympathy of their daughter; I would have been more interested if the screenplay had preserved their sweet romanticism and cut back on the slapstick.

Before Sunrise ★ ★ ★
R, 100 m., 1995

Ethan Hawke (Jesse), Julie Delpy (Celine), Erni Mangold (Palm Reader), Dominik Castell (Street Poet). Directed by Richard Linklater and produced by Anne Walker-McBay. Screenplay by Linklater and Kim Krizan.

They Meet Cute on a train in Austria. They start talking. There is a meeting of the minds (our most erotic organs), and they like each other. They're in their early twenties. He's an American with a Eurail pass, on his way to Vienna to catch a cheap flight home. She's French, a student at the Sorbonne, on her way back to Paris. They go to the buffet car, drink some coffee, keep talking, and he has this crazy idea: Why doesn't she get off the train with him in Vienna, and they can be together until he catches his plane?

This sort of scenario has happened, I imagine, millions of times. It has rarely happened in a nicer, sweeter, more gentle way than in Richard Linklater's *Before Sunrise*, which I could call a *Love Affair* for Generation X, except that Jesse and Celine stand outside their generation, and especially outside its boring insistence on being bored.

There is no hidden agenda in this movie. There will be no betrayals, melodrama, phony violence, or fancy choreography in sex scenes. It's mostly conversation, as they wander the city of Vienna from midafternoon until the following dawn. Nobody hassles them. *Before Sunrise* is so much like real life—like a documentary with an invisible camera—that I found myself remembering real conversations I had experienced with more or less the same words.

Jesse and Celine are played by Ethan Hawke and Julie Delpy. You may remember him from *Dead Poets Society*, *White Fang*, or especially *Reality Bites*, in which he played a character who is 180 degrees different from this one. She starred in Kieslowski's *White*, as the wife who eventually regrets dumping her husband. Here she is ravishingly beautiful and, more important, warm and matter-of-fact, speaking English so well the screenplay has to explain it (she spent some time in the States).

What do they talk about? Nothing spectacular. Parents, death, former boyfriends and girlfriends, music, and the problem with reincarnation when there are more people alive now than in all previous times put together (if there is a finite number of souls, are we living in a period of a five-to-one split?). Linklater's dialogue is weirdly amusing, as when Jesse suggests they should think of their time together as a sort of "time travel," and envisions a future in which she is with her boring husband and wonders, "What would some of those guys be like that I knew when I was young," and wishes she could

travel back in time to see—and so here she is, back in time, seeing.

A sexual attraction is obviously present between them, and Linklater handles it gently, with patience. There is a wonderful scene in the listening booth of a music store, where each one looks at the other, and then looks away, so as not to be caught. The way they do this—the timing, the slight embarrassment—is delicate and true to life. And I liked their first kiss, on the same Ferris wheel used in *The Third Man*, so much I didn't mind that they didn't know Orson Welles and Joseph Cotten had been there before them.

The city of Vienna is presented as a series of meetings and not as a travelogue. They meet amateur actors, fortune-tellers, street poets, friendly bartenders. They spend some time in a church at midnight. They drink wine in a park. They find a way to exchange personal information by holding imaginary phone calls with imaginary best friends. They talk about making love. There are good arguments for, and against.

This is Linklater's third film, after *Slacker* (1991) and *Dazed and Confused* (1993). He's onto something. He likes the way ordinary time unfolds for people, as they cross paths, start talking, share their thoughts and uncertain philosophies. His first movie, set in Austin, Texas, followed one character until he met a second, then the second until he met a third, and so on, eavesdropping on one life and conversation after another. The second film was a long night at the end of a high school year, as the students regarded their futures. Now *Before Sunrise*, about two nice kids, literate, sensitive, tentative, intoxicated by the fact that their lives stretch out before them, filled with mystery and hope, and maybe love.

Note: The "R" rating for this film, based on a few four-letter words, is entirely unjustified. It is an ideal film for teenagers.

*   *   *

From the Movie Answer Man:

Q. *I wonder whether you'd be interested in my story. I recently saw the movie Before Sunrise, where Ethan Hawke and Julie Delpy meet each other on a train, start talking, and end up spending the night walking around Vienna, Austria. Caught up in the romance of it all, I boarded a train from Philly to Charlottesville, Virginia (I had to go there anyway.) On the train I met a woman dressed exactly like Julie Delpy and about as beautiful. So began a rather romantic trip that began with her asking me to come to Atlanta with her and ended with my return to law school two days later.*

But now the story takes an interesting twist, and could probably be called After Sunrise. Since I had

missed some school, I felt the need to explain to a professor where I had been. Unfortunately, I was too embarrassed to relate the full details, so I informed him I was sick. Two weeks later I was asked to leave the school for lying to a professor.

My legal career is probably now over. So why do I write to you? To be honest, I don't know—but the link between the movie, and my life seemed so strong I felt someone in the industry should know. Make of it what you will. (Daryl Elfield, Berkeley, Calif.)

A. I am always getting letters from people who wonder if the movies these days are not a baleful influence on young people. In your case, Before Sunrise sparked a grand gesture of romanticism, which would have been wonderful if the consequences were not so dire. I hope you have the right to appeal.

Having been a college student myself, I relished the way you worded this phrase: "I felt the need to explain to a professor where I had been." My guess is, this felt need was inspired by the professor's curiosity about your absence from his classes. In a similar situation I, too, might have hesitated to reveal the whole truth. On the other hand, rules are rules. In law school I am sure it is especially important to enforce the honor code, since, as we all know, no lawyer has ever said he was sick to get out of anything.

Curious about your case, I made a few telephone calls.

The woman you met on the train was Jessica Turner, a Spanish teacher from Fryeburg, Maine. I talked to her to check out your story.

"I hadn't seen the movie when we met," she told me, "but we saw it together after we got off the train in Atlanta. I really was wearing one of those black dresses, like the woman in the movie. Actually, I started talking to him. I had stopped to see a friend in Baltimore, who packed me a bagel and wrapped it up with a note that said, 'Don't talk to strangers.' I saw Daryl sitting at the next table on the train and told him what my napkin said. We started talking, he told me all about the movie, and when we got to Charlottesville, I asked him if he wanted to stay on the train and spend some time in Atlanta."

"I feel really awful about what happened. I vaguely remember him saying that his professor would never believe his story."

Then I talked with Alison Kitch, one of your law professors, at Washington and Lee University, in Lexington, Virginia.

"I had Daryl in my contract law class last fall," she said. "I am quite sympathetic with what happened to him. But he indeed broke the rules. He got thrown out for doing what the honors book says you will be thrown out for: He lied. If he had only told his professor he missed class because he met a young woman on a train and spent two days with her in Atlanta, he might have gotten a bad grade, but he wouldn't have been thrown out of school. If you believe in the honor system, then you believe students ought to do what they sign up to do."

Professor Kitch said you are "smart and resourceful," and she is sure you will land on your feet. She added: "If you have to be stuck somewhere, Vienna seems like a better place than Atlanta."

I also talked with Eric Chaffin, who represented you before the honors committee. He confirmed the facts of the case, and added helpfully, "It's made me really want to see that movie."

Finally, Daryl, I talked with you personally. "I have a sales job right now," you said gloomily. "I'm applying to other law schools and hope to be accepted to one."

Will you see Jessica again?

"We plan to see each other in June."

"Daryl's taking me to a wedding," Jessica Turner told me. "It's in Boston. This time, he's going to fly."

Before the Rain ★ ★ ★ ★

NO MPAA RATING, 114 m., 1995
(See related Film Clip, p. 882.)

Rade Serbedzija (Aleksandar), Katrin Cartlidge (Anne), Gregoire Colin (Kiril), Labina Mitevska (Zamira). Directed by Milcho Manchevski and produced by Judy Counihan, Cedomir Kolar, Sam Taylor, and Cat Villiers. Screenplay by Manchevski.

If you are the average consumer of news in North America, you have been hearing about the Bosnians, the Serbians, and the Croats for years now, and you are not sure quite where they all are, or why they are fighting, or which are the people and which are the places. They are basically all a lot of people with mustaches who hate each other, and the UN can't do anything about it.

It's not entirely your fault. The news reports concentrate on today's violent developments; we get stories we can't understand unless we already know so much that we don't need them to begin with. Yet if I were to tell you that *Before the Rain* provides a context for those stories, you would still probably be indifferent, because it's simply not your war.

There is another reason to see *Before the Rain.* This is one of 1995's best films, a brilliant directorial debut for a young man named Milcho Manchevski, born in Macedonia, educated at Southern Illinois University, now a New Yorker who made award-winning MTV videos before returning home to make this extraordinary film. Work like this is what keeps me going, month after month and film after film: After the junk, this is a reminder of the nobility that film can attain.

The movie is made in three parts, two in Macedonia, one in London. The story circles back on itself, something like *Pulp Fiction,* and there is a paradox, a character who seems to be dead at a time he is still alive. Manchevski was not influenced by Tarantino; they were making their films simultaneously, and in *Before the Rain* the circular structure has a deeper purpose: It shows that

the cycle of hate and bloodshed will go on year after year, generation after generation, unless somehow men find the will to break with it.

The London sequence is the most chilling for North American armchair news viewers who think Bosnia is not their concern. I cannot describe it without giving away its shattering surprise. It involves a photographer named Aleksandar (Rade Serbedzija), born in Macedonia but now a citizen of the world, who leaves the war in Bosnia in disgust and returns to London, where a married British woman, Anne (Katrin Cartlidge), has long been his lover. We think this segment will deal with their story, and so it does, but in an unexpected way which shows that no war is really very far away, and no man is an island.

The first and third parts of the film take place in Macedonia, which, like Bosnia and Serbia, was part of Yugoslavia. The fighting has not reached there, but there is great tension between Muslims and Orthodox Christians, and the atmosphere, Manchevski feels, is heavy with anticipation and foreboding, as before a heavy rain. In the first part, an Albanian Muslim girl is suspected of having killed a Christian, and takes refuge in the cell of a beardless youth who, as a monk, has taken a vow of silence. In the third segment, Aleksandar returns to his homeland to see the Muslim woman he once loved, and almost has his throat slit by her grandson.

Manchevski tells his story in a clear, ironic, elliptic style: This is like an art film about war, in which passions replace ideas. The character of Aleksandar is the most compelling one in the film; played by Serbedzija, the best-known movie star in Yugoslavia, he has a worldly, weary attractiveness, something like Bruno Ganz in *Wings of Desire.* The first and second parts of the film, while working on their own, also function as a setup for the extraordinary payoff, in which he goes home to find that home as he recalls it no longer exists, that childhood playmates are now bitter enemies, rehashing the details of crimes so old they are merely hearsay.

Aleksandar's return is fueled by guilt. "I killed—my camera killed—a man," he explains. While shooting in a war zone, "I complained I wasn't getting anything exciting, so a guard pulled his gun and shot his prisoner for me." He finally decides to remove himself from this circle of hatred, and Manchevski has said in interviews that the seeming "time paradoxes" in his film—the moments when things happen that shouldn't

be able to happen—are his way of showing that we are perhaps not trapped by time, that sometimes there is an opening, an escape.

The construction of Manchevski's story is intended, then, to demonstrate the futility of its ancient hatreds. There are two or three moments in the film—I will not reveal them—where hatred of others is greater than love of one's own. Imagine a culture where a man would rather kill his daughter than allow her to love a man from another culture, and you will have an idea of the depth of bitterness in this film, the insane lengths to which men can be driven by belief and prejudice.

Being There ★ ★ ★ ★

PG, 130 m., 1980

Peter Sellers (Chance), Shirley MacLaine (Eve Rand), Melvyn Douglas (Ben Rand), Jack Warden (President), Richard Dysart (Dr. Allenby), Richard Basehart (Skrapinov). Directed by Hal Ashby and produced by Andrew Braunsberg. Screenplay by Jerzy Kosinski.

There's an exhilaration in seeing artists at the very top of their form: It almost doesn't matter what the form is, if they're pushing their limits and going for broke and it's working. We can sense their joy of achievement—and even more so if the project in question is a risky, off-the-wall idea that could just as easily have ended disastrously.

Hal Ashby's *Being There* is a movie that inspires those feelings. It begins with a cockamamie notion, it's basically one joke told for two hours, and it requires Peter Sellers to maintain an excruciatingly narrow tone of behavior in a role that has him onscreen almost constantly. It's a movie based on an idea, and all the conventional wisdom agrees that emotions, not ideas, are the best to make movies from. But *Being There* pulls off its long shot and is a confoundingly provocative movie.

Sellers plays a mentally retarded gardener who has lived and worked all of his life inside the walls of an elegant Washington town house. The house and its garden are in a decaying inner-city neighborhood, but what goes on outside is of no concern to Sellers: He tends his garden, he watches television, he is fed on schedule by the domestic staff, he is content.

Then one day the master of the house dies. The household is disbanded. Sellers, impeccably dressed in his employer's privately tailored wardrobe, wanders out into the city. He takes along the one possession he'll probably need: His remote-control TV channel switcher. He uses it almost immediately; surrounded by hostile street kids, he imperturbably tries to switch channels to make them go away. He hasn't figured out that, outside his garden, life isn't television.

And that is the movie's basic premise, lifted intact from a Jerzy Kosinski novel. The Sellers character knows almost nothing about real life, but he has watched countless hours of television and he can be pleasant, smile, shake hands, and comport himself; he learned from watching all those guests on talk shows. He knows nothing about *anything*, indeed, except gardening. But when he stumbles into Washington's political and social upper crust, his simple truisms from the garden ("Spring is a time for planting") are taken as audaciously simple metaphors. This guy's a Thoreau! In no time at all, he's the closest confidant of a dying billionaire industrialist (Melvyn Douglas)—and the industrialist is the closest confidant of the president.

This is, you can see, a one-joke premise. It has to be if the Sellers performance is to work. The whole movie has to be tailored to the narrow range within which Sellers's gardener can think, behave, speak, and make choices. The ways in which this movie could have gone out of control, could have been relentlessly boring on the one hand, or manic with its own audacity on the other, are endless. But the tone holds. That's one of the most exhilarating aspects of the joy you can sense, as Ashby pulls this off: Every scene needs the confidence to play the idea completely straight.

There are wonderful comic moments, but they're never pushed so far that they strain the story's premise. Some of them involve: a battle between the CIA and the FBI as to which agency destroyed the gardener's files; Shirley MacLaine unsuccessfully attempts to introduce Sellers to the concept of romance; Sellers as a talk-show guest himself (at last!), and Sellers as the hit of a Washington cocktail party. The movie also has an audacious closing shot that moves the film's whole metaphor into a brand-new philosophical arena.

What is *Being There* about? I've read reviews calling it an indictment of television. But that doesn't fit; Sellers wasn't warped by television, he was retarded to begin with, and has TV to thank for what abilities he *has* to move in society. Is it an indictment of soci-

ety, for being so dumb as to accept the Sellers character as a great philosophical sage? Maybe, but that's not so fascinating either. I'm not really inclined to plumb this movie for its message, although I'm sure that'll be a favorite audience sport. I just admire it for having the guts to take this weird conceit and push it to its ultimate comic conclusion.

Belle Epoque ★ ★ ★ ½
NO MPAA RATING, 108 m., 1993

Fernando Fernan Gomez (Manolo), Jorge Sanz (Fernando), Maribel Verdu (Rocio), Ariadna Gil (Violeta), Miriam Diaz-Aroca (Clara), Penelope Cruz (Luz), Mary Carmen Ramirez (Manolo's Wife), Michel Galabru (Her Manager). Directed and produced by Fernando Trueba. Screenplay by Rafael Azcona.

When *Belle Epoque* won its Academy Award as best foreign film of 1993, the director, Fernando Trueba, accepted with brevity and wit: "I would like to believe in God in order to thank him, but I just believe in Billy Wilder, so . . . thank you, Mr. Wilder."

Something of the spirit of the film is contained in those remarks, and something of the spirit of Wilder's *Some Like It Hot* is contained in *Belle Epoque*. Both films are largely concerned with sex—but not in sweaty, lustful terms. They appreciate the comic possibilities when a man is ruled by his libido.

The movie takes place in a sunny, rural district of Spain in 1931, between the end of the monarchy and the rise of fascism—just as the Spanish Republic was having its brief moment in the sun.

The opening sequence is worthy of Buñuel, patron saint of all Spanish films. A young army deserter has been arrested and is being marched down a country road by two national guardsmen, who are lifelong friends, civilians puffed up by the glory of their uniforms. They get into an argument over their duties. One is shot, and then the other, overcome by grief, kills himself. The incident has nothing to do, really, with their prisoner, who now finds himself at liberty in the middle of nowhere, but liable to be charged with murder.

The young man is Fernando (Jorge Sanz). Like many of his generation, he finds himself forced to take sides in the war that is tearing his country apart—the Spanish Civil War which, in its three-way confrontation of democracy, communism, and fascism, was called the rehearsal for World War II. Wandering across the countryside, Fernando

comes across the shabby but comfortable villa of old Manolo (Fernando Fernan Gomez), an artist who declares himself an anarchist. Manolo understands that Fernando is a deserter, but doesn't care; he is happy to have a visitor, and the two men form a quick friendship. The local priest, of a philosophical bent, joins in their nightly discussions.

Then it is time for Fernando to leave. Manolo takes him to the Madrid train, which is bringing the old man's four daughters out from the city for a visit. One by one the daughters alight from the train, each more fetching than the last, and when the train pulls out Fernando cannot bring himself to get aboard. He stays behind, and Manolo, understanding everything, invites him back to the house again.

Now unfolds a genial house party, with Fernando bewitched by first one daughter and then another, while old Manolo looks on benevolently; he would obviously not mind welcoming this young man into the family.

The daughters include Clara (Miriam Diaz-Aroca), recently widowed but outgrowing her grief; Violeta (Ariadna Gil), who we gather is a lesbian; Rocio (Maribel Verdu), sensuous and high-spirited; and Luz (Penelope Cruz), the youngest, who is innocent but wishes she were not. At one time or another all of them intrigue Fernando, while old Manolo pretends he doesn't notice and engages the young man in nightly conversation.

Manolo's dilemma is that he is an anarchist with nothing to rebel against. Everything is more or less as he wants it. As an artist, he is self-employed. As a father, he is blessed. He can't even work up a case against the village priest, who is too open-minded to make a respectable opponent. Manolo's underlying happiness warms the entire film. We know that terrible times are ahead for Spain; that in the years to come the country will be laid waste by war and then frozen in the long, closed Franco regime. But here is a brief, beautiful time before all of that begins.

Like the otherwise dissimilar *Sirens*, from around the world in Australia, *Belle Epoque* celebrates sensuality and the human body. It is a reminder that sex can be kind and gentle, tender and beautiful. American films link "sex and violence" so compulsively that we can hardly imagine an attractive woman who isn't hiding an ice pick behind her back.

Maybe the American men who control movies are afraid of women. Fernando

Trueba isn't, and neither is his hero. Seeing this film and *Sirens* in the same season, I was reminded that the movies once considered eroticism an end in itself, and not simply the prelude to a slasher scene. Here is a film so inviting you would love to sit in the sun with old Manolo and his friend the priest, and talk about the great matters of life. And about his daughters.

Benny and Joon ★ ★ ★
PG, 100 m., 1993

Johnny Depp (Sam), Mary Stuart Masterson (Joon), Aidan Quinn (Benny), Julianne Moore (Ruthie), Oliver Platt (Eric), C.C.H. Pounder (Dr. Garvey). Directed by Jeremiah Chechik and produced by Susan Arnold and Donna Roth. Screenplay by Barry Berman.

Benny and Joon is a film that approaches its subjects so gingerly it almost seems afraid to touch them. The story wants to be about love, but is also about madness, and somehow it weaves the two together with a charm that would probably not be quite so easy in real life.

The title characters are two young adults, Benny (Aidan Quinn) and his kid sister, known as Joon (Mary Stuart Masterson). He works to support them. She stays at home and paints, during her good periods, and rages at him, during her bad times. She is schizophrenic, although the screenplay doesn't ever say the word out loud. When she takes her medication and stays calm and things go smoothly, their lives are blessedly uneventful.

One of Benny's few pleasures is a monumental, long-running poker game, at which the stakes are all sorts of things other than money. One night Joon loses a big bet, and is forced to provide temporary room and board for a strange, goofy relative of one of the other players. This is Sam (Johnny Depp), who is sane, but lives in a strange, blissful moonscape all his own.

The first time we see Sam, riding on the bus, he's reading a book about the silent clown Buster Keaton. This is not idle curiosity. Sam has somehow determined to internalize the genius of Keaton, Chaplin, and the other early screen comedians, and although he never says *that* out loud, either, it becomes clear in a gradual, unforced way, as he incorporates little bits from their films into his daily life.

If I had been reading the screenplay of *Benny and Joon*, I would have started to form ominous misgivings at about this point, since

the conceit of bringing a character like Sam into the story seems a little too precious. But Depp pulls it off. In *Edward Scissorhands* he demonstrated two of the skills that are crucial to his performance in *Benny and Joon:* He was able to build an essentially wordless performance out of expression and gesture, and he had natural physical grace.

Here, without ever explaining himself, he simply behaves sometimes in the real world in the way Keaton and Chaplin behaved in their movie worlds. There is a moment at a lunch counter, for example, when he sticks two forks into two dinner rolls, holds them under his chin, and moves them to suggest that the rolls are his feet and he is dancing. It's a steal from *The Gold Rush*, but done with an offhand charm that makes it work all over again.

Sam charms Joon out of her self-absorption, and before long, inevitably, they fall in love. But this is not a romance made in heaven, because neither Sam nor Joon is fitted with all the tools useful for surviving in the modern world. Benny is enraged at the news that they love each other, because he believes Joon cannot live independently—and also because, having devoted his life to caring for her, he feels a certain possessiveness. A psychiatrist (C.C.H. Pounder, from *Bagdad Café*) also has serious reservations.

Because *Benny and Joon* is the kind of movie it is, the problems of reality, while occasionally present, are not entirely given their due. Sam exists so resolutely in his own world that it is even a little startling when, at one point, he quietly asks, "How sick is she?" We can glimpse for a second, under his clown façade, his own take on reality. Then his charming persona slides back into place.

Most people would side with Benny in his opposition to the talk of marriage, but the movie suggests that love and magic can overcome madness, and for at least the length of the film I was prepared to accept that. Much of the credit for that goes to Depp, who takes a character that might have seemed unplayable on paper, and makes him into the kind of enchanter who might be able to heal Joon. Mary Stuart Masterson, from *Fried Green Tomatoes* and many other good films, usually plays commonsensical, sane characters; this time she shows Joon able to swing in an instant from calm to rage, picking on little things that set her off. It's a convincing performance. And Aidan Quinn, in a somewhat thankless role as the movie's reality base and opponent of love, never plays a scene simply

for its obvious point, but lets us see that his love for his sister underlies all of his decisions.

Benny and Joon is a tough sell. Younger moviegoers these days seem to shy away from complexities, which is why the movie and its advertising all shy away from any implication of mental illness. The film is being sold as an offbeat romance between a couple of lovable kooks. I was relieved to discover it was about so much more than that.

Best Boy ★ ★ ★ ★
NO MPAA RATING, 111 m., 1980

A documentary produced, directed, and edited by Ira Wohl.

Sometimes there are movies that absorb you so completely that you forget you're watching them: They're simply happening to you. Ira Wohl's *Best Boy* is a movie like that. To see it is to participate in the lives of other people and to learn just a little more about being human. *Best Boy*, which won the 1980 Academy Award as best documentary, is the story of an only son named Philly, whose parents have always been too protective of him. But as the movie opens, it is time for Philly to go out a little more on his own—to go down to the corner for an ice cream cone, for example, or to look forward to his first day of school. Philly is fifty-two years old. He is mentally retarded, but otherwise, as a psychiatrist explains in the film, "quite normal." He is also warm and lovable, and when Wordsworth wrote that heaven was all about us when we were children, did he guess that would also be true for someone like Philly, who will never really leave childhood?

Best Boy deals intelligently with real people and their problems. It is not simply a documentary; it contains the surprises of true drama, and it is put together so thoughtfully that it takes what could have been a case study and turns it into a cliffhanger. That is largely due to the complete access that the filmmaker, Ira Wohl, had to his subject. Philly is Wohl's cousin, and Philly's parents are Wohl's aunt and uncle. All the time he was growing up, Ira knew Philly—he played with him, presumably, when he was four or five and Philly seemed to be about the same age. Philly stayed four or five. As Wohl grew older, he realized that sooner or later Philly's parents would die, and that Philly's total dependence on them would leave him defenseless.

Philly had been at home almost all his life. The movie begins as his parents make the first reluctant, tentative steps to allow him a little more independence—to set him free. *Best Boy* moves very delicately around this subject, and with good reason: As we watch it, we realize that the parents have come to depend on Philly, too. He provided them with a rationale for their own lives and choices. He is their crutch as well as their burden. And there is yet another drama that unfolds within the film—unfolds so subtly we barely realize it is there, and yet concludes so inevitably that it casts a light back on all the scenes that went before. Philly's father is dying. There is a time in the film when the father clearly knows that and no one else in the film does, but we, strangers, share his secret with him.

You see what I mean when I say *Best Boy* isn't a case study. It's not about what should be done with Philly, and it has little to do with the "problem" of mental retardation. It is so specifically about Philly and his family and their daily choices in life that we almost feel adopted into the family. And we get to like Philly so much! He is sweet and cheerful, patient and good-humored, with a child's logic that cuts right through so much of the confusion adults surround him with. There is a wonderful scene with a psychiatrist, who is trying to administer a series of questions Philly obviously feels are silly. There is a visit to the theater, where Philly is allowed backstage to meet Zero Mostel, and they sing "If I Were a Rich Man" together. Why is it, the movie asks but never answers, that Philly can remember songs better than speech?

Best Boy suffers, I suppose, from being labeled a documentary: Some small-minded people make it a policy never to watch one. But at the Toronto Festival of Festivals, where the patrons are asked to vote for their favorite film, it astonished everyone by defeating all the features in the festival and placing first. It's a wonderfully positive experience.

Betrayal ★ ★ ★ ★
R, 95 m., 1983

Jeremy Irons (Jerry), Ben Kingsley (Robert), Patricia Hodge (Emma). Directed by David Jones and produced by Sam Spiegel. Screenplay by Harold Pinter.

Love stories have beginnings, but affairs . . . affairs have endings, too. Even sad love stories begin in gladness, when the world is young and the future reaches out cheerfully forever. Then, of course, eventually you get Romeo and Juliet dead in the tomb, but that's the price you have to pay. Life isn't a free ride. Think how much *more* tragic a sad love story would be, however, if you could see into the future, so that even *this* moment, *this* kiss, is in the shadow of eventual despair.

The absolutely brilliant thing about *Betrayal* is that it is a love story told backward. There is a lot in this movie that is wonderful—the performances, the screenplay by Harold Pinter—but what makes it all work is the structure. When Pinter's stage version of *Betrayal* first appeared, back in the late 1970s, there was a tendency to dismiss his reverse chronology as a gimmick. Not so. It is the very heart and soul of this story. It means that we in the audience know more about the unhappy romantic fortunes of Jerry and Robert and Emma at *every moment* than they know about themselves. Even their joy is painful to see.

Jerry is a youngish London literary agent, clever, good-looking, confused about his feelings. Robert, his best friend, is a publisher. Robert is older, stronger, smarter, and more bitter. Emma is Robert's wife and becomes Jerry's lover. But that is telling the story chronologically. And the story begins at the end, with Robert and Emma fighting, and with Robert slapping her, and with Emma and Jerry meeting in a pub for a painful reunion two years after their affair is over. Each additional scene takes place further back in time, and the sections have uncanny titles: Two years earlier. Three years earlier. We aren't used to this. At a public preview of the film, some people in the audience actually *resisted* the backward timeframe, as if the purpose of the playwright was just to get on with the story, damn it all, and stop this confounded fooling around.

The *Betrayal* structure strips away all artifice. It shows, heartlessly, that the very capacity for love itself is sometimes based on betraying not only other loved ones, but even ourselves. The movie is told mostly in encounters between two of the characters; all three are not often on screen together, and we never meet Jerry's wife. These people are smart and they talk a lot—too much, maybe, because there is a peculiarly British reserve about them that sometimes prevents them from quite saying what they mean. They lie and they half-lie. There are universes left unspoken in their unfinished sentences. They are all a little embarrassed that the messy urges of sex are pumping away down there beneath their civilized deceptions.

The performances are perfectly matched. Ben Kingsley (of *Gandhi*) plays Robert, the publisher, with such painfully controlled fury that there are times when he actually is frightening. Jeremy Irons, as Jerry, creates a man whose desires are stronger than his convictions, even though he spends a lot of time talking about his convictions, and almost none acknowledging his desires. Patricia Hodge, as Emma, loves them both and hates them both and would have led a much happier life if they had not been her two choices. But how could she know that when, in life, you're required by the rules to start at the beginning?

Beverly Hills Cop ★ ★ ½
R, 105 m., 1984

Eddie Murphy (Axel Foley), Judge Reinhold (Detective Billy Rosewood), John Ashton (Sergeant Taggart), Lisa Eilbacher (Jenny), Ronny Cox (Lieutenant Bogomil). Directed by Martin Brest and produced by Don Simpson and Jerry Bruckheimer. Screenplay by Daniel Petrie.

Eddie Murphy looks like the latest victim of the Star Magic Syndrome, in which it is assumed that a movie will be a hit simply because it stars an enormously talented person. Thus it is not necessary to give much thought to what he does or says, or to the story he finds himself occupying. *Beverly Hills Cop* is a movie with an enormously appealing idea—a tough black detective from Detroit goes to Beverly Hills to avenge the murder of a friend—but the filmmakers apparently expected Murphy to carry this idea entirely by himself.

Murphy plays a street-wise rebel who is always getting in trouble with his commanding officer because he does things his own way. The movie opens with an example of that: Murphy is single-handedly running a sting operation when the cops arrive unexpectedly, setting off a wild car-truck chase through the city streets. Even while we're watching the thrilling chase, however, stirrings of unease are beginning to be felt: Any movie that *begins* with a chase is not going to be heavy on originality and inspiration. Then Murphy's old friend comes to town, fresh from a prison term and six months of soaking up the rays in California. The friend has some negotiable bonds with him, and then some friends of the guy who owns the bonds turn up and murder Murphy's friend. That makes Eddie mad, and he drives his ancient beater out to Beverly Hills, where it sort of stands out among the Porsches and Mercedeses. He also meets a childhood friend (Lisa Eilbacher) who now works for an art dealer.

At this point, the movie can go in one of two directions. It can become a perceptive and pointed satire about American attitudes, showing how the ultrachic denizens of Beverly Hills react to this black cop from Detroit. Or it can go for broad, cheap laughs, and plug into a standard plot borrowed from countless TV crime shows. *Beverly Hills Cop* doesn't pause a moment before taking the low road. We figure that out right away, when Murphy tries to register in a hotel and is told there isn't any room. He loudly pulls both ranks and race, claiming to be a correspondent from *Rolling Stone* and accusing the desk clerk of racism. This is (a) not funny, and (b) not convincing, because Beverly Hills desk clerks were not born yesterday. If the people who made this movie had been willing to listen to the ways that real people really talk, they could have made the scene into a jewel instead of an embarrassment.

Meanwhile, the plot thickens. It turns out that the killers of Eddie's friend were employees of the evil Victor Maitland (Steven Berkoff), a Beverly Hills criminal whose art gallery—where Eilbacher works—is a front for cocaine smuggling. When Murphy tries to move against Maitland, he comes up against the Beverly Hills Cops, including an Abbott and Costello team that supplies unnecessary pratfalls, successfully undermining the credibility of any police scene that threatens to work. But wait a minute. What's this movie about, anyway? Is it a comedy or an action picture? Audiences may expect a comedy, but the closing shoot-out seems inspired by the machine gun massacre at the end of Brian De Palma's *Scarface*, and the whole business with the cocaine is so very, very tired that when we see the boss and his henchmen in the warehouse, we feel like we've switched to another movie—maybe a dozen other movies. Murphy is one of the smartest and quickest young comic actors in the movies. But he is not an action hero, despite his success in *48 HRS*, and by plugging him into an action movie, the producers of *Beverly Hills Cop* reveal a lack of confidence in their original story inspiration. It's like they had a story conference that boiled down to: "Hey gang! Here's a great idea! Let's turn it into a standard idea and fill it with clichés, and take out the satire and put in a lot of machine guns!"

Big ★ ★ ★
PG, 102 m., 1988

Tom Hanks (Josh Baskin), Elizabeth Perkins (Susan Lawrence), Robert Loggia (MacMillan), Jared Rushton (Billy Kopeche). Directed by Penny Marshall and produced by James L. Brooks and Robert Greenhut. Screenplay by Anne Spielberg and Gary Ross.

Sooner or later, they're going to get this right. *Big* was no less than the fourth almost simultaneous variation on the same theme—a kid trapped in an adult body. How did four Hollywood studios simultaneously find themselves making essentially the same story? I guess each one thought its was the best, and refused to back down. And so we got *Like Father, Like Son* and *Vice Versa* and *18 Again* and now *Big*, which is a streamlined edition.

Instead of having a father and son exchange bodies, this one does away with the second character and simply gives us a thirteen-year-old who wishes he was big, and gets his wish. That's a useful inspiration, because it spares the filmmakers from the task of cutting back and forth between two different stories (dad in kid's body goes out with teen-age girl while kid in dad's body dates sexpot). Instead, we follow one character on his journey across the generation gap, and because there's more time to develop his dilemma, the movie is more persuasive.

Big describes the adventures of Josh Baskin, who, in a brief opening sequence, is a normal, pint-sized adolescent. He has a crush on one of the girls in his class—a girl who stands a head taller than he does. I had forgotten (or repressed) my memories of those strange days in the seventh grade when all the girls suddenly become amazons, but they all came crashing back during the movie's most poignant scene. In a carnival, Josh manages to stand in line next to the girl of his dreams, and it looks like he'll be able to sit next to her on the ride—but when they get to the front of the line, the carnival guy tells him he's not tall enough to go on the ride.

This is a species of humiliation beyond the limits of human endurance. As the girl gets on the ride with a taller boy, Josh wanders off forlorn and lonely, to a remote corner of the midway where he finds a strange fortune-telling machine. He puts in a quarter, wishes he were big, and wakes up the next morning as Tom Hanks.

Hanks carries most of the movie, and does it well; as a thirteen-year-old in a thirty-year-

old body, he is able to suggest such subtle things as a short attention span, a disregard for social niceties, and an ability to hop, skip, and jump through an office lobby. Through a stroke of good luck, he gets hired by a toy company, where his childlike innocence soon gets him a promotion to vice president in charge of product development. He and the company president (Robert Loggia) are the only two guys in the place who really like to play with toys, and there is a brilliant comic sequence where the two of them play "Chopsticks" by dancing on a giant computerized piano keyboard.

The movie is never quite able to deal successfully with the fact that the kid's mother thinks he has been kidnapped—it's cruel the way that plot thread is left dangling. But as Hanks slowly adjusts to his incredible good fortune, he attracts the attention of Elizabeth Perkins, a company executive who falls genuinely in love with his childlike innocence, little realizing it is real.

Big is a tender, soft-hearted, and cheerful movie, well-directed by Penny Marshall and with a script by Anne Spielberg and Gary Ross that has a lot of fun with simple verbal misunderstandings. (When the kid says, "What's a market research report?" Loggia nods and barks, "Exactly!") Hanks finds a vulnerability and sweetness for his character that's quite appealing.

In the sweepstakes of generation-gap movies, *Big* is not as funny as *Vice Versa*, and Hanks does not have as much fun with physical humor as Judge Reinhold did in that movie. But both films are way ahead of the other two contenders, and this one may be the only one of the four that could really be identified with by a thirteen-year-old kid.

The Big Chill ★ ★ ½
R, 108 m., 1983

Tom Berenger (Sam), Glenn Close (Sarah), William Hurt (Nick), Jeff Goldblum (Michael), Meg Tilly (Chloe), Kevin Kline (Harold), Mary Kay Place (Meg), JoBeth Williams (Karen). Directed by Lawrence Kasdan. Screenplay by Kasdan and Barbara Benedek.

I was going through some old papers the other night, from cardboard boxes that were packed at the end of college and have followed me around ever since. To open them up was like walking into a time capsule. There they were, the little campus literary magazines and the yellowing issues of the University of Illinois' *Daily Illini*, and a photo of a political demonstration on the steps of the student union.

On the other hand, I was going through my mail the next day and I got a letter from a teen-ager who wanted to know why they were making so many movies about the 1960s. "Who cares what happened in the olden days?" I think "olden days" was an attempt at humor.

I wrote back that the 1960s were big in the movies right now because the people who make the movies were students in the 1960s, and that the teen-agers of 2001 would no doubt be sick and tired of the olden days of the 1980s. And then I thought about *The Big Chill*, a movie in which survivors of the 1960s ask themselves how they could possibly be in their thirties. This is the second movie on almost exactly the same theme—a weekend reunion among college friends from the 1960s, during which they relive the past, fear the present, and regret the interim. They could have called it *Son of the Return of the Secaucus Seven.*

It's a good movie. It's well acted, the dialogue is accurately heard, and the camera is extremely attentive to details of body language. It observes wonderfully well how its veterans of the 1960s have grown up into adulthood, consumerhood, parenthood, drunkenhood, adulteryhood, and regrethood. These people could all be wearing warm-up jackets with *poignancy* stenciled on the backs.

The movie begins at a funeral. One of the old college friends has killed himself, for reasons that never become clear. The others gather for his funeral and stay for a weekend in a big old summer house. We get to meet them: the intellectual, the failed writer, the confused TV star, the woman who wants to have a baby and can't tear her eyes away from the biological clock. They eat, they drink, they pair up in various combinations, and they ask themselves questions like, Who were we? Who are we now? What happened to us? What will happen to us?

Because they are all graduates of the University of Michigan at Ann Arbor, they phrase these questions with style, of course. The dialogue sounds like a series of bittersweet captions from *New Yorker* cartoons. And at the end, of course, nothing is really discovered, nothing is really settled, and they go back into holding patterns until the next funeral.

The Big Chill is a splendid technical exercise. It has all the right moves. It knows all the right words. Its characters have all the right clothes, expressions, fears, lusts, and ambitions. But there's no payoff and it doesn't lead anywhere. I thought at first that was a weakness of the movie. There also is the possibility that it's the movie's message.

The Big Easy ★ ★ ★ ★
R, 106 m., 1987

Dennis Quaid (Remy McSwain), Ellen Barkin (Anne Osborne), Ned Beatty (Jack Kellom), John Goodman (Andre De Soto), Lisa Jane Persky (McCabe), Ebbe Roe Smith (Ed Dodge), Tom O'Brien (Bobby McSwain), Charles Ludlam (Lamar Parmentel). Directed by Jim McBride and produced by Stephen Friedman. Screenplay by Daniel Petrie, Jr.

The Big Easy happens to be a great thriller. I say "happens," because I believe the plot of this movie is only an excuse for its real strength: the creation of a group of characters so interesting, so complicated, and so original that they make a lot of other movie people look like paint-by-number characters.

The movie takes place in New Orleans, that most mysterious of American cities, a city where you have the feeling you will never really know what goes on down those shadowy passages into those green and humid courtyards so guarded from the street. The heroes of the film are two law enforcement officials: Remy (Dennis Quaid), a homicide detective, and Anne (Ellen Barkin), a special prosecutor for the D.A. They meet after the death of a Mafia functionary, and of course they are immediately attracted to each other.

So far, no surprises. But when they go out to dinner and the restaurant owner won't think of accepting their money, Anne accuses Remy of being on the take and he accuses her of not understanding how the system operates. Later we learn more about the system in New Orleans and come to understand more about Remy. He is an honest cop in the ways that really count and a dishonest cop in small ways he has been able to rationalize. He doesn't have a problem, for example, with the department's illegal "widows and orphans fund," because he's using the money to send his kid brother through college.

There are more killings. There also is, between Anne and Remy, one of the most erotic love scenes I have ever seen in a movie—all the more erotic because the two lovers do not perform like champions in the sexual Olympics, but come to bed with all the insecurity of people who are almost afraid to believe it could, this time, be for real.

The background of their story is populated with characters so well-drawn and with character actors so finely chosen that the movie is fascinating from moment to moment, even when nothing much seems to be happening.

My favorite supporting performance in the movie is by Charles Ludlam, as a defense attorney, impeccable in his Panama hat and summer suit, talking a mile a minute in a shrill Cajun shriek, like a cross between Truman Capote and F. Lee Bailey. Another slick Southerner is created by Ned Beatty, in his finest performance in years, as the police captain who sincerely wants to do the right thing and sincerely cannot.

All of these characters inhabit the most convincing portrait of New Orleans I've ever seen. The authentic local Cajun music on the sound track and the instinctive feel for the streets and alleys, the lives and the ways of doing business, the accents and the evasions, make the city itself into a participant in what happens.

In the middle of this riotous gumbo of colorful life, Quaid and Barkin construct a relationship that, by itself, would be enough for a whole movie. They love each other. They are disillusioned. They face each other as enemies in court. They eye each other warily in a wonderful scene at a fish boil and Cajun hootenanny thrown by Quaid's friends.

The movie indeed ends with the obligatory scene of climactic violence that is required in all thrillers, but it's well-handled and the actions at least do seem to be consistent with the characters.

The movie was directed by Jim McBride, whose previous film was *Breathless*, with Richard Gere, a high-style pastiche of 1940s crime movies and 1980s art direction. *The Big Easy* seems to be by a different man, a director not only in full mastery of his materials but in full sympathy with his characters. Forget it's a thriller. See it because you want to meet these people.

The Big Red One ★ ★
PG, 113 m., 1980

Lee Marvin (Sergeant), Mark Hamill (Griff), Robert Carradine (Zab), Bobby Di Cicco (Vinci), Kelly Ward (Johnson), Siegfried Rauch (Schroeder), Stephane Audran (Walloon). Directed and written by Samuel Fuller and produced by Gene Corman.

Sam Fuller's *The Big Red One* is a lot of war stories strung together in a row, almost as if the director filmed it for the thirty-fifth reunion of his old Army outfit, and didn't want to leave anybody out. That's one of the most interesting things about it—the feeling that the movie's events are included, not because they help the plot or make a point, but just because they happened.

Some of them happened to Fuller himself, he tells us, and there's a kid in the movie who's obviously supposed to be young Sam. Other scenes are based on things Fuller heard about. Some of them are brutal and painful, some of them are romantic, a lot of them are corny. The movie takes no position on any of them: This movie is resolutely nonpolitical, is neither pro- nor anti-war, is deliberately just a record of five dogfaces who found themselves in the middle of the action.

The movie's title refers to the U.S. Army's First Infantry Division, and the action follows one rifle squad through the entire war. The squad leader is a hard-bitten sergeant, played by Lee Marvin with the kind of gravel-voiced, squint-eyed authority he had more than a decade before in *The Dirty Dozen*. His four squad members are kids in their teens, and his job is to whip them into shape. He does. The squad is so efficient, or competent, or just plain lucky, that it survives to see action in half the major theaters of the war in Europe. At a rough count, they fight in North Africa, Tunis, Sicily, Normandy, Omaha Beach, rural France, Belgium, Czechoslovakia, and Germany. Halfway through this litany, we begin to suspect that *The Big Red One* is supposed to be something more than plausible.

The squad fights in so many places, stays together in one piece for so long, experiences so many of the key events of World War II (from the invasion of Europe to the liberation of the Nazi death camps) that of course these characters are meant to be symbols of all the infantrymen in all the battles. But Fuller, who fought in the First Division, seems determined to keep his symbols from illustrating a message. They fight. They are frightened. Men kill, other men are killed. What matters is if you're still alive. "I don't cry because that guy over there got hit," Fuller said in an interview, "I cry because I'm gonna get hit next."

This leads to a deliberately anecdotal structure for the film. One battle ends, another begins. A little orphan kid appears out of the smoke, is befriended, braids flowers

into the netting of a helmet, is forgotten for the rest of the film. What we have is a series of experiences so overwhelming that the characters can't find sense or pattern in them, and so simply try to survive them through craft and experience.

Is this all Fuller got out of the war? He seems to believe it's all anybody really gets, that the vast patterns of war's meaning are really just the creations of novelists, filmmakers, generals, and politicians, and that for the guy under fire there is no pattern, just the desperately sincere desire to get out in one piece.

The Big Red One is Sam Fuller's first film in more than a decade, and by far the most expensive and ambitious film he's ever made. It's like a dream come true, the capstone of a long career. Fuller began as a newspaperman in New York, he fought in the war, he went to Hollywood and he directed a lot of B-action pictures that are considered by connoisseurs to be pulp landmarks: *I Shot Jesse James, Pickup on South Street, Hell and High Water, Shock Corridor*. His previous film, hardly seen in this country, was a 1972 West German production with the marvelous title *Dead Pigeon on Beethoven Street*.

While this is an expensive epic, he hasn't fallen to the temptations of the epic form. He doesn't give us a lot of phony meaning, as if to justify the scope of the production. There aren't a lot of deep, significant speeches. In the ways that count, *The Big Red One* is still a B-movie—hard-boiled, filled with action, held together by male camaraderie, directed with a lean economy of action. It's one of the most expensive B-pictures ever made, and I think that helps it fit the subject. "A" war movies are about War, but "B" war movies are about soldiers.

The Big Town ★ ★ ★ ½
R, 110 m., 1987

Matt Dillon (J.C. Cullen), Diane Lane (Lorry Dane), Tommy Lee Jones (George Cole), Bruce Dern (Mr. Edwards), Lee Grant (Ferguson Edwards), Tom Skerritt (Phil Carpenter), Suzy Amis (Maggie Donaldson), Del Close (Deacon Daniels). Directed by Ben Bolt and produced by Martin Ransohoff. Screenplay by Robert Roy Pool.

This story has been told a hundred times, and yet, when it is told well, it is always fun to watch it being told again. The kid comes from the small town to the big city. He has a

gift. He signs up as a professional, working for some pretty tough people. He meets a good girl. He meets a bad girl. He meets a villain. He wants more independence than his employers will give him. At the end of the story, we don't have to be movie producers to know that he will reject the bad girl, embrace the good girl, defeat the villain, triumph in his big test, and win his independence.

This story could be about baseball, jazz, open-heart surgery, computer programming, tap-dancing, or mind-reading. In *The Big Town*, it's about gambling. Matt Dillon plays the farm boy from Iowa who keeps winning at the crap tables because he knows the odds cold, and also because he has amazing good luck. Suzy Amis is the good girl, a waitress supporting her small son. Diane Lane plays the bad girl, a stripper who is married to Tommy Lee Jones, who is the villain. The employers are Lee Grant and Bruce Dern, a married couple who are professional gamblers with a string of dice-players, or "arms," under contract.

Add a few character touches and you've got it. For example, Dern was blinded by acid years ago, and is looking for the man who did it—a man with a heart tattooed on the inside of his wrist. Lane married Jones because she thought she'd get control of half of his business, but she was wrong. And Lee Grant used to be in love with the Iowa gambler who sent Matt Dillon to the big city to work for her.

Why am I persisting in describing so much of the plot? So you can see that the story has little to do with the brilliance of this film. *The Big Town* is compulsively watchable not because of its plot, which is predictable down to the smallest detail, but because of its acting, its direction, and its style. This is a great-looking movie that never steps wrong, and Matt Dillon uses it to demonstrate once again that he is a master of unforced, natural acting. In a 1950s period film that's wall-to-wall with clichés, he never seems less than absolutely at home.

Dillon has some kind of spontaneous rapport with the camera. He never seems aware of it, never seems aware that he's playing a character; his acting is graceful and fluid, and his scenes always seem to start before the first shot, so that we see him in the middle of a motion. *The Big Town* requires Dillon to spend a lot of time shooting craps, and you wouldn't think it would be possible to bring anything new to the sight of a man throwing dice onto a table, but Dillon does it. He has little moves, subtle small touches of body language, that make every throw important. (That's a neat trick, since he hardly ever loses.)

The actors around him also are good, especially Tommy Lee Jones as the evil vice boss, who has his best moments when he simply stands and looks at Dillon with eyes filled with hate. Suzy Amis, a newcomer, is fresh and appealing as the waitress who loves this small-town boy, and Diane Lane is able to seem sincere to Dillon while letting us know she's calculating every move.

The look of the movie is effective in its studied artificiality. It's set in Chicago's South Loop, under the el tracks, in a series of exteriors and sets that are supposed to represent both sides of only a block or two—this is the 1950s backlot look, brought to a location. The photography and the wall-to-wall period music on the sound track (Ivory Joe Hunter, Big Joe Turner, Little Willie John, Ray Charles, Red Sovine) get the right balance between the wickedness of the big city and the dreams of the small-town kid. The story is predictable, but the style had me on the edge of my seat.

Bill & Ted's Bogus Journey ★ ★ ★
PG-13, 90 m., 1991

Keanu Reeves (Ted), Alex Winter (Bill), William Sadler (Grim Reaper), Joss Ackland (De Nomolos), George Carlin (Rufus). Directed by Pete Hewitt and produced by Scott Kroopf. Screenplay by Ed Solomon and Chris Matheson.

There were parts of *Bill & Ted's Bogus Journey* I probably didn't understand, but that's all right, because there were even more parts that Bill and Ted didn't understand. This is a movie that thrives on the dense-witted idiocy of its characters, two teen-age dudes who go on amazing journeys through time and space with only the dimmest perception that they are not still playing video games.

I missed the enormously popular movie that introduced these characters, *Bill & Ted's Excellent Adventure*, and felt myself blessed at the time. But now I'm not so sure. Their *Bogus Journey* is a riot of visual invention and weird humor that works on its chosen sub-moronic level, and on several others as well, including some fairly sophisticated ones. It's the kind of movie where you start out snickering in spite of yourself, and end up actually admiring the originality that went into creating this hallucinatory slapstick.

The movie begins far in the future, where students at Bill & Ted's University have the opportunity to chat personally with Thomas Edison and Beethoven, and to study such artistic classics as the "Star Trek" TV series. An evil overlord of time, named De Nomolos and played by that gravel-voiced, white-haired villain Joss Ackland, vows to rewrite history by destroying Bill and Ted (played as before by Alex Winter and Keanu Reeves). He has invented robots that look and act exactly like the two heroes, and are just as dumb, and he sends them rocketing back through time in a telephone booth.

Bill and Ted are meanwhile trying to win a rock band contest with their own group, Wyld Stallyns, which includes a couple of girl musicians they picked up in the fifteenth century. Startled by the appearance of their robot doubles, they commence their own journeys through time and space in a desperate attempt to destroy them, save themselves, preserve the book of history, stay cool, and meet cute chicks.

The funniest thing that happens to them is their showdown with the Grim Reaper (William Sadler), who looks just as he does in Ingmar Bergman's *The Seventh Seal*. In that film (as most of the audience for this one will probably not know), Death played chess with a medieval knight, with the knight's soul at stake. This time the dudes challenge the Reaper to a pocket video game, and beat him, even after he tries to weasel out with an offer of best of three.

Death, having lost, has to accompany Bill and Ted on their journey and do what they tell him, and this leads to some of the funniest moments I have seen in any movie in a long time, including one where the Reaper does a little comparison shopping for scythes at the hardware store.

One of the stops on the bogus journey is Heaven, created with great imagination and a lot of light and echoing sound effects and a most peculiar conversation with the Deity. Bill and Ted handle this summit meeting as they handle everything else in the film, like two dudes for whom "Pee-wee's Playhouse" would be too slow and intellectual.

All of the actors (including George Carlin, who turns up in an important supporting role) have a lot of fun with this material, and it turns into more delicate fun, based on more subtle timing, than you might imagine. Many of Sadler's laughs as the Grim Reaper come from simple physical cringing, as he conveys his embarrassment and lost dignity.

Of Bill and Ted, I can say that I have not seen Alex Winter much before (he was in *Rosalie Goes Shopping*), but I have seen Keanu Reeves in vastly different roles (the FBI man in *Point Break*, for example), and am a little astonished by the range of these performances. Like Sean Penn, who immortalized the word "awesome" in a *Bill & Ted*-like performance in *Fast Times at Ridgemont High*, Reeves brings more artistry to this cretinous role than might at first meet the eye.

Who is the movie intended for? Your basic *Bill & Ted* audience, for starters—upward-bound young moviegoers looking for something one notch more challenging than *Teenage Mutant Ninja Turtles*. But also for lovers of fantasy, whimsy, and fanciful special effects. This movie is light as a feather and thin as ice in spring, but what it does, it does very nicely.

Bird ★ ★ ★ ½
R, 160 m., 1988

Forest Whitaker (Charlie "Bird" Parker), Diane Venora (Chan Parker), Michael Zelniker (Red Rodney), Samuel E. Wright (Dizzy Gillespie), Keith David (Buster Franklin), Michael McGuire (Brewster), James Handy (Esteves), Damon Whitaker (Young Bird), Morgan Nagler (Kim), Arlen Dean Snyder (Mr. Heath). Produced and directed by Clint Eastwood. Written by Joel Oliansky.

In two documentaries about Charlie Parker I haven't seen a lot of Parker. In an age when archives are filled with newsreel footage and videotape on even the most obscure of public figures, Parker seems always to have been somewhere else when the cameras were on. There is a shot of him accepting a Downbeat award at a banquet, where the master of ceremonies solemnly informs him that jazz is colorblind (if so, then why the reassurance?), and another brief clip of him playing with Dizzy Gillespie. There are a few minutes of silent footage, too, and that's it. No complete performances on film. No interviews. No home movies.

That's one reason why Clint Eastwood's *Bird*, a musical biography of Charlie Parker, is so valuable. It supplies us with images to go with the music, and it provides an idea of the man, more than thirty years after his death. If we are to judge by Forest Whitaker's substantial performance, Parker was a large, warm, gentle man who was comfortable with himself and loved his work. He was haunted all of his days by drug addiction—he got hooked as a teen-ager and never got off—but for many years he doesn't seem to have been filled with the rages of most addicts. He seems to have regarded addiction as a burden to carry, and been resigned to carrying it while not wishing it on anybody else. He carried on as long and as well as he could, and only in the last years was he finally overcome with despair. But addiction took a dreadful physical toll. When he died, a coroner estimated his age at sixty-five. He was thirty-four.

Bird is a long, complex, ambitious movie, and it contains a lot of great music. Charles (Bird) Parker was one of the great fountainheads of jazz, a creator of bebop whose improvisations and joyful discoveries on the saxophone created a sound that is absolutely distinctive. He stood as a bridge between the swing era and the cool modern jazz of the 1950s, and even as his career collapsed into disarray, his influence continued to grow. At the end, Bird was denied a cabaret license because of his drug use, and couldn't even play in Birdland, the famous club named after him. But wherever and whenever he did play, other musicians gathered, because he taught them what they were working for.

Eastwood might seem like an unlikely choice to direct this film, but not if you consider his origins as a West Coast kid, growing up in the 1940s and buying into the Parker legend. Two of the themes running through much of Eastwood's work—and especially the fourteen films he has directed—are a love of music and a fascination with characters who are lonely, heroic drifters. There is a connection between the Charlie Parker of *Bird* and the alcoholic guitar player in *Honkytonk Man*. They are both men who use music as a way of insisting they are alive and can feel joy, in the face of the daily depression and dread they draw around themselves.

The film follows the general drift of Charlie Parker's life, but does not pay much attention to specific details (it glosses over all but his last marriage, for example). It shows the kid growing up in love with jazz, and sneaking in to hear his heroes play. It shows the almost overnight acceptance given to Parker's talent. It shows him joining bands, forming bands, taking delight in stunts like the time he toured the South with a band including Red Rodney, a white sideman who was passed off as "Albino Red" because integrated bands were forbidden. It shows him touring the West Coast and hearing some simple truths one night from Dizzy Gillespie, who told him that the difference be-

tween them was that Diz took care of business, and Charlie took care of screwing up. And it shows his relationship with Chan Parker, a white woman who loved jazz and understood Parker enough to be the best of his enablers—all of those who cared so much for Parker that they were willing to coexist with his drugs.

If Clint Eastwood were not a major movie star, he would be known as one of the most successful American directors of recent years (since *Play Misty for Me,* in 1971). His films are often bittersweet, and most at home in poverty. His heroes, usually played by himself, are loners who depend upon a strong personal code in the face of an uncaring world. The difference between Charlie Parker and the other Eastwood protagonists is that Parker was an artist, and so, on top of all the other adventures and struggles, there is the music, which comes from somewhere inside and is inexplicable.

Bird wisely does not attempt to "explain" Parker's music by connecting experiences with musical discoveries. This is a film of music, not about it, and one of the most extraordinary things about it is that we are really, literally, hearing Charlie Parker on the sound track. Eastwood and Lennie Niehaus, his music coordinator, began with actual Parker recordings, some of them from Chan Parker's private collection. They isolated the Parker tracks, scrubbed them electronically, recombined them with contemporary sidemen, and created a pure, clean, new stereophonic sound track on which Charlie Parker's saxophone is unmistakably present.

The movie is all of a piece—the music, the visual look, the tone of Forest Whitaker's performance. Eastwood has gone for a mostly somber, indoor, nighttime look, with a lot of shadows and warm, muted lighting. This is a world where breakfast is a meal held in the late afternoon, where hotel rooms are home, where work is play, and everything else is work. Whitaker occupies this world as a large, friendly, sometimes taciturn man who tries to harm nobody and who cannot understand why the world would not let him play his music. Neither can we.

Birdy ★ ★ ★ ★
R, 120 m., 1985

Nicolas Cage (Al), Matthew Modine (Birdy). Directed by Alan Parker and produced by Alan Marshall. Screenplay by Sandy Kroopf and Jack Behr.

The strangest thing about *Birdy,* which is a very strange and beautiful movie indeed, is that it seems to work best at its looniest level, and is least at ease with the things it takes most seriously. You will not discover anything new about war in this movie, but you will find out a whole lot about how it feels to be in love with a canary.

The movie is about two friends from South Philadelphia. One of them, Al, played by Nicolas Cage, is a slick romeo with a lot of self-confidence and a way with the women. The other, nicknamed Birdy (Matthew Modine), is goofy, withdrawn, and absolutely fascinated with birds. As kids, they are inseparable friends. In high school, they begin to grow apart, separated by their individual quests for two different kinds of birds. But they still share adventures, as Birdy hangs upside-down from elevated tracks to capture pigeons, or constructs homemade wings that he hopes will let him fly. Then the war comes. Both boys serve in Vietnam and both are wounded. Cage's face is disfigured, and he wears a bandage to cover the scars. Modine's wounds are internal: He withdraws entirely into himself and stops talking. He spends long, uneventful days perched in his room at a mental hospital, head cocked to one side, looking up longingly at a window, like nothing so much as a caged bird.

Because *Birdy* is not told in chronological order, the story takes a time to sort itself out. We begin with an agonizing visit by the Cage character to his friend Birdy. He hopes to draw him out of his shell. But Birdy makes no sign of recognition. Then, in flashbacks, we see the two lives that led up to this moment. We see the adventures they shared, the secrets, the dreams. Most importantly, we go inside Birdy's life and begin to glimpse the depth of his obsession with birds. His room turns into a birdcage. His special pets—including a cocky little yellow canary—take on individual characteristics for us. We can begin to understand that his love for birds is sensual, romantic, passionate. There is a wonderful scene where he brushes his fingers against a feather, showing how marvelously it is constructed, and how beautifully.

Most descriptions of *Birdy* tend to dwell on what seems to be the central plot, the story of the two buddies who go to Vietnam and are wounded, and about how one tries to help the other return to the real world. I felt that the war footage in the movie was fairly routine, and that the challenge of dragging Birdy back to reality was a good deal less interesting than the story of how he arrived at the strange, secret place in his mind. I have seen other, better, movies about war, but I have never before seen a character quite like Birdy.

As you may have already guessed, *Birdy* doesn't sound like a commercial blockbuster. More important are the love and care for detail that have gone into it from all hands, especially from Cage and Modine. They have two immensely difficult roles, and both are handicapped in the later scenes by being denied access to some of an actor's usual tools; for Cage, his face; for Modine, his whole human persona. They overcome those limitations to give us characters even more touching than the ones they started with.

The movie was directed by Alan Parker. Consider this list of his earlier films: *Bugsy Malone*, *Fame*, *Midnight Express*, *Shoot the Moon*, *Pink Floyd: The Wall*. Each one coming out of an unexpected place, and avoiding conventional movie genres. He was the man to direct *Birdy*, which tells a story so unlikely that perhaps even my description of it has discouraged you—and yet a story so interesting it is impossible to put this movie out of my mind.

Bitter Moon ★ ★ ★
R, 139 m., 1994

Peter Coyote (Oscar), Emmanuelle Seigner (Mimi), Hugh Grant (Nigel), Kristin Scott-Thomas (Fiona), Victor Banerjee (The Sikh). Directed and produced by Roman Polanski. Screenplay by Polanski, Gerard Brach, and John Brownjohn.

The returns are in from Europe and the coasts, and the critics have found Roman Polanski's *Bitter Moon* an embarrassment: It is too melodramatic, too contrived, too overwrought, too overacted. Polanski has come unhinged. His portrait of a doomed marriage may be high porn but it is low art.

What bothers some of the critics, I suspect, is the audacity Polanski exhibits by casting his own wife, Emmanuelle Seigner, in the central role—as a voracious seductress with black widow tendencies, whose amusement is to blind men in the headlights of her sexuality, and step on the gas. But *Bitter Moon* is nothing if it is not audacious, Polanski is far beyond concern over matters of taste, and his wife at least never seems miscast in a role which would have stopped many another actress cold in her tracks.

His story unfolds aboard an ocean liner, where an embittered husband, paralyzed and in a wheelchair, buttonholes a complete stranger and begins to tell him the story of his marriage. The stranger would like to escape, but cannot. For one thing he grows fascinated by the story. For another he is mesmerized by the man's wife, who has perfected that trick of looking him boldly in the eye until, by looking away, he concedes sexual supremacy. Hour after hour, day after day, the sordid story unspools, and in flashbacks we see a romance that turns into a dangerous obsession.

Oscar, the man in the wheelchair, is played by Peter Coyote, as a sardonic, self-loathing drunk who frankly holds out the bait of his wife as a lure to keep the stranger listening. Nigel, the stranger, is a well-behaved, bashful Englishman (played by Hugh Grant, as much the same character he also plays in *Sirens* and *Four Weddings and a Funeral*). Seigner is Mimi, Oscar's wife, a bold exhibitionist. And Kristin Scott-Thomas is Fiona, Nigel's wife—a cold, distant, somewhat dry woman who would seem to offer little competition for Mimi's juicy come-ons. As Oscar describes how he met Mimi, we see their marriage in long flashbacks. At first it is a romance, pure and simple. Then boredom begins to creep in—and, worse, antidotes to boredom. Mimi likes sadomasochistic fun and games. Oscar is fascinated. The two of them retreat into their marriage and pull the door closed behind them; in a kind of game of sexual chicken, they go farther and farther, acting out kinky fantasies until finally . . . well, we find out how Oscar ended up in the wheelchair.

These stories should act upon Nigel as a warning, but, predictably, he is fascinated. He starts telling lies and making excuses to Fiona, so he can spend more time with Oscar . . . and, it is hinted, Mimi. At first it seems that Oscar is the puppetmaster, but then it appears that he and Mimi may be up to a new game, with Nigel as the prize. We can't be sure, and that is one of the movie's pleasures: Somehow we know that although anything else may happen, Nigel will probably not end up with Mimi.

The word *lurid* was coined to describe films like this. Like all stories dealing with the extremes of sex, it arrives at moments when we can barely prevent ourselves from laughing. (There is a reason for this: S&M combines humorless scenarios with absurd choreography.) It is the easiest thing in the world to walk out of a movie like *Bitter Moon* shaking our heads wearily and complaining about Polanski's bad taste, grotesque situations, and fevered imagination. The purpose, of course, is to prove that *we* won't fall for it—that we are much too mature, serious, and well balanced to be taken in by his juvenile fantasizing. Well, of course *Bitter Moon* is wretched excess. But Polanski directs it without compromise or apology, and it's a funny thing how critics may condescend to it, but while they're watching it you could hear a pin drop.

The Black Marble ★ ★ ★ ½
PG, 110 m., 1980

Robert Foxworth (Sergeant Valnikov), Paula Prentiss (Sergeant Zimmerman), Harry Dean Stanton (Philo Skinner), Barbara Babcock (Madeline Whitfield), John Hancock (Clarence Cromwell), Raleigh Bond (Captain Hooker), Judy Landers (Pattie Mae), Pat Corley (Itchy Mitch). Directed by Harold Becker and produced by Frank Capra, Jr. Screenplay by Joseph Wambaugh.

The Black Marble is a delightfully twisted comedy, backing into itself, starting out in one direction, ending up somewhere else, constantly surprising us with its offbeat characters. It's so many things at once it's a juggling act: It's a police movie with lots of authentic details; it's a bizarre comedy about a kidnapped prize dog; it's a shaggy romance; it's got the most excruciating chase sequence I can remember; it's goofy, but it moves us.

The movie centers around several days in the life of a Los Angeles police sergeant named Valnikov (Robert Foxworth), an incurably romantic Russian who has been drinking too much since his partner's suicide. He gets a new partner, Sgt. Natalie Zimmerman, played by Paula Prentiss as a combination of Sally Kellerman and Lucille Ball. His new partner thinks Valnikov is insane. Maybe she's right.

The case they begin working on together involves a prize bitch that has been kidnapped and is being held for $85,000 ransom. Valnikov goes to interview the kidnapped dog's grieving owner, an attractive woman of a certain age. And, in a delightful scene that illustrates the movie's gift of being able to slide ever so lightly from drama into cheerful comedy, he winds up on the sofa with the woman, drying her tears and vowing, "Don't worry; I promise I'll get your doggie back."

The dry tone Foxworth brings to the pronunciation of such lines is one of the movie's charms. He is mustachioed, mournful-eyed, usually hung over, and filled with ancient Russian dreams and curses. It is inevitable, of course, that he and the sexy Zimmerman fall in love, and they have a wonderful seduction scene in his apartment. He puts sweepingly romantic Russian folk music on his stereo. They dance. "Translate the lyrics for me!" she whispers into his ear. He does. It does not bother either of them that there *are* no lyrics since the song is instrumental.

Meanwhile, a parallel plot involves the evil dog kidnapper, played by that uniquely malevolent character actor Harry Dean Stanton, who looks and talks like Robert Mitchum's mean kid brother. Stanton is a veterinarian who has never hurt a dog in his life. But he needs the ransom to pay a gambling debt before he is killed. Coughing, wheezing, and spitting through an endless chain of cigarettes, he makes telephone threats to the dog's owner, who counters with descriptions of her own financial plight, unpaid bills, and tax problems.

When Valnikov and the kidnapper finally meet face to face, they get into what is undoubtedly the most painful chase sequence I can remember, a chase that requires them to climb mesh fences separating a series of savage and terrified dogs that snap maniacally at their legs. The chase is another scene illustrating the curious way in which *The Black Marble* succeeds in being funny, painful, and romantic, sometimes simultaneously. The movie's not altogether a comedy, although we laugh; it's a love story that kids itself and ends up seriously; it contains violence but is not really violent. What it always does is keep us off balance. Because we can't anticipate what's going to happen next, the movie has a persistent interior life; there's never the sense that a scene is included because it's expected.

The performances go to show you that a good actor in a bad film can have a very hard time appearing to be any good. Foxworth's previous screen credits include *The Omen, Part II* and *Prophecy*. Neither film gave me the slightest reason to look forward to him in *The Black Marble*, but he's wonderful here. He gives his character weariness and craziness and then covers them both with warmth. He and Prentiss have so much fun with the long seduction scene that we can sense the joy of acting craftsmanship going into it.

The movie's the second production by Joseph Wambaugh, the L.A. cop who became a best-selling novelist only to see Hollywood doing terrible things to his novels.

Wambaugh vowed to produce his own books. The industry had its doubts, especially when Wambaugh hired a little-known British director, Harold Becker, to direct his first project, *The Onion Field*. But that was a strong, edgy, effective movie, and now Wambaugh and Becker are back with this unusual and distinctive comedy. Because it is uneven and moves so easily among its various tones and moods, it's possible, I suppose, to fault it on form: This isn't a seamless piece of work, but it's infectious and charming.

Black Rain ★ ★ ★ ½
NO MPAA RATING, 113 m., 1990

Yoshiko Tanaka (Yasuko), Kazuo Kitamura (Shigematsu), Etsuko Ichihara (Shigeko), Shoichi Ozawa (Shokichi), Norihei Miki (Kotaro), Keisuke Ishida (Yuichi). Directed by Shohei Imamura and produced by Hisa Iino. Screenplay by Toshiro Ishido and Imamura.

Black Rain is by Japan's great director Shohei Imamura, who shoots in a beautifully textured black and white to tell the story of survivors of the Hiroshima atomic bomb who were contaminated by the fallout. For years after the terrible day of the attack, they lived in fear of developing radiation poisoning or cancer—and finally, one by one, many of them did. The mushroom cloud hovered over every day of their lives.

This is not, however, an antinuclear message movie. It is a film about how the survivors of that terrible day internalized their experiences, how they came to see themselves as flawed because they carried the seeds of radiation sickness. Only a Japanese—perhaps only Imamura—could have made a film in which the bomb at Hiroshima is simply the starting point for an unforgiving critique of Japanese society itself.

His story, based on the novel by Masuji Ibuse, involves Yasuko, a young woman, on the day the bomb falls. She suffers no obvious or visible effects from the blast, but like everyone in her village—across a wide bay from Hiroshima—she has been touched by fallout from the mushroom cloud. And as time passes, the radiation poisoning ticks inside of her like a time bomb.

Imamura's depiction of the day of the blast itself is sudden, graphic, and unforgiving. It is an ordinary day in the isolated community where the story takes place, and then it becomes extraordinary as the sky fills with the light of a thousand suns. We see a railroad car literally blown apart by the force of

the blast, and then there are shots of survivors, wandering dazedly among the wreckage of a once-familiar world. The immediate impulse of the Japanese in the aftermath of such a cataclysm, Imamura shows in his film, is to re-establish the rhythms and values of traditional life. By returning to old ways, the wound can be healed and even denied.

That process would assume that Yasuko, who is of the appropriate age, would find the right man and marry. Her family tries to help arrange this process. But it is not so simple, since eligible men do not want a bride who may be infected with the lingering aftereffects of the fallout. Yasuko's uncle produces a document that allegedly certifies that the young woman is healthy, but, of course, what was really known about fallout in those days? Prudent would-be grooms take no chances with a woman whose health may be suspect.

As Yasuko grows older and is still unmarried, she becomes an affront to her family and community; the area is still very much bound by traditional beliefs, including the one that women of such an age should not be single. She does have a suitor, a young man she loves, and who loves her, but he is not of the right class or background to be an appropriate husband. Yet this is a delicate matter: Does the fact of her radiation poisoning "devalue" her to such an extent that they are more equal in status? And how long can her aunt and uncle maintain the fiction that she was not harmed by the blast?

Societies all over the world have sometimes blamed sick people for their illnesses; Susan Sontag's book *Illness as Metaphor* explores the ways in which we sometimes believe people get the diseases they deserve. Imamura's anger in *Black Rain* is directed not so much at those who dropped the bomb on Hiroshima as at the way his Japanese characters immediately started behaving as if somehow it had been their own fault. Some of the characters in this movie seem almost to be apologizing for having been beneath the fallout, and that makes Imamura angry—provides him, indeed, with the impulse for this film.

Black Rain premiered at the Cannes Film Festival in May 1989, but was released more than a year later in the U.S., perhaps to avoid confusion with the 1989 Michael Douglas thriller of the same name. There is irony in the fact that both movies concern Japan, Douglas's showing it as a canny, aggressive society with criminals who are up-to-date by anybody's standards, Imamura's concerned with ancient traits in the collective national personality.

It must have taken no small amount of courage for Imamura to make this film, which carries an insight many Japanese may not want to heed and many foreigners may not be able to believe. It's also interesting that he chose to shoot in black and white. He made that decision, I think, because the scenes of the atomic bomb explosion and its immediate aftermath would have been so gory in color that they would have wiped out all the subtlety of what he wanted to say. This is a film, after all, about people who want to conduct their lives and businesses as usual, to deal with the atomic holocaust by denying it. Imamura's message is that—do what you will—it cannot be denied.

The Black Stallion ★ ★ ★ ★
G, 120 m., 1980

Kelly Reno (Alec Ramsey), Mickey Rooney (Henry Dailey), Teri Garr (Alec's Mother), Clarence Muse (Snoe), Hoyt Axton (Alec's Father), Michael Higgins (Neville). The black stallion is portrayed by Cass-ole, owned by San Antonio Arabians. Directed by Carroll Ballard and produced by Francis Ford Coppola, Fred Roos, and Tom Sternberg. Screenplay by Melissa Mathison, Jeanne Rosenberg and William D. Wittliff.

The first half of *The Black Stallion* is so gloriously breathtaking that the second half, the half with all the conventional excitement, seems merely routine. We've seen the second half before—the story of the kid, the horse, the veteran trainer, and the big race. But the first hour of this movie belongs among the great filmgoing experiences. It is described as an epic, and earns the description.

The film opens at sea, somewhere in the Mediterranean, forty or so years ago, on board a ship inhabited by passengers who seem foreign and fearsome to a small boy. They drink, they gamble, they speak in foreign tongues, they wear caftans and beards and glare ferociously at anyone who comes close to their prize possession, a magnificent black stallion.

The boy and his father are on board this ship for reasons never explained. The father gambles with the foreigners and the boy roams the ship and establishes a shy rapport with the black stallion, and then a great storm sweeps over the ocean and the ship catches fire and is lost. The boy and the stallion are thrown free, into the boiling sea. The horse somehow saves the boy, and in the calm of the next morning they both find themselves thrown onto a deserted island.

This sequence—the storm, the ship's sinking, the ordeal at sea—is a triumphant use of special effects, miniature models, back projection, editing, and all the tricks of craft that go into the filming of a fantasy. The director, Carroll Ballard, used the big water tank at Cinecitta Studios in Rome for the storm sequences; a model ship, looking totally real, burns and sinks headfirst, its propellers churning slowly in the air, while the horse and boy struggle in the foreground.

The horse in this film (its name is Cass-ole) is required to perform as few movie horses ever have. But its finest scene is the quietest one, and takes place on the island a few days after the shipwreck. Ballard and his cinematographer, Caleb Deschanel, have already established the mood of the place, with gigantic, quiet, natural panoramas. The boy tries to spear a fish. The horse roams restlessly from the beaches to the cliffs. And then, in a single shot that is held for a long time, Ballard shows us the boy inviting the horse to eat out of his hand.

It is crucial here that this action be seen in a *single* shot; lots of short cuts, edited together, would simply be the filmmakers at work. But the one uninterrupted shot, with the horse at one edge of the screen and the boy at the other, and the boy's slow approach, and the horse's skittish advances and retreats, shows us a rapport between the human and the animal that's strangely moving.

All these scenes of the boy and horse on the island are to be treasured, especially a montage photographed underwater and showing the legs of the two as they splash in the surf. There are also wonderfully scary sequences, such as one in which the boy awakens to find a poisonous snake a few feet away from him on the sand. This scene exploits the hatred and fear horses have for snakes, and is cut together into a terrifically exciting climax.

But then, as all good things must, the idyll on the island comes to an end. The boy and the horse are rescued. And it's here that the film, while still keeping our interest, becomes more routine. The earlier passages of the film were amazing to look at (they were shot, with great difficulty and beauty, on Sardinia). Now we're back to earth again, with scenes shot around an old racetrack in Toronto.

And we've seen the melodramatic materials of the movie's second half many times before. The boy is reunited with his mother, the horse returns home with him, and the boy meets a wise old horse trainer who admits, that, yes, that Arabian *can* run like the wind—but the fool thing doesn't have any papers. The presence of Mickey Rooney, who plays the trainer, is welcome but perhaps too familiar. Rooney has played this sort of role so often before (most unforgettably in *National Velvet*) that he almost seems to be visiting from another movie. His Academy Award nomination for the performance is probably a recognition of that.

Still, the melodrama is effective. Everything depends on the outcome of the big race at the film's end. The young boy, of course, is the jockey (the Elizabeth Taylor role, so to speak). Ballard and Deschanel are still gifted at finding a special, epic look for the movie; one especially good scene has the stallion racing against time, in the dark before dawn, in the rain.

The Black Stallion is a wonderful experience at the movies. The possibility remains, though, that in these cynical times it may be avoided by some viewers because it has a G rating—and G movies are sometimes dismissed as being too innocuous. That's sure not the case with this film, which is rated G simply because it has no nudity, profanity, or violence—but it does have terrific energy, beauty, and excitement. It's not a children's movie; it's for adults *and* for kids.

Blade Runner ★ ★ ★
R, 114 m., 1982
(See *The Director's Cut*, p. 840.)

Harrison Ford (Deckard), Rutger Hauer (Batty), Sean Young (Rachel), Edward James Olmos (Gaff), M. Emmet Walsh (Bryant), Daryl Hannah (Pris). Directed by Ridley Scott and produced by Michael Deeley. Screenplay by Hampton Fancher and David Peoples.

The strangest thing about the future is that *this* is now the future that was once foretold. Twenty years ago, we thought of "now" as "the year 1987," and we wondered what life would be like. Little could we have guessed that there would be no world government, that the cars would look like boxes instead of rocket ships, and that there would still be rock 'n' roll on the radio. *Blade Runner* asks us to imagine its own future, in "the year 2020." The movie takes place in a Los Angeles that looks like a futuristic Tokyo, with gigantic billboards showing smiling Japanese girls drinking Coca-Cola. I would have predicted

L.A. would be Hispanic, but never mind, it looks sensational. The city is dominated by almost inconceivably huge skyscrapers. People get around in compact vehicles that fly, hover, climb, and swoop. (In a lot of fictional futures, people seem to zip around the city in private aircraft; can you imagine the traffic problems?) At ground level, however, the L.A. of the future is an urban jungle.

The movie stars Harrison Ford as a cop who moves confidently through the city's mean streets. He is laconic, cynical, competent. He has a difficult assignment. A group of "replicants," artificial people who seem amazingly human, have escaped from "off-world," and are trying to inflict themselves on Earth. Ford's job is to track them down and eliminate them. Anyone who has read this far can predict what happens next: He falls in love with one of the replicants. She may not be quite human, but, oh, you kid.

This basic story comes from a Philip K. Dick novel with the intriguing title, *Do Androids Dream of Electric Sheep?* The book examined the differences between humans and thinking machines, and circled warily around the question of memory: Does it make an android's personal memories less valid if they are inspired by someone else's experiences—especially if the android does not know that? Ford says he originally signed on for *Blade Runner* because he found such questions intriguing. For director Ridley Scott, however, the greater challenge seemed to be creating that future world. Scott is a master of production design, of imagining other worlds of the future *(Alien)* and the past *(The Duellists)*. He seems more concerned with creating his film worlds than populating them with plausible characters, and that's the trouble this time. *Blade Runner* is a stunningly interesting visual achievement, but a failure as a story.

The special effects were supervised by Douglas Trumbull, whose credits include *2001* and *Silent Running,* and who is about as good as anyone in the world at using miniatures, animation, drawings, optical effects, and other ways of tricking the eye. The visual environments he creates for this film are wonderful to behold, and there's a sense of detail, too; we don't just get the skyways and the monolithic skyscrapers and the skytaxis, we also get notions about how restaurants, clothes, and home furnishings will look in 2020 (not too different). *Blade Runner* is worth seeing just to witness this artistry. The movie's weakness, however, is that

it allows the special-effects technology to overwhelm its story. Ford is tough and low-key in the central role, and Rutger Hauer and Sean Young are effective as two of the replicants, but the movie isn't really interested in these people—or creatures. The obligatory love affair is pro forma, the villains are standard issue, and the climax is yet one more of those cliffhangers, with Ford dangling over an abyss by his fingertips. The movie has the opposite trouble as the replicants: Instead of flesh and blood, its dreams are of mechanical men.

Note: Reader Richard Doerflinger writes to observe that the movie reverses the original vision of Philip K. Dick's novel, which was about an under-*populated future. In a world short of humans, the hero might well be attracted to androids, but "Scott reverses the premise that makes the story coherent."*

Blaze ★ ★ ★ ½
R, 120 m., 1989

Paul Newman (Earl K. Long), Lolita Davidovich (Blaze Starr), Jerry Hardin (Thibodeaux), Gailard Sartain (LaGrange), Jeffrey DeMunn (Tuck), Garland Bunting (Doc Ferriday), Richard Jenkins (Picayune), Brandon Smith (Arvin Deeter), Jay Chevalier (Wiley Braden). Directed by Ron Shelton and produced by Gil Friesen and Dale Pollock. Screenplay by Shelton.

Toward the end of *Blaze,* the following exchange takes place between the film's two central characters:

Earl K. Long: "Would you still love me just as much if I wasn't the fine governor of the great state of Louisiana?"

Blaze Starr: "Would you still love *me* if I had little tits and worked in a fish house?"

The true and final answer to this question is withheld by the makers of *Blaze* almost until the movie's last scene; "love" is a big word, after all. But right from the opening passages of the film we can tell that these two characters like each other an awful lot: Earl, the boozy, wheeler-dealer governor of Louisiana, and Blaze, the hillbilly girl who became a famous stripper. They like each other for several reasons, including the obvious ones (she likes his power; he likes her body), but also because they are alike in so many ways. They're students of human nature who were born honest and have had to struggle with the consequences of that misfortune ever since.

Blaze is based on the autobiography of Blaze Starr, who can still to this day be glimpsed in

Baltimore, where she remains, the movie's closing credits inform us, "a part of the local cultural scene." It is a good question whether she was ever as naive, or her career ever as simple, as this movie makes it look. But never mind. The heart of the movie is a public relationship between a woman who was not respectable and a man who didn't give a damn what people said.

Paul Newman is an ideal choice to play Earl K. Long. Portraying the fine governor of the great state with his hair a little mussed, his gut sticking out over his belt buckle, and his voice a little slurred by large amounts of bourbon, he seems completely at home. The role fits him like an old flannel shirt. After the disappointment of *Fat Man and Little Boy,* in which Newman seemed vaguely out of focus as a military man, *Blaze* shows him as the kind of instinctively humorous man he plays the best, the kind of man whose response to hypocrisy is a delighted horselaugh, because he has been proven right once again in his theory that his enemies are full of it.

Although Newman is a delight, the best surprise in the movie is the performance of a new actress named Lolita Davidovich, who plays Blaze Starr. She has a comfortability in the role that is just right. Unlike a lot of new or beginning actors who project tension or concentration or a sense of how important they think every scene has to be, Davidovich acts like she's inside that flannel shirt along with Newman. It's important that she have that quality because *Blaze* is not by its nature a tense, wound-up story. It's about a couple of slightly frayed people who were a little peculiar, but who were not dumb, and who insisted on surviving on their own terms. The movie was directed by Ron Shelton, whose previous film was *Bull Durham,* and there is a similar sensibility in both films: Shelton's characters define their identities through their eccentricities.

During the course of the movie, the hillbilly girl who took the name Blaze Starr makes her way through a series of striptease parlors to the big time on Bourbon Street in New Orleans, where one night the long black limousine of the fine governor of the great state pulls up outside the club where she's working. The governor is instantly captivated by Blaze, but he doesn't know how much he likes her until she turns down his offer of a date: "Damn, but I'm attracted to strong-willed women," he tells one of his cronies. Blaze's mother has advised her never to believe it when a man says, "Trust me." She asks Earl if she can trust him. "Hell, no," he says. And so she does.

The development of their relationship is seen against a backdrop of Louisiana state politics in the late 1950s, as Long tries to hold together the populist, working-class, Democratic Party coalition first cobbled together by his late brother, Huey ("Every man a king") Long. The great threat to Earl's sovereignty is the "votin' rights bill" for blacks, which his cronies fear he will support in the legislature. They think it could lead to the destruction of their power base. Earl indeed favors the bill, and has long had his own peculiar and indirect ways of supporting the black cause; there is a scene in the movie where he creates jobs for black doctors and nurses in a state hospital by pretending to be shocked that black patients are being cared for by whites. Long is not a great reformist crusader, but within the realpolitik of the segregated South, he was a pragmatist who contributed to progress.

He was also a man constantly under indictment on tax charges, constantly under suspicion of "payrolling" and graft, and denounced from the pulpits of the state for his immoral liaison with Blaze Starr. He never bothered to deny his friendship with Blaze, and indeed often seemed to confuse his politics and sexuality (as in a wonderful scene where he is stricken temporarily impotent and admonishes his disobedient member to "stop acting like a payroller").

Blaze is the affectionate story of two colorful people who had the nerve to stick together even though that didn't suit everybody's notions of propriety. Whether it tells the whole story of their relationship is an open question; I imagine Blaze Starr could write a second volume of autobiography if she had a mind to. But this is a movie made up of feelings and moments, and not a work of political history. Newman and Davidovich create their characters with a rough affection that shines through, and by the end of the film we are prepared to concede that, yes, they might have loved each other even if she'd been a skinny waitress and he not the fine governor of the great state.

Blink ★ ★ ★ ½
R, 106 m., 1994

Madeleine Stowe (Emma Brody), Aidan Quinn (John Hallstrom), James Remar (Thomas Ridgely), Peter Friedman (Dr. Ryan Pierce), Bruce A. Young (Lt. Mitchell), Laurie Metcalf (Candice), Matt Roth (Crowe), Paul Dillon (Neal Booker). Directed by Michael Apted and produced by David Blocker. Screenplay by Dana Stevens.

Blink takes the damnedest story and tells it about characters so real they could almost be from a documentary. It sets the action in a Chicago that harbors a serial killer right out of Hollywood—but in the midst of its thriller plot is a portrait of the city that is closely and accurately observed. And the movie contains a love story about two people who, far from falling into each other's arms, might really prefer to be left alone.

The movie stars Madeleine Stowe as Emma Brody, a blind woman who plays violin in a band called the Drovers, which works the North Side bars of Chicago. She's not your average movie blind woman, all trembling and sensitive. She's independent, tough, smart, cynical, and likes to take a drink from time to time. Shortly after the movie opens, she is given a corneal transplant, and finds that she can see for the first time. But her mind is overwhelmed by the torrent of visual images, and in defense it begins to edit what she sees; sometimes she may witness something that doesn't "register" until hours later. That man in the hallway, for example, who may have murdered her upstairs neighbor.

I don't have the slightest idea if this phenomenon is possible in real life; I'll give the story the benefit of the doubt. The plot does, of course, sound like typically lurid and melodramatic thriller material. And it is. I was surprised, however, to find it in such a good movie. A lot of the good things come out of the relationship between Stowe and Aidan Quinn, as a cop named Hallstrom who gets assigned to the case after she reports she "may" have been a witness to the murder. Quinn and Stowe are able to bring to their characters a certain no-B.S. edge that I recognize as very Chicago. Their rough edges and the way they speak—taking delight in saying exactly what's on their minds—sounds all the more authentic because in so many thrillers the characters talk as if they watch too many daytime soap operas.

The film's director is Michael Apted, who brings a couple of special qualities to the material. He was born in Britain but works in the United States and says Chicago is his big-city location of choice (he made *Continental Divide* here, with its Royko-esque columnist). Rare for a major director, Apted continues to make documentaries; the *35 Up* series is his, where he visits the same group of British people every seven years. In *Blink*, he is very perceptive about the way a certain kind of Chicagoan lives—the kind, let's say, who lives mid-North in an ethnic neighborhood, and works at night, and knows the bar scene, and reads the paper for the rock and blues reviews, and doesn't like Chicago-style pizza because why pay extra for a thick crust? There aren't a lot of skyline and Magnificent Mile shots in this movie, which is more interested in streetscapes around the corner of North and Milwaukee.

The Quinn and Stowe characters get the notes just right. And the movie portrays Chicago cops with a certain attention to detail; these aren't the wisecrackers of New York or the storm troopers of Los Angeles, but ordinary hard-working guys with a job to do and a bar to go to after they've done it.

The cop is tempted to dismiss his "witness" to the murder, since, after all, how much can you rely on a woman who was recently blind and "thinks" she might have belatedly seen something? But the violinist persists. Other things happen to convince her she is right. The cop begins to doubt his own doubts. And of course they're drawn to one another. But not in the usual Hollywood way, in which they're so attracted that they eventually can't resist going to bed with each other. No, this is more of a Chicago thing, in which they go to bed with each other so much that they eventually can't resist being attracted.

The love-hate friendship between Stowe and Quinn is one of the more authentic relationships I've seen in a genre movie. It feels right. And then on top of it you have the developing thriller plot, with more "visions" and an ominous possible killer, and, inevitably, a scene in which the young woman is too trusting and goes where she shouldn't go. But even then, the screenplay by Dana Stevens has some surprises, and this doesn't end like most of the movies about women in danger and big, strong policemen.

The people in this movie are so good, there's a temptation to put down the thriller material. But even here Apted has some surprises. His cinematographer, Dante Spinotti, and his visual-effects supervisor, Art Durinski, cook up some visuals to let us understand what the woman can see—and what she can't see. And these have the effect of making us identify with her, making us strain along with her to decide what she can trust about what she sees. *Blink* is an uncommonly good thriller.

Blood Simple ★ ★ ★ ★
R, 96 m., 1985

John Getz (Ray), Frances McDormand (Abby), Dan Hedaya (Julian Marty), M. Emmet Walsh (Detective), Samm-Art Williams (Meurice). Directed by Joel Coen and produced by Ethan Coen. Screenplay by Coen and Coen.

A lot has been written about the visual style of *Blood Simple*, but I think the appeal of the movie is more elementary. It keys into three common nightmares: (1) You clean and clean, but there's still blood all over the place; (2) You know you have committed a murder, but you are not sure quite how or why; (3) You know you have forgotten a small detail that will eventually get you into a lot of trouble. *Blood Simple* mixes those fears and guilts into an incredibly complicated plot, with amazingly gory consequences. It tells a story in which every individual detail seems to make sense, and every individual choice seems logical, but the choices and details form a bewildering labyrinth in which there are times when even the murderers themselves don't know who they are.

Because following the plot is one of this movie's most basic pleasures, I will not reveal too much. The movie begins with a sleazy backwoods bar owner's attempt to hire a scummy private detective to murder his wife. The private eye takes the money and then pulls a neat double-cross, hoping to keep the money and eliminate the only witness who could implicate him. Neat. And then it *really* gets complicated.

The movie has been shot with a lot of style, some of it self-conscious, but deliberately so. One of the pleasures in a movie like this is enjoying the low-angle and tilt shots that draw attention to themselves, that declare themselves as being part of a movie. The movie does something interesting with its timing, too. It begins to feel inexorable. Characters think they know what has happened; they turn out to be wrong; they pay the consequences, and it all happens while the movie is marching from scene to scene like an implacable professor of logic, demonstrating one fatal error after another.

Blood Simple was directed by Joel Coen, produced by his brother, Ethan, and written by the two of them. It's their first film, and has the high energy and intensity we associate with young filmmakers who are determined to make an impression. Some of the scenes are virtuoso, including a sequence in which a dead body becomes extraordinarily hard to dispose of, and another one in which two people in adjacent rooms are trapped in the same violent showdown. The central performance in the movie is by the veteran character actor M. Emmet Walsh, who plays the private eye like a man for whom idealism is a dirty word. The other actors in the movie are all effective, but they are obscured, in a way, by what happens to them: This movie weaves such a bloody web that the characters are upstaged by their dilemmas.

Is the movie fun? Well, that depends on you. It is violent, unrelenting, absurd, and fiendishly clever. There is a cliché I never use: "Not for the squeamish." But let me put it this way. *Blood Simple* may make you squeam.

Blown Away ★ ★   NEW
R, 120 m., 1994
(See related Film Clip, p. 879.)

Jeff Bridges (Dove), Tommy Lee Jones (Gaerity), Suzy Amis (Kate), Lloyd Bridges (Max), Forest Whitaker (Franklin), Stephi Lineburg (Lizzy), John Finn (Captain Roarke). Directed by Stephen Hopkins and produced by John Watson, Richard Lewis, and Pen Densham. Screenplay by Joe Batteer and John Rice.

At one point, early in *Blown Away*, a tearful student at MIT is about to be blown up because her computer has been rigged with a bomb that will explode, the dialogue explains, "when the hard drive runs out of available bytes" or when she stops typing. No points for guessing which will come first, since at typing speed she would have to pound the keyboard for many long months to exhaust the memory of most hard discs.

But wait. A mad bomber is loose in Boston, and there are more diabolical schemes afoot. A member of the bomb squad is listening to a stereo which, alas, has been rigged with a bomb, so that if he removes his earphones his head will be blown off. The only recourse is for the threatened cop (Forest Whitaker) and his partner (Jeff Bridges) to separately and simultaneously cut two wires. The tension mounts as they do the countdown: "Three . . . two . . . one . . ." No points for figuring out that at the speed of electricity, if one of them is the smallest fraction of a second behind the other one . . .

But wait. There's more. A retired cop (Lloyd Bridges) is chained to a piece of playground equipment and wired to a bomb. And still more. The mad bomber (Tommy Lee Jones) holds a remote control device that will blow up Jeff Bridges's girlfriend while she plays violin for the Boston Pops. And still more. Jones has rigged an abandoned ship with a Rube Goldberg device in which bottles topple over, and balls roll down chutes, and switches and levers are triggered, and eventually a bomb will be set off. And there's more. And more.

Blown Away is the kind of movie that people should be sentenced to see if they complain that *Speed* is implausible. Its central enigma is supposed to be: How can bomb squad member Jeff Bridges stop mad bomber Tommy Lee Jones before he blows up everyone Bridges loves, and half of Boston along with them? In actual fact, the puzzle is: How does Jones have enough time to rig such intricate and labyrinthine schemes? What does he *really* want to do, get revenge or win the Westinghouse Science Search?

The movie is essentially a thriller about brave cops against a mad bomber, but there's a back story about how the characters played by Bridges and Jones met twenty years ago in Ireland, where Jones was a bomber and Bridges was his student. In an attempt to offend not even the IRA, the movie explains that Jones was "too crazy" for them, and indeed when Jones hatches a plan to bomb civilians, Bridges blows the whistle on him. Jones ends up in prison, and Bridges escapes to the United States, where he changes his name, becomes a cop, and eventually falls in love with the violinist (Suzy Amis). Then Jones tracks him down and starts setting his elaborate traps.

Conventional wisdom has it that a thriller is only as good as its villain. Jones is one of the best villains in the business, but here he has two problems. (1) He is saddled with all the Irish political apparatus, which provides a "motivation" when none is really needed. (2) He is a loner, so all of his scenes are with his enemies, leading to a one-note performance. In *Under Siege*, where he was also a mad bomber of sorts, he got to play other notes, as a deceptively friendly impostor, and as a group leader.

Bridges and Amis establish a nice relationship together, but we sense it's in the movie only because Amis and her daughter need to be set up as a target. Same thing with Forest Whittaker, as Bridges's partner. All of the dramatic scenes are just filler between explosions; they should either have been taken more seriously, or left out.

Meanwhile, we're left with a veritable anthology of mad bomber clichés, of which my favorite is an occurrence of the Moe Rule, from *Ebert's Little Movie Glossary*. This is the rule which states that, in any bomb movie, a hero will eventually have to decide which wire to cut, and will recite "Eeny, meeny, miney, moe . . ." with moe defined as the wire to be cut. In *Blown Away*, Bridges varies this by using "She loves me, she loves me not." This formula would not produce the same wire as the Moe Rule, which only goes to show you how much danger these guys live with.

Blow Out ★ ★ ★ ★
R, 107 m., 1981

John Travolta (Jack), Nancy Allen (Sally), John Lithgow (Burke), Dennis Franz (Manny Karp), Peter Boydon (Sam), Curt May (Donohue). Directed by Brian De Palma and produced by George Litto. Screenplay by De Palma.

There are times when *Blow Out* resembles recent American history trapped in the "Twilight Zone." Episodes are hauntingly familiar, and yet seem slightly askew. What if the "grassy knoll" recordings from the police radio in Dallas had been crossed with Chappaquiddick and linked to Watergate? What if Jack Ruby had been a private eye specializing in divorce cases? What if Abraham Zapruder—the man who took the home movies of President John F. Kennedy's death—had been a sound-effects man? And what if Judith Exner—remember her?—had been working with Ruby? These are some of the inspirations out of which Brian De Palma constructs *Blow Out,* a movie which continues his practice of making cross-references to other movies, other directors, and actual historical events, and which nevertheless is his best and most original work.

The title itself, of course, reminds us of *Blow Up,* the 1966 film by Michelangelo Antonioni in which a photographer saw, or thought he saw, a murder—and went mad while obsessively analyzing his photographs of the "crime." *Was* there a dead body to be found on that fuzzy negative? Was there even such a thing as reality? In *Blow Out,* John Travolta plays the character who confronts these questions. He's a sound man for a sleazy Philadelphia B-movie factory. He works on cheap, cynical exploitation films. Late one night, while he's standing on a bridge re-

cording owls and other night sounds, he becomes a witness to an accident. A car has a blowout, swerves off a bridge, and plunges into a river. Travolta plunges in after it, rescues a girl inside (Nancy Allen), and later discovers that the car's drowned driver was a potential presidential candidate. Still later, reviewing his sound recording of the event, Travolta becomes convinced that he can hear a gunshot just before the blowout. Was the accident actually murder? He traces down Nancy Allen, discovers that she was part of a blackmail plot against the candidate, and then comes across the trail of a slimy private eye (Dennis Franz) who wanted to cause a blowout, all right, but didn't figure on anybody getting killed.

The plot thickens beautifully. De Palma doesn't have just a handful of ideas to spin out to feature length. He has an abundance. We meet a gallery of violent characters, including Burke (John Lithgow), a dirty-tricks specialist who seems inspired by G. Gordon Liddy. The original crime is complicated by a series of other murders, designed to lay a false trail and throw the police off the scent of political conspiracy.

Meanwhile, the Travolta character digs deeper. For him, it's a matter of competence, of personal pride. Arguing with a cop about his tapes, Travolta denies that he's just imagining things: "I'm a *sound* man!" He stumbles across a series of photos of the fatal accident. In a brilliantly crafted sequence, we follow every step as he assembles the film and his recording into a movie of the event, doggedly extracting what seem to be facts from what looks like chaos.

De Palma's visual images in *Blow Out* invite comparison to many Alfred Hitchcock films, and indeed De Palma invited such comparisons when the posters for *Dressed to Kill* described him as "Master of the Macabre." In *Blow Out* there are such Hitchcock hallmarks as a shower scene (played this time for laughs rather than for the chills of *Dressed to Kill*), several grisly murders in unexpected surroundings, violence in public places, and a chase through Philadelphia on the anniversary of the ringing of the Liberty Bell. This last extended chase sequence reminds us of two Hitchcock strategies: His juxtaposition of patriotic images and espionage, as in *North by Northwest* and *Saboteur,* and his desperate chases through uncaring crowds, reminders of *Foreign Correspondent* and *Strangers on a Train.*

But *Blow Out* stands by itself. It reminds

us of the violence of *Dressed to Kill,* the startling images of *The Fury,* the clouded identities of *Sisters,* the uncertainty of historical "facts" from *Obsession,* and it ends with the bleak nihilism of *Carrie.* But it moves beyond those films, because this time De Palma is more successful than ever before at populating his plot with three-dimensional characters. We believe in the reality of the people played by John Travolta, Nancy Allen, John Lithgow, and Dennis Franz. They have all the little tics and eccentricities of life. And although they're caught in the mesh of a labyrinthine conspiracy, they behave as people probably would behave in such circumstances—they're not pawns of the plot.

Best of all, this movie is inhabited by a real cinematic intelligence. The audience isn't condescended to. In sequences like the one in which Travolta reconstructs a film and sound record of the accident, we're challenged and stimulated: We share the excitement of figuring out how things develop and unfold, when so often the movies only need us as passive witnesses.

Blue ★ ★ ★ ½
R, 98 m., 1994

Juliette Binoche (Julie), Benoit Regent (Olivier), Florence Pernel (Sandrine), Charlotte Very (Lucille), Helene Vincent (Journalist), Philippe Volter (Real Estate Agent), Claude Duneton (Doctor), Hugues Quester (Patrice [Julie's Husband]). Directed by Krzysztof Kieslowski and produced by Marin Karmitz. Screenplay by Kieslowski and Krzysztof Piesiewicz.

There is a kind of movie in which the characters are not thinking about anything. They are simply the instruments of the plot. And another kind of movie in which we lean forward in our seats, trying to penetrate the mystery of characters who are obviously thinking a great deal. *Blue* is the second kind of film: The story of a woman whose husband dies, and who deals with that fact in unpredictable ways.

The woman, named Julie, is played by Juliette Binoche, who you may remember from *The Unbearable Lightness of Being* or *Damage.* In both of those films she projected a strong sexuality; this time, she seems to be beyond sex, as if it no longer has any reality for her. She lives in France and is married to a famous composer, who is killed in an auto crash early in the film. Now she must pick up the pieces of her life.

She doesn't do that in the ways we think

she might. She is sad and shaken, but this is not a film about a grieving widow, and indeed by the way she behaves we can guess things about her marriage. One of her first acts, after the initial shock wears off, is to call a man who was a colleague of both her and her husband, and seduce him. "You have always wanted me," she says. "Here I am."

This sequence is not played for shock, nor does it even seem especially disrespectful to the dead husband: She seems to be testing, to see if she can still feel. She cannot. She walks out on the man and moves to the center of Paris, to what she hopes is an anonymous apartment on an anonymous street. She doesn't want to see anybody she knows. She wants to walk through the streets free of her history, her memories, her identities. She wants to begin again, perhaps—or to be free of the need to begin.

Binoche has a face that is well suited to this kind of role. Because she can convince you that she is thinking and feeling, she doesn't need to "do" things in an obvious way. In the opening moments of *Damage*, she saw the Jeremy Irons character for the first time, and they were both struck by a powerful physical passion. She projected this passion, not by overacting or acting at all, but (as nearly as I can tell) by looking at the camera and projecting the feeling without obvious external signs.

Here, too, her feelings are a mystery which her face will help us to solve. The film has been directed by Krzysztof Kieslowski, born in Poland, now working in France, and in the opinion of some the best active European filmmaker (he made *The Double Life of Veronique* two years ago). He trusts the human face, and watching his film I remembered a conversation I had with Ingmar Bergman many years ago, in which he said there were many moments in films which could only be dealt with by a closeup of a face—the right face—and that too many directors tried instead to use dialogue or action.

Think of how we read the thoughts of those closest to us, in moments when words will not do. We look at their faces, and although they do not make any effort to mirror emotions there, we can read them all the same, in the smallest signs. A movie that invites us to do the same thing can be very absorbing.

Eventually there is a surprise. Julie meets a woman she did not know existed—her husband's mistress. The two women must deal with this discovery together. Watching this film, it was impossible not to think about *Intersection*, the Hollywood weeper starring Richard Gere, Sharon Stone, and Lolita Davidovich in an uncannily similar story of two women dealing with their love of the same man. That film was an insult to the intelligence. This one, similar in superficial ways, is a challenge to the imagination. It's as if European films have a more adult, inward, knowing way of dealing with the emotions, and Hollywood hasn't grown up enough.

Blue Chips ★ ★ ★
PG-13, 107 m., 1994

Nick Nolte (Pete), Mary McDonnell (Jenny), J.T. Walsh (Happy), Ed O'Neill (Ed), Alfre Woodard (Lavada McRae), Bob Cousy (Vic), Shaquille O'Neal (Neon). Directed by William Friedkin and produced by Michele Rappaport. Screenplay by Ron Shelton.

A lot of college basketball coaches seem caught in a catch-22. If they don't win, they get fired. To win, they need great players. To recruit great players, they may have to offer them illegal inducements. If they get caught doing that, they get fired. It's a vicious circle.

Pete Bell, the coach played by Nick Nolte in William Friedkin's new film *Blue Chips*, has so far remained entirely honest. But he's just had his first losing season, after a career that has brought his teams two national titles. So maybe it's only a matter of time until he unleashes the rabid alums who, as "friends of the program," shower cash and cars on likely prospects, and new tractors and homes on their parents.

The movie is told almost entirely from Nolte's point of view, and he makes an immensely likable character right from the top, where he viciously chews out his losing team and stalks from the room—only to return, chew them out some more, and walk out again—only to come back a third time with afterthoughts.

He has never cheated on the recruiting rules and he doesn't want to start now. But the walls are closing in on him. He's after some hot high school prospects who are fairly frank about their requirements. "The way I see it," says one towering prospect from French Lick, Ind., "I'm a white, blue chip prospect and I think that should be worth about thirty thousand dollars. In one of those athletic bags." Plus a new tractor for

his dad's farm. A black inner-city kid from Chicago has a mom (Alfre Woodard) who would like a decent job and a home with a lawn.

No problem, if Nolte will only give an okay to the wealthy, obnoxious head of the alumni association's unofficial booster club (J.T. Walsh). He already has the football team on the payroll, and seems driven to corrupt the basketball team as well.

The movie contains a certain amount of basketball, but for once here's a sports movie where everything doesn't depend on who wins the big game. It's how they win it. We follow Nolte on his recruiting trips, including one to Algiers, La., where he goes after a seven-foot-four phenom named Neon Bodeaux (Shaquille O'Neal, from the Orlando NBA franchise). Neon doesn't even want a payoff, but eventually gets a new Lexus anyway.

The movie shows Nolte struggling with his conscience and with an ex-wife (Mary McDonnell) who he still loves, and who loves him enough to tutor Neon. He also has a close friendship with the school's athletic director, played by former Celtics great Bob Cousy in a surprisingly on-target performance. (The Cousy character doesn't know anything about any illegal recruiting tactics—and doesn't want to know.) And there's an adversary in a sportswriter (Ed O'Neill) who smells a rat.

The screenplay is by Ron Shelton, who also wrote *White Men Can't Jump* and *Bull Durham* and obviously knows the world of sports inside-out. The story is populated with familiar faces from the world of basketball, including Larry Bird as the coach's old friend, and former Las Vegas coach Jerry Tarkanian as the leader of a pack of hungry coaches competing for the best young prospects.

What Friedkin brings to the story is a tone that feels completely accurate; the movie is a morality play, told in the realistic, sometimes cynical terms of modern high-pressure college sports. The underlying theme, I think, is that since top-level intercollegiate athletic programs are profit centers for their universities and feeding programs for the pro leagues, maybe the players *should* simply be paid and the pretense of amateurism dropped. Look at the once-amateur Olympics.

The J.T. Walsh character, who is seen as unprincipled and hateful, nevertheless has one speech that is nearly irrefutable, as he points out how much money the coach, the team, and the school make, and then adds, "Goddamn it, Coach, we *owe* those kids!" And at the end of the film, after the coach makes his decision and the final credits are rolling up the screen, we reflect that *Blue Chips* projects a certain cynicism even in the midst of its bedrock morality. The message seems to be that although one man can take a stand, the system has been too corrupt for too long to change.

Blue Collar ★ ★ ★ ★
R, 114 m., 1978

Richard Pryor (Zeke), Harvey Keitel (Jerry), Yaphet Kotto (Smokey), Ed Begley, Jr. (Bobby Joe), Harry Bellaver (Eddie Johnson), George Memmoli (Jenkins). Directed by Paul Schrader and produced by Don Guest. Screenplay by Paul and Leonard Schrader.

Detroit. Dawn. The next shift arrives for work. On the sound track, music of pounding urgency, suggesting the power of the machines that stamp out car doors from sheets of sheel. The camera takes us into the insides of an automobile factory, takes us close enough to almost smell the sweat and shield our eyes against the sparks thrown off by welding torches.

Blue Collar is about life on the Detroit assembly lines, and about how it wears men down and chains them to a lifetime installment plan. It is an angry, radical movie about the vise that traps workers between big industry and big labor. It's also an enormously entertaining movie; it earns its comparison with *On the Waterfront*. And it's an extraordinary directing debut for Paul Schrader, whose credits include *Taxi Driver* and *Rolling Thunder*.

Schrader tells the story of three workers, buddies on and off the job, who are all more or less in the same boat. They work, they drink after work in the bar across the street, they go home to mortgages or bills or kids who need braces on their teeth. One day they get fed up enough to decide to rob the safe in the office of their own union. What they find there is only a few hundred bucks— and a ledger that seems to contain the details of illegal loans of union funds.

The three guys are played by Richard Pryor, Harvey Keitel, and Yaphet Kotto, and they're all three at the top of their forms. Pryor, in particular, is a revelation: He's been good in a lot of movies, but almost always as himself, fast-talking, wise-cracking,

running comic variations on the themes suggested by his dialogue. This time, held in rein by Schrader, he provides a tight, convincing performance as a family man.

Yaphet Kotto plays his opposite, an excon who likes to throw all-night parties with lots of sex, booze, and grass. And Harvey Keitel is their white friend, always behind on his loan company payments, who comes home one day to discover that his daughter has tried to bend paper clips over her teeth to convince her friends at school that she's got the braces she should have.

Schrader goes for a nice, raunchy humor in the scenes involving the three guys: The movie is relaxed and comfortable with itself, and we get the precise textures and tones of the society they live in. We understand their friendship, too, because it defies one of the things the movie passionately charges: That unions and management tacitly collaborate on trying to set the rich against the poor, the black against the white, the old against the young, to divide and conquer.

The burglary caper begins innocently enough with Pryor's demand, at a union meeting, that the company repair his locker: He's cut his hand trying to get the damn thing open. But the union representatives seem indifferent to Pryor and just about everyone else, and so Pryor marches into the office of the shaggy, white-maned union leader who was a radical himself, once, back in the 1930s. And while the great statesman is feeding him several varieties of lies, Pryor sees the office safe and gets his idea.

The burglary itself finds the right line between humor and suspense, and then the movie's anger begins to burn. Because when the three men discover that the ledger may be more important than any money in the safe, they're torn between using it for blackmail, or using it to expose the corruption of their own union. Schrader gradually reveals his total vision in the film's second hour: A friendship that was sound and healthy suddenly goes sour. The system drives a wedge between them, as Pryor is offered a union job, Keitel becomes an FBI informer, and Kotto is killed in a scene of great and gruesome power.

It took a measure of courage to make *Blue Collar*, and especially to follow its events through to their inevitable conclusion. The movie could have copped out in its last thirty minutes, and given us a nice, safe Hollywood ending. Instead, it makes criticisms of mass production that social critics like Harvey

Swados and Paul Goodman might have agreed with. This isn't a liberal movie but a radical one, and one I suspect a lot of assembly-line workers might see with a shock of recognition.

It took courage to make the movie that honest. But it also took a special filmmaking gift to make it burst with humor, humanity, and suspense as well. Like *On the Waterfront*, it's both an indictment and an entertainment, working just as well on its human levels as with its theoretical concerns. Paul Schrader has been a Hollywood wonder kid ever since negotiating a $450,000 deal for his first screenplay, *The Yakuza*. After *Taxi Driver* and *Obsession*, he was able to demand that he direct his own work, and *Blue Collar* is a stunning debut, taking chances and winning at them.

The Blue Kite ★ ★ ★ ★   NEW
NO MPAA RATING, 138 m., 1994

Yi Tian (Tietou, infant), Zhang Wenyao (Tietou, child), Chen Xiaoman (Tietou, adolescent), Lu Liping (Mum), Pu Quanxin (Dad), Li Xuejian (Uncle Li [Li Guodong]), Guo Baochang (Stepfather [Lao Wu]). Directed by Tian Zhuangzhuang and produced by Longwick Film Production Ltd. and Beijing Film Studio. Screenplay by Xiao Mao.

I don't know if there really is an ancient Chinese curse that says, "May you live in interesting times," but after seeing *The Blue Kite* I can certainly understand the feeling behind it. During a period which has given us one great Chinese film after another, here is one of the most extraordinary, a sweep of modern Chinese history seen through the eyes of a single family.

Much of the story takes place in the apartments around a small courtyard in Beijing, where the hero, Tietou ("Iron Head"), is born in the early 1950s. His father is a librarian. Times are hard, food is scarce, but spirits are high and we sense the extraordinary camaraderie with which this family and their friends pull together. Events from the outside world, such as the death of Stalin, seem remote compared to the urgency of their daily lives. And as their lives unfold, we become so familiar with the details of life in their small apartment that, if we walked in, we would know where to sit at the table, and how the sleeping arrangements would be made.

But the outside world does intrude into this secure corner, in a scene that is chilling because it shows how lives can be altered by random chance. Political correctness has come to China, and the library staff is called into a meeting. Apparently it has not been self-critical enough, and has not been able to find any reactionaries in its midst. While the discussion continues, Tietou's father leaves the room to visit the toilet. When he returns, he is aware, in a sudden silence, that all eyes are upon him: He has been chosen as the reactionary.

He must leave Beijing and go to work on a collective farm, for "reeducation." And after he has gone, life will never be as secure or safe for Tietou and his mother. We follow their lives through two more marriages—as she is wed first to an army officer who is an old friend of the family, and later to a good man who is an intellectual.

The Blue Kite follows its characters from the 1950s until the late 1960s, and the Cultural Revolution. And during all of that time, it demonstrates, ordinary life was impossible because a series of political manias swept the land, and zealots sought out those who did not conform, and punished them. At times there is a looking-glass quality to the political movements: Citizens are found guilty because of behavior which only yesterday was proper and correct.

If there had been movies at the time of the American Revolution or the Civil War, they might have had the same excitement as this one, which springs so directly from daily experience and recent memory. No wonder the Chinese government disapproves of the film, and tried to prevent it from being finished and shown. Not enough years have passed for the wounds to heal, and although China is now caught in a capitalist fever, *The Blue Kite* is a reminder of a time, only a few years ago, when mobs marched through the streets, banging on pans and denouncing fellow citizens for reactionary behavior.

Take, for example, the woman who owns the apartments around the courtyard. She tries to follow first one wind of political orthodoxy and then another, but she can't win, and although she tries to be a good landlady she finds that her class itself makes her guilty. And we see how the pressures of that time caused friends to testify against one another, caused family members to be betrayed, caused the unpredictability of political fashions to make everyone a little crazy.

The Blue Kite was directed by Tian Zhuang-zhuang, who is not concerned with big political issues except as they impact on small

lives. It is the very everyday, ordinary quality of his story that makes his film important. To some degree *The Blue Kite* parallels the times and events of another extraordinary Chinese film, *Farewell My Concubine,* but that film came cloaked in the exoticism of the sexual and personal intrigues at the Peking Opera. *The Blue Kite* is a movie about people who never go to the opera, who live in one room, but whose lives would nevertheless be warm and rewarding if society would only leave them alone.

Because I have written about the implications of *The Blue Kite,* I may have given the impression it is an ideological, intellectual movie. Nothing could be more wrong. It is a film made out of daily lives and universal impulses—to form and care for a family, to watch over a child, to be able to depend on parents. The story is narrated by Tietou, who at one point confesses that the more he considers what happened to his family, the less he understands it. It is a shame the Chinese government will not allow this film to be shown in China, because I suspect it would touch a nerve something like *Forrest Gump* touched here. It gives us a protagonist who is buffeted by the winds of politics and chance—but whose basic human values and needs never change.

The Blues Brothers ★ ★ ★
R, 133 m., 1980

John Belushi (Jake Blues), Dan Aykroyd (Elwood Blues), Ray Charles (Ray), Aretha Franklin (Waitress), James Brown (Rev. James), Cab Calloway (Curtis), Charles Napier (Good Ol' Boy), Henry Gibson (Nazi), John Candy (Burton Mercer), Murphy Dunne (Piano Player), Carrie Fisher (Mystery Lady). Directed by John Landis and produced by Robert K. Weiss. Screenplay by Dan Aykroyd and Landis.

The Blues Brothers is the Sherman tank of musicals. When it was being filmed in Chicago in 1979—with dozens of cars piling up in intersections, caroming down Lake Shore Drive and crashing through the Daley Center—it seemed less like a film than a war. The movie feels the same way. It's a big, raucous powerhouse that proves against all the odds that if you're loud enough, vulgar enough, and have enough raw energy, you can make a steamroller into a musical, and vise versa.

This is some weird movie. There's never been anything that looked quite like it; was it dreamed up in a junkyard? It stars John Be-

lushi and Dan Aykroyd as the Blues Brothers, Jake and Elwood, characters who were created on "Saturday Night Live" and took on a fearsome life of their own. The movie tells us something of their backgrounds: They were reared in a sadistic West Side orphanage, learned the blues by osmosis, and, as the movie opens, have teamed up again after Jake's release from the Joliet pen.

The movie's plot is a simple one, to put it mildly. The brothers visit their old orphanage, learn that its future is in jeopardy because of five thousand dollars due in back taxes, and determine to raise the money by getting their old band together and putting on a show. Their odyssey takes them to several sleazy Chicago locations, including a Van Buren flophouse, Maxwell Street, and lower Wacker Drive. They find their old friends in unlikely places, like a restaurant run by Aretha Franklin, a music shop run by Ray Charles, and a gospel church run by James Brown.

Their adventures include run-ins with suburban cops, good ol' boys, and Nazis who are trying to stage a demonstration. One of the intriguing things about this movie is the way it borrows so freely and literally from news events. The plot develops into a sort of musical *Mad Mad Mad Mad World,* with the Blues Brothers being pursued at the same time by avenging cops, Nazis, and an enraged country and western band led by Charles Napier, that character actor with the smile like Jaws. The chase is interrupted from time to time for musical numbers, which are mostly very good and filled with high-powered energy.

Aretha Franklin occupies one of the movie's best scenes, in her South Side soul food restaurant. Cab Calloway, as a sort of road manager for the Blues Brothers, struts through a wonderful old-style production of *Minnie the Moocher.* The Brothers themselves star in several improbable numbers; the funniest has the band playing in a country and western bar where wire mesh has been installed to protect the band from beer bottles thrown by the customers.

I was saying the musical numbers interrupt the chases. The fact is, the whole movie is a chase, with Jake and Elwood piloting a used police car that seems, as it hurdles across suspension bridges from one side to the other, to have a life of its own. There can rarely have been a movie that made so free with its locations as this one. There are incredible, sensational chase sequences under the elevated train tracks, on overpasses, in subway tunnels under the Loop, and literally through Daley Center. One crash in particular, a pileup involving maybe a dozen police cars, has to be seen to be believed: I've never seen stunt coordination like this before.

What's a little startling about this movie is that all of this works. *The Blues Brothers* cost untold millions of dollars and kept threatening to grow completely out of control. But director John Landis (of *Animal House*) has somehow pulled it together, with a good deal of help from the strongly defined personalities of the title characters. Belushi and Aykroyd come over as hard-boiled city guys, total cynics with a world-view of sublime simplicity, and that all fits perfectly with the movie's other parts. There's even room, in the midst of the carnage and mayhem, for a surprising amount of grace, humor, and whimsy.

Blue Sky ★ ★ ★
PG-13, 101 m., 1994

Jessica Lange (Carly Marshall), Tommy Lee Jones (Hank Marshall), Powers Boothe (Vince Johnson), Carrie Snodgress (Vera Johnson), Amy Locane (Alex Marshall), Chris O'Donnell (Glenn Johnson), Mitchell Ryan (Ray Stevens), Dale Dye (Colonel Mike Anwalt). Directed by Tony Richardson and produced by Robert H. Solo. Screenplay by Rama Laurie Stagner, Arlene Sarner, and Jerry Leichtling.

Blue Sky is such an ungainly mixture of politics, emotion, and nostalgia that it's a wonder the movie works at all—but it does. It's set in the late 1950s, at a time when nuclear tests were stirring up doubts and fears, and it stars Tommy Lee Jones as Major Hank Marshall, an army career officer who is also a leading nuclear scientist. His science is sound, but his family life is a soap opera, led by his wife, Carly (Jessica Lange), and two teenage daughters.

Carly is the kind of service wife who inspires the other women on the base to lock up their husbands. She pores over *Life* magazine reports from the Cannes film festival and then sunbathes topless on the beach and daydreams that she might have gone to Hollywood and become a Bardot or a Monroe, if things had just worked out a little differently.

As the movie opens, the Marshalls are transferred to Alabama, where the base commander, Vince Johnson (Powers Boothe), finds himself at the officers' club doing a dance with Carly that is just this side of vertical foreplay. He soon assigns Hank Marshall to fly out to Nevada to supervise some underground testing, and Hank, who is not a fool, asks his wife, "How did David steal Bathsheba away from her husband?"

The answer, of course, is that he sent him away to do battle. And in Nevada Hank finds himself concerned with the safety of underground tests, especially after one vents radioactivity into the atmosphere, and probably poisons two civilian cowboys who are too close. The Atomic Energy Commission and the army, caught in a Cold War frenzy, don't want any publicity about the bad side effects of testing. And meanwhile General Johnson has been doing a little underground testing of his own, with Carly Marshall.

Johnson's wife (Carrie Snodgress) knows exactly what is going on. She's been through this before. "You know what you mean to me?" she asks Carly. "One less Christmas card."

But when her son (Chris O'Donnell) and the Marshalls' older daughter (Amy Locane) also begin to wander off-limits together, it all becomes very tricky, especially after Marshall flies back to Alabama with a demand that the government look for the two contaminated cowboys. For reasons both public and private, Johnson has him committed to a mental hospital. And that barely scratches the surface of a plot which also invests a lot of energy into remembering what it was like to live in the 1950s.

Blue Sky is the last film directed by the late Tony Richardson, whose work includes *Loneliness of the Long Distance Runner, Tom Jones,* and *The Loved One.* It was caught in the financial collapse of Orion Pictures, and was finally released in 1994, after a couple of years on the shelf. That means it was made before Tommy Lee Jones got his Oscar nominations for *Under Siege* and *The Fugitive* and became a hot star. Here we can see him in a subdued role, as an intelligent, principled man who is married to a troubled woman but loves her.

A lot of *Blue Sky* involves the domestic turmoil of the Marshalls, who have lived on a lot of army bases and seen Carly make a display of herself on all of them. Hank tends to objectify the situation. "What we call love," he tells his daughters, "is really the exchange of energy over time. It's simple quantum mechanics." Very nice, but is that a consolation when she has a few drinks and starts doing her sexpot act? "I made a decision a long time ago, just to love her basic qualities," he tells his girls. But the older girl tells her sister: "He's blind and she's crazy. They're perfect for each other."

The strange thing is, that's exactly right. And we see the value of her craziness in the movie's third act, which I will not describe here. Jessica Lange's character has seemed basically just very disturbed until these closing scenes, when we sense an instinctive intelligence and a fierce idea of justice which must be what her husband sensed in her all along.

The relationship between Hank and Carly is interesting precisely because it never does play out the way we expect it to. She is promiscuous and yet loyal to her husband; he is cheated on, and yet proud and strong; as a couple, they have strengths neither has alone. And in an odd way, they do raise their children well, although it is hard to see how. *Blue Sky* is the kind of movie that is constantly surprising us with the originality of its developments. We think we know some of this material, and where it will lead, and how it can be resolved, and we are wrong.

Blue Steel ★ ★
R, 95 m., 1990

Jamie Lee Curtis (Megan Turner), Ron Silver (Eugene Hunt), Clancy Brown (Nick Mann), Elizabeth Pena (Tracy Perez), Louise Fletcher (Shirley Turner), Philip Bosco (Frank Turner). Directed by Kathryn Bigelow and produced by Edward R. Pressman and Oliver Stone. Screenplay by Bigelow and Eric Red.

Squint a little to see the structure lurking beneath the details, and *Blue Steel* is a sophisticated update of *Halloween,* the movie that first made Jamie Lee Curtis a star. She plays the competent, strong woman who finally has to defend herself because nobody else can. Her life is endangered by a man who seems unstoppable, unkillable: No matter what happens to him, he picks himself up, pulls himself together, and continues his inexorable pursuit.

Curtis plays a New York cop who graduates from the police academy in the pretitle sequence, and the movie's villain is Ron Silver, a commodities broker who goes off the deep end. The plot is a little of *Fatal Attraction,* a little of *Jagged Edge,* and a little of *Wall Street.* It works because it's so audacious in combining elements that don't seem to belong together.

As the movie opens, Curtis shoots and kills a stickup man on her first day on the job.

As the man drops dead in a supermarket, his gun spins out of control over the tile floor and is picked up and pocketed by Silver—a customer who hit the deck when the shooting started. He is already a deeply troubled man, and the sight of Curtis—a uniformed female cop—shooting a man dead is the image that pushes him over the edge.

It goes without saying that Curtis gets in trouble with her superiors at the department (the only reason commanding officers appear in cop movies is to wrongheadedly strip the heroes of their badges and guns). In the meantime, however, her social life picks up: Silver arranges to meet her "by accident," and they begin to date. She really likes the guy. And of course she never suspects that he was present in the supermarket or has a weirdo reason for being attracted to her—not even when dead people begin turning up around New York with her name engraved on the bullets they were shot with.

The movie is not simply a series of violent encounters—not at first, anyway. There's a half-realized subplot involving Curtis's parents (Louise Fletcher and Philip Bosco), and some vague psychological hints about why Bosco hates the idea of his daughter becoming a cop. The movie's weakest scene is the one where Curtis and her father leave his home for the sole purpose of not being there when Silver arrives, so she can be chilled when she finds him there on her return. The manipulation here is so awkward the scene should have been rewritten on the spot.

Other moments are much more convincing. What happens is that no one—especially not the men of the police department—believes Curtis's version of events. Nor do they believe that a respectable commodities broker could possibly be a mass murderer. The Silver character is intelligent enough to set up situations so that Curtis is seen in the worst possible way, until finally she seems to be the killer herself. But what does Silver want? In a truly diabolical twist, it appears that he wants to be murdered by this woman cop; he was truly unhinged by the experience in the supermarket. Silver does a good job of gradually revealing the demented depths of his character.

Blue Steel was directed by Kathryn Bigelow, whose previous credit was the well-regarded *Near Dark*. Does that make it a fundamentally different picture than if it had been directed by a man? Perhaps, in a way. The female "victim" is never helpless here, although she is set up in all the usual

ways ordained by male-oriented thrillers. She can fight back with her intelligence, her police training, and her physical strength. And there is an anger in the way the movie presents the male authorities in the film, who are blinded to the facts by their preconceptions about women in general and female cops in particular.

The bottom line, however, is that *Blue Steel* is an efficient thriller, a movie that pays off with one shock and surprise after another, including a couple of really serpentine twists and a couple of superior examples of the killer-jumping-unexpectedly-from-the-dark scenes. I always feel dumb after I jump during one of those scenes. But I always jump.

Blue Velvet ★
R, 120 m., 1986

Kyle MacLachlan (Jeffrey Beaumont), Isabella Rossellini (Dorothy Valiens), Dennis Hopper (Frank Booth), Laura Dern (Sandy Williams), Hope Lange (Mrs. Williams), Dean Stockwell (Gar), George Dickerson (Detective Williams). Directed by David Lynch and produced by Richard Roth. Screenplay by Lynch.

Blue Velvet contains scenes of such raw emotional energy that it's easy to understand why some critics have hailed it as a masterpiece. A film this painful and wounding has to be given special consideration. And yet those very scenes of stark sexual despair are the tip-off to what's wrong with the movie. They're so strong that they deserve to be in a movie that is sincere, honest, and true. But *Blue Velvet* surrounds them with a story that's marred by sophomoric satire and cheap shots. The director is either denying the strength of his material or trying to defuse it by pretending it's all part of a campy in-joke.

The movie has two levels of reality. On one level, we're in Lumberton, a simple-minded small town where people talk in television clichés and seem to be clones of 1950s sitcom characters. On another level, we're told a story of sexual bondage, of how Isabella Rossellini's husband and son have been kidnapped by Dennis Hopper, who makes her his sexual slave. The twist is that the kidnapping taps into the woman's deepest feelings. She finds that she is a masochist who responds with great sexual passion to this situation.

Everyday town life is depicted with a dead-pan irony; characters use lines with corny double meanings and solemnly recite platitudes. Meanwhile, the darker story of sexual

bondage is told absolutely on the level in cold-blooded realism.

The movie begins with a much-praised sequence in which picket fences and flower beds establish a small-town idyll. Then a man collapses while watering the lawn, and a dog comes to drink from the hose that is still held in his unconscious grip. The great imagery continues as the camera burrows into the green lawn and finds hungry insects beneath—a metaphor for the surface and buried lives of the town.

The man's son, a college student (Kyle MacLachlan), comes home to visit his dad's bedside and resumes a romance with the daughter (Laura Dern) of the local police detective. MacLachlan finds a severed human ear in a field, and he and Dern get involved in trying to solve the mystery of the ear. The trail leads to a nightclub singer (Rossellini) who lives alone in a starkly furnished flat.

In a sequence that Hitchcock would have been proud of, MacLachlan hides himself in Rossellini's closet and watches, shocked, as she has a sadomasochistic sexual encounter with Hopper, a drug-sniffing pervert. Hopper leaves. Rossellini discovers MacLachlan in the closet and, to his astonishment, pulls a knife on him and forces him to submit to her seduction. He is appalled but fascinated; she wants him to be a "bad boy" and hit her.

These sequences have great power. They make *9½ Weeks* look rather timid by comparison, because they do seem genuinely born from the darkest and most despairing side of human nature. If *Blue Velvet* had continued to develop its story in a straight line, if it had followed more deeply into the implications of the first shocking encounter between Rossellini and MacLachlan, it might have made some real emotional discoveries.

Instead, director David Lynch chose to interrupt the almost hypnotic pull of that relationship in order to pull back to his jokey, small-town satire. Is he afraid that movie audiences might not be ready for stark S&M unless they're assured it's all really a joke?

I was absorbed and convinced by the relationship between Rossellini and MacLachlan, and annoyed because the director kept placing himself between me and the material. After five or ten minutes in which the screen reality was overwhelming, I didn't need the director prancing on with a top hat and cane, whispering that it was all in fun.

Indeed, the movie is pulled so violently in opposite directions that it pulls itself apart. If the sexual scenes are real, then why do we need the send-up of the "Donna Reed Show"? What are we being told? That beneath the surface of Small Town, U.S.A., passions run dark and dangerous? Don't stop the presses.

The sexual material in *Blue Velvet* is so disturbing, and the performance by Rossellini is so convincing and courageous, that it demands a movie that deserves it. American movies have been using satire for years to take the edge off sex and violence. Occasionally, perhaps sex and violence should be treated with the seriousness they deserve. Given the power of the darker scenes in this movie, we're all the more frustrated that the director is unwilling to follow through to the consequences of his insights. *Blue Velvet* is like the guy who drives you nuts by hinting at horrifying news and then saying, "Never mind."

There's another thing. Rossellini is asked to do things in this film that require real nerve. In one scene, she's publicly embarrassed by being dumped naked on the lawn of the police detective. In others, she is asked to portray emotions that I imagine most actresses would rather not touch. She is degraded, slapped around, humiliated, and undressed in front of the camera. And when you ask an actress to endure those experiences, you should keep your side of the bargain by putting her in an important film.

That's what Bernardo Bertolucci delivered when he put Marlon Brando and Maria Schneider through the ordeal of *Last Tango in Paris*. In *Blue Velvet*, Rossellini goes the whole distance, but Lynch distances himself from her ordeal with his clever asides and witty little in-jokes. In a way, his behavior is more sadistic than the Hopper character.

What's worse? Slapping somebody around, or standing back and finding the whole thing funny?

Blume in Love ★ ★ ★ ★
R, 116 m., 1973

George Segal (Blume), Susan Anspach (Nina), Kris Kristofferson (Elmo), Marsha Mason (Arlene), Shelley Winters (Mrs. Cramer), Donald F. Muhich (Analyst), Paul Mazursky (Hellman). Directed, produced, and written by Paul Mazursky.

Paul Mazursky's *Blume in Love* begins with a busted-up Southern California marriage.

The marriage belonged to Blume, divorce lawyer, and his wife Nina, a social worker. It busted up all of a sudden one weekday afternoon when Nina came home with a cold and found Blume in bed with his secretary. Why, you may ask (Blume certainly does), could his wife not forgive this indiscretion—especially as Blume is madly in love with Nina and must have her back or die? ("And I don't want to die," he reasons, "so I have to get her back.")

Well, maybe Nina was sort of halfway ready for the marriage to end. She's into her own brand of self-improvement and women's lib, and isn't sure she approves of marriage anymore. She takes up with an out-of-work (for twelve years) musician who lives in a VW truck with his dreams. She gets into yoga and learns to play the guitar and to rely on herself instead of men.

Little good that does Blume, whose love for her becomes a consuming passion. It is complicated by the fact that he gets to like the musician, too: thinks, in fact, that the bearded Elmo is the nicest man he has ever met. Blume even goes so far as to start a beard himself. But nothing will work for him, because of the fact he refuses to accept: Nina simply does not love him anymore. Does not. Period. Blume is driven into a frenzy of love, desire, frustration.

This material, so far, doesn't exactly sound like the stuff of a great film. It sounds more like the brainy, funny dissections of California dreamin' that Mazursky carried out in three previous films, *I Love You, Alice B. Toklas, Bob & Carol & Ted & Alice*, and *Alex in Wonderland*. Those were all fine films—Mazursky is one of the best directors of comedy in Hollywood—but they were all more concerned with the laugh than with reality.

With *Blume in Love*, however, he seems to have pulled off what everybody is always hoping for from Neil Simon: a comedy that transcends its funny moments, that realizes we laugh so we may not cry, and that finally is about real people with real desperations. He's done that in a number of scenes, and yet somehow even during the movie's gloomiest moments he keeps some sort of hope alive. That's probably because Blume is played by the charming George Segal, who seems intrinsically optimistic. No matter what Nina says, he cannot quite give up on her, because he knows she must eventually love him again—because he loves her.

He carries this hope with him on a trip to Venice, which is where the film opens; she's asked him to go away somewhere for a couple of weeks, while she thinks. They had their first and second honeymoons in Venice, but now Blume wanders through Piazza San Marco in the autumn, stranded with a few other lonely tourists looking for love. The story is told in flashbacks from Venice, and it ends there. It ends with a note so unashamedly romantic that Mazursky gets away with "Tristan and Isolde" as his soundtrack music. He's right. The ending would not be believable at all, except as hyperbole.

Nina—thin, earnest, determined to do the right thing and no longer be mastered by mere emotion—is played with a very complex charm by Susan Anspach. We have to like her even though she doesn't like Blume, whom we're cheering for. We do, and we like her boyfriend as much as Blume does. The itinerant musician is played by Kris Kristofferson, who gives evidence once again that he has a real acting talent—particularly in the scene where he hits Segal and then bursts into tears, and in the scene where he tells Segal he's hitting the road again.

Blume in Love has a quality that's hard to analyze but impossible to miss: It sets up an intimate rapport with its audiences.

Bob Roberts ★ ★ ★
R, 103 m., 1992

Tim Robbins (Bob Roberts), Giancarlo Esposito (Bugs Raplin), Ray Wise (Chet MacGregor), Gore Vidal (Sen. Brickley Paiste), Alan Rickman (Lucas Hart III). Directed by Tim Robbins and produced by Forrest Murray. Screenplay by Robbins.

Bob Roberts isn't simply another satire about slimy political schemes. It's a satire about a whole mind-set, about the anything-goes greed of the 1980s, when decent American values were replaced by the cold cynicism of management experts. The bottom line became the only line. Winning was everything. The self-promotion spawned by the aggressive new M.B.A. programs made business into a new kind of jungle—one where the animals ate even when they weren't hungry.

Bob Roberts, the hero of Tim Robbins's new film, is a "populist" candidate for the Senate in Pennsylvania. He's a self-made millionaire who sings folk songs to his audiences, songs with titles like "The Times They Are A-Changin' Back." For him, as for others, populism no longer means the solidarity of the working class; it means its division—race against race, worker against worker, with hate being stirred up to obscure the real enemy: the profit-takers who are raping the companies and leaving them stripped and dead.

Roberts, played by Robbins, is a tall, open-faced man with an infectious grin that can turn, in an instant, into a mask of anger. His message to his supporters is that greed is good. From certain angles, in a certain light, he looks uncannily like another two-faced populist, Citizen Kane. His opponent is a weary old liberal senator named Brickley Paiste (Gore Vidal), whose message seems irrelevant. Voters don't want to hear about right or wrong. They have one question: What's in it for me?

The movie is shot as if it were a documentary. The cameras are sometimes on when they're not supposed to be. We eavesdrop on conversations we're not meant to hear. We begin to understand the sinister implications of the Bob Roberts campaign. His campaign bus isn't just a headquarters; it's a trading center. He's got brokers buying and selling day and night. His connections are unsavory. There are rumors about arms deals and savings-and-loan scandals. His campaign manager (Alan Rickman) is a study in realpolitik: Anything is justified if it will win votes. There is even an attack on poor old Paiste for dating teen-age girls. There are photos for proof. Paiste protests: "That's my daughter's best friend. My daughter was cut out of the picture." Nobody listens and nobody cares.

I like *Bob Roberts*—I like its audacity, and its freedom to say the obvious things about how our political process has been debased—but if it had been only about campaign tactics and techniques, I would have liked it more. There is another thread in the movie that doesn't work as well. It involves an investigative journalist named Bugs Raplin (Giancarlo Esposito), who has inside dirt on Roberts, and is eventually framed through a singularly unlikely chain of events. Even before the movie's unconvincing ending, Bugs has been a distraction because the character behaves like some kind of goofball; he may have the facts, but he doesn't seem trustworthy, and the movie would have been more effective if it had treated this part of the plot more realistically.

Apart from that, though, *Bob Roberts* is quite a package. Watching it might be an education for some voters, who will recognize in the movie political techniques they see being practiced all the time in real life. There is an eerie quality to Roberts's down-home fascism, the way he strums that guitar and

unashamedly looks like a Woody Guthrie, a Bob Dylan, a folk-singing regular guy, while his lyrics give us the litany of greed.

Tim Robbins made this movie mostly by himself. He wrote it, directed it, and stars in it, and maybe that uncanny visual resemblance to the young Orson Welles is poetic justice. It's quite an achievement. Robbins has a range from the endearing baseball rookie in *Bull Durham* to the cold Hollywood executive in *The Player*, and here he uses his very attractiveness—his open nature, his sunny smile—to show the hazards of choosing a political candidate on the basis of his ability to make us feel comfortable.

Body Double ★ ★ ★ ½
R, 110 m., 1984

Craig Wasson (Jake), Melanie Griffith (Holly), Gregg Henry (Sam), Deborah Shelton (Gloria). Directed and produced by Brian De Palma. Screenplay by Robert H. Averch and De Palma.

Body Double is an exhilarating exercise in pure filmmaking, a thriller in the Hitchcock tradition in which there's no particular point except that the hero is flawed, weak, and in terrible danger—and we identify with him completely. The movie is so cleverly constructed, with the emphasis on visual storytelling rather than dialogue, that we are neither faster nor slower than the hero as he gradually figures out the scheme that has entrapped him. And the casting of a Hitchcockian average guy also helps.

The movie stars Craig Wasson, an openfaced actor with an engaging smile, as its hero, an unemployed actor named Jake. He isn't smart, he isn't dumb, he isn't perfect, he isn't bad. He is an ideal choice to set up as a witness to a murder. Jake needs a place to stay, and another actor (Gregg Henry) offers him a job house-sitting in a weird, modernistic home on stilts up in the hills above Los Angeles. The other actor also points out all the sights—including a shapely neighbor who does a nightly striptease dance in front of her open window. Jake is only human. For two nights, he uses a telescope to watch the striptease. He also begins to suspect that the woman may be in danger. In sequences inspired by *Rear Window*, he begins to follow the woman (Deborah Shelton), but he keeps his distance because he's caught in the same dilemma as Jimmy Stewart was in the Hitchcock picture: He is, after all, technically a Peeping Tom, and he wouldn't know the

woman was in danger if he hadn't been breaking the law.

Since the plot is so important in *Body Double*, and because the movie contains so many nice surprises, I won't reveal very much more of the story. Let me describe in a carefully vague way, however, some of the pleasures of the movie. After a murder does indeed seem to have been committed, Jake's path leads him into the world of pornographic filmmaking. He wants to meet and hire a porno superstar (Melanie Griffith) who he thinks can help him figure out the mystery. His attempts lead to a series of very funny conversations, as the blond porno actress talks to him with a Runyonesque mixture of jaded sophistication and startling ignorance. The speech in which she explains exactly what she will, and will not, do in a movie is shocking, sad, and curiously moving. *Body Double*'s excursion into the world of pornography (we see some fairly mild porno scenes, shot by De Palma himself) is part of a veritable anthology of styles in this movie. The film opens with a satire on vampire movies, includes a Hitchcockian cat-and-mouse sequence, and even borrows some of the clichés of 1940s thrillers, including a detailed recapitulation at the end, complete with flashbacks. There is also a sharp 1940s look to the cinematography, which uses dramatic lighting, tilted cameras, and carefully constructed shots to make the style part of the story.

But the movie is not just an exercise in style. It is also a genuinely terrifying thriller, in which an almost clockwork plot brings the hero and the killer together without a single logical glitch. De Palma is at home in this genre. Although his *Scarface* was more of a serious social commentary, thrilling suspense movies are his specialty, and his credits include *Carrie*, *Obsession*, and *Dressed to Kill*. With *Body Double*, he has his most airtight plot. He also has, once again, his almost unique courage to go over the top—to push scenes beyond the edge of common sense and into cheerfully heightened and impassioned overkill. The burial sequence next to the Hollywood reservoir, for example, or the photography in the tunnel during one of Jake's attacks of claustrophobia, are so uninhibited that they skirt the dangerous edge of being ridiculous. But because the story's so strong, they're not. They work.

The Bodyguard ★ ★ ★
R, 129 m., 1992

Kevin Costner (Frank Farmer), Whitney Houston (Rachel Marron), Gary Kemp (Sy Spector), Bill Cobbs (Devaney), Ralph Waite (Herb Farmer), Tomas Arana (Portman). Directed by Mick Jackson and produced by Lawrence Kasdan, Jim Wilson, and Kevin Costner. Screenplay by Kasdan.

The ads for *The Bodyguard* make it look like a romance, but actually it's a study of two lifestyles: of a pop music superstar whose fame and fortune depends on millions of fans, and of a professional bodyguard who makes his living by protecting her from those fans. The movie does contain a love story, but it's the kind of guarded passion that grows between two people who spend a lot of time keeping their priorities straight.

The star is Rachel Marron, played by Whitney Houston, as rich and famous as . . . Whitney Houston. The bodyguard is Frank Farmer (Kevin Costner), who got his training in the Secret Service and still blames himself for the fact that Ronald Reagan got shot, even though he had an excellent excuse for being away from work that day. Now Farmer hires himself out at $3,000 a week to guard celebrities, and is careful not to get involved.

Of course, that's easy at the outset. He is hired by Marron's manager after the singer gets death threats, which at first she's not told about. It's not love at first sight. The conventions of this genre require, of course, that the star and bodyguard have to get off on the wrong foot; she doesn't want him meddling with her life-style and freedom, and he doesn't have any respect for an uncooperative client.

Eventually the tension between them melts, and there is a sort of love affair, based mostly on mutual proximity (they never talk about much but their professional relationship, and the skills of his job). There's an odd, effective dating scene where she leaves her mansion to visit his cluttered, grim little apartment (and a peculiar moment with a samurai sword and a scarf that is undeniably erotic, although I'm still trying to figure out why).

Meanwhile, Frank gets to know some of the members of Rachel's retinue, including her son, her sister, her manager, and her obnoxious press agent (Gary Kemp), who is full of himself, among other things. These people are supported by Rachel, and live with her on her terms, creating eddies of jealousy and palace intrigue. She is aware of her power, and tells Farmer she is essentially a nice person who is considered a bitch by a lot of people, and wishes that weren't so. Houston is effective at suggesting both sides of that personality.

The death threats keep coming in. There is a frightening scene at a charity concert, where Rachel essentially places her personal safety in the hands of a mob, and Farmer, with all of his skills, is powerless to protect her. I was less impressed by the scenes where he wires her estate with security cameras, and at one point goes crashing through her shrubbery in pursuit of a suspicious van. What's he going to do? Leap onto the roof and hammer his way in through the windshield?

The movie was written by Lawrence Kasdan *(Body Heat, Grand Canyon)* and directed by Mick Jackson, and it contains a little of the Hollywood insider cynicism that Kasdan suggested in the Steve Martin character in *Grand Canyon*. The willingness of the press agent to risk anything for publicity is noted, as well as the star's sense of personal invulnerability. This is Houston's screen debut, and she is at home in the role; she photographs wonderfully well and has a warm smile, and yet is able to suggest selfish and egotistical dimensions in the character. Costner hugs her with his eyes open, scanning the room for surprise attacks.

The movie was made as a thriller, I suppose, because of box-office considerations. I felt a little cheated by the outcome, although I should have been able to predict it, using my Law of Economy of Characters, which teaches that no movie contains any unnecessary characters, so that an apparently superfluous character is probably the killer. I thought the basic situation in *The Bodyguard* was intriguing enough to sustain a film all by itself: On the one hand, a star who grows rich through the adulation that fans feel for her, and on the other hand, a working man who, for a salary, agrees to substitute his body as a target instead of hers. Makes you think.

Body Snatchers ★ ★ ★ ★
R, 87 m., 1994

Terry Kinney (Steve Malone), Meg Tilly (Carol Malone), Gabrielle Anwar (Marti Malone), Reilly Murphy (Andy Malone), Billy Wirth (Tim Young), Christine Elise (Jenn Platt), Forest Whitaker (Dr. Collins). Directed by Abel Ferrara and produced by Robert H. Solo. Screenplay by Stuart Gordon, Dennis Paoli, and Nicholas St. John.

Sometimes I'll be looking at someone I know, and a wave of uncertainty will sweep over me. I'll see them in a cold, objective light: "Who is this person—really?" Everything I know about others is based on trust, on the assumption that a "person" is inside them, just as a person clearly seems to be inside me. But what if everybody else only *looks* normal? What if, inside, they're something else altogether, and my world is a laboratory, and I am a specimen?

These spells do not come often, nor do they stay long, nor do I take them seriously. But they reflect a shadowy feeling many people have from time to time. And the classic story of the body snatchers taps into those fears at an elemental level. Since Jack Finney wrote his original novel in the 1940s, his vision of pod people has been filmed three times: in 1956 and 1978 as *Invasion of the Body Snatchers*, by Don Siegel and Philip Kaufman, and now simply as *Body Snatchers*, by Abel Ferrara. The first film fed on the paranoia of McCarthyism. The second film seemed to signal the end of the flower people and the dawn of the Me Generation. And this one? Maybe fear of AIDS is the engine.

Ferrara's version is set on an army base in the South, and told through the eyes of a teen-age girl named Marti (Gabrielle Anwar) who has moved there with her family. Her dad (Terry Kinney) is a consultant. She doesn't get along well with her stepmother (Meg Tilly), although she likes her stepbrother (Reilly Murphy). Before the family even arrives on the base, Marti has been grabbed by a runaway soldier in a gas station rest room, who shakes her and says: "They're out there!"

And they are. It gradually becomes clear that visitors from outer space have arrived near the army base, unloading pods, which they store in a nearby swamp. The pods send out tentacles toward sleeping humans, the tendrils snaking up into noses and ears and open mouths and somehow draining out the life force, while the pod swells into a perfect replica of the person being devoured. When the process is complete, the leftover body is a shell, and the new pod person looks and sounds just like someone you know and trust.

There is a catch. They don't look quite right around the eyes. And they don't seem to possess ordinary human emotions, like jealousy. Their goal is to occupy the human race, rent-free. And of course, once Marti understands what is happening, she can't get anyone to believe her.

Ferrara, a talented but uneven director, is capable of making one of the best films of the year (*Bad Lieutenant*, 1993) and one of the worst (*Dangerous Game*, 1993). Here, working in a genre unfamiliar to him, he finds the right note in scene after scene. There is horror here—especially in the gruesome scenes that show us exactly how the pods go about their sneaky business—but there is also ordinary human emotion, as Marti and her boyfriend deal with the fact that people are changing into pods all around them.

Ferrara and his writers are also clever in placing the body-snatching story in the middle of a preexisting family crisis. Marti and her stepmother do not get along, and there is a sense in which the teen-age girl already feels that her "real" mother has been usurped by an impostor, and her father subverted. Even her little brother is an enigma: She likes him, but resents having to share love and space with him. So if some of these people turn out to be pods, the psychological basis for her revulsion has already been established.

Ferrara's key scenes mostly take place at night, on the army base, where most of the other people are already podlike in their similar uniforms, language, and behavior. There is a crafty connection made between the army's code of rigid conformity and the behavior of the pod people, who seem like a logical extension of the same code.

Most important, for a horror film, there are scenes of genuine terror. One shot in particular, involving a helicopter, is as scary as anything in *The Exorcist* or *The Silence of the Lambs*. And the fright is generated, not by the tired old slasher trick of having someone jump out of the screen, but by the careful establishing of situations in which we fear, and then our fears are confirmed.

Body Snatchers had its world premiere in May of 1993 in the official competition of the Cannes Film Festival, where the outspoken Ferrara did not endear himself by claiming that Jane Campion's *The Piano* was such a favorite "the jury gave her the award when she got off the plane." Certainly *Body Snatchers* is not the kind of movie that wins festivals: It is a hard-boiled entry in a disreputable genre. But as sheer moviemaking, it is skilled and knowing, and deserves the highest praise you can give a horror film: It works.

The Bonfire of the Vanities ★ ★ ½
R, 126 m., 1990

Tom Hanks (Sherman McCoy), Bruce Willis (Peter Fallow), Melanie Griffith (Maria Ruskin), Kim Cattrall (Judy McCoy), Saul Rubinek (Jed Kramer), Morgan Freeman (Judge White), Alan King (Arthur Ruskin). Directed and produced by Brian De Palma. Screenplay by Michael Cristofer.

Tom Wolfe's saga about Sherman McCoy has by now become one of America's favorite urban legends, a cautionary tale about a "master of the universe" who was earning millions on Wall Street and enjoying the pleasures of his wife, his mistress, and his seductive lifestyle, when he made one fatal wrong turn off the expressway and found himself in the South Bronx.

There, in a ludicrous comedy of errors, his mistress ran their car into a black youth she thought was attacking them. The youth died, and the case became an overnight sensation. Sherman, whose life was graced with every material and sensual excess, found himself plunged into a publicity circus, suffered the indignity of being jailed, and became the target of white political opportunists and black self-promoters who saw him as a convenient and hateful symbol.

The Bonfire of the Vanities, Wolfe's novel about McCoy, was savage and sarcastic, especially in the way it dissected the motives of every single character. Brian De Palma's movie is lacking in just that quality; it is not subtle or perceptive about the delicate nuances of motive that inspire these people. My notion is that Wolfe sees every single one of his characters in exactly the same light, as selfish, grasping swine who want to get their hands on everything they can, and whose approaches are suggested by the opportunities they find around them in whatever walk of life they occupy. The movie doesn't seem to despise anyone all that much.

Sherman McCoy, who makes millions and lives in a Park Avenue duplex, is no less selfish than the others in the novel, but he is not much of a survivor. He does well on the sedate battlefield of Wall Street, but when he runs into *real* fighters—cops, neighborhood activists, politicians, newspaper reporters, publicity hounds, ambulance-chasing lawyers, and his neighbors on the co-op board—he finds he's no match.

The Wolfe novel goes inside the characters' minds and lifestyles, showing how they think and what they value. The movie sees mostly the exteriors, and although it is narrated by one of the characters—Peter Fallow, the journalist, played by Bruce Willis—he provides few insights and little verbal grace, serving mostly just to hurry the story along. And yet it is enough of a story, and the actors are colorful enough in their different ways, that *The Bonfire of the Vanities* is an entertaining film, even if it misses the droll qualities of the book.

Tom Hanks stars as Sherman McCoy, but is more acted upon than acting in this movie. He has two typical expressions here: crafty cunning and disbelief shading into horror. He is never really developed as a character we feel we know, and he seems to inhabit his lifestyle rather than possess it. He generates no sympathy—but then he isn't supposed to. Much more interesting is Melanie Griffith, as Maria, his sexy mistress, who is utterly carnal, self-serving, and shameless.

The weakest character in the movie is Fallow, the journalist, played by Willis. He is supposed to be a drunk, and so the movie opens with him waving a bottle as he emerges from a limousine. But the movie makes no attempt to turn him into an interesting character with a personality—he doesn't have the moxie or the smarts to be the kind of reporter he's representing. He just mopes about, sighing and shrugging and raising his eyebrows. The Fallow created by Wolfe in the book was a great fictional character, a shameless, free-loading con artist who uses the McCoy story as a ploy to keep his job.

Other important characters are glimpsed as if at a distance. It helps to have read the book to understand the motives of the white lawyer who suddenly materializes at the side of the victim's grieving mother. And without having read the book, it is impossible to know the true motives of the two black youths who materialize in the shadows of the expressway and strike terror into the hearts of Sherman and Maria; they are played simply as menacing symbols. De Palma misses a bet, too, with the character of the black minister and community leader—obviously inspired by Al Sharpton—by making him a comic blowhard rather than the scheming, intelligent grafter of the Wolfe novel. One of the more effective characters is played by Morgan Freeman, pounding away on his gavel as Sherman's angry judge. He has a delicious final speech that is filled with irony—he has arrived at the right verdict, but because of Sherman's lies about a crucial piece of evidence.

If *The Bonfire of the Vanities* lacks the texture and detail that would make it realistic, at least it does work well in a certain glossy way. Sharp satirical points are made, often as throwaways, and there are little moments of truth, as when Fallow takes Ruskin (Alan King), Maria's husband, out to dinner. Kim Cattrall goes way over the top as Sherman's wife, Judy, but sometimes that works, as when she tries to give a dinner party while her world crumbles around her. (A famous scene from the book, in which she explains to their child that daddy makes his millions by taking crumbs from other people's cakes, is overplayed and underlined until it dies.)

What we have here, I think, is a movie that will be enjoyed most by those who haven't read the Tom Wolfe novel. In its glittering surfaces and snapshot performances, it provides a digest version of the Wolfe story, filled with obvious ironies and easy targets. Those who have read the book will be constantly distracted because they know so much more than the movie tells them about the characters. The beauty of the Wolfe book was the way it saw through its time and place, dissecting motives and reading minds. The movie sees much, but it doesn't see through.

Boomerang ★ ★ ★
R, 118 m., 1992

Eddie Murphy (Marcus Graham), Robin Givens (Jacqueline), Halle Berry (Angela), Martin Lawrence (Tyler), David Alan Grier (Gerard), Eartha Kitt (Lady Eloise), Grace Jones (Strange), Geoffrey Holder (Nelson). Directed by Reginald Hudlin and produced by Brian Grazer and Warrington Hudlin. Screenplay by Barry W. Blaustein and David Sheffield.

In May of 1991, at the Cannes Film Festival, Eddie Murphy joined the audience that saw John Singleton's *Boyz N the Hood,* and afterward he led the cheering. I wondered exactly what he was doing there; superstars never attend film festivals unless they have films in competition. And they certainly never sit in ordinary audiences. I wondered if perhaps, after two misguided flops in a row—*Another 48 HRS* and *Harlem Nights*—and the resulting bad rap, Murphy was seeking out new influences to redirect his career.

If that was the case, then *Boomerang* is powerful evidence that he's back on track. It shows a kinder, gentler, funnier Eddie Murphy than we've seen in recent years—a comic actor who can go for the little laughs as well

as the big ones, and build a character at the same time. In the movie, he's Marcus Graham, top executive in a cosmetics company, whose free time is spent in the tireless pursuit of women. He seduces them and dumps them with no compassion, until one day a female executive (Robin Givens) becomes his boss and starts treating him in exactly the same way.

The story for *Boomerang* is credited to Murphy, who may have seen this as an amends after *Harlem Nights,* a shockingly sexist movie that included one scene where the Murphy character shot a woman dead while she was making love to him. This time the tables are turned. As Givens seduces Murphy, dumps him, picks him up again, casts him away again, the whole demeanor of his character changes; he loses the bouncy step and the self-confident chuckle, and begins to hang his head and drag his feet.

The subplot, predictable but enjoyable all the same, involves another woman in the same firm, played by Halle Berry. She dates Murphy's best friend, but there are no sparks, and they keep insisting they're "just friends" even though everyone believes them the first time. Eventually, one night Murphy and Berry realize they're in love. By this time, Murphy has been so thoroughly traumatized and enlightened by the Givens episode that he knows how to do all the right things.

The movie was directed by Reginald Hudlin and coproduced by his brother, Warrington; they made the original, inspired *House Party.* Here, with a larger budget, they show the same gift for funny one-liners that strike out of the blue. Many of them come from an odd but brilliantly cast trio of key supporting actors: Eartha Kitt, Grace Jones, and Geoffrey Holder. Kitt is Lady Eloise, aging figurehead of a cosmetics conglomerate, who is sex-mad in her seventies and sees Murphy as the prize she wins for taking over his company. Jones plays a supermodel named Strange who arrives at a product introduction cracking a whip while four half-nude bodybuilders pull her chariot. And Holder is the director who makes some of the most inappropriate commercials in television history.

Both Givens and Berry are right for their roles: Givens as the kind of man-eater who uses traditionally male strategies with great carnal delight, Berry so warm and charming you want to cuddle her. But the real surprise of the movie is Eddie Murphy, who finds his character and stays with him. The plot of

Boomerang reminded me most of those tables-are-turned 1950s executive suite comedies that used to star people like Rosalind Russell. To work, they needed a mastery of light comedy, and Murphy has it here. Whatever he was thinking during the dark days of his career slump, it seems to have paid off handsomely.

The Boost ★ ★ ★ ½
R, 95 m., 1988

James Woods (Lenny), Sean Young (Linda), John Kapelos (Joel), Steven Hill (Max), Kelle Kerr (Rochelle), John Rothman (Ned), Amanda Blake (Barbara), Grace Zabriskie (Cheryl). Directed by Harold Becker and produced by Daniel H. Blatt. Screenplay by Darryl Ponicsan.

The Boost is not simply about drugs. It is also about the hedonistic lifestyles of the 1980s, especially in go-go areas like the Los Angeles real estate market, in which fortunes are won and squandered in a matter of months and there is unspeakable pressure to keep up appearances. The movie is a modern-day version of *Death of a Salesman,* with James Woods selling leveraged tax shelters. He's out there on a smile, a shoeshine, and a line of cocaine.

Woods is one of the most intense, unpredictable actors in the movies today. You watch his characters because they seem capable of exploding—not out of anger, but out of hurt, shame, and low self-esteem. They're wounded, but they fight back by being smarter than anyone else, and using jokes and sarcasm to keep people at arm's length. That's the case with Lenny, the guy he plays in this movie. Lenny doesn't care if you like him or not, just so long as you see that he has a big house, an expensive car, and a wife so beautiful that— in his words—"How did she wind up with a runt like me?"

As the movie opens, Lenny is calling names in the phone book to peddle some kind of half-baked "investment opportunity." He meets a pleasant enough young prospect, invites him to dinner, and then explodes halfway through the meal, all of his resentments pouring out. Lenny hurts. But one day he meets a kind, philosophical older man (Steven Hill) who hires him to come out to L.A. and sell tax shelters to people with windfall profits.

Lenny is an overnight success. All he needed was the veneer of respectability—the expensive suits, the Mercedes—to cover his desperation. He's flying high. When he decides to invest in some cockamamie Mexican nightclub, his wife, Linda (Sean Young), cautions him that they are overextended. He doesn't care. He's rich and the money is pouring in and he's invincible, and then Congress changes the tax laws and his business evaporates overnight.

It's at that point that he tries cocaine for the first time. He's given his first taste by a free-spending friend (John Kapelos) who owns a chain of car washes. He likes it. It puts him back on top of the world. And as Lenny and Linda hit the skids, they're looking up all the way down. Cocaine makes their failures seem like temporary setbacks in a master plan. It makes them feel great. They never figure out the truth in George Carlin's famous line: "What does cocaine make you feel like? It makes you feel like having some more cocaine."

As Lenny and Linda head for the bottom, the movie turns into one of the most convincing and horrifying portraits of drug addiction I've ever seen. The director, Harold Becker, has directed Woods in two of his best movies (*The Onion Field* and *The Black Marble*). In this even darker story, he never insists too much; he simply observes. Lenny and Linda lose their expensive house. They move out of their middle-class high-rise apartment. They spend some time working in a sporting-goods store on the beach, trying to go straight and dry out. Lenny attends some kind of a rehabilitation program (offscreen) and comes back temporarily sober, but he's walking a tightrope.

"I've got the problem," he says. "Linda was only keeping me company." Linda thinks the same thing—and so when the car-wash king and his wife visit her at the beach, she tries a line of cocaine, gets stoned, falls down some stairs, and has a miscarriage. And then they really hit the skids. The movie portrays with almost effortless conviction the world of apartments-by-the-week in the seamy neighborhoods of Hollywood, where everybody has two occupations—the one he hopes someday to work at, and dealing drugs. Lenny, who was born desperate, becomes completely strung out, disoriented, paranoid. And *still* he clings to the delusion that he'll be back on top someday, that drugs are somehow the answer.

I received a letter the other day from a documentary filmmaker who is working on a TV program about mystical experiences. "Alcoholism and drug addiction in the twentieth century," he wrote, "may be related to the human desire for transcendence." Yes, and in other centuries, too, but in a reverse sort of way: If you're a drunk or an addict, you've got to transcend that before you can move along to other kinds of transcendence. Lenny's problem, in the closing scenes of *The Boost*, is that every detail of his life is governed in one way or another by his need to drink or take drugs. He's not transcending. He's maintaining. All he can hope for is a miracle.

Bopha! ★ ★ ★ ½
PG-13, 120 m., 1993

Danny Glover (Micah Mangena), Malcolm McDowell (De Villiers), Alfre Woodard (Rosie Mangena), Marius Weyers (Van Tonder), Maynard Eziashi (Zweli Mangena), Malick Bowens (Pule Rampa), Michael Chinyamurindi (Solomon). Directed by Morgan Freeman and produced by Lawrence Taubman. Screenplay by Brian Bird and John Wierick.

He is a proud South African police sergeant, the second generation in the job, and he wants his son to follow him onto the force. In classes for new cadets, he tells them they'll be called "pig," and then he explains that the word's initials stand for Pride, Integrity, and Guts and Glory. He is good at his job and believes in it. And he is black.

His name is Micah Mangena, and Danny Glover plays him in *Bopha!* as a man who sums up much of the anguish of modern South Africa. As his story opens, in 1980, he works in a drowsy rural area where relationships between whites and blacks, and police and civilians, seem fairly good—at least from the official point of view. Mangena has a good working relationship with his white captain, who is not a bad man, and he is proud to provide a good standard of living for his wife (Alfre Woodard) and their only son (Maynard Eziashi).

Then there is trouble. The local students strike against a government decree that they be taught in Afrikaans instead of English. Both are European tongues, but Afrikaans is spoken only in South Africa, while English seems to them the language of the winds of change from outside, the language of freedom.

Mangena gets orders from his boss to raid a secret protest meeting they've heard about—a fairly innocent meeting, they're sure. "Use minimum force," the white man says. The raid goes as planned, and the area would probably have remained relatively tranquil, but a few days later new faces appear in the district: De Villiers (Malcolm McDowell), the hard-line officer from the Special Branch, and his thuggish assistant. They insist on extreme measures, eventually involving torture and death, to put down the protests. And then the black policeman's whole world comes crashing down around his ears, for his son is one of the protesters.

Bopha!, based on a play by Percy Mtwa, is the first film directed by Morgan Freeman, whose acting career has included two Oscar nominations *(Street Smart* and *Driving Miss Daisy)* and who starred in *The Power of One* (1992), a much more innocent film about South Africa. Like that film, *Bopha!* was shot on location in Zimbabwe, and captures the beauty as well as the unhappiness of southern Africa. Unlike it—unlike almost all the recent films about South Africa—*Bopha!* is told primarily through black eyes, and that is one of its greatest values.

I've admired such films as *Cry Freedom* and *A Dry White Season* while at the same time wondering why they saw South Africa through white eyes. *Cry Freedom* begins as the story of a black leader named Steven Biko, but he is killed halfway through, and the story focuses on his friend, a white newspaper editor. One is reminded of the bit player who thought *Hamlet* was about a gravedigger who meets a prince. To see South Africa in terms of white masters and black victims is comforting, but too simple; apartheid was a cruel system in which some of the spoils went to blacks, who were happy to have them, and it does not escape notice that Sergeant Mangena's house is the nicest in the township, with two bedrooms, electricity, and a refrigerator.

Mangena is not a bad man. He works hard, loves his family, is proud of his uniform, believes what he does is necessary. Indeed, most of it is. The law must be enforced. But to the degree that the law enforces apartheid, it places him in a terrible position: "He is," Freeman observed at the Toronto Film Festival, "a watch dog, trained to bark at trouble. He may be a sergeant, but the lowliest white member of the force can give him orders."

This is what the son sees, and acts on, while Mangena assumes that all is well, and that he knows his son's mind. And as violence envelops the once-peaceful area, as the brutality of the Special Branch tactics becomes inescapable, Mangena learns, but slowly. It is a great performance by Danny Glover, the portrait of a proud man who discovers his pride was entrusted to the wrong things. Alfre Woodard, who struggles to preserve her family in the middle of the rising anarchy, is also very strong here, and the film's ending has some of the power of classical tragedy.

I had some problems with the very end of the film. It seemed to me there should have been one more scene, explaining how the policeman arrives at his final destination. There was a sense that the viewer was required to read his mind. Perhaps that was the idea.

Born on the Fourth of July ★ ★ ★ ★
R, 144 m., 1989

Tom Cruise (Ron Kovic), Willem Dafoe (Charlie), Kyra Sedgwick (Donna), Raymond J. Barry (Mr. Kovic), Jerry Levine (Steve Boyer), Frank Whaley (Timmy), Carolina Kava (Mrs. Kovic), Abbie Hoffman (Strike Organizer), Oliver Stone (News Reporter), Tom Berenger (Recruiting Sergeant), Rob Camilletti (Tommy Finnelli), Sean Stone (Young Jimmy). Directed by Oliver Stone and produced by A. Kitman Ho and Stone. Screenplay by Stone and Ron Kovic.

For some time we've been reading in the papers about public apologies by governments of the Eastern bloc. The Russians admit they were wrong to invade Afghanistan and Czechoslovakia. The East Germans tear down the wall and denounce the secret luxuries of their leaders. The Poles and Hungarians say Marxism doesn't work very well. There is a temptation for an American reading these articles to feel smug. And yet— hold on a minute here. We had our own disastrous foreign policy mistake: the war in Vietnam. When is anybody going to get up before Congress and read an apology to the Vietnamese?

Never, is the obvious answer. We hail the Soviet bloc for its honesty but see no lessons for ourselves. And yet we have been issuing our own apologies, of a sort. A film like Oliver Stone's *Born on the Fourth of July* is an apology for Vietnam uttered by Stone, who fought there, and Ron Kovic, who was paralyzed from the chest down in Vietnam. Both of them were gung-ho patriots who were eager to answer their country's call to arms. When they came back home, they were still patriots— hurt and offended by the hostility they experienced from the antiwar movement.

Eventually both men turned against the war, Kovic most dramatically. He and his wheelchair were thrown out of the 1972 Republican convention, but in 1976 he addressed the Democratic convention, and if you want to you could say his 1976 speech was the equivalent of one of those recent breast-beatings in the Supreme Soviet. We do apologize for our mistakes in this country, but we let our artists do it, instead of our politicians.

Kovic came back from the war with a shattered body, but it took a couple of years for the damage to spread to his mind and spirit. By the time he hit bottom he was a demoralized, spiteful man who sought escape in booze and drugs and Mexican whorehouses. Then he began to look outside of himself for a larger pattern to his life, the pattern that inspired his best-selling autobiography, *Born on the Fourth of July*.

The director, Oliver Stone, who based his earlier film *Platoon* on his own war experiences, has been trying to film the Kovic book for years. Various stars and studios were attached to the project, but it kept being canceled, and perhaps that's just as well, because by waiting this long Stone was able to use Tom Cruise in the leading role. Nothing Cruise has done earlier will prepare you for what he does in *Born on the Fourth of July*. He has been hailed for years now as a great young American actor, but only his first film, *Risky Business*, found a perfect match between actor and role. *Top Gun* overwhelmed him with a special-effects display, *The Color of Money* didn't explain his behavior in crucial final scenes, *Cocktail* was a cynical attempt to exploit his attractive image. Almost always he seemed to be holding something in reserve, standing back from his own presence. In *Born on the Fourth of July*, his performance is so good that the movie lives through it—Stone is able to make his statement with Cruise's face and voice and doesn't need to put everything into the dialogue.

The movie begins in the early 1960s, indeed with footage of John Kennedy on the television exhorting, "Ask not what your country can do for you; ask what you can do for your country." Young Ron Kovic, football star and high school hero, was the kind of kid waiting to hear that message. And when the Marine recruiters came to visit his high school, he was ready to sign up. There was no doubt in his mind: There was a war in Vietnam, and his only worry was that he would miss the action. He knew there was a danger of being wounded or killed, but hell, he wanted to make a sacrifice for his country.

His is the kind of spirit all nations must have from time to time. The problem with the Vietnam War is that it did not deserve it. There was no way for a patriotic small-town kid to know that, however, and so we follow young Kovic through boot camp and into the battlefield. In these scenes, Cruise still looks like Cruise—boyish, open-faced—and I found myself wondering if he would be able to make the transition into the horror that I knew was coming. He was.

Oliver Stone was in combat for a year. In *Platoon*, he showed us firefights so confused we (and the characters) often had little idea where the enemy was. In *Born on the Fourth of July*, Stone directs a crucial battle scene with great clarity so that we can see how a mistake was made by Kovic. That mistake, which tortures him for years afterward, probably produced the loss of focus that led to his crippling injury.

The scenes which follow, in a military hospital, are merciless in their honesty. If you have even once, for a few hours perhaps, been helpless in a sickbed and unable to summon aid, all of your impotent rage will come flooding back as the movie shows a military care system that is hopelessly overburdened. At one point, Kovic screams out for a suction pump that will drain a wound that might cost him his leg. He will never have feeling in the leg—but, God damn it, he wants to keep it all the same. It's his. And a hospital orderly absentmindedly explains about equipment shortages and "budget cutbacks" in care for the wounded vets.

Back in civilian life, Kovic is the hero of a Fourth of July parade, but there are peaceniks on the sidewalks, some of them giving him the finger. He feels more rage. But then his emotional tide turns one night in the backyard of his parents' home. He gets drunk with a fellow veteran and finds they can talk about things nobody else really understands. It is from this scene that the full power of the Cruise performance develops. Kovic's life becomes a series of confusions—bar brawls, self-pity, angry confrontations with women he will never be able to make love with in the ordinary way. His parents love him but are frightened of his rage. Eventually it is suggested that he leave home.

In a scene of Dantean evil, Stone shows Kovic in Mexico with other crippled veterans, paying for women and drugs to take away the pain, and finally, shockingly, abandoned in the desert with another veteran with no way to get back to their wheelchairs or to town. It's the sort of thing that happens to people who make themselves unbearable to other people who don't give a damn about them. (In a nod toward *Platoon,* the other crippled veteran in the desert is played by Willem Dafoe, costar of that film; the other costar, Tom Berenger, is the Marine who gives the recruitment speech in the opening scenes.)

Born on the Fourth of July is one of those films that steps correctly in the opening moments and then never steps wrongly. It is easy to think of a thousand traps that Oliver Stone, Ron Kovic, and Tom Cruise could have fallen into with this film, but they fall into none of them.

Although this film has vast amounts of pain and bloodshed and suffering in it, and is at home on battlefields and in hospital wards, it proceeds from a philosophical core—it is not a movie about battle or wounds or recovery, but a movie about an American who changes his mind about the war. The filmmakers realize that is the heart of their story and are faithful to it, even though they could have spun off in countless other directions. This is a film about ideology, played out in the personal experiences of a young man who paid dearly for what he learned. Maybe instead of anybody getting up in Congress and apologizing for the Vietnam War, they could simply hold a screening of this movie on Capitol Hill and call it a day.

The Bostonians ★ ★ ★
PG, 120 m., 1984

Christopher Reeve (Basil Ransom), Vanessa Redgrave (Olive Chancellor), Madeleine Potter (Verena Tarrant), Jessica Tandy (Mrs. Birdseye), Nancy Marchand (Mrs. Burrage). Directed and produced by Ismail Merchant, James Ivory, and Ruth Prawer Jhabvala. Screenplay by Merchant, Ivory, and Jhabvala.

One of the qualities I like best in the novels of Henry James is the way his characters talk and talk about matters of passion and the heart, and never quite seem to act. One of his favorite words, in many of his books, is "intercourse," by which, significantly, he seems to mean conversation, although you can never quite be sure. James's novels run long and deep, and because he was writing for a 19th century that was not always open to the kinds of passions felt by his characters, he beat a lot, if you will, around the bush, so to speak, with lots of commas and asides and subtle hints of unspeakable practices.

The Bostonians is a novel with a lot of

asides, and hundreds of pages of hints. We can summarize it boldly: It is about a sweet and somewhat inconsequential young woman who has inspired crushes in two of her admirers. One of her would-be lovers is a straight-spoken lawyer from the South, who wants to sweep her off her feet and make her his wife. The other is a woman, who does not seem quite in touch with the true nature of her feelings; today she would know she was a lesbian, but in the world of James it is necessary for her to displace her feelings—to convince herself that she is in love with the young woman's politics. Those politics are mostly secondhand, made up of things the young woman has been told by others. The story is set at the birth of the suffragette movement, and women meet in each others' homes to talk about the right to vote and, by extension, the right to lead full lives. *The Bostonians* shows us several of those women, including the veteran leader Mrs. Birdseye (wonderfully played by Jessica Tandy) and the younger firebrand Olive Chancellor (Vanessa Redgrave).

Chancellor is in love with Verena Tarrant (Madeleine Potter). That is clear to us, but not as clear to Chancellor. She promotes the young woman as a lecturer and campaigner, filled with visions of her role in social reform—a role that will necessarily require her to become Chancellor's associate, and have little to do with men. Then the tall Southern lawyer (Christopher Reeve) arrives on the scene, and the movie turns into a tug-of-war in which nobody is quite frank about the real nature of the battle.

The Bostonians is by the veteran producer-director-writer team of Ismail Merchant, James Ivory, and Ruth Prawer Jhabvala, who collaborated on a 1979 film version of Henry James's *The Europeans.* This is a much better film, intelligent and subtle and open to the underlying tragedy of a woman who does not know what she wants, a man who does not care what he wants, and a girl who does not need what she wants.

The Bounty ★ ★ ★ ★
PG, 130 m., 1984

Anthony Hopkins (Captain William Bligh), Mel Gibson (Fletcher Christian), Tevaite Vernette (Mauatua), Laurence Olivier (Admiral Hood), Edward Fox (Captain Greetham), Daniel Day Lewis (Fryer). Directed by Roger Donaldson and produced by Bernard Williams. Screenplay by Robert Bolt.

The relationship between Fletcher Christian and Captain William Bligh is one of the most familiar in the movies: We've seen it acted between Clark Gable and Charles Laughton, and between Marlon Brando and Trevor Howard, but it's never before been quite as intriguing as in *The Bounty,* the third movie based on the most famous mutiny in the history of the sea. The movie suggests that Bligh and Christian were friends, of all things, and that Bligh—far from being the histrionic martinet of earlier movies—was an intelligent, contemplative man of great complications. The story is well-known, and simple: HMS *Bounty* sets sail for the South seas, has a difficult voyage that frays everyone's tempers, and then anchors at a Polynesian island. During the trip, the original first mate has been replaced by the young Fletcher Christian, whom Bligh decides to trust. But Christian tires of the voyage and of the dangers and probable death that lie ahead. He falls in love with a native girl and leads a mutiny of sailors who choose to stay on their island paradise.

Bligh is played by Anthony Hopkins in one of the most interesting performances of 1984: He is unyielding, but not mindlessly rigid; certain he is right, but not egotistical; able to be realistic about his fate and his chances, and yet completely loyal to his ideas of a British naval officer's proper duties. When Fletcher Christian leads a mutiny against his command, it is not seen simply as a revolt against cruel authority (as in the earlier movies) but as a choice between a freer lifestyle, and Bligh's placing of duty above ordinary human nature.

Every *Bounty* movie seems to shape its Fletcher Christian somewhat to reflect the actor who plays him. Gable's Christian was a man of action, filled with physical strength and high spirits. Brando's was introverted and tortured. Mel Gibson's is maybe the hardest to figure of the three. He is a man of very few words (the screenplay gives him little to say, and almost no philosophizing), quiet, observant, an enigma. Only in the arms of the woman he comes to love, the Tahitian girl Mauatua, does he find the utter simplicity that perhaps he was looking for when he went to sea. It is a decision of some daring to give Gibson so noticeably little dialogue in this movie, but it works.

This *Bounty* is not only a wonderful movie, high-spirited and intelligent, but something of a production triumph as well. Although this third *Bounty* film was originally conceived as a big-budget, two-part epic to be directed by David *(Doctor Zhivago)* Lean, the current version was prepared and directed after only a few months' notice by a talented young New Zealander named Roger Donaldson, whose previous credits included the brilliant *Smash Palace*, a critical hit and commercial failure. What's interesting is that Donaldson's film doesn't feel like a secondhand treatment; he directs with flair and wit, and the spectacular scenes (like a stormy crossing of the Cape) never allow the special effects to steal the film away from the actors.

The sea voyage is done with the sort of macho confidence that a good sea movie needs, and the land portions do an interesting job of contrasting the proper, civilized British (represented by Laurence Olivier, as an admiral) with the cheerful absolute freedom of Polynesia. The romance between Gibson and the beautiful Tevaite Vernette, as his island lover, is given time to develop instead of just being thrown in as a plot point. And the Polynesians, for once, are all allowed to go topless all the time (the movie nevertheless gets the PG rating, qualifying under the *National Geographic* loophole in which nudity doesn't count south of the equator). *The Bounty* is a great adventure, a lush romance, and a good movie.

Boyfriends and Girlfriends ★ ★ ★
PG, 102 m., 1988

Emmanuelle Chaulet (Blanche), Sophie Renoir (Lea), Anne-Laure Meury (Adrienne), Eric Viellard (Fabien), Francois-Eric Gendron (Alexandre). Written and directed by Eric Rohmer and produced by Margaret Menegoz.

Paris is not all crowded together into a cozy warren of colorful streets nestled on the banks of the Seine. And Parisians are not all colorful intellectuals, bohemians, artists, and tradesmen, so authentic they make you feel like a stage American. France, in fact, is not all like France. Parts of it are glossy new architectural enclaves where young yuppies meet to chirp and preen. That is the France of Eric Rohmer's film, *Boyfriends and Girlfriends*. The movie takes place in a modern suburb of Paris, so close you can sometimes see the Eiffel Tower in the distance, so far away it is almost another country. This is a clean, well-lighted environment, in which all the fixtures of a Paris neighborhood have been picked up, shaken well, dusted, sterilized, painted, and set down again. The sidewalk cafes, for example, have just the

right little porcelain sugar bowls and round white chairs. All they lack is a sidewalk.

In this environment, Rohmer places several young professionals, who range in age from, say, twenty-four to thirty-two. One woman works in a social agency. Another works in a travel bureau. The men have more abstract jobs that require them to venture into Paris itself. But their true home is here in this brand-new environment that seems designed to set off their new slacks and sweaters without throwing too much light on their opinions. *Boyfriends and Girlfriends* is one of a series of "proverbs" that Rohmer has been working through, after his earlier series of six "moral tales" such as *My Night at Maud's* and *Claire's Knee*. The moral tales presented their characters with actual and tricky moral dilemmas (for example, should one act selfishly on a desire to touch Claire's knee if that indulgence would interfere with Claire's otherwise happily innocent existence?). The proverbs, on the other hand, are skimpier affairs, lightweight little whimsies designed to illustrate some sort of everyday truth in an ironic way.

The proverb that inspired *Boyfriends and Girlfriends* is "The friends of my friends are my friends" (which in French was the original title of the movie, and in English would make a more intriguing one than *Boyfriends and Girlfriends*).

The movie is essentially about bad timing. Two young women are friends. Not deep, lifelong soul sisters, to be sure, but friends. They see a handsome young man. One likes him, the other gets him, and then, in a sense, they trade, with an additional boyfriend and a few other friends thrown into the mixture. All of the permutations are unimportant because we are not dealing with the heart here, but with fashion.

There is a sense in which none of these characters can feel deeply, although they can admittedly experience transient periods of weeping and moaning over their cruel fates. That's because their relationships are based essentially on outward appearances; they choose lovers as fashion accessories. In conversation, they find they have "a lot in common," but that's easy to explain: They all hold exactly the same few limited opinions.

When one girl thinks she has a boy and another girl gets him, there is a sense of betrayal, all right, but it's not the kind of passionate betrayal that leads to murder or suicide. It's the kind of betrayal that leads to dramatic statements like "I'm not ever going to speak to you again!"

Rohmer knows exactly what he is doing here. He has no great purpose, but an interesting small one: He wants to observe the everyday behavior of a new class of French person, the young professionals whose values are mostly materialistic, whose ideas have been shaped by popular culture, who do not read much, or think much about politics, or have much depth. By the end of this film, you may know his characters better than they will ever know themselves. In *My Night at Maud's*, a man sat by the bedside of a woman all night long while they talked and talked and talked. The sad thing about the people in *Boyfriends and Girlfriends*, we sense, is that in such a situation they would have little to talk about. And if the boy actually got into the bed, even less.

Boys on the Side ★ ★ ★ ½   NEW
R, 118 m., 1995

Whoopi Goldberg (Jane DeLuca), Mary-Louise Parker (Robin), Drew Barrymore (Holly), Matthew McConaughey (Abe Lincoln), Billy Wirth (Nick), Anita Gillette (Elaine), James Remar (Alex), Estelle Parsons (Louise). Directed by Herbert Ross and produced by Arnon Milchan, Steven Reuther, and Ross. Screenplay by Don Roos.

The very last shot in *Boys on the Side* is of an empty room. As the camera pans around it, we remember who was in it, and how much we grew to care about them. We may be a little surprised by how that happened, because the movie starts out seeming contrived and routine, and only gradually gathers power, until by the end it is completely involving.

The opening is a Meet Cute. A singer named Jane (Whoopi Goldberg) gets fired from her job in a crummy New York club, and decides to head out west in search of her destiny. She answers an ad from a woman named Robin (Mary-Louise Parker) who has a car and is looking for someone to share the driving.

Robin is, Jane decides, "the whitest human in America." How white? She once sang "Close to You" in a talent contest, and *The Way We Were* is her favorite film. But Jane needs the ride, and so they team up and hit the road, and so far nothing of great interest has happened, and we're anticipating this will be another one of those Goldberg roles where she gives white folks lessons in black appreciation.

The first glimmer of strangeness comes in

Pittsburgh, where they stop off to visit Jane's friend Holly (Drew Barrymore). Holly's boyfriend Nick (Billy Wirth) is a textbook example of a drugged-out paranoid who ministers to his own inadequacy by beating on his woman. The Goldberg character waltzes in between them, but suddenly it is quiet Robin, a former realtor, who commands the room—approaching the domestic violence as if it were a house closing. Jane, Holly, and even the drug-dealing loser fall silent in amazement as she somehow brokers them into a truce.

It doesn't quite last—Holly has to get Nick's attention with a baseball bat and then tape him to a chair before they can escape—but soon the three women are in the same car, heading west, and we realize this is not going to be a sitcom, a buddy movie, or a road movie but a story that develops on its own unexpected terms. The director is Herbert Ross *(Steel Magnolias)* and the writer is Don Roos *(Single White Female)*, and with the actresses they create three true originals.

There are elements of the plot that are shamelessly contrived—including the whole setup explaining why they think they need to go on the lam. But we don't care, because by then the movie has entered so deeply into these three lives that what really matters is only what they think about each other.

It is clear from the first scene or two that the Goldberg character is a lesbian. Less clear is whether the Parker character knows that, or how she feels about it. Parker, too, has a secret, which will not be revealed here. And the catalyst in the group is the Drew Barrymore character, filled with crazy energy, high spirits, and deep broodings.

Those who know Barrymore from her adolescent headlines in the supermarket trash press may not realize that in movies like *Guncrazy* (1992), she has been developing into an actress of great natural zest and conviction. The difficult emotional scenes in *Boys on the Side* belong to Goldberg and Parker, but it is Barrymore whose spirit somehow draws them together into a family. (She can also be very funny. Her take on some lesbians: "They're very emotional, they love uniforms, and don't break their hearts. Especially UPS uniforms.") And the movie gets a lot of comedy out of the Barrymore character's tempestuous love affair with a Tucson cop named Abraham Lincoln (Matthew McConaughey), who is an absolute straight arrow, and at one point does the most incredible thing and then explains, "I

take this name seriously! I cannot tell a lie." The others groan: "That was George Washington, schmuck!"

As for the other two women, they just get stronger and stronger as the movie goes on. Goldberg so often wastes her time (in movies like *Sister Act 2*) that her work here is a reminder of such great past roles as *The Color Purple* and *The Long Walk Home*. It is an exercise in restraint: She is wise, grown-up, and calm. She never reaches for an effect, never goes for a laugh that isn't right there in her hand, and deals with her character's lesbianism in a way that can perhaps be called good manners: Yes, she is gay, but she doesn't believe in imposing her choice on others, and it is only gradually that we realize what the stillness of her heart can contain.

The Parker character is a series of revelations, some sad, some delightful; the way she handles the violent Nick is one of the bravura scenes in recent movies, and we get the impression the other actors want to applaud as much as the audience does. Later she has a couple of big emotional scenes that are played on exactly the right notes. Look, for example, at the way she sees a piano that is a gift, and bites her lower lip. A tiny gesture, but the right one.

The reviews for *Boys on the Side* mentioned *Fried Green Tomatoes* and *Thelma and Louise*, because it shares their assorted themes: female bonding, unexpressed love, women on the run. But this movie is not a collection of parts from other films. It's an original, and what it does best is show how strangers can become friends, and friends can become like family.

To get to know someone is very difficult, but if you really do, they should be able to tell you almost anything, and ask you almost anything, and that is where *Boys on the Side* is leading us. By the end, it has prepared its ground so completely that the final powerful scenes can be played very quietly. Some people sing a song. A room is empty, and the camera remembers who was in it. And we miss them.

The Boy Who Could Fly ★ ★ ★
PG, 114 m., 1986

Lucy Deakins (Milly), Jay Underwood (Eric), Bonnie Bedelia (Charlene), Fred Savage (Louis), Colleen Dewhurst (Mrs. Sherman), Fred Gwynne (Uncle Hugo), Louise Fletcher (Psychiatrist). Directed by Nick Castle and produced by Gary Adelson. Screenplay by Castle.

Here is a sweet and innocent parable about a boy who could fly—and about a girl who could fly, too, when the boy held her hand. The lesson the girl learns in this film is that anything is possible, if only you have faith. The movie could have been directed fifty years ago by Frank Capra, except that in the Capra version, the boy wouldn't have been autistic and the girl wouldn't have been grieving because of the recent suicide of her father, who was dying of cancer. Parables have harder edges these days.

The movie takes place in a small town with picket fences, shade trees, and mean boys who won't let little kids ride their tricycles around the block. Into a run-down house on one of these streets, a small family moves: a mother, teen-age daughter, and little brother. The girl looks out her bedroom window to the house next door, and there she sees, poised on the roof, a teen-age boy with his arms outstretched, poised to fly.

She learns his story. When he was five, his parents died in an airplane crash. At the exact moment of the crash, he started to try to fly, as if he could have saved them. But can he really fly? The boy lives with an alcoholic uncle, who swears he has seen the kid fly. But the uncle sees a lot of things, not all of them real.

The Boy Who Could Fly surrounds this situation with small stories of everyday life. The mother (Bonnie Bedelia) goes back to her old job in the insurance industry and discovers she has to learn to use a computer. Her daughter (Lucy Deakins) goes to high school and makes friends with an understanding teacher (Colleen Dewhurst). The little brother (a small, fierce tyke named Fred Savage) plots to overcome the bullies who live around the corner. And next door, the strange boy (Jay Underwood) lives in his world of dreams and silence.

Can anything break through to him? Yes, as it turns out, one power on Earth is strong enough to penetrate his autism, and that power is adolescent love.

He gets a crush on his new neighbor. She cares for him. One day, he saves her life. She believes he can really fly, but nobody else does, and then the kid is taken away from his drunken uncle and placed in an institution, which could crush his spirit.

The movie develops along lines that we can more or less anticipate, and it ends on a note of high sentimentality. What's good about it are the performances, especially by Deakins, a warm and empathetic teen-ager,

Savage, a plucky little kid who could play Dennis the Menace, and Bedelia, a widow still mourning her husband.

Movies like this can be insufferable if they lay it on too thick. *The Boy Who Could Fly* finds just about the right balance between its sunny message and the heartbreak that's always threatening to prevail.

Boyz N the Hood ★ ★ ★ ★
R, 107 m., 1991

Cuba Gooding, Jr. (Tre Styles), Ice Cube (Doughboy), Morris Chestnut (Ricky Baker), Larry Fishburne (Furious Styles), Tyra Ferrell (Mrs. Baker). Directed by John Singleton and produced by Steve Nicolaides. Screenplay by Singleton.

There must be few experiences more wounding to the heart than for a parent to look at a child and fear for its future. In inner-city America, where one in every twenty-one young men will die of gunshot wounds, and most of them will be shot by other young men, it is not simply a question of whether the child will do well in school, or find a useful career: It is sometimes whether the child will live or die.

Watching her bright young son on the brink of his teen-age years, seeing him begin to listen to his troublesome friends instead of to her, the mother in *Boyz N the Hood* decides that it is best for the boy to go live with his father. The father works as a mortgage broker, out of a storefront office. He is smart and angry, a disciplinarian, and he lays down rules for his son. And then, out in the streets of south-central Los Angeles, the son learns other rules.

As he grows into his teens, his best friends are half brothers, one an athlete, the other drifting into drugs and alcohol. They've known each other for years—and have steered clear, more or less, of the gangs that operate in the neighborhood. They go their own way. But there is always the possibility that words will lead to insults, that insults will lead to a need to "prove their manhood," that with guns everywhere, somebody will be shot dead.

These are the stark choices in John Singleton's *Boyz N the Hood*, one of the best American films of recent years. The movie is a thoughtful, realistic look at a young man's coming of age, and is also a human drama of rare power—Academy Award material. Singleton is a director who brings together two attributes not always found in the same film: He has a subject, and he has a style. The film

is not only important, but also a joy to watch, because his camera is so confident and he wins such natural performances from his actors.

The movie's hero, who will probably excel in college and in a profession, if he lives to get that far, is an intelligent seventeen-year-old named Tre Styles (Cuba Gooding, Jr.). His father, Furious Styles (Larry Fishburne), grew up in the neighborhood, survived it, and understands it in two different ways: as a place where young men define their territory and support themselves by violence, and as a real estate market in transition—where, when prices and lives there find their bottom, investors will be able to buy cheap and then make money with gentrification.

Furious Styles also knows the dangers for his son—of gangs, of drugs, of the wrong friends. He lays down strict rules, but he cannot be everywhere and see everything. Meanwhile, Singleton paints the individual characters of the neighborhood with the same attention to detail that Spike Lee used in *Do the Right Thing*. He's particularly perceptive about the Baker family—about the mother (Tyra Ferrell) and her two sons by different fathers, Doughboy (rap artist Ice Cube) and Ricky (Morris Chestnut). Both live at home, where it is no secret in the family that the mother prefers Ricky. He's a gifted athlete who seems headed for a college football scholarship.

Doughboy is not a bad person, but he is into booze and drugs and will sooner or later find bad trouble. He spends most of his days on the front steps, drinking, plotting, feeding his resentments. They live in a neighborhood where violence is a fact of life, where the searchlights from police helicopters are like the guard lights in a prison camp, where guns are everywhere, where a kid can go down to the corner store and not come home alive. In painting the cops as an occupying force, Singleton is especially hard on one self-hating black cop, who uses his authority to mishandle young black men.

In the course of one summer week or two, all of the strands of Tre's life come together to be tested: his girlfriend, his relationship with his father, his friendships, and the dangers from the street gangs of the area. Singleton's screenplay has built well; we feel we know the characters and their motivations, and so we can understand what happens, and why.

A lesser movie might have handled this material in a perfunctory way, painting the

characters with broad strokes of good and evil, setting up a confrontation at the end, using a lot of violence and gunfire to reward the good and punish the rest. Singleton cares too much about his story to kiss it off like that. Look, for example, at the scene late in the film—the morning-after scene—where Doughboy walks across the street and speaks quietly to Tre; he knows what is likely to happen, and yet wants his friend to escape the trap, to realize his future.

Boyz N the Hood has maturity and emotional depth: There are no cheap shots, nothing is thrown in for effect, realism is placed ahead of easy dramatic payoffs, and the audience grows deeply involved. By the end of *Boyz N the Hood*, I realized I had seen not simply a brilliant directorial debut, but an American film of enormous importance.

The Brady Bunch Movie ★ ★
PG-13, 90 m., 1995

Shelley Long (Carol Brady), Gary Cole (Mike Brady), Christine Taylor (Marcia), Jennifer Elise Cox (Jan), Olivia Hack (Cindy), Christopher Daniel Barnes (Greg), Paul Sutera (Peter), Jesse Lee (Bobby), Henriette Mantel (Alice), Michael McKean (Mr. Ditmeyer). Directed by Betty Thomas and produced by Sherwood Schwartz and Lloyd J. Schwartz with David Kirkpatrick. Screenplay by Laurice Elehwany, Rick Copp, Bonnie Turner, and Terry Turner.

The Bradys at 4222 Clinton Way are caught in a time warp. For them, it's always the early 1970s, and dad Mike in his polka-dot ties and mom Carol in her orange Formica kitchen (well-stocked with salt, sugar, and white flour) like it just that way. They're raising their bunch in happy harmony, and hardly a day goes by without Dad sharing one of his optimistic little homilies about life: "Alone, we can only move buckets. But together, we can drain rivers!"

It is the nature of sitcoms to seem trapped in time. We channelsurf, and Lucy and Desi and Ralph and Alice are still firmly at home in the 1950s, in those apartments we have come to know like our own homes. And the Bunkers are still at it in their living room, and so is the Cosby family; the topical jokes don't seem dated for them, and their fashions never seem out of style, and it is forever 1954, or 1981.

The joke in *The Brady Bunch Movie* is that time *has* marched on for the rest of the Bradys' neighborhood. While the Bradys blissfully exist inside their bubble of the 1970s, the neighbors eye them suspiciously—and sometimes with outright hostility. For the first time in the movie we finally meet the Ditmeyers, their neighbors. Mrs. Ditmeyer has a drinking problem and lusts after the older Brady boys, and Mr. Ditmeyer (Michael McKean) has erected a spite fence to block out their annoying activities. (When little sister Cindy [Olivia Hack] ventures next door, he snarls: "Hey, kid—go yodel in your own backyard! Hop back on the Swiss Miss package where you belong!")

Of course, she's only *there* to warn him about the live electric wire that has fallen in his driveway, so is it *her* fault if he picks it up? Certainly not! And one of the running jokes in the movie is the unconscious passive hostility the Bradys unleash all around them: They're so wholesome, so darnright nice, they don't even realize they are driving people mad. (And they're so plastic, do they even have human bodily functions? One neighbor who has actually seen the inside of their house suspiciously tells a friend, "I didn't even *see* a toilet.")

The plot is made up out of the bits and pieces of what might have been sitcom story lines. The Bradys overlooked paying their real estate taxes, and now they stand to lose their idyllic home on Clinton Way. For the neighbors, that's just fine; Mr. Ditmeyer has plans to raze the neighborhood, and all of the other homeowners are blissful about the prospect of selling out and making big profits on their homes. But not Carol and Mike Brady (Shelley Long and Gary Cole). They want to stay right where they are.

Innocent of the forces massed against them, the Bradys wonder how they can raise twenty thousand dollars in a week, and the kids pool their lunch money and discuss fund-raising schemes. Nothing seems to work until they learn of a talent contest with a twenty-thousand-dollar first prize, and enter it, as a sort of 1970s Partridge Family singing group dressed like refugees from ancient reruns of "American Bandstand."

A lot of the humor in the movie comes from the burning jealousy Jan feels for her popular older sister, Marcia (Christine Taylor), with her long blond hair that must be brushed five thousand times every morning. In her restless dreams, she whacks off Marcia's flowing locks with kitchen shears, but even then Marcia is the winner, as her parents compliment her on how great she looks with her new shorter style. ("It was *my* idea!"

Jan screams in her nightmare. *"Mine!"*) Meanwhile, Marcia's so innocent she invites her best friend for a sleep-over, and doesn't recognize a lesbian pass ("Sorry . . . I thought that was *my* leg!").

There are also lots of jokes about how the parents are slightly adrift from the grim mainstream of modern life, with their sunny values, blind optimism, and blinkered view of the harsh 1990s realities all around them. The director, Betty Thomas, is best when she is establishing the bland, seamless, plain vanilla cocoon that protects the Bradys from bad news and evil influences.

Unfortunately, the movie itself seems to lean too far toward the Brady vision. Even its "modern" side is too innocent. The film establishes a bland, reassuring, comforting Brady reality—a certain muted tone that works just fine, but needs, I think, a bleaker contrast from outside to fully exploit the humor. *The Brady Bunch Movie* is rated PG-13, which is a compromise: The Bradys themselves live in a PG universe, and the movie would have been funnier if when they venture outside it was obviously *Wayne's World*.

Bram Stoker's Dracula ★ ★ ★
R, 130 m., 1992

Gary Oldman (Dracula), Winona Ryder (Mina Murray/Elisabeta), Anthony Hopkins (Prof. Abraham Van Helsing), Keanu Reeves (Jonathan Harker), Richard E. Grant (Dr. Jack Seward), Cary Elwes (Lord Arthur Holmwood). Directed by Francis Ford Coppola. Produced by Coppola, Fred Fuchs, and Charles Mulvehill. Screenplay by James V. Hart.

Think of the monstrous ego of the vampire. He thinks himself so important that he is willing to live forever, even under the dreary conditions imposed by his condition. Avoiding the sun, sleeping in coffins, feared by all, he nurses his resentments. In *Bram Stoker's Dracula*, the new film by Francis Ford Coppola, the vampire shakes his fist at heaven and vows to wait forever for the return of the woman he loves. It does not occur to him that after the first two or three centuries he might not seem all that attractive to her.

The film is inspired by the original Bram Stoker novel, although the author's name is in the title for another reason (Universal owns the rights to plain *Dracula*). It begins, as it should, with the tragic story of Vlad the Impaler, who went off to fight the Crusades and returned to find that his beloved wife, hearing

he was dead, had killed herself. And not just killed herself, but hurled herself from a parapet to a stony doom far below, in one of the many spectacular shots that are the best part of this movie.

Vlad cannot see the justice in his fate. He has marched all the way to the Holy Land on God's business, only to have God play this sort of a trick on him. (Vlad is apparently not a student of the Book of Job.) He embraces Satan and vampirism, and the action moves forward to the late Victorian Age, when mankind is first beginning to embrace the gizmos (phonographs, cameras, the telegraph, motion pictures) that will dispel the silence of the nights through which he has waited fearfully for centuries.

Coppola's plot, from a screenplay by James V. Hart, exists precisely between London, where this modern age is just dawning, and Transylvania, which still sleeps unhealthily in the past. We meet a young attorney (Keanu Reeves) who has been asked to journey out to Dracula's castle to arrange certain real estate transactions. The previous man who was sent on this mission ran into some sort of difficulties . . . health or something . . . all rather vague.

Reeves's carriage, driven by a man whose hands are claws, hurtles at the edges of precipices until he is finally discharged in the darkness to be met and taken to Dracula's castle. There, everything is more or less as we expect it, only much more so. Count Dracula (Gary Oldman) waits here as he has for centuries for the return of his dead bride, and when he sees a photograph of Reeves's fiancée, Mina Murray (Winona Ryder), he knows his wait has been rewarded at last. She lives again.

Back in London, we meet other principals, including the fearless vampire killer Prof. Abraham Van Helsing (Anthony Hopkins), and Lucy Westenra (Sadie Frost), a free spirit who has three suitors and is Mina's best friend. When Dracula appears in town, Van Helsing's antennae start to quiver. And the movie descends into an orgy of visual decadence, in which what people do is not nearly as degraded as how they look while they do it.

Coppola directs with all the stops out, and the actors perform as if afraid they will not be audible in the other theaters of the multiplex. The sets are grand opera run riot—Gothic extravaganza intercut with the Victorian London of gaslights and fogbound streets, rogues in top hats and bad girls in bustiers. Keanu Reeves, as a serious young man of the future, hardly knows what he's up against with Count Dracula, and neither do we, since Dracula cheerfully changes form—from an ancient wreck to a presentable young man to a cat and a bat and a wolf.

Vampire movies, which run in the face of all scientific logic, are always heavily laden with pseudoscience. Hopkins lectures learnedly on the "nosferatu," yet himself seems capable of teleportation and other tricks not in the physics books. And the Ryder character finds herself falling under the terrible spell of the vampire's need. Many women are flattered when a man says he has been waiting all of his life for them. But if he has been waiting four centuries?

The one thing the movie lacks is headlong narrative energy and coherence. There is no story we can follow well enough to care about. There is a chronology of events, as the characters travel back and forth from London to Transylvania, and rendezvous in bedrooms and graveyards. But Coppola seems more concerned with spectacle and set pieces than with storytelling; the movie is particularly operatic in the way it prefers climaxes to continuity.

Faced with narrative confusions and dead ends (why *does* Dracula want to buy those London properties in such specific locations?), I enjoyed the movie simply for the way it looked and felt. Production designers Dante Ferreti and Thomas Sanders have outdone themselves. The cinematographer, Michael Ballhaus, gets into the spirit so completely he always seems to light with shadows. Oldman and Ryder and Hopkins pant with eagerness. The movie is an exercise in feverish excess, and for that if for little else, I enjoyed it.

Braveheart ★ ★ ★ ½

R, 178 m., 1995
(See related Film Clip, p. 875.)

Mel Gibson (William Wallace), Sophie Marceau (Princess Isabelle), Patrick McGoohan (King Edward I), Catherine McCormack (Murron), Brendan Gleeson (Hamish), James Cosmo (Campbell), David O'Hara (Stephen), Angus McFadyen (Robert the Bruce), Peter Hanly (Prince Edward). Directed by Mel Gibson and produced by Gibson, Alan Ladd, Jr., and Bruce Davey. Screenplay by Randall Wallace.

Mel Gibson's *Braveheart* is a full-throated, red-blooded battle epic about a legendary Scots warrior who led his nation into battle against the English in the years around 1300. It's an ambitious picture, big on simple emotions like love, patriotism, and treachery, and it avoids the travelogue look of so many historical swashbucklers: Its locations look green, wet, vast, muddy, and rugged.

Not much is known about William Wallace, known as Braveheart, except that in an old epic poem he unified the clans of Scotland and won famous battles against the English before being captured, tortured, and executed as a traitor. Wallace's dying cry, as his body was stretched on the rack, was "Freedom!" That isn't exactly based on fact (the concept of personal freedom was a concept not much celebrated in 1300), but it doesn't stop Gibson from making it *his* dying cry, and it fits in with the whole glorious sweep of *Braveheart,* which is an action epic with the spirit of the Hollywood swordplay classics, and the grungy ferocity of *The Road Warrior.*

What people are going to remember from the film are the battle scenes, which are frequent, bloody, and violent. Just from a technical point of view, *Braveheart* does a brilliant job of massing men and horses for large-scale warfare on film. Gibson deploys what look like thousands of men on horseback, as well as foot soldiers, archers, and dirty tricks specialists, and yet his battle sequences don't turn into confusing crowd scenes: We understand the strategy, and we enjoy the tactics even while we're doubting some of them (did thirteenth-century Scots really set battlefields aflame?).

Gibson is not filming history here, but myth. William Wallace may have been a real person, but Braveheart owes more to Prince Valiant, Rob Roy, and Mad Max. Once we understand that this is not a solemn historical reconstruction (and that happens pretty fast), we accept dialogue that might otherwise have an uncannily modern tone, as when Braveheart issues his victory ultimatum to the English: "Scotland's terms are that your commander present himself in front of our army, put his head between his legs, and kiss his ass." Uh, huh.

In the film, Wallace's chief antagonist is King Edward I ("Longshanks"), played by Patrick McGoohan with sly cunning; he is constantly giving his *realpolitik* interpretation of events, and that's all the more amusing since he's usually guessing wrong. Edward's son, the Prince of Wales (Peter Hanly), is an effete fop who marries a French woman only for political reasons. "I may have to conceive the child myself!" Longshanks says, and indeed under the medieval concept of "prima notta," or "first night," nobles were allowed a first chance to sleep with the wives of their lessers.

The princess, played by the French actress Sophie Marceau, does not much admire her husband, who spends most of his time hanging about moon-eyed with his best friend (until the king, in a fit of impatience, hurls the friend out the castle window). Edward, smarting from defeats, dispatches the princess to offer his terms to Braveheart, but soon she's spilling all the state secrets, "because of the way you look at me."

The princess is the second love in Wallace's life; the first, his childhood sweetheart Murron (Catherine McCormack), marries him in secret (so the local English lord won't claim his rights). The two spend their wedding night outdoors, and the backlit shot as they embrace gains something, I think, from the frost on their breaths. These characters come from hardened stock. (When Wallace has a reunion with his childhood pal Hamish, they hurl rocks at each other for entertainment; later, when a Scotsman has his wound cauterized, all he says is, "That'll wake you up in the morning, boy!")

It is sometimes seen as an egotistical gesture when actors direct themselves, especially in heroic epics costing (so they say) $53 million. The truth is, given this material, I do not know that anyone could have directed it better. Gibson marshals his armies of extras, his stunt men, and his special effects, and creates a fictional world that is entertaining and thrilling.

And as Braveheart, Gibson plays his role with flamboyance, and cuts it with sly humor. He is an amazing battlefield strategist, inventing new strategies and weapons, outsmarting the English at every turn, leading his men into battle with his face painted blue, like a football fan. There is a scene where he is so pumped up with the scent of battle that his nostrils flare; not many actors could get away with that, but Gibson can.

Brazil ★ ★

R, 130 m., 1985

Jonathan Pryce (Sam Lowry), Robert De Niro (Tuttle), Katherine Helmond (Ida Lowry), Ian Holm (Kurtzmann), Bob Hoskins (Spoor), Michael Palin (Jack Lint). Directed by Terry Gilliam and produced by Arnon Milchan. Screenplay by Tom Stoppard, Charles McKeown, and Gilliam.

Just as Orwell's *1984* is an alternative vision of our times, so *Brazil* is an alternative to Orwell. The movie happens in a time and place that seem vaguely like our own, but with different graphics, hardware, and politics. Society is controlled by a monolithic organization, and citizens lead lives of paranoia and control. Thought police are likely to come crashing through the ceiling and start bashing at dissenters. Life is mean and grim.

The hero of *Brazil* is Sam Lowry (Jonathan Pryce), a meek, desperate little man who works at a computer terminal all day. Occasionally he cheats; when the boss isn't looking, he and his fellows switch the screens of their computers to reruns of exciting old TV programs. Sam knows his life is drab and lockstep, but he sees no way out of it, and his only escape is into his fantasies—into glorious dreams of flying high above all the petty cares of the world, urged on by the vision of a beautiful woman.

His everyday life offers no such possibilities. Even the basic mechanisms of life support seem to be failing, and one scene early in the movie has Robert De Niro, in a walk-on, as an illegal free-lance repairman who defies the state by fixing things. De Niro makes his escapes by sliding down long cables to freedom, like Spider-Man. For Sam, there seems to be no escape.

But then he gets involved in an intrigue that involves the girl of his dreams, the chief executive of the state, and a shadowy band of dissenters. All of this is strangely familiar; the outlines of *Brazil* are much the same as those of *1984*, but the approach is different. While Orwell's lean prose was translated, last year, into an equally lean and dour film, *Brazil* seems almost like a throwback to the psychedelic 1960s, to an anarchic vision in which the best way to improve things is to blow them up.

The other difference between the two worlds—Orwell's, and the one created here by director and co-writer Terry Gilliam—is that Gilliam has apparently had no financial restraints. Although *Brazil* has had a checkered history since it was made (for a long time, Universal Pictures seemed unwilling to release it), there was a lot of money available to make it, and the movie is awash in elaborate special effects, sensational sets, apocalyptic scenes of destruction, and a general lack of discipline. It's as if Gilliam sat down and wrote out all of his fantasies, heedless of production difficulties, and then they were filmed—this time, heedless of sense.

The movie is very hard to follow. I have seen it twice, and am still not sure exactly who all the characters are, or how they fit. Perhaps I am not supposed to be clear; perhaps the movie's air of confusion is part of its paranoid vision. There are individual moments that create sharp images (shock troops drilling through a ceiling, De Niro wrestling with the almost obscene wiring and tubing inside a wall, the movie's obsession with bizarre ductwork), but there seems to be no sure hand at the controls.

The best scene in the movie is one of the simplest, as Sam moves into half an office and finds himself engaged in a tug-of-war over his desk with the man through the wall. I was reminded of a Chaplin film like *Modern Times,* and reminded, too, that in Chaplin economy and simplicity were virtues, not the enemy.

The Breakfast Club ★ ★ ★
R, 95 m., 1985

Emilio Estevez (Andrew Clark), Anthony Michael Hall (Brian Johnson), Judd Nelson (John Bender), Molly Ringwald (Claire Standish), Ally Sheedy (Allison Reynolds), Paul Gleason (Teacher), John Kapelos (Janitor). Directed by John Hughes and produced by Ned Tanen and Hughes. Screenplay by Hughes.

The Breakfast Club begins with an old dramatic standby. You isolate a group of people in a room, you have them talk, and eventually they exchange truths about themselves and come to new understandings. William Saroyan and Eugene O'Neill have been here before, but they used saloons and drunks. *The Breakfast Club* uses a high school library and five teen-age kids.

The movie takes place on a Saturday. The five kids have all violated high school rules in one way or another, and they've qualified for a special version of detention, all day long, from eight to four, in the school library. They arrive at the school one at a time. There's the arrogant, swaggering tough guy (Judd Nelson). The insecure neurotic (Ally Sheedy) who hides behind her hair and her clothes. The jock from the wrestling team (Emilio Estevez). The prom queen (Molly Ringwald). And the class brain (Anthony Michael Hall). These kids have nothing in common, and they have an aggressive desire *not* to have anything in common. In ways peculiar to teen-agers, who sometimes have a studious disinterest in anything that contradicts their self-image, these kids aren't even

curious about each other. Not at first, anyway. But then the day grows longer and the library grows more oppressive, and finally the tough kid can't resist picking on the prom queen, and then there is a series of exchanges.

Nothing that happens in *The Breakfast Club* is all that surprising. The truths that are exchanged are more or less predictable, and the kids have fairly standard hang-ups. It comes as no surprise, for example, to learn that the jock's father is a perfectionist, or that the prom queen's parents give her material rewards but withhold their love. But *The Breakfast Club* doesn't need earthshaking revelations; it's about kids who grow willing to talk to one another, and it has a surprisingly good ear for the way they speak. (Ever notice the way lots of teen-age girls, repeating a conversation, say "she goes . . ." rather than "she says . . ."?)

The movie was written and directed by John Hughes, who also made 1984's *Sixteen Candles.* Two of the stars of that movie (Ringwald and Hall) are back again, and there's another similarity: Both movies make an honest attempt to create teen-agers who might seem plausible to other teen-agers. Most Hollywood teen-age movies give us underage nymphos or nostalgia-drenched memories of the 1950s. The performances are wonderful, but then this is an all-star cast, as younger actors go; in addition to Hall and Ringwald from *Sixteen Candles,* there's Sheedy from *WarGames* and Estevez from *Repo Man.* Judd Nelson is not yet as well known, but his character creates the strong center of the film; his aggression is what breaks the silence and knocks over the walls. The only weaknesses in Hughes's writing are in the adult characters: The teacher is one-dimensional and one-note, and the janitor is brought onstage with a potted philosophical talk that isn't really necessary. Typically, the kids don't pay much attention.

Note: The "R" rating on this film refers to language; I think a PG-13 rating would have been more reasonable. The film is certainly appropriate for thoughtful teen-agers.

Breaking Away ★ ★ ★ ★
PG, 100 m., 1979

Dennis Christopher (Dave), Dennis Quaid (Mike), Daniel Stern (Cyril), Jackie Earle Haley (Moocher), Paul Dooley (Dad), Barbara Barrie (Mom), Robyn Douglass (Katherine). Directed and produced by Peter Yates. Screenplay by Steve Tesich.

Here's a sunny, goofy, intelligent little film about coming of age in Bloomington, Indiana. It's about four local kids, just out of high school, who mess around for one final summer before facing the inexorable choices of jobs or college or the Army. One of the kids, Dave (Dennis Christopher), has it in his head that he wants to be a champion Italian bicycle racer, and he drives his father crazy with opera records and ersatz Italian.

His friends have more reasonable ambitions: One (Dennis Quaid) was a high school football star who pretends he doesn't want to play college ball, but he does; another (Jackie Earle Haley) is a short kid who pretends he doesn't want to be taller, but he does; and another (Daniel Stern) is one of those kids like we all knew, who learned how to talk by crossing Eric Sevareid with Woody Allen.

There's the usual town-and-gown tension in Bloomington, between the jocks and the townies (who are known, in Bloomington, as "cutters"—so called after the workers in the area's limestone quarries). There's also a poignant kind of tension between local guys and college girls: Will a sorority girl be seen with a cutter? Dave finds out by falling hopelessly in love with a college girl named Kathy (Robyn Douglass), and somehow, insanely, convincing her he's actually an Italian exchange student.

The whole business of Dave's Italomania provides the movie's funniest running joke: Dave's father (Paul Dooley) rants and raves that he didn't raise his boy to be an Eye-talian, and that he's sick and tired of all the eenees in the house: linguini, fettucini . . . even Jake, the dog, which Dave has renamed Fellini. The performances by Dooley and Barbara Barrie as Dave's parents are so loving and funny at the same time that we remember almost with a shock, that *every* movie doesn't have to have parents and kids who don't get along.

The movie was directed as a work of love by Peter Yates, whose big commercial hits have included *Bullitt* and *The Deep*. The Oscar-winning original screenplay was written by Steve Tesich, who was born in Yugoslavia, was moved to Bloomington at the age of thirteen, won the Little 500 bicycle race there in 1962, and uses it for the film's climax. Yates has gone for the human elements in *Breaking Away*, but he hasn't forgotten how to direct action, and there's a bravura sequence in which Dave, on a racing bicycle, engages in a high-speed highway duel with a semitrailer truck.

In this scene, and in scenes involving swimming in an abandoned quarry, Yates does a tricky and intriguing thing: He suggests the constant possibility of sudden tragedy. We wait for a terrible accident to happen, and none does, but the hints of one make the characters seem curiously vulnerable, and their lives more precious.

The whole movie, indeed, is a delicate balancing act of its various tones: This movie could have been impossible to direct, but Yates has us on his side almost immediately. Some scenes edge into fantasy, others are straightforward character development, some (like the high school quarterback's monologue about his probable future) are heartbreakingly true. But the movie always returns to light comedy, to romance, to a wonderfully evocative instant nostalgia.

Breaking Away is a movie to embrace. It's about people who are complicated but decent, who are optimists but see things realistically, who are fundamentally comic characters but have three full dimensions. It's about a Middle America we rarely see in the movies, yes, but it's not corny and it doesn't condescend. Movies like this are hardly ever made at all; when they're made this well, they're precious cinematic miracles.

The Bridges of Madison County
★ ★ ★ ½
PG-13, 135 m., 1995   NEW

Clint Eastwood (Robert Kincaid), Meryl Streep (Francesca Johnson), Annie Corley (Caroline), Victor Slezak (Michael), Jim Haynie (Richard Johnson). Directed by Clint Eastwood and produced by Eastwood and Kathleen Kennedy. Screenplay by Richard LaGravenese.

This kind of certainty comes but once in a lifetime.

—Robert to Francesca

Clint Eastwood's *The Bridges of Madison County* is not about love and not about sex, but about an idea. The film opens with the information that two people once met and fell in love, but decided not to spend the rest of their lives together. The implication is: If they *had* acted on their desire, they would not have deserved such a love.

Almost everybody knows the story by now. Robert James Waller's novel has been a bestseller for three years. Its prose is not distinguished, but its story is compelling: He provides the fantasy of total eroticism within perfect virtue, elevating to a spiritual level the common erotic fantasy in which a virile stranger materializes in the kitchen of a quiet housewife and takes her into his arms. Waller's gift is to make the housewife feel virtuous afterward.

It is easy to analyze the mechanism, but more difficult to explain why this film is so deeply moving—why Clint Eastwood and Meryl Streep have made it into a wonderful movie love story, playing Robert and Francesca. We know, of course, that they will meet, fall in love, and part forever. It is necessary that they part. If the story had ended "happily" with them running away together, no one would have read Waller's book and no movie would exist. The emotional peak of the movie is the renunciation, when Francesca does *not* open the door of her husband's truck and run to Robert. This moment, and not the moment when the characters first kiss, or make love, is the film's passionate climax.

When Eastwood announced that he had bought the novel and planned to direct and star in the movie, eyebrows were raised. Readers had already cast it in their minds, and not with Eastwood—or with Meryl Streep, for that matter. There is still a tendency to identify Eastwood with his cowboy and cop roles, and to forget that in recent years he has grown as both an actor and director into one of the most creative forces in Hollywood. He was taking a chance by casting himself as Robert Kincaid, but it pays off in a performance that is quiet, gentle, and yet very masculine. And Streep wonderfully embodies Francesca Johnson, the Italian woman who finds herself with a husband and children, living on a farm in the middle of a flat Iowa horizon. The two of them construct their performances not out of grand gestures, but out of countless subtle little moments of growing love; a time comes when they are solemn in the presence of the joy that has come to them.

Kincaid is a photographer for *National Geographic*, shooting a story on the covered bridges of the district. Francesca's husband and children have left home for several days to go to the state fair. Photographer and housewife meet, and an awkward but friendly conversation leads to an offer of iced tea; then she shyly asks him to stay for dinner.

One of the story's mysteries is just when each of them becomes erotically aware of the other, and there is a moment, when he goes out to get beer from the car and she pauses while preparing salad, when she not-quite-smiles to herself. She seems happy; there is a lift in her heart. In another scene, she answers the telephone and, standing behind him, adjusts his collar, brushes his neck with her finger, and then leaves her hand resting on his shoulder. Very quietly.

Eastwood and his cinematographer, Jack N. Green, find a wonderful play of light, shadow, and candlelight in the key scenes across the kitchen table, with jazz playing softly on a radio. They understand that Robert and Francesca are not falling in love with one another, exactly—that takes time, when you are middle-aged—but with the *idea* of their love, with what Robert calls "certainty." One of the sources of the movie's poignancy is that the flowering of the love will be forever deferred; they will *know* they are right for one another, and not follow their knowledge.

Robert wants her to leave with him. The notion is enormously attractive to her. Life on the farm is "not what I dreamed of when I was a girl." She envies his life of travel. Not understanding quite how tied she is to the land, he suggests her husband could take her "on a safari." Her smile shows what a wild idea that is. "What's he like?" Robert asks. "He's very clean . . . hard-working . . . gentle . . . a good father . . ."

And he is. The story never makes the mistake of portraying Richard Johnson as a bad husband. But we have seen, in an early scene, that there is no conversation around the Johnson family dinner table. With Robert Kincaid, there is much conversation; they talk of their ideals, and she says, "But how can you live for just what you want?" And, quietly, "We are the choices that we have made, Robert." And they talk on, quoting Yeats, smoking Camels, dancing to the radio.

All of the scenes involving Eastwood and Streep find the right notes and shadings. The surrounding story—involving Francesca's son and daughter, finding her diaries and reading her story after her death—is not as successful. I know this framing mechanism, added by writer Richard LaGravenese, is necessary; the whole emotional tone of the romance depends on it belonging to the lost past. And yet Annie Corley and Victor Slezak, as Caroline and Michael, never seem quite real, and his shock at his mother's behavior, in particular, seems forced, like a story device. The payoff at the end—as they reassess their own lives—seems perfunctory.

But the central story glows. I've seen the movie twice now, and was even more involved the second time, because I was able to pay more attention to the nuances of voice and gesture. Such a story could so easily be vulgarized, could be reduced to obvious elements of seduction, sex, and melodramatic parting. Streep and Eastwood weave a spell, and it is based on that particular knowledge of love and self that comes with middle age. Younger characters might have run off together. Older ones might not have dared to declare themselves. *The Bridges of Madison County* is about two people who find the promise of perfect personal happiness, and understand, with sadness and acceptance, that the most important things in life are not always about making yourself happy.

Bright Angel ★ ★ ★ ½
R, 94 m., 1991

Dermot Mulroney (George), Lili Taylor (Lucy), Sam Shepard (Jack), Valerie Perrine (Aileen), Burt Young (Art), Bill Pullman (Bob). Directed by Michael Fields and produced by Paige Simpson and Robert MacLean. Screenplay by Richard Ford.

There is a moment in every good movie when it becomes clear that the director knows what he is doing. In Michael Fields's *Bright Angel*, that moment comes when the son and the father come home, and find that the mother has been fooling around with another man. The other man is a kid from the local military base, and he doesn't want any trouble, no sir, and he can see that the father is capable of causing a lot of trouble. The voices are what to listen for in this scene—the words, and the music, as the situation balances on the edge of violence.

The mother eventually leaves home, and the son and his father exist in an uneasy camaraderie. The father, played by Sam Shepard, is a spare, angry man. He has good advice to give, and even some love, but his life has been spoiled by disappointment and he cannot create a harbor for his lonely, doubting son.

That is the end of the first movement in *Bright Angel*, which is loosely based on short stories by Richard Ford, who takes the image of the West—the freedom of the open prairies—and makes it seem like such a closed-in place, so drained of freedom, and threatening.

The movie's central story begins as the kid, named George and played with solemn strength by Dermot Mulroney, walks into the local café and runs into Lucy, played by Lili Taylor. She is a vague leftover hippie, belonging to no time and place, who is drifting through on a mission to visit a guy who might testify against her brother, and pay him not to. George and Lucy begin to talk, and like lost souls fall into one another's orbits. They set off together to find the man, and find not only him but a strange criminal ménage centering on a man filled with sarcastic anger (Burt Young). You can look at these people and smell violence.

There were times during *Bright Angel* when I was reminded of *Drugstore Cowboy*, another movie about drifters on the edge of society. These are characters who have no plans. Or rather, they have a lot of plans, but no will or means to make the plans happen. They live in motel rooms, or in houses that do not seem to have permanent inhabitants. They drive cars where a fender or a door will be a different color than the rest of the car—waiting for a paint job that will never come. They smoke a lot, have no pets, are capable of murder.

Like the young characters in *Drugstore Cowboy*, George and Lucy are in over their heads. They are innocents, and if they think they are in love, actually they are just holding on to each other to keep from going under. The movie takes them on an odyssey from one place that is nowhere in particular, to another place that is also nowhere in particular. They are in terrible danger—the danger of the Road Runner, hurrying ahead, not looking down to see if there is anything beneath their feet.

Movies like this (I am also reminded of Terence Malick's *Badlands* and *Days of Heaven*) depend so much on actors for the right tone, and Lily Taylor and Dermot Mulroney are perfectly matched to the material (you may remember her from *Mystic Pizza*, where she played Jojo, who inherited the pizza sauce recipe). Their characters seem to feed on each other's energy; they're in such need that without each other's support they might simply fly off into emptiness.

The movie surrounds them with characters from *film noir*—hard people waiting in those unfriendly rooms for deliveries to arrive and decisions to be made, and other people, junkheads so fried that their conversations seem like free association. And around all of this is the West, which used to be the frontier, but has now been passed by and surrounded.

Bright Lights, Big City ★ ★ ★ ½
R, 107 m., 1988

Michael J. Fox (Jamie), Kiefer Sutherland (Tad), Phoebe Cates (Amanda), Swoosie Kurtz (Megan), Frances Sternhagen (Clara), Tracy Pollan (Vicky), John Houseman (Mr. Vogel), Charlie Schlatter (Michael), Jason Robards (Alex Hardy), Dianne Wiest (Mother). Directed by James Bridges and produced by Mark Rosenberg and Sydney Pollack. Screenplay by Jay McInerney.

What does cocaine make you feel like? It makes you feel like having some more cocaine.
—George Carlin

And that is what Jamie Conway feels like, all day, every day. The chasm between his professional existence and his private life is laughable, and it's growing impossible to keep up the charade that he even cares about the things he's supposed to be doing. He works for a high-powered New York magazine, and the only two things that keep him on the job are guilt and the need for money. He needs the money because he puts it into his nose. He needs the guilt because it's his only link to his ambitions.

Bright Lights, Big City is the record of Jamie's search for the bottom. It takes place over the course of a week or so, a chaotic week in which people, events, and even whole days drift in and out of focus. He is completely out of control. The irony is that he still looks halfway okay, if you don't look too hard. He's together enough to sit in a club and drink double vodkas and engage in absentminded conversation with transparent people. He drinks prodigious amounts of booze, punctuated by cocaine.

It's hard to classify a guy like this. Is he (a) an alcoholic, using the coke so he can stay awake and drink more? Or (b) a cokehead, using the booze to level off? Those are the two choices on Jamie's multiple-part exam. There are no other parts of his life worth serious discussion. His "life" consists, in fact, of the brief window that opens every day between his hangover and oblivion.

Jamie is played by Michael J. Fox, red-eyed and puffy-faced, and trembling with fear every morning when the telephone rings. He once lived in Kansas City and dreamed of becoming a writer, and it was there he met and married Amanda (Phoebe Cates), his pretty young wife. They met in a bar. The movie deliberately never makes clear what, if anything, they truly had to share. In New York, she finds overnight success as a model, and drifts away from him. That's no surprise; the movie makes it pretty clear that Jamie is the kind of port where the tide is always going out.

Now Jamie hauls himself, filled with nausea and self-loathing, into the magazine office every day. He works as a fact-checker. He could care less. He had dreams once. He can barely focus on them. One day he's cornered at the water cooler by the pathetic old drunk Alex Hardy (Jason Robards), who once wrote good fiction and knew Faulkner, and now exists as the magazine's gin-soaked fiction editor.

Alex drags Jamie out to a martini lunch, where the conversation is the typical alcoholic mixture of resentment against those who have made it, and self-hatred for drinking it all away. Jason Robards has always been a great actor, but there is a fleeting moment in this scene that is as good as anything he has ever done. It is a totally blank look. A moment when we can look into the face and eyes of his character and see that nobody, literally nobody, is at home. It's as if his mind has stalled. By supplementing booze with cocaine, Jamie is going to be able to reach Alex's state of numbed incomprehension decades more quickly.

There is one glimmer of hope in Alex's life. He has dinner one night with a bright college student (Tracy Pollan) who is the cousin of his drinking buddy (Kiefer Sutherland). At a restaurant, he goes into the toilet and then decides not to use cocaine: "Let's see if I can get through one evening without chemicals," he muses. He likes her. She is intelligent and kind. Several days later, at the end of a lost weekend of confusion and despair, he looks at himself in a mirror and says, "I need help." He telephones her in the middle of the night. His conversation is disconnected and confused, but what he is really doing is calling for help.

Maybe she can help him, maybe not. The movie ends with Jamie staggering out into the bright dawn of a new day and, in a scene a little too contrived for my taste, trading his dark glasses for a loaf of bread. *Bright Lights, Big City* is a *Lost Weekend* for the 1980s, a chronicle of wasted days and misplaced nights. It was directed by James Bridges, whose *Urban Cowboy* was in many ways an earlier version of the same story. Fox is very good in the central role (he has a long drunken monologue that is the best thing he has ever done in a movie). To his credit, he never seems to be having fun as he journeys through clubland. Few do, for long. If you know someone like Jamie, show him this movie, and don't let him go to the john.

Bring Me the Head of Alfredo Garcia
★ ★ ★ ★
R, 112 m., 1974

Warren Oates (Bennie), Isela Vega (Elita), Kris Kristofferson (Paco), Gig Young (Killer). Directed by Sam Peckinpah and produced by Martin Baum. Screenplay by Gordon T. Dawson and Peckinpah.

Sam Peckinpah's *Bring Me the Head of Alfredo Garcia* is a weird, horrifying film that somehow transcends its unlikely material. It's the story of a drunken and violent odyssey across Mexico by a dropout bartender who, if he returns Alfredo Garcia's head, stands to be paid a million dollars. The head accompanies him in a burlap bag, tossed into the front seat of a beat-up old Ford convertible, and it gathers flies and symbolic meaning at about the same pace.

The movie is some kind of bizarre masterpiece. It's probably not a movie that most people would like, but violence, with Peckinpah, sometimes becomes a psychic ballet. His characters don't look for it, they don't like it, and they negotiate it with weariness and resignation. They're too beat up by life to get any kind of exhilaration from a fight. They've been in far too many fights already, and lost most of them, and the violence they encounter is just another cross to bear.

That's the case with Bennie, the antihero of *Bring Me the Head of Alfredo Garcia*. He's played by Warren Oates, one of that breed of movie actors who attract us, somehow, through their negative qualities. He's like some of the characters played by Jack Nicholson or Bruce Dern; we like him because he's suffered so much more than we ever will (we hope) that no matter what horrors he goes through, or inflicts, we still care about him.

Bennie is a bartender and plays a little piano, and he hears about the head of Alfredo Garcia from a couple of bounty hunters who pass through his saloon. They're played, by the way, by the unlikely team of Gig Young and Robert Webber, who between them define dissipation. Garcia's head is worth a million bucks because Garcia, it turns out, has impregnated the daughter of a rich Mexican industrialist. The millionaire is almost a caricature of macho compulsiveness; he simultaneously puts a price on the head of the culprit, and looks forward with pride to the birth of a grandson.

Bennie sees the million dollars as his ticket out of hell, and on the way to finding it he runs across Alfredo Garcia's former lover, Elita (Isela Vega, looking as moistly erotic as anyone since young Anna Magnani). They fall in love, or something; their relationship is complicated by Bennie's crude shyness and her own custom of being abused by men. The most perversely interesting relationship in the movie, however, is the friendship that grows between Bennie and Alfredo's head, once Bennie has gotten possession of it. That's made somewhat easier by the fact that Alfredo, it turns out, is already dead. But there is a gruesome struggle over his grave, and once Bennie finally gets the head he has to kill to protect his prize. His drive across Mexico is fueled by blood and tequila, and about halfway through it we realize why Peckinpah set his movie in the present, instead of in the past; this same material wouldn't have worked as a historical Western. The conventions of the genre would have insulted us from the impact of what happens. There would have been horses and watering holes and clichés. Instead, we get unforgettable scenes of Warren Oates with that grisly burlap bag and the bottle next to him in the front seat, and the nakedness of his greed is inescapable.

Somewhere along the way Oates, as Bennie, makes a compact with the prize he begins to call "Al." They both loved the same woman, they are both being destroyed by the same member of an upper class, they're both poor bastards who never asked for their grief in life. And slowly, out of the haze of the booze and the depths of his suffering, Bennie allies himself with Al and against the slob with the money. *Bring Me the Head of Alfredo Garcia* is Sam Peckinpah making movies flat out, giving us a desperate character he clearly loves, and asking us to somehow see past the horror and the blood to the sad poem he's trying to write about the human condition.

Broadcast News ★ ★ ★

R, 125 m., 1987

William Hurt (Tom Grunick), Albert Brooks (Aaron Altman), Holly Hunter (Jane Craig), Lois Chiles (Jennifer Mack), Joan Cusack (Blair Litton), Robert Prosky (Bureau Chief). Directed, produced, and written by James L. Brooks.

Broadcast News is as knowledgeable about the TV news-gathering process as any movie ever made, but it also has insights into the more personal matter of how people use high-pressure jobs as a way of avoiding time alone with themselves. The movie was described as being about a romantic triangle, but that's only partly true. It is about three people who toy with the idea of love, but are obsessed by the idea of making television.

Deadline pressure attracts people like that. The newspapers are filled with them, and also ad agencies, brokerages, emergency rooms, show business, sales departments, and police and fire stations. There's a certain adrenaline charge in delivering on a commitment at the last moment, in rushing out to be an instant hero or an instant failure. There's a kind of person who calls you up to shout into the phone, "I can't talk to you now—I'm busy!" This kind of person is always busy, because the lifestyle involves arranging things so you're always behind. Given plenty of time to complete a job, you wait until the last moment to start—guaranteeing a deadline rush.

I know all about that kind of obsession (you don't think I finished this review early, do you?). *Broadcast News* understands it from the inside out, and perhaps the most interesting sequence in the whole movie is a scene where a network news producer sweats it out with a videotape editor to finish a report that is scheduled to appear on the evening news in fifty-two seconds. In an atmosphere like that, theoretical questions get lost. The operational reality, day after day, is to get the job done and beat the deadline and make things look as good as possible. Positive feedback goes to people who deliver. Yesterday's job is forgotten. What have you got for me today?

Right at the center of *Broadcast News* is a character named Jane Craig (Holly Hunter), who is a newswriter-producer for the Washington bureau of one of the networks. She is smart and fast and cherishes certain beliefs about TV news—one of them being that a story should be covered by the person best-qualified to cover it. One of her best friends is Aaron Altman (Albert Brooks), a bright, aggressive reporter. He's one of the best in the business, but he's not especially good on camera. During a trip south she meets Tom Grunick (William Hurt), a sportscaster who cheerfully admits he has little education, is not a good reader, and doesn't know much about current events. But he has been hired for the

Washington bureau because he looks good and has a natural relationship with the camera.

The Hunter character is only human. She is repelled by this guy's credentials, but she likes his body. After he comes to Washington, he quickly gains the attention of the network brass, while the Brooks character goes into eclipse. Hunter is torn between the two men: Brooks, who says he loves her and is the better reporter, and Hurt, who says he wants to learn, and who is sexier.

The tricky thing about *Broadcast News*—the quality in James L. Brooks's screenplay that makes it so special—is that all three characters have a tendency to grow emotionally absentminded when it's a choice between romance and work. Frankly, they'd rather work. After Hunter whispers into Hurt's earpiece to talk him through a crucial live report on a Middle East crisis, he kneels at her feet and says it was like sex, having her voice inside his head. He never gets that excited about sex. Neither does she.

Much of the plot of *Broadcast News* centers around a piece that Hurt reports about "date rape." Listening to one woman's story, he is so moved that a tear trickles down his cheek. It means a great deal to Hunter whether that tear is real or faked. Experienced TV people will question why Hunter, a veteran producer, didn't immediately notice the detail that bothers her so much later on. But in a way, *Broadcast News* is not about details, but about the larger question of whether TV news is becoming show business.

Jack Nicholson has an unbilled supporting role in the movie as the network's senior anchorman, an irascible man who has high standards himself, but is not above seeing his ratings assisted by coverage that may be questionable. The implication is that the next anchor will be a William Hurt-type, great on camera, but incapable of discerning authenticity from fakery. Meanwhile, the Albert Brooks types will end up doing superior journalism in smaller "markets" (the TV word for "cities"), and the Holly Hunter types will keep on fighting all the old deadlines, plus a new one, the biological clock.

Broadcast News has a lot of interesting things to say about television. But the thing it does best is look into a certain kind of personality and a certain kind of relationship. Like *Terms of Endearment*, the previous film by James Brooks, it does not see relationships as a matter of meeting someone you like and falling in love. Brooks, almost alone among major Hollywood filmmakers, knows that some people have higher priorities than love, and deeper fears.

Broadway Danny Rose ★ ★ ★ ½
PG, 86 m., 1984

Woody Allen (Danny Rose), Mia Farrow (Tina Vitale), Nick Apollo Forte (Lou Canova). Directed by Woody Allen and produced by Robert Greenhut and Charles H. Joffe. Screenplay by Allen.

The first time we see him, he's talking fast, and his arms are working like a guy doing an imitation of an air traffic controller. His hands keep coming in for landings. This is Broadway Danny Rose, the most legendary talent agent in New York, the guy who will represent you after you've been laughed off every stage in the Catskills. He represents blind xylophonists, piano-playing birds, and has-been crooners with drinking problems. He's the kind of guy that comics sitting around on their day off tell stories about. He also is Woody Allen, but he is less like Woody Allen than some of the other characters Allen has played. After the autobiography of *Stardust Memories*, after the whimsy of *A Midsummer Night's Sex Comedy*, and the antiseptic experimentation of *Zelig*, this movie has Allen creating a character and following him all the way through a crazy story. After a period when Allen seemed stuck in self-doubt and introspection, he loosens up and has a good time.

Broadway Danny Rose, like all of Allen's best movies, is a New York movie. It starts at the Carnegie Deli, with comedians sitting around a table trading Danny Rose stories, and then it flashes back to the best Danny Rose story of them all, about how Danny signed up this has-been alcoholic tenor and carefully nurtured his career back to the brink of stardom. Riding the nostalgia boom, Danny takes the guy and books him into Top Forty concerts, until finally he gets him a date at the Waldorf—and Milton Berle is in the audience, looking for guests for his TV special. Except the crooner has a complicated love life. He has a wife, and he also has a girlfriend. He wants Danny Rose to be the "beard" and take the girlfriend to the concert. Otherwise he won't feel right. But then the crooner and the girl have a fight, and the girl goes back to her Mafioso boyfriend, and Danny Rose winds up at a mob wedding with a gun in his face.

All of this is accomplished with wonderfully off-the-wall characterizations. Allen makes Danny Rose into a caricature, and then, working from that base, turns him back into a human being: By the end of the film, we see the person beneath the mannerisms. Nick Apollo Forte, an actor I've never seen before, plays the has-been crooner with a soft touch: he's childish, he's a bear, he's loyal, he has a monstrous ego. The real treasure among the performances, however, is Mia Farrow's work as Tina Vitale, the crooner's girlfriend. You would think that Mia Farrow would be one of the most instantly recognizable actresses in the movies with those finely chiseled features and that little-girl voice. But here she is a chain-smoking, brassy blonde with her hair piled up on top of her head, and a pair of fashionable sunglasses, and dresses that look like they came from the boutique in a Mafia resort hotel.

Broadway Danny Rose uses all of the basic ingredients of Damon Runyon's Broadway: the pathetic acts looking for a job, the guys who get a break and forget their old friends, the agents with hearts of gold, the beautiful showgirls who fall for Woody Allen types, the dumb gangsters, big shots at the ringside tables (Howard Cosell plays himself). It all works.

A Bronx Tale ★ ★ ★ ★
R, 121 m., 1993

Robert De Niro (Lorenzo), Chazz Palminteri (Sonny), Lillo Brancato (Calogero, age 17), Francis Capra (Calogero, age 9), Taral Hicks (Jane), Kathrine Narducci (Rosina), Clem Caserta (Jimmy Whispers), Joe Pesci (Carmine). Directed by De Niro and produced by Jane Rosenthal, Jon Kilik, and De Niro. Screenplay by Palminteri.

A boy comes of age in an Italian-American neighborhood in the Bronx. His father gives him a piece of advice: "Nothing is more tragic than a wasted talent." A street-corner gangster gives him another piece of advice: "Nobody really cares." These pieces of advice seem contradictory, but the boy finds that they make a nice fit.

The movie starts when he is nine. Sitting on his front stoop, he sees Sonny, the gangster, shoot a man in what looks like a fight over a parking space. Then Sonny looks him in the eyes, hard, and the kid gets the message: "Don't squeal!" Sonny (Chazz Palminteri) wants to do something for the kid, and offers a cushy $150-a-week paycheck to his father, Lorenzo (Robert De Niro). Lorenzo turns him down. He is a working man,

proud that he supports his family by driving a bus. He doesn't like the Mafia and doesn't want the money.

The kid, whose name is Calogero but who is called C, idolizes Sonny. He likes the way Sonny exercises a quiet authority, and talks with his hands, and dresses well. When C is seventeen, he goes to work for Sonny, against his father's wishes. And in the year when most of the film is set, he learns lessons that he will use all of his life.

A Bronx Tale was written for the stage by Palminteri, who plays Sonny with a calm grace in the film, but was Calogero in real life. There have been a lot of movies about neighborhood mafiosi (Martin Scorsese's *GoodFellas* was the best), but this movie isn't like the others. It doesn't tell some dumb story about how the bus driver and the mobster have to shoot each other, or about how C is the hostage in a tug-of-war. It's about two men with some experience of life, who love this kid and want to help him out.

Lorenzo, the bus driver, gives sound advice: "You want to see a real hero? Look at a guy who gets up in the morning and goes off to work and supports his family. That's heroism." But Sonny gives sound advice, too. One of the things he tells C is that you cannot live your life on the basis of what other people think you should do, because when the chips are down, nobody really cares. You're giving them a power they don't really have. That sounds like deep thinking for a guy who hangs on the corner and runs a numbers racket, but Sonny, as played by Palminteri, is a complex, lonely character, who might have been a priest or a philosopher had not life called him to the vocation of neighborhood boss.

It is 1968. Blacks are moving into the next neighborhood. C's friends entertain themselves by beating up on black kids who ride past on their bikes. C has other things on his mind. On his father's bus, he has seen a lovely black girl named Jane (Taral Hicks), and been struck with the thunderbolt of love. From the way she smiles back, she likes him, too. When he discovers that they go to the same school, he knows his fate is to ask her out.

But he is troubled, because in 1968 this is not the thing for a kid from his neighborhood (or hers) to do. He questions both his father and Sonny, posing a hypothetical case, and although neither bursts into liberalspeak about the brotherhood of man, both tell him about the same thing, which is that you have to do what you think is right, or live with the consequences.

C's romance is a sweet subplot of the movie, which is filled with life and memories. There are, for example, the characters in Sonny's crowd, including a guy who is such bad luck he has to go stand in the bathroom when Sonny is rolling the dice. And another guy with a complexion so bad he looks like raisin bread. And strange visitors from outside the neighborhood—bikers and hippies and black people—who remind us that C lives in a closed and insular community.

The climax of the film finds C inside a car he does not want to occupy, going with his friends to do something he doesn't want to do. This part is very true. Peer pressure is a terrible thing among teen-age boys. It causes them to do things they desperately wish they could avoid. They're afraid to look chicken, or different. C is no exception. His whole life hinges on the outcome of that ride.

A Bronx Tale is a very funny movie sometimes, and very touching at other times. It is filled with life and colorful characters and great lines of dialogue, and De Niro, in his debut as a director, finds the right notes as he moves from laughter to anger to tears. What's important about the film is that it's about values. About how some boys grow up into men who can look at themselves in the mirror in the morning, and others just go along with the crowd, forgetting after a while that they ever had a choice.

The Brother from Another Planet
★ ★ ★ ½
PG, 110 m., 1984

Joe Morton (The Brother), Maggie Renzi (Noreen), Fisher Stevens (Card Trickster), John Sayles (Man in Black). Directed by John Sayles and produced by Sayles and Maggie Renzi. Screenplay by Sayles.

When the movies started to talk, they began to lose the open-eyed simplicity with which they saw the world. *The Brother from Another Planet* tells the story of a man who cannot talk, but who can read minds, listen carefully, look deep into eyes, and provide a sort of mirror for our society. That makes it sound serious, but like all the most serious movies, it's a comedy.

The film stars Joe Morton as a visitor from outer space, who looks like a black human being, unless you look carefully at the three funny toes on his feet. He arrives on

Earth in a spaceship that looks borrowed from the cheapest B space operas from the 1950s, swims ashore, and finds himself on Manhattan Island. At first he is completely baffled. Before long, everyone he meets is just as baffled. It is strange to deal with people who confound all your expectations: It might even force you to reevaluate yourself.

The brother is not looking for trouble, is not controversial, wants only to make sense of this weird new world. Because his instinctive response to most situations is a sort of blank reserve, people project their own feelings and expectations upon him. They tell him what he must be thinking, and behave as if they are right. He goes along.

The movie finds countless opportunities for humorous scenes, most of them with a quiet little bite, a way of causing us to look at our society. The brother runs into hookers and connivers, tourists from Indiana, immigrant shopkeepers, and a New York weirdo who, in one of the movie's best scenes, shows him a baffling card trick, and then demonstrates another trick that contains a cynical grain of big-city truth. The brother walks through this menagerie with a sometimes bemused, sometimes puzzled look on his face. People seem to have a lot of problems on this planet. He is glad to help out when he can; for example, curing video games by a laying on of hands. His right hand contains the power to heal machines, and it is amazing how quickly people accept that, if it is useful to them.

The Brother from Another Planet was written and directed by John Sayles, who is a one-man industry in the world of the American independent film. His credits include *Return of the Secaucus Seven, Lianna,* and *Baby, It's You,* and in this film—by using a central character who cannot talk—he is sometimes able to explore the kinds of scenes that haven't been possible since the death of silent film. There are individual moments here worthy of a Keaton, and there are times when Joe Morton's unblinking passivity in the midst of chaos really does remind us of Buster.

There is also a curious way in which the film functions as more subtle social satire than might seem possible in a low-budget, good-natured comedy. Because the hero, the brother, has literally dropped out of the skies, he doesn't have an opinion on anything. He only gradually begins to realize that on this world he is "black," and that his color makes a difference in some situations.

He tries to accept that. When he is hurt or wronged, his reaction is not so much anger as surprise: It seems to him so unnecessary that people behave unkindly toward one another. He is a little surprised they would go to such an effort. His surprise, in its own sweet and uncomplicated way, is one of the most effective elements in the whole movie.

Brother's Keeper ★ ★ ★
NO MPAA RATING, 104 m., 1993

Directed, produced, and edited by Joe Berlinger and Bruce Sinofsky.

For as long as anyone in the central New York hamlet of Munnsville (population 500) could remember, the Ward boys had run a dairy farm outside of town. Everybody knew them—by sight, anyway—and figured them for harmless old coots. They didn't bathe or shave overmuch, and rode into town arrayed on their tractor. They lived in a two-room shack that few of their neighbors had much desire to visit, or get downwind from.

Then, on a June morning in 1990, William Ward, at sixty-four the second-oldest brother, was discovered dead in bed. He had been feeling poorly for quite some time, and given his general condition, it was reasonable to assume he died of natural causes. But a hotshot local lawman smelled foul play, and within a day the youngest brother, Delbert, fifty-nine, was charged with murder. *Brother's Keeper* is an extraordinary documentary about what happened next, as a town banded together to stop what it saw as a miscarriage of justice.

"Hell," one of the townspeople observes, "when they asked Delbert if he was ready to waive his rights, he didn't know the difference between that and waving to someone on the road."

The Ward boys are none of them any too bright, although it's a good question whether they are retarded or simply completely out of touch with modern life. Their cows and pigs live in greater comfort on their farm than they do, not to mention the poultry they raise in an old school bus. They farmed for many decades, keeping to themselves, working long hours, sitting in front of a TV at night, turning in early.

The controversy over the Wards quickly hit the national media. It had everything: quaint rural hayseeds, dark hints of fratricide, doubts over the due process of law. Connie Chung and other media stars turned up to interview the Ward boys, and so did documentary filmmakers Joe Berlinger and Bruce Sinofsky and their cinematographer, Douglas Cooper.

They kept coming back, for more than a year; the passage of the seasons provides an undercurrent for the film. They filmed hearings and trials, community meetings, and even the benefits held to raise money for Delbert's defense. The irony was that after trouble found the Wards, they became more popular and accepted in Munnsville than ever before, and it's quite a sight, seeing them square dancing at a fund-raiser and loading up their plates at the buffet table.

Berlinger and Sinofsky were patient with Delbert and his two surviving brothers, Roscoe, seventy, and Lyman, sixty-two. They won their trust, and soon it was a common sight in Munnsville to see the brothers followed by the small camera team. We gradually begin to get a sense of the three men, whose values and daily rhythms reflect lives of hard manual labor as they might have been lived centuries ago.

The film wisely never takes a position on the actual guilt of Delbert (and I would not dream of revealing the outcome of his legal process, which unfolds as a courtroom drama). Instead, it tries to see into their lives, to understand that for unlearned men who had lived so close to the harsh realities of farming, life and death itself had a more fundamental meaning. Did Delbert smother William with a pillow, as the prosecution charged, in order to put him out of his misery—as he might have put down a sick animal? Or did William die in his sleep? Or are there darker possibilities?

Brother's Keeper, 1992's best documentary, has an impact and immediacy that most fiction films can only envy. It tells a strong story, and some passages are truly inspirational, as the neighbors of Munnsville become determined that Delbert will not be railroaded by some ambitious prosecutor more concerned with bringing charges than with understanding the reality of the situation. Seeing this film, I got a new appreciation for how deeply the notion of civil liberties is embedded in our national consciousness. None of the people on the Delbert Ward defense committee ever went to law school. But they know a lot more about fair play and due process than the people in this film who did.

The Buddy Holly Story ★ ★ ★ ½
PG, 113 m., 1978

Bill Jordan (Riley Randolph), Maria Richwine (Maria Elena Holly), Conrad Janis (Ross Turner), Dick O'Neill (Sol Zuckerman), Gary Busey (Buddy Holly), Don Stroud (Jesse), Charles Martin Smith (Ray Bob). Directed by Steve Rash and produced by Fred Bauer. Screenplay by Robert Gittler.

On February 3, 1959, a small plane crashed outside Mason City, Iowa, killing Buddy Holly, Ritchie Valens, and J.P. (The Big Bopper) Richardson. Don McLean sang about that day in "American Pie." He called it the day the music died.

Walking out of *The Buddy Holly Story*, you wonder if maybe he wasn't right. It's no use trying to guess how things might have turned out if Holly hadn't been on that flight. He might have continued to develop as the most original rock and roll artist of his generation. He might, on the other hand, have gradually become a Paul Anka or a Barry Manilow, a polished performer of comfortably mainstream pop. The movie makes a pretty good case for the first possibility.

It also involves us as show-biz biographies rarely do. This is one rock and roll movie with a chance of being remembered, one with something to say and the style and energy to say it well. That's partly because it had good material to start with; Holly's life provides a microcosm of rock and roll's transformation into the dominant music of the last decades. But it's also because of Gary Busey's remarkable performance as Buddy Holly. If you're a fan of Holly and his music, you'll be quietly amazed at how completely Busey gets into the character. His performance isn't an imitation, a series of "impressions." It's a distillation of how Holly *seemed*, and how he sounded. That's all the more impressive because the movie doesn't use dubbing from the original records: Busey himself sings Holly's arrangements. And the movie's many concert scenes don't use post-dubbing, which almost always result in a flat and unconvincing sound. Busey did the material live.

That's crucial, in a way, because if *The Buddy Holly Story* doesn't convince (or remind) us that Holly's music was good, and important, the movie itself fails. Busey and the filmmakers do convince us, without even seeming to try. Walking out of the theater, I overheard a teen-age couple expressing surprise that Holly had composed "It's So Easy to Fall in Love." They thought it was a Linda Ronstadt original.

More performers than Ronstadt learned from Holly. All the important rockers of the last thirty years, and particularly the Beatles, benefited from Holly's fusion of basic rock and roll, deeper musical sophistication, and lyrics that came with a sincere intensity ("I *was* Buddy Holly," John Lennon once said.) Most albums cut in 1958 or 1959 sound dated today, even the good ones. Holly's old albums still sound fresh.

The movie follows the events of Holly's life, more or less, from his beginnings in Lubbock, Texas, through his early hit records, his quick national fame, his performances on "The Ed Sullivan Show," his marriage, his death. Rock historians have pointed out the ways in which the screenplay alters the facts (Holly's parents were not opposed to his musical career; his romance with his wife, Maria, was whirlwind, not the stubborn courtship in the movie; the decision to take a plane that last night was made, not because the bus broke down, but because Holly and the others wanted to get their laundry done).

Details like that don't matter much. The movie gets the feel right, and there's real energy in the concert scenes, especially the tricky debut of Buddy Holly and the Crickets as the first white act in Harlem's famous Apollo Theater. And the supporting performances are convincing; they're not walk-ons, as they tend to be in show biz movies. Don Stroud and Charles Martin Smith are just right as the down-home Crickets. Maria Richwine brings a sweetness, an understanding to the role of Holly's wife, and Gloria Irricari, as her aunt, steals a wonderful scene. And Dick O'Neill, as the white booker who thought Holly was black when he booked him into the Apollo, does an inspired double-take.

When all of this has been said, there are still the songs to be considered. "That'll Be the Day." "Peggy Sue." "Oh, Boy!" "Words of Love." "True Love Ways." "It's So Easy." "It Doesn't Matter Anymore." Gary Busey sings them with a style that does Holly justice. And that's saying something. They live, and the movie's concert sequences have the immediacy and energy of documentary footage—which is essentially what they are.

Bugsy ★ ★ ★ ★
R, 135 m., 1991

Warren Beatty (Bugsy Siegel), Annette Bening (Virginia Hill), Harvey Keitel (Mickey Cohen),

Ben Kingsley (Meyer Lansky), Elliott Gould (Harry Greenberg), Joe Mantegna (George). Directed by Barry Levinson and produced by Mark Johnson, Levinson, and Warren Beatty. Screenplay by James Toback.

He's a real smoothie, Warren Beatty, and when he plays one in a movie he is almost always effective. But his title role in *Bugsy* is more than effective; it's perfect for him—showing a man who not only creates a seductive vision, but falls in love with it himself. Beatty plays Benjamin "Bugsy" Siegel, who if he were not a gangster might have been honored on a postage stamp by now as the father of Las Vegas.

Siegel ventured west with some of the eastern mob's investment funds in the early 1940s, and fell in love almost immediately with a leggy starlet named Virginia Hill (Annette Bening). He also fell in love with the movies, and with his slick good looks even got a screen test, although his best scenes were all to be played in mob boardrooms.

His great role in history came to him as he stood in a sleazy, low-rent casino in Vegas, which was then an obscure crossroads in a state that permitted legalized gambling. Ben Siegel had a vision of a Las Vegas that was not an obscure backwater, but a town with big, classy casinos that had name acts in their show rooms. Nobody shared his vision. But he knew that if he built it, they would come. And he did build one casino, the Flamingo, its name inspired by Virginia Hill's legs. He spent so much of the mob's money on it, in fact, that he was rubbed out before he could see the modern city spring from his dream.

This story is told in *Bugsy*, not as history, but as a romance. The screenplay by James Toback, developed with Beatty and then directed by Barry Levinson, shows Siegel as a smooth, charming, even lovable guy, even though he was also a coldhearted killer. The two sides of his character hardly seem to acknowledge one another; on the one hand, he is a family man with a wife and children, who goes to work every day. On the other hand, he is an adulterer whose business involves killing people, and who defies the Mafia itself by spending more of its money than he has quite gotten around to accounting for.

Watching Beatty and Annette Bening in this movie, it is impossible not to be reminded of the famous ad line for *Bonnie and Clyde* (1967), the greatest moment in Beatty's career: "They're young, they're in love . . . and they kill people." Hill does not kill, but

she is as hard and calculating, and seductive, as the Bonnie Parker character, and there are times here when Bugsy and Virginia and Bonnie and Clyde all seem to be playing the same tunes on their libidos.

Levinson is back in the same period he used for key scenes of his last picture, *Avalon*, and the 1940s look roomy and plush here; it was a decade that had many of the same inventions we now take for granted, like automobiles and telephones, but back then they were full size and made out of materials that would not break. Bugsy moves into a big Beverly Hills house (he makes the owner an offer he cannot refuse), he hangs out in the right restaurants and clubs, he makes the right contacts, he gets a lot of publicity, and his image is summed up in a headline: Gangster or Star?

It's a question the mob is asking, too. Levinson's movie strikes a different tone than the *Godfather* pictures, but like them, it shows the Mafia as essentially a business, depending on discipline. Levinson and Toback are interested in a different strata of organized crime than Francis Coppola and Mario Puzo, however; the *Godfather* pictures were mostly about Italian-Americans, and most of the key characters in *Bugsy* are Jewish. There's Ben Kingsley, as Meyer Lansky, the only Mafia leader who perhaps fully understood what made Bugsy tick; Harvey Keitel, as Mickey Cohen, an unforgiving killer; and Elliott Gould, as Harry Greenberg, the hapless friend for whom Bugsy will walk a mile, but no further.

For Toback, the screenplay touches on obsessions that are deep in his previous work. His first notable screenplay was *The Gambler* (1976), starring James Caan as a compulsive bettor, and in Toback's own movies as a director (*Fingers, Exposed, The Pick-Up Artist*) are the twin themes of men obsessively attracted to women, and men driven to extend themselves financially to the point of actual physical danger, usually from criminals.

Here, Bugsy Siegel scarcely seems to comprehend the danger he is hurtling toward. Distracted by his passionate love affair, besotted by his vision of a gambling temple in the desert, he listens to the warnings of Lansky and others, but does not seem to understand them. Meanwhile, the movie develops a sly, fascinating subplot involving Virginia Hill's own tangled motives. Does she really love Bugsy or money? Does she really know?

Bugsy moves with a lightness that belies its

strength. It is a movie that vibrates with optimism and passion, with the exuberance of the con man on his game. Bugsy Siegel is not a good man and no doubt does not deserve a good end, but somehow we are carried along with him because he seems so innocent (even of his own bloody sins). At the end of the movie there's one of those "crawls," as Hollywood calls them, where we're told what eventually happened—how Las Vegas became a $200 billion industry, how Virginia Hill finally died. It's the kind of crawl you'd get at the end of a movie about a great man. This time, with Bugsy, you don't get a lump in your throat, but you do think, Jeez, it's too bad the guy didn't at least live to see Glitter Gulch.

Bugsy Malone ★ ★ ★ ½
G, 94 m., 1976

Jodie Foster (Nightclub Singer), Scott Baio (Bugsy Malone), John Cassisi (Boss), Paul Murphy (Hit Man). Directed by Alan Parker and produced by Alan Marshall. Screenplay by Parker.

At first the notion seems alarming: a gangster movie cast entirely with kids. Especially when we learn that *Bugsy Malone* isn't intended as a kid's movie so much as a cheerful comment on the childlike values and behavior in classic Hollywood crime films. What are kids doing in something like this? But then we see the movie and we relax. *Bugsy Malone* is like nothing else. It's an original, a charming one, and it has yet another special performance by Jodie Foster, who at thirteen was already getting the roles that grown-up actresses complained weren't being written for women anymore. She plays a hard-bitten nightclub singer and vamps her way through a torch song by Paul Williams with approximately as much style as Rita Hayworth brought to *Gilda*. She starts on stage, drifts down into the audience, arches her eyebrows at the fat cats (all about junior high school age), and, in general, is astonishingly assured. And her performance seems just right in the film; *Bugsy Malone* depends almost totally on tone, and if you put kids in these situations and directed them just a little wrongly the movie would be offensive. But it's not, and it's especially right with Foster.

It tells a gangster story we know almost by heart, about the tough new gang that wants to take over the territory. Da Boss (a kid named John Cassisi who looks like he was born wearing a carnation in the lapel of his pinstripe) recruits hired guns to help protect his turf. Bugsy Malone (Scott Baio in training for John Garfield) is the guy he's gotta have. But maybe even Bugsy can't help, because the other gang has a dreaded new weapon. In Al Capone's day, it was machine guns. In Bugsy's movie, it's marshmallow guns. They open up on you with one of these, and you got more than egg on your face. Old-fashioned weapons like custard pies are useless in a one-on-one situation.

Halfway through *Bugsy Malone*, I started wondering how anyone ever came up with this idea for a movie. Alan Parker, who wrote and directed it, claims his inspiration came while he was watching *The Godfather.* I dunno, I think the movie has more insights into kids than into gangsters.

When kids play, it's real. That's one of the things we lose when we grow up: the ability to turn the backyard into the OK Corral. The kids in *Bugsy Malone* don't behave as if the material is camp or a put-on. For them, it's real—especially the indignity of catching a marshmallow in your ear. And so in an uncanny way the movie works as a gangster movie and we remember that the old Bogart and Cagney classics had a childlike innocence, too. The world was simpler then. Now it's so complicated maybe only a kid can still understand the Bogart role.

Bull Durham ★ ★ ★ ½
R, 108 m., 1988

Kevin Costner (Crash Davis), Susan Sarandon (Annie Savoy), Tim Robbins ("Nuke" LaLoosh), Trey Wilson (Skip), Robert Wuhl (Larry), William O'Leary (Jimmy). Directed by Ron Shelton and produced by Thom Mount and Mark Burg. Screenplay by Shelton.

"Some days, you win. Some days, you lose. And some days, it rains."—Baseball proverb

Bull Durham is a baseball version of *Wall Street,* in which everybody's takeover bid is for someone else's heart. The movie was promoted as a romantic comedy, but Susan Sarandon has a great scene right at the outset where she corrects that notion. She holds a little meeting between two of the new members of the local minor league ball club and explains that every year she chooses one player to spend the season with, and they are the two current finalists. The rest of the movie involves, in one way or another, a three-way contest to see (a) who really loves whom, (b) who really can trust whom, and

(c) whether the answers to (a) and (b) involve the same two persons.

A lot of baseball is played along the way. *Bull Durham* was written and directed by Ron Shelton, who spent some time in the minor leagues, and this is a sports movie that knows what it is talking about. There are quiet little scenes that have the ring of absolute accuracy, as when a player is called into the office and told his contract is not being picked up, and the blow is softened by careful mention of a "possibility of a coaching job in the organization next season . . ." And there probably isn't a coaching job and nobody wants it anyway, but by such lies can sad truths be told.

The movie stars Kevin Costner as Crash Davis, an aging catcher and minor league veteran who knows the ropes, and Tim Robbins as "Nuke" LaLoosh, a hot young pitcher who has one hell of a fastball but no control and no maturity. Costner has been brought to the club to provide some seasoning for the rookie, and so inevitably they get into a fight before they've even been introduced. Costner has observed that Robbins has great control—unless he thinks about what he's doing. One moment of thought, and the ball gets pitched into the stands. So Costner stands outside a bar and taunts Robbins to hit him in the chest with his best fastball—something, of course, that once he starts thinking about it, Robbins is absolutely unable to do.

That kind of baseball philosophy provides a sound background for the movie, which has its foreground in Susan Sarandon's bedroom. I don't know who else they could have hired to play Annie Savoy, the Sarandon character who pledges her heart and her body to one player a season, but I doubt if the character would have worked without Sarandon's wonderful performance. Annie could have been portrayed as a lot of things—as a tramp, maybe, or a pathetic case study—but Sarandon portrays her as a woman who, quite simply, loves baseball and baseball players and wants to do her thing for the home team. Why does she limit her love affairs to one season? Anyone who has ever been a minor league baseball fan knows the answer to that one: Anybody who's any good goes up to the big leagues after a year, and Annie, of course, is only interested in the best players.

The romantic triangle unfolds during a season in which it never seems to matter very much how well the Durham Bulls are doing.

They lose, they win, they spend a lot of time on buses and in hotel rooms, and meanwhile, Sarandon and Costner begin to realize that she is more than a groupie and he is more than a catcher. They find each other dropping the names of writers and making references to things they should not necessarily know, and finally one day Costner explodes in frustration: "Who *are* you, anyway?" Perhaps he suspects that if he finds the answer to that question, she will steal his heart away.

The kid pitcher is a lot less subtle about all of this. He enjoys being Annie's lover, for a time, but when he gets to a winning streak, he starts believing all those old stories about conserving your precious bodily fluids, and he becomes chaste as a monk. Costner, of course, is feeding him the stories. Meanwhile, we're getting to know some of the other members of the team and management, in a low-key, Altman-style directorial approach that fills up the background with a lot of atmosphere and action.

Bull Durham is a treasure of a movie because it knows so much about baseball and so little about love. The movie is a completely unrealistic romantic fantasy, and in the real world the delicate little balancing act of these three people would crash into pieces—but this is a movie, and so we want to believe in love, and we want to believe that once in a while lovers can get a break from fate. That's why the movie's ending is so perfect. Not because it seems just right, but because it seems wildly impossible and we want to believe it anyway.

Bullets Over Broadway ★ ★ ★ ½ |NEW|
R, 98 m., 1994
(See related Film Clip, p. 871.)

John Cusack (David Shayne), Jack Warden (Julian Marx), Chazz Palminteri (Cheech), Joe Viterelli (Nick Valenti), Jennifer Tilly (Olive Neal), Rob Reiner (Sheldon Flender), Mary-Louise Parker (Ellen), Dianne Wiest (Helen Sinclair), Harvey Fierstein (Sid Loomis), Jim Broadbent (Warner Purcell), Tracey Ullman (Eden Brent). Directed by Woody Allen and produced by Robert Greenhut. Screenplay by Allen and Douglas McGrath.

As Woody Allen's *Bullets Over Broadway* opens, an earnest young playwright has finally found financing for his latest dreary exercise in social responsibility. It's 1929, the world's in tumult, and the playwright is proudly left wing. But the guy putting up the money is a rich gangster who couldn't care less which wing he is—just as long as the gangster's girlfriend gets a big role in the play.

All by itself, this could be the set-up for a good comedy. But Allen has a master stroke up his sleeve, in the form of the gun moll's bodyguard, a hard-nosed killer who insists on attending all the play's rehearsals. He sits back in the darkness of the theater, a large dark lump of menace with a gun tucked under his armpit, and then, one day, from out of the shadows, his voice is heard. He has a suggestion about the crappy dialogue.

The bodyguard is named Cheech, and he is played by Chazz Palminteri on a note of menace combined with natural intelligence. He is not a playwright. He has hardly seen a play before. But as he sits there, day after day, watching the cast struggle with unsayable lines and unplayable ideas, he can see what's wrong. Hell, anyone could.

The twist involving the bodyguard is what makes *Bullets Over Broadway* more than what it could have been, a funny but routine backstage comedy. Allen follows the simple logic of this character until it leads to a moment both shocking and incredibly funny; when I saw the movie, the audience laughed uproariously, because taboos were being broken even as inexorable logic was being followed.

Allen's cast re-creates some of the same madcap zaniness that's always associated with the Broadway of the late 1920s, when every night's foibles were rehashed the next day at the Algonquin Round Table. John Cusack plays David Shayne, the playwright, as a young man of terrifying seriousness, who nevertheless is cheerfully willing to compromise his art for success. He is the target of a seduction attempt by Helen Sinclair (Dianne Wiest), a fading star with an alcohol problem, who loves to discuss her role over drinks. (In a speakeasy, she orders two martinis. He's flattered that she knows his drink—until she explains that both martinis are for her.)

The other members of the play cast are peculiar in that focused, self-obsessed way that only actors seem able to obtain. There's leading man Warner Purcell, for example, played by Jim Broadbent as a man with serious eating and romantic disorders. He starts out consuming only hot water "with a little lemon" and ends up eating everything in sight, ballooning to alarming proportions while dangerously falling in love with the gangster's girl. And there's Eden Brent (Tracey Ullman), loud, confident, and with a loose flywheel. And of course the shrill-voiced, spectacularly untalented Olive Neal (Jennifer Tilly), the gun moll, whose presence on stage is a serious handicap for any scene.

Allen and his cowriter, Douglas McGrath, play the backstage stuff for laughs, and get a lot of them, especially with the food subplot involving Broadbent. (He's the large, genial actor you may remember as the bartender in *The Crying Game*.) But when the second level of the screenplay gets cooking, darker and more forbidden areas of humor open up.

What, for example, is the responsibility of the artist to his art? We've heard of artists who would "kill for their art"—but would they really? And should they?

There's the sneaky suspicion that some of this subplot in *Bullets Over Broadway* may refer obliquely to events in Allen's life. The heart has its reasons, he argued at a famous press conference, and in the movie that's echoed with "an artist creates his own moral universe." Only gradually do we realize that the only artist in *Bullets Over Broadway* who takes art *really* seriously is Cheech, the bodyguard.

Bullets Over Broadway shares a kinship with a more serious film by Allen, *Crimes and Misdemeanors*, in which a man committed murder and was able, somehow, almost to justify it. Now here is the comic side of the same coin. The movie is very funny and, in the way it follows its logic wherever it leads, surprisingly tough.

Burden of Dreams ★ ★ ★ ★
NO MPAA RATING, 94 m., 1982

Featuring Werner Herzog, Klaus Kinski, Claudia Cardinale, Jason Robards, and Mick Jagger. Directed and produced by Les Blank, with Maureen Gosling.

Les Blank's *Burden of Dreams* is one of the most remarkable documentaries ever made about the making of a movie. There are at least two reasons for that. One is that the movie being made, Werner Herzog's *Fitzcarraldo*, involved some of the most torturous and dangerous on-location shooting experiences in film history. The other is that the documentary is by Les Blank, himself a brilliant filmmaker, who is unafraid to ask difficult questions and portray Herzog, warts and all.

The story of Herzog's *Fitzcarraldo* is already the stuff of movie legend. The movie was shot on location deep within the rain forests of South America, one thousand miles from civilization. When the first version of the film was half-finished, its star, Jason Robards, was rushed back to New York with amoebic dysentery and forbidden by his doctors to return to the location. Herzog replaced Robards with Klaus Kinski (star of his *Aguirre, the Wrath of God*), but meanwhile, co-star Mick Jagger left the production because of a commitment to a concert tour. Then the Kinski version of *Fitzcarraldo* was caught in the middle of a border war between tribes of Indians. The whole production was moved twelve hundred miles, to a new location where the mishaps included plane crashes, disease, and attacks by unfriendly Indians. And all of those hardships were on top of the incredible task Herzog set himself to film: He wanted to show his obsessed hero using teams of Indians to pull an entire steamship up a hillside using only block and tackle!

Blank and his associate, Maureen Gosling, visited both locations of Herzog's film. Their documentary includes the only available record of some of the earlier scenes with Robards and Jagger. It also includes scenes in which Herzog seems to be going slowly mad, blaming the evil of the jungle and the depth of his own compulsions. In *Fitzcarraldo*, you can see the incredible strain as men try to pull a steamship up a sharp incline, using only muscle power and a few elementary principles of mechanics. In *Burden of Dreams*, Blank's camera moves back one more step, to show the actual mechanisms by which Herzog hoped to move his ship. A giant bulldozer is used to augment the block-and-pulley, but it proves barely equal to the task, and at one point the Brazilian engineer in charge of the project walks off, warning that lives will be lost.

What drives Herzog to make films that test his sanity and risk his life and those of his associates? Stanley Kauffmann, in the *New Republic*, argued that, for Herzog, the purpose of film is to risk death, and each of his films is in some way a challenge hurled at the odds. Herzog has made films on the slopes of active volcanoes, has filmed in the jungle and in the middle of the Sahara, and has made films about characters who live at the edges of human achievement. *Burden of Dreams* gives us an extraordinary portrait of Herzog trapped in the middle of one of his wildest dreams.

Buster ★ ★ ★
R, 93 m., 1988

Phil Collins (Buster Edwards), Julie Walters (June Edwards), Larry Lamb (Bruce), Stephanie Lawrence (Granny), Ellen Beaven (Nicky), Michael Attwell (Harry), Ralph Brown (Ronnie), Martin Jarvis (Inspector Mitchell), Anthony Quayle (Sir James McDowell). Directed by David Green and produced by Norma Heyman. Screenplay by Colin Shindler.

Two of the key words in *Buster* are spoken softly, almost as an aside, and might be easy to miss. Spoken by one criminal to another, they are, "No shooters!" A "shooter" is Cockney slang for a gun, and the words come during the preparations for the crime that came to be known as the Great Train Robbery. The fact that Britain's crime of the century was carried out by unarmed men has contributed to its place in folklore, and helps to set the mood for this almost elegiac crime story.

The Royal Mail train from London to Glasgow was stopped and robbed on the night of Aug. 8, 1963, by a group of fifteen men who took loot that would be valued today at $35 million. The crime has inspired several earlier movies, notably *Robbery* (1967), a superior thriller starring Stanley Baker. All of the men were eventually captured except for one, Ronnie Biggs, who now enjoys a life of exile in Brazil. *Buster* tells the story of one of the more obscure Great Train Robbers, Ronnie (Buster) Edwards, who was safely in exile in Mexico but came back home to face the music because he missed his wife. The movie is a love story.

Buster, like *Robbery,* opens with the logistics of the robbery. But it sees it almost entirely through the eyes of Buster Edwards, who lives with his wife, June, and their little daughter in a flat that rents for three pounds a week. June would like them to have a nice bungalow of their own, but Buster doesn't have the money. "You could always borrow it from a bank," she suggests. "That's what I do for a living," he says. "I meant legally," she says.

Buster is played with surprising effectiveness by the rock star Phil Collins, who looks and sounds like a gentler Bob Hoskins. In the movie's opening sequence, he throws a garbage can through the window of a clothing store in order to steal a mannequin that is wearing a suit he fancies. This seems like a reckless act, but Buster seems to believe he is

protected by a cloak of invulnerability. As his wife (Julie Walters) tells her mother, he's led a life of crime and served only two weeks in jail.

Yes, but he's never felt the heat the way it comes down after the Great Train Robbery. The papers are full of the crime, and the Conservative government of the day, still smarting from the Profumo Affair, is eager to bring the robbers to justice. Buster and June go into hiding in a series of "safe houses" and have a series of close calls before finally fleeing to Mexico with their daughter. Meanwhile, Buster's share of the loot dwindles as a series of middlemen and payoff artists take their shares.

The center of the movie is occupied, not by the crime, but by the relationship between Buster and June, and we are inclined to believe him when he says he has done everything just for the love of his family. They come closest to breaking apart under the pressure in Mexico, where life in the sun makes June desperately homesick. Faced with a menu of Mexican food, she yearns for steak and fries, and wistfully observes, "We never used to be able to afford it." Now that they can, they're in the wrong country to order it.

June eventually returns to England, and Buster eventually follows. One of the last scenes in the film shows them kissing hungrily before he walks out the door to be handcuffed and led away. A coda at the end of the film might seem corny to some audiences. It shows Buster and June, years later, running a flower stall in London, having retired from crime. The scene may be corny, but it is true, and the next time you go to London, if you stop at the flower kiosk outside Waterloo Station, you can buy a bouquet from Buster Edwards. Be sure to count your change.

The Butcher's Wife ★ ★ ½
PG-13, 99 m., 1991

Demi Moore (Marina), Jeff Daniels (Dr. Alex Tremor), George Dzundza (Leo Lemke), Frances McDormand (Grace), Margaret Colin (Robyn Graves), Mary Steenburgen (Stella Kefauver). Directed by Terry Hughes and produced by Wallis Nicita and Lauren Lloyd. Screenplay by Ezra Litwak and Marjorie Schwartz.

The Butcher's Wife wants to be a whimsical, heartwarming fantasy, and it almost succeeds, but it is betrayed by its own need to

put a Hollywood spin on a plot that doesn't need one. It begins by asking us to make a romantic leap of faith, and after we've made it, the movie says, uh, hold on, think again, she fell for the wrong guy and it's time to make another leap. The plot mechanics of the second leap drag the movie back to earth again.

The movie commences with a real glow, though. On a lonely tower on the headland of some forgotten island off the coast of the southern United States, a beautiful young woman stands, the wind in her hair, and looks out to sea and toward her future. Her name is Marina, and she has been aware of a psychic gift since her earliest years. Among the things she "knows" is that her future husband will one day appear to her, and indeed, in no time at all a small boat is approaching the shore with a lone fisherman in it.

A voice inside of her announces that this is the man who is to be her husband, and so she wades into the water, climbs onto the boat, embraces the startled man, and informs him of this fact. He is inclined to agree with her, and within two days they are wed. The man's name is Leo Lemke. He is a butcher in Greenwich Village, and Marina journeys north with him and takes up her place behind the butcher's counter. She is happy to be the butcher's wife.

Up until this point, and for a few scenes afterward, *The Butcher's Wife* proceeds with a serene certainty. The movie has faith in its whimsy, and so do we. Demi Moore is warm and cuddly as Marina, a simple, soft-spoken woman with a Southern accent and a direct way of speech that seems to cut through confusions and difficulties. George Dzundza is a stalwart butcher, friendly and sensible and loving. He has been a bachelor until into his forties, and if he had not taken that fishing trip down South, he would be a bachelor still. But now a bride has dropped out of the heavens for him, and the very stars themselves seem to bless his marriage.

Then the movie loses faith in the momentum of its original inspiration and falls back upon the devices of screenwriting formulas. The butcher, you see, is stout and balding and almost as homely as Gene Hackman. So, obviously, in the Hollywood mind, he has not evolved high enough on the ladder of personal attractiveness to deserve Demi Moore. A mistake must have been made. The plot develops a compulsion to reassign her to a more handsome man, and that's where the movie goes wrong.

There is a psychiatrist who works across the street, in this Greenwich Village street that was built on a sound stage and contains mostly characters in the story. He is played by Jeff Daniels, is insecure about how much good he is doing his patients, but is basically a nice guy. He begins to hear repercussions about this psychic woman who has moved in behind the butcher's counter. She starts giving advice to his patients, and they start heeding the advice. This is not good for business.

Among the patients who are being improved by psychic insights is Stella Kefauver (Mary Steenburgen), a shrinking violet who has always harbored a dream to sing in a nightclub. Dare to realize your dream! the butcher's wife advises. And one day she does, in one of the movie's best scenes, singing a torch song with such grace and feeling that we are inspired to look at Mary Steenburgen all over again. But then the psychiatrist and the butcher's wife meet to discuss these matters, and, of course, it is clear that sooner or later they will end up in each other's arms.

All of this should be painful for the butcher, who had my complete sympathy. The screenplay labors and produces an explanation that eventually accounts for the reassignment of the various romantic partners. But I was disappointed that *The Butcher's Wife* lost faith in its original romantic inspiration. Is it not possible for a portly butcher to have a ripe young wife? Is it not possible for a clean-cut psychiatrist to fall in love with a slightly faded rose? This movie takes us back to the days of the high school prom, in which couples seemed to choose each other on the basis of a pecking-order of personal attractiveness, so that the king and queen of the prom were the two best-looking people in class, and over in the corner were all the nerds and wallflowers.

The fatal mistake of *The Butcher's Wife* is to allow itself to become sidetracked by the process of partner reassignment. There is an unspoken cruelty to the way Marina ditches Leo, and the movie fudges it. There is also a lot of unnecessary dialogue explaining things that need never have happened in the first place. If Marina had stayed by Leo's side, there behind the meat counter, and had contented herself with helping others make the same leap of faith she made, this movie might have been a little classic, instead of a big manipulative machine.

Bye Bye Brazil ★ ★ ★ ★
NO MPAA RATING, 100 m., 1979

Jose Wilker (Lord Gypsy), Betty Faria (Salome), Fabio Junior (Cico), Zaira Zambelli (Desdo), Principe Nabor (Swallow). Directed by Carlos Diegues and produced by L.C. Barreto. Screenplay by Diegues.

It's rare to come across truly great movie images, and we share them like treasured souvenirs—images like Jack Nicholson in the football helmet in *Easy Rider*, the bone turning into a spaceship in *2001*, the peacock spreading its feathers in the snow in *Amarcord*, and the helicopter assault in *Apocalypse Now*.

To the short list of great images, a film named *Bye Bye Brazil* adds one more. A small, raggedy troupe of traveling entertainers is putting on a show in a provincial Brazilian town. The townspeople sit packed together in a sweaty, smoky room, while the magician creates for brief moments the illusion that both he and his audience are more sophisticated than they are. It is time for the climax of his act, and he springs a completely unexpected image on his audience, and on us: Bing Crosby sings "White Christmas" while it snows on his amazed patrons.

That moment provides more than an image. It provides a neatly summarized little statement about *Bye Bye Brazil*, a film which exists exactly on the fault line between Brazil's modern civilization and the simple backwaters of its provinces. The film sees Brazil as a nation where half-assimilated Western culture (in the form of Bing Crosby, public address systems, and politicians) coexists with poverty, superstition, simple good nature, and the permanent fact of the rain forest.

The movie is about the small troupe of entertainers, who travel the backroads in a truck that contains living quarters, a generator, and the props for their nightly shows. The troupe is led by Lord Gypsy, a young man who is half-hippie, half-nineteenth-century medicine show huckster. At his side is Salome, a damply sultry beauty who is his assistant but also has a tendency to do business on her own. Swallow, a strongman, doubles as crew and supporting act.

These three pick up two hitchhikers, a young accordion player and his pregnant wife. And then *Bye Bye Brazil* tells the story of the changing relationships among the five people, and their checkered success with roadshow vaudeville.

Having said that, I've conveyed almost no notion of this movie's special charms. It shows us a society that most American audiences never have seen in the movies, the world of very old, very small Brazilian towns perched precariously along the roads that link them to far-away, half-understood cities.

Television has not come to most of these towns. Electricity is uncertain. The traveling entertainers provide more than music and magic; they provide a link with style that is more fascinating to the audiences than the magician's tricks. People do not pay to see the show, so much as to wonder at these strange performers who speak the same language but could be from another planet.

Bye Bye, Love ★ ★
PG-13, 106 m., 1995

Matthew Modine (Dave), Randy Quaid (Vic), Paul Reiser (Donny), Janeane Garofalo (Lucille), Amy Brenneman (Susan), Eliza Dushku (Emma), Ed Flanders (Walter), Maria Pitillo (Kim), Lindsay Crouse (Grace). Directed by Sam Weisman and produced by Gary David Goldberg, Brad Hall, and Sam Weisman. Screenplay by Goldberg and Hall.

Bye Bye, Love is a soppy sitcom that would like to pass as the quasi-heartfelt story of three divorced dads and their problems with the single life. It is possible to juggle lots of family stories (see Ron Howard's wonderful *Parenthood*), but this movie seems unfinished, as if the ingredients are there, but not much consideration was given to whether they fit, or were necessary.

The movie opens at a McDonald's, in a long and shameless product placement. *Bye Bye, Love* looks, in fact, like a McDonald's commercial for its first ten minutes, as the restaurant serves as neutral turf where ex-wives can drop off the kids for their ex-husbands' visitation rights. Nothing in this endless sequence has the poignancy and wit of one perfect line from the similar *Divorce American Style* (1967): "Come to Uncle Daddy!"

We meet three guys who are not handling divorce very well. Dave (Matthew Modine) has a young girlfriend, and also keeps half the moms of his son's soccer team on the line. Vic (Randy Quaid) is furious that his ex-wife is spending money on new tires for the car. Donny (Paul Reiser) still carries a torch for his ex-wife, and frets over his bad communication with his teenage daughter. During the next two days, as each father deals with weekend child custody and his own shaky social life, the movie will try, and fail, to deliver as a comedy. Something is wrong with the pacing, I think. Look at the episode, for example, where Dave plans dinner with a new girlfriend, Kim (Maria Pitillo), who takes him seriously and hopes this is the evening she'll make real progress with Dave and his kids. The doorbell rings, and two other "soccer moms" turn up with their kids. Dave pretends it's just a coincidence, but Kim suspects he wants to be surrounded by women to avoid a commitment. There's the material here for a sequence that's both biting and funny, but it never develops.

There's no real payoff, either, in Vic's date from hell (Janeane Garofalo), who drives him to the point of catatonia during an endless evening in an Italian restaurant. She's one of those people who reads the menu forever, and then orders and sends back five entrées before deciding to eat her date's dinner. What's her problem? An eating disorder? Insanity? Hostility toward this harmless man? The evening drags on and on—much too long—until the dinner date stops being a

scene and starts being a problem with the screenplay.

Donny's problems are also ineptly constructed. There's a subplot involving his teenage daughter (Eliza Dushku), who resents him, goes to a party, drives drunk, and ends up sulking in the tree house of their former family home, after which, of course, in order to talk with her, Donny has to climb up a trellis and creep out on a limb, which snaps, leaving him dangling. Give us a break. This character has already survived a scene where he prowls the lawn of his ex-wife's new home, jealously watching her with her new lover, and is inevitably caught when the lawn sprinkler system turns on. (Movie sprinkler systems never fail in a situation like that.)

These sitcom gag scenes are not improved by the cheap emotional insights they eventually produce. Nor does it help much that the movie intercuts dilemmas from life with a forty-eight-hour radio broadcast by a radio psychiatrist (Rob Reiner), leading to a particularly contrived payoff after Vic breaks into his studio.

The press notes are filled with information about how the writers researched their story, found a real McDonald's that functions as a child transfer center on weekends, etc. But then why did they translate all their insights into the manufactured contrivances of sitcoms? In the scene where Donny is cooking dinner for his daughter, for example, I can believe he has trouble removing the top of a can of spaghetti sauce, but was there no one to restrain the filmmakers before they made him open a hole in the lid with a power drill?

It's been said that European films are about adults, and American films are about adults acting like children. You see some truth in that statement when you watch *Bye Bye, Love*. None of the characters is emotionally complex, or very smart, or motivated by reasons more complex than the movie's paint-by-numbers screenplay. We know from other movies that Modine, Quaid, and Reiser can play intelligent, complex characters. Here it's like they're running through sand.

C

Cabaret ★ ★ ★ ½
PG, 119 m., 1972

Liza Minnelli (Sally Bowles), Michael York (Brian Roberts), Joel Grey (Master of Ceremonies), Helmut Griem (Maximilian von Heune), Fritz Wepper (Fritz Wendel). Directed by Bob Fosse and produced by Cy Feuer. Screenplay by Jay Allen.

Cabaret explores some of the same kinky territory celebrated in Visconti's *The Damned.* Both movies share the general idea that the rise of the Nazi party in Germany was accompanied by a rise in bisexuality, homosexuality, sadomasochism, and assorted other activities. Taken as a generalization about a national movement, this is certainly extreme oversimplification. But taken as one approach to the darker recesses of Nazism, it may come pretty close to the mark. The Nazi gimmicks like boots and leather and muscles and racial superiority and outdoor rallies and Aryan comradeship offered an array of machismo-for-rent that had (and has) a special appeal to some kinds of impotent people.

Cabaret is about people like that, and it takes place largely in a specific Berlin cabaret, circa 1930, in which decadence and sexual ambiguity were just part of the ambience (like the women mud-wrestlers who appeared between acts). This is no ordinary musical. Part of its success comes because it doesn't fall for the old cliché that musicals have to make you happy. Instead of cheapening the movie version by lightening its load of despair, director Bob Fosse has gone right to the bleak heart of the material and stayed there well enough to win an Academy Award for Best Director.

The story concerns one of the more famous literary inventions of the century, Sally Bowles, who first came to life in the late Christopher Isherwood's *Berlin Stories,* and

then appeared in the play and movie *I Am a Camera* before returning to the stage in this musical, and then making it into the movies a second time—a modern record, matched only by Eliza Doolittle, I'd say.

Sally is brought magnificently to the screen in an Oscar-winning performance by Liza Minnelli, who plays her as a girl who's bought what the cabaret is selling. To her, the point is to laugh and sing and live forever in the moment; to refuse to take things seriously—even Nazism—and to relate with people only up to a certain point. She is capable of warmth and emotion, but a lot of it is theatrical, and when the chips are down she's as decadent as the "daringly decadent" dark fingernail polish she flaunts.

Liza Minnelli plays Sally Bowles so well and fully that it doesn't matter how well she sings and dances, if you see what I mean. In several musical numbers (including the stunning finale *Cabaret* number), Liza demonstrates unmistakably that she's one of the great musical performers of our time. But the heartlessness and nihilism of the character is still there, all the time, even while we're being supremely entertained.

Sally gets involved in a triangular relationship with a young English language teacher (Michael York) and a young baron (Helmut Griem), and if this particular triangle didn't exist in the stage version, that doesn't matter. It helps define the movie's whole feel of moral anarchy, and it is underlined by the sheer desperation in the cabaret itself.

Here the festivities are overseen by a master of ceremonies (Joel Grey, whose performance received an Oscar for Best Supporting Actor) whose determination to keep the merriment going, at whatever psychic cost, has a poignant compulsiveness. When the song *Cabaret* comes at the end, you realize for the first time that it isn't a song of happi-

ness, but of desperation. The context makes the difference. In the same way, the context of Germany on the eve of the Nazi ascent to power makes the entire musical into an unforgettable cry of despair.

Cactus ★ ★ ★
NO MPAA RATING, 95 m., 1987

Isabelle Huppert (Colo), Robert Menzies (Robert), Norman Kaye (Tom), Monica Maughan (Bea), Banduk Marika (Banduk), Sheila Florance (Martha). Directed by Paul Cox and produced by Jane Ballantyne and Cox. Screenplay by Cox, Norman Kaye, and Bob Ellis.

One of the first shots in *Cactus* is a long, unbroken take in which the camera pans from a veranda across a lush landscape, all green and semi-tropical, while on the sound track we hear the loud cry of an exotic bird. The sound seems too loud, somehow, but what is being set up here is the condition of blindness, in which sounds take on an extraordinary importance.

The heroine of the film is a young French woman (Isabelle Huppert), who has come out to Australia on holiday. There is the suggestion that she has left an unhappy marriage behind in France. She has an accident, loses the sight of one eye, and is threatened with the loss of the other. The doctors offer her a choice. If she has the bad eye removed, the remaining eye may retain its function. Otherwise, "sympathetic blindness" may occur, and she will be totally blind.

No matter how this sounds, *Cactus* is not a docudrama, not a movie about medical problems. It is a movie about how we see, and what we choose to see. While she is trying to decide what to do, Huppert meets a young man who is blind. They talk, they understand each other, they fall in love. She seriously considers the option of choosing blindness, so that she will be able to share the world of her lover.

These episodes take place within the arms of a large, sheltering family. The woman's friends are middle-aged, literate, political. There are moments that have little to do with the movie's central problem; moments when friends gather to drink, talk, and listen to music. During those scenes, *Cactus* has an interesting, subtle technique. The visuals are always alive and inviting—rooms filled with unusual objects, landscapes jammed with life. And the sound track is filled, too, with words and music. Both senses, sight and sound, are calling out to be recognized.

Cactus was directed by Paul Cox, who is not one of the best-known of the new generation of Australian filmmakers, but in many ways is the most inventive, the most individual. His films are always about people who are cut off from normal relationships, and who try to improvise substitutes.

Lonely Hearts (1981) was about two people who met through a singles group, and found out why each was single. *Man of Flowers* (1983) was about a lonely, reclusive millionaire who paid a young woman to pose for him, so that he could fill his empty room with company. *My First Wife* (1984) was about a woman who decided that she could scarcely be lonelier outside marriage than inside it.

Cactus is not as satisfying as those three films, perhaps because its themes are not as clear. I was so distracted by the reality of the woman's choice—sight or blindness—that I found it hard to pull back to the larger question of how she should choose to communicate with the man she loved. In a way, the woman's choice is one we all have to make. Because there is such a gulf between all people, to bridge it we have to take on some of the blindness of others, and they have to share ours; two people who see things exclusively their own way may never be able to share the world. That is the issue in *Cactus;* the blindness is simply the way Cox chooses to dramatize it.

Although the movie is less than completely satisfying, it is worth seeing, as everything by Cox is worth seeing, because there is always the sense in his films of an active intelligence at work. He doesn't make routine genre pictures; he begins with complicated people and watches them as they live. Sometimes he seems as mystified by the results as we are.

Caddyshack ★ ★ ½
R, 99 m., 1980

Chevy Chase (Ty Webb), Rodney Dangerfield (Al Czervik), Ted Knight (Judge Smails), Michael O'Keefe (Danny), Bill Murray (Carl), Sarah Holcomb (Maggie). Directed by Harold Ramis and produced by Douglas Kenney. Screenplay by Brian Doyle-Murray, Ramis, and Kenney.

Caddyshack never finds a consistent comic note of its own, but it plays host to all sorts of approaches from its stars, who sometimes hardly seem to be occupying the same movie. There's Bill Murray's self-absorbed craziness, Chevy Chase's laid-back bemusement, and Ted Knight's apoplectic overplaying. And then there is Rodney Dangerfield, who wades into the movie and cleans up.

To the degree that this is anybody's movie, it's Dangerfield's—and he mostly seems to be using his own material. He plays a loud, vulgar, twitching condo developer who is thinking of buying a country club and using the land for housing. The country club is one of those exclusive WASP enclaves, a haven for such types as the judge who founded it (Knight), the ne'er-do-well club champion (Chase), and the manic assistant grounds keeper (Murray).

The movie never really develops a plot, but maybe it doesn't want to. Director Harold Ramis brings on his cast of characters and lets them loose at one another. There's a vague subplot about a college scholarship for the caddies, and another one about the judge's nubile niece, and continuing warfare waged by Murray against the gophers who are devastating the club. But Ramis is cheerfully prepared to interrupt everything for moments of comic inspiration, and there are three especially good ones: The caddies in the swimming pool doing a Busby Berkeley number, another pool scene that's a scatalogical satire of *Jaws,* and a sequence in which Dangerfield's gigantic speedboat devastates a yacht club.

Dangerfield is funniest, though, when the movie just lets him talk. He's a Henny Youngman clone, filled with one-liners and insults, and he's great at the country club's dinner dance, abusing everyone and making rude noises. Surveying the crowd from the bar, he uses lines that he has, in fact, stolen directly from his nightclub routine ("This steak still has the mark of the jockey's whip on it"). With his bizarre wardrobe and trick golf bag, he's a throwback to the Groucho Marx and W.C. Fields school of insult comedy; he has a vitality that the movie's younger comedians can't match, and they suffer in comparison.

Chevy Chase, for example, has some wonderful moments in this movie, as a studiously absent-minded hedonist who doesn't even bother to keep score when he plays golf. He's good, but somehow he's in the wrong movie: His whimsy doesn't fit with Dangerfield's blatant scenery-chewing or with the Bill Murray character. Murray, as a slob who goes after gophers with explosives and entertains sexual fantasies about the women golfers, could be a refugee from *Animal House.*

Maybe one of the movie's problems is that the central characters are never really involved in the same action. Murray's off on his own, fighting gophers. Dangerfield arrives, devastates, exits. Knight is busy impressing the caddies, making vague promises about scholarships, and launching boats. If they were somehow all drawn together into the same story, maybe we'd be carried along more confidently. But *Caddyshack* feels more like a movie that was written rather loosely, so that when shooting began there was freedom—too much freedom—for it to wander off in all directions in search of comic inspiration.

California Split ★ ★ ★ ★
R, 109 m., 1974

George Segal (Bill Denny), Elliott Gould (Charlie Waters), Ann Prentiss (Barbara Miller), Gwen Welles (Susan Peters), Edward Walsh (Lew), Joseph Walsh (Sparkle), Bert Remsen ("Helen Brown"). Directed by Robert Altman and produced by Altman and Joseph Walsh, based on a screenplay by Walsh.

They meet in a California poker parlor. One wins, despite a heated discussion with a loser over whether or not a dealt card hit the floor. They drink. They become friends after they are jointly mugged in the parking lot by the sore loser.

They did not know each other before, and they don't know much about each other now, but they know all they need to know: They're both compulsive gamblers, and the dimensions of the world of gambling equal the dimensions of the world they care anything about. It is a small world and a flat one, like one of those maps of the world before Columbus, and they are constantly threatened with falling over the edge.

They're the heroes (or at least the subjects) of *California Split*, the magnificently funny, cynical film by Robert Altman. Their names are Bill and Charlie, and they're played by George Segal and Elliott Gould with a combination of unaffected naturalism and sheer raw nervous exhaustion. We don't need to know anything about gambling to understand the odyssey they undertake to the tracks, to the private poker parties, to the bars, to Vegas, to the edge of defeat, and to the scene of victory. Their compulsion is so strong that it carries us along. The movie will be compared with *M*A*S*H*, the first big hit by Altman (who is possibly our best and certainly our most diverting American director). It deserves that comparison, because it resembles *M*A*S*H* in several big ways: It's funny, it's hard-boiled, it gives us a bond between two frazzled heroes trying to win by the rules in a game where the rules require defeat. But it's a better movie than *M*A*S*H* because here Altman gets it all together. Ever since *M*A*S*H*, he's been trying to make a kind of movie that would function like a comedy but allow its laughs to dig us deeper and deeper into the despair underneath.

Bill and Charlie are driven. We laugh at their hangovers, their bruises (treated with hot shaving cream), the kooky part-time prostitutes who serve them breakfasts of Froot Loops and beer. We move easily through the underworld of their friends, casually introduced through Altman's gift of overlapping dialogue and understated visual introductions, so that we're not so much shown a new character as encouraged to assume we knew him all along. And because Joseph Walsh's screenplay is funny and Segal and Gould are naturally engaging, we have a good time.

But then there are moments that take on bleaker meanings. At one point, for example, at the ragged edge of sleep, boozed out, defeated, Bill and Charlie cling desperately to a bar and very seriously bet with each other on the names of the Seven Dwarfs (There was Droopy . . . Sleepy . . . Dumbo?). And at another time, cornered with their winnings in still another parking lot by still another mugger, this one armed, they hand over half their winnings and bet him that's all they have.

He takes it and runs; they win; they could have been killed but their gambler's instinct forced them to make the try. At the end of *California Split* we realize that Altman has made a lot more than a comedy about gambling; he's taken us into an American nightmare, and all the people we met along the way felt genuine and looked real. This movie has a taste in its mouth like stale air-conditioning, and no matter what time it seems to be, it's always five in the morning in a second-rate casino.

As always, Altman fills his movie with quirky supporting roles—people who have somehow become caricatures of themselves. At the private poker game, Segal stands at the bar, surveys the table, and quietly describes every player. He's right about them, although he (and we) have never seen them before. We know he's right because these people wear their styles and destinies on their faces.

So do the hookers (played with a kind of tart-next-door wholesomeness by Ann Prentiss and Gwen Welles). So does "Helen Brown," one of their customers who's a middle-aged man who likes drag as much as he's terrified of the cops (inspiring a scene of true tragicomedy). Altman's movies always seem full, somehow; we don't have the feeling of an empty screen into which carefully drawn characters are introduced, but of a camera plunging into a boiling sea of frenzied human activity.

What Altman comes up with is sometimes almost a documentary feel; at the end of *California Split* we know something about organized gambling in this country we didn't know before. His movies always seem perfectly at home wherever they are, but this time there's an almost palpable sense of place. And Altman has never been more firmly in control of his style. He has one of the few really individual visual styles among contemporary American directors; we can always see it's an Altman film. He bases his visual strategies on an incredibly attentive sound track, using background noises with particular care so that our ears tell us we're moving through these people—instead of that they're lined up talking to us. *California Split* is a great movie and it's a great experience, too; we've been there with Bill and Charlie.

Camille Claudel ★ ★ ★ ½
R, 149 m., 1989

Isabelle Adjani (Camille Claudel), Gerard Depardieu (Auguste Rodin), Laurent Grevill (Paul), Alain Cuny (Camille's father), Madeleine Robinson (Camille's mother), Katrine Boorman (Jessie Lipscomb), Daniele Lebrun (Rose Beuret). Directed by Bruno Nuytten and produced by Bernard Artigues. Screenplay by Nuytten and Marilyn Goldin.

She is above all a lonely woman, because she chooses to do with her life what her society says no decent woman should do. She chooses to love whom she will, and she wants to be an artist—to create sculptures out of clay, just as if she were a man. It is hard to say which of her choices is the most offensive. And when she goes mad, it is impossible to say whether the seeds of madness were there from the beginning. Or whether she was driven to madness by a society that could not accept a woman who lived for herself.

Camille Claudel has until now occupied only the footnotes of late nineteenth-century art. She was one of the mistresses of Auguste Rodin, the willful sculptor who is known to everyone if only for "The Thinker." She was often his model, and for a time she worked as his collaborator.

She left behind many sculptures, which can be seen here or there, not much remarked, while Rodin's work has been enshrined in the pantheon. She spent the last thirty years of her life in a madhouse.

The film *Camille Claudel* is more concerned with her personality and passions than with her art, and so it is hard to judge, from the evidence on the screen, how good a sculptor she really was. This is not a movie about sculpture. Those who have seen her work report that some of it has a power that is almost disturbing—that there is an urgency in her figures suggesting she was not simply shaping them but using them to bring her own emotions to life.

Certainly the pressures against an independent woman artist were sufficient in her late nineteenth-century Paris that she would not have bothered to be a sculptor unless she absolutely had to.

The first time we see her she is grubbing in the dirt of a Paris construction site, down there in a ditch like a burrowing animal, looking for good clay that she can use in her work. She straightens up and, as she rubs the sweat from her face with a filthy hand, we see her as a very young woman with eyes that see more than this ditch she stands in: She sees, already, the figures she will mold from this clay.

Camille is played by Isabelle Adjani, who was nominated for an Academy Award for her work, and one of the mysteries of this performance is how Adjani, now in her thirties, is able so convincingly to span this woman's lifetime and seem to be the right age at all times. She is certainly convincing in the early scenes as a young, open, determined woman who has somehow got it into her head that not only men should be sculptors.

As an academy student seeking a new teacher, she meets Auguste Rodin (Gerard Depardieu), who looms like a colossus over the art world of his time, not least because of his ability at self-promotion; Rodin was one of the inventors of the artist as celebrity, rejecting the myth of the lonely recluse in the wretched garret and consciously occupying the spotlight. At first he pays little attention to her, even though he has a reputation as a womanizer. She observes his long-time mistress, Rose Beuret (Daniele Lebrun), and wonders if they are married. She works on a piece of marble he has given her and creates a foot, a wonderful foot that he acknowledges as well-made. They fall into each other's orbit, he is bewitched, they make love, she becomes pregnant, he will not leave Rose, and she begins the long descent into madness.

Rodin is simply not capable of being faithful to one woman. Nor is he much interested in a woman who dares to think of herself as his artistic rival. Such a woman can be allowed to grow only so far, to be encouraged so much, before she must be slapped back down into her place in his bed. Is this rejection what drives Camille mad, or is it the fundamental contradiction between what she is and the time she lives in? We follow her gradual decay as she moves into shabby lodgings and goes without food or fuel to pay for her art. This behavior concerns her parents, who begin to wonder if she has lost her senses, especially when she begins to drink and to neglect the impression she makes on people.

Adjani is possessed in this movie. It is not one of those leisurely costume dramas in which people in beautiful clothing move through elegant rooms. Her eyes always look haunted, and even in the moments of luxury and romance there is the suggestion in her body language of that feral creature down in the ditch, grubbing for clay. She makes sculptures because she must—because the figures in her work are trapped within her, and if she does not release them she will burst.

Depardieu plays a Rodin who is genial, assured, and malevolent. He will go only so far for a woman before he must pull back and be sure that his ego is served.

Has there ever been another actor, in any language, who seems so unself-consciously assured in such a variety of roles? Depardieu works all the time, always well, and just within the last few years he has been not only Rodin but also the hunchback peasant of *Jean de Florette* and the love-struck car salesman of *Too Beautiful for You.*

Artistic biographies are notoriously difficult to film because what an artist does takes place within his mind, and the camera can see only the outside. Sculptors are at least a little easier to deal with than writers or musicians; instead of Balzac or Mozart furiously scribbling on a piece of paper, we can at least see the knife shaping the block of clay. But *Camille Claudel* is not really about sculpture anyway. It is about a woman who tried to place sculpture before everything until she met a man who did the same thing.

Candyman ★ ★ ★
R, 101 m., 1992

Virginia Madsen (Helen Lyle), Tony Todd (Candyman), Xander Berkeley (Trevor Lyle), Kasi Lemmons (Bernadette Walsh), Vanessa Williams (Anne-Marie McCoy). Directed by Bernard Rose and produced by Steve Golin, Sigurjon Sighvatsson, and Alan Poul. Screenplay by Rose.

Urban legends tap our deepest fears, and one of the most subterranean involves the call for help that is laughed at or ignored. We cry out again and again, only to be dismissed by our friends, or the 911 operator, or strangers on the shore. At the beginning of Bernard Rose's *Candyman,* we hear an urban legend about a woman in a high-rise public housing project, who calls 911 but is not taken seriously. Not long after, her body is found, savagely slashed to death. The Candyman has struck again.

Who is the Candyman? According to the movie, he is a powerful supernatural being who haunts Cabrini Green, the housing complex on Chicago's near west side. He lures victims with candy, or puts razor blades in Halloween treats—the details are vague and dreamlike—and his lair is an abandoned apartment on one of Cabrini's upper floors.

All of this information is carefully written down by two researchers from the University of Illinois (Virginia Madsen and Kasi Lemmons), as part of a research project that also touches on such matters as alligators in sewers. Madsen, trapped in an unhappy marriage with a philandering professor, throws herself into her work, dragging Williams along as they interview the neighbors of the Candyman's latest victim. Oddly enough, their stories seem to support the legend—even though the theory is that these urban tales never quite check out.

Rose is a director who likes stories about supernatural invasions of real life. His brilliant *Paperhouse* (1989), about a young girl whose drawings seemed to influence the life of a boy in her feverish dreams, used images of razor-sharp reality to suggest that the dreams were as real as the rest of the movie. *Candyman,* from Rose's own screenplay, based on a Clive Barker story, does the same thing. We think we'll discover that the Candyman is actually a real, live human being—a killer using the legend as a cover. What we do discover is more frightening, and more intriguing. He may literally be a product of the imagination.

What if urban legends became real if enough people believed in them? What if the sheer psychic weight of faith from thousands of people were enough to create a supernatural reality? If everyone believed there were alligators in the sewers, would there be? Are gods the result of man's faith in them? Would the Candyman therefore take a dim view of a researcher's attempts to debunk him?

Madsen and Lemmons, courageous and plucky, make sympathetic heroines as they walk up and down the dangerous stairwells of Cabrini Green, crawling through empty apartments looking for a monster. And Rose has been clever in his use of locations. Just as urban legends are based on the real fears of those who believe in them, so are certain urban locations able to embody fear. Empty apartments in the upper floors of public housing projects are, it is widely believed, occupied by gangs. We perceive a real threat to the women, at the same time they're searching for what they think is an imaginary one.

Then the plot thickens. Rose evokes Hitchcock's favorite formula, the Innocent Victim Wrongly Accused. Just as the Candyman's victim called 911 and was not believed, so Madsen is arrested by the police and her story scornfully dismissed. It's all kind of intriguing. Elements of the plot may not hold up in the clear light of day, but that didn't bother me much. What I liked was a horror movie that was scaring me with ideas and gore, instead of simply with gore.

Candyman: Farewell to the Flesh ★ ★

R, 99 m., 1995

Tony Todd (Candyman), Kelly Rowan (Annie Tarrant), Timothy Carhart (Paul McKeever), Veronica Cartwright (Octavia), William O'Leary (Ethan Tarrant), Fay Hauser (Pam Carver), Joshua Gibran Mayweather (Matthew). Directed by Bill Condon and produced by Sigurjon Sighvatsson and Gregg D. Fienberg. Screenplay by Rand Ravich and Mark Kruger.

In the original *Candyman* (1992), a couple of Ph.D.s from the University of Illinois theorized that the Candyman was an urban legend, brought to life by the faith of all the people who believed in him. But it turned out there was a much more Gothic and supernatural explanation, and we learn more about his origins in the new *Candyman: Farewell to the Flesh.*

The Candyman stories, based on books by Clive Barker, are an attempt to make an intelligent fable out of a bogeyman, and Bernard Rose's 1992 film did a good job of it, with Virginia Madsen and Kasi Lemmons as the researchers who track down tales of a slasher with a hook for a hand. He was terrorizing Chicago's Cabrini-Green housing project, but in the second film he has moved back home to New Orleans, and started preying on his own descendants instead of innocent bystanders.

In the new film, directed by Bill Condon, there's once again an attempt to establish a real world in which Candymen aren't possible. Kelly Rowan stars as a New Orleans schoolteacher whose father was killed years earlier, Candyman-style. Now her brother has been accused of killing a Candyman expert, and a student in her class has started drawing the Candyman. How does the kid know about him?

The movie doesn't develop, alas, with the patience and restraint of the earlier film. It's got one of those sound tracks where everyday sounds are amplified into gut-churning shockaramas, and where we are constantly being startled by false alarms. There's a scene, for example, where a character walks up behind the teacher, and the sound track explodes. My notes read: "Scream! Shock! Rumble! Crack!"—followed, of course, by the guy saying, "Sorry, I thought you heard me."

The movie also pulls the old "It's only a cat" routine, where a shrieking, snarling presence from out of frame turns out, yes, to only be a cat. There is even an "it's only a raven" sequence, no doubt in honor of Clive Barker's predecessor in the macabre, Edgar Allan Poe.

The story proceeds. Characters near and dear to Kelly are slashed Candyman-style. Eventually, led by the little student from her class who seems tuned in to the Candyman, she is led to an old plantation, where all is explained. Read no further if you would rather not know that the Candyman turns out to have been a slave who fell in love with his master's daughter, and she with him. When she became pregnant, the enraged plantation owner set a mob on the slave, which cut off his arm and smeared him with honey, so that he was stung by thousands of bees, which is how he got the name Candyman.

Is there an entomologist among us? Are bees attracted by honey? I would have guessed they'd be rather blasé about it, and would be more quickly attracted if the victim had been smeared with one of those perfumes they advertise on the cable TV. Never mind. The slave, whose name is Daniel Robitaille, sees his bee-stung face in his lover's mirror, and somehow his spirit goes into the mirror, so that if you look in a mirror and say "Candyman" five times, that's going to be more or less the last thing you do. (I have tried this, and it doesn't work.)

The story goes to some lengths to develop sympathy for the terrible tortures he was subjected to, as a victim of racism who dared to love a white woman. (Because the Candyman is played by Tony Todd, who has more than a passing resemblance to O.J. Simpson, there are several scenes that have a curious double resonance.)

I suppose that Clive Barker would be happy to explain for us how *Candyman: Farewell to the Flesh* is a statement against racism, and maybe it is, although it sure does go the long way around. The message may be that because slaves were mistreated, we pay the price today, perhaps every time we look in the mirror and see our racism reflected back at us. (Hey, I didn't take those EngLit symbology classes for nothing.)

Like many movies with morals at the end, however, it has its slasher and eats him, too. If the last fifteen minutes of the movie are devoted to creating understanding for Daniel Robitaille, the first eighty-five are devoted to exploiting fears of slasher attacks by tall black men, with or without a hook for a hand. And the flashback is rather overelaborate: Did the mob vote against lynching Robitaille, deciding, "Naw, let's just cut off his hand and smear him with honey, so he can become an urban legend"? If not, it seems they went to a lot more trouble than most mobs in those sad days.

I am left with questions. Why did the Candyman prey on innocent young black victims who had done him no harm? Which is he: a mythical force brought to reality by psychic mind power, or an immortal being fueled by the life force of bees who lives in mirrors? I spend my days pondering questions such as these, so you won't have to.

Cape Fear ★ ★ ★
R, 130 m., 1991

Robert De Niro (Max Cady), Nick Nolte (Sam Bowden), Jessica Lange (Leigh Bowden), Juliette Lewis (Danielle Bowden), Joe Don Baker (Claude Kersek), Robert Mitchum (Lieutenant Elgart), Gregory Peck (Lee Heller), Martin Balsam (Judge). Directed by Martin Scorsese and produced by Barbara De Fina. Screenplay by Wesley Strick.

The way he sees the character of Sam Bowden is the key to why Martin Scorsese wanted to remake the 1962 thriller *Cape Fear.* Bowden, played by Nick Nolte, is a defense attorney who is threatened by a man from his past—a rapist who has finished a fourteen-year prison sentence and wants revenge for what he believes (correctly) was a lousy defense. In the original film, Sam Bowden was a good man trying to defend his family from a madman. In the Scorsese version, Bowden is flawed and guilty, and indeed everyone in this film is weak in one way or another, and there are no heroes. That's the Scorsese touch.

The movie, filmed near Fort Lauderdale, Florida, shows Nolte at the head of a troubled family. He and his wife (Jessica Lange) have been through counseling because of his infidelities, and now he seems to be in the opening stages of a new affair. They live in a rambling house on a lot of land, but there isn't space enough for their daughter (Juliette Lewis), who hates it when they fight, and locks herself in her bedroom to brood and watch MTV. This is a family with a lot of problems even before Max Cady arrives on the scene.

Cady is played by Robert De Niro, in a role filled by Robert Mitchum in 1962. Covered with tattoos spelling out dire biblical warnings, Cady is an iron-pumping redneck who learned to read in prison ("I started with Dick, Jane, and Spot, and went on to law books"). He drives into town in a Mustang convertible and offers to teach Bowden something about the law. And soon everywhere Bowden looks, he sees the ominous, threatening presence of Max Cady: outside a restaurant, in a movie theater, on the wall bordering his property.

But Cady is clever and stays just this side of the law; he doesn't actually trespass, and he doesn't do physical harm to Bowden. It's almost a game with Cady to taunt Bowden to the breaking point. Bowden goes to the cops, to a lawyer, to a private investigator, and as he seeks help we begin to realize that no one in this universe is untainted. Among the corrupt are Robert Mitchum, as a cop who hints that the lawyer should take the law into his own hands, and Gregory Peck, as a lawyer who represents Cady.

What we are looking at here is a *film noir* version of the classic Scorsese hero, who in film after film is a man tortured by guilt and the weakness of the flesh, and seeking forgiveness and redemption. And in this new version of Max Cady, Scorsese gives us not simply a bad man, but an evil one—a man whose whole purpose is to show Sam Bowden that he is a criminal, too.

A strata of evil underlies the whole film and is dramatized in the character of Danielle, the Bowdens' daughter, who is going on sixteen and is attracted to the menace and implied sexuality of Max Cady. It's as if she likes anybody who can bug her parents. In a tense, disturbing scene, Cady poses as a drama teacher and Danielle goes along even after she knows who he really is—allowing herself to be verbally seduced because evil and danger are attractive to her.

Nolte's character is more complex. He is not a bad man, but not a very good one, and he finally agrees with his private eye (Joe Don Baker) that maybe three guys should be hired to pound some sense into Max Cady. When Cady thrashes the three goons and comes looking for the Nolte character, we realize the complexity of this movie. Unlike the simplistic version of this scene we have seen in a hundred thrillers, what Scorsese gives us is a villain who has been wronged, seeking to harm a hero who has sinned.

I think the movie wanders a little toward the end, during a sensational climax in a tempest-tossed houseboat. The final struggle between Bowden and Cady passes beyond the plausible into the apocalyptic, and Cady delivers one-liners and bitter aphorisms long after he should be crazed by pain. But the final struggle between the two men is visually sensational, and once again Scorsese avoids the simplistic moralism of a conventional thriller; the key to the passage is the close-up of Bowden trying to wash the blood from his hands.

Cape Fear is impressive moviemaking, showing Scorsese as a master of a traditional Hollywood genre, able to mold it to his own themes and obsessions. Yet as I look at this $35 million movie with big stars, special effects, and production values, I wonder if it represents a good omen from the finest director now at work.

This is the first film in a production deal Scorsese has with Universal and Steven Spielberg's Amblin Entertainment, and represents his access to budgets much larger than he has worked with in the past. The result seems to be a certain impersonality in a film by this most personal of directors—the Scorsese touch on a genre piece, rather than a film torn out of the director's soul. Most directors would distinguish themselves by making a film this good. From the man who made *Taxi Driver*, *Raging Bull*, *After Hours*, and *GoodFellas*, this is not an advance.

Carlito's Way ★ ★ ★ ½
R, 141 m., 1993

Al Pacino (Carlito), Sean Penn (Kleinfeld), Penelope Ann Miller (Gail), John Leguizamo (Benny Blanco), Ingrid Rogers (Steffie), Luis Guzman (Pachanga). Directed by Brian De Palma and produced by Martin Bregman, Willi Baer, and Michael S. Bregman. Screenplay by David Koepp.

Ten years after they made *Scarface*, Al Pacino and director Brian De Palma are back with *Carlito's Way*, another large-canvas portrait of a professional criminal. Carlito Brigante is older and wiser, however, than *Scarface*'s Tony Montana, and for a time seems to be luckier.

He's a New Yorker with a Puerto Rican background, a drug dealer who was big in the barrio before he got sent up for thirty years. We meet him at the legal hearing that will free him after only five years, on a technicality. His lawyer, a flashy lowlife named Kleinfeld (Sean Penn), sits by with a smirk as Carlito expansively addresses the judge and courtroom on the lessons to be learned by his release.

The speech paints him as a self-righteous blowhard and something of a showboat, but we begin to see a deeper side of Carlito as he returns to the streets where he was once famous. Facing thirty years in prison, where he expected to die, he got a chance to do some thinking, and now he decides he wants to go straight. A friend has offered him a share in a car rental business in the Bahamas.

To finance his investment, Carlito takes a job at a flashy nightclub, where he's thrown into contact with all the people he should avoid the most. And he meets a young punk who always introduces himself as "Benny Blanco from the Bronx" (John Leguizamo), the kind of hothead Carlito once was. Benny brings out the worst in him.

The movie is narrated by Carlito himself, who explains his hopes, his strategies, and especially his mistakes. One of those is surely to have chosen Kleinfeld as his lawyer. The acting here, by Sean Penn, is a virtuoso tour de force—one of those performances that takes on a life of its own. Penn is hardly recognizable beneath a head of balding, curly hair. He gives the lawyer a spoiled narcissism, a sneakiness and smarminess, and we watch him steadily losing control to cocaine and greed.

Carlito, on the other hand, tries to be a stand-up citizen. He looks up an old girlfriend named Gail (Penelope Ann Miller), who says she dances on Broadway but neglects to explain it's in a strip club. They love each other, after their fashion, but we never sense much depth in their relationship; each one is caught up in the details of personal survival.

Brian De Palma in his best films is a muscular director who relishes over-the-top behavior, and here he paints a gallery of colorful gangsters and lowlifes. The hoods in the movie look borrowed from a production of *Guys and Dolls*, the nightclubs look recycled from *Saturday Night Fever*, and Al Pacino himself seems to be inspired by his Oscar-winning role in *Scent of a Woman* (there are times when his Puerto Rican accent migrates uncannily toward the voice of the crusty military man he played in that film).

The film is fascinated by the mechanisms that propel a man back into the criminal life despite his best intentions to escape it. Carlito wants only to keep his nose clean, make some money, and get out of town. But his values, his friends, and his circles are criminal, and the screenplay paints him into an inevitable corner—he's betrayed by his compulsion to stand by his friends.

Two of the set pieces in the film are among De Palma's best work. One involves an insane scheme by the lawyer to rescue a hood from the Riker's Island prison barge. The other is a cat-and-mouse chase leading to a shootout in Grand Central Station. There have been a lot of shootouts in railroad stations in the movies, mostly routine, but De Palma finds endless variations as Carlito tries to elude his pursuers. And the visuals are as striking as the ambush in Chicago's Union Station that was a high point of De Palma's *The Untouchables.*

Carlito's Way, like *Scarface,* is first and last a character study, a portrait of a man who wants to be better than he is. In *Scarface,* the hero's ambitions led only to power, lust, and greed. Here something more complicated is taking place; Carlito has grown enough to see himself from the outside, to understand some of the mistakes he made, to plot a way to escape from what seems like the inevitable fate of people in his position. Yet step by step and scene by scene, his fate is sealed.

Carmen ★ ★ ★ ★
PG, 152 m., 1984

Julia Migenes-Johnson (Carmen), Placido Domingo (Don Jose), Ruggero Raimondi (Escamillo), Faith Esham (Micaela), Jean-Philippe Lafont (Dancairo). Directed by Francesco Rosi and produced by Patrice Ledoux.

Bizet's *Carmen* is what movies are all about. It's one of the few modern movies that requires one of those legendary Hollywood advertising men who'd cook up copy like, for example . . .

Cheer! As Bizet's towering masterpiece blazes across the screen! Cry bravo! To passion, romance, adventure! From the bullrings of Spain to the innermost recesses of her gypsy heart, Carmen drives men mad and immortalizes herself as a romantic legend! Thrill! To the golden voice of Placido Domingo, and the tempestuous screen debut of the smouldering Julia Migenes-Johnson!

The temptation, of course, is to approach a film like this with hushed voice and bended knee, uttering reverent phrases about art and music. But to hell with it: This movie is the *Indiana Jones* of opera films, and we might as well not beat around the bush. *Carmen* is a Latin soap opera if ever there was one, and the sheer passionate joy of Bizet's music is as vulgar as it is sublime, as popular as it is clas-

sical. *Carmen* is one of those operas ideally suited to the movies, and this version by Francesco Rosi is exciting, involving, and entertaining.

You are doubtless already familiar with the music. The sound track was recorded in Paris with Lorin Maazel conducting the National Orchestra of France. Placido Domingo is in great voice, and a relatively unknown American soprano named Julia Migenes-Johnson not only can sing the title role but, perhaps just as importantly, can look it and act it. There is chemistry here, and without the chemistry—without the audience's belief that the scornful gypsy Carmen could enslave the soldier Don Jose—there would only be an illustrated sound track. After the recording was completed, the movie was shot on locations in Spain by Francesco Rosi, the Italian director of *Three Brothers* and *Christ Stopped at Eboli.* He has discovered lush, sun-drenched villages on hillsides, and a bullring of such stark Spanish simplicity that the ballet within the ring for once seems as elegant as the emotions it is reflecting. He also has found moonlight, rich firelight, deep reds and yellows—colors so glowing that the characters seem to warm themselves at his palette.

Opera films are traditionally not successful. They play in festivals, they find a small audience of music lovers, maybe they make some money in Italy. Domingo broke that pattern with his *La Traviata* (1983), directed by Franco Zeffirelli. It had good long runs around the United States, and even broke through to audiences beyond the core of opera lovers. But we Americans are so wary of "culture." Opera for many of us still consists of the fat lady on "The Ed Sullivan Show." And for many of the rest, it is something that inhabits a cultural shrine and must be approached with reverence. Maybe it takes the movies, that most popular of art forms, to break that pattern. Rosi, Domingo, and Migenes-Johnson have filmed a labor of love.

Carrie ★ ★ ★ ½
R, 98 m., 1976

Sissy Spacek (Carrie), William Katt (Her Prom Date), Piper Laurie (Her Mother). Directed by Brian De Palma and produced by Paul Monash. Screenplay by Lawrence D. Cohen.

Brian De Palma's *Carrie* is an absolutely spellbinding horror movie, with a shock at the end that's the best thing along those lines

since the shark leaped aboard in *Jaws.* It's also (and this is what makes it so good) an observant human portrait. This girl Carrie isn't another stereotyped product of the horror production line; she's a shy, pretty, and complicated high school senior who's a lot like kids we once knew. There is a difference, though. She has telekenesis, the ability to manipulate things without touching them. It's a power that came upon her gradually, and was released in response to the shrill religious fanaticism of her mother. It manifests itself in small ways. She looks in a mirror, and it breaks. Then it mends itself. Her mother tries to touch her and is hurled back against a couch. But then, on prom night . . .

Well, what makes the movie's last twenty minutes so riveting is that they grow so relentlessly, so inevitably, out of what's gone before. This isn't a science-fiction movie with a tacked-on crisis, but the study of a character we know and understand. When she fully uses (or is used by) her strange power, we know why. This sort of narrative development hasn't exactly been De Palma's strong point, but here he exhibits a gift for painting personalities; we didn't know De Palma, ordinarily so flashy on the surface, could go so deep. Part of his success is a result of the very good performances by Sissy Spacek, as Carrie, and by Piper Laurie, as Carrie's mother. They form a closed-off, claustrophobic household, the mother has translated her own psychotic fear of sexuality into a twisted personal religion. She punishes the girl constantly, locks her in closets with statues of a horribly bleeding Christ, and refuses to let her develop normal friendships.

At school, then, it's no wonder Carrie is so quiet. She has long blond hair but wears it straight and uses it mostly to hide her face. She sits in the back of the room, doesn't speak up much, and is the easy butt of jokes by her classmates. Meanwhile, the most popular girl in the class devises a truly cruel trick to play on Carrie. It depends on Carrie being asked to the senior prom by the popular girl's equally popular boyfriend—he's one of your average Adonises with letters in every sport. He's not in on the joke, though, and asks Carrie in all seriousness.

And then De Palma gives us a marvelously realized scene at the prom—where Carrie does, indeed, turn out to be beautiful. There's a little something wrong, though, and De Palma has an effective way to convey it: As Carrie and her date dance, the camera moves around them, romantically at first, but then too fast, as if they're spinning out of control.

I wouldn't want to spoil the movie's climax for you by even hinting at what happens next. Just let me say that *Carrie* is a true horror story. Not a manufactured one, made up of spare parts from old Vincent Price classics, but a real one, in which the horror grows out of the characters themselves. The scariest horror stories—the ones by M.R. James, Edgar Allan Poe, and Oliver Onions— are like this. They develop their horrors out of the people they observe. That happens here, too. Does it ever.

Casper ★ ★ ★
PG, 96 m., 1995

Christina Ricci (Kat), Bill Pullman (Dr. Harvey), Cathy Moriarty (Carrigan), Eric Idle (Dibs), Don Novello (Father Guido Sarducci), and the voices of: Malachi Pearson (Casper), Joe Nipote (Stretch), Joe Alaskey (Stinkie), Brad Garrett (Fatso), Mr. Rogers (Himself), Terry Murphy (Herself). Directed by Brad Silberling and produced by Colin Wilson. Screenplay by Sherri Stoner and Deanna Oliver.

It's easy to see why Casper the Friendly Ghost has such an appeal for small children. They have so much in common with him, since they, too, feel invisible and misunderstood, and remember little of their earlier lives. He is reassuring; in a universe of scary ghosts it's nice to know there's one on your side. The Casper comics did not survive into the current age of megadoom superheroes, but their memory did, and now here is *Casper*, a high-tech special effects extravaganza starring his friendliness.

There's been a lot of speculation about the coming age of computerized performances in the movies when we will see whole characters made up of bits and bytes. Jessica Rabbit was such a creation, and now Casper and his uncles—Stretch, Stinkie, and Fatso—dominate a movie that essentially stars computer programming. Ghosts offer, to be sure, certain advantages to the programmers, since their bodies are soft and changeable, but their faces display a full range of emotion and they are as real as the human characters in the film—which is, I suppose, a two-edged compliment.

As the movie opens, a rich man's daughter named Carrigan (Cathy Moriarty) learns that her father has left her nothing in his will except for crumbling Whipstaff Manor in Maine. She's enraged, until her assistant, Dibs

(Eric Idle), discovers a secret message suggesting that a vast treasure may be hidden there. They leave immediately for Maine— where, of course, it turns out that Whipstaff Manor is haunted.

She determines to get rid of the ghosts, and the movie has a lot of fun with scenes involving an exorcist (Don Novello as Father Guido Sarducci) and a ghostbuster (Dan Aykroyd). Nothing works. Meanwhile, Casper, the resident ghost, pulls himself away from watching "Mr. Rogers' Neighborhood" long enough to learn, on the news, about a ghost psychiatrist who specializes in helping spirits come to peace with themselves, so they won't need to haunt any longer.

Casper draws the program to Carrigan's attention in an insistent if ghostly way, and soon the psychiatrist (Bill Pullman, from *While You Were Sleeping*) is on the case, along with his daughter Kat (Christina Ricci, from *The Addams Family*). Kat and Casper soon become fast friends, and Casper is telling her what it's like to be a ghost: "You know that tingling feeling when your foot falls asleep? I think I'm made of that." Unfortunately, the presence of flesh and blood in Whipstaff Manor draws Casper's uncles from an ectoplasm, and things get exciting.

There are funny lines in the movie, as when the politically correct ghost psychiatrist observes, "You can call them ghosts or, as I prefer, the living impaired." The uncles could be a vaudeville team. And Moriarty makes a ferocious antagonist, clicking around Whipstaff in her high heels and trying to claim it as her own.

But the real stars of the movie are the special effects and animation artists. The story is more or less what you'd expect, and there is only so much you can do with a relationship between a little girl and a ghost. But Whipstaff comes alive with amazing achievements in art direction, set design, and gizmos like a chair that will brush your teeth while hurtling you down a rail at terrifying speeds. The use of special effects also allows sight gags that couldn't be done any other way, as when a car squeals to a stop on the edge of a towering cliff, just in the nick of time, and then a relieved character opens the door and steps out into nothingness.

Like *The Flintstones* and *The Addams Family, Casper* is an attempt to bring cartoons to life while incorporating them with real actors and sets. As a technical achievement it's impressive, and entertaining. And there is even a little winsome philosophy, as when Casper

sadly tells Kat, "I guess when you're a ghost, life just doesn't matter that much anymore."

Casualties of War ★ ★ ★
R, 120 m., 1989

Michael J. Fox (Eriksson), Sean Penn (Meserve), Don Harvey (Clark), John C. Reilly (Hatcher), John Leguizamo (Diaz), Thuy Thu Le (Oahn), Erik King (Brown), Jack Gwaltney (Rowan), Ving Rhames (Lieutenant Reilly), Dan Martin (Hawthorne). Directed by Brian De Palma and produced by Art Linson. Screenplay by David Rabe.

Casualties of War is a film based, we are told, on an actual event. A five-man patrol of American soldiers in Vietnam kidnapped a young woman from her village, forced her to march with them, and then raped her and killed her. One of the five refused to participate in the rape and murder, and it was his testimony that eventually brought the others to a military court-martial and prison sentences. The movie is not so much about the event as about the atmosphere leading up to it—the dehumanizing reality of combat, the way it justifies brute force, and penalizes those who would try to live by a higher standard.

The film begins as Eriksson, a young infantryman (Michael J. Fox), arrives in Vietnam and is assigned to a unit filled with veterans. They've been in combat, on and off, for months, and Meserve, the sergeant (Sean Penn), is a short-timer with less than a month to go before he can return home. Meserve is a good soldier, strong, violent, and effective. He is capable of heroism and has leadership ability. But he has lost, or he never had, the fundamental moral standards that most of us would like to believe are a product of his, and our, civilization.

On the night before he is scheduled to lead his men on a long-range reconnaissance patrol, Meserve is prevented by the MPs from going to a nearby village where he plans to visit a prostitute. Enraged, he involves his men in a plan to enter the village secretly and kidnap a young woman (not a prostitute), who will be brought along on the mission to service the sexual needs of all five men. When he explains this plan, Eriksson, the Fox character, doesn't believe he really means it. But he means it, all right.

In the field, the five men break into two groups: Eriksson and Diaz, who make a private agreement to "support" each other in refusing to go along with the rape, and the other three men, who are gung ho in favor of it. Meserve is the ringleader and is played by Sean Penn with such raw, focused power that it is easy to see how a weak person would be intimidated by him. Penn has a denial system that allows him to describe the kidnapped girl as a "Viet Cong prisoner," but actually he isn't even very concerned about justifying what he's doing. "What happens in the bush stays in the bush," one of the group members says.

When the actual moment of the gang rape arrives, Eriksson refuses to go along. He tries, in a tentative and agonizing way, to argue that "this isn't what it's supposed to be about over here." Meserve lashes him verbally: He is not loyal to the group, he loves the Cong, he's probably a queer, and so on. Diaz, hearing this, caves in and refuses to support Eriksson's stand. Four of the men rape the girl, and later the same four pump bullets into her.

This whole sequence of scenes is harrowing because it makes it so clear how impotent Eriksson's moral values are in the face of a rifle barrel. The other men either never had any qualms about what they are doing, or have lost them in the brutalizing process of combat. They will do exactly what they want to do, and Eriksson is essentially powerless to stop them. The movie makes it clear that when a group dynamic of this sort is at work, there is perhaps literally nothing that a "good" person can do to interrupt it. And its examination of the realities of the situation is what's best about the movie.

What is not so good are the scenes before and after the powerful central material. The movie begins and ends some time after the war, with the Fox character on a train—where he sees an Asian woman who reminds him of the victim. The dialogue he has with this woman in the movie's last scene is so forced and unnatural, and tries so hard to cobble an upbeat ending onto a tragic story, that it seems to belong in another movie. I also felt that the aftermath of the crime—Eriksson's attempts to bring charges—developed unevenly. Confrontations with two commanding officers are effective (they explain, obscenely and profanely, why he has no business pressing charges), but then the outcome seems sketchy and tacked on. Perhaps the movie would have been more effective if it had just recorded the incident, and ended as the group returned to base. That much would have contained everything important that the movie has to say; the narrative sandwich around it is simply distracting.

Casualties of War, written by the playwright David Rabe, is the first film by director Brian De Palma since *The Untouchables*. More than most films, it depends on the strength of its performances for its effect—and especially on Sean Penn's performance. If he is not able to convince us of his power, his rage, and his contempt for the life of the girl, the movie would not work. He does, in a performance of overwhelming, brutal power. Michael J. Fox, as his target, plays a character most of us could probably identify with, the person to whom murder or murder is unthinkable, but who has never had to test his values in the crucible of violence. The movie's message, I think, is that in combat human values are lost and animal instincts are reinforced. We knew that already. But the movie makes it inescapable, especially when we reflect that the story is true, and the victim was real.

Cat People ★ ★ ★ ½
R, 118 m., 1982

Nastassja Kinski (Irena Gallier), Malcolm McDowell (Paul Gallier), John Heard (Oliver Yates), Annette O'Toole (Alice Perrin), Ruby Dee (Female), Ed Begley, Jr. (Joe Creigh). Directed by Paul Schrader and produced by Charles Fries. Screenplay by Alan Ormsby.

It is a preposterous idea. Untold centuries ago, when all the world was a desert of windwhipped, blood-orange sand, and leopards lounged lazily in barren trees and arrogantly ruled all they could see, a few members of the puny race of human beings made their own accommodation with the fearsome beasts. They sacrificed their women to them. And the leopards did not kill the women, but mated with them. From those mists of prehistory, the race they created lives even today: The Cat People.

These people have had a hard time of it. They have the physical appearance of ordinary humans, except for something feline around the eyes and a certain spring in their step. They have all the mortal appetites, too, but there are complications when they make love, because in the heat of orgasm they are transformed into savage black leopards and kill their human lovers. They should mate only with their own kind. But as our story opens, there are only two Cat People—and, like their parents before them, are brother and sister.

This is the stuff of audacious myth, combining the perverse, the glorious, and the

ridiculous. The movies were invented to tell such stories. Paul Schrader's *Cat People* moves boldly between a slice-of-life in present-day New Orleans and the windswept deserts where the Cat People were engendered, and his movie creates a mood of doom, predestination, forbidden passion, and, to be sure, a certain silliness. It's fun in the way horror movies should be fun; it's totally unbelievable in between the times it's scaring the popcorn out of you.

Nastassja Kinski stars as the young sister, Irena. She is an orphan, reunited in New Orleans with her long-lost brother, Paul (Malcolm McDowell). She also is a virgin, afraid of sex and liquor because they might unleash the animal inside of her. (Little does she suspect that is literally what would happen.) She is tall, with a sensual mouth, wide-set green eyes, and a catlike walk. She catches the attention of the curator at the New Orleans zoo (John Heard). He senses danger in her. He also senses that this is the creature he has been waiting for all his life—waiting for her as the leopards in their cells wait, expecting nothing, ready for anything.

We have here, then, a most complex love triangle. Kinski fears her brother because she fears incest. She fears the curator but loves him. To love him is, eventually, to kill him. The curator is in love with the idea of her threat, but does not realize she *really* will turn into a leopard and rend his flesh. There are some supporting characters: Annette O'Toole is the sensible friend who senses danger, and Ed Begley, Jr. is the lackadaisical custodian whose arm is ripped from its socket. You shouldn't mess with leopards.

Schrader tells his story in two parallel narratives. One involves the deepening relationships among the sister, the brother, and the curator. The other, stunningly photographed, takes place in an unearthly terrain straight from Frank Herbert's *Dune* books. The designer, Ferdinando Scarfiotti, and the veteran special-effects artist, Albert Whitlock, have created a world that looks completely artificial, with its drifting red sands and its ritualistic tableau of humans and leopards—and yet looks realistic in its fantasy. In other words, you know this world is made up, but you can't see the seams; it's like the snow planet in *The Empire Strikes Back*.

Cat People moves back and forth between its mythic and realistic levels, held together primarily by the strength of Kinski's performance and John Heard's obsession. Kinski is something. She never overacts in this movie, never steps wrong, never seems ridiculous; she just steps onscreen and convincingly underplays a leopard. Heard also is good. He never seems in the grip of an ordinary sexual passion, but possesses one of those obsessions men are willing (and often are called upon) to die for. *Cat People* is a good movie in an old tradition, a fantasy-horror film that takes itself just seriously enough to work, has just enough fun to be entertaining, contains elements of intrinsic fascination in its magnificent black leopards, and ends in one way just when we were afraid it was going to end in another.

The Cement Garden ★ ★ ★
NO MPAA RATING, 108 m., 1994

Andrew Robertson (Jack), Charlotte Gainsbourg (Julie), Alice Coultard (Sue), Ned Birkin (Tom), Sinead Cusack (Mother), Hanns Zischler (Father), Jochen Horst (Derek). Directed by Andrew Birkin and produced by Bee Gilbert and Ene Vanaveski. Screenplay by Birkin.

Ian McEwan is a British author who specializes in twisted stories of deviate and devious secrets. His *The Comfort of Strangers*, made into a 1991 movie by Paul Schrader, was about honeymooners in Venice who fall into the sadomasochistic clutches of a two diabolical exiles, with dire consequences. Now comes the film of his *The Cement Garden*, equally perverse, but in a completely different way.

The movie takes place mostly inside and outside a barren, concrete-walled house on the outskirts of an English town. It seems to be situated on the banks of the town dump. In this house live a vile, coughing father; a sweet, inoffensive mother; and four children. One day the father takes offense at the weeds in his choked back garden, and determines to pave the entire area with cement. The work is too much for him, and he dies of a heart attack.

The mother (Sinead Cusack) soldiers on for a few more weeks before she too succumbs from an obscure complaint, after warning her children on her deathbed of such dangers as being carted off to orphanages. So the children decide to keep her death a secret, and conceal her body in the basement inside an old steel locker. They cover her with leftover cement.

All of this is simply the setup for McEwan's story, which toys with the possibility of incest between the two older children, the

girlish Jack (Andrew Robertson) and the wicked Julie (Charlotte Gainsbourg). Jack is what the British call a compulsive wanker, and Julie is a tease who takes delight in leading her brother into situations where he feels intrigued but uncomfortable.

Meanwhile, the children attempt to keep the secret of their parents' deaths. Weekly allotments of funds from their mother's bank account keep them in food, the authorities don't suspect anything, and there are no neighbors. But there is a gentleman caller, Derek (Jochen Horst), a slick and slimy sort in a red sports convertible, who has designs on Julie but little understands her designs on him.

The film was directed by Andrew Birkin, whose *Burning Secret* (1988) starred Klaus Maria Brandauer as a decadent German who befriends a young boy as a way of seducing his mother (Faye Dunaway). Birkin and McEwan seem destined for one another. Creating a gloomy claustrophobia inside the wretched house, Birkin uses nuance, timing, and Edward Shearmer's unsettling music to create an atmosphere in which outside values cease to matter, and life becomes a series of skirmishes between hostility and temptation. There is a little of *The Lord of the Flies* lurking here somewhere.

The movie is not really about sex or incest, I think, but about power—and particularly about the power that some adolescent girls learn to use to seek out the weaknesses of insecure teen-age boys. Usually there is some kind of monitor around—parents, teachers, the community—but inside this house there are no rules, and so the stronger will eventually prevail over the weaker or less certain.

In an Ian McEwan story nothing is quite as it seems, and many of the characters have a perfectly amoral willingness to break society's rules. That is the case here. *The Cement Garden* is not a pleasant film, nor is there any reassurance at the end—no promise that all will eventually be well. It's more of a seduction, like the events of the plot. It leads us into a world where some secrets are hidden and others indulged, and there is no restraint on its dark impulses.

The Cemetery Club ★ ★ ★
PG-13, 107 m., 1992

Ellen Burstyn (Esther Moskowitz), Olympia Dukakis (Doris Silverman), Diane Ladd (Lucille Rubin), Danny Aiello (Ben Katz), Lainie Kazan (Selma), Jeff Howell (Paul). Directed by Bill

Duke and produced by David Brown, Sophie Hurst, and Bonnie Palef. Screenplay by Ivan Menchell.

The Cemetery Club opens with a happy gathering—the wedding of a much-married friend, at which three women dance with their husbands. A year later, all three women are widows, sixtyish and uneasily facing the future. In the case of Esther Moskowitz (Ellen Burstyn), single life is especially ominous. She was married for thirty-nine years and hardly knows what it is like to be on her own.

The other survivors are Doris Silverman (Olympia Dukakis), strong-willed and easily offended, and Lucille Rubin (Diane Ladd), who would like to be seen as a merry widow but is secretly as lonely as the others. Together, they go out to the cemetery to stand near the tombstones of their departed partners and talk to them. But eventually one of them rebels: "We can't go on like this forever, living in the past. I feel like I'm in a cemetery club."

The movie, which is a sometimes uneasy compromise between comedy and drama, now becomes the story of the three lives, lived in a middle-class Jewish community where everybody knows each other, and attractive widows are likely to have complimentary glasses of V-8 juice sent over to their table at the delicatessen.

Esther, the Burstyn character, seems the most unlikely candidate for a second marriage, but lightning strikes one day when Ben Katz (Danny Aiello) walks into her life, likes her looks, and eventually asks her out. She resists, but he is persuasive, and soon she has tumbled into a love affair, only to have it seemingly end unhappily when Ben gets cold feet.

The scenes between Burstyn and Aiello are at the heart of the movie, and are sweet and warming—especially when they confess to each other about the scars that have accumulated on their bodies during years of wear and tear. Meanwhile, her affair causes some concern to the other women; Ladd is disappointed she didn't get the man, while Dukakis feels the romance is a little hasty and disrespectful to the memory of the dead husband.

The screenplay is by Ivan Menchell, based on his stage play, unseen by me. My guess is that the play had a more consistent tone. The movie has a serious undertone, lightened from time to time by scenes that don't quite seem to fit, as if the revisions were designed to lighten the mood of an essentially thoughtful piece.

Still, I liked it, partly because of the honesty of the love story, as Aiello struggles with issues we can hardly guess about. And I enjoyed the life-affirming counterpoint of Selma, the much-married character played by Lainie Kazan, who seems to be a gold-digger but comes through with some sound and sensible advice for Burstyn.

Sometimes at the movies I get the impression that Hollywood love stories are all about people too young to get driver's licenses. Here is a film open to a whole range of possibilities for older characters, and as Burstyn, Dukakis, and Ladd plot their strategies and exchange their hopes and fears, it's refreshing to know they realize that love is much more complicated than most young lovers ever dream.

Chances Are ★ ★ ★ ½
PG, 108 m., 1989

Cybill Shepherd (Corinne Jeffries), Robert Downey, Jr. (Alex Finch), Ryan O'Neal (Philip Train), Mary Stuart Masterson (Miranda), Christopher McDonald (Louie Jeffries), Josef Sommer (Judge Fenwick), Henderson Forsythe (Ben Bradlee), Lester Lanin (Conductor). Directed by Emile Ardolino and produced by Mike Lobell. Screenplay by Perry and Randy Howze.

Chances Are comes from the same gene bank as all the other mind-swap and reincarnation movies, but it's smart and entertaining. It proves the underlying thesis of all film criticism, which is that movies are not about their stories, they're about *how* they're about their stories. Plots are easy. Style is everything. *Chances Are* is a lighthearted romance about reincarnation told with wit and a certain irony.

Movies like this depend to a great degree on the personal styles of their actors: If we don't warm to the people on the screen and care about their feelings, then the plot is just the clanking and grinding of vast interchangeable machines. All four of the leading actors in *Chances Are* devote themselves to the material as if they really believed in it, and that's why this silly story works yet once again. The difference between good and bad acting in a romantic comedy is that in the good performances the characters somehow convince us that their hearts are actually at risk.

Cybill Shepherd stars in *Chances Are* as a Washington, D.C., professional woman whose husband is killed in a traffic accident in the early 1960s. She never quite gets over that loss. Years pass, and then decades, and she still treasures her love in her heart. She was pregnant when she became a widow, and she raises her daughter (Mary Stuart Masterson) and leads her life and never remarries. Her love is so constant that she remains oblivious to the fact that the family's best friend (Ryan O'Neal) has always been in love with her.

Meanwhile, we get another one of those standard movie fantasies of Heaven, in which everyone walks around on white clouds and speaks English and looks like someone painted by Norman Rockwell. And we discover that it's time for the soul of Shepherd's dead husband to be recycled back to Earth again. Through a heavenly mix-up, however, the soul is not inoculated with a special forgetfulness serum, and so the scene is set for the reincarnated husband to recognize his wife again.

When we meet the reborn husband (Robert Downey, Jr.), he is a student at Yale, where Shepherd's daughter also goes to school, of course. (Why don't they ever try a variation on this theme, and have the reborn husband come back as a yak breeder from Tibet?) Downey and Masterson start dating, she brings him home to meet her mom, and, of course, suddenly all of his memories come flooding back and he realizes that Shepherd is his wife and he is her reincarnated husband.

It's really at this point that the movie begins; everything earlier has just been laying the foundations. It is also at this point that I had better stop describing the details, because *Chances Are* has a lot of fun with the implications of its plot. If Downey is indeed the reborn husband, for example, then he is dating his own daughter. If he is not, then Shepherd will be guilty of stealing her daughter's boyfriend. And so on. Director Emile Ardolino *(Dirty Dancing)* approaches these paradoxes in a time-honored way, with lots of swinging bedroom doors and mistaken identities under the covers.

Although Cybill Shepherd gets top billing, and deserves it, in a way this movie belongs to Robert Downey, Jr. He is at the center of the action, trying to juggle the emotions of both women (while O'Neal stands on the sidelines, in love with Shepherd but still upstaged, after all these years, by the dead husband). If Downey were not able to bring a certain weight and conviction to his performance, everything else in the movie would collapse, but Downey is convincing and good.

His career before this movie was uneven, ranging from a strong, harrowing dramatic performance as a self-destructive cocaine addict in *Less Than Zero* to an obnoxious goofball in *The Pickup Artist*. He costars with James Woods in *True Believer,* where he is almost acted off the screen by Woods, but then here he is filled with confidence at the emotional center of *Chances Are*. He's uneven, but he's got the stuff.

The movie itself is surprisingly affecting, perhaps because Shepherd never goes for easy laughs but plays her character seriously: This Yale student, after all, may actually harbor the soul of her late husband, and that is an awesome possibility. By the end of the movie, all of the confusing possibilities have been sorted out with impeccable romantic logic, and the movie somehow provides a happy ending for everyone. (Of course it does. Just once, couldn't the yak dealer from Tibet be killed in a second traffic accident, leaving the widow to discover him a third time, reborn as a canasta player in a New Jersey retirement home?)

Chariots of Fire ★ ★ ★ ★
PG, 123 m., 1981

Ben Cross (Harold Abrahams), Ian Charleson (Eric Liddell), Nigel Havers (Lord Andrew Lindsay), Ian Holm (Coach Mussabini), Sir John Gielgud (Master of Trinity), Lindsay Anderson (Master of Caius), David Yelland (Prince of Wales), Nicholas Farrell (Aubrey Montague). Directed by Hugh Hudson and produced by David Puttnam. Screenplay by Colin Welland.

This is strange. I have no interest in running and am not a partisan in the British class system. Then why should I have been so deeply moved by *Chariots of Fire,* a British film that has running and class as its subjects? I've toyed with that question since I first saw this remarkable film in May 1981 at the Cannes Film Festival, and I believe the answer is rather simple: Like many great films, *Chariots of Fire* takes its nominal subjects as occasions for much larger statements about human nature.

This is a movie that has a great many running scenes. It is also a movie about British class distinctions in the years after World War I, years in which the establishment was trying to piece itself back together after the carnage in France. It is about two outsiders—

a Scot who is the son of missionaries in China, and a Jew whose father is an immigrant from Lithuania. And it is about how both of them use running as a means of asserting their dignity. But it is about more than them, and a lot of this film's greatness is hard to put into words. *Chariots of Fire* creates deep feelings among many members of its audiences, and it does that not so much with its story or even its characters as with particular moments that are very sharply seen and heard.

Seen, in photography that pays grave attention to the precise look of a human face during stress, pain, defeat, victory, and joy. Heard, in one of the most remarkable sound tracks of any film in a long time, with music by the Greek composer Vangelis Papathanassiou. His compositions for *Chariots of Fire* are as evocative, and as suited to the material, as the different but also perfectly matched scores of such films as *The Third Man* and *Zorba the Greek*. The music establishes the tone for the movie, which is one of nostalgia for a time when two young and naturally gifted British athletes ran fast enough to bring home medals from the 1924 Paris Olympics.

The nostalgia is an important aspect of the film, which opens with a 1979 memorial service for one of the men, Harold Abrahams, and then flashes back sixty years to his first day at Cambridge University. We are soon introduced to the film's other central character, the Scotsman Eric Liddell. The film's underlying point of view is a poignant one: These men were once young and fast and strong, and they won glory on the sports field, but now they are dead and we see them as figures from long ago.

The film is unabashedly and patriotically British in its regard for these two characters, but it also contains sharp jabs at the British class system, which made the Jewish Abrahams feel like an outsider who could sometimes feel the lack of sincerity in a handshake, and placed the Protestant Liddell in the position of having to explain to the peeved Prince of Wales why he could not, in conscience, run on the Sabbath. Both men are essentially proving themselves, their worth, their beliefs, on the track. But *Chariots of Fire* takes an unexpected approach to many of its running scenes. It does not, until near the film's end, stage them as contests to wring cheers from the audience. Instead, it sees them as *efforts*, as endeavors by individual runners—it tries to capture the exhilaration of running as a celebration of the spirit.

Two of the best moments in the movie: A

moment in which Liddell defeats Abrahams, who agonizingly replays the defeat over and over in his memory. And a moment in which Abrahams' old Italian-Arabic track coach, banned from the Olympic stadium, learns who won his man's race. First he bangs his fist through his straw boater, then he sits on his bed and whispers, "My son!"

All of the contributions to the film are distinguished. Neither Ben Cross, as Abrahams, nor Ian Charleson, as Liddell, are accomplished runners but they are accomplished actors, and they *act* the running scenes convincingly. Ian Holm, as Abrahams' coach, quietly dominates every scene he is in. There are perfectly observed cameos by John Gielgud and Lindsay Anderson, as masters of Cambridge colleges, and by David Yelland, as a foppish, foolish young Prince of Wales. These parts and others make up a greater whole.

Chariots of Fire is one of the best films of recent years, a memory of a time when men still believed you could win a race if only you wanted to badly enough.

Child's Play ★ ★ ★
R, 87 m., 1988

Catherine Hicks (Karen Barclay), Chris Sarandon (Mike Norris), Alex Vincent (Andy Barclay), Brad Dourif (Charles Lee Ray), Dinah Manoff (Maggie Peterson), Tommy Swerdlow (Jack Santos). Directed by Tom Holland and produced by David Kirschner. Screenplay by Don Mancini, John Lafia, and Holland.

What is it about dolls that makes them seem so sinister? Why is it that kids in the movies always seem to share some evil secret with their dolls? And why is it that when you see a doll on a shelf, its eyes seem to move by themselves? I think that when we were kids, we all secretly believed our dolls were up to something while we were asleep. And the movies can exploit that fear, because most of us are not aware that we carry it around as part of the subconscious trauma that makes life so interesting.

Child's Play is a cheerfully energetic horror film of the slam-bang school, but slicker and more clever than most, about an evil doll named Charles Lee Ray, or "Chuckie." This doll has been possessed by the mind and soul of the Lake Shore Strangler, a Chicago mass murderer who studied voodoo from a black magician. After the strangler is shot by a cop and left for dead in a toy store, he gathers enough energy to utter a voodoo incantation, after which ominous clouds roll in the sky and

lightning strikes the store, causing one of the several large explosions in this movie.

Cut to Karen Barclay (Catherine Hicks), a widow who works as a salesclerk at Carson, Pirie, Scott. Her kid wants a new kind of doll he's seen advertised on TV, but she can't afford the $100 price tag, so she buys one cheap from a peddler in the alley. No prizes for guessing if the Lake Shore Strangler has possessed this doll. Once Chuckie the Doll is home, he stays quiet around the adults but strikes up a friendship with Karen's son, Andy (Alex Vincent). Chuckie gets Andy to do favors for him, like carrying him into the living room so he can see the toy store explosion on the late news. And when the babysitter gets nosy, Chuckie plants a claw hammer between her eyebrows and sends her crashing through a window to the ground far below.

Film Note: The claw hammer scene is a case study of the False Alarm, a basic device in all horror movies of the Mad Slasher subgenre. Whenever there is a scare, and the scare turns out to amount to nothing, the movie takes a beat and *then* hits with the *real* scare. What's that noise behind the plant stand? Let's creep over and see. Gently . . . ah, nothing there! Relief. And then comes the Whammo! Moment. The next time you see one of these movies, wait for the False Alarm, and then start the countdown at the exact moment you hear the sigh of relief. The Whammo! Moment usually comes on the count of four. *Child's Play* is better than the average False Alarm movie because it is well-made, contains effective performances, and has succeeded in creating a truly malevolent doll. Chuckie is one mean SOB. The movie also has an intriguing plot device, which is that of course nobody will believe that the doll is alive. Little Andy tries to tell them, but they won't believe him. Then his mom realizes that Chuckie is moving and talking even though his batteries are not included. They won't believe her. After the police detective (Chris Sarandon) is nearly strangled by the little demon, who wrecks his squad car, he finally believes that Chuckie is for real. (Curiously, in the next scene, he meets with the mom but doesn't even mention what has just happened to him; in a movie like this, it takes a lot to hold your attention.)

Second Film Note: The movie ends with superb demonstrations of two other conventions in all Mad Slasher movies. The first is that once you kill the monster, he is never really dead. He looks dead, he's burned to a crisp and riddled with bullet holes, but then at a moment of peace and quiet we get another Whammo! Moment, and the godawful thing is still alive. The second convention of these movies is that the door is always left open for a sequel. *Child's Play* handles that with an ironic touch. The movie's last shot is of an open door.

China Moon ★ ★ ★ ½
R, 99 m., 1994

Ed Harris (Kyle Bodine), Madeleine Stowe (Rachel Munro), Benicio Del Toro (Lamar Dickey), Pruitt Taylor Vince (Daryl Jeeters), Roger Aaron Brown (Police Captain), Charles Dance (Rupert Munro). Directed by John Bailey and produced by Barrie M. Osborne. Screenplay by Roy Carlson.

China Moon is one of those labyrinthine police procedurals where you're constantly trying to outthink the plot, and you can't. It's an ingenious story line that folds back on itself in a way that I, at least, did not anticipate. And apart from its puzzle it also offers convincing performances by Ed Harris, as a veteran cop hopelessly besotted by a young woman he meets, and Madeleine Stowe, as the besotter.

Harris plays Kyle Bodine, a homicide detective who's so good at his job that in an opening sequence he's able to read a crime scene almost as well as Sherlock Holmes. He works backward from the evidence to the mind of the perpetrator and lectures Lamar (Benicio Del Toro), his rookie partner, on the basic truth of crime, which is that criminals are scared and dumb and they always forget something.

Bodine, a lonely bachelor, is drinking in a bar one night when he meets the lovely Rachel Munro (Madeleine Stowe), who smilingly deflects his come-ons, but admits she is charmed. Not long after, Bodine and Lamar are called to the Munro family home, where her husband (Charles Dance, as your basic suave rich pig) has been beating her. Bodine handles the case while concealing from Munro and his partner that he has met Rachel before. And then they begin to see each other secretly.

And that's almost all of the plot you're going to get from me, because from here on out, almost nothing in *China Moon* is quite as it seems. A murder is committed, Bodine gets involved in a cover-up, and then events get very complicated in a surprising way, and . . . That's enough. What pleased me about *China Moon* was its unusual combination of

human chemistry, especially in the relationship between the cop and the battered wife, and the cool expertise of its police work. The cops in this movie are skilled and smart, and we learn enough of their procedures to really get involved when the investigation turns into a duel between experts.

One of the pleasures of Roy Carlson's screenplay and John Bailey's direction is the success with which they conceal a key element of the story. In lesser movies of this genre, the surprise is almost always given away by what *Ebert's Little Movie Glossary* defines as the Law of Economy of Characters. This rule states that movie budgets are unable to accommodate any major characters who are not important to the story, so that any seemingly unnecessary character will turn out to be the villain. *China Moon* conceals its villain by seemingly having no unnecessary characters; everybody in the movie is accounted for in an expected way, so that the surprise, when it comes, is truly a surprise.

This is Madeleine Stowe's second superior thriller in a row, after *Blink*, and shows her once again playing a woman as smart as she is beautiful. There are some scenes here that require her to do some tricky emotional footwork (we don't know entirely *how* tricky until the movie is over), and she finds the right notes. Her performance works at the time, and holds up in retrospect.

Ed Harris shows a new side this time: He's sweet and charming as the cop, and we sort of believe that this lonely and battered woman would be attracted to him. Sure, she's married to the bank president, and he lives in a house trailer, but something happens between them that's convincing, and it underlies the whole effect of the movie, right up to the final shot.

The China Syndrome ★ ★ ★ ★
PG, 122 m., 1979

Jane Fonda (Kimberly Wells), Jack Lemmon (Jack Godell), Michael Douglas (Richard Adams), Scott Brady (Herman DeYoung), James Hampton (Bill Gibson), Peter Donat (Don Jacovich), Wilford Brimley (Ted Spindler). Directed by James Bridges and produced by Michael Douglas. Screenplay by Mike Gray, T.S. Cook, and Bridges.

The China Syndrome is a terrific thriller that incidentally raises the most unsettling questions about how safe nuclear power plants really are. It was received in some quarters as a

political film, and the people connected with it make no secret of their doubts about nuclear power. But the movie is, above all, entertainment: well-acted, well-crafted, scary as hell.

The events leading up to the "accident" in *The China Syndrome* are indeed based on actual occurrences at nuclear plants. Even the most unlikely mishap (a stuck needle on a graph causing engineers to misread a crucial water level) really happened at the Dresden plant outside Chicago. And yet the movie works so well not because of its factual basis, but because of its human content. The performances are so good, so consistently, that *The China Syndrome* becomes a thriller dealing in personal values. The suspense is generated not only by our fears about what might happen, but by our curiosity about how, in the final showdown, the characters will react.

The key character is Godell (Jack Lemmon), a shift supervisor at a big nuclear power plant in Southern California. He lives alone, quietly, and can say without any self-consciousness that the plant is his life. He believes in nuclear power. But when an earthquake shakes his plant, he becomes convinced that he felt an aftershock—caused not by an earthquake but by rumblings deep within the plant.

The quake itself leads to the first "accident." Because a two-bit needle gets stuck on a roll of graph paper, the engineers think they need to lower the level of the water shield over the nuclear pile. Actually, the level is already dangerously low. And if the pile were ever uncovered, the result could be the "China syndrome," so named because the superheated nuclear materials would melt directly through the floor of the plant and, theoretically, keep on going until they hit China. In practice, there'd be an explosion and a release of radioactive materials sufficient to poison an enormous area.

The accident takes place while a TV news team is filming a routine feature about the plant. The cameraman (Michael Douglas) secretly films events in the panicked control room. And the reporter (Jane Fonda) tries to get the story on the air. Her superiors refuse, influenced by the power industry's smoothly efficient public relations people. But the more Fonda and Douglas dig into the accident, the less they like it.

Meanwhile, obsessed by that second tremor, Lemmon has been conducting his own investigation. He discovers that the X-rays used to check key welds at the plant have been falsified. And then the movie takes off in classic thriller style: The director, James

Bridges, uses an exquisite sense of timing and character development to bring us to the cliffhanger conclusion.

The performances are crucial to the movie's success, and they're all the more interesting because the characters aren't painted as anti-nuclear crusaders, but as people who get trapped in a situation while just trying to do their jobs. Fonda is simply superb as the TV reporter; the range and excellence of her performance are a wonder. Douglas is exactly right as the bearded, casually anti-establishment cameraman. And Jack Lemmon, reluctant to rock the boat, compelled to follow his conscience, creates a character as complex as his Oscar-winning businessman in *Save the Tiger*.

Chinatown ★ ★ ★ ★
R, 131 m., 1974
(See also *The Two Jakes*.)

Jack Nicholson (J.J. Gittes), Faye Dunaway (Evelyn Mulwray), John Huston (Noah Cross), Perry Lopez (Escobar), John Hillerman (Yelburton), Darrell Zwerling (Hollis Mulwray), Diane Ladd (Ida Sessions), Roman Polanski (Man with Knife). Directed by Roman Polanski and produced by Robert Evans. Screenplay by Robert Towne.

Roman Polanski's *Chinatown* is not only a great entertainment, but something more, something I would have thought almost impossible: It's a 1940s private-eye movie that doesn't depend on nostalgia or camp for its effect, but works because of the enduring strength of the genre itself. In some respects, this movie actually could have been made in the 1940s. It accepts its conventions and categories at face value and doesn't make them the object of satire or filter them through a modern sensibility, as Robert Altman did with *The Long Goodbye*. Here's a private-eye movie in which all the traditions, romantic as they may seem, are left intact.

At its center, of course, is the eye himself: J.J. Gittes, moderately prosperous as a result of adultery investigations. He isn't the perenially broke loner like Philip Marlowe, inhabiting a shabby office and buying himself a drink out of the office bottle. He's a successful investigator with a two-man staff, and he dresses well and is civilized and intelligent. He does, however, possess the two indispensable qualities necessary for any traditional private eye. He is deeply cynical about human nature, and he has a personal code and sticks to it.

There is also, of course, the woman, who comes to the private eye for help but does not quite reveal to him the full dimensions of her trouble. And there are the other inevitable ingredients of the well-crafted private-eye plot, as perfected by Raymond Chandler and Dashiell Hammett and practiced by Ross Macdonald. There's the woman's father, and the skeletons in their family closet, and the way that a crime taking place now has a way of leading back to a crime in the past.

These plots work best when they start out seeming impossibly complicated and then end up with watertight logic, and Robert Towne's screenplay for *Chinatown* does that with consummate skill. But the whole movie is a tour de force; it's a period movie, with all the right cars and clothes and props, but we forget that after the first ten minutes. We've become involved in the movie's web of mystery, as we always were with the best private-eye stories, whether written or filmed. We care about these people and want to see what happens to them.

And yet, at the same time, Polanski is so sensitive to the ways in which 1930s' movies in this genre were made that we're almost watching a critical essay. Godard once said that the only way to review a movie is to make another movie, and maybe that's what Polanski has done here. He's made a perceptive, loving comment on a kind of movie and a time in the nation's history that are both long past. *Chinatown* is almost a lesson on how to experience this kind of movie.

It's also a triumph of acting, particularly by Jack Nicholson, who is one of the most interesting actors now working and who contributes one of his best performances. He inhabits the character of J.J. Gittes like a second skin; the possession is so total that there are scenes in the movie where we almost have telepathy; we *know* what he's thinking, so he doesn't have to tell us. His loyalty is to the woman, but on several occasions, evidence turns up that seems to incriminate her. And then he must pull back, because his code will not admit clients who lie to him. Why he's this way (indeed, even the fact that he's this way) is communicated by Nicholson almost solely in the way he plays the character; dialogue isn't necessary to make the point.

The woman is Faye Dunaway, looking pale and neurotic and beautiful, and justifying for us (if not always for him) J.J.'s trust in her. And then there are all the other characters, who revolve around a complicated scheme to float a bond issue and build a dam to steal water from Los Angeles, in a time of drought. Because the film depends so much on the exquisite unraveling of its plot, it would be unfair to describe much more; one of its delights is in the way that dropped remarks and chance clues gradually build up the portrait of a crime.

And always at the center, there's the Nicholson performance, given an eerie edge by the bandage he wears on his nose after it's slit by a particularly slimy character played by Polanski himself. The bandage looks incongruous, we don't often see a bandaged nose on a movie private eye, but it's the kind of incongruity that's creepy and not funny. The film works similar ground: Drifting within sight of parody every so often, it saves itself by the seriousness of its character.

Chocolat ★ ★ ★
PG-13, 105 m., 1989

Isaach De Bankole (Protee), Giulia Boschi (Aimee Dalens), Francois Cluzet (Marc Dalens), Cecile Ducasse (France Dalens [Child]), Jean-Claude Adelin (Luc Segalen), Kenneth Cranham (Jonathan Boothby). Directed by Claire Denis and produced by Alain Belmondo and Gerard Crosnier. Screenplay by Claire Denis and Jean-Pol Fargeau.

Of all the places I have visited, Africa is the place where the land exudes the greatest sadness and joy. Outside the great cities, the savannah seems ageless, and in the places where man has built his outposts, he seems to huddle in the center of a limitless space.

The land seems smaller at night than during the day. The horizon draws closer, containing strange rustlings and restlessness and the coughs of wild beasts, and voices carry a great distance—much farther than the lights from the verandah.

Chocolat evokes this Africa better than any other film I have ever seen. It knows how quiet the land can be, so that thoughts can almost be heard—and how patient, so that every mistake is paid for sooner or later. The film is set in a French colony in West Africa in the days when colonialism was already doomed but did not yet realize it. At an isolated outpost of the provincial government, a young girl lives with her father and mother and many Africans, including Protee, the houseboy, who embodies such dignity and intelligence that he confers status upon himself in a society that will allow him none.

The story is told partly through the eyes of the young girl, and the film opens in the present, showing her as an adult in 1988, going back to visit her childhood home. But what is most important about the story are the things the young girl could not have known, or could have understood only imperfectly. And the central fact is that Protee is the best man, the most capable man, in the district—and that her mother and Protee feel a strong sexual attraction to one another.

Protee moves through the compound almost silently, always prompt, always courteous, always tactful. He sees everything. His mistress is a French woman in her thirties, attractive, slender, with a few good dresses and the ability to provide a dinner party in West Africa with some of the chic of Paris. She has a workable marriage with her husband, whom she loves after the fashion of a dutiful bourgeois wife. But when the husband goes away on government business, the silence in the compound seems charged with tension; the man and woman who are left in charge become almost painfully aware of each other.

Daily life for the young girl is a little lonely for a child, but she shares secrets with Protee, too, and as she moves around the compound she has glimpses of a vast, unknown reality reaching out in all directions from the little patch of alien French society which has been planted there.

One day there is great excitement. An airplane makes an emergency landing in the district, bearing various visitors who seem exotic in this quiet place. One of them, young and bold, makes an implied proposition to the Frenchwoman. She is not interested, and yet there is a complicated dynamic at work here: She is drawn to Protee, yet cannot have him because of the racist basis of her society. And as is often the case, the master resents the servant, as if prejudice and segregation were the fault of the class that is discriminated against. In a way so subtle that some viewers of the film may miss it, the French woman behaves with the visiting male in such a way as to take revenge on Protee, whom she taunts because she cannot embrace.

Chocolat is a film of infinite delicacy. It is not one of those steamy, melodramatic interracial romances where love conquers all. It is a movie about the rules and conventions of a racist society, and how two intelligent adults, one black, one white, use their mutual sexual attraction as a battleground on which, very subtly, to hurt each other. The woman of course has the power; all of French colonial

society stands behind her. But the man has the moral authority, as he demonstrates in the movie's most important scene, which is wordless, brief, and final.

Chocolat is one of those rare films with an entirely mature, adult sensibility; it is made with the complexity and subtlety of a great short story, and it assumes an audience that can understand what a strong flow of sex can exist between two people who barely even touch each other. It is a deliberately beautiful film—many of the frames create breathtaking compositions—but it is not a travelogue and it is not a love story. It is about how racism can prevent two people from looking each other straight in the eyes, and how they punish each other for the pain that causes them.

Choose Me ★ ★ ★ ½
R, 106 m., 1984

Genevieve Bujold (Dr. Love), Keith Carradine (Mickey), Lesley Ann Warren (Eve), Patrick Bauchau (Zack), Rae Dawn Chong (Pearl). Directed by Alan Rudolph and produced by Carolyn Pfeiffer and David Blocker. Screenplay by Rudolph.

Apart from its other qualities, which are many, Alan Rudolph's *Choose Me* is an audaciously intriguing movie. Its main purpose, indeed, may be to intrigue us—as other films aim to thrill or arouse or mystify. There is hardly a moment in the whole film when I knew for sure what was going to happen next, yet I didn't feel manipulated; I felt as if the movie were giving itself the freedom to be completely spontaneous.

The movie begins with strangers talking to each other. One of the strangers is a radio talk show host. Her name is Dr. Love, and she gives advice to the lovelorn over the radio (most of her advice seems to be variations on "That's not my problem"). One of her regular callers, we learn, is a woman named Eve who owns a bar. One day a mental patient named Mickey, a guy whose past seems filled with mysterious connections to the CIA, the space program, and the Russians, walks out of a closed ward and into the bar and meets Eve. A few days later, Dr. Love, hoping to do some research into the ways that we ordinary folk live, adopts an assumed name and goes looking for a roommate. She finds Eve and moves in with her, and neither woman knows who the other woman really is. They also don't make the connection that Eve is a regular caller to the

radio program (highly unlikely, since Dr. Love speaks with an accent). None of this is really as hard to follow as it sounds. And since one of the pleasures of this movie is the leisurely and logical way it explores the implications of mistaken identity, I'm not going to write another word about the confusions the characters get involved in.

Choose Me is a deliberate throwback to the *film noir* of the 1940s—to those movies made up of dark streets and wet pavements, hookers under streetlamps, pimps in shiny postwar Studebakers, and people who smoke a lot. It's also about lonely people, but it's not one of those half-witted TV movies about singles bars and single women. It's about smart, complicated people who are trying to clear a space for themselves and using romance as an excavating tool. The performances are key to this strategy. The best thing in the movie is Genevieve Bujold's performance as Dr. Love. She is interesting, if detached, as the radio personality, but when love finally does touch her life, she is so unabashedly open and confessional and redfaced and sincere that we want to hug her. Bujold just gets better and better; coming so soon after her good work in *Tightrope*, this is a reminder of how many different kinds of roles she can play so well.

Keith Carradine is the drifter with the dangerous past. We are never quite sure how seriously to take him, and that's the idea behind his performance, I think: He is able to quite sincerely tell two different women he loves them and wants to marry them, and the funny thing is, we believe him, both times. Eve, the former hooker who owns a bar, is played by Lesley Ann Warren. It's another good performance, nervous and on-edge; she's the kind of woman who seeks a different man every night as a protection against winding up with the same guy for a whole lifetime in a row. There are other intriguing characters in this story, most notably Rae Dawn Chong as a cute young alcoholic with a weird marriage, a naive way of trusting strangers, and dreamy plans of becoming a poet someday. Her husband (Patrick Bauchau) begins to get real tired of seeing the Carradine character, who through a series of misunderstandings seems to specialize in robbing him of poker pots, dates, and the attentions of his wife.

All of these people interact throughout the whole movie without *Choose Me* ever settling into familiar patterns. It's as if Rudolph wanted to tell a story as it might actually have happened, with coincidental meetings, dumb misunderstandings, random chance, and the endless surprises of human nature. At the end of the movie we haven't learned anything in particular, but we have met these people and their loneliness and punch-drunk optimism, and we have followed them a little time through the night.

A Chorus Line ★ ★ ★ ½
PG-13, 117 m., 1985

Michael Blevins (Mark), Yamil Borges (Morales), Sharon Brown (Kim), Gregg Burge (Richie), Michael Douglas (Zack), Cameron English (Paul), Tony Fields (Al), Nicole Fosse (Kristine), Vicki Frederick (Sheila), Jan Gan Boyd (Connie), Michelle Johnston (Bebe), Janet Jones (Judy), Pam Klinger (Maggie), Audrey Landers (Val), Terrence Mann (Larry), Charles McGowan (Mike), Alyson Reed (Cassie), Justin Ross (Greg), Blane Savage (Don), Matt West (Bobby). Directed by Richard Attenborough and produced by Cy Feuer and Ernest Martin. Screenplay by Arnold Schulman.

Show business is the only business that reminds us there is no business like it. And it never tires of that message. If there were as many books about books as there are musicals about musicals, there wouldn't be room on the shelf for books about anything else. *A Chorus Line* is the quintessential backstage musical, a celebration of the lives and hard times of the gypsy dancers who turn up by the hundreds to audition for a handful of jobs on Broadway. It takes years of brutal hard work to become a good enough dancer to dare go to an audition, and then the reward is usually a brusque "thank you" and a sweaty ride home on the subway. In order to succeed as a Broadway dancer, applicants need a limitless capacity to absorb rejection, and *A Chorus Line* celebrates that masochism in song and dance.

A Chorus Line has spent more than a decade on stages all over the world; its story is by now well known. A choreographer is casting eight dancers for a new musical he hopes to stage, and during one long and truthful day he auditions dozens of dancers before he makes his final selection. Richard Attenborough's film treatment of this story sticks to the outlines of the stage version, by and large, although he leaves the stage to fill in the details of the choreographer's old romance, and he leaves out some of the original songs to make room for some new ones.

The result may not please purists who want a film record of what they saw on stage, but this is one of the most intelligent and compelling movie musicals in a long time—and the most grown-up, since it isn't limited, as so many contemporary musicals are, to the celebration of the survival qualities of geriatric actresses.

Most of the scenes take place inside a theater. Zack (Michael Douglas), the choreographer, sits behind a writing platform somewhere out there in the darkness. Occasionally he lights a cigarette, and the ash glows as he takes the measure of the dancers on the stage. He can see them. They can't see him. He communicates by microphone. They step hesitantly to the edge of the stage, blinded by the spotlight, and talk into the void. Well, if that isn't the life they wanted, why did they volunteer for it?

Platoons of dancers are brought on stage, winnowed, dismissed. Finally there are sixteen left, and Zack asks each one of them to talk on a personal level—talk about when they were born, and where, and what their lives have been like, and what their dreams are. Many of the dancers have the most extraordinary difficulties in doing this, and one of them is frank: "Give me the lines, and I can play anybody. Just don't ask me to talk about myself."

Meanwhile, backstage drama is taking shape. An unexpected dancer has appeared for the auditions—Cassie (Alyson Reed), Zack's former girlfriend. They met in the theater, courted in the theater, broke up because Zack's job left no time for a personal life. Cassie was a star, but now she simply needs a job.

The movie opens up the play by going offstage for flashbacks to their affair, but the flashbacks are notable mostly for the way they focus on the theatrical lives of this couple—the way their private lives seem valid only to the degree that they reflect acceptance from the audience. The underlying tension in the movie circles around Zack's eventual decision: Will his heart or his profession make the eventual decision about Cassie? Douglas plays Zack on a staccato, harsh note; this is a workaholic who walks around with a lot of anger. That makes it all the more effective when he occasionally relents and gives one of the dancers a break; softening momentarily before putting his mask on again.

I thought Zack's most revealing moment came when he made the cut from sixteen dancers to eight, reading out eight names

and then, when the eight were assembled downstage with smiles on their faces, thanking them and dismissing them; he had chosen the eight he did not name. Was this a misguided attempt to tell the rejected eight that they were also winners? Or was it simply cruelty? We are left to answer for ourselves.

Such questions are intercut with song and dance, with virtuoso solo numbers (my favorite was Charles McGowan's "I Can Do That!") and ensemble production numbers, leading up to a big and splashy finale, in which all of the dancers who originally auditioned are back on stage, together once again.

That leads to my one major difference with Attenborough's approach. Since *A Chorus Line* is a musical about itself, and since the whole hard, bitter, romantic truth of the story is that many are called but few are chosen, the roll call at the end strikes a false note of triumph. Better, perhaps, to have eight dancers on stage, and then cut to the others putting on their street clothes, waiting at bus stops, explaining to friends how they didn't get the job, or going to their dance classes yet again. I think the message of the play is that you don't get called back for a grand finale; you simply go to another audition.

Christiane F. ★ ★ ★ ½
R, 130 m., 1981

Natja Brunkhorst (Christiane), Thomas Haustein (Detlev), Jens Kuphal (Axel), Reiner Wolk (Leiche). Directed by Ulrich Edel and produced by Bernd Eichinger and Hans Weth.

This is one of the most horrifying movies I have ever seen. The fact that it's based on actual events makes it heartbreaking. *Christiane F.* is the portrait of a young girl who between her thirteenth and fifteenth years went from a fairly average childhood into the horrors of drug addiction, prostitution, and life on the brink of death.

The movie has become notorious in Europe, where both the film and book versions of Christiane's adventures have been bestsellers. The real Christiane first came to light as a witness in the trial of a man accused of having sex with minors. A reporter at the trial was intrigued by her appearance on the witness stand and tracked her down. His tape-recorded interviews with her became the basis for a twelve-part series in *Stern*, the German news magazine, which inspired the movie.

It is one of the most unremittingly grim portraits of drug addiction ever filmed. The only American equivalent that comes to mind is Shirley Clarke's *The Connection* (1961), but in that film the hell of heroin addiction was tempered by the story construction of the film, which evolved as a well-told play. *Christiane F.* simply evolves as one lower plateau of suffering after another, until Christiane hits a low bottom.

The movie opens with Christiane as an unexceptional young teen-ager, given to such minor vices as playing rock records too loud and staying out too late. She lives in an apartment with her mother and resents the regular presence of her mother's boyfriend. With friends, she experiments with alcohol and pot, and then, after a rock concert (David Bowie, playing himself), she sniffs some heroin, "just out of curiosity." She likes the feeling it gives her. She tries to get it again. She has young friends who are already junkies, but she disregards their warnings that she'll get hooked. She mindlessly repeats the addict's ageless claim: "I can't get hooked if I just use a little, only once in a while. I can control my using." She cannot. Before long, she's shooting heroin, and not much longer after that she is selling her body to buy it.

This is a common story in the big cities of the world. It is relatively unusual among girls as young as Christiane (I hope), but even more unusual is the fact that she finds her own way into the heroin-and-hooker underground, without being enslaved by a pimp. The movie is relentless in depicting the drug culture of West Berlin. We see unspeakable sights: a junkie leaping over a toilet stall to yank the needle from Christiane's arm and plunge it into his own, stealing her fix; Christiane and her boyfriend trying to withdraw cold turkey and vomiting all over one another; the discovery of dead overdose victims; and, unforgettably, the pale, sad faces of the junkies lined up in a subway station, all hope gone from their once-young eyes.

Christiane F. made lots of the "best ten" lists of European critics in 1982, but I found it hard to judge its artistic quality because of the shockingly bad dubbing job. The film has been dubbed into mid-Atlantic British, by voices that are often clearly too old and in slang that is ten to fifteen years out of date. New World should ask for its money back from the dubbers. And yet—the movie still works. After a time we forget the bad dubbing, because the images are so powerful, the horrors so strong and the performances (by a cast of young unknowns) so utterly, bleakly, realistic. This is a movie of hell.

Christine ★ ★ ★
R, 110 m., 1983

Keith Gordon (Arnie), John Stockwell (Dennis), Alexandra Paul (Leigh), Robert Prosky (Garage Owner), Harry Dean Stanton (Junkins). Directed by John Carpenter and produced by Richard Kobritz. Screenplay by Bill Phillips.

I've seen a lot of movies where the teen-age guy parks in a car with the girl he loves. This is the first one where he parks with a girl in the car he loves. I knew guys like this in high school. They spent their lives customizing their cars. Their girlfriends were accessories who ranked higher, say, than foam-rubber dice, but lower than dual carbs.

The car is named *Christine*. It's a bright red 1958 Plymouth Fury, one of those cars that used to sponsor the "Lawrence Welk Show," with tail fins that were ripped off for the *Jaws* ad campaign. This car should have been recalled, all right—to hell. It kills one guy and maims another before it's off the assembly line. Its original owner comes to a sad end in the front seat. And later, when Christine is twenty-one years old and rusting away, Arnie buys her. Arnie is a wimp. He's the kind of guy you'd play jokes on during lunch period, telling him the class slut wanted to talk to him, and then hiding his lunch tray while she was telling him to get lost. The kind of guy who was always whining, "Come on, guys—the joke's over!" But after Arnie buys Christine, he undergoes a strange metamorphosis. He becomes cool. He starts looking better. He stops with the greasy kid stuff. He starts going out with the prettiest girl in the school. That's where he makes his mistake. Christine gets jealous.

The entire movie depends on our willingness to believe that a car can have a mind of its own. I have believed in stranger things in the movies. Christine can drive around without a driver, play appropriate 1950s rock songs, lock people inside, and repair its own crushed fenders. The car is another inspiration from Stephen King, the horror novelist who specializes in thrillers about everyday objects. We saw his *Cujo*, about a rabid St. Bernard, and any day now I expect him to announce *Amityville IV: The Garage Door-Opener.*

Christine is, of course, utterly ridiculous. But I enjoyed it anyway. The movies have a love affair with cars, and at some dumb elemental level we enjoy seeing chases and crashes. In fact, under the right circumstances there is nothing quite so exhilarating as seeing a car crushed, and one of the best scenes in *Christine* is the one where the car forces itself into an alley that's too narrow for it.

Christine was directed by John Carpenter, who made *Halloween*, and his method is to take the story more or less seriously. One grin and the mood would be broken. But by the end of the movie, Christine has developed such a formidable personality that we are actually taking sides during its duel with a bulldozer. This is the kind of movie where you walk out with a silly grin, get in your car, and lay rubber halfway down the freeway.

A Christmas Story ★ ★ ★
PG, 94 m., 1983

Melinda Dillon (Mrs. Parker), Darren McGavin (The Old Man), Peter Billingsley (Ralphie). Directed by Bob Clark and produced by Rene Dupont and Clark. Screenplay by Jean Shepherd, Leigh Brown, and Clark.

Of course. That's what I kept saying during *A Christmas Story*, every time the movie came up with another one of its memories about growing up in the 1940s. Of course, any nine-year-old kid in the '40s would passionately want, for Christmas, a Daisy Brand Red Ryder repeating BB carbine with a compass mounted in the stock. Of course. And of course, his mother would say, "You'll shoot your eye out." That's what mothers always said about BB guns. I grew up in downstate Illinois. The hero of this film, Ralphie, grew up in Gary, Ind. Looking back over a distance of more than thirty years, the two places seem almost identical—Middle American outposts where you weren't trying to keep up with the neighbors, you were trying to keep up with Norman Rockwell.

The movie is based on a nostalgic comic novel named *In God We Trust, All Others Pay Cash*, by Jean Shepherd, the radio humorist, who also narrates it. He remembers the obvious things, like fights with the bullies at school, and getting into impenetrable discussions with younger kids who do not quite know what all the words mean. He remembers legendary schoolteachers and hiding in the cupboard under the sink and having fantasies of defending the family home with a BB gun.

But he also remembers, warmly and with love, the foibles of parents. The Old Man in *A Christmas Story* is played by Darren McGavin as an enthusiast. Not an enthusiast of anything, just simply an enthusiast. When he wins a prize in a contest, and it turns out to be a table lamp in the shape of a female leg in a garter, he puts it in the window, because it is the most amazing lamp he has ever seen. Of course. I can understand that feeling. I can also understand the feeling of the mother (Melinda Dillon), who is mortified beyond words.

The movie's high point comes at Christmastime, when Ralphie (Peter Billingsley) goes to visit Santa Claus. Visits to Santa Claus are more or less standard in works of this genre, but this movie has the best visit to Santa I've ever seen. Santa is a workaholic, processing kids relentlessly. He has one helper to spin the kid and deposit him on Santa's lap, and another one to grab the kid when the visit is over, and hurl him down a chute to his parents below. If the kid doesn't want to go, he gets Santa's boot in his face. Of course.

Chuck Berry Hail! Hail! Rock 'n' Roll
★ ★ ★ ★
PG, 120 m., 1987

Featuring Chuck Berry, Keith Richards, Eric Clapton, Robert Cray, Etta James, Johnnie Johnson, Julian Lennon, and Linda Ronstadt. Directed by Taylor Hackford and produced by Stephanie Bennett. Music produced by Keith Richards.

I expected *Chuck Berry Hail! Hail! Rock 'n' Roll!* to be a great concert film, and it is. What I did not expect was that it would also be a tantalizing mystery, a study of Chuck Berry that makes him seem as shrouded and enigmatic as Charles Foster Kane. Here is a sixty-year-old man singing *Sweet Little Sixteen,* and he sings it with total conviction, and we have no idea what he means, or ever meant, by it.

The argument of this film is that Chuck Berry was a crucial figure in the development of rock 'n' roll, that fusion of black gospel and rhythm and blues with mainstream pop and teen-age trauma. A good case is made, especially when Eric Clapton and Keith Richards explain precisely which chords and guitar strategies Berry used, and how you can still hear them today. There is a moment in the film when Berry and Richards are rehearsing, and Berry makes Richards do the same passage over and over again until he duplicates an effect that was first heard on records thirty years ago. It still sounds exactly right.

The film is a documentary about the six-

tieth birthday concert that Berry performed in his hometown of St. Louis in 1987. The concert was the inspiration of Richards, lead guitarist for The Rolling Stooes, who says he wanted to repay Berry for all the things the Stones and other rock groups have stolen from him. The way he wanted to do that was by producing a concert in which Berry would be backed by Richards and—for once—a first-rate, well-rehearsed band.

We quickly learn that this is not the way Berry has been operating in recent years. In testimony from Bruce Springsteen (who once opened for Berry) and in documentary footage of Berry himself, we learn that Berry has reduced his public appearances to an absolute routine. He travels alone, arrives backstage minutes before showtime, requires a local back-up band that knows his hit songs, walks onstage, does his thing, collects his money, and gets out of town.

Money seems to be very important to Berry. He discusses his original decision to become a full-time musician entirely in terms of money; he describes his guitar as "tax-deductible," and he shows off some vintage Cadillacs that he refuses to sell until he gets his price. He never discusses his music with a tenth of the interest he has for his bank account.

And yet the man is a terrific musician, and his songs retain an elemental, driving power that defines rock 'n' roll. There is a lot of concert footage in the film, and the audience I saw it with was rocking in their seats. Although Berry is a tough customer during the rehearsals (at one point, he shouts at Richards, "I been doin' it my way for sixty years"), the concert is a magnificent celebration of Berry's work as a composer and performer.

Berry is all over the stage, doing his famous duck walk, assaulting the microphone, nailing the beat, exuding the kind of forbidden anarchic sexuality that startled the bland teen-agers of the 1950s. He sings, he says, about the things that mattered to kids: school, romance, and cars.

Berry is backed up onstage by a band including Johnnie Johnson, the piano player who led the original trio where Berry got his start. There is some speculation that Johnson may have helped originate Berry's style, but he seems happier in the background, pounding out the beat. Richards oversees the band and plays lead guitar to Berry's rough rhythm, and there are several guest artists including Clapton, Julian Lennon,

Robert Cray, Linda Ronstadt, and, stealing the show, Etta James.

It's one hell of a concert, a joyous celebration of the music, yet always lurking just offstage is the sense of Berry's obsessive privacy about his personal life. One of the movie's quietest moments is unforgettable. We see Berry's wife on camera. She introduces herself. She is asked a question. We hear Berry's voice from off camera: "OK, that's enough." The screen goes black, and we never see her again. Behind the man who helped create a music that let it all hang out, there is another man who plays it all very close to the vest.

Cinema Paradiso ★ ★ ★ ½
NO MPAA RATING, 113 m., 1989

Philippe Noiret (Alfredo), Jacques Perrin (Salvatore), Salvatore Cascio (Salvatore as a Child), Marco Leonardi (Salvatore as an Adolescent), Agnese Nano (Elena), Antonella Attili (Young Maria), Isa Danielli (Anna), Pupella Maggio (Old Maria), Leopoldo Trieste (Father Adelfio). Directed by Giuseppe Tornatore and produced by Franco Cristaldi. Screenplay by Tornatore.

There is a village priest in *Cinema Paradiso* who is the local cinema's most faithful client. He turns up every week, like clockwork, to censor the films. As the old projectionist shows the movies to his audience of one, the priest sits with his hand poised over a bell, the kind altar boys use. At every sign of carnal excess—which to the priest means a kiss—the bell rings, the movie stops, and the projectionist snips the offending footage out of the film. Up in the projection booth, tossed in a corner, the lifeless strips of celluloid pile up into an anthology of osculation, an anthology that no one will ever see, not in this village, anyway.

Giuseppe Tornatore's *Cinema Paradiso,* which won the Oscar for best foreign language film, takes place in Sicily in the final years before television. It has two chief characters: old Alfredo (Philippe Noiret), who rules the projection booth, and young Salvatore (Salvatore Cascio), who makes the booth his home away from an indifferent home. As the patrons line up faithfully, night after night, for their diet of films without kisses, the boy watches in wonder as Alfredo wrestles with the balky machine that throws the dream images on the screen. At first Alfredo tries to chase Salvatore away, but eventually he accepts his presence in the booth and thinks of him almost as his child. Salvatore certainly considers the old man his father and (this is the whole point) the movies his mother.

I wonder if a theater has ever existed that showed such a variety of films as the Cinema Paradiso does in this movie. Giuseppe Tornatore tells us in an autobiographical note that the theater in his hometown, when he was growing up, showed everything from Kurosawa to the Hercules movies, and in *Cinema Paradiso,* we catch glimpses of Charlie Chaplin, John Wayne, and, of course, countless Hollywood melodramas in which men and women look smolderingly at one another, come closer, seem about to kiss, and then (with the jerk of a jump cut) are standing apart, exchanging a look of deep significance.

We become familiar with some of the regular customers at the theater. They are a noisy lot—rude critics, who shout suggestions at the screen and are scornful of heroes who do not take their advice. Romances are launched in the darkness of the theater, friendships are sealed, wine is drunk, cigarettes smoked, babies nursed, feet stomped, victories cheered, sissies whistled at, and God only knows how this crowd would react if they were ever permitted to see a kiss.

The story is told as a flashback; it begins with a prominent film director (Jacques Perrin) learning in Rome that old Alfredo is dead and making a sentimental journey back to his hometown. Then we see the story of the director's childhood (he is portrayed by Cascio) and his teen-age years, where he is played by Marco Leonardi. The earliest parts of the movie are the most magical. Then things grow predictable: There are not many rites of passage for an adolescent male that are not predictable, and not many original ways to show the death of a movie theater, either.

Tornatore's movie is a reminder of the scenes in Truffaut's *Day for Night,* where the young boy steals a poster of *Citizen Kane.* We understand that the power of the screen can compensate for a deprived life, and that young Salvatore is not apprenticing himself to a projectionist, but to the movies. Once that idea has been established, the film begins to reach for its effects, and there is one scene in particular—a fire in the booth—that has the scent of desperation about it, as if Tornatore despaired of his real story and turned to melodrama.

Yet anyone who loves movies is likely to love *Cinema Paradiso,* and there is one scene where the projectionist finds that he can reflect the movie out of the window in his booth and out across the town square, so that the images can float on a wall, there in the night above the heads of the people. I saw a similar thing happen one night in Venice in 1972 when they showed Chaplin's *City Lights* in the Piazza San Marco to more than ten thousand people, and it was then I realized the same thing this movie argues: Yes, it is tragic that the big screen has been replaced by the little one. But the real shame is that the big screens did not grow even bigger, grow so vast they were finally on the same scale as the movies they were reflecting.

Circle of Friends ★ ★ ★ ½
PG-13, 112 m., 1995   **NEW**

Chris O'Donnell (Jack), Minnie Driver (Benny), Geraldine O'Rawe (Eve), Saffron Burrows (Nan), Alan Cumming (Sean), Colin Firth (Simon Westward), Aidan Gillen (Aidan), Mick Lally (Dan Hogan). Directed by Pat O'Connor and produced by Arlene Sellers, Alex Winitsky, and Frank Price. Screenplay by Andrew Davies.

The most delirious part of romance comes when the two lovers begin to idealize each other. Much more important than physical love is the conviction that the other person is special, unique—a *good* person. Falling in love involves the conviction that the other person is, in some way, a hero. If you don't feel that way about the person you love, maybe it's because you think you don't deserve a hero. If so, beware the substitute.

Pat O'Connor's *Circle of Friends* is based on such beliefs. Early in the film, a young man named Jack makes a determination about a young woman named Benny. "You're really *there,*" he says, and she looks him straight in the eye and says, "Well . . . yes, I am." And she is. Benny, played by a luminous actress named Minnie Driver, is not beautiful in conventional terms—her two best friends are "prettier"—but Jack sees more deeply inside her, and what he finds is thrilling: nothing less than a soul mate.

Benny feels the same way about Jack (Chris O'Donnell), not for something superficial, like the fact that he's on the rugby team at the Dublin university they both attend, but because they can take long walks together and never stop talking, talking about what's most important to them. O'Donnell *(Scent of a Woman)* is crucial to the movie's success, because he so convincingly embodies the personal qualities the plot demands: He is her hero, and that's why it hurts her so much when he disappoints her—not so much because he "cheated" on her, as because he wasn't true to his best nature.

Circle of Friends is heart-warming and poignant, a love story that glows with intelligence and feeling. It's set in Ireland in the 1950s, and is another of those recent Irish films where the young characters are articulate, mature for their years, concerned about serious things, and with poetry in their hearts.

Because of its time and place, it is very much concerned with moral issues—with virginity, "going all the way," mortal sins, and the specter of temptation. "Which is it to be?" a priest asks young women in a sermon. "Will your body be a garden for Jesus, or a vessel of sin?" Somehow, one of Benny's friends complains, it's always up to the girls—as if boys can't make the same decision. Some of the dialogue, by Andrew Davies, based on the novel by Maeve Binchy, has a ring of perfect accuracy:

Benny in confession: "I've had impure thoughts, father."

Priest: "Did you entertain them?"

And there is another line that's just right, as Jack's father talks to his son after first meeting Benny: "There's a lot to be said for these big, soft girls." She is big and soft, tallish, with unruly hair and a face that's a little too wide for conventional beauty, but there are moments in this movie when she out-dazzles every other woman in the room, and that's because of her brains, her personality, and her smile.

As the movie opens, we meet Benny at home in a small town, where her father is the haberdasher. They confidently expect her to someday marry Sean (Alan Cumming), the store manager, an unctuous and shifty type. Benny grows older and goes off to university, taking the bus in to Dublin every day, and soon she has eyes only for Jack.

Meanwhile, a parallel story involves Benny's friend Nan (Saffron Burrows), superficially glamorous, and Simon (Colin Firth), a member of the Protestant land-owning class, whose family intends him to marry for money. Nan knows just what she wants, and it's not "one of these college boys." She wants an older, sophisticated man, and thinks Simon fits her needs. She goes after him with guile and charm, and he succumbs—or seems to, until the plot involves itself in betrayals and renunciations.

One of the pleasant things about this film

is that the characters are allowed to be intelligent and to think for themselves. Too many recent American movies about young people, lovers and otherwise, celebrate their self-congratulatory stupidity. It's as if Hollywood is terrified of putting people on the screen who might be smarter than anyone in the audience. Benny, as played by Minnie Driver, is a role model: She knows her mind and her heart, and she knows what she requires from a man before she will offer him either one. "I know I may look like a rhinoceros," she tells Jack, after he delays asking her to dance at a party, "but I'm quite thin-skinned, really. Don't mess me about. I'll flatten you."

Circle of Friends is a real treasure. Pat O'Connor, the director, also made the 1984 *Cal,* which won Helen Mirren the best actress award at Cannes. Here, again, he shows an instinctive feeling for characters who are not flighty, not silly, but, as Jack observes about Benny, really *there.*

City of Hope ★ ★ ★ ★
R, 129 m., 1991

Vincent Spano (Nick), Joe Morton (Wynn), Tony Lo Bianco (Joe), Barbara Williams (Angela), Angela Bassett (Reesha), David Strathairn (Asteroid), John Sayles (Carl). Directed by John Sayles and produced by Sarah Green and Maggie Renzi. Screenplay by Sayles.

John Sayles's *City of Hope* is like a wheel of torture to which the characters are chained. It goes around and around, sometimes through fire, sometimes through ice, and there is no way for them to free themselves. The film takes place in a fictional big city in New Jersey, where everyone is connected and where all the connections seem tainted by greed, graft, dishonesty, and corruption. Some of the players are on one side of the law and some on the other, but there is little to choose between them.

Sayles's method of telling the story of this city and the people trapped there is audacious. He fills his canvas with many characters—I didn't count, but I'm told there are thirty-six—and follows them through their days and nights as they run into one another, make deals, tell lies, seek happiness, and find mostly compromise and disappointment.

There are idealists in this city, but we watch as their idealism is shattered, as they learn the ways of clout and bribery, arson and perjury. The central character is a young man named Nick (Vincent Spano), whose

father (Tony Lo Bianco) is a local contractor. That means Nick has a cushy union job that requires him to sit around all day on a construction site, doing nothing, and eventually even this task is too much for him, and he walks off the job.

He leaves not because he is lazy, but because his ego can no longer deal with the pain of being paid to do nothing. "You don't *have* to just sit around all day!" his father shouts at him. "I could arrange for you to have some more responsibility." Yes, but that's not what Nick wants, either. He wants . . . well, if he could put it in words, his wish would be to live in a world with different rules. But in this world he drifts and falls into a romance with a woman named Angela (Barbara Williams), who has a kid and used to be married to a cop who beat her.

We meet the cop. We meet a couple of cops, one worried by his partner's dangerous temper. We meet the mayor, and the local fat cats, and a small-time crook (Sayles) who runs an auto repair shop, and a black alderman (Joe Morton) who wants to protect a housing development against developers who want to use urban renewal to make a fortune.

We meet a lot of people, and the surprise is that Sayles is able to make it so clear who they are, how they relate to one another, and why they matter. This movie is like a mapped-out version of *Slacker,* the independent film that wandered through Austin, Texas, allowing the camera to follow first one character, then another, drifting in and out of lives and conversations. Sayles is not working at random, and he advances his plot toward a conclusion of some urgency, but his camera seems to have the same random drift. He's telling us that it doesn't matter where he looks in this New Jersey town, he'd find more of the same sickness and greed. He's suggesting he doesn't need a plot to organize his indictment; it's there to be seen.

John Sayles is a director of many different genres and moods, and a festival of his work would show astonishing diversity, from *The Return of the Secaucus Seven* to *Eight Men Out,* from *Lianna* to *Matewan,* from *Baby, It's You* to *The Brother From Another Planet.* I felt that with both *Matewan,* about a bitter southern labor dispute, and *Eight Men Out,* about the Black Sox scandal, he allowed his large casts to grow too diffuse; we weren't always sure who was who or how they related. With *City of Hope,* he uses the large canvas and his most complex story with complete

assurance, and this time we get wrapped up; we care.

The movie is not simply story-driven, or only concerned with the politics and plotting of its characters. There is great attention to nuances of dialogue in scenes like the one where the Sayles character spars with a policeman who knows he has information. There is emotional subtlety in the scenes involving Spano and Williams, who are faced with creating the idealism necessary for love in a city where idealism is mocked. There is enormous power in the scenes between Spano and Lo Bianco—a man who wants to do the right thing and finds he is not strong enough.

One strong thread of the plot involves the dilemma of the black alderman, played by Morton as a reformer who finds he cannot really get anything accomplished unless he goes along. He's trapped between the white establishment and black militants, and turns for advice to a retired black mayor of a nearby town (Ray Aranha), who talks about the hard lessons that destroyed his own idealism.

City of Hope is a powerful film, and an angry one. It is impossible not to find echoes of its despair on the front pages every day. It asks a hard question: Is it possible for a good person to prevail in a corrupt system, just simply because right is on his side? The answer, in the short run, is that power is stronger than right. The notion of a long run, of course, is all that keeps hope alive.

City Slickers ★ ★ ★ ½
PG-13, 108 m., 1991

Billy Crystal (Mitch Robbins), Daniel Stern (Phil Berquist), Bruno Kirby (Ed Furillo), Patricia Wettig (Barbara Robbins), Helen Slater (Bonnie Rayburn), Jack Palance (Curly). Directed by Ron Underwood and produced by Irby Smith. Screenplay by Lowell Ganz and Babaloo Mandel.

City Slickers comes packaged as one kind of movie—a slapstick comedy about white-collar guys on a dude ranch—and it delivers on that level while surprising me by being much more ambitious, and successful, than I expected. This is the proverbial comedy with the heart of truth, the tear in the eye along with the belly laugh. It's funny, and it adds up to something.

The movie opens with three professional guys mired in their discontent. Billy Crystal plays Mitch, who sells time for a radio station, and is happy, more or less, although his wife tells him he has lost his smile. Daniel

Stern labors for his father-in-law's supermarket, and is married to a woman so insufferable that he has developed psychosomatic narcolepsy as a form of dealing with her. Bruno Kirby, the third pal, is obsessed with the passage of time and proves himself by pursuing young women and egging his pals on to harebrained vacation ideas.

It's his notion that this year they should try a dude ranch—but a "real one," where along with other city slickers they'll be cowboys for a couple of weeks, and move a real herd of real cattle across real plains to Colorado, also real. The setup of the movie—the three buddies and their various forms of misery—is funny, but the dude ranch possesses a certain mythic quality, reinforced by the theme from *The Magnificent Seven*, which plays under the Western action, sometimes ironically, sometimes even heroically.

The city slickers are choosing, half ironically, to follow in the footsteps of the great movie cattle rides of the past. They're fans of *Red River*, the John Wayne classic where the Duke shouts "Move 'em out!" and the cowboys are seen in a montage, waving their hats and shouting with glee. The herd at this dude ranch exists solely for the purpose of being moved back and forth by tenderfoots, but the trail boss does indeed seem like a survivor from an earlier time. He's Curly (Jack Palance), with a cigarette permanently pasted into his mug.

The plot unfolds along fairly predictable lines. The three city dudes meet up with their fellow urban cowboys, including two black Baltimore dentists and a good-looking blonde who has been abandoned by her boyfriend. They ride out one morning at dawn, saddle sore but plucky, and along the way there are the obligatory showdowns with macho professional cowboys, stubborn cattle, and nature.

What brings these scenes to life is the quality of the dialogue, by Lowell Ganz and Babaloo Mandel *(Parenthood)*, with additional lines that sound a lot like Crystal. There are moments of insight, of secrets sincerely shared, of the kind of philosophical speculation that's encouraged by life on the range. (What do guys talk about when they're on a cattle drive to Colorado? How to program the VCR, of course.)

Ron Underwood's direction is professional and focused; all of the subplots, like Crystal's love for a baby calf he helps deliver, pay off at the end. There is also the kind of crazy heroism that can be indulged in only by guys who don't understand the real dangers they're in, and the dreamy nights around the campfire when they stand back and look at their lives, their marriages, and the meaning of it all.

City Slickers is like *Parenthood* in the way it deals with everyday issues of living in an unforced way that doesn't get in the way of the humor, and yet sets the movie up for a genuine emotional payoff at the end. And the male bonding among Crystal, Stern, and Kirby is unforced and convincing. There are so many ways this movie could have gone wrong—with gratuitous action scenes, forced dialogue, or contrived showdowns—that it's sort of astonishing, how many ways it finds to go right.

Claire's Knee ★ ★ ★ ★
PG, 103 m., 1971

Jean-Claude Brialy (Jerome), Aurora Cornu (Aurora), Beatrice Romand (Laura), Laurence de Monaghan (Claire). Directed by Eric Rohmer and produced by Pierre Cottrell. Screenplay by Rohmer.

Now if I were to say, for example, that *Claire's Knee* is about Jerome's desire to caress the knee of Claire, you would be about a million miles from the heart of this extraordinary film. And yet, in a way, *Claire's Knee* is indeed about Jerome's feelings for Claire's knee, which is a splendid knee.

Jerome encounters Claire and the other characters in the film during a month's holiday he takes on a lake between France and Switzerland. He has gone there to rest and reflect before he marries Lucinda, a woman he has loved for five years. And who should he run into but Aurora, a novelist who's also been a little in love with for a long time.

Aurora is staying with a summer family that has two daughters: Laura, who is sixteen and very wise and falls in love with Jerome, and Claire, who is beautiful and blonde and full of figure and spirit. Jerome and Aurora enter into a teasing intellectual game, which requires Jerome to describe to Aurora whatever happens to him during his holiday. When they all become aware that Laura has fallen in love with the older man, Jerome encourages her in a friendly, platonic way. They have talks about love and the nature of life, and they grow very fond of each other, although of course the man does not take advantage of the young girl.

But then Claire joins the group, and one day while they are picking cherries, Jerome turns his head and finds that Claire has climbed a ladder and he is looking directly at her knee. Claire herself, observed playing volleyball or running, hand-in-hand, with her boyfriend, is a sleek animal, and Jerome finds himself stirring with desire.

He doesn't want to run away with Claire, or seduce her, or anything like that; he plans to marry Lucinda. But he tells his friend Aurora that he has become fascinated by Claire's knee; that it might be the point through which she could be approached, just as another girl might respond to a caress on the neck, or the cheek, or the arm. He becomes obsessed with desire to test this theory, and one day has an opportunity to touch the knee at last.

As with all the films of Eric Rohmer, *Claire's Knee* exists at levels far removed from plot (as you might have guessed while I was describing the plot). What is really happening in this movie happens on the level of character, of thought, of the way people approach each other and then shy away. In some movies, people murder each other and the contact is casual; in a work by Eric Rohmer, small attitudes and gestures can summon up a universe of humanity.

Rohmer has an uncanny ability to make his actors seem as if they were going through the experiences they portray. The acting of Beatrice Romand, as sixteen-year-old Laura, is especially good in this respect; she isn't as pretty as her sister, but we feel somehow she'll find more enjoyment in life because she is a . . . well, a better person underneath. Jean-Claude Brialy is excellent in a difficult role. He has to relate with three women in the movie, and yet remain implicitly faithful to the unseen Lucinda. He does, and since the sexuality in his performance is suppressed, it is, of course, all the more sensuous. *Claire's Knee* is a movie for people who still read good novels, care about good films, and think occasionally.

Clash of the Titans ★ ★ ★ ½
PG, 118 m., 1981

Harry Hamlin (Perseus), Judi Bowker (Andromeda), Burgess Meredith (Ammon), Laurence Olivier (Zeus), Maggie Smith (Thetis), Neil McCarthy (Calibos). Directed by Desmond Davis and produced by Charles H. Schneer and Ray Harryhausen, with special effects created by Harryhausen.

Clash of the Titans is a grand and glorious romantic adventure, filled with grave heroes, beautiful heroines, fearsome monsters, and awe-inspiring duels to the death. It is a lot of fun. It was quite possibly intended as a sort of Greek mythological retread of *Star Wars* (it has a wise little mechanical owl in it who's a third cousin of R2-D2), but it's also part of an older Hollywood tradition of special-effects fantasies, and its visual wonderments are astonishing.

The story, on the other hand, is robust and straightforward. Perseus (Harry Hamlin) is locked into a coffin with his mother and cast into the sea, after she has angered the gods. But Zeus (Laurence Olivier) takes pity and sees that the coffin washes ashore on a deserted island, where Perseus grows to manhood and learns of his mission in life. The mission, in a nutshell, is to return to Joppa and rescue Andromeda (Judi Bowker) from a fate worse than death: marriage to the hideously ugly Calibos, who was promised her hand in marriage before he was turned into a monster by the wrath of the gods. Calibos lives in a swamp and dispatches a gigantic, scrawny bird every night to fetch him the spirit of the sleeping Andromeda in a gilded cage. If Perseus is to marry Andromeda, he must defeat Calibos in combat and also answer a riddle posed by Cassiopeia, Andromeda's mother. Those who answer the riddle incorrectly are condemned to die. Love was more complicated in the old days.

There are, of course, other tests. To follow the bird back to the lair of Calibos, the resourceful Perseus must capture and tame Pegasus, the last of the great winged horses. He must also enter the lair of Medusa, who turns men to stone with one glance, and behead her so that he can use her dead eyes to petrify the gargantuan monster Kraken, who is unchained from his cage on the ocean floor so that he can ravish Joppa in general and Andromeda in particular.

All of this is gloriously silly. But because the movie respects its material, it even succeeds in halfway selling us this story; movies that look like *Clash of the Titans* have a tendency to seem ridiculous, but this film has the courage of its convictions. It is also blessed with a cast that somehow finds its way past all the monsters and through all the heroic dialogue and gets us involved in the characters. Harry Hamlin is a completely satisfactory Perseus, handsome and solemn and charged with his own mission. Judi Bowker is a beautiful princess and a great screamer, especially in the scene where she's chained

to the rock and Kraken is slobbering all over her. Burgess Meredith has a nice little supporting role as Ammon, an old playwright who thinks he may be able to turn all of this into a quick epic. And Laurence Olivier is just as I have always imagined Zeus: petulant, but a pushover for a pretty face.

The real star of the movie, however, is Ray Harryhausen, who has worked more than forty years as a creator of special effects. He uses combinations of animation, miniatures, optical tricks, and multiple images to put humans into the same movie frames as the most fantastical creatures of legend, and more often than not, they look pretty convincing: when Perseus tames Pegasus, it sure looks like he's dealing with a real horse (except for the wings, of course).

Harryhausen's credits include *Mighty Joe Young, Jason and the Argonauts,* and *The Golden Voyage of Sinbad,* but *Clash of the Titans* is his masterwork. Among his inspired set-pieces: the battle in the Medusa's lair, with her hair writhing with snakes; the flying-horse scenes; the gigantic prehistoric bird; the two-headed wolf-dog, Dioskilos; the Stygian witches; and, of course, Kraken, who rears up from the sea and causes tidal waves that do a lot of very convincing damage to a Greek city that exists only in Harryhausen's art. The most lovable special-effects creation in the movie is little Bubo, a golden owl sent by the gods to help Perseus in his trials. Bubo whistles and rotates his head something like R2-D2 in *Star Wars,* and he has a similar personality, too, especially at the hilarious moment when he enters the film for the first time.

Clash of the Titans is a family film (there's nothing in it that would disturb any but the most impressionable children), and yet it's not by any means innocuous: It's got blood and thunder and lots of gory details, all presented with enormous gusto and style. It has faith in a story-telling tradition that sometimes seems almost forgotten, a tradition depending upon legends and myths, magical swords, enchanted shields, invisibility helmets, and the overwhelming power of a kiss.

Clean and Sober ★ ★ ★ ½
R, 124 m., 1988

Michael Keaton (Daryl Poynter), Kathy Baker (Charlie Standers), Morgan Freeman (Craig), M. Emmet Walsh (Richard Dirks), Tate Donovan (Donald Towle), Henry Judd Baker (Xavier), Claudia Christian (Iris), J. David

Krassner (Miller), Dakin Matthews (Bob), Mary Catherine Martin (Cheryl Ann), Pat Quinn (June). Directed by Glenn Gordon Caron and produced by Tony Ganz and Deborah Blum. Written by Tod Carroll.

It's the kind of thing that could happen to anybody. Just plain rotten luck, really. He picks up a girl in a bar, and they do some cocaine together, and the next morning when he wakes up, she's dead. She had a heart attack or something. How was it his fault? What happens to the hero of *Clean and Sober* during the next several weeks of his life is that he decides that although it could have happened to anyone, he doesn't want it to happen to himself anymore.

The guy is named Daryl Poynter, and he is played by Michael Keaton with a kind of wound-up, edgy tension that is just right for the character. He's a hotshot Philadelphia real estate salesman, but by the time the movie opens there is nothing in his life of any importance, really, but cocaine. He doesn't even question the fact. It's not that he needs cocaine to function—because he doesn't function, really, he just goes through the motions—but that he needs cocaine to still himself from the savage, restless angers of his need for the drug.

It doesn't go over very well that the girl woke up dead in his bed. The police are interested. Even though it was her "fault" ("I didn't give her cocaine; she gave me cocaine," he argues), the girl's father plasters his neighborhood with posters branding him as a murderer. At work, things are not too good, either, because he has borrowed $92,000 from an escrow account and invested it in the market, hoping to make a lot of money. He has lost most of the money, instead.

So he needs a place to hide out, and when he hears on the radio about a confidential, anonymous drug rehabilitation program, he figures that might be a good place to disappear into. What he doesn't count on is that the program is run by a hard-headed counselor (Morgan Freeman) who has heard everybody's story before, and sees right through him.

Clean and Sober is the story of how the Keaton character is forced to look at the fact that his life is wildly out of control, and that cocaine addiction is the cause, not the solution. He fights this discovery every step of the way, and is far from being a model client in the rehab center. He steals phone calls to ask friends to send him cocaine in overnight

Federal Express packages; he slips out of the center on wild, undefined missions; and, of course, he thinks he's God's gift to women—especially to one of his cute fellow patients.

She's played by Kathy Baker, as a woman who has two addictions, one to booze, the other to the man she lives with, who beats her and then comes whining to her for forgiveness, telling her he's nothing without her. Her self-esteem has been so seriously wounded by her alcoholism that she clings to this relationship, perhaps believing that this loser is the only man who will accept her.

In his first few days in the center, Keaton finds himself at war with Morgan Freeman, the counselor. This is because Freeman has met so many, many others just like him, and knows the alibis and evasions, and knows that unless this guy gets serious, he is going to go right back out and get screwed up again. The relationships between the counselor and the patients are at the heart of the central portion of the movie, which also shows Keaton going to an Alcoholics Anonymous meeting and trying, on Freeman's orders, to get himself a "sponsor"—a veteran AA member who will advise and help him. Of course, Keaton goes for the prettiest woman at the meeting, but eventually he winds up with wise, lethargic M. Emmet Walsh, who looks at him quizzically because he knows what a lost cause he could easily be.

Clean and Sober is not the story of an ideal recovery from drug or alcohol addiction, because Keaton is not an ideal candidate for recovery. He tells too many lies, especially to himself, and he doesn't much like to accept advice. He is still somewhat seduced by the notion that he can do some repairs on his old lifestyle and it will still work. But by the end of the movie there is some hope that he may be able to get straight.

The subject matter of this film is commonplace in our society—for every celebrity who checks into the Betty Ford Center, there are thousands of ordinary people who check in somewhere else, or who pick up the phone and call AA. Everybody knows somebody like this. But the actual process of surrender and recovery is hardly ever the subject of films, maybe because it seems too depressing. One of the strengths Michael Keaton brings to *Clean and Sober* is his wild, tumultuous energy, which makes his character seem less a victim than an accident causing itself to happen. Surrounded by superb supporting performances—especially by Kathy Baker, who also costarred with Morgan

Freeman as the prostitute in *Street Smart*—Keaton makes this general story into a particular one, and a touching one.

Clean, Shaven ★ ★ ★ ½
NO MPAA RATING, 80 m., 1995

Peter Greene (Peter Winter), Megan Owen (Mrs. Winter), Jennifer MacDonald (Nicole), Molly Castelloe (Melinda Frayne), Robert Albert (Jack McNally), J. Dixon Byrne (Dr. Michaels). Directed and produced by Lodge H. Kerrigan. Screenplay by Kerrigan.

Clean, Shaven is an attempt to enter completely into the schizophrenic mind of a young man who is desperately trying to live in the world, on whatever terms will "work" in his condition. It is a harrowing, exhausting, painful film, and a very good one—a film that will not appeal to most filmgoers, but will be valued by anyone with a serious interest in schizophrenia or, for that matter, in film.

I was on a program the other day with Tom Wolfe, the author and social critic, who was defending novels as the only medium which truly allows us to enter into another person's point of view. We can go inside the heads of written characters, he said, in a way that doesn't work with movies or the theater. In many cases he may be right, because movies more often encourage us to be voyeurs than to identify with characters. But a film like *Clean, Shaven* is a shattering exception to his rule, since it restricts itself almost entirely to the way a schizophrenia victim must negotiate the horrors of everyday life.

The movie is about Peter (Peter Greene), who has a car but apparently no home, and has perhaps recently been released from treatment, although that is left vague. He wants to make a trip to see his daughter, from a marriage made before his condition developed. We follow every step of his excruciating journey, in a performance by Greene of great power and nerve.

There are terrors we can hardly imagine; he breaks out the glass of some of the car windows, and fills in the holes with taped newspapers. He wraps the rearview mirrors of the car with paper. Driven by some deep need, he tries to cut his hair and shave, and both operations produce painful cuts to which he seems oblivious.

The movie's sound track is sometimes harsh and obtrusive: We hear voices, some from the radio, some from inside his head or his memories. Power lines seem to emanate a low buzzing presence. The sound track is

entirely subjective; in a restaurant, his head is filled with noise until the moment when he begins to put a lot of sugar into his coffee, and then there is complete silence, as if his absorption in the task has quieted the sounds for a moment.

There are a few quiet scenes outside his presence. We meet his mother, who calls his ex-wife and tells her, "Peter's back." He stops at his mother's house, and she expresses concern for him, but we can see at once she has a long, exhausting history of dealing with his condition. She gives him the makings of a sandwich, and he constructs it with the care a child might lavish on building blocks. Eventually he does confront his young daughter.

What suffuses every moment of the movie is the constant agony he is in, because of the way his condition causes the everyday world of sensation to assault him. There is a gruesome moment when he cuts a fingernail loose from his finger (many viewers will close their eyes), as if the pain will for a moment free him from the greater pain of being alive.

The movie is, more than anything else, an uncompromising experiment in creating, for the viewer, an idea of what schizophrenia is like. The writer and director, Lodge H. Kerrigan, has made a leap of imagination that is both courageous and empathetic: He doesn't see Peter from the outside, as a danger or a threat, but from the inside, as a suffering man who still retains those instincts that make us human, including love for our children. That society cannot see him with the same empathy is perhaps inevitable. Peter is the kind of man we quickly cross the street to avoid. Now we understand how much he needs to avoid us, as well.

Clerks ★ ★ ★
R, 92 m., 1994

Brian O'Halloran (Dante Hicks), Jeff Anderson (Randal), Marilyn Ghiglotti (Veronica), Lisa Spoonauer (Caitlin), Jason Mewes (Jay), Kevin Smith (Silent Bob). Directed by Kevin Smith and produced by Scott Mosier and Smith. Screenplay by Smith.

Hardly anybody ever works in the movies, except at jobs like cops, robbers, drug dealers, and space captains. One of the many charms of Kevin Smith's *Clerks* is that it clocks a full day on the job. Its hero, Dante Hicks, is a clerk in a convenience store, and his friend Randal works next door in the video store.

Both stores are in a strip mall in Asbury Park, New Jersey—marginal operations with ill-paid and disenchanted employees.

The movie has the attitude of a gas station attendant who tells you to check your own oil. It's grungy and unkempt, and Dante and Randal look like they have been nourished from birth on beef jerky and Cheetos. They are tired and bored, underpaid and unlucky in love, and their encounters with customers feel like a series of psychological tests.

Dante, played by Brian O'Halloran on a perfect note of defensive detachment, has that gift for getting through a bad job by running his private life at the same time. He's twenty-two, a college dropout, dating the talkative Veronica (Marilyn Ghigliotti), and is alarmed to read in the paper that his former girlfriend, Caitlin, is engaged to an "Asian studies major." Meanwhile, his life is going nowhere, and he has had to cancel his hockey game to work on his day off.

His day begins at dawn. He sleeps in his clothes closet. He drinks his coffee out of the lid of the cookie jar. When the store's steel shutters won't roll up, he uses shoe polish to write a big sign: I ASSURE YOU WE ARE OPEN. He gets in desultory conversations with customers who are opposed to cigarettes, or looking for porno mags, or claim that the vacant-eyed guy leaning against the building is a heavy metal star from Russia.

Randal (Jeff Anderson), next door, is working in the kind of video store with a stock so bad that he goes to another store when he wants to rent a video. He has customers with questions like, "Do you have that one with that guy who was in that movie last year?" And he discusses deep cinematic questions with Dante, such as: When Darth Vader's second *Death Star* was destroyed, it was still under construction, so doesn't that mean a lot of innocent workers were killed?

Many of Dante's customers are very strange. One is obsessed with finding a dozen perfect eggs. Another finds an unprecedented use for the rest room. A guy named Silent Bob (Kevin Smith himself) is permanently posted outside the store; he's allegedly a drug dealer, but business seems very bad.

Considering that Smith shot the entire movie in and around the convenience store, he shows ingenuity in finding fresh setups. There's a danger that the movie could reduce itself to a series of people standing around talking, but look at the way he handles the conversation between Dante and Veronica, who paints her nails while they

talk. Or consider the hockey game, which is finally played on the store roof.

Clerks, which contains no nudity or violence, was originally classified NC-17 by the MPAA just on the basis of its language—which includes the kind of graphic descriptions of improbable sex acts which guys sometimes indulge in while killing vast amounts of celibate time. (One sexual encounter does take place during the movie, offscreen, and after it becomes clear exactly what happened, we are all pretty much in agreement, I think, that offscreen is where it belongs.)

Quentin Tarantino has become famous as a video store clerk who watched all the movies in his store, and then went out and directed *Reservoir Dogs* and *Pulp Fiction.* Kevin Smith has done him one better, by working behind the counter and then making a movie about the store itself. Within the limitations of his bare-bones production, Smith shows great invention, a natural feel for human comedy, and a knack for writing weird, sometimes brilliant, dialogue. Much has been written about Generation X and the films about it. *Clerks* is so utterly authentic that its heroes have never heard of their generation. When they think of "X," it's on the way to the video store.

The Client ★ ★ ½

PG-13, 117 m., 1994
(See related Film Clip, p. 879.)

Susan Sarandon (Reggie Love), Tommy Lee Jones (Roy Foltrigg), Mary-Louise Parker (Dianne Sway), Anthony LaPaglia (Barry Muldano), J.T. Walsh (McThune), Anthony Edwards (Clint Von Hooser), Brad Renfro (Mark Sway), Will Patton (Sergeant Hardy). Directed by Joel Schumacher and produced by Arnon Milchan and Steven Reuther. Screenplay by Akiva Goldsman and Robert Getchell.

The Client takes place in a steamy southern Gothic world of corruption, evil, and cynicism—John Grisham country, somewhere between Memphis and Yoknapatawpha County. In the center of this world stands young Mark Sway (Brad Renfro), a tough eleven-year-old whose life is in danger because he has information that could harm powerful people. He's on his own, but he's smart enough to know he needs a good lawyer.

So, he wanders through an office building, opening doors and poking around, until he finds someone who looks truthworthy. Her name is Reggie Love (Susan Sarandon),

and she's been through some hard times in a checkered personal life, but the kid is right and she's a good lawyer. Soon she will be defending not only his life but her own.

The creation of these two characters is at the heart of Grisham's accomplishment in *The Client.* They are original and genuinely interesting, and the roles have been cast well. Brad Renfro is a movie newcomer who seems to be a natural actor. He's from Knoxville, Tennessee, inexperienced except for school productions, but he has an unforced conviction and a lot of backbone, and provides a strong center for the film. As Reggie Love, the filmmakers cast Susan Sarandon, who is also right for the role: Weary and world-worn, but also tough, and warm enough to understand her client's difficult emotional needs. She has a special reason for earning the boy's trust: Earlier in her imperfect life, she lost custody of her own children.

Against these heroes, the movie provides two categories of villains. There are the corrupt gangsters and politicians who fear the young boy will destroy them with information. And there is a publicity-seeking federal prosecutor (Tommy Lee Jones), nicknamed "Reverend" because of his penchant for quoting scripture at press conferences, often inaccurately.

If Grisham is good at creating original, believable characters, he is all too good at dreaming up bizarre situations to place them in. His astonishing writing career is well known by now: How the southern lawyer began to write fiction in his spare time, and within a few years became the nation's best-selling author. He can write, to be sure. But his plots sometimes seem amateurish and overcontrived, and anyone who could follow all of the events in *The Firm* (1993) should probably share their explanation with the rest of us, as a public service.

In *The Client,* Grisham's story provides a starting point for some quietly realistic, emotionally convincing scenes for director Joel Schumacher *(Flatliners, Falling Down).* But in the last hour the action wanders less convincingly into Hardy Boys antics where the kid and his lawyer turn into amateur sleuths and risk their lives to solve the big case.

Much depends on the whereabouts of a missing body—which, if it can be produced, will overthrow an evil cabal of mafioso, mob lawyers, and politicians. After Mark and Reggie find the body, at great but unconvincing risk, the movie concludes with such unseemly haste that Jones, as the prosecutor, calls a press conference to boast of the location of the body before he has even gone there to see for himself if it is there. At moments like this, the movie betrays its willingness to go for effect even at the cost of credibility, and like other Grisham plots this one doesn't really stand up to close examination.

Still, there are wonderful moments in it, many of them between Sarandon and Renfro, and others involving a desperate lawyer named Romey (Walter Olkewicz), whose suicide attempt, thwarted by Renfro, sets up the plot. (It also inspires the hero's kid brother to fall into a convenient movie coma, which leads to several bedside scenes we have seen before.)

Tommy Lee Jones is fun, too. It is curious how he maintains his air of impenetrability while becoming a movie star. He never seems to reach for effect, but erects a wall of mystery that makes him the most interesting character in most scenes. That is not to say he underacts; quite the contrary. As Roy Foltrigg, the publicity-seeking prosecutor, he hambones his way through scene after scene. But we are always acutely aware that it's a performance, and that beneath the façade are two wiser presences: the character, who knows he's putting on a show, and the actor, who watches, amused, from a distance. What interests me most about Tommy Lee Jones's performances is the way these layers of watchfulness seem to form.

Sarandon and Renfro make easy, natural allies, and the scene where they meet for the first time is played so well we forget how unlikely it is. There are also courtroom scenes, which, like all movie courtroom scenes since time immemorial (and many scenes in real courtrooms), seem constructed out of arrangements of lovingly arranged clichés, but which work because of the inherent drama. Both the young boy and his lawyer know their lives are in danger if he testifies about what he knows, and Schumacher exploits that danger with pauses and silences and precisely worded dialogue.

Still, *The Client* is not as satisfying as it should be. Much of the blame, I think, goes to Grisham, who having created genuine characters and placed them in a fascinating fictional situation, loses control and goes over into melodrama just when human developments would have been enough. When I've met three-dimensional characters in a movie and grown to believe them, I always resent it when they shrink by a dimension,

and start creeping around in an action climax. Just when you really care what they'll do or say next, they become interchangeable parts from a thriller. The setup in *The Client* is done so well, it deserves a better payoff.

Cliffhanger ★ ★ ★
R, 118 m., 1993

Sylvester Stallone (Gabe Walker), John Lithgow (Qualen), Michael Rooker (Hal Tucker), Janine Turner (Jessie Deighan), Rex Linn (Travers), Caroline Goodall (Kristel). Directed by Renny Harlin and produced by Alan Marshall and Harlin. Screenplay by Michael France and Sylvester Stallone.

Sylvester Stallone has had a rough career lately, with thrillers that didn't thrill and comedies that weren't funny. *Cliffhanger*, his new action epic, arrives with a faint scent of urgency surrounding it; if this one flops, Sly may be in trouble.

My guess is that it won't flop, because it delivers precisely what it promises. It's a big-budget extravaganza with a lot of stunts and special effects, starring Stallone as a professional mountain climber and rescue expert, who gets roped into a scheme masterminded by criminal skyjackers.

True, there's not a moment in the plot that I could believe. That didn't bother me for an instant. *Cliffhanger* is a device to entertain us, and it works, especially during those moments when Stallone is hanging by his fingernails over a three-mile fall, and the bad guys are stomping on him.

The movie begins with a clever midair theft and crash landing: sort of a cross between *The Pursuit of D.B. Cooper* and *Alive!* A gang of expert criminals, led by John Lithgow, hijacks a U.S. Treasury plane carrying millions of dollars in large bills. Their cockeyed plan is to transfer the money to another plane, and indeed one of the crooks transfers from one plane to another on a wire rope. This feat, which was actually performed by a stuntman, is one of the movie's most breathtaking moments.

But then the plan goes wrong; there is a crash, and Lithgow and his partners find themselves stranded on top of a snow-covered mountain, with all of the cash but no way to get down. So they send out a phony distress signal, which is picked up by Stallone and another rescue man, played by Michael Rooker.

That sets up the main thread of the plot, as the crooks and the good guys chase each

other over the mountainside and through a series of bluffs, showdowns, and fights to the finish, all taking place on the edge of suitably vertiginous precipices.

The movie adds a back-story involving Stallone and Rooker, which sets up some quarrels on the mountainside. During an opening sequence, Rooker unwisely takes his new girlfriend on a difficult climb, and when she gets into a tough spot Stallone tries to rescue her, with unfortunate results (she screams all the way down). Did Stallone do the right thing, or was his judgment hasty? He and Rooker have it out, while also trying to deal with the skyjackers.

Movies like this need good villains, and Lithgow makes a satisfactory one. Like a lot of recent movie villains (most of them played by Alan Rickman or Charles Dance), Lithgow seems subtly effete and dangerously intellectual, and speaks with a slight British accent. He also of course cares for nothing but the money and his own skin, and in the great tradition of all cliffhangers he eventually has to face Stallone, mano-a-mano. It is one of the achievements of the movie to convince us that Lithgow and Stallone are a good match.

The movie was directed by Renny Harlin, who directed one of the Die Hard movies and one of the Freddy movies and knows his way around a thriller. The credits mention a lot of stuntpersons, who deserve any credit they can get, because many of the most hazardous stunts in this movie were obviously not faked. That stuntman who makes the midair transfer between two planes deserves a gold medal. And at one point, we can clearly see that Stallone himself is dangling over a nightmarish fall. Movies like this are machines for involving us and thrilling us. *Cliffhanger* is a fairly good machine.

Close Encounters of the Third Kind: The Special Edition ★ ★ ★ ★
PG, 152 m., 1980

Richard Dreyfuss (Roy Neary), Francois Truffaut (Claude Lacombe), Teri Garr (Ronnie Neary), Melinda Dillon (Jillian Guiler). Directed and written by Steven Spielberg and produced by Julia Phillips and Michael Phillips.

Close Encounters of the Third Kind: The Special Edition is the movie Steven Spielberg wanted to make in the first place. The changes Spielberg has made in his original 1978 film are basic and extensive, adding up to essentially a new moviegoing experience. Spielberg's changes fall into four categories:

• He's provided an entirely new conclusion, taking us inside the alien spaceship that visits at the end of the film.

• He's provided more motivation for the strange behavior of the Richard Dreyfuss character—who is compelled by "psychic implanting" to visit the Wyoming mountain where the spaceship plans to land.

• He's added additional manifestations of UFO intervention in earthly affairs—including an ocean-going freighter deposited in the middle of the Gobi Desert.

• In addition to the sensational ending, he's added more special effects throughout the film. One shot seems like a lighthearted quote from Spielberg's own *Jaws*. In that film, a high-angle shot showed the shadow of the giant shark passing under a boat. In this one, a high-angle shot shows the shadow of a giant UFO passing over a pickup truck.

Spielberg's decision to revise the original version of *Close Encounters* is all but unprecedented. Some directors have remade their earlier films (Hitchcock did British and American versions of *The Man Who Knew Too Much*), and others have thought out loud about changes they'd like to make (Robert Altman wanted to edit a nine-hour version of *Nashville* for TV). And countless directors, of course, have given us sequels—"part two" of their original hits.

Spielberg's *Special Edition* is sort of a *Close Encounters: Part 1½*. It is also a very good film. I thought the original film was an astonishing achievement, capturing the feeling of awe and wonder we have when considering the likelihood of life beyond the Earth. I gave that first version a four-star rating. This new version gets another four stars: It is, quite simply, a better film—so much better that it might inspire the uncharitable question, "Why didn't Spielberg make it this good the *first* time?"

His changes fall into three categories. He has (1) thrown away scenes that didn't work, like the silly sequence in which Dreyfuss dug up half of his yard in an attempt to build a model of the mountain in his vision; (2) put in scenes he shot three years ago but did not use, such as the Gobi sequence and Dreyfuss flipping out over the strange compulsion that has overtaken him, and (3) shot some entirely new scenes.

The most spectacular of these is the new ending, which shows us what Dreyfuss sees when he enters the spacecraft. He sees a sort of extraterrestrial cathedral, a limitless interior space filled with columns of light, countless sources of brilliance, and the machinery of an unimaginable alien technology. (The new special effects were designed by the underground artist R. Cobb, I understand; no credit is given.) This new conclusion gives the movie the kind of overwhelming final emotional impact it needed; it adds another dimension to the already impressive ending of the first version.

The movie gains impact in another way. Spielberg has tightened up the whole film. Dead ends and pointless scenes have been dropped. New scenes do a better job of establishing the characters—not only of Dreyfuss, but also of Francois Truffaut, as the French scientist. The new editing moves the film along at a faster, more absorbing pace to the mind-stretching conclusion. *Close Encounters*, which was already a wonderful film, now transcends itself; it's one of the great moviegoing experiences. If you've seen it before, I'm afraid that now you'll have to see it again.

Close to Eden ★ ★ ★
NO MPAA RATING, 106 m., 1992

Badema (Pagma, Gombo's Wife), Bayaertu (Gombo, a Sheep Farmer), Vladimir Gostukhin (Sergei), Babushka (Grandma), Larissa Kuznetsova (Marina, Sergei's Wife), Jon Bochinski (Stanislas, Sergei, and Marina's Son), Bao Yongyan (Bourma, Gombo, and Pagma's Daughter), Wurinile (Bouin, Gombo, and Pagma's Son), Wang Zhiyong (Van Biao, a Chinese Pianist), Baoyinhexige (Bayartou, the Uncle), Nikolai Vachtiline (Nikolai, Sergei's Friend). Directed by Nikita Mikhalkov and produced by Michel Seydoux, Jean-Louis Piel, and Rene Cleitman. Screenplay by Roustam Ibraguimbekov.

Close to Eden is the kind of movie that has no reason for existence, except to keep the viewer bemused. It does that with such sly charm that when it's over, you don't even think to ask why it was made. You're simply pleased that it was. The movie occupies no known category (I have never seen a film about modern-day Mongols, especially those who play accordions), and although you can possibly extract a message from it, why bother?

The time is the present day, although we don't know that for a while. The place is beautiful: endlessly rolling wheat fields near the border between China and Russia. The first shot is of a man pursuing a woman.

Both are on horseback, and the man has a long, netted hook that makes him look like a cross between a polo player and a butterfly collector. Is he trying to net the woman? Not at all. The woman is his wife, and local custom has it that if he catches her and they are overcome with romantic impulses, he sticks the pole into the ground as a request for privacy from his neighbors—none of whom live within miles, anyway.

Another child results from their pursuit. They now have three, which is over the family limit in China. They don't seem much concerned. They live in a utilitarian round house that is set down into the ground and looks a little like a circus tent. They raise sheep and cattle. The man's old mother lives with them. Sometimes a drunken neighbor stops by with presents, such as a Rambo poster, which he swears is a likeness of his brother in America.

One day a Russian truck driver passes through the vast and empty district, falls asleep at the wheel, and ends up stuck on the edge of a lake. The Mongols take him in, and slaughter a sheep for his benefit. We learn from this scene that we would not like to slaughter our own sheep. After dinner there is entertainment: The older daughter serenades them on an accordion that is about as big as she is.

The truck driver speaks of television. The Mongol determines that the family needs a set (which, in answer to your obvious question, will be driven by a generator hooked to his windmill). He goes into town to buy the TV. Scenes of big city life. A return to the steppes. There are only two shows on the air. One of them is Bush welcoming Gorbachev to the family of nations. So it goes.

Close to Eden is as slight as a breeze, as charming as a sly old con man. It shows a way of life we can barely imagine; surely Eden, had it been like this, would have needed no apples. One of the strongest qualities in the film is the joy of living shared by husband and wife, who love each other. There is a tacked-on epilogue that I fear contains the message, which is that civilization is corrupting, but the real message comes earlier, and it is, be nice to people, enjoy yourself, and don't worry too much about the family limit.

Coal Miner's Daughter ★ ★ ★
PG, 125 m., 1980

Sissy Spacek (Loretta Lynn), Tommy Lee Jones (Mooney Lynn), Beverly D'Angelo

(Patsy Cline), Levon Helm (Ted Webb), Phyllis Boyens (Clara Webb). Directed by Michael Apted and produced by Bernard Schwarts. Screenplay by Tom Rickman.

What improbable lives so many Americans lead, compared to the more orderly and predictable careers of the Swedes, say, or the French. It's not just that we're the most upwardly mobile society in history, we're the most mobile, period: We go to ruin as swiftly and dramatically as we hit the jackpot. No wonder one of our favorite myths involves a rags-to-riches story in which success then destroys the hero.

Look at country music star Loretta Lynn. If we can believe *Coal Miner's Daughter* (and I gather that, by and large, we can), here's a life which began in the poverty of the coalfields of Kentucky and led almost overnight to show-business stardom. And what's astonishing is that it wasn't even really planned that way: Loretta learned to play on a pawnshop guitar, her husband thought she could sing, and one day she just sorta found herself on stage. The movie's about Loretta Lynn's childhood, her very early marriage, her quick four kids, her husband's move to Washington State looking for a job, her humble start in show business, her apparently quick rise to stardom, and then the usual Catch-22 of self-destructiveness.

We're not surprised, somehow, that right after the scenes where she becomes a superstar, there are scenes where she starts using pills, getting headaches, and complaining that everybody's on her case all the time. We fiercely want to believe in success in this country, but for some reason we also want to believe that it takes a terrible human toll. Sometimes it does—and that always makes for a better story. Straightforward success sagas, in which the heroes just keep on getting richer, are boring. We want our heroes to suffer. We like to identify—it makes stars more human, somehow, if they get screwed by Valium, too.

What's refreshing about *Coal Miner's Daughter* is that it takes the basic material (rags to riches, overnight success, the onstage breakdown, and, of course, the big comeback) and relates them in wonderfully human terms. It's fresh and immediate. That is due most of all to the performance by Sissy Spacek as Loretta Lynn. With the same sort of magical chemistry she's shown before, when she played the high school kid in *Carrie,* Spacek at twenty-nine has the ability

to appear to be almost any age onscreen. Here she ages from about fourteen to somewhere in her thirties, always looks the age, and never seems to be wearing makeup. I wonder if she does it with her posture; early in the film, as a poor coal miner's kid, she slouches and slinks around, and then later she puts on dignity with the flashy dresses she wears onstage.

The movie is mostly about Lynn's relationships with her husband, Mooney (played by Tommy Lee Jones), and her first close show-business friend and mentor, Patsy Cline (Beverly D'Angelo). Both of these relationships are developed in direct, understated, intelligent ways; we are spared, for example, a routine portrait of Mooney Lynn as Official Show Biz Husband, and given instead a portrait of a recognizable human being who is aggressive, confident, loving, and fallible. The fact that this movie felt free to portray Mooney as hard-nosed is one of the most interesting things about it: Loretta Lynn, who had a certain amount of control over the project, obviously still has her feet on the ground and didn't insist that this movie be some kind of idealized fantasy.

We are left to speculate, of course, on whether Lynn's rise to stardom was really as picaresque as *Coal Miner's Daughter* suggests. She seems to get on the Grand Ole Opry mighty fast, and Patsy Cline seems to adopt her almost before she knows her. But then the amazing thing about Loretta Lynn's life seems to be how fast everything happened, and how wide open the avenues to success are in this country—if you're talented and, of course, lucky.

The most entertaining scenes in the movie are in the middle, after the coal mines and before the Top 40, when Loretta and Mooney are tooling around the back roads trying to convince country disc jockeys to play her records. The scene with Mooney taking a publicity photo of Loretta is a little gem illustrating the press agent that resides within us all.

So, anyway . . . how good *is* this movie? I think it's one of those films people like so much while they're watching it that they're inclined to think it's better than it is. It's warm, entertaining, funny, and centered around that great Sissy Spacek performance, but it's essentially pretty familiar material (not that Loretta Lynn can be blamed that Horatio Alger wrote her life before she lived it). The movie isn't great art, but it has been made with great taste and style; it's more

intelligent and observant than movie biographies of singing stars used to be. That makes it a treasure to watch, even if we sometimes have the feeling we've seen it before.

Cobb ★ ★

R, 128 m., 1994

Tommy Lee Jones (Ty Cobb), Robert Wuhl (Al Stump), Lolita Davidovich (Ramona), Lou Myers (Willie), J. Kenneth Campbell (Professor Cobb), Rhoda Griffis (Ty Cobb's Mother), Eloy Casados (Louis Prima), Paula Rudy (Keely Smith). Directed by Ron Shelton and produced by David Lester. Screenplay by Shelton.

Ty Cobb was by many accounts a mean-tempered, vicious, drunken, wife-beating, racist SOB who was impossible to spend any length of time with, and the movie *Cobb* faithfully represents those qualities, especially the last one. Being locked up with this movie for 123 minutes is like taking a three-day bus trip sitting next to Hunter S. Thompson.

That is not to say the movie is without redeeming qualities. On the contrary, this is one of the most original sports biopics I've seen, if only because it tells the truth, or tries to—and because it contains one of Tommy Lee Jones's best performances. It's the kind of film where you admire the craftsmanship and artistry while questioning the wisdom of the project itself.

Ty Cobb was "the greatest baseball player of all time"—a fact repeated many times in the movie. He was the first member of the Baseball Hall of Fame, the holder of a lifetime batting average of .367 that has still never been approached, and the inventor of the modern game of baseball. And he made a fortune in the stock market.

He was also the kind of guy that the other Hall of Famers locked out of their hotel rooms after the annual ceremony. A base runner who sharpened the spikes on his shoes and sent twelve men to the hospital in one season. Who went into the stands to punch out a heckler who, it turned out, had no hands. Who pistol-whipped a man to death. Who was divorced for wife-beating, whose daughter would not speak to him, who grabbed a mike in Reno to snarl about "niggers, Jews, and dagos," and who kept himself alive with alarming mixtures of morphine, lithium, insulin, and bourbon.

Cobb remains a towering American figure because no one else ever did on a baseball diamond what he did. He lived until 1961, which means he died at a time when celebrities were still routinely sheltered from scandal. If nobody could stand him, nobody made it a point to say so.

Now comes *Cobb*, written and directed by Ron Shelton, a former baseball player whose filmmaking credits include two of the best movies about sports ever made, *Bull Durham* and *White Men Can't Jump*. Shelton approaches the problem of Cobb from an oblique angle, through the eyes of a sportswriter named Al Stump (Robert Wuhl). Hired by Cobb to ghostwrite his autobiography, Stump hangs on for a wild, drunken ride down snowy roads and through Nevada casinos, from the Hall of Fame dinner to grungy roadside motels and a final rendezvous with death.

Al Stump really exists, and really did ghost Cobb's autobiography, shaping it into a standard rags-to-riches saga. He has also written a recent book telling the "real story." In the closing moments of *Cobb*, his character, who has written two books—one true, one laundered—decides to publish the lies. "I didn't lie so the children could have a hero," he tells us. "I lied for myself. I needed him to be a hero." Scribbling notes in the dark, I wrote down "hogwash!" The movie never ever shows us why Stump needed Cobb to be a hero.

Its problem, indeed, is that it doesn't know what to do with Stump in the first place. Cobb is a magnificently evil and deranged character, ranting and raving, shooting bullet holes through walls and ceilings, making a public nuisance of himself, crashing automobiles, disrupting meetings, and participating in an ugly sexual assault at gunpoint. He has been deeply damaged, and we find out why as the story gradually emerges about the death of his father—who was killed by Cobb's mother, or maybe by her lover.

Cobb wants Stump to put only the good stuff in his book, and so he conceals many of the seamy details. To work them into the movie Shelton hits on the clever idea of a newsreel about Cobb's life. We see it at the beginning of the film, and then it's played again at a Hall of Fame dinner in his honor—only this time, the drunken Cobb hallucinates that the newsreel is showing what *really* happened, and so we see the murder, the scandals, the domestic violence, the misery.

Cobb is there, in the round, and convincing. Oliver Cromwell once urged a painter to make an honest portrait, "warts and everything," and *Cobb* makes its hero look like all warts, with a batting average attached. Cobb is fine. The movie's weakness is that it gives Stump no place to go, no way to develop.

Awestruck by Cobb's greatness, he puts up with drunken rages and violent escapades like a battered wife. As their odyssey takes them from state to state, they fall into almost a domestic arrangement: Stump as biographer, chauffeur, stenographer, and nurse, "the only thing keeping the bastard alive," occasionally making shrill threats to leave, but never following through on them. Does he learn anything? Served with divorce papers, he pulls a gun on the process server and puts some bullets through the walls, emulating his hero.

Shelton works hard to inspire even marginal sympathy for Cobb, and it is to Tommy Lee Jones's credit that some does develop, for example during a maudlin visit to the crypt Cobb has built for his reunion after death with a family that cannot stand him alive. Cobb is a lonely, unpleasant alcoholic, and Stump, by the end of the movie, is just as lonely and alcoholic, but does not have it within himself to be unpleasant on such a heroic scale.

I've seen the movie twice. The first time, I found Cobb so unpleasant and Stump such a toady that I couldn't understand why anyone would want to make a movie about them. The second time I was able to focus more clearly on the strength of Jones's performance. I suppose if I rode a Greyhound long enough sitting next to Hunter Thompson, I might get to appreciate his fine points, too, if he didn't shoot me first.

Cocoon ★ ★ ★
PG-13. 115 m., 1985

Wilford Brimley (Ben), Steve Guttenberg (Jack), Brian Dennehy (Walter), Hume Cronyn (Joe), Don Ameche (Art), Maureen Stapleton (Mary), Jessica Tandy (Alma), Jack Gilford (Bernie), Tahnee Welch (Kitty). Directed by Ron Howard and produced by Richard D. Zanuck, David Brown, and Lili Fini Zanuck. Screenplay by Tom Benedek.

Cocoon is one of the sweetest, gentlest science-fiction movies I've seen, a hymn to the notion that aliens might come from outer space and yet still be almost as corny and impulsive as we are. It is also the first film since *On Golden Pond* to deal at length with old people, and you can tell by their performances that these older actors have been waiting a long time to get something nice and meaty and silly to sink their choppers into.

The movie opens with the suggestion that aliens have landed on Earth. Then we see apparently normal human beings renting a boat and a beachfront estate. Meanwhile, in a nearby retirement home, three of the old guys have started sneaking onto the estate to take illegal swims in a big enclosed pool. One day, they discover some large, mossy rocks on the bottom of the pool. That doesn't stop them. They dive in, and before long they feel terrific—and curiously youthful.

The rocks are actually cocoons collected from the bottom of the sea by aliens, who left them behind 10,000 years ago when they were forced to evacuate Atlantis in a hurry. The pool has been charged with a life force to reawaken the cocoons, and the force works on elderly humans, too. When the leader of the aliens (Brian Dennehy) finds the old guys in the pool, he doesn't zap them with extraterrestrial weaponry. He smiles and tells them to go ahead and keep using the pool—but not to tell anyone else.

That's impossible. The old guys can't keep a secret long in a retirement home, and before long this literal fountain of youth has totally changed the lifestyles of the senior citizens. The old guys are played by three wonderful actors: Hume Cronyn, Don Ameche, and, best of all, Wilford Brimley, who has a way of investing each word with such simple truth that his dialogue seems more weighted, more real, than the other dialogue in the movie.

Brimley is sort of a ringleader. He is also a homespun philosopher, who goes fishing with his grandson and talks about the meaning of life and death. Others in the retirement home are not so serene, especially the stubborn Jack Gilford, who does not want to feel young and does not want to go swimming and thinks we should all be satisfied with the time allotted us on this planet. The introduction of the mysterious pool and its life force tests Gilford's friendships with the others, and it also puts strains on the marriage between Cronyn and Jessica Tandy. The scenes involving these characters are the best scenes in the movie.

But I also liked the treatment of the aliens, especially the Dennehy character, who observes that every 10,000 years he's entitled to do something silly. Dennehy eventually offers the old folks eternal life, under certain rather difficult conditions, and the way they consider his offer is rather thought provoking—especially in the scenes between Brimley and his grandson. That's really the payoff of the movie, right there, but the ending is too drawn-out. We could also do without the romance between the boat's human captain (Steve Guttenberg) and the beautiful alien (Tahnee Welch). But the good parts in *Cocoon* are warm and sort of tender.

Cocoon: The Return ★ ★ ½
PG, 116 m., 1988

Don Ameche (Art Selwyn), Wilford Brimley (Ben Luckett), Courteney Cox (Sara), Hume Cronyn (Joe Finley), Jack Gilford (Bernie Lefkowitz), Steve Guttenberg (Jack Bonner), Barret Oliver (David), Maureen Stapleton (Mary Luckett), Elaine Stritch (Ruby), Jessica Tandy (Alma Finley), Gwen Verdon (Bess McCarthy), Tahnee Welch (Kitty), Tyrone Power, Jr. (Pillsbury), Mike Nomad (Doc). Directed by Daniel Petrie and produced by Richard D. Zanuck, David Brown, and Lili Fini Zanuck. Screenplay by Stephen McPherson.

At the end of *Cocoon*, a group of senior citizens were lifted into the sky by a beam of light from a hovering spacecraft, and taken to live on a planet where nobody ever got tired, and nobody ever grew old. Now they are back on earth. Why did they return from their other-worldly paradise? It is too easy to give the cynical answer—because they were needed for the sequel—but I am afraid the movie comes up with no better justification.

The central weakness of *Cocoon: The Return* is that the film lacks any compelling reason to exist. Yes, it is a heartwarming film. Yes, the performances are wonderful, and yes, it's great to see these characters back again. But that's about it. If you've seen *Cocoon*, the sequel gives you the opportunity to see everybody saying good-bye for the second time.

The locale, once again, is a retirement community in Florida. Steve Guttenberg, as the skipper who fell in love with an alien being (Tahnee Welch) in the previous movie, is still chugging around on his glass-bottom boat casting winsome glances at the sky. In the bedroom of one of the local Little Leaguers, a strange event takes place. The kid tries to turn off his TV set, but the screen remains bright—and then suddenly he sees his grandfather (Wilford Brimley), one of the old-timers who disappeared into space. He's coming back for a visit, Gramps says.

If you want to get technical about it, there is a motive for the spacecraft's return: The "cocoons" that were deposited on the bottom of the bay have been discovered by oceanographers and are being disturbed. While an alien team sets about recovering one of their kidnapped fellows, we see a series of reunions between the human travelers and those they left behind.

In the process, all of the same problems, questions, and dilemmas that concerned the characters in the first movie are taken out and dusted off again. For example, which is better, to live forever on another world, or get sick and die on this one, but at least get to see your grandson playing baseball? To see the familiar sunsets over the tacky but comfortable retirement villages of the Florida coast, or live forever in a silver city beneath three alien moons? In a way, both *Cocoon* pictures consider the same dilemma that the angels struggled with in Wim Wenders's *Wings of Desire:* Is it better to live forever as a spirit who can feel nothing, or for a finite time as a creature who can breathe and hurt and die?

My answer would be, take me to the silver city and I'll think it over for a few thousand years. Dying now would be a permanent solution to a temporary problem. But the folks in *Cocoon: The Return* don't all see it that way, and each couple makes up its own mind. Don Ameche wants to get back on the spaceship, for example, because, to his wonderment, he and his middle-aged wife (Gwen Verdon) are expecting a child, and he wants to live long enough to see it grow up. Jessica Tandy, on the other hand, would rather stay here on earth and take a job as a teacher in a day-care center—"the first job anybody has ever offered me."

While these decisions are being arrived at, the movie provides a series of love affairs, misunderstandings, philosophical conversations, and tragedies small and large. There is also a subplot involving the kidnapped alien, who has fun at first with its captors, but was "awakened" too soon, and begins to pine away and die. Also, of course, there is another opportunity for Guttenberg and Welch to share the strange experience of "merging," which not only passes for sex on the other planet, but replaces it—with no complaints, by all accounts.

The last half of the movie feels kind of strange. It's all so elegiac, so filled with farewells and bittersweet moments of philosophy. The movie lacks the creative energy of the first one, in which the discovery of the alien "cocoons" created genuine tension,

and there was such joy in the scenes where the old men (Brimley, Ameche, and Hume Cronyn) were suddenly made young again. This time, once again, we are invited to share the victory of the elderly cast over the effects of aging, and the best thing in the movie is probably the vitality of the actors. But at the end of the film, as those who wish to leave are carried up once more into the sky, we on earth are left with the question, was this trip necessary?

Code of Silence ★ ★ ★ ½
R, 102 m., 1985

Chuck Norris (Eddie Cusack), Henry Silva (Luis Comacho), Bert Remsen (Commander Kates), Mike Genovese (Tony Luna), Molly Hagan (Diana Luna), Nathan Davis (Felix Scalese), Ralph Foody (Cragie). Directed by Andy Davis and produced by Raymond Wagner. Screenplay by Michael Butler, Dennis Shryack, and Mike Gray.

Chuck Norris is often identified with grade-zilch karate epics, but *Code of Silence* is a heavy-duty thriller—a slick, energetic movie with good performances and a lot of genuine human interest. It grabs you right at the start with a complicated triple-cross, and then it develops into a stylish urban action picture with sensational stunts. How sensational? How about an unfaked fight on top of a speeding elevated train, ending when both fighters dive off the train into the Chicago River? The stunts are great, but not surprising; Chuck Norris is famous for the stunts he features in all of his movies. What is surprising is the number of interesting characters in *Code of Silence*. The screenplay doesn't give us the usual cardboard clichés; there's a lot of human life here, in a series of carefully crafted performances. For once, here's a thriller that realizes we have to care about the characters before we care about their adventures.

Norris stars as a veteran Chicago vice cop named Cusack. He's a straight arrow, an honest cop that his partners call a "one-man army." As the film opens, he's setting up a drug bust, but an Italian-American gang beats him to it, stealing the money and the drugs and leaving a roomful of dead gangsters. That sets off a Chicago mob war between the Italian-American factions, and as bodies pile up in the streets, Cusack begins to worry about the daughter of a Mafia chieftain—a young artist named Diana (Molly Hagan) who wants nothing to do with her father's business, but finds she can't be a bystander. After an elaborate cat-and-mouse chase through the Loop, she's kidnapped and Cusack wants to save her.

Meanwhile, the movie has an interesting subplot about a tired veteran cop (Ralph Foody) who has mistakenly shot and killed an Italian-American kid while chasing some mobsters through a tenement. The veteran's young partner (Joseph Guzaldo) watches him plant a gun on the dead kid and claim that the shooting was in self-defense. It's up to the freshman, backed up by Cusack, to decide what he'll say at the departmental hearing.

The movie has a knack for taking obligatory scenes and making them more than routine. Among the small acting gems in the movie is the performance of Chicago actor Nathan Davis as Felix Scalese, a wrinkled, wise old Mafia godfather who sits on his yacht and counsels against a mob war—to no avail. Mike Genovese plays the mob chief whose daughter is kidnapped, and his first scene, as he wishes his wife a happy birthday while hurrying out the door to do battle, is wonderfully timed. Foody has some nice scenes as the tired old cop, hanging around a bar talking big and looking scared.

Holding all of the performances together is Norris's work as Cusack. Bearded, dressed in jeans for undercover street duty, and driving a battered old beater, Norris seems convincing as a cop—with, of course, the degree of heroic exaggeration you need in a role like this. By the end of the film, when he is reduced to functioning as a one-man army, we can't really believe the armored robot tank that he brings into action, but, what the hell, we accept it. Norris resembles Clint Eastwood in his insistence on the barest minimum of dialogue; there's a scene where he quietly, awkwardly tries to comfort the mobster's daughter, and it rings completely true. He also seems to be doing a lot of his own stunts, and although the credits list a lot of stuntmen and they were all obviously kept busy, it looks to me like that's really Norris on top of that elevated train.

The movie was directed by Andy Davis, who was a cinematographer on Haskell Wexler's 1968 Chicago film *Medium Cool,* and returned to some of the same locations to film this picture. Davis's directorial debut was the low-budget *Stony Island* (1977), which had moments of truth and insight but nothing like the assurance he shows this time; *Code of Silence* is a thriller so professional

that it has the confidence to go for drama and humor as well as thrills. It may be the movie that moves Norris out of the ranks of dependable action heroes and makes him a major star.

The Color of Money ★ ★ ½
R, 119 m., 1986

Paul Newman (Eddie), Tom Cruise (Vincent), Mary Elizabeth Mastrantonio (Carmen), Helen Shaver (Janelle), John Turturro (Julian), Bill Cobbs (Orvis). Directed by Martin Scorsese and produced by Irving Axelrad and Barbara De Fina. Screenplay by Richard Price.

If this movie had been directed by someone else, I might have thought differently about it because I might not have expected so much. But *The Color of Money* is directed by Martin Scorsese, the most exciting American director now working, and it is not an exciting film. It doesn't have the electricity, the wound-up tension of his best work, and as a result I was too aware of the story marching by.

Scorsese may have thought of this film as a deliberately mainstream work, a conventional film with big names and a popular subject matter; perhaps he did it for that reason. But I believe he has the stubborn soul of an artist, and cannot put his heart where his heart will not go. And his heart, I believe, inclines toward creating new and completely personal stories about characters who have come to life in his imagination—not in finishing someone else's story, begun twenty-five years ago.

The Color of Money is not a sequel, exactly, but it didn't start with someone's fresh inspiration. It continues the story of "Fast Eddie" Felson, the character played by Paul Newman in Robert Rossen's *The Hustler* (1961). Now twenty-five years have passed. Eddie still plays pool, but not for money and not with the high-stakes, dangerous kinds of players who drove him from the game. He is a liquor salesman, a successful one, judging by the long, white Cadillac he takes so much pride in. One night, he sees a kid playing pool, and the kid is so good that Eddie's memories are stirred.

This kid is not simply good, however. He is also, Eddie observes, a "flake," and that gives him an idea: With Eddie as his coach, this kid could be steered into the world of big-money pool, where his flakiness would throw off the other players. They wouldn't be inclined to think he was for real. The challenge, obviously, is to train the kid so he

can turn his flakiness on and off at will—so he can put the making of money above every other consideration, every other lure and temptation, in the pool hall.

The kid is named Vincent (Tom Cruise), and Eddie approaches him through Vincent's girlfriend, Carmen (Mary Elizabeth Mastrantonio). She is a few years older than Vince and a lot tougher. She likes the excitement of being around Vince and around pool hustling, but Eddie sees she's getting bored. He figures he can make a deal with the girl; together, they'll control Vince and steer him in the direction of money.

A lot of the early scenes setting up this situation are very well handled, especially the moments when Eddie uses Carmen to make Vince jealous and undermine his self-confidence. But of course these scenes work well, because they are the part of the story that is closest to Scorsese's own sensibility. In all of his best movies, we can see this same ambiguity about the role of women, who are viewed as objects of comfort and fear, creatures that his heroes desire and despise themselves for desiring. Think of the heroes of *Mean Streets, Taxi Driver,* and *Raging Bull* and their relationships with women, and you sense where the energy is coming from that makes Vincent love Carmen, and distrust her.

The movie seems less at home with the Newman character, perhaps because this character is largely complete when the movie begins. "Fast Eddie" Felson knows who he is, what he thinks, what his values are. There will be some moments of crisis in the story, as when he allows himself, to his shame, to be hustled at pool. But he is not going to change much during the story, and maybe he's not even free to change much, since his experiences are largely dictated by the requirements of the plot.

Here we come to the big weakness of *The Color of Money*: It exists in a couple of time-worn genres, and its story is generated out of standard Hollywood situations. First we have the basic story of the old pro and the talented youngster. Then we have the story of the kid who wants to knock the master off the throne. Many of the scenes in this movie are almost formula, despite the energy of Scorsese's direction and the good performances. They come in the same places we would expect them to come in a movie by anybody else, and they contain the same events.

Eventually, everything points to the ending of the film, which we know will have to be a showdown between Eddie and Vince, between Newman and Cruise. The fact that the movie does not provide that payoff scene is a disappointment. Perhaps Scorsese thought the movie was "really" about the personalities of his two heroes, and that it was unnecessary to show who would win in a showdown. Perhaps, but then why plot the whole story with genre formulas and only bail out at the end? If you bring a gun onstage in the first act, you've gotta shoot somebody by the third.

The side stories are where the movie really lives. There is a warm, bittersweet relationship between Newman and his long-time girlfriend, a bartender wonderfully played by Helen Shaver. And the greatest energy in the story is generated between Cruise and Mastrantonio—who, with her hard edge and her inbred cynicism, keeps the kid from ever feeling really sure of her. It's a shame that even the tension of their relationship is allowed to evaporate in the closing scenes, where Cruise and the girl stand side by side and seem to speak from the same mind, as if she were a standard movie girlfriend and not a real original.

Watching Newman is always interesting in this movie. He has been a true star for many years, but sometimes that star quality has been thrown away. Scorsese has always been the kind of director who lets his camera stay on actors' faces, who looks deeply into them and tries to find the shadings that reveal their originality. In many of Newman's close-ups in this movie, he shows an enormous power, a concentration and focus of his essence as an actor.

Newman, of course, had veto power over who would make this movie (because how could they make it without him?), and his instincts were sound in choosing Scorsese. Maybe the problems started with the story, when Newman or somebody decided that there had to be a young man in the picture; the introduction of the Cruise character opens the door for all of the preordained teacher-pupil clichés, when perhaps they should have just stayed with Newman, and let him be at the center of the story. Then Newman's character would have been free (as the Robert De Niro characters have been free in other Scorsese films) to follow his passions, hungers, fears, and desires wherever they led him—instead of simply following the story down a well-traveled path.

Color of Night ★ ½
R, 123 m., 1994

NEW

Bruce Willis (Capa), Jane March (Rose), Rubén Blades (Martinez), Lesley Ann Warren (Sondra), Scott Bakula (Bob Moore), Brad Dourif (Clark), Lance Henriksen (Buck), Kevin J. O'Connor (Casey). Directed by Richard Rush and produced by Buzz Feitshans and David Matalon. Screenplay by Matthew Chapman and Billy Ray.

Color of Night approaches badness from so many directions that one really must admire its imagination. Combining all the worst ingredients of an Agatha Christie whodunit and a sex-crazed slasher film, it ends in a frenzy of recycled thriller elements, with a chase scene, a showdown in an echoing warehouse, and not one but two clichés from *Ebert's Little Movie Glossary:* the Talking Killer and the Climbing Villain. I am compelled to admit that the use of the high-powered industrial staple gun is original.

The film stars Bruce Willis as an East Coast psychologist who loses his faith in analysis after he talks tough to a patient and she hurls herself through the window of his skyscraper office, falling to the ground far below in the best suicide effect since *The Hudsucker Proxy.* (The pool of bright red blood under her body turns black, as Willis develops psychosomatic color blindness right there on the spot.)

Desperate for a change, Willis heads for Los Angeles, where his best friend (Scott Bakula) has a psychiatric practice that finances a luxurious lifestyle. He is a guest one night at a group therapy session run by the friend. The group is an updated, kinky version of one of those collections of eccentrics so beloved by Dame Agatha, who in plot exercises like *The Mousetrap* introduced a roomful of weirdos so that all of them could have their turn at being the Obvious Suspect.

In no time at all a suspect is required: Willis's friend is found murdered in his high-security mansion, and of course there is a reason why each member of the group seems guilty. The group includes Sondra (Lesley Ann Warren), a nymphomaniac with a nervous giggle and a careless neckline; Clark (Brad Dourif), who lost his job at a law firm after he started compulsively counting everything; Buck (Lance Henrickson), an ex-cop who foams at the mouth with anger at the least provocation; Casey (Kevin J. O'Connor), a neurotic artist; and Ricky, a young

man with a gender identity problem, of whom the less said the better.

Willis, who wants to retire from psychology, takes over the group at the urging of Martinez, the detective in charge of the murder investigation, who is played by Rubén Blades as an anthology of Latino cop shtick (during a chat with Willis on a sidewalk, he slams a passerby against a car and frisks him while continuing the conversation). The therapy group is of course a seething hotbed of neurosis and suspicion, and the screenplay (by Matthew Chapman and Billy Ray) sends Willis to visit each of the group members in turn, so they can spread paranoia about the other members while establishing themselves as possible suspects.

Meanwhile, a beautiful young woman materializes in Willis's life. She is Rose (Jane March, from *The Lover*), who seems to come from nowhere, who is lovely, who adores him, and who quickly joins him in a swimming pool sex scene that contained frontal nudity by Willis before the film was trimmed to satisfy the MPAA's censors. (The best possible argument for including Willis's genitals would have been that the movie, after all, contains everything else.)

Readers of *Ebert's Little Movie Glossary* will guess that Rose is explained by the Law of Economy of Characters, which teaches that there are no unnecessary characters in a movie. Either she is there simply to supply him with a partner in the sex scenes, or she is somehow involved with the mystery surrounding the murder. How and why and if this is true, I will not reveal.

There is, indeed, not much I can say about the rest of the movie without revealing plot points so subtle and cleverly concealed that they would come as astonishing surprises to Forrest Gump. So let's move on to the chase scene, in which a bright red car with blacked-out windows tries to force Willis off the road. It fails, but comes back for more, and there is a scene where Willis's car is driving on a street next to a parking garage, and a high-angle shot shows the red car on the roof of the garage, stalking him.

It is clear that from this angle the driver of the car cannot possibly see over the edge of the garage, and thus could not have any idea of where Willis's car is, but wait, there's more: A little later, the red car pushes another car off the top of the parking garage, so that the falling car barely misses Willis. How could the person in the red car know where a pedestrian six floors below would be by the time he pushes a car over the edge? Answer: This movie will do anything for a cheap action scene, and so we should not be surprised, a little later, when people who should be perfectly happy to remain at ground level go to a lot of trouble to climb a tower so that one can almost fall off, and the other can grab him, during and after heated dialogue in which the plot is explained.

Miss Christie would have loved the explanations. Her plots always ended with puzzled questions and serene answers ("The dog did not bark because the poisoned dagger . . ."), and so does this one. By the end of *Color of Night* I was, frankly, stupefied. To call the movie absurd would be missing the point, since any shred of credibility was obviously the first thing to be thrown overboard. The movie has ambitions to belong to the genre of *Jagged Edge, Fatal Attraction, Basic Instinct, Single White Female,* and other twisto-thrillers, but why did it aim so low? The movie is so lurid in its melodrama and so goofy in its plotting that with just a little more trouble it could have been a comedy.

The Color Purple ★ ★ ★ ★
PG-13, 155 m., 1985

Danny Glover (Mister), Whoopi Goldberg (Celie), Margaret Avery (Shug Avery), Oprah Winfrey (Sofia), Willard Pugh (Harpo), Akosua Busia (Nettie), Adolph Caesar (Old Mister), Rae Dawn Chong (Squeak), Dana Ivey (Miss Millie). Directed by Steven Spielberg and produced by Kathleen Kennedy, Frank Marshall, Quincy Jones, and Spielberg. Screenplay by Menno Meyjes.

There is a moment in Steven Spielberg's *The Color Purple* when a woman named Celie smiles and smiles and smiles. That was the moment when I knew this movie was going to be as good as it seemed, was going to keep the promise it made by daring to tell Celie's story. It is not a story that would seem easily suited to the movies.

Celie is a black woman who grows up in the rural South in the early decades of this century, in a world that surrounds her with cruelty. When we first see her, she is a child, running through fields of purple flowers with her sister. But then she comes into clear view, and we see that she is pregnant, and we learn that her father has made her pregnant, and will give away the child as he has done with a previous baby.

By the time Celie is married—to a cruel, distant charmer she calls only "Mister"—she will have lost both her children and the ability to bear children, will have been separated from the sister who is the only person on earth who loves her, and will be living in servitude to a man who flaunts his love for another woman.

And yet this woman will endure, and in the end she will prevail. *The Color Purple* is not the story of her suffering but of her victory, and by the end of her story this film had moved me and lifted me up as few films have. It is a great, warm, hard, unforgiving, triumphant movie, and there is not a scene that does not shine with the love of the people who made it.

The film is based on the novel by Alice Walker, who told Celie's story through a series of letters, some never sent, many never received, most addressed to God. The letters are her way of maintaining sanity in a world where few others ever cared to listen to her. The turning point in the book, and in the movie, comes after Celie's husband brings home the fancy woman he has been crazy about for years—a pathetic, alcoholic juke-joint singer named Shug Avery, who has been ravaged by life yet still has an indestructible beauty.

Shug's first words to Celie are: "You are as ugly as sin." But as Shug moves into the house, and Celie obediently caters to her husband's lover, Shug begins to see the beauty in Celie, and there is a scene where they kiss, and Celie learns for the first time that sex can include tenderness, that she can dare to love herself. A little later, Celie looks in Shug's eyes and allows herself to smile, and we know that Celie didn't think she had a pretty smile until Shug told her so. That is the central moment in the movie.

The relationship between Shug and Celie is a good deal toned down from the book, which deals in greater detail with sexual matters. Steven Spielberg, who made the movie, is more concerned with the whole world of Celie's life than he is with her erotic education. We meet many members of the rural black community that surrounds Celie. We meet a few of the local whites, too, but they are bit players in this drama.

Much more important are people like Sofia (Oprah Winfrey), an indomitable force of nature who is determined to marry Harpo, Mister's son by a first marriage. When we first see Sofia, hurrying down the road with everyone trying to keep up, she looks like someone who could never be stopped. But she is stopped, after she tells the local white mayor to go to hell, and the saddest story in the movie is the way her spirit is forever dampened by the beating and jailing she receives. Sofia is counterpoint to Celie: She is wounded by life, Celie is healed.

Shug Avery is another fascinating character, played by Margaret Avery as a sweet-faced, weary woman who sings a little bit like Billie Holiday and has long since lost all of her illusions about men and everything else. Her contact with Celie redeems her; by giving her somebody to be nice to, it allows her to get in touch with what is still nice inside herself.

Mister, whose real name is Albert, is played by Danny Glover, who was the field hand in *Places in the Heart.* He is an evil man, his evil tempered to some extent by his ignorance; perhaps he does not fully understand how cruel he is to Celie. Certainly he seems outwardly pleasant. He smiles and jokes and sings, and then hurts Celie to the quick—not so much with his physical blows as when he refuses to let her see the letters she hopes are coming from her long-lost sister.

And then, at the center of the movie, Celie is played by Whoopi Goldberg in one of the most amazing debut performances in movie history. Goldberg has a fearsomely difficult job to do, enlisting our sympathy for a woman who is rarely allowed to speak, to dream, to interact with the lives around her. Spielberg breaks down the wall of silence around her, however, by giving her narrative monologues in which she talks about her life and reads the words in the letters she composes.

The wonderful performances in this movie are contained in a screenplay that may take some of the smoking edges off Walker's novel, but keeps all the depth and dimension. The world of Celie and the others is created so forcibly in this movie that their corner of the South becomes one of those movie places—like Oz, like Tara, like Casablanca—that lay claim to their own geography in our imaginations. The affirmation at the end of the film is so joyous that this is one of the few movies in a long time that inspires tears of happiness, and earns them.

Colors ★ ★ ★
R, 120 m., 1988

Sean Penn (Danny McGavin), Robert Duvall (Bob Hodges), Maria Conchita Alonso (Louisa Gomez), Randy Brooks (Ron Delaney), Grand Bush (Larry Sylvester), Don Cheadle (Rocket). Directed by Dennis Hopper and produced by Robert H. Solo. Screenplay by Michael Schiffer.

There are many good moments in *Colors,* but the one I will remember the longest is in the scene where a group of Los Angeles gang members is trying to explain why the gang is so important to them. Talking to a social worker, they describe the feeling of belonging—of feeling for the first time in their lives that they were part of a "family" that cared for them and was ready to die for them.

The product of their family is, of course, tragic. Their gang deals in drugs, defends its turf, and uses murder to enforce its authority. Sometimes innocent bystanders are shot dead in the middle of a party, or while standing on their own lawns. Because the gangs represent a good deal of what little authority and structure survives in their neighborhoods, they help to set the tone for a segment of society—a tone of desperation, despair, and reckless, doomed grandiose gestures. Because there are so many gangs, so well-entrenched, the police are all but helpless to bring about any fundamental change in the situation.

That helplessness of the police is the central subject of Dennis Hopper's *Colors,* which stars Sean Penn and Robert Duvall as two cops, one newly assigned to the gang unit, one a veteran. But what makes *Colors* special is not the portraits of the cops, but the movie's willingness to look inside the gangs. Almost without exceetion, American movies about gangs have either romanticized them in fantasies *(West Side Story, Warriors)* or viewed them from outside, as a monolithic, dangerous unit. This movie tries to understand a little of the tragic gang dynamic, to explain why in some devastated inner-city neighborhoods they seem to offer the only way for young men to find power and status.

The story of the two cops, on the other hand, is not exactly new. We have the streetsmart veteran (Duvall), who has a realistic assessment of the situation and knows that he sometimes has to bend the rules to get results. And then we have the hotheaded younger cop (Penn), who has a simplistic us-against-them mentality, and wants to bust heads and make arrests. That leads into scenes where the cops come dangerously close to losing their street authority because they're fighting with each other instead of presenting a unified front to the gangs.

If the situation is not new, it is redeemed by the performances. Robert Duvall and Sean Penn are two of the best actors in America, bringing a flavor and authority to their roles that make them specific. A lot of their acting in this movie is purely physical, as when Penn disarms, frisks, and handcuffs a suspect, seeming sure and confident at every

moment. Other moments, when the two actors are talking to each other, contain that electricity that makes you think these words are being said for the first time.

The plot involves the attempts of the two cops to come to terms with a gang that is involved, we discover, in dealing drugs. During the course of the film they follow the brief life of the younger brother of one of the gang members, who seems for a time to have a chance to escape gang society. And there is a brief, doomed romance between Penn and Maria Conchita Alonso, as a Chicano who loves him but cannot reconcile his status as a cop and her perception of how cops like Penn treat her people.

The movie has some flaws. The story is needlessly complicated, and at times we're not sure who is who on the gang side. And some of the action seems repetitious; Hopper, trying to show the routine, makes it feel routine. But *Colors* is a special movie: Not just a police thriller, but a movie that has researched gangs and given some thought to what it wants to say about them.

Come Back to the 5 & Dime, Jimmy Dean, Jimmy Dean ★ ★ ★
PG, 109 m., 1982

Sandy Dennis (Mona), Cher (Sissy), Karen Black (Joanne), Sudie Bond (Juanita), Kathy Bates (Stella Mae), Marta Heflin (Edna). Directed by Robert Altman and produced by Scott Bushnell. Screenplay by Ed Graczyk.

If Robert Altman hadn't directed this movie, the reviews would have described it as Altmanesque. It's a mixture of the bizarre and the banal, a slice of lives that could never have been led, a richly textured mixture of confessions, obsessions, and surprises.

The movie takes place in a worn-out Woolworth's in a small Texas town not far from the locations where James Dean shot *Giant* in 1955. The story begins twenty years later, at a reunion of the local James Dean fan club; the members swore a solemn vow to get together after two decades, and they drift in one by one, greeted by the tired waitress who's still on duty. There's Sandy Dennis, the flaky, visionary local woman who's convinced that she bore a son by James Dean. Then Cher walks in—looking not like the glamorous Cher of television, but like a small-town sexpot unsure of her appeal. The last arrival is Karen Black, who drove in all the way from California, and is not

surprised when nobody recognizes her at first.

The fan club members and a few local good ol' girls join in a long afternoon of memories, nostalgia, self-analysis, accusation, shocking revelations, and anger, while heat-lightning flickers offscreen. And their memories trigger flashbacks to the time twenty years earlier when the proximity of James Dean served as a catalyst in all of their lives, giving some the courage to realize their dreams and others, the timid ones, the courage at least to dream them.

Jimmy Dean was a Broadway play before it was a movie, and Altman, who directed it first on stage, stays pretty close here to Ed Graczyk's script. He works just as closely with David Gropman's extraordinary stage set, on which the movie was shot. Gropman has actually created two dime stores, one a mirror-image of the other. They're separated by a two-way mirror, so that at times we're looking at the reflection of the "front" store, and at other times, the glass is transparent and we see the second store. Altman uses the front as the present and the back as the past, and there are times when a foreground image will dissolve into a background flashback. In an age of sophisticated optical effects, this sort of dissolve looks routine—until you learn that Altman isn't using opticals, he's actually shooting through the two-way mirror. His visual effects sometimes require fancy offscreen footwork for his actors to be in two places during the same shot.

Jimmy Dean's script also requires some fancy footwork, as we reel beneath a series of predictable revelations in the last twenty minutes. This is not a great drama, but two things make the movie worth seeing: Altman's visual inventiveness and the interesting performances given by everyone in the cast. Although Sandy Dennis and Karen Black in many ways have more difficult roles, Cher is the one I watched the most because her performance here is a revelation. After years and years of giving us "Cher," she gives us a new character here, in a fine performance that creates sympathy for a sexpot who doubts her own sensuality.

Come See the Paradise ★ ★ ★
R, 133 m., 1991

Dennis Quaid (Jack McGurn), Tamlyn Tomita (Lily Kawamura), Sab Shimono (Mr. Kawamura), Shizuko Hoshi (Mrs. Kawamura), Stan

Egi (Charlie Kawamura), Ronald Yamamoto (Harry Kawamura). Directed and written by Alan Parker.

Here is a movie about people who insist they are Americans, even when small and evil-minded people in power would treat them as if they were not. Most of the characters in *Come See the Paradise* are Japanese-Americans who were thrown into prison camps at the outset of World War II, even though there was no evidence that they were less patriotic, less "American," than members of other ethnic groups such as the Germans or the Italians. Their imprisonment was essentially racist, translated into laws that said they were not entitled to the same constitutional rights as their fellow citizens.

Another character in the film is an Irish-American who is a left-wing labor organizer. He gets involved in a stupid and illegal action against a movie theater chain, flees from the East to the West Coast, and changes his name. But he cannot change his ideas, and after he gets a job in a fish cannery, he is soon supporting the right of his fellow workers to strike. That means he, too, is not an "American"—at least not in the eyes of the company goons.

Although we make much of our traditions of freedom in this country, we are not so clever at understanding what freedom really means. Even George Bush, for example, cannot understand that among the rights symbolized by the American flag is the right to burn it—or honor it, if that is our choice. I have always wondered why the people who call themselves "American" most loudly are often the ones with the least understanding of the freedoms that word should represent.

When the country is threatened, our civil liberties are among the first casualties—as if we can fight the enemy by taking away our own freedoms before the enemy has a chance to. That is what happened in the early days of World War II, when a wave of racism swept the Japanese-Americans out of their homes and businesses, confiscated their savings and investments, and shipped them away in prison trains to concentration camps that were sometimes no more than barns and stables. Later on, some of these same Japanese-Americans fought with valor in the same war, perhaps because they understood better than their captors what they were fighting for.

Come See the Paradise tells a story of this period in terms of a romance between the labor organizer and a young Japanese-American

woman. Her name is Lily (Tamlyn Tomita), and she is the daughter of a businessman who runs a little chain of Japanese-language movie theaters. When the Irishman, Jack McGurn (Dennis Quaid), flees to San Francisco after getting in trouble in New York, he finds a job as a projectionist in one of the theaters, and then he meets the daughter and they fall in love with each other almost immediately. (On their first date, he leans across the table and asks to kiss her, and she gives permission. It's a sweet scene, reminiscent of some of the Hollywood movies being made at about the same time.)

Lily's father, of course, opposes the marriage. Jack goes to confront him, in one of the movie's strongest scenes, and when the old man remains inflexible, the two young people run away to get married out of state (marriages between members of different races were illegal in California at the time). In a scene that is gloriously romantic and highly improbable, they find themselves at someone else's wedding party, where they dance the night away.

Then Pearl Harbor is attacked and war is declared. By executive order of Franklin Roosevelt, Lily, her family, and everyone they know find themselves herded away to prison camps. One of her brothers later volunteers for the U.S. Army and another becomes militantly pro-Japanese, but the saddest figure is the father, who is accused by his own people of being a spy, and literally fades away into death, sitting sadly in a chair and gazing at nothing.

Lily and Jack have had a daughter, who goes into the camp with her mother, while Jack goes into the Army, but not before one of the most lacerating scenes in the film, when Jack takes his little daughter to meet Santa Claus, and Santa refuses to let the child sit on his lap. "She's an American," Jack informs Santa, grabbing him, "and you will sit here and listen to what she wants for Christmas or I will kill you."

Come See the Paradise has been criticized in a few places because it uses a technique that is common in movies about minority groups: A convenient Caucasian provides the point of view, so that the audience will have someone to identify with. I didn't appreciate that approach in *Glory*—why couldn't the story of these black Civil War soldiers be seen through their own eyes, rather than through the eyes of their white commanding officer? But with *Come See the Paradise* the introduction of the Quaid character seemed some-

what less contrived because the film's director, Alan Parker, is making a statement not limited to the story of his Japanese-American characters. The theme of the whole movie is that all of its characters are Americans, too. That people of various colors and political beliefs are all equally Americans, and if there is not room for them here, then there is no purpose for this society. By adding the Quaid character, he is able to show in one story how eager we sometimes are to deprive people of their rights for both racial and political reasons.

The story itself is rather sweet, when it is not angry. It's told in a flashback from shortly after the war, when Lily is describing the events of those days to her daughter, now just barely old enough to ask questions. The love affair between Jack and Lily is tender and romantic, and if Lily's father dies after he loses all pride and self-esteem, at least her mother lives long enough to finally accept and embrace her little half-Japanese granddaughter. *Come See the Paradise* is a fable to remind us of how easily we can surrender our liberties, and how much we need them.

Coming Home ★ ★ ★ ★
R, 127 m., 1978

Jane Fonda (Sally Hyde), Jon Voight (Luke Martin), Bruce Dern (Bob Hyde), Robert Carradine (Bill Munson), Penelope Milford (Vi Munson), Robert Ginty (Sergeant Mobley). Directed by Hal Ashby and produced by Jerome Hellman. Screenplay by Waldo Salt and Robert C. Jones.

Sally Hyde makes an ideal wife for a Marine: She is faithful, friendly, sexy in a quiet way, and totally in agreement with her husband's loyalties. Since his basic loyalty is to the Marine Corps, that presents difficulties at times. ("You know what they tell them," a girlfriend says. "'If the Marine Corps had wanted you to have a wife, they would have issued you one.'") Still, she's reasonably happy in the spring of 1968, as her husband prepares to ship out for a tour of duty in Vietnam. There's every chance he'll get a promotion over there. And the war, of course, is for a just cause, isn't it? It has to be, or we wouldn't be fighting it.

That is the Sally Hyde at the beginning of Hal Ashby's *Coming Home*, an extraordinarily moving film. The Sally Hyde at the end of the film—about a year later—is a different person, confused in her loyalties, not sure of her beliefs, awakened to new feelings within her. She hasn't turned into a political activist or a hippie or any of those other radical creatures of the late 1960s. But she is no longer going to be able to accept anything simply because her husband, or anybody else, says it's true.

Coming Home considers a great many subjects, but its heart lies with that fundamental change within Sally Hyde. She is played by Jane Fonda as the kind of character you somehow wouldn't expect the outspoken, intelligent Fonda to play. She's reserved, maybe a little shy, of average intelligence and tastes. She was, almost inevitably, a cheerleader in high school. She doesn't seem to have a lot of ideas or opinions. Perhaps she even doubts that it's necessary for her to have opinions—her husband can have them for her.

When her husband (Bruce Dern) goes off to fight the war, though, she finds herself on her own for the first time in her life. There's no home, no high school, no marriage, no Officers' Club to monitor her behavior. And she finds herself stepping outside the role of a wife and doing . . . well, not strange things, but things that are a little unusual for her. Like buying a used sports car. Like renting a house at the beach. Like volunteering to work in the local Veterans' Administration hospital. That's where she meets Luke (Jon Voight), so filled with his pain, anger, and frustration. She knew him vaguely before; he was the captain of the football team at her high school. He went off to fight the war, came home paralyzed from the waist down, and now, strapped on his stomach to a table with wheels, uses canes to propel himself furiously down hospital corridors. In time, he will graduate to a wheelchair. He has ideas about Vietnam that are a little different from her husband's.

Coming Home is uncompromising in its treatment of Luke and his fellow paraplegics, and if that weren't so the opening sequences of the film wouldn't affect us so deeply. Luke literally runs into Sally on their first meeting, and his urine bag spills on the floor between them. That's the sort of embarrassment he has to learn to live with—and she too, if she is serious about being a volunteer.

She is, she finds. Luke in the early days is a raging troublemaker, and the hospital staff often finds it simpler just to tranquilize him with medication. Zombies are hardly any bother at all. Sally tries to talk to Luke, gets to know him, invites him for dinner. He begins to focus his anger away from himself and toward the war; he grows calmer, re-

gains maturity. One day, softly, he tells her: "You know there's not an hour goes by that I don't think of making love with you."

They do eventually make love, confronting his handicap in a scene of great tenderness, beauty, and tact. It is the first time Sally has been unfaithful. But it isn't really an affair; she remains loyal to her husband, and both she and Luke know their relationship will have to end when her husband returns home. He does, too soon, having accidentally wounded himself, and discovers from Army Intelligence what his wife has been up to. The closing scenes show the film at its most uncertain, as if Ashby and his writers weren't sure in their minds how the Dern character should react. And so Dern is forced into scenes of unfocused, confused anger before the film's not very satisfying ending. It's too bad the last twenty minutes don't really work, though, because for most of its length *Coming Home* is great filmmaking and great acting.

And it is also greatly daring, since it confronts the relationship between Fonda and Voight with unusual frankness—and with emotional tenderness and subtlety that is, if anything, even harder to portray.

Consider. The film has three difficulties to confront in this relationship, and it handles all three honestly. The first is Voight's paralysis: "You aren't one of these women that gets turned on by gimps?" he asks. She is not. The second is the sexual and emotional nature of their affair, an area of enormous dramatic danger, which the movie handles in such a straightforward way, and with such an obvious display of affection between the characters, that we accept and understand.

The third is the nature of the *friendship* between Voight and Fonda, and here *Coming Home* works on a level that doesn't depend on such plot elements as the war, the husband, the paralysis, the time and place, or anything else. Thinking about the movie, we realize that men and women have been so polarized in so many films, have been made into so many varieties of sexual antagonists or lovers or rivals or other couples, that the mutual human friendship of these two characters comes as something of a revelation.

The Commitments ★ ★ ★
R, 117 m., 1991

Robert Arkins (Jimmy Rabbitte), Michael Aherne (Steven Clifford), Andrew Strong (Deco Cuffe), Angeline Ball (Imelda Quirke), Maria Doyle (Natalie Murphy), Johnny Murphy (Joey Fagan), Dave Finnegan (Mickah Wallace), Bronagh Gallagher (Bernie McGloughlin). Directed by Alan Parker and produced by Roger Randall-Cutler and Lynda Myles. Screenplay by Dick Clement, Ian La Frenais, and Roddy Doyle.

Alan Parker's *The Commitments* is a loud, rollicking, comic extravaganza about a rock band from the poorest precincts of North Dublin that decides to play soul music. The organizer of the band is the lean, ingenious Jimmy Rabbitte (Robert Arkins), whose suggestion is greeted with puzzlement by his friends. They like soul music, yes, but they don't particularly identify with it. Rabbitte's logic is persuasive: "The Irish are the blacks of Europe. Dubliners are the blacks of Ireland. North Dubliners are the blacks of Dublin."

The movie is based on a novel by Roddy Doyle, a North Dublin schoolteacher, but it is founded on charm. Parker introduces a Dickensian gallery of characters, throws them all into the pot, keeps them talking, and makes them sing a lot. The result is a movie that doesn't lead anywhere in particular and may not have a profound message—other than that it's hell at the top, however low the top may be. But the movie is filled with life and energy, and the music is honest. *The Commitments* is one of the few movies about a fictional band that's able to convince us the band is real and actually plays together.

Jimmy Rabbitte is the mercurial force at the center of the group, holding it together, but the real star of the music in the movie is a large, shambling, unkempt young man named Deco Cuffe (Andrew Strong). After Rabbitte has disappointing luck at a series of auditions for his new band (there's a funny montage showing the would-be talent knocking at his door), he finds Deco at a wedding party, where he picks up the microphone and begins to sing while the band is on break.

Strong's discovery in real life was scarcely less of a happy chance: He is the sixteen-year-old son of a Dublin singer who Parker was using to rehearse with, and when the father grew hoarse, the son stepped in, and Parker cast him on the spot. He's one of those oversize, big-voiced natural talents, with the look of Meat Loaf and the verbal style of Joe Cocker, and he gives the music in the movie a driving energy.

Meanwhile, backstage stories multiply. The oldest member of the group is Joey Fagan (Johnny Murphy), who claims to have toured America with all of the greats, from Wilson Pickett to Little Richard, and he is indeed an accomplished session musician. But he is even more accomplished at sessions between the sheets, and with great smoothness and subtlety he makes his way through all three women who sing backup for the band. Parker has fun letting that level of the story sort of happen in the background; like Robert Altman, he is able to capture the spontaneous nature of real life by letting several stories unfold at the same time.

The Commitments is so much fun that maybe it's unfair of me to expect anything more. But I was rather disappointed that the movie seemed to dissipate toward the end. The band is created with great conviction, we feel we really know several of its members, and then Parker seems to choose music over story, as the band members quarrel offstage but spend most of their time onstage, playing.

Could there have been something more? Parker never promises us a profound human drama here, and the band is so good that maybe music was the best way to go. But I was left with sort of an empty feeling, as if after the characters were developed into believable people, Parker couldn't find anywhere to go with them. As film, this is not one of the major works by the man who directed *Midnight Express, Birdy, Shoot the Moon,* and *Mississippi Burning.* But as music and human comedy, it works just fine.

Conan the Barbarian ★ ★ ★
R, 129 m., 1982

Arnold Schwarzenegger (Conan), James Earl Jones (Thulsa Doom), Max von Sydow (King Osric), Sandahl Bergman (Valeria), Ben Davidson (Rexor). Directed by John Milius and produced by Buzz Feitshans and Raffaella de Laurentiis. Screenplay by Milius and Oliver Stone.

Not since Bambi's mother was killed has there been a cannier movie for kids than *Conan the Barbarian.* It's not supposed to be just a kids' movie, of course, and I imagine a lot of other moviegoers will like it—I liked a lot of it myself, and with me, a few broadswords and leather jerkins go a long way. But *Conan* is a perfect fantasy for the alienated

preadolescent. Consider: Conan's parents are brutally murdered by the evil Thulsa Doom, which gets *them* neatly out of the way. The child is chained to the Wheel of Pain, where he goes around in circles for years, a metaphor for grade school. The kid builds muscles so terrific he could be a pro football player. One day he is set free. He teams up with Subotai the Mongol, who is an example of the classic literary type—the Best Pal—and with Valeria, Queen of Thieves, who is a *real* best pal.

Valeria is everything you could ever hope for in a woman, if you are a muscle-bound preadolescent, of course. She is lanky and muscular and a great sport, and she can ride, throw, stab, fence, and climb ropes as good as a boy. Sometimes she engages in sloppy talk about love, but you can tell she's only kidding, and she quickly recovers herself with cover-up talk about loyalty and betrayal—emotions more central to Conan's experience and maturity.

With the Mongol and the Queen at his side, Conan ventures forth to seek the evil Thulsa Doom and gain revenge for the death of his parents. This requires him to journey to the mysterious East, where he learns a little quick kung-fu, and then to the mountainside where Doom rules his slave-priests from the top of his Mountain of Power. There are a lot of battles and a few interesting nights at crude wayside inns and, in general, nothing to tax the unsophisticated. *Conan the Barbarian* is, in fact, a very nearly perfect visualization of the Conan legend, of Robert E. Howard's tale of a superman who lived beyond the mists of time, when people were so pure, straightforward, and simple that a 1930s pulp magazine writer could write about them at one cent a word and not have to pause to puzzle out their motivations.

The movie's casting is ideal. Arnold Schwarzenegger is inevitably cast as Conan, and Sandahl Bergman as Valeria. Physically, they look like artist's conceptions of themselves. What's nice is that they also create entertaining versions of their characters; they, and the movie, are not without humor and a certain quiet slyness that is never allowed to get out of hand. Schwarzenegger's slight Teutonic accent is actually even an advantage, since Conan lived, of course, in the eons before American accents.

The movie is a triumph of production design, set decoration, special effects and makeup. At a time when most of the big box-office winners display state-of-the-art tech-

nology, *Conan* ranks right up there with the best. Ron Cobb, the sometime underground cartoonist who did the production design on this film (and on *Alien*) supervises an effort in which the individual frames actually do look like blowups of panels from the Marvel Comics "Conan" books. Since this Conan could have so easily looked ridiculous, that's an accomplishment.

But there is one aspect of the film I'm disturbed by. It involves the handling of Thulsa Doom, the villain. He is played here by the fine black actor James Earl Jones, who brings power and conviction to a role that seems inspired in equal parts by Hitler, Jim Jones, and Goldfinger. But when Conan and Doom meet at the top of the Mountain of Power, it was, for me, a rather unsettling image to see this Nordic superman confronting a black, and when Doom's head was sliced off and contemptuously thrown down the flight of stairs by the muscular blond Conan, I found myself thinking that Leni Reifenstahl could have directed the scene, and that Goebbels might have applauded it.

Am I being too sensitive? Perhaps. But when Conan appeared in the pulps of the 1930s, the character suggested in certain unstated ways the same sort of Nordic superrace myths that were being peddled in Germany. These days we are more innocent again, and Conan is seen as a pure fantasy, like his British cousin, Tarzan, or his contemporary, Flash Gordon. My only reflection is that, at a time when there are *no* roles for blacks in Hollywood if they are not named Richard Pryor, it is a little unsettling to see a great black actor assigned to a role in which he is beheaded by a proto-Nordic avenger.

That complaint aside, I enjoyed *Conan.* Faithful readers will know I'm not a fan of Sword & Sorcery movies, despite such adornments as Sandahl Bergman—having discovered some time ago that heaving bosoms may be great, but a woman with a lively intelligence and a sly wit is even greater.

The problem with *Conan* is the problem with all S & S movies. After the initial premise (which usually involves revenge) is established, we suspect there's little to look forward to *except* the sets, special effects, costumes, makeup, locations, action, and surprise entrances. Almost by definition, these movies exclude the possibility of interesting, complex characters. I'd love to see them set loose an intelligent, questing, humorous hero in one of these prehistoric sword-swingers. Someone at least as smart as, say, Alley Oop.

Conan the Destroyer ★ ★ ★
PG, 103 m., 1984

Arnold Schwarzenegger (Conan), Grace Jones (Zula), Wilt Chamberlain (Bombaata), Mako (The Wizard), Tracey Walter (Malak), Sarah Douglas (Queen). Directed by Richard Fleischer and produced by Raffaella de Laurentiis. Screenplay by Stanley Mann.

What you can see in *Conan the Destroyer,* if you look closely, is the beginning of a movie dynasty. This is the film that points the way to an indefinite series of Conan adventures—one that could even replace Tarzan in supplying our need for a noble savage in the movies. Tarzan was more or less stuck in Africa; Conan can venture wherever his sword and sorcery can take him. The first Conan movie, *Conan the Barbarian,* was a dark and gloomy fantasy about the shadows of prehistory. This second film is sillier, funnier, and more entertaining. It doesn't take place before the dawn of time, but instead in that shadowy period of movie history occupied by queens and monsters, swords and castles, warriors and fools. There's more Prince Valiant and King Arthur than *Quest for Fire.*

And Conan is defined a little differently, too. He doesn't take himself as seriously. He's not just a muscle-bound superman, but a superstitious half-savage who gets very nervous in the presence of magic. Arnold Schwarzenegger, who plays Conan again, does an interesting job of defining his pop hero: Like James Bond, Conan now stands a little aside from the incessant action around him, and observes it with a bit of relish. The story this time involves the usual nonsense. Conan is recruited by an imperious queen (Sarah Douglas, looking vampirish) to take a virgin princess (Olivia D'Abo) on a mission to an enchanted crystal palace guarded by a monster, etc. He will be joined on his quest by the head of the queen's palace guard (Wilt Chamberlain). And along the way he rescues a savage woman warrior (Grace Jones) and earns her undying gratitude.

Let's face it. The Conan series does not require extraordinary acting ability, although Schwarzenegger provides a sound professional center to the story, and the film would be impossible if he couldn't carry off Conan. The characters around him, however, are basically atmosphere, and that frees the filmmakers to abandon the usual overexposed Hollywood character actors and go for really interesting types like Chamberlain and Jones.

And Grace Jones is really sensational. She has all the flash and fire of a great rock stage star, and it fits perfectly into her role as Zula, the fierce fighter. Sarah Douglas provides the necessary haughty iciness as the queen, Chamberlain gives a good try at the thankless role of the turncoat guard, and only D'Abo is a disappointment: Her princess seems to have drifted in from a teen-age sitcom.

Conan the Destroyer is more entertaining than the first Conan movie, more cheerful, and it probably has more sustained action, including a good sequence in the glass palace. Compared to the first Conan movie, which was rated R for some pretty gruesome violence, this one is milder. That's part of the idea, I think: They're repackaging Conan as your friendly family barbarian.

Continental Divide ★ ★ ★
PG, 103 m., 1981

John Belushi (Souchak), Blair Brown (Nell), Allen Goorwitz (Howard), Carlin Glynn (Sylvia), Tony Ganios (Possum), Val Avery (Yablonowitz). Directed by Michael Apted and produced by Bob Larson. Written by Lawrence Kasdan.

Here is a movie that is supposed to be about a newspaperman—a columnist for the *Chicago Sun-Times,* in fact—who is like no newspaperman I know, but exactly like every newspaperman would like to be. In my opinion, that makes it accurate. *Continental Divide* stars John Belushi as the journalist, obviously inspired by Mike Royko. He likes to walk along the lakeshore with the towers of the city outlined behind him against the lonely sky at dusk, a notebook stuck in his pocket and a cigarette stuck in his mug, on his way to rendezvous with stoolie aldermen and beautiful women.

The movie takes this character, played by Belushi with a surprising tenderness and charm, and engages him in an absolute minimum of newspaper work before spiriting him off to the Rocky Mountains for what the movie is *really* about, a romance with an eagle expert. The movie opens as if it's going to be a tough Chicago slice-of-life, with Belushi getting tips from an insider about city graft and payola, but then the columnist is beaten up by a couple of cops on an alderman's payroll. The managing editor suggests this might be a good time for Belushi to spend a few weeks out of town, and so the columnist heads for the Rockies to get an interview with a mysterious and beautiful woman (Blair Brown)

who has generated worldwide curiosity by becoming a hermit to spy on the habits of bald eagles.

The whole center section of the movie takes place in the mountains, and if nothing very original happens there, we are at least reminded of several beloved movie clichés that seemed, until this film, to belong exclusively in the comedies that Katharine Hepburn and Spencer Tracy used to make together. After the city slicker Belushi crawls wearily up a mountainside (losing his booze and cigarette supply in the process), he meets the beautiful birdwatcher and falls instantly in love. She's having none of it. She's one of those independent women who marches from crag to aerie in her L.L. Bean boots and designer wardrobe.

Because Belushi's grizzled mountain guide already has disappeared down the mountain, the two of them are destined to spend the next two weeks together in a cabin. This sets up a classic situation in which the girl talks tough but starts to fall for the big lunkhead. And there are the obligatory switches on male-female roles as Brown climbs mountains and Belushi stays home and makes goulash. Occasionally, a mountain lion attacks.

This all sounds predictable, of course, and yet this movie's predictability is one of its charms. It's rare these days to find a film that is basically content to be about a colorful man and an eccentric woman who are opposites and yet fall madly in love. It is even rarer to find a movie cast with performers who are offbeat and appealing and do not have obvious matinee-idol appeal. Belushi's character in this movie is quite unlike his self-destructive slob in *National Lampoon's Animal House;* it shows the gentleness and vulnerability that made him so appealing in some of Second City's quieter skits. Brown is also a revelation. She has been in several other movies without attracting a great deal of attention, but here she is unmistakably and wonderfully a star, a tousled-haired, big-eyed warm person who does not project sex appeal so much as warmth and humor. In other words, she has terrific sex appeal.

One of Belushi's special qualities was always an underlying innocence. Maybe he created his Blues Brothers persona in reaction to it. He's an innocent in this movie, an idealist who's a little kid at heart and who wins the love of Brown not by seducing her but by appealing to her protective qualities. That's the secret of the character's appeal. We're cheering for the romance because

Belushi makes us protective, too, and we want him to have a woman who'd be good for him.

What about the movie's view of journalism? It's really just a romanticized backdrop, *The Front Page* crossed with "Lou Grant" and modernized with a computerized newsroom. The newspaper scenes in the movie were shot on location in the *Sun-Times* features department, and one of the quietly amusing things about *Continental Divide*'s view of newspaper life is that in the movie it's more sedate and disciplined than the real thing. In the "real" *Sun-Times* features department, there's a lot of informality and chaos and good-natured confusion and people shouting at one another and eating lunch at their desks. In the movie, the extras (recruited from the *Sun-Times* staff) forget about real life and sit dutifully at their video display terminals, grinding out the news.

The newspaper's managing editor is played by Allen Goorwitz, a gifted character actor who usually plays manic overcompensators, but who this time is reasonable, calm, civilized, compassionate, and understanding, just like my boss. The movie's city of Chicago is populated by colorful old newsstand operators, muggers who apologize before taking your watch, and city council bosses who make sure their shady deals don't get into the official transcript. The newsies and muggers are fiction. The movie itself is fun: goofy, softhearted, fussy, sometimes funny, and with the sort of happy ending that columnists like to find for their stories and hardly ever find themselves.

The Conversation ★ ★ ★ ★
PG, 113 m., 1974

Gene Hackman (Harry Caul), John Cazale (Stan), Allen Garfield (Bernie Moran), Frederic Forrest (Mark), Cindy Williams (Ann), Michael Higgins (Paul). Directed by Francis Ford Coppola and produced by Fred Roos. Screenplay by Coppola.

As he is played by Gene Hackman in *The Conversation*, an expert wiretapper named Harry Caul is one of the most affecting and tragic characters in the movies; he ranks with someone like Willy Loman in *Death of a Salesman* or the pathetic captives of the middle class in John Cassavetes's *Faces*. Hackman is such a fine actor in so many different roles, from his action roles like *The French Connection* to this introverted, frightened, paranoid who is "the best bugger on the West Coast." He is,

indeed, maybe the best wiretapper in the country, but he hasn't gone back to the East Coast since a bugging assignment there led to the deaths of three people. He tries to force himself not to care. He goes to confession and begs forgiveness for not paying for some newspapers, but not for bringing about a murder—because the murder, you see, was none of his business. He is only a professional. He does his job and asks no questions: doesn't *want* to know the answers.

His latest job has been a tactical masterpiece. The assignment: Bug a noon-hour conversation between two young people as they walk in a crowded plaza. He does it by tailing them with a guy who's wired for sound, and also by aiming parabolic microphones at them from buildings overlooking the plaza. This gives him three imperfect recordings of their conversation, which he can electronically marry into one fairly good tape. He is a good craftsman, and, although the film doesn't belabor his techniques, it does show us enough of how bugging is done to give us a cynical education.

It's a movie not so much about bugging as about the man who does it, and Gene Hackman's performance is a great one. He does not want to get involved (whenever he says anything like that, it sounds in italics)—but he does. After he has recorded the conversation, he plays it again and again and becomes convinced that a death may result from it, if he turns the tape in. The ways in which he interprets the tape, and the different nuances of meaning it seems to contain at different moments, remind us of Antonioni's *Blow Up*. Both movies are about the unreality of what seems real: We have here in our hands a document that is maddeningly concrete and yet refuses to reveal its meaning. And the meaning seems to be a matter of life and death.

The movie is a thriller with a shocking twist at the end, but it is also a character study. Hackman plays a craftsman who has perfected his skill at the expense of all other human qualities; he lives in paranoia in a triple-locked apartment, and is terrified when it turns out his landlady has a key. She explains she might have to get in in case of some emergency—his furniture might burn up or something. He explains that none of his possessions is important to him—except his keys.

He has no friends, but he does have acquaintances in the bugging industry, and they're in town for a convention. One of

them (played by Allen Garfield) is a truly frightening character. He's the one who talks about the three murders, and he's the one whose hateful envy reveals to us how good Harry Caul really is. A boozy scene in Harry's workshop, with some colleagues and their random dates, provides a perfect illustration of the ways in which even Harry's pathetically constrained social life is expressed through his work.

The Conversation is about paranoia, invasion of privacy, bugging—and also about the bothersome problem of conscience. The Watergate crew seems, for the most part, to have had no notion that what they were doing was objectively wrong. Harry wants to have no notion. But he does, and it destroys him.

The Cook, the Thief, His Wife and Her Lover ★ ★ ★ ★
NO MPAA RATING, 120 m., 1990

Richard Bohringer (Richard), Michael Gambon (Albert), Helen Mirren (Georgina), Alan Howard (Michael), Tim Roth (Mitchel), Ciaran Hinds (Cory), Gary Olsen (Spangler), Ewan Stewart (Harris). Directed by Peter Greenaway and produced by Kees Kasander. Screenplay by Greenaway.

Rarely has a movie title been more—or less—descriptive than Peter Greenaway's *The Cook, the Thief, His Wife and Her Lover.* On one level you can describe the movie simply in terms of the characters and the lustful and unspeakable things they do to one another. On another level, there is no end to the ideas stirred up by this movie, which was threatened with an X rating in America while creating a furor in Great Britain because of its political content. So, which is it? Pornographic, a savage attack on Margaret Thatcher, or both? Or is it simply about a cook, a thief, his wife, and her lover?

The thief's thuggish personality stands astride the movie and browbeats the others into submission. He is a loud, large, reprehensible criminal, played by Michael Gambon as the kind of bully you can only look at in wonder that God does not strike him dead. He presides every night over an obscene banquet in a London restaurant, where the other customers exhibit remarkable patience at his hoglike behavior. He surrounds himself with his cronies, hit men, and hangers-on, and with his long-suffering wife (Helen Mirren), for whom martyrdom has become a lifestyle. No behavior is too crude for the thief, who delights in making animal noises, who humiliates his underlings, who beats and degrades his wife, and whose treatment of the chef in the opening scene may send some patrons racing for the exits before the real horror show has even begun.

At another table in the restaurant sits the lover (Alan Howard), a book propped up so that he can read while he eats. He ignores the crude displays of the thief; his book distracts him. Then one night his eyes meet the eyes of the thief's wife. Lightning strikes, and within seconds they are making passionate love in the ladies' room. The sex scenes in this movie are as hungry and passionate as any I have seen, and yet they are upstaged by the rest of the film, which is so uncompromising in its savagery that the sex seems tranquil by comparison.

Night after night the charade goes on— the thief acting monstrously, the cook being humiliated, the wife and her lover meeting to make love in the toilet, the kitchen, the meat room, the refrigerator, anywhere that is sufficiently inappropriate and uncomfortable. (Greenaway gives a nightmare tinge to these scenes by using a different color scheme for every locale—red for the dining room, white for the toilets—and having the color of the character's costumes change as they walk from one to another.) Then the thief discovers that he is a cuckold, and in a rage orders his men to shove a book on the French Revolution down the lover's throat, one page at a time. That is the prelude to the movie's conclusion, which I will merely describe as cannibalism, to spare your feelings.

So. What is all this about? Greenaway is not ordinarily such a visceral director, and indeed his earlier films (*The Draughtsman's Contract, A Zed and Two Noughts, In the Belly of the Architect*) have specialized in cerebral detachment. What is his motivation here? I submit it is anger—the same anger that inspired large and sometimes violent British crowds to demonstrate against Margaret Thatcher's poll tax that whipped the poor and coddled the rich. Some British critics read the movie this way:

Cook = Civil servants, dutiful citizens.

Thief = Thatcher's arrogance and support of the greedy.

Wife = Britannia.

Lover = Ineffectual opposition by leftists and intellectuals.

This provides a neat formula and allows us to read the movie as a political parable. (It is easily as savage as Swift's "modest proposal" that if the Irish were starving and overcrowded, they could solve both problems by eating their babies.) But I am not sure Greenaway is simply making an Identikit protest movie, leaving us to put the labels on the proper donkeys. I think *The Cook, the Thief, His Wife and Her Lover* is more of a meditation on modern times in general. It is about the greed of an entrepreneurial class that takes over perfectly efficient companies and steals their assets, that marches roughshod over timid laws in pursuit of its own aggrandizement, that rapes the environment, that enforces its tyranny on the timid majority— which distracts itself with romance and escapism to avoid facing up to the bullyboys.

The actors in this movie exhibit a rare degree of courage. They are asked to do things that few human beings would have the nerve or the stomach for, and they do them because they believe in the power of the statement being made. Mirren, Gambon, and Howard are three of the most distinguished actors in Britain—among them, they've played most of the principal roles in Shakespeare— and here they find the resources to not only strip themselves of all their defenses, but to do so convincingly.

This isn't a freak show; it's a deliberate and thoughtful film in which the characters are believable and we care about them. Gambon makes the thief a study in hatefulness. At the end of the film, I regretted it was over because it let him too easily off the hook. Mirren's character transformation is almost frightening—she changes from submissive wife to daring lover to vicious seeker of vengeance. And watch the way she and Howard handle their sex scenes together, using sex not as joy, not as an avenue to love, but as sheer escapism; lust is their avenue to oblivion.

The Cook, the Thief, His Wife and Her Lover is not an easy film to sit through. It doesn't simply make a show of being uncompromising—it is uncompromised in every single shot from beginning to end. Why is it so extreme? Because it is a film made in rage, and rage cannot be modulated. Those who think it is only about gluttony, lust, barbarism, and bad table manners will have to think again. It is a film that uses the most basic strengths and weaknesses of the human body as a way of giving physical form to the corruption of the human soul.

Congo ★ ★ ★
PG-13, 102 m., 1995

NEW

Dylan Walsh (Peter Elliot), Laura Linney (Karen Ross), Ernie Hudson (Monroe Kelly), Tim Curry (Herkermer Homolka), Grant Heslov (Richard), Joe Don Baker (R.B. Travis), Adewale Akinnuoye-Agbaje (Kahega), Amy (Herself). Directed by Frank Marshall and produced by Kathleen Kennedy and Sam Mercer. Screenplay by John Patrick Shanley.

Congo is a splendid example of a genre no longer much in fashion, the jungle adventure story. Perhaps aware that its material was already dated when Stewart Granger made *King Solomon's Mines* in 1950, the filmmakers have cheerfully turned it into an action comedy, and the actors have gone a step further, treating it like one of those movies like *Beat the Devil* that is a put-on of itself. The result is not a movie that is very good, exactly, but it's entertaining and funny. False sophisticates will scorn it. Real sophisticates will relish it.

The movie begins with a ludicrous setup featuring Joe Don Baker, chewing the scenery (and I believe even the foundations of the sound stage) as a megalomaniac tycoon who needs a rare African diamond to build a laser system that will "dominate the communications industry!" His son Charlie seems to have discovered the diamond lode before his satellite transmission is knocked off the air by what look like killer gorillas.

Baker convinces an assistant, Karen (Laura Linney), to go into the jungle to find out what happened to Charlie, and to bring back the diamonds. The diamonds seem more important than his son. She accuses him of not being human. "I'll be human later!" he barks.

For very complicated reasons, Karen merges her mission with an expedition being mounted by a "primologist" (Dylan Walsh), who has taught an ape to communicate by using American Sign Language to activate a speech synthesizer. Also along for the ride is a shadowy, sinister figure named Herkermer Homolka (Tim Curry), who introduces himself as a "Rumanian philanthropist," but has in fact staged a lifelong quest for the jewels of the lost city of Zinj. He has the Peter Lorre role.

Are you following this? I realize only a very particular kind of filmgoer is likely to relate to this movie: one raised on Saturday matinees, with a good sense of the absurd and an appreciation for movie clichés. Curry's first appearance gets a laugh, for example, even before he says anything, because he glowers so pregnantly.

And an ideal audience will also enjoy the scene where Charlie looks over his shoulder, sees something, and screams before the screen turns black. And the scene where Karen kicks open the door of a DC-3 and shoots down anti-aircraft fire with a flare gun. And lines like, "Why are they putting on parachutes?" And, in the middle of the jungle, the classic, ominous line, "Two of our porters have run away." And the shot of the hand of a corpse clutching a big diamond.

The key actor in the African sequences is Ernie Hudson, as Monroe Kelly, the local guide, who described himself as "a great white hunter who happens to be black." In a droll performance that is perfectly suited to the material, Hudson resembles Clark Gable and, yes, Stewart Granger in his ability to maintain a sardonic detachment and calm courage while (a) being attacked by killer apes as (b) the ground opens up under him during a volcanic earthquake, and (c) rivers of molten lava head in his direction.

Many of the other best moments belong to Amy the trained gorilla, played by herself, who enjoys a martini on the plane ("She's allowed one; it will calm her down") and later amazes the African gorillas by informing them, in synthesized speech, that her name is Amy and they are ugly.

The closing action sequences, involving the lost city of Zinj, the volcanic eruption, and the attack of the killer apes, are in the tradition of the Indiana Jones movies, although the traffic direction isn't as good and a lot more porters disappear without being accounted for. The movie was directed by Frank Marshall, who has worked with Steven Spielberg on his action extravaganzas, and is based on a novel by Michael Crichton, who is said to be unhappy about what they've done with his book. Since it is impossible to imagine this material being played for anything but laughs, maybe he should be grateful.

Cop ★ ★ ★
R, 110 m., 1988

James Woods (Lloyd Hopkins), Lesley Ann Warren (Kathleen McCarthy), Charles Durning (Dutch), Charles Haid (Whitey Haines), Raymond J. Barry (Gaffney), Randi Brooks (Joanie), Steven Lambert (Bobby Franco), Christopher Wynne (Jack Gibbs), Jan McGill (Jen Hopkins), Vicki Wauchope (Penny

Hopkins). Directed by James B. Harris and produced by Harris and James Woods. Screenplay by Harris.

Anyone without a history of watching James Woods in the movies might easily misread *Cop.* They might think this was simply a violent, sick, contrived exploitation picture—and that would certainly be an accurate description of its surfaces. But Woods operates in this movie almost as if he were writing his own footnotes. He uses his personality, his voice, and his quirky sense of humor to undermine the material and comment on it, until *Cop* becomes an essay on this whole genre of movie. And then, with the movie's startling last shot, Woods slams shut the book.

The film stars Woods, who is the most engaging and unconventional of leading men, as a brilliant but twisted cop. He's a lone ranger, and he likes to shoot first and ask questions later. In the movie's unsettling opening scene, he kills a man who is possibly innocent, and then lets his partner clean up the mess while he tries to pick up the dead man's date. No wonder Woods is considered a danger to public safety, even by his own superiors. He makes Dirty Harry look cool and reflective.

Before long a plot begins to emerge. A dead body has been discovered, and Woods, working backward from the date of the crime and piecing together apparently unrelated clues, becomes convinced that the dead woman is the latest of a long string of murders by the same serial killer. His superiors don't want to hear about it. The last thing Los Angeles needs is another mass murderer.

But Woods persists. He interviews a kinky cop, and cross-examines a feminist bookstore owner (Lesley Ann Warren), whose high school yearbook may contain the clue to the mystery. Can it be that events fifteen years ago in high school have triggered a series of killings which have continued ever since? It can in Woods's mind, and he stays on the case even after the department has stripped him of his badge and gun because of . . . well, because basically he represents a danger to the community.

The screenplay of *Cop* was based by the director, James B. Harris, on a thriller by James Ellroy. It contains echoes of the great *film noir* stories of the 1940s, where the supporting cast is filled with various sleazebags and weirdos who are ticked off, one by one, by the hero. The difference this time is that Woods is as sleazy and weird as any of them,

and not above breaking and entering and stealing evidence and making love to potential witnesses in order to get information (or, for that matter, simply in order to get laid). He wants to solve this case, but not so much because he wants to punish evildoing as because he is one stubborn S.O.B. and he doesn't like to be told not to do something.

James Woods was born to play this role. He uses a curious and effective technique to get laughs, of which the movie has plenty. Instead of saying funny things, he knows how to throw in a pause, just long enough for the audience to figure out what he's really thinking, so that when he says a straight line, it's funny. The result is creepy; he invites us into his mind, and makes us share his obsession.

Cop is a very violent movie, all the more so because it is so casual about the violence most of the time. It sees its events through the mind of a man who should never have been a cop, and who has been a cop much too long. Yet the Woods character is not stupid and not brutal, just several degrees off from normal.

As we follow him through his "case of the yearbook murders," we can figure out the clues and sometimes arrive at conclusions before he does, but we can never quite figure out what is driving him on this case. There are strange psychological clues, as in the unforgettable scene where he tells his little daughter a bedtime story that's based on straight police procedure, but by the end, the character still remains an enigma. It's as if Woods and Harris watched a Dirty Harry movie one night and decided to see what would happen if Harry were *really* dirty.

Corrina, Corrina ★ ★ ½   NEW
PG, 115 m., 1994

Whoopi Goldberg (Corrina Washington), Ray Liotta (Manny Singer), Tina Majorino (Molly Singer), Wendy Crewson (Jenny Davis), Larry Miller (Sid), Erica Yohn (Grandma Eva), Jenifer Lewis (Jevina), Joan Cusack (Jonesy). Directed by Jessie Nelson and produced by Steve Tisch, Paula Mazur, and Nelson. Screenplay by Nelson.

Corrina, Corrina has its heart in the right place, and its characters are some of the nicest people I've met at the movies lately, but the movie seems to exist under a cloud of gloom, and I kept hoping for sunshine.

The story involves Manny Singer (Ray Liotta), a jingle writer for an advertising agency, whose wife has died, leaving him with a seven-year-old daughter named Molly (Tina Majorino). He desperately needs a nanny, and interviews several applicants, all deeply flawed in the ways Movie Reject Nannies always are, before settling on Corrina Washington (Whoopi Goldberg).

The time is 1959, and the movie implies that Corrina, a recent college graduate, can't find any other job because she is black. She is overqualified for this one, but has many qualifications for being Manny's partner in life, one of them being her suggestion to take the "t" off of "shouldn't," so it rhymes with "puddin'," and he wins the Jell-O account.

The Singer household is a cavern of gloom when Corrina first enters it. Molly has decided to stop talking, and Manny spends most of his time looking dazed and confused, and smoking too many cigarettes. Corrina smokes, too, and this leads to a lot of intimate cigarette behavior, in which the two adults, shy about communicating in other ways, light up together. They also spend a lot of time discussing jazz. (There is a running gag about how Molly is stealing their cigarettes because she heard a government health warning on TV; the movie would have been improved by the elimination of this subplot, with its cutesy payoff.)

The opening hour of the film is morose and sad, as the two adults and the child create a series of small social embarrassments, awkwardnesses, and apologies. But Corrina is slowly able to win the little girl's trust, and soon she is talking again. The plot contrives for Corrina to find herself staying over for dinner on several occasions, and Manny is surprised at her comments about music and literature. There are also well-written philosophical discussions between Corrina and Molly, who blames herself for her mother's death. A family unit is obviously being formed here, and there's a nice little moment when Manny is hurrying out the door and Corrina gives Molly instructions, and Manny blurts out, "Listen to your mother!"

Molly smiles secretly at that, because she has determined that Corrina should, indeed, marry her daddy and move in full-time. It takes the adults longer to figure that out, and the screenplay, by director Jessie Nelson, seems sort of shy about the emotional details. Liotta plays Manny as closed-off and absent, and Goldberg plays Corrina as prescient and tactful, and eventually the two find themselves in each other's arms—but more through a logical decision, somehow, than because of love or passion.

The movie has a lively subplot involving Corrina's home life; she lives with her sister and her sister's kids, who become Molly's playmates. The energy in this household provides some needed sunshine, but the movie also supplies the usual obligatory scenes in which Corrina's sister, Manny's mother, and a nosy neighbor all express their disapproval of interracial romance. Those scenes seem almost pro forma; there's no real emotional confrontation over the subject, and indeed the whole movie seems kind of muted.

There's a lot I liked in the film, including the intelligence of some of the dialogue, but *Corrina, Corrina* seemed to be trying to do both too much, and too little. It deals with death, loss, healing, romance, and communication, but in ways that are predictable, however well handled. And it seems almost as shy as the characters about the charged issues of race and romance. After it was over I felt that, yes, it was warm and good-hearted, but there was more of a story there to be told.

The Cotton Club ★ ★ ★ ★
R, 121 m., 1984

Richard Gere (Dixie Dwyer), Gregory Hines (Sandman Williams), Diane Lane (Vera Cicero), Lonette McKee (Lila Rose Oliver), Bob Hoskins (Owney Madden), James Remar (Dutch Schultz), Fred Gwynne (Frenchy). Directed by Francis Ford Coppola and produced by Robert Evans. Screenplay by William Kennedy and Coppola.

After all the rumors, all the negative publicity, all the stories of fights on the set and backstage intrigue and imminent bankruptcy, Francis Ford Coppola's *The Cotton Club* is, quite simply, a wonderful movie. It has the confidence and momentum of a movie where every shot was premeditated—and even if we know that wasn't the case, and this was one of the most troubled productions in recent movie history, what difference does that make when the result is so entertaining?

The movie takes place in New York in the 1920s and 1930s, where Irish and Jewish gangsters battled the Italians for the rackets. Most of their intrigues were played out in public, in flashy settings like the Cotton Club, a Harlem nightclub that featured the nation's most talented black entertainers on stage—playing before an all-white audience. By telling us two love stories, Coppola shows us both sides of that racial divide. He begins by introducing Dixie Dwyer (Richard Gere), a

good-looking young musician who saves the life of a gangster and is immediately recruited into the hood's inner circle. There he meets the gangster's teen-age girlfriend (Diane Lane), and they immediately fall in love—but secretly, because they'll live longer that way. Then we meet Sandman Williams (Gregory Hines), a black tap dancer who dreams of appearing at the Cotton Club, and falls in love with a member of the chorus line (Lonette McKee), a mulatto who talks about her secret life among people who think she is white.

The two love stories are developed against a background of a lot of very good jazz, some great dancing, sharply etched character studies of the gang bosses, and a couple of unexpected bursts of violence that remind us, in their sudden explosion, of moments in Coppola's *Godfather* films. Indeed, there's a lot of *The Godfather* in *The Cotton Club,* especially in the movie's almost elegiac sadness: We get the feeling of time passing, and personal histories being written, and some people breaking free and other people dying or surrendering to hopelessness.

There's another reminder of *The Godfather* movies, and that's in the brilliant, indepth casting. There's not an uninteresting face or a boring performance in this movie, but two supporting characters really stand out: Bob Hoskins, as a crooked club owner named Madden, and Fred Gwynne, as a towering hulk named Frenchy. They are friends. They also are criminal associates. Hoskins is a bantamweight filled with hostility; Gwynne is a giant with a deep voice and glowering eyes. After Gwynne is kidnapped and Hoskins pays the ransom, the scene between the two of them begins as a routine confrontation and unfolds into something surprisingly funny and touching.

Coppola has a way, in this film, of telling all the different stories without giving us the impression he's jumping around a lot. Maybe the music helps. It gives the movie a continuity and an underlying rhythm that makes all of the characters' lives into steps in a sad ballet. We like some of the characters, but we don't have much respect for them, and the movie doesn't bother with clear distinctions between good and evil. *The Cotton Club* is a somewhat cynical movie about a very cynical time, and along with the music and the romance there is racism, cruelty, betrayal, and stunning violence. Romance with a cutting edge.

The performances are well-suited to the material. Richard Gere is especially good as

Dixie Dwyer, maybe because the camera has a way of seeing him off-balance, so that he doesn't dominate the center of each shot like a handsome icon; Coppola stirs him into the action. Diane Lane, herself still a teen-ager, is astonishing as the party girl who wants to own her own club. Gregory Hines and his brother, Maurice, create a wonderful moment of reconciliation when they begin to tap dance and end by forgiving each other for a lifetime's hurts. And Hoskins, the British actor who played the unforgettable mob chief in *The Long Good Friday,* is so wound-up and fierce and funny as the mobster that he takes a cliché and turns it into an original.

The Cotton Club took months to shoot, and they claim they have another 200,000 feet of footage as good as this movie. I doubt it. Whatever it took to do it, Coppola has extracted a very special film out of the checkered history of this project.

Country ★ ★ ★ ½
PG, 108 m., 1984

Jessica Lange (Jewell Ivy), Sam Shepard (Gil Ivy), Wilford Brimley (Otis Stewart), Matt Clark (Tom McMullen), Therese Graham (Marlene Ivy), Levi L. Knebel (Carlisle Ivy). Directed by Richard Pearce and produced by William D. Wittliff and Jessica Lange. Screenplay by Wittliff.

The opening moments of *Country* show a woman frying hamburgers and wrapping them up and sending them out to her men, working in the fields. The movie is using visuals to announce its intentions: It wants to observe the lives of its characters at the level of daily detail and routine, and to avoid pulling back into "Big Country" cliché shots. It succeeds. This movie observes ordinary American lives carefully, and passionately. The family lives on a farm in Iowa. Times are hard, and times are now. This isn't a movie about symbolic farmers living in some colorful American past. It is about the farm policies of the Carter and Reagan administrations, and how the movie believes that those policies are resulting in the destruction of family farms. It has been so long since I've seen a Hollywood film with specific political beliefs that a funny thing happened: The movie's anger moved me as much as its story.

The story is pretty moving, too. We meet the members of the Ivy family: Jewell Ivy (Jessica Lange), the farm wife; her husband, Gil (Sam Shepard); her father, Otis (Wilford Brimley); and the three children, espe-

cially Carlisle (Levi L. Knebel), the son who knows enough about farming to know when his father has given up. The movie begins at the time of last year's harvest. Some nasty weather has destroyed part of the yield. The Ivys are behind on their FHA loan. Ordinarily, that would be no tragedy; farming is cyclical and there are good years and bad years, and eventually they'll catch up with the loan. But this year is different. An FHA regional administrator, acting on orders from Washington, instructs his people to enforce all loans strictly, and to foreclose when necessary. He uses red ink to write his recommendation on the Ivys' loan file: *Move toward voluntary liquidation.* Since there is no way the loan can be paid off, the Ivys will lose the land that Jewell's family has farmed for one hundred years. The farm agent helpfully supplies the name of an auctioneer.

All of this sounds just a little like the dire opening chapters of a story by Horatio Alger, but the movie never feels dogmatic or forced because *Country* is so clearly the particular story of these people and the way they respond. Old Otis is angry at his son-in-law for losing the farm. Jewell defends her husband, but he goes into town to drink away his impotent rage. There are loud fights far into the night in a house that had been peaceful. The boy asks, "Would somebody mind telling me what's going on around here?"

The movie's strongest passages deal with Jewell's attempts to enlist her neighbors in a stand against the government. The most touching scenes, though, are the ones showing how abstract economic policies cause specific human suffering, cause lives to be interrupted, and families to be torn apart, all in the name of the balance sheet. *Country* is as political, as unforgiving, as *The Grapes of Wrath.*

The movie has, unfortunately, one important area of weakness, in the way it handles the character of Gil (Shepard). At the beginning we have no reason to doubt that he is a good farmer. Later, the movie raises questions about that assumption, and never clearly answers them. Gil starts drinking heavily, and lays a hand on his son, and leaves the farm altogether for several days. The local farm agent tells him, point blank, that he's a drunk and a bad farmer. Well, is he? In an affecting scene where Gil returns and asks for the understanding of his family, his drinking is not mentioned. It's good that the movie tries to make the character more complex and interesting—not such a noble hero—but if he really is a drunk and a bad farmer, then

maybe that's why he's behind on the loan. The movie shouldn't raise the possibility without dealing with it.

In a movie with the power of *Country,* I can live with a problem like that because there are so many other good things. The performances are so true you feel this really is a family; we expect the quality of the acting by Lange, Shepard, and gruff old Brimley, but the surprise is Levi L. Knebel, as the son. He is so stubborn and so vulnerable, so filled with his sense of right when he tells his father what's being done wrong, that he brings the movie an almost documentary quality; this isn't acting, we feel, but eavesdropping.

Cousins ★ ★ ★ ½
PG-13, 110 m., 1989

Ted Danson (Larry Kozinski), Isabella Rossellini (Maria Hardy), William Petersen (Tom Hardy), Sean Young (Tish Kozinski), Norma Aleandro (Edie), Lloyd Bridges (Larry's Father), Keith Coogan (Larry's Son), Gina DeAngelis (Aunt Sofia). Directed by Joel Schumacher and produced by William Allyn. Screenplay by Stephen Metcalfe.

Cousins is a celebration of carnal desire, wrapped up in a comedy so that nobody is too badly hurt. In the real world, this kind of fooling around would turn family reunions into emotional bloodbaths—but here everybody smiles, and the sun always seems to be shining. When it's over, you start asking yourself what it was really about. But while it's playing you don't think in those terms because you're having too much fun.

The movie centers around three weddings, where a big, boisterous American family gets together for dancing, drinking, gossip, and shoving matches. At the first wedding, two distant relatives (William Petersen and Sean Young) sneak off for a little hanky-panky in the middle of the afternoon. They return long after the party's over, with some lame excuse about the car breaking down.

Their disappearance has given time for their spouses (Isabella Rossellini and Ted Danson) to meet each other, and to start to like each other. Danson is a job-hopper who teaches ballroom dancing, lives upstairs over a Chinese restaurant, and isn't too concerned about his wife's possible infidelity: "Everybody has to do what they feel they have to do." But Rossellini does take it seriously, and the next day she tracks Danson down at his work to ask him if he thinks her husband and his wife are having an affair.

This is, of course, the beginning of their own affair—although they're not ready to admit that for a while.

The movie is intelligently directed by Joel Schumacher, who places these two affairs in the center of a lot of detail; this isn't one of those shallow movies that's about nothing except love, and instead we get inside the lives of these people—Petersen as the womanizing BMW salesman, Rossellini as the woman who has stopped loving him but wants to be faithful to him, Danson as a warmhearted misfit, Young as a woman who wandered into the wrong marriage by mistake.

And there are some other family members who are very important to the action, especially Danson's gruff old codger of a father (Lloyd Bridges), who has most of the best one-liners in the movie, and Danson's punkster son from an earlier marriage (Keith Coogan). Acting as kind of a chorus in the background are Rossellini's mother (Norma Aleandro), who loses one husband and gains another during the course of the movie, and Aunt Sofia (Gina DeAngelis), who is perfect as the bitter relative who attends every family event and mutters darkly in the background about everything she sees there ("That dress, you would wear to a hooker's wedding").

Rossellini and Danson are at the center of the story, however, because theirs is the romance based on true love, and they try, up to a point, to deny their feelings. And Rossellini is the key to everything. She is so huggable in this movie, so funny, so sweet, that she brings sunshine into scenes that might otherwise seem contrived. She has one moment almost impossible to describe, when she and Danson have agreed to meet "accidentally" at a restaurant by bringing their families there. And as she looks up and is "surprised" to see Danson there, her joy and embarrassment and good humor all bubble up at once, and she almost breaks out laughing as she tries to go through with the charade.

Rossellini has the role in *Cousins* that was played by Marie-Christine Barrault in *Cousin, Cousine,* the warmhearted 1975 French comedy that inspired this Hollywood remake. Both actresses share some of the same qualities: sunny good humor and instinctive warmth in a merry, *zaftig* package. And they both have particularly winning smiles. Rossellini has previously been in only six or seven movies, and the one that made the biggest impression (the gothic comedy *Blue Velvet*) was scarcely designed to bring out her

warmth. But in *Cousins* she has the kind of qualities that viewers really respond to.

Danson is less perfectly cast as her lover; this is his most believable and likable role, and yet there is a certain reserve about him that never quite seems to fit, and maybe William Petersen, who plays the other man, would have seemed warmer. Still, the material is so strong that we're inclined to believe that if Rossellini likes him, she must know what she's doing. Petersen is very good as the womanizing salesman, tormented by guilt but a sinner anyway. Sean Young, as Danson's wife, is brittle and distant; we never really get to know her.

We do, though, have a lot of fun with Lloyd Bridges and Keith Coogan, as Danson's father and son. Bridges has three or four lines that are explosively funny, and Coogan, a self-styled "video performance artist," makes an avant-garde version of a wedding movie that brings things to a screeching halt.

Cousins is basically a rambling, warmhearted but artificial construction that seems more convincing because of the riot of life that surrounds the manipulated central characters. We don't really believe what's happening—adultery is never this simple, and seldom this life-affirming—but the movie gets away with murder because it's funny; because the dialogue has been written with an ear for the funny things people say, especially when they're being serious; and because of Rossellini.

Cries and Whispers ★ ★ ★ ★
R, 106 m., 1973

Harriet Andersson (Agnes), Kari Sylwan (Anna), Ingrid Thulin (Karin), Liv Ullmann (Maria), Erland Josephson (Lakaren), Henning Moritzen (Joakim). Directed, produced, and written by Ingmar Bergman.

Cries and Whispers is like few movies we'll ever see. It is hypnotic, disturbing, frightening. It envelops us in a red membrane of passion and fear, and in some way that I do not fully understand, it employs taboos and ancient superstitions to make its effect. We slip lower in our seats, feeling claustrophobia and sexual disquiet, realizing that we have been surrounded by the vision of a filmmaker who has absolute mastery of his art. *Cries and Whispers* is about dying, love, sexual passion, hatred, and death—in that order.

The film inhabits a manor house set on a vast country estate. The rooms of the house open out from each other like passages in the

human body; with the exception of one moment when Agnes, the dying woman, opens her window and looks at the dawn, the house offers no views. It looks in upon itself.

Three women stay in the house with Agnes (Harriet Andersson), waiting for her to die. She is in the final stages of cancer and in great pain. The women are Karin and Maria, her sisters, and Anna, the stout, round-cheeked servant. In elliptical flashbacks (intended to give us emotional information, not to tell a story), we learn that the three sisters have made little of their lives. Karin (Ingrid Thulin) is married to a diplomat she despises. Maria (Liv Ullmann) is married to a cuckold, and so she cuckolds him (what is one to do?). Agnes, who never married, gave birth to a few third-rate watercolors. Now, in dying, she discovers at last some of the sweetness of life.

The sisters remember that they were close in childhood, but somehow in growing up they lost the ability to love, to touch. Only Anna, the servant, remembers how. When Agnes cries out in the night, in fear and agony, it is Anna who cradles her to her bosom, whispering soft endearments. The others cannot stand to be touched. In a moment of conjured nostalgia, Maria and Karin remember their closeness as children. Now, faced with the fact of their sister's death, they deliberately try to synthesize feeling and love. Quickly, almost frantically, they touch and caress each other's faces, but their touching is a parody and by the next day they have closed themselves off again.

These two scenes—of Anna embracing Agnes, and of Karin and Maria touching like frightened kittens—are two of the greatest Bergman has ever created. The feeling in these scenes—I should say, the way they force us to feel—constitutes the meaning of this film. It has no abstract message; it communicates with us on a level of human feeling so deep that we are afraid to invent words for the things found there.

The camera is as uneasy as we are. It stays at rest mostly, but when it moves it doesn't always follow smooth, symmetrical progressions. It darts, it falls back, is stunned. It lingers on close-ups of faces with the impassivity of God. It continues to look when we want to turn away; it is not moved. Agnes lies thrown on her deathbed, her body shuddered by horrible, deep gasping breaths, as she fights for air, for life. The sisters turn away, and we want to, too. We know things are this bad—but we don't want to know. Bergman's camera stays and watches.

The movie is drenched in red. Bergman has written in his screenplay that he thinks of the inside of the human soul as a membranous red. Color can be so important; in *Two English Girls,* a movie about the absence of passion, Francois Truffaut kept red out of his compositions until the movie's one moment of unfeigned feeling, and then he filled his screen with red.

All of *Cries and Whispers* is occupied with passion—but the passion is inside, the characters can't get it out of themselves. None of them can, except Anna (Kari Sylwan). The film descends into a netherworld of the supernatural; the dead woman speaks (or is it only that they think they hear her?). She reaches out and grasps for Karin (or does Karin move the dead arms?—Bergman's camera doesn't let us see).

The movie, like all supernatural myths, like all legends and fables (and like all jokes—which are talismans to take the pain from truth) ends in a series of threes. The dead woman asks the living women to stay with her, to comfort her while she pauses within her dead body before moving into the great terrifying void. Karin will not. Maria will not. But Anna will, and makes pillows of her breasts for Agnes. Anna is the only one of them who remembers how to touch and love. And she is the only one who believes in God.

We saw her in the morning, praying. We learned that she had lost her little daughter, but is resigned to God's will. Is there a God in Bergman's film, or is there only Anna's faith? The film ends with a scene of astonishing, jarring affirmation: We see the four women some months earlier, drenched with the golden sun, and we hear Anna reading from Agnes's diary: "I feel a great gratitude to my life, which gives me so much." And takes it away.

Crimes and Misdemeanors ★ ★ ★ ★
PG-13, 107 m., 1989

Caroline Aaron (Barbara), Alan Alda (Lester), Woody Allen (Cliff Stern), Claire Bloom (Miriam Rosenthal), Mia Farrow (Halley Reed), Joanna Gleason (Wendy Stern), Anjelica Huston (Dolores Paley), Martin Landau (Judah Rosenthal), Jenny Nichols (Jenny), Jerry Orbach (Jack Rosenthal), Sam Waterston (Ben). Directed by Woody Allen and produced by Robert Greenhut. Screenplay by Allen.

Woody Allen's *Crimes and Misdemeanors* is a thriller about the dark nights of the soul. It shockingly answers the question most of us have asked ourselves from time to time: Could I live with the knowledge that I had murdered someone? Could I still get through the day and be close to my family and warm to my friends knowing that because of my own cruel selfishness, someone who had loved me was lying dead in the grave?

This is one of the central questions of human existence, and society is based on the fact that most of us are not willing to see ourselves as murderers. But in the world of this Woody Allen film, conventional piety is overturned, and we see into the soul of a human monster. Actually, he seems like a pretty nice guy.

He's an eye doctor with a thriving practice, he lives in a modern home on three acres in Connecticut, he has a loving wife and nice kids and lots of friends, and then he has a mistress who is going crazy and threatening to start making phone calls and destroy everything. This will not do. He has built up a comfortable and well-regulated life over the years and is respected in the community. He can't let some crazy woman bring a scandal crashing around his head.

Crimes and Misdemeanors tells his story with what Allen calls realism, and what others might call bleak irony. He also tells it with a great deal of humor. Who else but Woody Allen could make a movie in which virtue is punished, evildoing is rewarded, and there is a lot of laughter—even subversive laughter at the most shocking times?

Martin Landau stars in the film as the opthalmologist who has been faithful to his wife (Claire Bloom) for years—all except for a passionate recent affair with a flight attendant (Anjelica Huston). For a few blessed months he felt free and young again, and they walked on the beach, and he said things that sounded to her like plans for marriage. But he is incapable of leaving his wife, and when she finally realizes that she becomes enraged.

What can the doctor do? It's a *Fatal Attraction* situation, and she's sending letters to his wife (which he barely intercepts) and calling up from the gas station down the road threatening to come to his door and reveal everything. In desperation, the doctor turns to his brother (Jerry Orbach), who has Mafia connections. And the brother says that there's really no problem, because he can make one telephone call and the problem will go away.

Are we talking . . . murder? The doctor can barely bring himself to say the word. But his brother is more realistic and certainly more honest, and soon the doctor is forced to ask, and answer, basic questions about his own values. Allen uses flashbacks to establish the childhood of both brothers, who grew up in a religious Jewish family with a father who solemnly promised them that God saw everything, and that, even if He didn't, a good man could not live happily with an evil deed on his conscience.

The story of the doctor's dilemma takes place at the center of a large cast of characters—the movie resembles Allen's *Hannah and Her Sisters* in the way all of the lives become tangled. Among the other important characters are Allen himself, as a serious documentary filmmaker whose wife's brother (Alan Alda) is a shallow TV sitcom producer of great wealth and appalling vanity. Through his wife's intervention, Allen gets a job making a documentary about the Alda character—and then both men make a pass at the bright, attractive production assistant (Mia Farrow). Which will she choose? The dedicated documentarian or the powerful millionaire?

Another important character is a rabbi (Sam Waterston), who is going blind. The eye doctor treats him and then turns to him for moral guidance, and the rabbi, who is a good man, tells him what we would expect to hear. But the rabbi's blindness is a symbol for the dark undercurrent of *Crimes and Misdemeanors,* which seems to argue that God has abandoned men, and that we live here below on a darkling plain, lost in violence, selfishness, and moral confusion.

Crimes and Misdemeanors is not, properly speaking, a thriller, and yet it plays like one. In fact, it plays a little like those *film noir* classics of the 1940s, like *Double Indemnity,* in which a man thinks of himself as moral, but finds out otherwise. The movie generates the best kind of suspense, because it's not about what will happen to people, it's about what decisions they will reach. We have the same information they have. What would we do? How far would we go to protect our happiness and reputation? How selfish would we be? Is our comfort worth more than another person's life? Woody Allen does not evade this question, and his answer seems to be, yes, for some people. Anyone who reads the crime reports in the daily papers would be hard put to disagree with him.

Crimson Tide ★ ★ ★ ½
R, 116 m., 1995

Denzel Washington (Hunter), Gene Hackman (Ramsey), Matt Craven (Zimmer), George Dzundza (COB), Viggo Mortensen (Weps), James Gandolfini (Lt. Bobby Dougherty), Rocky Carroll (Lt. Westergaurd), Jaime P. Gomez (Ood Mahoney). Directed by Tony Scott and produced by Don Simpson and Jerry Bruckheimer. Screenplay by Michael Schiffer.

There's an early scene in *Crimson Tide* when the characters are playing a trivia game, remembering the stars of early submarine movies like *Run Silent, Run Deep*. It's clever, showing how the crew members of the U.S. nuclear submarine *Alabama* have formed many of their images of the silent service at the movies. It's also daring: This movie is inviting comparison with the classics, and although it doesn't mention *Das Boot* or *The Hunt for Red October*, it could have: This movie is in the same skillful tradition.

The tradition includes a strong commander, and the *Alabama* possesses a legend: Captain Ramsey (Gene Hackman), who trained under the legendary Admiral Hyman Rickover, father of the nuclear submarine, and is now nearing the end of his active duty. Ramsey, known for chewing up subordinates, is also famous for his little dog, a Jack Russell terrier that is allowed to lift its little leg wherever it pleases.

As the movie opens, the *Alabama* gets a new second in command: Hunter (Denzel Washington). In an early interview with Ramsey, the old-timer strikes a vaguely sinister note; Hackman is a master at seeming genial and friendly while masking deeper, darker thoughts. The sub sets out to sea, and during a discussion around the dinner table, Hunter makes the mistake of telling Ramsey, "In my humble opinion, in the nuclear world the true enemy is war itself."

These words will haunt him. Ramsey tests the younger man, and when a fire breaks out in the sub's galley, the captain chooses that moment to order an onboard drill. Hunter questions the decision, saying he would have attended to the fire first, before calling a drill. Ramsey says he saw the fire as an opportunity to test the ability of his men to function under chaotic conditions. And, he adds, while the junior officer is free to disagree, he should never do so in front of the men: "We're here to preserve democracy, not to practice it."

A coded message is received. Russian rebel troops have seized control of nuclear missile silos, and the *Alabama* is placed on full war alert. Its job, if it receives a verified command message, will be to fire its nuclear missiles at the land-based targets in a preemptive strike. Meanwhile, in an exchange of missiles with an enemy sub, the *Alabama*'s radio apparatus is temporarily disabled, but not before a confirmed message has been received ordering the sub to ready its missiles for firing.

Now deep silence reigns beneath the ocean. The sub, cut off from its chain of command, may be the only deterrent to a Russian nuclear attack. Should the captain seize the initiative and order a launch? He can do that only if his second-in-command agrees, and Hunter doesn't. That's the basic setup in *Crimson Tide*, an uncommonly intelligent dramatization about the choices, dangers, and duties of nuclear warfare.

The movie has the usual trappings of submarine adventure pictures: emergency flooding, near-hits, the danger of sinking below a safe depth. Director Tony Scott *(Top Gun)* handles these scenes with skill, and yet they're not at the heart of Michael Schiffer's screenplay. Instead, the movie develops along ideological lines, as Ramsey and Hunter—both absolutely convinced they're right—attempt to gain control of the submarine. Is the captain guilty of a procedural violation, or is his second guilty of mutiny?

Oddly enough, *Crimson Tide* develops into an actors' picture, not just an action movie. There are a lot of special effects, high-tech gadgets, and violent standoffs, yes, but the movie is really a battle between two wills. Hackman and Washington are wellmatched, and although my sympathies were with the Washington character (faced with the prospect of a billion deaths, it is best to err on the side of caution), I could understand the logic of the senior officer. Hackman's Ramsey is not a warmonger or a mad dog, but an officer so obsessed with following orders that even an incomplete one has a message, just for him.

In a large supporting cast, George Dzundza stands out as the COB (the Chief of the Boat), the officer who must side with Hunter or Ramsey, and who places proper procedure higher than his opinion of either man's position. His best scene comes as he monitors a depth gauge that shows the *Alabama* sinking to hull-crushing pressures. As it appears inevitable that the sub will be destroyed,

he makes an interesting actor's choice: Instead of allowing his voice to grow tense or exciting, he flattens it into a disinterested monotone of resignation. That works even better to underline the tension.

What's unique about *Crimson Tide* is that it doesn't offer clear-cut choices between good and evil. Hackman may be violating procedures, but perhaps he has good reasons. Washington, fearing to unleash war, may leave his country unprotected. Even the ending is intriguingly evenhanded. This is the rare kind of war movie that not only thrills people while they're watching it, but invites them to leave the theater actually discussing the issues.

Critters ★ ★ ★
PG-13, 97 m., 1986

Dee Wallace Stone (Helen), M. Emmet Walsh (Harv), Billy Green Bush (Jay Brown), Scott Grimes (Brad Brown), Nadine Van Der Velde (April Brown), Don Opper (Charlie McFadden), Terrence Mann (Johnny Steele). Directed by Stephen Herek and produced by Rupert Harvey. Screenplay by Herek and Domonic Muir.

If perfect fools can hold driver's licenses, why can't creatures from outer space be just as dumb? And if they *are* bounty hunters, why shouldn't they be trigger-happy—firing at everything that moves, like a television set, for example? We always assume that visitors from other worlds will be far more intelligent than we are, but maybe they'll just turn out to have faster means of intergalactic travel.

In the opening scenes of *Critters*, a spaceship is approaching a barren asteroid which has been converted into a prison. It carries on board several of the dreaded Cripes, who are furry little bowling balls with dozens of rows of sharp teeth. The Cripes escape, take over the ship, and land on earth. And bounty hunters follow them here, while the nasty little critters are terrorizing the countryside.

What this gives us is a truly ambitious ripoff of not one but four recent science-fiction movies: *Gremlins, E.T., The Terminator,* and *Starman*. We get the critters from the first and the hunters from the third, and from *Starman* the notion that an alien can assume the outward appearance of a human being. (That is a particularly attractive quality for an alien to have, especially in a low-budget picture, because then you can hire an actor and claim he is inhabited by an alien, and you can save a lot of money on special effects.) From *E.T.*, there is Dee Wallace Stone, who played Henry Thomas's mother in that film and is now the equally dubious and harried mother of young Scott Grimes, a plucky kid who goes into battle against the invaders.

The movie takes place in a small town and the surrounding countryside, where the vicious little furballs start attacking everything that moves. They have a lot of tricks at their command: They can eat you like a piranha, shoot darts at you from their foreheads, and curl up into a ball and roll away. That leads up to the big scene in the bowling alley, where we expect that someone's going to reach down and pick up a critter instead of a ball, but as it turns out, that scene contains other surprises.

We meet the folks in the area. There's the friendly farmer (Billy Green Bush), his wife (Stone), son (Grimes), and daughter (Nadine Van Der Velde). They live on a farm that gives the critters their first haven, and there's the obligatory scary scene where the father goes down in the basement with his flashlight to see what's making the noise.

Meanwhile, the local lawman (that dependably slimy character actor M. Emmet Walsh) notices that strange things are happening in his territory. Two strangers from out of town have turned up and started to blast everybody away, and dang if one of them doesn't look exactly like the local minister! The other one soon assumes the outward appearance of the village idiot.

All of these plot threads move inexorably toward the final showdown, but what's interesting is the way the movie refuses to be just a thriller. The director, Stephen Herek, likes to break the mood occasionally with a one-liner out of left field, and he gives the critters some of the funniest lines. What makes *Critters* more than a rip-off are its humor and its sense of style. This is a movie made by people who must have had fun making it.

Crocodile Dundee ★ ★
PG-13, 98 m., 1986

Paul Hogan (Mike Dundee), Linda Kozlowski (Sue Charlton), John Meillon (Wally), Michael Lombard (Sam Charlton), Mark Blum (Richard). Directed by Peter Faiman and produced by John Cornell. Screenplay by Hogan, Ken Shadie, and Cornell.

They made this kind of movie better in the 1930s, when audiences were more accus-tomed to the reliable old story line: Aggressive female newspaper reporter from New York tracks down legendary wilderness guide in Outback, is saved from crocodiles, falls in love, asks living legend to return with her to New York, there to meet her millionaire daddy and her fiancé, a wimp. Clark Gable and Carole Lombard could have made this movie. Maybe they did.

Crocodile Dundee knows the words to this story, but not the music. All of the clichés are in the right places, and most of the gags pay off, and there are moments of real amusement as the Australian cowboy wanders around Manhattan as a naive sightseer. The problem is, there's not one moment of chemistry between the two stars—Paul Hogan as "Crocodile" Dundee and Linda Kozlowski as the clever little rich girl. The movie feels curiously machine-made, as if they had all the right ingredients and simply forgot to add the animal magnetism.

The movie got a lot of attention because of Paul Hogan, a former truck driver who has become one of Australia's top TV stars, and is known over here for those Australian tourism commercials where he reminds us about who won the 1986 America's Cup. He's a lean, tanned, weathered man with a perpetual squint, and he looks right at home when he's stabbing crocodiles and strangling snakes. His co-star is not as well cast; Linda Kozlowski always looks a little too made up, a little too formal, to be able to really unwind and accept this sweaty folk hero. When she smiles at him, it's politely, not passionately. Maybe she's downwind.

The story begins with a New York newspaper sending her on assignment to interview Dundee, who allegedly lost a leg to a crocodile and then crawled for hundreds of miles through the Outback. She spends more money on this story than most newspapers earmark for a gubernatorial election. She hires a helicopter, pays a $2,500 fee to Dundee's partner, and later—after she brings the Croc back to New York—puts him in a $900-a-day suite at the Plaza. What she doesn't do is get the story.

The Manhattan scenes are the best, as Dundee scares off muggers, unmasks transvestites, hitches rides with mounted policemen, and sleeps on the floor of his hotel room. Many of the best scenes have the same whimsical quality as *The Gods Must Be Crazy*, in which a character with a truly direct and open mind is able to see right through the strange conventions of civilization.

What doesn't work is the love story. If we don't believe in the chemistry between Crocodile and the woman reporter, we certainly don't believe her fiancé, a simpering and supercilious jerk who tries to pull the old foreign language menu trick on the guy from the sticks. The ending of the movie (which I would not dream of revealing) involves a love scene on a subway platform. If these were two lovers we really cared about, the scene, as written, could have had the impact of that moment in *An Officer and a Gentleman* where Richard Gere carries Debra Winger off the factory floor. As it's acted in this movie, alas, the scene is so unconvincing that the lovers are upstaged by the other people on the train platform.

Cronos ★ ★ ★
NO MPAA RATING, 92 m., 1994

Federico Luppi (Jesus Gris), Ron Perlman (Angel), Claudio Brook (Dieter), Margarita Isabel (Mercedes), Tamara Shanath (Aurora), Daniel G. Cacho (Tito). Directed by Guillermo del Toro and produced by Bertha Navarro and Arthur Gorson. Screenplay by del Toro.

Cronos begins with the legend of a fourteenth-century Spanish alchemist who invents a device both elegant and horrifying: a small golden machine, looking like a scarab beetle from Fabergé, which unfolds its beautiful claws and sinks them into the flesh of its user, injecting a substance that will impart immortality. Centuries later, we learn, a Mexican earthquake shakes down the building where the alchemist . . . was still alive.

The body of the alchemist is found dead in the rubble, its heart pierced by a stake, of course. The Cronos Device, hidden inside an ancient wooden statue of an archangel, is purchased by an antique dealer named Jesus Gris (Federico Luppi), who finds the diabolical toy, winds it up, and watches with terror as it attaches itself to his skin and makes him, he later discovers, immortal.

This is the stuff of classic horror films, and *Cronos*, written and directed by a twenty-nine-year-old Mexican named Guillermo del Toro, combines it with a colorful Latin magic realism. There is also an undercurrent of fatalism and sadness in the film, flowing from the relationship of the old antique dealer and his granddaughter Aurora (Tamara Shanath), who loves the old man even after an embalmer makes some gruesome alterations on his undead body.

Elsewhere in the city, a dying industrialist

(Claudio Brook, favorite Mexican actor of Luis Buñuel) obtains the journal of the ancient Spanish alchemist and learns of the Cronos Device. He imports his American nephew (Ron Perlman, of TV's "Beauty and the Beast") to track down and obtain the device, setting the plot into motion. Perlman brings a comic element into the film, whistling "We Wish You a Merry Christmas" in a way that for the first time finds sinister undertones in the tune.

But *Cronos* is not really about plot. It is about character. One of the curious things about immortality in fiction is that it almost always seems to be possessed by those unworthy of it. The typical immortal is not a young and cheerful person who wishes to spend eternity doing good, but an old, embittered miser who wants to live long enough to see compound interest make him a billionaire. There is always something shameful, in these stories, about being unwilling to die when your time has come.

Those dark feelings are at the heart of del Toro's story, made more poignant because the antique dealer is a good man who has had immortality with all of its inconveniences thrust upon him, while the industrialist is a cadaverous monster, and the nephew is a goon. The heart of the story is the love that persists between the little granddaughter and the immortal old man, after everything begins to go horribly wrong.

All good horror movies have a sense of humor, usually generated by the tension between their terrible subjects and the banality of everyday life (see the embalming scene for a demonstration). What Latin horror films also have is an undercurrent of religiosity: The characters, fully convinced there is a hell, may have excellent reasons for not wanting to go there. The imagery is also enriched by an older, church-saturated culture, and for all its absurdity *Cronos* generates a real moral conviction. If, as religion teaches us, the purpose of this world is to prepare for the next, then what greater punishment could there be, really, than to be stranded on the near shore?

Crooklyn ★ ★ ★ ½
PG-13, 132 m., 1994

Alfre Woodard (Carolyn), Delroy Lindo (Woody), David Patrick Kelly (Tony Eyes), Zelda Harris (Troy), Carlton Williams (Clinton), Sharif Rashid (Wendell), Tse-Mach Washington (Joseph), Spike Lee (Snuffy). Directed and produced by Spike Lee. Screenplay by Joie Susannah Lee, Cinque Lee, and Spike Lee.

Spike Lee's *Crooklyn* is a memory of growing up in Brooklyn in the early 1970s, a time that now seems like a golden age before crack, guns, and gangs ruled the inner-city streets. It tells the story of the Carmichaels, a family with four boys and a girl, who live in a brownstone on a street where everybody knows everybody else, and who have their problems, just like everybody else, but also possess a lot of life and love.

The early scenes in the film plunge into the middle of family life, and it's only gradually that we realize the story is focusing on Troy (Zelda Harris), the young daughter in the family. Her father, Woody (Delroy Lindo), is a musician who once made good money playing pop music but is now concentrating on more serious composition, with no income. Her mother, Carolyn (Alfre Woodard), is a high school teacher whose struggles to make ends meet lead to family arguments. And her brothers are a rambunctious bunch who can turn the house upside down.

Crooklyn was written by Lee with his sister, Joie Susannah Lee, and his brother, Cinque Lee. They say it isn't literal autobiography, but was "inspired" by their memories. Some of those memories have the specificity of real life, however, including a showdown between Carolyn and a son who *will not* clean up his plate of black-eyed peas. And there are family quarrels, as when Carolyn temporarily throws Woody out of the house for bouncing checks and not contributing to the family income. One particularly poignant scene has the oldest son, Clinton (Carlton Williams), deciding whether to attend his father's all-important solo piano recital, or use his ticket to the Knicks' all-important playoff game. He goes to the game, but when he comes home the Knicks' victory somehow doesn't seem as important as it should.

Spike Lee is one of the few directors willing to try experimental visual approaches in his films, and some viewers may be confused by a tactic he uses in a sequence where Troy goes south to Virginia to spend summer vacation with her more affluent relatives. Their world, of split-level suburban homes with attached garages, surrounded by green lawns, seems utterly alien to her as a city girl.

Lee finds the visual equivalent for that alienation by filming the southern scenes in a squeezed format; the effect is the same as when a wide-screen movie is projected without the correct lens. Some viewers may think the projectionist has made a mistake. But the device is deliberate, and although it's distracting, it is also interesting, showing that every detail of the relatives' lives—from their furniture to their snippy little dog—could be from Mars as far as Troy is concerned.

One of the undercurrents of *Crooklyn* is that trouble was all around the Carmichaels in the early 1970s, but it could still be managed. A neighbor (David Patrick Kelly) is an eccentric recluse who never seems to clean his apartment. The kids retaliate by dumping garbage on his stoop. Then everybody shouts at one another. Today, we reflect, the neighbor might draw a gun.

In another wonderfully observed scene, Troy goes to the local store with a nine-year-old friend, who is going to teach her to shoplift. She gets caught with a bag of potato chips, and gets a lecture from the store owner that will, I believe, forever cure her of shoplifting. The message here may be that many growing children do at one time or another succumb to peer pressure and experiment with things like shoplifting, but that the community, as well as the parents, can teach them it is wrong. Today, I'm afraid, it would be treated as a bigger deal, perhaps with less happy results.

Although the Lees say the movie should not be read as straight autobiography, some of the scenes have the directness and pain of real memory. There's a night, for example, when the mother, exhausted and worried, tells the kids to clean up the kitchen before they go to bed. They do not, and in the middle of the night, in a rage, she awakens them and marches them downstairs. She has obviously reached some kind of a breaking point. The children are frightened and confused, and the movie doesn't process their feelings into some kind of neat package; when things like that happen, they hurt, and are remembered. Later in the film, we discover some of the things that might have been on Carolyn's mind.

Lee's choice of actors is a complete success. The children seem like siblings, and interact in a natural, habituated way. Alfre Woodard, as Carolyn, finds the right balance between wife, mother, and overtaxed human being. She makes the character into a good person without ever laying it on too thick. Delroy Lindo is a surprise as the father. He played West Indian Archie, the Harlem gambling kingpin, in Lee's *Malcolm X,* and that was a brilliant performance—

but nothing in it suggested the patience, the sensitivity, and the depth he brings to Woody Carmichael. There are scenes late in the film where Woody's tact and empathy have to fill enormous voids, and they do.

Crooklyn is not a neat package with a tidy payoff at the end. It contains the messiness of life. As it ends, the children are still children, and whatever life holds for them is still ahead. Most movies about children insist on arriving at a conclusion, when childhood is a beginning. Someday Spike Lee may make a movie about how he went to NYU and became a filmmaker, or Joie Susannah Lee (who wants to direct) will tell the story of her teen-age years. Then these beginnings will be enriched as we know more of the story.

For now, we can know that in a house something like this brownstone, in a family something like the Carmichaels, some remarkable children grew up. And we can see in the movie that their society *let* them grow up. Lee's wonderful opening title sequence shows the children's street games that flourished in Brooklyn in the 1970s. Today, he says, those games have died, and he had to teach them to the actors who played the children. They have died because the kids in comparable neighborhoods today are afraid to go outside and play in the streets. *Crooklyn* is not in any way an angry film. But thinking about the difference between its world and ours can make you angry, and I think that was one of Lee's purposes here.

Crossroads ★ ★ ★ ½
R, 98 m., 1985

Ralph Macchio (Eugene Martone), Joe Seneca (Willie Brown), Jami Gertz (Frances), Joe Morton (Scratch's Assistant), Robert Judd (Scratch), Harry Carey, Jr. (Bartender). Directed by Walter Hill and produced by Mark Carliner. Screenplay by John Fusco.

Crossroads borrows so freely and is a reminder of so many other movies that it's a little startling, at the end, to realize how effective the movie is and how original it manages to feel despite all the plunderings. The movie stars Ralph Macchio as a bright teenager who studied classical guitar at Juilliard and worships as his heroes the great old blues musicians of the 1930s and 1940s. One day he tracks down a survivor of that era, a harmonica player named Willie Brown (Joe Seneca) in a nursing home. Macchio helps him escape, and they hit the road, hoboing

their way down South to a crossroads where Seneca once made a deal with the devil.

With the devil? You bet. *Crossroads* is a cheerful cross between a slice of life and a supernatural fable. And at the end, it's up to the kid to pick up his guitar and outplay the devil's man, to save Seneca's soul. This story is a combination of no less than two reliable genres. It borrows, obviously, from Macchio's 1984 *The Karate Kid,* which was also the story of a young man's apprenticeship with an older master. It also borrows from the countless movies in which everything depends on who wins the big fight, match, game, or duel in the last scene. The notion of the showdown with the devil may have been suggested by the country song "Devil Went Down to Georgia."

And yet the remarkable thing is how fresh all this material seems, and how entertaining it is. Just when I'm ready to despair of a movie coming up with a fresh plot, a movie like *Crossroads* comes along to remind me that acting, writing, and direction can redeem any plot, and make any story new. The foundation for *Crossroads* is the relationship between the boy and the old man, and here we have two performances that are well suited to one another. Macchio, once again, as in *The Karate Kid,* has an unstudied, natural charm. A lot of young actors seem to take themselves seriously, but not many have Macchio's gift of seeming to take other things seriously. We really believe, in this movie, that he is a fanatic about the blues, and has read all the books and listened to all the records.

Seneca does a terrific job as a rock-solid, conniving, no-nonsense old man who doesn't take this kid seriously at first, and uses him as a way to get out of the nursing home and back down South to the crossroads, where he has a longstanding rendezvous. The kid knows that Willie was a partner of the legendary blues musician Robert Johnson and he makes a deal with the old man. He'll help him return to that crossroads if the old man will teach him a lost Johnson song.

Along the way, the two men pick up a third partner, a tough young runaway named Frances (Jami Gertz), and there is a brief, sweet romance between the two young people before she leaves one morning, perhaps because it is better for the old man and the young one to move on toward their mutual destiny.

Gertz is a newcomer: this was her second major movie in 1985, after a somewhat thankless role in *Quicksilver,* in which she worked for a bicycle messenger service. She's just

right for this movie, with the toughness required by the character, and yet with the tenderness and the romantic notes that remind us that this is really a myth. Another good performance in the movie is by Joe Morton, who played *The Brother from Another Planet* and this time is the devil's assistant, sinister and ingratiating.

The film was directed by Walter Hill, who specializes in myths, in movie characters who seem to represent something greater than themselves. Detailed character studies are not his strong point; he makes movies like *The Warriors, 48 HRS,* and *Streets of Fire,* in which the characters seem made out of the stuff of legend. In *48 HRS,* though, he also found the human qualities in the Nick Nolte and Eddie Murphy characters, and he does that again this time, making Seneca and Macchio so individual, so particular, that we aren't always thinking that this movie is really about an old man and a boy and the devil.

A word about the music. Ry Cooder did most of the sound track, drawing from many blues scores, and the movie is wonderful to listen to: confident and sly and not all tricked up for Hollywood. The closing scene, the dueling guitars, presents a challenge that perhaps no film composer could quite solve (what's the right approach to music as a weapon?), but somehow Cooder actually does pull off the final showdown.

The Crow ★ ★ ★ ½
R, 102 m., 1994

Brandon Lee (Eric), Ernie Hudson (Albrecht), Michael Wincott (Top Dollar), David Patrick Kelly (T-Bird), Angel David (Skank), Rochelle Davis (Sarah), Bai Ling (Myca), Lawrence Mason (Tin Tin). Directed by Alex Proyas and produced by Edward R. Pressman and Jeff Most. Screenplay by David J. Schow and John Shirley.

The Crow is, of course, the movie Brandon Lee was making when he was accidentally shot dead during the filming of a scene. It is not without irony that the story involves a hero who returns from the dead—just as, in a sense, Lee did with the release of this film. It is a stunning work of visual style—the best version of a comic book universe I've seen—and Brandon Lee clearly demonstrates in it that he might have become an action star, had he lived.

The story begins with a resurrection from the dead. A rock star named Eric Draven (Lee) is murdered, along with his fiancée, on the eve of their wedding. His soul is escorted to the next world (according to the narration) by a crow; but when a spirit is unhappy there because of unsettled business on Earth, sometimes the crow will bring him back again. And so a year later, on Halloween Eve, Eric reappears on Earth, vowing vengeance on those who committed the murders—and the evil kingpin who ordered them.

That's about all there is to the story. Flashbacks re-create the original murder, and then Eric, led by the crow, tracks the mean, rainy, midnight streets on his lonely quest. He has fashioned for himself some death's-head makeup, and since he is already dead, of course bullets cannot harm him (except sometimes—which is always the catch in comic book stories).

The story exists as an excuse for the production values of the film, which are superb. The director, Alex Proyas, and his technical team have created a world that will remind you of *Blade Runner*'s forlorn urban wasteland, and of *Batman*'s Gothic extravagances, yet this world is grungier and more forbidding than either. It's not often that movies can use miniatures and special effects and sets and visual tricks to create a convincing place, rather than just a series of obvious sets. But *The Crow* does.

The visual style, by cinematographer Dariusz Wolski, obviously owes a great deal to the study of comic books (or "graphic novels," as they like to be called). The camera swoops high above the city, or dips low for extreme-angle shots. Shadows cast fearsome daggers into the light. Buildings are exaggerated in their architectural details, until they seem a shriek of ornamentation. The superhero comic books of the 1940s, especially *Batman*, grew up at the same time as *film noir*, and borrowed some of the same visual language. But comic books were not simply drawn versions of *film noir;* for one thing, the films tended to use their extreme-angle shots for atmosphere and storytelling, and would hold them for a time, while comics are meant to be read quickly, and give the equivalent of cinematic quick-cutting. *The Crow*, with its fast pace and its countless camera setups, evokes comics much more than the more good-looking but more leisurely *Batman* movies. It also reflects a bleak modern sensibility, with little room for *Batman*'s comic villains.

The actors are adapted in appearance to this graphic *noir* vision; their appearances are as exaggerated as the shots they appear in. For example: The bosoms of women in comic books always seem improbably perfect but sketched in—drawn by a pen, not made of flesh—and the villainess Myca (Bai Ling) in this story has the same look. As the half-sister of the villain, she represents a drawn image, not a person, and so do many of the other characters, including a thin, angular Brandon Lee behind his makeup.

The sound track is wall-to-wall with heavy metal music (by the Cure, Stone Temple Pilots, Violent Femmes, Pantera, Nine Inch Nails, etc.). At times the film looks like a violent music video, all image and action,no content. If it had developed more story and characterization, however, it might not have had quite the same success in evoking a world where the bizarre reality, not the story, is the point.

The scene in which Brandon Lee was accidentally shot is not in the film, but the fact of his death cannot help provide a melancholy subtext to everything he does on screen, and to all of his speeches about death and revenge. It is a sad irony that this film is not only the best thing he accomplished, but is actually more of a screen achievement than any of the films of his father, Bruce Lee. Both careers seemed cut short just as early potential was being realized. There was talk of shelving *The Crow*, but I'm glad they didn't. At least what Brandon Lee accomplished—in a film that looks to have been hard, dedicated labor—has been preserved.

Crumb ★ ★ ★ ★
R, 119 m., 1995
(See related Film Clip, p. 892.)

`NEW`

Directed by Terry Zwigoff and produced by Lynn O'Donnell and Zwigoff.

People who have been damaged by life can make the most amazing adjustments in order to survive and find peace. Sometimes it is a toss-up whether to call them mad, or courageous. Consider the case of R. Crumb. He was the most famous comics artist of the 1960s, whose images like "Keep on Truckin'" and "Fritz the Cat" and his cover for the Janis Joplin "Cheap Thrills" album helped to fix the visual look of the decade. He was also a person hanging onto sanity by his fingernails, and it is apparently true that his art saved his life.

Crumb, which is one of the most remarkable and haunting documentaries ever made, tells the story of Robert Crumb, his brothers Max and Charles, and an American childhood which looks normal in the old family photographs but concealed deep wounds and secrets. It is the kind of film that you watch in disbelief, as layer after layer is peeled away and you begin to understand the strategies that have kept Crumb alive and made him successful, when one of his brothers became a recluse in an upstairs bedroom and the other passes his time quite literally sitting on a bed of nails.

Movies like this do not usually get made because the people who have lives like this usually are not willing to reveal them. *Crumb* was directed by Terry Zwigoff, who had two advantages: He had known Crumb well for many years, and he was himself so unhappy and suicidal during the making of the film that in a sense Crumb let him do it as a favor.

Of Crumb's importance and reputation there is not much doubt. His original illustrations and the first editions of his 1960s and 1970s underground comic books command high prices. His new work is shown in galleries, and is in important collections. No less an authority that Robert Hughes, the art critic of *Time* magazine, appears in *Crumb* to declare him "the Brueghel of the last half of the twentieth century."

But *Crumb* is not really about the art, although it will cause you to look at his familiar images with a new eye. It is about the artist, who grew up in a dysfunctional family led by a father who was an overbearing tyrant—a depressive, sadistic bully who, according to this film, beat his sons and lost few opportunities to demean them. (There were also two sisters, who declined to participate in the film.)

All three brothers retreated into fantasies in an attempt to cope with their home life. It was Charles, the oldest, who first started to draw comic strips, and then Robert began to copy him. The brothers seem to have had strong fantasy relationships with comic characters; Charles began to pretend he was Long John Silver. And while it is one thing to learn that Robert masturbated while looking at comics, especially his own, it is another to learn that his prime erotic fixation was with Bugs Bunny.

Many of the people in Crumb's life talk with great frankness about him, including his brothers, his mother, his first wife, Dana (who says he began to develop a "new vision" in 1966 after experimenting with drugs), and his present wife, Aline Kominsky, who recounts bizarre details of his lifestyle with acceptance and understanding. We learn most from Robert himself, however.

He was intensely unhappy in high school, nursed deep grudges against his contemporaries, and uses high school enemies as the models for many of the unattractive caricatures in his work. It is surprising to learn how closely autobiographical some of his drawings are; in his comics men are fixated by callipygian women, and dream of riding them piggy-back, and then we see Robert doing the same thing at a gallery opening. He pages through the faces in a high school yearbook, and then we see their look-alikes in his cartoons.

If Robert was unhappy in high school, Charles found it an ordeal from which he never really recovered. In a trip to the family home, occupied by Charles and his mother, we visit the upstairs room that he rarely left, and with Robert essentially acting as the interviewer, he remembers, "I was good-looking, but there was something wrong with my personality; I was the most unpopular kid in school." On a visit to Max, we find him living as a monk, drawing a long linen tape through his body to clean his intestines, and showing recent oil paintings of considerable skill (he still has his mail-order test from the Famous Artists School).

Mrs. Crumb, interviewed while sprawled on a sofa and worrying darkly about the window shades, seems complacent about the fact that Charles never leaves the house: "At least he's not out taking illegal drugs or making some woman miserable."

Zwigoff shows us details of many Crumb comic strips which are intensely violent, sadistic, and hateful toward women. And he interviews such voices of sanity as Dierdre English, former editor of *Mother Jones,* who finds his work pornographic—"an arrested juvenile vision." So it is, and her voice expresses not Puritanism but concern and simple observation. Yet as I left the film I felt that if anyone had earned the right to express Crumb's vision, it was Crumb, since his art is so clearly a coping mechanism that has allowed him to survive, and deal with his pain. *Crumb* is a film that gives new meaning to the notion of art as therapy.

Cry-Baby ★ ★ ★
PG-13, 85 m., 1990

Johnny Depp (Cry-Baby), Amy Locane (Allison), Susan Tyrrell (Ramona), Polly Bergen (Mrs. Vernon-Williams), Iggy Pop (Belvedere), Ricki Lake (Pepper), Traci Lords (Wanda), Kim McGuire (Hatchet-Face). Directed by John Waters and produced by Rachel Talalay. Screenplay by Waters.

It is only now that I am in a condition to appreciate the 1950s. At the time, I was too cynical. I read *Mad* magazine and listened to Stan Freberg and Bob & Ray, and viewed all manifestations of 1950s teen-age culture with the superiority of one who had read *Look Homeward, Angel* and knew, even then, that you could not go home again.

Now things are different. Battered and weary after the craziness of the 1960s, the self-righteousness of the 1970s, and the greed of the 1980s, I want to go home again, oh, so desperately—home to that land of drive-in restaurants and Chevy Bel-Airs, making out and rock 'n' roll and drag races and Studebakers, Elvis and James Dean and black leather jackets. Not that I ever owned a black leather jacket. Even today, I do not have the nerve. Black leather suggests a degree of badness I could never aspire to.

Feelings like these are what John Waters's *Cry-Baby* is about. The movie takes place in 1954 in Baltimore, at the dawn of rock 'n' roll (one is reminded of the opening scenes of *2001,* at the dawn of man, an event less remarked at the time). The teen-age culture is divided into three camps: the drapes, the squares, and the nerds. The drapes slick their hair in ducktails and wear black leather jackets and are proud to be juvenile delinquents. The squares wear crew cuts and want to go to college. The nerds are not made much of in *Cry-Baby,* but in my memory they were the kids who wore slide rules in their pockets and collected science-fiction magazines and grew up, one suspects, to be John Waters.

The movie tells the story of Cry-Baby himself, played by teen idol Johnny Depp as a juvenile delinquent who forever has a tear sliding halfway down his cheek, a reminder of a grief he will live with forever, a teen-age tragedy that has left its mark on his soul, a lost romance. Into his life comes Allison (Amy Locane), the good girl who has a crush on Cry-Baby and feels strange stirrings in her loins from the promise that he is as bad as they say. The movie's bad guy is the good guy, Baldwin (Stephen Mailer), who loves Allison in the right way, which is to say he loves her so boringly he might as well not love her at all.

The movie's very large cast (large enough to accommodate Polly Bergen and Traci Lords, David Nelson and Iggy Pop) includes Cry-Baby's grandparents (Iggy Pop and Susan Tyrrell), a rockabilly family that lives on the wrong side of the tracks and includes musicians who seem to be on the edge of inventing rock 'n' roll, if someone does not invent it for them. It also includes various parents, schoolmates, local tramps and sluts, and the straight-arrow types without which the 1950s would have lost their point of reference.

If there is one constant in recent social history, it is that we feel nostalgia for yesterday's teen-age badness even while we fear today's. As I was reading an alarmist newsweekly cover story on rap music recently, I found myself wishing that the hysterical old maids who wrote it could have been taken first to see *Cry-Baby* so that they could gain some insight into themselves.

In every generation teen-agers find a way to express themselves and annoy adults. And the adults of that generation find in this teen-age behavior alarming signs of the collapse of civilization as they know it. *Cry-Baby,* which is a good many things (including a passable imitation of a 1950s teen-age exploitation movie), is above all a reminder of that process. Today's teen-agers will grow up to be tomorrow's adults, and yet in every generation teen-agers and adults seem to have as little knowledge of that ancient fact as the caterpillar has of the butterfly. It is an additional irony that in human culture we have learned little from the insects, and the butterflies turn into the worms.

Cry Freedom ★ ★ ½
PG, 154 m., 1987

Kevin Kline (Donald Woods), Penelope Wilton (Wendy Woods), Denzel Washington (Steve Biko), John Thaw (Kruger), Sophie Mgcina (Evalina), Joseph Marcell (Moses). Directed and produced by Richard Attenborough. Screenplay by John Briley.

Cry Freedom begins with the story of a friendship between a white liberal South African editor and an idealistic young black leader who later dies at the hands of the South African police. But the black leader is dead and buried by the movie's halfway point, and the rest of the story centers on the editor's desire to escape South Africa and publish a book.

You know there is something wrong with the premise of this movie when you see that the actress who plays the editor's wife is billed above the actor who plays Biko. This movie promises to be an honest account of the turmoil in South Africa, but turns into a routine cliff-hanger about the editor's flight across the border. It's sort of a liberal yuppie version of that Disney movie where the brave East German family builds a hot-air balloon and floats to freedom. The problem with this movie is similar to the historic dilemma in South Africa: Whites occupy the foreground and establish the terms of the discussion while the eighty percent non-white majority remains a shadowy, half-seen presence in the background.

Yet *Cry Freedom* is a sincere and valuable movie, and despite my fundamental reservations about it, I think it probably should be seen. Although everybody has heard about apartheid, and South Africa remains a favorite subject of campus protest, few people have an accurate mental picture of what the country actually looks like and feels like. It is a place, not an issue, and *Cry Freedom* helps to visualize it. The movie was mostly shot across the border in Zimbabwe, the former nation of Southern Rhodesia, which serves as an adequate stand-in; we see the manicured lawns of the whites, who seem to live in country club suburbs, and the jerry-built "townships" of the blacks, and we sense the institutional racism of a system where black maids call their employers "master," and even white liberals accept that without a blink.

The film begins with the story of Donald Woods, editor of the *East London* (South Africa) *Daily Dispatch,* and Steve Biko, a young black leader who has founded a school and a clinic for his people, and continues to hold out hope that blacks and whites can work together to change South Africa. In the more naive days of the 1960s and 1970s, Biko's politics are seen as "black supremacy," and Woods writes sanctimonious editorials describing Biko as a black racist. Through an emissary, Biko arranges to meet Woods, and eventually the two men become friends and Woods sees black life in South Africa at first hand (something few white South Africans have done).

Although Biko is played with quiet power by Academy Award-nominee Denzel Washington, he is seen primarily through the eyes of Woods (Kevin Kline). There aren't many scenes in which we see Biko without Woods, and fewer still in which his friendship with Woods isn't the underlying subject of the scene. No real attempt is made to show daily life in Biko's world; although we move into the Woods home, meet his wife, children, maid, and dog, and share his daily routine,

there is no similar attempt to portray Biko's daily reality.

There is a reason for that. *Cry Freedom* is not about Steve Biko. It is Donald Woods's story from beginning to end, describing how he met Biko, how his thinking was changed by the man, how he actually witnessed black life at first hand (by patronizing a black speakeasy in a township and having a few drinks), and how, after he was placed under house arrest by the South African government, he engineered the escape from South Africa. The story has a happy ending: Donald Woods and his family made it safely to England, where he was able to publish two books about his experience. (The bad news is that Steve Biko was killed.)

For the first half of this movie, I was able to suspend judgment. Interesting things were happening, the performances were good, and it is always absorbing to see how other people live. Most of the second half of the movie, alas, is taken up with routine cloak-and-dagger stuff, including Woods's masquerade as a Catholic priest, his phony passport, and his attempt to fool South African border officials. These scenes could have been recycled out of any thriller from any country in any time, right down to the ominous long shots of the men patroling the border bridge, and the tense moment when the guard's eyes flick up and down from the passport photo.

Cry Freedom is not really a story of today's South Africa, and it is not really the story of a black leader who tried to change it. Like *All the President's Men,* it's essentially the story of heroic, glamorous journalism. Remember *Ace in the Hole,* that Kirk Douglas movie where the man was trapped in the cave, and Douglas played the ambitious reporter who prolonged the man's imprisonment so he could make his reputation by covering the story? I'm not saying the Donald Woods story is a parallel. But somehow the comparison did arise in my mind.

The Crying Game ★ ★ ★ ★
R, 108 m., 1992

Stephen Rea (Fergus), Jaye Davidson (Dil), Forest Whitaker (Jody), Miranda Richardson (Jude), Adrian Dunbar (Maguire), Breffini McKenna (Tinker), Joe Savino (Eddie). Directed by Neil Jordan and produced by Stephen Woolley. Screenplay by Jordan.

Some movies keep you guessing. Some movies make you care. Once in a long while a

movie comes along that does both things at the same time. It's not easy. Neil Jordan's *The Crying Game* keeps us involved and committed through one plot twist after another. It was one of the best films of 1992.

Jordan's wonderful film does what Hitchcock's *Psycho,* a very different film, also did: It involves us deeply in its story, and then it reveals that the story is really about something else altogether. We may have been fooled, but so was the hero, and as the plot reveals itself we find ourselves identifying more and more with him. The movie doesn't make it easy; we have to follow him through a crisis of the heart, but the journey is worth it.

The movie opens in Northern Ireland, where a British soldier (Forest Whitaker) is kidnapped by the IRA. In a secluded forest hideout, he is guarded by a team including Fergus (Stephen Rea), who has become a committed terrorist and yet is still a person with kindness in his soul. The soldier may be executed if the British government doesn't release IRA prisoners. Meanwhile, he must be guarded, and as Fergus spends a long night with him, they get to know and even like one another. The soldier shows Fergus a snapshot of his girlfriend, back in London, and asks him to look her up someday—if, as the soldier suspects, he is going to die soon.

This is a version of the classic Irish short story *A Guest of the Nation,* by Frank O'Connor, in which IRA men in the 1920s make the mistake of becoming friendly with the man they will have to kill. But the movie resolves this dilemma with an unexpected development. And then, the next time we see Fergus, he is in London, under a new name, working as a laborer on a construction site.

He still has the snapshot. He goes looking for the soldier's girlfriend, and finds her working in a beauty salon. On an impulse he goes in to get his hair cut. After work she goes to a nearby pub. They begin a conversation, using the bartender as a middle man in one of the many unexpected narrative touches in an entirely original film. The girlfriend, named Dil (Jaye Davidson), is an original, too, with a delightful dry way of understating herself, of keeping her cool while seeming amused at the same time. She reminds us there is such a thing as verbal style; too much modern movie dialogue is flat and plot-driven.

Fergus and Dil are attracted to one another. But there are fundamental unacknowledged deceptions between them—not least, the fact that Fergus is the man who shares responsibility for the boyfriend's death. The most fascinating passages in the film follow the development of their relationship, which becomes an emotional fencing match as it survives one revelation after another. Then the IRA tracks Fergus to his hiding place, and has another job for him to do.

The peculiar thing about *The Crying Game* is that this story outline, while true, hardly suggests the actual content of this film. It is much more complex and labyrinthine—both in terms of simple plotting, and in terms of the matters of the heart that follow. Most movie love stories begin as a given; we know from the first frame who will be together in the last. Here, there are times when we know nothing, and times when we know less than that. Yet because we care about the characters—we can't help liking them—it's surprising, how the love story transcends all of the plot turns to take on an importance of its own.

One of the keys to the movie is the casting. The ironic, vulnerable Dil is a real original, a person who arrives on the screen not as a writer's notion but with a convincing, engaging personality. Stephen Rea, as Fergus, is an essentially good person who has gotten involved in a life that requires him to be violent and ruthless. He doesn't have much heart for it; maybe Dil has deeper resources. And Miranda Richardson has a key role as an IRA terrorist who toys with Fergus, early and late, confusing sexual power with political principles.

Neil Jordan first came to view as the writer-director of *Mona Lisa* (1987), with Bob Hoskins as the chauffeur who has a love-hate relationship with a prostitute (Cathy Tyson). His films since then have been widely varied, from the odd supernatural comedy *High Spirits* to last year's winsome fable *The Miracle*, which many liked more than I did. Now comes *The Crying Game*, one of a very few films that want to do something unexpected and challenging, and succeed even beyond their ambitions.

A Cry in the Dark ★ ★ ★
PG-13, 120 m., 1988

Meryl Streep (Lindy Chamberlain), Sam Neill (Michael Chamberlain), Charles "Bud" Tingwell (Muirhead), Bruce Myles (Parker), Dennis Miller (Sturgess), Neil Fitzpatrick (Phillips). Directed by Fred Schepisi and produced by Veriuty Lambert. Screenplay by Robert Caswell and Schepisi.

I had an argument about capital punishment with some friends, and I wish I could have taken them to see this movie. I was against the death penalty in principle, of course, but what really bothered me was the thought that a convicted person could be put to death on the basis of circumstantial evidence. There's just too much that can go wrong—as *A Cry in the Dark* and another 1988 movie, *The Thin Blue Line*, both demonstrate.

A Cry in the Dark takes place in Australia, and is based on the famous recent case of Lindy Chamberlain, the mother who said her baby daughter had been dragged away and killed by one of the wild Australian dogs named dingoes. No one else saw the tragic event take place, and the initial rush of sympathy for the parents was replaced, after a few weeks, by a malicious whispering campaign.

Did Lindy Chamberlain in fact murder her own baby and only then blame the dogs? The evidence against her began to pile up. A mark on a cloth looked like her bloody handprint. Blood was found sprayed all over the underside of the dashboard on the family car. A dingo was not big enough to carry away a human baby. Worst of all, Lindy Chamberlain did not seem sufficiently distraught by the death. Charges were eventually filed against her, she was found guilty and sentenced to life in prison, and she served three and a half years behind bars—even giving birth to another child there—before she was released. An appeals court quashed her conviction on September 15, 1988, declaring it a miscarriage of justice.

Why was Mrs. Chamberlain compelled to maintain her composure—even an icy facade—in press interviews and on TV? Why didn't she weep for her baby? There is the implication in *A Cry in the Dark* that if Lindy had behaved "correctly" in the media, the investigation that led to her conviction might never have been carried forward. In trying to help us understand Mrs. Chamberlain, Meryl Streep, the star of the movie, faces the formidable challenge of making an unlikable woman seem sympathetic. It appears that Mrs. Chamberlain was not naturally prone to outbursts of emotion in public. She kept things bottled up. After she was charged with murdering her child, anger took over, filling her with a deep bitterness that was evident in her face and voice.

And there was another matter, the matter of the religious beliefs of Lindy and Michael Chamberlain (who is solidly played by Sam Neill). They were Seventh-day Adventists in a country where that religion is in a small minority and widely misunderstood. While they spoke of reconciling themselves to the will of God, the public maliciously whispered that she had sacrificed her child in some sort of cult ceremony—an event that is unthinkable in terms of the Adventist religion. Whatever she did, she and her husband were religious, emotional, and social outsiders, and the press and the law were after them like a pack of dingoes.

A Cry in the Dark takes the time to marshal the case against Lindy Chamberlain, and the time to destroy it. The blood under the dashboard proved to be rust-proofing. Dingoes could indeed kill and carry a human baby. And additional physical evidence (the coat the baby was wearing when she disappeared) turned up years later, and corroborated Mrs. Chamberlain's story.

Fred Schepisi, who directed and cowrote the film, has used Australian public opinion as a sort of Greek chorus in the background. He cuts away to tennis games, saloons, filling stations, and dinner parties where the Australian public tries Lindy and finds her guilty (one hostess finally bans the subject at her dinner table, declaring that the case is not going to ruin another one of her parties). Schepisi is successful in indicting the court of public opinion, and his methodical (but absorbing) examination of the evidence helps us understand the state's circumstantial case.

In the lead role, Meryl Streep is given a thankless assignment: to show us a woman who deliberately refused to allow insights into herself. She succeeds, and so, of course, there are times when we feel frustrated because we do not know what Lindy is thinking or feeling. We begin to dislike the character, and then we know how the Australian public felt. Streep's performance is risky, and masterful.

The final point of the movie, I suppose, is that when passions run high enough, a court is likely to decide almost anything about anybody—especially an unlikable, unpopular member of a minority group who is charged with an unspeakable crime. When you combine that possibility with the uncertainty of circumstantial evidence and the human lust for revenge, you get a situation in which the death penalty can result in irrevocable tragedy. Lindy Chamberlain spent three and a half years in prison for a murder she did not commit, but at least she did not die for it.

The Cure ★ ★ ½
PG-13, 95 m., 1995

Joseph Mazzello (Dexter), Brad Renfro (Erik), Annabella Sciorra (Linda), Diana Scarwid (Gail), Bruce Davison (Dr. Stevens), Nicky Katt (Pony). Directed by Peter Horton and produced by Mark Burg and Eric Eisner. Screenplay by Robert Kuhn.

There are three moments of perfect truth in *The Cure*. There are several passages that are very moving. And then there's an impossible story that plays like a cross between a Disease of the Week movie and *The Goonies*. It's possible that viewers in their earlier teens—the target audience—will like it a lot. I was derailed by the silly stuff, and by the movie's conviction that it's funny to play practical jokes about death.

The movie takes place in a small Minnesota town where young Erik (Brad Renfro) has recently moved with his newly divorced mom (Diana Scarwid). Next door, behind a tall wooden fence, lives a boy named Dexter (Joseph Mazzello), who contracted AIDS through a blood transfusion. They're about the same age, but Dexter, who is very small, explains cheerfully: "If you look at the lower limit of what's considered normal for my age, I'm only four inches shorter."

Bullies at the school torment Erik as a "faggot" for being friends with Dexter, and Erik's own mother advises him to keep his distance, which she defines as seven feet. But the two boys become best friends, and Dexter's mother (Annabella Sciorra) comes to love the rough-edged kid who has befriended her son. Strange, how real the Sciorra character seems, and how unconvincing Erik's mom is (she spends the movie drinking, smoking, and being mean-spirited).

Meanwhile, the boys are inspired by a movie they see on TV (*Medicine Man*, with Sean Connery finding a miracle cure in the jungle). Erik involves Dexter in harebrained home-brew AIDS cures, including experiments with "The Periodic Table of the Candies." (The theory here is that combinations of candies can cure AIDS; in practice, the scene plays like product placement for Butterfinger bars.)

These scenes have a sweetness and a natural quality, helped by convincing performances by Renfro, the nonpro actor discovered in *The Client*, and Mazzello, who never makes a play for sympathy. I liked their theoretical discussion of whether a lion or a shark would win in a fight.

But, come on—are we really supposed to believe it when the kids read in a supermarket tabloid that a New Orleans doctor has discovered a cure for AIDS, and then they run away from home to float 1,200 miles down the Mississippi to find him? Wouldn't there be a media storm and a manhunt? How far do you think two kids would get on a raft, towing an inflatable crocodile behind them?

The plot then provides a couple of shifty pleasure-boat types who agree to carry them as passengers (see same objections as above), and, yes, the plot actually involves a chase into an Abandoned Warehouse, the desperate screenwriter's friend. The speedboat trip is somewhat redeemed by a priceless exchange between young Dexter and a bimbo picked up along the way. (He: "You misspelled your tattoo. It doesn't say 'Angel.' It says 'Angle.'" She: "I'm aware of that now.")

The three perfect scenes are clustered toward the end. One comes after an unconvincing scene in which Dexter uses his disease to scare off a bad guy, and then is shaken to realize his blood is "poison." Another comes when a doctor (Bruce Davison) explains why he believes in miracles. The third is a confrontation between the two mothers.

Those scenes have a greatness to them. But they fit uneasily into the same movie with stock villains, phony showdowns, and the unlikely trip down the river. And then there's that series of practical jokes that Erik and Dexter play in the hospital; they're a miscalculation so enormous they destroy what should have been the most important scenes in the movie.

Curly Sue ★ ★ ★
PG, 98 m., 1991

James Belushi (Bill Dancer), Kelly Lynch (Grey Ellison), Alisan Porter (Curly Sue), John Getz (Walter McCormick), Fred Dalton Thompson (Bernard Oxbar). Directed and produced by John Hughes. Screenplay by Hughes.

Curly Sue is a cornball, soupy, syrupy, sentimental exercise in audience manipulation, but that's the good news, because this is a movie that works. I don't know how and I don't know why, but somehow the film got around my guard, overcame my cynicism, and left me sitting there with a grin on my face.

The movie is a fantasy from beginning to end. It was filmed in the real world, but could not possibly have taken place there.

No matter. It exists on its own terms, without apologies. It stars James Belushi as a down-and-out drifter who travels the highways of America with a pint-size little con woman named Curly Sue (Alisan Porter). Pulling cons to get money for food, they stage an "accident" in which Belushi is apparently hit by a car driven by a cynical, hard-driving Chicago lawyer (Kelly Lynch).

She buys them dinner before being dragged away by her drippy boyfriend (John Getz), but the next day, after she *really* hits Belushi a second time with her car, she invites them home. That's partly because she hasn't been able to get Curly Sue's winsome little face out of her mind. And then you can more or less guess what happens, as she falls in love with the tyke, finds herself attracted to Belushi, and eventually goes through a complete change of heart.

This is a story that could have been written by Damon Runyon, illustrated by Norman Rockwell, and filmed by Frank Capra. That it has been written and directed by John Hughes should not come as much of a surprise, because he has a knack for stories that tug at the heartstrings, exploiting basic human sentiment. Sometimes his stories work *(Planes, Trains and Automobiles)*, sometimes they don't *(Dutch)*, and sometimes the box office says they work better than I thought they did *(Home Alone)*, but when you are working with broad-based comic sentimentality, there is a fine line to be found, and this time Hughes finds it.

What happened to me was, at some point during *Curly Sue*, I simply caved in and accepted the story. Yes, it's impossible; yes, the characters are living in a fantasy world; yes, it's shamelessly sentimental. But I started to care about them. And then the quiet humor and the warmth of the actors began to work some kind of charm.

The audience I saw it with seemed to go through the same process. Let me try to describe a strange thing that happened. At a crucial moment in the movie, after the Lynch character has fallen for Curly Sue and is beginning to fall for Belushi, her snotty boyfriend picks up the phone and asks for the number of the Department of Children and Family Services. He's gonna turn in the kid out of pure spite. And the audience was so wrapped up in this development that at least a third of them sighed right out loud. That reaction was so widespread that it got a second reaction—laughter, because the audience was tickled at itself for having cared so much. And the good feeling that came out of the sigh and the laughter generated as much warmth in that theater as I've experienced in a movie in a long time.

So, sure, if you're a hard-bitten intellectual and you're into serious films and don't like to get taken for a sucker with cornball manipulation, this isn't your film. Hey, I feel like that myself most of the time. But if occasionally you come down with an attack of warmheartedness and let a sentimental movie slip past you, then *Curly Sue* is likely to blindside you. It's not great and it's not deep, but it sure does have a heart.

Cyrano de Bergerac ★ ★ ★ ½
PG, 138 m., 1990

Gerard Depardieu (Cyrano de Bergerac), Anne Brochet (Roxanne), Vincent Perez (Christian de Neuvillette), Jacques Weber (Comte De Guiche), Roland Bertin (Raguenea), Philippe Morier-Genoud (Le Bret). Directed by Jean-Paul Rappeneau and produced by Rene Cleitman and Michel Seydoux. Screenplay by Jean-Claude Rappeneau and Jean-Claude Carriere.

It is entirely appropriate that Cyrano—whose very name evokes the notion of grand romantic gestures—should have lived his life bereft of romance. What is romanticism, after all, but a bold cry about how life should be, not about how it is? And so here is Cyrano de Bergerac, hulking, pudding-faced, with a nose so large he is convinced everyone is laughing at him—yet he dares to love the fair Roxanne. I have made it one of my rules in life never to have anything to do with anyone who does not instinctively love Cyrano, and I am most at home with those who identify with him.

The "real" Cyrano, if there was such a creature beneath the many layers of myth that have grown up around the name, lived in France from 1619 to 1655, and wrote stories about his magnificent voyages to the moon and the sun. He inspired the Cyrano we love, a more modern creation, the work of Edmond Rostand, who wrote a play in 1897 that may not have been great literature, but has captured the imagination of everyone who has read it and has been recycled countless times.

Steve Martin and Daryl Hannah starred in the wonderful modern-dress comedy *Roxanne* (1987), inspired by the outlines of Rostand's story, and now here is a magnificently lusty, brawling, passionate, and tempestuous classical version, directed by Jean-Paul Rappeneau. Cyrano is played by Gerard Depardieu, the most popular actor in France, who won the best actor award at the 1990 Cannes festival for his work.

You would not think he would be right for the role. Shouldn't Cyrano be smaller, more tentative, more pathetic—instead of this outsize, physically confident man of action? Depardieu is often said to be "wrong" for his roles. His physical presence makes a definite statement on the screen, and then his acting genius goes to work and transforms him into whatever is required for the role—into a spiritual priest, a hunchbacked peasant, a Medieval warrior, a car salesman, a businessman, a sculptor, a gangster.

Here he plays Cyrano, gadfly and rabblerouser, man about town, friend of some, envied by many, despised by a powerful few, and hopelessly, oh, most painfully and endearingly, in love with Roxanne (Anne Brochet). But his nose is too large. Not quite as long as Steve Martin's was, perhaps, but long enough that when he looks in the mirror he knows it would be an affront to present the nose anywhere in the vicinity of the fair Roxanne with an amorous purpose attached to it.

Now here is the inoffensive clod Christian de Neuvillette (Vincent Perez), Cyrano's friend. He is a romantic, too, but not in Cyrano's league. For him, love is a fancy. For Cyrano, a passion. Yet, if Cyrano cannot have Roxanne, then he will help his friend, and so he ghost-writes letters and ghost-recites speeches in the moonlight, and because Roxanne senses that the words come from a heart brave and true, she pledges herself to Christian. The irony—which only the audience can fully appreciate—is that anyone with a heart so pure she could love a cheesy lump like Christian because of his language could certainly love a magnificent man like Cyrano for the same reason, and regardless of his nose.

The screenplay by Rappeneau and the skilled veteran Jean-Claude Carriere spins this love story in a web of court intrigue and scandal, with Cyrano deeply involved on the wrong (that is, the good) side. And all leads up to the heartbreaking final round of revelations and truth-telling, and at last to Depardieu's virtuoso dying scene, which has to be seen to be believed.

What other actor would have had the courage to go with such determination so far over the top, to milk the pathos so shamelessly, to stagger and groan and weep and moan until it would all be funny, if it were not, paradoxically, so very effective and sad? Only the French could conceive and write, and perhaps only Depardieu could deliver, a dying speech that rises and falls with pathos and defiance for so long, only to end with the assertion that when he is gone, he will be remembered for . . . what? His heart? Courage? Bravery? No, of course not. Nothing half so commonplace: for his panache.

Cyrano de Bergerac is a splendid movie not just because it tells its romantic story and makes it visually delightful and centers it on Depardieu, but for a better reason: The movie acts as if it believes this story. Depardieu is not a satirist—not here, anyway. He plays Cyrano on the level, for keeps. Of course, the material is comic. But it is the frequent mistake of amateurs to play comedy for laughs, when the great artists know there is only one way to play it, and that is very seriously indeed. But with panache.

D

Daddy Nostalgia ★ ★ ★ ½
PG, 105 m., 1991

Dirk Bogarde (Daddy), Jane Birkin (Caroline), Odette Laure (Miche), Emmanuelle Bataille (Juliette), Charlotte Kady (Barbara). Directed by Bertrand Tavernier and produced by Adolphe Viezzi. Screenplay by Colo Tavernier O'Hagan.

The operation has been a success from the surgeon's point of view, but that leaves little consolation for the patient who knows he is going to die soon. All he can hope for are a few weeks or months of respite from pain. He is a British businessman somewhere in his sixties, who lives with his French wife in a retirement apartment on the Riviera, and he returns there to die.

Then something remarkable happens. His daughter arrives from England. They have not been close over the years, and often he was too distracted to really notice her. But now, as they begin to talk, the seasons of his life begin to take shape in her mind. They begin to know one another.

This is a wonderful story, but *Daddy Nostalgia* is not a very good title for it. I like the British title better: *These Foolish Things*. That refers to the song that haunts the movie, with some of the most bittersweet lyrics ever written, about how these foolish things remind me of you. Bertrand Tavernier's whole movie is told in the tone of that song, as a fond, elegiac memory.

The father is played by Dirk Bogarde. This is his first screen appearance in at least ten years, and he says it will be his last. He began in movies as a brash young man, but has aged into the perfect person to play this role. As in such movies as *Death in Venice* and *Providence*, he is a gentle man, a little regretful of lost opportunities, sentimental, and quietly brave. The daughter is Jane Birkin,

angular and quick, a British actress who has long lived in Paris. Both she and Bogarde are fluent in French, which in the movie is sort of a joke between them; English people with a private language.

And then there is another character in the movie who is at the heart of what *Daddy Nostalgia* is really about, even though she doesn't speak much at all. This is Bogarde's wife and Birkin's mother, played by Odette Laure as a stolid, resigned woman who sits in the kitchen and smokes endless cigarettes and drinks a lot of Coca-Cola and is deeply bitter. If you think enough about this character, the entire message of *Daddy Nostalgia* begins to shift.

It is easy enough to describe it as the leave-taking between two people who finally get to know one another: The father and daughter who allowed great silences to grow up in their lives, and who now cross those silences and become friends at the end. But what about the wife? In flashbacks from Birkin's point of view, we see a quiet, shy little daughter, sitting on the stairs as her glamorous parents whisk past on their way to parties and dinners. She was neglected then. But at some point, the Bogarde character lost interest in his wife. For years they have not really spoken to one another. And now this autumn relationship with his daughter is a flirtation of sorts—she is another young woman he wants to charm, even now, when he is about to die.

Tavernier directed this film from a screenplay by his former wife, Colo Tavernier O'Hagen. There must be elements of autobiography in it for both of them—especially when you remember his two earlier films, *A Week's Vacation* (1982) and *Sundays in the Country* (1989). Both told of children going to visit their fathers with a mixture of love and anger, and both showed fathers who were admirable and lovable but also self-centered and flawed.

It's that extra complication that makes *Daddy Nostalgia* so much more than just a sweet leave-taking. The movie knows that even as we die, we hang onto our weaknesses as fondly as our strengths. That dying people are selfish, all the more so because their resources are dwindling, and that even some of their good, generous, loving actions are done with complex motives. On one level, this is a heart-warming movie. On another, it is a wise and even a bitter one.

Damage ★ ★ ★ ★
R, 111 m., 1993

Jeremy Irons (Dr. Stephen Fleming), Juliette Binoche (Anna Barton), Miranda Richardson (Ingrid), Rupert Graves (Martyn), Ian Bannen (Edward Lloyd), Leslie Caron (Elizabeth Prideaux). Directed and produced by Louis Malle. Screenplay by David Hare.

One of the most sublime and hazardous moments in human experience comes when two people lock eyes and realize that they are sexually attracted to one another. They may not act on the knowledge. They may file it away for future reference. They may deny it. They may never see each other again. But the moment has happened, and for an instant all other considerations are insignificant.

Early in Louis Malle's *Damage*, such a moment takes place between Dr. Stephen Fleming, a British government official, and Anna Barton, a young woman he has met at a reception. They speak briefly, their eyes meet, and then each holds the other's gaze for one interminable second after another, until so much time has passed that we, in the audience, realize we are holding our breath.

There might have been a moment when they could have broken the spell, but both chose not to, continuing the moment far beyond the bounds of propriety or reason—particularly since Anna (Juliette Binoche) has just told Stephen (Jeremy Irons) that she is his son's fiancée.

This moment is followed by another that is remarkable for being so abrupt. Stephen sits at his desk. The telephone rings. A voice: "It's Anna." He replies: "Tell me where you are and I'll be there within an hour." And so begins their love affair, passionate and obsessive, reckless and heedless of harm to others. It is not that they want to hurt anyone, and it is not even that they want a sexual dalliance. This is something different. Indeed, they both love Martyn (Rupert Graves), Stephen's son, and plans for the marriage of Martyn and Anna continue uninterrupted.

Damage is not about romance but about obsession, about erotomania on the part of the older man, and about complex and hidden feelings on the part of the young woman. She is attracted to Stephen, yes, but there is more than that. When she was young she suffered a traumatic loss, and she describes herself as "damaged." She would not hurt him, not by an overt act, but her presence will eventually lead to harm. Watching this movie is like watching an emotional traffic accident as it unfolds.

The film is based on the bestseller by Josephine Hart, which had a certain undeniable power, but the right place for this material is the screen, I think, because it can show exactly how the two look at one another. This is a movie about sight; from the first moment the two meet, it is filled with what is seen and what is not seen, as Stephen suffers though a dinner party with his wife, his son, Anna, and her mother—and some observe, and some do not, what has happened.

Casting is everything here. Stephen could easily come to seem like a fool, and some actors could have played him no other way. Jeremy Irons, gaunt and consumed, brings no fleshy pleasure to the role. Love makes him look like a condemned man, and he feels guilty about sleeping with his son's fiancée, but he must, he cannot help himself, and so he does. The heart knows what it must have.

Juliette Binoche also embodies qualities that are essential to the film. She is attractive, but not in a conventional movie way; her face is solemn and serious, and she is capable of showing nothing and yet suggesting multitudes. Godard chose her for the title role of his *Hail Mary*, Andre Techine cast her as a sexual tigress in *Rendezvous*, and in Phil Kaufman's *The Unbearable Lightness*

of Being, she was the young woman who the doctor saw for a moment in a train station, and who came to stay with him, and who he could not deny. It is clear that all three directors saw her as somehow outside the norm, as an actress who could portray sexuality without descending to its usual displays.

Louis Malle is a director who has specialized in varieties of forbidden sex. His credits include *Pretty Baby*, about a photographer's child model, and *Murmur of the Heart*, about incest. His screenplay is by the playwright David Hare, who does an excellent job of surrounding these people with convincing characters whose very ordinariness underlines the madness of their actions. Miranda Richardson plays Jeremy Irons's wife, and is magnificently angry in the film's powerful closing scenes. Leslie Caron is Anna's mother, who knows her daughter well, and sees what is happening. And Rupert Graves is warm and likable as the son, who must seem worthy of Anna's love, but irrelevant.

Damage, like *Last Tango in Paris* and *The Unbearable Lightness of Being*, is one of those rare movies that is about sexuality, not sex; about the tension between people, not "relationships"; about how physical love is meaningless without a psychic engine behind it. Stephen and Anna are wrong to do what they do in *Damage*, but they cannot help themselves. We know they are careening toward disaster. We cannot look away.

Dances With Wolves ★ ★ ★ ★
PG-13, 181 m., 1990

Kevin Costner (Lieutenant Dunbar), Mary McDonnell (Stands With a Fist), Graham Greene (Kicking Bird), Rodney A. Grant (Wind in His Hair), Floyd Red Crow Westerman (Ten Bears), Tantoo Cardinal (Black Shawl), Annie Costner (Christine). Directed by Kevin Costner and produced by Jim Wilson and Costner. Screenplay by Michael Blake.

They meet at first in the middle of the prairie, holding themselves formally and a little awkwardly, the infantry officer and Sioux Indians. There should be instant mistrust between them, but they take each other's measure and keep an open mind. A civilized man is a person whose curiosity outweighs his prejudices, and these are curious men.

They know no words of each other's languages. Dunbar, the white man, tries to pantomime a buffalo. Wind in His Hair, the chief, looks at the charade and says, "His mind is

gone." But Kicking Bird, the holy man, thinks he understands what the stranger is trying to say, and at last they exchange the word for "buffalo" in each other's languages. These first halting words are the crucial moments in Kevin Costner's *Dances With Wolves*, a film about a white man who goes to live with Indians and learns their civilization at first hand.

In real life, such contacts hardly ever took place. The dominant American culture was nearsighted, incurious, and racist, and saw the Indians as a race of ignorant, thieving savages, fit to be shot on sight. Such attitudes survived until so recently in our society—just look at the B Westerns of the 1940s—that we can only imagine how much worse they were one hundred years ago. In a sense, *Dances With Wolves* is a sentimental fantasy, a "what if" movie that imagines a world in which whites were genuinely interested in learning about a Native American culture that lived more closely in harmony with the natural world than any other before or since. But our knowledge of how things turned out—of how the Indians were driven from their lands by genocide and theft—casts a sad shadow over everything.

The movie, which won the Academy Award as the best picture of 1990, is a simple story, magnificently told. It has the epic sweep and clarity of a Western by John Ford, and it abandons the contrivances of ordinary plotting to look, in detail, at the way strangers get to know one another. The film is seen from the point of view of Dunbar (Costner), a lieutenant in the Union Army, who runs away from a field hospital as his foot is about to be amputated and invites death by riding his horse in a suicidal charge at the Confederate lines. When he miraculously survives, he is decorated and given his choice of any posting, and he chooses the frontier, because "I want to see it before it's gone."

He draws an isolated outpost in the Dakotas, where he is the only white man for miles around. He is alone, but at first not lonely; he keeps a journal and writes of his daily routine, and after the first contact with the Sioux, he documents the way they slowly get to know one another. Dunbar possesses the one quality he needs to cut through the entrenched racism of his time: He is able to look another man in the eye, and see the man, rather than his attitudes about the man.

As Dunbar discovers the culture of the Sioux, so do we. The Indians know the white man is coming, and they want to learn more about his plans. They have seen other invaders in these parts: the Spanish, the Mexicans, but they always left. Now the Indians fear the white man is here to stay. They want Dunbar to share his knowledge, but at first he holds back. He does not wish to discourage them. And when he finally tells how many whites will be coming ("As many as the stars in the sky"), the words fall like a death knell.

At first, Dunbar and the Indians meet on the open prairie. One day they bring along Stands With a Fist (Mary McDonnell), a white woman who as a girl came to live with the tribe after her family was killed. She remembers a little English. With a translator, progress is quicker, until one day Dunbar comes to live with the tribe, and is eventually given the name Dances With Wolves.

There are some of the plot points we would expect in a story like this. The buffalo hunt (thrillingly photographed). A bloody fight with a hostile tribe. The inevitable love story between Dunbar and Stands With a Fist. But all is done with an eye to detail, with a respect for tradition, and with a certain sweetness of disposition. The love story is especially delicate; this isn't one of those exercises in romantic cliché, but a courtship conducted mostly through the eyes, through these two people looking at one another. There is a delicate, humorous sequence showing how the tribe observes and approves of the romance when the chief's wife, Black Shawl (Tantoo Cardinal), tells her husband it is time for Stands With a Fist to stop mourning her dead husband and accept this new man into her arms.

Meanwhile, we get to know many members of the Sioux tribe, most especially Kicking Bird (Graham Greene), Wind in His Hair (Rodney A. Grant), and the old wise man Ten Bears (Floyd Red Crow Westerman). Each has a strong personality; these are men who know exactly who they are, and at one point, after Dunbar has killed in battle beside them, he realizes he never knew who "John Dunbar" was, but he knows who Dances With Wolves is. Much of the movie is narrated by Dunbar, and his speech at this point is a center for the film: He observes that the battle with the enemy tribe was not fought for political purposes, but for food and land, and it was fought to defend the women and children who were right there in the midst of battle. The futility he felt on his suicidal day as a Union officer has been

replaced by utter clarity: He knows why he was fighting, and he knows why he was willing to risk losing his life.

Dances With Wolves has the kind of vision and ambition that is rare in movies today. It is not a formula movie, but a thoughtful, carefully observed story. It is a Western at a time when the Western is said to be dead. It asks for our imagination and sympathy. It takes its time, three hours, to unfold. It is a personal triumph for Kevin Costner, the intelligent young actor of *Field of Dreams*, who directed the film and shows a command of story and of visual structure that is startling; this movie moves so confidently and looks so good it seems incredible that it's a directorial debut. Costner and his cinematographer, Dean Semler, are especially gifted at explaining things visually. Many of their most important points are made with a glance, a close-up, a detail shot.

In 1985, before he was a star, Costner played a small role in a good Western called *Silverado* simply because he wanted to be in a Western. Now he has realized his dream by making one of the best Westerns I've seen. The movie makes amends, of a sort, for hundreds of racist and small-minded Westerns that went before it. By allowing the Sioux to speak in their own tongue, by entering their villages and observing their ways, it sees them as people, not as whooping savages in the sights of an infantry rifle.

Dance With a Stranger ★ ★ ★ ★
R, 102 m., 1985

Miranda Richardson (Ruth Ellis), Rupert Everett (David Blakely), Ian Holm (Desmond Cussen), Matthew Carroll (Andy), Tom Chadbon (Anthony Findlater), Jane Bertish (Carole Findlater). Directed by Mike Newell and produced by Roger Randall Cutler. Screenplay by Shelagh Delaney.

Ruth Ellis and David Blakely were a tragedy waiting to happen. She was a B-girl, pouring drinks and massaging men's egos in a sleazy little 1950s London nightclub. He was a rich young brat, whose life centered around his career as a race driver. They met one boozy night in the club, and there was an instant spark of lust between them—Ruth, whose profession was to keep her distance from men, and David, who had never felt love in his life.

Dance With a Stranger is the story of their affair, which led to one of the most famous British murder trials of the decade. After

Ellis shot Blakely dead in the street outside a pub, she was brought to trial, convicted, and executed with heartless speed; her trial began on June 20, 1955, and she was hanged on July 19—the last woman to receive the death penalty in England.

In the thirty years since Blakely and Ellis died, the case has fascinated the British, perhaps because it combines sexuality and the class system, two of their greatest interests. Blakely was upper-class, polished, affected, superior. Ellis was a working-class girl who made herself up to look like Marilyn Monroe and used the business of bar hostess as a way to support her young son and maintain her independence from men. Ironically, she was finally undone by her emotional dependence on Blakely, who gave and then withdrew his affection in a way that pushed her over the edge.

Their story is told by Mike Newell in a film of astonishing performances and moody, atmospheric visuals. Ruth Ellis is the emotional center of the film, and she is played by a newcomer, Miranda Richardson, as a woman who prides herself on not allowing men to hurt her, and who almost to the end cannot believe that the one man she loves would hurt her the most.

We see her first in the nightclub, where her blond Monroe looks supply the only style in the whole shabby room. We meet her regular "friends," including Desmond Cussen (Ian Holm), a quiet, loyal bachelor who adores her in an unpossessive way. Then Blakely (played by Rupert Everett) walks into her life, and in an instant there is erotically charged tension between them; the way they both flaunt their indifference is a clue. Their relationship falls into a pattern: lust, sex, tears, quarrels, absences, and then lust and sex again. Newell tells the story only in terms of the events and characters themselves. There are no detours into shallow psychology; just the patterns of attraction and repulsion.

For Ruth Ellis, a woman living at a time when women's options were cruelly limited, the obsession with Blakely becomes totally destructive. She loses her job. She grows more dependent as he grows more cold and unpredictable, and everything is complicated by their mutual alcoholism. Cussen, the inoffensive, long-suffering admirer, takes her in, and she makes an effort to shape up, but Blakely sounds chords in her that she cannot ignore.

By the end of the movie, Blakely has done

things to her that she cannot forgive. And they are not the big, melodramatic things like the violence that breaks out between them. They are little unforgivable things, as when he raises her hopes and then disappoints her. By the end, he is hardly even hurting her intentionally. He drinks in the company of fawning friends, he ignores responsibilities, he disappears into his own drunken absent-mindedness, and forgets her. And then one night outside a pub, she reminds him, once and for all.

Dangerous Liaisons ★ ★ ★
R, 120 m., 1988

Glenn Close (Marquise de Merteuil), John Malkovich (Vicomte de Valmont), Michelle Pfeiffer (Madame de Tourvel), Swoosie Kurtz (Madame de Volanges), Keanu Reeves (Chevalier Danceny), Mildred Natwick (Madame de Rosemonde), Uma Thurman (Cecile de Volanges). Directed by Stephen Frears and produced by Norma Heyman and Hank Moonjean. Screenplay by Christopher Hampton.

Dangerous Liaisons is a story of two people who lack the courage to admit they love each other, and so spend their energies destroying the loves of others. They describe as cynicism what is really depravity, and are so hardened to the ordinary feelings of life that only one emotion can destroy them. That emotion is love, of course.

The two people live in 18th-century France, at a time just before the Revolution, when the decadence of the aristocracy has become an end in itself. The Marquise de Merteuil lives in a world of drawing rooms and boudoirs, where she swoops down like a hawk upon the innocent and the naive, wrecking their idealism with a triumphant laugh to herself. Her partner and confidant is the Vicomte de Valmont, who was once her lover and is now her weapon against young women presumptuous enough to love. In their private scorekeeping, nothing counts more than a heart destroyed, and hopes laid to waste.

One day the Marquise (Glenn Close) comes to the Vicomte (John Malkovich) with an assignment. She has lost a lover, who has left her to marry an innocent young woman named Cecile (Uma Thurman). She wishes the Vicomte to seduce the young woman before she can bear her virginity to the marital bed. The Vicomte accepts the dare, and dispatches himself to the country—where,

however, he eventually sets his sights on another young woman instead.

She is the virtuous Madame de Tourvel (Michelle Pfeiffer), who wishes to be faithful to her husband. Certainly there is nothing overpoweringly attractive in the lecherous Vicomte, who is a little cadaverous and has a reputation as a cad. But the Vicomte persists, and he uses a weapon that sometimes works against the pure and the good: He presents himself as frankly evil, and thus inspires a spark of lust to stir within the woman herself. He plays on her curiosity about what it would be like to be a bad girl.

All this intrigue goes more or less according to plan, especially when the Marquise sics another young man on the unsuspecting Cecile, then uses that as an excuse to arrange for Cecile to visit the country home where, wouldn't you know, Valmont and Madame de Tourvel are staying. The seduction of Cecile comes easily. But the seduction of Madame de Tourvel, when it is finally arrived at, is a surprise for everyone, because it happens that Valmont and Tourvel actually do really fall in love.

This is too much for the Marquise; as her instrument, Valmont may make love to whomsoever he pleases, but he is not to *fall* in love with anyone. All of the pretend emotions of the game of seduction turn into the real emotions of the game of betrayal.

Dangerous Liaisons, based on Christopher Hampton's London and New York stage hit *Les Liaisons Dangereuses* (and on the scandalous 18th-century novel by Choderlos de Laclos), is a mannered, elegant film in which the languorous intrigues of the opening scenes set up the violent passions of the later ones. It is a film in which the surfaces are usually calm, and only the flash of an eye or a slightly raised voice betrays the most terrible struggles going on beneath.

It is played to perfection by Close and Malkovich in the central roles; their arch dialogues together turn into exhausting conversational games, tennis matches of the soul. The other key roles, played by Pfeiffer and Thurman, are trickier, because they involve characters who should not be entirely aware of what is really happening. Both actresses are well cast for their roles, and for Pfeiffer, in a year which saw her in such various assignments as *Married to the Mob* and *Tequila Sunrise*, the movie is more evidence of her versatility—she is good when she is innocent, and superb when she is guilty.

If there is anything lacking in the movie, it

may be a certain gusto. The director, Stephen Frears, is so happy to make this a tragicomedy of manners that he sometimes turns away from obvious payoffs. I am not suggesting he should have turned the material toward the ribald, or gone for easy laughs, but there are times when he holds back and should have gone for the punch line. *Dangerous Liaisons* is an absorbing and seductive movie, but not a compelling one.

Dark Eyes ★ ★ ½
NO MPAA RATING, 118 m., 1987

Marcello Mastroianni (Romano), Silvana Mangano (Elisa), Marthe Keller (Tina), Elena Sofonova (Anna), Pina Cei (Elisa's Mother), Vsevolod Larionov (Pavel). Directed by Nikita Mikhalkov and produced by Silvia D'Amico Bendico and Carlo Cucchi. Screenplay by Alexander Adabachian and Mikhalkov.

Some stories need to be told after they are over. We need to know that all the events are past and gone in order to feel the same nostalgia as the storyteller. When a story is happening "now," there is always the possibility of surprise and happiness. But when a story happened "then," and it is a love story, then even the happy moments feel bittersweet, and, of course, that is the whole point of the story.

Dark Eyes is a story told by a man who sits at a table in the lounge of an ocean liner, the bottle in front of him, the glass in his hand, his voice steady as if he has rehearsed these same facts many times before. He is a middle-aged man with sad eyes and a weary face. His listener is about the same age, but not so sad and not so weary. Neither one seems to much care about the ship's destination.

The man telling the story is Marcello Mastroianni, the most complete of movie actors, his face never seeming composed for the screen but acting simply as a window for his words. He tells the stranger that once he was married, comfortably if not ecstatically, to a rich wife (Silvana Mangano). They were not in love, but they were content with one another. Then he went on a visit to a spa, and there he saw a young lady, and danced with her, and fell in love with her, and had one of those holiday romances that fade like postcards in the memory. After all, nothing could come of it; they were both married.

The problem with this romance, Mastroianni tells his listener, is that it did not fade. Back home again, he found he was still in love with the woman (Elena Sofonova).

She grew stronger in his memory. He could not forget her. She was a Russian, and eventually he went to Russia in search of her, and found her, and they shared perfect love and vowed to divorce their spouses to marry each other. She went to tell her husband, and he returned to Italy to tell his wife, but at home he found his wife had lost all of her money, and his sense of loyalty was such that he could not leave her under those circumstances, and so . . .

Mastroianni continues with his story, but I will stop here, before all the twists and turns, the ironies, and the final heartbreak. *Dark Eyes* tells one of those stories where you think you know everything, but you do not, and at the end of the story you know that everyone is very unhappy, but you cannot see precisely what they should have done differently. The movie is based on stories by Chekhov, and has been directed by a Russian, Nikita Mikhalkov, who is not afraid of large romantic gestures and tragic coincidences. You realize after a while that it doesn't matter that Mastroianni can do nothing, that his tragedy is in the past; the telling of the story is the whole point, and he travels the world with his sad tale, telling it probably again and again, for the whole importance of his life has been reduced to his great loss.

This is a beautiful film, lavishly shot on location at Italian and Russian spas and in great houses. The nineteenth-century period is important, not simply because it recalls a time before telephones (which could have solved the whole tragedy), but because it recalls a state of mind before telephones, a time when people did not much believe in easy solutions. The movie is intriguing because of its moral complexity. After it's over, you find yourself asking hard questions about who did right and who did wrong, and you're confronted with the ironic possibility that maybe it didn't matter, that maybe everyone was doomed from the start.

The ending of this film is a real stunner. If you see *Dark Eyes*, ask yourself this question afterward: How would it have felt if the movie had provided the encounter we anticipate will be the last scene, but isn't? Would it have been simply corny? Or too heartbreaking to be endured?

Dark Obsession ★ ★ ★
NC-17, 87 m., 1991

Gabriel Byrne (Sir Hugo Buckton), Amanda Donohoe (Lady Virginia Buckton), Struan

Rodger (Peter), Douglas Hodge (Jamie), Peter Sands (Colonel), David Delve (Alec), Michael Hordern (Lord Crewne), Ian Carmichael (Exeter). Directed by Nick Broomfield and produced by Tim Bevan. Screenplay by Tim Rose Price.

The film opens in solemn ceremony, as a group of men in military formal wear offer a toast to the queen. It is followed by countless other toasts, until finally this cream of the British aristocracy is galloping around the banquet hall on each other's shoulders, in a boozy game of horses and riders. Later that night, as they all drive home together, the car of the drunken Sir Hugo hits a woman in the middle of the street. She is not killed instantly, but Sir Hugo deliberately leaves her for dead. She dies the next day, and is described in the papers as a hit-and-run victim.

Actually there were four witnesses to Sir Hugo's crime, but they take a solemn oath not to reveal what happened. And Hugo (played by Gabriel Byrne as a monstrously selfish, jealous rich man) carries on his life as usual. There is his wife, whom he suspects of adultery, and his small child, about to be packed away to boarding school, and his doddering father, who complains, "Are they roping me off?" on the days when the public is admitted for tours of the ancestral home.

The fact is, the hit-and-run was murder in more ways than one. The victim (identified as the cook of a friend of Sir Hugo's) looked, for one moment on the dark, rainy street, very much like his wife. And perhaps at that moment he avoided braking, when he could have saved the woman, because in his drunken state he was running down his wife instead. It is hard to say. And of course, sober, Sir Hugo is the soul of probity and decorum. Like many members of his class and generation, he is obsessive about performing all of his public acts in the absolutely correct way, while being completely permissive with himself about what he does in private.

Dark Obsession, a film of murder, sexual jealousy, and refined decadence, is only fitfully a murder mystery. A crime has taken place, and there is an attempt to solve it, and one of Sir Hugo's young friends is tortured by his conscience because of the bloody secret he has been pledged to keep. But the business of the crime plugs along in the background, while Hugo and his family carry out the daily pathology of lives that have become lies. About the only thing that cheers up these dreadful people is that they think they

are better than everyone else. But even within their own closed circle they are snobs: "I do so want you to feel a member of the family," Hugo's mother tells his wife, making it clear than after several years of marriage she does not believe this feeling has yet been obtained.

The movie was written by Tim Rose Price and directed by Nick Broomfield, whose previous films include the documentary *Soldier Girls,* and whose approach to this material is documentary as well. He wants to show us how the very fabric of the lives of these aristocrats has undercut their human perspective, has convinced them they are above and beyond the law. When they toast the queen, it is almost because they think she needs it.

Broomfield's sequences have the feeling of carefully crafted set pieces, as in a scene that takes place at night, at a party in the ancestral country home. The garden, the pool, the gardener's shed, the disused gazebo—these all become, not architectural details, but destinations for elaborate games of hide-and-seek, as lords and ladies slip off into the night for furtive couplings. There is a particularly painful encounter between Sir Hugo and his wife, which is probably responsible for the film's NC-17 rating, but which is helpful, I think, in establishing the ways in which he can feel himself to be a man.

If you want to understand the British ruling class, the Cockney-born Michael Caine once explained to me, it will help to know that they were all shipped off to boarding school at the age of five, and spent the next ten years in a same-sex society, being beaten about once a week. The opening scene of *Dark Obsession* begins about where Caine's explanation left off.

D.A.R.Y.L. ★ ★ ★
PG, 99 m., 1985

Barret Oliver (Daryl), Mary Beth Hurt (Joyce Richardson), Michael McKean (Andy Robinson), Daniel Bryan Corkill (Turtle), Josef Sommer (Dr. Stewart), Kathryn Walker (Ellen Lamb). Directed by Simon Wincer and produced by John Heyman and Burtt Harris. Screenplay by David Ambrose.

They know there is something odd about the kid when he starts doing his own laundry. That's not natural for a grade-schooler. Daryl has some other strange attributes. He is unfailingly polite, obsessively honest, and bats 1.000 in Little League. Finally his friend, Turtle, pulls him aside and explains that adults don't like it when a kid is too perfect. It makes them nervous. They need to connect with him so they can relax around him. Daryl nods gravely, and his next time at bat, he strikes out.

Daryl's history is strange. He was discovered by the side of the road, a neatly dressed little boy with amnesia. He didn't know who his parents were, or what his last name was, or where he lived. He is placed with a foster family, and by halfway through the movie *D.A.R.Y.L.* he is beginning to develop into a more typical kid, with real human emotions. That is against the game plan, unfortunately, because Daryl is both more and less than human. He is a prototype of a secret government attempt to combine a computer brain with a genetically cloned body, creating a humanoid who can use his five senses as input for his silicon mind.

D.A.R.Y.L. is sort of *Charly* in reverse. Instead of a retarded man who is allowed, through science, to have a brief glimpse of what it would be like to be normal, what we have here is a super-intelligent thinking machine who gets a taste of being a real little boy. It's an intriguing premise, and the movie handles it with skill. The boy is played by Barret Oliver with an earnest, touching solemnity. The people around him (including his foster parents, Mary Beth Hurt and Michael McKean) are out of a Norman Rockwell drawing: loving, generous, loyal. His best friend Turtle (Daniel Bryan Corkill) is tactful in trying to get this odd kid to act normal.

Tacked onto this small-town story, the details of the intrigue seem almost unnecessary. The movie contains the usual hardnosed military men, visionary scientists, and officious cops. They've lost track of their expensive *D.A.R.Y.L.*, and want to find him and deprogram him. Daryl fights back by borrowing a supersecret fighter plane (as the movie is borrowing its ending from Clint Eastwood's *Firefox*), and the ending is really sort of neat; it's high-tech and heartwarming at the same time.

D.A.R.Y.L. is a good movie that could have been better. Maybe they should have screened *Charly* before making it. That would have reminded them that the scientific parts of their story are more or less predictable, and that the human elements are what keep us involved.

Daughters of the Dust ★ ★ ★
NO MPAA RATING, 113 m., 1992

Cora Lee Day (Nana Peazant), Alva Rogers (Eula Peazant), Barbara-O (Yellow Mary), Trula Hoosier (Trula), Umar Abdurrahamn (Bilal Muhammed), Adisa Anderson (Eli Peazant). Directed by Julie Dash and produced by Dash and Arthur Jafa. Screenplay by Dash.

Julie Dash's *Daughters of the Dust* is a tone poem of old memories, a family album in which all of the pictures are taken on the same day. It tells the story of a family of African-Americans who have lived for many years on a Southern offshore island, and of how they come together one day in 1902 to celebrate their ancestors before some of them leave for the North. The film is narrated by a child not yet born, and ancestors already dead also seem to be as present as the living.

The film doesn't tell a story in any conventional sense. It tells of feelings. At certain moments we are not sure exactly what is being said or signified, but by the end we understand everything that happened—not in an intellectual way, but in an emotional way. We learn of members of the Ibo people who were brought to America in chains, how they survived slavery and kept their family memories and, in their secluded offshore homes, maintained tribal practices from Africa as well. They come to say good-bye to their land and relatives before setting off to a new land, and there is the sense that all of them are going on the journey and all of them are staying behind, because the family is seen as a single entity.

Daughters of the Dust was made by Dash over a period of years for a small budget (although it doesn't feel cheap, with its lush color photography, its elegant costumes, and the lilting music of the sound track). She made the film as if it were partly happening now, partly blurred racial memories; I was reminded of the beautiful family picnic scene in *Bonnie and Clyde* where Bonnie goes to say good-bye to her mother.

There is no particular plot, although there are snatches of drama and moments of conflict and reconciliation. The characters speak in a mixture of English, African languages, and a French patois. Sometimes they are subtitled; sometimes we understand exactly what they are saying; sometimes we understand the emotion but not the words. The fact that some of the dialogue is deliberately difficult is not frustrating, but comforting; we relax like children at a family picnic, not

understanding everything, but feeling at home with the expression of it.

The movie would seem to have slim commercial prospects, and yet by word of mouth it attracted steadily growing audiences. People tell each other about it. "I've seen it three times," a woman told me the night I saw it at the Film Center of the Chicago Art Institute. "I get something new out of it every time." It is all a matter of notes and moods, music and tones of voice, atmosphere and deep feeling. If Dash had assigned every character a role in a conventional plot, this would have been just another movie—maybe a good one, but nothing new. Instead, somehow she makes this many stories about many families, and through it we understand how African-American families persisted against slavery, and tried to be true to their memories.

Dave ★ ★ ★ ½
PG-13, 110 m., 1993

Kevin Kline (Dave Kovic/Bill Mitchell), Sigourney Weaver (Ellen Mitchell), Frank Langella (Bob Alexander), Kevin Dunn (Alan Reed), Ving Rhames (Duane Stevensen), Ben Kingsley (Vice President Nance), Charles Grodin (Murray Blum), Faith Prince (Alice). Directed by Ivan Reitman and produced by Lauren Shuler-Donner and Reitman. Screenplay by Gary Ross.

Dave takes that old plot about an ordinary person who is suddenly thrust into a position of power, and finds a fresh way to tell it. The movie's about a nice guy who runs an employment agency and is otherwise undistinguished, except that he happens to look exactly like the president of the United States. When the president wants to sneak away for a quickie with his mistress, Dave is recruited by the Secret Service to act as a stand-in. Then the president has a stroke, and Dave is hired on a more or less permanent basis.

When I first heard this story line, I imagined that *Dave* would be completely predictable. I was wrong. The movie is another proof that it isn't what you do, it's how you do it: Ivan Reitman's direction and Gary Ross's screenplay use intelligence and warmhearted sentiment to make *Dave* into a wonderful, lighthearted entertainment.

The movie opens with the White House occupied by President Bill Mitchell, who seems to have been inspired by George Bush. (The first lady, played by Sigourney Weaver, incorporates elements of both Barbara Bush and Hillary Clinton.) The "first marriage" is over in all but name; Bill and Ellen Mitchell appear together in public, but hardly even talk in private, because she's so angry about his philandering and general wimpiness.

The president is played by Kevin Kline, who also plays good old Dave Kovic, a man who cannot rest when one of his clients needs a job. He's thrilled when he's asked to stand in for the president, and enjoys the experience immensely (who would not enjoy getting a standing ovation simply for existing?). But when Mitchell has his stroke, the White House chief of staff, an evil genius played by Frank Langella, decides not to turn over the reins of power to the vice president (kind, decent Ben Kingsley), but instead to use Dave Kovic as a permanent front man.

Dave dimly understands that this is wrong, but allows himself to be persuaded, and settles into the role with great enjoyment. We in the audience are waiting to see how long it will take the first lady to catch on, and one of the movie's charms is the way it toys with our expectations. Ellen Mitchell, as played by Weaver, is a smart and proud woman with a good heart; she detests Mitchell's two-timing politics and personal infidelity, and spends so little time with him that perhaps Langella can make the deception work.

The plot unfolds with elements that would be at home in a Frank Capra movie, which Reitman crosses here with some sly political satire. But the heart of the film is really the relationship between Dave and the first lady, who wander about their cavernous and lonely private quarters in the White House like a couple of moonstruck teen-agers.

Both Kline and Weaver are good at playing characters of considerable intelligence, and that's the case here. The movie may be built on subtle variations of the Idiot Plot (in which the characters skillfully avoid tripping over obvious conclusions), but they bring such particular qualities to their characters that we almost believe them.

We also almost believe the way the movie resolves everything; there's poetic justice in the way both private and public agendas are fulfilled. Much depends on the supporting performances, and Langella is superb as the oily, dishonest manipulator who thinks he can run the country as a puppet-master. I also enjoyed Kevin Dunn as Langella's right-hand man, Kingsley as a vice president of great dignity and forbearance, and the always dependable Charles Grodin in a small but essential role as Dave's best friend.

The subtext of *Dave* resembles the messages of many of the Capra movies: If people in power only behaved sensibly and with good will, a lot of our problems would solve themselves. Of course, it's not that simple. But watching *Dave*, there were moments when I found myself asking, why isn't it?

Dawn of the Dead ★ ★ ★
R, 126 m., 1979

With David Emge, Ken Foree, Scott H. Reiniger, and Gaylen Ross. Directed by George A. Romero and produced by Richard P. Rubenstein. Screenplay by Romero.

Dawn of the Dead is one of the best horror films ever made—and, as an inescapable result, one of the most horrifying. It is gruesome, sickening, disgusting, violent, brutal, and appalling. It is also (excuse me for a second while I find my other list) brilliantly crafted, funny, droll, and savagely merciless in its satiric view of the American consumer society. Nobody ever said art had to be in good taste.

It's about a mysterious plague that sweeps the nation, causing the recently dead to rise from their graves and roam the land, driven by an insatiable hunger for living flesh. No explanation is offered for this behavior—indeed, what explanation would suffice?—but there is a moment at which a survivor solemnly intones: "When there is no more room in hell, the dead will walk the Earth."

Who's that a quotation from? From George A. Romero, who wrote and directed *Dawn of the Dead* as a sequel to his *Night of the Living Dead*, which came out in 1968 and now qualifies as a cult classic. If you have seen *Night*, you will recall it as a terrifying horror film punctuated by such shocking images as zombies tearing human flesh from limbs. *Dawn* includes many more scenes like that, more graphic, more shocking, and in color. I am being rather blunt about this because there are many people who will *not* want to see this film. You know who you are. Why are you still reading?

Well . . . maybe because there's a little of the ghoulish voyeur in all of us. We like to be frightened. We like a good creepy thrill. It's just, we say, that we don't want a movie to go *too* far. What's too far? *The Exorcist? The Omen?* George Romero deliberately intends to go too far in *Dawn of the Dead*. He's dealing very consciously with the ways in which images can affect us, and if we sit through the film (many people cannot) we make some curious discoveries.

One is that the fates of the zombies, who are destroyed wholesale in all sorts of terrible ways, don't affect us so much after a while. They aren't being killed, after all: They're already dead. They're even a little comic, lurching about a shopping center and trying to plod up the down escalator. Romero teases us with these passages of humor. We relax, we laugh, we see the satire in it all, and then—*pow!* Another disembowelment, just when we were off guard.

His story opens in a chaotic television studio, where idiotic broadcasters are desperately transmitting inaccurate information (one hopes the Emergency Broadcast System will do a whole lot better). National Guard troops storm public housing, where zombies have been reported. There are ten minutes of unrelieved violence, and then the story settles down into the saga of four survivors who hijack a helicopter, land on the roof of a suburban shopping center, and barricade themselves inside against the zombies.

Their eventual fates are not as interesting as their behavior in the meantime; there is nothing quite like a plague of zombies to wonderfully focus your attention on what really matters to you. Romero has his own ideas, too, and the shopping center becomes a brilliant setting for a series of comic and satiric situations: Some low humor, some exquisitely sly.

But, even so, you may be asking, how can I defend this depraved trash? I do not defend it. I praise it. And it is not depraved, although some reviewers have seen it that way. It is *about* depravity. If you can see beyond the immediate impact of Romero's imagery, if you can experience the film as being more than just its violent extremes, a most unsettling thought may occur to you: The zombies in *Dawn of the Dead* are not the ones who are depraved. They are only acting according to their natures, and, gore dripping from their jaws, are blameless.

The depravity is in the behavior of the healthy survivors, and the true immorality comes as two bands of human survivors fight each other for the shopping center: *Now* look who's fighting over the bones! But *Dawn* is even more complicated than that, because the survivors have courage, too, and a certain nobility at times, and a sense of humor, and loneliness and dread, and are not altogether unlike ourselves. A-ha.

The Day After Trinity ★ ★ ★ ★
NO MPAA RATING, 88 m., 1980

A documentary produced and directed by
Jon Else. Written by David Peoples, Janet
Peoples, and Else.

There is a scene in *The Day After Trinity*
showing the world's first atomic device being
hoisted atop a steel frame tower that looks
barely adequate to hold a windmill. The
scene is not shot gracefully. The bomb looks
like a giant steel basketball with some tubes
and wires stuck onto it. In the background,
the sky is a washed-out blue. In the next
shot, the bomb is back on the ground again
and a man is posing next to it, somewhat self-
consciously. In 1945, the Russians would
have killed for this footage.

On the sound track, the narrator reads
sections of a personal diary kept by one of
the scientists at Los Alamos, New Mexico,
where the government ran its top-secret project to develop the atom bomb: *Gadget is in
place . . . should we have the chaplain here?* It is
all somewhat banal until, on reflection, it
becomes emotionally shattering. The greatest achievement of *The Day After Trinity* is
that it counts down those final days before
nuclear weapons became a fact of our lives.

This is a documentary that develops more
suspense than most of the thrillers I have
seen. It includes photographs and film footage from the Los Alamos laboratory, and it
begins and ends with the story of J. Robert
Oppenheimer, the brilliant scientist who was
the "father of the atomic bomb" and then, a
few years later, was branded as a security risk
by Senator Joseph McCarthy. It includes newsreel footage of World War II, including the
devastation of Hiroshima and Nagasaki, and
more footage of Oppenheimer after the war
and testifying before the McCarthy committee. And there are present-day interviews
with some of the scientists who worked at
Los Alamos.

All of this is gripping, especially the second thoughts of Oppenheimer and others
about the wisdom of dropping the bomb. Of
the wisdom of *developing* the bomb there
seems to have been no doubt: The bomb was
theoretically possible, it was technologically
feasible, if we did not build it, the Russians
would, and so we built it first, hurrah! Oppenheimer's brother, Frank, remembers that Robert's initial reaction to the first nuclear explosion (the "Trinity" blast), was, "it worked!" It
wasn't until after Hiroshima, he says, that it
occurred to him that it killed people.

The most riveting sections of the film deal
with the establishment of Los Alamos and
the weeks and days leading up to the Trinity
test. The New Mexico base was a jerry-built
collection of temporary housing, muddy
streets, 6,000 people, and paranoid secrecy.
But it seems to have been a glorious time for
the people who were there: It was like a summer camp for Ph.D.s, with Glenn Miller
records playing on the jukebox and bright
young nuclear whiz kids given the full resources of the government.

Those who were there on the day of Trinity remember that nobody really knew what
would happen. One scientist took side bets
that New Mexico would be incinerated. In
the event, it was just a very big bang. A woman
who was driving through the desert with
her sister remembers that her sister saw the
blast from hundreds of miles away; her sister
was blind. Today, physicist Robert Wilson
asks himself why he—why *they*—didn't just
all walk away from the bomb after they saw
what it could do. But of course they did not.

Day for Night ★ ★ ★ ★
PG, 116 m., 1974

Francois Truffaut (Ferrand), Jean-Pierre
Aumont (Alexandre), Jacqueline Bisset (Julie),
Jean-Pierre Leaud (Alphonse), Valentina
Cortese (Séverine). Directed by Francois
Truffaut and produced by Marcel Bébert.
Screenplay by Truffaut, Jean-Louis Richard,
and Suzanne Shiffman.

Movies about movies usually don't quite get
things right. The film business comes out
looking more romantic and glamorous (or
more corrupt and decadent) than it really is,
and none of the human feeling of a movie set
is communicated. That is not the case with
Francois Truffaut's funny and touching
film, *Day for Night*, which is not only the best
movie ever made about the movies but is also
a great entertainment.

A movie company, especially if it's away
from home on a location somewhere, is a
family that's been thrown into close and
sometimes desperate contact; strangers become friends and even intimates in a few
weeks, and in a few more weeks they're scattered to the winds. The family is complicated by the insecurities and egos of the
actors, and by the moviemaking process
itself: We see the result, but we don't see the
hours and days spent on special effects, on
stunts, on making it snow or making it rain

or making an allegedly trained cat walk from
A to B. *Day for Night* is about all of these
aspects of moviemaking; about the technical
problems, the boredom between takes (a
movie set is one of the most boring places on
earth most of the time), and about the romances and intrigues. It's real; this is how a
movie set really looks, feels, and smells. Truffaut's story involves a movie company on
location in Nice. They're making a melodrama called *Meet Pamela*, of which we see
enough to know it's doomed at the box office. But good or bad, the movie must be
made; Truffaut, who plays the director in his
own film, says at one point: "When I begin a
film, I want to make a great film. Halfway
through, I just hope to finish the film."

His cast includes a beautiful American
actress (Jacqueline Bisset); an aging matinee
idol (Jean-Pierre Aumont), and his former
mistress, also past her prime (Valentina Cortese); the young, lovestruck male lead (Jean-
Pierre Leaud), and the entire crew of script
girls, camera operators, stunt men, and a
henpecked production manager. (And if you
have ever wondered what the key grip does
in a movie, here's your chance to find out.)
Truffaut sets half a dozen stories in motion,
and follows them all so effortlessly it's almost as if we're gossiping with him about his
colleagues. The movie set is a microcosm:
there is a pregnancy and a death; a love affair
ended, another begun, and a third almost but
not quite destroyed; and new careers to be
nourished and old careers to be preserved.

Truffaut was always a master of quiet
comedy, and there are fine touches like the
aging actress fortifying herself with booze
and blaming her lack of memory on her
makeup girl. Then there's the young male
lead's ill-fated love for Jacqueline Bisset; she
is happily married to a doctor, but unwisely
extends her sympathy to the youth, who
repays her by very nearly destroying her marriage as well as himself. And all the time
there is the movie to be made: Truffaut gives
us a hilarious session with the "trained" cat,
and shows us without making a point of it
how snow is produced on a set, how stunt
drivers survive car crashes, and how third-
floor balconies can exist without buildings
below them.

What we see on the screen is nothing at all
like what happens on the set—a truth the
movie's title reflects. ("Day for night" is the
technical term for "night" scenes shot in
daylight with a special filter. The movie's
original French title, *La Nuit Americaine*, is

the French term for the same process—acknowledging their debt to Hollywood.)

The movie is just plain fun. Movie buffs will enjoy it like *Singin' in the Rain* (that perfect musical about the birth of talkies), but you don't have to be a movie buff to like it. Truffaut knows and loves the movies so much he's infectious; one of *Day for Night*'s best scenes is a dream in which the adult director remembers himself, as a little boy, slinking down a darkened street to steal a still from *Citizen Kane* from in front of a theater. We know who the little boy grew up to be, and that explains everything to us about how he feels now.

The Day of the Jackal ★ ★ ★ ★
PG, 150 m., 1973

Edward Fox (The Jackal), Terence Alexander (Lloyd), Michel Auclair (Colonel Rolland), Alan Badel (The Minister), Tony Britton (Inspector Thomas), Denis Carey (Casson), Olga Georges-Picot (Denise), Cyril Cusack (The Gunsmith). Directed by Fred Zinnemann and produced by John Woolf. Screenplay by Kenneth Ross.

Fred Zinnemann's *The Day of the Jackal* is one hell of an exciting movie. I wasn't prepared for how good it really is: it's not just a suspense classic, but a beautifully executed example of filmmaking. It's put together like a fine watch. The screenplay meticulously assembles an incredible array of material, and then Zinnemann choreographs it so that the story—complicated as it is—unfolds in almost documentary starkness.

The "jackal" of the title is the code name for a man who may (or may not) be a British citizen specializing in professional assassinations. He allegedly killed Trujillo of the Dominican Republic in 1961 and, now, two years later, he has been hired by a group of Frenchmen who want de Gaulle assassinated. His price is $500,000; he says, "and considering that I'm handing you France, I wouldn't call that expensive."

Zinnemann, working from Frederick Forsyth's bestseller, tells both sides of the story that unfolds during the summer of 1963. The jackal prepares two disguises and three identities, gets a legal passport by applying in the name of a child who died in 1931, and calls on European experts for his materials. An old gunsmith hand-makes a weird-looking lightweight rifle with silencer, sniper scope, and explosive bullets. A forger provides French identity papers and a driver's license

(and comes to an unexpected end). And then the jackal enters France.

Meanwhile, the government has received information that an attempt will be made on de Gaulle's life. The general absolutely insists that he will make no changes in his public schedule, and that any attempt to prevent an assassination must be made in secret. The French police cooperate "unofficially" with the top police forces of other nations in attempting an apprehension. But they don't even know who the jackal is.

How can they stop him? The movie provides a fascinating record of police investigative work, which combines exhaustive checking with intuition. But the jackal is clever, too, particularly when he's cornered. Some of the movie's finest moments come after the jackal's false identity is discovered and his license plates and description are distributed. He keeps running—and always convincingly; this isn't a movie about a killer with luck, but about one of uncommon intelligence and nerve.

Playing the jackal, Edward Fox is excellent. The movie doesn't provide much chance for a deep characterization, but he projects a most convincing persona. He's boyishly charming, impeccably groomed, possessed of an easy laugh, and casually ruthless. He will kill if there's the slightest need to. Fox's performance is crucial to the film, of course, and the way he carries it off is impressive.

The others on the case are uniformly excellent, especially Tony Britton as a harried police inspector and Cyril Cusack, in a nicely crafted little vignette, as the gunsmith. The movie's technical values (as is always the case with a Zinnemann film) are impeccable. The movie was filmed at great cost all over Europe, mostly on location, and it looks it. A production of this scope needs to appear absolutely convincing, and Zinnemann has mastered every detail—including the casting of a perfect de Gaulle look-alike.

The Day of the Jackal is two and a half hours long and seems over in about fifteen minutes. There are some words you hesitate to use in a review, because they sound so much like advertising copy, but in this case I can truthfully say that the movie is spellbinding.

Days of Heaven ★ ★ ★ ★
PG, 95 m., 1978

Richard Gere (Bill), Brooke Adams (Abby), Sam Shepard (The Farmer), Linda Manz (Linda), Robert Wilke (Foreman), Jackie

Shultis (Linda's Friend), Stuart Margolin (Mill Foreman). Directed by Terence Malick and produced by Bert and Harold Schneider. Screenplay by Malick.

Can any description of Terence Malick's *Days of Heaven* quite evoke the sense of wonder this film inspires? It's about a handful of people who find themselves shipwrecked in the middle of the Texas Panhandle—grain country—sometime before World War I. They involve themselves in a tragic love triangle, but their secrets seem insignificant, almost pathetic, seen against the awesome size of their world. Our wonder is that they endure at all in the face of the implacable land.

The land is farmed by a sick young man (Sam Shepard) who is widely believed to be on the edge of death. In the autumn, he and his foreman hire crews of itinerant laborers who ride out from the big cities on the tops of boxcars: swaggering, anonymous men who will follow the harvest north from Texas to Canada. Others pass through to entertain them and live off their brief periods of wage earning: aerial barnstormers, circus troupes, all specks on the great landscape.

We meet three people who set out together from the grime of Chicago, looking for harvest work: A strong young man (Richard Gere), his kid sister (Linda Manz), and the woman he lives with and also claims, for convenience, as his sister (Brooke Adams). They arrive at the farm of the sick young man, who falls in love with the older "sister."

Because they are so poor, because the farmer has a house, land, and money, the three keep quiet about his mistake and eventually the farmer and the "sister" marry. Her "brother"—her man—works on the farm and observes the marriage from a resentful, festering distance. The younger girl also observes, and the film's narration comes from her comments, deeply cynical, pathetically understated.

So goes the story of *Days of Heaven*, except that Malick's film doesn't really tell a story at all. It is an evocation of emptiness, loneliness, desolation, the slow accumulation of despair in a land too large for its inhabitants and blind to their dreams. Willa Cather wrote novels about such feelings—*The Lost Lady, Death Comes for the Archbishop*, the middle section of *The Professor's House*—and now Malick joins her company. This is a huge land we occupy. The first people to settle it must have wondered if they could ever really possess it.

Malick's vision of the land, indeed, is so sweeping that an ordinary, human-scale "story" in the foreground would be a distraction. We get a series of scenes, like tableaux, as the characters involve themselves in their mutual tragedy. The visual compositions often place them against vast backdrops (this is one of the most beautifully photographed films ever made), but Malick finds terror, too, in extreme close-ups of grasshoppers, of a germinating seed, of the little secrets with which nature ultimately builds her infinite secret.

When it develops that the girl has really fallen in love with her new husband, that she is not a con artist but just another victim, we might expect, in another movie, all sorts of blame and analysis. A director not sure of this material could have talked it away. But Malick brings a solemnity to his revelations, as the farmer gradually discovers the deception, as the laborer discovers his loss, as the little sister loses what little childhood she had.

Days of Heaven is a unique achievement—I can't think of another film anything like it. It's serious, yes, very solemn, but not depressing. More than anything else, it wants to re-create its time and place, as if Malick believes the decisions of his characters (and maybe his very characters themselves) come out of the time and place, and are caused by them.

So many movies are jammed with people talking to each other all the time, people obsessed with the conviction they're saying something. The people of *Days of Heaven* are so overwhelmed by the sheer force of nature, by the weight of the land, the bounty of the harvest, the casual distraction of fire and plague, the sharp, involuntary impulses of their passions, that they hardly know what to say. When you look at it that way, who does?

Days of Thunder ★ ★ ★
PG-13, 106 m., 1990

Tom Cruise (Cole Trickle), Robert Duvall (Harry Hogge), Randy Quaid (Tim Daland), Nicole Kidman (Dr. Claire Lewicki), Cary Elwes (Russ Wheeler), Michael Rooker (Rowdy Burns), John C. Reilly (Buck Bretherton), Don Simpson (Aldo Benedetti), Donna Wilson (Darlene). Directed by Tony Scott and produced by Don Simpson and Jerry Bruckheimer. Screenplay by Robert Towne.

Days of Thunder is an entertaining example of what we might as well call the Tom Cruise Picture, since it assembles most of the same elements that worked in *Top Gun, The Color of Money,* and *Cocktail* and runs them through the formula once again. Parts of the plot are beginning to wear out their welcome, but the key ingredients are still effective. They include:

1. The Cruise Character, invariably a young and naive but naturally talented kid who could be the best, if ever he could tame his rambunctious spirit.

2. The Mentor, an older man who has done it himself and been there before and knows talent when he sees it, and who has faith in the kid even when the kid screws up because his free spirit has gotten the best of him.

3. The Superior Woman, usually older, taller, and more mature than the Cruise character, who functions as a Mentor for his spirit, while the male Mentor supervises his craft.

4. The Craft, which the gifted young man must master.

5. The Arena, in which the young man is tested.

6. The Arcana, consisting of the specialized knowledge and lore that the movie knows all about, and we get to learn.

7. The Trail, a journey to visit the principal places where the masters of the craft test one another.

8. The Proto-Enemy, the bad guy in the opening reels of the movie, who provides the hero with an opponent to practice on. At first the Cruise character and the Proto-Enemy dislike each other, but eventually through a baptism of fire they learn to love one another.

9. The Eventual Enemy, a *real* bad guy who turns up in the closing reels to provide the hero with a test of his skill, his learning ability, his love, his craft, and his knowledge of the Arena and the Arcana.

The archetypal Tom Cruise Movie is, of course, *Top Gun,* in which the young fighter pilot, a natural, was tutored by a once-great pilot and emotionally nurtured by an older female flight instructor before testing his wings against the hot dogs of his unit, in preparation for a final showdown against the Enemy. In *The Color of Money,* the young pool player, a natural, was tutored by a once-great pool hustler and emotionally nurtured by an older female who had been around the block a few times, in preparation for a two-part showdown with (a) his hated opponent on the professional pool circuit, and (b) his Mentor himself. In *Cocktail,* the young bar-tender, a natural, was tutored by an older bartender, before eventually meeting first an older female who taught him a thing or two, and then a younger but still more mature female who taught him how to forget them.

In *Days of Thunder,* all of these elements are present in an entertainment of great skill but predictable construction. The Craft is stock-car racing. The Mentor is played by Robert Duvall, as a veteran racing-team leader. The Superior Woman is a physician (Nicole Kidman), who is attracted to the raw energy of the hero but forces him to grow up by laying down the line of responsible behavior. The Arena is the auto-racing track, and the Arcana includes such lore as "slipstreaming," RPMs, tire temperature, and whether to pass on the outside or the inside. The Proto-Enemy is a driver named Rowdy (Michael Rooker), who challenges the hero to racing duels including one that winds them both up in the hospital. The Eventual Enemy (Cary Elwes) is a driver named Wheeler who would like to run the hero into the wall and kill him. And the Trail, of course, is the Southern stock-car circuit, ending in the holy city of Daytona.

Days of Thunder was directed by Tony Scott, the same man who started this whole cycle by directing *Top Gun,* and it shows the same mastery of the photography of fast machines. The movie's handicap is that auto racing is visually a boring sport unless you are standing close to the cars or they are crashing into each other. The rest consists of long shots of lots of anonymous cars dashing confusingly around the track, medium shots of two cars trying to pass one another, and closeups of drivers looking as if they are experiencing proctoscopy.

As *Days of Thunder* sees it, the principal strategy in stock-car racing consists of trying to sideswipe your opponent and push him into the wall, and Cruise's car scrapes the wall for easily half of the time it is on the track. Most of this racing footage is loud and fast enough to be exciting, however, and the off-track sequences are served by Robert Duvall's usual laconic, sensitive performance, Randy Quaid as a used-car dealer who has faith in the kid, and Michael Rooker as the perfect Proto-Enemy (he can look hateful and then turn it around with a smile). Nicole Kidman has little to do as the physician, and doesn't make much of an impression. And Tom Cruise is so efficiently packaged in this product that he plays the same role as a saint in a Mexican village's holy day procession:

It's not what he does that makes him so special, it's the way he manifests everybody's faith in him.

Dazed and Confused ★ ★ ★
R, 97 m., 1993

Jason London (Pink), Joey Lauren Adams (Simone), Milla Jovovich (Michelle), Shawn Andrews (Pickford), Rory Cochrane (Slater), Adam Goldberg (Mike). Directed by Richard Linklater and produced by James Jacks, Sean Daniel, and Linklater. Screenplay by Linklater.

The years between thirteen and eighteen are among the most agonizing in a lifetime, yet we remember them with a nostalgia that blocks out much of the pain. This is a truth well understood by *Dazed and Confused*, Richard Linklater's film about the last day of school and the long night that follows it.

The film is art crossed with anthropology. It tells the painful underside of *American Graffiti*. In a small town, classes let out for the summer, and upperclassmen go looking for next year's new high school students, so they can paddle them—an initiation inspired, I guess, by high school fraternities.

We follow a large number of teen-agers, boys and girls, popular and not, "good" and "troubled," as they drive aimlessly around town, drink beer, hang out, trade adolescent life-truths, lust, experiment with sex, fight, and in general try to invest their passage into adulthood with a significance it does not seem to have. "If I ever say these were the best years of my life," one of the kids says, "remind me to kill myself."

Linklater does not impose a plot on his material. *Dazed and Confused* (the title comes from a song) is not about whether the hero gets the girl, or the nerd loses his virginity, or the bully gets beaten up. It doesn't end in a tragic car crash, although it does end in some quiet moments of truth, which are not pressed too hard.

The film's real inspiration, I think, is to depict some high school kids from the 1970s with such unblinking attention that we will realize how romanticized most movie teenagers are. A lot of these kids are asking, with Peggy Lee, "Is that all there is?"

Linklater's style is to introduce some characters, linger with them for a while, and then move on to different characters, eventually circling back so that all the stories get told simultaneously. His previous film, *Slacker* (1991), applied a more extreme version of this style to a large group of characters in Austin,

Tex. The film would follow one character, then veer off to follow another, so that we got glimpses of many lives.

Here, in addition to limiting his characters and following through on their stories, he quietly introduces an observation. It is always the case in any group of males—students, fraternity brothers, military men, businessmen—that the ones most zealous about male-bonding rituals, especially those involving drinking and quasi-sexual "initiations," are the most troubled. They secretly feel like outsiders. As their targets, they choose misfits who are too dumb or too smart, who are different in any way, who do not reflect the mediocrity of the crowd.

The kids who enforce this system usually turn out to be losers, and indeed part of their desperation—part of the reason they cling to status in teen-age society—is that they already feel themselves losing. The most pathetic character in *Dazed and Confused* is a graduate from a few years back, in his twenties now, who still hangs out with the kids because he senses that the status he had at seventeen was his personal high point. This is a good film, but it would not cheer people up much at a high school reunion.

The Dead ★ ★ ★
PG, 83 m., 1987

Anjelica Huston (Gretta), Donal McCann (Gabriel), Rachel Dowling (Lily), Dan O'Herlihy (Mr. Browne), Donal Donnelly (Freddy), Cathleen Delany (Aunt Julia), Helena Carroll (Aunt Kate), Ingrid Craigie (Mary Jane), Frank Patterson (Bartell D'Arcy). Directed by John Huston and produced by Wieland Schulz-Keil and Chris Sievernich. Screenplay by Tony Huston.

Better pass boldly into that other world, in the full glory of some passion, than fade and wither dismally with age. The words are from James Joyce's *The Dead*, sometimes called the greatest short story ever written in English. The thoughts belong to a middle-aged man, Gabriel Conroy, and when he thinks them he is lying next to his sleeping wife in a Dublin hotel room, and the snow is falling all over Ireland. He has spent a musical evening at the home of his aunts, Julia and Kate, in the company of the same old friends who gather every Christmas to sing the same songs and tell the old stories and cluck over the fact that poor Freddy Malins has turned up drunk again, to the embarrassment of his mother.

Most of the story is devoted to the party—

who is there, and what happens, and what they say. But Joyce is somehow able to use words to suggest some great silence beneath the chatter, deeper feelings that go unexpressed in all the holiday cheer. The story ends as Gabriel and his wife, Gretta, ride across Dublin to their hotel, and she confesses to him that one of the songs reminded her of a boy who loved her when she was seventeen, a boy named Michael Furey, who was ill. When she made plans to go up to Dublin to convent school, he begged her not to go, and came and stood outside her window in the winter rain. A week later he was dead.

After Gretta tells the story, Gabriel realizes that there is a large part of his wife's life that he did not even suspect existed. She goes to sleep, and he lies beside her in the dark. Joyce writes: "Generous tears filled Gabriel's eyes. He had never felt like that himself toward any woman, but he knew that such a feeling must be love." He can see through the window that it is snowing, and he knows it is snowing all over Ireland, even on the grave where Michael Furey lies.

I have described so much of the Joyce story because I want to illustrate what a hard challenge John Huston set for himself when he decided to make a film of *The Dead*. It is easy enough to film all the details of the party, all the comings and goings, the toasts and the songs. But all of those scenes are there for only one reason: to establish the surface of a commonplace, satisfactory life, so that the closing moments of the story can shock us by showing what hidden depths of loneliness and passion can exist secretly in the hearts of people we think we know.

The key emotional moment in *The Dead* does not belong to Gretta, who still mourns for her dead young lover. It belongs to Gabriel, who weeps for the man his wife once loved, a man he never met or even heard of before tonight. To cry for a stranger is to shed tears for the human condition, to weep because in giving us consciousness, God also gave us the ability to know loss and to mourn it.

There is no way in the world that any filmmaker can reproduce the thoughts inside Gabriel's head at the end of *The Dead*. And that must have been something Huston knew when he decided to make this film. Then why did he make it anyway? I think I know the answer. He made it because he came of Irish blood and lived for many years in Ireland. He made it because the film would be written by his son, Tony, and would star his daughter, Anjelica. And he made it because he knew he was dying, and it would be his last film.

And there was one last reason, which can be glimpsed in the words I began with: "Better pass boldly into that other world, in the full glory of some passion, than fade and wither dismally with age." Huston was an old man when he died, but he had not withered dismally with age because he still had the courage and the imagination to attempt to make an impossible film of the greatest story that he had ever read. Look at Huston's *The Dead* and you will not see a successful film, but you will see a grand gesture, and you will see the best film that Huston could possibly have made. And now the snow falls upon every part of the lonely churchyard on the hill where John Huston lies buried.

Dead Again ★ ★ ★ ★
R, 107 m., 1991

Kenneth Branagh (Church/Strauss), Emma Thompson (Grace/Margaret), Andy Garcia (Gray Baker), Derek Jacobi (Madson), Andy Garcia (Gray Baker), Hanna Schygulla (Inga). Directed by Kenneth Branagh and produced by Charles H. Maguire. Screenplay by Scott Frank.

Dead Again is like *Ghost* for people who grew up on movies that were not afraid of grand gestures. This is a romance with all the stops out, a story about intrigue, deception, and bloody murder—and about how the secrets of the present are unraveled through a hypnotic trance that reveals the secrets of the past. I am a particular pushover for movies like this, movies that could go on the same list with *Rebecca, Wuthering Heights,* or *Vertigo.*

Murder! screams the first word on the screen. Headlines tell of a Hollywood scandal in the 1940s involving the death of the beautiful young wife of a European composer. We cut to the present day. The musical score by Patrick Doyle is ominous and insinuating. We see a threatening old Gothic mansion, we meet a cynical private eye, there is a beautiful woman who has lost her memory, a devious hypnotist who wants to regress her in a search for clues. And of course the murder in the 1940s holds the clue to the woman's amnesia.

Dead Again is Kenneth Branagh once again demonstrating that he has a natural flair for bold theatrical gesture. If *Henry V,* the first film he directed and starred in, caused people

to compare him with Olivier, *Dead Again* will inspire comparisons with Welles and Hitchcock—and the Olivier of Hitchcock's *Rebecca.* I do not suggest Branagh is already as great a director as Welles and Hitchcock, although he has a good start in that direction. What I mean is that his spirit, his daring, is in the same league. He is not interested in making timid movies.

This film is made of Grand Guignol setting and mood, music and bold stylized camera angles, coincidence and shock, melodrama and romance. And it is also suffused with a strange, infectious humor; Branagh plays it dead seriously, but sees that it is funny. Consider, for example, the character of Madson (Derek Jacobi), the old antiques dealer who dabbles in hypnotism on the side. As he regresses his clients in a search for the details of their earlier lives, he has a little sideline, auto-suggesting that they keep a lookout for any interesting antiques they see along the way, so that he can track them down and snap them up cheap.

The movie stars Branagh and his wife, Emma Thompson, in dual roles. In the present day, they are Church, a detective specializing in tracking down missing heirs, and Grace, a young woman who has lost her memory. In black-and-white flashbacks to the lush Hollywood of the postwar 1940s, they are Strauss, a composer who fled from Hitler and is now the toast of Los Angeles, and Margaret, Strauss's beautiful new wife. Lurking in the background of the Hollywood marriage is Inga, the sinister German maid (Hanna Schygulla), and her little boy. Inga is forever lurking on a stair landing, eavesdropping on conversations while painful emotions churn in her memories.

Margaret, the new bride, is not happy with the ominous Inga lurking in the shadows, but Strauss cannot dismiss her because she did, after all, save him from Hitler and deliver him safely to America. But if Margaret is jealous of Inga, Strauss is jealous, too—of Gray Baker (Andy Garcia), the sleek, darkly handsome newspaper reporter who falls for Margaret on the day of her wedding to the older man. Are they having an affair? Can Strauss trust her?

The plot shuttles back and forth between past and present, as the sins of one generation are visited on the next. The dual roles are a way of suggesting that the uneasy spirits of the 1940s characters might have found new hosts in the present to resolve their profound psychic unease. And the old hypno-

tist, established in the baroque shadows of his cluttered antique shop, may hold the key to everything (the photography here is right out of *The Third Man*).

The screenplay, by Scott Frank, is oldfashioned (if you will allow that to be a high compliment). It takes grand themes—murder, passion, reincarnation—and plays them at full volume. Yet there is room for wit, for turns of phrase, for subtle little sardonic touches, for the style that transforms plot into feeling. Kenneth Branagh's direction, here as in *Henry V* (1989), shows a flair for the memorable gesture, for theatricality, for slamming the screen with a stark emotional image and then circling it with suspicions of corruption. When his characters kiss, we do not feel they do so merely to give or receive sexual pleasure; no, they are swept into each other's arms by a great passionate tidal force greater than either one of them, a compulsion from outside of time. You get the idea.

Dead Calm ★ ★ ★
R, 97 m., 1989

Nicole Kidman (Rae Ingram), Sam Neill (John Ingram), Billy Zane (Hughie Warriner), Rod Mudlinar (Russell Bellows), Joshua Tilden (Danny), George Shevtsov (Doctor), Michael Long (Specialist Doctor). Directed by Phillip Noyce and produced by Terry Hayes, Doug Mitchell, and George Miller.

The key image of *Dead Calm* is of two ships drawing near each other in the middle of a vast, empty expanse of ocean. The emotions generated by this shot, near the beginning of the film, underlie everything that follows, making us acutely aware that help is not going to arrive from anywhere, that the built-in protections of civilization are irrelevant, and that the characters will have to settle their own destinies.

On board a sailing yacht are a married couple who hope the cruise will help them deal with the death of their son. On board the other ship—a sinking schooner—is a young man who seems to be the only survivor of a tragic incident of food poisoning. He jumps into a lifeboat and rows for his life toward the yacht, where he is taken aboard. The husband, curious, goes to inspect the schooner, leaving his wife alone with the castaway, who of course turns out to be a homicidal killer.

Almost the entire movie involves these three characters, in a violent game of psychological strategy. Sam Neill stars as the husband, who is stranded on the sinking ship when the killer sails away. Nicole Kidman is the wife, who has to outsmart and outfight the madman. And Billy Zane is the killer, wild-eyed and off-balance. The plot splits into two for most of the movie, with the woman on board the yacht with the killer, while her husband finds himself trapped in the hold of the sinking ship with the water rapidly rising above nose level. The counterpoint is effective.

A plot like this is probably impossible without two ancient movie traditions, the Talking Killer and the Undead Dead. Time and again in the movie, the story would be over if someone—anyone—simply pulled the trigger. There is a moment when the wife temporarily has the upper hand against this madman who had assaulted and beaten her and left her husband to drown, and what does she do? *She ties him up!* And with the knot in front, too—where he can get at it. Later in the film, after he appears to be dead, he reappears, of course, and has to be fought a second time.

And yet *Dead Calm* generates genuine tension because the story is so simple and the performances are so straightforward. This is not a gimmick film (unless you count the husband's method of escaping from the sinking ship), and Nicole Kidman and Billy Zane do generate real, palpable hatred in their scenes together.

Note: The film is based on a 1963 novel by Charles Williams, which inspired an ill-fated Orson Welles project that was suspended in 1970 and then abandoned in 1973 with the death of his leading man, Laurence Harvey. I haven't read the novel, but the story is worthy of a robust craftsman like John D. MacDonald—all except for the unnecessary prologue in the hospital, which he would have junked.

Dead Poets Society ★ ★
PG, 130 m., 1989

Robin Williams (John Keating), Robert Sean Leonard (Neil Perry), Ethan Hawke (Todd Anderson), Josh Charles (Knox Overstreet), Gale Hansen (Charlie Dalton), Dylan Kussman (Richard Cameron), Allelon Ruggiero (Steven Meeks), James Waterston (Gerard Pitts). Directed by Peter Weir and produced by Steven Haft, Paul Junger Witt, and Tony Thomas. Screenplay by Tom Schulman.

Peter Weir's *Dead Poets Society* is a collection of pious platitudes masquerading as a coura-

geous stand in favor of something—doing your own thing, I think. It's about an inspirational, unconventional English teacher and his students at "the best prep school in America," and how he challenges them to question conventional views by such techniques as standing on their desks. It is, of course, inevitable that the brilliant teacher will eventually be fired from the school, and when his students stood on their desks to protest his dismissal, I was so moved, I wanted to throw up.

The film makes much noise about poetry, and there are brief quotations from Tennyson, Herrick, Whitman, and even Vachel Lindsay, as well as a brave excursion into prose that takes us as far as Thoreau's *Walden*. None of these writers are studied, however, in a spirit that would lend respect to their language; they're simply plundered for slogans to exhort the students toward more personal freedom. At the end of a great teacher's course in poetry, the students would love poetry; at the end of this teacher's semester, all they really love is the teacher.

The movie stars Robin Williams as the mercurial John Keating, teacher of English at the exclusive Welton Academy in Vermont. The performance is a delicate balancing act between restraint and schtick. For much of the time, Williams does a good job of playing an intelligent, quick-witted, well-read young man. But then there are scenes in which his stage persona punctures the character—as when he does impressions of Marlon Brando and John Wayne doing Shakespeare. There is also a curious lack of depth to his character; compared to such other great movie teachers as Miss Jean Brodie and Professor Kingsfield, Keating is more of a plot device than a human being.

The story in *Dead Poets Society* is also old stuff, recycled out of the novel and movie *A Separate Peace* and other stories in which the good die young and the old simmer in their neurotic and hateful repressions. The key conflict in the movie is between Neil (Robert Sean Leonard), a student who dreams of being an actor, and his father (Kurtwood Smith), a domineering parent who orders his son to become a doctor, and forbids him to go on stage. The father is a strict, unyielding taskmaster, and the son, lacking the will to defy him, kills himself. His death would have had a greater impact for me if it had seemed like a spontaneous human cry of despair, rather like a meticulously written and photographed set piece.

Other elements in the movie also seem to have been chosen for their place in the artificial jigsaw puzzle. A teen-age romance between one of the Welton students and a local girl is given so little screen time, so arbitrarily, that it seems like a distraction. And I squirmed through the meetings of the "Dead Poets Society," a self-consciously bohemian group of students who hold secret meetings in the dead of night in a cave near the campus.

The society was founded, we learn, by Mr. Keating when he was an undergraduate, but in its reincarnate form it never generates any sense of mystery, rebellion, or daring. The society's meetings have been badly written and are dramatically shapeless, featuring a dance-line to Lindsay's "The Congo" and various attempts to impress girls with random lines of poetry. The movie is set in 1959, but none of these would-be bohemians have heard of Kerouac, Ginsberg, or indeed of the beatnik movement at all.

One scene in particular indicates the distance between the movie's manipulative instincts, and what it claims to be about. When Mr. Keating is being railroaded by the school administration (which makes him the scapegoat for his student's suicide), one of the students acts as a fink and tells the old fogies what they want to hear. Later, confronted by his peers, he makes a hateful speech of which not one word is plausible except as an awkward attempt to supply him with a villain's dialogue. Then one of the other boys hits him in the jaw, to great applause from the audience. The whole scene is utterly false, and seems to exist only so that the violence can resolve a situation which the screenplay is otherwise unwilling to handle.

Dead Poets Society is not the worst of the countless recent movies about good kids and hidebound, authoritarian older people. It may, however, be the most shameless in its attempt to pander to an adolescent audience. The movie pays lip service to qualities and values which, on the evidence of the screenplay itself, it is cheerfully willing to abandon. If you are going to evoke Henry David Thoreau as the patron saint of your movie, then you had better make a movie he would have admired. Here is one of my favorite sentences from Thoreau's *Walden*, which I recommend for serious study by the authors of this film: ". . . instead of studying how to make it worth men's while to buy my baskets, I studied rather how to avoid the necessity of selling them." Think about it.

The Dead Pool ★ ★ ★ ½
R, 94 m., 1988

Clint Eastwood (Harry Callahan), Liam Neeson (Peter Swan), Patricia Clarkson (Samantha Walker), Evan Kim (Juan), David Hunt (Harlan Rook). Directed by Buddy Van Horn and produced by David Valdes. Screenplay by Steve Sharon.

The little twitch comes and goes so fast it's easy to miss. It's in the corner of Dirty Harry's face, and it betrays the seething anger hidden beneath his mask of calm. It's not even anger, really, that seethes inside there—but indignation that criminals are going free while the San Francisco Police Department devotes itself to public relations. What's interesting about the twitch is that it comes at just the right moment, early in the movie, and the audience is waiting for it, and there's actually a cheer when they see it.

Rarely can the mental states of a series movie character have become more familiar than those of Dirty Harry. *The Dead Pool* is the fifth in the series, and most of the people watching it will have seen the other four. They know of Harry's impatience with bureaucracy, and his willingness to go it alone, one-on-one, with the criminals in his path. Like the fans of a familiar opera, Dirty Harry fans wait for the key moments.

After the twitch, we know that before long there will be two more: the moment when Det. Harry Callahan is called on the carpet in his superior's office and given a severe dressing down, and the moment, not long after, when he is suspended from active duty. Unless my memory fails, Harry has solved all of his cases while on suspension.

The balancing act in a good Dirty Harry movie is between the familiar notes, which must remain the same every time, and the new angles in every new case. *The Dead Pool*, which is as good as the original *Dirty Harry*, has lots of new angles, and a lot of things to say, especially about horror films, television news, and the burden of being a celebrity.

The title comes from a macabre gambling game that is being played in San Francisco as the movie opens: A list of eight celebrities has been distributed, and people place bets on which of the eight will be the first to die. The winner takes the pool. And before long, of course, Harry Callahan's name is on the list.

One of the players of the game is Peter Swan (Liam Neeson), a monomaniacal British horror film director who is making a rock video in San Francisco. One of the names on the list is the drug-addicted rock star who is starring in the video. When the rock star is found dead, the director is naturally a prime suspect—but Harry thinks the plot runs deeper than that, and he is right.

In the course of his investigation, he crosses paths with Samantha Walker (Patricia Clarkson), an aggressive TV reporter who is constantly shoving her camera in Harry's face. One day Harry grabs her camera and throws it as far as he can, but in no time the two of them are having candlelit dinners and discussing the problems of fame—problems Harry has thought about much more deeply and interestingly than Samantha.

As the movie develops, we get point-of-view glimpses that clue us in to the fact that someone is killing the members of the Dead Pool and trying to frame the hapless Peter Swan. These shots arrive at some sort of climax in a brilliant and inspired scene in which Harry's car is pursued up and down the hills of San Francisco by another car that is filled with powerful plastic explosives. The gimmick is that the other car is a model, only about a foot long, and so the suspense is intermixed with a hilarious parody of the chase scene in *Bullitt*. (It is highly doubtful that such a small car could travel that fast, but what the hell.)

The best thing about *The Dead Pool* is the best thing about almost all of Clint Eastwood's movies—the film is smart, quick, and made with real wit. It's never just a crude action movie, bludgeoning us with violence. It's self-aware, it knows who Dirty Harry is and how we react to him, and it has fun with its intelligence. Also, of course, it bludgeons us with violence.

The Dead Zone ★ ★ ★ ½
R, 103 m., 1983

Christopher Walken (Johnny), Brooke Adams (Sarah), Herbert Lom (Dr. Weizak), Tom Skerritt (Sheriff), Martin Sheen (Candidate). Directed by David Cronenberg and produced by Debra Hill. Screenplay by Jeffrey Boam.

The Dead Zone does what only a good supernatural thriller can do: It makes us forget it is supernatural. Like *Rosemary's Baby* and *The Exorcist*, it tells its story so strongly through the lives of sympathetic, believable people that we not only forgive the gimmicks, we accept them. There is pathos in what happens to the Christopher Walken character in this movie and that pathos would never be felt if we didn't buy the movie's premise.

Walken plays a high school teacher whose life is happy (he's in love with Brooke Adams), until the night an accident puts him into a coma for five years. When he "returns," he has an extrasensory gift. He can touch people's hands and "know" what will happen to them. His first discovery is that he can foresee the future. His second is that he can change it. By seeing what "will" happen and trying to prevent it, he can bring about a different future. Of course, then he's left with the problem of explaining how he knew something "would have" happened, to people who can clearly see that it did not. Instead of ignoring that problem as a lesser movie might have, *The Dead Zone* builds its whole premise on it.

The movie is based on a novel by Stephen King and was directed by David Cronenberg, the Canadian who started with low-budget shockers (*The Brood, It Came From Within*) and worked up to big budgets (*Scanners*). It's a happy collaboration. No other King novel has been better filmed (certainly not the dreadful *Cujo*), and Cronenberg, who knows how to handle terror, also knows how to create three-dimensional, fascinating characters.

In that he gets a lot of help from Walken, whose performance in this movie in a semireputable genre is the equal of his work in *The Deer Hunter*. Walken does such a good job of portraying Johnny Smith, the man with the strange gift, that we forget this is science fiction or fantasy or whatever, and just accept it as this guy's story.

The movie is filled with good performances: Adams, as the woman who marries someone else during Johnny's coma, but has a clear-eyed, unsentimental love for him at a crucial moment; Tom Skerritt, as the local sheriff who wants to enlist this psychic to solve a chain of murders; Herbert Lom as a sympathetic doctor; and Martin Sheen as a conniving populist politician. They all work together to make a movie that could have been just another scary thriller, and turn it into a believable thriller—which, of course, is even scarier.

Dear America: Letters Home From Vietnam ★ ★ ★ ★
PG-13, 86 m., 1988

Directed by Bill Couturie and produced by the Couturie Co. and Vietnam Veterans Ensemble Theater Company. Screenplay by Richard Dewhurst and Couturie.

Surf's up, and the Beach Boys are singing. American kids dive into the waves and come up wet and grinning, and there's a cooler of beer waiting under the palm trees. It looks like Vietnam is going to be a fun place. The opening scenes of *Dear America: Letters Home From Vietnam* are so carefree, so lighthearted, that it doesn't even seem strange that most of the soldiers look exactly like the kids they are—high school graduates drafted straight into war.

On the sound track, we hear the voices of these soldiers, in the words they wrote home. They speak of patriotism, of confidence, of new friendships. In their letters there is a sense of wonder at this new world they have found, a world so different from the American cities and towns they left behind. And then gradually the tone of their letters begins to change.

There have been several great movies about Vietnam. This is the one that completes the story, that has no plot except that thousands of young men went to a faraway country and had unspeakable experiences there, and many of them died or were wounded for life in body or soul. This movie is so powerful precisely because it is so simple—the words are the words of the soldiers themselves, and the images are taken from their own home movies, and from TV news footage of the war.

There are moments here that cannot be forgotten, and most of them are due to the hard work of the filmmaker, director Bill Couturie, who has not taken just any words and any old footage, but precisely the right words to go with the images. Couturie began with an anthology of letters written home by U.S. soldiers in Vietnam. Then he screened the *entire* archive of TV news footage shot by NBC-TV from 1967 to 1969—two million feet of film totaling 926 hours. He also gained access to footage from the Department of Defense, including previously classified film of action under fire. Much of the footage in this film has never been seen publicly before, and watching it, you know why.

What Couturie and his researchers have done is amazing. In many cases, they have matched up individual soldiers with their letters—we see them as we hear their words, and then we discover their fates. "I tell you truthfully I doubt if I'll come out of this alive," a private named Raymond Griffiths writes home to his girlfriend. "In my original squad, I'm the only one left unharmed." He died in action on the Fourth of July, 1966.

There are amateur 8-mm home movies here, of GIs clowning in front of the camera, and cracking beers, and cleaning their weapons. There are frightening firefights, and unflinching shots of men in the process of dying. And there are chilling scenes such as the one when General William Westmoreland greets the survivors from a bloodbath, and his words are the words of an automaton, with utterly no emotion in his voice as he "chats" with his troops. He is so false, it seems like a bad performance. If this footage had been shown on TV at the time, he might have been forced to resign.

The movie follows a chronology that roughly corresponds to a soldier's year in Vietnam. From the first days of swimming in the surf to the last exhausted days of fear and despair, it never looks away. And the words of the soldiers have the eloquence of simple truth. One soldier writes of the bravery of men who rescued their comrades under enemy fire. Another writes of a momentary hush in a tank battle on Christmas Eve, and of hearing someone begin to sing "Silent Night" and others joining in.

The words in the letters are read by some forty different actors and actresses, whose voices you can sometimes identify, until you stop thinking in those terms. The voices include Robert De Niro, Martin and Charlie Sheen, Kathleen Turner, Tom Berenger, Brian Dennehy, Howard Rollins, Jr., Sean Penn, Matt Dillon, Michael J. Fox. The music on the sound track is all from the period, and then, at the end of the movie, there is a heartbreaking flash-forward to the Vietnam War Memorial in Washington fifteen years later, and we hear Bruce Springsteen's "Born in the USA" as Ellen Burstyn reads from a letter that the mother of a dead veteran left at the foot of the wall of names:

"Dear Bill, Today is February 13, 1984. I came to this black wall again to see and touch your name, William R. Stocks, and as I do I wonder if anyone ever stops to realize that next to your name, on this black wall, is your mother's heart. A heart broken fifteen years ago today, when you lost your life in Vietnam.

"They tell me the letters I write to you and leave here at this memorial are waking others up to the fact that there is still much pain left, after all these years, from the Vietnam War.

"This I know. I would rather have had you for twenty-one years, and all the pain that goes with losing you, than never to have had you at all. Mom."

Choose any film as the best movie ever made about Vietnam, and this is the other half of the same double feature. Francois Truffaut once wrote that it was impossible to make an "anti-war film," because any war film, no matter what its message, was sure to be exhilarating. He did not live to see this film.

Death and the Maiden ★ ★ ★
R, 100 m., 1995
(See related Film Clip, p. 890.)

Sigourney Weaver (Paulina Escobar), Ben Kingsley (Dr. Roberto Miranda), Stuart Wilson (Gerardo Escobar). Directed by Roman Polanski and produced by Thom Mount and Josh Kramer. Screenplay by Rafael Yglesias and Ariel Dorfman.

It is a dark and stormy night. In an isolated house on a deserted landscape, a woman waits alone. The opening moments of *Death and the Maiden* are so intriguing that almost any continuation would be a disappointment—but movies have to be about something, and so slowly the purity of the situation settles down into the business of the plot. But not before the woman, played by Sigourney Weaver, has made an indelible impression.

She is angry and deeply troubled. She is expecting someone, and has a chicken in the oven and a bottle of wine prepared. Then she hears a news bulletin on the radio, and her mood turns to rage. She eats her own dinner, savagely jabbing it with a knife, and dumps the rest in the garbage. She is acutely aware of the night outside. When the man she is waiting for appears, he has been given a lift by a stranger. She conceals herself in the bedroom, and pretends to be asleep. The two men talk and drink. She creeps out into the night, steals the stranger's car, and drives away.

The visitor is distraught to have his car taken—to be marooned, in thanks for his good deed. The two men sit on the steps and continue their conversation. One man is her husband, Gerardo Escobar (Stuart Wilson). The other is a neighbor named Dr. Roberto Miranda (Ben Kingsley). The men become friendly, confiding. It is very late, there is no way to leave the house, and so the visitor agrees to bed down on the couch in the living room. He seems drunk, convivial, but the moment the husband disappears a chemical change seems to take place, and he is thoughtful and self-possessed.

He goes to sleep. The woman approaches

the house quietly, steals into the living room, and is able to surprise the visitor and tie him up before he can resist. She believes he is a torturer—the man who raped her fourteen times when she was a political prisoner. She never saw him, because she was blindfolded, but she knows his voice, his way of using little phrases like "itty bitty," and even his smell. She *knows* it is him.

That is the setup for Roman Polanski's film, based on the play by Ariel Dorfman. In the movie's long night of the soul, the man, bound to a chair, will protest his innocence. The woman will jeer at him and cross-examine him. And her husband will waver first in one direction and then in the other, because this Dr. Miranda is a charming man and a very intelligent one, and if there is a way for him to talk his way to freedom, he will find it.

Death and the Maiden is said to be based on events in Chile, but it could take place in any of the many countries where rule is by force and intimidation. It is, to some degree, about actual guilt: Is this the man who raped and tortured her? To another degree, it is about the nature of guilt and human identity: If this *is* the same man, has he perhaps changed? Was he a product of the times—even a victim of the times, which forced some to be torturers no less than requiring others to be victims?

If he is guilty, does he repent? Is there forgiveness for his crime? Does the woman, by making him a captive and taunting him, descend to his level? Is her husband in some way caught up in a male bonding with this man against women—an instinctive camaraderie that requires him to join forces with any man against any woman?

All of these questions lurk tantalizingly under the surface of *Death and the Maiden*, making it richer than its materials might promise. The story is not about *whether* this is the same man who tortured her, but about the question: What then? There is even the subtle suggestion that—if he was the man—he was not as cruel to her as he might have been, might even have shown her some twisted kindness, during those dark days when an evil society forced captors and their prisoners to enact the rites of torture.

Yes, and it is even more complex than that. Because the whole story leads up to a long monologue by the doctor, brilliantly delivered by Ben Kingsley, so that we must answer not only the question of his guilt or innocence, but the question of its meaning.

By the time the film arrives at its answers, they have become questions. The most difficult question is, how must we punish the evil? If a man kills, must he then be killed? The most compelling argument against capital punishment, for me, is not that society should not execute, but that society should not make anyone into an executioner.

Death and the Maiden is all about acting. In other hands, even given the same director, this might have been a dreary slog. Kingsley makes it come alive with his insinuating performance as the accused rapist: He makes his character so smart we have a certain admiration for his struggle. He is powerless, except for his wits, but they are formidable. The logic of the story places him at its center, but without the Sigourney Weaver performance it would still probably not work. There must have been the temptation to play up the rage of her character, but she brings so many other colors to this woman. There are times, during the dialogue, when we feel we have almost been transported back through time to the actual events she remembers.

What of the third character, the husband? Played convincingly by Wilson as a man who would genuinely like to know the truth, he is a surrogate for us: a jurist who will chair a panel to get to the bottom of those tragic years. But his wife knows (and the man strapped to the chair knows) that no panel can answer, or understand, the nature of the situation. Only the torturer and the tortured have shared that information, and perhaps only by changing places can they understand it. Always assuming, of course, that she has strapped the right man to the chair.

Deathtrap ★ ★ ★
R, 116 m., 1982

Michael Caine (Sidney Bruhl), Christopher Reeve (Clifford Anderson), Dyan Cannon (Myra Bruhl), Irene Worth (Psychic). Directed by Sidney Lumet, produced by Burtt Harrisand. Screenplay by Jay Presson Allen.

Deathtrap is a wonderful windup fiction machine with a few modest ambitions: It wants to mislead us at every turn, confound all our expectations, and provide at least one moment when we levitate from our seats and come down screaming. It succeeds, more or less. It's a thriller that depends on all sorts of surprises for its effects, and you may continue reading in the confidence that I'll reveal none of them.

That doesn't leave me much to write about, however. Let's see. I can tell you something about how the movie begins. Michael Caine plays a very successful Broadway playwright whose latest mystery is a total flop. We see him at the outset, standing at the back of the house, a gloomy witness to a disastrous opening night. (It's a Broadway in-joke that the play he's watching is being performed on the stage set of *Deathtrap*.) Caine gets drunk and goes home to his farmhouse in Connecticut and sinks into despair. There is perhaps, however, some small shred of hope. In the mail the next day Caine receives a manuscript from a former student (Christopher Reeve). It is a new thriller, and Caine sees at once that it's a masterpiece. It could run for years and earn millions of dollars. As he talks with his wife (Dyan Cannon) about it, he slowly develops the idea that he could *steal* the play, kill Reeve, and produce the hit himself.

A plausible plan? Perhaps. Caine and Cannon invite Reeve to come for a visit to the country. They grill him, subtly, and discover that absolutely no one else knows he has written the play. The stage is set for murder, betrayal, and at least an hour and a half of surprises. The tables are turned so many times in this movie that you would think they were on wheels.

Anyway, that's all I'll say about the plot. It is fair to observe, however, that *Deathtrap* is a comic study of ancient and honorable human defects, including greed, envy, lust, pride, avarice, sloth, and falsehood. Interest in the movie depends on its surprises, but its delight grows basically out of the human characteristics of its performers. They do a very good job. Thrillers like this don't always bother to pay attention to the human nature of their characters (for example, the Agatha Christie omnibus whodunits, with their cardboard suspects). *Deathtrap*, however, provides a fascinating, quirky character in Sidney Bruhl, played by Caine, and two strong supporting performances in his goofy, screaming wife (Cannon, looking great) and his talented, devious student (Reeve, who has a light, handsome comic touch not a million miles removed from Cary Grant's). The dialogue is witty without being Neil Simonized. The sets are so good they're almost distracting (a windmill appears to operate in close association with the Bruhls' bed). The only distraction is a strange character played by Irene Worth—a next-door neighbor who's a busybody, snooping psychic who sniffs down false leads. We don't know why she's even in the play, until it's much too late.

Deathtrap is not a great film and will not live forever, but if you're an aficionado of whodunits and haven't seen this one, it'll be a treat. It's more fiendishly complicated than, for example, Caine's similar outing in *Sleuth*. It plays absolutely fair, more or less, and yet fools us every time, more or less. And perhaps its greatest gift is the sight of three lighthearted comic actors having a good time chewing on the dialogue, the scenery, and each other.

Death Wish ★ ★ ★
R, 94 m., 1974

Charles Bronson (Paul Kersey), Hope Lange (Joanna Kersey), Vincent Gardenia (Frank Ochoa), Steve Keats (Jack Toby), William Redfield (Sam Kreutzer), Stuart Margolin (Ames), Jack Wallace (Policeman). Directed by Michael Winner and produced by Dino de Laurentiis. Screenplay by Wendell Mayes.

Death Wish is a quasifascist advertisement for urban vigilantes, done up as a slick and exciting action movie; we like it even while we're turned off by the message. It gives us Charles Bronson in a role that starts out by being somewhat out of character: He plays a liberal, an architect, a former conscientious objector. But he turns into the familiar Bronson man of action after his wife is murdered and his daughter reduced to catatonia by muggers.

His immediate reaction is one of simple grief. Then something happens which suggests a different kind of response. His office sends him to Arizona on a job, and he meets a land developer who's a gun nut. The man takes Bronson to his gun club, watches him squeeze off a few perfect practice rounds, and slips a present into his suitcase when he heads back to New York. It's a .32-caliber revolver.

Alone in his apartment, Bronson examines snapshots from his recent Hawaiian vacation with his wife. Then he examines the gun. He goes out into the night, is attacked by a mugger and shoots him dead. Then he goes home and throws up. But the taste for vengeance, once acquired, has a fascination of its own. And the last half of *Death Wish* is essentially a series of cat-and-mouse games, in which Bronson poses as a middle-aged citizen with a bag of groceries and then murders his attackers.

They are, by the way, everywhere. Director Michael Winner gives us a New York in the grip of a reign of terror; this doesn't look like 1974, but like one of those bloody future cities in science-fiction novels about anarchy in the twenty-first century. Literally every shadow holds a mugger; every subway train harbors a killer; the park is a breeding ground for crime. Urban paranoia is one thing, but *Death Wish* is another. If there were really that many muggers in New York, Bronson could hardly have survived long enough to father a daughter, let alone grieve her.

The movie has an eerie kind of fascination, even though its message is scary. Bronson and Winner have worked together on several films, and they've perfected the Bronson persona. He's a steely instrument of violence, with few words and fewer emotions. In *Death Wish* we get just about the definitive Bronson; rarely has a leading role contained fewer words or more violence.

And Winner directs with a cool precision. He's one of the most efficient directors of action and violence. His muggings and their surprise endings have a sort of inevitable rhythm to them; we're set up for each one almost like the gunfights in Westerns. There's never any question of injustice, because the crimes are attempted right there before our eyes. And then Bronson becomes judge and jury—and executioner.

That's what's scary about the film. It's propaganda for private gun ownership and a call to vigilante justice. Even the cops seem to see it that way; Bronson becomes a folk hero as the New York Vigilante, and the mugging rate drops fifty percent. So the police want to catch Bronson, not to prosecute him for murder, but to offer him a deal: Get out of town, stay out of town, and we'll forget this. Bronson accepts the deal, and in the movie's last scene we see him taking an imaginary bead on a couple of goons in Chicago.

Deep Cover ★ ★ ★ ½
R, 112 m., 1992

Larry Fishburne (John Q. Hull), Jeff Goldblum (David Jason), Victoria Dillard (Betty McCutcheon), Charles Martin Smith (Carver), Sydney Lassick (Gopher). Directed by Bill Duke and produced by Pierre David. Screenplay by Henry Bean and Michael Tolkin.

Deep Cover has a title that reflects its own relationship to the genre of movies about cops, drugs, and violence. It deals in the same familiar materials, but in such an unexpected way that the movie is really a drama, disguised as a thriller. The ads make it look like a hundred other recent movies. It is different from all of them.

Larry Fishburne stars in, surprisingly, his first lead role, although he has been in movies since he appeared in *Apocalypse Now* (1979) as a fifteen-year-old, and played the key role of the father in *Boyz N the Hood* (1991). He plays a cop who is assigned to go undercover and ingratiate himself with an important ring of cocaine dealers. He finds this hard to do; as a child he witnessed his own father killed while pulling a stickup, and his psychic well-being depends heavily on his self-image as a cop—as a good guy, a straight arrow.

He is talked into taking the assignment by a cold federal agent played by Charles Martin Smith, who overcomes his resistance by quoting from a psychological profile: "You score almost like a criminal. You resent authority and have a rigid moral code but no underlying system of values. Look at all your rage and repressed violence. Undercover, your faults will become virtues."

Fishburne is reluctantly recruited and goes undercover as a street buyer of cocaine. He is able to work his way into the circle of a midlevel drug distributor, played with a nice, off-balance craziness by Jeff Goldblum. And eventually he infiltrates the highest levels of the organization, which is bringing drugs in from Latin America.

All of that is more or less routine, the stuff of many other movies. What sets *Deep Cover* apart is its sense of good and evil, the way it has the Fishburne character agonize over the moral decisions he has to make. Most drug movies are so casual about their shootings and killings that you'd hardly think it even hurt to get shot. Fishburne, faced with a situation where he might have to kill somebody, is deeply torn, and he suffers agonizingly through the aftermath. He engages in bitter arguments with Smith over the morality of the actions the government wants him to take. And as the child of an alcoholic who was shot while drunk, he doesn't drink or use drugs, until a crucial turning point in the movie.

Deep Cover was directed by Bill Duke, who directed a lot of television before getting his first feature assignment (*A Rage in Harlem*, 1991). He consciously goes back to traditions of 1940s *film noir* here; he has Fishburne narrate the story much as Fred MacMurray did in *Double Indemnity* (1944), and allows the language of the narration to be poetic and colorful. That's part of the process elevating the story from the mundane to the mythic.

The screenplay is by Henry Bean and Michael Tolkin. Bean is unknown to me, but Tolkin wrote and directed *The Rapture*, about a woman who moves from promiscuity to deep religious belief, and wrote Robert Altman's *The Player*, about a Hollywood executive whose studio power struggle seems to threaten him more deeply than a murder investigation. Tolkin is clearly interested in characters who do wrong and then have to live with the consequences of their actions. Unlike the countless movie characters whose only goal is to kill their enemies and obtain their goals, the Fishburne character is placed in the middle of moral dilemmas that torture him, and then left to figure his own way out of them.

This fresh material inspires the actors. Fishburne is strong and complex, in a role that marks him for more leading work. Goldblum whirls through scenes with wacky dialogue ("Let's have dinner!" he shouts to a victim during a bloody chase scene. "We'll have shrimp!") Victoria Dillard, as a dealer in African art who also launders money, has to make a moral about-face much as the central character in *The Rapture* did. Among the many unexpected aspects of this movie, which is seemingly just another drug thriller, is the way its characters constantly ask themselves what the right course is—and if they can afford to take it.

The Deer Hunter ★ ★ ★ ★
R, 183 m., 1978

Robert De Niro (Michael), John Cazale (Stan), John Savage (Steven), Christopher Walken (Nick), Meryl Streep (Linda), George Dzundza (John), Chuck Aspegren (Axel). Directed by Michael Cimino and produced by Barry Spikings, Michael Deeley, Cimino, and John Peverall. Screenplay by Deric Washburn.

Michael Cimino's *The Deer Hunter* is a three-hour movie in three major movements. It is a progression from a wedding to a funeral. It is the story of a group of friends. It is the record of how the war in Vietnam entered several lives and altered them terribly forever. It is not an anti-war film. It is not a pro-war film. It is one of the most emotionally shattering films ever made.

It begins with men at work, at the furnaces of the steel mills in a town somewhere in Ohio or Pennsylvania. The klaxon sounds, the shift is over, the men go down the road to a saloon for a beer. They sing "I Love You *Bay*-bee" along with the jukebox. It is still morning on the last day of their lives that will belong to them before Vietnam.

The movie takes its time with these opening scenes, with the steel mill and the saloon and especially with the wedding and the party in the American Legion Hall. It's important not simply that we come to know the characters, but that we feel absorbed into their lives, that the wedding rituals and rhythms feel like more than just ethnic details. They do.

The opening moment is lingered over; it's like the wedding celebration in *The Godfather*, but celebrated by hard-working people who have come to eat, dance, and drink a lot and wish luck to the newlyweds and to say good-bye to the three young men who have enlisted in the army. The party goes on long enough for everyone to get drunk who is ever going to, and then the newlyweds drive off and the rest of the friends go up into the mountains to shoot some deer. There is some Hemingwayesque talk about what it means to shoot deer: We are still at a point where shooting something is supposed to mean something.

Then Vietnam occupies the screen, suddenly, with a wall of noise, and the second movement of the film is about the experiences that three of the friends (Robert De Niro, John Savage, and Christopher Walken) have there. At the film's center comes one of the most horrifying sequences ever created in fiction, as the three are taken prisoner and forced to play Russian roulette while their captors gamble on who will, or will not, blow out his brains.

The game of Russian roulette becomes the organizing symbol of the film: Anything you can believe about the game, about its deliberately random violence, about how it touches the sanity of men forced to play it, will apply to the war as a whole. It is a brilliant symbol because, in the context of this story, it makes any ideological statement about the war superfluous.

The De Niro character is the one who somehow finds the strength to keep going and to keep Savage and Walken going. He survives the prison camp and helps the others. Then, finally home from Vietnam, he is surrounded by a silence we can never quite penetrate. He is touched vaguely by desire for the girl that more than one of them left behind, but does not act decisively. He is a "hero," greeted shyly, awkwardly, by the hometown people.

He delays for a long time going to the VA hospital to visit Savage, who has lost his legs. While he is there he learns that Walken is still in Vietnam. He had promised Walken—on a drunken moonlit night under a basketball hoop on a playlot, the night of the wedding—that he would never leave him in Vietnam. They were both thinking, romantically and naively, of the deaths of heroes, but now De Niro goes back in an altogether different context to retrieve the living Walken. The promise was adolescent stuff, but there is no adolescence left when De Niro finds Walken still in Saigon, playing Russian roulette professionally.

At about this point in a review it is customary to praise or criticize those parts of a film that seem deserving: the actors, the photography, the director's handling of the material. It should be said, I suppose, that *The Deer Hunter* is far from flawless, that there are moments when its characters do not behave convincingly, such as implausible details involving Walken's stay and fate in Vietnam, and unnecessary ambiguities in the De Niro character. It can also be said that the film contains greatly moving performances, and that it is the most impressing blending of "box office" and "art" in American movies since *Bonnie and Clyde, The Godfather*, and *Nashville*. All of those kinds of observations will become irrelevant as you experience the film: It gathers you up, it takes you along, it doesn't let up.

The Deer Hunter is said to be about many subjects: About male bonding, about mindless patriotism, about the dehumanizing effects of war, about Nixon's "silent majority." It is about any of those things that you choose, if you choose, but more than anything else it is a heartbreakingly effective fictional machine that evokes the agony of the Vietnam time.

If it is not overtly "anti-war," why should it be? What *The Deer Hunter* insists is that we not *forget* the war. It ends on a curious note: The singing of "God Bless America." I won't tell you how it arrives at that particular moment (the unfolding of the final passages should occur to you as events in life) but I do want to observe that the lyrics of "God Bless America" have never before seemed to me to contain such an infinity of possible meanings, some tragic, some unspeakably sad, some few still defiantly hopeful.

Defence of the Realm ★ ★ ★
PG, 94 m., 1987

Gabriel Byrne (Nick Mullen), Greta Scacchi (Nina Beckman), Denholm Elliott (Vernon Bayliss), Ian Bannen (Dennis Markham), Fulton Mackay (Victor Kingsbrook), Bill Paterson (Jack Macleod). Directed by David Drury and produced by Robin Douet and Lynda Myles. Screenplay by Martin Stellman.

Defence of the Realm is a newspaper thriller about a touchy investigation into British security matters. The story ends the way many newspaper stories end—inconclusively—but the movie ends with a shocking event that suggests the British and their U.S. allies would do anything to defend the American nuclear presence in the U.K.

The movie stars Gabriel Byrne as a young, ambitious newspaper reporter who covers a scandal involving an MP who has the bad judgment to patronize the same call girl used by a KGB agent. Is he a security risk, or does he only seem to be one? Byrne's paper doesn't ask too many questions before putting the story on page one and forcing the politician's resignation.

But there's an older, more experienced hand at the newspaper—a veteran political reporter played by Denholm Elliott, that most dependable and believable of British character actors. He believes the MP may have been framed by people who wanted to silence his embarrassing questions in Parliament. Byrne half-listens to him, and halfway wants to go with the story just because it's so spicy. Upstairs on the executive floor, the proprietor of the paper likes the scandal because it increases circulation.

The film moves quickly and confidently into a net of intrigue, and the director, David Drury, does a good job of keeping us oriented even though the facts in the case remain deliberately confusing. In one especially effective scene, he shows Byrne pretending to be a policeman in order to get quotes from the wife of the disgraced MP; her simple, quiet dignity when she discovers the deception is a rebuke to him.

So is the dogged professionalism of the veteran reporter, who has an anonymous source who insists the MP is innocent. But then the old-timer dies suspiciously, and it's up to Byrne to decide whether there's a deeper story involved, or only a coincidence.

Defence of the Realm reminded me sometimes of *All the President's Men*, but this is a bleaker, more pessimistic movie, which assumes that a conspiracy can be covered up, and that the truth will not necessarily ever be found. The real target of the movie is the American nuclear presence in Britain, and the exciting framework of the newspaper story is an effective way to make a movie against nuclear arms without ever really addressing the point directly.

The acting is strong throughout, but Elliott is especially effective. What is it about this actor, who has been in so many different kinds of movies and seems to make each role special? You may remember him as the Thoreau-quoting father in *A Room With a View*, or as Ben Gazzara's lonely friend in *Saint Jack*. Here he is needed to suggest integrity and scruples, and does it almost simply by the way he looks.

Gabriel Byrne, a relative newcomer, is quietly effective as the reporter, and Greta Scacchi, as a woman who gets involved on both sides of the case, shows again that she can project the quality of knowing more than she reveals. *Defence of the Realm* ends on a bleak and cynical note—unless you count the somewhat contrived epilogue—and gets there with intelligence and a sharp, bitter edge.

Defending Your Life ★ ★ ★ ½
PG, 111 m., 1991

Albert Brooks (Daniel Miller), Meryl Streep (Julia), Rip Torn (Bob Diamond), Lee Grant (Lena Foster), Buck Henry (Dick Stanley). Directed by Albert Brooks and produced by Michael Grillo. Screenplay by Brooks.

A recent survey indicated that most Americans believe in heaven and hell, and of those who believe, the overwhelming majority expect to find themselves in heaven after they die. Since many of them obviously deserve to go to the other place, if only for owning cars with burglar alarms that go off in the middle of the night, a movie like *Defending Your Life* makes perfect sense.

It is Albert Brooks's notion in this film that after death we pass on to a sort of heavenly way station where we are given the opportunity to defend our actions during our most recent lifetime. The process is like an American courtroom, with a prosecutor, defense attorney, and judge, but the charges against us are never quite spelled out. The basic question seems to be, are we sure we did our best, given our opportunities?

In the movie, Brooks plays Dan Miller, a successful exec who takes delivery of a new BMW and plows it into a bus while trying to adjust the CD player. He awakens in a place named Judgment City, which resembles those blandly modern office and hotel complexes around big airports. He's given a room in a clean but spartan place that looks franchised by Motel 6.

At first, Dan is understandably dazed at finding himself dead, but the staff takes good care of him. He's dressed in a flowing gown, whisked around the property on a bus, and told he can eat all he wants in the cafeteria (where the food is delicious but contains no calories). Then he meets his genial, avuncular defense attorney (Rip Torn), and his hard-edged prosecutor (Lee Grant). It's time for the courtroom, in which we see flashbacks to Dan's life as he tries to explain himself.

This is a perfect story notion for Brooks, whose movies always involve his insecurities about himself, his relationships, and his material possessions (who can forget the moment in *Lost in America* when he mercilessly blasted his wife for gambling away their nest egg?). But his notion would finally have no place to go if Brooks didn't add a romantic subplot, in which he falls in love with another sojourner in Judgment City.

She is a sweet, open-faced, serene young woman named Julia and played by Meryl Streep, who is the only actress capable of providing the character's Streepian qualities. They fall into like with one another. Dan visits her hotel and is dismayed to discover that she has much better facilities than he does—Four Seasons instead of Motel 6— and he wonders if maybe your hotel assignment is a clue about how well you lived your past life. But nobody in Judgment City will give him a straight answer to a question like that.

The movie is funny in a warm, fuzzy way, and it has a splendidly satisfactory ending, which is unusual for an Albert Brooks film (his inspiration in his earlier films is bright but seems to wear thin toward the third act). The best thing about the movie, I think, is the notion of Judgment City itself. Doesn't it make sense that heaven, for each society, would be a place much like the earth that it knows? We're still stuck with images of angels playing harps, which worked fine for Renaissance painters. But isn't our modern world ready for images in which the angels look like Rotarians and CEOs?

Stanley Kubrick's *2001* ended with the astronaut leaving the solar system and finding himself, quite unexpectedly, in a spotless hotel room. The usual explanation for that scene is that a superior race from elsewhere in the universe had constructed this room for him as a place where he would feel at home, while they studied him—much as a zoo throws in some trees for the monkeys. The best joke in *Defending Your Life* is that heaven is run along the lines that would be recommended by a good MBA program.

The Delta Force ★ ★ ★
R, 129 m., 1985

Chuck Norris (Major McCoy), Lee Marvin (Colonel Alexander), Robert Forster (Abdul), Martin Balsam (Ben Kaplan), Joey Bishop (Harry Goldman), Lainie Kazan (Sylvia Goldman), George Kennedy (Father O'Malley), Hanna Schygulla (Ingrid), Bo Svenson (Captain). Directed by Menahem Golan and produced by Golan and Yoram Globus. Screenplay by James Bruner and Golan.

Some of the opening moments of *The Delta Force* had me ready to laugh. Here was a movie about an airplane hijacking, and who was on the passenger list? Why, George Kennedy, of course—fresh from four *Airport* movies and *Earthquake*—and Shelley Winters, going on her first vacation since the *Poseidon* sank. I thought this was going to be another hilarious disaster movie, but I was wrong. *The Delta Force* settles down into a well-made action film that tantalizes us with its parallels to real life.

The movie was inspired by the June 1985 hijacking of the TWA airplane and the hostage crisis after the passengers were held captive in Beirut. (In the movie, the airline is renamed ATW—real subtle.) Many of the moments in the film are drawn directly from life, as when an American serviceman is beaten to death by terrorists, and his body is dumped on the runway, or when a terrorist holds a gun to the head of the pilot during a press conference.

The docudrama approach gives an eerie conviction to the movie, although later, after Chuck Norris and Lee Marvin arrive on the scene, there's not much we would mistake for reality. The movie caters directly to our national revenge fantasies; in *The Delta Force*, the hijacking ends the way we might have wanted it to.

The story establishes the plane and its passengers, and then intercuts the hijacking with the movements of the Delta Force, a crack U.S. commando unit that specializes in anti-terrorist missions. Delta is led by grizzled old Lee Marvin, and its best fighter is a hot dog played by Chuck Norris, who once again this time is depicted as a man who yearns only for retirement, but cannot resist the call to action, and arrives at the last moment in his trusty pickup truck. (If I were Chuck Norris's agent, I'd insist that his next movie include a new way of introducing him into the plot.)

There are a couple of hazards here that the movie has to face. The action inside the airplane has a tendency to degenerate into a retread of the old *Airport* movies, but director Menahem Golan wisely has his cast keep their acting fairly low-key. And the action involving Norris has a tendency to resemble his activities in *Missing in Action* and *Invasion USA*. Golan does nothing to fight this tendency—indeed, he relishes it, in scenes like the one where Norris drives his rocket-firing motorcycle right through the window of a terrorist hideout, and socks the bad guy on the jaw. This is the second movie in a row where Norris has possessed X-ray vision; in *Invasion USA* he drove his pickup into a department store to stop a terrorist attack. How does he know what's on the other side of the barriers he crashes through?

It's a funny thing about action movies. When they don't work, we have a lot of fun picking holes in them, like the fallacy of the hero's X-ray vision. When they do work, though, we forgive them their inconsistencies. *The Delta Force* works. It is taut and exciting and well-tuned to the personalities of Marvin and Norris, who work together here like a couple of laconic veterans of lots of tough jobs.

The movie also has the one other attribute that any good thriller needs: A first-rate performance by the actor playing the villain. As Abdul, the chief terrorist, an American actor named Robert Forster gives a frightening, good performance, intense and uncompromising. He makes the threat real, and keeps *The Delta Force* from becoming just an action comic book.

Desperately Seeking Susan ★ ★ ★
PG-13, 103 m., 1985

Rosanna Arquette (Roberta), Madonna (Susan), Aidan Quinn (Dez), Mark Blum (Gary), Robert Joy (Jim), Laurie Metcalf (Leslie). Directed by Susan Seidelman and produced by Sarah Pillsbury and Midge Sanford. Screenplay by Leora Barish.

Desperately Seeking Susan is a movie that begins with those three words, in a classified ad. A time and place are suggested where Susan can rendezvous with the person who is desperately seeking her. A bored housewife (Rosanna Arquette) sees the ad and becomes consumed with curiosity. Who is Susan and who is seeking her, and why? So Arquette turns up at the rendezvous, sees Susan (Madonna), and inadvertently becomes so involved in her world that for a while she even *becomes* Susan.

This sounds complicated, but, believe me, it's nothing compared to the complexities of this movie. *Desperately Seeking Susan* is a screwball comedy based on several cases of mistaken identity. Susan, for example, is a punk drifter who is in a hotel room with a mobster the first time we see her. Shortly after, the mobster is killed and the mob hit man comes back looking for Susan, who may be a witness. But meanwhile, Susan has sold the jacket that is her trademark, and the housewife has bought it, and then the housewife has banged her head and become a temporary amnesia victim, and there are people who see her jacket and think she's Susan.

But enough of the plot. I wouldn't even dream of trying to explain how Arquette ends up being sawed in half by a nightclub magician. The plot isn't the point, anyway; once you realize the movie is going to be a series of double-reverses, you relax and let them happen. The plot is so unpredictable that, in a way, it's predictable; that makes it the weakest part of the movie.

What I liked in *Desperately Seeking Susan* was the cheerful way it hopped around New York, introducing us to unforgettable characters, played by good actors. For example, Aidan Quinn plays a guy who thinks Arquette is Susan, his best friend's girl. He lets her spend the night, and inadvertently feeds her amnesia by suggesting that she *is* Susan. Laurie Metcalf plays Arquette's yuppie sister-in-law. Robert Joy plays Susan's desperately seeking lover. Peter Maloney is the broken-down magician. New York underground characters such as Richard Hell, Anne Carlisle, and Rockets Red Glare also surface briefly. The director is Susan Seidelman, whose previous film, *Smithereens*, was a similar excursion through the uncharted depths of New York.

Desperately Seeking Susan does not move with the self-confidence that its complicated plot requires. But it has its moments, and many of them involve the different kinds of special appeal that Arquette and Madonna are able to generate. They are very particular individuals, and in a dizzying plot they somehow succeed in creating specific, interesting characters.

Diamonds Are Forever ★ ★ ★
PG, 119 m., 1971

Sean Connery (James Bond), Jill St. John (Tiffany Case), Charles Gray (Blofeld), Lana Wood (Plenty O'Toole), Jimmy Dean (Willard Whyte), Bruce Cabot (Saxby), Bernard Lee (M), Desmond Llewelyn (Q). Directed by Guy Hamilton and produced by Albert R. Broccoli and Harry Saltzman.

The cultists like the early James Bond movies best, but I dunno. They may have been more tightly directed films, but they didn't understand the Bond mythos as fully as *Goldfinger* and *Diamonds Are Forever*. We see different movies for different reasons, and *Diamonds Are Forever* is great at doing the things we see a James Bond movie for.

Not the least of these is the presence of Sean Connery, who was born to the role: dry, unflappable (even while trapped in a coffin at a crematorium), with a mouth that does as many kinds of sly grins as there are lascivious possibilities in the universe. There's something about his detachment from danger that props up the whole Bond apparatus, insulating it from the total ridiculousness only an inch away.

In *Diamonds Are Forever,* for example, Bond finds himself driving a moon buggy (antennae wildly revolving and robot arms flapping) while being chased across a desert—never mind why. The buggy looks comical, but Connery does not; he is completely at home, as we know by now, with every form of transportation. Later, after outsmarting five Las Vegas squad cars in a lovely chase scene, he nonchalantly flips his Mustang up on two wheels to elude the sixth. But not a sign of a smile. There is an exhiliration in the way he does it, even more than in the stunt itself.

The plot of *Diamonds Are Forever* is as complicated as possible. That's necessary in order to have somebody left after nine dozen bad guys have been killed. It has been claimed that the plot is too complicated to describe, but I think I could if I wanted to. I can't imagine why anyone would want to, though. The point in a Bond adventure is the moment, the surface, what's happening now. The less time wasted on plot, the better.

Diary of a Mad Housewife ★ ★ ★
R, 95 m., 1970

Carrie Snodgress (Tina Balser), Richard Benjamin (Jonathan Balser), Frank Langella (George). Directed and produced by Frank Perry. Screenplay by Eleanor Perry.

Frank Perry's *Diary of a Mad Housewife* is about a long-suffering young woman who has somehow gotten herself married to the most supercilious dope in Manhattan. He's egotistical, cruel, insecure, immature, and bitchy. He sides with "his" children against his wife. He considers her a household drudge, good for housework during the day, and, maybe, a "little roll in de hay" at night. He humiliates her in public, and humiliates himself, too, by his shameless social-climbing. Does she hate him? Not exactly.

She's a masochistic type who sees her husband as, somehow, her fate in life. She enjoys martyrdom, I guess; I can't imagine any other reason why she'd put up with this monster she's married to. And that's at the base of our initial irritation with the film; she stays with this guy we can't stand, and so we have trouble admiring her. We even begin to doubt her sanity, until she falls into a love affair with a writer. And then *he* turns out to be such an egotistical, selfish, cruel type that we just about give up on her. She has what's known, I believe, as self-destructive tendencies. Not that she'd ever try suicide; that'd be too easy, and end the delight of suffering. What makes the movie work, however, is that it's played entirely from the housewife's point of view, and that the housewife is played brilliantly by Carrie Snodgress. We're irritated by the things the character puts up with, but Miss Snodgress is beautifully good at putting up with them.

Still, when you've finished watching this movie you start getting mad at Richard Benjamin. He overplays his character so much that he nearly destroys the role; nobody, but nobody, is that supercilious. Near the beginning of the movie there's a scene when the whole family is in an elevator, and Benjamin gives instructions to his wife about packing a suitcase. He describes everything in highly specific brand names, and with such precision that the dialogue passes beyond reality and becomes satire. You can see it as a caption under a *New Yorker* cartoon.

But then, then . . . you start thinking about the title and the point of view of the movie, and you realize this is indeed a diary; that we're getting the housewife's version of

the story. So of course she seems noble and long-suffering, and of course he's a witless bastard—because that's the way she sees it. And of course his dialogue is extreme and hers isn't, because in her version of the story, she's sane, and he's not.

Dick Tracy ★ ★ ★ ★
PG, 105 m., 1990

Warren Beatty (Dick Tracy), Al Pacino (Big Boy Caprice), Madonna (Breathless Mahoney), Glenne Headly (Tess Trueheart), Charlie Korsmo (Kid), Seymour Cassel (Sam Catchem), James Keane (Pat Patton), Charles Durning (Chief Brandon), Mandy Patinkin (88 Keys), Paul Sorvino (Lips Manlis), Dustin Hoffman (Mumbles), Dick Van Dyke (D.A. Fletcher). Directed and produced by Warren Beatty. Screenplay by Jim Cash and Jack Epps, Jr.

There was always something inbred about the *Dick Tracy* comic strip, some suggestion that all of its characters had been mutated by the same cosmic rays, and then locked together in a bizarre loony bin of crime. *Tracy* was the first comic strip I encountered after I outgrew funny animals, and what struck me was that the physical appearance of the characters always mirrored their souls, or occupations. They looked like what they were, and what you saw was what you got, from the square-jawed Tracy barking into his wrist radio, to Pruneface, Flattop, and the others.

Warren Beatty's production of *Dick Tracy* approaches the material with the same fetishistic glee I felt when I was reading the strip. The Tracy stories didn't depend really on plot—they were too spun-out for that— and of course they didn't depend on suspense—Tracy always won. What they were about was the interaction of these grotesque people, doomed by nature to wear their souls on their faces. We see this process at work in one of the film's first scenes, where a poker game is in progress, and everyone around the table looks like a sideshow attraction, from Little Face, whose features are at the middle of a sea of dissipation, to The Brow, always deep in shallow thought.

Another of the movie's opening shots establishes, with glorious excess, the Tracy universe. The camera begins on a window, and pulls back, and moves up until we see the skyline of the city, and then it seems to fly through the air, turning as it moves so that we sweep above an endless urban vista. Skyscrapers and bridges and tenements and elevated railways crowd each other all the way to the distant horizon, until we realize this is the grandest and most squalid city that ever was. It's more than a place. It's the distillation of the idea of City—of the vast, brooding, mysterious metropolis spreading in all directions forever, concealing millions of lives and secrets.

And then the camera moves in on one of those buildings, and as we see people again we realize that everything we have seen before—every skyscraper, every bridge—was created in a movie studio. *Dick Tracy* is a masterpiece of studio artificiility, of matte drawings and miniatures and optical effects. It creates a world that never could be. There is a scene where a giant locomotive roars down upon the fleeing figure of a small boy, and he jumps in front of it and we actually flinch. The whole fearsome train is actually a model and the running figure has been combined with it in an optical process, but don't tell that to anyone watching the movie because they won't believe you.

Into this theater of the night comes striding the peculiar figure of a man in a yellow hat and a yellow raincoat—Dick Tracy. When Chester Gould first conceived him all those years ago, did it seem unlikely that a police detective would wear yellow? Maybe not, since Tracy didn't live in a city but in a comic strip, and the primary colors had to jump off the page. Beatty's decision to shoot *Dick Tracy* only in the seven basic colors of comic strips is a good one, because this is a movie about creatures of the imagination, about people who live in rooms where every table lamp looks like a Table Lamp and every picture on the wall represents only a Picture on the Wall. It was necessary for Tracy to wear the essence of hats and coat, and so of course they were yellow; anything less would have been too ordinary.

Tracy in the comics was always an enigma, a figure without emotion or complexity. Warren Beatty plays his Tracy as a slightly more human figure, a cop who does have a personality, however slight. To the degree that the human side of Tracy peeks through, I believe, the character is diminished; the critics who have described Tracy as too shallow have missed the entire point, which is that we are not talking about real people here, but about archetypes. Tracy should be as square as his jaw.

Surrounding him are the characters who provide the real meat of the movie, and the scene-stealer is Big Boy Caprice, played by

Al Pacino with such grotesque energy that we seem to have stumbled on a criminal from Dickens. Consider the scene where Big Boy rehearses the chorus line in his nightclub. He dashes and darts behind the girls, pushing them, slapping them, acting more like a dog trainer than a choreographer. There is an edge of cruelty to his behavior, and later we see that some of his cruelty is directed toward himself. Unlike most of the villains of modern movies, he does not flaunt his evil, but is ashamed of it, and this Victorian trait makes him more interesting.

In the shadows around Big Boy are a gallery of other human grotesqueries—characters who have been named for their physical abnormalities, like Lips Manlis and Shoulders, or for other handicaps, like Mumbles (Dustin Hoffman), who talks so fast he cannot be heard. Because these characters are glimpsed rather quickly, their makeup can be more bizarre; the characters who are onscreen all the time look more normal, and among them are the two women in Tracy's life, the faithful Tess Trueheart (Glenne Headley) and the seductive Breathless Mahoney (Madonna).

Pop sociologists have made a specialty out of Madonnaology, claiming she changes images so quickly that she is always ahead of her audience, always on the cutting edge. Her very appearance in each new tour is a clue to her latest message about pop imagery, we're told. Her mistake in *Dick Tracy,* I think, is that she frankly reaches back to Marilyn Monroe and tries to make Breathless into a Monroe clone, right down to the lighting and costuming in some numbers, which seems inspired by Monroe in *Some Like It Hot.* It doesn't work. She's not Monroe and she's not Madonna, either. Breathless should have come out of a new place in her mind.

That's not a crucial flaw in the movie because Tracy himself is so bloodless that we barely believe he can be seduced. The deepest emotional attachment in the detective's life, indeed, is not even Tess Trueheart, but Kid (Charlie Korsmo), an orphan Tracy takes under his wing, and the movie's emotional high point is probably when Kid decides to call himself Dick Tracy, Jr.

Last summer's *Batman,* a movie I found disappointing, was at least a triumph of special effects—of set design and art direction. *Dick Tracy,* which is a sweeter, more optimistic movie, outdoes even *Batman* in the visual departments. This is a movie in which

every frame contains some kind of artificial effect. An entire world has been built here, away from the daylight and the realism of ordinary city streets. And *Dick Tracy* also reflects the innocence of the comic strip that inspired it. Unlike the movie version of *Batman,* which hyped up the level of its violence to a degree that could have been truly disturbing to younger viewers, the PG-rated *Dick Tracy* contains no obscenity, no blood, and no "realistic" violence. It is one of the most original and visionary fantasies I've seen on a screen.

Die Hard ★ ★
R, 132 m., 1988

Bruce Willis (John McClane), Alan Rickman (Hans Gruber), Bonnie Bedelia (Holly McClane), Reginald Veljohnson (Sgt. Al Powell), Paul Gleason (Deputy Chief). Directed by John McTiernan and produced by Lawrence Gordon and Joel Silver. Screenplay by Jeb Stuart and Steven E. de Souza.

The idea has a certain allure to it: A cop is trapped inside a high-rise with a team of desperate terrorists. He is all that stands between them and their hostages. Give the terrorist leader brains and a personality, make one of the hostages the estranged wife of the cop, and you've got a movie.

The name of the movie is *Die Hard,* and it stars Bruce Willis in another one of those Hollywood action roles where the hero's shirt is ripped off in the first reel so you can see how much time he's been spending at the gym. He's a New York cop who has flown out to Los Angeles for Christmas, and we quickly learn that his marriage was put on hold after his wife (Bonnie Bedelia) left for the Coast to accept a great job offer. She is now Assistant to the President of the multinational Nakatomi Corp., and shortly before Willis makes his entrance at the office party, the terrorists strike.

They, too, are a multinational group, led by a German named Hans Gruber (Alan Rickman), who is well-dressed and has a neatly trimmed beard and talks like an intellectual and thinks he is superior to the riffraff he has to associate with. He has a plan that has been devised with clockwork precision, involving the theft of millions of dollars in negotiable bonds, and it is only after Willis starts causing trouble that he allows the situation to escalate beyond his original plans.

The terrorists are skilled and well-armed, and there are a lot of them. Willis's strategy involves keeping them off guard with lightning attacks from his hiding place, on an upper floor of the building that is still under construction. This plan involves the deployment of a great many stunts and special effects, as when Willis swings through a plateglass window on the end of a fire hose, or when he drops plastic explosives down the elevator shaft of the building.

On a technical level, there's a lot to be said for *Die Hard*. It's when we get to some of the unnecessary adornments of the script that the movie shoots itself in the foot. Willis remains in constant radio contact with a police officer on the ground (Reginald Veljohnson), who tries to keep his morale up. But then the filmmakers introduce a gratuitous and unnecessary additional character, the deputy police chief (Paul Gleason), who doubts that the guy on the other end of the radio is really a New York cop at all.

As nearly as I can tell, the deputy chief is in the movie for only one purpose: to be consistently wrong at every step of the way, and to provide a phony counterpoint to Willis's progress. The character is so willfully useless, so dumb, so much a product of the Idiot Plot Syndrome, that all by himself he successfully undermines the last half of the movie. Thrillers like this need to be well-oiled machines with not a single wasted moment. Inappropriate and wrongheaded interruptions reveal the fragile nature of the plot and prevent it from working.

Without the deputy chief and all that he represents, *Die Hard* would have been a more than passable thriller. With him, it's a mess, and that's a shame, because the film does contain superior special effects, impressive stunt work and good performances, especially by Alan Rickman as the terrorist. Here's a suggestion for thriller-makers: You can't go wrong if all of the characters in your movie are at least as intelligent as most of the characters in your audience.

Die Hard 2: Die Harder ★ ★ ★ ½
R, 124 m., 1990

Bruce Willis (John McClane), Bonnie Bedelia (Holly McClane), William Atherton (Thornberg), Reginald Veljohnson (Al Powell), Franco Nero (Esperanza), William Sadler (Stuart), John Amos (Grant), Dennis Franz (Carmine Lorenzo). Directed by Renny Harlin and produced by Lawrence Gordon, Joel Silver, and Charles Gordon. Screenplay by Steven E. de Souza and Doug Richardson.

Die Hard 2, subtitled *Die Harder*, enters Bruce Willis in a decathlon of violence, and he places first in every event, including wrestling for guns, jumping onto conveyor belts, being ejected from cockpits, leaping onto the wings of moving airplanes, and fighting with the authorities. This is one of those thrillers like the *Indiana Jones* series that I categorize as Bruised Forearm Movies, because when the movie is over your forearm is black-and-blue from where your date has grabbed it during the moments of suspense.

Why is Bruce Willis so effective in a movie like this? Maybe because he combines a relatively athletic physique with the appearance and manner of everyman. The title of the movie describes the basic plot device: Here is a man who will not give up, who will not admit defeat, who doggedly carries on in the face of adversity. The dangers and tests he faces would daunt a James Bond, but for this open-faced cop with the receding hairline, there is no choice. After all: "My wife is on that plane!"

Again this time he plays a cop on vacation. He's in Washington's Dulles airport, waiting for his wife's flight to land, on a crowded evening during the Christmas season. And scheduled into the same airport at the same time is a military jet bringing a South American drug tyrant to justice. A skilled band of terrorists, led by a former CIA operative, plans to seize control of airport operations by electronically bypassing the control tower. They'll shut off the airport lights, leave dozens of planes circling overhead, and then cause one flight to crash as a warning. What they want is a fully fueled standby plane, ready to spirit the dictator to freedom.

Willis, who has a cop's practiced eye, spots one of the conspirators, follows him into a luggage handling area, and discovers that a plot is afoot. But he can't convince the chief of airport security (Dennis Franz), who resents an outside cop on his turf. After a killing and various other hints (including a plane crash), the security chief finally admits he may have a problem on his hands, but even then Willis's work is not over, and by the end of the movie he is single-handedly taking on whole planeloads of mercenaries in a fight to the finish.

Because *Die Hard 2* is so skillfully constructed and well-directed, it develops a momentum that carries it past several credibility gaps that might have capsized a lesser film. For example, how about the scene where the tower informs the circling airplanes that they'll be out of radio contact for a couple of hours and should just keep circling? Why can't those planes simply establish radio contact with other ground transmitters and be diverted to alternate airports? Because then Willis's wife (Bonnie Bedelia) wouldn't be up there in the sky and in mortal danger, that's why.

A more serious problem involves the whole rescue operation itself. When Noriega was taken captive and returned to the United States to stand trial, there was little serious effort to save him: At the end, he was a refugee in his own country, reduced to seeking asylum in the residence of a Vatican diplomat. Would anyone have the means, the money, and the will to mount such a vast and complicated terrorist operation simply to save one drug-connected dictator? Even if he does bear an uncanny resemblance to Fidel Castro? I doubt it.

But, on the other hand, I don't care. *Die Hard 2* is as unlikely as the Bond pictures and as much fun. It tells a story we can identify with, it has a lot of interesting supporting characters, it handles the action sequences with calm precision, and it has a couple of scenes that are worth writing home about.

One of those is a plane crash. Not everybody's favorite image, I'll grant you (and this is a feature that will be severely edited before it becomes an in-flight movie). Watching the plane burst into flames on a runway, I knew intellectually that I was watching special effects, probably a fairly large and detailed model photographed in slow motion. But no matter. The crash was scarily convincing.

Another shot, more fun, is harder to describe without giving away a plot point. But it involves placing the camera's eye hundreds of feet straight up in the air and then catapulting Willis up until his nose almost touches the lens before he begins to fall to earth again. Not only is this shot sensationally effective in terms of the story, but as a visual it is exhilarating: I love it when a director finds a new way to show me something.

The director of *Die Hard 2* is a Finn named Renny Harlin, whose other credits include *Nightmare on Elm Street 4* and the Andrew Dice Clay picture, *Ford Fairlane*. Like the Dutch-born Paul Verhoeven (*Robocop, Total Recall*), he has taken Hollywood commercial moviemaking, shaken it, and given it a new energy. Given the enormous success of the original *Die Hard* (a movie I didn't enjoy nearly as much as this one), producer Lawrence Gordon and his partners must have crossed their fingers before risking this sequel with a relatively untried director. But they did the right thing: This is a terrific entertainment.

Die Hard With a Vengeance ★ ★ ★
R, 130 m., 1995

Bruce Willis (John McClane), Jeremy Irons (Simon), Samuel L. Jackson (Zeus), Graham Greene (Joe Lambert), Colleen Camp (Connie Kowalski), Anthony Peck (Ricky Walsh), Larry Bryggman (Chief Cobb), Sam Phillips (Katya). Directed by John McTiernan and produced by McTiernan and Michael Tadross. Screenplay by Jonathan Hensleigh.

There was a time when the James Bond movies started with one sensational stunt sequence, and we were grateful for it. Now there are movies that are essentially nothing but sensational stunt sequences, one after another, each one a feat of staging, until we're reeling in our seats from input overload. *Die Hard With a Vengeance* is the kind of movie where, toward the end, you start looking for the kitchen sink.

The movie, third in the *Die Hard* series, stars Bruce Willis as detective John McClane, this time on the New York police force—or, more accurately, suspended from it. There's a scene where the chief takes out McClane's badge and shoves it across the desk, and McClane asks, "Does this mean I'm back on active duty?" and I heard knowledgeable chuckles in the audience from those who appreciate the fine old traditions, such as that all hero cops are rogues who are either under suspension or heading for it.

After the frighteningly realistic bombing of a Manhattan department store, McClane gets a call from a mad bomber named Simon (Jeremy Irons), ordering him to stand on a Harlem street corner wearing a sandwich board bearing a motto that one would particularly hope not to be wearing in Harlem. McClane's life is saved by a local store-owner named Zeus (Samuel L. Jackson), who is then included in Simon's strange game of cat and mouse.

The pattern of the movie is particularly suited to a series of stunts and violent action sequences. Simon, who seems to be everywhere and see everything, sends McClane and Zeus hurtling around Manhattan on one death-defying mission after another (at one point piloting a cab down the sidewalks of Central Park). Bombs seem to be everywhere in the city—on a subway train, for starters, and then allegedly in a city school.

Simon is not, however, only a mad bomber. He has a purpose behind his behavior, and a private army at his command. And it turns out he has a motive for singling out McClane, since it was McClane who dropped Simon's brother off that Los Angeles highrise in the first *Die Hard* movie.

Willis and Jackson inhabit most of the scenes, usually together. Their dialogue is heavy on obligatory talk about racism, even though there is not the slightest sign that either one holds racist feelings; I dunno, I guess the use of the N-word makes action heroes feel macho. They work well together as actors, Jackson's observant detachment a good counterpoint to Willis's manic desperation. And there's a running gag, as Simon sets them puzzles and Jackson solves them (although I was not quite clear how they used the three- and five-gallon jugs to measure exactly four gallons of water; a fourth grader can probably enlighten me).

Toward the end of the movie there is, of course, a scene where a member of the bomb squad is sweating over an infernal machine, one big enough to blow up several city blocks and equipped, as they all are, with a helpful digital countdown. He even has to decide which wires to snip. (There could be a little film festival on one of the cable channels, consisting of scenes where experts defuse bombs.)

The motivation behind Simon's plan is ingenious, and I will not discuss it, except to say I am a little hazy about how the trucks got to Canada. Jeremy Irons, as the madman, is in the great tradition of the British actor as villain; like Alan Rickman, Anthony Hopkins, Gary Oldman, and Tim Roth, he uses a certain clipped precision of speech that makes everything he says sound resentful.

Irons's performance and all of the others take second place, however, to sequences in which two men slide down a cable from a bridge to a ship, a wall of water chases a truck through an aqueduct, a subway car careens out of control through a station, and cars hurtle through the air like airplanes. *Die Hard With a Vengeance* is basically a wind-up action toy, cleverly made and delivered with high energy. It delivers just what it advertises, with a vengeance.

Note: A movie based on urban bombings creates, of course, unavoidable reminders of the Oklahoma City tragedy. During press interviews about *Die Hard With a Vengeance*, Willis requested that he not be asked about Oklahoma City because he didn't want to trivialize that tragedy by discussing it in terms of this movie. That seems to me like a sane response.

Dim Sum ★ ★ ★
PG, 88 m., 1985

Laureen Chew (Geraldine Tam), Kim Chew (Mrs. Tam), Victor Wong (Uncle Tam), Ida F.O. Chung (Auntie Mary), Cora Miao (Julia), John Nishio (Richard). Directed by Wayne Wang and produced by Tom Sternberg, Wang, and Danny Yung. Screenplay by Terrel Seltzer.

Director Wayne Wang says his favorite image in *Dim Sum* is the sight of the shoes left outside the living-room door in the Tam household in San Francisco's Chinatown. They are Western shoes, taken off as the characters enter a home that is still run according to Chinese values by old Mrs. Tam, a sweet widow with a strong but quietly concealed will. After the success of *Chan Is Missing*, his first slice-of-life about Chinese-Americans, Wang was looking for another story, and when he saw some shoes left outside a Chinese home, he knew he had his viewpoint, and only had to create his characters.

He has created some unforgettable ones, including Mrs. Tam (Kim Chew), a sixtyish woman whose husband is dead and whose children have left home, all except for the youngest daughter; Geraldine Tam (Laureen Chew), the daughter, who says she wants to get married but feels she should stay with her mother, and Uncle Tam (Victor Wong), a jolly, worldly bartender who would marry Mrs. Tam if Geraldine would only get out of the way.

These three characters dance a subtle little emotional ballet during the film, as we gradually become aware of their true motives. Mrs. Tam is given to sadly shaking her head and bemoaning the fact that her daughter is thirty and still single, but there are clues that she enjoys the fact that Geraldine has stayed at home with her. That way, she will not have to deal with Uncle Tam, who, for that matter, may only be paying lip service to his desire to marry her. Meanwhile, Geraldine has a boyfriend in Los Angeles who has been waiting patiently to marry her, and perhaps Geraldine uses her mother as an excuse to avoid the idea of marriage.

What is remarkable is the way Wang deals with this complex set of emotions, in a movie that is essentially a comedy. Some of the scenes in *Dim Sum* are as quietly funny as anything I've seen, especially Mrs. Tam's birthday party, a long conversation she has over the back fence with a neighbor, and the way Uncle Tam effortlessly mixes his Chinese wisdom with the lessons he has learned as a bartender.

The movie is not heavily plotted, and that's good; a heavy hand would spoil this fragile material. Wang's camera enters quietly and observes as his characters lead their lives, trying to find a compromise between too much loneliness and too much risk. At the end, everyone is more or less happy, and more or less sad, and in this movie that is satisfactory.

Note: Although this is no doubt not what Wang had in mind, I couldn't help thinking, as I watched Dim Sum, *that the movie's characters and situations could be effortlessly spun off into a wonderful TV sitcom.*

Diner ★ ★ ★ ½
R, 110 m., 1982

Steve Guttenberg (Eddie), Daniel Stern (Shrevie), Mickey Rourke (Boogie), Kevin Bacon (Fenwick), Timothy Daly (Billy), Ellen Barkin (Beth). Directed by Barry Levinson and produced by Jerry Weintraub. Screenplay by Levinson.

Women are not strange, not threatening, not mysterious, unless you happen to be a man. Young men in particular seem to regard women with a combination of admiration, desire, and dread that is quite out of their control. This is especially true in the late 1950s, a decade during which the Playmate of the Month was more alien than E.T. is today. Women were such a puzzling phenomenon to 1950s young men that, after a date, the best way for males to restore their equilibrium was to regroup with the guys for the therapeutic consumption of cheeseburgers, greasy fries, black coffee, chocolate malteds, Lucky Strikes, and loud arguments about football teams and pop singers. *Diner* is a story about several such young men, who live in Baltimore. They share one awkward problem: They are growing up, painfully and awkwardly, at an age when they are supposed to have already grown up. Adolescence lasts longer for some people than society quite imagines. These guys are best friends for the time being, although in the fall they will go separate ways, to schools and jobs and even marriage, and it's possible they will never be this close again. They cling to one another for security, because out there in the real world, responsibility lurks, and responsibility is spelled *woman.* They have plans, but their plans are not as real as their dreams.

Diner is structured a lot like *American Graffiti* and Fellini's *I Vitelloni.* It's episodic, as the young men venture out for romantic and sexual adventures, practical jokes, drunken Friday evenings, and long mornings of hangovers and doubt. Some of the movie's situations seem quite implausible, but they all fit within the overall theme of fear of women. One bizarre sequence, for example, involves a young man who insists that his fiancée pass a tough quiz about pro football before he'll agree to marry her. He's serious: If she flunks, the wedding is off. This situation doesn't seem possible to me, but it's right symbolically, since what the man is really looking for in a wife is one of the guys—a woman who will agree to become an imitation man.

Another character, already married, is much more realistic. He has absolutely no communication with his wife and no way to develop any, since he sees her only as a "wife" and not as a friend, a companion, or even a fellow human being. Her great failure is an inability to regard his life with the proper reverence; when she gets his record collection out of alphabetical order, it's grounds for a fight. He's flabbergasted that she hasn't memorized the flip sides of all the Top 40 hits of 1958, but he never even suspects that he doesn't know what's inside her mind.

Diner is often a very funny movie, although I laughed most freely not at the sexual pranks but at the movie's accurate ear, as it reproduced dialogue with great comic accuracy. If the movie has a weakness, however, it's that it limits itself to the faithful reproduction of the speech, clothing, cars, and mores of the late 1950s, and never quite stretches to include the humanity of the characters. For all that I recognized and sympathized with these young men and their martyred wives, girlfriends, and sex symbols, I never quite believed that they were three-dimensional. It is, of course, a disturbing possibility that, to the degree these young men denied full personhood to women, they didn't *have* three-dimensional personalities.

Dirty Harry ★ ★ ★
R, 103 m., 1971

Clint Eastwood (Harry), Harry Guardino (Bressler), Reni Santoni (Chico), Andy Robinson (Killer), John Vernon (Mayor). Directed and produced by Don Siegel. Screenplay by Harry Julian Fink.

There is a book named *From Caligari to Hitler* that tries to penetrate the German national subconscious by analyzing German films between 1919 and the rise of the Nazis. I have my doubts about the critical approach (it gets cause and effect backwards), but if anybody is writing a book about the rise of fascism in America, they ought to have a look at *Dirty Harry.* The film is directed by Don Siegel, and like *Coogan's Bluff* it considers the role of a cop in society with lots of dynamite action and enough wry cynicism to keep the blood from getting too thick. It is photographed all over San Francisco, and is filled with good character actors.

The presence of Eastwood in an action role is enough to explain the movie's popularity, but when you see it you discover that the movie has a message with a vengeance. It is loosely based on 1970's headlines, and makes Eastwood a cop who is assigned to find a mysterious killer named Scorpio. The killer has kidnapped and killed various girls, he has tried to extract $200,000 ransom from the city, and in the film's climax he hijacks a school bus. The gimmick is that Eastwood is so filled with hatred for Scorpio that he violates the poor fiend's civil rights. While attempting to find out where a kidnapped girl is, for example, Eastwood gets no less than four amendments wrong. And so the city has to set Scorpio free—even though they have a murder weapon and a confession.

Eastwood doesn't care; he says to hell with the Bill of Rights and stalks out of the district attorney's office. But when Scorpio hijacks the school bus, it is Eastwood again, who is asked to be bag man and carry the ransom. This time he refuses. He wants Scorpio on his own. We've already seen him twisting Scorpio's broken arm ("I have a right to a lawyer!" Scorpio shouts), and soon we will see him kill Scorpio in cold blood. Then, in a thoughtful final scene, Eastwood takes his police badge and throws it into a gravel pit.

It is possible to see the movie as just another extension of Eastwood's basic screen character: He is always the quiet one with the painfully bottled-up capacity for violence, the savage forced to follow the rules of society. This time, by breaking loose, he did what he was always about to do in his earlier films. If that is all, then *Dirty Harry* is a very good example of the cops-and-killers genre, and Siegel proves once again that he understands the Eastwood mystique.

But wait a minute. The movie clearly and unmistakably gives us a character who understands the Bill of Rights, understands his legal responsibility as a police officer, and nevertheless takes retribution into his own hands. Sure, Scorpio is portrayed as the most vicious, perverted, warped monster we can imagine—but that's part of the same stacked deck. The movie's moral position is fascist. No doubt about it.

I think films are more often a mirror of society than an agent of change, and that when we blame the movies for the evils around us we are getting things backward. *Dirty Harry* is very effective at the level of a thriller. At another level, it uses the most potent star presence in American movies—Clint Eastwood—to lay things on the line. If there aren't mentalities like Dirty Harry's at loose in the land, then the movie is irrelevant. If there are, we should not blame the bearer of the bad news.

Dirty Rotten Scoundrels ★ ★ ★
PG, 110 m., 1988

Steve Martin (Freddy Benson), Michael Caine (Lawrence Jamieson), Glenne Headly (Janet Colgate), Anton Rodgers (Inspector Andre), Barbara Harris (Fanny Eubanks), Ian McDiarmid (Arthur), Dana Ivey (Mrs. Reed), Meagen Fay (Lady From Oklahoma). Directed by Frank Oz and produced by Bernard Williams. Screenplay by Dale Launer, Stanley Shapiro, and Paul Henning.

There's something about the very words "dirty rotten scoundrel" that makes being one OK. They evoke an earlier age of simpler evils, back before everyone was playing for keeps. And the movie *Dirty Rotten Scoundrels* evokes a more innocent time in the movies, too; it's a remake of the David Niven comedy *Bedtime Story* about a roguish Riviera con man bilking rich tourists out of more money than they needed in the first place.

The movie stars Michael Caine in the Niven role, as Lawrence Jamieson, a suave, aloof confidence man who seems so noble, so regal, so aloof, that gullible tourists from Nebraska have no difficulty believing he is a king in exile. Steve Martin plays Freddy Benson, a scruffy American who works the lower end of the scam ladder, accepting donations for his allegedly ailing grandmother.

They meet on a train, sort of, when Jamieson observes Benson pulling his crude routine on a tourist. When the slick European discovers that the gauche American is planning to locate in his own home territory—the wealthy Riviera resort town of Beaumont-sur-Mer—he decides to do anything possible to keep him out of town. Jamieson's theory is that bad crooks pollute the water for sophisticated con men like himself.

Freddy keeps turning up, however, like a bad penny, and finally Jamieson decides out of desperation that he must work with him. They do a couple of cons together, and then they make a wager of $50,000 on who will be the first to con a rich visiting American (Glenne Headly). So their pride is at stake—and a lot more than pride, it turns out.

The plot is mostly an excuse for a series of bizarre set pieces in which one con man tries to corner the other one in an outrageous trap. My favorite sequence came when Caine played an incredibly wealthy European aristocrat, and saddled Martin with the hapless role of Ruprecht, his brother. Ruprecht is so maladroit that he has to eat with a cork on the end of his fork, to prevent damage if he stabs himself in the eye. (For added protection, he also wears an eyepatch.)

The plot develops into a *Sting*-like series of cons within cons, as the two confidence men surpass themselves in their attempts to outsmart the surprisingly elusive Headly. Caine goes the high road, with visual and verbal humor. Martin does more pratfalls than in any of his movies since *The Jerk*, and he has one absolutely inspired scene in a jail cell. He knows the name of only one local citizen who might bail him out: Lawrence Jamieson. And as he tries to remember his name, his mind and body undergo the most fearsome contortions. Martin, who seems to be improvising the scene, tries to drag the missing name from his stubborn subconscious, one syllable at a time.

The plot of *Dirty Rotten Scoundrels* is not as complex as a movie like *The Sting*, and we can see some of the surprises as soon as they appear on the horizon. But the chemistry between Martin and Caine is fun, and Headly provides a resilient foil, as a woman who looks like a pushover but somehow never seems to topple.

Disclosure ★ ★
R, 125 m., 1994   **NEW**

Michael Douglas (Tom Sanders), Demi Moore (Meredith Johnson), Donald Sutherland (Bob Garvin), Caroline Goodall (Susan Hendler), Dennis Miller (Mark Lewyn), Roma Maffia (Catherine Alvarez). Directed by Barry Levinson and produced by Levinson and Michael Crichton. Screenplay by Paul Attanasio.

Disclosure contains an inspiring, terrific shot of Demi Moore's cleavage in a Wonder Bra, surrounded by 125 minutes of pure goofiness leading up to, and resulting from, this moment. Advertised as the first movie about the sexual harassment of men by women in the workplace, it is an exercise in pure cynicism, with little respect for its subject—or for its thriller plot, which I defy anyone to explain. The "theme" is basically a launch pad for sex scenes. And yet the movie is so sleek, so glossy, so filled with possessoporn (toys so expensive they're erotic), that you can enjoy it like a Sharper Image catalog that walks and talks.

The film takes place inside the Seattle R&D headquarters of a vast high-tech corporation. The male employees have not had their consciousness raised. ("I definitely have lift-off," one says, after Demi Moore walks by.) Michael Douglas plays Tom Sanders, an executive involved in the manufacture of a new computer product. There are problems on the assembly line that may jeopardize a merger.

Working to protect himself, Douglas uses Corridor, a new virtual reality database that is some software program, all right. Users stand in the center of a network of light beams that track their movements. They wear a headset that creates the illusion that they are wandering the corridors of a Greco-Roman temple lined with filing systems. They reach out a hand, and files come into view, which can be searched and accessed. In other words, for hundreds of thousands of dollars, busy executives can do the work of file clerks.

The company is about to be acquired by a larger firm, and the boss (Donald Sutherland) stands to make $100 million. So he doesn't want to hear any bad news. Meanwhile, Douglas expects a promotion—and is shocked to learn it will go instead to a former lover named Meredith Johnson (Demi Moore). The day she gets the job, she calls him to her office for a seven P.M. conference, pours his favorite wine, and segues directly into an attempted rape. He fights her off (although not without being tempted long enough, of course, to let the confrontation develop into a satisfactory movie sex scene). The next day, she accuses him of sexual harassment, and his life and career seem about to be destroyed.

Okay. That part you already know, from the publicity surrounding the Michael Crichton best-seller that inspired the movie. And, of course, there are office hearings and confrontations as the company tries to get to the bottom of the charges without allowing a public scandal. Douglas is defended by a bright, high-powered attorney named Catherine Alvarez (Roma Maffia), who is the subject of one of the movie's cleverest lines: "She'd change her name to 'TV Listings' to get it in the paper." But things look bad for him until he starts getting anonymous tips via e-mail, and another level of conspiracy is revealed.

A lot of that is obligatory material in thrillers about sex and conspiracy in the corridors of power. What's unusual this time is the Nancy Drew stuff: evidence obtained by means so lame and unlikely we laugh even while it's happening. What are the odds, for example, that Michael Douglas could overhear Demi Moore's evil schemes by eavesdropping outside an exercise room, where Moore climbs a Stairmaster while helpfully, and loudly, divulging her secrets to a henchman? And what about the plot's answering-machine gimmick—a textbook *deus ex machina*?

Without these contrivances there would be no way for Douglas to defend himself, or for the plot to advance. There are also anonymous e-mail messages from "A Friend," although they are not very helpful, and (as it turns out) could easily be tracked. Late in the film, some sort of labyrinthine scheme involving the Sutherland character is hinted at, without ever becoming clear; it's a distraction, because there are references to things that are not explained.

Disclosure loves its high-tech look. The corporation occupies offices where every wall is made of glass, and lives are lived in public. There's a lot of computer stuff in the movie, which makes us feel clever, unless we know anything about computers, in which case it makes the movie feel dumb. (How likely is it, data base fans, that a corporation would trust all of its records to a prototype of new software?) There's a neat scene where Douglas dons the virtual reality headpiece and goes hunting through the files, while his enemies materialize in the cyberspace behind him. Looks great. But techheads will be rolling in the aisles.

As the movie started, I expected a sexy docudrama about sexual harassment. What I got was more of a thriller and whodunit, in which the harassment theme gets misplaced. Too bad, since the best scenes involve the attorneys for Moore and Douglas, and especially the scenes where Douglas's attorney sets out in chilling detail what a lawsuit is likely to do to his life. There's also an intriguing subplot involving Douglas's relationship with his wife (Caroline Goodall). Much could have been made of this material. Much has been made of it. But not the same much.

The Discreet Charm of the Bourgeoisie
★ ★ ★ ★
PG, 100 m., 1972

Fernando Rey (Ambassador), Stephane Audran (Mrs. Scnechal), Delphine Seyrig (Mrs. Thevenot), Bulle Ogier (Florence), Jean-Pierre Cassel (Senechal), Michel Piccoli (Secretary of State). Directed by Luis Buñuel and produced by Serge Silberman. Screenplay by Buñuel and Jean-Claude Carriere.

"The best explanation of this film is that, from the standpoint of pure reason, there is no explanation."—Buñuel's preface to *The Exterminating Angel*

There is never quite an explanation in the universe of Luis Buñuel. His characters slip in and out of each other's fantasies, driven by compulsions that are perhaps not even their own. Buñuel doesn't like characters who have free will; if they inhabit his films, they will do what he tells them. And his fancies are as unpredictable as they are likely to be embarrassing.

His theme is almost always entrapment. His characters cannot get loose. He places them in either literal or psychological bondage, and forces them to watch with horror as he demonstrates the underlying evil of the universe. Buñuel is the most pessimistic of filmmakers, the most negative, certainly the most cynical. He is also the most obsessive, returning again and again to the same situations and predicaments; it's as if filmmaking, for him, is a grand tour of his favorite fetishes.

The Discreet Charm of the Bourgeoisie (which won the Oscar as 1972's best foreign film) has nothing new in it; but Buñuel admirers don't want anything new. They want the same old stuff in a different way, and Buñuel doesn't—perhaps cannot—disappoint them. The most interesting thing about *Discreet Charm* is the way he neatly reverses the situation in his *Exterminating Angel* (1962).

In that film, one of my favorites, a group of dinner guests finds itself in an embarrassing predicament: After dinner, no one can leave the drawing room. There is nothing to prevent them; the door stands wide open. But, somehow, they simply . . . can't leave. They camp out on the floor for several days of gradually increasing barbarism, black magic, death, suicide, and visits from a bear and two sheep (which they capture and barbecue).

The film, as Buñuel noted in his opening title, makes no sense. Not that it needs to; it gives us an eerie feeling, and we look at his trapped characters with a mixture of pity and the notion that they got what was coming to them. In *The Discreet Charm of the Bourgeoisie*, Buñuel reverses the mirror; this time, his characters are forever sitting down to dinner—but they never eat.

The consummation of their feast is prevented by a series of disasters—some real, some dreams, some obviously contrived to feed some secret itch of Buñuel's. At first there is a simple misunderstanding; the guests have arrived on the wrong night. Later, at an inn, their appetites are spoiled when it develops that the owner has died and is laid out in the next room. Still later, there are interruptions from the army, the police . . . and the guests' own dreams. All of the fantasies of public embarrassment are here, including a scene in which the guests sit down to eat and suddenly find themselves on a stage in front of an audience.

The movie isn't about anything in particular, I suppose, although devoted symbolmongers will be able to make something of the ambassador who is a cocaine smuggler and the bishop who gets off by hiring himself out as a gardener. Buñuel seems to have finally done away with plot and dedicated himself to filmmaking on the level of pure personal fantasy.

Since the form of a movie is so much more important than the content anyway, this decision gives Buñuel's immediately preceding films (*Tristana, Belle de Jour*) a feeling almost of relief. We are all so accustomed to following the narrative threads in a movie that we want to *make* a movie make "sense," even if it doesn't. But the greatest directors can carry us along breathlessly on the wings of their own imaginations, so that we don't ask questions; we simply have an experience. Ingmar Bergman's *Cries and Whispers* did that; now here comes old Buñuel to show that he can, too.

Diva ★ ★ ★ ★
R, 123 m., 1981

Wilhelmenia Wiggins Fernandez (Cynthia,) Frédéric Andrei (Jules), Richard Bohringer (Gordorish), Thay An Luu (Alba), Jacques Fabbri (Saporta), Chantal Deruaz (Nadia). Directed by Jean-Jacques Beineix and produced by Irene Silberman. Screenplay by Beineix and Jean Van Hamme.

The opening shots inform us with authority that *Diva* is the work of a director with an enormous gift for creating visual images. We meet a young Parisian mailman. His job is to deliver special-delivery letters on his motor scooter. His passion is opera, and, as *Diva* opens, he is secretly tape-recording a live performance by an American soprano. The camera sees this action in two ways. First, with camera movements that seem as lyrical as the operatic performance. Second, with almost surreptitious observations of the electronic eavesdropper at work. His face shows the intensity of a fanatic: He does not simply admire this woman, he adores her. There is a tear in his eye. The operatic performance takes on a greatness, in this scene, that is absolutely necessary if we're to share his passion. We do. And, doing so, we start to like this kid.

He is played by Frédéric Andrei, an actor I do not remember having seen before. But he could be Antoine Doinel, the subject of *The 400 Blows* and several other autobiographical films by Francois Truffaut. He has the same loony idealism, coexisting with a certain hard-headed realism about Paris. He lives and works there, he knows the streets, and yet he never quite believes he could get into trouble. *Diva* is the story of the trouble he gets into. It is one of the best thrillers of recent years but, more than that, it is a brilliant film, a visual extravaganza that announces the considerable gifts of its young director, Jean-Jacques Beineix. He has made a film that is about many things, but I think the real subject of *Diva* is the director's joy in making it. The movie is filled with so many small character touches, so many perfectly observed intimacies, so many visual inventions—from the sly to the grand—that the thriller plot is just a bonus. In a way, it doesn't really matter what this movie is about; Pauline Kael has compared Beineix to Orson Welles and, as Welles so often did, has made a movie that is a feast to look at, regardless of its subject.

But to give the plot its due: *Diva* really gets under way when the young postman slips his tape into the saddlebag of his motor scooter. Two tape pirates from Hong Kong know that the tape is in his possession, and, since the American soprano has refused to ever allow any of her performances to be recorded, they want to steal the tape and use it to make a bootleg record. Meanwhile, in a totally unrelated development, a young prostitute tape-records accusations that the Paris chief of police is involved in an international white-slavery ring. The two cassette tapes get exchanged, and *Diva* is off to the races.

One of the movie's delights is the cast of characters it introduces. Andrei, who plays the hero, is a serious, plucky kid who's made his own accommodation with Paris. The diva herself, played by Wilhelmenia Wiggins Fernandez, comes into the postman's life after a most unexpected event (which I deliberately will not reveal, because the way in which it happens, and *what* happens, are enormously surprising). We meet others: A young Vietnamese girl who seems so blasé in the face of Paris that we wonder if anything truly excites her; a wealthy man-about-town who specializes in manipulating people for his own amusement; and a grab bag of criminals.

Most thrillers have a chase scene, and mostly they're predictable and boring. *Diva's* chase scene deserves ranking with the all-time classics, *Raiders of the Lost Ark*, *The French Connection*, and *Bullitt*. The kid rides his motorcycle down into the Paris Metro system, and the chase leads on and off trains and up and down escalators. It's pure exhilaration, and Beineix almost seems to be doing it just to show he knows how. A lot of the movie strikes that note: Here is a director taking audacious chances, doing wild and unpredictable things with his camera and actors, just to celebrate moviemaking.

There is a story behind his ecstasy. Jean-Jacques Beineix has been an assistant director for ten years. He has worked for directors ranging from Claude Berri to Jerry Lewis. But the job of an assistant director is not always romantic and challenging. Many days, he's a glorified traffic cop, shouting through a bullhorn for quiet on the set, and knocking on dressing room doors to tell the actors they're wanted. Day after day, year after year, the assistant director helps set up situations before the director takes control of them. The director gives the instructions, the assistant passes them on. Perhaps some assistants are always thinking of how *they* would do the shot. Here's one who finally got his chance.

Divine Madness ★ ★ ★ ½
R, 94 m., 1980

Bette Midler, with the Harlettes (Jocelyn Brown, Ula Hedwig, Diva Gray) and Irving Sudrow as the Head Usher. Directed and produced by Michael Ritchie. Written by Jerry Blatt, Bette Midler, and Bruce Vilanch.

Think of a concert film and you think of a camera bolted to the floor in front of the stage and shooting straight up into the singer's nostrils, which are half-concealed by the microphone. Those films are all right as recordings of song performances, but as cinema they stink. Some directors have broken out of the mold by making documentaries about the event of a concert; the best of those films is still Michael Wadleigh's *Woodstock* (1970).

Here Michael Ritchie, whose background is almost entirely in dramatic features *(Downhill Racer, The Candidate, The Bad News Bears)*, tries a new approach. There are times in Ritchie's *Divine Madness* when he seems to be trying to turn a live Bette Midler stage concert into a Hollywood genre musical. He opens as if *Divine Madness* is going to be a traditional concert film—Bette charges on stage, the audience cheers, there's an electric performance feel. But from that beginning, Ritchie subtly moves into the material until there are times when we almost forget we're watching an actual concert performance.

Ritchie's first decision was to declare an absolute ban on visible cameras. At no moment during *Divine Madness* do we see any cameras or any members of Ritchie's crew onstage, even though twenty cameras were used to shoot the performance. Ritchie and Midler used a week of rehearsal to choreograph the camera moves and time them to Midler's own abundant energy. So instead of looking beyond the performer and being distracted by cinematographers carrying handheld cameras and sneaking around in their Adidas, we see only the stage, Midler, and her backup singers, the Harlettes. Ritchie also uses camera techniques that are rarely seen in concert films. There are, for example, crane shots in this movie—shots where the camera swoops up to look down on Midler or to circle down and toward her. That's especially effective during the Magic Lady sequence, in which Bette portrays a sort of dreamy bag lady on a park bench. This sequence comes closest to capturing the feel of a studio musical. That's not to say that *Divine Madness* loses the impact of a live concert performance. This movie is amazingly alive and involving, and Midler, who has become one of the great live performers, has an energy that steamrollers through an incredible variety of material.

When you think about *Divine Madness* after it's over, you realize what a wide range of material Midler covers. She does rock 'n' roll, she sings blues, she does a hilarious stand-up comedy routine, she plays characters (including a tacky show-lounge performer who enters in a motorized wheelchair outfitted with a palm tree), she stars in bizarre pageantry, and she wears costumes that Busby Berkeley would have found excessive. That's one reason *Divine Madness* doesn't drag: Midler changes pace so often that there's never too much of the same thing.

Is there a weakness in the film? I think there's one—a curious one. I don't think Ritchie intercuts enough close-up shots of the audience. That may seem like a curious objection, since I've already praised *Divine Madness* for sometimes feeling more like a movie musical than a concert documentary. But you can use people in an audience as characters. Richard Lester did in the original Beatles film, *A Hard Day's Night* (and who can ever forget that blond girl weeping and screaming?).

With a Midler concert, the audience is part of the show. Intercutting selected audience shots with the stage material could have set up a nice byplay in some of the numbers. But Ritchie keeps the audience mostly in long shot; it looks like a vast, amorphous mass out there in the dark. Since the film was actually edited together from three different concert performances, maybe he was concerned about matching audiences. But close-ups would have eliminated that problem.

No matter, though, really. Bette Midler is a wonderful performer with a high and infectious energy level and a split-second timing instinct that allows her to play with raunchy material instead of getting mired in it. She sings well, but she performs even better than she sings: She's giving a dramatic performance in music, and *Divine Madness* does a good job of communicating that performance without obscuring it in the distractions of most concert documentaries.

D.O.A. ★ ★ ★
R, 100 m., 1988

Dennis Quaid (Dexter Cornell), Meg Ryan (Sydney Fuller), Charlotte Rampling (Mrs. Fitzwaring), Daniel Stern (Hal Petersham), Jane Kaczmarek (Gail Cornell), Christopher Neame (Bernard), Robin Johnson (Cookie Fitzwaring), Rob Knepper (Nicholas Lang). Directed by Rocky Morton and Annabel Jankel and produced by Ian Sander and Laura Ziskin. Screenplay by Charles Edward Pogue.

Are we in the middle of something new here? Are thrillers abandoning supermen and embracing everyman? For a decade or more we've had the spectacle of the violent man of action, smashing everything that stands in his way. The only question was how long it would take him to kill everyone he didn't like. But lately, there's been a return of a quieter, more intriguing kind of thriller—in which ordinary people get caught up against their will in mysteries they don't understand.

D.O.A. is a movie like that, in which a college professor learns he has been poisoned, and has twenty-four hours to live—twenty-four hours to find his killer. Look at some other movies that came out at about the same time. In *Masquerade*, Meg Tilly plays a la-de-dah rich girl who falls blissfully in love, unaware that she is surrounded by a pack of vipers. *Frantic* stars Harrison Ford as an American doctor whose wife is kidnapped from their Paris hotel, all because of a baggage mix-up at the airport. In *The House on Carroll Street*, Kelly McGillis overhears a conversation and is plunged into the midst of Nazi schemes.

What all of these movies have in common is that the hero is passive, and wants only to be left alone. But other people have other plans, and the hero is swept along by the tide. This is, of course, the classic definition of *film noir*, those 1940s thrillers in which ordinary people discovered the evil that lurked beneath the surface of society, and *D.O.A.* itself is inspired by a 1949 thriller starring Edmond O'Brien.

The plot is irresistible from the first frame onward. A man staggers into a police station to report a murder. A cop asks him who was murdered. "I was," he says. The man is a college English professor (Dennis Quaid), who has been told that his body contains a radioactive substance that will give him only twenty-four hours to live. During that time he must discover the identity of his killer, a problem made more complicated because he

is being sought by the police on framed-up murder charges.

His search leads him into more bizarre corners than you would expect to find at the University of Texas at Austin, where the movie is set during the Christmas season. There are all sorts of suspects. The bright young student, for example, who commits suicide after Quaid delays in reading his novel. The jealous assistant professor who is enraged because Quaid has tenure and he does not. The mysterious mother of the dead student. Quaid's own ex-wife. And so on.

Although the plot follows the broad outlines of a 1940s whodunit, Charles Edward Pogue's screenplay adds a lot of campus atmosphere and academic intrigue. The Quaid character once published a brilliant first novel, we learn, and for a time was a promising writer, but he has produced nothing for four years. "They didn't kill me; I was dead already," he says at one point, equating, as only a writer could, death and writer's block. The whole story plays sly variations on the theme of "publish or perish."

It is required, of course, that the hero of a story like this fall in love along the way, in order to have company on his quest. Quaid's companion is a bright young student (Meg Ryan) who first flirts with him, then is frightened of him, and finally believes in him. Together, they travel a bloody road that leads from ancient family secrets to a deadly tar pit. The family with the secrets is headed by a mysterious widow (Charlotte Rampling), who may have poisoned Quaid in revenge for her beneficiary's suicide. Then again, maybe not. Everything is settled in an ending that seems contrived and is the movie's weakest link.

D.O.A. is a witty and literate thriller, with a lot of irony to cut the violence. Quaid is convincing as the chain-smoking English professor, Meg Ryan is true-blue as the stalwart coed, and Rampling looks capable of keeping her victims alive just to toy with them. The film was directed by Rocky Morton and Annabel Jankel, who created Max Headroom. This is their first feature, showing an almost sensuous love for the shadows and secrets of *film noir*.

Doc Hollywood ★ ★ ★
PG-13, 99 m., 1991

Michael J. Fox (Ben Stone), Julie Warner (Lou), Barnard Hughes (Dr. Hogue), Woody

Harrelson (Hank), David Ogden Stiers (The Mayor), George Hamilton (Dr. Halberstrom), Bridget Fonda (Nancy Lee). Directed by Michael Caton-Jones and produced by Susan Solt and Deborah D. Johnson. Screenplay by Jeffrey Price, Peter S. Seaman, and Daniel Pyne.

On the basis of the movie's trailer, I was expecting *Doc Hollywood* to be a comedy. And it is a comedy. But it surprised me by also being a love story, and a pretty good one—the kind where the lovers are smart enough to know all the reasons why they shouldn't get together, but too much in love to care.

The movie stars Michael J. Fox, an actor who knows how to be quiet and attractive without seeming to work at it, as a recent medical school graduate on his way from Washington to Los Angeles. He's looking forward to a high-paying job as a plastic surgeon. It's a good field. "After all," one of his colleagues tells him, "the surgery is neat, the pay is good, and no one dies on you." Fox feels a little guilt about going into the field, but he also feels a lot of ambition, and he's looking forward to that California paycheck.

On his coast-to-coast drive, however, he gets sidetracked in the South Carolina hamlet of Grady ("Squash Capital of the South"), where his car plows through the fence of the local judge, and he's sentenced to work-release at the hospital. The locals quickly organize themselves into a conspiracy to convince "Doc Hollywood" to settle in Grady. He is absolutely opposed to the idea. But that's before he meets Lou (Julie Warner), who drives an ambulance and is studying for the bar and is drop-dead wonderful.

Doc Hollywood is not a cranked-up, assembly-line comedy—it would rather be sweet than clever—and although its general contours are familiar, a lot of the local color is not. The film was directed by Michael Caton-Jones, who has a knack for finding the right character actors here to create the local color. Instead of the usual clichéd rednecks and homespun philosophers, he uses good character actors like David Ogden Stiers (as the local mayor and head of the recruiting effort), Bernard Hughes (as the aging local doctor), Woody Harrelson (who cannot decide if he would rather beat up Fox or just sell him some insurance), Bridget Fonda (as the local sexpot), and George Hamilton (perfectly cast as a plastic surgeon, and reminding us that his talent, while narrowly defined, is inimitable).

The town of Grady (actually Micanopy, Florida) is also a character in the movie, with its statue of a local hero holding a squash in his hand. Like all small towns in Hollywood movies, this one has a parade, an anniversary celebration, and a fireworks display during the course of the story, but Caton-Jones has fun with the parade (lots of marching squashes), and the carnival provides the backdrop for a small, tender, perfectly choreographed and photographed love scene; while Fox and Warner dance to Patsy Cline's "Crazy," all of the people drop out of the background and only the bright lights remain.

The chemistry does work between Fox and Warner (who is making her movie debut after TV work such as "Star Trek: The Next Generation"). They're good together, partly because the screenplay by Jeffrey Price, Peter S. Seaman, and Daniel Pyne doesn't give them sappy things to say; they hold reasonable conversations from which, eventually, romance blossoms.

Love stories are among the trickiest kinds of movies to make. Stories of sex and passion are easier. What love needs is an ability to idealize the loved one, and to feel narcissistic bliss because one is loved by such a paragon. Dialogue and plot and all the rest take second place to the conviction that two people only have eyes for one another. Fox and Warner create that feeling, which is why *Doc Hollywood* is a sweetheart of a movie.

The Doctor ★ ★ ★ ½
PG-13, 128 m., 1991

William Hurt (Jack), Christine Lahti (Anne), Elizabeth Perkins (June), Mandy Patinkin (Murray), Adam Arkin (Eli), Wendy Crewson (Dr. Abbott). Directed by Randa Haines and produced by Laura Ziskin. Screenplay by Robert Caswell.

Anyone who has ever been through the medical system—even with the very best of treatment—will identify with this film. *The Doctor* tells the story of an aloof, self-centered heart surgeon who treats his patients like names on a list. Then he gets sick himself, and doesn't like it one bit when he's treated like a mere patient. "It may interest you to know that I happen to be a resident surgeon on the staff of this hospital!" he barks at a nurse who wants him to fill out some forms just like the ones he has already filled out. He still has to fill out the forms.

The role is played in a detailed, observant way by William Hurt, who is able to make this egocentric surgeon into a convincing human being. In the wrong hands, this material could have been simply a cautionary tale, but Hurt and his director, Randa Haines, who also collaborated on *Children of a Lesser God*, make it into the story of a specific, flawed, fascinating human being.

As the movie opens, Hurt pipes rock 'n' roll into his operating theater while literally holding the hearts of his patients in his hands. He leads a comfortable life in Marin County with his wife (Christine Lahti) and two sons, but is not very close to his family. (In one revealing scene, he's standing in the living room when a son races in. "Say hello to your father," Lahti says, and the kid automatically picks up the phone.) In his lectures to the interns at the hospital, Hurt warns that personal feelings have nothing to do with the science of medicine. Then he discovers otherwise.

His problem starts as a small, nagging cough. He ignores it until one day he coughs up blood. He goes to an eye, ear, nose, and throat expert (played with cold precision by Wendy Crewson), and discovers that there is a tumor in his throat. It is malignant. He needs radiation therapy. If it doesn't work, he may need surgery. In that case, it's impossible to predict how his vocal cords will respond. He could lose the power of speech.

This is devastating news, which he receives with disbelief. How could a master of medicine like himself become its victim? As his treatment progresses, he doesn't much like how his own hospital treats him, as he wastes time in waiting rooms, tangles with the bureaucracy, and is repelled by Crewson's frigid bedside manner. For the first time, he grows close to a patient: June (Elizabeth Perkins), who has a brain tumor. They meet every day while they're having their treatments.

The broad outlines of the story progress more or less as expected. Threatened with his own mortality, he turns to June not for romantic reasons but as a fellow traveler on the same path. Their scenes together are handled with quiet tact and gentleness. Although his wife desperately tries to break through to him, she can't reach him ("I've spent so much time pushing her away, I don't know how to let her get close," he confesses). He continues to work at his own practice, and finds that for the first time he actually, personally, cares about his patients.

In structure, *The Doctor* is similar to *Regarding Henry*, another 1991 summer release. Both movies are about successful professional men who are monsters until a devastating event forces them to reshape their personalities. The difference is that Hurt, Haines, and writer Robert Caswell are able to find the details, the intonations, and shadings of voice and tone, that make their doctor into a plausible, convincing person. In *Regarding Henry*, I could always hear the hum of the plot mechanism, right offstage.

I imagine audiences will relate strongly to *The Doctor*, because most people have had experiences similar to those in the movie. I personally have been blessed with what I consider particularly expert and caring medical attention, and I have no complaints. But I have a memory.

A few years ago I was struck low by food poisoning, and checked into the hospital as sick as a whipped dog. Wearing one of those hospital gowns designed to remove the last vestige of dignity from the patient, I was taken by wheelchair to get some tests and was parked by an elevator. I lacked even the strength to lift my head. Sure enough, half the people who went by recognized me from TV. But they didn't talk to me. They talked about me. "Look, there's the guy on TV! Jeez, he looks terrible!" In *The Doctor*, there's a scene where the Hurt character is being wheeled toward surgery, and some doctors hold a technical conversation practically across his cart. He lifts his head, contributes some expert advice, and then, when they look at him in surprise, says "Yes! There's a person here!" I felt like cheering.

Dog Day Afternoon ★ ★ ★ ½
R, 120 m., 1975

Al Pacino (Sonny), Charles Durning (Moretti), James Broderick (FBI Man), John Cazale (Sal), Chris Sarandon (Leon), Judith Malina (Sonny's Mother). Directed by Sidney Lumet and produced by Martin Bregman and Martin Elfand. Screenplay by Frank Pierson.

There's a point midway in *Dog Day Afternoon* when a bank's head teller, held hostage by two very nervous stick-up men, is out in the street with a chance to escape. The cops tell her to run. But, no, she goes back inside the bank with the other tellers, proudly explaining, "My place is with my girls." What she means is that her place is at the center of live TV coverage inspired by the robbery. She's enjoying it.

Criminals become celebrities because their crimes provide fodder for the media. Many of the fashionable new crimes—hijacking,

taking hostages—are committed primarily as publicity stunts. And a complex relationship grows up among the criminals, their victims, the police, and the press. Knowing they're on TV, hostages comb their hair and killers say the things they've learned on the evening news. That's the subject, in a way, of Sidney Lumet's pointed film. It's based on an actual bank robbery that took place in New York in the 1970s. And it seems to borrow, too, from that curious episode in Stockholm when hostages, barricaded in a bank vault with would-be robbers, began to identify with their captors. The presence of reporters and live TV cameras changed the nature of those events, helped to dictate them, made them into happenings with their own internal logic.

But Lumet's film is also a study of a fascinating character: Sonny, the bank robber who takes charge, played by Al Pacino as a compulsive and most complex man. He's street-smart, he fought in Vietnam, he's running the stick-up in order to get money for his homosexual lover to have a sex-change operation. He's also married to a chubby and shrill woman with two kids, and he has a terrifically possessive mother (the Freudianism gets a little thick at times). Sonny isn't explained or analyzed—just presented. He becomes one of the most interesting modern movie characters, ranking with Gene Hackman's eavesdropper in *The Conversation* and Jack Nicholson's Bobby Dupea in *Five Easy Pieces*.

Sonny and his zombie-like partner, Sal, hit the bank at closing time (a third confederate gets cold feet and leaves early). The stick-up is discovered, the bank is surrounded, the live TV mini-cams line up across the street, and Sonny is in the position, inadvertently, of having taken hostages. Sal (John Cazale) is very willing to shoot them, a factor in all that follows.

There are moments when *Dog Day Afternoon* comes dangerously close to the clichés of old Pat O'Brien gangster movies and the great Lenny Bruce routine inspired by them (the Irish cop shouts into his bullhorn "Come on out, Sonny, and nobody's gonna get hurt," and Sonny's mother pleads with him from the middle of the street). But Lumet is exploring the clichés, not just using them. And he has a good feel for the big-city crowd that's quickly drawn to the action. At first, Sonny is their hero, and he does a defiant dance in front of the bank, looking like a rock star playing to his fans. When it be-

comes known that Sonny's bisexual, the crowd turns against him. But within a short time (New York being New York), gay libbers turn up to cheer him on.

The movie has an irreverent, quirky sense of humor, and we get some notion of the times we live in when the bank starts getting obscene phone calls—and the giggling tellers breathe heavily into the receiver. There's also, in a film that's probably about fifteen minutes too long, an attempt to take a documentary look at the ways police and banks try to handle situations like this. And through it all there's that tantalizing attraction of instant celebrityhood, caught for an instant when a pizza deliveryman waves at the cameras and shouts, "Hey, I'm a star!"

Dogfight ★ ★ ★
R, 95 m., 1991

River Phoenix (Birdlace), Lili Taylor (Rose), Richard Panebianco (Berzin), Anthony Clark (Okie), Mitchell Whitfield (Benjamin), Holly Near (Rose Sr.). Directed by Nancy Savoca and produced by Peter Newman and Richard Guay. Screenplay by Bob Comfort.

Dogfight isn't a love story so much as a story about how a young woman helps a confused teen-age boy to discover his own better nature. The fact that his discoveries take place on the night before he ships out to fight the war in Vietnam only makes the story more poignant.

The film takes place in San Francisco in 1963, a few weeks before the Kennedy assassination. River Phoenix plays Birdlace, a young marine who has been given a final night's shore liberty with his friends from boot camp. They decide to hold a "dogfight," a particularly cruel contest in which they pool their money, rent a bar, and have a competition to see who can find the ugliest date. The marine with the best "dog" wins the cash.

Phoenix finally settles on Rose (Lili Taylor) in desperation. She isn't very ugly (and indeed, in the tradition of such characters, she grows more lovely as the night wears on), but she's the best he can do. Rose is a vulnerable, poetic young girl who listens to Joan Baez records and writes poetry and has a sensitive nature. She agrees to go out with Birdlace mostly because she feels sorry for him.

Then she finds out about the "dogfight," and in a scene of enormous power she attacks the young man—not for what he has done to her, but for what they have all done to their other victims. Then she walks out. But he follows her home, apologizes awkwardly, and they begin a conversation that leads to an evening on the town. They even have dinner in a nice restaurant, snubbing the headwaiter who tries to snub them.

To fully appreciate *Dogfight*, it helps to see it as the record of a particular time. In November 1963, John Kennedy was still president, "Vietnam" was not yet a familiar word, hair was short, and the counterculture was still idealistic and tentative—more concerned with realization than revolution. And also, more in 1963 than today, male bonding sometimes consisted of the real or imaginary humiliation of women.

That, I think, is why Rose even considers still talking to Birdlace after she finds out about the "dogfight." Some viewers of the film question her forgiveness of him; I think that, in 1963, she might have been more flexible than a woman of subsequent years could possibly have been.

What does happen between Rose and Birdlace is a long night of great tenderness and poignancy, directed by Nancy Savoca from Bob Comfort's screenplay with great care and love. (Savoca's previous film was *True Love*, in 1989, the story of a couple getting married in the midst of confusion, doubt, and almost universally mistaken motives.) Maybe you have to be a little idealistic to even enjoy this movie—to understand what it means to her, to play her folk records and sit in her room and feel poetic and lonely.

River Phoenix and Lili Taylor are well cast here. Taylor (who played the girl who composed her own songs in *Say Anything*, and was also in *Mystic Pizza* and the wonderful sleeper *Bright Angel*) has a solemn face, a serious smile, and a stillness that reads as sympathy. Phoenix, who sometimes plays rebels and misfits, here plays a kid who wants only to conform, and finds to his surprise he is just a little too good to do that.

I wonder if you will like *Dogfight*'s final scene. Some people have found it tacked on. I felt the movie needs it—grows because of it. I won't reveal what happens. I will say it is handled with great delicacy, that the buildup is just right, and that Savoca and Comfort were right to realize that, in the final moments, nothing needs to be explained.

Dolores Claiborne ★ ★ ★
R, 131 m., 1995

NEW

Kathy Bates (Dolores Claiborne), Jennifer Jason Leigh (Selena St. George), Judy Parfitt (Vera Donovan), Christopher Plummer (Detective Mackey), David Strathairn (Joe St. George), Eric Bogosian (Peter), John C. Reilly (Constable Stamshaw), Ellen Muth (Young Selena). Directed by Taylor Hackford and produced by Hackford and Charles Mulvehill. Screenplay by Tony Gilroy.

Under a gray and brooding sky, Stephen King's Maine brings forth yet another labyrinthine tragedy in *Dolores Claiborne*. This is a horror story, all right, but not a supernatural one; all of the elements come out of such everyday horrors as alcoholism, wife beating, child abuse, and the sin of pride. The nonsupernatural movies based on King stories (*Stand by Me, Misery, The Shawshank Redemption*, and this one) are curious in that they deal with unhappy situations, and yet somehow don't turn audiences off—maybe because the characters are so strongly drawn.

Here we have a story involving a hardworking housekeeper named Dolores (Kathy Bates) and the daughter she hasn't seen for fifteen years, a New York magazine writer named Selena (Jennifer Jason Leigh). One day Selena gets a fax of an article from the Bangor paper, about a woman suspected of murder. Scrawled across the cover page are the words, "Isn't this your mother?"

Although she has a big assignment in Arizona she desperately wants to cover, Selena ventures to the Maine island where her mother awaits possible booking for the crime. She arrives in the kind of town where the motels close all winter, everybody knows each other, and people still say, "Oh, my gravy!" But the prosecuting attorney is from the mainland, and has cold eyes. His name is Mackey (Christopher Plummer), and his accent starts out folksy but turns chilling.

We in the audience have already seen the fatal event, in the title sequence, and it sure did *look* like Dolores pushed that poor old lady down the stairs, and then was fixing to bash her head in with a marble rolling pin, just when the mailman interrupted the crime. But maybe there is another way of looking at the murder—and at the death, fifteen years ago, of Dolores's husband and Selena's father, a mean drunk who died after falling down a well.

Dolores worked for ages for the old lady, a perfectionist named Vera Donovan (Judy Parfitt), who demanded "six clothespins, not five" on every sheet, and wanted them hung outside on the line, even in deepest winter. Maybe she had a motive for killing her. The mother and her daughter move back into the ramshackle family home, and we discover that Selena uses a lot of booze, pills, and cigarettes to keep the lid on the kinds of stresses that are caused by cigarettes, pills, and booze. She has little regard for her mother, and may even believe the woman had something to do with the father's death.

More than this I dare not say. *Dolores Claiborne* is the kind of movie where every corner of the house and lawn contains its own flashback to long-ago events which look differently, depending on your angle. And much depends on what happened on a day when there was a six-minute total eclipse of the sun (King is big on eclipses), and how the drunken dad (David Strathairn) ended up down that well.

Given the level of melodrama in this story, it's surprising how much it turns into a two-character drama. Bates and Leigh are well matched here, as mother and daughter with a long history and deep hurts and suspicions. There is no false sentimentality, and—more importantly—no false theatrics in their relationship: They are bitter, taciturn Maine people, with a lot of shared hurt. So complete is their chemistry that a subplot involving Selena's New York job and editor is an unnecessary addition.

It's sometimes distracting to tell a story in flashbacks and memories; the story line gets sidetracked. The director, Taylor Hackford, is successful, however, in making the present seem to flow into and out of the past. He is helped by the uncanny resemblance between Leigh and Ellen Muth, the actress who plays her as a young girl. And a key story thread is made much more convincing by a couple of key speeches, wonderfully delivered by Judy Parfitt as the exacting but not evil old lady. (The movie assigns her one of several repetitions of the movie's dialogue riff, which is, "Sometimes, being a bitch is all a woman has to hold on to.")

Sticklers for detail may wonder about the final scene before a local magistrate. Isn't a lot being taken for granted, not only about the current death but also about the past one? It seemed to me the plot stirred up more than it settled, but Tony Gilroy's screenplay satisfied me with one perfect speech by Leigh, which ends, "Whatever you did, I know you did it for me."

Stephen King fans hoping for ghouls and satanic subplots and bizarre vastations may be disappointed by *Dolores Claiborne*. I was surprised how affecting the movie was, mostly because Bates and Leigh formed such a well matched and convincing pair. Does this movie creep up on you? Oh, my gravy.

Dominick and Eugene ★ ★ ★ ½
PG-13, 111 m., 1988

Tom Hulce (Dominick), Ray Liotta (Eugene), Jamie Lee Curtis (Jennifer), Robert Levine (Dr. Levinson), Todd Graff (Larry Higgins), Bill Cobbs (Jesse Johnson), Tommy Snelfire (Mickey), David Strathairn (Mickey's Father). Directed by Robert M. Young and produced by Marvin Minoff and Mike Farrell. Screenplay by Alvin Sargent and Corey Blechman.

Dominick was dropped on his head when he was young, and now he is a little "slow," but not so slow that he can't hold down a good job as a garbageman, and use his salary to send his brother through medical school. Eugene, the brother, is an overworked intern who is on duty long hours at a stretch, and hardly has time for a girlfriend, but does have time to love and care for Dominick. Their parents are dead, and the two brothers live upstairs over a deli in Pittsburgh, where Dominick dreams of the day he'll be able to see Hulk Hogan in person.

This might possibly sound like one of those tearjerker plots that inspire you to start giggling halfway through (there is nothing quite so funny as melodramatic pathos). But *Dominick and Eugene* is a special movie, a movie that somehow negotiates its plot without becoming corny or ridiculous, and leaves us feeling surprisingly moved.

The film stars Tom Hulce in the crucial role of Dominick, a friendly, outgoing young man whose retardation has left him well able to function, but not always able to understand other people's motives. He is completely trusting, likes everyone, and expects everyone to like him, but it doesn't work that way with one of the stops on his garbage route. There's a young boy there named Mickey (Tommy Snelfire) who shares his love of comic books, and they trade back issues until Mickey's drunken father (David Strathairn) tells Dominick, "Stop hanging around my kid!"

Dominick's feelings are hurt. And there are other complications in his life. His brother, Eugene (Ray Liotta), turns up one day with a date (Jamie Lee Curtis), and Dominick fears that Eugene will run away and leave him. Larry (Todd Graff), the guy who works with him on the garbage truck, fills his head with bad ideas all the time, including the suggestion that Eugene may run away to Atlantic City and gamble away all of their money.

The director, Robert M. Young, regards this situation with an evenhanded point of view. We see Dominick's world through his own eyes, and then we see the world of Eugene at the hospital. Attention is paid to Eugene's relationship with Jamie Lee Curtis; they're both so busy, so ambitious, and so overworked as medical students that they seem to realize there is no place in their plans for each other. Sometimes Eugene grows frustrated with Dominick, and sometimes his temper explodes, but they have a loving relationship.

Then one day Dominick sees something. Little Mickey's drunken father mistreats him, and throws him down the basement steps, and as Dominick accidentally witnesses this act there is a long, painful close-up on his face and we realize he is remembering something. The way in which Tom Hulce projects his thoughts, in this scene and others, is surprisingly effective. His performance is a courageous one, completely uninhibited and without any fear of looking silly. Many actors protect themselves, refuse to go "too far," worry about their image; Hulce dedicates himself absolutely to this character.

I was also impressed by Ray Liotta's work as Dominick's brother. You may remember Liotta from *Something Wild*, where he was the mysterious, violent husband who turned up unexpectedly two-thirds of the way through. Liotta's ability to suggest an undercurrent of danger is present in this role, too, but channeled in a different direction. What comes out more strongly is his tenderness, his willingness to meet Tom Hulce's lack of inhibition and go with it. Jamie Lee Curtis has a fairly thankless role as an intelligent observer admitted into the family circle, but she is right for it, and projects a kind of fierce careerism that doesn't quite mask her emotions.

Dominick and Eugene is a message movie with several different messages, but it never feels like a messenger. In the way it shows the two brothers caring for each other, it captures a tenderness and intimacy that few love stories ever reach. It reminded me sometimes of *Midnight Cowboy*, another movie in which two men learned to take care of one another and make allowances for each other's weaknesses. The danger is that any description of the plot will make it sound so melodramatic that its genuine human qualities get overlooked. It's quite an experience.

Don Juan DeMarco ★ ★
PG-13, 97 m., 1995

Marlon Brando (Jack Mickler), Johnny Depp (Don Juan), Faye Dunaway (Marilyn Mickler), Geraldine Pailhas (Dona Ana), Bob Dishy (Dr. Paul Showalter), Rachel Ticotin (Dona Inez), Talisa Soto (Dona Julia). Directed by Jeremy Leven and produced by Francis Ford Coppola, Fred Fuchs, and Patrick Palmer. Screenplay by Leven.

In a new book about how he makes movies, the director Sidney Lumet speculates that Marlon Brando has a way of testing his directors. Brando does a scene twice, he writes, once really putting his soul into it, the second time using only technique. He waits to see if the director can tell the difference between the two takes. If the director fails the test, Brando walks through the rest of the movie.

I don't know if that speculation is true, but maybe Jeremy Leven, the director of *Don Juan DeMarco*, failed the test. Brando doesn't so much walk through this movie as coast, in a gassy, self-indulgent performance no one else could have gotten away with. Having long since proved he can be one of the best actors in movie history, he now proves he can be one of the worst.

That's a shame, really, because *Don Juan DeMarco* is the kind of delicate, oddball fantasy that could have been charming, without Brando's petulant presence spoiling the fun. It stars Johnny Depp, who in *Benny and Joon* and *Arizona Dreams* showed the kind of delicate touch an actor needs to slip into the darkness of the soul and find human comedy there.

Like both of those films, this one deals with mental illness: Depp plays a character who is convinced he is Don Juan, the world's greatest lover. He gets other people to believe it, too, in dialogue so steamy that maybe only Depp could have delivered it, with his deadpan sincerity and big honest eyes. "What do you know of love?" he asks a psychiatrist. "Have you ever loved a woman until milk leaked from her—as if she had just given birth to love itself, and now must feed it or burst?"

The psychiatrist admits he has not. He

doubts Don Juan has, either. Don Juan finds himself in the mental hospital for a ten-day evaluation process, after being committed because he has, in the diagnosis of the experts, "obsessive-compulsive disorder with eroto-manic features." When the first psychiatrist washes his hands of the case, Don Juan is assigned to a distinguished man nearing retirement: Jack Mickler, played by Brando.

The problem with Brando these days is that we have read so much about his acting techniques and shortcuts that it is hard to see anything else. He wears a hearing aid. Is it intended to add a touch of realism to his character—or is he being fed his lines by a dialogue coach? He adds little touches of busyness, like eating during a scene, and we're aware that he's done it before (M&Ms in *The Formula*, nuts in *The Freshman*). And there are moments so bizarre we wonder if the director actually suggested them, or whether Brando had a brainstorm, and everybody was afraid to tell him it wasn't such a hot idea.

One of these moments comes during a curious bedroom scene with Faye Dunaway, who plays his loving wife. We are given to understand the moment is postcoital. What does Brando do? Light a cigarette? Turn on the TV? Cuddle? Nooooooo . . . what he does is blow kernels of popcorn into the air through a paper tube, so that Dunaway can try to catch them in her mouth. She catches one, finally, and seems so happy you wonder how much film they burned trying to get the trick right. The next time I see Dunaway, I'm going to ask her if, during that scene, she was wondering if acting with Brando was really worth the trouble.

We can guess what the movie might have been in the scenes where Brando is not around. The Depp character, given ten days to convince the psychiatrist of his sanity, insists on elaborating his fantasies. We learn that, as Don Juan, he once fought a duel over his mother's honor. And that he was sold into slavery to a sultan. While imprisoned in the sultan's harem, he made love to every woman there, leading him, in a later scene, to answer a lover's question by telling her that, "including you," he has made love to 1,502 women—"a sum substantially greater than the one she had in mind."

Don Juan's poetry has a hypnotic effect on those around him. After all the female nurses develop crushes on him, he's assigned a hulking male nurse named Rocco (Tiny Lister), and soon has *him* dancing in the patient's ward. Depp must be one of the few actors who can get away with sincerely speaking lines like: "Women sense that I search out the beauty that dwells within them, until it overwhelms everything else. And then they cannot avoid their desire to release that beauty, and envelop me in it." He has an openness to fantasy that makes his strange characters—also including Edward Scissorhands and Ed Wood—touching and convincing. Actors often talk about how they'd like to work with Brando. This kid could teach him some things.

The Doors ★ ★ ½
R, 135 m., 1991

Val Kilmer (Jim Morrison), Frank Whaley (Robby Krieger), Kevin Dillon (John Densmore), Meg Ryan (Pamela Courson), Kyle MacLachlan (Ray Manzarek), Kathleen Quinlan (Journalist). Directed by Oliver Stone and produced by Bill Graham, Sasha Harari, and A. Kitman Ho. Screenplay by J. Randal Johnson and Stone.

F. Scott Fitzgerald wrote that the problem with American lives is that they have no second act. The problem with Jim Morrison's life was that it had no first and third. His childhood was lost in a mist of denial—he never quite forgave his father for being an admiral—and his maturity was interrupted by an early death, caused by his relentless campaign against his own mind and body. What he left behind was a protracted adolescence, during which he recorded some great rock 'n' roll.

If we can trust Oliver Stone's new biographical film, *The Doors*, life for Jim Morrison was like being trapped for months at a time in the party from hell. He wanders out of the sun's glare, a curly-haired Southern California beach boy with a cute pout and a notebook full of poetry. He picks up a beer, he smokes a joint, and then life goes on fast-forward as he gobbles up drugs and booze with both hands, while betraying his friends and making life miserable for anyone who loves him. By the age of twenty-seven he is dead. Watching the movie is like being stuck in a bar with an obnoxious drunk when you're not drinking.

The songs he left behind, it is true, are wonderful. Many of them are on the sound track of *The Doors*, which combines Morrison's original vocals and new vocals by Val Kilmer so seamlessly that there is never, not even for a moment, the sensation that Kilmer is not singing everything we hear. That illusion is strengthened by Kilmer's appearance. He looks so uncannily like Jim Morrison that we feel this is not a case of casting, but of possession.

The performance is the best thing in the movie—and since nearly every scene centers on Morrison, that is not small praise. Val Kilmer has always had a remarkable talent, which until now has been largely overlooked, but if you want to see why Stone thought he could be convincing as a rock star, look at *Top Secret!*, the *Airplane!*-style spoof of spy movies in which Kilmer plays Elvis Presley. Because of Kilmer, and because of extraordinary location work with countless convincing extras, the concert scenes in *The Doors* play with the authenticity of a documentary.

If the songs are timeless and the concert footage is convincing, however, the scenes from life are more painful than in any other backstage movie I can remember. The typical showbiz biopic describes a sort of parabola, in which the talented kid wins early fame, begins to self-destruct, hits bottom, and then makes his big comeback and goes on, of course, to have a movie made about him. Jim Morrison becomes a star very quickly, and then self-destructs as efficiently as he can. It is not a pretty picture. He must have been one of those people with a constitutional inability to handle drugs or booze in any quantity. For him there is no moderation; he isn't seeking to get high, he's looking for oblivion.

He knows it. His poetry and lyrics—and a lot of the dialogue in the movie—glorify death. He's infatuated with it, mesmerized by death as the ultimate trip and as the ultimate loyalty test: If you love him, you will die with and/or for him. He's like Edgar Allen Poe on acid, crawling along the ledges outside hotel windows, or begging his lovers to stab him in the heart. This kind of narcissism has its source, of course, in self-loathing, and the early scenes of Jim preening and posturing before the camera like a male pinup eventually segue into scenes where he hides behind a beard and dark glasses, hibernating in hotel rooms on long, lonely binges.

Oliver Stone, who as a young man once tried to pitch an early version of this screenplay to Morrison himself, has a natural feel for the Los Angeles beach and rock scene in the years when The Doors were first establishing themselves as "the band from Venice." Morrison materializes on the beach like a young god from the sea, falls in love with a hippie chick (Meg Ryan), and reads his poetry, which as poetry is sophomoric, but translates easily into haunting song lyrics, helped by the mournful quality of his voice. Whatever else you can say about Morrison and The Doors, there is no denying their sound: Their records, especially "Light My Fire" and "L.A. Woman," have become a part of our shared consciousness.

Stone shows the band working out some early arrangements and playing early gigs at rock clubs on the Sunset Strip, and then, just as in life, Jim Morrison becomes a superstar at about the same time he becomes unreliable as a stage performer. He carries a bottle with him everywhere, gulping big slugs of booze as if it were pop. He uses drugs. They do not help his personality, and he becomes mean-spirited and autocratic to those who depend on him, and obnoxious to the public—except, of course, for those moments when lightning strikes and his underlying talent flashes out.

The band grows weary of him—of the missed dates, the no-shows, the late arrivals, and endless recording sessions in which a drunken or hungover Morrison indulges himself in expensive retakes. Keyboardist Ray Manzarek (Kyle MacLachlan), who first told him he had potential as a singer, drifts into a kind of passive-aggressive trance, sitting stone-faced during Morrison's outbursts. Others threaten to quit. Listening to the final version of one of his best albums, Morrison tells the musicians, "That's not bad for a bunch of guys who weren't even talking to each other the day the album was recorded."

Prancing and preening onstage as a sex god, Morrison is bedeviled by impotence in real life; the drugs have done their work. In the movie's most extraordinary scene, he encounters an older rock journalist (Kathleen Quinlan) who is heavily into sadomasochism and the trappings of witchcraft, and who, through heroic measures including pain, ritual, and the mutual drinking of blood, succeeds in stimulating Morrison to the point where he actually achieves potency—although, if the movie is to be trusted, it was his last hurrah.

Quinlan's character is almost the only one able to break through the fog of Morrison's indulgences to create a distinctive screen persona for herself (the character is miles different from anything she has played before, and brilliantly conceived and executed). The other principals in Morrison's life, even his wife as played by Ryan, are supporting

characters who drift in and out of focus during his long, sad binge.

The experience of watching *The Doors* is not always very pleasant. There are the songs, of course, and some electrifying concert moments, but mostly there is the mournful, self-pitying descent of this young man into selfish and boring stupor. Having seen this movie, I am not sad to have missed the opportunity to meet Jim Morrison, and I can think of few fates more painful than being part of his support system. The last hour of the film, in particular, is a dirge of wretched excess, of drunken would-be orgies and obnoxious behavior, of concerts in which the audiences waited for hours for the spectacle of Morrison stumbling onstage to fake a few songs or, notoriously, to expose himself.

In the end, Stone leaves a large question unanswered: How was Morrison able to leave the country after being sentenced to a jail term for public indecency? But leave he did, to die of an "apparent heart attack" in Paris, where he lies buried to this day, his tomb a mecca for his fans, who have spray-painted all of the neighboring tombs with exhortations and obscenities. Even in death, Jim Morrison is no fun to be around.

Do the Right Thing ★ ★ ★ ★
R, 120 m., 1989

Danny Aiello (Sal), Ossie Davis (Da Mayor), Ruby Dee (Mother Sister), Richard Edson (Vito), Giancarlo Esposito (Buggin Out), Spike Lee (Mookie), Bill Nunn (Radio Raheem), John Turturro (Pino), Paul Benjamin (ML), Frankie Faison (Coconut Sid). Directed, produced, and written by Spike Lee.

Spike Lee's *Do the Right Thing* is the kind of film people find they have to talk about afterward. Some of them are bothered by it—they think it will cause trouble. Others feel the message is confused. Some find it too militant, others find it the work of a middle-class director who is trying to play street-smart. All of those reactions, I think, are simply different ways of avoiding the central fact of this film, which is that it comes closer to reflecting the current state of race relations in America than any other movie of our time.

Of course it is confused. Of course it wavers between middle-class values and street values. Of course it is not sure whether it believes in liberal pieties, or militancy. Of course some of the characters are sympathetic and others are hateful—and of course some of the likable

characters do bad things. Isn't that the way it is in America today? Anyone who walks into this film expecting answers is a dreamer or a fool. But anyone who leaves the movie with more intolerance than they walked in with wasn't paying attention.

The movie takes place during one long, hot day in the Bedford-Stuyvesant neighborhood of Brooklyn. But this is not the typical urban cityscape we've seen in countless action movies about violence and guns and drugs. People live here. It's a neighborhood like those city neighborhoods in the urban movies of the Depression—people know each other, and accept each other, and although there are problems there is also a sense of community.

The neighborhood is black, but two of the businesses aren't. Sal's Famous Pizzeria has been on the same corner since before the neighborhood changed, and Sal (Danny Aiello) boasts that "these people have grown up on my pizza." And in a nearby storefront that had been boarded up for years, a Korean family has opened a fruit and vegetable stand. Nobody seems to quite know the Koreans, but Sal and his sons are neighborhood fixtures—they know everybody, and everybody knows them.

Sal is a tough, no-nonsense guy who basically wants to get along and tend to business. One of his sons is a vocal racist—in private, of course. The other is more open toward blacks. Sal's ambassador to the community is a likable local youth named Mookie (Spike Lee), who delivers pizzas and also acts as a messenger of news and gossip. Mookie is good at his job, but his heart isn't in it; he knows there's no future in delivering pizzas.

We meet other people in the neighborhood. There's Da Mayor (Ossie Davis), a kind of everyman who knows everybody. Buggin' Out (Giancarlo Esposito), a vocal militant. Radio Raheem (Bill Nunn), whose boom box defines his life, and provides a musical cocoon to insulate him from the world. Mother Sister (Ruby Dee), who is sort of the neighborhood saint. And there's the local disk jockey, whose program provides a running commentary, and a retarded street person who wanders around selling photos of Martin Luther King and Malcolm X, and then there are three old guys on the corner who comment on developments, slowly and at length.

This looks like a good enough neighborhood—like the kind of urban stage the proletarian dramas of the 1930s liked to start with. And for a long time during *Do the Right Thing*, Spike Lee treats it like a backdrop for a Saroyanesque slice of life. But things are happening under the surface. Tensions are building. Old hurts are being remembered. And finally the movie explodes in racial violence.

The exact nature of that violence has been described in many of the articles about the film—including two I wrote after the movie's tumultuous premiere at the Cannes Film Festival—but in this review I think I will not outline the actual events. At Cannes, I walked into the movie cold, and its ending had a shattering effect precisely because I was not expecting it. I would like you to have the experience for yourself, and think about it for yourself. Since Spike Lee does not tell you what to think about it, and deliberately provides surprising twists for some of the characters, this movie is more open-ended than most. It requires you to decide what you think about it.

Do the Right Thing is not filled with brotherly love, but it is not filled with hate, either. It comes out of a weary urban cynicism that has settled down around us in recent years. The good feelings and many of the hopes of the 1960s have evaporated, and today it would no longer be accurate to make a movie about how the races in America are all going to love one another. I wish we could see such love, but instead we have deepening class divisions in which the middle classes of all races flee from what's happening in the inner city, while a series of national administrations provides no hope for the poor. *Do the Right Thing* tells an honest, unsentimental story about those who are left behind.

It is a very well-made film, beautifully photographed by Ernest Dickerson, and well-acted by an ensemble cast. Danny Aiello has the pivotal role, as Sal, and he suggests all of the difficult nuances of his situation. In the movie's final scene, Sal's conversation with Mookie holds out little hope, but it holds out at least the possibility that something has been learned from the tragedy, and the way Aiello plays this scene is quietly brilliant. Lee's writing and direction are masterful throughout the movie; he knows exactly where he is taking us, and how to get there, but he holds his cards close to his heart, and so the movie is hard to predict, hard to anticipate. After we get to the end, however, we understand how, and why, everything has happened.

I believe that any good-hearted person,

white or black, will come out of this movie with sympathy for all of the characters. Lee does not ask us to forgive them, or even to understand everything they do, but he wants us to identify with their fears and frustrations. *Do the Right Thing* doesn't ask its audiences to choose sides; it is scrupulously fair to both sides, in a story where it is our society itself which is not fair.

The Double Life of Veronique ★ ★ ★ ½
NO MPAA RATING, 96 m., 1991

Irene Jacob (Veronique/Veronika), Halina Gryglaszewska (The Aunt), Kalina Jedrusik (The Gaudy Woman), Aleksander Bardini (Orchestra Conductor), Wladyslaw Kowalski (Veronika's Father), Jerzy Gudejko (Antek). Directed by Krzysztof Kieslowski and produced by Leonardo de la Fuente. Screenplay by Kieslowski and Krzysztof Piesiewicz.

It is important to resist the temptation to figure out every last detail of *The Double Life of Veronique*, the mysterious and poetic new film by Krzysztof Kieslowski. That way lies frustration. The parts do not quite fit, and anyway this is not a puzzle to be assembled. It is a romance about those moments we all sometimes have when we think we see ourselves at a distance. Is there, we wonder, more than one me? Why haven't I ever seen a portrait in a gallery that looks exactly like me—or anyone I know? How would I feel if I did?

The movie is about two young women, one named Veronique, one named Veronika, both played by Irene Jacob. They never quite meet, although their paths almost cross one day. One lives in France, the other in Poland. They were born on the same day. They have identical heart problems. They are both wonderful singers. One dies, the other doesn't.

The movie could have been truly confusing if it cut back and forth between the two women, both played by the same actress, but it doesn't. We follow the Polish Veronika until she shockingly collapses during a music recital, and then we pick up the thread in Paris. This is the reverse of what Luis Buñuel once did when he had two different actresses play the same woman interchangeably. With Kieslowski we are also a little confused: Is this the same woman? Did she not really die? We listen for clues. Then we realize there are none. First we saw one woman, now we see the other.

There is a long central section in the film that is a triumph of narrative technique. Ver-

onique receives a tape in the mail. She listens to it, and eventually is able to identify it as the sounds in a train station—a particular station. She has received other clues, from a secret admirer who seems to challenge her to find him. She follows the clues, using enormous ingenuity, but when she finally meets the admirer she is chagrined, because there was nothing there, really, but the game, and somehow she felt there would be truth and illumination at the end of her quest. Perhaps this part of the film is a parable for the puzzle that Kieslowski has set us.

Sometimes I play a game in my life, which consists of returning to an exact place and time and duplicating an exact action. Here I am again, I think, following my own footsteps. This café, on a rainy morning in Paris in the winter. The same waiter, the same order, the same book in my hand. And next year I will do this again. The problem with these games is that they are locked in time. I can always repeat my action next year, but never last year. I cannot make an appointment in the past. Something like that game is what *The Double Life of Veronique* is about, with the addition that only the filmmaker, only Kieslowski, knows both of the women.

Are they the same woman? No. Why are they so similar? Perhaps because there are only so many differences that are possible. Why does the second woman seem to feel a fleeting moment of pain when the first one dies? Kieslowski is not interested in the answers to such questions, because they would be meaningless speculations. But the *possibility* of such connections between lives is infinitely interesting. To think about them is to touch the mystery of consciousness.

When I do think I see myself at a distance, by the way, I never hurry to catch up. What if I were right? What would we say to each other?

Down and Out in Beverly Hills ★ ★ ★
R, 103 m., 1986

Nick Nolte (Jerry Baskin), Richard Dreyfuss (Dave Whiteman), Bette Midler (Barbara Whiteman), Little Richard (Orvis Goodnight), Tracy Nelson (Jenny Whiteman), Elizabeth Pena (Carmen). Directed and produced by Paul Mazursky. Screenplay by Mazursky and Leon Capetanos.

Buddy Hackett once said that the problem with Beverly Hills is, you go to sleep beside your pool one day and when you wake up you're seventy-five years old. *Down and Out in Beverly Hills* understands that statement inside-out.

It tells the story of a rich family that lives in the timeless comfort of a Beverly Hills mansion—in the kind of house where they use *Architectural Digest* for pornography. One day a bum wanders down the alley and into their backyard and tries to drown himself in their swimming pool. After he is saved, he changes their lives forever.

In its broad outlines, this story is borrowed from Jean Renoir's classic film *Boudo Saved from Drowning*. But this isn't just a remake. The director, Paul Mazursky, makes his whole film depend on the very close observation of his characters. Mazursky knows Beverly Hills (he lives there, on the quiet cloistered flatlands below Sunset Boulevard), and he knows the deceptions and compromises of upper-middle-class life (his credits include *An Unmarried Woman* and *Bob & Carol & Ted & Alice*). With great attention and affection, he shows us the lives that are disrupted by the arrival of the derelict—this seedy failure whose whole life is an affront to the consumer society.

The film's heroes are the Whitemans, Dave and Barbara (Richard Dreyfuss and Bette Midler), and the bum, Jerry Baskin. He is played by Nick Nolte as the kind of guy who didn't set out in life to be a failure, but just sort of drifted from one plateau down to the next one, until finally he was spending most of his time talking to his dog.

It is, indeed, the dog's disappearance that inspires Nolte's suicide attempt, and it will be the Whitemans' own amazing dog, named Matisse, that gets some of the loudest laughs in the movie. Maybe Mazursky is trying to tell us something about the quality of human relationships in Beverly Hills.

The Dreyfuss character is a coat-hanger manufacturer. He didn't set out in life to be rich (one of his favorite conversational gambits involves his own good luck and assurances that it could have happened to you as easily as to him—nice if you are him, but not if you are you). Here he is, living in a manicured mansion, exploiting wetback labor, sleeping with the Mexican maid, driving a Rolls convertible, selling 900 million coat hangers to the Chinese, and yet, somehow, something is missing. And almost from the first moment he sets eyes on the Nolte character, he realizes what it is: the authenticity of poverty.

The movie has a quiet, offhand way of introducing us to the the rich man's milieu. We meet his wife, whose life involves long sessions with masseurs, yogis, and shrinks (even her dog has a doggie psychiatrist). We meet his daughter (Tracy Nelson), a sunny-faced, milk-fed child of prosperity. We meet the Whitemans' neighbor, played by Little Richard with an incongruous mixture of anger and affluence (he complains that he doesn't get full service from the police; when he reports prowlers, they don't send helicopters and attack dogs).

We meet Carmen (Elizabeth Pena), the maid, who greets her employer lustily in her servant's quarters, but who grows, during the movie, from a soap opera addict into a political radical. We also meet the extended family and friends of the Whitemans, each one a perfectly written vignette, right down to the dog's analyst.

Down and Out in Beverly Hills revolves around the fascination that Dreyfuss feels for Nolte's life of dissipation and idleness. He is drawn to the shiftless sloth like a moth to a flame. A bum's life seems to have more authenticity than his own pampered existence. And, indeed, perhaps the last unreachable frontier of the very rich, the one thing they cannot buy, is poverty. Dreyfuss spends a night down on the beach with Nolte and his bum friends, and there is a breathtaking moment at sundown when Nolte (who claims to be a failed actor) recites Shakespeare's lines beginning "What a piece of work is a man!"

Certain predictable things happen. Nolte not only becomes Dreyfuss's good buddy, but is enlisted by all of the women in the household—the wife, the daughter, and the maid—as a sex therapist. Dreyfuss will put up with almost anything, because he really likes this guy, and Nolte's best hold on them is the threat to leave. Mazursky makes the most of that paradox, and gradually we see the buried theme of the movie emerging, and it is the power of friendship. What these people all really lacked, rich and poor, sane and crazy alike, was the power to really like other people.

The movie should get some kind of award for its casting. Dreyfuss, who has been so good in the past as a hyperactive overachiever, succeeds here in slightly deflecting that energy. He has the success, but is bedazzled by it, as if not quite trusting why great wealth should come to him for doing so little. He channels his energy, not into work, but into enthusiasms—and Nolte becomes his greatest enthusiasm.

For Bette Midler, Barbara Whiteman is the perfect character, all filled with the distractions of living up to her level of consumption. Nolte in some ways has the subtlest role to play, although when we first see it, it seems the broadest. His shiftless drifter has to metamorphose into a man who understands his hosts so deeply that he can play them like a piano.

The supporting roles are so well filled, one after another, that we almost feel we recognize the characters before they're introduced. And Mike, the dog, should get an honorary walk-on at the Oscars.

Perhaps I have made the movie sound too serious. Mazursky has a way of making comedies that are more intelligent and relevant than most of the serious films around; his last credit, for example, was the challenging *Moscow on the Hudson*. So let me just say that *Down and Out in Beverly Hills* made me laugh longer and louder than any film I've seen in a long time.

Down by Law ★ ★ ★
R, 95 m., 1986

Tom Waits (Zack), John Lurie (Jack), Roberto Benigni (Roberto), Nicoletta Braschi (Nicoletta), Ellen Barkin (Bobbie). Directed by Jim Jarmusch. Screenplay by Jarmusch.

It's a sad and beautiful world.
—Line of dialogue

Down by Law is a movie about cheap whiskey and black coffee, all-night drunks and lost jobs, and the bad times you can have with good-time girls. It tells the story of a pimp, an unemployed disc jockey, and a bewildered Italian tourist, and how they escape from jail together and wind up slogging through the Louisiana bayous looking for a decent place to have breakfast. It's like a collage made out of objects from old gangster movies, old blues songs, and old jailhouse stories. At the end, it's like that line of dialogue. It's a sad and beautiful world, someone says, and someone else should say, yeah, but so what?

The movie was directed by Jim Jarmusch. You may remember his *Stranger than Paradise* (1984), a deadpan black-and-white comedy in which three strangely assorted friends decided it was too cold in Cleveland in the winter, and went to Florida and lost all their money at the dog races. *Down by Law* has the same sort of feeling; it's about two people who choose to be losers and a third who has bought the American Dream.

The movie stars Tom Waits, whose sandpaper voice sounds like he's pushing his words through three layers of hangovers. The other two guys are played by John Lurie, who was the Hungarian-American poker player in *Stranger than Paradise*, and Roberto Benigni, a previously unknown Italian actor who resembles a cross between Father Guido Sarducci and Woody Allen. They meet in the same Louisiana jail cell through a series of misadventures in which two of the guys are framed and the third is severely misunderstood.

No cell is large enough to hold these three. Lurie and Waits hate each other, but hate is nothing compared to the emotions they feel for the Italian, who commits the unpardonable sin of being cheerful and constantly pleased with himself. Eventually the three prisoners escape, and the movie follows them through the swamps as they slog through every cliché Jarmusch can remember.

In notes accompanying the film, Jarmusch is at pains to explain that he never saw the Louisiana bayou country before he went to shoot a movie there. What he has seen are lots of movies, and *Down by Law* is an anthology of pulp images from the world of *film noir*. On the surface, it's grim and relentless, but there's a thread of humor running through everything, and that takes the curse off. We are never quite sure that Jarmusch intends us to take anything seriously, and there are times when the actors seem to be smiling to themselves as they growl through their lines.

Lurie is known from the previous film, and from his work as a musician. Tom Waits is a star playing himself. The discovery in the picture is the redoubtable Roberto Benigni, who has an irrepressible, infectious manner, and is absolutely delighted to be himself. I don't know where he came from and I can't imagine what he's going to do next, but he could have a long comic career ahead of himself; he's like a show-off kid who gets you laughing and then starts laughing at himself, he's so funny, and then tries to top himself no matter what.

Down by Law is a true original that kind of grows on you. Maybe it goes on a little too long, and maybe it depends too much on its original inspiration—these three misfits and the oddballs they meet along the way—instead of trying to be about something. It doesn't have the inspired perfection of

Stranger than Paradise, in which every shot seemed inevitable, but it's a good movie, and the more you know about movies the more you're likely to like it.

Dragnet ★ ★ ★
PG-13, 100 m., 1987

Dan Aykroyd (Friday), Tom Hanks (Pep Streebeck), Christopher Plummer (Whirley), Harry Morgan (Bill Gannon), Alexandra Paul (Connie Swail), Jack O'Halloran (Emil Muzz), Elizabeth Ashley (Jane Kirkpatrick), Dabney Coleman (Jerry Caesar). Directed by Tom Mankiewicz and produced by David Permut and Robert K. Weiss. Screenplay by Aykroyd, Alan Zweibel, and Mankiewicz.

From the loud, confident opening chords of the famous "Dragnet" theme music, I was filled with confidence that this 1987 *Dragnet* knew what it was doing. My confidence lasted several seconds. Then the original music segued into some kind of dreadful disco rap unmusic, and my heart sank. How could they? How could they possibly make a movie called *Dragnet* and think that *anything* had to be done to the music?

They make the same mistake at the end, over the closing titles. I guess it was some kind of a business deal, and they wanted to make a lot of money with the music video or something. Hollywood is so greedy these days. God forbid that whoever wrote the original "Dragnet" theme should make a dime, when it can be cloned and corrupted for profit.

In between, the movie's pretty good. To be more precise, it is great for an hour, good for about twenty-five munutes, and then heads doggedly for the Standard 1980s High Tech Hollywood Ending, which means an expensive chase scene and a shoot-out. God, I'm tired of chases and shoot-outs.

The movie takes the basic ingredients of the "Dragnet" TV shows, kids them, and plugs them into a bizarre plot about a cult of Los Angeles pagans who hold weird satanic rites. Dan Aykroyd stars as Joe Friday, nephew of the original, and he was born to play this role, with his off-the-rack brown suit, his felt fedora, and his square jaw with the Chesterfield pasted into it. Tom Hanks is his partner, the nonconforming Detective Streebeck, game for anything but puzzled by Aykroyd's straight-arrow squareness.

There's a series of "pagan murders" in L.A..and the two cops get on the trail, which leads to a phony TV preacher, some highly

placed creeps, and an absolutely hilarious pagan-rite scene, in which oddly assorted would-be pagans stomp around in thighhigh sheepskins, while the Virgin Connie Swail (Alexandra Paul) is prepared for a sacrifice.

That's what she's always called, the Virgin Connie Swail. Friday falls in love with her, and his heart beats so hard that he stays on the case even after Chief Gannon (the legendary Harry Morgan) lifts his badge. Among other familiar faces involved in the case is Jack O'Halloran, as Emil Muzz, the big killer (you may remember him as Moose Malloy in the Mitchum version of *Farewell, My Lovely*).

Aykroyd's performance is the centerpiece of the film. He must have practiced for hours, even days, to perfect the rapid-fire delivery he uses to rattle off polysyllabic utterances of impenetrable but kaleidoscopic complexity. Listening to him talk in this movie is a joy.

It's an open question, I think, how much they really wanted to kid the old "Dragnet" shows. Jack Webb's visual style was built around a series of deadpan close-ups and clipped one-liners, and there's a little of that in this movie, but they never make a real point of it or have a lot of fun with it. The visuals are a lot looser than Webb would have enjoyed. And the color photography, of course, is all wrong; this is a movie that begs to be in black-and-white.

Still, it's fun, a lot of the time. Several individual shots are hilarious, including a long shot in pantomime of the two partners trying to show Harry Morgan how the pagans did their dance. Hanks and Aykroyd have an easy, unforced chemistry, growing out of their laconic delivery and opposite personalities, and the movie is filled with nice supporting turns, especially from Elizabeth Ashley and Dabney Coleman, as crooked officials.

This would have been a great movie if they'd bothered to think of an ending for it. And used the original "Dragnet" theme. The end of the film cries out—*cries* out, mind you—for the simple, stark, authority of *dum-de-dum-dum*. I wanted to hear it so badly I walked out of the screening singing the notes out loud, to drown out the disco Drano from the screen.

The Draughtsman's Contract ★ ★ ★ ★
R, 103 m., 1983

Anthony Higgins (Mr. Neville), Janet Suzman (Mrs. Herbert), Anne Louise Lambert (Mrs. Talmann). Directed by Peter Greenaway and produced by David Payne. Screenplay by Greenaway.

What we have here is a tantalizing puzzle, wrapped in eroticism and presented with the utmost elegance. I have never seen a film quite like it. *The Draughtsman's Contract* seems to be telling us a very simple story in a very straightforward way, but after it's over you may need hours of discussion with your friends before you can be sure (if even then) exactly what happened.

The film takes place in 1694, in the English countryside. A rich lady (Janet Suzman) hires an itinerant artist to make twelve detailed drawings of her house. The artist (Anthony Higgins) strikes a hard bargain. In addition to his modest payment, he demands "the unrestricted freedom of her most intimate hospitality." Since the gentleman of the house is away on business, the lady agrees, and thus begins a pleasant regime divided between the easel and the boudoir.

All of this is told in the most precise way. All of the characters speak in complete, elegant, literary sentences. All of the camera strategies are formal and mannered. The movie advances with the grace and precision of a well-behaved novel. There is even a moment, perhaps, when we grow restless at the film's deliberate pace. But then, if we are sharp, we begin to realize that strange things are happening under our very noses.

The draughtsman demands perfection. There must be no change, from day to day, in the view he paints. He aims for complete realism. But little changes do creep in. A window is left open. A ladder is found standing against a wall. There are things on the lawn that should not be on the lawn. The lady's daughter calls on the artist and suggests that a plot may be under way and that her father, the lord of the manor, may have been murdered. Furthermore, the artist may be about to be framed for the crime. As a payment for her friendship, the daughter demands the same payment in "intimate hospitality" as her mother. Now the artist is not only draughtsman but lover to mother and daughter *and* the possible object of a plot to frame him with murder.

There is more. There is a lot more, all allowed to unfold at the same deliberate pace. There is a mysterious statue in the garden. An eavesdropper. Misbehaved sheep. The raw materials of this story could have been fashioned into a bawdy romp like *Tom Jones*. But the director, Peter Greenaway,

has made a canny choice. Instead of showing us everything, and explaining everything, he gives us the clues and allows us to draw our own conclusions. His movie is like a crossword puzzle for the senses.

Dreamchild ★ ★ ★
PG, 94 m., 1985

Coral Browne (Mrs. Hargreaves), Ian Holm (Reverend Dodgson), Peter Gallagher (Jack Dolan), Caris Corfman (Sally Mackeson), Nicola Cowper (Lucy), Jane Asher (Mrs. Liddell). Directed by Gavin Miller and produced by Rick McCallum and Kenith Trodd. Screenplay by Dennis Potter.

It probably comes as no surprise that the man who wrote *Alice's Adventures in Wonderland* was not an absolute paragon of normality. His biographers have recently revealed that the Rev. Charles Dodgson (who wrote under the pen name Lewis Carroll) had an obsession with young girls, which he satisfied through hundreds of photographic studies and through lots of chummy friendships and correspondence. *Dreamchild* deals with his obsession as a problem that he tried to resolve in basically healthy ways, but it does argue that the writing of *Alice* created lifelong problems for the girl who inspired it.

According to this movie, which is fiction inspired by fact, the original Alice was a girl named Alice Liddell. She suffered Dodgson's attentions for a time and allowed herself to be rowed up and down a river by him one sunny afternoon, but she was more interested in playing with her friends than in having the original manuscript of *Alice* read to her. "But I wrote this just for you!" protests the anguished clergyman (played with a nice, quiet intensity by Ian Holm).

Dreamchild is not, in any event, a psychological case study. It's too much fun for that. The movie begins some seventy years after the book was published. The young girl, now eighty years old, is known as Mrs. Alice Hargreaves (Coral Browne) and is sailing for America to receive an honorary degree on the centennial of Dodgson's birth. She is accompanied by a young traveling companion named Lucy (Nicola Cowper), and on arrival in New York in 1932 she is surrounded by a mob of aggressive newspaper reporters. One of them (Peter Gallagher) succeeds in pushing his way into Mrs. Hargreaves's life and Lucy's heart.

What happens next is sort of sweet. As the reporter and Lucy gradually fall in love, Har-

greaves at first is violently opposed to their relationship. She is, indeed, a rather unpleasant old lady—inflexible and dogmatic, with definite ideas about the proper conduct of young people.

But she is much more complex than we think, as we learn by sharing her private nightmares and fantasies. In her mind, the world of Alice's Wonderland still has a scary reality, and we see the original fantasy figures (the king and queen, the Cheshire cat, and so on) as grotesque caricatures designed not to delight a little girl, but to frighten her.

The movie uses these fantasy sequences as counterpoint for more realistic flashbacks in which we meet Dodgson, see Alice as a young girl, and begin to sense some of the pathetic extremes to which Dodgson went to satisfy his passion for her, which was platonic but nonetheless bothering. We begin to realize, as old Mrs. Hargreaves herself begins to realize, that her whole life has been shaped by things that happened seventy years before.

Dreamchild is a remarkable film in many ways, not least because it gives itself such freedom of style and subject matter. For example, all the creatures in Alice's fantasies appear as muppetlike creations done by Jim Henson and his Creature Shop, but they are not Muppets. The movie has some subtle points to make with them.

At the same time, *Dreamchild* is not unremittingly grim, and it is not just a case study. The newspaper world of New York in the 1930s is re-created with style and humor, and the love story between the two young people is handled with a lot of cheerful energy. *Dreamchild* is an ambitious movie that tries to do a lot of things, and does most of them surprisingly well.

Dream Lover ★ ★ ★
R, 103 m., 1994

James Spader (Ray Reardon), Madchen Amick (Lena Reardon), Bess Armstrong (Elaine), Fredric Lehne (Larry), Larry Miller (Norman), Kathleen York (Martha), Blair Tefkin (Cheryl), Scott Coffey (Billy). Directed by Nicholas Kazan and produced by Sigurjon Sighvatsson, Wallis Nicita, and Lauren Lloyd. Screenplay by Kazan.

She is everything he has always desired—which means, in today's American movies, she is also everything he should fear. He spills wine on her at a gallery opening. She overreacts angrily. But when they meet a week later in a supermarket, she apologizes. And by then he is fascinated.

It's one of those instant relationships that begins with a cup of coffee and ends, hours later, with deep talk of eternal truths. There is passion, too. But he doesn't have her telephone number, and so he stakes out her loft, waiting for her to come home, wondering who she is, really. On their next meeting she is cool. He calls her on it. She confesses that she's trying to keep her distance because . . . she likes him too much. This is a weakness a man finds easy to forgive.

Nicholas Kazan's *Dream Lover,* like many films of the '90s, is an allegory about the dangers of love and sex. These movies teach a lesson: When you find the lover of your dreams, the reward is not happiness, but danger, betrayal, and death. Be careful what you dream of; you may get it.

The man, named Ray Reardon, is played by James Spader as a polished architect on the rebound from an earlier unhappy relationship. The woman, named Lena, is played by Madchen Amick with a tantalizing mixture of beauty and danger. Some of her best scenes in the movie come when she is lying, perfectly and seamlessly. It is clear to us that she is lying, and probably clear to Ray, too—but she does it so well it's almost like a game.

Dream Lover has been written and directed by Nicholas Kazan, who is consistent in his interest in dangerous marriages; his previous screenplay, *Reversal of Fortune,* was based on the possibility that Klaus von Bulow tried to murder his wife. Here he creates an intrigue that seems all the more seductive because, to some degree, it's a game both partners are playing.

The movie isn't simply about how Ray is deceived by Lena. It's about how, at some level, he cooperates in his own deception. At first he's so besotted by her that he ignores the questions that should occur to him about a person who apparently has no past and no friends. Later, fueled by jealousy, he begins to dig into her past—something she makes it relatively easy for him to do, for sinister reasons of her own. Spader is good at projecting the feeling that somehow her perfidy hasn't diminished her sex appeal.

As for Madchen Amick, a stunning beauty with an edgy intelligence, Kazan has given her a role that grows more interesting as it deepens. This isn't a one-level thriller in which she tries to keep a secret and her husband tries to discover it. It's more delicately complicated: She allows him to discover secrets, then plausibly lies to him about them, then reveals hints of other secrets, playing him like a piano until she gets what she wants.

The ending of all of this, I'm afraid, doesn't live up to the rest. The movie's last five minutes are a disappointment, in which Kazan wraps things up with an irony that is much too neat. But the movie's rewards are not really intended for the ending, anyway; it's the sensuous, deadly game of romantic cat-and-mouse that makes *Dream Lover* worth seeing.

Dressed to Kill ★ ★ ★
R, 105 m., 1980

Michael Caine (Dr. Elliott), Angie Dickinson (Kate Miller), Nancy Allen (Liz Blake), Keith Gordon (Peter Miller), Dennis Franz (Detective Marino), David Margulies (Dr. Levy). Directed by Brian De Palma and produced by George Litto. Screenplay by De Palma.

When Alfred Hitchcock died, the obituaries puzzled over the fact that Hitchcock had created the most distinctive and easily recognizable visual style of his generation—but hadn't had a great influence on younger filmmakers. The obvious exception is Brian De Palma, who deliberately set out to work in the Hitchcock tradition, and directed this Hitchcockian thriller that's stylish, intriguing, and very violent.

The ads for De Palma's *Dressed to Kill* describe him as "the master of the macabre," which is no more immodest, I suppose, than the ads that described Hitchcock as "the master of suspense." De Palma is not yet an artist of Hitchcock's stature, but he does earn the right to a comparison, especially after his deliberately Hitchcockian films *Sisters* and *Obsession.* He places his emphasis on the same things that obsessed Hitchcock: precise camera movements, meticulously selected visual details, characters seen as types rather than personalities, and violence as a sudden interruption of the most mundane situations.

He also has Hitchcock's delight in bizarre and unexpected plot twists, and the chief delight of the first and best hour of *Dressed to Kill* comes from the series of surprises he springs on us. Although other key characters are introduced, the central character in these early scenes is Kate Miller (Angie Dickinson), an attractive forty-fiveish Manhattan woman who has a severe case of unsatiated lust. De Palma opens with a deliberately shocking shower scene (homage to Hitch), and then follows the woman as her sexual fantasies become unexpectedly real during a lunchtime trip to the museum.

The museum sequence is absolutely brilliant, tracking Dickinson as she notices a tall, dark, and handsome stranger. She makes eye contact, breaks it, tries to attract the stranger's attention by dropping her glove, and then is tracked *by* the stranger. To her, and our, astonishment, this virtuoso scene (played entirely without dialogue) ends in a passionate sexual encounter in the back of a taxicab.

Later, she wakes up in the stranger's apartment, and De Palma shamelessly manipulates her, and us, by springing a series of plot surprises involving embarrassment and guilt: What would *you* do if you were a cheating wife and had just forgotten your wedding ring in a stranger's apartment? The plot now takes several totally unanticipated turns, and I, of course, would not dream of revealing them. Indeed, I'll be vague about the plot from now on, because De Palma's surprises are crucial to his effect.

The movie's other characters include Michael Caine, who's the psychiatrist of two of the characters in the film. Then there's Nancy Allen, who's wonderfully offbeat as a sweet Manhattan hooker who discovers a body and gets trapped in the investigation. And there's Keith Gordon: He's one of those teen-age scientific geniuses, and he invents brilliant gimmicks to investigate the crime.

Some people are going to object to certain plot details in *Dressed to Kill,* particularly the cavalier way it explains a homocidal maniac's behavior by lumping together transsexuality and schizophrenia. But I doubt that De Palma wants us to take his explanations very seriously; the pseudoscientific jargon used to "explain" the case reminds me of that terrible psychiatric explanation at the end of *Psycho*—a movie De Palma has been quoting from all along.

Dressed to Kill is an exercise in style, not narrative; it would rather look and feel like a thriller than make sense. Its plot has moments of ludicrous implausibility, it nearly bogs down at one point near the end and it cheats on us with the old "it was only a dream!" gimmick. But De Palma has so much fun with the conventions of the thriller that we forgive him and go along. And there are really nice touches in the performances: Dickinson's guilt-laden lust, Caine's analytical detachment, Allen's street-wise cool in life and death situations,

Gordon's wise-guy kid. De Palma earns the title of master, all right . . . but Hitch remains the grand master.

The Dresser ★ ★ ★ ★
PG, 118 m., 1984

Albert Finney (Sir), Tom Courtenay (Norman), Edward Fox (Oxenby), Zena Walker (Her Ladyship). Directed and produced by Peter Yates. Screenplay by Ronald Harwood.

Much of mankind is divided into two categories, the enablers and the enabled. Both groups accept the same mythology, in which the enablers are self-sacrificing martyrs and the enabled are egomaniacs. But the roles are sometimes reversed; the stars are shaken by insecurities that are subtly encouraged by enablers who, in their heart of hearts, see themselves as the real stars. It's human nature. Ever hear the one about the guy who played the gravedigger in *Hamlet*? He was asked what the play was about, and he answered, "It's about this gravedigger . . ."

The Dresser is about a guy like that, named Norman. He has devoted the best years of his life to the service of an egomaniacal actor, who is called Sir even though there is some doubt he has ever been knighted. Sir is an actor-manager who runs his own traveling theatrical troupe, touring the provinces to offer a season of Shakespeare. One night he plays King Lear. The next night, Othello. The next, Richard III. Most nights he has to ask his dresser what role he is playing. Dressers in the British theater do a great deal more than dress their employers. In *The Dresser,* Norman is also Sir's confidant, morale booster, masseur, alter ego, and physician, nursing him through hangovers with medicinal amounts of brandy. Norman has been doing this job for years, and Sir is at the center of his life. Sir, however, takes Norman very much for granted, and it is this difference between them that provides the emotional tension.

The Dresser is a backstage movie, based on a backstage play, but the movie leaves the theater for a few wonderful additions to the play, as when Sir commands a train to stop, and the train does. Mostly, though, the action is in a little provincial theater, where tonight's play is *King Lear,* and Sir looks as if he had spent the last week rehearsing the storm scene. It is Norman's job to whip him into shape. Sir is seriously disoriented. He is so hung over, shaky, and confused that he can't even remember how the play begins—indeed, he starts putting on the makeup for

Othello. There are other problems for Norman to handle, such as Sir's relationships with his wife, his adoring stage manageress, and a young actress he is considering for Cordelia (she is slim, and would be easier to carry onstage). There are also an angry supporting player and a quaking old trouper who is being pressed into service as the Fool.

The minor characters are all well-drawn, but *The Dresser* is essentially the story of two people, and the movie has been well-cast to make the most of both of them; no wonder both actors won Oscar nominations. Norman is played by Tom Courtenay, who had the role on stage in London and New York and will also be remembered from all those British Angry Young Men films like *Billy Liar* and *Loneliness of the Long Distance Runner.* He is perfect for playing proud, resentful, self-doubting outsiders. Sir is played by Albert Finney, who manages to look far older than his forty-seven years and yet to create a physical bravura that's ideal for the role. When he shouts "Stop . . . that . . . train!" we are not too surprised when the train stops.

On the surface, the movie is a wonderful collection of theatrical lore, detail, and superstition (such as the belief that it is bad luck to say the name "Macbeth" aloud—safer to refer always to "the Scottish tragedy"). The physical details of makeup and costuming are dwelled on, and there is a great backstage moment when the primitive thunder machine is rattled to make a storm. Beneath those details, though, a human relationship arrives at a crisis point and is resolved, in a way. Sir and Norman come to the end of their long road together, and, as is the way with enablers and enabled, Norman finally understands the real nature of their relationship, while Sir, of course, can hardly be bothered. This is the best sort of drama, fascinating us on the surface with color and humor and esoteric detail, and then revealing the truth underneath.

Drive, He Said ★ ★ ★
R, 90 m.,1971

William Tepper (Hector), Karen Black (Olive), Michael Margotta (Gabriel), Bruce Dern (Coach Builion), Robert Towne (Richard), Harry Jaglom (Conrad). Directed by Jack Nicholson and produced by Steve Blauner and Nicholson. Screenplay by Jeremy Larner and Nicholson.

Jack Nicholson's *Drive, He Said* is a disorganized but occasionally brilliant movie about

two college students and the world they, and we, inhabit. Their campus is a microcosm of the least reassuring aspects of contemporary America; the two overwhelming mental states are paranoia and compulsive competitiveness. Sufferers from both conditions are obsessed by the fear that something might be gaining on them. In *Drive, He Said,* the paranoic student is afraid of the draft, the System, and They, whoever They are. The other student is a star basketball player, or, as his friends tell him, "You stay after school to run around in your underwear." His fears are more general and vague and, therefore, more frightening.

The movie has a sort of jumpy, nervous rhythm, as if it were on speed, and sometimes that works but it's finally just distracting. The problem is that the stories of the two main characters don't mesh. They're roommates, to be sure, but that's a tenuous connection. And when the paranoid (Michael Margotta) has his three big adventures—freaking out at the draft physical, attacking a faculty wife, and freeing all the animals in a biology lab—the scenes feel like set pieces, unrelated to the movie.

The movie that surrounds them involves Hector (played with laconic charm by William Tepper), who plays basketball not because he's a jock but because he enjoys the self-testing that the game involves. By the time we meet him, he has become a star and a prime choice for the pro draft, but, well, somehow the whole thing is falling apart on him.

One of his problems is the faculty wife, played by Karen Black. He has been having an affair with her, but she breaks it off just as he discovers, uncomfortably, that he might be in love. And then it turns out she's pregnant. This is a real-life experience of the most unsettling sort, and makes it difficult for him to take basketball as seriously as his coach thinks he should.

The coach is an intense competitor who positively believes in all the values, moral and physical, that have been preached by all coaches since the dawn of time-outs. Bruce Dern's performance as the coach, by the way, is a small masterpiece of accurate observation.

The performances, indeed, are the best thing in the movie. Nicholson himself is a tremendously interesting screen actor, and he directs his actors to achieve a kind of intimacy and intensity that is genuinely rare. But if Nicholson is good on the nuances, he's weak on the overall direction of his film. It doesn't hang together for us as a unified piece of work.

I have a notion he may have been trying for an effect similar to that in his three previous films as an actor *(Easy Rider, Five Easy Pieces,* and *Carnal Knowledge),* which were deliberately episodic and depended on the cumulative effect of the episodes for a structure that occurred to us only gradually. But the episodes refuse to come together in *Drive, He Said,* and what we're left with are some very good scenes in search of a home.

Driving Miss Daisy ★ ★ ★ ★
PG, 99 m., 1989

Morgan Freeman (Hoke Colburn), Jessica Tandy (Daisy Werthan), Dan Aykroyd (Boolie Werthan), Patti Lupone (Florine Werthan), Esther Rolle (Idella), Joann Havrilla (Miss McClatchey), William Hall, Jr. (Oscar), Alvin M. Sugarman (Dr. Well), Clarice F. Geigerman (Nonie). Directed by Bruce Beresford and produced by Richard D. Zanuck and Lili Fini Zanuck. Screenplay by Alfred Uhry.

Driving Miss Daisy is a film of great love and patience, telling a story that takes twenty-five years to unfold, exploring its characters as few films take the time to do. By the end of the film, we have traveled a long way with the two most important people in it—Miss Daisy Werthan, a proud old Southern lady, and Hoke Colburn, her chauffeur—and we have developed a real stake in their feelings.

The movie spans a quarter-century in the lives of its two characters, from 1948, when Miss Daisy's son decides it is time she stop driving herself and employ a chauffeur, to 1973, when two old people acknowledge the bond that has grown up between them. It is an immensely subtle film, in which hardly any of the most important information is carried in the dialogue, and in which body language, tone of voice, or the look in an eye can be the most important thing in a scene. After so many movies in which shallow and violent people deny their humanity and ours, what a lesson to see a film that looks into the heart.

The movie contains a performance nominated for an Academy Award by Morgan Freeman, as Hoke, and an Academy Award–winning role by Jessica Tandy, who at the age of eighty creates the best performance of her career as Miss Daisy. As the movie opens, Miss Daisy still lives in proud self-sufficiency, with only her cook to help out, and she drives herself around in a big new 1948 Packard.

One day she drives the Packard over the wall and into the neighbor's yard, and her son (Dan Aykroyd) lays down the law: It is time that she have a chauffeur.

She refuses. She needs no such thing. It is a nuisance to have servants in the house, anyway—they're like children, always underfoot. But her son hires a chauffeur anyway, and in their first interview he tells Hoke that it is up to him to convince Miss Daisy to let herself be driven. Thus commences a war of wills that continues, in one way or another, for twenty-five years, as two stubborn and proud old people learn to exist with one another.

Hoke's method is the employment of infinite patience, and Morgan Freeman's performance is a revelation, based on close observation and quiet nuance. Hoke is not obsequious. He is not ingratiating. He is very wise. His strategy is to express verbal agreement in such a way that actual agreement is withheld. If Miss Daisy does not want to be driven to the Piggly Wiggly, very well then, Hoke will not drive her. He will simply follow her in the car. The car by this time is a shiny new 1949 Hudson, and Hoke somehow defuses the situation by making the car itself the subject, rather than himself. It is a shame, he observes, that a fine new car like that is left sitting in the driveway, not being used. It's good for a car to be driven. . . .

Eventually Miss Daisy agrees to be driven, and eventually, over the years, she and Hoke begin to learn about one another. Neither one is quick to reveal emotion. And although Miss Daisy prides herself on being a Southern Jewish liberal, she is not always very quick to see the connections between such things as an attack on her local synagogue and the Klan's attacks on black churches. Indeed, much of Hoke's relationship with her consists of helping her to see certain connections. When she goes to listen to a speech by Martin Luther King, for example, she has Hoke drive her—but although she has an extra ticket it never occurs to her to invite him to come inside. "Things have changed," she observes complacently in another scene, referring to race relations in the South, and he replies that they have not changed all *that* much.

"Is Morgan Freeman the greatest American actor?" Pauline Kael once asked, reviewing his performance as a steel-eyed pimp in *Street Smart* (1987). It is when you compare that performance with his own in *Driving Miss Daisy* and another film, *Glory,* that you begin to understand why the question can be asked. The three performances have almost nothing in common; all three are works of the imagination in which Freeman creates three-dimensional characters that are completely convincing. In *Street Smart,* he created an aura of frightening violence. In *Lean on Me,* early in 1989, he was school principal Joe Clark, a man of unassailable self-confidence and bullheaded determination. In *Glory,* he was an ignorant grave digger who becomes a soldier in the Civil War. In *Miss Daisy,* he is so gentle, so perceptive, so patient, it is impossible to get a glimpse of those other characters.

It is a great performance, and matched by Miss Tandy's equally astonishing range, as she ages from a sprightly and alert widow in her sixties to an infirm old woman drifting in and out of senility in her nineties. Hers is one of the most complete portraits of the stages of old age I have ever seen in a film.

Driving Miss Daisy was directed by Bruce Beresford, an Australian whose sensibilities seem curiously in tune with the American South. His credits include the superb *Tender Mercies* and *Crimes of the Heart,* as well as the underrated and overlooked 1986 film about an aborigine teen-ager, *The Fringe Dwellers.* Working from a screenplay by Alfred Uhry, based on Uhry's play (and on Uhry's memories of a grandmother and a chauffeur in his own family), Beresford is able to move us, one small step at a time, into the hearts of his characters. He never steps wrong on his way to a luminous final scene in which we are invited to regard one of the most privileged mysteries of life: the moment when two people allow each other to see inside.

Drop Zone ★ ★ ½
R, 102 m., 1994

Wesley Snipes (Peter Nessip), Gary Busey (Ty Moncrief), Yancy Butler (Jessie Crossman), Michael Jeter (Earl Leedy), Corin Nemec (Selkirk), Kyle Secor (Swoop), Malcolm-Jamal Warner (Terry Nessip), Rex Linn (Bobby). Directed by John Badham and produced by D.J. Caruso, Wallis Nicita, and Lauren Lloyd. Screenplay by Peter Barsocchini and John Bishop.

Drop Zone is one of those thrillers where the action is so interesting that you almost forgive (or even forget) the plot. The movie is virtually one stunt after another, many of them taking place in midair, and during the pure action sequences you simply suspend your interest in the story and look at the amazing sights before you. The movie is the most elaborate feature ever made about sky-diving, with aerial photography and stunts so good that the stuff on the ground almost, but not quite, gets forgiven.

The movie stars Wesley Snipes as Pete Nessip, a hard-charging U.S. marshal, and Gary Busey as Ty Moncrief, the leader of a renegade gang of skydivers who have an audacious scheme to sell the secrets of the DEA to drug lords. But first they need to spring computer mastermind Earl Leedy (Michael Jeter) from prison, and that leads to a scene in a 747 at 38,000 feet where the bad guys snatch Leedy from his federal escort and parachute with him through a gaping hole in the side of the plane.

The stunt is so audaciously planned and executed that it doesn't look like an escape bid, and the missing persons are all presumed dead—by everyone except Nessip (an anagram for Snipes, although why they overlooked Pissen is beyond me). Everyone tells him it's impossible to jump out of a 747 at 38,000 feet and live (and I am prepared to believe this), but he's offended, because his brother (Malcolm-Jamal Warner) has been accused of endangering the airplane, and he is even a suspect himself. ("Give me your gun and your badge," his superior says; not the first time we've heard *that* in a movie.)

The marshal decides to sniff around for suspects in the world of championship-level skydiving, and soon picks up a promising trail. He's aided in his search by Jessie Crossman (Yancy Butler), who runs her own skydiving school, makes her own rules, and treats Nessip to a dangerous thrill on his first ride, by pushing him out of the plane without a parachute.

Soon Jessie points Pete to the legendary Fourth of July jump in Washington, D.C.—allegedly the only night of the year when skydivers can violate the capitol's protected air space. And he realizes that Busey and his gang have not only survived their jump from the 747, but now plan another audacious scheme. They jump to the top of a federal building, use the computer nerd to hack into secret files, and then escape by parachuting into the bed of a moving semitrailer truck on the streets below.

Logic, that tiresome spectre at the feast of fantasy, here raises its skeletal hand and asks a few questions, like (1) Why does the computer whiz need to be in the building to crack the computers? Hasn't he ever heard of a

modem? And (2) Wouldn't people in central Washington be likely to notice skydivers parachuting into a semi driving down a major street?

Drop Zone shrugs off those and all other questions as it hurtles to a conclusion. The director, John Badham *(WarGames)*, possibly believes that his aerial sequences are so compelling that the rest of the plot can be hurried through. And there are moments here of real beauty, terror, and excitement, as incredible skydiving stunts unfold on the screen. (The movie's technical advisers and stunt jumpers are among the world's best.)

I've seen better movies involving skydiving *(Point Break* was one, in 1991, also starring Busey), but never one in which the aerial material was so well done and photographed. For that, I'm almost prepared to forgive the jumpy screenplay, and such incredible events as when a character is able to jump out of an airplane and hold onto the bottom sill of the doorway. (Would you fall straight down from a flying plane?)

But I can't quite forgive them, because the movie should have cared more. Should have given us better characters and smarter dialogue, as *Point Break* did. And spared us the scene where Jessie sternly lectures on safety, having earlier pushed the novice out of the plane without a chute, counting on her own skills to save him. *Drop Zone* is an example of a superb production harnessed to a shallow script.

Drugstore Cowboy ★ ★ ★ ★
R, 100 m., 1989

Matt Dillon (Bob), Kelly Lynch (Diane), James Le Gros (Rick), Heather Graham (Nadine), Max Perlich (David), James Remar (Gentry), Grace Zabriskie (Bob's Mother), Beah Richards (Drug Counselor), William S. Burroughs (Tom the Priest). Directed by Gus Van Sant, Jr., and produced by Cary Brokaw. Screenplay by Van Sant and Daniel Yost.

Drugstore Cowboy is one of the best films in a long tradition of American outlaw road movies—a tradition that includes *Bonnie and Clyde, Easy Rider, Midnight Cowboy,* and *Badlands.* It is about criminals who do not intend to be particularly bad people, but whose lives run away with them. The heroes of these films always have a weakness, and in *Drugstore Cowboy* the weakness is drug abuse.

The movie stars Matt Dillon in one of the great recent American movie performances, as the leader of a pack of two young couples

who are on the prowl in Washington and Oregon. It is 1971 and they are the rear guard of the love generation. They drift from one rented apartment or motel room to another, in an aimless migration in search of drugs. They will use almost anything, but their favorites are prescription drugs, and they have developed a smooth method of stealing them from drugstores.

We see them at work. The four enter a store separately. One of them creates a commotion—pretending to have a fit, let's say. Under cover of the confusion, Dillon sneaks behind the prescription counter and scoops up as many drugs as he can identify. What drugs they can't use, they sell. And when they aren't stealing or on the road, their lives fall into a listless routine of getting high, watching TV, smoking, talking, waiting.

Sex is not high on Dillon's list of enthusiasms. Like a lot of drug abusers, he is more turned on by drugs than sex—by the excitement of setting up a job, the fear during the actual stealing, and the payoff afterward when he gets high. He has apparently been with the same girlfriend (Kelly Lynch) since they were in high school, and at some point along the road they got married, but their eyes are turned toward drugs, not each other. They travel with a goofy sidekick (James Le Gros) and his girlfriend, a pathetic teen-age drifter (Heather Graham). Together, they're a family.

Strangely enough, it is the family feeling that makes *Drugstore Cowboy* so poignant and effective. This is not a movie about bad people, but about sick people. They stick together and try to help one another in the face of the increasing desperation of their lives. The movie is narrated by Dillon, whose flat voice doesn't try to dramatize the material; he could be telling his story at an AA meeting. He knows that it is sad, but he also knows that it is true, and he is not trying to glamorize it, simply trying to understand it.

There is humor in their lives—craziness almost always breeds humor—and there is also deeply buried hurt, as in the scene where the Dillon character goes to visit his mother (Grace Zabriskie). Up until this point in the movie we have seen him primarily through his own eyes and have grown to like him, a little, for the resourceful way he is trying to lead his team of losers. Then his mother refuses to let him into the house—not because she doesn't love him, but because she knows him too well and knows he will steal anything to get money for drugs. The way he has to stand there and accept this, and try to shrug it off, provides one of the most painful scenes in the movie.

Life falls into a rhythm of excitement and ennui. And their lives drift imperceptibly from bad to worse. There is a way in which desperate people can accept the conditions of their lives up to a point, and then there is the unmistakable day when that point has been passed. For this family, that day comes when the teen-age girl overdoses and they are stuck with a corpse in their room at a motel where a deputy sheriffs' convention is being held. It is a tribute to the sure hand of the director, Gus Van Sant, Jr., that this scene works through irony and desperation, instead of through the cheap laughs another director might have settled for.

Drugstore Cowboy is a story told with a threat of insane logic that makes it one of the most absorbing movies in a long time. It is a logic that many drug abusers would understand. It goes like this: I feel bad and drugs make me feel good, although they are also why I feel bad. But since they make me feel good now and bad later, I will worry about later when the time comes. Eventually, for the Dillon character, the time does come, and he tells his wife that he is heading back to Seattle to get into some kind of a program and try to kick drugs. He has the intelligence to see that things are out of control, that he can no longer make them hold together, that he has lost the fight and had better surrender before his corpse is somebody else's problem.

The movie then inserts a small supporting performance by William Burroughs that is like a guest appearance by Death. Sitting in a fleabag hotel room, playing a defrocked priest addicted to heroin, Burroughs talks to Dillon in a gallows voice about drugs. We sense two things about the character: that he should have died long ago, and that death would not have been unwelcome compared to his earthly purgatory. This cameo appearance has been criticized by some writers as the movie's single flaw. It's distracting to see Burroughs in a fiction film, they say. But with his skull shining through his eyes and his dry voice and his laugh like a smoker's cough, Burroughs creates a perfect moment. The Dillon character looks at him and sees one of the fates he is free to choose.

Like all truly great movies, *Drugstore Cowboy* is a joyous piece of work. I believe that the subject of a film does not determine whether it makes us feel happy or sad. I am unutterably depressed after seeing stupid comedies that insult my ingelligence, but I felt exhilarated after seeing *Drugstore Cowboy* because every person connected with this project is working at top form. It's a highwire act of daring, in which this unlikely subject matter becomes the occasion for a film about sad people we come to care very deeply about.

At the end of the film, the Dillon character seems to have broken out of drugs. His wife is still on the road. "Are you crazy?" she asks him when he says he wants to kick his habit. She cannot imagine life without drugs. He can. That is the difference between them, and in painting that difference, this movie shows the distance between hope and despair.

A Dry White Season ★ ★ ★

R, 106 m., 1989

Donald Sutherland (Ben du Toit), Janet Suzman (Susan), Zakes Mokae (Stanley), Jurgen Prochnow (Captain Stolz), Susan Sarandon (Melanie), Marlon Brando (McKenzie), Winston Ntshona (Gordon), Thoko Ntshinga (Emily). Directed by Euzhan Palcy and produced by Paula Weinstein. Screenplay by Colin Welland and Palcy.

When you are safe and well-off, and life has fallen into a soothing routine, there is a tendency to look the other way when trouble happens—especially if it hasn't happened to you. Say, for example, that you are a white schoolmaster in South Africa, and live in a comfortable suburban home with your wife and two children. Suppose your African gardener's son disappears one day. How do you feel? You feel sorry, of course, because you have humanitarian instincts. But what if it appears that the boy was the victim of police brutality and may be imprisoned illegally? What do you do then? In a country where the gardener has little hope of lodging an effective appeal, do you stick your neck out and help him?

That is the question posed to Ben du Toit (Donald Sutherland) in the opening passages of *A Dry White Season*. His answer is almost instinctive: "Best to let it go," he tells the gardener. "No doubt they'll see they made a mistake and release him. There's nothing to be done." This is a sensible answer, if the boy is not your son. But Gordon Ngubene (Winston Ntshona), the gardener, cannot accept it. With the help of an African lawyer, he tries to get some answers, to find out why and how his son disappeared. And it is not very long until Gordon has disappeared, too.

A Dry White Season is set in the 1970s, at the time when the schoolchildren of Soweto, an African township outside Johannesburg, held a series of protests. They wanted to be educated in English, not Afrikaans (a language spoken only in South Africa and mostly by whites). The protests resulted in the deaths of many marchers, but the government weathered the storm and clapped a lid on the possibility of a civil uprising, as it always has.

In 1989 we have arrived at another season of protest in South Africa, where, to the general amazement of almost everyone involved, peaceful antigovernment marches were permitted by the government in Cape Town and Johannesburg. As someone who has visited South Africa and studied for a year at the University of Cape Town, I wonder what the average American reader makes of the headlines. How does he picture South Africa? What does he think life is like there? Does he see these marches in the same context as American freedom marches? Does he ask how six million whites can get away with ruling twenty-four million Africans?

This film, based on a novel by Andre Brink, provides a series of bold images to go with the words and the concepts in the stories out of South Africa. Like *A World Apart* (1988), it is set mostly in the pleasant world of white suburbia, an easy commute from the skyscrapers of downtown (some Americans, I believe, still see South Africa in images from old Tarzan movies, and do not know the country is as modern and developed as any place in Europe or North America). We meet the schoolteacher, a decent and quiet man, a onetime Springbok sports hero, who finds it easy not to reflect overlong on the injustices of his society. He disapproves of injustice in principle, of course, but finds it prudent not to rock the boat.

Then disaster strikes into the life of the gardener, who also loves his family, and who also lives a settled family life, in a township outside the city. Jonathan, the gardener's son, is a clever lad, and the schoolteacher is helping him with a scholarship. Jonathan is arrested almost at random and jailed with many other demonstrators, and then a chain of events is set into motion that leads Ben du Toit into a fundamental difference with the entire structure of his society.

The movie follows him step by step as he sees things he can hardly believe, and begins to suspect the unthinkable—that the boy and his father have been ground up inside the justice system and spit out as "suicides."

He meets with the African lawyer (Zakes Mokae) and with the gardener's wife (Thoko Ntshinga). He finds one catch-22 being piled on another. (After her husband is reported dead, the widow no longer has a legal right to stay in her house and must be deported to a "homeland" she has never seen, from where it will be impossible to lodge a legal protest.)

As a respected white man, the schoolteacher is allowed access to the system—until it becomes obvious that he is asking the wrong questions and adopting the wrong attitude. Then he is ostracized. He loses his job. Shots are fired through his windows. His wife (Janet Suzman, brittle and unforgiving) is furious that he has betrayed his family by appearing to be a "kaffir lover." His daughter finds him a disgrace. Only his young son seems to understand that he is wearily, doggedly, trying to do what is right.

A Dry White Season is a powerfully serious movie, but the director, Euzhan Palcy, provides a break in the middle, almost as Shakespeare used to bring on pantomime before returning to the deaths of kings. A famous South African lawyer, played by Marlon Brando, is brought in to lodge an appeal against the finding that one of the dead committed suicide. The Brando character knows the appeal is useless, that his courtroom appearance will be a charade, and yet he goes ahead with it anyway—using irony and sarcasm to make his points, even though the outcome is hopeless.

Brando, in his first movie appearance since 1980, has fun with the role in the way that Charles Laughton or Orson Welles would have approached it. He allows himself theatrical gestures, droll asides, astonished double takes. His scenes are not a star turn, but an effective performance in which we see a lawyer with a brilliant mind, who uses it cynically and comically because that is his form of protest.

At the center of the film, Donald Sutherland is perfectly cast and quietly effective as a man who will not be turned aside, who does not wish misfortune upon himself or his family, but cannot ignore what has happened to the family of his friend. Like *A World Apart* and *Cry Freedom,* the movie concentrates on a central character who is white (because the movie could not have been financed with a black hero), but *A Dry White Season* has much more of the South African black experience in it than the other two films.

It shows daily life in the townships, which are not slums but simply very poor places where determined people struggle to live decently. It hears the subtleties of voice when an intelligent African demeans himself before a white policeman, appearing humble to gain a hearing. It shows some of the details of police torture that were described in Joseph Lelyveld's *Move Your Shadow,* the most comprehensive recent book about South Africa. It provides mental images to go with the columns of text in the newspapers. American network TV coverage of South Africa all but ended when the government banned the cameras (proving that the South African government was absolutely right that the networks were interested only in sensational footage, and not in the story itself). Here are some pictures to go with the words.

Here is also an effective, emotional, angry, subtle movie. Euzhan Palcy, a gifted filmmaker, is a thirty-two-year-old from Martinique, whose first feature was the masterpiece about poor black Caribbean farm workers, *Sugar Cane Alley.* Here, with a larger budget and stars in the cast, she still has the same eye for character detail. This movie isn't just a plot trotted out to manipulate us, but the painful examination of one man's change of conscience. For years he has been blind, perhaps willingly. But once he sees, he cannot deny what he feels is right.

Dumb and Dumber ★ ★
PG-13, 106 m., 1994

Jim Carrey (Lloyd), Jeff Daniels (Harry), Lauren Holly (Mary), Mike Starr (Joe Mentalino), Karen Duffy (J.P. Shay), Teri Garr (Helen). Directed by Peter Farrelly and produced by Charles B. Wessler, Brad Krevoy, and Steve Stabler. Screenplay by Peter Farrelly, Bennett Yellin, and Bobby Farrelly.

The purpose of a comedy is to make you laugh, and there is a moment in *Dumb and Dumber* that made me laugh so loudly I embarrassed myself. I just couldn't stop. It's the moment involving the kid who gets the parakeet. *But* because the first sentence of this review was lifted out and reprinted in an ad, I hasten to add that I did not laugh as loudly again, or very often. It's just as well. If the whole movie had been as funny as that moment, I would have required hospitalization.

The movie is more silliness from Jim Carrey, who is beginning to grow on me. It's strange. His mannerisms, instead of becoming more wearisome from film to film, grow more endearing. I hated him in *Ace Ventura,* enjoyed him in *The Mask,* and felt positively fond of him here. He plays a limousine driver whose roommate (Jeff Daniels) runs a dog-grooming service, although business is bad for both of them and they live in a dump. (At one point a gangster suggests trashing their apartment, and decides they wouldn't notice it.)

As the movie opens, Carrey is driving a beautiful but troubled young woman (Lauren Holly) to the airport. He has fallen instantly in love with her. When he notices that she has left a briefcase on the terminal floor, he races into the building and snatches it—thus foiling a kidnap ransom payment. Trying to chase after her onto a flight to Aspen, he has a nasty accident that is the movie's second big laugh, although not nearly so big as the parakeet.

After developments that will be familiar to students of sitcom and other formula comedy, Carrey and Daniels find themselves heading west in their dogmobile (a van that looks like a shaggy dog). They intend to drive to Aspen, find the woman, and return the briefcase. Along the way they have the usual obligatory run-in with some tough guys in a diner, are pulled over by the usual cop, and are chased by gangsters, etc., etc.

The cop gets a bad surprise when he tests what he thinks is an open bottle of beer, but that gag misfires because its final shot is just plain not funny. That happens several times in *Dumb and Dumber:* The movie sets up a potentially good joke (like the one involving a megadose of laxative) and then doesn't know how to pay it off.

The plot is lame, but that doesn't matter, because *Dumb and Dumber* is essentially pitched at the level of an *Airplane!*-style movie, with rapid-fire sight gags. Some of them work, like the karate fight that ends with a guy getting his heart handed to him in a doggie bag. Some of them don't, like a curious scene where Carrey is hugging a girl and lifts the back of her skirt for no apparent reason: It seems creepy.

For Jeff Daniels, the role is a departure from his usual deadpan comedy roles and straight drama. He fits right in. The relationship between the two guys creates a lot of the fun, as they discuss their grim lifestyle and their bizarre plans to improve it. The elements are here for a better movie, and Jim Carrey, I am now convinced, is a true original. In *The Mask,* he had the screenplay and production to back him up. Here, the filmmaking is more uncertain.

E

Earth Girls Are Easy ★ ★ ★
PG, 100 m., 1989

Geena Davis (Valerie), Jeff Goldblum (Mac), Jim Carrey (Wiploc), Damon Wayans (Zeebo), Julie Brown (Candy), Michael McKean (Woody), Charles Rocket (Ted), Larry Linville (Dr. Bob), Rick Overton (Dr. Rick). Directed by Julien Temple and produced by Tony Garnett. Screenplay by Julie Brown, Charlie Coffey, and Terrence E. McNally.

In my fantasies about visitors from outer space, I always imagine them as strange and wondrous creatures that are eons ahead of us in intellectual and emotional development. But what if they are simply hot-shot space jockeys looking for a good time—like a bunch of Air Force fliers on a Saturday night? That is more or less the emotional level reached by the fur-covered aliens in *Earth Girls Are Easy*, a lighthearted and goofy musical comedy about a love affair between an extraterrestrial and a manicurist.

The manicurist is played by Geena Davis, in her first film appearance after she won the supporting actress Oscar for *The Accidental Tourist*. Although two movies could not possibly be more different, the characters played by Davis are actually somewhat similar: optimistic, openhearted, trusting women who can't help themselves when they see a guy in trouble.

As the movie opens, Valerie, the Davis character, is a manicurist in trouble. Her boyfriend (Charles Rocket) doesn't seem to be interested any longer. The boss at her beauty salon (Julie Brown) suggests a complete change of image, and makes her over into a platinum blonde. This does not work, since it turns out her boyfriend already has another woman on the hook. But the next day her love life begins to look up, when three aliens crash-land their spaceship in her swimming pool.

The aliens are nice guys, but hungry and clumsy and covered with fur. Valerie accidentally strands them on earth when she sinks their ship in her pool, and so to make it up to them she offers the most precious thing she can think of, a complete head-to-toe beauty makeover. The aliens emerge as three fairly good-looking guys (led by Jeff Goldblum), and after they all go out for a night on the town, romance blossoms between the Davis and Goldblum characters.

A lot of the humor in *Earth Girls Are Easy* depends on the ways the aliens misunderstand the everyday details of Earth culture. This is fairly familiar subject matter in the movies (as in *Starman* and *My Stepmother Is an Alien*), but *Earth Girls* peps it up by setting the movie in a day-glo, instantly disposable Southern California culture where even aliens *with* their fur would not attract a whole lot of attention.

The movie was directed by Julien Temple, who has had a considerable underground reputation ever since his cult Sex Pistols movie, *The Great Rock and Roll Swindle*, a decade earlier. His previous film was the strange, difficult *Absolute Beginners*, in which he shows a visual style that was willing to go to any length to make a point. Preparing for *Earth Girls*, he seems to have studied *Little Shop of Horrors* and the works of John Waters, and gives us a science fiction musical where the art direction is so flamboyant it should almost be billed along with the actors.

The movie's sense of fun is infectious, and saves the material when it starts to sag. Geena Davis is a manifestly happy young woman, and her joy of performance spills over into her character and inspires the actors around her, so that although the movie sometimes gets giggly it never gets distracted or loses its energy level. *Earth Girls Are Easy* is silly and predictable and as permanent as a feather in the wind, but I had fun watching it.

Edward Scissorhands ★ ★
PG-13, 105 m., 1990

Johnny Depp (Edward Scissorhands), Winona Ryder (Kim), Dianne Wiest (Peg), Anthony Michael Hall (Jim), Kathy Baker (Joyce), Vincent Price (The Inventor), Alan Arkin (Bill). Directed by Tim Burton and produced by Denise Di Novi and Burton. Screenplay by Caroline Thompson.

The director, Tim Burton, wages valiant battle to show us new and wonderful things. In a Hollywood that placidly recycles the same old images, Burton uses special effects and visual tricks to create sights that have never been seen before. That is the good news. The disappointment is that Burton has not yet found the storytelling and character-building strength to go along with his pictorial flair.

That was true even of his *Batman,* which was the all-time box office champion, but could have been a better film, I believe, if there had been anyone in it to inspire our emotional commitment. Even comic characters can make us care. Unlike Richard Donner's original *Superman*, which actually had a heart beneath its special effects, Burton's *Batman* occupied a terrain in which every character was a grotesque of one sort or another, and all of their actions were inspired by shallow, melodramatic motivations.

That movie was stolen by a supporting character—Jack Nicholson's Joker—and now comes *Edward Scissorhands*, another inventive effort in which the hero is strangely remote and iaccessible. He is intended, I think, as an everyman, a universal figure like one of the silent movie clowns, who exists on a different plane from the people he meets in his adventures. One problem is that the other people are as weird, in their ways, as he is: Everyone in this film is stylized and peculiar, so he becomes another exhibit in the menagerie, instead of a commentary on it.

The movie takes place in an entirely artificial world, where a haunting gothic castle crouches on a mountaintop high above a storybook suburb, a goofy sitcom neighborhood where all of the houses are shades of pastels and all of the inhabitants seem to be emotional clones of the Jetsons. The warmest and most human resident of this suburb is the Avon lady (Dianne Wiest), who comes calling one day at the castle—not even its forbidding facade can deter her—and finds it occupied only by a lonely young man named Edward (Johnny Depp).

His story, told in a flashback, is a sad one. He was created by a mad inventor (Vincent Price), who was almost finished with his task when he died, leaving Edward with temporary scissors in place of real hands. One look at Edward and we see that scissors are inconvenient substitutes for fingers: His face is a mass of scars, and he tends to shred everything he tries to pick up.

The Avon lady isn't fazed. She bundles Edward into her car and drives him back down the mountain to join her family, which includes daughter Kim (Winona Ryder) and husband Bill (Alan Arkin). The neighbors in this suburb are insatiably curious, led by a nosy parker named Joyce (Kathy Baker). The movie then develops into a series of situations that seem inspired by silent comedy, as when Edward tries to pick up a pea.

Successful satire has to have a place to stand, and a target to aim at. The entire world of *Edward Scissorhands* is satire, and so Edward inhabits it, rather than taking aim at it. Even if he lived in a more hospitable world, however, it is hard to tell what satirical comment Edward would have to make, because the movie makes an abrupt switch in his character about two-thirds of the way through. Until then he's been a gentle, goofy soul, a quixotic outsider. Then Burton and his writer, Caroline Thompson, go on autopilot and paste in a standard Hollywood ending.

You know what that is. The hero and the villain meet, there is a deadly confrontation, and no prizes for guessing who wins. Except in pure action films, situations used to be solved by dialogue and plot developments. No more. Now someone is killed, and that's the solution, and the movie is over. In *Edward Scissorhands*, the villain is a neighborhood lout named Jim (Anthony Michael Hall), who doesn't like guys with scissors for hands and picks on Edward until finally

there is a trumped-up fight to the finish up at the castle. This conclusion is so lame it's disheartening. Surely anyone clever enough to dream up Edward Scissorhands should be swift enough to think of a payoff that involves our imagination.

All of Burton's movies look great. *Pee-wee's Big Adventure* was an unalloyed visual delight, and so was *Beetlejuice*. And *Batman* gave us a Gotham City that was one of the most original and atmospheric places I've seen in the movies. But shouldn't there be something more? Some attempt to make the characters more than caricatures? All of the central characters in a Burton film—Pee-wee, the demon Betelgeuse, Batman, the Joker, or Edward Scissorhands—exist in personality vacuums; they're self-contained oddities with no connection to the real world. It's saying something about a director's work when the most well-rounded and socialized hero in any of his films is Pee-wee Herman.

Ed Wood ★ ★ ★ ½

R, 120 m., 1994

NEW

Johnny Depp (Ed Wood), Martin Landau (Bela Lugosi), Sarah Jessica Parker (Dolores Fuller), Bill Murray (Bunny Breckinridge), Patricia Arquette (Kathy O'Hara), Jeffrey Jones (Criswell), G.D. Spradlin (Reverend Lemon), Vincent D'Onofrio (Orson Welles). Directed by Tim Burton and produced by Denise DiNovi and Burton. Screenplay by Scott Alexander and Larry Karaszewski.

Edward D. Wood, Jr., must have been the Will Rogers of filmmaking: He never directed a shot he didn't like. It takes a special weird genius to be voted the Worst Director of All Time, a title that Wood has earned by acclamation. He was so in love with every frame of every scene of every film he shot that he was blind to hilarious blunders, stumbling ineptitude, and acting so bad that it achieved a kind of grandeur. But badness alone would not have been enough to make him a legend; it was his love of film, sneaking through, that pushes him over the top.

Wood's most famous films are *Plan 9 from Outer Space* (during which his star, Bela Lugosi, died and was replaced by a double with a cloak pulled over his face), and *Glen or Glenda*, in which Wood himself played the transvestite title roles. It was widely known even at the time that Wood himself was an enthusiastic transvestite, and when Tim Burton, director of the *Batman* movies, announced a project named *Ed Wood*, I

assumed it would be some kind of a camp send-up, maybe a cross between *Rocky Horror* and *Sunset Boulevard*.

I assumed wrong. What Burton has made is a film which celebrates Wood more than it mocks him, and which celebrates, too, the zany spirit of 1950s exploitation films—in which a great title, a has-been star, and a lurid ad campaign were enough to get bookings for some of the oddest films ever made. It was a decade when there were still lots of drive-in movie theaters, cut-price fleapits, and small-town bijous that thrived on grade Z double features.

The people who made many of those films may have been hucksters and con-men, but they were not devoid of a sense of humor, and often their movies had more life and energy than their betters. America's theaters hadn't been centralized and computerized, and you couldn't book two thousand screens with a single keystroke, and Ed Woods could thrive.

Burton's career has always shown a fondness for touching outsiders, like Beetlejuice and Edward Scissorhands, Batman and Jack Skellington (the lonely star of *The Nightmare Before Christmas*). In *Ed Wood*, he gives us a hero who is not merely an outsider, but one who attracts even more desperate cases to himself. Played with warmth and enthusiasm by Johnny Depp, Wood is a guy who simply *must* make movies—and who is so bedazzled by Hollywood legend that he mistakes poor Bela Lugosi, long past his prime and mired in drug addiction, as a star.

There are others who fall into his orbit: Bunny Breckinridge (Bill Murray), a camp queen who would have stood out like a sore thumb in anyone else's pictures, but fit right into Wood's. And the amazing Criswell (Jeffrey Jones), amazing primarily for being able to find employment for no apparent talent. And Tor Johnson (George "The Animal" Steele), physically inept but gifted in Wood's eyes. And Vampira (Lisa Marie), the midnight movie hostess whose cleavage always looked clammy. And then Lugosi (a brilliant performance by Martin Landau), as a man who was half Wood's headliner, half his patient. When Wood assembled his casts, they looked like a cartoon portrait from *Mad* magazine.

In Burton's version, Wood is a man who not only accepts reality, but celebrates it. Far from being secretive about his love of dressing in women's clothes, he treats it as the most natural thing in the world, putting on an angora sweater, skirt, and high heels to help himself relax while directing a scene. "Are you a homosexual?" he's asked. "No!" he replies cheerfully, "I'm a cross-dresser!"

Depp plays Wood as a man deliriously happy to be making movies. He rarely makes two takes of the same shot because the first one always looks great to him. (In one take Tor Johnson misses the door and walks into a wall, shaking the set, but when the cameraman in amazement asks Wood if he doesn't want another shot, he replies thoughtfully, "You know, in actuality Lobo would have to struggle with that problem every day.")

Wood's partner in his uncertain career is his long-suffering fiancée Dolores Fuller (Sarah Jessica Parker), whose misfortune is to view his situation clearly ("I see the usual gang of misfits and dope addicts are here"). She bravely tries to deal with his cross-dressing, however, and pitches in to act along with the usual gang (Wood's salaries were so low and infrequent that his actors bordered on volunteers).

I am uncertain how much of the movie is based on actual fact, and how much has been invented by Burton and his writers, Scott Alexander and Larry Karaszewski. But I relished the process by which Wood's project *Grave Robbers from Outer Space* became *Plan 9 from Outer Space* after he raised the money from a church group that objected to grave-robbing, in the title, anyway. There is a wonderful scene where Wood grows angered when the church leaders try to meddle with his vision, and stomps into Musso and Frank's legendary grillroom on Hollywood Boulevard, wearing women's clothes and a wig. He spots Orson Welles (Vincent D'Onofrio) alone at a booth, turns to him for encouragement, and gets it—along with the movie's funniest line of dialogue.

The movie's black-and-white photography convincingly recaptures the look and feel of 1950s sleaze, including some of the least convincing special effects in movie history. There are also running gags involving Wood's ability to write almost any piece of stock footage into almost any script.

At the heart of the movie is Wood's friendship with Lugosi, a man he truly adores, and who comes to depend on him. We see Lugosi alone and lonely in a flimsy little tract house, inhabiting the deepening gloom of his obscurity and addiction (his first scene in the movie shows him trying on a coffin for size), and Wood is able to lift the gloom, if only briefly, in a final series of roles which gave

him double immortality: as the star of some of the best horror movies ever made, and then of some of the worst.

The Efficiency Expert ★ ★ ★
PG, 97 m., 1992

Anthony Hopkins (Wallace), Ben Mendelsohn (Carey), Toni Collette (Wendy), Alwyn Kurts (Mr. Ball), Dan Wyllie (Fletcher), Bruno Lawrence (Robert). Directed by Mark Joffe and produced by Richard Brennan and Timothy White. Screenplay by Max Dann and Andrew Knight.

There is a precision in the way Anthony Hopkins presents himself, a crisp manner of speech combined with a certain formality of expression, that can make him seem fearsome *(Silence of the Lambs)* or hidden *(Howards End)* or, in *The Efficiency Expert,* somehow needy. He plays a man who advises others how to plan their lives, yet who hasn't a clue about his own.

The movie takes place in Australia, in the 1960s, in a family-owned factory that makes moccasins, all sorts of moccasins, from leather loafers to those feathery puffball slippers for women who eat bonbons in bed. The company is named Ball's, and Mr. Ball (Alwyn Kurts) is a benevolent geezer who has been running the factory more or less as a pleasant pastime for his employees. Now he is concerned that he might be about to run out of money, and so Ball brings in Wallace (Hopkins), who will prowl the premises with his clipboard and make recommendations.

Not much seems to be happening in the factory, although moccasins are apparently manufactured somehow. The employees spend most of their time having lunch and tea, and taking off early for personal excursions. They live in such a fool's paradise, they don't even bother to conceal their laziness from Wallace. Ball's is like the wire factory run by Gregory Peck in *Other People's Money,* where tradition and paternalism and family feeling count for a lot more than mundane topics like quotas and profits.

We meet some of the eccentrics who populate the factory, including employees who essentially seem to have located their own private activities on the premises, and others for whom slot-car racing is a lot more important than anything one could possibly do to earn a living. And there is a love triangle, or quadrangle, involving the boss's daughter and two men who are after her—the honest Carey (Ben Mendelsohn) and the avaricious

Kim (Russell Crowe, who was the best friend in *Proof* but here only wants to marry the boss's daughter for the obvious reasons). The fourth person in the equation is the openhearted Wendy (Toni Collette), who loves Carey even though he hardly cares or notices.

Wallace, meanwhile, is about to lose his own wife and home, but is so wrapped up in his work that he hardly knows he is married. He wanders about the factory, contemplating reforms and hunting down missing ledgers, which prove old Mr. Ball has been supporting his workers by selling off his assets. That has to stop. Or does it?

All of this seems inspired by one of those black-and-white British comedies from the 1950s—*The Man in the White Suit,* perhaps, or *I'm All Right, Jack.* But Hopkins (who made this movie soon after winning the Oscar for *Lambs*), has a light in his eye that nudges the story to another level. It is about eccentricity, yes, and paternalism and romance and goofy supporting characters, but it's also about forgetting your stopwatch and pausing to hear the music. It's interesting, the way Hopkins's face relaxes as the movie continues and his character learns, perhaps for the first time, that time-and-motion studies are about people, not facts.

84 Charlie Mopic ★ ★ ★
R, 95 m., 1989

Jonathan Emerson (LT), Nicholas Cascone (Easy), Jason Tomlins (Pretty Boy), Christopher Burgard (Hammer), Glenn Morshower (Cracker), Richard Brooks (OD), Byron Thames (MoPic). Directed by Patrick Duncan and produced by Michael Nolin. Screenplay by Duncan.

Patrick Duncan's *84 Charlie Mopic* was directed by a veteran of combat in Vietnam, and Duncan is at such pains to provide us with the infantryman's point of view that he literally takes a 16mm camera along on a reconnaissance mission in the field. The premise of the movie is that a documentary ("mopic") is being made about a patrol—and all of the footage in the film is seen through a camera being carried along by a filmmaker assigned to the unit.

It's a style that makes the action feel immediate and unrehearsed; the other soldiers address the camera as if they're talking to the man who's carrying it, and the effect is that they're talking to us. The strength here is that the movie seems to happen as we watch it. The trade-off is that the director has less freedom to pick and choose his shots for dramatic effect; once he establishes the point of view, he's stuck with it.

The first-person point of view has rarely been used for an entire film (Robert Montgomery made the camera into a private eye in *Lady in the Lake*, and Orson Welles once wanted to film *Heart of Darkness* through the eyes of various protagonists including a bird), but Duncan's angle in *84 Charlie Mopic* is intriguing: By explaining the presence of the camera, he gives a realistic basis to the technique, instead of using it as pure style.

The story of *84 Charlie Mopic* is not original, nor was it meant to be. Anyone who has seen a fair number of war films will recognize the various types of characters in the platoon—the natural leader, the newcomer, the scared youngster—but what is original to this film is the sense of reality that Duncan is able to recapture. The types are familiar but what happens to them is not predictable, and the story takes the sudden, unexpected turns of real warfare rather than the manufactured developments of a Hollywood plot. As the patrol gets lost in the Central Highlands of Vietnam and finds itself in deeper and deeper trouble, we begin to feel the senselessness of their mission; their training helps them only to a point, and then they are in the hands of luck, or fate.

All of this is seen through the eyes of "MoPic," the cameraman, and what makes his subjective camera convincing is that he is not simply recording the action, but trying to make a documentary which can be used as a training film for other infantrymen. The six members of the reconnaissance unit are more or less experienced in the field, and they share their experience and lore with the camera; it's like giving a briefing to trainees. The film is filled with dozens of tiny details that only a field veteran like Duncan would know about—the danger of smoking, for example, when cigarettes can be smelled on the wind for hundreds of yards, and instantly identified as American tobacco. This kind of minutiae somehow adds up to more suspense than any number of mysterious shadows in the jungle.

The subjective camera is probably responsible for many of the weaknesses of *84 Charlie Mopic*, as well as its strengths. Duncan knows more about war than he knows about dramatic construction, and this shows in the way he builds the various relationships in the movie. There are a few too many speeches which are "overheard" by the camera—speeches that provide background information which the characters would probably not provide in quite that way. There are conflicts and tensions within the group, and sometimes we can feel them being created and manipulated by the script. If the genius of the movie is to show the unit through a camera, the movie's failure is to trust that approach enough. The development of the conflicts and character backgrounds should have been more subtle and offhand, as they might have been in real life.

Still, *84 Charlie Mopic* deserves a place by itself among the films about Vietnam. It is a brave and original attempt to record nothing more or less than the actual daily experience of a unit on patrol, drawn out of the memories of men who were there. I've never seen a combat movie that seemed this close to actual experience, to the kinds of hard lessons that soldiers are taught by their enemies. The filmmakers have earned their right to shoot with a subjective camera—because the eyes we are really seeing through are their own.

The Electric Horseman ★ ★ ★
PG, 120 m., 1979

Robert Redford (Sonny), Jane Fonda (Hallie), Valerie Perrine (Charlotta), Willie Nelson (Wendell), John Saxon (Hunt Sears), Nicolas Coster (Fitzgerald). Directed by Sydney Pollack and produced by Ray Stark. Screenplay by Robert Garland.

The Electric Horseman is the kind of movie they used to make. It's an oddball love story about a guy and a girl and a prize racehorse, and it has a chase scene and some smooching and a happy ending. It could have starred Tracy and Hepburn, or Gable and Colbert, but it doesn't need to because this time it stars Robert Redford and Jane Fonda.

The movie almost willfully wants to be old-fashioned. It's got bad guys from a big corporation, and big kisses seen in silhouette in the sunset, and it works Fonda and Redford for all the star quality they've got. But *The Electric Horseman* doesn't try to be completely guileless. It has a bunch of contemporary themes and causes to dress up its basic situation—which is, let's face it, Girl meets Boy (and Horse). And although we are never for a moment in doubt about the happy ending, there *is* a certain basic suspense as Redford and Fonda head for the hills and the evil corporation follows by helicopter.

The movie begins with Redford in the process of downfall. He plays a former five-time national champion rodeo cowboy named Sonny, who has retired from competition and signed on as the spokesman for a cereal named "Ranch Breakfast." This is some cereal. It is fortified, we gather, not only with vitamins, minerals, and bran, but also with leather, nails, and sagebrush. Redford makes personal appearances on behalf of the cereal, wearing a garish electrified cowboy suit that plugs into the saddle of his horse. The cowboy outfit isn't the only thing that's lit up: Redford's drunk most of the time, and ignominiously falls off his horse during a halftime show.

Things come to a climax during a big Las Vegas convention sponsored by the conglomerate that owns Ranch Breakfast. Redford's supposed to ride onstage on a multimillion-dollar champion racehorse. But he has a run-in with the president of the conglomerate, discovers that the horse is drugged and on steroids, and decides to make his own personal gesture of defiance. He rides onstage, all right—and right offstage, too, and down the Vegas strip, and out into the desert.

Jane Fonda plays a TV newswoman who's covering the convention, and she does some clever detective work to figure out where Redford might be headed. And then the movie's more or less predictable: Fonda finds Redford, grows to share his indignation at how the horse has been treated, and trades her loyalty for exclusive rights to the story. It turns out to be a really big story, of course, as the conglomerate tries to track down its racehorse and the TV networks get in a race to find Redford.

If you spend much time scrutinizing the late show on television, some of this material might not sound dazzlingly original. The device of the famous runaway with a journalist in hot pursuit, for example, is straight out of *It Happened One Night*—and as Fonda calls her office from remote pay phones, we're reminded of Clark Gable in exactly the same situations. The notion of the last of the cowboys heading for the hills and being tracked by helicopters is also familiar; it's from *Lonely Are the Brave*, with Kirk Douglas, and some of the shots look hauntingly familiar.

The relationship between Fonda and Redford is also pretty basic stuff, in which the gruff outdoorsman and the perfect lady grow to respect each other while sharing the rigors of life on the run. Bogart and Hepburn made that relationship a classic in *The African Queen,* but Redford and Fonda have much the same chemistry. Remember that scene on the boat with Hepburn putting her chin in her hand and giving Bogart the old once-over? Fonda does that to Redford, and it's about as erotic as six of your average love scenes.

Both Redford and Fonda have identified themselves with a lot of the issues in this movie (which are—I have a list right here— the evils of corporate conglomeratism, the preservation of our wild lands, respect for animals, the phoniness of commercialism, the pack instinct of TV journalism, and nutritious breakfasts). But although this is a movie filled with messages, it's not a message movie. The characters and plot seem to tap-dance past the serious stuff and concentrate on the human relationships.

If *Electric Horseman* has a flaw, it's that the movie's so warm and cozy it can hardly be electrifying. The director, Sydney Pollack, gives us solid entertainment, but he doesn't take chances and he probably didn't intend to. He's an ideal choice for orchestrating Redford and Fonda; he directed Fonda in *They Shoot Horses, Don't They?* and has made a subsidiary career out of directing Redford (in *This Property is Condemned, Jeremiah Johnson, The Way We Were,* and *Three Days of the Condor*). He has grown up with them, he respects the solidity of their screen personas, and he seems to understand (as the directors of Bogart, Hepburn, Gable, et al., did in the forties) that if you have the right Boy and the right Girl and the right story, about all you have to do is stay out of the way of the Horse.

El Mariachi ★ ★ ★
R, 80 m., 1993

Carlos Gallardo (El Mariachi), Consuelo Gomez (Domino), Jaime De Hoyos (Bigoton), Peter Marquardt (Mauricio), Reinol Martinez (Azul), Ramiro Gomez (Cantinero). Directed by Robert Rodriguez. Produced by Rodriguez and Carlos Gallardo. Screenplay by Rodriguez.

El Mariachi, an enormously entertaining movie, stands in danger of being upstaged by its budget, which was seven thousand dollars. Yes, seven thousand dollars, or about what it costs to cater lunch for a day on a Schwarzenegger picture. A movie's budget, no matter how high or how low, is not a reason to go to see it. *Hudson Hawk* was bad even though it cost tens of millions, and *El Mariachi* is good even though it was made for what Hollywood considers walking-around money.

The movie was cowritten, directed, photographed, and edited by Robert Rodriguez, a twenty-three-year-old from Austin, Texas, who shot on location in a Mexican border town and tells the story of a young mariachi, a rambling guitar player, who arrives one day looking for work. He is dressed in black and carries a guitar case, and a killer arrives in the same town on the same day, dressed the same way. All the mariachi (Carlos Gallardo) wants to do is sing and play his guitar, but soon he's thrust into the middle of someone else's blood feud.

Rodriguez shoots this story in a lively visual style that brings a lot of energy even to routine shots. He probably overuses such devices as wide-angle lenses, zooms, speeded-up action, and weird camera placements, but I'm inclined to forgive him his excesses because they add to the exuberance of the film. Today's major films are often shot in such portentous visual styles that they fairly march to their conclusions, but Rodriguez isn't afraid to reach all the way back to silent comedy for shots that punch up the humor and the action. If it works, why knock it?

The story is the stuff of pulp novels, old TV Westerns, and Victorian melodrama. The mariachi is a harmless romantic who only wants to sing, but people start shooting at him. He defends himself, while trying to figure out why he is the center of attention. A sexy barmaid named Domino (Consuelo Gomez) believes his story and befriends him, and before long they are falling in love, which adds another complication: Domino is the object of the local warlord's unrequited lust, and the warlord's men have confused the mariachi with the other man in black.

This story of coincidences and mistaken identities is so obviously contrived that it's almost a parody of itself, but the film's style saves it and gives it charm. Shooting with amateur actors on real locations, plundering his surroundings for his shots and props, Rodriguez gets a gritty, sweaty, dusty feel that drips with atmosphere. Although *El Mariachi* is peopled with stereotypes and told with broad strokes, there is somehow an authenticity about it; it feels committed to its story.

The actors are all adequate for their roles, and Gallardo and Gomez, both completely inexperienced, are more than that. She has the kind of dark, flashing eyes that can dart from love to suspicion in an instant, and he is enough of a mope to seem convincing as an innocent mariachi, and enough of a hero to rise to the occasion. (Rodriguez met Gallardo in boarding school, and has been using him as star and collaborator in home movies since they were kids.)

El Mariachi is already gathering a legend around it, about how Rodriguez sold his body to medical science to raise money to buy film, and wrote the screenplay while working as a guinea pig for cholesterol medication. Now he is at work on another film about the mariachi, this one with such an enormous budget that it would pay for the catered lunches on an entire movie by Schwarzenegger.

El Norte ★ ★ ★
R, 141 m., 1983

Zaide Silvia Gutierrez (Rosa), David Villalpando (Enrique), Ernesto Gomez Cruz (Father), Alicia del Lago (Mother), Trinidad Silva (Monty). Directed by Gregory Nava and produced by Anna Thomas. Screenplay by Nava and Thomas.

From the very first moments of *El Norte,* we know that we are in the hands of a great movie. It tells a simple story in such a romantic and poetic way that we are touched, deeply and honestly, and we know we will remember the film for a long time. The movie tells the story of two young Guatemalans, a brother and sister named Rosa and Enrique, and of their long trek up through Mexico to *el Norte*— the United States. Their journey begins in a small village and ends in Los Angeles, and their dream is the American Dream.

But *El Norte* takes place in the present, when we who are already Americans are not so eager for others to share our dream. Enrique and Rosa are not brave immigrants who could have been our forefathers, but two young people alive now, who look through the tattered pages of an old *Good Housekeeping* for their images of America. One of the most interesting things about the film is the way it acknowledges all of the political realities of Latin America and yet resists being a "political" film. It tells its story through the eyes of its heroes, and it is one of the rare films that grants Latin Americans full humanity. They are not condescended to, they are not made to symbolize something, they are not glorified, they are simply themselves.

The movie begins in the fields where Arturo, their father, is a *bracero*—a pair of arms. He goes to a meeting to protest working conditions and is killed. Their mother disappears. Enrique and Rosa, who are in their late teens, decide to leave their village and go to America. The first part of the film shows their life in Guatemala with some of the same beauty and magical imagery of Gabriel Garcia Marquez's *One Hundred Years of Solitude*. The middle section shows them going by bus and foot up through Mexico, which is as harsh on immigrants from the South as America is. At the border they try to hire a "coyote" to guide them across, and they finally end up crawling to the promised land through a rat-infested drainage tunnel.

The final section of the film takes place in Los Angeles, which they first see as a glittering carpet of lights, but which quickly becomes a cheap motel for day laborers, and a series of jobs in the illegal, shadow job market. Enrique becomes a waiter. Rosa becomes a maid. Because they are attractive, intelligent, and have a certain naive nerve, they succeed for a time, before the film's sad, poetic ending.

El Norte is a great film, one of 1983's best, for two different kinds of reasons. One is its stunning visual and musical power; the approach of the film is not quasi-documentary, but poetic, with fantastical images that show us the joyous hearts of these two people.

The second reason is that this is the first film to approach the subject of "undocumented workers" solely through *their* eyes. This is not one of those docu-dramas where we half-expect a test at the end, but a film like *The Grapes of Wrath* that gets inside the hearts of its characters and lives with them.

The movie was directed by Gregory Nava and produced by Anna Thomas, who wrote it together. It's been described by *Variety* as the "first American independent epic," and it is indeed an epic film made entirely outside the studio system by two gifted filmmakers (their credits include *The Confessions of Amans,* which won a Gold Hugo at the Chicago Film Festival, and *The Haunting of M,* one of my favorite films from 1979). This time, with a larger budget and a first-rate cast, they have made their breakthrough into the first ranks of filmmaking.

Emmanuelle ★ ★ ★
x, 92 m., 1975

Sylvia Kristel (Emmanuelle), Alain Cuny (Mario), Marika Green (Bee), Daniel Sarky (Jean), Jeanne Colletin (Ariane), Christine Boisson (Marie-Ange). Directed by Just Jaeckin and produced by Yves Rousset-Rouard. Screenplay by Jean-Louis Richard.

Emmanuelle is a silly, classy, enjoyable erotic film that became an all-time box-office success in France. It's not remotely significant enough to deserve that honor, but in terms of its genre (soft-core skin flick) it's very well done: lushly photographed on location in Thailand, filled with attractive and intriguing people, and scored with brittle, teasing music. Now that hard-core porno has become passé, it's a relief to see a movie that drops the gynecology and returns to a certain amount of sexy sophistication.

There have been movies influenced by other movies, and directors influenced by other directors, but *Emmanuelle* may be the first movie influenced by magazine centerfolds. Its style of color photography seems directly ripped off from the centerfolds in *Penthouse,* including even the props and decor. Its characters (French diplomats and—especially—their women in Thailand) inhabit a world of wicker furniture, soft pastels, vaguely Victorian lingerie, backlighting, forests of potted plants, and lots of diaphanous draperies shifting in the breeze. It's a world totally devoid of any real content, of course, and Emmanuelle is right at home in it. She's the young, virginal wife of a diplomat, and has just flown out from Paris to rejoin him. Her husband refuses to be possessive, and indeed almost propels her into a dizzying series of sexual encounters that range from the merely kinky to the truly bizarre. In the midst of this erotic maelstrom, Emmanuelle somehow retains her innocence.

The director, Just Jaeckin, correctly understands that gymnastics and heavy breathing do not an erotic movie make, nor does excessive attention to gynecological detail. Carefully deployed clothing can, indeed, be more erotic than plain nudity, and the decor in *Emmanuelle* also tends to get into the act. Jaeckin is a master of establishing situations; the seduction of Emmanuelle on the airplane, for example, is all the more effective because of its forbidden nature. And the encounter after the boxing match (Emmanuelle is the prize for the winning fighter and tenderly licks the sweat from his eyebrow) is given a rather startling voyeuristic touch (the spectators don't leave after the fight).

The movie's first hour or so is largely given over to lesbian situations, but then Emmanuelle comes under the influence of the wise old Mario (played by Alain Cuny, the French actor immortalized as Steiner, the intellectual who committed suicide in Fellini's *La Dolce Vita*). She is turned off at first by his age, but with age, she is assured, comes experience, and does it ever. Mario delivers himself of several profoundly meaningless generalizations about finding oneself through others and attaining true freedom, and then he introduces her to a series of photogenic situations. Mario's philosophy is frankly foolish, but Cuny delivers it with such solemn, obsessed conviction that the scenes become a parody, and *Emmanuelle*'s comic undertones are preserved.

What also makes the film work is the performance of Sylvia Kristel as Emmanuelle. She's a slender actress who isn't even the prettiest woman in the film, but she projects a certain vulnerability that makes several of the scenes work. The performers in most skin flicks seem so impervious to ordinary mortal failings, so blasé in the face of the most outrageous sexual invention, that finally they just become cartoon characters. Kristel actually seems to be present in the film, and as absorbed in its revelations as we are. It's a relief, during a time of cynicism in which sex is supposed to sell anything, to find a skin flick that's a lot better than it probably had to be.

Enemies, a Love Story ★ ★ ★ ½
R, 119 m., 1989

Ron Silver (Herman), Anjelica Huston (Tamara), Lena Olin (Masha), Margaret Sophie Stein (Yadwiga), Alan King (Rabbi Lembeck), Judith Malina (Masha's mother). Directed and produced by Paul Mazursky. Screenplay by Roger L. Simon and Mazursky.

Enemies, a Love Story is a movie about a man who ends up being married to three women at the same time, and it should not surprise you that he is not a happy man. He is not surprised. Happiness is not a part of his repertory.

His name is Herman, and there are times when he wonders why he is even alive. He was a Polish Jew during World War II, but he was saved from the camps and certain death because Yadwiga, his family's servant, hid him from the Nazis in the hayloft of a barn. Now it is 1949, and he is living in Coney Island with the woman, having married her and brought her to America after the war.

She is a good woman with a trusting heart, and she adores him. But he does not feel fulfilled by her, and he cheats on her with the zaftig and naughty Masha, his mistress, who lives in the Bronx. Yadwiga reminds him of the past, which cools his passion, and another problem is, she worships him so slavishly that making love with her is like attending devotions to himself.

With Masha it is different. She is a passionate woman, a Jew who also escaped the Nazis, but she doesn't live in the past, and they share a sexual obsession that helps them to exist only in the present—while they're making love, at any event. Masha knows about Yadwiga but doesn't much care. Then she gets pregnant. Herman wants to do the right thing and so he marries her.

This is complicated enough, but then Herman's true first wife, Tamara, unexpectedly turns up in New York. He had been told by eyewitnesses that she died in the camps. But they were wrong. She escaped to Russia and now here she is in New York, scaring the daylights out of poor Yadwiga when she turns up at their door. Yadwiga recognizes her instantly and assumes she is a ghost.

So, three wives. "In America," his first wife, Tamara, tells him, "they have a thing called a manager. That is what you need. I will be your manager, because you are incapable of making your decisions for yourself." She is absolutely correct. She knows him so well that when she first tells her he is married to Yadwiga, she immediately wants to know about the mistress she is sure he must also have.

Paul Mazursky's *Enemies, a Love Story,* based on the novel by Isaac Bashevis Singer, contains the clue to this story in its title. Who are the enemies? The women that Herman loves. Why are they his enemies? Because love presumes commitment, and Herman is not capable of commitment, is not even capable of forming a working faith in the future. Many others have suffered much more at the hands of the Nazis than he did— he was lucky, up there in his hayloft—but he has lived under the threat of death for so long that no relationship can have any meaning for him. As he scurries between his three women, desperately trying to keep all three happy or at least placated, what drives him is not love but guilt.

Guilt he understands. Love is the enemy. Singer is said to have based his novel on several similar stories abouu Jewish survivors of the Nazis who came to New York City to start over again. In the foreword to his novel, he writes, "The characters are not only Nazi victims, but victims of their own personalities and fates." And that is really the point he has to make: that these people, having been delivered more or less miraculously from death, are nevertheless left with the same character flaws and weaknesses they would have possessed if there had been no Nazis. In other words, they are still possessed of their full, fallible humanity.

Enemies, a Love Story is such an intriguing film because it refuses to be tamed, to settle down into a nice, comforting parable with a lesson to teach us. It is about the tumult of the heart, and Mazursky tells its story without compromise. There is no key to tell us how to feel. No easy laughs as Herman races from one woman to another, but no cheap pathos, either, at their fates. Indeed, this is not even a movie about how the women are victimized; each one receives more or less what her fate has dictated for her, and Herman, who suffers so grievously, is punished mostly by his own knowledge of what a rat he is.

The movie stars four actors in an ensemble that fits so well together that much can be shown without being said. Ron Silver is Herman, harried, desperate, making up lies on pay phones and always hushing one woman while reassuring another. Margaret Sophie Stein is Yadwiga, blond and blue-eyed and forever waxing the floor to make up for being totally intimidated by her husband. Lena Olin (she wore the bowler hat in *The Unbearable Lightness of Being*) is the carnal Masha, whose insouciance disguises a surprising grief. And Anjelica Huston is Tamara, the first wife, the wisest, not only because she knows Herman better than the others, but because she knows herself.

Enemies, a Love Story has been described here and there as a sad movie. That is a very limited view. Parts of it are very funny, as Herman tries to get away with his desperate juggling act. Parts are ironic. Parts, especially the scenes with Huston, are heartwarming in a strange way, because they show one human being accepting the weaknesses of another. Of course there is sadness in the story, and of course such a story cannot end happily. But reflect that these people are lucky to be alive at all, and their stories become almost triumphant. Because a person has survived a great evil does not make a great person—only a lucky one. And if you think Herman's not lucky, well, life's like that. You take your chances.

The Englishman Who Went Up a Hill But Came Down a Mountain [NEW]
★ ★ ★
PG, 100 m., 1995

Hugh Grant (Reginald Anson), Tara Fitzgerald (Betty of Cardiff), Colm Meaney (Morgan the Goat), Ian McNeice (George Garrad), Ian Hart (Johnny Shellshocked), Kenneth Griffith (Reverend Jones), Tudor Vaughn (Thomas Twp), Hugh Vaughn (Thomas Twp, Too). Directed by Christopher Monger and produced by Sarah Curtis. Screenplay by Monger.

Her Majesty's Ordnance Survey Office has for more than a century been mapping the British Isles down to the smallest lane, hill, and footpath. Country walkers can buy a map so detailed it includes clumps of trees. These maps are of incalculable importance to the people whose lands they detail, since they touch on old wounds: feuds, battles, disputed place names, historical perceptions.

The Englishman Who Went Up a Hill But Came Down a Mountain begins as two surveyors for the O.S. arrive in a small village in Wales. Their purpose: to measure the local "mountain," which they cannot quite pronounce without sounding as if they are muffling a sneeze.

"Mountain" is in quotation marks because there is some doubt as to whether the elevation actually qualifies for that name. Mountains must be at least a thousand feet high. Anything smaller is a large hill. The locals are aghast: Their "mountain" has been a mountain since time immemorial, and any suggestion that it is otherwise would be a calamity. Indeed, the local pastor (Kenneth Griffith) considers the elevation very nearly as ecclesiastical as Ararat.

The surveyors are named Reginald and George, and are played by Hugh Grant (in his first film after *Four Weddings and a Funeral*) and Ian McNeice. The instant they walk into the local inn, run by Morgan the Goat (Colm Meaney), they are nailed as outsiders; their accents would give them away even if it were not for their clothing, which in Reginald's case seems to have been supplied by a theatrical costumer with fanciful ideas about the surveying trade.

The men set up their instruments and get a first reading, of 930 feet. The townspeople are apoplectic. The surveyors emphasize that the reading is "preliminary," and that they will not have a more accurate reading until they can triangulate the local elevation with a nearby mountain whose height is known. That elevation, in turn, was measured by being compared with *another* elevation, and so on back into the dim origins of the O.S. "But . . . who measured the *first* mountain?" a local wonders. "God, my boy."

In plot and atmosphere, *The Englishman Who Went Up a Hill But Came Down a Mountain* is a fond throwback to the British comedies of the 1950s in which earnest citizens went about their daily lives little realizing how eccentric they were. The British dote on eccentricity; one of their recent scientific surveys triumphantly concluded that the eccentric are happier and live longer than you and I (since we, of course, are not eccentric). Every character in this movie, with the possible exception of the fresh-cheeked local lass Betty of Cardiff (Tara Fitzgerald), is crazy as a bedbug, and none of them know it, and that is why they are so funny.

Reginald is played by Grant as another of his self-effacing, shy, stuttering, apologetic, and hapless chaps who bumble through somehow. He prefaces every sentence with various warm-up exercises, subvocalized huffs, and throat-clearings, mostly. He wants most desperately not to offend. The locals are most definitely offended, especially when additional surveys do not succeed in raising the height of the mountain to more than 986 feet.

Reverend Jones, the clergyman, is dismayed. A passionate man of considerable age, he confuses the height of the mountain with revelation, and rails from the pulpit against the forces arrayed against it. At last, during a town meeting, the locals hit upon a brilliant plan, which I will not reveal here, to *raise* the mountain. And torrential rains set in—a Welsh secret weapon, preventing the surveyors from completing their last measurements and packing their bags. Meanwhile, of course, Reginald falls in love with the local girl.

The Englishman Who Went Up a Hill But Came Down a Mountain is a movie with the same charms as *Local Hero* (in which Scottish townspeople conspired to outfox visiting Americans). That it is "true" adds only to the charm, and at the film's end, when we see an actual stone set on the site at the time of the Ordnance Wars, that seems entirely appropriate. The people in this movie are so crazy they could only be real.

E.T.—The Extra-Terrestrial ★ ★ ★ ★
PG, 115 m., 1982

Henry Thomas (Elliott), Dee Wallace (Mary), Peter Coyote (Keys), Robert MacNaughton (Michael), Drew Barrymore (Gertie). Directed by Steven Spielberg and produced by Spielberg and Kathleen Kennedy. Screenplay by Melissa Mathison.

This movie made my heart glad. It is filled with innocence, hope, and good cheer. It is also wickedly funny and exciting as hell. *E.T.—The Extra-Terrestrial* is a movie like *The Wizard of Oz*, that you can grow up with and grow old with, and it won't let you down. It tells a story about friendship and love. Some people are a little baffled when they hear it described: It's about a relationship between a little boy and a creature from outer space that becomes his best friend. That makes it sound like a cross between *The Thing* and *National Velvet*. It works as science fiction, it's sometimes as scary as a monster movie, and at the end, when the lights go up, there's not a dry eye in the house.

E.T. is a movie of surprises, and I will not spoil any of them for you. But I can suggest some of the film's wonders. The movie takes place in and around a big American suburban development. The split-level houses march up and down the curved drives, carved out of hills that turn into forest a few blocks beyond the backyard. In this forest one night, a spaceship lands, and queer-looking little creatures hobble out of it and go snuffling through the night, looking for plant specimens, I guess. Humans arrive—authorities with flashlights and big stomping boots. They close in on the spaceship, and it is forced to take off and abandon one of its crew members. This forlorn little creature, the *E.T.* of the title, is left behind on Earth—abandoned to a horrendous world of dogs, raccoons, automobile exhausts, and curious little boys.

The movie's hero is one particular little boy named Elliott. He is played by Henry Thomas in what has to be the best little boy performance I've ever seen in an American film. He doesn't come across as an overcoached professional kid; he's natural, defiant, easily touched, conniving, brave, and childlike. He just *knows* there's something living out there in the backyard, and he sits up all night with his flashlight, trying to coax the creature out of hiding with a nearly irresistible bait: Reese's Pieces. The creature, which looks a little like Snoopy but is very,

very wise, approaches the boy. They become friends. The E.T. moves into the house, and the center section of the film is an endless invention on the theme of an extra-terrestrial's introduction to bedrooms, televisions, telephones, refrigerators, and six-packs of beer. The creature has the powers of telepathy and telekinesis, and one of the ways it communicates is to share its emotions with Elliott. That's how Elliott knows that the E.T. wants to go home.

And from here on out, I'd better not describe what happens. Let me just say that the movie has moments of sheer ingenuity, moments of high comedy, some scary moments, and a very sad sequence that has everybody blowing their noses.

What is especially wonderful about all of those moments is that Steven Spielberg, who made this film, creates them out of legitimate and fascinating plot developments. At every moment from its beginning to its end, *E.T.* is really *about* something. The story is quite a narrative accomplishment. It reveals facts about the E.T.'s nature; it develops the personalities of Elliott, his mother, brother, and sister; it involves the federal space agencies; it touches on extra-terrestrial medicine, biology, and communication, and *still* it inspires genuine laughter and tears.

A lot of those achievements rest on the very peculiar shoulders of the E.T. itself. With its odd little walk, its high-pitched squeals of surprise, its tentative imitations of human speech, and its catlike but definitely alien purring, E.T. becomes one of the most intriguing fictional creatures I've ever seen on a screen. The E.T. is a triumph of special effects, certainly; the craftsmen who made this little being have extended the boundaries of their art. But it's also a triumph of imagination, because the filmmakers had to imagine E.T., had to see through its eyes, hear with its ears, and experience this world of ours through its utterly alien experience in order to make a creature so absolutely convincing. The word for what they exercised is empathy. *E.T.—The Extra-Terrestrial* is a reminder of what movies are for. Most movies are not for any one thing, of course. Some are to make us think, some to make us feel, some to take us away from our problems, some to help us examine them. What is enchanting about *E.T.* is that, in some measure, it does all of those things.

Evil Dead 2: Dead by Dawn ★ ★ ★
NO MPAA RATING, 96 m., 1987

Bruce Campbell (Ash), Sarah Berry (Annie), Dan Hicks (Jake), Kassie Wesley (Bobby Joe), Theodore Raimi (Henrietta). Directed by Sam Raimi and produced by Robert G. Tapert. Screenplay by Raimi and Scott Spiegel.

Evil Dead 2: Dead by Dawn is a comedy disguised as a blood-soaked shock-a-rama. It looks superficially like a routine horror movie, a vomitorium designed to separate callow teenagers from their lunch. But look a little closer and you'll realize that the movie is a fairly sophisticated satire. Level One viewers will say it's in bad taste. Level Two folks like ourselves will perceive that it is about bad taste.

The plot: Visitors to a cottage in the Michigan woods discover a rare copy of the *Book of the Dead* and accidentally invoke evil spirits. The spirits run amok, disemboweling and vivisecting their victims. The hero battles manfully with the dread supernatural forces, but he is no match for the unspeakably vile creatures in the basement, in the woods, and behind every door.

This story is told with wall-to-wall special effects. Skeletons dance in the moonlight. Heads spin on top of bodies. Hands go berserk and start attacking their owners. After they are chopped off, they have a life of their own. Heads are clamped into vises and squashed. Blood sprays all over everything. Guts spill. Slime spews. If nauseating images of horrific gore are not, as they say, your cup of tea, the odds are good you will not have a great time during this movie.

On the other hand, if you know it's all special effects, and if you've seen a lot of other movies and have a sense of humor, you might even have a great time seeing *Evil Dead 2*. I did—up to a point. The movie devours ideas at such a prodigious rate that it begins to repeat itself toward the end, but the first forty-five minutes have a kind of manic, inspired genius to them.

Consider, for example, the scene where the hero severs his hand from his body and the hand takes on a life of its own, attacking him. Leave out the blood and the gore and a few of the details, and this entire sequence builds like a tribute to the Three Stooges. Consider the scene where the hero attaches a chainsaw to what's left of his amputated arm. Disgusting, right? But the director, Sam Raimi, approaches it as a sly jab at *Taxi Driver*.

I'm not suggesting that *Evil Dead 2* is fun merely because you can spot the references to other movies. It is fun because (a) the violence and gore are carried to such an extreme that they stop being disgusting and become surrealistic; (b) the movie's timing aims for comedy, not shocks; and (c) the grubby, low-budget intensity of the film gives it a lovable quality that high-tech movies wouldn't have.

There is one shot in the film that is some kind of masterpiece. There is a force out there in the woods. We never see it, but we see things from its point of view. In one long and very complex unbroken point-of-view shot, this force roars through the woods, flattens everything, crashes through the cabin door, and roars through room after room with invincible savagery, chasing the hero until . . . but I wouldn't dream of giving away the joke.

Evil Under the Sun ★ ★ ★
PG, 102 m., 1982

Peter Ustinov (Hercule Poirot), Colin Blakely (Sir Horace Blatt), Jane Birkin (Christine Redfern), Nicholas Clay (Patrick Redfern), Maggie Smith (Daphne Castle), Roddy McDowall (Rex Brewster), Sylvia Miles (Myra Gardener), James Mason (Odell Gardener). Directed by Guy Hamilton and produced by John Brabourne and Richard Goodwin. Screenplay by Anthony Shaffer.

The delicious moments in an Agatha Christie film are supposed to come at the end, when the detective (in this case, the redoubtable Hercule Poirot) gathers everyone in the sitting room and toys with their guilt complexes before finally fingering the murderer. Well, there are delicious moments in the final fifteen minutes of *Evil Under the Sun,* but what I especially liked about this Christie were the opening scenes—the setup. They had a style and irreverence that reminded me curiously of *Beat the Devil,* with Bogart and Robert Morley chewing up the scenery. *Evil Under the Sun* is not, alas, as good as *Beat the Devil,* but it is the best of the recent group of Christie retreads (which include *Murder on the Orient Express, Death on the Nile,* and *The Mirror Crack'd*).

It begins in the usual way, with a corpse. It continues in obligatory fashion with the gathering of a large number of colorful and eccentric suspects in an out-of-the-way spot, which just happens to also be the destination of Hercule Poirot. It continues with the discovery of another corpse, with the liberal distribution of gigantic clues and with Poirot's lip-smacking summary of the evidence. It's the cast that makes *Evil* more fun than the previous manifestations of this identical plot. As Poirot, Peter Ustinov creates a wonderful mixture of the mentally polished and physically maladroit. He has a bit of business involving a dip in the sea that is so perfectly timed and acted it tells us everything we ever wanted to know about Poirot's appetite for exercise. He is so expansive, so beaming, so superior, in the opening scenes that he remains spiritually present throughout the film, even when he's not onscreen.

All of the rest of the cast are suspects. They include Maggie Smith, a former actress who now runs an elegant spa in the Adriatic Sea; Diana Rigg, as her jealous contemporary; Sylvia Miles and James Mason, as a rich couple who produce shows on Broadway; Jane Birkin and Nicholas Clay as a young couple constantly arguing over his roving eye; Colin Blakely as a rich knight who's been taken by a gold digger; Emily Hone as the young new wife; and Roddy McDowall as a bitchy gossip columnist who knows the dirt about everybody. The newly discovered corpse belongs to one of the above. The murderer is one (or more) of the above. Nothing else I could say about the crime would be fair.

I can observe, however, that one of the delights of the movies made from Agatha Christie novels is their almost complete lack of passion: They substitute wit and style. Nobody really cares who gets bumped off, and nobody really misses the departed. What's important is that all the right clues be distributed, so that Poirot and the audience can pick them up, mull them over, and discover the culprit. Perhaps, then, one of the reasons I liked *Evil Under the Sun* was that this time, when Ustinov paused in his summation (after verbally convicting everyone in the room), and it was clear he was about to finger the real killer, I guessed the killer's identity, and I was right. Well, half right. That's better than I usually do.

Exit to Eden ½★
R, 113 m., 1994

Dana Delany (Lisa), Paul Mercurio (Elliot), Rosie O'Donnell (Sheila), Dan Aykroyd (Fred), Hector Elizondo (Martin), Stuart Wilson (Omar), Iman (Nina), Sean O'Bryan (Tommy). Directed by Garry Marshall and produced by Alexandra Rose and Marshall. Screenplay by Deborah Amelon and Bob Brunner.

There is a scene in *Exit to Eden* in which the hero butters Dana Delany's breast, sprinkles it with cinnamon, and licks it before taking bites from a croissant. I'm thinking: The breast or the croissant, make up your mind.

The whole movie is like that. It's supposed to be a kinky sex comedy, but it keeps getting distracted. On the first page of my notes, I wrote "Starts slow." On the second page, I wrote "Boring." On the third page, I wrote "Endless!" On the fourth page, I wrote "Bite-size shredded wheat, skim milk, cantaloupe, frozen peas, toilet paper, salad stuff, pick up laundry."

The movie is based on a novel by Anne Rice, who is said to know a lot about bizarre sexual practices. Either she learned it all after writing this book, or the director, Garry Marshall, just didn't have his heart in it. The movie is not only dumb and ill-constructed, but tragically miscast. The actors look so uncomfortable they could be experiencing alarming intestinal symptoms.

You know me. I'm easy on actors. These are real people with real feelings. When I see a bad performance, I'm inclined to blame anyone but the actors. In the case of *Exit to Eden* I'm inclined to blame the actors. Starting with Rosie O'Donnell. I'm sorry, but I just don't get Rosie O'Donnell. I've seen her in three or four movies now, and she has generally had the same effect on me as fingernails on a blackboard. She's harsh and abrupt and staccato and doesn't seem to be having any fun. She looks mean.

In *Exit to Eden*, she has the misfortune to star in a subplot involving an unnecessary, stupid, boring police investigation. The movie acts as if we care about this dumb case, involving a suspect who may be hiding out in an island resort devoted to S&M. I was reminded of those old nudist camp movies that pretended to be documentaries about volleyball.

Rosie and her partner, played by Dan Aykroyd, turn up on the island, which is managed by a woman named Lisa (Dana Delany). Oh, it's quite a place. They have a merry-go-round with humans instead of wooden horses. A sticky buns booth. Dialogue like, "Baking *and* bondage? I could do both?!" The male customers look like Chippendale dancers. The female customers look like mud wrestlers. Here is a typical exchange:

"Wow! You're a CEO!"

"Yes, I am."

Come on, Garry Marshall, what's going on here? You're a smart guy. You made *Flamingo Kid* and *Pretty Woman*. Didn't you realize (a) that the whole police plot had to go, and O'Donnell and Aykroyd along with it?

And (b) that sex is funny when it's taken seriously, but boring when it's treated as funny? What were your thoughts the first time Rosie turned up in the leather dominatrix uniform? Did you have maybe slight misgivings that you were presiding over one of the more misguided film projects of recent years?

I don't know what kinds of people would sign up for a vacation resort that specializes in sadomasochism, bondage, and discipline. But I imagine they'd want their money's worth. The lifeless, listless charades presided over by Delany are practically family entertainment. The late Harriet Nelson could have attended this camp with only the occasional "Oh, my!"

And of all the actresses I can imagine playing the role of boss dominatrix, Dana Delany is the last. She's a cute, merry-faced type—perfect for the dominatrix's best friend. For the lead, let's see. How about Faye Dunaway? Linda Fiorentino? Sigourney Weaver? See what I mean?

The Exorcist ★ ★ ★ ★
R, 121 m., 1973

Ellen Burstyn (Chris), Linda Blair (Regan), Jason Miller (Father Karras), Max von Sydow (Father Merrin), Kitty Winn (Sharon), Lee J. Cobb (Kinderman). Directed by William Friedkin and produced by William Peter Blatty. Screenplay by Blatty.

1973 began and ended with cries of pain. It began with Ingmar Bergman's *Cries and Whispers*, and it closed with William Friedkin's *The Exorcist*. Both films are about the weather of the human soul, and no two films could be more different. Yet each in its own way forces us to look inside, to experience horror, to confront the reality of human suffering. The Bergman film is a humanist classic. The Friedkin film is an exploitation of the most fearsome resources of the cinema. That does not make it evil, but it does not make it noble, either.

The difference, maybe, is between great art and great craftsmanship. Bergman's exploration of the lines of love and conflict within the family of a woman dying of cancer was a film that asked important questions about faith and death, and was not afraid to admit there might not be any answers. Friedkin's film is about a twelve-year-old girl who either is suffering from a severe neurological disorder or—perhaps has been possessed by an evil spirit. Friedkin has the answers; the problem is that we doubt he believes them.

We don't necessarily believe them ourselves, but that hardly matters during the film's two hours. If movies are, among other things, opportunities for escapism, then *The Exorcist* is one of the most powerful ever made. Our objections, our questions, occur in an intellectual context after the movie has ended. During the movie there are no reservations, but only experiences. We feel shock, horror, nausea, fear, and some small measure of dogged hope.

Rarely do movies affect us so deeply. The first time I saw *Cries and Whispers*, I found myself shrinking down in my seat, somehow trying to escape from the implications of Bergman's story. *The Exorcist* also has that effect—but we're not escaping from Friedkin's implications, we're shrinking back from the direct emotional experience he's attacking us with. This movie doesn't rest on the screen; it's a frontal assault.

The story is well-known; it's adapted, more or less faithfully, by William Peter Blatty from his own bestseller. Many of the technical and theological details in his book are accurate. Most accurate of all is the reluctance of his Jesuit hero, Father Karras, to encourage the ritual of exorcism: "To do that," he says, "I'd have to send the girl back to the sixteenth century." Modern medicine has replaced devils with paranoia and schizophrenia, he explains. Medicine may have, but the movie hasn't. The last chapter of the novel never totally explained in detail the final events in the tortured girl's bedroom, but the movie's special effects in the closing scenes leave little doubt that an actual evil spirit was in that room, and that it transferred bodies. Is this fair? I guess so; in fiction the artist has poetic license.

It may be that the times we live in have prepared us for this movie. And Friedkin has admittedly given us a good one. I've always preferred a generic approach to film criticism; I ask myself how good a movie is of its type. *The Exorcist* is one of the best movies of its type ever made; it not only transcends the genre of terror, horror, and the supernatural, but it transcends such serious, ambitious efforts in the same direction as Roman Polanski's *Rosemary's Baby*. Carl Dreyer's *The Passion of Joan of Arc* is a greater film—but, of course, not nearly so willing to exploit the ways film can manipulate feeling.

The Exorcist does that with a vengeance. The film is a triumph of special effects. Never for a moment—not when the little girl is possessed by the most disgusting of spirits, not when the bed is banging and the furniture flying and the vomit is welling out—are we less than convinced. The film contains brutal shocks, almost indescribable obscenities. That it received an R rating and not the X is stupefying.

The performances are in every way appropriate to this movie made this way. Ellen Burstyn, as the possessed girl's mother, rings especially true; we feel her frustration when doctors and psychiatrists talk about lesions on the brain and she *knows* there's something deeper, more terrible, going on. Linda Blair, as the little girl, has obviously been put through an ordeal in this role, and puts us through one. Jason Miller, as the young Jesuit, is tortured, doubting, intelligent.

And the casting of Max von Sydow as the older Jesuit exorcist was inevitable; he has been through so many religious and metaphysical crises in Bergman's films that he almost seems to belong on a theological battlefield the way John Wayne belonged on a horse. There's a striking image early in the film that has the craggy von Sydow facing an ancient, evil statue; the image doesn't so much borrow from Bergman's famous chess game between von Sydow and Death (in *The Seventh Seal*) as extend the conflict and raise the odds.

I am not sure exactly what reasons people will have for seeing this movie; surely enjoyment won't be one, because what we get here aren't the delicious chills of a Vincent Price thriller, but raw and painful experience. Are people so numb they need movies of this intensity in order to feel anything at all? It's hard to say.

Even in the extremes of Friedkin's vision there is still a feeling that this is, after all, cinematic escapism and not a confrontation with real life. There is a fine line to be drawn there, and *The Exorcist* finds it and stays a millimeter on this side.

Exotica ★ ★ ★ ★
R, 103 m., 1995
(See related Film Clip, p. 872.)

NEW

Bruce Greenwood (Francis), Mia Kirshner (Christina), Don McKellar (Thomas), Arsinee Khanjian (Zoe), Elias Koteas (Eric), Sarah Polley (Tracey), Victor Garber (Harold), Calvin Green (Customs Officer). Directed by Atom Egoyan and produced by Egoyan and Camelia Frieberg. Screenplay by Egoyan.

Exotica is a movie labyrinth, winding seductively into the darkest secrets of a group of people who should have no connection with one another, but do. At the beginning, the film seems to be about randomly selected strangers. By the end, it is revealed that these people are so tightly wound up together that if you took one away, their world would collapse.

Christina (Mia Kirshner) works in a "gentleman's club," so called because few gentlemen go there. She has a regular client named Francis (Bruce Greenwood). He pays her an hourly rate to come and "dance" seductively at his table. No touching is allowed in this club, but Francis has no desire to touch. What he needs from Christina is not physical. And Christina . . . what does she need? We sense an odd private bond between them.

Eric is the deejay in the club, spinning suggestive fantasies about the dancers, drumming up business for the tables. He was once Christina's lover. Now he watches jealously, possessively, as she lingers for hours with Francis. Zoe owns the club. It was started by her late mother, whose "sense of freedom" she admired so much that she even dresses in her mother's clothes. Zoe is pregnant, sweet, honest; she sees the club as a place where lonely people can be less lonely for a few hours. No one there is lonelier than her.

Who are these other characters? Who is the customs officer, and what is his real connection with the man who picks him up at the ballet—the man who owns a pet shop? Why does he steal precious eggs from the man's incubator? And why does Francis hire a baby sitter to stay at his house when he goes to the gentleman's club, since he has no children?

It's easy for a director to play these games all night, setting up mysteries and then revealing deeper mysteries inside of them. That is not Atom Egoyan's game. His plot for *Exotica* coils back upon itself, revealing one layer of mystery after another, but this is not an exercise in style. It is a movie about people whose lives, once we understand them, reveal a need and urgency that only these mysteries can satisfy.

Egoyan, a Canadian director whose imagination and originality have not always been under such masterful control, has been moving toward *Exotica* in his other recent films, like *The Adjuster* (1992). Of that film, he wrote, "I wanted to make a movie about believable people doing believable things in an unbelievable way." It was a good film, but you could see the gears turning. *Exotica* is his best yet, a film in which the characters seem completely real even while they seem to be acting without any apparent explanation—and then seem even more real when we understand them.

Many of the actors come from his stock company. Elias Koteas, who was the adjuster, now plays the deejay; in the earlier film he served others, but this time he serves only himself. Arsinee Khanjian (Egoyan's wife) is Zoe, the club owner, suffusing the sleazy surroundings with a gentle innocence. Mia Kirshner, an actress new to me, combines sexual allure with a kindness that makes her all the more appealing. Indeed, the intriguing thing about Egoyan's work here is how he sets the story in a hothouse of sex, and then works around the sex, getting to the feelings, revealing how most of the characters are much nicer than at first they seem.

In the months after *Pulp Fiction* opened, I talked to a lot of people who were stimulated by its plot structure, the way it played with apparent paradoxes. Those people are likely to admire the plot of *Exotica* even more: We begin with desperation and need, and move to satisfaction and fulfillment, and at the same time Egoyan astonishingly finds a way to add melodrama, blackmail, and an ingenious deception. The movie is a series of interlocking surprises and delights, and, at the end, it is heartbreaking as well. It's quite a performance, announcing Egoyan's arrival in the first rank of filmmakers.

Experience Preferred . . . But Not Essential ★ ★ ★
PG, 77 m., 1983

Elizabeth Edmonds (Annie), Sue Wallace (Mavis), Geraldine Griffith (Doreen), Karen Meagher (Paula), Ron Bain (Mike), Alun Lewis (Hywel). Directed by Peter Duffell and produced by David Puttnam and Chris Griffin. Screenplay by June Roberts.

This movie is so slight and charming you're almost afraid to breathe during it, for fear of disturbing the spell. It's about ordinary people in an ordinary setting, but because the setting is a small resort hotel in Wales, and the time is the summer of 1962, there's also the strange feeling that we've entered another time and place, where some of the same rules apply, but by no means all of them.

The movie tells the story of a young woman named Annie (Elizabeth Edmonds) who comes to work for the summer in a hotel, and finds that she's entered a cozy little backstairs world with its own sets of loyalties and jealousies. All of the other waitresses at the hotel have their own stories, some funny, some sad, and Annie feels a little left out. "I'm the only one here without a past," she complains, but of course one of the reasons for spending your summer working in a hotel is to accumulate a past. The other women are suspicious of her because she's a student, but as the waitresses cram into the servants' quarters, three to a room and sometimes two to a bed, a sort of democracy sets in, and Annie is accepted.

The movie uses a wonderfully offhand style for filling us in on the characters. There's the gallant cook, who immediately takes a liking to Annie. And the redheaded bartender, who makes it a nightly habit to sleepwalk in the nude. And the conceited young waiter whose idea of a courtship is to belt his girl in the eye every once in a while. And the pretty hostess of the dining room, who owes her position and her private boudoir to the favors she supplies the hotel's owner. ("How did you get such a nice room?" Annie asks her, innocently.)

There's not much of a plot. Things just sort of happen. Young men and women work from dawn to dusk and then collapse into each other's arms, almost but not quite too exhausted for sex. And the sexual customs of the pre-Pill era take on a certain quaintness, and a certain desperation, as couples grimly try to walk the line between lust and prudence. *Experience Preferred* is charming precisely because of its inconsequential air. It's funny because it goes for whimsical little insights into human nature rather than for big, obvious jokes. It's charming because it doesn't force the charm.

Exposed ★ ★ ★ ½
R, 100 m., 1983

Nastassja Kinski (Elizabeth), Rudolph Nureyev (Daniel), Harvey Keitel (Rivas), Ian McShane (Miller), Bibi Andersson (Margaret), Pierre Clementi (Vic). Directed and produced by James Toback. Screenplay by Toback.

This movie contains moments so exhilarating they reawakened me to the infinite possibilities of movies. Yet this movie loses itself in its closing sequences and meanders through the details of a routine terrorist plot. Somewhere between its greatness and its wandering there must be a compromise, and I would strike it this way: *Exposed* contains the most exciting evidence I have seen so far that Nastassja Kinski is the next great female superstar. I do not say that she is a great actress; not yet, and perhaps not ever. I do not compare her with Meryl Streep or Kate Nelligan, Jill Clayburgh or Jessica Lange. I am not talking in those terms of professional accomplishment. I am talking about the mysterious, innate quality that some performers have to cast a special spell, to develop a relationship with the camera that you can call stardom or voodoo or magic, because its name doesn't really matter.

Kinski has it. There are moments in this film (two virtuoso scenes, in particular, and then many other small moments and parts of scenes) when she affects me in the same way that Marilyn Monroe must have affected her first viewers, in movies like *The Asphalt Jungle* or *All About Eve.* She was not yet a star and audiences did not even know her name, but there was a quality about her that could not be dismissed. Kinski has that quality. She has exhibited it before in better films, such as *Tess,* and in ambitious, imperfect films such as *Cat People* and *One from the Heart.* Now here is *Exposed,* written and directed by James Toback, who in screenplays such as *The Gambler* and his brilliant, little-seen directing debut *Fingers,* has specialized in characters who live on the edge.

There are two sequences in *Exposed* where he pulls out all the stops. In one of them, Kinski (who plays a college dropout, lonely and sexually frustrated) dances all by herself in a nearly empty apartment. In another one, she meets a violinist (Rudolph Nureyev), they fall instantly into a consuming passion, and after he has tantalized her with a violin bow they make sudden, passionate love. The sheer quality of Kinski's abandon in these two scenes made me realize how many barriers can sometimes exist between a performance and an audience: Here there are none.

The movie is wonderful for its first hour or more. It follows Kinski through a brief, unhappy love affair with her professor (played by Toback), shows her moving to New York, has her discovered by a photographer and becoming a world-famous model (because she is Kinski, this is believable), and brings her up through the love affair with Nureyev. At this moment, *Exposed* seems poised on the brink of declaring itself one of the most riveting character portraits ever made.

And that is the moment where it falters, and loses itself in the details of a plot involving Harvey Keitel, as the leader of an underground terrorist cell in Paris. It's as if Toback didn't trust the strength of this character he had created (or, more likely, didn't know when he wrote his thriller that Kinski would bring the character so completely to life). The rest of the movie is okay, I suppose, in a somewhat familiar way. But its special quality is lost in plot details. Too bad. But if a movie can electrify me the way this one did, not once but twice and then some, I'm prepared to forgive it almost anything.

Extreme Prejudice ★ ★ ★
R, 104 m., 1987

Nick Nolte (Jack Benteen), Powers Boothe (Cash Bailey), Michael Ironside (Major Hackett), Maria Conchita Alonso (Sarita Cisneros), Rip Torn (Sheriff Pearson), Clancy Brown (Sergeant McRose). Directed by Walter Hill and produced by Buzz Feitshans. Screenplay by Deric Washburn.

The story elements in *Extreme Prejudice* are so ancient they sound like ad copy: Two strong men, one good, one evil, battle each other for justice—and for the heart of the woman they both love. Walter Hill is the right director for this material. He specializes in male action movies where the characters are all a little taller, leaner, meaner, and more obscene than in real life.

Hill doesn't really try to avoid the clichés in a story like this. He simply turns up the juice. Like his *Southern Comfort, 48 HRS,* and *The Warriors,* this is a movie that depends on style, not surprises. He doesn't want to make a different kind of movie; he wants to make a familiar story look better than we've seen it look recently. And yet there is a big surprise in *Extreme Prejudice* in the appearance and character of Nick Nolte.

When last seen, Nolte had successfully overcome his early pretty-boy image and turned into one of the shabbier ruins on the landscape of American leading men. His performance in *Teachers* needed a diagnosis, not a review. But then, about halfway through *Down and Out in Beverly Hills,* he underwent some kind of metamorphosis. He shaved off the beard and emerged as a weathered, older, more attractive actor; for the first time, I realized that he had the materials to become a big-league star like Cooper or Gable.

In *Extreme Prejudice,* he is working in the Cooper tradition. He is leaner than before, his face chiseled like some Western artifact, and he wears his Texas Ranger hat down on his forehead, so his eyes are always in shadow. He works the border, trying to control the drug trade, and at night he comes home exhausted to the bed of his girl (Maria Conchita Alonso).

She is restless with this arrangement. Her previous lover was Cash Bailey (Powers Boothe), once Nolte's best friend, now a drug baron who controls the flow across the border. Cash moves with impunity back and forth in a private helicopter and offers Alonso more than a Ranger's salary can buy. One day, she packs up and goes to live with him. Meanwhile, Nolte's territory is invaded by an unofficial, top-secret cadre of American combat veterans who apparently are working for a U.S. military covert operations team. Their mission remains murky (they screw up a mysterious bank heist), but they seem to be after Cash, too. That leads to the shoot-out at Cash's Mexican fortress, not to mention a lot of last-minute switching of sides and loyalties.

The specifics of the plot you can do without. You've seen this movie before, right down to the dozing guards who permit the enemy gunmen to walk right into the stronghold.

What makes the film good are Hill's style and the acting. Everything is cranked up about ten degrees. Nolte is quiet and tough, Boothe gives a great performance as a slimy drug merchant with some residual charm, and Alonso was born for her role as the passionate señorita trapped between two men who will kill for her.

The love triangle is sort of a broad, bloody version of *The Third Man*, where Orson Welles and Joseph Cotten were childhood friends who ended up on opposite sides of the law and in love with Alida Valli. The conflict in these triangles is always the same: The woman knows the bad guy is a slimy snake, but she loves him, anyway. That breaks the good guy's heart and leaves him free to kill his childhood buddy. Then you get the poignant ending.

Hill has made a lot of movies in the last fifteen years, and I guess it's too late to hope that he'll develop a real interest in his female characters. They're the pawns of his male buddies, and everything else boils down to the way the characters walk, the way they look at each other, the personal tics they develop, and the new ways the stunt men find for people to die. *Extreme Prejudice* offers a lot of technique, some strong acting, and the absolute confidence of a good director who knows what he wants to do and doesn't care if that limits him.

Eye of the Needle ★ ★ ★
R, 118 m., 1981

Donald Sutherland (Faber), Kate Nelligan (Lucy), Christopher Cazenove (David), Ian Bannen (Canter). Directed by Richard Marquand and produced by Stephen Friedman. Screenplay by Stanley Mann.

Eye of the Needle resembles nothing so much as one of those downbeat, plodding, quietly horrifying, and sometimes grimly funny war movies that used to be made by the British film industry, back when there was a British film industry. They used to star Stanley Baker or Trevor Howard. This one stars Donald Sutherland, as the kind of introverted psychopath who should inhabit only black-and-white movies, although the color here is sometimes gloomy enough to suffice. I admired the movie. It is made with quiet competence, and will remind some viewers of the Alfred Hitchcock who made *The 39 Steps* and *Foreign Correspondent*. It is about a German spy, the "Needle," who dropped out of sight in Germany in 1938 and now inhabits a series of drab bed-sitting-rooms in England while he spies on the British war effort. He is known as the Needle because of his trademarked way of killing people by jabbing a stiletto into their rib cages. He kills with a singular lack of passion; this is Jack the Ripper crossed with J. Alfred Prufrock. As played by Sutherland, the Needle is a very lonely man. We are given hints to explain his isolation: He was raised by parents who did not love him, he was shipped off to boarding schools, he spent parts of his childhood in America, where he learned English. None of these experiences fully explains his ruthlessness, but then perhaps it is just a spy's job to be ruthless.

The plot is part espionage, part cliffhanger. The Needle discovers phony plywood "airplanes" intended to look, from the air, like Patton's invasion force—a ruse to throw off the Germans. His assignment is to personally deliver news of the actual Allied invasion plans to Hitler. This he intends to do with every fiber of his being, and yet we never get the feeling that the this man is a patriotic Nazi. He is more of a dogged functionary. In his attempts to rendezvous with a Nazi submarine, he's shipwrecked on an isolated island occupied only by a lighthouse-keeper and by a young married couple—a woman (Kate Nelligan), her legless husband (Christopher Cazenove), and their son. The last third of the movie turns into a bloody melodrama, as the Needle kills the husband and the lighthouse-keeper and threatens the woman, first in a psychological way and then with violence. But before the final standoff, he pretends to be merely a lost sailor. And the woman, frustrated by her husband's drunkenness and refusal to love, becomes attracted to the stranger. They make love. She grows fond of him. Does he grow fond of her? We can never be sure, but he tells her things he has told to no one else.

Some people will find the movie slow going. I preferred to think of it as deliberate. It is effective, I think, to develop a plot like this at a deliberate pace, instead of rushing headlong through it. That gives us time to meditate on the character of the Needle, and to ponder his very few, enigmatic references to his own behavior. We learn things about him that he may not even know about himself, and that is why the film's final scene is so much more complex than it seems. "The war has come down to the two of us," Sutherland tells Nelligan, and in the final exchange of desperate looks between the man and the woman there is a whole universe left unspoken. The movie ends with Nelligan regarding a man who is either a treacherous spy or an unloved child, take your choice.

Eyewitness ★ ★ ★
R, 102 m., 1981

William Hurt (Daryll Deever), Sigourney Weaver (Tony Sokolow), Christopher Plummer (Joseph), James Woods (Aldo), Irene Worth (Mrs. Sokolow), Pamela Reed (Linda). Directed and produced by Peter Yates. Screenplay by Steve Tesich.

Somebody was explaining the difference between European and American movies to me the other day: European movies are about people, but American movies are about stories. It's an interesting idea, especially when it's applied to a thriller like *Eyewitness*, which is good precisely because it pays more attention to its people than its story. Does that make it European? Well, it was directed by Peter Yates, who is British but has directed some of the most "American" movies of the past decade, from *Bullitt* to *Breaking Away*. It is definitely set in America—from the bowels of a Manhattan boiler room to the newsroom of a TV station. But it's about such interesting, complicated, quirky, and sometimes funny people that it must at the least be mid-Atlantic.

The movie stars William Hurt as a janitor

who stumbles across evidence that could lead to the solution of a murder investigation. But he doesn't go to the police with it because he's too complicated, too introspective, too distrustful of his own discovery . . . and, mostly, he's too much in love from afar with a TV news reporter (Sigourney Weaver). Maybe he can win her attention by giving her the scoop?

There are other complications. Sigourney Weaver is engaged to an Israeli agent (Christopher Plummer) who is involved in secret international negotiations to smuggle Jews out of the Soviet Union. His plan involves clandestine payments to a Vietnamese agent who got rich on the black market in Saigon and has now moved to Manhattan. The other characters include James Woods, as Hurt's eccentric and unpredictable fellow janitor, and Steven Hill and Morgan Freeman as a couple of cops who wearily track down leads in the case (their best line: "When

Aldo was a little boy, he must have wanted to grow up to be a suspect").

The development and solution of the murder mystery are handled with professional dispatch by Yates and his writer, Steve Tesich (who also wrote *Breaking Away*). A final shoot-out in a midtown riding stable has a touch of Hitchcock to it; the old master always loved to mix violence with absolutely inappropriate settings. But what makes this movie so entertaining is the way Yates and Tesich and their characters play against our expectations.

Examples. Weaver is not only a TV newswoman, but also a part-time serious pianist and the unhappy daughter of her domineering parents. Hurt is not only a janitor but also a sensitive soul who can talk his way into Weaver's heart. Woods is not only a creepy janitor but also the enthusiastic promoter of a marriage between his sister and Hurt. Hurt and the sister (Pamela Reed) carry on the

courtship because they are both too embarrassed to tell the other one they're not in love. Plummer is the most complicated character of all, and it's a very good question whether he's a villain. It all depends on how you view his own personal morality.

I've seen so many thrillers that, frankly, I don't always care how they turn out—unless they're really well-crafted. What I like about *Eyewitness* is that, although it *does* care how it turns out, it cares even more about the texture of the scenes leading to the denouement. There's not a scene in this movie that exists only to provide us with plot information. Every scene develops characters. And they're developed in such offbeat fidelity to the way people do behave that we get all the more involved in the mystery, just because, for once, we halfway believe it could really be happening.

F

The Fabulous Baker Boys ★ ★ ★ ½
R, 114 m., 1989

Jeff Bridges (Jack Baker), Michelle Pfeiffer (Susie Diamond), Beau Bridges (Frank Baker), Ellie Raab (Nina), Xander Berkeley (Lloyd), Jennifer Tilly (Monica), Dakin Matthews (Charlie), Ken Lerner (Ray), Albert Hall (Henry). Directed by Steve Kloves and produced by Paula Weinstein and Mark Rosenberg. Screenplay by Kloves.

There is a scene in *The Fabulous Baker Boys* where Michelle Pfeiffer, wearing a slinky red dress, uncurls on top of a piano while singing "Makin' Whoopee." The rest of the movie is also worth the price of admission. Pfeiffer stars in the film with Jeff and Beau Bridges, who play the halves of a cocktail lounge piano duet. Their act is growing relentlessly more hopeless when they decide to liven things up by hiring a girl singer. The singer is Pfeiffer. Things liven up.

The Fabulous Baker Boys is a new version of an old show-biz formula about the long-time partners whose relationship is threatened when one of them falls in love with the sexy new singer. *Young Man With a Horn* did a version of this material, and so have lots of other movies, but rarely with such intriguing casting and such a sure hand for the material. There's probably some autobiographical truth lurking beneath the rivalry of the Bridges brothers, old wounds from the twenty years they have both been working in the movies. And Pfeiffer quite simply has one of the roles of a lifetime as the high-priced call girl who wants to become a low-priced lounge singer.

The movie takes place in that shadowy area of show business where people make a living, even a fairly decent living, but they always seem to be marking time. Night after night, the Baker Boys sit down at their twin pianos in the lounges of fading Seattle supper clubs and pretentious motels, and go through an act they could do in their sleep. The audience, drunks in search of melancholy, doesn't even bother to listen.

The problem is, the fabulous Baker Boys are getting dated. They're doing tired material and arrangements that sound like elevator music. And the jobs aren't coming their way anymore. Deciding to add a singer to the act, they conduct a long series of auditions, during which they meet nearly every woman in town who should not consider a singing career. And then Pfeiffer walks in.

She's not an experienced singer. She doesn't quite know how to handle herself or her voice. But she has that ineffable vocal quality that causes people to listen because they might be missing something. And she looks like a million bucks. She's been a hooker, yes, but we know from a hundred other movies that she has a good heart and that the tough come-on is all an act.

Working with the girl singer, the Baker Boys begin to play real music again. This re-opens an old wound. Jack Baker (Jeff Bridges) is, in fact, a brilliant jazz pianist, who has turned his back on the music he loves out of some twisted love-hate loyalty to his brother, Frank (Beau Bridges). Frank easily handles the business side of the partnership, and could easily go through the same hackneyed act night after night for years. So the girl inevitably comes between them. And Jack inevitably falls in love with her.

The Fabulous Baker Boys doesn't do anything very original, but what it does, it does wonderfully well. It was written and directed by a first-timer, Steve Kloves, and even though the screenplay depends on formulas, we begin to forget that; we begin to care about these people, especially when the relationship between the brothers turns inward and

they start looking hard at what they both really need from life.

This is one of the movies they will use as a document years from now when they begin to trace the steps by which Michelle Pfeiffer became a great star. I cannot claim that I spotted her unique screen presence in her first movie, which, I think, was *Grease II*, but certainly by the time she made *Ladyhawke*, *Tequila Sunrise, Dangerous Liaisons,* and *Married to the Mob*, something was going on, and this is the movie of her flowering—not just as a beautiful woman, but as an actress with the ability to make you care about her, to make you feel what she feels.

All of those qualities are here in this movie, and so is the "Makin' Whoopee" number, which I can only praise by adding it to a short list: Whatever she's doing while she performs that song isn't merely singing—it's whatever Rita Hayworth did in *Gilda* and Marilyn Monroe did in *Some Like It Hot,* and I didn't want her to stop.

The Falcon and the Snowman ★ ★ ★ ★
R, 131 m., 1985

Timothy Hutton (Christopher Boyce), Sean Penn (Daulton Lee), Pat Hingle (Mr. Boyce), Joyce Van Patten (Mrs. Boyce), David Suchet (Alex), Boris Leskin (Mikhail). Directed by John Schlesinger and produced by Gabriel Katska and Schlesinger. Screenplay by Steven Saillian.

A few years ago there were stories in the papers about a couple of California kids who were caught selling government secrets to the Russians. The stories had an air of unreality about them. Here were a couple of middle-class young men from suburban backgrounds, who were prosecuted as spies and traitors and who hardly seemed to have it quite clear in their own minds how they had gotten into the spy business. One of the many strengths of *The Falcon and the Snowman* is that it succeeds, in an admirably matter-of-fact way, in showing us exactly how these two young men got in way over their heads. This is a movie about spies, but it is not a thriller in any routine sense of the word; it's just the meticulously observant record of how naiveté, inexperience, misplaced idealism, and greed led to one of the most peculiar cases of treason in American history.

The movie stars Timothy Hutton as Christopher Boyce, a seminarian who has a crisis of conscience, drops out of school, and ends up working almost by accident for a message-routing center of the CIA. Sean Penn is his best friend, Daulton Lee. Years ago, they were altar boys together, but in recent times their paths have diverged; while Boyce was studying for the priesthood, Lee was setting himself up as a drug dealer. By the time we meet them, Boyce is earnest and clean-cut, just the kind of young man the CIA might be looking for (it doesn't hurt that his father is a former FBI man). And Lee, with a mustache that makes him look like a failed creep, is a jumpy, paranoid drug dealer who is one step ahead of the law.

The whole caper begins so simply. Boyce, reading the messages he is paid to receive and forward, learns that the CIA is engaged in dirty tricks designed to influence elections in Australia. He is deeply offended to learn that his government would be interfering in the affairs of another state, and the more he thinks about it, the more he wants to do something. For example, supply the messages to the Russians. He doesn't want to be a Russian *spy*, you understand, just to bring this injustice to light. Lee has some contacts in Mexico, where he buys drugs. One day, in a deceptively casual conversation by the side of a backyard swimming pool, the two friends decide to go into partnership to sell the information to the Soviet Embassy in Mexico City. Lee takes the documents south and launches them both on an adventure that is a lark at first, and then a challenge, and finally just a very, very bad dream.

These two young men have one basic problem. They are amateurs. The Russians don't necessarily like that any better than the Americans would; indeed, even though the Russians are happy to have the secrets that are for sale, there is a definite sense in some scenes that the key Russian contact agent,

played by David Suchet, is almost offended by the sloppy way Penn deals in espionage. The only thing Penn seems really serious about is the money.

The Falcon and the Snowman never steps wrong, but it is best when it deals with the relationship between the two young American spies. The movie was directed by John Schlesinger, an Englishman whose understanding of American characters was most unforgettably demonstrated in *Midnight Cowboy,* and I was reminded of Joe Buck and Ratso Rizzo from that movie as I watched this one. There is even a quiet, understated quote to link Ratso with the Penn character: a moment in a parking garage when Penn defies a car to pull in front of him, and we're reminded of Ratso crossing a Manhattan street and hurling the line "I'm *walking* here!" at a taxi that dares to cut him off. Instead of relying on traditional methods for creating the suspense in spy movies, this one uses the energy generated between the two very different characters, as the all-American Boyce gradually begins to understand that his partner is out of control. *The Falcon and the Snowman,* like most good movies, is not really about its plot but about its characters. These two young men could just as easily be selling stolen IBM programs to Apple, instead of CIA messages to the Russians; the point is that they begin with one set of motives and then the implacable real world supplies them with another, harder, more unforgiving set of realities.

Just as with *Midnight Cowboy,* it's hard to say who gives the better performance this time: Sean Penn, with his twitching intensity as he angles for respect from the Russians, or Timothy Hutton, the straight man, earnestly telling his girlfriend that she should remember he really loves her—"no matter what you may hear about me in a few days from now."

Falling Down ★ ★ ★
R, 112 m., 1993

Michael Douglas (D-FENS), Robert Duvall (Prendergast), Barbara Hershey (Beth), Rachel Ticotin (Sandra), Tuesday Weld (Mrs. Prendergast). Directed by Joel Schumacher and produced by Arnold Kopelson, Herschel Weingrod, and Timothy Harris. Screenplay by Ebbe Roe Smith.

A lot of the reviews for *Falling Down* are going to compare it to earlier movies about white men who go berserk: *Joe,* for example, or *Death Wish.* Some will even find it racist

because the targets of the film's hero are African-American, Latino, and Korean— with a few whites thrown in for balance. Both of these approaches represent a facile reading of the film, which is actually about a great sadness that turns into madness, and can afflict anyone who is told, after many years of hard work, that he is unnecessary and irrelevant.

The movie stars Michael Douglas, in a performance of considerable subtlety and some courage, as a Los Angeles man who a few years ago thought he had it all figured out. He was a well-paid defense worker, he had a wife and child, the sun came up every morning, and what was there to worry about? But already there must have been danger signals, and we learn later in the film that he had flashes of violence against his wife and child, that he is divorced, that a court order prevents him from approaching them.

On the morning the film begins, he is stuck in traffic on the freeway. Nothing is moving. Exhaust fumes rise all around him. The director, Joel Schumacher, deliberately shoots this scene as a homage to the famous opening of Fellini's *8½,* but instead of finding himself floating up into the sky, like Fellini's hero, the man gets out of his car, slams the door, and goes walking alone across Los Angeles. This is not always a safe thing for a crew-cut white man, wearing a shirt and a tie.

The man has no name in the film; he becomes known to the police as D-FENS, after his license plate. He is already unhinged when he starts his walk, but eventually the tools of violence fall into his hands, and he uses them. In a grocery store, he asks for change for the telephone, and is refused by the Korean proprietor. He tries to buy a can of pop, but the change from a dollar would not be enough for a phone call. His frustration rages, until he grabs the owner's baseball bat and starts swinging, taking down piles of junk foods, cans of diet soda.

He keeps walking. During the course of his day he will meet, and confront, Latino gang members who want to steal his briefcase, fast-food workers who tell him it's too late for breakfast, a neo-Nazi gun-shop owner, and other characters who seem placed in his way to fuel his anger.

Eventually he comes to the attention of the police, as Prendergast (Robert Duvall), a cop in his last day on the job, puts together scattered reports to deduct that the same goofy white guy is causing a series of disturbances. Prendergast is, in his own way, an example of the same syndrome afflicting the Douglas character. He feels impotent, unnecessary, obsolete. His superior officer tells him frankly he is sick of him. The story builds to a final confrontation between Douglas and Duvall—between a man who has snapped, and a man who has held together, under many of the same pressures.

If this film had been made ten or twenty years ago, it might have been an audience-pleaser in which we cheered as the white hero shot up druggies or got vengeance on rapists. Schumacher and his screenwriter, Ebbe Roe Smith, have not made a revenge movie, and the film isn't constructed to inspire cheers when Douglas pulls the trigger. Maybe it will play that way for some audiences, but more thoughtful viewers are likely to pick up on Douglas's anomie—his soul-sickness that has turned to madness, his bafflement at becoming obsolete and irrelevant.

Because the character is white, and many of his targets are not, the movie could be read as racist. I prefer to think of it as a reflection of the real feelings of a lot of people who, lacking the insight to see how political and economic philosophies have affected them, fall back on easy scapegoating. If you don't have a job and the Korean shop owner does, it is easy to see him as the villain. It takes a little more imagination to realize that you lost your job because of the greedy and unsound financial games of the go-go junk-bond years.

What is fascinating about the Douglas character, as written and played, is the core of sadness in his soul. Yes, by the time we meet him, he has gone over the edge. But there is no exhilaration in his rampage, no release. He seems weary and confused, and in his actions he unconsciously follows scripts that he may have learned from the movies, or on the news, where other frustrated misfits vent their rage on innocent bystanders.

Nor does Schumacher build to some kind of easy audience-pleasing climax. The way the movie ends is the way it must, in real life—not the way it would in *Death Wish VII*. And the values and style of the Duvall character reflect, not a triumphant cop, but simply a guy who still believes in trying to roll with the punches and make the best of things. *Falling Down* does a good job of representing a real feeling in our society today. It would be a shame if it is seen only on a superficial level.

Falling from Grace ★ ★ ★ ★
PG-13, 101 m., 1992

John Mellencamp (Bud Parks), Mariel Hemingway (Alice Parks), Claude Akins (Specs Parks), Dub Taylor (Grandpa Parks), Kay Lenz (P.J. Parks). Directed by John Mellencamp and produced by Harry Sandler. Screenplay by Larry McMurtry.

Thomas Wolfe told us, "You can't go home again," and people who have never read a word of his novels remember that warning, perhaps because it is so obviously true. And still people try to go back home. In *Falling From Grace*, John Mellencamp's powerful and perceptive movie, a country-rock star returns to his small town in Indiana, hoping to throw back a few brews and hang out with his old buddies at the pool hall. It doesn't work out that way.

The Mellencamp character left more than memories behind in Indiana. He also left an alcoholic father (Claude Akins), whose idea of an ideal male role falls somewhere between patriarch and rapist. And he left behind an old girlfriend (Kay Lenz), who has now married the hero's brother but who has spent a lot of years thinking the singer should have taken her along when he left for the big time.

John Mellencamp, of course, is a rock star who comes from Indiana himself, and often goes back there—so often it is unlikely *Falling From Grace* is autobiographical except in its broadest and least personal outlines. What he has done, I imagine, is to combine Larry McMurtry's uncommonly good original screenplay with his own small-town insights, and the experiences of all sorts of other people he's met or worked with on the road. They all come together in this story where old wounds never heal.

One of the strangest truths about high school reunions is that all of the old jealousies and resentments of years before are still remembered so clearly; the people who sat together in the school lunchroom now sit together at the reunion banquet, as if the years in between haven't made a difference. We get that same sense of wounded memory in the opening scenes of *Falling From Grace*, as Mellencamp's private plane arrives at the local airport, disgorging the singer, his wife (Mariel Hemingway), and his entourage.

Word quickly gets around town that Mellencamp is back, and it is especially quick to reach Kay Lenz, the sister-in-law. The situation resembles, I suppose, a script from

"Dallas" or "Dynasty" (returning rock star still feels chemistry with sexy old flame, now married to his brother), but McMurtry doesn't write it that way. His screenplay is too intelligent, and too observant.

Kay Lenz has many of the best scenes in the movie. She plays a woman who has achieved some degree of material comfort (she lives in one of the best houses in town), but no psychic or emotional satisfaction. She fools around all the time, and everyone in town knows it, and she doesn't care that they know.

The Mellencamp character comes back to town with the idea that everyone will be more or less happy to see him. He is wrong. His friends and relatives have spent a long time thinking about his life in the fast lane, and there are a lot of jealousies and resentments. Lenz is particularly angry. She knows she was smart enough and pretty enough for him to take along when he made his break, and if he's going to come back she isn't going to simply smile and bite the bullet.

While Hemingway, as the singer's wife, sits around bored and ignored, and pawed by the singer's randy father—who treats her like a toy that his son brought home for Dad—Mellencamp and Lenz engage in a hostile and risky flirtation. This could have been soap opera material, but McMurtry's screenplay is based on a lot of psychological insight, and we see how old issues and old wounds are still able to affect the present and change lives.

A lot of rock stars and other showbiz heroes have the notion that because they're successful in other areas, they can direct a movie, too. Usually they're wrong. But Mellencamp turns out to have a real filmmaking gift. His film is perceptive and subtle, and doesn't make the mistake of thinking that because something is real, it makes good fiction. The characters created here with McMurtry are three-dimensional and fully realized—and the Lenz character is probably even better-seen than Mellencamp's. At the end of the movie we are left with the possibility that although you may be able to go home again, it might be a good idea not to.

Fame ★ ★ ★ ½
R, 133 m., 1980

Eddie Barth (Angelo), Irene Cara (Coco), Lee Curreri (Bruno), Laura Dean (Lisa), Antonia Franceschi (Hilary), Boyd Gaines (Michael), Albert Hague (Shorofsky), Tresa Hughes (Mrs.

Finsecker). Directed by Alan Parker and produced by David De Silva and Alan Marshall. Screenplay by Christopher Gore.

Mrs. Seward, the draconian rhetoric teacher who drilled literacy into generations of Urbana (Ill.) high school students, used to tell us we were having the best four years of our lives. We groaned. *Fame* is a movie that she might have enjoyed. It's about a dozen or so talented kids who enter New York's High School of the Performing Arts as freshmen and emerge four years later as future Freddie Prinzes and Benny Goodmans, Leonard Bernsteins and Mrs. Sewards.

Fame is a genuine treasure, moving and entertaining, a movie that understands being a teen-ager as well as *Breaking Away* did, but studies its characters in a completely different milieu. It's the other side of the coin: A big-city, aggressive, cranked-up movie to play against the quieter traditions of *Breaking Away*'s small Indiana college town. *Fame* is all New York City. It's populated by rich kids, ghetto kids, kids with real talent, and kids with mothers who think they have real talent. They all go into the hopper, into a high school of kids who are worked harder because they're "special"—even if they're secretly not so sure they're so special.

The movie has the kind of sensitivity to the real lives of real people that we don't get much in Hollywood productions anymore. Anyone who ever went to high school will recognize some of *Fame*'s characters: the quiet little girl who blossoms, the class genius who locks himself up in the basement with his electronic equipment, the kid who can't read but is a naturally gifted performer, the wiseass, the self-destructive type, the sexpot, the rich kid, and on and on. The cast has been recruited from New York's most talented young performers, some of them almost playing themselves. The teachers are familiar too: self-sacrificing, perfectionist, cranky, love-hate objects.

If the character types seem familiar, the movie's way of telling their stories is not. This isn't a movie that locks its characters into a conventional plot. Instead, it fragments the experiences of four years into dozens of vignettes, loosely organized into sections titled "The Auditions," "Freshman Year," and so on. We get to know the characters and their personalities gradually, as we see them in various situations. The effect is a little like high school itself; you come in as a total stranger and by the time you leave, the school has become your world.

If the kids in *Fame* are like high school kids anywhere, they're also different because they *are* talented, and the movie's at its best when it examines the special pressures on young people who are more talented than they are mature, experienced, or sure of themselves. The ghost that hovers over everyone in this school is a former graduate, Freddie Prinze, who had the talent but never figured out how to handle it.

The movie's director, Alan Parker, seems to have a knack for isolating just those moments in the lives of his characters when growth, challenge, and talent are all on the line at once. Where did he find his insights into talented young people? Probably while he was directing his first film, the wonderful *Bugsy Malone* (1976), which was a gangster musical with an all-kid cast. *Fame* is a perfect title for this movie; it establishes an ironic distance between where these kids are now and where they'd like to be someday, and then there's also the haunting suggestion that some of the ones who find fame will be able to handle it, and some will not.

Family Business ★ ★ ★
R, 73 m., 1989

Sean Connery (Jessie), Dustin Hoffman (Vito), Matthew Broderick (Adam), Rosana DeSoto (Elaine), Janet Carroll (Margie), Victoria Jackson (Christin), Bill McCutcheon (Doheny), Deborah Rush (Michele Dempsey), Marilyn Cooper (Rose), Salem Ludwig (Nat). Directed by Sidney Lumet and produced by Lawrence Gordon. Screenplay by Vincent Patrick.

What does Sidney Lumet's *Family Business* want to be? A caper movie, or a family drama? I ask because the movie seems to pursue both goals with equal success until about the three-quarter mark, and then leaves leftover details of the caper hanging disconcertingly in midair. I was distracted during the movie's important final scenes by a large unanswered question, which I'll get to later.

Good news first. The movie stars Sean Connery, Dustin Hoffman, and Matthew Broderick as three generations of the same family, all touched in one way or another by crime. Connery, the grandfather, is a Scotsman whose arrest record is as long as his arm. He lives by one of those macho criminal codes in which you haven't proven anything unless you've proven it with your fists, and as the movie opens he's in jail after getting in a bar brawl with an off-duty policeman.

Hoffman is Connery's son, half Scots and half Sicilian ("He'd be five inches taller with a Scots mother," Connery observes), and Broderick is Hoffman's son, half Jewish. The movie makes such a point of the hereditary makeup of the three men, I guess, because the caper involves breaking into a genetic-engineering laboratory and stealing some DNA research material. The idea for the caper comes from Broderick, a Westinghouse Scholar who has never been involved in crime before. Hoffman is adamantly opposed to it—he still bears the wounds of his childhood with a criminal father—but Connery is enthusiastic, and Hoffman finally decides to come along out of concern for the safety of his son.

All of the scenes establishing the characters and setting up the caper are joyful to watch, mostly because of the rich comic exaggerations of the Connery character, who makes such a contrast to his uptight son and all-American grandson. The caper itself is a disappointment (they have a key card and a security code, after all, so we're not talking brain surgery). The aftermath gets interesting when Broderick makes a stupid mistake and is collared by the cops—and Connery and Hoffman have to decide whether to turn themselves in to help the kid avoid a prison term.

It's going to be tricky explaining that big question that I think the movie leaves hanging. Without revealing too much, here goes. There is a crucial scene in which Connery corners the Chinese-American scientist who had originally hired them to steal the DNA material. The scientist tells him something which, if brought out in open court, would certainly lead to the whole case being seen in a different light. But the movie ignores this new material, and goes in another direction, leaving us patiently waiting for a big courtroom scene that never arrives. They should have either left the scientist out, or dealt with his information.

The closing scenes of the movie are a disappointment for more reasons than one. What happens to Connery is sudden, unprepared, and dramatically unsatisfactory. And then what happens between Hoffman and Broderick seems to belong in a different kind of movie. *Family Business* tries to play it down the middle, when it probably should have jumped in one direction or the other, toward a pure caper, or toward a family drama. The problem with capers and courtrooms is, once evidence is on the table, the audience can hardly think of anything else until it's disposed of.

Fanny and Alexander ★ ★ ★ ★
R, 197 m., 1983

Pernilla Allwin (Fanny Ekdahl), Bertil Guve (Alexander Ekdahl), Jan Malmsjo (Bishop Vergerus), Erland Josephson (Isak Jacobi), Kabi Laretei (Aunt Emma), Gunn Wallgren (Helena Ekdahl), Ewa Froling (Emilie Ekdahl), Gunnar Bjornstrand (Filip Landahl). Directed by Ingmar Bergman and produced by Jorn Donner. Screenplay by Bergman.

There was a time when Ingmar Bergman wanted to make films reflecting the whole of human experience. He asked the big questions about death, sex, and God, and he wasn't afraid of the big, dramatic image, either. Who else (except Woody Allen) has had the temerity to show a man playing chess with Death? Bergman was swinging for the fences in those deliberately big, important films. But he has discovered that a better way to encompass all human experience is to be specific about a small part of it and let the audience draw its own conclusions. In *The Seventh Seal* (1956), he portrayed Death as a symbolic grim reaper. But in *Cries and Whispers* (1973), by showing one particular woman dying painfully while her sisters and her maid stood by helplessly, he said infinitely more about death.

His film *Fanny and Alexander* is one of the most detailed and specific he's ever made, and therefore one of the most universal. It comes directly out of his experiences as a Swede in his mid-sixties who was born into a world of rigid religious belief, grew up in a world of war and turmoil, and is now old enough, wise enough, and resigned enough to develop a sort of philosophical mysticism about life. In its chronology, the film covers only a handful of years. But in its buried implications about life, I believe, it traces the development of Bergman's thought from his school days until the day before yesterday.

Fanny and Alexander is a long film that contains many characters and many events. Very simply: In a Swedish provincial town in the early years of this century, two children are growing up within the bosom of a large, jolly extended family. Their father dies and their mother remarries. Their new stepfather is a stern, authoritarian clergyman who means well but is absolutely incapable of understanding the feelings of others. Escape from his household leads them, by an indirect path, into the life of an old Jewish antique dealer whose life still has room for the mysticism and magic of an earlier time.

Not everything is explained by the end of the film, but everything is reconciled.

Bergman has confessed that a great deal of the movie is autobiographical—if not literally, then in terms of its feelings. He had, for example, a father who was a strict clergyman. But it's too easy to assume the bishop in the movie represents only Bergman's father: Can he not also represent Bergman himself, who is seen within the circle of his collaborators as an authoritarian figure with a tendency to know what is right for everyone else? Bergman has hinted that there's a little of himself, indeed, in *all* the male characters in his movies. Looking for Bergman's autobiography in his characters is one thing. I think we also can see *Fanny and Alexander* as the autobiography of his career. The warm humanism of the early scenes reflects his own beginnings in naturalism. The stern aestheticism of the middle scenes reflects his own middle period, with its obsession with both philosophical and stylistic black-and-white. The last third of the film, like the last third of his career, admits that there are more things in heaven and on Earth than dreamed of in his philosophy.

Fanny and Alexander is a big, exciting, ambitious film—more of a beginning than, as Bergman claims, the summary of his career. If you've followed him on his long trek of discovery, this will feel like a film of resolution. If you're coming fresh to Bergman, it may, paradoxically, seem to burst with the sort of invention we associate with young first-time directors. It's a film for all seasons.

Farewell My Concubine ★ ★ ★ ★
R, 156 m., 1993

Leslie Cheung (Cheng Dieyi), Zhang Fengyi (Duan Xiaolou), Gong Li (Juxian), Lu Qi (Guan Jifa), Ying Da (Na Kun), Ge You (Master Yuan), Li Chun (Xiao Si, Teen-age), Lei Han (Xiao Si, Adult), Tong Di (Old Man Zhang). Directed by Chen Kaige and produced by Hsu Feng. Screenplay by Lilian Lee and Lu Wei.

Farewell My Concubine is two films at once: an epic spanning a half century of modern Chinese history, and a melodrama about life backstage at the famed Peking Opera. The idea of viewing modern China through the eyes of two of the opera's stars would not, at first, seem logical: How could the birth pangs of a developing nation have much in common with the death pangs of an ancient and ritualistic art form? And yet the film flows with such urgency that all its connections

seem logical. And it is filmed with such visual splendor that possible objections are swept aside.

The film opens on a setting worthy of Dickens, as two young orphan boys are inducted into the Peking Opera's harsh, perfectionist training academy. The physical and mental hardships are barely endurable, but they produce, after years, classical performers who are exquisitely trained for their roles.

We meet the delicate young Douzi (Leslie Cheung), who is assigned to the transvestite role of the concubine in a famous traditional opera, and the more masculine Shitou (Zhang Fengyi), who will play the king. Throughout their lives they will be locked into these roles onstage, while their personal relationship somehow survives the upheavals of World War II, the communist takeover of China, and the Cultural Revolution.

Under the stage names of Cheng Dieyi (Leslie Cheung) and Duan Xiaolou (Zhang Fengyi), the two actors become wildly popular with Peking audiences. But they are politically unsophisticated, and Cheng in particular makes unwise decisions during the Japanese occupation, leading to later charges of collaborating with the enemy.

Their personal relationship is equally unsettled. Dieyi, a homosexual, feels great love for Xiaolou, but the "king" doesn't share his feelings, and eventually marries the beautiful prostitute Juxian, played by China's leading actress, Gong Li. Dieyi is resentful and jealous, but during long years of hard times Juxian stands heroically by both men.

That the Peking Opera survives at all during five decades of upheaval is rather astonishing; apparently its royalist and bourgeois origins are balanced against its long history as a Chinese cultural tradition, so that even the Red Chinese accept it in all of its anachronistic glory. What almost does it in, however, is the Cultural Revolution, as shrill young ideologues impose their instant brand of political correctness on the older generations, and characters are forced to denounce one another. Xiaolou even denounces Dieyi as a homosexual, and Dieyi counterattacks by denouncing his friend's wife as a prostitute.

The movie's director is Chen Kaige, who knows about the Cultural Revolution at first hand. Born in 1952, he was sent in 1969 to a rural area to do manual labor; the scenes involving the Peking Opera's youth training programs may owe something to this experience. The son of a filmmaker, he was a Red Guard and a soldier before enrolling in film school, and at one point actually denounced his own father, an act for which he still feels great shame. (The father, sentenced to hard labor for several years, worked with his son as artistic director of this film.)

Farewell My Concubine won the Grand Prix at Cannes in 1993, but Chen Kaige returned home to find his film first shown, then banned, then shown again and banned again in China. His particular offense was to show a suicide taking place in 1977, a year in which, government orthodoxy holds, life in China did not justify such measures. The Chinese authorities were also uneasy about the homosexual aspects in the story.

What is amazing, given the conditions under which the film was made, is the freedom and energy with which it plays. The story is almost unbelievably ambitious, using no less than the entire modern history of China as its backdrop, as the private lives of the characters reflect their changing fortunes: The toast of the nation at one point, they are homeless outcasts at another, and nearly destroyed by their political naïveté more than once. (It is perhaps an unfair quibble that although they must be sixtyish by the end of the story, they look only somewhat older than when they were young men.)

The Peking Opera itself is filmed in lavish detail; the costumes benefit from the rich colors of the world's last surviving three-strip Technicolor lab, in Shanghai, and the backstage intrigues and romances are worthy of a soap opera. Leslie Cheung's concubine is never less than convincing, and his private life—he is essentially raised by the opera as a homosexual whether or not he consents—contains labyrinthine emotional currents. Gong Li, as the prostitute, is sometimes glamorous, sometimes haggard, and always at the mercy of two men whose work together has defined their individual personalities.

The epic is a threatened art form at the movies. Audiences seem to prefer less ambitious, more simpleminded stories, in which the heroes control events, instead of being buffeted by them. *Farewell My Concubine* is a demonstration of how a great epic can function. I was generally familiar with the important moments in modern Chinese history, but this film helped me to feel and imagine what it was like to live in the country during those times. Like such dissimilar films as *Dr. Zhivago* and *A Passage to India*, it took me to another place and time, and made it emotionally comprehensible.

Farewell, My Lovely ★ ★ ★ ★
R, 95 m., 1975

Robert Mitchum (Philip Marlowe), Charlotte Rampling (Velma), John Ireland (Lieutenant Nulty), Sylvia Miles (Mrs. Nulty), Jack O'Halloran (Moose Malloy), Anthony Zerbe (Brunette), Harry Dean Stanton (Billy Rolfe), Walter McGinn (Tommy Ray). Directed by Dick Richards and produced by George Pappas and Jerry Bruckheimer. Screenplay by David Zelag Goodman.

Los Angeles, 1941. A run-down street of seedy shop fronts and blinking neon signs. Music from a lonely horn. The camera pans up to a second-story window of a flophouse. In the window, his hat pushed back, his tie undone, Philip Marlowe lights another cigarette and waits for the cops to arrive. He is ready to tell his story.

These opening shots are so evocative of Raymond Chandler's immortal Marlowe, archetypical private eye, haunting the underbelly of Los Angeles, that if we're Chandler fans we hold our breath. Is the ambience going to be maintained, or will this be another campy rip-off? Half an hour into the movie, we relax. *Farewell, My Lovely* never steps wrong. It is, indeed, the most evocative of all the private-detective movies we have had in the last few years. It is not as great as Roman Polanski's *Chinatown*, which was concerned with larger subjects, but in the genre itself there hasn't been anything this good since Hollywood was doing Philip Marlowe the first time around. One reason is that Dick Richards, the director, takes his material and character absolutely seriously. He is not uneasy with it, as Robert Altman was when he had Elliott Gould flirt with seriousness in *The Long Goodbye*. Richards doesn't hedge his bet.

And neither does Robert Mitchum, in what becomes his definitive performance. Mitchum is one of the great screen presences. He was born to play the weary, cynical, doggedly romantic Marlowe. His voice and his face and the way he lights his cigarette are all exactly right, and seem totally effortless. That's his trademark. In a good Mitchum performance, we are never aware he is acting. And it is only when we measure the distances between his characters that we can see what he is doing. Mitchum is at home on the kinds of streets Philip Marlowe worked: streets of one-room furnished flats and pink stucco hotels, out-of-town newsstands and seedy bars, and always the drowsy commonness of the flatlands leading up to the baroque mansions in the hills and canyons.

Farewell, My Lovely gets all of this just right—Angelo Graham's art direction is a triumph—and then places Mitchum's Marlowe in the center of it and leads him through one of Chandler's tortuous plots. Although everything does finally tie together in this one (as it never did in Chandler's labyrinthine *The Big Sleep*), it doesn't matter that much. What's important is the gallery of characters Marlowe encounters, each grotesque and beautiful in his own way. The most touching is Moose Malloy, played by an ex-prizefighter named Jack O'Halloran. Moose towers over everyone in the film, both in stature and in the immensity of his need. Seven years ago he fell in love with a hooker named Velma and they were going to be married, but something went wrong during a bank job, and Moose took the rap. When he gets out of prison, he hires Marlowe to find his Velma.

Marlowe's quest for Velma, a faded memory from a hopeless love affair, leads him, as we might have known, into a case a lot larger and more important than he could have suspected. There is an odyssey through a lurid whorehouse and a killing in a ghetto bar, and a midnight rendezvous that ends in another death, and always there is Lieutenant Nulty, of the Los Angeles Police Department, trying to figure out why Marlowe winds up attached to so many dead bodies. Richards's approach, with screenplay by David Zelag Goodman, is to start the story at the end with Marlowe trying to explain things to Nulty and then flash back to the beginning and let Marlowe elaborate on the story voice-over. It is a strategy that is often distracting in movies. But not this time, because it borrows from Chandler's own first-person narrative. And it provides great one-liners, as when the elusive Velma (Charlotte Rampling) sizes Marlowe up and down and he says, "She threw me a look I caught in my hip pocket."

Farewell, My Lovely is a great entertainment and a celebration of Robert Mitchum's absolute originality. The day after you view it, you might find yourself quoting lines to friends, which is always the test in these cases, because most of the time private-eye stories have no meaning at all unless it is in the way their heroes behave in the face of the most unsettling revelations about human nature. This time Philip Marlowe behaves very well.

Farewell to the King ★ ★ ★
PG, 113 m., 1989

Nick Nolte (Learoyd), Nigel Havers (Botanist), Frank McRae (Tenga), Gerry Lopez (Gwai), Marilyn Tokuda (Yoo), Choy Chang Wing (Lian), James Fox (Ferguson). Directed by John Milius and produced by Albert S. Ruddy and Andre Morgan. Screenplay by Milius.

The opening image in *Farewell to the King* shows a man walking out on World War II. His lifeboat has been washed ashore on a tropical island somewhere in the Pacific, and while his fellow survivors are captured and executed by the Japanese, he plunges into the jungle, staggering and hallucinating, until he is found by a native tribe. When the movie rejoins his life three years later, he is the king of the tribe, and is trying to steer it clear of any contact with the war.

This image—of the white man deep in the jungle, ruling a tribe—must be a compelling one for John Milius, who wrote and directed *Farewell to the King.* In his screenplay for Francis Coppola's *Apocalypse Now,* Milius created a similar character for Marlon Brando. Learoyd, the character played by Nick Nolte in this film, is like Kurtz, the Brando character: He has gone both AWOL and native, and lives in a jungle fastness, catered to by a tribe that sees him as a sort of god.

There is probably a deep-seated personal impulse at work here. Does Milius imagine his characters shouldering the White Man's Burden, or does he see them escaping a corrupt civilization to live in an unspoiled natural society? With Kurtz, we never knew, but the Nolte character in *Farewell to the King* gladly embraces his new situation and wants to drop out of Western civilization if he can. At a key point in the film, he shows a visiting British officer a secret valley in the heart of the island, where a sort of Shangri-la has grown up, isolated from the corruptions of the outside. He feels it is his mission to protect this sacred place from the Japanese *and* the Allies.

It is tempting to consider the politics of this movie, which waver between benevolent despotism and anthropological zeal. But perhaps Milius really has no message. The spirit of the film seems closer to the work of Conrad or Melville than to contemporary politics: Here is an extraordinary man, the story says, who finds himself in an extraordi-

nary situation and takes advantage of it. I was reminded a little of Van Wyk, the Dutchman in Conrad's *End of the Tether* who runs his corner of the Pacific more or less the way he wants to, and knows enough about his fellow Europeans to keep them at arm's length.

In a film like this, the central performance is crucial, and Nick Nolte is absorbed by the character. Just a few days before seeing *Farewell to the King* I saw Nolte as a painter—a manipulator and player in the New York art world—in the Martin Scorsese segment of *New York Stories.* Now here he was half-naked in the jungle, dandling an infant on his knee. The strength of Nolte as an actor is that he seemed to feel at home in both environments; he was an inhabitant, not a visitor.

The plot, based on a novel by Pierre Schoendoerffer, is much more predictable than the situation. Learoyd, the Nolte character, is a full-blown tribal king by the time we see him again, and the movie bypasses any attempt to show how he won that status, preferring instead to move ahead to a more conventional action scenario. British commandos, led by Nigel Havers, are parachuted onto the island to try to enlist the American and his tribesmen in the war against the Japanese. Learoyd wants nothing to do with them.

"You cannot turn your back on this war," Havers warns him, and sure enough, he is right. Milius then unfolds a more or less predictable series of action scenes in which Learoyd turns into a superhuman fighting machine, blasting countless foes to smithereens before finally announcing, "From this day forward, I will raise my hand against no man." This vow is less impressive than it might have been, since there are few enemies left alive to raise his hand against. And then there is a sequel revealing whether Learoyd realizes his dream of living apart from civilization.

What is most interesting about *Farewell to the King* is its impulse to tell this story at all. It could so easily have become ridiculous, or merely violent, but Milius keeps edging back toward the philosophy of his hero. Learoyd is given several speeches in which he explains why he believes what he believes, and the movie never becomes only an action film. There is a contradiction somewhere, I suppose, in the story of a pacifistic isolationist who kills in order to defend his vision, but what the heck, nobody's perfect.

Farinelli ★ ★ `NEW`
R, 110 m., 1995

Stefano Dionisi (Farinelli/Carlo Broschi), Enrico Lo Verso (Riccardo Broschi), Elsa Zylberstein (Alexandra), Caroline Cellier (Margaret Hunter), Marianne Basler (Countess Mauer), Jacques Boudet (Philip V), Graham Valentine (Prince of Wales), Pier Paolo Capponi (Father). Directed by Gerard Corbiau and produced by Vera Belmont, Linda Gutenberg, Aldo Lado, Dominique Janne, and Stephane Thenoz. Screenplay by Andree and Gerard Corbiau.

Descending from above the stage on a chariot, wearing an elaborate and vaguely Aztecan golden headdress, Farinelli caused women to swoon as he sang operatic arias. He used handkerchiefs to wipe the sweat from his brow, then threw the silks to his audience. He was responsible, one listener tells him, "for my first musical orgasm." He was also responsible, in my opinion, for Tom Jones, Engelbert Humperdinck, and Liberace, whose Vegas acts are the direct descendants of his European concert tours, and for Elvis's late period, as well as David Bowie, Freddie Mercury, and all the other peacocks of rock 'n' roll. He founded a style.

Carlo Broschi (1705–82), known as Farinelli, was the most famous castrato of his age—one of those unfortunate boys whose testicles were removed before puberty, to prevent his sweet, pure voice from ever changing. "The combination of the larynx of a youth and the chest and lungs of a man produced a powerful voice of great range and sound," according to my encyclopedia. But, as a playmate warns him before he is hauled away for the operation, "Your death is in your voice." (At the time, "death" had many meanings, especially in romantic poetry.)

There is something about a sexually ambiguous man that drives some women into a frenzy; his very unavailability is a goad. In *Farinelli,* we see how the singer's irresistible lure was used in a bait-and-switch routine with his untalented brother, Riccardo. Farinelli would seduce a female admirer, and then Riccardo would supply the missing parts.

Was Farinelli happy in this lifestyle? Yes, apparently he was. He was rich, famous, and adored—so idolized, in fact, that he was often willing to allow his artistic ambition to be sidetracked by the romantic and financial needs of his brother. The greatest composers in Europe wanted to write for his voice, but for many years his principal composer was Riccardo, who was no Handel (as Handel himself points out several times in the movie).

Farinelli, one of the 1995 Oscar nominees in the foreign film category, is onto an interesting story, all right, but it leaves us feeling, like some of Farinelli's lovers, that something is missing. What, exactly, is the point of the story? To depict an interesting lifetime? It does. To tell us something meaningful about music, and about how it was taken so seriously that for more than a century few people seriously challenged the practice of castration? Here it is less successful, confusing music with fame, fame with sexuality.

All of the elements are in place, including the long-running feud between Riccardo and Handel (who once told him, "Without your brother, you are nothing but silence"). But while a film like *Amadeus* was able to create real poignancy in the mixed envy and admiration a lesser composer felt for a genius, *Farinelli* never convinces us that Riccardo really understands how bad he is—and Farinelli never understands how good Handel is. There should be some kind of moment of musical epiphany, I think, to show music not as a profession but as an opening to the sublime.

In real life (the *Columbia Encyclopedia* reports), Farinelli spent from 1737 to 1759 as the official court singer to Philip V of Spain: "His sole duty was to sing the same four songs every night to the king, from whom he received an astronomical fee." Here again, Farinelli predicted the Vegas superstars, who essentially sing their same old chestnuts night after night, year after year, belting them out as if songs had genetically imprinted themselves upon their cortexes. There is a kind of death in life in such an existence, in being rewarded so well for doing endlessly what one, perhaps, would rather not be doing at all. How does Don Ho feel as he cranks up for "Tiny Bubbles"?

Note: I am informed by Melissa Maier of the Multnomah County Library in Portland, Oregon, that a recording exists called "The Last Castrato," featuring Alessandro Moreschi (1858–1922), who sang for the Vatican. "It is," she says, "an eerie sound." In Farinelli *computerized techniques are used to blend female and male voices to produce the singing voice. It is eerie, too; a mechanical production in which the singer does not seem to sing so much as play host to his voice.*

Fatal Attraction ★ ★ ½
R, 120 m., 1987

Michael Douglas (Dan Gallagher), Glenn Close (Alex Forrest), Anne Archer (Beth Gallagher), Ellen Hamilton Latzen (Ellen), Stuart Pankin (Jimmy), Ellen Foley (Hildy), Fred Gwynne (Arthur). Directed by Adrian Lyne and produced by Stanley R. Jaffe and Sherry Lansing. Screenplay by James Dearden.

Fatal Attraction is a spellbinding psychological thriller, and could have been a great movie if the filmmakers had not thrown character and plausibility to the winds in the last act to give us their version of a grown-up *Friday the 13th*.

Because the good things in the movie, including the performances, are so very good, it's a shame that the film's potential for greatness was so blatantly compromised. The movie is so right for so long that you can almost feel the moment when the script goes "click" and sells out.

The story stars Michael Douglas as a lawyer who has been happily married for nine years, has a six-year-old daughter, loves his wife, and has no particular problems on the day when he meets an intriguing blonde (Glenn Close) at a business party. She makes it her business to get to know him, and one weekend when Douglas's wife and daughter are out of town visiting his in-laws, he invites the blonde out to dinner.

She finds him willing to be seduced, and they have wild, passionate sex. Their couplings take place in a freight elevator, on the kitchen sink, and, I think, in bed; the film was directed by Adrian *(9½ Weeks)* Lyne, whose ideas of love and genital acrobatics seem more or less equivalent.

Douglas has made it clear that he's a happily married man and that he sees their meeting as a one-night stand ("Two adults who saw an opportunity and took advantage of it"), but Close doesn't see it that way. The moment sex is over for her, capture begins, and she starts a series of demands on Douglas's time and attention.

He tells her to get lost. She grows pathological. She visits him at the office, calls him at home in the middle of the night, throws acid on his car, visits his wife under the pretext of buying their apartment. Desperate to keep his secret and preserve his happy marriage, Douglas tries to reason with her, threaten her, and even hide from her, but she is im-

placable. (And you should read no further if you plan to view the movie—or perhaps, come to think of it, you should.)

The early and middle passages of the movie are handled with convincing psychological realism; James Dearden's dialogue sounds absolutely right, especially the way he allows the Close character to bait her hook with honeyed come-ons and then set it with jealousy, possessiveness, and finally guilt (after she says, inevitably, that she is pregnant). With the exception of the silly sex scenes, *Fatal Attraction* never steps wrong until its third act—and then it steps very wrong.

First, let me suggest how I hoped the movie would continue. Having created a believable and interesting marriage between Michael Douglas and Anne Archer (who is wonderful as his wife), and having drawn Glenn Close as a terrifying and yet always plausible other woman, I hoped the film would continue to follow its psychological exploration through to the end.

I wanted, for example, to hear a good talk between Douglas and Archer, in which truth was told and the strength of the marriage was tested. I wanted to see more of the inner workings of Close's mind. I wanted to know more about how Douglas really felt about the situation; although he grows to hate Close, is he really completely indifferent to the knowledge that she carries his child?

The movie does not explore any of those avenues, although the filmmakers clearly have the intelligence to do so. Instead, the last third of the movie collapses into pathetic melodrama. The big scene of truth between Douglas and Archer is short-changed and feels unfinished. There is a pathetic sequence in which Close captures their daughter and scares her with a roller-coaster ride, while a frantic Archer gets in a car crash and breaks her arm. Give me a break.

And then there is the horror movie conclusion, complete with the unforgivable *Friday the 13th* cliché that the villain is never *really* dead. The conclusion, by the way, operates on the premise that Douglas cares absolutely nothing for his unborn child.

Fatal Attraction was produced by Stanley R. Jaffe and Sherry Lansing, and it seems to repeat a pattern for them. In 1984 they made *Firstborn*, with Teri Garr as a divorced mother who falls in love with Peter Weller as a man who is very wrong for her family. The first two-thirds of that film are also psychologically sound and dramatically fascinating, and then it degenerates into a canned formula of violence and an idiotic chase scene. Now they throw away the ending of *Fatal Attraction*. What's the matter here? Do they lack the courage to follow their convictions through to the end? They seem to have a knack for finding thoughtful, sensitive screenplays about interesting adults, and then adding gruesome Hollywood horror formulas to them. *Fatal Attraction* clearly had the potential to be a great movie. I walked out feeling cheated and betrayed.

Father of the Bride ★ ★ ★
PG, 105 m., 1991

Steve Martin (George Banks), Diane Keaton (Nina Banks), Kimberly Williams (Annie Banks), Kieran Culkin (Matty Banks), George Newbern (Bryan MacKenzie), Martin Short (Franck Eggelhoffer). Directed by Charles Shyer and produced by Nancy Meyers, Carol Baum, and Howard Rosenman. Screenplay by Frances Goodrich, Albert Hackett, Meyers, and Shyer.

The most surprising discovery audiences are making about Steve Martin at this stage of his career is that he is a warm actor—warm, and yet not ingratiating. My image of Martin, formed from his stage persona and his early movies, was of a chilly wise guy of undeniable intelligence but little empathy. And yet look at his best recent screen roles, in the movies *All of Me, Roxanne, Parenthood, L.A. Story, Father of the Bride,* and *Housesitter.* He's one of the most empathetic men on the screen.

In *Father of the Bride,* his character is inspired by a 1950 Spencer Tracy role, and it's fair to say he is as likable as Tracy. Perhaps more to the point, he plays a role much like the one played by Alan Alda in *Betsy's Wedding,* and although Alda has made a career out of playing nice guys and usually does it convincingly, I liked Martin better.

The screenplay is predictable, and if you've seen the trailer you have, in some sense, seen the movie. The screenplay is based on confirmations, not surprises; everything we think will happen, does. In that sense it is like a successful wedding. Martin and Diane Keaton play the rather amazingly happily married parents of a young woman (Kimberly Williams) and a small boy (Kieran Culkin, of the Culkin child dynasty). Their daughter goes off to study in Europe for a semester, and comes home glowing with joy and announcing her engagement. The father

of the bride is not pleased by the prospect of losing his little girl. He is even less pleased when he finds out what the wedding will cost.

A recent newspaper story about the escalating costs of weddings told of a father who offered his daughter a choice: a nice ceremony, or a condo. This is not far off. The wedding in *Father of the Bride* is priced out at $250 a head, and, of course, the bare minimum guest list initially comes to something like six hundred people. At this point, in one of the movie's funniest scenes, Martin and Keaton join Williams in going through their card file, seeing who they can leave out. ("He died? That's great!")

Martin Short has a hilarious star character role as Franck Eggelhoffer, the wedding coordinator, who speaks with an accent that seems to be part central European and part nasal congestion, and who agrees wholeheartedly that the wedding should not be too fancy, although his definition of moderation somehow includes three live swans. He handles Martin almost with pity; from long experience, he knows what the father is in for, and forgives him even the tuxedo, which Martin insists is a black Armani and the coordinator has good reason to believe is dark blue polyester.

The best moments in the movie are not, however, the passages of obvious comedy (I didn't much go for the extended set piece that involved Martin visiting his in-laws' bathroom and ending up in the swimming pool). This is a movie with heart, and there are little moments in it when Martin is deeply moved by the fact that this perfect creature he brought into the world is now going to start a family of her own.

There is, for example, a touching moment when he touches his heart as if it will burst. Another moment when Keaton gently corrects his original vision of the wedding ceremony (lots of balloons in the back yard, and Martin standing at the barbecue grill wearing a chef's hat). And the poignancy of a moment when Martin realizes his daughter now listens to her fiancé, not her old dad, for helpful suggestions.

Father of the Bride is not as ambitious or as insightful as *Parenthood,* the film it should probably be linked with in Martin's career. Its truths are more sweet and gentle. But it's one of those movies with a lot of smiles and laughter in it, and a good feeling all the way through. The movie was directed by Charles Shyer and produced by Nancy Meyers, and

their previous credits include two films in the same vein, *Irreconcilable Differences* and *Baby Boom* (which starred Keaton as a career woman who suddenly finds herself a mother). There are no great revelations or stunning insights in their films. Just everyday life, warmly observed.

Fearless ★ ★ ★
R, 124 m., 1993

Jeff Bridges (Max Klein), Isabella Rossellini (Laura Klein), Rosie Perez (Carla Rodrigo), Tom Hulce (Brillstein), John Turturro (Dr. Bill Perlman), Benicio Del Toro (Manny Rodrigo). Directed by Peter Weir and produced by Paula Weinstein and Mark Rosenberg. Screenplay by Rafael Yglesias.

Is this, I wonder, the way it would be? The airplane has lost hydraulic pressure and is falling through the sky. Some of the passengers scream, others pray, some hold hands and exchange words of love. One man seems serenely apart from the crowd. He walks up the aisle to a small boy who is traveling alone, and tries to comfort him. The man believes his life is coming to an end, but he is at peace with that fact.

Everyone who has flown has pictured the possibility of an unsuccessful flight. The 1992 movie *Alive* did a masterful special-effects job of showing what might happen on an airplane crash-landing onto a snow field. Now *Fearless* is eerily convincing in its portrait of the last moments of a flight, and its aftermath. For there is an aftermath. Not everyone is killed, and the man who is so serene is one of the survivors.

His name is Max Klein (Jeff Bridges). He is a hero, helping save the lives of others after the crash. Then he walks away from it and checks into a motel. In a sense, he is walking away from his entire life. All of the worries and cares, the hopes and responsibilities have been wiped away.

But it is not that simple. The FBI finds him, and then he returns home to his wife (Isabella Rossellini), and the airline provides him with a psychiatrist (John Turturro), and there is a lawyer (Tom Hulce) who thinks there may be big money for Max, and for the widow of his business partner, who was killed in the crash. "Did you *see* him die?" the lawyer asks. "That could be worth extra money. . . ."

One person understands Max's peculiar state of mind, in these weird days of his second chance at life. Her name is Carla

Rodrigo (Rosie Perez), and she also survived the crash. They feel a bond through having survived an experience that is impossible to describe for anyone who was not there. They grow so close that at times it seems they will fall in love, or have an affair, but finally it isn't that kind of closeness. Meanwhile, Max's wife tries to understand, but grows frustrated by his distant behavior. Is it her fault that her husband nearly died? Or is still alive?

Fearless, directed by Peter Weir *(Witness, Dead Poets Society)*, was written by Rafael Yglesias, and based on his novel. It is unusual for being essentially philosophical and introspective, rather than romantic; it doesn't allow either the troubled marriage or the possible affair to distract from its real subject, which is the fragility of everyday life.

Jeff Bridges, who despite his Oscar nominations has never really been recognized for the subtle depth of his acting, is a good choice for the role of Max. He plays him matter-of-factly. There are no mystical overtones or gratuitous emotional displays in the performance, just the serious comings and goings of a man who has escaped death by such a slender chance that all of life's assumptions have come into question.

Rosie Perez, who played Woody Harrelson's girlfriend in *White Men Can't Jump* and Marisa Tomei's best friend in *Untamed Heart*, is emerging as one of the great new originals in the movies. Her tough Brooklyn accent just a little softened this time, she strikes a no-nonsense, in-your-face note that makes her character quirky and unique. It's an example of imaginative casting; this same crash survivor could have been soulful, or neurotic, or weepy. By making her colorful and outspoken, the filmmakers create an unexpected dynamic; we see that she isn't Rossellini's rival for her husband's heart, but for his soul.

Fearless is like a short story that shines a bright light, briefly, into a corner where you usually do not look. It makes you realize how routine life can become; how it is actually possible to be bored despite the fact that a universe has evolved for aeons in order to provide us with the five senses by which we perceive it. If we ever really fully perceived the cosmic situation we are in, we would drop unconscious, I imagine, from shock. That is a little of what *Fearless* is about.

Fear of a Black Hat ★ ★ ★
R, 87 m., 1994

Larry B. Scott (Tasty-Taste), Mark Christopher Lawrence (Tone-Def), Rusty Cundieff (Ice Cold), Kasi Lemmons (Nina Blackburn). Directed by Rusty Cundieff and produced by Darin Scott. Screenplay by Cundieff.

The world of rap music is ripe for a satirical bashing, and *Fear of a Black Hat* is often right on target. It treats rap with the same droll dubiousness that *This is Spinal Tap* provided for heavy metal. It's not as fearless and sharp-edged as it could be, but it provides a lot of laughs, and barbecues a few sacred cows. After rap was marshmallow-bombed by *CB4* a year ago, this movie at least knows how to hit where it hurts.

The movie is so similar in approach to *Spinal Tap* it could almost be considered homage. It pretends to be a documentary about a rap group named NWH (Niggaz With Hats). The producer, a pretty walking sound bite named Nina Blackburn (Kasi Lemmons), comes from a much different world than the NWH band members (or thinks she does). Her questions are softballs, lobbed underhand to the band members, who reply with clichés and hyperbole so lovingly manufactured they're sometimes hard to tell from the statements of real rappers.

Rap music is faced with an essentially comic paradox, which is that the art form must find a way to safely exist in the mass media while at the same time projecting angry, antisocial attitudes. It's a neat trick to denunciate society and collect Grammys with the same album. This leads to some fancy verbal footwork in *Fear of a Black Hat*, as Ice Cold (Rusty Cundieff), the band's most articulate spokesman, explains how their song "Kill Whitey" was misunderstood and unfairly criticized as racist, when in fact it was a subtle artistic statement.

Cundieff, who wrote and directed the movie, has some inspired riffs as he attempts to explain NWH's material. He accounts for the group's name by rewriting history on the spot, explaining that in the days of slavery, field hands were not allowed to wear hats in the sun, and thus were too tired at the end of the day to revolt. Give them hats, and a revolution was born.

The NWH band members are surrounded by toadying whites, including a series of managers. (They always have white managers, they explain, because their man-

agers are always being killed, and so it would be wrong to subject a brother to such a risk.) Record company executives kowtow to them. And yet the band is going downhill with dizzying speed, and at one gig makes it onto the marquee only as "Guest Artist."

A truly uncompromising satire on this subject could probably not be filmed at this time, I suppose. You can almost feel *Fear of a Black Hat* pulling back in sensitive areas, going so far and no further. Nor does the movie really have much to say about the music itself—music which, like the heavy metal of *Spinal Tap*, takes itself more seriously than anyone with common sense is likely to take it (rap and heavy metal are both more about attitudes than about melody). But the movie is funny and fresh, and filled with wicked little moments like the uneasy meeting of five or six rappers who all have "Ice" in their names.

Fellini's Roma ★ ★ ★ ★
R, 128 m., 1973

Featuring Peter Gonzales, Stefano Majore, Britta Barnes, Pia de Doses, Fiona Florence, Marno Maitland, Giovannoli Renato, Anna Magnani, Gore Vidal, and Federico Fellini. Directed by Federico Fellini. Screenplay by Bernardino Zapponi and Fellini.

Federico Fellini first included his name in the title of one of his movies with *Fellini Satyricon* (1969), and then for legal reasons: A quickie Italian version of the *Satyricon* being palmed off in international film markets as the real thing. Once having savored the notion, however, Fellini found it a good one, and so we have *Fellini's Roma*, which was followed by *Fellini Casanova*.

The name in the title doesn't seem conceited or affected, as it might from another director (*Peckinpah's Albuquerque?*). This *is* Fellini's Rome and nobody else's, just as all of his films since *La Dolce Vita* have been autobiographical musings and confessions from the most personal—and the best—director of his time. Any connection with a real city on the map of Italy is libelous. Fellini's Rome gets its suburbs trimmed when he goes for a haircut.

The movie isn't a documentary, although sometimes he lets it look like one. It's a rambling essay, meant to feel like free association. There's a very slight narrative thread, about a young man named Fellini who leaves the little town of Rimini and comes to the great city and is overwhelmed by its pleasures of body and spirit. He moves into a mad boarding house that would make a movie all by itself; he dines with his neighbors in great outdoor feasts when the summer heat drives everyone into the piazzas; he attends a raucous vaudeville show and he visits his first whorehouse . . . and then his second.

This material, filmed with loving attention to period detail, exists by itself in the movie; there's no effort to link the naive young Fellini with the confident genius who appears elsewhere in the movie. It's as if Fellini, the consummate inventor of fantasies, didn't grow out of his young manhood—he created it from scratch.

The autobiographical material is worked in between pseudo-documentary scenes that contain some of the most brilliant images Fellini has ever devised. The movie opens with a monumental Roman traffic jam that, typically, becomes important because Fellini has deigned to photograph it. He swoops above it on a crane, directing his camera, his movie, and the traffic. A blinding rainstorm turns everything into a hellish apparition, and then there's a final shot, held just long enough to make its point, of the autos jammed around the Colosseum.

The image is both perfect and natural; as someone commented about Fellini's 8½, his movies are filled with images, and they're all obvious. If Bergman is the great introvert of the movies, forever probing more and more deeply, Fellini is the joyous exponent of surfaces and excess, of letting more hang out than there is.

The obviousness of his images gives his movies a curious kind of clarity; he isn't reaching for things to say, but finding ways to say the same things more memorably. The decadence of Rome has been one of his favorite subjects throughout his career, and who could forget Anita Ekberg in the fountain, or the Mass procession at dawn, in *La Dolce Vita*?

But in *Roma*, he is even more direct, more stark: An expedition to inspect progress on the Rome subway system suddenly becomes transcendent when workmen break through to an underground crypt from pre-Christian times. The frescoes on the walls are so clear they might have been painted yesterday—until the air of the modern city touches them.

Rome, the eternal city, has historically been as carnal as it has been sacred. Fellini won't settle for one or the other; he uses scenes of carnality to symbolize a blessed state, and vice versa. Nothing could be more eternal, more patient, and more resigned than Fellini's use of a weary prostitute standing beside a highway outside Rome. She is tall, huge-bosomed, garishly made up, and her feet are tired. She stands among the broken stones of the Roman Empire, expecting nothing, hoping for nothing.

The prostitute, so often used as a symbol of fleeting moments and insubstantial experiences, becomes eternal; and the Church, always the symbol of the unchanging, the rock, becomes temporal. In his most audacious sequence, Fellini gives us an "ecclesiastical fashion show," with roller-skating priests, and nuns whose habits are made of blinking neon lights. What is unreal, and where is the real? Fellini doesn't know, and he seems to believe that Rome has never known. Rome has simply endured, waiting in the hope of someday finding out.

Fellini's Roma was attacked in some circles as an example of Fellini coasting on his genius. I find this point of view completely incomprehensible. Critics who would force Fellini back into traditional narrative films are missing the point; Fellini isn't just giving us a lot of flashy scenes, he's building a narrative that has a city for its protagonist instead of a single character.

The only sly thing is that the city isn't Rome—it's Fellini, disguised in bricks, mortar, and ruins. Fellini, who cannot find his way between the flesh and the spirit, who cannot find the connection between his youth and his greatness, and whose gift is to make movies where everything is obvious and nothing is simple. That was the dilemma that the Fellini character faced in *8½*, when he couldn't make sense of his life, and it's the dilemma we all face every day, isn't it?

Ferris Bueller's Day Off ★ ★ ★
PG-13, 103 m., 1986

Matthew Broderick (Ferris), Alan Ruck (Cameron Frye), Mia Sara (Sloane), Jeffrey Jones (Ed Rooney), Cindy Pickett (Mrs. Bueller), Jennifer Grey (Katie Bueller), Lyman Ward (Mr. Bueller), Edie McClurg (Secretary), Charlie Sheen (Young Punk). Directed by John Hughes and produced by Hughes and Tom Jacobson. Screenplay by Hughes.

Here is one of the most innocent movies in a long time, a sweet, warmhearted comedy about a kid who skips school so he can help his best friend win some self-respect. The therapy he has in mind includes a day's visit to Chicago, and after we've seen the Sears Tower and a parade down Dearborn Street, the Art Institute and the Board of Trade, architectural landmarks and lunch on Rush Street, and a game at Wrigley Field, we've got to concede that the city and state film offices have done their job. If *Ferris Bueller's Day Off* fails on every other level, at least it works as a travelogue.

It does, however, work on at least a few other levels. The movie stars Matthew Broderick as Ferris, a bright kid from the North Shore who fakes an illness so he can spend a day in town with his best friend, Cameron (Alan Ruck). At first, it seems as if skipping school is all he has in mind—especially after he talks Cameron into borrowing his dad's antique red Ferrari, a car the father loves more than Cameron himself.

The body of the movie is a lighthearted excursion through the Loop, including a German-American Day parade in which Ferris leaps aboard a float, grabs a microphone, and starts singing "Twist and Shout" while the polka band backs him up. The kids fake their way into a fancy restaurant for lunch, spend some time gawking at the masterpieces in the Art Institute, and then go out to Wrigley Field, where, of course, they are late and have to take left-field seats (the movie gets that detail right; it would be too much to hope that the kids could arrive in the third inning and find seats in the bleachers).

There is one great, dizzying moment when the kids visit the top of the Sears Tower and lean forward and press their foreheads against the glass, and look straight down at the tiny cars and little specks of life far below, and begin to talk about their lives. And that introduces, subtly, the buried theme of the movie, which is that Ferris wants to help Cameron gain self-respect in the face of his father's materialism.

Ferris is, in fact, a bit of a preacher. "Life goes by so fast," he says, "that if you don't stop and look around, you might miss it." He's sensitive to the hurt inside his friend's heart, as Cameron explains how his dad has cherished and restored the red Ferrari and given it a place of honor in the house—a place denied to Cameron.

Ferris Bueller was directed by John Hughes, the philosopher of adolescence, whose credits include *Sixteen Candles*, *The Breakfast Club*, and *Pretty in Pink*. In all of his films, adults are strange, distant creatures, who love their teen-agers, but fail completely to understand them. That's the case here, all right: All of the adults, including a bumbling high school dean (Jeffrey Jones) are dim-witted and one-dimensional. And the movie's solutions to Cameron's problems are pretty simplistic. But the film's heart is in the right place, and *Ferris Bueller* is slight, whimsical, and sweet.

A Few Good Men ★ ★ ½
R, 130 m., 1992

Tom Cruise (Lt. J.G. Daniel Kaffee), Jack Nicholson (Col. Nathan R. Jessep), Demi Moore (Lt. Cmdr. JoAnne Galloway), Kevin Bacon (Capt. Jack Ross), Kiefer Sutherland (Lt. Jonathan Kendrick), Kevin Pollak (Lt. Sam Weinberg), Wolfgang Bodison (Lance Cpl. Harold Dawson), James Marshall (Pfc. Lowden Downey). Directed by Rob Reiner and produced by David Brown, Reiner, and Andrew Scheinman. Screenplay by Aaron Sorkin.

Rob Reiner's *A Few Good Men* is one of those movies that tells you what it's going to do, does it, and then tells you what it did. It doesn't think the audience is very bright. There is a scene in the film that is absolutely wrong. In it, a lawyer played by Tom Cruise previews his courtroom strategy to his friends. The strategy then works as planned—which means that an element of surprise is missing from the most important moment in the movie, and the key scene by Jack Nicholson is undermined, robbed of suspense, and made inevitable.

That's a shame, because in many ways this is a good film, with the potential to be even better than that. The flaws are mostly at the screenplay level; the film doesn't make us work, doesn't allow us to figure out things for ourselves, is afraid we'll miss things if they're not spelled out.

The story is based on fact, as transmuted into a Broadway play by Aaron Sorkin. A marine at the Guantanamo Naval Air Station in Cuba dies after a hazing incident. Two young marines are charged with the death, but a nosy navy legal ace in Washington (Demi Moore) suspects there's more to the story and wants to investigate. She's prodded by her own superior to assign a lazy navy lawyer (Cruise) to the case, perhaps because he has an unblemished record of settling out of court, and can be counted on to handle the case without generating public embarrassment.

After Moore and Cruise meet with the ac-cused young marines, she realizes they have a sticky case on their hands, because the un-written marine code means that the two won't talk, even to save themselves. One of them, a black kid played by Wolfgang Bodi-son, is so fiercely proud of the corps that he would rather go to prison for years. The other, a rather dim and easily impressed white farm boy, goes along.

Cruise is all for settling the case out of court and getting back to his beloved softball games. Moore won't let him. A third friend, played by Kevin Pollak, joins in strategy ses-sions as they gather evidence that eventually leads to a disturbing conclusion: Although hazing is officially against the law and ma-rine policy, the Guantanamo commander, a crusty old dog played by Jack Nicholson, may have tacitly approved the attack on the dead marine.

The movie's setup scenes have good en-ergy to them. Cruise is well cast and effective here as an untried lieutenant, the son of a great man, who has to be taught to take his job seriously and live up to his heritage. Demi Moore is attractive and determined as his superior, who tries to teach him.

Given decades of Hollywood convention, we might reasonably expect romance to blos-som between them, providing a few gratu-itous love scenes before the courtroom fi-nale, but no: They're strictly business—so much so that it seems a little odd that these two good-looking, unmarried young people don't feel any mutual attraction. I have a friend, indeed, who intuits that the Demi Moore character was originally conceived of as a man, and got changed into a woman for Broadway and Hollywood box office rea-sons, without ever quite being rewritten into a woman.

Everything leads up, in any event, to the courtroom scene, which concludes the movie, with Kevin Bacon playing the prosecutor as-signed to convict the two young marines. We have already met the Jack Nicholson charac-ter in Cuba, where he is particularly good at sexist verbal brutality, which he aims espe-cially at Moore. We know he will turn up again, and he does, in a denouement that would have had greater power if the movie didn't telegraph it.

What happens is that the movie brings us to the brink of a courtroom breakthrough, and then we get the scene that undermines everything, as Cruise explains to his friends what he hopes to do, how he hopes to do it, and how he thinks it will work. When Nich-olson's big courtroom scene develops, we re-alize with sinking hearts that it is following the movie's scenario. That robs us of plea-sure two ways: (1) We are not allowed the pleasure of discovering Cruise's strategy for ourselves, and (2) Nicholson's behavior seems scripted and inevitable, and is robbed of shock value.

The movie is reduced then, to a lesser pleasure, that of watching good actors do good work. Nicholson is always fun to watch, as he barks and snarls and improvises new obscenities. Cruise is an effective contrast, as the immature young officer who discovers himself. Wolfgang Bodison, the stubborn defendant, gives the most interesting perfor-mance in the movie, because we can see the battle going on inside, and the movie allows it to happen almost as a separate scenario. But the movie doesn't quite make it, because it never convinces us that the drama is hap-pening while we watch it; it's like the defense team sneaked an advance look at the script.

Field of Dreams ★ ★ ★
PG, 107 m., 1989

Kevin Costner (Ray Kinsella), Amy Madigan (Annie Kinsella), Gaby Hoffman (Karin Kinsella), Ray Liotta (Shoeless Joe Jackson), Timothy Busfield (Mark), James Earl Jones (Terence Mann), Burt Lancaster (Dr. "Moon-light" Graham), Frank Whaley (Archie Graham), Dwier Brown (John Kinsella). Directed by Phil Alden Robinson and produced by Lawrence Gordon and Charles Gordon. Screenplay by Robinson.

The farmer is standing in the middle of a cornfield when he hears the voice for the first time: "If you build it, he will come." He looks around and doesn't see anybody. The voice speaks again, soft and confidential: "If you build it, he will come." Sometimes you can get too much sun, out there in a hot Iowa cornfield in the middle of the season. But this isn't a case of sunstroke.

Up until the farmer (Kevin Costner) starts hearing voices, *Field of Dreams* is a com-pletely sensible film about a young couple who want to run a family farm in Iowa. Ray and Annie Kinsella (Costner and Amy Madigan) have tested the fast track and had enough of it, and they enjoy sitting on the porch and listening to the grass grow. When the voice speaks for the first time, the farmer is baf-fled, and so was I: Could this be one of those religious pictures where a voice tells the humble farmer where to build the cathedral?

It's a religious picture, all right, but the religion is baseball. And when he doesn't understand the spoken message, Ray Kinsella is granted a vision of a baseball diamond, right there in his cornfield. If he builds it, the voice seems to promise, Joe Jackson will come and play on it—Shoeless Joe, who was a member of the infamous 1919 Black Sox team but protested until the day he died that he played the best he could.

As *Field of Dreams* developed this fantasy, I found myself being willingly drawn into it. Movies are often so timid these days, so afraid to take flights of the imagination, that there is something grand and brave about a movie where a voice tells a farmer to build a baseball diamond so that Shoeless Joe Jackson can materialize out of the cornfield and hit a few fly balls. This is the kind of movie Frank Capra might have directed and James Stewart might have starred in—a movie about dreams.

It is important not to tell too much about the plot. (I was grateful I knew nothing about the movie when I went to see it, but the ads gave away the Shoeless Joe angle.) Let it be said that Annie Kinsella supports her husband's vision, and that he finds it necessary to travel east to Boston so he can enlist the support of a famous writer (James Earl Jones) who has disappeared from sight, and north to Minnesota to talk to what remains of a doctor (Burt Lancaster) who never got the chance to play with the pros.

The movie sensibly never tries to make the slightest explanation for the strange events that happen after the diamond is constructed. There is, of course, the usual business about how the bank thinks the farmer has gone haywire and wants to foreclose on his mortgage (the Capra and Stewart movies always had evil bankers in them). But there is not a corny, stupid payoff at the end. Instead, the movie depends on a poetic vision to make its point.

The director, Phil Alden Robinson, and the writer, W.P. Kinsella, are dealing with stuff that's close to the heart (it can't be a coincidence that the author and the hero have the same last name). They love baseball, and they think it stands for an earlier, simpler time when professional sports were still games and not industries. There is a speech in this movie about baseball that is so simple and true that it is heartbreaking. And the whole attitude toward the players reflects that attitude. Why do they come back from the great beyond and materialize here in this

cornfield? Not to make any kind of vast, earth-shattering statement, but simply to hit a few and field a few, and remind us of a good and innocent time.

It is very tricky to act in a movie like this; there is always the danger of seeming ridiculous. Kevin Costner and Amy Madigan create such a grounded, believable married couple that one of the themes of the movie is the way love means sharing your loved one's dreams. Jones and Lancaster create small, sharp character portraits—two older men who have taken the paths life offered them, but never forgotten what baseball represented to them in their youth.

Field of Dreams will not appeal to grinches and grouches and realists. It is a delicate movie, a fragile construction of one goofy fantasy after another. But it has the courage to be about exactly what it promises. "If you build it, he will come." And he does.

52 Pick-Up ★ ★ ★ ½
R, 111 m., 1986

Roy Scheider (Harry Mitchell), Ann-Margret (Barbara Mitchell), Vanity (Doreen), John Glover (Alan Raimy), Clarence Williams III (Bobby Shy), Lonny Chapman (Jim O'Boyle), Kelly Preston (Cini), Doug McClure (Mark Averson). Directed by John Frankenheimer and produced by Menahem Golan and Yorum Globus. Screenplay by Elmore Leonard and John Steppling.

The old golden-age Warner Brothers crime dramas knew something that most modern movies have forgotten: Heroes are great, but a movie is only as good as its villain. John Frankenheimer's *52 Pick-Up* provides us with the best, most reprehensible villain of 1986, and uses his vile charm as the starting point for a surprisingly good film.

The villain's name is Raimy, and he is played by John Glover as a charming blackmailer with the looks of an aging British juvenile and a conscience with parts on order. He tries to pull a slick job on a rich businessman named Harry (Roy Scheider). He shows him videotapes of an affair Harry is having with a topless dancer. He wants $110,000.

Harry thinks it over, decides not to pay, and confesses everything to his wife, Barbara (Ann-Margret). She is very hurt, and in a scene of powerful understatement she says she had guessed the truth for a long time, but she just doesn't know why he had to tell her. Then Raimy turns up with another video-

tape. This one shows the topless dancer being murdered with Harry's gun.

This plot is not startlingly original (although there are some unexpected developments later in the film). What makes it special is the level at which it is told. The screenplay is based on an Elmore Leonard novel, and retains Leonard's gift for terse, colorful dialogue. It also isolates the key ingredient in Leonard's best novels, which is the sight of a marginal character being pushed far beyond his capacity to cope. In *52 Pick-Up*, there are actually three such characters, and by the end of the movie they are all desperately confused and frightened.

One is Raimy, a well-dressed sleazebag who makes porno movies and is capable of cold-blooded murder but caves in completely at the thought of his own destruction. One is Harry, an ordinary amoral businessman who rises to the challenge and figures out a way to outsmart his blackmailers by using their own character defects against them. The third is a sweaty little guy named Leo (Robert Trebor), who works for Raimy and went along with the crime but, holy God, never figured anyone was actually going to get hurt.

The problem with so many action adventures is that nobody in the movies ever seems scared enough. People are getting killed in every other scene, and they stay cool. If the movies were like real life and this kind of torture and murder were going on, everybody would be throwing up every five minutes—like they do in John D. MacDonald's novels. *52 Pick-Up* creates that sense of hopelessness and desperation, and it does it with those three performances—three guys who are in way over their heads, and know it all too well.

There are three other good performances in the movie, by Ann-Margret, Vanity, and Clarence Williams III (as a black pimp who is a lot more experienced about violence and death than his cheerful white partners). Is it still necessary to be surprised when Ann-Margret is good in a role, as if she were still making *Viva Las Vegas*? She has grown into a dependable serious actress, and here she does a delicate job of finding the line between anger at what her husband has done and pride in how he is trying to fix it. Vanity has a smaller role, as a prostitute with crucial information, and she does what all good character actors can do—she gives us the sense that she's fresh from intriguing off-screen action.

The story of *52 Pick-Up* is basically revenge melodrama. No thriller fan is going to be very astonished by what happens. What matters is the energy level, and the density of detail in the performances. This is a well-crafted movie by a man who knows how to hook the audience with his story—it's John Frankenheimer's best work in years. And if we can sometimes predict what the characters will do, there's the fascination of seeing them behave like unique and often very weird individuals; they aren't clones. I have gotten to the point where the one thing I know about most thrillers is that I will not be thrilled. *52 Pick-Up* blind-sided me.

Firefox ★ ★ ★ ½
PG, 136 m., 1982

Clint Eastwood (Mitchell Gant), Freddie Jones (Kenneth Aubrey), David Huffman (Buckholz), Warren Clarke (Pavel Upensky), Ronald Lacey (Semelovsky), Kenneth Colley (Colonel Kontarsky), Stefan Schnabel (First Secretary). Directed and produced by Clint Eastwood. Screenplay by Alex Lasker and Wendell Wellman.

Clint Eastwood's *Firefox* is a slick, muscular thriller that combines espionage with science fiction. The movie works like a well-crafted machine, and it's *about* a well-crafted machine. The *Firefox* of the title is a top-secret Russian warplane capable of flying six times the speed of sound while remaining invisible on radar. Eastwood's mission, if he chooses to accept it: Infiltrate the Soviet Union disguised as a Las Vegas drug smuggler, and then steal the Firefox by flying it to the West.

This is one of those basic movie plots that can generate a lot of entertainment if it's handled properly. *Firefox* knows the territory. It complicates things slightly by making Eastwood a Vietnam veteran who is sometimes overcome by the hallucination that he's still in combat. The movie calls it Post-Combat Stress Syndrome. But the CIA man who recruits him explains that the government isn't much worried, because you don't have the syndrome while you're *in* combat, you see, but only afterward. Somebody ought to compile a textbook of psychology as practiced in movies.

Anyway, Eastwood trains for the mission, is disguised with a mustache and horn-rim glasses, and survives some uncomfortable moments at Moscow customs before he makes it into Russia. Then he makes contact with a confederation of spies and double agents who lead him to a Jewish dissident

who is such a brilliant scientist that he is still being allowed to work on Firefox. Why does the dissident *want* to work on it? Because he knows how Eastwood could steal the plane. All of these scenes include obligatory shots, which are kind of fun to anticipate, if you're a fan of the Alistair Maclean–James Bond–"Mission: Impossible"–*Guns of Navarone* genre. The one indispensable scene is probably the Introduction of the MacGuffin. A MacGuffin, you will remember, was what Alfred Hitchcock called that element of the plot that everybody thinks is important. In this case, it's the Firefox, a long, sleek, cruel-looking machine that looks like a cross between a guided missile and a DeLorean. Eastwood and the camera circle it lovingly; this is the sexiest shot in a movie without a romantic subplot. The movie's climax involves Eastwood's attempt to fly this plane north to the Arctic Circle, make a refueling rendezvous, and then take it on home. His flight is intercut with comic opera scenes involving members of the Russian high command, who argue and bicker while looming over an illuminated map that casts an eerie underlight on their faces, making them look like ghouls from old E.C. comics.

Does Eastwood make it out in one piece? Does he bring along the plane? I wouldn't dream of giving away the plot. But I will say that the movie's climax is a sensational high-altitude dogfight between two different Fire-foxes, and that as Eastwood occupies the Firefox cockpit, surrounded by video screens and computer displays of flight patterns and missile trajectories, it looks as if Dirty Harry has died and gone to Atari heaven. The special effects are really pretty good in this movie. The planes looked surprisingly real to me, and the choreography of the dogfight was not only realistic but understandable. There's one sensational chase sequence that's an homage to *Star Wars*. Remember the *Star Wars* scene where the two ships chased each other between the towering walls of the city in space? Eastwood and his Russian pursuer rocket through a crevice between two ice cliffs, and it looks great even while we're realizing it's logically impossible. I guess that goes for the whole movie.

The Firm ★ ★ ★
R, 153 m., 1993

Tom Cruise (Mitch McDeere), Jeanne Tripplehorn (Abby McDeere), Gene Hackman (Avery Tolar), Hal Holbrook (Oliver Lambert),

Ed Harris (Wayne Tarrance), Holly Hunter (Tammy Hemphill), David Strathairn (Ray McDeere). Directed by Sydney Pollack and produced by Scott Rudin and John Davis. Screenplay by David Rabe, Robert Towne, and David Rayfiel.

Watching *The Firm*, I realized that law firms have replaced army platoons as Hollywood's favorite microcosm. The new law thrillers have the same ingredients as those dependable old World War II action films: a cross section of ethnic and personality types, who fight with each other when they're not fighting the enemy. The law movies have one considerable advantage: The female characters participate fully in all the action, instead of just staying home and writing letters to the front.

In *The Firm*, a labyrinthine 153-minute film by Sydney Pollack, Tom Cruise plays Mitch McDeere, a poor boy who is ashamed of his humble origins, now that he has graduated from Harvard Law fifth in his class. He gets offers from all the top law firms in New York and Chicago, but finally settles on a smaller firm headquartered in Memphis. His decision is salary-driven; he sees money as security, although later in the film he is unable to say how rich he'd have to be to feel *really* secure.

Mitch moves to Memphis with his wife, Abby (Jeanne Tripplehorn, the peculiar psychiatrist in *Basic Instinct*). They are provided with a house and a shiny new Mercedes—both bugged, as it turns out. And gradually McDeere begins to realize that his new law firm is in league with the devil. An FBI man spills the beans: Only a quarter of the clients are aboveboard, and the rest are thieves, scoundrels, and money-launderers, with the firm's partners acting as bagmen shipping the money to offshore banks.

Some movies about the law oversimplify the legal aspects. This one milks them for all they're worth. Without revealing too much of the plot, I can say that McDeere is eventually being blackmailed simultaneously by both the FBI and the firm's security chief (kindly old Wilford Brimley, very effective in a rare outing as a villain). To save himself, he has to use both brain and muscle, outrunning killers and outthinking lawyers, to save both his life and his license to practice law.

The story is fairly clear in its general outlines, but sometimes baffling on the specifics. Based on the novel by John Grisham, as adapted by three of the most expensive screenwriters in the business (David Rabe, Robert Towne, and David Rayfiel), *The Firm* takes two and a half hours to find its way through a moral and legal maze. By the end, despite McDeere's breathless explanations during phone calls in the middle of a chase sequence, I was fairly confused about his strategy. But I didn't care, since the form of the movie was effective even when the details were vague.

Sydney Pollack, the director, likes to make long, ambitious movies *(Out of Africa, Havana),* and he's comfortable working with familiar stars; he uses them as character-building shorthand. One glimpse of Hal Holbrook as the head of the firm, for example, and we know it's a shady outfit. Holbrook almost always plays the seemingly respectable man with dark secrets. One look at Gene Hackman, as the law partner who becomes Cruise's mentor, and we know he's a flawed but fundamentally decent man, because he always is. One look at Cruise and we feel comfortable, because he embodies sincerity. He is also, in many of his roles, just a little slow to catch on; his characters seem to trust people too easily, and so it's convincing when he swallows the firm's pitches and pep talks.

The movie is virtually an anthology of good small character performances. Ed Harris, sinister with a shaved head, needs only a couple of brief scenes to convincingly explain the FBI's case against the firm—and to reveal its cheerful willingness to subject a potential witness to unendurable pressure. Another effective performance is by David Strathairn, as the brother McDeere hasn't told the firm about, because he's doing time for manslaughter. Strathairn is emerging as one of the most interesting character actors around (he was the slow-witted movie usher in *Lost in Yonkers,* and the local boy who came courting in *Passion Fish).* There are also colorful performances by Gary Busey, as a fast-talking private eye, and by Holly Hunter, as his loyal secretary, who witnesses a murder and then becomes McDeere's courageous partner.

The large gallery of characters makes *The Firm* into a convincing canvas; there are enough believable people here to give the McDeeres a convincing world to occupy. And Pollack is patient with his material. He'll let a scene play until the point is made a little more deeply. That allows an actor like Gene Hackman to be surprisingly effective in scenes where he subtly establishes that, despite everything, he has a good heart. A

late, tricky scene between Hackman and Tripplehorn is like a master class in acting.

The parts of *The Firm* are probably better than the whole, however. The movie lacks overall clarity, and in the last half hour audiences are likely to be confused over what's happening, and why. As I said, that didn't bother me overmuch, once I realized the movie would work even if I didn't always follow it. But with a screenplay that developed the story more clearly, this might have been a superior movie, instead of just a good one with some fine performances.

First Blood ★ ★ ★
R, 94 m., 1982

Sylvester Stallone (Rambo), Richard Crenna (Trautman), Brian Dennehy (Teasle), David Caruso (Mitch). Directed by Ted Kotcheff and produced by Buzz Feitshans. Screenplay by Michael Kozoll, William Sackheim, and Q. Moonblood.

Sylvester Stallone is one of the great physical actors in the movies, with a gift for throwing himself so fearlessly into an action scene that we can't understand why somebody doesn't *really* get hurt. When he explodes near the beginning of *First Blood,* hurling cops aside and breaking out of a jail with his fists and speed, it's such a convincing demonstration of physical strength and agility that we never question the scene's implausibility. In fact, although almost all of *First Blood* is implausible, because it's Stallone on the screen, we'll buy it.

What we can't buy in this movie is the message. It's handled in too heavy-handed a way. Stallone plays a returned Vietnam veteran, a Green Beret skilled in the art of jungle survival and fighting, and after a small-town police force sadistically mishandles him, he declares war on the cops. All of this is set up in scenes of great physical power and strength—and the central sections of the movie, with Stallone and the cops stalking each other through the forests of the Pacific Northwest, have a lot of authority. But then the movie comes down to a face-off between Stallone and his old Green Beret commander (Richard Crenna), and the screenplay gives Stallone a long, impassioned speech to deliver, a speech in which he cries out against the injustices done to him and against the hippies who demonstrated at the airport when he returned from the war, etc. This is all old, familiar material from a dozen other films—clichés recycled as formula. Bruce Dern did it in *Coming Home* and William

Devane in *Rolling Thunder.* Stallone is made to say things that would have much better been implied; Robert De Niro, in *Taxi Driver,* also plays a violent character who was obviously scarred by Vietnam, but the movie wisely never makes him talk about what happened to him. Some things are scarier and more emotionally moving when they're left unsaid.

So the ending doesn't work in *First Blood.* It doesn't necessarily work as action, either. By the end of the film, Stallone has taken on a whole town and has become a one-man army, laying siege to the police station and the hardware store and exploding the pumps at the gas station. This sort of spectacular conclusion has become so commonplace in action movies that I kind of wonder, sometimes, what it would be like to see one end with a whimper rather than a bang.

Until the last twenty or thirty minutes, however, *First Blood* is a very good movie, well-paced, and well-acted not only by Stallone (who invests an unlikely character with great authority) but also by Crenna and Brian Dennehy, as the police chief. The best scenes come as Stallone's on the run in the forest, using a hunting knife with a compass in the handle, and living off the land. At one point he's trapped on a cliffside by a police helicopter, and we really feel for this character who has been hunted down through no real fault of his own. We feel more deeply for him then, in fact, than we do later when he puts his grievances into words. Stallone creates the character and sells the situation with his presence itself. The screenplay should have stopped while it was ahead.

A Fish Called Wanda ★ ★ ★ ★
R, 108 m., 1988

John Cleese (Archie), Jamie Lee Curtis (Wanda), Kevin Kline (Otto), Michael Palin (Ken), Maria Aitken (Wendy), Tom Georgeson (George), Patricia Hayes (Mrs. Coady). Directed by Charles Crichton and produced by Michael Shamberg. Screenplay by Cleese and Crichton.

This may be a purely personal prejudice, but I do not often find big-scale physical humor very funny. When squad cars crash into each other and careen out of control, as they do in nine out of ten modern Hollywood comedies, I stare at the screen in stupefied silence. What is the audience laughing at? The creative bankruptcy of filmmakers who have to turn to stunt experts when their own ideas run out?

I do, on the other hand, laugh loudly at comedies where eccentric people behave in obsessive and eccentric ways, and other, equally eccentric, people do everything they can to offend and upset the first batch. In *A Fish Called Wanda*, for example, a character played by Kevin Kline is very particular about one thing: "Don't you *ever* call me stupid!" He is then inevitably called stupid on a number of occasions, leading to the payoff when his girlfriend explains to him in great detail why and how he is stupid, and lists some of the stupid things he believes. ("The London Underground is not a political movement.")

I also like it when people have great and overwhelming passions—passions that rule their lives and are so outsized they seem like comic exaggerations—and then their passions are deliberately tweaked. In *A Fish Called Wanda*, for example, Michael Palin is desperately in love with a tank of tropical fish, and so Kevin Kline, who is equally desperate about discovering the whereabouts of some stolen jewels, eats the fish, one at a time, in an attempt to force Palin to talk. (The fact that Kline also stuffs French fries up Palin's nose gives the scene a nice sort of fish-and-chips symmetry.)

Another thing I like is when people are appealed to on the basis of their most gross and shameful instincts, and surrender immediately. When Jamie Lee Curtis wants to seduce an uptight British barrister, for example, she simply wears a low-cut dress and blinks her big eyes at him and tells him he is irresistible, and this illustrates a universal law of human nature, which is that every man, no matter how resistible, believes that when a woman in a low-cut dress tells him such things she must certainly be saying the truth.

Many of these things that I like come together in *A Fish Called Wanda*, which is the funniest movie I have seen in a long time; it goes on the list with *The Producers*, *This Is Spinal Tap*, and the early Inspector Clouseau movies.

One of its strengths is its mean-spiritedness. Hollywood may be able to make comedies about mean people (usually portrayed as the heroes), but only in England are the sins of vanity, greed, and lust treated with the comic richness they deserve. *A Fish Called Wanda* is sort of a mid-Atlantic production, with flawless teamwork between its two American stars (Curtis and Kline) and its British Monty Python veterans (Cleese and Palin). But it is not a compromise; this is essentially a late-1950s-style British comedy in which the

Americans are employed to do and say all of the things that would be appalling to the British characters.

The movie was directed by Charles Crichton, who co-wrote it with Cleese, and Crichton is a veteran of the legendary Ealing Studio, where he directed perhaps its best comedy, *The Lavender Hill Mob*. He understands why it is usually funnier to *not* say something, and let the audience know what is not being said, than to simply blurt it out and hope for a quick laugh. He is a specialist at providing his characters with venal, selfish, shameful traits, and then embarrassing them in public. And he is a master at the humiliating moment of public unmasking, as when Cleese the barrister, in court, accidentally calls Jamie Lee Curtis "darling."

The movie involves an odd, ill-matched team of jewel thieves led by Tom Georgeson, a weaselly thief who is locked up in prison along with the secret of the jewels. On the outside, Palin, Kline, and Curtis plot with and against each other, and a great deal depends on Curtis's attempts to seduce several key defense secrets out of Cleese.

The film has one hilarious sequence after another. For classic farce, nothing tops the scene in Cleese's study, where Cleese's wife almost interrupts Curtis in mid-seduction. Curtis and Kline are both behind the draperies while the mortified Cleese tries to explain a bottle of champagne and a silver locket. The timing in this scene is as good as anything since the Marx Brothers.

And then there is the matter of the three murdered dogs. One friend of mine said she wouldn't see *A Fish Called Wanda* because she heard that dogs die in it (she is never, of course, reluctant to attend movies where people die). I tried to explain to her that the death of a pet is, of course, a tragic thing. But when the object is to inspire a heart attack in a little old lady who is a key prosecution witness, and when her little darling is crushed by a falling safe, well, you've just got to make a few sacrifices in the name of comedy.

Fitzcarraldo ★ ★ ★ ★
PG, 157 m., 1982

Klaus Kinski (Fitzcarraldo), Claudia Cardinale (Molly), Jose Lewgoy (Don Aquilino), Miguel Angel Fuentes (Cholo). Directed by Werner Herzog. Screenplay by Herzog.

Werner Herzog's *Fitzcarraldo* is a movie in the great tradition of grandiose cinematic

visions. Like Coppola's *Apocalypse Now* or Kubrick's *2001*, it is a quest film in which the hero's quest is scarcely more mad than the filmmaker's. Movies like this exist on a plane apart from ordinary films. There is a sense in which *Fitzcarraldo* is not altogether successful—it is too long, we could say, or too meandering—but it is still a film that I would not have missed for the world. The movie is the story of a dreamer named Brian Sweeney Fitzgerald, whose name has been simplified to "Fitzcarraldo" by the Indians and Spanish who inhabit his godforsaken corner of South America. He loves opera. He spends his days making a little money from an ice factory and his nights dreaming up new schemes. One of them, a plan to build a railroad across the continent, has already failed. Now he is ready with another: He seriously intends to build an opera house in the rain jungle, twelve hundred miles upstream from the civilized coast, and to bring Enrico Caruso there to sing an opera.

If his plan is mad, his method for carrying it out is madness of another dimension. Looking at the map, he becomes obsessed with the fact that a nearby river system offers access to hundreds of thousands of square miles of potential trading customers—if only a modern steamship could be introduced into that system. There is a point, he notices, where the other river is separated only by a thin finger of land from a river that already is navigated by boats. His inspiration: Drag a steamship across land to the other river, float it, set up a thriving trade, and use the profits to build the opera house—and then bring in Caruso! This scheme is so unlikely that perhaps we should not be surprised that Herzog's story is based on the case of a real Irish entrepreneur who tried to do exactly that.

The historical Irishman was at least wise enough to disassemble his boat before carting it across land. In Herzog's movie, however, Fitzcarraldo determines to drag the boat up one hill and down the other side in one piece. He enlists engineers to devise a system of blocks-and-pulleys that will do the trick, and he hires the local Indians to work the levers with their own muscle power. And it is here that we arrive at the thing about *Fitzcarraldo* that transcends all understanding: Werner Herzog determined to literally drag a real steamship up a real hill, using real tackle and hiring the local Indians! To produce the movie, he decided to do personally what even the original Fitzgerald never attempted.

Herzog finally settled on the right actor to play Fitzcarraldo, author of this plan: Klaus Kinski, the shock-haired German who starred in Herzog's *Aguirre, the Wrath of God* and *Nosferatu*, is back again to mastermind the effort. Kinski is perfectly cast. Herzog's original choice for the role was Jason Robards, who is also gifted at conveying a consuming passion, but Kinski, wild-eyed and ferocious, consumes the screen. There are other characters important to the story, especially Claudia Cardinale as the madam who loves Fitzcarraldo and helps finance his attempt, but without Kinski at the core it's doubtful this story would work.

The story of Herzog's own production is itself well-known, and has been told in Les Blank's *Burden of Dreams*, a brilliant documentary about the filming. It's possible that every moment of *Fitzcarraldo* is colored by our knowledge that Herzog was "really" doing the things we see Fitzcarraldo do. (The movie uses no special effects, no models, no opticals, no miniatures.) Perhaps we're even tempted to give the movie extra points because of Herzog's ordeal in the jungle. But *Fitzcarraldo* is not all sweat and madness. It contains great poetic images of the sort Herzog is famous for: An old phonograph playing a Caruso record on the deck of a boat spinning out of control into a rapids; Fitzcarraldo frantically oaring a little rowboat down a jungle river to be in time to hear an opera; and of course the immensely impressive sight of that actual steamship, resting halfway up a hillside.

Fitzcarraldo is not a perfect movie, and it never comes together into a unified statement. It *is* meandering, and it is slow and formless at times. Perhaps the conception was just too large for Herzog to shape. The movie does not approach perfection as *Aguirre* did. But as a document of a quest and a dream, and as the record of man's audacity and foolish, visionary heroism, there has never been another movie like it.

See also Burden of Dreams, *a documentary on the making of* Fitzcarraldo.

Five Easy Pieces ★ ★ ★ ★
R, 98 m., 1970

Jack Nicholson (Robert Dupea), Karen Black (Rayette), Susan Anspach (Catherine), Billy Green Bush (Elton), Helena Kallianiotes (Hitchhiker), Ralph Waite (Carl Dupea), William Challee (Nicholas Dupea), John Ryan (Spicer). Directed by Bob Rafelson and produced by Richard Wechsler and Rafelson. Screenplay by Adrien Joyce.

The title of *Five Easy Pieces* refers not to the women its hero makes along the road, for there are only three, but to a book of piano exercises he owned as a child. The film, one of the best American films, is about the distance between that boy, practicing to become a concert pianist, and the need he feels twenty years later to disguise himself as an oil-field rigger. When we sense the boy, tormented and insecure, trapped inside the adult man, *Five Easy Pieces* becomes a masterpiece of heartbreaking intensity.

At the outset, we meet only the man—played by Jack Nicholson with the same miraculous offhandedness that brought *Easy Rider* to life. He's an irresponsible roustabout, making his way through the oil fields, sleeping with a waitress (Karen Black) whose every daydreaming moment is filled with admiration for Miss Tammy Wynette. The man's name is Robert Eroica Dupea. He was named after Beethoven's Third Symphony and he spends his evenings bowling and his nights wearily agreeing that, yes, his girl sings "Stand By Your Man" just like Tammy.

In these first marvelous scenes, director Bob Rafelson calls our attention to the grimy life textures and the shabby hopes of these decent middle Americans. They live in a landscape of motels, highways, TV dinners, dust, and jealousy, and so do we all, but they seem to have nothing else. Dupea's friends are arrested at the mental and emotional level of about age seventeen; he isn't, but thinks or hopes he is.

Dupea discovers his girl is pregnant (his friend Elton breaks the news out in the field, suggesting maybe it would be good to marry her and settle down). He walks out on her in a rage, has a meaningless little affair with a slut from the bowling alley, and then discovers more or less by accident that his father is dying. His father, we discover, is a musical genius who moved his family to an island and tried to raise them as Socrates might have. Dupea feels himself to be the only failure.

The movie bares its heart in the scenes on the island, where Dupea makes an awkward effort to communicate with his dying father. The island is peopled with eccentrics, mostly Dupea's own family, but including a few strays. Among their number is a beautiful young girl who's come to the island to study piano with Dupea's supercilious brother. Dupea seduces this girl, who apparently suggests the early life he has abandoned. He does it by playing the piano; but when she says she's moved, he says he isn't—that he played better as a child and that the piece was easy anyway.

This is possibly the moment when his nerve fails and he condemns himself, consciously, to a life of self-defined failure. The movie ends, after several more scenes, on a note of ambiguity; he is either freeing himself from the waitress or, on the other hand, he is setting off on a journey even deeper into anonymity. It's impossible to say, and it doesn't matter much. What matters is the character during the time covered by the film: a time when Dupea tentatively reapproaches his past and then rejects it, not out of pride, but out of fear.

The movie is joyously alive to the road life of its hero. We follow him through bars and bowling alleys, motels and mobile homes, and we find him rebelling against lower-middle-class values even as he embraces them. In one magical scene, he leaps from his car in a traffic jam and starts playing the piano on the truck in front of him; the scene sounds forced, described this way, but Rafelson and Nicholson never force anything, and never have to. Robert Eroica Dupea is one of the most unforgettable characters in American movies.

The Five Heartbeats ★ ★ ★
R, 120 m., 1991

Robert Townsend (Duck), Michael Wright (Eddie), Leen (J.T.), Harry J. Lennix (Dresser), Tico Wells (Choirboy), Diahann Carroll (Eleanor Potter), Tressa Thomas (Duck's Baby Sister). Directed by Robert Townsend and produced by Loretha C. Jones. Screenplay by Townsend and Keenen Ivory Wayans.

Robert Townsend's *The Five Heartbeats* takes the notion of a musical biopic one step further than usual. His movie is not only the rags to riches story of a group of guys from the neighborhood who become big stars, but also the story of what happens to them next. Their ultimate destination is not simply stardom, which is fairly easy for them to attain, but maturity and happiness, which are a lot harder.

The Five Heartbeats are a singing group, loosely patterned on groups like the Dells and the Temptations. They start out singing for fun in living rooms and on street corners, they perform in local amateur nights, they gain an audience of friends and neighbors, and then they're spotted by a talent scout who wants two things—to make them stars, and to rip them off.

The broad outlines of this story are familiar from a lot of other showbiz biographies, maybe because this is more or less the way it happens with a lot of performers. What Townsend adds that's special is the way he sees each of the five group members as an individual with his own problems and destiny. This is not only a biography with music, but also a thoughtful look at the way five young men from a poor but nurturing black neighborhood find success and deal with it.

The screenplay, by Townsend and Keenen Ivory Wayans, begins some twenty-five or thirty years ago with a bunch of kids, two of them brothers, who are already very different individuals. There's Duck, the natural leader (Townsend), who has a cool head for the group's best interests. Eddie (Michael Wright), the lead singer, who has the biggest talent but also the biggest problems, including drugs. J.T. (Leon), Duck's brother, who is a ladies' man, incapable of settling down. Dresser (Harry J. Lennix), smooth and flashy. And Choirboy (Tico Wells), whose father is a minister who thinks jazz and rock 'n' roll are the work of the devil.

Townsend tells their stories in an interlocking series of episodes that's confusing at first—the opening twenty minutes or so are hard to follow—and then settles down, as if he's found his way. I doubt if the movie was shot in chronological order, but it certainly picks up confidence and power as it goes along, until by the end we really care about these guys, especially in a couple of scenes where they have to make decisions for a lifetime.

The big dramatic interest centers around Eddie, who has the real star power in the group, and whose ability to break out of a song and really let go has the fans in the front rows swooning. But Eddie is not simply the star; he's also the one with the most vulnerable ego, the biggest problems with self-regard, the almost inevitable attraction to drugs. He begins to screw up and miss dates, and eventually the group has to drop him—leading to a painful scene outside a club, where the Heartbeats are getting into their limo as Eddie comes stumbling up like a bum. Eddie's ultimate fate is the counterpoint for everything else in the movie.

The other characters are all sharply seen, in moments involving family and romance, pregnancies and heartbreaks, redemptions and breakthroughs. There is one obligatory scene showing racial prejudice against the group (they're touring the South when they're stopped by racist state troopers), and it seems a little tacked on, as if the only purpose of the Southern trip was to justify the scene; it's a retread from the much more effective similar scenes in *Bird*.

This is Townsend's first traditional feature film; his directorial debut, some four years ago, was *Hollywood Shuffle*, a series of comic sketches that parodied the clichéd ways Hollywood has used black characters in the movies. Most of those sketches were under ten minutes; this time, at feature length, Townsend shows a real talent, and, not surprisingly, an ability to avoid most clichés, to go for the human truth in his characters.

The Flamingo Kid ★ ★ ★ ½
PG-13, 100 m., 1984

Matt Dillon (Jeffrey Willis), Hector Elizondo (Arthur Willis), Molly McCarthy (Ruth Willis), Martha Gehman (Nikki Willis), Richard Crenna (Phil Brody), Jessica Walter (Phyllis Brody), Carole R. Davis (Joyce Brody). Directed by Garry Marshall and produced by Michael Phillips. Screenplay by Neal Marshall and Garry Marshall.

"When I was eighteen, my father was ignorant on a great many subjects," Mark Twain once said, "but by the time I was twenty-five, it was amazing the things the old man had learned." Here is a movie that condenses that process into one summer. The summer begins with a kid from a poor Brooklyn neighborhood taking a job as a cabana boy at a posh beach club out on Long Island. That's against the advice of his father, a plumber, who wants his son to get a job where he can learn about hard work. By the middle of the summer, the kid has started to idolize a flashy car dealer who's the champion of the gin rummy tables. By Labor Day, he has found out more about the car dealer than he wanted to know. And he has come to love and understand his father in a new way.

The Flamingo Kid stars Matt Dillon as the teen-ager, Hector Elizondo as his father, and Richard Crenna as the car dealer. There are other characters—in particular, a bikinied goddess who helps sell Matt on life at the beach—but these are the three characters who stand at the heart of the story. Elizondo is a hard-working man who still remembers how to dream, but knows that life has few openings for dreamers. In some of the movie's most poetic passages, he reveals a lifelong obsession with ships, and the ways of harbor pilots. Crenna, on the other hand, is a man who firmly believes "You are what you wear," and values his status as the club's gin rummy champion as if it really meant something.

Dillon is a revelation in this movie. Perhaps because of his name, Matt Dillon has risked being confused with your average teen-age idol, the kind the pimple magazines put on their covers. Yet he has been an extraordinarily sensitive actor ever since his first appearance, in the unsung 1977 movie about alienated teen-agers, *Over the Edge*. In two movies based on novels by S.E. Hinton, *Tex* and *Rumble Fish,* he had the kind of clarity, the uncluttered relationship with the camera, that you see in only a handful of actors: He was a natural. He is here, too. His role in *The Flamingo Kid* could easily have been turned into an anthology of twitches and psychic anguish as he wrestles with the meaning of life. But Dillon has the kind of acting intelligence that allows him to play each scene for no more than that particular scene is really about; he's not trying to summarize the message in every speech. That gives him an ease, an ability to play the teen-age hero as if every day were a whole summer long.

We fall into the rhythm of the beach club. Into the sunny days where all the members have lots of time to know and envy each other, and time is so plentiful that it can take hours for a nasty rumor to sweep through the cabanas. Dillon hurries from one member to another with drinks, towels, club sandwiches, messages. He feels acutely that he does not belong at this level of society—and when Richard Crenna takes notice of him, and even more when Crenna's daughter invites him home for dinner, Dillon feels that he's cutting loose from the boring life back in Brooklyn. But this will be a summer of learning, and by autumn he will have learned how wise and loving his own father is, and how easy it is to be deceived by surfaces. Along the way to that lesson, *The Flamingo Kid* has a lot of fun (I hope I haven't made this social comedy sound dreary), and at the end it has a surprisingly emotional impact.

Flashback ★ ★ ★
R, 108 m., 1990

Dennis Hopper (Huey Walker), Kiefer Sutherland (John Buckner), Carol Kane (Maggie), Cliff De Young (Sheriff Hightower), Paul Dooley (Donald R. Stark), Richard Masur

(Barry), Michael McKean (Hal), Kathleen York (Sparkle). Directed by Franco Amurri and produced by Marvin Worth. Screenplay by David Loughery.

I've heard people complaining recently that once you've seen the coming attractions trailer for a movie, you've seen the movie. That's the way I felt after seeing the trailer for Franco Amurri's *Flashback*, but the film itself is a pleasant surprise—deeper and more original than the formula that the trailer seemed to promise.

The movie stars Dennis Hopper as Huey Walker, once famous, now forgotten, who once got his picture on the cover of *Life* magazine as an "activist clown," but has now been in hiding for twenty years. Kiefer Sutherland is the straight-arrow young FBI man assigned to return him to Spokane for trial.

What was Huey Walker's crime? When Spiro T. Agnew was on whistle-stop through the Pacific Northwest in 1968, Walker uncoupled his railroad car—so when the train pulled out, Agnew was left waiting at the station. This was a gag good enough to make Walker a hero of the counterculture at the time, but now his time has long since passed, and he is just another sad drifter, moving along every time anyone begins to suspect his true identity.

Walker is finally betrayed to the FBI by an anonymous phone caller, and that's when John Buckner, the Sutherland character, is called into play. His job is to accompany the aging hippie as he goes back home to face the music. And, of course, the two men take the train. No points for correctly predicting that history will repeat itself.

Flashback seems to be settling down into a combination of two recent movies, one good, one bad: *Midnight Run*, where Robert De Niro had to return Charles Grodin cross country, and *Rude Awakening*, where two aging 1960s hippies were dumped into 1989. But then, just when the movie seems content to settle into its formula, the screenplay by David Loughery gets inventive, instead.

Huey, played on a perfect note of spaced-out wackiness by Dennis Hopper, begins to play psychological games with Sutherland. He discovers the FBI man is only twenty-six years old, and begins to taunt him about his conservative appearance and rigidly correct opinions. Before long Sutherland has unwound enough to play a game of chess with his captive, and then Hopper convinces him he's slipped a tab of acid into his mineral water.

The FBI man begins to trip out, and the old hippie shaves his beard, cuts his hair, and changes places with him—so that when they arrive at an intermediate stop, it's Hopper who presents himself as the agent, and the zonked-out Sutherland who looks like the radical. This is all lots of fun, as Hopper and Sutherland develop an edgy back-and-forth rivalry, but it's also all predicted in the trailer. In fact, on the basis of the trailer, you'd predict that the movie would continue as a series of gags involving mistaken identity.

That's not what happens, and I'm reluctant to say what *does* happen, because the movie takes such an interesting U-turn into what develops into a halfway serious contrast between the values of the Summer of Love and the greed of the Me Decade. The movie sounds its new note at about the time Maggie, an unreformed 1960s hippie played by Carol Kane, enters into the picture. We learn some surprising things about Sutherland, Hopper begins to think some surprising thoughts about Maggie, and there are moments when *Flashback* is actually touching.

The best thing in the movie is the Hopper performance, which is quick and smart and oddly engaging. It's hard to play a character with charisma, since the charisma has to seem to come from the character and not from the actor, but Hopper does it here. He's convincing, and his dialogue actually sounds like the sorts of things an unrepentant hippie might say—not like the clichés someone might write for him. Credit is obviously due to the filmmakers, but Hopper puts the right spin on a difficult character, and makes the movie special. How long has it been since a movie gave us not only everything the trailer promised, but more?

Flatliners ★ ★ ★
R, 111 m., 1990

Kiefer Sutherland (Nelson), Julia Roberts (Rachel), Kevin Bacon (Labraccio), William Baldwin (Joe), Oliver Platt (Steckle), Kimberly Scott (Winnie Hicks), Joshua Rudoy (Billy Mahoney), Benjamin Mouton (Rachel's Father). Directed by Joel Schumacher and produced by Michael Douglas and Rick Bieber. Screenplay by Peter Filardi.

One of the things you learn in medical school, it is said, is how to think like God. No one can teach you that, but unless you somehow learn it, you'll never be comfortable looking people in the eye and telling them what their chances are. The characters in *Flatliners* are

all medical students, and their egos are so healthy that during the course of the movie they engage in a competition to see who can look God himself in the eye.

Here's their plan. It starts with those stories about people who are pronounced dead but then are brought back to life—and how a lot of them report the same blissful afterlife experience. They talk about a tunnel of light, peaceful music, and the presence of loved ones welcoming them to the other side. And they talk about being outside their own bodies, looking down, conscious of the efforts to revive them but feeling detached, because death is so sweet.

The young heroes of *Flatliners* want to visit that land of light and music, and return to tell the story. So they devise a dangerous experiment in which, one after another, they'll deliberately create a condition of clinical death, sample the afterlife experience, and then be brought back to life by emergency measures. The audacity of this experiment is terrifying and intriguing, and let's face it: It's a great idea for a movie.

Flatliners was mostly shot in the neo-Gothic gloom of turn-of-the-century locations in and around the University of Chicago. Gargoyles and shadows and gloomy stained-glass windows surround the deadly experiments, as the students, urged on by ringleader Kiefer Sutherland, tamper with God's plans for them. One after another, they take what they hope is a round-trip into eternity. The risks are many: not only death, of course, but even expulsion from medical school.

What they find on the other side is not the proper business of a reviewer to reveal. How they come back, however, deserves some comment, because the movie engages in plot manipulation that is unworthy of the brilliance of its theme. Each student tries to one-up the others, to stay away a little longer, to go a little deeper into whatever is there. And so each resuscitation attempt is a little trickier. Eventually the movie falls into a disappointing pattern, in which we're supposed to once again hold our breath while yet another voyager balances between life and death. One resuscitation is suspenseful. Two are fine. More than two wear out their welcome.

The cast, talented young actors, inhabit the shadows with the right mixture of intensity, fear, and cockiness. In addition to Sutherland, there are Julia Roberts (her first role after *Pretty Woman*), Kevin Bacon, William Baldwin (Alec's brother), Oliver Platt, and Kimberly Scott. There were some hazards in this project—with the wrong note, they could easily look silly—and yet they take their chances and pull it off. *Flatliners* is an original, intelligent thriller, well-directed by Joel Schumacher. I only wish it had been restructured so we didn't need to go through the same crisis so many times.

The Flintstones ★ ★ ½
PG, 92 m., 1994

John Goodman (Fred Flintstone), Elizabeth Perkins (Wilma Flintstone), Rick Moranis (Barney Rubble), Rosie O'Donnell (Betty Rubble), Kyle MacLachlan (Cliff Vandercave), Halle Berry (Miss Stone), Elizabeth Taylor (Pearl Slaghoople). Directed by Brian Levant and produced by Bruce Cohen. Screenplay by Tom S. Parker, Jim Jennewein, and Steven E. de Souza.

If *The Flintstones* had been able to devise a story as interesting as its production values, it would have been some kind of wonderful. This is a great-looking movie, a triumph of set design and special effects, creating a fantasy world halfway between suburbia and a prehistoric cartoon. The frame is filled with delightful and inventive notions, all based on the idea that modern America might somehow be reconstructed out of rocks. Just watching it is fun. Following the plot is not so much fun.

It's strange: The parts of the movie you'd think would have been the trickiest are the ones that work best. Led by John Goodman, the actors successfully impersonate the classic cartoon characters, and look and sound convincing. And the world they inhabit is just right. But the story is confusing, not very funny, and kind of odd, given the target audience of younger children and their families. Do kids really care much about office politics, embezzlement, marital problems, difficulties with adoption, aptitude exams, and mothers-in-law?

John Goodman stands foursquare at the center of the story as Fred Flintstone, a repository of good nature, insecurity, and rock-headed stubbornness. Nagged at home by his mother-in-law (Elizabeth Taylor, looking terrific), who spurs his wife, Wilma (Elizabeth Perkins), to discontent, he is generally happy at work. But he keeps hearing how he should be bringing home a bigger paycheck.

His best friends are Barney and Betty Rubble (Rick Moranis and Rosie O'Donnell), who desperately hope to adopt a baby. When

Fred is able to help them out, Barney repays him when an aptitude test is administered down at Slate & Co., where they both work. (Here, as elsewhere, there are lots of stone-age jokes, as Fred chips his multiple-choice answers into a slab of stone with a chisel.) Not telling his friend, Barney substitutes his own answers for Fred's, and Fred wins a promotion to the head office, where boss Cliff Vandercave (Kyle MacLachlan) and his slinky secretary Miss Stone (Halle Berry) quickly see how they can use his stupidity to cheat the workers and embezzle company funds.

The plot is a too-laborious working out of all of those threads, none of which really generate much interest. A simpler story, involving human relationships and adventures instead of office shenanigans, would have been more interesting for kids, and probably for older audiences, too.

Still, there is a lot to praise here. The best way to describe the look of this movie is to say that the physical world of the cartoon series and the comic strip has been translated to live action with no compromise. The cars that run on foot-power, for example, look as clunky and heavy as in the original drawings, but somehow plausible, too (and there's a great early scene where the Flintstones motor out to the drive-in to see a movie—*Tar Wars*, of course). All sorts of consumer products and office equipment and supplies are reproduced in stone, and the costumes are a combo of caveman chic and suburban ready-to-wear. On the heels of *Jurassic Park*, it's also fun to see a variety of prehistoric dinosaurs.

As I watched the movie, though, my attention strayed from the story to the settings. The plot was so artificially contrived and cobbled together that it didn't provide energy to the characters; they seemed stuck in it, reciting arbitrary dialogue in the midst of a production that should have inspired more energy and excitement. Maybe kids just plain won't mind; they'll disregard the story and enjoy the stone-age gags. But *The Flintstones* does so well with the hard part of creating its world that it's a shame the easier part—putting a story into it—doesn't measure up.

Flirting ★ ★ ★ ★
NO MPAA RATING, 102 m., 1992

Noah Taylor (Danny Embling), Thandie Newton (Thandie Adjewa), Nicole Kidman

(Nicola Radcliffe), Bartholomew Rose ("Gilby Fryer"), Felix Nobis (Jock Blair), Josh Picker ("Baka" Bourke), Kiri Paramore ("Slag" Green). Directed by John Duigan and produced by George Miller, Doug Mitchell, and Terry Hayes. Screenplay by Duigan.

Flirting is one of those rare movies with characters I cared about intensely. I didn't simply observe them on the screen; I got involved in their decisions and hoped they made the right ones. The movie is about two teenagers at private schools in Australia in the 1960s, a white boy and an African girl, who fall in love and do a little growing up, both at the same time.

The boy is Danny (Noah Taylor), awkward, a stutterer, the target of jokes from some of his classmates. He has a fine offbeat mind, which questions authority and doubts conventional wisdom. He is gawky in that way teen-age boys can be before the parts grow into harmony with the whole. The girl is Thandie (Thandie Newton), very pretty, very smart, attracted to Danny because alone of the boys in her world he possesses a sense of humor and rebellion. She first sees him during a get-together between their twin schools, which are on either side of a lake, and looks at him boldly until he meets her gaze. Not long after, they are on opposing debate teams, and carry on a subtle little flirtation by disagreeing with the arguments of their own sides.

The girl's mother was British; her stepmother is African, like her father, who is a diplomat. Uganda is newly independent and is approaching the agony of the Idi Amin years. Events far away in Africa will decide whether the boy and girl will be able to carry on a normal teen-age flirtation, or whether she will be swept away by the tide of history. Meanwhile, their eyes wide open, with joy and solemnity, they try to honor their love.

The movie is not about "movie teenagers," those unhappy creatures whose interests are limited and whose values are piggish. Most movies have no idea how thoughtful and responsible many teen-agers are—how seriously they take their lives, how carefully they agonize over personal decisions. Only a few recent films, like *Say Anything* and *Man in the Moon*, have given their characters the freedom that *Flirting* grants—for kids to grow up by trying to make the right choices.

In *Flirting*, every scene serves a purpose. We go to classrooms and dormitories, to

Parents' Day and sporting events, and we see the wit and daring with which Thandie and Danny arrange to meet under the eyes of their teachers. We also get a sense of the schools; the boys' school, where one of the teachers is too fond of caning, and another too fond of building model airplanes, and the girls' academy, where one of the older girls (Nicole Kidman) is responsible for Thandie, but secretly admires her willingness to break the rules.

Scene after scene is written with delicacy and wit. For example, a scene in which the young lovers' parents meet. Neither set of parents knows their child is dating at all; the way they all behave in this social setting, in a time and place where interracial dating raises eyebrows, is written with subtlety and tact. The adult actors bring a kind of awkward grace to the scene that is somehow very moving. The little nonconversation between Danny's parents, after they are alone again, is priceless.

Race itself is not the issue in *Flirting*, however; the movie is a coming-of-age drama (and comedy) about the ways in which these two young people balance lust with mutual respect, and how the girl, who is wiser and more mature, is also enormously tactful in guiding and protecting the boy that she loves. There is a scene in which they explore one another sexually, but it is not a "sex scene" in any conventional sense of the term, and the way it is handled is a rebuke to the way so many movies cheapen physical love.

Flirting came to me out of the blue, without advance notice, and I was deeply affected by it. Then I discovered it is a sequel to an earlier Australian film, *The Day My Voice Broke*, unseen by me, and that Danny will be seen again in a third film still to be made by the writer-director, John Duigan. I have gone searching for the first film, which I remember having heard good things about, but I know from experience that it is possible to see *Flirting* all by itself.

So often we settle for noise and movement from the movie screen, for stupid people indulging unworthy fantasies. Only rare movies like *Flirting* remind us that the movies are capable of providing us with the touch of other lives, that when all the conditions are right we can grow a little and learn a little, just like the people on the screen. This movie is joyous, wise, and life-affirming, and certainly one of 1992's best films.

Fool for Love ★ ★ ★
R, 107 m., 1985

Sam Shepard (Eddie), Kim Basinger (May), Harry Dean Stanton (Old Man), Randy Quaid (Martin). Directed by Robert Altman and produced by Menahem Golan and Yoram Globus. Screenplay by Sam Shepard.

At the center of Sam Shepard's *Fool for Love* are two people whose hurts are so deep, whose angers are so real, that they can barely talk about what they really feel. That does not stop them from talking, on and on into the hurtful night, and eventually we can put together their stories, using what they have said, and especially what they have not said.

One of the characters is a blond slattern named May, whose natural beauty has been rearranged into a parody of the classic movie baby doll—Brigitte Bardot, say. The other character is named Eddie, and he is a cowboy who drives through the empty Texas reaches in the obligatory pickup truck with the obligatory rifle rack behind his head and the obligatory horse trailer behind. One night May is working behind the counter of a restaurant in a crumbling motel, and she sees Eddie's pickup coming down the road. She runs and hides. Standing in the shadows of the rundown motel is an older man (Harry Dean Stanton) who simply waits and watches.

Shepard's method is direct. He allows his characters to talk around what they're really thinking, and occasionally the talk escalates into brief, incisive bursts of action—even violence. Eventually we learn that the older man is the father of both Eddie and May, that they had different mothers, that the old man commuted between two families, and that Eddie and May eventually met under circumstances that were later determined to be incestuous.

These developments would provide the ingredients for a basic story of redneck passion, and there are times when *Fool for Love* wants to strike those very notes. We feel we might be looking at the characters in a story by William Faulkner or Erskine Caldwell, and the visual compositions look inspired by the lurid covers of 1940s paperback novels. The deliberately trashy surface, however, conceals deeper levels of feeling, and by the end of *Fool for Love* we have witnessed some sort of classic tragedy, set there in the Texas backlands.

Robert Altman's movie version of Shepard's play stars Shepard himself, in a strong performance as Eddie. But he doesn't dominate the story as much as you might think.

The central performance in the movie is really Kim Basinger's, as May. Although she has played sexpots before—has indeed specialized in them—nothing prepared me for the dimensions she was able to find in this one. What's astonishing is that *Fool for Love* is essentially a male drama, told from a male point of view, and yet Basinger is able to suggest so much with her performance that she steals the center of the stage right away from the man who wrote the lines and is playing opposite her.

Part of her impact is probably because the director is Altman. Few other major directors are more interested in women, and in his films like *Thieves Like Us, Three Women,* and *Come Back to the 5 & Dime, Jimmy Dean, Jimmy Dean,* he has shown women in settings very similar to this one: unfulfilled women, conscious of the waste of their lives, living in backwaters where their primary pastime is to await the decisions of men.

Altman does a brilliant job of visualizing this particular backwater. From the opening aerial shots of the godforsaken motel, he creates a tangibly real, dusty, forlorn world. Some of his shots are so beautiful it's hard to figure how he obtained them: That ominous dark sky lowering over the motel, for example, looks almost like a painting. Altman is also up to some of the same visual tricks he used in *Jimmy Dean,* including the use of windows and mirrors to give us two planes of action at the same time. And he has a wonderfully subtle way of showing us the Harry Dean Stanton character in both the past and the present.

This is Altman's fourth movie in a row based on a play. It comes after *Jimmy Dean, Streamers,* and the extraordinary *Secret Honor,* about Richard Nixon (he has filmed three other plays for cable television). After a career as one of the most free-swinging of all modern movie directors (*M*A*S*H, McCabe and Mrs. Miller, Nashville*) it is interesting to see him embracing the discipline of a play script. Having made movies that were all over the map, he now inhabits interiors—of rooms, and of people's minds. With *Fool for Love,* he has succeeded on two levels that seem opposed to each other. He has made a melodrama, almost a soap opera, in which the characters achieve a kind of nobility.

Forget Paris ★ ★ ★ ½
PG-13, 100 m., 1995

Billy Crystal (Mickey), Debra Winger (Ellen), Joe Mantegna (Andy), Cynthia Stevenson (Liz), Richard Masur (Craig), Julie Kavner (Lucy), William Hickey (Arthur), Robert Costanzo (Waiter). Directed and produced by Billy Crystal. Screenplay by Crystal, Lowell Ganz, and Babaloo Mandel.

Billy Crystal's *Forget Paris* is a more or less deliberate attempt to repeat the success of *When Harry Met Sally*, his 1989 romantic comedy. Its ingredients look as if they were devised to appeal to all audiences: This is the first film to find a way to combine professional basketball with April in Paris. By all rights the movie should be a pale imitation of its betters, but sometimes lightning does strike twice, and this is a wonderful film, filled with romantic moments that ring true, and with great big laughs.

The movie stars Crystal as Mickey, a popular NBA referee who is known as skilled and fearless (in an opening sequence, he nullifies a sensational game-winning last-second shot by Charles Barkley). When his father dies, Mickey accompanies the body to France, because the old man, who made few friends after the Second World War was over, wanted to be buried with the dead of his army company. At the Paris airport, the body is lost, causing Mickey to scream: "What do you mean, what did it look like? My coffin was the one with the red yarn on the handle!"

He is screaming at Ellen (Debra Winger), an American in Paris, who works for the airline. She likes his sense of humor. (When customs later quarantines the body for health reasons, he screams, "He's dead! He has no health!") They meet again at the cemetery, one thing leads to another, he stays in Paris an extra day, and she takes him sightseeing. (Looking at Rodin's *The Thinker*, Mickey muses, "The Thinker is thinking, 'Goddamn that Rodin! Three drinks, and I'm nude.'")

This whole story of their first meeting and gradual courtship is told as a series of flashbacks, in a conversation between an old friend of Mickey's (Joe Mantegna) and his fiancée (Cynthia Stevenson). They're in a restaurant, waiting for others to arrive, and as each new couple joins the table it adds details to the saga of Mickey and Ellen. No prizes for guessing which couple arrives last.

Mickey and Ellen were made in heaven for one another. Unfortunately, their lifestyles were made in hell, and although falling in love is easy for them (despite various obligatory difficulties), living together is not. Ellen is not thrilled by her first glimpse of Mickey's bachelor pad, which is "kind of a shrine for watching ESPN." Nor does she much like sitting around at home while Mickey commutes within the far-flung empire of the NBA. The pattern of the movie consists of fights and separations, followed by reunions and reconciliations, all recounted by the pals around the restaurant table.

It all works. Even the seemingly artificial device of having the friends tell the story works, especially since Mantegna is a sportswriter and his story about Mickey could be a warning to Stevenson that life with him could also be difficult. What works especially well is the prickly relationship between Mickey and Ellen, who are both bright and quirky, and so have interesting fights.

What everyone remembers about *When Harry Met Sally*, of course, is Meg Ryan's virtuoso scene in a restaurant, where she fakes an orgasm and the woman at the next table tells the waiter, "I'll have whatever she's having." *Forget Paris* wisely doesn't attempt to duplicate that scene, but comes up with a classic of its own, involving Winger and a pigeon, that builds into one of the great slapstick moments.

And then of course there is Paris. No other city has so many associations with movie romance, and when Mickey realizes he is looking at the Pont Neuf, which figured in *An American in Paris*, of course we hear Gene Kelly singing "Our Love Is Here to Stay" on the sound track.

What's weird is to see scenes of Paris romance intercut with Mickey's daytime job. The movie convincingly places Crystal in the middle of NBA action, using cameos by a lot of stars; there is a great moment when Kareem gets ejected from his own farewell game by the lovelorn Mickey.

Crystal has made a career out of being smart, quick, and glib. It takes a smart actress, like Winger, to match with him, and here, as in the otherwise completely different *Shadowlands*, she is the right woman for a man so wrapped up in his work that he has no life. Of course, their relationship isn't simple; as Mickey observes, "Marriages don't work when one partner is happy and the other is miserable. They only work when both are miserable."

For Keeps ★ ★ ★
PG-13, 98 m., 1988

Molly Ringwald (Darcy), Randall Batinkoff (Stan), Kenneth Mars (Mr. Bobrucz), Miriam Flynn (Mrs. Elliot), Conchata Ferrell (Mrs. Bobrucz), Sharon Brown (Lila), Jack Ong (Reverend Kim), Sean Frye (Wee Willy), Allison Roth (Ambrosia), Trevor Edmond (Ace). Directed by John G. Avildsen and produced by Jerry Belson and Walter Coblenz. Screenplay by Tim Kazurinsky and Denise DeClue.

The movies of Molly Ringwald have been responsible for a revolution in the way Hollywood regards teen-agers. Before Ringwald (and her mentor, John Hughes) there were horny teen-agers, dead teen-agers, teen-age vampires, and psychotic crack-ups. More recently teen-age movies have been working their way through some of the aspects of the normal lives of American teen-agers, and in *For Keeps*, Ringwald plays a popular high school senior who gets pregnant and gets married.

Because she is Ringwald, and because this is a movie, her experience of these adventures is probably a good deal more pleasant than the average American teen-age girl could look forward to. There is a line in the movie that could apply to the movie itself, when a high school teacher asks the very pregnant Ringwald to drop out of school and take night classes, because she's so popular that other girls might want to imitate her and get pregnant themselves.

If the movie lacks something, it is a sense of the real pain, shame, and suffering that someone like this high school senior might undergo with a pregnancy. She seems too sound, too well-adjusted, too resilient. And yet there is a certain bottom line of honesty in this movie, and if it is about the joy of young love, it is also about the pressures of young responsibility. (I hope impressionable teen-age viewers will devote careful attention to the scenes where Molly is stuck at home in her walk-up apartment while her young husband is out having a beer with his buddies.)

In the film, Ringwald and her boyfriend, played by Randall Batinkoff, begin to sleep together and almost immediately have to face the pregnancy. In a plot that centers around national holidays, she blurts out the news at Thanksgiving, and they decide to get married at Christmas. Both of these decisions are met with varying degrees of horror by their parents—by Miriam Flynn, as

Ringwald's divorced and bitter mother, and by Kenneth Mars and Conchata Ferrell, as Batinkoff's loving, conventional parents.

The movie is perhaps a bit too willing to play Batinkoff's parents for laughs, and I could have done without a scene of a toppling Christmas tree. But the moments between Ringwald and Batinkoff are well-written and played with a quiet, touching sensitivity; we recognize elements of real life in their relationship.

The movie was written by Tim Kazurinsky and Denise DeClue, whose previous collaboration was the wonderful *About Last Night. . . .* That movie, based very loosely on a play by David Mamet, was about swinging singles in their twenties and thirties. This one, an original, has the same feel for plausible dialogue and the same knack for finding scenes that reveal personalities, instead of simply advancing the plot. Consider, for example, the sequence after the birth, when Ringwald suffers from post-partum depression; this is the sort of touching realism you wouldn't expect from a "teen-age movie," and yet it lends weight and importance to the sequences that follow.

I also liked the way in which her husband was shown as unready to accept the responsibilities of marriage and fatherhood, and then the way the movie subtly suggests that Ringwald isn't ready, either—but as the woman, she's the one who gets stuck at home with the kid. All of this is made more dramatic because of a subplot about the husband's full-ride college scholarship, Ringwald's own college potential, and the lack of campus facilities for married freshmen.

The ending of the movie is too contrived, as all of the threads come together—marriage, parenthood, scholarships, family acceptance, college plans. And yet *For Keeps* is an intriguing movie that succeeds in creating believable characters, keeping them alive, and steering them more or less safely past the clichés that are inevitable with this kind of material. It's a movie with heart, and that compensates for a lot of the predictability. The one thing it lacks, perhaps, is a notice at the end advising teen-agers that for every young couple like this one, there are a thousand broken hearts.

Forrest Gump ★ ★ ★ ★
PG-13, 135 m., 1994

Tom Hanks (Forrest Gump), Robin Wright (Jenny Curran), Gary Sinise (Lieutenant Dan), Mykelti Williamson (Bubba), Sally Field (Mama Gump), Michael Humphreys (Young Forrest), Hanna Hall (Young Jenny). Directed by Robert Zemeckis and produced by Wendy Finerman, Steve Tisch, and Steve Starkey. Screenplay by Eric Roth.

I've never met anyone like Forrest Gump in a movie before, and for that matter I've never seen a movie quite like *Forrest Gump.* Any attempt to describe him will risk making the movie seem more conventional than it is, but let me try. It's a comedy, I guess. Or maybe a drama. Or a dream.

The screenplay by Eric Roth has the complexity of modern fiction, not the formulas of modern movies. Its hero, played by Tom Hanks, is a thoroughly decent man with an IQ of seventy-five, who manages between the 1950s and the 1980s to become involved in every major event in American history. And he survives them all with only honesty and niceness as his shields.

And yet this is *not* a heartwarming story about a mentally retarded man. That cubbyhole is much too small and limiting for *Forrest Gump.* The movie is more of a meditation on our times, as seen through the eyes of a man who lacks cynicism and takes things for exactly what they are. Watch him carefully and you will understand why some people are criticized for being "too clever by half." Forrest is clever by just exactly enough.

Tom Hanks may be the only actor who could have played the role. I can't think of anyone else as Gump, after seeing how Hanks makes him into a person so dignified, so straight-ahead. The performance is a breathtaking balancing act between comedy and sadness, in a story rich in big laughs and quiet truths.

Forrest is born to an Alabama boardinghouse owner (Sally Field), who tries to correct his posture by making him wear braces, but who never criticizes his mind. When Forrest is called "stupid," his mother tells him, "Stupid is as stupid does," and Forrest turns out to be incapable of doing anything less than profound. Also, when the braces finally fall from his legs, it turns out he can run like the wind.

That's how he gets a college football scholarship, in a life story that eventually becomes a running gag about his good luck. Gump the football hero becomes Gump the Medal of Honor winner in Vietnam, and then Gump the Ping-Pong champion, Gump the shrimp boat captain, Gump the millionaire stockholder (he gets shares in a new "fruit company" named Apple Computer), and Gump the man who runs across America and then retraces his steps.

It could be argued that with his IQ of seventy-five Forrest does not quite understand everything that happens to him. Not so. He understands everything he needs to know, and the rest, the movie suggests, is just surplus. He even understands everything that's important about love, although Jenny, the girl he falls in love with in grade school and never falls out of love with, tells him, "Forrest, you don't know what love is." She is a stripper by that time.

The movie is ingenious in taking Forrest on his tour of recent American history. The director, Robert Zemeckis, is experienced with the magic that special effects can do (his credits include the *Back to the Future* movies and *Who Framed Roger Rabbit*), and here he uses computerized visual legerdemain to place Gump in historic situations with actual people.

Forrest stands next to the schoolhouse door with George Wallace, he teaches Elvis how to swivel his hips, he visits the White House three times, he's on the Dick Cavett show with John Lennon, and in a sequence that will have you rubbing your eyes with its realism, he addresses a Vietnam-era peace rally on the Mall in Washington. Special effects are also used in creating the character of Forrest's Vietnam friend Lt. Dan (Gary Sinise), a Ron Kovic type who quite convincingly loses his legs.

Using carefully selected TV clips and dubbed voices, Zemeckis is able to create some hilarious moments, as when LBJ examines the wound in what Forrest describes as "my butt-ox." And the biggest laugh in the movie comes after Nixon inquires where Forrest is staying in Washington, and then recommends the Watergate. (That's not the laugh, just the setup.)

As Forrest's life becomes a guided tour of straight-arrow America, Jenny (played by Robin Wright) goes on a parallel tour of the counterculture. She goes to California, of course, and drops out, tunes in, and turns on. She's into psychedelics and flower power, antiwar rallies and love-ins, drugs and needles. Eventually it becomes clear that between them Forrest and Jenny have covered all of the landmarks of our recent cultural history, and the accommodation they arrive at in the end is like a dream of reconciliation for our society. What a magical movie.

48 HRS ★ ★ ★ ½
R, 100 m., 1982

Nick Nolte (Cates), Eddie Murphy (Reggie), James Remar (Ganz), Sonny Landham (Billy Bear), Annette O'Toole (Elaine). Directed by Walter Hill and produced by Lawrence Gordon and Joel Silver. Screenplay by Roger Spottiswoode, Hill, Larry Gross, and Steven E. de Souza.

Sometimes an actor becomes a star in just one scene. Jack Nicholson did it in *Easy Rider*, wearing the football helmet on the back of the motorcycle. It happened to Faye Dunaway when she looked sleepily out of a screen window at Warren Beatty in *Bonnie and Clyde*. And in *48 HRS*, it happens to Eddie Murphy. His unforgettable scene comes about halfway through *48 HRS*. He plays a convict who has done thirty months for theft and still has six months to go—but he gets a forty-eight hour prison leave through the efforts of Nick Nolte, a hungover hot dog of a detective who's on the trail of some cop killers and figures Murphy can help. Murphy thinks there's a bartender who may have some information. The thing is, the bar is a redneck country joint, the kind where urban cowboys drink out of longneck bottles and salute the Confederate flag on the wall. Murphy has been jiving Nolte about how he can handle any situation. Nolte gives him a chance. And Murphy, impersonating a police officer, walks into that bar, takes command, totally intimidates everybody, and gets his information. It's a great scene—the mirror image of that scene in *The French Connection* where Gene Hackman, as Popeye Doyle, intimidated the black regulars in a Harlem bar.

Murphy has other good moments in this movie, and so does Nolte, who gives a wonderful performance as a cynical, irresponsible, and immature cop who's always telling lies to his girlfriend and sneaking a jolt of whiskey out of his personal flask. The two men start out suspicious of each other in this movie and work up to a warm dislike. But eventually, grudgingly, a kind of respect starts to grow.

The movie's story is nothing to write home about. It's pretty routine. What makes the movie special is how it's made. Nolte and Murphy are good, and their dialogue is good, too—quirky and funny. Character actor James Remar makes a really slimy killer, genuinely evil. Annette O'Toole gets third billing as Nolte's lover, but it's another one of those thankless women's roles. Not only could O'Toole have phoned it in—she does, spending most of her scenes on the telephone calling Nolte a no-good bum. The direction is by Walter Hill, who has never been any good at scenes involving women and doesn't improve this time. What he is good at is action, male camaraderie and atmosphere. His movies almost always feature at least one beautifully choreographed, unbelievably violent fight scene (remember Charles Bronson's bare-knuckle fight in *Hard Times*?), and the fight scene this time is exhausting.

Where Hill grows in this movie is in his ability to create characters. In a lot of his earlier movies *(The Warriors, The Driver, Long Riders, Southern Comfort)* he preferred men who were symbols, who represented things and so didn't have to be human. In *48 HRS*, Nolte and Murphy are human, vulnerable, and touching. Also mean, violent, and chauvinistic. It's that kind of movie.

For Your Eyes Only ★ ★
PG, 127 m., 1981

Roger Moore (James Bond), Carole Bouquet (Melina), Topol (Columbo), Julian Glover (Kristatos), Cassandra Harris (Lisl), Janet Brown (Prime Minister). Directed by John Glen and produced by Albert R. Broccoli. Screenplay by Richard Malbaum and Michael Wilson.

For Your Eyes Only is a competent James Bond thriller, well-crafted, a respectable product from the 007 production line. But it's no more than that. It doesn't have the special sly humor of the Sean Connery Bonds, of course, but also doesn't have the visual splendor of such Roger Moore Bonds as *The Spy Who Loved Me*, or special effects to equal *Moonraker*. And in this era of jolting, inspired visual effects from George Lucas and Steven Spielberg, it's just not quite in the same league. That will no doubt come as a shock to Producer Albert (Cubby) Broccoli, who has made the James Bond series his life's work.

Broccoli and his late partner, Harry Saltzman, all but invented the genre that Hollywood calls "event films" or "special effects films." The ingredients, which Bond popularized and others imitated, always included supervillains, sensational stunts, sex, absurd plots to destroy or rule the world, and, of course, a hero. The 007 epics held the patent on that formula in the late '60s and early '70s, but they are growing dated. *For Your Eyes Only* doesn't have any surprises. We've seen all the big scenes before, and when the villains turn out to be headquartered in an impregnable mountaintop fortress, we yawn. After *Where Eagles Dare* and *The Guns of Navarone* and the hollow Japanese volcano that Bond himself once infiltrated, let's face it: When you've seen one impregnable mountaintop fortress, you've seen 'em all.

The movie opens with James Bond trapped inside a remote-controlled helicopter being guided by a bald sadist in a wheelchair. After Bond triumphs, the incident is never referred to again. *This* movie involves the loss of the secret British code controlling submarine-based missiles. The Russians would like to have it. Bond's mission: Retrieve the control console from a ship sunk in the Aegean. The movie breaks down into a series of set pieces. Bond and his latest Bondgirl (long-haired, undemonstrative Carole Bouquet) dive in a mini-sub, engage in a complicated chase through the back roads of Greece, crawl through the sunken wreck in wet suits, are nearly drowned and blown up, etc. For variety, Bond and Bouquet are dragged behind a powerboat as shark bait, and then Bond scales the fortress mountain. A fortress guard spots Bond dangling from a rope thousands of feet in the air. What does he do? Does he just cut the rope? No, sir, the guard descends part way to tantalize Bond by letting him drop a little at a time. The rest is predictable.

In a movie of respectable craftsmanship and moderate pleasures, there's one obvious disappointment. The relationship between Roger Moore and Carole Bouquet is never worked out in an interesting way. Since the days when he was played by Sean Connery, agent 007 has always had a dry, quiet, humorous way with women. Roger Moore has risen to the same challenge, notably opposite Barbara Bach in *The Spy Who Loved Me*. But Moore and Bouquet have no real chemistry in *For Your Eyes Only*. There's none of that kidding byplay. It's too routine. The whole movie is too routine.

Four Friends ★ ★ ★ ★
R, 114 m., 1981

Craig Wasson (Danilo Prozor), Jodi Thelen (Georgia Miles), Jim Metzler (Tom Donaldson), Michael Huddleston (David Levine), Reed Birney (Louie Carnahan), Julie Murray (Adrienne Carnahan), Miklos Simon (Mr.

Prozor). Directed by Arthur Penn and produced by Penn and Gene Lasko. Screenplay by Steven Tesich.

Somewhere in the middle of *My Dinner with André*, Andre Gregory wonders aloud if it's not possible that the 1960s were the last decade when we were all truly alive—that since then we've sunk into a bemused state of self-hypnosis, placated by consumer goods and given the illusion of excitement by television. Walking out of *Four Friends*, I had some of the same thoughts. This movie brings the almost unbelievable contradictions of that decade into sharp relief, not as nostalgia or as a re-creation of times past, but as a reliving of all of the agony and freedom of the weirdest ten years any of us is likely to witness.

The movie is told in the form of a loose-knit autobiography, somewhat inspired by the experiences of Steve Tesich, the son of Yugoslavian parents who moved to this country as a boy and lived in the neighborhoods of East Chicago, Indiana, that provide the film's locations. If the film is his emotional autobiography, it is also perhaps the intellectual autobiography of Arthur Penn, the film's director, whose *Bonnie and Clyde* was the best American film of the 1960s and whose *Alice's Restaurant* (1970) was an earlier examination of that wonderful and haunted time.

Their movie tells the stories of four friends. When we meet them, they're entering their senior year of high school. It is 1961. That is so long ago that nobody has yet heard of the Beatles. One of the friends is a young woman (Jodi Thelen), who imagines she is the reincarnation of Isadora Duncan, and who strikes attitudes and poses in an attempt to appear altogether too much of an artistic genius for East Chicago to contain. The other three friends are male classmates. They all love the girl in one way or another, or perhaps it's just that they've never seen anyone like her before. In the ten years to follow, these four people will have lives that were not imaginable in 1961. They will have the opportunity to break out of the sedate conservatism of the Eisenhower era and into the decade of "alternative life-styles."

The movie is ambitious. It wants to take us on a tour of some of the things that happened in the 1960s, and some of the ways four midwestern kids might have responded to them. It also wants to be a meditation on love, and on how love changes during the course of a decade. When Thelen turns up at the bedroom window of her "real" true love (Craig

Wasson) early in the movie and cheerfully offers to sleep with him, Wasson refuses, not only because he's a high school kid who's a little afraid of her—but also because he's too much in love with his idea of her to want to make it real. By the time they finally do come back together, years later, they've both been through bad scenes, through madness, drug abuse, and the trauma of the war in Vietnam. They have also grown up, some. The wonder is not that *Four Friends* covers so much ground, but that it makes many of its scenes so memorable that we learn more even about the supporting characters than we expect to.

There are individual scenes in this movie that are just right. One of them involves a crowd of kids walking home in the dusk after school. Another happens between Wasson and Miklos Simon, who plays his gruff, defensive Yugoslavian father, and who finally, painfully, breaks down and smiles after a poker-faced lifetime. A relationship between Wasson and a dying college classmate (Reed Birney) is well drawn, to remind us of undergraduate friendships based on idealism and mutual discovery. And the scene where Wasson and Thelen see each other after many years is handled tenderly and with just the right notes of irony.

Four Friends is a very good movie. Like *Breaking Away*, the story of growing up in Bloomington, Indiana (for which Tesich also wrote the original screenplay), this is a movie that remembers times past with such clarity that there are times it seems to be making it all up. Did we really say those things? Make those assumptions? Live on the edge of what seemed to be a society gone both free and mad at once? Some critics have said the people and events in this movie are not plausible. I don't know if they're denying the movie's truth, or arguing that from a 1980s point of view the '60s were just a bad dream. Or a good one.

1492: Conquest of Paradise ★ ★ ★
PG-13, 152 m., 1992

Gérard Depardieu (Christopher Columbus), Armand Assante (Sanchez), Sigourney Weaver (Queen Isabella), Angela Molina (Beatrix), Fernando Rey (Antonio), Tcheky Karyo (Pinzon), Frank Langella (Don Luis). Directed by Ridley Scott and produced by Scott and Alain Goldman. Screenplay by Roselyne Bosch.

Ridley Scott's *1492: Conquest of Paradise* sees Christopher Columbus as more complex

and humane than in the other screen treatments of the character. His Columbus is an enlightened revision of the traditional figure, treating Indians the same as Spanish noblemen and seeming content with the notion that nature, not the Catholic God, is their deity.

Columbus is also a good deal more convincing as a human being. As played by Gérard Depardieu, he seems huge and shaggy and dogged, just the kind of man who would get an idea in his head and refuse to surrender it. We are familiar with many of the stages in his story, such as his defense of his voyage before hostile scholars, and his careful courting of Queen Isabella as his patron, but Depardieu makes them seem new.

That is even true of the inevitable scene in which Columbus uses a piece of fruit to illustrate his belief that the world was round. This time it is an orange. In the dreary previous version of this story, *Christopher Columbus: The Discovery*, released in August of 1992, it was an apple. I am waiting for someone to make it a potato, since Europe before the discovery of America had no potatoes—a fact I have been husbanding for years in case I am ever a guest on "Jeopardy."

What disappoints me a little about Scott's version is that he seems to hurry past Columbus's actual voyage of discovery. There is intrigue in the Old World and adventure and violence in the New, but the crucial journey that links them seems reduced to its simplest terms: The three ships sail, the crews grow restless, there is mutiny in the air, Columbus quiets it, and then land is sighted. (In the previous film version, Columbus helpfully offered to be beheaded if land was not sighted in three days, an embellishment of history that Scott and screenwriter, Roselyne Bosch, wisely omit.)

The theory that the world was round was held in intelligent circles long before Columbus was born, and ships capable of sailing across the Atlantic had been available for a long time (Europeans were already rounding Africa on their way to Asia, and the Vikings preceded Columbus to North America by centuries). What prevented Europe from expanding into the new continent was essentially superstition and conservatism, a strong impulse to leave things as they were. It was an impulse that Columbus was constitutionally unable to accept, and that Isabella apparently found seductive.

Ridley Scott is a visually oriented director who finds great beauty in his vision of the

New World, including a breathtaking shot in which the ocean mists rise to reveal a verdant shore. He shot his film on location in Costa Rica, where the Native Americans are depicted as dignified and gentle, people who inspire Columbus to wonder whether they might not be an improvement on the inbred backbiting nobles of the Spanish court. I am personally not convinced that Columbus was as enlightened as he seems in this movie, but perhaps historical figures exist in order to be reinterpreted every so often in terms of current needs.

The screenplay is the result of extended research by Bosch (who observes in the film's notes that Catholics in Isabella's Spain could be burned at the stake for eating meat on "Holy Friday"). She continues Columbus's story for a decade after his discovery of America, as he brings news of his triumph back to Spain, returns to the New World as a viceroy, and then struggles with the land, violent noblemen, opponents in Spain, and even a hurricane before being returned in disgrace to prison. There is a happy ending; Isabella grants his wish to visit the American mainland, and he dies after dictating his memoirs to his son.

One of Depardieu's most touching moments in the film is a close-up as he hears his fellow Italian Amerigo Vespucci described as the discoverer of the mainland, although here the movie plays fast and loose with the facts, since Columbus, who visited South America before Vespucci did, is given a sad line in which he asks how much farther it was (and "America" was not named after Vespucci until the year after Columbus's death).

What I would someday like to see is a film much closer to the bone than this one, one in which the physical rigors of the voyage and the first settlements were depicted more realistically. Scott's version is particularly handicapped by a score by Vangelis that alternates between breathless angelic choirs and brooding jungle music. The sound track instructs us what to think about many of the shots; the quasi-ecclesiastical strains seem to suggest the Church will indeed save many souls in the New World, while the Indian themes suggest that these simple forest people were already well on the way to inventing New Age music.

Still, in its own way and up to a certain point, *1492* is a satisfactory film. Depardieu lends it gravity, the supporting performances are convincing, the locations are realistic, and we are inspired to reflect that it did

indeed take a certain nerve to sail off into nowhere just because an orange was round.

The Fourth Protocol ★ ★ ★ ½
R, 119 m., 1987

Michael Caine (John Preston), Pierce Brosnan (Petrofsky), Ned Beatty (Borisov), Joanna Cassidy (Vassilieva), Julian Glover (Brian Harcourt-Smith), Michael Gough (Sir Bernard Hemmings), Ray McAnally (General Karpov), Ian Richardson (Sir Nigel Irvine). Directed by John Mackenzie and produced by Timothy Burrill. Screenplay by Frederick Forsyth.

August 1987. I am writing this review in the Scottish Highlands, where the peace is broken only by the occasional low-level flyby of a jet fighter plane. I was walking yesterday along the banks of Loch Tummell, and I came to a lively waterfall that was tumbling through the woods. The birds were singing and the sun was doing its best to penetrate the mist, and then the sky was shattered by the arrogant roar of a warplane, swooping low over the hills, then gone in an instant.

The flights are part of a joint defense exercise by the United States and Royal Air Forces, and they fly on nearly every clear day. Folks up here don't like them much. It's like being subjected to a daily version of one of those moronic displays where the Blue Angels demonstrate how much noise they can make.

There are a lot of U.S. military bases on British soil, including the famous one at Greenham Common where anti-nuclear protesters have been camping out for years. If there were a nuclear accident at one of those bases, it would seriously undermine our welcome over here. The low-level training missions are no doubt important for security, but they have contributed to a good deal of grumbling among the citizens who live in their path. That grumbling, in a way, is what *The Fourth Protocol* is about.

The Fourth Protocol involves a Soviet plan to smuggle the elements for a nuclear device into Britain, assemble it, and detonate it right next to a U.S. base. The explosion would be so huge that its precise location would be obliterated, and it would look exactly like an American accident. Result: pressure for the Yankees to go home and a strategic victory for the Russians.

The key Russian operative is played by Pierce Brosnan, in what certainly is the best performance he has ever given, as a dark, brooding man with an outwardly cheerful

disposition and a perfect British accent. The only person who seems capable of anticipating his plan, and stopping it, is Michael Caine as a British intelligence officer who is in political trouble with his bosses because he's too independent.

This is essentially the same character Caine played in the second movie role of his career, *The Ipcress File* (1965). This time, though, he's older, less cocksure, and more wily in getting his way. After his superiors take him off the case, he simply works on it in a different way. Eventually he puts the pieces together and realizes what the Soviets are up to, and then the movie becomes a race against time.

The Fourth Protocol is based on a novel by Frederick Forsyth, whose *Day of the Jackal* also made a terrific thriller. The stories have similar structures: The villain is as strongly drawn as the heroes, and there is a sympathetic woman character who loves the villain—unwisely, as it turns out. The woman in *The Fourth Protocol* is a Russian intelligence agent played by Joanna Cassidy, who does not work often enough in the movies but always is a strong, sure center for every scene. (Remember her in *Under Fire*, as the foreign correspondent caught between Nick Nolte and Gene Hackman?) This time she arrives with the key element Brosnan needs for his bomb, and if his treatment of her is unkind, consider what will happen to everyone within a forty-mile radius.

The Fourth Protocol is first-rate because it not only is a thriller, but it also pays attention to its characters and shows how their actions grow out of their personalities. Like Michael Caine's other 1987 British spy film, *The Whistle Blower*, it is effective not simply because it's a thriller but also because for long stretches it simply is a very absorbing drama.

The Fourth War ★ ★ ★
R, 95 m., 1990

Roy Scheider (Jack Knowles), Jurgen Prochnow (Valachev), Tim Reid (Lieutenant Colonel Clark), Lara Harris (Elena), Harry Dean Stanton (General Hackworth), Dale Dye (Sergeant Major), Bill MacDonald (M.P. Corporal). Directed by John Frankenheimer and produced by Wolf Schmidt. Screenplay by Stephen Peters.

I don't know when production began on John Frankenheimer's *The Fourth War*, but its timing is interesting: In period, it's the last Cold War movie, and in spirit, the first post–Cold War thriller. The suspense centers around whether someone will screw up detente. Some of the new geopolitical dialogue sounds a little strange to the ear, as when an American colonel stands near the border between West Germany and Czechoslovakia and fearlessly barks, "What we have here is primarily a public relations role!" No specific reference is made in the movie to the Gorbachev era, but it's clear that the primary purpose of the American border patrols is to avoid shooting themselves in the foot.

That prepares the canvas for the arrival of Col. Jack Knowles (Roy Scheider), who has been the army's loose cannon and maybe its loose screw ever since the war in Vietnam. Knowles has so many decorations you can't see his uniform, but he has never been known for his sound judgment in command positions. The army has posted him as far away from trouble as possible—Guam was a typical duty—but now he has finally been returned to a frontline command. It has something to do with how an old Vietnam buddy (Harry Dean Stanton) has faith that he's regained his senses.

The faith is premature. Knowles is a hothead and a lone wolf, and his war, as they like to say in the movie ads, is not over. It is his misfortune, and perhaps the misfortune of the entire planet, that he has been positioned on the Czech border exactly opposite an equally short-tempered Russian named Colonel Valachev (Jurgen Prochnow). On the first day of his new command, Knowles has to stand by impotently and watch as a would-be refugee is shot down within yards of freedom. Then Valachev hovers overhead in a Soviet helicopter and, in Knowles's words, "sticks his rockets in my face."

Nobody sticks his rockets in the face of Col. Jack Knowles, and before long Knowles is sneaking across the border on unauthorized solo missions to sabotage enemy installations and stick his own rockets, so to speak, in Valachev's face. Knowles's dangerous activities do not go unnoticed by his second in command (Tim Reid), and there are reprimands from Harry Dean Stanton back at division headquarters, but now Valachev has engaged himself in the dangerous game, and the two men refuse to back down. There are moments when the possibility of accidental war seems very real.

The Fourth War is essentially a psychological study of a man coming apart at the hinges. Knowles, played by Scheider, is an embittered, alcoholic loser who was a hero once, a long time ago and far away. Now appropriate conditions no longer exist for his kind of hot-dog heroism. Although the movie centers on well-made action scenes and contains a couple of tidy surprises, its strength comes from the portrait of this soldier on the edge. Scheider has a role not unlike Laurence Harvey's in Frankenheimer's masterpiece *The Manchurian Candidate*. He is a victim of his programming. He reacts to Soviet troops the way Harvey reacted to a hand of solitaire.

The supporting performances are where the movie's sanity resides. Tim Reid, as the second in command, plays the role as a textbook officer who knows he's on thin ice and does everything by the book. Stanton, as the general, has a long, angry speech in one scene, and as he slams his words into Scheider's silence, we're reminded of what a powerful actor he is.

Movies like *The Fourth War* are a reminder that Hollywood is running low on dependable villains. The Nazis were always reliable, but World War II ended forty-five years ago. Now the Cold War is winding down, and just when *Lethal Weapon 2* introduced South African diplomats as the bad guys, de Klerk came along to make that approach unpredictable. Drug dealers are wearing out their welcome. Bad cops are a cliché. Suggestions?

Four Weddings and a Funeral ★ ★ ★ ½
R, 116 m., 1994

Hugh Grant (Charles), Andie MacDowell (Carrie), Kristin Scott Thomas (Fiona), Simon Callow (Gareth), James Fleet (Tom), John Hannah (Matthew), Corin Redgrave (Hamish). Directed by Mike Newell and produced by Duncan Kenworthy. Screenplay by Richard Curtis.

Four Weddings and a Funeral, delightful and sly, is a comedy about people who seem to live out their lives in public, attending weddings. No doubt they have everyday lives as well, but the film doesn't supply them. Even in the case of the central character, a likable, shy, perennial best man named Charles (Hugh Grant), we're never told what he does for a living. Of course, the film is British, and in Britain it is considered bad form to ask anyone what they do, so perhaps the film simply doesn't know.

The movie is about an extended group of friends. Some of them probably met at school, and others have married into their various families, and they all know each other, more or less. Occasionally a new face pops up: Carrie, for example, the sparkling American girl who is a guest at the first wedding, turns up again at the second, and is scheduled to be married at the third.

Carrie, played by Andie MacDowell, is one of those women who is not quite as confident as she seems. She's smart and beautiful, but she is engaged to marry an older man named Hamish (Corin Redgrave) who is so thick, confident, and overbearing that you figure no one would marry him who didn't need to. Sure, she says she loves him. But she is clearly falling for Charles, and he for her.

Their flirtation begins at the first ceremony, and their romance is consummated during the celebration that follows—and reconsummated after the second wedding. She does most of the aggressing, because Charles is too reticent to ever come right out and say what he really feels—not even if the happiness of a lifetime depends on it.

While Charles and Carrie fall in love, the movie introduces us in a haphazard way to a lot of the other members of the crowd. It's like being at a wedding. We glimpse people across a room, we meet them, we forget their names, we are reminded, and then we make a connection and figure out who they're with—or not with, as the case may be. Among the regulars at all of the weddings, we grow especially fond of Gareth (Simon Callow), who eats too much and drinks too much, whose vest is too tight and manner too jolly, but who is, we can see, true blue. Eventually we catch on that he is gay, although in this as in most other personal matters, the movie is subtle enough that we have to read social clues, just as we would at a wedding.

Other regulars at the ceremonies include Henrietta (Anna Chancellor), who used to date Charles and now would plainly like to start dating him again. Charles is doubly afflicted: He cannot tell a woman he likes her, and he also cannot tell her he dislikes her. He ends up back in Henrietta's orbit through a combination of loneliness, absentmindedness, and alcohol, and is engaged to her basically because he has given up on his earlier ideals and is willing to settle for less.

Four Weddings and a Funeral has been directed by Mike Newell, with the same kind of lighthearted enchantment that made his *Enchanted April* (1991) and 1993's *Into the West* so seductive. Here, with his large cast, he moves nimbly through the crowd, making introductions with his camera. Luckily, many of the scenes are set in large houses with room for the characters to creep away and engage in private drama.

Hugh Grant, the star of the film, has been in a lot of movies, but this may be the one that makes him finally familiar to American audiences. He has a self-deprecating manner, a kind of endearing awkwardness, that makes you understand why a woman might like him—and why he might drive her mad while tap-dancing around his real feelings. MacDowell is much more open and direct ("more American," the movie must feel), and so it's intriguing to realize that while she is in love with a man she can say anything to, she's engaged to a man she basically has to lie to all the time.

Like Kenneth Branagh's *Peter's Friends*, this film forms a community that eventually envelops us. Also like that film, it's about how a homosexual character becomes a focus for much of what is best among the other characters, who are mostly straight; the gay man in both films is a center of good feeling, and helps create a sense of family. By the end of the movie, you find yourself reacting to the weddings, and the funeral, almost as you do at real events involving people you didn't know very well, but liked, and wanted to know better.

The Fox and the Hound ★ ★ ★
G, 83 m., 1981

With the voices of Pearl Bailey (Big Mama), Kurt Russell (Copper), Mickey Rooney (Tod), Sandy Duncan (Vixey), Pat Buttram (Chief), Jack Albertson (Slade). Directed by Art Stevens, Ted Berman, and Richard Rich and produced by Wolfgang Reitherman and Stevens. Screenplay by Larry Clemmons and others.

In all the old familiar ways, *The Fox and the Hound* looks like a traditional production from Walt Disney animators. It has cute little animals and wise old owls. It has a villain in the shape of a mountainous grizzly bear, and comic relief in a long-standing feud between a woodpecker and a caterpillar. And it has songs that contain such uncontroversial wishes as, "If only the world wouldn't get in the way . . . If only the world would let us play." And yet, for all of its familiar qualities, this movie marks something of a departure for the Disney studio, and its movement is in an interesting direction. *The Fox and the Hound* is one of those relatively rare Disney animated features that contains a useful lesson for its younger audiences. It's not just cute animals

and frightening adventures and a happy ending; it's also a rather thoughtful meditation on how society determines our behavior.

The movie is a fable about a small puppy named Copper and an orphaned fox named Tod. At the outset we sense something unusual—after the camera traces a gloomy path through the shadows of the forest, a mother fox and her baby come running terrified out of the woods, chased by hunters and hounds. Will the mother and child escape? They almost do. But then the mother hides her baby and sacrifices her life to draw attention away from him. This is the cruel world, without any magical cartoon escapes.

The little fox is taken under the wing, so to speak, by wise old Big Mama Owl, who arranges for the baby to be adopted by a kindly farm woman. It's at this point that the puppy comes into the plot. Puppy and fox become great friends in their childhoods and pledge to be loyal to each other forevermore. But then the quickly growing hound is taken away to be trained as a hunter, and the next time the two friends meet, the hound is savagely trying to chase down the fox. After they are almost killed by the bear, there is a reconciliation of sorts. They realize (and perhaps the kids in the audience will realize, too) how quickly our better impulses can be drowned out by the noise of society. The message is not heavy-handed, nor does it need to be, because the lessons in the movie are so firmly illustrated by the lives of the animals.

Although *The Fox and the Hound* is the first Disney animated feature to have been made mostly by a newer generation of artists at the studio, the film's look still is in the tradition of *The Rescuers* (1977) and other Disney work in the 1970s. That means we don't get the painstaking, frame-by-frame animation of individual leaves and flowers and birds that made *Snow White* magical back when animator man-hours were cheaper. But we do get a lot of life and energy on the screen.

The star of the movie's sound track is Pearl Bailey as Big Mama Owl. She sings three songs, dispenses advice with a free hand, and struts around in the forest as a sort of feathered Ann Landers. The animators have done a wonderful job of giving their cartoon owl some of Pearlie Mae's personality traits, but the two leading characters (with Mickey Rooney as the fox and Kurt Russell as the hound) are more straightforward.

The bottom line, I suppose, is: Will kids

like this movie? And the answer is, sure, I think so. It's a fast-moving, colorful story, and as I watched the animated images on the screen, I was suddenly reminded of a curious belief I held when I was a kid. I believed that cartoons looked more real than "live" features, because everything on the screen had sharper edges. I outgrew my notion, but I'm not sure that represents progress.

Foxes ★ ★ ★
R, 106 m., 1980

Jodie Foster (Jeanie), Scott Baio (Brad), Sally Kellerman (Mary), Randy Quaid (Jay), Lois Smith (Mrs. Axman), Adam Faith (Bryan), Cherie Currie (Annie), Marilyn Kagan (Madge), Kandice Stroh (Dierdre). Directed by Adrian Lyne and produced by David Puttnam and Gerald Ayres. Screenplay by Ayres.

God help us if many American teen-agers are like the ones in this movie—but God love *them*, for that matter, for surviving in the teen-age subculture of Los Angeles. *Foxes* is a movie about four teen-age girls who live in the San Fernando Valley, who come from broken or unhappy homes, who are surrounded by a teen-age subculture of sex, dope, booze, and rock 'n' roll . . . and who aren't bad kids, not really.

They run in a pack, sleeping over at each other's homes, going to school together, hanging out together, forming a substitute family because home doesn't provide a traditional one. They form the fierce loyalties that all teen-agers depend upon—loyalties of friendship that run deeper than the instant romances and sudden crushes that are a dime a dozen. They live in a world where sixteen-year-old kids are somehow expected to live in adult society, make decisions about adult vices, and yet not be adult. That's what's scariest about *Foxes:* Our knowledge that alcohol, pot, and pills *are* available to teen-agers unwise enough to go looking for them, and that they can provide emotional overloads far beyond the ability of the kids to cope.

One of the kids in the movie does cope fairly well, though. She's Jeanie, played by Jodie Foster as a sort of teen-age mother hen, a young girl who's got problems of her own but is intelligent, balanced, and enough of a survivor to clearly see the mistakes the others are making. That doesn't mean she rejects her friends. She runs with the pack and she takes her chances, but she's not clearly doomed. And some of the others are.

The movie follows its four foxes through several days and several adventures. It's a loosely structured film, deliberately episodic to suggest the shapeless form of these teen-agers' typical days and nights. Things happen on impulse. Stuff comes up. Kids stay out all night, or run away, or get drunk, or get involved in what's supposed to be a civilized dinner party until it's crashed by a mob of greasers.

The subject of the movie is the way these events are seen so very differently by the kids and their parents. And at the heart of the movie is one particular, wonderful, and complicated parent-child relationship, between Jodie Foster and Sally Kellerman. They only have a few extended scenes together, but the material is written and acted with such sensitivity that we really understand the relationship. And we understand Kellerman, as an attractive woman in her thirties, divorced from a rock promoter, who is trying to raise a sixteen-year-old, attend college, and still have a love life of her own. Kellerman has a line that evokes whole lives, when she talks about "all those desperately lonely, divorced UCLA undergraduates."

The parallels here are obvious. The Kellerman character, we suspect, got swept up in the rock and drug subculture, got married too young, got pregnant immediately, and now, the mother of a sixteen-year-old, is *still* in the process of growing up herself. She doesn't want her kid to go through what she went through. But kids grow up so fast these days that, oddly enough, these two women are almost in the same boat.

Foxes is an ambitious movie, not an exploitation picture. It's a lot more serious, for example, than the hit *Little Darlings*. It contains the sounds and rhythms of real teenage lives; it was written and directed after a lot of research, and is acted by kids who are to one degree or another playing themselves. The movie's a rare attempt to provide a portrait of the way teen-agers really do live today in some suburban cultures.

Frances ★ ★ ★ ½
R, 139 m., 1983

Jessica Lange (Frances Farmer), Sam Shepard (Harry York), Bart Burns (Farmer). Directed by Graeme Clifford and produced by Jonathan Sanger. Screenplay by Eric Bergren, Christopher Devore, and Nicholas Kazan.

Graeme Clifford's *Frances* tells the story of a small-town girl who tasted the glory of Hol-lywood and the exhilaration of Broadway and then went on to lead a life during which everything went wrong. It is a tragedy without a villain, a sad story with no moral except that there, but for the grace of God, go we. The movie is about Frances Farmer, a beautiful and talented movie star from the 1930s and 1940s who had a streak of independence and a compulsion toward self-destruction, and who went about as high and about as low as it is possible to go in one lifetime. She came out of Seattle as a high school essay-contest winner and budding intellectual. She was talented and pretty enough to make her way fairly easily into show business, where she immediately gravitated to the left-wing precincts of the Group Theater and such landmark productions as Clifford Odets's *Waiting for Lefty*. She also became a movie star, and there was a time when her star shone so brightly that it seemed it would last forever.

It did not. She was a stubborn, opinionated star who fought with the studio system, defied the bosses, drank too much, took too many pills, and got into too much trouble. Her strong-willed mother stepped in to help her, and that's when Frances's troubles really began. The mother orchestrated a series of hospitalizations in bizarre mental institutions, where Frances Farmer was brutally mistreated and finally, horrifyingly, lobotomized. She ended her days as a vague, pleasant middle-aged woman who did a talk show in Indianapolis and finally died of alcoholism.

Jessica Lange plays Frances Farmer in a performance that is so driven, that contains so many different facets of a complex personality, that we feel she has an intuitive understanding of this tragic woman. She is just as good when she portrays Farmer as an uncertain, appealing teen-ager from the Northwest as she is when she plays her much later, snarling at a hairdresser and screaming at her mother. All of those contradictions were inside Farmer, and if she had learned to hide or deal with some of them she might have lived a happier life.

The story of Frances Farmer makes a fascinating movie, if only because it's such a contrast to standard show-business biographies. They usually come in two speeds: rags to riches, or rags to riches to victim. *Frances* never really lays blame for the tragedy of Farmer's life. It presents a number of causes for Farmer's destruction. (A short list might include her combative personality, her shrewish mother, the studio system, betrayal by her lovers, alcoholism, drug abuse, psychiatric malpractice, and the predations of a mad lobotomist.) But the movie never comes right out and says what it believes "caused" Farmer's tragedy. That is good, I think, because no simple explanation will do for Farmer's life. The movie is told from her point of view, and from where she stood, she was surrounded. On one day she had one enemy, and on another day, another enemy. Always, of course, her worst enemy was herself. The movie doesn't let us off the hook by giving us someone to blame. Instead, it insists on being a bleak tragedy, and it argues that sometimes it is quite possible for everything to go wrong. Since most movies are at least optimistic enough to provide a *cause* for human tragedy, this one is sort of daring.

It is also well made by Clifford, whose credits as a film editor include such virtuoso work as *McCabe and Mrs. Miller* and *Don't Look Now*. In his debut as a director Clifford has made a period picture that wears its period so easily that we're not distracted by it, a movie that is bleak without being unwatchable.

There are a few problems with his structure, most of them centering around an incompletely explained friend of Farmer's, played by Sam Shepard as a guy who seems to drift into her life whenever the plot requires him. Kim Stanley plays Farmer's mother on a rather thankless note of shrillness, and the lobotomist in the picture seems to have wandered over from a nearby horror film. (He apparently gave the same impression in real life.) But Lange provides a strong emotional center for the film, and when it is over we're left with the feeling that Farmer never really got a chance to be who she should have been, or to do what she should have done. She had every gift she needed in life except for luck, useful friends, and an instinct for survival. She could have been one of the greatest movie stars of her time. As it is, when I was asked to name a few of Frances Farmer's best films, I had to admit that, off-hand, I couldn't think of one.

Frantic ★ ★ ★
R, 115 m., 1988

Harrison Ford (Richard Walker), Emmanuelle Seigner (Michelle), Betty Buckley (Sondra Walker), John Mahoney (Embassy Official), Jimmie Ray Weeks (Embassy Security).

Directed by Roman Polanski and produced by Thom Mount and Tim Hampton. Screenplay by Polanski and Gerard Brach.

The first thing I noticed were the tones of the voices, low, flat, and weary. Just like people should sound after the twelve-hour flight from San Francisco to Paris. They are happy to be in Paris, but would be happier to be in bed. This was where they spent their honeymoon, twenty years ago, and now Dr. Richard Walker and his wife, Sondra, have returned for a medical convention.

There is some confusion with the luggage; apparently she picked up the wrong bag at the airport. But everything else seems to be going perfectly when Walker steps into his hotel shower. The phone rings, his wife answers it and says something, but he can't hear her because the water is running. By the time he steps out of the shower, she has disappeared.

That's the setup for *Frantic*, Roman Polanski's thriller and a professional comeback for the director of *Rosemary's Baby* and *Chinatown*, who was previously reduced to serving as gun-for-hire on the dreary *Pirates*. Every scene of this film feels like a project from Polanski's heart—a film to prove he is still capable of generating the kind of suspense he became famous for. And every scene, on its own, seems to work. It is only the total of the scenes that is wrong; the movie goes on too long, adds too many elaborations, tacks on too many complications, until the lean and economical construction of the first hour begins to drift into self-parody.

The movie stars Harrison Ford as the visiting American doctor, who is unable to convince the hotel, police, and American Embassy officials that his wife (Betty Buckley) is truly missing. He tries to track her down on his own, with only a few clues. After finding a drunk who saw his wife being forced into a car, he opens the "wrong" suitcase she picked up at the airport and finds a phone number that may be a lead.

The movie then develops into a cat-and-mouse game played out in Paris nightclubs, airports, and parking garages. Along the way, Ford teams up with the young woman (Emmanuelle Seigner) who brought the suitcase into the country. She's a mercenary courier, who was hired to carry the suitcase, doesn't know what was in it, but wants the 10,000 francs she was promised.

I will not reveal any additional plot details. I will say, however, that the nature of the mystery becomes clear to the audience some

time before it becomes clear to Ford, and that the movie begins to lose its tightly wound tension about the time the Seigner character enters the plot. Until then, it develops with chilling logic, one step at a time. After the doctor and the girl become partners, it falls into more conventional patterns. And the series of endings—one false climax after another—is too contrived to be exciting.

Still, to watch the opening sequences of *Frantic* is to be reminded of Polanski's talent. Here is one of the few modern masters of the thriller and the *film noir*, whose career in exile has drifted aimlessly. *Frantic* would have benefited from the coldhearted cutting of some scenes and the trimming of others (such as a dance sequence in a nightclub that continues until it is inexplicable). But perhaps Polanski was so happy to be back where he belonged, making a big-budget thriller with a big star, that he lost his objectivity. It's understandable. And even with its excesses, *Frantic* is a reminder of how absorbing a good thriller can be.

Free Willy ★ ★ ★ ½
PG, 113 m., 1993

Jason James Richter (Jesse), Lori Petty (Rae), August Schellenberg (Randolph), Michael Madsen (Glen), Jayne Atkinson (Annie), Michael Ironside (Dial), Richard Riehle (Wade). Directed by Simon Wincer and produced by Jennie Lew Tugend and Lauren Shuler-Donner. Screenplay by Keith A. Walker and Corey Blechman.

Free Willy tells the story of a boy and his whale, and if that sounds like an unwieldy adaptation of the sturdy old formula about a boy and his dog, it is. Whales are not as charismatic as dogs, not as easily trained, and cannot be hugged. Yet *Free Willy* works its way around the physical reality of its animal lead, and somehow becomes one of the summer of 1993's best family pictures.

The movie stars Jason James Richter as Jesse, a twelve-year-old who is going through a stormy period in his life. He has just moved into a foster home, and although his new parents (Michael Madsen and Jayne Atkinson) are patient and loving, he finds it necessary to test them by rebelling. He's unruly, insulting, distant, and disappears for hours at a time.

One day Jesse is caught spraying graffiti at the ramshackle "adventure park" near his home, and is ordered to clean the graffiti as punishment. Washing his work off the walls of the seaquarium, he becomes aware of

Willy, an Orca whale who has recently been captured. And one night, running away from home and sitting in the moonlight near Willy's tank, he finds that the whale seems to react to the sound of his harmonica.

It's the start of a beautiful friendship. The boy and the whale both feel homeless, cut off from their real families—Willy because he has been captured, Jesse because (as a social worker patiently explains) his birth mother has gone away and there is no reason to believe she will ever return. Eventually two friendly workers at the park, a trainer named Rae (Lori Petty, from *A League of Their Own*) and a handyman named Randolph (August Schellenberg) discover that Jesse has reached the creature that will pay attention to no one else. And Jesse becomes, overnight, not a future delinquent but a whale trainer.

The scenes with the whale are very convincing. The filmmakers have used a combination of a real whale and various animatronic whales to create a convincing, seamless illusion; there's a scene where Willy saves Jesse from drowning, and it's impossible to tell the real and artificial whales apart. The film also does what it can to give Willy a personality. In fact, it goes a little too far; by the end of the movie, Willy spontaneously figures out how to nod his head for "yes" and shake it from side to side for "no," skills which I suspect a real Orca would have little interest in developing.

The plot involves the larcenous, villainous owners of the park, who first want to exploit the relationship between Jesse and Willy, and then want to kill Willy for the insurance money. That sets into motion the predictable, but no less effective, conclusion, in which the threads of boy, whale, and family are all woven together nicely.

Free Willy has a kind of gentle sweetness that I found very appealing. It is about change—about a young boy discovering himself—and about adventure. And the "save the whales" subplot makes it more than just an adventure, or a caper. The screenplay is written with a certain intelligence; the relationship between Jesse and his foster parents, for example, has the ring of truth. The movie is sure to be appealing to younger viewers (they may find it more accessible and certainly less frightening than *Jurassic Park*), and it's smart enough to keep older viewers involved, too.

French Kiss ★ ★
PG-13, 103 m., 1995

Meg Ryan (Kate), Kevin Kline (Luc), Timothy Hutton (Charlie), Jean Reno (Jean-Paul), Susan Anbeh (Juliette), Francois Cluzet (Bob), Renee Humphrey (Lilly), Michael Riley (Campbell). Directed by Lawrence Kasdan and produced by Tim Bevan, Eric Fellner, Meg Ryan, and Kathryn F. Galan. Screenplay by Adam Brooks.

Some may question the casting of Kevin Kline as a Frenchman in *French Kiss*, but not I. Few French actors would have been capable of playing such a romantic wimp, and few Frenchmen, for that matter, would likely be interested in Meg Ryan's act as a neurotic woman who has been dumped by her fiancé in favor of a French "goddess." The characters in this movie may look like adults, but they think like teenagers.

The story: Kate (Meg Ryan) is engaged to Charlie (Timothy Hutton), but he has cold feet about marriage. He flies to Paris for a medical convention. Kate can't go along because she is so afraid of flying she flunked out of trauma school. A few days later, Charlie calls Kate and tells her (in a singularly unconvincing and badly written scene) that he cannot marry her because he has found the woman of his dreams.

Kate now overcomes her fears and flies off to France to win Charlie back. On the plane she meets Luc (Kevin Kline), an unshaven French jewel thief, who hides a diamond bracelet in her luggage and then must follow her halfway across France to get it back again. As an excuse he pretends to help her win her man back—but along the way, of course, they fall in love, and we have to wait until they figure that out.

Doris Day could have made this movie. She probably did. And she would have brought to it the same qualities Ryan brings, of spunk and vulnerability and charm. Only the charisma of Ryan and Kline make some of the scenes work at all, and as for the relationship between Hutton and the goddess (Susan Anbeh), it's all but inexplicable. No French woman with money, breeding, world-class model looks, and big hair is much interested in marrying an American doctor, especially one with no conversation.

Yet the movie is not without its charms. It takes place mostly in Paris and Cannes, two of the most photogenic cities on earth, and Owen Roizman's cinematography makes love to the locations. Ryan does a breathtaking job with the age-old transformation scene, turning from a caterpillar into a butterfly by ditching her sweats and putting on one of those French designer dresses that look like sexual gift wrapping. And Kline manages a plausible French accent, although his word order is usually English, a giveaway. (The movie provides yet another example of the Kevin Kline Mustache Principle, which observes that Kline always wears facial hair when playing goofballs, but shaves for serious roles.)

The movie wants to have some fun with nationalities. It gives us a snotty French hotel clerk and an insouciant French cop, and when Ryan has trouble with her passport (she is not quite either Canadian or American), she has to deal with Canadian and U.S. consular officials. All of those scenes could have been pushed a little further, I think, except that the movie is so firmly aimed at romance that director Lawrence Kasdan and his writer, Adam Brooks, hold back on the comic freedoms of supporting characters.

And the underlying problems remain. Kline's Frenchman is somehow not worldly enough, and Ryan's heroine never convinces us she ever loved her fiancé in the first place. Hutton and Anbeh have thankless roles; once the movie gets to France, their basic purpose is to be glimpsed from afar by Ryan. A movie about this kind of material should either be about people who feel true passion, or it should commit itself as a comedy. Compromise is pointless.

The French Lieutenant's Woman
★ ★ ★ ½
R, 124 m., 1981

Meryl Streep (Sarah and Anna), Jeremy Irons (Charles and Mike), Hilton McRae (Sam), Emily Morgan (Mary), Charlotte Mitchell (Mrs. Tranter), Lynsey Baxter (Ernestina). Directed by Karel Reisz and produced by Leon Clore. Screenplay by Harold Pinter.

Reading the last one hundred pages of John Fowles's *The French Lieutenant's Woman* is like being caught in a fictional labyrinth. We think we know where we stand in the story, and who the characters are and what possibilities are open to them, and then Fowles begins an astonishing series of surprises. He turns his story inside out, suggesting first one ending, then another, always in a way that forces us to rethink everything that has gone before. That complex structure was long thought to make Fowles's novel unfilmable. How could his fictional surprises, depending on the relationship between reader and omniscient narrator, be translated into the more literal nature of film? One of the directors who tried to lick *The French Lieutenant's Woman* was John Frankenheimer, who complained: "There is no way you can film the book. You can tell the same story in a movie, of course, but not in the same way. And how Fowles tells his story is what makes the book so good." That seemed to be the final verdict, until the British playwright Harold Pinter tackled the project.

Pinter's previous screenplays, such as *Accident* and *The Go-Between*, are known for a mastery of ambiguity, for a willingness to approach the audience on more than one level of reality, and what he and director Karel Reisz have done with their film, *The French Lieutenant's Woman*, is both simple and brilliant. They have frankly discarded the multilayered fictional devices of John Fowles, and tried to create a new cinematic approach that will achieve the same ambiguity. Fowles made us stand at a distance from his two doomed lovers, Sarah and Charles. He told their story, of a passion that was forbidden by the full weight of Victorian convention, and then he invited us to stand back and view that passion in terms of facts and statistics about . . . well, Victorian passions in general. Pinter and Reisz create a similar distance in their movie by telling us two parallel stories. In one of them, Sarah Woodruff (Meryl Streep) still keeps her forlorn vigil for the French lieutenant who loved and abandoned her, and she still plays her intriguing cat-and-mouse game with the obsessed young man (Jeremy Irons) who must possess her.

In the other story, set in the present, two actors named Anna and Mike are playing Sarah and Charles. And Anna and Mike are also having a forbidden affair, albeit a more conventional one. For the length of the movie's shooting schedule, they are lovers offscreen as well as on. But eventually Mike will return to his family and Anna to her lover.

This is a device that works, I think. Frankenheimer was right in arguing that just *telling* the Victorian love story would leave you with . . . just a Victorian love story. The modern framing story places the Victorian lovers in ironic relief. Everything they say and do has another level of meaning, because we know the "real" relationship between the actors themselves. Reisz opens his film with a shot that boldly states his approach: We see Streep in costume for her role as Sarah, attended by a movie makeup woman. A clapboard marks the scene, and *then* Streep walks into the movie's re-creation of the British coastal village of Lyme Regis.

"It's only a movie," this shot informs us. But, of course, it's *all* only a movie, including the story about the modern actors. And this confusion of fact and fiction interlocks perfectly with the psychological games played in the Victorian story by Sarah Woodruff herself.

The French lieutenant's woman is one of the most intriguing characters in recent fiction. She is not only apparently the victim of Victorian sexism, but also (as Charles discovers) its manipulator and master. She cleverly uses the conventions that would limit her, as a means of obtaining personal freedom and power over men. At least that is one way to look at what she does. Readers of the novel will know there are others.

The French Lieutenant's Woman is a beautiful film to look at, and remarkably well-acted. Streep was showered with praise for her remarkable double performance, and she deserved it. She is offhandedly contemporary one moment, and then gloriously, theatrically Victorian the next. Opposite her, Jeremy Irons is authoritative and convincingly bedeviled as the man who is frustrated by both of Streep's characters. The movie's a challenge to our intelligence, takes delight in playing with our expectations, and has one other considerable achievement as well: It entertains admirers of Fowles's novel, but does not reveal the book's secrets. If you see the movie, the book will still surprise you, and that's as it should be.

Frenzy ★ ★ ★ ★
R, 116 m., 1972

Jon Finch (Richard Blaney), Barry Foster (Rusk), Barbara Leigh-Hunt (Brenda Blaney), Anna Massey (Babs Mulligan), Alec McCowen (Chief Inspector Oxford), Vivien Merchant (Mrs. Oxford). Directed by Alfred Hitchcock. Associate producer William Hill. Screenplay by Anthony Shaffer.

Alfred Hitchcock's *Frenzy* is a return to old forms by the master of suspense, whose newer forms have pleased movie critics but not his public. This is the kind of thriller Hitchcock was making in the 1940s, filled with macabre details, incongruous humor, and the desperation of a man convicted of a crime he didn't commit.

The only 1970s details are the violence and the nudity (both approached with a certain grisly abandon that has us imagining *Psycho* without the shower curtain). It's almost as if Hitchcock, at seventy-three, was consciously attempting to do once again what he did better than anyone else. His films since *Psycho* struck out into unfamiliar territory and even got him involved in the Cold War *(Torn Curtain)* and the fringes of fantasy *(The Birds)*. Here he's back at his old stand.

Frenzy, which allegedly has a loose connection with a real criminal case, involves us in the exploits of a murderer known as The Necktie Killer (Barry Foster). And involvement is the sensation we feel, I think, since we know his identity from the beginning and sometimes cannot help identifying with him. There is a scene, for example, in which he inadvertently gets himself trapped in the back of a potato truck with a sack containing the body of his latest victim. We know he is a slimy bastard, but somehow we're sweating along with him as he crawls through the potatoes trying to regain a bit of incriminating evidence. He is the killer but, as is frequently the case with Hitchcock, another man seems much more guilty. This is Richard Blaney (Jon Finch), an ex-RAF hero who is down on his luck and has just lost his job. Through a series of unhappy coincidences which I'd better not give away, he's caught red-handed with the evidence while the killer walks away.

Hitchcock sets his action in the crowded back alleys of Covent Garden, where fruit and vegetable vendors rub shoulders with prostitutes, third-rate gangsters, bookies, and barmaids. A lot of the action takes place in a pub, and somehow Hitchcock gets more feeling for the location into his films than he usually does. With a lot of Hitchcock, you have the impression every frame has been meticulously prepared. This time, the smell and tide of humanity slops over. (There is even one tide in the movie which does a little slopping over humanity itself—but never mind.)

It's delicious to watch Hitchcock using the camera. Not a shot is wasted, and there is one elaborate sequence in which the killer goes upstairs with his victim. The camera precedes them up the stairs, watches them go in a door, and then backs down the stairs, alone, and across the street to look at the outside of the house. This shot is not for a moment a gimmick; the melancholy of the withdrawing camera movement is one of the most touching effects in the film, despite the fact that no people inhabit it.

There's a lot of humor, too, including two hilarious gourmet meals served to the Chief Inspector (Alec McCowen) by his wife (Vivien Merchant). There is suspense, and local color ("It's been too long since the Christie murders; a good colorful crime spree is good for tourism") and, always, Hitchcock smacking his lips and rubbing his hands and delighting in his naughtiness.

Fresh ★ ★ ★ ★
R, 109 m., 1994

Sean Nelson (Fresh), Giancarlo Esposito (Esteban), Samuel L. Jackson (Sam), N'Bushe Wright (Nichole), Ron Brice (Corky), Jean LaMare (Jake), Jose Zuniga (Lieutenant Perez), Luis Lantigua (Chuckie). Directed by Boaz Yakin and produced by Lawrence Bender and Randy Ostrow. Screenplay by Yakin.

Characters are never at a loss for words in the movies. They talk quickly, never hesitating or repeating themselves. Kids are especially articulate, like well-trained little word machines. Movies are getting to be more and more like television, where there's never a moment to spare. *Fresh* isn't like that. Here's a movie filled with drama and excitement, unfolding a plot of brilliant complexity, in which the central character is solemn and silent, saying only what he has to say, revealing himself only strategically.

Fresh is a twelve-year-old boy who lives in Brooklyn. He is a runner for drug dealers. Because he is smart and honest, they respect him. Fresh lives with eleven other children in the spotless, orderly apartment of his aunt, who is a saint, he agrees, but who is helpless against the dangers that children face in the streets. Sometimes he sees his dad, an alcoholic who lives in a camper and supports himself by hustling chess games for cash. Sometimes he sees his sister, who has moved out of their aunt's apartment to live with a dealer. Her days pass in a sad haze of drugs.

Fresh knows a lot about drugs, and has a good relationship with a local dealer named Esteban, who is not a bad man as drug dealers go, and who is proud of Fresh—thinking of him almost like a son. Fresh's life, and the city that formed it, are drawn carefully in the early scenes of *Fresh*, which was written and directed by Boaz Yakin, a sometime writer of Hollywood thrillers *(The Rookie),* who dropped out, moved to Paris, and told himself he would return to the movies only when he had something to say, and control over how it was said. *Fresh* meets those qualifications.

You may think, having seen an urban thriller or two, that you can guess how *Fresh* feels and sounds. You would be wrong. The sound track is not filled with loud, angry music. The plot is not manic but focused and perceptive. Fresh, the central character, is played in an extraordinary performance by Sean Nelson, as a boy who sees and understands much, and keeps his own counsel.

It is important that the film establish its world. We will need to understand it in order to appreciate the remarkable last act of this movie, in which Fresh pulls off a plan that is part scam and part revenge—an unforgiving retribution against the system that is destroying the lives of those he loves.

The early scenes are fascinating. Fresh is doted on by the dealers (Giancarlo Esposito is engaging as Esteban). A great future is predicted for him. He doesn't use drugs himself, and his opinion of those who do is indifference laced with contempt—except in the case of his older sister (N'Bushe Wright), who makes his heart weep. Fresh saves his money, and has a lot of it. He has some friends his own age, especially Chuckie (Luis Lantigua), who talks too much—a mistake Fresh never makes.

To fill the great vacuum in his life, the need for love and discipline, he returns to his father (Samuel L. Jackson), a man who might have been a great chess champion, and is still almost unbeatable in the rough school of New York street chess. His father, who is never far from a bottle purchased with his winnings, does the best he can for Fresh, using chess as a metaphor for life. It is during one of his chess lectures that Fresh conceives the audacious scheme he pulls off. Seeing the movie at the 1994 Cannes Film Festival, I thought I was hearing some chess advice. Seeing it the second time, I realized that the actual outcome of the movie was being predicted.

Fresh is barely old enough to be noticing girls, but there is one he does notice, and as she smiles sweetly at him, he feels his heart sing for perhaps the first time in his life. It is the outcome of this first schoolyard crush that influences all the rest of the movie. The movie is well constructed; no event is unmotivated, and Yakin's screenplay establishes all of the emotional reasons, too, so that nothing is unexplained, even what seems at first like the gratuitous death of a dog.

Sudden, violent death is a fact of life in America today. Guns have made our cities unsafe for children. What *Fresh* does is bring a new perspective to those facts, in the form of both drama and thriller. This is not an action film, not a clever, superficial thriller, but a story of depth and power, in which the dangerous streets are seen through the eyes of a twelve-year-old who reacts with the objectivity he has learned from chess, and the anger taught to him by his life.

The Freshman ★ ★ ★ ½
PG, 102 m., 1990

Marlon Brando (Carmine Sabatini), Matthew Broderick (Clark Kellogg), Bruno Kirby (Victor Ray), Penelope Ann Miller (Tina Sabatini), Frank Whaley (Steve Bushak), Jon Polito (Chuck Greenwald), Paul Benedict (Arthur Fleeber), Richard Gant (Lloyd Simpson). Directed by Andrew Bergman and produced by Mike Lobell. Screenplay by Bergman.

There have been a lot of movies where stars have repeated the triumphs of their past—but has any star ever done it more triumphantly than Marlon Brando does in *The Freshman*? He is doing a reprise here of his most popular character, Don Vito Corleone of *The Godfather*, and he does it with such wit, discipline, and seriousness that it's not a rip-off and it's not a cheap shot; it's a brilliant comic masterstroke.

The Brando character is named Carmine Sabatini this time, but in every other respect he's the Godfather. He looks like him, talks like him, and most of all has the easy air of great authority long exercised. In the film, he has a job for a young man who has just started in film school. He wants him to pick up a package at the freight terminal of the airport and deliver it to a certain address. Of course we're thinking it's drugs—that's what the young man assumes—but actually this delivery is of a most peculiar nature. It is a giant lizard.

The young man is played by Matthew Broderick. He has got off to an uncertain start in New York City after all of his possessions and money were stolen by a thief (Bruno Kirby) who met him in Grand Central Station and offered him a ride. Now he's in trouble at New York University's film school, where the professor (Paul Benedict) doesn't want to hear excuses; he only wants to hear how all of his students have purchased his book. So when Kirby wanders by, Broderick chases him down the street, collars him, and demands his possessions back. Kirby offers him better than that. He offers him a job.

The job involves a trip to Little Italy and the cloistered world behind the anonymous shop front of a social club where Carmine Sabatini keeps his office. On the wall is a photograph of Mussolini, there for nostalgia's sake ("It is like you might have a photo of the Beatles," Sabatini explains to the young man). The job offer is made, and accepted (after the don symbolically crushes some nuts in his hand), and before Broderick realizes it he has been swept up into the embrace of this Mafia family.

Penelope Ann Miller plays the don's daughter, Tina. A man with a machine gun is posted above the entrance to their home. Over the fireplace is the *Mona Lisa*. It's not a copy, as Broderick assumes. "Remember when it was sent over here to tour all of the museums?" Miller asks. "It never went back." She pushes a button, and we hear Nat King Cole singing "Mona Lisa" on the stereo system.

The Freshman was written and directed by Andrew Bergman, an unconventional comedy talent whose credits include co-authoring the screenplay for *Blazing Saddles* and writing *The In-Laws*. What he has created in *The Freshman* is a comedy of the peculiar, the oblique, and the offbeat. Very little is predictable in *The Freshman*—not the job Broderick is asked to do, not the relationship he finds himself in, and certainly not the climactic scene in which some very rich people sit down to a strange banquet while Maximilian Schell acts as maitre d' and Bert Parks serenades them with a version of "Maggie's Farm" that is unlike any that has ever been performed before.

When Brando finished filming *The Freshman* last September, he attacked the movie in a notorious interview in the *Toronto Globe and Mail*, claiming it was trash and that he was retiring from acting. A few days later, he retracted his statements and conceded that the movie might be all right, after all. Who knows what his motives were for either statement? Who ever knows with Brando? The fact is that while he's on the screen, few actors have a more complete command of their work, and in *The Freshman* he walks a tightrope above the hazards of bad laughs.

Think how many ways this performance could have gone wrong. Think of the criticism Brando risked receiving, from those ready to attack him for cashing in on his most famous performance by reprising it for a comedy. Brando must have known the dangers, but he must have had confidence in himself, too—enough to go ahead anyway, and to win a considerable gamble.

The other actors, perhaps aware of the chances Brando was taking, seem a little in awe of him—which is as it should be. Broderick is fine in the central role as the earnest film student, and Bruno Kirby has a lot of fun as the fast-talking street kid who knows all the angles. And Bert Parks must have been saving up his ideas for this movie ever since they terminated him at the Miss America pageant. *The Freshman* plays like a celebration of a lot of talented people who have all decided to try to get away with something.

Fried Green Tomatoes ★ ★ ★
PG-13, 130 m., 1992

Kathy Bates (Evelyn Couch), Mary Stuart Masterson (Idgie Threadgoode), Mary-Louise Parker (Ruth Jamison), Jessica Tandy (Ninny Threadgoode), Stan Shaw (Big George), Cicely Tyson (Sipsey), Chris O'Donnell (Buddy Threadgoode). Directed by Jon Avnet and produced by Avnet and Jordan Kerner. Screenplay by Fannie Flagg and Carol Sobieski.

I have a built-in resistance to movies where a couple of people sit around in the present, discussing a story that took place in the past, and then we get flashbacks showing the earlier story. I usually can't see what the point is: Why not just tell that story from the past and be done with it? And my blood always curdles a little toward the end of these flashback movies, when . . . hold on . . . can you believe it . . . *the person telling the story is actually that young person from all those years ago that (gasp!) the story actually happened to!*

Sometimes flashbacks work. They worked in *Citizen Kane*, for example. Usually they do not. Look at Bette Midler's *For the Boys*, which creeps with unendurable inevitability to a foregone conclusion. One of the reasons Jon Avnet's *Fried Green Tomatoes* survives the flashback structure is that it devises an interesting character to be the listener to the long-ago tale.

She is Evelyn Couch (Kathy Bates), dowdy, unhappily married, dripping with low self-esteem, who during a visit to a nursing home meets a sparkling old lady named Miz Threadgoode (Jessica Tandy). They start to talking, and before long Evelyn looks forward to her Wednesday visits, at which the old lady makes a continued story out of

the sensational events of half a century ago in the town of Whistle Stop, Georgia.

You have been to Whistle Stop before, in a dozen other books and movies. It is one of those Southern towns where decent folks get along fine with the Negroes, but the racist rednecks are forever driving up in their pickups and waving shotguns around and causing trouble. In this case, one of the rednecks is the violent, drunken husband of a young woman named Ruth (Mary-Louise Parker). Ruth actually shouldn't have ought to married him in the first place, especially according to Idgie Threadgoode (Mary Stuart Masterson), who wears pants and a tie and cuts her hair short and has a crush on Ruth.

The two women set up in business together as the Whistle Stop Café (breaded fried green tomatoes a speciality), with the help of Big George (Stan Shaw), a black man whose mother, Sipsey (Cicely Tyson), raised Idgie. But when the women insist on serving Big George at the café, the local Klansmen get riled, and when Ruth's evil husband disappears and is assumed murdered, the lynch mob decides Big George was the killer.

Well, what *did* happen to the drunken lout? That is the payoff of old Miz Threadgoode's story. But the murder and even the subsequent trial are not really the subject of *Fried Green Tomatoes*, which is really about nonconformity in an intolerant society. It's pretty clear that Idgie is a lesbian, and fairly clear that she and Ruth are a couple, although given the mores of the South at the time a lot goes unspoken, and we are never quite sure how clear things are to Ruth. It is also clear that they consider Sipsey and George better company than most of the white folks in town, and that, by deciding for themselves who they are and how they will lead their lives, Idgie and Ruth are a threat to the hidebound locals.

All of that makes an interesting story, but what is also interesting is the way the story gradually gives the Kathy Bates character the courage to deal with her own life. She is a compulsive overeater whose husband, Mr. Couch, was apparently named after the piece of furniture he favors while watching the complete seasons of all of America's professional sports teams on the TV. Even after she takes some of those titillating "Complete Woman" suggestions and turns up at the door wrapped in Saran Wrap, she's still not able to interest her husband.

Fried Green Tomatoes is fairly predictable, and the flashback structure is a distraction, but the

strength of the performances overcomes the problems of the structure. I especially liked Mary Stuart Masterson's work, but then I nearly always do (see her in *Some Kind of Wonderful*). And I enjoyed the vigor with which Jessica Tandy told her long-ago tale, about a woman not completely unlike herself.

The Friends of Eddie Coyle ★ ★ ★ ★
R, 102 m., 1973

Robert Mitchum (Eddie Coyle), Peter Boyle (Dillon), Richard Jordan (Dave Foley), Steven Keats (Jackie), Alex Rocco (Scalise), Joe Santos (Artie Van). Directed by Peter Yates and produced and written by Paul Monash.

Someone remarks of Eddie, about halfway through *The Friends of Eddie Coyle*, that for a two-bit hood, he has fingers in a lot of pies. Too many, as it turns out. Without ever rising to the top, Eddie has been employed in organized crime for most of his life. He's kind of a utility infielder, ready to trade in some hot guns, drive a hijacked truck, or generally make himself useful.

Eddie got the nickname "Fingers" some years ago after a gun deal. The buyers he supplied got caught. Their friends slammed Eddie's fingers in a drawer. He understood. There is a certain code without which it would be simply impossible to go on doing business.

But as the movie opens, Eddie is in trouble, and it looks like he'll have to break the code. He's facing a two-year stretch in New Hampshire, and he wants out of it. He doesn't want to leave his wife and kids and see them go on welfare. He is, at heart, just a small businessman; he deals in crime but is profoundly middle class. He thinks maybe he can make a deal with the state's attorney and have a few good words put in for him up in New Hampshire.

The movie is as simple as that. It's not a high-strung gangster film, it doesn't have a lot of overt excitement in it, and it doesn't go in for much violence. He gives us a man, invites our sympathy for him, and then watches almost sadly as his time runs out. And *The Friends of Eddie Coyle* works so well because Eddie is played by Robert Mitchum, and Mitchum has perhaps never been better.

He has always been one of our best screen actors: sardonic, masculine, quick-witted, but slow to reveal himself. He has never been in an absolutely great film; he doesn't have masterpieces behind him like Brando or Cary Grant. More than half his films have been conventional action melodramas, and it is a rare summer without at least one movie in which Mitchum wears a sombrero and lights bombs with his cigar. But give him a character and the room to develop it, and what he does is wonderful. Eddie Coyle is made for him: a weary middle-aged man, but tough and proud; a man who has been hurt too often in life not to respect pain; a man who will take chances to protect his own territory.

The movie is drawn from a knowledgeable novel by George V. Higgins, himself a state's attorney, and has been directed by one of the masters of this sort of thing, Peter Yates *(Robbery, Bullitt)*. Paul Monash's screenplay stays close to the real-life Massachusetts texture of the novel, and the dialogue sounds right. The story isn't developed in the usual movie way, with lots of importance being given to intricacies of plot; instead, Eddie's dilemma occurs to him as it occurs to us, and we watch him struggle with it.

If the movie has a flaw, it's that we don't really care that much about the bank robberies that are counterpointed with Eddie's situation. We're interested in him. We can get the bank robberies in any summer's caper picture. It's strange that a movie's interest should fall off during its action scenes. But this is Eddie Coyle's picture, and Mitchum's.

Fright Night ★ ★ ★
R, 106 m., 1985

Roddy McDowall (Peter Vincent), Chris Sarandon (Jerry, the Vampire), William Ragsdale (Charley), Amanda Bearse (Amy), Stephen Geoffreys (Evil Ed). Directed by Tom Holland and produced by Herb Jaffe. Screenplay by Holland.

The best line in *Fright Night* belongs to Roddy McDowall, who plays a broken-down old hambone actor who used to star in vampire movies. "The kids today," he complains, "don't have the patience for vampires. They want to see some mad slasher running around and chopping off heads." He's right. Vampires, who are doomed to live forever, have outlived their fashion. They've been replaced by guys in ski masks who hack their way through Dead Teen-ager Movies.

Fright Night is an attempt to correct that situation. It stars William Ragsdale as an impressionable teen-ager who becomes convinced that vampires have moved in next door. It doesn't take a detective to figure that out. The vampires almost flaunt their unholy natures, performing weird rites in

front of open windows and disposing of the bodies of their victims in plastic garbage bags. They are safe in the knowledge that nobody believes in vampires anymore.

The kid calls the cops. The vampires have a plausible explanation for their activities. The kid claims there has to be a coffin somewhere down in the basement. The cops warn him to stop wasting their time. And then, when the vampires start getting really threatening, the kid has no place to turn—except to old Peter Vincent (McDowall), the former B-movie actor who has just been fired from his TV job as host of the local Creature Features.

McDowall knows all about vampires: How to detect them, how to repel them, how to kill them. He also knows all about being behind on the rent, being evicted, and being out of work. For 500 bucks, he agrees to have a go at the vampires, and that sets up the second half of *Fright Night*.

The first part of the movie is basically funny. The second half unleashes lots of spectacular special effects devised by Richard Edlund, the same man who created the effects for *Ghostbusters*. Since part of the fun with vampire movies is how bad the special effects usually are, Edlund has to walk a narrow line, and he does. He gives us satisfactory scenes of transformations and decompositions, and seems to know his way around vampires, but he doesn't overwhelm the action.

The center of the movie, however, is the Roddy McDowall character, whose name, Peter Vincent, is obviously supposed to remind us of Peter Cushing and Vincent Price. Throw in Christopher Lee, and you'd have a quorum. McDowall's performance is wickedly funny, and he must have enjoyed it, chewing the scenery on his horror movie TV program and then chewing real scenery down in the vampire's basement. *Fright Night* is not a distinguished movie, but it has a lot of fun being undistinguished.

The Fringe Dwellers ★ ★ ★ ½
PG-13, 98 m., 1987

Kristina Nehm (Trilby), Justine Saunders (Mollie), Bob Maza (Joe), Kylie Belling (Noonah), Denis Walker (Bartie), Ernie Dingo (Phil). Directed by Bruce Beresford and produced by Sue Milliken. Screenplay by Bruce and Rhoisin Beresford.

There always seem to be too many people in Trilby's home. She is a teen-age girl who

lives in an aborigine shantytown in Australia, and who sometimes goes downtown to peer into the window of the travel agency and dream of Paris, London, and New York. At home, there are parents and brothers and sisters and uncles and aunts and cousins in a riotous, disorganized, and loving extended family. They all love Trilby, but she is a quiet child, proud and stubborn, determined that she will make something of her life.

Trilby's determination is the central story in *The Fringe Dwellers*, a gentle and powerful movie by Bruce Beresford, who made it between *Tender Mercies* and *Crimes of the Heart*. In all three films, he shows a strong instinct for people living on the outside of society, on their own terms, drawing strength when they can from the people who love them.

The Fringe Dwellers is probably the most interesting of the three, because it shows us a world we know little about: Aborigines in an uncertain relationship with white society in Australia. Trilby and her younger brother are both doing well in school. An older sister has a gift for nursing, and is well-regarded at the local hospital. But Trilby's parents belong to an earlier generation—their lives are still sometimes ordered by myths that go back to the traditional aborigine culture—and they are not, truth to tell, all that eager to embrace white society.

Trilby feels trapped by the communal life in the shantytown. She convinces her parents to buy a new home in a white housing development, even though they can hardly afford it. But all of the uncles and aunts and cousins and neighbors follow them there (her parents can't resist inviting them to move in), and she still doesn't have a room of her own.

The film unfolds in a series of brief episodes. Trilby and three other aborigines go into a soda shop and have to sit through rude stares and half-audible racist jokes from the white kids, which is bad, but then a white man assures everyone they have "a perfect right" to be there, and that's worse. "I don't want anyone speaking up for me," Trilby says.

In school, she slaps a white girl and is reprimanded. If she had been white, she tells her boyfriend, she would have been expelled: "They're going easy because they feel sorry for me." Through many small glimpses like this, we begin to know her as a young woman who wants to be judged entirely on her own.

The Fringe Dwellers is a movie filled with life and laughter, as well as hurtful silences. There is a remarkable scene between the mother and daughter in which some of the mother's heritage and wisdom is expressed. There are perhaps a dozen fringe characters, including an old cousin who feels his time has come to return to the Outback lands of his ancestors. And then there are the modern problems, as when Trilby gets pregnant.

Will the baby lock her into repeating the lifetime cycle of poverty? Here Beresford provides a mysterious, unexplained scene (which I will not reveal), which seems to answer that question with a much larger question. The scene, like a couple of others in the movie, seems to imply that aborigines really do have inherited psychic powers. This is a common theme in Australian films; stories may begin with racial prejudice as their subjects, but they tend to skew off into mystical speculations about the ancient traditions and metaphysical gifts of aborigines. These traditions and gifts may, for all I know, be real, but the function they play in the movies is the Australian equivalent of American truisms about how blacks have natural rhythm.

In *The Fringe Dwellers*, Trilby's life is touched by the supernatural—an old crone foretells the future in a disturbing scene— but it is controlled much more by Trilby's own determination. She is played by Kristina Nehm, in an extraordinary screen debut; this young actress is not only beautiful and graceful, but is able to express a great deal more than she says—which is the point. She is surrounded by wonderful performances, especially by Justine Saunders as her mother. And at the end of the movie, I found myself truly interested in what eventually would happen to her, and whether she would realize her dream. There aren't many movie characters I can really care about, but here is one.

The Fugitive ★ ★ ★ ★
PG-13, 133 m., 1993

Harrison Ford (Dr. Richard Kimble), Tommy Lee Jones (Deputy U.S. Marshal Gerard), Jeroen Krabbe (Dr. Charles Nichols), Joe Pantoliano (Renfro), Andreas Katsulas (Sykes), Sela Ward (Helen Kimble), Daniel Roebuck (Biggs), L. Scott Caldwell (Poole), Tom Wood (Newman). Directed by Andrew Davis and produced by Arnold Kopelson. Screenplay by Jeb Stuart and David Twohy.

Andrew Davis's *The Fugitive* is a tense, taut, and expert thriller that becomes something more than that: an allegory about an innocent man in a world prepared to crush him.

Like the cult television series that inspired it, the film has a Kafkaesque view of the world. But it is larger and more encompassing than the series: Davis paints with bold visual strokes so that the movie rises above its action-film origins and becomes operatic.

The story involves a cat-and-mouse game between a man unjustly accused of having murdered his wife, and a law officer who tracks him with cunning ferocity. This was, of course, Hitchcock's favorite theme, touching on the universal dread of the innocent man wrongly accused. The man is Dr. Richard Kimble (Harrison Ford), a respected Chicago surgeon, who returns home one night to find his wife fatally beaten by a one-armed man who flees after a struggle. All of the evidence points to Kimble's guilt, and his story of the intruder is brushed away in a courtroom scene of such haste and finality that, like a lot of the film, it only looks realistic while actually functioning on the level of a nightmare.

Kimble is sentenced to death, but escapes during a collision between his prison bus and a train. The crash sequence is as ambitious and electric as any I have seen, with Kimble fleeing for his life while a locomotive bears down on him (the echo here is of Harrison Ford's famous sequence in *Raiders of the Lost Ark* in which he is nearly crushed by a giant stone ball).

Free for the time being, but isolated in a cold winter landscape of hostile stones, icy water, and barren trees, Kimble is pursued in a manhunt directed by a deputy U.S. marshal (Tommy Lee Jones). It seems incredible that he could remain free, and even pursue attempts to prove his innocence, but he does, in a film that never relaxes its tension even for an instant. This is pure filmmaking on a master scale.

Tommy Lee Jones has become one of the great craggy presences of the screen, often cast as a villain, but with a half-masked amusement that borders on contempt for lesser beings: He has the charm of a hangman promising to make things as comfortable as possible. In *The Fugitive*, his role is more complex than at first it seems. As the chase continues, he gradually becomes convinced of the innocence of his prey, but this conviction is wisely never spelled out in dialogue, and remains ambivalent, expressed in the look in his eyes, or his pauses between words.

Ford is once again the great modern movie everyman, dogged, determined, brave, and not demonstrative. As an actor, nothing he does seems merely for show, and in the face of this melodramatic material he deliberately plays down, lays low, gets on with business instead of trying to exploit the drama in meaningless acting flourishes.

The director, Andrew Davis, has come up through a series of superior action films. His gift was apparent in one of his earlier features, the Chuck Norris thriller *Code of Silence*, which remains Norris's best film and one of the best, most atmospheric uses of Chicago locations ever achieved. Davis's good films continued with the Steven Seagal thriller *Above the Law*, *The Package* with Gene Hackman, and 1992's superb *Under Siege*. Here he transcends genre and shows an ability to marry action and artistry that deserves comparison with Hitchcock, yes, and also with David Lean and Carol Reed.

The device of the film is to keep Kimble only a few steps ahead of his pursuers. It is a dangerous strategy, and could lead to laughable close calls and near-misses, but Davis tells the story of the pursuit so clearly on the tactical level that we can always understand why Kimble is only so far ahead, and no farther. As always, Davis uses locations not simply as the place where action occurs, but as part of the reason for the action. Consider his virtuoso opening chase sequence, which after the train crash leads to a series of drainage tunnels (echoes here of *The Third Man*) and finally to a spectacular dam, where Kimble risks death for a chance of freedom, and dives into the cascading waters in a moment that can only be called Wagnerian.

Jones's "Deputy," as he likes to be called, has much more dialogue than Kimble, and in the screenplay by Jeb Stuart and David Twohy it always serves an intelligent purpose. You never have the feeling the characters are saying things simply to give us information; instead, a little at a time, they reveal the way they are thinking. Jones is surrounded by good character actors, who for once sound like Chicago cops in their words and inflections, instead of like transplants from a TV police drama. Strangely, although the film is relentlessly manipulative, it plays like real events. Nothing can really be believed in retrospect, but Davis and his actors ground all the action and dialogue in reality, so we don't consider the artifice while it's happening.

Thrillers are a much-debased genre these days, depending on special effects and formula for much of their content. *The Fugitive* has the standards of an earlier, more classic time, when acting, character, and dialogue were meant to stand on their own, and where characters continued to change and develop right up until the last frame.

Full Metal Jacket ★ ★ ½
R, 121 m., 1987

Matthew Modine (Private Joker), Arliss Howard (Cowboy), Vince D'Onofrio ("Gomer" Pyle), Dorian Harewood (Eightball), Lee Ermey (Sergeant Hartman), Adam Baldwin (Animal Mother), Kevyn Major Howard (Rafterman), Ed O'Ross (Lieutenant Touchdown). Directed and produced by Stanley Kubrick. Screenplay by Kubrick, Michael Herr, and Gustav Hasford.

Stanley Kubrick's *Full Metal Jacket* is more like a book of short stories than a novel. Many of the passages seem self-contained, and some of them are masterful, and others look like they came out of the bottom drawer. This is a strangely shapeless film from the man whose work usually imposes a ferociously consistent vision on his material.

The movie is about Vietnam, and was shot on stages and outdoor sets in England. To say it's one of the best-looking war movies ever made on sets and stages is not quite enough praise, after the awesome reality of *Platoon*, *Apocalypse Now*, and *The Deer Hunter*. The crucial last passages of the film too often look and feel like World War II films from Hollywood studios. We see the same sets from so many different angles that after the movie we could find our own way around Kubrick's Vietnam.

That would not be a problem if his material made the sets irrelevant. It does not, especially toward the end of the film. You can only watch so much footage of a man crouched behind a barrier, pinned down by sniper fire, before the situation turns into a cinematic cliché. We've been here before, in other war movies, and we keep waiting for Kubrick to spring a surprise, and he never does.

The opening passages of *Full Metal Jacket* promise much more than the film is finally able to deliver. They tell the story of a group of Marine grunts undergoing basic training on Parris Island, and the experience comes down to a confrontation between the Gunnery Sergeant (Lee Ermey) and a tubby misfit (Vince D'Onofrio) who is nicknamed Gomer Pyle. These are the two best performances in the movie, which never recovers after they leave the scene.

Ermey plays a character in the great tradition of movie drill instructors, but with great brio and amazingly creative obscenity. All situations in the Marines and in war seem to suggest sexual parallels for him, and one of the film's best moments has the recruits going to bed with their rifles and reciting a traditional U.S. Marine Corps love poem to them.

In scene after scene, the war/sex connection is reinforced, and it parallels the personal battle between Ermey and D'Onofrio, who at first fails all of the tasks in basic training, and then finds he has one skill; he is an expert marksman. It is likely that in a real boot camp D'Onofrio would have been thrown out after a week, but Kubrick's story requires him to stay, and so he does, until the final showdown between the two men.

In that showdown, and at several other times in the film, Kubrick indulges his favorite close-up, a shot of a man glowering up at the camera from beneath lowered brows. This was the trademark visual in *A Clockwork Orange*, and Jack Nicholson practiced it in *The Shining*. What does it mean? That Kubrick thinks it's an interesting angle from which to shoot the face, I think. In *Full Metal Jacket*, it promises exactly what finally happens, and spoils some of the suspense.

There is a surprise to come, however: The complete abandonment of the sexual metaphor once the troops are in Vietnam. The movie disintegrates into a series of self-contained set pieces, none of them quite satisfying. The scene in the press room, for example with the lecture on propaganda, seems to reflect some of the same spirit as *Dr. Strangelove*. But how does it connect with the curious scene of the Vietnamese prostitute—a scene with a riveting beginning but no middle or end? And how do either lead to the final shoot-out with a sniper?

Time and again in the film, we get great shots with no payoffs. In one elaborate setup, for example, Kubrick shows us a cameraman and a soundman being led by their shirttails as they pan down a line of exhausted Marines. At first the shot has power. Then the outcome is that several soldiers deliver neat one-liners, all in a row, all in their turns, all perfectly timed, and the effect is so contrived that the idea of actual battle is completely lost.

Kubrick seems to want to tell us the story of individual characters, to show how the war affected them, but it has been so long since he allowed spontaneous human nature into his films that he no longer knows how.

After the departure of his two most memorable characters, the sergeant and the tubby kid, he is left with no characters (or actors) that we really care much about, and in a key scene at the end, when a Marine feels joy after finally killing someone, the payoff is diminished because we don't give a damn about the character.

The movie has great moments. Ermey's speech to his men about the great Marine marksmen of the past (Charles Whitman and Lee Harvey Oswald among them) is a masterpiece. The footage on the Parris Island obstacle course is powerful. But *Full Metal Jacket* is uncertain where to go, and the movie's climax, which Kubrick obviously intends to be a mighty moral revelation, seems phoned in from earlier war pictures. After what has already been said about "Vietnam" in the movies, *Full Metal Jacket* is too little and too late.

Funny Farm ★ ★ ★ ½
PG, 98 m., 1988

Chevy Chase ((ndy), Madolyn Smith (Elizabeth), Kevin O'Morrison (Sheriff Ledbetter), Joseph Maher (Michael Sinclair), Jack Gilpin (Bud Culbertson), Caris Corfman (Betsy Culbertson), William Severs (Newspaper Editor), Mike Starr (Crocker). Directed by George Roy Hill and produced by Robert L. Crawford. Screenplay by Jeffrey Boam.

Funny Farm is one of those small miracles that start out like a lot of other movies and then somehow find their own way, step after step, to an original comic vision. *Funny Farm* is funny, all right, but it's more than funny, it's likable. It enlists our sympathies with the characters even while cheerfully exploiting their faults. And at the end, I had a goofy grin on my face because the movie had won me over so completely I was even willing to accept the final gag about the two ducks.

The movie stars Chevy Chase and Madolyn Smith as a married couple who decide to move to a small New England town so he can write his novel and they can breathe the fresh country air and mow their own lawn. Chase has been a sportswriter for years, but now he figures that with the typewriter placed just exactly right next to the big open window on the second floor overlooking the lawn, conditions will be perfect for the creation of a bestseller.

Conditions are not perfect. The birds sing too loudly. The mailman speeds by in a cloud of dust hurling letters from the window of his pickup. There are snakes in the lake and a corpse buried in the garden and it costs twenty cents to make a call from the pay phone in the kitchen. And the townspeople, they discover, are drawn more from Stephen King than Norman Rockwell. By wintertime, Chase is withdrawn and bitter, drinking heavily, and sleeping past noon, while his wife has sold a children's novel about a city squirrel who moves to the country and has the same name as her husband.

None of this, I imagine, sounds as good as it plays. *Funny Farm* has a good screenplay by Jeffrey Boam, and yet in other hands it might have yielded only a routine movie. George Roy Hill, the director, makes it better than that because he finds the right tone and sticks to it—a sort of bemused wonder at the insanity of it all, in a movie that doesn't underline its gags or force its punch lines but just lets everything develop naturally. Notice, for example, the timing in the sequence where the sheriff first comes to chat about the corpse in the garden.

Chevy Chase is not exactly playing a fresh kind of role here—his hero is a variation of the harassed husband he's been playing for years—but he has never been better in a movie. He has everything just right this time, and he plays the character without his usual repertory of witty asides and laconic one-liners. It's a performance, not an appearance. Madolyn Smith makes a good foil for him, although she isn't given enough to do in scenes of her own, and one scene in particular—a visit to an antique shop—felt suspiciously truncated.

The gallery of townspeople has to be seen to be believed. They are almost all meanspirited, crafty, suspicious, and greedy, and happy to be just exactly who they are. The sheriff travels by taxi because he flunked his driving test, the lady who runs the antique shop seems to be selling nothing except her own precious and irreplaceable family heirlooms, and down at the local cafe, there's a competition to see who can eat the most stir-fried lamb testicles.

Funny Farm is kind of a loony, off-center comedy version of Hill's *The World According to Garp*, another movie about strange people

in bizarre situations. *Garp* made too much of its significance, however, while the comedy in this film is light as a feather. The final sequence, in which the townspeople are bribed to act "normal," while Chase hands out Norman Rockwell covers from the *Saturday Evening Post* for them to admire, has a kind of inspired lunacy that is so fragile you almost don't want to laugh for fear of breaking the mood.

F/X ★ ★ ★ ½
R, 108 m., 1985

Bryan Brown (Rollie Tyler), Cliff DeYoung (Lipton), Brian Dennehy (Lieutenant Leo McCarthy), Trey Wilson (Lieutenant Murdoch), Mason Adams (Mason), Martha Gehman (Andy), Diane Venora (Ellen), Jerry Orbach (DeFranco), Tim Gallin (Adams). Directed by Robert Mandel and produced by Dodi Fayed and Jack Wiener. Screenplay by Robert T. Megginson and Gregory Fleeman.

F/X is Hollywood shorthand for "effects," or special effects, the art form that creates bullet holes and gaping wounds, fake shotgun blasts, and severed limbs.

In the movie, Bryan Brown plays a special-effects man whose customized truck is a mobile effects lab. He can create his illusions almost anywhere, and is in big demand from the Hollywood studios. Then one day he gets an unusual request from the federal government. As part of their witness relocation and protection program, they want to fake the murder of an organized-crime leader. Their reasoning: If everybody thinks DeFranco is dead, nobody will try to kill him, and he will survive and be able to testify in court.

This premise is only the beginning of the movie's ingenuity. Like *Jagged Edge*, this is one of those tightly constructed plots in which the hero is almost the last person to find out anything. Who can he trust? Who is really on his side, who is lying to him, who is trying to kill him? One of the pleasures of *Jagged Edge* was that we could watch the central character, the lawyer played by Glenn Close, use all of her intelligence and intuition and still walk right into danger, because she could not believe that people could be such deceptive swine.

The same thing happens in *F/X*, and I will have to tread carefully to avoid giving away too much of the plot. Briefly, there are large, basic questions about who wants DeFranco, the underworld leader, killed, and who wants him alive. There are other fundamental questions about whether special effects have indeed been used, or whether he actually was killed. And there are great ominous possibilities that the special-effects man himself might be next on the hit list.

The movie moves quickly through a large gallery of players. At the center of everything is Rollie Tyler, the effects man, given a nice, laconic professionalism by Bryan Brown, whose Australian accent reminds us that he was not brought up to automatically trust the U.S. government in all matters.

The Broadway veteran Jerry Orbach plays DeFranco as an expensively barbered creep. Halfway through the movie, the dependable character actor Brian Dennehy turns up as a city cop not in on the scam. Cliff DeYoung is the slippery Lipton, mastermind of the federal scheme. Martha Gehman is Andy, the loyal assistant of the effects man, and Diane Venora is his doomed girlfriend.

I mention so many of these actors because, more than most thrillers that depend on tightly constructed plots, *F/X* also depends on good, well-observed performances. This movie takes a lot of delight in being more psychologically complex than it has to be. It contains fights and shoot-outs and big chase scenes, but they're all firmly centered on who the characters are and what they mean to one another. And by the end of the film when everything comes down to the events in a large, scary, and isolated mansion, the movie is able to use the personalities of the characters as part of the payoff.

Every year should bring a few good thrillers, to balance out all the failed and shallow attempts. The irony of *F/X*, which is a very good thriller indeed, is that it avoids the pitfall of so many thrillers; it doesn't degenerate into a mindless display of special effects. The effects in this film just happen to be the ways the hero has of expressing himself.

G

The Gambler ★ ★ ★ ★
R, 111 m., 1974

James Caan (Axel), Paul Sorvino (Hips), Lauren Hutton (Billie), Morris Carnovsky (A.R. Lowenthal), Jacqueline Brooks (Naomi), Burt Young (Carmine). Directed by Karel Reisz and produced by Irwin Winkler and Robert Chartoff. Screenplay by James Toback.

"Jeez, Axel, I never seen such bad cards," Axel Freed's friend tells him consolingly. They're standing in the kitchen of a New York apartment, and gray dawn is seeping through the smoke. Axel has never seen such bad cards either. His disbelief that anyone could draw so many lousy poker hands in a row has led him finally $44,000 into debt. He doesn't have the money, but it's been a bigtime game, and he has to find it somewhere or be in heavy trouble.

And that's how Karel Reisz's *The Gambler* begins: with a problem. The way Axel solves his problem is only fairly difficult. He borrows the money from his mother, who is a doctor. But then we discover that his problem is greater than his debt, because there is some final compulsion within him that won't let him pay back the money. He needs to lose, to feel risk, to place himself in danger. He needs to gamble away the forty-four grand on even more hopeless bets because in a way it isn't gambling that's his obsession—it's danger itself.

"I play in order to lose," he tells his bookie at one point. "That's what gets my juice going. If I only bet on the games I know, I could at least break even." But he doesn't want that. At one point, he's driven to bet money he doesn't really have on college basketball games picked almost at random out of the sports pages.

And yet Axel Freed is not simply a gambler, but a very complicated man in his mid-thirties who earns his living as a university literature teacher. He teaches Dostoyevski, William Carlos Williams, Thoreau. But he doesn't seem to teach their works so much as what he finds in them to justify his own obsessions. One of the students in his class has Axel figured out so completely that she always has the right answer, when he asks what Thoreau is saying, or what Dostoyevski is saying. They're saying, as Axel reads them, to take risks, to put the self on the line.

"Buffalo Bill's defunct," he says, quoting the e e cummings poem, and the death of the nineteenth-century age of heroes obsesses him. In that earlier age, he could have tested himself more directly. His grandfather came to America flat broke, fought and killed to establish himself, and still is a man of enormous vitality at the age of eighty. The old man is respectable now (he owns a chain of furniture stores), but the legend of his youth fascinates Axel, who recites it poetically at the eightieth-birthday party.

Axel finds nothing in 1974 to test himself against, however. He has to find his own dangers, to court and seduce them. And the ultimate risk in his life as a gambler is that behind his friendly bookies and betting cronies is the implacable presence of the Mafia, the guys who take his bets like him, but if he doesn't pay, there's nothing they can do. "It's out of my hands," his pal Hips explains. "A bad gambling debt has got to be taken care of." And that adds an additional dimension to *The Gambler*, which begins as a portrait of Axel Freed's personality, develops into the story of his world, and then pays off as a thriller. We become so absolutely contained by Axel's problems and dangers that they seem like our own. There's a scene where he soaks in the bathtub and listens to the last minutes of a basketball game, and another scene where he sits in the stands and watches a basketball game he has tried to fix (while a couple of hit men watch him), and these scenes have a quality of tension almost impossible to sustain.

But Reisz sustains them, and makes them all the more real because he doesn't populate the rest of his movie with stock characters.

Axel Freed, as played by James Caan, is himself a totally convincing personality, and original. He doesn't derive from other gambling movies or even from other roles he's played.

And the people around him also are specific, original creations. His mother Naomi (Jacqueline Brooks) is a competent, independent person who gives him the money because she fears for his life, and yet understands that his problem is deeper than gambling. His grandfather, marvelously played by Morris Carnovsky, is able to imply by his behavior why he fascinates Axel so. The various bookies and collectors he comes across aren't Mafia stereotypes. They enforce more in sorrow than in anger. Only his girlfriend (Lauren Hutton) fails to seem very real. Here's still another demonstration of the inability of contemporary movies to give us three-dimensional women under thirty.

There's a scene in *The Gambler* that has James Caan on screen all by himself for two minutes, locked in a basement room, waiting to meet a Mafia boss who will arguably instruct that his legs be broken. In another movie, the scene could have seemed too long, too eventless.

But Reisz, Caan, and screenwriter James Toback have constructed the character and the movie so convincingly that the scene not only works, but works two ways: first as suspense, and then as character revelation. Because as we look into Axel Freed's caged eyes we see a person who is scared to death and yet stubbornly ready for this moment he has brought down upon himself.

Gandhi ★ ★ ★ ★
PG, 188 m., 1982

Ben Kingsley (Mahatma Gandhi), Candice Bergen (Margaret Bourke-White), Edward Fox (General Dyer), John Gielgud (Lord Irwin), Trevor Howard (Judge Broomfield), John Mills (The Viceroy), Martin Sheen (Walker), Rohini Hattangady (Kasturba Ghandi), Ian Charleson (Charlie Andrews), Athol Fugard (General Smuts). Directed and produced by Richard Attenborough. Screenplay by John Briley.

In the middle of this epic film there is a quiet, small scene that helps explain why *Gandhi* is such a remarkable experience. Mahatma Gandhi, at the height of his power and his fame, stands by the side of a lake with his wife of many years. Together, for the benefit of a visitor from the West, they reenact their marriage vows. They do it with solemnity, quiet warmth, and perhaps just a touch of shyness; they are simultaneously demonstrating an aspect of Indian culture and touching on something very personal to them both. At the end of the ceremony, Gandhi says, "We were thirteen at the time." He shrugs. The marriage had been arranged. Gandhi and his wife had not been in love, had not been old enough for love, and yet love had grown between them. But that is not really the point of the scene. The point, I think, comes in the quiet smile with which Gandhi says the words. At that moment we believe that he is fully and truly human, and at that moment, a turning point in the film, *Gandhi* declares that it is not only a historical record but a breathing, living document.

This is the sort of rare epic film that spans the decades, that uses the proverbial cast of thousands, and yet follows a human thread from beginning to end: *Gandhi* is no more overwhelmed by the scope of its production than was Gandhi overwhelmed by all the glory of the British Empire. The movie earns comparison with two classic works by David Lean, *Lawrence of Arabia* and *Dr. Zhivago*, in its ability to paint a strong human story on a very large canvas.

The movie is a labor of love by Sir Richard Attenborough, who struggled for years to get financing for his huge but "non-commercial" project. Various actors were considered over the years for the all-important title role, but the actor who was finally chosen, Ben Kingsley, makes the role so completely his own that there is a genuine feeling that the spirit of Gandhi is on the screen. Kingsley's performance is powerful without being loud or histrionic; he is almost always quiet, observant, and soft-spoken on the screen, and yet his performance comes across with such might that we realize, afterward, that the sheer moral force of Gandhi must have been behind the words. Apart from all its other qualities, what makes this movie special is that it was obviously made by people who believed in it.

The movie begins in the early years of the century, in South Africa. Gandhi moved there from India in 1893, when he was twenty-three. He already had a law degree, but, degree or not, he was a target of South Africa's system of racial segregation, in which Indians (even though they are Caucasian, and thus should "qualify") are denied full citizenship and manhood. Gandhi's reaction to the system is, at first, almost naive; an early scene on a train doesn't quite work only because we can't believe the adult Gandhi would still be so ill-informed about the racial code of South Africa. But Gandhi's response sets the tone of the film. He is nonviolent but firm. He is sure where the right lies in every situation, and he will uphold it in total disregard for the possible consequences to himself.

Before long Gandhi is in India, a nation of hundreds of millions, ruled by a relative handful of British. They rule almost by divine right, shouldering the "white man's burden" even though they have not quite been requested to do so by the Indians. Gandhi realizes that Indians have been made into second-class citizens in their own country, and he begins a program of civil disobedience that is at first ignored by the British, then scorned, and finally, reluctantly, dealt with, sometimes by subterfuge, sometimes by brutality. Scenes in this central passage of the movie make it clear that nonviolent protests could contain a great deal of violence. There is a shattering scene in which wave after wave of Gandhi's followers march forward to be beaten to the ground by British clubs. Through it all, Gandhi maintains a certain detachment; he is convinced he is right, convinced that violence is not an answer, convinced that sheer moral example can free his nation—as it did. "You have been guests in our home long enough," he tells the British, "Now we would like for you to leave."

The movie is populated with many familiar faces, surrounding the newcomer Kingsley. Where would the British cinema be without its dependable, sturdy, absolutely authoritative generation of great character actors like Trevor Howard (as a British judge), John Mills (the British viceroy), John Gielgud, and Michael Hordern? There are also such younger actors as Ian Bannen, Edward Fox, Ian Charleson, and, from America, Martin Sheen as a reporter and Candice Bergen as the photographer Margaret Bourke-White.

Gandhi stands at the quiet center. And Ben Kingsley's performance finds the right note and stays with it. There are complexities here; *Gandhi* is not simply a moral story with a happy ending, and the tragedy of the bloodshed between the Hindu and Muslim populations of liberated India is addressed, as is the partition of India and Pakistan, which we can almost literally feel breaking Gandhi's heart.

I imagine that for many Americans, Mahatma Gandhi remains a dimly understood historical figure. I suspect a lot of us know he was a great Indian leader without quite knowing why and—such is our ignorance of Eastern history and culture—we may not fully realize that his movement did indeed liberate India, in one of the greatest political and economic victories of all time, achieved through nonviolent principles. What is important about this film is not that it serves as a history lesson (although it does) but that, at a time when the threat of nuclear holocaust hangs ominously in the air, it reminds us that we are, after all, human, and thus capable of the most extraordinary and wonderful achievements, simply through the use of our imagination, our will, and our sense of right.

The Garden of the Finzi-Continis
★ ★ ★ ★
R, 90 m., 1971

Dominique Sanda (Micol), Lino Capolicchio (Giorgio), Helmut Berger (Alberto), Fabrio Tesel (Malnate), Romolo Valli (Giorgio's Father). Directed by Vittorio de Sica and produced by Gianni Hecht Lucari. Screenplay by Ugo Pirro and Vittorio Bonicelli.

The Garden of the Finzi-Continis, as nearly as I can tell, is not an enclosed space but an enclosed state of mind. Eager for an afternoon of tennis, the young people ride into it on their bicycles one sunny Sunday afternoon. The Fascist government of Mussolini has declared the ordinary tennis clubs off limits for Italian Jews—but what does that matter, here behind these tall stone walls that have faithfully guarded the Finzi-Contini family for generations?

Micol, the daughter, welcomes her guests

and gives some of them a little tour: That tree over there is said to be five hundred years old and might even have been planted by the Borgias. If it has stood for all those years in this garden, she seems to believe, what is there to worry about in the world outside?

She is a tall blond girl with a musical laugh and a way of turning away from a man just as he reveals himself to her. Giorgio, who has been helplessly in love with her since they were both children, deceives himself that she loves him. But she cannot quite love anyone, although she carries on an affair with a tall, athletic young man who is about to be drafted into the army. Giorgio's father says of the Finzi-Continis: "They're different. They don't even seem to be Jewish."

They're different because wealth and privilege and generations of intellectual and social position have bred them into a family as proud as it is vulnerable. The other Jews in the town react to Mussolini's edicts in various ways: Giorgio is enraged; his father is philosophical. But the Finzi-Continis hardly seem to know, or care, what is happening. They are above mere edicts; they chose to live behind their walls long before the Fascists said they must.

This is the situation as Vittorio de Sica sketches it for us at the outset of *The Garden of the Finzi-Continis*, which was a true surprise from a director who had seemed to lose his early genius. De Sica's previous two or three films (especially the disastrous *A Place for Lovers*) were embarrassments from the director of *Bicycle Thief* and *Shoeshine*.

But here he returned with a film that seems to owe little to his previous work. It is not neorealism; it is not a comic mixture of bawdiness and sophistication; it is most of all not the dreamy banality of his previous few films. In telling of the disintegration of the Jewish community in one smallish Italian town, de Sica merges his symbols with his story so that they evoke the meaning of the time.

It was a time in which many people had no idea what was really going on. Giorgio's younger brother, sent to France to study, finds out to his horror about the German concentration camps. There has been no word of them in Italy, of course. Italy in those final prewar years is painted by de Sica as a perpetual wait for something no one admitted would come: war and the persecution of the Jews.

The walled garden of the Finzi-Continis

is his symbol for this waiting period. It seems to promise that nothing will change, and even the Jews who live in the village seem to cling to the apparent strength of the Finzi-Continis as assurance of their own power to survive.

In presenting the garden to us, de Sica uses an interesting visual strategy; he never completely orients us visually, and so we don't know its overall size and shape. Therefore, visually, we can't count on it: We don't know when it will give out. It's an uneasy feeling to be inside an undefined space, especially if you may need to hide or run, and that's exactly the feeling de Sica gets.

The ambiguity of the garden's space is matched by an understated sexual ambiguity. Nothing happens overtly, but de Sica uses looks and body language to suggest the complex varieties of sexual attractions among his characters. When Micol is discovered by Giorgio with her sleeping lover, she does a most interesting thing. She covers him, not herself, and stares at Giorgio until he goes away.

The thing is, you can't count on anything. And nothing permanent can be permitted to take place during this period of waiting. De Sica's film creates a feeling of nostalgia for a lost time and place, but it isn't the nostalgia of looking back. It's the nostalgia of the time itself, when people still inhabiting their world could sense it slipping away, and already missed what they had not yet lost.

Gates of Heaven ★ ★ ★

NO MPAA RATING, 85 m, 1978

A documentary produced, directed, and written by Errol Morris.

There are many invitations to laughter during this remarkable documentary, but what *Gates of Heaven* finally made me feel was an aching poignancy about its subjects. They say you can make a great documentary about almost anything, if only you see it well enough and truly, and this film proves it. *Gates of Heaven*, which has no connection with the unfortunate *Heaven's Gate*, is a documentary about pet cemeteries and their owners. It was filmed in Southern California, so of course we immediately anticipate a sardonic look at peculiarities of the Moonbeam State. But then *Gates of Heaven* grows ever so much more complicated and frightening, until at the end it is about such large issues as love, immortality, failure, and the dogged elusiveness of the American Dream.

The film was made by a California filmmaker named Errol Morris, and it has been the subject of notoriety because Werner Herzog, the West German director, promised to eat his shoe if Morris ever finished it. Morris did finish it, and at the film's premiere in Berkeley, Herzog indeed boiled and ate his shoe.

Gates of Heaven is so rich and thought-provoking, it achieves so much while seeming to strain so little, that it stays in your mind for tantalizing days. It opens with a monologue by a kind-looking, somewhat heavyset paraplegic, with a slight lisp that makes him sound like a kid. His name is Floyd McClure. Ever since his pet dog was run over years ago by a Model A Ford, he has dreamed of establishing a pet cemetery. The movie develops and follows his dream, showing the forlorn, bare patch of land where he founded his cemetery at the intersection of two superhighways. Then, with cunning drama, it gradually reveals that the cemetery went bankrupt and the remains of 450 animals had to be dug up. Various people contribute to the story: One of McClure's investors, a partner, two of the women whose pets were buried in his cemetery, and an unforgettable old woman named Florence Rasmussen, who starts on the subject of pets, and switches, with considerable fire, to her no-account son. Then the action shifts north to the Napa Valley, where a go-getter named Cal Harberts has absorbed what remained of McClure's dream (and the 450 dead pets) into his own pet cemetery, the Bubbling Well Pet Memorial Park. It is here that the movie grows heartbreaking, painting a portrait of a lifestyle that looks chillingly forlorn, and of the people who live it with relentless faith in positive thinking.

Harberts, a patriarch, runs his pet cemetery with two sons, Phil and Dan. Phil, the older one, has returned home after a period spent selling insurance in Salt Lake City. He speaks of having been overworked. Morris lets the camera stay on Phil as he solemnly explains his motivational techniques, and his method of impressing a new client by filling his office with salesmanship trophies. He has read all of Clement Stone's books on "Positive Mental Attitude," and has a framed picture of Stone on his wall. Phil looks neat, presentable, capable. He talks reassuringly of his positive approach to things, "mentally wise." Then we meet the younger brother, Dan, who composes songs and plays them on his guitar. In the late afternoon, when no one is at the pet cemetery, he hooks up his 100-watt speakers and blasts his songs all over the valley. He has a wispy mustache and looks like a hippie. The family hierarchy is clear. Cal, in the words of Phil, is "El Presidento." Then Dan comes next, because he has worked at the cemetery longer. Phil, the golden boy, the positive thinker, is maintaining his P.M.A. in the face of having had to leave an insurance business in Salt Lake City to return home as third in command at a pet cemetery.

The cemetery itself is bleak and barren, its markers informing us, "God is love; dog is god backwards." An American flag flies over the little graves. Floyd McClure tells us at the beginning of the film that pets are put on Earth for two reasons: to love and to be loved. At the end of this mysterious and great movie, we observe the people who guard and maintain their graves, and who themselves seem unloved and very lonely. One of the last images is of old Cal, the patriarch, wheeling past on his forklift, a collie-sized coffin in its grasp.

The Gauntlet ★ ★ ★
R, 111 m., 1977

Clint Eastwood (Ben Shockley), Sondra Locke (Gus Mally), Pat Hingle (Josephson), William Prince (Blakelock), Bill McKinney (Constable), Michael Cavanaugh (Feyderspiel). Directed by Clint Eastwood and produced by Robert Daley. Screenplay by Michael Butler and Dennis Shryack.

The Gauntlet is classic Clint Eastwood: fast, furious, and funny. It tells a cheerfully preposterous story with great energy and a lot of style, and nobody seems more at home in this sort of action movie than Eastwood. He plays a cop again this time, but not a supercop like Dirty Harry Callahan. He's a detective from Phoenix, and no hero: He drives up in front of police headquarters, opens his car door, and a whiskey bottle crashes to the street.

Eastwood hasn't compiled the most stellar record in the department, but somehow the police commissioner thinks he's the right man for the next assignment: Fly to Las Vegas, take custody of a hooker there, and bring her back to Phoenix to be a witness in an important court case. It sounds routine to Eastwood, until he flies to Vegas, takes custody, and discovers that the Mafia is quoting sixty-to-one odds against his witness leaving Nevada alive. Maybe, he begins to suspect, this isn't a totally typical witness. . . .

The witness (played by Sondra Locke) isn't a totally typical hooker, either. She's a college graduate, spunky, pleasant. She tells Eastwood he'd be wise to catch the next flight home, because there's a contract out on her. Eastwood's too stubborn. He's taken the assignment and he'll carry it out through hell and high water (which turn out to be just about the only two things he doesn't have to survive on this mission).

The return trip gets off to a slightly shaky start when they survive an auto bomb. Then, after Eastwood commandeers an ambulance, they're involved in a high-speed chase with three gunmen. They take refuge in Locke's house, which is promptly surrounded by dozens of police marksmen, who open fire, achieving overkill so completely that (in one of the movie's many mixtures of humor and violence), the house simply topples over. Still ahead of them are nights in the desert, an encounter with Hell's Angels, a fight on a moving freight train, a chase in which their motorcycle is pursued by a rifle marksman in a helicopter . . . and then the grand finale, in which Eastwood hijacks a passenger bus, armor-plates it, and drives himself and his witness through downtown Phoenix against a hail of machine-gun fire. You see what I mean about the plot's being cheerfully preposterous.

Eastwood directed himself again this time, and he's a good action craftsman (as *The Outlaw Josey Wales* demonstrated). He's also good at developing relationships; despite the movie's barrage of violence, there's a nice pacing as his cop and hooker slog through their ordeals and begin to like and respect one another. As in most Eastwood movies, by the way, the woman's role is a good one: Eastwood has such a macho image that maybe people haven't noticed that his female sidekicks (like Tyne Daly, Dirty Harry's partner in *The Enforcer*) have minds of their own and are never intended to be merely decorative.

The Gauntlet will no doubt be attacked in various quarters because of its violence, but it's a harmless, pop-art type of violence, often with a comic quality. The wall of gunfire during the final bus ride up the steps of the Hall of Justice, for example, is an extravaganza of sound and action during which, incredibly, no one is killed. Eastwood himself fires his pistol only twice: once at a door, and once at a gas tank.

George Stevens: A Filmmaker's Journey
★ ★ ★ ½
PG, 113 m., 1985

A documentary written, produced, and directed by George Stevens, Jr. Edited by Catherine Shields. Music by Carl Davis.

The last shot of *Citizen Kane* showed the dead tycoon's storerooms, vast spaces filled with the jumble of a lifetime. One of the early shots in this documentary about George Stevens has something of the same quality. We see the memorabilia of his long career: cowboy hats, leather-bound scripts, cans of film, albums of photographs, Oscars, diaries, belt buckles—everything with a story, and half the stories already forgotten.

The voice on the sound track is the filmmaker's son, telling us about his famous father. One of the things the father told him, one day when they were driving past the warehouse where all of these memories were stored, was, "That'll all be yours when I'm gone." As he rummaged through the souvenirs of his father's lifetime, he made some extraordinary discoveries: Not only the prints and scripts of such classics as *Giant*, *A Place in the Sun*, and *Alice Adams*, but also documentary footage of Stevens on the set of his movies, and rare color footage Stevens shot for himself while he was leading a newsreel unit during World War II.

More than most men, Stevens seems to have been concerned to leave behind a record of his career. He began in movies almost at the beginning, as an assistant on the early silent films, and his first work as a director was on the Laurel and Hardy films. We see some of his earliest footage, and then we begin to hear the voices of the people who knew him then, and worked with him: Old directors like Rouben Mamoulian and John Huston, stars like Katharine Hepburn and Warren Beatty, writers like Irwin Shaw. Hepburn gave Stevens his real start, rescuing him from grade B features and second-unit work because she was impressed by his enthusiasm for *Alice Adams*. It became his first prestigious production, but then there was a flood of others: the definitive Astaire-Rogers musical *Swing Time*, the audacious *Gunga Din*, and *Woman of the Year*, and Stevens began to build a reputation as a man who saw his own way through the standard scripts he was handed, freeing his actors so that *Gunga Din*, for example, became a high-spirited comic masterpiece instead of just another swashbuckler.

The film contains a lot of home movies and private documentary footage; Stevens shot the only color footage of the landing at Normandy, and we also see moments of Stevens at work, always quietly professional, thoughtful, not the flamboyant self-promoter so many other directors of his generation became. Stevens, more than anyone else, fashioned the image of James Dean. He directed some of Elizabeth Taylor's most memorable scenes. And he pressed on in the face of daunting odds to direct such movies as *The Greatest Story Ever Told*. Shooting in Utah, he was faced with the first snowstorms in a generation, and when he asked the cast and crew to pitch in and shovel snow, they respected him enough that they did it.

A Filmmaker's Journey is a film biography of a movie director, and it inevitably shares some of the conventions of the genre. We see the clips of great scenes, we hear the memories of old colleagues. Two things distinguish the film: The quiet professionalism with which the materials have been edited together, and the feeling that George Stevens, Jr., really is engaging in a rediscovery of his father through the making of this film. By the end of the film, we are less aware of George Stevens as a filmmaker than as a good and gifted man who happened to use movies as a means of expressing his gifts.

Germinal ★ ★ ★
R, 160 m., 1994

Renaud (Etienne Lantier), Gérard Depardieu (Maheu), Miou-Miou (Maheude), Jean Carmet (Bonnemort), Judith Henry (Catherine Maheu), Jean-Roger Milo (Chaval), Laurent Terzieff (Souvarine), Jean-Pierre Bisson (Rasseneur). Directed and produced by Claude Berri. Screenplay by Berri and Arlette Langmann.

In 1884, the French author Emile Zola traveled to a poor rural district of France to observe the living and working conditions of striking coal miners. The novel he wrote about that experience, *Germinal*, was instrumental in winning justice for the workers, who existed in a condition little better than slavery. Claude Berri's ambitious new epic *Germinal* re-creates Zola's story.

Zola, who began as a writer at a time when most novels were inspired by imagination and romance, helped pioneer a style of detailed realism, piling fact upon fact so that his books seemed drawn from real life. Berri's film has been made in the same spirit, and the elaborate sets showing the villages and mines are so convincing the movie almost seems shot on nineteenth-century locations.

The story is a simple one. We meet the Maheu family, who live crowded together in a cold and smoky cottage not far from the mines. They do backbreaking work to earn their living, and expect their children to do the same; indeed, the mother frankly states that one of the reasons for having children is so that they can work and bring more money to the family.

The wages in the local pits seem carefully calculated, down to the last franc, to support life and the ability to work while not providing one franc more. The miners are unable ever to gather enough capital to leave the district, or to make a different choice of work. They are trapped between servitude and starvation.

The film observes the daily life of the family, led by the burly Maheu (Gérard Depardieu) and his fierce, determined wife (Miou-Miou, in a powerful performance). Their daughter, Catherine (Judith Henry), also works in the mines. Etienne Lantier (Renaud), a man from out of the district, comes seeking work. He has some education, and is an organizer for a new miners' union. He is quickly attracted to Catherine, and she to him, but he does not act on his feelings, and she unexpectedly goes to live with a worthless local man named Chaval (Jean-Roger Milo). Perhaps she wants to spite her family, perhaps she wants to escape their crowded home, perhaps her life has made her feel so worthless that she believes she is worthy only to marry a brute.

In the mines, working conditions are hazardous. The miners are responsible for shoring up the shafts with timber, but are not paid for this work, so every moment spent timbering comes out of their own pockets. Understandably, they prefer to dig coal. Also understandably, there are many mine accidents, each one expensive for the rich owners, who propose a scheme in which timbering will be paid for, but the price paid for coal will be reduced. The result will be even smaller wages.

Berri lays this groundwork against a backdrop of the daily life in the district, as season follows season and the workers struggle to maintain even simple humanity in the face of their grim conditions. Meanwhile, we see the lives of the mine owners and managers, with their great houses, their Paris fashions, their carriages, their banquets and parties. Berri is fond of cutting back and forth between poverty and affluence, as Zola was in his novel, and the message is unmistakable: The owners are stealing the fruits of the workers' labor.

The film climaxes, as it must, with a dreadful mine accident, and Berri shows panic and desperation as the mine begins to flood and the workers are cornered like rats. Catherine and Etienne, who had never before expressed their feelings for one another, find themselves trapped together, and in a scene both melodramatic and moving, they finally say what is in their hearts.

The film will seem filled with unrelieved gloom for many audience members. There are also some unplanned smiles—as when the hefty Depardieu is sponging down and we cannot help observing that he, at least, doesn't seem to be underfed. The overall effect of the movie is much the same as the effect of Zola's novel: to present a time and place so realistically in fiction that the audience will be able to share the experience. For me, *Germinal* provided visual and dramatic images of nineteenth-century history that I understood in only an abstract way.

Geronimo: An American Legend
★ ★ ★ ½
PG-13, 115 m., 1993

Jason Patric (Lieutenant Charles Gatewood), Gene Hackman (Brigadier General George Crook), Robert Duvall (Al Sieber), Wes Studi (Geronimo), Matt Damon (Lieutenant Britton Davis), Rodney A. Grant (Mangas), Kevin Tighe (Brigadier General Nelson Miles). Directed by Walter Hill and produced by Hill and Neil Canton. Screenplay by John Milius and Larry Gross.

Within a few days of each other, I saw *Schindler's List* and *Geronimo*, and it occurred to me that both films are about holocausts, about entire populations murdered because of their race. But Americans are not quick to describe our treatment of the Indians as genocide, and even a somewhat revisionist film like *Geronimo* is careful to describe the conflicts between the U.S. government and Indian "hostiles" as a war. It was a war carried out with most of the power on our side, and our justification—that the land belonged to us and we therefore had the divine right to cleanse it of an alien race—is, of course, Hitler's argument. One of the unanswerable questions in this film comes when Geronimo asks why there is not enough land for everyone.

Indians are these days called Native Americans, although they are immigrants to this continent like everyone else, and should more properly be called First Americans. They lived on the land for a thousand years or more before the U.S. Army came to dispossess and contain them, a process that Geronimo and his small bands of Apache warriors were able to frustrate through many years of brilliant guerrilla warfare. Geronimo was never defeated, although he surrendered twice and finally died a natural death at eighty, a prosperous Oklahoma farmer.

Walter Hill's *Geronimo*, a film of great beauty and considerable intelligence, covers the same ground as many other movies about Indians, but in a new way. The screenplay by John Milius and Larry Gross shows the daily lives of the Army's few professional Indian fighters who actually had some understanding of their foe, in particular a scout named Al Sieber (Robert Duvall) and a young lieutenant named Charles Gatewood (Jason Patric).

They worked under Brig. Gen. George Crook (Gene Hackman), who developed a grudging respect for Geronimo, and the movie follows their stories for several years as they track and hunt Geronimo's warriors, sometimes negotiate with him, betray and are betrayed, and finally see the leader and his handful of surviving followers put aboard a train that would take them away from their land forever.

Geronimo himself, played by Wes Studi, is seen as a man of considerable insight, able to live off the land and launch deadly raids, yet contemplative about his role. He was responsible for the deaths of many white settlers, including women and children, but he points out to Crook with perfect logic that the "white eyes" had also killed many Indians, including women and children.

American history has come slowly to share Geronimo's perspective. Looking in two editions of the *Columbia Encyclopedia*, one published in 1950, one in 1993, I find that the 1950 reference to his "brutal raids" has been dropped, and that a charge that he "broke his word" has now been replaced by the information that the federal government broke its word to him.

The fact that Geronimo has been seen in movies mostly in long shot, as a "murdering redskin," is a reflection of the ancient truth that the histories of war are written by the victors. Even this film sees him primarily as an outsider, and takes a white point of view, showing us white men who are better or worse only in relation to their contemporaries.

Al Sieber, the professional scout, makes no apologies for doing his job, and finds Lt. Gatewood a "real sad case: You don't love who you're fighting for, and you don't hate who you're fighting against." Yet Sieber lives according to a code that makes him willing to risk his life to protect an Indian from Texas bounty hunters. And Gen. Crook argues with a straight face that "The U.S. Army is the best friend the Indians have ever had," which sounds strange until we realize that he operates within the law in a land where rewards were paid for Apache scalps—and many white killers discovered that any Indian scalp looked Apache, and that peaceful Indians were easier to kill.

Hill is a director who specializes in action films about men. *Geronimo* is too visually striking and too thoughtful, however, to be described in such a limiting way. The photography by Lloyd Ahern paints the Texas and Mexican landscapes in dusty, bloody crimsons. The music by Ry Cooder speaks of loneliness. There are no artificial climaxes caused by "victories" or "defeats," but instead the sadness of one race taking the land and pride of another.

The film is narrated by a young observer, Lt. Britton Davis (Matt Damon), a West Point graduate who accompanies Gatewood as they bring Geronimo to an army settlement; later, after Geronimo resumes his war, they go looking for him again. Davis acts in the film like a witness from the future, seeing how those who understood the situation, like Gatewood, were ignored and reviled because they did not fit in easily with the current sentiments in Washington.

I wish in a way the film had told more of the story of Geronimo's exile—of his removal to Florida, where he was told his band would be joined by their women and children, a lie. And his later removal to Oklahoma, where he was kept as an army prisoner but later became a Christian, bought land, farmed it, and wrote his autobiography. He was quite a celebrity in his later years, and even rode in Theodore Roosevelt's inaugural parade. I wonder what he was thinking.

Getting It Right ★ ★ ★ ★
R, 102 m., 1989

Jesse Birdsall (Gavin Lamb), Helena Bonham Carter (Minerva Munday), Peter Cook (Mr. Adrian), John Gielgud (Sir Gordon Munday), Jane Horrocks (Jenny), Lynn Redgrave (Joan), Shirley Anne Field (Anne), Pat Heywood (Mrs. Lamb), Bryan Pringle (Mr. Lamb). Directed by Randal Kleiser and produced by Joanathan D. Krane and Kleiser. Screenplay by Elizabeth Jane Howard.

Getting It Right is a late-1980s version of all those driven, off-center London films like *Darling, Georgy Girl*, and *Morgan*—movies in which a wide-eyed innocent journeys through the jungle of the eccentric, the depraved, and the blasé, protected only by a good heart and limitless naïveté.

The movie tells the story of Gavin Lamb, a hairdresser who shampoos the coiffures and the miseries of his ancient clients, and returns every night to the home of his parents—where his mother serves awesomely inedible dinners promptly at the stroke of six. Gavin is thirty-one and still a virgin, and his bedroom is a sanctuary where he keeps his precious collection of recorded music, meticulously arranged.

At first we can't get a reading on Gavin Lamb. He is pleasant, friendly, a little standoffish. Life doesn't seem to have happened to him yet. The character is played close to the vest by Jesse Birdsall, a young actor who manages to look thoroughly ordinary most of the time, and sublimely crafty the rest of the time. It's a performance a little like Dustin Hoffman's in *The Graduate*, where society is criticized by the character's very indifference to it.

One day Gavin is taken to a party that seems to be a last-gasp attempt to resurrect Swinging London. It's held in the spectacular penthouse of a garish divorcée (Lynn Redgrave), whose red wig and outlandish costumes look like a conscious attempt to keep people at arm's length. But she likes Gavin, and takes pity on him, and invites him to a secret inner sanctum in the vast apartment—the only room, apparently, where she feels free to take off her wig and be herself. Her secret identity turns out to be sweet and tender, and Gavin is started down the road toward losing his virginity and gaining his independence.

There is another woman at the party—a girl, really—who is dark and intense and small and determined. Her name is Minerva

Munday (Helena Bonham Carter) and her father is fearsomely old and rich and eccentric (Sir John Gielgud has great relish with the role). Suddenly Gavin is catapulted out of his safe orbit of the hairdressing salon and life with Mum and Dad, and finds his romantic life more eventful than he could have dreamed.

Getting It Right is a character film, not a plot film, and so the point is not what happens, but who it happens to. The screenplay is by Elizabeth Jane Howard, based on her own novel, and it shows a novelist's instinct for character and dialogue. This is not one of those mechanically plotted forced marches through film school script formulas, but a story that lives and breathes and gives the characters the freedom to surprise us.

Smaller roles, like Peter Cook's cameo as the owner of the hairdressing salon, are enriched with asides that suggest the entire character. And some of the characters sneak up on us—like Jenny (Jane Horrocks), who is Gavin's assistant at the salon. He has barely looked at her in two years, but now, emboldened by his late flowering, he looks at everyone in a new light, and Jenny begins to blossom.

Getting It Right was directed by Randal Kleiser, whose big hit film *Grease*, in 1978, has been followed by a career with no discernible pattern (can the same director have made *The Blue Lagoon*, *Flight of the Navigator*, and *Big Top Pee-wee*?).

With this film, however, Kleiser has gotten everything right; he is often dealing with the most delicate nuances, in which the whole point of some scenes depends on subtle reactions or small shifts of tone, and he doesn't step wrong. Look, for example, at his control of a scene where Gavin takes a date to a birthday party for a gay friend who breaks up with his lover right there on the spot; the scene is poignant, and yet still works as the comedy of embarrassment. There is a delicious delight seeing the film find its way into the lives of so many bright, lonely, mixed-up people. And *Getting It Right* does not box them into a plot, but allows them to be themselves.

Gettysburg ★ ★ ★
PG, 238 m., 1993

Confederate Cast: Tom Berenger (Longstreet), Martin Sheen (Robert E. Lee), Stephen Lang (George E. Pickett), Richard Jordan (Armistead). Union Cast: Jeff Daniels (Colonel Chamberlain), Sam Elliott (Buford), C. Thomas Howell (Tom Chamberlain), Kevin Conway (Kilrain). Directed by Ronald F. Maxwell and produced by Robert Katz and Moctesuma Esparza. Screenplay by Maxwell.

Most war movies use battle as a backdrop to little human dramas. We learn of the private lives of the soldiers, their loves and fears. Personalities are sketched, weaknesses revealed, rivalries established which will all be settled under fire. Then we get the action scenes. *Gettysburg* avoids all of those war movie clichés. This is a film, pure and simple, *about* the Battle of Gettysburg in the summer of 1863, about the strategies, calculations, mistakes, and heroism that turned the tide of the Civil War decisively against the South. The movie is some four hours long and every minute is devoted to either battle itself, or the planning and preparation for battle. Typical eve-of-battle romance is so far from the minds of the filmmakers that there is not a single woman in the cast.

The movie was made at great cost by Turner Pictures, which, after releasing it theatrically through its New Line subsidiary, broadcast it on the TNT cable channel. It should really be seen on a large screen. The movie was shot on the actual locations, in the Gettysburg National Park, and it deployed thousands of Civil War reenactment buffs, in costumes authentic down to the last button, to reproduce the actions of the two sides on those three bloody days when 158,000 men went into battle and 43,000 were killed.

Of the several set pieces in the film, none is more harrowing than an early defense of a crucial wooded ridge by Union troops from Maine, under the command of Col. Joshua Lawrence Chamberlain (Jeff Daniels). His men control the heights, but are badly outnumbered and low on ammunition. Yet they repel repeated charges, taking deep casualties, in sequences so desperate, bloody, and protracted that for once we sense the sheer physical exhaustion of combat, the combination of fear, fatigue, and determination.

Much is made in the second half of the film of the fatal decision by Gen. Robert E. Lee (Martin Sheen) to send his Confederate troops into what became a suicidal attack across an open field to entrenched and superior Union forces. The night before the first attack, his aide Longstreet (Tom Berenger) pleads with him to reconsider, but Lee seems seized by an almost mystical faith in his cause and his men. Inspired by him, they march joyfully into battle, many of them to certain death.

One of the film's best performances, as the Confederate Brig. Gen. Lewis Armistead, is by Richard Jordan. He has a long nighttime speech about death, delivered with deep feeling and tremendously effective, and it is his farewell as an actor: This was Jordan's last performance before he fell ill with a brain tumor and died. In the film, he dies in glory, stabbing his hat through with his sword and raising it above his head, crying "Virginians! Who will go with me?" and mounting a wall to be struck with fatal gunfire.

The film, written and directed by Ronald F. Maxwell, is made of countless vignettes, almost all of them informed by military strategy and considerations. We understand, step by step, what the objectives are on each side. We listen to intelligence briefings as the two armies discover they are closer to one another than they thought. In a time before aerial reconnaissance, we watch as the opposing generals seem to depend on a sixth sense, buttressed by fragmentary scouting reports, to intuit where the enemy is, and where he is moving.

And most of all, we experience the horrifying reality of battle itself. What Lee called on his men to do was walk a mile across open ground, in the face of withering fire, and engage Union troops who were fortified behind a stone wall. That they would do this— that they still had the will to fight when they got there—is evidence of the deep, almost fanatical conviction that both sides brought into the war.

Maxwell deserves credit for not hedging his bets. This is a film that Civil War buffs will find indispensable, even if others might find it interminable. I began watching with comparative indifference, and slowly got caught up in the majestic advance of the enterprise; by the end, I had a completely new idea of the reality of war in the nineteenth century, when battles still consisted largely of men engaging each other in hand-to-hand combat. And I understood the Civil War in a more immediate way than ever before.

Ghost ★ ★ ½
PG-13, 128 m., 1990

Patrick Swayze (Sam Wheat), Demi Moore (Molly Jensen), Whoopi Goldberg (Oda Mae Brown), Tony Goldwyn (Carl Brunner), Rick

Aviles (Willie Lopez), Gail Boggs (Oda Mae's Sister Louise), Armelia McQueen (Oda Mae's Sister Clara), Vincent Schiavelli (Subway Ghost). Directed by Jerry Zucker and produced by Lisa Weinstein. Screenplay by Bruce Joel Rubin.

The thing about ghost stories is that they usually have such limited imaginations. If a spirit were indeed able to exist in two realms at the same time—to occupy the spirit world while still involving itself in our designs here in the material universe—wouldn't it be aghast with glory and wonder? Wouldn't it transcend the pathetic little concerns of daily life? To put it another way: If you could live in the mind of God, would you still be telling your girlfriend she's wearing the T-shirt you spilled the margarita on?

Ghost is no worse an offender than most ghost movies, I suppose. It assumes that even after death we devote most of our attention to unfinished business here on earth, and that danger to a loved one is more important to a ghost than the infinity it now inhabits. Such ideas are a comfort to us. We like to picture our dear ones up there on a cloud, eternally "looking down" on us, so devoted that they would rather see what we're cooking for dinner than have a chat with Aristotle or Elvis.

In *Ghost*, Patrick Swayze plays an investment counselor who is killed by a mugger one night, but remains on the scene in his spirit form to observe, as his young girlfriend (Demi Moore) weeps and mourns and then attempts to piece her life together. Swayze has an important piece of information he needs to get to her: His death was not an act of random urban violence, but a contract murder. He was about to stumble across a multimillion-dollar computer theft by a sneaky colleague (Tony Goldwyn), and that's why he was murdered. Now Moore is in danger, too.

This plot takes place in the world of upscale Manhattan yuppies. Swayze and Moore inhabit a loft apartment so luxurious that he must be making a fortune at his job (or maybe she's doing well with her art pottery business). That's why, after Swayze's death, Moore doesn't believe it when a self-appointed psychic (Whoopi Goldberg) contacts her with messages from beyond the grave. What's amazing is that Goldberg really is able to hear every word Swayze says to her—even though she has no previous record of genuine psychic powers.

That's how we get around to the descrip-

tion of the T-shirt with the margarita stains. Swayze has to feed Goldberg so much personal information that Moore is forced to believe that the communications are genuine. This he does to a fault. One of the irritations of *Ghost* is that the Moore character is such a slow study. Over and over again, Goldberg tells her things only her boyfriend could possibly have known, and over and over again, Moore disbelieves her—she trusts the villain, instead. We are treading here on the edge of the Idiot Plot.

Ghost does, however, make a nice mixture of horror and humor, especially in the scenes involving Goldberg and her sisters (Gail Boggs and Armelia McQueen). The film's biggest puzzlement involves the exact status of Swayze's spiritual sojourn in this world. Is he in heaven's holding pattern? Must he protect his girlfriend before he can ascend that tunnel of light into the sky? What about his ability to interact with the physical world? At first he walks right through everything, but later, after tutelage from his fellow dead, he learns simple parlor tricks—like picking up a penny—and, of course, by the end of the movie he is able to beat the hell out of the bad guy.

The movie's single best scene—one that does touch the poignancy of the human belief in life after death—comes when Swayze is able to take over Goldberg's body, to use her physical presence as an instrument for caressing the girlfriend that he loves. (In strict logic this should involve us seeing Goldberg kissing Moore, but, of course, the movie compromises and shows us Swayze holding her—too bad, because the logical version would actually have been more spiritual and moving.) Then there is the obligatory action climax, necessary in all mass-market entertainments these days, and a particularly ridiculous visitation from the demons of hell. *Ghost* contains some nice ideas, and occasionally, for whole moments at a time, succeeds in evoking the mysteries that it toys with.

Ghostbusters ★ ★ ★ ½
PG, 107 m., 1984

Bill Murray (Venkman), Dan Aykroyd (Stantz), Harold Ramis (Spengler), Sigourney Weaver (Dana), Ernie Hudson (Winston), Rick Moranis (Louis). Directed and produced by Ivan Reitman. Screenplay by Dan Aykroyd and Harold Ramis.

Ghostbusters is a head-on collision between two comic approaches that have rarely worked

together very successfully. This time, they do. It's (1) a special-effects blockbuster, and (2) a sly dialogue movie, in which everybody talks to each other like smart graduate students who are in on the joke. In the movie's climactic scenes, an apocalyptic psychic mindquake is rocking Manhattan, and the experts talk like Bob and Ray.

This movie is an exception to the general rule that big special effects can wreck a comedy. Special effects require painstaking detail work. Comedy requires spontaneity and improvisation—or at least that's what it should feel like, no matter how much work has gone into it. In movies like Steven Spielberg's *1941*, the awesome scale of the special effects dominated everything else; we couldn't laugh because we were holding our breath. Not this time. *Ghostbusters* has a lot of neat effects, some of them mind-boggling, others just quick little throwaways, as when a transparent green-slime monster gobbles up a mouthful of hot dogs. No matter what effects are being used, they're placed at the service of the actors; instead of feeling as if the characters have been carefully posed in front of special effects, we feel they're winging this adventure as they go along.

The movie stars Bill Murray, Dan Aykroyd, and Harold Ramis, three graduates of the Second City/*National Lampoon*/"Saturday Night Live" tradition. They're funny, but they're not afraid to reveal that they're also quick-witted and intelligent; their dialogue puts nice little spins on American clichés, and it uses understatement, irony, in-jokes, vast cynicism, and cheerful goofiness. Rarely has a movie this expensive provided so many quotable lines.

The plot, such as it is, involves an epidemic of psychic nuisance reports in Manhattan. Murray, Ramis, and Aykroyd, defrocked parapsychologists whose university experiments have been exposed as pure boondoggle, create a company named Ghostbusters and offer to speed to the rescue like a supernatural version of the Orkin man. Business is bad until Sigourney Weaver notices that the eggs in her kitchen are frying themselves. Her next-door neighbor, Rick Moranis, notices horrifying monsters in the apartment hallways. They both apparently live in a building that serves as a conduit to the next world. The ghostbusters ride to the rescue, armed with nuclear-powered backpacks. There is a lot of talk about arcane details of psychic lore (most of which the ghostbusters are inventing on the spot), and then an earthshaking showdown between good and evil, during which Manhattan is menaced by a monster that is twenty stories high, and about which I cannot say one more word without spoiling the movie's best visual moment.

Ghostbusters is one of those rare movies where the original, fragile comic vision has survived a multimillion-dollar production. It is not a complete vindication for big-budget comedies, since it's still true, as a general rule, that the more you spend, the fewer laughs you get. But it uses its money wisely, and when that, ahem, monster marches down a Manhattan avenue and climbs the side of a skyscraper . . . we're glad they spent the money for the special effects because it gets one of the biggest laughs in a long time.

Gladiator ★ ★ ★
R, 98 m., 1992

James Marshall (Tommy Riley), Brian Dennehy (Boss), Robert Loggia (Manager), Cuba Gooding, Jr. (Lincoln), John Heard (Tommy's Father), T.E. Russell (Spits), Anthony Fitzpatrick (Collector). Directed by Rowdy Herrington and produced by Frank Price and Steve Roth. Screenplay by Lyle Kessler and Robert Mark Kamen.

All boxing movies deplore the sport to some extent. They regret the blood and mayhem even while they glorify it. *Gladiator* goes one step beyond, with its hero who hates the game and ends up bare-knuckled in the ring with the evil fight promoter who is trying to enslave him. Don King would not enjoy this story.

The movie stars James Marshall as Tommy Riley, a white hope from Chicago's Bridgeport neighborhood, whose mom has died and whose dad has landed them in an unfurnished flat with gambling collectors knocking on the door. Tommy transfers to a school where some of the students want to pound him to a pulp, and a boxing manager (Robert Loggia) spots him and offers him quick money to fight.

Tommy needs the money to bail out his father, and so he gets ensnared in the underground world of a shadowy fight promoter (Brian Dennehy), who stages illegal fights, fixes the odds, and makes money off the gambling. The idea of the illegal boxing arena is a storytelling masterstroke; it explains the small crowds at the same time it permits the boxers to fight dirty.

And they do. Hitting below the belt is just a warm-up for these violent street brawlers,

who also kick their opponents' jaws, rub acid in their eyes, and keep punching opponents who are already unconscious. Tommy, a talented Golden Gloves amateur, is repelled by the dangerous level of violence encouraged in the illegal ring, but Dennehy buys up his father's gambling debts and makes other threats to keep him fighting. He knows what buttons to push.

James Marshall, as Tommy, is a member of the River Phoenix school of studied detachment. He is so aloof, indeed, that at times he seems like a neutral observer of his own life. I can see what he's trying to do, and sometimes it works, but he pushes his cool too far.

The film places its boxing story in a surprisingly realistic milieu; when he isn't dealing out punishment, Riley goes to high school, discusses Mark Twain, is encouraged by a helpful teacher, finds a girlfriend, and becomes pals with a local black fighter (Cuba Gooding, Jr., from *Boyz N the Hood*). The movie was coproduced by Frank Price, who produced *Boyz*, and it exhibits nimble footwork in avoiding the cliché of a black-white showdown in the final fight; Dennehy himself climbs into the ring with Tommy Riley, so at last the hero of a fight film is boxing his real opponent.

Gladiator was directed by Rowdy Herrington, a filmmaker with a natural feel for pumped-up action. His credits include the stalker film *Jack's Back* and the ludicrous but not unentertaining *Road House*, which was about the toughest bouncers in the world. What he has here is a story that probably cannot be believed on any conceivable level, and yet, to give him his due, he tells it with such conviction that it works anyway.

Glengarry Glen Ross ★ ★ ★ ½
R, 100 m., 1992

Al Pacino (Ricky), Jack Lemmon (Shelley), Alec Baldwin (Blake), Ed Harris (Dave), Alan Arkin (George), Jonathan Pryce (James), Kevin Spacey (John). Directed by James Foley and produced by Jerry Tokofsky and Stanley R. Zupnik. Screenplay by David Mamet.

The shabby real estate office in *Glengarry Glen Ross* seems likely to become one of the movie places we will remember, like the war room in *Dr. Strangelove* or Hannibal Lecter's cell. It is divided into two parts: a glassed-in area where the office manager lives, along with his precious "leads"—cards with the names of people who might want to buy real

estate—and the rest of the office, given over to the desks of the salesmen, who try to sound rich and confident over the phone, but whose eyes are haunted with despair.

Hour after hour, they make calls to sell real estate that no one wants to buy. They are making no money. It is worse than that; they are about to lose their jobs. Blake (Alec Baldwin), the slick hotshot from downtown, arrives to give them a chalk talk and a warning. There is a new sales contest. First prize is a Cadillac. Second prize, a set of steak knives. Third prize is, you're fired: "Hit the bricks, pal, and beat it, 'cause you are going *out!*"

The movie is based on a play by David Mamet, who once briefly worked in such a boiler room. He knows the way these people talk, and turns their jargon into a version of his own personal language, in which the routine obscenities and despair of everyday speech are transcribed into a sad music. Their struggle takes on a kind of nobility.

Look at Shelley (the Machine) Levine, for example. Played by Jack Lemmon, he was once a hotshot salesman, winning the office sweepstakes month after month. Now he is making no sales at all, and his wife is in the hospital, and it's heartbreaking to hear his lies, about how he would feel wrong, not sharing this marvelous opportunity.

Lemmon has a scene in this movie that represents the best work he has ever done. He makes a house call on a man who does not want to buy real estate. The man knows it, we know it, Lemmon knows it—but Lemmon keeps trying, not registering the man's growing impatience to have him out of his house. There is a fine line in this scene between deception and breakdown, between Lemmon's false jollity and the possibility that he may collapse right on the man's rug, surrendering all hope.

The other salesmen are assembled in a well-balanced cast that rehearsed Mamet's dialogue for weeks, getting to know the music of the words while working on the characters. Kevin Spacey is the office manager, unblinking and cold, playing by the rules. The salesmen are played by Al Pacino, Ed Harris, Alan Arkin, and Lemmon. They are all in various stages of breakdown. There is a duet between Harris and Arkin that is one of the best things Mamet has written. They speculate about the near-legendary "good leads" that Spacey allegedly has locked in his office. What if someone broke into the office and stole the leads? Harris and Arkin discuss it, neither one quite saying out loud what's on his mind.

There are other duets. Lemmon and Spacey have a scene in a car, in the rain, where Lemmon tries to buy the goddamn leads from Spacey. And Pacino and Jonathan Pryce, who plays a possible customer, have a masterful scene in a restaurant booth, in which Pacino subtly tries to seduce Pryce into buying, by playing on what he senses is latent homosexuality.

In *Death of a Salesman*, Arthur Miller made the salesman into a symbol for the failure of the American dream. In Miller's play, Willy Loman was out there all alone, on a shoeshine and a dream. *Glengarry Glen Ross* is a version for modern times. Produced on stage in the good times of the 1980s, filmed in the hard times of the 1990s, it shows the new kind of American salesmanship, which is organized around offices and corporations. No longer is a salesman self-employed, going door-to-door. Now individual effort has been replaced by teamwork. The shabby Chicago real estate office, huddled under the "el" tracks, could be any white-collar organization in which middle-aged men find themselves faced with sudden and possibly permanent unemployment.

Having said that, I must not forget to mention the humor in the film. Mamet's dialogue has a kind of logic, a cadence, that allows people to arrive in triumph at the ends of sentences we could not possibly have imagined. There is great energy in it. You can see the joy with which these actors get their teeth into these great lines, after living through movies in which flat dialogue serves only to advance the story. The film was directed by James Foley (*At Close Range*), whose timing and camera help underline the humor; a line of dialogue will end with a reaction shot that mirrors our own reaction—surprised, blindsided, maybe a little stunned, but entertained by the zing of anger and ego in the words. Meanwhile nobody is buying any real estate, and it is raining, and the "el" thunders by like a mystery train to hell.

Gloria ★ ★ ★
PG, 123 m., 1980

Gena Rowlands (Gloria Swenson), John Adames (Phil), Buck Henry (Jack), Julie Carmen (Jeri Dawn). Directed by John Cassavetes and produced by Sam Shaw. Screenplay by Cassavetes.

Well, it's a cute idea for a movie, and maybe that's why they've had this particular idea so often. You start with tough-talking, street-wise gangster types, you hook them up with a little kid, you put them in fear of their lives, and then you milk the situation for poignancy, pathos, excitement, comedy, and anything else that turns up. It's the basic situation of *Little Miss Marker,* the Damon Runyon story that has been filmed three times. And now John Cassavetes tells it again in *Gloria.* The twists this time: The tough-talking gangster type is a woman, and the kid is Puerto Rican. Cassavetes has cast his wife, Gena Rowlands, in the title role, and it's an infectious performance—if infectious is the word to describe a chain-smoking dame who charges around town in her high heels, dragging a kid behind her.

The kid is also well cast. He's a youngster named John Adames who has dark hair and big eyes and a way of delivering his dialogue as if daring you to change one single word. Precisely because the material of this movie is so familiar, almost everything depends on the performances. And that's where Cassavetes saves the material and redeems the corniness of his story. Rowlands propels the action with such appealing nervous energy that we don't have the heart to stop and think how silly everything is.

The movie begins with a two-bit hoodlum (Buck Henry, an inexplicable casting choice) barricaded in an apartment with his Puerto Rican wife (Julie Carmen) and their kids. Men are going to come through the door at any moment with guns blazing. There's a knock on the door. It's Rowlands, as the neighbor, with the somehow inevitable name of Gloria Swenson. She wants to borrow sugar. She winds up with the kid. She doesn't want the kid. She doesn't like kids, she tells Henry: "Especially your kids." But the kid tags along. There's a shoot-out, the kid's family is dead, and things get even more complicated when it turns out that Henry gave his kid a notebook that has information in it the mob will kill to retrieve. That's the premise for the rest of the movie, which is a cat-and-mouse chase through the sleazier districts of New York and New Jersey.

Cassavetes has a nice eye for locale. There's a crummy flophouse where the clerk tells Rowlands, "Just pick a room. They're all open." There's a garishly decorated love nest that Rowlands occasionally occupies with a mobster. There are bus stations, back alleys, dimly lit hallways, and the kinds of bars that open at dawn and do most of their business by 9 A.M. (That provides one of the movie's best scenes. Gloria and the kid argue, Gloria tells the kid to split if that's the way he feels, and then she marches into the bar, orders a beer, lights a cigarette and says to the bartender: "Listen. There are reasons why I can't turn around and look . . . but is there a little kid heading in here?")

Cassavetes remains one of the most consistently interesting Hollywood mavericks. He makes money by acting, and immediately spends it producing his own films. Most of them are passionately indulgent of the actors, who sometimes repay his indulgence with inspired performances. Rowlands won an Oscar nomination for Cassavetes's *A Woman Under the Influence.* His next picture starred Ben Gazzara in *The Murder of a Chinese Bookie* (1978), which has become an unseen, lost film—better, if the truth be known, than *Gloria,* which is fun and engaging but slight. What saves this movie is Cassavetes's reliance on a tried-and-true plot construction. For once, his characters aren't all over the map in nonstop dialogue, as they were in *Husbands,* the talkathon he made in 1970 with Peter Falk, Gazzara, and himself. *Gloria* is tough, sweet, and goofy.

Glory ★ ★ ★ ½
R, 122 m., 1989

Matthew Broderick (Robert Gould Shaw), Denzel Washington (Trip), Cary Elwes (Cabot Forbes), Morgan Freeman (Rawlins), Jihmi Kennedy (Sharts), Andre Braugher (Searles), John Finn (Mulcahy). Directed by Edward Zwick and produced by Freddie Fields. Screenplay by Kevin Jarre.

The story goes that the author of *Glory,* Kevin Jarre, was walking across Boston Common one day when he noticed something about a Civil War memorial that he had never noticed before. Some of the soldiers in it were black. Although the American Civil War is often referred to as the war to free the slaves, it had never occurred to Jarre—or, apparently, to very many others—that blacks themselves fought in the war. The inspiration for *Glory* came to Jarre as he stood looking at the monument.

It tells the story of the 54th Regiment of the Massachusetts Volunteer Infantry, made up of black soldiers—some Northern freemen, some escaped slaves—and led by whites including Robert Gould Shaw, the son of Boston abolitionists. Although it was widely believed at the time that blacks would not make good soldiers and would not submit to discipline under fire, the 54th figured in one of the bloodiest actions of the war, an uphill attack across muddy terrain against a Confederate fort in Charleston, South Carolina. The attack was almost suicidal, particularly given the battlefield strategies of the day, which involved disciplining troops to keep on marching into withering fire. The 54th suffered a bloodbath. But its members remained disciplined soldiers to the end, and their performance on that day—July 18, 1863—encouraged the North to recruit other blacks to its ranks, one hundred thousand in all, and may have been decisive in turning the tide of the war.

Glory tells the story of the 54th Regiment largely through the eyes of Robert Gould Shaw (Matthew Broderick), who in an early scene in the film is seen horrified and disoriented by the violence of the battlefield. Returned home to recover from wounds, he is recruited to lead a newly formed black regiment and takes the job even though his own enlightened abolitionist opinions still leave room for doubts about the capability of black troops.

It is up to the troops themselves to convince him they can fight—and along the way they also gently provide him with some insights into race and into human nature, a century before the flowering of the civil rights movement. Among the men who turn into the natural leaders of the 54th are Trip (Denzel Washington), an escaped slave, and John Rawlins (Morgan Freeman), first seen in the film as a grave digger who encounters the wounded Shaw on the field of battle.

These men are proud to be soldiers, proud to wear the uniform, and also too proud to accept the racism they see all around them, as when a decision is made to pay black troops less than white. Blacks march as far, bleed as much, and die as soon, they argue. Why should they be paid less for the same work?

Robert Gould Shaw and his second in command, Cabot Forbes (Cary Elwes), eventually see the logic in this argument and join their men in refusing their paychecks. That action is a turning point for the 54th, fusing the officers and men together into a fighting unit with mutual trust. But there are countless smaller scenes that do the same thing, including one in which Shaw is pointedly told by one of his men that when the war is over, nothing much will have changed: "You'll go back to your big house."

Glory has been directed by Edward Zwick, designed by Norman Garwood, and photographed by Freddie Francis with enormous attention to period detail, as in such small touches as the shoes issued to the troops (they don't come in right and left, but get to be that way after you've worn them long enough). These little details lead up to larger ones, as when the children of poor black sharecroppers look on in wonder as black soldiers in uniform march past their homes. And everything in the film leads up to the final bloody battle scene, a suicidal march up a hill that accomplishes little in concrete military terms but is of incalculable symbolic importance.

Watching *Glory,* I had one recurring problem with the film. I didn't understand why it had to be told so often from the point of view of the 54th's white commanding officer. Why did we see the black troops through his eyes—instead of seeing him through theirs? To put it another way, why does the top billing in this movie go to a white actor? I ask, not to be perverse, but because I consider this primarily a story about a black experience and do not know why it has to be seen largely through white eyes. Perhaps one answer is that the significance of the 54th was the way in which it changed white perceptions of black soldiers (changed them slowly enough, to be sure, that the Vietnam War was the first in American history in which troops were not largely segregated). *Glory* is a strong and valuable film no matter whose eyes it is seen through. But there is still, I suspect, another and quite different film to be made from this same material.

The Go-Between ★ ★ ★ ½
PG, 116 m., 1971

Julie Christie (Marian), Alan Bates (Ted Burgess), Dominic Guard (Leo, as a Boy), Michael Gough (Mr. Maudsley). Directed by Joseph Losey and produced by John Heyman. Screenplay by Harold Pinter.

There was a time, fairly recent, when the British upper classes thought it was a shade embarrassing to have to work for a living. Boys from middle-class families might attend the same school as upper-class boys, but they were tarnished, somehow, by their parents' direct contact with money. Money was something that needed to pass through a few sets of intervening hands, to let the sweat dry, before it could be spent by the aristocracy.

In a famous essay about English boarding schools, George Orwell delineated this delicate, cruel class distinction. He came from a white-collar family that made less than many blue-collar families, and yet had to present certain "standards" to the world. One of these was the necessity to send its children away to schools which, although they were shabby by Eton standards, were at least private. The children were the ones who suffered directly at the hands of class snobbism, of course, and sometimes their personalities were marked for life.

Joseph Losey's *The Go-Between* is about class distinction and its warping effect upon the life of one small boy. The story is set in the days before World War I, privileged days that seemed to stretch endlessly before the British upper class. The boy, Leo, comes to spend a summer holiday at the home of a rich friend. And he falls in hopeless schoolboy love with the friend's older sister (Julie Christie).

The sister is engaged to marry well, but she is in love with a roughshod tenant farmer (Alan Bates), and she enlists the boy to carry messages back and forth between them. The boy has only a shadowy notion at first about the significance of the messages, but during the summer he is sharply disillusioned about love, fidelity, and his own place in the great scheme of things.

Losey and his screenwriter, Harold Pinter, are terribly observant about small nuances of class. In the family's matriarch (Margaret Leighton) they give us a woman who seems to support the British class system all by herself, simply through her belief in it. They show a father and a fiancé who are aware of the girl's affair with the farmer, but do nothing about it. They are confident she will do the "right thing" in the end, and she does. "Why don't you marry Ted," the boy asks the young woman. "Because I can't," she replies. "Then why are you marrying Trimmington?" "Because I must."

She understands, and she is tough enough to endure. Indeed, at the end of the film she turns up years later as an old lady very much in the image of her mother. The victim is the boy, who is scarred sexually and emotionally by his summer experience. When we see him at the film's end, he is a sort of bloodless eunuch, called in to perform one last errand for the woman.

Losey's production is elegantly costumed and mounted and has the same eye for details of character that distinguished his two previous films with Pinter (*The Servant* and *Accident*). One visual device is distracting, however, he keeps giving us short flash-forwards to the end of the film. On the one hand, this eventually gives the ending away.

On the other, it imposes a ponderous significance on the events that go before, diluting their freshness.

If the film had been told in straight chronology followed by an epilogue, it would have been more effective. In fact, the epilogue could have been lost altogether with no trouble; everything that will become of this boy in his adult life is already there, by implication, at the end of his summer holiday.

The Godfather ★ ★ ★ ★
R, 171 m., 1972

Marlon Brando (Don Vito Corleone), Al Pacino (Michael Corleone), James Caan (Sonny Corleone), Robert Duvall (Tom Hagen), Richard Castellano (Clemenza). Directed by Francis Ford Coppola and produced by Albert S. Ruddy. Screenplay by Mario Puzo.

We know from Gay Talese's book *Honor Thy Father* that being a professional mobster isn't all sunshine and roses. More often, it's the boredom of stuffy rooms and a bad diet of carry-out food, punctuated by brief, terrible bursts of violence. This is exactly the feel of *The Godfather*, which brushes aside the flashy glamour of the traditional gangster picture and gives us what's left: fierce tribal loyalties, deadly little neighborhood quarrels in Brooklyn, and a form of vengeance to match every affront.

The remarkable thing about Mario Puzo's novel was the way it seemed to be told from the inside out; he didn't give us a world of international intrigue, but a private club as constricted as the seventh grade. Everybody knew everybody else and had a pretty shrewd hunch what they were up to.

The movie (based on a script labored over for some time by Puzo and then finally given form, I suspect, by director Francis Ford Coppola) gets the same feel. We tend to identify with Don Corleone's family not because we dig gang wars, but because we have been with them from the beginning, watching them wait for battle while sitting at the kitchen table and eating chow mein out of paper cartons.

The Godfather himself is not even the central character in the drama. That position goes to the youngest, brightest son, Michael, who understands the nature of his father's position while revising his old-fashioned ways. The Godfather's role in the family enterprise is described by his name; he stands outside the next generation which will carry on and, hopefully, angle the family into legitimate enterprises.

Those who have read the novel may be surprised to find Michael at the center of the movie, instead of Don Corleone. In fact, this is simply an economical way for Coppola to get at the heart of the Puzo story, which dealt with the transfer of power within the family. Marlon Brando, who plays the Godfather as a shrewd, unbreakable old man, actually has the character lead in the movie; Al Pacino, with a brilliantly developed performance as Michael, is the lead.

But Brando's performance is a skillful throwaway, even though it earned him an Academy Award for best actor. His voice is wheezy and whispery, and his physical movements deliberately lack precision; the effect is of a man so accustomed to power that he no longer needs to remind others. Brando does look the part of old Don Corleone, mostly because of acting and partly because of the makeup, although he seems to have stuffed a little too much cotton into his jowls, making his lower face immobile.

The rest of the actors supply one example after another of inspired casting. Although *The Godfather* is a long, minutely detailed movie of some three hours, there naturally isn't time to go into the backgrounds and identities of such characters as Clemenza, the family lieutenant; Jack Woltz, the movie czar; Luca Brasi, the loyal professional killer; McCluskey, the crooked cop; and the rest. Coppola and producer Al Ruddy skirt this problem with understated typecasting. As the Irish cop, for example, they simply slide in Sterling Hayden and let the character go about his business. Richard Castellano is an unshakable Clemenza. John Marley makes a perfectly hateful Hollywood mogul (and, yes, he still wakes up to find he'll have to cancel his day at the races).

The success of *The Godfather* as a novel was largely due to a series of unforgettable scenes. Puzo is a good storyteller, but no great shakes as a writer. The movie gives almost everything in the novel except the gynecological repair job. It doesn't miss a single killing; it opens with the wedding of Don Corleone's daughter (and attendant upstairs activity); and there are the right number of auto bombs, double crosses, and garrotings.

Coppola has found a style and a visual look for all this material so *The Godfather* becomes something of a rarity: a really good movie squeezed from a bestseller. The decision to shoot everything in period decor (the middle and late 1940s) was crucial; if they'd tried to save money as they originally planned, by bringing everything up-to-date, the movie simply wouldn't have worked. But it's uncannily successful as a period piece, filled with sleek, bulging limousines and postwar fedoras. Coppola and his cinematographer, Gordon Willis, also do some interesting things with the color photography. The earlier scenes have a reddish-brown tint, slightly overexposed and feeling like nothing so much as a 1946 newspaper rotogravure supplement.

Although the movie is three hours long, it absorbs us so effectively it never has to hurry. There is something in the measured passage of time as Don Corleone hands over his reins of power that would have made a shorter, faster moving film unseemly. Even at this length, there are characters in relationships you can't quite understand unless you've read the novel. Or perhaps you can, just by the way the characters look at each other.

The Godfather, Part II ★ ★ ★
R, 200 m., 1974

Al Pacino (Michael), Robert Duvall (Tom Hagen), Diane Keaton (Kay), Robert De Niro (Don Vito Corleone), John Cazale (Fredo), Lee Strasberg (Hyman Roth), G.D. Spradlin (Senator Geary). Directed by Francis Ford Coppola and produced by Gray Frederickson and Fred Ross. Screenplay by Coppola and Mario Puzo.

Moving through the deep shadows and heavy glooms of his vast estate, Michael Corleone presides over the destruction of his own spirit in *The Godfather, Part II*. The character we recall from *The Godfather* as the best and brightest of Don Vito's sons, the one who went to college and enlisted in the Marines, grows into a cold and ruthless man, obsessed with power. The film's closing scenes give us first a memory of a long-ago family dinner, and then Michael at mid-life, cruel, closed, and lonely. He's clearly intended as a tragic figure.

The Corleone saga, as painted by Francis Ford Coppola and Mario Puzo in two films totaling nearly seven hours, has been a sort of success story in reverse. In a crazy way, *The Godfather* and its sequel belong in the same category with those other epics of immigrant achievement in America, *The Emigrants* and *The New Land*. The Corleone family worked hard, was ambitious, remembered friends, never forgave disloyalty, and started from humble beginnings to become the most powerful Mafia organization in the country. If it were not that the family business was crime, these films could be an inspiration for us all.

Coppola seems to hold a certain ambivalence toward his material. Don Vito Corleone as portrayed by Marlon Brando in *The Godfather* was a man of honor and dignity, and it was difficult not to sympathize with him, playing with his grandchild in the garden, at peace after a long lifetime of murder, extortion, and the rackets. What exactly were we supposed to think about him? How did Coppola feel toward the Godfather?

The Godfather, Part II moves both forward and backward in time from the events in *The Godfather*, in an attempt to resolve our feelings about the Corleones. In doing so, it provides for itself a structural weakness from which the film never recovers, but it does something even more disappointing: It reveals a certain simplicity in Coppola's notions of motivation and characterization that wasn't there in the elegant masterpiece of his earlier film.

He gives us, first of all, the opening chapters in Don Vito's life. His family is killed by a Mafia don in Sicily, he comes to America at the age of nine, he grows up (to be played by Robert De Niro), and edges into a career of crime, first as a penny-ante crook and then as a neighborhood arranger and power broker: a man, as the movie never tires of reminding us, of respect.

This story, of Don Vito's younger days, occupies perhaps a fourth of the film's 200 minutes. Coppola devotes the rest to Michael Corleone, who has taken over the family's business after his father's death, has pulled out of New York, and consolidated operations in Nevada, and has ambitions to expand in Florida and Cuba. Michael is played, again and brilliantly, by Al Pacino, and among the other familiar faces are Robert Duvall as Tom Hagen, the family's lawyer; Diane Keaton as Michael's increasingly despairing wife Kay; and John Cazale as the weak older brother Fredo.

Coppola handles a lot of this material very well. As in the earlier film, he reveals himself as a master of mood, atmosphere, and period. And his exposition is inventive and subtle. The film requires the intelligent participation of the viewer; as Michael attempts to discover who betrayed him and attempted his assassination, he tells different stories to different people, keeping his own counsel,

and we have to think as he does so we can tell the truth from the lies.

Pacino is very good at suggesting the furies and passions that lie just beneath his character's controlled exterior. He gives us a Michael who took over the family with the intention of making it "legitimate" in five years, but who is drawn more and more deeply into a byzantine web of deceit and betrayal, all papered over with code words like respect, honor, and gratitude. By the film's end he has been abandoned by almost everyone except those who work for him and fear him, and he is a very lonely man.

But what was his sin? It was not, as we might have imagined or hoped, that he presided over a bloody enterprise of murder and destruction. No, Michael's fault seems to be pride. He has lost the common touch, the dignity he should have inherited from his father. And because he has misplaced his humanity he must suffer.

Coppola suggests this by contrast. His scenes about Don Vito's early life could almost be taken as a campaign biography, and in the most unfortunate flashbacks we're given the young Vito intervening on behalf of a poor widow who is being evicted from her apartment. The don seems more like a precinct captain than a gangster, and we're left with the unsettling impression that Coppola thinks things would have turned out all right for Michael if he'd had the old man's touch.

The flashbacks give Coppola the greatest difficulty in maintaining his pace and narrative force. The story of Michael, told chronologically and without the other material, would have had really substantial impact, but Coppola prevents our complete involvement by breaking the tension. The flashbacks to New York in the early 1900s have a different, a nostalgic tone, and the audience has to keep shifting gears. Coppola was reportedly advised by friends to forget the Don Vito material and stick with Michael, and that was good advice.

There's also some evidence in the film that Coppola never completely mastered the chaotic mass of material in his screenplay. Some scenes seem oddly pointless (why do we get almost no sense of Michael's actual dealings in Cuba, but lots of expensive footage about the night of Castro's takeover?), and others seem not completely explained (I am still not quite sure who really did order that attempted garroting in the Brooklyn saloon).

What we're left with, then, are a lot of good scenes and good performances set in the midst of a mass of undisciplined material and handicapped by plot construction that prevents the story from ever really building.

There is, for example, the brilliant audacity of the first communion party for Michael's son, which Coppola directs as counterpoint to the wedding scene that opened *The Godfather*. There is Lee Strasberg's two-edged performance as Hyman Roth, the boss of the Florida and Cuban operations; Strasberg gives us a soft-spoken, almost kindly old man, and then reveals his steel-hard interior. There is Coppola's use of sudden, brutal bursts of violence to punctuate the film's brooding progress. There is Pacino, suggesting everything, telling nothing.

But Coppola is unable to draw all this together and make it work on the level of simple, absorbing narrative. The stunning text of *The Godfather* is replaced in *Part II* with prologues, epilogues, footnotes, and good intentions.

The Godfather Part III ★ ★ ★ ½
R, 162 m., 1990

Al Pacino (Michael Corleone), Diane Keaton (Kay), Talia Shire (Connie), Andy Garcia (Vincent Mancini), Sofia Coppola (Mary Corleone), Eli Wallach (Don Altobello), Joe Mantegna (Joey Zasa). Directed and produced by Francis Ford Coppola. Screenplay by Mario Puzo and Coppola.

And so here we are back again now, in the rich, deep brown rooms inhabited by the Corleone family, the rooms filled with shadows and memories, and regretful decisions that people may have to die. We have been taught this world so well by Francis Ford Coppola that we enter it effortlessly; has there ever before been a film saga so seductive and compelling, so familiar to us that even after years we remember all of the names of the players? Here, for example, is a new character, introduced as "Sonny's illegitimate son," and, yes, we nod like cousins at a family reunion, yes, he *does* seem a lot like Sonny. He's the same kind of hotheaded, trigger-happy lunatic.

The Godfather Part III continues the Corleone family history right down to the early 1980s, as the sins of the parents are visited upon the children. Despite every attempt to go legit, to become respectable, the past cannot be silenced. The family has amassed unimaginable wealth, and as the film opens

Michael Corleone (Al Pacino) is being invested with a great honor by the church. Later that day, at a reception, his daughter announces a Corleone family gift to the church and the charities of Sicily, "a check in the amount of $100 million." But the Corleones are about to find, as others have throughout history, that money can't buy you love. Sure, you can do business with evil men inside the church, for all men are fallible and capable of sin. But God does not take payoffs.

Michael is older now, and walks with a stoop. He has a diabetic condition. He has spent the years since *The Godfather Part II* trying to move the family out of crime and into legitimate businesses. He has turned over a lot of the old family rackets to a new generation, to people like Joey Zasa (Joe Mantegna), who is not scrupulous about dealing dope, who is capable of making deals that would offend the fastidious Michael. It is Michael's dream, now that he senses his life is coming to a close, that he can move his family into the light.

But the past is seductive. Because Michael knows how to run a Mafia family, there is great pressure on him to do so. And throughout *Godfather III* we are aware of the essential tragedy of this man, the fact that the sins that stain his soul will not wash off—especially the sin of having ordered the death of his brother, Fredo. Michael is positioned in the story between two characters who could come from *King Lear*—his daughter, Mary (Sofia Coppola), whom he loves and wants to give his kingdom to, and Sonny's son, Vincent (Andy Garcia), who sees the death of his enemies as the answer to every question. Michael is torn between the futures represented by the two characters, between Mary, quiet and naive, and the hot-blooded Vincent. And when Vincent seduces Mary and makes her his own, Michael's plans begin to go wrong.

There is also Kay Corleone (Diane Keaton), of course, still the woman Michael loves and the mother of his children. He wants their son, Anthony, to join the family business. She defends his ambition to be an opera singer. They face each other like skilled opponents. Perhaps she even still loves him, too, or would if she did not know him so well. She is the only person who can tell Michael what she really thinks, and in one of those dark, gloomy rooms she lets him know that it doesn't matter what grand order he is invested in by the church, he is at heart still a gangster. The best scenes in *Godfather III* are

between these two, Michael and Kay, Pacino and Keaton, fiercely locked in a battle that began many years ago, at that wedding feast where Michael told Kay he was not part of his family business.

The plot of the movie, concocted by Coppola and Mario Puzo in a screenplay inspired by headlines, brings the Corleone family into the inner circles of corruption in the Vatican. Actual events—the untimely suddenness of John Paul I's death, the scandals at the Vatican Bank, the body of a Vatican banker found hanging from a London bridge—are cheerfully intertwined with the Corleone's fictional story, and it is suggested that the Vatican lost hundreds of millions in a fraud directed by the Mafia. We eavesdrop on corrupt Vatican officials, venal cardinals scheming in the vast Renaissance palaces that dwarf them, and we travel to Sicily so that Michael Corleone can consult with Don Tommasino, his trusted old friend, to discover who is plotting against him within the Mafia council.

They are so seductive, these Byzantine intrigues. Alliances are forged with a pragmatic decision, betrayed with sudden violence. Always there is someone in a corner, whispering even more devious advice. This trait of operatic plotting and betrayal is practiced beautifully by Connie Corleone (Talia Shire), Michael's sister, who has turned in middle age into a fierce, thin-faced woman in black, who stands in the deepest shadows, who schemes and lobbies for her favorites—especially for Vincent, whom she wants Michael to accept and embrace.

In the *Godfather* movies Coppola has made a world. Because we know it so intimately, because its rhythms and values are instantly recognizable to us, a film like *The Godfather Part III* probably works better than it should. If you stand back and look at it rationally, this is a confusing and disjointed film. It is said that Coppola was rewriting it as he went along, and indeed it lacks the confident forward sweep of a film that knows where it's going.

Some of the dialogue scenes, especially in the beginning, sound vaguely awkward; the answers do not fit the questions, and conversations seem to have been rewritten in the editing room. Other shots—long shots, into the light so we cannot see the characters' lips—look suspiciously like scenes that were filmed first and dubbed later. The whole ambitious final movement of the film—in which two separate intrigues are intercut with the progress of an opera being sung by

Anthony—is intended to be suspenseful, but is so confusing we are not even sure which place (Sicily, Rome, London?) one of the intrigues is taking place in. The final scene of the movie, which is intended to echo Marlon Brando's famous death scene, is perfunctory and awkward.

And yet it's strange how the earlier movies fill in the gaps left by this one and answer the questions. It is, I suspect, not even possible to understand this film without knowing the first two, and yet, knowing them, *Part III* works better than it should, evokes the same sense of wasted greatness, of misdirected genius. Both Don Vito Corleone and Don Michael Corleone could have been great men. But they lacked that final shred of character that would have allowed them to break free from their own pasts. Or perhaps their tragedies were dictated by circumstances. Perhaps they were simply born into the wrong family.

The Gods Must Be Crazy ★ ★ ★
PG, 109 m., 1984

N!xau (Xixo), Marius Weyers (Andrew Steyn), Sandra Prinsloo (Kate Thompson), Louw Verwey (Sam Boga), James Uys (The Reverend). Directed and produced by Jamie Uys. Screenplay by Uys.

Here's a movie that begins with a Coke bottle falling from the heavens, and ends with a Jeep up in a tree. *The Gods Must Be Crazy* is a South African movie that arrived in Europe with little fanfare in 1982, broke box office records in Japan and South America and all over Europe, and even became a cult hit here in North America, where there has not been much of a demand for comedies from South Africa.

The film begins in the Kalahari Desert. A pilot in a private plane throws his empty Coke bottle out the window. It lands near a Bushman who is on a hunting expedition. He has never seen anything like it before. He takes it back to his tribe, where it is put to dozens of uses: It becomes a musical instrument, a patternmaker, a fire starter, a cooking utensil, and, most of all, an object of bitter controversy. Everybody in the tribe ends up fighting over the bottle, and so the Bushman, played by the Xhosa actor N!xau (the exclamation point represents a click), decides there is only one thing to do: He must return the bottle to the gods. This decision sends him on a long odyssey toward more settled lands on the edges of the desert, where the movie develops into a somewhat more conventional comedy.

We meet some of the new characters: A would-be schoolteacher, a goofy biologist, and an insurgent leader. They are all intent on their own lives and plans, but in one way or another, the Xhosa and his Coke bottle bring them together into unexpected combinations. And the director, Jamie Uys, has the patience to develop some really elaborate sight gags, which require a lot of preparation but pay off with big laughs—particularly the sequence with an indecisive, back-and-forth Jeep.

The star of the movie is N!xau, who is so forthright and cheerful and sensible that his very presence makes some of the gags pay off. In any slapstick comedy, the gags must rest on a solid basis of logic: It's not funny to watch people being ridiculous, but it is funny to watch people doing the next logical thing, and turning out to be ridiculous. N!xau, because he approaches Western society without preconceptions, and bases all of his actions on logical conclusions, brings into relief a lot of the little tics and assumptions of everyday life. I think that reveals the thought that went into this movie: It might be easy to make a farce about screwball happenings in the desert, but it's a lot harder to create a funny interaction between nature and human nature. This movie's a nice little treasure.

The Gods Must Be Crazy II ★ ★ ★
PG, 98 m., 1990

N!xau (Xixo), Lena Farugia (Dr. Ann Taylor), Hans Strydom (Dr. Stephen Marshall), Eiros (Xiri), Nadies (Xisa), Erick Bowen (Mateo), Treasure Tshabalala (Timi), Pierre Van Pletzen (George), Lourens Swanepoel (Brenner). Directed by Jamie Uys and produced by Boet Troskie. Screenplay by Uys.

I was looking at the laserdisk of *Mr. Hulot's Holiday* the other day—that wonderful Jacques Tati comedy about a whimsical fisherman who takes his holiday by the sea. And I realized how much the movie's opening scenes benefitted from the character of his automobile, one of those ancient and obscure European models that was so small his head almost stuck out of the top of it like in a cartoon. *The Gods Must Be Crazy II* gets the same sort of effect with a quirky little airplane barely large enough to contain two passengers and a tank of gas.

The airplane isn't the only point of connection between the two movies. I do not

mean to compare the great Tati with Jamie Uys, the director of both *The Gods Must Be Crazy* movies—that wouldn't be fair—but there's something of the same spirit in the work of the two men, and in these gloomy times it is welcome. Most movie humor these days springs from verbal or physical insult, ridicule, or unfunny "jokes" based on special effects and violence. The biggest laughs come when a character gets killed in an unexpected way.

Tati didn't work like that and neither does Uys. *The Gods Must Be Crazy II* is the work of a patient craftsman who gets his laughs out of the careful construction of elaborate physical and plot situations. Some of his buildups last for most of a movie, and his punch lines are usually inspired by character traits, not dumb gags. Uys's style sheds a sweet and gentle light on this new comedy, which is a sequel to the surprising international success—and, I think, a better film.

The location once again is an unspecified part of Southern Africa (Botswana, probably, but why are there Cuban troops on patrol?). The hero of the first film, Xixo (N!xau), is seen in the opening scenes with two of his children hunting on the veld. The children, a girl and her younger brother, get into big trouble when they climb into a water tank being pulled by the truck of game poachers. The truck drives off, separating them from their father and taking them steadily away from the area they know. Meanwhile, we meet two other characters, a scientist (Lena Farugia) and a naturalist and pilot (Hans Strydom).

The movie's method is to alternate scenes involving the children, the scientists, the poachers, and two soldiers—one local, one Cuban. What Uys does is weave all of these characters into a simple story about survival in the bush and depend upon the moment-to-moment charm of his situations rather than on heavy plotting.

The airplane is a sight to behold. Because I saw it fly in the movie, I assume such planes actually exist—but it's so tiny it looks like a joke, and at one point it actually takes off while the pilot is running along, holding it up to replace a broken wheel. Once the woman scientist and her pilot are marooned in the bush, the plane figures in a lot of gags—the plane becomes this movie's equivalent of the Jeep in the previous movie. Meanwhile, the misadventures of the kids become a cliffhanger as Uys finds countless ways to develop their dilemma.

I read a news story recently that made an amazing claim: The video of *Lethal Weapon 2* is more popular among children, it said, than the video of *Batman*. This amazed me because I would have thought both movies were too dark, gloomy, and depressing for kids—that they'd be attracted to sunnier and more cheerful films. I guess I'm out of step, and today's kids are suffering from a malaise that prepares them for violent action pictures and revenge tragedies in which a masked hero atones for the mugging of his parents. But if you happen to know any kids who have not yet given up on life, who like happy movies better than grim and violent ones, they're likely to enjoy *The Gods Must Be Crazy II*. And so did I.

Godspell ★ ★ ★ ★
G, 102 m., 1973

Victor Garber (Jesus), David Haskell (John, Judas), Jerry Sroka (Jerry), Lynne Thigpen (Lynne), Katie Hanley (Katie), Robin Lamont (Robin), Gilmer McCormick (Gilmer), Joanne Jonas (Joanne), Merrell Jackson (Merrell), Jeffrey Mylett (Jeffrey). Directed by David Greene.

The thing about *Godspell* that caught my heart was its simplicity, its refusal to pretend to be anything more than it is. It's not a message for our times, or a movie to cash in on the Jesus movement, or even quite a youth movie. It's a series of stories and songs, like the Bible is, and it's told with the directness that simple stories need: with no tricks, no intellectual gadgets, and a lot of openness.

This was the quality that attracted me to the stage version. I had to be almost dragged to the play, because its subject matter sounded so depressingly contemporary. But after I finally got into the theater and sat down and let *Godspell* relax me, I found myself simply letting it happen. For a musical based on the Gospel according to St. Matthew, *Godspell* is strangly irreverent, wacky, and endearing.

The stage version has been opened up into a movie by taking the whole of New York as a set. Except for the scenes at the beginning and end—which show the city as a temple of mammon and a rat nest—the movie is populated only by its cast; we don't see anybody else, and the ten kids dance, sing, and act out parables in such unlikely places as the World Trade Center and a tugboat. This is a new use for New York, which looks unusually clean; even its tacky skyscrapers edge toward grandeur when the vast long shots engulf them.

Against this wilderness of steel and concrete, the characters come on like kids at a junior high reunion, clothed in comic book colors and bright tattered rags. Only two have names: Jesus, and a character who plays both John (who ushered Jesus into the Bible) and Judas (who hastened him out). The other eight characters, who seem to represent an on-the-spot gathering of disciples, are just themselves.

What's nice about the casting—which gives us all new faces—is that the characters don't look like professional stage youths. Remember *West Side Story*, where all the allegedly teen-age dancers looked like hardened theatrical professionals in greaser wigs? *Godspell*'s cast is not only young but is allowed to look like a collection of individuals. These could conceivably be real people, and their freshness helps put the material over even when it seems pretty obvious. For some blessed reason the director, David Greene, has resisted any temptation to make the movie visually fancy. With material of this sort, there must have been an impulse to go for TV-commercial trendiness, but Greene's style is unforced, and goes well with the movie's freshness and basic colors.

The movie characters, like the stage characters, are given little watercolor designs on their faces by Jesus. A girl gets a little yellow flower, a boy gets a tiny red star, and so on. It was necessary in the stage version to exaggerate this makeup to make it visible, but the movie underplays it and it was gentle and nice. It occurred to me, about an hour into the film, that maybe young people will pick up on this. Tattoos were big in the '70s—little butterflies and stars—so why not facepaint zigzags and pinwheels and flowers? Anything to brighten up this miserable world: Which is what *Godspell* is saying, anyway.

Note: Not yet available on videocassette.

The Golden Child ★ ★ ★
PG-13, 94 m., 1986

Eddie Murphy (Chandler), Charlotte Lewis (Kee Nang), Charles Dance (Sardo), Victor Wong (Old Man), J.L. Reate (Golden Child), "Tex" Cobb (Til Randall), James Hong (Dr. Wong). Directed by Michael Ritchie and produced by Edward S. Feldman and Robert D. Wachs. Screenplay by Dennis Feldman.

There are a lot of moments to remember in *The Golden Child*, but the one I will treasure

the longest happens when Eddie Murphy gets behind the wheel of a beat-up station wagon and is led by a sacred parrot to the lair of the devil.

Maybe you had to be there. The parrot, which has already made the round-trip between Tibet and Los Angeles twice, chirps merrily and flies off down a dusty road. Murphy leans down to look up at it through his windshield, and the way he looks at it is what started me laughing. There is just something about the tilt of his head that seems entirely appropriate for a man who is following a sacred parrot. Murphy is exactly right in that moment, but then he is exactly right all through this movie, which is utterly ridiculous and jolly good fun.

The advance rumors about *The Golden Child* were not encouraging. I heard Paramount feared it had a bomb on its hands, but what were they worried about? The preview audience laughed all through the movie. No wonder, because this film—insignificant and lightweight and monumentally silly—is entertaining from beginning to end. Although it contains the usual scatological language, the sex and violence are mild.

Murphy plays the hero, a professional searcher for lost children. After agents from hell kidnap a holy child from Tibet, Murphy is recruited to recover the child, find a magic dagger, defeat Satan's henchmen, beat up some Hell's Angels, pass several death-defying trials by fire, follow the sacred parrot, and fall in love with the beautiful heroine who must first be brought back from the dead. You know, the usual stuff.

The movie's opening shots should have had a subtitle flashing "Raiders Rip-off!" Hollywood must have a whole industry supplying temples and gongs to the spawn of Indiana Jones. But from the moment Murphy appears on the screen, he makes the movie all his own; the special effects are basically just comic props. Murphy slides through the picture with easy wisecracks and unflappable cool, like a hip Bob Hope.

A lot of the time, he seems to improvise his wise-ass one-liners—I haven't seen the script, and so I can't say for sure. What's amazing is that his dialogue always seems to fit. A lot of stand-up comedians throw off the pacing in a movie by going for improv at the wrong moments (Robin Williams is sometimes an example). Murphy usually seems to have the perfect reaction, even when he's shocked to catch a wise old seer picking his nose. Maybe the director, Michael Ritchie,

deserves some of the credit for that; he let Williams wreck his *The Survivors* with inappropriate one-liners, but this time everything flows.

The movie's plot is an anthology of clichés from every Oriental swashbuckler in history; just off the top of my head I can remember a bottomless cavern, a 300-year-old woman with a dragon's tail, a child whose touch turns bad men into good ones, an evil spirit that turns into a serpent, several dozen temple guards, countless karate fights, secret rooms beneath the stores in Chinatown, and, of course, the preternaturally beautiful heroine.

Her name is Kee Nang, and she is played by Charlotte Lewis, the London schoolgirl who starred in Roman Polanski's *Pirates*. That movie won her an audience of dozens; this one will likely do a lot better. She is very beautiful, and since that is her role in this movie, she fulfills it flawlessly. She also does a good job of keeping a straight face while Murphy uses her as the subject of speculation, rejection, romance, and betrayal, and while she uses her effortless mastery of kung fu to protect him.

No silly swashbuckler is any better than its villain, and the leader of the evil forces is played by Charles Dance, last seen as Meryl Streep's coldly intellectual husband in *Plenty*. He, too, has to keep a straight face through this movie, in scenes such as the one where Murphy outsmarts him at airport customs and the scene where he turns into a rat. There's also good work from Victor Wong, who plays a wise old man in several different costumes and accents.

The Golden Child may not be the Eddie Murphy movie we were waiting for, but it will do. It is funnier, more assured and more tailored to Murphy than *Beverly Hills Cop* and it shows a side of his comic persona that I don't think has been much appreciated: his essential underlying sweetness. Murphy's comedy is not based here on hurt and aggression, but on affection and an understanding that comes from seeing right through the other characters. His famous laugh is not aimed as a weapon at anybody, but is truly amused. He is perfectly suited to survive this cheerfully ridiculous movie, and even lend it a little charm.

The Goodbye Girl ★ ★ ★
PG, 110 m., 1977

Richard Dreyfuss (Elliott Garfield), Marsha Mason (Paula McFadden), Quinn Cummings

(Lucy McFadden), Paul Benedict (Mark), Barbara Rhoades (Donna), Theresa Merritt (Mrs. Crosby). Directed by Herbert Ross and produced by Ray Stark. Screenplay by Neil Simon.

Neil Simon's *The Goodbye Girl* is a funny movie with its heart finally in the right place, but all sorts of unacknowledged complications lurk just beneath its polished surface. The surface is pure Simon, which means that it's a funny-sad-tough-warm story about basically nice people who are given just three snappy one-liners too many to be totally human. But this time Simon has slipped in some subtleties we might miss the first time around.

The story's about three people we can instantly identify with. There's the former actress (Marsha Mason) and her cute ten-year-old daughter (Quinn Cummings), and the would-be actor from Chicago (Richard Dreyfuss). Until the moment before the movie opens, Miss Mason has been living with another actor in an apartment on New York's Upper East Side, where apartments are harder to find than cabs, which are harder to find than plumbers who make house calls on Sunday (which is a Simon kind of progression).

Miss Mason and her daughter come home to find that her roommate, that rat, has jumped the boat. He leaves a note explaining that he's got a great role in the new Bertolucci picture in Europe—and lotsa luck, kid. That's bad enough. Worse is when she finds out that the apartment has been sublet to this actor from Chicago, who's paid three months' rent and, reasonably enough, expects to move in, especially since at the moment he's standing in the rain.

After the two of them shout at each other for a sufficient period of time, she does allow him to move in (he gets the smaller bedroom). And then we know the basic plot structure: Total warfare in the apartment will de-escalate into a guarded truce, followed by alternating forays of warmth and decency, until the kid acts as a catalyst and they fall in love.

Wonderful. Not so wonderful is the way the Marsha Mason character is written and acted. She's hardly ever sympathetic. Sure, she's been burned by a lot of guys—but she's so hard-edged you wonder how she met them in the first place. She sees the situation strictly in economic terms, consistently behaves as a bitch, and gives Dreyfuss no reason for getting to like her.

Dreyfuss, on the other hand, is great. Eccentric, yes, since Simon always gives his characters off-the-wall touches to make them human (he meditates, plays his guitar in the middle of the night, sleeps in the nude, eats health food, etc.). But he's a nice guy. He's trapped in this weird off-off-off-Broadway production of Shakespeare's *Richard III*, and the director is convinced Richard should be played as a gay (the scenes involving the production, performance, and reception of the play are the funniest in a movie since Mel Brooks staged *Springtime for Hitler*). He fears, rightly, that the play could be the end of his New York career, and his fears are played against the unsympathetic Mason character and her basically lovable daughter.

He finally wins the mother through her child ("Listen, I can't stand you, but you got a ten-year-old in there I'm nuts about . . ."). But why does he want to? Simon short-circuits the first scene in which Mason says a decent and warm word by having Dreyfuss fall asleep so he doesn't hear it. He never really provides the dialogue and situations we need to *like* the female character—and so, in a funny way, we *aren't* rooting for them to get together. When they do, though, the movie works best. The first hour is awkward at times and never quite involving, but some of the later scenes, especially a dinner on a rooftop and the way Dreyfuss receives the disastrous reviews of his play, are really fine. It's strange: We leave the movie having enjoyed its conclusion so much that we almost forgot our earlier reservations. But they were there, and they were real.

GoodFellas ★ ★ ★ ★
R, 148 m., 1990

Robert De Niro (James Conway), Ray Liotta (Henry Hill), Joe Pesci (Tommy DeVito), Lorraine Bracco (Karen Hill), Paul Sorvino (Paul Cicero), Frank Sivero (Frankie Carbone), Catherine Scorsese (Tommy's Mother). Directed by Martin Scorsese and produced by Irwin Winkler. Screenplay by Nicholas Pileggi and Scorsese.

There really are guys like this. I've seen them in restaurants and I've met them on movie sets, where they carefully explain that they are retired and are acting as technical consultants. They make their living as criminals, and often the service they provide is that they will not hurt you if you pay them. These days there is a certain guarded nostalgia for their brand of organized crime, because at least the mob would make a deal with you for your life, and not just kill you casually, out of impatience or a need for drugs.

Martin Scorsese's *GoodFellas* is a movie based on the true story of a mid-level professional criminal named Henry Hill, whose only ambition, from childhood on, was to be a member of the outfit. We see him with his face at the window, looking across the street at the neighborhood Mafiosi, who drove the big cars and got the good-looking women and never had to worry about the cops when they decided to hold a party late at night. One day the kid goes across the street and volunteers to help out, and before long he's selling stolen cigarettes at a factory gate and not long after that the doorman at the Copacabana knows his name.

For many years, it was not a bad life. The rewards were great. The only thing you could complain about was the work. There is a strange, confused evening in Hill's life when some kidding around in a bar leads to a murder, and the guy who gets killed is a "made man"—a man you do not touch lightly, because he has the mob behind him—and the body needs to be hidden quickly, and then later it needs to be moved, messily. This kind of work is bothersome. It fills the soul with guilt and the heart with dread, and before long Henry Hill is walking around as if there's a lead weight in his stomach.

But the movie takes its time to get to that point, and I have never seen a crime movie that seems so sure of its subject matter. There must have been a lot of retired technical consultants hanging around. Henry Hill, who is now an anonymous refugee within the federal government's witness protection program, told his life story to the journalist Nicholas Pileggi, who put it into the best-seller *WiseGuy*, and now Pileggi and Scorsese have written the screenplay, which also benefits from Scorsese's firsthand observations of the Mafia while he was a kid with his face in the window, watching the guys across the street.

Scorsese is in love with the details of his story, including the Mafia don who never, ever talked on the telephone and held all of his business meetings in the open air. Or the way some guys with a body in the car trunk will stop by to borrow a carving knife from one of their mothers, who will feed them pasta and believe them when they explain that they got blood on their suits when their car hit a deer. Everything in this movie reverberates with familiarity; the actors even inhabit the scenes as if nobody had to explain anything to them.

GoodFellas is an epic on the scale of *The Godfather,* and it uses its expansive running time to develop a real feeling for the way a lifetime develops almost by chance at first, and then sets its fateful course. Because we see mostly through the eyes of Henry Hill (Ray Liotta), characters swim in and out of focus; the character of Jimmy Conway (Robert De Niro), for example, is shadowy in the earlier passages of the film and then takes on a central importance. And then there's Tommy DeVito (Joe Pesci), always on the outside looking in, glorying in his fleeting moments of power, laughing too loudly, slapping backs with too much familiarity, pursued by the demon of a raging anger that can flash out of control in a second. His final scene in this movie is one of the greatest moments of sudden realization I have ever seen; the development, the buildup, and the payoff are handled by Scorsese with the skill of a great tragedian.

GoodFellas isn't a myth-making movie, like *The Godfather.* It's about ordinary people who get trapped inside the hermetic world of the mob, whose values get worn away because they never meet anyone to disagree with them. One of the most interesting characters in the movie is Henry Hill's wife, Karen (Lorraine Bracco), who is Jewish and comes from outside his world. He's an outsider himself—he's half-Irish, half-Italian, and so will never truly be allowed on the inside—but she's so far outside that at first she doesn't even realize what she's in for. She doesn't even seem to know what Henry does for a living, and when she finds out, she doesn't want to deal with it. She is the co-narrator of the film, as if it were a documentary, and she talks about how she never goes anywhere or does anything except in the company of other mob wives. Finally she gets to the point where she's proud of her husband for being willing to go out and steal to support his family, instead of just sitting around like a lot of guys.

The parabola of *GoodFellas* is from the era of "good crimes," like stealing cigarettes and booze and running prostitution and making book, to bad crimes involving dope. The godfather in the movie (Paul Sorvino) warns Henry Hill about getting involved with dope, but it's not because he disapproves of narcotics (like Brando's Don Corleone); it's because he seems to sense that dope will spell trouble for the mob, will unleash street anar-

chy and bring in an undisciplined element. What eventually happens is that Hill makes a lot of money with cocaine but gets hooked on it as well, and eventually spirals down into the exhausted paranoia that proves to be his undoing.

Throbbing beneath the surface of *Good-Fellas,* providing the magnet that pulls the plot along, are the great emotions in Hill's makeup: a lust for recognition, a fear of powerlessness, and guilt. He loves it when the headwaiters know his name, but he doesn't really have the stuff to be a great villain—he isn't brave or heartless enough—and so when he does bad things, he feels bad afterward. He begins to hate himself. And yet, he cannot hate the things he covets. He wants the prizes, but he doesn't want to pay for the tickets.

And it is there, on the crux of that paradox, that the movie becomes Scorsese's metaphor for so many modern lives. He doesn't parallel the mob with corporations or turn it into some kind of grotesque underworld version of yuppie culture. Nothing is that simple. He simply uses organized crime as an arena for a story about a man who likes material things so much that he sells his own soul to buy them—compromises his principles, betrays his friends, abandons his family, and finally even loses contact with himself. And the horror of the film is that, at the end, the man's principal regret is that he doesn't have any more soul to sell.

Good Morning, Vietnam ★ ★ ★ ★
R, 119 m., 1988

Robin Williams (Adrian Cronauer), Forest Whitaker (Edward Garlick), Tung Thanh Tran (Tuan), Chintara Sukapatana (Trinh), Bruno Kirby (Lieutenant Hauk), Robert Wuhl (Marty Lee Dreiwitz), J.T. Walsh (Sergeant Dickerson), Noble Willingham (General Taylor). Directed by Barry Levinson and produced by Mark Johnson and Larry Brezner. Screenplay by Mitch Markowitz.

Like most of the great stand-up comedians, Robin Williams has always kept a certain wall between himself and his audience. If you watch his concert videos, you see him trying on a bewildering series of accents and characters; he's a gifted chameleon who turns into whatever makes the audience laugh. But who is inside?

With George Carlin, Richard Pryor, Steve Martin, Billy Crystal, Eddie Murphy, we have an idea—or think we do. A lot of their humor

depends on confessional autobiography. With Robin Williams, the wall remains impenetrable. Like Groucho Marx, he uses comedy as a strategy for personal concealment.

Williams's best movies *(Popeye, The World According to Garp, Moscow on the Hudson)* are the ones where he is given a well-written character to play, and held to the character by a strong director. In his other movies, you can see him trying to do his stand-up act on the screen, trying to use comedy to conceal not only himself from the audience—but even his character. The one-liners and ad-libs distance him from the material and from his fellow actors. Hey, he's only a visitor here.

What is inspired about *Good Morning, Vietnam,* which contains far and away the best work Williams has ever done in a movie, is that his own tactics are turned against him. The director, Barry Levinson, has created a character who *is* a stand-up comic—he's a fast-talking disc jockey on Armed Forces Radio during the Vietnam War, directing a non-stop monologue at the microphone. There is absolutely no biographical information about this character. We don't know where he comes from, what he did before the war, whether he's ever been married, what his dreams are, what he's afraid of. Everything in his world is reduced to material for his program.

Levinson used Mitch Markowitz's script as a starting point for a lot of Williams's monologues, and then let the comedian improvise. Then he put together the best parts of many different takes to create sequences that are undeniably dazzling and funny. Williams is a virtuoso.

But while he's assaulting the microphone, Levinson is doing something fairly subtle in the movie around him. He has populated *Good Morning, Vietnam* with a lot of character actors who are fairly complicated types, recognizably human, and with the aid of the script, they set a trap for Williams. His character is edged into a corner where he *must* have human emotions, or die.

The character (his name is Adrian Cronauer) resists. At one point his Jeep breaks down in the middle of the jungle in Viet Cong territory, and he starts using one-liners on the trees. He meets a Vietnamese girl he likes, and uses one-liners on her, too, in a genuine exercise in cynicism since she doesn't understand any of his humor. He runs afoul of top Army brass that doesn't approve of his anti-establishment tone on the radio, and he wisecracks at them, too, trying to insist that he's always on stage, that nothing is real, that the whole war is basically just material.

And then things happen. To impress the girl and her brother, he starts teaching an English-language class for the Vietnamese. He finds that he likes them. He witnesses (and barely survives) a particularly gruesome terrorist attack. He gets thrown off the radio. He meets some kids who are going into battle, and who admire him, and in their eyes he sees something that makes him start to take himself a little more seriously. By the end of the movie, Cronauer has turned into a better, deeper, wiser man than he was at the beginning; the movie is the story of his education.

I know there are other ways to read this material. *Good Morning, Vietnam* works as straight comedy, and it works as a Vietnam-era *M*A*S*H*, and even the movie's love story has its own bittersweet integrity. But they used to tell us in writing class that if we wanted to know what a story was really about, we should look for what changed between the beginning and the end. In this movie, Cronauer changes. War wipes the grin off of his face. His humor becomes a humanitarian tool, not simply a way to keep him talking and us listening.

In a strange, subtle way, *Good Morning, Vietnam* is not so much about war as it is about stand-up comedy, about the need that compels people to get up in front of the room and try to make us laugh—to control us.

Why do comics do that? Because they need to have their power proven and vindicated. Why do they need that? Because they are the most insecure of earth's people (just listen to their language—they're gonna kill us, unless they die out there). How do you treat low self-esteem? By doing estimable things and then saying, hey, I did that! What happens to Cronauer in this movie? Exactly that. By the end of the film he doesn't wisecrack all the time because he doesn't need to. He no longer thinks he's the worthless (although bright, fast, and funny) sack of crap that got off the plane. In the early scenes of the movie, the character's eyes are opaque. By the end, you can see what he's thinking.

A Goofy Movie ★ ★ ★
G, 77 m., 1995

With the voices of: Bill Farmer (Goofy), Jason Marsden (Max), Jim Cummings (Pete), Kellie Martin (Roxanne), Rob Paulsen (PJ), Wallace Shawn (Principal Mazur), Jenna Von Oy (Stacey), Frank Welker (Bigfoot). Directed by Kevin Lima and produced by Dan Rounds. Screenplay by Jymn Magon, Chris Matheson, and Brian Pimental.

About two-thirds of the way through the screening of *A Goofy Movie* last Saturday morning, something goofy happened. The movie was suddenly upside-down, and you could see the jagged lines of the optical sound track zipping along on the right side of the screen.

This was not a good sign. As Goofy would say, "Gorsh!" I was in a theater with about two hundred kids, who made loud noises of protest, confusion, and delight. Eventually the movie was stopped, and the manager explained that there was a "technical difficulty," and gave us all passes for a future screening. Since we had gotten into *this* screening for free, this was a good deal.

But now I am faced with a deadline, and a review to write. What to do? It occurred to me that since I had seen a movie in progress, I should write a review in progress, simply by supplying you with the notes, written and mental, that I had taken during the movie's first hour. Such as:

—Is Goofy a human, or a dog? I once met Bill Farmer, who does the voice of Goofy, and he gave me the definitive answer: "Pluto is definitely a dog. Goofy is sort of the missing link between dog and man."

—The movie is not really about Goofy, but about his teenage son, Max. Today's kids are so youth-oriented that Goofy is too old for them to identify with. Max wears shades and wants to take his best girl/dog, Roxanne, to a rock concert.

—All the animated characters in Disney movies have a thumb and three, not four, fingers. Is it true that Walt thought this was a good idea because it makes it impossible for them to flip the bird?

—What does the bathroom look like in Goofy's house, and how does he use it?

—At one point there is a moving truck in the movie, and on its side is painted: "Starving House Pets Movers." Nice touch.

—I realized the human-potential movement has gotten completely out of hand when I heard Goofy telling Max they needed to spend more "quality time" together.

—Another sad sign of the times we live in: For the first time in cartoon history, Goofy locks his car after he parks it.

—Cute moment: During a fishing trip together, Goofy suggests they play car games. "I'm thinking of a person," Goofy tells Max. "You have to guess who it is." "Is it a male?" asks Max. "Yes," says Goofy. "Walt Disney?" says Max. "Right," says Goofy.

That's as far as I got before the movie went upside-down. How many stars would I give *A Goofy Movie*? Well, at the time they stopped the show, the star-meter was clicking over at just a shade under three stars, but let's round it off to three and call it a day. That may be a goofy way to rate a movie, but goofy is as goofy does.

Note: I later saw the rest of the movie, and was rather surprised how much I enjoyed it. It's not one of Disney's mega-million blockbusters, but it has a charm of its own.

The Goonies ★ ★ ★
PG, 114 m., 1985

Sean Astin (Mikey), Josh Brolin (Brand), Jeff Cohen (Chunk), Corey Feldman (Mouth), Kerri Green (Andy), Martha Plimpton (Stef), and Ke Huy Quan (Data). Directed by Richard Donner and produced by Donner and Harvey Bernhard. Executive producer, Steven Spielberg. Screenplay by Chris Columbus.

The Goonies is a smooth mixture of the usual ingredients from Steven Spielberg action movies, made special because of the high-energy performances of the kids who have the adventures. It's a fantastical story of buried pirate treasure, told with a slice-of-life approach that lets these kids use words Bogart didn't know in *Casablanca*. There used to be children's movies and adult movies. Now Spielberg has found an in-between niche, for young teen-agers who have fairly sophisticated tastes in horror. He supervises the formula and oversees the production, assigning the direction to stylish action veterans (this time, it's Richard Donner, of *Superman* and *Ladyhawke*).

Goonies, like *Gremlins*, walks a thin line between the cheerful and the gruesome, and the very scenes the adults might object to are the ones the kids will like the best: Spielberg is congratulating them on their ability to take the heavy-duty stuff. The movie begins with an assortment of engaging boys, including a smart kid, a kid with braces, a fat kid, an older brother, and an Asian kid whose clothing conceals numerous inventions. Along the way they pick up a couple of girls, whose function is to swap spit and get bats in their hair. The kids find an old treasure map and blunder into the hideout of a desperate gang of criminals—two brothers, led by a Ma Barker type. There is a third brother, a Quasimodish freak, who is kept chained down in the cellar, where he watches TV. The tunnels to the treasure begin under the hideout. The kids find the tunnels while fleeing from the bad guys, and then go looking for the treasure with the crooks on their tails. There are lots of special effects and among the set pieces are the same kinds of booby traps that Indiana Jones survived in *Raiders* (falling boulders, sharp spikes), and a toboggan ride on a water chute that will remind you of the runaway train in *The Temple of Doom.*

If the ingredients are familiar from Spielberg's high-powered action movies, the kids are inspired by *E. T.* The single most important line of dialogue in any Spielberg movie is probably the line in *E. T.* when one kid calls another kid "penis-breath." The dialogue hears and acknowledges the precocious way that kids incorporate vulgarity into their conversations, especially with each other; the line in *E. T.* created such a shock of recognition that the laughs swept away any objections.

This time, his kids say "shit" a lot, and it is a measure of Spielberg's insight that the word draws only a PG rating for the movie; Spielberg no doubt argues that most kids talk like that half the time, and he is right. His technique is to take his thirteen- and fourteen-year-olds and let them act a little older than their age. It's more refreshing than the old Disney technique, which was to take characters of all ages and have them behave as if they were twelve.

Another Spielberg trademark, faithfully achieved by Donner, is a breakneck narrative speed. More things happen in his movie than in six ordinary action films. There's not just a thrill a minute; there's a thrill, a laugh, a shock, and a special effect. The screenplay has all the kids talking all at once, all the time, and there were times, especially in the first reel, when I couldn't understand much of what they were saying. The movie needs to be played loud, and with extra treble.

During *Goonies,* I was often exhilarated by what was happening. Afterward, I was less enthusiastic. The movie is totally manipulative, which would be okay, except it doesn't have the lift of a film like *E. T.* It has the high energy without the sweetness. It uses what it knows about kids to churn them up, while *E. T.* gave them things to think about, the values to enjoy. *The Goonies,* like *Gremlins,* shows that Spielberg and his directors are absolute masters of how to excite and involve an audience. *E. T.* was more like *Close Encounters*; it didn't simply want us to feel, but also to wonder, and to dream.

Gordy ★ ★
G, 89m., 1995   **NEW**

Doug Stone (Luke MacAllister), Kristy Young (Jinnie Sue MacAllister), Michael Roescher (Hanky Royce), Deborah Hobart (Jessica Royce), Ted Manson (Henry Royce), Jim Meskiman (President's Voice), James Donadio (Gilbert Sipes), Tom Lester (Cousin Jake), Tom Key (Brinks). Directed by Mark Lewis and produced by Sybil Robson. Screenplay by Leslie Stevens.

In the opening scenes of *Gordy,* some men in a truck come to a struggling family farm to load up a mother pig and her piglets and cart them away. "Can't blame folks for selling their livestock; they need cash," they say, as if the natural inclination of farmers would be to support their animals until they die of old age.

These are no ordinary pigs, however, as we discover when we meet Gordy, a piglet who luckily misses being shipped to the fattening farm. Gordy is some pig. He speaks English, for example—in a high-pitched voice that's intercut with all sorts of snorts and squeaks. And he trots around on his little feet like a pig with a mission. He's determined to find his family and save them from hickory smoking.

Gordy (who was born not far from the historical town of Hope, Arkansas) hits the road, and is soon adopted by a little girl who sings with her father in a country band. Her name is Jinnie Sue MacAllister (Kristy Young), and she moves Gordy into her bunk in the family motor home. In one of those movie moments kids always especially like, her dad, a widower named Luke (Doug Stone), gets a good-night kiss from the pig and thinks it's his daughter.

The odyssey continues. Luke's band plays at the governor's mansion, where a young boy named Hanky (Michael Roescher) falls into the pool and nearly drowns—until he is rescued, of course, by the quick-thinking Gordy. The pig becomes a hero (he even gets a call from President Clinton), and is adopted as the trademark of a company owned by Hanky's rich grandfather. Meanwhile, he still wants to find his family before they end up arrayed in slices on either side of a short stack.

Pigs are not my favorite animals, but I am aware of the arguments that they are among the most intelligent of the barnyard animals (they're smarter than horses, according to Johnny Carson, who had a long-running debate on the subject with Ed McMahon). Gordy, however, has a certain (very limited) charm, and the human story—which has the single parents of Hanky and Jinnie Sue falling in love to country music—has a cornball appeal.

This is not the kind of film that rewards deep analysis. I rate it at two stars, but I'd recommend it for kids. I can't recommend it for people like me, but there are many other kinds of people in the world, some of them children who believe that pigs can talk, and for them *Gordy* is likely to be very entertaining. You know who you are.

Gorillas in the Mist ★ ★ ★
PG-13, 130 m., 1988

Sigourney Weaver (Dian Fossey), Bryan Brown (Bob Campbell), Julie Harris (Roz Carr), John Omirah Miluwi (Sembagare), Iain Cuthbertson (Dr. Louis Leakey), Constantin Alexandrov (Van Vecten). Directed by Michael Apted and produced by Arnold Glimcher and Terence Clegg. Screenplay by Anna Hamilton Phelan.

Gorillas in the Mist tells us what Dian Fossey accomplished and what happened to her, but it doesn't tell us who she was, and at the end that's what we want to know. Here is a movie that has gone to great lengths to be technically accomplished—the shots of the apes are everything we could wish for—but the screenplay has been skimped on, and there is a person missing here somewhere. We leave feeling that when Fossey was buried in her beloved jungle, the third act of the movie was buried there, too.

The film tells a life story that many people already know. Dian Fossey was a woman of average achievement and no particular scientific background, but she loved animals and she was deeply disturbed by reports that the mountain gorillas of central Africa were being threatened with extinction. With absolute determination, she convinced Louis Leakey, the guru of African anthropologists, to allow her to man a jungle camp and conduct a census of the gorillas. And over the years she grew into one of the great experts on these fearsome but manlike beasts, learning to imitate their behavior so well that they accepted her in their midst.

Fossey's work was featured in *National Geographic* and on TV documentaries. She became a romantic figure, out there almost alone in the wild, protecting "her" gorillas against poachers who sold gorilla hands to be made into ashtrays. Then, in 1985, she was found murdered in her camp, and as more came to be known about her there were many likely suspects. Fossey had grown fanatical about her animals, had all but waged war against the pygmy tribes that were killing them. She had alienated the trappers who procured animals for zoos. And she had made powerful enemies in a government that needed all the foreign currency it could find—and made lots of money off of gorillas.

Who killed her? The movie does not say, and that's as it should be. This is not a whodunit. But why did she become the ferocious and antisocial recluse of her later years? Why did she prize her relationships with gorillas above those with humans? Why did she choose to stay in the jungle rather than to join the man she loved? I can imagine good answers to all of these questions—I think the fate of Dian Fossey was more or less inevitable, and admirable—but in the movie the transitions in her emotional state are made so abruptly that we become conscious of the story being told.

Fossey is played in the movie by Sigourney Weaver, who makes her passionate and private, and has an exquisite tenderness and tact in her delicate scenes with wild animals. It is impossible to imagine a more appropriate choice for the role. But she grows away from us as the movie reaches its conclusion. A woman we have come to know turns into a stranger, and even if that is what happened to Dian Fossey—even if she did pull a cocoon of obsession around her—we deserve to see that happening, and to understand it. The screenplay simply presents it as an accomplished fact.

There is also a rather canned feeling to the romance in the central scenes of the film, when a *National Geographic* photographer (Bryan Brown) turns up in the jungle, and the two people fall in love. He arrives, they become lovers, and then he tells her that he has an assignment on the other side of the world and he wants her to come along. He cannot, he says, stay in the jungle forever; he has a job to do. She tells him she will not leave, and that if he does, he need not ever return or ever write. Was this argument not inevitable from the moment they first met? Did the photographer expect this woman to leave? Did she expect him to stay? They

never really talk with one another, and so we're not sure.

The movie's best scenes involve her gradual acceptance by the gorillas. Here it is hard to say who should get the most credit—those who photographed real animals in the jungle, or those who used special effects to create animals, and parts of animals, for particular shots. I imagine that some of the close-ups of a gorilla's hand clasping Weaver's were done with Rick Baker's special-effects creations. I imagine some of the gorillas in the jungle are real, and some are men inside gorilla suits. But the work is done so seamlessly that I could never be sure. Everything looked equally real to me, and the delicacy with which director Michael Apted developed the relationships between woman and beasts was deeply absorbing. There were moments when I felt a touch of awe. Those moments, which are genuine, make the movie worth seeing.

But what we are really dealing with here are two stories that do not fit together very easily. Do we care more about the public Dian Fossey or the private? Is her work more important or her madness? In these modern times we demand the whole life, we say we are realists and don't want the autobiography cleaned up for a "screen version," but the result is a movie that is much more depressing and shapeless than it should be. The parabolas are wrong; Fossey's work fills us with joy, but her fate fills us with confusion and dismay. Perhaps an old-fashioned Hollywood cop-out would actually have been more satisfactory here, with Fossey against the bad guys and everyone assigned his role, and some kind of a happy ending. I left *Gorillas in the Mist* feeling cheated somehow, as if the story had no more insight into Dian Fossey than she apparently had into herself.

Gorky Park ★ ★ ★ ½
R, 128 m., 1983

William Hurt (Arkady Renko), Lee Marvin (Jack Osborne), Joanna Pacula (Irina), Brian Dennehy (Kirwell), Ian Bannen (Iamskoy). Directed by Michael Apted and produced by Gene Kirkwood and Howard W. Koch, Jr. Screenplay by Dennis Potter.

Mystery fans talk about the "police procedural," a crime novel that follows police work, step by meticulous step, from the opening of a case to its eventual resolution. The crimes aren't always solved, but then the solution isn't really the point. Instead,

"procedurals" are a way to study human nature under stress, to see how a society works from the inside out and the bottom up. There are procedurals set all over the world, from Ed McBain's 87th Precinct on the East coast to the Martin Beck thrillers in Stockholm, but Martin Cruz Smith's *Gorky Park* was the first good police procedural set in Russia. It used the procedural approach to show us an honest cop under pressure, a system that functioned only through corruption, and a conflict between socialism and Russia's homegrown capitalism.

This is the movie of that book, and it has all of the same strengths. It begins with a shocking murder (three corpses found frozen in the snow with their faces and fingerprints removed). There are no clues. A police inspector named Renko (William Hurt) is assigned to the case, and makes it his personal crusade. He recruits a physical anthropologist to try to re-create the missing faces on the bodies. He prowls the black market, where deals are made in Western currency. He meets a beautiful young woman and a mysterious American businessman. And he learns about the obsessive power of sable fur coats.

The investigation of the crime has a fascination of its own, but what makes *Gorky Park* really interesting is its views of Soviet cops, criminals, bureaucrats, and ordinary citizens. As Renko gets closer and closer to a solution to the case, his investigation leads him to powerful circles in the Soviet Union. And his heart, of course, leads him closer to the girl, who may have all of the necessary information but has been so warped by paranoia that she refuses to betray those she thinks are her friends.

The movie is directed with efficiency by Michael (*Coal Miner's Daughter*) Apted, who knows that pacing is indispensable to a procedural. Too long a pause for anything—romance, detail, speculation, explanation—and the spell is broken. He uses actors who are able to bring fully realized characters to the screen, so we don't have to stand around waiting for introductions. That involves a certain amount of typecasting. Lee Marvin, gravel-voiced, white-haired, expensively dressed, is perfect for the businessman. Joanna Pacula, a young Polish actress in her first Western role, is beautiful, vulnerable, wide-eyed, and fresh—and as an exile stranded in Paris when her Warsaw theater was closed by Poland's martial law, she doesn't have to fake her paranoia about the Soviet state.

William Hurt, as Renko, is probably the

key to the picture. He makes this cop into a particular kind of person, cold, at times willfully blinded by duty, sublimating his feelings in his profession, until this case breaks him wide open. By the end of *Gorky Park*, we realize that it's not the solution that matters, but what the case itself forces the people to discover about themselves.

Grand Canyon ★ ★ ★ ★
R, 134 m., 1992

Danny Glover (Simon), Kevin Kline (Mack), Steve Martin (Davis), Mary McDonnell (Claire), Mary-Louise Parker (Dee), Alfre Woodard (Jane). Directed by Lawrence Kasdan and produced by Kasdan, Charles Okun, and Michael Grillo. Screenplay by Kasdan and Meg Kasdan.

Lawrence Kasdan's *Grand Canyon* begins in much the same way as *The Bonfire of the Vanities*, as a white man driving a luxury car strays off his usual route and finds himself threatened by black youths in a deserted urban landscape. But at that point the two stories take different paths, because this is a film about possibilities, not fears. At first, to be sure, the white man (Kevin Kline) believes he is going to be killed by the ominous black muggers, one of whom displays a gun. But then a tow truck arrives, driven by another black man (Danny Glover), who talks to the leader of the would-be thieves and defuses the situation.

The dialogue in this scene, and throughout the movie, does not simply exist to push along the plot. It is the way we really think and talk in various situations. "Do you respect me, or do you respect my gun?" the gang leader asks Glover, who looks him in the eye and says, "You don't have that gun, there's no way we're having this conversation." And that honesty somehow satisfies the man with the gun.

Honesty is all through *Grand Canyon*, which is about several characters who would never, in the ordinary course of events, meet one another. Kline plays a wealthy immigration attorney attached to the entertainment industry; Glover is a divorced, hardworking tow truck driver. A few days after the street incident, Kline seeks out Glover for a cup of coffee because, he says, he wants to thank the man who saved his life. He doesn't want it to be just a chance meeting in the night.

This impulse—to break down the barriers society erects between people—is what *Grand Canyon* is about. It takes place in a Los Angeles that is painted as ominous and threatening, an alienating landscape where rich people pile up bulwarks of money and distance to protect them from the dangers of poverty and despair. But the Kline character believes that he has been granted a new life, and he wants to lead it a little differently this time. Like the characters in two other Kasdan movies, *The Big Chill* and *The Accidental Tourist*, he finds that the nearness of death can be an inspiration to live more thoughtfully.

His wife (Mary McDonnell) feels the same way. Their son is about to leave for college, and as the empty nest looms, a miracle falls into her life: She hears crying in the bushes along her daily jogging route, and finds an abandoned baby. She brings it home and wants to keep it. Kline is opposed at first to the notion of raising another child, but eventually comes around to the logic of the situation: Just as Glover appeared from nowhere to save Kline, so Kline's wife appeared to save the baby.

Grand Canyon is not all about coincidences. Much of it is about daily life in a big American city. Glover tells Kline he's worried about his sister's son, who seems to be getting involved with gangs. Kline says he knows a man who owns an apartment building in a better neighborhood. But that neighborhood turns out to have its own sorts of dangers, including policemen who believe that the sight of a jogging young black man is automatically suspicious.

It is uncanny, the way the movie tunes in to the kinds of fears that are all around us in the cities—even those we're not always aware of. In a film that vibrates with an impending sense of danger, the single most terrifying scene is a driving lesson. Kline takes his son out for a drive, during which they are going to practice left turns, and as this scene develops, there is something about Owen Roizman's camera work and James Newton Howard's music that creates a frightening undercurrent. It's only a *driving lesson*, for chrissakes, but by the end of it Kline is explaining to his son that you only have a split second to act, or you'll get creamed. How many of those split-second choices do we make every day without even thinking about them?

Various kinds of romance act as counterpoint to the dangers in this film. Kline arranges a blind date between Glover and Alfre Woodard, a single woman who works in his office, and later that evening, the two of them, realizing he hardly really knows either one, surmise they may be the only two black people he knows. McDonnell falls in love with the baby she has found. A regard develops between Kline and Glover. And so on.

There is another character in *Grand Canyon*, a producer of violent action pictures, played by Steve Martin. Early in the movie, he's complaining because an editor has left out the "money shot" (a bus driver getting his brains sprayed on a windshield). Then a mugger shoots Martin in the leg, and he feels real pain, and has a great awakening and vows not to make any more violent movies. We doubt that he will keep his promise. But the symbolism is there: In a time when our cities are wounded, movies like *Grand Canyon* can help to heal.

The Great Gatsby ★ ★ ½
PG, 146 m., 1974

Robert Redford (Gatsby), Mia Farrow (Daisy Buchanan), Bruce Dern (Tom Buchanan), Karen Black (Myrtle Wilson), Scott Wilson (George Wilson), Sam Waterston (Nick Carraway), Lois Chiles (Jordan Baker), Howard Da Silva (Meyer Wolfsheim), Robert Blossom (Mr. Gatz), Edward Herrmann (Klipspringer). Directed by Jack Clayton and produced by David Merrick. Screenplay by Francis Ford Coppola.

The Great Gatsby is a superficially beautiful hunk of a movie with nothing much in common with the spirit of F. Scott Fitzgerald's novel. I wonder what Fitzgerald, whose prose was so graceful, so elegantly controlled, would have made of it: of the willingness to spend so much time and energy on exterior effect while never penetrating to the souls of the characters. It would take about the same time to read Fitzgerald's novel as to view this movie—and that's what I'd recommend.

The movie is "faithful" to the novel with a vengeance—to what happens in the novel, that is, and not to the feel, mood, and spirit of it. Yet I've never thought the events in *The Great Gatsby* were that important to the novel's success; Fitzgerald, who came out of St. Paul to personify the romance of an age, was writing in a way about himself when he created Gatsby. The mundane Midwestern origins had been replaced by a new persona, by a flash and charisma that sometimes only concealed the despair underneath. For Fitzgerald, there was always something unattainable; and for Gatsby, it was Daisy Buchanan, the lost love of his youth, forever symbolized by that winking green beacon at the end of her dock.

The beacon and the other Fitzgerald symbols are in this movie version, but they communicate about as much as the great stone heads on Easter Island. They're memorials to a novel in which they had meaning. The art director and set decorator seem to have ripped whole pages out of Fitzgerald and gone to work to improve on his descriptions. Daisy and her husband, the ruthless millionaire Tom Buchanan, live almost drowning in whites, yellows, and ennui. Tom's mistress Myrtle and her husband, the shabby filling station owner George, live in a wasteland of ashes in Fitzgerald's novel; in the movie, they seem to have landed on the moon.

All of this unfeeling physical excess might have been overcome by performances. But the director, Jack Clayton, having assembled a promising cast, fails to exploit them very well. When the casting of Robert Redford as Jay Gatsby was announced, I objected because he didn't fit my notion of Gatsby: He was too substantial, too assured, even too handsome. I saw him as Tom Buchanan, and somebody else as Gatsby (Jack Nicholson, maybe, or Bruce Dern—who plays Tom). Having seen the movie, I think maybe I was wrong: Redford could have played Gatsby. I'm not even sure it's his fault he doesn't. The first time Clayton shows us Gatsby, it's a low-angle shot of a massive figure seen against the night sky and framed by marble: This isn't the romantic Gatsby on his doomed quest, it's Charles Foster Kane. A scene where Gatsby reaches out as if to snatch the green beacon in his hand is true to the book, but the movie's literal showing of it looks silly.

These hints of things to come lead up to two essential scenes in which Clayton fails to give us a Gatsby we care about. The first is the initial meeting between Gatsby and Nick (Gatsby wants Nick, his neighbor and Daisy's cousin, to invite her to tea so they can meet again). Redford is so inarticulate and formal in this scene with Nick that we laugh; it's the first time we hear him talk, and he's so mannered that the acting upstages the content of the scene. Doesn't that have to be Clayton's fault? We know Redford has range enough to have played the scene in several better ways. And then the actual reunion between Gatsby and Daisy—the moment on which the rest of the movie is going to depend—gives us Gatsby's toothpaste grin and Daisy's stunned reaction and holds both for so long that any

tension reduces itself to the ridiculous. It doesn't even feel as if Gatsby's happy to see Daisy—more that he assumes she's overjoyed to see him.

The message of the novel, if I read it correctly, is that Gatsby, despite his dealings with gamblers and bootleggers, is a romantic, naive, and heroic product of the Midwest—and that his idealism is doomed in any confrontation with the reckless wealth of the Buchanans. This doesn't come through in the movie. When Nick, at his last meeting with Gatsby, tells him how much he admires him ("You're worth the whole crowd of them"), we frankly don't know why unless we've read the book. Oh, we're *told*, to be sure: The sound track contains narration by Nick that is based pretty closely on his narration in the novel. But we don't feel. We've been distanced by the movie's overproduction. Even the actors seem somewhat cowed by the occasion; an exception is Bruce Dern, who just goes ahead and gives us a convincing Tom Buchanan. We don't have to be told the ways in which Tom is indifferent to human feeling, because we can sense them.

But we can't penetrate the mystery of Gatsby. Nor, to be honest, can we quite understand what's so special about Daisy Buchanan. Not as she's played by Mia Farrow, all squeaks and narcissism and empty sophistication. In the novel, Gatsby never understands that he is too good for Daisy. In the movie, we never understand why he thought she was good enough for him. And that's what's missing.

That, and one other small item: How could a screenplay that plundered Fitzgerald's novel so literally, that quoted so much of the narration and dialogue, have ended with a rinky-dink version of "Ain't We Got Fun" instead of the most famous last sentence of any novel of the century? Maybe because the movie doesn't ever come close to understanding it: "And so we beat on, boats against the current, borne back ceaselessly into the past."

The Great Mouse Detective ★ ★ ★
G, 102 m., 1986

Featuring the voices of Vincent Price, Barrie Ingham, Val Bettin, Susanne Pollatschek, Candy Candido, Diana Chesney, Evan Brenner, Alan Young, and Melissa Manchester. Directed by John Musker, Ron Clements, Dave Michener, and Bunny Mattison.

Philosophers have the notion of parallel universes—whole worlds that are right next to our own, but in a different dimension, so that we can't see them, even while our actions are mirrored with infinite variations. Movie animators have a similar notion, which is that human lives are mirrored on a smaller scale by the parallel lives of the little cartoon characters who live down there closer to the floor.

Near the beginning of *The Great Mouse Detective*, the camera moves through London, passing many of the familiar landmarks, before finally tilting down and moving in toward a little doorway down near to the ground. Inside there's a busy little mouse, a craftsman, hard at work. Like so many domesticated cartoon animals, he is the very soul of bourgeois respectability (I always liked it in the "Tom & Jerry" cartoons when they showed the floor lamps and chintz-covered sofas inside the mouse holes).

Before long, however, a mysterious figure appears who disrupts this image of comfortable domesticity. And then *The Great Mouse Detective* launches its story, which depends on the conceit that London in those days housed not only a great human detective (Sherlock Holmes), but also a mouse who was every bit as good a detective.

The Sherlock Holmes legend is such a durable story that all sorts of filmmakers have adapted it to their own ends, styles, and genres. Just in recent years, we've seen Billy Wilder's *The Private Life of Sherlock Holmes*, Gene Wilder's *Sherlock Holmes' Younger Brother*, Nicholas Meyer's *The Seven Percent Solution*, and Steven Spielberg's *Young Sherlock Holmes*—which told the story of the schooldays of Sherlock and young Watson, surrounded by props and special effects borrowed from other Spielberg extravaganzas.

Here is the Disney version, told on a mouse scale in cartoon form, with a freedom and creativity of animation that reminded me of the earlier Disney feature-length cartoons. In recent decades, Disney and the other animators had started to cut corners; the old-style full animation of such classics as *Pinocchio* was simply too expensive to duplicate any more, with its endless man-hours of drawing. So we began to get backgrounds that didn't move, and actions that seemed recycled out of other actions. Now, however, computer animation has taken most of the drudgery and much of the expense out of animation, and the result is a movie like this, that looks more fully animated than anything in some thirty years.

The movie's story is the usual silliness about evil villains and abducted geniuses. Although the detective in the movie is not called Sherlock Holmes (or Sherlock Mouse, for that matter), he is obviously cut from the same cloth, right down to his ever-present pipe. And there is a Doctor Watson character, who befriends a bewildered waif in the street, and takes it to the great detective, who scents one of his greatest cases.

What's fun is the carefree way the animators swing through their story, using the freedom of the cartoon form to blend nineteenth-century realism with images that seem borrowed from more recent special-effects pictures. For a long time, I was down on the full-length animated efforts of Disney and others, because they didn't seem to reflect the same sense of magic and wonderment that the original animated classics always had. Who, for example, could ever equate *101 Dalmations* with *Snow White*? But now, maybe thanks to computers, animated movies are beginning to sparkle again.

The Great Santini ★ ★ ★
PG, 118 m., 1980

Robert Duvall (Bull Meechum), Blythe Danner (Lillian Meechum), Michael O'Keefe (Ben Meechum), Lisa Jane Persky (Mary Anne Meechum), Stan Shaw (Toomer Smalls), Theresa Merritt (Arrabelle Smalls). Directed by Lewis John Carlino and produced by Charles A. Pratt. Screenplay by Carlino.

Like almost all of my favorite films, *The Great Santini* is about people more than it's about a story. It's a study of several characters, most unforgettably the Great Santini himself—played by Robert Duvall. Despite his name, he is not a magician or an acrobat but a lieutenant colonel in the Marines with the real name of Bull Meechum. He sees himself as the Great Santini, an ace pilot, great Marine, heroic husband and father and, in general, a sterling man among men. His family is expected to go along with this— and to go along with him, as he's transferred to a duty camp in South Carolina in the early 1960s.

There are five other members of the Meechum family. His wife (Blythe Danner) is a sweet Southern girl who calls her kids "sugar" and understands her maverick husband with a love that is deep but unforgiving. His oldest son (Michael O'Keefe) is just turning eighteen and learning to stand up to a father who issues "direct orders," calls

everyone "sports fan," and expects to be called "sir." There are two daughters and one more son, but the movie's main relationship is between the father and the oldest boy.

Santini, you understand, is one hell of a guy. All he understands is competition. He's a royal pain in the ass to his Marine superiors, because he's always pulling damn fool stunts and making a spectacle out of himself. But he's a great pilot and he's said to be a good leader (even though his first briefing session for the men under him in South Carolina leaves them totally bewildered). Santini wants to win at everything, even backyard basketball with his son.

But the son is learning to be his own man. And there's a subplot involving a friendship between O'Keefe and the intense actor Stan Shaw, who plays the son of the family's black maid. Marine kids grow up nowhere and everywhere, we learn, and in South Carolina these two kids go shrimping together, trade lore together, become friends. It's a nice relationship, although a little tangential to the main thrust of the movie.

It's Robert Duvall who really makes the movie live—Duvall and Blythe Danner in a stunning performance that nothing she's done before (in *1776, Hearts of the West*, etc.) prepares us for. Although *The Great Santini* is set about ten years before *Apocalypse Now*, Duvall is playing essentially the same character in both films—we remember his great scene in *Apocalypse*, shouting that napalm smells to him like victory, as he gives his gung-ho speeches in this movie.

Duvall and O'Keefe go hard at each other, in the father-son confrontation, and there's an especially painful scene where the father bounces a basketball off his son's head, egging him on. But this movie is essentially a comedy—a serious, tender one, like *Breaking Away*, which is also about a son getting to know his father.

There are wonderful little moments in the dialogue (as when the Great Santini's daughter wonders aloud if females are allowed full Meechum family status, or are only sort of one-celled Meechums). There are moments straight out of left field, as when Duvall and the family's new maid (the formidable Theresa Merritt) get into an impromptu shoulder-punching contest. There are moments so unpredictable and yet so natural they feel just like the spontaneity of life itself. And the movie's conclusion is the same way: sentimental without being corny, a tearjerker with dignity.

The Great Santini is a movie to seek out and to treasure.

Green Card ★ ★ ★
PG-13, 108 m., 1991

Gerard Depardieu (George), Andie MacDowell (Bronte), Bebe Neuwirth (Lauren), Gregg Edelman (Phil), Robert Prosky (Bronte's lawyer), Jessie Keosian (Mrs. Bird). Directed and produced by Peter Weir. Screenplay by Weir.

Hollywood has, since time immemorial, defined the Meet Cute as a comic situation contrived entirely for the purpose of bringing a man and a woman together, after which they can work out their destinies for the remainder of the film. The classic Meet Cute involves the hero and heroine crashing into each other outside a department store, while all of their Christmas shopping falls to the ground. He helps her pick up her packages, they start to talk, and the rest is history—or formula comedy, anyway.

The package gambit is such a familiar Hollywood standby that *Green Card* has fun employing it as an alibi. The main characters— a Frenchman and an American woman who have to pretend their marriage is the real thing—solemnly explain to an immigration official that they met when they ran into each other, their packages fell to the ground, etc.

Actually the whole movie is a slightly more sophisticated application of the same formula. The Frenchman, played by Gerard Depardieu, needs a green card if he is to be able to stay in America. The woman, played by Andie MacDowell, needs a husband if she is to rent a desirable Manhattan apartment. They are introduced by a friend, they go through the fiction of a marriage ceremony, and then when immigration comes sniffing around, they have to put on a convincing show of really being married.

A movie like *Green Card* can supply two kinds of pleasures: those caused when it observes its formula, and those created when it violates it. The movie was written and directed by Peter Weir *(Dead Poets Society, Witness)*, who constructs it lovingly according to sturdy old principles: The couple is at first indifferent to one another, then hostile, then in love, then in denial, and then, of course, they break up—right before they get together. All of these stops are observed, but, at the same time, Weir has added some nice touches, including the unconventional characters themselves.

Depardieu, the leading actor in France, here making his American debut, is a large, shaggy, untidy man who brings to every role a kind of effortless charm. He occupies a considerable psychic space on the screen. It is not hard to figure out his practical reasons for wanting to marry MacDowell. But her character has its work cut out: Would an attractive young woman, smart and with a great job, actually marry a stranger just to get an apartment? In Manhattan, this movie argues, the answer is yes—especially if the apartment incorporates a large solarium. We accept the marriage of convenience for the purposes of the plot, but the screenplay still has some explaining to do.

Weir is good with his actors and good, too, at putting a slight spin on some of the obligatory scenes. When Depardieu meets MacDowell's parents, for example, the scene doesn't develop along standard lines of outrage and bluster. Instead, Conrad McLaren, as her father, grasps the situation instantly, and proves to be a good judge of character. I also liked the scene where Depardieu goes to a party and meets MacDowell's friends. Of course, they are snotty, and, of course, it is mentioned that Depardieu is a composer, and, of course, there is a piano there, and Depardieu is asked to play one of his compositions. But what happens then is perhaps the best scene in the movie.

Green Card is not blindingly brilliant, and is not an example of the very best work of the director who made *The Year of Living Dangerously* or the actor who starred in *Cyrano de Bergerac*. But it is a sound, entertaining work of craftsmanship, a love story between two people whose meet is not as cute as it might have been.

The Green Room ★ ★ ★
PG, 90 m., 1978

Francois Truffaut (Julien), Nathalie Baye (Cecelia). Directed by Francois Truffaut. Screenplay by Truffaut and Jean Gruault.

The films of Francois Truffaut seem divided into two categories, which I admire for completely different reasons. On one side are the films affirming life, films like *Small Change*, *Day for Night*, and *Stolen Kisses*. On the other side are the films involving his obsession with death, films like *The Bride Wore Black*, *Two English Girls*, and *The Story of Adele H.* Truffaut's *The Green Room* most defi-

nitely belongs in the second category, and is in fact the closest he has come to suggesting that his own interest in death may be a morbid preoccupation. The film is based on one of the most death-obsessed stories in the English language, *The Altar of the Dead*, in which Henry James told the story of a man who worshiped the memory of his dead wife to the point of madness.

In the James story, and in the Truffaut film, the character arrives at a crisis when he falls in love with a woman who is undeniably still alive. How can the new love be reconciled with the adoration of the departed wife? The solution is appropriately macabre. The living woman is invited to join the man in worship at the altar of the dead—to become a fellow mourner.

That is the basic situation in James's version. What fascinates Truffaut about the story is where it leads from there, for the woman is obsessed with the dead, too, and has her own departed ones to worship. The man builds an altar, a shrine, photographs, and candles on every wall and in every corner, and he offers to admit the woman's dead to the shrine. But then he discovers that one of her dead is one of his old enemies—a man whose memory would desecrate his own dead. Thus his grief is betrayed as monstrously selfish.

Truffaut tells this story with necrophilic relish, and plays the leading role himself. Nathalie Baye, a young French actress who is usually unforced and natural, plays the woman, an equally obsessed person—but one who eventually wants to break away from the lure of the dead and admit love into her life again. To the man, of course, that is too much of a challenge. A perfect love can exist only with the dead, because it is always on the terms set down by the living.

The Green Room is, as you have intuited by now, a very somber and depressed film. But it is not depressing, because its characters are such grotesques, such caricatures, that we marvel at them instead of sympathizing. They carry their death obsessions so far that they almost exorcise them. Unlike the heroine of *Adele H.*, whose urge toward self-destruction was conceited, narcissistic, and a device to dramatize her own plight, the characters in *The Green Room* are so simple they are comic in a Dickensian sense; they exaggerate one attribute so absurdly that they lose all other human dimensions.

The Green Room should be seen by: admirers of Henry James, admirers of Truffaut,

and admirers of crumbling old cemeteries where the tombs gape openly at passersby. As an admirer of all three of these subjects, no doubt I admired the film more than others might. I especially enjoyed the scene where the gates are bolted shut and Truffaut is locked among the graves overnight.

Gregory's Girl ★ ★ ★
PG, 93 m., 1982

Gordon John Sinclair (Gregory), Dee Hepburn (Dorothy), Chic Murray (Headmaster), Jake D'Arcy (Phil), Alex Norton (Alec), John Bott (Alistair). Directed by Bill Forsyth and produced by Clive Parsons and Davina Boling. Screenplay by Forsyth.

There was a little item in the paper not long ago that should have been front page news. It was about a survey reporting that physically handsome men were less successful in business, made less money, married younger, and had less "desirable" spouses than men of average or below-average looks. The sociologists who announced these conclusions speculated that the handsome guys tended to get sidetracked in high school, spending more time on social life and less time on studies; they tended to depend on their golden boy charm instead of plowing ahead through college; and they tended, because they were more sexually active at younger ages, to marry sooner and therefore to marry women who were looking for marriage rather than careers. On the average, therefore, the weird kid with acne who's president of Chem Club will do better in the long run than the prom king.

Bill Forsyth's *Gregory's Girl* is a charming, innocent, very funny little movie about the weird kid. It is set in Scotland, where the teen-agers are quieter, more civilized and more naive than, let's say, those in *The Class of 1984*. And it is about Gregory (Gordon John Sinclair), a gangling adolescent who has started to shoot up all of a sudden and finds he is hopelessly uncoordinated on the soccer field. Gregory looks sort of like an immensely likable stork. He loses his place on the soccer team to another student who is a good deal faster and more coordinated. The other student happens to be a girl. Her name is Dorothy (Dee Hepburn), and Gregory instantly falls deeply in love with her. Nothing like this has ever hit him before, and romance becomes for him almost a physical illness. Dorothy is sweet to him, but distant, because she not only suspects Gregory's feelings but is way ahead of him in her analysis of the whole situation.

The movie takes place mostly in a pleasant suburb of Glasgow, where the kids hang about and trade endless speculation on the impossibility of being sixteen and happy at the same time. Gregory turns for romantic advice to his younger sister, who is much more interested in ice cream. His sister, in fact, is oblivious to boys, although one pays her an earnest compliment: "She's only ten, but she has the body of a woman of thirteen." Meanwhile, Gregory consoles his best friend, who is fifteen and a half and has never known love.

This movie is a reminder that we tend to forget a lot of things about adolescence. For example: That it is no use telling a teen-ager what his faults are, because he is painfully aware of every possible fault in the minutest detail; that boys are absolutely helpless in the throes of teen-age romance, whereas girls tend to retain at least some perspective; that it is an unwritten law of the universe that no sixteen-year-old ever falls instantly in love with the right person at the right time.

The movie has a lot of gentle, civilized fun with insights like that. And along the way, Gregory the stork is led on a wild goose chase with a swan at the end. The movie contains so much wisdom about being alive and teen-aged and vulnerable that maybe it would even be painful for a teen-ager to see it; it's not much help, when you're suffering from those feelings of low self-esteem and an absolutely hopeless crush, to realize that not only are you in pain and suffering an emotional turmoil, but you're not even unique. Maybe only grown-ups should see this movie. You know, people who have gotten over the pains of unrequited love (hollow laugh).

Gremlins ★ ★ ★
PG, 111 m., 1984

Hoyt Axton (Rand Peltzer), Zach Galligan (Billy), Phoebe Cates (Kate), Scott Brady (Sheriff Frank), Polly Holliday (Mrs. Deagle). Directed by Joe Dante and produced by Michael Finnell. Executive producer Steven Spielberg. Screenplay by Chris Columbus.

Gremlins is a confrontation between Norman Rockwell's vision of Christmas and Hollywood's vision of the blood-sucking monkeys of voodoo island. It's fun. On the one hand, you have an idyllic American small town, with Burger Kings and Sears stores clustered merrily around the village square,

and on the other hand you have a plague of reprehensible little beasties who behave like a rodent road company of Marlon Brando's motorcycle gang in *The Wild One*.

The whole movie is a sly series of send-ups, inspired by movie scenes so basic they reside permanently in our subconscious. The opening scene, for example, involves a visit to your basic Mysterious Little Shop in Chinatown, where, as we all know, the ordinary rules of the visible universe cease to operate and magic is a reality. Later on, after a kid's father buys him a cute little gremlin in Chinatown, we have a new version of your basic Puppy for Christmas Scene. Then there are such basic movie characters as the Zany Inventor, the Blustering Sheriff, the Clean-Cut Kid, the Cute Girlfriend, and, of course, the Old Bag.

The first half of the movie is the best. That's when we meet the little gremlins, which are unbearably cute and look like a cross between a Pekingese, Yoda from *Empire*, the Ewoks from *Jedi*, and kittens. They have impossibly big eyes, they're cuddly and friendly, and they would make ideal pets except for the fact that they hate bright lights, should not be allowed to get wet, and must never be fed after midnight. Well, of course, it's *always* after midnight; that's the tip-off that this isn't a retread of *E.T.* but comes from an older tradition, the fairy tale or magic story. And in the second half of the movie, after the gremlins have gotten wet, been fed after midnight, etc., they turn into truly hateful creatures that look like the monster in *Alien*.

The movie exploits every trick in the monster-movie book. We have scenes where monsters pop up in the foreground, and others where they stalk us in the background, and others when they drop into the frame and scare the Shinola out of everybody. And the movie itself turns nasty, especially in a scene involving a monster that gets slammed in a microwave oven, and another one where a wide-eyed teen-age girl (Phoebe Cates) explains why she hates Christmas. Her story is in the great tradition of 1950s sick jokes, and as for the microwave scene, I had a queasy feeling that before long we'd be reading newspaper stories about kids who went home and tried the same thing with the family cat.

Gremlins was hailed as another *E.T.* It's not. It's in a different tradition. At the level of Serious Film Criticism, it's a meditation on the myths in our movies: Christmas, families, monsters, retail stores, movies, boogey-

men. At the level of Pop Moviegoing, it's a sophisticated, witty B movie, in which the monsters are devouring not only the defenseless town, but decades of defenseless clichés. But don't go if you still believe in Santa Claus.

The Grey Fox ★ ★ ★ ½
PG, 92 m., 1983

Richard Farnsworth (Bill Miner), Jackie Burroughs (Kate Flynn), Wayne Robson (Shorty), Ken Pogue (Jack Budd). Directed by Phillip Borsos and produced by Peter O'Brian. Screenplay by John Hunter.

Here's a lovely adventure: a movie about a stubborn, indomitable character who robs people because that's what he knows best. A man should work at his craft, shouldn't he? *The Grey Fox* tells the story of Bill Miner, a man who was thrown into prison in the heyday of the Old West, was kept behind bars for thirty-three years, and who finally emerged, confused but interested, into the twentieth century, where the movie begins in 1901. Bill Miner robbed stagecoaches. What's he supposed to do with a train? He's a whiskery old man, stubborn as a mule, and his pride hasn't grown any smaller during those years in jail. He heads for his sister's place to look for work and a roof over his head, but he doesn't get along with his brother-in-law and he also doesn't much like picking oysters for a living. He leaves. He hits the road, drifting aimlessly, a man without a mission—until the night in 1903 when he sees Edwin S. Porter's *The Great Train Robbery*. That famous movie is only eleven minutes long, but long enough to make everything absolutely clear to Miner, who realizes he has a new calling in life, as a train robber.

All of this could, of course, be an innocuous Disney movie, but it's well-written and directed, and what gives it zest and joy is the performance by Richard Farnsworth, who plays Miner. Maybe you'll recognize Farnsworth when you see him on the screen. Maybe not. His life has been one of those careers that makes you realize Hollywood is a company town, where you can make a living for years and never be a star. Farnsworth has been in more than three hundred movies. He was a stuntman for thirty years. He's had speaking roles in movies ranging from *The Cowboys* to *Resurrection*. He was even in "Roots" on TV. And yet there is absolutely no mention of his name in Leslie Halliwell's *Filmgoer's Companion*. Farnsworth is one of those unstudied, graceful, absolutely natural actors who has spent a lifetime behaving exactly as he feels. I think he is incapable of a false or a dishonest moment. He makes Miner so proud, so vulnerable, such a noble rascal, that the whole movie becomes just a little more complex because he's in it.

There's one scene where you can really see Farnsworth's gift for conviction. It's a love scene with a feminist lady photographer named Kate Flynn (Jackie Burroughs), who is touring the West to document its changing times. Bill and Kate are instantly attracted to one another. And their love scene together is a warm, amusing masterpiece of quiet affection. Miner doesn't deny his age; he triumphs with it. He's not handsome but he's damned attractive, and knows it. Kate Flynn can see that this man has six times the worth of an ordinary man, and adores him. The scene is a treasure, even when you don't know whether to laugh or cry.

The director, Phillip Borsos, is able to make this a human story and still keep it exciting as an action picture. And he gives it a certain documentary feel; *The Grey Fox* is apparently based, to some degree, on truth. That doesn't matter half as much as that Farnsworth bases his performance on how he sees the truth of Bill Miner.

Greystoke ★ ★ ★
PG, 129 m., 1984

Christopher Lambert (Tarzan), Ralph Richardson (Earl of Greystoke), Ian Holm (Captain D'Arnot), Andie MacDowell (Jane Porter). Directed by Hugh Hudson and produced by Hudson and Stanley S. Canter. Screenplay by P.H. Vazak and Michael Austin.

One of the most unforgettable mothers in the history of literature is named Kala, and she is an ape. Some people will immediately know that Kala is the great ape who adopted a shipwrecked orphan and raised him as her own, until he became Tarzan, Lord of the Apes. Other people will not know that, and for them, the movie *Greystoke* may be missing a certain resonance. I think it helps, in seeing this movie, to draw on a background of rainy Saturday afternoons when you were ten and had your nose buried in *Tarzan* books.

Greystoke, the Legend of Tarzan, Lord of the Apes is the most faithful film adaptation of the Tarzan legend ever made. That isn't saying much, because most of the forty or so Tarzan movies were laughable quickies with Tarzan trying not to be upstaged by cute

chimps. *Greystoke* takes the legend seriously, and it's worthy of being taken seriously, I think, because the story of Tarzan has become one of the most durable of all the myths of the twentieth century. The obvious challenge for this movie is to convince an audience that it is actually looking at a little human baby being nurtured by wild animals. *Greystoke* passes that test. The movie combines footage of real animals with footage of human actors disguised by the special-effects makeup of Rick Baker, and I was hard-pressed to tell the difference. The movie has an extended opening sequence that takes place entirely in the jungle, without spoken dialogue, and that captures the central mystery of the Tarzan legend as well as anything I've ever seen.

Unfortunately, there's one other aspect of Tarzan that *Greystoke* doesn't capture as well. The Tarzan adventures were all inspired by the imagination of a pulp writer named Edgar Rice Burroughs, who was not a stylist or a philosopher but was certainly a great plotter and knew how to entangle Tarzan in cliff-hanging melodrama. *Greystoke* isn't melodrama and doesn't try to be, and I missed that. After the great early jungle scenes, it has the grown-up Tarzan (Christopher Lambert) being discovered by a Belgian explorer (Ian Holm) who returns him to his ancestral Scottish home, Greystoke Manor, where he meets his grandfather (Ralph Richardson) and also a young lady named Jane (Andie MacDowell). The movie has fun showing Tarzan's introduction to civilization; there's a spine-tingling moment when he growls into Jane's ear. The characters also are well-drawn, especially Ralph Richardson's Earl of Greystoke, who childishly slides down a staircase on a silver tray, and who has a touching death scene that was acted not long before Richardson himself died.

But where's the action? Shouldn't there be some sort of pulp subplot about the ant men, or the jewels of Opar, or a wild elephant on a rampage? *Greystoke* is the story of the legend of Tarzan, but it doesn't contain an adventure *involving* Tarzan. Who would have guessed there'd ever be a respectable Tarzan movie?

The Grifters ★ ★ ★ ★
R, 119 m., 1991

Anjelica Huston (Lily Dillon), John Cusack (Roy Dillon), Annette Bening (Myra Langtry), Pat Hingle (Bobo Justus), Henry Jones (Simms),

J.T. Walsh (Cole), Charles Napier (Hebbing). Directed by Stephen Frears and produced by Martin Scorsese, Robert Harris, and James Painten. Screenplay by Donald E. Westlake.

Con men are more appealing than run-of-the-mill villains, who want to take your money because they are stronger or more dangerous than you are. Con men want to take it because they're smarter than you are. And there is hardly ever a con man who isn't likable, because, after all, if he can't win your confidence, how can he take your money? Movies about con men are seductive because the audience is on both sides of the moral issues: We want to see justice done, of course, but at the same time we're intrigued by the audacity of this character who is trying to out-think his opposition.

You can see some of that seductiveness at work in David Mamet's *House of Games* (1987), where a woman psychologist grows fascinated by a con man and asks him to teach her some of the tricks of his trade. Does he ever. The con man is sweet and almost gentle as he devastates his victim. In a sense, he really does like her. In Stephen Frears's *The Grifters*, there aren't any outsiders to be seduced, because the three central characters are all confidence tricksters. So they seduce each other.

The movie is based on a 1950s novel, but it's set in the present day. There are a few details that don't translate very well—today's con man probably wouldn't stay in a colorful fleabag hotel, but in a downtown executive suite—but the underlying story is universal. It involves the archetypal triangle of the lover, the loved one, and the authority figure who would separate them. The lover is Roy Dillon (John Cusack), a con man in his twenties, who isn't very good and pulls mostly small-time cons. The loved one is Myra Langtry (Annette Bening), who looks young and sexy, but is probably older than she looks and certainly more dangerous than Roy realizes. And the authority figure is Roy's mother, Lily (Anjelica Huston), who has been pulling cons since a very early age and considers everyone a potential victim. That list would certainly include her son.

Myra has knocked around the country a good deal, working as a sexy decoy for big-time con operators. Lily has an arrangement with a major sports gambling operation and travels from one racetrack to another, placing large bets at the last minute to improve the odds. Roy isn't in their league. He's still pulling nickel-and-dime stuff like walking into a bar and getting change for a twenty dollar bill and then switching to a smaller bill. One day, a bartender catches him at it and beats him up so badly that he almost dies.

It's in his hospital room that the two women meet and unsheathe their claws. Roy doesn't realize it, but he's doomed right from the moment of their meeting, because, for each of these women, it is more important to win than to love, and poor, dumb, sentimental Roy doesn't play in that league. He loves too easily, perhaps, and the movie suggests Oedipal possibilities long before the shocking final confrontation.

The Grifters is the first American production by Stephen Frears, one of the best new British directors. His credit list is short but distinguished: *My Beautiful Laundrette, Prick Up Your Ears, Sammy and Rosie Get Laid,* and *Dangerous Liaisons.* All four films deal with labyrinths of passion, with characters deceiving others about the true nature of their loves. The story of *The Grifters* comes from a pulp novel by the recently rediscovered Jim Thompson, a poet of *film noir,* whose books exist in a world of cynicism and despair, where characters put up a big front but are being gnawed inside by fear, guilt, and low self-esteem. The screenplay is by another distinguished crime novelist, Donald Westlake, and, for once, here is a new movie that exudes the *film noir* spirit from its very pores, instead of just adding a few cosmetic touches to a modern chase-and-crash story.

The performances are all insidiously powerful. Cusack provides a sympathetic center for the film, as a kid with a burning ambition to be good at the con game, but with no particular talent and without the ruthlessness he will need. Anjelica Huston was an Academy Award nominee as his mother, who had this child when she was a teen-ager, and who has never fully accepted the fact that he is her son. And Annette Bening has some of that same combination of sexiness, danger, and vulnerability you could see in Gloria Grahame in movies like *The Big Heat* and *In a Lonely Place.*

One of the strengths of *The Grifters* is how everything adds up, and it all points toward the conclusion of the film, when all secrets will be revealed and all debts collected. This is a movie of plot, not episode. It's not just a series of things that happen to the characters, but a web, a maze of consequences; by the end, when Roy and his mother are facing

each other in their last desperate confrontation, the full horror of their lives is laid bare.

Why do confidence operators do what they do? Why do they need to win our love and trust, and then betray us? In *The Grifters*, it's pretty clear that they're locked into an old pattern of trust and betrayal that goes back to childhood, and that they're trying to get even. Poor Roy. He thinks he wants to be a great con man, and all he really wants is to find just one person he can safely love, one person who isn't trying to con him.

Gross Anatomy ★ ★ ★
PG-13, 107 m., 1989

Matthew Modine (Joe Slovak), Daphne Zuniga (Laurie Rorbach), Christine Lahti (Rachel Woodruff), Todd Field (David Schreiner), John Scott Clough (Miles Reed), Alice Carter (Kim McCauley), Robert Desiderio (Dr. Banks), Zakes Mokae (Dr. Banumbra). Directed by Thom Eberhardt and produced by Howard Rosenman and Debra Hill. Screenplay by Ron Nyswaner and Mark Spragg.

Gross Anatomy contains scenes of laughter and scenes of romance, but the scenes that I identified with the most involved performance anxiety. This is a film that follows a group of students through their first year of medical school, and they seem to be taking an examination every ten minutes. The university atmosphere is reproduced with relentless accuracy, right down to the most subtle intonations in the voices of the professors setting the exams and asking the questions. And all of the dialogue has the ring of truth.

Watching the film, I began to ask myself what I was feeling. I was absorbed by the story, I cared about the characters, and yet I felt a growing unease, which I finally identified: The movie was reawakening fears that I thought I had buried years ago, those fears that the final exam was being held tomorrow and I'd never studied for the course, and I was going to fail miserably and humiliate myself and disappoint my family and flunk out of school and get drafted and die.

Because the movie gets that right, almost everything else in the plot seems to fall naturally into place. This is not a movie about medical school or medicine so much as it's a movie about being under relentless pressure. Early in their first semester, the students figure out they have to master about 3,500 pages of material a week, and attend lectures

and anatomy laboratory, and somehow find time to eat and sleep. We can taste their exhaustion as they get up at five in the morning and march like zombies through one unrelenting day after another. Their lives are a race between total exhaustion and fear of failure.

There is one student, however, who seems unaffected by the pressure. He's Joe Slovak (Matthew Modine), a bright, cocky kid with a chip on his shoulder, who claims he doesn't care much about his future patients or anything else except making a lot of money. The only thing he takes seriously is his love for his lab partner (Daphne Zuniga), and she's almost too busy to have time for him.

Most of the classroom scenes take place in the anatomy laboratory, where the students dissect corpses with the most minute attention to detail, under the guidance of two doctors played by Zakes Mokae and Christine Lahti. He is a serene African who advises the students not to revise their exam papers, "because your first instincts are almost always right," and she is a stern, unforgiving administrator whose idea of an orientation lecture is to remind the students that medicine is the profession with the highest rates of alcoholism, drug addiction, divorce, and suicide.

Slovak, the Modine character, gets under her skin because he refuses to even pretend as if he cares. He's bright, he gets good grades, but he has an attitude about everything. He's sarcastic, and he insists on always getting the last word. He cares about the other members on his lab team (including not only Zuniga but also Todd Field as a worried loser, John Scott Clough as a compulsive perfectionist, and Alice Carter as an Asian woman determined to finish the year despite an unexpected pregnancy). But he doesn't care about sucking up to faculty members or playing campus politics.

Most of the major events in the movie can be anticipated, but they are played with a genuine grace. I especially admired the scene where Zuniga finally tells Modine, "All right, you've got me," and the one in which Lahti finally levels with her best student about her real hopes and fears. There is not much in this movie that hasn't been seen before, especially on TV medical shows, but the level of the direction, by Thom Eberhardt, gives the material more weight and importance, and the actors make their characters into particular people whose decisions begin to seem important to us.

Groundhog Day ★ ★ ★
PG, 103 m., 1993

Bill Murray (Phil), Andie MacDowell (Rita), Chris Elliott (Larry), Stephen Tobolowsky (Ned), Brian Doyle-Murray (Buster), Marita Geraghty (Nancy). Directed by Harold Ramis and produced by Trevor Albert and Ramis. Screenplay by Danny Rubin and Ramis.

There is an old belief that everyone is rewarded with the heaven or hell that he deserves. For Phil, the nasty, self-centered weatherman played by Bill Murray in *Groundhog Day*, that hell reveals itself one morning in the Groundhog Capital of Punxsutawney, Pennsylvania. He has journeyed there to do a remote broadcast about his namesake, the groundhog Punxsutawney Phil, who every year informs the nation whether it will have six more weeks of winter.

Now the alarm goes off in Murray's bed-and-breakfast room, and he awakens to find it is . . . Groundhog Day, all over again. It will be Groundhog Day again tomorrow, too, and on the day after that. In another sense, tomorrow will never come. Groundhog Day will repeat itself over and over and over again, apparently until the end of time, and Phil will be permanently condemned to cover it. He's trapped in some kind of time warp.

As Phil figures out the rules of his dilemma, we do, too. His world is inhabited by the same people every day, but they don't know that Groundhog Day is repeating itself. He is the only one who can remember what happened yesterday. That gives him a certain advantage: He can, for example, find out what a woman is looking for in a man, and then the "next" day he can behave in exactly the right way to impress her.

Luckily there is a woman close at hand to practice on. She's Rita (Andie MacDowell), Phil's long-suffering producer, who has had to put up with his tantrums, demands, surliness, and general lack of couth. As day follows day, Phil is gradually able to see the error of his ways, and improve his behavior until finally, to her surprise, a Groundhog Day dawns when she finally likes him.

The movie is basically a comedy, but there's an underlying dynamic that is a little more thoughtful. Like *Scrooged*, Murray's dreary 1988 film, this is a movie about a grouch in the process of self-redemption: A supernatural force is showing him his weaknesses. Another movie that comes to mind is *It's a Wonderful Life*, although that film showed James Stewart how bad life would have been without his help, and this one shows Murray that people might actually have been cheerier without his contributions.

Groundhog Day was directed and co-written by Harold Ramis, Murray's fellow Ghostbuster and a partner from their Second City days. The film is lovable and sweet. If *Scrooged* seemed to reflect a dour discontent, this one is more optimistic about the human race, and the Murray character is likable by the end. That's a mixed blessing, since Murray is funnier in the early scenes in which he is delivering sardonic weather reports and bitterly cursing the fate that brought him to Punxsutawney in the first place.

Formula comedies are a dime a dozen. Those based on an original idea are more rare, and *Groundhog Day*, apart from everything else, is a demonstration of the way time can sometimes give us a break. Just because we're born as SOBs doesn't mean we have to live that way.

Grumpy Old Men ★ ★
PG-13, 105 m., 1993

Jack Lemmon (John), Walter Matthau (Max), Ann-Margret (Ariel), Burgess Meredith (Grandpa), Daryl Hannah (Melanie), Kevin Pollak (Jacob), Ossie Davis (Chuck). Directed by Donald Petrie and produced by John Davis and Richard C. Berman. Screenplay by Mark Steven Johnson.

Jack Lemmon and Walter Matthau go together like a couple of old shoes, broken in and comfortable, but still able to take a shine. Their rhythms of speech and their body language create a kind of harmony. Each fills in for the other. *The Odd Couple* could have been written for them, and *Grumpy Old Men* probably was.

They play a couple of neighbors in a snowbound Wabasha, Minnesota, neighborhood. They've been feuding for years, mostly because they like each other so much. They trade insults, dismissals, snubs, and dire imprecations. Then they go ice fishing together. That means they go separately, but adjacently, so they can glower at one another.

They live in the kind of neighborhood where everybody spends all of their time either out in front of the house, shoveling snow, or inside the house, peering out through the curtains. Neither John Gustafson (Lemmon) nor Max Goldman (Matthau) seems to have much actually *inside* the house to hold their attention. Their lifeblood is gossip and jealousy.

Things heat up nicely when a woman named Ariel moves into the neighborhood. Played by Ann-Margret, she's single, a professor, and likes to career around the neighborhood on a snowmobile. She comes calling, first to one of the old coots and then to the other. Both, of course, fall instantly into love. She likes John more, but when she thinks she's been rejected, she goes out with Max, which inspires a lot of supercilious sneering.

We perhaps have a slight problem with credibility here. We're asked to believe that Ariel's entire universe of dating possibilities is limited to John and Max. That sure wouldn't be the case in my neighborhood. But what the heck. Meanwhile, the movie offers various subplots, mostly involving ice fishing. A genial old guy named Chuck (Ossie Davis) runs the bait and refreshment stand down by the lake, and for a time it looks as if he might have a chance with Ariel, but the screenplay puts a sudden end to that possibility.

Grumpy Old Men is mostly made up out of spare parts from other movies. The neighborhood seems inspired by those sunny 1940s comedies and 1950s sitcoms in which the neighbors were all part of one big, nosy, inquisitive family. The patter between the two old guys is so smooth it could be part of a vaudeville act. And the milieu is so folksy it could be part of a Christmas card.

That business of peering out the windows extends even to the next generation. Lemmon has a daughter named Melanie (Daryl Hannah), and Matthau has a son named Jacob (Kevin Pollak). Their destinies in life have kept them apart up until now, despite an adolescent crush they've not outgrown, but one night, when Melanie is in her dad's house, and she happens to look out and notice that Jacob is gazing upon her from the house next door . . . well, in another neighborhood that might be cause to draw the shades, but in Grumpyville, it could be the beginning of a beautiful romance.

The movie is too pat and practiced to really be convincing, and the progress of Ariel's relationships with the two grumps seems dictated mostly by the needs of the screenplay. But Matthau and Lemmon are fun to see together, if for no other reason than just for the essence of their beings.

Guarding Tess ★ ★ ★ ½
PG-13, 98 m., 1994

Shirley MacLaine (Tess Carlisle), Nicolas Cage (Doug Chesnic), Austin Pendleton (Earl), Edward Albert (Barry Carlisle), James Rebhorn (Howard Shaeffer), Richard Griffiths (Frederick). Directed by Hugh Wilson and produced by Ned Tanen and Nancy Graham Tanen. Screenplay by Wilson and Peter Torokvei.

Sometimes you can hear an entire relationship reflected in the intonation of a single word. At the beginning of *Guarding Tess*, a man carries a tray upstairs to a closed bedroom door, takes his gun from a holster, places it on a table next to the door, knocks, and says "breakfast." In the way he says it, you know that he has had a long and not pleasant relationship with the person on the other side of the door. You also know that he is determined to perform his job correctly.

The man is a Secret Service agent, Doug Chesnic, head of a detail assigned to protect a former first lady named Tess Carlisle. She is "beloved" by her fellow Americans, as all former first ladies of course are, with the possible exception of Nancy Reagan. But in private she's a real piece of work: demanding, stubborn, sarcastic, able to get under the skin and find the weak points. Chesnic has been assigned to her for a tour of three years, and when his tour is up he requests a change of scenery. She doesn't agree.

Chesnic is played by Nicolas Cage, who is able to imply a mind-set. This is a professional who knows his job, does it well, is proud, and resents having to perform little domestic chores for his client. But he is vulnerable to her; she has an unerring instinct about which buttons to push and how far to go.

Tess is played by Shirley MacLaine. I hope she will think it a compliment that I have never seen her in a role that I sense is closer to herself. I've interviewed her many times, and I know that trick she has of looking intently at you and making an intuitive remark designed to penetrate your defenses, and then asking a pointed question and waiting patiently for an answer that is usually not easy to provide.

Here she creates Tess Carlisle as a woman who once had the world as her stage, and now operates out of an upstairs bedroom in a comfortable farmhouse in Ohio. She is not elderly, or weak, or unintelligent, but she is

lonely: During the film we see no friends, and her only relationships seem to be with her Secret Service guards, her cooks, her secretary, her chauffeur, and other employees. Accustomed to having power on a vast scale, she now micromanages every detail of her shrunken realm. When Doug plucks the rose from her breakfast tray to wear in his lapel, she notices it immediately and demands her rose back.

Worse, she complains about the rose thievery in a telephone call to the current president, who sounds a lot like Bill Clinton and provides many of the movie's best moments in his anguished return calls to Agent Chesnic ("Goddamn it, Doug, I'm supposed to be handling the problems of the free world here, and I'm dealing with a Secret Service man who's stealing flowers from a little old lady.") When Tess learns that Doug has requested reassignment after his three years with her, she takes care of that with a call to the president, too, and Doug is back on the farm in Ohio.

What adds an interesting texture to *Guarding Tess* is the matter-of-fact detail with which the director and cowriter, Hugh Wilson, regard the daily routine inside the Carlisle home. There is an easy camaraderie between Chesnic and the household staff members, including her chauffeur, Earl (Austin Pendleton), her male nurse (Richard Griffiths), and her neurotic, barely functioning secretary (Susan Blommaert). As Special Agent *in Charge*, as he particularly insists he is, Chesnic enforces all rules and regulations, and that leads to showdowns with Tess—when she wants to sit on the wrong side of the backseat of her car, for example, in violation of security procedures.

As the story unfolds we begin to sense a deep current of feeling between Tess and Agent Chesnic. It isn't love, God forbid, but a certain respect for a tough opponent, and even some grudging affection. The movie seems to be headed in a direction not unlike *Driving Miss Daisy*, until it takes an unanticipated turn which I had better not reveal here, except to say that the melodrama, when it comes, is handled well enough that it doesn't break the earlier mood of the movie but only underlines it.

MacLaine and Cage are really very good here. MacLaine is playing a woman probably intended to be ten or fifteen years older than her, and she does it without affecting any of the mannerisms of "age" that often make such performances feel false. She is alert, she

is smart, she knows what's going on, she keeps her secrets, and if she has been reduced to playing mind games with her bodyguard, at least she plays them cleverly. Cage, who can cheerfully go over the top (see *Wild at Heart* and *Honeymoon in Vegas*) is restrained here, yet very likable. We feel for this man who has no life of his own—except to guard a woman who has no life of *her* own.

Guelwaar ★ ★ ★ ★
NO MPAA RATING, 115 m., 1994

Omar Seck (Gora), Mame Ndoumbe Diop (Nogoy Marie Thioune), Thierno Ndiaye (Pierre Henri Thioune [Guelwaar]), Ndiawar Diop (Barthelemy), Moustapha Diop (Aloys), Marie-Augustine Diatta (Sophie), Samba Wane (Gor Mag). Directed by Ousmane Sembene and produced by Sembene and Jacques Perrin. Screenplay by Sembene.

Most moviegoers hardly ever get the opportunity to see a film like *Guelwaar*, and even fewer take advantage of it. Does anyone care that Ousmane Sembene, the foremost African filmmaker, has made a film that tells a simple story and yet touches on some of the most difficult questions of our time? Moviegoers have little curiosity. Most of them have never seen a film about Africans, by Africans, in modern Africa, shot on location. They see no need to start now (and this indifference extends, of course, to African-Americans). Movies can show us worlds and societies we will never otherwise glimpse, but most of the time we prefer to watch slick fictions with lots of laughs and action.

Enough of the sermon. What about the movie. *Guelwaar* is the name of a man who is dead at the beginning of Sembene's film. He was, we gather, quite a guy—a district leader in Senegal who made a fiery speech against foreign aid. He felt it turned those who accepted it into slaves. Soon after, he was found dead, and by the end of the film we more or less know why he died, although this is not a whodunit.

It is, in fact, the story of his funeral. His family gathers: The older son flies home from France; a daughter who works as a prostitute returns from Dakar, the capital; and the youngest son is still in the village. Then there is a problem. Guelwaar's body disappears from the morgue.

Sembene uses this disappearance, and the search for the body, to tell us a story about modern Senegal, which is a former French colony on the west coast of Africa, with a population of about eight million. In the district where the story takes place, the majority of people are Islamic, but there is a sizable Roman Catholic minority, including Guelwaar's family. At first it is suspected that the body has been snatched by members of a fetishistic cult who might use it in their ceremonies, but there is a much more mundane explanation: Through a mixup at the morgue, Guelwaar has been confused with a dead Muslim, and has already been buried in the Islamic cemetery.

Sembene tells this story in a series of conversations which reveal, subtly and casually, how things work in modern Senegal. The Catholics and Muslims live side by side in relative harmony, but when a controversy arises there are always troublemakers who attempt to fan it up into sectarian hatred. As the Catholics march out to the cemetery to try to retrieve the body, they are met by a band of angry Muslims who intend to defend the graves of their ancestors from sacrilege.

One of the few cool heads belongs to a district policeman, himself a Muslim, but fair-minded. He thinks it sensible that the misplaced body should be reburied in its rightful grave. He sets up a meeting between the priest and the Imam of the district, both reasonable men, although sometimes hotheaded. There are moments of hair-trigger tension, when the wrong word could set off a bloody fight which might spread far beyond this small local case. And when the situation is almost resolved, an officious government official arrives ("Park the Mercedes in the shade"), and tries to play to the crowd.

The struggle over the body and its burial provides Sembene's main plot line. But curling around and beneath it are many other matters. One of the most interesting encounters in the film is between the priest and a prostitute (a friend of the sister from Dakar), who tells him she is proud to be helping a brother through medical school, and to not be a beggar. She has arrived in the village wearing a revealing costume. The priest listens silently, and then simply says, "Try to put on something more decent." He does not condemn her for her prostitution, and indeed the passionate message of Sembene's film is that anything is better than begging—or accepting aid.

We learn that for long years the country fed and provided for itself. Now a drought has caused starvation. But even more fatally, Sembene suggests, the country's political bureaucracy has grown fat and distant, fed on corruption, enriched by stealing and reselling the aid shipments from the West. In a shocking scene late in the film, sacks of grain and rice (marked "Gift of the USA") are thrown in the road, and the people walk over them, in an homage to Guelwaar, who spoke against aid.

Guelwaar's words are: "Make a man dependent on your charity and you make him your slave." He argues that aid has destroyed the Senegalese economy and created a ruling class of thieves. And he shows how these facts have been obscured because political demagogues have fanned Muslim-Catholic rivalries, so that the proletariat fights among itself instead of against its exploiters.

The film is astonishingly beautiful. The serene African landscape is a backdrop for the struggle over the cemetery, and the sere colors of the landscape frame the bright colors of the African costumes. We see something of the way the people live, and what their values are, and how their traditional ways interact with the new forms of government. And it is a joy to listen to the dialogue, in which intelligent people seriously discuss important matters; not one Hollywood film in a dozen allows its characters to seem so in control of what they think and say.

Sembene's message is thought-provoking. He does not blame the hunger and poverty of Senegal on buzz-words like colonialism or racism. He says they have come because self-respect has been worn away by thirty years of living off foreign aid. Like many stories that are set in a very specific time and place, this one has universal implications.

Ousmane Sembene is seventy-one years old. This is his seventh feature. Along the way he has also made many short subjects, founded a newspaper, written a novel. I am happy to have seen two of his other films (*Black Girl* and *Xala*), and with *Guelwaar* he reminds me that movies can be an instrument of understanding, and need not always pander to what is cheapest and most superficial.

Guilty as Sin ★ ★ ★
R, 107 m., 1993

Rebecca De Mornay (Jennifer Haines), Don Johnson (David Greenhill), Stephen Lang (Phil Garson), Jack Warden (Moe), Dana Ivey (Judge Tompkins), Ron White (Diangelo). Directed by Sidney Lumet and produced by Martin Ransohoff. Screenplay by Larry Cohen.

Don Johnson finds a role that he's peculiarly right for in *Guilty as Sin*. He plays a smooth, silky ladies' man with an undertone of menace, the kind of man who checks himself in every mirror and likes what he sees. When a woman in a bar asks what he does, he replies, "I don't do anything. Women support me." Then he lets her pay for the drink he's already drinking. He exudes self-confidence, but threaten him and he gets hysterically flustered; he has a scene here that casts him in such an unfavorable light that it must have taken him some determination to go through with it.

In the film, he's a man charged with having pushed his rich wife to death through a window. He appeals to an ace Chicago criminal lawyer (Rebecca De Mornay) for help: He looks guilty as sin, yes, but he insists he's innocent. At first she's repelled by his oily sexuality, but then she grows intrigued; flushed with success from her last big case, she's attracted to the challenge of defending an unattractive womanizer who, if he didn't push his wife through that window, was probably capable of it.

Guilty as Sin then proceeds on two levels. It is a courtroom procedural, with all of the usual presentation of evidence and lawyers' strategies. And it is a battle of the will between De Mornay and Johnson. Several times during the film, the director, Sidney Lumet, holds them in close-up profile, facing each other from opposite sides of the screen, eyes locked, engaged in a fierce mental duel with an undertone of sexual attraction. De Mornay hates and fears this man, but he's a hypnotic snake whose very amorality is fascinating to her.

The plot, by Larry Cohen, is a little different from most of the recent courtroom thrillers. We're usually in on the facts of the case, and there's even a flashback to show us exactly what the Johnson character really did do on the day in question. But the facts aren't really the issue in this story: It's how people understand them, and how they act on them. When De Mornay takes a huge risk and plants some evidence, for example, Johnson knows that's what she has done—but is prevented from saying so because of the delicate legal trap he's in. The movie becomes a deadly chess game; we know, and the characters know, most of the facts, but what nobody knows is how they'll act on them.

Movies like this require great attention, as we separate the threads of reality from the tactics of courtroom defense. One element that bothered me involved a woman who is brought forward as a last-minute witness in

Johnson's defense. She claims she was with him when the wife went out the window, and she's apparently telling the truth. (As the respectable wife of a Chicago Bears lineman, she argues she'd have to be crazy to lie.) Yet from what we know, her story, which creates a courtroom bombshell, can't be true. What's the explanation for her testimony? The movie never provides one.

What it does provide are a couple of intriguing character studies. Most movies in this genre depend on sex as a motivator, and in a more conventional version of this story De Mornay would probably make the mistake of sleeping with her client. *Guilty as Sin* is aiming for more complex motivations. As the true extent of Johnson's twisted scheme becomes revealed, as De Mornay becomes trapped between what she sees as justice and the mistakes she's made, the movie becomes truly engrossing on a psychological level.

There are some supporting characters—Jack Warden as her trusted investigator, Stephen Lang as her busy boyfriend, jealous on cue—but essentially *Guilty as Sin* is about two people of intelligence and strong will, playing a game with very high stakes. The plot is preposterous, the logic is sometimes faulty, but Lumet and his actors don't step wrong in the central thrust of the story. And De Mornay's inescapable resemblance to Hillary Rodham Clinton provides a subtext that, while probably not intended, adds a certain intriguing tone to the whole enterprise.

Guilty by Suspicion ★ ★ ★ ½
PG-13, 105 m., 1991

Robert De Niro (David Merrill), Annette Bening (Ruth), George Wendt (Bunny Baxter), Patricia Wettig (Dorothy Nolan), Sam Wanamaker (Felix Graff), Martin Scorsese (Joe Lesser). Directed by Irwin Winkler and produced by Arnon Milchan. Screenplay by Winkler.

Which should come first, your friend or your country? Honest people find they can take first one side and then the other—depending somewhat on which friend and which country. But for the people who were caught in the Hollywood witch-hunt beginning in the late 1940s, the decision meant, in many cases, betraying your ideals, or losing your job.

The House Un-American Activities Committee, convinced that Hollywood was a hotbed of subversion, held hearings into the alleged communist connections of many directors, writers, and actors. Many of them had been members of the Communist Party or its front groups, especially in the late 1930s, when Stalin's Russia was seen as an ally against fascism. Most of those who testified before HUAC admitted their own political activities (for that matter, membership in any political party was perfectly legal, then as now, protected by the Bill of Rights).

But HUAC wanted more than personal confessions. They wanted their witnesses to "name names," to list people they had seen at party meetings, or had heard were party members. Since this was hearsay evidence and the committee usually knew the names anyway, this process did not really further the campaign against subversion. It was a brutal process by which one group was offered public shame and humiliation at the hands of another.

The HUAC members, drunk with the power they had over the rich and famous, gloried in the publicity they got by quizzing big stars like John Garfield, playwrights like Arthur Miller and Lillian Hellman, and directors like Dalton Trumbo. The Hollywood studios fell right in line, blacklisting those people who would not "cooperate." So the classic debating question had become a nightmare reality: Choose your friends or your country.

Few governmental agencies have been more "un-American" than HUAC, more opposed to what the nation stands for. But red-baiting gave it such publicity and clout that before long, a senator named McCarthy had seen the possibilities, and moved from Hollywood to the really big targets, waving a sheet of paper in the air and claiming it held the names of five hundred highly placed communists in the federal government.

Guilty by Suspicion is a movie that tells the story of that time, a story that even today divides those who named names and those who did not. History has vindicated those who refused to betray their principles, but how would any of us have responded at the time—when to defy the committee meant virtual unemployment in show business?

The movie tells the story of a fictional director named David Merrill, played by Robert De Niro as a man who is not a fanatic or hero, but balks at betraying his friends before a group he has no respect for. As the film opens, Merrill has come back from Europe for a conference with Darryl F. Zanuck (Ben Piazza), head of 20th Century Fox. He has heard things about the hearings, but thinks he won't be involved, because he's no subversive. Sure, he went to a couple of party meetings back in the 1930s, when it was commendable in Hollywood to embrace antifascist groups, but the party threw him out "for arguing too much, I think."

He finds that things are not going to go easily. The studio suggests he see a lawyer named Graff (played by Sam Wanamaker, himself a blacklist victim). The lawyer explains how everything can be handled behind closed doors. All he has to do is name some names, to "cooperate," and he'll be cleared to work on his new Fox project. If he doesn't cooperate, there will be public hearings, scandal, and no Fox project.

One of the names HUAC wants him to name is that of his friend Bunny (George Wendt), a writer. Merrill can't do that. He can't betray a friend that way. And so the Fox project is canceled and he drifts into a nightmare world where nobody will tell him exactly what the rules are, but he cannot find a job anywhere.

Merrill has been estranged from his wife (Annette Bening), but now, broke and needing encouragement, he moves back in with her and their son, sleeping on the couch. He makes a trip to New York, where old Broadway friends shun him when they discover he's blacklisted. He has to listen as Bunny, broken and in tears, confesses that now the committee wants him to name Merrill. And he is the witness to a suicide as a once-famous actress (Patricia Wettig) drives her car over a cliff, distraught by the blacklist.

Work, when it comes, is furtive. Another blacklisted director (Martin Scorsese) has decided to leave the country, and wants Merrill to finish editing his film. A sleazy B movie producer hires Merrill under a pseudonym to direct a Western, then fires him when the secret is discovered. Only the cowboy hero sticks up for him. (This scene, like many moments and much of the dialogue, is inspired by an actual event; Gary Cooper, no communist, balked at anyone being blackmailed into betraying his friends.) Finally the day comes when Merrill has to face HUAC in public hearings. He still cannot see himself as a fighter: "What the hell, maybe I'll talk. I'm tired of not working."

Guilty by Suspicion is not only a powerful statement against the blacklist, but also one of the best Hollywood movies I've seen. The filmmaker, Irwin Winkler, making his directing debut, has been an important producer for years (his credits, often with partner Robert Chartoff, include the *Rocky* pictures, *The Right Stuff*, *Raging Bull*, and Oscar nominee *GoodFellas*). He has a matter-of-fact approach to the business that feels much more authentic than the glitzy showbiz tinsel Hollywood usually dishes up. Notice, for example, the cool professionalism with which the two directors (played by De Niro and Scorsese) discuss how a sequence will be edited.

Or the carefully measured dialogue with which the Zanuck character lays out the choices: Here is a man who has no regard for the blacklist, but also no desire to commit professional suicide.

Guilty by Suspicion is about a period that is now some forty years ago (although some blacklist members did not work again until the 1970s). But it teaches a lesson we are always in danger of forgetting: that the greatest service we can do our country is to be true to our conscience.

H

Hair ★ ★ ★ ★
R, 118 m., 1979

John Savage (Claude), Beverly D'Angelo (Sheila), Dorsey Wright (Hud), Cheryl Barnes (Hud's Fiancee), Treat Williams (Berger), Annie Golden (Jeannie), Don Dacus (Woof). Directed by Milos Forman and produced by Lester Persky and Michael Butler. Screenplay by Michael Weller.

I walked into *Hair* with the gravest doubts that this artifact of 1960s social shock would transfer to our current, sleepier times. In the 1960s we went to angry musicals; now we line up for *La Cage aux Folles.* My doubts disappeared with the surge and bold authority of the first musical statement: *This is the dawning of the Age of Aquarius!*

So maybe it isn't, really, and maybe the sun set on that particular age back around the time they pinched the Watergate burglars. But Milos Forman's *Hair* opens with such confidence and joy, moves so swiftly and sustains itself so well that I wonder why I had any doubts. *Hair* is, amazingly, not a period piece but a freshly conceived and staged memory of the tribulations of the mid-sixties.

It is also a terrific musical. The songs, of course, were good to begin with: The glory of "Hair" and "Let the Sun Shine In" and "Age of Aquarius" and the sly, silly warmth of "Black Boys/White Boys." But to the original music, the film version adds a story that works well with it, airy and open photography, and glorious choreography by Twyla Tharp.

I said I lost my doubts about *Hair* during "Age of Aquarius." To be more precise, they disappeared during Tharp's opening scene in Central Park, when the dancers were joined by the horses of mounted policemen. Anyone who can sit through that opening dance

sequence and not be thrilled should give up musicals.

The original play, you may recall, didn't exactly have what you could call much of a plot. The screenplay, by Michael Weller, remedies that, but not too much. Weller provides a framework structured around the experiences of a young Midwestern farmboy (John Savage) who takes the bus to Manhattan to be inducted into the army and makes instant friends with a family of hippies living in Central Park.

Savage is just right as the shy, introspective kid who feels suspicious of the hippies—and, indeed, of any alternative lifestyle. But he knows nobody else in New York, so he hangs around with these kids and suddenly a vision enters his life: a beautiful girl on horseback (Beverly D'Angelo), a debutante passing through Central Park and probably out of his life.

She comes from an incredibly wealthy family, he learns. They have nothing in common. But she's drawn, sort of, to the easy freedom of the hippies. And the leader of the hippies (Treat Williams, of *Jesus Christ Superstar*) leads them all in a high-spirited invasion of the girl's debutante party. It's one of the movie's best scenes, somehow finding a fresh way to handle the old cliché of the uninvited street people at a millionaire's party.

The movie also evokes the stylistic artifacts of the flower-power time. The love beads and vests and headbands and fringed jackets and all the other styles that were only yesterday, already look more dated than costumes from the 1940s. And it remembers the conflicts in lifestyles, mostly strikingly in scenes between the young black man (Dorsey Wright) who has joined the hippies, and the mother of his child (Cheryl Barnes), whom he left behind.

The movie's final sequences center on Savage's induction, leading to the hilarious "Black Boys/White Boys" number, an omnisexual showstopper. Twyla Tharp's choreography here is wonderfully happy and grin-inducing, as enlisted men rub legs under the table.

This number, like a lot of the movie, is loosely structured around the political attitudes of the Vietnam era, but the politics isn't heavy-handed. The movie's ideas are handled with grace and style. And it's interesting how it recalls *Hair*'s myths of the 1960s—especially the image of the youth culture as a repository, simultaneously, of ancient American values and the new values aborning in the Age of Aquarius.

That this time and spirit could be evoked so well and so naturally is a tribute to the director, Forman. His accomplishment is all the more remarkable when you reflect that when *Hair* first occupied a stage, the Russians were in the process of occupying Forman's native Czechoslovakia, and he was in the process of becoming a filmmaker without a country.

He has since, however, shown an uncanny feeling for the textures of American life, in his *Taking Off,* with its runaway children, in his *One Flew Over the Cuckoo's Nest,* and now in *Hair.* Maybe it's just as well that this version had to wait a decade to be filmed so Forman could be hired to do it. He brings life to the musical form in the same way that *West Side Story* did, the last time everyone was saying the movie musical was dead.

Hairspray ★ ★ ★
PG, 89 m., 1988

Ricki Lake (Tracy Turnblad), Shawn Thompson (Corny Collins), Sonny Bono (Franklin Von Tussle), Colleen Fitzpatrick

(Amber Von Tussle), Debbie Harry (Velma Von Tussle), Divine (Edna and Arvin), Ruth Brown (Maybell), Michael St. Gerard (Link Larkin), Leslie Ann Powers (Penny), Jerry Stiller (Wilbur Turnblad), Pia Zadora (Beatnik Girl). Directed by John Waters and produced by Rachel Talalay. Screenplay by Waters.

"If you remember the sixties, you weren't there."
—Dennis Hopper

Yeah, but those were the *late* sixties. Everybody remembers the early sixties, that season of innocence when a man could be named Chubby Checker and still be a star. The early sixties were before the Beatles, LSD, Vietnam, and hippies. They were, in fact, a lot like the late fifties, except that the cars were not as stylish and people were joining the Peace Corps, and in every town large enough to support a TV station there was a version of "The Hop."

"The Hop" was the name of the show on Channel 3 in Champaign-Urbana, Illinois, where I grew up. It had other names in other towns, but it always had the same format: A studio full of pimply-faced teen-agers in ducktails and ponytails, pumping away to mainstream rock music under the benevolent supervision of the local clone of Dick Clark.

Everybody I knew watched "The Hop." Nobody I knew ever appeared on it. Where did they get these kids? Did they hire professional teen-agers from other towns? Nobody I knew dressed as cool or danced as well as the kids on "The Hop," and there was a sinking feeling, on those long-ago afternoons in front of the TV, that the parade had passed me by.

John Waters's *Hairspray* is a movie about that time and those kids and the sinking feeling. It takes place in 1962 in Baltimore, where a program known as "The Corny Collins Show" is at the center of many local teen-age fantasies. The kids on Corny's show are great dancers, with hair piled in grotesque mounds atop their unformed little faces. They are "popular." They are on the "Council," a quasi-democratic board of teen-agers who advise Corny on matters of music, and supervise auditions for kids who want to be on the show.

One kid who hungers to be on the show is Tracy (Ricki Lake), who is fat, but who can dance better than Amber (Colleen Fitzpatrick), who is not. Tracy dances in front of her TV set and knows all the right moves, and is tolerated in her fantasies by her parents, who are played by Jerry Stiller and Divine.

The plot of the movie loosely involves Ricki's attempts to win a talent show and win a place on the Council, and the attempts that are made to stop her by Amber and her ambitious parents (Sonny Bono and Debbie Harry). It is some kind of commentary on the decivilizing eighties that Stiller and Divine and Bono and Harry, who would have qualified as sideshow exhibits in the real sixties, looked, in the context of this movie, like plausible parents. The supporting cast includes various local weirdos, including Pia Zadora as a "beatnik chick" (I quote from the credits). If nothing else is worth the price of renting this movie, perhaps you will be persuaded by the prospect of Pia Zadora reading from Allen Ginsberg's "Howl."

The movie carries a social message as sort of a sideline: "The Corny Collins Show" is racially segregated, and Ricki and her black friends help to change that situation, gate-crashing a Corny Collins night at the local amusement park. But basically the movie is a bubble-headed series of teen-age crises and crushes, alternating with historically accurate choreography of such forgotten dances as the Madison and the Roach.

The movie probably has the most to say to people who were teen-agers in the early sixties—but they are, I suppose, the last people likely to see this movie. It will also appeal to today's teen-agers, who will find that every generation has its own version of Corny Collins, and its own version of the Council, designed to make you feel like a worthless reject on the trash heap of teen-age history. If there is a message in the movie, it is that John Waters, who could never in a million years have made the Council, did, after all, survive to make the movie.

Half Moon Street ★ ★ ★
R, 90 m., 1986

Sigourney Weaver (Lauren Slaughter), Michael Caine (Lord Bulbeck), Ram John Holder (Lindsay Walker), Niall O'Brien (Captain Twilley), Patrick Kavanagh (General Newhouse), Nadim Sawalha (Karim Hatami), Michael Elwyn (Tom Haldane). Directed by Bob Swaim and produced by Geoffrey Reeve. Screenplay by Swaim and Edward Behr.

I was reflecting, as the lights went down before *Half Moon Street*, that I could not recall a single bad performance by either of the stars, Michael Caine and Sigourney Weaver. Caine's record is all the more remarkable because he has emerged untouched from some of the worst movies of the last twenty years with his unshakable self-confidence and quiet good humor. In a certain sense, it didn't even matter what *Half Moon Street* was about, or whether it was much good, because I was so curious to see what Caine and Weaver would be like together.

The movie stars Weaver as the wonderfully named Dr. Lauren Slaughter, an American academic who specializes in China and works for a cold-war think tank in London. She is tall, smart, calculating, and concerned with her own advantage. When she writes an article for the potty general who runs her organization and it turns up in the *Spectator* under his name, she doesn't go along with the program: She lets him know he's a spineless pig. And when she reflects that she is doing the work of her inferiors for starvation wages, she takes action.

It happens this way: She meets a man at a party, and he sends her a videotape documentary about a high-priced call-girl agency. She looks at the tape, considers the possibilities, and goes to interview for a job. She is completely open about the whole thing. She entertains clients using her real name, and when she is asked at an academic gathering what she does with her evenings, she replies that she has dinner with rich men.

One night she recognizes one of her clients. He tries to introduce himself as Sam Weller, but she has read her Dickens, smiles at that, and calls him by his name—Lord Bulbeck. He is a government spokesman on defense in the House of Lords and a lonely man who lives alone in a large house and says he doesn't have the time to find sex and companionship through ordinary channels.

That's fine with her. They make love, start talking, begin to like one another, and, before long, they have crossed over that great divide between asking each other what they like in bed and asking each other how they like their omelets. There is a certain instant compatibility between them. They are both friendly and outgoing people with something cold at their cores, and the device of the escort agency rather suits them: It provides a reason why they are in bed that does not involve such complicated issues as love and affection.

Dr. Slaughter meets other clients, including rich Middle Easterners who set her up in an expensive flat in Mayfair. She continues to work at the think tank, where she doesn't much mind that certain people know about her moonlighting. Bulbeck gets involved in tricky negotiations involving a Middle East peace settlement, and of course the Special Branch monitors all of his activities. It checks out Dr. Slaughter and eavesdrops on his private moments with her, and that is as it should be.

What makes *Half Moon Street* so intriguing up to this point is the literal and almost offhand honesty that grows between the Weaver and Caine characters. Their feelings are clear, their motives are clear, and with their eyes wide open they're falling in love.

This whole aspect of the movie is essentially the contribution of the director, Bob Swaim, and his co-writer, Edward Behr. In Paul Theroux's original novel, *Doctor Slaughter*, Lord Bulbeck was older and less amusing, and Dr. Slaughter was very alone in the world she had made for herself. The love that grows between the bright young woman and the gentle middle-aged man provides a subject that wasn't there in the Theroux version, and so it's sort of a shock when the plot reintroduces itself.

The plot has to do with Middle Eastern intrigues, spy rings, terrorists, and plans to sabotage Lord Bulbeck's peace initiative. And it leads to the movie's closing sequence, in which we lose the particular charms of the growing romance and find ourselves back in those familiar movie clichés where everything is settled with violence. God, it's boring to have to wait through an obligatory series of scenes until all of the right people have been killed and the movie can be over.

The last scene in *Half Moon Street* is particularly unconvincing, because for a long time this movie seemed so unorthodox that I expected a tough and realistic ending in which at least one of the wrong people would get killed. No such luck. And so I was right: The movie is interesting primarily because of the interaction between Weaver and Caine. Swaim deserves credit for the intelligence and wit of the first eighty or ninety minutes, but must also take the blame for the ending, which is a complete surrender to generic conventions.

Halloween ★ ★ ★ ★
R, 93 m., 1978

With Donald Pleasence, Jamie Lee Curtis, P.J. Soles, and Nancy Loomis. Directed by John Carpenter and produced by Irving Yablans. Screenplay by Carpenter and Debra Hill.

"I enjoy playing the audience like a piano."
—Alfred Hitchcock

So does John Carpenter. *Halloween* is an absolutely merciless thriller, a movie so violent and scary that, yes, I *would* compare it to *Psycho*. It's a terrifying and creepy film about what one of the characters calls Evil Personified. Right. And that leads us to the one small piece of plot I'm going to describe. There's this six-year-old kid who commits a murder right at the beginning of the movie, and is sent away, and is described by his psychiatrist as someone he spent eight years trying to help, and then the next seven years trying to keep locked up. But the guy escapes. And he returns on Halloween to the same town and the same street where he committed his first murder. And while the local babysitters telephone their boyfriends and watch *The Thing* on television, he goes back into action.

Period: That's all I'm going to describe, because *Halloween* is a visceral experience—we aren't seeing the movie, we're having it happen to us. It's frightening. Maybe you don't like movies that are *really* scary: Then don't see this one. Seeing it, I was reminded of the favorable review I gave a few years ago to *The Last House on the Left*, another really terrifying thriller. Readers wrote to ask how I could possibly support such a movie. But it wasn't that I was supporting it so much as that I was describing it: You don't want to be scared? Don't see it. Credit must be paid to filmmakers who make the effort to really frighten us, to make a good thriller when quite possibly a bad one might have made as much money. Hitchcock is acknowledged as a master of suspense; it's hypocrisy to disapprove of other directors in the same genre who want to scare us too.

It's easy to create violence on the screen, but it's hard to do it well. Carpenter is uncannily skilled, for example, at the use of foregrounds in his compositions, and everyone who likes thrillers knows that foregrounds are crucial: The camera establishes the situation, and then it pans to one side, and something unexpectedly looms up in the foreground. Usually it's a tree or a door or a bush. Not always. And it's interesting how he paints his victims. They're all ordinary, everyday people—nobody's supposed to be the star and have a big scene and win an Academy Award. The performances are all the more absorbing because of that; the movie's a slice of life that is carefully painted (in drab daylights and impenetrable night-

times) before its human monster enters the scene.

We see movies for a lot of reasons. Sometimes we want to be amused. Sometimes we want to escape. Sometimes we want to laugh, or cry, or see sunsets. And sometimes we want to be scared. I'd like to be clear about this. If you don't want to have a really terrifying experience, don't see *Halloween*.

Hamlet ★ ★ ★ ½
PG, 120 m., 1990

Mel Gibson (Hamlet), Glenn Close (Gertrude), Alan Bates (Claudius), Paul Scofield (The Ghost), Ian Holm (Polonius), Helena Bonham-Carter (Ophelia), Stephen Dillane (Horatio). Directed by Franco Zeffirelli and produced by Dyson Lovell. Screenplay by Christopher De Vore and Zeffirelli.

I had a professor in college who knew everything there was to know about *Romeo and Juliet*. Maybe he knew too much. One day in class he said he would give anything to be able to read it again for the first time. I feel the same way about *Hamlet*. I know the play so well by now, have seen it in so many different styles and periods and modes of dress, that it's like listening to a singer doing an old standard. You know the lyrics, so the only possible surprises come from style and phrasing.

The style of Franco Zeffirelli's *Hamlet*, with Mel Gibson in the title role, is robust and physical and—don't take this the wrong way—upbeat. Gibson doesn't give us another Hamlet as Mope, a melancholy Dane lurking in shadows and bewailing his fate. We get the notion, indeed, that there was nothing fundamentally awry with Hamlet until everything went wrong in his life, until his father died and his mother married his uncle with unseemly haste. This is a prince who was healthy and happy and could have lived a long and active life if things had turned out differently.

Part of that approach may come from Zeffirelli, whose famous film version of *Romeo and Juliet* also played on the youth and attractiveness of its characters, who were bursting with life and romance until tragedy separated them. The approach may also come from Gibson himself, the most good-humored of contemporary stars, whose personal style is to deflect seriousness with a joke, and who doesn't easily descend into self-pity and morose masochism. He gives us a Hamlet who does his best to carry on, until he is overwhelmed by the sheer weight of events.

Zeffirelli sets his film in a spectacular location—a castle on an outcropping of the stark coast in northern Scotland, perched on top of a rock nearly surrounded by the sea. There is mud here, and rain and mist, and the characters sometimes seemed dragged down by the sheer weight of their clothing. This is a substantial world of real physical presence, fleshed out by an unusual number of extras; we have the feeling that this throne rules over real subjects, instead of existing only in Shakespeare's imagination.

Right at the outset, Zeffirelli and his collaborator on the shooting script, Christopher De Vore, take a liberty with *Hamlet,* by shifting some dialogue and adding a few words to create a scene that does not exist in the original: the wake of Hamlet's father, with Hamlet, Gertrude, and Claudius confronting each other over the coffin. In film terms, this scene makes the central problem of *Hamlet* perfectly clear and dramatically strengthens everything that follows. It sets up not only Hamlet's anguish, but the real attraction between his mother and his uncle, which is seen in this version to be at least as sexual as it is political.

The cast is what is always called "distinguished," which usually, but not always, means "British," includes at least three actors who have played Hamlet themselves: Alan Bates, as Claudius; Paul Scofield, as the ghost of Hamlet's father; and Ian Holm, as Polonius. Holm is especially effective in the "to thine own self be true" speech, evoking memories of his great work as the track coach in *Chariots of Fire,* and I enjoyed Bates's strength of bluster and lust, as a man of action who will have what he desires and not bother himself with the sorts of questions that torture Hamlet.

The women of the play, Glenn Close, as Gertrude, and Helena Bonham-Carter, as Ophelia, are both well cast. Close, in particular, adds an element of true mothering that is sometimes absent from Gertrude. She loves her son and cares for him, and is not simply an unfaithful wife with a short memory. Indeed, there are subtle physical suggestions that she has loved her son too closely, too warmly, creating the buried incestuous feelings that are the real spring of Hamlet's actions. Why has she remarried with such haste? Perhaps simply so the kingdom's power vacuum will be filled; she seems a sensible sort, and indeed everyone in this version

seems fairly normal, if only Hamlet could rid himself of his gnawing resentment and shameful desires long enough to see it.

Bonham-Carter is a small and darkly beautiful actress who is effective at seeming to respond to visions within herself. As Ophelia she has a most difficult role to play, because a character who has gone mad can have no further relationship with the other characters but must essentially become a soloist. All of her later scenes are with herself.

That leaves Hamlet and his best friend, Horatio (Stephen Dillane), as those who are not satisfied with the state of things in the kingdom, and Dillane, with his unforced natural acting, provides a good partner for Gibson. As everything leads to the final sword fight and all of its results, as Hamlet's natural good cheer gradually weakens under the weight of his thoughts, the movie proceeds logically through its emotions. We never feel, as we do sometimes with other productions, that events happen arbitrarily. Zeffirelli's great contribution in "popularizing" the play has been to make it clear to the audience why events are unfolding as they are.

This *Hamlet* finally stands or falls on Mel Gibson's performance, and I think it will surprise some viewers with its strength and appeal. He has not been overawed by Shakespeare, has not fallen into a trap of taking this role too solemnly and lugubriously. He has observed the young man of the earlier and less troubled scenes, and started his performance from there, instead of letting every nuance be a foreshadow of what is to come. It's a strong, intelligent performance, filled with life, and it makes this into a surprisingly robust *Hamlet.*

Hangin' With the Homeboys ★ ★ ★
R, 89 m., 1991

Doug E. Doug (Willie), Mario Joyner (Tom), John Leguizamo (Johnny), Nestor Serrano (Vinny). Directed by Joseph B. Vasquez and produced by Richard Brick. Screenplay by Vasquez.

Hangin' With the Homeboys was originally set for release in May and June of 1991, but then *Boyz N the Hood* made its big splash, and *Straight Out of Brooklyn* got a lot of publicity, and *Hangin'* was held over until fall. The theory must have been that audiences would confuse the titles—or that maybe the market wasn't big enough to support three films about young inner-city men looking for di-

rection in their lives. The fact is, the films aren't that similar—except that all three are good and honest portraits of a generation unsure of what to do with itself.

Boyz took place in the "hood" of Los Angeles, where palm trees and carports confer a superficial middle-class look to the poor neighborhoods. *Brooklyn* took place in the world of projects and unemployment. *Hangin'* takes place in the South Bronx, in a high-energy big-city world where the characters talk faster and live a roller-coaster experience where it is just barely plausible they could have all of these adventures in one twenty-four-hour period.

The movie is about four friends, two blacks, two Hispanics (although one of the Puerto Ricans renames himself "Vinnie" and wants to pose as Italian). They set out one evening looking for action, and find it in various forms, but at the same time they also discover a few truths before the sun comes up.

The cast is relatively unknown, but experienced and talented, and includes the stand-up comics Doug E. Doug and Mario Joyner, character actors John Leguizamo and Nester Serrano, and TV actresses Kimberly Russell and Mary B. Ward. The day may come when this movie, like *American Graffiti* and *Diner,* will be remembered because so many in its cast went on to become famous.

There are no star turns in the story, however; the movie adopts a loose, improvisational style as the homeboys try to crash a party, cruise the streets of Manhattan looking for action, pick up a couple of girls, and begin to realize that their entire lives could be as aimless as this night—unless they get organized.

The screenplay by Joseph B. Vasquez, who also directed, is fairly conventional in giving each character a problem to solve and then pushing him toward a solution, but the movie doesn't feel traditional because Vasquez doesn't hammer his points home; he lets them develop naturally. I liked the way one character is quietly encouraged by a girl to take a chance and go back to school, and the way another one—who sees racism in every slight, real or imagined—is able to start learning that he is not always a victim.

Vasquez, like many in his generation of filmmakers, owes a great deal to the techniques of John Cassavetes, who perfected this sort of male-bonding movie. He's helped by his actors, who sometimes seem to be improvising even when they're probably not.

I liked the whole way the gate-crashing party scene developed, with the guys trying to fake invitations into a party where everybody knows everybody—and nobody knows them.

One of the undercurrents in this movie is that these four young men are all essentially good. That needs to be said in films like this, and such films need to be seen. Our society is so racially divided that the sight of four "homeboys" approaching on the street is adequate to strike terror in the hearts of many white (and not a few nonwhite) citizens. Young urban males are often seen only in terms of the fears they inspire, instead of for who they really are. These are nice kids. Maybe that's the message.

Hannah and Her Sisters ★ ★ ★ ★
PG-13, 107 m., 1985

Woody Allen (Mickey), Michael Caine (Elliot), Mia Farrow (Hannah), Carrie Fisher (April), Barbara Hershey (Lee), Lloyd Nolan (Hannah's Father), Maureen O'Sullivan (Hannah's Mother), Daniel Stern (Dusty), Max von Sydow (Frederick), Dianne Wiest (Holly). Directed by Woody Allen and produced by Robert Greenhut. Screenplay by Allen.

Woody Allen's *Hannah and Her Sisters*, the best movie he has ever made, is organized like an episodic novel, with acute self-contained vignettes adding up to the big picture.

Each section begins with a title or quotation on the screen, white against black, making the movie feel like a stately progression through the lives of its characters. Then the structure is exploded, time and again, by the energy and the passion of those characters: an accountant in love with his wife's sister, a TV executive who fears he is going to die, a woman whose cocaine habit has made her life a tightrope of fear, an artist who pretends to be strong but depends pitifully on his girlfriend.

By the end of the movie, the section titles and quotations have made an ironic point: We try to organize our lives according to what we have read and learned and believed in, but our plans are lost in a tumult of emotion.

The movie spans two years in the lives of its large cast of characters—New Yorkers who labor in Manhattan's two sexiest industries, art and money. It begins and ends at family Thanksgiving dinners, with the dinner in the middle of the film acting as a turning point for several lives.

It is hard to say who the most important characters are, but my memory keeps returning to Elliot, the accountant played by Michael Caine, and Lee, the artist's girlfriend, played by Barbara Hershey. Elliot is married to Hannah (Mia Farrow), but has been blind-sided with a sudden passion for Lee. She lives in a loft with the tortured artist Frederick (Max von Sydow), who treats her like his child or his student. He is so isolated from ordinary human contact that she is actually his last remaining link with reality.

Lee and Hannah have a third sister, Holly (Dianne Wiest). They form parts of a whole. Hannah is the competent, nurturing one. Lee is the emotional, sensuous earth mother. Holly is a bundle of tics and insecurities. When they meet for lunch and the camera circles them curiously, we sense that in some ways the movie knows them better than they will ever know themselves. And to talk about the movie that way is to suggest the presence of the most important two characters in the movie, whom I will describe as Woody Allen and Mickey.

Mickey is the character played by Allen; he is a neurotic TV executive who lives in constant fear of death or disease. He was married to Hannah at one time. Even after Hannah's marriage to Elliot, Mickey remains a member of the family, circling its security with a winsome yearning to belong.

The family itself centers on the three women's parents, played by Maureen O'Sullivan and Lloyd Nolan as an aging show-business couple who have spent decades in loving warfare over his cheating and her drinking and their mutual career decisions.

If Mickey is the character played by Woody Allen in the movie, Allen also provides another, second character in a more subtle way. The entire movie is told through his eyes and his sensibility; not Mickey's, but Allen's. From his earlier movies, especially *Annie Hall* and *Manhattan*, we have learned to recognize the tone of voice, the style of approach.

Allen approaches his material as a very bright, ironic, fussy, fearful outsider; his constant complaint is that it's all very well for these people to engage in their lives and plans and adulteries because they do not share his problem, which is that he sees through everything, and what he sees on the other side of everything is certain death and disappointment.

Allen's writing and directing style is so strong and assured in this film that the actual filmmaking itself becomes a narrative voice, just as we sense Henry James behind all of his novels, or William Faulkner and Iris Murdoch, behind theirs.

The movie is not a comedy, but it contains big laughs, and it is not a tragedy, although it could be if we thought about it long enough. It suggests that modern big-city lives are so busy, so distracted, so filled with ambition and complication that there isn't time to stop and absorb the meaning of things. Neither tragedy nor comedy can find a place to stand; there are too many other guests at the party.

And yet, on reflection, there is a tragedy buried in *Hannah and Her Sisters*, and that is the fact of Mickey's status as the perennial outsider. The others get on with their lives, but Mickey is stuck with his complaints. Not only is he certain there is no afterlife, he is very afraid that this life might also be a sham. How he ever married Hannah in the first place is a mystery; it must have been an intermediate step on his journey to his true role in life, as the ex-husband and hanger-on.

There is a scene in the movie where Michael Caine confronts Barbara Hershey and tells her that he loves her. She is stunned, does not know what to say, but does not categorically deny that she has feelings for him. After she leaves him, he stands alone on the street, ecstatic, his face glowing, saying "I've got my answer! I've got my answer!"

Underlying all of *Hannah and Her Sisters* is the envy of Mickey (and Woody) that anyone could actually be happy enough and lucky enough to make such a statement. And yet, by the end of the movie, in his own way, Mickey has his answer, too.

Hard Choices ★ ★ ★ ½
NO MPAA RATING, 90 m., 1986

Margaret Klenck (Laura), Gary McCleery (Bobby), John Seitz (Sheriff Johnson), John Sayles (Don), John Snyder (Ben), Martin Donovan (Josh). Directed by Rick King and produced by Robert Mickelson and Earle Mack. Screenplay by King.

Many movies start out strong and end in confusion and compromise. *Hard Choices* starts out like a predictable action picture, and grows and grows until at the end it astonishes us. It gives its characters a freedom very few movies are willing to relinquish—the freedom to surprise us by moving in unexpected directions. The movie develops in ways we anticipate, and then there is a startling turning point, a moment when one of the characters makes a radical decision and acts on it, and from that moment on, *Hard Choices* never lets go.

Any review of this film has to be a tight-wire act. This isn't a case of "not giving away the ending," it's a case of preserving a crucial surprise so that it can strike you with the same impact it struck me with. The people who released this film cared so little about their surprise that they actually revealed it in film clips supplied to television reviewers. I'm not going to repeat that mistake, because at a time when a reasonably intelligent movie-goer can predict eighty percent of what's going to happen in a movie, *Hard Choices* is a treasure.

The movie takes place in the backwoods of Tennessee, where Bobby (Gary Mc-Cleery), the hero, is a fifteen-year-old kid with good prospects for making something out of his life. His older brothers are into drugs and robberies. When they can't get the drugs they need, their insides fill up with a desperate vacuum, and they decide to rob a drugstore. They take their kid brother along. Everything goes wrong and a cop is killed and the three of them are caught and arrested, and the decision is made to try Bobby as an adult, for murder. There goes his life.

In jail, Bobby is not treated with the brutality that has become a cliché in movies like this. The local sheriff even has a sort of grudging sympathy for the kid. Meanwhile, a woman who works with juvenile offenders hears about his case; she travels to the small town and gets to know Bobby and becomes convinced that he did not want to go along on the robbery, did not pull the trigger, and was, in fact, an innocent bystander. The woman decides to do what she can to help Bobby.

This woman, played by Margaret Klenck, provides the central turning point in the movie. Until she appears, the story has developed along fairly routine lines. After she appears, there's nothing we can really count on. I don't want to say anything more about what actually happens in the movie, or what Klenck does. But look at her performance and you will see great screen action.

I've never seen Klenck before; I gather from the publicity material that she appeared for six years as Edwina Lewis on the TV soap opera "One Life to Live." What she does here is so deeply absorbing and yet so quiet that at first we don't even realize what's happening. She appears on screen wrapped in a cloak of conventionality. Everything is "normal" about her; how she looks, how she talks, how she behaves. And then, gradually,

we realize that this woman is a true outsider, a person who works in the system but is not of the system, a person with an outlaw soul.

There are several other good performances in the movie, one by John Seitz, who turns the thankless role of the sheriff into a three-dimensional middle-aged guy with feelings; another by McCleery, as the kid, who has to survive a lot of tense and anguished scenes in the beginning before he can establish the interior rhythms of his character. One role is especially well-written: An intellectual, philosophical drug dealer, played by John Sayles, who does not remind us of any drug dealer we've ever seen in a movie before.

Hard Choices is a sleeper. That means it doesn't have any stars and was made on a small budget and got haphazard distribution around the country and will never be heard of by most people. No wonder it has a low profile; it's intelligent, surprising, powerful, and true to itself, and that sure puts it outside the mainstream. It's a classic example of a movie waiting to be discovered on video.

Hardcore ★ ★ ★ ★
R, 106 m., 1979

George C. Scott (Jake VanDorn), Peter Boyle (Andy Mast), Season Hubley (Niki), Dick Sargent (Wes DeJong), Leonard Gaines (Ramada), David Nichols (Kurt), Gary Rand Graham (Tod), Larry Block (Burrows). Directed by Paul Schrader and produced by Buzz Feitshans. Screenplay by Schrader.

Hardcore is said to be the story of a father's search for a daughter who has disappeared into the underworld of pornography and prostitution. That does indeed describe its beginning and ending. But there are moments in between when it becomes something much more interesting: The story of a tentative, trusting human relationship between the father and the young prostitute he enlists in his search.

The man is played by George C. Scott, the girl by Season Hubley. They have moments in the movie when they talk, really talk, about what's important to them—and we're reminded of how much movie dialogue just repeats itself, movie after movie, year after year. There's a scene in *Hardcore* where the man (who is a strict Calvinist) and the prostitute (who began selling herself in her early teens) talk about sex, religion, and morality, and we're almost startled by the belief and simple poetry in their words.

This relationship, between two people

with nothing in common, who meet at an intersection in a society where many have nothing in common, is at the heart of the movie, and makes it important. It is preceded and followed by another of those story ideas that Paul Schrader seems to generate so easily. His movies are about people with values, in conflict with society. He wrote *Taxi Driver* and *Rolling Thunder* and wrote and directed *Blue Collar*. All three are about people prepared to defend (with violence, if necessary) their steadfast beliefs.

The Scott character is a fundamentalist from Grand Rapids, Michigan—Schrader's own hometown. The opening scenes establish the family setting, at Christmas, with a fairly thick theological debate going on around the dinner table. (The small boy listening so solemnly, Schrader has said, can be taken for himself.) A few days later, Scott's daughter leaves home for a church rally in California. She never returns. Scott hires a private detective (Peter Boyle) to try to find her, and Boyle does find her—in an 8-millimeter porno movie. Can it be traced? Boyle says not: "Nobody made it. Nobody sold it. Nobody *sees* it. It doesn't exist."

But Scott vows to follow his daughter into the sexual underworld and bring her back. His efforts to trace her, through San Francisco and Los Angeles and San Diego, make *Hardcore* into a sneakily fascinating guided tour through massage parlors, whorehouses, and the world of porno movies. Schrader sometimes seems to be having it both ways, here: Scott is repelled by the sex scenes he explores, but is the movie?

That doesn't matter so much after he meets Niki (Season Hubley), who might know some people who might know where his daughter is. She is in many ways like all the other lost young girls who drift to California and disappear. But she has intelligence and a certain insight into why she does what she does, and so their talks together become occasions for mutual analysis.

She has a deep psychological need for a father figure, a need she thinks Scott can meet. She also has insights into Scott's own character, insights his life hasn't previously made clear to him. There's a scene near the waterfront in San Diego that perfectly illuminates both of their personalities, and we realize how rare it is for the movies to show us people who are speaking in real words about real things.

The movie's ending is a mess, a combination of cheap thrills, a chase, and a shoot-out, as if Schrader wasn't quite sure how to escape from the depths he found. The film's last ten minutes, in fact, are mostly action, the automatic resolution of the plot; the relationship between Scott and Hubley ends without being resolved, and in bringing his story to a "satisfactory" conclusion, Schrader doesn't speak to the deeper and more human themes he's introduced. Too bad. But *Hardcore*, flawed and uneven, contains moments of pure revelation.

The Hard Way ★ ★ ★ ½
R, 111 m., 1991

Michael J. Fox (Nick Lang), James Woods (John Moss), Stephen Lang (Party Crasher), Annabella Sciorra (Susan), John Capodice (Grainy), Penny Marshall (Angie). Directed by John Badham and produced by William Sackheim and Rob Cohen. Screenplay by Daniel Pyne and Lem Dobbs.

There is nothing very remarkable about *The Hard Way*, except for its comic energy, but the energy of this movie is everything, reminding me of the wisecracking, hard-boiled, screwball comedies of the 1940s, back when they assumed the audience knew how to listen fast. You have to listen really fast during this movie, but what you get is an earful of James Woods in full flower, and Michael J. Fox so hyper he ventilates.

Woods plays the kind of role that, if they hadn't been able to hire him, they would have had to shut down the movie. Who else could play this rapid-fire, angry, violent, foul-mouthed, insecure, sneaky, and lying but lovable rascal? He's the toughest cop in New York, the kind who rams his police car into the back of a truck because he's late for a date. I have seen some James Woods movies I didn't enjoy, but it's hard to remember them—the names of few other actors give you more of a guarantee that you will not be bored and will possibly be electrified.

This time he plays John Moss, a homicide detective on the trail of the Party Crasher (Stephen Lang), a mass murderer who specializes in shooting his victims in the middle of discos, usually after inviting the police to attend. Moss almost catches the Crasher as the movie opens—there's a typical Woods scene that has him hanging onto the door of a speeding truck while the Crasher is at the wheel—but after he's nearly killed, his commander takes him off the case.

What's his new assignment? A Hollywood action star named Nick Lang (Michael J.

Fox) wants more authenticity in his performances, and when he sees a clip of Woods in the TV news, he knows this is his man. He wants to move into the life of this cop, to follow him everywhere, to study his methods and mannerisms, to live in his apartment and see what makes him tick. He even gets to be friends with his girlfriend (Annabella Sciorra). Woods wants no part of this plan, and informs his commander in blunt and colorful language. The commander tells him it's an order.

This is essentially just another version of the reliable old cop partner movie, in which the veteran is assigned to take a rookie under his wing. But the filmmakers crank up the energy until the movie takes on a life of its own. The director, John Badham, knows how to make genre pictures; his credits include *Stakeout* and *WarGames*. The screenplay, by Daniel Pyne and Lem Dobbs, is clever and funny and provides Woods with some genuinely funny vulgarities. The stunts and action direction, the second unit work, and the special effects are all seamless and exciting—especially a climactic scene that manages to parody *North by Northwest* while substituting a billboard in Times Square for Mount Rushmore.

But mostly what we're talking about here is energy. There is a certain exhilarating, high-altitude buzz you get from actors who are working well at the limits of their ability, and I got it during *The Hard Way*. Faced with a plot that was potentially predictable, Woods and Fox seem to have agreed to crank up the voltage, to take the chance of playing every scene flat-out. They also take some chances with their images, or at least Fox does (Woods has always gloried in his role as a manic killer rat from speed city). The result is funny, fun, exciting and, when you look beneath the glossy surface, an example of professionals who know their crafts and enjoy doing them well.

Harlan County, U.S.A. ★ ★ ★ ★
PG, 103 m., 1976

A documentary directed and produced by Barbara Kopple.

One moment among many in *Harlan County, U.S.A.*: The striking miners are holding an all-day rally and picnic. A big tent has been pitched, and it's filled with people—some of them familiar to us by now, others new. There are speeches and songs and union battle cries, and then an old woman takes

the microphone. The words she sings are familiar: *They say in Harlan County, there are no neutrals there. You'll either be a union man or a thug for Sheriff Blair.* And then the whole tent-full joins in the chorus: *Which side are you on?*

The woman who is leading the singing wrote the song fifty years ago, during an earlier strike in the county the miners call "Bloody Harlan." And here it is 1973, in a county where the right of workers to organize has presumably long since been won, and the song is not being sung out of nostalgia. It is being sung by striking coal miners in Harlan County, where it still applies.

That's the most uncomfortable lesson we learn in Barbara Kopple's magnificent documentary: That there are still jobs for scabs and strike breakers, that union organizers still get shot at and sometimes get killed, and that in Harlan County, Kentucky, it still matters very much which side you're on. And so a song we know best from old Pete Seeger records suddenly proves itself still frighteningly relevant.

The movie, which won the 1976 Academy Award for best feature-length documentary, was shot over a period of eighteen months in eastern Kentucky, after the miners at the Brookside mine voted to join the United Mine Workers. The Duke Power Company refused to sign the UMW contract, fought the strike, and was fought in turn by the miners and—most particularly—their wives.

Barbara Kopple and her crew stayed in Harlan County during that entire time, living in the miners' homes and recording the day-by-day progress of the strike. It was a tumultuous period, especially since the mine workers' union itself was deep in the midst of the Tony Boyle-Jock Yablonsky affair. But what emerges from the film is not just a document of a strike, but an affecting, unforgettable portrait of a community.

The cameras go down into the mines to show us the work, which is backbreaking, dirty, and brutal. We get to meet many of the miners, and to notice a curious thing about the older ones: They tend to talk little, as if their attentions are turned inward to the source of the determination that takes them back down the mine every day. Their wives, on the other hand, seem born to lead strikes. The film shows them setting up committees, organizing picket lines, facing (and sometimes reciprocating) violence, and becoming eloquent orators.

Ms. Kopple is a feminist, and her work

includes *Year of the Women*. In *Harlan County*, though, she doesn't seem to have gone looking for examples of capable, competent, strong women: They were simply inescapable. There are talents, energies, and intelligences revealed in this film that could, if we would tap them, transform legislatures and bring wholesale quantities of common sense to public life. There are tacticians, strategists, and philosophers in *Harlan County, U.S.A.* who make the UMW theoreticians look tame—and the company spokesmen look callow and inane.

The movie is a great American document, but it's also entertaining; Kopple structures her material to provide tension, brief but vivid characterizations, and dramatic confrontations (including one incredibly charged moment when the sheriff attempts to lead a caravan of scabs past the picket line). There are gunshots in the film, and a death, and also many moments of simple warmth and laughter. The many union songs on the sound track provide a historical context, and also help Kopple achieve a fluid editing rhythm. And most of all there are the people in the film, those amazing people, so proud and self-reliant and brave.

Harry and Tonto ★ ★ ★ ★
PG, 115 m., 1974

Art Carney (Harry), Ellen Burstyn (Shirley), Chief Dan George (Indian), Geraldine Fitzgerald (Jessie). Directed and produced by Paul Mazursky. Screenplay by Mazursky and Josh Greenfield.

Paul Mazursky's *Harry and Tonto* tells the story of a feisty seventy-two-year-old who is carried forcibly from his New York apartment one step ahead of the wrecker's ball. He was happy with his life in the city (apart from the four muggings so far this year) and content to talk to his old cronies and to his cat, Tonto. But life without a home isn't easy. He goes for a while to live with his son on Long Island, where he's welcomed, sort of, into a household on the edge of insanity. One of his grandsons thinks the other one is crazy. The other won't respond because, you see, he has taken a vow of silence. Harry sizes up the situation, packs Tonto in a carrying case, and hits the road. The road becomes a strange and wonderful place for Harry, mostly because of his own resilient personality. He's played by Art Carney as a man of calm philosophy, gentle humor, and an acceptance of the ways people can be. He is also not a man

in a hurry. When he can't carry Tonto onto an airplane, he takes the bus. When the bus can't wait for Tonto to relieve himself, he buys a used car and picks up hitchhikers.

One of them is a young girl who becomes his friend. She talks of her life, and he talks of his, including his long-ago romance with a member of the Isadora Duncan troupe. The last he'd heard of her, she was living in Peru, Indiana, as the wife of a pharmacist. The girl talks him into stopping in Indiana and looking the old woman up. And he does so, in a scene of rare warmth and tenderness. The woman, Jessie (played by Geraldine Fitzgerald), has a very shaky memory, but she does recall being a dancer, and in the calm of the recreation room at her nursing home, the old couple dances together one last time.

And then Harry's back on the road to Chicago, where he has a daughter who runs a bookstore. He spends a few days with her, walking on the beach and talking things over. His silent grandson has broken his vow and flown to Chicago to try to talk the old man into coming back to New York. But, no, Harry doesn't think he will. ("You're talking now?" he asks his grandson. "Garbo speaks," the kid shrugs.)

He heads vaguely westward. His young hitchhiker has fallen in love with his grandson, and they think they'll aim for a commune in Colorado. Harry gives them a lift because that's more or less where he's going, but he declines, just now, to join the commune. He gives them his car, hitches a ride with a Las Vegas hooker, is (to his vast surprise) seduced by her, has a good time in Vegas, and, alas, is arrested for having a few too many.

This leads to the film's most hilarious scene. Harry is tossed into a cell already occupied by an ancient Indian (Chief Dan George) who has been arrested for practicing medicine without a license. The two old men gravely discuss recent television shows and the problem of bursitis, and the chief cures Harry's aching shoulder in return for an electric blender. Chief Dan George is so solemn, so understated, with Mazursky's dialogue that the result is a great comic scene.

Harry and Tonto drift on West toward the Pacific, and we begin to get the sense that this hasn't been your ordinary road picture, but a sort of farewell voyage by a warm and good old man who is still, at seventy-two, capable of being thankful for the small astonishments offered by life. The achievement is partly Mazursky's, partly Carney's.

Mazursky has established himself as the master of a kind of cinema he calls "serious comedy"—movies that make us laugh and yet have a special attitude toward their material and American society. His earlier films have included *Bob & Carol & Ted & Alice* and the remarkable *Blume in Love*.

Art Carney has, of course, fashioned a distinguished career for himself on the stage after all those years as Norton on "The Honeymooners." Here, he flowers as a movie star. The performance is totally original, all his own, and worthy of the Academy Award it received. It's not easy to make comedies that work as drama, too. But Carney's acting is so perceptive that it helps this material succeed.

Havana ★ ★ ★
R, 145 m., 1990

Robert Redford (Jack Weil), Lena Olin (Bobby Duran), Alan Arkin (Joe Volpi), Raul Julia (Arturo Duran), Tomas Milian (Menocal), Daniel Davis (Marion Chigwell), Mark Rydell (Meyer Lansky), Richard Farnsworth (Professor). Directed by Sydney Pollack and produced by Pollack and Richard Roth. Screenplay by Judith Rascoe and David Rayfiel.

Sydney Pollack's *Havana*, which is a good movie, tells much the same story as *Casablanca*, which is a better movie. The difference between the two movies is instructive. *Casablanca* benefits from being part of our common mythology; lines from its dialogue have entered into our everyday speech, and Bogart and Bergman are remembered for that movie more than for any other. But look at it again and you will be surprised what a large role the supporting characters play. The very world of *Casablanca* is unthinkable without Paul Henreid, Claude Rains, Sydney Greenstreet, Peter Lorre, and, of course, Dooley Wilson.

Havana tells a similar story, of a man and a woman whose love is in conflict with the political dilemma of their times. It has a similar romantic triangle: The woman must choose between a good man who is politically correct, and a flawed man who seeks redemption through her. There are other parallels: The heroes of both films get a lot of their income from gambling, the actresses in both films are Swedish, gangsters control the world the characters live in. The most obvious difference between the two films—and this is the reason *Havana* is not better—is that *Casablanca* allows its key supporting character, the political idealist, to emerge more fully, and *Havana* sees him more as a backdrop to the stars.

Havana stars Robert Redford as Jack Weil, professional gambler come to Cuba in the waning days of the corrupt Batista regime, determined to find a high-stakes poker game and make a big score. He has a theory that high-rollers get reckless in times of political turmoil. Soon after he arrives in Havana—city of neon signs, garish casinos, corrupt officials and flashy Detroit convertibles—he meets Roberta Duran (Lena Olin), and of all of the gin rummy joints in the world, why did she have to walk into this one?

She is the wife of Arturo Duran (Raul Julia), a Communist with ties to Fidel Castro, who is up in the mountains, preaching revolution over a shortwave radio. Arturo is a good man. Jack Weil, on the other hand, is a cynical man, a manipulator who has played poker so long all his values can be expressed in a five-card hand. Their attraction is strongly physical, and when it appears that Arturo has been murdered by the police, she seeks consolation in Jack's arms. There is a moment when they plan to flee the country together and live happily in America. Then the political situation reaches a head, and Jack discovers that he may have values, after all.

There are so many parallels here with *Casablanca* that it's a wonder the screenplay, by Judith Rascoe and David Rayfiel, based on a story by Rascoe, doesn't credit the original 1942 screenplay. But the parallels don't make *Havana* a bad movie, and indeed there are powerful scenes here, as Redford and Olin make their characters complex and believable.

The central sequence of the film is one where Redford, foolhardy with love and idealism, drives his big Cadillac convertible out into the rebel-held countryside to look for Olin and try to save her from the coming storm. The sequence is implausible, and it's unlikely he could have survived that drive, but it's the kind of grand heroic gesture a story like this requires, and the scene they play together when they finally meet again is one of the best in the movie.

There are other good scenes, many of them involving Pollack's convincing, juicy re-creation of pre-Castro Havana (he filmed on sets and locations in the Dominican Republic). He peoples his Havana with bit players who embody some of the same seedy realism we remember from Greenstreet and Lorre in *Casablanca*. Guys like Joe Volpi

(Alan Arkin), who runs the local casino for the Mafia; the secret police chief Menocal (Tomas Milian), who has two scenes of startling power; Marion Chigwell (Daniel Davis), the CIA spook who pretends to be a travel writer; and, borrowed from real life, mob boss Meyer Lansky (Mark Rydell), who washes a lot of his dirty linen in public in a foolhardy scene where he chews out the casino boss while Redford is listening.

All of these characters, drifting through the background, lend color and authenticity to the story. Often they add echoes from *Casablanca*, too, as when Menocal's residual humanity reminds us of the local police official, Claude Rains, in *Casablanca*, or when Chigwell's prissiness recalls the whining of Lorre, as the man who needed a stronger man to help him.

But the key figure in the supporting cast should be Arturo Duran, the idealistic revolutionary played by Raul Julia, and here the screenplay lets us down. Duran, like the resistance leader played by Henreid in *Casablanca*, comes from a sophisticated, wealthy background. He has cast his lot with the masses. His attraction for women is idealistic, rather than physical; women are attracted to his goodness. And it is essential that the movie convince us of this, or the ending will not work. *Havana* did not convince me.

Remember, for a moment, the great ending of *Casablanca*. Movie legend has it that the screenplay was being rewritten day by day, that Ingrid Bergman had no idea whether she would eventually end up with Bogart or Henreid. Perhaps, but of course the movie could only end one way, because if Bogart and Bergman had placed their love ahead of Henreid's anti-Nazi ideals, we could not have liked them, and they could not have faced each other. So it is essential that the Henreid character be seen in a strong, courageous light.

That doesn't happen with the Julia character in *Havana*. Somehow he fails to emerge, to convince, to move us. We know that he's on the right side, we know what "should" happen in the movie, and yet his dialogue and screen time aren't enough to do the trick. Perhaps the sheer psychic presence of Redford's starring role tended to diminish Julia's presence in the movie. Too bad. For the hero's sacrifice to have any meaning at the end, the reasons for it must be clear and convincing. And although our minds may understand why the characters do what they do in *Havana*, there's a way in which our

hearts almost believe the lovers should have said the hell with it and jumped on that last plane to Las Vegas.

Hear My Song ★ ★ ★ ½
R, 104 m., 1992

Adrian Dunbar (Micky O'Neill), Ned Beatty (Josef Locke), William Hootkins (Mr. X), Tara Fitzgerald (Nancy), Shirley-Anne Field (Her Mother), David McCallum (Police Chief). Directed by Peter Chelsom and produced by Alison Owen-Allen. Screenplay by Chelsom and Adrian Dunbar.

There really was a Josef Locke, a legendary Irish singer who found it prudent to disappear for several years while the British tax boys were looking for him. And on that intriguing shred of fact, *Hear My Song* builds a romantic comedy of great charm. Locke is absent for most of the picture, but the search for him, like the search for Harry Lime in *The Third Man*, makes him grow in stature the longer he is absent from the screen.

The movie is set in Liverpool, where Micky, the inventive owner of a failing pub, keeps it open through increasingly desperate measures, such as advertising a concert by "Franc Cinatra." He is approached one day by a mysterious Mr. X, who claims to be the missing Josef Locke. The tenor's fans are legion in Liverpool, and so the owner (Adrian Dunbar) books Mr. X, who puts on a plausible deception but is unmasked as an impostor.

The pub patrons are outraged, but Micky has bigger problems at home, where his fiancée's mother (Shirley-Anne Field) was once, long ago, in love with Locke. She too was deceived by Mr. X, and so Micky feels he must go to Ireland on a mission of honor to find the real Josef Locke, wherever he may be. He has his work cut out for him; the locals in Ireland are so secretive they make Appalachian hillbillies look like talk show guests. But Dunbar appeals to them with the same kind of know-it-all charm used by Denis Lawson, as the man who seemed to hold every job in *Local Hero*.

All of this sounds like fodder for thirty minutes of sitcom, but not the way *Hear My Song* is directed by Peter Chelsom. He comes from that small band of British and Irish directors who embrace human comedy, who love the quirks and weaknesses of their characters, and like to make their points in small, sly asides. Within five minutes the movie has created the sense of a tight-knit community, and within half an hour it has created the considerable miracle of making us care whether Micky can find Josef Locke.

Locke, when he is found, is played by Ned Beatty, who won an Academy Award for his supporting work in *Network*, and who might seem an unlikely choice for an Irish tenor but plays the role with the robust presence of a man who, finding himself on a stage, would know exactly what to do there. The ending goes on a bit too long, but then, when you've spent a whole movie looking for a man, you're probably reluctant to leave him without an encore.

Hear My Song was cowritten by Chelsom and Dunbar, is their first feature, and is a labor of love as well as wit. Large parts of it are based on fact, according to the film's notes; not only was there a real Jo Locke who fled the British tax men, but there was a Mr. X, who teased club audiences for years with the ad line, "Is he or isn't he?" Chelsom was raised in the seaside town of Blackpool, where Locke performed for nineteen seasons, and many of the characters in the pub are drawn more or less from life.

I was in a discussion the other day about the concept of a "small film." We use the term as shorthand, but what does it mean? That a movie has no major explosions or special effects, I suppose, and contains no superstars. But perhaps also that it prefers to look at people closely and with love, instead of destroying dozens of them in high-speed chases. *Hear My Song* is the very soul of a great small film.

Heartbreakers ★ ★ ★ ½
R, 98 m., 1985

Peter Coyote (Arthur Blue), Nick Mancuso (Eli Kahn), Carole Laure (Liliane), Max Gail (King), Carol Wayne (Cathy), James Laurenson (Terry Ray), Jamie Rose (Libby), Kathryn Harrold (Cyd). Directed by Bobby Roth and produced by Bob Weis and Roth. Screenplay by Roth.

You can only play the field so long. Then you get stuck in it. You become a person so adept at avoiding commitment that it eventually becomes impossible for you to change your own rules, and so there you are, trapped in your precious freedom. Bobby Roth's *Heartbreakers* is about a group of people like that, a mixed bag of loners that includes a couple of artists, a businessman, a gallery owner, an aerobics instructor, and a model who specializes in telephone sex. During the course of a few weeks, their lives cross in ways that

make it particularly hard for each one of them to deny his own unhappiness.

The movie stars Peter Coyote as an angry young artist and Nick Mancuso as his best friend, a businessman who is confused about women and a great many other things. They've been pals for a long time, through good times and bad, but the one thing they've never been able to do is break down and talk about what they're really feeling. During the course of the film, they both fall in love with a beautiful young woman (Carole Laure) who works in an art gallery, and whose body is available but whose mind always seems to be somewhere else.

These three characters are in a movie populated with a lot of other interesting characters, the sort of mixed bag of people who find themselves thrown together in a big city like Los Angeles. Kathryn Harrold plays Coyote's longtime lover, who finally can't take his irresponsibility any longer and moves in with another artist (Max Gail), who is big and powerful but surprisingly gentle—his character is developed against type, in interesting ways. Jamie Rose plays an aerobics instructor who is attracted to Mancuso, but he is attracted to Laure, although not in a way that is likely to get him anywhere.

All of the threads of these lives seem to come together during one long night that Mancuso and Coyote spend with the busty, mid-thirties blonde who models for Coyote's kinky paintings. She is played by Carol Wayne, who had regular walk-ons on the Johnny Carson program until she drowned in Mexico not long after completing her work on this movie. Her performance is so good, so heartbreaking, if you will, that it pulls the whole movie together; her character's willingness to talk about what she really feels places the other characters in strong contrast.

When we first see her, she's an enigma at the edge of the screen—a seemingly dumb blonde who dresses up in leather to model for Coyote's strange, angry paintings. Later, the two men, adrift and unhappy about their respective love lives, end up in her apartment, and what begins as a *ménage à trois* ends up as her own startlingly direct confessional. She makes a frank assessment of her body, her appearance, her prospects. She talks about what she hoped for from life, and what she has received. There is an uncanny feeling that, to some degree, we are listening here to the real Carol Wayne, the real person beneath the image on the Carson show. It is one of the best movie scenes in a long time.

The rest of the movie is also very good, in the way it examines the complex relationships in its Los Angeles world of art, sex, and business, and in the way it shows how arid the Mancuso-Coyote buddy relationship is. The people in this movie might seem glamorous if you glimpsed just a small corner of their lives. But *Heartbreakers* sees them whole, and mercilessly.

The Heartbreak Kid ★ ★ ★ ½
PG, 106 m., 1972

Charles Grodin (Lenny), Cybill Shepherd (Kelly), Jeannie Berlin (Lila), Eddie Albert (Mr. Corcoran), Audra Lindley (Mrs. Corcoran). Directed by Elaine May and produced by Edgar J. Scherick. Screenplay by Neil Simon.

We know as early as the wedding scene—which opens the film—that Elaine May's *The Heartbreak Kid* was directed with a sure feeling for how comedy can edge over into satire and then tragedy. Both of Lila's parents are determined to give her away. They flank her, each clutching an arm, and attempt to march down the aisle in their living room. But it won't do: The folding chairs are too close together.

The honeymoon which follows is, to put it mildly, a disaster. Lenny begins to tire of his new bride during the drive to Miami Beach. She smears egg salad all over her face while eating a sandwich. She sings the same songs over and over. Somewhat ominously, she has saved herself for her wedding night.

In Miami Beach, disaster strikes. Lila gets a terrific sunburn and is confined to the hotel room, immersed in lotion and pain. Lenny goes down to the beach alone, spreads out his towel, stretches out, and is confronted by his destiny. His destiny is named Kelly. She is a blond Nordic goddess from Minnesota, dedicated to twisting men around her little finger as a form of mild amusement. Lenny is thunderstruck with love and decides on the spot that he must divorce Lila, journey to Minnesota, and marry this creature.

That is the premise of *The Heartbreak Kid*, and maybe only Elaine May and the author of the screenplay, Neil Simon, could make such a hurtful situation funny, and still somewhat true. The movie is about how we do violence to each other with our egos—how everybody does, except for the poor nebbishes like Lila. She does violence only to egg salad. The movie has a way of making us laugh while it hurts, because it makes Lenny into such a blunt object of egotism, desire, and upward mobility.

But in a lot of ways the most interesting character in the movie is Kelly (as played by Cybill Shepherd). She's so inapproachably beautiful that, in a way, all she *can* do with men is tease and taunt them—they're too hypnotized to treat her as if she were alive and accessible. She has a couple of husky athletes to carry her books, and a rich daddy who'd do anything for her (he's actually helpless when she smiles at him). And, inside, she hungers for love more, even, than Lenny.

Lenny is headed for heartbreak, all right, I don't think he really believes in the possibility of love—not for himself. He's into the acquisition of inaccessible goals; maybe the only reason he married Lila was because she *did* save herself. Now there are new peaks to climb. But Lenny's victories are so lonely; we see him at the movie's end, confronted with the fact that he would rather desire than possess.

Jeannie Berlin (Elaine May's daughter) is wonderful as Lila. She has enough acting confidence to be able to go too far and still make us believe; she can get away with smearing that egg salad around for several seconds after common sense says she should stop. Charles Grodin, as her husband, is good as a kind of Dustin Hoffman-as-overachiever; in this role we can find the genesis of many of his later roles.

The movie doesn't constantly bow to Neil Simon's script (as most movie versions of his work do). Elaine May is willing to improvise, to indulge (and exploit) quirks in acting style, and to examine social hypocrisy with a kind of compulsive ferocity. It's a comedy, but there's more in it than that; it's a movie about the ways we pursue, possess, and consume each other as sad commodities.

Heartbreak Ridge ★ ★ ★
R, 130 m., 1986

Clint Eastwood (Highway), Marsha Mason (Aggie), Everett McGill (Major Powers), Moses Gunn (Sergeant Webster), Eileen Heckart (Little Mary), Bo Svenson (Roy Jennings), Mario Van Peebles (Stitch), Peter Koch (Swede). Directed and produced by Clint Eastwood. Screenplay by James Carabatsos.

Clint Eastwood's *Heartbreak Ridge* uses an absolutely standard plot, and makes it special with its energy, its colorful characters, and its almost poetic vulgarity. We have seen

this story in a hundred other movies, where the combat-hardened veteran, facing retirement, gets one last assignment to train a platoon of green kids and lead them into battle. But Eastwood, as the producer, director, and star, caresses the material as if he didn't know B movies have gone out of style.

He plays a gunnery sergeant named Tom Highway, universally known as Gunny, a hard-drinking loser who has sacrificed everything—wife, family, friends, reputation—on the altar of the Corps. We meet him in a title sequence that seems directly inspired by *Dirty Harry;* he's in a drunk tank, smoking a cigar and telling tall tales, when a brawny giant attacks him. Eastwood hands his cigar to a bystander, creams the bully, and reaches for his cigar again (just as Dirty Harry finishes eating his hot dog after the opening shoot-out).

The opening scene promises his fans that *Heartbreak Ridge* will provide the violent Eastwood persona they have come to love. What's surprising is that Eastwood doesn't let Tom Highway stride through the picture beating up everybody in sight, and winning the war single-handedly. Instead, the movie is more of a tour through Highway's memories, a last hurrah for a combat veteran who won the Medal of Honor when he was a kid, and has been trying to lose it ever since.

Highway gets assigned to his old outfit, has a reunion with the veteran master sergeant he fought with in Korea, and is chewed out by the Annapolis grad (Everett McGill) who now heads the battalion and wants to run everything by the book. Highway is assigned to a platoon of misfits and malcontents, including a bright black kid (Mario Van Peebles), who wants to be a rock-and-roll singer, and a gigantic Swede (Peter Koch), who he is going to have to fight if he wants to win control of his new command.

There is also the reunion with his former wife (Marsha Mason), who couldn't take the weeks and months of waiting at home, watching the evening news for a glimpse of her husband in Vietnam. We can almost predict her dialogue; Highway was always more married to the Corps than he was to her.

The movie has a brisk, rough-and-tumble pace, with a knock-down fight every fifteen minutes or so. Highway may be over fifty, but of course he can still outfight any man alive, and there is one brutal scene in which he stands his ground and simply outtalks an opponent, his words as hard as his fists.

Nothing in *Heartbreak Ridge* is very subtle,

and I wasn't surprised to learn that the shooting schedule lasted less than eight weeks—lightning speed for a movie including basic training and combat scenes. There is a certain raw energy in filmmaking at this pace, however; the actors swagger through their roles instead of chewing them, and there is never more subtlety than the plot can support.

It's easy to spot Eastwood, the director, as he cuts corners. The battalion only seems to support two platoons, for example, and its base seems limited to a few quonset huts. Even the climactic battle scenes are budget-basement: Highway leads his men into action on Grenada, where they liberate some medical students.

And yet *Heartbreak Ridge* has as much energy and color as any action picture of 1986, and it contains truly amazing dialogue. Some people may be offended by the scatological and ancestral generalities in Highway's speech, but I was mostly amused by his flights of verbal invention. (The U.S. Marine Corps intended to use this film at benefits for its "Toys for Tots" program, but withdrew its support after screening it, presumably because the characters talked too much like Marines.)

Heartbreak Ridge is Eastwood's thirteenth picture as a director, and by now he is a seasoned veteran behind the camera. He has starred in all but one of his films, and who knows Eastwood better? This time he makes himself look old, ragged, and scarred, with a lot of miles behind him. He uses harsh lighting to make his face into a fierce icon. He speaks in a low rasp. He seems to be aiming for the kind of scuzzy, fast-paced vitality of a low-budget Sam Fuller picture, and he gets it. *Heartbreak Ridge* doesn't aim as high as most current high-tech action movies, but it hits its target.

Heartland ★ ★ ★ ★
PG, 95 m., 1981

Conchata Ferrell (Elinore Randall), Rip Torn (Clyde Stewart), Barry Primus (Jack), Lilia Skala (Grandma), Megan Folsom (Jerrine). Directed by Richard Pearce and produced by Annick Smith, Michael Hausman, and Beth Ferris. Screenplay by Ferris.

Richard Pearce's *Heartland* is a big, robust, joyous movie about people who make other movie heroes look tentative. It takes place in 1910, out in the unsettled frontier lands of Wyoming, and it's about a determined young widow who packs up her daughter and moves out West to take a job as the housekeeper on a ranch. At first she is completely baffled by the rancher who has hired her ("I can't talk about anything with that man"), but in the end she marries him and digs in to fight an endless battle with the seasons, the land, and the banks.

A movie newcomer named Conchata Ferrell plays the widow, Elinore Randall. She's a big-boned, clear-eyed, wide-hipped woman of about thirty who makes us realize that most of the women in Westerns look as if they're about to collapse under the strain. She is extremely clear about her motivations. She gives a full day's work for a full day's pay, but she is tired of working for others, and would like to own her own land someday. She does not, however, speak endlessly about her beliefs and ambitions, because *Heartland* is a movie of few words. That is partly because of the character of Clyde Stewart (Rip Torn), the rancher she goes to work for. He hardly ever says anything. He is a hard man, a realist who knows that the undisciplined Western land can break his back. But he is not unkind, and in the scene where he finally proposes to marry her, his choice of words contains understated wit that makes us smile.

Everything in this movie affirms life. Perhaps that is why *Heartland* can also be so unblinking in its consideration of death. The American West was not settled by people who spent all their time baking peach cobbler and knitting samplers, and this movie contains several scenes that will shock some audiences because of their forthright realism. We see a pig slaughtered, a calf birthed, cattle skinned, and a half-dead horse left out in the blizzard because there is simply nothing to feed it.

All of *Heartland* is stunningly photographed on and around a Montana ranch. (The movie is based on the real life of a settler named Elinore Randall Stewart.) It contains countless small details of farming life, put in not for "atmosphere" but because they work better than dialogue to flesh out the characters. The desolation of the frontier is suggested in small vignettes, such as one involving a family that could get this far and no farther, and lives huddled inside a small wagon. Among the many scenes that delight us with their freshness is one moment right after the wedding, when Ferrell realizes she got married wearing her apron and work boots, and another when she is about to give birth and her husband rides off into the

storm to fetch the midwife from the next farm. We settle back here in anticipation of the obligatory scene in which the midwife arrives and immediately orders everyone to boil hot water, lots of it—but this time we're surprised. The husband returns alone; the midwife was not at her farm. Quiet little developments like that help expose the weight of cliché that holds down most Westerns.

In a movie filled with wonderful things, the very best thing in *Heartland* is Conchata Ferrell's voice. It is strong, confident, clear as a bell, and naturally musical. It is a fine instrument, bringing authenticity to every word it says. It puts this movie to a test, because we could not quite accept that voice saying words that sounded phony and contrived. In *Heartland,* we never have to.

Hearts of Darkness ★ ★ ★ ½
NO MPAA RATING, 97 m., 1991

Featuring Francis Ford Coppola, Eleanor Coppola, Martin Sheen, Marlon Brando, Dennis Hopper, and Robert Duvall. A documentary directed and written by Fax Bahr and George Hickenlooper, with footage and commentary by Eleanor Coppola.

The making of a film has never been documented with more penetration and truth than in *Hearts of Darkness*, which chronicles the agony and the ecstasy of Francis Ford Coppola's *Apocalypse Now.* That is because no other documentary has ever had access to materials that are normally off limits: shots that were never used, scenes that were abandoned, private arguments between the director and his actors, cries for help and confessions of despair, and even conversations between Coppola and his wife that she secretly tape-recorded.

The film strips Coppola bare of all defenses and yet reveals him as a great and brave filmmaker. It also reveals the ordeal he put his actors and crew through, on location in the Philippines, and what he endured at their hands. We see a drunken and bloodied Martin Sheen improvising a breakdown while the room is charged with the possibility that he will attack Coppola or his camera. Sheen being given first aid after a serious heart attack. Coppola screaming in outrage that Sheen's condition has been leaked to the trade papers and the news could pull the plug on the production: "Even if he dies, I don't want to hear anything but good news until it comes from me." Dennis Hopper, his mind adrift on drugs, unable to remember his lines and yet impro-

vising brilliantly. Marlon Brando, at $1 million a week, turning up without preparation and engaging in endless debates with Coppola about his character. Brando beginning a scene, then wandering off while the camera is still running, and mumbling, ". . . and that's all the dialogue I can think of today."

Apocalypse Now premiered in 1979 at Cannes, shared the Palme d'Or, and went on to become one of the great mythic productions in film history. It told a story about Vietnam that was inspired by Joseph Conrad's great novella *Heart of Darkness*, about a journey up the Congo River in search of a man named Kurtz. In the film, Sheen commands a Navy patrol boat that penetrates a Vietnamese river in search of Colonel Kurtz (Brando), who has set himself up as the god of a tribe of jungle Indians.

Apocalypse Now is one of the greatest films ever made, and legends have grown up around it. Coppola, at a tumultuous press conference at Cannes in 1979, famously said, "My film is not about Vietnam. My film is Vietnam." He also confessed he did not think the ending worked. Now we see what he was talking about.

The script, written by John Milius and originally set to be directed by George Lucas, went through so many changes that finally Coppola was writing it as he shot it, and actors were improvising. The production was bedeviled by monsoons, destroyed sets, huge cost overruns, health problems, and logistical nightmares, as when the Philippine government of Ferdinand Marcos tried to rent Coppola the same helicopters it was using to fight rebels ten miles away. Brando put Coppola under enormous pressure by turning up without having read *Heart of Darkness* and refusing to be shot except in shadow.

And Coppola, in conversations he did not know were being recorded, shouted in despair to his wife, Eleanor: "I tell you from the bottom of my heart that I am making a bad film." And again, "We are all lost. I have no idea where to go with this."

Yet Coppola's vision somehow remained secure. Milius, flown to the Philippines by a desperate United Artists to try to bring sanity back to the script, remembers that he walked in prepared to convince Coppola that the war was lost and they had to salvage what they could. After ninety minutes, he says, "Francis had me convinced this would be the first film to win the Nobel Prize."

Hearts of Darkness, written and directed

by Fax Bahr and George Hickenlooper, is based on documentary footage that Eleanor Coppola shot at the time, and on recent interviews with both Coppolas, plus Milius, Lucas, and actors Martin Sheen, Frederic Forrest, Robert Duvall, Dennis Hopper, Timothy Bottoms, and Larry Fishburne, who incredibly was only fourteen when he played one of the patrol boat crew. Eleanor's secret tape recordings were also made available, and the result is fascinating, harrowing film history. We feel for once we are witnessing the true story of how a movie got made.

See also Burden of Dreams, *Les Blank's documentary about the no-less-legendary filming of Werner Herzog's* Fitzcarraldo.

Heat and Dust ★ ★ ★
R, 130 m., 1983

Julie Christie (Anne), Zakir Hussain (Inder Lal), Greta Scacchi (Olivia), Shashi Kapoor (The Nawab). Directed by James Ivory and produced by Ismail Merchant. Screenplay by Ruth Prawer Jhabvala.

Forster suggested in *A Passage to India* that the subcontinent would forever be beyond the understanding of Western minds, and that attempts to impose European ways upon it were bound to be futile and likely to be ridiculous. *Heat and Dust* makes the same argument by telling us two love stories, one set in the 1920s, the other set in the present day.

The heroine of the earlier love story is Olivia Rivers (Greta Scacchi), a free spirit whose independent ways do not fit in with the hidebound values of the British. Her husband demands that she conform, that she stay with the other British wives, share their values and interests, and keep India itself at arm's length. Olivia does not see it that way. She explores on her own. She becomes fascinated by India. Eventually she has an affair with the local Nawab (Shashi Kapoor), who is beguiling, attractive, cheerfully sophisticated, and possibly a murderer. When she becomes pregnant with his child, the whole fabric of British-Indian relationships is torn, because—depending on the point of view—*both* of the lovers have lowered themselves.

The second love story involves Olivia's great-niece, Anne (Julie Christie). Fascinated by hints about the long-ago family scandal, she follows Olivia's footsteps out to India and does her own exploring and has her own affair. There comes a moment in the movie when we realize, with a little shock, what the movie is really about. It's an effective scene; soon after Anne arrives at a decision about her own pregnancy, she visits the isolated cottage where the disgraced Olivia went for her confinement.

As Anne dreamily moves among the memories of the past, we realize that India and England, the East and the West, are not quite the issues here: that both women were made social outcasts from both societies in two different periods, simply because of biological facts. East is East and West is West, and never the twain shall meet—except possibly in a shared enthusiasm for sexist double standards.

Heat and Dust contains wonderful sights and sounds and textures. It is seductive, treating both of its love stories with seriousness; these are not romances, but decisions to dissent. It is fully at home in its times and places (the director, James Ivory, and the producer, Ismail Merchant, have spent twenty years making films about the British in India). And when it is over, we're a little surprised to find that it is angry, too. Angry that women of every class and every system, women British and Indian, women of the 1920s and of the 1980s, are always just not quite the same caste as men.

Heaven and Earth ★ ★ ★ ½
R, 138 m., 1993

Hiep Thi Le (Le Ly), Tommy Lee Jones (Steve Butler), Joan Chen (Mama), Dr. Haing S. Ngor (Papa), Debbie Reynolds (Eugenia). Directed by Oliver Stone and produced by Stone, Arnon Milchan, Robert Kline, and A. Kitman Ho. Screenplay by Stone.

She is born into a time of tranquillity, in which the people of her village live as they have for many centuries. All is ordered; everyone has his place, including the ancestors who are buried on land that has been in the same family since time immemorial. Then a warplane streaks across the sky, and in an instant all she knows is destroyed. Her name is Le Ly, and her destiny will take her from the rice fields of the Central Highlands to the suburban split-levels of California.

Oliver Stone has made films about Vietnam from the point of view of a combat infantryman and a disabled veteran, and now in *Heaven and Earth* he completes his trilogy by viewing the war through the eyes of a Vietnamese woman. The story is factual, as were Stone's *Platoon* (1986), inspired by his own combat in Vietnam, and *Born on the Fourth of July* (1989), based on the autobiography of Ron Kovic. *Heaven and Earth* is based on two books by Le Ly Hayslip, who is now a successful Vietnamese-American businesswoman in California.

Stone is not known for his films about women. From *Salvador* through *Talk Radio, Wall Street, The Doors,* and *JFK,* he has made films about men to whom women were a pleasant but not central element of life. This is the first time he has tried to place himself inside a woman's imagination, and that he succeeds so well is due partly, I think, to an extraordinary performance by Hiep Thi Le, in the leading role. She was born in Vietnam, came to America as a child, knows both worlds, and is able to reflect the disorientation of a woman whose life and values are placed in turmoil.

Seeing the war through her eyes, watching as foreign troops march across the fields of her family, we are asked by Stone to see how fundamentally wrongheaded the American strategy in Vietnam was. The overarching goal was to win the "hearts and minds" of the Vietnamese people. To this end, we uprooted them from the land of their ancestors, and herded them into "strategic hamlets" designed to keep the Viet Cong out, although they functioned more like enclosures to keep the occupants in. This experience actually encouraged them to identify with the Cong, who understood the same values.

For ordinary farmers who wanted only to tend their crops, the war brought horrible choices. We watch as Le Ly's village is visited both by Viet Cong propagandists and American and South Vietnamese advisers. We see her savagely mistreated by men from both sides, who effortlessly translate their patriotic zeal into the act of rape. We see her separated from her family, joining aimless columns of refugees, and finding herself in Saigon as part of an economy where the Americans have all the money, and what a lot of them are buying is sex and drugs.

Into her life one day comes a tall, craggy American named Steve Butler (Tommy Lee Jones), who does not want her as a prostitute, but as a bride. He is gentle, understanding, persistent, although perhaps if she had been less desperate she should have been able to distinguish a disturbing note when he vowed, "I want an *oriental* wife." His image of her is hopelessly entangled with his own guilt and fear, his inner demons, his need for a woman who will simultaneously forgive him and surrender to him.

Le Ly returns to America as Mrs. Steve Butler, to a land where the supermarket shelves seem to reach endlessly in every direction and the in-laws regard her as something between a scandal and a pet. (One of her American relatives is played, in a bit of wicked casting, by Debbie Reynolds.) Le Ly has trouble adjusting, but not as much trouble as her husband, who finds that his training and twenty years as a "military adviser" have left him hopelessly unsuited to civilian life. In these scenes, Jones draws on an earlier character, the Vietnam veteran he played in Lynne Littman's underrated *Rolling Thunder* (1977). He shows his gift for creating characters who are never more frightening than when they are being nice.

In a time when few American directors are drawn toward political controversy, Stone seeks it out. He loves big subjects and approaches them fearlessly. The Vietnam War is the most important event in recent American history, but only Stone has made it his business as a filmmaker.

Movies are not the best way to make a reasoned argument. For that you need the written word, which can be pinned down, footnoted, double-checked, and debated. Movies traffic in emotions. They are about the ways things look and feel. In *Platoon*, *Born on the Fourth of July*, and now *Heaven and Earth*, Stone has tried to let us look through eyes that saw three elements of the war. The first film was about a patriotic young American who went to fight it. The second saw the confused and demoralized aftermath of the war through the eyes of a paralyzed veteran whose country wished to forget him. Now comes a woman who represents all of the ordinary people who wanted only to get on with their ordinary lives.

It is no secret that Stone thinks the Vietnam War was a tragedy for everyone concerned. But he doesn't make the Viet Cong into the good guys here; they are brutal, arbitrary, sadistic. Americans also commit atrocities (we see possible informers being forced to watch their friends being dropped out of helicopters). The conclusion seems to be that Vietnam was a particularly unwholesome and misguided war, one which those who did not come from the land were inevitably destined to lose.

But Le Ly is also, of course, an outsider when her husband brings her to America. There is one area where I wish Stone had given us more information, and that involves her later life in the United States. She has stayed here, written two books, and prospered. We see the beginnings of that process, as she borrows money from fellow Vietnamese to start a deli. To lose everything, to come to a strange land and make herself a success, was her victory, in her war.

Heavenly Creatures ★ ★ ★ ½
R, 99 m., 1994   **NEW**

Melanie Lynskey (Pauline Parker), Kate Winslet (Juliet Hulme), Sarah Peirse (Honora Parker), Diana Kent (Hilda Hulme), Clive Merrison (Henry Hulme), Simon O'Connor (Herbert Rieper). Directed by Peter Jackson and produced by Jim Booth. Screenplay by Jackson.

New Zealand was stunned in 1952 by a brutal murder carried out by two teenage girls, ages fifteen and sixteen, who crushed the skull of one of their mothers with a rock. It was whispered at the time that the girls had a lesbian relationship; but since almost everyone involved, including the girls, knew very little about what that might entail, the subject was suppressed. Tried and sentenced, the girls served five years in prison before being paroled on the condition that they never see each other again.

Their story, based on facts but interpreted with a great deal of freedom, is the inspiration for *Heavenly Creatures*, a film by Peter Jackson. The film would be remarkable anyway, but comes with a new footnote attached: One of the girls, Juliet Hulme, has been identified as Anne Perry, the bestselling British crime novelist. Watching her on the "Today" program, talking forthrightly about the events of forty years ago, I got the impression of a sensible, thoughtful woman, for whom the original murder was as much an enigma as everyone else.

The movie shows the crime as resulting from a tragic confluence of coincidences: Two girls, both emotionally unstable in just the right way to complement each other's weaknesses, are outsiders in a Christchurch girls' school. They become fast friends, bound by a fascination for the macabre. Simple, stolid Pauline is dazzled by Juliet, who thinks nothing of correcting the French teacher during class. But Pauline has status in Juliet's eyes, too, not least because of a scar on her leg, after an operation for bone disease: "All the best people have had chest and bone disease! It's all frightfully romantic!"

Almost everything is frightfully romantic in the lives of these girls, who become inseparable, sharing crushes on the tenor Mario Lanza and such movie stars as Orson Welles. They become intoxicated by their friendship, rushing headlong everywhere, with squeals and giggles, giddy with delight at the private world they are creating. Their parents are out of the loop—especially Juliet's mother, a psychologist who is much more concerned with proving her own fading sexuality than with communicating with her daughter.

The girls are separated when one contracts tuberculosis. They begin to write each other long, detailed letters, involving the events in an imaginary country they have created, with dream castles and heroic figures they identify with. Jackson uses fantasy sequences to make this world as real for us as it is to the girls, who inhabit it as an alternative to the daily lives they find dreary.

Adults grow disturbed by the closeness of the girls; lesbianism is suspected by people for whom the very word itself cannot be spoken. Indeed we can see, in awkward little scenes where they wrestle together or exchange "accidental" kisses, that there is a strong bond between Juliet and Pauline, but whether it is homosexual or asexual is not for anyone in this movie to ask, or understand. In any event, it is decided the girls "see too much" of each other, and would "benefit by a change," and in terror at being separated the girls plan and carry out a horrible murder—ironically, of the mother who is kinder and more open.

Casting is a delicate matter in telling a story like this, and in Melanie Lynskey as Pauline and Kate Winslet as Juliet, Jackson has found the right two actresses. There is a way Lynskey has of looking up from beneath glowering eyebrows that lets you know her insides are churning. And Juliet, superficially so "bright" and normal, laughs too much, agrees too quickly, always exists just this side of hysteria.

The insight of *Heavenly Creatures* is that sometimes people are capable of committing acts together that they could not commit by themselves. A mob can be as small as two persons. Reading in the paper about a crowd of teenage boys who beat an innocent youth to death, I was reminded of this film. Sometimes tragedies happen because each person is waiting for someone else to say "no!"

In the case of Pauline and Juliet, that truth is complicated by their own emotional maladjustments. What makes Jackson's film enthralling and frightening is the way it shows these two unhappy girls, creating out of their imaginations an alternative world so safe and attractive they thought it was worth killing for.

Henry and June ★ ★ ★
NC-17, 134 m., 1990

Fred Ward (Henry Miller), Uma Thurman (June Miller), Maria de Medeiros (Anais Nin), Richard E. Grant (Hugo), Kevin Spacey (Osborn), Jean-Philippe Ecoffey (Eduardo). Directed by Philip Kaufman and produced by Peter Kaufman. Screenplay by Philip Kaufman and Rose Kaufman.

Henry Miller was the most notorious author of his generation, but unlike his predecessors in scandal like Lawrence and Joyce there was always some doubt about the quality of his writing. Yes, he was dirty, but was he very good? The irony about *Henry and June,* this odd film about Miller and his wife and the triangle they formed for a time with Anais Nin, is that circumstances force me to put the question in the opposite way: Yes, it's good, but is it very dirty?

This is the film that finally inspired the revision of the American movie ratings, and was the first film assigned to the new category of NC-17—admission limited to adults only. Why? Not because of its sexual content, I suspect, so much as because of the matter-of-fact way it accepts the unconventional sexual maneuvering of its three couples. Americans seem more comfortable with sex when it's lurid and thrill-soaked, as in the R-rated works of David Lynch. When adults are seen freely and calmly making unorthodox sexual decisions, we get all aflutter: Good heavens, they're taking this for granted!

Censors by their nature are happier with sex when it is presented as sin, with red neon signs flickering through the slats on the window, and the music panting with passion. That shows the artists think their material is as excitingly immoral as the censors do. When an artist presents sexual material in an everyday manner, however, censors are offended, because that makes their jobs seem like less of a big deal. So they grow grave and perturbed, and we get the NC-17 rating when, for this film, an R would have been just fine.

What we have here is essentially a story of innocents abroad. Miller was the quintessential expatriate in that he never really felt at home anywhere except in America, and his restlessness in Paris, his astonishment at the sexual freedoms of the French, always seemed a little like the reaction of the proverbial farm boy in gay Paree. Read his books and you will find them dripping with the wonderful American qualities of enthusiasm, exaggeration, naivete, and envy. Read between the lines of his scenes of sexual descriptions, his breathless accounts of the exploits of his inexhaustable hero, and you will find a soldier boy writing home to his pals that they sure got a lot of loose wimmen in Paree.

Philip Kaufman's *Henry and June* is based loosely on a period in the 1930s when Miller fell into the orbit of Anais Nin, the great free spirit of her Parisian literary generation, the inexhaustable diarist who seldom had an unrecorded experience and who indeed, is seen here writing journal entries while between the sheets, if not literally while engaged in the acts she is recording.

Miller was in Paris with the intention of becoming a great author, pure and simple, and he rented a garret and filled it with the sound of typewriting and clouds of cigarette smoke, which is what all writers were then required to do. In between, he hung out in cafés and moved in bohemian circles and became an intellectual—which is the word for someone whose primary activity consists of describing his secondary activities.

Miller was married at the time to June, an American expected in Paris momentarily, but he had an affair, or sort of an affair, with Nin, and then when June arrived, she and Anais got along very well and Miller, for a time, formed the third part of the triangle. What they did in bed, doubly and triply, is depicted by Kaufman in scenes of wit and some restraint; this is not a "sex film," which is why the tarnished X-rating would have been so wrong for it.

Fred Ward is at the center of the film. He is an actor who specializes in being particularly American, and in films like *The Right Stuff, Uforia,* and *Miami Blues,* he has provided the kind of open-eyed, virile innocence that Miller projected in many of his books. If he does not always seem at home in *Henry and June,* perhaps it is because it is almost impossible to play a writer. Either you show him not writing, which misses the point, or you show him typing away furiously and racing into cafés with his manuscript, which makes him seem like some nutty kid you knew in high school.

June is played by Uma Thurman, from *Dangerous Liaisons,* as an enigma: How did she get to be so much cooler and more worldly than Miller, and what does she really think about her husband? Anais Nin is played by Maria De Medeiros, petite and large-eyed, absorbed in herself, a mystery, seeking material, it almost seems, as fodder for her journals. The three characters and their friends meet, talk, love, talk, argue, talk, are hurt, shift their loyalties, and in general seem to be test-driving new experiences. They lead the kinds of lives that make them seem very grown-up at the time, and very young later.

Henry and June is likely to be a little puzzling for those not familiar with Nin and Miller. It's hard to find the purpose of the film, not always easy to care about the characters, and what we learn about the written work of the two writers in the movie does not send us to a bookstore in search of volumes we have missed. And yet the film has a charm, the same charm that Miller had: The wide-eyed eagerness in the face of experience, the touching belief that in the physical we can find the spiritual.

Henry V ★ ★ ★ ½
NO MPAA RATING, 138 m., 1989

Kenneth Branagh (Henry V), Derek Jacobi (Chorus), Emma Thompson (Katharine), Michael Maloney (Dauphin), Robbie Coltrane (Falstaff), Richard Briers (Bardolph), Judi Dench (Mistress Quickly), Alec McCowen (Ely), Ian Holm (Fleullen), Richard Innocent (Burgundy), Fabian Cartwright (Cambridge). Directed by Kenneth Branagh and produced by Stephen Evans. Screenplay by Branagh.

Shakespeare's *Henry V* is a favorite play of the British in times of national crisis, and in 1944, during the darkest days of World War II, Laurence Olivier directed and starred in it as a patriotic call to the barricades. Perhaps it is no coincidence that another hot-blooded Turk of the London stage, Kenneth Branagh, directed and starred in this new film version in 1989, as Britain stood poised uneasily on the banks of the new Europe, its toe dipped shyly into the waters of monetary union.

There is no more stirring summons to arms in all of literature than Henry's speech to his troops on St. Crispian's Day, ending with the lyrical "We few, we happy few, we band of brothers." To deliver this speech successfully is to pass the acid test for anyone daring to perform the role of Henry V in public, and as Kenneth Branagh, as Henry, stood up on the dawn of the Battle of Agincourt and delivered the famous words, I was emotionally stirred even though I had heard them many times before. That is one mark of a great Shakespearean actor: to take the familiar and make it new.

Branagh is not yet thirty, and yet already the publicity machines are groaning to make him into the "new Olivier." Before his *Henry V*, he had made only one other movie (he was the sunburned young husband in *High Season*), but he has triumphed on the London stage in such talismanic roles as Jimmy Porter in Osborne's *Look Back in Anger* and his stock could not be higher. It was a risk to make this film, and it could have been a disastrous failure, but instead it is a success.

That it is not a triumph is because Branagh the director is not yet as good as Branagh the actor. He knows better how to play Henry V than how to get him on the screen, and his pacing could be improved. The film begins slowly, bogs down in the seemingly endless battle scenes, and then drags to its conclusion through Henry's endlessly protracted and coy courtship of Katharine.

Branagh himself seems to know that the opening sequences—involving a rebellion in the English court—are in trouble, and he attempts to speed them along with distractingly intrusive music, which only gets in the way of the words. Part of the problem is in Shakespeare, who dawdles with diplomatic matters before getting to the heart of his story. Olivier dealt with this problem in his 1944 film by facing it humorously. As the French ambassador and others squabble over boundaries and treaties, a frisky wind blows their documents around the stage. In Branagh, all is solemn and hard to follow.

One of the wonders of Shakespeare's prose is that, spoken by actors who understand the meaning of the words, it is almost as comprehensible today as when it was first written. In the Olivier film, the actors are better at making the words make sense, perhaps because, for Olivier, clarity of communication ranked above anything else in a performance. Branagh and his actors go for emotion or styles of delivery at the cost of clarity, and so the new *Henry V* is more appropriate for viewers familiar with the play; Olivier's version was literally intended for everyone.

And yet, these observations aside, Branagh has made quite a film here. His Henry V has a spectacular entrance, backlit and framed by huge palace doors, and is a king from beginning to end (the youthful transgressions with Falstaff are firmly behind him). He is not a tall and dashing king—Branagh looks something like Jimmy Cagney—but he is a brave and stubborn one, and Branagh's direction wisely goes for realism in the battle scenes. They are not wars of words but of swords.

The famous British victory over the French at the Battle of Agincourt was Henry's and Medieval England's greatest triumph (although Shakespeare could not resist improving on the facts in the scene where Henry is informed of ten thousand French deaths as opposed to only twenty-nine on the English side). In the film, Branagh seems determined to account for every French death, and the battle wears on, steel against steel and horse against man, endlessly. There is too much of it—as if, having spent all the money for those extras and all those costumes, he wanted to get his money's worth. And yet, at the end, when the exhausted king confesses, "I know not if the day be ours or no," we share his exhaustion and his despair at bloodshed.

Branagh's approach depends on blood and thunder, as opposed to Olivier's insouciance. Even though Olivier made his film in the midst of a world war, it is probably true to say that we live in a more violent time today. Certainly our films are more violent, and in a sense Branagh is only keeping up with the state of the art when he soaks his battles in blood and mud. What happens as a result is that the scenes in court seem to exist on a different level of reality—especially the long scene of flirtation and proposal between Henry and Katharine, which ends the film. We have seen so much real blood that we have no patience for affected social gamesmanship, and the movie would probably play better if Henry had simply swept Katharine into his arms and forgotten the elaborate phrase-making.

What works best in the film is the overall vision. Branagh is able to see himself as a king, and so we can see him as one. He schemes, he jests, and he deceives his soldiers during his famous tour of the field on the night before the battle. In victory he is humble, and in romance uncertain. Olivier, who was thirty-seven in 1944, wrote that Henry V was the kind of role he couldn't have played when he was younger: "When you are young, you are too bashful to play a hero; you debunk it." For Branagh, twenty-eight is old enough.

Henry: Portrait of a Serial Killer ★ ★ ★ ½
NO MPAA RATING, 90 m., 1986

Michael Rooker (Henry), Tom Towles (Ottis), Tracy Arnold (His Sister). Directed by John McNaughton and produced by Waleed Ali. Screenplay by Richard Fire.

Filmed in 1986 and trapped in the movie rating system for three years, a movie named *Henry* finally came into wider view in the autumn of 1989. The story of a pathological mass murderer, it was told in such flat, unforgiving realism that it inspired angry debates after its screenings at film festivals and midnight cult screenings. Some viewers feel it is evil incarnate; others say it is superb filmmaking. The MPAA denied it an R rating (and said, indeed, that no possible cuts could qualify it for an R movie), so it was eventually released with no rating at all.

Henry was filmed during the winter of 1985–86 by a Chicago director named John McNaughton, on a budget of $125,000, using unknown actors from the free-wheeling Organic Theater Company. Loosely inspired by the confessions, since recanted, of a self-described mass murderer named Henry Lucas, the film uses a slice-of-life approach to create a docu-drama of chilling horror.

Unlike typical "slasher" movies, *Henry* does not employ humor, campy in-jokes, or a colorful antihero. Filmed in the gray slush and wet winter nights of Chicago's back alleys, honky-tonk bars, and drab apartments, it tells of a drifter who kills strangers, efficiently and without remorse. The movie contains scenes of heartless and shocking violence, committed by characters who seem to lack the ordinary feelings of common humanity.

Henry drifted in a cinematic no-man's-land after it was first seen publicly in a video version at the 1986 Chicago film festival. It played at midnight screenings in New York (where the *Village Voice*'s Elliott Stein called it one of the best American films of the year) but could not gain mass distribution without the R rating.

The title role in *Henry* is played with unrelenting power by Michael Rooker, who has since gone on to major Hollywood movies (he was the redneck who confronts Gene Hackman in *Mississippi Burning,* and the killer in *Sea of Love*). Organic Theater veteran Tom Towles plays the equally chilling role of Ottis, a casual friend who casually drifts into murder, and Tracy Arnold is Ottis's sister, a teen-age stripper who knows Henry killed his mother, and finds the fact intriguing.

In the film Henry becomes the roommate of Ottis, a parolee working in a gas station, and then the sister arrives from out of town and moves in. She is fascinated by Henry's stories of violence. Ottis, who may have a homosexual interest in Henry, eventually goes along with him in a series of brutal killings, including one where they pretend to have car trouble and then shoot a good samaritan, and another where they invade a home and videotape the murder of an entire family. The videotape scene appalls many viewers, but at least it shows *Henry* dealing honestly with its subject matter, instead of trying to sugar-coat violence as most "slasher" films do.

The director, McNaughton, is a onetime Chicago ad executive who dropped out for a few years to work in a traveling carnival, build sailboats in New Orleans, and tend bar in Homewood before getting into film by directing music videos. He raised the budget for *Henry* from Waleed Ali, a Chicago home-video executive, who wanted a horror film but was reportedly surprised when McNaughton gave him the real thing instead of an easy teenage exploitation film. Ali's surprise has been reflected wherever the film has been shown.

At the Telluride festival, where I saw it in September 1989, some said the film was too violent and disgusting to be endured. Others said it was justified because of its uncompromising honesty in a world where most horror films cheapen death by trivializing it. The division seemed to be between those who felt the film did its job brilliantly, and those who felt its job should not have been done at all.

The Hidden ★ ★ ★
R, 98 m., 1987

Michael Nouri (Tom Beck), Kyle MacLachlan (Lloyd Gallagher), Ed O'Ross (Cliff Willis), Clu Gulager (Ed Flynn), Claudia Christian (Brenda Lee), Clarence Felder (John Masterson). Directed by Jack Sholder and produced by Robert Shaye. Screenplay by Bob Hunt.

The Hidden opens with a brutal bank robbery and a violent chase scene, and for a moment I thought I was in for another routine cop movie, but then I saw the funny look in the eyes of the bank robber, and I wasn't so sure. Here was a guy who seemed to be receiving secret transmissions. Aiming his car at a police barricade, he allowed a little smile to flicker on his lips, and when the cops aimed a hail of bullets at him, he took dozens

of hits and yet still stayed on his feet and laughed at them.

Back at headquarters, Michael Nouri plays the cop assigned to the case. He wants to catch this guy, who has been responsible for an incredible string of violent crimes, but he's not so happy when an FBI man turns up and assigns himself to the case. The federal agent is played by Kyle MacLachlan, the clean-cut kid from *Blue Velvet,* and he looks just as clean-cut this time, but he, too, has a strange light in his eyes. Nouri discovers the key to this mystery about half an hour after we've figured it out for ourselves. Both the killer and the so-called FBI agent are from another planet. "Are we talking spaceman here?" Nouri asks, and we are.

The Hidden takes this situation and makes a surprisingly effective film out of it, a sleeper that talks like a thriller and walks like a thriller, but has more brains than the average thriller. It also has a sense of humor, and some subtle acting by MacLachlan, whose assignment is to play a character who is always just a beat out of step.

Jeff Bridges had a similar challenge in *Starman,* where he played an alien who cloned a human body and then tried to find his way around in it. MacLachlan takes a different approach, playing his alien with a certain strange reserve, as if he's trying the controls very lightly, afraid of going into a spin.

At first, Nouri naturally assumes this FBI guy is simply another weirdo. As he gradually begins to believe the story, his problem is to deal with his fellow cops, who don't believe in spacemen. Meanwhile, the killer moves from one host body to another, taking a guided tour of earth life-forms (his hosts include a dog and a stripper). The movie was directed by Jack Sholder, whose previous film was *A Nightmare on Elm Street, Part Two.* I don't know what I was expecting, but certainly not this original and efficient thriller.

Hidden Agenda ★ ★ ★
R, 108 m., 1990

Frances McDormand (Ingrid), Brian Cox (Kerrigan), Brad Dourif (Paul), Mai Zetterling (Moa). Directed by Ken Loach and produced by Eric Fellner. Screenplay by Jim Allen.

The tragedy of Northern Ireland is like a broken record. There was another incident just as this movie opened in the spring of 1991—the shooting death of young Fergal Caraher. The British authorities say he was shot while in a car trying to run a roadblock.

Witnesses say he was shot without provocation. Thousands marched at his funeral. An investigation is promised.

Ken Loach's lacerating new film *Hidden Agenda* centers on an incident uncannily like the Caraher shooting. Two men in a car are shot without warning by British security forces. There is a great outcry. An investigation is promised. The movie, set in the recent past, is inspired by the Stalker Affair, in which a senior British police official, John Stalker, was assigned to investigate a killing by British security officials—and then suddenly removed from the investigation after uncovering evidence that the shooting was unjustified. That was a conclusion the Thatcher government could not tolerate.

Hidden Agenda is put together like a political thriller, like *Z* or *No Way Out,* but it adds a gritty everyday realism. The story is seen through the eyes of two Americans assigned to investigate charges that British security forces have sanctioned murder as a tactic in their struggle against Irish nationalism. The Americans (Frances McDormand and Brad Dourif) are members of a human rights group like Amnesty International, and are idealists out of their depth in the dangerous world they have entered. They become pawns in the political struggle when an IRA man slips a tape recording to them—an explosive tape with evidence that could not only lead to a murder conviction, but also suggest that a British right-wing group had run a "dirty tricks" campaign against national leaders.

Brian Cox plays the character based on Stalker. He's a career professional, a policeman who prides himself on ethical behavior, and he finds himself distinctly unwelcome in Northern Ireland. A senior Ulster policeman all but threatens him with death if he proceeds in his investigation, and tacitly concedes that the police have had to use illegal tactics to counter the terrorism of the IRA. But Cox persists, meeting with shadowy IRA figures in the back rooms of pubs and trying to get to the bottom of a killing that many powerful people would rather he forget.

The movie is set in everyday surroundings—hotel lobbies, car parks, pubs, and restaurants—and the participants are not the slick spies of Bond thrillers but ordinary, weatherbeaten people, often a little shabby. They have the look of weariness about them, as if the struggle has gone on too long and brought too much unhappiness. By contrast, the Ulster police official is all spit and polish, with a voice that's particularly grating when he tries to sound reasonable.

It quickly becomes apparent that the Amnesty investigators are in way over their heads, in a situation they do not understand, and that British security knows everything they're doing. It is also apparent that the corruption they are attempting to find extends all the way up to the highest levels of the British government. One of the most astonishing things about this film is the way it uses real names, dates, and places—charging a secret right wing group with attempting to bring down not only the Labour government of Harold Wilson, but the Conservative government of Edward Heath, which followed, and which the group found too soft for their taste. The implication is that Margaret Thatcher became prime minister at least partly through this group's efforts.

Hidden Agenda has understandably touched off a ferocious controversy in Great Britain. For Americans, it works more as a thriller than as political polemic, and indeed toward the end—when the dialogue threatens to overwhelm the action—the going gets thick. There is also the problem of that tape recording, which is seen as so important by everyone involved. Surely it could have been duplicated by the dozens and mailed all over the world? Questions like that are bothersome, and yet in its own terms and for much of the way, this is a superior thriller.

Hideaway ★ ★ ★
R, 112 m., 1995

NEW

Jeff Goldblum (Hatch), Christine Lahti (Lindsey), Alicia Silverstone (Regina), Jeremy Sisto (Vassago), Alfred Molina (Jonas), Rae Dawn Chong (Rose Orwetto), Kenneth Welsh (Detective Breech), Suzy Joachim (Dr. Kari Dovell). Directed by Brett Leonard and produced by Jerry Baerwitz, Agatha Hanczakowski, and Gimel Everett. Screenplay by Andrew Kevin Walker and Neal Jimenez.

In its end titles, *Hideaway* lists an "archemythologist," which is undoubtedly the most intriguing credit since *A River Runs Through It* thanked its trout wrangler. Not only does it list an archemythologist, it needs one: The movie is a expedition into the deepest caverns of after-death spookiness, with a hero zapped back to life after lingering just a little too long on the distant shore.

As the movie opens, Hatch and Lindsey (Jeff Goldblum and Christine Lahti) are driving down a tricky mountain road in the rain. Their teenage daughter is in the backseat. A giant semi looms out of the darkness and forces them off the road, and although they survive a plunge into a mountain stream, Hatch is dead by the time Lindsey drags him to the shore.

Cut to an operating theater, where the ominously bearded Dr. Jonas (Alfred Molina) determines to bring him back using his "very special resuscitative medicine program." In the kind of dialogue that makes me cackle with glee, one of his aides demurs: "But doctor, remember what happened the last time we tried that. . . ." Jonas waves him off and goes to work on Hatch, who is soon sitting up in bed and joking with his brave wife and sulky daughter.

But it is not, of course, going to be as simple as that, and soon Hatch is having terrifying dreams and hallucinations, in which he kidnaps and kills innocent victims. One day, after imagining he has victimized a young girl, he finds her photo in the morning paper. She's listed as missing, and the circumstances match up with his dream. How can this be?

I personally would not dream of telling you. If you happen to see the ads for the movie, however, *they* will inform you that the Life Force of the dead Hatch was somehow mixed, on the Other Side, with the essence of a vicious killer who was also resurrected after being left on hold too long. Could this killer possibly be related to the alarming Dr. Jonas? The doctor has one of the movie's best lines: "Even as a child, Jerry was psychotic—but, he was my son!"

Good taste will get you nowhere in watching this movie. It belongs in the category of Wretched Excess, which is a category I am quite able to enjoy. I can think of carloads of movies with more probity and higher intent than *Hideaway*. But what *Hideaway* delivers is the sort of experience I occasionally crave at the movies: lurid, overwrought melodrama, and an ending that shoots for the moon.

It helps, in a movie like this, if the actors are first-rate. Jeff Goldblum and Christine Lahti transform scenes that in other hands might have simply been laughable: She, in particular, is good at playing an intelligent, patient, resourceful woman whose husband is obviously going around the bend. First he dies. Then he comes back to life. Then he starts slicing his palm with a razor blade, because that helps him plug into his shadowy psychic connection. Who wouldn't get fed up? As their daughter, Regina, complains to a teenage pal about her dad: "He's, like, really on edge—dying and all, you know."

The movie, directed by Brett Leonard from a screenplay by Andrew Kevin Walker and Neal Jimenez, is based on a novel by Dean R. Koontz. It likes a sly understatement now and again, as in this exchange:

"He's dead."

"Yes, but, uh . . . not from . . . being dead."

Then there's the movie's climax, which has visual fantasies unmatched since the forces of heaven and hell held their apocalyptic struggle in *Raiders of the Lost Ark*. A younger daughter of Hatch and Lindsey died some years ago, and now her spirit leads the forces of good against the powers of darkness in a showdown which must be seen to be believed.

Look, I'm not saying this is a great movie, or even a distinguished one. I'm saying: You want horror, you want psychic abandon, you want Rae Dawn Chong reading Jeff Goldblum's Tarot cards and not liking what she sees, you see this movie, you get your money's worth. *Hideaway* is for people who like movies as much as they like films.

Higher Learning ★ ★ ★
R, 127 m., 1995

NEW

Omar Epps (Malik Williams), Kristy Swanson (Kristen Connor), Michael Rapaport (Remy), Ice Cube (Fudge), Laurence Fishburne (Professor Phipps), Jason Wiles (Wayne), Regina King (Monet), Jennifer Connelly (Taryn), Tyra Banks (Deja). Directed by John Singleton and produced by Singleton and Paul Hall. Screenplay by Singleton.

You gotta get that 'We are the World' crap outta your head. 'Cause it ain't gonna happen on this campus.

—dialogue in *Higher Learning*

The college campus in John Singleton's new film is a racial and ideological war zone, where students rarely talk to other students who are not more or less just like themselves. Early in the film, a black freshman is given a tour of the turfs staked out by various racial groups: "There's Chinatown . . . the Black Hole . . . Disneyland . . . South of the Border . . ." The enforced segregation of the past has been replaced by a new, voluntary xenophobia, and the result is a dreary place in which people define themselves by negatives.

The institution is named Columbus University (named after the Dead White European Male whose "discovery" of America led to genocide, etc., etc.). It is not safe to walk the campus grounds after dark. The Students for a Non-Sexist Society has mottos like "Dead Men Don't Rape." And this is not some futurist Orwellian nightmare, but a more or less realistic picture of the Politically Correct modern campus. It is easy to imagine that in a faculty office David Mamet's *Oleanna* is taking place.

Into this sanctuary of self-enforced apartheid a new freshman class is enrolled. It includes a young black man named Malik (Omar Epps), a young white woman named Kristen (Kristy Swanson), and a young white man named Remy (Michael Rapaport). They are here, allegedly, to learn, but most of their most important lessons will be taught by the campus itself. The only classroom we enter is ruled by the most conservative character in view: Professor Phipps (Laurence Fishburne), the pipe-smoking West Indian who refuses to play favorites and has the quaint idea that all students should be judged only on the basis of their performance.

Singleton's film is interesting for a lot of reasons, but especially because he stands outside this campus system and looks at it with a detached eye. Like Spike Lee's *School Daze*, Singleton's *Higher Learning* is idealistic in a way that seems refreshingly dated: He believes the campus should allow students from different races and places to get to know one another, instead of compartmenting them into rigid self-righteousness. At a time when some believe only blacks should teach black studies and DWEMs should hardly be taught at all, this is almost radical.

Singleton himself, twenty-six when he made this film, was only a few years out of USC, and his film is at home on the campus. Looking through the eyes of the incoming freshmen, we go through the process of moving in, meeting roommates, taking the first classes, and socializing. For Kristen, the first week is a nightmare. She meets a cute guy at a beer blast, goes home with him, and is a victim of date rape. Singleton's handling of this scene is perceptive; he shows the outcome predicted even in its earliest stages ("You think we should let Kristen go with Billy? 'Cause she doesn't even drink"). It shows Billy's own confusion, and the way booze contributes to it. And it sets up a subplot, as the shattered Kristen is befriended by Taryn (Jennifer Connelly), head of a fem-

inist group and a lesbian who Kristen will eventually consider as a possible lover.

Taryn doesn't "recruit" Kristen exactly, although she has her eye on her. The first night that Kristen seems attracted, Taryn even warns her: "Don't say yes simply because you're fascinated." Singleton is making a larger point, about how young freshmen seek role models on a campus, and are singled out by older students who take advantage of their naïveté. Malik, the black student, is soon in conversation with Fudge (Ice Cube), a "professional student" who has been on campus six years and affects an Afrocentric position. And Remy, the scared young white kid with the confused eyes, is singled out by a clever, demented neo-Nazi skinhead (Cole Hauser), who correctly guesses he might be capable of violence.

Each of these older students is supporting a position. Fudge sees himself at war with white America, and quizzes Malik on whether he would stand during the national anthem "in a football stadium, with sixty thousand eyes on you." Taryn believes men can basically not be trusted. The skinhead envisions race war as a worthy goal, believes the campus is a good place to start, and suspects his freshman recruit might be crazy enough to pull a trigger.

Standing apart from all of these factions, in a performance all the more effective because it is so subtle, is Laurence Fishburne as Professor Phipps. He persists in seeing each student as an individual, apart from his or her group. He has only one standard for grading. Malik, recruited to the campus as a potential track star, feels himself out of his depth in Phipps's class and tries to play the black card, but Phipps isn't playing: He would not be doing Malik a favor, he explains, by holding him to a lower standard. So Malik works harder, tutored by his new girlfriend Deja (Tyra Banks), and is eventually able to turn in a decent paper.

Meanwhile, a sense of impending doom hangs over the campus. All of these groups with all of their agendas are headed for a collision. Singleton does a good job of cutting back and forth among many stories; this is not a "black movie" but sees the whole campus population as its subject. He handles the subplot involving the neo-Nazis especially effectively; skinheads lend themselves to parody, but in Cole Hauser and Michael Rapaport, Singleton has cast two effective actors who bring a chilling plausibility to their characters. Rapaport plays a

big, confused kid who looks like a rabbit caught in headlights, and Hauser, with his cynical charm and insinuating drawl, is like a snake charmer.

Higher Learning is Singleton's third film, after the great *Boyz N the Hood* (1991) and the more meandering, romantic *Poetic Justice* (1993). He may be following, in some way, the threads of his own autobiography, in these three films about teenagers in South Central Los Angeles, young people working for the post office, and now freshmen in college. He sees with a clear eye and a strong will, and is not persuaded by fashionable ideologies. His movies are thought-provoking because he uses familiar kinds of characters and then asks hard questions about them.

Higher Learning has no easy answers. In an opening scene, when the black freshman gets on an elevator with the young white student, she instinctively clutches her purse tighter. In a closing scene, we see them able to talk with one another in the aftermath of a campus tragedy. She doesn't remember the moment in the elevator. He does. But life goes on, and why does a campus exist, except for learning?

High Hopes ★ ★ ★

NO MPAA RATING; 110 m., 1989

Philip Davis (Cyril), Ruth Sheen (Shirley), Edna Dore (Mrs. Bender), Philip Jackson (Martin), Heather Tobias (Valerie), Lesley Manville (Laetitia), David Bamber (Rupert). Written and directed by Mike Leigh and produced by Simon Channing-Williams and Victor Glynn. Screenplay by Leigh.

The characters in *High Hopes* exist on either side of the great divide in Margaret Thatcher's England, between the new yuppies and the die-hard socialists.

Cyril and Shirley, quasi-hippie survivors of the 1970s, live in comfortable poverty in a small flat, supported by Cyril's earnings as a motorcycle messenger. Cyril's sister, Valerie, lives in an upscale home surrounded by Modern Conveniences with her husband, Martin, who sells used cars. In their language, their values, and the way they furnish their lives, each couple serves as a stereotype for their class: Cyril and Shirley are what Tories think leftists are like, and Valerie and Martin stand for all the left hates most about Thatcherism.

Sometimes these two extremes literally live next door to each other. Cyril and Valerie's mother, a bitter, withdrawn old woman named Mrs. Bender, lives in solitude in the last council flat on a street that has otherwise been gentrified. Her next-door neighbors are two particularly frightening examples of the emerging social class the British call Hooray Henrys (and Henriettas). Paralyzed by their affected speech and gestures, they play out a grotesque parody of upper-class life in their own converted row house, which they like to forget was recently public housing for the poor.

All of these lives, and a few others, collide during the course of a few days in *High Hopes*, which was written and directed by Mike Leigh with the participation of the actors, who developed their scenes and dialogue in improvisational sessions. Leigh is a legendary figure in modern British theater, for his plays and television films that mercilessly dissect the British class system, using as their weapon the one emotion the British fear most, embarrassment.

Leigh has made only one other film, the brilliant *Bleak Moments,* some eighteen years ago. He cannot easily find financing for his films because, at the financing stage, they do not yet have scripts; he believes in developing the material as he goes along.

The backing for *High Hopes* came partly from Channel Four, the innovative alternative British TV channel, and with its money he has produced one of those rare films in which anger and amusement exist side by side—in which the funniest scenes are also the most painful ones.

Consider, for example, the dilemma of the old mother, Mrs. Bender, when she locks herself out of her council house. She naturally turns for help to her neighbors. But Rupert and Laetitia, who live next door, are upwardly mobile yuppies who treat the poor as a disease they hope not to catch. As the old woman stands helplessly at the foot of the steps, grasping her shopping cart, her chic neighbor supposes she must, after all, give her shelter, and says, "Hurry up, now. Chop, chop!"

Mrs. Bender calls her daughter, Valerie, who can hardly be bothered to come and help her, until she learns that her mother is actually inside the yuppie house next door. Then she's there in a flash, hoping to nose about and see what they've "done" with the place. Some of her dialogue almost draws blood, as when she looks into Rupert's leather-and-brass den and shouts, "Mum, look what they've done with your coal-hole!"

This sort of materialism and pride in possessions is far from the thoughts of Cyril and Shirley, the left-wing couple, who still sleep on a mattress on the floor and decorate their flat with posters and cacti. Lacking in ambition, they make enough from Cyril's messenger job to live on, and they smooth over the rough places with hashish. They are kind, and the movie opens with them taking a bewildered mental patient into their home; he has been wandering the streets of London, a victim of Thatcher's dismantled welfare state. (America and Britain are indeed cousins across the waters; we are reminded that the Reagan administration benevolently turned thousands of our own mentally ill out onto the streets.)

Most of the action in *High Hopes* centers around two set pieces, both involving the mother: the crisis of the lost keys, and then the mother's birthday party, which the hysterical Valerie stages as a parody of happy times. As the confused Mrs. Bender sits in bewilderment at the head of the table, her daughter shouts encouragement at her with a shrill desperation. The evening ends with a bitter quarrel between the daughter and her husband, while Cyril and Shirley pack the miserable old lady away home.

High Hopes is not a movie with a simple message; it's not left-wing propaganda in which all kindness resides with the Labourites and all selfishness with the Conservatives. Leigh shows us a London that exists beyond such easy distinctions, and it is possible he is almost as angry at Cyril and Shirley—laidback, gentle, ineffectual potheads—as at the movie's cruel upward-strivers.

Much of the movie's concern seems to center around Shirley's desire to have a child, and Cyril's desire that they should not. Their conflict is not the familiar old one of whether or not to "bring" a child into "this world." It seems to center more around the core of Cyril's laziness. He cannot be bothered. Of course, he stands for all good things and opposes all bad ones, in principle—but in practice, it's simpler to light up a joint.

High Hopes is an alive and challenging film, one that throws our own assumptions and evasions back at us. Leigh sees his characters and their lifestyles so vividly, so mercilessly, and with such a sharp satirical edge, that the movie achieves a neat trick: We start by laughing at the others, and end by feeling uncomfortable about ourselves.

High Season ★ ★ ★
R, 104 m., 1988

Jacqueline Bisset (Katherine), James Fox (Patrick), Irene Papas (Penelope), Paris Tselios (Yanni), Sebastian Shaw (Basil Sharp), Kenneth Branagh (Rick), Lesley Manville (Carol). Directed by Clare Peploe and produced by Clare Downs. Screenplay by Clare and Mark Peploe.

High Season reminds me a little of the neglected John Huston comedy *Beat the Devil,* with its assortment of eccentric exiles up to mischief far from home. The film takes place on the Greek island of Rhodes, where once a Colossus stood, but where now the most controversial sculpture is dedicated to the Unknown Tourist. For many years a celebrated British photographer (Jacqueline Bisset) has lived on the island with her daughter, and as the story opens, her past and future are both about to catch up with her.

She lives in a lazy white house in a small town that, until now, has not been discovered by the tourists. But now they have started to arrive in numbers, and that has created a schism in the most prominent local family. The son, Yanni (Paris Tselios) wants to turn the ancient family store into a T-shirt shop, while his mother (the immortal Irene Papas) wants to drive all tourists from the island—by force, if necessary.

Yanni has commissioned a trendy sculptor to create the monument to the Unknown Tourist. And because the sculptor is played by James Fox, we can all but relax, sure that something wickedly funny will come of all of this. The Fox brothers (James and Edward) are masters of a certain note of brave British dissipation. They play characters who are capable of doing fine things, if only they had the will. In this case, James Fox's arrival on the island precipitates a small crisis, since Bisset is his former wife.

Other newcomers also arrive; one of the great pleasures of a film like this is in the introduction of the new characters. We meet, for example, Basil Sharp (Sebastian Shaw), the legendary British art expert who is an old friend of Bisset's. He has come out to have a look at an invaluable Roman vase he once gave her—and also to arrange a political defection. He confides in her that he has long been a Russian spy, and is preparing to meet Soviet agents and defect to Russia. (Sharp's character—and indeed his name—are obviously inspired by the scandal of Anthony Blunt, keeper of Her Majesty's picture collection until he was unmasked as a Soviet agent.)

Sharp's escape is with the approval of the British authorities, who feel they simply cannot deal with the scandal of another high-placed spy. Is it only coincidence that at the same time he arrives on the island, a famous international art dealer also turns up? And also a confused and forlorn young British couple? They have no place to stay until Papas unexpectedly rents them a room.

With all of the actors in place, the delights of the screenplay begin to unfold. The movie was directed by Clare Peploe and written by her and her brother, Mark, who were involved in such Michelangelo Antonioni projects as *The Passenger*. Nothing in their previous work would suggest they'd make a light-footed social satire like *High Season*, but the movie is completely assured as it juggles its characters and a labyrinthine plot involving the vase, the spy case, and the assorted old and new romances.

The best movies of this sort always include some sort of scene in which one or more of the decadent heroes voices regret at a misspent life. In *High Season*, Sebastian Shaw does a masterful job of looking back over his life of art, finance, and espionage, and his confessional scene with Bisset is one of the best pieces of work along that line I've ever seen.

I also enjoyed the playful way that the Peploes contrived a sequence involving a long, long night during which the precious vase and several hearts are tampered with. The ingeniousness with which they weave their tangled plot created real questions in my mind—which were resolved in one of those deeply satisfying endings in which everything has an answer and yet nobody turns out to have been quite blameless. *High Season* is an example of a rare species, the intelligent silly movie.

Hoffa ★ ★ ★ ½
R, 138 m., 1992

Jack Nicholson (Jimmy Hoffa), Danny DeVito (Bobby Ciaro), Armand Assante (Mafia Leader), J.T. Walsh (Frank Fitzsimmons), Kevin Anderson (Bobby Kennedy). Directed by Danny DeVito and produced by Edward R. Pressman, DeVito, and Caldecot Chubb. Screenplay by David Mamet.

It comes as a shock, about halfway through *Hoffa*, to discover that the Teamsters leader has a wife and daughter. They turn up during a crowd scene. But this film about Jimmy Hoffa has no time to show him meeting his wife, courting her, marrying her, setting up housekeeping, or fathering a child. That is

almost as it should be: *Hoffa* shows a man who lives, breathes, wakes, sleeps, and dies for the union.

We see him for the first time as he waits outside a roadhouse in suburban Detroit. He is waiting for his death, and almost seems to know it, placing a handgun carefully between his feet in the backseat of the car. He is with his friend Bobby, and we see how they met, many years before, when Jimmy talked his way into Bobby's cab and gave him the Teamsters pitch.

Hoffa says he knows all about driving a truck. The long hours, the overtime, the unpaid downtime, the trucks killing drivers who go to sleep, the owners who think a guy can drive for twenty-four hours straight. He talks the language. We see him on picket lines, haunting loading docks, living on cigarettes and coffee, shouting angrily at management and its hired Pinkertons. And we see him winning a key strike by enlisting the aid of the Mafia, paying off the syndicate by promising that certain trucks would lose their way and end up being unloaded by the Mob.

Does the movie agree, then, that Jimmy Hoffa was a tool of organized crime? Not at all. It argues that Hoffa would take any help he could get, anywhere he could find it, to organize the drivers and put pressure on the owners. He was a union pragmatist. What is peculiar then, and what makes this movie so fascinating and frightening, is that we can never quite glimpse the idealism that should be in there somewhere. No light of inner conviction burns in his eyes. Some horrible wrong must have been done this man at an early age, and organizing the Teamsters is his way of getting even—his lonely, angry vendetta.

Jack Nicholson is an actor who can reflect almost anything in his face. One reason his performance is so good as Hoffa is that he reveals almost nothing. The first time we see him, the physical resemblance is striking: the heavy, hooded face, the hair cut high on the sides, and most of all the eyes—reptilian, like a very old, remorseless turtle. He is filled with vindictiveness, not idealism. He organizes the way some guys kick dogs or get in fights, because it releases the terrible pressures inside.

The movie is directed by Danny DeVito, who also plays the key role of Bobby Ciaro, a trucker Hoffa meets on the road. Bobby is afraid to join the Teamsters. He could lose his job just by talking to this guy. Your secret is safe with me, Hoffa promises him, and

then betrays it at a key moment, costing Bobby his job but gaining himself a sidekick. And Bobby is at his side until the end, a faithful yes-man and lapdog, who looks at Hoffa and sees a great man.

I am not sure if Bobby Ciaro is based on a real-life person, but this movie needs him as a window into Hoffa, who is portrayed as a loner, a self-contained strategist who cold-bloodedly sets about finding the weak points of his enemies. We see Jimmy through Bobby's eyes. It's a good question whether Jimmy ever really sees himself. The film's one weakness is that it never answers that; I would have appreciated more insight into Hoffa's own feelings.

The production is lavish with period details—the old trucks, the shabby roadside gas stations, the weather-beaten loading docks, the cigarettes, one after another in a lifelong chain. The truckers' world contrasts with the world of power inhabited by the insiders: the old-world elegance of the Mafia meeting places, for example, or the rooms where men of power in the government reside. The movie makes its best points for union organizing just by contrasting the cabs and road stops of the drivers with the world of privilege.

Real names are used. The movie has two villains, Bobby Kennedy (Kevin Anderson) and Frank Fitzsimmons (J.T. Walsh), who for different reasons want to destroy Hoffa—Kennedy, because he has a personal vendetta against this foul-mouthed man who insults his family, Fitzsimmons because, having taken over leadership of Hoffa's union, he has no wish to give it back. You could argue that the third villain is the Mafia, as personified in a character played by Armand Assante, but actually the gangsters in this movie operate in a more objective, businesslike way than the public officials. The Mafia sponsors the murder of Hoffa at the end of the film, but it's nothing personal. It's because Hoffa's anger finally got the better of his negotiating ability.

Why is it, in the movies and in life, that guys who are marked men go to sit in lonely places where they can be gunned down? Don't they know what's coming? Maybe they welcome it. Maybe they're tired. David Mamet's screenplay does not allow his characters the words for such introspection; Hoffa and the men of his world respond to power and strategy, not emotion. Winning is everything, which means that eventually losing is everything.

Hoffa shows DeVito as a genuine filmmaker. Here is a movie that finds the right look and tone for its material. Not many directors would have been confident enough to simply show us Jimmy Hoffa instead of telling us all about him. This is a movie that makes its points between the lines, in what is not said. It's not so much about what happened to Jimmy Hoffa, as about the fact that something eventually would.

Hollywood Shuffle ★ ★ ★
R, 82 m., 1987

Robert Townsend (Bobby Taylor), Anne-Marie Johnson (Lydia), Helen Martin (Grandmother), Starletta Dupois (Mother), Craigus R. Johnson (Stevie), Domenick Irrera (Manvacum). Directed and produced by Robert Townsend. Screenplay by Townsend.

The story behind *Hollywood Shuffle* is more thrilling than anything on the screen. It's the story of Robert Townsend, young black actor from Chicago, talented, ambitious, who wins supporting roles in *Cooley High, Streets of Fire*, and *A Soldier's Story* but fails to gain stardom in a Hollywood where most roles for blacks are stereotypes and the rest go to people named Murphy, Pryor, and Glover.

In the ordinary course of events, Townsend would continue to make the weary rounds from one casting agent to another, auditioning for one forgettable role after another, paying the rent by waiting tables, until he was finally discovered or—more likely—quit the business and got a daytime job.

Townsend knew that routine as well as anyone, but he decided to break out of it. So he made his own movie. The saga of his production was well-publicized: He begged cinematographers for leftover film, borrowed every dollar he could find, talked cast and crew into working for deferred payments, and somehow made an expensive-looking movie for less than $100,000. Comparisons have been drawn to Spike Lee, another young black filmmaker who broke the rules and had his first hit with *She's Gotta Have It*.

It's a cliché that young novelists write their first novels about young novelists writing their first novels. Townsend's *Hollywood Shuffle* falls within this tradition. It is a movie about a young man much like Townsend, who makes the rounds, fights stereotypes, and dreams of the day when there will be a black Rambo.

The movie begins with Townsend working in a hot dog stand owned by a couple of negative thinkers who don't believe he can be successful as an actor. He defies their expectations and gets a job in a movie, but then he walks off the set; with his grandmother and his younger brother looking on, he just can't bring himself to mouth the street-talk clichés of his character, a gang member. This action inspires a series of fantasies in which Townsend sees himself in war movies, Westerns, and slice-of-life dramas, and even imagines a TV show in which two soul brothers are the feuding critics and give movies the finger as well as their thumbs.

There are a lot of good laughs in *Hollywood Shuffle*, and the movie certainly functions as a showcase for Townsend—who has a strong screen presence. The movie has its problems, however. Many of the skits run on too long after we've long since gotten the jokes. Some of the supporting performances are wooden and under-written. And many of the stereotypes Townsend protests against haven't been used in Hollywood movies in decades. His attacks on them will be the first time some viewers have seen the stereotypes at all.

I suspect many of these problems are the direct result of the movie's low budget, hurried shooting schedule, and limited supply of film. When one take of a scene was acceptable, Townsend must have been inclined to accept it, rather than to waste precious film stock in trying to make it better. Under the circumstances, *Hollywood Shuffle* is an artistic compromise but a logistical triumph, announcing the arrival of a talent whose next movie should really be something.

Home Alone ★ ★ ½
PG, 103 m., 1990

Macaulay Culkin (Kevin), Joe Pesci (Harry), Daniel Stern (Marv), John Heard (Peter), Roberts Blossom (Marley), Catherine O'Hara (Kate), John Candy (Gus Polinski). Directed by Chris Columbus and produced by John Hughes. Screenplay by Hughes.

Home Alone is a splendid movie title because it evokes all sorts of scary nostalgia. Being left home alone, when you were a kid, meant hearing strange noises and being afraid to look in the basement—but it also meant doing all the things that grown-ups would tell you to stop doing, if they were there. Things like staying up to watch Johnny Carson, eating all the ice cream, and sleeping in your parents' bed.

Home Alone is about an eight-year-old hero who does all of those things, but unfortunately, he also single-handedly stymies two house burglars by booby-trapping the house. And they're the kinds of traps that any eight-year-old could devise, if he had a budget of tens of thousands of dollars and the assistance of a crew of movie special effects people.

The movie's screenplay is by John Hughes, who sometimes shows a genius for remembering what it was like to be young. His best movies, like *Sixteen Candles, The Breakfast Club, Ferris Bueller's Day Off*, and *Planes, Trains and Automobiles*, find a way to be funny while still staying somewhere within the boundaries of remote plausibility. This time, he strays so far from his premise that the movie suffers.

If *Home Alone* had limited itself to the things that might possibly happen to a forgotten eight-year-old, I think I would have liked it more. What I didn't enjoy was the subplot involving the burglars (Joe Pesci and Daniel Stern), who are immediately spotted by little Kevin (Macaulay Culkin), and made the targets of his cleverness.

The movie opens in the Chicago suburbs with a houseful of people on the eve of a big family Christmas vacation in Paris. There are relatives and kids everywhere, and when the family oversleeps and has to race to the airport, Kevin is somehow overlooked in the shuffle. When he wakes up later that morning, the house is empty. So he makes the best of it.

A real kid would probably be more frightened than this movie character, and would probably cry. He might also try calling someone, or asking a neighbor for help. But in the contrived world of this movie, the only neighbor is an old coot who is rumored to be the Snow Shovel Murderer, and the phone doesn't work. When Kevin's parents discover they've forgotten him, they find it impossible to get anyone to follow through on their panicked calls—for the simple reason that if anyone did so, the movie would be over.

The plot is so implausible that it makes it hard for us to really care about the plight of the kid. What works in the other direction, however, and almost carries the day, is the gifted performance by young Macaulay Culkin, as Kevin. Culkin is the little boy who co-starred with John Candy in *Uncle Buck*, and here he has to carry almost the whole movie. He has lots of challenging acting scenes, and he's up to them. I'm sure he got lots of help from director Chris Columbus, but he's got the stuff to begin with. He's such a confident and gifted little actor that I'd like to see him in a story I could care more about.

Home Alone isn't that story. When the burglars invade Kevin's home, they find themselves running a gamut of booby traps so elaborate they could have been concocted by Rube Goldberg—or by the berserk father in *Last House on the Left*. Because all plausibility is gone, we sit back, detached, to watch stunt men and special effects guys take over a movie that promised to be the kind of story audiences could identify with.

A Home of Our Own ★ ★ ★
PG, 104 m., 1993

Kathy Bates (Frances Lacey), Edward Furlong (Shayne Lacey), Soon-Teck Oh (Mr. Munimura), Tony Campisi (Norman), Clarissa Lassig (Lynn Lacey), Sarah Schaub (Faye Lacey). Directed by Tony Bill and produced by Dale Pollock and Bill Borden. Screenplay by Patrick Duncan.

A Home of Our Own is a sentimental and fairly unlikely story about a widow who packs her kids into a jalopy and takes John Prine's advice: "Blow up your TV, throw away your papers, head for the country, and build you a home." The TV blows up more or less by itself.

The widow (Kathy Bates) is a proud woman who believes in paying her own way, and refuses any form of charity. When she sees that her oldest son (Edward Furlong) is in the early stages of what may develop into a criminal career, she realizes Los Angeles is not the place for raising children. Since she's just been fired from her job for smacking the foreman when he got fresh, the time is ripe for her to pack their possessions into the family car and head in the general direction of Idaho.

This situation, set in the 1960s, could be the setup for a sitcom, or a retread of an old Disney family yarn. It ends up being a lot more, partly because Kathy Bates brings a solid, no-nonsense clarity to what could have been a marshmallow role, and partly because the director, Tony Bill, is too smart to go for heart-wrenching payoffs until the very end of the film, when they work so well that I actually felt some tears in my eyes.

It doesn't make a movie good just because you sniff a little. But it makes it hard to dismiss. Recognizing that *A Home of Our Own* is manipulative, I must be honest enough to admit that it successfully manipulated me; that when the family is helped in its darkest

hour by the goodness of neighbors, there is something enormously moving about it all.

The Bates character, named Frances Lacey, is still angry at her late husband for having died on her. She lambastes him from time to time, but confides to her son Shayne (Furlong) that he was, in fact, a reasonably good man. Now she is left with her "tribe," which she calls her tribe about six times too often in the film. Pointing the old car for the horizon, she knows in her bones that she will find a house for them—that they'll never have to live under a landlord's roof again.

They're penniless, but she trusts in providence, and providence provides a half-finished little frame house across the street from a nursery run by a Japanese-American man named Mr. Munimura (Soon-Teck Oh). The house was abandoned, we learn, when his son did not return alive from the Korean War. She bargains with him. In return for deed to the house and some land, she will supply him with housecleaning and chores to be supplied by her tribe. He is at first astonished, then dubious, then convinced.

Mrs. Lacey gets a job as a waitress in the local bowling alley, sometimes gratefully accepting tools as tips, and the family sets to work winterizing its humble quarters. The tribe has generally good spirits, but their poverty leads to humiliations at school, and unhappiness at home, especially during a Christmas scene that even Dickens might have found depressing.

Tony Bill is a director not shy of tearjerking; his films include the fine *My Bodyguard* (1980) as well as the shamelessly sentimental *Six Weeks* (1982) and *Crazy People* (1990). During *A Home of Our Own* I was aware that the situation had been carefully crafted out of clichés and stereotypes, and yet the film was able to bring them to life, and Bates and Furlong were believable even when the tribe seemed to be posing for Save the Children posters. This is not a great movie, but it has a big heart.

Home of the Brave ★ ★ ★ ½
NO MPAA RATING, 90 m., 1986

A concert documentary directed by Laurie Anderson and produced by Paula Mazur. Screenplay by Anderson.

Laurie Anderson once spoke, in a wondering voice, of the plight of human sperm: "Hundreds of thousands of tiny specks, all knowing exactly the same thing." Her performances are filled with insights like that.

She doesn't make them to supply us with information, but to create a tone, an attitude. She is engulfed by the enormous mysteries of nature, and yet the human life around her seems more and more banal. Civilization is an assembly line to hell.

In retaliation, she weaves dream-images out of songs and symbols and electronic noises. She calls herself a "performance artist" rather than a musician. And although all musicians are performance artists, I think I know what she means. She does not give concerts. She attempts to create in her audiences a more open, wondering state of mind.

Home of the Brave is a ninety-minute documentary based on one of her performances. Large parts of it will be familiar to anyone who has seen her in person, but the film has a somewhat different feel than her live performances. As a backdrop to her music, Anderson uses a large rear-projection screen that sometimes relays messages made up of technological clichés and sometimes uses film loops to show the same images over and over.

The images have a hypnotic quality. Crudely drawn sheep jump over and over, again and again, or boats steam past a rusty bridge or—as she talks about the sperm—we see little tadpoles earnestly swimming upstream, one of them breaking away every once in a while for a loop-the-loop. The images are deliberately crude and machine-made. The film loops are so short that they announce themselves. We can see that the same images are being recycled in a circle, and the feeling is sort of poignant: All those sperm, all that effort, all for nothing.

In front of these images, the Laurie Anderson Band performs. With her short, spiky hair and her athletic grace, Anderson sometimes seems more like a craftsman than a singer. She moves in a kind of robot choreography, and she likes to seem deadpan. She takes the hand-held mike and wanders the stage, reciting parables and slices of bizarre information. She likes phrases such as "This just in . . . ," as if she were at the anchor desk for the death of the world. She uses strange lighting effects to create instants of magic.

She was one of the first to use voice synthesizers, which lower the tone of her voice while maintaining the same speed of speech. The effect is sort of big-brotherish; she seems official, detached, a voice made from a machine, speaking words as objects. Behind her, the rhythms are seductive, statements made over and over until they lull us into her mind state.

There are times when Anderson seems like an anti-performance artist, times when she cuts off a song or interrupts a progression just as it is threatening to develop into melody and entertainment. But the effect is not dry and antiseptic, as it is with some ultra-modern music. Every song has a soul of wit and an edge of rebellion.

It's strange. You can't put your finger on it, but after you see it, you have the feeling that your perception of things has been skewed slightly. Anderson is saying: We're surrounded by bankrupt images and music that is fascist noise, and they're pouncing away at us, trying to break us down, to kill the spark, but if we keep two things we will be able to survive and complete our journeys. Those two things are a sense of wonder and the ability to laugh back.

Homeward Bound: The Incredible Journey ★ ★ ★
G, 84 m., 1993

Ben (Shadow), Rattler (Chance), Tiki (Sassy). Animal Voices: Michael J. Fox (Chance), Sally Field (Sassy), Don Ameche (Shadow). Directed by Duwayne Dunham and produced by Franklin R. Levy and Jeffrey Chernov. Screenplay by Caroline Thompson and Linda Woolverton.

So there I was, sitting in a theater with a lot of kids, watching an animal picture. Worse, an animal picture where the animals talked. And even worse, not an animated movie, but a live-action film where the animals' lips don't even move when they talk. How do they do it? Ventriloquism, or telepathy?

The movie was about a wise old dog and an impetuous young pup and a snotty cat. Their human owners are about to go to San Francisco on business, and leave the animals with a friend who lives on a ranch on the other side of the mountains. But will the animals understand that they are not being abandoned? Or will they think they're trapped in a nightmarish four-footed remake of *Home Alone*?

I started to think of possible titles. *Bone Alone*? I asked myself what I was doing watching this movie. And then a funny thing happened. I got hooked by the story. I started to like the thing. The pets decide to return home by crossing a mountain range. Along the way they have a lot of amazing adventures, few of them possible, most of them fun.

Homeward Bound: The Incredible Journey is a movie frankly designed for kids, and yet it has a certain craftsmanship and an undeni-

able charm, and if you find yourself watching it with a child you may end up liking it almost as much. You will almost certainly not be as disturbed when the cat, named Sassy, gets swept over a waterfall and is given up for drowned, because you know the unwritten rule in this genre is that kitty will turn up, wet and mad, a little farther downstream.

The animal actors—Ben the wise one, Rattler the brash one, and Tiki the spoiled feline—are given voices by Don Ameche, Michael J. Fox, and Sally Field. Sometimes the voices are just a little too smooth, but some of the lines are good, especially Tiki's. And the adventures are exciting almost precisely in proportion to their impossibility. By the time one dog lures a mountain lion onto the end of a log and the other dog jumps on the other end to catapult the dangerous beast into the river, we have given up looking for credibility, and are waiting for the animals to start solving mathematical equations and picking out simple tunes on the piano.

The director, Duwayne Dunham, and his cinematographer, Reed Smoot, must have had considerable patience to put together all of the complicated stunts in this movie. The animals must have, too. The movie is based on a 1963 Disney picture named *The Incredible Journey*, unseen by me. In that one, I gather, the animals did not speak. I'm not sure if they did tricks with mountain lions.

Homicide ★ ★ ★ ★
R, 102 m., 1991

Joe Mantegna (Bobby Gold), William H. Macy (Tim Sullivan), Natalija Nogulich (Chava), Ving Rhames (Randolph), Rebecca Pidgeon (Miss Klein), Vincent Guastaferro (Senna), Lionel Mark Smith (Olcott), Jack Wallace (Frank). Directed by David Mamet and produced by Michael Hausman and Edward R. Pressman. Screenplay by Mamet.

There is a moment in David Mamet's *Homicide* when the hero does not know he is being overheard. He is a police detective, using the telephone in the library of a wealthy Jewish doctor who has complained about shots being fired on a nearby rooftop. The detective does not take the charges very seriously; he resents being pulled off a glamorous drug bust because the doctor, who has clout, has asked for him.

Standing at the phone, the detective unleashes a tightly knit, brilliantly arranged, flawlessly executed stream of four-letter obscenities and anti-Semitic remarks. Only

David Mamet could write, and perhaps only his favorite actor Joe Mantegna could deliver, this dialogue so bluntly and forcibly, and yet with such verbal slickness that it has the freedom of a jazz improvisation. It's so well done, it gets an audience response just on the basis of the delivery.

Then the cop turns around and he sees that he is not alone in the room. The doctor's daughter has heard every foul, bitter word. She knows something we also know: This cop himself is Jewish. And because she heard him, she forces him to listen to himself. To hear what he's really saying.

Homicide is about a man waking up to himself. As the movie opens, Detective Bobby Gold, the Mantegna character, is a cop who places his job first and his personal identity last. He does not think much about being Jewish. He gets in a scrape with a superior officer, who is black, and when the officer calls him a "kike," he is ready to fight—but we sense his anger grows more out of departmental rivalries than a personal sense of insult. Throughout the movie, Mamet's characters use the bluntest street language in their racial and sexual descriptions, as if somehow getting the ugliness out into the open is progress. (The language in this film, like the dialogue in Sidney Lumet's 1990 *Q & A*, is staccato gutter dialect.)

Gold is angry with the doctor because the doctor's mother got murdered, and the murder resulted in Gold being pulled off the big case. The mother, a stubborn old lady, ran a corner store in a black ghetto. She didn't need the money, but she refused to budge from the store, and she is shot dead in a robbery. Bobby, speeding toward the drug bust with his partner (William H. Macy), happens on the scene of the crime accidentally. "This isn't my case," he keeps saying. "I'm not here. You didn't see me." But the old woman's son, who has the clout downtown, wants him assigned to the case. Since Bobby Gold is Jewish, the doctor thinks, maybe he'll really care.

The doctor has the wrong man. What Mamet is trying to do in *Homicide*, I think, is combine the structure of a thriller with the content of a soul-searching conversion process. The two cases get all mixed up throughout the film—the black drug dealer on the run, and the murdered old lady—and in a sense Bobby is not going to be able to figure out who did anything until he decides who *he* is.

The movie crackles with energy and life, and with throwaway slang dialogue by Mamet, who takes realistic speech patterns and simplifies them into a kind of hammer-and-nail poetry. This is his third film as a writer-director (after *House of Games* and *Things Change*), and he is a filmmaker with a clear sense of how he wants to proceed. He uses the elements of traditional genres—the con game, the mistaken identity, the personal crisis, the cop picture—as a framework for movies that ask questions like, Who's real? Who can you trust? What do people really want?

Here he has several of his favorite actors, who have grown up in Mamet stage productions: Mantegna, Macy, Jack Wallace, J.J. Johnston—substantial guys with good haircuts who smoke cigarettes like they need to. This isn't a cast of aging teen idols. These are men, middle-aged, harassed, run down. They've seen it all. We sense that Bobby Gold is not in touch with his Jewishness because, like a lot of his partners, he has let the job take over from the person. Gold has become so hard-boiled, he doesn't even know how he sounds, until he hears himself through that woman's ears.

Honeymoon in Vegas ★ ★ ★ ½
PG-13, 95 m., 1992

James Caan (Tommy), Nicolas Cage (Jack), Sarah Jessica Parker (Betsy/Donna), Pat Morita (Mahi), Peter Boyle (Chief), Johnny Williams (Johnny Sandwich), John Capodice (Sally Molars), Robert Costanzo (Sidney Tomashefsky), Anne Bancroft (Bea Singer). Directed by Andrew Bergman and produced by Mike Lobell. Screenplay by Bergman.

There is a cheerfully rising tide of goofiness in Andrew Bergman's *Honeymoon in Vegas* that is typical of his work. This is the writer-director of *The Freshman*, in which the members of a gourmet diners' club proposed to eat a threatened species of lizard, and so perhaps we should not be surprised this time when the hero finds himself unexpectedly part of a team of skydiving Elvis impersonators. What is surprising is how, by that point in the film, it seems more or less logical.

The movie begins with a man (Nicolas Cage) who is terrified of marriage. He promised his late mother on her deathbed that he would never marry, and he has honored his pledge, but now he stands to lose his cherished partner (Sarah Jessica Parker) unless he proposes or gets off the pot, and so he suggests they fly to Vegas, just like that, and find one of those little instant-wedding chapels.

She agrees, but in Vegas, Cage gets cold feet, and meanwhile an astonishing thing happens. A professional gambler (James Caan) sees Parker in the lobby of a casino, and is overwhelmed by her resemblance to his own dead wife. He must have her. He cannot live without her. Thinking fast, he lures Cage into a poker game with steadily escalating stakes, until the only way Cage can possibly meet his losses is by agreeing to Caan's terms, and Caan wants . . . a weekend with Parker.

The plot is dumb enough to be a sitcom, but Bergman isn't dumb enough to make it one; he has a way of finding comedy in the urgency of driven characters, and here he traps Parker between two desperate men: her lover, who does not relish the idea of having his legs broken, and the gambler, who is obsessed with the idea that she is his wife reincarnated.

The story goes through many more permutations, which I will not spoil for you, except to note that when Caan and Parker arrive in Hawaii, and the distraught Cage follows them, there is an inspired scene involving Peter Boyle as a Hawaiian chief who somehow amazingly resembles Marlon Brando. Since Brando starred in *The Freshman* (a very funny performance) and then inexplicably trashed the movie in an interview, this is Bergman's sweet revenge.

Now about the Elvis impersonators. They are holding a convention at the Vegas hotel when Cage and Parker check in, and provide a funny backdrop for a lot of scenes, before the big payoff in which Cage, for reasons far too complex to be explained here, finds himself parachuting into Vegas at night while dressed as Elvis. Andrew Bergman has a gift for touches like that, in which the story line takes amazing twists and turns to include wonderfully bizarre developments.

Nicolas Cage is one of those actors some people like and others find excessive. I tend to like him, especially when he is consumed by love, as he was in *Moonstruck* and is again here. He sweats and squirms in the key scene, as he tries to explain to Parker that, yes, he loves her, but no, he can't pay his poker losses, and so, yes, maybe she should play along with this sinister gambler's weird obsession.

The plot loses its way in some of the later moments, as when Caan suddenly turns from a smoothie into a sinister, uptight threat (maybe it would have been funnier if he had simply continued to be a nice guy, to Cage's mounting frustration). But by then the movie

has already inspired enough laughter to pay its way, and that's with the skydiving Elvis impersonators still to come.

Honkytonk Man ★ ★ ★
PG, 123 m., 1982

Clint Eastwood (Red Stovall), Kyle Eastwood (Whit), John McIntire (Grandpa), Alexa Kenin (Marlene), Verna Bloom (Emmy). Directed and produced by Clint Eastwood.

Clint Eastwood produced and directed *Honkytonk Man*, and stars in it as a Depression-era loser who drifts through the South with his young nephew, aiming eventually to get to Nashville and maybe get on the Grand Ol' Opry. The movie's credits say the screenplay is by Clancy Carlile, based on his own novel, but in speculating on what drew Eastwood to this project, I came across this entry in Ephraim Katz's *Film Encyclopedia:*

"Eastwood, Clint. Actor, director. Born on May 31, 1930, in San Francisco. A child of the Depression, he spent his early boyhood trailing a father who pumped gas along dusty roads all over the West Coast. . . ."

The entry goes on to list the usual odd jobs (logger, steel-furnace stoker) that all actors seem to hold down on their way to stardom, but I'd read enough to support my intuition that *Honkytonk Man* means a lot to Eastwood in ways that may not be immediately apparent. This is a sweet, whimsical, low-key movie, a movie that makes you feel good without pressing you too hard. It provides Eastwood with a screen character who is the complete opposite of the patented Eastwood tough guys and provides a role of nearly equal importance for his son, Kyle, as a serious, independent and utterly engaging young nephew named Whit. What happens to them on the road is not quite as important in this movie as what happens between them.

The movie starts with Eastwood drunk behind the wheel of a big 1930s touring car, knocking over the windmill on his latest return to the old homestead. He's sort of a Hank Williams type. His family has seen this act before. They put him to bed and hide the bottle. The next day, with an ominous cough, Eastwood talks about his dream of heading for Nashville and cashing in some old IOUs. He's a singer and a songwriter, luckless but not untalented, and he thinks he could make it onto the Opry. He wants to take the kid along. After some hesitation, the kid's mother (Verna Bloom) agrees, mostly because she hopes her son can ride herd on Eastwood and keep him reasonably sober. She makes her son promise not to drink or fool around with women (thus putting her finger unerringly on one thing he did the night before, and another that he hopes to do as soon as possible). Old grandpa (John McIntire) also decides to go along for the ride; he's got some people in Tennessee he hasn't seen in forty years.

The road part of the picture is picaresque, photographed through a haze of romance and nostalgia, and spiced up with a visit to a gambling house and an encounter with a very individualistic young woman (Alexa Kenin) who also decides to join the traveling party. She has an amazing gift for couching the most ordinary sentiments in romantic prose. The movie's best scenes are the ones Eastwood plays in Nashville, during an audition at the Opry and, later, in a recording studio. He sings his songs with the kind of bone-weariness that doesn't hurt the right kind of country song, and there's a special moment in the studio when a supporting musician lends a hand. The movie turns out to be about realizing your dreams after all, which is sort of a surprise in a story where even the high points are only bittersweet.

This is a special movie. In making it, Eastwood was obviously moving away from his Dirty Harry image, but that's nothing new; his spectacular success in violent movies tends to distract us from his intriguing and challenging career as the director and star of such offbeat projects as *Bronco Billy* and *Play Misty For Me*. He seems to have a personal stake in this story, and we begin to feel it, too. Sometimes the simplest country songs are just telling the facts.

Hoop Dreams ★ ★ ★ ★
PG-13, 165 m., 1994
(See related essay, p. 901.)

Directed by Steve James and produced by Frederick Marx, James, and Peter Gilbert. Screenplay by James, Marx, and Gilbert.

A film like *Hoop Dreams* is what the movies are for. It takes us, shakes us, and makes us think in new ways about the world around us. It gives us the impression of having touched life itself.

Hoop Dreams is, on one level, a documentary about two black kids named William Gates and Arthur Agee, from Chicago's inner city, who are gifted basketball players and dream of someday starring in the NBA. On another level, it is about much larger subjects: about ambition, competition, race,

and class in our society. About our value structures. And about the daily lives of people like the Agee and Gates families, who are usually invisible in the mass media, but have a determination and resiliency that is a cause for hope.

The movie spans six years in the lives of William and Arthur, starting when they are in the eighth grade, and continuing through the first year of college. It was intended originally to be a thirty-minute short, but as the filmmakers followed their two subjects, they realized this was a much larger, and longer, story. And so we are allowed to watch the subjects grow up during the movie, and this palpable sense of the passage of time is like walking in their shoes.

They're spotted during playground games by a scout for St. Joseph's High School in suburban Westchester, a basketball powerhouse. Attending classes there will mean a long daily commute to a school with few other black faces, but there's never an instant when William or Arthur, or their families, doubt the wisdom of this opportunity: St. Joseph's, we hear time and again, is the school where another inner-city kid, Isiah Thomas, started his climb to NBA stardom.

One image from the film: Gates, who lives in the Cabrini Green project, and Agee, who lives on Chicago's South Side, get up before dawn on cold winter days to begin their daily ninety-minute commute to Westchester. The street lights reflect off the hard winter ice, and we realize what a long road—what plain hard work—is involved in trying to get to the top of the professional sports pyramid. Other high school students may go to "career counselors," who steer them into likely professions. Arthur and William are working harder, perhaps, than anyone else in their school—for jobs which, we are told, they have only a 0.00005 percent chance of winning.

We know all about the dream. We watch Michael Jordan and Isiah Thomas and the others on television, and we understand why any kid with talent would hope to be out on the same courts someday. But *Hoop Dreams* is not simply about basketball. It is about the texture and reality of daily existence in a big American city. And as the film follows Agee and Gates through high school and into their first year of college, we understand all of the human dimensions behind the easy media images of life in the "ghetto."

We learn, for example, of how their extended families pull together to help give kids a chance. How if one family member is

going through a period of trouble (Arthur's father is fighting a drug problem), others seem to rise to periods of strength. How if some family members are unemployed, or if the lights get turned off, there is also somehow an uncle with a big backyard, just right for a family celebration. We see how the strong black church structure provides support and encouragement—how it is rooted in reality, accepts people as they are, and believes in redemption.

And how some people never give up. Arthur's mother asks the filmmakers, "Do you ever ask yourself how I get by on $268 a month and keep this house and feed these children? Do you ever ask yourself that question?" Yes, frankly, we do. But another question is how she finds such determination and hope that by the end of the film, miraculously, she has completed her education as a nursing assistant. *Hoop Dreams* contains more actual information about life as it is lived in poor black city neighborhoods than any other film I have ever seen.

Because we see where William and Arthur come from, we understand how deeply they hope to transcend—to use their gifts to become pro athletes. We follow their steps along the path that will lead, they hope, from grade school to the NBA.

The people at St. Joseph's High School were not pleased with the way they appear in the film, saying among other things that they were told the film would be a nonprofit project to be aired on PBS, not a commercial venture. The filmmakers responded that they, too, thought it would—that the amazing response which found it a theatrical release was a surprise to them. The movie simply turned out to be a masterpiece, and its intended noncommercial slot was not big enough to hold it. The St. Joseph suit reveals understandable sensitivity, because not all of the St. Joseph people come out looking like heroes.

It is as clear as day that the only reason Arthur Agee and William Gates are offered scholarships to St. Joseph's in the first place is because they are gifted basketball players. They are hired as athletes as surely as if they were free agents in pro ball; suburban high schools do not often send scouts to the inner city to find future scientists or teachers.

Both sets of parents are required to pay a small part of the tuition costs. When Gates's family cannot pay, a member of the booster club pays for him—because he seems destined to be a high school all-American. Arthur at first does not seem as talented. And when he has to drop out of the school because his parents have both lost their jobs, there is no sponsor for him. Instead, there's a telling scene where the school refuses to release his transcripts until the parents have paid their share of his tuition.

The morality here is clear: St. Joseph's wanted Arthur, recruited him, and would have found tuition funds for him if he had played up to expectations. When he did not, the school held the boy's future as hostage for a debt his parents clearly would never have contracted if the school's recruiters had not come scouting grade school playgrounds for the boy. No wonder St. Joseph's feels uncomfortable. Its behavior seems like something out of Dickens. The name Scrooge comes to mind.

Gene Pingatore, the coach at St. Joseph's, felt he was seen in an unattractive light. I thought he came across fairly well. Like all coaches, he believes athletics are a great deal more important when they really are, and there is a moment when he leaves a decision to Gates that Gates is clearly not well prepared to make. But it isn't Pingatore but the whole system that is brought into question: What does it say about the values involved, when the pro sports machine reaches right down to eighth-grade playgrounds?

But the film is not only, or mostly, about such issues. It is about the ebb and flow of life over several years, as the careers of the two boys go through changes so amazing that, if this were fiction, we would say it was not believable. The filmmakers (Steve James, Frederick Marx, and Peter Gilbert) shot miles of film, 250 hours in all, and that means they were there for several of the dramatic turning points in the lives of the two young men. For both, there are reversals of fortune—life seems bleak, and then is redeemed by hope and even sometimes triumph. I was caught up in their destinies as I rarely am in a fiction thriller, because real life can be a cliff-hanger, too.

Many filmgoers are reluctant to see documentaries, for reasons I've never understood; the good ones are frequently more absorbing and entertaining than fiction. *Hoop Dreams*, however, is not only a documentary. It is also poetry and prose, muckraking and exposé, journalism and polemic. It is one of the great moviegoing experiences of my lifetime.

Hoosiers ★ ★ ★ ★
PG, 114 m., 1987

Gene Hackman (Norman Dale), Barbara Hershey (Myra Fleener), Dennis Hopper (Shooter), Sheb Wooley (Cletus), Fern Parsons (Opal Fleener), Chelcie Ross (George), Robert Swan (Rollin), Michael O'Guinne (Rooster). Directed by David Anspaugh and produced by Carter De Haven and Angelo Pizzo. Screenplay by Pizzo.

I was a sportswriter once for a couple of years in downstate Illinois. I covered mostly high school sports, and if I were a sportswriter again, I'd want to cover them again. There is a passion to high school sports that transcends anything that comes afterward; nothing in pro sports equals the intensity of a really important high school basketball game.

Hoosiers knows that. This is a movie about a tiny Indiana high school that sends a team all the way to the state basketball finals in the days when schools of all sizes played in the same tournaments and a David could slay a Goliath. The school in the movie is so small that it can barely field a team, especially after the best player decides to drop out. Can schools this small actually become state champs? Sure. That's what high school sports are all about.

Hoosiers is a comeback movie, but it's not simply about a comeback of this small team, the Hickory Huskers. It's also about the comeback of their coach, a mysterious middle-age guy named Norman Dale (Gene Hackman), who seems to be too old and too experienced to be coaching in an obscure backwater like Hickory.

And it's also the comeback story of Shooter, the town drunk (played by Dennis Hopper, whose supporting performance won an Oscar nomination). Everybody in this movie seems to be trying to start over in life, and, in a way, basketball is simply their excuse.

Hoosiers has the broad overall structure of most sports movies: It begins with the problem of a losing team, introduces the new coach, continues with the obligatory training sequences and personality clashes, arrives at the darkest hour, and then heads toward triumph. This story structure is almost as sacred to Hollywood as basketball is to Indiana.

What makes *Hoosiers* special is not its story, however, but its details and its characters. Angelo Pizzo, who wrote the original screenplay, knows small-town sports. He knows all about high school politics and how the school board and the parents' groups always think they know more about basketball than the coach does. He knows about gossip, scandal, and vengeance. And he knows a lot about human nature.

All of this knowledge, however, would be pointless without Hackman's great performance at the center of this movie. Hackman is gifted at combining likability with complexity—two qualities that usually don't go together in the movies. He projects all of the single-mindedness of any good coach, but then he contains other dimensions, and we learn about the scandal in his past that led him to this one-horse town. David Anspaugh's direction is good at suggesting Hackman's complexity without belaboring it.

Hickory High School is where Hackman hopes to make his comeback, but he doesn't think only of himself. He meets Shooter (Hopper), the alcoholic father of one of his team members, and enlists him as an assistant coach with one stipulation: no more drinking. That doesn't work. In a way, Hackman knows it won't work, but by involving Shooter once again in the life of the community, he's giving him a reason to seek the kind of treatment that might help.

Hackman finds that he has another project on his hands, too: the rehabilitation of his heart. He falls in love with a teacher at the school (Barbara Hershey), and their relationship is interesting, as far as it goes, although it feels like key scenes have been cut out of the romance. Maybe another movie could have been made about them; this movie is about basketball.

The climax of the movie will come as no great surprise to anyone who has seen other sports movies. *Hoosiers* works a magic, however, in getting us to really care about the fate of the team and the people depending on it. In the way it combines sports with human nature, it reminded me of another wonderful Indiana sports movie, *Breaking Away*. It's a movie that is all heart.

Hope and Glory ★ ★ ★
PG-13, 118 m., 1987

Sebastian Rice Edwards (Bill), Geraldine Muir (Sue), Sarah Miles (Grace), David Hayman (Clive), Sammi Davis (Dawn), Derrick O'Connor (Mac), Susan Wooldridge (Molly), Jean-Marc Barr (Bruce), Ian Bannen (Grandfather). Directed, produced, and written by John Boorman.

Maybe there is something in the very nature of war, in the power of guns and bombs, that appeals to the imagination of little boys. Bombers and fighter planes and rockets and tanks are thrilling at that age when you are old enough to understand how they work, but too young to understand what they do. John Boorman's *Hope and Glory* is a film about that precise season in the life of a young British boy who grows up in a London suburb during World War II.

The boy (Sebastian Rice Edwards), probably meant to be Boorman himself, is bright and curious, and although he is sad when his dad goes away in uniform, there are certain consolations, such as the nightly German air raids that leave real pieces of shrapnel in the garden—some of them still hot from explosions, and all of them very collectible.

For his mother (Sarah Miles, in one of the best performances of her career), life is not so simple, but it has its consolations. Left to raise the family after her husband is drafted, she deals distractedly with rebellion in the ranks of her children, particularly from a teen-age daughter whose sexual awakening has been hastened by the arrival of Canadian troops who are training in the neighborhood.

Hope and Glory is first of all a painstaking re-creation of the period. All the cars and signs and clothes look right, and there are countless small references to wartime rationing, as when the older sister draws seams on her legs to make fake nylons. But after re-creating the period, Boorman also reconstructs the very feeling that was in the air.

The nightly routine of air raids quickly loses its novelty, and Miles has to shake her sleepyheads to get them out of bed and into the backyard bomb shelter. One night, they don't make it, and crouch in the hall closet as the bombs fall closer and closer. The next one, they whisper, will either hit them or not—but it misses, and hits the house of a mean old lady down the street, creating a great fire and drawing lots of exciting fire engines.

There is something almost perverse in the way Boorman defines his point of view. He is not concerned in this film about the tragedy of war, or the meaning of war, but only with the specific experience of war for a grade school boy. Drawing from his own autobiographical memories, he has not given the little boy in the movie any more insights than such a little boy should have. His approach is especially effective in a scene where the boy witnesses his sister making out with a soldier; he looks, and does not quite understand, and

looks away, perhaps sensing that this is a chapter that has not yet opened for him.

Toward the end of the film, the locale changes; the family goes to stay in the country with Miles's grandparents, and existence there seems more idyllic than in the city. Probably this is the way Boorman remembers it; going to the country is not an escape from bombs, but a chance to float on the river and run in the pastures.

Wartime is always a time, on the domestic front, of personal upheaval. There is a quiet, touching subplot in *Hope and Glory* about a choice Sarah Miles made when she got married. She married out of common sense, not out of love, and although she is still best friends with the man she loved, she is faithful to her absent husband. This situation leads to one of the film's best scenes, when the daughter confesses her love for a Canadian airman—and reveals that she is pregnant. The mother tells her daughter she must be true to her heart, and follow love wherever it leads, and we know that is exactly what she did not do.

Hope and Glory was an enormous success in England, where every frame must have its special memories for British audiences. Through American eyes, it is a more universal film, not so much about war as about memory. When we are young, what happens is not nearly as important as what we think happens. Perhaps that's true even when we are not so young.

Hotel Terminus ★ ★ ★
NO MPAA RATING, 267 m., 1988

A documentary directed by Marcel Ophuls and produced by Ophuls and Bernard Farrel. Edited by Albert Jurgenson and Catherine Zins.

Meandering through *Hotel Terminus*, I felt two sensations that do not ordinarily go together. One was a sense of outrage, and the other was the hypnotic rhythm of a repetitive process. The movie records a tireless search by Marcel Ophuls, a documentary filmmaker who went looking for anyone who could tell him about Klaus Barbie, the Nazi war criminal from France who became known as the "Butcher of Lyons." By the end of the film we know a lot about Barbie, and a lot about Ophuls.

Over and over during the course of the film, people protest that Ophuls is asking questions about things that happened "over forty years ago." If that were true, it would

not be a reason to avoid asking the questions. But it is not true. The whole point of the movie is that Klaus Barbie's war did not end with everyone else's, with the defeat of Nazi Germany.

Barbie was one of the lucky ones whose skills (mostly torture and interrogation) were useful to the postwar Allies in their fight against communism. So he was sheltered from charges of war crimes, used by various agencies (most notably the U.S. counterintelligence corps), and eventually provided with a new identity and resettled in South America—where he continued to practice his torturer's trade.

Barbie was eventually located and denounced by anti-Nazi groups, was extradited by Bolivia, stood trial in Germany, was convicted of war crimes including the sentencing of forty-one orphans to Nazi war camps, and is serving a life sentence. *Hotel Terminus* is not about his capture, trial, and conviction. It is about how people remember him.

Some remember what they want to remember, others remember what they cannot forget. In the film's most harrowing monologue, a woman describes how Barbie methodically tortured one particular prisoner—the woman's father. In other interviews, we learn that Barbie "made the Gestapo respectable" in Lyons by joining it, that he may have betrayed various Resistance fighters, that he enjoyed hitting people, and also that he was a "nice" man, an intelligent man, and a man who was useful to the Allies after the war. As we listen to retired American intelligence agents describe how they used him, there is the impression that he was just the man they needed, a man not too squeamish to do the dirty jobs they were reluctant to do themselves.

Ophuls is a man with a highly developed sense of irony, and in editing more than 120 hours of interviews into a 267-minute film, he has often selected moments that are rich with self-contradiction. One man, for example, observes that his dog liked Barbie, "and you can't fool a dog." Of course you can fool a dog—and its owner. Other interview subjects are almost absurd as they do verbal handstands to avoid admitting what they almost certainly knew, did, and said.

I felt outrage as I viewed these scenes, and I noticed a curious thing within myself: At times I was more outraged at the "good citizens"—the retired American spies, the postwar officials—than I was at Barbie.

That was because I accepted that Barbie was evil, but I did not want to accept that our side would leap to shelter him and work for him. It is easier when all the Nazis are Germans, but harder when we cannot isolate the evil of Nazism in the historical past, and have to accept that officials of several U.S. administrations and even the Vatican were willing to protect this man.

The other sensation I felt was the hypnotic rhythm of Ophuls's reporting process. Long films create a time of their own. Films like *Shoah, Little Dorrit,* and *Hotel Terminus* cut us loose from the expectation of a beginning, middle, and end, and leave us adrift for long periods in the center of the film with no shore in sight. Without a story structure to guide us, we become the accomplices of the director—his passengers. We go where he goes. Ophuls asks the same questions again and again, until we grow as angry as he does by the evasions of the answers. When he grows sarcastic (ridiculing one man who will not talk to him by interviewing the cabbages in his garden), it is a relief—we're fed up, too. By the end of *Hotel Terminus,* we have become absorbed somewhat into the filmmaking process; in a strange way, we have gone on the same quest as Ophuls.

Hotel Terminus is not a great film, like Ophuls's *The Sorrow and the Pity,* his masterful indictment of the French who collaborated with the Nazis. It is almost deliberately a film in a minor key, a stubborn film, a gadfly's film, the film of a man who agrees with you that the Nazis were monsters, but adds that he hopes you won't mind if he clears up a few other details as well, such as the utter embarrassment of the postwar history of Klaus Barbie. *The Sorrow and the Pity* was the film of a man who held his audience spellbound. *Hotel Terminus* is the film of a man who continues the conversation after others would like to move on to more polite subjects. It is a stubborn, angry, nagging, sarcastic assault on good manners, and I am happy Ophuls was ill-tempered enough to make it.

Hot Shots, Part Deux ★ ★ ★
PG-13, 87 m., 1993

Charlie Sheen (Topper Harley), Lloyd Bridges (Tug Benson), Valeria Golino (Ramada Rodham Hayman), Richard Crenna (Colonel Denton Walters), Brenda Bakke (Michelle Rodham Huddleston), Miguel Ferrer (Harbinger). Directed by Jim Abrahams and produced by Bill Badalato. Screenplay by Abrahams and Pat Proft.

There is a love scene in *Hot Shots, Part Deux* in which the hero, a dashing Navy commando played by Charlie Sheen, is dining with a beautiful espionage expert played by Valeria Golino. They are having spaghetti in an Italian restaurant, and somehow they each get one end of a long strand of pasta into their mouths, and suck it in until their faces come closer, and closer . . . and they kiss.

This is, of course, a famous shot stolen from *Lady and the Tramp.* So is the next shot, in which Sheen lovingly uses his nose to push a meatball in the direction of his lady love. One of the pleasures of watching a spoof like this is to spot the references; it's like a quiz on pop art.

The Golina character is named Ramada Rodham Hayman. The other principal female character in the movie, played by Brenda Bakke, is named Michelle Rodham Huddleston. So it goes. The movie is directed by Jim Abrahams, who was one of the perpetrators of *Airplane!* (1980), the satirical parody that spawned this and many other films, including *Top Secret!, The Naked Gun,* and the original *Hot Shots.*

The current film takes *Rambo III* as its starting place, with lots of loving little touches. The Sheen character, patterned on the Stallone original, is a pumped-up man of few words, who at the beginning of the film has left his life of action and violence to live a life of contemplation with monks in a remote Eastern land. He is tracked down there by his old commanding officer, played by Richard Crenna in a repeat of Crenna's role in *Rambo III.* Sheen wants to stay where he is, until Crenna tells him a story that makes him realize he is needed for a dangerous mission in the Middle East. The story is *Goldilocks and the Three Bears.*

Sheen, named Topper Harley in the movie, is needed there to rescue Americans who were sent in to rescue other Americans who were sent in to rescue other Americans. Why is his participation essential? "You are the best of what we have left!" In the unnamed Arab country, we see a Saddam Hussein look-alike living a life of blissful domesticity, interrupted by moments of mayhem and torture. And we join Sheen on the mission, which is constructed out of countless jokes based on the *Rambo* movies and other commando epics.

There are also the usual in-jokes. Proceeding down an Asian river in a gunboat, Sheen passes another boat headed in the opposite direction. On it is his father, Martin Sheen, who starred, of course, in *Apocalypse Now,* and is apparently still inside that movie as we see him. "Loved you in *Wall Street,*" the father shouts, as the boats pass.

Movies like this are more or less impervious to the depredations of movie critics. Either you laugh, or you don't. I laughed. Will this genre ever run out of steam? *Hot Shots, Part Deux* doesn't have the high-voltage nonstop comedy of *Airplane!* and *Top Secret!,* still the best of their kind, and it isn't as hard on Stallone as it could have been. But as long as the Hollywood assembly lines keep groaning, there will probably be a function for these corrective measures.

The Hot Spot ★ ★ ★
R, 130 m., 1990

Don Johnson (Harry Madox), Virginia Madsen (Dolly Harshaw), Jennifer Connelly (Gloria Harper), Charles Martin Smith (Lon Gulik), William Sadler (Frank Sutton), Jerry Hardin (George Harshaw). Directed by Dennis Hopper and produced by Paul Lewis. Screenplay by Nona Tyson and Charles Williams.

A guy comes in from out of town. He doesn't have a past, at least not one he wants to talk about. He gets a job in a used car lot. It's one of those typical small towns from the movies of the 1940s and 1950s, the kind of backwater where the other guy on the job is a nerd, and the boss is a blowhard with a bum ticker—but the boss's wife is this great broad with blonde hair and big eyelashes and when she gets up in the morning, she puts on her negligee just when the other women in town are taking theirs off. Oh, and the bookkeeper at work is this innocent young girl who is intimidated, for mysterious reasons, by the vicious creep who lives in a shack outside of town.

I feel at home in movies like *The Hot Spot.* They come out of that vast universe formed by the historic meeting of B movies and the idea of *film noir*—films about the soft underbelly of the human conscience. There are certain conventions to be observed, and *The Hot Spot* knows them and observes them. The hero has to smoke and look laconic and be trying to suppress something in his past. It helps if he drives a Studebaker. The boss's wife has to have learned all of her moves by studying old movies. The plot has to provide that the bad guys don't commit all of the crimes; the hero, for example, robs the bank.

Dennis Hopper, who directed *The Hot Spot*, grew up in the movies at a time when films like this were familiar—back in the days when there was time for luxuries like a supporting cast and a plot, back before high-tech violence and machine-gun editing came to dominate crime movies. As an actor, he was directed by *film noir* veterans like Nicholas Ray and Henry Hathaway. And maybe his sensibility is attuned to this kind of material, to the notion that an ordinary guy can stumble into some pretty strange stuff. The movie has been compared in some quarters to the work of David Lynch, but it's less self-hating and more stylistically exuberant.

The movie is all style and tone, and a lot of the tone is set by the performance of Virginia Madsen as Dolly Harshaw, the boss's wife. It's the kind of work that used to be done by Lana Turner or Barbara Stanwyck—the tough woman with the healthy sexual interest, who sizes a guy up and makes sure he knows what she likes in a man. Jennifer Connelly, as the innocent bookkeeper down at the office, is perfectly cast as her opposite. She's got the Teresa Wright role, the good girl who has been bruised by an uncaring world. Hopper regards both women with the visual imagination of a cheesecake photographer, which is kind of refreshing. Male superstars have come to dominate action movies so thoroughly that it's rare to find a movie with the time and inclination to linger on beautiful women.

The plot is silly, as such plots always are. It stars Don Johnson as Harry Madox, the stranger from out of town, and he figures out a way to steal money from the bank, and he also finds himself embroiled in violence when the creep in the shack outside of town starts messing with the young girl. And, of course, the boss's wife also has a connection to the creep, and the key to everything is in the shameful secrets of the past.

A film this simple can best be appreciated by a fairly sophisticated viewer, I think. Your average workaday moviegoer will relate to it on Level One and think it contains clichés and stereotypes. Only movie lovers who have marinated their imaginations in the great B movies from RKO and Republic will recognize *The Hot Spot* as a superior work in an old tradition—as a manipulation of story elements as mannered and deliberate, in its way, as variations on a theme for the piano.

Household Saints ★ ★ ★ ★
R, 124 m., 1993

Vincent Phillip D'Onofrio (Joseph Santangelo), Tracey Ullman (Catherine), Lili Taylor (Teresa), Victor Argo (Lino Falconetti), Judith Malina (Joseph's Mother), Michael Imperioli (Leonard Villanova). Directed by Nancy Savoca and produced by Richard Guay and Peter Newman. Screenplay by Savoca and Guay.

Saints are a great inconvenience. They interfere with the plans of ordinary people. When a modern family finds itself with a saint in its midst, there is a tendency to send for the psychiatrist. *Household Saints* is about Italian-Americans in New York City who begin with a form of madness they are comfortable with, and end with a madness only a saint could understand.

Like many stories of miracles, this one begins with a pinochle game. The local butcher, Joseph Santangelo, has fallen in love with Catherine, the daughter of his card-playing buddy, Lino Falconetti. The stakes in their game go higher and higher one night, until finally Joseph wants to play for the right to marry Catherine. Lino agrees, and loses, and goes home and orders his daughter to fix a nice dinner because the Santangelos are coming over.

"I want you to make a meal so good a man would get married to eat like that every night," he says. "I got news for you," she says. "Nobody gets married for the food." And particularly not her cooking, which is so haphazard that Joseph's mother insults the cooking right there at the table.

But Joseph (Vincent D'Onofrio) and Catherine (Tracey Ullman) do get married. And gradually they change. As young people they look like the "before" pictures in an ad for a beauty school. Catherine is particularly careless, with her lank hair and her tendency to spend the day locked up with a book. But eventually prosperity touches them. Joseph grows a mustache and goes to a better barber. Catherine tints her hair and uses makeup.

It is a constant trial, living with Joseph's shrill and hateful mother (Judith Malina), who spends Catherine's first pregnancy pumping her full of horrifying old wives' tales—superstitions about all the things that can lead to miscarriages or the birth of monsters. When Mrs. Santangelo finally dies, Catherine paints the dark old apartment in bright pastels and buys Tupperware, and the family enters the twentieth century.

To them a daughter is born. Teresa (Lili Taylor) is a quiet, serious girl who grows up as a devout Catholic. She is attracted to that uncompromising thread of Catholicism that challenges her to become a saint. She prays, meditates, and spends her days in penance and good works. She develops a special devotion to her namesake, St. Teresa, known as the Little Flower of Jesus. She agrees with the saint that it is not necessary to do great things in the world to be holy; one can do God's work anywhere, and there is grace to be won by scrubbing floors.

Teresa is a child who would be completely understood by her superstitious grandmother. Her parents have become modernized, however, and while of course they are Catholics, they don't see any need to get carried away with things. When Teresa shyly announces her hope to enter the convent, her father explodes: "I don't want no daughter of mine lining the Pope's pockets."

By now it is about 1970. Change is in the air. Teresa enrolls in college, where most of the students are on the floor in sit-ins, not prayer. She meets a young man named Leonard Villanova (Michael Imperioli), who explains that he has a Life Plan: "First, I get the St. John's law degree. Then I want a Lincoln Continental. I want a family, and a town house on the upper East Side, and I want membership in all those clubs that always turned up their noses at the Italians." He plans a career in "television law." Teresa is impressed: "You mean like Perry Mason?"

Household Saints is a wonderful movie, without a second that isn't blessed by the grace of its special humor and tenderness. But the closing scenes are transcendent, as Teresa drifts away from the Villanova Plan and into a plan of her own, for loving Jesus. The fact is that modern people *do* worship false gods, and that a life devoted to getting a big car and a town house is seen as eminently more sane than a life devoted to God. You can decide for yourself if Teresa goes mad. In an earlier age, people would have known how to think of her.

This warmhearted jewel of a movie was directed by Nancy Savoca, whose previous films are *True Love* and *Dogfight* (which also starred the priceless Lili Taylor). She treasures eccentricity in people. Another director might have started right off with the story of Teresa. But Savoca's subject is larger: She wants to show how, in only three generations, an Italian family that is comfortable with the mystical turns into an American family that is threatened by it. And she wants to explore the possibilities of sainthood in these secular days. That she sees great humor in her subject is perfect; it is always easier to find the truth through laughter.

There will be people who question Teresa's devotion to the Little Flower. For me, the movie rang one bell of memory after another. I went to Catholic school in the 1950s—that age of Latin, incense, and mystery before Vatican II repainted the Church in politically correct pastels. I know this movie is closer to the literal truth of those days than many non-Catholics will believe. When was it, I wonder, that it became madness to want to be a saint?

Housekeeping ★ ★ ★ ★
PG, 117 m., 1988

Christine Lahti (Sylvie), Sara Walker (Ruth), Andrea Burchill (Lucille), Anne Pitoniak (Aunt Lily), Barbara Reese (Aunt Nona). Directed by Bill Forsyth and produced by Robert F. Colesberry. Screenplay by Forsyth.

In a land where the people are narrow and suspicious, where do they draw the line between madness and sweetness? Between those who are unable to conform to society's norm, and those who simply choose not to, because their dreamy private world is more alluring? That is one of the many questions asked, and not exactly answered, in Bill Forsyth's *Housekeeping*, which was one of the strangest and best films of 1988.

The movie, set some thirty or forty years ago in the Pacific Northwest, tells the story of two young girls who are taken on a sudden and puzzling motor trip by their mother to visit a relative. Soon after they arrive, their mother commits suicide, and before long her sister, their Aunt Sylvie, arrives in town to look after them.

Sylvie, who is played by Christine Lahti as a mixture of bemusement and wry reflection, is not an ordinary type of person. She likes to sit in the dusk so much that she never turns the lights on. She likes to go for long, meandering walks. She collects enormous piles of newspapers and hundreds of tin cans—carefully washing off their labels and then polishing them and arranging them in gleaming pyramids. She is nice to everyone and generally seems cheerful, but there is an enchantment about her that some people find suspicious.

Indeed, even her two young nieces are divided. One finds her "funny," and the other loves her, and eventually the two sisters will take separate paths in life because they differ about Sylvie. At first, when they are younger, she simply represents reality to them. As they grow older and begin to attend high school, however, one of the girls wants to be "popular," and resents having a weird aunt at home, while the other girl draws herself into Sylvie's dream.

The townspeople are not evil, merely conventional and "concerned." Parties of church ladies visit, to see if they can "help." The sheriff eventually gets involved. But *Housekeeping* is not a realistic movie, not one of those disease-of-the-week docudramas with a tidy solution. It is funnier, more offbeat, and too enchanting to ever qualify on those terms.

The writer-director, Bill Forsyth, has made all of his previous films in Scotland (they make a list of whimsical, completely original comedies: *Gregory's Girl, Local Hero, Comfort and Joy, That Sinking Feeling*). For his first North American production, he began with a novel by Marilynne Robinson that embodies some of his own notions, such as that certain people grow so amused by their own conceits that they cannot be bothered to pay lip service to yours.

In Christine Lahti, he has found the right actress to embody this idea. Although she has been excellent in a number of realistic roles (she was Gary Gilmore's sister in *The Executioner's Song*, and Goldie Hawn's best friend in *Swing Shift*), there is something resolutely private about her, a sort of secret smile that is just right for Sylvie. The role requires her to find a delicate line; she must not seem too mad or willful, or the whole charm of the story will be lost. And although there are times in the film when she seems to be indifferent to her nieces, she never seems not to love them.

Forsyth has surrounded that love with some extraordinary images, which help to create the magical feeling of the film. The action takes place in a house near a lake that is crossed by a majestic, forbidding railroad bridge, and it is a local legend that one night decades ago, a passenger train slipped ever so lazily off the line and plunged down, down into the icy waters of the frozen lake. The notion of the passengers in their warm, well-lit carriages, plunging down to their final destination, is one that Forsyth somehow turns from a tragedy into a notion of doomed beauty. And the bridge becomes important at several moments in the film, especially the last one.

The pastoral setting of the film (in British Columbia) and the production design by Adrienne Atkinson are also evocative; it is important that the action takes place in a small, isolated community, in a place cut off from the world where whimsies can flourish and private notions can survive. At the end of the film, I was quietly astonished; I had seen a film that could perhaps be described as being about a madwoman, but I had seen a character who seemed closer to a mystic, or a saint.

House of Games ★ ★ ★
R, 102 m., 1987

Lindsay Crouse (Margaret Ford), Joe Mantegna (Mike), Mike Nussbaum (Joey), Lilia Skala (Dr. Littauer), J.T. Walsh (Businessman), Jack Wallace (Bartender). Directed by David Mamet and produced by Michael Hausman. Screenplay by Mamet.

This movie is awake. I have seen so many films that sleepwalk through the debris of old plots and secondhand ideas that it was a constant pleasure to watch *House of Games*, a movie about con men that succeeds not only in conning its viewers, but also in creating a series of characters who seem imprisoned by the need to con or be conned.

The film stars Lindsay Crouse as a psychiatrist who specializes in addictive behavior, possibly as a way of dealing with her own compulsions. One of her patients is a gambler who fears he will be murdered over a bad debt. Crouse walks through lonely night streets to the neon signs of the House of Games, a bar where she thinks she can find the gambler who has terrorized her client. She wants to talk him out of enforcing the debt.

The gambler (Joe Mantegna) has never heard anything like this before. But he offers her a deal: If she will help him fleece a high-roller Texan in a big-stakes poker game, he will tear up the marker. She does so. She also becomes fascinated by the back-room reality of these gamblers who have reduced life to a knowledge of the odds. She comes back the next day, looking for Mantegna. She tells him she wants to learn more about gamblers and con men, about the kind of man he is. By the end of this movie, does she ever.

House of Games was written and directed by David Mamet, the playwright *(Glengarry Glen Ross)* and screenwriter *(The Untouchables)*, and it is his directorial debut. Originally it was intended as a big-budget movie with an established director and major stars, but Mamet took the reins himself, cast his wife in the lead and old acting friends in the other important roles, and shot it on the rainy streets of Seattle. Usually the screenwriter is insane to think he can direct a movie. Not this time. *House of Games* never steps wrong from beginning to end.

The plotting is diabolical and impeccable, and I will not spoil the delight of its unfolding by mentioning the crucial details. What I can mention are the performances, the dialogue, and the setting. When Lindsay Crouse enters the House of Games, she enters a world occupied by characters who have known each other so long and so well, in so many different ways, that everything they say is a kind of shorthand. At first we don't fully realize that, and there is a strange savor to the words they use. They speak, of course, in Mamet's distinctive dialogue style, an almost musical rhythm of stopping, backing up, starting again, repeating, emphasizing, all the time with the hint of deeper meanings below the surfaces of the words. The leading actors, Joe Mantegna and Mike Nussbaum, have appeared in countless performances of Mamet plays over the years, and they know his dialogue the way other actors grow into Beckett or Shakespeare. They speak it as it is meant to be spoken, with a sort of aggressive, almost insulting, directness. Mantegna has a scene where he "reads" Lindsay Crouse— where he tells her about her "tells," those small giveaway looks and gestures that poker players use to read the minds of their opponents. The way he talks to her is so incisive and unadorned it is sexual.

These characters and others live in a city that looks, as the Seattle of *Trouble in Mind* did, like a place on a parallel time track. It is a modern American city, but like none we have quite seen before; it seems to have been modeled on the paintings of Edward Hopper, where lonely people wait in empty public places for their destinies to intercept them. Crouse is portrayed as an alien in this world, a successful, best-selling author who has never dreamed that men like this exist, and the movie is insidious in the way it shows her willingness to be corrupted.

There is in all of us a fascination for the inside dope, for the methods of the confidence game, for the secrets of a magic trick. But there is an eternal gulf between the shark and the mark, between the con man and his victim. And there is a code to protect the secrets. There are moments in *House of Games* when Mantegna instructs Crouse in the methods and lore of the con game, but inside every con is another one.

I met a woman once who was divorced from a professional magician. She hated this man with a passion. She used to appear with him in a baffling trick where they exchanged places, handcuffed and manacled, in a locked cabinet. I asked her how it was done. The divorce and her feelings meant nothing compared to her loyalty to the magic profession. She looked at me coldly and said, "The trick is told when the trick is sold." The ultimate question in *House of Games* is, who's buying?

The House on Carroll Street ★ ★ ★
PG, 101 m., 1988

Kelly McGillis (Emily), Jeff Daniels (Cochran), Mandy Patinkin (Salwen), Jessica Tandy (Miss Venable), Jonathan Hogan (Alan), Remak Ramsay (Senator Byington), Ken Welsh (Hackett), Christopher Rhode (Stefan). Directed and produced by Peter Yates. Screenplay by Walter Bernstein.

There is a kind of movie sequence which Alfred Hitchcock always did well, and which most later directors have chosen not to do at all. It involves the hero discovering information by being nosy. Little or no dialogue is used. Most of what the hero sees is in longshot, and we can sometimes not quite make out all of the details. Half-heard words float on the air. What is being spied on is none of the hero's business, but he cannot resist the human need to be a spy, and neither can we.

The crucial developments in *The House on Carroll Street* are established with such a sequence, and so well is it handled that it casts a sort of spell over the movie. The time is the early 1950s, the height of McCarthyism. The heroine (Kelly McGillis) is a young woman who has just lost her job at a magazine, after refusing to testify before the House Un-American Activities Committee. Desperate for work, she takes a job reading aloud to an old lady. One afternoon, walking in the lady's garden, she sees some figures moving in the tall back windows of the house on the other side of the yard.

She is intrigued. She moves closer, hiding behind the branch of a tree. She overhears an argument. She can tell that something is wrong, but does not know what it could be. Later, on the street, she sees a young man who was standing in the window. She tries to engage him in conversation, but he resists. Eventually, piecing together a clue here and a word there, she becomes convinced that the people in the house are smuggling Nazi

war criminals into the United States, and that they have friends in high places.

There is more. Because the McGillis character is presumably a dangerous radical, she is being tailed by the FBI (there is a hint here of the opening scenes of *Notorious*). The important friends of the Nazis might want to smear her as a Commie, to confuse the trail. The Nazis begin to suspect what she knows. The old lady becomes a valuable ally. And in another echo from *Notorious*, she and one of the FBI men fall in love.

He's played by Jeff Daniels, that dependable, open-faced middle American from *Something Wild* and *Terms of Endearment*. Hey, maybe she is a Commie, but she sure is pretty. He is attracted to her, is disturbed when she is harassed by a search of her home, begins to trust her, and eventually becomes her ally in the fight against the Nazis and their protectors.

As thriller plots go, *The House on Carroll Street* is fairly old-fashioned, which is one of its merits. This is a movie where casting is important, and it works primarily because McGillis, like Ingrid Bergman in *Notorious*, seems absolutely trustworthy. She becomes the island of trust and sanity in the midst of deceit and treachery. The movie advances slowly enough for us to figure it out along with McGillis (or sometimes ahead of her), and there is a nice, ironic double-reverse in the fact that the government is following a good person who seems evil, and discovers evil people who seem good.

What is particularly welcome about the movie is that it's not high-tech. It not only takes place in the 1950s, but is happy there. We don't get the slam-bang cynicism of most characters in modern movies, and after a while I began to figure out why. This movie takes place so long ago that the characters in it have never had their imaginations boiled by full immersion in the thriller culture of recent decades. They're still sort of sweet and innocent, and believe everybody is basically good, and are shocked when they're wrong. Maybe that's the movie's ultimate twist.

House Party ★ ★ ★
R, 105 m., 1990

Christopher Reid (Kid), Christopher Martin (Play), Robin Harris (Pop), Tisha Campbell (Sidney), A.J. Johnson (Sharane), Martin Lawrence (Bilal), George Clinton (D.J.). Full Force: Stab, Zilla, and Pee Wee as played by The George Brothers: Paul Anthony, B. Fine, and Bowlegged Lou, respectively. Directed by Reginald Hudlin and produced by Warrington Hudlin. Screenplay by Reginald Hudlin.

House Party is first of all a musical, and best approached in that spirit. To call it a teen-age movie would confuse the characters with the subject. Yes, it's about a crowd of black teen-agers who go to the same school and hang out together, and it's about their loves and rivalries, and a party one of the kids is having at his house. But the plot is an excuse to hang a musical on, and the movie is wall-to-wall with exuberant song and dance.

Original Hollywood musicals have fallen on hard times. The golden age is long gone, and now we get either retreads of Broadway shows or rock concert films. Only occasionally, in a film like *Saturday Night Fever, Dirty Dancing,* or even *The Little Mermaid,* do we get a film where the dramatic developments coexist with original and creative sound-track music.

In the case of *House Party,* the musical is a canvas used by the director, Reginald Hudlin, to show us black teen-agers with a freshness and originality that's rare in modern movies. We hardly ever see black teen-agers at all in films, and when we do they're painted in images that are either negative and threatening or impossibly clean-cut. Hudlin's teen-agers are neither: They're normal, average kids with the universal desire to go to a party and dance.

The movie's hero is Kid (Christopher Reid), a bright goofball with a haircut that makes Eraserhead look like a marine. He lives with his father (Robin Harris), a gruff but lovable disciplinarian who doesn't want to seem unreasonable but does believe a kid should do his homework before partying at night. And when a kid gets in trouble, he should be grounded.

Kid doesn't want to be grounded. Like all teen-agers, he believes that life literally exists one day at a time, and that an opportunity missed today—especially an opportunity to meet the girlfriend of his dreams—is missed forevermore. He sneaks out of the house, leading to a long night of mild slapstick as he's chased by his father, by the police, and by three tough athletes from his school he has unwisely offended. The chases serve to punctuate the music and the dancing.

A lot of the energy in the movie comes from the natural, unaffected performance of Christopher Reid as the teen-ager who will do anything to get to that dance. He has an engaging, off-center rhythm that suggests he plans to think his way through life instead of making a frontal assault. In his encounters with the jocks from his high school, he tries to talk his way out of tight spots, and his seduction technique with girls is almost entirely verbal; he'll *convince* them they like him. To their credit, the girls, Sidney (Tisha Campbell) and Sharane (A.J. Johnson), look at times like they almost believe him. In matters of romance, teen-age boys can take themselves so dreadfully seriously that Kid must come as a change-of-pace.

House Party is a first feature for writer-director Reginald and producer Warrington Hudlin, brothers from East St. Louis, and is based on a shorter film Reginald made while a student at Harvard. Like his older contemporary Spike Lee, he is a black filmmaker who is concerned with his black characters on their own terms, and doesn't feel the need felt by an earlier generation of directors to relate his characters and plots to white society. His characters don't represent anything but themselves, and there are moments of refreshing honesty here, as when two teen-age boys discuss the disadvantages of dating a girl from a project (one problem: her relatives always seem to be hanging around watching the TV).

There is a certain deadening way in which some critics have taken to evaluating recent films about blacks, in which points are given for positive image reinforcement, useful themes, and the promotion of middle-class values. To describe *House Party* in those terms would be unfair and would miss the whole point of the movie's energy and exuberance. It was refreshing for a change to see a story about young blacks that didn't revolve around social problems, thriller elements, drugs, or any particular form of seriousness. *House Party* is silly and high-spirited and not particularly significant, and that is just as it should be.

Housesitter ★ ★ ★
PG, 108 m., 1992

Steve Martin (Newt Davis), Goldie Hawn (Gwen), Dana Delany (Becky), Julie Harris (Edna Davis), Donald Moffat (George Davis), Peter MacNicol (Marty), Richard B. Shull (Ralph), Laurel Cronin (Mary). Directed by Frank Oz and produced by Brian Grazer. Screenplay by Mark Stein.

It is an old truth of acting that comedy is harder than tragedy. It may be true. It is certainly true that much of the humor in *Housesitter* is generated by the carefully modulated performancee of Steve Martin and Goldie Hawn. Their relationship in the movie is made of nuances and denials, and at any moment they could have brought the movie tumbling down to the level of a sitcom, but they never do.

The film fits broadly into that old category of romances about people who don't know they're falling in love with one another. They think they dislike each other, in fact—but we know better. The formula is usually a drone because the characters have to be unusually stupid to avoid realizing they're in love. But Mark Stein's screenplay for *Housesitter* avoids that trap by adding a whole additional level to the story: Both of these characters are lying most of the time, deliberately, and although they both know it, the lies mask their real feelings.

Martin plays Newt Davis, an architect who has designed his dream house and in the opening credits asks his childhood sweetheart (Dana Delany) if she will marry him and move into it. She says she will not. Heartbroken, he blurts out his sorrows one boozy night to a waitress named Gwen (Goldie Hawn), whose last name and most of the other facts about her are much in doubt during the film.

Learning of the new house, sitting empty and forlorn in a quaint little village, Gwen takes a bus there, introduces herself around town as Newt's wife, and furnishes the place, on credit. By the time Newt is horrified to discover her deception, Gwen has succeeded in making friends of Newt's parents *and* his former love. She has also told a few lies.

The genius of the film is that Newt immediately becomes attracted by the idea of extending the lies in order to get what he wants—a promotion and the love of Delany. Gwen agrees to help him. They will pretend to a phony marriage, stage a phony divorce, and manipulate and cheat the fates. But of course, things do not work out quite that way.

There is much more to the plot, but the charm of the movie comes in the performances—in the way Martin and Hawn lie to themselves and each other—and in the dialogue, which is endlessly inventive as one lie piles upon another, and the characters test each other with a high-wire act of falsehood. They are helped in this by sturdy supporting performances by Delany, Donald Moffat and Julie Harris as Newt's parents, and by

Richard B. Shull and Laurel Cronin as a couple of street people who are pressed into service as Gwen's parents.

Martin is very good here; in movies like *Parenthood* and *Planes, Trains and Automobiles* he has developed into a sort of upper-middle-class American everyman, crazy on the inside, normal on the outside, needy all over. But Goldie Hawn's performance is the keystone of the movie, and she is wonderful as Gwen, who hardly ever says anything that is quite the truth. The way she modulates her feelings—making her emotional state clear without telegraphing it and without going for laughs that would ruin the underlying drama—is subtle and effective. This is one of her best performances.

Housesitter is finally just a sweet and funny movie, rather than a comic masterpiece, but I think that's fine. It's what the movie wants to be. It's sympathetic, perceptive, cynical on the surface, warm at heart. The only question it leaves unanswered is whether you wouldn't get awfully cold in a New England winter, walking down that glass-enclosed passage to the bedroom.

Howards End ★ ★ ★ ★
PG, 140 m., 1992

Anthony Hopkins (Henry Wilcox), Vanessa Redgrave (Ruth Wilcox), Emma Thompson (Margaret Schlegel), Helena Bonham Carter (Helen Schlegel), Joseph Bennett (Paul Wilcox), James Wilby (Charles Wilcox), Sam West (Leonard Bast). Directed by James Ivory and produced by Ismail Merchant. Screenplay by Ruth Prawer Jhabvala.

Howards End, a film at once civilized and passionate, is named for a house in the English countryside. It has been in the Wilcox family for a long time—or, more properly, in the family of Mrs. Wilcox, who makes it the center of her life and retreats to its peace when the noise of life in London with Mr. Wilcox grows too deafening.

In America, where we change our address as easily as we change our telephone number, the meaning of such a house is harder to understand. We do not often grow up in the same rooms where our grandparents were born. But in a country such as England, until quite recently, many families had such houses in their histories, and *Howards End* is about the passing of the traditional and humanist values that could flourish in such places.

The story of the house and the people who pass through it is told by E.M. Forster, in the best of his novels and one of the last (after *A Passage to India, A Room With a View, Where Angels Fear to Tread,* and *Maurice*) to be filmed.

The year is 1910. Mrs. Wilcox (Vanessa Redgrave) develops an admiration for Margaret Schlegel (Emma Thompson), who belongs to a musical family with a British mother and a German father (but not "Germans of the dreadful sort," Forster confides). She finds she can talk to Margaret—she recognizes a spark in the girl that reminds her of herself. When she dies, her family is horrified to discover a scrawled, unsigned coda to her will, leaving the house to Margaret. They burn the scrap of paper ("Mother couldn't have meant it"), and agree to say nothing about it.

But life has a way of correcting errors. Margaret, who is young and beautiful by our standards but old enough to be on the edge of spinsterhood by the standards of her day, catches the eye of the bereaved Mr. Wilcox, a very rich, shy, abrupt industrialist played by Anthony Hopkins. He proposes, or more exactly croaks out some tortured syllables that seem to express esteem and desire. She interprets, and accepts. And she comes home to Howards End.

But this is not a melodrama about inheritances. It is a film about values. Other characters are involved, especially Margaret's sister, Helen (Helena Bonham Carter), and the desperately poor and unhappy Mr. Leonard Bast (Sam West), who meets the Schlegels through an incident of a lost umbrella, and becomes the victim of their attempts to help him. Mr. Wilcox, asked for advice on Mr. Bast's job prospects, advises him to leave a thriving company and join one that soon goes bankrupt, and when the girls cry out that poor Mr. Bast is now worse off than he was before, Wilcox replies, not complacently, "The poor are the poor, and one's sorry for them—but there it is."

The fiery Helen will not stand for this, and indeed produces poor Mr. Bast at Wilcox's daughter's wedding fete on the lawns of Howards End, where Bast, the leper at the feast, discovers along with everyone else that his slovenly wife knows Mr. Wilcox far better than she should. This development leads to the story's angry outcry against hypocrisy, as Helen denounces her sister and Margaret denounces her husband—not for immorality, but for failing to apply to himself the same standards he would apply to others.

Howards End is one of the best novels of the twentieth century. Read it. This film adaptation, by the team of director James Ivory, writer Ruth Prawer Jhabvala, and producer Ismail Merchant, is one of the best movies of the year—one of the best collaborations ever by these three, who specialize in literate adaptations of novels of manners *(A Room With a View, The Bostonians, Mr. and Mrs. Bridge).*

Howards End is such a good story, partly because Forster himself was a master storyteller who was particularly gifted at strong endings, and partly because the splendid cast embodies the characters so fully that the events actually seem to be happening to them, instead of unfolding from a screenplay.

Emma Thompson is superb in the central role: quiet, ironic, observant, with steel inside. Helena Bonham Carter has never been better than she is here, as the hothead who commits her mind and body to the radical new social ideas of the day. Anthony Hopkins gives a heartbreaking performance as a man who wants to change and wants to love, but finally cannot quite bring himself to break through the hidebound, reactionary impulses that protect him from his better nature. And Vanessa Redgrave, as the dying Mrs. Wilcox, casts a spell over the whole movie; if we do not believe in her values, and understand what she sees in Margaret and why she wants her to have the house, we miss the whole point.

What a beautiful film it is: not an over-decorated "period" adaptation, but a film in which the people move easily through town and country homes and landscapes that frame and define them. The house used as Howards End in the film is the very same house, I am informed, that Forster used as a model in writing his novel. It is easy to imagine standing on the lawn and understanding what such a house could mean. Paul Goodman once wrote, "As an architect draws, men live," by which, among other things, he possibly meant that good houses inspire good lives. Here is a house that sets such a test that a whole society is challenged.

The Hudsucker Proxy ★ ★
PG, 111 m., 1994

Tim Robbins (Norville Barnes), Jennifer Jason Leigh (Amy Archer), Paul Newman (Sidney J. Mussburger), Charles Durning (Waring Hudsucker), John Mahoney (Chief), Jim True (Buzz). Directed by Joel Coen and produced by Ethan Coen. Screenplay by Ethan Coen, Joel Coen, and Sam Raimi.

Two little creatures are perched on my shoulders, one whispering into each ear. One carries a pitchfork. The other has gossamer wings. They are dictating this review of *The Hudsucker Proxy:*

Angel: This is the best-looking movie I've seen in years, a feast for the eyes and the imagination. The art direction and set design are breathtaking, re-creating the world of 1930s screwball comedy in which towering skyscrapers and vast boardrooms were the playing fields for the ambitions of corrupt executives, ambitious kids, unsung geniuses, and lady newspaper reporters with nails as sharp as their wisecracks.

Devil: But the problem with the movie is that it's all surface and no substance. Not even the slightest attempt is made to suggest that the film takes its own story seriously. Everything is style. The performances seem deliberately angled as satire.

Angel: But those performances are right on target. Tim Robbins stars, as a mailroom clerk who finds himself thrust into the presidency of the giant Hudsucker Corp. Paul Newman is the gray eminence behind the scenes, who engineers Robbins's ascendancy because he believes the kid is hopelessly incompetent and will drive the stock price down—just what Newman desires. And Jennifer Jason Leigh has been studying Rosalind Russell in *His Girl Friday*, and has the part down perfect: the hard-bitten, fast-talking girl reporter who sits on your desk, lights a cigarette, and lays down the law.

Devil: So what? Was there anyone in this movie to really care about? And did the screwball aspects of the story ever take hold? Screwball comedy needs a certain looseness, an anarchic spirit that's alien to the meticulous productions of the Coen brothers, Joel and Ethan, who in this film as in their others *(Blood Simple, Raising Arizona, Miller's Crossing, Barton Fink)* seem to be so much in love with old movies that they shape their own ideas into the forms of films made before they were born.

Angel: Which brings me back to why I want to see the movie again. There is a grandness to the very conception of *The Hudsucker Proxy*, which sets the stage in the opening sequence, as an executive jumps out of a skyscraper and the camera precedes him in a headlong fall down what looks like a couple of hundred stories of terrifying free-fall, be-

fore . . . but you know the scene I mean. It was exhilarating.

Devil: But to what purpose other than pure style? And isn't there a glitch between the movie's look and style, which are clearly 1930s Art Deco, and its claim to be set in the 1950s?

Angel: Who really cares about stuff like that? Putting it in the 1950s allowed the Coens to have a lot of fun with the brainstorm of the Robbins character, who invents the hula hoop and makes untold billions for Hudsucker. And the hula hoop, in turn, provides an excuse for a montage showing hoopery sweeping across America—a filmmaking device which the Coens somehow are able to exploit and kid at the same time.

Devil: Wouldn't it have been a little more fun, though, if the hula hoop came as a surprise? The ads and the poster for the Coens' movie shows Robbins holding a big hula hoop, so walking into the theater, you know the secret. It's typical of their approach: They obviously think their plot is unimportant except as a clothesline for the visuals. And wasn't there something dead at the heart of all of this? A kind of chill in the air? A feeling that the movie was more thought than art, more calculated than inspired? Doesn't the viewer spend more time admiring the sights on the screen than caring about them? Isn't there something wrong when you walk out of a movie humming the sets?

Angel: That's the tired old rap against the Coens, that they're all technique and no heart. How many movies do have heart these days? Not many. Most movies recycle tired old formulas; even a so-called Generation X rebel picture like *Reality Bites* is just a retread of a 1930s romantic comedy that could have played on the same double bill with whatever inspired *The Hudsucker Proxy*. One good reason to go to the movies is to feast the eyes, even if the brain remains unchallenged. And *Hudsucker* is a pleasure to regard.

Devil: Unless . . . you want something more from a movie.

. . . The debate goes on. Just before they vaporized into thin air, the Angel advised me to give *The Hudsucker Proxy* four stars, and the Devil, whispering that the Coens are talented but need to be prodded to go beyond their technical mastery, wickedly advised me to cut them off with zero. Having weighed all their advice, I have taken a middle position.

Hugh Hefner: Once Upon a Time ★ ★ ★
NO MPAA RATING, 91 m., 1992

A documentary on Hugh Hefner, narrated by James Coburn. Directed by Robert Heath and produced by Gary H. Grossman and Heath.

This is the authorized version of Hugh Hefner's life, and must be viewed in that light. The founder of the Playboy empire obviously worked closely with the filmmakers, giving them hours of interviews and access to his archives. And Hefner is a man who has worked as his own personal archivist all of his life—he began a cartoon autobiography of himself in grade school and has continued the record, in one form or another, ever since.

What we are getting here is Hefner as he wants to be remembered. He says that, in a way, he wrote his "Playboy Philosophy" in the 1960s to explain himself to his mother. His mother is still alive, at ninety-seven, and maybe this movie is for her, too. Hef was raised in a strict Methodist home with old-fashioned values and no hugging, and after decades spent in reaction to that upbringing, he has come full circle and is now the head of a family with a pop, a mom, two sons, and maybe a baby sister on the way. Mom is the 1988 Playmate of the Year, of course, but lots of guys meet nice girls at work.

The movie's style is smooth and professional. James Coburn's narration sounds like an ad for a luxury car. But the materials of the movie are very personal: childhood snapshots, home movies, yearbook pictures, Hef in high school, Hef in college, Hef at his first job, Hef inventing the Playboy mystique and living right at the heart of it, and finally Hef growing older, as we all must, and having a stroke that slaps him in the face with his mortality, and then, in his sixties, marrying a second time and starting a second family. Full circle.

There are two sequences in the film that contain, I believe, the key to Hefner's public persona. We learn that as "Hugh" he was shy and unpopular the first two years in high school, and then he "reinvented" himself—the word is in the movie—as "Hef," the high school wit and cartoonist, actor and editor, who made the others laugh and entertained them. All the time he was at one remove from this process, turning himself and his friends into cartoons (there are several shots in which high school photos dissolve into his Archie and Jughead caricatures of the same friends).

It was a role that suited him, and later we see him presiding over parties at the Playboy Mansion—where, one of his friends recalls, "there was a bar, but Hef didn't drink. There was a fabulous buffet, but you never saw him eating. It was all for his friends." Hefner himself says, over and over, that his last two years of high school were the happiest years of his life. And there you have the key: Hefner's Playboy image was an extension of Hef, the upperclassman at Chicago's Steinmetz High School, throwing neat parties for his friends with lots of good eats and drinks and movies and pop music—and as the friends had a great time, Hef stood back and watched, and recorded it all in his magazine.

"Classes were great at Steinmetz," Hef told the students during a visit there last week, "but extracurricular activities were fabulous." It was the same in the magazine: The articles and interviews and political controversy were the classes. They were good. After class was out, there were the Playmates and the party jokes and the recipes for exotic libations and the specs on new sports cars. And instead of going over to Hef's house after school to spin some platters, Hef's new classmates (his readers) were invited, symbolically, over to Hef's mansion.

Jules Feiffer, an early guest, observes in the film that he dreamed of bedding dozens of Playmates, but never had sex in the mansion. His story is revealing. If the image was of a nonstop orgy, the reality was more like a 1940s after-school party, in which the guys could look at the girls and dream, but in the meantime there were pinball machines and a pool, a bowling alley and a neat fire pole to slide down, movies and a hi-fi system, and permanent icebox-raiding privileges. The Playmates were, literally, well named.

The party lasted from the late 1950s until the late 1980s, but all of the times were not good. The movie goes into some detail about the two great tragedies of the Playboy story: the suicide of Hefner's private secretary, Bobbie Arnstein, in the midst of a drug probe, and the murder of Playmate of the Year Dorothy Stratten by her insanely jealous husband. Arnstein was charged with buying and selling cocaine, and Hefner argues in the movie that, while she did use cocaine, she was targeted only because a politically motivated prosecution was after bigger game and wanted her to testify against Hefner. She refused to, and, facing jail, killed herself. Later the probe was dropped, with no charges ever filed.

Hefner does not say in the movie whether he ever used cocaine. Drugs in general were discouraged at the mansion because of the legal risks, but Hefner admits to an addiction to pep pills that kept him working for forty-hour stretches. His drug use was the opposite of recreational; until the stroke, he was a workaholic.

The Stratten story is more complex because Dorothy was in love with movie director Peter Bogdanovich at the time of her death, and Bogdanovich wrote an anguished book blaming her death on the Playboy mystique. Not true, Hefner says; she had outgrown her sleazy husband and he might have killed her if *Playboy* had never existed.

What *if Playboy* had never existed? Would we live in a different world? Possibly. Historians will someday conclude, I believe, that for better or worse, *Playboy* was the most influential magazine of its time. *Hugh Hefner: Once Upon a Time* gives the founder's view of that phenomenon. There are many other views, some far less favorable. But American society was never quite the same after we all went over to Hef's house after school.

The Hunt for Red October ★ ★ ★ ½
PG, 134 m., 1990

Sean Connery (Marko Ramius), Alec Baldwin (Jack Ryan), Scott Glenn (Bart Mancuso), Sam Neill (Captain Borodin), James Earl Jones (Admiral Greer), Joss Ackland (Andrei Lysenko), Richard Jordan (Jeffrey Pelt), Peter Firth (Ivan Putin), Tim Curry (Dr. Petrov), Jeffrey Jones (Skip Tyler). Directed by John McTiernan and produced by Mace Neufeld. Screenplay by Larry Ferguson and Donald Stewart.

The movies have one sure way of involving us that never fails. They give us a character who is right when everybody else is wrong and then invite us to share his frustration as he tries to talk some sense into the blockheads. In *The Hunt for Red October,* that character is Jack Ryan, the intelligence man who believes he knows the real reason why a renegade Soviet skipper is trying to run away with a submarine.

The skipper's name is Ramius, and he is the most respected man in the Soviet underwater navy. He has trained most of the other captains in the fleet, and now he has been given the controls of an advanced new submarine named Red October—a sub that uses a revolutionary new drive and that is almost completely silent. American intelligence tracks the Red October as it leaves its Soviet shipyard, but then the sub seems to disappear—and, soon after, the entire Soviet navy mobilizes itself into a vast cat-and-mouse game in the North Atlantic.

The Soviets would like their American counterparts to believe that Ramius is a madman who wants to hide his sub off the American coast and aim its nuclear missiles at New York or Washington. They ask the U.S. Navy to help them track and destroy the Red October. But Ryan (Alec Baldwin) believes that would be a tragic mistake. He tells his superior, an admiral played by James Earl Jones, that Ramius is actually trying to defect and to bring his submarine along with him.

That is the setup for John McTiernan's film, as it was for Tom Clancy's best-selling novel, and in both cases it is also the starting point for a labyrinthine plot in which, half of the time, we have to guess at the hidden reasons for Ramius's actions. It is a tribute to the movie, which has much less time than Clancy did at book length, that it allows the plot its full complexity and yet is never less than clear to the audience.

Many military thrillers, especially those set in the Cold War period, rely on stereotyping and large, crude motivations to move their stories along. *The Hunt for Red October* has more fun by suggesting how easily men can go wrong, how false assumptions can seem seductive, and how enormous consequences can sometimes hang by slender threads. Ryan's knowledge of Ramius's personality, for example, upon which so much depends, is based almost entirely on one occasion when they dined at the same table. Everything else is simply a series of skilled hunches.

McTiernan, whose previous films were *Predator* and *Die Hard,* showed a sense of style and timing in those movies, but what he adds in *The Hunt for Red October* is something of the same detached intelligence that Clancy brought to the novel. Somehow we feel this is more than a thriller; it's an exercise in military and diplomatic strategy in which the players are all smart enough that we can't take their actions for granted.

The Hunt for Red October has more than a dozen important speaking roles, in addition to many more cast members who are crucial for a scene or two, and any film with a cast this large must depend to some extent on typecasting. We couldn't keep the characters straight any other way. What McTiernan does is to typecast without stereotyping. Sean Connery makes a convincing Ramius, and yet, with his barely concealed Scots accent, he is far from being a typical movie Soviet. Alec Baldwin, as the dogged intelligence officer, has the looks of a leading man, but he dials down his personality—he presents himself as a deck-bound bureaucrat who can't believe he has actually gotten himself into this field exercise. And Scott Glenn, as the commander of a U.S. submarine that finds itself within yards of the silent Red October, is leaner, younger, and has more edge than most of the standard movie skipper types.

The production design lends a lot to the movie's credibility. I'm told that the interiors of submarines in this movie look a good deal more high-tech and glossy than they do in real life—that there would be more grease around on a real sub—and yet, for the movie screen, these subs look properly impressive with their awesome displays of electronic gadgetry. The movie does not do as good a job of communicating the daily and hourly reality of submarine life as *Das Boot* did, but perhaps that's because we are not trapped and claustrophobic inside a sub for the whole movie. There are cutaways to the White House and CIA headquarters in Langley, to the Kremlin, and to the decks of ships at sea.

If there's one area where the movie is truly less than impressive, it's the underwater exterior shots. Using models of submarines, the filmmakers have attempted to give an impression of these behemoths maneuvering under the sea. But the outside of a submarine is not intrinsically photogenic, and what these shots most look like are large, gray, bloated whales seen through dishwater.

And yet that lapse doesn't much matter. *The Hunt for Red October* is a skillful, efficient film that involves us in the clever and deceptive game being played by Ramius and in the best efforts of those on both sides to figure out what he plans to do with his submarine—and how he plans to do it. The movie is constructed so we can figure that out along with everybody else, and that leaves a lot of surprises for the conclusion, which is quite satisfactorily suspenseful. There was only one question that bothered me throughout the movie. As one whose basic ideas about submarines come from Commander Edward Beach's classic *Run Silent, Run Deep,* in which the on-board oxygen supply was a source of constant concern, I kept asking myself if those Russian sailors should be smoking so much down there in the depths of the ocean.

Husbands and Wives ★ ★ ★ ½
R, 108 m., 1992

Woody Allen (Gabe Roth), Mia Farrow (Judy Roth), Sydney Pollack (Jack), Judy Davis (Sally), Juliette Lewis (Rain), Liam Neeson (Michael), Blythe Danner (Rain's Mother). Directed by Woody Allen and produced by Robert Greenhut. Screenplay by Allen.

The opening sequence in Woody Allen's *Husbands and Wives* is a long, unbroken shot done in documentary style. The camera swoops here and there, nervously darting around the room to watch the action as two long-married couples deal with the news that one couple has decided to get divorced. With the invention of the Steadicam, this kind of sequence can be done with a relatively smooth camera style, but that's not what Allen wants. He wants a jerky, harried camera (we imagine the cinematographer sweating as he tries to keep up with the action), a camera as confused as the characters, who keep interrupting each other and denying what they hear.

Sydney Pollack and Judy Davis play the couple who are divorcing. They are relaxed, reasonable; this is an amicable move that will allow them both to "grow"—and to "grow," in psychobabble, is of course more important than to commit, to compromise, to share, to sacrifice. The news of the divorce comes as a devastating blow to the other couple, played by Woody Allen and Mia Farrow. They thought their friends were so happy! The news is also a threat—because if this happy couple can split up, what couple is safe?

For many people, the real-life troubles between Allen and Farrow were the same sort of blow. It wasn't that they had an ideal marriage (they weren't married, for one thing), but they'd built an interesting relationship that allowed each partner to work and remain independent, while somewhere in the middle was their love and the children they were raising. They seemed so . . . adult about the whole thing.

But what *Husbands and Wives* argues is that many "rational" relationships are actually not as durable as they seem, because somewhere inside every person is a child crying me! me! me! We say we want the other person to be happy. What we mean is, we want them to be happy with us, just as we are, on our terms.

Look at the scene in the movie where the Allen character runs into his old pal (Pollack) on the street, and they continue their conversation inside a convenience store. Pollack has now left his wife of many years, and is living with a sexy aerobics instructor. She has the bounce and body of a centerfold, and is into self-improvement, by which she means anything that can be learned from those magazines with full-page ads for fruit juicers. It would appear to Allen (and to the audience) that the bond between the older man and the younger woman consists primarily of sex, but as Pollack talks, his voice rapid and confidential, we get a better glimpse of his thinking. He sees this young woman as his second chance, his lost youth—what he deserves! Yes! His right to be happy! "With my wife, I always felt like I was taking an audition." The girl loves him for—we can see this coming—himself. Which is really all any of us wants to be loved for.

Later, of course, the sexy aerobics instructor turns into a real person, one who delivers boring monologues about astrological signs. It is not enough that she adore the Pollack character and have firm thighs and high breasts and clean blond hair. She must also not be stupid. This is a man who is hard to satisfy.

The thought process that goes into this relationship is at the very heart of *Husbands and Wives*. And it is mirrored in the movie's other key development, as the Allen and Farrow characters also find themselves splitting up, and Allen, who plays a fiftyish professor of English, finds himself attracted to his twenty-year-old student (Juliette Lewis). She has a pattern of neurotic involvement with older men, but the Allen character is blind to it. What older man, accepted by a younger woman despite his balding gray hair, wants to know that he is attractive because of flaws, not despite them—that his lover is actually attracted to the decay of mortality?

The best scenes in *Husbands and Wives* are between the characters played by Allen and Farrow. If we can judge by the subsequent events in their lives, some of this dialogue must have cut very close to the bone. They talk about trust and being faithful, and what they're "really looking for," and they skate skittishly around the minefields of sex and lust. Both married couples in the film are really asking the same question: Is this all there is? Must we abandon our fantasies of the perfect partner in order to accept the comfort and truth of our real one?

In the film, the Allen character realizes that the twenty-year-old is, in some way, a mirage: She will give him the vision of a romantic oasis, but will not slake his thirst. He backs away. In real life, Allen apparently did not back away, and to some degree *Husbands and Wives* is his apologia for the relationship he has entered into with Farrow's adopted daughter.

All of that will work itself out over time, and will end happily, or unhappily, as such things do. What he is saying in *Husbands and Wives* has little to do with the wisdom of any particular relationship. Beneath the urgency of all the older characters—both men, both women, and even the older dating partners they experiment with—is the realization that life is short, that time is running out, that life sells you a romantic illusion and neglects to tell you that you can't have it, because when you take any illusion and make it flesh, its hair begins to fall out, and it has BO, and it asks you what your sign is. True love involves loving another's imperfections, which are the parts that tend to endure. Woody Allen's character discovers that in *Husbands and Wives*, although perhaps not in time to help its creator.

I

Iceman ★ ★ ★ ★
PG, 99 m., 1984

Timothy Hutton (Dr. Shephard), John Lone (Iceman), Lindsay Crouse (Dr. Diane Brady). Directed by Fred Schepisi and produced by Norman Jewison and Patrick Palmer. Screenplay by John Drimmer and Chip Proser.

Iceman begins in almost exactly the same way as both versions of *The Thing*, with a team of Arctic scientists chopping a frozen mammal out of the ice. But somehow we're more interested in this discovery because the frozen object isn't simply a gimmick at the beginning of a horror picture; it is presented with real curiosity and awe.

What is it? As a helicopter lifts the discovery aloft, we can glimpse its vague, shadowy outline through the block of forty-thousand-year-old ice. It seems almost to be a man, with its arms outstretched. If we remember Fellini's *La Dolce Vita*, we're reminded of its famous opening scene, as the helicopter flew above Rome with the statue of Christ. In both cases, a contrast is made between the technological gimmicks of man and an age-old mystery. In both cases, also, we're aware that we are in the hands of a master director. *Iceman* is by Fred Schepisi, the Australian who made *The Chant of Jimmy Blacksmith* and Willie Nelson's *Barbarosa*. Both of those movies were about men who lived entirely apart from modern society, according to rules of their own, rules that we eventually realized made perfect sense (to them, at least). Now Schepisi has taken that story idea as far as it will go.

The block of ice is thawed. As each drop of water trickles down a stainless-steel table to the floor, we feel a real excitement. We're about to discover something, just as we were when the apes found the monolith in *2001*. Inside the block of ice is a Neanderthal man,

perfectly preserved, frozen in an instant with his hands pushing out and his mouth open in a prehistoric cry of protest. Such a discovery is at least theoretically possible; mastodons have been found in Russia, frozen so quickly in a sudden global catastrophe that the buttercups in their stomachs had still not been digested. Why not a man? Of course, the man's cell tissue would have been destroyed by the freezing process, right? Not according to *Iceman*, which advances an ingenious theory.

The scene in which the Neanderthal is brought back to life is one of those emergency room dramas we're familiar with from the TV medical shows, with medics pounding on the chest and administering electrical shocks. Then the movie leaves the familiar, and begins an intriguing journey into the past of the man. The Neanderthal (his name sounds like "Charlie") is placed in a controlled environment. Two scientists (Timothy Hutton and Lindsay Crouse) establish a relationship with him. Elementary communication is started—although here the movie makes a basic error in showing the scientists teaching Charlie to speak English, when of course they would want to learn his language instead.

The rest of the movie develops a theory about how Charlie was frozen and what he was looking for when that surprising event took place. There is also an argument between two branches of science: Those who are more interested in what they can learn from Charlie's body and those who want to understand his mind. This conflict seems to have been put in to generate suspense (certainly no responsible scientist, presented with a living Neanderthal man, would suggest any experiment that would endanger his life). But never mind; before it turns into conflict between good and evil, *Iceman* departs in an unexpected, mystical direction.

This movie is spellbinding storytelling. It begins with such a simple premise and creates such a genuinely intriguing situation that we're not just entertained, we're drawn into the argument. What we feel about Charlie reflects what we feel about ourselves. And what he knows—that we've forgotten—illuminates the line between man the fire-builder, and man the stargazer. Think how much more interesting *The Thing* would have been if its frozen life form had been investigated rather than destroyed, and you have an idea of *Iceman*'s appeal.

The Idolmaker ★ ★ ★
PG, 117 m., 1980

Ray Sharkey (Vince Vacarri), Tovah Feldshuh (Brenda Roberts), Peter Gallagher (Caesare), Paul Land (Tommy Dee), Joe Pantoliano (Gino Pilate). Directed by Taylor Hackford and produced by Gene Kirkwood and Howard W. Koch, Jr. Screenplay by Edward Di Lorenzo.

At the core of *The Idolmaker*, making it a better film than it might otherwise have been, is the hungry, lonely ego of the movie's hero, Vince Vacarri. He has all the skills necessary to become a rock 'n' roll idol, especially in the late-1950s world of Top Forty payola and prefabricated stars. But he doesn't have the looks. He so desperately wants stardom, though, that he tries to have it vicariously, through the "idols" he painstakingly manufactures. Maybe that makes *The Idolmaker* sound more serious than it is, but it's that core of obsession in the Ray Sharkey performance that takes a movie that might have been routine and makes it interesting. This is not a dazzlingly original idea, but the movie understands its passions well enough to entertain us with them.

The "idolmaker" of the title is based, I understand, on the real-life character of Bob

Marcucci (listed as the film's "technical adviser"). He is the Philadelphia Svengali who discovered, coached, and managed Frankie Avalon and Fabian, quarterbacking them to stardom. If this movie can be believed, he was a rock 'n' roll puppetmaster, supplying the lines, the songs, the delivery and—most importantly—the stage mannerisms and "look" of his personalities.

The movie moves the story to Brooklyn, and borrows heavily from the clichés of show-biz rags-to-riches movies: Not only is it lonely at the top in this movie . . . it's lonely at the bottom, too, for practice. The Sharkey character manufactures his first rock star (Paul Land) out of a little raw talent, an unshaped stage presence, and sheer energy. One of the movie's most engaging scenes shows Land at a high school record hop, doggedly pantomiming his first record while Sharkey, backstage, goes through the same motions.

Land does a good job of playing the movie's first rock singer—a spoiled, egotistical creation renamed "Tommy Dee." We can predict what will happen. He'll be pushed to the top by Sharkey, develop an inflated opinion of himself, and think he did it all alone. That's exactly what happens, but Land moves through these stages with a conviction that makes them seem fairly new, even while we're recognizing them.

Meanwhile, Sharkey has another discovery waiting in the wings. He spots a busboy (Peter Gallagher) in his brother's restaurant. The guy can't keep time, can't sing, and has one enormous hairy eyebrow all the way across his face. No problem: Sharkey pounds rhythm into him, grooms him, renames him Caesare and fast-talks him onto the movie's version of "American Bandstand." It turns out that this kid *does* have a natural rapport with the prepubescent girls in his audiences, and he's on his way.

None of this would work if *The Idolmaker* didn't have convincing actors playing the two rock singers. It does. Land and Gallagher are actually convincing as teen idols. They can also act well enough to modulate their stage performances—they start out terrible and work their way up to levels that Fabian himself must only have dreamed about. And the movie has fun with its production numbers. The songs are all standard late-fifties rock dreck (but newly composed for the movie), but the stage performances are a little sneaky. They're not as ridiculous as many of the late-fifties adolescent heroes

actually were; they seem to owe a lot not only to Elvis (naturally) but also to such performers of a decade later as Mick Jagger.

All of this is not to say that *The Idolmaker* is a masterpiece. But it is a well-crafted movie that works, that entertains, and that pulls us through its pretty standard material with the magnetism of the Ray Sharkey performance. Because we sense his hungers, his isolations, and his compulsive needs, we buy scenes that might otherwise have been unworkable.

I Like It Like That ★ ★ ★
R, 94 m., 1994

Lauren Velez (Lisette Linares), Rita Moreno (Rosaria), Griffin Dunne (Stephen Price), Jon Seda (Chino Linares), Jesse Borrego (Alexis), Lisa Vidal (Magdalena), Tookie Smith (Val), Tomas "Tommy" Melly (Li'l Chino). Directed by Darnell Martin and produced by Ann Carli and Lane Janger. Screenplay by Martin.

Darnell Martin's *I Like It Like That* is centered on one of those New York City blocks where life seems to be lived mostly in the street, everybody minds everybody else's business, and reality exists somewhere between a soap opera and a sitcom. It's like *Do the Right Thing* crossed with "Roseanne."

The movie's heroine, Lisette (Lauren Velez), has been married for ten years to Chino (Jon Seda), who has a roving eye and is being pursued by the lustful Magdalena (Lisa Vidal). When Chino steals a stereo and is put in jail, Lisette is determined to raise the money for bail. So she goes to a fly-by-night modeling agency, where she stumbles into a real job, working with Stephen (Griffin Dunne), a WASP producer specializing in Latino music.

Stephen thinks he only needs a fake "date" to convince a couple of hot Puerto Rican singers that he's the real thing. But Lisette, who understands the music and the culture, soon muscles into a better job, as his assistant. And when the neighborhood guys tell Chino that his wife is cheating with her new boss, Chino (now out on bail) retaliates with Magdalena.

This is not exactly a riveting plot, but what makes the film interesting is the way Martin sees the details. Instead of going for obvious contrasts between the two men in Lisette's life, she sees the similarities: In one way or another, they both always have their eye on the clock. Neither one believes she is as smart and capable as she obviously is. And both make their decisions with their libidos, not their intelligence.

Lisette has another brother in her life, the transvestite Alexis (Jesse Borrego), who lives downstairs, runs a store specializing in lucky candles, and has an unhappy relationship with their parents (their mother is played by Rita Moreno). Alexis lends her lots of good advice, but the character seems more like a subplot than a convincing part of the story.

Martin, a first-time director who was previously an assistant director for Spike Lee, is good at creating a sense of life and excitement in the neighborhood, where even minor street people are sharply drawn. Inside Lisette's apartment, she shows a state of nonstop interruption, as the couple's three untamed kids cause constant havoc and Lisette locks herself in the bathroom for a moment's solitude. (One of her neighbors is that old movie standby, the outraged woman pounding on the ceiling with a broom handle.)

It's clear, though, that Martin is far less interested in Lisette's role as a mother than in her prospects as a record producer, and the scenes between mother and children leave us with unanswered doubts about the quality of her parenting. The kids are there mostly for atmosphere, and Lisette doesn't seem to have convincing relationships with them.

What's good is the way Lisette fights for what she deserves—in relationships and in work. She's in the face of the scheming Magdalena, and with Griffin Dunne she has a couple of scenes (including an office seduction) in which the exec is startled by her directness. *I Like It Like That* looks more unconventional than it is, but Martin puts a spin on the material with lots of human color and high energy.

Il Ladro di Bambini ★ ★ ★
NO MPAA RATING, 116 m., 1993

Enrico Lo Verso (Antonio), Valentina Scalici (Rosetta), Guiseppe Ieracitano (Luciano), Florence Darel (Martine), Marina Golovine (Nathalie), Fabio Alessandrini (Grignani). Directed by Gianni Amelio and produced by Angelo Rizzoli. Screenplay by Amelio, Sandro Petraglia, and Stefano Rulli.

The Italian title *Il Ladro di Bambini* translates as *The Thief of Children*, and the movie's English title is *Stolen Children*, but both titles have to be read with great irony, because here is a film about a man who only steals children away from great unhappiness, and allows them to see for a few days that life can contain joy, as well. Like *Cinema Paradiso*, but in a different way, the movie tells a heart-warming story about an older man who acts as a parent and friend for kids who need one.

The movie opens in Milan, where Rosetta, an eleven-year-old girl, and her brother Luciano, a year younger, live with their mother, who forces the girl to work as a child prostitute. This element of the story, tragic and unsavory, is not dwelled on; the movie properly begins when the two children are taken away from the mother and placed in the care of Antonio (Enrico Lo Verso), a young policeman, whose job is to take them to a children's home.

The cop doesn't much relish the job, especially after his partner cooks up a scam where Antonio will do the work while the partner takes an unscheduled vacation. Antonio believes he doesn't care for children—and the kids return the favor. After years of emotional and physical abuse, they are withdrawn, sullen, and suspicious.

But that will change during the course of the story. The children are turned away from the church-run children's home, apparently out of fear that their past might infect the other students. Naively taking the case into his own hands, without authorization, Antonio next takes them to Sicily. As they travel all the way down the length of Italy, stopping even for a feast at the home of Antonio's parents, a bond grows between the three travelers.

The movie is a road picture, in a sense; the people and experiences along the way are part of the education of Antonio, Rosetta, and Luciano, and what we see through the car windows is a cross-section of modern Italy, good and bad. But what happens in the car is more important, as Antonio learns to love the children, and they learn to trust an adult for the first time in their lives.

There are no big episodes, until the end. Instead, the director and cowriter, Gianni Amelio, takes small events, the daily routine, and shows how the behavior of the travelers gradually changes. There is also a magical day at the beach, where the children from a dark, oppressive slum breathe fresh air and run on the sand in the sunshine, and Antonio realizes how much he has come to care for them.

With child abuse in all the headlines, it is unlikely this story could be told today as an American movie; our thinking on such subjects has been poisoned by too many talk shows and tabloids, and the cop's genuine love might seem suspect. But somehow the fact that the film is Italian creates the right perspective on the material. It seems more innocent, more filled with grace, more plausible.

Unknown to Antonio and the children, however, a scandal is brewing over their "disappearance." The policeman has operated outside the rules, on his own authority, and although we see that he has done nothing wrong, the authorities assume he has stolen the children, and a manhunt gets under way. The resolution is as satisfactory as in any film since, oh, *Cinema Paradiso*.

Maybe Hollywood films have grown so slick and sophisticated that simple stories like this can no longer be told in the big commercial genres. I don't know. I do know that in the early months of 1993, the best films I've seen have mostly been from other countries. *Il Ladro di Bambini*, *Like Water for Chocolate*, *Léolo*, and *The Last Days of Chez Nous* all have a freshness and daring that's in contrast to the assembly-line stories. Here is a movie with the spontaneity of life; watching it is like living it.

I'll Do Anything ★ ★ ★
PG-13, 115 m., 1994

Nick Nolte (Matt Hobbs), Whittni Wright (Jeannie Hobbs), Albert Brooks (Burke Adler), Julie Kavner (Nan Mulhanney), Joely Richardson (Cathy Breslow), Tracey Ullman (Beth Hobbs), Jeb Brown (Male D Person), Joely Fisher (Female D Person). Written and directed by James L. Brooks and produced by Brooks and Polly Platt. Screenplay by Brooks.

Are you like me? Do you like people who try to put a spin on words, instead of talking flat-footed? Do you like people who would *prefer* to be nice, even if they don't know how? Do you like people who feel some weird compulsion to tell the truth? Then *I'll Do Anything* might just grow on you. It's one of those off-center comedies that gets its best moments simply by looking at people and seeing how funny, how pathetic, how sometimes wonderful they can be.

The movie is about Hollywood and the people on all rungs of the ladder who struggle to survive there. It's not as cynical as *The Player*, but just as knowing about the industry. The writer-director is James L. Brooks, who has been researching this film, I imagine, for thirty years, starting with his days on "The Mary Tyler Moore Show" and including the movies *Terms of Endearment*, *Broadcast News*, and the animated sitcom "The Critic."

His original goal was to make a Hollywood musical, maybe a *Singin' in the Rain* for an older, wiser, more corrupt generation. But a funny thing happened on the way to opening day. Test audiences *hated* the songs, and so Brooks bit the bullet and took them out, did some extra shooting to fill the gaps, and has now released *I'll Do Anything* in a nonmusical form. This sounds like some kind of desperate formula for averting complete ruin, but Brooks has somehow pulled it off. Maybe because his original screenplay was so strongly written, this doesn't feel like a movie with parts on order; it's a bright, edgy, funny story about people who have all the talent they need, but not all the luck.

The film stars Nick Nolte as Matt Hobbs, an actor who has won Emmy nominations for TV docu-dramas but whose career has never really taken off. Now he's at an all-time low, financially desperate. Going to auditions, he drifts into the sphere of a driven, oral-compulsive producer named Burke Adler, played by Albert Brooks as a fundamentally all right guy who has carefully studied how big-time Hollywood jerks behave, and tries unconvincingly to imitate them: "I don't make movies for theaters that serve cappuccino in the lobby!"

Adler's assistant, Cathy Breslow, played by Joely Richardson, has always admired Hobbs's work and tries to get him involved in one of her boss's projects. And Adler's researcher and girl Friday, in certain ways the most interesting character in the movie, is Nan Mulhanney (Julie Kavner), who tells Adler the truth. The plain, unvarnished truth. He finds this irresistible, and falls in love with her, perhaps because he secretly knows he's an ass and can identify with somebody who agrees with him. (She: "You only think you feel that way because you're on the verge of failure and you're without a core." He: "See? No one else gets me!")

Hobbs was once married, but his wife (Tracey Ullman) has left him, and now he finds himself beginning to like Cathy, who is herself a basket case, always thinking about something else, doubting herself, unable to trust her own opinions. In one of the film's many quirky moments of truth, on the morning after she sleeps with Hobbs for the first time, she's asked point-blank in a casting meeting: "Would you sleep with him?" She thinks it over, and says, "No." Is this a lie? It's hard to say. The movie understands that there's not always a perfect match between what one *would* do and what one *does* do.

Suddenly Hobbs's life undergoes a fundamental change: His former wife announces that she is leaving their six-year-old daughter with him. This child, played by Whittni Wright with frightening self-confidence, has been carefully raised by the ex-wife to be a little monster—not simply spoiled, but articulate and clever about being spoiled, and quite capable of creating dramatic scenes in public to get her way. Hobbs is beside himself. An understanding neighbor in his apartment building helps out, but Hobbs has no idea how to relate to any child, and especially to this one, and there is a moment when he admits complete defeat.

What Brooks does with this large and strange cast is to put it together in various ways and see what happens. Hobbs, for example, becomes Adler's driver at the same time he is auditioning for the lead in Adler's new movie. Neither finds this especially peculiar. The two women deal with the two men as women are often able to do, effortlessly seeing through their defenses and cutting straight to the ego.

There are a couple of dialogue scenes in the movie that have to be heard to be believed. One consists of a production meeting at which the participants run down a list of top male Hollywood stars—mercilessly skewering each one's biggest weakness. Real names and real weaknesses are used. ("Bob Hoskins: Turns into a fur ball when he takes off his shirt. Jeff Daniels: a bean pole. Tommy Lee Jones: Shame about his complexion.") Another scene takes place when Ullman, as the ex-wife, brings the daughter to her father, and then briefs her against the dangers of the world in a truly horrifying way: "Brush your teeth before you go to bed every night, or your gums will bleed and you'll choke to death in your sleep."

I have no idea how *I'll Do Anything* would have played as a musical. Maybe we'll be able to find out someday, when the "Restored Director's Cut" appears on laserdisc. It is helpful, I think, to simply forget about the missing songs, and recognize that *I'll Do Anything* is a complete movie without them—smart, original, subversive.

I Love You to Death ★ ★ ★
R, 97 m., 1990

Kevin Kline (Joey), Tracey Ullman (Rosalie), Joan Plowright (Nadja), River Phoenix (Devo), William Hurt (Harlan), Keanu Reeves (Marlon), James Gannon (Lieutenant Schooner), Jack Kehler (Wiley). Directed by Lawrence Kasdan

and produced by Jeffrey Lurie and Ron Moler. Screenplay by John Kostmayer.

I Love You to Death is like an acting class in which the students are presented with impossible situations and asked how they would handle them. The students in this case are accomplished actors—Kevin Kline, William Hurt, Tracey Ullman, and Joan Plowright, among others—but what was each one thinking in the scene where the dead man walks downstairs? How do you carry on a polite conversation with someone who has a bullet hole clean through him, but hasn't noticed? Particularly if you were involved in his attempted murder?

The movie's plot is so unlikely that of course it is based on fact. The story was in the news a couple of years ago, about how the wife of a pizzeria owner decided to kill her husband because he was cheating on her. After the murder attempt failed, the husband refused to press charges against his wife because he felt she had done the right thing. After all, he *was* guilty, wasn't he? My memory is hazy about what happened then. They lived happily ever after, most probably.

In the movie version, written by John Kostmayer and directed by Lawrence Kasdan, this story is developed into a domestic black comedy of droll and macabre dimensions. And it is told in a series of scenes in which most of the characters are either lying to each other, lying to themselves, or incapable of coherent thought. The few moments of honesty and lucidity have a fascination all their own, since under those conditions the characters tend to become tongue-tied with embarrassment.

The result is an actor's dream, a film in which the truth of almost every scene has to be excavated out of the debris of social inhibition. I am not so sure this is a dream film for an audience, however; the moviegoer eager for plot and drama is likely to grow impatient and think nothing much is happening on the screen, when in fact volumes are happening inside the minds and consciences of the characters.

The movie begins with a happy day at the pizzeria in Tacoma, where Joey (Kevin Kline) and his wife Rosalie (Tracey Ullman) take care of business with the help of Devo (River Phoenix), who is very, very far out, but who occasionally focuses on the object of his devotion, Rosalie. Joey is a ladies' man. Cheerfully shouldering his kit of plumber's tools, he sallies forth daily to do "odd jobs" in the

rental apartments the family owns—most of them occupied by willing females whose plumbing is in fine repair. It should be obvious to anyone that Joey is cheating, but Rosalie remains blissfully blind to the evidence. She trusts her Joey.

The moment of her awakening is a painful one. She feels betrayed and double-crossed. She confides in her mother (Joan Plowright), and they agree, without hesitation, that the death penalty is called for in this case. They dispatch the faithful Devo to a local pool hall, where two low-life drugheads (William Hurt and Keanu Reeves) are bent low over the pool table, for support. They agree to shoot Joey, for a price. Meanwhile, Rosalie and her mother have fed the philandering husband several helpings of spaghetti laced with three large bottles of sleeping pills.

The drugheads arrive, hold a confused conference at the bedside, and shoot the slumbering victim. Then, while everyone is conferring downstairs, Joey appears, still alive. The movie's most difficult and intriguing scene now follows. It takes place almost entirely in the eyes of the actors, and in their pauses and silences, and is an exquisite exercise in guilty embarrassment. It is an almost impossible scene to pull off, but somehow they all accomplish it.

Another good thing about the movie is Tracey Ullman's low-key, plain-Jane approach to the wife. It's all the more effective because Kevin Kline has for some reason adopted a comic opera accent and mannerisms as the husband, and is hard to believe except in the scenes where he is almost dead. Ullman finds the stubborn vindictiveness inside her character, who is so sunny when she trusts her husband and so unforgiving when she discovers she was deceived. Joan Plowright might seem like an unlikely choice as the mother, but gets some of the movie's biggest laughs. William Hurt could have walked through the role of the spaced-out hit man, but takes the time to make the character believable and even, in a bleary way, complex.

Nothing in Lawrence Kasdan's previous career (*Body Heat, The Big Chill, Silverado, The Accidental Tourist*) seems like preparation for this film, but then what could? It is the first time Kasdan has directed from a screenplay he didn't write, and I assume he was attracted to it for the obvious reason—because it seemed all but impossible to do. I am not sure if the film is a success because I am not sure what it is trying to do. It founders in embarrassment, but not boringly.

I, Madman ★ ★ ★
R, 90 m., 1989

Jenny Wright (Virginia), Clayton Rohner (Richard), Randall William Cook (Malcolm), Stephanie Hodge (Mona), Michelle Jordan (Colette), Vance Valencia (Sergeant Navarro), Mary Baldwin (Librarian), Rafael Nazario (Hotel Clerk). Directed by Tibor Takacs and produced by Rafael Eisenman. Screenplay by David Chaskin.

She works in a used-book store and brings home lurid pulp thrillers to read at night, alone, while she's snuggled up on the sofa and a violent electrical storm is raging outside. She's reading one now, titled *Much of Madness, More of Sin.*

It's about a mad scientist who is rejected by the woman he loves. She doesn't like his facial features. He'll show her. He takes a scalpel and removes his offending features, and comes calling on her with a hole where his face used to be.

This is some book. She turns a page. The lightning crackles outside. Something creaks in the hallway. The night is late and the single lamp leaves deep shadows in the room. And I'm thinking that I love movies that begin this way because they understand that horror movies can be fun. They don't have to be vomitoriums about mad slashers and dead teen-agers.

Tibor Takacs's *I, Madman* places its terrors where they belong, in the midst of everyday life. Virginia, the heroine (Jenny Wright), works days in the bookstore and would like to spend her evenings with her boyfriend, but he's a cop and always seems to be on a dope stakeout somewhere. So she reads. And the movie slips between reality and imagination—between the book she's reading and the things that really seem to be happening in her life.

The novel about the mad scientist is by a man named Malcolm Brand. We find out a little more about him than Virginia does. We learn, for example, that he lives in a fleabag hotel and conducts experiments in creating life. He wants to cross a monkey with a jackal and create a new race. His books may be autobiographical. And he may still be alive—or at least, alive in a sense. (Malcolm is played in the movie by special-effects man Randall William Cook, who designed the grotesque makeup and then convinced the director to let him wear it himself.)

Life goes on. There are strange visitors to the used-book store. In the streets outside,

bizarre crimes are committed. Is Malcolm Brand killing people in order to steal their lips and noses so that he can stitch his own face back together again?

I, Madman contains the usual elements in a modern thriller, including the lonely woman, late at night, in danger. It gets the usual mileage out of the standard False Alarm scene, where the door creaks open and the heroine is terrified—but it's only her boyfriend. What's original about this movie is the fun it has with the thin line between reality and imagination, between what Virginia is reading and what is really happening.

Jenny Wright seems to enjoy the role, especially the parts where she curls up on the sofa and turns the pages while her eyes pop out of her head. Movies like this always have a scene where nobody will believe the heroine. She knows, she just *knows* that a madman is loose in the neighborhood—but everyone says it's only her hyperthyroid imagination.

Climaxes in thrillers have gotten pretty standard recently, involving chases and shoot-outs and a lot of blood. *I, Madman* has some surprises for her. There's that old trunk up in the attic of the used-book store—the one that turns out to be from the estate of the late Malcolm Brand. It has holes punched in the top, almost as if there's something inside that needs to breathe. Something with big teeth and very long arms.

Imaginary Crimes ★ ★ ★ ½   **NEW**
PG, 107 m., 1994

Harvey Keitel (Ray Weiler), Fairuza Balk (Sonya), Elisabeth Moss (Greta), Vincent D'Onofrio (Mr. Webster), Chris Penn (Jarvis), Seymour Cassel (Eddie), Kelly Lynch (Ray's Late Wife), Diane Baker (Abigale Tate), Amber Benson (Margaret). Directed by Anthony Drazan and produced by James G. Robinson. Screenplay by Kristine Johnson and Davia Nelson.

Ray Weiler, the character played by Harvey Keitel in *Imaginary Crimes,* is a con man. He spins fabulous stories of vast deposits of gold and uranium, just waiting to be harvested, and talks investors into sinking money into his foolhardy schemes. He is usually just this side of the law. Occasionally he strays to the other side; it is not a distinction that means much to him, since he knows in his heart that success is just around the corner.

It is important that we understand that about his heart: That in some fundamental way, Ray really does believe in his dreams.

Like many great con men, the person he has conned most thoroughly is himself. He has certainly not conned his two daughters, Sonya and Greta, who have lived through so many of his schemes that they are openly dubious about almost everything he says.

Ray is a widower, trying to raise the two girls—the older, played by Fairuza Balk, who is a gifted high school student, and the younger (Elizabeth Moss), who is learning fast. Their late mother (Kelly Lynch) is seen in flashbacks, looking dubious as Ray unveils gadgets that are "going to revolutionize the mining industry." Now, the family of three stays one step ahead of the landlord and the bill collectors, and the girls are skilled at not answering the door, and letting the phone ring.

Imaginary Crimes, based on an autobiographical novel by Sheila Ballantyne, is one of those movies like *King of the Hill* or *This Boy's Life* that show children adapting to the difficult circumstances of their home life—to parents who are distant or difficult—and surviving. It regards Ray, the Keitel character, as neither monster nor lovable character, but simply as a very difficult case. And it suggests that in many ways the girls benefited by having such a strange father—although, of course, his behavior is not admirable.

Ray is the central character, but Sonya is the one through whose eyes we see, and she is played by Fairuza Balk as a strong, outgoing, realistic girl, who has secret dreams of being a writer. She is encouraged by her high school English teacher (Vincent D'Onofrio), who reads her stories of chaotic family life and guesses that they are based on fact. He encourages her to attend college, and when she says, "You don't know my father," he shyly says, "Well, in a way, I do."

Sonya, of course, has a crush on the teacher, and spies on him at home, but the movie doesn't move in an obvious direction; she isn't perceived as troubled, and he isn't seen as improper in his behavior toward her. Instead, he is like so many good teachers who at a crucial point in a student's life can give just the right push.

Meanwhile, Ray's business schemes are going from bad to worse. His long-suffering partner (Seymour Cassel) half believes that a new tract of land does contain mineral wealth, and so does their investor, Jarvis (Chris Penn). But Ray has not quite obtained all the rights he says he has, and Jarvis can be a dangerous man. (Penn plays the role on the right note of concealed menace; like his brother Sean, he can be quietly powerful.)

The obvious points of the movie are made quickly: that Ray is a liar and a con man, and his daughters are being raised in a world of self-deception and uncertainty. The deeper points emerge more slowly: When there is real love in a family, it can absorb many wounds. As Sonya's teacher wryly tells her one day about her father, "He is one hell of a source for material, isn't he?" Here is the movie to prove it.

Imagine: John Lennon ★ ★ ★
R, 103 m., 1988

A documentary directed by Andrew Solt and produced by David L. Wolper and Solt. Written by Sam Egan and Solt. Narrated by John Lennon.

When John Lennon was killed on Dec. 8, 1980, he left behind some 200 hours of film and video footage, most of it never publicly seen, a lot of it in the category of home movies. The people who made *Imagine: John Lennon* had access to all of it, and so this is not a return visit to the familiar Beatles footage we've seen before in documentaries like *The Beatles Story.* Although *Imagine* begins in Lennon's childhood and of course includes the Beatles period, the emphasis is on the years after the Beatles broke up and he merged with Yoko Ono.

I use that word—merged—deliberately, because the movie portrays John and Yoko not so much as man and wife, business partners or artistic collaborators, but as two people who had spent so much time alone together on various planes of awareness that they had started to act as if they were one—like twins, or an old married couple. The effect is of a psychic barrier between John and Yoko and the rest of the world; they're inside looking out.

Those final years were the end of a long journey for the restless boy from Liverpool who had a lonely, unsettled youth, who was raised by a beloved aunt, who was violent and moody and then burst forth into one of the greatest songwriters of modern times. Lennon was above all an artist—his music will live as long as songs are sung—but the Beatles made him into a cultural hero as well, a star who lived inside a bubble of wealth, fame, and adulation, and could rarely feel alone and off-guard. It was a form of heroism that led him to live in New York as if he were an ordinary person—insisting on walking the streets, going to movies, going to the park with his son, as if those freedoms were the right of anyone, even an ex-Beatle. That delusion was ended by Mark David Chapman.

Imagine is not an obituary, however, but a memory. What it remembers most clearly were those enchanted and befuddled days of hippies and flower power, be-ins and the love generation, when John and Yoko spent their honeymoon in bed together, holding press conferences to advise people to grow their hair and work for peace. The whole time comes rushing back in one long sequence where John and Yoko have a debate with Al Capp, the right-wing creator of "Li'l Abner," about the effectiveness of their "bed-in." Capp is a performer, aware all the time that he's being filmed. In the face of his debating points, John seems bewildered and a little petulant.

The revealing moments in this exchange are there because they were filmed by outsiders, by documentarians who were trying to look through the lens and see what was happening. Other moments in the film are revealing precisely because they were *not* filmed self-consciously. They are the home movies, sometimes seemingly made by turning on the camera and sitting in front of it, sometimes perhaps made by John or Yoko or friends. In the sequence which opens the film and provides its framework, we see John at Tittenhurst, his country manor in England, in 1971, sitting at a piano, composing and singing. There is something so simple and pure about these images that they set the tone for the whole film.

At other times, however, the home movies are deceptive—they show less than they seem. When people film themselves, or each other, they are acutely aware of the camera, and much of their behavior is self-conscious performance. It's the opposite of *cinéma vérité.* It's only when an unobtrusive, observant third party is holding the camera that we get a truly documentary vision. And the underlying problem with *Imagine* is that John and Yoko are holding the camera too much of the time—symbolically, anyway. The film shows the face they turned to the world, not the faces they turned to each other.

Much has been made of the fact that *Imagine* acts as a response to Albert Goldman's much-attacked biography of John Lennon, which paints him in his final years as an anorexic, drug-addicted puppet of Yoko Ono. In this movie, we were told, we would see him as a happy, healthy, productive family man. And there are shots that seem to show that person. But there are also moments when he does seem thin and ill, and times when he is clearly speaking from a drug-induced unreality. The film skirts so lightly over the touchy subject of John's decision to leave Yoko and live for a time with May Pang that, unless we know the story, we'd never understand it on the basis of this information.

Imagine was made with Yoko Ono's cooperation but without her imprimatur, and the result is the portrait of a man who was complex, sometimes confused, not always very happy, but a great artist all the same. Yoko Ono appears in the film not as his puppetmaster, but as his fellow-journeyer; whatever their reality, they shared it.

The most touching moments in the film come when it records direct testimony from those who knew Lennon the best. They look straight into the camera and speak simply and directly: his aunt Mimi; Cynthia Lennon, his first wife, and Julian Lennon, their son; Yoko Ono, and Sean Lennon, their son. They miss him, and perhaps we feel anger at Chapman for shooting him. But there is an extraordinary sequence in the film that almost seems to address that anger.

At Tittenhurst in 1971, a confused young drifter had been hanging around, in the delusion that Lennon's songs were messages to him. We see Lennon talking to the man, telling him he only writes for himself and for his friends and to make money and do a good job. He can't, he says, be everything to everybody. And then he tells the drifter he looks hungry, and invites him in for a meal. If you treat every confused drifter with that much humanity, you risk tragedy, as Lennon finally discovered. But his openness to the lonely and confused young man reveals, I think, the spirit of his greatest songs.

Immortal Beloved ★ ★ ★ ½ `NEW`
R, 123 m., 1995

Gary Oldman (Ludwig van Beethoven), Jeroen Krabbe (Anton Felix Schindler), Isabella Rossellini (Anna Marie Erdody), Johanna Ter Steege (Johanna Reiss), Marco Hofschneider (Karl van Beethoven), Miriam Margolyes (Nanette Streicher), Barry Humphries (Clemens Metternich), Valeria Golino (Giulietta Guicciardi), Christopher Fulford (Caspar van Beethoven). Directed by Bernard Rose and produced by Bruce Davey. Screenplay by Rose.

There is an image in *Immortal Beloved* as evocative as any I can remember—as complete as the sled in *Citizen Kane,* or the shadowy doorway in *The Third Man.* A boy runs through the forest at night to a perfectly still lake and floats on his back. The camera pulls back and we see the stars of the sky reflected in the water. And then it seems as if the boy is floating in the firmament—lost in the stars. On the sound track, we hear the "Ode to Joy" from Beethoven's Ninth Symphony.

Movies that attempt to match visual images to great music are often asking for trouble. Remember the "1812 Overture" playing in Ken Russell's biopic of Tchaikovsky, the cannon roars illustrated by images of soldiers' heads being blown off. What Bernard Rose has accomplished in *Immortal Beloved* is a film that imagines the mental states of Beethoven with a series of images as vivid and convincing as a dream.

The film unfolds like a biographical puzzle. Beethoven after his death left a letter addressed to his "immortal beloved," with no hint as to who that person was. As a last testament this document may have been faulty, but as a biographical puzzle it was a masterstroke, inspiring two centuries of fevered speculations, of which this film is the latest and most romantic. I doubt Rose has solved the puzzle of the unnamed beloved, but I care not, because he has done something more valuable: He has created a fantasy about Beethoven that evokes the same disturbing, ecstatic passion we hear in his music.

The film opens with Schindler (Jeroen Krabbe), Beethoven's confidante, beginning a search for the immortal beloved. As he visits first one and then another possible source of information, it is impossible not to be reminded of the hapless reporter who sought the meaning of "Rosebud" in *Citizen Kane.* As he visits the important women in Beethoven's life, we see flashbacks to the composer's disorderly and precarious existence, and we hear music, magnificent music.

Unusual for the director of a musical biography, Rose has paid as much attention to the music as to the biography. Most biopics about classical composers dredge up obscure, low-rent recordings of the music. Not this one. The film's musical supervisor is Sir Georg Solti, conducting the London Orchestra, with soloists such as Murray Perahia and Yo Yo Ma. If there are moments when we doubt Beethoven was thinking exactly *these* images as he composed, there are others

when the momentum of the story takes over, and we identify with a tortured genius whose deafness cut him off from the immortal sounds he was giving to mankind.

Beethoven is played in the film by Gary Oldman, who at first seems an unlikely choice: too small, too driven, too insinuating. Then we see that he is right. He is a man on the edge of madness, obsessed with women, even more obsessed with Karl (Marco Hofschneider), the young nephew he hopes to turn into a prodigy. He wages a lifelong campaign of hate against Karl's mother, Johanna (Johanna Ter Steege), telling his brother Caspar (Christopher Fulford) she is a foul slut. The movie proposes an interesting explanation of Beethoven's hatred of her and love for her son, one which sensible biographers will question, but that fits perfectly with the terms of the story.

If Johanna is, by default, one of the three most important women in Beethoven's life, the other two are Countess Giulietta Guicciardi (Valeria Golino), who becomes his student and patron; and the older, wiser Countess Anna Marie Erdody (Isabella Rossellini), who stands up to Beethoven after he has gone into court to wrest young Karl away from Johanna, his mother.

In the scenes with Giulietta we see Beethoven's status as the most sought-after lion of the European musical scene; in his day, a great composer was the equivalent of today's rock stars, swooned over and showered with attention. He becomes the countess's piano teacher, but does not always play the game according to her world's rules: "A mistake is nothing," he tells her, "but the fact that you thump out the notes without the least sensitivity to their meaning is unforgivable, and your lack of passion is unforgivable. I shall have to beat you." She thinks he is teasing until he slaps her so hard that tears well in her eyes.

The scenes with the Rossellini character are among the best in the film, because here he finds a haven from his debts, from his troubles with the law, from his wars with his relatives, from his fawning admirers and mocking rivals. She sees most clearly his curious obsession with young Karl, which takes an odd turn: Beethoven stops composing entirely for five years in order to supervise Karl's education as a music virtuoso, despite the boy's tearful pleas to be allowed to become a soldier.

Beethoven's deafness is a subject through much of the film, including a precarious scene

where the Rossellini character leads him from the stage after he grows confused during a public performance, and another in which he places his head against the wood of a pianoforte to hear the music. He tries desperately to conceal his deafness, fearing it would destroy his livelihood, and on the sound track Rose sometimes reproduces what he can hear: low rumbles curiously like the music of the whales.

This is the fourth film by the young British director Bernard Rose, after *Paperhouse* (1989), *Chicago Joe and the Showgirl* (1990), and *Candyman* (1992). The first was a masterpiece, a haunting fantasy about the secret mental worlds of children. The second, set in World War II, was a fanciful re-creation of a relationship between a GI and a British girl, both living in their delusions. The third was about a legendary figure said to haunt Chicago public housing projects. In all three films Rose shows a remarkable gift for visualizing his themes: His films are stimulating to *look* at.

Here, in the shopworn genre of the musical biopic, he makes everything new. *Immortal Beloved* has clearly been made by people who feel Beethoven directly in their hearts, and are not approaching him through a classroom or historical setting. Beethoven writes to Schindler at one point, arguing: "It is the power of music to carry one directly into the mental state of the composer. The listener has no choice. It is like hypnotism." The viewer of *Immortal Beloved* likewise has no choice, and for the same reason.

Impulse ★ ★ ★
R, 109 m., 1990

Theresa Russell (Lottie), Jeff Fahey (Stan), George Dzundza (Lieutenant Joe Morgan), Alan Rosenberg (Charley Katz), Nicholas Mele (Rossi), Eli Danker (Dimarjian), Charles McCaughan (Frank Munoff), Lynne Thigpen (Dr. Gardner). Directed by Sondra Locke and produced by Albert S. Ruddy and Andre Morgan. Screenplay by John De Marco and Leigh Chapman.

Theresa Russell is an actress who likes characters who dance on the edge, who dare themselves to get into situations they'll have to think fast to escape from. The character she plays in *Impulse* seems at first to come out of the same mold as other recent female cops in the movies, but there's a twist to her—she's attracted to the dark impulses of the people she meets in her work, and she envies the sinners their freedom to sin. Sometimes it seems like the cops have to go home just when the fun is beginning.

Russell works for the vice squad as an undercover cop. She dresses in miniskirts and wears a lot of chains and works the bars and the sidewalks where the johns are. Her job is to guide them lustfully into the arms of the law, and when her backup support arrives to read the guy his rights, she's outta there.

The problem is, it's a dangerous and lonely job with a high frustration factor. Her boss on the force (George Dzundza) is a woman-hating creep who is mad at her because she broke up with him. His eyesight seems to be Pavlovian; when he sees a woman who looks like a hooker, he assumes she is a hooker—even if in fact she is an undercover cop. Yes, he likes it when Russell busts somebody. Sure, she's a good cop. But would she dress up that way if she were a nice girl?

Some nights the action gets a little dicey. Some nights she almost gets killed. Some nights adrenaline is pumping through her veins and she is expected to go quietly home and be a good girl until it's time to put on the push-up bra again. On one of those nights, tired and depressed, Russell goes into a bar and when a guy offers to buy her a drink, she accepts.

She knows what the score is. She's dressed like a hooker. He's dressed like a business-man with two hundred bucks in his pocket that he has just decided not to spend on flowers for his wife. But the thing is, she enjoys the power over men that this role gives her. All she has to do is wear the right blouse and smile the right way, and the brains of otherwise sensible men send Code Blue to their genitals. Just once, just tonight, with the warm coil of whiskey in her stomach, she decides to go back to the guy's place and maybe take the money and see what it's like.

It is here that the plot steps in. If *Impulse* had been a French movie, no doubt we would have continued to explore the twists and tastes of the woman's character, but in a Hollywood movie, personalities take second place to manipulation, and so we go on hold while the movie explains uninteresting details such as: The guy who picks her up is a criminal, and her colleagues on the force are working on his case, and it's all tied up with a lot of drug money, and so on.

And yet the movie gets interesting again, because of the corner Russell paints herself into. She makes some mistakes that become

increasingly unwise and complicated, and the question is, can she think fast enough to stay ahead of some experienced cops who are likely to see straight through the whole tissue of lies at any moment?

Impulse is the second feature directed by Sondra Locke, whose first film, *Rat Boy*, quickly dropped from view. She seems to have learned a lot about directing since then. The movie is good to look at and painfully intense at times—not so much when the plot is squeezing in as when we're invited to identify with Russell when she's looking for trouble. You know the feeling? It's something you're not supposed to do, and you could get in trouble if you're caught, but you want to, and you're tired, and nobody loves you, and there's this seductive stirring inside you, and temptation has thrown an arm over your shoulder and is signaling the bartender with the other hand.

It's this impulse that makes the movie interesting and worth seeing. The other stuff—the relationship with Jeff Fahey as the good cop, the details of the criminal situation—are taken off the shelf, given a quick polish, and stuck in where they fit. Robert Bresson made a movie once named *Pickpocket*, about a man with a criminal personality. The movie followed the pickpocket and watched him, and that was enough. Would anybody in the audience have been seriously disappointed if *Impulse* had simply followed the Russell character? What if Locke hadn't felt the need to solve the plot and tie up the loose ends? What if nobody ever found out what Russell did and she was left to think about it? Isn't that what usually happens in life? And isn't it more fun, and more dangerous, that way?

In Country ★ ★ ★
R, 120 m., 1989

Bruce Willis (Emmett Smith), Emily Lloyd (Samantha Hughes), Joan Allen (Irene), Kevin Anderson (Lonnie), John Terry (Tom), Peggy Rea (Mamaw), Judith Ivey (Anita). Directed by Norman Jewison and produced by Jewison and Richard Roth. Screenplay by Frank Pierson and Cynthia Cidre.

Norman Jewison's *In Country* is constructed like a short story, not a novel. It sneaks up on us with a series of incidents from daily life—moments that don't seem to be leading anywhere in particular, until we're blindsided by the surprising emotional impact of the closing scene. It's not about conflict be-

tween characters, but about people in the process of learning about themselves.

The film's central character is a seventeen-year-old girl named Samantha (Emily Lloyd), who is living in the small town of Hopewell, Kentucky, with her uncle. He's a guy named Emmett (Bruce Willis), who fought in Vietnam and has spent the years since then wandering in sort of detached silence and watching a lot of television. Samantha's father was killed in Vietnam before she was born. Her mother (Joan Allen) has remarried.

In the course of the story, Sam is confronted by no less a question than the meaning of birth and parenthood. She wants to know more about her father, and finds some of his letters home. There are some old photographs, too, of a soldier barely older than she is now—a nineteen-year-old in a private's uniform. Sometimes she talks to the photograph, telling her father of some of the things he missed by being killed in Vietnam, things like listening to Springsteen.

Other events happen, connected to the notion of parents and children. Sam's own mother visits with her young daughter. One of Sam's friends gets pregnant and has to decide what to do. All of these events seem to circle the key questions in Sam's life: Who was her father, and what did his life and death mean? "Honey," her mother tells her in the movie's saddest line, "I married him four weeks before he left for the war. I was nineteen. I hardly even remember him."

Sam begins to wonder if her uncle Emmett, the Vietnam survivor, can provide the key to her questions. Emmett isn't the kind of stereotyped Vietnam veteran who has become a staple in action movies—the crazed nut case who runs amok with a machine gun. He has disappeared inside his own passivity, and seems content to let his life slip through his fingers. She tries to awaken him with questions and even through a dance the local people sponsor in "belated appreciation" for the boys who fought the war.

All of these episodes (and others involving Sam's grandparents) create emotional momentum without revealing where they're leading us. The movie is not constructed in the usual ways with clear milestones in the plot. It is only at the end, when Sam and Emmett and Sam's grandmother (Peggy Rea) go to visit the Vietnam Veterans Memorial in Washington, that we see what the movie has been leading up to. It's there, in a scene of amazing emotional impact, that Jewison releases all the emotional tension, all the sadness and bewilderment that has been piling up during the film.

In Country is based on the novel by Bobbie Ann Mason, and Jewison is faithful to its accumulation of small incidents involving ordinary people. It is the fact that the ending is so low-key that makes it work so well ("Let's go get us some of that barbecue," the grandmother suggests after they've finished their visit to the memorial). The film should almost list the Vietnam Memorial in its credits, it works so effectively as a focus for the emotion.

Emily Lloyd is astonishing in the film's leading role. A young actress from London with only two previous roles in her credits *(Wish You Were Here* and *Cookie)*, she masters not only the Kentucky accent but the whole feeling of Sam—her gawkiness, her energy, the power of her curiosity. Bruce Willis has less-showy scenes (the character of Emmett is the opposite of every other character Willis has ever played), but he is well-cast, almost disappearing into the sad, silent survivor. The movie is like a time bomb. You sit there interested, absorbed, sometimes amused, sometimes moved, but wondering in the back of your mind what all of this is going to add up to. Then you find out.

Indecent Proposal ★ ★ ★
R, 119 m., 1993

Robert Redford (John Gage), Demi Moore (Diana Murphy), Woody Harrelson (David Murphy), Seymour Cassel (Mr. Shakelford), Oliver Platt (Jeremy). Directed by Adrian Lyne and produced by Sherry Lansing. Screenplay by Amy Holden Jones.

Like *Pretty Woman*, a movie it resembles in subtle ways, *Indecent Proposal* is a fantasy about characters who are allowed to try out amorality and see if they like it. The screenplay is a cleverly contrived mechanism inspired by that old joke with the punch line, "We've already established that. Now we're talking price." In this case, the price is a million dollars.

The movie opens with a dreamy narration about how Diana and David (Demi Moore and Woody Harrelson) have been in love since high school, and have stuck together through thick and thin and architecture school, until . . . well, until they go broke, and David is threatened with the loss of his

masterpiece, a house on the beach in Santa Monica.

We see the house, which in my opinion is so architecturally undistinguished that the filmmakers should have ordered another one, but never mind: David gets the bright idea of taking their last five thousand dollars and going to Vegas, hoping to win enough money to save the day. He does not. But while they are there, Diana catches the eye of John Gage, a handsome billionaire (Robert Redford) who offers them a million dollars if he can spend one night with her.

Well, what would *you* say to an offer like that? I ask not because I imagine you have been weighing such offers, but because the movie is deliberately designed to place the viewer in the position of assessing his or her own ideas about marital fidelity, and putting a price tag on them. Since seeing the movie, I've been involved in half a dozen discussions on the subject. Most people have said there's no way they would accept such an offer. Some people have said there are *some* ways in which, you know what, they just possibly might. Only one person was unkind enough to suggest that if the choice was between being faithful to Woody Harrelson or sinning with Robert Redford, Bob could keep his million and she'd consider it anyway.

The movie is ingenious in the way it surrounds its essentially crass subject matter with a camouflage of romantic scenery. Redford is, first of all, a splendid salesman, avoiding strong-arm tactics, seducing the couple into seriously considering the choice. The actual night of adultery is wisely kept off screen. And because the actors are all well-known stars, they elevate the subject to a more symbolic level (if the actors had been unknowns, we'd probably view the choice in a completely different light).

I mentioned *Pretty Woman* earlier. I could also have mentioned *The Crying Game*. What those movies and *Indecent Proposal* all do brilliantly is allow the audience to be voyeurs while acceptable people do unacceptable things. We might not admit we'd be intrigued by the idea of sleeping with a hooker, or accepting a million bucks for a night of sex, or accepting Jaye Davidson on rather unexpected terms. But we *are* intrigued by movies in which the plots somewhat plausibly present Richard Gere, Demi Moore, or Stephen Rea with such a choice. In the immortal words of a folk song by Bob Gibson:

But what the hell, honey—
Since you've already got my money . . .

Indecent Proposal was directed by Adrian Lyne, whose credits include two other excursions into the thickets of sexual danger, *9½ Weeks* and *Fatal Attraction*. This movie is a kinder and gentler exploration of love and lust. It even becomes plausible, for a time, that Moore and Redford would feel romantic inclinations, especially after Harrelson finds he is not quite as broad-minded as he imagined.

There are large challenges to logic in the film (for example, even apart from how Harrelson eventually seems determined to spend the million, why has he forgotten his lawyer's 5 percent?). The plot is manipulative, with Harrelson almost pushing his wife into Redford's arms. But there is also a genuine romantic spirit at work here, and I liked the scene toward the end with Moore, Redford, and his chauffeur (Seymour Cassel) saying things without quite saying them.

Indecent Proposal is in a very old tradition, in which love is put to the test of need and desire, and triumphs in the end, although not without a great many moments when it seems quite willing to cave in to passion. It is artificial and manipulative, and in the real world this sort of thing would never happen in this way, but then that's why we watch them: We want to leave the real world, for a couple of hours, anyway.

Indiana Jones and the Last Crusade
★ ★ ★ ½
PG-13, 125 m., 1989

Harrison Ford (Indiana Jones), Sean Connery (Dr. Henry Jones), Denholm Elliott (Marcus Brody), Alison Doody (Dr. Elsa Schneider), John Rhys-Davies (Sallah). Directed by Steven Spielberg and produced by Robert Watts. Screenplay by Jeffrey Boam.

There is a certain style of illustration that appeared in the boys' adventure magazines of the 1940s—in those innocent publications that have been replaced by magazines on punk lifestyles and movie monsters. The illustrations were always about the same. They showed a small group of swarthy men hovering over a treasure trove with greedy grins on their bearded faces, while in the foreground, two teen-age boys peered out from behind a rock in wonder and astonishment. The point of view was always over the boys' shoulders; the reader was invited to share this forbidden glimpse of the secret world of men.

Indiana Jones and the Last Crusade begins with just such a scene; Steven Spielberg must have been paging through his old issues of *Boys' Life* and *Thrilling Wonder Tales* down in the basement. As I watched it, I felt a real delight, because recent Hollywood escapist movies have become too jaded and cynical, and they've lost the feeling that you can stumble over astounding adventures just by going on a hike with your Scout troop.

Spielberg lights the scene in the strong, basic colors of old pulp magazines, and of course when the swarthy men bend over their discovery, it seems to glow with a light of its own, which bathes their faces in a golden glow. This is the kind of moment that can actually justify a line like *It's mine! All mine!*—although Spielberg does not go so far.

One of the two kids behind the boulder is, of course, the young Indiana Jones. But he is discovered by explorers plundering an ancient treasure, and escapes just in the nick of time. The sequence ends as an adult claps a battered fedora down on Indiana's head, and then we flash forward to the era of World War II.

The opening sequence of this third Indiana Jones movie is the only one that seems truly original—or perhaps I should say, it recycles images from 1940s pulps and serials that Spielberg has not borrowed before. The rest of the movie will not come as a surprise to students of Indiana Jones, but then how could it? The Jones movies by now have defined a familiar world of death-defying stunts, virtuoso chases, dry humor, and the quest for impossible goals in unthinkable places.

When *Raiders of the Lost Ark* appeared, it defined a new energy level for adventure movies; it was a delirious breakthrough. But there was no way for Spielberg to top himself, and perhaps it is just as well that *Last Crusade* will indeed be Indy's last film. It would be too sad to see the series grow old and thin, like the James Bond movies.

Even in this third adventure, some of the key elements are recycled from *Raiders*. This time, Indy's quest is to find the Holy Grail, the cup Jesus Christ is said to have used at the Last Supper. (To drink from the cup is to have eternal youth.) The Holy Grail reminds us of the Ark of the Covenant in the first film, and in both cases the chase is joined by Nazi villains.

The new element this time is the way Spielberg fills in some of the past of the Jones character. We learn his real name (which I would not dream of revealing here), and we meet his father, Professor Henry Jones, who is played by Sean Connery on exactly the right note. Like the fathers in classic boys' stories, Dr.

Jones is not a parent so much as a grown-up ally, an older pal who lacks three dimensions because children are unable to see their parents in that complexity. I kept being reminded of the father in the Hardy Boys books, who shook his head and smiled at the exploits of his lovable tykes and only rarely "expressed concern" or "cautioned them sternly." Since the Hardy Boys were constantly involved, at a tender age, with an endless series of counterfeiters, car thieves, kidnap rings, Nazi spies, and jewel thieves, their father's detachment seemed either saintly or mad—and Connery has fun with some of the same elements.

Harrison Ford is Indiana Jones again this time, of course, and what he does seems so easy, so deadpan, yet few other actors could maintain a straight and a credible presence in the midst of such chaos. After young Indy discovers his life's mission in the early scenes, the central story takes place years later, when Professor Jones (the world's leading expert on the Grail) is kidnapped by desperados who are convinced he knows the secret of where it is now hidden.

He does. And Indy, working from his father's notebook, follows a trail from America to the watery catacombs beneath Venice, and then to the deserts of the Holy Land, where there is a sensational chase scene involving a gigantic Nazi armored tank. He is accompanied on his mission by Dr. Elsa Schneider (Alison Doody), a scientist he meets in Venice, but the character is a disappointment after the fire of Karen Allen in the first movie, and even the sultriness of Kate Capshaw in the second.

Spielberg devises several elaborate set pieces, of which I especially liked the rat-infested catacombs and sewers beneath Venice (I tried not to remember that Venice, by definition, has no catacombs). The art direction looks great in a scene involving a zeppelin, and an escape from the airship by airplane. And the great tank in the desert is a fearsome and convincing construction.

If there is just a shade of disappointment after seeing this movie, it has to be because we will never again have the shock of this material seeming new. *Raiders of the Lost Ark* now seems more than ever a turning point in the cinema of escapist entertainment, and there was really no way Spielberg could make it new all over again. What he has done is take many of the same elements, and apply all of his craft and sense of fun to make them work yet once again. And they do.

Indiana Jones and the Temple of Doom

★ ★ ★ ★
PG, 118 m., 1984

Harrison Ford (Indiana Jones), Kate Capshaw (Willie Scott), Ke Huy Quan (Short Round), Amrish Puri (Mola Ram), Philip Stone (Captain Blumburtt), Roshan Seth (Chattar Lal). Directed by Steven Spielberg and produced by George Lucas. Screenplay by Willard Huyck and Gloria Katz.

Steven Spielberg's *Indiana Jones and the Temple of Doom* is one of the greatest Bruised Forearm Movies ever made. You know what a Bruised Forearm Movie is. That's the kind of movie where your date is always grabbing your forearm in a viselike grip, as unbearable excitement unfolds on the screen. After the movie is over, you've had a great time but your arm is black-and-blue for a week. This movie is one of the most relentlessly nonstop action pictures ever made, with a virtuoso series of climactic sequences that must last an hour and never stop for a second. It's a roller-coaster ride, a visual extravaganza, a technical triumph, and a whole lot of fun. And it's not simply a retread of *Raiders of the Lost Ark*, the first Indiana Jones movie. It works in a different way, and borrows from different traditions.

Raiders was inspired by Saturday afternoon serials. It was a series of cliff-hanging predicaments, strung out along the way as Indiana Jones traveled from San Francisco to Tibet, Egypt, and other romantic locales. It was an exotic road picture. *Indiana Jones* mostly takes place on one location, and belongs more to the great tradition of the Impregnable Fortress Impregnated. You know the kind of fortress I'm talking about. You see them all the time in James Bond pictures. They involve unbelievably bizarre hideaways, usually buried under the earth, beneath the sea, on the moon, or inside a volcano. They are ruled over by megalomaniac zealots who dream of conquest, and they're fueled by slave labor. Our first glimpse of an Impregnable Fortress is always the same: An ominous long shot, with Wagnerian music, as identically uniformed functionaries hurry about their appointed tasks.

The role of the hero in a movie like this is to enter the fortress, steal the prize, and get away in one piece. This task always involves great difficulty, horrendous surprises, unspeakable dangers, and a virtuoso chase sequence. The very last shots at the end of the sequence are obligatory: The fortress must be destroyed. Hopefully, there will be great walls of flame and water, engulfing the bad guys as the heroes race to freedom, inches ahead of certain death.

But enough of intellectual film criticism. Let's get back to Indiana Jones. As *Temple of Doom* opens, Indiana is in a nightclub somewhere in Shanghai. Killers are after him. He escapes in the nick of time, taking along a beautiful nightclub floozy (Kate Capshaw), and accompanied by his trusty young sidekick, Short Round (Ke Huy Quan). Their getaway leads them into a series of adventures: A flight over the Himalayas, a breathtaking escape from a crashing plane, and a meeting with a village leader who begs Indiana to find and return the village's precious magic jewel—a stone which disappeared along with all of the village's children. Indiana is a plucky chap and agrees. Then there's a dinner in the palace of a sinister local lord. The dinner scene, by the way, also is lifted from James Bond, where it's an obligatory part of every adventure: James is always promised a sure death, but treated first to an elegant dinner with his host, who boasts of his power and takes inordinate pride in being a sophisticated host. After Indiana and Willie retire for the night, there's the movie's only slow sequence, in which such matters as love are discussed. (Make some popcorn.) Then the movie's second half opens with a breathtaking series of adventures involving the mines beneath the palace—mines that have been turned into a vision of hell.

The set design, art direction, special effects, and sound effects inside this underground Hades are among the most impressive achievements in the whole history of Raiders and Bond-style thrillers. As dozens of little kids work on chain gangs, the evil maharajah keeps them in slavery by using the sinister powers of the missing jewel and its two mates. Indiana and his friends look on in astonishment, and then Indiana attempts to steal back the jewel. Some of the film's great set pieces now take place: Human victims are lowered into a subterranean volcano in a steel cage, weird rituals are celebrated, and there is a chase scene involving the mine's miniature railway. This chase has to be seen to be believed. Spielberg has obviously studied Buster Keaton's *The General*, that silent classic that solved the obvious logistic problem of a chase on railway tracks (i.e., what to do about the fact that one train seemingly always has to be behind the other one). As Indiana and friends hurtle in the little out-of-control mine car, the pursuers are behind, ahead, above, below, and beside them, and the scene will wring you out and leave you breathless. *Indiana Jones and the Temple of Doom* makes no apologies for being exactly what it is: Exhilarating, manic, wildly imaginative escapism.

No apologies are necessary. This is the most cheerfully exciting, bizarre, goofy, romantic adventure movie since *Raiders*, and it is high praise to say that it's not so much a sequel as an equal. It's quite an experience. You stagger out with a silly grin—and a bruised forearm, of course.

The Indian Runner ★ ★ ★
R, 126 m., 1991

David Morse (Joe), Viggo Mortensen (Frank), Valeria Golino (Maria), Patricia Arquette (Dorothy), Charles Bronson (Father), Sandy Dennis (Mother), Dennis Hopper (Caesar). Directed by Sean Penn and produced by Don Phillips. Screenplay by Penn.

The faded home movies show two brothers, little boys, playing in the sun and blinking up at the camera. One is more aggressive than the other, and you can see he has a temper. Many years later, those same two personalities are still locked into the same two brothers, and everything is in place for a family tragedy that has been a long time coming.

As *The Indian Runner* opens, the peaceful brother, Joe (David Morse), is a deputy sheriff in a small country town. The other brother, Frank (Viggo Mortensen), has decided to come back to town in the aftermath of his latest run-in with the law. Frank says he wants to make a fresh start, and Joe tells his wife that he's prepared to help him. That's what brothers are for.

But some people simply seem constitutionally incapable of changing, of accepting help, of shedding their criminal natures. Frank seems to be one of them. He's filled with pipe dreams and vague plans, and he can sweet-talk a young woman like Dorothy (Patricia Arquette), who he's living with these days and who is bearing his child. But when his violent temper flashes out of control, Frank forgets his plans and resolutions, and his life falls into pieces again.

That is the story of *The Indian Runner*, the thoughtful, surprisingly effective directing debut of Sean Penn, who also wrote the screenplay. He says his script was inspired by "Highway Patrolman," the Bruce Springsteen song, but maybe it was also inspired, in part, by the two sides of Sean Penn's own character: Here, in one person, is not only the media caricature of a hothead who gets in public shoving matches, but also the young man who is one of the three or four best actors of his generation.

Is there a flash point inside Penn that sometimes cannot be controlled? Maybe there was, although in the last few years he has seemed calmer and happier. But certainly he knows about the duality of human nature—and in these two brothers he has dramatized the pull between one who is responsible to his core, and another who cannot help getting in trouble.

It's impressive, how thoughtfully Penn handles this material. The good brother isn't a straight arrow, and the bad brother isn't romanticized as a rebel without a cause, and there are no easy solutions or neat little happy endings for this story. It's as intractable as life itself. And Penn surrounds his brothers with supporting characters who are so well realized, I'll remember them as long as I remember the leads.

Charles Bronson plays the boys' father. It is a performance of quiet, sure power. After his recent string of brainless revenge thrillers, I wondered if Bronson had sort of given up on acting and was just going through the motions. Here he is so good it is impossible to think of another actor one would have preferred in his place. And Sandy Dennis, another unexpected casting choice, fits well as his wife. There are also strong performances by Valeria Golino, as Morse's wife, and by Arquette—a girl confused by half-baked romantic notions, who sees Frank as a knight when nobody else can see anything but a loser.

Sean Penn announced after this film that he would not act anymore—at least, not if he could support himself as a director. He's too good an actor to lose. But *The Indian Runner* proves he was right when he thought he could direct.

Indian Summer ★ ★ ★
PG-13, 98 m., 1993

Alan Arkin (Uncle Lou), Matt Craven (Jamie Ross), Diane Lane (Beth Warden), Bill Paxton (Jack Belston), Elizabeth Perkins (Jennifer Morton), Kevin Pollak (Brad Berman), Sam Raimi (Stick Coder). Directed by Mike Binder and produced by Jeffrey Silver and Robert Newmyer. Screenplay by Binder.

Indian Summer starts out like one of those reunion movies where friends from long ago gather again to settle old scores, sort out old romances, open old wounds, and make new beginnings. All of those rituals have been performed by the end of the film, but curiously enough, the movie isn't really about what happens. It's about how it feels. This is a story more interested in tone and mood than in big plot points.

The film takes place at Camp Tamakwa, on the wooded shores of an Ontario lake, where an aging camp director known to everyone as Uncle Lou (Alan Arkin) has invited some of his favorite campers to return for an autumn reunion before the camp is boarded up for good. From all over North America they gather—a recent widow, a rich clothing retailer, a reformed hippie, a new millionaire and his twenty-one-year-old fiancée, and the others. Uncle Lou enforces the camp rules: boys in one cabin, girls in another, reveille at dawn. The old campers find their names scratched on the weathered camp walls, and remember their first kisses, practical jokes, erections, and other milestones that took place under the watchful eye of Tamakwa, the Indian weather god.

Stories like this are usually constructed in a fairly rigid fashion. The first act is devoted to introductions, and plot problems are assigned to various characters. The second act develops the problems, and the third act solves them, with appropriate surprises. By the end we can expect that one couple will break up, one will begin a new romance, one will find a new truth, and at least one old secret will be revealed. Oh, and a skeleton will be taken out of the closet.

All of those things happen in *Indian Summer*, but in a strangely low-key way. The movie was written and directed by Mike Binder, who probably attended just such a camp—maybe even this one (the credits indicate that Camp Tamakwa is a real place). He scores his points, but he's not a slam-dunker. The prevailing feeling of the film is warm and gentle, and there are no really bad people or terrible secrets. The biggest emotional payoff comes when Uncle Lou admits that once, decades ago, he refused to hire a counselor because he was black—and if there was one day in his whole life he wishes he could take back and handle differently, it is that day.

The film's cast is a *Big Chill*-style assortment: Diane Lane, Elizabeth Perkins, Kevin Pollack, Matt Craven, and Bill Paxton as the only kid who was ever sent home from camp in disgrace, but who has been invited back by Uncle Lou for reasons that are eventually revealed. Lou considers these campers representative of the camp's Golden Age. These days, he complains, he doesn't understand the kids anymore; "I try to teach them how to light a one-match fire, and they look at me like I'm crazy. Any kid who needs to wear one of those Walkmans when he's in the middle of the North Woods is a mystery to me."

Watching the film, I was reminded of seeing *Enchanted April* for the first time. During that film, apart from enjoying its pleasures, I was seized with a great desire to actually go and spend a vacation in the same corner of Italy the movie's characters had discovered. Watching *Indian Summer*, I was possessed by an impulse to get into the car one day and drive to the shores of Bankson Lake, near Paw Paw, Michigan, to see if the weathered cabins of St. Joseph's Boys Camp still remain. It was there, during three or four summers, that I gathered memories that *Indian Summer* awakened with a fierce poignancy.

It is human nature to form groups and be loyal to them. There are real groups, like families and army units, and artificial groups, like friends you make on a cruise, or the other kids at summer camp. The artificial groups create instant traditions (all camps have their songs and legends), and in remembering them you are pulled back for a moment to a summer when all life seemed to be ahead of you. Now that it isn't, that summer seems more precious, and that promise more elusive, than ever before.

I Never Promised You a Rose Garden
★ ★ ★
R, 90 m., 1977

Kathleen Quinlan (Deborah), Bibi Andersson (Dr. Fried), Ben Piazza (Mr. Blake), Lorraine Gary (Mrs. Blake), Michael McGuire (McPherson), Reni Santoni (Hobbs), Susan Tyrrell (Kitty), Robert Viharo (Anterrabae). Directed by Anthony Page and produced by Terence F. Deane, Daniel H. Blatt, and Michael Hausman. Screenplay by Gavin Lambert and Lewis John Carlino.

I'm becoming suspicious of movies that assure us mental illness can be cured if the victim "wants" to be cured, or assume that mental illness is not illness at all—because in an insane world the only sane people are the crazies. *I Never Promised You a Rose Garden* doesn't altogether avoid the first assumption, but it firmly rejects the second, and it gives us a heroine so convincingly real we finally believe perhaps she *could* cure herself.

The heroine is well known to the millions of readers of Joanne Greenberg's novel, which began as a cult paperback and became a durable bestseller. She is Deborah, sixteen, schizophrenic, child of an affluent home, but inhabitant of a personal fantasy. After a suicide attempt, she spends three years in a mental institution, coming close to self-destruction more than once, but finally surviving through her own efforts and those of a psychiatrist who really attempts to understand her.

We are given only sketchy information about what drove her to attempt suicide—her parents didn't understand her, she's filled with guilt because she believes she tried to kill a younger sister—but her fantasies are shown in much greater detail. As visualized in the film, they seem to be inspired by the paintings of Frank Frazetta: A race of muscular young people, clothed in furs and feathers, ride giant horses across the desert and want her to join them.

This alternative universe is so much more romantic and seductive than the real world, which for Deborah becomes Ward D of the mental institution. It's a women's ward, filled with the "worst" cases. Some of the patients do indeed seem to be totally within their private hells, but others (like the loud and often cheerful Kitty) have a reservoir of common sense. Deborah is wary, here, and often silent; she's properly afraid of the sinister male attendant Hobbs, but the turning point in her cure comes when she can admit of the other attendant, McPherson: "I like him. He treats me like I'm a real person." That touch of reality from outside is the first crack in the totality of her fantasies.

The psychiatrist is Dr. Fried, played by Bibi Andersson with sympathy and fortitude: She listens, encourages, supports, suggests, doesn't push. And over a period of three years Deborah is finally able to open herself to the world outside her dreams, to send her phantom gods galloping out into the desert without her.

I Never Promised You a Rose Garden has been compared, of course, to *One Flew Over the Cuckoo's Nest*, which first defied a kind of unwritten Hollywood superstition. That superstition was that movies about mental illness wouldn't succeed at the box office, that they were too depressing. *Cuckoo's Nest* wasn't filmed for years because of that taboo, and *Rose Garden* probably couldn't have been made if it hadn't been for *Cuckoo's Nest*'s great success.

One big difference between the two movies is that R.P. McMurphy, in *Cuckoo,* was, in fact, sane. Deborah is not. *Cuckoo* celebrates McMurphy's cosmic sanity, and so has room for the dimensions of Jack Nicholson's manic performance. *Rose Garden* celebrates, instead, very small victories (and one of its most poignant moments comes when Deborah, burning herself with a cigarette, realizes with triumph that she actually feels pain—that her mind has let the reality in).

This is difficult material to bring to life, but a young actress named Kathleen Quinlan does it with heart and sensitivity. There were opportunities here for climbing the walls and chewing the scenery, I suppose, but her performance always finds the correct and convincing human note.

And it's the skill with which Miss Quinlan (and Bibi Andersson) follow that thread of characterization that makes the movie work. Otherwise, those desert fantasies and all those feathers and fur might have been fatally distracting. But because Deborah seems to regard them with a sober fatalism, we can almost accept them; and because she never expresses any emotions that don't seem to grow right out of the situations she finds herself in, we always accept her.

I Never Sang for My Father ★ ★ ★ ★
PG, 92 m., 1971

Melvyn Douglas (Tom), Gene Hackman (Gene), Dorothy Stickney (Margaret), Estelle Parsons (Alice, The Sister), Elizabeth Hubbard (Peggy). Directed and produced by Gilbert Cates. Screenplay by Robert Anderson.

At the beginning and again at the end of *I Never Sang for My Father,* we see a grainy snapshot of an old man and a middle-aged man, arms thrown about each other's shoulders, peering uncertainly into the camera as if they're not quite sure what drew them out into the sunshine to pose this day. And we hear Gene Hackman's voice: "Death ends a life. But it does not end a relationship." This film takes that simple fact and uses it to make a poignant and ultimately tragic statement about parents and children, life and death, and all the words that go unspoken. The man is played by Melvyn Douglas, and Hackman plays his son, and the film is about the fierce love they bear for each other, and about their inability to communicate that love, or very much of anything else.

The story takes place at a time when the old man's life is ending, but he won't admit it, and when the younger man's life is about to permit a new beginning. The old man is eighty-one, and a long time ago he was the mayor and the school board president—one of the town's most important citizens. But now he has largely been forgotten, left to live a comfortable life in the rambling old family home. He lives there with his wife and his memories, and a fierce possessiveness for his son.

What he wants from the son is a show of devotion. He doesn't communicate with him; indeed, he spends a lot of time falling asleep in front of the television set. But he wants him there, almost as a hostage, because he has a hunger for affection left over from his own neglected childhood. The son tries to go through the motions. But his own wife died a year ago, and now, at forty-four, he has decided to marry a woman doctor who lives in California. This will mean leaving the hometown, and that would be heresy to his father.

The situation becomes urgent when the old man's wife dies. He seems to accept the death as an inconvenience, transferring his grief to memories of his own mother's death half a century before. But his dependence upon his son becomes almost total. His daughter (Estelle Parsons) comes home for the funeral; in a fit of rage, the old man had banished her for marrying a Jew. Now she explains to Hackman, with an objectivity that sounds cruel but springs from love, that an arrangement is going to have to be made about their father. He can't live in the big house by himself.

The trouble is, his pride makes him refuse to hire the housekeeper he could easily afford. He expects his son to watch over him. And Hackman has not gathered the courage to reveal his marriage plans. He goes to look at a couple of old people's homes, but he finds them depressing and he knows his father would never, ever, go to one. So there you have the son's dilemma. The father should not live alone. A nursing home seems impossible. For a moment, the children consider gaining power of attorney and insisting on a housekeeper. But then, in a scene of remarkable emotional impact, the son watches as his father finally breaks down and reveals his grief, and the son invites him to come and live in California. But that, of course, is also unacceptable to the old man, whose pride will not allow him to admit that others could make his decisions, and whose stub-

bornness makes him insist on having everything his way, no matter what.

These bare bones of plot hardly give any hint of the power of this film. I've suggested something of what it's about, but almost nothing about the way the writing, the direction, and the performances come together to create one of the most unforgettably human films I can remember.

Robert Anderson's screenplay is from his autobiographical play, and it rings with truth. His dialogue is direct and revealing, without the "literary" touches or sophistication that could have sabotaged the characters. Eugene O'Neill was writing a different kind of dialogue for different purposes in *Long Day's Journey into Night,* a somewhat similar work that comes to mind. But for Anderson's story, which depends on everyday realism and would find symbolism dangerous, the unadorned dialogue is essential.

Gilbert Cates's direction also respects the fact that this is a movie not about visual style or any other fashionably cinematic selfconsciousness. With the exception of an inappropriate song which sneaks onto the sound track near the film's beginning, Cates has directed solely to get those magnificent performances onto the screen as movingly as possible. Much of the film is just between the two of them and the characters seem to work so well because Douglas and Hackman respond to each other in every shot; the effect is not of acting, but as if the story were happening right now while we see it.

The film tells us that death ends a life, but not a relationship. That's true of all close and deep human relationships; when one person dies, the other continues long afterwards to wonder what could have been said between them, but wasn't.

I Never Sang for My Father has the courage to remain open-ended; the father dies, but the problems between father and son remain unresolved. That is really more tragic than the fact of death, because death is natural, but human nature cries out that parents and children should understand each other.

Infra-Man ★ ★ ½
PG, 92 m., 1976

Li Hsiu-hsien, Wang Hsieh, Yuan Man-tzu, Terry Liu, Tsen Shu-yi, Huang Chien-lung, Lu Sheng. Directed by Hua Shan and produced by Rumme Shaw.

Within the first four mintues of *Infra-Man,* (a) a giant flying lizard attacks a school bus,

(b) the Earth cracks open, (c) Hong Kong is destroyed by flames, (d) mountains disintegrate to reveal the forms of reptilian monsters with blinking yellow eyes, (e) the Professor announces that a twenty-million-year-old woman is unleashing the hibernating monsters upon civilization, (f) the Science Headquarters is shaken by a second quake, (g) the Mutants awake, and (h) the Professor, obviously shaken, informs a secret meeting of world leaders, "This situation is so bad that it is the worst that ever has been!"

No doubt about it: This is a case for Infra-Man. In his secret laboratory far beneath the Science Headquarters, the Professor explains to a brave volunteer: "We will wire your arms and legs with powerful transistors and death rays. You will be powered by a tiny nuclear reactor. Unfortunately, the operation will be very painful and you may die."

And so we're off and running, in the best movie of its kind since *Invasion of the Bee Girls*. I'm a pushover for monster movies anyway, but *Infra-Man* has it all: Horrendous octopus men, a gigantic beetle man with three eyes who sprays his victims with sticky cocoons, savage robots with coiled spring necks that can extend ten feet, a venomous little critter that looks like a hairy mutant footstool, elaborately staged karate fights, underground throne rooms, damsels in distress, exploding volcanoes, ann a whipcracking villainess named Princess Dragon Mom (Philip Wylie, please note).

The movie's totally, almost joyfully absurd, and a victim of John Carter's Syndrome. You remember J.C.S., based on the logical oversight in Edgar Rice Burrough's books about John Carter of Mars. After whole chapters of galloping across the Martian desert on his Martian steed and fighting off enemies in sword fights, John Carter finally says to hell with it, pulls out a ray gun, and fries everybody.

Same here. Gigantic mutant monsters with built-in death rays attack Infra-Man, who can hurl lightning bolts from the soles of his feet, and what do they do? They have a karate fight. After ten minutes of chopping and socking and doing acrobatic flips, THEN they zap each other.

No matter, *Intra-Man* contains terrific moments. In one cliff-hanging scene, for example, the Professor has Infra-Man wired up on the operating table when Science Headquarters is attacked by gigantic mutant arms. That's right, arms: no body, just arms. The arms squirm all over the headquarters,

knocking off the power supply. The Professor shouts into his radio: "You have one minute to restore power before Infra-Man dies!"

His aide struggles toward a red power switch. He is knocked unconscious by an arm. Shot of a stopwatch ticking away the seconds. He regains consciousness, struggles some more. The arm attacks again. With ten seconds to go, soldiers burst into the room with a power saw and cut the arm in half. The switch is thrown and Infra-Man lives.

There are other good things. Lines like, "We are doing this for the children of the world." Or, "The clouds will cut off the sun and deprive Infra-Man of his power source." Or, "Drop the Earthling to her doom—she will melt at 3,000 degrees." The movie even looks good: It's a classy, slick production by the Shaw Brothers, the Hong Kong kung fu kings. When they stop making movies like *Infra-Man*, a little light will go out of the world.

The Inner Circle ★ ★ ★
PG-13, 134 m., 1992

Tom Hulce (Ivan), Lolita Davidovich (Anastasia), Bob Hoskins (Beria), Bess Meyer (Kathy at Sixteen), Feodor Chaliapin, Jr. (Professor Bartnev), Alexandre Zbruev (Stalin). Directed by Andrei Konchalovsky and produced by Claudio Bonivento. Screenplay by Konchalovsky and Anatoly Usov.

There is a convention in the movies that little guys are harmless. *The Inner Circle* argues otherwise. Its subject is the littlest of guys, and yet, in his own modest way and with his limited means, he creates as much suffering and unhappiness as he can. What is monstrous about him is how little he understands about his corrupt values, until it's too late.

His name is Ivan, and he is a film projectionist in Stalin's Russia. The big guys file in and settle into the overstuffed leather armchairs and the lights go down and that's him, back in the booth, projecting the film and hoping to heaven that nothing goes wrong. He lives in a tiny flat with his wife, Anastasia; they share their space with a Jewish family. One day the forces of the government come crushing down on the Jewish father, who propels himself across the room so hard that his forehead smashes on the wall, leaving a bloodstain.

Ivan is happy to have the extra space after the Jews are gone, and moves a piece of fur-

niture in front of the stain. Anastasia would like to adopt the little daughter of their Jewish neighbors, but Ivan has bigger things to occupy his mind. He has caught the attention of Comrade Stalin, and has been chosen as Stalin's official projectionist inside the Kremlin. His body seems to swell as he makes this announcement, and it is clear that working for Stalin is more important to him than any consideration of his wife, or the child, or indeed his own life. He is a born toady.

The Inner Circle, which is said to be inspired by a real, if very insignificant, person, is a film that must have been boiling up inside of Andrei Konchalovsky for years. Born in Russia, raised as a child of the Cold War, Konchalovsky opted for the West and has been making American movies (*Runaway Train, Shy People*) for some time. Now he returns to the atmosphere that must have shaped his young manhood, and makes a frightening film about the climate of fear in a dictatorship.

Ivan is played by Tom Hulce (*Amadeus*), whose performance will probably grate on some people's nerves because he is so ingratiating, so obnoxiously humble, so lacking in ordinary signs of character. I think the performance is on the money; he is taking some risks by playing Ivan as the little worm that he is, and we must not mistake the messenger for the message.

Much of the film involves the bureaucracy of the Kremlin, where Ivan is suddenly brought one day as a substitute projectionist. As he stands proudly beside his projector, explaining to Comrade Stalin why it has broken down and how he could fix it, we understand, in the looks exchanged by the others in the room, that death or disappearance is a daily fact of their lives—that by talking so frankly, Ivan could bring disaster down on his own head, or on the heads of those he implicates. But this is one of Stalin's good days, and he expansively embraces the little nonentity, elevating him to what Ivan blissfully considers his inner circle.

The progress of Ivan in the Kremlin is counterpointed with his wife's more humane progress in the opposite direction. Anastasia (played with great character by Lolita Davidovich) cannot forget her love for the small daughter of their former flatmates, and follows the little girl to a state orphanage, even pretending to be a nurse in order to be near to her. She is on very thin ice, and when Ivan discovers her deception, he explodes: It is unthinkable that anyone could endanger the status of Stalin's projectionist for so inconsequential a thing as a little girl!

The Inner Circle is about states of mind under totalitarianism; about how a dictatorship, by denying the humanity of its subjects, inspires abject boot-licking in some, even as it inspires others to acts of heroism. The movie obviously has a deep, strong meaning for Konchalovsky, and he offers it as his way of explaining the decades of collective compromise his native Russia is only now freeing itself from. The movie is fascinating in its details (such as the scenes where Stalin watches Hollywood newsreels of the progress of World War II), and it works as a story. But it also works, powerfully, as an insight into a shameful period of history.

Innerspace ★ ★ ★
PG, 120 m., 1987

Dennis Quaid (Tuck Pendleton), Martin Short (Jack Putter), Meg Ryan (Lydia Maxwell), Kevin McCarthy (Scrimshaw), Fiona Lewis (Dr. Canker), Vernon Wells (Mr. Igoe), Robert Picardo (The Cowboy). Directed by Joe Dante and produced by Michael Finnell. Screenplay by Jeffrey Boam and Chip Proser.

I would have loved to eavesdrop on the script conferences for *Innerspace*. Here is an absurd, unwieldy, overplotted movie that is nevertheless entertaining—and some of the fun comes from the way the plot keeps laying it on.

The movie stars Dennis Quaid as a daring but irresponsible test pilot who signs up for a bizarre mission: He will be placed inside a capsule, which will be reduced in size until it is smaller than a molecule, and then the capsule will be injected into a rabbit. (If the experiment is a success, future surgeons could operate from inside their patients' diseased organs.)

High-tech thieves want to steal the technology of Quaid's employers, and send a squad of hit men to steal the syringe that contains his capsule. A scientist flees with the syringe to a nearby shopping mall, where in desperation he plunges the needle into Martin Short, and injects Quaid's capsule where the sun don't shine.

Are you following this? Quaid uses a communications system to talk from within Short's head. At first Short thinks he's hearing things, but then Quaid tells him the whole story, and enlists Short's aid in a desperate effort to

outwit the bad guys and restore Quaid to normal size before his oxygen runs out.

There are complications—a lot of them—mostly centering around Meg Ryan, as Quaid's estranged girlfriend. Short, with Quaid inside of him, has to convince Ryan of what's happening. And in the process, of course, he gets a crush on her—with Quaid eavesdropping on every word and heartbeat. It's a new twist on the old gag about the Siamese twin who wanted a moment alone with his girl.

This plot is not only unbelievable, but almost unworkable, especially when much is made of the intrigues of the villains. The complications grow so labyrinthine that the movie drags at times; it could have benefited from some fairly severe editing. And yet I liked *Innerspace* all the same, for the special effects and especially for the performances by Quaid and Short.

This was Short's comeback film after the unhappy experience of *The Three Amigos*. At last he shows what he can do in a film, realizing the promise of his peculiar but fascinating work on "Saturday Night Live." He gives us a little of his SNL schtick in a weird, off-balance dance, but basically he's playing a very confused straight man in this film, and he is always fun to watch.

Working inside Short in his tiny capsule, Quaid has a tougher role because he can't get physical. All of his actions have to be taken through the instrument of Short's body, and there are wonderful scenes where he uses rhetoric to inspire this nerd to act like a hero.

I wish I knew more about how they achieved the special effects. Some of the scenes inside the human bloodstream look like fairly straightforward, computer-generated animation. But there is a sequence involving the heart that has an uncanny reality to it, as if Quaid's capsule had been combined with actual footage of a beating heart, taken with miniaturized cameras.

Innerspace never quite knows whether to be a comedy or a thriller, and I never quite cared which way it went. The performances are so engaging and the effects are so enthusiastic that even when the movie runs long, it's only because it has too many ideas. In fact, it has one idea too many, leading to a howling logical error: When Quaid wants a drink, he asks Short to chug some Jack Daniel's—and then intercepts the booze on its way past the miniaturized capsule. But Quaid himself is as small as a molecule of the whiskey he wants to drink. I've felt that way myself some mornings.

Note: Then again, I'm not a molecular scientist. A couple of readers have written to point out that Quaid's ship is about the size of a blood cell, which would be millions of times larger than a molecule.

Insignificance ★ ★ ★
R, 110 m., 1985

Theresa Russell (The Actress), Tony Curtis (The Senator), Gary Busey (The Ballplayer), Michael Emil (The Professor), Will Sampson (Elevator Man). Directed by Nicolas Roeg and produced by Jeremy Thomas. Screenplay by Terry Johnson.

The premise is not too unlikely. Imagine that during one hot and steamy night in a New York City hotel room, the lives of these people crossed paths: Marilyn Monroe, Senator Joe McCarthy, Joe DiMaggio, and Albert Einstein. The key linking element is, of course, Monroe, a woman of such undefinable and ethereal appeal that her real life did indeed encompass such husbands as DiMaggio and Arthur Miller, such admirers as Norman Mailer and Laurence Olivier, such friends as Jack Kennedy and Robert Mitchum. Her address book, which disappeared mysteriously after she died, no doubt included names from such unexpected corners of America that DiMaggio, Einstein, and McCarthy would only have been starters.

But imagine, all the same, that long and steamy night and that hotel room, and you have the substance of *Insignificance*, which was first a play on the London stage and is now one of the last sorts of films I would have expected Nicolas Roeg to direct. Roeg is a master of baroque visuals and tangled plot lines. His *Don't Look Now* still has people trying to explain that Venetian dwarf in the red raincoat, and his credits include at least one good film, *Eureka*, that was not quite sure whether it was a dream.

Insignificance is a film in which almost all the audacity is contained by the premise—that these four most famous figures of the 1950s met during one long night. Grant Roeg that much, and he gives us a fairly realistic film most of the rest of the way. The characters are never actually given their real names in the film, but there seems to be little doubt who they're meant to be, especially when Einstein and Monroe work out the theory of relativity together, using a flashlight, a few simple props, and some almost perfect dialogue.

Monroe is played in the film by Theresa

Russell, who is *still* only about twenty-six years old, and who already has appeared in such landmarks as *Straight Time, The Last Tycoon,* and *Bad Timing.* She doesn't really look very much like Monroe, but what does it matter? The blond hair and the red lips are there, and so is the manner, which has been imitated so often, and so badly, that the imitators prove that Monroe was a special case. Russell doesn't imitate. She builds her performance from the ground up, and it works to hold the movie together.

Tony Curtis has a lot of fun as the hard-drinking, paranoic senator. He has turned, in his middle years, into a glorious ham, willing to take the chance of appearing ridiculous in order to reach for the farther edges of a performance. His theories about the Russians in this film are little masterpieces of dialogue. Gary Busey is the ballplayer, stolid and not quite comprehending his famous wife, and Michael Emil is a wonderful Einstein, sweet and childlike, and closest of all of them to Monroe's own personality.

I am not quite sure, however, what the point of the movie is. It's more of an acting and writing tour de force than a statement on sports, politics, sex symbol, or relativity. It begins by imagining its remarkable meetings, and ends by having created them. It's all process, no outcome. I think in this case that's OK.

Interiors ★ ★ ★ ★
PG, 93 m., 1978

Kristin Griffith (Flyn), Mary Beth Hurt (Joey), Richard Jordan (Frederick), Diane Keaton (Renata), E.G. Marshall (Arthur), Geraldine Page (Eve), Maureen Stapleton (Pearl), Sam Waterston (Mike). Directed by Woody Allen and produced by Charles H. Joffe. Screenplay by Allen.

Yes, the opening *does* remind us of Bergman: The static shots, held for a moment's contemplation, of the rooms and possessions of a family. But then people enter the rooms, and their lives and voices have a particularly American animation; Woody Allen is right to say that his drama, *Interiors,* belongs more in the tradition of Eugene O'Neill than of Ingmar Bergman. But what's this? Here we have a *Woody Allen* film, and we're talking about O'Neill and Bergman and traditions and influences? Yes, and correctly. Allen, whose comedies have been among the cheerful tonics of recent years, is astonishingly assured in his first drama.

He gives us a time of crisis in a family, and develops it in counterpoint with the countless smaller joys and crises that are a family. He is very spare: Every scene counts, and the dialogue has the precision of a J.D. Salinger short story. There's nothing thrown in for effect unless the effect contributes specifically to the direction of the complete film.

Allen's central character is the family's mother, Eve, played by Geraldine Page as a heartbreaking showdown between total self-confidence in the past and catastrophic breakdown in the present. She is a designer, and her rooms are some, but not all, of the interiors of the title. She aims for a cool perfectionism in her rooms, for grays and greens and pale blues, for a look of irreproachable sterility. Her science and art is to know the correct place for a lamp, within a fraction of an inch.

She is married to a wealthy lawyer (E.G. Marshall). She has three daughters: A poet (Diane Keaton), a movie star (Kristin Griffith), and a searcher for meaningful occupation (Mary Beth Hurt). Keaton lives with an alcoholic would-be novelist (Richard Jordan). Hurt lives with a filmmaker (Sam Waterston). Marshall announces that he wants a trial separation from Page, and later introduces a woman he's met on a cruise and wants to marry (Maureen Stapleton).

There you have them, the eight people of this movie. Allen, who thought nothing in *Annie Hall* of producing Marshall McLuhan from behind a theater lobby display for a comic walk-on, isolates his characters in *Interiors* so thoroughly, we're reminded of O'Neill's family in *Long Day's Journey into Night,* coming and going in an old house with no access to any world outside.

There are hurts in this family that have been buried for years, and guilts that still hold it together. One daughter finally blurts out an accusation against her mother, who had thought herself so perfect and yet was as capable as anyone of pettiness and cruelty. We get the feeling, indeed, that the family has been together much too long, and that family life is not necessarily a blessing.

If there is a common wish shared by all the characters in the film, it's to live a life of their own. The father, defending to his daughters his decision to marry a woman they call a "vulgarian," argues not unreasonably that he's paid the bills and maintained the household for years—that now, in his early sixties, he's *earned* his right to some years of his own choosing.

The others have earned their rights, too,

but each at the expense of the others. That is how each sees it, anyway. The same charge passes again and again around the family circle: That if the others had not been so demanding, or selfish, or jealous, or vindictive, then *this* person would have been set free to realize himself or herself.

Allen treats these themes in scenes that have an elegant economy of expression. The scene around the dinner table, for example, as the father announces his decision to leave, is handled in a way that etches the feelings of every member of the family, in just the right tones of anger, disbelief, or defiance. Scenes involving the daughters and their men suggest in different ways that the problems of this family will not end in this generation.

The funniest and saddest scene begins with the father's second marriage; Maureen Stapleton is wonderful as the "vulgarian," sweeping in with her red gown and finding Page's rooms "so gray. . . ." The dinner table conversation this time allows Allen to regard the Stapleton character with a mix-ture of tenderness and satire so delicately balanced, it's virtuoso.

The wonderment is that it's "serious." Yes, it is, but to be serious is not always to be good, and a movie both serious and bad is a great depression for everyone. *Interiors* becomes serious by intently observing complex adults as they fend and cope, blame and justify. Because it illuminates some of the ways we all act, it is serious but not depressing; when it's over, we may even find ourselves quietly cheered that Allen has seen so clearly how things can be.

Interview With the Vampire
★ ★ ★   NEW
R, 115 m., 1994

Tom Cruise (Lestat), Brad Pitt (Louis), Antonio Banderas (Armand), Stephen Rea (Santiago), Christian Slater (Malloy), Kirsten Dunst (Claudia). Directed by Neil Jordan and produced by Stephen Woolley and David Geffen. Screenplay by Anne Rice.

Although one of the characters in *Interview With the Vampire* begs to be transformed into a vampire, and eagerly awaits the doom of immortality, the movie never makes vampirism look like anything but an endless sadness. That is its greatest strength. Vampires throughout movie history have often chortled as if they'd gotten away with something. But the first great vampire movie, *Nosferatu* (1922), knew better, and so does this one.

The movie is true to the detailed vision that has informed all of Anne Rice's novels, and which owes much to the greater taste for realism that has crept into modern horror fiction. It is a film about what it *might really be like* to be a vampire. The title sets the tone, and in the opening scenes, set in San Francisco, the two hundred-year-old vampire Louis de Pointe du Lac (Brad Pitt) submits to an interview by a modern journalist (Christian Slater), just as any serial killer or terrorist bomber might sit down to talk to "60 Minutes."

His story begins in the late 1700s, in New Orleans, that peculiar city where even today all things seem possible, and where, after losing his wife and daughter, he threw himself into a life of grief and debauchery. His path crossed that of the vampire Lestat (Tom Cruise), who transformed him into a vampire, and ever since he has wandered the world's great cities, feeding on the blood of his victims.

The initial meeting between Louis and Lestat takes the form of a seduction; the vampire seems to be courting the younger man, and there is a strong element of homoeroticism in the way the neck is bared and the blood is engorged. Parallels between vampirism and sex, both gay and straight, are always there in all of Rice's novels; the good news is that you can indulge your lusts night after night, but the bad news is that if you stop, you die.

Tom Cruise, who initially seemed to many people an unlikely choice to play Lestat, is never less than convincing, and his slight British accent, combined with makeup that is dramatic without being obtrusive, disguises the clean-cut star—makes him seem unwholesome in an odd, insinuating way. Brad Pitt, whose role is probably larger, and who has been at home as the depraved hero of films like *Kalifornia,* here seems more like an innocent, a young man who makes unwise choices, and lives (and lives, and lives) to regret them.

One of the creepier aspects of the story is the creation of the child vampire, Claudia, played by Kirsten Dunst, who is about twelve years old. The character was six in the novel, but even twice as old she is disturbing, trapped in her child's body as she ages, decade after decade. Dunst, perhaps with the help of Stan Winston's subtle makeup, is somehow able to convey the notion of great age inside apparent youth.

The movie's unique glory is in its look, created by cinematographer Phillipe Rousselot and production designer Dante Ferretti.

Ferretti's credits include Scorsese's *The Age of Innocence* and Gilliam's *The Adventures of Baron Munchausen,* and here he combines the elegance of the former and the fantastic images of the latter into a vampire world of eerie beauty. The action, of course, largely takes place at night, in old southern plantations and French Quarter dives, along gloomy back streets and in decadent boudoirs, and it truly takes flight after the action moves on board a transatlantic sailing ship, and then into the catacombs of Paris. There are scenes set in a vast underground columbarium, where the vampires sleep on shelves reaching up into the gloom, that is one of the great sets of movie history.

In Paris, Louis meets the vampires Armand (Antonio Banderas) and Santiago (Stephen Rea), and begins to understand he is a member of an international clandestine society. Vampires, of course, need regular supplies of fresh blood, and the details involving its procurement are dismaying to the creatures, who, to live, must constantly feed off the lives of others. Their sadness is manifest in Rice's screenplay and the moody direction by Neil Jordan *(The Crying Game),* who take this subject, with its abundant possibilities for looking ridiculous, and play it as tragedy. Although much has been said about the film's level of violence (and although the R rating is quite correct), those who have seen other horror films will not be particularly shocked.

My complaint about the film is that not very much happens, in the plot sense. The movie is more about the history and reality of vampirism than about specific events, although some action does center around the fate(s) of Lestat. A stronger plot engine might have drawn us more quickly to the end, but on a scene-by-scene basis, *Interview With the Vampire* is a skillful exercise in macabre imagination.

In the Line of Fire ★ ★ ★ ½
R, 123 m., 1993

Clint Eastwood (Frank Horrigan), John Malkovich (Mitch Leary), Rene Russo (Lilly Raines), Dylan McDermott (Al D'Andrea), Gary Cole (Bill Watts), Fred Dalton Thompson (Harry Sargent), John Mahoney (Sam Campagna). Directed by Wolfgang Petersen and produced by Jeff Apple. Screenplay by Jeff Maguire.

Thrillers are as good as their villains, and *In the Line of Fire* has a great one—a clever,

slimy creep who insidiously burrows his way into the psyche of the hero, a veteran Secret Service agent named Horrigan (Clint Eastwood). The creep, who likes to play mind games with his opponents, makes a series of phone calls threatening to assassinate the president. He chooses Horrigan because he knows the agent still feels guilty about failing to save the life of John F. Kennedy thirty years ago.

The would-be killer has an all-American name, Mitch, and is played by John Malkovich as an intelligent, twisted man who uses disguises, fake I.D., and an ingratiating manner to get close to the president. He tells Horrigan more or less what he plans to do and when, but Horrigan's hands are tied. The president is running for reelection, and his chief of staff (Fred Dalton Thompson) doesn't want him to look like a coward. So after Horrigan sounds a couple of false alarms, he's taken off the White House detail, and has to break rules in order to stay on Mitch's trail.

In its broad outlines, *In the Line of Fire* has a story similar to many of Eastwood's Dirty Harry movies, in which a psycho killer plays games with the cop, who is ordered off the case and then continues as a free-lancer, helped by a loyal partner. The movie even supplies a typical Eastwood sidekick, a woman agent played by Rene Russo who is tough and capable, and able to fall in love.

Despite the familiar plot elements, however, *In the Line of Fire* is not a retread but a smart, tense, well-made thriller—Eastwood's best in the genre since *Tightrope* (1984). The director is Wolfgang Petersen *(Das Boot),* who is able to unwind the plot like clockwork while at the same time establishing the characters as surprisingly sympathetic.

Horrigan, the Secret Service man, still blames himself for the Kennedy assassination. He feels he somehow could have made a difference. Mitch has done his research, knows all about Horrigan, and insidiously slithers into his mind with words aimed like poison darts. Soon the assassination attempt becomes a two-handed game, in which Horrigan is as much of an outsider as Mitch, and must protect the president almost against his will—and the will of his politically ambitious staff.

Rene Russo, as Lilly, another agent, finds an interesting variation on the role of associate and lover. Her relationship with Horrigan begins on a rocky note, when he drops a couple of sexist statements, essentially accusing the service of tokenism for hiring women. Well, okay, he's an unreconstructed chauvinist pig, but eventually their respect for each other grows, and there is a wonderfully played moment when they concede they are attracted to one another.

Meanwhile, the plot advances relentlessly. After seeing *The Firm*, which was good but needlessly labyrinthine, it was a pleasure to follow the twists and turns of Jeff Maguire's screenplay for *In the Line of Fire*. It doesn't waste a line. Horrigan takes the clues that Mitch provides him, uses intuition and experience, breaks agency policy when necessary, and eventually finds himself testing the willingness that all Secret Servicemen are supposed to have—to take a bullet in place of the president.

Eastwood is perfect for the role, as a man of long experience and deep feelings. He is set off by an inspired performance by Malkovich, who is quiet and methodical and very clever, and devises a sneaky plan to work his way close to the president with an ingenious murder weapon. The movie's climax is exciting not only because of its action, but also because of its flawless logic.

What's surprising is how much time the movie finds for small touches of realistic detail and emotion. The conversations between Eastwood and Russo—about work, jazz, strategy, and romance—sound as if they're taking place between real people. The locations look convincing, especially Air Force One and some shots supposedly inside the White House. The special effects are good at inserting a young Eastwood into 1963 footage of Kennedy, establishing the character's deep need to stop the new assassination he feels is coming. And the direction of the final scenes is as spectacular as it is skillful.

Yes, it's unlikely that Mitch the killer would jump into that elevator (it's an example, in fact, of the Fallacy of the Climbing Killer, in which villains always make the mistake of heading for a high place). But it allows an earlier situation to come around again as a sensational payoff. Most thrillers these days are about stunts and action. *In the Line of Fire* has a mind.

In the Mouth of Madness ★ ★
R, 95 m., 1995

Sam Neill (John Trent), Julie Carmen (Linda Styles), Jurgen Prochnow (Sutter Cane), Charlton Heston (Jackson Harglow). Directed by John Carpenter and produced by Sandy King. Screenplay by Michael De Luca.

Stephen King has a lot of fun playing with the line between reality and fiction—his *Misery* was the story of a fan who takes a horror writer's work a little too seriously—and now here is a movie to turn the tables on King.

John Carpenter's *In the Mouth of Madness* begins with the disappearance of a horror writer named Sutter Cane, whose latest book has caused some of its readers to go mad. The book is a best-seller, and when stores sell out, they're besieged by angry mobs. (It is a sign of our times, I suppose, that citizens are fanned into a frenzy by the book even before they read it.)

Enter an insurance-fraud investigator named John Trent (Sam Neill), who is sitting in the window of a coffee shop one day when a man across the street picks up an ax, walks through traffic, and slams the ax through the shop window. (This shot, showing the man approaching in the background while a quiet conversation proceeds unaware in the foreground, is one of the movie's best.) Turns out the would-be ax murderer is Sutter Cane's former agent.

As an epidemic of apparent paranoid schizophrenia spreads, fueled by the latest Cane novel, we meet Cane's publisher (Charlton Heston) and his book editor, named Linda Styles (Julie Carmen). She hires Trent to investigate the apparent disappearance of Cane; she wants a fraud investigator because she suspects everything is not as it seems. No kidding.

Now the movie lifts off into fantasy, as Trent and Styles go in search of Cane. There are lots of cross-references to Stephen King, as when Trent cleverly pieces together a map of New Hampshire out of the covers of Cane's books, and when a town named Hobb's Corner figures heavily, just as Castle Rock is the locale of many of King's stories.

As Trent and Styles drive through the night, strange nightmarish apparitions appear by the roadside: innocent ones, like kids on bicycles, and more disturbing ones, like ghouls. They arrive at a town that is not on any map, check into an inn with weird creatures in the basement, and are constantly startled by threats that leap in from out of frame, the oldest trick in the horror movie book.

It's about here—still fairly early in the film—that *In the Mouth of Madness* begins to lose its way. The notion of a book that drives its readers mad is intriguing (especially in a movie where no one thinks to take it off sale), but after the heroes arrive in Hobb's Corner

what we essentially have is a horror house movie, in which the protagonists creep along while creatures leap at them.

The novelist Sutter Cane (Jurgen Prochnow) does eventually turn up, with lines like "More people believe in my work than believe in the Bible," but not much is done to develop him, and the movie does what no horror movie can afford to do, which is to play tennis without a net. Stories like this need rules; it's not enough to send the beleaguered hero on a roller-coaster ride through shocking images.

One wonders how *In the Mouth of Madness* might have turned out if the script had contained even a little more wit and ambition. The fact that the book was driving its readers mad might have provided an opening for some entertaining satire. The Charlton Heston character, a publisher who stands to make millions by selling the book, might have been expanded into more of a hypocrite. What about the government? Is a book that makes you paranoid protected by free speech?

The movie starts out with lots of intriguing ideas, and then sidesteps most of them in order to provide a special effects sideshow that looks inspired by the *Nightmare on Elm Street* series. Ironically, at about the same time we got the new *Elm Street* movie, *Wes Craven's New Nightmare*, about a movie director who finds that his horror films are seeping over into real life. It covers similar ground in a much more original way—*and* it has better special effects.

In the Name of the Father ★ ★ ★
R, 127 m., 1994

Daniel Day-Lewis (Gerry Conlon), Pete Postlethwaite (Guiseppe Conlon), Emma Thompson (Gareth Peirce), John Lynch (Paul Hill), Corin Redgrave (Police Official), Don Baker (IRA Man). Directed and produced by Jim Sheridan. Screenplay by Terry George and Sheridan.

The Guildford Four were framed; there seems to be no doubt about that. A feckless young Irishman named Gerry Conlon and three others were charged by the British police with being the IRA terrorists who bombed a pub in Guildford, England, in 1974, and a year later they were convicted and sentenced to life. But great doubts grew up about their guilt; it was proven that evidence in their favor had been withheld, and in 1989 their convictions were overturned.

In the Name of the Father tells this story in

angry, dramatic detail, showing that the British police were so obsessed with the need to produce the IRA bombers that they seized on flimsy hearsay evidence and then tortured their prisoners to extract confessions. The film is based on Conlon's autobiography, *Proved Innocent*, and in its general thrust is factual—although the director, Jim Sheridan, cheerfully explained to the *London Daily Telegraph* at the time of the film's release how he changed facts, characters, and dates to suit his fictional purposes.

As he tells it, the story becomes a tragedy of errors. The film's rambling opening scenes are important in setting up what follows: Conlon (Daniel Day-Lewis), a young man from Belfast, finds himself in England with some friends, halfheartedly looking for work, sleeping in a shared squatter's pad, drinking, and doing drugs. Conlon is not a model citizen. One night he robs a prostitute of her earnings, and returns to Ireland, flashing the money and buying drinks for family and friends. A former friend fingers him to the police, and he's snatched from his bed in a predawn raid—along with his astonished father, who had nothing to do with anything, and also eventually found himself serving a life sentence.

It is Conlon's bad luck that his visit to the Guildford area coincided with the bombing, and that his newfound wealth looked suspicious. The IRA is a tightly disciplined organization whose members are not accustomed to getting rich off their work, or throwing money around, but never mind: Conlon is a splendid suspect, and when a sadistic British policeman (Corin Redgrave) gets finished with him, he's a confessed murderer.

The movie does a harrowing job of showing how, and why, a man might be made to confess to a bombing he didn't commit. The early sequences of the movie are a Kafkaesque nightmare for Conlon, who finds himself snatched from his bed and locked up for the rest of his life. It's a nightmare for us, too, because Conlon behaves so stupidly, avoiding the obvious things he could say and do to defend himself.

The greater part of the movie takes place in prison, where Conlon and his father (Pete Postlethwaite) are housed in the same cell. His father, a hard-working, honest man, is filled with indignation. Conlon is more filled with self-pity and despair, but gradually, inspired by his father, he begins trying to prove his innocence, and is lucky to convince a stubborn lawyer (Emma Thompson) to take

his case. She works for years, and even so might not have made much progress if a police evidence technician hadn't mistakenly given her a report she was never meant to see.

Convinced by the film's documentary detail, we assume all these facts are based on truth, and it is a little surprising to discover that the sadistic British policeman is a composite of several officers, that Conlon and his father were never in the same cell—and that the crucial character of Joe McAndrew (Don Baker), an IRA man who confesses to the Guildford bombings, is a fictional invention. All the same, the main thrust of the story is truthful: British courts found that Conlon and the others were jailed unjustly.

The film's dramatic thrust doesn't simply go from wrong to right, however. It's more the story of how Gerry Conlon changes and grows during those years in prison. He is shown in the early scenes to be an aimless drifter—a dimmer and more genial version, in fact, of the unbalanced, angry homeless man in Mike Leigh's *Naked*, a British film made at about the same time. In prison, Conlon educates himself and the law educates him; by the time of his release, he is sober, intelligent, radicalized. Seeing this process happen is absorbing, especially since so much of it is inspired by the love of the father for his son.

And yet the film is somehow less than it should be. The urgency of the early scenes is lost when the story turns to prison life, and I began to feel that dialogue and events were repeating themselves. Points about the prison years and the fight for an appeal are made too painstakingly, and there is much dialogue when a little would have done. I had the feeling that if ten or twelve minutes had been edited from the film, from the scenes behind bars, that would have made a big difference.

Some of the weaknesses of script and structure are obscured by the power of Day-Lewis's performance; he proves here once again that he is one of the most talented and interesting actors of his generation. Sheridan was the director of *My Left Foot*, for which Day-Lewis won the Academy Award for Best Actor. Here is a story with similar appeal, and yet somehow the story doesn't coil and spring; it simply unfolds.

Into the West ★ ★ ★ ½
PG, 91 m., 1993

Gabriel Byrne (Papa Riley), Ellen Barkin (Kathleen), Ciaran Fitzgerald (Ossie), Ruaidhri [Rory] Conroy (Tito), David Kelly (Grandfather), Johnny Murphy (Tracker), Colm Meaney (Barreller), John Kavanagh (Hartnett). Directed by Mike Newell and produced by Jonathan Cavendish and Tim Palmer. Screenplay by Jim Sheridan.

If I were to tell you that *Into the West* was about two boys and their magical white horse, you would, of course, think it was a children's film. But it is more than that, although children will enjoy it. The movie is set in a world a little too gritty for innocent animal tales. It concerns two young gypsy boys growing up in the high-rise slums of Dublin with their father, who loves them but has grown distant and drunken since their mother died.

One day, their grandfather, who still travels the roads in the ancient way in his horse-drawn gypsy caravan, gives them the gift of a horse. The horse is named Tir na nOg, which means "Land of Eternal Youth," the grandfather explains, although he may be making it up as he goes along. Where are two city boys to keep a horse? In their apartment? Of course! But of course the neighbors complain, and the police are called, and one thing leads to another.

Then the horse is stolen by a rich man, who obtains spurious papers for it. The boys see it on television, go to where it is racing, and ride off with it. The rich man offers a ten-thousand-pound reward, and all of Ireland follows the story as the two boys and their horse outwit the combined efforts of the rich and powerful.

The subtext of the movie involves the gypsy culture in modern Ireland. Known also as tinkers and travelers, the gypsies are often discriminated against, and charged with any crimes that take place even vaguely near to them. For their grandfather (David Kelly), the traveling life is still rich and satisfying, but for their father (Gabriel Byrne), it has been replaced by a form of imprisonment in a high-rise ghetto. The father enlists two friends (Ellen Barkin and Colm Meaney), who remind him of the ancient strengths of the travelers, and what is regained is not only a horse, but a family and a tradition.

Into the West is one of many interesting

films to come from Ireland recently: remember, for example, *My Left Foot, Hear My Song, The Miracle, The Commitments,* and *The Crying Game.* It was written by Jim Sheridan, who wrote and directed *My Left Foot,* and is directed by Mike Newell, who made *Dance With a Stranger* and *Enchanted April.* Sheridan and Newell are not interested in simply shaping the material into an easy, commercial form. They're interested in the relationships beneath the surface, and in the way the father is redeemed through the adventure.

And yet there is a lot of adventure, as the magnificent horse seems almost able to read the boys' minds, and they think fast, too, the older one (Ciaran Fitzgerald) guiding his younger brother (Rory Conroy) as they avoid the main roads, ford streams to throw off the bloodhounds, and at one point even escape certain capture by taking a detour through the house of some strangers.

Texture is everything in a movie like this. The bare story itself could be simplistic and silly: cops chasing a couple of kids on a horse. But when relationships are involved, and social realities, and a certain level of magical realism, then the story grows and deepens until it really involves us. Kids will probably love this movie, but adults will get a lot more out of it.

I.Q. ★ ★ ★ ½
PG, 106 m., 1994

NEW

Meg Ryan (Catherine Boyd), Tim Robbins (Ed Walters), Walter Matthau (Albert Einstein), Lou Jacobi (Godel), Gene Saks (Podolsky), Joe Maher (Liebknecht), Stephen Fry (James), Charles Durning (Louis Bamberger). Directed by Fred Schepisi and produced by Carol Baum and Schepisi. Screenplay by Andy Breckman and Michael Leeson.

I.Q. begins, like almost all romantic comedies, with a Meet Cute: A garage mechanic named Ed is thunderstruck with love at his first sight of a young woman. Alas, she has been driven into his garage by her fiancé, a brilliant academic. Even more unfortunately, she thinks it is important to marry a genius, and although the mechanic may be smart, he doesn't have any intellectual credentials.

The woman, whose name is Catherine (Meg Ryan), has reason to want a genius for a husband: He will fit in better around the family dinner table, since she lives with her uncle, who is Albert Einstein (Walter Matthau). The mechanic is, so to speak, no Ein-

stein. Played by Tim Robbins, he knows all there is to know about cars, however, and a great deal about human nature—enough to sense he has a chance with her.

Human nature is allegedly the specialty of her fiancé, who is played by the tall and deflatable British actor and author Stephen Fry. His entrance is behind the wheel of a little MG sports car; he's too large for it, so his head comes up above the windshield, and he looks like one of those cartoon men who drive little roadsters. His idea of a honeymoon is a vacation in the Belgian Congo, among pygmies. Her idea is to make love under a waterfall in Hawaii that feels like a million kisses on her skin. You see what they're up against.

Matthau as Einstein is a stroke of casting genius. He looks uncannily like the great mathematician. Whether he acts like him or not I am not in a position to say, but he certainly doesn't act like himself: He has left all his Matthauisms behind, and created this performance from scratch, and it's one of the year's genuine comic gems.

Einstein has three old mathematician buddies who all dote on his niece. They're played by the veteran characters actors Lou Jacobi (who cried, "You cut the turkey without me!" in *Avalon*), Gene Saks, and Joe Maher. They form sort of a chorus, giving Einstein someone to talk with as he wrestles with the challenge of his niece's future happiness. He is much perturbed. Admittedly, the Stephen Fry character is a genius. But he is also so much less than that: a pompous twit, in fact. And the Tim Robbins character, grease-stained although he may be, is stalwart and true, ingenious and engaging.

The elderly brain trust conspires to make Robbins seem like a genius. They supply him with a fictitious identity and various brilliant-sounding discoveries, including, if I recall correctly, bright ideas for cold fusion. And then, at parties and in a lecture hall, they go through a hilarious repertory of secret signs, signals, and twitches, to prompt him with the correct answers.

Meg Ryan is one of the most radiant actresses now at work, and the charm she brings to *I.Q.* reminded me of her work in *When Harry Met Sally* and *Joe Vs. the Volcano.* She projects a certain stubbornness, an unwillingness to be pushed, that makes her right for this role: Sure, she likes this big lunk at the garage, but that doesn't mean she has to marry him.

One of the charms of *I.Q.* is that the young

lovers conduct their courtship almost on stage; it's like an Elizabethan comedy, in the way that all the subsidiary characters observe everything and feel free to provide a running commentary. The old guys get a terrific act going, and so do the other guys down at the garage, and what everybody sees is that these two people are perfect for one another. *I.Q.* is a romantic comedy with its heart in the right place, and all of the other pieces distributed correctly, too.

Ironweed ★ ★ ★
R, 143 m., 1988

Jack Nicholson (Francis Phelan), Meryl Streep (Helen), Carroll Baker (Annie Phelan), Michael O'Keefe (Billy), Diane Venora (Peg), Fred Gwynne (Oscar Reo), Margaret Whitton (Katrina). Directed by Hector Babenco and produced by Keith Barish and Marcia Nasatir. Screenplay by William Kennedy.

At first the shape simply seems to be some old debris blown up against the side of a building, but then the shape stirs and we see that it is a man. At first we cannot quite make out his face, and when we can, and we see that the character is played by Jack Nicholson, there is a shock, for even in that first moment he seems to have been enveloped by the character. A little later in *Ironweed,* when we see Meryl Streep, there is a similar shock, not so much because of her appearance as because of her voice, which is an amalgam of high-class breeding and low-class usage.

Nicholson and Streep play drunks in *Ironweed,* and actors are said to like to play drunks, because it gives them an excuse for overacting, but there is not much visible "acting" in this movie; the actors are too good for that. Nicholson plays a man haunted by guilt from his past. He dropped and killed his baby son years ago, and has never forgiven himself. He left home soon after, and dropped like a stone until he hit the gutters of Albany, his hometown, where he still lives. Streep's guilt is less dramatic; she let herself down, or that is what she believes, for she does not understand that it is not her own fault she is a drunk.

Ironweed, directed by the Brazilian Hector Babenco, whose familiarity with the human sewers of Sao Paulo and Rio de Janeiro made *Pixote* one of the best films of 1981, is a movie of moods, locales, and voices. It is not much on plot, and even when something dramatic happens—when the Nicholson character returns home after many years to face his family—the scene is played for the silences as much as for the noises. It is probably a fault of the film that it contains so little drama; we quickly sense that hopelessness is a condition of this movie, that since alcoholism has been accepted as a fact of life, none of the other facts will be able to change. The movie generates little suspense and no relief.

And yet it is worth seeing as a chamber piece, an exercise in which two great actors expand their range and work together in great sympathy. Both Nicholson and Streep have moments as good as anything they have done. Nicholson's come in a graveyard scene at the beginning of the film, and in the long stretch after he returns to his home. Streep's come in a barroom fantasy scene, in which she sings as she remembers singing long ago, and in a confessional scene in a church where she tells the Virgin she is not a drunk, no matter what people say.

Nicholson's homecoming is all the more effective because Carroll Baker is so good as his wife, who has never remarried, who in her way does not blame him for what he has made of their lives, because he had his reasons. Baker was not nearly this impressive in her "first" career, many years ago, in movies ranging from *Baby Doll* to *The Carpetbaggers*. It may seem surprising to say that Baker holds the screen against Jack Nicholson, and yet she does.

The movie was shot mostly on location in upstate New York, and is set in the last years of the Depression. Its visual look is heightened realism, but Babenco also uses imaginary scenes, as he did in *Kiss of the Spider Woman*. As the drunk, hallucinatory Nicholson sees the face of a trolley driver he accidentally killed years ago, we begin to understand some of the chaos within his soaked brain.

Ironweed was released while *Barfly*, another movie about a Skid Row couple, was still playing around the country. Do the movies bear comparison? *Barfly*, with Mickey Rourke and Faye Dunaway, has more energy, more life and humor, and is more directly about advanced alcoholism. *Ironweed* carries a weight of memory and guilt, with drunkenness as a backdrop. I enjoyed *Barfly* more as a movie, but both films are well-acted. The difference is that in *Barfly* the characters scream a lot, and in *Ironweed* they listen a lot, to things we cannot hear.

It Could Happen to You ★ ★ ★ ½ [NEW]
PG, 101 m., 1994

Nicolas Cage (Charlie Lang), Bridget Fonda (Yvonne Biasi), Rosie Perez (Muriel Lang), Wendell Pierce (Bo Williams), Isaac Hayes (Angel), Victor Rojas (Jesu), Seymour Cassel (Jack Gross). Directed by Andrew Bergman and produced by Mike Lobell. Screenplay by Jane Anderson.

It Could Happen to You tells the kind of story you vaguely remember reading about in the papers. Or maybe you didn't. But it's the kind of story you easily *could* have read about, and if you had read it, you'd probably think, Jeez, why didn't this happen to me? The movie's original title, which I like better than this one, was *Cop Gives Waitress $2 Million Tip*, and I think we can all imagine ourselves as the waitress in a situation like this, although the cop might be more of a stretch.

The movie is about a cop named Charlie (Nicolas Cage), who orders coffee for himself and his partner in a greasy spoon, and has enough for the coffee but not for a tip. So he tells the waitress, named Yvonne (Bridget Fonda), that he'll give her half of his winnings if the lottery ticket in his billfold is a winner. The next day, his number is drawn, and his share is $4 million, so of course Yvonne is due $2 million.

But it isn't that simple to Charlie's wife, Muriel (Rosie Perez). She's a screamer. She screams and goes manic when the winning number is read on the TV, and she screams twice as loud when Charlie finally tells her what he has done. "Do you love me?" she asks. "Then stiff her! Stiff her! And smell the flowers—for me!" She talks like that. And she hardly ever stops.

Charlie thinks he has a moral obligation to the waitress. His partner (Wendell Pierce) is not so sure. If he won, he says, he'd buy the Knicks, and put himself in at forward. Charlie wavers, and plays a little game with his conscience by offering Yvonne a choice: Twice the tip amount, or half the lottery, if he won. She takes the lottery. He tells her he won. The way she gradually assimilates this news is one of the best things in the movie.

It Could Happen to You was written by Jane Anderson, and directed by Andrew Bergman, who is one of the genuine comic talents in American movies; his credits include *The Freshman* and *Honeymoon in Vegas*, which also starred Cage, who at one point was involved with parachuting Elvis impersonators. This movie isn't funny in the same way as those

earlier titles—it's heavier on human nature and sentiment—but it has the same vast amusement with human nature.

And in Rosie Perez's work as Muriel it has another almost indescribable performance from this loud little dynamo. It has been observed that Rosie Perez always seems to give the same performance, and it's true that her characters in *Do the Right Thing, White Men Can't Jump*, and *Untamed Heart* all struck more or less the same note, although she was more subdued in *Fearless*.

I don't mind the same performance, though, because I'm still not tired of it. Strutting, waving her arms, posing for imaginary cameras, changing emotional gears with dizzying speed, she plays every possible variation on the themes of greed and jealousy. Her take on her husband's generosity, for example, is: "They should put you in a straitjacket and take you to the loony bin on Staten Island that Geraldo Rivera is always exposing." Eventually he placates her with the possibility that she will soon be famous for their generosity, and will be in demand for celebrity endorsements.

Cage and Fonda are of course more or less destined to fall in love with one another, but Bergman never goes for heavy-handed schmaltz, and the whole movie has the same lighthearted, big-city spirit as the *New York Post* headlines that follow the story. The movie is not so much about romance as about goodheartedness, which is a rarer quality, and not so selfish. And Cage has a certain gentleness that brings out nice soft smiles on Fonda's face.

The title has been lifted from the song "Young at Heart," which begins with the promise, "Fairy tales can come true." And the fairy tale element is underscored by a narration by a man with the significant name of Angel, who is played by Isaac Hayes and hangs around at the sides of a lot of scenes, telling us the story. One of the lessons we learn is that everyone gets more or less what they deserve in life, in the long run—even Muriel, who meets a sly old slickster named Jack Gross (Seymour Cassel). "Charlie!" she shrieks soon after their first deep conversation, "Jack is going to help us plot our Investment Strategy!!!" (When Perez does dialogue, you can hear the capitalized words and see the extra exclamation points.)

Coming home after seeing the movie, I plundered the press releases, hoping to find some mention that this story was, indeed, based on true events. Apparently not. Funny.

I could have sworn I read all about it, somewhere.

Note: Many readers inform me that it was based on a real case. I am much relieved.

I've Heard the Mermaids Singing
★ ★ ★ ½
NO MPAA RATING, 85 m., 1987

Sheila McCarthy (Polly Vandersma), Paule Baillargeon (Gabrielle St-Peres), Ann-Marie McDonald (Mary Joseph), John Evans (Warren), Brenda Kamino (Japanese waitress), Richard Monette (Critic). Directed by Patricia Rozema and produced by Rozema and Alexandra Raffe. Screenplay by Rozema.

"I have heard the mermaids singing, each to each. I do not think that they will sing to me."
—T.S. Eliot, "The Love Song of
J. Alfred Prufrock"

Don't we all know that feeling? That feeling that other people in other places are singing in the sunshine, but here in the shadows of our own miserable existence, the parade has passed us by. It is a key discovery of adult life that almost everyone else feels the same way, too, and that anyone who believes he's leading the parade is either stupid, mistaken, or a saint.

Polly (Sheila McCarthy), the heroine of *I've Heard the Mermaids Singing*, is a thirty-one-year-old Toronto woman who does not think the mermaids will sing to her. The most important thing in her life is photography, and sometimes she even dreams of the pictures she will take. But no one else has seen her work, and to all outward signs she is a winsome and lonely woman with few skills. Sometimes she gets office work through a temporary agency, but she isn't very good,

and so it is with a certain amazement that she finds an employer who actually likes her.

The employer's name is Gabrielle (Paule Baillargeon), and she is an elegant French-Canadian woman who runs an art gallery in Toronto. Polly calls her "the Curator," and idolizes her. The Curator is able to overlook Polly's little lapses, such as turning letters into a sticky sea of correction fluid. And one night at a Japanese restaurant, she actually offers Polly a full-time job. Polly recalls that wonderful night, and other nights, on a homemade videotape that serves as the narration for the movie.

I've Heard the Mermaids Singing then develops into a much more subtle character study than the opening scenes might have prepared us for. Gabrielle, the Curator, reveals that her greatest regret in life is her inability to become a great painter; she sells the work of others, but she cannot paint. Polly asks to see some of her attempts, and is overwhelmed by them. But of course Polly has no confidence in her own taste, and so she smuggles one of the Curator's paintings into a show, where it is laboriously praised in impenetrable ArtSpeak by a hilarious caricature of a critic.

If the critic has validated the Curator's work, Polly thinks, maybe there is hope for her own photographs. So she sends them to Gabrielle anonymously, only to have them shot down as hopelessly inept. Her spirit is crushed. But there are more discoveries for her to make. She finds, for example, that Gabrielle has a lover, a woman named Mary, and that Mary, not Gabrielle, actually created the painting that the critic liked. It may be that the Curator lacks not only talent, but taste.

It is only gradually, while we're watching

this movie, that we realize it is as much about Gabrielle as Polly, and that we are permitted to make discoveries about Gabrielle that Polly herself only dimly suspects. The movie was written and directed by Patricia Rozema, who uses a seemingly simple style to make some quiet but deep observations. What happens to Polly in the movie is easy to anticipate: She learns to trust in mermaids. What happens to Gabrielle is that she is closely observed and skillfully dissected.

When the movie is over, we leave thinking of Polly, and I have even read reviews in which the movie is treated entirely as Polly's story. That is partly because of Sheila McCarthy's extraordinary performance in the role; she has one of those faces that speaks volumes, and she is able to be sad without being depressing, funny without being a clown. She strikes just the right off-center note for the narration of the film; she must not seem too sure of herself, because the movie must not seem too sure of what it wants to say. It works by indirection, and Polly is actually only the instrument for the real story here, of a lonely and proud woman whose surfaces are flawless but whose sadness is deep.

If you see this movie and then have occasion to read "The Love Song of J. Alfred Prufrock," which contains lines that strike some readers with the force of a blow, reflect that the narrator of the poem is more like Gabrielle than Polly. More like the Curator, who has measured out her life in coffee spoons, who has seen the moment of her greatness flicker, who lacks the strength to force the moment to its crisis, who grows old. Polly is, I suspect, intended to be out there with the mermaids, neither stupid nor mistaken, but a saint.

J

Jacknife ★ ★ ★
R, 120 m., 1989

Robert De Niro (Megs), Kathy Baker (Martha), Ed Harris (Dave), Tom Isbell (Bobby). Directed by David Jones and produced by Robert Schaffel and Carol Baum. Screenplay by Stephen Metcalfe, based on his play *Strange Snow*.

There is a sense in which *Jacknife* is a continuation of *The Deer Hunter*, the 1978 movie in which a group of friends from a working-class town in Pennsylvania went off to fight the war in Vietnam. *Jacknife* begins some fifteen years after the war is over, and it takes place in a small town in Connecticut, but many of its shots and moods feel the same as in the earlier film, and the theme is the same, too: The idea that if your buddy gets left behind, you have to go back and get him.

The buddy who gets left behind this time is named Dave (Ed Harris). He doesn't get left behind in Vietnam, though. He gets left behind in the America that he has returned to. While other veterans return to jobs or families or education, Dave returns to a life that is empty except for the booze and the cigarettes that keep him company in lonely bars.

Dave lives with his sister, Martha (Kathy Baker). She is a schoolteacher in her thirties, and her life is on hold. Months pass into years in the house they inherited from their parents, where Martha's role is to put Dave's dinner on the table, do his laundry, change his sheets, give him money from time to time, and accept him exactly as he is. Her problem is, until Dave's life changes, hers cannot change, either. She is a classic case of an enabler; she's a one-woman support system allowing Dave to continue to drink and throw his life away.

The buddy who comes back to rescue Dave is named Megs (Robert De Niro). He doesn't have to come far—only across town. He turns up early one morning to remind Dave they have a date to go fishing together. It's a long-standing date, with a lot of significance to it, but we don't learn of the significance until later. Dave is in bed with a hangover, but Martha lets Megs in. He has never really noticed her before; maybe he's never even seen her. Now he likes what he sees.

Megs is their deliverance. If he is successful, he will be able to get Dave moving again, help him break out of the vicious cycle of booze-hangover-booze. And if Dave becomes self-supporting, Martha will be free. Free for Megs, maybe. What Megs represents is change, in a situation that has grown old with habit and stagnation.

There are not too many surprises in *Jacknife*, and not even the revelations in the flashbacks, the scenes showing what happened in the war, are really surprises. But this is not a movie of plot; it's a movie of character. It's about how these three people create a triangle of pain and possible healing. It's not a buddy movie, where the woman looks on while the two guys work things out. It's very much a triangle, in which a drunk has to learn to let go of his sister, a spinster has to learn to let go of her routine, and a loner has to learn to let go of his detachment from life.

All three performances are right for the characters. De Niro makes a good choice for Megs because of the reserve he brings to the role. This is a man not doing something he wants to do, but something he has to do. Harris, staring at his cigarette, sitting hour after hour at the end of the bar, is able to project an unhappiness and frustration so deep that when he explodes, as he sometimes does, we are almost relieved. And Baker's schoolteacher is not a drab wallflower who suddenly turns into a sexpot; she's a calm, competent woman who has gotten trapped in something that her guilt will not let her escape from.

Jacknife has some effective scenes that take place in a veterans' encounter group, where the lesson is that life goes on, and that today cannot be lived out in painful memories of the past. That's the same message Megs has for Dave. To a degree, this lesson is both familiar and predictable. *Jacknife* redeems it in the specifics of the performances. De Niro, Harris, and Baker seem to be oblivious to the "message" and lose themselves in the personalities of their characters. And so the movie works.

Jack's Back ★ ★ ★
R, 95 m., 1988

James Spader (John/Rick), Cynthia Gibb (Christine), Rod Loomis (Dr. Tannerson), Rex Ryon (Jack Pendler), Robert Picardo (Dr. Battera). Directed by Rowdy Herrington and produced by Tim Moore and Cassian Elwes. Screenplay by Herrington.

Exactly a century has passed since Jack the Ripper committed his monstrous crimes, and now a copycat killer is duplicating them—each murder one hundred years to the day after the Ripper's crime. This sounds depressingly like the premise for an exploitation film, and the title *Jack's Back* does nothing to encourage our hopes, but the surprising thing is that this is actually a good movie, with intriguing work by James Spader.

He plays two characters, twin brothers, one an earnest medical student, the other a rebel who has had some trouble with the law. Without revealing any more of the film's surprises, I can tell you that the good brother discovers one of the victims, and that the other brother eventually finds himself considered the police department's prime suspect for the murders. The movie develops into a thriller in which the second twin has to run from the police, clear his name, and somehow prevent the real killer from murdering the woman who has loved both twins.

All of this sounds contrived. Of course it is contrived. A movie like this is nothing without contrivance, and one of its pleasures is to watch the plot gimmicks as they twist inward upon themselves, revealing one level of surprise after another. By the end of the film we are more or less sure we understand everything that has happened, but even then there is one more surprise—and not the one you're no doubt expecting.

But apart from the pleasures of the plot, what makes *Jack's Back* worth seeing is the work of James Spader, a young actor who I believe has as much promise as anyone of his generation. He was the slick, detached drug dealer in *Less Than Zero*, projecting an easy charm that masked a cold contempt for his clients. And he has played villains in three other recent films: He was the guy who gave Charlie Sheen the insider tips in *Wall Street* and the nasty store employee in *Mannequin* and the ambitious yuppie who wanted Diane Keaton's job in *Baby Boom*. I don't have any statistics to prove this, but my notion is that actors who play villains early in their careers often turn out to have more interesting careers than those who always play the lead. They find more interesting places inside themselves, and they carry a hint of complexity and secretiveness even into heroic roles; look at Jack Nicholson, for example. *Jack's Back* is Spader's first chance to play a good guy, and he plays two of them—the good twin, and the bad twin who reveals positive qualities. It's the kind of dual role an actor loves because it allows him to do the same thing in two different ways.

Look carefully at a couple of the early scenes. There's a small moment in an emergency clinic when Spader comforts a wounded elderly woman, making the scene original and not a recycled docudrama—and then ending with a friendly, kidding one-liner that puts everything into context. And then notice later in the movie, when, as the other twin, Spader does a kind of leisurely dance around Cynthia Gibb, who is engaging and believable as the heroine. Does he like her? Does he frighten her? An actor who can make us ask those questions is doing his job.

Jack's Back was written and directed by Rowdy Herrington, who pays adequate homage to the requirements of the thriller, espe-

cially in a couple of truly shocking moments. But he's up to something more than a routine shock movie here. He's taken the trouble to make three-dimensional characters, and paused here and there to provide scenes that make the characters seem real and complicated, instead of just pawns in a movie formula.

Jack the Bear ★ ★ ★
PG-13, 98 m., 1993

Danny DeVito (John Leary), Robert J. Steinmiller, Jr. (Jack Leary), Miko Hughes (Dylan Leary), Gary Sinise (Norman Strick), Art LaFleur (Mr. Festinger), Stefan Gierasch (Grandpa Glickes), Erica Yohn (Grandma Glickes). Directed by Marshall Herskovitz and produced by Bruce Gilbert. Screenplay by Steven Zaillian.

There is an age in the lives of all children when they wish their parents were invisible. Everything about them is acutely embarrassing. How many parents have had to park the car around the corner while picking the kids up after school, because to be picked up by one's parents is, of course, the ultimate admission of wimphood?

If there is anything worse than parents who are hopelessly outdated, it is parents who are somehow cool. Imagine, for example, the humiliation of having a father who is the host of the midnight monster bash on the local TV channel, and appears in ghoul makeup with blood dripping from his fangs, or an ax embedded in his skull. That is the weekly ordeal of Jack Leary (Robert J. Steinmiller, Jr.) in *Jack the Bear*, an odd new movie in which his father is not even the strangest man on their block.

The father is John Leary (Danny DeVito), a man whose cheerful overacting on the tube every Saturday night is counterbalanced by long hours spent sitting at the kitchen table with a quart of booze. John is depressed for many reasons. His wife has been killed in an accident, leaving him with Jack and a younger son, Dylan, to raise on his own. He has been fired by one television station after another, ending up near the bottom of the ladder. And his in-laws make unannounced visits during which they are appalled by the way he runs his home.

Oh, and there is a neo-Nazi living across the street. Norman Strick (Gary Sinise) is a peculiar man who seems to live with his parents, although no one ever sees them, and spends his energy keeping kids off his lawn

and looking sinister. When he circulates a petition for the local white-supremacist candidate, the DeVito character drunkenly attacks him on television, after which Norman retaliates by abducting one of the children.

By this point in the movie, all hope of a consistent tone has already been long abandoned. *Jack the Bear* lives in a world that makes the midnight monster madness look sane by comparison. Some scenes in the movie are closely observed slices of real life, while others are lurid and melodramatic, and at least some seem pure fantasy. You have to stay on your toes.

And yet I liked it—barely. The subplot involving the neo-Nazi is a mistake—a dead end that has nothing to do with the movie's real subject, the difficulty of being a member of an unconventional household. Norman the Nazi may have come from the novel by Dan McCall, which is the basis for Steven Zaillian's screenplay, but that is not reason enough to leave him in the movie, especially since the outcome of his part of the story is an anticlimactic nonevent.

What works is, first of all, the DeVito performance as a driven man in a ridiculous job who loves his children but has lost his bearings. There is a lot of the child in his character. Halloween is his favorite holiday because he gets to dress up in costumes. The neighbor kids love to come over to hear his ghost stories. His drinking is mainly fueled by worry; he would like to be a better dad, but feels he has let his children down.

Steinmiller is also good as young Jack, especially in a bittersweet sequence where he develops a crush on a girl at school (Reese Witherspoon, from the wonderful *Man in the Moon*). She's a head taller than Jack, but accepts his invitation to come over for dinner one Friday night, an event that galvanizes the entire household and puts the DeVito character into high gear. The way this dinner date and its sequel are handled is the best thing in the movie, remembering so well what it is like to be at the edge of adolescence and at the mercy of raging emotions. There are also scenes of great poignancy in which the father and his older son talk frankly about the mysteries of life.

Jack the Bear is not an ordinary movie, and I never had the feeling I knew what would happen next. The characters are clearly seen, and despite the bizarre elements, there is always a feeling that DeVito and the two young boys make up a real family. If the focus had stayed there, the movie would have been better, I think. The addition of Norman and all of his demented activities is a dead end—a distraction that keeps this from being a much better film.

Jacob's Ladder ★ ★ ★ ½
R, 115 m., 1990

Tim Robbins (Jacob), Elizabeth Pena (Jezzie), Danny Aiello (Louis), Matt Craven (Michael), Pruitt Taylor Vince (Paul), Jason Alexander (Geary). Direced by Adrian Lyne and produced by Alan Marshall. Screenplay by Bruce Joel Rubin.

This movie left me reeling with turmoil and confusion, with feelings of sadness and despair. Those are the notes it strives for. *Jacob's Ladder* enters into the hallucinations of a desperate mind, and lives there. It evokes a paranoid-schizophrenic state as effectively as any film I have ever seen. Despite an ending that is intended as victorious, the movie is a thoroughly painful and depressing experience—but, it must be said, one that has been powerfully written, directed, and acted.

The story stars Tim Robbins, previously the pleasant young hero of such films as *Bull Durham,* as an American soldier in Vietnam who undergoes a shocking battle experience. The actual nature of the experience is withheld until the end of the film—and even then, we cannot be completely sure we know the truth—but it appears to send him back into civilian life as a psychological time bomb.

Years pass. He gains a doctoral degree, but does not use it. Instead, after a first marriage fails and a young son is killed in an accident, he goes to work for the post office, and starts to live with a woman he meets there. Then terrible things begin to happen to him. He is nearly run down by a subway train. Almost run over in the streets. Faceless demons pursue him. His doctor is killed in an automobile explosion. So is a friend.

He begins to suspect that he and his Vietnam friends were victims of some kind of misbegotten Army experiment. That day of their bloody battlefield experience, they all grew dizzy and their heads began to spin, and then he cannot remember what happened next. He was wounded, yes, and airlifted to a hospital—and what then? Flashbacks throughout the film follow his emergency treatment. But what is the secret of what happened? He gathers a group of fellow veterans, and they talk to a lawyer about representing them, but then the veterans and the lawyer back out.

I am ordinarily more than a little impatient with movies that deal with hallucinations, with dream states and delusions, because I feel artificially manipulated; the filmmakers are jerking my chain, and often it's a lazy substitute for the bother of constructing an intelligent screenplay. *Jacob's Ladder* is so well made, however, that I didn't feel impatient this time, because I didn't have the opportunity. The movie lives right on the raw edge of insanity and carries us along with it.

Coming out of the film, riding down in the elevator with some fellow critics, I got involved in a conversation about the underlying reality of the film. Was it all a flashback—or a flash-forward? What was real, and what was only in the hero's mind? Are even the apparently "real" sequences the product of his imagination? More than this I should not say, because the film should have the opportunity to toy with you as it toyed with us.

Making a chart of the real and the imagined is not the point of *Jacob's Ladder,* anyway. This movie is the portrait of a mental state, as Orson Welles's *The Trial* and Ken Russell's *Altered States* were. The screenplay is by Bruce Joel Rubin, who also wrote the completely different *Ghost,* and I've read an essay by him in which he talks about his original ideas for the film, and the way they were translated into visuals by the director, Adrian Lyne.

Judging by the essay, Lyne has done a good job of determining what could be translated, and what could be safely left behind. Rubin's original material, with its visions of demons and heaven and hell, has been replaced by the more frightening notion that paradise and the inferno are all about us here on earth, and that we participate in one or the other almost by choice.

The key performances in the film are by Robbins and Elizabeth Pena, who plays the woman he lives with. It's difficult to evaluate their work because the movie sets them the task of behaving in an utterly realistic, slice-of-life manner in many scenes (even some which are later revealed as hallucinations), and then coasting away into fearsome fantasy in other scenes. Pena achieves the difficult task here of creating a believable and even sympathetic woman, while, at the same time, suggesting dimensions which the hero can only guess at.

Most films tell stories. *Jacob's Ladder* undoubtedly contains a story, which can be ex-

tracted with a certain amount of thought. (Since the ending can be read in two different ways, however, the extraction process could result in two different stories.) That isn't the point. What *Jacob's Ladder* really wants to do is to evoke the feeling of a psychological state in the audience. We are intended to feel what the hero feels.

A lesser film would have ended with some dumb denouement in a courtroom, or some shoot-out with government security guys. This is a film about no less than life and death, and Jacob seems to stand at the midpoint of a ladder that reaches in two directions. Up to heaven, like the ladder that God put down for the biblical Jacob in Genesis. Or down to hell, in drug-induced hallucinations. This movie was not a pleasant experience, but it was exhilarating in the sense that I was able to observe filmmakers working at the edge of their abilities and inspirations. Not every movie has to be fun.

Jacquot ★ ★ ★ ½
NO MPAA RATING, 118 m., 1993

Philippe Maron (Jacquot 1), Edouard Joubeaud (Jacquot 2), Laurent Monnier (Jacquot 3), Brigitte de Villepoix (Mother), Daniel Dublet (Father), and with Jacques Demy. Directed by Agnes Varda and produced by Perrine Bauduin and Danielle Vaugon. Screenplay by Varda, based on the memories of Jacques Demy.

Agnes Varda and Jacques Demy, who together and separately had been making films for thirty years, began a new one in April 1990. It was about Demy's childhood memories. If you have seen his *The Umbrellas of Cherbourg,* a musical set in a garage and featuring singing mechanics, you may have guessed that Demy grew up as the son of an auto mechanic. *Umbrellas* won all the awards—the prize at Cannes, the foreign language Oscar—and Demy made such others as *Lola* and *Donkey Skin,* often centering around the songs he remembered from his youth.

Meanwhile Varda made films, too, often films based on her own life, such as *Daguerreotypes,* about the people who lived on her street in Paris, the rue Daguerre. She starred their son Matthew in *Kung Fu Master* (1989), about a young boy's coming of age. This new film would be her film about Demy's memories. As they began it, they both knew that he was dying of a brain tumor.

"The film was shot exactly where Jacques

Demy spent his childhood," Varda says, "in the garage of his father and in other places where, later, he was to film sequences." He wrote the storyline by telling his childhood memories to Agnes. But he refused to write the screenplay or dialogue because he wanted it to be her film. His health was failing through 1990 but he was able to visit the location, to appear in a few scenes, to see most of the rushes before he died in October 1990.

And now here is *Jacquot*, a love film, a film a woman has made about the memories of the man she lived with for thirty-three years, as she imagines them. The film uses three young actors to re-create the life of Jacques Demy from 1939, when he was eight, through the wartime years and his adolescence, to the years when he learns that he loves film and must be a director. It begins with a Punch and Judy show, which Demy saw and immediately imitated, making his own theater and figures out of cardboard. It continues as he goes to the movies, and is struck by their magic when he sees Walt Disney's *Snow White and the Seven Dwarfs*.

From the beginning he knew he had to make his own films. He is given a cheap little toy projector and a worn-out old 8mm Chaplin film, which he views again and again, until he muses, "I wish I could erase the film and make my own." And he does so, soaking the film in hot water and scraping off the images with a knife, so that he can draw his own crude animated images directly on the film. This is the single-mindedness of all great directors, the willingness to erase even Chaplin to make room for their own visions.

In a junk shop he finds a hand-wound camera, and uses it to film his own stop-action animated stories, taking hours to move his cardboard puppets ever so slightly between every frame of film. He mails the exposed film off to the Pathe labs and waits breathlessly . . . and waits . . . and waits six full months until the developed film is returned, and he is crushed to discover that every frame is blank. "I have to learn about the f-stop," he says.

At last he gets a better camera. He films the screenplay in the instruction book that comes with the camera, casting his playmates, costuming them, ordering them around with the confidence of a born director. He goes all the time to the cinema. He tells his friends which directors are good and which cannot be depended on.

His father wants him to go to a trade school. He wants to go to the high school

and become a film director. His father insists that he learn a trade. He spends hated months learning about a machine shop, while every free moment is spent in an attic room with his camera and his experiments. In a moment of betrayal that Jacques Demy still remembered months before he died, his art teacher comes to visit his parents and agrees that the boy has talent, but advises against a career in film because "many are called but few are chosen."

But Jacques Demy was chosen. The film begins and ends with Demy on the beach, looking out at the sea, and then with closeups of the grains of sand that run out through his fingers. It is not a sad film, however. It is a film about a boy lucky enough to discover how he wanted to spend his life, and able to spend it that way.

Jagged Edge ★ ★ ★ ½
R, 108 m., 1985

Glenn Close (Teddy Barnes), Jeff Bridges (Jack Forester), Peter Coyote (Thomas Krasny), Robert Loggia (Sam Ransom). Directed by Richard Marquand and produced by Martin Ransohoff. Screenplay by Joe Eszterhas.

Directors like to talk about playing the audience like a piano, about making movies that are efficient machines for assaulting our emotions. *Jagged Edge* is a movie like that, a murder thriller which dangles one clue after another before our eyes, daring us to decide who committed the murder. The machinery in this movie is so efficient that we don't know the answer until the very last shot—and I'll be getting back to that last shot in a moment.

The film stars Jeff Bridges as a powerful San Francisco publisher whose wife is brutally murdered in their isolated oceanside home. After an investigation reveals that he stood to inherit his wife's entire fortune, he is arrested and charged with the murder. Glenn Close plays his defense attorney. At first, she insists she has retired from courtroom cases, but then Bridges convinces her that he is innocent. And before long, she is also convinced that they are in love.

The Close character stands at the center of the film. Is she defending the man she loves against the unjust charges against him? Or is she defending a cold-blooded killer, who might murder her just as he murdered his wife? There are moments in *Jagged Edge* when each of these possibilities seems convincing,

but most of the time we just don't know. There's a lot of evidence on both sides.

Close's courtroom opponent is the assistant D.A. (Peter Coyote). They worked together a few years ago on a case where, she believes, he concealed evidence in order to win a conviction. Is he concealing evidence this time? There comes a time when we think he may be. And by then the film's tension is so tightly wound that we, and Close, don't know what to believe.

Jagged Edge is supremely effective at what it sets out to do—toy with the audience. It's another effective thriller from Richard Marquand, who made *Eye of the Needle*. The performances are good and the plot is watertight, as a whodunit must be. I have only one quarrel with the film, but it's a fairly substantial one. The movie *only* wants to keep us guessing. The characters are developed only in ways intended to string us along. Any behavior is possible if it will further the plot. There's no sense of reality beneath the gleaming surface.

Even that would be all right, if the movie didn't reveal the identity of the real killer in the final shot. Here's my theory: In a movie which exists only to tantalize us with clues and deceptive evidence, we *shouldn't* find out who the killer was—because that should be what we're arguing about as we leave the theater. Once the killer is unmasked, his crime reflects on everything else we know about his character, and that's more realism than you really need in a well-oiled machine.

Note: As this movie went into wide release, a strange thing happened. People started to get confused about the identity of the real killer. Even though there is a close-up of his face, the shot is taken from such an oblique angle that some viewers were confused, and I got letters and phone calls suggesting at least three possible villains. I imagine a VCR freeze-frame will solve the mystery.

Jamon Jamon ★ ★ ★ ½
NO MPAA RATING, 90 m., 1994

Penelope Cruz (Silvia), Anna Galiena (Carmen), Javier Bardem (Raul), Stefania Sandrelli (Conchita), Juan Diego (Manuel), Jordi Molla (Jose Luis). Directed by Bigas Luna and produced by Andres Vicente Gomez. Screenplay by Cuca Canals and Luna.

Jamon Jamon is the funniest sexy movie, or the sexiest comedy, since *Like Water for Chocolate*. The movie is an outrageous throwback to the days when directors took crazy chances, counting on their audience to keep up with them. It comes from Spain, land of Luis Buñuel and Pedro Almodovar, and is in their wicked anarchic spirit; it sees sex as a shortcut to the ridiculous in human nature.

The movie, which won the Silver Lion at the 1993 Venice Film Festival, takes place in a steamy little provincial town, where the richest family owns the underwear factory. The most famous local landmark is a billboard of a bull with a pair of cajones you can see for miles. Jose Luis, the son of the underwear people, falls in love with Silvia, the pneumatic and sensuous daughter of Carmen, who runs the local bordello.

Jose's rich mother, Conchita, horrified that her son might marry the daughter of a prostitute, decides to take matters into her own hands. She hires Raul, who works in the local ham factory, to seduce Silvia away from Jose Luis. Raul is chosen because he is also the model for the family's underwear ads, and looks promising in briefs.

The plot thickens. Conchita, the rich woman, grows so distracted by Raul that she begins an affair with him, if affair is the word for events so carnal they suggest years of marital deprivation. Meanwhile, it turns out that the young suitor, Jose Luis, is better known to Silvia's mother than he should be. "If you marry my daughter," Carmen tells him, "I don't want to see you around here anymore!" Jose Luis begs for one last visit upstairs with Carmen. The logic here is unassailable: Since Silvia is ostensibly a virgin, it is only proper that Jose Luis meet his needs in a discreet manner. If that means continuing as the client of his future mother-in-law, well, business is business.

There is more. There is much more. I do not know how to even begin describing the scene with the garlic and the pig. Or how to explain why and how Raul and his friend decide to go bullfighting in the nude at midnight. Nor can I adequately describe what happens to the "cajones" on the billboard, except to suggest that John Wayne Bobbitt would probably not enjoy this film.

Jamon Jamon, a title that translates as "Ham Ham," is a movie that combines lurid melodrama with vast improbabilities, sexy soap opera with heartfelt romance, and cheerful satire with heedless raunch. As is only proper, it stars actors of considerable physical appeal, most particularly Penelope Cruz as Silvia, Anna Galiena as Carmen, and Stefania Sandrelli (from Bertolucci's *The Conformist*) as Conchita. Javier Bardem, as Raul,

is well cast as the town stud. And Jordi Molla, as Jose Luis, is appropriately hapless.

Jamon Jamon is a kind of movie I have a great fondness for. It is frankly outrageous, it has the courage to offend, it is not afraid of sex, and it goes over the top in almost every scene. It takes a certain kind of moviegoer, I suppose, to enjoy a film like this; of course it's in bad taste, of course it's vulgar, of course it flies in the face of all that is seemly, and of course that is the idea.

Jason's Lyric ★ ★ ★
R, 119 m., 1994

NEW

Allen Payne (Jason Alexander), Jada Pinkett (Lyric Greer), Forest Whitaker (Maddog), Bokeem Woodbine (Joshua Alexander), Suzzanne Douglas (Gloria Alexander), Treach (Alonzo), Lisa Carson (Marti), Eddie Griffin (Rat), Lahmard Tate (Ron). Directed by Doug McHenry and produced by McHenry and George Jackson. Screenplay by Bobby Smith, Jr.

Long ago, on a traumatic night in childhood, something happened to forever scar the lives of two brothers named Jason and Joshua. And *Jason's Lyric* tells the story of how those two brothers grew up—one a criminal, the other dutiful and strong—against the backdrop of a love story so sweetly romantic it almost steals the show.

The story takes place in Houston, where Jason and Joshua were raised by their mother (Suzzanne Douglas) after the death of their father (Forest Whitaker), a Vietnam veteran whose loss of a leg and subsequent alcoholism earned him the nickname "Maddog." The father was not a bad man to begin with (there is a winsome scene where his widow recalls one of their first dates), but the war destroyed him, even before he died in the event which haunts Jason's nightmares. Now years have passed and Jason (Allen Payne) has a good job at a TV store, while Joshua (Bokeem Woodbine) has just been released from his latest prison term.

The two brothers love one another, but have come to live in different worlds. Joshua is quickly drawn into the orbit of Alonzo (Treach), the local gangster, while Jason falls instantly in love with Lyric (Jada Pinkett), who walks into the store one day. She's hard to get. "If we're meant to meet again, we will," she says, and when he finds her behind the counter of a soul food restaurant, he follows her home, giving her a bouquet of roses,

from which she deigns to select one, with a smile.

Lyric is Alonzo's sister. She is also best friends with his girl, Marti (Lisa Carson), the brash, buxom owner of the restaurant, who has sized up her world and decided Alonzo is the best she can do. But when she sees the light in her girlfriend's eyes, she knows Lyric's found the real thing.

And she has. The love story in *Jason's Lyric* is a reminder of how rarely, these days, genuine warm romantic passion is seen on the screen. (I place the emphasis on "warm" and "romantic" to distinguish their relationship from the calisthenics, jousts, and suppressed hostility in so many recent movies, where people make love as if they were being punished for their sins.) "Meet me when the sun leaves footprints across the sky," Lyric says, and she and Jason sit on an abandoned bridge, watching the sun set, and dreaming of getting on a bus and going—well, anywhere.

Anywhere to get out of the inexorably building tragedy in their lives, where Alonzo enlists Joshua in his gang, for a bank robbery that these particular gang members are way too unstable to pull off. The movie develops two plot threads—the robbery and the romance—and plays them against flashbacks to the tragedy of years ago. And we realize how rarely in the movies we *really* care about what's going to happen, and yet are in genuine suspense about what it will be.

The movie was directed by Doug McHenry and produced by McHenry and George Jackson; their credits include *New Jack City*. Here they use Bobby Smith, Jr.'s, screenplay, with its richly drawn supporting characters, to paint a canvas that glows with life. The word "lyric" in the title is well used, because McHenry is not shy about lyrical touches, including a touching picnic in a grand old bus terminal, and a quotation from John Donne ("Come live with me and be my love") that is so right, we wonder why lovers never quote poetry to one another anymore.

The performances are strong, and particularly so because Jason, the "good brother," is not portrayed as the sort of wimp that this genre usually calls for. Just because he is responsible and hardworking and wears a "dumb uniform" on the job doesn't make him soft; we gradually realize that he's harder than his ex-con brother. Allen Payne is both tough and sweet in the role, and has powerful chemistry with the enigmatic, teasing, tender character played by Jada Pinkett; they really seem to like one another, which is not a feeling you always pick up in screen romances.

Bokeem Woodbine, as the troubled brother, has a more thankless role—it's not easy to be the source of all a plot's problems—but the way he gets us involved with the character is to show that his Joshua does love Jason, and their mother, and doesn't want to hurt them—although in his drinking and violence he is obviously the heir of Maddog.

The movie takes time for small excursions into the lives of the surrounding characters. There is a sort of Greek chorus, an old man whose jazzy recitations comment on the action. And I enjoyed the friendship between Lyric and Marti, Alonzo's girlfriend, who is confiding and verbal and explains her theories about women's breasts, men's needs, man's fate, and sizing up the situation.

The very last shots in the movie are, I think, a little uncertain—as if there was some doubt which way the story should turn. It finally turns in the way it should. *Jason's Lyric*, like *New Jack City* and *Sugar Hill*, has the boldness to go for big dramatic themes, for love, tragedy, and redemption. It's not some little plot-bound genre formula. It's invigorating, how much confidence it has, and how much space it allows itself.

Jaws ★ ★ ★ ★
PG, 124 m., 1975

Roy Scheider (Brody), Robert Shaw (Quint), Richard Dreyfuss (Hooper), Lorraine Gary (Ellen Brody), Murray Hamilton (Mayor). Directed by Steven Spielberg and produced by Richard Zanuck and David Brown. Screenplay by Peter Benchley and Carl Gottlieb.

Steven Spielberg's *Jaws* is a sensationally effective action picture—a scary thriller that works all the better because it's populated with characters that have been developed into human beings we get to know and care about. It's a film that's as frightening as *The Exorcist*, and yet it's a nicer kind of fright, somehow more fun because we're being scared by an outdoor-adventure saga instead of by a brimstone-and-vomit devil.

The story, as I guess everyone knows by now, involves a series of attacks on swimmers by a great white shark, the response of the threatened resort island to its loss of tourist business, and, finally, the epic attempt by three men to track the shark and kill it. There are no doubt supposed to be all sorts of levels of meanings in such an archetypal story, but

Spielberg wisely decides not to underline any of them. This is an action film content to stay entirely within the perimeters of its story, and none of the characters has to wade through speeches expounding on the significance of it all. Spielberg is very good, though, at presenting those characters in a way that makes them individuals. Before the three men get on that leaky old boat and go forth to do battle with what amounts to an elemental natural force, we know them well enough to be genuinely interested in the ways they'll respond. There's Brody (Roy Scheider), the police chief, who came to the island from New York looking, so he thought, for a change from the fears of the city. There's Quint (Robert Shaw), a caricature of the crusty old seafaring salt, who has a very particular personal reason for hating sharks. And there's Hooper (Richard Dreyfuss), the rich kid turned oceanographer, who knows best of all what a shark can do to a man, and yet is willing to get into the water with one.

All three performances are really fine. Scheider is the character most of us identify with. He's actually scared of the water, doesn't like to swim and, when he sees the giant shark swim past the boat for the first time, we believe him when he informs Quint, very sincerely, "We need a bigger boat." Shaw brings a degree of cheerful exaggeration to his role as Quint, stomping around like a cross between Captain Queeg and Captain Hook, and then delivering a compelling five-minute monologue about the time the *Indianapolis* went down and he was one of more than a thousand men in the water. By the time rescue came, two-thirds of them had been killed by sharks.

Probably the most inspired piece of casting in the movie is the use of Richard Dreyfuss as the oceanographer. He made this film soon after playing the driven, scheming, overwhelmingly ambitious title character in *The Apprenticeship of Duddy Kravitz,* and the nice kid, college-bound, in *American Graffiti.* Here he looks properly young, engaging, and scholarly, and introduces the technical material about sharks in a way that reinforces our elemental fear of them.

Which brings us to the shark itself. Some of the footage in the film is of an actual great white shark. The rest uses a mechanical shark patterned on the real thing. The illusion is complete. We see the shark close up, we look in its relentless eye, and it just plain feels like a shark. *Jaws* is a great adventure movie of the kind we don't get very

often any more. It's clean-cut adventure, without the gratuitous violence of so many action pictures. It has the necessary amount of blood and guts to work—but none extra. And it's one hell of a good story, brilliantly told.

Jean de Florette ★ ★ ★ ½
PG, 121 m., 1987
(See also *Manon of the Spring*)

Gerard Depardieu (Jean de Florette), Yves Montand (Cesar Soubeyran), Daniel Auteuil (Ugolin), Elisabeth Depardieu (Aimee), Ernestine Mazurowna (Manon). Directed by Claude Berri and produced by Pierre Grunstein. Screenplay by Berri and Gerard Brach.

If you were to walk into the middle of *Jean de Florette,* you would see a scene that might mislead you.

In the middle of a drought, a farmer is desperate to borrow a mule to help haul water from a nearby spring. He asks his neighbor for the loan of the animal. The neighbor is filled with compassion and sympathy, but simply cannot do without his mule, which he needs in order to farm his own land and provide for his own family. As the neighbor rejects the request, his face is so filled with regret you'd have little doubt he is one of the best of men.

Actually, he is a thief. And what he is stealing is the joy, the hope, and even the future of the man who needs the mule. *Jean de Florette* is a merciless study in human nature, set in Provence in the 1920s. It's the story of how two provincial French farmers systematically destroy the happiness of a man who comes out from the city to till the land.

The man from the city is Jean de Florette, a hunchback tax collector played by Gerard Depardieu, that most dependable of French actors. When he inherits a little land in Provence, he is only too happy to pack up his loyal wife and beautiful child and move to the country for a new beginning. He wants to raise vegetables and rabbits on the land, which, according to the map, includes a freshwater spring.

His neighbors have other ideas. The old local farmer (Yves Montand) and his nephew (Daniel Auteuil) long have had their eyes on that land, and they realize that if they can discourage the newcomer they can buy the land cheap. So they do what is necessary. They block the spring with concrete, conceal its location, and wait to see what happens.

At first, nothing much happens. There are steady rains, the vegetables grow, and the rabbits multiply. Then comes the drought, and Depardieu is forced to bring water from a neighboring well, using his mule and his own strength, turning himself into a beast of burden. From morning to night he plods back and forth under the burning sun, and his wife helps when she can, but the burden is too much and the land surely will die. It is then that he asks for the loan of Auteuil's mule, and is turned down.

The director, Claude Berri, does not tell this story as a melodrama; all of the motives are laid out well in advance, and it is perfectly clear what is going to happen. The point of the film is not to create suspense, but to capture the relentlessness of human greed, the feeling that the land is so important the human spirit can be sacrificed to it.

To create this feeling, Berri stands well back with his camera. There are not a lot of highly charged close-ups, to turn the story into a series of phony high points. Instead, many of the shots are surrounded by the landscape and the sky, and there is one enormously dramatic set piece when the sky fills up with rain clouds, and the thunder roars and the rain seems about to come. And then, as Depardieu and his family run outside to feel it against their faces, the rain falls elsewhere and Depardieu shakes his fist at the heavens and asks God why he has been forsaken.

But God has not double-crossed him, his neighbors have. And the enormity of their crime is underlined by the deliberate pace of this film, which is the first installment of a two-part epic (the second part is *Manon of the Spring*). We realize here that human greed is patient, and can wait years for its reward. And meantime daily life goes on in Provence, and neighbors pass the time of day and regret that it is impossible to make a loan of a mule.

Jefferson in Paris ★ ★
PG-13, 142 m., 1995

`NEW`

Nick Nolte (Thomas Jefferson), Gwyneth Paltrow (Patsy Jefferson), Estelle Eonnet (Polly Jefferson), Thandie Newton (Sally Hemings), Greta Scacchi (Maria Cosway), Simon Callow (Richard Cosway), Seth Gilliam (James Hemings), Jean-Pierre Aumont (D'Hancarville), James Earl Jones (Madison Hemings). Directed by James Ivory and produced by Ismail Merchant. Screenplay by Ruth Prawer Jhabvala.

Thomas Jefferson fathered six children by his wife, Martha, and, according to revisionist historians, several more by his slave Sally Hemings. Yet if you visit his home at Monticello, outside Charlottesville in Virginia, you will come away with the impression that he was a bachelor. Everything is arranged for a single man, including the bed, barely large enough for one, and the toys: adjustable chairs and desks, ingenious writing instruments, closets that seem to hang their own clothes, and staircases which (in an era of grand flights of stairs) are wide enough only for one person at a time.

After the guide has told you about Jefferson's first marriage, and his deathbed promise to Martha that he would never marry again, you wait for Sally Hemings's name to be mentioned, but it never is. If you ask about her, your guide will explain that there is no definitive evidence that Jefferson ever had children by Hemings.

Of course, the chance that Jefferson would leave such definitive evidence is minute, and in a state where slaves had no legal standing except as property there was no way for them to do it. So we are left with the debate between the traditional historians and those who say they are Jefferson's black descendants.

Jefferson in Paris, the film by the team of Ismail Merchant, James Ivory, and Ruth Prawer Jhabvala, has no doubt that Jefferson fathered at least one child by Sally Hemings. What the movie doesn't know is what, if anything, he thought about it. The Jefferson in this movie is such a remote figure that you wonder, by the movie's end, if he actually knew he was having sex at the time. Perhaps his mind was preoccupied with architecture or philosophy.

The movie takes place during a period in the mid-1780s, when Jefferson (Nick Nolte), author of the Declaration of Independence, replaced Benjamin Franklin as the representative of the new United States at the court of Louis XVI and Marie Antoinette. His wife is already dead. He lives the life of a man about town, carrying on a flirtation with Maria Conway (Greta Scacchi), the beautiful wife of a world-class fop (Simon Callow). If she leaves her husband, will he marry her? She asks about the deathbed promise, and he regards her solemnly and says, "You and I are alive, and the earth belongs to us, to the living." Ah, yes, but that doesn't answer her question, and indeed there seems something considered and remote about his passion, as if his mind were elsewhere.

Jefferson's oldest daughter, Patsy (Gwyneth Paltrow), is in Paris with him. Another of his daughters dies in Virginia, and he sends for his youngest, Polly (Estelle Eonnet), to join him. With her comes her young slave, Sally Hemings (Thandie Newton, from *Flirting*), a quadroon who was his late wife's half sister on, needless to say, her father's side.

Sally is only fifteen at the time she arrives in Paris. Soon Jefferson is making her little presents, such as a necklace, and she is visiting him in his bedroom for flighty flirtations. Their closeness is obvious to Patsy, who calls it "unspeakable," and eventually Maria sees enough to realize her own future with Thomas is limited.

Still, considering that the relationship of slave and master is really the reason *Jefferson in Paris* was made, the filmmakers seem to have few ideas about the nature of their feelings. Does Sally "love" Jefferson, or only act seductively around him because of his importance and power? How does he feel about her? She is pregnant by the end of the film, but the sex scene is, of course, off-camera, and later as he discusses Sally's plight, Jefferson seems almost to talk as if she might have gotten pregnant by herself. Newton's performance is also hard to read; she adopts an odd dialect, behaves childishly, seems more like a caricature of an ingratiating slave than like a woman who was apparently to interest Jefferson so much that he went on to have several more children with her, over a period of years.

Of course, the Sally Hemings matter is only a part of the film. We also get glimpses of the decadence of the French court (Marie Antoinette appearing in bizarre theatricals), and there are discussions about the politics of the time, including several about slavery, in which Jefferson seems confused about exactly what he thinks: It is bad, yes, but then it is the law, although of course it should not be the law. . . .

Sally Hemings's brother James (Seth Gilliam) is also part of the household, and quite aware that under French law he is a free man. Jefferson therefore pays him, and Sally, salaries ("Yours to do with as you wish," he tells her; "would you like me to keep it for you?"). When Jefferson offers James and Sally their choice of freedom or returning to Monticello, Sally cries: "Where's I going?" The implication is that the paternalistic Jefferson thinks they'll be better off staying with him, "the best master in Virginia," according to his daughter. (James Hemings's confrontations with Jefferson and Sally are the best-written scenes in the film; the character seems willing to confront questions that the movie otherwise allows to slip quietly past.)

The film is lavishly produced and visually splendid, like all the Merchant-Ivory productions *(Howards End, Remains of the Day)*. But what is it about? Revolution? History? Slavery? Romance? No doubt a lot of research and speculation went into Jhabvala's screenplay, but I wish she had finally decided to jump one way or the other. The movie tells no clear story and has no clear ideas; it is all elaborate glimpses of a private man who, as the architect of his own home, did not see why anyone would ever want to walk upstairs side-by-side.

Jeremiah Johnson ★ ★ ★
PG, 108 m., 1972

Robert Redford (Jeremiah Johnson), Will Geer (Bear Claw), Stefan Gierasch (Del Gue), Allyn Ann McLerie (Crazy Woman), Delle Bolton (Swan), Charles Tyner (Robidoux). Directed by Sydney Pollack and produced by Joe Wizan. Screenplay by John Milius and Edward Anhalt.

If Thoreau had been a violent man, angry and unforgiving, *Jeremiah Johnson* might have been made from one of his books. Like *Walden*, it's the story of a man who goes alone into the wilderness to live by his hands and wits. It is good at showing us this man and the ways by which he survives; but not so good when it ventures into Indian myth and magic, and edges up to vast universal questions.

There's a sense in which movies like this should be rough-hewn and a little inarticulate. When a man makes up his mind to go into the mountains and say to hell with civilization, it's cheating a little to frame him against spectacular landscapes as if he were a particularly heroic tour guide. It may also be cheating to cast Robert Redford in the title role; he projects a kind of intellectual, winsome handsomeness that doesn't really belong in such a simple character.

Still, the movie does approach its subject with a certain dogged honesty; it agrees for the most part to coexist with the rhythms of the wilderness, and not go for big, phony climaxes (it is so studiously low-keyed, indeed, that it seems to end four or five times before it really does). The humor is direct and folksy, as when an old trapper asks Jeremiah if he can skin a grizzly. Jeremiah says he can, and

so the trapper lures a grizzly into the cabin with Jeremiah, jumps out the back window and shouts, "Start skinnin'!"

The humor is direct, and so is the violence. Director Sydney Pollack approaches his scenes head-on. He doesn't deal in the choreography of violence, like Peckinpah, or the fetish of violence, like the Kubrick of *A Clockwork Orange*. Instead, his violent scenes are brutally short and forcible. Death occurs suddenly, and is absorbed by the emptiness of the mountain range.

The story follows Jeremiah as he makes a roughly circular journey through high mountain ranges and passes. He nearly starves the first winter, until the old trapper (Will Geer, looking like Father Christmas in his fur parka) has mercy on him. He forms brief friendships and partnerships with some of the other outcasts of the mountains; he has hostile encounters with Crow Indians and friendly ones with Flatheads; and as the result of a misunderstanding he finds himself married to the daughter of a Flathead chief. The marriage sets up the movie's most absorbing sequences. Jeremiah has earlier become a sort of guardian for a young boy, and now the three of them set up housekeeping. Pollack gets a kind of poetic documentary rhythm going as they clear a space, cut some trees, and build a cabin. Their long weeks of work are followed by a clumsy football game in which the three of them, so different from one another, show that they've become a family.

It is after this section of the movie that things begin to go a little wrong. Without telling you everything that happens (because that would remove the necessary shock value), I can say that Jeremiah runs up against a host of impenetrable wilderness mysteries, undying Indian blood feuds, and, yes, fate itself. In the end he becomes a mysterious and legendary figure, a man of the mountains, who is too symbolic to suit me.

Still, as the portrait of a man who turns his back on society, *Jeremiah Johnson* is a finely felt and beautiful film. And the scenery is particularly beautiful. I say that with a certain sense of pain; I made a vow never to praise a movie because "the scenery is beautiful." The scenery is always beautiful in movies. Liking a movie because of its beautiful scenery is like buying a car because its tires are round. And yet . . . the movie was shot on location in the national forests of Utah, and there are moments in it that make *Doctor Zhivago* look cramped for space.

Jesus of Montreal ★ ★ ★ ½
R, 119 m., 1990

Lothaire Bluteau (Daniel Coloumbe), Catherine Wilkening (Mireille), Johanne-Marie Tremblay (Constance), Remy Girard (Martin), Robert Lepage (Rene), Gilles Pelletier (Father Leclerc), Yves Jacques (Richard Cardinal). Directed by Denys Arcand and produced by Roger Frappier and Roger Gendron. Screenplay by Arcand.

The Passion Play has been a success for more than forty years in the famous Montreal basilica, but the passage of time has made it seem old-fashioned, and modern audiences are growing restless. It's time for an overhaul. So the priest in charge hires some new actors—younger, more inventive—to stage a revised and updated version. And they make the mistake of taking their material literally.

The teachings of Christ, it has often been observed, would be radical and subversive if anyone ever took them literally. And they would be profoundly offensive to those who build their kingdoms in this world and not in the next. The actors who rewrite the Passion in *Jesus of Montreal* create a play that is good theater and perhaps even good theology, but it is not good public relations. And although audiences respond well and the reviews are good, the church authorities are reluctant to offend the establishment by presenting such an unorthodox reading of the sacred story. So they order the play to be toned down.

But by the time they act, a curious thing has happened to the actors. They have come to believe in their play; to be shaped by the roles they play. *Jesus of Montreal* does not try to force a parallel between the Passion of Christ and the experiences of these actors, and yet, certain similarities do appear, and Daniel (Lothaire Bluteau), the actor who plays Christ, discovers that his own life is taking on some of the aspects of Christ's. By the end of the film, we have arrived at a Crucifixion scene that actually plays as drama, and not simply as something which has been forced into the script.

Jesus of Montreal was written and directed by Denys Arcand, the best of the new generation of Quebec filmmakers. His previous film was *The Decline of the American Civilization*, in which a group of Montreal intellectuals gathered to prepare a meal and talk about the meanings of their lives; it was sort of a conversational version of *The Big Chill*. This film is much more passionate, and angrier. It suggests that most establishments, and especially the church, would be rocked to their foundations by the practical application of the maxims of Christ.

Many of the scenes have obvious parallels in the New Testament. In one, an actress from the troupe appears at an audition for a TV commercial and is asked to take off her clothes—not because nudity is required in the commercial, but more because the casting director wants to exercise his power. Arriving late at the audition, Daniel, the Christ figure, shouts out to his friend to leave her clothes on, and then, when the advertising people try to have him ejected, he goes into a rage, overturning lights and cameras. It is a version, of course, of Christ and the moneylenders in the temple.

Another way in which *Jesus of Montreal* parallels the life of Christ is in the way a community grows up around its central figure. Filled with a vision they believe in, nourished by the courage to carry on in the face of the authorities, these actors persist in presenting their play even in the face of religious and legal opposition. It's interesting the way Arcand makes this work as theology and drama at the same time; in a sense, *Jesus of Montreal* is a movie about the theater, not about religion.

Pay close attention to Lothaire Bluteau in the title role. He is considered the most powerful actor to come out of Canada in years, with his emaciated good looks and his burning intensity, and he has received strong reviews for his stage work in London. He's an actor of the Mickey Rourke-Eric Roberts-James Woods school, consumed with fire, intense in his concentration, and he is just right for this role.

As for the film itself, I was surprised at how absorbed I became, even though, right from the beginning, I assumed I would see some kind of modern parallel of the Passion. Arcand doesn't force the parallels, and his screenplay is not simply an updated paraphrase of the New Testament. It's an original and uncompromising attempt to explore what really might happen if the spirit of Jesus were to walk among us in these timid and materialistic times.

The Jewel of the Nile ★ ★ ★
PG, 105 m., 1985

Michael Douglas (Jack Colton), Kathleen Turner (Joan Wilder), Danny DeVito (Ralph), Avner Eisenberg (Holy Man), Spiros Focas

(Omar). Directed by Lewis Teague and produced by Michael Douglas. Screenplay by Mark Rosenthal and Lawrence Konner.

The Jewel of the Nile is more silliness in the tradition of *Romancing the Stone*, which in its turn was a funny action comedy inspired by the Indiana Jones epics. We walk into the theater expecting absolutely nothing of substance, and that's exactly what we get, served up with high style. The movie reassembles three key cast members—Michael Douglas, Kathleen Turner, and Danny DeVito—and goes on to a fourth inspired casting decision with the addition of Avner Eisenberg as a holy man of gentle goofiness.

Movie industry gossip had it that Kathleen Turner didn't particularly want to make this sequel, and that even Michael Douglas, who produces as well as stars, thought it might be best to quit while he was ahead. But the original contract specified a sequel, and it's to everybody's credit that *The Jewel of the Nile* is an ambitious and elaborate attempt to repeat the success of the first movie; it's not just a rip-off.

Even so, it lacks some of the pleasures of *Romancing*, especially the development of the romance between Douglas and Turner. This time, as the movie opens, they're old friends, unwinding in Cannes and reminiscing about the good times they had in South America. Perhaps sensing that there is nowhere to go with this essentially stable relationship, the movie plunges them almost immediately into Middle East intrigue.

A fabulously wealthy Arab (Spiros Focas) invites Turner to travel with him to his homeland, for reasons as vague as they are fascinating. Douglas temporarily drops out; after a manufactured spat, he decides he'd rather sail his boat through the Mediterranean. Turner is quickly involved in danger as the Arab reveals plans to usurp the role of a legendary holy man, and Douglas becomes an ally of the great spiritual leader, who is known as the Jewel of the Nile. (Danny DeVito is somewhat lost in all of this, and left for long stretches of the film to wander through the desert and suffer meaningless tortures in lieu of a clearly defined role.)

The Jewel of the Nile expends amazing resources on some of its scenes, including a gigantic spiritual meeting in the desert that is staged as a cross between a rock concert and the Nuremberg Rally. What makes the Middle Eastern stuff work, however, is the performance of Eisenberg, who is a true comic

discovery. He has some of the same cynical innocence we sensed in the Harold Ramis character in *Ghostbusters:* he's very wise and very innocent. Some of his best moments involve his bewildering cross-cultural dialogue: he speaks in vast metaphysical concepts which are unexpectedly interrupted with 1985 slang and pop sociology.

Meanwhile, Douglas and Turner have fun with two of the broadest roles in recent memory. They fight, they make up, they wisecrack in the face of calamity. And they make an ideally matched comedy team. Just as Woody Allen and Diane Keaton always seem to be on the same wavelength in their comic dialogues, so do Douglas and Turner, in their own way, seem well matched. It seems clear that they like each other and are having fun during the parade of ludicrous situations in the movie, and their chemistry is sometimes more entertaining than the contrivances of the plot.

My favorite moment between them comes as they hang by their hands over a rat-pit, while acid gnaws away at the ropes which suspend them above certain doom. Sure, this scene owes something to *Raiders of the Lost Ark*. But what's new about it this time is the dialogue, the way they break down and confess they love each other and make marriage plans as death inexorably approaches. And then, when DeVito appears and might possibly save them, there is some business with a ladder that is followed by dialogue so perfectly timed that I laughed not so much in amusement as in delight at how well the mechanisms of the scene fell together.

For all of those pleasures, *The Jewel of the Nile* is a slight and lightweight entertainment. How could it be otherwise? And it is not quite the equal of *Romancing the Stone*. That's not a surprise. For what it is, though, it's fun. And for what it's worth, Douglas and Turner could keep on working in this tradition forever, giving us a 1980s version of the Crosby and Hope *Road* pictures. I guess they don't want to, though, and perhaps that's just as well. What I hope is that a casting director sees Avner Eisenberg for what he is, the most intriguing comedy discovery in a long time.

JFK ★ ★ ★ ★
R, 188 m., 1991

Kevin Costner (Jim Garrison), Sissy Spacek (Liz Garrison), Joe Pesci (David Ferrie), Tommy Lee Jones (Clay Shaw), Gary Oldman

(Lee Harvey Oswald), Jay O. Sanders (Lou Ivon), Donald Sutherland ("X"), Michael Rooker (Bill Broussard), Laurie Metcalf (Susie Cox), Brian Doyle-Murray (Jack Ruby), Ed Asner (Guy Bannister), Jack Lemmon (Jack Martin), John Candy (Dean Andrews), Kevin Bacon (Willie O'Keefe). Directed by Oliver Stone and produced by A. Kitman Ho and Stone. Screenplay by Stone and Zachary Sklar.

Oliver Stone's *JFK* builds up an overwhelming head of urgency that all comes rushing out at the end of the film in a tumbling, angry, almost piteous monologue—the whole obsessive weight of Jim Garrison's conviction that there was a conspiracy to assassinate John F. Kennedy. With the words come images, faces, names, snatches of dialogue, flashbacks to the evidence, all marshaled to support his conclusion that the murder of JFK was not the work of one man.

Well, do you know anyone who believes Lee Harvey Oswald acted all by himself in killing Kennedy? I don't. I've been reading the books and articles for the last twenty-five years, and I've not found a single convincing defense of the Warren Commission report, which arrived at that reassuring conclusion. It's impossible to believe the Warren report because the physical evidence makes its key conclusion impossible: One man with one rifle could not physically have caused what happened on November 22, 1963, in Dallas. If one man could not have, then there must have been two. Therefore, there was a conspiracy.

Oliver Stone's *JFK* has been attacked by those who believe Stone has backed the wrong horse in the Kennedy assassination sweepstakes—by those who believe the hero of this film, former New Orleans District Attorney Jim Garrison, was a loose cannon who attracted crackpot conspiracy theories the way a dog draws fleas.

The important point to make about *JFK* is that Stone does not subscribe to all of Garrison's theories, and indeed rewrites history to supply his Garrison character with material he could not have possessed at the time of these events. He uses Garrison as the symbolic center of his film because Garrison, in all the United States in all the years since 1963, is the only man who has attempted to bring anyone into court in connection with the fishiest political murder of our time.

Stone's film is truly hypnotically watchable. Leaving aside all of its drama and emotion, it is a masterpiece of film assembly. The writing, the editing, the music, the photography, are all used here in a film of enormous complexity to weave a persuasive tapestry out of an overwhelming mountain of evidence and testimony. Film students will examine this film in wonder in the years to come, astonished at how much information it contains, how many characters, how many interlocking flashbacks, what skillful interweaving of documentary and fictional footage. The film hurtles for 188 minutes through a sea of information and conjecture, and never falters and never confuses us.

That is not to say that we are quite sure, when it is over and we try to reconstruct the experience in our minds, exactly what Stone's final conclusions are. *JFK* does not unmask the secrets of the Kennedy assassination. Instead, it uses the Garrison character as a seeker for truth who finds that the murder could not have happened according to the official version. Could not. Those faded and trembling images we are all so familiar with, the home movie Abraham Zapruder took of the shooting of Kennedy, have made it forever clear that the Oswald theory is impossible—and that at least one of the shots *must* have come from in front of Kennedy, not from the Texas Schoolbook Depository behind him.

Look at me, emphasizing the word "must." The film stirs up that kind of urgency and anger. The CIA and FBI reports on the Kennedy assassination are sealed until after most of us will be long dead, and for what reason? Why can't we read the information our government gathered for us on the death of our president? If Garrison's investigation was so pitiful—and indeed it was flawed, underfunded, and sabotaged—then where are the better investigations by Stone's attackers? A U.S. Senate select committee found in 1979 that Kennedy's assassination was probably a conspiracy. Why, twelve years later, has the case not been reopened?

Stone's film shows, through documentary footage and reconstruction, most of the key elements of those 1963 events. The shooting. The flight of Air Force One to Washington. Jack Ruby's murder of Oswald. And it shows Garrison in New Orleans, watching the same TV reports we watched, and then stumbling, hesitantly at first, into a morass of evidence suggesting that various fringe groups in New Orleans, pro- and anti-Castro, may have somehow been mixed up with the CIA and various self-appointed soldiers of fortune in a conspiracy to kill JFK.

His investigation leads him to Clay Shaw, respected businessman, who is linked by various witnesses with Lee Harvey Oswald and other possible conspirators. Some of those witnesses die suspiciously. Eventually Garrison is able to bring Shaw to trial, and although he loses his case, there is the conviction that he was onto something. He feels Shaw perjured himself, and in 1979, five years after Shaw's death and ten years after the trial, Richard Helms of the CIA admits that Shaw, despite his sworn denials, was indeed an employee of the CIA.

Most people today, I imagine, think of Garrison as an irresponsible, publicity-seeking hothead who destroyed the reputation of an innocent man. Few know Shaw perjured himself. Was Garrison the target of the same kind of paid misinformation floated in defense of Michael Milkin? A good PR campaign can do a better job of destroying a reputation than any Louisiana D.A. Stone certainly gives Garrison a greater measure of credibility than he has had for years, but the point is not whether Garrison's theories are right or wrong—what the film supports is simply his seeking for a greater truth.

As Garrison, Kevin Costner gives a measured yet passionate performance. "You're as stubborn as a mule," one of his investigators shouts at him. Like a man who has hold of an idea he cannot let go, he forges ahead, insisting that there is more to the assassination than meets the eye. Stone has surrounded him with an astonishing cast, able to give us the uncanny impression that we are seeing historical figures. There is Joe Pesci, squirming and hyperkenetic as David Ferrie, the alleged getaway pilot. Tommy Lee Jones as Clay Shaw, hiding behind an impenetrable wall of bemusement. Gary Oldman as Lee Harvey Oswald. Donald Sutherland as "X" (actually Fletcher Prouty), the high-placed Pentagon official who thinks he knows why JFK was killed. Sissy Spacek, in the somewhat thankless role of Garrison's wife, who fears for her family and marriage. And dozens of others, including Jack Lemmon, Ed Asner, Walter Matthau, and Kevin Bacon in small, key roles, their faces vaguely familiar behind the facades of their characters.

Stone and his editors, Joe Hutshing and Pietro Scalia, have somehow triumphed over the tumult of material here and made it work—made it grip and disturb us. The achievement of the film is not that it answers the mystery of the Kennedy assassination, because it does not, or even that it vindicates

Garrison, who is seen here as a man often whistling in the dark. Its achievement is that it tries to marshal the anger that ever since 1963 has been gnawing away on some dark shelf of the national psyche. John F. Kennedy was murdered. Lee Harvey Oswald could not have acted alone. Who acted with him? Who knew?

Jimmy Hollywood ★ ★ ½
R, 110 m., 1994

Joe Pesci (Jimmy Alto), Christian Slater (William), Victoria Abril (Lorraine), Jason Beghe (Detective), John Cothran, Jr. (Detective), Hal Fishman, Jerry Dunphy, Andrea Kutyas (Anchorpeople). Directed by Barry Levinson and produced by Mark Johnson and Levinson. Screenplay by Levinson.

Barry Levinson's *Jimmy Hollywood* has a wonderful opening shot in which Jimmy Alto, would-be actor, walks down Hollywood Boulevard reciting the name of every star on the pavement, by memory. There are people who can do this. And there are a lot of people like Jimmy (Joe Pesci), holding on desperately to the leftover dreams of many years ago, still hoping to be "discovered."

Pesci's own life is a case in point: He had given up hopes of an acting career and resigned himself to real life in 1980, when Martin Scorsese and Robert De Niro discovered him and cast him in his career-making role in *Raging Bull*. That stroke of luck is still awaiting Jimmy Alto, who hangs out in coffee shops, lives in an apartment where the rent is paid by his girlfriend, and sometimes gets a job as a waiter. His hair, curly and blond, is about the only feature that looks the same as his aging publicity photo. But he has been close to glory: "I was up for the role of Cliff on 'Matlock,'" he tells a short-order cook. "But they felt I was a little too strong for Andy Griffith."

Jimmy's best friend is William (Christian Slater), a harmless, dim-witted street person who plays the sidekick in Jimmy's nonstop talk show. Life is a monologue for Jimmy, who has opinions on everything, from the mummy movies on the late show to the Hollywood epidemic of street crime. One day the car radio is stolen from Jimmy's beater, and when Jimmy finds out that the cops don't much care, he decides to become a video vigilante. He'll capture the perps on videotape.

That sets up the story gimmick in *Jimmy Hollywood*, which is that Jimmy teams up with William to tape the bad guys, send the tapes to TV stations, and represent himself as a shadowy vigilante organization named "S.O.S."—which stands for "Save Our Streets," and is inspired, he explains, by the initials of "Steven O. Selznick," whose name was David, but why sweat the details?

Leadership of the S.O.S. is the greatest role in Jimmy Alto's life, and he plays it to the hilt, monopolizing the Los Angeles media with a crimestoppers campaign that grows more daring and dangerous. Lorraine (Victoria Abril), his long-suffering Latina girlfriend, thinks he has taken leave of his senses, which of course he has, but the movie knows that an unemployed actor who thinks he has finally found a great role cannot be reasoned with.

Jimmy Hollywood was written and directed by Barry Levinson (*Rain Man, Good Morning, Vietnam*), who has probably had a lot of Jimmy Altos through his office. In Pesci, Slater, and Abril he has actors who find the right tone for the material. But the plot weighs them down. They'd be at home in a human comedy about their dreams and other ways of killing time. When they get caught up in the whirlwind of Levinson's plot mechanism, they lose their goofy street credibility and become characters in a sitcom: Events drive them, and the scale of the story escalates, until finally nothing can be believed—which is a shame, because for the first hour we believed in them.

John Cassavetes knew how to make movies like this without letting the plot take over. His *Minnie and Moskowitz* was about a lonely museum curator (Gena Rowlands) and a parking lot attendant (Seymour Cassel), and Moskowitz could be Jimmy Alto's first cousin: a guy on the outside physically, but on the inside in his mind. The whole point of such characters is that they drift. And it is important that they drift in a recognizable version of real life (romanticized, to be sure).

Jimmy Hollywood goes wrong when Jimmy starts pulling off stunts that would make you famous in the movies but would get you killed in real life. Once the story cuts loose from its base of realism, it doesn't much matter what happens; Jimmy, William, and Lorraine, who seemed so real in her cluttered apartment, become plot devices, not people.

Too bad. I felt my heart sinking when I saw the plot machinery gearing up. There's probably a theory that audiences demand heavy plotting—that unless there's some kind of dumb, manipulated crisis as a climax, they'll lose interest. I wonder how valid that is. Today's audiences have been exposed to so many hours of TV and film that they can sense it when a movie cuts loose from its convictions and goes on automatic pilot. Here were characters who might have really amounted to something, and we can see the movie dying right under their feet.

Joe Vs. the Volcano ★ ★ ★ ½
PG, 94 m., 1990

Tom Hanks (Joe), Meg Ryan (Patricia/Angelica/DeDe), Lloyd Bridges (Graynamore), Robert Stack (Dr. Ellison), Abe Vigoda (Chief of the Waponis), Dan Hedaya (Waturi), Barry McGovern (Luggage salesman), Ossie Davis (Marshall), Amanda Plummer (Dagmar). Directed by John Patrick Shanley and produced by Stephen Goldblatt. Screenplay by Shanley.

Gradually, through the opening scenes of *Joe Vs. the Volcano*, my heart began to quicken, until finally I realized a wondrous thing: I had not seen this movie before. Most movies, I have seen before. Most movies, you have seen before. Most movies are constructed out of bits and pieces of other movies, like little engines built from cinematic erector sets. But not *Joe Vs. the Volcano*. It is not an entirely successful movie, but it is new and fresh and not shy of taking chances, and the dialogue in it is actually worth listening to because it is written with wit and romance.

The movie announces its individuality in its opening shot, which is of a loathsome factory—a vast block of ugliness set down in the middle of a field of mud. Into this factory every morning trudge the broken spirits and unhealthy bodies of its employees, among them ashen-faced Joe (Tom Hanks), who has felt sick for years and believes the buzzing fluorescent tubes above his desk may be driving him mad.

The factory is a triumph of production design (by Bo Welch, who also designed *Beetlejuice*). It is a reminder that most movies these days are rigidly realistic in their settings, as if a law had been passed against flights of fancy like this factory that squats obscenely in the center of the screen. The entire movie breaks that law and allows fantasy back into the movies again. Like *Metropolis, The Wizard of Oz, Ghostbusters,* or *Batman,* this movie isn't content to photograph the existing world—it goes to the trouble of creating its own.

In the factory, Joe hunches in his little corner, quailing at the attacks of his boorish boss (Dan Hedaya) and hardly daring a peek at the office secretary (Meg Ryan), whose huge typewriter seems ready to crush her. He hates his job. Hates, hates, hates it. He barely has the strength to crawl out to a doctor's appointment, where he learns that a Brain Cloud is spreading between the hemispheres of his brain. He will feel terrific for four or five months, and then he will die.

The death sentence is a liberation. Joe quits his job and is almost immediately offered another one. A man named Graynamore (Lloyd Bridges) owns an island that is rich in a rare mineral. The island is inhabited by natives who must be placated. They need a human sacrifice for their volcano. Since Joe is going to die anyway, Graynamore reasons, why shouldn't he go out in style by leaping into the volcano?

Sounds good to Joe. And meanwhile the movie has been developing into a duet between whimsy and romance. The writer-director, John Patrick Shanley, is the same man who wrote Norman Jewison's wonderful *Moonstruck* and wrote the astonishingly bad *The January Man*. Now he is back on the track again. The best thing about his direction is his own dialogue. The characters in this movie speak as if they would like to say things that had not been said before, in words that had never been used in quite the same way.

En route to the island, Joe meets one of Graynamore's daughters and then the other. Both are also played by Meg Ryan, who has three different kinds of fun with her three characters: grungy, waspish, and delectable. They set sail for the South Seas. Everything leads to the moment when they stand on the lip of the fiery volcano, wondering whether they should risk fate by jumping in. Only in this movie could jumping into a volcano be considered risking fate, rather than certain death.

Joe Vs. the Volcano achieves a kind of magnificent goofiness. Tom Hanks and Meg Ryan are the right actors to inhabit it, because you can never catch them going for a gag that isn't there: They inhabit the logic of this bizarre world and play by its rules. Hanks is endearing in the title role because, in the midst of these astonishing sets and unbridled flights of fancy, he underplays. Like a Jacques Tati, he is an island of curiosity in a sea of mystery.

Some of the movie's sequences are so picaresque they do themselves in: The native tribe, for example, is a joke that Shanley is unable to pull off. What's strongest about the movie is that it actually does possess a philosophy, an idea about life. The idea is the same idea contained in *Moonstruck:* At night, in those corners of our minds we deny by day, magical things can happen in the moon shadows. And if they can't, (a) they should, and (b) we should always, in any event, act as if they can.

Johnny Got His Gun ★ ★ ★ ★
R, 111 m., 1971

Timothy Bottoms (Joe Bonham), Kathy Fields (Kareen), Jason Robards (Joe's Father), Diane Varsi (Fourth Nurse), Donald Sutherland (Jesus Christ), Eduard Franz (General Tillery). Directed by Dalton Trumbo and produced by Bruce Campbell. Screenplay by Trumbo.

I've never much liked anti-war films. They've never much stopped war, for one thing. For another, they attract hushed and reverential praise which speaks of their universality and the urgency of their messages. Most anti-war films come so burdened with universality and urgency that the ads for them read like calls to sunrise services.

Dalton Trumbo's *Johnny Got His Gun* smelled like that kind of anti-war film. It came out of the Cannes Film Festival with three awards and a slightly pious aroma, as if it had been made for joyless Student Peace Union types of thirty-five years ago. But it isn't like that at all. Trumbo has taken the most difficult sort of material—the story of a soldier who lost his arms, his legs, and most of his face in a World War I shell burst—and handled it, strange to say, in a way that's not so much anti-war as pro-life. Perhaps that's why I admire it. Instead of belaboring ironic points about the "war to end war," Trumbo remains stubbornly on the human level. He lets his ideology grow out of his characters, instead of imposing it from above. In this sense, his film resembles Joseph Losey's *King and Country* which also turned its back on the war in order to consider one ordinary, unremarkable soldier.

Trumbo's soldier is Joe Bonham (Timothy Bottoms), who comes from an American background that is clearly modeled on Trumbo's own. The boy works in a bakery, supports his mother and sisters after his father's death, is in love with an open-faced and sweet Irish girl, and enlists in the army be-

cause "it's the sort of thing a fellow ought to do, when his country is in trouble." Months later, he's sent on a patrol into no-man's land to bury a corpse that was offending a colonel's nose. A shell lands near him, and he wakes up in a hospital.

The army is convinced he has no conscious mind. They decide to keep him alive simply to learn from him. But he can think, and gradually the enormity of his injuries is revealed to him. He is literally the prisoner of his mind, for years, until he finds a way of communicating with a sympathetic nurse (Diane Varsi).

Trumbo uses flashbacks and fantasies to make Joe alive for us, while he exists in a living death. The most charming flashback is the first, when Joe and his girl kiss in her living room and are interrupted by her father. He's an old Wobbly who sends them both into the bedroom, and there is a love scene of such tenderness and beauty that its echoes resound through the entire film. Other scenes develop Joe's relationship with his father (Jason Robards) and with Jesus Christ (Donald Sutherland), whom he consults in fantasies. Christ really doesn't have much to suggest; he has no answers, in Joe's fantasies, because there are no answers.

The movie ends with no political solutions and without, in fact, even a political position. It simply states a case. Here was a patriotic young man who went off and was grievously wounded for no great reason, and whose conscious mind remains a horrible indictment of the system that sent all the young men away to kill each other. The soldier's own answer to his situation seems like the only possible one. He wants them to put him in a sideshow, where, as a freak, he can cause people a moment's thought about war. If they won't do that, he wants them to kill him. The army won't do either, of course.

Johnny Handsome ★ ★ ★ ½
R, 100 m., 1989

Mickey Rourke (John Sedley), Ellen Barkin (Sunny Boyd), Elizabeth McGovern (Donna McCarty), Morgan Freeman (Lieutenant Drones), Forest Whitaker (Dr. Resher), Lance Henriksen (Rafe Garrett), Scott Wilson (Mikey Chalmette). Directed by Walter Hill and produced by Charles Roven. Screenplay by Ken Friedman.

"Film noir: *a motion picture with an often grim urban setting, photographed in somber tones and permeated by a feeling of disillusionment, pessimism, and despair."*—Random House Dictionary

And, they might have added, you can't really get inside a *film noir* unless you are a romantic, a person who sees life in terms of the grand gesture and fate as a pair of dice. After I saw *Johnny Handsome*, I was unfortunate enough to encounter a couple of pragmatic modern nonromantic types, who assumed without even asking me that I had not approved of the movie. They were bright young things who found the movie filled with "stereotypes." I wish the professors who teach about stereotypes in undergraduate literature classes would remember to add that they are not necessarily a bad thing—that sometimes a film is better because it returns to its roots.

Johnny Handsome comes out of the *film noir* atmosphere of the 1940s, out of movies with dark streets and bitter laughter, with characters who live in cold-water flats and treat saloons as their living rooms. It is set in New Orleans, a city with a *film noir* soul, and it stars Mickey Rourke as a weary loser who has just about given up on himself. They call him "Johnny Handsome" because his face has been horribly disfigured since birth, and as the movie opens he and his best friend have been double-crossed by a couple of crooks who kill the friend, steal the loot, and leave Johnny to take the rap.

In jail, he's offered a deal if he'll identify his accomplices. He refuses, because it is the underworld code that you do not rat on your associates, and also because he plans to kill them when he gets back on the street. But then an interesting thing happens to him. In the jail, a thoughtful surgeon (Forest Whitaker) suggests that plastic surgery could turn Johnny into a reasonably average-looking guy, and speech therapy could make him into a passable candidate for rehabilitation.

Johnny has nothing to lose and undergoes the surgery (which, true to the tradition of movies like this, is a snap). Out on parole, he goes straight with a job down on the docks. And he meets a girl (Elizabeth McGovern) who loves him. But Johnny has a problem: He has spent so many years walking around feeling distrustful and grotesque and unlovable that he has a hard time handling success. The movie presents him with a clear choice: He can go straight, keep his nose clean, and be happy with this woman. Or he can return to crime and carry out his revenge against the hoods who double-crossed him.

Because we live in a time of simple-minded action pictures, with audiences that are less adventurous than those of the 1940s and stars who like to look good at the end, there is the assumption that Johnny will take the direction of growth and happiness (not without some setbacks, of course). But Walter Hill, who directed this film, and Mickey Rourke, who seems to seek out difficult projects, would not have been interested in a simple modern approach. This is dark material, and they head for the shadows.

The movie is filled with real style. Matthew F. Leonetti, the cinematographer, finds a gritty loneliness in the seedy quarters of New Orleans, and the Ry Cooder music is a cross between the blues and a sob. The movie benefits from strong supporting performances by an unusually distinguished cast (also including Ellen Barkin as one of the double-crossers, and Morgan Freeman as a cop who can't wait for Johnny to fail). And Hill (who made *48 HRS* and *Streets of Fire*) directs with an almost rude disregard for modern Hollywood convention. This is a movie in the true tradition of *film noir*—which someone who didn't write a dictionary once described as a movie where an ordinary guy indulges the weak side of his character, and hell opens up beneath his feet.

Johnny Mnemonic ★ ★
R, 98 m., 1995

NEW

Keanu Reeves (Johnny), Dina Meyer (Jane), Ice-T (J-Bone), Takeshi (Takahashi), Denis Akiyama (Shinji), Dolph Lundgren (Street Preacher), Henry Rollins (Spider), Barbara Sukowa (Anna). Directed by Robert Longo and produced by Don Carmody. Screenplay by William Gibson.

Johnny Mnemonic is one of the great goofy gestures of recent cinema, a movie which doesn't deserve one nanosecond of serious analysis, but has a kind of idiotic grandeur that makes you almost forgive it. Based on a story by William Gibson, the father of cyberpunk fiction, it has the nerve to pose as a futuristic fable when in fact all of its parts were bought off the shelf at the Used Movie Store.

The movie takes place a few decades in the future, when the world is in the grip of a high-tech virus caused indirectly by the high-speed cyber lifestyle. It stars Keanu Reeves as a data courier, who has a "wet-wired brain" (no wisecracks please) into which vast amounts of priceless computer data can be uploaded. Then he travels incognito to his destination, where the data is downloaded. If he doesn't get his brain emptied out fast enough, it melts down and he dies.

As a method of data transfer, this sucks. Even today, it would be faster, easier, and safer to encrypt the data and send it by modem, and by Johnny Mnemonic's time the world will be wired with fiber-optic cables allowing enormous files to be squirted around the world in seconds.

So why would you pump everything into Keanu Reeves's brain and then have a bunch of bad guys from the Yakuza and other crime organizations chase him from China to Newark? Because it's a movie, stupid. And because, in a concept recycled from hundreds of other movies, he wants to make "one more final run" in order to "pay for getting my memory back." (As Johnny explains in dialogue that I think is supposed to be poignant, "I had to dump a chunk of long-term memory—my childhood.")

The plot of this movie is breathtakingly derivative. In essence: The hero is entrusted with a valuable cargo, which he must get from A to B without being killed by the bad guys or stepping in anything. There are a pretty girl, evil villains, a weird prophet, and of course a violent final shootout in an Abandoned Flame Factory. (You know what an Abandoned Flame Factory is; you've seen them a zillion times in the movies. It's a big clanky warehouse where the hero and the villain stalk each other for an ultimate confrontation, while pointless and sourceless sheets of flame burst out as handy background visuals.)

This plot could plug equally well into a Western, a war movie, a samurai film, or *Ace Ventura IV*. It is not about anything. Or, more to the point, it is the excuse for the special effects. And *those* are good in this movie—really good.

I liked the visuals, for example, when Johnny is getting his multi-gigabyte download (the one that gives him nosebleed). And I especially liked a virtual-reality sequence where Johnny sort of goes inside the Internet and handles the visualized programming instructions with his hands, which are wearing remote-control gloves. All good stuff.

The problem is, *Johnny Mnemonic* uses the cyber-visuals entirely as atmosphere. Take them away, and the plot could be a 1946 B picture, right down to and including the concocted deadly deadline after a machine in Newark airport scans him and announces,

"Neural seepage! Fatal within twenty-four hours! Seek medical attention immediately!"

The fiction of Gibson is much prized on the campus, where, I am tempted to say, its fans know more about cyberspace than about fiction. That's why it's puzzling that this movie is so dumb about computers. Where did it get the notion that the best way to get information from Beijing to Newark would be to hand it to a courier and have him travel the distance? Hey, a lot of people went to a lot of trouble to invent computers and modems and satellites just to make trips like that unnecessary. There have also been great advances in the art of the cinema since this plot was first recycled—but that's another story.

Jo Jo Dancer, Your Life Is Calling
★ ★ ★
R, 97 m., 1986

Richard Pryor (Jo Jo), Debbie Allen (Michelle), Paula Kelly (Satin Doll), Billy Eckstine (Johnny Barnett), Art Evans (Arturo), J.J. Barry (Sal), Barbara Williams (Dawn), Carmen McRae (Grandmother), Diahnne Abbott (Mother), Scoey Mitchell (Father), E'Lon Cox (Little Jo Jo). Directed and produced by Richard Pryor. Screenplay by Rocco Urbisci, Paul Mooney, and Pryor.

Richard Pryor says that *Jo Jo Dancer, Your Life Is Calling* is not really his autobiography, and I believe him. But the movie is clearly inspired by the journey he has taken since that day in 1980 when he almost killed himself in a drug-related accident. There is pain in this movie, and truth, and also a lot of warmth and nostalgia. There is a certain incompleteness in the ending of the film, however; it seems to close without a third act. But Pryor has said there may be a sequel, and perhaps that's where the rest of the story will be told.

Jo Jo Dancer begins when its hero already is an entertainment superstar. We track him restlessly around his luxurious Hollywood home as he calls a drug dealer and sets up a party, all the time claiming that he's off drugs. He throws bottles and paraphernalia into the fireplace, screams to himself that he's gotta stop, and then decides to do cocaine one last time. The rest of the scene is borrowed from the headlines, as Jo Jo is raced into an emergency room with burns over most of his body.

He faces a turning point. Will he choose to live, or die? Jo Jo's alter ego separates from

his body, looks down at the bandages, and says, "Jo Jo, what have you done to us this time?" And then the alter ego embarks on a trip back through Jo Jo's life and the memories that will die if the body dies.

We see little Jo Jo being raised in a small Ohio town, where his grandmother runs a whorehouse, and his mother is one of the girls. We see the affection he receives, but also the conflicting signals about sex, race, and booze. Later, after his mother has married, there is tension at home after Jo Jo announces that he thinks he could become a nightclub comedian. There are painful scenes of his first stumbling attempts to entertain an audience, and then the night when he talks back to a drunk and begins to find his own onstage voice.

This early show-business material supplies the most heartfelt material in the film, and some of its best characters, especially a stripper named Satin Doll (Paula Kelly), who befriends Jo Jo and gets him his first job. Backstage, we meet the boozy old emcee (Art Evans), and the veteran trouper (Billy Eckstine). There is a great sequence where Pryor, dressed in drag, pulls out a fake pistol and tries to bluff the club's Mafia owners into paying him his salary.

There's an abrupt transition from these early scenes, which seem bathed in a glow of nostalgia and gratitude, and later scenes in which Jo Jo starts to make it big and is introduced to the Beverly Hills cocaine scene. Along the way, there have been several wives, one too frightened to leave her hometown, one so mercenary she comes along only for the money, one a white girl who likes cocaine too much. None of the relationships seems real, because Jo Jo doesn't seem real himself.

That's a point Pryor makes at the end of the film, in an onstage routine that represents his comeback nightclub act after he recovers from his accident. These passages are a reminder of *Richard Pryor Live on the Sunset Strip* and *Richard Pryor Here and Now*, his two post-cocaine concert films. He talks about always feeling that he didn't belong, always needing the instant confidence that came from booze and drugs, until finally they took away everything they had promised him.

The problem with the final onstage scene is that it's too self-contained. It doesn't take the dramatic chances that the rest of the movie is so willing to risk. It shows Pryor the performer, instead of continuing the story of Jo Jo the character. The structure of the

movie leads us to a place where we expect some sort of redemption and re-evaluation from the character, but it's not there and we miss it. Maybe the sequel will show Jo Jo learning to live without drugs.

All the same, Pryor has taken some major risks in this movie. He has played straight and honest with his story, but he also has shown that he has a real gift as a director; the narrative scenes in the movie have a conviction and an interest that grow and hold us. This isn't a heartfelt amateur night, but a film by an artist whose art has become his life.

The Journey of Natty Gann ★ ★ ★
PG, 101 m., 1985

Meredith Salenger (Natty Gann), John Cusack (Harry Slade), Ray Wise (Natty's Father). Directed by Jeremy Kagan and produced by Mike Lobell. Screenplay by Jeanne Rosenberg.

There is one sense in which I cannot stand any movie involving a child and an animal. I am acutely aware of the possibilities for manipulating the story in order to gain unearned emotional payoffs. There is another sense in which I cannot resist a story about a child and an animal—if it is done intelligently, bravely, and without cheap sentiment.

The Journey of Natty Gann falls into the second category. It begins with potentially lethal ingredients: A young girl is joined by a glorious wolf on a cross-country odyssey in search of her missing father. Along the way, she is befriended by another teen-age drifter, threatened by tough kids and railway cops, and faced with one setback after another. This is the sort of story that used to be routinely trashed by the Walt Disney people, who would turn it into sentimental melodrama. Amazingly, then, *The Journey of Natty Gann* is a Disney production, more evidence of the fresh winds blowing through the studio.

The movie stars Meredith Salenger, a solemn-faced newcomer, as Natty Gann, the young teen-age daughter of a Chicago working-class stiff (Ray Wise). The time is the Depression. Jobs are scarce and dollars are few. When Wise gets a chance at a good-paying lumberman's job in the Northwest, he decides to take it. The bus is pulling out, Natty is nowhere to be found, and he decides to leave her in the care of a boarding-house owner and send for her later.

It appears to Natty that he is never going

to send for her, and the reformatory beckons. She hops on a freight train and heads west in a forlorn search for her father, and most of the movie concerns her adventures along the way. Her great moment comes when she is lost and alone in a rainstorm in a forest, and a wolf approaches her and, amazingly, curls up at her side. With the wolf as a companion, she is understandably protected from many of the dangers of the road, and she makes it out West and also makes a friend, Harry (John Cusack), another teen-ager riding the rails.

The film's photography is magnificent, as the girl, the boy, and the wolf make their way through the Rockies and into the Northwest. More to the point is the relationship between Natty and her wolf. The movie was written by Jeanne Rosenberg, co-author of *The Black Stallion,* and again this time there is a real, fundamental feeling for the reality of a relationship between a human and a beast. The wolf looks longingly into the forest, but stays by the girl's side, and there is a thrilling sequence in which both of them jump a freight train—a close call.

This is the kind of movie that younger teen-agers might like a lot, if they have not already been broken down by the corrupt cynicism of so many Hollywood "teen-age" movies. It is about dreams and fears and dangers, love and determination. And it does justice to those qualities.

The Joy Luck Club ★ ★ ★ ★
R, 135 m., 1993

The Mothers: Kieu Chinh (Suyuan), Tsai Chin (Lindo), France Nuyen (Ying Ying), Lisa Lu (An Mei). The Daughters: Ming-Na Wen (June), Tamlyn Tomita (Waverly), Lauren Tom (Lena), Rosalind Chao (Rose). Directed by Wayne Wang and produced by Wang, Amy Tan, Ronald Bass, and Patrick Markey. Screenplay by Tan and Bass.

The Joy Luck Club comes rushing off the screen in a torrent of memories, as if its characters have been saving their stories for years, waiting for the right moment to share them. That moment comes after a death and a reunion that bring the past back in all of its power, and show how the present, too, is affected—how children who think they are so very different are deeply affected by the experiences of their parents.

The movie, based on Amy Tan's 1989 best-selling novel, tells the story of four women who were born in China and eventually came to America, and of their daughters. Around these eight women circle innumerable friends and relatives, both there and here, Chinese and not, in widening circles of experience. What is about to be forgotten are the origins of the women, the stories of how they were born and grew up in a time and culture so very different from the one they now inhabit.

The Joy Luck Club of the title is a group of four older Chinese ladies who meet once a week to play mah-jongg, and compare stories of their families and grandchildren. All have made harrowing journeys from prerevolutionary China to the comfortable homes in San Francisco where they meet. But those old days are not often spoken about, and sometimes the whole truth of them is not known.

June (Ming-Na Wen), the narrator, is the daughter of one of the women, Suyuan (Kieu Chinh). After her mother's death, she decides to take a trip to China, to meet for the first time two half-sisters who still live there. The movie opens at a farewell party, and then, in a series of flashbacks, tells the secrets and stories of all four of the "aunties." In a screenplay remarkable for its complexity and force, *The Joy Luck Club* moves effortlessly between past and present, between what was, and how it became what is. Many different actresses are used to play the daughters and mothers at different ages, and there are many stories, but the movie proceeds with perfect clarity.

We see that the China of the 1930s and 1940s, before the revolution, was an unimaginably different place than it is today. Women were not valued very highly. Those with independent minds and spirits were valued even less than the docile, obedient ones. Life was cheap, especially in wartime. A mother's ability to care for her children was precarious. In many cases, issues from those hard days still affect later generations: The ability of the mothers to relate to their daughters depends on things that have never been said out loud.

How, for example, could June's mother have told of abandoning her firstborn twin girls by the roadside? Suyuan, starving and sick, was sure she would die, and felt her girls would have a better chance of survival if they were not linked to the "bad luck" of a dead mother.

Other stories fall equally hard on Americanized ears. There is the auntie who became the fourth wife of a rich man, and when she bore him the son he desired so much, the boy child was taken from her by the second wife. There are humorous stories, too, including the auntie who prayed before her arranged marriage for a husband "not too old," and got a ten-year-old boy ("Maybe I prayed too hard!").

In America, the mothers find it hard to understand the directions their daughters are taking. Some marry whites, who have bad table manners. They move out of the old neighborhood into houses that seem too modern and cold. One daughter despairs of ever satisfying her mother, who criticizes everything she does.

These stories are about Chinese and Chinese-American characters, but they are universal stories. Anyone with parents or children, which is to say, everyone, will identify with the way that the hopes of one generation can become both the restraints and the inspirations of the next.

The movie is a celebration, too, of the richness of Asian-American acting talent; all of the performers here have appeared in many other films and plays, and I could list their credits, from the old days of *South Pacific* and *The World of Suzie Wong* to recent films like *1,000 Pieces of Gold* and *Come See the Paradise.* But often they were marginalized, or used in "exotic" roles, or placed in stories that were based on what made them different from the dominant culture, instead of what makes them human and universal. *The Joy Luck Club* is like a flowering of talent that has been waiting so long to be celebrated.

Judge Dredd ★ ★
R, 91 m., 1995

Sylvester Stallone (Judge Dredd), Armand Assante (Rico), Rob Schneider (Fergie), Jurgen Prochnow (Judge Griffin), Max Von Sydow (Judge Fargo), Diane Lane (Judge Hershey), Joanna Miles (McGruder), Joan Chen (Ilsa). Directed by Danny Cannon and produced by Charles M. Lippincott and Beau E.L. Marks. Screenplay by William Wisher and Steven E. De Souza.

The first voice we hear in *Judge Dredd* belongs to James Earl (Darth Vader) Jones, reading the words that crawl up the screen, describing a future world in which most of the Earth is a wasteland, and humans huddle in closed, violent megacities. Jones's voice, along with the words crawling up the screen, are a reminder of *Star Wars.* The fact that he has to read them is a reminder that in 1977, when *Star Wars* came out, audiences didn't need to have them read. We are getting closer to the wasteland every day.

The movie is based on a comic book series about that future time, when anarchy reigns, and the citizens massacre one another in "block wars," using machine guns to fight violent battles just for the fun of it, I guess, since the movie never really provides their motivation. The only force for law and order are the Judges—heavily armed and armored cops who double as judge and jury, and often execute criminals right on the spot.

Dredd is played by Sylvester Stallone, who is ideal for a role like this, because he's smart and funny enough to pull it off. The screenplay gives him little help, however, with a love interest (Diane Lane) who never really connects, a comic sidekick named Fergie (Rob Schneider) who seems badly out of tune, and a tag line ("I knew you'd say that") that doesn't exactly rank with "Make my day" or even "I'll be back."

The special effects are messy and cluttered, but atmospheric; they show us a megacity that looks like a cross between the cities in *Blade Runner* and *Total Recall,* with buildings towering into the sky and gangs rumbling in the streets and helpful neon signs that say things like "Store."

Judge Dredd and his partner Judge Hershey (Diane Lane) patrol the streets and shoot it out with bad guys, and Dredd arrests Fergie for being in the apartment of some violent outlaws Dredd has just killed.

"But I had only been there five minutes!" Fergie cries.

"You could have jumped out of the window."

"Forty floors up? That would be suicide!"

"But it's legal," says Dredd, who is an unbending law enforcer until he, himself, is convicted of the murder of a TV newsman. How do they know he did it? Well, the guns of the future imprint each bullet with the DNA of the person who fired it, and so Dredd is shipped off to the Aspen Prison Colony. Then we learn from Senior Judge (Max von Sydow) that Dredd was cloned, and has an identical brother (Armand Assante) who could have also supplied the same DNA. This is an angle the Simpson defense team should not overlook.

The movie cheerfully borrows from everywhere. In addition to the movies already mentioned, it lifts bits of *Mad Max* and *The Hills Have Eyes* in a subplot involving the Angel Family, who live in a cave in the hinterlands and barbecue their human victims. One of the Angel brothers has a dial implanted in his forehead, so his anger level can be adjusted. Nice touch. His I.Q. seems set on defrost.

Judge Dredd never slows down enough to make much sense; it's a *Blade Runner* for audiences with attention deficit disorder. Stallone survives it, but his supporting cast, also including an uninvolved Joan Chen and a tremendously intense Jurgen Prochnow, isn't well used. Only Assante, as the rogue Judge who frames his brother, holds up under the material, although the movie doesn't exploit the brother angle, maybe because that would have involved dialogue of more than one sentence at a time.

Ju Dou ★ ★ ★ ½
NO MPAA RATING, 93 m., 1991

Gong Li (Ju Dou), Li Baotian (Yang Tianqing), Li Wei (Yang Jinshan), Zhang Yi (Yang Tianbai, infant), Zheng Jian (Yang Tianbai, youth). Directed by Zhang Yimou and produced by Zhang Wenze, Yasuyoshi Tokuma, and Hu Jian. Screenplay by Liu Heng.

Sex, it is said, is the only luxury with which the poor are as well supplied as the rich. But, within the rigid Chinese feudal society depicted by *Ju Dou,* that is not quite the case. The movie, which is set in the 1920s but might as well be set a century earlier, tells the story of a wealthy old textile man who marries a juicy young bride and hires a desperate young nephew and enslaves both of them with his cruel will.

The old man owns a factory where he dips bolts of cloth in great vats of bright dyes, and then hangs them on long poles to dry. The cloth is bold and brilliant, the colors of passion, but nothing to compare to the emotional tumult taking place beneath the old villain's roof. He is sadistic and impotent, and entertains himself by tormenting his bride while the nephew listens in the middle of the night. The nephew is too poor, of course, to afford a wife, and the bride too poor to take the husband of her choice. But one day she deliberately reveals herself to the young man, he is easily seduced, and they have a child, which she convinces the old man is his own.

The infant grows into a hateful, strong-willed little monster, while the old man grows older and eventually cripples himself in an accident. He has a cart built, in which he pushes himself around his domain, while the nephew and wife continue their affair. Their deception becomes even more dangerous when the child grows old enough to understand what is going on; ironically, he resembles the sour merchant more than the lusty young man who fathered him.

The ending of *Ju Dou* is as lurid and melodramatic as anything conceived by Edgar Allan Poe or filmed by Buñuel, and it exhibits justice completely untempered by mercy. But long before the gory finale, the Chinese censors had apparently already decided to suppress this film, which was directed by a young turk named Zhang Yimou. The film was suppressed in China, but went on the international festival circuit, and won a best director award at Cannes and the Gold Hugo at Chicago before becoming one of 1990's Oscar nominees in the foreign language category, over the official objections of the Chinese.

Why did the Chinese film establishment find *Ju Dou* so offensive? It is tempting for us to read it as a political parable, to see the old merchant as an example of the old order of Maoism, and the hateful little boy as a symbol of the Red Guard. But the Chinese might just as easily have been offended by the sexuality, which is frank for a Chinese film and for a puritanical society.

The film appealed to me for two reasons. First, because of its unabashed, lurid melodrama, in which the days are filled with scheming and the nights with passion and violence. Second, because of its visual beauty. When the Technicolor company abandoned its classic three-strip process for reproducing color on film, two of its factories were closed down, but the third was packed up and sold to China, and that is why the bright colors in the vats of the textile mill will remind you of a brilliance not seen in Hollywood films since the golden age of the MGM musicals. Not that this story would have been very easily set to music.

Juice ★ ★ ★
R, 90 m., 1992

Omar Epps (Q), Khalil Kain (Raheem), Jermaine Hopkins (Steel), Tupac Shakur (Bishop), Cindy Herron (Yolanda). Directed by Ernest R. Dickerson and produced by David Heyman, Neal H. Moritz, and Peter Frankfurt. Screenplay by Gerard Brown and Dickerson.

There's a scene in *Grand Canyon,* a film released shortly before *Juice,* that's like a setup for the second movie's whole tragic story. In the earlier film, an older black man confronts a group of young punks on the street. One punk has a gun. He asks the older man, "Do you respect me, or do you respect my gun?" The answer is: "You don't have that gun, there's no way we're having this conversation."

That is a dangerous answer, but an honest one, and *Juice* is like a mirror image of the *Grand Canyon* scene; it tells the story of the young men—how they got into a criminal situation, and how they got the gun. It tells one of those stories with the quality of a nightmare, in which foolish young men try to out-macho one another until they get trapped in a violent situation that will forever alter their lives.

The movie was directed and cowritten by Ernest Dickerson, the cinematographer on Spike Lee's films, and like Lee's *Do the Right Thing* it is filled with details of the daily life, fashions, music, and language of a black neighborhood. It introduces its four central characters as they get up in the morning and venture out from poor but supportive homes into New York streets where, as they perceive it, the person with a gun commands respect. At first the movie seems meandering, following these young men through their daily routines, listening to their talk, looking at the street life in their neighborhood, watching the ambition of one nicknamed Q (Omar Epps), who dreams of being a disc jockey in a club.

Then the focus tightens, as everything turns wrong, when Bishop (Tupac Shakur) gets his hands on a gun and decides the four of them should stick up the corner store. There is a sense in which the existence of the gun leads to the necessity of using it; without the cheap handgun, there would be no crime, and lives would be saved. Q doesn't want anything to do with the stickup; his mind is focused on a DJ contest at a local club. But Bishop has the stronger personality and badgers them all into coming along.

The best shot in the movie takes place in a club where Q has just done a successful gig as a DJ and is filled with joy, until he sees the unsmiling faces of his friends in the crowd and realizes he has to leave, now, and commit the stickup. What happens next depends too much on surprise for me to reveal it, but the movie generates a real tension in its closing passages, as it shows its characters trapped in a plot that seems to be unfolding according to its own merciless logic.

Much of the strength of the film comes from the actors, Epps, Shakur, Khalil Kain as Raheem, whose enthusiasm for the stickup ends tragically, and Jermaine Hopkins as Steel, a pudgy innocent. They are able to make us know their characters, which is important if *Juice* is to be more than just a morality play. It is also interesting the way Dickerson's story makes them—and the street culture of cheap handguns—the instruments of their own downfall. There are a lot of cops in the movie, but for a change they are seen not as villains but as street troops in the fight against crime.

It's a common criticism of cinematographers that when they direct their own films, they pay too much attention to style, not enough to the story. The scene-setting opening moments of *Juice* seem almost too picturesque, but then we feel the underlying logic of the story, and Dickerson finds a rhythm that uses the visuals instead of just flaunting them. *Juice*, like *Boyz N the Hood* and *Straight Out of Brooklyn*, is like a reaction to years of movies that have glamorized urban violence. There is a real terror in the faces of these kids as they realize that people have died, that guns kill, and that your life can be ruined, or over, in an instant.

Julia and Julia ★ ★ ★
R, 98 m., 1988

Kathleen Turner (Julia), Gabriel Byrne (Paolo), Sting (Daniel), Gabriele Ferzetti (Paolo's Father), Angela Goodwin (Paolo's Mother), Lidia Broccolino (Carla), Alexander Van Wyk (Marco). Directed by Peter Del Monte and produced by Francesco Pinto and Gaetano Stucchi. Screenplay by Silvia Napolitano, Sandrea Petraglia, and Del Monte.

Julia and Julia tells one of those nightmare stories, like *The Trial*, where the hero is condemned to live in a world in which absolutely nothing can be counted on. The story unfolds as a series of surprises, and since even the first surprise is crucial to the plot, I frankly don't see any way to review the film without spoiling some of the effect. I will, however, carry on, but I advise you not to read any further if you plan to see the film.

The story begins on the wedding day of its heroine, Julia, who is played by Kathleen Turner as a sweet and rather moony young woman not at all like the smart, aggressive characters she usually creates. It is a beautiful day in Italy, in a sunlit garden where even the trees seem to bow in happiness, but a few

hours later Julia and her new husband (Gabriel Byrne) are involved in a road accident, and Byrne is killed.

You see what I mean about not reading any further. Yet how can I review the film at all without discussing such details? And there are more to follow. Turner, an American, decides to stay in Italy. She moves into a small apartment across the street from the large flat that was to be her home. Time passes. One day something strange happens, which the movie shows but does not explain. She passes through some kind of dimension into a different time scheme, a parallel path in which things turned out differently, and her husband did not die, and they have a small boy.

The sequence in which she discovers this is wonderful. She goes to her little flat, which is occupied by a strange woman who insists she has always lived there. She sees lights in the large flat across the street, which she had always refused to sell. Trembling, she climbs the stairs to find Byrne at home with their son, and everyone treating her as if she had been with them all along and none of her tragic memories had ever taken place.

She is, of course, shattered. She does not know how this could have happened, and there is no one she can discuss it with without appearing insane (although I kept wishing she wouldn't internalize everything). She is pathetically grateful to have her happiness back until one moment, completely without warning, when she is plunged back into her other, tragic lifetime. Then she is flipped back to happiness again, sort of like a pingpong ball of fate, and there is the complication of a lover (played by Sting), whom she apparently has taken in her "happy" lifetime. (The rule at the center of these paradoxes is that she always remembers all of the sad lifetime, but only remembers those parts of the happy one that we actually see her experiencing.)

What's going on here? Don't ask me—and don't ask the movie, either. Even the simplest explanation, of parallel time tracks, is one I've borrowed out of old science-fiction novels. *Julia and Julia* wisely declines to offer any explanation at all, preferring to stay completely within Julia's nightmares as she experiences them.

The construction of the story is ingenious and perverse, and has a kind of inner logic of its own, and if there is a flaw, it's that no woman could endure this kind of round-trip more than once, if that much, before being emotionally shattered. I was reminded of Kathleen Turner's work in *Peggy Sue Got Married*, in which she traveled back in time to her own adolescence; think how much more disturbing it would be to travel sideways into the happiness you thought you'd lost.

This is the kind of movie that proves unbearably frustrating to some people, who demand explanations and resent obscurity. I have seen so many movies in which absolutely everything could be predicted that I found *Julia and Julia* perversely entertaining.

Note: This movie wins a footnote in cinematic history as the first feature shot entirely in High-Definition Television and then transferred to film. How does it look? There are a few moments when quick movements seem to trail their shadows behind them, but in general, the quality is comparable to a 16-millimeter print blown up to 35-millimeter. Although the film lacks the sharpness and clarity of a true 35-millimeter print, the result is much better than any previous TV-to-film transfer I've seen.

Jungle Fever ★ ★ ★ ½
R, 132 m., 1991

Wesley Snipes (Flipper Purify), Annabella Sciorro (Angie Tucci), Spike Lee (Cyrus), Ossie Davis (Doctor Purify), Ruby Dee (Lucinda Purify), Samuel L. Jackson (Gator Purify), John Turturro (Paulie Carbone), Lonette McKee (Drew), Anthony Quinn (Mike). Directed, produced, and written by Spike Lee.

Jungle Fever is Spike Lee's term for unhealthy sexual attraction between the races—for relationships based on stereotypes. Too often, he believes, when blacks and whites go to bed with one another, they are motivated, not by love or affection, but by media-based myths about the sexual allure of the other race. Lee has explained this belief in countless interviews, and yet it remains the murkiest element in his new film, which is brilliant when it examines the people who surround his feverish couple, but uncertain when it comes to the lovers themselves.

The victims of *Jungle Fever* are Wesley Snipes, as Flipper, an affluent, married, successful architect, and Anabella Sciorro, as Angie, a temporary office worker. He is African-American; she is Italian-American. She comes to work in his Manhattan office one day, their eyes meet, and the fever starts. Their halting, tentative conversations expand into "working late," eating Chinese food from the take-out, and finally having sex right there on top of the blueprints.

Because I have heard Lee discuss the film, I know he believes that the Snipes and Sciorro characters are blinded to other issues by each other's blackness and whiteness—that she is intrigued by the myth of black male prowess, that he is fascinated by the ideal of white female beauty. But, in fact, neither of these notions is really established in the film, which is least successful and focused in the scenes between its two principals. We never really believe the attraction they feel for one another, we never really understand their relationship, and their romance seems to be mostly an excuse for the other events in the movie to happen—the events that make the film special.

It's as if Lee himself, as a screenwriter, could see these characters only as stereotypes—could not, or would not, get inside of them. They lunge hungrily at one another, but his camera looks away from their passion, is already moving on to the real subjects of his film, which he finds in the communities that the two characters came from.

The black architect comes from a traditional, God-fearing Harlem family. His father (Ossie Davis) is a self-righteous former preacher called the Good Reverend Doctor by one and all. His mother (Ruby Dee) is loving and sensible. There is another son, Gator (Samuel L. Jackson), who is a crackhead, who has gone as far down as Flipper has gone up. Flipper is married to Drew (Lonette McKee), and he loves her, but that has nothing to do with the fever.

The office worker comes from an Italian-American family in Bensonhurst. Angie is engaged to Paulie (John Turturro), who works all day in the luncheonette owned by his father (Anthony Quinn), a hidebound old man who sits around upstairs praying to the photograph of his wife. When word gets back to the local communities about the new romance, it does not go over well. Flipper's wife is enraged and his father deeply offended (not least by the adultery), and all of Angie's relatives and friends react with shock.

But Lee does not leave it at that. He keeps burrowing, finding the truth beneath the pain, in dialogue of brutal honesty, as when Drew reveals her own deepest reasons for being hurt by her husband: She herself is half-white, has always suspected Flipper married her for her lighter skin color, now fears that color is also why he left her. And back in the luncheonette, inhabited by a stable of Italian-American regulars, the news that Paulie's girl is dating a black man is re-

ceived with anger and yet ambiguity by his friends, including one so swarthy that he himself has experienced rejection, yet is doubly racist as a result.

The mysteries and traps of pigmentation have always fascinated Lee, who told uncomfortable truths about them in his second film, *School Daze*, and again this time gives us a lot of frank talk. The best single scene in the movie comes as Drew and her friends sit around talking about black men, in hard truths ranging from sorrow and anger to humor. This scene was improvised over a period of two days by Lee and the actresses, who were asked to contribute their own deepest feelings on the subject.

Meanwhile, there is another story in *Jungle Fever*, the story of Gator, the brother who is a crackhead. Lee shows how drugs can split a family down the middle, so that while one brother is a white-collar success, another is trapped in a hell of addiction. The most harrowing sequence in the movie follows Flipper as he searches for Gator through the demonic sewers where crackheads gather—until finally there is a scene out of Dante, in a crackhouse where the moments of release are surrounded by a great bottomless pall of despair.

As in *Do the Right Thing*, Lee tells his larger story in terms of these many smaller stories—including a subtle development that takes place when the luncheonette operator is told by Angie that she is dating a black man. The Turturro character takes this news surprisingly well, perhaps because he is not much in love with Angie himself, and has developed a soft spot for the sweet black woman who has a nice word for him every morning as she stops in for her coffee and Danish. When he tells the regulars he plans to ask her out, they beat him up almost as an automatic reflex, but he goes off to ring her doorbell anyway.

We sense that this relationship will probably not flower; she does not really see him as someone she can take seriously, and yet Lee seems to be suggesting that at least the Turturro character does not suffer from jungle fever—that he simply finds himself attracted to this woman, admires her, and wants to go out with her. If this relationship had been more fully developed, perhaps we could have contrasted it with the doomed love between Flipper and Angie.

But Lee seems least certain when it comes to the intricacies of the heart. *Jungle Fever* contains two sequences—the girl talk and the crackhouse visit—of amazing power. It contains humor and insight and canny psychology, strong performances, and the fearless discussion of things both races would rather not face. The one area where it is least certain is "jungle fever," which Lee uses as his starting point and then leaves behind as quickly as possible.

Junior ★ ★ ★ ½
PG-13, 110 m., 1994

Arnold Schwarzenegger (Dr. Alexander Hesse), Danny DeVito (Dr. Larry Arbogast), Emma Thompson (Dr. Diana Reddin), Frank Langella (Noah Banes), Pamela Reed (Angela), Judy Collins (Naomi), James Eckhouse (Ned Sneller), Aida Turturro (Louise). Directed and produced by Ivan Reitman. Screenplay by Kevin Wade and Chris Conrad.

The wonder is not that Arnold Schwarzenegger plays a pregnant person in *Junior*, but that he plays one so well. He has an uncanny idea of what will and won't work, and since you expect almost nothing to work, the result is a sort of deliverance. As an actor with big muscles and a balky Austrian accent, you'd think he would be limited, and yet he knows himself so well that it gives him freedom: Is a pregnant Arnold any harder to believe, really, than Arnold as Conan the Barbarian?

He begins in *Junior* as a scientist named Hesse, with no charm and no personality, an automaton whose only reaction, when his research funding is yanked, is to pack his bags and head back to Europe. Even his partner, a fellow researcher named Arbogast (Danny DeVito), doesn't like him ("You have all the warmth and charm of a walleyed pike"). But Arbogast is convinced they're on the trail of a fertility drug that will make millions, and in a last-ditch effort he convinces Hesse to experiment by trying the drug on himself.

This is a dubious procedure, because Arnold must first be implanted with a fertilized human egg—unusual for a woman, unheard of for a man. It's a good thing Arbogast is a persuasive talker; DeVito plays him with a conspiratorial charm, talking about the "beauty of the plan" as if it's something anyone would be lucky to participate in. The two doctors borrow an egg, Arnold donates the sperm, they inject the result into his body, and Arnold starts taking daily doses of their miracle drug.

The experiment is not only a success, but Schwarzenegger actually becomes pregnant.

The movie wisely never even attempts to explain how this is possible in a person without a womb; hard science is not the strong point here. The movie's comedy, and some other scenes that are sort of touching, all come out of the man's experience as he begins to feel motherly toward his unborn child.

I know this sounds odd, but Schwarzenegger is perfect for the role. Observe his acting carefully in *Junior*, and you'll see skills that many "serious" actors could only envy. He never reaches for an effect. He never grabs for a joke. He never wrings an emotion out of reluctant material. He plays the role absolutely straight, trusting the material to make the points and get the laughs. This is probably the only way this story could have worked, but not every actor would have known that.

Schwarzenegger is helped mightily by being flanked by three superb comic actors: DeVito, whose crazy enthusiasm makes the scheme almost halfway convincing; Emma Thompson, as the scientist who takes over Schwarzenegger's old lab and makes an unexpected contribution to the experiment; and Pamela Reed, as DeVito's ex-wife, who is pregnant herself, possibly by a member of Aerosmith. DeVito and Thompson turn their scenes into a seminar for the study and exercise of the double take; the way they react to developments is funnier than the developments themselves. One of Thompson's gifts, which is precious here, is a way of cheerfully making the best of obviously catastrophic situations.

The movie's plot is more or less preordained by the progress of a pregnancy. We follow Arnold through morning sickness, cramps, visits to the ultrasound lab, and natural childbirth classes, all given a spin by the need to keep his condition as secret as possible. The writers, Kevin Wade and Chris Conrad, are endlessly inventive with explanations: When the director of an expectant mom's center (Judy Collins) finds it odd that her newest client is a muscle-bound six-footer, Arnold haltingly reveals that he is an East German athlete, victimized by illegal hormone treatments.

The most unexpected thing about the movie is not that it's funny, which we expect, but that it's sweet. It's one of those films you sit through with an almost continuous smile. It's goofy and ridiculous and preposterous, and yet it makes you feel good, and there is something oddly heartwarming about the sight of this macho guy melting with feelings of protectiveness and maternal concern. The

scenes with the Thompson character have a special spin, too, because in a complicated way both of these characters have to work both sides of the emotional fence.

Junior was directed by Ivan Reitman *(Ghostbusters)*, who also directed two other Schwarzenegger comedies, *Kindergarten Cop* (1990) and *Twins* (1988). They make a good team. They both understand that in movie acting, what matters more than range, sometimes, is accuracy. There may be a lot of roles Arnold Schwarzenegger could not play. But there are also roles no one else could play, and they don't all involve a guy firing missiles at a skyscraper. A lot of actors can hold big machine guns and stand convincingly in front of special effects and explosions. Not many can stand in front of a camera and be nine months pregnant, and actually make us care.

Note: In an unexpected way, Junior *is a good family movie, for parents and adolescents to see together, and then to discuss in terms of male and female roles and responsibilities.*

Jurassic Park ★ ★ ★
PG-13, 123 m., 1993

Sam Neill (Grant), Laura Dern (Ellie), Jeff Goldblum (Malcolm), Richard Attenborough (Hammond), Bob Peck (Muldoon), Martin Ferrero (Gennaro), B.D. Wong (Wu), Wayne Knight (Nedry). Directed by Steven Spielberg and produced by Kathleen Kennedy and Gerald R. Molen. Screenplay by Michael Crichton and David Koepp.

When young Steven Spielberg was first offered the screenplay for *Jaws*, he said he would direct the movie on one condition: that he didn't have to show the shark for the first hour. By slowly building the audience's apprehension, he felt, the shark would be much more impressive when it finally arrived.

He was right. I wish he had remembered that lesson when he was preparing *Jurassic Park*, his new thriller set in a Pacific-island theme park where real dinosaurs have been grown from long-dormant DNA molecules. The movie delivers all too well on its promise to show us dinosaurs. We see them early and often, and they are indeed a triumph of special effects artistry, but the movie is lacking other qualities that it needs even more, such as a sense of awe and wonderment, and strong human story values.

It's clear, seeing this long-awaited project, that Spielberg devoted most of his effort to creating the dinosaurs. The human characters are a ragtag bunch of half-realized, sketched-in personalities who exist primarily to scream, utter dire warnings, and outwit the monsters.

Richard Attenborough, as the millionaire who builds the park, is given a few small dimensions—he loves his grandchildren, he's basically a good soul, he realizes the error of tampering with nature. But there was an opportunity here to make his character grand and original, colorful and oversize, and instead he comes across as unfocused and benign.

As the film opens, two dinosaur experts (Sam Neill and Laura Dern) arrive at the park, along with a mathematician played by Jeff Goldblum, whose function in the story is to lounge about uttering vague philosophical imprecations. Also along are Attenborough's grandchildren, and a lawyer, who is the first to be eaten by a dinosaur.

Attenborough wants the visitors to have a preview of his new park, where actual living prehistoric animals dwell in enclosures behind tall steel fences, helpfully labeled "10,000 volts." The visitors set off on a tour in remote-controlled utility vehicles, which stall when an unscrupulous employee (Wayne Knight) shuts down the park's computer program so he can smuggle out some dinosaur embryos. Meanwhile, a tropical storm hits the island, the beasts knock over the fences, and Sam Neill is left to shepherd the kids back to safety while they're hunted by towering meat-eaters.

The plot to steal the embryos is handled on the level of a TV sitcom. The Knight character, an overwritten and overplayed blubbering fool, drives his Jeep madly through the storm and thrashes about in the forest. If this subplot had been handled cleverly—with skill and subtlety, as in a caper movie—it might have added to the film's effect. Instead, it's as if one of the Three Stooges wandered into the story.

The subsequent events—after the creatures get loose—follow an absolutely standard outline, similar in bits and pieces to all the earlier films in this genre, from *The Lost World* and *King Kong* right up to 1993's *Carnosaur*. True, because the director is Spielberg, there is a high technical level to the execution of the clichés. Two set pieces are especially effective: a scene where a beast mauls a car with screaming kids inside, and another where the kids play hide-and-seek with two creatures in the park's kitchen.

But consider what could have been. There

is a scene very early in the film where Neill and Dern, who have studied dinosaurs all of their lives, see living ones for the first time. The creatures they see are tall, majestic leaf-eaters, grazing placidly in the treetops. There is a sense of grandeur to them. And that is the sense lacking in the rest of the film, which quickly turns into a standard monster movie, with screaming victims fleeing from roaring dinosaurs.

Think back to another ambitious special-effects picture from Spielberg, *Close Encounters of the Third Kind* (1977). That was a movie about the *idea* of visitors from outer space. It inspired us to think what an awesome thing it would be if Earth were visited by living alien beings. You left that movie shaken and a little transformed. It was a movie that had faith in the intelligence and curiosity of its audience.

In the sixteen years since it was made, however, big-budget Hollywood seems to have lost its confidence that audiences can share big dreams. *Jurassic Park* throws a lot of dinosaurs at us, and because they look terrific (and indeed they do), we're supposed to be grateful. I have the uneasy feeling that if Spielberg had made *Close Encounters* today, we would have seen the aliens in the first ten minutes, and by the halfway mark they'd be attacking Manhattan with death rays.

Because the movie delivers on the bottom line, I'm giving it three stars. You want great dinosaurs; you got great dinosaurs. Spielberg enlivens the action with lots of nice little touches; I especially liked a sequence where a smaller creature leaps suicidally on a larger one, and they battle to the death. On the monster movie level, the movie works and is entertaining. But with its profligate resources, it could have been so much more.

Notes: (1) The movie's much-ballyhooed new digital sound system is a disappointment. It does a great job of rendering the special effects, all right—roars and rumbles and screams and breaking glass. But much of the dialogue is unintelligible. In an opening sequence, neither I nor five people I spoke to could understand anything one character said. I noticed the same phenomenon last month at Cannes, during a demonstration of another new digital sound system. The human voice doesn't benefit from being jacked up to such keening fidelity that it no longer breaks down into understandable words. (2) This movie is rated PG-13, "for intense science fiction terror." Take the warning seriously. Several sequences are much too violent and nightmare-inspiring for younger viewers.

Just Cause ★ ★
R, 102 m., 1995

Sean Connery (Armstrong), Laurence Fishburne (Tanny Brown), Kate Capshaw (Laurie Armstrong), Blair Underwood (Bobby Earl), Ruby Dee (His Grandmother), Ed Harris (Blair Sullivan). Directed by Arne Glimcher and produced by Lee Rich, Glimcher, and Steve Perry. Screenplay by Jeb Stuart and Peter Stone.

Just Cause starts out strong and then, boy, does it jump the rails. It's the kind of movie where you look at the screen and start imagining the pushpins holding the three-by-five cards to the corkboard in a Hollywood office, as the filmmakers try to keep the plot straight. When the movie's over, you realize that the first hour only *seemed* convincing: The whole movie is made out of thin air.

As the movie opens, a Harvard law professor named Armstrong (Sean Connery) is attacking capital punishment in a campus debate. Then an elderly black woman (Ruby Dee) hands him a letter from her son, who is on Florida's death row for a murder he says he didn't commit. Armstrong tries to hand the letter back, but she looks him fiercely in the eye, and says, "No, no, you keep it. It's got your name on it." This is the best scene in the movie.

Armstrong goes home, where his wife, Laurie (Kate Capshaw), is masterminding a party for their young kids. She reads the letter. Then she encourages him to take the case, even though he hasn't practiced law in twenty-five years: "Every once in a while, you gotta get a little bloody. It's good for the soul." This seems curious. Not many mothers of small children encourage the other half of a May-December marriage to take complicated pro bono cases on Florida's death row. Later, her words make sense—or at least they are explained.

Armstrong flies south to meet Bobby Earl, the prisoner (Blair Underwood), and we get flashbacks showing how Bobby was arrested on suspicion of the kidnapping, rape, and murder of a little girl. In a harrowing scene, a local black cop named Tanny Brown (Laurence Fishburne) beats a confession out of him, at one point clicking a pistol in Bobby's mouth in a version of Russian roulette. Armstrong's investigation shows that Bobby Earl was railroaded, that the forensic evidence doesn't hold up, and that he got a pathetic defense from a local attorney (Ned Beatty), who whines: "I lost half of my business defending that SOB—and he got the chair! Can you imagine what it would have been like if he'd been acquitted?"

By now we feel we're on pretty sound ground. We are not, although I must be cautious not to give away plot details, since this movie is, finally, all plot. There are a couple of good clues early on that everything is not as it appears. For example, the movie illustrates the Law of Conservation of Star Power, which teaches, "In a thriller, a star who receives second billing to the hero, and whose role seems clear at the end of the first hour, will be revealed as the opposite of what he seems." The movie also makes good use of the Tangled Web Syndrome, which is found in thrillers where all of the events of today are revealed to have their roots in long-ago events.

But enough. Most people will want to see this movie because of the presence of Sean Connery in the leading role, and on that score, if on no other, they will get their money's worth. When it comes to expressing quiet wrath, Connery is an actor like few others, and here, where he is a mild-mannered law professor and family man, he keeps his action side well concealed until an absurd climax that has him all but wrestling alligators. I especially enjoyed the scenes where he moseys through a hostile southern town, keeping his cool while the local crackers insult him, and always remembering to thank them "for your time."

If his role is the strong center of the film, none of the other actors have an easy time of it. That's because the corkscrews of the plot prevent them from being consistent from beginning to end. Reflect, after you see the film, about how hard it must have been for a couple of the actors to describe 180-degree turns in their motivations. The movie depends on an audience with a short attention span, since if we remember some of the events of the first thirty minutes clearly, we will be asking tricky questions long after the movie is over.

My basic complaint with *Just Cause* is that it's simply an exercise in plot manipulation. Take out the violence and perversion, take out the nasty serial killer in the next cell (played by Ed Harris with Hannibal Lecter's lighting and camera angles), take out the police brutality and the victimized children, and what you're left with is pure Agatha Christie. There is no psychological depth, no real motivation, no human values to weigh: just characters jerked here and there, like puppets in an arbitrary plot. I was serious about those three-by-five cards. They're what writers and directors use to keep everything straight in a movie like this. The audience could use some, too.

K

Kagemusha ★ ★ ★ ★
PG, 160 m., 1980

Tatsuya Nakadai (Shingen and Kagemusha), Tsutomu Yamazaki (Nobukado), Kenichi Hagiwara (Katsuyori), Jinpachi Nezu (Bodyguard), Shuji Otaki (Fire General). Directed by Akira Kurosawa and produced by Kurosawa and Tomoyuki Tanaka. Screenplay by Kurosawa and Masato Ide.

Kagemusha, we learn, means "shadow warrior" in Japanese, and Akira Kurosawa's great film tells the story of a man who becomes the double, or shadow, of a great warrior. It also teaches the lesson that shadows or appearances are as important as reality, but that men cannot count on either shadows or reality.

Kagemusha is a samurai drama by the director who most successfully introduced the genre to the West (with such classics as *The Seven Samurai* and *Yojimbo*), and who, at the age of seventy, made an epic that dares to wonder what meaning the samurai code—or any human code—really has in the life of an individual man. His film is basically the story of one such man, a common thief who, because of his astonishing resemblance to the warlord Shingen, is chosen as Shingen's double. When Shingen is mortally wounded in battle, the great Takeda clan secretly replaces him with the double—so their enemies will not learn that Shingen is dead. Thus begins a period of three years during which the kagemusha is treated by everyone, even his son and his mistresses, as if he were the real Shingen. Only his closest advisers know the truth.

But he is not Lord Shingen. And so every scene is undercut with irony. It is important that both friends and enemies believe Shingen is alive; his appearance, or shadow, creates both the respect of his clan and the cau-

tion of his enemies. If he is unmasked, he is useless; as Shingen's double, he can send hundreds of men to be killed, and his own guards will willingly sacrifice their lives for him. But as himself, he is worthless, and when he *is* unmasked, he's banished into the wilderness.

What is Kurosawa saying here? I suspect the answer can be found in a contrast between two kinds of scenes. His film contains epic battle scenes of astonishing beauty and scope. And then there are the intimate scenes in the throne room, the bedroom, the castles, and battlefield camps. The great battle scenes glorify the samurai system. Armies of thousands of men throw themselves heedlessly at death, for the sake of pride. But the intimate scenes undermine that glorious tradition; as everyone holds their breath, Shingen's double is tested in meetings with his son, his mistresses, and his horse. They know him best of all. If they are not fooled, all of the panoply and battlefield courage is meaningless, because the Takeda clan has lost the leader who is their figurehead; the illusion that he exists creates the clan's reality.

Kurosawa made this film after a decade of personal travail. Although he is often considered the greatest living Japanese director, he was unable to find financial backing in Japan when he first tried to make *Kagemusha*. He made a smaller film, *Dodeskaden*, which was not successful. He tried to commit suicide, but failed. He was backed by the Russians and went to Siberia to make the beautiful *Dersu Uzala* (1976), about a man of the wilderness. But *Kagemusha* remained his obsession, and he was finally able to make it only when Hollywood directors Francis Ford Coppola and George Lucas helped him find U.S. financing.

The film he finally made is simple, bold, and colorful on the surface, but very thought-

ful. Kurosawa seems to be saying that great human endeavors (in this case, samurai wars) depend entirely on large numbers of men sharing the same fantasies or beliefs. It is entirely unimportant, he seems to be suggesting, whether or not the beliefs are based on reality—all that matters is that men accept them. But when a belief is shattered, the result is confusion, destruction, and death. At the end of *Kagemusha*, for example, the son of the real Lord Shingen orders his troops into a suicidal charge, and their deaths are not only unnecessary but meaningless, because they are not on behalf of the sacred person of the warlord.

There are great images in this film: Of a breathless courier clattering down countless steps, of men passing in front of a blood-red sunset, of a dying horse on a battlefield. But Kurosawa's last image—of the dying kagemusha floating in the sea, swept by tidal currents past the fallen standard of the Takeda clan—summarizes everything: ideas and men are carried along heedlessly by the currents of time, and historical meaning *seems* to emerge when both happen to be swept in the same way at the same time.

Kalifornia ★ ★ ★
R, 117 m., 1993

Brad Pitt (Early Grayce), Juliette Lewis (Adele Corners), David Duchovny (Brian Kessler), Michelle Forbes (Carrie Laughlin), Sierra Pecheur (Mrs. Musgrave), Gregory Mars Martin (Walter Livesy). Directed by Dominic Sena and produced by Steve Golin, Aris McGarry, and Joni Sighvatsson. Screenplay by Tim Metcalfe.

Be careful what you ask for. You may get it.
—Old saying

Once in a very long while I see a film that cuts through the surface of movie violence and says something important about the murderous energies at loose in society. *Kalifornia* is such a film—terrifying and horrifying, yes, but also unflinchingly honest, and so well acted that for most of the film I abandoned any detachment and just watched it as if I were observing the lives of real people.

The film brings together four people who are, by themselves, fairly recognizable types. But while an ordinary film would simply plug them into a story, this film forces them to actually deal with one another, so that we see a confrontation between voyeurs who are turned on by violence (as long as it's at arm's length) and those who are actually capable of killing.

The movie introduces us to two couples. Brian and Carrie are smart, ambitious yuppies. Early and Adele are wretched white trash. Brian (David Duchovny) is a writer with an interest in mass murderers. Carrie (Michelle Forbes) is a photographer, a would-be Mapplethorpe with a low, no-nonsense voice and a certain cool detachment. They want to move to California, and Brian suggests a cross-country tour of the sites of famous mass murders. She can take the pictures, he can write the text, and they can get a book out of it.

Early and Adele, played by Brad Pitt and Juliette Lewis in two of the most harrowing and convincing performances I've ever seen, live in a slovenly rented trailer. He's on parole. She's a slack-jawed child-woman who repeats clichés that seem to have been imperfectly learned from television. The landlord is on their case about the rent.

Brian and Carrie need someone to share the gas and driving for their trip out West. They put up a card on the bulletin board at the university. Bad luck: Early, who has been sent over to the campus by his parole officer to take a job as a janitor, sees the card and decides it's time to take off for California with Adele. Of course, that's a parole violation, but what the hell: Before he leaves, he murders and buries his landlord to teach him a lesson about bugging people for the rent.

Most of the film takes place on the road, as the writer and photographer gradually become aware of the nature of the people who are sharing the ride. It is here that the movie reveals its greatness. A lesser film would simply be a thriller in which the protagonists would desperately scheme to escape from the killers in their car. *Kalifornia* is much more subtle than that. It's about the strange fascination that some people feel for those who seem tougher and more "authentic." Usually those who romanticize in that way have never had to deal with anyone who hurts others just for the entertainment value.

There's a deep class difference between the two couples—between Brian, with his yuppie sportswear, and Early, with his greasy hair and careless tattoos and smelly socks. And between the feminist Carrie and Adele, who observes curiously, "I used to smoke, but Early broke me of it." The yuppies, though, with their liberals' reluctance to show bad manners, try to "accept" these two strangers and to make allowances for their behavior.

A certain bond even grows between Brian and Early. Brian, for example, has never fired a gun. Early has. Brian is fascinated by Early's gun (Carrie is terrified). Early lets him shoot out some windows in an abandoned factory, and Brian is like a kid with a toy. It's also exciting—a rush, a high—when the two guys go out drinking one night, and when a guy in the bar takes offense to Brian's appearance, Early steps in and kicks the guy almost to death.

Early is not stupid, and has a better sense of Brian than Brian has of him. As Carrie gradually discovers that Early beats Adele and is probably a sociopath, Brian is being halfway seduced by Early's lawlessness. Not that he wants to get involved, of course. But it's intriguing to be so close to it.

Gradually, by slow, logical steps, the director, Dominic Sena, and the writer, Tim Metcalfe, reveal to Brian and Carrie the full reality of the situation they've gotten themselves into. Here's a middle-class couple who thought it would be a gas to revisit the scenes of mass murders, and whaddaya know? They end up with a real mass murderer, right in the same car, and it isn't fun. Not at all.

Dominic Sena is a director unknown to me, but he shows the kind of mastery of material here that I've seen in other early films such as Martin Scorsese's *Mean Streets*, Terence Malick's *Badlands*, John McNaughton's *Henry: Portrait of a Serial Killer*, and Carl Franklin's *One False Move*. The suspense screws up tighter than a drumhead. The characters remain believable; we have a conflict of personalities, not stereotypes. The action coexists seamlessly with the message.

A woman sitting behind me at the screening objected out loud, from time to time, to the movie's "depravity." If she hates it so much, I wondered, why doesn't she leave? Afterward, she admitted it was "very well made," but that she feared "the wrong people could see it and get bad ideas." I think the point of *Kalifornia* is that it's altogether too comforting to believe that people need inspiration to hurt and kill. Some people, the movie says, are simply evil. They lack all values and sympathy. And they don't need anybody to give them ideas.

The Karate Kid ★ ★ ★ ★
PG, 126 m., 1984

Ralph Macchio (Daniel), Noriyuki "Pat" Morita (Miyagi), Elisabeth Shue (Ali), Martin Kove (Kreese), William Zabka (Johnny). Directed by John G. Avildsen and produced by Jerry Weintraub. Written by Robert Mark Kamen.

I didn't want to see this movie. I took one look at the title and figured it was either (a) a sequel to *Toenails of Vengeance*, or (b) an adventure pitting Ricky Schroeder against the Megaloth Man. I was completely wrong. *The Karate Kid* was one of the nice surprises of 1984—an exciting, sweet-tempered, heartwarming story with one of the most interesting friendships in a long time. The friends come from different worlds. A kid named Daniel (Ralph Macchio) is a New Jersey teen-ager who moves with his mother to Los Angeles. An old guy named Miyagi (Pat Morita) is the Japanese janitor in their apartment building. When Daniel starts to date the former girlfriend of the toughest kid in the senior class, the kid starts pounding on Daniel's head on a regular basis. Daniel tries to fight back, but this is a Southern California kid, and so of course he has a black belt in karate. Enter Mr. Miyagi, who seems to be a harmless old eccentric with a curious hobby: He tries to catch flies with chopsticks. It turns out that Miyagi is a karate master, a student not only of karate fighting but of the total philosophy of the martial arts. He agrees to take Daniel as his student.

And then begins the wonderful center section of *The Karate Kid,* as the old man and the kid from Jersey become friends. Miyagi's system of karate instruction is offbeat, to say the least. He puts Daniel to work shining cars, painting fences, scrubbing the bottoms of pools. Daniel complains that he isn't learning karate, he's acting as free labor. But there is a system to Mr. Miyagi's training.

The Karate Kid was directed by John G. Avildsen, who made *Rocky*. It ends with the same sort of climactic fight scene; Daniel faces his enemies in a championship karate tournament. But the heart of this movie isn't in the fight sequences, it's in the relationships. And in addition to Daniel's friendship with Miyagi, there's also a sweet romantic liaison with Ali (Elisabeth Shue), who is your standard girl from the right side of town and has the usual snobbish parents.

Macchio is an unusual, interesting choice for Daniel. He's not the basic handsome Hollywood teen-ager but a thin, tall, intense kid with a way of seeming to talk to himself. His delivery always sounds natural, even offhand; he never seems to be reading a line. He's a good, sound, interesting lead, but the movie really belongs to Pat Morita, an actor who has been around a long time (he was Arnold on "Happy Days") without ever having a role anywhere near this good. Morita makes Miyagi into an example of applied serenity. In a couple of scenes where he has to face down a hostile karate coach, Miyagi's words are so carefully chosen they don't give the other guy any excuse to get violent; Miyagi uses the language as carefully as his hands or arms to ward off blows and gain an advantage. It's refreshing to see a completely original character like this old man. *The Karate Kid* is a sleeper with a title that gives you the wrong idea: It's one of 1984's best movies.

The Killing Fields ★ ★ ★ ★
R, 139 m., 1984

Sam Waterston (Sydney Schanberg), Dr. Haing S. Ngor (Dith Pran), John Malkovich (Al Rockoff), Craig T. Nelson (Military Attaché), Athol Fugard (Dr. Sundesval). Directed by Roland Joffe and produced by David Puttnam. Screenplay by Bruce Robinson.

There's a strange thing about stories based on what the movies insist on calling "real life." The haphazard chances of life, the unanticipated twists of fate, have a way of getting smoothed down into Hollywood formulas, so that what might once have happened to a real person begins to look more and more like what might once have happened to John Wayne. One of the risks taken by *The Killing Fields* is to cut loose from that tradition, to tell us a story that does not have a traditional Hollywood structure, and to trust that we'll find the characters so interesting that we won't miss the cliché. It is a risk that works, and that helps make this into a really affecting experience.

The "real life" story behind the movie is by now well-known. Sydney Schanberg, a correspondent for the *New York Times*, covered the invasion of Cambodia with the help of Dith Pran, a local journalist and translator. When the country fell to the communist Khmer Rouge, the lives of all foreigners were immediately at risk, and Schanberg got out along with most of his fellow Western correspondents. He offered Pran a chance to leave with him, but Pran elected to stay. And when the Khmer Rouge drew a bamboo curtain around Cambodia, Pran disappeared into a long silence. Back home in New York, Schanberg did what he could to discover information about his friend; for example, he wrote about four hundred letters to organizations like the Red Cross. But it was a futile exercise, and Schanberg had given up his friend for dead, when one day four years later word came that Pran was still alive and had made it across the border to a refugee camp. The two friends were reunited, in one of the rare happy endings that come out of a period of great suffering.

As a human story, this is a compelling one. As a Hollywood story, it obviously will not do because the last half of the movie is essentially Dith Pran's story, told from his point of view. Hollywood convention has it that the American should fight his way back into the occupied country (accompanied by renegade Green Berets and Hell's Angels, and Rambo, if possible), blast his way into a prison camp, and save his buddy. That was the formula for *Uncommon Valor* and *Missing in Action*, two box-office hits, and in *The Deer Hunter* one friend went back to Vietnam to rescue another. Sitting in New York writing letters is not quite heroism on the same scale. And yet, what else could Schanberg do? And, more to the point, what else could Dith Pran do, in the four years of his disappearance, but try to disguise his origins and his education, and pass as an illiterate peasant—one of the countless prisoners of Khmer Rouge work camps? By telling his story, and by respecting it, *The Killing Fields* becomes a film of an altogether higher order than the Hollywood revenge thrillers.

The movie begins in the early days of the journalistic coverage of Cambodia. We meet Schanberg (Sam Waterston) and Pran (played by Dr. Haing S. Ngor, whose own story is an uncanny parallel to his character's), and we sense the strong friendship and loyalty that they share. We also absorb the conditions in the country, where warehouses full of Coca-Cola are blown up by terrorists who know a symbolic target when they see one. Life is a routine of hanging out at cafes and restaurants and official briefings, punctuated by an occasional trip to the front, where the American view of things does not seem to be reflected by the suffering that the correspondents witness.

The whole atmosphere of this period is suggested most successfully by the character of an American photographer, played by John Malkovich as a cross between a dopehead and a hard-bitten newsman. He is not stirred into action very easily, and still less easily stirred to caring, but when an occasion rises (for example, the need to forge a passport for Pran), he reveals the depth of his feeling. As the Khmer Rouge victory becomes inevitable, there are scenes of incredible tension, especially one in which Dith Pran saves the lives of his friends by some desperate fast talking with the cadres of adolescent rebels who would just as soon shoot them. Then there is the confusion of the evacuation of the U.S. Embassy and a last glimpse of Dith Pran before he disappears for four years.

In a more conventional film, he would, of course, have really disappeared, and we would have followed the point of view of the Schanberg character. But this movie takes the chance of switching points of view in midstream, and the last half of the film belongs to Dith Pran, who sees his country turned into an insane parody of a one-party state, ruled by the Khmer Rouge with instant violence and a savage intolerance for any reminders of the French and American presence of the colonial era. Many of the best scenes in the film's second half are essentially played without dialogue, as Pran works in the fields, disguises his origins, and waits for his chance.

The film is a masterful achievement on all the technical levels—it does an especially good job of convincing us with its Asian locations—but the best moments are the human ones, the conversations, the exchanges of trust, the waiting around, the sudden fear, the quick bursts of violence, the desperation. At the center of many of those scenes is Dr. Haing S. Ngor, a non-actor who was recruited for the role from the ranks of Cambodian refugees in California, and who brings to it a simple sincerity that is absolutely convincing. Sam Waterston is effective in the somewhat thankless role of Sydney Schanberg, and among the carefully drawn vignettes are Craig T. Nelson as a military attaché and Athol Fugard as Dr. Sundesval.

The American experience in Southeast Asia has given us a great film epic *(Apocalypse Now)* and a great drama *(The Deer Hunter)*. Here is the story told a little closer to the ground, of people who were not very important and not very powerful, who got caught up in events that were indifferent to them, but never stopped trying to do their best and their most courageous.

Killing Zoe ★ ★ ½
R, 96 m., 1994

Eric Stoltz (Zed), Julie Delpy (Zoe), Jean-Hugues Anglade (Eric), Tai Thai (Francois), Bruce Ramsey (Ricardo), Kario Salem (Jean), Salvador Xurev (Claude), Gary Kemp (Oliver). Directed by Roger Roberts Avary and produced by Samuel Hadida. Screenplay by Avary.

Killing Zoe is Generation X's first bank caper movie, an ultraviolent screamfest about a soft-spoken American who gets involved with a gang of drug-crazed Parisian thieves and blunders into a hostage situation. It must have been even more exhausting to make this film than it is to watch it. But it's made with a kind of manic joy that makes me suspect its writer-director, Roger Roberts Avary, might develop into a considerable filmmaker, once he thinks of something to say.

The movie stars Eric Stoltz as Zed, a shaggy-haired American safecracking expert who met the Frenchman Eric (Jean-Hugues Anglade) during a student exchange program. They have remained fast friends since those carefree schooldays, when they robbed minimarts together, and now Zed has flown to Paris to open the safe of the bank Eric plans to rob.

First, though, Eric meets Zoe (Julie Delpy), a hooker who is sent to his room by a helpful cab driver. Zoe is, of course, not "really" a prostitute, but a student, very beautiful, who takes a client now and then to pay for her tuition. I looked at the credits and, yep, sure enough, the movie's executive producer is Quentin Tarantino; the trademark of his projects is that the only way guys meet girls is if they're hookers—but very nice hookers, of course, like the Patricia Arquette character in Tarantino's screenplay *True Romance*, who had only been hooking for three days, I think, before she met Mr. Right.

Anyway, Zed and Zoe make blissful love. (Zed supplies her with an orgasm the likes of which she has never experienced before—another clue that this movie benefits from a certain postadolescent male sexual idealism.) Then Eric turns up and violently throws the naked Zoe out of Zed's room. Zed, very curiously, hardly stirs in protest at this behavior, which says something about him or about Avary, and I guess it's Avary, because later Zed is going to be quite solicitous of Zoe.

So. Eric takes Zed on a heroin-fueled tour of the Parisian underworld, a shadowy Hades of jazz clubs and dark streets. This is the kind of movie that treats drugs approximately the same way Wimpy treats hamburgers. And the next day, still hung over and confused, Eric and his ragtag gang take Zed along to the bank heist—where they screw things up, kill someone, and have to take everyone in the bank hostage.

Will it surprise anyone that one of the hostages is Zoe? Hardly, given the movie's title. Zoe works days as a bank clerk. Her tuition must really be high. Avary's screenplay is carefully constructed to isolate Zed downstairs in the vault area, so he doesn't know that Eric is going berserk upstairs, terrifying everyone, as a bloodbath develops and police ring the building.

Watching this movie, it occurred to me that after years of waiting we are finally harvesting the fruit of the film generation. Avary, who is a few years younger than Tarantino, "began his career," as his bio puts it, "making aggressive Super-8 shorts at the age of thirteen." I love that "aggressive." *Killing Zoe* looks exactly like the first feature of a guy who grew up devouring videos, who loves movies, and who jumped at the chance to make one. When his producer found an empty bank building (in Los Angeles, where much of the film was actually shot), Avary naturally said, Hey! Let's make a heist movie!

If you look at it like that—as an action-packed bloodbath mostly shot on a few sets with a low budget and hard-working actors—*Killing Zoe* is commendable. Like an earlier generation that started with 1960s exploitation pictures (Coppola, Scorsese, Hopper, De Palma, Nicholson), Avary is getting his foot in the door. That's great, but I just hope he realizes it's going to take more than kinetic energy to string out a whole career.

His characters are thin and undeveloped, his attitudes toward violence and drugs owe more to scene-setting than to substance, and the ending of his movie can be justified only in the heady atmosphere of a desperate story conference. And reading the movie's press notes is like a short course in hype, except Avary seems to be hyping himself: "Being inside the bank is like being inside Eric's brain," he's quoted. "Zoe means 'life' in Latin, so the title of the movie can be interpreted as *Killing Life*." "Eric can be likened to the Reagan/Bush years—they kept everyone happy through hysteria."

Et cetera. Avary, who was thirteen when the Reagan-Bush years began, may be relieved to learn that not everyone was happy then, and that when it comes to keeping people happy through hysteria, his own filmmaking style owes more than a little to the methods and attributes of Reagan and Bush.

But you know what? I like this guy. A couple of days ago I was surfing through the messages on CompuServe, and I found one in the ShowBiz Forum headed "Live in LA?" "If you do," the message said, "be sure to see 'Killing Zoe'! It's a terrific movie," etc. Idly, I looked up to see who sent the message. It was Roger Avary. Anyone with that kind of zeal and fighting spirit for his work, is sooner or later going to do something great. You mark my words.

Kindergarten Cop ★ ★ ★
PG-13, 110 m., 1990

Arnold Schwarzenegger (Kimble), Penelope Ann Miller (Joyce), Pamela Reed (Phoebe), Linda Hunt (Miss Scholwski), Richard Tyson (Crisp), Carroll Baker (Eleanor Crisp). Directed by Ivan Reitman and produced by Reitman and Brian Grazer. Screenplay by Murray Salem, Herschel Weingrod, and Timothy Harris.

Kindergarten Cop is made up out of parts that shouldn't fit, but somehow they do, making a slick entertainment out of the improbable, the impossible, and Arnold Schwarzenegger. He plays a cop who finds himself teaching kindergarten as part of an undercover effort to locate a little boy and his mother. There is no way that Schwarzenegger can plausibly teach class, but that doesn't prevent him from finding warmhearted possibilities in the role—and it doesn't get in the way of several big laughs, either.

The movie opens with Arnold and his cop partner (Pamela Reed) on the trail of a vicious swine of a drug dealer and momma's boy, played with smarmy conviction by Richard Tyson. Tyson and his mother (Carroll Baker) are eager to discover the whereabouts of his ex-wife and their son. So is Arnold, because he dreams of nailing this creep, and also because he believes that the ex-wife may have $3 million of Tyson's drug earnings.

The trail leads to a storybook town in the Pacific Northwest, where Schwarzenegger and Reed believe the little boy is attending kindergarten. Reed used to be a schoolteacher, and so they convince the local school authorities to let her teach the kindergarten class—hoping to pick up clues, even though the little boy and his mother have changed their names. Then Reed gets food poisoning, and it's up to Arnold to face the screaming hordes of five-year-olds.

Kindergarten Cop was directed by Ivan Reitman, whose best work, like *Ghostbusters*, shows an ability to mix the absurd with the dramatic, so that we're laughing as the suspense reaches its peak. That happens this time. The scenes involving Schwarzenegger and the kindergarten kids are the best things in the movie, not only because the kids say the darnedest things, but also because Arnold's strong point here is gentle comedy, often with himself as the foil.

Contrasting with the classroom stuff is a low-key little romance involving Arnold and one of the other teachers (Penelope Ann Miller), a parallel story involving the vicious drug dealer and his mom, who journey to the small town for the obligatory, but quite effective, violent climax. Reitman juggles the light stuff, the heartwarming scenes, the comedy, and the violence with endless invention, so that the movie doesn't seem to be shifting gears even when it is.

Movies like this are often no stronger than their villains, and Tyson and Baker make a scary and effective team. He's a spoiled-rotten mother's pet who has never grown up, and whose love for his son is basically narcissistic. She is a bitch on wheels. The other key performances are also effective, and it was interesting for me to observe, while seeing the movie in a large audience, what genuine affection the public has for Schwarzenegger. He has a way of turning situations to his advantage and creates an entertaining relationship with his young students in this movie.

Warning: This is not a film appropriate for young children. Despite the title and the ad campaign, which make it look like a sweet and jolly funfest, the movie contains images sure to be terrifying to grade-schoolers, such as a man setting the school on fire, small children kidnapped and terrorized, a father slapping his child, and so forth. In context and for mature viewers, the scenes have a purpose and the movie works. But it'll be nightmare time for young children who see it.

King Lear ★ ★ ★
PG, 138 m., 1972

Paul Scofield (King Lear), Irene Worth (Goneril), Jack MacGowran (Fool), Alan Webb (Gloucester), Cyril Cusack (Albany), Patrick Magee (Cornwall), Robert Lloyd (Edgar), Tom Fleming (Kent), Susan Engel (Regan), Annelise Gaboid (Cordelia). Directed by Peter Brook. Screenplay by Brook.

Peter Brook's *King Lear* occupies a barren kingdom frozen in the middle of a winter that chills souls even more than bodies. He is not his own master; he gives away his power and then discovers, with a childlike surprise, that he can no longer exercise it. Burdened by senility and a sense of overwhelming futility, he collapses gratefully into death.

It is important to describe him as Brook's Lear, because he is not Shakespeare's. *King Lear* is the most difficult of Shakespeare's plays to stage, the most complex and, to my mind, the greatest. There are immensities of feeling and meaning in it that Brook has not even touched. And for Shakespeare's difficulties of staging, he has substituted his own cinematic decorations.

This is not to say that his film is not a brave and interesting effort in its own right. Peter Brook is not constitutionally able to direct "screen versions" of someone else's work. The vision must be his own, even if that means Shakespeare finishes second; this is not so much a film of *King Lear* as a film about it, with Brook's critical analysis of the play suggesting his directorial strategy.

His approach was suggested by *Shakespeare Our Contemporary*, a controversial book by the Polish critic Jan Kott. In Kott's view, *King Lear* is a play about the total futility of things. The old man Lear stumbles ungracefully toward his death because, simply put, that's the way it goes for most of us. To search for meaning of philosophical consolation is to kid yourself.

I suppose every age has attempted to redefine Shakespeare in terms of its own preoccupations, and the Brook-Kott version of *Lear* is certainly fashionable and modern. But it gives us a film that severely limits Shakespeare's vision, and focuses our attention on his more nihilistic passages while ignoring or sabotaging the others.

There is a great deal of goodness in *King Lear*. There is the old king himself, "more sinned against than sinning," whose cruelties are the result of misplaced love. There is Cordelia, the most touchingly sincere heroine in all of Shakespeare. There is Edgar, totally devoted to the father who has disowned him, and Kent, who serves Lear out of love. And there are the moments when Lear shakes off his sense of doom and hurls taunts at the gods, or tells his beloved Cordelia that their suffering will pass and they will once again live like the songbirds and dabble in the gossip of the court. Lear even seems to die convinced that Cordelia lives; she does not, but his last conscious impulse is one of hope and faith. Perhaps that is Shakespeare's final thought: that the ability to hope is what makes us human, even if, in fact, our hopes are futile.

This is a great humanistic assertion, and it has no place in the Peter Brook film. He omits or rearranges dialogue and scenes in order to make the evil daughters, Regan and Goneril, ambiguous in their villainy. He gives us a Cordelia who is not as perfect as she should be. He gives us a Lear who is only a figure of pity, not (as he was in Shakespeare) also sometimes a figure of greatness. He gives us a world so grim we might as well be dead.

Lear is played by Paul Scofield, whose beard and large, sad eyes make him look distractingly like the middle-aged Hemingway. Perhaps because of Brook's direction, Scofield's readings are often uninflected and exhausted. He reads Shakespeare's poetry the way Mark Twain said women use profanity: "They know the words, but not the music." The acting style suits Brook's ideas about the play, but leaves Lear diminished as a character.

Shakespeare's *Lear* survives in his play and will endure forever. Brook's *Lear* is a new conception, a rethinking, and a critical commentary on the play. It is interesting precisely because it contrasts so firmly with Shakespeare's universe; by deliberately omitting all faith and hope from Lear's kingdom, it paradoxically helps us to see how much is there.

The King of Comedy ★ ★ ★
PG, 101 m., 1983

Robert De Niro (Rupert Pupkin), Jerry Lewis (Jerry Langford), Diahnne Abbott (Rita), Sandra Bernhard (Masha), Ed Herlihy (Himself). Directed by Martin Scorsese. Screenplay by Paul Zimmerman.

Martin Scorsese's *The King of Comedy* is one of the most arid, painful, wounded movies I've ever seen. It's hard to believe Scorsese made it; instead of the big-city life, the violence and sexuality of his movies like *Taxi Driver* and *Mean Streets*, what we have here is an agonizing portrait of lonely, angry people with their emotions all tightly bottled up. This is a movie that seems ready to explode—but somehow it never does. That lack of release seriously disturbed me the first time I saw *The King of Comedy*. I kept straining forward, waiting for the movie to let loose, and it kept frustrating me. Maybe that was the idea. This is a movie about rejection, with a hero who never admits that he has been rejected, and so there is neither comic nor tragic release—just the postponement of pain.

I left that first screening filled with dislike for the movie. Dislike, but not disinterest. Memories of *The King of Comedy* kept gnawing at me, and when people asked me what I thought about it, I said I wasn't sure. Then I saw the movie a second time, and it seemed to work better for me—maybe because I was able to watch without any expectations. I knew it wasn't an entertainment, I knew it didn't allow itself any emotional payoffs, I knew the ending was cynical and unsatisfying, and so, with *those* discoveries no longer to be made, I was free to simply watch what was on the screen.

What I saw the second time, better than the first, were the performances by Robert De Niro, Jerry Lewis, Diahnne Abbott, and Sandra Bernhard, who play the movie's most important characters. They must have been difficult performances to deliver, because there's almost no feedback in this movie. The actors can't bounce emotional energy off each other, because nobody *listens* in this film; everybody's just waiting for the other person to stop talking so they can start. And everybody's so emotionally isolated in this movie that they don't even seem able to guess what they're missing.

The movie stars De Niro, as Rupert Pupkin, a nerdish man in his thirties who fantasizes himself as a television star. He practices in his basement, holding condescending conversations with life-size cardboard cutouts of Liza Minnelli and Jerry Lewis. His dream is to get a stand-up comedy slot on the late-night talk show hosted by Lewis (whose name in the movie is Jerry Langford). The movie opens with Rupert's first meeting with Jerry; he barges into Jerry's limousine and is immediately on an obnoxious first-name basis. Jerry vaguely promises to check out Rupert's comedy routine, and

the rest of the movie is devoted to Rupert's single-minded pursuit of fame. He arrives at Jerry's office, is politely brushed off, returns, is ejected, arrives at Jerry's country home with a "date" in tow, is ejected again, and finally decides to kidnap Jerry.

This *sounds* like an entertaining story, I suppose, but Scorsese doesn't direct a single scene for a payoff. The whole movie is an exercise in *cinema interruptus;* even a big scene in a bar, where Rupert triumphantly turns on the TV set to reveal himself on television, is deliberately edited to leave out the payoff shots—reaction shots of the amazed clientele. Scorsese doesn't want laughs in this movie, and he also doesn't want release. The whole movie is about the inability of the characters to get any kind of a positive response to their bids for recognition.

The King of Comedy is not, you may already have guessed, a fun movie. It is also not a bad movie. It is frustrating to watch, unpleasant to remember, and, in its own way, quite effective. It represents an enormous departure for Scorsese, whose movies teemed with life before he filmed this emotional desert, and whose camera used to prowl restlessly before he nailed it down this time. Scorsese and De Niro are the most creative, productive director/actor team in the movies right now, and the fact that they feel the freedom to make such an odd, stimulating, unsatisfying movie is good news, I guess. But *The King of Comedy* is the kind of film that makes you want to go and see a Scorsese movie.

The King of Marvin Gardens ★ ★ ★
R, 104 m., 1972

Jack Nicholson (David Staebler), Bruce Dern (Jason Staebler), Ellen Burstyn (Sally), Julia Anne Robinson (Jessica), Scatman Crothers (Lewis), Charles Levine (Grandfather). Directed and produced by Bob Rafelson. Screenplay by Jacob Brackman.

Bob Rafelson's *The King of Marvin Gardens* is a perversely satisfying movie—it works after going out of its way not to—and a very eccentric one. It backs into its real subject in much the same way that *Five Easy Pieces,* Rafelson's previous film, did. Only after it's over do some of its scenes and moments fall into place; for much of the way we've been disoriented and the story has been suspended somewhere in midair. As someone wrote about a totally dissimilar movie, Paul Morrissey's *Trash,* it's the kind of film you want

to walk out of, and then when it's over you want to see it again.

The movie opens and closes with autobiographical monologues being delivered by an all-night talk jockey (Jack Nicholson) into the loneliness of the FM airwaves. He works in a darkened studio, stopping sometimes to search for words, and it's evident that his broadcasts tear something loose from deep inside. It's possible, indeed, that he says more on the radio (or into his tape recorder) in this movie than he ever gets around to saying in the actual situations he finds himself in. He's tentative, unsure, private. His radio fantasies often involve his brother, Jason (Bruce Dern), who lives in Atlantic City, New Jersey, and does mysterious but glorious things there. After a long silence, Jason himself calls his brother and tells him to hustle down to Atlantic City because there are big deals cooking. They're going to buy an island near Hawaii and develop it into a resort. Sure.

Most of the movie takes place in Atlantic City, where the metaphor of a Monopoly game is employed a little too persistently, I thought. There's the Boardwalk, of course, and Marvin Gardens itself; but there are also Jason's attempts to buy a hotel, and the fact that he's in jail when we first meet him. This stuff is worked in quietly enough by Jacob Brackman's script, however, that it doesn't really distract.

Jason is living with a blonde on the far side of the hill (Ellen Burstyn) and her stepdaughter, a blonde coming up fast on this side (Julia Anne Robinson). A great deal of the movie is about the unacknowledged sexual competition between the two women, but this (like a few other things) becomes important only gradually. Most of the action seems to involve a disagreement between Jason, who turns out to be a minor hood, and the mysterious Lewis, who is the black rackets boss and moneyman in town. Jason's deals are based on reckless confidence in Lewis's money, and Lewis isn't going along.

Until the movie's end, when everything falls together with a really stunning force, Rafelson and Brackman seem to be going for a series of set-pieces. There is an unhappy lobster dinner with two Japanese investors reputed to have money; they wear their lobster-proof bibs happily, but don't come through. There's the matter of the older blonde marching into the hotel next door to take a bath ("Hell, you told me you *owned* the damn place," she says, then Jason explains the deal is still at the stage of "negotiations over language").

And there is a truly fine scene, almost surrealistic, in which the stepmother concedes the sexual sweepstakes to her stepdaughter and throws all of her clothes and makeup apparatus into a bonfire on the beach. Even her false eyelashes. "They're made out of mink hairs, did you know that?" she says. "For twenty years I've been wearing animal hairs on my face."

The movie's performances are as good as we've come to expect from the somewhat incestuous BBS Productions. Rafelson had directed three movies for the company before this one, and Nicholson had acted in three and directed one (*Drive, He Said*, in which Dern was wonderfully uptight and focused as the basketball coach). These people have worked together often enough that they have a kind of BBS feel for scenes, if you will; Nicholson and Dern work with each other as easily as any two actors. Ellen Burstyn succeeds in a difficult task; she has to make her performance striking enough to justify the movie's ending, but she can't push *too* far or we'll know too much, too soon.

For the rest, all I can say is that *The King of Marvin Gardens* is an original, individual, and often frustrating movie that takes a lot of chances and wins on about sixty percent of them. There are scenes (including a simulated Miss America pageant in a deserted hall and a horseback confrontation between Nicholson and Dern) that are hopelessly affected. There are others, including Dern's blurted-out declaration of his love for his brother, that are deeply affecting.

King of the Gypsies ★ ★ ★
R, 112 m., 1978

Sterling Hayden (King Zharko Stepanowicz), Shelley Winters (Queen Rachel), Susan Sarandon (Rose), Judd Hirsch (Groffo), Eric Roberts (Dave), Brooke Shields (Tita), Annette O'Toole (Persa). Directed by Frank Pierson and produced by Dino and Federico De Laurentiis. Screenplay by Pierson.

It's impossible to see *King of the Gypsies* and not to be reminded of *The Godfather*. The film stories have uncanny parallels, and that's all the more interesting because Peter Maas's book *King of the Gypsies* is based on fact: Reality is chasing fiction this time.

Both stories deal with grizzled, wise, and unshakably traditional old patriarchs. Both have sons who cannot quite fill their father's shoes. Instead of the still younger son in *The Godfather*, *King of the Gypsies* gives us a grandchild—but in both films this character is powerfully lured by the attractions of middle-class American affluence, he leaves the ethnic group to take a WASP girl as his lover, and he eventually does accept the responsibility of leading his clan.

The movies even feel rather the same, with their elegiac music, their ancient rituals, their stately processions of classic autos, their obsessions with the secrets of the clan. It must have taken a certain amount of courage for Frank Pierson, the screenwriter and director, to venture into territory already inhabited by cinematic landmarks, and yet he gets away with it: *King of the Gypsies* is poetic and violent and memorable, and it gives us the first authentic movie glimpse of American gypsy culture.

The story's about a transfer of power within the Stepanowicz family, gypsies living in the New York area. The old patriarch, the gypsy king, is dying (although Sterling Hayden plays the role with so much zest it's hard to believe that). The son (Judd Hirsch) is an alcoholic, a horse player, an unfit man to become king. But the grandson (Eric Roberts) is another story: He's smart, cunning, handsome, and ambitious. Unfortunately, he's also halfway assimilated into mainstream culture. He's not at all sure he even wants to be king of the gypsies.

He is sure, though, that his father is cruel and worthless, and that his mother (Susan Sarandon) should try to free herself from him. She doesn't; life outside the gypsy society is unthinkable to her. In one of the movie's central confrontations, she faces her son after having sold her daughter into marriage for $6,000 to pay her husband's gambling debts.

In *The Godfather*, Al Pacino was lured away from the Mafia clanship by the WASP attractions of Diane Keaton. In *King of the Gypsies*, Eric Roberts falls for Annette O'Toole. As an outsider, she presents a basic threat not only to the gypsy society but also to the continuity of the Stepanowicz family.

Peter Maas's original book revealed things that gypsies would no doubt much rather have kept secret. Frank Pierson explores some of those same secrets, but his film isn't just an exposé; it has a sense of life and humor, as when Sarandon takes her son into a jewelry store and trains him as a con man by having him swallow a diamond.

The movie is above all an elegy to a passing way of life, to a society of people who've endured and prevailed as outsiders in so different Western cultures. Gypsies have lived by choice outside the law, have been blamed no doubt for countless things they did not do, have preserved a fierce pride. *King of the Gypsies* suggests that gypsy culture may finally fall, not to laws and discrimination and persecution, but to that most insidious influence of all, the seductive middle-class way of life.

King of the Hill ★ ★ ★ ★
PG-13, 102 m., 1993

Jesse Bradford (Aaron), Jeroen Krabbe (Mr. Kurlander), Lisa Eichhorn (Mrs. Kurlander), Joseph Chrest (Ben), Spalding Gray (Mr. Mungo), Elizabeth McGovern (Lydia), Karen Allen (Miss Mathey), Adrien Brody (Lester). Directed by Steven Soderbergh and produced by Albert Berger, Barbara Maltby, and Ron Yerxa. Screenplay by Soderbergh.

Steven Soderbergh's *King of the Hill* is the story of a twelve-year-old boy who is left on his own in St. Louis during the Great Depression, and not only survives but thrives, and learns a thing or two. His parents are absent for excellent reasons: His mother is in a TB sanitarium, and his father, a door-to-door salesman, having failed to find much of a market for wickless candles, has left town to travel for a watch company. His younger brother has been shipped away to relatives. That leaves young Aaron (Jesse Bradford) behind in his family's rooms in the Empire Hotel, a transient hotel not quite nice enough to qualify as a brothel.

As a hero, Jesse has some of the qualities of Huckleberry Finn, David Copperfield, or Oliver Twist. He's plucky, smart, and knows his way around people. It is a sad truth that he could not survive in today's unkinder world, but in the 1930s, he finds it possible to support himself and even attend a prestigious local school, all because of his gift of gab and his genius at creative lying.

King of the Hill is based on a 1972 memoir by A.E. Hotchner, who presumably lived through experiences something like these, and who grew up to be the biographer of Ernest Hemingway and Doris Day, as well as others, indicating, among other things, an impressive reach. It's curious that Steven Soderbergh chose this story for his third film, since it has no apparent connection with his first two: *sex, lies and videotape*, which was a sensational debut, and *Kafka*, which was a ponderous and uncompelling follow-up. Now, with the kind of material you'd never dream of associating with him, he has made his best film.

Some of the credit goes to Bradford, a young actor who looks thoroughly normal and yet has that rare ability to convince us he is thinking when he seems to be doing nothing. His family has fallen on desperate times. His father (Jeroen Krabbe), an immigrant from Germany, is bedeviled by bill collectors and landlords, and tries everything he can think of to make money. Nothing works. His mother (Lisa Eichhorn) is capable and loving, but too ill to help out, and finally has to go to the sanitarium. After the little brother leaves, his father gives him an earnest lecture, tells him he will send money and be back as soon as possible, and leaves him on his own.

The St. Louis where he must survive seems, here, like a glorious city, one of those places that are tough and devious, where you can break your heart or make your fortune. Young Aaron knows his way around the Empire Hotel, with its bribable bellboys and its semipermanent guests such as the elusive Mr. Mungo (Spalding Gray), who lives across the hallway, occasionally sobering up enough to entertain a prostitute (Elizabeth McGovern) who is slightly less hapless than he is.

The movie follows Aaron's adventures as he talks his way into a private school, creating out of whole cloth a story about his family. He charms a rich girl and is even invited to her house, but he also survives on the streets, and at one point learns to drive, on the spot, when his father's car must be hidden from the collection agency.

This material could make many different kinds of movies. *King of the Hill* could have been a family picture, or a heartwarming TV docudrama, or a comedy. Soderbergh must have seen more deeply into the Hotchner memoir, however, because his movie is not simply about what happens to the kid. It's about how the kid learns and grows through his experiences. It's about growing up, not just about having colorful adventures. And despite the absence of Aaron's family for much of the picture, it's about the support a family can give—even, if it's believed in, when it isn't there.

A Kiss Before Dying ★ ★ ★
R, 93 m., 1991

Matt Dillon (Jonathan Corliss), Sean Young (Ellen/Dorothy Carlsson), Max von Sydow

(Thor Carlsson), Diane Ladd (Mrs. Corliss), James Russo (Dan Corelli). Directed by James Dearden and produced by Robert Lawrence. Screenplay by Dearden.

Ambitious young men are almost always dangerous in the movies. They hunger, and brood, and dream, and they will allow nothing to stand in their way. They're a familiar type, almost always achieved by overacting: Asked to project resentment, hurt, and ambition, all at once, your average actor goes over the top. It is one of the strengths of James Dearden's *A Kiss Before Dying* that Matt Dillon is able to make his character self-contained, impassive, and so all the more dangerous.

Dillon plays Jonathan, a poor kid from the wrong side of the tracks, who as a child used to sit in his bedroom and gaze morosely at the endless freight trains rumbling past, all of them emblazoned with the logo of Carlsson Copper. One day, he apparently said to himself, those trains will be mine. We meet him next at the University of Pennsylvania, where he is dating Dorothy (Sean Young), one of two twin daughters of crusty old Thor Carlsson (Max von Sydow), a proud millionaire. And then the film springs a surprise on us, which I will not reveal—and even so, do not read any further unless you want to know that Dorothy is found dead, an apparent suicide.

Dorothy's twin is Ellen, also played by Sean Young, and soon she and Jonathan are in love. They both work in the same homeless rescue agency, picking up street kids and giving them counseling and a place to spend the night. But Jonathan doesn't see social work as a permanent career, and he ingratiates himself with the uncompromising old man, goes fishing with him, agrees with everything he says, and is eventually given a job in the family firm.

Ellen is in love, but she is obsessed with the notion that her twin did not commit suicide. There are all sorts of clues if you know where to look: For example, Dorothy was wearing new shoes, purchased just before she died. Is that the action of a suicidal person? And then there are the mysterious deaths of Dorothy's former friends and co-students. Did they know something? Are their deaths a coincidence?

Veteran filmgoers, familiar with the Rule of Economy of Characters, will have guessed that Jonathan, the Dillon character, is not in the film simply to stand by while Ellen finds the real killer. *A Kiss Before Dying* generates

most of its suspense, in fact, by allowing us to know things about Jonathan that Ellen doesn't know. Dearden, the director, wrote *Fatal Attraction* and got substantial mileage out of the same idea—that a character is in mortal danger from a lover. In *Fatal Attraction* there was an additional twist, in that the audience was not quite so sure of the facts, but the strength of *A Kiss Before Dying* is that the Matt Dillon character is so private, so controlled by inner needs no one else in the film is allowed to see, that he is almost two persons, all by himself.

This is Matt Dillon's first film since *Drugstore Cowboy*, and demonstrates again that he is one of the best actors working in movies. He possesses the secret of not giving too much, of not trying so hard that we're distracted by his performance. Dillon was never trained as an actor, was a junior high school kid when he was cast in an unsung but powerful movie named *Over the Edge*, and has turned out to have a natural affinity with the camera. There was a brief period when his career was endangered by quasi-Teen Idol status, but he just kept working, choosing interesting roles and good directors, and today he and the slightly older Sean Penn are the best actors in their age group.

About Sean Young I am not quite so sure. In her best work like *The Boost* (1988), she is convincing—angry, obsessed, fearful. But here her character seems to know too much of the story; she has a detachment that's not appropriate, a way of seeming to know, as we do, what the real outcome is going to be. It undermines the concern we feel for her.

And yet *A Kiss Before Dying* works, in most of its scenes, because it is fueled by the need of the Dillon character. Dearden helps it work because he doesn't press his point. The film opens and closes with close-ups of Dillon as a small boy, looking at those trains going by, and Dillon is too good an actor to feel any need to improve on the emotions we associate with those wide little eyes.

Kiss of Death ★ ★
R, 101 m., 1995

David Caruso (Jimmy Kilmartin), Nicolas Cage (Little Junior Brown), Helen Hunt (Bev), Kathryn Erbe (Rosie), Samuel L. Jackson (Calvin), Stanley Tucci (Frank Zioli), Michael Rapaport (Ronnie), Ving Rhames (Omar). Directed by Barbet Schroeder and produced by Schroeder and Susan Hoffman. Screenplay by Richard Price.

Kiss of Death is a hard-boiled crime movie featuring "NYPD Blue's" David Caruso in his first big-screen starring role. He's opposite Nicolas Cage, who plays the weirdest villain since Dennis Hopper slithered into *Blue Velvet*. The direction is by Barbet Schroeder *(Reversal of Fortune)*, the screenplay is by novelist Richard Price *(Clockers)*, it's a loose remake of the 1947 movie where Richard Widmark pushed the wheelchair down the stairs, and with a pedigree like that it shouldn't be disjointed and uncompelling, but it is.

It's about professional car thieves in Queens. Caruso plays Jimmy Kilmartin, who used to be a drunk and a thief. Now that he and his wife have sobered up and started a family, he wants to stay on the straight and narrow. But one night his cousin Ronnie comes pounding on the door, desperate, because he has a carrier truck of stolen cars and if he doesn't get someone to drive it the mob will kill him. Against his better judgment, Jimmy goes along, and gets caught in a bust that results in the shooting of a cop.

He ends up serving time, but won't rat on his friends, out of his own highly personal code, which seems glued together out of Mafia honor and his twelve-step program. Meanwhile, everybody is betraying him, especially Ronnie, who gets the wife drunk and seduces her, setting up Jimmy's motive for a dangerous game of double-cross revenge.

There is plot and more plot in *Kiss of Death*. By the time it's over you may wish you had taken notes to keep track of who is doing what, and with which, and to whom. A lot of the scheming centers around Little Junior Brown, the Nicolas Cage character. The first time we see Junior, he's bench-pressing a stripper in his father's topless bar, called Baby Cakes. This is the kind of "gentleman's club" where you wonder why any of the customers ever come back again, since if they look sideways at anyone they get pounded by Junior.

A little of Little Junior Brown goes a long way. The part has been overwritten by Price, who gives Junior so many traits that Cage is run ragged keeping up with the weirdness. Junior is a bodybuilder, and has severe asthma, and adores his father, and can't stand the taste of metal in his mouth, and compresses his rules for living into "agonyms," which is how he says "acronyms." He also likes to debate philosophy, although, in his business, when he asks, "What's worse? Losing a wife, or a father?" he isn't dealing in abstractions.

Junior talks like a guy who reads the "Increase Your Word Power" page in *Reader's Digest;* every sentence has one extra word, as in "the difficult becomes the repulsively impossible." At first he hates Jimmy. Then he gets to like him, and eventually he confides in him: "I never told anybody about me and the metal-tasting before. I hated it in prison. I couldn't get plastic forks."

One problem with Junior is that the things he says don't match the things he does; he's too dumb to be as smart as he is. But Cage is a real movie actor and plays the role with style and bravado. David Caruso, on the other hand, is a serious problem in the lead. Sure, he's the good guy, which is a disadvantage in this movie, but he should project more of a sense of menace. When he gets into showdowns with tough guys, you don't see why they should take him seriously. He seems too laid-back and unfocused, and is not able to carry this movie. He doesn't compel us to identify with him as he winds through the labyrinthine plot.

The conflict in *Kiss of Death* is triangular, involving not only Jimmy against the mob, but also the law vs. the mob, with Jimmy in the middle. He has a lot of trouble with an unforgiving cop (Samuel L. Jackson), and with a district attorney (Stanley Tucci), whose word is meaningless.

Since one of the motifs in the movie is the way Jimmy stands by his word, the message may be that an honest man can't stand with the cops or the robbers. Jimmy winds up wearing a wire at times and places where common sense indicates it would be discovered, and is saved only by the Bathroom Rule, which indicates toilets in movies are never used for biological purposes, but only to dispose of wires, guns, evidence, etc.

When I'm watching a movie as complex as *Kiss of Death*, I look forward to the ending, since the filmmakers have to somehow tie together all the loose ends. The climax of *Kiss of Death*, set in Baby Cakes, is so ludicrous it could be comedy, with characters arriving, leaving, and being killed or saved according to an elaborate plot-driven timetable. Those who remember the original *Kiss of Death* will be waiting for somebody to push a wheelchair down the stairs, but in a plot like this, that would be wretched excess.

Kiss of the Spider Woman ★ ★ ★ ½
R, 119 m., 1985

William Hurt (Luis Molina), Raul Julia (Valentin), Sonia Braga (Leni/Marta/Spider Woman), Jose Lewgoy (Warden). Directed by Hector Babenco and produced by David Weidman. Screenplay by Leonard Schrader.

Kiss of the Spider Woman tells one of those rare and entrancing stories where one thing seems to happen while another thing is really happening. There are passages in the movie that seem to be absolutely self-contained, and then a word or gesture will reveal that they have depths we can only guess. By the end of the film, what started out as a contest between two opposite personalities has expanded into a choice between two completely different attitudes toward life. And the choice is not sexual, although for a long time it seems so. It is between freedom and slavery.

The movie opens in a prison cell, somewhere in South America. A man is telling a story. The story is a lurid intrigue that seems pieced together from fragments and memories of countless old *film noir* melodramas— from those movies of the 1940s where the woman had lips that could kill, and the men were dying to kiss them. Only gradually does the reality of the film reveal itself: We are in a cramped, depressing prison cell, and the storyteller is a prisoner, trying to pass the days by escaping into fantasy.

His name is Luis. He is played by William Hurt as an affected homosexual, a window dresser who has been jailed for sex offenses. His cellmate is Valentin (Raul Julia), a bearded, macho political prisoner who has nothing but contempt for Luis's stories—not to mention his sexuality and his politics. But as Luis calmly explains, unless someone gives him a key to walk out of his prison, he will continue to escape in any way he can.

As he continues to weave his verbal movie plots, the movie uses fantasy scenes to depict them. There is a Nazi crime melodrama, and a thriller about a spider woman, and the woman in both of them is played by the same actress (Sonia Braga). Later in the film, she will also appear as Valentin's lover; reality and fantasy are by then thoroughly mixed.

What *Kiss of the Spider Woman* at first seems to be about is the changing nature of the relationship between two very different men who have been locked together in the same cell. They are opposites in every way. But they share the same experiences, day after day, and that gives them a common bond. Gradually, an affection grows between them, and we assume that the movie will be about the ways in which they learn to accept each other. Only gradually, mysteriously, do we realize that the movie is about a good deal more. Details of the plot are revealed so subtly and so surprisingly that I will say nothing more, except that the film does not lead in the directions we anticipate.

The performances are wonderful. The director, Hector Babenco, is a Brazilian, but he has directed his American stars in English without falling prey to the occasional loss of tone you sometimes hear as foreigners work in unfamiliar languages. William Hurt, who won the Academy Award and best actor award at Cannes for this film, creates a character utterly unlike anyone else he has ever played—a frankly theatrical character, exaggerated and mannered—and yet he never seems to be reaching for effects. Raul Julia, sweaty and physical in the early scenes, gradually reveals a poetry that makes the whole movie work. And Sonia Braga, called upon to satirize bad acting, makes a perfect spider woman.

Every decade seems to be dominated by the cinema of a different country (in addition to Hollywood, of course, a country of its own). In the 1950s it was Italy. In the 1960s, France. In the 1970s, Germany. In the 1980s, Brazil and Australia seem to be the centers of the most exciting work. Babenco's previous credits include the heartbreaking *Pixote* about a child growing up on the streets of São Paulo. *Kiss of the Spider Woman* is another film of insights and surprises.

Klute ★ ★ ★ ½
R, 114 m., 1971

Jane Fonda (Bree Daniel), Donald Sutherland (John Klute), Charles Cioffi (Frank Ligouri), Dorothy Tristan (Arlyn Page). Directed and produced by Alan J. Pakula. Screenplay by Andy K. and Dave Lewis.

What is it about Jane Fonda that makes her such a fascinating actress to watch? She has a sort of nervous intensity that keeps her so firmly locked into a film character that the character actually seems distracted by things that come up in the movie. You almost have the feeling, a couple of times in *Klute*, that the Fonda character had other plans and was just leaving the room when this (whatever it is) came up.

The movie is about a skilled, intelligent, cynical, and personally troubled New York call girl who does not, for once, have a heart of gold. She never feels anything when she's with a man, she tells her shrink, but she does experience a sense of professional pride when she's able to satisfy a client. And some of her clients have very complicated needs, which challenge the girl's imaginative acting ability. One old garment industry tycoon, for example, has spent all his life making clothes. But he fantasizes an idealistic sort of pre-World War I existence in Europe, in Vienna maybe, and the girl describes it to him in quiet, warm images while she disrobes. He never touches her.

The girl's name is Bree, and the movie should probably be titled *Bree* instead of *Klute*, because the Fonda character is at the center. John Klute (played by Donald Sutherland) is a policeman who has come to New York, free-lance, to try to settle a missing persons case. It appears that the missing man may still be alive, and may be the source of obscene letters and telephone calls Bree has been receiving. Bree initially refuses to talk to Klute, but she eventually does confide in him, mostly because she's frightened by midnight prowlers and wants his protection. The film examines their somewhat strange relationship, and at the same time functions on another level as a somewhat awkward thriller.

There are scary shots of the prowler, for example, and shots of hands gripping a mesh fence—shots that are not very satisfactory because the wrong point of view is established. One thing about a thriller is that the threat should always be seen from the point of view of the threatened. We don't like looking over the killer's shoulder at his victim; shots like that interfere with our desire to identify with the victim and be scared in a satisfactory way.

Klute doesn't scare us very satisfactorily, maybe because it's kind of schizo. The director is Alan Pakula, whose concern is all too much with plot, and it gets in the way of the unusual and interesting relationship between Bree and Klute. But how *do* you develop a relationship between a prostitute with hang-ups and a square suburban cop? *Klute* does it by making the cop into a person of restraint and dignity, a man who is genuinely concerned about this girl he's met. His attitude is what makes their love relationship so absorbing. Usually, in the movies, it's just assumed the lovers were drawn toward each other by magnetism or concealed springs or something.

The scenes between Fonda and Sutherland are very good, then, and Bree is further developed in scenes showing her trying to get out of the trade and into something straight.

She takes acting lessons, she auditions to model for cosmetics ads. She talks to her shrink (in scenes that sound improvised and exhibit Fonda's undeniable intelligence).

Intelligence. I suppose that's the word. In *Klute* you don't have two attractive acting vacuums reciting speeches at each other. With Fonda and Sutherland, you have actors who understand and sympathize with their characters, and you have a vehicle worthy of that sort of intelligence. So the fact that the thriller stuff doesn't always work isn't so important.

Koyaanisqatsi ★ ★ ★
NO MPAA RATING, 87 m., 1983

Produced and directed by Godfrey Reggio.

ko·yaa·nis·qatsi, n. (Hopi). 1. crazy life. 2. life in turmoil. 3. life disintegrating. 4. life out of balance. 5. a state of life that calls for another way of living.

I give the definition because it is the key to the movie. Without it, you could make a sincere mistake. *Koyaanisqatsi* opens with magnificent images out of nature: great canyons and limitless deserts and a world without man. Through the use of speeded-up images, clouds climb the sides of mountains and speed across the sky, their shadows painting the landscape. Then the movie turns to images of smokestacks, factories, and expressways. There is an assumption on the part of the filmmaker, Godfrey Reggio, that we'll immediately get the message. And the message, I think, is that nature is wonderful, but that American civilization is a rotten despoiler that is creating a "crazy life."

But I am irreverent, and given to my own thoughts during the film. After I have admired its visionary photography (this is a beautiful movie) and fallen under the spell of its music (an original sound track by the distinguished composer Philip Glass), there is still time to think other thoughts, such as:

This film has one idea, a simplistic one. It contrasts the glory of nature with the mess made by man. But man *is* a messy beast, given to leaving reminders of his presence all over the surface of planet Earth. Although a Hopi word is used to evoke unspoiled nature, no Hopis are seen, and the contrast in the movie doesn't seem to be between American Indian society and Los Angeles expressways, but between expressways and a beautiful world *empty* of man. Thanks, but no thanks.

I had another problem. *All* of the images in this movie are beautiful, even the images of man despoiling the environment. The first shots of smokestacks are no doubt supposed to make us recoil in horror, but actually I thought they looked rather noble. The shots of the expressways are also two-edged. Given the clue in the title, we can consider them as an example of life out of control. Or—and here's the catch—we can marvel at the fast-action photography and reflect about all those people moving so quickly to their thousands of individual destinations. What a piece of work is a man! And what expressways he builds!

Koyaanisqatsi, then, is an invitation to knee-jerk environmentalism of the most sentimental kind. It is all images and music. There is no overt message except the obvious one (the Grand Canyon is prettier than Manhattan). It has been hailed as a vast and sorrowful vision, but to what end? If the people in all those cars on all those expressways are indeed living crazy lives, their problem is not the expressway (which is all that makes life in L.A. manageable) but perhaps social facts such as unemployment, crime, racism, drug abuse, and illiteracy—issues so complicated that a return to nature seems like an elitist joke at their expense. Having said that, let me add that *Koyaanisqatsi* is an impressive visual and listening experience, that Reggio and Glass have made wonderful pictures and sounds, and that this film is a curious throwback to the 1960s, when it would have been a short subject to be viewed through a marijuana haze. Far-out.

The Krays ★ ★ ★ ½
R, 119 m., 1990

Billie Whitelaw (Violet Kray), Gary Kemp (Ronald Kray), Martin Kemp (Reginald Kray), Susan Fleetwood (Rose), Charlotte Cornwell (May), Jimmy Jewel (Cannonball Lee). Directed by Peter Medak and produced by Dominic Anciano and Ray Burdis. Screenplay by Philip Ridley.

You meet kids like this in grade school sometimes. Kids who seem naturally mean-spirited and sadistic, who take pleasure in causing pain. When they twist your arm behind your back; they really are trying to break it. The strange thing about the schoolyard bully is that, nine times out of ten, he can put on an angelic face whenever he wants to. Comb his hair and put him in a tie, age him thirty years, and he'll look like a model citizen. Maybe he'll beat his wife or rough up his kids—maybe life

is hell for his family—but he places great importance on seeming respectable.

The Krays is a movie about a couple of men like that. They were well-dressed, well-behaved, sleek, carefully groomed mother's boys who grew up to become the most sadistic criminals in the modern history of London. They ruled the East End, the Cockney neighborhoods stretching along the Thames beyond the Tower of London. But their fame spread far beyond the modest streets where they were born and lived, and by the end of their reign, they were regulars on the nightclub and show biz circuits. There is something about gangsters that interests a lot of people. It's probably related to the fascination of playing with fire.

Before the Kray twins, British crime was simply not down to the American standard. Neither the cops nor the robbers carried guns, and most crimes were done with cunning and stealth rather than by brute force. Criminals looked down on those who lacked the intelligence to figure out a nonviolent way to steal. But there were signs that urban violence was creeping across the Atlantic. In his famous essay "The Decline of the English Murder," George Orwell complained that the devious spouse-poisoners and acid-bath murderers of his youth had given way to a new generation of killers totally lacking in imagination, people who simply shot those they disliked, instead of plotting for years to squirrel their remains in a geranium bed.

Billie Whitelaw, who plays the twins' mother in *The Krays*, thinks maybe they learned some of their lessons through the study of Hollywood gangster movies. Certainly they were born with the pathology and innate sadism to be good students. The movie shows them observing the existing protection rackets in the East End and then muscling in and taking over by the simple expedient of being unimaginably more vicious than any of their competitors.

The violence in the movie is effective because it is matter-of-fact, business as usual. It's not the entertaining, even exhilarating fantasy-violence of a big-budget action picture, but the mean, low-key violence of a man who wants to hurt you so you'll pay him money. The most chilling scene in the movie is one where a former associate of the Krays has his mouth disfigured with a sharp knife, so quickly he hardly realizes he's being attacked.

The movie's visuals place the Krays in the dingy, drab world of the East End, of narrow

streets crowded with tenements, of working-men's cafés, of cinemas and bingo halls, pubs, and shabby nightclubs. But there is one haven of cheer and respectability—their home, which is ruled over by Violet, their loving mother, and also contains the less consequential figures of their father and Charlie, their brother. Violet will hear no evil of her boys, and it's something to see her straighten the ties and pat the cheeks of her glistening little killers.

The twins are played by brothers, Gary and Martin Kemp, as a sort of psychic double act. They share a secret wavelength, one on which Ronnie, who is truly pathological, uses subtle force to bring Reggie along with him. Whitelaw, who knew the Krays, believes that Reggie, without Ronnie, would have developed into an ordinary low-level criminal. It was Ronnie, with his deeper sickness, who turned the two of them into a fearsome unit.

The role of the mother is central to the film. She dotes, confides, encourages, loves, forgives. The twins continue to live at home at an age long after what seems appropriate, and when Ronnie brings home a male lover, little notice is taken. Reggie moves out when he marries, but never seems far from home, and the gang's council meetings are held upstairs over the parlor.

The Krays was directed by Peter Medak, whose best previous film was *The Ruling Class* (1971), with Peter O'Toole as a British lord whose eccentricity shaded over into madness. This movie shares the sense of unspeakable secrets just beneath the surface. It's a gangster film by definition, but really it's a study of human pathology. Most people we meet in the course of a lifetime are basically good folks who want to live and let live. A few have something missing inside, maybe the ability to have any empathy for the feelings of others. To get what they want, they cause pain. Usually such people were mistreated as children, and are bullies to compensate for shame and low self-esteem. The strange thing about the Krays is that they were doted on as children, and their self-esteem seems robust and unquestioning. And they have such a nice mother.

Kung Fu Master ★ ★ ★
R, 80 m., 1989

Jane Birkin (Mary Jane), Mathieu Demy (Julien), Charlotte Gainsbourg (Lucy), Lou Doillon (Lou), Eva Simonet (The Friend), Judy Campbell (The Mother), David and Andrew

Birkin (The Father and Brother). Directed and produced by Agnes Varda. Screenplay by Varda and Jane Birkin.

Agnes Varda's *Kung Fu Master* is a French film that tells the story of a love affair between a forty-year-old woman and a fourteen-year-old boy. The subject is disturbing, and yet Varda treats it with a rare sympathy and empathy, perhaps inspired by the fact that the boy in the film is played by her own son, Mathieu Demy. The movie was cowritten by Jane Birkin, an English actress who has lived in Paris for years and who plays the older woman—a woman who falls in love with the innocence and honesty of this young man.

Of course their relationship is doomed, and in a way, of course, they know that. It is wisely never made clear in the film exactly how far the relationship goes in a physical sense, but on the emotional side we can see that the boy is at first bold and audacious in his approach to the older woman, but then begins to tune out as his attention wanders.

A film like this cannot be described in terms of its plot. Everything depends on the look in an eye, the tone of voice. Varda's true subject seems to be the way in which "pure" love, classical romanticism, can exist as an idea in a vacuum, but can survive in the real world only for a moment before practical considerations mercilessly wipe it out. There is a degree of deliberate daring in her choice of this subject matter. Like Louis Malle's *Murmur of the Heart* (1971), which dealt with incest, *Kung Fu Master* is on one level an experiment—to see if this shocking subject matter can be made palatable.

It can be, or at least it is here (one doubts if things would work so smoothly in the real world). The film opens with a chance meeting between the woman and the boy at a birthday party for the woman's teen-age daughter. They meet on the stairs and talk. Nothing comes of it. They meet again and talk again, and then the boy makes a bold approach to her. She is shocked and amused—and intrigued. Gradually, surprising herself, she permits the relationship to continue.

Julien, the boy, is a loner who feels left out of his adolescent society. He spends a great deal of time riveted to Kung Fu Master, a video arcade game in a neighborhood café, where he has developed considerable skill at manipulating an animated karate master who must save a damsel in distress. His approach to Mary Jane, the woman, has the same directness. Although she is not ostensibly in distress, she is lonely and isolated, and for a time they fill each other's needs.

Mary Jane's daughter, of course, is offended and shocked by the entire episode. She can barely believe a woman of her mother's age has romantic feelings at all, let alone for a boy. One of the hardest scenes to believe is the one where the woman takes the boy to meet her family. It works only as wish-fulfillment. In the real world, the family and society in general would disapprove of this liaison—but the lovers try to hide from society. Picking up the boy at school, the woman plays the role of a responsible adult. And at one point they go off for a holiday on an island where the world is far away.

What redeems this movie and allows it to work is that it is about feelings, not actions. Varda draws an invisible line at physical frankness in the film, so there is never a moment when we feel embarrassment for the characters (or the actors). The fill is really about the phenomenon of the romantic crush—about how another person can suddenly seem to embody an ideal for us, especially if that person is distant enough or different enough that we do not have to deal with his or her real-life situation.

The crush also involves projection, as we see ourselves in the other person. And here perhaps the woman sees her own innocent idealism in the boy, and the boy identifies with her somewhat dreamy isolation. Apart from the difference in their ages, they really are well-suited to one another, at least as long as they can dream and are not distracted by pragmatic reality.

Agnes Varda is one of the most individual and intriguing of contemporary French directors, in part because each of her films seems to satisfy a different need. Her previous film, the masterful *Vagabond*, was so different in tone from *Kung Fu Master* that it's hard to believe it comes from the same director. It told the story of an unhappy young woman who left her boring job for a carefree life on the road, and gradually sank, one small step at a time, down the scale of social acceptability until she became a vagrant. That film suggested that we may all be closer to the gutter than we think, if we lose our discipline and our support systems. This one suggests we may all be closer to our ideal but impossible love if we lose our fears.

L

La Bamba ★ ★ ★
PG-13, 108 m., 1987

Lou Diamond Phillips (Ritchie Valens), Esai Morales (Bob Morales), Rosana De Soto (Connie Valenzuela), Elizabeth Pena (Rosie Morales), Danielle von Zerneck (Donna Ludwig), Joe Pantoliano (Bob Keene). Directed by Luis Valdez and produced by Taylor Hackford and Bill Borden. Screenplay by Valdez.

La Bamba opens with a sequence that at first seems like a memory. Some teen-age boys are playing basketball in a school yard. Far overhead, a light plane drones through the sky. The colors of this scene are all washed out, as in an old memory, and the voices sound far away. There is slow motion. Another airplane appears. The basketball game continues. We are lulled by the feeling of a slow summer afternoon. Then the two planes collide and fall into the school yard below.

Because *La Bamba* is the story of Ritchie Valens, we assume this is his memory. But he was not present when the planes fell, and the scene represents how he might have imagined it. One of his friends was killed that day. He always assumed that if he had been in the school yard, he would have been killed, too. That was why he never liked to take airplanes.

The scene itself is very effective. But I wonder if it is the right way to open *La Bamba.* Everyone who goes to the movie will know that Valens died in an airplane crash with Buddy Holly and the Big Bopper on February 3, 1959, the day the music died. The opening scene is followed by several other references to Valens's fear of flying, and the effect is to put the whole movie under a cloud, to weigh down every scene with the knowledge of impending death.

That robs *La Bamba* of a quality I think it could use: the sense of fun. This is a sincere,

well-acted movie about the short life of a minor rock & roll star, and by the time it's over we almost have the feeling Valens would have been surprised not to have died in a crash.

He is played by Lou Diamond Phillips as a serious, introspective, intensely focused young man who wanted to play his music more than anything else in life. His dedication amounts almost to an obsession. He never seems to really let go.

Valens had only three hit songs. His public career lasted less than six months. He died before he was eighteen. There isn't a wealth of material to draw from as there was for *The Buddy Holly Story.* So Luis Valdez, the director, fleshes out the story with information about Valens's family, especially his hardworking, cheerful mother (Rosana De Soto) and his half brother (Esai Morales), who both supports him and resents him.

Valens's real surname was Valenzuela. He was a Mexican-American, raised for a time in migrant labor camps, and he idolized the older brother who would appear from time to time on a glamorous motorcycle. But he admired music more and began to sing wherever he could find work in Los Angeles in the late 1950s. After the family moved into the city, and Valens got a girlfriend—a blond Anglo named Donna, whose parents didn't approve of Valens, inspiring "Donna," one of his hits. He had some of the usual adventures of growing up, and the movie makes much of a trip he and his brother took to Tijuana, where Valens was less interested in the girls than in the band (in the movie it is, of course, playing "La Bamba").

Once Valens is discovered by a minor record producer (Joe Pantoliano), his career goes surprisingly well. He records a song, it is a hit, he is invited by Alan Freed to appear in one of his pioneering rock & roll stage

shows in Brooklyn and two other hits follow fairly quickly. Valens makes one crucial artistic decision: Although he doesn't speak Spanish, he insists on recording "La Bamba" in Spanish, using the irrefutable logic that if Nat King Cole could record in Spanish, he could, too.

Valens's last tour is handled in an almost perfunctory manner. We know how the movie will end, anyway. The Big Bopper circulates backstage, saying "Hello, baby!" to everyone he meets. Buddy Holly sings "Crying, Waiting, Hoping." They go out to the airport in a snowstorm, Holly flips a coin, and Valens calls heads and wins his place on the fated plane. Still to come, no doubt, is a movie about the Big Bopper. And why not one called *Rock & Roll Pilot* ("He Was at the Controls the Day the Music Died!")?

This is a good small movie, sweet and sentimental, about a kid who never really got a chance to show his stuff. The best things in it are the most unexpected things: the portraits of everyday life, of a loving mother, of a brother who loves and resents him, of a kid growing up and tasting fame and leaving everyone standing around at his funeral shocked that his life ended just as it seemed to be beginning.

La Belle Noiseuse ★ ★ ★ ★
NO MPAA RATING, 240 m., 1992

Michel Piccoli (Frenhofer), Jane Birkin (Liz), Emmanuelle Béart (Marianne), Marianne Denicourt (Julienne), David Bursztein (Nicolas), Gilles Arbona (Porbus). Directed by Jacques Rivette and produced by Pierre Grise. Screenplay by Pascal Bonitzer, Christine Laurent, and Rivette.

Some movies are worlds that we can sink into, and *La Belle Noiseuse* is one of them. It is a four-hour movie, but not one second too long, in which the process of art and the process of life come into a fascinating conflict. There is something fundamentally sensual about the relationship between an artist and a model, not because of the nudity and other superficial things, which are obvious, but because the artist is trying to capture something intimate and secret from another person and put it on the canvas. It is possible to have sex with someone and not know them, but it is impossible to draw them well and not know them well.

The movie is about an artist in his sixties, who has not painted for many years. In his studio is an unfinished canvas, a portrait of his wife, which leans against the wall like a rebuke for the passion that has died between them. They are still happily married, but their relationship is one of understanding, not hunger. One day a young admirer brings his girlfriend to meet the artist and his wife. Something stirs within the older man, and he asks the girl to pose for him. She agrees, indifferently, and as he begins his portrait a subtle dance of seduction begins.

To understand the dynamic, you will have to picture the actors. The artist is played by Michel Piccoli, veteran of dozens of important French movies, he of the intimidating bald forehead, the vast eyebrows, the face of an aging satyr. The young woman is played by Emmanuelle Béart *(Manon of the Spring)*, whose beauty may come from heaven but whose intelligence is all her own. Watching her here, we realize that it would not have been enough simply to cast a beautiful woman in the role, for the artist is entrapped by her mind, not her appearance. The artist's wife is played by Jane Birkin (the daughter in *Daddy Nostalgia*), who knows her husband well enough to warn Béart against him, but not well enough to warn herself.

The sittings begin, and the artistic process takes over. And the film's director, Jacques Rivette, takes a big risk, which works brilliantly. He shows the preliminary sketches, the pencil drawings, charcoals and watercolor washes, in great detail. The camera looks over the shoulder of the artist and regards his hand as he draws. Sometimes the camera is on the hand for four or five minutes at a time. This may sound boring. It is more thrilling than a car chase. We see a human being taking shape before us. And as the artist tries one approach and then another, we see the process of his mind at work.

It is said that artistic processes take place on the right side of the brain, the side that is liberated from mundane considerations like the passage of time. I know for myself that when I draw, I drop out of time and lose all consciousness of its passing. I even fail to hear people who are talking to me because the verbal side of my mind is not engaged. Most films are a contest between the right and left brains, in which dialogue and plot struggle to make sense, while picture, mood, music, and emotion struggle toward a reverie state. In *La Belle Noiseuse,* the right side, the artistic side, of the viewer's mind is given the freedom to take over, and as the artist draws, something curious happens. We become the artist ourselves, in a way, looking at the model, taking up the tools, plunging into the preliminary drawings.

The artist and his model do not get along very well. He is almost sadistic in his treatment of her, addressing her curtly, asking her to assume uncomfortable poses, keeping an impolite distance between her concerns and his own. She hates him. He does not care. It is a battle of the wills. But Jacques Rivette is an old and wise man, and so this movie doesn't develop along simplistic lines in which love soon rears its inquisitive head. Here is where Béart's intelligence comes in—hers, and her character's. The battle between the two people becomes one of imagination, a chess game of the emotions, in which small moves can have great consequences.

You may think you can guess what will happen. The artist will fall in love with his model. The wife and the boyfriend will be jealous. There will be sex scenes. Perhaps to some degree you are right. To a much larger degree, however, *La Belle Noiseuse* will surprise you, because this is not a movie that limits its curiosity to the question of where everybody's genitals will turn up.

The reason the movie benefits from its length is twofold. First, Rivette takes all of the time he needs to show the actual physical process of drawing. These passages are surprisingly tactile; we hear the whisper of the pencil on the paper, the scratch of the drawing pen, and we see that drawing is a physical process, not, as some people fancy, an exercise in inspiration. Second, having given the artist time to discover his model on his canvas, Rivette then gives himself the time to discover his own models. While the artist and model in the film are investigating one another, Rivette stands at his own canvas and draws both of them.

La Cage aux Folles ★ ★ ★ ★
R, 91 m., 1979

Ugo Tognazzi (Renato), Michel Serrault (Zaza), Michel Galabru (Charrier), Claire Maurier (Simone), Remy Laurent (Laurent), Benny Luke (Jacob). Directed by Edouard Molinaro and produced by Marcello Danon. Screenplay by Francis Veber and Molinaro.

La Cage aux Folles are "birds of a feather," which are precisely and hilariously what do not flock together in this wonderful comedy from France. It's about the gay owner of a scandalous nightclub in St. Tropez, his transvestite lover, and how the owner reacts after his son returns home one day and announces he's going to marry . . . a girl!

But that's not *really* what it's about: This is basically the first sitcom in drag, and the comic turns in the plot are achieved with such clockwork timing that sometimes we're laughing at what's funny and sometimes we're laughing at the movie's sheer comic invention. This is a great time at the movies.

The nightclub owner is played by Ugo Tognazzi, that grizzled Italian veteran of so many macho roles, and he has lived for twenty years with a drag queen (Michel Serrault) who stars in the club. They're like an old married couple, nostalgic and warm one minute, fighting like cats and dogs the next. Tognazzi sired the son all those years ago and has raised him with the help of "Auntie" Serrault and their live-in "maid," a wickedly funny black transvestite who has perhaps the movie's funniest moment.

Tognazzi and Serrault have trouble at first accepting the notion that their treasured young man is going to get married. They have more trouble, however, accepting the notion that the intended bride is the daughter of the Minister of Moral Standards—and that the in-laws are planning to come to dinner.

This dilemma inspires the film's hilarious middle section, in which Tognazzi's garishly bizarre apartment is severely redecorated in crucifixes and antiques, and Serrault is gently asked by the son if he'd mind being gone for the evening: "I told them my father was a Cultural Attaché; what'll they think when they find out he lives with a drag queen?"

Tognazzi, meanwhile, goes to visit the woman who bore his son two decades ago, to ask her to portray the mother for one night. She agrees. Too bad, because in the course of the uproariously funny dinner party, at least two reputed mothers are produced, one of them suspiciously hairy around the chest.

Describing a comedy is always a risky business; the bare plot outline is, of course, no hint as to how funny a film is, and to steal the jokes is a misdemeanor. What I can say, though, is that *La Cage aux Folles* gets the audience on its side with immediate ease; it never betrays our confidence; it astonishes us with the inspiration and logic it brings to ringing changes on the basic situation.

And it contains several classic sequences. The best is perhaps the one in which Tognazzi coaches Serrault on how to act "macho," an attribute that apparently consists of knowing how to butter your toast with manly firmness. There's also that extended dinner scene that begins with the Minister of Moral Standards discovering that . . . Greek boys . . . are doing . . . *something* . . . on his soup plate . . . and builds from there.

Ladybird, Ladybird ★ ★ ★ ★ | NEW
NO MPAA RATING, 102 m., 1995

Crissy Rock (Maggie), Vladimir Vega (Jorge), Sandie LaVelle (Mairead), Mauricic Venegas (Adrian), Ray Winstone (Simon), Clare Perkins (Jill), Jason Stracey (Sean), Luke Brown (Mickey). Directed by Ken Loach and produced by Sally Hibbin. Screenplay by Rona Munro.

> *Ladybug, ladybug,*
> *Fly away home.*
> *Your house is on fire,*
> *And your children will burn.*
> —nursery rhyme

This is the story of a troublesome woman. A woman with a big heart and a big temper, who has had four children by four different fathers, and lost custody of all of them because she cannot function responsibly. Or, looking at it differently, it is the story of a woman persecuted by British social workers who slap her down every time she almost has her life together. The strength of the film is that there is truth to both interpretations: Yes, she is treated cruelly by social workers— and, yes, she is her own worst enemy.

The woman's name is Maggie, and she is played by a former barmaid and stand-up comic named Crissy Rock who has never acted before. It is the strongest performance in any film of its year; seeing the movie for the first time at the Telluride Film Festival in September 1994, I walked out of the theater and saw Rock standing there, and wanted to comfort her, she had embodied Maggie's suffering so completely. The Oscar nominations were incomplete because they did not take this performance into account.

If you hang around bars where a lot of steady drinking goes on, you will have met someone like Crissy. She is short, blond, pudgy, in her thirties, with a nice face tending to fat. She's a "character." On karaoke night, she grabs the mike and brings down the house. She's good company, tells jokes, gets bawdy, holds her own. She likes to laugh, but there is sadness inside, and after too many drinks she may start to sob. She's in the bar looking for comfort, reassurance, a sense of belonging, and so she's a pushover for guys who buy her a drink and seem to care.

One night she meets a man who really does care. His name is Jorge (Vladimir Vega), and he is an immigrant from Paraguay with "political problems" at home. He seems almost improbably nice, and for once she dares to hope: Maybe this man will treat her better than the others, who were abusive, irresponsible, drunks, and dopeheads. He watches her singing, and is attracted to her spirit. Soon they are a couple, and she begins to hope.

We see how hopeless she is as a mother— and as a responsible adult. She was abused as a child, never learned basic survival and social skills, and exists in chaos, moving from one flat to another, treating each meal as a fresh challenge, as if food itself baffles her. We see her exploding; she has a fierce temper, a knack for blowing up when she should lay low. One day she does something that is shockingly irresponsible, and her four children are taken away from her by the social workers. She deserves to lose them. But because *Ladybird, Ladybird* sees her so clearly, we can understand why she acted as she did. Not forgive, but understand.

Now starts her long ordeal. She wants her children back, but sees the photograph of one of them in the newspaper, offered for adoption. Jorge sticks by her, and soon she is pregnant again, but now the social workers watch her like a hawk, and she loses that baby to them—and then another, in a scene where the social workers enter the maternity ward and all but rip the infant from her womb, while a nurse breaks down and sobs.

To witness Crissy Rock in these scenes is to see acting of such elemental power and truth it can hardly be borne. She screams, she cries, she rages against her fate. The rawness of her need and grief is like an open wound. And yet at the same time we acknowledge that she seems unfit to be a mother, although perhaps Jorge could make a new start for her, and his sweetness and good sense could teach her hard lessons of maturity and balance.

The social workers are monstrous precisely because they seem to apply rules without any regard for the human beings in front of them—and yet we can see their reasoning, as Maggie explodes again and again. She is white, her children are of various races, and now her new husband is a foreigner with questionable British immigration papers; the workers never say anything overtly racist, they are too correct for that, but sometimes you can guess what they're thinking.

Ken Loach directed the film. After twenty-five years of specializing in working-class British life *(Kes, Poor Cow)*, he has recently made a cluster of particularly fine movies: *Riff-Raff*, about the floating population of construction workers; *Raining Stones*, about an unemployed man trying to buy a communion dress for his daughter; and now *Ladybird, Ladybird*, which could have been a predictable tear-jerking docu-drama, but is too honest to stack the deck. What we see here is not a "problem," not a "solution," but simply a painful record from life. The movie is "based on a true story." I never doubted that for a second.

Lady Sings the Blues ★ ★ ★
R, 144 m., 1972

Diana Ross (Billie Holiday), Billy Dee Williams (Louis McKay), Richard Pryor (Piano Man), James Callahan (Reg Hanley), Paul Hampton (Harry), Virginia Capers (Mama Holiday). Directed by Sidney J. Furie and produced by Berry Gordy. Screenplay by Terence McCloy, Chris Clark, and Suzanne de Passa.

My first reaction when I learned that Diana Ross had been cast to play Billie Holiday was a quick and simple one: I didn't think she could do it. I knew she could sing, although not as well as Billie Holiday and certainly not in the same way, but I couldn't imagine Diana Ross reaching the emotional highs and lows of one of the more extreme public lives of our times. But the movie was financed by Motown, and Diana Ross was Motown's most cherished property, so maybe the casting made some kind of commercial sense. After all, Sal Mineo played Gene Krupa.

All of those thoughts were wiped out of my mind within the first three or four minutes of *Lady Sings the Blues,* and I was left with a feeling of complete confidence in a dramatic performance. This was one of the great performances of 1972.

And there is no building up to it. The opening scene is one of total and unrelieved anguish; Billie Holiday is locked into prison, destitute and nearly friendless, and desperately needing a fix of heroin. The high, lonely shriek which escapes from Ross in this scene is a call from the soul, and we know this isn't any "screen debut" by a Top 40 star; this is acting.

It was probably inevitable that the movie itself would follow the tried-and-true formula of most of the musical biographies of the last twenty years. The genre is well-established, and since most of the musicians they've made movies about have had unhappy private lives, there's the problem of making downhill look like uphill, at least sometimes. This is usually handled (and it is again this time) by showing the performer hitting bottom, rebounding into the arms of friends, being nursed back to health, and making a spectacular comeback performance at Carnegie Hall, or at least the Palace. The formula is so firmly established that stars even seem to follow it consciously, and we're left with tantalizing possibilities: Did Judy Garland play the Palace for the last time to give the proper form to her biography? You gotta go out in triumph, no matter what happens before.

Lady Sings the Blues has most of the clichés we expect—but do we really mind clichés in a movie like this? I don't think so. There's the childhood poverty, the searching for love, the unhappy early sexual experiences, the first audition, the big break, the years of climbing to the top, the encounter with hard drugs, the fall, the comeback, the loyal lover . . . we know the scenes by heart.

What brings the movie alive is the performance that Diana Ross, and director Sidney J. Furie, bring to the scenes. As a gangly adolescent set out to work as a maid in a whorehouse, Ross somehow manages to look gangly and adolescent. When she is transformed into a great beauty later in the film, it *is* a transformation, because she was brave enough, and good enough, to really look awful at first: "You got a long way to go," the madam tells her accurately, "before anybody gonna pay $2 for an hour of your time."

The movie is filled with many of the great Billie Holiday songs, and Ross handles them in an interesting way. She doesn't sing in her own style, and she never tries to imitate Holiday, but she sings somehow in the manner of Holiday. There is an uncanny echo, a suggestion, and yet the style is a tribute to Billie Holiday, not an impersonation. The songs do slow the movie down quite a bit, and it feels long at over two hours, but the Billie Holiday music is really the occasion, so I suppose I shouldn't complain.

La Femme Nikita ★ ★ ★
R, 117 m., 1991

Anne Parillaud (Nikita), Jean-Hugues Anglade (Marc), Tcheky Karyo (Bob), Jeanne Moreau (Amande), Jean Reno (Nikita's Friend). Directed and produced by Luc Besson. Screenplay by Besson.

Here is a version of the Pygmalion legend for our own violent times—the story of a young woman who is transformed from a killer in the streets to a government assassin. *La Femme Nikita* is a smart, hard-edged psycho-romantic thriller by the young French director Luc Besson *(Subway),* who follows a condemned woman as she exchanges one doom for another.

The woman is played by Anne Parillaud, who projects a feral hostility in the opening scenes, as she joins a crowd of drug-addled friends in holding up a drugstore. Cornered by the police, she takes advantage of a cop's momentary lapse of attention to grab his gun and shoot him point-blank in the face. She has no hope of escape; she is simply so antisocial and strung out that she doesn't care if she kills or dies.

The courts, of course, sentence her to death, but then a strange thing happens. Her death is faked, and she finds herself inside a secret government program that takes people with no hope and remakes them into programmed hit-men. She is given a new identity, new values, new skills. It doesn't happen overnight. Her controller, a tough spymaster, has to tame her like a circus animal; she is so filled with anger and violence that she will bite and kick him rather than listen gratefully now that he has spared her life. Finally, after three years, she is ready to graduate, to leave the secret training place and live an ordinary life in society until the government needs her.

It is then that she meets a simple, warm, humorous man—a check-out clerk in a grocery store. She likes him at first sight, takes him home, makes him her boyfriend, and begins to feel tenderness and trust, which for her are brand-new emotions. Then the inevitable government call comes. And the rest of the movie is about the ways in which she carries out her deadly assignment while still yearning to be true to the new emotion of love.

Parillaud is the right actress for this role. In the early scenes she barely seems aware she is a woman; she has lived rough in the streets with homeless drug addicts until all gentleness has been bleached from her soul. One of the movie's skills is the way it shows her slowly learning that she is a woman, and how to be a woman, and how to enjoy that. There is a short, touching scene with Jeanne Moreau, as an instructor in the government killing school, who seats Parillaud in front of a mirror and teaches her about makeup and grooming, hair care and eyeliner, and we see the grubby street waif turn into an attractive woman.

La Femme Nikita begins with the materials of a violent thriller, but transcends them with the story of the heroine's transformation. It is a surprisingly touching movie with the same kind of emotional arc as *Awakenings*; the character is in a trance of deprivation and poverty, neglect and drugs, until she is awakened by her violent act and its unexpected result. But, as she awakens to love and sweetness, to the touch of a man who knows nothing about her past, to questions of trust, she also awakens to a world in which, sooner or later, she will have to pay a price for her life and freedom.

La Lectrice ★ ★ ★ ★
R, 98 m., 1989

Miou-Miou (Constance/Marie), Christian Ruche (Jean/Philippe), Sylvie Laporte (Françoise), Michel Raskine (Agency Man), Brigitte Catillon (Eric's Mother/Jocelyn), Regis Royer (Eric), Simon Eine (Hospital Professor), Christian Blanc (Old Teacher). Directed by Michel Deville and produced by Rosalinde Deville. Screenplay by Rosalinde and Michel Deville.

Constance is in bed with her boyfriend when he asks her to read aloud to him. As she reads, she begins to imagine herself as the heroine of the story. The story Constance reads is about Marie, a young woman who needs employment and takes an ad in the paper, offering to read aloud to people. Marie finds that a surprising number of clients want to take advantage of her services—and, as she reads for them, she begins to enter into their lives.

This is the elegant, Chinese-box structure of Michel Deville's *La Lectrice,* and one of the pleasures of the film is the way Deville moves up and down through the various levels of the story, and then sideways through the sometimes devious motives of the clients who hire the reader. Only someone who loves to read would understand how one person can become another, can enter into the life of a person in a book. That is what happens in this movie.

Marie is played by Miou-Miou as a solemn woman who comes to care about her clients. There are several, each one with a different problem (and probably with a different "real" reason why he wants to be read aloud to). There is a young boy who has been gravely injured in an accident and fears for his potency. He wants Marie to read him passionate poetry—and he falls in love with her, identifying her with the poems. An old woman, once filled with fire and conviction, hires Marie to read to her, for one last time, the writers like Tolstoy and Marx who once inspired her. A busy mother hires Marie to read *Alice in Wonderland* to her small daughter. And a rich investor probably wants her to read him pornography, but is reluctant to say so, and so gets respectable erotica instead.

Each client's book reflects the nature of his or her fantasy, and Marie understands that immediately. As she reads to them, a curious process begins to take place. She becomes, in a way, the author of the books. The teen-ager idealizes her as a romantic. The old lady thinks she is an intellectual. The little girl sees her as a mother figure. And the businessman, of course, wants to sleep with her. What is intriguing is that Marie herself starts to identify with the books, and so is almost able to see herself as lover, confidante, mother, and prostitute.

La Lectrice is a movie in love with words—deliriously intoxicated by the stories and images in the pages that Marie reads. But making a movie about reading is like writing a symphony about looking at paintings: How do you make the leap from one medium to another? In Francois Truffaut's *Fahrenheit 451,* another film about the love of books, the final scene showed human beings who had "become" books in order to preserve their contents in an age of book-burning. One was *David Copperfield,* another was *Pride and Prejudice,* walking back and forth in the snow, reciting the words to themselves. In *La Lectrice,* the words become real in a different way—by having an actual ef-

fect. Because the love poems make the teenager amorous, because the eroticism arouses the businessman, the books become like magical talismans.

I hope I have not made *La Lectrice* sound too difficult or dryly intellectual. This is a sensuous film from beginning to end, a film that is all the more seductive because it teases the imagination. As the reader becomes the books she reads, we become the people she reads to. And so, in our imaginations, we see her in all her roles. In some scenes she is sweet, in others thoughtful, in others carnal. The film is a demonstration that we can rarely understand the secret minds of people, so therefore upon their exteriors we project our own fantasies. When the movie was over, I wanted to go out and find the novel by Raymond Jean that the screenplay is based on. I didn't want to read it. I wanted someone to read it to me.

The Land Before Time ★ ★ ★
G, 71 m., 1988

With the voices of: Pat Hingle (Narrator), Helen Shaver (Littlefoot's Mother), Gabriel Damon (Littlefoot), Candice Houston (Cera), Burke Barnes (Daddy Topps), Pat Hingle (Rooter), Judith Barsi (Ducky), Will Ryan (Petrie). Directed by Don Bluth and produced by Bluth, Gary Goldman, and John Pomeroy. Screenplay by Stu Krieger, based on a story by Judy Freudberg and Tony Geiss.

The love affair between small children and prehistoric dinosaurs is a phenomenon of the toy industry, which cannot manufacture brontosauruses and tyrannosaurus rexes fast enough to meet the demand. Kids love dinosaurs, I think, for the same reason they have always felt an emotional identification with movie creatures like Godzilla and Frankenstein's monster. Kids and monsters have lots in common: They are clumsy and are always knocking things over, they feel as if they cannot control themselves, they do not fit easily into the adult world, and they are usually misunderstood.

In *The Land Before Time* the filmmakers make a strategic error, I think, by making their dinosaurs into children. This destroys the distinction between the two species. The dinosaurs in this movie are just as human as the kitten in *Oliver & Co.,* the mouse in *An American Tail,* and all the animated dogs and rabbits and woodpeckers since time immemorial. One of the reasons kids like dino-

saurs is that they are *not* human. They are deliciously alien.

I do not know what kind of movie could have been made from truly reptilian dinosaurs, but I'll bet it would have been interesting. The opening shots of *The Land Before Time,* before the dinosaurs start to speak English, have an eerie fascination. We see a tribe of brontosauruses roaming the parched land, looking for green leaves, which they call "tree stars." There are none to be found, because the climate has changed, and so these peaceful vegetarians head west, seeking a fabled green valley where they hope to find food. They are pursued by their enemies, the sharp-toothed, meat-eating tyrannosaurus rexes. The story is told through the eyes of Littlefoot, a baby brontosaurus who barely escapes being eaten in the first few minutes of the movie.

Littlefoot's saga is an adventure recycled directly out of other movies of this genre, and indeed I was not surprised to discover that the authors of the story also wrote *An American Tail.* Both films involve a childlike creature who is separated from its parents. In this film, Littlefoot's father is nowhere to be found, and his mother dies in an earthquake and the orphan has to undergo a long and perilous journey before finding happiness at the end. The perilous middle sections of both films are fairly rough, as natural forces and predators attempt to destroy the little hero, who joins up with the infants of four other dinosaur species to make his long trek. Both films could have been written by Jack London.

As a backdrop to the series of hazards, the visual look of *The Land Before Time* is apocalyptic. All but the last scenes take place in a blasted heath of red skies, parched land, withered trees, barren wastes, and thorn thickets. But the animation treats this wasteland gently, with little details such as the sparkling drops of water that fall from a leaf, or the ways in which the clumsy, childlike movements of the little creatures are lovingly created.

The Land Before Time does have some charming scenes to counterbalance its grim determinism. Director Don Bluth surpasses himself in a witty ballet in which several prehistoric birdlike creatures fight over a trove of cherries; the animation here is brilliant. There is also a sequence in which Littlefoot and several of his pals get stuck in a tar pit, and a moment at which a clumsy pterodactyl learns to fly. Bluth works in the time-honored

Disney tradition, in which body movements are particularly convincing and the backgrounds are not simply static panoramas.

I guess I sort of liked the film, although I wonder why it couldn't have spent more time on natural history and the sense of discovery, and less time on tragedy.

The Last Boy Scout ★ ★ ★
R, 107 m., 1991

Bruce Willis (Joe Hallenbeck), Damon Wayans (Jimmy Dix), Chelsea Field (Sarah Hallenbeck), Noble Willingham (Sheldon Marcone), Taylor Negron (Milo), Danielle Harris (Darian Hallenbeck), Halle Berry (Cory). Directed by Tony Scott and produced by Joel Silver and Michael Levy. Screenplay by Shane Black and Greg Hicks.

The Last Boy Scout opens with a sequence of such sudden and unexpected violence that the audience is stunned into uneasy silence. The movie never looks back. Perhaps propelled by the determination of its star, Bruce Willis, to erase the box-office curse of *Hudson Hawk*, this film panders with such determination to the base instincts of the action crowd that it will, I am sure, be an enormous hit.

It was produced by Joel Silver, who has made violence toward women a key element in his films, and cheerfully expands its horizons to violence toward children—providing the Willis character with a foul-mouthed thirteen-year-old daughter who is hauled around by bad guys with a gun pointed at her temple. (The film is rated R, proving that violence alone cannot earn the NC-17 rating.)

It is some kind of a tribute to Tony Scott, who directed the film, and especially to Shane Black and Greg Hicks, who wrote the screenplay, that this material survives its own complete cynicism and somehow actually works. Watching it, I felt like some weatherbeaten innocent from an earlier, simpler time. My distaste is irrelevant. This movie is the future. It assumes the average audience now has no standards except those of the mob.

The only consistent theme of the film is its hatred of women. The two heroes (Willis and Damon Wayans) have a wife and a girlfriend, respectively, who cheat on them—the wife with Willis's best friend, the girlfriend by prostituting herself. Both men are at home in this screenplay, which hates women with a particular viciousness; the verbal violence begins by calling them bitches and whores and worse, over and over again, and

the message is that a man can only really trust another man. The end of the movie is peculiar in the way it insists on this; the hero, reconciled with his cheating wife, embraces her and whispers vile obscenities into her ear. We are intended to read them as tender. Then he strolls off lovingly with his buddy.

I am a reporter. I must report not only the film's willingness to degrade women and children. I must also report the film's slick, clever professionalism. As I said before, this film works. Despite any objection I may have felt, it plays well with an audience (although some of the people around me seemed disturbed by an extended scene in which Willis and his child curse each other). The movie has a lot of laughs, its action sequences are thrilling, its surprises are startling, and it shows a real ingenuity in the ways by which it gets Willis into, and out of, trouble.

The plot involves Willis as an ex-Secret Service agent (he once stopped several bullets intended for Jimmy Carter), who is now a flea-bitten private eye. He's hired to protect a stripper (Halle Berry) who is getting threats, and after Berry is ambushed, Willis begins an uneasy partnership with her boyfriend, a disgraced NFL star (Wayans) who was booted out of the league for gambling.

The plot leads to bigger game, all the way up to a corrupt team owner (Noble Willingham) who wants to buy legislators and legalize gambling on pro football. Willingham is surrounded by sleazy and depraved henchmen (Taylor Negron is magnificently despicable as the worst of them), and there is a plot involving high explosives, kidnappings, high-tech chases, long moments spent on the brink of death, graphic beatings, and the involvement of the young child in the most savage of the violence, to flavor it with a novel edge. The original screenplay for *The Last Boy Scout* set a record for its purchase price; that was probably because of the humor of the locker-room dialogue, since the plot itself could have been rewritten by any film school graduate out of the *Lethal Weapon* movies.

The story depends heavily on the device of the Talking Killer, which I have written about elsewhere: the killer who needs only pull the trigger to end the movie, but chooses instead to boast and stall until the hero can somehow outsmart him. The many ways in which Willis outsmarts Talking Killers in this film provide some of its best moments, and there is also excitement in the climactic scene inside the football stadium (although I imagine the average NFL crowd, confronted

with a machine-gun battle inside the stadium, would flee rather than cheer on cue).

The Last Boy Scout is a superb example of what it is: a glossy, skillful, cynical, smart, utterly corrupt, and vilely misogynistic action thriller. How is the critic to respond? To give it a negative review would be dishonest, because it is such a skillful and well-crafted movie. To be positive is to seem to approve its sickness about women. I'll give it three stars. As for my thumb, I'll use it and my forefinger to hold my nose.

The Last Days of Chez Nous ★ ★ ★ ½
R, 96 m., 1993

Lisa Harrow (Beth), Bruno Ganz (J.P.), Kerry Fox (Vicki), Miranda Otto (Annie), Kiri Paramore (Tim), Bill Hunter (Beth's Father). Directed by Gillian Armstrong and produced by Jan Chapman. Screenplay by Helen Garner.

It is one of those households that implies a criticism of the ways other people choose to live. They're free spirits, don't you know, and not bound by the ordinary rules. Beth is Australian, and her husband, J.P., is from France. She is an author, and he is a . . . well, categories, like jobs, would be too limiting for him. He is a self-appointed lord of his domain, willful and spoiled, and expert on everything, especially according to himself. That they love each other is a victory of will over nature. Beth has a teen-ager, Annie.

The film opens as Beth's younger sister, Vicki, comes to live with them after an unsuccessful time of traveling. Not long after, to make ends meet, they take in a boarder, Tim, who plays the piano. Days tumble one after another, most of them centered in the kitchen, where J.P. fancies himself a great cook, and is certainly good at drinking wine while chopping away at helpless vegetables.

The Last Days of Chez Nous is a title that hints not only at the ending of Gillian Armstrong's new film, but also at the tone, which is a certain bitter irony. The household is about to break up, but then again was it really a household anyway—or only Beth's idea of one? "Chez nous" translates as "our house," but it turns out that J.P. and Beth may have different notions of who that encompasses.

The movie is not strongly plotted. Like life, it is a little disorganized, moments of anger and passion occurring side by side with joy, boredom, and the reassuring rhythms of daily life. J.P. and Beth seem to be in love, depending on your definition, but J.P. needs more than one woman to satisfy his ego, and sees himself as such a wonderful fellow that Beth would have to be small-minded to deny him. Looking at him, trying to read his eyes, Beth begins to realize that she may not really know this egotistical foreigner.

Sex is an undercurrent in *Chez Nous* even at the most mundane moments. Annie and Tim begin to like each other. And then, unmistakably to anyone but Beth, her husband and her younger sister begin to feel careless tides pulling them together. Beth takes a few weeks off to drive through the Outback with her aging father, hoping desperately that it isn't too late for them to begin communicating, and while she is gone Vicki and J.P. begin to sleep together.

Neither one thinks much about how Beth will react when she gets back. They don't plan on her finding out. But their moral carelessness is matched by bad planning, and when their secret is revealed, Beth has to decide how she thinks about it. We in the audience have no idea what she will do. The movie is not about ordinary categories of romance and family melodrama, but about these particular and strange individuals, who are smart enough that they don't fall into the usual clichés of guilty betrayal and wounded feelings.

Armstrong, whose first success was *My Brilliant Career*, the movie that introduced Judy Davis, has a gift here for finding the tones of everyday life, for creating bright and untidy people and showing them coping with the dissolution of a household and of a lot of their certainties. The difference between drama and melodrama is that in melodrama the characters fall into categories, and here we would have the Faithless Husband, the Wronged Wife, the Betraying Sister, and the Bystanding Children. Even in real life, many people prefer to play such roles, finding them easier than thinking for themselves. But *The Last Days of Chez Nous* is a drama, and so none of the characters plays an expected part, and what we get is astonishing: Movie characters who think for themselves.

Bruno Ganz, his native German accent edging uncomfortably into a French one, plays one of those large, shambling men who regard life as a feast being held especially for them. Lisa Harrow, as Beth, seems to have married him in the hope of never again being bored. They have, it is true, created an interesting household. Kerry Fox, as the younger sister, is one of those people who absent-

mindedly wreak havoc in ordinary lives because they never stop to think about the consequences of their actions; she sometimes hardly seems aware that she is acting. And in the corner, the daughter and the boarder play two-handed piano, and seem blindingly normal compared to the others.

I like movies like this because I get to meet people who it would be entertaining to know—at a certain distance. I can imagine sitting in their kitchen, watching them prepare dinner, and knowing that at least some of the drama surrounding that process was being created just for my entertainment. You see people like this and you know they will go down in flames, but always in the kind of accident where there are miraculous survivals.

The Last Detail ★ ★ ★
R, 104 m., 1974

Otis Young (Mulhall), Jack Nicholson (Buddusky), Randy Quaid (Meadows), Carol Kane (Prostitute), Michael Moriarty (Marine OD). Directed by Hal Ashby and produced by Gerald Ayres. Screenplay by Robert Towne.

Meadows is a big hulk of a kid who compulsively shoplifts candy bars and peanut butter sandwiches and eats them for consolation. He has been in the navy only long enough to get busted for stealing a charity box with forty bucks inside, for which he has been sentenced to eight years in the Portsmouth naval brig. Buddusky and Mulhall are the two navy lifers assigned to transport him to Portsmouth, and *The Last Detail* is the story of how they travel there on a series of trains, buses, and drunks. It's a very good movie—and the best thing in it is Jack Nicholson's performance as Buddusky. Nicholson, always one of the most interesting of actors, does in *The Last Detail* what he did in *Easy Rider*. He creates a character so complete and so complex that we stop thinking about the movie and just watch to see what he'll do next.

What he tries to do is show the kid a good time. Now a good time, by Buddusky's standards, is not everybody's idea of a good time. It involves great volumes of time spent drinking great volumes of beer. It involves bitching about the system instead of doing something about it. But it also involves some small measure of human sympathy: Buddusky is personally affronted that the kid is going to be locked up for eight years before his life as a man has even begun.

Mulhall (Otis Young), the other member

of this shore patrol, is a serious black man who has spent a lot of years working for his seniority and his retirement rights, and is not going to forfeit everything just by letting one dumb kid escape. But he goes along, within limits, and they take off the kid's handcuffs and try to give him some taste of life. They get him drunk in Washington and take him to a red-light house in New York—and the funny thing is, the kid goes along mostly to please them.

He might be described as a totally unformed youth. He's played superbly by Randy Quaid, who you might remember as the kid with the bottle in his sport-coat pocket in *The Last Picture Show*—the grinning kid in the corner who took Cybill Shepherd skinny-dipping in the next county. His character is the only one that changes in the movie. What happens is that he learns in a very tentative way to assert himself—even to value himself, and make a token protest against his fate.

The direction is by Hal Ashby. How good this movie really is can be gauged by comparing it to *Cinderella Liberty*, another navy movie based on a novel by the same author, Darryl Ponicsan. Both movies have similar world views, and the stories in both move somewhat relentlessly toward inevitable conclusions. But *Cinderella Liberty* just can't be believed, and in *The Last Detail*, we always have the sense that these people are plausible individuals: each limited in his own way, but each somehow coping with life. The movie is ultimately pretty sad, but for most of the way it alternates between being poignant and being very funny. Nicholson plays comedy better than most comedians, because with him the humor seems to well up from the real experiences of his character.

The Last Emperor ★ ★ ★ ★
PG-13, 160 m., 1987

John Lone (Pu Yi, adult), Joan Chen (Wan Jung), Peter O'Toole (Reginald Johnston), Ying Ruocheng (Governor), Victor Wong (Chen Pao Shen), Dennis Dun (Big Li), Ryuichi Sakamoto (Amakasu), Maggie Han (Eastern Jewel). Directed by Bernardo Bertolucci and produced by Jeremy Thomas. Screenplay by Mark Peploe and Bertolucci.

The boy was three when he first sat on the Dragon Throne as emperor of China, and seven when he abdicated. He had barely reached what in the West is considered the age of reason, and already events beyond his control had shaped his life forever. Bernardo Bertolucci's *The Last Emperor* tells the story of this child, named Pu Yi, in an epic that uses the life of one man as a mirror that reflects China's passage from feudalism through revolution to its current identity crisis.

This is a strange epic because it is about an entirely passive character. We are accustomed to epics about heroes who act on their society—Lawrence of Arabia, Gandhi—but Pu Yi was born into a world that allowed him no initiative. The ironic joke was that he was emperor of nothing, for there was no power to go with his title, and throughout the movie he is seen as a pawn and victim, acted upon, exploited for the purposes of others, valued for what he wasn't rather than for what he was.

The movie reveals his powerlessness almost at once; scenes of his childhood in the Forbidden City are intercut with scenes from later in his life, when the Chinese communists had taken power, and he was seized and held in a re-education camp, where a party official spent a decade talking him through a personal transition from emperor to gardener—which was Pu Yi's last, and perhaps happiest, occupation.

But the process in the communist jail actually starts many years earlier, in one of the most poignant scenes in the film, when young Pu Yi is given a bicycle and excitedly pedals it around the Forbidden City until he reaches its gates to the outer world, and is stopped by his own guards. He is an emperor who cannot do the one thing any other little boy in China could do, which was to go out of his own house.

Bertolucci is able to make Pu Yi's imprisonment seem all the more ironic because this entire film was shot on location inside the People's Republic of China, and he was even given permission to film inside the Forbidden City—a vast medieval complex covering some 250 acres and containing 9,999 rooms (only heaven, the Chinese believed, had 10,000 rooms). It is probably unforgivably bourgeois to admire a film because of its locations, but in the case of *The Last Emperor,* the narrative cannot be separated from the awesome presence of the Forbidden City, and from Bertolucci's astonishing use of locations, authentic costumes, and thousands of extras to create the everyday reality of this strange little boy.

There is a scene early in the film when Pu Yi, seated on the Dragon Throne, attended by his minders and servants, grows restless,

as small boys will do. He leaps impatiently from his seat and runs toward the door of the throne room, where at first a vast billowing drapery (a yellow one—the color reserved for only the emperor) obstructs the view. Then the curtain is blown aside, and we see an incredible sight, thousands of the emperor's minions, all of them traditionally costumed eunuchs, lined up in geometric precision as far as the eye can see, all of them kowtowing to the boy.

After he formally abdicates power in 1912, Pu Yi remains on the throne, a figurehead maintained in luxury for the convenience of the real rulers of China. A Scottish tutor named Reginald Johnston (Peter O'Toole) comes out to instruct him in the ways of Europe, and the youth (played in manhood by John Lone) becomes an anglophile, dreaming of "escaping" to Cambridge. Johnston advises him to escape instead into marriage, and he takes an empress (Joan Chen) and a concubine. In 1924, he is thrown out of the Forbidden City, and moves with his retinue back to his native Manchuria, then controlled by the Japanese. In a scene of great elegant irony, Bertolucci shows him in Western clothes, a cigarette in hand, leaning on a piano and crooning "Am I Blue?"

As World War II grows closer, Pu Yi grows increasingly irrelevant, except to the Japanese, who set him up briefly as their puppet in Manchuria. His wife becomes an opium addict and begins a dalliance with a lesbian Japanese spy, his old tutor returns to England, he gives himself over to a life of depravity and drifting, and then everything changes for him when the communists take control of China and he is captured by Russians who turn him over to their new allies.

We might expect the communists to sentence Pu Yi to death (a fate he himself confidently expected), but instead there is the re-education process, complicated by the fact that this grown man has never done anything for himself and does not know how to tie his own shoes or turn off the tap after filling a glass with drinking water. When we see him at the end of the film, he is working as a gardener in Peking, and seems happy, and we assume that for him, at least, re-education was a success because it was essentially education in the first place, for a man whose whole life was directed toward making him impotent and irrelevant.

In Orson Welles's *Citizen Kane,* one of the tycoon's friends says, "I was there before the beginning—and now I'm here after the end."

The Last Emperor ends with an extraordinary sequence, beyond the end, in which an elderly Pu Yi goes to visit the Forbidden City, which is now open to tourists. He sneaks past the velvet rope and climbs onto the Dragon Throne. Once that would have been a fatal offense. And the old man who was once the boy on that throne experiences a complex mixture of emotions. It is an inspired ending for the film, which never makes the mistake of having only one thing to say about the life of a man who embodied all the contradictions and paradoxes of twentieth-century China.

There aren't a lot of action scenes in *The Last Emperor,* and little enough intrigue (even the Japanese spy isn't subtle: "I'm a spy, and I don't care who knows it," she tells the empress on their first meeting). As in *Gandhi,* great historical changes take place during *The Last Emperor,* but, unlike Gandhi, the emperor has no influence on them. His life is a sad irony; his end is a bittersweet elegy. But it is precisely because so little "happens" in this epic that its vast and expensive production schedule is important. When we see those thousands of servants bowing to a little boy, for example, the image is effective precisely because the kowtowing means nothing to the boy, and the lives of the servants have been dedicated to no useful purpose.

Everything involving the life of Pu Yi was a waste. Everything except one thing—the notion that a single human life could have infinite value. In its own way, the Dragon Throne argued that, making an emperor into a god in order to ennoble his subjects. And in its own way, the Chinese revolution argued the same thing by making him into a gardener.

Last Exit to Brooklyn ★ ★ ★ ½
R, 102 m., 1990

Stephen Lang (Harry Black), Jennifer Jason Leigh (Tralala), Burt Young (Big Joe), Peter Dobson (Vinnie), Jerry Orbach (Boyce), Stephen Baldwin (Sal), Alexis Arquette (Georgette), Zette (Regina), Ricki Lake (Donna). Directed by Uli Edel and produced by Bernd Eichinger. Screenplay by Desmond Nakano.

Love stories are about people who find love in happy times. Tragedies are about people who seek love in unhappy times. *Last Exit to Brooklyn* makes a point of taking place in the early 1950s, when all the escape routes had been cut off for its major characters. The union official cannot admit to being left wing. The strike leader cannot reveal he is homosexual. The father cannot express his love for his child, the prostitute cannot accept her love for the sailor, and the drag queen is not able to love himself. There isn't even any music to release these characters—rock 'n' roll is still in the future, and the pop ballads of the era mock the passions of everyday life. The characters drink and some of them do drugs, but they don't get high—they simply find the occasional release of oblivion.

The movie takes place in one of the gloomiest and most depressing urban settings I've seen in a movie. These streets aren't mean; they're unforgiving. Vast blank warehouse walls loom over the barren pavements, and vacant lots are filled with abandoned cars where mockeries of love take place. When Hubert Selby, Jr., wrote the book that inspired this movie twenty-five years ago, it was attacked in some quarters as pornographic, but it failed the essential test: It didn't arouse prurient interest, only sadness and despair.

Why do I respond so strongly to movies like this—or Barfly, Taxi Driver, The Cook, the Thief, His Wife and Her Lover, and Christiane F., which was the previous film by the makers of Last Exit to Brooklyn? Most people hate movies like this. I think perhaps it is because no attempt is being made to force the characters and stories into comforting endings. The movies don't let me off the hook. These are fellow human beings who suffer, who are limited in their freedom to imagine greater happiness for themselves, and yet in their very misery they embody human striving. There is more of humanity in a prostitute trying to truly love, if only for a moment, than in all of the slow-motion romantic fantasies in the world.

The movie takes place in a Brooklyn neighborhood torn by a bitter strike; most of the men work at the factory and are unemployed by the dispute, but for Harry Black (Stephen Lang), a worker who has been hired to run the strike office, these are good times. He has an expense account to stock kegs of beer in the office, he has a telephone, and best of all he has an excuse to spend long hours away from the wife he does not love or understand. He is a homosexual, and he doesn't understand that, either, but strange feelings fill him when the neighborhood drag queen sashays by.

One of the striking workers is Big Joe (Burt Young), whose daughter (Ricki Lake) is pregnant. "She ain't pregnant—she's just fat!" Big Joe insists even in the eighth month, and yet when he discovers it is true, he finds it his duty to beat up the responsible boy—beat him up and then embrace him as a future son-in-law and then beat him up some more at the wedding. He accepts the boy as his daughter's husband, and so the beatings are not really intended as hostile acts, you understand—just the price you have to pay in pain for the freedom of sex.

Sex and pain are linked throughout the movie. When Tralala (Jennifer Jason Leigh), the local prostitute, lures the boys from the Brooklyn Naval Yard into the vacant lots where she works, it's not for sex—it's so neighborhood guys can mug the young draftees and roll them. Tralala gets beaten up a lot, too, both physically and mentally. She has been witness to so many loveless acts of sex that her own body is a thing apart. "I've got the best boobs in the West," she cries, as if they were not a part of her but some kind of award she won in a contest. When one sailor takes her seriously and falls for her, she moves into a Manhattan hotel with him for a few days' mockery of a real relationship. He's naive enough to believe it's love. She's almost sad enough.

But love and sex do not connect in this movie. When Harry Black, the strike leader, finally admits he is gay and expresses his love for the drag queen, he finds, as the sailor does, that the person he loves cares only for money. Eventually both Harry and Tralala end up in vacant lots, brutally punished, because of sex. The only difference is that Harry is attacked because he tries to have sex, and Tralala is punished through sex—through a horrifying gang rape.

Is there any love in this movie? Yes, in a sense. There is a rather simpleminded boy who wanders through the film and idolizes Tralala and yearns after her in a goofy way, but she doesn't know what to do about him. How do you explain to an admirer that his love is misplaced—that really you don't deserve it?

The performances are strong, true, and not a little courageous. One of the best is by Jerry Orbach (the mafioso brother in Crimes and Misdemeanors), who plays a union leader. At a time when McCarthyism is rampant and strikes are seen as a symptom of communist agitation, he tries to handle hotheads on both sides, and there is the sense that he is successful partly because he sticks to business; his personality doesn't have a sexual component.

Last Exit to Brooklyn was banned as a book and resulted in several obscenity cases in both America and England. Remembering the book and now looking at the movie, I wonder what really upset people: Was it the sex or just the lovelessness? The drugs or just the despair? The violence, or its pointlessness? Don't most books prosecuted for sexual obscenity celebrate sex? This one argues that it's not worth the trouble—that you'll end up by breaking your heart.

Last House on the Left ★ ★ ★ ½
R, 82 m., 1972

David Hess (Krug), Ludy Gratham (Phyllis), Sandra Cassell (Mari), Marc Sheffler (Junior), Jeramie Rain (Sadie), Fred Lincoln (Weasel), Gaylord St. James (Dr. Collingwood), Cynthia Carr (Mrs. Collingwood). Directed by Wes Craven and produced by Sean S. Cunningham. Screenplay by Craven.

Last House on the Left is a tough, bitter little sleeper of a movie that's about four times as good as you'd expect. There is a moment of such sheer and unexpected terror that it beats anything in the heart-in-the-mouth line since Alan Arkin jumped out of the darkness at Audrey Hepburn in Wait Until Dark.

I don't want to give the impression, however, that this is simply a good horror movie. It's horrifying, all right, but in ways that have nothing to do with the supernatural. It's the story of two suburban girls who go into the city for a rock concert, are kidnapped by a gang of sadistic escaped convicts and their sluttish girlfriend, and are raped and murdered. Then, in a coincidence even the killers find extreme, the gang ends up spending the night at the home of one of the girls' parents.

The parents accidentally find out the identities of the killers, because of a stolen locket and some blood-stained clothing in their baggage. Enraged, the father takes on the gang single-handedly and murders them. Does any of this sound familiar? Think for a moment. Setting aside the modern details, this is roughly the plot of Ingmar Bergman's The Virgin Spring.

The story is also based on a true incident, we're told at the beginning of the movie, but I have my doubts; I think the producers may simply be trying one of those "only the names have been changed" capers. What does come through in Last House on the Left is a powerful narrative, told so directly and strongly that the audience (mostly in the mood for just another good old exploitation film) was rocked back on its psychic heels.

Wes Craven's direction never lets us out from under almost unbearable dramatic tension (except in some silly scenes involving a couple of dumb cops, who overact and seriously affect the plot's credibility). The acting is unmannered and . . . natural, I guess. There's no posturing. There's a good ear for dialogue and nuance. And there is evil in this movie. Not bloody escapism, or a thrill a minute, but a fully developed sense of the vicious natures of the killers. There is no glory in this violence. And Craven has written in a young member of the gang (again borrowed on Bergman's story) who sees the horror as fully as the victims do. This movie covers the same philosophical territory as Sam Peckinpah's *Straw Dogs,* and is more hard-nosed about it: Sure, a man's home is his castle, but who wants to be left with nothing but a castle and a lifetime memory of horror?

The Last Metro ★ ★ ★
NO MPAA RATING, 133 m., 1980

Catherine Deneuve (Marion Steiner), Gerard Depardieu (Bernard Granger), Jean Poiret (Jean-Loup), Heinz Bennent (Lucas Steiner), Andrea Ferreol (Arlette), Paulette Dubost (Germaine), Jean-Louis Richard (Daxlat). Directed by Francois Truffaut. Screenplay by Truffaut, Suzanne Schiffman, and Jean-Claude Grumberg.

Francois Truffaut said he wanted to satisfy three old dreams by making *The Last Metro.* He wanted to take the camera backstage in a theater, to evoke the climate of the Nazi occupation of France, and to give Catherine Deneuve the role of a responsible woman. He has achieved the first and last dreams, but he doesn't evoke the occupation well enough to make *The Last Metro* more than a sentimental fantasy.

The film takes place backstage, and below-stage, at a theater in Paris. The theater's director is a German Jew (Heinz Bennent) who already has fled from Nazi Germany and now, with the occupation of Paris, goes into permanent hiding in the basement of his theater. Upstairs, his wife (Deneuve) spreads the rumor that he has fled to South America. Then she relays his instructions as the theater attempts to save itself from bankruptcy by presenting a new production.

There are many other characters in the

movie, which at times resembles Truffaut's history of a film production in *Day for Night.* Gerard Depardieu plays the leading man for the new production. The supporting cast includes a young woman who will do anything for a job in the theater, an older woman of ambiguous sexuality, an avuncular stage manager, a gay director, and a powerful critic who is such an evil monster that he must surely have been inspired by a close Truffaut friend. Most of the movie's events take place within the walls of the theater; this is a backstage film, not a war film. We see the rehearsals under way, with Bennent downstairs listening through an air duct. There are the romantic intrigues among the cast members. There are occasional walk-throughs by Nazis. There are moments of great danger, somewhat marred by the fact that Truffaut does not resolve them realistically. And there is an unforgivably sentimental ending that ties up everything without solving anything.

The problem, I think, is that Truffaut sees the Nazi presence in Paris simply as a plot device to create tension within his theatrical troupe. It is ever so much more dramatic if the show must go on despite raids, political directives, and an electrical blackout that requires the stagehands to power a generator by bicycle-power. It's all too cute. Nobody seems to *really* understand that there's a war on out there. And yet, within the unfortunate limitations that Truffaut sets for himself, he does deliver an entertaining movie. Catherine Deneuve is as beautiful as ever, and as enigmatic (it is typical of her performance that at the end we have to wait for the screenplay to tell us who she does, or does not, really love). Depardieu is gangly and sincere, a strong presence. Bennent, as the husband downstairs, is wan and courageous in the Paul Henreid role. And the most fascinating character in the cast is of course the villain, Daxlat, the pro-Nazi critic. He at least seems in touch with the true evil that the others, and Truffaut, see as backdrop.

The Last of the Mohicans ★ ★ ★
R, 120 m., 1992

Daniel Day-Lewis (Hawkeye), Madeleine Stowe (Cora), Russell Means (Chingachgook), Eric Schweig (Uncas), Jodhi May (Alice), Steven Waddington (Heyward). Directed by Michael Mann and produced by Mann and Hunt Lowry. Screenplay by Mann and Christopher Crowe.

Much has been made about how authentic *The Last of the Mohicans* is, about how the cast learned wilderness survival skills and how every bow, arrow, canoe, and moccasin was constructed according to the ancient ways. That's the kind of publicity Cecil B. DeMille used to churn out, as if he had created a brand-new world from scratch, like God.

I am the first to confess I know little about how people really lived in the first decades of the European settlement of North America, but while I was watching *The Last of the Mohicans,* I was haunted by memories of another movie—*Black Robe* (1991), set in the earliest days of the French settlement of Quebec. This was a long and depressing film by Bruce Beresford, who went to great pains to re-create the actual living conditions in North America at the time of his story. The architectural details of the Indian dwellings, their methods of hunting and food-procurement, the way they used absolute cooperation and trust of each other as a weapon against the deadly climate—all were made clear in the movie.

Black Robe did not involve me in its story, but its visual picture of life in those days has stayed with me. Watching *The Last of the Mohicans,* I could not get it out of my mind. As the handsome frontiersman Hawkeye (Daniel Day-Lewis) decides whether to join the troops being raised by the British to fight the French, as he falls in love with the daughter of a British officer (Madeleine Stowe), as he sides with the Mohicans who have adopted him and they face the threat of the Huron tribe that opposes them, I was acutely conscious of the Saturday matinee traditions that were being exploited.

I was also aware that I was enjoying the movie more than the earlier film. Michael Mann, who directed *The Last of the Mohicans,* says that his first conscious movie memory was of the 1936 film version of the same story, starring Randolph Scott, and indeed Philip Dunne's screenplay for that movie is cited as a source for this one. It is also inspired, of course, by the novel by James Fenimore Cooper, whose frontier fantasies were competently demolished in a hilarious essay by Mark Twain, who noted that whenever the plot required a twig to be stepped on, a Cooper character was able to find a twig and step on it, no matter what the difficulty.

Mann's film is quite an improvement on Cooper's all-but-unreadable book, and a worthy successor to the Randolph Scott version. In Daniel Day-Lewis he has found the right actor to play Hawkeye, even though no other role ever played by Day-Lewis *(My Left Foot, A Room With a View, My Beautiful Laundrette)* would remotely suggest that. There are just enough historical and political details; the movie touches quickly on the fine points of British-French-Indian-settler conflicts, so that they can get on to the story we're really interested in, about the hero who wins the heart of the girl.

The scenes of forest fighting in *The Last of the Mohicans* follow all the usual Hollywood rules; the hero rarely misses, and the villains rarely hit anyone needed later in the story. Remembering the sickening thuds of weapon against bone in *Black Robe*, I realized I was looking at a sanitized entertainment, but for the time being I didn't care.

I was also not much disturbed by the movie's predigested history. (How many people, even after seeing this movie, could correctly report that the French and Indian Wars were not between the French and the Indians?) We live in an age of pop images, in which these are the parts that get remembered: Hawkeye, a white man, adopted by Indians, standing between the two civilizations at a time when the Indians were richer and more powerful than the settlers; his decision to escort the British officer's daughter and her sister to the fort where their father awaits them; their adventures along the way, leading to death, bloodshed, and a stirring final shot of the couple gazing out toward the horizon—toward all those millions of unspoiled square miles to be turned into shopping malls by the issue of their loins.

L.A. Story ★ ★ ★
PG-13, 95 m., 1991

Steve Martin (Harris), Victoria Tennant (Sara), Richard E. Grant (Roland), Marilu Henner (Trudi), Sarah Jessica Parker (SanDeE). Directed by Mick Jackson and produced by Daniel Melnick and Michael Rachmil. Screenplay by Steve Martin.

There are some big laughs in Steve Martin's *L.A. Story*, but also a certain delicacy of tone that is bewitching. Somehow the film evokes an elusive side of Los Angeles that isn't often seen in the movies. We know all about the weirdo Southern California lifestyle, the obsessions with food and physical appearance and lifestyle, and we know all the standard show biz types. We've seen movies about

those subjects many times before (and, for that matter, Martin doesn't neglect them).

But there is also a bewitching Los Angeles, a city I glimpsed on my first visit there many years ago, where, after my team won in the Rose Bowl, I was driven up to Mulholland Drive and the whole city lay glittering beneath, and for a kid from downstate Illinois, there was something enchanting going on down there—there was the promise of not merely success and the fulfillment of lust, but even of happiness and the fulfillment of dreams.

None of that has much to do with the reality of the city, I am aware, and sometimes the dreams seem buried by car washes and minimalls, smog and traffic, and urban wretchedness. But *L.A. Story* is a lighthearted fantasy that asks us to just accept one small possibility, and promises us we may find contentment if we keep an open mind. That possibility is that a giant electrical traffic warning billboard might one day start sending personal messages to a TV weatherman, suggesting how he can make improvements in his life.

The weatherman is named Harris K. Telemacher (Martin), and he specializes in goofy weather reports that have little connection with actual climatic conditions. He makes enough money at his job to move in an affluent circle of beautiful people who seem prepared to sit in the sunshine ordering cappucino for the rest of their lives. Then Telemacher is fired, and discovers that his mistress (Marilu Henner) is having an affair, and with relief and a certain feeling of freedom he walks out of the relationship and takes stock of his life, inspired by the sentient highway sign. (He is not without his own difficulties in believing that the sign is on the level; the first time it talks to him, he looks around in paranoid despair, convinced he's on "Candid Camera.")

The sign urges him to telephone a number that's been given to him by a friendly Valley Girl in a clothing store, and before long he finds himself in an energetic relationship with SanDeE (Sarah Jessica Parker), who, like many Southern Californians, spells her name as if it were an explosion at the type foundry. SanDeE has a carefree and liberating air, but eventually Telemacher has to admit that the woman he's really attracted to is Sara (Victoria Tennant), a British journalist in town to do a story on L.A. lifestyles.

These stories of love provide the fragile narrative thread on which Martin (who wrote) and Mick Jackson (who directed)

weave their spell. There are scenes that, in other hands, might have seemed obvious (for example, the daily routine of shooting at other drivers while racing down the freeway), but somehow there is a fanciful edge in the way they do it, a way they define all of their material with a certain whimsical tone.

The film is astonishing in the amount of material it contains. Martin has said he worked on the screenplay, on and off, for seven years, and you can sense that as the film unfolds. It isn't thin or superficial; there is an abundance of observation and invention here, and perhaps because the filmmakers know they have so much good material, there's never the feeling that anything is being punched up, or made to carry more than its share. I was reminded of the films of Jacques Tati, in which, calmly, serenely, an endless series of comic invention unfolds.

Steve Martin shows again in this film that he has found the right comic presence for the movies; the lack of subtlety in early films like *The Jerk* has now been replaced by a smoothness and unforced intelligence. The other cast members are basically in support of that character, although Sarah Jessica Parker has figured out a Valley Girl airhead right down to the ground. What you feel here, as you feel in the work of Tati and some of the comedians of the silent era, is that the whole film is the work of comedy—that it isn't about jokes, or a funny individual, but about creating a fictional world which is funny on its own terms.

The Last Picture Show ★ ★ ★ ★
R, 114 m., 1971

Timothy Bottoms (Sonny), Jeff Bridges (Duane), Cybill Shepherd (Jacy Farrow), Ben Johnson (Sam the Lion), Cloris Leachman (Ruth Popper), Ellen Burstyn (Lois Farrow), Eileen Brennan (Genevieve), Bill Thurman (Coach Popper). Directed by Peter Bogdanovich and produced by Bert Schneider and Stephen J. Friedman. Screenplay by Larry McMurtry and Bogdanovich.

There was something about going to the movies in the 1950s that will never be the same again. It was the decade of the last gasp of the great American movie-going habit, and before my eyes in the middle 1950s the Saturday kiddie matinee died a lingering death at the Princess Theater on Main Street in Urbana. For five or six years of my life (the years between when I was old enough to go alone, and when TV came to town) Saturday afternoon at the Princess was a descent into a dark magical cave that smelled of Jujubes, melted Dreamsicles, and Crisco in the popcorn machine. It was probably on one of those Saturday afternoons that I formed my first critical opinion, deciding vaguely that there was something about John Wayne that set him apart from ordinary cowboys. The Princess was jammed to the walls with kids every Saturday afternoon, as it had been for years, but then TV came to town and within a year the Princess was no longer an institution. It survived into the early 1960s and then closed, to be reborn a few years later as the Cinema. The metallic taste of that word, cinema, explains what happened when you put it alongside the name "Princess."

Peter Bogdanovich's *The Last Picture Show* uses the closing of another theater on another Main Street as a motif to frame a great many things that happened to America in the early 1950s. The theater is the Royal, and along with the pool hall and the all-night cafe it supplies what little excitement and community survives in a little West Texas crossroads named Anarene.

All three are owned by Sam the Lion, who is just about the only self-sufficient and self-satisfied man in town. The others are infected by a general malaise, and engage in sexual infidelities partly to remind themselves they are alive. There isn't much else to do in Anarene, no dreams worth dreaming, no new faces, not even a football team that can tackle worth a damn. The nourishing myth of the Western (*Wagonmaster* and *Red River* are among the last offerings at the Royal) is being replaced by nervously hilarious TV programs out of the East, and defeated housewives are reassured they're part of the "Strike It Rich" audience with a heart of gold.

Against this background, we meet two high school seniors named Sonny and Duane, who are the co-captains of the shameful football squad. We learn next to nothing about their home lives, but we hardly notice the omission because their real lives are lived in a pickup truck and a used Mercury. That was the way it was in high school in the 1950s, and probably always will be: A car was a mobile refuge from adults, frustration, and boredom. When people in their thirties say today that sexual liberation is pale compared to a little prayerful groping in the front seat, they are onto something.

During the year of the film's action, the two boys more or less survive coming-of-age. They both fall in love with the school's only beauty, a calculating charmer named

Jacy who twists every boy in town around her little finger before taking this skill away with her to Dallas. Sonny breaks up with his gum-chewing girlfriend and has an unresolved affair with the coach's wife, and Duane goes off to fight the Korean War. There are two deaths during the film's year, but no babies are born, and Bogdanovich's final pan shot along Main Street curiously seems to turn it from a real location (which it is) into a half-remembered backdrop from an old movie. *The Last Picture Show* is a great deal more complex than it might at first seem, and this shot suggests something of its buried structure. Every detail of clothing, behavior, background music, and decor is exactly right for 1951—but that still doesn't explain the movie's mystery.

Mike Nichols's *Carnal Knowledge* began with 1949, and yet felt modern. Bogdanovich has been infinitely more subtle in giving his film not only the decor of 1951, but the visual style of a movie that might have been shot in 1951. The montage of cutaway shots at the Christmas dance; the use of an insert of Sonny's foot on the accelerator; the lighting and black-and-white photography of real locations as if they were sets—everything forms a stylistic whole that works. It isn't just a matter of putting in Jo Stafford and Hank Williams.

The Last Picture Show has been described as an evocation of the classic Hollywood narrative film. It is more than that; it is a belated entry in that age—the best film of 1951, you might say. Using period songs and decor to create nostalgia is familiar enough, but to tunnel down to the visual level and get that right, too, and in a way that will affect audiences even if they aren't aware how, is one hell of a directing accomplishment. Movies create our dreams as well as reflect them, and when we lose the movies we lose the dreams. I wonder if Bogdanovich's film doesn't at last explain what it was that Pauline Kael, and a lot of the rest of us, lost at the movies.

The Last Seduction ★ ★ ★ ★
NO MPAA RATING, 110 m., 1994

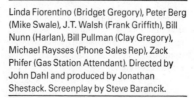

Linda Fiorentino (Bridget Gregory), Peter Berg (Mike Swale), J.T. Walsh (Frank Griffith), Bill Nunn (Harlan), Bill Pullman (Clay Gregory), Michael Raysses (Phone Sales Rep), Zack Phifer (Gas Station Attendant). Directed by John Dahl and produced by Jonathan Shestack. Screenplay by Steve Barancik.

There is a kind of deliciousness to the great movie villains. By setting out to do evil, they tempt our own darker natures. By getting away with it, they alarm us: Is there nothing safe or sacred? In crime pictures and thrillers, the villains are almost always more interesting than the heroes, and there is a kind of unconscious sigh in the audience when a really intriguing villain is defeated. Harry Lime doesn't even appear in the first eighty minutes of *The Third Man*, and yet is more fascinating than anyone on the screen.

John Dahl's *The Last Seduction* knows how much we enjoy seeing a character work boldly outside the rules. It gives us a diabolical evil woman, and goes the distance with her. We keep waiting for the movie to lose its nerve, and it never does: This woman is bad from beginning to end, she never reforms, she never compromises, and the movie doesn't tack on one of those contrived conclusions where the morals squad comes in and tidies up.

The woman is named Bridget Gregory, although she goes under other names as the plot develops. She is played by Linda Fiorentino, with a hard voice and cold eyes and a certain fearsome sexiness; she plays Bridget as the kind of woman who has the same effect on a man as a bucket of ice in the bathtub. Her motivation is simple: She wants to get her hands on large amounts of money, and is willing to play any game with any man who will help her. "Are you still a lawyer?" she asks her attorney. "Yeah," he says. "Are you still a self-serving bitch?"

As the movie opens, she and her husband have made a big haul—$700,000 in illegal funds. Then he makes the big mistake of hitting her in the face. He knows it's a mistake: "Hey, you can hit me anywhere, hard." During the course of the movie she will accept his invitation, in her own way.

The plot takes her to a small town, where she meets a guy named Mike (Peter Berg). He tries to pick her up in a bar. This is one of the more unwise moves in his life. She rejects him, then casually decides to toy with him, and eventually ends up recruiting him as an accessory to murder. He never quite catches on to the full depth of her deception.

It would not be fair to *The Last Seduction* to say much more about the plot, which only gradually reveals itself even to Bridget (she has a gift for improvising, moving from one crime to another as a jazzman might sample various melodic lines). Like Billy Wilder's classic *Double Indemnity*, where Barbara Stanwyck mesmerized Fred MacMurray with his own lust, *The Last Seduction* is about the way even a smart guy gets dumb when he starts thinking tumescently.

The Last Seduction is the second amazing film I've seen by John Dahl, whose *Red Rock West* was a sleeper hit in early 1994. Who is this guy? He makes movies so smart and cynical that the American movie industry doesn't know how to handle him.

I loved *Red Rock West* when I saw it in 1993 at the Toronto Film Festival, but distributors wouldn't touch it, and it went to cable and video without a theatrical release. Then a theater in San Francisco started showing it, and set a house record, and soon it had returned from its video grave to play in theaters all over the country. Then came *The Last Seduction*, with the same story: passed over by distributors, played on cable, etc. And then it opened in London and got some of the best reviews of the year, before finally arriving in American theaters.

What is it? Do distributors think American audiences are so dumb they can't appreciate a smart woman who unspools a criminal plan of diabolical complexity, while treating men like disposable diapers? Are they afraid of a female character who is *really* evil—not just pretend-bad, like the saucy heroines of the glossy Hollywood slasher movies? (There's a pop psychology theory that women are weak in American movies because Hollywood executives are terrified of strong women.)

The great quality in *The Last Seduction* is the dry humor with which Linda Fiorentino puts across the role. Look at this movie just a little sideways, and it's a comedy, although you can never quite catch Dahl or Fiorentino smiling. It must have been a lot of fun for her to play the role; there are several scenes where the men in the movie simply cannot believe she's really serious. "You mean this broad is really going to go through with that?" She is.

Fiorentino has played other roles like this. She has a quality about her. In *VisionQuest* (1985), a silly wrestling movie, there was nothing silly about her scenes. In Martin Scorsese's *After Hours*, she was the black widow waiting in the net that the hapless hero stumbled into. What's crucial is that she plays these roles with relish: She seems to enjoy the freedom a script like *The Last Seduction* gives her, and the result is a movie that is not only ingenious and entertaining, but liberating, because we can sense the story isn't going to be twisted into conformity with some stupid formula.

Last Tango in Paris ★ ★ ★ ★
x, 127 m., 1972

Marlon Brando (Paul), Maria Schneider (Jeanne), Darling Legitimus (Concierge), Jean-Pierre Leaud (Tom). Directed by Bernardo Bertolucci and produced by Alberto Grimaldi. Screenplay by Bertolucci and Franco Arcalli.

Bernardo Bertolucci's *Last Tango in Paris* is one of the great emotional experiences of our time. It's a movie that exists so resolutely on the level of emotion, indeed, that possibly only Marlon Brando, of all living actors, could have played its lead. Who else can act so brutally and imply such vulnerability and need?

For the movie is about need; about the terrible hunger that its hero, Paul, feels for the touch of another human heart. He is a man whose whole existence has been reduced to a cry for help—and who has been so damaged by life that he can only express that cry in acts of crude sexuality.

Bertolucci begins with a story so simple (which is to say, so stripped of any clutter of plot) that there is little room in it for anything but the emotional crisis of his hero. The events that take place in the everyday world are remote to Paul, whose attention is absorbed by the gradual breaking of his heart. The girl, Jeanne, is not a friend and is hardly even a companion; it's just that because she happens to wander into his life, he uses her as an object of his grief.

The movie begins when Jeanne, who is about to be married, goes apartment-hunting and finds Paul in one of the apartments. It is a big, empty apartment, with a lot of sunlight but curiously little cheer. Paul rapes her, if rape is not too strong a word to describe an act so casually accepted by the girl. He tells her that they will continue to meet there, in the empty apartment, and she agrees.

Why does she agree? From her point of view—which is not a terribly perceptive one—why not? One of the several things this movie is about is how one person, who may be uncommitted and indifferent, nevertheless can at a certain moment become of great importance to another. One of the movie's strengths comes from the tragic imbalance between Paul's need and Jeanne's almost unthinking participation in it. Their difference is so great that it creates tremendous dramatic tension; more, indeed, than if both characters were filled with passion.

They do continue to meet, and at Paul's insistence they do not exchange names. What has come together in the apartment is almost an elemental force, not a connection of two beings with identities in society. Still, inevitably, the man and the girl do begin to learn about each other. What began, on the man's part, as totally depersonalized sex develops into a deeper relationship almost to spite him.

We learn about them. He is an American, living in Paris these last several years with a French wife who owned a hotel that is not quite a whorehouse. On the day the movie begins, the wife has committed suicide. We are never quite sure why, although by the time the movie is over we have a few depressing clues.

The girl is young, conscious of her beauty and the developing powers of her body, and is going to marry a young and fairly inane filmmaker. He is making a movie of their life together; a camera crew follows them around as he talks to her and kisses her—for herself or for the movie, she wonders.

The banality of her "real" life has thus set her up for the urgency of the completely artificial experience that has been commanded for her by Paul. She doesn't know his name, or anything about him, but when he has sex with her it is certainly real; there is a life in that empty room that her fiancé, with all of his *cinema verité,* is probably incapable of imagining.

She finds it difficult, too, because she is a child. A child, because she hasn't lived long enough and lost often enough to know yet what a heartbreaker the world can be. There are moments in the film when she does actually seem to look into Paul's soul and half-understand what she sees there, but she pulls back from it; pulls back, finally, all the way—and just when he had come to the point where he was willing to let life have one more chance with him.

A lot has been said about the sex in the film; in fact, *Last Tango in Paris* has become notorious because of its sex. There is a lot of sex in this film—more, probably, than in any other legitimate feature film ever made—but the sex isn't the point, it's only the medium of exchange. Paul has somehow been so brutalized by life that there are only a few ways he can still feel.

Sex is one of them, but only if it is debased and depraved—because he is so filled with guilt and self-hate that he chooses these most intimate of activities to hurt himself beyond all possibilities of mere thoughts and words. It is said in some quarters that the sex in the movie is debasing to the girl, but I don't think it is. She's almost a bystander, a witness at the scene of the accident. She hasn't suffered enough, experienced enough, to more than dimly guess at what Paul is doing to himself with her. But Paul knows, and so does Bertolucci; only an idiot would criticize this movie because the girl is so often naked but Paul never is. That's their relationship.

The movie may not contain Brando's greatest performance, but it certainly contains his most emotionally overwhelming scene. He comes back to the hotel and confronts his wife's dead body, laid out in a casket, and he speaks to her with words of absolute hatred—words which, as he says them, become one of the most moving speeches of love I can imagine.

As he weeps, as he attempts to remove her cosmetic death mask ("Look at you! You're a monument to your mother! You never wore makeup, never wore false eyelashes . . ."), he makes it absolutely clear why he is the best film actor of all time. He may be a bore, he may be a creep, he may act childish about the Academy Awards—but there is no one else who could have played that scene flat-out, no holds barred, the way he did, and make it work triumphantly.

The girl, Maria Schneider, doesn't seem to act her role so much as to exude it. On the basis of this movie, indeed, it's impossible to really say whether she can act or not. That's not her fault; Bertolucci directs her that way. He wants a character who ultimately does not quite understand the situation she finds herself in; she has to be that way, among other reasons, because the movie's ending absolutely depends on it. What happens to Paul at the end must seem, in some fundamental way, ridiculous. What the girl does at the end has to seem incomprehensible—not to us; to her.

What is the movie about? What does it all mean? It is about, and means, exactly the same things that Bergman's *Cries and Whispers* was about, and meant. That's to say that no amount of analysis can extract from either film a rational message. The whole point of both films is that there is a land in the human soul that's beyond the rational—beyond, even, words to describe it.

Faced with a passage across that land, men make various kinds of accommodations. Some ignore it; some try to avoid it through temporary distractions; some are lucky enough to have the inner resources for a successful journey. But of those who do

not, some turn to the most highly charged resources of the body; lacking the mental strength to face crisis and death, they turn on the sexual mechanism, which can at least be depended upon to function, usually.

That's what the sex is about in this film (and in *Cries and Whispers*). It's not sex at all (and it's a million miles from intercourse). It's just a physical function of the soul's desperation. Paul in *Last Tango in Paris* has no difficulty in achieving an erection, but the gravest difficulty in achieving a life-affirming reason for one.

The Last Temptation of Christ ★ ★ ★
R, 160 m., 1988

Willem Dafoe (Jesus), Harvey Keitel (Judas), Paul Greco (Zealot), Steven Shill (Centurion), Barbara Hershey (Mary Magdalene), Harry Dean Stanton (Paul), David Bowie (Pontius Pilate), Verna Bloom (Mary the Mother), Andre Gregory (John the Baptist). Directed by Martin Scorsese and produced by Barbara De Fina. Screenplay by Paul Schrader.

Christianity teaches that Jesus was both God and man. That he could be both at once is the central mystery of the Christian faith, and the subject of *The Last Temptation of Christ*. To be fully man, Jesus would have had to possess all of the weakness of man, to be prey to all of the temptations—for as man, he would have possessed God's most troublesome gift, free will. As the son of God, he would of course have inspired the most desperate wiles of Satan, and this is a film about how he experienced temptation and conquered it.

That, in itself, makes *The Last Temptation of Christ* sound like a serious and devout film, which it is. The astonishing controversy that has raged around this film is primarily the work of fundamentalists who have their own view of Christ and are offended by a film that they feel questions his divinity. But in the father's house are many mansions, and there is more than one way to consider the story of Christ—why else are there four Gospels? Among those who do not already have rigid views on the subject, this film is likely to inspire more serious thought on the nature of Jesus than any other ever made.

That is the irony about the attempts to suppress this film; it is a sincere, thoughtful investigation of the subject, made as a collaboration between the two American filmmakers who have been personally most attracted to serious films about sin, guilt, and

redemption. Martin Scorsese, the director, has made more than half of his films about battles in the souls of his characters between grace and sin. Paul Schrader, the screenwriter, has written Scorsese's best films *(Taxi Driver, Raging Bull)* and directed his own films about men torn between their beliefs and their passions *(Hardcore,* with George C. Scott as a fundamentalist whose daughter plunges into the carnal underworld, and *Mishima,* about the Japanese writer who killed himself as a demonstration of his fanatic belief in tradition).

Scorsese and Schrader have not made a film that panders to the audience—as almost all Hollywood religious epics traditionally have. They have paid Christ the compliment of taking him and his message seriously, and have made a film that does not turn him into a garish, emasculated image from a religious postcard. Here he is flesh and blood, struggling, questioning, asking himself and his father which is the right way, and finally, after great suffering, earning the right to say, on the cross, "It is accomplished."

The critics of this film, many of whom did not see it, raised a sensational hue and cry about the final passages, in which Christ on the cross, in great pain, begins to hallucinate and imagines what his life would have been like if he had been free to live as an ordinary man. In his reverie, he marries Mary Magdalene, has children, grows old. But it is clear in the film that this hallucination is sent to him by Satan, at the time of his greatest weakness, to tempt him. And in the hallucination itself, in the film's most absorbing scene, an elderly Jesus is reproached by his aging Apostles for having abandoned his mission. Through this imaginary conversation, Jesus finds the strength to shake off his temptation and return to consciousness to accept his suffering, death, and resurrection.

During the hallucination, there is a very brief moment when he is seen making love with Magdalene. This scene is shot with such restraint and tact that it does not qualify in any way as a "sex scene," but instead is simply an illustration of marriage and the creation of children. Those offended by the film object to the very notion that Jesus could have, or even imagine having, sexual intercourse. But, of course, Christianity teaches that the union of man and wife is one of the fundamental reasons God created human beings, and to imagine that the son of God, as a man, could not encompass such thoughts within his intelligence is itself a kind of insult. Was he less than the rest of us? Was he not fully man?

There is biblical precedent for such temptations. We read of the forty days and nights during which Satan tempted Christ in the desert with visions of the joys that could be his if he renounced his father. In the film, which is clearly introduced as a fiction and not as an account based on the Bible, Satan tries yet once again at the moment of Christ's greatest weakness. I do not understand why this is offensive, especially since it is not presented in a sensational way.

I see that this entire review has been preoccupied with replying to the attacks of the film's critics, with discussing the issues, rather than with reviewing *The Last Temptation of Christ* as a motion picture. Perhaps that is an interesting proof of the film's worth. Here is a film that engaged me on the subject of Christ's dual nature, that caused me to think about the mystery of a being who could be both God and man. I cannot think of another film on a religious subject that has challenged me more fully. The film has offended those whose ideas about God and man it does not reflect. But then, so did Jesus.

The Late Show ★ ★ ★
PG, 94 m., 1977

Art Carney (Ira Wells), Lily Tomlin (Margo), Bill Macy (Charlie Hatter), Eugene Roche (Ron Birdwell), Joanna Cassidy (Laura Birdwell), John Considine (Lamar), Howard Duff (Harry Regan), Ruth Nelson (Mrs. Schmidt). Directed by Robert Benton and produced by Robert Altman. Screenplay by Benton.

It's hard enough for a movie to sustain one tone, let alone half a dozen, but that's just what Robert Benton's *The Late Show* does. It's the story of a strangely touching relationship between two people. It's a violent crime melodrama. It's a comedy. It's a commentary on the private-eye genre, especially its 1940s manifestations. It's a study of the way older people do a balancing act between weariness and experience. It's a celebration of that uncharted continent, Lily Tomlin.

And most of all, it's a movie that dares a lot, pulls off most of it, and entertains us without insulting our intelligence. What's quietly astonishing is that all of it starts with a woman coming to a private eye about a missing cat. The woman is played by Lily Tomlin, who somehow provides scatterbrained eccentricism with a cutting edge.

The cat has been missing a couple of days, and she's worried. The private eye is played by Art Carney, who has seen it all twice, when once would have been too much.

He takes the case maybe because he could use the money, maybe because he's intrigued by the client, maybe because he's bored, maybe because he's been taking cases so long it's second nature. He doesn't give a damn about the cat. But then, in a series of plot developments so labyrinthine we should be taking notes, the missing cat leads to a mysterious robbery, a missing stamp collection, a fence with a house full of stolen goods, and a dead body that's in the . . .

But, no, I won't say where the body is, because the way Benton reveals it and then lets Lily Tomlin discover it (when all she was after was a Coke) is one of the movie's many pleasures. A friend of mine objected to the body, and to the movie's violence, as being unnecessary in a comedy. Well, *The Late Show* is a long way from being only a comedy, and the introductory shot of that body redeems any amount of gratuitous movie violence.

It's the case with most good detective fiction that the puzzle seems impossible to solve until the last chapter, when everything is made transparently clear. That's true here, with Art Carney providing a brilliant analysis of the connections and coincidences just when it's most irrelevant. But the plot's incidental to the movie's center, which has to do with Carney and Lily Tomlin.

You see, they're allowed to be people here. They're allowed to play characters who have no particular connection with clichés or stereotypes or characters who were successful in a box-office hit last year. Yes, Carney's a private eye, but a particular one: Overweight and wheezing, hard of hearing, given to comments that only obliquely refer to the problem at hand.

And Lily Tomlin . . . well, her character employs a form of reasoning that has nothing to do with logic but a lot to do with the good reasons we have for behaving as we do. An example. Art Carney pretends to be mortally ill (never mind why). He is not (never mind why). His ruse has saved their lives (never mind how). Lily Tomlin is not pleased: She could have had a heart attack! Does he think it's funny, playing with his own friend's *emotions* that way? Doesn't he have any *consideration*?

Benton's screenplay is filled with lines that perfectly define their moments (and be-

long so securely to the characters that they seem to come from them, as some of them probably did). The way in which Tomlin explains why today is the *pits*, for example. The way Carney wonders if it would kill her, for chrissakes, to wear a dress once in a while. The way Carney's sometime partner talks to himself before he dies. The way the fence offers a bribe of a stereo set.

The Late Show is one of three movies from the seventies that had their spiritual origins in the classic private-eye films. The other two were Dick Richards's *Farewell, My Lovely* (in which Robert Mitchum demonstrated that he was born to play Philip Marlowe), and Robert Altman's *The Long Goodbye*, (in which Elliott Gould demonstrated that he was not).

Altman produced *The Late Show*, which is probably another way of saying he made it possible to be filmed, and Benton has brilliantly realized it. Maybe these three films about an all but extinct occupation are telling us something: That the more we become plastic and bland, the more we become fascinated by a strata in our cities we'd like to believe still exists, a society of loners and eccentrics, people brave and crazy and doomed, old private eyes and cat lovers. If they're OK, we're OK.

Laws of Gravity ★ ★ ★
R, 100 m., 1992

Peter Greene (Jimmy), Edie Falco (Denise), Adam Trese (Jon), Arabella Field (Celia), Paul Schulze (Frankie), Saul Stein (Sal). Directed by Nick Gomez and produced by Bob Gosse and Larry Meistrich. Screenplay by Gomez.

Seems like every week there's a story in the paper about how somebody got shot in the street outside a tavern on Saturday night. It was a fight over guns, or money, or drugs, or love, or some damn thing nobody can now quite remember. *Laws of Gravity* is, in a way, the story of all of those killings. It is about the desultory lives of a group of friends who do a little shoplifting and a lot of drinking and sitting around in the kitchen and talking, and about how bad things, in addition to happening to good people, also happen to dumb people.

The movie covers a few days in the lives of Denise and Jimmy, who are married, and Jon and Celia, who are going together, or something; it's one of those relationships in which two people, who don't have much going for themselves to begin with, find that by joining forces, they can create a synergy in which each can bring out the worst in the other.

They hang out in bars and on the street. They talk all the time. They never shut up. You could call them criminal, but not criminals—they're not ambitious or well-enough organized to qualify for professional standing. They go into drugstores and steal shampoo, stuff like that. Then they fight over whether they stole crappy shampoo. They are in and out of a bar where they know everybody. If they read Elmore Leonard, which is doubtful, they would say, "Hey, he's telling our story!"

One day Sal turns up. He has some guns for sale. The guys buy the guns. Denise thinks this is crazy, especially since Jimmy is on parole and this is not going to look good if the guns turn up at the wrong time in the wrong way. All of this does add up to a plot, an eventually interesting one in fact, but story is not the point here. *Laws of Gravity* is about behavior, and its eye and ear are what make the movie worth seeing.

Much has been made of the fact that Nick Gomez, who wrote and directed this film, did it on a budget of around $35,000, in a few weeks, working with actors who saw it as a labor of love. Sometimes I think stories of low-budget heroics backfire on filmmakers; the average audience would probably prefer that the movie cost more. Besides, there's always some kid like Robert Rodriguez who comes along and says his film, *El Mariachi*, cost $7,000, and then $35,000 looks like a wastrel squandering his inheritance.

The point with *Laws of Gravity*, no matter what it cost, is that the screenplay and the acting do such an accurate job of achieving the movie's goals. What Gomez wants to do, I guess, is to show us exactly how his characters look and sound—how they talk all the time, screaming at each other a lot, in what sometimes sounds like a movie inspired by the Rosie Perez performance in *White Men Can't Jump*. By the end of the film, we know these people fairly well, and we can understand with an almost ruthless clarity how sometimes people get themselves shot outside of taverns.

A League of Their Own ★ ★ ★
PG, 124 m., 1992

Tom Hanks (Jimmy Dugan), Geena Davis (Dottie Hinson), Lori Petty (Kit Keller), Madonna (Mae Mordabito), Rosie O'Donnell (Doris Murphy), Megan Cavanaugh (Marla

Hooch), Tracy Reiner (Betty Horn), Bitty Schram (Evelyn Gardner). Directed by Penny Marshall and produced by Robert Greenhut and Elliot Abbott. Screenplay by Lowell Ganz and Babaloo Mandel.

Until seeing Penny Marshall's *A League of Their Own*, I had no idea that an organization named the All-American Girls' Professional Baseball League ever flourished in this country, even though I was twelve when it folded up shop, and therefore of an age to collect Bob Feller and Robin Roberts baseball cards and listen to the Cardinals on the radio. The league was founded in 1943, when it briefly appeared that men's baseball would be a casualty of the war, and once the men came marching home it's a wonder the AAGPBL survived until 1954. Then it was consigned to oblivion; history is written by the victors.

At the time, it seemed as if the AAGPBL might mean the financial survival of the major league baseball franchises and their owners. The movie gives us a Chicago candy-bar mogul in place of the Wrigleys, and shows his agents scouting the countryside for women who could play ball. In a rural area of Oregon, the scout finds two sisters, Dottie and Kit (Geena Davis and Lori Petty), one who can catch and hit, the other who can throw but is a sucker for high fastballs. He brings them back to Chicago for tryouts with a lot of other hopefuls, including would-be team members played by Madonna, Rosie O'Donnell, and Megan Cavanaugh.

A coach is needed for the team, which is based in Rockford. The owner (Garry Marshall) recruits Jimmy Dugan (Tom Hanks), a onetime home-run king whose alcoholism has wrecked his career and left him without prospects. For the first few weeks of the season, Dugan can hardly focus on the field, but then he starts to take an interest in his girls, and excitement builds. By the end of the season, Rockford is in the World Series against Racine (no great achievement, since there are only four teams in the league), and the movie, like all sports movies, ends with a great play at the last moment.

A League of Their Own follows many of the time-honored formulas of sports movies, and has a fair assortment of stock characters (the plain girl who gains confidence, the brash girl with the heart of gold, the jealous sisters), but it has another level that's a lot more interesting.

What happened during World War II was that American society, after years of perpet-

uating the image of the docile little woman who sat at home caring for her lord and master, suddenly found that it needed women who were competent to do hard, skilled work. Rosie the Riveter became a national emblem, Hollywood threw out its romance formulas and started making movies about strong, independent females, and it was discovered that women could actually excel at professional sports.

The movie remembers this period from the present; it begins with Dottie Hinson, the Geena Davis character, now older, taking a trip to Cooperstown for ceremonies honoring the AAGPBL. What we learn about Dottie is that she never took women's baseball all that seriously. She was the best player of her time, and yet, in her mind, her life was simply on hold until her husband came back from the war. Dugan, the coach, tells her she lights up when she plays baseball—that something comes over her. But she doesn't seem aware of it.

This ambiguity about a woman's role is probably in the movie because it was directed by a woman, Penny Marshall. A man might have assumed that these women knew how all-important baseball was. Marshall shows her women characters in a tug-of-war between new images and old values, and so her movie is about transition—about how it felt as a woman to suddenly have new roles and freedom.

The movie has a real bittersweet charm. The baseball sequences, we've seen before. What's fresh are the personalities of the players, the gradual unfolding of their coach, and the way this early chapter of women's liberation fit into the hidebound traditions of professional baseball. By the end, when the women get together again for their reunion, it's touching, the way they have to admit that, whataya know, they really were pioneers.

Leap of Faith ★ ★ ★
PG-13, 106 m., 1992

Steve Martin (Jonas Nightengale), Debra Winger (Jane), Lolita Davidovich (Marva), Liam Neeson (Will), Lukas Haas (Boyd), Meat Loaf (Hoover). Directed by Richard Pearce and produced by Michael Manheim and David V. Picker. Screenplay by Janus Cercone.

The caravan comes tooling down the highway, a couple of custom buses and big semis, carrying salvation to the needy. It's a high-tech revival show, starring Jonas Nightengale, faith healer and preacher, who can pick a stranger at random out of his audience, and tell him the most amazing things about himself. And then he takes up a collection. That's the most important part of the show.

Leap of Faith is the first movie to reveal the actual methods used by some revivalists and faith healers to defraud their unsuspecting congregations. Earlier movies, from features like *Elmer Gantry* and *Uforia* to the documentary *Marjoe*, have had an equally jaundiced view of barnstorming evangelists, but this is the first exposé of the high-tech age, showing how electronics and computers are used to fabricate miracles on demand.

Steve Martin stars, as a preacher who has conned so many people in so many ways that he hardly knows when he's conning himself. As the movie opens, one of the trucks breaks down with engine trouble, and they pull off into a Southwestern backwater to throw a few unscheduled shows until replacement parts arrive. It seems like an ordinary enough town. He doesn't realize it's his personal crossroads.

The role is an unusual one for Martin, who plays it straight (this is not a comedy) and yet satirizes the character at the same time. Or is it satire? I've seen faith healers on TV as bizarre as Nightengale, with his prancing, posturing delivery, his show-biz antics, his glittering suits, his backup gospel choir. What I haven't seen, although I've read about it in court cases, is the way faith healers use computerized data bases, informers, and overheard conversations to gather miraculous insights into the innocents in their congregations. There's a tiny earpiece in the preacher's ear, so that a backstage helper can whisper instructions: "Woman in red, sixth row aisle seat . . . has back problems."

Debra Winger plays the woman backstage at the computer, the wizard of this particular Oz. Like her boss, she sees the show as good, honest entertainment. People pay their money, and they leave with a few laughs, a few tears, some great music, and maybe a little more hope than they walked in with. Where's the harm in that? When the local sheriff (Liam Neeson) tries to shut down the show because times are hard, the drought is killing the crops, and people don't have money to throw away on con men, it's Winger's job to charm him. She tries to. He charms her, too, and it's clear that in another time and another place, they could easily fall in love. But maybe not this time.

The preacher meets someone in the town, too. A waitress (Lolita Davidovich) with a crippled brother. He sees her as a conquest.

Or maybe as something more. The boy sees the preacher as a man who can possibly heal his crippled leg. The preacher tries to warn him off, tries to give the kid a break. He knows the truth about his own miracles, or thinks he does.

Leap of Faith, directed by Richard Pearce from a screenplay by Janus Cercone, begins as an exposé, develops into a social commentary, and ends . . . without really ending. It's strange, the way this movie opens and builds so strongly, and then has such an unsatisfying ending. I'm not talking about what happens just before the end, but about the way the screenplay never really develops that, never completes the arc of the preacher's character. Maybe the ending is seen as open; I see it as inconclusive, a cop-out.

And yet the movie itself has considerable qualities, among them Martin's performance as Nightengale. This isn't the sleek, groomed, prosperous Steve Martin we've seen in movies like *L.A. Story*. It's Martin as a seedy, desperate, bright, greedy man without hope. It's quite a performance, when the spirit takes him and he leaps about on stage, pumping energy into his lethargic audience with show-biz cunning. Debra Winger, who is not in nearly enough films, does a wonderful job of grounding the movie in reality; she sees everything that is happening, has made her compromises with a lot of it, and wonders if enough of her integrity is left to make her a woman worth loving.

Their performances—and Neeson's and Davidovich's—provide the movie with a convincing center. The behind-the-scenes stuff is fascinating, as we see spotters gathering information from the unsuspecting congregation so the preacher can pump it back to them later. All of that is fascinating, and what happens at the end could have been too, if the movie had hung around long enough to deal with it.

Legends of the Fall ★ ★ ★
R, 133 m., 1995

NEW

Brad Pitt (Tristan), Anthony Hopkins (Colonel Ludlow), Aidan Quinn (Alfred), Julia Ormond (Susannah), Henry Thomas (Samuel), Karina Lombard (Isabel Two), Tantoo Cardinal (Pet), Gordon Tootoosis (One Stab). Directed by Edward Zwick and produced by Zwick, Bill Wittliff, and Marshall Herskovitz. Screenplay by Susan Shilliday and Wittliff.

Legends of the Fall is the kind of movie where you have to make a conscious effort to keep

the words "Big Sky Country" out of the first paragraph of the review. It's an epic Western saga about a beautiful woman from back East, and the three sons of a Montana rancher who loved her and fought for her, told against the backdrop of World War I. This is the kind of story that usually appears in an interminable series of paperback novels with the titles embossed in silver, but in fact this material is based on a slim novella by Jim Harrison, who must be mighty surprised how much his stuff adapts to the screen just like Margaret Mitchell and John Jakes.

It's not that the movie is bad. It's pretty good, in fact, with full-blooded performances and heartfelt melodrama. It's that the material is so cheerfully old-fashioned it makes *Giant* look subtle. This is the kind of big, robust Western love story that just begs to be filmed—which, come to think of it, it has been.

The movie stars Anthony Hopkins as Colonel Ludlow, whose distaste for the U.S. Cavalry's treatment of the Indians has led him to carve out an empire of his own in Montana. His wife, having borne him three sons, has repaired to the comforts of the East, leaving the colonel to see them grow to manhood. There's Alfred (Aidan Quinn), the oldest and most responsible. Tristan (Brad Pitt), the middle son, whose idea of entertainment is to awaken hibernating bears and cut out their still-beating hearts. And there's Samuel (Henry Thomas), the youngest.

The movie opens with portentous narration by One Stab (Gordon Tootoosis), the Indian who is the colonel's most trusted friend. One Stab talks in the same kind of slightly hoarse, slightly musical profundity used by many Indians in the movies. Just as all airline pilots are said to have speech patterns influenced by Chuck Yeager, so many movie Indians seem to model their vocal style on the late Chief Dan George. We have a feeling One Stab's narration will not be able to entirely avoid the words of the movie's title, and we are correct.

Soon Samuel returns from the East with Susannah, a young woman who is his fiancée. She is played by Julia Ormond, a young British actress who looks, here, uncannily like Ingrid Bergman. She is strong, capable, beautiful, and high-spirited, able to ride, rope, and shoot, and when Tristan, the Brad Pitt character, saunters in covered with sweat, blood, and horsehair, we can tell just by the way her nostrils flare that riding, roping, and shooting are not necessarily even her best sports.

The colonel hates war and the army, and wants his boys to settle down in Montana and run the ranch. But Samuel is much disturbed. He is a virgin who seeks advice from his brothers, and perhaps feels uncertain about his prowess. Maybe that, along with patriotism, is involved in his decision to go to Canada and enlist when World War I breaks out. The colonel is outraged, but the other two sons enlist, too, and we are asked to decide which is the more unlikely: that all three would end up on the same battlefield, or that Tristan would not be required by the British to cut his flowing blond locks.

I dare not reveal too much of the plot, except to hint that in one way or another Susannah figures in the lives of all three of the sons, against a background of the changing West, as cities grow and prohibition benefits a thriving criminal class. The colonel meanwhile grows older and more infirm, in one of those strange Anthony Hopkins performances that steals every scene with its air of brooding, motionless menace.

The movie is a showcase for acting, and in addition to Ormond and Hopkins, it also shows how strong Aidan Quinn and Brad Pitt are, in roles that have inescapable parallels to the Rock Hudson and James Dean characters in *Giant.* There is even a time when Pitt goes away "forever," just as Dean's character threatened to do, although in an act of sensational one-upmanship this movie sends Pitt all the way to New Guinea for some practical anthropology.

Legends of the Fall is not a Serious movie, despite the profound sentiments of its narration and the classical ironies of its plot. It is a high-class horse opera—with the emphasis on *opera,* with an abundance of operatic coincidences, passions, loves, losses, overwrought arias, and heart-wrenching soliloquies. On that basis it is enormously entertaining, a throwback to the days when Hollywood didn't apologize for passionate stories involving three brothers whose fates are intertwined with that of a legendary woman, as they're all outlined against the Big Sky.

Léolo ★ ★ ★ ★
NO MPAA RATING, 107 m., 1993

Gilbert Sicotte (Narration), Maxime Collin (Léolo), Ginette Reno (Mother), Julien Guiomar (Grandfather), Pierre Bourgault (The Word Tamer), Giuditta Del Vecchio (Bianca), Andrée Lachapelle (Psychiatrist). Directed by Jean-Claude Lauzon and produced by Lyse Lafontaine and Aimee Danis. Screenplay by Lauzon.

Léolo is an enchanting, disgusting, romantic, depressing, hilarious, tragic movie, and it is quite original—one of 1993's best. I have never seen one like it before. It cannot be assigned a category, or described in terms of other films. I felt alive when I was watching it. If you are one of those lonely film lovers who used to attend foreign films, who used to seek out the offbeat and the challenging, and who has given up on movies because they all seem the same, crawl out of your bunker and look at this one. It will remind you that movies can be wonderful.

Directed by Jean-Claude Lauzon, a young nonconformist from Quebec, it tells the story of the young manhood of Leo, who grows up in an insanely dysfunctional but colorful and not altogether harmful family in Montreal. Leo despises his father, so much so that he has created a fantasy in which his mother was somehow impregnated by a tomato from Sicily, which bore the sperm of the man he imagines was his real father. Leo insists he is therefore Italian, and should be called Léolo.

The film is narrated by him, in a sense. In fact, the narration comes out of a journal he keeps as a child, a journal that falls into other hands some years later—into the hands of an old man who treasures the written word, and plunders garbage cans to save it from destruction. This is the same man who once, visiting Léolo's vast and awesomely maternal mother, stopped the kitchen table from tilting by placing an old book under one of the legs—which is how the only book in Léolo's house got there.

Léolo has a way he can dream, and in his dreams he is visited by his Muse. The rest of his time is fairly grim. It is believed in his household that a bowel movement a day keeps the doctor away, and so he spends long hours locked in the toilet, making convincing sound effects to cover his other activities, which include reading naughty Parisian magazines and plotting the murder of his grandfather.

The grandfather is a vile old codger who is conducting a mercenary relationship with the beautiful young neighbor who Léolo persists in thinking of as virginal, and someday destined to become his own. The scene in which Léolo attempts to actually carry out his death plan, using perfectly understood principles of pulleys and levers but faulty craftsmanship, is one of the more astonishing I have seen.

A streak of madness runs, or more accurately gallops, through Léolo's family. They are all either in the madhouse or headed that way. Léolo is a self-raised boy (his mother's maternalism is as misguided as it is smothering), aware of the family curse, and also clever at keeping his own secrets within the claustrophobic household. He is not a cute Hollywood child, or a *Home Alone* brat, or a little plastic monster. He is a fully formed, difficult, complicated individual, who sees himself clearly, sees through his family, and uses fantasy as an escape and a tonic.

Jean-Claude Lauzon, who wrote as well as directed, made his debut in 1987 with *Night Zoo,* a movie that was sensationally well-received in Canada (eleven Genie awards—the equivalent of the Oscar) but left some observers, myself included, less than convinced. Yet I remember it clearly after six years, perhaps because Lauzon's films contain images no other film would dare to show. In *Night Zoo,* for example, the young hero grants his father's dying wish by breaking into the zoo so the old man can hunt big game before he dies.

If I was not sure about *Night Zoo,* I have not the slightest doubt about *Léolo.* It is a work of genius—and the best kind of genius, too, which is deranged genius. Lauzon takes no hostages. He has only scorn for sure-fire box office formulas. He makes his films from scratch. It is amazing how many notes he plays in this 107-minute film. How there is broad burlesque, fanciful dreaming, seamy sex, dire poverty, hope for the future, despair. The structure of the film is another amazement, gradually revealing itself, so that the more we know about how and why the story is being told, the more poignant it becomes.

There is a beer in England that advertises itself as "refreshing the parts the others do not reach." I commend this motto to the distributors of *Léolo,* because here is a film that does exactly the same thing.

Less Than Zero ★ ★ ★
R, 100 m., 1987

Andrew McCarthy (Clay), Jami Gertz (Blair), Robert Downey, Jr. (Julian), James Spader (Rip), Tony Bill (Bradford Easton), Nicholas

Pryor (Benjamin Wells), Donna Mitchell (Elaine Easton), Michael Bowen (Hop), Sarah Buxton (Markie). Directed by Marek Kanievska and produced by Jon Avnet and Jordan Kerner. Screenplay by Harley Peyton.

George Carlin was once asked how cocaine made you feel, and he answered: "It makes you feel like having some more cocaine." That inescapable fact is at the bottom of *Less Than Zero,* a movie that knows cocaine inside out and paints a portrait of drug addiction that is all the more harrowing because it takes place in the Beverly Hills fast lane, in a world of wealth, sex, glamour, and helpless self-destruction.

The movie is about three very rich kids who graduate from the same high school. How rich? As a graduation present, the father of one of the kids sets him up in the recording industry. The character's name is Julian, and he is played by Robert Downey, Jr., as a slick, smart, charming young man who takes less than a year to lose everything. His best friend in high school was Clay, played by Andrew McCarthy. Clay, who wears a tie even in Southern California, goes off to an Ivy League university, leaving behind his girlfriend, Blair (Jami Gertz). By Thanksgiving, Downey and Gertz are sleeping together and doing cocaine together, and by Christmas, a terrified Gertz is calling McCarthy and begging him to come home and rescue Downey, who is in very big trouble.

The problem is, you cannot rescue someone who is addicted to drugs. You can lecture them, to no point, and plead with them, to no avail, but essentially, an outsider is powerless over someone else's addiction. Downey is clearly out of control and headed for bottom. He has lost the recording studio, spent all his money, made a half-hearted stab at a rehab center, gone back to using, and been banished from his home by his father, who practices tough love and tells him, "You can lead your life any way you want, but stay the hell out of mine."

The first hint of this movie's power comes during a Christmas party scene. McCarthy, back from the East, tries to talk to his old friend and his former girlfriend, but they're stoned, and talk too fast and too loud, almost mechanically, and have tiny attention spans. Later, Gertz begs McCarthy to help Downey but what can he do? And then the movie's long middle section functions almost as a documentary of the Beverly Hills fast track, of private clubs that open at midnight, of expensive cars and smooth drug dealers and glamorous hangers-on, and the quiet desperation of a society of once-bright, once-attractive, once-promising young people who talk about a lot of things but essentially think only about cocaine.

The movie's three central performances are flawless: by Jami Gertz, as the frightened girl who witnesses the disintegration of her friend; by Andrew McCarthy, as the quiet, almost cold, witness from outside this group; and especially by Robert Downey, Jr., whose acting here is so real, so subtle, and so observant that it's scary.

His life in the film revolves around the will of a fourth character, his drug dealer (James Spader). He owes the dealer $50,000 and has no money and no prospects, and the most frightening thing about his situation is that the Spader character is actually fairly reasonable, as these characters go. "I'm not the problem," Spader tells McCarthy. "Julian is the problem." He has extended much more credit than he would usually permit, out of "friendship," but now Downey is at the end of the line.

The movie's last thirty minutes are like a kick in the gut, as Downey spirals through the ultimate results of his addiction. He appeals to his father, to his friends, and even to his dealer, and the fact is, he gets more help than perhaps he deserves. He makes firm resolutions to stop using, and vague plans to "get back into rehab," and his friends stand by him as much as they can. The movie's outcome reflects, more or less accurately, what awaits most cocaine addicts who do not get clean.

If this description of *Less Than Zero* makes it sound like a downbeat retread of *The Lost Weekend,* that's because I haven't described the movie's visual style. Director Marek Kanievska and cinematographer Ed Lachman have photographed Beverly Hills, Bel Air, and Palm Springs the way they look in high-priced fashion ads and slick TV commercials. The water in the pools is always an azure blue. The homes look like sets. The people look like models. The discos look like music videos. The whole movie looks brilliantly superficial, and so Downey's predicament is all the more poignant: He is surrounded by all of this, he is in it and of it, and he cannot have it. All he wants to have is a good time, but he is trapped in a paradox: Cocaine is the good time that takes itself away.

Lethal Weapon ★ ★ ★
R, 110 m., 1987

Mel Gibson (Martin Riggs), Danny Glover (Roger Murtaugh), Gary Busey (Joshua), Mitchell Ryan (The General), Tom Atkins (Michael Hunsaker), Darlene Love (Trish Murtaugh), Traci Wolfe (Rianne Murtaugh). Directed by Richard Donner and produced by Donner and Joel Silver. Screenplay by Shane Black.

Lethal Weapon is another one of those Bruised Forearm Movies, like *Raiders of the Lost Ark,* a movie where you and your date grab each other's arm every four minutes and you end up black and blue and grinning from ear to ear. It's a buddy movie about two homicide cops who chase a gang of drug dealers all over Southern California, and the plot makes an amazing amount of sense, considering that the action hardly ever stops for it.

The cops are played by Danny Glover, as a homebody who has just celebrated his fiftieth birthday, and Mel Gibson, as a crazed, wild-eyed rebel who has developed a suicidal streak since his wife was killed in a car crash. In the space of less than forty-eight hours, they become partners, share a family dinner, kill several people, survive a shoot-out in the desert, battle with helicopters and machine guns, toss hand grenades, jump off buildings, rescue Glover's kidnapped daughter, drive cars through walls, endure torture by electric shock, have a few beers, and repair the engine on Glover's boat—not in that order.

The movie's so tightly wound up, it's like a rubber band ready to snap. Richard Donner, the director, throws action scenes at us like hardballs, and we don't know when to duck. All of the elements of this movie have been seen many times before—the chases, the explosions, the hostage negotiations—but this movie illustrates a favorite belief of mine, which is that the subject of a movie is much less important than its style. I'm a guy who is bored by shoot-outs and chase scenes. I've seen it all. But this movie thrilled me from beginning to end.

Part of that is because I cared about the characters. Glover has had important roles for several years (in movies as different as *Places in the Heart* and *The Color Purple*), but this movie makes him a star. His job is to supply the movie's center of gravity, while all the nuts and weirdos and victims whirl around him. He's a family man, concerned about those gray hairs he sees in the mirror, not interested in taking unnecessary chances.

Gibson is the perfect counterpoint, with his wild hair, his slob clothing, and his emotional misery. It's a running gag in the movie that Gibson is so suicidal he doesn't care if he lives or dies—and that gives him a definite advantage in showdown situations. That's what happens in a scene where Gibson is up on a rooftop trying to reason with a jumper. I won't spoil the scene; I'll just say the scene ends with one of the few genuinely unexpected surprises in any recent action film.

The supporting cast is strong, and has to be, to stand out in the midst of the mayhem. Gary Busey, slimmed down and bright of eye, makes an appropriately hateful killer. And Traci Wolfe, as Glover's good-looking daughter, is cute when she gets a teen-age crush on Gibson. But most of the attention focuses on Glover and Gibson, and they work easily together, as if they were having fun, their eccentric personal rhythms supplying a counterpoint to the movie's roar of violence.

Now about that matter of style. In a sense, a movie like *Lethal Weapon* isn't about violence at all. It's about movement and timing, the choreography of bodies and weapons in time and space. In lesser movies, the people stand there and shoot at each other and we're bored. In a movie with the energy of this one, we're exhilarated by the sheer freedom of movement; the violence becomes surrealistic and less important than the movie's underlying energy level.

Richard Donner has directed a lot of classy pictures. My favorites are *Inside Moves, Ladyhawke*, and the original *Superman*, which is still the best. This time he tops himself.

Lethal Weapon 2 ★ ★ ★ ½
R, 111 m., 1989

Mel Gibson (Martin Riggs), Danny Glover (Roger Murtaugh), Joe Pesci (Leo Getz), Joss Ackland (Arjen Rudd), Derrick O'Connor (Pieter Vorstedt), Patsy Kensit (Rika Van Den Haas), Darlene Love (Trish Murtaugh) Traci Wolfe (Rianne Murtaugh), Damon Hines (Nick Murtaugh), Ebonbie Smith (Carrie Murtaugh), Steve Kahan (Captain Murphy), Mary Ellen Trainor (Psychiatrist). Directed by Richard Donner and produced by Donner and Joel Silver. Screenplay by Jeffrey Boam.

Lethal Weapon 2 is that rarity, a sequel with most of the same qualities as the original. After anemic retreads like *Ghostbusters II, Star Trek V,* and *The Karate Kid, Part III,* I walked into the movie with a certain dread—

but this is a film with the same off-center invention and wild energy as the original.

The heroes once again are a couple of cops who form an odd couple: Riggs (Mel Gibson), who lives in a trailer by the beach and delights in making people think he's crazy, and Murtaugh (Danny Glover), a stolid middle-class family man with retirement plans. In the original *Lethal Weapon*, their relationship was the center of the film, and in the sequel they define it further—it's a balancing act between exasperation and trust.

But sequels do not live by repeating the same scenes and lessons as the films that inspired them. There has to be a new angle—and *Lethal Weapon 2* finds one in the creation of a band of diabolical villains. It's my contention that the James Bond films sink or swim on the quality of their villains, and that's true here, too: These aren't just violent bad guys, but particular characters, well-acted and malevolently conceived.

What Riggs and Murtaugh stumble over is a complex plot, never quite explained, by which South African diplomats are dealing illegally in gold and other contraband. It is unclear exactly what their plan is, but they are ruthless in its execution, led by Joss Ackland as a white-haired ambassador with steel eyes, and Derrick O'Connor as his lantern-jawed hitman.

Riggs and Murtaugh stumble onto their scheme through the help of the movie's most memorable character, a fast-talking pip-squeak named Leo (Joe Pesci). He's an accountant who has figured out a foolproof way to launder vast quantities of illegal drug money: half a billion dollars, he claims at one time. What's better, he's found a way to use the profits to obtain illegal income tax deductions.

"OK, OK, OK, OK," he says, with a wide chipmunk grin. "I like you guys, so I'll tell you how it's done." He's a government witness they're supposed to protect, but instead they drag him into the center of danger. And the movie is filled with invention as it devises clever forms for the danger to take.

There is, for example, the tricky situation Murtaugh finds himself in when he sits on the toilet and discovers that if he stands up, a bomb will explode. And the close call when Riggs's trailer is attacked by helicopter gunships. And the several astonishing chase scenes in the movie, which succeeded in entertaining me even though I am heartily sick of chase scenes in general.

The creation of the Leo Getz character is

the movie's masterstroke; instead of recycling scenes in which the two partners fight with each other, *Lethal Weapon 2* provides a third character who can exasperate both men. Pesci, who was brilliant as the younger brother in *Raging Bull*, provides an entirely different kind of character here—ingratiating, slimy, self-deprecating, lovable. He gives us a counterpoint to the violence, and Gibson and Glover both have fun playing off of him.

Lethal Weapon 2 was directed by Richard Donner, who also made the first film and whose credits include the first, and best, *Superman* movie. Unlike a lot of directors specializing in high-tech action comedies, he doesn't seem exhausted or cynical. There's an alertness to his scenes, and a freshness to the dialogue by Jeffrey Boam. This doesn't seem like a sequel, but like a movie in which new discoveries are always possible.

Lethal Weapon 3 ★ ★ ★
R, 110 m., 1992

Mel Gibson (Martin Riggs), Danny Glover (Roger Murtaugh), Joe Pesci (Leo Getz), Rene Russo (Lorna Cole), Stuart Wilson (Jack Travis), Darlene Love (Trish Murtaugh), Traci Wolfe (Rianne Murtaugh). Directed by Richard Donner and produced by Donner and Joel Silver. Screenplay by Jeffrey Boam and Robert Mark Kamen.

The freshness of the first two *Lethal Weapon* movies shows signs of settling down into a formula in this third excursion by stars Mel Gibson and Danny Glover, and director Richard Donner. They know what they're doing and how to do it, but we miss the sense of invention that brightened the earlier movies. Parts one and two seemed to wing it; this one falls back on experience and craftsmanship.

Perhaps as a reflection of that, *Weapon 3* depends more on chases, explosions, and set pieces than it does on character development. The story again involves the partnership of Riggs and Murtaugh (Gibson and Glover), buddies in the long tradition of movie cop partners. This time Glover is only eight days from retirement, a sure sign in any cop movie that his life will be repeatedly in danger. And Gibson is the irrepressible clown, talking them both into danger.

They have the same freewheeling relationship, but the movie doesn't pause for the little human set pieces, like the dinner at Murtaugh's house in the first film, or the various scenes set in Riggs's shambles of a house trailer. Even though Joe Pesci is back again as Leo Getz, the hyperkinetic hustler from the second movie, he isn't given much to do. He has some funny scenes, and yet if you really think about the story, he isn't *necessary* to it.

Yet there are elements in the movie that make it worth seeing, and that set it aside from the routine movies in this genre. One new addition is Rene Russo as Lorna Cole, a sergeant from Internal Affairs who starts out suspecting Riggs and Murtaugh of various chicaneries, and ends up as their partner. She's one tough woman, a karate expert who can dispatch three tough guys single-handedly, and there is a funny scene in which the Russo and Gibson characters start by comparing each other's battle scars and get into a game of one-upmanship not unlike strip poker.

Richard Donner has always been skilled at working special effects and big production numbers into his action movies, and this time there is a sensational wrong-way chase down an expressway between two armored trucks, and a showdown at a construction site that ends up on fire while a berserk villain goes after the heroes with a bulldozer.

The bad guy is Jack Travis (Stuart Wilson), an ex-cop who seems to exist primarily to give Riggs and Murtaugh a purpose in their lives. He is not in the great tradition of *Weapon* villians—he's a disappointment after Joss Acklund as the South African diplomat in the second movie—but the final showdown is as berserk, outrageous, and over-the-top as the best action sequences from earlier in the series.

The screenplay is tailored to Mel Gibson's conversational style, or maybe he threw in some of the touches on his own. He's a punster, in love with wordplay, and his dialogue is livelier and more varied than the monosyllabic caveman speech of many movie cops. He and Glover have their patter down pat by now, until maybe it's too smooth. Part of the effect comes from our familiarity with the characters. If *Lethal Weapon 3* were the first film in a series, it wouldn't be a very promising beginning. It gets the job done as the third time around, but I have a feeling maybe after this one Murtaugh really should consider retirement.

Let Him Have It ★ ★ ★ ½
R, 114 m., 1992

Chris Eccleston (Derek Bentley), Paul Reynolds (Chris Craig), Tom Courtenay (William Bentley), Tom Bell (Fairfax), Eileen Atkins (Lilian Bentley), Clare Holman (Iris Bentley). Directed by Peter Medak and produced by Luc Roeg and Robert Warr. Screenplay by Neal Purvis and Robert Wade.

Two frightened boys are cornered on a rooftop by a policeman. They were trying to break into a building. One of the boys has a gun. The policeman, cool and collected, reaches out a hand and asks the boy to hand the gun over. The other boy says, "Let him have it." The boy with the gun pulls the trigger and the officer drops dead.

What did those four words, "Let him have it," really mean? There are two possibilities: "Hand over the gun!" Or, "Shoot him!" Because a jury settled on the second possibility, a retarded youth named Derek Bentley was put to death in a British prison a few years after World War II.

The Bentley case has stirred uneasily in the British psyche ever since, refusing to rest. Over the years the conviction has grown that a harmless young man, mentally incapable of responsibility for his own actions, got into the wrong place at the wrong time and said tragically the wrong words.

Let Him Have It is a sad human document directed by Peter Medak, whose previous film, *The Krays*, was also based on true British crime material. The films, which seem so different, have two similarities: They show criminals coming from ordinary working-class homes, and they show a stronger personality leading a weaker one. *The Krays* was about the most notorious gangsters in recent British history, twin brothers who ruled the East End in a reign of terror and violence. *Let Him Have It* is about a gentle youth, mentally subnormal, who falls in with a crowd of boys he admires, and is badgered by one of them into going along on a break-in.

Derek Bentley is played by Chris Eccleston as a likable teen-ager, inoffensive, fond of his family, able to deal with life in its ordinary aspects, but incapable of standing up to his friend Chris (Paul Reynolds). Chris and his whole circle live in a postwar Britain of poverty and rationing, and their fantasies are fueled by the Hollywood gangster pictures at the local cinema. They practice wearing hats, smoking cigarettes, carrying guns, just like their heroes. It is play-acting, in a way, although the guns are real, and there is a chilling scene when a boy is found in school carrying one.

Perhaps Chris is not so much a criminal as an impressionable kid, play-acting. Perhaps he wants somebody to come along on the job for moral support, and Derek is weak-willed enough to be forced to agree. The events of Derek's last night of freedom are poignant in their unfolding. He lives happily at home with loving parents (Tom Courtenay and Eileen Atkins) and a loyal sister (Clare Holman), and the living room of his little house is uncannily like the domestic hearth from which the Krays set forth. The wireless plays, the chairs are centered around the fireplace, the parents look up fondly as a child goes out into the night to commit a crime. Courtenay, who played a wronged young man himself in one of his greatest films *(The Loneliness of the Long Distance Runner)*, is touching here as an ordinary dad who loves his boy.

In his reconstruction of the trial, Medak is unforgiving, showing a legal system less concerned with justice than with proving itself correct. The judges in their wigs and majesty gaze down on hapless Derek Bentley, who wants to please, who fears death, who can find no voice for his own view of things in this merciless system. And so he goes to his death.

There have been a lot of films about capital punishment. They all say the same thing. No matter what arguments can be made in its favor, if the law makes a mistake, an innocent life is lost. Few lives were more innocent than Derek Bentley's.

Lianna ★ ★ ★ ½
R, 110 m., 1983

Linda Griffiths (Lianna), Jane Hallaren (Ruth), Jon DeVries (Dick), Jo Henderson (Sandy), John Sayles (Jerry). Directed by John Sayles. Produced by Jeffrey Nelson and Maggie Renzi. Screenplay by Sayles.

Movies are good at showing us people who make great changes in their lives, but not so good at showing us the consequences of those changes. It's easier to present the sudden dramatic revelation than to follow through into all the messy complications in everyday life. John Sayles's *Lianna*, the story of a woman who discovers in her early thirties that she is a lesbian, follows through. Instead of being the simple, dramatic story of a woman who "comes out," it is the complex, interesting story of what happens then.

The woman is named Lianna (Linda Griffiths). When she was an undergraduate, she fell in love with her teacher—a pattern she is about to repeat. Her husband is a film professor and the father of their two small children. He tends to treat her like one of the children, lecturing to the general audience at the dinner table as if his wife was about as bright as the kids. He is a boor. Lianna, unhappy, tries to change her life. She signs up for a night class in child psychology, and finds herself attracted to the professor, a woman who has a quick sense of humor and really seems to care about her students.

The woman, Ruth (Jane Hallaren), has been a lesbian for years, and is attracted to Lianna. But it is Lianna who makes the first, subtle moves, staying after class for a moment's chat, just as perhaps she did years ago with her husband. The two women become lovers fairly quickly, and although there are love scenes, the movie is not really about that side of their relationship. If *Personal Best* was an exploration of the physical aspects of lesbianism, *Lianna* explores the consequences. They are many. Lianna's husband throws her out and tries to block access to their children. Lianna's oldest friend, Sandy, is suddenly cold and distant. Ruth, a little surprised at the intensity of the affair, confesses that she has a long-standing relationship with another woman in another city. Lianna rents a room off-campus and begins a lifestyle that is free, yes, but also lonely and filled with guilt.

As *Lianna* looks into the large and small things that have changed in the life of its heroine, we become increasingly aware of the perception of the filmmaker, John Sayles, who wrote, directed, and edited. In this movie and his previous work, *Return of the Secaucus Seven,* he seems in touch with the kinds of changes that some Americans in their thirties are going through; his movies are cinematic versions of Gail Sheehey's *Passages.* He is attentive to what is said, what is worn, what attitudes are taken, what goes unsaid—and he is particularly interested, in both movies, in the ways that a generation raised to "do your own thing" now tries to decide when personal freedom ends and responsibility begins.

It's in that particular area that *Lianna* is a little shaky. It never quite dealt, I thought, with the issue of Lianna's two children. Although Lianna's lover is a child psychologist and Lianna herself seems to be a responsible and loving mother as the film opens, the kids are sort of left hanging. There are a couple of brief scenes with the kids, but no real resolution of the questions that a newly gay mother would have to answer. (Since the husband is presented as such a twerp, this absence of

follow-through is doubly bothering.) Still, in many other scenes, including two in which Lianna has a subtly class-conscious affair with a woman in the armed services, *Lianna* is an intelligent, perceptive movie. And the performances, especially by Griffiths and Hallaren, are so specific that we're never looking at "lesbians"—only at people.

Licence to Kill ★ ★ ★ ½
PG-13, 135 m., 1989

Timothy Dalton (James Bond), Carey Lowell (Pam Bouvier), Robert Davi (Franz Sanchez), Talisa Soto (Lupe Lamora), Anthony Zerbe (Milton Krest), Frank McRae (Sharkey), Everett McGill (Killifer), Wayne Newton (Professor Joe Butcher), Benicio Del Toro (Dario), Anthony Starke (Truman-Lodge). Directed by John Glen and produced by Albert R. Broccoli and Michael G. Wilson. Screenplay by Wilson and Richard Maibaum.

The James Bond movies have by now taken on the discipline of a sonnet or a kabuki drama: Every film follows the same story outline so rigidly that we can predict almost to the minute such obligatory developments as (1) the introduction of the villain's specialized hit man; (2) the long shot which establishes the villain's incredibly luxurious secret hideout; (3) the villain's fatal invitation to Bond to spend the night; (4) the moment when the villain's mistress falls for Bond; (5) the series of explosions destroying the secret fortress; and (6) the final spectacular stunt sequence.

Connoisseurs evaluate the elements in a Bond picture as if they were movements in a symphony, or courses in a meal. There are few surprises, and the changes are evolutionary, so that the latest Bond picture is recognizable as a successor to the first, *Dr. No,* in 1962. Within this framework of tradition, *Licence to Kill* nevertheless manages to spring some interesting surprises. One is that the Bond character, as played now for the second time by Timothy Dalton, has become less of a British icon and more of an international action hero. The second is that the tempo has been picked up, possibly in response to the escalating pace of the Rambo and Indiana Jones movies. The third is that the villain has fairly modest aims for a change: He doesn't want to rule the world; he only wants to be a cocaine billionaire.

I've grown uneasy lately about the fashion of portraying drug smugglers in glamorous lifestyles; they're viewed with some of the

same glamour as gangsters were in films of the 1930s. Sure they die in the end, but they have a lot of fun in the meantime. In *Licence to Kill,* however, the use of a drug kingpin named Sanchez (Robert Davi) and his henchmen (Anthony Zerbe, Frank McRae) is apparently part of an attempt to update the whole series and make it feel more contemporary.

There are still, of course, the obligatory scenes. The film still begins with a sensationally unbelievable stunt sequence (Bond and friend lasso plane in midair, then parachute to a wedding ceremony.) But then the action switches to the more-or-less recognizable modern world in and around Key West, Florida, where the British agent finds himself involved in an operation to capture Sanchez and cut his pipeline of cocaine.

Like all Bond villains, Sanchez has unlimited resources and a beautiful mistress. His operation uses an underwater shark-nabbing company as its cover, and keeps a few sharks on hand just so they can dine on federal agents. After Bond's friend, Felix Leiter, is mistreated by the bad guys, 007 begins a savage personal vendetta against Sanchez, which involves elaborate and violent stunt sequences in the air, on land, and underwater.

He is aided in his campaign by the beautiful Pam Bouvier (Carey Lowell), introduced as "Miss Kennedy, my executive secretary," and saved more than once by Sanchez's beautiful mistress, Lupe Lamora (Talisa Soto). Both women are as beautiful as the historical Bond standard, but more modern—more competent, intelligent, and capable, and not simply sex objects. This is no doubt part of the plan, announced before Dalton's first Bond picture, to de-emphasize the character's promiscuous sex life. Compared to his previous films, 007 is practically chaste this time.

My favorite moments in all the Bond pictures involve The Fallacy of the Talking Killer, in which the villain has Bond clearly in his power, and then, instead of killing him instantly, makes the mistake of talking just long enough for Bond to gather his wits and make a plan. The fallacy saves Bond's life two or three times in this movie—especially once when all that Davi has to do is slice his neck.

Licence to Kill ends, as all the Bond films do, with an extended chase and stunt sequence. This one involves some truly amazing stunt work, as three giant gasoline trucks speed down a twisting mountain road, while a helicopter and a light aircraft also join in the chase. There were moments when I was straining to spot the trickery, as a big semi rig spun along tilted to one side to miss a missile aimed by the bad guys. But the stunts all look convincing, and the effect of the closing sequence is exhilarating.

On the basis of this second performance as Bond, Timothy Dalton can have the role as long as he enjoys it. He makes an effective Bond—lacking Sean Connery's grace and humor and Roger Moore's suave self-mockery, but with a lean tension and a toughness that is possibly more contemporary. The major difference between Dalton and the earlier Bonds is that he seems to prefer action to sex. But then so do movie audiences, these days. *Licence to Kill* is one of the best of the recent Bonds.

Life Is Sweet ★ ★ ★ ★
NO MPAA RATING, 102 m., 1991

Alison Steadman (Wendy), Jim Broadbent (Andy), Claire Skinner (Natalie), Jane Horrocks (Nicola), Stephen Rea (Patsy), Timothy Spall (Aubrey). Directed by Mike Leigh and produced by Simon Channing-Williams. Screenplay by Leigh.

Most movies begin by knowing everything about their characters. *Life Is Sweet* seems to make discoveries as it goes along; it really feels as if the story is as surprising to the characters as it is to us. The filmmaker, Mike Leigh, works in a unique way: He assembles his actors, and then they spend weeks or months devising the screenplay by improvising together. When it's finished, they start shooting, having invented the characters from the inside out.

With *Life Is Sweet*, that approach combines more humor and more poignancy into the same story than most screenwriters would have dared for. There are scenes here that are funnier than those of any other movie of 1991, and other scenes that weep with the pain of sad family secrets, and when it's over we have seen some kind of masterpiece. This is one of the best films of 1991.

The story takes place in a small home in a London suburb, where the parents, Wendy and Andy (Alison Steadman and Jim Broadbent), live with twin daughters who are twentyish (Claire Skinner and Jane Horrocks). These daughters are like the night and day. Nicola, played by Horrocks, hides behind glasses, tangled hair, and cigarettes, and affects a great contempt for all things

conventional, progressive, or healthy. Natalie, played by Skinner, is clean-cut, cheerful, and dutiful. Each sister is a rebuke to the other.

Andy, the father, was athletic when he was younger, but is now going comfortably to seed. He and Wendy were married when they were quite young, and have grown up together, learning some hard lessons along the way, but now they seem to have settled into a comfortable accommodation with one another, inspired partly by Andy's lunatic schemes, and partly by the way Wendy is both horrified and amused by them. There is a moment when Andy leads his wife out into the front of the house with her eyes covered, and then—ta da!—unveils them to reveal his latest scheme for independent living, a mobile hot dog stand.

In his day job, Andy works in the food preparation industry, and hates it. When he trips over a spoon and breaks a leg, there is a wonderful illustration of the way the humor develops in this film. He brings the spoon home with him, hangs it in a place of shame on the wall, and accuses it of treachery in the warmest and most personal terms. It is hard to imagine a screenwriter coming up with this dialogue, but it feels both original and exactly right—the sort of things that would come out of an improvisational investigation.

The funniest passage in the movie actually has little to do with the rest of it; it involves a family friend (the feckless Timothy Spall) who opens a grotty French restaurant on the high road, hires one of the girls as his waitress, and then gets doggedly drunk while waiting for customers and reviewing his implausible menu.

Meanwhile, at home, in such a subtle way we don't at first realize it, the movie reveals its more serious undertones. Nicola really is seriously disturbed—convinced she is ugly and fat—and the sunny cheerfulness of her sister acts only as a daily depressant. The twins know almost everything about each other, but several important secrets have never been openly discussed, and now they are, as the family's underlying problems come out into the open.

I do not want to reveal too much. I especially want to avoid spoiling for you the extraordinary impact of an outburst by Wendy, the mother, who tells her girls some of the sorts of things children do not realize about parents. By the end of *Life Is Sweet* we are treading close to the stuff of life itself—to the way we all struggle and make do, compro-

mise some of our dreams and insist on the others. Watching this movie made me realize how boring and thin many movies are; how they substitute plots for the fascinations of life.

Life Is Sweet has been the greatest success so far in the long, brave career of Mike Leigh, who made a film named *Bleak Moments* that made my "best of the year" list in 1972. He then did not make another film until *High Hopes* in 1989 (that also made my "best ten" list—so he's never made a film that didn't). Film financiers are understandably slow to back a film that doesn't have a screenplay, but Leigh has persisted in his collaborations with actors, working usually on the British stage and TV, where in his own brave and stubborn way he has finally become something of a hero.

What is amazing is that a man can labor against the market forces of the stage and screen for twenty years and still retain his sense of humor. And yet that is what he has done. *Life Is Sweet* is as funny, spontaneous, and free as if it had been made on a lark by a millionaire. This is an almost miraculous coming-together of actors, material, a time and a place, and an attitude. See it, and you will sense the freedom with which movies can be made when they are freed from the lockstep of the assembly line.

Life Stinks ★ ★ ★
PG-13, 91 m., 1991

Mel Brooks (Goddard Bolt), Lesley Ann Warren (Molly), Jeffrey Tambor (Vance Crasswell), Stuart Pankin (Pritchard), Howard Morris (Sailor), Rudy DeLuca (J. Paul Getty). Directed and produced by Mel Brooks. Screenplay by Brooks, Ron Clark, Rudy DeLuca, and Steve Haberman.

It may take more skill and intelligence to live without money than to make and spend a great deal of it, and that is the buried message of *Life Stinks*, a warmhearted new comedy from Mel Brooks. It's easy to sit inside an air-conditioned car and feel scorn for some poor wretch who is trying to earn a quarter for wiping a rag across the windshield. But if we were out there on the streets without a home or money, what bright ideas would we come up with? Donald Trump can make millions selling condos to other millionaires, but could he make ten bucks in a day if he had to start from scratch?

The conventional wisdom in these situations is that the poor and homeless should get a grip on themselves, should pull themselves up by their bootstraps. But if they have no boots, what then? Wasn't it Voltaire who said that the law, in its magnificent equality, prohibits the rich as well as the poor from sleeping under bridges and begging in the streets? What Brooks does with this idea is tell a fable of a rich urban developer who finds himself on the streets, in the ghetto, wondering where his next meal is coming from.

Brooks plays the rich man himself. His name is Goddard Bolt, and he intends to buy a large, wretchedly poor area of Los Angeles, tear it down, and start over—at immense profit to himself. His archenemy in business is a predatory capitalist named Vance Crasswell (played by Jeffrey Tambor with oily superiority). They get in a bidding and bluffing war, and it finally all comes down to a bet: The Brooks character bets he can live for thirty days, by his wits, as a homeless bum—without ever stepping foot outside the area.

This is a premise Brooks and his writers have borrowed from *Sullivan's Travels*, the 1941 Preston Sturges classic in which Joel McCrea plays a Hollywood director who goes on the road as a bum. But the streets are a little meaner in 1991 than they were in 1941, and the affluent are stingier. It is sometimes all Brooks can do to make his movie seem like a comedy, when the desperation of the homeless is so evident in every scene.

But he pulls it off. He gets mileage out of his own efforts to emulate the panhandlers he sees—he wipes a windshield; he dances and hopes people will toss coins into his hat—and he makes some friends on the street, who steer him toward the nearest soup kitchen. And he meets some kindred spirits, like Molly (Lesley Ann Warren), who lives in an alley she has furnished as her living room. The movie's best scene is one in which, together, they transform poverty into fantasy, in a dance inspired by the old MGM musicals.

Life Stinks is a new direction in Brooks's directing career. The typical note in most of his earlier work was cheerful vulgarity, as he went for the laugh, no matter what. He has made some of the funniest movies I've ever seen, including *The Producers, Blazing Saddles,* and *Young Frankenstein.* This is not one of them. It has its laughs, but it's a more thoughtful film, more softhearted toward its characters. It's warm and poignant.

Brooks, as usual, is his own best asset. As an actor, he brings a certain heedless courage to his roles. His characters never seem to pause for thought; they're cocky, headstrong, confident. They charge ahead into the business at hand. There is a certain tension in *Life Stinks* between the bullheaded optimism of the Brooks character, and the hopeless reality of the streets, and that's what the movie is about.

Light of Day ★ ★ ★ ½
PG-13, 107 m., 1987

Michael J. Fox (Joe Rasnick), Gena Rowlands (Jeanette Rasnick), Joan Jett (Patti Rasnick), Jason Miller (Ben Rasnick), Michael McKean (Bu Montgomery), Thomas G. Waites (Smittie), Cherry Jones (Cindy). Directed by Paul Schrader and produced by Rob Cohen and Keith Barish. Screenplay by Schrader.

Early in *Light of Day,* a brother and sister go to their mother's birthday dinner at their parents' home. The atmosphere is charged with tension. At the table, the father sits silently in the calm before the storm. The mother begins to ask the blessing, and then her prayer turns into something more specific: She begins to ask God to forgive her daughter.

All hell breaks loose. The daughter runs from the table, and the brother follows her out of the house, trying to make peace. We can see that the two women are bitter enemies, although the mother probably would not see it that way; she uses prayer as a weapon, just as much as her daughter uses alienation and aggression.

This scene sets up the emotional conflict in *Light of Day,* which shows a family tearing itself apart despite the best efforts of the son, who wants to hold things together at almost any cost. This is a family drama, all right—but not one of those neat docudramas in which every character comes attached to a fashionable problem, and all the problems are solved in the same happy ending. The family in *Light of Day* is more like your average everyday unhappy family, in which the biggest problem is that some of the members quite simply hate each other.

Writer-director Paul Schrader tells his story against a working-class background in Cleveland. The parents (Gena Rowlands and Jason Miller) have worked hard for their share of suburban respectability. The children (Michael J. Fox and Joan Jett) play every night in a rock band, and although Fox has a daytime job in a factory, Jett's life is on hold until the sun goes down; she says rock 'n' roll is the most important thing in the world, and she means it.

Because she means it, life is not very healthy for her little boy, a son born out of wedlock by a father she refuses to name. It is this child that has driven the wedge between mother and daughter. And soon it becomes the focus of her relationship with her brother. When their band goes on a tour—sometimes playing for no more than a few bucks and free drinks—the child is left in cheap motel rooms, and Fox doesn't approve of that. Jett, filled with anger and defiance, won't listen to his objections, and Fox stands by helplessly, trying to be all things to all people.

His family is clearly a matriarchy, a battleground between two strong women. The father, played by Miller as a sensitive wimp, has long since given up, and now Fox is trying to play the peacemaker, the responsible one, almost the parent. Fox obviously idolizes his sister (and, in a way, his mother), and so there are painful moments, very well acted, in which he hurts because he cannot help these people he loves.

The movie is subtle in its construction. Schrader doesn't telegraph his ending in the first half-hour, and indeed the movie's one fault is that it sometimes seems without a clear direction. At first the film seems to be a blue-collar story. Then a family drama. Then a rock 'n' roll movie. But then we see that the rock band is going nowhere, and the center of the story turns back to the family, after the mother becomes seriously ill. And it's the illness that provides the payoff, in strong and painful bedside scenes between Gena Rowlands, Fox, and Jett.

This mother may be sick, but she knows exactly what she's doing, and Rowlands's acting is powerfully, heartbreakingly effective. The mother uses love, truth, insight, and a measure of cynical calculation in an attempt to control what will happen to her family if she dies. She has always been a controller, and the possibility of death only inspires her to new efforts.

Light of Day is told like a short story by Henry James or Raymond Carver, in which the last few moments and the final words throw everything else into focus. And there is so much pain and anger in the film's ending that we can speculate that this is the real material that Schrader only touched on in *Hardcore,* his 1979 film about a runaway daughter's rebellion against her strict fundamentalist family.

Light of Day arrived with an advance reputation as a rock 'n' roll film, and yet Joan Jett, the movie's one certified rocker, gives the most surprisingly good performance. In the bedside scene with Rowlands, she is acting in the big leagues; Rowlands is inspired and Jett rises to the same inspiration, and there's a rare, powerful chemistry. Fox, playing a weak, conciliatory character, is the right balance for these two strong women, and Miller, kept in the background in most of his scenes, has one searching speech in which he tries to explain what has happened to his family.

Schrader has been one of the most consistently interesting writers and directors of the last decade. Try to find the thread connecting his screenplays, such as *Taxi Driver* and *Raging Bull*, and his films as a director, such as *Blue Collar*, *Hardcore*, *American Gigolo*, *Cat People*, and *Mishima*, and what you come up with are wildly different characters with one thing in common: Their pasts keep them imprisoned, and shut them off from happiness in the present. Here is his most direct and painful statement of that theme.

Light Sleeper ★ ★ ★
R, 103 m., 1992

Willem Dafoe (John LeTour), Susan Sarandon (Ann), Dana Delany (Marianne), David Clennon (Robert), Mary Beth Hurt (Teresa). Directed by Paul Schrader and produced by Linda Reisman. Screenplay by Schrader.

People get into situations like this. They start doing drugs when they're young, and then they start dealing drugs in order to pay for them, and then if they survive, the day comes when they get off drugs, because eventually one day you either get off drugs or you die. And then they are left with selling the drugs, because the money is easy and it is the only life they know, and their résumé for a straight job would have a gap representing their adult lifetime.

John LeTour, the hero of *Light Sleeper*, Paul Schrader's brooding, lonely film, delivers drugs to clients in Manhattan. He works for a dealer named Ann, who runs her operation as a business, but dreams of getting into another one—maybe she'll start a cosmetics firm. It's the daydream of anyone who is being paid too much to do something that no longer matters to them; they'll quit one day, and do what they really want to do. But somehow they can never afford that. Maybe a catastrophe would be a blessing in disguise.

Schrader knows this world of insomnia, craving, and addiction. And he knows all about people living in a cocoon of themselves. *Light Sleeper* is the third in his trilogy about alienated night workers, after *Taxi Driver* (he wrote the screenplay, Martin Scorsese directed) and *American Gigolo*, about a man who supplies sex at great cost to himself. Now comes this story about the man who delivers drugs. There are many parallels in the three films; all involve the men in misguided efforts to save or connect with a self-destructive woman, and all end in violence. But, perhaps because he is growing older and wiser, the characters over the years have become better people. The zombie craziness in Travis Bickle, the De Niro character in *Taxi Driver* (1973), has mellowed into a certain gentle resignation in Willem Dafoe's gifted portrait of John LeTour in *Light Sleeper*.

LeTour has been off drugs for a couple of years. He still drinks, and never really got involved in going to meetings. He does his job for money. He has clients who worry him, including one completely strung out guy who has holed up in an apartment with booze and drugs and is going off the deep end. His last trip to this guy's house—where he brutally tells him he's hit bottom, and kicks the guy back down to the floor while making a call to turn him in—is a scene of perfect insight into the world of addiction.

One day LeTour accidentally runs into a woman he loved and lost because of drugs (Dana Delany). She is afraid of him; she keeps edging away, because she's been clean and sober for five years, and she thinks his shaky status might be catching. He pursues her. He tries to tell her he's cleaned up his act. He goes sometimes to a psychic (Mary Beth Hurt), who sees an aura of death around him, and he appeals to her desperately for help and advice. *Light Sleeper* isn't about the help he can get from psychics, however; it's about desperation that makes him project healing qualities upon anyone who is halfway sympathetic.

The movie is familiar with its life of night and need. It finds the real human qualities in a person like Ann, the dealer (Susan Sarandon)—who, in a crisis, reacts with loyalty and quick thinking. It is filled with great weariness and sadness; the party has been over for a long time, and these old druggies, now approaching middle age, have been left behind. Because they were survivors, because they were more intelligent and honest

than most, this is the thanks they get: They continue to work in the scene long after they should have been replaced by a new generation of losers.

I've talked to some people who had this or that complaint about the plot of *Light Sleeper*, often that they didn't like the way the ending seemed like an ironic echo of *Taxi Driver*. This movie isn't about plot; it's about a style of life, and the difficulty of preserving self-respect and playing fair when your income depends on selling people stuff that will make them hate you. In film after film, for year after year, Paul Schrader has been telling this story in one way or another, but never with more humanity than this time.

Like Water for Chocolate ★ ★ ★
R, 113 m., 1993

Lumi Cavazos (Tita), Marco Leonardi (Pedro), Regina Torne (Mama Elena), Mario Ivan Martinez (John Brown), Ada Carrasco (Nacha), Yareli Arizmendi (Rosaura). Directed and produced by Alfonso Arau. Screenplay by Laura Esquivel.

In Mexico, so I have learned, hot chocolate is made with water, not milk. The water is brought to a boil and then the chocolate is spooned into it. A person in a state of sexual excitement is said to be "like water for chocolate." And now here is a movie where everyone seems at the boil, their lives centering around a woman whose sensual life is carried out in the kitchen, and whose food is so magical it can inspire people to laugh, or cry, or run naked from the house to be scooped up and carried away by a passing revolutionary.

Like Water for Chocolate creates its own intense world of passion and romance, and adds a little comedy and a lot of quail, garlic, honey, chilies, mole, cilantro, rose petals, and cornmeal. It takes place in a Mexican border town, circa 1910, where a young couple named Tita and Pedro are deeply in love. But they are never to marry. Mama Elena, Tita's fearsome and unbending mother, forbids it. She sees the duty of her youngest daughter to stay always at home and take care of her. Tita is heartbroken—especially when Pedro marries Rosaura, her oldest sister.

But there is a method to Pedro's treachery. During a dance at the wedding, he whispers into Tita's ear that he has actually married Rosaura in order to be always close to Tita. He still loves only her. Weeping with sadness and joy, Tita prepares the wedding cake, and as her tears mingle with the granulated sugar, sifted cake flour, beaten eggs, and grated peel of lime, they transform the cake into something enchanting that causes all of the guests at the feast to begin weeping at what should be an occasion for joy.

The movie is narrated by Tita's greatniece, who describes how, through the years, Aunt Tita's kitchen produces even more extraordinary miracles. When Pedro gives her a dozen red roses, for example, she prepares them with quail and honey, and the recipe is such an aphrodisiac that everyone at the table is aroused, and smoke actually pours from the ears of the middle sister, Gertrudis. She races to the outhouse, which catches fire, and then, tearing off her burning clothes, is swept into the saddle of a passing bandolero. (She returns many years later, a famous revolutionary leader.)

Like Water for Chocolate is based on a bestselling novel by Laura Esquivel, and has been directed by her husband, Alfonso Arau. Like *Bye Bye Brazil* and parts of *El Norte,* it continues the tradition of magical realism that is central to modern Latin film and literature. It begins with the assumption that magic can change the fabric of the real world, if it is transmitted through the emotions of people in love. And Lumi Cavazos, as Tita, is the perfect instrument for magic, with her single-minded, lifelong devotion to Pedro— a love that transcends even their separation, when the evil Mama Elena dispatches Pedro and Rosaura to another town, where their baby dies for lack of Tita's cooking.

The movie takes the form of an old family legend, and the source is apparently Esquivel. It gains the poignancy of an old story that is already over, so that the romance takes on a kind of grandeur. What has survived, however, is a tattered but beautiful old book containing all of Aunt Tita's recipes, and who has not felt some sort of connection with the past when reading or preparing a favorite recipe from a loved one who has now passed on?

Imagine, for example, melting some butter and browning two cloves of garlic in it. Then adding two drops of attar of roses, the petals of six roses, two tablespoons of honey, and twelve thinly sliced chestnuts to the mixture, and rubbing it all over six tiny quail and browning them in the oven. Serve, of course, with the remaining rose petals. And stand back.

The Lion King ★ ★ ★ ½
G, 87 m., 1994

With the voices of: Jonathan Taylor Thomas (Young Simba), Matthew Broderick (Adult Simba), James Earl Jones (Mufasa), Jeremy Irons (Scar), Moira Kelly (Adult Nala), Niketa Calame (Young Nala), Ernie Sabella (Pumbaa), Whoopi Goldberg (Shenzi). Directed by Roger Allers and Rob Minkoff and produced by Don Hahn. Screenplay by Irene Mecchi, Jonathan Roberts, and Linda Woolverton.

My generation grew up mourning the death of Bambi's mother. Now comes *The Lion King,* with the death of Mufasa, the father of the lion cub who will someday be king. The Disney animators know that cute little cartoon characters are not sufficient to manufacture dreams. There have to be dark corners, frightening moments, and ancient archetypes like the crime of regicide. *The Lion King,* which is a superbly drawn animated feature, is surprisingly solemn in its subject matter, and may even be too intense for very young children.

The film is another in a series of annual media events from Disney, which with *The Little Mermaid, Beauty and the Beast,* and *Aladdin* reinvented its franchise of animated feature films. The inspiration for these recent films comes from the earliest feature cartoons created by Walt Disney himself, who in movies like *Dumbo,* with the chaining of Mrs. Jumbo, and *Snow White and the Seven Dwarfs,* with its wicked stepmother, tapped into primal fears and desires. Later Disney films drifted off into the neverland of innocuous "children's movies," which were harmless but not very exciting. These four recent animated features are once again true "family films," in that they entertain adults as well as children.

The Lion King is the first Disney animated feature not based on an existing story. In another sense, it is based on half the stories in classical mythology. It tells the tale of the birth, childhood, and eventual manhood of Simba, a lion cub. The cub's birth is announced in the opening sequence of the movie, called "The Circle of Life," which is an evocative collaboration of music and animation to show all of the animals of the African veld gathering to hail their future king. The cute little cub is held aloft from a dramatic spur of rock, and all his future minions below hail him, in a staging that looks like the jungle equivalent of a political rally.

Of course, this coming together of zebra and gazelle, monkey and wildebeest fudges on the uncomfortable fact that many of these animals survive by eating one another. And all through *The Lion King* the filmmakers perform a balancing act between the fantasy of their story and the reality of the jungle. Early scenes show Simba as a cute, trusting little tyke who believes everyone loves him. He is wrong. He has an enemy— his uncle Scar, the king's jealous brother, who wants to be king himself one day.

Villains are often the most memorable characters in a Disney animated film, and Scar is one of the great ones, aided by a pack of yipping hyenas who act as his storm troopers. With a voice by Jeremy Irons, and facial features suggestive of Irons's gift for sardonic concealment, Scar is a mannered, manipulative schemer who succeeds in bringing about the death of the king. Worse, he convinces Simba that the cub is responsible, and the guilty little heir slinks off into the wastelands. (The movie makes a sly reference to a famous earlier role by Irons. When Simba tells him, "You're so weird," he replies "You have no idea," in exactly the tone he used as Claus von Bulow in *Reversal of Fortune.*)

It is an unwritten law that animated features have comic relief, usually in the form of a duet or trio of goofy characters who become buddies with the hero. This time they are a meerkat named Timon (voice by Nathan Lane) and a warthog named Pumbaa (Ernie Sabella), who cheer up Simba during his long exile.

The movie has a large cast of other colorful characters, including a hornbill named Zazu (Rowan Atkinson), who is confidant and adviser to King Mufasa (James Earl Jones). And there are the three hyenas (with voices by Whoopi Goldberg, Cheech Marin, and Jim Cummings), who are a tumbling, squabbling, yammering team of dirty-tricks artists.

The early Disney cartoons were, of course, painstakingly animated by hand. There has been a lot of talk recently about computerized animation, as if a computer program could somehow create a movie. Not so. Human animators are responsible for the remarkably convincing portrayals of Scar and the other major characters, who somehow combine human and animal body language. But computers did assist with several remarkable sequences, including a stampede in which a herd seems to flow past the camera.

Despite the comic relief from the hyenas,

the meerkat, and the warthog, *The Lion King* is a little more subdued than *Mermaid, Beauty,* and *Aladdin.* The central theme is a grim one: A little cub is dispossessed and feels responsible for the death of its father. An uncle betrays a trust. And beyond the gently rolling plains of the great savanna lies a wasteland of bones and ashes. Some of the musical comedy numbers break the mood, although with the exception of "Circle of Life" and "Hakuna Matata," the songs in *The Lion King* are not as memorable as those in *Mermaid* and *Beauty.*

Basically what we have here is a drama, with comedy occasionally lifting the mood. The result is a surprising seriousness; this isn't the mindless romp with cute animals that the ads might lead you to expect. Although the movie may be frightening and depressing to the very young, I think it's positive that *The Lion King* deals with real issues. By processing life's realities in stories, children can prepare themselves for more difficult lessons later on. The saga of Simba, which in its deeply buried origins owes something to Greek tragedy and certainly to *Hamlet,* is a learning experience as well as an entertainment.

Listen Up: The Lives of Quincy Jones ★ ★ ★ ½
PG-13, 111 m., 1990

With Quincy Jones and appearances by Ray Charles, Miles Davis, Billy Eckstine, Ella Fitzgerald, Herbie Hancock, Michael Jackson, Frank Sinatra, and Sarah Vaughan. Directed by Ellen Weissbrod and produced by Courtney Sale Ross.

There is a moment in *Listen Up: The Lives of Quincy Jones* where he pays a visit to the house on Chicago's South Side where he spent his earliest years. He remembers a lot of pain from those days, but it isn't connected to specific images until he sees and touches the scenes of his childhood. The texture of a hot-air register feels familiar to his hand, and suddenly memories come rushing back from more than fifty years earlier, and he walks through the house in a cloud of associations.

He did not spend a happy time here. His mother was mentally ill, and he remembers angers and rages and, most of all, the absence of a mother's love. On one of his birthdays, she threw his cake off the back porch. She was eventually sent away for care, and the family moved to Seattle—from an all-

black to an all-white environment—and it was there that Jones picked up his first musical instrument, and was revealed as such a natural musician that he was playing with big bands when he was only fifteen.

The illness of Jones's mother was treatable ("It turned out what she really needed was only a lot of Vitamin B," he told me sadly in an interview), and eventually mother and family were reconciled. The past has been forgiven, but the scars are still there, and we learn in *Listen Up* of a man who feels his loss of a mother's love when he was young has made it all but impossible for him to trust women and have long-term relationships with them.

The yearning that he feels—a yearning from childhood that can never be answered, because the child itself no longer exists—has expressed itself in many ways in his life: in an outpouring of original songs. In musical scores for the movies, after Richard Brooks hired him for *In Cold Blood* and Jones became the first black composer to score for mainstream films. In his arrangements and the albums he has produced for musicians as varied as Ella Fitzgerald, Michael Jackson, Frank Sinatra, and Barbra Streisand. In thirty Grammy awards. In seven Oscar nominations. In his work as executive producer of *The Color Purple.*

Yet we learn in this film that the private Quincy Jones has not always been as happy as his smiling public image on talk shows and the Grammys. *Listen Up* is an extraordinarily frank story of a life that has also contained broken marriages, children who harbor some resentments, and health problems, including two harrowing brain surgeries and a nervous breakdown. The odds against both surgeries were one hundred to one, Jones mentions in the film, and the scar of one of them is still slightly visible above his right temple.

Listen Up is the stronger because of its honesty. This isn't a once-over-lightly PR job, but a movie about the peaks and valleys of a man's life. Director Ellen Weissbrod and producer Courtney Sale Ross have looked unblinkingly at the sad as well as the happy times, and some of the most poignant moments in the movie come as Jolie Jones, Quincy's oldest daughter, talks quietly about her father.

There are many other witnesses as well. People who never talk for documentaries talk for this one: Frank Sinatra, Ray Charles, the shy Michael Jackson (whose interview takes place partly in darkness). Because the

filmmakers wanted to avoid the usual captions and subtitles of documentaries, each subject is asked to identify himself, and this leads to some humor, as when Ray Charles smiles that it's been a long time since anybody had to ask who he was.

The movie is constructed in an unusual kaleidoscopic way. Instead of moving ponderously from one subject to another, and following chronological order, the filmmakers organize their material more like a jazz composition. The interview subjects are like soloists improvising on a theme and, occasionally, stepping in to comment on someone else's observations. The result is not an orderly, routine documentary, but an original work that may be a little off-putting at first, but grows on you. By the end of this film, I felt I knew Quincy Jones better than I had ever expected to, and that now that I knew the bad things, I admired the good things even more.

Little Big League ★ ★ ★ ½

PG, 120 m., 1994

Luke Edwards (Billy Heywood), Timothy Busfield (Lou Collins), Ashley Crow (Jenny Heywood), Jason Robards (Thomas Heywood), Dennis Farina (George O'Farrell), John Ashton (Mac Macnally), Kevin Dunn (Arthur Goslin). Directed by Andrew Scheinman and produced by Mike Lobell. Screenplay by Gregory K. Pincus and Adam Scheinman.

Baseball was made for kids; grown-ups only screw it up.
—Bob Lemmon, quoted in *Little Big League*

Little Big League is a movie about a twelve-year-old kid who inherits the Minnesota Twins and decides to manage them himself. The last thing I was expecting was that the movie would take baseball seriously. But it does. It's one of those rare baseball movies that has a real feel for the game, instead of using it as a backdrop for bizarre characters.

The kid's name is Billy Heywood (Luke Edwards). He has a close relationship with his millionaire grandfather (Jason Robards), who owns the Twins, and they spend a lot of time talking strategy. Billy is not one of the stars of his local Little League team, but his judgment is sound and he's always the final authority on details about the rules. He seems to have absorbed the complete history of the game, and is able to tell you what great players of the past did when faced with tricky situations.

The grandfather dies, and leaves little Billy "my very favorite thing: the Minnesota Twins." Of course, grandfather didn't expect to die quite so soon, and probably imagined that Billy would be happy to leave the day-to-day management of the team to professionals. But after the manager (Dennis Farina) exhibits a hotheaded attitude and makes too many mistakes, Billy grows convinced that he should manage the team personally. His mother (Ashley Crow) wonders why he can't get a job carrying papers, like everyone else.

We're in a world of pure fantasy here. But somehow *Little Big League* works an alchemy that almost makes us believe this kid could manage a team. Luke Edwards plays Billy as a solemn, smart, thoughtful kid who seems grown-up for his years. His strategy in dealing with the players is to speak in simple, honest terms. He has one especially effective speech about how they should be grateful for the privilege of getting to play baseball: to step up to the plate where the Babe swung his bat, or stand in the same batter's box once occupied by Joe DiMaggio.

The movie is canny in the way it shows how major-league professionals react to this information. The director, Andrew Scheinman, is aware that his material is a mine field of hazards, and that a mistake in tone could take a serious moment and make it ludicrous. He doesn't step wrong. His strategy is to have the adult ballplayers act more or less the way real adults might behave, in such an impossible situation.

In the case of Billy's inspirational lockerroom speech, they listen impassively and do not respond much at all. In other situations, they ignore the kid, disregard his advice, tell him to get lost. But Billy really does know a lot about baseball, and by the end of the season he has won their grudging respect. It does not come easily, and there is a touchy moment when Billy walks out to the mound to remove a hulking, bearded pitcher (Bradley Jay Lesley) from the game. In his dealings with the team, he is helped out a lot by two veterans: Mac (John Ashton), the veteran coach, who acts as an adviser and right-hand man, and Lou Collins (Timothy Busfield), a veteran first baseman who also happens to be dating Billy's widowed mother.

More than once, watching *Little Big League,* I found myself monitoring my feelings: Is this movie really *working?* It was. Unlike *Major League II,* which used baseball only as an excuse for sitcom situations and recycled characters, *Little Big League* has the same mystical regard for the game as movies like *Field of Dreams* and *Bull Durham.* And even when Billy is dreaming up some cockamamie stunt or trick play that he learned about in an old record book, we find ourselves saying, hey, if it worked once, maybe it will work again.

There's also a subtext in the movie. Billy starts out as a normal kid with normal friends, but by midway through the season he gets a big head, and starts forgetting his "appointments" with his old playmates. To apologize, he offers them autographed balls. This is no way to behave, but the kid is under a lot of pressure, and one of the best sequences in the film shows how Lou, his mother's fiancé, subtly deals with being benched. He understands Billy and respects him in spite of everything, and is able to help the kid learn a lesson.

Like *Free Willy, The Secret Garden, Searching for Bobby Fischer* and *The Man in the Moon,* this is a "family movie" that doesn't condescend. It takes its twelve-year-old hero as seriously as he takes baseball, and nothing is "dumbed down" for the PG audience. One of the qualities of the film is that it doesn't feel predictable. Of course, it ends with a Big Game. All sports movies do. But for once the outcome is not necessarily certain.

Little Big Man ★ ★ ★ ★
PG, 157 m., 1971

Dustin Hoffman (Jack Crabb), Faye Dunaway (Mrs. Pendrake), Martin Balsam (Merriweather), Richard Mulligan (General Custer), Chief Dan George (Old Lodge Skins), Jeff Corey (Wild Bill Hickok). Directed by Arthur Penn and produced by Stuart Millar. Screenplay by Calder Willingham.

Arthur Penn's *Little Big Man* is an endlessly entertaining attempt to spin an epic in the form of a yarn. It mostly works. When it doesn't—when there's a failure of tone or an overdrawn caricature—it regroups cheerfully and plunges ahead. We're disposed to go along; all good storytellers tell stretchers once in a while, and circle back to be sure we got the good parts.

It is the very folksiness of Penn's film that makes it, finally, such a perceptive and important statement about Indians, the West, and the American dream. There's no stridency, no preaching, no deep-voiced narrators making sure we got the point of the last massacre. All the events happened long, long ago, and they're related by a 121-year-old man who just wants to pass the story along. The yarn is the most flexible of story forms. Its teller can pause to repeat a point; he can hurry ahead ten years; he can forget an entire epoch in remembering the legend of a single man. He doesn't capture the history of a time, but its flavor. *Little Big Man* gives us the flavor of the Cheyenne nation before white men brought uncivilization to the West. Its hero, played by Dustin Hoffman, is no hero at all but merely a survivor.

Hoffman, or Little Big Man, gets around pretty well. He touches all the bases of the Western myth. He was brought West as a settler, raised as a Cheyenne, tried his hand at gunfighting and medicine shows, scouted for the cavalry, experimented with the hermit life, was married twice, survived Custer's Last Stand, and sat at the foot of an old man named Old Lodge Skins, who instructed him in the Cheyenne view of creation.

Old Lodge Skins, played by Chief Dan George with such serenity and conviction that an Academy Award was mentioned, doesn't preach the Cheyenne philosophy. It is part of him. It's all the more a part of him because Penn has allowed the Indians in the film to speak ordinary, idiomatic English. Most movie Indians have had to express themselves with an "um" at the end of every other word: "Swap-um wampum plenty soon," etc. The Indians in *Little Big Man* have dialogue reflecting the idiomatic richness of Indian tongues; when Old Lodge Skins simply refers to Cheyennes as "the Human Beings," the phrase is literal and meaningful and we don't laugh.

Despite Old Lodge Skins, however, Little Big Man doesn't make it as an Indian, or as a white man, either, or as anything else he tries. He looks, listens, remembers, and survives, which is his function. The protagonists in the film are two ideas of civilization: the Indian's and the white man's. Custer stages his bloody massacres and is massacred in turn, and we know that the Indians will eventually be destroyed as an organic community and shunted off to reservations. But the film's movement is circular, and so is its belief about Indians.

Penn has adopted the yarn form for a reason. All the characters who appear in the early stages of the film come back in the later stages, fulfilled. The preacher's wife returns as a prostitute. The medicine-quack, already lacking an arm, loses a leg (physician, heal thyself). Wild Bill Hickok decays from a has-been to a freak show attraction. Custer fades from glory to madness. Only Old Lodge Skins makes it through to the end not merely intact, but improved.

His survival is reflected in the film's structure. Most films, especially ones with violence, have their climax at the end. Penn puts his near the center; it is Custer's massacre of an Indian village, and Little Big Man sees his Indian wife killed and his baby's head blown off. Penn can control violence as well as any American director (remember *Bonnie and Clyde* and *The Left Handed Gun*). He does here. The final massacre of Custer and his men is deliberately muted, so it doesn't distract from Old Lodge Skins's "death" scene.

But Custer stays dead, and Old Lodge Skins doesn't quite die ("I was afraid it would turn out this way"). So he leaves the place of death and invites Little Big Man home to have something to eat. Custer's civilization will eventually win, but Old Lodge Skins's will prevail. William Faulkner observed in his Nobel Prize speech that man will probably endure—but will he prevail? It's probably no accident that we don't smile when Old Lodge Skins explains the difference between Custer and the Human Beings.

Little Dorrit ★ ★ ★ ★
G, 357 m., 1988

Alec Guinness (William Dorrit), Sarah Pickering (Little Dorrit), Cyril Cusack (Frederick Dorrit), Amelda Brown (Fanny), Derek Jacobi (Arthur Clennam), Joan Greenwood (Mrs. Clennam), Roshan Seth (Mr. Pancks). Directed by Christine Edzard and produced by John Brabourne and Richard Goodwin. Screenplay by Edzard based on the novel by Charles Dickens.

I turned on the TV late one night, just in time to catch the closing moments of Truffaut's *Fahrenheit 451*. You remember the scene. In a world where the printed word has been forbidden, a little colony of book-lovers lives by the side of a lake in the woods. Each one has dedicated his life to memorizing the contents of one book. They walk slowly back and forth on paths through the snow, reciting the words over and over, and their voices form a litany of familiar passages.

Little Dorrit is like a film made in the same spirit. It is a six-hour epic, with 242 speaking roles, and yet it was crafted almost by hand.

The director, Christine Edzard, and the co-producer, her husband Richard Goodwin, live and work in a converted warehouse in London's dockland. When they are not making films, they manufacture dollhouses. They built the sets for this film inside their warehouse, they sewed all of the costumes on premises, they used their dollhouse skills to build miniature models which are combined with special effects to create a backdrop of Victorian London. And to their studio by the side of the Thames, they lured such actors as Alec Guinness, Derek Jacobi, Cyril Cusack, and Joan Greenwood to appear in a film that was made mostly out of the love of Charles Dickens.

I myself have spent some time in the company of Dickens. I read *Nicholas Nickleby* not long ago, and then *Our Mutual Friend*, and now here is this six-hour film version of *Little Dorrit*, which is so filled with characters, so rich in incident, that it has the expansive, luxurious feel of a Victorian novel. Dickens created worlds large enough that you could move around in them. He did not confine himself to the narrow focus of a few neurotic characters and their shell-shocked egos; he created worlds, in the closing words of *Little Dorrit*, where "the noisy and the eager, and the arrogant and the froward and the vain, fretted, and chafed, and made their usual uproar."

Little Dorrit opens with the information that the story will be told in two parts, the first through the eyes of Arthur Clennam, the second through the eyes of Little Dorrit. The two parts of the film contain many of the same scenes, seen from different points of view and remembered differently, so that half a line of throwaway dialogue in the first version may turn out, in the second version, to have been absolutely crucial. The use of two different points of view is not simply a conceit of the filmmakers, but creates a real romantic tension, because it is clear from the outset that Clennam and Little Dorrit are in love with each other—and neither one has any way of admitting that fact.

The film opens in Marshalsea Prison, where the heroine's father, William Dorrit (Alec Guinness) has been confined for twenty years for nonpayment of debt. Although her older sister despises the debtor's prison, Dorrit (Sarah Pickering) has grown to love it, as the only home she has ever known. On its stairs she received her education—learned to read and write, learned her English history in the form of stories told of kings and queens. She is not too proud to be poor.

Near the beginning of the film, Dorrit goes to work in an old, gloomy house occupied by the grasping Mrs. Clennam (Joan Greenwood), who lives there with Flintwinch, her bitter steward (Max Wall). It is there that Dorrit first lays eyes on the old lady's son, Arthur (Derek Jacobi), who has plugged away honorably in life without getting much of anywhere. And it is there that Dorrit discovers the clue to an ancient inheritance that the mother is determined to keep from her son.

Arthur's first glimpse of Dorrit is only momentary. But he wants to know who that young girl was. He wants to know in a tentative, almost frightened voice that lets us know, immediately, that he has fallen irrevocably into love with her. But there are great barriers, of course. One of them is the difference in their ages—although that was not so big a problem in Victorian times, when poor young ladies were often married off for reasons of money rather than love. A greater problem is Dorrit's self-image. Since her father, who she dearly loves, lives in a debtor's prison, her place is at his side. The third problem, of course, is that Arthur and Dorrit can barely endure to be in the same room together, because they love each other so much and cannot admit it.

I saw *Little Dorrit* all in the same day. I think that is a good way to see it, although many people will want to split it into two different evenings. Very long films can create a life of their own. We lose our moorings. We don't know exactly where we stand within the narrative, and so we can't guess what will happen next. People appear and reappear, grow older and die, and we accept the rhythm of the story rather than requiring it to be speeded up.

This kind of timing imparts tremendous weight to the love story. During the course of the film, we ourselves come to love Little Dorrit and Arthur Clennam (who is a good man and a very lonely one). We see all their difficulties. We know all of their fears. We identify with all of their hesitations. When they are finally able to bring themselves to admit that they are in love, it is a joyous moment. And when old Dorrit comes to the time when he must die, Alec Guinness plays the scene with the kind of infinitely muted pathos that has you wiping your eyes even as you're admiring his acting craft.

Many good novels, it is said, begin with a funeral and end with a wedding. *Little Dorrit* more or less travels that route, with another funeral at the end. It is never simply a love story, and it is not structured melodramatically. It is about the accumulation of incident. We are told that old Dorrit, the Guinness character, lives in the prison for twenty years. We begin to feel those years, as he sits in his chair by the window and we inventory the pathetically short list of his possessions. We see the hopelessness and waste of the Victorian debtor system, which Dickens helped to reform with novels such as this. But we also see the hope that could exist in a city where people lived cheek by jowl, rich by poor, everyone in sight of the street.

Little Man Tate ★ ★ ★ ½
PG, 99 m., 1991

Adam Hann-Byrd (Fred Tate), Jodie Foster (Dede Tate), Dianne Wiest (Jane Grierson), David Pierce (Garth), Debi Mazar (Gina), P.J. Ochlan (Damon Wells), Harry Connick, Jr. (Eddie). Directed by Jodie Foster and produced by Scott Rudin and Peggy Rajski. Screenplay by Scott Frank.

Jodie Foster says there is an element of autobiography in *Little Man Tate,* the first film she chose to direct. It's the story of a six-year-old who happens to be a genius, and also happens to be a little boy. Math problems solve themselves in his mind, and he plays piano at a concert level, and when he reads the paper he gets depressed by the news. But he also needs his mom, feels tongue-tied when a lot of adults are looking at him, and gets homesick when he stays away from home overnight.

I know Foster is telling the truth when she says there is a little of her own story in the story of Fred Tate, because I met her when she was only a few years older than the little man in her film. She had been appearing in movies since she was three, but child actors are commonplace and that isn't what made her special. What was impressive was how smart, cool, and observant she was for her age; how she discussed the motivations of her characters and the quirks of her directors.

I was interviewing her for *Freaky Friday* or one of those other Disney movies she made. She met me at a health food place on Sunset Boulevard—no publicist in tow—and ordered something with a lot of alfalfa sprouts in it. The next time I saw her, she was already thirteen, and translating from French to English and back again at the Cannes Film Festival, where she starred in *Taxi Driver.*

I mention these meetings for a reason. I sensed a quality in Jodie Foster that I also sense in Fred Tate: a certain balance, a certain perspective on the strangeness of life. Despite spending twenty-five of her twenty-eight years in show business, Foster is sane, focused, and not much impressed by showbiz glitter. Fred Tate is the same way: He looks at things with a level eye, he is not neurotic, he handles a roller-coaster childhood without going nuts.

And that's one reason why *Little Man Tate* isn't precisely the movie you'd expect. The child genius (Adam Hann-Byrd) is not treated as a sideshow stunt, nor as a cute gimmick, but as a miniature human being who brings out the worst, and best, of those around him. As the movie opens, he is amazing his mother, Dede (Foster), by reading the bottom of his cereal bowl when he is hardly big enough to lift it. Soon he is painting, playing piano, and attracting the attention of Jane Grierson (Dianne Wiest), a child psychologist who runs a school for gifted kids.

What Foster and her screenwriter, Scott Frank, know about gifted kids is that you mustn't forget they're still kids. One of my favorite characters in the movie is an adolescent "mathemagician" with a lightning mind but an obnoxious personality, who wears a magician's cape at all times and in all places. He's hard on Fred when he first comes to the Grierson school, but eventually confides that he has no friends, and that if it weren't for his brains, "I'd just be another asshole with a cape."

Wiest plays the psychologist as someone who knows everything about children in theory and nothing in practice. She has an oddly formal way of speaking to Fred, as if she were giving dictation, and she doesn't have a clue about the needs of a kid his age. Foster, as the mother, may not know much about the theory of child geniuses, but she knows her little boy and is fiercely protective of him, and although sparks fly between the two women, eventually there is a rapprochement based on their mutual love of Fred.

The movie has enough plot, but not too much; it's loosely centered around a brainy Olympics for smart kids. Foster, who has worked with many different kinds of directors, seems attracted to a kind of film she hasn't really ever appeared in: the sunny French comedy of truth, as practiced by Truffaut, where the laughs are built on insights, and the movie ends in a resolution rather than a climax. *Little Man Tate* is the kind of movie you enjoy watching; it's about interesting people finding out about themselves. And as Jodie Foster creates this little man who sees a lot and knows a lot but is only gradually beginning to understand a lot, we can hear echoes, perhaps, of a young girl who once found it more interesting to study French than get her picture in the fan magazines.

The Little Mermaid ★ ★ ★ ★
G, 82 m., 1989

With the voices of: Jodi Benson (Ariel), Kenneth Mars (Triton), Pat Carroll (Ursula), Buddy Hackett (Scuttle), Samuel E. Wright (Sebastian), Rene Auberjonois (Louis), Christopher Daniel Barnes (Eric), Jason Marin (Flounder), Edie McClurg (Carlotta), Ben Wright (Grimsby), Will Ryan (Seahorse). Directed by John Musker and Ron Clements and produced by Howard Ashman and Musker. Screenplay by Musker and Clements.

Walt Disney's *The Little Mermaid* is a jolly and inventive animated fantasy—a movie that's so creative and so much fun it deserves comparison with the best Disney work of the past. It's based on the Hans Christian Andersen tale about a mermaid who falls in love with a prince, but the Disney animators have added a gallery of new supporting characters, including an octopus named Ursula who is their most satisfying villainess since the witch in *Snow White.*

Watching *The Little Mermaid,* I began to feel that the magic of animation had been restored to us. After the early years of Walt Disney's pathfinding feature-length cartoons, we entered into a long dark age in which frame-by-frame animation was too expensive, and even the great Disney animation team began using shortcuts. Now computers have taken the busywork out of the high-priced hands of humans, who are free to realize even the most elaborate flights of imagination. And that's certainly what they do in this film.

The movie opens far beneath the sea, where the god Triton rules over his underwater kingdom. All obey his commands—except for his daughter, Ariel, a mermaid who dreams of far-off lands. One day Ariel makes a forbidden visit to the surface of the sea, and there she sees a human for the first time—a handsome young prince. She saves him from drowning, but he remembers nothing about the experience except for her voice, which he falls in love with. Triton is angry at Ariel's disobedience, but she can think of nothing but the prince, and eventually she strikes an unwise bargain with the evil Ursula, an octopus who can disguise herself in many different forms. Ursula will take away Ariel's tail and give her human legs so she can follow the prince onto the land—but in exchange Ariel must give up her haunting singing voice, and if the prince doesn't kiss her within three days, she will become Ursula's slave.

Two key elements in the storytelling make *The Little Mermaid* stand apart from lesser recent animated work. One is that Ariel is a fully realized female character who thinks and acts independently, even rebelliously, instead of hanging around passively while the fates decide her destiny. Because she's smart and thinks for herself, we have sympathy for her scheming. The second element involves the plot itself: It's tricky and clever, and involves some suspense as Ariel loses her voice and very nearly loses her prince to the diabolical Ursula (who assumes the form of a *femme fatale* and hijacks Ariel's beautiful voice).

As the plot thickens and the melodrama unwinds, the animators introduce a gallery of new characters who are instantly engaging. Ariel is accompanied most places, for example, by Sebastian, a crab with extraordinary wisdom, by Flounder, a fish who cannot always be counted upon, and by Scuttle, a busybody sea gull who looks and sounds a good deal like Buddy Hackett. They provide comic relief, especially in a sequence that mixes comedy and danger in the best Disney tradition, as Sebastian finds himself captured by a French chef who attempts to cook and serve the little blighter.

What's best about *The Little Mermaid* is the visual invention with which the adventures are drawn. There is a lightness and a freedom about the setting—from Triton's underwater throne room to storms at sea and Ursula's garden of captured souls (they look a little like the tourists buried in Farmer Vincent's backyard in *Motel Hell*). The colors are bright, the water sparkles with reflected light, and there is a sense that not a single frame has been compromised because of the cost of animation.

The songs are good, too. *The Little Mermaid* contains some of the best Disney music since the glory days. My favorite song is a laidback reggae number named *Under the Sea*, sung by Samuel E. Wright in such a splendid blend of animation and music that I recommend it to the cable music channels. The movie was written and directed by John Mus-ker and Ron Clements, who made the entertaining *The Great Mouse Detective* (1986), and the songs are by Alan Menken and the coproducer, Howard Ashman, who did *Little Shop of Horrors*.

Something seems to have broken free inside all of these men, and the animating directors they worked with: Here at last, once again, is the kind of liberating, original, joyful Disney animation that we remember from *Snow White, Pinocchio*, and the other first-generation classics. There has been a notion in recent years that animated films are only for kids. But why? The artistry of animation has a clarity and a force that can appeal to everyone, if only it isn't shackled to a dimwitted story. *The Little Mermaid* has music and laughter and visual delight for everyone.

Little Odessa ★ ★
R, 98 m., 1995

NEW

Tim Roth (Joshua Shapira), Edward Furlong (Reuben Shapira), Moira Kelly (Alla Shustervich), Vanessa Redgrave (Irina Shapira), Maximilian Schell (Arkady Shapira), Paul Guilfoyle (Boris Volkoff), Natasha Andreichenko (Natasha), David Vadim (Sasha). Directed by James Gray and produced by Paul Webster. Screenplay by Gray.

In the opening moments of *Little Odessa*, a hit man played by Tim Roth walks quickly across a street toward a man on a park bench, and shoots him dead. Then he goes to a telephone to report that the job has been done. He learns that his next job will take him to the Brighton Beach neighborhood of Brooklyn. Not there, he says. He can't go back there.

But he does, and we learn that he has been running from this neighborhood—settled by Jews from Russia—and from his past, ever since he was banished by his father for committing an earlier murder, maybe his first. Still living there are his father, his mother, a kid brother, and the girl he walked out on when he fled Brighton Beach.

It is, we gather, risking his life to go back there, but the hit man, named Joshua Shapira, is not too clever about escaping notice. He checks into a local hotel for several days. He visits a social club, and sits in the window. Soon even his kid brother Reuben (Edward Furlong) knows he's back, and they meet at Nathan's on the boardwalk, on a cold winter day. He looks up the girl, Alla (Moira Kelly), and they go to a movie. And he returns home to visit his dying mother (Vanessa Redgrave), but his father (Maximilian Schell) throws him out, crying, "Murderer!"

Soon Joshua is involved again in the local crime scene; he has been hired to do a killing, others are hoping to kill him, and there are old scores to settle. One of them is with his father, who takes off his belt to beat the younger brother, and who is eventually humiliated by Joshua—made to disrobe in a vacant field and anticipate his own death. This scene, inspired perhaps by an equally unpleasant but more plausible scene in *Miller's Crossing*, brings the film to a shuddering halt.

The whole undercurrent of child abuse in the movie is unconvincing, and doesn't provide much of an explanation for Joshua becoming a hit man. I felt as if the whole crime plot of the movie had been imposed on the underlying story, to make the project more commercial.

Tim Roth is an amazingly versatile actor; compare this character from Brooklyn with his Cockney thief in *Pulp Fiction* and his foppish con man in *Rob Roy*. He does what he can with his character, but the story, written and directed by James Gray, is neither a family drama nor a crime melodrama, but a series of disconnected scenes that play like exercises—some of them very good ones. Consider, for example, the kid brother. Edward Furlong is a skillful actor, but what can he do with a role that requires him to materialize uncannily at key moments, just so he can witness things it is unlikely he would even know about? Or what about the father, played by Schell, who is written as such a hamhanded heavy that he bursts through credibility? And what, given the movie's Jewish milieu, are we to make of a closing scene in which a furnace is used as a crematorium? There is symbolism there, I'm sure, but I don't feel like working it out, and I don't think the movie has earned it.

James Gray, the filmmaker, was twenty-five years old when he made this, his first film. It plays a little as if he put everything into it that he ever wanted to say, or do, in a movie—even a closing shoot-out sequence that uses such stagy choreography it feels more like film school than any possible sequence of real events. Watching a subtle play of shadows on sheets hanging on a clothes line, it seemed to me that the movie had raised too many serious issues to turn into a visual exercise at the end. It's a set piece when a dramatic scene is needed.

Some individual passages are very well done. A quiet, sad discussion, for example, between the father and his mistress. A conversation between Joshua and the girl he left behind. A final talk between Joshua and his mother. None of these need a contrived crime plot to make them work, and when *Little Odessa* is over you wonder if it wasn't really meant to be a family drama—and that the idea of making the son a hit man was an afterthought, to make the project more attractive to investors.

A Little Princess ★ ★ ★ ½
G, 98 m., 1995

NEW

Liesel Matthews (Sara Crewe), Eleanor Bron (Miss Minchin), Liam Cunningham (Father/ Prince Rama), Rusty Schwimmer (Amelia Minchin), Arthur Malet (Charles Randolph), Vanessa Lee Chester (Becky), Errol Sitahal (Ram Dass). Directed by Alfonso Cuaron and produced by Mark Johnson. Screenplay by Richard LaGravenese and Elizabeth Chandler.

A Little Princess is another magical family film based on a book by Frances Hodgson Burnett, whose work also inspired *The Secret Garden*. Both films approach the characters of her children with calm solemnity and delight, placing them in vast, wonderful, frightening houses, and allowing them to discover some of the lessons of life there. Unlike the insipid devices of most family films, Miss Burnett's plots understand that children take stories very seriously indeed, and that all stories are really about the uncertain place of the child in the mysterious world of adults.

A Little Princess, which opens just before World War I, tells the story of Sara Crewe (Liesel Matthews), who until the age of ten or eleven is raised by her father in India. Then her father finds it his duty to go off and fight in the war, and he places Sara in a magnificent private school in New York, run by a forbidding headmistress named Miss Minchin (Eleanor Bron), who is impressed by Captain Crewe's wealth and assigns little Sara to a suite so luxurious it could have been decorated by Cecil Beaton.

Miss Minchin's school, like most of the places in the movie, is obviously a set, and no less fascinating for that. It crouches at the end of a street like the palace of a Victorian robber baron, and inside, the glistening hardwood floors reflect the light of high stained-glass windows. But all is not an idyll here, and in her first moments at the school Sara

notices Becky (Vanessa Lee Chester), a black girl in a simple dress, mopping the floor.

Sara soon becomes the most popular girl in school, because of her ability to spin fantasies out of mundane materials. Give her a boring child's book to read aloud, and in her hands it will become a legend from India. Most of the girls quickly idolize her, and one who doesn't, a spiteful little snob with long hair, is warned by Sara, in what sounds like a display of supernatural prescience, "I wouldn't brush my hair as much if I were you."

Then one day Sara's birthday party is interrupted with an ominous omen: "Go to your room and get a simple black dress." There has been a major reversal in her life, and soon she's sharing attic quarters with Becky. What happens then depends on large servings of coincidence, fate, melodrama, and adventure, and is thoroughly satisfactory in all of those departments. Miss Minchin of course reveals herself as a cold snob, and Eleanor Bron's performance is all the more effective because it is cool and contained, instead of going over the top into cartoon exaggeration. "If you fail to meet the standards of this institution," she informs Sara at one low point, "you will be expelled. The streets of this city are not kind to homeless orphans."

A Little Princess was directed by the Mexican-born Alfonso Cuaron, and produced by Mark Johnson, formerly Barry Levinson's producer on such films as *Good Morning, Vietnam* and *Avalon*. I mention both because it is well directed *and* produced: Cuaron's version of magic realism consists of seeing incredibly fanciful sets and situations in precise detail, and Johnson has provided him with the freedom and logistical support to create such places as the street where Miss Minchin's School looms so impressively.

Imagination is a precious gift, and too many films hammer it down into submissiveness. Children sit transfixed before films and TV shows which substitute action for fancy; cartoon characters fly through space and blast each other endlessly, providing kids with the impression of a story without the substance.

Movies like *A Little Princess* and *The Secret Garden* contain a sense of wonder, and a message: The world is a vast and challenging place, through which a child can find its way with pluck and intelligence. It is about a girl who finds it more useful to speak French than to fire a ray gun. I know there are more

kids this season who want to see *Judge Dredd, Die Hard III,* and *Batman Forever,* than *The Little Princess,* and I feel sorry for them.

Little Vera ★ ★ ★
R, 109 m., 1989

Natalya Negoda (Vera), Andrei Sokolov (Sergei), Ludmila Zaitzeva (Mother), Andrei Fomin (Andrei), Alexander Negreba (Viktor), Yuri Nazarov (Father), Alexandra Tabakova (Lena), Alexandra Linov (Mikhail). Directed by Vasily Pichul and produced by Gorky Film Studios. Screenplay by Maria Khmelik.

Little Vera comes advertised as the first Soviet film to deal frankly with youth rebellion, discontent with the system, and sex. Its star, Natalya Negoda, has gained a measure of fame by being the first Russian actress to appear nude in a fairly explicit sex scene. To help launch the film in America, she posed nude for *Playboy* and told her story to *People* magazine. The strangest thing about this process is that it has made a truly revolutionary Soviet film look like another one of those "one summer of happiness" sex romps from Scandinavia.

The strategy of selling a foreign film on its sexual content is tried and true, but *Little Vera* is not a sexy film, and its star is not the new Bardot or Loren. The sex in *Little Vera* is sweaty and passionate but not erotic, and the film's real fascination comes from its portrait of everyday life in the Soviet Union—life that contains few surprises, but has never before been shown with such frankness and honesty in a Russian film.

The film takes place in a provincial city where Vera, a restless teen-ager, lives in a cramped three-room apartment with her alcoholic father and her thoroughly disillusioned mother. A brother has moved to Moscow. Life in the family is a drab routine: The self-pitying, unemployed father gets up in the morning and starts to drink, and the mother and daughter plan their days around his rages and remorses. Not surprisingly, Vera seeks to escape from this life, and she leaves the apartment with relief, dressed in a miniskirt, to hang out with a group of non-conformist teen-agers who like to listen to rock 'n' roll and bait the authorities.

Among the scenes in *Little Vera* that we have not seen in a Soviet movie before is one where policemen with guard dogs break up a meeting of teen-agers. The film is frankly on the side of youth and against authority, and the cops are seen as repressive agents of a humorless system. Vera herself finds what cheer she can in the arms of Sergei, whom she has met at a dance. He is an "intellectual," a nonconformist, but it is hard for him to express his free spirit when he must move into Vera's flat with her warring parents. (The housing shortage in the USSR is actually one of the film's most important themes; none of the characters can count on a moment's privacy.)

Vera and Sergei share a few moments of happiness, including one ironic interlude on the beach where they pause in their lovemaking to discuss their goals, and Vera says: "In our country, we have but one goal—communism." This line, in all its sarcasm, has reportedly become as famous in the Soviet Union as "Plastics, Benjamin, plastics!" became after the release of *The Graduate* in this country.

Life in the cramped apartment becomes impossible. The drunken father fights with Sergei, who moves out, and Vera attempts suicide. Her brother, visiting from Moscow, screams in anguish over his impossible family situation, but what the film makes clear is that much of the unhappiness comes from a social system which has given people no clear tasks, few areas to exercise personal ambition, cramped living quarters, no privacy, and too much bootleg booze.

The irony is that *Little Vera* is being sold as a sex film. Eroticism in Soviet films reminds me of Dr. Johnson's famous line about a dog standing on its hind legs: "It is not done well, but one is surprised to find it done at all." What this film does express, strongly and clearly, is a deep discontent among Russians who have lived in an incompetently managed society for too long. The angers in this film are the same ones that have produced Mikhail Gorbachev. For an American, *Little Vera* confirms what we already knew: Life for the poor, the unemployed, and the alcoholic is as bad in Russia as it is here.

Little Women ★ ★ ★ ½

PG, 115 m., 1994

Winona Ryder (Jo March), Gabriel Byrne (Friedrich Bhaer), Trini Alvarado (Meg March), Susan Sarandon (Mrs. March), Samantha Mathis (Older Amy March), Kirsten Dunst (Younger Amy March), Claire Danes (Beth March), Christian Bale (Laurie), Eric Stoltz (John Brooke). Directed by Gillian Armstrong and produced by Denise DiNovi. Screenplay by Robin Swicord.

The very title summons up preconceptions of treacly do-gooders in a smarmy children's story, and some of the early shots in *Little Women* do little to discourage them: In one of the first shots, the four little women and their mother somehow manage to arrange their heads within the frame with all of the spontaneity of a Kodak ad. But this movie is not smarmy, not do-gooding, and only a little treacly; before long I was beginning to remember, from many years ago, that Louisa May Alcott's *Little Women* was a really *good* novel—one that I read with great attention.

Of course, I was eleven or twelve then, but the novel seems to have grown up in the meantime—or maybe director Gillian Armstrong finds the serious themes and refuses to simplify the story into a "family" formula. *Little Women* may be marketed for children and teenagers, but my hunch is it will be best appreciated by their parents. It's a film about how all of life seems to stretch ahead of us when we're young, and how, through a series of choices, we choose and narrow our destiny.

The story is set in Concord, Massachusetts, and begins in 1862, in a winter when all news is dominated by the Civil War. The March family is on its own; their father has gone off to war. Times are hard, although it's hard not to smile when we find out how hard. "Firewood and lamp oil were scarce," we hear, while seeing the Marches living in what passes for poverty: a three-story colonial, decorated for a Currier and Ives print, with the cheerful family cook in the kitchen and the Marches sitting around the fire, knitting sweaters and rolling bandages.

The movie doesn't go the usual route of supplying broad, obvious "establishing" scenes for each of the girls; instead, we gradually get to know them, we sense their personalities, and we see how they relate to one another. The most forcible personality in the family is the tomboy daughter Jo, played in a strong and sunny performance by Winona Ryder. She wants to be a writer, and stages family theatricals in which everyone—even the long-suffering cat—is expected to play a role.

The others include wise Meg (Trini Alvarado), as the oldest; winsome Amy (Kirsten Dunst), as the youngest; and Beth, poor little Beth (Claire Danes), as the sickly one, who survives a medical crisis but is much weakened ("Fetch some vinegar-water and rags! We'll draw the fever down from her head!"). There isn't a lot of overt action in their lives, but then that's typical of the nineteenth-century novel about women, which

essentially shows them sitting endlessly in parlors, holding deep conversations about their hopes, their beliefs, their dreams, and, mostly, their marriage destinies.

The March girls have many other interests (their mother, played by Susan Sarandon, is what passed 130 years ago for a feminist), but young men and eligible bachelors rank high on the list. Their young neighbor is Laurie (Christian Bale), a playmate who is allowed to join their amateur theatricals as an honorary brother, and who eventually falls in love with Jo. Then there's Laurie's tutor, the pleasant Mr. Brooke (Eric Stoltz), who is much taken with Meg, but is dismissed by Jo as "dull as powder."

Jo, who moves to New York and starts to write lurid Victorian melodramas with titles like *The Sinner's Corpse,* falls under the eye of a European scholar, Friedrich Bhaer (Gabriel Byrne), who takes her seriously enough to criticize her work. He knows she can do better—why, she could write a novel named *Little Women* if she put half a mind to it. "I'm hopelessly flawed," Jo sighs. But she is not. And late in the film, when she tells Friedrich that, yes, it's all right for him to love her, Winona Ryder's face lights up with a smile so joyful it illuminates the theater.

Little Women grew on me. At first I was grumpy, thinking it was going to be too sweet and devout. Gradually I saw that Gillian Armstrong (whose credits include *My Brilliant Career* and *High Tide*) was taking it seriously. And then I began to appreciate the ensemble acting, with the five actresses creating the warmth and familiarity of a real family.

The buried issues in the story are quite modern: How must a woman negotiate the right path between society's notions of marriage and households, and her own dreams of doing something really special, all on her own? One day their mother tells them: "If you feel your value lies only in being merely decorative, I fear that someday you might find yourself believing that's all you really are. Time erodes all such beauty, but what it cannot diminish is the wonderful workings of your mind." Quite so.

Local Hero ★ ★ ★ ★

PG, 112 m., 1983

Burt Lancaster (Happer), Peter Riegert (Mac), Peter Capaldi (Danny), Fulton McKay (Ben), Denis Lawson (Urquhart). Directed by Bill Forsyth and produced by David Puttnam. Screenplay by Forsyth.

Here is a small film to treasure; a loving, funny, understated portrait of a small Scottish town and its encounter with a giant oil company. The town is tucked away in a sparkling little bay, and is so small that everybody is well aware of everybody else's foibles. The oil company is run by an eccentric billionaire (Burt Lancaster) who would really rather have a comet named after him than own all the oil in the world. And what could have been a standard plot about conglomerates and ecology, etc., turns instead into a wicked study of human nature.

The movie opens in Houston, but quickly moves to the fishing village of Ferness. The oil company assigns an earnest young American (Peter Riegert) and a whimsical Scot (Peter Capaldi) to go to Ferness, and buy it up, lock, stock, and beachline, for a North Sea oil-refining complex. This is a simpler job than it appears, since a lot of the locals are all too willing to soak the oil company for its millions of dollars, sell the beach, and go in search of the bright lights of Edinburgh. But there are complications. One of them is old Ben, the cheerful philosopher who lives in a shack on the beach. It turns out that the beach has been the legal property of Ben's family for four centuries, ever since an ancestor did a favor for the king. And Ben doesn't want to sell: "Who'd look after the beach then? It would go to pieces in a short matter of time."

The local negotiations are handled by the innkeeper, Urquhart (Denis Lawson). He also is the accountant, and sort of the mayor, I guess, and is so much in love with his pretty wife that they're forever dashing upstairs for a quickie. Meanwhile, Riegert and Capaldi fall under the spell of the town, settle into its rhythms, become wrapped up in its intrigues, and, in general, are co-opted by a place whose charms are seductive.

What makes this material really work is the low-key approach of the writer-director, Bill Forsyth, who also made the charming *Gregory's Girl* and has the patience to let his characters gradually reveal themselves to the camera. He never hurries, and as a result, *Local Hero* never drags: Nothing is more absorbing than human personalities, developed with love and humor. Some of the payoffs in this film are sly and subtle, and others generate big laughs. Forsyth's big scenes are his little ones, including a heartfelt, whiskey-soaked talk between the American and the innkeeper, and a scene where the visitors walk on the beach and talk about the mean-ing of life. By the time Burt Lancaster reappears at the end of the film, to personally handle the negotiations with old Ben, *Local Hero* could hardly have anything but a happy ending. But it's a fairly close call.

The Lonely Passion of Judith Hearne
★ ★ ★
R, 110 m., 1988

Maggie Smith (Judith Hearne), Bob Hoskins (James Madden), Wendy Hiller (Aunt D'Arcy), Marie Kean (Mrs. Rice), Ian McNeice (Bernard), Alan Devlin (Father Quigley), Rudi Davies (Mary). Directed by Jack Clayton and produced by Peter Nelson and Richard Johnson. Screenplay by Nelson.

The most intimate moment in *The Lonely Passion of Judith Hearne* is one played between the heroine and a bottle of whiskey. She retreats to her lonely room in a sad Dublin boardinghouse and locks the door, then runs to her closet and finds the bottle where it has been hidden away during all the recent days of happiness, waiting quietly until she would need it again. She pours the drink quickly, and then all is chaos once again in her life, as we sense it has been so many times before.

Maggie Smith brings precise body language to this scene. She does not play it eagerly, or desperately, but with well-rehearsed precision, showing us that for the alcoholic Miss Hearne, this is a ritual. Smith's goal in the scene is to show us, without telling us, that this is not the first time Judith Hearne has admitted despair. And as the whiskey takes hold and the lonely spinster begins to sing to herself, her boozy joy is all the more depressing because it comes from defeat, not victory.

The realities of Miss Hearne's life are made clear a little at a time. She is poor, but respectable. She lives in rooming houses. She has few friends, and the family she is closest to tolerates her out of pity. She gives piano lessons, and dreams that someday a white knight will come riding out of the mist—a man to sweep her off her feet and make everything right again. In this dream she is frequently disappointed, and then the bottle comes out of the closet and her downward spiral continues. Since the only apparent joy in her life comes from drunkenness, there is even the possibility that she sets up her own failures—to give herself an excuse to drink.

This time, though . . . this time may be different. As *The Lonely Passion of Judith Hearne* opens, she has moved into another boardinghouse, and at breakfast she meets the brother of the landlady. His name is James (Bob Hoskins), and he has just come back from spending many years in America. She thinks America must be a wonderful place, and before long she thinks James must be a wonderful person. He seems lonely, too, and after some shy verbal sparring they go to Mass together and to the picture show.

Eventually it becomes clear that James is interested in Judith primarily for the money he thinks she must have—money she might invest in his own dream of an American-style hot dog stand, to cater to all the Yankee tourists in Dublin. There is even talk of marriage between the two people, before Judith finally sees through to James's real motives. Then she gets drunk, of course, but that is not the end of the movie, only the midpoint, because then James must question his own motives.

We sense that this sort of scenario has repeated itself, in one version or another, for many years in Judith Hearne's life. But since James is, in some ways, her last chance, the cruelty of his betrayal hits her harder and almost destroys her. And her suffering leads up to a crucial scene in which she is at last able to tell James, and herself, the exact reality of her life. The movie implies that by seeing herself clearly, she can begin to mend.

For Maggie Smith, the movie is a triumph, a performance to compare with *The Prime of Miss Jean Brodie* of twenty years ago. Bob Hoskins is very good, too, but his character is less clearly seen, and it might have been wise for the screenplay to make his actual feelings for Judith Hearne more clear. The movie's ending is courageous and moving, I suppose, but since it deals more with Judith's fate than with her drinking, it rather evades the issue. Courage and clarity will not heal Judith unless they come after sobriety—without which, for her, even the best intentions will end with another ritualistic search for the bottle in the back of the closet.

The Long Goodbye ★ ★ ★
R, 112 m., 1973

Elliott Gould (Philip Marlowe), Nina van Pallandt (Eileen Wade), Sterling Hayden (Roger Wade), Mark Rydell (Marty Augustine), Henry Gibson (Dr. Verringer), David Arkin (Harry). Directed by Robert Altman and produced by Elliott Kastner. Screenplay by Leigh Brackett.

Robert Altman's *The Long Goodbye* attempts to do a very interesting thing. It tries to be all genre and no story, and it almost works. It makes no serious effort to reproduce the Raymond Chandler detective novel it's based on; instead, it just takes all the characters out of that novel and lets them stew together in something that feels like a private-eye movie.

The private eye is, I suppose, a fairly obsolete institution in our society. I'm not talking about the divorce case specialists and the missing persons guys; I'm thinking of the Chandler, Dashiell Hammett, Ross Mac-Donald kind of hired eye whose occupation takes him into glamorous danger and who subscribes to a weary private credo. The private eye as a fiction device was essentially a way to open doors; the best novels of Chandler and the others are simply hooks for a cynical morality.

Altman seems to understand this. He knows we don't care any more about the plot than he does; he agrees with Hitchcock that it doesn't even matter what the plot is about (as long as it's something). The important thing is the way the characters spar with each other. But Altman has added a twist: Instead of making his private eye into a cool, competent professional, he makes him into a 1950s anachronism. Philip Marlowe has been in a lot of movies, but never one in which he was more confused than he is in this one.

The story, or whatever you want to call it, involves a murder, a missing person, and an alcoholic writer with a bewitching blonde wife. There are also some gangsters and a cat. The writer and his wife are played with really fine style by Sterling Hayden and Nina van Pallandt—who not only demonstrates that she can act, but also that a real woman is infinitely more interesting on the screen than some starlet beauty-school graduate who should be leading the pompon team.

The middle of this mess is inhabited by Elliott Gould, as the chain-smoking, mumbling, disorganized Marlowe. It's a good performance, particularly the virtuoso ten-minute stretch at the beginning of the movie when he goes out to buy food for his cat. Gould has enough of the paranoid in his acting style to really put over Altman's revised view of the private eye.

Altman doesn't string his scenes together to tell a taut story, but he directs each scene as if were. There's an especially memora-ble scene involving Philip Marlowe and a gangster (played by Mark Rydell, who is usually a director). The gangster smacks his girlfriend with a pop bottle and then snarls at Marlowe: "Now that's someone I *love*. Think what could happen to you." The scene sounds rather grim in print, I know, but in the movie it has a kind of hard-boiled desperation to it. It feels like it belongs in a private eye's life and so does the whole movie—right up to the ending, which is really off the wall.

The Long Good Friday ★ ★ ★ ★
R, 118 m., 1982

Bob Hoskins (Harold Shand), Helen Mirren (Victoria), Eddie Constantine (Charlie), Derek Thompson (Jeff), Bryan Marshall (Harris), Paul Freeman (Collin). Directed by John Mackenzie and produced by Barry Hanson. Screenplay by Barrie Keeffe.

Harold is as hard as a rock and he will crush you. He runs the London docks and he wants to put together the biggest real estate deal in Europe. He has Mafia money from America and the tacit cooperation of the London criminal organization. He's short, barrel-chested, with his thinning hair combed forward above a round face and teeth that always seem to be grinding. He cannot believe that in one weekend his whole world can come apart. Harold Shand is a hood, but he lives in a penthouse, anchors a world-class yacht in the Thames, has the love of an intelligent and tactful mistress, and talks obsessively about the ten years of peace he has helped negotiate in the London underground. Then a bomb blows up his Rolls Royce, killing his chauffeur. Another bomb demolishes the lovingly restored landmark pub he owns. A third bomb is found inside Harold's Mayfair casino, but fails to detonate. Who is after him? Who is his enemy? And why has the enemy chosen this worst of all possible times to come after him—the Easter weekend when an American Mafioso is in town to consider investing millions in his real estate project?

The Long Good Friday, which is a masterful and very tough piece of filmmaking, eventually does answer these questions. But the point of the film isn't to analyze Harold Shand's problems. It's to present a portrait of this man. And I have rarely seen a movie character so completely alive. Shand is an evil, cruel, sadistic man. But he's a mass of contradictions, and there are times when we understand him so completely we almost feel affectionate. He's such a character, such an overcompensating Cockney, sensitive to the slightest affront, able to strike fear in the hearts of killers, but a pushover when his mistress raises her voice to him. Shand is played by a compact, muscular actor named Bob Hoskins, in the most-praised film performance of the year from England. Hoskins has the energy and the freshness of a younger Michael Caine, if not the good looks, of course. There are scenes where he hangs his enemies upside down from meat hooks and questions them about the bombings, and other scenes, moments later, where he solemnly kids with the neighborhood juvenile delinquents and tries to soft-talk the American out of his millions.

He's an operator. He's a con man who has muscled his way to the top by knowing exactly how things work and what buttons to push, and now here he is, impotent before this faceless enemy. *The Long Good Friday* tells his story in a rather indirect way, opening with a montage of seemingly unrelated events, held together by a hypnotic music theme. Everything is eventually explained. It's all a big misunderstanding, based on stupid decisions taken by Shand's underlings and misinterpreted by the IRA. But although we know the real story, and Harold Shand does, the IRA never does—and the movie's final shots are, quite simply, extraordinary close-ups, held for a long time, of Shand's ratlike face in close-up, as his eyes shift from side to side, and his mouth breaks into a terrified grin, and he realizes how it feels to get a dose of his own medicine. This movie is one amazing piece of work, not only for the Hoskins performance but also for the energy of the filmmaking, the power of the music, and, oddly enough, for the engaging quality of its sometimes very violent sense of humor.

Longtime Companion ★ ★ ★ ½
R, 96 m., 1990

Stephen Caffrey (Fuzzy), Patrick Cassidy (Howard), Brian Cousins (Bob), Bruce Davison (David), John Dossett (Paul), Mark Lamos (Sean), Dermot Mulroney (John), Michael Schoeffling (Michael), Campbell Scott (Willy). Directed by Norman Rene and produced by Stan Wlodkowski. Screenplay by Craig Lucas.

"He is survived," the obituaries sometimes say, "by his longtime companion." The phrase is taken by everybody to mean "lover," but newspapers prefer the euphemism, and only in the age of AIDS have they even finally admitted that homosexuals do not live, or die, alone. Norman Rene's *Longtime Companion* is a film that begins on the day when an obscure story in the *New York Times* first mentions a disease that seems to be striking homosexual men, and it ends after AIDS has profoundly affected all their lives—mostly, but not entirely, for the worse.

That first small cloud on the horizon was a story about a "gay cancer" that doctors were reporting among some of their homosexual patients. Within a few months, the *Village Voice* was providing in-depth reporting on the "gay plague," which eventually was named AIDS. But at the beginning, the characters in the story have difficulty in believing that a disease could seem to single them out.

The movie has been written by Craig Lucas as a series of scenes, sometimes separated by months or years, in the lives of several ordinary homosexual men, and it is the very everyday quality of their lives—work and home, love and cooking, and weekends—that provides the bedrock for this film. The emphasis is on the notion of "longtime." During the course of the movie some characters will fall in love and others will break up, but most of them will be steadfast in their friendships, and they will stand by each other in a series of crises. Of course, others simply disappear when AIDS arrives to interfere with their personal priorities, but not everyone is a saint, and some of the events in this film require, or inspire, a quality of sainthood.

The movie is told in chronological order, so that at every moment we know as much as the characters do about AIDS. At first they can't believe it at all. Then they can't believe it could strike anyone they know—or themselves. Then they begin to ask themselves uneasy questions about less-than-prudent episodes in their lives: Are long-forgotten indiscretions about to come back and take a deadly toll? Is AIDS the revenge of the past?

When a friend gets sick, it is hard to ask what the matter is, easy to pretend it is "something else." A friend loses weight and inevitable questions arise. Lovers ask each other hard questions about fidelity and do not always get honest answers. One by one, over the period of years, the circle of friends grows smaller. Of course, many will survive, but there seems to be no sensible pattern in who is chosen, and no guarantee that a man will not care for his friend only to need help himself before long. Few films have done a

better job of illustrating the virtue of "visiting the sick"—that cardinal act of mercy most neglected in an America that likes to let hospitals take care of that sort of hard work.

The central scene in the film—one of the most emotionally affecting scenes in any film on dying—involves Bruce Davison as the lover of a dying man. The struggle has been long and painful, but now it is almost over, and what Davison has to do is hold the hand of his friend and be with him when he dies. The fight has been so brave that it is hard to end it. "Let go," Davison whispers. "It's all right. You can let go now." The scene plays for a long, quiet time, and it is about the absolute finality of death, but it is also about why we are alive in the first place. Man is the only animal that knows it will die. This scene shows how that can be the source of courage and spiritual peace.

One of the particular strengths of *Longtime Companion* is that it does not identify its characters only through their sexual preferences. It would seem bizarre to watch a movie in which heterosexual men were defined only by the fact that they like to sleep with women—but many films about gays have made the opposite error and limited their characters as a result. *Longtime Companion* is about friendship and loyalty, about finding the courage to be helpful, and the humility to be helped.

The Long Walk Home ★ ★ ★ ½
PG, 97 m., 1991

Sissy Spacek (Miriam Thompson), Whoopi Goldberg (Odessa Cotter), Dwight Schultz (Norman Thompson), Ving Rhames (Herbert Cotter), Dylan Baker (Tunker Thompson), Erika Alexander (Selma Cotter). Directed by Richard Pearce and produced by Howard W. Koch, Jr., and Dave Bell. Screenplay by John Cork.

The Long Walk Home tells the stories of two women and their families at a critical turning point in American history. One of the women is black, a maid in an affluent neighborhood, a hard-working woman who goes home after a long day and does all of the same jobs all over again for her family. The other woman is white, the wife of a successful businessman. She works, too. She doesn't have a paid job, but in 1955 in Montgomery, Alabama, it was full-time work to please a husband who thought a woman's place was in the home, and who had a great many other thoughts on

the proper places of just about everybody in his narrow world.

These characters are confronted by a historic moment. One day in Montgomery, a black woman named Rosa Parks, who had worked hard and was tired, refused to stand up in the back of the segregated bus when there was an empty seat in the front. Her action, born out of a long weariness with the countless injustices of discrimination, inspired the Montgomery Bus Boycott, which was led by a young local preacher named Martin Luther King, Jr., and which grew into the civil rights movement.

For a woman like Odessa Cotter (Whoopi Goldberg), however, the eventual verdict of history could not have been easily guessed on the day she decided to join thousands of other Montgomery blacks in refusing to take the bus. She simply knew how she felt and acted on it, and started to walk to work every day. That meant getting up a couple of hours earlier in the morning, and getting home long after dark, and it meant blisters on her heels. It also meant inconvenience for her employer, Miriam Thompson (Sissy Spacek), who had a house to keep and a husband to feed, and who took her duties as a wife very solemnly—suppressing the obvious reality that he was a jerk.

Odessa is not eager for her employer to discover she is honoring the boycott—she doesn't want to risk losing her job—but one day Miriam finds out, and decides that she will give the maid a ride in her car a couple of days a week. This decision, of course, would enrage Miriam's husband, a self-satisfied bigot named Norman (Dwight Schultz), but Miriam doesn't tell him, and when he finds out, she defends her action as part of her job as a dutiful housewife.

In the meantime, she and her husband grow in different ways because of the boycott. Miriam is no activist, but she can see as a wife and a mother what the boycotting black women are going through, and begins to sympathize with them. Her husband is taken by a relative to a White Citizens' Council meeting, where rabble-rousers depict the boycotters as dangerous subversives (any true American would, of course, prefer to stand in the back of the bus than sit in the front—if he were black, that is).

The movie leads up to an inevitable confrontation between the white husband and wife, and to a climax of surprising power. But the general lines of the plot are not what make the movie special. We know going in more or less what will happen, both with the boycott and with these characters. What involved me was the way John Cork's screenplay did not simply paint the two women as emblems of a cause, but saw them as particular individuals who defined themselves largely through their roles as wives and mothers.

This movie would not have been made quite the same way ten or twenty years ago. The focus would have been on the liberalism of the white woman and the courage of the black woman, and most of the scenes would have involved the white family. *The Long Walk Home* takes the time to develop both families, to show that in addition to being heroic but abstract media images, the maids like Odessa were also individuals with all the usual human hopes and worries, not least of which was losing a job.

Because the movie does center some of its important scenes inside the black household, it's all the more surprising that it uses the gratuitous touch of a white "narrator"— apparently to reassure white audiences that the movie is "really" intended for them. The narrator is Spacek's teen-age daughter, who has no role of any importance in the movie and whose narration adds nothing except an unnecessary point of view. When she talks about her memories of "my mother," we want to know why Goldberg's daughter doesn't have equal time. She probably has more interesting memories.

That objection aside, *The Long Walk Home* is a powerful and affecting film, so well played by Goldberg and Spacek that we understand not just the politics of the time but the emotions as well. In a way, this movie takes up where *Driving Miss Daisy* leaves off. Both are about affluent white southern women who pride themselves on their humanitarian impulses, but who are brought to a greater understanding of racial discrimination— gently, tactfully, and firmly—by their black employees.

Miss Daisy and Miss Miriam are not revolutionaries. Neither are Hoke Colburn and Odessa Cotter. But the situation had gotten to the point where something had to be done, because people, after all, must be permitted fairness and dignity, and these two movies tell two small and not earth-shaking stories about ordinary people, black and white, who managed to talk and managed to listen, and made things a little better.

Looking for Mr. Goodbar ★ ★ ★
R, 136 m., 1977

Diane Keaton (Theresa), Tuesday Weld (Katherine), William Atherton (James), Richard Kiley (Mr. Dunn), Richard Gere (Tony), Alan Feinstein (Martin), Tom Berenger (Gary), Priscilla Pointer (Mrs. Dunn). Directed by Richard Brooks and produced by Freddie Fields. Screenplay by Brooks.

There's one crucial thing that *Looking for Mr. Goodbar* doesn't make clear: Just because you find Mr. Goodbar doesn't necessarily mean you were looking for him. The heroine of Judith Rossner's bestseller *was* looking. Theresa was turned on to a particular flavor of self-destructive sexual experience, one involving possible danger to herself, and she played a role in bringing about her own death.

In Richard Brooks's film version, that masochistic impulse isn't considered as openly. He gives us a Theresa who drinks too much, sleeps around too much, and takes too many drugs—but she seems more of a hedonist than a masochist. She's looking for a combination of good times, good sex, and a father figure, for psychological reasons the movie makes all too abundantly clear. But she isn't looking for danger, mistreatment, or death. Maybe Brooks thought audiences would find Rossner's masochistic heroine too hard to understand. He has rewritten the story, in any event, into a cautionary lesson: Promiscuous young women who frequent pick-up bars and go home with strangers are likely to get into trouble.

Brooks hasn't improved the story by changing its focus, and he's distracted from the heart of the narrative by several unnecessary scenes. Theresa's fantasies, for example, are handled in ways that annoy viewers more than they intrigue them. And her home life—its broadly painted Freudian details right out of soap operas—could have just simply been dropped.

But, all the same, Brooks hasn't directed a bad picture. *Looking for Mr. Goodbar* is very much worth seeing, particularly for the Diane Keaton performance. And it's not fair to praise her while damning Brooks (as so many critics have done). Brooks and Keaton must have worked together to create such a great performance; it's just a shame that it's surrounded by perhaps half an hour of material that only distracts.

The performance creates a character who would have been unthinkable in the movies of thirty years ago: A young woman who spends her days teaching first grade to a classroom of deaf-mutes and her nights making herself available in singles bars. Women weren't allowed to be that complicated in the "women's pictures" that *Mr. Goodbar* has come such a long way from. They were ladies or they were tramps. Now they're allowed to be both, which has done wonders for the quality of the tramps you meet these days.

Diane Keaton suggests the motivation for her character almost independently from all those heavy-handed scenes in which her father stomps around the living room, and we get flashbacks of her tragic childhood. She suggests that Theresa is driven by a need to communicate on her own terms—and that those terms require her to have an advantage. She's great in a classroom of deaf-mutes, and great, too, with the men she picks up—men who are inarticulate because of insecurity, cultural short-changing, or too much booze. She delights in working people over verbally—in kidding them, mocking them, putting them down, playing games with them. On the physical level, though, she needs constant reassurance.

This Theresa is a different woman from the Judith Rossner character, but she's an interesting one. And Keaton plays her wonderfully, with a light touch you'd think would be impossible with this material. She's always moving. She choreographs every situation, and only eventually do we realize she's dancing out of the way. Her voice is liquid and funny, tossing off asides because they cut more deeply that way. The performance and the character are fully realized, even in this movie that finds room for so many loose ends and dead ends.

Then there's that ending that bothers me. On a New Year's Eve, she makes a fatal decision in choosing the next guy she's going to take home. *We* know she's made the wrong decision because Brooks abandons her point of view to show us a scene in which the guy is established as unbalanced and hostile. But she doesn't know that and gets killed because she doesn't. Her lack of knowledge is exactly the issue here: In the book, Theresa might have picked up the guy *because* she knew he'd be trouble.

What we get (and I quote from someone walking out of the screening ahead of me) is "another one of those movies that are supposed to be all filled with significance because the person gets killed at the end." What we might have gotten is a movie about a character obsessed, and fascinated, by what the end might be. Even a movie about how she got to be that way.

Look Who's Talking ★ ★ ★
PG-13, 96 m., 1989

John Travolta (James), Kirstie Alley (Mollie), Olympia Dukakis (Rosie), George Segal (Albert), Abe Vigoda (Grandpa), Bruce Willis (Voice of Mikey). Mikey played at different ages by Jason Schaller, Jaryd Waterhouse, Jacob Haines, and Christopher Aydon. Directed by Amy Heckerling and produced by Jonathan D. Krane. Screenplay by Heckerling.

If I were sitting at home and watching TV, and I saw a commercial for this movie, I don't think I'd want to see it. For starters, I wouldn't want to see a movie where the thoughts of an infant were spoken aloud for it by Bruce Willis. Then I'd reflect that John Travolta had appeared in several disappointments recently and that Kirstie Alley's movies had not exactly set the world on fire.

As a movie critic, however, I am not permitted such thoughts—at least not officially—and so one afternoon not long ago I found myself feeling very good during a screening of Look Who's Talking. This fairly unlikely idea for a movie turns into a warm and lovable comedy—although I still don't think it needed the voice-overs from the baby.

The movie stars Kirstie Alley (best known as the bar manager from "Cheers") as an accountant who's having an affair with a boorish, self-centered businessman (George Segal). She gets pregnant, he double-crosses her, and suddenly she's a single mom. She encounters Travolta through one of those standard movie Meet Cutes, when she goes into labor and he's the taxi driver who races her to the hospital.

The rest of the movie, lightweight and warmhearted, is about how Travolta falls in love with both the mother and the child. It's easy to see what appeals to him: Alley glows with health and good cheer in this movie, and the baby (played by four different infants) is, I must confess, adorable. Reviewing a baby's "performance" in a movie is meaningless, since babies do what they do without paying much attention to their directors, but there are scenes in this movie (including one where Travolta waltzes around with the kid) where the filmmakers just plain lucked out and got some of the best baby-moments I've ever seen in a movie.

If the baby isn't predictable, the story is, right down to the moment when Travolta is the baby sitter while Alley goes out on a date with a fellow accountant. We've seen all this stuff before and, yep, they even throw in the obligatory toupee scene, where the baby lifts the rug off the poor guy's head.

But as a silly entertainment, Look Who's Talking is full of good feeling, and director Amy Heckerling (Fast Times at Ridgemont High) finds a light touch for her lightweight material. Travolta demonstrates, twelve years after Saturday Night Fever, that he is a warm and winning actor when he's not shoehorned into the wrong roles. And Kirstie Alley finds the kind of role she must have been looking for, a role that lets us see the person who was always there, beneath all those hours of TV images.

Lorenzo's Oil ★ ★ ★ ★
PG-13, 135 m., 1993

Nick Nolte (Augusto Odone), Susan Sarandon (Michaela Odone), Peter Ustinov (Professor Nikolais), Zack O'Malley Greenburg (Lorenzo), Kathleen Wilhoite (Deirdre Murphy), Gerry Bamman (Doctor Judalon), Margo Martindale (Wendy Gimble). Directed by George Miller and produced by Doug Mitchell and Miller. Screenplay by Miller and Nick Enright.

You may have heard that Lorenzo's Oil is a harrowing movie experience. It is, but in the best way. It takes a heartbreaking story and pushes it to the limit, showing us the lengths of courage and imagination that people can summon when they must. The performances, by Susan Sarandon and Nick Nolte, are daring, too: They play a married couple sometimes too exhausted and obsessed to even be nice to one another. But they share a common goal. They want to save their son's life.

When doctors urge a dying patient to have patience while research continues into the cure for their disease, what they are saying is, please be patient enough to wait until after your death while we work on this. That is not much consolation for the parents when the patient is their little boy, stricken in the dawn of life. Some assume that the doctors know best—as, indeed, usually they do. Some strike out with anger or denial.

Augusto and Michaela Odone, the real-life models for the parents in Lorenzo's Oil, went through all of those stages when their son was diagnosed with adrenoleukodystrophy (ALD), a rare nerve disease that strikes only little boys and was always fatal. They decided to take matters into their own hands.

Knocking on doors, haunting research libraries, reading everything, talking to the parents of other sick children, using intuition, they actually discovered a treatment for the disease, employing humble olive oil.

The last frames of Lorenzo's Oil provide a montage of young boys who are healthy and active today because of the work of the Odones. One doesn't know whether to laugh or weep; their good fortune comes after hundreds of other children were gradually imprisoned inside their own bodies, blind, deaf, unable to touch or taste, because of the disease that was strangling their nervous systems.

The movie has been directed and co-written by George Miller (Road Warrior, The Witches of Eastwick), a filmmaker who is also a medical doctor. He does not insult the intelligence of the audience by turning this story into a disease-of-the-week docudrama. We follow the thought process of Augusto Odone as he asks questions, makes connections, and uses common sense: If his son's body is breaking down the fatty sheath that protects the nerves, is there a way to replace the fat, or frustrate the process?

While Augusto spends months in research libraries (where the librarians eventually share his quest), his wife maintains a stubborn, even mad, conviction that her boy will get well. The child is moved home to the living room, which is converted into a hospital ward. Nurses are hired around the clock. Convinced that her boy is alive and alert inside the shell of his body, Michaela reads to him by the hour, and hires other readers—firing one employee after another for not sharing her unbending vision.

There is probably as much dialogue in this movie as in two other films. Augusto and Michaela talk to each other in rapid-fire, impatient bursts; there is no time to lose if their child is to be saved. The screenplay incorporates a great deal of technical information, somehow making it comprehensible, so that we can understand the reasoning when scientists like the distinguished Professor Nikolais (Peter Ustinov) debate the Odones.

Nikolais represents the larger medical establishment, which Miller does not portray as a bunch of conservative, unfeeling clods. He shows the doctors and researchers doing their jobs conscientiously, and doubting the claims of the Odones because, after all, they are not the first parents of a dying child to grasp at any straw.

I was distracted at first by the Italian accent Nolte uses in the film, not because it is badly done (he sounds much like the real Odone, who has appeared on talk shows), but because it seems odd to hear Nolte with an accent. But eventually the accent issue fell by the side; this is an immensely moving and challenging movie, and it is impossible not to get swept up in it.

Losing Isaiah ★ ★ ½
R, 108 m., 1995

Jessica Lange (Margaret), Halle Berry (Khaila), Mark John Jeffries (Isaiah), David Strathairn (Charles Lewin), Samuel L. Jackson (Kadar Lewis), Daisy Eagan (Hannah), Cuba Gooding, Jr. (Eddie Hughes), Joie Lee (Marie Spencer), La Tanya Richardson (Caroline Jones). Directed by Stephen Gyllenhaal and produced by Howard W. Koch, Jr., and Naomi Foner. Screenplay by Foner.

The papers are filled with heartbreaking stories of tugs of war over children. Natural parents sue for custody, adoptive parents sue to keep the children they have grown to love, divorced couples fight desperately for possession of the children. The public takes sides in these wrenching melodramas, but really there can be no winners, only survivors. And God help the children.

Losing Isaiah, inspired by various actual cases, tells the story of a cocaine-addicted black woman named Khaila (Halle Berry) who, in a drugged haze, stumbles out of a crack house and abandons her son in a cardboard box in an alley. The next morning, realizing her mistake, she races outside, but it is too late; the child has disappeared, and for several years she believes it is dead.

But it has been saved. Garbage men have heard its cries, and taken it to an emergency room, where at first it seems about to die. That's all right with the hospital workers, who have seen a lot of crack babies, and do not believe in taking "extraordinary measures" to save them. But then a white social worker named Margaret Lewin (Jessica Lange) takes pity: "If you're not going to help him, you might as well just throw him back in the dumpster."

The baby lives, and is eventually adopted by Lange and her husband, Charles (David Strathairn). They have a teenage daughter of their own. The baby is difficult and hyperactive; it makes a scene at the older girl's school musical. But the Lewins love it. And so the situation remains until the baby is three or four.

Meanwhile, Khaila has been through drug rehabilitation and is clean, sober, and working as a housekeeper and child minder for an affluent white family. Then one day she learns, almost by accident, that her son is still alive. And eventually, with the help of a social worker and an attorney (Samuel L. Jackson), she sues for custody. That leads to a courtroom confrontation and agonizing drama behind the scenes, in a ritual that has become familiar in many real cases.

Who does the baby belong with? The parents it has bonded with? Or its natural mother? Did the mother forfeit her rights on that drugged-out night, or has she earned them back again with her recovery? What about the arguments that black children belong in black homes? The movie, directed by Stephen Gyllenhaal and written by Naomi Foner, deals with all of those issues, but in a finally unsatisfactory way.

The problem, obviously, is that there *are* no satisfactory answers—no way a solution can be found without causing great pain. There are many individual scenes in the film that have great power, as when Khaila quietly visits the Lewins' neighborhood to see her child at a distance. But there are other scenes that ring false, such as a confrontation in a washroom outside the courtroom, where the filmmakers have stacked the cards by making Khaila look fresh and flawless, and Margaret ratty and tearful, her hair straggling into her eyes.

The movie has been carefully written so as not to offend the opinions of anyone in the audience. No matter what side you are on, you will find your viewpoint expressed. The filmmakers apparently have no firm ideas of their own about the rightness and wrongness of the alternatives (why did they make the movie?), and the conclusion dispenses understanding and love on all sides, while finding a solution which does indeed allow the movie to end, but really solves nothing.

Lost in America ★ ★ ★ ★
R, 90 m., 1985

Albert Brooks (David Howard), Julie Hagerty (Linda Howard), Garry K. Marshall (Casino Boss), Art Frankel (Job Counselor). Directed by Albert Brooks and produced by Marty Katz. Screenplay by Brooks and Monica Johnson.

Every time I see a Winnebago motor home, **I** have the same fantasy as the hero of *Lost in America.* In my dream, I quit my job, sell ev-

erything I own, buy the Winnebago, and hit the open road. Where do I go? Look for me in the weather reports. I'll be parked by the side of a mountain stream, listening to Mozart on compact discs. All I'll need is a wok and a paperback.

In *Lost in America,* Albert Brooks plays an advertising executive in his thirties who realizes that dream. He leaves his job, talks his wife into quitting hers, and they point their Winnebago down that long, lonesome highway. This is not, however, a remake of *The Long, Long Trailer.* Brooks puts a different spin on things. For example, when movie characters leave their jobs, it's usually because they've been fired, they've decided to take an ethical stand, or the company has gone broke. Only in a movie by Brooks would the hero quit to protest a "lateral transfer" to New York. There's something intrinsically comic about that: He's taking a stand, all right, but it's a narcissistic one. He's quitting because he wants to stay in Los Angeles, he thinks he deserves to be named vice president, and he doesn't like the traffic in New York.

Lost in America is being called a yuppie comedy, but it's really about the much more universal subjects of greed, hedonism, and panic. What makes it so funny is how much we can identify with it. Brooks plays a character who is making a lot of money, but not enough; who lives in a big house, but is outgrowing it; who drives an expensive car, but not a Mercedes-Benz; who is a top executive, but not a vice president. In short, he is a desperate man, trapped by his own expectations.

On the morning of his last day at work, he puts everything on hold while he has a long, luxurious telephone conversation with a Mercedes dealer. Brooks has great telephone scenes in all of his movies, but this one perfectly captures the nuances of consumerism. He asks how much the car will cost—including *everything.* Dealer prep, license, sticker, add-ons, extras, *everything.* The dealer names a price.

"That's *everything?*" Brooks asks.

"Except leather," the dealer says.

"For what I'm paying, I don't get leather?" Brooks asks, aghast.

"You get Mercedes leather."

"*Mercedes* leather? What's that?"

"Thick vinyl."

This is the kind of world Brooks is up against. A few minutes later, he's called into the boss's office and told that he will not get the promotion he thinks he deserves. Instead, he's going to New York to handle the Ford account. Brooks quits, and a few scenes later, he and his wife (Julie Hagerty) are tooling the big Winnebago into Las Vegas. They have enough money, he conservatively estimates, to stay on the road for the rest of their lives. That's before she loses their nest egg at the roulette tables.

Lost in America doesn't tell a story so much as assemble a series of self-contained comic scenes, and the movie's next scene is probably the best one in the movie. Brooks the adman tries to talk a casino owner (Garry K. Marshall) into giving back the money. It doesn't work, but Brooks keeps pushing, trying to sell the casino on improving its image. ("I'm a high-paid advertising consultant. These are professional opinions you're getting.") There are other great scenes, as the desperate couple tries to find work to support themselves: An interview with an unemployment counselor, who listens, baffled, to Brooks explaining why he left a $100,000-a-year job because he couldn't "find himself." And Brooks's wife introducing her new boss, a teen-age boy.

Lost in America has one strange flaw. It doesn't seem to come to a conclusion. It just sort of ends in midstream, as if the final scenes were never shot. I don't know if that's the actual case, but I do wish the movie had been longer and had arrived at some sort of final destination. What we do get, however, is observant and very funny. Brooks is especially good at hearing exactly how people talk, and how that reveals things about themselves. Take that line about "Mercedes leather." A lot of people would be very happy to sit on "Mercedes leather." But not a Mercedes owner, of course. How did Joni Mitchell put it? "Don't it always seem to go, that you don't know what you've got, till it's gone."

Lost in Yonkers ★ ★ ★
PG, 110 m., 1993

Richard Dreyfuss (Louie), Mercedes Ruehl (Bella), Irene Worth (Grandma), Brad Stoll (Jay), Mike Damus (Arty), David Strathairn (Johnny). Directed by Martha Coolidge and produced by Ray Stark. Screenplay by Neil Simon.

Their mother has died and their father thinks he might be able to find work in the war industries of the South, and so Jay and Arty go to live with their grandmother in Yonkers in the opening moments of Neil Simon's *Lost in*

Yonkers. This is a fairly standard opening for Simon, who often sees life through the wide-open eyes of teen-age boys. But the film of Simon's Broadway play has a special quality to it. All of the performances are good, but one of them, by Mercedes Ruehl, casts a glow over the entire film.

Ruehl plays Aunt Bella, the daffy, movie-loving younger daughter of the formidable Grandma (Irene Worth). There is a possibility, subscribed to by everybody but never quite put into words, that she is mentally ill. She's certainly flighty. She overflows with enthusiasms, and then is brought low by tormenting doubts, and her optimism has hard sailing into the gales of Grandma's scorn.

For the boys, Aunt Bella is a pal in a strange new land. Jay (Brad Stoll) and Arty (Mike Damus), fifteen and thirteen, are fascinated by the half-heard family legends they now see being demonstrated. They've heard a lot, for example, about Uncle Louie (Richard Dreyfuss), the black sheep of the family, who is said to be a "henchman," although the exact nature of his duties is much in doubt. And they have gathered, from the tone of their father's voice, that Grandma, his mother-in-law, is not among his favorite persons. No wonder. She is cold, strict, forbidding, and unforgiving. It must be God's special justice that she has been given two such trials as Bella and Louie as her children.

The boys move into Grandma's apartment upstairs from her candy store, and begin to settle into the unpredictable life of the eccentric family. Aunt Bella lives in a fantasy world of movies, which she describes to them in loving detail. And they meet her boyfriend Johnny (David Strathairn), who is an usher at the movie palace, and seems to be mentally unbalanced in an opposite direction from Bella: She is expansive, he is introspective, so they make a nice fit. Meanwhile, Uncle Louie seems embroiled in the Yonkers version of a mob war, and gives them stern warnings against playing with firearms—especially his.

Both Mercedes Ruehl and Irene Worth played the same roles on Broadway, and here they are well served by the director, Martha Coolidge, who avoids the trap of letting their characters become larger than life. *Lost in Yonkers* is material Coolidge seems comfortable with, perhaps because she also directed *Rambling Rose*, another film in which a strange and rare woman was at the center of an unconventional family.

All of the material is seen through the eyes

of the boys, especially Jay, the older, who will do a lot of growing up during this summer—as will Aunt Bella, who sometimes seems like his contemporary. The film is a series of small discoveries and victories, over life, over handicaps, and especially over Grandma's autocracy.

The key role is Ruehl's. The first time we see her, she is bravely cheerful, as if she believes the happy endings in the movies she loves so much. Only gradually do we begin to understand the darker side of her character, the unhealthy way in which her mother has suppressed her natural exuberance. By the end of the movie, when Aunt Bella is finally able to find a way to live life on her own terms, we're almost surprised how much we've come to care about her.

Louie Bluie ★ ★ ★ ½
NO MPAA RATING, 75 m., 1985

A documentary featuring Howard Armstrong and Ted Bogan. Directed and produced by Terry Zwigoff.

It was back in 1970 when the Earl called me up and said I should be at his bar on Monday night because he had something special, a band called Martin, Bogan, and the Armstrongs. "Don't ask any questions," he said. "Just be here." I was there, and I returned week after week for more than a year, along with a loyal cult who packed the place.

Martin, Bogan, and one of the Armstrongs were black men in their sixties and seventies (the other Armstrong, a son, played bass). They looked like a blues band, but they didn't play the blues, and in fact it was hard to figure out exactly what they did play. They did all the Mills Brothers standards, such as "Lazy River" and "Paper Doll," and they sang "Lady Be Good" and an unprintable version of "Sweet Georgia Brown." Howard Armstrong stood up and did fiddle solos on songs such as "Turkey in the Straw," and brought the house down.

Sixteen years later, those Monday sessions blur into a smoky series of hot summer nights when the sweet lyrics of Armstrong's fiddle danced above Martin's guitar and Bogan's mandolin, and they took turns on the vocals, including Martin's composition of "The Barnyard Dance" and Armstrong's pseudo-Hawaiian love songs. Toward the end of the evening, Ted Bogan would sing "Summertime" with such unadorned purity that you knew, quite simply, that you would never, ever, hear that great song sung better by anyone, anywhere.

Martin, Bogan, and the Armstrongs stopped playing together in the mid-1970s, and a few years later the Earl of Old Town closed its doors. When I would run into Earl Pionke, I would ask him about them and he would have vague reports that they were in Detroit, or Tennessee. Then word came that Carl Martin, who always scowled the fiercest when he was singing the funniest lyrics, had died.

And that was the situation when I went to the 1985 Telluride Film Festival, up in the San Juan range of the Rockies, and there on Main Street I saw Howard Armstrong with his beret and all that hip jewelry around his neck, checking out the scene and giving free advice to Ted Bogan, who was nodding and not listening, just like he always did when Armstrong talked to him during the sets at the Earl.

The story of how they got to Telluride is an amazing one, and it explains the existence of *Louie Bluie*, an equally amazing music documentary film.

Terry Zwigoff, a music lover who went on to produce and direct *Louie Bluie*, was an avid collector of old jazz and blues recordings. He liked the sound on an old 1930s disc that was by somebody named Louie Bluie who never recorded before or since, and after years of searching he found out that Louie Bluie was Howard Armstrong, and his group, one of the first (and now one of the last) of the traditional black string bands, was still around.

Zwigoff tracked down Armstrong, who had moved to Detroit, and talked Armstrong and Bogan into appearing in a film, and *Louie Bluie* is that film, filled with music and life and humor, but also with an extraordinary portrait of Howard Armstrong, who is an artist, poet, composer, violin virtuoso, storyteller, and tireless womanizer (according to many of his stories).

The movie is loose and disjointed, and makes little effort to be a documentary about anything. Mostly, it just follows Armstrong around as he plays music with Bogan, visits his Tennessee childhood home, and philosophizes on music, love, and life. The film occasionally turns to the pages of the semi-pornographic journals Armstrong has kept through the years, filled with lurid cartoons and bawdy poems and his observations of life. Armstrong is a natural artist, and he remembers making his first colors out of dyes wrung out of crepe paper.

There is a lot of music in the movie, including some I could do without. (Armstrong likes his Hawaiian and German songs much better than I do.) There is also an enigma to consider: the relationship of Bogan and Armstrong, who have known each other and played together for almost seventy years, despite the fact that Armstrong is almost always on Bogan's case, and Bogan's eyes always seem to be looking for the nearest exit. *Louie Bluie* peers into the areas where nothing is certain, except that these people live and strive and laugh and make music. It is a wonderful film.

Love Affair ★ ★ ★
PG-13, 107 m., 1994

`NEW`

Warren Beatty (Mike Gambril), Annette Bening (Terry McKay), Katharine Hepburn (Aunt Ginny), Garry Shandling (Kip), Chloe Webb (Marisa), Pierce Brosnan (Ken Allen), Kate Capshaw (Lynn Weaver). Directed by Glenn Gordon Caron and produced by Warren Beatty. Screenplay by Robert Towne and Beatty.

Love Affair depends on grace and style to make its effect, and that's just as well, because most of the people seeing this movie are going to know how it turns out. If they haven't seen the original *Love Affair* (1939) with Irene Dunne and Charles Boyer, or the remake, *An Affair to Remember* (1957) with Deborah Kerr and Cary Grant, they've seen *Sleepless in Seattle* (1993), which was *about* people who loved the earlier films.

No, there aren't going to be many people in the audience who don't know what's supposed to happen on May 8 on top of the Empire State Building. When Warren Beatty is pacing around up there, indeed, we almost expect him to be part of a crowd, with Boyer, Grant, and Tom Hanks, all partners in misery. That's why it's kind of surprising that this new *Love Affair* works as well as it does.

Part of the effect may be the teasing parallels with real life. When Warren Beatty tells Annette Bening, "You know, I've never been faithful to anyone in my whole life," you have the strangest feeling these words might have passed between them on an earlier occasion. And when the chemistry between them really seems to be working, no wonder: This is one of the most famously happy couples in Hollywood.

The story stars Beatty as Mike Gambril, a playboy sportscaster who is engaged to a millionaire talk show hostess. Bening plays Terry McKay, who is working as an interior designer for a zillionaire (Pierce Brosnan). They Meet Cute on a flight across the Pacific, and when their plane develops engine trouble and makes an emergency landing on a tiny atoll, they continue their journey aboard a screwy Russian cruise ship, before landing in Tahiti, where Beatty's legendary aunt (Katharine Hepburn) lives in a magnificent house on the side of the hill. To say that these are the sorts of things that only happen in the movies would be an understatement.

What's interesting about the screenplay, written by Robert Towne and Beatty, is that the movie's key turning point takes place, not between Beatty and Bening, but between Bening and Hepburn. Sure, Bening likes the guy, but she distrusts him, and it's not until she sees the real Mike through the eyes of his aunt that she can take him seriously as a potential partner.

Hepburn's scenes steal, and almost stop, the show. She has been old for a long time (she is in her eighties), but this is the first time she has also looked small and frail. Yet the magnificent spirit is still there, and the romantic fire, and she's right for this eccentric old woman, living alone in unimaginable splendor, and feeling an instant connection with the young woman her nephew has brought home.

Part of the magic of the Hepburn scenes is set up by the location, and Conrad Hall's cinematography. There are scenes in the movie—including Beatty and Bening walking across a vast, lush green meadow—that are so radiant your jaw drops open. It's as if nature itself is a coconspirator in the romance. The director, Glenn Gordon Caron, is better known for hard-edged material like *Clean and Sober*, but maybe that's because there's not much work in Hollywood these days for filmmakers who still believe in the Semi-Obligatory Lyrical Interlude.

The rest of the movie is a slow edging up to the big final scene, the emotionally fraught meeting between Mike and Terry. Watching it, I realized it was a classic example of what *Ebert's Little Movie Glossary* identifies as the Idiot Plot; that's a plot that works only because everybody in it behaves like an idiot. One word, and all the misunderstanding would be at an end, so of course that one word is never spoken.

Funny thing. This is one of the few Idiot Plots that works. Yes, there is a monumental and tragic misunderstanding between Mike and Terry. Yes, their happiness stands to be destroyed because both of them are pussy-footing around, and not saying what needs to be said. But the movie toys with that, and with us, in delicately written dialogue that allows them to say, and not say, everything that needs to be said, and needs not to be said.

For a time the love story seemed to be a threatened genre in Hollywood. Women characters in movies were more likely to stab you than kiss you. Then came *Sleepless in Seattle* and *Only You* and now *Love Affair*, all movies about nice people getting into goofy misunderstandings because they love one another so much. You have to be in the right mood to enjoy movies like this. Or maybe they put you in the mood.

Love Field ★ ★ ½
PG-13, 104 m., 1993

Michelle Pfeiffer (Lurene Hallett), Dennis Haysbert (Paul Cater), Brian Kerwin (Ray Hallett), Stephanie McFadden (Jonell), Louise Latham (Mrs. Enright). Directed by Jonathan Kaplan and produced by Sarah Pillsbury and Midge Sanford. Screenplay by Don Roos.

She is a Dallas housewife who worships Jacqueline Kennedy, and is stuck in a drab marriage with a husband whose idea of communication is to ask her to get him another beer out of the icebox. When she learns that the Kennedys plan to visit Dallas, she's beside herself. She gets a neighbor lady in a wheelchair to come with her to the airport, figuring that the wheelchair will allow them both to get up close. This is the most important day of her life.

We know what happened then. *Love Field* depicts the moment of the assassination in a creepy, effective way, by showing the woman driving through the streets of Dallas and realizing that something has gone wrong. People aren't behaving normally. There is a crowd outside the TV store, looking at something on the sets in the windows.

When the woman, whose name is Lurene and who is played by Michelle Pfeiffer, realizes that the president is dead, her heart goes out to the first lady; she identifies so strongly with her that she cares more for Jackie's husband than for her own. She decides she *must* attend the funeral. Her husband tells her she's crazy (a blanket diagnosis he applies to most of her actions).

So she takes the bus to Washington. And along the way, as she meets a black man (Dennis Haysbert) and his young daughter, she finds herself blundering into a drama

much bigger than she counted on. Lurene has an active imagination. She sees plots where they do not exist. She convinces herself the man is kidnapping the little girl, and when she realizes her error she is so contrite that somehow together the three of them end up in a car that isn't theirs, heading east together.

It's at about this time that *Love Field* accumulates more plot than it really needs. We already have the Jackie-worshipper on her pilgrimage. Now we also have a road movie, involving a possible but unstated romantic attraction, and a little girl, and cops chasing the couple, and bystanders getting involved, and a race against the deadline of the funeral.

Maybe I'm wrong, but I think this basic situation would have worked better as a simple human story, instead of being tricked up with so many Hollywood formulas and gimmicks. The whole business of the car and the chase and the danger that Pfeiffer puts Haysbert in is all essentially just screenwriting. We grow impatient at the contrivance. We want the people, not twists and turns.

And yet there are real qualities to this movie, not least Michelle Pfeiffer's performance, which takes a woman who could have become a comic target and invests her with a certain dignity: Within her limitations and almost against her nature, she grows and and almost against her nature, she grows and changes during these few days, and will never be the same again.

The Haysbert character is also carefully drawn, as a Southern black man of thirty years ago, who is acutely aware of the racism and danger she hardly seems to notice. Some of the best lines in Don Roos's screenplay involve Pfeiffer making blithe assumptions about the nature of American reality, and Haysbert adding quiet, subtle footnotes.

Seeing this film for the second time, I was more than ever aware, however, that the essential truth of the characters was being undercut by all the manufactured gimmicks of the plot. The ancient formula for a movie in trouble was, "cut to the chase." Nothing has changed. And when *Love Field* turns from an odyssey into a chase, it loses its way. By the end, the Kennedy funeral, which should provide the whole focus, is really only a McGuffin.

Love Letters ★ ★ ★ ½
R, 98 m., 1984

Jamie Lee Curtis (Anna), James Keach (Oliver), Amy Madigan (Wendy), Matt Clark

(Mr. Winter). Directed by Amy Jones and produced by Roger Corman. Screenplay by Jones.

Love Letters teaches this lesson: Passion can exist between two people who know their relationship is wrong, but love cannot exist, because love demands to know that it is right. The movie stars Jamie Lee Curtis, in the best performance she has ever given, as Anna, a bright young woman who has an affair with a married man. She tries to make herself see their relationship as existing above conventional morality, but she can't, not after she sees the man's wife and kids.

The affair begins at a crossroads in her life. She's an announcer for a public radio station in San Francisco, and within a period of a few weeks her mother dies, and she gets a job offer from a larger station. She doesn't take the job, though, because something else happens. She meets a photographer (James Keach), who is a sensitive, intelligent, married man, and feels powerfully drawn to him. And she finds her mother's love letters, which reveal that her mother once had an affair. The old letters are used as a counterpoint to the events in the present. They're read on the sound track in the voice of the man who wrote them—a man we don't meet until the movie is almost over. They are letters about love, separation, loneliness, and loyalty. Anna learns to her astonishment that her mother continued the affair for years and years during her marriage, finally ending it only because she had decided to stay with her husband.

We meet the husband, Anna's father. He is a self-pitying alcoholic who believes he was never good enough for Anna's mother, and who smothers Anna with neurotic demands. What happens then is fascinating, and the movie treats it with great intelligence. Anna is already attracted to the James Keach character. Now, reading the old love letters, she begins to develop a romantic idea about affairs. She hates her father, and so, perhaps, did her mother. Her mother cheated on her father—and so will she, by having an affair with Keach. She will become the same kind of noble, romantic outsider that the author of the love letters must have been.

All of this is handled with as much subtlety as Ingmar Bergman brought to similar situations in *Scenes from a Marriage*. This isn't a soap opera romance; it's an investigation into how we can intellectualize our way into situations where our passions are likely to take over. Anna and the photographer spend happy times together. They are "in love." Anna thinks she only wants an affair, but she grows possessive in spite of herself. And when she spies on Keach's family, she sees that his wife is a good woman and there is love in their home. Her life refuses to parallel the love letters.

Love Letters was written and directed by Amy Jones, whose previous credit was *The Slumber Party Massacre.* This is perhaps another case of a young filmmaker beginning with exploitation movies and finally getting the chance to do ambitious work. What she accomplishes here is wonderful. She creates a story of passion that is as absorbing as a thriller. She makes a movie of ideas that never, ever, seems to be just a message picture. And she gives Jamie Lee Curtis the best dramatic role of her career; this role, side-by-side with Curtis's inspired comic acting in *Trading Places,* shows her with a range we couldn't have guessed from all her horror pictures. *Love Letters* is one of those treasures that slips through once in a while: A movie that's as smart as we are, that never goes for cheap shots, that's about passion but never blinded by it.

The Lover ★ ★
R, 103 m., 1992

Jane March (Young Girl), Tony Leung (Chinese Man), Frederique Meininger (Mother), Arnaud Giovaninetti (Elder Brother). Directed by Jean-Jacques Annaud and produced by Claude Berri. Screenplay by Gérard Brach and Annaud.

Marguerite Duras's novel *The Lover* tells the story of a passionate secret sexual adventure between a young French girl and an older Chinese man in Indochina in the 1920s. She says it is autobiographical, but I suspect it is the autobiography of her imagination, not of her real life. The elements in the story are the basic stuff of common erotic fantasies: sex between strangers separated by age, race, and social convention, and conducted as a physical exercise without much personal communication.

Perhaps these adventures really took place, in one form or another. It hardly matters. Jean-Jacques Annaud's film treats them in much the same spirit as *Emmanuelle* or the *Playboy* and *Penthouse* erotic videos, in which beautiful actors and elegant photography provide a soft-core sensuality. As an entry in that genre, *The Lover* is more than capable,

and the movie is likely to have a long life on video as the sort of sexy entertainment that arouses but does not embarrass.

Is *The Lover* any good as a serious film? Not really. Annaud and his collaborators have got all of the physical details just right, but there is a failure of the imagination here; we do not sense the presence of real people behind the attractive facades of the two main characters.

They are a French teen-ager (Jane March), living in a provincial area of Indochina and sent to Saigon to attend boarding school, and a rich Chinese aristocrat in his thirties (Tony Leung). They are attracted to each other in the first place by the kind of unconditional erotic magnetism that the French call a thunderbolt: they look, they see, they lust. Soon they are meeting regularly in an anonymous room in a Chinese district of the city, where their sexual encounters can only be described as inventive and thorough.

Life goes on outside the walls of this cocoon. The girl hates her life—hates the bloody-mindedness of her teachers and fellow students, and the descent of her dysfunctional family into depravity. Of the man we learn less; he comes from a proud old family, and his bride will be selected for him according to the ancient ways. The secret love affair is of course forbidden by the mores of the time; both races hold strong feelings against interracial romance. But the movie treats those attitudes less with indignation than with relief; because society prevents these two lovers from being seen together in public, the movie doesn't have to deal with their roles in society. Like classic pornography, it can isolate them in a room, in a bed: They are bodies that have come together for our reveries.

I wanted to know more. I believe true eroticism resides in the mind; what happens between bodies is more or less the same, but what it means to the occupants of those bodies is another question. What do these two people really think about one another? Do they love in the romantic sense? Is each escaping from the idea of a more personal relationship? Is this a purely sexual arrangement? At the end, as the girl leaves Saigon and her ship passes the dock, she sees the man get out of his limousine and look at her departing ship. Years later, he visits Paris, without result. What did they lose? What would have been possible between them, in another world—or even in this one? The film does not seem to know.

Love Story ★ ★ ★ ★
PG, 100 m., 1970

Ali MacGraw (Jenny Cavilleri), Ryan O'Neal (Oliver Barrett IV), Ray Milland (Oliver Barrett III), John Marley (Phil Cavilleri). Directed by Arthur Hiller and produced by Howard G. Minsky. Screenplay by Erich Segal.

I read *Love Story* one morning in about fourteen minutes flat, out of simple curiosity. I wanted to discover why five and a half million people had actually bought it. I wasn't successful. I was so put off by Erich Segal's writing style, in fact, that I hardly wanted to see the movie at all. Segal's prose style is so revoltingly coy—sort of a cross between a parody of Hemingway and the instructions on a soup can—that his story is fatally infected.

The fact is, however, that the film of *Love Story* is infinitely better than the book. I think it has something to do with the quiet taste of Arthur Hiller, its director, who has put in all the things that Segal thought he was being clever to leave out. Things like color, character, personality, detail, and background. The interesting thing is that Hiller has saved the movie without substantially changing anything in the book. Both the screenplay and the novel were written at the same time, I understand, and if you've read the book, you've essentially read the screenplay. Nothing much is changed except the last meeting between Oliver and his father; Hiller felt the movie should end with the boy alone, and he was right. Otherwise, he's used Segal's situations and dialogue throughout. But the Segal characters, on paper, were so devoid of any personality that they might actually have been transparent. Ali MacGraw and Ryan O'Neal, who play the lovers on film, bring them to life in a way the novel didn't even attempt. They do it simply by being there, and having personalities.

The story by now is so well-known that there's no point in summarizing it for you. I would like to consider, however, the implications of *Love Story* as a three-, four- or five-handkerchief movie, a movie that wants viewers to cry at the end. Is this an unworthy purpose? Does the movie become unworthy, as *Newsweek* thought it did, simply because it has been mechanically contrived to tell us a beautiful, tragic tale? I don't think so. There's nothing contemptible about being moved to joy by a musical, to terror by a thriller, to excitement by a Western. Why shouldn't we get a little misty during a story about young lovers separated by death?

Hiller earns our emotional response because of the way he's directed the movie. The Segal book was so patently contrived to force those tears, and moved toward that object with such humorless determination, that it must have actually disgusted a lot of readers. The movie is mostly about life, however, and not death. And because Hiller makes the lovers into individuals, of course we're moved by the film's conclusion. Why not?

Love Streams ★ ★ ★ ★
PG-13, 141 m., 1984

Gena Rowlands (Sarah Lawson), John Cassavetes (Robert Harmon), Diahnne Abbott (Susan), Seymour Cassel (Jack Lawson), Margaret Abbott (Margarita). Directed by John Cassavetes and produced by Menahem Golan and Yoram Globus. Screenplay by Ted Allan and Cassavetes.

John Cassavetes's *Love Streams* is the kind of movie where a woman brings home two horses, a goat, a duck, some chickens, a dog, and a parrot, and you don't have the feeling that the screenplay is going for cheap laughs. In fact, there's a tightening in your throat as you realize how desperate an act you're witnessing, and how unhappy a person is getting out of the taxi with all those animals. The menagerie scene occurs rather late in the film, after we've already locked into Cassavetes's method. This is a movie about mad people, and they are going to be acting in crazy ways, but the movie isn't going to let us off the hook by making them funny or picaresque or even symbolic (as in *King of Hearts*). They are, quite simply, desperate.

The brother, Robert (played by Cassavetes), is a writer who lives up in the Hollywood Hills in one of those houses that looks like *Architectural Digest* Visits a Motel. He writes trashy novels about bad women. A parade of hookers marches through his life; he gathers them by the taxi load, almost as a hobby, and dismisses them with lots of meaningless words about how he loves them, and how they're sweethearts and babies and dolls. The circular drive in front of his house is constantly filled with the cars of the lonely and the desperate. He is an alcoholic who stays up for two or three days at a stretch, as if terrified of missing one single unhappy moment. The sister, Sarah (Gena Rowlands), is as possessive as her brother is evasive. She is in the process of a messy divorce from her husband (Seymour Cassel), and her daughter is in flight from her. Rowlands thinks that

maybe she can buy love: First she buys the animals, later she talks about buying her brother a baby, because that's what he "needs."

At least Cassavetes and Rowlands can communicate. They share perfect trust, although it is the trust of two people in the same trap. There are other characters in the movie that Cassavetes talks at and around, but not with. They include a bemused young singer (Diahnne Abbott) who goes out with Cassavetes but looks at him as if he were capable of imploding, and a former wife (Michele Conway) who turns up one day on the doorstep with a small boy and tells him: "This is your son." The way Cassavetes handles this news is typical of the movie. The woman wonders if maybe he could baby sit for a weekend. He says he will. He brings the kid into the house, scares him away, chases him halfway down Laurel Canyon, brings him back, pours him a beer, has a heart-to-heart about "Women, Life and Marriage," and then asks the kid if he'd like to go to Vegas. Cut to Vegas. Cassavetes dumps the kid in a hotel room and goes out partying all night. He is incapable of any appropriate response to a situation requiring him to care about another human being. He fills his life with noise, hookers, emergencies, and booze to drown out the insistent whisper of duty.

The movie is exasperating, because we never know where we stand or what will happen next. I think that's one of its strengths: There's an exhilaration in this roller-coaster ride through scenes that come out of nowhere. This is not a docudrama or a little psychological playlet with a lesson to be learned. It is a raw, spontaneous life, and when we laugh (as in the scene where Cassavetes summons a doctor to the side of the unconscious Rowlands), we wince.

Viewers raised on trained and tame movies may be uncomfortable in the world of Cassavetes; his films are built around lots of talk and the waving of arms and the invoking of the gods. Cassavetes has been making these passionate personal movies for twenty-five years, ever since his *Shadows* helped create American underground movies. His titles include *Minnie and Moskowitz* (in which Rowlands and Cassel got married), *Faces*, *A Woman Under the Influence*, *The Killing of a Chinese Bookie*, *Gloria*, *Opening Night*, and *Husbands*. Sometimes (as in *Husbands*) the wild truth-telling approach evaporates into a lot of empty talk and play-acting. In *Love Streams*, it works.

Lucas ★ ★ ★ ★
PG-13, 99 m., 1985

Corey Haim (Lucas), Kerri Green (Maggie), Charlie Sheen (Cappie), Courtney Thorne-Smith (Alise), Guy Bond (Coach). Directed by David Seltzer and produced by Lawrence Gordon and David Nicksay. Screenplay by Seltzer.

The first loves of early adolescence are so powerful because they are not based on romance, but on ideals. When they are thirteen and fourteen, boys and girls do not fall in love with one another because of all the usual reasons that are celebrated in love songs; they fall in love because the other person is perfect. Not smart or popular or good-looking, but *perfect*, the embodiment of all good.

The very name of the loved one becomes a holy name, as you can see in *Lucas*, when the hero says, "Maggie. Is that short for Margaret?" And then hugs himself to find that it is, because he suddenly realizes that Margaret is the most wonderful name in all the world.

Everybody grows up, and sooner or later love becomes an experience that has limits and reasons. *Lucas* is a movie that takes place before that happens. It is about a very smart kid who looks a little too short and a little too young to be in high school, and when you tell him that, he nods and solemnly explains that he is "accelerated."

One summer day, while riding his bike through the leafy green of a suburb north of Chicago, he sees a red-haired girl practicing her tennis swing. He stops to speak to her, and before long they are fast friends who sit cross-legged in the grass, knees touching knees, and talk about things that begin with capital letters, like Life and Society and Art.

Lucas loves Maggie, but she is just a little older and more mature than he, and has her eye on a member of the football team. Lucas believes, of course, that the whole value system of football and cheerleaders and pep rallies is corrupt. Maggie says she agrees. But how can she argue when the football hero notices her, breaks up with his girlfriend, and asks her if he can have a kiss?

To describe this situation is to make *Lucas* sound like just one more film about teen-age romance. But it would be tragic if this film got lost in the shuffle of "teen-age movies." This is a movie that is as pure and true to the adolescent experience as Truffaut's *The 400 Blows*. It is true because it assumes all of its characters are intelligent, and do not want to hurt one another, and will refuse to go along with the stupid, painful conformity of high school.

The film centers around the character of Lucas, a skinny kid with glasses and a shock of unruly hair and a gift for trying to talk himself into situations where he doesn't belong. Lucas is played by Corey Haim, who was Sally Field's son in *Murphy's Romance,* and he does not give one of those cute little boy performances that get on your nerves. He creates one of the most three-dimensional, complicated, interesting characters of any age in any recent movie, and if he can continue to act this well he will never become a half-forgotten child star but will continue to grow into an important actor. He is that good.

But the film's other two major actors are just as effective. Kerri Green, who was in *The Goonies,* is so subtle and sensitive as Maggie that you realize she isn't just acting, she understands this character in her heart. As the football hero, Charlie Sheen in some ways has the most difficult role, because we're primed to see him in terms of clichés—

the jock who comes along and wins the heart of the girl. Sheen doesn't play the character even remotely that way. It is a surprise to find that he loves Lucas, that he protects him from the goons at school, that although he has won Maggie away from Lucas, he cares very deeply about sparing the kid's feelings.

The last third of the movie revolves around a football game. So many films have ended with the "big match" or the "big game," that my heart started to sink when I saw the game being set up. Surely *Lucas* wasn't going to throw away all its great dialogue and inspired acting on another formula ending? Amazingly, the movie negotiates the football game without falling into predictability. Lucas finds himself in uniform and on the field under the most extraordinary circumstances, but they are plausible circumstances, and what happens then can hardly be predicted.

There are half a dozen scenes in the movie so well-done that they could make little short films of their own. They include: The time Lucas and Maggie listen to classical music and discuss her name; the scene between

Maggie and the football hero in the high school's laundry room; the scene in which Lucas is humiliated at a school assembly, and turns the situation to his advantage; the way in which he takes the news that he will not be going to the dance with Maggie; and the very last scene in the whole movie, which is one of those moments of perfect vindication that makes you want to cry.

Lucas was written and directed by David Seltzer, who has obviously put his heart into the film. He has also used an enormous amount of sensibility. In a world where Hollywood has cheapened the teen-age years into predictable vulgarity, he has remembered how urgent, how innocent, and how idealistic those years can be. He has put values into this movie. It is about teen-agers who are learning how to be good to each other, to care, and not simply to be filled with egotism, lust, and selfishness—which is all most Hollywood movies think teen-agers can experience. *Lucas* is one of the year's best films.

M

Mac ★ ★ ★ ½
R, 121 m., 1993

John Turturro (Mac), Michael Badalucco (Vico), Carl Capotorto (Bruno), Katherine Borowitz (Alice), John Amos (Nat), Olek Krupa (Polowski), Ellen Barkin (Oona). Directed by John Turturro and produced by Nancy Tenenbaum and Brenda Goodman. Screenplay by Turturro and Brandon Cole.

John Turturro's *Mac* is inspired by the story of his own father, a hard-working Italian-American from Queens who began as a carpenter and ended as a contractor, and whose voice can be heard on his son's answering machine in the very last moment of the film. Turturro plays Mac himself, as a man who works hard and holds himself to high standards, and sometimes loses his temper when others don't see things his way. Mac can be a hard man to live with, but he represents something real in the modern American character, and at the end of the film we feel that Mac's qualities are needed in an age when people would rather make money out of money than houses out of lumber.

The movie opens at the funeral of Mac's own father. His sons line up beside the casket to pay their respects, and then, shockingly, the old man rises up to lecture them. He is not happy with the workmanship on his coffin, or with much of anything else, and his restless need to excel has brought him back from the dead, still complaining.

It is a fantasy scene in an otherwise realistic movie that exists close to the daily lives of the characters. The time is the early 1950s, and in Queens, as across the nation, there is a housing boom. America has come home from the war and moved to the suburbs, and Mac and his brothers work for a construction gang run by a Polish guy who has his eye firmly fixed on the bottom line.

The brothers are more or less willing to go along. Not Mac, who likes to say there are two ways to do any job, "the right way and my way, and they're both the same." Told to work more quickly and use fewer nails, he is likely to take a hammer and flail at the wood, undoing his work in a frenzy because he cannot compromise. The other brothers, Vico (Michael Badalucco) and Bruno (Carl Capotorto), are more easygoing, but Mac is the one who has inherited his father's fierce pride.

The movie exists close to the ground, to the wet, muddy construction sites where we can almost feel the relief when it's lunch time and the gang stretches out on a grassy slope, eating sandwiches and engaging in desultory talk. But Mac always seems focused, and never sees himself simply as a hired hand. He dreams of the day when he'll run his own contracting business, and eventually he does, at first with his brothers and then, inevitably, by himself. His fights with his brothers are mostly over money and standards; the family life centers around home, where Mac lives until well into his twenties, adjusting to the implied disintegration of his mother, who is mostly an offscreen, despairing voice.

Then he meets Alice (Katherine Borowitz), a young woman, along the way, and they get married and start a family and despair of ever selling some houses that he's built too close to the rich aromas of a dairy farm. But eventually the houses do sell, and there is a scene late in the film as Mac stands in front of one of the houses with his son, and states simply, "I built that." The whole movie has been pointing to that moment, and we know that the son would grow up to be the maker of this film.

Turturro has been acting in the movies now for nearly a decade, at first in smaller supporting roles in films like *To Live and Die in L.A.*, and then in such major films as *Do the Right Thing, Miller's Crossing* (where his character begged for his life and then double-crossed the man who spared him), *Jungle Fever,* and the title role of *Barton Fink*. There is no mistaking him for anyone else; he is tall and gawky and brooding, and can seem goofy *(Barton Fink)* as well as touchingly ordinary (the man who runs the neighborhood sandwich shop in *Jungle Fever*).

Here, as Mac, we sense we're seeing a character close to the bone, and that although he makes movies instead of houses, some of the members of his crew have probably had occasion to hear him explain that if the job's worth doing, it's worth doing well.

Macbeth ★ ★ ★ ★
R, 139 m., 1972

Jon Finch (Macbeth), Francesca Annis (Lady Macbeth), Martin Shaw (Banquo), Nicholas Selby (Duncan), John Stride (Ross), Stephen Chase (Malcolm), Paul Shelley (Donalbain), Terence Bayler (Macduff). Directed by Roman Polanski and produced by Andrew Braunsberg. Screenplay by Polanski and Kenneth Tynan.

We have all heard it a hundred times, Macbeth's despairing complaint about life: ". . . it is a tale told by an idiot, full of sound and fury, signifying nothing." But who has taken it more seriously than Roman Polanski, who tells his bloody masterpiece at precisely the level of the idiot's tale?

Macbeth always before seemed reasonable, dealing with a world in which wrongdoing was punished and logic demonstrated. Macbeth's character was not strong enough to stand up under the weight of the crime he committed, so he disintegrated into the fantasies of ignorant superstition, while his flimsy wife went mad.

It all seemed so clear. And at the proper moment, the forces of justice stepped forward, mocked the witches' prophecies which deluded poor Macbeth and set things right for the final curtain. There were, no doubt, those who thought the play was about how Malcolm became king of Scotland.

But in this film Polanski and his collaborator, Kenneth Tynan, place themselves at Macbeth's side and choose to share his point of view, and in their film there's no room at all for detachment. All those noble, tragic Macbeths—Orson Welles and Maurice Evans and the others—look like imposters now, and the king is revealed as a scared kid.

No effort has been made to make Macbeth a tragic figure, and his death moves us infinitely less than the murder of Macduff's young son. Polanski places us in a visual universe of rain and mist, of gray dawns and clammy dusks, and there is menace in the sound of hoofbeats but no cheer in the cry of trumpets. Even the heroic figure of Macduff has been tempered; now he is no longer the instrument of God's justice, but simply a man bent on workaday revenge. The movie ends with the simple fact that a job has been done: Macbeth got what was coming to him.

Polanski has imposed this vision on the film so effectively that even the banquet looks like a gang of highwaymen ready to wolf down stolen sheep. Everyone in the film seems to be pushed by circumstances; there is small feeling that the characters are motivated by ideas. They seem so ignorant at times that you wonder if they understand the wonderful dialogue Shakespeare has written for them. It's as if the play has been inhabited by Hell's Angels who are quick studies.

All of this, of course, makes Polanski's *Macbeth* more interesting than if he had done your ordinary, respectable, awe-stricken tiptoe around Shakespeare. This is an original film by an original film artist, and not an "interpretation." It should have been titled *Polanski's Macbeth*, just as we got *Fellini Satyricon*.

I might as well be honest and say it is impossible to watch certain scenes without thinking of the Charles Manson case. It is impossible to watch a film directed by Roman Polanski and not react on more than one level to such images as a baby being "untimely ripped from his mother's womb." Indeed, Polanski adds his own grim conclusion after Shakespeare's, with a final scene in which Malcolm, now crowned king, goes to consult the same witches who deceived Macbeth. Polanski's characters resemble

Manson: They are anti-intellectual, witless, and driven by deep, shameful wells of lust and violence.

Why did Polanski choose to make *Macbeth*, and why this *Macbeth*? I have no way of guessing. This is certainly one of the most pessimistic films ever made, and there seems little doubt that Polanski intended his film to be full of sound and fury—which it is, to the brim—and to signify nothing.

It's at that level that Polanski is at his most adamant: The events that occur in the film must not be allowed to have significance. Polanski and Tynan take only small liberties with Shakespeare, and yet so successfully does Polanski orchestrate *Macbeth*'s visual content that we come out of the film with a horrified realization. We didn't identify with either Macbeth or Macduff in their final duel. We were just watching a sword-fight.

McCabe and Mrs. Miller ★ ★ ★ ★
R, 120 m., 1971

Warren Beatty (McCabe), Julie Christie (Mrs. Miller), Rene Auberjonois (Shehan), Hugh Millais (Butler), Michael Murphy (Sears), William Devane (Lawyer). Directed by Robert Altman and produced by David Foster and Mitchell Brower. Screenplay by Altman and Brian McKay.

McCabe rides into the town of Presbyterian Church under a lowering sky, dismounts, takes off his buffalo-hide coat, puts on his bowler hat, and mumbles something under his breath that we can't quite make out, but the tone of voice is clear enough. This time, he's not going to let the bastards grind him down. He steps off through the mud puddles to the only local saloon, throws a cloth on the table, and takes out a pack of cards, to start again. His plan is to build a whorehouse with a bathhouse out in back, and get rich. By the end of the movie, he will have been offered $6,250 for his holdings, and he will be sitting thoughtfully in a snowbank, dead, as if thinking it all over.

And yet Robert Altman's *McCabe and Mrs. Miller* doesn't depend on that final death for its meaning. It doesn't kill a character just to get a trendy existential feel about the meaninglessness of it all. No, McCabe doesn't find it meaningless at all, and once Mrs. Miller explains the mistake he made in his reasoning, he rides all the way into the next town to try to sell his holdings for half what he was asking, because he'd rather not die.

Death is very final in this Western, because the movie is about life. Most Westerns are about killing and getting killed, which means they're not about life and death at all. We spend a time in the life of a small frontier town, which grows up before our eyes out of raw, unpainted lumber and tubercular canvas tents. We get to know the town pretty well, because Altman has a gift for making movies that seem to eavesdrop on activity that would have been taking place anyway.

That was what happened in *M*A*S*H*, where a lot of time didn't have to be wasted in introducing the characters and explaining the relationships between them, because the characters already knew who they were and how they felt about each other. In a lot of movies, an actor appears on the screen and has no identity at all until somebody calls him "Smith" or "Slim," and then he's Smith or Slim. In *McCabe and Mrs. Miller*, Altman uses a tactfully unobtrusive camera, a distinctive conversational style of dialogue, and the fluid movements of his actors to give us people who are characters from the moment we see them; we have the sense that when they leave camera range they're still thinking, humming, scratching, chewing, and nodding to each other in the street.

McCabe and Mrs. Miller are an organic part of this community. We are aware, of course, that they're played by Warren Beatty and Julie Christie, but rarely have stars been used so completely for their talents rather than their fame. We don't ever think much about McCabe being Warren Beatty, and Mrs. Miller being Julie Christie; they're there along with everybody else in town, and the movie just happens to be about their lives.

Because the movie is about a period in the lives of several people (and not about a series of events that occur to one-dimensional characters), McCabe and Mrs. Miller change during the course of the story. Mrs. Miller is a tough Cockney madam who convinces McCabe that he needs a competent manager for his whorehouse: How would *he* ever know enough about managing women? He agrees, and she lives up to her promise, and they're well on their way to making enough money for her to get out of this dump of a mining town and back to San Francisco, where, she believes, a woman of her caliber belongs.

All of this happens in an indoor sort of a way, and by that I don't mean that the movie looks like it was shot on a sound stage. The outdoors is always there, and people are always coming in out of it and shaking the rain from their hats, and we see the trees whipping in the wind through the windows. But it's a wet autumn and then a cold winter, so people naturally congregate in saloons and grocery stores and whorehouses, and the climate forces a sense of community. Then the enforcers come to town: The suave, Scottish-accented Butler, who kills people who won't sell out to the Company, and his two sidekicks. One of them is slack-jawed and mean, and the other is a nervous blond kid with the bare makings of a mustache. On the suspension bridge that gets you across the river to the general store, he kills another kid—a rawboned, easygoing country kid with a friendly smile—and it is one of the most affecting and powerful deaths there ever has been in a Western.

The final hunt for McCabe takes place in almost deserted streets, because the church is burning down and everybody is out at the edge of town trying to save it. The church burns during a ghostly, heavy daylight snow-storm: fire and ice. And McCabe almost gets away. Mrs. Miller, who allowed him into her bed but always, except once, demanded five dollars for the privilege, caught on long before he did that the Company would rather kill him than go up $2,000. She is down at the foot of town, in Chinatown, lost in an opium dream while the snow drifts against his body. *McCabe and Mrs. Miller* is like no other Western ever made.

Madame Bovary ★ ★ ★
NO MPAA RATING, 124 m., 1991

Isabelle Huppert (Emma Bovary), Jean-François Balmer (Charles Bovary), Christophe Malavoy (Rodolphe Boulanger), Jean Yanne (Monsieur Homais, pharmacist), Lucas Belvaux (Leon Dupuis). Directed by Claude Chabrol and produced by Marin Karmitz. Screenplay by Chabrol.

Madame Emma Bovary is one of the two or three most famous characters in French literature—but for her attitude, more than for anything she says or does. She is famed for the vain, romantic longings that were all that stirred her selfish and shallow personality. She is the kind of person who believes there must be more to life than this, but never stops to wonder why there is so little to herself.

When Flaubert wrote about her in 1856, he was dramatizing a modern type that survives right down to the present. What is the

difference between Madame Bovary's dreams of being swept off her feet at a neighbor's ball, and the jaded Club Med regular who hopes to meet somebody really interesting this year? Those who believe that the solution to their boredom is external to themselves move restlessly from one disappointment to the next.

Claude Chabrol, the French New Wave veteran, specializes in lust, greed, adultery, and crimes of passion. Period films are not his specialty. But here, with Isabelle Huppert in the title role, he makes a *Madame Bovary* that has been acclaimed in France, even though the novel was considered all but unfilmable. Huppert's key contribution to the role is a defiant passivity. She is bored, she is discontented with her good but stupid husband, she dreams of dancing all night, she is repressing a great deal of anger but very little insight. Huppert here is a first cousin to the famous character she played in Chabrol's *Violette Noziere*, where once again a woman placed her own desires ahead of common decency.

The story is well known. Emma, daughter of a prosperous local landowner, marries Charles Bovary, the region's doctor (Jean-François Balmer). She does it basically to get off her father's farm. Bovary moves her into the town and provides her with a good house, nice clothes, and mindless devotion. She is discontented. Finally something different happens in her life. She is taken to the ball of a district aristocrat, and there she meets the dashing Rodolphe Boulanger (Christophe Malavoy), who has an affair with her and promises to elope with her.

Of course, he does not really mean to. But Emma believes him, and places herself deeply in debt with the local milliner for a traveling costume she cannot pay for. She plans to be long gone when the bill comes due—she has little feeling for her husband—but when Boulanger abandons her, she is faced with the consequences of her actions.

Madame Bovary is not a very good or likable character, and yet, like her contemporary, the vain and selfish Scarlett O'Hara, she has become a favorite of millions of readers. The difference between Bovary and O'Hara is in how they react to misfortune, and their different styles say a great deal about the differences between France and America: Emma kills herself, while Scarlett plants potatoes.

Isabelle Huppert is a great movie star, but of a type that could not flourish in Holly-

wood, because her greatness is in her secrets, not her surfaces. From her first two films, *The Lacemaker* and *Violette Noziere* (both 1977), she has played silent, introverted types who burn with great passions. Her most recent great role was in Chabrol's *Story of Women*, as a wartime collaborationist and abortionist who essentially just wanted money to buy things and never thought about the moral consequences. She has played many other, more extroverted, even cheerful, roles, but Chabrol was quite right to find Emma Bovary within her. Who else could do so little and yet project such a burning need—such a cry for deliverance from the bondage of self?

Madame Sousatzka ★ ★ ★ ★
PG-13, 120 m., 1988

Shirley MacLaine (Madame Sousatzka), Navin Chowdhry (Manek Sen), Peggy Ashcroft (Lady Emily), Shabana Azmi (Sushila), Twiggy (Jenny), Leigh Lawson (Ronnie Blum), Geoffrey Bayldon (Cordle), Lee Montague (Vincent Pick). Directed by John Schlesinger and produced by Robin Dalton. Screenplay by Ruth Prawer Jhabvala and Schlesinger, from the novel by Bernice Rubens.

The Indian boy comes every afternoon for piano lessons from Madame Sousatzka, who cannot disguise the love in her voice as she teaches him not only about music, but also about how to sit, how to breathe, how to hold his elbows, and how to think about his talent. Behind her, in the shadows of her musty London apartment, are the photographs of earlier students who were taught the same lessons before they went out into the world—where some of them became great pianists and others became just players of the piano.

Madame Sousatzka believes that this boy, Manek, can be a great pianist, a virtuoso—but we have no objective way to know if she is a great teacher of great musicians, or just a piano teacher who is deluding herself and the boy. That doesn't matter. *Madame Sousatzka* is not a one-level movie in which everything leads up to the cliché of the crucial first concert. This is not a movie about success or failure; it is a movie about soldiering on, about continuing to do your best, day after day, simply because you believe in yourself—no matter what anyone else thinks. Madame believes this sixteen-year-old boy can be a great pianist, and that she—no one else—is the person to guide him on the right path to his destiny.

Madame Sousatzka is a film about her efforts to protect the boy from all the pressures and temptations around him, while simultaneously shoring up the ruins of her own world. As played by Shirley MacLaine, in one of the best performances of her career, she is a faded, aging woman who possesses great stubbornness and conviction. Once, long ago, she failed in her own concert debut. Her own mother pushed her too fast, too soon, and she broke down in the middle of her debut concert and fled from the stage.

That humiliation is still in her nightmares, and still shapes her attitude toward her students. They must not be allowed to perform in public until they are ready. Unfortunately, Madame is hardly ever prepared to admit they are ready, and so sooner or later all of her pupils are forced to make a break with her. Their departures have made her career a series of heartbreaks, and populated the shelves of photographs in her apartment.

Manek, her latest student, is played by Navin Chowdhry as a teen-ager who apart from his talent is a fairly normal young man. He travels by skateboard despite Madame's explicit orders that he is not to endanger his hands, he enjoys playing the piano and yet is not obsessed by it, and he has a lively interest in the model (Twiggy) who lives upstairs in Madame's eccentric rooming house. His mother (Shabana Azmi) is divorced, and supports them by making gourmet Indian pastries for the food department of Harrod's. She has an admirer, but Manek is jealous of her boyfriend, and wants to make his concert debut so that he—not some strange man—can support his mother. He is encouraged in his ambition by a predatory booking agent who overhears his playing and wants to use him immediately—creating a war of wills between Madame and her pupil.

Madame Sousatzka was directed by John Schlesinger, who plays it in a very particular kind of London household. The shabby rooming house is on a once-distinguished street that has now been targeted by realtors for gentrification. The house is owned by Lady Emily (Dame Peggy Ashcroft), a sweet-tempered old lady who lives in the basement and peacefully coexists with her tenants, who include Madame, the model, and Cordle (Geoffrey Bayldon), a decayed civil servant type with occasional, furtive homosexual adventures. Although the movie creates affection for the little community within the house, this is not a film about how the developers must be defeated—and you will be relieved to learn that the young pianist does not star in a benefit for Lady Emily.

The film is not about preserving the present, but about being prepared to change, and by the end of the film Lady Emily and Cordle have found that they can live quite comfortably in a little riverside flat, while Madame resolutely soldiers on in the house, undeterred by the noise and dirt of construction. But she has changed in a more important way, by being able to understand for the first time, a little anyway, why a student must eventually be allowed to go out into the world and take his chances.

MacLaine's approach to the role is interesting. She deliberately ages herself, and has put on weight for the role, so that there is relatively little of the familiar Shirley MacLaine to be seen on the screen. Even those traces soon disappear into the role of a woman who loves music, loves to teach, loves her students, and is crippled only by her traumatic failure on the stage. It might have embittered her, but it has not; she holds onto her students not out of resentment but out of pride, and fear.

The screenplay, by Ruth Prawer Jhabvala and Schlesinger, takes the time to be precise about teaching; we may feel by the end that we've had a few lessons ourselves. It is about discipline, about patience, about love of music. Manek tells Sousatzka at one point that when he goes on a stage, he will feel a small core of strength inside himself that she has given him. It is all, besides technique, that any teacher has to offer. *Madame Sousatzka* is an extraordinary movie that loves music and loves the people it is about, and has the patience to do justice to both.

Mad Dog and Glory ★ ★ ★ ½
R, 97 m., 1993

Robert De Niro (Wayne), Uma Thurman (Glory), Bill Murray (Frank), David Caruso (Mike), Mike Starr (Harold), Tom Towles (Andrew), Kathy Baker (Lee). Directed by John McNaughton and produced by Barbara De Fina and Martin Scorsese. Screenplay by Richard Price.

Mad Dog and Glory is one of the few recent movies where it helps to pay close attention. Some of the best moments come quietly and subtly, in a nuance of dialogue or a choice of timing. The movie is very funny, but it's not broad humor; it's humor born of personality quirks and the style of the performances.

The movie begins when Wayne, a timid Chicago cop (Robert De Niro), walks in on a convenience store holdup and accidentally saves the life of Frank, an expansive gangster (Bill Murray). Frank is not your average hood. He not only owns a comedy club, he performs in it. He also collects bets, which is why he controls a young woman named Glory (Uma Thurman), who is trying to work off her brother's gambling debt. One day she turns up at Wayne's house and explains that Frank is giving her to him for a week, in gratitude.

This is a present Wayne does not want. Indeed, he is beginning to see that his entire relationship with Frank is a big mistake, since there is no way to be this gangster's friend without being drawn into his activities. Wayne doesn't even think of himself as a real cop. He's shy and fears he is a coward. He works for the department as an evidence technician, and frames his photos of dead bodies as if they were art; he's a would-be Weejee.

The screenplay by Richard Price *(The Wanderers, The Color of Money)* avoids the temptation to paint this situation in broad strokes. A dumb comedy might have been made of the situation, but this is a smart one. It's about a man who begins the movie with no friends, and quickly gets one he doesn't want and another, Glory, who terrifies him. She gives him kissing lessons, but he is uncertain about his bedroom skills, and when she tries to get his shirt off he explains that he should do some sit-ups. "Right now?" she asks. She can't believe her ears. "No . . . I mean generally."

The director, John McNaughton, is best known for the chilling *Henry: Portrait of a Serial Killer.* This movie is completely different in theme, and yet it has the same quiet way of developing characters. The camera watches people while they gradually reveal themselves. Nothing is simply told to the audience.

For De Niro, Murray, and Thurman, what happens is sort of magical. De Niro is known for his ability to get into characters by changing himself physically, and here, somehow, he seems to have shrunk. He seems shorter, more tentative. Murray, reining in his rapid-fire comic gift, comes across as the kind of guy who would love to be gentle and nice, but was born with the wrong genes. Thurman, so elegant in other pictures, here becomes almost mousy in some scenes; Glory has low self-esteem, as indeed she should if she allows herself to be made into a thank-you note.

Mad Dog and Glory is the kind of movie I like to see more than once. The people who made it must have come to know the characters very well, because although they seem to fit into broad outlines, they are real individuals—quirky, bothered, worried, bemused. By the end of the film, when the friendship between Wayne and Frank has come to blows, even the fight is handled differently. For some reason it reminded me of Jimmy Breslin's observation that hoods never bury their victims deep enough because they don't like to get mud on their shoes.

Made in America ★ ★ ★
PG-13, 115 m., 1993

Whoopi Goldberg (Sarah Mathews), Ted Danson (Hal Jackson), Will Smith (Tea Cake Walters), Nia Long (Zora Mathews), Paul Rodriguez (Jose), Jennifer Tilly (Stacy). Directed by Richard Benjamin and produced by Arnon Milchan, Michael Douglas, and Rick Bieber. Screenplay by Holly Goldberg Sloan.

I've been thinking about Whoopi Goldberg's appeal, which is real but elusive, and I think it has something to do with a directness of style. There are no false highs and lows in her performances, no flourishes for effect. She seems to respond directly to the situation at hand. This quality provides a leveling effect for *Made in America*, a movie that could have been all over the map emotionally, but turns out to be surprisingly effective.

In the movie, Goldberg plays Sarah Mathews, who runs an African-American bookstore in Oakland, and is raising Zora, a daughter of college age (Nia Long). Goldberg's husband died many years ago, and Zora has always assumed he was her father. Then she discovers by accident that she was the product of artificial insemination. And in a raid on a sperm bank computer, she discovers that her biological father is a white man. And, to her horror, he's one of the biggest jerks in town, Hal Jackson, the corn-pone car dealer who makes a fool of himself in his TV ads.

Zora is devastated. So is Sarah, who specified to the sperm bank that the father be black. So, when he finds out, is Hal Jackson (Ted Danson), a committed bachelor with no interest in planning, starting, or retrospectively discovering, a family.

The movie's setup is not subtle. Character touches are added with a trowel. What purpose is served, for example, by showing that the Goldberg character rides her bicycle through traffic without the slightest caution, cutting in front of cars and trucks as if they were not there? Of course that sets up her accident, which sends her to the hospital and leads to further important plot developments, but it's so goofy—such an obviously phony gimmick—that the writers should have found another way to get her to the hospital.

The strange thing is, after a while it doesn't matter. The ham-handed first forty-five minutes of the movie set up a situation that the rest of the film handles with increasing effectiveness. The Danson character, a grotesque caricature when we first see him, calms down into a nice guy with a heart. And once the dust has settled from all the busyness of the setup, *Made in America* becomes actually heartwarming.

A lot of that is because of Goldberg. As the plot swoops and turns, as melodramatic revelations are followed by manufactured brushes with death, she forges steadily onward, her eye on the main line of the screenplay, which has to do with what it means to be a parent, or a child. Her daughter's self-image is seriously affected by the discovery of a white father, just as Danson finds it astonishing to possess any child at all. Since we can more or less guess where the plot is heading (there is a surprise, but the main lines are clear), the movie stands or falls on how much emotional honesty and human comedy it can find between the lines.

It finds a lot. Once the Danson character has toned down his original excesses, once the daughter has discovered that nature can be color blind, once the mother has drawn everyone together with her sanity, the movie proceeds to its conclusion with warmth and conviction. This isn't a great movie, but it sure is a nice one.

Mad Love ★ ★ ★
PG-13, 99 m., 1995

Chris O'Donnell (Matt), Drew Barrymore (Casey), Matthew Lillard (Eric), Richard Chaim (Duncan), Robert Nadir (Coach), Joan Allen (Margaret), Jude Ciccolella (Richard), Amy Sakasitz (Joanna). Directed by Antonia Bird and produced by David Manson. Screenplay by Paula Milne.

Mad Love is not the first story about two teenagers who fall in love against their parents' wishes. *Romeo and Juliet* wasn't even the first. And it's not the first movie about two troubled kids who hit the road in an attempt to run away to their dreams. But it's the first one in a while that turns realistic, and shows one of the kids trying to react responsibly when the situation gets out of hand. That makes it more interesting, because it's about real problems, not movie problems.

The movie takes place in a Seattle suburb, where Casey (Drew Barrymore) is the alluring new girl in school. Matt (Chris O'Donnell) is her good-looking classmate, who lives across the lake, and finds his telescope trained less often on the stars than on Casey's house. He contrives a Meet Cute, and after a little awkwardness they like each other, and before much longer they are in love.

There are complications. Matt lives with his father and kid brother, after his mother disappeared in a traumatic departure that still hurts. "She left you!" Matt tells his dad at one point, trying to blame him. "No—she left us!" Matt has become the surrogate parent, fixing breakfast and handling household duties, while his dad disappears into his work.

There are problems, too, on the other side of the lake, although they take longer to emerge. Casey's father, a strict and domineering type, doesn't want her getting serious about Matt. He doesn't think she's ready for a relationship, and his reason makes a certain sense: She's a manic-depressive, and needs healing and treatment.

Matt doesn't know that. And most of the time Casey is fine. When the situation explodes and she's placed in an institution, Matt does what most movie characters do in a similar situation: He diagnoses the institution as the problem, and helps Casey escape. Then they hit the road with what money they can scrape together, living in a series of fleabag motels or sleeping under the stars.

At this point in many films, the road trip turns criminal, and the two misunderstood lovers turn into recycled Bonnies and Clydes. Barrymore's own movie *Gun Crazy* had a little of that, although it was pointed in another direction. But *Mad Love* breaks with formula and continues to view its characters with the complexity they deserve. The movie, directed by Antonia Bird *(Priest)* and written by Paula Milne, shows Matt gradually realizing the full dimensions of Casey's condition, and trying to do the right thing. It's not a movie about young lovers or "mad love," but about a young man growing up and taking responsibility.

It is becoming increasingly clear what a good actress Drew Barrymore is. In *Boys on the Side* she entered the movie with the energy of a natural force, and stayed around to reveal a deep emotional seriousness, under her character's initial goofiness. Here, she has a couple of scenes that could have gone badly wrong—a blowup in a restaurant, and a confrontation with Matt—and she plays them just right, not too dramatically or strangely, but with the right balance of bravado and fear.

Chris O'Donnell just continues to grow. Actors who look like him often get cast as the school jock, but he avoids stereotyping and goes for intelligently written roles (as in *Scent of a Woman*). He doesn't have the showy scenes in *Mad Love*, but he has the crucial ones, as he plays his romantic obsession against the side of his personality that needs to care and nurture.

Mad Love has a few glitches—I thought Casey's father was written and played too broadly—and it might have found a way around that ancient movie belief that patients can only be cured by being yanked out of the hospital. But the movie deals seriously with mental illness, and also with that overwhelming mental and physical condition known as being a teenager in love.

Mad Max Beyond Thunderdome
★ ★ ★ ★
R, 115 m., 1985

Mel Gibson (Mad Max), Tina Turner (Aunty Entity), Frank Thring (Collector), Angelo Rossitto (Master), Paul Larsson (Blaster), Angry Anderson (Ironbar). Directed and produced by George Miller. Co-directed by George Ogilvie. Screenplay by Miller and Terry Hayes.

It's not supposed to happen this way. Sequels are not supposed to be better than the movies that inspired them. The third movie in a series isn't supposed to create a world more complex, more visionary, and more entertaining than the first two. Sequels are supposed to be creative voids. But now here is *Mad Max Beyond Thunderdome*, not only the best of the three Mad Max movies, but one of the best films of 1985.

From its opening shot of a bizarre vehicle being pulled by camels through the desert, *Mad Max Three* places us more firmly within its apocalyptic postnuclear world than ever before. We are some years in the future; how many, it is hard to say, but so few years that

the frames and sheet metal of 1985 automobiles are still being salvaged for makeshift new vehicles of bizarre design. And yet enough years that a new society is taking shape. The bombs have fallen, the world's petroleum supplies have been destroyed, and in the deserts of Australia, mankind has found a new set of rules and started on a new game.

The driver of the camels is Mad Max (Mel Gibson), former cop, now sort of a free-lance nomad. After his vehicle is stolen and he is left in the desert to die, he makes his way somehow to Bartertown, a quasi-Casablanca hammered together out of spare parts. Bartertown is where you go to buy, trade, or sell anything—or anybody. It is supervised by a Sydney Greenstreet-style fat man named the Collector (Frank Thring), and ruled by an imperious queen named Aunty Entity (Tina Turner).

And it is powered by an energy source that is, in its own way, a compelling argument against nuclear war: In chambers beneath Bartertown, countless pigs live and eat and defecate, and from their waste products, Turner's soldiers generate methane gas. This leads to some of the movie's most memorable moments, as Mad Max and others wade knee-deep in piggy-do.

Tina Turner herself lives far above the masses, in a birds'-nest throne room perched high overhead. And as Mad Max first visits Turner's sky palace, I began to realize how completely the director, George Miller, had imagined this future world. It has the crowding and the variety of a movie crossroads, but it also has a riot of hairstyles and costume design, as if these desperate creatures could pause from the daily struggle for survival only long enough to invent new punk fashions. After the clothes, the hair, the crowding, the incessant activity, the spendthrift way in which Miller fills his screen with throwaway details, Bartertown becomes much more than a movie set—it's an astounding address of the imagination, a place as real as Bogart's Casablanca or Orson Welles's Xanadu or the Vienna of *The Third Man*. That was even before the movie introduced me to Thunderdome, the arena for Bartertown's hand-to-hand battles to the death.

Thunderdome is the first really original movie idea about how to stage a fight since we got the first karate movies. The "dome" is a giant upside-down framework bowl. The spectators scurry up the sides of the bowl, and look down on the fighters. But the combatants are not limited to fighting on the

floor of the arena. They are placed on harnesses with long elastic straps, so that they can leap from top to bottom and from side to side with great lethal bounds. Thunderdome is to fighting as three-dimensional chess is to a flat board. And the weapons available to the fighters are hung from the inside of the dome: Cleavers, broadaxes, sledge-hammers, the inevitable chainsaw.

It is into Thunderdome that Mad Max goes for his showdown with Aunty Entity's greatest warrior, and George Miller's most original creation, a character named Master-Blaster, who is actually two people. Blaster is a giant hulk of a man in an iron mask. Master is a dwarf who rides him like a chariot, standing in an iron harness above his shoulders. The fight between Mad Max and Master-Blaster is one of the great creative action scenes in the movies.

There is a lot more in *Mad Max Beyond Thunderdome*. The descent into the pig world, for example, and the visit to a sort of postwar hippie commune, and of course the inevitable final chase scene, involving car, train, truck, cycle, and incredible stunts. This is a movie that strains at the leash of the possible, a movie of great visionary wonders.

The Madness of King George ★ ★ ★ ★
NO MPAA RATING, 110 m., 1995

Nigel Hawthorne (George III), Helen Mirren (Queen Charlotte), Ian Holm (Willis), Amanda Donohoe (Lady Pembroke), Rupert Graves (Greville), Rupert Everett (Prince of Wales), Alan Bennett (Second M.P.). Directed by Nicholas Hytner and produced by Stephen Evans and David Parfitt. Screenplay by Alan Bennett.

WILLIS: *My patients acquire a better conceit of themselves.*
GEORGE: *I'm the king of England! A man can have no better conceit of himself than that!*
—dialogue between the king and his doctor

The Madness of King George tells the story of the disintegration of a fond and foolish old man, who rules England, yet cannot find his way through the tangle of his own mind. The parallel with *King Lear* is clear, and there is even a moment when George III reads from the play: "I fear I am not in my perfect mind." But the story of George is not tragedy, because tragedy requires a fall from greatness, and George III is not great, merely lovable and confused.

The film opens in 1788, some years after the American colonies have thrown off George's rule. He presides over an establishment that wishes him gone—his own son, the Prince of Wales, waits impatiently in the wings—and over a court scandalized by his erratic behavior. He awakes before dawn, runs in his nightshirt through the fields, pounces on a lady-in-waiting—and, worse still, cannot remember the names of his enemies. His queen, Charlotte, keeps up a brave front ("Smile and wave! It's what you're paid for!" she hisses at the Prince of Wales). When George forces his court to sit through an interminable session of "Greensleeves" being rung on bells and then asks to hear it again, troubled looks are exchanged: The king is losing it.

Alan Bennett's play, now filmed with its original stage star, Nigel Hawthorne, still in the title role, is a fond portrait of this befuddled old man. The action takes place in 1788, when the king was fifty. He lived on until 1820, blind and hopelessly insane the last ten years of his life, but the film wisely focuses on his middle age, when there were periods of clarity, and he struggled bravely to keep his wits and his throne.

The film shows both court and parliament acutely attuned to the weathers of the king's mind. The Prince of Wales (Rupert Everett) schemes with the opposition leader, Charles Fox (Jim Carter), to displace his father ("If a few ramshackle colonists in America can send him packing, why not me?"). Fox's archenemy, William Pitt (Julian Wadham), the king's loyal prime minister, schemes to keep George and his policies in power. And the loving, loyal Queen Charlotte (Helen Mirren), is denied access to her husband by the Prince of Wales—a cruel, foppish man, who complains, with a prescient bow to the present holder of his title, "To be Prince of Wales is not a position; it is a predicament."

All of this could be the material for a solemn historical biopic, but Bennett's play, and the direction by Nicholas Hytner, are more lighthearted than analytical, and the performance by Nigel Hawthorne as the ailing king is barbed and yet lovable: Madness burns in his eyes, but also sweetness and vulnerability, and when he lashes out at his court and accosts its ladies, we sense his suffering.

Medical science at the time could not offer much help: Great attention is lavished on the condition of the king's stools, and particularly their color. The king performs royally upon the pot, but, as a doctor observes sadly, "One may produce a copious, regular evacuation every day of the week and still be a stranger to reason." (Future historians were able to deduce from the medical records that George's mental state was caused by porphyria, a metabolic imbalance.)

What saves the king, at least for a time, is the materilization of a man named Willis (Ian Holm), who has revolutionary ideas about mental health. During a period of George's greatest confusion, the serious face of Willis swims into view, along with his portentious words: "I have a farm. . . ." On that farm he hopes to shock the king into sanity, and the king is shocked, all right:

George: *I am the king!*
Willis: *No, sir! You are the patient!*

The battle of wills between these two strong men is the centerpiece of the movie, and hugely entertaining. Willis, whose approach seems to embody some of the theories of modern psychology, tries to break the king down so he can build him up again. The king resists, aghast that a commoner would so treat the royal personage: "I am the verb, sir! I am not the object!" Holm is perfect for the role, stern, unyielding, and dotty.

It is only when strings are pulled to reunite the king with Queen Charlotte that the pieces fall into place. Reduced from grandeur to a sad little old man, he finds that his mind has cleared, and "I have remembered how to seem myself." The sequence during which he pulls himself together and astounds Parliament is triumphant, and funny.

I am not sure anyoné but Nigel Hawthorne could have brought such qualities to this role. Having seen him onstage in London at about the same time the movie was released, in *The Clandestine Marriage*, a play written during George's reign, I was struck again by the way he projects a ferocious façade, and then peeks out from behind it, winking. Through the movie, he punctuates George's dialogue with little verbal tics like "What-what!" and "Yes-yes!" When George emerges briefly from his madness, one of the signs, for those who love him, is the reappearance of "What-what!" The way Hawthorne delivers the line makes it seem, for a moment, as if George has defeated insanity with eccentricity—which, of course, is the madness of the sane.

Major Payne ★ ★ ★

PG-13, 97 m., 1995

NEW

Damon Wayans (Major Payne), Karyn Parsons (Dr. Emily Walburn), Steven Martini (Cadet Alex Stone), Andrew Harrison Leeds (Cadet Dotson), Joda Blaire-Hershman (Cadet Bryan), Stephen Coleman (Cadet Leland), Damien Wayans (Cadet Williams), Chris Owen (Cadet Wulinger). Directed by Nick Castle and produced by Eric L. Gold and Michael Rachmil. Screenplay by Dean Lorey, Damon Wayans, and Gary Rosen.

Major Payne likes to think of himself as a killing machine. That's why he's devastated to be passed over for promotion and mustered out of the service. Surely, he begs his commanding officer, there must be another war to fight? Somebody else to kill? "Sorry, Payne," he's told. "There's nobody else to kill. You've killed them all."

Back in civilian life and unemployed, he tries out for the police force, but gets carried away during a "real life simulation" and hammers an actor who is portraying a perpetrator. Then an old friend finds him a job as the officer in charge of the junior ROTC cadet training corps at a private school in Virginia. This is not the job he was born to fill.

Payne is played in the movie by Damon Wayans, in the best work he's done since the inspired "In Living Color" TV series. Although the plot of the movie is a familiar formula, the dialogue and performance are not; it's a smart, funny job of poking fun at all those movies where sadistic drill instructors terrorized their green recruits.

In this case, according to the school's doddering headmaster (a bug collector played by William Hickey), the recruits are literally green: They wear green uniforms, he knows, but he's not sure exactly why. The only person on the school faculty with a clue about real life is a cute teacher named Dr. Emily Walburn (Karyn Parsons), who makes Payne get all mushy-mouthed when she sweet-talks him.

The members of the junior ROTC corps are your usual mixed bag, even more mixed: There must be a three-foot difference in height between the shortest and the tallest, and when Payne screams at one of them, "What's the matter, cadet? Are you deaf?" the answer, of course, is that he is deaf. That doesn't faze Payne, who relies on the kid's lip-reading skills to get his harrowing threats across.

One of the funny things about the movie is that the dialogue of the Payne character is truly artful in its ability to paint horrifying pictures and utter dire insults. When Dr. Walburn asks him, at one point, if he understands "positive reinforcement," Payne nods and says, "Is that like when you break the neck of a POW after torturing him, so he doesn't have to spend the rest of his life with a colostomy bag?"

Hmmm. Reading through that line, I can see how it might not sound howlingly funny, out of context. The context is the whole key to the character in this film: Wayans presents Payne as a tunnel-visioned "killing machine" who applies his values as single-mindedly to school kids as to recruits on a practice range. "War has made me very paranoid," he says, "and when a man gets to eyeballing me too much, it makes my Agent Orange act up." And when his cadets complain about conditions in the quonset hut they're expected to occupy, he buries them up to their necks in mud to make them grateful for their former quarters. Even more terrifying is his personal interpretation of *The Little Engine That Could.*

The key to this kind of comedy is to go all the way with it, and Wayans creates a comic character out of narrowness, obsession, and blind commitment. Of course, the arc of the story line is familiar; we know the pretty teacher will soften him, and that he will grow fond of the cadets, and no prizes for guessing who wins the big all-Virginia ROTC competition.

Wayans is one of the most talented comic actors around, especially when he lets go and swings for the fences. In some of his earlier film work, including *Mo' Money* (1992), he was softening the edges too much. His best work, including the "Men on Film" segments of "In Living Color," depend on outrageous behavior, and as Major Payne he is plenty outrageous.

Making Mr. Right ★ ★ ★ ½
PG-13, 98 m., 1987

John Malkovich (Jeff/Ulysses), Ann Magnuson (Frankie), Glenne Headly (Trish), Ben Masters (Steve), Laurie Metcalf (Sandy), Robert Trebor (Tuxedo Salesman). Directed by Susan Seidelman and produced by Mike Wise and Joel Tuber. Screenplay by Floyd Byars and Laurie Frank.

Making Mr. Right is about a scientist who invents a remarkably lifelike android in his own image and about an ad executive who

begins to like the android more than the scientist. These raw materials easily could have been turned into a fairly dreary movie, but not this time. Instead, we get a smart, quick-witted, and genuinely funny movie.

A lot of the movie's smarts come from John Malkovich, who plays the dual role of the scientist and the android, and a newcomer named Ann Magnuson, who plays the account executive with a pert intelligence that reminded me of Susan Hayward or Gloria Grahame. Both actors see right through their roles, know what's funny and what's important, and are able to put a nice spin even on the obligatory scenes.

That's true, for example, during the sweet, tentative moments when the android begins to fall for the woman. Malkovich provides just the right amount of inept clumsiness for the android, which sometimes has trouble getting its mind-body coordination in line. Like Jeff Bridges in *Starman,* he's able to meet the tricky challenge of moving in an uncoordinated way without looking merely ridiculous.

Magnuson is fun, too, with her high heels and designer outfits, clipboards and speculative looks. She has an instantly combative relationship with the scientist who invented the android, and it's made trickier because as the android grows more human, the scientist subtly grows more robotic.

Making Mr. Right was directed by Susan Seidelman, whose previous credits are *Smithereens,* which I didn't much like, and *Desperately Seeking Susan,* which was much more assured. With this film, she hits her stride as a comedy director who would rather be clever than obvious, who allows good actors such as Malkovich to go for quiet effects rather than broad, dumb clichés.

Another comedy depending on dual and mistaken identities is *The Secret of My Success.* Seeing the two movies is instructive because they take such different approaches to the challenge of identity. *Secret* has lots of moments when characters don't realize exactly who they're talking to, and it creates those moments out of the stupidity of the characters. In *Mr. Right,* there are scenes where the scientist and the android are mistaken for one another, and Seidelman uses the misunderstandings to make comic points about the personalities of her characters: They make wrong assumptions because of who they are, instead of because of how stupid they are. It makes all the difference in the world.

Seidelman also has fun populating the outskirts of her plot with good character actors, especially Robert Trebor as the tuxedo salesman. You may remember him as the smarmy, sweating porno store operator in *52 Pick-Up.* The distance between these two good performances is impressive.

At one point in *Making Mr. Right,* we see a theater marquee in the background advertising *The Parent Trap.* That was, of course, the movie where Hayley Mills played twins, thanks to trick photography. Malkovich is often seen onscreen with himself in this movie, but I never noticed any seams or glitches, and I was grateful to Seidelman for not providing any moments that were intended merely to exploit the trick.

Malcolm X ★ ★ ★ ★
PG-13, 201 m., 1992

Denzel Washington (Malcolm X), Angela Bassett (Betty Shabazz), Albert Hall (Baines), Al Freeman, Jr. (Elijah Muhammad), Delroy Lindo (West Indian Archie), Spike Lee (Shorty). Directed by Spike Lee and produced by Marvin Worth and Lee. Screenplay by Arnold Perl and Lee.

Spike Lee's *Malcolm X* is one of the great screen biographies, celebrating the whole sweep of an American life that began in sorrow and bottomed out on the streets and in prison, before its hero reinvented himself. Watching the film, I understood more clearly how we do have the power to change our own lives, how fate doesn't deal all of the cards. The film is inspirational and educational—and it is also entertaining, as movies must be before they can be anything else.

Its hero was born Malcolm Little. His father was a minister who preached the beliefs of Marcus Garvey, the African-American leader who taught that white America would never accept black people, and that their best hope lay in returning to Africa. Years later, Malcolm would also become a minister and teach a variation on this theme, but first he had to go through a series of identities and conversions and hard lessons of life.

His father was murdered, probably by the Klan, which had earlier burned down the family house. His mother was unable to support her children, and Malcolm was parceled out to a foster home. He was the brightest student in his classes, but was steered away from ambitious career choices by white teachers who told him that, as a Negro, he should look for something where he could "work with his hands." One of his early jobs was as a Pullman porter, and then, in Harlem, he became a numbers runner and small-time gangster.

During that stage of his life, in the late 1940s, he was known as "Detroit Red," and ran with a fast crowd including white women who joined him for sex and burglaries. Arrested and convicted, he was sentenced to prison; the movie quotes him that he got one year for the burglaries and seven years for associating with white women while committing them. Prison was the best thing that happened to Detroit Red, who fell into the orbit of the Black Muslim movement of Elijah Muhammad, and learned self-respect.

The movie then follows Malcolm as he sheds his last name—the legacy, the Muslims preached, of slave-owners—and becomes a fiery street-corner preacher who quickly rises until he is the most charismatic figure in the Black Muslims, teaching that whites are the devil and that blacks had to become independent and self-sufficient. But there was still another conversion ahead: During a pilgrimage to Mecca, he was embraced by Muslims of many colors, and returned to America convinced that there were good people of peace in all races. Not long after, in 1965, he was assassinated—probably by members of the Muslim sect he had broken with.

This is an extraordinary life, and Spike Lee has told it in an extraordinary film. Like *Gandhi*, the movie gains force as it moves along; the early scenes could come from the lives of many men, but the later scenes show a great original personality coming into focus. To understand the stages of Malcolm's life is to walk for a time in the steps of many African-Americans, and to glimpse where the journey might lead.

Denzel Washington stands at the center of the film, in a performance of enormous breadth. He never seems to be trying for an effect, and yet he is always convincing; he seems as natural in an early scene, clowning through a railroad club car with ham sandwiches, as in a later one, holding audiences spellbound on street corners, in churches, on television, and at Harvard. He is as persuasive early in the film, wearing a zoot suit and prowling the nightclubs of Harlem, as later, disappearing into a throng of pilgrims to Mecca. Washington is a congenial, attractive actor, and so it is especially effective to see how he shows the anger in Malcolm, the unbending dogmatic side, especially in the early Muslim years.

Lee tells his story against an epic background of settings and supporting characters (the movie is a gallery of the memorable people in Malcolm's life). Working with cinematographer Ernest Dickerson, Lee paints the early Harlem scenes in warm, sensuous colors, and then uses cold, institutional lighting for the scenes in prison. In many of the key moments in Malcolm's life as a public figure, the color photography is intercut with a black-and-white, quasi-documentary style that suggests how Malcolm's public image was being shaped and fixed.

That image, at the time of his death, was of a man widely considered racist and dogmatic—a hate-monger, some said. It is revealing that even Martin Luther King, seen in documentary footage making a statement about Malcolm's death, hardly seems overcome with grief. The liberal orthodoxy of the mid-1960s taught that racism in America could be cured by legislation, that somehow the hopeful words in the folk songs would all come true. Malcolm doubted it would be that simple.

Yet he was not the monolithic ideogogue of his public image, and one of the important achievements of Lee's film is the way he brings us along with Malcolm, so that anyone, black or white, will be able to understand the progression of his thinking. Lee's films always have an underlying fairness, an objectivity that is sometimes overlooked.

A revealing scene in *Malcolm X* shows Malcolm on the campus of Columbia University, where a young white girl tells him her heart is in the right place, and she supports his struggle. "What can I do to help?" she asks. "Nothing," Malcolm says coldly, and walks on. His single word could have been the punch line for the scene, but Lee sees more deeply, and ends the scene with the hurt on the young woman's face. There will be a time, later in Malcolm's life, when he will have a different answer to her question.

Romantic relationships are not Lee's strongest suit, but he has a warm, important one in *Malcolm X*, between Malcolm and his wife, Betty (Angela Bassett), who reminds her future husband that even revolutionary leaders must occasionally pause to eat and sleep. Her sweetness and support help him to find the gentleness that got lost in Harlem and prison.

Al Freeman, Jr., is quietly amazing as Elijah Muhammad, looking and sounding like the man himself, and walking the screenplay's tightrope between his character's importance and his flaws. Albert Hall is also

effective, as the tough Muslim leader who lectures Malcolm on his self-image, who leads him by the hand into self-awareness, and then later grows jealous of Malcolm's power within the movement. And there is a powerful two-part performance by Delroy Lindo, as West Indian Archie, the numbers czar who first impresses Malcolm with his power, and later moves him with his weakness.

Walking into *Malcolm X*, I expected an angrier film than Spike Lee has made. This film is not an assault but an explanation, and it is not exclusionary; it deliberately addresses all races in its audience. White people, going into the film, may expect to meet a Malcolm X who will attack them, but they will find a Malcolm X whose experiences and motives make him understandable and finally heroic. A reasonable viewer is likely to conclude that, having gone through similar experiences, he might also have arrived at the same place. Black viewers will not be surprised by Malcolm's experiences and the racism he lived through, but they may be surprised to find that he was less one-dimensional than his image, that he was capable of self-criticism and was developing his ideas right up until the day he died.

Spike Lee is not only one of the best filmmakers in America, but one of the most crucially important, because his films address the central subject of race. He doesn't use sentimentality or political clichés, but shows how his characters live, and why.

Empathy has been in short supply in our nation recently. Our leaders are quick to congratulate us on our own feelings, slow to ask us to wonder how others feel. But maybe times are changing. Every Lee film is an exercise in empathy. He is not interested in congratulating the black people in his audience, or condemning the white ones. He puts human beings on the screen, and asks his audience to walk a little while in their shoes.

The Mambo Kings ★ ★ ★ ½
R, 111 m., 1992

Armand Assante (Cesar Castillo), Antonio Banderas (Nestor Castillo), Cathy Moriarty (Lanna Lake), Maruschka Detmers (Delores Fuentes), Desi Arnaz, Jr. (Desi Arnaz, Sr.). Directed by Arne Glimcher and produced by Arnon Milchan and Glimcher. Screenplay by Cynthia Cidre.

The Mambo Kings tells the story of two brothers who flee from Havana in the early

1950s, arrive in New York, and dream of making themselves famous musicians. In some ways this story is as old as the movies, but *The Mambo Kings* is so filled with energy, passion, and heedless vitality that it seems new, anyway. It's the kind of movie where an opening sequence, with its shot of dancers swooning as the camera flies above them, lets you know you may not be surprised, but you are probably not going to be bored.

The film stars Armand Assante and Antonio Banderas as the Castillo brothers, musicians who are fairly well known on the local club circuit but find it prudent to leave Havana hastily after making enemies of the wrong people. In New York, they find work as meat-cutters, but dream of making it big, and there is a wonderful scene where Assante climbs up on the stage with the legendary Tito Puente and insinuates himself into a performance with sheer gall.

He's good. The boys form their own band and begin to get some bookings, while Assante falls for a brassy nightclub cigarette girl (Cathy Moriarity) and his brother begins to romance a beauty named Delores (Maruschka Detmers). There is unresolved tension between Delores and the Assante character, which the movie introduces but never really deals with, and evidence of other loose ends. The first-time director, New York art dealer Arne Glimcher, based his film on the Pulitzer Prize-winning novel *The Mambo Kings Play Songs of Love* by Oscar Hijuelos. Glimcher's screen transition, written by Cynthia Cidre, allows some weaknesses in narrative clarity, but what's more important is the enormous vitality they bring to the project. *The Mambo Kings* is energizing to watch; Michael Ballhaus's photography glows with sensuality.

One sequence that could easily have gone wrong, but doesn't, involves the Mambo Kings being discovered by Desi Arnaz, the Cuban bandleader whose TV stardom made him the hero of musicians like the Castillo brothers. One day he walks into a club, hears them, likes them, and the next thing they know they're guesting on "I Love Lucy." Arnaz is played in the movie by his son, Desi Arnaz, Jr., and through clever editing Assante and Banderas actually seem to be playing a black-and-white TV scene with the real Lucille Ball.

The plot line, involving the rise and fall of the band and the tangled romantic lives of the brothers, is not precisely original. The movie depends more on its music; the sound

track is terrific, and the ballad "Beautiful Maria of My Soul" is gloriously romantic. And it depends on the strong personalities of Assante, a greatly underrated actor who seems to specialize in ethnic characters, and Banderas, the Spanish star of several Pedro Almodóvar films. Assante, who last played a Puerto Rican drug dealer in *Q & A*, here makes a virtue of sleek machismo, and his assurance in a scene where he glides Detmers onto the dance floor is the kind of romantic scene the movies loved in the 1940s, but have been shy about in recent years.

Manhattan ★ ★ ★ ½
R, 96 m., 1979

Woody Allen (Isaac Davis), Diane Keaton (Mary Wilke), Michael Murphy (Yale), Mariel Hemingway (Tracy), Meryl Streep (Jill), Anne Byrne (Emily), Karen Ludwig (Connie), Michael O'Donoghue (Dennis). Directed by Woody Allen and produced by Charles H. Joffe. Screenplay by Allen and Marshall Brickman.

The overture is filled with brash confidence: Gershwin's "Rhapsody in Blue," played over powerful black-and-white visions of Manhattan and its skyline, and the mighty bridges leaping out to it from the provinces. The voice is filled with uncertainty and hesitation: "Chapter One. . . ."

The voice is Woody Allen's, of course, and we find ourselves laughing—actually laughing *already*—on the words "Chapter One," because the Allen character is so firmly established in our imaginations that we supply the rest of the joke ourselves. "Chapter One," yes, but Woody's the definitive vulnerable artist with giant dreams, and so of course he begins with confidence but will be mired in self-doubt long, long before Chapter Two.

A great deal of the success of Allen's *Manhattan* depends on how well he has established that Woody persona. Because we believe we know him (or the character he plays), we supply additional dimensions to the situations on the screen. A movie that might seem sketchily fleshed-out in other hands becomes a great deal more resonant in Allen's: This is a variation on a familiar theme.

And the Gershwin is a masterstroke. Woody Allen populates his film with people who are at odds with their own visions of themselves. They've been so sold, indeed, on the necessity of seeming true and grave and ethical that even their affairs, their deceptions, have to be discussed in terms of "values" and "meanings"—the dialogue in this film was

learned in psychoanalysis. Their rationalizations double back upon themselves, and then, clear as a bell on the sound track, there are the Gershwin songs. "S'Wonderful" and "Embraceable You" and "Sweet and Low Down" and "I've Got a Crush on You" . . . written as if love were *simple*, for chrissakes, and you actually could "fall" in love when we all know it's more a matter of pulling yourself up, hand over hand, out of a pit of snapping emotions. In Allen's earlier films, middle-class society was usually the contrast to the Woody character's hang-ups and fantasies. This time, brilliantly, he sets his entire story in a "real" world—and uses the music as the counterpoint. No wonder it's deliberately loud and dominating; Gershwin is the second most important person in this film.

Allen's humor has always been based on the contrast between his character ("Woody," spectacled, anemic, a slob, incredibly bright and verbal, tortured by self-doubt) and his goals (writing a great novel, being like Bogart, winning the love of beautiful women). The fact that he thinks he can achieve his dreams (or that he *pretends* he thinks he can) makes him lovable. It is amazing, for example, how many women believe they are unique because they find Woody sexy.

What Allen does in *Manhattan* is to treat both the Woody character and the goals with more realism, and to deal with them in an urban social setting we can recognize. He was already doing this in *Annie Hall*, the comedy the critics said was "really" serious—as if comedy were not already serious enough. His earlier movies were made from farce, slapstick, stand-up verbal wit, satire, and the appeal of the Woody character. *Annie Hall* and *Manhattan* are made from his observations about the way we talk and behave, and the fearsome distances between what we say and what we mean, and how we behave and how we mean to behave.

The story follows several characters through several affairs. Woody himself is twice-divorced as the movie opens—most recently from a lesbian who is writing a book that will tell all about their marriage. He is having an affair with a seventeen-year-old girl (Mariel Hemingway). His best friend, Yale (Michael Murphy), is married and is having an affair with a girl he met at a party (Diane Keaton). But Murphy has doubts about the relationship, and so subtly tries to shift Keaton to Allen, who in the meantime thinks he wants to ditch the seventeen-year-old. Inevitably, Woody and Keaton begin to fall in love, and their courtship is photographed against magnificent Manhattan backdrops. And once this is all set up, of course, it goes topsy-turvy.

The relationships aren't really the point of the movie: It's more about what people say during relationships—or, to put it more bluntly, it's about how people lie by technically telling the truth. *Manhattan* is one of the few movies that could survive a sound track of its dialogue; a lot of it, by Allen and Marshall Brickman, has the kind of convoluted intellectual cynicism of the early Nichols and May (and a lot of the rest of it consists of great one-liners).

Manhattan has been almost routinely praised by the New York critics as "better than *Annie Hall.*" I don't think so. I think it goes wrong in the very things the New York critics like the most—when, in the last forty-five minutes or so, Allen does a subtle turn on his material and gets serious about it. I'm most disturbed by the final scene between Woody and Mariel Hemingway. It's not really thought out. Allen hasn't found the line between the irony the scene needs and the sentiment he wants his character to feel. The later scenes involving the Michael Murphy character are also not as good as the early ones; the character is seen correctly for humor, but hasn't been developed completely enough to bear the burden of confession.

And yet this is a very good movie. Woody Allen is . . . Woody, sublimely. Diane Keaton gives us a fresh and nicely edged New York intellectual. And Mariel Hemingway deserves some kind of special award for what's in some ways the most difficult role in the film. It wouldn't do, you see, for the love scenes between Woody and Mariel to feel awkward or to hint at cradle-snatching or an unhealthy interest on Woody's part in innocent young girls. But they don't feel that way: Hemingway's character has a certain grave intelligence, a quietly fierce pride, that, strangely enough, suggest that even at seventeen she's one Woody should be thinking of during Gershwin's "Someone to Watch Over Me."

Note: The video version of Manhattan *was released with black bands at the top and bottom to preserve the wide-screen composition of the film. This unusual decision reflects Allen's perfectionism—and provides an eye-opening demonstration of how much is lost when other wide-screen formats are squeezed into the video frame.*

Manhattan Murder Mystery ★ ★ ★
PG, 108 m., 1993

Woody Allen (Larry Lipton), Diane Keaton (Carol Lipton), Jerry Adler (Paul House), Alan Alda (Ted), Anjelica Huston (Marcia Fox), Ron Rifkin (Sy), Joy Behar (Marilyn). Directed by Woody Allen and produced by Robert Greenhut. Screenplay by Allen and Marshall Brickman.

The man in the apartment down the hallway is so awfully nice. He has one of those deep, expansive voices, and a face that breaks naturally into a smile, and the kind of big, disorganized body that's somehow reassuring. Therefore, obviously, he must be hiding something. And when his wife dies of a heart attack, it cannot be as simple as that. There must be more to it. Something deep, dark, and ominous.

This is the way Carol's mind works. She can't help it; she was probably raised on Nancy Drew. She drives her husband nuts. He wants her to shut up and go to sleep, but all night and all day her mind is at work, threading together facts and possibilities into an obsessive theory: This nice guy has killed his wife, and unless she does something about it, he'll get away with murder.

This is the kind of plot you might expect on "Murder, She Wrote." In the hands of Woody Allen, in his comedy *Manhattan Murder Mystery*, what happens is more or less what would happen in a 1930s novel about an amateur detective. But how it happens is more or less the way it would happen in one of the *Thin Man* comedies, where Manhattanites are stacked side by side in luxury apartment buildings where the walls are just thin enough to arouse suspicions, but too thick to permit proof.

The movie stars Diane Keaton as Carol Lipton, who can put two and two together working with one two. Woody Allen plays her husband, Larry, who believes that God created neighbors to mind their own business and man should leave it that way. The neighbor, the friendly, avuncular Mr. House, is played by Jerry Adler. One day, he and his wife run into the Liptons in the hallway, and a conversation leads to an invitation to drinks. There's a warm conversation about the joys of many years of wedded bliss. The next day, Mrs. House is being carried out of her apartment feet first. Heart failure.

But that's funny, Carol Lipton frets. Mrs. House didn't *say* anything about heart problems. Larry tells her to mind her own busi-

ness. She can't. She shadows Mr. House to a movie theater, and sees him in deep conversation with a young "model type." They're talking money. Obviously, this guy murdered his wife and is going to run off with his bit of fluff on the side.

The plot of *Manhattan Murder Mystery* proceeds as if Carol not only read the Nancy Drew books, but studied them for spycraft. She sneaks into the Houses' apartment, in a scene that's structured for suspense because she might be caught there. I knew it was contrived, and that's why I liked it; Allen is playing here with the conventions of the genre, with the delicious danger of being caught flat-footed inside someone else's apartment with no alibi. The Keaton character has the courage and recklessness of the innocent. She even hides under the bed.

Both Allen and Keaton are playing clones of the characters they played in *Annie Hall*. This could be, in a way, the same couple, fifteen years down the road, still caught in the paradox of her energy and daring, and his neurotic timidity.

Their dialogue is pure Allen, and elevates the material to a sort of ironic commentary on itself. Some of the lines are as perfect as the spider as big as a Buick. This one, for example: "There's nothing wrong with you that a little Prozac and a big polo mallet wouldn't cure." Or Allen, trying to put his foot down as the man of the household when she stays up all night sorting out her theories: "I'm your husband; I'm commanding you to sleep. Sleep! I command it. I command it. Sleep! I forbid you to go. I'm forbidding." She leaves. "Is that what you do when I forbid you?"

The investigation broadens from comedy into farce when the couple enlists the help of some friends (Alan Alda and Anjelica Huston) in their would-be investigation. The Huston character, the well-named Marcia Fox, is afire with theories and strategies, and is a keen egger-on. Alda plays the best-buddy character, a fixture in many of Allen's films, and gets involved despite his qualms. The climax would make Miss Marple proud.

Allen has been called a filmmaker whose subject is Manhattan first and the world second, if at all, and certainly the situation in *Manhattan Murder Mystery* is one that any high-rise apartment dweller (like Allen himself) will naturally identify with. People who live closely together are likely to find out more about each other than they really ought to know. Sometimes there is even a sort of conspiracy of silence, in which neighbors know their secrets are mutual, and so both sides affect to notice nothing. To actually notice—worse, to pry—is a violation of the code, and it is that violation that seems to disturb the Allen character even more than possible danger. A similar situation was exploited in Allen's *Another Woman*, the film where Gena Rowlands unexpectedly began to hear the secrets of strangers through the air shaft.

Manhattan Murder Mystery is an accomplished balancing act. It is, on one level, a recycling of ancient crime formulas about nosy neighbors. On another, it's about living in the big city. On still another, it's about behavior and taboos and breaking the rules. And always with Woody fretfully convinced that it would be safer for everybody if they just stayed at home and pretended there were no neighbors; that the world was inhabited by one fearful neurotic and his crazy wife, who thankfully therefore didn't have anyone to practice on.

The Manhattan Project ★ ★ ★
PG-13, 118 m., 1986

John Lithgow (John Mathewson), Christopher Collet (Paul Stephens), Cynthia Nixon (Jenny Anderman), Jill Eikenberry (Elizabeth Stephens). Directed by Marshall Brickman and produced by Brickman and Jennifer Ogden. Screenplay by Brickman and Thomas Baum.

The kid is really smart, but like a lot of smart kids he has learned to hide it, to lay back and observe and keep his thoughts to himself. When the new scientist arrives in town and starts to date the kid's mother, and then tries to make pals by taking the kid on a tour of the research lab where he works, the kid keeps his eyes open and his mouth shut. But he knows the lab is devoted to nuclear weapons research, and he's kind of insulted that the scientist would try to deceive him.

That's the setup for *The Manhattan Project*, a clever, funny, and very skillful thriller about how the kid builds his own atomic bomb. This is not, however, another one of those teen-age movies about bright kids and science projects. There have been some good movies in that genre—I liked *WarGames* and *Real Genius*—but this isn't really a teen-age movie at all, it's a thriller. And it's one of those thrillers that stays as close as possible to the everyday lives of convincing people, so that the movie's frightening aspects are convincing.

The kid is played by Christopher Collet. He is very, very smart. We know that not just because we are told so, but because the movie has lots of subtle, sometimes funny little ways of demonstrating it—as when the kid solves a puzzle in three seconds flat, just as we were trying to understand it.

The kid lives with his mother (Jill Eikenberry) in an upstate New York college town. John Lithgow plays the scientist who moves into the town and starts to date Eikenberry and makes friends with the kid. The movie is very sophisticated about the relationship between Collet and Lithgow. This isn't a case of the two men competing for the affections of the mother; indeed, there are times when these two bright, lonely males seem to have more in common with each other.

In particular, the Lithgow character isn't allowed to fall into clichés. He isn't a mad scientist, and he isn't a heartless intellectual: He's just a smart man trying to do his job well and still have some measure of simple human pleasure.

After Collet is given his tour of the "research center," he tells his girlfriend (Cynthia Nixon) that he's a little insulted that they thought they could fool him. He knows a bomb factory when he sees one. And so, to prove various things to various people, the kid figures out a way to sneak into the plant, steal some plutonium, and build his own nuclear bomb. He wants to enter it in a New York City science fair.

I love it when movies get very detailed about clever schemes for outsmarting people. *The Manhattan Project* invites us to figure out things along with Collet, as he uses his girlfriend as a decoy and outsmarts the security guards at the plant. Inside, he has it all figured out: how to baffle the automatic alarms, how to anticipate what the guards are going to do, how to get in and out without being detected.

The long closing sequence is probably too predictable, as Lithgow and the federal authorities try to convince the kid to take his bomb out of the science fair and allow them to disarm it before he vaporizes the city. Even here, the movie doesn't depend on ordinary thriller strategies; a lot depends not only on the relationship between the kid and the scientist, but on how they think alike and share some of the same goals.

The Manhattan Project was cowritten and directed by Marshall Brickman, the sometime Woody Allen collaborator (*Annie Hall*, *Manhattan*) whose own films include *Love-*sick and *Simon*. This movie announces his arrival into the first ranks of skilled American directors. It's a *tour de force*, the way he combines everyday personality conflicts with a funny, oddball style of seeing things, and wraps up the whole package into a tense and effective thriller. It's not often that one movie contains so many different kinds of pleasures.

The Man in the Moon ★ ★ ★
PG-13, 99 m., 1991

Sam Waterston (Matthew Trant), Tess Harper (Abigail Trant), Gail Strickland (Marie Foster), Reese Witherspoon (Dani Trant), Jason London (Court Foster), Emily Warfield (Maureen Trant). Directed by Robert Mulligan and produced by Mark Rydell. Screenplay by Jenny Wingfield.

When this movie was over, I sat quietly for a moment so that I could feel the arc of its story being completed in my mind. They had done it: They had found a path all the way from the beginning to the end of this material, which is so fraught with peril, and never stepped wrong, not even at the end, when everything could have come tumbling down. *The Man in the Moon* is a wonderful movie, but it is more than that; it is a victory of tone and mood. It is like a poem.

The film takes place on a farm outside a small country town in the 1950s. Two teenage girls are being raised by parents who are strict, but who are also loving and good. One of the girls, Dani, is fourteen years old and has just passed uncertainly into young womanhood. Her sister, Maureen, is about seventeen. On hot summer nights they sleep on the screened-in porch and have girl talks, and Dani laments that she will never be as beautiful and popular as her sister. Of course, all kid sisters feel that way.

A widow moves onto the farm next door with her son, Court, who is about seventeen. One day he happens upon Dani down at the swimming hole. They fight at first, but then they make up and become friends. Dani, of course, develops an enormous crush on this boy, and for a day or two he seems to feel the same emotions she does. Dani asks Maureen how to kiss, and Maureen gives her lessons. She "practices" on her hand. Then Court kisses her, and she confesses it was the first time she has ever been kissed by a boy. "How was it?" he asks. "Perfect," she says.

The moment is perfect, too, but there is an even better one when she tells him, "I want to know what your hopes are." This isn't just a movie about teen-age romance; it's a movie about idealism—about how we idealize what and who we love—and a movie about the meaning of life. Yes, the Meaning of Life, which is a topic teen-agers discuss a good deal as their insides churn with hope and doubt, and which adults discuss less and less, the more they could benefit from it.

The way the scenes between Dani and Court are handled is typical of the entire movie, which takes material we may have seen many times before and makes it true and fresh. Maybe it is because of the acting—Reese Witherspoon as Dani and Jason London as Court do justice to the slightest nuance of the scene. Maybe it is the direction, by Robert Mulligan, whose long career includes another fine movie about a young girl, *To Kill a Mockingbird*. Or maybe it is because everyone involved with the film knew that the script, by Jenny Wingfield, was not going to sell out at the end, was not going to contrive an artificial ending, or go for false sentiment, or do anything other than exactly what the material cries out for.

There are some complications surrounding that "perfect" kiss. One of them is that the girls' mother (Tess Harper) is in the last weeks of pregnancy. Another is that the older sister has just had a particularly nasty date with a crude local boy. Another is that their father (Sam Waterston) is fairly strict—not because he is mean, but because he loves them. Another, inevitably and painfully, is that when Court sees the older girl, he forgets about the kid sister with whom he shared the perfect kiss. Life is so direct sometimes in the way it hurts us—and the younger we are, the more universal the hurt.

Now something happens in the story that I cannot tell. It must catch you unprepared. And then the magnificent concluding passages of this film are about how deeply one can be hurt, how hard it is to forgive, how impossible it is to share the deepest feelings. *The Man in the Moon* is like a great short story, one of those masterpieces of language and mood where not one word is wrong or unnecessary. It flows so smoothly from start to finish that it hardly even seems like an ordinary film. Usually I am aware of the screenwriter putting in obligatory scenes. I can hear the machinery grinding. Not this time. Although, in retrospect, I can see how carefully the plot was put together, how meticulously each event was prepared for, as I watched the film I was only aware of life passing by.

Of the performances, it is enough to say that each one creates a character that could not be improved on. Tess Harper and Sam Waterston are convincing parents here; they aren't simply stick figures in a plot, used only to move events along, but people we believe could really have raised these girls. There is a moment when Waterston hugs his youngest girl, and the way it arrives and the way it plays are heartbreakingly touching. There is a moment when Harper intuits something about her older girl, and the way she acts on her intuition is so tactful we feel she is giving the girl a lesson on how to be a mother. And Gail Strickland, as the boy's mother, creates moments that are as difficult as they are true.

Then there are the two sisters, Reese Witherspoon and Emily Warfield. Like all sisters of about the same age, they share almost all of their secrets, but the ones they cannot share are the ones that hurt deeply. Their intimate moments together—talking about boys, about growing up—have a special intimacy. But the silences and the hurt body language of some of their later scenes speak of an intimacy betrayed, and are even more special. There is a scene where Court comes over and is asked to stay for dinner, and the way he has eyes only for Maureen—he all but ignores Dani—reflects, we remember, exactly the cruel and thoughtless ways that teen-agers deal with affairs of the heart.

Robert Mulligan is a director whose titles range from *Inside Daisy Clover* to *Blood Brothers* to *The Other*. He made *Summer of '42*, also a story of the intensity of young love, and his *Same Time, Next Year* and *Clara's Heart* were also, in a way, about how time and age affect romance. Although his work is uneven, he has always been a serious and sincere artist—both in the early days of the partnership with Alan J. Pakula that produced *Mockingbird*, and since.

Nothing else he has done, however, approaches the purity and perfection of *The Man in the Moon*. As the film arrived at its conclusion without having stepped wrong once, I wondered whether he could do it—whether he could maintain the poetic, bittersweet tone, and avoid the sentimentalism and cheap emotion that could have destroyed this story. Would he maintain the integrity of this material? He would, and he does.

Man of Iron ★ ★ ★ ★
NO MPAA RATING, 140 m., 1980

Jerzy Radziwilowicz (Tomczyk), Krystyna Janda (Agnieszka), Marian Opania (Winkiel), Lech Walesa (As himself). Directed by Andrzej Wajda. Screenplay by Aleksander Scibor-Rylski.

As a youth of thirteen, the Polish filmmaker Andrzej Wajda lived in a small town where he witnessed German troops lead thousands of Polish army officers to their deaths in concentration camps. As a young student after the war, he lived through the repressive Stalinist years. In the 1950s he made his first films, betraying a spirit that the Party ideologues found too individualistic for their taste. In a speech in 1981 at American University in Washington, D.C., he quoted from "the best review I've ever had." It was from a confidential 1976 Polish censor's report:

. . . politically and ideologically he is not on our side. He has taken the position, often found among artists, of a "neutral judge" of history and today's times—believing that he has the right . . . to apply the gauge of humanism and morals to all the problems of the world and that he doesn't need Marxism nor any other philosophical-social system to do it.

Wajda is at it again, judging history, applying the gauge of humanism, not requiring Marxism, in *Man of Iron*, his extraordinary film about the birth of the Polish Solidarity labor movement. This film is a marriage between a fictional story and actual events, and Wajda took his cameras and his actors right into the firestorm of the Gdansk demonstrations to record the victorious Solidarity agreement at the Lenin Shipyard.

Wajda is in a strange position in Poland. He and Krystof Zanussi are the only two Polish directors still in Poland who have international reputations. He is honored all over the world, but at home the authorities are a little reluctant to give him his head; his films do not promote domestic tranquility.

Man of Iron, filmed during the tumultuous days of relative freedom when Solidarity seemed to hold all the cards, was permitted to be flown out of Warsaw during the closing days of the 1981 Cannes Film Festival, where it won the Grand Prize.

It's a sequel of sorts to Wajda's *Man of Marble* (1976), although you needn't have seen the earlier film, which was about a labor leader during the years of repressive policies in Poland. This film is about the same man's son, who is a Solidarity leader a few steps down in influence from Lech Walesa. Wajda follows his fictional characters into the center of real events (it's sometimes hard to tell where fiction ends and documentary begins), and he uses a broadcast newsman as an interviewer—a technique that allows his film to go places and ask questions that would be difficult to cover in "pure" fiction.

Exactly the same two techniques—the use of a character who is a journalist, and the juxtaposition of a fictional story with actual events—were used by Haskell Wexler in *Medium Cool,* the film about the 1968 Democratic convention demonstrations in Chicago. The approach leaves some ragged edges, but when you are filming at the cutting edge of history you can't stop for rewrites.

Wajda's film is not a polemic, however. That humanist streak, complained of by the state censors, sneaks through even at the expense of the Solidarity politics he wants to celebrate. Wajda is an artist first, a reporter second or third, and not really a very good propagandist. And the best things in *Man of Iron* are the purely personal moments, the scenes where Wajda is concerned with the human dimensions of his characters rather than their ideological struggles.

Those dimensions come through most clearly in the character of Winkiel (Marian Opania), the alcoholic journalist who is sent by the party bosses in Warsaw to spy on Solidarity in the guise of a radio reporter. Winkiel had his own values once. Meeting the son of the old labor leader, he remembers the father. Arriving in Gdansk, Winkiel discovers to his horror that the area has been declared dry because of the troubles—he can't get booze. A party agent slips him a bottle of vodka, but Winkiel breaks it on the bathroom floor, and in a scene that will profoundly affect the way we understand his later actions, he desperately tries to soak up some of the vodka with a towel. He is a man whose spirit is broken, a man prepared to be a spy. The most moving of the several stories in *Man of Iron* concerns his gradual rediscovery of his old values, until he finally decides to side with the workers and to abandon his undercover role.

Man of Iron is a fascinating and courageous document—a film of dissent made because of, or in spite of, the upheaval in Poland.

In that speech in 1981, Wajda closed with these words: *Someone once asked me a naive question. It's a question often asked of very old writers: Do you feel that you've helped to make history? My answer is this. I don't know whether I helped make it. I know I didn't stand with my hands folded. I didn't look on indifferently as history was being made.*

Manon of the Spring ★ ★ ★ ★
PG, 113 m., 1987
(See also *Jean de Florette*)

Yves Montand (Cesar Soubeyran), Daniel Auteuil (Ugolin), Emmanuelle Beart (Manon), Hippolyte Girardot (Schoolteacher), Elisabeth Depardieu (Aimee), Gabriel Bacquier (Victor). Directed by by Claude Berri and produced by Pierre Grunstein. Screenplay by Berri and Gerard Brach.

There is something to be said for a long story that unfolds with an inexorable justice. In recent movies, we've become accustomed to stories that explode into dozens of tiny, dim-witted pieces of action, all unrelated to each other. Cars hurtle through the air, victims are peppered with gunshot holes, heroes spit out clever one-liners, and at the end of it all, what are we left with? Our hands close on empty air.

Manon of the Spring, which is the conclusion of the story that began with *Jean de Florette,* is the opposite kind of movie. It moves with a majestic pacing over the affairs of four generations, demonstrating that the sins of the fathers are visited upon the children. Although *Manon* is self-contained and can be understood without having seen *Jean de Florette,* the full impact of this work depends on seeing the whole story, right from the beginning; only then does the ending have its full force.

In the first part of the story, as you may recall, a young hunchbacked man from Paris (Gerard Depardieu) came with his wife and daughter to farm some land he had inherited in a rural section of France. The locals did not greet him kindly, and one of the local patriarchs (Yves Montand) sabotaged his efforts by blocking the spring that fed his land. The young man worked morning to night to haul water for his goats and the rabbits he wished to raise, but in the end the effort killed him. Montand and his worthless nephew (Daniel Auteuil) were then able to buy the land cheaply.

Montand's plot against the hunchback was incredibly cruel, but the movie was at pains to explain that Montand was not gratuitously evil. His most important values centered around the continuity of land and family, and in his mind, his plot against Depardieu was justified by the need to defend the land against an "outsider." As *Manon of the Spring* opens, some years later, the unmarried and childless Montand is encouraging his nephew to find a woman and marry, so the family name can be continued.

The nephew already has a bride in mind: the beautiful Manon (Emmanuelle Beart), daughter of the dead man, who tends goats on the mountainside and lives in poverty, although she has received a good education. Unfortunately for the nephew, he has a rival for her affections in the local schoolteacher. As the story unfolds, Manon discovers by accident that the nephew and his uncle blocked her father's spring—and when she accidentally discovers the source of the water for the whole village, she has her revenge by cutting off the water of those who killed her father.

All of this takes place with the implacable pace of a Greek tragedy. It sounds more melodramatic than it is, because the events themselves are not the issue here—the director, Claude Berri, has a larger point he wants to make, involving poetic justice on a scale that spans the generations. There are surprises at the end of this film that I do not choose to reveal, but they bring the whole story full circle, and Montand finally receives a punishment that is perfectly, even cruelly, suited to his crime.

Apart from its other qualities, *Manon of the Spring* announces the arrival of a strong and beautiful new actress from France in Emmanuelle Beart. Already seen in *Date With an Angel,* a comedy in which she supplied the only redeeming virtue, she is very effective in this central role, this time as a sort of avenging angel who punishes the old man and his nephew by giving them a glimpse of what could have been for them, had they not been so cruel.

The Man Who Would Be King
★ ★ ★ ★
PG, 129 m., 1975

Sean Connery (Daniel Dravot), Michael Caine (Peachy Carnahan), Christopher Plummer (Kipling), Saeed Jaffrey (Billy Fish), Shakira Caine (Roxanne). Directed by John Huston and produced by John Foreman. Screenplay by Huston and Gladys Hill.

John Huston's *The Man Who Would Be King* is swashbuckling adventure, pure and simple, from the hand of a master. It's unabashed and thrilling and fun. The movie invites comparison with the great action films like *Gunga Din* and *Mutiny on the Bounty,* and with Huston's own classic *The Treasure of the Sierre Madre:* We get strong characterizations, we get excitement, we even get to laugh every once in a while.

The action epics of the last twenty years seem to have lost their sense of humor; it's as if once the budget goes over five million dollars, directors think they have to be deadly serious. *Lawrence of Arabia* was a great movie, but introspective and solemn, and efforts such as *Doctor Zhivago* and *War and Peace* never dared to smile. Huston's movie isn't like that. It reflects his personality and his own best films; it's open, sweeping, and lusty—and we walk out feeling exhilarated.

Huston waited a long time to make this film, and its history is a Hollywood legend. He originally cast Bogart and Gable, but then Bogart died, and the project was shelved until 1975. Maybe it's just as well. We need movies like this more now than we did years ago, when Hollywood wasn't shy about straightforward action films. And Huston's eventual casting of Michael Caine and Sean Connery is exactly right.

They work together so well, they interact so easily and with such camaraderie, that watching them is a pleasure. They never allow themselves to be used merely as larger-than-life heroes, photographed against vast landscapes. Kipling's story, and Huston's interpretation of it, requires a lot more than that; it requires acting of a subtle and difficult sort, even if the sheer energy of the movie makes it look easy.

The two of them play former British soldiers who vow to march off into Afghanistan or somewhere and find a kingdom not yet touched by civilization. With their guns and training, they think they'll be able to take over pretty easily, manipulate the local high priests, and set themselves up as rulers. They tell their plan to an obscure colonial editor named Kipling (played very nicely by Christopher Plummer) and then they set off into the mountains. After the obligatory close calls, including an avalanche that somehow saves their lives, they find their lost land and it's just as they expected it would be.

The natives aren't too excited by their new rulers at first, but a lucky Masonic key chain saves the day—never mind how—and Connery finds himself worshiped as a deity. He even gets to like it, and condescends to Caine, who remains a Cockney and unimpressed. The movie proceeds with impossible coincidences, untold riches, romances and betrayals, and heroic last words and—

best of all—some genuinely witty scenes between Connery and Caine, and when it's over we haven't learned a single thing worth knowing and there's not even a moral, to speak of, but we've had fun. It's great that someone still has the gift of making movies like this; even Huston, after thirty years, must have wondered whether he still knew how.

The Man Without a Face ★ ★ ★
PG-13, 114 m., 1993

Mel Gibson (McLeod), Margaret Whitton (Catherine), Fay Masterson (Gloria), Gaby Hoffmann (Megan), Geoffrey Lewis (Chief Stark), Richard Masur (Carl), Nick Stahl (Chuck). Directed by Mel Gibson and produced by Bruce Davey. Screenplay by Malcolm MacRury.

The most striking element in Mel Gibson's *The Man Without a Face* is the intelligence of the language. Listening to the people talk in this movie, I was made aware that many American movies play dumb; they have their characters talk in a simplified way, and so of course they have to think that way, too. How many modern movie characters are allowed to be as smart as the average audience member?

In the movie, Gibson plays McLeod, a character of great complexity, a former teacher, his face and body horribly burnt in an automobile accident, who lives alone in a big house on an island off Maine, and supports himself as a freelance illustrator. To the island's inhabitants and summer people, he is "Hammerhead" and other cruel nicknames. Because he stays so resolutely to himself, rumors circulate about him. He killed his wife, some say. Others say it was a young boy. He did time in prison.

To his house one day comes a young adolescent named Chuck (Nick Stahl), who wants to go to a prep school and asks McLeod to be his tutor. At first McLeod is distant and abrupt with him. He sets him meaningless tasks: "Right here, I want a hole dug. Three feet, cubic." He has him write essays. Eventually McLeod relaxes around the boy, and they become friends.

Chuck comes from a disorganized background. His mother (Margaret Whitton) has had three children, each by a different husband, and is working on a potential new spouse, known to Chuck as "the Hairball." Chuck is often at war with his older and younger sisters, and sometimes with his

mother, too, but the movie avoids the clichés of the "unhappy home" and shows that the family is no more dysfunctional, alas, than many others.

It's society that's dysfunctional, viewing with suspicion any friendship between a solitary older man and a young boy—especially because of the disturbing rumors about the man's past, and the circumstances of his injury. Eventually the local police chief (Geoffrey Lewis) steps in, among fears that molestation has taken place. And Chuck is threatened with the loss of his teacher and friend.

Here is what I mean about the movie not being willfully dumb. Given this setup, nine out of ten Hollywood movies would cut straight to some kind of contrived courtroom scene, in which good and evil would come swinging out of their appropriate corners and the movie would end like all courtroom dramas. *The Man Without a Face* cares too much about its theme to use formula shortcuts. And its theme is not molestation, or guilt and innocence, but trust—trust, and the way a good teacher must allow a good student to figure things out on his own.

The movie is Gibson's debut as a director, and shows him not only with a good visual sense, but with what is even rarer, the confidence to know what needs to be told and what can be left unsaid. The mystery of his character's past, for example, is left deliberately unclear, so that when the boy confronts him near the end of the film, the teacher can give him an important lesson: We must be willing to decide the truth for ourselves, based on what we believe and have experienced, instead of allowing others to do it for us.

One of the special qualities of the film is the performance by Nick Stahl, as the boy. The screenplay by Malcolm MacRury, based on the novel by Isabelle Holland, makes him into a smart, bold kid—one with enough self-confidence that we can guess he'll turn out well in life.

His early meetings with McLeod are interesting because he stands up to this apparently fearsome man, speaks firmly, lets him know what's on his mind. Stahl is much more interesting than most actors his age, because he knows what many actors never learn, how to do no more than necessary. He doesn't believe that his face has to mirror every emotion; he takes a no-nonsense approach to the material that's fresh and interesting.

Gibson's performance is interesting as a

reminder of his versatility; not many actors can fit comfortably in both *Lethal Weapon* and *Hamlet,* and here he finds just the right note for McLeod: not a caricature, not a softy, not pathetic, but fiercely sure of what is right and wrong. There are times in the movie where McLeod could make things easy for himself simply by saying things that his pride and ethics will not let him say. He does not say them. That is admirable, but even more admirable is that Gibson, as director, doesn't give himself a soppy speech explaining why he doesn't say them. He lets us figure it out. That is the essence of the story and, we eventually realize, the essence of teaching, too.

Map of the Human Heart ★ ★ ★

R, 95 m., 1993

Jason Scott Lee (Avik), Robert Joamie (Young Avik), Anne Parillaud (Albertine), Annie Galipeau (Young Albertine), Patrick Bergin (Walter Russell), Clotilde Courau (Rainee Russell), John Cusack (Clark), Jeanne Moreau (Sister Banville). Directed by Vincent Ward and produced by Tim Bevan and Ward. Screenplay by Louis Nowra.

Map of the Human Heart tells a soaring story of human adventure—adventure of the best kind, based not on violence, but on an amazing personal journey. It is incredible sometimes what distances can be traveled in a single human life, and this is a movie about a man who could not have imagined his end in his beginning.

The story begins in the 1930s in the Arctic north, where a young Eskimo boy is fascinated by the mapmaking activities of a visiting British cartographer named Russell (Patrick Bergin). The boy is named Avik (played as a boy by Robert Joamie, and as a man by Jason Scott Lee). Because Avik says "Holy Boy!" when he means "Holy Cow!" he comes to be known as Holy Boy in the movie.

The mapmaker arrives at the Eskimo settlement by airplane, an astonishing sight, and when he leaves he takes the boy with him—because Avik has tuberculosis, and can be treated in Montreal. The city itself is an unbelievable sight for Avik, who did not imagine such places existed. And in the hospital, he makes a lifelong friend—Albertine, played as a girl by Annie Galipeau and later, as a woman, by Anne Parillaud (from *La Femme Nikita*).

She is half-Indian, half-white. Avik is half-Eskimo, half-white. And the movie shows

them standing halfway between their two worlds. For Avik, the meeting with Russell will change his life forever, setting in motion a chain of events that eventually leads to Britain during World War II, where Avik becomes an aerial photographer on bombing missions against Germany. And it is in England that he meets Albertine once again—only to find that she is involved with Russell.

This sort of romantic triangle could easily have collapsed into soapy melodrama, but Vincent Ward is too intelligent to go for the obvious treatment of this story. He doesn't allow his characters cheap sentiment, and indeed as Avik and Albertine renew their love from so long ago, we see two of the most astonishing romantic scenes I've ever seen in a movie—one on top of a barrage balloon, the other inside the hollow ceiling of the Royal Albert Hall.

The entire story of Avik is told in flashback. The movie begins in the present, with a new mapmaker (John Cusack) visiting the Eskimo village, where Avik, now an old man, tells him his story. The device at first seems unnecessary, but by the end of the film, as we see how Ward uses it to come full circle, it becomes a strength.

Ward is a young New Zealander whose previous film was also strange and original. *Navigator* (1988) was about medieval adventurers in the time of the plague, who begin to tunnel to what a mystic tells them is salvation, and somehow find their way through a time warp into a modern city—where they begin to climb the spires of a cathedral.

Oddly enough, this theme is very similar to *Map of the Human Heart,* where once again the hero flees disease and finds his destiny in a modern city. Where *Navigator* was sometimes bleak and obtuse, however, *Map of the Human Heart* is a juicier, more involving film.

Much of its power comes from the charisma of the actors. Jason Scott Lee, a newcomer who also stars in *Dragon: The Bruce Lee Story,* brings a joy and freshness to the early scenes, and makes a good contrast to the older Avik, who has lost his way. Anne Parillaud, once again, as in *La Femme Nikita,* is a combination of warmth and steely courage, and she is best in those scenes where she feels empathy for Avik, so far from home. And Patrick Bergin handles a difficult role with delicacy; he is not precisely the villain, and in some ways is a hero in this story, but when the heart is involved all motives can grow murky.

Robert Joamie and Annie Galipeau, the actors who play the young characters, also have special qualities. When Avik and Albertine become friends in the hospital, for example, there is a magical scene, played in a tent made of bed sheets, in which they exchange their deepest secrets. And when Avik leaves the hospital, he takes with him an odd photograph—Albertine's X rays, which will figure throughout the film. It almost makes sense, later, that they communicate through notes on aerial photographs, which Avik takes and Albertine catalogs, and that in turn is the link that leads to an extraordinary scene involving the fire-bombing of Dresden.

One of the best qualities of *Map of the Human Heart* was that I never quite knew where it was going. It is a love story, a war story, a lifetime story, but it manages to traverse all of that familiar terrain without doing the anticipated. The screenplay, by Louis Nowra, based on a story by Ward, deals with familiar emotions but not in a familiar way. The best movies seem to reinvent themselves as they move along, not drawing from worn-out sources, and *Map of the Human Heart* is one of 1993's best films.

The Marriage of Maria Braun
★ ★ ★ ★

R, 120 m., 1979

Hanna Schygulla (Maria Braun), Klaus Lowitsch (Hermann Braun), Ivan Desny (Oswald), Gottfried John (Willi), Gisela Uhlen (Mother), R.W. Fassbinder (Peddler). Directed and produced by Rainer Werner Fassbinder. Screenplay by Peter Marthescheimer and Pea Frohlicj.

Rainer Werner Fassbinder had been working his way toward this film for years, ever since he began his astonishingly prodigious output with his first awkward but powerful films in 1969. His films were always about sex, money, and death, and his method was often to explore those three subjects through spectacularly incompatible couples (an elderly cleaning woman and a young black worker, a James Dean look-alike and a thirteen-year-old girl, a rich gay about town and a simpleminded young sweepstakes winner).

Whatever his pairings and his cheerfully ironic conclusions, though, there was always another subject lurking in the background of his approximately thirty-three (!) features. He gave us what he saw as the rise and second fall of West Germany in the three postwar decades—considered in the context of the overwhelming American influence on his country.

With the masterful epic *The Marriage of Maria Braun,* he made his clearest and most cynical statement of the theme, and at the same time gave us a movie dripping with period detail, with the costumes and decor he was famous for, with the elegant decadence his characters will sell their souls for in a late-1940s economy without chic retail goods.

Fassbinder's film begins with a Germany torn by war and ends with a gas explosion and a soccer game. His ending may seem arbitrary to some, but in the context of West German society in the 1970s it may only be good reporting. His central character, Maria Braun, is played with great style and power by Hanna Schygulla, and Maria's odyssey from the war years to the consumer years provides the film's framework.

The film opens as Maria marries a young soldier, who then goes off to battle and presumably is killed. It follows her during a long period of mourning, which is punctuated by a little amateur hooking (of which her mother tacitly approves) and then by a tender and very carefully observed liaison with a large, strong, gentle black American soldier whom she really likes—we guess.

The soldier's accidental death, and her husband's return, are weathered by Maria with rather disturbing aplomb, but then we begin to see that Maria's ability to feel has been atrophied by the war, and her ability to be surprised has withered away. If war makes any plans absolutely meaningless, then why should one waste time analyzing coincidences?

Fassbinder has some rather bitter fun with what happens in the aftermath of the soldier's death (the lovestruck, or perhaps just shellshocked, husband voluntarily goes to prison, and Maria rises quickly in a multinational corporation). The movie is more realistic in its treatment of characters than Fassbinder sometimes is, but the events are as arbitrary as ever (and why not—events only have the meanings we assign to them, anyway).

The mini-apocalypse at the end is a perfect conclusion (an ending with "meaning" would have been obscene for this film) and then I think we are left, if we want it, with the sum of what Fassbinder has to say about the rebuilding of Germany: We got the stores opened again, but we don't know much about the customers yet.

Mary Shelley's Frankenstein ★ ★ ½   NEW
R, 128 m., 1994

Robert De Niro (Creature), Kenneth Branagh (Victor), Tom Hulce (Henry), Helena Bonham Carter (Elizabeth), Aidan Quinn (Walton), Ian Holm (Victor's Father), Richard Briers (Grandfather), John Cleese (Professor Waldman). Directed by Kenneth Branagh and produced by Francis Ford Coppola, James V. Hart, and John Veitch. Screenplay by Steph Lady and Frank Darabont.

The monster has always been the true subject of the Frankenstein story, and Kenneth Branagh's new retelling understands that. *Mary Shelley's Frankenstein* has all of the usual props of the Frankenstein films, brought to a fever pitch: the dark and stormy nights, the lightning bolts, the charnel houses of spare body parts, the laboratory where Victor Frankenstein stirs his steaming cauldron of life. But the center of the film, quieter and more thoughtful, contains the real story.

The Creature (Robert De Niro) has escaped his captivity and wandered into a pastoral setting where a little family lives peacefully. It is cold, and he creeps into the barn, feeding from the same trough as the pigs, and looking longingly through the window to the peaceful scene around the hearth. In the night he prepares firewood for his unwitting hosts. The family gradually becomes aware that some sort of forest spirit is befriending them—and the old grandfather, who is blind, actually invites the Creature in to sit by the fire.

This Creature, more than those in any of the earlier films, is acutely aware that in appearance he is a hideous monster. He also knows more about his origins. He reads Frankenstein's original journal, and learns how he was constructed from parts of dead bodies. And he is thoughtful: "Yes, I speak, and read, and think, and know the ways of man," he says, with an echo of Caliban. And he asks, "What of my soul? Do I have one? What of these people of which I am composed?"

The whole issue of the Branagh film is concentrated here: Has Frankenstein created a monster, or a man? De Niro brings a real pathos to the role, and there is agony when he asks the scientist, "Did you ever consider the consequences of your actions?" And his loneliness is palpable: "For the sympathy of one living being I would make peace with all."

But the film surrounding these scenes is less satisfactory. Branagh has always been a director cheerfully willing to shoot for the moon, to pump up his scenes with melodrama and hyperbole, and usually I enjoy that (as in *Dead Again* and *Henry V*). Here, however, faced with material that *begins* as lurid melodrama, he goes over the top.

The movie is bracketed with an unnecessary prologue and epilogue, taken from the original novel, during which an Arctic expedition encounters Frankenstein and his monster wandering far from home on the frozen wastes. Presumably this material is there to allow the headstrong explorer (Aidan Quinn) to learn from Frankenstein the hazards of indulging one's will. But that's a point the movie has already made.

The story leading up to Frankenstein's desire to create life involves his love affair with Elizabeth (Helena Bonham Carter), his sister by adoption. Carter continues to blossom as a passionate English rose, and Branagh, as Frankenstein, is convincingly obsessed with her (they kiss as the camera whirls around them like a homage to *Vertigo*). But as a blood-soaked Caesarean birth is accompanied by lightning bolts pulverizing trees, we begin to wish Branagh would turn the volume down. (One sequence I did like involved the harnessing of lightning to give the Creature life; it's inspired by the 1935 *Bride of Frankenstein*.)

I admired the scenes with De Niro so much I'm tempted to give *Mary Shelley's Frankenstein* a favorable verdict. But it's a near miss. The Creature is on target, but the rest of the film is so frantic, so manic, it doesn't pause to be sure its effects are registered.

M*A*S*H ★ ★ ★ ★
R, 116 m., 1970

Donald Sutherland (Hawkeye), Elliott Gould (Trapper John), Tom Skerritt (Duke), Sally Kellerman (Hot Lips Hoolihan), Robert Duvall (Major Burns), Jo Ann Pflug (Lieutenant Dish), Rene Auberjonois (Dago Red). Directed by Robert Altman and produced by Ingo Preminger. Screenplay by Ring Lardner, Jr.

One of the reasons *M*A*S*H* is so funny is that it's so desperate. It is set in a surgical hospital just behind the front lines in Korea, and it is drenched in blood. The surgeons work rapidly and with a gory detachment, sawing off legs and tying up arteries, and making their work possible by pretending they don't care. And when they are at last out of the operating tent, they devote their lives to remaining sane. The way they do that, in *M*A*S*H*, is to be almost metaphysically cruel. There is something about war that inspires practical jokes and the heroes (Donald Sutherland, Elliott Gould, and cronies) are inspired and utterly heartless. They sneak a microphone under the bed of Major "Hot Lips" Hoolihan, and broadcast her lovemaking to the entire camp. They drug a general and photograph him in a brothel.

We laugh, not because *M*A*S*H* is Sgt. Bilko for adults, but because it is so true to the unadmitted sadist in all of us. There is perhaps nothing so exquisite as achieving (as the country song has it) sweet mental revenge against someone we hate with particular dedication. And it is the flat-out, poker-faced hatred in *M*A*S*H* that makes it work. Most comedies want us to laugh at things that aren't really funny; in this one we laugh precisely because they're not funny. We laugh, that we may not cry.

But none of this philosophy comes close to the insane logic of *M*A*S*H*, which is achieved through a peculiar marriage of cinematography, acting, directing, and writing. The movie depends upon timing and tone to be funny. I had an opportunity to read the original script, and I found it uninteresting. It would have been a failure, if it had been directed like most comedies; but Ring Lardner, Jr., wrote it, I suspect, for exactly the approach Robert Altman used in his direction, and so the angle of a glance or the timing of a pause is funnier than any number of conventional gag lines. This is true, for example, in the football game between the surgeons and the general's team. The movie assumes, first of all, that we are intimate with the rules of football. We are. The game then becomes doubly funny, not just because the *M*A*S*H* boys have recruited a former pro as a ringer for their side, but because their victory depends upon legal cheating (how about a center-eligible play?). The audience's laughter is triumphant, because our guys have outsmarted the other guys. Another movie might have gone for purely physical humor in the scene (big guy walks over little guy, etc.) and blown it.

The performances have a lot to do with the movie's success. Elliott Gould and Donald Sutherland are two genuinely funny actors; they don't have to make themselves ridiculous to get a laugh. They're funny because their humor comes so directly from their personalities. They underplay everything (and Sutherland and Gould trying to

downstage each other could eventually lead to complete paralysis).

Strangely enough, they're convincing as surgeons. During operations, covered with blood and gore, they mutter their way through running commentaries that sound totally professional. Sawing and hacking away at a parade of bodies, they should be driving us away, but they don't. We can take the unusually high gore-level in *M*A*S*H* because it is originally part of the movie's logic. If the surgeons didn't have to face the daily list of maimed and mutilated bodies, none of the rest of their lives would make any sense. When they are matter-of-factly cruel to "Hot Lips" Hoolihan, we cannot quite separate that from the matter-of-fact way they've got to put wounded bodies back together again. "Hot Lips," who is all Army professionalism and objectivity, is less human because the suffering doesn't reach her.

I think perhaps that's what the movie is about. Gould and Sutherland and the members of their merry band of pranksters are offended because the Army regulars don't feel deeply enough. "Hot Lips" is concerned with protocol, but not with war. And so the surgeons, dancing on the brink of crack-ups, dedicate themselves to making her *feel* something. Her façade offends them; no one could be unaffected by the work of this hospital, but she is. And so if they can crack her defenses and reduce her to their own level of dedicated cynicism, the number of suffering human beings in the camp will go up by one. And even if they fail, they can have a hell of a lot of fun trying. Also, of course, it's a distraction.

Mask ★ ★ ★ ½
PG-13, 120 m., 1985

Cher (Rusty Dennis), Eric Stoltz (Rocky Dennis), Sam Elliott (Gar), Estelle Getty (Evelyn), Richard Dysart (Abe), Laura Dern (Diana). Directed by Peter Bogdanovich and produced by Martin Starger. Screenplay by Anna Hamilton Phelan.

When we see him for the first time, it's a glimpse through his bedroom window, half-reflected in a mirror. A second later, we see him more clearly, this teen-age boy with the strange face. We are shocked for a second, until he starts to talk, and then, without effort, we accept him as a normal kid who has had an abnormal thing happen to him. The name of his disease is craniodiaphyseal dyaplasia, and it causes calcium deposits on his skull that force his face out of shape.

"What's the matter?" he likes to ask. "You never seen anyone from the planet Vulcan before?"

The kid's name is Rocky Dennis, and his mother is named Rusty. She is not your normal mom, either. She rides with a motorcycle gang, abuses drugs, shacks up with gang members, and has no visible means of employment. But within about ten minutes, we know that she is the ideal mom for Rocky. That's in the scene where the school principal suggests that Rocky would be better off in a "special" school, and she tells the principal he is a jerk, her son is a good student with good grades, and here is the name of her lawyer.

Movies don't often grab us as quickly as *Mask* does. The story of Rocky and Rusty is absorbing from the very first, maybe because the movie doesn't waste a lot of time wringing its hands over Rocky's fate. *Mask* lands on its feet, running. The director, Peter Bogdanovich, moves directly to the center of Rocky's life—his mother, his baseball cards, his cocky bravado, his growing awareness of girls. Bogdanovich handles *Mask* a lot differently than a made-for-TV movie would have, with TV's disease-of-the-week approach. This isn't the story of a disease, but the story of some people. And the most extraordinary person in the movie, surprisingly, is not Rocky, but his mother. Rusty Dennis is played by Cher as a complicated, angry, high-energy woman with a great capacity to love her son and encourage him to live as fully as he can. Rocky is a great kid, but because he succeeds so well at being a teen-ager, he is not a special case like, say, the Elephant Man. He is a kid with a handicap. It is a tribute to Eric Stoltz, who plays the role beneath the completely convincing makeup of Michael Westmore, that we accept him on his own terms.

Cher, on the other hand, makes Rusty Dennis into one of the most interesting movie characters in a long time. She is up front about her lifestyle, and when her son protests about her drinking and drugging, she tells him to butt out of her business. She rides with the motorcycle gang, but is growing unhappy with her promiscuity, and is relieved when the guy she really loves (Sam Elliott) comes back from a trip and moves in. She is also finally able to clean up her act, and stop drinking and using, after Rocky asks her to; she loves him that much.

Mask is based on a true story, and that doesn't come as a surprise: Hollywood wouldn't have the nerve to make a fictional tearjerker like this. The emotional peak of the movie comes during a summer that Rocky spends as an assistant at a camp for the blind. He falls in love with a blind teenager (Laura Dern), who feels his face and says he looks all right to her, and they have some of that special time together that only teen-agers can have: time when love doesn't mean sex so much as it means perfect agreement on the really important issues, like Truth and Beauty. Then the girl's parents come to pick her up, and their reaction to Rocky comes as a shock to us, a reminder of how completely we had accepted him.

Mask is a wonderful movie, a story of high spirits and hope and courage. It has some songs in it, by Bob Seger, and there was a lot of publicity about the fact that Peter Bogdanovich would rather the songs were by Bruce Springsteen. Let me put it this way: This is a movie that doesn't depend on its sound track. It works because of the people it's about, not because of the music they listen to.

The Mask ★ ★ ★
PG-13, 100 m., 1994

NEW

Jim Carrey (Stanley Ipkiss), Cameron Diaz (Tina Carlyle), Richard Jeni (Charlie Schumacher), Peter Riegert (Lieutenant Kellaway), Amy Yasbeck (Peggy Brandt), Peter Greene (Dorian Tyrel), Max (Milo). Directed by Charles Russell and produced by Bob Engelman. Screenplay by Mike Werb.

The opening shots of *The Mask* look like they were salvaged from a desperately low-budget 1950s science fiction movie. Marine salvage operations lead to the rupture of an ancient chest that has rested for ages on the bottom of the bay, and a curious wooden mask floats to the surface.

Not long after, disconsolate bank teller Stanley Ipkiss, a genial nerd played by Jim Carrey, is staring into the dark waters and contemplating suicide. He has just been bounced from a nightclub—the latest in a long series of humiliations. But he has a good heart, and when he sees the mask floating with some rubbish, he thinks it is a drowning victim and jumps in to save it. All he brings to shore is the mask. But then, later that night . . .

Transformation scenes are, of course, the soul of comic book fiction. Billy Batson shouts "Shazam!" and Clark Kent darts into a phone booth and Bruce Wayne becomes Batman, and in every case an insignificant

wimp becomes a superhero. No wonder adolescent boys respond to these stories so powerfully. Consider what happens to Stanley when he puts on the mask. He is instantly transformed into a maniacal whirlwind of energy, dressed in a 1940s-style zoot suit—a cross between the Joker and Aladdin's genie, with elements of the Shadow.

The Mask is a perfect vehicle for the talents of Jim Carrey, who underwhelmed me with *Ace Ventura, Pet Detective* but here seems to have found a story and character that work together with manic energy. One of the key design decisions on the movie must have involved the Mask character's makeup. It transforms Carrey's features into a much larger, comic-bookish parody, but at the same time the features are still able to move in a lifelike way. The notes with the film explain that makeup expert Greg Cannom realized Carrey's exaggerated facial expressions are part of his essence, and didn't want them lost behind makeup.

The result is a movie character who seems half real, half animated. And the director, Charles Russell, is able to use special effects to move effortlessly between what might be possible and what is certainly not, as the Mask whirls like a beebop dervish and triumphantly prevails in situations which would have baffled poor Stanley Ipkiss.

The story begins with Stanley as a hapless bank clerk, who is hopelessly besotted by a beautiful customer, Tina Carlyle (Cameron Diaz). She flirts with him in the bank while taking a secret videotape of the vault for her boss, the slimy Dorian Tyrel (Peter Greene), who runs the Coco Bongo Club, where of course Tina is the slinky chanteuse.

Cameron Diaz is a true discovery in the film, a genuine sex bomb with a gorgeous face, a wonderful smile, and a gift for comic timing. This is her first movie role, after a brief modeling career. It will not be her last. Her chemistry with the Carrey character holds together a plot that is every bit as derivative as it can be, and when she dances with the Mask the result is one of those scenes when movie magic really works.

The story otherwise involves Richard Jeni as Charlie, Stanley's best friend at the bank, who introduces him to the mysteries of the Coco Bongo Club; Peter Riegert as a cop who notices the Mask's tie seems to be made of the same material as Stanley's unspeakable pajamas; and Milo, Stanley's dog, who is at least as clever as his master.

The art design on the movie goes for the

lurid 1940s *film noir* look of a lot of superhero comic books, and the Coco Bongo club looks recycled out of *Gilda* and a dozen other movies with elegant nightclubs. Stanley's apartment resembles a teenage boy's bedroom; all that's missing is a sign on the outside of the door saying "Keep Out! This means you!" The look of the film is as much fun as anything else.

I was not one of the admirers of *Ace Ventura, Pet Detective*. Millions were, however. I thought the story surpassed stupidity, and not in interesting ways. But I could sense some of Carrey's unrestrained energy and gift for comic invention, and here—where the story and the decor and the idea of the mask provide an anchor for his energy— Carrey demonstrates that he does have a genuine gift. It is said that one of the indispensable qualities of an actor is an ability to communicate the joy he takes in his performance. You could say *The Mask* was founded on that.

Masquerade ★ ★ ★
R, 91 m., 1988

Rob Lowe (Tim Whalan), Meg Tilly (Olivia Lawrence), Kim Cattrall (Brooke Morrison), Doug Savant (Mike McGill), John Glover (Tony Gateworth), Dana Delany (Anne Briscoe), Erik Holland (Chief of Police), Brian Davies (Granger Morrison), Barton Heyman (Tommy McGill), Bernie McInerney (Harland Fitzgerald). Directed by Bob Swaim and produced by Michael I. Levy. Screenplay by Dick Wolf.

"The problem with us," one of her relatives tells her, "is that we have too much money." They do. The whole family is rich, and now here is young Olivia, fresh out of school, single, an orphan, with a bank balance of $200 million. She's a target for every gold digger in the Hamptons. But even Olivia should not have to endure the way men treat her in *Masquerade*, which is a thriller in the shape of a Chinese puzzle box: Every time she solves one mystery, there's another one hidden inside it.

The movie's first mystery is Olivia herself, played by Meg Tilly in a very particular way that was slightly distracting at first, until I began to realize how well-chosen it was for the part. Tilly, who can be sharp-edged and observant, is a little dreamy this time. She talks in a breathy voice that seems filled with afterthoughts, and she comes across as innocent and passive.

Her character has not had an easy life. Her father died when she was twelve, and her mother has died just a few months before the story opens. She lives in a mansion in the Hamptons (one of her nine homes) with her mother's fourth husband, a drunken lout played with cheerful hatefulness by John Glover. She hates him, but there's no way to get him out of the house; he's protected by her mother's will.

Back home after school, Olivia drifts into a round of idle days and evenings filled with parties and dances. She runs into Mike (Doug Savant), the boy she promised to marry when she was twelve. He's now one of the local cops, forever on the other side of the divide between the rich and the poor. "Some dreams don't die," he tells her, but she tells him gently that it wasn't meant to be. Then one night at a dance she meets Tim (Rob Lowe), the handsome skipper of the racing sailboat owned by a local millionaire.

Tim has been sleeping with the millionaire's wife, but it's love at first sight when he sees Olivia. Before long they're holding hands on the beach and even committing the ultimate transgression: public fraternization between members and employees at the yacht club. Glover, the stepfather, is savage in his disapproval of the penniless sailor. He goes away for the weekend, the young couple sleep together in her house, Glover unexpectedly bursts in drunkenly, there is a struggle, and Tim shoots him dead.

That's what happens, all right, but what really happens is a lot more complicated. Because *Masquerade* depends so surely upon its many surprises, I won't reveal any more of the plot, except to say that Olivia tries to cover up for the man she loves, and Mike, the local cop, seems to go along with the cover-up for complicated motives going back to his original love for her.

If all of this sounds needlessly complicated (sort of a "Deathstyles of the Rich and Famous"), director Bob Swaim and writer Dick Wolf are sure-footed in their storytelling. One by one, the curtains of deception and intrigue are pulled back, and the most tantalizing thing about their method is that they always keep young Olivia in the dark. While evil currents swirl around her, while the people she trusts turn treacherous, she remains in a kind of innocent cocoon, gullible and deluded. That's why Meg Tilly's acting style is the right choice for the movie. Her dreaminess, which at first seems distracting, becomes an important part of the

suspense, because while she drifts in her romantic reverie, a sweet smile on her face, we're mentally screaming at her to wake up and smell the coffee.

The other performances are mostly adequate. Rob Lowe is rather boxed in by the complicated things the plot does with his character, and Doug Savant goes through some interesting changes as the local cop. I was disappointed, though, by John Glover's evil stepfather. Glover was a superb villain in John Frankenheimer's *52 Pick-Up* (1986), suave and oily, but this time he overplays the drunk routine and lurches around the house so grotesquely that we fear more for his balance than Tilly's life.

This was Bob Swaim's third film, after the great *La Balance* and the intriguing *Half Moon Street*. Like both of those films, it has its roots in the crime melodramas of the 1940s—when movies were about attractive victims, rather than attractive killers. The notion of placing a complete innocent at the center of the frame, and then surrounding her with menace, is a little old-fashioned, in a way; many recent films have preferred all-powerful heroes and heroines who destroy anyone who crosses them. But in Roman Polanski's *Frantic*, Peter Yates's *The House on Carroll Street*, and *Masquerade*, we see a rebirth of the innocent bystander.

Matinee ★ ★ ★ ½
PG, 100 m., 1993

John Goodman (Lawrence Woolsey), Cathy Moriarty (Ruth Corday), Simon Fenton (Gene Loomis), Omri Katz (Stan), Kellie Martin (Sherry), Lisa Jakub (Sandra). Directed by Joe Dante and produced by Michael Finnell. Screenplay by Charlie Haas.

I've looked at a couple of 1950s monster movies lately, and was struck by their innocence. Sure, they showed death rays from outer space, and great cities trampled by giant grasshoppers. But it was so optimistic, in a way, to assume that doom would arrive in such a comprehensible form, that we would die of things we could see coming, instead of from invisible viruses, and poverty, and global pollution.

Matinee, a delightful comedy and one of the most charming movies in a long time, takes place exactly at a moment when that innocence may have ended. The time is November 1962. President Kennedy has gone on television to warn that Cuba is armed with nuclear missiles, and that the U.S. Navy

is blockading the island against an approaching Russian fleet. Meanwhile, in Key West, which is just over the horizon from Cuba, another drama is unfolding. An exploitation filmmaker has arrived in town with his latest sleazo production, *Mant*—the story of a man who has mutated into a giant ant.

After the Cuban missile crisis and other shocks to our system, such as Vietnam, it became harder to get worked up over B-movie heroes who started to grow tentacles. But this is an earlier time, and for a local kid name Gene (Simon Fenton), the arrival of the famous Lawrence Woolsey (John Goodman) is a great day for Key West. Gene reads all the fanzines about monsters of moviedom, and considers Woolsey a great man.

They say if you go to the movies long enough you will finally see yourself on the screen. I had that experience during *Matinee*, because in many ways I was just like that kid Gene. At the age of twelve, I was fascinated by science fiction, baffled by girls, and starstruck by show business. Like Gene, I tried to meet the celebrities who came through my town, although I was never lucky enough to talk my way into the confidence of a big-time sleaze king like Woolsey, and get a behind-the-scenes glimpse as he prepared for a premiere.

Woolsey, portrayed by Goodman as an affable man who genuinely enjoys his work, is a combination of dozens of exploitation filmmakers who prospered in the 1950s by adding showmanship to their cheapo productions. For the premiere of *Mant*, Woolsey wires the theater seats with electrical buzzers, sets up equipment to blow dry-ice vapors at the audience, and hires a guy to dress up like a giant ant and run up and down the aisles.

All of these techniques were actually used in the 1950s, often by the legendary William Castle, who once allowed the audience to choose between two possible endings of the same horror film. In *Matinee*, they come together to produce a premiere showing of great hilarity, as the audience leaps from its seats on cue, and the awfulness of *Mant* is equaled only by its demented craziness.

The story of the premiere is intercut with events in the real world. Gene's father is a navy officer on board one of the ships in the blockade. American jets fly overhead, ominously low. TV bulletins relate a countdown to possible nuclear war. And Sherry, the prettiest girl in school (Kellie Martin), wants to go out with Simon, but meanwhile her former boyfriend, a juvenile delinquent, warns the hero not to get close to his girl.

Simon goes to the *Mant* matinee with friends, and discovers to his horror that Sherry is also there. His troubles are only starting. The guy hired to get inside the giant ant costume is . . . the former boyfriend. And so on.

There are a lot of big laughs in *Matinee*, and not many moments when I didn't have a wide smile on my face. I loved, for example, the character of Ruth Corday, played by Cathy Moriarty. She's a big, flashy blonde who is Goodman's girlfriend and leading lady, and she never stops complaining because she can see this guy is mostly dreams and hot air. But she's a good sport, and puts on a nurse uniform to sit in the lobby and get the kids to sign "medical consent forms" saying they won't sue if they keel over after seeing the giant ant.

Once again, this is a detail straight from movie history. A producer named Joe Solomon made millions from an inconsequential sex-education film named *Mom and Dad* by stationing a nurse in the lobby, and parking an ambulance outside to rush shock victims to the emergency room. What would the makers—or the audiences—of those 1950s movies have thought of *Texas Chainsaw Massacre?* Or *Basic Instinct,* for that matter?

Matinee was directed by Joe Dante, whose credentials are right for making this film. His credits include *Piranha, The Howling,* and *Gremlins,* and in his portrayal of the Goodman character is a lot of the enjoyment Dante must feel in his own work. The Hollywood game today is often played as high-finance sweepstakes, but in a gentler time there was still room for a guy with a few bucks and a big imagination to make a little movie and sell it with showmanship and flimflam. At the end of *Matinee,* we sense that time is coming to a close, along with a lot of the other elements of American innocence.

Maurice ★ ★ ★
R, 140 m., 1987

James Wilby (Maurice), Hugh Grant (Clive), Rupert Graves (Scudder), Denholm Elliott (Dr. Barry), Simon Callow (Mr. Ducie), Billie Whitelaw (Mrs. Hall), Ben Kingsley (Lasker-Jones). Directed by James Ivory and produced by Ismail Merchant. Screenplay by Kit Hesketh-Harvey and Ivory.

Maurice tells the story of a young English homosexual who falls in love with two completely different men—and in their differences is the whole message of the movie, a

message I do not agree with. Yet because the film is so well made and acted, because it captures its period so meticulously, I enjoyed it even in disagreement.

This is the first film from the team of James Ivory and Ismail Merchant since *A Room with a View,* and is based once again on a novel by E.M. Forster. Both books are about the gulf between idealistic romance and immediate physical passion, but otherwise they could not be more dissimilar. *Maurice,* written in 1913, was Forster's attempt to deal in fiction with his own homosexuality, and he suppressed the novel until after his death.

The story takes place in the years before World War I, when homosexuality was outlawed in Britain, and exposure meant disgrace and ruin. At Cambridge, two undergraduates become close friends, and then one day, in a moment of risk, one tells the other that he loves him.

The man declaring his love is Clive (Hugh Grant), an aristocrat who can look forward to a lifetime of wealth, privilege, and perhaps public office. The man he loves is Maurice (James Wilby), also well-born, who may go into the stock market. At first Maurice is shocked and repelled by what his friend says, but later that night he climbs in the window to give him a quick, passionate kiss and whisper, "I love you."

From the first, their ideas about love are opposite. Clive is not much interested in the physical expression of love; he thinks it will "lower" them. His notions are more platonic and idealistic. Maurice, once he has been introduced to the idea of love between men, becomes a passionate romantic, and before long Clive, the pursuer, becomes the pursued.

Clive fears exposure and disgrace. He sees homosexuality as something to be battled and overcome, and he breaks off with Maurice to marry, assume his family responsibilities, and go into politics. At first Maurice is shattered, and there are tragicomic scenes in which he seeks help from a hypnotist and the family doctor. Then he has a physical encounter of astonishing passion with Scudder (Rupert Graves), the rough-hewn gamekeeper on Clive's estate, and eventually both men determine to risk everything, throw their reputations to the wind, and live together as lovers.

Merchant and Ivory tell this story in a film so handsome to look at and so intelligently acted that it is worth seeing just to regard the production. Scene after scene is perfectly

created: a languorous afternoon floating on the river behind the Cambridge colleges; a desultory cricket game between masters and servants; the daily routine of college life; visits to country estates and town homes; the settings of the rooms. The supporting cast (Ben Kingsley, Simon Callow, Billie Whitelaw, Denholm Elliott) is unusually strong, and although some people might find Wilby unfocused in the title role, I thought he was making the right choices, portraying a man whose real thoughts were almost always elsewhere.

The problem in the movie is with the gulf between his romantic choices. His first great love, Clive, is a person with whom he has a great deal in common. They share minds as well as bodies. Scudder, the gamekeeper, is frankly portrayed as an unpolished working-class lad, handsome but simple. In the England of 1913, with its rigid class divisions, the two men would have had even less in common than the movie makes it seem, and the real reason their relationship is daring is not because of sexuality but because of class.

Apart from their sexuality, they have nothing of substance to talk about with each other in this movie. No matter how deep their love, I suspect that within a few weeks or months the British class system would have driven them apart.

In ignoring this reality, Forster and Ivory seem to be making the idealistic statement that love conquers all. Sometimes it does. Not usually. Physical sexuality is an important part of everyone, but, especially after the first passion has cooled, it is not the most important part. There comes a time when people need to simply talk to one another, to coexist as companions, and I doubt if that time could ever come between Maurice and Scudder.

By arguing that their decision to stay together was a good and courageous thing, *Maurice* seems to argue that the most important thing about them was their homosexuality. Perhaps in the dangerous atmosphere of homophobia in the England of seventy-five years ago, that might have seemed the case. But this film was made in 1987, and shares the same limited insight.

Maverick ★ ★ ★
PG, 129 m., 1994

Mel Gibson (Maverick), Jodie Foster (Annabelle), James Garner (Zane Cooper), Graham Greene (Joseph), James Coburn (The Commodore), Alfred Molina (Angel).

Directed by Richard Donner and produced by Bruce Davey and Donner. Screenplay by William Goldman.

The Western is truly making a comeback when a movie like *Maverick* can be made. After years in which no Westerns at all were produced in America, we began to get a few tentative, serious looks at the genre; movies like *Silverado, Dances With Wolves, Posse, Unforgiven,* and *Tombstone*. Now comes *Maverick*, the first lighthearted, laugh-oriented family Western in a long time, and one of the nice things about it is, it doesn't feel the need to justify its existence. It acts like it's the most natural thing in the world to be a Western.

The film is inspired, of course, by the 1950s TV series starring James Garner, who played a cheerful gambler who preferred to charm and con people rather than shoot them, although he was able to handle a sidearm when that seemed absolutely inescapable. Garner is back for the movie version, playing a marshal named Zane Cooper, and the Bret Maverick role is played by Mel Gibson.

It is a tribute to Gibson, I think, that he can play scenes side-by-side with the man who originated the character, and produce much the same effect, as a smiling card shark who hopes to win money by playing poker and not get shot in the process. What with their sideburns and their easy smiles, the two men even look sort of related. Their costar is Jodie Foster, as a sexy poker player named Annabelle Bransford. I imagine there were few professional female poker players in the Old West, and fewer still who looked like Foster, but *Maverick* is clearly not striving for grim realism.

As the movie opens, Maverick is desperately trying to win another five thousand dollars to finance his entry in a world series of poker, to be held in St. Louis. This is difficult because he finds himself in games with players like Angel (Alfred Molina), who likes to shoot people who win money from him; Chief Joseph (Graham Greene), an Indian with a future in public relations; and the Commodore (James Coburn), who has been conning people longer, and better, than Maverick can ever hope to.

The screenplay is by William Goldman, who wrote *Butch Cassidy and the Sundance Kid* for Paul Newman and Robert Redford, but its spirit owes more to the next Newman and Redford collaboration, *The Sting*. As one deception follows another, we catch on that nothing is as it seems, that the plot will unpeel layers like an onion, that revelations are made only to be unmasked. It's fun, although at 129 minutes the movie is probably a little too long.

One of the pleasures of the film is watching the actors used by director Richard Donner to populate his backgrounds. There are unbilled celebrity cameos by stars of his earlier pictures, including Danny Glover *(Lethal Weapon)* and Margot Kidder *(Superman)*. Fans of the Western will also appreciate the presence of such legendary Western stars as Denver Pyle, Dub Taylor, and Bert Remsen.

One difference between *Maverick* and a vintage Western comedy is that the stunts and some of the showdowns are staged more elaborately. There's a runaway stagecoach scene, with Gibson being dragged behind the coach and then pulling his way up to the front and controlling the team, that's as well done as anything I've seen in that line. And a fast-draw competition with a cocky young gunfighter generates the kind of suspense similar scenes had in *Tombstone*.

Is there an audience for the movie? Do people remember "Maverick" on TV well enough to care about the movie? I'm not sure. The movie doesn't require you to have ever seen a TV "Maverick" to enjoy this story. But there's a twist at the end you'll like more if you were a fan of the series.

May Fools ★ ★ ★
R, 105 m., 1990

Michel Piccoli (Milou), Miou-Miou (Camille), Michel Duchaussoy (Georges), Dominique Blanc (Claire), Harriet Walter (Lily), Bruno Carette (Grimaldi), Francois Berleand (Daniel), Martine Gautier (Adele). Directed by Louis Malle and produced by Vincent Malle. Screenplay by Louis Malle and Jean-Claude Carriere.

A colleague of mine has a simple test for the worth of a movie. He asks himself, "Is this movie more interesting than a documentary of the same actors having a meal together?" Often the answer is "no." But how would the test apply to *May Fools*, a French movie which has a great many scenes in which the actors have meals together, and carry on the same sorts of conversations I imagine they might have in real life?

Many of the reviews of the film have criticized it on the basis of its plot and its message. I like it because of the time I got to spend with the characters as they dealt with family matters over a period of days. It was intrinsically interesting, not because of what it was about, but simply because of what it was.

The movie takes place in May of 1968, a month that has a special ring to the French ear. That was the month that the revolution seemed poised to overthrow bourgeois society—the month the radicals shut down the Cannes Film Festival, the students occupied the streets of Paris, and rumors flew that de Gaulle was going to flee the country. I was in Paris during that time, and collected a few black-and-blue marks across the back of my legs, souvenirs of police truncheons when I made the mistake of trying to sightsee in the middle of a riot. For many Parisians, it appeared that society was up for grabs.

In the country, it was quieter, and *May Fools* takes place on a small farm that has been in the same family for generations. The matriarch, much loved and also feared, rules the household. Her children, some well into middle age, have moved away—all except for Milou (Michel Piccoli), a genial man who likes to go fishing and ride his bicycle and oversee the vineyards in a desultory sort of way.

One day, the mother drops dead. The family gathers for her funeral at the same moment in history when the radicals are trying to shut down French society. Among the survivors is Milou's daughter, Camille (Miou-Miou), who suggests the estate be divided into three and sold. Milou is shocked to think that the family's history would be so casually converted into cash, but the others point out that they have subsidized his idyllic existence in the country with their own hard work in the city.

Rumors of the outer world penetrate into the house, which is given over to a wake. One of the mourners is a sometime correspondent for *Le Monde*, who makes dire predictions about the future of France. Everyone seems to be on strike, and the mother cannot be properly buried because even the morticians are out. Most of the characters in the movie are solidly middle-class and conservative, but a few wayward rebels turn up, including a granddaughter who is a lesbian, and a passing truck driver who joins the wake as it turns gradually into a party.

Many meals are consumed. Some love affairs are considered, others consummated. A picnic is held on the grass, and for a second it seems that revolutionary fervor will inspire these people, half drunk on wine, to experiment with free love. But they are not quite ready for such a big step. Secrets are revealed, charges are traded, confessions are heard, and there are even a couple of small miracles, as the deceased seems to be not altogether dead.

May Fools was directed by Louis Malle and written by Malle and that best of modern French screenwriters, Jean-Claude Carriere. It is a movie that is reluctant to announce its intentions. What *is* Malle trying to say here? The revolution comes to nothing, the family neither caves in nor rises to heroism, and the happiest person in the film is arguably the maid, Lily, who is unexpectedly included in the will.

I think perhaps Malle is gently trying to make a movie about imperfect but interesting people, the goodness of whose souls is tested by the coincidence of a public and private crisis at the same time. No great lessons are learned, no great statements made, but by the end of the film, we have spent some interesting time with these people and know them better. What more can you ask of any weekend in the country, or of any group of people? This is a movie that may be precisely as interesting as watching the actors having dinner with one another.

Mean Streets ★ ★ ★
R, 110 m., 1974

Robert De Niro (Johnny Boy), Harvey Keitel (Charlie). Directed by Martin Scorsese and produced by Jonathan T. Taplin. Screenplay by Scorsese and Mardik Martin.

Martin Scorsese's *Mean Streets* isn't so much a gangster movie as a perceptive, sympathetic, finally tragic story about how it is to grow up in a gangster environment. Its characters (like Scorsese himself) have grown up in New York's Little Italy, and they understand everything about that small slice of human society except how to survive in it. The two most important characters, Charlie and Johnny Boy, move through the Mafia environment almost because it's expected of them. Charlie is a Catholic with pathological guilt complexes, but because the mob is the family business, he never quite forces himself to make the connection between right and wrong and what he does. Not that he's very good at being a Mafioso: He's twenty-seven, but he still lives at home; he's a collector for his uncle's protection racket, but the collections don't bring in much. If he has any luck

at all, he will be able to take over a bankrupt restaurant.

He is, at least fitfully, a realist. Johnny Boy, on the other hand, is a violent, uncontrolled product of romanticized notions of criminal street life. Little Italy is all around him, and yet he seems to have formed his style and borrowed half his vocabulary from the movies. He contains great and ugly passions, and can find no way to release them except in sudden violent bursts. Charlie is in love with Johnny Boy's sister, and he also feels a dogged sense of responsibility for Johnny Boy: He goes up on a roof one night when Johnny is shooting out streetlights and talks him down. At least Johnny releases his angers in overt ways. Charlie suppresses everything, and sometimes in desperation passes his hand through a flame and wonders about the fires of hell. He takes his Catholicism literally.

Scorsese places these characters in a perfectly realized world of boredom and small joys, sudden assaults, the possibility of death, and the certainty of mediocrity. He shot on location in Little Italy, where he was born and where he seems to know every nuance of architecture and personality, and his story isn't built like a conventional drama: It emerges from the daily lives of the characters. They hang out. They go to the movies. They eat, they drink, they get in sudden fights that end as quickly as a summer storm. Scorsese photographs them with fiercely driven visual style. We never have the sense of a scene being set up and then played out; his characters hurry to their dooms while the camera tries to keep pace. There's an improvisational feel even in scenes that we know, because of their structure, couldn't have been improvised.

Scorsese got the same feel in his first feature, *Who's That Knocking at My Door?* (1967). *Mean Streets* is a sequel, and Scorsese gives us the same leading actor (Harvey Keitel) to assure the continuity. In the earlier film, he was still on the edge of life, of sex, of violence. Now he has been plunged in, and he isn't equal to the experience. He's not tough enough to be a Mafia collector (and not strong enough to resist). Johnny Boy is played by Robert De Niro and it's a marvelous performance, filled with urgency and restless desperation.

The movie's scenes of violence are especially effective because of the way Scorsese stages them. We don't get spectacular effects and skillfully choreographed struggles. Instead, there's something realistically clumsy

about the fights in this movie. A scene in a pool hall, in particular, is just right in the way it shows its characters fighting and yet mindful of their suits (possibly the only suits they have). The whole movie feels like life in New York; there are scenes in a sleazy nightclub, on fire escapes, and in bars, and they all feel as if Scorsese has been there.

Melvin and Howard ★ ★ ★ ½
R, 95 m., 1980

Paul Le Mat (Melvin Dummar), Jason Robards (Howard Hughes), Mary Steenburgen (Lynda Dummar), Pamela Reed (Bonnie Dummar), Michael J. Pollard (Little Red), Charles Napier (Man with Envelope), Robert Ridgely (TV Host), Melvin Dummar (Depot Counterman). Directed by Jonathan Demme and produced by Art Linson and Don Phillips. Screenplay by Bo Goldman.

Melvin Dummar is the man who claimed he gave a lift to a doddering old hitchhiker, loaned him a quarter, and was left $156 million in the hitchhiker's will. If he was telling the truth, the hitchhiker was Howard Hughes. But Jonathan Demme's wonderful comedy *Melvin and Howard* doesn't depend on whether the so-called Mormon Will was really written by Hughes. That hardly matters. This is the story of a life lived at the other end of the financial ladder from Hughes. It sees Dummar as the kind of American hero who is celebrated for being so extraordinarily ordinary.

For what, after all, constitutes heroism? And why shouldn't Dummar be considered a hero? We learn from this movie that he ventured single-handedly into the jungle of American consumerism, and lived. We see his major battles. Here's a guy who was married three times (twice to the same woman, the second time with the "Hawaiian War Chant" playing in an all-night Vegas chapel). He had three cars and a boat repossessed, he went from being Milkman of the Month to hauling his first wife off a go-go stage, he loved his children, did not drink or smoke, and stood at the brink of losing his gas station franchise on the very day when a tall, blond stranger dropped what looked a lot like Hughes's last will and testament into his life.

The genius of *Melvin and Howard* is that it is about Melvin, not Howard. The film begins and ends with scenes involving the Hughes character, who is played by Jason Robards as a desert rat with fading memories of happiness. Dummar stops in the desert to answer a call of nature, finds Hughes lying in the sagebrush, gives him a ride in his pickup truck, and gets him to sing. For reasons of his own, Hughes sings "Bye, Bye Blackbird": *Got no one to love and understand me . . . oh, what hard-luck stories they all hand me.*

Robards is a chillingly effective Hughes. But this movie belongs to Paul Le Mat, as Dummar. Le Mat played the round-faced hot-rodder in *American Graffiti*, and Dummar is the kind of guy that character might have grown up to be. He is pleasant, genial, simple of speech, crafty of mind, always looking for an angle. He angles for Milkman of the Month, he plots to get his wife on a TV game show, he writes songs like "Santa's Souped-Up Sleigh," he plays the slots at Vegas and goes through his life asking only for a few small scores.

When he gets a big score—named the beneficiary of a $156 million will that seems to have been signed by Hughes—he hardly knows what to do. Long-lost relatives and new-found friends turn up by the dozens, and press conferences are held in front of his gas station. There is a court trial, but the movie never really addresses itself to the details of the Hughes will court case. It goes instead for the drama and for the effect on Dummar and his family.

This is a slice of American life. It shows the flip side of Gary Gilmore's Utah. It is a world of mobile homes, Pop Tarts, dust, kids, and dreams of glory. It's pretty clear how this movie got made. The producers started with the notion that the story of the mysterious Hughes will might make a good courtroom thriller. Well, maybe it would have. But my hunch is that when they met Dummar, they had the good sense to realize that they could get a better—and certainly a funnier—story out of what happened to him between the day he met Hughes and the day the will was discovered. Dummar is the kind of guy who thinks they oughta make a movie out of his life. This time, he was right.

Memories of Me ★ ★ ★ ½
PG-13, 103 m., 1988

Billy Crystal (Abbie), Alan King (Abe), JoBeth Williams (Lisa), David Ackroyd (Assistant Director), Phil Fondacaro (Bosco), Robert Pastorelli (Broccoli). Directed by Henry Winkler and produced by Alan King, Billy Crystal, and Michael Hertzberg. Screenplay by Eric Roth and Crystal.

Two of the most intriguing words in show business are "No—really!" They usually come right after a compliment, as in, "You're looking great! No—really!" The effect is of complete insincerity, since if the subject really *were* looking great, there wouldn't be any need to insist on it. This kind of double-reverse English, in which what is said is the opposite of what is meant, lies at the heart of Henry Winkler's *Memories of Me,* a comedy about a man who has never been able to talk seriously with his father. No—really.

Billy Crystal stars in the movie as Abbie, a high-powered New York surgeon who begins to take his life more seriously after he has a heart attack. He has been alienated for years from his father, Abe, a character who has become known as the King of the Extras out in Hollywood. Abbie has vague memories of Abe telling him bedtime stories, and then there is a great silence over many years. When he thinks of his father at all, Abbie thinks of him as an embarrassment. But now the heart attack has caused him to examine his life more closely, and so, almost against his will, he goes out West to visit his father.

The moment we see Abe, we recognize him. He's the life of the party, one of those ebullient types who keeps people at a distance while professing friendship. He slaps you on the back so he doesn't have to look in your eyes. Almost from the moment Abbie sees Abe, he's making plans to go back home to New York. But somehow, he stays. And eventually he begins to notice some disturbing things about his father. One day, for example, Abe is playing an extra in a daytime medical soap opera. He's a patient, and all he has to do is lie still and keep quiet. But he starts talking. Another day, dressed up like a big red lobster, he inexplicably starts reciting a speech from a play he was in years ago.

What's going on here? Alzheimer's? His son the doctor talks him into a complete medical examination, and the brain scan reveals a problem, "a little pimple on a blood vessel in the brain." Sometimes, Abe gets a little confused. He starts playing the wrong tapes. Someday, maybe tomorrow, maybe years from now, there could be much bigger trouble. Abe is dying.

But so what? Everybody is dying. That's Abe's approach to the problem. And the movie itself is not one of those depressing tear-jerker docudramas where everybody goes around describing symptoms. Most of the movie's scenes are upbeat, and some of them are hilarious, as Abbie and his fiancée (JoBeth Williams) follow Abe into the world of Hollywood extras. They have their own club, right off Hollywood Boulevard. They stick up for each other in times of trouble. They're always performing, always "on," and Abe is the leader of the pack.

The best moments in the movie involve tightly knit dialogue scenes between Alan King and Billy Crystal, who cowrote the movie. Their timing has the almost effortless music of two professionals who have spent their lifetimes learning how to put the right spin on a word. Much of it involves paradox, as when King observes that his wife was crazy: "That's why I divorced her."

"But," says Crystal, "she divorced you."

"See what I mean?"

Memories of Me is a surprise, a warmhearted comedy that somehow creates believable characters without sacrificing big laughs. It is hard to imagine how two egos as secure as King's and Crystal's could have coexisted on the set—and indeed there are moments that feel like improvised one-upmanship—but Henry Winkler, the director, is able to find the strong story line from beginning to end, and so we do care when the film arrives at its touching conclusion. Crystal is very good in a role that must have been second nature to him; King, playing the more complicated character, is a genuine revelation. As the King of the Extras, he pulls off the neat trick of showing us why his son avoided him for so many years—and why he was wrong.

Memphis Belle ★ ★ ★
PG-13, 101 m., 1990

Matthew Modine (Dennis Dearborn), Eric Stoltz (Danny Daly), Tate Donovan (Luke Sinclair), D.B. Sweeney (Phil Rosenthal), Billy Zane (Val Kozlowski), Sean Astin (Richard "Rascal" Moore), Harry Connick, Jr. (Clay Busby). Directed by Michael Caton-Jones and produced by David Puttnam and Catherine Wyler. Screenplay by Monte Merrick.

Memphis Belle tells the story of the journey of several brave young Americans through an anthology of aviation movie clichés. Not a trick is missed—not even the faithful dog lifting its loyal head from the grass when a missing plane finds its way back to base. This movie is said to be based on a World War II documentary by William Wyler, but, in another sense, it is based on *The Battle of Britain, One of Our Aircraft Is Missing,* and countless other formula thrillers about the air war in Europe.

The task of the filmmakers is thankless.

They have to introduce a dozen crew members of the Memphis Belle, and then somehow make them all memorable within the cramped confines of a plot where most of them have to wear oxygen masks most of the time. The movie begins while we see the young men playing football, and a voice-over narration names them and provides them with thumbnail character sketches. Then, later, we learn what assignments they have on board the Memphis Belle when the pilot holds a roll-call and they sign in, giving their names and battle stations.

The crew, we learn, has survived twenty-four bombing raids over Germany. One more, and they get to go home. The voice-over narration is by an Army Air Force P.R. man (John Lithgow), assigned to stage-manage the final raid for *Life* magazine. And given the fact that these man have flown twenty-four missions together, I hardly thought it necessary for them to introduce themselves by name to their pilot—but then the introductions were really for us, and the roll-call was an economical way to explain their various jobs—copilot, radioman, navigator, tail-gunner, bombardier, etc.

Michael Powell used exactly the same strategy to introduce the bomber crew members in his wartime drama *One of Our Aircraft Is Missing*, with the difference that he used a Wellington bomber, because its crew of six was easier for the audience to keep straight. He was right. The Flying Fortress used in *Memphis Belle* has such a large crew that the movie is fatally slowed as the screenplay works its way around and around the characters, trying to keep them all alive.

Each character is a different cliché: The cool and calculated captain, the jittery gunner and his practical-joking sidekick, the superstitious one, etc. On the ground, the characters are equally machine-made, from the taciturn commanding officer to the heartless general to the shameless flack. It would be safe to say there is not a single development in this movie that cannot accurately be predicted by any audience member familiar with the requirements of the genre.

And yet, despite everything I have said, I found *Memphis Belle* entertaining, almost in spite of my objections. That's because it exploits so fully the universal human tendency to identify with a group of people who are up in an airplane and may not be able to get down again. As the flak flies, as enemy fighters attack, as wings are shredded, as engines catch on fire and gun turrets are blown off, I found myself: (a) mentally ticking off the clichés, but (b) physically on the edge of my seat. It was a classic case of divided loyalties—the intelligence maintaining its distance while the emotions became engaged.

In a perverse sort of way, one of the appeals of *Memphis Belle* is in its adherence to dependable old clichés. This isn't a high-tech pinball machine like *Top Gun*, but a movie about people in a fairly primitive piston-engine aircraft. Their uniforms are not glossy aluminum underwear, but leather jackets and fur-lined helmets and wool sweaters. When petrol must be moved from one wing to another, by God, they crawl back to the pump handle and pump it themselves.

This human element in the experience of the *Memphis Belle* crew somehow compensates for a lack of human dimension in the characters. We can't really tell the crew members apart, and don't much care to, but we can identify with them. As they fly on their bombing mission, I reflected that such high-altitude bombing was seen at the time as inhuman. But at least the World War II flight crews flew their missions and took their chances. These days wars can be fought by pushing a button. It is somehow more fair when the combatants have to risk their lives to push the buttons.

Menace II Society ★ ★ ★ ★
R, 97 m., 1993

Tyrin Turner (Caine), Larenz Tate (O-Dog), Jada Pinkett (Ronnie), MC Eiht (A-Wax), Marilyn Coleman (Grandmama), Arnold Johnson (Grandpapa), Samuel L. Jackson (Tat Lawson). Directed by the Hughes brothers and produced by Darin Scott. Screenplay by Tyger Williams.

Caine, the young man at the center of *Menace II Society*, is not an evil person in the usual sense of the word. He has a good nature and a quick intelligence, and in another world he might have turned out happy and productive. But he was not raised in a world that allowed that side of his character to develop, and that is the whole point of this powerful film.

Caine, like so many young black men from the inner city, has grown up in a world where the strong values of an older generation are being undermined by the temptations of guns, drugs, and violence. As a small boy he sees his father murder a man over a trivial matter. He sees his mother die of an overdose. He takes an older neighborhood man as his mentor, only to see him go to prison. By the time he is in high school, Caine wears a beeper on his belt and is a small-time drug dealer. The film's narration tells us he is society's nightmare: "He's young, he's black, and he doesn't give a ———."

We see that it is more complicated than that. The tragedy of Caine's life is that he cannot stand back a little and get a wider view, and see what alternatives are available to him. He adopts the street values that are based on a corruption of the word "respect." He wants respect, but has done nothing to deserve it. For him, "respect" is the product of intimidation: If you back down because you fear him, you "respect" him.

The movie opens as Caine and O-Dog, his heedless, violent friend, enter a Korean grocery store to buy a couple of beers. The grocer and his wife, who don't want trouble, ask them to make their purchase and leave. Caine and O-Dog engage in a little meaningless verbal intimidation, aware that because they are young and black they can score some points from the couple's fear. "I feel bad for your mother," the grocer says as they are about to leave. That is all O-Dog needs to hear, and he murders the grocer and then forces his wife to hand over the store's security videotape before killing her, too.

Caine is shocked by this sudden violent development. He sees it in terms of his own misfortune: He went out to get a beer, and now he's an accessory to murder. During the course of the movie, O-Dog will use the videotape for entertainment at parties, freeze-framing the moment of the grocer's death. Eventually dozens of people will know who killed the grocer, but nobody will be charged with the crime, because such violence is so common and the laws are such that many murders simply slip through the fingers of the police.

There are people in Caine's life who care for him. A friend who has an athletic scholarship. A teacher at school. His God-fearing grandparents, who eventually throw him out of the house. His mentor's girlfriend, who wants him to move to Atlanta with her and start over.

But Caine's world is narrow and limited. He has the values of his immediate circle, and the lack of imagination: He cannot quite envision a world for himself outside of the limited existence of guns, cars, drugs, and swagger. This movie, like many others, reminds us that murder is the leading cause of death among young black men. But it doesn't blame the easy target of white racism for that: It looks unblinkingly at a street culture that offers its members few choices that are not self-destructive.

If *Boyz N the Hood* was the story of a young man lucky enough to grow up with parents who cared, and who escapes the dangers of the street culture, *Menace II Society* is, tragically, about many more young men who are not so lucky. The movie was directed by Allen and Albert Hughes, twin brothers, and is based on the screenplay they wrote with their friend, Tyger Williams. The brothers were twenty-one when they finished the film, but already they had a track record of many music videos. Their mother gave them a video camera when they were twelve, they told me at the Cannes Film Festival, and that pointed them away from the possibilities they show in their film, and toward their current success.

The message here is obvious: Many of the victims of street and gang violence are a great loss to society, their potential destroyed by a bankrupt value system. The Hughes twins, given a chance, reveal here that they are natural filmmakers. *Menace II Society* is as well-directed a film as you'll see from America in 1993, an unsentimental and yet completely involving story of a young man who cannot quite manage to see a way around his fate.

It's impressive, the way the filmmakers tell Caine's story without making him seem either the hero or victim; he is presented more as a typical example. He is not bad, but he does bad things and clearly would do more. We are not asked to sympathize with him, but to a degree we do, in the sense of the empathetic prayer, "There, but for the grace of God, go I." It is clear that, given the realities of the society in which he is raised, Caine's fate is likely.

The film is filled with terrific energy. The performances, especially those by Tyrin Turner as Caine, Larenz Tate as O-Dog, and Jada Pinkett as Ronnie, the caring girlfriend, are filled with life and conviction. Because *Menace II Society* paints such an uncompromised picture, and offers no easy hope or optimistic conclusion, it may be seen as a very negative film in some quarters. "If you hate blacks, this movie will make you hate them more," Allen Hughes said during his Cannes visit. "But true liberals will get something sparked in their heads."

That is true. If *Menace II Society* shows things the way they often are—and I believe it does—then the film is not negative for de-picting them truthfully. Anyone who views this film thoughtfully must ask why our society makes guns easier to obtain and use than any other country in the civilized world. And that is only the most obvious of the many questions the film inspires.

Mephisto ★ ★ ★ ★
NO MPAA RATING, 135 m., 1981

Klaus Maria Brandauer (Henrik Hofgon), Krystyna Janda (Barbara Bruckner), Ildiko Bansagi (Nicolette Von Hiebuhr), Karin Boyd (Juliette Martens). Directed and produced by Istvan Szabo. Screenplay by Szabo and Peter Dobel.

There are times in *Mephisto* when the hero tries to explain himself by saying that he's only an actor, and he has that almost right. *All* he is, is an actor. It's not his fault that the Nazis have come to power, and that as a German-speaking actor he must choose between becoming a Nazi and being exiled into a foreign land without jobs for German actors. As long as he is acting, as long as he is not called upon to risk his real feelings, this man can act his way into the hearts of women, audiences, and the Nazi power structure. This is the story of a man who plays his life wearing masks, fearing that if the last mask is removed, he will have no face.

The actor is played by Klaus Maria Brandauer in one of the greatest movie performances I've ever seen. The character, Henrik, is not sympathetic, and yet we identify with him because he shares so many of our own weaknesses and fears. Henrik is not a very good actor or a very good human being, but he is good enough to get by in ordinary times. As the movie opens, he's a socialist, interested in all the most progressive new causes, and is even the proud lover of a black woman. By the end of the film, he has learned that his liberalism was a taste, not a conviction, and that he will do anything, flatter anybody, make any compromise, just to hear applause, even though he knows the applause comes from fools.

Mephisto does an uncanny job of creating its period, of showing us Hamburg and Berlin from the 1920s to the 1940s. And I've never seen a movie that does a better job of showing the seductive Nazi practice of providing party members with theatrical costumes, titles, and pageantry. In this movie, not being a Nazi is like being at a black-tie ball in a brown corduroy suit. Hofgon, the actor, is drawn to this world like a magnet.

From his ambitious beginnings in the provincial German theater, he works his way up into more important roles and laterally into more important society. All of his progress is based on lies. He marries a woman he does not love, because her father can do him some good. When the rise of the Nazis destroys his father-in-law's power, he leaves his wife. He continues all this time to maintain his affair with his black mistress. He has a modest, but undeniable, talent as an actor, but prostitutes it by playing his favorite role, Mephistopheles in *Faust*, not as he could but as he calculates he should.

The obvious parallel here is between the hero of this film and the figure of tragedy who sold his soul to the devil. But *Mephisto* doesn't depend upon easy parallels to make its point. This is a human story, and as the actor in this movie makes his way to the top of the Nazi propaganda structure and the bottom of his own soul, the movie is both merciless and understanding. This is a weak and shameful man, the film seems to say, but then it cautions us against throwing the first stone.

Mephisto is not a German but a Hungarian movie, directed by the talented Istvan Szabo, who has led his country's cinema from relative obscurity to its present position as one of the best and most innovative film industries in Europe. Szabo, in his way, has made a companion film to Fassbinder's *The Marriage of Maria Braun*. The Szabo film shows a man compromising his way to the top by lying to himself and everybody else, and throwing aside all moral standards. It ends as World War II is under way. The Fassbinder film begins after the destruction of the war, showing a woman clawing her way out of the rubble and repeating the same process of compromise, lies, and unquestioning materialism.

Both the man in the Szabo film and the woman in the Fassbinder film maintain one love affair all through everything, using their love (he for a black woman, she for a convict) as a sort of token contempt for a society whose corrupt values they otherwise completely accept. The fact that they *can* still love, of course, makes it impossible for them to quite deceive themselves. That is the price they pay for their deals with the devil.

Mermaids ★ ★ ★
PG-13, 110 m., 1990

Cher (Mrs. Flax), Bob Hoskins (Lou Landsky), Winona Ryder (Charlotte Flax), Michael

Schoeffling (Joe), Christina Ricci (Kate Flax), Caroline McWilliams (Carrie). Directed by Richard Benjamin and produced by Lauren Lloyd, Wallis Nicita, and Patrick Palmer. Screenplay by June Roberts.

I had the feeling, watching *Mermaids*, that it was originally headed in another direction. The material is "funny" instead of funny, and we don't laugh so much as we squirm with recognition and sympathy. It's a story told by a teen-age girl whose mother avoids becoming known as the town tramp only because she changes towns so often. In the movies, eccentric parents can be palmed off as colorful originals. In life, especially to an adolescent, they can be excruciating embarrassments.

The mom in *Mermaids* goes by the name of Mrs. Flax, and is played by Cher. Not only played *by* Cher, but in an eerie sense, played *as* Cher, with perfect makeup and a flawless body that seems a bit much to hope for, given the character's lifestyle and diet. Mrs. Flax has a personality trait that leads her to seek doomed love affairs with hopeless men, and then move to another town when her life crashes down around her. Little attempt is made to present her as a plausible character; this is one of those movies sidetracked by the David Lynch Syndrome, in which characters exhibit a tacky trait of consumerism that is exaggerated out of all proportion (the meals served by Mrs. Flax, for example, consist entirely of artistic arrangements of "fun foods").

She has two daughters; a teen-ager, Charlotte (Winona Ryder), and a grade-schooler, Kate (Christina Ricci). As the movie opens, Kate is practicing her swimming, and will eventually see if she can match the world record for holding her breath underwater. That supplies one of the movie's many clues to the symbolism of its title, as well as suggesting the desperation Mrs. Flax inspires in her children. The older daughter, Charlotte, has been driven nearly mad by her mother's incessant moves (eighteen by last count). She's never gone long to the same school, or made many friends, or experienced much normal life outside the hothouse of Mrs. Flax's fevered existence.

After yet another romantic disaster, the family moves again, to Massachusetts, where Charlotte makes friends with a young man named Joe (Michael Schoeffling), who has some kind of handyman job at a Roman Catholic convent that is just over the way. Charlotte is rather attracted to the nuns, to their quiet ways and cheerful encouragement, but she is more attracted to Joe, who perhaps possesses the secret of exactly what it is adults do when they're alone—what her mother does with all those men, for example.

This story is told by the director, Richard Benjamin, within a veritable thicket of art direction, which creates an odd world in which the realistic and the bizarre exist side by side. The movie makes a comparatively sedate companion piece for *Edward Scissorhands*, which also creates a fantasy universe out of exaggerated details of 1990-type popular culture. The central pop culture detail here is Cher, who, like Bette Midler in the somewhat similar *Stella*, does not entirely suffer her famous persona to disappear inside the role.

Her life begins to change, however, in Massachusetts, after she is discovered by Lou (Bob Hoskins), a husky salt-of-the-earth type, who sizes up the situation and decides that what Mrs. Flax and her daughters need is a transfusion of normalcy. He tries to contribute some balance to the family routine and has luck on the days when Mrs. Flax is not warring with him, while meanwhile a crisis develops in Charlotte's life: She is kissed by Joe, and becomes convinced she is pregnant.

It was here that I began to suspect that the movie may have lightened the vision it found in the original novel by Patty Dann. There are all sorts of gothic props around, including the monastery and a sinister river next to it, which suggest that terrible things could happen, but disasters are narrowly averted so that the movie can have one of those happy endings Hollywood likes so much right now. The plot of *Mermaids* seems to march toward that ending with great determination, looking neither right nor left at the way the events seem to impact on the lives of the characters.

And yet, perversely perhaps, I found this an interesting movie. I didn't give a bean how it turned out, and I found a lot of it preposterous, but I enjoyed that quality. Why do we look at movies? To learn lessons and see life reflected back at us? Sometimes. But sometimes we simply sit there in the dark, stupefied by the spectacle. *Mermaids* is not exactly good, but it is not boring. Winona Ryder, in another of her alienated outsider roles, generates real charisma. And the movie is saying something about Cher as elusive as it is intriguing.

Metropolitan ★ ★ ★ ½
PG-13, 98 m., 1990

Carolyn Farina (Audrey Rouget), Edward Clements (Tom Townsend), Christopher Eigeman (Nick Smith), Taylor Nichols (Charlie Black), Allison Rutledge-Parisi (Jane Clarke), Dylan Hundley (Sally Fowler), Isabel Gillies (Cynthia McLean), Bryan Leder (Fred Neff), Will Kempe (Rick von Sloneker), Elizabeth Thompson (Serena Slocum). Directed and produced by Whit Stillman. Screenplay by Stillman.

Metropolitan holds a mirror up to the lives and values of a group of New York preppies during the debutante season. They live in a world I dimly knew existed, but one as alien to me as if they belonged to a tribe in the Amazon. Yet their motives are universally recognizable: They want to be accepted, admired, and loved. They're teen-agers, many of them from wealthy homes, and they go to the right schools and want to be seen in the right places with the right people.

They are acutely aware that they are anachronisms. Even as they put on their tuxedos and venture out into the cold Christmas weather to attend debutante balls at the Plaza, they realize (in the words of the butler in Elaine May's *A New Leaf*) that they are carrying on in their own lifetimes a tradition that was dead before they were born.

They are, one of the kids says, the children of the UHB—the "urban haute bourgeoisie." They dress well and hold parties in the Park Avenue apartments of their parents, where they try to sound intellectual about Jane Austen and French socialists, and then play "truth games," like the one where you have to answer even the most embarrassing question with absolute veracity.

Into this tightly knit group comes a newcomer, Tom Townsend (Edward Clements), who lives on the West Side and wears a London Fog raincoat instead of a dark blue overcoat, and who says he doesn't believe in deb parties and the whole preppie value system. Nick (Christopher Eigeman), the most aware and cynical of the group, argues with him: "Deb parties are a way of getting invited to all of the best places and being supplied with food, drink, and companionship at very little cost to yourself. What could possibly be the matter with that?" Besides, Tom is told, there is a shortage of "escorts," and he'll actually be doing these poor girls a favor by coming along to their parties.

One of the girls develops an obvious crush on Tom, but he is oblivious to her; indeed, he seems to have an uncanny gift for thoughtless statements that hurt her feelings. He has a crush on the elusive Serena Slocum, once glimpsed at a dance, never forgotten. She has a reputation among the group members for being fast—probably not deserved—and another legendary character often talked about is the mysterious Rick von Sloneker (Will Kempe), said to have driven a girl to suicide.

These fabled people do eventually turn up in *Metropolitan*, but not before we've fallen into the seductive rhythms of the deb season—into bursts of hurt feelings or sudden crushes, punctuated by long, desultory conversations and deep confidences. The movie was written and directed by Whit Stillman, who, in his mid-thirties, is obviously still fascinated by the coming-of-age process he went through as a preppie. He has made a film F. Scott Fitzgerald might have been comfortable with, a film about people covering their own insecurities with a façade of social ease. And he has written wonderful dialogue, words in which the characters discuss ideas and feelings instead of simply marching through plot points as most Hollywood characters do.

Not very much happens in *Metropolitan*, and yet everything that happens is felt deeply, because the characters in this movie are still too young to have perfected their defenses against life. They care very much about what others think of them, their feelings are easily hurt, their love affairs are really forms of asking for acceptance.

It is strange how the romances of the teenage years retain a poignancy all through life—how a girl who turns you down when you're sixteen retains an aura in your memory even long after you, and she, have ceased to be who you were then. When I attended my high school reunion I discovered in the souvenir booklet assembled by the reunion committee that one of the girls in my class had a crush on me all those years ago. I would have given a great deal to have had that information at the time. This is a movie about people who are still living through that time, whose reunions and souvenir booklets are still ahead of them, along with their futures, and disappointments and pains that the whole world of debs and dances can scarcely prepare them for.

Miami Rhapsody ★ ★ ★
PG-13, 95 m., 1995

[NEW]

Sarah Jessica Parker (Gwyn), Gil Bellows (Matt), Antonio Banderas (Antonio), Mia Farrow (Nina), Paul Mazursky (Vic), Kevin Pollak (Jordan), Barbara Garrick (Terri), Carla Gugino (Leslie), Naomi Campbell (Kaia). Directed by David Frankel and produced by Barry Jossen and Frankel. Screenplay by Frankel.

Miami Rhapsody has been dismissed in some quarters as an imitation Woody Allen movie, but since the imitation and the movie are both so entertaining, I don't see what the problem is. Allen himself has made unabashed pastiches in the style of Fellini *(Stardust Memories)*, Bergman *(Interiors)*, and German Expressionism *(Shadows and Fog)*, and now here is David Frankel's take on Allen's comedies about the moral qualms of the affluent.

Just to make clear he knows exactly what he's doing, Frankel stars Mia Farrow, Allen's former muse, in a key role. And he opens the picture with a closeup of another character delivering a monologue to her psychiatrist. This is Woodyland, all right, and my guess is that if this *were* a Woody Allen film, it would be reviewed as a pretty good one. Not great, but pretty good.

The movie stars Sarah Jessica Parker as Gwen, the middle child of the Marcus family, affluent Jewish Miamians. She is engaged to be married to Matt (Gil Bellows), a zoologist who dreams of living in the rain forest, presumably with Gwen, and studying the intimate lives of simians. But before that can happen, Gwen finds herself doing a little psychological zoology involving the intimate lives of her family.

At her sister's wedding, she's told by her father, Vic (Paul Mazursky), that he suspects her mother, Nina (Farrow), is having an affair. This turns out to be quite true; Nina confesses to having fallen for Tony (Antonio Banderas), the handsome Latin American male nurse who is caring for *her* mother in a nursing home. Gwen has always considered her parents' marriage perfect, and her faith in the institution of marriage is shaken by Nina's secret, which turns out to be the tip of the iceberg.

In quick succession, Gwen discovers that Vic himself is having an affair with his travel agent. That her brother Jordan (Kevin Pollack) is cheating with his partner's wife (Naomi Campbell). That even her newly married sister Leslie (Carla Gugino), bored with her

football-hero husband and appalled by his stinginess, is seeing an old boyfriend. How can it be possible, Gwen wonders, for her to commit to an institution that everyone around her is undermining? And . . . could it just possibly be true that the handsome Tony would rather date Gwen than her mother?

I realize this plot synopsis makes *Miami Rhapsody* sound like a screwball comedy with couples popping in and out of bed. What is rather impressive is the way Frankel, who wrote as well as directed, is able to bring levels of truth, poignancy, and pain to what begins as a fairly mechanical plot. He does this by making most of the characters self-aware; if they're doing wrong, to some degree they realize that, and learn from it. And in Gwen's grandmother, a Holocaust survivor who never speaks but yet somehow casts rays of cheerfulness and love on all about her, he provides a moral center: a person whose example causes most of the characters to think twice before descending into heedless selfishness.

Of course, not all of the marriages should probably be saved. The football star (Bo Eason), who seems like a nice guy until he gets married, turns out to be so self-absorbed he doesn't see why any of his money should be spent by his wife. We understand why she strays. But the other adulterers really belong with their original spouses, and with the moral neatness of a comedy by Shakespeare, Frankel manages to restore order and balance by the end.

Frankel's dialogue is smart and topical, although it aims at a slightly lower intellectual level than Allen's screenplays, maybe because the movie is set in Miami, where people are more likely to discuss politics than philosophy. "You kids tend to put me up on a pedestal," Farrow complains to Parker, who replies, "You lowered it the year you voted for Bush."

Miami itself is almost one of the characters in the film. Jack Wallner's cinematography uses its tropical colors and Art Deco architecture to create a pulsing backdrop, and there's the sense that the characters are just a little warmer, faster, and more lustful here than they might be up north. Parker has a line that could have been spoken by the Allen of *Annie Hall*: "I look at marriage the same way I look at Miami: It's hot and stormy and sometimes a little dangerous—but if it's so awful, then why is there so much traffic?"

Micki & Maude ★ ★ ★ ★
PG-13, 115 m., 1984

Dudley Moore (Rob Salinger), Amy Irving (Maude Salinger), Ann Reinking (Micki Salinger), Richard Mulligan (Leo Brody), Lu Leonard (Nurse Verbeck). Directed by Blake Edwards and produced by Tony Adams. Screenplay by Jonathan Reynolds.

The key to the whole thing is Dudley Moore's absolutely and unquestioned sincerity. He loves both women. He would do anything to avoid hurting either woman. He wants to do the right thing but, more than that, he wants to do the kind thing. And that is how he ends up in a maternity ward with two wives who are both presenting him with baby children. If it were not for those good qualities in Moore's character, qualities this movie goes to great lengths to establish, *Micki & Maude* would run the risk of turning into tasteless and even cruel slapstick. After all, these are serious matters we're talking about. But the triumph of the movie is that it identifies so closely with Moore's desperation and his essentially sincere motivation that we understand the lengths to which he is driven. That makes the movie's inevitable climax even funnier.

As the movie opens, Moore is happily married to an assistant district attorney (Ann Reinking) who has no desire to have children. Children are, however, the only thing in life that Moore himself desires; apart from that one void, his life is full and happy. He works as a reporter for one of those TV magazine shows where weird people talk earnestly about their constitutional rights to be weird: For example, nudists defend their right to bear arms. Then he meets a special person, a cello player (Amy Irving) who has stepped in at the last moment to play a big concert. She thinks he has beautiful eyes, he smiles, it's love, and within a few weeks Moore and Irving are talking about how they'd like to have kids. Then Irving gets pregnant. Moore decides to do the only right thing, and divorce the wife he loves to marry the pregnant girlfriend that he also loves. But then his wife announces that she's pregnant, and Moore turns, in this crisis of conscience, to his best friend, a TV producer wonderfully played by Richard Mulligan. There is obviously only one thing he can do: become a bigamist.

Micki & Maude was directed by Blake Edwards, who also directed Moore in *10,* and who knows how to build a slapstick climax

by one subtle development after another. There is, for example, the fact that Irving's father happens to be a professional wrestler, with a lot of friends who are even taller and meaner than he is. There is the problem that Moore's original in-laws happen to pass the church where he is having his second wedding. Edwards has a way of applying absolute logic to insane situations, so we learn, for example, that after Moore tells one wife he works days and the other one he works nights, his schedule works out in such a way that he begins to get too much sleep.

Dudley Moore is developing into one of the great movie comedians of his generation. *Micki & Maude* goes on the list with *10* and *Arthur* as screwball classics. Moore has another side as an actor, a sweeter, more serious side, that shows up in good movies like *Romantic Comedy* and bad ones like *Six Weeks,* but it's when he's in a screwball comedy, doing his specialty of absolutely sincere desperation, that he reaches genius. For example: The last twenty minutes of *Micki & Maude,* as the two pregnant women move inexorably forward on their collision course, represents a kind of filmmaking that is as hard to do as anything you'll ever see on a screen. The timing has to be flawless. So does the logic: One loose end, and the inevitability of a slapstick situation is undermined. Edwards and Moore are working at the top of their forms here, and the result is a pure, classic slapstick that makes *Micki & Maude* a real treasure.

A Midnight Clear ★ ★ ★
R, 107 m., 1992

Peter Berg (Bud Miller), Kevin Dillon (Mel Avakian), Arye Gross (Stan Shutzer), Ethan Hawke (Will Knott), Gary Sinise ("Mother" Wilkins), Frank Whaley ("Father" Mundy). Directed by Keith Gordon and produced by Dale Pollock and Bill Borden. Screenplay by Gordon.

The opening shots of *A Midnight Clear* have a clarity and force that linger after, casting a spell over the entire movie. They show a group of young men in Jeeps, making their way through the deep snow in an almost primeval forest. Everything is dark or blinding white; the snow crunches, reluctantly accepting the trespassers. We can see at once that this is a war movie—we know from the costumes it is World War II—but somehow the film is able to suggest some hidden pur-

pose, and we know it will not simply tell a war story.

The screenplay is by the director, Keith Gordon, based on a novel by the brooding William Wharton, whose *Birdy* was also about young men changed forever by war. As the characters begin to speak, we think at first we have re-entered the world of the mundane, that this will be another one of those movie platoons with an obligatory ethnic balance (Miller, Avakian, Shutzer, Knott). But as we get to know them, we see that they have formed new personality links more important than their backgrounds, and it is significant that one of the soldiers is nicknamed Mother, and another Father.

These are bright soldiers, we learn—smarter than average, although inexperienced and ill-trained for this mission, which requires them to patrol into the woods, locate the enemy, and report back about him. The enemy, it turns out, is much better at locating them, and in one breathtaking scene some of the patrol members stand transfixed in the rifle sights of Nazi soldiers—who then fade back into the forest without shooting at them.

What's happening here? It is the Christmas season of 1944, late in the war. Germany has obviously lost. One of the Americans speculates that perhaps the Germans intend to surrender to them. There are other hints: Christmas carols drifting on the wind. A snowball fight. Eventually it becomes clear that the Germans—as young and inexperienced as the Americans—want to give up the fight, but need a way to save face at the same time. A mock combat encounter, perhaps, followed by a surrender.

And here the story again stops following the usual war movie lines, and takes its own way, which I will not describe. Wharton seems to believe that the conditions of battle are such that insanity is a reasonable response, and as his characters cope, each in his own way, with the unreality of the forest and the war, and film moves toward a conclusion that is not at all what we were expecting.

The cast is first-rate, filled with young actors like Peter Berg, Kevin Dillon, Ayre Gross, Ethan Hawke, and Gary Sinise as Mother. The director, Keith Gordon, is about the same age as many of his actors, and this is his second film, after the interesting but not successful *Chocolate War.* Both films are about the dynamics of groups of young men, and about how at different times they select different leaders, because they have different needs about where to be led. *A*

Midnight Clear is a little too much of a parable for my taste—there are times when the characters seem to be acting out of the author's need, rather than their own—but it's a good film, and Gordon is uncanny in the way he suggests the eerie forest mysteries that permeate all of the action.

Midnight Run ★ ★ ★ ½
R, 123 m., 1988

Robert De Niro (Jack Walsh), Charles Grodin (Jonathan Mardukas), Yaphet Kotto (Alonzo Mosely), John Ashton (Marvin Dorfler), Dennis Farina (Jimmy Serrano), Joe Pantoliano (Eddie Moscone), Richard Foronjy (Tony Darvo), Robert Miranda (Joey), Jack Kehoe (Jerry Geisler), Wendy Phillip (Gail). Produced and directed by Martin Brest. Screenplay by George Gallo.

Jack Walsh is a bounty hunter, a former cop who now works for bondsmen, bringing back clients who have tried to jump bail. Jonathan Mardukas is an accountant who embezzled millions of dollars from the mob in Vegas, and then jumped bail. Oddly enough, what these two men have most in common is the way they see themselves as more ethical than the system.

The two men are played in *Midnight Run* by Robert De Niro and Charles Grodin, an odd couple who spend most of the movie trying to survive a cross-country trip while the FBI is trying to capture them and the Mafia is trying to kill them. Along the way, of course, they discover that despite their opposite natures, they really do like and respect one another.

This sounds like a formula, and it is a formula. But *Midnight Run* is not a formula movie, because the writing and acting make these two characters into specific, quirky individuals whose relationship becomes more interesting even as the chase grows more predictable. Whoever cast De Niro and Grodin must have had a sixth sense for the chemistry they would have; they work together so smoothly, and with such an evident sense of fun, that even their silences are intriguing.

De Niro does not usually appear in movie comedies, and when he does, as in *Brazil*, it's usually in some sort of bizarre disguise. Here he proves to have comic timing of the best sort—the kind that allows dramatic scenes to develop amusing undertones while still working seriously on the surface. It's one thing to go openly for a laugh. It's harder to do what he does, and allow the nature of the character to

get the laughs, while the character himself never seems to be trying to be funny.

De Niro is often said to be the best movie actor of his generation. Grodin has been in the movies just about as long, has appeared in more different titles, and is of more or less the same generation, but has never received the recognition he deserves—maybe because he often plays a quiet, self-effacing everyman. In *Midnight Run*, where he is literally handcuffed to De Niro at times, he is every bit the master's equal, and in the crucial final scene, it is Grodin who finds the emotional truth that defines their relationship.

The movie develops that relationship during and between a series of virtuoso action sequences, after De Niro finds Grodin in New York and sets out to return him to Los Angeles. Grodin is afraid of flying, so the two men set out on a long cross-country odyssey that involves train trips, a shoot-out at the Chicago bus terminal, hitchhiking, riding the rails in boxcars, and being attacked by helicopters.

Their pursuers come in waves. The FBI is led by agent Alonzo Mosely (Yaphet Kotto), who is enraged because De Niro has stolen his FBI identification and is posing as a federal agent. The Mafia team is deployed by Jimmy Serrano (Dennis Farina), who grows increasingly enraged as his hit squads miss their targets.

And all the time, De Niro and Grodin feud with each other as Grodin schemes to escape. He knows that if he is ever returned to custody, the mob will have him killed in prison, and so his strategy is to convince De Niro he was only an embezzler in order to combat the mob. Oddly enough, this seems to be the truth, and fits in with De Niro's story—he's an ex-cop who left the force because of all the bureaucratic interference with his crusade against evil.

What *Midnight Run* does with these two characters is astonishing, because it's accomplished within the structure of a comic thriller. The director, Martin Brest, came to this project after *Beverly Hills Cop*, but if the action in the two films is comparable, the characters are a lot more interesting this time. It's rare for a thriller to end with a scene of genuinely moving intimacy, but this one does, and it earns it.

A Midsummer Night's Sex Comedy
★ ★
PG, 88 m., 1982

Woody Allen (Andrew), Mia Farrow (Ariel), Jose Ferrer (Leopold), Julie Hagerty (Dulcy), Tony Roberts (Maxwell), Mary Steenburgen (Adrian). Directed by Woody Allen and produced by Robert Greenhut. Screenplay by Allen.

The further north you go in summer, the longer the twilight lingers, until night is but a finger drawn between the dusk and the dawn. Such nights in northern climes are times of revelry, when lads and maids frolic in the underbrush to the pipes of Pan. Woody Allen's *A Midsummer Night's Sex Comedy* sneaks up rather suspiciously on this tradition; his men and women are rationalists, belong to such professions as finance, medicine, and psychiatry, and are nonchalant in the face of such modern inventions as flying bicycles. And yet here they all are, out in the country for the weekend. They gather at a little cottage somewhere in upstate New York, arriving by carriage or primitive auto, and in no time at all they are deeply unhappy about each other's sex lives. The host and hostess are Woody Allen and Mary Steenburgen. He is a stockbroker and she is his shy and sweet wife. The guests include Jose Ferrer, as an egotistical scientist, Mia Farrow, as his fiancée, Tony Roberts as a doctor, and Julie Hagerty as his abundantly sexed nurse.

During the course of their long weekend, many themes emerge, but the most common one is the enigma of male jealousy. Look at these three men, each one paired with the wonderful woman of his dreams. Allen, a part-time crackpot inventor, has a wife who loyally supports his experiments. Ferrer, an aging genius with a monstrous ego, has a beautiful young woman to hang on his arm. Roberts, an insatiable satyr, has a nubile nurse panting with desire. Are all three men happy and satiated? Not a chance. It is the most inevitable thing in the world that each man should be consumed with lust for one or more of the other women. It is not enough to have a bird in the hand; one must also have another bird in the bush. Or, as David Merrick once observed, "It is not enough for me to succeed. My enemies must fail."

From this simple and intriguing little situation, Woody Allen spins a rondelet of sexual intrigue and frustration. The basic developments: Allen pines away with the thought that he could once have made love to Farrow, but declined the chance. Ferrer conspires to meet Hagerty in the woods. Roberts attempts to seduce Farrow. And, through it all, Steenburgen steadfastly hopes for the best from everybody. To pass the time in between assignations and intrigues, the couples picnic, go for walks in the woods and express curiosity in Allen's latest inventions, which, in addition to the flying bicycle, include a metal sphere that can provide a magic lantern show that remembers the past and foresees the future.

This all sounds very charming and whimsical, and it is—almost paralyzingly so. *A Midsummer Night's Sex Comedy* is so low-key, so sweet and offhand and slight, there are times when it hardly even seems happy to be a movie. I am not quite sure what Allen had in mind when he conceived this material, but in addition to the echoes of Shakespeare and of Bergman's *Smiles of a Summer Night*, there are suggestions of John Cheever's *Wapshots*, Doctorow's *Ragtime*, and Jean Renoir films in which nice people do nice things to little avail. This is not a "Woody Allen film," then. It is not a brash comedy, it does not really contain the Woody Allen persona, and I guess Woody wanted it that way; he says he wants to try new things instead of giving people the same old stuff all the time. It is our misfortune that he arrived at that decision just after making *Annie Hall* and *Manhattan*, two wonderful films that brought his same old stuff to an exciting new plateau.

Now, with *Stardust Memories* and this film, he seems rudderless. I don't object to *A Midsummer Night's Sex Comedy* on grounds that it's different from his earlier films, but on the more fundamental ground that it's adrift. There doesn't seem to be a driving idea behind it, a confident tone to give us the sure notion that Allen knows what he wants to do here. It's a tip-off that the story is lacking in both sex and comedy. If the film seems at a loss to know where to turn next, the ending is particularly unsatisfactory. It involves a moment of fantasy or spirituality in which one of the movie's most rational characters dies and turns into a spirit of light, and bobs away on the twilight breeze. I don't object to the development itself, but to the way Allen handles it, so briefly and incompletely that it ends the film with what can only be described as a whimsical anticlimax.

There are nice small moments here and reflective, quiet performances, and a few laughs and smiles. But when we see Woody pedaling furiously to spin the helicopter blades of his flying bicycle, we're reminded of what we're missing. Woody doesn't have to be funny in every shot and he doesn't have to become another Mel Brooks, but he should allow himself to be funny when he feels like it, without apology, instead of receding into cuteness. I had the feeling during the film that Woody Allen was soft-pedaling his talent, was sitting on his comic gift, was trying to be somebody that he is not—and that, even if he were, would not be half as wonderful a piece of work as the real Woody Allen.

Mighty Morphin Power Rangers™: The Movie ½ ★   [NEW]
PG, 88 m., 1995

Paul Freeman (Ivan Ooze), Jason David Frank (Tommy, White Ranger), Steve Cardenas (Rocky, Red Ranger), David Yost (Billy, Blue Ranger), Johnny Yong Bosch (Adam, Black Ranger), Amy Jo Johnson (Kimberly, Pink Ranger), Karan Ashley (Aisha, Yellow Ranger), Paul Schrier (Bulk), Jason Narvy (Skull), Gabrielle Fitzpatrick (Dulcea). Directed by Bryan Spicer and produced by Haim Saban, Shuki Levy, and Suzanne Todd. Screenplay by Arne Olsen and John Kamps.

Mighty Morphin Power Rangers™: The Movie is about as close as you can get to absolute nothing and still have a product to project on the screen. The movie is like those synthetic foods that have no fat, no sugar, no vitamins, and no calories, but they come in bright packages and you can chew them.

What depresses me inutterably is that children, who are fresh and inquisitive, will go to this movie and, for eighty-eight minutes, the movie will do what it can to deaden their imaginations. The movie is like a little unkindness done to its victims. Its status as a product is underlined by the curious practice of adding the trademark symbol after every occurrence of the name in all of the advertising and promotion. (No room for an apostrophe after "Morphin," though.)

The movie stars six teenaged characters who have been marketed on TV and in toy stores. They have names, but no discernible personalities. None of them ever says anything more interesting than "You guys!" As teenagers, they are skilled in-line skaters and karate fighters, but they don't get their *real* powers until they turn into faceless clones in Power Ranger™ uniforms with plastic masks and helmets.

Is that the message? Faceless conformity is the way to success? Certainly the Rangers™ are not individuals in or out of uniform, but I wonder if they don't represent a triumph of merchandising over creativity. Children's heroes have traditionally been individualistic and eccentric. The Rangers™ are not, properly speaking, even characters. They are color-coded products.

In the movie, their city of Angel Grove is under threat from Ivan Ooze, an evil villain who has been imprisoned for six thousand years inside a buried egg. Curious that six thousand years ago he would have had an English name. Liberated from his prison by construction workers, he wages war on Zordon, the Power Rangers'™ leader, who is an old man whose face is projected as a hologram inside a big glass jar.

Ooze has strange powers, including the ability to raise reinforcements by hawking up gobs of spit, which transform themselves into ooze-monsters. The movie also features various very large animated monsters that walk stiffly down phony-looking streets and do battle with one another in the tradition of the worst Japanese monster movies. Other action scenes involve the Power Rangers™ using badly choreographed martial arts moves on platoons of enemies, while mindless rock music drones on the sound track.

Ivan Ooze is the only character in the movie with any personality or interest. Some of his dialogue seems to have been slipped into the film by the writers as an antidote to their own boredom; the kids who go to this movie are unlikely to make much of Ooze's complaint that by being imprisoned in his egg, "I missed the Black Plague, the Spanish Inquisition, and the Brady Bunch reunion."

Paging through the movie's press kit, I came across the following quote attributed to Amy Jo Johnson, who portrays Kimberly, the Pink Power Ranger: "*Mighty Morphin Power Rangers™: The Movie* is a mix between *Star Wars* and *The Wizard of Oz.*" I wonder if Amy Jo actually said "TM" when she was delivering that wonderfully fresh and spontaneous quote, which is so much longer and more involved than anything she says in the movie. More to the point, I wonder if she has ever seen *Star Wars* or *The Wizard of Oz.*

The Mighty Quinn ★ ★ ★
R, 98 m., 1989

Denzel Washington (Xavier), James Fox (Elgin), Robert Townsend (Maubee), Mimi Rogers (Hadley), M. Emmet Walsh (Miller), Sheryl Lee Ralph (Lola), Art Evans (Jump),

Esther Rolle (Ubu Pearl), Norman Beaton (Governor Chalk). Directed by Carl Schenkel and produced by Sandy Lieberson, Marion Hunt, and Ed Elbert. Screenplay by Hampton Fancher, based on the novel *Finding Maubee* by A.H.Z. Carr.

The Mighty Quinn is a spy thriller, a buddy movie, a musical, a comedy, and a picture that is wise about human nature. And yet with all of those qualities, it never seems to strain: This is a graceful, almost charmed, entertainment. It tells the story of a police chief on an island not unlike Jamaica, who gets caught in the middle when a wealthy developer is found murdered. Everyone seems to believe the chief's best friend, a no-account drifter named Maubee, committed the crime. Everyone but the chief and the chief's wife, who observes laconically, "Maubee is a lover, not a killer."

The film stars Denzel Washington, in one of those roles that creates a movie star overnight. You might have imagined that would have happened to Washington after he starred in *Cry Freedom,* as the South African hero Steven Biko. He got an Oscar nomination for that performance, but it didn't even begin to hint at his reserves of charm, sexiness, and offbeat humor. In an effortless way that reminds me of Robert Mitchum, Michael Caine, or Sean Connery in the best of the Bond pictures, he is able to be tough and gentle at the same time, able to play a hero and yet not take himself too seriously. He plays Xavier Quinn, a local boy who once played barefoot with Maubee and got into the usual amount of trouble, but who grew up smart, went to America to be trained by the FBI, and has now returned as the police chief. The people of his district call him *The Mighty Quinn,* after the Bob Dylan song, and there is something both affectionate and ironic in the nickname. He knows everybody in town, knows their habits, and is on good terms even with the island governor (Norman Beaton), a cheerfully corrupt hack who only wants to keep the lid on things.

The murder is a great embarrassment. It is likely to discourage tourism, and perhaps there are more sinister reasons for sweeping the crime under the carpet and blaming Maubee. Quinn is the only one who wants to press an investigation, and it takes him into the decadent lives of the local establishment. He encounters Elgin, the suave local fixer (played by the elegant James Fox, that British specialist in the devious and the evasive). He is pow-

erfully attracted to Elgin's restless wife (Mimi Rogers), and has a private encounter with her that is charged with eroticism precisely because he wants to resist her seductiveness.

Most troublesome of all, he encounters a shambling, overweight, genial American who wanders around with a camera and always seems to be in the wrong place at the right time. This character, Miller, is played by M. Emmet Walsh, one of Hollywood's greatest character actors, who in this movie seems to combine the Sydney Greenstreet and Peter Lorre roles: He is comic relief at first, sinister malevolence later.

As his investigation makes its way through this moral quicksand, Quinn also weathers trouble at home. His wife, Lola (Sheryl Lee Ralph), is rehearsing with a reggae trio and is just a shade too emasculating to make a man truly comfortable around her. A local beauty (Tyra Ferrell) wants to steal Quinn away from her. An old crone (Esther Rolle), who is the island's resident witch, makes prophecies of dire outcomes. And the carefree Maubee himself (played by Robert Townsend) turns up to taunt Quinn with his innocence.

This story, rich enough to fuel one of the great and complicated old Warner Bros. plots, is enriched still further by wall-to-wall music, including a lot of reggae and even a couple of appearances by Rita Marley. And the photography by Jacques Steyn is natural and amused, allowing us to ease into the company of these people instead of confronting us with them.

Denzel Washington is at the heart of the movie, and what he accomplishes is a lesson in movie acting. He has obligatory action scenes, yes, and confrontations that are more or less routine. He handles them easily. But watch the way he and Mimi Rogers play their subtle romantic encounter. The scene develops in three beats instead of two, so that the erotic tension builds. But coexisting with his macho side is a playfulness that allows him to come up behind a woman and dance his fingers along her bare arms, and sashay off again before she knows what has happened.

If Washington is the discovery in this movie, he is only one of its many wonderful qualities. I'd never heard of the director, Carl Schenkel, before, and I learned from the press releases only that he is Swiss and has directed a lot of commercials, but on the basis of this film, he's a natural. He is able in the moderate running time of 98 minutes to create a film that seems as rich and detailed

as one much longer. He uses his Jamaican locations and interiors so easily that the movie seems to really inhabit its world, instead of merely being photographed in front of it. And the music helps; reggae somehow seems passionate, lilting, and comforting, all at once. *The Mighty Quinn* was one of 1989's best films.

Miles From Home ★ ★ ★
R, 113 m., 1988

Richard Gere (Frank Roberts), Kevin Anderson (Terry Roberts), Brian Dennehy (Frank, Sr.), Penelope Ann Miller (Sally), Helen Hunt (Jennifer), Judith Ivey (Frances), Laurie Metcalf (Exotic Dancer), John Malkovich (Reporter). Directed by Gary Sinise and produced by Frederick Zollo and Paul Kurta. Screenplay by Chris Gerolmo.

Miles From Home opens with what looks like old TV news footage, in snowy black and white, of big Cadillacs speeding down dusty roads past prosperous cornfields. Then we see the stocky man in the oversize suit climbing out of the limo, and we remember the event: This is the famous visit that Nikita Khrushchev paid to an average American farm in Iowa. On the front porch steps, he shakes hands with the farmer while the farmer's two small boys stand uneasily at attention, their hair slicked down flat with brilliantine.

That was thirty years ago. Now, as the film turns into color, a fierce rainstorm is sweeping the plains, and the farmer's two sons, grown to men, struggle to move a big combine before it can get stuck in the mud. The brothers are named Frank and Terry Roberts, and in the summer of 1987 they have a weather problem—ironically, in view of the drought of 1988, it is too much rainfall. Their corn is soaked and some of it is rotting. Their yield will be disappointing. On the walls of the farmhouse where they were born are plaques and clippings naming their father the Farmer of the Year. But this is not the first bad year the sons have had, and they will lose the farm to the bank.

Those are the opening scenes of *Miles From Home,* a movie about the farm crisis that is sometimes too contrived, but finally very moving as the story of an angry reaction to the squeeze on small farmers. The movie stars Richard Gere as the older, angrier brother, and Kevin Anderson as the younger, sweeter kid who is carried along by Gere's headlong rage.

There is a quiet scene near the front of the film that sets up a lot of things. The brothers are holding a yard sale to raise some cash. A thoughtless, pretty city girl (Penelope Ann Miller) stops by with a girlfriend and observes to Anderson, "People would have to be pretty desperate to try to sell junk like this." Then she realizes it is Anderson's farm. Her eyes fill with tears as she starts to apologize, but then there is a charged silence between the two of them, as they realize they have fallen in love.

All right, so love at first sight is contrived and corny, an obvious plot device. Plots are as good as the actors who inhabit them, however, and Kevin Anderson and Penelope Ann Miller create a believable, warm chemistry here, one that will serve as the film's center when the Gere character flies out of control. That happens slowly, implacably, as Gere realizes he has failed the memory of his father and the farm. He blames himself, and there is a scene in a cemetery, Gere talking to his father's tombstone, before the furies inside of him break loose.

In an action that mirrors one of the key scenes in *Bonnie and Clyde,* he shoots out some of the windows of the farmhouse. Then he intimidates his kid brother to join him in a wilder plan to burn down the farmhouse and set the fields ablaze rather than see the farm fall into the hands of the bank. With the flames roaring against the sky, the two brothers set off on a doomed escape across the state of Iowa, where the symbolism of their act makes them folk heroes.

Many of the visuals in *Miles From Home* seem to echo compositions in Terence Malick's *Days of Heaven* (1978), one of Richard Gere's earliest films. But the story of the two fugitives becoming media heroes is a reminder of both *Bonnie and Clyde* and Malick's own earlier film, *Badlands,* with Martin Sheen and Sissy Spacek on the run. That film began with a murder; this one seems doomed at times to lead to one.

As Gere and Anderson use a series of stolen cars to move across the state, they meet a series of strange people—outsiders and rebels—who support them. There is a roadhouse stripper (Laurie Metcalf), and an entranced woman in a trailer park (Judith Ivey), and a lean reporter who wants to tell their story (John Malkovich). And there are all the people in the beer tent at a county fair, who know exactly who these two young men really are and protect them from the police.

With the exception of Gere, the cast of *Miles From Home* is largely populated with members and alumni of Chicago's Steppenwolf Theater. Malkovich, Ivey, and Metcalf are familiar faces in the movies, but this is only the second starring role for Kevin Anderson (after *Orphans*) and he is strong in it, especially in his scenes with Miller, in which he shares his growing fear that his brother is running wild, dangerously out of control.

The direction of the film is by another Steppenwolf member, Gary Sinise, who reflects the Steppenwolf tradition to go for broke emotionally. There are scenes in the film—like the first falling-in-love scene—that a filmmaker with less courage would have shot in a more understated style. Steppenwolf has always been in love with melodrama, and *Miles From Home* is, too.

Milk Money ★
PG-13, 105 m., 1994

NEW

Melanie Griffith (V), Ed Harris (Dad), Michael Patrick Carter (Frank), Malcolm McDowell (Waltzer), Anne Heche (Betty), Casey Siemaszko (Cash), Philip Bosco (Jerry the Pope), Adam LaVorgna (Brad). Directed by Richard Benjamin and produced by Kathleen Kennedy and Frank Marshall. Screenplay by John Mattson.

Sometimes they produce a documentary about the making of a movie. You know, like *The Making of Jurassic Park*. I would give anything within reason to see *The Making of Milk Money*, or, for that matter, to simply listen to recordings of the executive story conferences. In fact, it's funny . . . as I sit here in reverie . . . why, it's almost as if I can hear the voices now. . . .

Studio Executive A: So what's the premise?

Studio Executive B: We got kids, we got sex, we got romance, all in a family picture.

A: Can't have sex in a family picture.

B: Depends. Nobody actually *has* sex. Sure, you got a hooker, but she's a *good* hooker, with a heart of gold. Melanie Griffith is gonna play her.

A: Kind of like *Working Girl Turns a Trick?*

B: Cuter than that. We start with three twelve-year-old boys. They're going crazy because they've never seen a naked woman.

A: Whatsamatter? They poor? Don't they have cable?

B: Ever hear of the concept of "the willing suspension of disbelief"? I know the audience will find it hard to believe but it's true: These kids don't know what a naked woman

looks like. So they pool their pocket money and ride their bikes into the big city, and ask women on the street if they're hookers, until they find one who is. That's Melanie.

A: How much they got?

B: More'n a hundred bucks. So she shows them.

A: She strips? This has got to get a PG-13 rating.

B: Like I say, it's a family movie. She only strips to the waist. And we only see her from the back.

A (slightly disappointed): Oh. So that's ten minutes. Where do we go from here?

B: There's more to the plot. Melanie is in danger from the evil gangsters who control prostitution, and after her pimp is killed they think she has all of his money. So she needs to hide out. And one of the kids thinks she'd make an ideal wife for his dad. So he invites her out to the suburbs.

A: The dad's not married?

B: We got a nice touch here. The kid's mother died in childbirth. So all his life he's had this single father. He wants to fix up Dad with the hooker, see? He thinks she'd make a great mom.

A: So we get a Meet Cute?

B: Yeah. See, the kid moves the hooker into his tree house, and then tells his dad that she's his buddy's math tutor.

A: What's she wearing?

B: A kind of clingy minidress with a low neckline. High heels.

A: Is that what a math tutor wears?

B: You ever see *My Tutor*? *Private Lessons*? Any of those Sybil Danning or Sylvia Kristel pictures?

A: You got a point. So Dad doesn't catch on.

B: Naw. He falls for her. Also, this is a nice angle, he's a high school science teacher who is fighting to save the wetlands near the school from an evil developer who wants to pave it and turn it into a shopping center. Dad is played by Ed Harris.

A (nods approvingly): Ecology. Very good.

B: So the hooker is in the tree house, Dad thinks she's a math tutor, and meanwhile the evil gangster is cruising the streets of the suburb with another hooker, looking for her. And Dad fights against the encroachment of the wetlands and chains himself to his automobile so the bulldozers can't come in. And meanwhile we throw in some of those cute conversations where one person means one thing and another person means something else. You know, so that all of the people in the town know she's a hooker except for Dad, who takes her out to eat and scandalizes your standard table of gossiping local biddies.

A: This is nice, this is original.

B: We put in some nice Norman Rockwell touches. Like, the way the kid communicates between his bedroom and the hooker in the tree house is with one of those old tin-can telephones? You know, where you attach two tin cans with a string?

A: I was never able to get one of those to work when I was a kid.

B: Neither was I. But don't worry. No kid today has ever seen one before, so they won't know. Today's kids use cellular phones and beepers.

A: Good point.

B: And then we get the big climax.

A: What happens?

B: I don't want to spoil it for you, but let's just say the gangster doesn't get what he wants, and true love saves the day.

A: What about the wetlands?

B: The wetlands? Let me just say, from the point of view of the ultimate significance of this picture, the message for the family audience sort of thing, the wetlands are what this picture is all about.

A: Saving the wetlands. A good cause.

B: Of course, you don't mention the wetlands in the ads.

A: No, you mention the hooker in the ads. So what's the picture called? *Pocket Money?*

B: No, it's called *Milk Money.*

A: Why *Milk Money?*

B: You'll understand when you see the ads.

Miller's Crossing ★ ★ ★
R, 115 m., 1990

Gabriel Byrne (Tom Reagan), Marcia Gay Harden (Verna), John Turturro (Bernie Bernbaum), Jon Polito (Johnny Caspar), J.E. Freeman (Eddie Dane), Albert Finney (Leo). Directed by Joel Coen and produced by Ethan Coen. Screenplay by Joel and Ethan Coen.

The room. I keep thinking about the room. The office from which Leo pulls the strings that control the city. Leo, played by Albert Finney, is a large, strong man in late middle-age, and he lacks confidence in only one area. He is not sure he can count on the love of Verna, the young dame he's fallen for. That causes him to hesitate when he knows that Verna's brother, Bernie, should be rubbed out. He doesn't want to lose Verna. And his hesitation brings the city's whole criminal

framework crashing down in blood and violence.

But I think about the room. What a wonderful room. All steeped in dark shadows, with expensive antique oak furniture and leather chairs and brass fittings and vast spaces of flooring between the yellow pools of light. I would like to work in this room. A man could get something done in this room. And yet the room is a key to why *Miller's Crossing* is not quite as successful as it should be—why it seems like a movie that is constantly aware of itself, instead of a movie that gets on with business.

I do not really think that Leo would have such an office. I believe it is the kind of office that would be created by a good interior designer with contacts in England, and supplied to a rich lawyer. I am not sure a rackets boss in a big American city in 1929 would occupy such a space, even though it does set him off as a sinister presence among the shadows.

I am also not sure that the other characters in this movie would inhabit quite the same clothing, accents, haircuts, and dwellings as we see them in. This doesn't look like a gangster movie, it looks like a commercial intended to look like a gangster movie. Everything is too designed. That goes for the plot and the dialogue, too. The dialogue is well-written, but it is indeed written. We admire the prose rather than the message. People make threats, and we think about how elegantly the threats are worded.

Miller's Crossing comes from two traditions that sometimes overlap: the gangster movie of the 1930s and the *film noir* of the 1940s. It finds its characters in the first and its visual style in the second, but the visuals lack a certain stylish tackiness that *film noir* often had. They're in good taste. The plot is as simple as an old gangster movie, but it takes us a long time to figure that out, because the first thirty minutes of the film involve the characters in complicated dialogue where they talk about a lot of people we haven't met, and refer to a lot of possibilities we don't understand. It's the kind of movie you have to figure out in hindsight.

Don't get me wrong. There is a lot here to admire. Albert Finney is especially good as Leo, the crime boss, and Jon Polito was wonderful as Johnny Caspar, his rival, who keeps talking about "business ethics." One of the most interesting characters in the movie is Bernie Bernbaum (John Turturro), a two-timing bookie who pleads for his life in a

monologue that he somehow keeps afloat long past any plausible dramatic length.

The pleasures of the film are largely technical. It is likely to be most appreciated by movielovers who will enjoy its resonance with films of the past. What it doesn't have is a narrative magnet to pull us through—a story line that makes us really care what happens, aside from the elegant, but mechanical, manipulations of the plot. The one human moment comes when Leo finds out Verna really can't be trusted. Even then, I was thinking about *Farewell, My Lovely,* where a big mug named Moose finds out the same thing about a dame named Velma.

Miracle Mile ★ ★ ★
R, 88 m., 1989

Anthony Edwards (Harry Washello), Mare Winningham (Julie Peters), John Agar (Ivan Peters), Lou Hancock (Lucy Peters), Mykel T. Williamson (Wilson), Kelly Minter (Charlotta), Kurt Fuller (Gerstead), Denise Crosby (Landa). Directed by Steve DeJarnatt. Produced by John Daly and Derek Gibson. Screenplay by DeJarnatt.

Miracle Mile has the logic of one of those nightmares in which you're sure something is terrible, hopeless, and dangerous, but you can't get anyone to listen to you—and besides, you have a sneaking suspicion that you might be mistaken. The film begins as a low-key boy-meets-girl story, and then a telephone is answered by the wrong person and everything goes horribly wrong. Much of the movie's diabolical effectiveness comes from the fact that it never reveals, until the very end, whether the nightmare is real, or only some sort of tragic misunderstanding.

The opening scenes are sunny and sweet. Harry (Anthony Edwards) and Julie (Mare Winningham) are two young people in Los Angeles who have what the movies like to call a Meet Cute; they like each other's looks, and begin to talk, and it's love at first sight, and so Harry makes a date to pick up Julie after she gets off work at the all-night coffee shop where she's a waitress. So far, so good, but then Harry oversleeps and wakes up in the middle of the night, confused and befuddled, and races down to the coffee shop, only to find that Julie has already left for home.

That's when the pay telephone rings in the booth outside the restaurant. Harry answers it, and hears some kind of panicky warning that he can barely understand. It's something about how nuclear missiles have been launched, and it's too late to recall them, and the Russians are involved, and the irrevocable events leading up to World War III have been set into motion. The guy on the other end of the line doesn't know who he's talking to; he thinks he called his father, and doesn't know he got the wrong number—and then there's the sound of gunfire, and Harry is told by a new voice to ignore everything he just heard.

Well, what *did* he hear? Was it a genuine call, or some sort of a practical joke? Did the guy on the other end really know what he was talking about? Or did Harry perhaps get everything out of context, and misunderstand it? This is the device through which the movie generates its suspense; we can never be sure that telephone call was genuine.

At first, Harry doesn't know what to do. And the inhabitants of the all-night diner aren't much help. One is a drunk, one is a drag queen, one is the hard-boiled short-order cook, and then there's the impeccably groomed brunette at the counter who calmly takes out a portable phone, dials a secret number, and tells them all that things look bad—that an attack may be on the way. Is she crazy, or what?

The movie was written and directed by Steve DeJarnatt, who toys with our sense of reality by establishing a time limit early in the film; there's about an hour until the missiles arrive, if they're indeed arriving. What can be done in that time? Harry desperately tries to find Julie, the girl with whom he wants to share his last moments of life. He and the short-order cook organize some kind of half-baked attempt to get out of town. Then there's a plan to use a helicopter pilot to airlift some of the characters out of the target zone. All of these disorganized plans are accompanied by confusion, bad communications, misunderstandings, accidents, and outbursts of violence—and the clock keeps ticking.

Miracle Mile reminded me a little, at times, of Martin Scorsese's *After Hours*. Both show a city at night, sleeping, dreaming, disoriented, while a character desperately tries to apply logic where it will not work. *Miracle Mile* is not as good as the Scorsese film, perhaps because its danger is an impersonal nuclear attack rather than the random craziness of late-night street people. But the effect is sometimes the same, and there is real terror in a scene where word of the possible attack begins to spread through the city, and there are riots in the streets. What the movie

confirmed for me is something I've always suspected; that if there's ever an hour's warning that the nuclear missiles are on the way, thanks all the same, but I'd just as soon not know about it.

Miracle on 34th Street ★ ★ ★
PG, 114 m., 1994

NEW

Richard Attenborough (Kriss Kringle), Elizabeth Perkins (Dorey Walker), Dylan McDermott (Bryan Bedford), Mara Wilson (Susan Walker), J.T. Walsh (Ed Collins), James Remar (Jack Duff), Jane Leeves (Alberta Leonard), Simon Jones (Shellhammer), William Windom (C.F. Cole). Directed by Les Mayfield and produced by John Hughes. Screenplay by George Seaton and Hughes.

Little girls are more sophisticated than they used to be. When six-year-old Susan Walker sees a drunken Santa Claus, for example, she takes it right in stride: "Bombed? It's the pressure." Susan's mother is the PR director for Cole's, a big Manhattan department store, and so the kid knows the angles. "This seems like a pretty pointless exercise," she sighs at one point, while climbing into Santa's lap.

But of course her disbelief in Santa Claus will not last long, because she finds herself in a retread of *Miracle on 34th Street*, the 1947 classic about a department store Santa who may possibly be the genuine article. The movie has been remade by producer John Hughes and director Les Mayfield, who follow the original fairly closely, but with a quieter, more elegiac tone.

As in the earlier version, this *Miracle* begins with a charming old gentleman who is hired on sight and pressed into service after the department store's Santa gets drunk at the start of the annual New York Thanksgiving parade. The old man says his name is Kriss Kringle (spelled with two S's in the new version, for no good reason). Played in 1947 by Edmund Gwenn (who won the Oscar), he's portrayed this time by Richard Attenborough, whose eyes twinkle and whose beard, he proves, cannot be pulled off.

Kringle is such a hit in the parade that he gets the full-time job as Cole's Santa, and inspires good publicity by telling children the truth even when it means sending them across the street for cheaper prices at the evil Shopper's Express store ("Today! Free gum guns!"). In a touching twist on the earlier film, where Santa was able to talk to a Dutch girl in her own language, this Kringle uses sign language with a deaf girl.

Meanwhile, little Susan (Mara Wilson) is beginning to wonder if there might perhaps be a Santa Claus after all. If there is, she knows what she wants: a father, a brother, and a house of their own. Her own dad has not been seen for years, but Bryan (Dylan McDermott), a lawyer who lives next door, is in love with her mother, Dorey (Elizabeth Perkins). Dorey is a cynic, once wounded and twice shy, who doesn't believe in Santa, or love.

The movie follows the 1947 version into a courtroom where, after some shady tricks by a rival department store, an attempt is made to have old Kriss Kringle declared insane because he really does believe he's Santa Claus. Bryan defends him, with results just as satisfying as in the original, and then there is the happy ending, even more satisfying, because when Bryan and Dorey get married, it is in the very same Chicago church where I got married, and so it was not possible to achieve critical objectivity.

There will never really be a movie to replace the 1947 *Miracle on 34th Street,* nor a performance to replace Edmund Gwenn's, but this modern update is a sweet, gentle, good-hearted film that stays true to the spirit of the original and doesn't try to make everything slick and exploitative. You know it's a good movie when you start humming the songs, and this time, it was "Joy to the World."

Misery ★ ★ ★
R, 104 m., 1990

James Caan (Paul Sheldon), Kathy Bates (Annie Wilkes), Richard Farnsworth (Buster), Frances Sternhagen (Virginia), Lauren Bacall (Marsha Sindell). Directed by Rob Reiner and produced by Andrew Scheinman and Reiner. Screenplay by William Goldman.

Stephen King has a modest, but undeniable genius for being able to find horror in everyday situations. My notion is that he starts with a germ of truth from his own life, and then takes it as far as he can into the macabre and the bizarre. Take *Misery*, for example, the story of a writer who finds himself the captive of his self-proclaimed "No. 1 fan." The hero has not finished a novel to her liking, and now she has him in her grip and he is writing under a particularly painful and violent deadline.

I can only imagine what some of the more peculiar fan letters of a writer like King must read like, and perhaps one of them even suggested this story. *Misery* involves a writer named Paul Sheldon (James Caan) who has been prostituting his talent for years with a series of romantic historical potboilers about a character named Misery, who after great triumphs and travails has finally been killed off. Having assassinated the character he had come to hate, Sheldon holes up in a Colorado lodge to write a "real" novel, and when he finishes it, he packs it into his car and heads down a mountain road in a blizzard, loses control of his car, and ends up injured and in a snowbank.

He might easily have died, but he's rescued by a brusque, resourceful woman named Annie Wilkes (Kathy Bates), who digs him out, takes him home, nurses him back to health, and then is outraged to learn he has killed off Misery. That simply will not do, and so she holds her invalid prisoner while he writes a sequel bringing Misery back to life.

The world thinks Sheldon is dead. We follow the search for his body, which involves his literary agent (Lauren Bacall), the local backwoods sheriff (Richard Farnsworth), and the sheriff's wife (Frances Sternhagen). They are essentially the only other actors in the movie, which develops mostly as a two-hander between Caan and Bates.

They make an intriguing team. Caan, who has been hyper in some of his recent performances, is controlled and even passive here, the disbelieving captive of a madwoman. Bates, who has the film's key role, is uncanny in her ability to switch, in an instant, from sweet solicitude to savage scorn. Some of the things Stephen King invents for her to do to the writer are so shocking that they could be a trap for an actor—an invitation to overact. But she somehow remains convincing inside her character's madness.

The material in Misery is so much Stephen King's own that it's a little surprising that a director like Rob Reiner would have been interested in making the film. Reiner has started with literary properties before—like King's Stand by Me and William Goldman's The Princess Bride—but his strength is in putting a personal stamp on his films (which also include the cross-country romance The Sure Thing and the fake documentary This Is Spinal Tap). What he does with Misery is essentially simply respectful—he "brings the story to the screen," as the saying goes.

It is a good story, a natural, and it grabs us. But just as there is almost no way to screw it up, so there's hardly any way to bring it above a certain level of inspiration. Many competent directors could have done what

Reiner does here, and perhaps many other actors could have done what Caan does, although the Kathy Bates performance is trickier and more special. The result is good craftsmanship, and a movie that works. It does not illuminate, challenge, or inspire, but it works.

Mishima ★ ★ ★ ★
R, 121 m., 1985

Ken Ogato (Yukio Mishima), Mashayuki Shionoya (Morita), Hiroshi Mikami (First Cadet), Naoko Otani (Mother). Directed by Paul Schrader and produced by Mata Yamamoto and Tom Luddy. Screenplay by Paul and Leonard Schrader.

The Japanese author Yukio Mishima seems to have thought of his life as a work of art, and more than anyone since Hemingway he got other people to think of it that way, too. He was a brilliant self-promoter who not only wrote important novels and plays, but also cultivated the press, posed for beefcake photographs, and founded his own private army. He was an advocate of a return to medieval Japanese values, considered himself a samurai, and died on schedule and according to his own plan: After occupying an Army garrison with some of his soldiers, he disemboweled himself while being beheaded by a follower.

Mishima's life obviously supplies the materials for a sensationalistic film. Paul Schrader has not made one. Instead, his Mishima takes this most flamboyant of writers and translates his life into a carefully structured examination of three different Mishimas: public, private, and literary.

The film begins with the public Mishima, a literary superstar who begins the last day of his life by ritualistically donning the uniform of his private army. From time to time during the film, we return to moments from that final day, as Mishima is jammed somewhat inelegantly into a tiny car and driven by his followers to an appointment with a Japanese general. The film ends with Mishima holding the general hostage, and winning the right to address the troops of the garrison (who must have been just as astonished as if Norman Mailer turned up at West Point). Although the film ends with Mishima's ritual suicide, it is not shown in the graphic detail that's popular in recent films; Schrader wisely realizes that too much blood would destroy the mood of his film and distract attention from the idea behind Mishima's death.

Mishima's last day is counterpointed with black-and-white sequences showing his childhood and adolescence, and with gloriously stylized color dramatizations of scenes from his novels, *Temple of the Golden Pavilion, Kyoko's House,* and *Runaway Horses.* The scenes from the novels were visualized by designer Eiko Ishioka, who seems to have been inspired by fantasy scenes from early Technicolor musicals. They don't summarize Mishima's novels so much as give us an idea about them; as we see the ritualistic aspects of his fantasies, we are seeing Japan through his eyes, as he wished it to be.

The black-and-white biographical sequences show a little boy growing up into a complicated man. Young Yukio, raised by his mother and his grandmother, was a lonely outcast with a painful stammer, and we can see in the insecurities of his youth impulses that led him to build his muscles, to leap for literary glory, and to wrap himself in the samurai ethic.

Mishima is a rather glorious project, in these days of pragmatic commercialism and rank cynicism in the movie industry. Although a sensationalized version of his life might have had potential at the box office (and although Schrader, author of *Taxi Driver,* director of *American Gigolo,* would have been quite capable of directing it), this is a much more ambitious and intellectual film.

It challenges us to think about Mishima, instead of simply observing the strange channels of his life. What did he prove, on the day when his life ended according to plan? That he was willing to pay the ultimate price to transform his life into an artistic statement—and also, perhaps, that some of his genius was madness. Was it worth it? Who can say who is not Mishima?

Miss Firecracker ★ ★ ★ ½
PG, 102 m., 1989

Holly Hunter (Carnelle Scott), Mary Steenburgen (Elaine Rutledge), Tim Robbins (Delmount Williams), Alfre Woodard (Popeye Jackson), Scott Glenn (Mac Sam), Veanne Cox (Tessy Mahoney), Ann Wedgeworth (Miss Blue), Trey Wilson (Benjamin Drapper), Amy Wright (Missy Mahoney), Kathleen Chalfant (Miss Lily). Directed by Thomas Schlamme and produced by Fred Berner. Screenplay by Beth Henley, based on her play *The Miss Firecracker Contest.*

At first I was thinking the beauty contest in *Miss Firecracker* was too impossibly cornball to be true, but then I remembered the county fair queens of my youth—teen-age girls made up to within an inch of their lives, and trotted out in their formal gowns to parade in the heat of an August afternoon, downwind from the hog judging, which always took place at about the same time. These contests were run by selfless volunteers, usually men of a certain age whose obsession with the rules and regulations helped them to sublimate their lust for the fairway beauties. The one thing I could sense, even as a kid covering the canned-goods competition for the local paper, was that these girls were desperate to prove something, and it had little to do with glamour.

In *Miss Firecracker,* the playwright Beth Henley has taken such a contest, the Fourth of July pageant in Yazoo City, Mississippi, and turned it into another of those Southern Gothic romances where mansions crumble and young women weep bitter tears because their older sisters are prettier than they are. This is not new material, but Henley replaces some of the painful sincerity with a lighthearted goofiness that cheers things up, and the movie is performed with the kind of insight that could only have been achieved by actresses who once, for a moment however brief, dreamed of themselves stepping forward with a radiant smile to accept the crown and the roses.

The film stars Holly Hunter, fresh from *Broadcast News,* as Carnelle Scott, who was adopted by her cousins in the Williams family after becoming an orphan at eight. She is now somewhere in her twenties, works as a fish-gutter at the local catfish packing plant, and has earned the nickname of "Miss Hot Tamale" among the local swains. But she has never quite forgotten the glorious day in 1972 when her cousin Elaine (Mary Steenburgen) was named Miss Firecracker, and stepped forward in all her glory and a shocking red gown. This is the summer, Carnelle has vowed, when she will finally succeed her cousin as the Fourth of July queen.

The movie opens with an assembly of the key players. Carnelle's boy cousin, Delmount (Tim Robbins) has just arrived in town via freight train, and has a drunken plan to sell the crumbling Williams mansion to developers. Elaine has come home for a visit from Atlanta, where she lives with her husband; she is scheduled to deliver the keynote address at this year's pageant, "My Life as a Beauty." Meanwhile, Carnelle despairs of getting Elaine to loan her the winning red

dress, and turns in desperation to a local black seamstress named Popeye (Alfre Woodard), who has designed prize-winning costumes before—but for bullfrogs.

Carnelle is on her best behavior, turning a cold shoulder to the local boys in heat. She has determined to live down her image as a Hot Tamale, and finally amount to something. But then the carnival arrives in town for the Fourth of July, and she has a reunion with Mac Sam (Scott Glenn), the smooth-talking roustabout who developed a taste for tamales over the years. Will she be able to preserve—or at least restore—her virtue? Will Elaine lend her the red dress? Will Delmount succeed in his scheme to sell the homestead out from under them? Will Popeye design a winning dress that does not make anyone think of bullfrogs?

Miss Firecracker is not so much concerned with the answers to these questions as with the asking of them. Every story like this has problems with the last act, in which all of the threads of plot have to be pulled together, but *Miss Firecracker* wisely spends most of its energy on character development, instead. Apart from Hunter and Steenburgen, who create a tight little ballet of cousinly "love" and jealousy, the most interesting characters in the movie are Delmount and Popeye—who behave in the most peculiar ways, and seem serenely unaware of it. They are both congenital outsiders, who sensibly cannot quite understand why anyone would want to be Miss Firecracker. Their difference is, Popeye wants to help Carnelle all she can, and Delmount affects a careless indifference. The performances by Tim Robbins (the young pitcher in *Bull Durham*) and Alfre Woodard (nominated for an Oscar for *Cross Creek*) are the hidden treasures of the movie.

The director and the cinematographer, Thomas Schlamme and Arthur Albert, surround the plot with a lot of local atmosphere—the movie was shot on location with the cooperation of everyone in Yazoo City, and I think we see most of them on the screen—and also with a sort of moony, romantic glow. Many of the scenes are set at night, when hearts can be bared with greater safety, and love can declare itself free from lust. What finally makes *Miss Firecracker* special is that it is not about who wins the contest, but about how all beauty contests are about the need to be loved, and about how silly a beauty contest can seem if somebody really loves you.

Missing ★ ★ ★
R, 122 m., 1982

Jack Lemmon (Ed Horman), Sissy Spacek (Beth Horman), Melanie Mayron (Terry Simon), John Shea (Charles Horman), Charles Cioffi (Capt. Tower), David Clennon (Consul Putnam). Directed by Constantin Costa-Gavras and produced by Edward and Mildred Lewis. Screenplay by Costa-Gavras and Donald Stewart.

Much has already been written about the bravery of *Missing,* which dares, we are told, to make a specific attack on American policies in Chile during and after the Allende regime. I wish the movie had been even braver—brave enough to risk a clear, unequivocal, uncompromised statement of its beliefs, instead of losing itself in a cluttered mishmash of stylistic excesses. This movie might have *really* been powerful, if it could have gotten out of its own way.

The story involves the disappearance in the early 1970s of a young American journalist in a country (not named) that is obviously intended to be Chile. The young man and his wife (played by John Shea and Sissy Spacek) have gone down there to live, write, and absorb the local color. But then a civil war breaks out, martial law is declared, troops roam the streets, and one day soldiers come and take the young man away. The movie is the record of the frustrating attempts by Spacek and her father-in-law (Jack Lemmon) to discover what happened to the missing man. It suggests that the young American might have been on some sort of informal hit list of left-wing foreign journalists, that he was taken away and killed, and that (this is the controversial part) American embassy officials knew about his fate and may even have been involved in approving his death.

If that was indeed the case, then it is a cause for great anger and dismay. And the best scenes in *Missing*—the ones that make this movie worth seeing despite its shortcomings—are the ones in which Spacek and Lemmon hack their way through a bureaucratic jungle in an attempt to get someone to make a simple statement of fact. Those scenes are masterful. The U.S. embassy officials are painted as dishonest weasels, shuffling papers, promising immediate action, and lying through their teeth. Lemmon and Spacek are about as good an example of Ordinary Americans as you can find in a movie, and their flat voices and stubborn determination and even their initial dislike for one another all ring exactly true. If *Missing* had started with the disappearance of the young man, and had followed Spacek and Lemmon in a straightforward narrative as they searched for him, this movie might have generated overwhelming tension and anger. But the movie never develops the power it should have had, because the director, Constantin Costa-Gavras, either lacked confidence in the strength of his story, or had too much confidence in his own stylistic virtuosity. He has achieved the unhappy feat of upstaging his own movie, losing it in a thicket of visual and editing stunts.

Let's begin with the most annoying example of his meddling. *Missing* contains scenes that take place before the young man disappears. We see his domestic happiness with his wife and friends, we see him reading from *The Little Prince* and making plans for the future. The fact that this material is in the movie suggests, at least, that the story is being told by an omniscient author, one who can also tell us, if he wishes to, what happened to the victim. But he does not. Costa-Gavras shows us all sorts of ominous warnings of approaching trouble (including a lot of loose talk by American military men who are not supposed to be in the country, but are, and all but claim credit for a coup). He shows us a tragic aftermath of martial law, guns in the streets, vigilante justice, and the chilling sight of row after row of dead young men, summarily executed by the new junta. But he does not show us what happened to make the film's hero disappear. Or, rather, he shows us several versions—visual fantasies in which the young husband is arrested at home by a lot of soldiers, or a few, and is taken away in this way or that. These versions are pegged to the unreliable eyewitness accounts of the people who live across the street. They dramatize an uncertain human fate in a time of upheaval, but they also distract fatally from the flow of the film.

By the time *Missing* begins its crucial last half-hour, a strange thing has happened. We care about this dead American, and his wife and father, almost *despite* the movie. The performances of Spacek and Lemmon carry us along through the movie's undisciplined stylistic displays. But at the end of the film, there isn't the instant discharge of anger we felt at the end of Costa-Gavras's great *Z* (1968), because the narrative juggernaut of that film has been traded in for what is basically just a fancy meditation on the nature of reality. Something happened to the missing

young man (his story is based on real events). Somebody was guilty, and somebody was lying, and he was indeed killed. But *Missing* loses its way on the road to those conclusions, and at the end Lemmon and Spacek seem almost to mourn alone, while the crew is busy looking for its next shot.

Mississippi Burning ★ ★ ★
R, 127 m., 1988

Gene Hackman (Anderson), Willem Dafoe (Ward), Frances McDormand (Mrs. Pell), Brad Dourif (Deputy Pell), R. Lee Ermey (Mayor Tilman), Gailard Sartain (Sheriff Stuckey), Stephen Tobolowsky (Townley), Michael Rooker (Frank Bailey), Pruitt Taylor Vince (Lester Cowens), Badja Djola (Agent Monk), Kevin Dunn (Agent Bird). Directed by Alan Parker and produced by Frederick Zollo and Robert F. Colesberry. Screenplay by Chris Gerolmo.

Movies often take place in towns, but they rarely seem to live in them. Alan Parker's *Mississippi Burning* feels like a movie made from the inside out, a movie that knows the ways and people of its small Southern city so intimately that, having seen it, I know the place I'd go for a cup of coffee and the place I'd steer clear from. This acute sense of time and place—rural Mississippi, 1964—is the lifeblood of the film, which gets inside the passion of race relations in America, and was the best film of 1988.

The film is based on a true story, the disappearance of Chaney, Goodman, and Schwerner, three young civil rights workers who were part of a voter registration drive in Mississippi. When their murdered bodies were finally discovered, their corpses were irrefutable testimony against the officials who had complained that the whole case was a publicity stunt, dreamed up by Northern liberals and outside agitators. The case became one of the milestones, like the day Rosa Parks took her seat on the bus or the day Martin Luther King marched into Montgomery, on the long march toward racial justice in this country.

But *Mississippi Burning* is not a documentary, nor does it strain to present a story based on the facts. This movie is a gritty police drama, bloody, passionate, and sometimes surprisingly funny, about the efforts of two FBI men to lead an investigation into the disappearances. Few men could be more opposite than these two agents: Anderson (Gene Hackman), the good old boy who used to be a

sheriff in a town a lot like this one, and Ward (Willem Dafoe), one of Bobby Kennedy's bright young men from the Justice Department. Anderson believes in keeping a low profile, hanging around the barber shop, sort of smelling out the likely perpetrators. Ward believes in a show of force, and calls in hundreds of federal agents and even the National Guard to search for the missing workers.

Anderson and Ward do not like each other very much. Both men feel they should be in charge of the operation. As they go their separate paths, we meet some of the people in the town: The mayor, a slick country-club type, who lectures against rabble-rousing outsiders. The sheriff, who thinks he can intimidate the FBI men. And Pell (Brad Dourif), a shifty-eyed deputy who has an alibi for the time the three men disappeared, and it's a good alibi—except why would he have an alibi so good, for precisely that time, unless he needed one?

The alibi depends on the word of Pell's wife (Frances McDormand), a woman who has taken a lot over the years from this self-hating racist, a man who needs a gun on his belt by day and a hood over his head by night just to gather the courage to stand and walk. Anderson, the Hackman character, singles her out immediately as the key to the case. He believes the sheriff's department delivered the three men over to the local klan, which murdered them. If he can get the wife to talk, the whole house of cards crashes down.

So he starts hanging around. Makes small talk. Shifts on his feet in her living room like a bashful boy. Lets his voice trail off, so that in the silence she can imagine that he was about to say what a pretty woman she still was. Anderson plays this woman like a piano. And she wants to be played. Because Gene Hackman is such a subtle actor, it takes us a while to realize that he has really fallen for her. He would like to rescue her from the scum she's married to, and wrap her up in his arms.

McDormand is wonderful in the role. She could have turned her role into a flashy showboat performance, but chose instead to show us a woman who had been raised and trained and beaten into accepting her man as her master, and who finally rejects that role simply because with her own eyes she can see that it's wrong to treat black people the way her husband does. The woman McDormand plays is quiet and shy and fearful, but in the moral decision she makes, she represents a generation that finally said, hey, what's going on here is simply not fair.

The relationship between the McDormand and Hackman characters is counterpoint to the main current of the film, which involves good police work, interrogations, searches and—mostly—hoping for tips. There is reason to believe that the local black community has a good idea of who committed the murders, but the klan trashes and burns the home of one family with a son who might talk, and there is terror in the air in the black neighborhood.

Parker, the director, doesn't use melodrama to show how terrified the local blacks are of reprisals; he uses realism. We see what can happen to people who are not "good nigras." The Dafoe character approaches a black man in a segregated luncheonette and asks him questions. The black refuses to talk to him—and *still* gets beaten by the klan. Sometimes keeping your mouth shut can be sound common sense. Parker has dealt with intimidating bullies before in his work, most notably in *Midnight Express,* but what makes this film so particular is the way he understates the evil in it. There are no great villains and sadistic torturers in this film, only banal little racists with a vicious streak.

By the end of the film, the bodies have been found, the murderers have been identified, and the wheels of justice have started to grind. We knew the outcome of this case when we started watching. What we may have forgotten, or never known, is exactly what kinds of currents were in the air in 1964. The civil rights movement of the early 1960s was the finest hour of modern American history, because it was the painful hour in which we determined to improve ourselves, instead of others. We grew. The South grew, the whole nation grew more comfortable with the radical idea that all men were created equal and endowed with certain inalienable rights, among them life, liberty, and the pursuit of happiness.

What *Mississippi Burning* evokes more clearly than anything else is how recently in our past those rights were routinely and *legally* denied to blacks, particularly in the South. In a time so recent that its cars are still on the road and its newspapers have not started to yellow, large parts of America were a police state in which the crime was to be black. Things are not great for blacks today, but at least official racism is no longer on the law books anywhere. And no other movie I've seen captures so forcefully the look, the

feel, the very smell of racism. We can feel how sexy their hatred feels to the racists in this movie, how it replaces other entertainments, how it compensates for their sense of worthlessness. And we can feel something breaking free, the fresh air rushing in, when the back of that racism is broken.

Mississippi Masala ★ ★ ★ ½
R, 118 m., 1992

Denzel Washington (Demetrius), Sarita Choudhury (Mina), Roshan Seth (Jay [Her Father]), Sharmila Tagore (Kinnu [Her Mother]), Charles S. Dutton (Tyrone). Directed by Mira Nair and produced by Michael Nozik and Nair. Screenplay by Sooni Taraporevala.

The director Mira Nair made an unexpected discovery a few years ago: A lot of the independent motels in the Deep South are owned and operated by Asian Indians. Although they trace their roots back to India or Pakistan, many of them arrived in America via Uganda, where they had put down roots for two or three generations, showing a gift for running small businesses before Idi Amin ordered them all to leave in 1972. Nair, who is herself from India via Harvard, made her discovery while journeying in the South after the release of *Salaam Bombay!* (1988), her wonderful first film about a street child. She decided to make a movie about it.

Her film opens in Uganda, where an Indian lawyer's family lives in comfort and security until Amin confiscates the property of tens of thousands of Indians and orders them to leave immediately. The story continues in Greenwood, Mississippi, where the lawyer and his wife (Roshan Seth and Sharmila Tagore) own a shabby roadside motel. Their daughter, Mina (Sarita Choudhury), a child with sketchy memories of Africa, has grown into a ripe beauty of twenty-four, with an American accent that immediately suggests she does not share all of her family's ideas.

Driving a car one day, she crashes into the van of a young black man (Denzel Washington), and exchanges addresses and perhaps a subtle glance of curiosity. He's interested too, and eventually they go out on a date. This is not the sort of social life Mina's parents approve of; they expect their daughter to marry within their extended community of Indian exiles and forbid her to see Washington.

The ban only serves to underline the isolated nature of the young woman's life, and there are ironies in the racism and color con-

sciousness she faces. Within her own community, she is considered too dark-skinned to make a desirable wife (her mother explains that if you want to catch a husband, you can be dark and rich, or light and poor, but not dark and poor). Within the black community, the Indian woman is at first accepted with friendliness (Washington takes her to meet his family at a backyard picnic). But after all of the local Indian motel owners boycott Washington's rug-cleaning company, the blacks get angry, too.

What we are dealing with is more than a transplanted version of *Romeo and Juliet*. Both the black and Indian characters (and certainly the local whites, who are not much of a factor in this movie) have a vast and comfortable lack of curiosity about other races; they prefer to think of them in stereotypes, and have no desire to meet them as individuals. When the Indian woman and the black man meet and fall in love with one another, everyone on all sides falls obediently into place to condemn their relationship.

It was racism, of course, that brought the Indians to Africa in the first place, to build the railroads, and racism that kicked them out. And it was racism that brought Africans to America. But to be a victim of the racism of others does not inoculate anyone against the prejudice that can grow in his own heart.

All of these serious questions linger just under the surface of *Mississippi Masala,* which is, despite its subject, surprisingly funny and cheerful at times, and generates a full-blown romanticism. Denzel Washington is an actor of immense and natural charm, and he makes a good match with Sarita Choudhury, a newcomer who seems a little awkward in some of her scenes, but uses that feeling as part of her performance.

If I have a complaint about Nair's work, it's that she tries to cover too much ground. She knows a lot about her subject, but should have decided what was important and left out the rest. The scenes in Uganda, for example, are not necessary for narrative purposes, and her closing scenes (as the father returns to the home of twenty years earlier) upstage the conclusion of the love story.

She also has a lot of material about the daily lives of Indians in Mississippi, and while I find some of it amusing and all of it interesting, it also serves to keep the young lovers out of the foreground for extended periods of screen time. There are really three movies here—the exile from Uganda, the love story, and the lives of Indians in the

Deep South—and only screen time enough for one of them.

And yet I do not complain too much, because *Mississippi Masala* has the benefit of showing me people I had not met before, coping with the human currents that carried them all, blacks and Indians, out of Africa and across the ocean to Mississippi. The movie is about people who, having survived those upheavals, nevertheless have no curiosity about those outside their own social and racial circles—and about a few who do.

Mr. and Mrs. Bridge ★ ★ ★
PG-13, 127 m., 1991

Paul Newman (Walter Bridge), Joanne Woodward (India Bridge), Margaret Welsh (Carolyn Bridge), Kyra Sedgwick (Ruth Bridge), Blythe Danner (Grace Barron), Robert Sean Leonard (Douglas Bridge), Simon Callow (Dr. Alex Sauer). Directed by James Ivory and produced by Ismail Merchant. Screenplay by Ruth Prawer Jhabvala.

Mr. and Mrs. Bridge observes with great care and an almost frightening detachment the precise ways in which an emotionally paralyzed couple gets through life together. The movie is set in an affluent Kansas City neighborhood in the 1930s and 1940s. Manicured lawns surround generous white houses with green shutters, and inside the house of the Bridges lives a man who is absolutely sure he knows how life is best to be lived, but his knowledge is not bringing very much happiness to his family.

Mr. Bridge is a lawyer, played by Paul Newman in one of his most daring and self-effacing performances. Mrs. Bridge is a housewife, played by Joanne Woodward in a masterful observation of suppression and resignation. It is hard to say exactly what is the matter with Mr. Bridge—whether he is frightened of intimacy, or shy, or simply locked into his view of proper male behavior. Whatever his problem, it involves a subtle sort of psychological wife-beating, in which his wife is essentially his emotional captive. She can communicate with him only by following careful formulas involving what can be said, and how, and when.

Passion has perhaps never existed in this couple—not, at least, joyous passion. Even the first sexual experiences must have been largely physical, involving bodily functions more than personalities. Now life has settled into a routine. The children have nearly grown up, and are hardly known to their father. Their mother knows them better, but is afraid to reveal all she knows, or tell them all she wants to say. Mr. Bridge goes off to his office and does his job and associates in time-honored patterns of ritual with his fellow professional men, and Mrs. Bridge, "keeping house," reminds me of that woman that Stevie Smith wrote about—the woman out in the sea who seemed to be waving, but was not waving, but drowning.

The film is based on two novels by Evan S. Connell, adapted by another novelist, Ruth Prawer Jhabvala, for her longtime collaborators the director James Ivory and the producer Ismail Merchant. Their other work includes *A Room With a View* and *The Bostonians*, and it is not surprising that they were drawn to this carefully seen portrait of social behavior. The film does not have a plot in the ordinary sense of the word, perhaps because a plot would have appeared unseemly to Mr. Bridge; one does not, in his world, do this in order to have that happen. One exists as nearly as possible in the same admirable way, day after day.

Incidents happen. The Bridges have children who want to lead lives that do not correspond to the family values and timetable. They are absolutely forced to rebel in one way or another, because within the family there is no room for compromise. Mrs. Bridge has a friend (Blythe Danner) who is slowly cracking up; the alcoholism that is killing her is her only strategy for surviving. For Mrs. Bridge, this friend is an external sign of her own inner turmoil. Her own life is apparently ordered and serene, and seems placid and happy to the world, but in a way she is as desperate as her friend.

The movie is not heavy-handed. It does not present Mr. Bridge as a monster. He is as trapped in his world as everyone else. Very occasionally he permits himself the smallest of tight-lipped smiles, and once in a very long time, he will unbend a little. But essentially he is the captive of duty, and his duty as a professional white man in Kansas City in the late 1930s is to conform, to do what is expected, to present the proper appearances, and to beware of emotional extremes that could lead him to lose control.

Much is made of the excesses and silliness of the sixties, but it is because of that liberating decade that Mr. Bridge and his world will never quite exist again, and it is worth remembering that the young people of the 1960s were the children of parents who were often very much like the Bridges: parents who were playing out some ideal role of probity and respectability, and who were so wary of their own feelings that they disciplined their children for having feelings at all.

I hope I haven't made *Mr. and Mrs. Bridge* seem like a dreary or depressing film. Bad films are depressing. Good films, no matter what they're about, are exhilarating, and *Mr. and Mrs. Bridge* observes its characters with such attention and care that it is always absorbing. Most movies want us to care about what happens to the characters. This one simply wants us to care about them. The work of Woodward and Newman here is a classic example of a certain kind of acting, of studies of voice and behavior, of fleeting glances and subtle nuances of body language, of people who would almost rather drown than wave.

Mr. Baseball ★ ★ ★
PG-13, 111 m., 1992

Tom Selleck (Jack Elliot), Ken Takakura (Uchiyama), Aya Takanashi (Hiroko Uchiyama), Dennis Haysbert ("Hammer" Dubois), Toshi Shioya (Yoji Nishimura), Kohsuke Toyohara (Toshi Yamashita). Directed by Fred Schepisi and produced by Schepisi, Doug Claybourne, and Robert Newmyer. Screenplay by Gary Ross, Kevin Wade, and Monte Merrick.

Mr. Baseball is another one of those formula sports movies, in which the locale is changed but the recipe stays the same. I was able to anticipate almost everything that happened, as in the predictable hockey movie *The Mighty Ducks*. So why did I like it? Maybe because style is as important as story in a movie like this, and *Mr. Baseball* is not without a certain flair.

The movie stars Tom Selleck, convincing as a heavy-hitting first baseman who is traded to Japan by the New York Yankees. He's not a paragon of virtue. He drinks, chews, smokes cigars, womanizes, and has a bad attitude and a bum knee. Faced with calisthenics on his first day in Japan, he grumbles: "Athletes? We aren't athletes. We're baseball players."

He's the property of the Nagoya Dragons. The team is coached by Uchiyama (Ken Takakura, from *Black Rain*), a crusty old-timer who insists Selleck has a hole in his swing. Selleck is not prepared to take advice on this or any other baseball subject from a Japanese, and before long he's in hot water for disobeying orders, losing his temper, getting into fights, and insulting the management.

There is, of course, a woman. There always is in this formula. Her name is Hiroko (Aya Takanashi), and for once she is not a clone of the stereotyped quasi-geisha; she's an advertising professional who runs the club's endorsements, and makes Selleck appear in commercials he would rather not think about. They fall in love, but because of his ignorance of Japanese ways he is forever committing grave offenses against proper behavior, and she is forever vowing never to speak to him again.

The other major character is an African-American player named Hammer and played by Dennis Haysbert in the obligatory good-buddy role. He gives advice on such matters as taking off one's shoes before entering the clubhouse. Together, Selleck and Haysbert try to instill a fighting spirit into a club that avoids trying to steal extra bases because getting thrown out would be a loss of face.

The movie is directed by Fred Schepisi, an Australian who usually avoids genre films like this (his credits include *A Cry in the Dark* and *Russia House*). He gives this one some unexpected touches, of which the best is the handling of the crowd scenes. You can spot the phony crowds in most baseball movies (*The Babe* never seemed to have enough people in the stands), but here Schepisi uses a documentary approach to show real crowds at real games, and he joins the fictional action so seamlessly it's not only convincing, but exciting, as the Dragons go into the big series against their archrivals.

Schepisi and Selleck also do a nice, quiet job of making the title character convincing. He isn't overwritten or overplayed, and seems like what he is: A player of considerable but not unlimited ability who needs to do some growing up. He grows up, the games get played, the subplots resolve themselves satisfactorily, and although the movie sets no records for brilliance, it works.

Mister Johnson ★ ★ ★
PG-13, 101 m., 1991

Maynard Eziashi (Mister Johnson), Pierce Brosnan (Harry Rudbeck), Edward Woodward (Sargy Gollup), Beatie Edney (Celia Rudbeck). Directed by Bruce Beresford and produced by Michael Fitzgerald. Screenplay by William Boyd.

When the novelist Joyce Cary went out to Nigeria to join the British colonial civil service in 1913, there was no question in his mind, and in the minds of most British, that he was doing a good thing, representing the world's greatest democracy in an African backwater much in need of improvement. When Cary wrote *Mister Johnson*, the fourth of his African novels in 1939, some questions had begun to arise. The novel is about those questions.

Mister Johnson, directed by Bruce Beresford in his first film since *Driving Miss Daisy*, tells the story of an African civil servant, known to all as Mister Johnson, who works as a clerk in the office of the British district administrator. Mister Johnson, played by Maynard Eziashi in a performance of great humor, grace, and desperation, has adopted the values of Great Britain so enthusiastically that he even thinks of himself as British, and wears a white tropical suit and leather dress shoes even in the summer's fierce heat. He speaks of "our" standards and "our" institutions, and places his trust in his district officer while failing to understand that the purpose of British law in Nigeria is to protect the British and subdue Africans like himself.

He is a cheerful man, this Mister Johnson, hurrying through the district, flirting with the pretty girls, reprimanding laggards for not being up to his standards, and working efficiently for his boss, Harry Rudbeck (Pierce Brosnan). It is Brosnan's obsession to build a great road into the wilderness and connect his outpost with the capital. Perhaps he sees himself as a local version of an empire-builder of the earlier generation, Cecil Rhodes, who dreamed of an all-British route all the way from Cape Town to Cairo.

There is, alas, not enough money for the road, and it looks like work will have to be halted until Johnson suggests to Rudbeck that they juggle the books a little, robbing Peter to pay Paul, until the next year's budget comes through. Rudbeck agrees, but when the deception is discovered, of course, it is Johnson who must be dismissed for the bookkeeping infraction.

Loss of his position and status is a serious blow for Mister Johnson, who has a good many debts to pay. But he soon finds another job, working as a clerk for Sargy Gollup (Edward Woodward), the hard-drinking British owner of the local general store. Gollup has a drunken love-hate relationship with Africans, who he sometimes beats "for their own good," and the desperate Mister Johnson agrees with him—partly because he has no other choice, but also because in his increasingly confused mind, he identifies with him.

There is obviously going to be a tragedy here somewhere, and it is equally obvious that it is Mister Johnson who is going to suffer, despite all of the glories of British justice which he so admires. There is a genuine sadness in the scenes where Johnson forgives Harry Rudbeck for the sentence he has to carry out, and even sympathizes with him and tries to cheer him up.

There is also, of course, a savage irony in the fact that Rudbeck knows Johnson got into trouble in the first place by taking the rap for him. One of the subtleties of the film is the way this is never quite spelled out—not even by Rudbeck to his wife, Celia (Beatie Edney). Rudbeck maintains silence about his own guilt even while outwardly continuing to be a humane and reasonable administrator, and the film's last scenes take on a terrible sadness because of this silence.

I have seen *Mister Johnson* two times, and both times I admired its sense of time and place, and the thoughtful performances of Eziashi, Brosnan, and Woodward. Beresford's screenwriter is the novelist William Boyd, whose own novels, especially *An Ice-Cream War*, are set in British East Africa a few decades later. What they are doing here is quiet and rather tricky. They're not banging the audience over the head with the injustice of what happens to Johnson, but trying to re-create a moment in colonial history when many people, both white and black, believed in the rhetoric of official idealism, even while it was rotting from within.

The result is a very subtle film, one where the ideas are sometimes in danger of being overwhelmed by the sheer exuberance of Eziashi's performance. After seeing the film, I found myself asking what it was really about—was there a message, or only a careful reconstruction of a moment in history? There is a message, I now believe, but so subdued that some viewers may leave the film thinking it has said the opposite of what Beresford and Boyd intended—that it mocks, rather than celebrates, the martyrdom of Mister Johnson. The movie, like the Cary novel, allows us to find its truth in our own way.

Mr. Jones ★ ★ ★
R, 114 m., 1993

Richard Gere (Mr. Jones), Lena Olin (Libbie), Anne Bancroft (Dr. Holland), Tom Irwin (Patrick), Delroy Lindo (Howard), Bruce Altman (David), Lauren Tom (Amanda), Lisa Malkiewicz (Susan). Directed by Mike Figgis and produced by Alan Greisman and Debra

Greenfield. Screenplay by Eric Roth and Michael Cristofer.

There is a scene in *Mr. Jones* where the hero, played by Richard Gere, is experiencing manic euphoria. He is all-powerful, he is elated, everything has become clear at last! He walks into a symphony concert as the orchestra is playing Beethoven's "Ode to Joy." It's his theme song! He walks down the aisle and onto the stage, his arms waving, and tries to take over from the conductor.

In the next scene Mr. Jones is in a mental hospital, drugged into a stupor, but he fights against the drugs, against the whole depressing world of normality. He misses his euphoria. Only then does he have charm, wit, grace, intelligence. And only then is he invulnerable to the grief of the world. What is remarkable about *Mr. Jones* is how clearly it communicates his feelings.

Gere is the right actor for this role. He has always brimmed with a cocky self-confidence. He projects the sense that he can talk anybody into anything; he could have been a con man instead of an actor. In other movies he has used his charm in a conventional sense, to make friends, seduce women, get his way. But Gere has always been a risk-taker as an actor, and in *Mr. Jones* he is like a magician revealing his tricks: He shows you how he can turn up the heat, and turn it down again.

In the film we never really find out very much about Mr. Jones, except that he wanders into lives with a sad mixture of elation and dejection. At the mental hospital, he comes under the care of a psychiatrist named Libbie (Lena Olin), who finds herself falling for him with her eyes wide open. She knows it is wrong for a psychiatrist to get romantically involved with a patient, and she even knows she may be falling in love with the disease, not the man. But he's so charming. It's too bad about this aspect of the screenplay. The study of Mr. Jones is itself so interesting that we don't require the addition of a forbidden romance to make the movie work. The story is told so intelligently that we feel Libbie should know better. In a less ambitious movie, we might accept the romance as part of the whole commercial formula. But *Mr. Jones*, directed by Mike Figgis and written by Eric Roth and Michael Cristofer, seems too wise about mental illness to make such a mistake.

The movie does a good job of portraying the two worlds that Gere inhabits: the institution, and the outside. There are strong supporting performances by Lisa Malkiewicz, as a bank teller who gets swept off her feet and is still a little in love with him even after being his date to that fateful concert. Lauren Tom plays a fellow patient who never gets the help she needs. And Delroy Lindo is a man who seems to understand Jones more or less on his own terms, while recognizing that he needs help.

Gere spent time among mental patients in researching the role, and the filmmakers are obviously familiar with their subject. The question of the psychiatrist's liaison with her patient is even treated correctly; she knows she has behaved wrongly, and confesses to a superior (Anne Bancroft). It's just that the whole romantic subplot feels contrived, an add-on to a story that didn't need one.

Yet the movie is worth seeing, for Gere's transitions from highs to lows, which are done so convincingly that we really do feel in the presence of mental illness, with all of its seductive interior logic. There is often a strange quality about crazy people: They are filled with a glowing conviction that everything makes sense, and sometimes we almost envy them.

Mrs. Doubtfire ★ ★ ½
PG-13, 125 m., 1993

Robin Williams (Daniel Hillard/Mrs. Doubtfire), Sally Field (Miranda Hillard), Pierce Brosnan (Stu), Harvey Fierstein (Frank), Robert Prosky (Mr. Lundy), Lisa Jakub (Lydia Hillard), Matthew Lawrence (Chris Hillard), Mara Wilson (Natalie Hillard). Directed by Chris Columbus and produced by Marsha Garces Williams and Mark Radcliffe. Screenplay by Randi Mayem Singer and Leslie Dixon.

Mrs. Doubtfire tells the story of a divorced man who misses his children so desperately that he disguises himself as a middle-aged British nanny in order to be near them. The man's ex-wife and three kids are all, of course, completely fooled by the deception, leading to great poignancy when the man hears himself discussed in what appears to be his absence.

If this plot sounds to you like an elaborate scheme to create a comic role for an actor in drag, you would not be far off; Robin Williams, who is famous for his ability to do voices and impressions, would have had to be carried kicking and screaming away from the project. But the film is not as amusing as the premise, and there were long stretches when I'd had quite enough of Mrs. Doubtfire.

Williams stars in the movie as Daniel Hillard, an actor who specializes in dubbing the voices of cartoon characters. That means we get a title sequence showing him talking like a cat and a mouse, and since he's done such a brilliant job with characters like the genie in *Aladdin*, this is fun to see.

But soon the plot machinery begins to creak. His wife, Miranda (Sally Field), can no longer endure his little eccentricities, like hiring a private zoo for his son's birthday party. She files for divorce. The judge gives Daniel visitation rights only on Saturdays. And so he turns in desperation to his gay brother, Frank (Harvey Fierstein), a makeup expert, who helps disguise him as the redoubtable Mrs. Doubtfire, a younger but not slimmer Miss Marple.

The disguise is surprisingly good. Not good enough to fool one's own kith and kin, I suppose, but we can allow the movie its premise. Mrs. Doubtfire turns out to be the nanny from heaven, so firm, so helpful, so reassuring, that if Daniel had been at all like this, he'd still be married. The kids love him.

Act two. Time for complications. His exwife turns up with a new boyfriend (Pierce Brosnan), and Daniel, in drag, has to stand by and grind his teeth as the romance progresses. Daniel has been ordered to find work by the judge, and is employed as a shipping clerk at a TV station. (This is necessary for plot purposes, I guess; otherwise, why would a skilled and experienced voiceover actor not be able to make more money in his original field?)

All leads up to the movie's climactic comic set piece, when, for complicated reasons, both Daniel and Mrs. Doubtfire must be in the same restaurant at the same time, at different tables. Is this funny? Sort of. But it doesn't explode with humor the way it really should.

Everyone knows that Williams is a mercurial talent who loves to dart in and out of many different characters and voices. But a little of that goes a long way, and already has. There's a scene here, for example, where Williams "does" a dozen voices for an employment counselor, and the movie stops cold for this vaudeville act, just as the Marx Brothers movies always paused for Harpo's instrumental solos.

Any review of *Mrs. Doubtfire* must take into account Dustin Hoffman's transvestite comedy, *Tootsie*, which remains by far the better film: more believable, more intelligent, and funnier. *Tootsie* grew out of real wit and insight; *Mrs. Doubtfire* has the values and depth of a sitcom. Hoffman as an actor was able to successfully play a woman. Williams, who is also a good actor, seems more to be playing himself playing a woman.

Mrs. Parker and the Vicious Circle   NEW
★ ★ ★ ½
R, 124 m., 1994
(See related Film Clip, p. 881.)

Jennifer Jason Leigh (Dorothy Parker), Campbell Scott (Robert Benchley), Matthew Broderick (Charles MacArthur), Andrew McCarthy (Eddie Parker), Tom McGowan (Alexander Woollcott), Nick Cassavetes (Robert Sherwood), Gary Basaraba (Heywood Broun), Jake Johannsen (John Peter Toohey). Directed by Alan Rudolph and produced by Robert Altman. Screenplay by Rudolph and Randy Sue Coburn.

> *Guns aren't lawful;*
> *Nooses give;*
> *Gas smells awful;*
> *You might as well live.*
> —Dorothy Parker

And live she did, until her life itself became a long-running suicide note. When she died at seventy-four in 1967, nearly forty years had passed since she reigned at the Algonquin Round Table, that fabled shrine in a hotel dining room where New York's wits practiced their art on one another, and got drunk. Dorothy Parker was the wittiest of the Algonquin crowd, and the one whose work has survived the best, and probably she was the saddest, too; she never won her true love, drank too much, and her wonderful talent rarely broke free from the wisecracks and the booze. Her credo: "Let's go wild tonight! There's plenty of time to do nothing once you're dead."

The great achievement of Alan Rudolph's *Mrs. Parker and the Vicious Circle* is that it allows us to empathize with Dorothy Parker on her long descent. That is largely because of the performance by Jennifer Jason Leigh in the title role, as a small, pretty, tough alcoholic—a woman who found unhappiness in love affairs and two marriages (to the same man) and spent a lifetime in love with another man, who she never married.

That was the humorist Robert Benchley, whose short subjects used to play before feature films in the 1930s and 1940s, and who was once as famous as he is now forgotten. I read everything he wrote when I was young,

and thought Benchley had to be the nicest, as well as the funniest, man alive (Thurber was as funny, but not nice). Campbell Scott plays him in *Mrs. Parker* with a detached, almost studious niceness that is just right: If he tried any harder, he'd seem to *want* to be nice, and of course the Algonquin wits lived in fear of ever seeming to want to be anything.

As the story opens in the 1920s, Parker and Benchley are working for *Vanity Fair* magazine. Parker is fired because of the caustic tone of her reviews, Benchley resigns in sympathy, and they establish their own partnership, named the Utica Drop Forge and Tool Co. It consists of the two of them sitting at facing desks with twin typewriters, and it is significant that their typewriters are between them: They kept themselves apart with words. "I'm afraid I might lose you," she tells him at one point, and he replies gently, "You'd have to wear a pretty large hole in your pocket to lose me, Mrs. Parker."

In New York in the 1920s, before television, the written and spoken word was king, and the members of the Algonquin Round Table were known for their quick verbal skills. A legend grew up around them so potent that even today they are remembered for their wit (even if few people can quote any of it). They met every day for lunch and basically drank right on through until dawn; it is hard to see how they got any work done, but they did, and also hard to imagine how they kept up the level of their conversation, but perhaps they did not: Hours of conversation were distilled in the next morning's columns into perfectly edited little gems.

Rudolph follows the favorite approach of his producer, Robert Altman, in assembling a large number of characters and thrusting us into the middle of them. Since few people among the general movie audience today are likely to recognize Robert Sherwood, Edna Ferber, George S. Kaufman, Wolcott Gibbs, Heywood Broun, or Harold Ross, Rudolph doesn't pause to explain them. If you know who they are, you'll be happy to see them, and if you don't, they work as background to the film's heroine and the key men in her life: Eddie Parker (Andrew McCarthy), the alcoholic war hero she married twice; Charles MacArthur (Matthew Broderick), the dashing newsman and screenwriter who loved and dumped her; and dear, long-suffering Robert Benchley.

History does not record how the big round table in the center of the Algonquin dining

room came to be installed. Certainly it was not already there waiting for Parker and her crowd, and the movie's explanation is as good as any: The head waiter (Wallace Shawn), exasperated by all the famous people crowding around one tiny banquette, simply had a big round table wheeled in one day. Rudolph shoots the table from above, and then his camera circles it, so we hear snatches of countless bons mots; the screenplay sometimes reads as if it were lifted from *Bartlett's Familiar Quotations*.

Leigh's performance, at the center of almost every scene, shows us a woman in a world of men, who wore it as a badge of honor that she could outdrink and outtalk them. Using recordings of Parker's smoky voice, Leigh creates a low-pitched, ironic tone with a little cynicism and a lot of booze in it. When the film was premiered at the Cannes Film Festival, many viewers thought Leigh slurred a little too much; redubbing has made the dialogue easier to understand, and no less hung over.

Her relationship with Eddie, the husband, is seen here as a sad case: He was handsome and dashing, smiling and confident, and a wreck. Bad as Parker's own habits were, his were worse, and after the drugs took over she left him. Charles MacArthur, on the other hand, was a ladykiller (presumably until he met and married *his* true love, Helen Hayes). Unable to be faithful to Dorothy, he won her heart and then broke it.

These relationships, and her friendship with Benchley, are seen as being played out largely in public. For the Algonquin crowd, it was not enough to do: One had to be seen doing it, preferably with the Round Table looking on. The dining room worked for them as a saloon or pub works for some people, as a living room, an arena, a stage: All experience was reduced to one-liners, and in Parker's face you can see the pain lines growing, as she tries to hide her private grief with public bravado. A friend uneasily observes, "Dotty can't be suffering and still say all those funny things."

The *New Yorker* magazine was born, more or less, around the Round Table, and many of the regulars wrote for it, including Parker. Then talking movies required writers who could handle dialogue, and Parker joined many others in an exodus to Hollywood, where she spent her last decades in well-paid exile. One of Leigh's best scenes is the last one, in which she is asked by a reporter to supply her own epitaph. "What a morbid thing to ask a person!" she says, and then adds quietly: "You've just stolen my heart." (Once, on a happier occasion, she suggested for her tombstone: "Excuse my dust.")

Mrs. Parker and the Vicious Circle is the kind of movie best appreciated, I think, by those who already know the players around the Round Table, and have read some of their work. Others are likely to wonder what the fuss was about. Although some of the Algonquin wits survived into relatively modern times, their period remains forever the 1920s. It was a time when celebrities could become famous because they were smart and quick; today, few people talk as cleverly as the Algonquin crowd, and could hardly become popular doing so, because people have forgotten how to listen that fast.

Note: Perhaps in response to the release of this film, MGM has reissued classic short subjects by Benchley, Pete Smith, and others in a video package.

Mo' Better Blues ★ ★ ★
R, 129 m., 1990

Denzel Washington (Bleek Gilliam), Cynda Williams (Clarke Bentancourt), Joie Lee (Indigo Jones), Spike Lee (Giant), Wesley Snipes (Shadow Henderson), Giancarlo Esposito (Left Hand Lacey), Robin Harris (Butterbean Jones), Bill Nunn (Bottom Hammer), John Turturro (Moe Flatbush). Directed, produced, and written by Spike Lee.

Spike Lee's *Mo' Better Blues* is about a jazzman, but it's not really about jazz—it's about work, about being so wrapped up in your career that you don't have space for relationships, and you can't see where you're headed. It's a less passionate and angry film than Lee's previous work, *Do the Right Thing*, and less inspired, too. It's his fourth feature but suffers a little from the "second-novel syndrome," the pressure on an artist to follow up a great triumph. But it's a logical film to come at this point in Lee's career, since it's about the time and career pressures on a young artist.

The movie stars Denzel Washington as a trumpet player with the evocative name of Bleek. He leads a successful jazz group, but sometimes seems distracted and unhappy, maybe because he never really wanted to be a musician, maybe because he hasn't grown up enough to find himself. The movie gives us some insights into those possibilities in a prologue that shows Bleek as a young boy, growing up on a middle-class Brooklyn street,

being forced by his mother to practice his trumpet while the neighborhood kids stand on the sidewalk and taunt him because he can't come out and play softball. "Let the boy be a boy," Bleek's father says, but the mother will have none of it. There won't be any softball until he finishes his scales.

We flash forward to Bleek as a successful jazzman. As played by Washington, he is handsome, assured, and a dedicated ladies' man. There are two women in his life: Clarke Bentancourt (Cynda Williams), as sleek as her name, a seductive songstress; and Indigo Downes (Joie Lee), sometimes as blue as her name, less glamorous but steadier and more emotionally healthy. Bleek desires both of them and has enough time for neither, and eventually gets himself into one of those situations where they both show up at the nightclub on the same evening wearing the same red dresses—identical gifts from Bleek.

The band is on the brink of breaking out big, but needs better leadership than it gets from Bleek and his childhood friend and manager, Giant (Spike Lee). Giant is a compulsive gambler who is hopelessly incompetent to guide anyone's career, but through some sort of perverse logic, Bleek is loyal to him instead of to the friends who would really help him. That leads into physical and professional tragedy.

The middle sections of the movie take place in a world of jazz clubs and dressing rooms, stage door entrances, bars, coffee shops, and apartments—urban New York at night. There is a lot of music in the film, provided both by Bill Lee's score and by the Bleek group, which has been dubbed by the Branford Marsalis Quartet. The music is sensuous big-city jazz from around midnight, swirling through cigarette smoke and perfume and the musty smell of a saloon, and it's good to listen to. On stage, Washington looks at home with his horn, and Wesley Snipes is also strong as Shadow, a saxophone player who likes to hog the solos.

Backstage in the dressing room, in scenes that feel improvised, the musicians argue about the band, its leadership, its direction, and even the romantic preferences of its members. One sideman has a white girlfriend, and the others argue the pros and cons of that until he tells them it's none of their business. In this film, as in Lee's three earlier films, questions involving race are a good deal more sophisticated and complicated than the simplistic formulas from earlier decades.

At the center of everything stands Bleek, who in some ways resembles the heroine of Lee's first film, *She's Gotta Have It*. That was about a woman who kept three guys on the line because she didn't want any one of them to feel he possessed her. This time, it's Bleek who tries to juggle the two women—but he's representing irresponsibility, not independence. And there's a suggestion of a theme from *School Daze*, in which Lee examined subtle value systems within the black community, based on the relative lightness of skin tone: Clarke has "whiter" features than Indigo, and that may go into Bleek's emotional quandary, too. Clarke represents a superficial ideal of beauty as portrayed in the media, even though the darker Indigo is clearly the woman he should choose.

Lee has said he doesn't do "push-button" movies, and indeed *Mo' Better Blues* completely avoids the central cliché in almost all musical biopics. After Bleek gets into real trouble and can't play for a year, he walks into a nightclub to make his comeback, and we settle back for the obligatory scene in which he makes his triumphant return. But that's not the way things work out.

Lee avoids the usual formulas in that scene only to surprise us again, with an epilogue which mirrors the prologue. This time, though, some years have passed, and it's Bleek's own son who is practicing the trumpet. The symmetry of this ending feels awkward, especially since there seems to be an act missing—how did Bleek get from where he was, to where he is in the final scene?

Mo' Better Blues is not a supremely confident film like *Do the Right Thing*, which never took a wrong step. There are scenes that seem incompletely thought-out, improvised dialogue that sounds more like improvisation than dialogue, and those strange narrative bookends at the top and bottom of the movie. But the film has a beauty, grace, and energy all the same. Washington has been seen mostly in heavy dramatic roles *(Glory, Cry Freedom)*, and here, as in *The Mighty Quinn*, shows that he is gifted at comedy and romance. Cynda Williams, in her first film, is a luminous discovery; she has a presence that seems to occupy the screen by divine right. Joie Lee, in her most important role, isn't supposed to be as flashy, but succeeds in the challenge of drawing our sympathy away from the sexpot and toward the more substantial woman. And I liked Spike Lee's acting, too: He has a kind of off-center, driving energy that makes you into an accomplice even when he's marching straight for trouble. *Mo' Better Blues* is not a great film, but it's an interesting one, which is almost as rare.

The Moderns ★ ★ ★
NO MPAA RATING, 126 m., 1988

Keith Carradine (Nick Hart), Linda Fiorentino (Rachel Stone), John Lone (Bertram Stone), Wallace Shawn (Oiseau), Genevieve Bujold (Libby Valentin), Geraldine Chaplin (Nathalie de Ville), Kevin J. O'Connor (Hemingway), Elsa Raven (Gertrude Stein), Ali Giron (Alice B. Toklas). Directed by Alan Rudolph and produced by Carolyn Pfeiffer from a screenplay by Rudolph and John Bradshaw.

When I was in college we used to do "source studies" for the plays of Shakespeare, reading the books that were allegedly in his library and trying to figure out where he got his ideas. *The Moderns* is sort of a source study for the Paris of Ernest Hemingway in the 1920s; it's a movie about the raw material he shaped into *The Sun Also Rises* and *A Movable Feast,* and it also includes raw material for books by Gertrude Stein, Malcolm Cowley, and Clifford Irving. My source studies were always ungainly, disorganized and filled with wild surmises ("Shakespeare was undoubtedly referring to . . .") and *The Moderns* is equally puerile, but more fun.

It takes place at that enchanted moment in Paris when the Lost Generation created itself and then proceeded to create, promote, fabricate, and publicize modern literature, art, music, and attitudes. It tells the stories of an American painter in exile, the woman he loved and lost, and the millionaire he lost her to. Important roles are also played by his unscrupulous art dealer, by a busybody newspaperman on the English-language daily, and by Ernest Hemingway, Gertrude Stein, Alice B. Toklas, and others who are called by their real names even if the resemblance stops there.

The movie was directed and co-written by Alan Rudolph, who treats his Paris as something of a dream city; it's the same approach, but not the same look, as he used for the cities in *Choose Me* and *Trouble in Mind*—people drift in and out of each other's lives and conversations and eventually a plot develops, and it contains passion, greed, fear, envy, and lust, but hardly anybody ever raises a voice.

Keith Carradine stars as a starving artist who is stunned one day to see the woman he was married to (Linda Fiorentino) on the arm of a slick, sinister millionaire (John

Lone). He still loves her. Maybe she still loves him. One thing's for sure. When he turns up unexpectedly in her bathroom, if she didn't still feel something for him, she wouldn't have invited him into the tub. Meanwhile, Carradine needs money badly, and his art dealer (Genevieve Bujold) offers him a secret commission to forge three famous paintings. When he discovers that the paintings are connected to John Lone, he agrees to do it—and from that decision springs most of the plot, such as it is.

Rudolph's Paris is a place where people wander into scenes, say a line or two, and leave. Ernest Hemingway (Kevin J. O'Connor) appears in the backgrounds of several scenes, sometimes reciting earlier versions of his famous lines, to see how they sound. He climbs into the ring for a boxing match with another expatriate, and we see a cross between his actual fight with F. Scott Fitzgerald and the fictional fisticuffs in *The Sun Also Rises.* There are other scenes where Gertrude Stein and Alice B. Toklas receive the expatriate community in their legendary apartment where the walls were covered by some of the most famous and priceless of all twentieth-century paintings, and other moments where minor characters say things that are immediately borrowed by their betters and turned into legend. Drifting around within earshot of everything is the gossip columnist for the *Paris Trib* (Wallace Shawn), who claims to have invented modernism while losing his own soul.

The Moderns is not a great movie and is fairly sloppy and unsatisfying, but I never found a moment of it uninteresting, maybe because I have always been so intrigued by the Paris of the Lost Generation that I found the cross-references fun to spot and sometimes amusing. If there is a flaw in the movie, it's that Rudolph didn't find a way to use even more of the famous one-liners of the Lost Generation, instead of getting so bogged down in his fake-art plot. We learn in *The Autobiography of Alice B. Toklas* that when Ezra Pound came to Paris, "Gertrude Stein liked him but did not find him amusing. She said he was a village explainer, excellent if you were a village, but if you were not, not." She could have been reviewing this movie.

Mommie Dearest ★
PG, 129 m., 1981

Faye Dunaway (Joan Crawford), Diana Scarwid (Christina, adult), Steve Forrest (Greg

Savitt), Howard Da Silva (L.B. Mayer), Maaa Hobel (Christina, child), Rutanya Alda (Carol Ann). Directed by Frank Perry and produced by Frank Yablans. Screenplay by Yablans, Perry, Tracy Hotchner, and Robert Getchell.

I can't imagine who would want to subject themselves to this movie. *Mommie Dearest* is a painful experience that drones on endlessly, as Joan Crawford's relationship with her daughter, Christina, disintegrates from cruelty through jealousy into pathos. It is unremittingly depressing, not to any purpose of drama or entertainment, but just to depress. It left me feeling creepy. The movie was inspired, of course, by a best-selling memoir in which adopted daughter Christina Crawford portrayed her movie-star mother as a grasping, sadistic, alcoholic wretch whose own insecurities and monstrous ego made life miserable for everyone around her. I have no idea if the book's portrait is an accurate one, but the movie is faithful to it in one key sense: It made life miserable for me.

Mommie Dearest repeats the same basic dramatic situation again and again. Baby Christina tries to do the right thing, tries to be a good girl, tries to please Mommie, but Mommie is a manic-depressive who alternates between brief triumphs and long savage tirades, infecting her daughter with resentment and guilt. In scene after scene, we are invited to watch as Joan Crawford screams at Christina, chops her hair with scissors, beats her with a wire coat hanger and, on an especially bad day, tackles her across an end table, hurls her to the carpet, bangs her head against the floor, and tries to choke her to death. Who wants to watch this?

This material is presented essentially as sensationalism. The movie makes no attempt to draw psychological insights from the life of its Joan Crawford—not even through the shorthand Freudianism much beloved by Hollywood. Mommie is a monster, that's all, and there's some mention of her unhappy childhood. Christina is a brave, smiling, pretty, long-suffering dope who might inspire more sympathy if she were not directed (in both her childhood and adult versions) to be distant and veiled.

The movie doesn't even make narrative sense. Success follows crisis without any pattern. At one moment, Joan is in triumph after winning the Oscar for *Mildred Pierce.* In the very next scene she goes so berserk we want to scrape her off the screen with a spatula. The scenes don't build, they just happen. Another example: After an especially ugly fight, Joan sends Christina to a convent school. There's a scene where the mother superior welcomes her and promises to reform her. One scene later, Christina checks out of the school, and the nun wishes her godspeed. No mention of what happened in the school, how it affected Christina, or whether the nun changed her opinion of the girl.

The movie also offers few insights into Crawford's relationships with others. There's a loyal housekeeper, but never a scene where Crawford speaks personally with her. There is a lover and a third husband, both enigmas. Crawford's acting career is treated mostly in ellipses. The sets look absolutely great, Faye Dunaway's impersonation of Crawford is stunningly suggestive and convincing, and little Mara Hobel, as Baby Christina, handles several difficult moments very well. But to what end? *Mommie Dearest* is a movie that knows exactly how it wants to look, but has no idea what it wants to make us feel.

Mona Lisa ★ ★ ★ ★
R, 104 m., 1986

Bob Hoskins (George), Cathy Tyson (Simone), Michael Caine (Mortwell), Clarke Peters (Anderson), Kate Hardie (Cathy), Robbie Coltrane (Thomas). Directed by Neil Jordan and produced by Stephen Wooley and Patrick Cassavetti. Screenplay by Jordan and David Leland.

You can tell how much they will eventually like each other by how much they hate each other at first. His name is George. He's a short, fierce, bullet-headed foot-soldier in the London underworld, and he's just gotten out of prison. Her name is Simone. She's a tall, beautiful black woman who works as a high-priced call girl. George goes to Mortwell, who runs the mob, looking for a job. He is assigned to drive Simone around to expensive hotels and private homes and to wait for her while she conducts her business. He is also supposed to protect her if anything goes wrong.

At first he seems hopelessly unsuited to his job. He wears the wrong clothes, and stands out like a sore thumb in the lobbies of hotels like the Ritz. She can't believe she's been saddled with this misfit. He thinks she is stuck-up and cold, and puts on too many airs for a whore. They are at each other's throats day and night, fighting about everything, until eventually they realize they enjoy

their arguments; they are entertained by one another.

That's the setup for *Mona Lisa*, a British film set in the tattered precincts of Soho, where vice lords run sordid clubs where bewildered provincial girls sell themselves to earn money for drugs. Simone now operates at a higher level in the sex business, but she never forgets where she started, and sometimes she orders George to cruise slowly in the big Jaguar, as she searches for a young girl who used to be her friend when they were on the streets together, and who is still the slave, she fears, of a sadistic pimp. These nighttime journeys are a contrast to her usual routine, which involves visiting wealthy bankers, decadent diplomats, and rich Middle Eastern investors who live on the most expensive streets of Hampstead. George drives her, argues with her, speculates about her, and falls in love with her. And when she asks him to help find the missing girl, he risks his life for her.

Mona Lisa stars Bob Hoskins as George. You may remember him as the ferocious little mob boss in *The Long Good Friday*, where he had it all fixed up to go respectable and then someone started blowing up his pubs. Hoskins is one of the very best new British actors, and this is a great performance—it won him the best actor award at the 1986 Cannes Film Festival. Simone is played by Cathy Tyson, and she is elegant and cool and yet able to project the pain that is always inside. The relationship of their characters in the film is interesting, because both people, for personal reasons, have developed a style that doesn't reveal very much. They have walls, and friendship means being able to see over someone else's wall while still keeping your own intact.

The third major character in the movie, and the third major performance, is by Michael Caine, as Mortwell, the vice boss. In the more than twenty years since I first saw Caine in a movie, I don't believe I've seen him in a bad performance more than once or twice. And I've rarely seen him doing the same thing, which is strange, since in one way or another he usually seems to look and talk like Michael Caine—and yet with subtle differences that are just right for the role. In *Mona Lisa*, he plays one of his most evil villains, a slimebag who trades in the lives and happiness of naive young girls, and he plays the character without apology and without exaggeration, as a businessman. That's why Mortwell is so creepy.

The movie plot reveals itself only gradually. At first *Mona Lisa* seems to be a character study, the story of George and Simone and how they operate within the call-girl industry. After we find out how important the missing girl is to Simone, however, the movie becomes a thriller, as George descends into gutters to try to find her and bring her back to Simone. The movie's ending is a little too neat for my taste. But in a movie like this, everything depends on atmosphere and character, and *Mona Lisa* knows exactly what it is doing.

Monkey Trouble ★ ★ ★
PG, 92 m., 1994

Finster (Dodger), Thora Birch (Eva), Harvey Keitel (Azro), Mimi Rogers (Amy), Christopher McDonald (Tom), Adrian Johnson and Julian Johnson (Jack), Kevin Scannell (Peter). Directed by Franco Amurri and produced by Mimi Polk and Heide Rufus Isaacs. Screenplay by Amurri and Stu Krieger.

It's no mistake that the credits for *Monkey Trouble* give top billing to the monkey, named Finster. He steals the show with a fetching performance that goes beyond "training" and into acting itself. And the show is a quirky, bright, PG-rated adventure that's as entertaining as *Free Willy*. Better, maybe, since monkeys are a lot more charismatic than whales. This is a splendid family film.

The movie stars Thora Birch (from *Hocus Pocus*) as Eva, a troubled grade-schooler who isn't doing very well in school. At home, with her mom (Mimi Rogers) and stepfather (Christopher McDonald), she's resentful of a new baby brother, and mad because she can't have a dog. Her stepdad is allergic to animals, but that's only one reason; her mom also points out that she's not responsible enough to walk, feed, and clean up after a pet.

Meanwhile, we've gotten to know the swarthy, dishonest Azro (Harvey Keitel), a street entertainer who works the Venice Beach area of Los Angeles with his pet monkey, which has been trained to pick pockets and steal watches and jewelry. Azro is not a kind master, and when the monkey sees his chance, he runs away—to Eva's home, which he has scouted out during an exercise in housebreaking and thievery.

The girl and the monkey, which she names Dodger, form an immediate bond. Meanwhile, Azro is in trouble, because he's made a deal with some gangsters who want to use the monkey in a big heist. That sets up the fairly mechanical plot of the movie, which involves Eva hiding Dodger from her parents while Azro schemes to track down the monkey and get it back.

Okay. This is all more or less routine, right down to the bad guys in the black limousine, who seem to be a convenient shortcut for any screenwriter who needs instant villains on demand. What isn't routine is the performance by the monkey, an adult capuchin, which is small, cute, and very smart, and able to move more or less invisibly through the human world. And the plot isn't just about bad guys and chases; it involves the ways Eva learns to take responsibility for the monkey and herself in some tight scrapes.

It takes her awhile to figure out that Dodger is a trained pickpocket, who can get her into a lot of trouble. When she goes shopping, for example, he peeks out of her knapsack and shoplifts sardines. The resulting scene with the store manager is like a nightmare: She can't explain how she got the shoplifted goods without revealing the monkey. Another day, when she tries to earn some quick money with the monkey in a sidewalk performance, she's startled later to learn Dodger was collecting billfolds along with tips.

W.C. Fields used to refuse to appear with small children and animals, on the reasonable grounds that they always stole the scene. *Monkey Trouble* is an example of that, a movie that has taken the time and trouble to orchestrate such an excellent animal performance that the monkey's adventures are not only fun, but almost believable.

I wonder, though, why the filmmakers found it necessary to identify the Keitel character as a Gypsy, thus reinforcing all kinds of negative stereotypes. He could have had a nonspecific background and the movie would have worked just as well, without giving its young audiences a lesson in prejudice.

Monsieur Hire ★ ★ ★ ★
PG-13, 88 m., 1990

Michel Blanc (Monsieur Hire), Sandrine Bonnaire (Alice), Luc Thuillier (Emile), Andre Wilms (Police Inspector). Directed by Patrice Leconte and produced by Philippe Carcassonne and Rene Cleitman. Screenplay by Leconte and Patrick DeWolf.

Monsieur Hire's life is organized with the extreme precision of a man who fears that any deviation from routine could destroy him. He lives alone in a neatly ordered room

where everything has its place. He dresses carefully and conservatively and goes out every day to work by himself in a small office in the town, where he operates a mail-order business. He comes home to his dinner of a hard-boiled egg. He listens to the same piece of music over and over again. He speaks to people only to observe the formalities: "Good morning." "Nice day."

His sexual life is equally precise. Hour after hour, he stands in his darkened room, looking across the small courtyard of his building into the window of a young woman who lives directly opposite and one floor below. She never pulls her shades. He watches her dress, undress, read, eat, listen to the radio, make love. Hour after hour.

Another young woman is found dead in the neighborhood—her body cast aside in an overgrown vacant lot. Who committed the crime? There are no suspects, but in this neighborhood a man like Monsieur Hire is always a suspect. He has no friends, no associations, no "life." The neighbors have marked him out as peculiar. To look at him you would think it was absurd that he could kill anyone. But suspicion begins to grow.

The story of Monsieur Hire was first told in a novel by Georges Simenon, that endlessly observant Belgian who wrote more than three hundred books, many of them works of genius. This is one of his best stories, a study of character and loneliness. Reading the book some years ago, I formed a picture of Hire in my mind, and seeing this movie I was startled to see how closely my notions matched the appearance of Michel Blanc, who plays the title role.

He is a solemn man with a fringe of black hair around a face that is more than merely pale; he seems to have been sprouted in a basement. He is reclusive, solemn, absorbed with his own thoughts. As he watches the woman across the courtyard, we can only imagine what he is thinking. Somehow the conventional sexual fantasies do not seem to fit him; perhaps he is thinking what a slattern she is, or what an angel.

The woman (Sandrine Bonnaire) has a boyfriend. He is cold, distant, and cruel, and he treats her badly. She does what he says. He does not make her happy, but certain women are attracted to cruel men. Did the boyfriend commit the murder? The movie is not really concerned with the solution to the crime—much less concerned than the Simenon novel. Indeed, when the police inspector turns up in the movie, we're not sure at first who he is. Maybe he's a family friend?

Monsieur Hire is so delicate that you almost hold your breath during the last half-hour. Events of grave subtlety are taking place. The heart of the movie involves two difficult questions: What exactly does the young woman think about Monsieur Hire, and what does he think that she thinks? Of course, the woman knows that Hire is always at his window, watching. She sees him one day, illuminated by lightning. Still she does nothing to conceal herself, and so from that moment on there is a kind of communication between them. Each knows the other is aware.

Monsieur Hire, so middle-aged and nondescript, is certainly not her "type." But is his adoration appealing to her? Is he the one man in the world who regards her simply as she is and finds her wonderful? Does he want nothing more from her than to worship? Does this make her grateful to him, in a sense, considering the mistreatment she gets from the boyfriend? Will she lie to save Hire? Will she lie to save the boyfriend?

The concluding passages of the movie have the weight of sad, inevitable tragedy to them. But nothing prepares us for the movie's extraordinary final shot, in which a swift action contains a momentary pause, a look that seems torn out of the very fabric of life itself. What does the look say? What is this woman trying to communicate? The director, Patrice Leconte, knows that to explain the look is to destroy the movie. *Monsieur Hire* is a film about conversations that are never held, desires that are never expressed, fantasies that are never realized, and murder.

Moonlighting ★ ★ ★ ★
PG, 97 m., 1982

Jeremy Irons (Nowak), Eugene Lipinski (Banaszak), Jiri Stanislav (Wolski), Eugeniusz Haczkiewicz (Kudaj). Directed by Jerzy Skolimowski and produced by Mark Shivas and Skolimowski. Screenplay by Skolimowski.

Moonlighting is a wickedly pointed movie that takes a simple little story, tells it with humor and truth, and turns it into a knife in the side of the Polish government. In its own way, this response to the crushing of Solidarity is as powerful as Andrzej Wajda's *Man of Iron*. It also is more fun. The movie takes place in London, during the weeks just before and after the banning of the Solidarity movement in Poland. It begins, actually, in Warsaw, with a mystifying scene in which a group of plotters are scheming to smuggle some hardware past British customs. They're plotters, all right; their plot is to move into a small house in London and remodel it, knocking out walls, painting ceilings, making it into a showplace for the Polish government official who has purchased it. The official's plan is simplicity itself: By bringing Polish workers to London on tourist visas, he can get the remodeling done for a fraction of what British workman would cost him. At the same time, the workers can earn good wages that they can take back to Poland and buy bicycles with. The only thing nobody counts on is the upheaval after Solidarity is crushed and travel to and from Poland is strictly regulated.

Jeremy Irons, of *The French Lieutenant's Woman*, plays the lead in the film. He's the only Polish workman who can speak English. Acting as foreman, he guides his team of men through the pitfalls of London and safely into the house they're going to remodel. He advises them to keep a low profile, while he ventures out to buy the groceries and (not incidentally) to read the newspapers. When he finds out about the crisis in Poland, he keeps it a secret from his comrades. The daily life of the renovation project falls into a pattern, which the film's director, Jerzy Skolimowski, intercuts with the adventures of his hero. Jeremy Irons begins to steal things: newspapers, bicycles, frozen turkeys. He concocts an elaborate scheme to defraud the local supermarket, and some of the movie's best scenes involve the subtle timing of his shoplifting scam, which involves the misrepresentation of cash-register receipts. He needs to steal food because he's running out of money, and he knows his group can't easily go home again. There's also a quietly hilarious, and slightly sad, episode involving a salesgirl in a blue-jeans store. Irons, pretending to be more naive than he is, tries to pick the girl up. She's having none of it.

Moonlighting invites all kinds of interpretations. You can take this simple story and set it against the events of the last two years, and see it as a kind of parable. Your interpretation is as good as mine. Is the house itself Poland, and the workmen Solidarity—rebuilding it from within, before an authoritarian outside force intervenes? Or is this movie about the heresy of substituting Western values (and jeans and turkeys) for a home-grown orientation? Or is it about the manipulation of the working classes by the intelligentsia? Or is it simply a frontal attack

on the Communist Party bosses who live high off the hog while the workers are supposed to follow the rules?

Like all good parables, *Moonlighting* contains not one but many possibilities. What needs to be insisted upon, however, is how much *fun* this movie is. Skolimowski, a Pole who has lived and worked in England for several years, began writing this film on the day that Solidarity was crushed, and he filmed it, on a small budget and with a small crew, in less than two months: He had it ready for the 1982 Cannes Film Festival where it was a major success. It's successful, I think, because it tells an interesting narrative in a straightforward way. Skolimowski is a natural storyteller. You can interpret and discuss *Moonlighting* all night. During the movie, you'll be more interested in whether Irons gets away with that frozen turkey.

Moonstruck ★ ★ ★ ★
PG, 100 m., 1987

Cher (Loretta Castorini), Nicolas Cage (Ronny Cammareri), Vincent Gardenia (Cosmo Castorini), Olympia Dukakis (Rose Castorini), Danny Aiello (Johnny Cammareri), Julie Bovasso (Rita Cappomaggi), John Mahoney (Perry), Louis Guss (Raymond Cappomaggi), Feodor Chaliapin (Old Man). Directed by Norman Jewison and produced by Patrick Palmer and Jewison. Screenplay by John Patrick Shanley.

"When the moon hits your eye, like a big-a pizza pie—that's amore!"—Dean Martin

The most enchanting quality about *Moonstruck* is the hardest to describe, and that is the movie's tone. Reviews of the movie tend to make it sound like a madcap ethnic comedy, and that it is. But there is something more here, a certain bittersweet yearning that comes across as ineffably romantic, and a certain magical quality that is reflected in the film's title.

The movie stars Cher, as an Italian-American widow in her late thirties, but she is not the only moonstruck one in the film. There is the moonlit night, for example, that her wise, cynical mother (Olympia Dukakis) goes out for dinner by herself, and meets a middle-aged university professor (John Mahoney) who specializes in seducing his young students, but who finds in this mature woman a certain undeniable sexuality. There is the furtive and yet somehow sweet affair that Cher's father (Vincent Gardenia) has been

carrying on for years with the ripe, disillusioned Anita Gillette.

And at the heart of the story, there is Cher's astonishing discovery that she is still capable of love. As the movie opens, she becomes engaged to Mr. Johnny Cammareri (Danny Aiello), not so much out of love as out of weariness. But after he flies to Sicily to be at the bedside of his dying mother, she goes to talk to Mr. Johnny's estranged younger brother (Nicolas Cage), and is thunderstruck when they are drawn almost instantly into a passionate embrace.

Moonstruck was directed by Norman Jewison and written by John Patrick Shanley, and one of their accomplishments is to allow the film to be about all of these people (and several more, besides). This is an ensemble comedy, and a lot of the laughs grow out of the sense of family that Jewison and Shanley create; there are, for example, small hilarious moments involving the exasperation that Dukakis feels for her ancient father-in-law (Feodor Chaliapin), who lives upstairs with his dogs. (In the course of a family dinner, she volunteers: "Feed one more bite of my food to your dogs, old man, and I'll kick you 'til you're dead!")

As Cher's absent fiancé lingers at his mother's bedside, Cher and Cage grow even more desperately passionate, and Cher learns the secret of the hatred between the two brothers: One day Aiello made Cage look the wrong way at the wrong time, and he lost his hand in a bread-slicer. Now he wears an artificial hand, and carries an implacable grudge in his heart.

But grudges and vendettas and old wounds and hatreds are everywhere in this film. The mother knows, for example, that her husband is having an affair with another woman. She asks from the bottom of her heart why this should be so, and a friend replies, "Because he is afraid of dying." She sees at once that this is so. But does that cause her to sympathize with her husband? Hardly. One night he comes home. She asks where he has been. He replies, "Nowhere." She tells him she wants him to know one thing: "No matter where you go, or what you do—you're gonna die."

Some of these moments are so charged with tension they remind us of the great opening scenes of *Saturday Night Fever* (and the mother from that movie, Julie Bovasso, is on hand here as an aunt). But all of the passion is drained of its potential for hurt, somehow, by the influence of the moon, which has enchanted these people and protects them from the consequences of their frailties. Jewison captures some of the same qualities of Ingmar Bergman's *Smiles of a Summer Night,* in which nature itself conspires with lovers to bring about their happiness.

The movie is filled with fine performances—by Cher, 1987's Best Actress Oscar winner, never funnier or more assured; by Olympia Dukakis (who was named Best Supporting Actress) and Vincent Gardenia, as her parents, whose love runs as deep as their exasperation; and by Nicolas Cage as the hapless, angry brother, who is so filled with hurts he has lost track of what caused them. In its warmth and in its enchantment, as well as in its laughs, this is a fine comedy.

The Morning After ★ ★ ★
R, 103 m., 1986

Jane Fonda (Alex), Jeff Bridges (Turner), Raul Julia (Manero), Diane Salinger (Isabel), Richard Foronjy (Sergeant Greenbaum), Geoffrey Scott (Bobby), Bruce Vilanch (Bartender). Directed by Sidney Lumet and produced by Bruce Gilbert. Screenplay by James Hicks.

If an ordinary person woke up in the morning feeling the way a drunk feels with a hangover, they'd call an ambulance and check themselves into the emergency room. I'm not talking about your average garden-variety office-party hangover. I'm thinking of one of those mornings when you pick up the phone and somebody says hello and you're stuck for an answer.

That's how Jane Fonda feels in the first scene of *The Morning After.* She crawls out of bed and looks in the mirror and sloshes some gin into a glass and wonders about the guy she woke up with. She wonders things like, who is he? She has apparently had a lot of mornings like this. She doesn't realize how bad things really are until she notices the guy has a knife stuck in his chest.

Did she kill him? She knows no cop is going to believe her story. She wanders back out into the blinding Los Angeles light, and in a shot from high overhead, she looks like a laboratory animal, trapped in some kind of a test.

This feels like the beginning of an extraordinary thriller. Unfortunately, *The Morning After* never lives up to its early promise—not as a thriller, anyway. The plot has some yawning gaps in it, and thriller plots should be watertight. But *The Morning After* is worth

seeing anyway, because of the characters that it develops, and the performances of Fonda and Jeff Bridges in the two leads.

She plays an alcoholic actress who is long past her prime. He plays an ex-cop who happens to be repairing his car at the airport parking lot when she tumbles into his backseat and pleads with him to get her away from there, fast. The mere presence of Jeff Bridges in this movie is sort of a tease; we remember him from *Jagged Edge,* when he was one of the prime suspects, and we wonder if it's a coincidence that he happens along this time.

Bridges lives in a Quonset hut, where he fixes things like toasters. This is all Fonda needs. She moves in the fast lane—her friends are bartenders and drag queens, and her estranged husband (Raul Julia) is the classiest hairdresser in Beverly Hills. What does she need with a small-appliance repairman? But Bridges is sure and steady, and she needs a friend. Of course it goes without saying that they fall in love.

The plot of *The Morning After* is not nearly as good as the everyday lives of these characters; indeed, I can imagine a movie which would leave out the murder and simply follow the natural human development of the relationship between Fonda and Bridges. The thriller stuff isn't necessary, but as long as they put it in, couldn't they have worked just a little harder and made it plausible? Why, for example, didn't the cops find the bloody sheets under Fonda's sink?

The whole murder plot gets such sloppy handling that maybe I shouldn't have been surprised by the big scene in which the identity of the murderer is revealed. I've seen a lot of revelations in a lot of murder movies, but rarely one as unsubtle as this one, where the plot secrets are simply blurted out in an unlikely speech. (Maybe I should be more grateful; I understand that this very scene—implausible and awkward as it is—was re-shot because the original version was worse.)

It would be a mistake, however, to dismiss this movie just because the plot is so shaky. I think it's worth considering because of the performances. Fonda and Bridges are wonderful in the film, and their relationship, based on secrets and resentments and private agendas, gets really interesting. They feel good together, and they have some dialogue that seems more alive than most romantic talk in the movies.

I liked what they did with the characters, and I also liked what Sidney Lumet has done

with the look of the movie. He creates a Los Angeles made out of great flat planes of cold pastels, and threatening sunlit open spaces. He pins the hungover Fonda on this canvas like a butterfly on the wall, and the visuals make the whole first hour of the movie much more threatening than it deserves to be. Too bad they couldn't have done something about the screenplay.

Mortal Thoughts ★ ★ ★
R, 104 m., 1991

Demi Moore (Cynthia Kellogg), Glenne Headly (Joyce Urbanski), Bruce Willis (James Urbanski), John Pankow (Arthur Kellogg), Harvey Keitel (Detective John Woods), Billie Neal (Linda Nealon), Frank Vincent (Dominic Marino), Karen Shallo (Gloria Urbanski). Directed by Alan Rudolph and produced by John Fiedler and Mark Tarlov. Screenplay by William Reilly and Claude Kerven.

There is a part of me that would sit at home all day reading true crime books and doing nothing else. I'm particularly attracted to stories set in the present, among ordinary people who would not think of themselves as criminals, but who one day commit a violent crime and think they can get away with it. The papers are filled with these stories, about jealous spouses and secret lovers, ancient grudges and fatal miscalculations, teenage boyfriends and elderly recluses, usually with sex on their minds. When they are caught, as they almost always are, the perpetrators of these crimes turn into accomplished courtroom performers who begin to enjoy their overnight fame, to think of themselves as stars instead of defendants.

Alan Rudolph's *Mortal Thoughts* is a movie just like the true crime stories I enjoy the most. It's about two friends who work in the perfectly named Clip 'n' Dye Beauty Parlor in Bayonne, New Jersey. The owner, Joyce Urbanski (Glenne Headly) is married to Jim (Bruce Willis), an abusive lout of a husband who beats her, lies to her, and grabs money out of the cash register to go buy booze and drugs. Joyce's friend and business partner, Cynthia, is played by Demi Moore as a fascinated witness to the increasing violence in the Urbanski marriage. Her own marriage, to the boring but dedicated Arthur (John Pankow), seems to be just the opposite.

The two women engage in deadly but entertaining brinksmanship over the question of whether Jim, who everybody agrees is a reprehensible brute, should be murdered.

Joyce is frequently overheard saying she'd like to knock her husband off, and on one occasion, she even fills the sugar bowl with rat poison and tells Cynthia all about it—and Cynthia has to run upstairs to save Jim's life. She is thanked for her trouble by Jim's clumsy sexual advances and adolescent pawing.

Then one night, Jim and the two women go to a carnival, and Jim dies, or is murdered, and the women conspire to hide the body and cover up the death. We learn all of this a few years later, during a police interrogation being carried out by two detectives (Harvey Keitel and Billie Neal). They have the Demi Moore character in a small room, and are videotaping her as they lead her through the details of the crime.

There are a lot of unanswered questions, such as exactly how the husband was found dead, who found him, what happened then, and why. There is even another death to consider, although to discuss it would spoil a surprise for you, and indeed, this whole movie is an unfolding series of surprises and revelations. It begins as a case history, turns into a whodunit, and ends by trying to determine what was done, among other questions.

Like many crimes, the ones in this movie seem simple at first and only grow complicated the more you look at them. The screenplay, by William Reilly and Claude Kerven, is meticulously constructed so that the flashbacks during the testimony never reveal too much, and yet never seem to conceal anything. Nor is the screenplay simply ingenious; it is also very funny, in a mordant and blood-soaked way, as these two women scheme and figure and lie to the cops, to each other, and to themselves. There is a banality to their language and images that sets the correct tone.

The way Moore and Headly squirm to justify and defend themselves is deliciously fraudulent. Yet there is another level to *Mortal Thoughts* than either the guilt or innocence of the characters, or the wit with which Rudolph portrays their world. It is the level on which ordinary people cut themselves loose from ordinary morality, who commit crimes for their own convenience. Human life should be sacred, but we live in a world where people are killed simply to make life easier for their murderers. Maybe that's why the killers' alibis are often so pathetic, and their planning is so slipshod: If the murderers really took murder seriously, they'd take the time and trouble to get away with it.

Moscow on the Hudson ★ ★ ★ ★
R, 115 m., 1984

Robin Williams (Vladimir Ivanoff), Maria Conchita Alonso (Lucia Lombardo), Cleavant Derricks (Witherspoon), Alejandro Rey (Orlando Ramirez). Directed and produced by Paul Mazursky. Screenplay by Mazursky and Leon Capetanos.

Mike Royko likes to make fun of foreign-born taxi drivers. He uses a lot of phonetic spellings to show how funny dey speaka da Engleesh. Maybe he's missing out on some good conversations. Have you ever *talked* to a taxi driver from Iran or Pakistan or Africa? I have, and usually I hear a fascinating story about a man who has fled from poverty or persecution, who in some cases has left behind a thriving business, and who is starting out all over again in this country. I also usually get the name of a good restaurant.

I thought of some of those experiences while I was watching Paul Mazursky's *Moscow on the Hudson,* a wonderful movie about a man who defects to the United States. His name is Vladimir Ivanoff, he plays the saxophone in a Russian circus, and when the circus visits New York, he falls in love with the United States and defects by turning himself in to a security guard at Bloomingdale's. The Russian is played by Robin Williams, who disappears so completely into his quirky, lovable, complicated character that he's quite plausible as a Russian. The movie opens with his life in Moscow, a city of overcrowded apartments, bureaucratic red tape, long lines for consumer goods, secret pleasures like jazz records, and shortages so acute that toilet paper has turned into a currency of its own. The early scenes are eerily convincing, partly because Williams plays them in Russian. This isn't one of those movies where everybody somehow speaks English. The turning point of the movie occurs in Bloomingdale's, as so many turning points do, and Ivanoff makes two friends right there on the spot: Witherspoon, the black security guard (Cleavant Derricks), and Lucia, the Italian salesclerk (Maria Conchita Alonso).

They're a tip-off to an interesting casting decision by Mazursky, who populates his movie almost entirely with ethnic and racial minorities. In addition to the black and the Italian, there's a Korean taxi driver, a Cuban lawyer, a Chinese anchorwoman, all of them reminders that all of us, except for American Indians, came from somewhere else. Ivanoff

moves in with the security guard's family, which greatly resembles the one he left behind in Moscow, right down to the pious grandfather. He gets a job selling hot dogs from a pushcart, he works his way up to driving a limousine, and he falls in love with the salesclerk from Italy. That doesn't go so well. She dreams of marrying a "real American," and Ivanoff, even after he trims his beard, will not quite do.

Moscow on the Hudson is the kind of movie that Paul Mazursky does especially well. It's a comedy that finds most of its laughs in the close observations of human behavior, and that finds its story in a contemporary subject Mazursky has some thoughts about. In that, it's like his earlier films *An Unmarried Woman* (women's liberation), *Harry and Tonto* (growing old), *Blume in Love* (marriage in the age of doing your own thing), and *Bob & Carol & Ted & Alice* (encounter groups). It is also a rarity, a patriotic film that has a liberal, rather than a conservative, heart. It made me feel good to be an American, and good that Vladimir Ivanoff was going to be one, too.

Motel Hell ★ ★ ★
R, 106 m., 1980

Rory Calhoun (Farmer Vincent), Paul Linke (Bruce Smith), Nancy Parsons (Ida Smith), Nina Axelrod (Terry), Wolfman Jack (Reverend Billy), Elaine Joyce (Edith Olson). Directed by Kevin Connor and produced by Steven-Charles Jaffe and Robert Jaffe. Screenplay by Jaffe and Jaffe.

Motel Hell satirizes a whole sub-basement genre of American movies that a lot of lucky people may never even have seen. I call them Sleazoid Movies; films that deliberately test our sensibilities, and our stomachs, by the subhuman and nauseating behavior of the characters on the screen. The genre includes *The Texas Chainsaw Massacre, The Hills Have Eyes, The Honeymoon Killers, Night of the Living Dead,* and *Last House on the Left.*

These films are not to be confused with those of a neighboring genre, the Women in Danger films, which spew hatred of women. Sleazoid movies seem to exist on the edge of self-parody, and their ambition is to be to the cinema what the geek show is to the circus. They're not antiwoman, they're antitaste, and their characters sink into moronic, bestial savagery. They touch on the ultimate horror of people degraded into subhuman, animalistic behavior. Some of these films, I should add, are not without merit—although this isn't the place to launch into a defense of them.

What *Motel Hell* brings to this genre is the refreshing sound of laughter. This movie *is* disgusting, of course; it's impossible to satirize this material, I imagine, without presenting the subject matter you're satirizing. But *Motel Hell* is not nearly as gruesome as the films it satirizes, and it finds the right stylistic note for its central characters, who are simple, cheerful, smiling, earnest, and resourceful cannibals.

Motel Hell (the second "o" on the neon sign has gone out) is a ramshackle place that seems to be located in the same redneck backwoods where Russ Meyer's characters all live. It is operated by friendly Farmer Vincent (Rory Calhoun) and his sister (Nancy Parsons). The district is patrolled, none too adroitly, by a relative (Paul Linke), who is the sheriff, but sees nothing wrong with burying the victims of a motorcycle crash without benefit of investigation or autopsy.

That's just as well, because Farmer Vincent's specialty is burying people. He just doesn't wait until they're dead. He waylays unsuspecting travelers, knocks them unconscious, buries them up to their necks in his secret garden, fattens them up with cattle feed, and then slaughters them, smokes them in his smokehouse, and sells them as sausage at his roadside stand. His cheerful motto: "It takes all kinds of critters . . . to make Farmer Vincent's fritters."

All right now, of *course* this is disgusting. But hold on just a dagbone minute, as Farmer Vincent might say. It isn't simply the subject matter of Sleazoid Movies that makes them reprehensible, it's their low opinion of human nature, their acquiescence in the proposition that the world is essentially an evil place. *Motel Hell,* with Rory Calhoun looking like a Norman Rockwell model in his bib overalls, pushes this material so far in such unlikely directions that, incredibly, it works as satire. A lot of horror movies used to work that way. We went to be scared, sure, but we also went to laugh, enjoying the delicious self-indulgence with which Vincent Price or Christopher Lee hammed it up. But horror movies stopped being funny. And now they're mostly just depressing, disgusting exercises in depravity.

Motel Hell is a welcome change-of-pace; it's to *Chainsaw Massacre* as *Airplane!* is to *Airport.* It has some great moments, including a duel fought with chainsaws, a hero

swinging to the rescue on a meathook, and Farmer Vincent's dying confession of the shameful secret that he concealed for years. These moments illuminate the movie's basic and not very profound insight, which is that most of the sleazoids would be a lot more fun if they didn't take themselves with such gruesome solemnity.

Mountains of the Moon ★ ★ ★ ½
R, 135 m., 1990

Patrick Bergin (Richard Burton), Iain Glen (John Hanning Speke), Richard E. Grant (Oliphant), Fiona Shaw (Isabel), John Savident (Lord Murchison), James Villiers (Lord Oliphant), Adrian Rawlins (Edward). Directed by Bob Rafelson and produced by Daniel Melnick. Screenplay by William Harrison and Rafelson.

The astronauts of the nineteenth century were the explorers—those intrepid men, often British, who mounted expeditions from the club rooms of Pall Mall to the most exotic hinterlands of the world. When the astronauts came back from the moon, they told their stories to *Life* magazine. When the Victorians returned from their expeditions, they presented their findings in lectures before the Royal Geographical Society, and then they wrote their memoirs in large, leather-bound volumes. But make no mistake; they were some of the greatest celebrities of their age, the Robert Scotts and David Livingstones, and exploration was not only a rewarding but a democratic profession. Explorers did not need breeding or wealth to become famous—only luck and unholy determination.

Of all the British explorers of the nineteenth century, the most interesting is Richard Francis Burton (1821–90), who was also a linguist, a poet, and a pioneer of sexual studies who translated the *Kama Sutra* and an unexpurgated version of *The Arabian Nights* into English. For his pains, he became thoroughly disrespectable, and on his death his wife burned his translation of *The Perfumed Garden,* a masterpiece of Arabic erotica he had been laboring over for fourteen years.

The black-magic practitioner Aleister Crowley, who was one of the few men of the time more disreputable than Burton, wrote in his *Confessions* that Victorians like Burton "seethed with impotent rage" at their doom, which was to live within the repressions and evasions of the Victorian period. If the Bur-

tons were not banished altogether, their careers and lives were rewritten to give the age more proper heroes. A flamboyant original like Burton "was toned down into a famous traveler and translator," Crowley complained.

Now here is a movie to tone him up again. Bob Rafelson's *Mountains of the Moon* is centered on a series of expeditions led by Burton and John Hanning Speke, who marched for months through East Africa in their search for the source of the Nile. They were the first Europeans to set eyes on most of the lands they walked across, the first to see many African species of animals, birds, and insects, and the first to encounter tribal customs that had developed in an uninterrupted continuity since the birth of history. Burton was already famous for some of his other exploits, such as disguising himself as an Arab and slipping into the holy city of Mecca. Speke, a less dashing and more ambitious man, was not lacking in physical stamina but lacked Burton's fire. At first they were a good team. Later their differences destroyed them.

The movie is not one of those wide-screen epics that might have been directed by David Lean. It's wide screen, all right, and it's an epic, but it's a not a movie about adventure and action. It's an epic about the personalities of the men who endured incredible hardships because of their curiosity, egos, greed, or even because of their nobility. Rafelson (whose credits include *Five Easy Pieces*) fills his movie with unobtrusive period detail; he has not only the costumes and the settings right, but also the attitudes, as men in proper attire and an astonishing variety of facial hair crowd into the Geographical Society to hear lectures from the great explorers. These men look ancient and proper, but actually they are fans, and to them Richard Burton is a dashing hero—a man they envy because he has gotten out from under Victoria's skirts by thousands of dangerous miles.

To win their ovations, Burton and Speke were prepared to risk their lives in the unknown. We see their expeditions snaking across uncharted territories, where death by native attack was less of a threat than disease, famine, pestilence, or simply getting lost. When one expedition finally reaches a lake that may be a source of the Nile, Burton arrives carried on a stretcher, almost too sick to think. A diary by a member of Scott's expedition to the South Pole is titled *The Worst Journey in the World.* That could also be the diary of this expedition.

Back in London, Burton (Patrick Bergin) and Speke (Iain Glen) have a falling-out based on a lack of communication and a tragic misunderstanding. Speke takes credit for finding the source of the Nile; Burton is adamant that the evidence is not sufficient. An unscrupulous publisher tells Speke lies about Burton, and Speke acts on them, making unforgivable statements about his former friend. When he learns that they were lies— that Burton has the material to destroy him in a debate—he falls into despair. There is the suggestion, tantalizing and unresolved, that he may have been in love with Burton, a man whose sexual appetites seem to have been fueled as much by curiosity as by lust.

Mountains of the Moon is completely absorbing. It tells its story soberly and intelligently and with quiet style. It doesn't manufacture false thrills or phony excitement. It's the kind of movie that sends you away from the screen filled with curiosity to know more about this man Burton. Why, you ask yourself, has such an oversized character become almost forgotten? The movie is about the unquenchable compulsion of some men to see what is beyond the horizon, and about the hunger for glory. It is about stubbornness and pride. It is about a friendship that would have been infinitely less painful if the friends had not both been bullheaded and flawed. It is a tribute to this movie that, at the end, neither the filmmakers nor their audience have much interest in whether anyone found the source of the Nile.

Much Ado About Nothing ★ ★ ★
PG-13, 111 m., 1993

Denzel Washington (Don Pedro, Prince of Aragon), Kenneth Branagh (Benedick, of Padua), Robert Sean Leonard (Claudio, of Florence), Emma Thompson (Beatrice, an orphan), Kate Beckinsale (Hero), Keanu Reeves (Don John), Michael Keaton (Dogberry), Gerald Horan (Borachio), Richard Clifford (Conrade). Directed and produced by Kenneth Branagh. Screenplay by Branagh.

Sunshine and laughter, and merrymakers on a hillside sprinkled with flowers. In the opening scene of *Much Ado About Nothing*, Kenneth Branagh insists on the tone the movie will take: These are healthy, joyful young people whose high spirits will survive anything, even the dark double-crosses of Shakespeare's plot.

The story involves two sets of lovers. The first, Claudio and Hero, are destined to be almost torn apart by the treachery of others. The second, Benedick and Beatrice, are almost kept apart by the treachery of their own hearts. The plot is driven by the kinds of misunderstandings, deceptions, and cruel jokes that work only in stage comedy, or perhaps in P.G. Wodehouse, where people are always lurking in the shrubbery, eavesdropping on crucial conversations.

Branagh is nothing if not a film director of high spirits and great energy. His *Henry V* was a Shakespeare history filled with patriotism and poetry. His *Dead Again* hurtled headlong into the juiciness of the murder-and-reincarnation genre. His *Peter's Friends* was a reunion of old university chums whose youthful quirks had matured into full-blown eccentricities, for good or ill. That last film, oddly enough, has a tone somewhat in common with *Much Ado About Nothing*.

The play, set in Sicily and shot in Tuscany, involves a few crucial days in the lives of the followers of Don Pedro (Denzel Washington), Prince of Aragon, who returns victorious from battle with his half brother Don John (Keanu Reeves). They are now apparently on speaking terms, but Don John, wearing a wicked black beard, mopes about the edges of the screen, casting dark looks upon the merrymakers.

Claudio (Robert Sean Leonard), Don Pedro's follower, casts eyes on the beautiful Hero (Kate Beckinsale) and is immediately possessed by love. Her eyes reveal that she reciprocates. Meanwhile, the older Benedick (Branagh) and Beatrice (Emma Thompson) feel a powerful attraction, too, but it is expressed through barbed insults and verbal sparring. Sometimes when people are frightened by the love they feel, it comes out through mock hostility.

The film's action is a progression through a series of picnics, communal baths, dinners, banquets, dances, and courtships. Branagh sets the pace just this side of a Marx Brothers movie. While Benedick and Beatrice do their best to assure that they will never become a couple, the scheming Don John plots to destroy the love that has bloomed for Claudio and Hero. His evil plan involves the use of impostors to convince Claudio that Hero is a wanton woman, unfaithful to him with any man who comes to hand.

A play like *Much Ado About Nothing* is all about style. I doubt if Shakespeare's audiences at the Globe took it any more seriously than we do. It is farce and mime and wisecracks, and dastardly melodrama which all comes right in the end, of course, because this is a comedy. The key to the film's success is in the acting, especially in the sparks that fly between Branagh and Thompson as their characters aim their insults so lovingly that we realize, sooner than they do, how much they would miss their verbal duets.

Of the others, the actor who tries the hardest, to uncertain effect, is Michael Keaton, as Dogberry, the oafish constable. One of Shakespeare's characters made of low comedy and burlesque, Dogberry here becomes a recycled grotesque modeled on Keaton's performance in *Beetlejuice*. Does the approach work? Probably not as Shakespeare intended, because it seems to come from a universe other than the one inhabited by the other characters in the play. But viewed by itself—and Dogberry is after all a self-contained character—it's quite a piece of work, and Keaton gets points just for trying so hard.

Any modern film of Shakespeare must deal with the fact that many people in the audience will be unfamiliar with the play, and perhaps even with the playwright. Branagh deals with this fact by making *Much Ado* into a film that reinvents the story; this is not a film "of" a Shakespeare play, but a film that begins with the same materials and the wonderful language and finds its own reality. It is cheerful from beginning to end (since we can hardly take the moments of doom and despair seriously). It is entirely appropriate that it has been released in the springtime.

The Muppet Christmas Carol ★ ★ ★
G, 86 m., 1992

Michael Caine (Scrooge). Voices: Dae Goelz (Great Gonzo), Steve Whitmire (Rizzo and Kermit), Jerry Nelson (Tiny Tim Cratchit), Frank Oz (Miss Piggy), David Rudman (Peter Cratchit). Directed by Brian Henson and produced by Henson and Martin G. Baker. Screenplay by Jerry Juhl.

Curious that Charles Dickens's *A Christmas Carol* should be the best-beloved of all fictional Christmas stories. It's a tale of Gothic gloom relieved only at the end by the warmth of holiday cheer. In order to enjoy that Christmas turkey with Bob Cratchit and share in Scrooge's redemption, we have to pay heavy dues: Marley's ghost, the rattling of chains, lots of graveyards and skeletons, poverty and suffering, greed and cold, and finally the spirits of Christmas, climaxing with the Grim Reaper.

No wonder when my dad read me the story I preferred the one about Rudolph. And no wonder Disney has tried to lighten up this latest of at least a dozen film versions of the story by adding the Muppets (in the mid-1980s, they made a version starring Mickey Mouse). Even the Muppets seem a little awed by the solemnity of the tale; "Isn't this a little violent for some of the kids in the audience?" one of them asks, only to be reminded of the story's artistic importance.

The Muppet Christmas Carol is made with one principal human actor, Michael Caine, in the role of Ebenezer Scrooge. There are a few more humans, including Scrooge as a youth, but most of the other roles, great and small, are played by Muppets, who are credited in the opening titles: "Kermit the Frog as Bob Cratchit . . . Miss Piggy as Mrs. Cratchit . . . the Great Gonzo as Charles Dickens . . . Rizzo the Rat as Himself."

This leads to some logical leaps of faith, as when we see the Cratchit household and realize all the boy children are frogs and all the girl children are pigs. But it also helps to introduce a Muppetian jollity into the story (when Scrooge's bookkeeping rats complain about cold, for example, and he threatens to fire them, they switch immediately into beachwear and start singing "Island in the Sun").

Caine is the latest of many human actors (including the great Orson Welles) to fight for screen space with the Muppets, and he sensibly avoids any attempt to go for a laugh. He plays the role straight, and treats the Muppets as if they are real. It is not an easy assignment. Consider the moment when he is moved to tears by Tiny Tim. This scene plays one way when Tim is a lovable little tot on a crutch, and another way when he is a small frog made of green felt. Caine, whose technical skills on screen are the equal of any actor's, does as well as he can under the circumstances.

The movie, directed by Brian Henson, son of the late Muppet creator Jim Henson, follows the original fairly faithfully. Like the earlier three Muppet movies, it manages to incorporate the Muppets convincingly into the action; we may know they're puppets, but usually we're not much reminded of their limited fields of movement. Ever since Kermit rode a bicycle across the screen in *The Muppet Movie* in 1979, the Muppeteers have managed to bypass what you'd think would be the obvious limitations of the form. This time, they even seem to belong in Victorian London, created in atmospheric sets that combine realism and expressionism.

Like all the Muppet movies, this one is a musical, with original songs by Paul Williams (my favorite is the early chain-rattling duet by the Marley brothers). It could have done with a few more songs than it has, and the merrymaking at the end might have been carried on a little longer, just to offset the gloom of most of Scrooge's tour through his lifetime spent spreading misery. Will kids like the movie? The kids around me in the theater seemed to, although more for the Muppets than for the cautionary tale of Scrooge.

The Muppet Movie ★ ★ ★ ½
G, 94 m., 1979

Jim Henson (Kermit, Rowlf, Dr. Teeth, and Waldorf), Frank Oz (Miss Piggy, Fozzie Bear, Animal, and Sam), Jerry Nelson (Floyd Pepper, Crazy Harry, Robin the Frog, and Lew Zealand), Richard Hunt (Scooter, Statler, Janice, Sweetums, and Beaker), Dave Goelz (The Great Gonza, Zoot, and Dr. Bunsen Honeydew). Directed by James Frawley and produced by Jim Henson. Screenplay by Jerry Juhl and Jack Burns.

Jolson sang, Barrymore spoke, Garbo laughed, and now Kermit the Frog rides a bicycle. *The Muppet Movie* not only stars the Muppets but, for the first time, shows us their feet. And if you can figure out how they were able to show Kermit pedaling across the screen, then you are less a romantic than I am: I prefer to believe he did it himself.

He's pedaling on his way to Hollywood, and *The Muppet Movie* itself is one of those origin stories so beloved by comic books. We've learned how Spiderman came into his extraordinary powers, and now here are the earliest days of the Muppets.

Kermit, we learn, was born in a swamp. Well, maybe we coulda guessed it. And he was born with an ability somewhat unusual to frogs: a talent for playing the ukulele. We encounter him sitting on a log and singing one of the movie's several Paul Williams songs, and for just a second we wonder where Jim Henson is. That's because Kermit is quite clearly surrounded by water, and we can't for the life of us figure out where they hid the Muppeteer.

It turns out Henson was sitting in a watertight compartment and communicating with the rest of the crew via walkie-talkie, and that Kermit's hands on the ukelele were animated by remote control, and that all sorts of technology went into making the Muppets move, but after that first second we quit wondering: This is magic, after all, so who *wants* to know where Henson is?

Dom DeLuise, on the other hand, wants to know where Kermit is. DeLuise comes rowing through the swamp in a rowboat and hears Kermit's song and reveals himself to be a big Hollywood agent with a copy of *Variety* in his boat. And, wouldn't you know, *Variety* has an ad for singing frogs in it. So of course Kermit leaves his swamp behind and commences a cross-country odyssey to Hollywood to make his audition.

He makes his trip mostly in a late-1940s Studebaker, one of those models that looked like it was going in both directions simultaneously, and the trip would have been a happy one except for one thing: Kermit is pursued by an evil fast-food magnate (Charles Durning) who wants him to sign on as the trademark of a chain of French-fried frogs' legs restaurants. It is one of the movie's more poignant ironies that no sooner does Kermit obtain legs than humans find an unsavory use for them.

Durning and DeLuise are two of the several humans in the film. The format makes absolutely no distinction between the Muppets and other forms of life, so we meet such humans as Mel Brooks, Bob Hope, Carol Kane, Steve Martin, Richard Pryor, Telly Savalas, Orson Welles, and, in their last film appearance before their deaths, Edgar Bergen and Charlie McCarthy.

We also meet, of course, Miss Piggy, who falls instantly and incurably in love with Kermit. And we get to know all the Muppets better than we could on their television show. They turn out, somehow, to have many of the same emotions and motivations that we do. They are vain and hopeful, selfish and generous, complicated and true. They mirror ourselves, except that they're a little nicer.

The Muppets Take Manhattan ★ ★ ★
G, 94 m., 1984

With guest stars Dabney Coleman, Joan Rivers, Liza Minnelli, and John Landis. Directed by Frank Oz and produced by David Lazer. Written by Oz and Jim Henson.

Dear Kermit,

I hope you will take this in the right spirit. I know you've been tortured for some years now by an identity crisis, ever since you were discovered sitting on that log down in the swamp, strumming on your ukulele. Stardom happened almost overnight, and here you are in your third starring vehicle, *The Muppets Take Manhattan.* Yet you still don't know who you really are.

You are obviously not a frog. You have none of the attributes of a frog, except for your appearance and your name. In your first film, *The Muppet Movie,* you were sort of a greenish overgrown pop singer, an amphibian Frankie Avalon. In your second movie, *The Great Muppet Caper,* you were cast adrift in a plot that really belonged to the human guest stars. You basically had a supporting role, making the humans look good. Only in *The Muppets Take Manhattan,* your third film, do you really seem to come into your own. You take charge. You are the central figure in the plot, you do not allow yourself to get shouldered aside by Miss Piggy, and you seem thoroughly at home with the requirements of genre, stereotype, and cliché. In the 1940s, you would have been under contract to MGM.

The plot of your movie has been seen before. I doubt if that will come as news to you. *The Muppets Take Manhattan* is yet another retread of the reliable old formula in which somebody says "Hey, gang! Our senior class musical show is so good, I'll bet we could be stars on Broadway!" The fact that this plot is not original does not deter you, Kermit, nor should it. It's still a good plot.

I liked the scenes in which you persevered. I liked the way you went to New York and challenged the stubborn agents like Dabney Coleman, and upstaged Liza Minnelli in Sardi's. I especially liked the scenes where you supported yourself by waiting tables in a greasy spoon cafe with rats in the kitchen and a Greek owner who specialized in philosophical statements that didn't make any sense. I even liked Miss Piggy's scenes, especially her childhood memories. I gasped at the wedding scene, in which you finally married her. I refrained from speculating about your wedding night—and speculation is all your G-rated movie left me with.

In short, I liked just about everything about your movie. But what I liked best was your discovery of self. Kermit, you are no longer a frog with an identity crisis. You've found the right persona, old boy, and it will see you through a dozen more movies. It was clear to me from the moment you took your curtain call and basked in the spotlight. Kermit, this may come as a shock, but you're Mickey Rooney in a frog suit. Think about it. You're short. You're cute. You never say

die. You keep smilin'. You have a philosophy for everything. You appear only in wholesome, G-rated movies. And sex bombs like Liza Minnelli only kiss you on the cheek.

One word of advice. Dump Miss Piggy. Stage a talent search for a Liza Minnelli Muppet. Mickey Rooney made a lot of movies with Liza's mother before you were hatched, Kermit, and now it's your turn. Move fast, kid, before you croak.

Murder in the First ★ ★
R, 113 m., 1995

NEW

Christian Slater (James Stampill), Kevin Bacon (Henri Young), Gary Oldman (Associate Warden Glenn), Embeth Davidtz (Mary McCasslin), Bill Macy (William McNeil), Stephen Tobolowsky (Mr. Henkin), Brad Dourif (Byron Stampill), R. Lee Ermey (Judge Clawson). Directed by Marc Rocco and produced by Marc Frydman and Mark Wolper. Screenplay by Dan Gordon.

Murder in the First takes place in two worlds. One is cold, gray, and artificially lit. The other is as warm as a cedar's dream, all sunlight and furniture polish, brass and tweed. The film is about how a man who lives in one of these worlds might learn to trust a man who lives in the other one. It is a good idea, but the film depends on us believing in the two men, and that isn't easy.

The story unfolds during the same season that Joe DiMaggio was setting his record for hits in consecutive games; that's a favorite year for filmmakers, because it allows them to counterpoint DiMaggio's streak with their own characters' more obscure lives (see, for example, *Farewell, My Lovely*). The plot involves a man named Henri Young (Kevin Bacon) who has been cruelly treated by the California prison system, and a lawyer named James Stampill (Christian Slater) who is appointed to defend him.

Young, originally arrested for stealing five dollars to feed his starving little sister, was later kept in solitary confinement for three years, went berserk, killed another prisoner, and is now being tried for murder. Stampill says the system, not the prisoner, is guilty. As the movie opens, Young has been driven into a tiny corner of his mind by the brutal experience of solitary confinement, and peers out suspiciously at the world. It is Stampill's task to win his trust.

Stampill is a man who is always running. The first time we see him, he's chasing a San Francisco cable car. He's usually late. The

movie has no particular purpose for establishing this trait; it's just background, designed to flesh out a character who needs it. There is no shortage, however, of background for Young, who is played by Bacon as such a mass of suffering and victimization that Bacon needs every ounce of his considerable skill to keep from eating right through the scenery.

The scenery is, to be sure, awesome. Alcatraz is seen on its bleak, cruel rock, and the world inside is carefully re-created. The movie's art department really grows enthusiastic, however, in the courtroom: Whether this is a set or an actual location I do not know, but if *Architectural Digest* ever does an issue on the legal system, this is the cover photo. The courtroom is so interesting, in fact, that it almost upstages several important moments; we're looking at the chairs and wondering if they're real, and how much they cost. This is one terrific courtroom.

It is presided over by Judge Clawson (R. Lee Ermey, the former marine drill instructor who starred in Kubrick's *Full Metal Jacket*), who runs a tight ship, barks commands, has a quirky personality, and is fun to watch, although only a judge in a movie would allow the ending of this trial to unfold as it does. Other important characters include Gary Oldman as a sadistic Alcatraz warden who administers the inhuman punishment system, and a California state prison chief who doesn't have a clue what's going on. Bill Macy has the thankless role of the prosecuting attorney.

But most of the film is given over to the relationship between the accused and his lawyer, and Bacon and Slater spend a lot of time in two-shots together, holding intensity contests. Slater, who in certain shots here looks curiously like Kevin Costner, is an actor with talent, but he is too young to play this role, and not confident enough to dial down a little. Like DiMaggio the same summer, he wants a hit every time he goes to the plate. Hollywood sometimes goes on youth kicks like this, casting kids in their midtwenties in roles where a substantial character actor is called for. Eventually we stop believing in the story, and then we stop caring, and then we start admiring that great furniture.

Murder on the Orient Express ★ ★ ★
PG, 128 m., 1974

Albert Finney (Hercule Poirot), Lauren Bacall (Mrs. Hubbard), Martin Balsam (Bianchi),

Ingrid Bergman (Greta Ohlsson), Jacqueline Bisset (Countess Andrenyi), Jean-Pierre Cassel (Pierre Paul Michel), Sean Connery (Colonel Arbuthnot), John Gielgud (Beddoes), Wendy Hiller (Princess Dragomiroff), Anthony Perkins (Hector McQueen), Vanessa Redgrave (Mary Debenham), Richard Widmark (Ratchett), Rachel Roberts (Hildegarde Schmitt), Michael York (Count Andrenyi). Directed by Sidney Lumet and produced by John Brabourne and Richard Goodwin. Screenplay by Paul Deim.

There is a cry of alarm, some muffled French, a coming and a going in the corridor. Hercule Poirot, adjusting the devices that keep his hair slicked down and his mustache curled up, pauses for a moment in his train compartment. He lifts an eyebrow. He looks out into the hallway. He shrugs. The next morning, it's revealed that Ratchett, the hateful American millionaire, has been stabbed to death in his sleep. This is quite obviously a case for Poirot, the most famous detective in the world, and, over breakfast, he agrees to accept it. The list of suspects is long, but limited: It includes everybody on board the crack Orient Express, en route from Istanbul to Calais, and currently brought to a standstill by an avalanche of snow that has fallen across the track. Poirot arranges to begin a series of interviews and plunges himself (and the rest of us) into a net of intrigue so deep, so deceptive, and so labyrinthine that only Agatha Christie would have woven it. *Murder on the Orient Express* is a splendidly entertaining movie of the sort that isn't made any more: It's a classical whodunit, with all the clues planted and all of them visible, and it's peopled with a large and expensive collection of stars. Albert Finney, who plays Poirot, is the most impressive, largely because we can never for a moment be sure that he *is* Finney. His hair is slicked down to a patent-leather shine, his eyes have somehow become beady and suspicious, his French mustache is constantly quivering with alarm (real and pretended), and he scurries up and down the train like a paranoid crab. The performance is brilliant, and it's high comedy.

So is the movie, although it's careful never to make its essentially comic intentions get in the way of Miss Christie's well-oiled mystery. This isn't a "thriller," because we're not thrilled, or scared—only amused. The murder itself has a certain antiseptic, ritualistic quality, and the investigation is an exercise in sophisticated cross-examination and sput-

ters of indignation. What I liked best about this movie is its style, both the deliberately old-fashioned visual strategies used by director Sidney Lumet, and the cheerful overacting of the dozen or more suspects.

They form a suitably bizarre menagerie and at first glance have nothing in common with one another. Bear with me please, and I'll work my way through the all-stars: Lauren Bacall is a particularly obnoxious American, Ingrid Bergman is an African missionary, Michael York and Jacqueline Bisset are Hungarian royalty, Jean-Pierre Cassel is the conductor, Sean Connery is an English officer returning from India, Vanessa Redgrave is his constant companion, John Gielgud is a veddy, veddy proper man-servant to millionaire Richard Widmark, Wendy Hiller is an aloof Russian aristocrat, Anthony Perkins is Widmark's secretary, Rachel Roberts is a neo-Nazi ladies' maid, Martin Balsam is a director of the railroad line, and there are, believe it or not, others also under suspicion.

There are obviously big technical problems here: More than a dozen characters have to be introduced and kept alive, a very complicated plot has to be unraveled, and everything must take place within the claustrophobic confines of the railway car. Lumet overcomes his difficulties in great style, and we're never for a moment confused (except when we're supposed to be, which is most of the time).

There is hardly anything more I can tell you, or even hint, about the plot, except that nothing is as it seems (and you knew that already about a movie based on an Agatha Christie book). The movie provides a good time, high style, a loving salute to an earlier period of filmmaking, and an unexpected bonus: It ends with a very long scene in which Poirot asks everyone to be silent, please, while he explains his various theories of the case. He does so in great detail, and it's fun of a rather malicious sort watching a dozen high-priced stars keep their mouths shut and just listen while Finney masterfully dominates the scene.

Muriel's Wedding ★ ★ ★ ½
R, 105 m., 1995

NEW

Toni Collette (Muriel), Bill Hunter (Bill), Rachel Griffiths (Rhonda), Jeanie Drynan (Betty), Gennie Nevinson (Deidre), Matt Day (Brice), Daniel Lapaine (David Van Arkle), Sophie Lee (Tania). Directed by P.J. Hogan and produced by Lynda House and Jocelyn Moorhouse. Screenplay by Hogan.

When Muriel catches the bouquet at a friend's wedding, her friends are furious: "Throw it again—*you'll* never get married." She doesn't look like much of a catch, in a leopard-skin dress that stands out so much she's spotted by another wedding guest who is, unfortunately, a floorwalker at the store where Muriel shoplifted it. She's delivered home from the wedding by the police, but is spared arrest when her dad, a local politician with the backslapping ease of a much more successful man, treats the cops to a case of beer.

This is in Porpoise Spit, Australia ("Jewel of the North Coast"), and P.J. Hogan's *Muriel's Wedding* is another of those Australian films that walk a careful line between satire and misery. Like *Man of Flowers, High Tide, Sweetie, Proof,* and *Strictly Ballroom,* it is merciless in its portrait of provincial society, and yet has a huge affection for its misfit survivors. When Muriel (Toni Collette) is wounded, she retreats to her bedroom, drowning out reality with Abba songs. She is a large, big-boned young woman with unruly hair and a clueless look, and her friends from high school—swimsuit issue wannabes with promiscuous but grim sex lives—don't want her around anymore. They're planning a holiday on a tropical island and she will not enhance their appeal.

Muriel's home life is cheerless, with an undertone of tragedy in Betty, her mother (Jeanie Drynan), a thoroughly cowed woman who is treated by her children like a domestic slave and by her husband, Bill (Bill Hunter), as a household appliance who cooks and cleans. Bill is a failed politician who takes obscure Japanese investors to dinner in Chinese restaurants where he is owed free meals because of shady favors. His children are couch potatoes who sit, stunned, staring at the television. At least Muriel has had enough ambition to flunk out of secretarial school.

Then life changes, suddenly, when Muriel comes into some money (a blank check from her mother) and a high-spirited new friend named Rhonda (Rachel Griffiths), who has an infectious grin and faith in Muriel's potential. Muriel meets Rhonda on vacation on the very island where the snobs have gone, and the two are the hit of the talent night with their mimed version of "Waterloo." With Rhonda around, life suddenly has promise; the two girls move to Sydney, where Muriel finally has a sexual experience, not very successful (the boy unzips a chair instead of Muriel's pants, in a misunderstanding that must be seen to be understood). "When I lived in Porpoise Spit," Muriel tells Rhonda, "I sat in my room for hours and listened to Abba songs. Since I met you and moved to Sydney, my life is as good as an Abba song—as good as 'Dancing Queen.'"

For her, there is no higher praise. But Muriel is still unhappy, and because she identifies perfect happiness with getting married, she haunts wedding shops and eventually ends up in a marriage of convenience with an empty-eyed South African swimming star who needs a wife to get an Australian passport. (During their wedding, she lets out little simpering squeaks, and he looks at her with slack-jawed incredulity.)

Muriel's Wedding has a lot of big and little laughs in it, but also a melancholy undercurrent, which reveals itself toward the end of the film in a series of surprises and unexpected developments. The arc of its story involves Muriel's discovery of herself, and a developing faith that she can have a good time, make friends, and be valued. The film's good heart keeps it from ever making fun of Muriel, although there are moments that must have been tempting. And the casting of minor characters (including Muriel's sister with the naughty-naughty smirk) is flawless.

Murphy's Romance ★ ★ ★
PG-13, 107 m., 1985

Sally Field (Emma Moriarty), James Garner (Murphy Jones), Brian Kerwin (Bobby Jack), Corey Haim (Jake), Dennis Burkley (Freeman Coverly), Georgann Johnson (Margaret). Directed by Martin Ritt and produced by Laura Ziskin. Screenplay by Harriet Frank, Jr., and Irving Ravetch.

From the moment Sally Field pilots her battered old pickup into town and parks her kid out at the farm and walks into James Garner's drugstore and they lay eyes on each other for the first time, it's pretty clear that they are going to have to fall in love with each other and get married. All you have to do is look at them to see that.

Murphy's Romance takes almost two hours to arrive at the conclusion that takes us two minutes, but that doesn't mean this is a predictable movie. The whole point of this movie is how it looks at those characters, and listens to them, and allows them to live in a specific time and place. If they knew what we

know, it would spoil all the fun, as they flirt and pout and spar and circle each other, and survive the sudden and unexpected appearance of Sally Field's no-good ex-husband.

His name is Bobby Jack, and Field describes him in a sentence: "How come you were never as good on your feet as you were between the sheets?" He's an immature, sweet-talking con man without a responsible bone in his body. He turns up one day, and moves in, and Field lets him stay because it means a lot to their son, Jake.

At first it appears that Bobby Jack's arrival is going to cause problems for the budding relationship between Emma and Murphy (Field and Garner). But Emma keeps on inviting Murphy to stay to dinner, and Murphy reads the situation correctly: Emma may be stuck with Bobby Jack, but she is stuck on Murphy.

Murphy is quite a guy. He figures he has a lot of knowledge about human nature, and he's not shy about sharing it. He doesn't take himself too seriously, but he likes to pretend that he does. He speaks thoughtfully, moves deliberately, and lets you know what a character he is by parking his mint-condition 1928 Studebaker out in front of his drugstore. Garner plays this character in more or less his usual acting style, but he has been given such quietly offbeat dialogue by the screenwriters, Harriet Frank, Jr., and Irving Ravetch, that he comes across as a true original.

Sally Field is also not particularly original in her approach to the character Emma, who is a close relative of other Field heroines: plucky, quietly sensible in the face of calamity. Originality is not called for in this performance, anyway; it would have been a mistake to turn into a colorful character, instead of letting her proceed at her own speed. In the movie's key series of scenes—where Bobby Jack makes his move and Emma sneezes at him and then a surprise visitor turns up from Tulsa—the movie is saved from melodrama only by Field's matter-of-fact ability to take things as they come.

Then comes the ending, which is one of the most carefully and lovingly written passages in any recent movie. Much depends on exactly what Emma and Murphy say to each other, and how they say it, and what they don't say. The movie gets it all right.

Murphy's Romance was directed by Martin Ritt, who also directed Field's Oscar-winning performance in *Norma Rae* (and worked with her again in the less-than-suc-

cessful *Back Roads*). Ritt specializes in movies about the rural South and Southwest (his credits also include *Sounder, Hud,* and *Conrack*), and one of the strengths of *Murphy's Romance* is the freedom he feels to simply pause, occasionally, and soak in the local color. Two examples: Listen carefully to the man who calls the bingo numbers, and the old man Murphy gives a lift to one day. They have particular voices and deliberate word choices, and they seem completely authentic. So, to a surprising degree, does the whole movie.

The Music of Chance ★ ★ ★
NO MPAA RATING, 110 m., 1993

James Spader (Jack Pozzi), Mandy Patinkin (James Nashe), M. Emmet Walsh (Calvin Murks), Charles Durning (Bill Flower), Joel Grey (Willie Stone), Samantha Mathis (Tiffany), Christopher Penn (Floyd). Directed by Philip Haas and produced by Frederick Zollo and Dylan Sellers. Screenplay by Philip Haas and Belinda Haas.

To describe *The Music of Chance* as a journey into the Twilight Zone would be unfair—there's more to it—but would strike the right note. The movie tells a bizarre, disturbing story of two men who meet by chance, and find themselves trapped in a bargain that seems sealed by the powers of evil.

The movie opens, as all satanic stories do, on a fine, untroubled day. Mandy Patinkin plays a man named Nashe, who has just cut his ties with his earlier life, and is driving down the road, free and open to new experiences. He gives a lift to a stranger on the roadside (James Spader), who turns out to be a professional poker player named Pozzi, and tells of losing ten thousand dollars to a couple of guys he should have beaten. Nashe has ten thousand dollars and offers to back Pozzi in a rematch. Up to this point, the movie is strange, but plausible. We could be in David Mamet country. But the story, based on a novel by Paul Auster, has a stranger destination in mind.

The two men arrive at the gates of a mysterious country estate occupied by two old friends, Mr. Flower (Charles Durning) and Mr. Stone (Joel Grey). They are jolly and genial hosts, so cheerful indeed that there seems something the matter with them. They agree to a poker game, after first taking the visitors on a tour of their house, which contains an elaborate scale model of their corner of the world, and even little figures representing Stone and Flower. This model, which the movie never quite explains, works because it is left mysterious: Not knowing its function, we are ready to attribute anything to it.

The game proceeds. Pozzi, backed by Nashe, loses again. Credit is extended, and he loses still more. There is no way the two visitors can make good their debt, and so Flower and Stone, not so friendly now, suggest the men "work it off." They are put to work constructing an enormous stone wall, under the genial but unrelenting guidance of a foreman with the wonderful name of Calvin Murks, played by M. Emmet Walsh, that master of false jollity.

There is, no doubt, a metaphor here for something, although the movie wisely never tells us what it is. There are echoes not only of Rod Serling but of *Waiting for Godot* and the myth of Sisyphus, that luckless Greek assigned by the gods to spend eternity rolling a stone up a hill, so that he can watch it roll back down again. The director, Philip Haas, roots his story in gritty realism; there is a great deal about the mechanics of wall-building, and the off-duty hours of Nashe and Pozzi are used to develop their suspicions and resentments, particularly when a visiting hooker appears on the scene.

The Music of Chance is one of those movies you can argue about for hours. It refuses to reveal its meaning, yet seems convinced it has one. The acting is all perfectly straightforward (Durning and Grey are inspired in their cheery double act), the details are there to be seen, the wall is eventually built, and yet when you try to add up all the details, they seem as elusive as life itself.

My Beautiful Laundrette ★ ★ ★
R, 93 m., 1986

Daniel Day Lewis (Johnny), Saeed Jaffrey (Nasser), Roshan Seth (Papa), Gordon Warnecke (Omar), Shirley Ann Field (Rachel), Rita Wolf (Tania). Directed by Stephen Frears and produced by Sarah Radclyffe and Tim Bevan. Screenplay by Hanif Kureishi.

When people told me they'd seen *My Beautiful Laundrette* and it was a good movie, I had a tendency to believe them, for who would dare to make a bad movie with such an uncommercial title? The launderette in question is a storefront operation in one of the seedier areas of London, and it is losing money when a rich Pakistani decides to entrust its management to his nephew. But

this is not the saga of a launderette. It is the story of two kinds of outsiders in modern London.

The film opens with some uneventful days in the life of its hero, Omar, who is a young man in need of a job. His father is an alcoholic journalist, once important and successful, now never far from the gin bottle. His uncle Nasser is one of the more successful members of the Pakistani community in London, a businessman who owns a chain of parking garages and storefront retail shops. He enjoys success in British terms: He has a big house in the country, an expensive car, and a British mistress.

Because a man cannot stand by and see a member of his family fail for lack of opportunity, he gives Omar a job in a parking garage, and later turns the launderette over to him. He also suggests that Omar should get married, perhaps even to his own daughter.

There is some doubt, however, about whether Omar will ever get married. Earlier in the film, we have witnessed a strange scene. Omar and friends have been stopped by a gang of punk neo-fascist Paki-bashers, when Omar walks up fearlessly to their leader, Johnny, and greets him with affection. We discover that the two young men had been lovers, and before long Johnny abandons his gang to join with Omar in the operation of the launderette.

My Beautiful Laundrette refuses to commit its plot to any particular agenda, and I found that interesting. It's not about whether Johnny and Omar will remain lovers, and it's not about whether the launderette will be a success, and it's not about the drunken father or even about Nasser's daughter, who is so bored and desperate that during a cocktail party she goes outside and bares her breasts to Omar through the French doors: Anything to get away from the small talk.

The movie is not concerned with plot, but with giving us a feeling for the society its characters inhabit. Modern Britain is a study in contrasts, between rich and poor, between upper and lower classes, between native British and the various immigrant groups—some of which, like the Pakistanis, have started to prosper. To this mixture, the movie adds the conflict between straight and gay.

Their relationship encompasses some subtleties which the movie handles with great delicacy. Although Omar is a member of a non-white immigrant group and Johnny

is Anglo-Saxon, the realities of their lives are that Omar will probably turn out to be more successful and prosperous than Johnny. He has the advantage of his uncle's capital, his family connections, and his own gift at business. Johnny is a true outsider with small prospects of success.

There is another outsider in the movie who shares his dilemma. She is Rachel, Nasser's British mistress. Nasser remains married to his Pakistani wife, and although the two women are more or less known to one another, he keeps them in separate compartments of his life. There is a moment, though, during the opening ceremonies at the launderette, when the two women are accidentally in the same room at the same time, and it results in an extraordinary speech by Rachel, who with pride and dignity defends her position as Nasser's mistress by describing herself as a woman who has never had a break in life, who has always had to ask for what she wanted, and who deserves some small measure of happiness, just like everybody else.

A movie like this lives or dies with its performances, and the actors in *My Beautiful Laundrette* are a fascinating group of unknowns, with one exception—Shirley Anne Field, who plays Rachel, and who may be familiar from *Saturday Night and Sunday Morning* and other British films.

The character of Johnny may cause you to blink, if you've seen the wonderful *A Room with a View;* he is played by Daniel Day Lewis, the same actor who in that film plays the heroine's affected fiancé Cecil. Seeing these two performances side by side is an affirmation of the miracle of acting: That one man could play these two opposites is astonishing.

Omar is played by Gordon Warnecke, an actor unknown to me, as a bright but passive youth who hasn't yet figured out the strategy by which he will approach the world. He is a blank slate, pleasant, agreeable, not readily showing the sorrows and angers that we figure ought to be inside there somewhere. The most expansive character in the movie is Nasser (Saeed Jaffrey), an engaging hedonist who doesn't see why everyone shouldn't enjoy life with the cynical good cheer he possesses.

The viewer is likely to go through a curious process while watching this film. At first there is unfamiliarity: Who are these people, and where do they come from, and what sort of society do they occupy in England? We get oriented fairly quickly, and understand the values that are at work. Then we begin to wonder what the movie is about. It is with some relief that we realize it isn't "about" anything; it's simply some weeks spent with some characters in a way that tells us more about some aspects of modern Britain than we've seen before.

I mentioned *A Room with a View* because of the link with Daniel Day Lewis. There is another link between the two films. They are both about the possibility of opening up views—of being able to see through a window out of your own life and into other possibilities. Both films argue that you have a choice. You can accept your class, social position, race, sexuality, or prejudices as absolutes, and live entirely inside them. Or you can look out the window, or maybe even walk out the door.

My Bodyguard ★ ★ ★ ½
PG, 97 m., 1980

Chris Makepeace (Clifford), Adam Baldwin (Linderman), Matt Dillon (Moody), Ruth Gordon (Gramma), Martin Mull (Mr. Peache), John Houseman (Dobbs), Paul Quandt (Carson), Craig Richard Nelson (Griffith). Directed by Tony Bill and produced by Don Devlin. Screenplay by Alan Ormsby.

There is a terrifying moment in adolescence when suddenly some of the kids are twice as big as the rest of the kids. It is terrifying for everybody: For the kids who are suddenly tall and gangling, and for the kids who are still small and are getting beat up all the time. *My Bodyguard* places that moment in a Chicago high school and gives us a kid who tries to think his way out of it.

The kid's name is Clifford. He has everything going against him. He's smart, he's new in the school, he's slightly built. As he's played by Chris Makepeace, he is also one of the most engaging teen-age characters I've seen in the movies in a long time. Too many movie teen-agers have been sex-crazed (*Little Darlings*), animalistic food-fighters (*Meatballs*), or hopelessly romanticized (*The Blue Lagoon*). Clifford is basically just your normal, average kid.

He has just moved to Chicago with his family. His father (Martin Mull) is the new resident manager of the Ambassador East Hotel. His grandmother (Ruth Gordon) hangs out in the lobby and picks up old men in the bar. Life is great, backstage at a hotel (he gets his meals in the kitchen or sometimes in the Pump Room). But it's not so great at school. The movie sends Clifford to Lake View High

School, where he's immediately shaken down for his lunch money.

The extortionist (Matt Dillon) is the kind of kid we all remember from high school. He's handsome in an oily way, he's going through a severe case of adolescent sadism, he's basically a coward. His threat is that unless Clifford pays protection money, he'll sic the dreaded Linderman on him.

Linderman (Adam Baldwin) is a school legend, a big, hulking kid who allegedly killed his brother, raped a teacher, hit a cop, you name it. The movie's inspiration is to have Clifford *think* his way out of his dilemma—neutralizing Linderman by hiring him as a bodyguard. This is genius, and there's a wonderful scene where Clifford springs Linderman on the rest of the kids.

Then the movie takes an interesting turn. Clifford and Linderman become friends, and we learn some of the unhappy facts of Linderman's life. It turns out Linderman isn't the Incredible Hulk after all—he's just another kid going through growing pains and some personal tragedy. This whole middle stretch is the best part of the movie, developing a friendship in a perceptive and gentle way that's almost shocking in comparison with the idiotic, violent teen-agers so many movies have given us.

The ending is predictable (it's a showdown between Linderman and another tough kid). And there are some distractions along the way from Clifford's family. Martin Mull makes an interesting hotel manager, whimsical and charming. But the movie gets off track when it follows Ruth Gordon through some of her adventures, including a romantic collision with a hotel executive played by John Houseman. These scenes just don't seem part of the same movie: The hotel stuff is sitcom, while the stuff in the high school is fresh and inventive.

That seems to apply to the performances, too. One of the strengths of *My Bodyguard* is in the casting of the younger performers—Chris Makepeace, Adam Baldwin, Matt Dillon. They look right for their parts, but, more to the point, they *feel* right. Dillon exudes creepiness, Makepeace is plausible while thinking on his feet, Linderman is convincingly vulnerable and confused, and there's another kid, the solemn-faced, wide-eyed Paul Quandt, who steals a couple of scenes with his absolute certainty that the worst is yet to come.

My Bodyguard is a small treasure, a movie about believable characters in an unusual sit-

uation. It doesn't pretend to be absolutely realistic, and the dynamics of its big city high school are simplified for the purposes of the story. But this movie is fun to watch because it touches memories that are shared by most of us, and because its young characters are recognizable individuals, and not simplified cartoon figures like so many movie teen-agers.

My Brilliant Career ★ ★ ★ ½
NO MPAA RATING, 101 m., 1980

Judy Davis (Sybylia Melvyn), Sam Neill (Harry Beecham), Wendy Hughes (Aunt Helen), Robert Grubb (Frank Hawden), Max Cullen (Mr. McSwat), Pat Kennedy (Aunt Gussie). Directed by Gillian Armstrong and produced by Margaret Fink. Screenplay by Eleanor Witcombe.

What magic is it that sometimes allows young girls in backward districts to guess that they need not play along with the general ideas about a "woman's role"? I ask because three of my favorite writers—and now a fourth—discovered, more or less by themselves, that the possibilities in their lives were unlimited.

Two of the writers are famous: Willa Cather, who wrote of independent young women in Nebraska and points west, and Doris Lessing, whose *Children of Violence* series chronicles the liberation of a young woman from Rhodesia. The other two writers are not so well known, but the parallels in their lives are so astonishing that I'd like to sketch them, briefly, before moving on to an extraordinary film, *My Brilliant Career.* Their names are Olive Schreiner and Miles Franklin. They both led isolated childhoods in the nineteenth century, in the backwaters of the British Empire. And they both wrote novels about those lives at a very early age.

Olive Schreiner was raised on a farm in the Orange Free State, in South Africa. She learned Afrikaans along with English, read the Bible daily, and in her mid-teens wrote a classic novel, *The Story of an African Farm.* It was about the awakening of the spirit of a teen-age girl (herself, obviously) who did not see why her life had to be so limited just because she was a woman. Schreiner's later life was spent in intellectual and feminist circles in London (and for a time she filled the challenging position of being Havelock Ellis's mistress).

The other writer is someone I've just learned about recently: Miles Franklin, born in 1879 in rural Australia and raised on an isolated country station in the outback. At the age of sixteen she wrote a novel about her experiences, *My Brilliant Career.* It was published six years later in Edinburgh. Like Schreiner, Franklin became a feminist, traveled abroad in her twenties (and came to Chicago, where she and Alice Henry organized the Women's Trade Union League).

The Story of an African Farm is an established literary classic. *My Brilliant Career,* on the other hand, was relatively forgotten until a group of Australian women filmmakers made it into this remarkable film. It tells the story of a restless, high-spirited young woman whose temperament just isn't suited to the leftover Victorian standards of Australian country districts in the 1890s.

Franklin's novel is successful as a movie primarily because of a brilliant casting discovery. Judy Davis, who plays the film's heroine, is so fresh, unique, irreverent, and winning that she makes this material live. She's a young actress from Perth, a sometime pop and jazz singer, who was reportedly the second choice for the film's lead; if that's so, it was a completely fortunate second choice.

My Brilliant Career could have been just another feminist film. The director, Gillian Armstrong, could have gone to great lengths to explain the thinking and motivations of her character—and bored us in the meantime. But she doesn't. Instead, she makes her points through Judy Davis's presence and personality.

This isn't a movie that ends with any final answers or conclusions. Instead, it's about a young woman in a painful and continuing process of indecision. She's not considered by her family to be an ideal young woman at all—she's too independent, untamed, unreconciled to a woman's role. She doesn't automatically swoon at the attentions of every young man in the district. She's redhaired, freckled, feisty.

These qualities do appeal, however, to one young neighboring man, a farmer who's of two minds about her: He finds her independence appealing, and yet he tends to share the prevailing view about proper behavior for women. Can he overcome his narrow view and accept her? He does propose marriage. Can she overcome her headstrong independence and accept him? That's the film's key question, and *My Brilliant Career* is wise in never quite answering it.

The film is beautiful to look at. It was filmed on location in the outback, in warm natural colors, and the costumes and settings meticulously establish the period. But

Judy Davis's performance establishes it even more, because she creates a complicated character so naturally that we feel the conflicts instead of having to understand them intellectually. This is the best kind of movie of ideas, in which the movie supplies the people and emotions and *we* come up with the conclusions.

My Cousin Vinny ★ ★ ½
R, 119 m., 1992

Joe Pesci (Vinny Gambini), Ralph Macchio (Bill Gambini), Marisa Tomei (Mona Lisa Vito), Mitchell Whitfield (Stan Rothenstein), Fred Gwynne (Judge), Lane Smith (Prosecutor). Directed by Jonathan Lynn and produced by Dale Launer and Paul Schiff. Screenplay by Launer.

My Cousin Vinny is a movie that meanders along going nowhere in particular, and then lightning strikes. I didn't get much involved in it, and yet individual moments and some of the performances were really very funny. It's the kind of movie home video was invented for: not worth the trip to the theater, but slam it into the VCR and you get your rental's worth.

The film stars Joe Pesci as a New Yorker who thinks a black knit shirt under a black leather jacket, if set off by a gold chain around the neck, is elegant courtroom attire. He might be right if he were a defendant in the Bronx, but the movie takes place in Alabama, and he's the defense attorney. His cousin (Ralph Macchio) and a friend (Mitchell Whitfield), two innocent college students on their way to school, have been charged with the murder of a convenience store owner. The circumstantial evidence looks damning, but the worst thing they have going against them is Pesci's sweeping lack of legal experience.

Although the film is set in the South and has an early shot of a sign that says "Free Horse Manure," this is not another one of your Dixie-bashing movies. The judge (Fred Gwynne, his face longer than ever) and prosecutor (Lane Smith) are civilized men who aren't trying to railroad anybody. It's just that after gunshots were heard, three different witnesses made a positive identification on the two suspects, fleeing the store in a distinctive late-1960s Buick convertible.

Pesci, who is Macchio's cousin Vinny, has finally passed the bar on his sixth attempt. He has no courtroom experience, and indeed no experience at all except with a few personal-injury cases. He arrives in town

with his girlfriend, named Mona Lisa Vito and played by Marisa Tomei as a woman who has a certain legal potential trapped inside a street-smart personality. Pesci is so inexperienced he doesn't even know enough to stand when the judge enters the courtroom, and Whitfield, in desperation, hires another lawyer (Austin Pendleton) who thinks it a triumph if he can successfully complete a sentence.

The movie saves most of its best laughs for the long concluding courtroom sequence, in which one witness after another hammers together the prosecution case, and the innocent youths clearly seem headed for the electric chair. Gwynne's dour work in the courtroom scenes is especially good; in the annals of Judge Reaction Shots, which are a performance genre all their own, his work ranks high.

But we never feel much for, or about, the two accused prisoners. Macchio, who has been effective in movies like *The Karate Kid* and *Crossroads,* is used here essentially as a foil. He and Whitfield sit at the defense table and look worried, and that's about that.

Pesci and Tomei, on the other hand, create a quirky relationship that I liked. Neither one is played as a dummy. They're smart, in their own ways, but involved in a legal enterprise they are completely unprepared for. Tomei's surprise appearance as an expert witness on automobiles ("I come from an entire family of mechanics") is a high point, and left me feeling I would like to see this couple again. Maybe in a screenplay that was more focused.

My Dinner with André ★ ★ ★ ★
NO MPAA RATING, 110 m., 1981

Wallace Shawn (Wally), André Gregory (André), Jean Lenauer (Waiter), Roy Butler (Bartender). Directed by Louis Malle and produced by George W. George and Beverly Karp. Screenplay by Shawn and Gregory.

The idea is astonishing in its audacity: a film of two friends talking, just simply talking—but with passion, wit, scandal, whimsy, vision, hope, and despair—for 110 minutes. It sounds at first like one of those underground films of the 1960s, in which great length and minimal content somehow interacted in the dope-addled brains of the audience to provide the impression of deep if somehow elusive profundity. *My Dinner with André* is not like that. It doesn't use all of those words as a stunt. They are alive on the screen, breathing, pulsing, reminding us of endless, impassioned conversations we've had with those few friends worth talking with for hours and hours. Underneath all the other fascinating things in this film beats the tide of friendship, of two people with a genuine interest in one another.

The two people are André Gregory and Wallace Shawn. Those are their real names, and also their names in the movie. I suppose they are playing themselves. As the film opens, Shawn travels across New York City to meet Gregory for dinner, and his thoughts provide us with background: His friend Gregory is a New York theater director, well-known into the 1970s, who dropped out for five years and traveled around the world. Now Gregory has returned, with wondrous tales of strange experiences. Shawn has spent the same years in New York, finding uncertain success as an author and playwright. They sit down for dinner in an elegant restaurant. We do not see the other customers. The bartender is a wraith in the background, the waiter is the sort of presence they were waiting for in *Waiting for Godot*. The friends order dinner, and then, as it is served and they eat and drink, they talk.

What conversation! André Gregory does most of the talking, and he is a spellbinding conversationalist, able to weave mental images not only out of his experiences, but also out of his ideas. He explains that he had become dissatisfied with life, restless, filled with anomie and discontent. He accepted an invitation to join an experimental theater group in Poland. It was *very* experimental, tending toward rituals in the woods under the full moon.

From Poland, he traveled around the world, meeting a series of people who were seriously and creatively exploring the ways in which they could experience the material world. They (and Gregory) literally believed in mind over matter, and as Gregory describes a monk who was able to stand his entire body weight on his fingertips, we visualize that man and in some strange way (so hypnotic is the tale) we share the experience.

One of the gifts of *My Dinner with André* is that we share so many of the experiences. Although most of the movie literally consists of two men talking, here's a strange thing: *We* do not spend the movie just passively listening to them talk. At first, director Louis Malle's sedate series of images (close-ups, two-shots, reaction shots) calls attention to itself, but as Gregory continues to talk, the very simplicity of the visual style renders it invisible. And like the listeners at the feet of a master storyteller, we find ourselves visualizing what Gregory describes, until this film is as filled with visual images as a radio play—*more* filled, perhaps, than a conventional feature film.

What Gregory and Shawn talk about is, quite simply, many of the things on our minds these days. We've passed through Tom Wolfe's Me Decade and find ourselves in a decade during which there will apparently be less for everybody. The two friends talk about inner journeys—not in the mystical, vague terms of magazines you don't want to be seen reading on the bus, but in terms of trying to live better lives, of learning to listen to what others are really saying, of breaking the shackles of conventional ideas about our bodies and allowing them to more fully sense the outer world.

The movie is not ponderous, annoyingly profound, or abstract. It is about living, and Gregory seems to have lived fully in his five years of dropping out. Shawn is the character who seems more like us. He listens, he nods eagerly, he is willing to learn, but—something holds him back. Pragmatic questions keep asking themselves. He can't buy Gregory's vision, not all the way. He'd like to, but this is a real world we have to live in, after all, and if we all danced with the druids in the forests of Poland, what would happen to the market for fortune cookies?

The film's end is beautiful and inexplicably moving. Shawn returns home by taxi through the midnight streets of New York. Having spent hours with Gregory on a wild conversational flight, he is now reminded of scenes from his childhood. In *that* store, his father bought him shoes. In that one, he bought ice cream with a girl friend. The utter simplicity of his memories acts to dramatize the fragility and great preciousness of life. He has learned his friend's lesson.

My Family ★ ★ ★ ★

R, 122 m., 1995
(See related Film Clip, p. 883.)

Jimmy Smits (Jimmy), Esai Morales (Chucho), Eduardo Lopez Rojas (Jose), Jenny Gago (Maria), Constance Marie (Toni), Edward James Olmos (Paco), Lupe Ontiveros (Irene Sanchez), Jacob Vargas (Young Jose), Jennifer Lopez (Young Maria), Elpidia Carrillo (Isabel), Enrique Castillo (Memo), Maria Canals (Young Irene). Directed by Gregory Nava and produced by Anna Thomas. Screenplay by Nava and Thomas.

Gregory Nava's *My Family* is like a family dinner with everybody crowded around the table, remembering good times and bad, honoring those who went before, worrying about those still to come. It is an epic told through the eyes of one family, the Sanchez family, whose father walked north to Los Angeles from Mexico in the 1920s, and whose children include a writer, a nun, an ex-convict, a lawyer, a restaurant owner, and a boy shot dead in his prime.

Their story is told in images of startling beauty and great, overflowing energy; it is rare to hear so much laughter from an audience that is also sometimes moved to tears. Few movies like this get made because few filmmakers have the ambition to open their arms wide and embrace so much life. This is the great American story, told again and again, of how our families came to this land and tried to make it better for their children.

The story begins with a man named Jose Sanchez, who thinks it might take him a week or two to walk north from Mexico to "a village called Los Angeles," where he has a relative. It takes him a year. The relative, an old man known as El Californio, was born in Los Angeles when it was still Mexico, and on his tombstone he wants it written, "and where I lie it is *still* Mexico."

El Californio lives in a small house in East Los Angeles, and this house, tucked under a bridge on a dirt street that still actually exists, becomes a symbol of the family, gaining paint and windows and extra rooms and a picket fence, as the family grows. Jose (Jacob Vargas) crosses the bridge to the Anglo neighborhoods to work as a gardener, and there he meets Maria (Jennifer Lopez), who works as a nanny. They are married and have two children, and she is pregnant with a third, in the Depression year of 1932, when government troops round her up with tens of thousands of other Mexican-Americans (most of them, like Maria, U.S. citizens) and ship them in cattle cars to central Mexico, hoping they will never return.

"This really happened," says the narrator, Paco (Edward James Olmos), a writer who is telling the story of his family. But Maria fights her way back to her family, her baby in her arms. As the action moves from the 1930s to the late 1950s, we meet all the children: Paco; Irene, on her wedding day; Toni, who becomes a nun; Memo, who wants to go to law school; Chucho, who is attracted to the street life; and little Jimmy ("whose late arrival came as a great surprise").

Nava and his cowriter and producer, Anna Thomas, tell their stories in vivid sequences. Irene's wedding is interrupted by the arrival of a gang hostile to the hotheaded Chucho, and as they threaten each other Paco tells us "it was the usual macho bullshit." But eventually Chucho will lose his life because of it, and little Jimmy, seeing him die, will be scarred for many years.

Toni, meanwhile, becomes a nun, goes to South America, gets "political," and comes home to present her family with a big surprise, in one of the many scenes that mix social commentary with humor. Memo does become a lawyer (and tells his Anglo in-laws his name is "basically Spanish for 'Bill'").

In one of the movie's best sequences, Toni (Constance Marie), now an activist in L.A., becomes concerned by the plight of a young woman from El Salvador, who is about to be deported and faces death because of the politics of her family. She convinces Jimmy to marry her and save her from deportation, and in a sequence that is first hilarious and later quite moving, Jimmy does. (Instead of kissing the bride, he mutters "you owe me" ominously at his activist sister). This relationship, between Jimmy (Jimmy Smits) and Isabel (Elpidia Carrillo) leads to a love scene of great beauty, as they share their stories of pain and loss.

In the scenes set in the 1950s and 1980s, Jose and Maria are played by Eduardo Lopez Rojas and Jenny Gago. They wake up at night worrying about their children ("thank God for Memo going to law school," Paco says, "or they would have never gotten a night's sleep"). Jimmy, so tortured by the loss of his brother, is a special concern. But the family pulls together, and Paco observes, "In my home the difference between a family emergency and a party wasn't that big."

Nava, a Chicano whose earlier films include the great El Norte (1984), an Oscar nominee for its screenplay, has an inspired sense of color and light, and his movie has a visual freedom you rarely see on the screen. Working with cinematographer Ed Lachman, he uses color filters, smoke, shafts of sunlight, and other effects to make some scenes painterly with beauty and color—and he has used a painter, Patssi Valdez, to design the interior of the Sanchez home. The movie is not just in color, but in *colors*.

Through all the beauty, laughter, and tears,

the strong heart of the family beats, and everything leads up to a closing scene, between old Jose and Maria, that is quiet, simple, joyous, and heartbreaking. Rarely have I felt at the movies such a sense of time and history, of stories and lessons passing down the generations, of a family living in its memories. The story of the Sanchezes is the story of one Mexican-American family, but it is also in some ways the story of all families. Watching it, I was reminded of my own family's legends and heroes and stray sheep, and the strong sense of home. "Another country?" young Jose says, when he is told where Los Angeles is. "What does that mean—'another country'?"

My Father's Glory ★ ★ ★ ★
G, 110 m., 1991

Philippe Caubere (Joseph), Nathalie Roussel (Augustine), Didier Pain (Uncle Jules), Therese Liotard (Aunt Rose), Julien Ciamaca (Marcel), Joris Molinmas (Lili). Directed by Yves Robert and produced by Alain Poire. Screenplay by Lucette Andrei.

My Father's Glory is the first in a series of two films that creep up on you with small moments of warmth and charm. At first this film and its companion, *My Mother's Castle*, don't seem to be about much of anything. They meander. To a viewer accustomed to the machinery of plots, they play like a simple series of episodes. Then the episodes add up to a childhood. And by the end of the second film, the entire foundation for a life has been recreated, in memories of the perfect days of childhood. Of course the films are sentimental. Who would want it any other way?

My Father's Glory is based on the childhood of Marcel Pagnol, the French novelist and filmmaker whose twinned novels, *Jean de Florette* and *Manon of the Spring*, were turned into wonderful films a few years earlier. Those were stories based on melodrama and coincidence, telling of a poor city man who tries to make a living from the land, the bitter local farmers who hide the existence of a spring from him, and the shocking poetic justice that punishes a cruel old man. The films provided showcases for the considerable talents of Yves Montand and Gérard Depardieu, the two ranking stars of French cinema.

There are no recognizable stars in *My Father's Glory*—and no melodrama, either. The movie is narrated by the hero, Marcel, as an adult. We see him as a young man of ten or

twelve. His father, Joseph, is a schoolteacher in the city, and his mother, Augustine, is a paragon of domestic virtue. One summer they journey out to the hills of Provence to take a cottage and spend their vacation. These hills are to become the focus of Marcel's most enduring love affair. He loves the trees and the grasses, the small birds, and the eagle that nests high in a crag, the pathways up rock faces, and the way that voices carry from one side of a valley to another.

His guide and teacher for the lore of Provence is a local boy named Lili, who becomes his fast friend. Together they explore the countryside, which in this film seems bathed in a benevolent light and filled with adventures but not with dangers. The evenings are spent sitting around a battered old table in the yard, under a tree, eating the food that Augustine has prepared from the local markets and orchards.

There are others in his life: Uncle Jules, so full of secrets and wit, who becomes married to the charming Aunt Rose. And all of the local people, who seem through good luck to have found the place, the occupation, and the partner who will make them contented. The nights are filled with stars, and dreams of adventure. The days with Lili are spent learning the names and ways of all the living things that share the valley. Then autumn comes, and school begins again, and Marcel must leave his beloved hills.

The movie has a deliberate nostalgic tone. It is most definitely intended as a memory. The narrator's voice reminds us of that, but the nature of the events makes it clear, too. What do we remember from our childhoods? If we are lucky, we recall the security of family rituals, our admiration for our parents, and the bittersweet partings with things we love. Childhood ends, in a sense, the day we discover that summer does not last forever.

Because not much "happens" in these films, there is more time for things to happen. There is time to dash out of the rain and into a cave, and discover that a great eagle has gotten there first. Time to run through the dusty orchards and climb up hills to the top of the world. Time to admire the perfect handwriting of Joseph, as he writes out the lessons on the board. Time to bask in the snug bourgeois security of the family, which is blessed, for a time, with perfect happiness.

My Father's Glory was released first, before *My Mother's Castle*, the continuation. That is the best way to see them—the first film about memory becoming a memory itself, to be reawakened by the second. What is surprising about the two films is the way they creep up on you emotionally, until at the end of the second one, when we discover the meaning of the movie's title, there is a deeply moving moment of truth and insight. The films were directed by Yves Robert, whose previous titles, including *The Tall Blond Man with One Black Shoe*, did not prepare me for the joy and serenity of these films. Like all the best movies, these memories of Marcel Pagnol work by becoming our memories, as well.

My Favorite Year ★ ★ ★ ½
PG, 92 m., 1982

Peter O'Toole (Alan Swann), Mark Linn-Baker (Benjy Stone), Jessica Harper (K.C. Downing), Joseph Bologna (King Kaiser), Lainie Kazan (Belle Corroca), Lou Jacobi (Uncle Morty). Directed by Richard Benjamin and produced by Michael Gruskoff. Screenplay by Norman Steinberg and Dennis Palumbo.

"Live? I can't go on *live!!* I'm a movie star—not an actor!"

Alan Swann is imploring them: Say it isn't so! He's an alcoholic British matinee idol, veteran of countless swashbuckling epics in which he faced fleets of pirates and waves of savage barbarians. Now he is being asked to accept the worst challenge of all: to appear on live television.

My Favorite Year is the story of an era when most television was live, and the great television stars were inventing the medium out of their own imaginations every Saturday night. The year is 1954. The program is "King Kaiser's Comedy Hour," obviously inspired by the old Sid Caesar and Imogene Coca programs. The British star, Alan Swann, is played by Peter O'Toole, but he could be Errol Flynn or John Barrymore or even O'Toole himself. The movie is told from the point of view of a young production assistant named Benjy (Mark Linn-Baker). His job is to shadow the great Alan Swann, get him everything he wants except booze, keep him out of trouble, and deliver him intact to the studio in time for the broadcast. Along the way, Benjy adds a priority of his own, his continuing courtship of his would-be girlfriend, K.C. (Jessica Harper).

Through Benjy's eyes, we see Swann as the great man he was, as the pathetic drunk he is, and as the hero he could become—if he survives the live telecast. We also gain some understanding of King Kaiser (Joseph Bologna), who is a big, beefy, not-too-bright guy who has an absolutely accurate understanding of his own comic talent. Translated, that means he knows what will work. What will get a laugh. He has no taste, of course; when he offends a girl, he sends her steaks instead of flowers, and he sends a business associate a gift of tires. But he's a physical comedian with a gift for pumping the laughter out of this frail new medium, and he's backed up by a whole crew of talented writers.

Swann, meanwhile, is backed up only by memories of his greatness and fears of performing in front of a live audience. But as O'Toole plays this character, he becomes one of the great comic inventions of recent movies. Swann is a drunk, but he has an uncanny ability to pass from coma through courtliness to heroics without ever quite seeming to gain consciousness. A character like Swann could probably only be played by someone who is both a great actor and a great ham, and O'Toole is both.

My Favorite Year is not a perfect movie. I could have done without the entire romantic subplot between Benjy and K.C. But I liked the movie's ability to move from one unexpected comic situation to another. That produces one of the best scenes, when Benjy takes Swann home to Brooklyn to meet his mother and weird Uncle Morty (Lainie Kazan and Lou Jacobi in hilarious performances). There is, to be sure, a force running through the movie's disorganization, and that force is O'Toole's charisma. He is so completely charming, so doomed, so funny, and so pathetically invincible as Swann that this movie succeeds despite its occasional unnecessary scenes.

My Girl ★ ★ ★ ½
PG, 102 m., 1991

Dan Aykroyd (Harry Sultenfuss), Jamie Lee Curtis (Shelly DeVoto), Macaulay Culkin (Thomas J. Sennett), Anna Chlumsky (Vada Sultenfuss), Richard Masur (Phil Sultenfuss). Directed by Howard Zieff and produced by Brian Grazer. Screenplay by Laurice Elehwany.

She lives in a grim world for such a plucky little girl. Her mother died two days after she was born. Her father runs a funeral home. The embalming takes place in the basement. Her grandmother has Alzheimer's and is wrapped in a deep silence, except for the times when she starts singing the hit songs of forty years ago. No wonder Vada is a hypochondriac who is always running off to the family doctor with imaginary illnesses.

And yet in other ways Vada is fairly normal. She has a crush on the teacher who lives down the street. She goes biking with her best pal, Thomas J., and they talk about the meaning of life. She adores her dad, who is sort of distant, and, of course, she gets a little jealous when Dad hires a new cosmetologist and then it looks as if he might be thinking about getting married again.

Like *Man in the Moon*, another film that was released at about the same time, *My Girl* is about young romance, innocence, tragedy, and growth. The characters in *My Girl* are a few crucial years younger than those in *Man in the Moon*—Vada is eleven, and just this side of the great divide of adolescence—but both movies feature a swimming hole, and a first kiss, and a father who is strict but loving. And the key to both movies is in affecting, genuine performances.

Vada is played by Anna Chlumsky, a newcomer who does a good job of creating her smart, curious, gloomy character. Thomas J., her best pal, is Macaulay Culkin, in his first role since *Home Alone*, and once again he is a solemn, owl-eyed little boy who sees much and says little. The adults in movies like this are often turned into dotty caricatures, but it says a lot for the filmmakers (director Howard Zieff and writer Laurice Elehwany) that they see their adults as normal people with ordinary interests—like doing their jobs and maybe building a relationship.

The father is played by Dan Aykroyd, the new cosmetologist by Jamie Lee Curtis, and they're both lonely as the movie opens; Aykroyd hasn't dated in twenty years, and Curtis confides that she took the job at the funeral home ("even though I don't much like dead people") because she saw that a family lived there, and thought it would be good for her to be around a family. Vada is jealous as she begins to lose her father's full attention, but that gets taken care of, too, all in good time.

And then something tragic happens, just as it did in *Man in the Moon*, and young Vada has to learn to accept the hardness and hurt of life. The movie pays full respect to her loss; there isn't a hasty and emotional ending, but a conclusion that shows how Vada makes her accommodation with loss—and a scene in which a deep truth gets spoken.

The beauty in this film is in its directness.

There are some obligatory scenes (can we have any American movie about relationships in the summertime that does not involve a visit to a carnival, or any rivalry that doesn't eventually get expressed through bump-'em cars?). But there are also some very original and touching ones, such as a conversation between Curtis and Aykroyd, and another between the little girl and Thomas's mother. This is a movie that has its heart in the right place.

My Left Foot ★ ★ ★ ★
R, 103 m., 1989

Daniel Day-Lewis (Christy Brown), Brenda Fricker (Mrs. Brown), Alison Whelan (Sheila), Kirsten Sheridan (Sharon), Declan Croghan (Tom), Eanna MacLiam (Benny), Marie Conmee (Sadie), Cyril Cusack (Lord Castlewelland). Directed by Jim Sheridan and produced by Noel Pearson. Screenplay by Jim Sheridan and Shane Connaughton.

I am trying to imagine what it would be like to write this review with my left foot. Quite seriously. I imagine it would be a great nuisance—unless, of course, my left foot was the only part of my body over which I had control. If that were the case, I would thank God that there was still some avenue down which I could communicate with the world.

That is the story of Christy Brown, born in a large, poor, loving family in a Dublin slum and considered for the first ten years of his life to be hopelessly retarded. He was born with cerebral palsy, and his entire body was in revolt against him—all except for the left foot, with which one day he picked up a piece of chalk and wrote a word on the floor. Everyone was amazed except for Christy's mother, who had always believed he knew what was going on. She could see it in his eyes.

The story of Christy Brown is one of the great stories of human courage and determination. He belongs on the same list with Helen Keller—and yet it is hard to imagine Christy being good company for the saintly Miss Keller, since he was not a saint himself but a ribald, boozing, wickedly gifted Irishman who simply happened to be handicapped.

Jim Sheridan's *My Left Foot* is the story of Brown's life, based on his autobiography and on the memories of those who knew him. He was not an easy man to forget. Tiny and twisted, bearded and unkempt, he managed, despite his late start, to grow into a poet, a

novelist, a painter, and a lyrical chronicler of his own life. Like many geniuses, he was not an easy man to live with, and the movie makes that clear in its brilliant opening scene.

Perhaps concerned that we will mistake *My Left Foot* for one of those pious TV docudramas, the movie begins in the middle of one of Brown's typical manipulations. He is backstage in the library of a great British country home, where he is soon to be brought out to be given an award. He has a pint of whiskey hidden in his jacket pocket with a straw to allow him to sip it. But a hired nurse is watching him with a gimlet eye. Trying to get her out of the way for a second, he asks her for a light for his cigarette.

"But Mr. Brown," she says, "you know that smoking is not good for you."

"I didn't ask for a fucking psychological lecture," he replies. "I only asked for a fucking light."

It is the perfect opening scene because it breaks the ice. We know that it is all right to laugh with Christy and not to be intimidated by the great burden of his life. And as the movie develops, it is startling how much of it plays as comedy—startling unless we remember the universal Irish trait of black humor, in which the best laughter, the wicked laughter, is born out of hard times and bad luck.

My Left Foot charts Christy Brown's life from his earliest days until his greatest triumph, but the key scene in the movie may be one that takes place shortly after he is born. His father goes into the local pub to have a pint and consider the fact that his son has been born handicapped, and then he stubbornly makes the statement that no son of his will be sent to a "home." The decision to raise Christy as part of a large and loving family is probably what saved his life—for a man of such intelligence would have been destroyed by an institution. His brilliant mind, trapped inside his imperfect body, would have gone mad from calling for help.

Christy is played in the early scenes by Hugh O'Conor and from his teen-age years onward by Daniel Day-Lewis. The two actors fit Brown's life together into one seamless performance of astonishing beauty and strength. There is an early scene in which Christy's brothers and other neighbor kids are playing soccer in the street, and crippled Christy, playing goalie, defends the goal by deflecting the ball with his head. There is great laughter and cheering all around, but the heart of the scene is secure: This child is

not being protected in some sort of cocoon of sympathy, but is being raised in the middle of life, hard knocks and all. This is reinforced in other scenes where Christy's siblings dump him in a barrow and wheel him around to their games.

As he watched and listened, the boy was making the observations that would inform his life work. His novel *Down All the Days* and his other writings see Dublin street life with a clarity that is only possible because he was raised right in the middle of it and yet was always an outsider. As a painter, he saw Dublin in the same way: as a stage upon which people did things he was intimately familiar with and yet would never do himself.

Christy's life as a man was not easy. He was willful and arrogant, and right from the first time he tasted whiskey he knew there was at least one way to escape from the cage of his body. Like all men, he desired love, and there is a heartbreaking sequence in which he develops a crush on a teacher who works with him on speech therapy and loves Christy, but not in the romantic way that he imagines. Learning of her engagement, he creates a scene in a restaurant that in the power of its hurt and anger is almost unbearable.

He drank more. He was demanding. Like all bright people forced to depend on the kindness of others, he was filled with frustration. A woman did finally come into his life, a nurse who became his wife and loved him until the end, but by then happiness was conditional for Christy because he was an alcoholic. Since he could not obtain booze on his own—since it had to be brought to him and provided to him—there is the temptation to ask why his loved ones didn't simply shut him off. But of course that would have been a cruel exploitation of his weakness, and then too, Christy was a genius at instilling guilt.

My Left Foot is a great film for many reasons, but the most important is that it gives us such a complete picture of this man's life. It is not an inspirational movie, although it inspires. It is not a sympathetic movie, although it inspires sympathy. It is the story of a stubborn, difficult, blessed, and gifted man who was dealt a bad hand, who played it brilliantly, and who left us some good books, some good paintings, and the example of his courage. It must not have been easy.

My Mother's Castle ★ ★ ★ ★
PG, 98 m., 1991

Philippe Caubere (Joseph), Nathalie Roussel (Augustine), Didier Pain (Uncle Jules), Therese Liotard (Aunt Rose), Julien Ciamaca (Marcel). Directed by Yves Robert and produced by Alain Poire. Screenplay by Jerome Tonnere, Louis Nucera, and Robert.

And now here we are back again in the hills of Provence, in the second of two remarkable memory-films based on the childhood of the great French writer Marcel Pagnol. If you have seen *My Father's Glory*, the first of the films, these places will be familiar to you, along with some of the people and all of the feelings of Marcel, the young narrator, who has grown a year older and is now aware that there are girls in the world, in addition to hills and valleys and caves and eagles.

My Mother's Castle begins where *My Father's Glory* ended, after a brief look back. (It is best to see the films in order, even though this one is complete in itself.) The effect of the two films is a long, slow, subtle buildup to the enormous emotional payoff at the end of the second film, a moment when gratitude and regret come flowing into the heart of the narrator.

The time is the earlier decades of this century. The hero, Marcel, is now thirteen or fourteen. His father is a schoolteacher, much admired, and his mother is a sweet and loving woman who is still quite young and girlish, although she does not seem that way, of course, to her son. The family had been going every summer and during holidays to the countryside of Provence, and now old friends greet Marcel, including Lili, the local boy who taught him the ways of the countryside. But Lili is no longer the center of the universe; that position is soon taken by an imperious young lady who has read, perhaps, too many historical romances, and treats Marcel as her vassal.

The central set piece of the movie involves the journey the family must make to get to their summer cottage. The legal way is long and tiring, involving a walk that circles several great estates. There is a shortcut that reduces the walk by four-fifths, but it involves walking along the canal path that cuts through the estates, not only trespassing but also somehow getting through the locked gates as the path crosses each property line. Help comes in the form of a canal guard who was once a student of Marcel's father, Joseph. He has the keys, and sees no need for the family to take the long way around. He gives a key to Joseph, and on each visit the little family takes the shortcut, as the vast private houses look down frowningly upon them from the hills.

One house has a mean, bitter caretaker, and a dog that looks ferocious but would really rather sun itself than bite. Marcel's mother, Augustine, is terrified of dogs, and there comes a day when the dog and the caretaker frighten the family, and it was up to Joseph to somehow salvage his family's self-respect.

All of this sounds as simple as a children's film, I suppose, and yet there are deep currents of pain and memory flowing here, and these scenes set up an emotional payoff at the end of the film that brings the whole experience to a triumphant conclusion.

My Father's Glory and *My Mother's Castle* are linked autobiographical stories by Pagnol, who also wrote the two novels *Jean de Florette* and *Manon of the Spring*. Those stories were more epic in sweep; these are intimate and nostalgic. It is likely that no one, not even Pagnol, had a childhood quite this perfect, and yet all happy childhoods grow happier in memory, and it is the nature of film that we can share some of Pagnol's happiness.

My Own Private Idaho ★ ★ ★ ½
R, 105 m., 1991

River Phoenix (Mike Waters), Keanu Reeves (Scott Favor), James Russo (Richard Waters), William Richert (Bob Pigeon), Rodney Harvey (Gary), Chiara Caselli (Carmella). Directed by Gus Van Sant and produced by Laurie Parker. Screenplay by Van Sant.

Drama thrives on the weaknesses of its characters, but what can we make of a hero who suffers from narcolepsy? At precisely those moments when he is called to rise to the occasion, he goes to sleep. He misses most of the crucial developments in his own life, and must depend on the kindness of strangers even to pull him out of the middle of the road.

Mike Waters, the young drifter played by River Phoenix in Gus Van Sant's *My Own Private Idaho,* is a narcoleptic. To those who do not understand the disorder, it appears that he must be on drugs, or mentally deficient, or from another planet. His condition has given him a certain dreamy detachment; there is no use getting too deeply involved in events you may end up sleeping through. Mike works as a male prostitute, and it goes without saying that narcolepsy is not an asset in his line of work.

Watching the film, I was reminded of Dostoyevsky's *Crime and Punishment,* in which Raskolnikov, the murderer of the old lady, suffers from epileptic seizures. He has some of the same moods and traits as Mike Waters does here: Both live in unreal worlds, detached from the ordinary progress of time by their conditions. In a sense, their own lives are so elusive that what they do to the lives of others is not very meaningful. Mike is like a holy fool or a clown, and his only real attachment is to Scott Favor (Keanu Reeves), another hustler.

One comes from a rich family, the other from poverty. Neither background would account for the strange existence they now share, drifting through the automobiles and bedrooms of strangers, acting out fantasy roles, spending long hours in coffee shops, smoking and talking and killing time.

The characters have been compared by one critic to Prince Hal and Falstaff—to the errant heir and his lowlife companion. It's the strangest thing. Here is a movie about lowlife sexual outlaws, and yet they remind us of works by Shakespeare or Dostoyevsky, not William Burroughs or Andy Warhol. Maybe that's because Van Sant is essentially making a human comedy here, a story that may be sad and lonely in parts but is illuminated by the insight that all experience is potentially ridiculous; that if we could see ourselves with enough detachment, some of the things we take with deadly seriousness might seem more than faintly absurd.

The movie takes place in Portland and the open spaces of the Northwest—the same territory covered by *Drugstore Cowboy,* Van Sant's previous picture. Again he is looking into the lives of outlaws on the road. Life centers around who you get a ride from, where you spend the night, how much money you have in your pocket. There are no long-range plans.

Mike and Scott meet a variety of clients, including one who likes his apartment kept very, very clean. They encounter a young woman from Italy. They find themselves in Italy. It is almost hallucinatory, how one can be in Idaho today and Italy tomorrow, and have no money in either place, but if you make an object out of yourself, then people with more money and stronger wills are able to take you wherever they choose.

Although the central characters are prostitutes, the movie is not really about sex, which does not interest either Mike or Scott very much. What Mike wants is love, and by love what he really means is someone to hold him and care for him. He was deeply damaged as a child, and now he seeks shelter; it is a matter of indifference whether he finds it with a man or a woman. The achievement of this film is that it wants to evoke that state of drifting need, and it does. There is no mechanical plot that has to grind to a Hollywood conclusion, and no contrived test for the heroes to pass; this is a movie about two particular young men, and how they pass their lives.

Mystery Train ★ ★ ★ ½
R, 110 m., 1990

Masatoshi Nagase (Jun), Youki Kudoh (Mitzuko), Screamin' Jay Hawkins (Night Clerk), Cinque Lee (Bellboy), Nicoletta Braschi (Luisa), Elizabeth Bracco (DeeDee), Joe Strummer (Johnny), Rick Aviles (Will Robinson), Steve Buscemi (Charlie). Directed by Jim Jarmusch and produced by Jim Stark. Screenplay by Jarmusch.

Mystery train. The two most evocative words in the language, suggesting streamliners into the night and strangers whose eyes meet in the club car as the train's rhythm creates an erotic reverie. But trains are no longer quite like that in America, and the opening shots of Jim Jarmusch's new film show two young Japanese tourists in a faded Amtrak coach, listening to their Walkmans as the train pulls through the outskirts of Memphis.

The girl is an Elvis fan. Her boyfriend believes Carl Perkins was the true father of rock 'n' roll. They have come to visit the shrines of Memphis: The Sun recording studios, for example, where rock 'n' roll was born.

In the hands of another director, this setup would lead directly into social satire, into a comic put-down of rock tourism with a sarcastic visit to Graceland as the kicker. But Jarmusch is not a satirist. He is a romantic who sees America as a foreigner might—as a strange, haunting country where the urban landscapes are painted by Edward Hopper and the all-night blues stations provide a sound track for a life.

The tourists arrive in Memphis, drag their luggage through the cavernous train station, and walk to the Sun studios, where a guide rattles off her spiel about Elvis and Carl faster than an auctioneer could. Then they check into the Arcade Hotel, one of those fleabags that has grown exhausted waiting for the traveling salesmen who no longer come. This is a hotel out of a 1940s *film noir*, with neon signs and a linoleum lobby, and a night clerk who has seen it all and a bellboy whose eyes are so wide he might be seeing everything for the first time.

Other people will check into this hotel during the movie's long night of mystery. There is a woman who needs to spend the night somewhere before she flies away with the remains of her husband. She meets a woman who has just broken up with her boyfriend, and they decide to share a room for a night. Meanwhile, on the other side of town, some men are drinking too much and get into a disagreement, and drive off into the night in a pickup truck, and stick up a liquor store, and then they also head for the Arcade Hotel.

The sound track is from a local radio station, and Presley's version of "Blue Moon" is heard at one time or another during all three of these stories, providing a common link. An offscreen gunshot provides another link. And so does the ghost of Elvis, who seems to haunt the movie with his voice and his legend—and who appears to the woman whose husband has just died.

There is a strange appropriateness there. It is not her own husband who appears in the night, spectral and mysterious, but Elvis, and his legend seems to inspire the film. But this is not the Elvis of the supermarket tabloids, just as *Mystery Train* is not about dusty Amtrak coaches. The movie is about legends and people who believe in them. In fact it is the movie that believes most of all.

Jarmusch believes in an American landscape that existed before urban sprawl, before the sanitary sterility of the fast-food strips on the highways leading into town. His movies show us saloons where everybody knows each other, diners where the short-order cook is in charge, and vistas across railroad tracks to a hotel where transients are not only welcome, they are understood.

Mystery Train is Jarmusch's third film, after *Stranger than Paradise* and *Down by Law*. In all three there is the belief that America cannot be neatly packaged into safe and convenient marketing units, that there must be a life of the night for the drifters and the dropouts, the heroes of no fixed abode and no apparent place of employment. These are the people that songs like "Mystery Train" are about, and although in fact their lives may be flat and empty, in Jarmusch's imagination they are the real inhabitants of the city, especially after midnight.

Mystery Train is not a conventional narrative, and it is not how the story ends that is important, but how it continues. It is populated by dozens of small, well-observed moments of human behavior, such as the relationship between the night clerk (Screamin' Jay Hawkins) and the bellboy (Cinque Lee), or between the two teen-age Japanese tourists (Masatoshi Nagase and Youki Kudoh), whose entire image of American reality is formed out of popular culture.

The best thing about *Mystery Train* is that it takes you to an America you feel you ought to be able to find for yourself, if you only knew where to look. A place of people who are allowed to be characters, to be individuals, who do not have to graduate from Hamburger University to stand over a grill. The train is the perfect metaphor in this movie. It's not where it's been that's important, or even where it's going. It's the sound of that whistle as it finds its way through the night.

Mystic Pizza ★ ★ ★ ½
R, 104 m., 1988

Julia Roberts (Daisy Araujo), Annabeth Gish (Kat Araujo), Lili Taylor (Jojo Barboza), Vincent Phillip D'Onofrio (Bill Montijo), William R. Moses (Tim Travers), Adam Storke (Charles Gordon Winsor, Jr.), Conchata Ferrell (Leona Valsouano). Directed by Donald Petrie and produced by Mark Levinson. Screenplay by Amy Jones, Randy and Perry Howze, and Alfred Uhry.

There is a certain breathlessness about the summer after high school, which *Mystic Pizza* captures with an effortless charm. Childhood is officially behind. Adulthood is still a mystery, but one which it is now possible to begin solving. Romance still has the intensity of a teen-age crush, but for some teen-agers it also begins to require a certain idealism; the loved one must be not merely perfect, but good.

The movie takes place in a fishing town named Mystic, Conn., where many of the year-round people are Portuguese-American, and the summer people have names like Charles Gordon Winsor, Jr. It is about three girls who work in the Mystic Pizzeria, famous for the secret ingredients in its special sauce. Two of the girls are sisters, the third is their best friend, and the movie begins when the best friend walks away from the altar and leaves her fiancé standing there.

Her name is Jojo Barboza (Lili Taylor). She simply can't face marriage. She loves Bill (Vincent Phillip D'Onofrio), but she's not ready for a permanent commitment. Her problem is, like, he really turns her on, but he doesn't believe in sex until after marriage. Is she ready to marry him just to get him into bed? Not quite. Jojo doesn't plan to go on to college, and her dream is to someday inherit the secret pizza sauce from Leona (Conchata Ferrell), and run the pizzeria herself. Her friends are Daisy and Kat Araujo (Julia Roberts and Annabeth Gish), and one night they're drinking a few beers at a local hangout when Daisy sees Mr. Right walk in.

He's tall, preppy, cool, and able to almost hit three bull's-eyes on the dart board while drinking a shot of tequila before every dart. This may not seem like a skill that prepares him for life, but Daisy picks him up and before long they are more or less in love. He is a very rich kid named, of course, Charles Gordon Winsor, Jr. (Adam Storke), and he is in law school, he says, although actually he has been thrown out of law school for cheating, and that is why he can devote so much time to his dart game.

Kat, meanwhile, is baby-sitting for a thirty-year-old Yale graduate who is an architect rehabbing a local landmark. She's been accepted to Yale for the fall, and so they have that in common. Also reckless romanticism. His name is Tim (William R. Moses), his wife is in Europe, and Kat falls head over heels in idealism with him. They have long talks about Important Subjects, she impresses him with her intelligence, and she is so fresh and pretty that perhaps he is more easily impressed than he should be. She loves his baby, too. She projects herself into his life, declares him to be good and true, and tries not to think too much about his absent wife. Perhaps—she snatches at straws—they're going to be divorced.

Mystic Pizza takes these three couples and follows them through several months. Each romance turns into a hard lesson to be learned, but one of the nice qualities of this movie is how lightly it moves on its feet. It doesn't hammer its points home, it doesn't go for big, telegraphed scenes of heartbreak, and its single best scene is used to make a fairly subtle ethical point. The rich kid has brought the poor Portuguese-American girl home to have dinner with his family, and in the middle of the dinner the kid explodes at an "insult" to his girl and attacks all of the relatives for being complacent, racist, stupid snobs. Then he pulls the tablecloth out from under all the dishes and storms out of the house, perhaps expecting to be followed by an adoring girl who admires him for sticking up for her.

But Daisy is not stupid, and she can read people better than Charles Gordon Winsor, Jr. She accuses him, accurately, of staging an embarrassing scene for his own self-aggrandizement, and concludes by telling him that he is not good enough for her. This twist on the scene—passing up the obvious docudrama piety in order to make a more difficult point—is typical of what's best about this movie. The idea of three teen-age girls and their first post-high school romances is a cliché, but *Mystic Pizza* does not treat it as one.

I have a feeling that *Mystic Pizza* may someday become known for the movie stars it showcased back before they became stars. All of the young actors in this movie have genuine gifts. Julia Roberts is a major beauty with a fierce energy, Annabeth Gish projects intelligence and stubbornness like a young Katharine Hepburn, and Lili Taylor, who is given what's intended as a more comic role, finds human comedy in her ongoing problems with the earnest and chaste Bill. It's fun to watch them work. Of the men, Vincent D'Onofrio, as Bill, has the best part to work with as he stubbornly explains how he doesn't believe in sex without a commitment. Moses and Storke have less to work with; their roles are constructed out of obligatory emotions, in a movie that is really about women.

There are nice performances around the edges of this movie, too, by Conchata Ferrell (from *Heartland*) as the pizza cook with the secret, and by Louis Turenne as the local television gourmet, who turns up one fateful day to review the famous pizza. *Mystic Pizza* does create the feeling of a small resort town and the people who live there and, amazingly, given the familiar nature of a lot of the material, it nearly always keeps us interested. That's because the characters are allowed to be smart, to react in unexpected ways, and to be more concerned with doing the right thing than with doing the expedient or even the lustful thing. The movie isn't really about three girls in love; it's about three girls discovering what their standards for love are going to be.

N

Naked ★ ★ ★
NO MPAA RATING, 130 m., 1994

David Thewlis (Johnny), Lesley Sharp (Louise), Katrin Cartlidge (Sophie), Greg Cruttwell (Jeremy), Claire Skinner (Sandra), Peter Wight (Brian), Ewen Bremner (Archie), Susan Vidler (Maggie). Directed by Mike Leigh and produced by Simon Channing-Williams. Screenplay by Leigh.

The characters in Mike Leigh's *Naked* look as if they have lived indoors all of their lives, perhaps down in a cellar. Their pale, pasty skin looks cold to the touch in the film's blue-gray lighting. The film is shot in a high-contrast style that makes everything seem a little more bleak and narrow than it must. And if you listen carefully to the sound track, you become aware that it lacks much of the background ambiance of most movies; we are hearing voices, flat and toneless, in what sounds like an empty room.

All of these stylistic choices are right for *Naked*, and so is the title, which describes characters who exist in the world without the usual layers of protection. They are clothed, but not warmly or cheerfully. They are naked of families, relationships, homes, values, and, in most cases, jobs. They exist in modern Britain with few possessions except their words.

The central character in *Naked* is Johnny (David Thewlis), who as the movie opens has rough sex with a weeping girl in an alley in some barren northern city, and then steals a car and drives down to London. From the way he talks and certain things he refers to, we gradually conclude that he has had an education—is an "intellectual," in that his opinions are mostly formed from words, not feelings.

Something has gone terribly wrong in his life, leaving him stranded without connections, employment, or hope. He goes to the flat of an old girlfriend, who is away on holiday, and moves in, establishing a rapport of the damned with her flatmate Sophie (Katrin Cartlidge), who is so spaced out on drugs that she seems barely able to make the connection between what she says and what she thinks, if anything.

The "relationship" that develops between these two people is so pathetic that it can barely be watched. The "sex" they have is such a desperate attempt to feel something in the midst of their separate wastelands that it is much like watching them wound themselves. When others appear in the flat—especially the supercilious, hurtful Jeremy (Greg Cruttwell), the landlord—they are like visitors from adjacent circles in hell.

Nor do matters improve with the arrival of Sandra (Claire Skinner), whose name is on the lease. She has a job, and apparently thinks of herself as being normal and productive, and offers free advice and criticism, but the film invites us to see how precariously close she is to falling into the same abyss as her friends.

Mike Leigh's method of working is well known. He gathers his actors, suggests a theme, and asks them to improvise situations. A screenplay develops out of their work. This method has created in *Naked* a group of characters who could not possibly have emerged from a conventional screenplay; this is the kind of film that is beyond imagining, and only observation could have created it. Are there people like this? Yes, a great many, who have the ability and intelligence to lead functioning lives but lack the will and—in particular—the opening. Somehow they have slipped out of the picture. It is not easy to slip back in.

The movie won the best director award for Leigh at the 1993 Cannes Film Festival, and a best actor award for Thewlis, who was also honored by several critics' groups. His performance never steps wrong. He creates a kind of heroism in Johnny: It's not that we like him or approve of him, but that we must admire the dogged way he sticks to his guns and forges ahead through misery, anger, and despair. There is a scene here that is among the best Leigh has ever done. Johnny strikes up a conversation with a night watchman, who takes him on a midnight tour of a modern office building. The subtext is that the watchman will never do what the employees in the building do in the daytime, but owes his survival to his job of guarding it for them at night, from the likes of Johnny, who lacks even that much of a toehold.

This is a painful movie to watch. But it is also exhilarating, as all good movies are, because we are watching the director and actors venturing beyond any conventional idea of what a modern movie can be about. Here there is no plot, no characters to identify with, no hope. But there is care: The filmmakers care enough about these people to observe them very closely, to note how they look and sound and what they feel.

Leigh has said in an interview that while his earlier films (including *High Hopes* and *Life Is Sweet*) might have embodied a socialist view of the world, this one edges over into anarchy. I agree. It suggests a world in which the operating systems have become distant from such inhabitants as Johnny and the women in the flat. The world is indifferent to them, and they to it. To some degree, they don't even know what's hit them. Johnny has a glimmer. His response is not hope or a plan. It is harsh, sardonic laughter. Destruction is his only response.

The Naked Gun ★ ★ ★ ½

PG-13, 85 m., 1988

Leslie Nielsen (Lt. Frank Drebin), Priscilla Presley (Jane Spencer), Ricardo Montalban (Vincent Ludwig), George Kennedy (Capt. Hocken), O.J. Simpson (Nordberg), Nancy Marchand (L.A. Mayor), John Houseman (Driving Instructor), Reggie Jackson (Right-fielder). Directed by David Zucker and produced by Robert K. Weiss. Screenplay by Jerry Zucker, Jim Abrahams, and David Zucker.

Criticism quails in the face of *The Naked Gun*. The film is as transparent as a third-grader with a water gun, and yet it would be easier to review a new film by Ingmar Bergman, for there, at least would be themes to discuss and visual strategies to analyze. Reviewing *The Naked Gun*, on the other hand, is like reporting on a monologue by Rodney Dangerfield. You can get the words, but not the music.

The movie is as funny, let it be said, as any comedy of 1988, with the exception of *A Fish Called Wanda*. You laugh, and then you laugh at yourself for laughing. Some of the jokes are incredibly stupid. Most of them are dumber than that. And yet this is not simply a string of one-liners. There is a certain manic logic to the progression of the film, as the plot leads us from Yasser Arafat to Reggie Jackson, with a pause while Queen Elizabeth passes a hot dog to the person sitting on the other side of her at Dodger Stadium.

The movie stars Leslie Nielsen, star (it says here) of a thousand TV shows, as Lt. Frank Drebin, ace lawman who has been taken hostage at a summit conference of all of America's enemies. He frees himself and decks them with right crosses to the jaw, and makes a patriotic speech about the American Way. When he is returned by jet aircraft to American soil at last, the sun is shining, the band is playing, and the crowds are cheering—but they're not at the airport to greet him, they're there for Weird Al Yankovic.

And so on. *The Naked Gun* is the work of Zucker, Abrahams, and Zucker, the same firm that brought us *Airplane!* and the vastly underrated *Top Secret*. (In that one, a mortally wounded spy lay in a dark alley behind the Iron Curtain and handed a colleague an envelope that absolutely had to be postmarked no later than midnight. It was addressed to Publisher's Clearing House.)

These are the same guys behind the short-lived TV series "Police Squad," which has attained cult status on video, and *The Naked Gun* is in the same style of nonstop visual and spoken puns, interlaced with satire, slapstick, and scatalogical misunderstandings.

Do you even care about the plot? The critic knows his duty, and will press onward. Nielsen is soon investigating a fishy scam being masterminded by a criminal named Vincent Ludwig (played by Ricardo Montalban, who has said in publicity releases that he took the role for the money, and plans to buy a new Chrysler). Montalban's assistant is the sensuous Jane Spencer (Priscilla Presley, who has a light comic touch that works as a counterweight to the less subtle aspects of the movie, which are myriad).

Through complications too nonsensical to relate, Montalban's plans involve a plot to assassinate the Queen at a Dodgers home game, and Nielsen goes undercover—first posing as the opera star who sings "The Star-Spangled Banner," and then as the home-plate umpire. It's around here that Reggie Jackson shows up.

The wisdom of directing the assassination attempt at an actual public figure is questionable, but it must be said that the use of an Elizabeth look-alike inspires some very funny moments, most of them centering around the fact that she is appalled to be attending a baseball game.

Other famous walk-ons in the movie include not only Jackson but O.J. Simpson and, in a very funny sequence, the late John Houseman—who plays a driving instructor who is unflappable in the face of disaster. *The Naked Gun* is an utterly goofy movie and a lot of fun, and don't let anyone tell you all the jokes before you watch it.

The Naked Gun 2½: The Smell of Fear ★ ★ ★

PG-13, 85 m., 1991

Leslie Nielsen (Lt. Frank Drebin), Priscilla Presley (Jane Spencer), George Kennedy (Capt. Ed Hocken), O.J. Simpson (Nordberg), Robert Goulet (Quentin Hapsburg), Richard Griffiths (Dr. Meinheimer). Directed by David Zucker and produced by Robert K. Weiss. Screenplay by Zucker and Pat Proft.

The critical mind boggles at the opportunity to review *The Naked Gun 2½: The Smell of Fear*. What can usefully be said about this movie, other than the essential information that I laughed? The plot exists to be disregarded, the characters are deliberately constructed of cardboard, the sight gags are idiotic, and the dialogue is dumb. Really dumb. So dumb you laugh twice, once because of how stupid it is, and the second time because you fell for it.

The Naked Gun 2½ is not the best of the slapstick parody films by the Zucker-Abrahams-Zucker boys; that honor goes to *Top Secret!* (1984) with its inspired performance by Val Kilmer. The movie was a spoof of Elvis Presley musicals and cold war spy stories, both at the same time, and I still laugh when I remember the spy who is shot and lies dying in an alley, and pulls out a letter that must be mailed by midnight. It's for one of those Ed McMahon sweepstakes promotions.

Naked, etc., stars Leslie Nielsen, first utilized by the Zucker-Abrahams-Zucker team in their original *Airplane!* in 1980, and since developed into the superstar of this genre. Nielsen's secret is that he does almost nothing, and certainly nothing he seems to think is funny.

He is the wooden straight guy, unaware of all that's going on around him, completely lacking in insight, without charm, grace, or intelligence, a total square—in other words, everyman. In this movie he plays Lt. Frank Drebin, his character from the old "Police Squad!" TV series, who as the movie opens is a guest of honor at a White House dinner, at which a Barbara Bush lookalike is pummeled with doors and lobsters. Later, as the plot develops, he tries to rekindle his old love affair with Priscilla Presley, while getting to the bottom of an attempt to sabotage the national policy on ecology.

Sample dialogue reflecting the nature of their relationship:

He: How are the children?

She: We never had any children, Frank.

One of the knacks of the filmmakers is to find actors who can get laughs more or less by playing their images, as Zsa Zsa Gabor, Robert Goulet, and George Kennedy do in this movie. Another knack is the crude, unsubtle nature of their visual style, in which the favored camera angle is to stare a sight gag right in the eye. A third is the low blow, as in a hilarious restaurant scene where all of the pictures on the wall depict great catastrophes—some natural, some human, one political.

Hey, look. The same day I saw *Naked, etc.*, I saw a movie about a mother who seeks her long-lost son, and another movie about a savior from the future who has come back to save the human race. It was kind of fun to settle back for the third bill on the triple feature and know that for eighty-five minutes I might possibly laugh, and would certainly not be called upon to think.

Naked Gun 33⅓: The Final Insult ★ ★ ★
PG-13, 75 m., 1994

Leslie Nielsen (Lieutenant Frank Drebin), Priscilla Presley (Jane Spencer-Drebin), George Kennedy (Captain Ed Hocken), O.J. Simpson (Nordberg), Fred Ward (Rocco), Anna Nicole Smith (Tanya), Kathleen Freeman (Muriel), Ellen Greene (Louise). Directed by Peter Segal and produced by Robert K. Weiss and David Zucker. Screenplay by Pat Proft, Zucker, and Robert LoCash.

In preparing to write this review of *Naked Gun 33⅓: The Final Insult*, I went back into the yellowing archives and read my reviews of the first two *Naked Gun* movies. It was an unsettling experience. I found I was repeating myself.

From my review of *The Naked Gun: From the Files of Police Squad!* (1988): "You laugh, and then you laugh at yourself for laughing. Some of the jokes are incredibly stupid." From my review of *The Naked Gun 2½: The Smell of Fear* (1991): ". . . the dialogue is dumb. Really dumb. So dumb you laugh twice, once because of how stupid it is, and the second time because you fell for it."

In both reviews, I also fondly recalled the best joke from *Top Secret!* (1984), when the spy in the alley desperately begs that the letter be mailed by midnight, and then we see that it's addressed to the Publishers Clearing House sweepstakes.

What was going on here? Were two great minds (mine) running in the same paths? Was I plagiarizing myself? There is a clue, I think, in the opening words of the second review: "What can usefully be said about this movie, other than the essential information that I laughed?" The answer, obviously, is "not much," and so by recycling what few insights I had, I was able to spin out three or four paragraphs fairly painlessly. Careful readers will notice that I have just done it again.

Naked Gun 33⅓ once again stars the durable Leslie Nielsen as Lt. Frank Drebin, who, as the movie opens, is retiring from the Police Squad in order to spend more time with his new bride (Priscilla Presley). He's experiencing domestic difficulties; she tells a marriage counselor he doesn't want children, although as he points out, "Honey, you know how much I wanted to adopt that eighteen-year-old Korean girl."

Retirement is of course not going to be possible for Drebin, because of a threat from a terrorist named Rocco (Fred Ward), who plans to blow up the Academy Awards. Rocco's girlfriend, Tanya, is played by Anna Nicole Smith, the pneumatic Playmate of the Year whose dresses display her bosom in such a way that if anything falls off her fork she knows where to look for it.

The movie is once again largely the work of David Zucker, who complains in the press book that people still think he makes his films with his brother Jerry and friend Jim Abrahams (the "Zaz Boys"). Not so: He produced and cowrote this one, which has been directed by Peter Segal in exactly the style of the others, which is to say, nonstop sight gags and one-liners occupy the center of the action, while the sides and backgrounds are crammed with as many additional gags as the filmmakers can think of.

The movie's opening sequence, a takeoff on the train station shootout in *The Untouchables*, is hilarious, with as many as three out-of-control baby carriages rolling down the stairs at the same time. And there's a lot of other funny stuff, leading up to an Academy Awards ceremony in which real celebrities (Pia Zadora, Vanna White, Raquel Welch, Mary Lou Retton) play themselves as Lt. Drebin (posing as Phil Donahue) makes a shambles of the ceremony. Zadora's dance sequence may be the only work of choreography I have ever seen that includes the dialogue, "Phil Donahue is puking in the trombone."

It occurred to me, watching the film, that what Leslie Nielsen and Priscilla Presley do here is not easy, and is done well. It would be fatal to the movie if either one ever betrayed the slightest suggestion that they know funny things are going on. They play everything on a level of seriousness that would be appropriate, say, for a 1960s TV cop drama. Their timing is impeccable. And they provide the sure, strong center around which the madness revolves. And if you think *that* line comes from another one of my old reviews, you may be right.

Naked in New York ★ ★ ★
R, 91 m., 1994

Eric Stoltz (Jake Briggs), Mary-Louise Parker (Joanne White), Ralph Macchio (Chris), Jill Clayburgh (Shirley Briggs), Tony Curtis (Carl Fisher), Timothy Dalton (Elliot Price), Lynne Thigpen (Helen), Kathleen Turner (Dana Coles), Roscoe Lee Browne (Mr. Reid), Whoopi Goldberg (Tragedy Mask). Directed by Dan Algrant and produced by Frederick Zollo. Screenplay by Algrant and John Warren.

Naked in New York tells an old story in a fresh way. It's about a young man who graduates from college and moves to the big city and dreams of success. He doesn't have a big ego and he doesn't necessarily have a big talent, but he has big ideas, and as he narrates the film in a mildly ironic voice, we begin to like him. We also like the oddly assorted cast of characters that surrounds him.

His name is Jake Briggs (Eric Stoltz). He has had a confusing childhood; the first time we see him, as a baby, he is being rotated between his parents on the Lazy Susan in the center of a table in a Chinese restaurant. In college, he becomes a drama major. His teacher (Roscoe Lee Browne) admires his writing, but is concerned about his themes ("Perhaps you should see the people over at Health Services").

Jake is smart but not wise in the ways of the world. His girlfriend Joanne (Mary-Louise Parker) is, like many women of her generation, a couple of years ahead of him in her social development. She knows, for example, how to make small talk with a famous author (William Styron) at a cocktail party, while Jake can only inspire Styron's eyes to glaze over. Joanne is a photographer, who catches the eye of a lecherous gallery owner (Timothy Dalton) at about the time Jake leaves for New York with his best play under his arm.

Naked in New York is a first film written and directed by Dan Algrant, who based it on an autobiographical short film he wrote while a film student at Columbia. His teacher there, Martin Scorsese, is executive producer of the film, but it's not a Scorsese clone. It reminded me more of Woody Allen, with its insecure narrator describing his setbacks in life and love.

Algrant has assembled a surprising supporting cast for his film; in addition to Browne and Dalton, small roles are played by Tony Curtis, Kathleen Turner, and Jill Clayburgh—and see if you can spot Whoopi Goldberg. Cameo roles are often an excuse for a filmmaker to flaunt his good luck, and for the actors to run through their trademarked riffs, but here the casting seems exactly on target.

As Jake's play actually moves toward an off-Broadway production, Curtis finds precisely the right note for playing a jaded but not unkind producer, and Turner, as the sexually alert soap opera actress who is cast in the lead. Curtis is a smart actor with a sense of humor, and his performance here may suggest possibilities to other directors. He suggests a quality I've observed in many of the better older producers; his character combines competence and experience with a certain detachment, because he knows that most plays, hits and misses, will soon be forgotten.

Turner is funny, but, like Curtis, she contains the humor in the role and never seems to reach for a laugh. It is clear she has slept her way to the top and down the other side, and is ready for a new ascent. "Which are you, a man or a boy?" she asks Jake, after suggesting a weekend together. "Well, it doesn't matter. I'm partial to both." Algrant, using these famous actors in smaller roles, knows what many more-experienced directors sometimes forget: A cameo works only when it distills the essence of a character, and then is perfectly matched with the actor.

Meanwhile, Jake's life grows more complex. His best friend at college was Chris (Ralph Macchio), an actor, who has been responsible for shopping Jake's play to the Curtis character. Now it appears that Chris himself may be forced out of his role. That would be betrayal, Chris cries, but Jake is powerless. Curtis has cast Turner, who doesn't like young Chris, and that's that. Meanwhile, both friends are going through trials of their sexual identities. Chris thinks he may be gay. Jake thinks he may be losing his girlfriend to the older gallery owner.

What distinguishes *Naked in New York* is its confidence in its intelligence. It doesn't go for cheap shots or easy laughs, but patiently follows its hero through the labyrinth of his early career. The use of voice-over narration, which is sometimes an irritation, seems as right here as it does in Woody Allen's films, because the points of view of the director and the hero are the same. And Eric Stoltz is right for the character of Jake: Smart, unsure, self-deprecatory, Jake is not a giant but he has a talent, maybe, and we hope he does something with it.

Nashville ★ ★ ★ ★
R, 159 m., 1975

Henry Gibson (Haven Hamilton), Ronee Blakley (Barbara Jean), Timothy Brown (Tommy Brown), Gwen Welles (Sueleen Gay), Michael Murphy (John Triplette), Shelley Duvall (L.A. Joan), Lily Tomlin (Linnea Reese), Ned Beatty (Delbert Reese), Scott Glenn (Pfc. Glenn Kelly), Keith Carradine (Tom Frank), Geraldine Chaplin (Opal), Karen Black (Connie White), Barbara Harris (Albuquerque). Directed and produced by Robert Altman. Screenplay by Joan Tewkesbury.

Robert Altman's *Nashville*, which was the best American movie since *Bonnie and Clyde*, creates in the relationships of nearly two dozen characters a microcosm of who we were and what we were up to in the 1970s. It's a film about the losers and the winners, the drifters and the stars in Nashville, and the most complete expression yet of not only the genius but also the humanity of Altman, who sees people with his camera in such a way as to enlarge our own experience. Sure, it's only a movie. But after I saw it I felt more alive, I felt I understood more about people, I felt somehow wiser. It's that good a movie.

The movie doesn't have a star. It does not, indeed, even have a lead role. Instead, Altman creates a world, a community in which some people know each other and others don't, in which people are likely to meet before they understand the ways in which their lives are related. And he does it all so easily, or seems to, that watching *Nashville* is as easy as breathing and as hard to stop. Altman is the best natural filmmaker since Fellini.

One of the funny things about *Nashville* is that most of the characters never have entrances. They're just sort of there. At times, we're watching an important character and don't even know, yet, why he's important, but Altman's storytelling is so clear in his own mind, his mastery of this complex wealth of material is so complete, that we're never for a moment confused or even curious. We feel secure in his hands, and apart from anything else, *Nashville* is a virtuoso display of narrative mastery.

It concerns several days and nights in the lives of a very mixed bag of Nashville locals and visitors, all of whom, like the city itself, are obsessed with country music. Tennessee is in the midst of a presidential primary, and all over Nashville, there are the posters and sound trucks of a quasi-populist candidate, Hal Philip Walker, who seems like a cross between George Wallace and George McGovern. We never meet Walker, but we meet both his local organizer and a John Lindsay-type PR man. They're trying to round up country-western talent for a big benefit, and their efforts provide a thread around which some of the story is loosely wound.

But there are many stories here, and in the way he sees their connections, Altman makes a subtle but shrewd comment about the ways in which we are all stuck in this thing together. There are the veteran country stars like Haven Hamilton (Henry Gibson), who wears gaudy white costumes, is self-conscious about his short stature, is painfully earnest about recording a painfully banal Bicentennial song, and who, down deep, is basically just a good old boy. There is the reigning queen of country music, Barbara Jean (Ronee Blakley), who returns in triumph to Nashville after treatment at a burn center in Atlanta for unspecified injuries incurred from a fire baton (she's met at the airport by a phalanx of girls from TIT—the Tennessee Institute of Twirling—only to collapse again). There is the corrupted, decadent rock star, played by Keith Carradine, who is so ruthless in his sexual aggression, so evil in his need to hurt women, that he telephones one woman while another is still just leaving his bed, in order to wound both of them.

But these characters are just examples of the people we meet in *Nashville*, not the leads. Everyone is more or less equal in this film, because Altman sees them all with a judicious and ultimately sympathetic eye. The film is filled with perfectly observed little moments: The star-struck young soldier keeping a silent vigil by the bedside of Barbara Jean; the campaign manager doing a double take when he discovers he's just shaken the hand of Elliott Gould ("a fairly well-known actor," Haven Hamilton explains, "and he used to be married to Barbra Streisand"); the awestruck BBC reporter describing America in breathless, hilarious hyperbole; the way a middle-aged mother of two deaf children (Lily Tomlin) shyly waits for an assignation with a rock singer; the birdbrained cheerfulness with which a young groupie (Shelley Duvall) comes to town to visit her dying aunt and never does see her, being distracted by every male over the age of sixteen that she meets.

The film circles around three motifs without, thankfully, ever feeling it has to make a definitive statement about any of them. Since they're all still very open subjects, that's just as well. What Altman does is suggest the ways in which we deal with them—really, in unrehearsed everyday life, not thematically, as in the movies. The motifs are success, women, and politics.

Success: It can be studied most fruitfully in the carefully observed pecking order of the country-and-western performers. There are ones at the top, so successful they can afford to be generous, expansive, well-liked. There are the younger ones in the middle, jockeying for position. There are what can only be described as the professional musicians at the bottom, playing thanklessly but well in the bars and clubs where the stars come to unwind after the show. And at the very bottom, there are those who aspire to be musicians but have no talent at all, like a waitress (Gwen Welles) who comes to sing at a smoker, is forced to strip, and, in one of the film's moments of heartbreaking truthfulness, disdainfully flings at the roomful of men the sweat socks she had stuffed into her brassiere.

Women: God, but Altman cares for them while seeing their predicament so clearly. The women in *Nashville* inhabit a world largely unaffected by the feminist revolution, as most women do. They are prized for their talent, for their beauty, for their services in bed, but not once in this movie for themselves. And yet Altman suggests their complexities in ways that movies rarely have done before. The Lily Tomlin character, in particular, forces us to consider her real human needs and impulses as she goes to meet the worthless rock singer (and we remember a luminous scene during which she and her deaf son discussed his swimming class). Part of the movie's method is to establish characters in one context and then place them in another, so that we can see how personality—indeed, basic identity itself—is constant but must sometimes be concealed for the sake of survival or even simple happiness.

Politics: I won't be giving very much away by revealing that there is an attempted assassination in *Nashville*. The assassin, a loner who takes a room in a boarding house, is clearly telegraphed by Altman. It's not Altman's style to surprise us with plot. He'd rather surprise us by revelations of character. At this late date after November 22, 1963, and all the other days of infamy, I wouldn't have thought it possible that a film could have anything new or very interesting to say on assassination, but *Nashville* does, and the film's closing minutes, with Barbara Harris finding herself, to her astonishment, onstage and singing, "It Don't Worry Me,"

are unforgettable and heartbreaking. *Nashville*, which seems so unstructured as it begins, reveals itself in this final sequence to have had a deep and very profound structure—but one of emotions, not ideas.

This is a film about America. It deals with our myths, our hungers, our ambitions, and our sense of self. It knows how we talk and how we behave, and it doesn't flatter us but it does love us.

National Lampoon's Animal House
★ ★ ★ ★
R, 109 m., 1978

John Belushi (Bluto), Tim Matheson (Otter), John Vernon (Dean Wormer), Verna Bloom (Mrs. Wormer), Thomas Hulce (Pinto), Cesare Danova (Mayor), Donald Sutherland (Jennings), Mary Louise Weller (Mandy), Stephen Furst (Flounder), Mark Metcalf (Neidermeier). Directed by John Landis and produced by Marry Simmons and Ivan Reitman. Screenplay by Harold Ramis, Douglas Kenney, and Chris Miller.

"What we need right now," Otter tells his fraternity brothers, "is a stupid, futile gesture on someone's part." And no fraternity on campus—on any campus—is better qualified to provide such a gesture than the Deltas. They have the title role in *National Lampoon's Animal House*, which remembers all the way back to 1962, when college was simpler, beer was cheaper, and girls were harder to seduce.

The movie is vulgar, raunchy, ribald, and occasionally scatological. It is also the funniest comedy since Mel Brooks made *The Producers. Animal House* is funny for some of the same reasons the *National Lampoon* is funny (and Second City and Saturday Night Live are funny): Because it finds some kind of precarious balance between insanity and accuracy, between cheerfully wretched excess and an ability to reproduce the most revealing nuances of human behavior.

In one sense there has never been a campus like this movie's Faber University, which was apparently founded by the lead pencil tycoon and has as its motto "Knowledge is Good." In another sense, Faber University is a microcosm of . . . I was going to say *our society*, but why get serious? Let someone else discuss the symbolism of Bluto's ability to crush a beer can against his forehead.

Bluto is, of course, the most animalistic of the Deltas. He's played by John Belushi, and the performance is all the more remarkable

because Bluto has hardly any dialogue. He isn't a talker, he's an event. His best scenes are played in silence (as when he lasciviously scales a ladder to peek at a sorority pillow fight).

Bluto and his brothers are engaged in a holding action against civilization. They are in favor of beer, women, song, motorcycles, *Playboy* centerfolds, and making rude noises. They are opposed to studying, serious thought, the Dean, the regulations governing fraternities, and, most especially, the disgusting behavior of the Omegas—a house so respectable it has even given an ROTC commander to the world.

The movie was written by *National Lampoon* contributors (including Harold Ramis, who was in Second City at the same time Belushi was), and was directed by John Landis. It's like an end run around Hollywood's traditional notions of comedy. It's anarchic, messy, and filled with energy. It assaults us. Part of the movie's impact comes from its sheer level of manic energy: When beer kegs and Hell's Angels come bursting through the windows of the Delta House, the anarchy is infectious. But the movie's better made (and better acted) than we might at first realize. It takes skill to create this sort of comic pitch, and the movie's filled with characters that are sketched a little more absorbingly than they had to be, and acted with perception.

For example: Tim Matheson, as Otter, the ladies' man, achieves a kind of grace in his obsession. John Vernon, as the Dean of Students, has a blue-eyed, rulebook hatefulness that's inspired. Verna Bloom, as his dipsomaniacal wife, has just the right balance of cynicism and desperation. Donald Sutherland, a paranoic early sixties pothead, nods solemnly at sophomoric truisms and admits he's as bored by Milton as everyone else. And stalking through everything is Bluto, almost a natural force: He lusts, he thirsts, he consumes cafeterias full of food, and he pours an entire fifth of Jack Daniel's into his mouth, belches, and observes, "Thanks. I needed that."

He has, as I suggested, little dialogue. But it is telling. When the Delta House is kicked off campus and the Deltas are thrown out of school, he makes, in a moment of silence, a philosophical observation: "Seven years down the drain." What the situation requires, of course, is a stupid, futile gesture on someone's part.

Natural Born Killers ★ ★ ★ ★   NEW

R, 123 m., 1994
(See related Film Clips, p. 879 and 887.)

Woody Harrelson (Mickey Knox), Juliette
Lewis (Mallory Knox), Robert Downey, Jr.
(Wayne Gale), Tommy Lee Jones (McClusky),
Tom Sizemore (Jack Scagnetti), Rodney
Dangerfield (Mallory's Dad), Russell Means
(Indian), Edie McClurg (Mallory's Mom).
Directed by Oliver Stone and produced by
Jane Hamsher, Don Murphy, and Clayton
Townsend. Screenplay by David Veloz,
Richard Rutowski, and Stone.

Oliver Stone's *Natural Born Killers* might have
played even more like a demented nightmare
if it hadn't been for the O.J. Simpson case.
Maybe Stone meant his movie as a warning
about where we were headed, but because of
Simpson it plays as an indictment. We are
becoming a society more interested in crime
and scandal than in anything else—more
than in politics and the arts, certainly, and
maybe even more than sports, unless crime
is our new national sport.

If that's true, then Stone's movie is about
the latest all-Americans, Mickey and Mallory (Woody Harrelson and Juliette Lewis),
two mass murderers who go on a killing spree
across America, making sure everybody knows
their names, so they get credit for their crimes.
(Terrorists always claim "credit" rather
than "blame.") The movie is not simply
about their killings, however, but also about
the way they electrify the media and exhila-
rate the public. (One teenager tells the TV
cameras, "Mass murder is wrong. But if I
were a mass murderer, I'd be Mickey and
Mallory!")

The boom in courtroom TV has given us
long hours to study the faces of famous accused murderers; we have a better view than
the jury. Looking into their faces, I sense a
curious slackness, an inattention, as if the
trial is a mirage, and their thoughts far away.
If they're guilty, it's like they're rehearsing
their excuses for the crime. If they're innocent, maybe those empty expressions mean
the courtroom experience is so alien they
can't process it. Not once during his trial did
I see a shot of Simpson looking normal in any
way I can understand. His expression always
seems to be signifying, "Yes, but . . ."

Oliver Stone captures this odd emptiness,
this moral inattention, in the faces and behavior of Mickey and Mallory. They're on
their own frequency. The casting is crucial:
Woody Harrelson and Juliette Lewis are both

capable of being frightening, both able to
project amorality and disdain as easily as
Jack Lemmon projects ingratiation. There is
a scene where a lawman is trying to intimidate Lewis, and he throws his cigarette onto
the floor of her cell. She steps on it and rubs
it out with her bare foot. Set and match.

Natural Born Killers is not so much about
the killers, however, as about the feeding
frenzy they inspire. During the period of
their rampage, they are the most famous
people in America, and the media goes nuts.
There are Mickey and Mallory fan clubs and
T-shirts; tabloid TV is represented by a blood-
thirsty journalist played by Robert Downey,
Jr., who is so thrilled by their fame he almost
wants to embrace them. The people Mickey
and Mallory touch in the law industry are
elated to be handling the case; it gives them a
brush with celebrity, and a tantalizing whiff
of the brimstone that fascinates some cops.

Stone has never been a director known for
understatement or subtlety. He'll do anything to get his effect, and that's one of the
things I value about him. He understands
that celebrity killers have achieved such a
bizarre status in America that it's almost impossible to satirize the situation—to get beyond real life. But he goes for broke, in scenes
of carnage like a prison riot which is telecast
live while the "host" gets caught up in the
bloodlust.

Yet you do not see as much actual violence
as you think you do in this movie; it's more
the tone, the attitude, and the breakneck
pacing that gives you that impression. Stone
is not making a geek show, with close-ups of
blood and guts. Like all good satirists, he
knows that too much realism will weaken his
effect. He lets you know he's making a comedy. There's an over-the-top exuberance to
the intricate crosscut editing, by Hank Corwin
and Brian Berdan and, to the hyperactive
camera of Robert Richardson. Stylistically,
the film is a cinematic bazaar, combining
color and black and white, film and video,
35mm and Super 8, sitcom style and animated cartoons, fiction and newsreels. They're
throwing stuff at the screen by the gleeful
handfuls.

And look how this film blindsided the good
citizens of the MPAA classification board.
The review panel threatened the film with
the dreaded NC-17 rating, and after five appeals and some cutting, finally granted the R
rating. But read their parental warning: "For
extreme violence and graphic carnage, for
shocking images, and for strong language

and sexuality." They've got the fever! I could
point to a dozen more-violent recent films
that have left the MPAA unstirred, but Stone
has touched a nerve here, because his film
isn't about violence, it's about how we respond to violence, and that truly is shocking.

Stone's basic strategy is to find the current buzzwords and buzz ideas of crime and
violence, and project them through the looking glass into a wonderland of murderous
satire. It is a commonplace, for example,
that many violent criminals were abused as
children. All right, then, Stone will give us
abuse: We see Mallory's childhood, shot in
the style of a lurid TV sitcom, with Rodney
Dangerfield as her drunken, piggish father.
As he shouts and threatens violence, as he
ridicules Mallory's thoroughly cowed mother,
as he grabs his daughter and makes lewd
suggestions, we hear a sitcom laugh track
that grinds out mechanical hilarity. Everything is funny to the "live studio audience,"
because Dangerfield's timing is right for the
punch lines. Never mind how frightening
the words are. Who really listens to sitcoms,
anyway?

Everything is grist for Stone's mill. Look
at Tommy Lee Jones, as Warden McClusky
of Batongaville State Prison. He's seen too
many prison movies, and he's intoxicated by
the experience of being on TV. He rants, he
raves, he curses, he runs his prison like a
deranged slave plantation. And then here
comes Downey, as Wayne Gale, who hosts a
clone of "Hard Copy" or "America's Most
Wanted." Using a Robin Leach accent that
makes the whole thing into showbiz, he's so
thrilled to be in the same frame with these
famous killers that he hardly cares what happens to him. Watch his reaction in the final
bloody showdown, when he believes he is
immune because, after all, he has the camera.

Seeing this movie once is not enough. The
first time is for the visceral experience, the
second time is for the meaning. *Natural Born
Killers* is like a slap in the face, waking us up
to what's happening.

Watching the movie, it occurred to me
that I didn't meet or talk with anyone who
seemed genuinely, personally, angry that
Simpson (or anyone else) might have committed those sad murders. Instead, people
seem more intrigued and fascinated. The
word *grateful* comes to mind. The case has
given us all something to talk about. The
barking dog. The blood tests. The ice cream
that didn't melt. The matching glove. When
the subject came up at a party, you could

almost feel the relief in the room, as everyone joined in: At last, a topic we could all get worked up about! Once we were shocked that the Romans threw Christians to the lions. Now we figure out a way to recycle the format into a TV show. That's what *Natural Born Killers* is all about.

Necessary Roughness ★ ★ ★

PG-13, 104 m., 1991

Scott Bakula (Paul Blake), Hector Elizondo (Coach Gennaro), Robert Loggia (Coach Riggendorf), Harley Jane Kozak (Suzanne Carter), Sinbad (Andre Krimm), Fred Dalton Thompson (TSU President), Peter Navy Tuiasosopo (Manumana), Jason Bateman (Edison). Directed by Stan Dragoti and produced by Mace Neufeld and Robert Rehme. Screenplay by Rick Natkin and David Fuller.

I've seen versions of the plot of *Necessary Roughness* in almost every other movie ever made about an underdog sports team—but I fell for it again this time because it was well done and because the movie doesn't try to pump itself up into more than it is, a good-humored entertainment.

The film tells the story of a college football team that faces its new season under an incredible handicap: Only actual, bona fide students will be allowed to play on the team. No recruited superstars. No future pros who will be coddled in no-brainer classes. No players with under-the-table financial aid from the booster club. Just real students who try out for the team.

This is a big comedown for the Texas State Armadillos, who were last year's national college football champions before an investigation uncovered widespread corruption in the school's athletic program. The school had to give up its trophies and forfeit its victories, and for the new season the only returning player will be a guy who spent all of his time on the bench.

The Texas State president (Fred Dalton Thompson) can't even find anyone to lead the team, until he has a brainstorm: He offers the job to a veteran coach named Gennaro (Hector Elizondo), who has just finished attacking the school's ethics on national television. Gennaro accepts, naturally, because in a movie like this nobody is ever allowed to turn down a challenge.

Gennaro hires an old pal named Riggendorf (Robert Loggia) as his assistant. At first they plan to divide up offense and defense,

but when only seventeen students make the team, they decide it's time for a return to Iron Man football. And they recruit players in unlikely places: A thirty-four-year-old former Texas high school star (Scott Bakula) has never used his college eligibility, and he's drafted as quarterback. A school astronomy professor (Sinbad) has a year of eligibility left, and he joins the team, along with a kicker (Kathy Ireland) recruited from the women's soccer team.

You can see this movie's plot unfolding a mile away: The ragbag collection of misfits will lose almost all of their games, but will they finally pull themselves together and win the big one? What do you think? And will there be a love affair between Bakula and his standoffish journalism professor (Harley Jane Kozak)? All of these events are written in the stars.

The movie assembles an offbeat group of supporting talent, including a lineman from Samoa (Peter Navy Tuiasosopo) who makes the Refrigerator look like an ice chest. Not so successful is Larry Miller, as the priggish antisports dean; his scenes play on a different note than the rest of the movie and seemed shoehorned in. But Elizondo and Loggia, two veterans of many years of fine supporting work, seem to enjoy themselves playing the coaches. And as the Armadillos creep toward greatness, *Necessary Roughness* generates a genuine charm.

Neighbors ★ ★ ★

R, 90 m., 1981

John Belushi (Earl Keese), Kathryn Walker (Enid Keese), Cathy Moriarty (Ramona), Dan Aykroyd (Vic). Directed by John G. Avildsen and produced by Richard D. Zanuck and David Brown. Screenplay by Larry Gelbart.

If there's one quality that middle-class Americans have in common, it's a tendency to be rigidly polite in the face of absolutely unacceptable behavior. Confronted with obnoxious rudeness, we freeze up, we get a nervous little smile, we allow our eyes to focus on the middle distance, and we cannot believe this is happening to us. It's part of our desire to avoid a scene. We'd rather choke to death in a restaurant than break a plate to attract attention. *Neighbors* is about one such man, Earl Keese (John Belushi). He is a pleasant, low-key dumpling of a fellow. He lives an uneventful life with an uneventful wife (Kathryn Walker). Then the neighbors move in, and there goes the neighborhood. They are every-

thing we dread in neighbors. They are loud. They are blatant freeloaders. The man (Dan Aykroyd) is gung-ho macho. The woman (Cathy Moriarty, from *Raging Bull*) is oversexed and underloved. They park some kind of customized truck on their front lawn. They invite themselves to dinner.

There are compensations. For example, the woman seems to be a nymphomaniac. That would be more of a compensation for Earl if he were not terrified of aggressive women. Earl has not the slightest notion of how to deal with these next-door maniacs, and his wife's no help: She puts on her best smile and tries to handle the situation as if everyone were playing by Emily Post's rules. The story of the Keeses and their weird neighbors was first told in Thomas Berger's novel. It was obviously a launching pad for a movie, but what sort of movie? The relationships among these neighbors depend almost entirely on the chemistry of casting: For example, obnoxious Richard Benjamin could have moved in next to meek Donald Sutherland. In *Neighbors*, however, we get Belushi and Aykroyd. I think it was brilliant casting, especially since they divided the roles somewhat against our expectations. Belushi, the most animalistic animal in *Animal House*, plays the mild-mannered Keese. And Aykroyd, who often plays straight-arrows, makes the new neighbor into a loud neo-fascist with a back slap that can kill.

The movie slides easily from its opening slices of life into a surburban nightmare. We know things are strange right at the start, when Aykroyd extorts money from Belushi to get a carry-out Italian dinner, and then secretly cooks the spaghetti right in his own kitchen. Belushi sneaks out into the night to spy on Aykroyd and catches him faking it with Ragu, but is too intimidated to say anything. The whole movie goes like that, with Belushi so intimidated that he hardly protests even when he finds himself sinking into quicksand.

Meanwhile, the women are making their own strange arrangements, especially after the Keese's college-age daughter (Lauren-Marie Taylor) comes home from school and begins attracting Moriarty's attention. The movie operates as a satire of social expectations, using polite clichés as counterpoint to deadly insults (all delivered in pleasant conversational tones).

The first hour of *Neighbors* is probably more fun than the second, if only because the plot developments come as a series of surprises. After a while, the bizarre logic of the movie becomes more predictable. But *Neighbors* is a truly interesting comedy, an offbeat experiment in hallucinatory black humor. It grows on you.

Nell ★ ★ ★

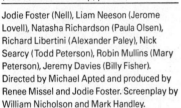

PG-13, 113 m., 1994
(See related Film Clip, p. 873.)

Jodie Foster (Nell), Liam Neeson (Jerome Lovell), Natasha Richardson (Paula Olsen), Richard Libertini (Alexander Paley), Nick Searcy (Todd Peterson), Robin Mullins (Mary Peterson), Jeremy Davies (Billy Fisher). Directed by Michael Apted and produced by Renee Missel and Jodie Foster. Screenplay by William Nicholson and Mark Handley.

One of the great movies of modern times is François Truffaut's *The Wild Child* (1969), about a child who is found living like an animal in the woods, and becomes the ward of a doctor who hopes to educate him. The story, set in the eighteenth century, is based on a real child, and it ends, like many such cases do, without much progress: The child learns to love, but never learns to speak. The truth is that speech must be learned very young, or not at all.

Nell, the story of a present-day wild child who grows up in a forest wilderness in North Carolina, gives us a character who *has* learned to speak, but not in a language anyone has ever heard before. When she is first discovered, she has been living alone in an isolated cabin, where first her twin and then her mother had died. It is speculated that the twins developed a private language, based on English, before one died.

This case history is useful for the story, because Nell must be able to speak if she is to give us her message—which is, as in many such stories, that the natural is better than the civilized. "You are hungry for silence," Nell tells her friends.

Despite its predictable philosophy, however, *Nell* is an effective film, and a moving one. That is largely because of the strange beauty of Jodie Foster's performance as Nell, and the warmth of the performance by Liam Neeson, as a doctor who finds himself somehow responsible for her. Along with Natasha Richardson, who has a somewhat thankless role as Neeson's partner in the case, they inhabit the characters so fully that it's only later, after withdrawing from the emotional experience, that we recognize the movie's fairly shaky premises.

The movie takes place in a wilderness where Nell was living with her mother. It's a little unclear how they survived; a motorcycle delivery boy drops off provisions, but, still, the movie glosses over a lot of details. No matter; what's important is that Nell lives alone and, once her existence is discovered, she is a potential victim as news helicopters swarm overhead and the curious come calling.

She is perfectly able to take care of herself in isolation, but unfamiliar with civilization. Of course civilization insists on finding her deprived. Neeson and Richardson, taken to the site by the local sheriff, establish their headquarters on a houseboat anchored near Nell's cabin, and begin to observe her and try talking with her. At first her language sounds like nonsense, but eventually a logic emerges, and finally Neeson is able to break down her reserve and win her confidence.

Of course Nell is a fully grown, attractive woman; bathing naked in the mist of a woodland river, she looks uncannily like a model for a Maxfield Parrish print. Neeson, as the doctor, is not blind to her charms. But somehow her innocence and his ethics (and Richardson's presence) defuse the situation, and even in a skinny-dipping episode (necessary to deal with Nell's "fear of men") there is a kind of chastity to the situation.

The villain is a psychologist played by Richard Libertini, who, like all such movie shrinks, knows nothing of human nature and would solve all problems by institutionalizing the subject. But to be locked in an asylum would destroy Nell, and besides, she's not mentally ill, she simply marches to a different drummer. Neeson tries gingerly to introduce her to towns, but visits to a supermarket and a pool hall go badly, and he realizes she must develop on her own terms.

There were scenes in *Nell* I had trouble believing (none more so than her courtroom speech on her own behalf), but other scenes generated a true beauty and mystery. And Jodie Foster is quite successful in creating a woman with completely alien speech cues and body language—a person who has not grown up learning how to let others know what she feels. The movie's insight is that Nell is more the solution than the problem. In real life, a wild child might not be quite so inspiring or pleasant to know. But in *Nell*, the result is a quiet poem to the more natural side of our natures.

Network ★ ★ ★ ★

R, 121 m, 1976

Faye Dunaway (Diana Christenson), William Holden (Alex Schumacher), Peter Finch (Howard Beale), Robert Duvall (Frank Hackett), Wesley Addy (Nelson Chaney), Ned Beatty (Arthur Jensen). Directed by Sidney Lumet and produced by Howard Gottfried. Screenplay by Paddy Chayefsky.

There's a moment near the beginning of *Network* that has us thinking this will be the definitive indictment of national television we've been promised. A veteran anchorman has been fired because he's over the hill and drinking too much and, even worse, because his ratings have gone down. He announces his firing on his program, observes that broadcasting has been his whole life, and adds that he plans to kill himself on the air in two weeks. We cut to the control room, where the directors and technicians are obsessed with getting into the network feed on time. There are commercials that have to be fit in, the anchorman has to finish at the right moment, the buttons have to be pushed, and the station break has to be timed correctly. Everything goes fine. "Uh," says somebody, "did you hear what Howard just said?" Apparently nobody else had.

They were all consumed with form, with being sure the commercials were played in the right order and that the segment was the correct length. What was happening—that a man has lost his career and was losing his mind—passed right by. It wasn't their job to listen to Howard, just as it wasn't his job to run the control board. And what *Network* seems to be telling us is that television itself is like that: an economic process in the blind pursuit of ratings and technical precision, in which excellence is as accidental as banality.

If the whole movie had stayed with this theme, we might have had a very bitter little classic here. As it is, we have a supremely well-acted, intelligent film that tries for too much, that attacks not only television but also most of the other ills of the 1970s. We are asked to laugh at, be moved by, or get angry about such a long list of subjects: sexism and ageism and revolutionary ripoffs and upper-middle-class anomie and capitalist exploitation and Neilsen ratings and psychics and that perennial standby, the failure to communicate. Paddy Chayefsky's script isn't a bad one, but he finally loses control of it. There's just too much he wanted to say. By the movie's end, the anchorman is obviously totally insane and is being exploited by blindly ambitious programmers on the one hand and corrupt businessmen on the other, and the scale of evil is so vast we've lost track of the human values.

And yet, still, what a rich and interesting movie this is. Lumet's direction is so taut, that maybe we don't realize that it leaves some unfinished business. It attempts to deal with a brief, cheerless love affair between Holden and Dunaway, but doesn't really allow us to understand it. It attempts to suggest that multinational corporations are the only true contemporary government, but does so in a scene that slips too broadly into satire, so that we're not sure Chayefsky means it. It deals with Holden's relationship with his wife of twenty-five years, but inconclusively.

But then there are scenes in the movie that are absolutely chilling. We watch Peter Finch cracking up on the air, and we remind ourselves that *this* isn't satire, it was a style as long ago as Jack Paar. We can believe that audiences would tune in to a news program that's half happy talk and half freak show, because audiences *are* tuning in to programs like that. We can believe in the movie's "Ecumenical Liberation Army" because nothing along those lines will amaze us after Patty Hearst. And we can believe that the Faye Dunaway character could be totally cut off from her emotional and sexual roots, could be fanatically obsessed with her job, because jobs as competitive as hers almost require that. Twenty-five years ago, this movie would have seemed like a fantasy; now it's barely ahead of the facts.

So the movie's flawed. So it leaves us with loose ends and questions. That finally doesn't bother me, because what it does accomplish is done so well, is seen so sharply, is presented so unforgivingly, that *Network* will outlive a lot of tidier movies. And it won several Academy Awards, including those for Peter Finch, awarded posthumously as best actor; Chayevsky for his screenplay; Beatrice Straight, as best supporting actress; and Faye Dunaway, as best actress. Watch her closely as they're deciding what will finally have to be done about their controversial anchorman. The scene would be hard to believe—if she weren't in it.

The Neverending Story ★ ★ ★
PG, 94 m., 1984

Barret Oliver (Bastian), Noah Hathaway (Atreyu), Tami Stronach (Empress), Moses Gunn (Cairon). Directed by Wolfgang Petersen and produced by Bernd Eichinger and Dieter Geissler. Screenplay by Petersen and Herman Weigel.

How's this for a threat? The kingdom of Fantasia is about to be wiped out, and the enemy isn't an evil wizard or a thermonuclear device, it's Nothingness. That's right, an inexorable wave of Nothingness is sweeping over the kingdom, destroying everything in its path. Were children's movies this nihilistic in the old days?

The only thing standing between Fantasia and Nothingness is the faith of a small boy named Bastian (Barret Oliver). He discovers the kingdom in a magical bookstore, and as he begins to read the adventure between the covers, it becomes so real that the people in the story know about Bastian. How could that be? Well, that's the very first question Bastian asks. This is a modern kid with quite a healthy amount of skepticism, but what can he do when he turns the page and the Child Empress (Tami Stronach) is begging him to give her a name so that Fantasia can be saved?

The idea of the story within a story is one of the nice touches in *The Neverending Story*. Another one is the idea of a child's faith being able to change the course of fate. Maybe not since the kids in the audience were asked to save Tinker Bell in *Peter Pan* has the outcome of a story been left so clearly up to a child's willingness to believe. There is a lot we have to believe in *The Neverending Story*, and that's the other great strength of this movie. It contains some of the more inventive special-effects work of a time when battles in outer space, etc., have grown routine. Look for example, at *The Last Starfighter*, where the special effects are competent but never original—all the visual concepts are ripped off from *Star Wars*—and then look at this movie, where an entirely new world has been created.

The world of Fantasia contains creatures inspired by Alice in Wonderland (a little man atop a racing snail), the Muppets (a cute dragon-dog that can fly), and probably B.C. (a giant made of stone, who snacks on quartz and rumbles around on his granite tricycle). Many of the special effects involve sophisticated use of Muppet-like creatures (there are scenes that reminded me of *The Dark Crystal*). They are, in a way, more convincing than animation, because they exist in three dimensions and have the same depth as their human co-stars. And that illusion, in turn, helps reinforce the more conventional effects like animation, back projection, and so on. The world of this movie looks like a very particular place, and the art direction involved a lot of imagination. The movie's director, Wolfgang Petersen, is accustomed to creating worlds in small places; his last film, *Das Boot (The Boat)*, took place almost entirely within a submarine.

Within the world of Fantasia, a young hero (Noah Hathaway) is assigned to complete a hazardous quest, sneak past the dreaded portals of some stone amazons, and reach the Ivory Tower, where he will receive further instructions from the empress. In most movies, this quest would be told in a straightforward way, without the surrounding story about the other little boy who is reading the book. But *The Neverending Story* is *about* the unfolding of a story, and so the framing device of the kid hidden in his school attic, breathlessly turning the pages, is interesting. It lets kids know that the story isn't just somehow happening, that storytelling is a neverending act of the imagination.

Never Say Never Again ★ ★ ★ ½
PG, 137 m., 1983

Sean Connery (James Bond), Klaus Maria Brandauer (Largo), Max von Sydow (Blofeld), Barbara Carrera (Fatima Blush), Kim Basinger (Domino), Bernie Casey (Felix Leiter). Directed by Irwin Kershner and produced by Jack Schwartzman. Screenplay by Lorenzo Semple, Jr.

Ah, yes, James, it is good to have you back again. It is good to see the way you smile from under lowered eyebrows, and the way you bark commands in a sudden emergency, and it is good to see the way you look at women. Other secret agents may undress women with their eyes. You are more gallant. You undress them, and then thoughtfully dress them again. You are a rogue with the instincts of a gentleman.

It has been several years since Sean Connery hung it up as James Bond, several years since *Diamonds Are Forever*, and Connery's announcement that he would "never again" play special agent 007. What complex instincts caused him to have one more fling at the role, I cannot guess. Perhaps it was one morning in front of the mirror, as he pulled in his gut and reflected that he was in pretty damn fine shape for a man over fifty. And then, with a bow in the direction of his friend Roger Moore, who has made his own niche as a different kind of Bond, Sean Connery went back on assignment again.

The movie is called *Never Say Never Again*. The title has nothing to do with the movie—except why Connery made it—but never mind, nothing in this movie has much to do with anything else. It's another one of those Bond plots in which the basic ingredients are thrown together more or less in fancy. We begin with a threat (SPECTRE has stolen two nuclear missiles and is holding the world at ransom). We continue with Bond, his newest gadgets, his mission briefing. We meet the beautiful women who will figure in the plot (Barbara Carrera as terrorist Fatima Blush; Kim Basinger as the innocent mistress of the evil Largo). We meet the villains (Max van Sydow as Blofeld; Klaus Maria Brandauer as Largo). We visit exotic locations, we survive near-misses, and Bond spars with the evil woman and redeems the good one. All basic.

What makes *Never Say Never Again* more fun than most of the Bonds is more complex than that. For one thing, there's more of a human element in the movie, and it comes from Klaus Maria Brandauer, as Largo. Brandauer is a wonderful actor, and he chooses not to play the villain as a cliché. Instead, he brings a certain poignancy and charm to Largo, and since Connery always has been a particularly human James Bond, the emotional stakes are more convincing this time.

Sean Connery says he'll never make another James Bond movie, and maybe I believe him. But the fact that he made this one, so many years later, is one of those small show-business miracles. There was never a Beatles reunion. Bob Dylan and Joan Baez don't appear on the same stage anymore. But here, by God, is Sean Connery as Sir James Bond. Good work, 007.

The New Age ★ ★ ★ ½
R, 112 m., 1994

NEW

Peter Weller (Peter Witner), Judy Davis (Katherine Witner), Patrick Bauchau (Jean Levy), Rachel Rosenthal (Sarah Friedberg), Adam West (Jeff Witner), Paula Marshall (Alison Gale), Bruce Ramsay (Misha), Tanya Pohlkotte (Bettina). Directed by Michael Tolkin and produced by Nick Wechsler and Keith Addis. Screenplay by Tolkin.

That's what we're good at—shopping and talking.
—dialogue from *The New Age*

Peter and Katherine Witner are conduits for vast amounts of money, which flow from their extravagant Beverly Hills salaries into the hands of the people they buy their lifestyle from. They live in a designer house with walls covered by "important" paintings, and their friends are as wealthy as themselves. Their personalities are made out of psychobabble and arrogance; they are obsessed with their toys, but hey, you're okay, I'm okay, and that's okay.

Then one day they both find themselves out of work, with only enough cash in the bank to finance about thirty more days of opulence before the whole structure of their lives comes crashing down. *The New Age*, Michael Tolkin's film about their dilemma, is a satire, but it avoids making them into easy targets. They're too vulnerable to really dislike; without their credit cards, they're like Boy Scouts without any way to start a campfire.

Tolkin knows the world of Peter and Katherine from the inside out, as he showed in his screenplay for *The Player,* another X-ray of the lifestyles of the rich and famous. *The New Age* also has something in common with the 1992 film Tolkin wrote and directed, *The Rapture*. It shows his characters caught up in the search for quick spiritual fixes. As their bank account shrinks, the Witners (played with frightening accuracy by Peter Weller and Judy Davis) turn to a series of gurus whose prescriptions run from meditation in the desert to all-night pool orgies.

This need to believe in *something* is almost required by the hedonistic lifestyles of the characters. While many spiritual programs advocate humility, the New Age beliefs of the Witners allow them to star as the objects of their own worship. If you feel right about yourself, if you think positive, if you send out the right aura, then success, of course, will come to you. The catch is that failure and poverty are therefore somehow your own fault, too.

At one point in the movie, the Witners are encouraged to get in touch with their own fears, and Peter utters a classic line: "I know what I fear the most. Having to work to make money." But work they do. The Witners pool their diminishing savings and borrow money to open a trendy boutique. One of their gurus (played by the droll voluptuary Patrick Bauchau) stands in the center of the empty storefront, tuning in to the space before advising them where to place the dressing room. Opening night is a great party, but soon the store is failing, and the few customers who do wander in are not much encouraged by the Witners' increasingly bizarre adaptation to the world of retail.

Tolkin gives us one richly detailed set piece after another, involving luncheons, openings, massages, telephone tag, psychic consultations, sex, heartfelt conversation, and pagan rituals led by a bald-headed woman who sees what others cannot see. Meanwhile, the material universe remains the one thing Peter and Katherine can really count on. This is the kind of movie where ancient Chinese sayings can find themselves in the same conversation with codependency. For the Witners, everything centers on themselves. "We were born when the economy was expanding," Peter says. But now that it's contracting, there's no room for people who consider their jobs primarily as a source of money to finance their "real" lives. Down and down they go, the Witners, auctioning their important paintings, losing their house and their cars, failing at business, all the time looking for spiritual fixes, as they wander through the New Age supermarket of southern California. It's like they have a disease named Overdrawn. One former friend of Katherine is frank about why she didn't invite them to her latest party: It makes people uncomfortable to be around failure.

The ending of the movie is perhaps a bit too manipulative. Maybe not. Tolkin is a director who is not afraid to push stories to their limits, and the final situation in which the Witners find themselves is one which was a real possibility right from the first. What's best about the movie is that Peter and Katherine are so smart. They understand everything that's happening, they're articulate, sardonic, witty, and savage about it, and yet there's not much they can do. "The reason you keep falling," one spiritual adviser explains to them, "is because there's no bottom." Thanks a whole lot.

New Jack City ★ ★ ★ ½
R, 97 m., 1991

Wesley Snipes (Nino Brown), Ice-T (Scotty Appleton), Chris Rock (Pookie), Judd Nelson (Nick Peretti), Mario Van Peebles (Detective Stone). Directed by Mario Van Peebles and produced by Doug McHenry and George Jackson. Screenplay by Thomas Lee Wright and Barry Michael Cooper.

There is a moment in *New Jack City* when Nino Brown, a character who has made millions by selling cocaine to poor blacks, relaxes in his suburban mansion. He has his own screening room and is viewing *Scarface*, the Al Pacino movie about a drug lord. Nino brags to his girlfriend that he will never make the mistakes the guy made in the movie—but as he stands in front of the screen, the image of Scarface's dead body is projected across his own.

In another movie, this moment might look like simple cinematic tricksmanship. In *New Jack City*, it has a special impact, because this ambitious film aims to be a similar record of the rise and fall of a big drug business. The movie was advertised (no doubt wisely) as a slam-bang action adventure, but in fact it's a serious, smart film with an impact that lingers after the lights go up.

The story involves the career of Nino (Wesley Snipes), a smart man with a certain genius for organization, as he ruthlessly takes over a Harlem apartment building and makes it the distribution headquarters for his cocaine business. He picks his lieutenants carefully, goes to elaborate lengths to enforce security, makes a lot of money, and seems invulnerable. He also surrounds himself with opulence and beauty. As played by Snipes, he has the threatening charisma of a great screen villain.

I've seen a lot of movies where the lifestyle of the drug lord looks seductive—until he's killed in the last reel, of course—but this isn't one of them. It's a character study of a bad man running an evil business, and by the end even his mistress is telling the cops she'll testify against him. The movie isn't a comic book that's been assembled out of the spare parts from other crime movies; it's an original, in-depth look at this world, written and directed with concern—apparently after a lot of research and inside information.

Against the clever Nino, the movie arrays some hard-edged street cops: Scotty (Ice-T) and Nick (Judd Nelson). They don't like each other, which is par for the formula, but the movie makes their rivalry intense and personal. Scotty is a genuinely interesting character, a cop who has been through cocaine himself and knows not only about addiction but about recovery. Nick is crazy and irresponsible, often on suspension, filled with hatred for drug dealers.

The buildup of the cop plot is done well, but is fairly standard stuff. What isn't standard is the payoff, as Nick rescues a young addict named Pookie (Chris Rock), who is so strung out on cocaine he can hardly lift his head. He gets the kid into a rehab center, lectures him on Narcotics Anonymous, and supports him through several NA meetings and a long recovery process. When Pookie is clean and sober, he wants to help the cop who helped him. Scotty has doubts, but reluctantly agrees to let Pookie infiltrate the crack house as an undercover spy.

This whole section of the movie takes on genuine urgency. That's partly because of the performances (Ice-T and Chris Rock are effortlessly authentic and convincing), but also because of the direction by Mario Van Peebles and the screenplay by Thomas Lee Wright and Barry Michael Cooper. There is no sense that this movie wants to play it safe, to coast, to be a retread of all the other movies about cops and drugs. And Van Peebles takes chances to give his film an authentic and gritty feel: He shoots on location, he uses a lot of street slang, he allows his cast to sound like their street characters and not like guys from a TV cop show. This is the movie where he comes of age as a director.

The movie's ending involves the usual chase and shoot-out material, but it's more effective than usual, maybe because by then we know the characters and care about them, so their actions are not simply moves from an arcade game. By the end of the film, we have a painful but true portrait of the impact of drugs on this segment of the black community: We see how they're sold, how they're used, how they destroy, what they do to people.

Truffaut once said it was impossible to make an antiwar movie, because the war sequences would inevitably be exciting and get the audience involved on one side or the other. It is almost as difficult to make an antidrug movie, since the lifestyle and money of the drug dealers looks like fun, at least until they're killed. This movie pulls off that tricky achievement. Nino, who looks at the dead body of Scarface and laughs, does not get the last laugh.

New Jersey Drive ★ ★ ★
R, 98 m., 1995

NEW

Sharron Corley (Jason Petty), Gabriel Casseus (Midget), Saul Stein (Roscoe), Gwen McGee (Renee Petty), Andre Moore (Ritchie), Donald Adeosun Faison (Tiny Dime), Conrad Meertins, Jr. (P-Nut), Devin Eggleston (Jamal). Directed by Nick Gomez and produced by Larry Meistrich and Bob Gosse. Screenplay by Gomez.

If the story in *New Jersey Drive* seems to drift, it's because the lives of its characters are aimless. They spend their days stealing cars, joyriding in them, and then selling, crashing, or abandoning them. Their lives have provided them with no other focus, and it is clear that sooner or later most of them are going to be in jail, or dead.

That is especially clear to Jason Petty (Sharron Corley), a fifteen-year-old who seems a little smarter and more prudent than the guys he runs with. He doesn't even particularly care about cars, but his best friend, Midget (Gabriel Casseus), lives for them, and so Jason goes along for the ride. He and his friends are still kids, but dangerous kids—and dangerous most of all to themselves, because what they're doing is stupid, and the cops have them beat on guns and strategy.

The cops in the movie are mostly white, and all of the other characters are black, so the stage is set for racial confrontation. But Nick Gomez, who wrote and directed the movie, isn't out to make all the cops into monsters and all the thieves into kids who are "really" victims. Both sides are a little more three-dimensional. He gives us a bad cop named Roscoe (Saul Stein), who takes revenge with an ambush when his own car is stolen, and who is under suspicion of murder during most of the movie. Roscoe and some other cops beat suspects and lay traps for them. On the other hand, the young thieves place lives in danger with their incredibly reckless driving. And you're really kind of asking for it when you steal a squad car.

Gomez is an interesting filmmaker. His first movie, *Laws of Gravity* (1991), was made for about $35,000 and did an uncanny job of portraying a group of two-bit white criminals, the kind who steal shampoo from a drugstore and then get into fights over whether they chose the right brand. That movie also went for texture and dialogue instead of plot: It was a study of how stupidity, boredom, and the lack of any kind of a vision or goal in life can lead to an existence that inexorably attracts trouble. It was essentially the story of how people end up getting shot dead outside taverns on Saturday night—how it's not an accident, but a fate they were hurtling toward.

With *New Jersey Drive*, Gomez has a more adequate budget (and Spike Lee as an executive producer), and he uses black characters instead of white ones, but basically his interest is the same: He wants to look at how an empty lifestyle leads to trouble. If the only choices you can imagine in life are stealing cars or standing around looking at other people driving stolen cars, how long you gonna stand around?

The movie is expert on how cars are stolen (it takes about ten seconds). It is also expert on how a smart and essentially prudent kid ends up inside a lot of stolen cars, and gets into a lot of trouble. Yes, the cops are out to get him—but at one point in the movie a neighborhood guy he hardly knows tries to shoot him dead because of an argument over nothing. "I just get tired of running," he finally says.

Gomez has a good ear for dialogue (we learn that "bouncing" is leaving), and a good feel for the way life is closing in on Jason, whose mother (Gwen McGee) tries hard to keep him in line but rarely knows where he is. She reasons with him and warns him of the danger he's in, but Jason can't hear her because all of his values are founded on approval by his peer group.

It's interesting the way *New Jersey Drive* doesn't really pull back for a wider view until the very end. Everyone in the movie—kids and cops—seems contained and absorbed by the lifestyles surrounding stolen vehicles. There's not racism in the cop's behavior as much as an us-against-them attitude, as if the cops and the thieves are fighting for control of the same turf. The message, which comes so late in the film it's hardly necessary, is that this is a war with no point, especially since you're going to lose.

New York, New York ★ ★ ★
PG, 163 m., 1977

Liza Minnelli (Francine Evans), Robert De Niro (Jimmy Doyle), Lionel Stander (Tony Harwell), Barry Primus (Paul Wilson), Mary Kay Place (Berenice), Georgie Auld (Frankie Harte). Directed by Martin Scorsese and produced by Irwin Winkler and Robert Chartoff. Screenplay by Earl Mac Rauch and Mardik Martin.

Martin Scorsese's *New York, New York* never pulls itself together into a coherent whole, but if we forgive the movie its confusions we're left with a good time. In other words: Abandon your expectations of an orderly plot, and you'll end up humming the title song. The movie's a vast, rambling, nostalgic expedition back into the big band era, and a celebration of the considerable talents of Liza Minnelli and Robert De Niro.

She plays a sweet kid with a big voice who starts as a band vocalist and ends up as a movie star. He plays an immature, aggres-

sive, very talented saxophone player whose social life centers around the saloon fights. A generation before Punk Rock, here's Punk Swing. They get married for reasons the movie never makes quite clear (oh, they're in love, all right, but he's so weird it's a miracle she'll have him). And then their marriage starts to disintegrate for reasons well hallowed in show-biz biographies: Her success, his insecurity, his drinking, their child.

De Niro comes on as certifiably loony from the start, and some of the movie's best scenes are counterpoint between his clowning and her rather touching acceptance of it. Maybe because he's really shy underneath, he likes to overact in social situations. He's egotistical, self-centered, inconsiderate, and all sorts of other things she should leave him because of, and there are times when the Minnelli character is so heroically patient that it's gotta be love. The movie doesn't really explore the nuances of their personalities, though; the characters are seen mostly by their surfaces, and they inhabit a cheerfully phony Hollywood back-lot New York. Scorsese, who knows how to shoot New York in California so it looks real (see *Mean Streets*), is going for a frankly movie feel with his sets and decors, and especially with his colors, which tend toward lurid rotogravure.

The look is right for the movie's musical scenes, and there are a lot of them: We start with a loving re-creation of V-J Day, with Tommy Dorsey's orchestra playing all the obligatory standards and De Niro trying with desperate zeal to pick up Minnelli. And then maybe half of the movie from then on will be music, mostly very good music (the movie's new songs deserve comparison with the old standards), and wonderfully performed. That Liza Minnelli has not been making an annual musical for the last decade is our loss; she's hauntingly good and so much more, well, human than Barbra Streisand.

It's a good thing the movie inhabits a familiar genre, though, because the fact that we've seen dozens of other musical biographies helps us fill in the gaps in this one. And there are a lot of them; the movie originally came in at something like four hours, and the cuts necessary to get it down to a more commercial length are responsible for a lot of confusion. The confusions, as I've suggested, can be forgiven because the movie has so many good things in it. And in the video version, to make amends, they've put back two musical numbers that weren't seen in the theater. But the ending is still puzzling. We've seen

De Niro, totally unable to deal with the fact that he's become a father, tearfully (and amusingly) end their marriage right there in the maternity ward. Six years pass, there are Liza's great final production numbers, and then they have a backstage reunion after her night of triumph. Great, we're thinking, we've been here before, we relish the obligatory romantic reunion scene in the dressing room. But, no, he leaves. Then he calls her from a pay phone: He can't stand the people she's with, but would she like to sneak out, meet by the stage door, eat some Chinese food, and talk about themselves? Sure, she would. He waits outside the door. She approaches it from inside, pauses, sees no one there, and goes back to her dressing room. End of movie (with a nicely evocative night street scene). But did she change her mind and *decide* not to go out and meet him, or did she expect him to be waiting *inside* the door—and assume the cocky S.O.B. had stood her up again? This particular confusion is hard to forgive.

So the movie's flawed. It's not Scorsese's best work, or De Niro's (there are scenes in which his personality quirks and bizarre behavior make him seem uncannily like his Travis Bickle in Scorsese's *Taxi Driver*). Liza Minnelli's musical numbers are wondrous, as I've said, but the movie doesn't provide her with a character as fully understood as *Cabaret* did. So I guess we go to *New York, New York* to enjoy the good parts, and spend just a moment regretting the absence of a whole.

New York Stories
PG, 130 m., 1989

Produced by Jack Rollins and Charles H. Joffe.

Life Lessons ★ ★ ★ ½

Nick Nolte (Lionel Dobie), Rosanna Arquette (Paulette), Patrick O'Neal (Philip Fowler). Directed by Martin Scorsese and produced by Barbara DeFina from a screenplay by Richard Price.

Life Without Zoe ★ ½

Heather McComb (Zoe), Talia Shire (Charlotte), Giancarlo Giannini (Claudio), Don Novello (Hector the Butler). Directed by Francis Coppola from a screenplay by himself and Sofia Coppola. Produced by Fred Roos and Fred Fuchs.

Oedipus Wrecks ★ ★

Woody Allen (Sheldon), Mae Questel (Mother), Mia Farrow (Lisa), Marvin Chatinover (Psychiatrist). Directed by Woody Allen and produced by Robert Greenhut. Screenplay by Allen.

New York Stories is an anthology—a gathering of short films by Martin Scorsese, Francis Coppola, and Woody Allen, all three taking New York City as a backdrop, although the Scorsese and Allen films could have been set in many big cities. Anthologies were popular in the 1940s *(Trio, Quartet)* and in the 1960s *(Boccacio 70, Yesterday, Today and Tomorrow),* but have fallen on hard times recently, perhaps because, in an age of megaproductions, the movie industry is not interested in short stories.

Of the three films, the only really successful one is *Life Lessons,* the Scorsese story of a middle-aged painter and his young, discontented girlfriend. The Coppola, an updated version of the story of Eloise, the little girl who lived in the Plaza Hotel, is surprisingly thin and unfocused. And the Allen, about a fifty-year-old man still dominated by his mother, starts well but then takes a wrong turn about halfway through.

Although Scorsese's film begins before the director is identified, there's not a moment's doubt whose work it is. His restless nature is obvious from the first shots; Nestor Almendros's camera moves almost unceasingly throughout the film, and most of the cuts are on movement, so that we rarely get the feeling that there is anything still and contented in the soul of his hero.

This is a man named Lionel Dobie (Nick Nolte), a large, shaggy painter who works in a loft, weaving back and forth in front of his canvas like a boxer, painting to very loud rock & roll. He uses a garbage-can lid as a palate, and there is a voluptuous scene in which the camera follows his brush back and forth from paint to canvas. Dobie lives with a twenty-two-year-old woman (Rosanna Arquette), whose bedroom is perched on a balcony below the ceiling. She wants to leave him, and in the long reaches of the night he looks up sometimes at her bedroom window like a middle-aged Romeo who has lost his Juliet.

Dobie is verbally clever but emotionally uncertain. In his attempts to keep the woman, he flatters her, makes promises of reform, explains that he can help her career, says he needs her. She has some canvasses of her own around the studio—anemic, unfocused, skeletal figures on muddy backgrounds—and she wants to know if she will ever be any good. But the one compromise Lionel Dobie

cannot bring himself to make is to lie about the quality of a painting.

The film moves easily in the New York art world of dealers and openings, seeing and being seen. The girl has a crush on a young "performance artist," and Dobie takes her to his show, which consists of bad stand-up comedy and flashing searchlights in an abandoned subway station. Dobie's gesture is intended to show he understands her, but in fact he has contempt for the performer ("You sing, you dance, you act—what's performance art?"). And the girl, uncertain what she wants but certain that she must escape his smothering possessiveness, drifts away.

Life Lessons seems the longest of these short films because it has the greatest density, the most to say. It is not about love. It is about how the girl is first attracted by Dobie's power, then grows restless because there is no role in it for her, except as cheerleader and sex trophy. It is about how Dobie really does have deep loneliness and need, but that it does not require *this* woman to satisfy them; he is so needy, any woman will do. The movie never steps wrong until the final scene, which Scorsese continues for just a few lines too many. Dobie sees another young woman at a party. She admires him. His eyes light up. The scene could have ended there; everything else is where we came in.

Francis Coppola's *Life Without Zoe,* the middle of the three stories, stars Heather McComb as Zoe, a precocious little rich girl who lives in the Sherry-Netherland Hotel and attends a private school where her classmates include not only the richest boy in the world, but several of the runners-up. Zoe's father (Giancarlo Giannini) is a famous classical flautist, and her mother (Talia Shire) is in the fashion industry. Neither one is at home much, and Zoe's best friend is the hotel butler (Don Novello, in the most engaging performance in the movie).

Coppola's film is set in the present day, but treats New York as if this were still the 1940s, and spoiled little girls in expensive dresses could move easily around the city under the benevolent eyes of doormen and cops. The plot involves some silliness about a missing diamond earring and a birthday party for the rich boy, and Zoe's indifferent mother ends up as her closest friend, although the movie never explains how or why. The entire sketch seems without purpose, unless it is to show off the elaborate costumes and settings; nothing holds together on an emotional or plot level.

Woody Allen's *Oedipus Wrecks* is his first pure comedy since *Broadway Danny Rose* (1984), which will please those who don't like his serious films, but it is also his weakest film of any sort. The movie stars Allen as a fifty-year-old banker whose tiny, inalienable mother (Mae Questel) still dominates his life, embarrassing him by showing his baby pictures to strangers and turning up unannounced at his office.

The banker is engaged to a divorcée with three children (Mia Farrow), and this his mother doesn't understand. One day, under circumstances it would be unfair to reveal, the mother disappears (this disappearance, I might add, is a true comic inspiration—the high point of the film). The banker is at first troubled by her disappearance, but later learns that he can live with it. It's not as if she got sick or died. She just . . . disappeared.

The movie goes wrong, I think, from the moment the mother returns (once again, I will not reveal the details). If you see the film, ask yourself this question: Knowing what you know of New York, could this mother reappear in this way and be received as the film shows her being received? Allen's mistake, I think, was to avoid dealing with the actual consequences that would result from such a startling manifestation. The last half of the film seems more odd and off-balance than funny. Perhaps it would have been better to build more satire into the mother's re-appearance, perhaps by having her come back like one of those miraculous holy images people are always seeing in screen doors, snowbanks, and the stains on their refrigerator doors.

Night on Earth ★ ★ ★
R, 128 m., 1992

Winona Ryder (Corky), Gena Rowlands (Victoria Snelling), Giancarlo Esposito (Yo-Yo), Armin Mueller-Stahl (Helmut Grokenberger), Rosie Perez (Angela). Written, directed, and produced by Jim Jarmusch.

Jim Jarmusch's *Night on Earth* assembles five moments in time, in taxicabs, in the middle of the night, in five of the world's cities. At the end we have learned no great lessons and arrived at no thrilling conclusions, but we have shared the community of the night, when people are unbuttoned and vulnerable—more ready to speak about what's really on their minds.

In Los Angeles, a casting agent tries to convince a tough young female cabbie that she might have a career in the movies. In New York, a black passenger becomes convinced that his driver, from East Germany, will never make it to Brooklyn without help. In Paris, a taxi driver from the Ivory Coast throws out some tipsy African diplomats and picks up a harsh, wounded blind girl. In Rome, a cabbie insists on describing his sexual peculiarities to the priest who is having a heart attack in the backseat. And in Helsinki, on the edge of a cold winter dawn, it is a toss-up whether the passengers or the drivers have a more tragic story to tell.

Jarmusch is a poet of the night. Much of *Night on Earth* creates the same kind of lonely, elegiac, romantic mood as *Mystery Train*, his film about wanderers in nighttime Memphis. Tom Waits's music helps to establish this mood, of cities that have been emptied of the waking. It's as if the minds and moods of these night people are affected by all of the dreams and nightmares that surround them.

Jarmusch is not interested in making each segment into a short story with an obvious construction. There are no zingers at the end. He's more concerned with character; with the relationship that forms, for example, between a tattooed, gum-chewing, chain-smoking young cab driver (Winona Ryder) and the elegant executive (Gena Rowlands) who wants to cast her for a movie. "I've got my life all mapped out," says the Ryder character, who hopes to work her way up to mechanic. "There must be lotsa girls who want to be in the movies. Not me." The movie doesn't insist that the cabbie is right or wrong; it simply reports her opinion.

As the film moves on from Los Angeles, Jarmusch creates a worldwide feeling of kinship; we will hear Spanish, German, French, Italian, Finnish, and even a little Latin. Only the venue remains the same: The inside of a taxi in the middle of the night. Many questions are not answered. What about the young blind woman in Paris, for example? Where is she coming from? Where is she going? Why does she want to walk alone on the edge of a canal? How was she so deeply wounded?

Her cab driver, an African, asks her shyly what sex is like for her—what it's like to make love with someone she can't see. He asks her what she thinks about colors. She is abrupt in her answers. She knows more about colors, and sex, than he ever will. Her entire organism is involved. "I can do everything you can do," she says. "Can you drive?" he asks. "Can you?" she shoots back.

The New York segment is the funniest. Armin Mueller-Stahl plays the East German, Giancarlo Esposito is the passenger who insists on driving himself, Rosie Perez (from *White Men Can't Jump*) is the shrill counterpoint voice from the backseat, and each man (named Helmut and Yo-Yo) thinks the other has a ludicrous name.

The segment in Rome is the least successful, although Robert Benyayin, a favorite of Jarmusch's, has fun with his zany monologue as he races through the empty streets before picking up the priest. The segment in Helsinki is the saddest, almost unbearably sad, as the driver hears what a bad day one of his passengers has had, and then tops him.

Jarmusch essentially empties the streets for his night riders. The cities are lonely and look cold; even in L.A., "it gets dark early in the winter." His characters seem divorced from the ordinary society of their cities; they're loners and floaters. We sense they have more in common with one another than with the daytime inhabitants of their cities. And their cabs, hurtling through the deserted streets, are like couriers on a mission to nowhere.

Nina Takes A Lover ★ ★

R, 106 m., 1995

NEW

Laura San Giacomo (Nina), Paul Rhys (Lover), Fisher Stevens (Paulie), Michael O'Keefe (Journalist), Cristi Conaway (Friend). Directed by Alan Jacobs and produced by Jacobs and Jane Hernandez. Screenplay by Jacobs.

Nina Takes a Lover is like a sophisticated, low-key yuppie version of those soft-core "couples tapes" in the romance section of the video store. It's not a sex movie, but it's not exactly anything else, either. And a lot of what's unique about it isn't apparent until the very end. You'll see what I mean.

The movie stars Laura San Giacomo, looking fetching and projecting a wary intelligence, as Nina, a San Francisco woman whose husband always seems to be away on business trips. One day she sees a guy on a park bench and makes a not exactly subtle bid for his attention, by crunching loudly on an apple. By day three they're sharing the apple, and by day four Eve has her Adam.

The guy's name is, uh, Lover. He's never called anything else. Played by Paul Rhys, he's a British photographer who finds Nina so attractive that when she doesn't turn up in the park one day, he tracks down the shoe store she owns, and they are soon becoming

good friends while perched on the stepladder in the stockroom. The customers are ignored a lot in this movie.

The heart of *Nina Takes a Lover* is their love affair, which can last, we gather, three weeks—until Nina's husband returns to town. Lover has a wife, but the details are vague, and her flat and his studio make convenient rendezvous points. The movie, written and directed by Alan Jacobs, depends on romantic clichés for many of its scenes, but there are a couple that generate authentic chemistry, including a prolonged dalliance during which Nina asks, at every pause, "What would make me a better lover?" The key to this scene is its honesty, and the ability of both San Giacomo and Rhys to play smart, and not simply portray dopey sexual hobbyists.

A counterplot of sorts takes place between Nina's friend, named Friend (Cristi Conaway), and an espresso shop owner named Paulie (Fisher Stevens). Friend likes Paulie and picks him up after he engages her in small talk ("There's a little of me in every cup"); this must be the first movie to recognize that as many pickups take place in coffee shops as bars these days. Friend invites Paulie to Nina's apartment, where he criticizes her coffee ("The key to making good espresso is tamping") and steals her underwear, leading to a later complication that leads nowhere.

Meanwhile, the affair between Nina and Lover takes on a certain urgency with the approaching end of their three-week idyll. Will they leave their spouses and stay with one another? Or will their dangerous games of truth-telling go too far?

Some viewers may foresee the ending of the movie. I did not, although it was clear enough in hindsight, and caused me to rethink what had gone before. It's original, all right, but I'm not sure it's the ending the film deserves. If the story had been less tricky and more what it seemed, the payoff might have been more moving. I was also underwhelmed by the device of having the participants tell all their story to a reporter (Michael O'Keefe) for the *San Francisco Chronicle*, although maybe that provided an excuse for some of the narration.

When the movie was over, I felt vaguely empty and cheated. I liked the acting, I admired a lot of the dialogue, and the movie looks good. Maybe I liked it enough to think these characters deserved more. As I said at the top, if you see it, you'll know what I mean.

9½ Weeks ★ ★ ★ ½
R, 113 m., 1985

Kim Basinger (Elizabeth), Mickey Rourke (John). Directed by Adrian Lyne and produced by Anthony Rufus Isaacs and Zalman King. Screenplay by Patricia Knop, King, and Sarah Kernochan.

9½ Weeks arrived in a shroud of mystery and scandal, already notorious as the most explicitly sexual big-budget movie since *Last Tango in Paris*. I went expecting erotic brinksmanship (how far *will* its famous stars go in the name of their art?) and came away surprised by how thoughtful the movie is, how clearly it sees exactly what really happens between its characters.

That's not to say the movie isn't sexy. I suppose a project of this sort depends crucially on the chemistry between its actors, and Kim Basinger and Mickey Rourke develop an erotic tension in this movie that is convincing, complicated, and sensual.

In the film, they play strangers who meet one day in a Chinese grocery store in Manhattan—Elizabeth, the smart, pretty assistant in a Soho art gallery, and John, the smiling, enigmatic currency trader. Their first meeting is crucial to the entire film, and it is a quiet masterpiece of implication. She waits by a counter. Senses someone is standing behind her. Turns, and meets his eyes. He smiles. She turns away. Is obviously surprised by how much power was in their exchange of glances. She hesitates, turns back, meets his eyes again, almost boldly, and then turns away again. And a few minutes later looks at him very curiously as he walks away along the street.

They meet again, of course, and that is the beginning of their relationship, as chronicled first in a best-selling novel and now in this movie by Adrian Lyne, the director of *Flashdance*. It is clear from the start that they aren't going to follow an orthodox pattern of courtship and romance. He offers her, quite boldly, an experimental erotic relationship. The first time he touches her seriously, it is to tie a blindfold around her eyes. They advance into arenas of lovemaking often described in the letters column in *Penthouse* magazine, and Elizabeth, for the most part, is prepared to let John call all the shots. He wants to be in control, and as she surrenders to him, she abandons herself into dreamy erotic absent-mindedness.

John is nothing if not inventive. In one scene, he blindfolds her and feeds her all kinds of strange foods, sweet and sour, different textures, each one a surprise to her lips, and it's astonishing the way the movie makes this visual scene so tactile. John calls her at unexpected times, orders her to unorthodox rendezvous, and as she follows his instructions they both seem to retreat more deeply into their obsession.

The movie contrasts their private life with the everyday world of her work: With the small talk and gossip of the art gallery, with a visit she pays to an old artist who lives like a hermit in the woods, with the intrigue as her ex-husband dates another woman in the gallery. This everyday material is an interesting strategy: It makes it clear that the private life of Elizabeth and John is a conscious game they're playing outside of the real world, and not just a fantasy in a movie where reality has been placed on hold.

Eventually, it is Elizabeth's hold on the real world that redeems the movie—makes it more than just a soft-core escapade—and sets up the thoughtful and surprising conclusion. So long as it is understood that she and John are engaged in a form of a game, and are conspiring in a sort of master-slave relationship for their mutual entertainment, Elizabeth has no serious objections. But as some of John's games grow more challenging to her own self-respect, she rebels. Does he want to engage her mind and body in an erotic sport, or does he really want to edge her closer to self-debasement? There are two times that Elizabeth draws the line, and a third time when she chooses her own independence and self-respect over what begins to look like his sickness.

That's what makes the movie fascinating: Not that it shows these two people entering a bizarre sexual relationship, but because it shows the woman deciding for herself what she will, and will not, agree to. At the end of *9½ Weeks*, there is an argument, not for sexual liberation, but for sexual responsibility.

I have a few problems with certain scenes in the film. There is a moment when John and Elizabeth run through the midnight streets of a dangerous area of Manhattan, chased by hostile people, and finally take refuge in a passageway where they make love in the rain. The scene owes more to improbable gymnastic events than to the actual capabilities of the human body.

There is another scene in which John and Elizabeth go into a harness shop, and John selects and purchases a whip, while the shop employees do double takes and Elizabeth stands wide-eyed, while he whooshes it through the air. There is no subsequent scene in which the whip is used. I do not argue that there should be; I only argue that in a movie like this, to buy a whip and not use it is like Camille coughing in the first reel and not dying in the last.

Any story like *9½ Weeks* risks becoming very ridiculous. The actors are taking a chance in appearing in it. Plots like this make audiences nervous, and if the movie doesn't walk a fine line between the plausible and the bizarre, it will only find the absurd. A lot of the success of *9½ Weeks* is because Rourke and Basinger made the characters and their relationship convincing.

Rourke's strategy is to never tell us too much. He cloaks himself in mystery, partly for her fascination, partly because his whole approach depends on his remaining a stranger. Basinger's strategy is equally effective, and more complicated. Physically, she looks sensuous and luscious; if you saw her in *Fool for Love*, you won't be surprised by the force of her appearance here. But if she'd just presented herself as the delectable object of all of these experiments, this would have been a modeling job, not an acting job.

In the early scenes, while she's at work in the gallery, she does a wonderful job of seeming distracted by this new relationship; her eyes cloud over and her attention strays. But one of the fascinations of the movie is the way her personality gradually emerges and finds strength, so that the ending of the film belongs completely to her.

The Hitcher is also about a sadomasochistic relationship between a stronger personality and a weaker one. Because it lacks the honesty to declare what it is really about, and because it romanticizes the cruel acts of its characters, it left me feeling only disgust and disquiet. *9½ Weeks* is not only a better film, but a more humanistic one, in which it is argued that sexual experimentation is one thing, but the real human personality is something else, something incomparably deeper and more valuable—and more erotic.

1984 ★ ★ ★ ½
R, 117 m., 1984

John Hurt (Winston Smith), Richard Burton (O'Brien), Suzanna Hamilton (Julia), Cyril Cusack (Charrington), Gregor Fisher (Parsons). Directed by Michael Radford and produced by Simon Perry. Screenplay by Radford.

George Orwell made no secret of the fact that his novel *1984* was not really about the future but about the very time he wrote it in, the bleak years after World War II when England shivered in poverty and hunger. In a novel where passion is depicted as a crime, the greatest passion is expressed, not for sex, but for contraband strawberry jam, coffee, and chocolate. What Orwell feared, when he wrote his novel in 1948, was that Hitlerism, Stalinism, centralism, and conformity would catch hold and turn the world into a totalitarian prison camp. It is hard, looking around the globe, to say that he was altogether wrong.

Michael Radford's brilliant film of Orwell's vision does a good job of finding that line between the "future" world of 1984 and the grim postwar world in which Orwell wrote. The movie's 1984 is like a year arrived at through a time warp, an alternative reality that looks constructed out of old radio tubes and smashed office furniture. There is not a single prop in this movie that you couldn't buy in a junkyard, and yet the visual result is uncanny: Orwell's hero, Winston Smith, lives in a world of grim and crushing inhumanity, of bombed factories, bug-infested bedrooms, and citizens desperate for the most simple pleasures.

The film opens with Smith rewriting history: His task is to change obsolete government documents so that they reflect current reality. He methodically scratches out old headlines, obliterates the photographs of newly made "unpersons," and attends mass rallies at which the worship of Big Brother alternates with numbing reports of the endless world war that is still going on somewhere, involving somebody. Into Smith's world comes a girl, Julia, who slips him a note of stunning force. The note says, "I love you." Smith and Julia become revolutionaries by making love, walking in the countryside, and eating strawberry jam. Then Smith is summoned to the office of O'Brien, a high official of the "inner party," who seems to be a revolutionary too, and gives him the banned writings of an enemy of the state.

This story is, of course, well known. *1984* must be one of the most widely read novels of our time. What is remarkable about the movie is how completely it satisfied my feelings about the book; the movie looks, feels, and almost tastes and smells like Orwell's bleak and angry vision. John Hurt, with his scrawny body and lined and weary face, makes the perfect Winston Smith; and Richard Burton, looking so old and weary in this

film that it is little wonder he died soon after finishing it, is the immensely cynical O'Brien, who feels close to people only while he is torturing them. Suzanna Hamilton is Julia, a fierce little war orphan whose rebellion is basically inspired by her hungers.

Radford's style in the movie is an interesting experiment. Like Chaplin in *Modern Times*, he uses passages of dialogue that are not meant to be understood—nonsense words and phrases, garbled as they are transmitted over Big Brother's primitive TV, and yet listened to no more or less urgently than the messages that say something. The 1954 film version of Orwell's novel turned it into a cautionary, simplistic science-fiction tale. This version penetrates much more deeply into the novel's heart of darkness.

Nine to Five ★ ★ ★
PG, 111 m., 1980

Jane Fonda (Judy Bernly), Lily Tomlin (Violet Newstead), Dolly Parton (Doralee Rhodes), Dabney Coleman (Franklin Hart, Jr.), Sterling Hayden (Tinsworthy), Elizabeth Wilson (Roz). Directed by Colin Higgins and produced by Bruce Gilbert. Screenplay by Higgins and Patricia Resnick.

Nine to Five is a good-hearted, simpleminded comedy that will win a place in film history, I suspect, primarily because it contains the movie debut of Dolly Parton. She is a natural-born movie star, a performer who holds our attention so easily that it's hard to believe it's her first film. The movie has some funny moments, and then it has some major ingredients that don't work, including some of its fantasy sequences. But then it also has Dolly Parton. And she contains so much energy, so much life and unstudied natural exuberance that watching her do anything in this movie is a pleasure. Because there have been so many Dolly Parton jokes (and doubtless will be so many more), I had better say that I'm not referring to her sex appeal or chest measurements. Indeed, she hardly seems to exist as a sexual being in the movie. She exists on another plane, as Monroe did: She is a center of life on the screen.

But excuse me for a moment while I regain my composure. *Nine to Five* itself is pleasant entertainment, and I liked it, despite its uneven qualities and a plot that's almost too preposterous for the material. The movie exists in the tradition of 1940s screwball comedies. It's about improbable events happening to people who are comic carica-

tures of their types, and, like those forties movies, it also has a dash of social commentary. The message has to do with women's liberation and, specifically, with the role of women in large corporate offices. Jane Fonda, Lily Tomlin, and Dolly Parton all work in the same office. Tomlin is the efficient office manager. Fonda is the newcomer, trying out her first job after a divorce. Parton is the boss's secretary, and everybody in the office thinks she's having an affair with the boss. So the other women won't speak to her.

The villain is the boss himself. Played by Dabney Coleman, he's a self-righteous prig with a great and sincere lust for Dolly Parton. She's having none of it. After the movie introduces a few social issues (day care, staggered work hours, equal pay, merit promotion), the movie develops into a bizarre plot to kidnap Coleman in an attempt to win equal rights. He winds up swinging from the ceiling of his bedroom, attached by wires to a garage-door opener. Serves him right, the M.C.P. This whole kidnapping sequence moves so far toward unrestrained farce that it damages the movie's marginally plausible opening scenes. But perhaps we don't really care. We learn right away that this is deliberately a lightweight film, despite its superstructure of social significance. And, making the necessary concessions, we simply enjoy it.

What I enjoyed most, as you have already guessed, was Dolly Parton. Is she an actress? Yes, definitely, I'd say, although I am not at all sure how wide a range of roles she might be able to play. She's perfect for this one—which was, of course, custom-made for her. But watch her in the scenes where she's not speaking, where the action is elsewhere. She's always in character, always reacting, always generating so much energy we expect her to fly apart. There's a scene on a hospital bench, for example, where Tomlin is convinced she's poisoned the boss, and Fonda is consoling her. Watch Dolly. She's bouncing in and out, irrepressibly. What is involved here is probably something other than "acting." It has to do with what Bernard Shaw called the "life force," that dynamo of energy that some people seem to possess so bountifully. Dolly Parton simply seems to be having a great time, ready to sweep everyone else up in her enthusiasm, her concern, her energy. It's some show.

Nobody's Fool ★ ★ ★ ½
R, 112 m., 1995
(See related Film Clip, p. 885.)

NEW

Paul Newman (Sully), Jessica Tandy (Miss Beryl), Bruce Willis (Carl Roebuck), Melanie Griffith (Toby Roebuck), Dylan Walsh (Peter), Pruitt Taylor Vince (Rub Squeers), Gene Saks (Wirf), Josef Sommer (Clive Peoples, Jr.). Directed by Robert Benton and produced by Scott Rudin and Arlene Donovan. Screenplay by Benton.

Sitting in the dark, watching Paul Newman's performance in *Nobody's Fool,* I jotted down the word "humility." It seemed to be the word that fit best. He is on-screen in virtually every scene of the movie, playing a sixty-year-old man named Sully who has spent most of his life drinking beer and avoiding responsibility and who now is thrown into daily contact with a son who doesn't trust him and a grandson who doesn't know him. Sully decides to change—or has change thrust upon him, which amounts to about the same thing.

I have been watching Paul Newman in movies all of my life. He is so much a part of the landscape of modern American film that sometimes he is almost invisible: He does what he does with simplicity and grace and a minimum of fuss, and so I wonder if people even realize what a fine actor he is. We remember the characters instead: Fast Eddie Felson, Hud, Butch Cassidy, the alcoholic lawyer in *The Verdict* . . .

In *Nobody's Fool,* Newman plays another heavy drinker, the kind of feckless free spirit you occasionally meet: a man who has never grown up, who despite his carefree disregard for the ordinary requirements of society, remains somehow so charming and innocent that people forgive him his sins. Sully has found an economic niche that supports his lifestyle. He does construction work for a local builder. He rents a room upstairs in the house of his eighth-grade teacher.

Of course, freedom has a price. He has long ago departed from his marriage, and his son has grown up almost a stranger to him. His "family," such as it is, consists of the regulars in a neighborhood bar: an old lawyer, a barmaid, a coworker who is mentally retarded. At one point in the film he talks about his ex-wife with his son, who says, "Mom's biggest fear is that your life was fun." To which he can honestly reply: "Tell her not to worry."

Sully works on and off for a local contrac-

tor named Carl Roebuck (Bruce Willis). And he has been conducting a sort of arm's-length flirtation with Carl's wife, Toby (Melanie Griffith). It involves a lot of wishful thinking on both sides. Sully's best friend is Rub Squeers (Pruitt Taylor Vince), a mildly retarded local handyman who helps out on jobs. One day the even pattern of Sully's life is interrupted when his son, Peter (Dylan Walsh), comes back into his life.

Peter is a college teacher. His marriage is breaking up, and he returns to his old hometown with one of his two children (his wife keeps the other, for the time being). He has no clear plan. Perhaps he will work with Sully on construction for a time. This does not sit well with Rub, who feels rejected, and quits so he can sit on his steps and sulk.

It is the middle of the winter in the small town, which seems almost uninhabited (director Robert Benton wisely focuses on the foreground characters in his story, and mostly avoids extras). Sully is engaged in a long-running duel with Roebuck, involving the theft and recapture of a snow blower. Otherwise, with work scarce, he hangs out in the local saloon with his drinking buddy Wirf (Gene Saks), who is also his lawyer in a seemingly endless string of cases involving workman's compensation and traffic violations.

In a sense, not much happens in *Nobody's Fool.* In another sense, great changes take place. Sully is a man who has put his truly important issues on hold for a very long time, while making a cause out of trivial issues. He will, for example, go to great lengths to steal the snow blower, or to score points off a dim-witted local policeman. But now, with Peter back, he finds that all the big issues of his early life—his marriage, his family—are staring him in the face again. Above all, he is challenged to be responsible to his young grandson as he never was to the boy's father.

The story, written by Benton from the novel by Richard Russo, unfolds according to its own logic. It has the patience to listen to silences. Above all, it benefits from the confidence of Newman's performance. He is not hammering the points home, not marching from one big scene to another, but simply living on the screen, and if the film's last shot is of Sully sound asleep, by then we understand why he has earned his rest.

The best moments in the film are based on relationships. Sully is quite fond, for example, of his landlady, old Miss Beryl (Jessica Tandy, in one of her last performances). He has a bantering relationship with Wirf, the

lawyer who seemingly has only this one fool for a client. His pipe dreams with Toby, which involve the two of them flying off to Hawaii, are important to him, because he is a romantic—and to her, because she trusts his goodness, and is fed up with her husband. And there are other characters, including a woman bartender and the local police chief, who help create the character of Sully by the way they respond to him.

At the center is Paul Newman. He is an exact contemporary of Marlon Brando, who is said to have invented modern film acting. Yes, and he probably did, stripping it of the mannerisms of the past and creating a hyper-charged realism. Like Brando, Newman studied the Method. Like Brando, Newman looked good in an undershirt. Unlike Brando, Newman went on to study life, and so while Brando broke through and then wandered aimlessly in inexplicable roles (especially since *The Godfather* twenty years ago), Newman continued to work on his craft. Having seen what he could put in, he went on to see what he could leave out. In *Nobody's Fool,* he has it just about figured out.

No Man's Land ★ ★ ★
R, 107 m., 1987

D.B. Sweeney (Benjy Taylor), Charlie Sheen (Ted Varrick), Lara Harris (Ann Varrick), Randy Quaid (Lieutenant Bracey), Bill Duke (Malcolm), R.D. Call (Frank Martin), Arlen Dean Snyder (Lieutenant Loos), M. Emmet Walsh (Captain Haun). Directed by Peter Werner and produced by Joseph Stern and Dick Wolf. Screenplay by Wolf.

The lieutenant wants the new patrolman to do undercover work for a couple of reasons: The kid knows all about Porsches, and he's so new on the force that he doesn't act like a cop. There are two things the lieutenant doesn't take into account: The kid really loves Porsches, and he doesn't think like a cop. By the end of *No Man's Land,* those two items have gotten everybody into a lot of trouble.

The young cop, played by D.B. Sweeney, is a fresh-faced rookie who spends all of his free time rebuilding old cars. The lieutenant wants him to infiltrate a Porsche dealership run by a rich kid (Charlie Sheen). The dealership seems to be a front for a car-theft and chop-shop operation, and the previous cop who infiltrated it has been murdered. The lieutenant is convinced that Sheen pulled the trigger.

Sweeney gets the job after he passes a couple of tests; he proves he knows all about repairing Porsches, and during a fast trip down the hairpin turns in the hills above Los Angeles, he proves to Sheen that he can drive one, too. You'd think that Sheen would be on the alert for another undercover cop, having just discovered one, but he trusts Sweeney and before long the two men have become friends.

It's a complicated friendship. Sweeney, from a working-class background, is impressed by Sheen's style and wealth, by the fancy discos and private clubs he hangs out in, and by the expensive cars he lets Sweeney drive. He is also impressed by Sheen's sister (Lara Harris), and after they fall in love, he becomes convinced that there's no way Sheen could have murdered a cop.

Randy Quaid, as the lieutenant, worries that his undercover guy is falling for a con job. "You're not going native, are you?" he asks. He's right; the kid hasn't been on the force long enough to develop good police instincts, and he falls under the influence of the charismatic Sheen. That leads him into a no man's land, halfway between the criminals and the law, and as he tries to do the right thing and juggle his conflicting loyalties, a tragic situation begins to develop.

No Man's Land is better than the average thriller because it is interested in these moral questions—in the way that money and beautiful women and fast cars look more exciting than good police work. The screenplay, by Dick Wolf, is subtle in the way it develops its temptations for Sweeney. He is seduced by Sheen's style and flash. And Sheen creates his character as a very complicated young man. True, he's rich, and doesn't need to steal and kill. But like the members of that Billionaire Boys' Club out in L.A., he is attracted to risk. And eventually he gets way in over his head.

The climax of the movie is fascinating in the way it uses a *really* corrupt cop to create a situation in which the two friends are faced with the consequences of their actions. By the end of the film, Sweeney and Sheen both possess all the facts, and in a way, they both understand all the facts. They think there must be a way they can work this thing out. But maybe there isn't. Like the *film noir* thrillers of the 1940s, *No Man's Land* is about ordinary people with flawed characters, who fall to temptation and pay for it.

The performances are very good, by Sheen (who played the narrator in *Platoon*), and

especially by Sweeney, who at first seems lost in his role, until we realize that's the character he's playing. The director is Peter Werner, who creates a real sense of materialistic subculture in which $60,000 automobiles are the proof of personal worth (offered a chance to steal another expensive import, Sheen scornfully says, "I only steal Porsches"). The movie has lots of scenes of Sheen and Sweeney stealing cars, and it dwells on the details of their crimes, and the reckless way they risk capture. This is a movie about how money and excitement generate a seduction that can change personal values; it's better and deeper than you might expect.

No Mercy ★ ★ ★
R, 107 m., 1986

Richard Gere (Eddie Jillette), Kim Basinger (Michel Duval), Jeroen Krabbe (Losado), George Dzundza (Stemkowski), Joe Basaraba (Collins), William Atherton (Deneneux). Directed by Richard Pearce and produced by D. Constantine Conte. Screenplay by Jim Carabatsos.

I could go two ways. I could say that *No Mercy* is a dumb formula thriller, or I could go the other way, and talk about the movie's style and energy. I think I'll go the second way, because whatever this movie is, it's not boring. It doesn't take shortcuts and it delivers on its grimy, breathless action sequences.

The plot has the footprints of other movies all over it: A cop's partner is murdered. A beautiful blonde is involved. The cop follows the blonde to New Orleans, and discovers she belongs to a sleazy vice boss. He tries to arrest her, they become handcuffed to one another, he loses the key, the villain's goons try to kill them, and they escape into the bayou country with nothing more than her torn blouse standing between them and the alligators. Meanwhile, they're falling in love. So what do you want for six bucks?

It's easy to make fun of the plot, but what's a plot for? In a thriller like *No Mercy*, it exists for one simple reason, to provide the characters with something to do while they attempt to make themselves interesting. And the really remarkable thing about this movie is the genuine chemistry that is generated, not only between Richard Gere and Kim Basinger, who are on either end of the handcuffs, but also between both of them and the movie's two principal bad guys: An effete rich Southerner played by William Ather-

ton, and a sadistic neo-Nazi vice lord, played by the Dutch actor Jeroen Krabbe.

Thrillers are often only as good as their villains. The Krabbe character seems seriously confused about time and place; I never understood what he was doing in the bayou with his Dr. Strangelove act, and I don't think his redneck followers did, either. But he makes a very satisfactory villain, especially after we learn that the Basinger character was heartlessly sold to him when she was only a child, and has been his slave ever since.

The Richard Gere character figures this out only belatedly. At first he thinks she's another one of this guy's hookers, used to lure his partner to his doom. But there is nothing like being handcuffed to Kim Basinger in the middle of a swamp to concentrate the mind, and eventually he can see that she is a victim. His realization comes at a delicately handled, understated turning point; he learns, almost by accident, that she has never learned to read, and we can see in his eyes that this touches him.

Gere is interesting all through the movie. As it happened, I'd just seen him again in *American Gigolo* a few days before I saw *No Mercy,* and so at first I was cross-referencing his standard mannerisms, like that way he struts across the screen. Then he sold me on the character, and I stopped thinking about Richard Gere and started caring about what was going to happen next.

With Basinger, that process was even easier. Although she fits all of the usual requirements for a movie sexpot, there is within her the genuine soul of an artist, and she throws herself into this role so convincingly that there is real pathos in her history. There is enough conviction in their relationship that it carries over even into the obligatory bloodbath that ends the film, and I found myself caring about them even while on another level I was running an inventory on the special effects.

The movie's climax, a shoot-out in a flophouse across the river from New Orleans, is an anthology of action clichés and a few fresher touches, such as the villain's ability to ram through walls. It's always a shame when a movie bothers to create interesting characters and then discards them in a high-tech climax. But up until then, *No Mercy* has been an above-average *film noir* and its creepy feeling for the backstreets of New Orleans and the sultry evil of its red-light suburbs got under my skin.

Norma Rae ★ ★ ★
PG, 114 m., 1979

Sally Field (Norma Rae), Ron Leibman (Reuben), Beau Bridges (Sonny), Pat Hingle (Father), Barbara Baxley (Mother), Gail Strickland (Bonnie). Directed by Martin Ritt and produced by Tamara Asseyev and Alex Rose. Screenplay by Irving Ravetch and Harriet Frank, Jr.

We're sometimes unfair to our movie actresses, and Sally Field's extraordinary performance in *Norma Rae* helps dramatize it. Most new actresses come up through television and its lame-brained sexist stereotyping. And most of the female TV stars have their moment of glory and then become unfairly categorized in our memories. Be honest: Didn't we think of Sally Field as the Flying Nun before this Oscar-winning performance?

For any actress, an opportunity to star on TV has to be great. But the opportunity to escape TV and appear in a challenging movie has to be a godsend. Jill Clayburgh got her chance with *An Unmarried Woman*. Here it's Sally Field's turn. And as the plain-spoken, spunky Southern textile worker in Martin Ritt's *Norma Rae,* she quite simply surpassed our expectations.

The performance is at the heart of the movie, because this isn't a film about labor unions or mill working conditions; it's about a woman of thirty-one learning to grow into her own potential.

She has a couple of kids—one out of wedlock, the other orphaned by a brawling father—and a few boyfriends here and there, and she's never taken much time to think about the value of her life. Like everyone in the town, she works in the textile mill, which has no union, pays minimum wages, has few benefits, and does little or nothing about brown lung disease.

Then a union organizer (Ron Leibman) from New York turns up in town. He finds precious little support, and almost none from Norma Rae; she's too absorbed in a whirlwind courtship and marriage with a local good ol' boy (Beau Bridges) who promises to bring his check home on Fridays and not chase around. She marries him, mostly out of affection and convenience.

But then the organizer begins to make a little sense to her. She grows less blind to the conditions at the mill. She gets angry when her father drops dead on an assembly line. She goes to a couple of meetings at which Leibman harangues his handful of recruits.

She becomes a recruit herself, a volunteer organizer, and eventually it's taking up all of her time.

Her new husband complains—but both she and the movie tend to ignore him. The marriage, indeed, seems almost peripheral to the movie's central story, which is about the way she slowly opens her eyes to herself and her world. Leibman puts it simply: "You're too smart to do what you're doing to yourself."

She eventually agrees. And we're sort of set up for a situation where Norma Rae and the organizer fall in love with each other. But they don't; the movie is steadfast in its determination to show Norma Rae growing because of her own thought and will—not under the influence of yet another sexual liaison.

That's what makes the movie so special. It has all sorts of plot problems (especially involving the marriage), and there are scenes that don't quite fit together, and moments that don't sound right. But the character of Norma Rae is so deeply seen and realized, and played by Sally Field with such conviction, that we accept her in spite of our doubts about other things. In the tenth year of her acting career, Sally Field has made a remarkable debut.

North
no stars
PG, 86 m., 1994

NEW

Elijah Wood (North), Jason Alexander (North's Dad), Julia Louis-Dreyfus (North's Mom), Marc Shaiman (Piano Player), Jussie Smollet (Adam), Taylor Fry (Zoe), Alana Austin (Sarah), Bruce Willis (Narrator). Directed by Rob Reiner and produced by Reiner and Alan Zweibel. Screenplay by Zweibel and Andrew Scheinman.

I have no idea why Rob Reiner, or anyone else, wanted to make this story into a movie, and close examination of the film itself is no help. *North* is one of the most unpleasant, contrived, artificial, cloying experiences I've had at the movies. To call it manipulative would be inaccurate; it has an ambition to manipulate, but fails.

The film stars Elijah Wood, who is a wonderful young actor (and if you don't believe me, watch his version of *The Adventures of Huck Finn*). Here he is stuck in a story that no actor, however wonderful, however young, should be punished with. He plays a kid with inattentive parents, who decides to go into

court, free himself of them, and go on a worldwide search for nicer parents.

This idea is deeply flawed. Children do not lightly separate from their parents—and certainly not on the evidence provided here, where the great parental sin is not paying attention to their kid at the dinner table. The parents (Jason Alexander and Julia Louis-Dreyfus) have provided little North with what looks like a million-dollar house in a Frank Capra neighborhood, all on dad's salary as a pants inspector. And, yes, I knew that is supposed to be a fantasy, but the pants-inspecting jokes are only the first of several truly awful episodes in this film.

North goes into court, where the judge is Alan Arkin, proving without the slightest shadow of a doubt that he should never, ever, appear again in public with any material even vaguely inspired by Groucho Marx. North's case hits the headlines, and since he is such an all-star overachiever, offers pour in from would-be parents all over the world, leading to an odyssey that takes him to Texas, Hawaii, Alaska, and elsewhere.

What is the point of the scenes with the auditioning parents? (The victimized actors range from Dan Aykroyd as a Texan to Kathy Bates as an Eskimo.) They are all seen as broad, desperate comic caricatures. They are not funny. They are not touching. There is no truth in them. They don't even work as parodies. There is an idiocy here that seems almost intentional, as if the filmmakers plotted to leave anything of interest or entertainment value out of these episodes.

North is followed on his travels by a mysterious character who appears in many guises. He is the Easter bunny, a cowboy, a beach bum, and a Federal Express driver who works in several product plugs. Funny, thinks North; this guy looks familiar. And so he is. All of the manifestations are played by Bruce Willis, who is not funny, or helpful, in any of them.

I hated this movie. Hated hated hated hated hated this movie. Hated it. Hated every simpering stupid vacant audience-insulting moment of it. Hated the sensibility that thought anyone would like it. Hated the implied insult to the audience by its belief that anyone would be entertained by it.

I hold it as an item of faith that Rob Reiner is a gifted filmmaker; among his credits are *This Is Spinal Tap, The Sure Thing, The Princess Bride, Stand by Me, When Harry Met Sally* and *Misery.* I list those titles as an incantation against this one. *North* is a bad film, but it is not by a bad filmmaker, and must represent some sort of lapse from which Reiner will recover—possibly sooner than I will.

North Dallas Forty ★ ★ ★ ½
R, 117 m., 1979

Nick Nolte (Phil Elliott), Mac Davis (Maxwell), Charles Durning (Coach Johnson), Dayle Haddon (Charlotte), Bo Svenson (Jo Bob), Steve Forrest (Conrad Hunter), G.D. Spradlin (B.A.), John Matuszak (O.W. Shaddock). Directed by Ted Kotcheff and produced by Frank Yablans. Screenplay by Yablans, Kotcheff, and Peter Gent.

North Dallas Forty is about pro football the way *Network* was about television. It's about the ways large and competitive institutions grind up people and spit them out. The guy who gets spit out in this movie is Phil Elliott, whose coach tells him he has the best hands in football, but a "bad attitude." Elliott is played by Nick Nolte in a muscular and compelling performance: After this movie, people began to take Nolte seriously.

The movie is not really a sports film. It doesn't share the patented formula of the routine sports movie, in which everything depends on the bravura final match, or game, or race. The film does lead up to an important game, yes—North Dallas plays Chicago for a divisional championship—but by then we're so involved in the human drama that we almost don't care who wins.

The drama revolves around the Nolte character and his best friend, a quarterback played by Mac Davis. They play football very hard and very well. Off the field, they regard the business of football with a profound cynicism, and they assault themselves with boozing, drugs, all-night partying, and bleak thoughts about what they will do when the day comes when they finally cannot play any longer.

Characters in the movie talk, at times, about words like "play" and "game." Is professional football a game? Not according to John Matuszak, in real life an Oakland Raider, who in one of the movie's most electrifying scenes has a shouting match with a coach in the locker room. At *some* point, he screams, football for the players must be more than a business—must be a cause, a spirit. In the fourth quarter, when you're cold and hurt and exhausted, the game plan means nothing, but your desire means everything.

The North Dallas management doesn't quite see it that way. The owners and coaches are detached, scientific, quite prepared to see a player shoot up pain-killers and run the risk of permanently crippling himself. Nolte himself is prepared to do that. But the management doesn't like him. He's a wiseass. He has the wrong attitude. He's childish. Their ideal football player would be someone like the fearsome Jo Bob Priddy (Bo Svenson), who is not in fact as good a player as Nolte, but has a magnificently simpleminded "correct" attitude.

The pressures put Nolte in a vise: He loves playing, he cannot envision himself not playing, he even understands the management attitude if only they knew it. But age and wear and cynicism are closing in, and he finds himself, half astonished, in love with a woman. She represents a kind of settling down that football has given him license to avoid, and the movie uses the relationship as a counterpoint to a week of training and a climactic game.

The football scenes are brutally real; the locker room scenes are totally authentic. There are obscenities and violence and pain, and a clear view of how the "adults"—the coaches—manipulate their strong, fearsome, and intimidated employees. "*We're* not the team," Nolte shouts at the owner. "*You're* the team. We're only the equipment—like the jockstraps and the helmets."

The movie is funny at times, especially during the lecture meetings where the players, openly contemptuous, listen to such dim inspirational insights as that, if God had really meant all men to be equal, he wouldn't have called us the human "race." God, for example, clearly meant for North Dallas to be more equal than Chicago.

Those kinds of details, and the scenes of the players' agents and the parties and the practice sessions, have a convincing documentary feel. Holding it all together, making it work, forcing us to get involved, is the Nolte character. It's a tribute to this movie that we would probably care as much about Nolte if he were *not* a football player. What he's facing is common in so many parts of American society; in so many of the things we do and the jobs we have, at some ultimate level we are just simply part of somebody else's business.

Nosferatu ★ ★ ★ ★
R, 63 m., 1979

Klaus Kinski (Count Dracula), Isabelle Adjani (Lucy Harker), Bruno Ganz (Jonathan Harker). Directed, produced, and written by Werner Herzog.

Set aside for the moment the details of the Dracula story. They've lost their meaning. They've been run through a thousand vampire movies too many. It's as easy these days to play Dracula as Santa Claus. The suit comes with the job. The kids sit on your knee and you ask them what they want and this year they want blood.

Consider instead Count Dracula. He bears a terrible cross but he lives in a wonderful sphere. He comes backed by music of the masters and dresses in red and black, the colors De Sade found finally the most restful. Dracula's shame as he exchanges intimacies and elegant courtesies with you is that tonight or sometime soon he will need to drink your blood. What an embarrassing thing to know about someone else.

Werner Herzog's *Nosferatu* concerns itself with such knowledge. *Nosferatu*. A word for *the vampire*. English permits "vampire movies"—but a "nosferatu movie?" Say "vampire" and your lips must grin. The other word looks like sucking lemons. Perfect. There is nothing pleasant about Herzog's vampire, and this isn't a movie for Creature Feature fans. There are movies for people who like to yuk it up and make barfing sounds, God love 'em, while Christopher Lee lets the blood dribble down his chin, but they're not the audience for *Nosferatu*. This movie isn't even scary. It's so slow it's meditative at times, but it is the most evocative series of images centered around the idea of the vampire that I have ever seen—since F.W. Murnau's *Nosferatu*, which was made in 1922.

That is why we're wise to forget the details of the basic Dracula story. *Nosferatu* doesn't pay them heed. It is about the mood and *style* of vampirism, about the terrible seductive pity of it all. There is a beautiful passage early in the film showing the hero, Jonathan Harker, traveling from his home village to the castle of Dracula. The count has summoned him because he is considering the purchase of another home. Harker makes the journey by horse path. He enters into a high mountain pass filled with tenuous cloud layers that drift by a little too fast, as if God were sucking in his breath. The music is *not* your standard creepy Loony Tunes, but a fierce melody of exhilaration and dread. Deeper and deeper rides Harker into the cold gray flint of the peaks. Some will say this passage goes on too long and that nothing happens during it. I wish the whole movie were this empty.

Before long, we are regarding the count himself. He is played totally without ego by Klaus Kinski. The *count* has a monstrous ego, of course—it is Kinski who has none. There is never a moment when we sense this actor enjoying what a fine juicy cornpone role he has, with fangs and long sharp fingernails and a cape to swirl. No, Kinski has grown far too old inside to play Dracula like that: He makes his body and gaunt skull transparent, so the role can flicker through.

Sit through *Nosferatu* twice, or three times. Cleanse yourself of the expectation that things will happen. Get with the flow. This movie works like an LP record: You can't love the music until you've heard the words so often they're sounds. It's in German with English subtitles. It would be just fine with no subtitles, dubbed into an unknown tongue. The need to know what Dracula is saying at any given moment is a bourgeois affectation. Dracula is *always* saying, "I am speaking with you now as a meaningless courtesy in preface to the unspeakable event that we both know is going to take place between us sooner rather than later."

Not Without My Daughter ★ ★ ★
PG-13, 116 m., 1990

Sally Field (Betty), Alfred Molina (Moody), Sheila Rosenthal (Mahtob), Roshan Seth (Houssein), Sarah Badel (Nicole), Mony Rey (Ameh Bozorg), Georges Corraface (Mohsen). Directed by Brian Gilbert and produced by Harry J. Ufland and Mary Jane Ufland. Screenplay by David W. Rintels.

Here is a perplexing and frustrating film, which works with great skill to involve our emotions, while at the same time making moral and racial assertions that are deeply troubling. On one level, it tells a story that almost anyone can identify with—a mother deprived of her child and her freedom by the rigid rules of an unbending religion. On another level, it applies a harsh assortment of negative qualities to a group of people we found ourselves at war with.

The film stars Sally Field as Betty, an ordinary American mom in all respects but one—she has married an Iranian who is a doctor at the local hospital. They have a young daughter and a settled middle-class life, but beneath the surface all is not well. Her husband, Moody (Alfred Molina) suffers from racist taunts at the hospital, and grows homesick when he telephones to his family back in Iran. Finally, he suggests a visit to his homeland.

Betty is not so sure. She reads about unrest in Iran. She is not sure of her welcome. Moody promises her—on the Koran—that she has nothing to fear. But soon after they land in Iran, she is plunged into a frightening and alien world. As a woman, she is an occasion of sin. It is forbidden for her to reveal so much as a lock of hair in public. The other members of her husband's family make little effort to communicate with her—other than to give orders or repeat religious truths. They are interested in her only as the mother of her husband's child; her role, it appears, is to be the infidel mother of an Islamic daughter.

At first Moody is supportive. But as the time draws near for their return to America, he undergoes a personality change, becoming angry and short with her, and finally admitting that they are not going back at all. He has lost his job at the hospital, and plans to stay in Iran. And as for Betty and their daughter? Why, they will stay, too. She is his wife and must obey him.

The movie then plunges us into a world of Islamic fundamentalism, which it depicts in shrill terms as one of men who beat their wives, of a religion that honors women by depriving them of what in the West would be considered basic human rights, of women who are willing or unwilling captives of their men. No attempt is made—deliberately, I assume—to explain the Muslim point of view, except in rigid sets of commands and rote statements. No Muslim character is painted in a favorable light; the local people who help the heroine are dissidents or outlaws. We are not even permitted to learn what they say, because the film declines to use subtitles to translate the considerable spoken dialogue of the Iranian characters. All is seen from the point of view of Betty, who is shown surrounded by harsh, cruel religious fanatics.

Islam is not a religion that reflects Western beliefs about human dignity. It seems to have little place for the concept of individual freedom—especially as it applies to women. The chilling death sentence pronounced against Salman Rushdie is an example of its regard for free speech, and Rushdie's attempts at compromise, as the price of buying his life, are understandable even while they are inutterably depressing. Yet, at the same time, we should stubbornly believe in a concept of fair play—even fair play for those who might not play fair with us. And *Not Without My Daughter* does not play fair with its Muslim characters. If a movie of such a vitriolic and spiteful nature were to be made in America about any other ethnic group, it would be denounced as racist and prejudiced. It is no excuse that some Muslims are our enemies. In a world that does not reflect our ideals, we must hold to them for ourselves.

Yet I recommend that the film be seen for two reasons. One reason is because of the undeniable dramatic strength of its structure and performances; it is impossible not to identify with this mother and her daughter, and Field is very effective as a brave, resourceful woman who is determined to free herself and her daughter from involuntary captivity.

The second reason is harder to explain. I think the movie should be seen because it is an invitation to thought. It can be viewed as simply a one-sided and bitter attack. But it also provides an opportunity for testing our own prejudices, our own sense of fairness. Must all movies be taken on their own terms, or do we retain the strength of mind to view them critically—to remain alert to prejudice and single-minded vitriol?

It is curious, in a way, that this movie is set in Iran. At the time its events take place—and at the time the film was made—Iran was our enemy and Iraq was our ally. Now times have changed, and Saddam Hussein, our so recent friend, is our enemy. Think of the box office possibilities if the movie had been set in Iraq! That would be right in keeping with the long sad human history of portraying enemies as godless, inhuman devils. But every soldier is somebody's child, and some, no doubt, hope to have children of their own, and movies fueled by hate are not part of the solution.

No Way Out ★ ★ ★ ★
R, 114 m., 1987

Kevin Costner (Tom Farrell), Gene Hackman (David Brice), Sean Young (Susan Atwell), Will Patton (Scott Pritchard), Howard Duff (Senator Duvall), George Dzundza (Sam Hesselman), Jason Bernard (Major Donovan), Iman (Nina Beka). Directed by Roger Donaldson and produced by Laura Ziskin and Robert Garland. Screenplay by Garland.

No Way Out is one of those thrillers like *Jagged Edge*, where the plot gives us a great deal of information, but the more we know, the less we understand. It's like a terrifying jigsaw puzzle. And because the story is so tightly wound and the performances are so good, I found myself really caring about the characters. That's the test of a good thriller: When you stop thinking about the mechanics of the plot and start caring about the people. The movie begins with the same basic situation that was always one of Alfred Hitchcock's favorites: An innocent man stands wrongly accused of a crime, and all the evidence seems to point right back to him. In *No Way Out*, there are a couple of neat twists. One is when the innocent man is placed in charge of the investigation of the crime.

The man is played by Kevin Costner in a performance I found a lot more complex and interesting than his work in *The Untouchables*. He plays a career Navy man who is assigned to the personal staff of the secretary of defense (Gene Hackman). Hackman and his devoted assistant (Will Patton) want Costner to handle some sensitive assignments for them involving the secretary's pet defense projects.

All of those details are handled in the first few minutes, and after the movie springs a genuine erotic surprise. Costner goes to a diplomatic reception to meet Hackman. There is a beautiful young woman at the party. Their eyes meet. The chemistry is right. They leave almost immediately, and the woman throws herself at Costner in hungry passion.

They have an affair. The woman (Sean Young) is friendly, but mysterious, and eventually Costner finds out why: She is also Hackman's mistress. And that leads to the night when Hackman attacks her in a jealous rage, and she dies. Because Costner saw Hackman going into her apartment as he was leaving, he knows who committed the crime. But there are reasons why he cannot say what he knows. And then Patton determines to mastermind a cover-up and enlists Costner.

At about this point you may be thinking I have revealed too much of the plot. I haven't. *No Way Out* is truly labyrinthine and ingenious. The director, Roger Donaldson, sometimes uses two or three suspense-building devices at the same time, such as when a search of the Pentagon coincides with Costner's attempt to obtain evidence against Hackman, and the slow progress of a computer that may, or may not, enhance a photograph that could hang Costner.

A lot of what goes on in the film is psychological and not merely plot-driven. For example, there's the interesting performance of Patton, who says early on that he would willingly sacrifice his life for Hackman and who is later revealed to have more than one reason for his devotion. There's another good performance by George Dzundza *(The Deer Hunter)* as the wheelchair-bound Pentagon computer expert, trying to be a nice guy without ever really understanding what he's in the middle of.

The movie contains some of the ingredients I have declared myself tired of in recent thrillers, including a couple of chases. But here the chases do not exist simply on their own accord; they grow out of the logic of the plot. And as the plot moves on it grows more and more complex, until a final twist that some people will think is simply gratuitous but that does fit in with the overall logic.

Movies such as this are very hard to make. For proof, look at the wreckage of dozens of unsuccessful thrillers every year. *No Way Out* is a superior example of the genre, a film in which a simple situation grows more and more complex until it turns into a nightmare not only for the hero but also for everyone associated with him. At the same time, it respects the audience's intelligence, gives us a great deal of information, trusts us to put it together, and makes the intellectual analysis of the situation one of the movie's great pleasures.

O

The Object of Beauty ★ ★ ★ ½
R, 97 m., 1991

John Malkovich (Jake), Andie MacDowell (Tina), Lolita Davidovich (Joan), Rudi Davies (Jenny), Joss Ackland (Mr. Mercer), Peter Riegert (Larry). Directed by Michael Lindsay-Hogg and produced by Jon S. Denny. Screenplay by Lindsay-Hogg.

Hiding from the hotel manager, slinking through the lobby like a hunted criminal, this is a man with a problem. His name is Jake and he lives in that world where money is made with money, but right now there is no money in his world. He put most of his funds into a cocoa deal in some Third World country where a revolution has stranded his cocoa on the docks and himself in a London hotel where he owes thousands of pounds and has not the slightest prospect of being able to pay.

Jake is played by John Malkovich as a man who maintains a cool, detached façade, no matter what. He lives with Tina (Andie Mac-Dowell), an elegant beauty who once, briefly, was a model, and has now cast her lot with Jake, although they "are not, in the classic sense, man and wife," as they are careful to explain. For that matter, they do not, in the classic sense, live anywhere in particular; life for them has been an existence of drifting from one expensive hotel and city to another, while Jake does his business on the phone.

Now it has come down to this: Presenting an American Express card in a restaurant and then making the sign of the cross while the cashier checks the credit. Or taking the stairs rather than the elevator to avoid the hotel manager and his unctuous security chief. They literally do not have a dime. They want to be rich and famous, but in this hotel they are famous for not being rich. They have one asset to their name: A small

bronze head, sculpted by Henry Moore, that might be worth $50,000 or so. It is Tina's, given to her by her first husband (to whom she is still, in the classic sense, married).

Working in the hotel is a maid (Rudi Davies), who is deaf, and who lives in a basement hovel with her young brother, a loutish punk. She falls in love with the Moore figure because it speaks to her. One day, she slips it into her pocket. Meanwhile, in desperation, Jake has suggested to Tina that they sell the Moore to raise cash. "But I love my little head!" she pouts, and so they decide on an insurance scam to "steal" it and collect the money—only to discover that someone has gotten in ahead of them and already stolen it.

The Object of Beauty, which has been quietly, intelligently written and directed by Michael Lindsay-Hogg, is only about these financial problems on a surface level. What's underneath is really the ability of these people to learn to love and trust one another. The movie is too cool and witty to descend to obviously sloppy emotion, but in Jake and Tina we see two hedonistic drifters who have finally been forced to take stock of who they really are, separately and as a couple.

Jake is played by Malkovich as a man who would really rather die than be embarrassed in public, and who places so much trust in the way money protects him that when he runs out, he gallantly offers Tina her freedom. He can understand why she would want him for better but not for worse. And he would rather set her free than ask her to stand by him. We are given a brief but completely revealing glimpse into his character during a brief telephone call he makes to his parents—an alcoholic mother and a father he still calls "sir"—and in an instant we understand that he has been denied both affection and respect by his parents, and would do anything rather than admit inadequacy.

By the end of the film, the plot has been worked out to everyone's satisfaction, but the plot isn't really that important. What is important are the ways that people love one another—not only Jake and Tina, but the maid and her brother, and even the hotel manager and the security chief. And we meet two other important characters: Tina's first husband (Peter Riegert), who does not seem to have suffered very much upon losing her, and her best friend Joan (Lolita Davidovich), whom she should not, in the classic sense, trust.

Like a John Cheever short story or a sociological snapshot by Tom Wolfe, *The Object of Beauty* is about people who have been so defined by their lifestyles that without those styles they scarcely exist. Jake and Tina are not really married, do not really live anywhere, do not really work at anything. This whole episode is a blessing in disguise for them: They are, at last, really something, even if it is only broke.

An Officer and a Gentleman ★ ★ ★ ★
R, 126 m., 1982

Richard Gere (Zack Mayo), Debra Winger (Paula Pokrifki), Lou Gossett, Jr. (Sergeant Foley), David Keith (Sid Worley), Robert Loggia (Byron Mayo), Lisa Blount (Lynette), Lisa Eilbacher (Casey Seeger). Directed by Taylor Hackford and produced by Martin Elfand. Screenplay by Douglas Day Stewart.

An Officer and a Gentleman is the best movie about love that I've seen in a long time. Maybe that's because it's not about "love" as a Hollywood concept, but about love as growth, as learning to accept other people for who and what they are. There's romance in this movie, all right, and some unusually erotic sex, but what makes the film so special is that the sex and everything else is presented within the context of its characters finding out who they are, what they stand for—and what they will *not* stand for.

The movie takes place in and around a Naval Aviation Officer Candidate School in Washington state. Every thirteen weeks, a new group of young men and women come here to see if they can survive a grueling session of physical and academic training. If they pass, they graduate to flight school. About half fail. Across Puget Sound, the local young women hope for a chance to meet an eligible future officer. They dream of becoming officers' wives, and in some of their families, we learn, this dream has persisted for two generations.

After the first month of training, there is a Regimental Ball. The women turn out with hope in their hearts and are sized up by the candidates. A man and a woman (Richard Gere and Debra Winger) pair off. We know more about them than they know about one another. He is a loner and a loser, whose mother died when he was young and whose father is a drunk. She is the daughter of an officer candidate who loved and left her mother twenty years before. They dance, they talk, they begin to date, they fall in love. She would like to marry him, but she refuses to do what the other local girls are willing to do—get pregnant or fake pregnancy to trap a future officer. For his part, the man is afraid of commitment, afraid of love, incapable of admitting that he cares for someone. All he wants is a nice, simple affair, and a clean break at the end of OCS.

This love story is told in counterpoint with others. There's the parallel affair between another candidate and another local girl. She *is* willing to trap her man. His problem is, he really loves her. He's under the thumb of his family, but he's willing to do the right thing, if she'll give him the chance.

All of the off-base romances are backdrops for the main event, which is the training program. The candidates are under the supervision of a tough drill sergeant (Lou Gossett, Jr.) who has seen them come and seen them go and is absolutely uncompromising in his standards. There's a love-hate relationship between the sergeant and his trainees, especially the rebellious, resentful Gere. And Gossett does such a fine job of fine-tuning the line between his professional standards and his personal emotions that the performance deserves its Academy Award.

The movie's method is essentially to follow its characters through the thirteen weeks,

watching them as they change and grow. That does wonders for the love stories, because by the end of the film we know these people well enough to care about their decisions and to have an opinion about what they should do. In the case of Gere and Winger, the romance is absolutely absorbing because it's so true to life, right down to the pride that causes these two to pretend they don't care for each other as much as they really do. When it looks as if Gere is going to throw it all away—is going to turn his back on a good woman who loves him, just because he's too insecure to deal with her love—the movie isn't just playing with emotions, it's being very perceptive about human behavior.

But maybe I'm being too analytical about why *An Officer and a Gentleman* is so good. This is a wonderful movie precisely because it's so willing to deal with matters of the heart. Love stories are among the rarest of movies these days (and when we finally get one, it's likely to involve an extra-terrestrial). Maybe they're rare because writers and filmmakers no longer believe they understand what goes on between modern men and women. *An Officer and a Gentleman* takes chances, takes the time to know and develop its characters, and by the time this movie's wonderful last scene comes along, we know exactly what's happening, and why, and it makes us very happy.

Of Mice and Men ★ ★ ★ ½
PG-13, 110 m., 1992

John Malkovich (Lennie), Gary Sinise (George), Ray Walston (Candy), Casey Siemaszko (Curley), Sherilyn Fenn (Curley's Wife), John Terry (Slim). Directed by Gary Sinise and produced by Russ Smith and Sinise. Screenplay by Horton Foote.

"And will there be rabbits, George?"

"Yeah, Lennie. There'll be rabbits."

There is a certain curse attached to the most familiar lines in literature. Because we know them so well, we tend to smile when we encounter them, and they can break the reality of the story they're trying to tell. What stage Hamlet has not despaired of getting through "To be, or not to be?" in one piece?

In John Steinbeck's novel *Of Mice and Men*, made into an enduringly popular 1939 movie, the lines about the rabbits have become emblems for the whole relationship between George and Lennie—the quiet-spoken farm laborer and the sweet, retarded cousin he has taken under his arm. I would

not have thought I could believe the line about the rabbits one more time, but this new version made me do it, as Lennie asks about the farm they'll own one day, and George says yes, it will be just as they've imagined it.

Lennie is played by John Malkovich and George is Gary Sinise, who also directed this film, using an adaptation by Horton Foote. The most sincere compliment I can pay them is to say that all of them—writer and actors—have taken every unnecessary gesture, every possible gratuitous note, out of these characters. The story is as pure and lean as the original fable that formed in Steinbeck's mind. And because they don't try to do anything fancy—don't try to make it anything other than exactly what it is—they have a quiet triumph.

The time is the Great Depression. Men ride the rails, living in hobo camps, looking for a day's work. Two of them are George and Lennie, who together might make a perfect person: Lennie with his great strength and simplicity, George with his intelligence and cunning. George does the thinking for them, and Lennie does a lot of the work. In the harvest season, they find themselves working on a place with a lot of other guys, and a foreman named Curley, and Curley's wife (who is never named by Steinbeck, nor here, either).

Curley's wife is sexy, and she knows it. Played by Sherilyn Fenn, she enjoys her little starring role on the farm—likes to know the eyes of the men follow her as she walks across the yard, just as in Paris a woman walks a little differently past a café. Curley (Casey Siemaszko), a sadistic brute, does not enjoy the show so much.

Lennie does not quite understand all of the implications of the situation, but he knows that he feels good when Curley's wife asks him to stroke her soft brown hair. George warns him to stay clear—she's trouble. But Curley's wife makes that hard. She enjoys teasing the dim-witted giant, as if he were a dog tied up just out of reach. One day she handles him wrong, and although he is only trying to be nice to her, he gets confused and frightened and doesn't know his own strength. And then the men and the hounds are after him, and George won't be able to settle this one with his quick thinking.

What is this story really about? There are a lot of possibilities, from the Lennie as Saint theory, to the feminist deconstruction that has no doubt been performed more lately.

The highest praise I can give the filmmakers is that none of them seem to have any theories at all. They give us characters, a milieu, some events. The central tragedy of the story is that these two men have formed a friendship that works—they have a synergy in which each takes according to his needs and gives according to his abilities—and when George isn't there Lennie gets into trouble through no fault of his own, and then the world slaps them down.

Sinise says *Of Mice and Men* was his favorite novel as a young man. It led him to a love of Steinbeck, and he eventually played Tom Joad on stage in the famous Steppenwolf production of *The Grapes of Wrath.* Then he directed his first movie, *Miles From Home,* about two brothers who grow up on a farm in Iowa. One is more sober and responsible, the other more reckless. They can't find the balance, and get into a lot of trouble. The buried theme is similar to *Of Mice and Men:* Two men together form a workable partnership, but neither is complete separately. You can sense how important this material is to Sinise. So important that in this movie he doesn't fool around with it; the story itself says all he wants to say.

Oh, God! ★ ★ ★ ½
PG, 104 m., 1977

George Burns (God), John Denver (Jerry Landers), Teri Garr (Bonnie Landers), Donald Pleasence (Dr. Harmon), Ralph Bellamy (Sam Raven), William Daniels (George Summers), Paul Sorvino (Reverend Williams), Dinah Shore (Dinah). Directed by Carl Reiner and produced by Jerry Weintraub. Screenplay by Larry Gelbart.

Carl Reiner's *Oh, God!* is a treasure of a movie: A sly, civilized, quietly funny speculation on what might happen if God endeavored to present himself in the flesh yet once again to forgetful Man. He comes back this time looking and talking a great deal like George Burns, an improvement on his earlier cinematic incarnations. And as his contact on Earth, he selects a common man—John Denver, to the manner born.

Part of the movie's charm is in the way it surprises us by treating its subject matter with affection and respect. I went expecting blasphemous jokes and cheap shots at religion, since serious subjects so rarely make it into comedies these days except as targets. But no: *Oh, God!* is lighthearted, satirical,

and humorous and (that rarest of qualities) in good taste.

It also makes you feel good, in the way some of the Frank Capra comedies did. The John Denver character becomes a contemporary version of Mr. Smith, John Doe, Mr. Deeds, and those other Capra heroes who prevailed because they were decent, honest, and true. Once Denver gets over his initial astonishment at being selected as God's spokesman, he makes a good job of it, justifying God's faith in the common man, which he, after all, put into production.

God is careful, throughout the movie, to make his reasoning clear. Why did he pick Denver? "You're like the lady who's the millionth person across the bridge and gets to meet the governor. You're better than some people, and worse than others, but you came across the bridge at the right time." The message God wants to remind his creatures of is a simple one: That things *can* turn out all right, although they will not necessarily or automatically do so. That we have everything here on Earth that we need to bring a happy ending to our story. And that we should try being a little nicer to one another.

Carl Reiner's credits as a director include the immortal *Where's Poppa?* (1970), a masterpiece of comic bad taste. So there was reason to anticipate a showdown again this time between the sacred and the profane. As an idea, indeed, *Oh, God!* must have seemed almost impossibly supplied with ways to go wrong. But it doesn't. Reiner is superb at establishing the right tone for this very difficult material, and the casting of George Burns as God is an inspiration.

"I took this form," God explains, "because if I showed myself to you as I am, you wouldn't be able to comprehend me." He chose his form well. God, as Burns, recalls some of his miracles (the 1969 Mets), some of his mistakes (tobacco, giraffes, and avocados—"I made the seeds too big"), and some common misconceptions about himself ("To tell you the truth, I spent the first five days thinking and created everything on the sixth"). And he has such quiet authority, such wonderfully understated humor, such presence. John Denver, too, is well-cast: Sincere, believable, with that face so open and goofy. They work with Reiner, and with Larry Gelbart's screenplay, to create a movie that takes a really risky comic gamble, and wins.

Oh, God! You Devil ★ ★ ★ ½
PG, 96 m., 1984

George Burns (God and Harry), Ted Wass (Bobby Shelton), Roxanne Hart (Wendy), Ron Silver (Gary). Directed by Paul Bogart and produced by Robert M. Sherman. Screenplay by Andrew Bergman.

The *God* pictures are ideal for sequels; after all, the leading character has no beginning and no end. But sequels have a way of ripping off profitable ideas without anything new to say. They grow so dreary and pale that we forget why we liked the original picture in the first place. That's why *Oh, God! You Devil* is such a delight. Here is George Burns's third God movie, and not only does it have as much humor, warmth, and good cheer as the first—it actually has a better story. The story involves a young man who was placed under God's protection when he was a little baby; he had a fever, and his father's prayers were answered. The kid has grown up into an unsuccessful musician, and one day while he's performing at some dumb wedding reception, he meets an unusual guest, one Harry O. Tophet, who is, of course, the devil. Harry makes the kid an offer he should, but does not, refuse, and before long the kid is the top rock superstar in the world.

Of course, there's a catch. He has to assume the identity of another musician—an existing superstar whose deal with the devil has just run out. And worst of all, he has to remember his previous life, including the wife he loved and the child they were expecting. This whole balancing act between success and loss is unexpectedly touching, and gives the movie a genuine human heart.

Meanwhile, the devil basks in his acquisition, and then God gets into the act when the rock star prays to be released from his deal with the devil.

It's here that we get what we've been waiting for all through the picture, the scenes where God and the devil, both played by George Burns, appear on the same screen. Dual appearances through trick photography are, of course, an old Hollywood standby, but what's fun here is the way Burns plays scenes with himself: This casting was made in heaven.

Oh, God! You Devil has two different kinds of successful elements. The Burns stuff is all superb, especially when the devil reflects whimsically about the evils he's unleashed upon the earth. But the other story—the story starring Ted Wass as the condemned rock star—has an authenticity of its own. Like Warren Beatty's *Heaven Can Wait*, it starts with a fantastical idea and then develops it along plausible human lines. For the first time in the God pictures, we care so much about the human characters that it really does make a difference what God does; it's not just a celestial vaudeville act.

Oleanna ★ ★
NO MPAA RATING, 89 m., 1994 | NEW |

William H. Macy (John), Debra Eisenstadt (Carol). Directed by David Mamet and produced by Patricia Wolff and Sarah Green. Screenplay by Mamet.

Experiencing David Mamet's play *Oleanna* on the stage was one of the most stimulating experiences I've had in a theater. In two acts, he succeeded in enraging all of the audience—the women with the first act, the men with the second. I recall loud arguments breaking out during the intermission and after the play, as the audience spilled out of an off-Broadway theater all worked up over its portrait of . . . sexual harrassment? Or was it self-righteous Political Correctness?

There are two characters in the cast: a professor named John (William H. Macy) and his student, Carol (Debra Eisenstadt). She is failing his class. She absolutely cannot accept a failing grade, and so she visits him in his office, where he is distracted by telephone calls about a house he and his wife hope to buy. He never really seems to hear or understand her problem.

In the second act, the student returns, with a new wardrobe and a more confident attitude. She is now a member of an unidentified "group." She has brought charges of sexual harassment against the professor, based on statements and physical behavior she found offensive. He stands to lose his tenure and his beloved house. He absolutely cannot accept these losses.

An objective observer might conclude that the professor's behavior is incorrect in the first act, and the student's in the second; that the play is Mamet's attempt to portray the situation from both points of view. Yet even the movie's press kit lacks this objectivity. (On the basis of the grammatical errors it contains, I doubt if the kit was personally reviewed by Mamet.) "There are two sides to every story and they are both Carol's," we read. And " . . . he instead turns their meeting into a platform from which he espouses

his own pedantic ideologies on education and life, but not her grade. Sentences fly, inner thoughts revealed and motives change with hair-pin precision."

Penetrating as best I can the illiteracy of these sentences, and others later in the synopsis, I gather that Carol was basically right, and John basically wrong. Sarah Green, the coproducer of the film, is quoted as believing *Oleanna* is "the most feminist play David has ever written. I absolutely identified with the woman's point of view."

But *what has the professor done?* It is made apparent in the first act that Carol is failing the course because she is either incapable or unprepared. Certainly the professor should not raise her grade simply because she is unhappy about it. Nor does he make an improper sexual advance—although his awkward movement at one point is later misinterpreted by Carol, and is the basis of the complaint which may destroy his career.

But then, you see, I am a man and Sarah Green is a woman. The most illuminating value of *Oleanna* is that it demonstrates so clearly how men and women can view the same events through entirely different prisms. With all the best will in the world, despite a real effort, I cannot see the professor as guilty. I see the student as a monstrous creature who masks her own inadequacies with a manufactured ideological attack: She is failing the course not because she is a bad student but because her teacher is a sexist pig.

Everything I have written refers to the stage version of the play. Now we come to the film, directed by Mamet himself and essentially unchanged from the theatrical version. To my astonishment, it is not a very good film. I am not sure why. The original characters are there, and the situation, and the dialogue, and even one of the actors (Macy) is the same as on the stage. But the material never really takes hold. It seems awkward. It lacks fire and passion. Watching it was like having a pale memory of a vivid experience.

Would the film seem more powerful to someone unfamiliar with the play? I obviously have no way of knowing. All I can say is that Mamet's play, so provoking that I bought and read the script, doesn't seem to have the same effect on the screen. Certainly it will inspire some of the same arguments in its audience, and may be worth seeing for that reason. But as a film, it is a disappointment.

Oliver & Co. ★ ★ ★
G, 73 m., 1988

With the voices of: Joey Lawrence (Oliver), Billy Joel (Dodger), Cheech Marin (Tito), Richard Mulligan (Einstein), Roscoe Lee Browne (Francis), Sheryl Lee Ralph (Rita), Dom Deluise (Fagin), Taurean Blacque (Roscoe), Carl Weintraub (Desoto), Robert Loggia (Sykes), Natalie Gregory (Jenny), William Glover (Winston), Bette Midler (Georgette). Directed by George Scribner. Inspired by Charles Dickens's *Oliver Twist*. Animation screenplay by Jim Cox, Timothy J. Disney, and James Mangold.

Walt Disney's *Oliver & Co.* is a safer version of *An American Tail*, with a kitten instead of a mouse trying to survive in the overwhelming streets of New York City. If children were disturbed in *An American Tail* by the hero's enforced separation from its parents, they may be relieved this time, since Oliver apparently has no parents and is on his own from a very early age. We see him for the first time in a cardboard box marked "Kittens $5," and later that night he is still there, even after having been marked down to "Free."

The kitten is swept out of its box by a torrential rainstorm, chased by savage dogs, finds refuge beneath the huge wheels of a truck, and is befriended the next day by a street-wise dog named Dodger (get it?). Together, they work a scam to steal some hot dogs from a vendor, but then the dog tries to make off with all of the wienies, and the kitten follows him back to a ramshackle houseboat where several dogs live with their owner, Fagin.

Fagin is a human who trains dogs to steal, just as the original Fagin in the Dickens story trained children to be pickpockets. That connection is about as close as *Oliver & Co.* gets to *Oliver Twist*, but since the connection is not insisted on and most smaller children will (alas) never have heard of Oliver Twist, I suppose it makes no difference.

The movie is filled with rousing action and chase scenes, and a properly menacing set of villains (the evil juice-loan vendor Sykes and his killer Dobermans). The animation, augmented by computers to do the detail work, is full-bodied and efficient, and if the street scenes still lack the kind of loving background detail and movement they had in the classic Disney movies, at least they contain an extraordinary number of subliminal plugs for Coca-Cola. Some of the action moments may be a little strong for younger kids (I'm not sure it was wise to demonstrate to them how a person can be strangled by being trapped by an automated car window). But the story is robust and muscular, the sentiments are not overdone, and the kitten is cute.

Once Around ★ ★ ★ ½
R, 115 m., 1990

Richard Dreyfuss (Sam Sharpe), Holly Hunter (Renata Bella), Danny Aiello (Joe Bella), Laura San Giacomo (Jan Bella), Gena Rowlands (Marilyn Bella). Directed by Lasse Hallstrom and produced by Griffin Dunne and Amy Robinson. Screenplay by Malia Scotch Marmo.

Did I like *Once Around*? I'm not sure. Did it bore me? Not for a moment. Is it a good film? Not in any conventional way; it's too much of a mess for that, and yet, at the same time, it's not a stupid film and not without feeling. What we have here is the untidiness of life, and it hasn't been made neat and simple and subjected to a formula screenplay. It's as confusing, as unsatisfying, as frustrating, and as occasionally wonderful as a big, emotional, unruly family—which is what it's about. The family and a slick salesman named Sam who marries into it.

The family, the Bellas, are complicated and close-knit, ruled by a father (Danny Aiello) who is smart, affectionate, and wise about affairs of the heart, although not wise enough to deal with this new in-law. He and his wife (Gena Rowlands) have had a loving and successful marriage of thirty-four years, but their children seem to be having a harder time with love—especially Renata (Holly Hunter), who has been living with a guy who confesses he has no desire to marry her.

On the rebound, and with her own sister's marriage fresh in her mind, Hunter goes to the Caribbean to take a course on selling condominiums. The hero of the meeting is a supersalesman named Sam Sharpe (Richard Dreyfuss), who has allegedly sold countless condos for untold piles of money. She takes one look at him and decides, in her words, that one day they will be kissing on an altar in the sight of God. She moves the place-cards around to be sure of sitting next to him at lunch, and by the time lunch is over, they're holding hands.

But, hold on, it's not exactly that kind of story. This man, Sam Sharpe, is some piece of work. He has an unfailing touch for saying the wrong thing in the wrong way at the

wrong time. All of his gestures are intended to be warm, kind, and generous, but he has the kind of style that grates the wrong way— he puts your teeth on edge while you're trying to smile back at him. And he is capable of the most amazingly vulgar expressions and offensive gestures, as when he orders belly dancers for birthday parties or insists, absolutely insists, on singing an obscure Lithuanian song at a party where that would be sensationally inappropriate.

We keep waiting for the other shoe to drop. What's the real story on this guy? Is he for real? Has he really sold all those condos? Can he be trusted? "We don't know a thing about him," Hunter's sister complains to their parents. And they don't. But we think we do— we think *Once Around* is going to fall into familiar screenplay modes, and that Sam will be unmasked as some kind of impostor.

The movie toys with our expectations, those and others. There is an ice-skating sequence in which we think we know exactly what's going to happen, twice, and the movie manipulates our expectations shamelessly. The most effective scenes are studies of social embarrassment, in which we cringe at the way Sam brings everything down to his own level of phony-sincere smarminess. The family can't stand him.

But Holly Hunter sticks by him, and gets pregnant by him, and insists in one speech, "This is my adventure and nobody can take it away from me!" What does she see in this guy? Maybe by the end of the movie we can understand, even though the scene involving baptism and reunion is, to put it charitably, less than convincing.

The movie is essentially all about acting. Richard Dreyfuss creates a character here who is so difficult, so impossible, so offensive, that it is easy to dislike the personality and forget how good the performance is. But this is some of Dreyfuss's best and riskiest work—he's out there on the edge, with this suntanned, chain-smoking, larger-than-life case study. Holly Hunter brings to this role the same vulnerable intensity she had in *Broadcast News*, and something new, a certain mystery, so that we're not always sure just what she thinks about this unwieldy personality she's married to. Danny Aiello has delicate scenes to negotiate as the patriarch, and watch his face as he tells his daughter how he feels about her husband, or how he responds during key moments in family ceremonies.

One of the great strengths of the movie is its dialogue, which is literate and original

without sounding "written." The screenplay is by Malia Scotch Marmo, the direction is by Lasse Hallstrom *(My Life as a Dog),* and I guess they had a lot to do with it. I'd be intrigued to learn how much input the producers, Amy Robinson and Griffin Dunne, had because in its underlying emotional rhythms this movie has a lot in common with *After Hours,* the Martin Scorsese film they produced in 1986. Both films create the sensation of accidents waiting to happen.

Watching the coming attractions trailer for *Once Around,* I observed to myself that it had not given me the slightest clue as to what this movie was about. Watching the movie, I have the same impression. It's an odd, eccentric, off-center study of some very strange human natures, and at every turn it confounds our expectations for them. It's untidy, unpredictable, and made me feel very uncomfortable at times. And it took me all the way through the process of writing this review to discover a surprising thing about this movie, which is that I loved it.

Once Upon a Time in America
★—short version
★ ★ ★ ★—original version
R, 137 m., 227 m., 1984

Robert De Niro (Noodles), James Woods (Max), Elizabeth McGovern (Deborah), Treat Williams (Jimmy), Tuesday Weld (Carol), Burt Young (Joe). Directed by Sergio Leone and produced by Arnon Milchan. Screenplay by L. Benvenuti, P. De Bernardo, E. Medioli, F. Arcalli, F. Ferrini, Leone, and S. Kaminski.

This was a murdered movie, now brought back to life on cassette. Sergio Leone's *Once Upon a Time in America,* which in its intended 227-minute version is an epic poem of violence and greed, was chopped by ninety minutes for U.S. theatrical release into an incomprehensible mess without texture, timing, mood, or sense. The rest of the world saw the original film, which I saw at the Cannes Film Festival. In America, a tragic decision was made. When the full-length version (now available in cassette form) played at the 1984 Cannes Film Festival, I wrote:

"Is the film too long? Yes and no. Yes, in the sense that it takes real concentration to understand Leone's story construction, in which everything may or may not be an opium dream, a nightmare, a memory, or a flashback, and that we have to keep track of characters and relationships over fifty years.

No, in the sense that the movie is compulsively and continuously watchable and that the audience did not stir or grow restless as the epic unfolded."

The movie tells the story of five decades in the lives of four gangsters from New York City—childhood friends who are merciless criminals almost from the first, but who have a special bond of loyalty to each other. When one of them breaks that bond, or thinks he does, he is haunted by guilt until late in his life, when he discovers that he was not the betrayer but the betrayed. Leone's original version tells this story in a complex series of flashbacks, memories, and dreams. The film opens with two scenes of terrifying violence, moves to an opium den where the Robert De Niro character is seeking to escape the consequences of his action, and then establishes its tone with a scene of great power: A ceaselessly ringing telephone, ringing forever in the conscience of a man who called the cops and betrayed his friends. The film moves back and forth in a tapestry of episodes, which all fit together into an emotional whole. There are times when we don't understand exactly what is happening, but never a time when we don't feel confidence in the film's narrative.

That version was not seen in American theaters, although it is now available on cassette. Instead, the whole structure of flashbacks was junked. The telephone rings once. The poetic transitions are gone. The movie has been wrenched into apparent chronological order, scenes have been thrown out by the handful, relationships are now inexplicable, and the audience is likely to spend much of its time in complete bewilderment. It is a great irony that this botched editing job was intended to "clarify" the film.

Here are some of the specific problems with the shortened version. A speakeasy scene comes before a newspaper headline announces that Prohibition has been ratified. Prohibition is then repealed, on what feels like the next day but must be six years later. Two gangsters talk about robbing a bank in front of a woman who has never been seen before in the film; they've removed the scene explaining who she is. A labor leader turns up, unexplained, and involves the gangsters in an inexplicable situation. He later sells out, but to whom? Men come to kill De Niro's girlfriend, a character we've hardly met, and we don't know if they come from the mob or the police. And here's a real howler: At the end of

the shortened version, De Niro leaves a room he has never seen before by walking through a secret panel in the wall. How did he know it was there? In the long version, he was told it was there. In the short version, his startling exit shows simple contempt for the audience.

Many of the film's most beautiful shots are missing from the short version, among them a bravura moment when a flash-forward is signaled by the unexpected appearance of a Frisbee, and another where the past becomes the present as the Beatles' "Yesterday" sneaks into the sound track. Relationships are truncated, scenes are squeezed of life, and I defy anyone to understand the plot of the short version. The original *Once Upon a Time in America* gets a four-star rating. The shorter version is a travesty.

Once Were Warriors ★ ★ ★ ½   NEW
R, 102 m., 1995

Rena Owen (Beth Heke), Temuera Morrison (Jake Heke), Mamaengaroa Kerr-Bell (Grace Heke), Julian (Sonny) Arahanga (Nig Heke), Taungaroa Emile (Boogie), Rachael Morris (Polly Heke), Joseph Kairau (Huata Heke), Clifford Curtis (Bully). Directed by Lee Tamahori and produced by Robin Scholes. Screenplay by Riwia Brown.

Jake Heke is a man with a hair-trigger temper, and its unpredictability is the most frightening thing about him. He likes to play the role of the genial, beer-swilling host, playing his guitar, singing songs, beloved by all, especially late at night by his drunken buddies. But let someone cross him, and he can lash out in the blink of an eye, the rage boiling over.

Jake and his wife, Beth, are Maoris, living in a housing development in New Zealand. They're both good-looking people, and Jake, with his sunny, sleepy-eyed, self-satisfied smile, seems like he's brimming with confidence. He is not. Beer fuels his resentments and insecurities, and masks his strength.

There is a scene early in *Once Were Warriors* where he gets into a fight in a bar, and inflicts incredible damage on a muscle-bound thug who seemed, until he met Jake, able to whip anybody in sight. This is a key scene because it establishes what Jake is capable of; all through the movie, we are waiting for that violence to be unleashed again.

Once Were Warriors shows Jake and Beth in good times and bad. They flirt, they sing boozy duets, they make love. But Jake is also

capable of turning in a flash into a brutal monster, and Beth wakes up one morning with her face a bloody mass of bruises. "It's the same old story," she tells a friend. "I've got to learn to keep my mouth shut." During the course of *Once Were Warriors*, she will slowly learn to stop blaming herself when she gets beaten.

Beth has a temper, too. Booze is the problem in the household, triggering terrifying personality changes. The kids learn to stay out of the way, especially the older ones: Boogie, the boy, joins a gang, and Grace, a beautiful teenager, retreats into her journal and into a friendship with a spaced-out boyfriend who lives with his drugs in an abandoned car. Huddled in their room one night with the sounds of anger crashing through the walls, Grace explains to her brother: "People show their true feelings when they're drunk."

The movie carved a reputation for itself on the festival circuit, leaving audiences shaken and silent at Telluride, Toronto, Honolulu, and Park City. It is powerful and chilling, and directed by Lee Tamahori with such narrative momentum that we are swept along in the enveloping tragedy of the family's life.

In Temuera Morrison, as Jake, the movie finds a leading actor as elemental, charismatic, and brutal as the young Marlon Brando; he has instinctive star power, and it's his likability that makes the violence of his character so shocking. Rena Owen, as Beth, supplies the moral center of the film, as a woman who finally calls a halt to the spiral of pain in her family.

The director's key achievement is to create a convincing sense of daily life in the household and neighborhood. This is not a narrow drama that focuses on a few themes; it paints a whole style of life, the good times with the bad, and perhaps no scene is more sad than the one where the family rents a car and sets off on a picnic, happy and in good spirits, only to have everything go wrong when Jake decides to stop for just one drink.

Mamaengaroa Kerr-Bell, as Grace, the pretty teenager, is also important to the film. She reflects a hope and optimism that somehow shines out even on the family's cloudiest days, and although her runaway boyfriend's hideout under an expressway seems grim and depressing, they are able to make it into a refuge where laughter and dreams are possible. Then everything goes bad for them, too.

Once Were Warriors has been praised as an attack on domestic violence and abuse. So it is. But I am not sure anyone needs to see this film in order to discover that such brutality is bad. We know that. I value it for two other reasons: its perception in showing how alcohol triggers sudden personality shifts, and its power in presenting two great performances by Morrison and Owen. You don't often see acting like this in the movies. They bring the Academy Awards into perspective.

One False Move ★ ★ ★ ★
R, 105 m., 1992

Bill Paxton (Dale "Hurricane" Dixon), Cynda Williams (Fantasia/Lila), Billy Bob Thornton (Ray Malcolm), Michael Beach (Pluto), Jim Metzler (Dud Cole), Earl Billings (McFeely). Directed by Carl Franklin and produced by Jesse Beaton and Ben Myron. Screenplay by Billy Bob Thornton and Tom Epperson.

Here is a crime movie that lifts you up and carries you along in an ominously rising tide of tension, building to an emotional payoff of amazing power. On the very short list of great movies about violent criminals, *One False Move* deserves a place of honor, beside such different kinds of films as *In Cold Blood*, *Henry: Portrait of a Serial Killer*, *Badlands*, *The Executioner's Song*, and *At Close Range*. It is a great film—one of the best of the year—and announces the arrival of a gifted director, Carl Franklin.

Yet no words of praise can quite reflect the seductive strength of *One False Move*, which begins as a crime story and ends as a human story in which everything that happens depends on the personalities of the characters. It's so rare to find a film in which the events are driven by people, not by chases or special effects. And rarer still to find a story that subtly, insidiously gets us involved much more deeply than at first we realize, until at the end we're torn by what happens—by what has to happen.

The movie was written by Billy Bob Thornton and Tom Epperson, who begin by telling one story—about three criminals on the run from Los Angeles to Arkansas—and end by telling two. The second story involves the interaction between a small-town Arkansas sheriff and two tough Los Angeles cops who fly out to join him in a trap for the fugitives. The movie pays full attention to the dynamics of both groups, the cops and the killers, and then quietly reveals a hidden connection between them—a secret that I will not reveal, because it generates such a moral and emotional force at the end of the film.

The film begins in Los Angeles, with a series of brutal murders of people in the drug underworld. Three people are involved: two men who have teamed up to steal drugs and money, and the girlfriend of one of them. They're played by Billy Bob Thornton, as a violent, insecure redneck type; Cynda Williams, as his lover, a black woman obviously deeply wounded in the past; and Michael Beach as the partner, a black man whose wire-rim glasses and impassive reserve conceal a capacity for sudden, cold violence.

Their original plan is to sell the drugs in Houston, but after they're identified as the fleeing murderers they change course, heading for the small Arkansas town where Williams was born and raised. The movie cuts ahead to the town, where we meet a cheerfully ambitious young sheriff, nicknamed "Hurricane" and played by Bill Paxton as the kind of guy who knows everybody in town and has never had to draw a gun in six years. He is mightily impressed when two Los Angeles detectives (Jim Metzler and Earl Billings) fly out to join him. He thinks he might be able to make the big time in L.A. himself some day.

The screenplay intercuts between these two story lines in a way that makes it increasingly important to us what will happen when the fugitives arrive in town. This isn't the usual formula of the cops and criminals drawing nearer, but a more subtle approach, in which secrets about the past that raise the stakes are gradually revealed.

One of the strengths of the film is the way it draws its interpersonal relationships. As the Thornton and Williams characters veer unhappily between protestations of love and outbursts of accusations, Beach sits quietly to one side—on a motel bed, in the backseat of the car—talking in a low, controlled voice. Most of what he says makes sense, and is disregarded. Meanwhile, in Arkansas, the two visiting cops, one black, one white, joke about the aspirations of the local lawman, who they see as a naive greenhorn. But his knowledge about the town goes very deep, and what he knows about the approaching fugitives will provide the key to the movie's last thirty minutes.

Carl Franklin's career has been mostly in acting until now, on stage and in several TV series. He directed some low-budget exploitation films, attended the American Film Institute, and then got *One False Move* as his first substantial film project. It is a powerful directing job. He starts with an extraordi-

nary screenplay and then finds the right tones and moods for every scene, realizing it's not the plot we care about, it's the people.

One of the unique qualities of the screenplay, and his direction, is that this is a film where the principals are three black people and three white people, and yet the movie is not about black-white "relationships" in the dreary way of so many other recent movies, which are motivated either by idealistic bonhomie or the clichés of ethnic stereotypes. Every character in this film, black and white, operates according to his or her own agenda. That's why we care so very much about what happens to them.

One Flew Over the Cuckoo's Nest
★ ★ ★
R, 129 m., 1975

Jack Nicholson (R.P. McMurphy), Louise Fletcher (Nurse Ratched), Will Sampson (The Chief), William Redfield (Harding), Brad Dourif (Billy), Sydney Lassick (Cheswick), Scatman Crothers (Turkle), Dean R. Brooks (Dr. Spivey), Danny DeVito (Martini). Directed by Milos Forman and produced by Saul Zaentz and Michael Douglas. Screenplay by Lawrence Hauben and Bo Goldman.

Milos Forman's *One Flew Over the Cuckoo's Nest* is a film so good in so many of its parts that there's a temptation to forgive it when it goes wrong. But it does go wrong, insisting on making larger points than its story really should carry, so that at the end, the human qualities of the characters get lost in the significance of it all. And yet there are those moments of brilliance. If Forman was preaching a parable, the audience seemed in total agreement with it, and I found that a little depressing: It's a lot easier to make noble points about fighting the establishment, about refusing to surrender yourself to the system, than it is to closely observe the ways real people behave when they're placed in an environment like a mental institution.

That sort of observation, when it's allowed to happen, is what's best about *One Flew Over the Cuckoo's Nest*. We meet a classic outsider—R.P. McMurphy, a quintessentially sane convict sent to the institution as a punishment for troublemaking—whose charisma and gall allow him to break through to a group of patients who've mostly fallen into a drugged lethargy. Their passive existence is reinforced by the unsmiling, domineering Nurse Ratched, who lines them up for compulsory tranquilizers and then leads them through group therapy in a stupor.

McMurphy has no insights into the nature of mental illness, which is his blessing. He's an extroverted, life-loving force of nature who sees his fellow patients as teammates, and defines the game as the systematic defiance of Nurse Ratched and the system she personifies. In many of the best scenes in the film, his defiance takes the shape of spontaneous and even innocent little rebellions: During exercise period, the patients mill around aimlessly on a basketball court until McMurphy hilariously tries to get a game going.

He also makes bets and outrageous dares, and does some rudimentary political organizing. He needs the votes of ten patients, out of a possible eighteen, to get the ward schedule changed so they can all watch the World Series—and his victory is in overcoming the indifference the others feel not only toward the Series but toward existence itself. McMurphy is the life force, the will to prevail, set down in the midst of a community of the defeated. And he's personified and made totally credible by Jack Nicholson, in another of the remarkable performances that have made him the most interesting actor to emerge in the last two decades. Nicholson, manically trying to teach basketball to an Indian (Will Sampson) who hasn't even spoken in twelve years, sometimes succeeds in translating the meaning of the movie and Ken Kesey's novel into a series of direct, physical demonstrations.

That's when the movie works, and what it's best at. If Forman had stayed at that level—introducing his characters and making them real, and then seeing how they changed as they bounced off one another—*One Flew Over the Cuckoo's Nest* might have been a great film. It's a good one as it is, but we can see the machinery working. Take, for example, the all-night orgy that finally hands McMurphy over to his doom. He's smuggled booze and broads into the ward, and everyone gets drunk, and then the hapless Billy (Brad Dourif) is cheerfully bundled into a bedroom with a willing girl. Billy stutters so badly he can hardly talk, but he's engaging and intelligent, and we suspect his problems are not incurable. The next morning, as Nurse Ratched surveys the damage, Billy at first defies her (speaking without a stutter, which is too obvious) and then caves in when she threatens to tell his mother what he's done. Nurse Ratched and Billy's mother

are old friends, you see (again, too obvious, pinning the rap on Freud and Mom). Billy commits suicide, and we're invited to stand around his pitiful corpse and see the injustice of it all—when all we've really seen is the plot forcing an implausible development out of unwilling subject matter.

Another scene that just doesn't work, because it's too heavily burdened with its purpose, occurs when McMurphy escapes, commandeers a school bus, and takes all the inmates of the ward on a fishing trip in a stolen boat. The scene causes an almost embarrassing break in the movie—it's Forman's first serious misstep—because it's an idealized fantasy in the midst of realism. By now, we've met the characters, we know them in the context of hospital politics, and when they're set down on the boat deck, they just don't belong there. The ward is the arena in which they'll win or lose, and it's not playing fair—to them, as characters—to give them a fishing trip.

Even as I'm making these observations, though, I can't get out of my mind the tumultuous response that *Cuckoo's Nest* received from its original audiences. Even the most obvious, necessary, and sobering scenes—as when McMurphy tries to strangle Nurse Ratched to death—were received, not seriously, but with sophomoric cheers and applause. Maybe that's the way to get the most out of the movie—see it as a simple-minded antiestablishment parable—but I hope not. I think there are long stretches of a very good film to be found in the midst of Forman's ultimate failure, and I hope they don't get drowned in the applause for the bad stuff that plays to the galleries.

101 Dalmatians ★ ★ ★
G, 79 m., 1961

With the voices of Rod Taylor (Pongo), Betty Lou Gerson (Cruella). Directed by Wolfgang Reitherman, Hamilton S. Luske, and Clyde Geronimi. Art direction and production design by Ken Anderson. Screenplay by Bill Peet.

All of Walt Disney's animated films have his signature on them, but *101 Dalmations* (1961) was one of the last to be made under his personal supervision. Seen thirty years later in a national rerelease, it's an uneven film, with moments of inspiration in a fairly conventional tale of kidnapping and rescue. This is not one of the great Disney classics—it's not in the same league with *Snow White* or *Pi-*

nocchio—but it's passable fun, and will entertain its target family audiences.

The movie tells the story of two London dalmatians and their human owners—who they refer to as "pets"—and a villainess named Cruella, who wants to buy all the dalmatian puppies she can find in order to turn them into fur coats. When the hero and heroine produce a litter of fifteen puppies, Cruella's appetite is whetted, and she hires a couple of thugs to kidnap them. The story continues in her ramshackle country mansion, where ninety-nine puppies are eventually held for a fate worse than death.

The rescue attempt involves the adult dogs, as well as a brave cat and advice from various neighboring dogs. The big last scene is a chase down snowy roads in the middle of winter. And there are some cute touches, as when word of the missing dogs is sent all over London by doggie telegraph. But the story seems somewhat perfunctory, the chase scene is not as inventive as the climaxes of other Disney feature cartoons, and the animators never solve the problem of making the puppies seem different from one another.

By the time the film was made, the golden days of full animation were already past. It was simply too expensive to animate every frame by hand, as Disney did in earlier days, and computer assistance was still in the future. In a film like *101 Dalmatians,* you can see certain compromises, as when the foreground figures are fully animated but the backgrounds look static and sometimes one-dimensional. The strong point is in movement, and the animal figures have a nice three-dimensional reality to them, as in a scene where a puppy crawls under a blanket and tucks itself in.

One sequence stands out from the others, as the puppies line up in front of the TV set to watch their favorite show, starring a brave dog. The interplay between the show and the pups is clever, and the TV show itself functions as a little added attraction; this is the first feature with the cartoon built in.

If there's one thing that's absolutely first-rate about the film, it's the character of Cruella, with a voice by Betty Lou Gerson, who achieves almost operatic effects with her sudden entrances and exits, accompanied by clouds of yellow cigarette smoke. She's in a league with the Wicked Stepmother and the other great Disney villainesses—but the rest of the movie is more ordinary.

1,000 Pieces of Gold ★ ★ ★
NO MPAA RATING, 105 m., 1991

Rosalind Chao (Lalu/Polly), Chris Cooper (Charlie), Michael Paul Chan (Hong King), Dennis Dun (Jim), Jimmie F. Skaggs (Jonas), Will Oldham (Miles). Directed and produced by Nancy Kelly. Screenplay by Anne Makepeace.

For some measure of the progress of women, consider *1,000 Pieces of Gold,* set in the nineteenth century and telling the story of a Chinese woman sold from man to man as if she were property. The film is based on the little-known fact that years after slavery was abolished in America, Asians were still held in involuntary servitude—sometimes by their own people. Inspired by true stories, the movie is angry and impassioned, but it is also, somewhat surprisingly, a romance.

Rosalind Chao, an actress of great character and presence, stars as a young woman named Lalu, born in China where girl babies were not highly valued and sold by her father to a Chinese "wife-trader" (Dennis Dun). He brings her to America and sells her as a wife to Hong King (Michael Paul Chan), another Chinese man, who runs a saloon in a dismal backwater of Idaho and plans to use her as a prostitute. Lalu reacts to his plans violently, with a knife, refusing to prostitute herself, and Hong King wisely observes that she does not seem cut out for the profession.

Lalu's innate self-esteem is her only protection in the wilderness. American laws deny Chinese men citizenship—they are wanted mostly for cheap labor—and women are viewed as even more insignificant. Lalu, nicknamed "China Polly" by the cowboys who cannot be bothered to pronounce her name, is saved from prostitution but then becomes Hong King's slave, until her husband's white partner, a genial alcoholic named Charlie (Chris Cooper), explains to her that slavery has been outlawed.

Charlie, a good man when he doesn't drink too much, is attracted to "Polly," but she dreams only of buying her freedom and returning to China. Then Hong King, short of funds and tired of living with a "hellcat," decides to auction his wife to the highest bidder—and Charlie, in a rare stroke of luck, wins her. She lives with him, but in fierce chastity, until Charlie is shot in an anti-Chinese race riot, and as she nurses him back to health she falls in love with him.

Meanwhile, the wife-trader, whose conscience has been bothering him, returns to the mining camp with enough money to buy Lalu's freedom. He hopes to marry her and take her back to China, but, seeing her living with a white man, he considers her hopelessly damaged and abandons his plans.

I gather that this development, like most of the film, is based on fact, but as a consequence *1,000 Pieces of Gold* paints an overwhelmingly negative portrait of Chinese men—from the father who betrays her, to the trader who sells her, to the saloon keeper who wants to prostitute her. The only man portrayed positively in the film is Charlie, the white. There must have been good Chinese men in America in those days, but you will not meet them in this film.

The story is told with power and high drama, however, and the love that grows between Lalu and Charlie, like all loves that smolder for a long time, becomes a great passion. And Rosalind Chao's performance is a wonder—the sort that, in a conventional Hollywood epic, would inspire Oscar speculation. She gives us a character who begins as a child in grief and confusion, and prevails in a strange land until she is finally able to stand free as her own woman. It's quite a story.

One-Trick Pony ★ ★ ★ ½
R, 98 m., 1980

Paul Simon (Jonah), Blair Brown (Marion), Rip Torn (Walter Fox), Joan Hackett (Lonnie Fox), Allen Goorwitz (Cal Van Damp), Mare Winningham (Modeena), Lou Reed (Steve), Harper Simon (Young Jonah). Directed by Robert M. Young and produced by Michael Tannen. Screenplay and original music by Paul Simon.

One-Trick Pony is a wonderful movie, an affectionate character study with a lot of good music in it, and it's being sold in all the wrong ways to Paul Simon "fans." True, you'll like it if you *are* a Paul Simon fan, but does Paul Simon have "fans" anymore? He has lots of admirers, people who follow his music—but they're not necessarily prepared to race out into the night to see this movie, as fans of, say, Bruce Springsteen might be willing to do. And that's sort of the point of *One-Trick Pony,* which tells the story of a folk singer who used to have a lot more fans than he does today.

It's ironic, the way the movie's ad campaign seemed to have exactly missed the point of the movie. Ironic, but not unusual.

And never mind: This movie was one of a lousy film year's few good films, a work that knows exactly what it's like to be a musician on tour. Jonah, the character Paul Simon wrote and plays, is a person drawn from life. If you are or ever have been a regular at a marginal local folk club, you've seen singers like Jonah many times.

He was very big in the 1960s. He wrote one of the songs that became an anthem for that decade. His music was an anti-war rallying point. But the sixties are long ago. And Jonah has continued to perform more or less in the same vein. He still travels the country by van, working with a small band. He still writes and arranges his own songs. He is still very good, for that matter—but he's out of date. He plays smaller and smaller clubs, and back home, in New York, his wife and child are both growing up without him.

There is a point, this movie argues, when a singer like Jonah stops being a brave individualist and becomes merely a middle-aged man hanging onto an obsolete self-image. That's the opinion held by Jonah's wife (Blair Brown), who loves him but wants a divorce. Jonah is sort of willing to try a change. He begins to deal with a "hitmaker" (Rip Torn) who sets him up with an arranger (Lou Reed) who can almost guarantee a Top 40 sound.

The movie does an effortless job of teaching us this aspect of the music business. We hear various versions of one of Jonah's songs: first as it sounds in a small club, then as it sounds during a very nervous audition session, and finally as it is gruesomely transformed, violins and all, into a prepackaged "hit." During this period we begin to feel sympathy with a certain nobility in Jonah's character. *One-Trick Pony* never forces its points, but we begin to understand why his way might be preferable to success.

The movie is filled with interesting, sharply drawn characters. Allen Goorwitz is brilliant in a hateful role as an egotistical monster who controls radio playtime. Joan Hackett, as Torn's sexually adventurous wife, goes after Jonah in simple, lustful boredom, but ends up trying to be his friend, to explain the realities of the situation they find themselves in. Brown plays the singer's wife as a complex woman who, in her thirties, still knows and feels why she married this man, but wonders how long he has to prove his point before her life is sidetracked.

And Simon is very good in the central role. The movie has a lot of music in it that he sings well and with love, but it also contains some very tricky dramatic moments. Halfway through, we begin to realize that it's about a lot more things than an aging folk hero. It is also about the generation that was young and politically active in the 1960s and now has been overtaken by the narcissism of the most brutally selfish and consumer-oriented period in American history. Many children of the sixties have been, of course, willing converts to the new culture of the Cuisinart. Others stick to what they used to believe in. In Jonah's case, it's folk music. Everybody's case is different.

On Golden Pond ★ ★ ★
PG, 109 m., 1981

Katharine Hepburn (Ethel Thayer), Henry Fonda (Norman Thayer, Jr.), Jane Fonda (Chelsea), Doug McKeon (Billy Ray), Dabney Coleman (Bill Ray). Directed by Mark Rydell and produced by Bruce Gilbert. Screenplay by Ernest Thompson.

Simple affection is so rare in the movies. Shyness and resentment are also seldom seen. Love is much talked-about, but how often do we really believe that the characters are in love and not simply in a pleasant state of lust and like? Fragile emotions are hard to portray in a movie, and the movies that reach for them are more daring, really, than movies that bludgeon us with things like anger and revenge, which are easy to portray.

On Golden Pond is a treasure for many reasons, but the best one, I think, is that I could believe it. I could believe in its major characters and their relationships, and in the things they felt for one another, and there were moments when the movie was witness to human growth and change. I left the theater feeling good and warm, and with a certain resolve to try to mend my own relationships and learn to start listening better. All of those achievements are small miracles for any movie, but especially for this one, which began as a formula stage play and still contains situations and characters that are constructed completely out of cardboard.

The story of *On Golden Pond* begins with the arrival of an old, long-married couple (Henry Fonda and Katharine Hepburn) at the lakeside cottage where they have summered for many years. They know each other very well. Hepburn, of course, knows Fonda better than he knows her—or himself, for that matter. Fonda is a crotchety, grouchy old professor whose facade conceals a great

deal of shyness, we suspect. Hepburn knows that. Before long, three more people turn up at the pond: Their daughter (Jane Fonda), her fiancé (Dabney Coleman), and his son (Doug McKeon).

That's the first act. In the second act, the conflicts are established. Jane Fonda feels that her father has never really given her her due—he wanted a son, or perhaps he never really understood how to be a father, anyway. Jane tells her parents that she's spending a month in Europe with Coleman, and, ah, would it be all right if they left the kid at the lake? Hepburn talks the old man into it. In the central passages of the movie, the old man and the kid grudgingly move toward some kind of communication and trust. There is a crisis involving a boating accident, and a resolution that brings everybody a lot closer to the realization that life is a precious and fragile thing. Through learning to relate to the young boy, old Fonda learns, belatedly, how to also trust his own daughter and communicate with her: The kid provides Henry with practice at how to be a father. There is eventually the sort of happy ending that some people cry through.

Viewed simply as a stage plot, *On Golden Pond* is so predictable we can almost hear the gears squeaking. Forty-five minutes into the movie, almost everyone in the audience can probably predict more or less what is going to happen to the characters, emotionally. And yet *On Golden Pond* transcends its predictability and the transparent role of the young boy, and becomes a film with passages of greatness.

This is because of the acting, first of all, but also because Ernest Thompson, who wrote such a formula play, has furnished it with several wonderful scenes. A conversation between old Henry Fonda and young Coleman is an early indication that this is going to be an unusual movie: A man who is forty-five asks a man who is eighty for permission to sleep in the same room with the man's daughter, and after the old man takes the question as an excuse for some cruel put-downs, the conversation takes an altogether unexpected twist into words of simple truth. That is a good scene. So are some of the conversations between Hepburn and Fonda. And so are some remarkable scenes involving the boating accident, in which there is no doubt that Hepburn, at her age, is doing some of her own stunts. It's at moments like this that stardom, acting ability, character, situation—and what the audience already

knows about the actors—all come together into an irreplaceable combination.

As everybody knows, this is the first film in which Hepburn and the two Fondas have acted in any combination with one another. Some reviews actually seem to dismiss the casting as a stunt. I believe it adds immeasurably to the film's effect. If Hepburn and Henry Fonda are legends, seen in the twilight of their lives, and if we've heard that Jane and Henry have had some of the same problems offscreen that they have in this story—does that make the movie simple gossip? No, not if the movie deals honestly with the problems, as this one does. As people, they have apparently learned something about loving and caring that, as actors, they are able to communicate, even through the medium of this imperfect script. Watching the movie, I felt I was witnessing something rare and valuable.

The Onion Field ★ ★ ★ ★
R, 126 m., 1979

John Savage (Karl Hettinger), James Woods (Greg Powell), Franklyn Seales (Jimmy Smith), Ted Danson (Ian Campbell), Ronny Cox (Pierce Brooks), David Huffman (Phil Halpin), Christopher Lloyd (Jailhouse Lawyer), Diane Hull (Helen Hettinger), Priscilla Pointer (Chrissie Campbell). Directed by Harold Becker and produced by Walter Coblenz. Screenplay by Joseph Wambaugh.

Since *The Onion Field* will inevitably inspire comparisons with *In Cold Blood*, we might as well begin with a basic one: Both the book and the film of *In Cold Blood* began with murder instead of ending with it.

The Onion Field does the same thing. It is also based on real events—the 1963 kidnappings of Los Angeles police officers Karl Hettinger and Ian Campbell, and the eventual cold-blooded murder of Campbell. And Joseph Wambaugh, who wrote the book and personally controlled the film production, didn't reorder the facts to give us a dramatic burst of gunfire at the end. Instead, he places the deadly event of the murder in an onion field at about where it should occur, midway between the criminal preparations that led up to it and the longest single criminal court case in California history, which lasted more than seven years.

For Wambaugh (himself a former policeman), the trial, too, was a crime—and the fact of Campbell's murder had to be considered in the context of the legal travesties that followed it. That attention to the larger context of the kidnap-killing is one thing that makes *The Onion Field* so much more than another cop drama. This movie is about people, about how they behave and why, and about how small accidents and miscalculations can place people in situations they never dreamed of. Life is a very fragile thing; *The Onion Field* knows that in its bones.

The film moves between two basic, completely dissimilar, sets of characters: the two police officers, and the two third-rate hoods who would eventually be convicted of the crime. The cops aren't seen in quite the same sharp focus as the criminals—perhaps because, until the night of the onion field, little they had done in their lives had prepared them for what would follow.

Campbell (Ted Danson), the one who is killed, is seen almost as a memory: a tall, good-looking, black-haired Scottish-American with an obsession for bagpipes. Hettinger (John Savage from *The Deer Hunter*) is seen at the beginning as a cheerful, open-faced young man who will only later, after the onion field, develop very deep hurts and complications.

The hoods are seen more clearly. There's Greg Powell (James Woods), a street-wise smartass with a quick line of talk and an ability to paint situations so other people see them his way. And then there's Jimmy Smith (Franklyn Seales), a disturbed, insecure young black who is a perfect recruit for Powell. They make a suitable team. Powell creates criminal scenarios out of his fantasies; Smith finds them real enough to follow; and in some convoluted way Powell then follows Smith into them.

The Onion Field makes these two characters startlingly convincing: It paints their manners, their speech, their environment, their indecisions in such a way that we can almost understand them as they blunder stupidly into their crimes.

It never quite captures the personality of Campbell, the man who will be killed, but in the aftermath of the killing it begins to develop disturbing insights into Hettinger, the survivor. In a dozen subtle ways he becomes an outcast in the department (he senses, perhaps correctly, that the other cops wonder how he could allow his partner to be killed). Eventually, punishing himself, seeking guilt, he becomes a shoplifter, and is caught and fired from the force. Savage's handling of a scene of near-suicide, late in the film, is so frightening we can hardly stand to watch it.

Those events take place as *The Onion Field* explores the bureaucratic nightmare of the criminal courts system. The case dragged on and on and on—Hettinger was called upon to testify in more than six different trials—and plea bargaining, delays, and continuances, and legal loopholes made the case into an impossible (and almost insoluble) tangle.

So there is a lot of ground for *The Onion Field* to cover. It covers it remarkably well, working both as a narrative and as Wambaugh's cry of protest against the complicated and maddening workings of the courts. The movie is actually a vindication for Wambaugh: He was so displeased with the Hollywood and TV treatments of his novels (especially *The Choirboys*) that he said he would never let this factual story be made into a movie unless he controlled the production.

He did, and he has made it into a strong and honorable film. His instinct in going with Harold Becker, a commercial director with little previous feature experience, was obviously a good one; the movie's craftsmanship is unobtrusive but fine. And the performances (especially James Woods's as Greg Powell) bring the characters into heartbreaking reality. This is a movie that, once seen, cannot be set aside.

Only You ★ ★ ★ ½
PG, 108 m., 1994

Marisa Tomei (Faith), Robert Downey, Jr. (Peter), Bonnie Hunt (Kate), Joaquim De Almeida (Giovanni), Fisher Stevens (Larry), Billy Zane (False Damon), Adam LeFevre (Real Damon), John Benjamin Hickey (Dwayne). Directed by Norman Jewison and produced by Jewison, Cary Woods, Robert N. Fried, and Charles Mulvehill. Screenplay by Diane Drake.

Norman Jewison's *Only You* is the kind of lighthearted romance that's an endangered species in today's Hollywood. It is total fantasy, light as a feather, contrary to all notions of common sense, it features a couple of stars who are really good kissers—and it takes place mostly in Venice, Rome, and the glorious Italian hillside town of Positano. What more do you want?

Movies like this were once written for Katharine Hepburn (*Summertime*), Audrey Hepburn (*Roman Holiday*), and Rossano Brazzi (*Three Coins in the Fountain*). Or remember Clark Gable and Sophia Loren in *It Happened in Naples*. There is a case to be made that no modern actors have quite the innocence or the faith to play such heedless lovers,

but Marisa Tomei and Robert Downey, Jr., somehow manage to lose all the baggage of our realistic, cynical age, and give us a couple of fools in love.

The movie begins when the heroine, Faith, is eleven. She and her cousin Kate ask a Ouija board who she will marry, and the answer is clear: She will marry a man named Damon Bradley. A few years later, a fortune-teller tells her the same thing. Such a coincidence cannot be ignored, and so "Damon Bradley" becomes a psychic beacon for the appropriately named Faith.

Years pass, however, and no Damon Bradley appears, and finally Faith, now played by Marisa Tomei, becomes engaged to a podiatrist (John Benjamin Hickey). Then, on the eve of her wedding, she receives a call from a friend of the groom's, who cannot attend the ceremony because he is on his way to Venice. The friend's name, of course, is Damon Bradley, and Faith abandons all her wedding plans, of course, to fly after him to Venice.

There she meets Peter, played by Robert Downey, Jr., and one of the questions posed by the movie is whether he is, in fact, really Damon Bradley. What is interesting is that he may be, even if he's not—a paradox you will understand after you see the movie. Whether he is or isn't hardly matters after Faith and Peter fall in love in Venice, or after they continue their romance in Rome, or after it nearly comes to pieces in Positano.

The screenplay by Diane Drake of course throws great hurdles in the way of the lovers, not least those caused by Faith's explicit belief in the childhood prophecy. All of this is sheer contrivance and artifice, which is part of the fun. There is a fine line between the Idiot Plot, so called because the characters act in defiance of common sense, and what we might call, in deference to Jewison's 1987 hit, the Moonstruck Plot—in which the characters also act in defiance of common sense, but we don't mind because it's fun.

Only You gives us two people who should fall in love and live happily together for the rest of their days. They know it, we know it, and all of their friends know it. We also know with a confidence bordering on certainty that they *will* fall in love. And so there is a special kind of movie pleasure in watching them pigheadedly postpone their bliss—especially when they do it on Italian locations lovingly photographed by Sven Nykvist.

I can think of many angst-laden young Hollywood stars, many of them accomplished actors, who could not have come within miles of the work done by Downey and Tomei in this movie. There is craft involved, yes, and even a certain inspiration, but what I reacted to more strongly was an ineffable sense of good nature: Tomei and Downey seem happy in their beings here, and happier together than apart. That is what must be present if we're to respond to a story like this. I have not read in the supermarket papers that they are "linked in real life," and so I must assume their chemistry comes from acting. All the more remarkable. (Or maybe not; many real-life couples sometimes seem fed up with one another on the screen.)

Norman Jewison, who directs *Only You* with a light, smiling touch, began his directing career just as movies like this were going out of style. He directed Doris Day in *The Thrill of It All* (1963), costarring James Garner, and in *Send Me No Flowers* (1964), with Rock Hudson, and I hope Marisa Tomei understands it is a compliment when I say that in *Only You* she has some of Doris Day's sunny warmth. I suppose Doris Day is out of fashion, and so are movies like *Only You*, but just because something is not done anymore doesn't mean it's not worth doing.

On the Road Again ★ ★ ★
PG, 119 m., 1980

Willie Nelson (Buck), Dyan Cannon (Viv), Amy Irving (Lily), Slim Pickens (Garland), Joey Floyd (Jamie), Mickey Rooney, Jr. (Cotton). Directed by Jerry Schatzberg and produced by Sydney Pollack and Gene Taft. Screenplay by Carol Sobieski, William D. Wittliff, and John Binder.

The plot of Willie Nelson's *On the Road Again** is just a slight touch familiar, maybe because it's straight out of your basic country and western song. To wit: The hero, a veteran country singer still poised at the brink of stardom after twenty-five years on the road, won't listen to his wife's pleas that he leave the road and settle down with her and their son. Meanwhile, the band's guitarist, who is also the singer's best friend, retires. A replacement is needed, and the singer hires the best friend's daughter.

She is a shapely young lady who has had a crush on the singer since she was knee-high to a grasshopper. Once they go out on the road again, the singer and the best friend's daughter start sleeping with one another. This situation causes anguish for the singer, the daughter, the best friend, the wife, the son, and the band. But after going down to Mexico to slug back some tequila and think it over, the singer returns to his wife and the best friend's daughter wisely observes: "Anything that hurts this many people can't be right."

This story is totally predictable from the opening scenes of *On the Road Again*, which is a disappointment; the movie is sly and entertaining, but it could have been better. Still, it has its charms, and one is certainly the presence of Willie Nelson himself, making his starring debut at the age of forty-seven and not looking a day over sixty. He's grizzled, grinning, sweet-voiced and pleasant, and a very engaging actor. (He gave promise of that with a single one-liner in his screen debut in *The Electric Horseman*, expressing his poignant desire for the kind of girl who could suck the chrome off a trailer hitch.)

The movie also surrounds Nelson with an interesting cast: Dyan Cannon is wonderful as Willie's long-suffering wife, a sexy forty-ish earth-woman with streaked hair and a wardrobe from L.L. Bean. She survives the test of her big scene, an archetypical C&W confrontation in which she charges onstage to denounce her husband and his new girlfriend.

Amy Irving is not quite so well-cast as the girlfriend; she has too many scenes in which she gazes adoringly at Willie—who, on the other hand, hardly ever gazes adoringly at her. Slim Pickens, who should be registered as a national historical place, is great as the best friend. And there is a hilarious bit part, a fatuous country singer, played by Mickey Rooney, Jr.

Mercifully, the movie doesn't drag out its tale of heartbreak into a C&W soap opera. Instead, director Jerry Schatzberg (*Scarecrow*) uses an easy-going documentary style to show us life on the band bus, at a family reunion, and backstage at big concerts. All of these scenes are filled to overflowing with colors; this is one of the cheeriest, brightest-looking movies I've ever seen, starting with Willie's own amazing costumes and including the spectrum at the concerts, reunions, picnics, etc. Half the movie seems to be shot during parties, and although we enjoy the texture and detail we sometimes wonder why so little seems to be happening.

The movie remains resolutely at the level of superficial cliché, resisting any temptation to make a serious statement about the character's hard-drinking, self-destructive lifestyle; this isn't a movie like *Payday*, in which Rip Torn re-created the last days of the dying Hank Williams. *On the Road Again* has the kind of problems that can be resolved with an onstage reconciliation in the last scene: Willie and Dyan singing a duet together and everybody knowing things will turn out all right.

If there's an edge of disappointment coming out of the movie, maybe it's inspired by that simplicity of approach to complicated problems. Willie Nelson has lived a long time, experienced a lot, and suffered a certain amount on his way to his current success, and my hunch is that he knows a lot more about his character's problems in this movie than he lets on. Maybe the idea was to film the legend and save the man for later.

*Retitled On the Road Again *for TV and cassette. Original Title:* Honeysuckle Rose.

Opening Night ★ ★ ★
PG-13, 146 m., 1978

Gena Rowlands (Myrtle Gordon), John Cassavetes (Maurice Aarons), Ben Gazzara (Manny Victor), Joan Blondell (Sarah Goode), Paul Stewart (David Samuels), Zohra Lampert (Dorothy Victor). Directed by John Cassavetes and produced by Al Ruban. Screenplay by Cassavetes.

John Cassavetes's *Opening Night* tells the story of an alcoholic actress going through the final agony of bottoming out, while surrounded by people whose lives she is making impossible, and who are not nearly as angry with her as they should be. Gena Rowlands plays the role at perfect pitch: She is able to suggest, even in the midst of seemingly ordinary moments, the controlled panic of a person who needs a drink, right here, right now.

The story takes place in the final days of the out-of-town tryout of a new play, which stars Rowlands as Myrtle Gordon, a famous actress idolized by her fans. Ben Gazzara plays the director, who doggedly tries to keep the doomed production on track, Joan Blondell is the playwright, and Cassavetes himself plays the leading man.

Everyone in the cast and on the production staff knows that Myrtle is a drunk, but to one degree or another they all go along with her fantasy, which is that she drinks because she is terrified of aging, and since the play is about an aging woman, the pain is simply too much for her to bear. Alcoholics can always tell you about the problems they're drinking over, but they can never quite see how the boozing and the problems might be related.

Opening Night is of a piece with two other films directed by Cassavetes and starring Rowlands: *A Woman Under the Influence* and *Love Streams*. In all three films Rowlands has a central role as a woman who is cracking up, but *Opening Night* is unusual in pinpointing alcoholism as the specific agent of her self-destruction, and rarely has a movie been so knowledgeable about the ways in which alcoholics—especially talented ones—manage to surround themselves with enablers who will buy into their neurosis and help them continue to drink. "I've seen a lot of drunks in my time," an admiring stage manager tells Myrtle as she weaves in the wings before her first entrance, "but I've never seen anyone as drunk as you who could stand up. You're great!"

In a scene at the beginning of the film, a young woman asks Myrtle for her autograph, and then runs after her limousine in the rain. As the limo speeds away, another car strikes the fan, who is killed, but she continues to appear to Myrtle throughout the film. The young girl is possibly an alcoholic hallucination (Myrtle has clearly reached the final stages before hospitalization), but Blondell, as the playwright, suggests that a spiritualist friend might be able to give counsel.

The scenes in which Myrtle consults first one and then another spiritualist are typical of Cassavetes's genius in filming madness. He gives us characters who are clearly breaking apart inside, and then sends them hurtling around crazily in search of quick fixes and Band-Aids. (In *Love Streams*, the hard-drinking Cassavetes surrounds himself with hookers, while Rowlands, as his sister, fills a taxicab with animals she has "rescued" from a pet store; in *A Woman Under the Influence*, a crowd of basket cases sits down to eat a big dinner that has been whipped together under the delusion that life is normal and everybody is having a great time.) Myrtle is too strung out and unhappy to even make sense of the spiritualists, who for their part are either too phony or too locked into their own terms of reference to notice what a sick woman they are dealing with.

As the play's opening night creeps closer, and Myrtle gets worse, Cassavetes gives us a series of frantic confrontations in which his characters try to deny the evidence before their very eyes. Blondell's long-suffering husband and producer (Paul Stewart, the butler in *Citizen Kane*) tries to keep up his wife's

spirits on the night of the big performance as curtain time comes and goes and Myrtle still has not appeared at the theater. Blondell is calmer than most playwrights would be under the circumstances ("I can't deny I'm disappointed, but worse things have happened to me").

Then follows a climax of pure Cassavetes psychic chaos. When Myrtle finally staggers into the theater and falls on her face, Gazzara gets her made up and costumed and sends her onto the stage, where a supporting actor literally supports her through the first act, and she and the Cassavetes character ad lib the second act as drunken farce, with the audience in on the joke. Then there is great applause, the curtain comes down, and Cassavetes's buddies like Peter Falk, Seymour Cassel, and Peter Bogdanovich play well-wishers.

What does this ending mean? Does it celebrate Myrtle's triumph, that she got through the evening despite being falling-over drunk? Is it a triumph? Will this play ever have another performance? Will Rowlands ever stop drinking? I would love to be able to ask Cassavetes what, exactly, the happy people milling around on stage are happy about. But Cassavetes, of course, is dead.

I love his films with the kind of personal urgency that you feel toward a beloved friend who is destroying himself. The films, taken together, are portraits of a crackup that is sustained, through courage and resiliency, for as long as humanly possible. Recovering alcoholics talk about "what it used to be like, what happened, and what it is like now." All of Cassavetes's films are about what it used to be like, and for his doomed characters, nothing ever happens to make it any different now.

Ordinary People ★ ★ ★ ★
R, 125 m., 1980

Donald Sutherland (Calvin), Mary Tyler Moore (Beth), Judd Hirsch (Berger), Timothy Hutton (Conrad), M. Emmet Walsh (Swim Coach), Elizabeth McGovern (Jeannine), Dinah Manoff (Karen). Directed by Robert Redford and produced by Ronald L. Schwary. Screenplay by Alvin Sargent.

Families can go along for years without ever facing the underlying problems in their relationships. But sometimes a tragedy can bring everything out in the open, all of a sudden and painfully, just when everyone's most vulnerable. Robert Redford's *Ordinary People* be-

gins at a time like that for a family that loses its older son in a boating accident. That leaves three still living at home in a perfectly manicured suburban existence, and the movie is about how they finally have to deal with the ways they really feel about one another.

There's the surviving son, who always lived in his big brother's shadow, who tried to commit suicide after the accident, who has now just returned from a psychiatric hospital. There's the father, a successful Chicago attorney who has always taken the love of his family for granted. There's the wife, an expensively maintained, perfectly groomed, cheerful homemaker whom "everyone loves." The movie begins just as all of this is falling apart.

The movie's central problems circle almost fearfully around the complexities of love. The parents and their remaining child all "love" one another, of course. But the father's love for the son is sincere yet also inarticulate, almost shy. The son's love for his mother is blocked by his belief that she doesn't really love him—she only loved the dead brother. And the love between the two parents is one of those permanent facts that both take for granted and neither has ever really tested.

Ordinary People begins with this three-way emotional standoff and develops it through the autumn and winter of one year. And what I admire most about the film is that it really *does* develop its characters and the changes they go through. So many family dramas begin with a "problem" and then examine its social implications in that frustrating semifactual, docudrama format that's big on TV. *Ordinary People* isn't a docudrama; it's the story of these people and their situation, and it shows them doing what's most difficult to show in fiction—it shows them changing, learning, and growing.

At the center of the change is the surviving son, Conrad, played by a wonderfully natural young actor named Timothy Hutton. He is absolutely tortured as the film begins; his life is ruled by fear, low self-esteem, and the correct perception that he is not loved by his mother. He starts going to a psychiatrist (Judd Hirsch) after school. Things are hard for this kid. He blames himself for his brother's death. He's a semi-outcast at school because of his suicide attempt and hospitalization. He does have a few friends—a girl he met at the hospital, and another girl who stands behind him at choir practice and who would, in a normal year, naturally become his girlfriend. But there's so much turmoil at home.

The turmoil centers around the mother (Mary Tyler Moore, inspired casting for this particular role, in which the character masks her inner sterility behind a facade of cheerful suburban perfection). She does a wonderful job of running her house, which looks like it's out of the pages of *Better Homes and Gardens*. She's active in community affairs, she's an organizer, she's an ideal wife and mother—except that at some fundamental level she's selfish, she can't really give of herself, and she *has*, in fact, always loved the dead older son more. The father (Donald Sutherland) is one of those men who wants to do and feel the right things, in his own awkward way. The change he goes through during the movie is one of the saddest ones: Realizing his wife cannot truly care for others, he questions his own love for her for the first time in their marriage.

The sessions of psychiatric therapy are supposed to contain the moments of the film's most visible insights, I suppose. But even more effective, for me, were the scenes involving the kid and his two teen-age girlfriends. The girl from the hospital (Dinah Manoff) is cheerful, bright, but somehow running from something. The girl from choir practice (Elizabeth McGovern) is straightforward, sympathetic, able to be honest. In trying to figure them out, Conrad gets help in figuring himself out.

Director Redford places all these events in a suburban world that is seen with an understated matter-of-factness. There are no cheap shots against suburban lifestyles or affluence or mannerisms: The problems of the people in this movie aren't caused by their milieu, but grow out of themselves. And, like it or not, the participants have to deal with them. That's what sets the film apart from the sophisticated suburban soap opera it could easily have become. Each character in this movie is given the dramatic opportunity to look inside himself, to question his *own* motives as well as the motives of others, and to try to improve his own ways of dealing with a troubled situation. Two of the characters do learn how to adjust; the third doesn't. It's not often we get characters who face those kinds of challenges on the screen, nor directors who seek them out. *Ordinary People* is an intelligent, perceptive, and deeply moving film.

Orlando ★ ★ ★ ½
PG-13, 93 m., 1993

Tilda Swinton (Orlando), Billy Zane (Shelmerdine), Lothaire Bluteau (The Khan), John Wood (Archduke Harry), Charlotte Valandrey (Sasha), Heathcote Williams (Nick Greene/Publisher), Quentin Crisp (Queen Elizabeth I). Directed by Sally Potter and produced by Christopher Sheppard. Screenplay by Potter.

Orlando is a film about a person who achieves in a lifetime what many people have dreamed of doing: viewing four centuries of experiences through the eyes of both sexes. Obviously it is a very long and unusual lifetime. Born as a man in the time of Elizabeth I, Orlando becomes a woman midway in the journey ("You see? Absolutely no difference!") and is still going strong as the film ends.

This is the kind of movie you want to talk about afterward. Directed with sly grace and quiet elegance by Sally Potter, it is not about a story or a plot, but about a vision of human existence. What does it mean to be born as a woman, or a man? To be born at one time instead of another? To be born into wealth, or into poverty, or into the traditions of a particular nation? Most of us will never know. We are stuck with ourselves, and as long as we live, will always see through the same eyes and interpret with the same sensibility. Yes, we can learn and develop, but so much of what makes us ourselves is implanted at an early age, and won't budge.

Orlando is inspired by the novel by Virginia Woolf, herself a writer who tried to break free of sex and class restraints. Stanley Kauffmann writes in *The New Republic* that the novel was originally written for, and inspired by, Vita Sackville-West, said to be one of Woolf's lovers. It comes out of that pre-de Beauvoir time in the earlier twentieth century when society still regarded women as second-class citizens, not fit to vote, but when many women were energetically assaulting society's quaint notions as quickly as they could.

Orlando, the omnisexual hero-heroine of the story, is played throughout by Tilda Swinton, who is definitely a woman and not particularly androgynous; her obvious femininity is explained in an early scene by a reference to the male fops and dandies of Elizabeth's reign, who in their fashions and vanities outdid their women. Orlando, as a man, owns an estate with a great home on it, and is told during a visit by the Queen that he can keep it forever—but only if he always remains young, fresh, and ageless. So, he does. (In a bow to the film's underlying theme, Elizabeth is played by Quentin Crisp, the octogenarian who wrote a famous book, *The Naked Civil Servant*, about his long years of shocking the British with his flamboyant homosexuality.)

Orlando drifts dreamily and bemused from one era to the next. The film skips ahead in leaps of about fifty years, as Orlando tries various careers (a stint as an ambassador in the Middle East is particularly educational) and relationships. There is a hitch when he becomes a she; as a woman, Orlando is informed by the authorities, she can no longer legally own her great estate (only men could then hold the title to property). If this were not bad enough, they explain there is another hitch: Having lived by then more than two hundred years, she must be presumed dead.

No matter. Life is perhaps simpler without the bother of property, and in modern times Orlando has a loving relationship with a modern man (Billy Zane) and samples a more bourgeois lifestyle. If Tilda Swinton had attempted to react to every turn and event in Orlando's life—to actively participate in everything—the movie might have grown tiresome. But her detachment and what can only be called her sweetness, provide the proper tone for the material. Given the gift of eternal youth, Orlando is able to temper it with the no less valuable gift of grateful bemusement.

Other People's Money ★ ★ ★ ½
PG-13, 106 m., 1991

Danny DeVito (Lawrence Garfield), Gregory Peck ("Jorgy" Jorgenson), Penelope Ann Miller (Kate Sullivan), Piper Laurie (Bea Sullivan), Dean Jones (William J. Coles). Directed by Norman Jewison and produced by Jewison and Ric Kidney. Screenplay by Alvin Sargent.

Danny DeVito is the right actor to play Larry the Liquidator. He doesn't have to say that he uses big piles of money to compensate for the lack of love in his life. We know. We can see it in Larry's eyes, which sparkle when he talks about accumulating other people's money, but turn into the large, brown eyes of an adoring spaniel whenever he gazes upon Kate Sullivan.

She is the attorney who stands between him and New England Wire & Cable, a second-generation family firm that has fallen on hard times but has no debt and a lot of cash. Larry wants to raid the company, break it up, strip the assets, and sell the profitable divisions. The company's president, an old-fashioned stalwart named Jorgy and played by Gregory Peck, wants to continue making wire and cable.

The situation is immensely complicated because Miss Sullivan (Penelope Ann Miller) is the daughter of Jorgy's assistant and companion (played by Piper Laurie). Kate, who is a foot taller than Larry the Liquidator, is blond, is sleek, is chic, and knows how to push all of Larry's buttons. From the moment she walks into his office determined to defeat him and save the company, he knows he is in love. He also knows he wants to win.

Larry is a smart man. That's one of his appeals. He is also immensely likable, except when he is trying to strip-mine the family firm. Kate finds him intriguing on first sight, but she wants to defeat him in the struggle for the company, and so Norman Jewison's *Other People's Money* turns into a wrestling match between lust and greed. Since these are two of the strongest motivations known to humankind, the movie is very funny and at the same time tremendously interesting.

We see something of Larry's life—the expensive corner office in the Manhattan tower, the block-long limousine, the townhouse, the butler. We see that it is empty of everything except a great deal of money. We see something of Kate's life—the high-powered law firm, the chic fashions, the handsome but empty guys who take her to the opera. We see that it is empty except for defending other people's money. They need each other and they know it, and they spar with this unspoken knowledge in a series of wonderful scenes, including a lunch in a Japanese restaurant and a telephone conversation during which he serenades her on his violin.

Meanwhile, the takeover bid climaxes in a shareholders' meeting inside the factory, at which both Jorgy and Larry make speeches. Gregory Peck's words and delivery here reminded me of the key scenes in a lot of the Frank Capra classics, where the little guy stood up and defended old-fashioned American values, and got a standing ovation, and the movie was over. In *Other People's Money*, after Peck sits down, DeVito stands up and defends greed. It is amazing how good an argument he makes.

The problem is, if he wins the company, will he lose the girl? Maybe the best single moment in the movie comes when he is sure he will never, ever, get to first base with Kate. He falls flat on his face onto the bedspread, stunned with grief and loss, and his butler tries to cheer him. Nothing will work. No material pleasure can possibly cure his agony. "How about a piece of that carrot cake you like?" the butler asks. The timing of DeVito's response to this question wins a roar of laughter.

I didn't like the very last scene of *Other People's Money*. It felt tacked on, manufactured, concocted out of a Hollywood studio's knee-jerk need to provide a smiley-face ending that was not in the spirit of the film. *Other People's Money* is a four-star movie that loses its way in the last, crucial scene, and for that it loses half a star, but that doesn't mean I didn't enjoy every moment right up until the happy ending, which is the unhappiest moment in the movie.

Outbreak ★ ★ ★ ½

R, 127 m., 1995

NEW

Dustin Hoffman (Colonel Sam Daniels, M.D.), Rene Russo (Dr. Robby Keough), Morgan Freeman (General Billy Ford), Kevin Spacey (Major "Casey" Schuler), Cuba Gooding, Jr. (Major Salt), Patrick Dempsey (Jimbo Scott), Donald Sutherland (General McClintock). Directed by Wolfgang Petersen and produced by Arnold Kopelson, Petersen, and Gail Katz. Screenplay by Laurence Dworet and Robert Roy Pool.

It is one of the great scare stories of our time, the notion that deep in the uncharted rain forests, deadly diseases are lurking, and if they ever escape their jungle homes and enter the human bloodstream, there will be a new plague the likes of which we have never seen.

Wolfgang Petersen's *Outbreak* is a clever, daunting thriller about such a possibility. It follows the career of a microscopic bug that kills humans within twenty-four hours after exposure, by liquefying the internal organs. Not a pretty picture. The bug is based on fact; an account of something similar can be found in Richard Preston's book, *The Hot Zone*. The thriller occupies the same territory as countless science fiction movies about deadly invasions and high-tech conspiracies, but has been made with intelligence and an appealing human dimension.

Outbreak opens thirty years ago in Africa, as American doctors descend on a small village that has been wiped out by a deadly new plague. They promise relief, but send instead a single airplane, which incinerates the village with a firebomb. The implication is that the microbe is too deadly to deal with any other way; there is no information about where the bug came from, or why it surfaced in this remote area, although the village witch doctor is quoted ominously: "It is not good to kill the trees."

Flash forward to the present. Dustin Hoffman and Rene Russo are a newly divorced couple, both experts in disease-causing microorganisms. He works for the army, and she has just taken a new job at the Centers for Disease Control in Atlanta. As we follow the disintegration of their relationship, Petersen intercuts scenes showing an African monkey being illegally imported into the United States. This monkey, of course, carries the deadly bug, and the smuggler, unable to sell it, releases it in a California woodland, although not before being infected.

Petersen now shows the disease being spread from one carrier to another, in a montage that would be funny if it were not so chilling: When the first carrier gets off a flight to Boston, he is flushed, sweating, trembling, and almost too weak to stand, but his girlfriend, of course, doesn't let his illness stand in the way of a long, deep, French kiss. Back in a small California town, an infected carrier sneezes in a movie theater, and the camera stalks the germs as they wend their way through the crowd. In a laboratory, a test tube breaks in a centrifuge, and a scientist is infected. And so on. I especially liked the moment when the smuggler takes one bite out of a cookie on an airplane, and a little kid asks him if he's planning to eat the rest of it.

Soon reports of a plague outbreak filter in from Boston and California. Hoffman is assigned to the case by his superior officer (Morgan Freeman). But as he and a colleague (Kevin Spacey) follow the trail of infection and its spread, we get glimpses of a deep conspiracy, involving Freeman's own commanding officer, a sinister general played by Donald Sutherland. For some reason, the army has secrets involving this bug. It also possesses an antidote, although after the microbe mutates into a different form, only the original carrier—the monkey—can serve as the source of an antibody.

Petersen and his writers, Laurence Dworet and Robert Roy Pool, now combine the conventions of several different kinds of thrillers into one gripping story. There is medical detective work, military conspiracy, marital and professional jealousy, and finally an action climax in which Hoffman and his daring helicopter pilot (Cuba Gooding, Jr.) fly all over California and even out to a ship at sea, in a race against time and against another deadly bomb drop.

Outbreak is the kind of movie you enjoy even while you observe yourself being manipulated. The Hoffman character has been recycled out of dozens of other movies; he's the military version of that old crime standby, the Cop With a Theory No One Believes In. Sutherland plays a role so familiar that he himself can be seen playing essentially the same character in a Soviet uniform, in the cable movie *Citizen X*. But the roles are well written and acted, and Morgan Freeman, as a general caught in the middle, brings something quite real, a general trapped between obeying instructions and his own better instincts.

It is a Hollywood law these days that all thrillers end with a chase. Mere dialogue-driven endings are too slow for today's attention-deprived audiences. I am not sure I believed the helicopter chase sequence in *Outbreak*, and I am sure I didn't believe the standoff between a helicopter and a bomber (in a scene with echoes of *Dr. Strangelove*). But by then the movie had cleverly aligned its personal, military, medical, and scientific plots into four simultaneous countdowns, and I was hooked.

The Outlaw Josey Wales ★ ★ ★
PG, 135 m., 1976

Clint Eastwood (Josey), Chief Dan George (The Old Indian), Sondra Locke (The Girl), John Vernon (Fletcher). Directed by Clint Eastwood and produced by Robert Daley. Screenplay by Phil Kaufman.

Clint Eastwood's *The Outlaw Josey Wales* is a strange and daring Western that brings together two of the genre's usually incompatible story lines. On the one hand, it's about a loner, a man of action and few words, who turns his back on civilization and lights out for the Indian nations. On the other hand, it's about a group of people heading West who meet along the trail and cast their destinies together. What happens next is supposed to be against the rules in Westerns, as if *Jeremiah Johnson* were crossed with *Stagecoach*: Eastwood, the loner, becomes the group's leader and father figure.

We meet his character, Josey Wales, just after the Civil War. He's an unreconstructed Southerner, bitter about the atrocities he's witnessed, refusing to surrender. When Northern troops cold-bloodedly murder some of his comrades, he mows down the Yankees with a Gatling gun and becomes a fugitive. So far, we're on familiar ground; Eastwood plays essentially the same character he's been developing since the *Dollar* Westerns. He says little, keeps his face in the shadows, has an almost godlike personal invulnerability, and lives by a code we have to intuit because he'd die rather than explain it aloud.

But then this character begins to come across other drifters and refugees in the unsettled postwar West. The first is an old Indian, played by Chief Dan George with such wonderfully understated wit that there should have been an Oscar nomination around somewhere. "I myself never surrendered," he explains to Josey Wales. "But they got my horse, and *it* surrendered." George achieves the same magical effect here that he did in *Harry and Tonto*, trading Mixmasters for Indian medicine in a jail cell: He's funny and dignified at once. He joins up with the outlaw Eastwood, and their relationship is a reminder of all those great second bananas from the Westerns of the 1940s—the grizzled old characters played by Gabby Hayes and Smiley Burnette. But Chief Dan George brings an aura to his role that audiences seem to respond to viscerally. He has his problems (he's humiliated, as an Indian, that he's grown so old he can no longer sneak up behind people), but he has a humanity that's just there, glowing. He's as open with his personality as Josey Wales is closed; it's a nice match.

Various, and inexhaustible, bounty hunters are constantly on the outlaw's trail, despite the Eastwood ability (in this movie as before) to wipe out six, eight, ten bad guys before they can get off a shot. Eastwood keeps moving West, picking up along the way a young Indian girl and then the survivors of a Kansas family nearly wiped out on their quest for El Dorado. The relationships in the group are easily established or implied. There's not a lot of talking, but everybody understands each other.

Eastwood is such a taciturn and action-oriented performer that it's easy to overlook the fact that he directs many of his movies—and many of the best, most intelligent ones. Here, with the moody, gloomily beautiful, photography of Bruce Surtees, he creates a magnificent Western feeling.

Out of Africa ★ ★ ★
PG, 153 m., 1985

Meryl Streep (Karen), Robert Redford (Denys), Klaus Maria Brandauer (Bror), Michael Kitchen (Berkeley), Malick Bowens (Farah), Joseph Thiaka (Kamante), Stephen Kinyanjui (Kinyanjui), Michael Gough (Delamere), Suzanna Hamilton (Felicity). Directed and produced by Sydney Pollack. Screenplay by Kurt Luedtke.

Earlier, there was a moment when a lioness seemed about to attack, but did not. The baroness had been riding her horse on the veld, had dismounted, had lost her rifle when the horse bolted. Now the lioness seemed about to charge, when behind her a calm voice advised the baroness not to move one inch. "She'll go away," the voice said, and indeed the lioness did skulk away after satisfying its curiosity.

That scene sets up the central moment in Sydney Pollack's *Out of Africa*, which comes somewhat later in the film. The baroness is on safari with the man who owned the cool voice, a big-game hunter named Denys. They happen upon a pride of lions. Once again, the man assumes charge. He will protect them. But then a lion unexpectedly charges from another direction, and it is up to the baroness to fell it, with one shot that must not miss, and does not. After the man and woman are safe, the man sees that the woman has bitten her lip in anxiety. He reaches out and touches the blood. Then they hold each other tightly.

If you can sense the passion in that scene, then you may share my enjoyment of *Out of Africa*, which is one of the great recent epic romances. The baroness is played by Meryl Streep. The hunter is Robert Redford. These are high-voltage stars, and when their chemistry is wrong for romances (as Streep's was for *Falling in Love*, and Redford's for *The Natural*), it is very wrong. This time, it is right.

The movie is based on the life and writings of Baroness Karen Blixen, a Danish woman who, despairing that she would be single forever, married her lover's brother, moved to Kenya in East Africa, ran a coffee plantation on the slopes of Kilimanjaro, and later, when the plantation was bankrupt and the dream was finished, wrote books about her experiences under the name Isak Dinesen.

Her books are glories—especially *Out of Africa* and *Seven Gothic Tales*—but they are not the entire inspiration for this movie.

What we have here is an old-fashioned, intelligent, thoughtful love story, told with enough care and attention that we really get involved in the passions between the characters.

In addition to the people Streep and Redford play, there is a third major character, Bror, the man she marries, played by Klaus Maria Brandauer. He is a smiling, smooth-faced, enigmatic man, who likes her well enough, but never seems quite equal to her spirit. After he gives her syphilis and she returns to Denmark for treatment, she is just barely able to tolerate his behavior—after all, he did not ask to marry her—until a New Year's Eve when he flaunts his infidelity, and she asks him to move out.

He turns up once more, asking for money, after Redford has moved his things into the baroness's farmhouse. The two men have a classic exchange. Brandauer: "You should have asked permission." Redford: "I did. She said yes."

The movie takes place during that strange blip in history when the countries of East Africa—Kenya, Uganda, the Rhodesias—were attracting waves of European settlers discontented with life at home in the years around World War I. The best land available to them was in the so-called white highlands of Kenya, so high up the air was cooler and there were fewer insects, and some luck could be had with cattle and certain crops.

The settlers who lived there soon settled into a hard-drinking, high-living regime that has been documented in many books and novels; they were sort of "Dallas" crossed with *Mandingo*. The movie steers relatively clear of the social life, except for a scene where Streep is snubbed at the local club, a few other scenes in town, and an extraordinary moment when she goes down on her knees before the British governor to plead for land for the Africans who live on her bankrupt farm.

Before that moment, she has not seemed particularly interested in Africans, except for an old overseer who becomes a close friend (and this is not true to the spirit of her book, where Africans are of great importance to her). Instead, she is much more involved in the waves of passion that sweep over the veld, as Redford passes through her life like a comet on a trajectory of its own.

He wants to move "his things" in, but does not want to move himself in. He wants commitment, but personal freedom. His ambiguity toward her is something like his ambiguity toward the land, which he penetrates with truck and airplane, leading tours while all the time bemoaning the loss of the virgin veld. Because *Out of Africa* is intelligently written, directed, and acted, however, we do not see his behavior as simply willful and spoiled, but as part of the contradictions he needs to stay an individual in a land where white society is strictly regimented.

The Baroness Blixen needs no such shields; she embodies sufficient contradictions on her own. In a land where whites are foreigners, she is a foreign white. She writes and thinks instead of gossiping and drinking. She runs her own farm. She scorns local gossip. In this hunter, she finds a spirit equal to her own, which is eventually the undoing of their relationship.

Out of Africa is a great movie to look at, breathtakingly filmed on location. It is a movie with the courage to be about complex, sweeping emotions, and to use the star power of its actors without apology. Sydney Pollack has worked with Redford before—notably in another big-sky epic, *Jeremiah Johnson*. He understands the special, somewhat fragile mystique of his star, who has a tendency to seem overprotective of his own image. In the wrong hands, Redford can look narcissistic. This time, he seems to have much to be narcissistic about.

Out of the Blue ★ ★ ★ ½
R, 94 m., 1982

Linda Manz (CeBe), Dennis Hopper (Don), Sharon Farrell (Kathy), Raymond Burr (Dr. Brean), Don Gordon (Charlie). Directed by Dennis Hopper and produced by Gary Jules Jouvenat. Screenplay by Leonard Yakir and Brenda Nielson.

Out of the Blue is one of the unsung treasures of independent films, a showcase for the maverick talents of two movie rebels: veteran actor Dennis Hopper, of *Easy Rider* and *Rebel Without a Cause,* and young, tough-talking Linda Manz, whose debut in *Days of Heaven* was so heartbreaking. Made in 1982, it never got a chance in commercial theaters. The movie is Hopper's comeback as a director. After the enormous international success of *Easy Rider* (1969) and the resounding thud of his next directorial effort, *Last Movie* (1971), he didn't direct again until this movie (he acted, in such films as *The American Friend* and *Apocalypse Now*). Originally hired just to act in *Out of the Blue,* he took over two weeks into production, rewrote the screenplay, found new locations and made this movie into a bitter, unforgettable poem about alienation.

Hopper is one of the movie's stars, playing an alcoholic truck driver whose semi-rig crashes into a school bus, kills children, and sends him to jail for six years. Manz plays his daughter, a leather-jacketed, punk teen-ager who combs her hair with shoe polish and does Elvis imitations. Her mother is played by Sharon Farrell as a small-town waitress who tries a reconciliation with Hopper when he gets out of prison but is undercut by her drug addiction. Manz is the centerpiece of the film. As she demonstrated in the magnificent pastoral romance *Days of Heaven,* she has a presence all her own. She's tough and hard-edged and yet vulnerable, and in this movie we can sometimes see the scared little kid beneath the punk bravado. She lives in a world of fantasy. All but barricaded into her room, surrounded by posters of Elvis and other teen heroes, she practices her guitar (she isn't very good) and dresses up in her dad's leather jacket. He's a hero to her. She doesn't buy the story that he was responsible for the deaths of those kids. And when he finally gets out of prison, she has a father at last—but only for a few days.

Hopper's touch as a director is especially strong in a pathetic scene of reunion, including the family's day at the overcast, gloomy beach, and a "party" that turns into a violent brawl dominated by the Hopper character's drunken friend (Don Gordon). The movie escalates so relentlessly toward its violent, nihilistic conclusion that when it comes, we believe it. This is a very good movie that simply got overlooked. When it premiered at the 1980 Cannes Film Festival, it caused a considerable sensation, and Manz was mentioned as a front-runner for the best actress award. But back in North America, the film's Canadian backers had difficulties in making a distribution deal, and the film slipped through the cracks.

P

The Package ★ ★ ★
R, 108 m., 1989

Gene Hackman (Johnny Gallagher), Joanna Cassidy (Eileen Gallagher), Tommy Lee Jones (Thomas Boyette), John Heard (Col. Glen Whitacre). Directed by Andrew Davis and produced by Beverly J. Camhe and Tobie Haggerty. Screenplay by John Bishop.

The Package is like one of those thrillers where you keep having to turn back to an earlier chapter to see if you missed something. It turns out you haven't. The movie's plot is so intricate that it seems there have to be loose ends, but there aren't any, and after it's over you rerun the events in your head, seeing at last how all the pieces fit together. Untangling the conspiracy is one of the story's pleasures.

The movie stars Gene Hackman in another one of those man-of-action roles he seems to play more convincingly than ever, now that he seems to be a little too old to be guys like this; both he and his characters seem to have the benefit of experience. He's the leader of a crack U.S. military unit in charge of security at an American-Soviet nuclear disarmament summit. When security seems to have been compromised and a carload of VIPs is ambushed, Hackman gets a lot of the blame. And he is rotated stateside, as the escort for a military prisoner (played with irony and menace by Tommy Lee Jones).

He has already picked up some hints that nothing—especially not the violent ambush—was quite as it seemed. And in a run-in before he leaves Europe, he encounters a specialist in undercover espionage (John Heard) who gives him the creeps. Hackman doesn't like spies. He doesn't think they're professional or quite honest, and the movie argues that he's right; we begin to witness small

moments and snatches of conversation that suggest there's a conspiracy to undermine the peace talks—a conspiracy of spies from both sides. But by then Hackman is on a military aircraft to America with his prisoner.

And it is here, this early in the film, that the surprises start, as the plot turns in upon itself, giving us a series of people with shifting identities and allegiances. Who is the prisoner—really? When Hackman is attacked in the washroom of the airport in Washington and the prisoner is spirited away, was that an escape, a kidnapping, or part of the same plot? Attempting to track down reality in a bewildering maze of possibilities, Hackman calls on one person he knows he can trust: his former wife (Joanna Cassidy), who now outranks him in the military.

It would not be fair to reveal very much more of the plot. In fact, this plot really consists of its revelations. Like *The Manchurian Candidate,* it creates a world in which little is as it seems, and long-buried conspiracies eventually pay off. The Hackman character realizes he has stumbled over a remarkably subtle plan to assassinate a world leader during a visit to Chicago—but we know of the plan before he does, and one of the movie's pleasures is the way we are allowed to figure things out for ourselves, along with Hackman or a little ahead of him.

The Package is directed by Andrew Davis. It is his third film in a row to involve strong action heroes and labyrinthine conspiracies set in Chicago (the others were *Code of Silence,* with Chuck Norris, and *Above the Law,* with Steven Seagal). Although shooting movies on location has been a Hollywood way of life for years, few directors get more out of a location than Davis. He doesn't seem to see cities as most other directors do; he contrives somehow to create a more convincing sense of actual places. By the time the mo-

ment for the would-be assassination has arrived, we have a good idea of the physical layout involved—the angles, the hiding places—but we also have an almost palpable sense of the city.

All three of Davis's movies have the same theme running just beneath the surface, one involving the loyalty of law-enforcement professionals to one another. He always has a character in his movies who is a veteran, street-smart cop with a strong sense of ethics, a man whose word can be absolutely counted on. And there's always a conspiracy somewhere else in the legal apparatus; all of Davis's movies involve diabolical schemes by top security people. What sets *The Package* apart from the earlier films is that there's less emphasis on violent action and more on the unfolding of the plot.

Hackman is very good in the leading role, but then Gene Hackman is so good, so often, that he sometimes seems like a natural force in danger of being taken for granted. What I noticed in this film was the way he made his character into a particular human being. There's not a lot to build on. The plot is so important, the pacing is so urgent, that the pure character moments are rare. So he works with his dialogue, finding ways to make it sound like his ingrained style of speech. There's never the sense he's reading dialogue; he has a habitual ease with the words, almost a weariness in the way he handles his business, that convinces us he's been doing his job for a long time.

I often complain that modern thrillers leave out the third act. There's the setup, the development, and then, instead of a payoff, we get a routine chase and shoot-out. *The Package* does end in a race against time, but Davis bases the race so firmly on who the characters are and what their goals are that it doesn't feel contrived. The whole movie, in fact, is smarter than most contemporary thrillers. It gives us credit for being able to figure things out, and it contains characters who are devilishly intelligent. Almost smart enough, we think for a while, to really pull this thing off.

Pale Rider ★ ★ ★
R, 113 m., 1985

Clint Eastwood (Preacher), Michael Moriarty (Hull Barret), Carrie Snodgress (Sarah Wheeler), Christopher Penn (Josh LaHood), Richard Dysart (Coy LaHood), Sydney Penny (Megan Wheeler), Richard Kiel (Club), Doug McGrath (Spider). Directed and produced by Clint Eastwood. Screenplay by Michael Butler and Dennis Shryack.

Clint Eastwood has become an actor whose moods and silences are so well-known that the slightest suggestion will do to convey an emotion. No actor is more aware of his own instrument, and Eastwood demonstrates that in *Pale Rider*, a film he dominates so completely that only later do we realize how little we really saw of him.

Instead of filling each scene with his own image and dialogue, Eastwood uses sleight of hand: We are shown his eyes, or a corner of his mouth, or his face in a shadow, or his figure with strong light behind it. He has few words. The other characters in the movie project their emotions upon him. He may indeed be the Pale Rider suggested in the title, whose name was death, but he may also be an avenging spirit, come back from the grave to confront the man who murdered him. One of the subtlest things in the movie is the way it plays with the possibility that Eastwood's character may be a ghost, or at least something other than an ordinary mortal.

Other things in the movie are not so subtle. In its broad outlines, *Pale Rider* is a traditional Western, with a story that has been told, in one form or another, a thousand times before. In a small California mining town, some independent miners have staked a claim to a promising lode. The town is ruled by a cabal of evil men, revolving around the local banker and the marshal, who is his hired gun. The banker would like to buy out the little miners, but, lacking that, he will use force to drive them off their land and claim it for his company.

Into this hotbed rides the lone figure of Eastwood, wearing a clerical collar and preferring to be called "Preacher." There are people here he seems to know from before. The marshal, for example, seems to be trying to remember where he has previously encountered this man. Eastwood moves in with the small miners, and becomes close with one group: a miner (Michael Moriarty) who lives with a woman (Carrie Snodgress) and her daughter (Sydney Penny). He urges the miners to take a stand and defend their land, and agrees to help them. That sets the stage for a series of violent confrontations.

As the film's director, Eastwood has done some interesting things with his vision of the West. Instead of making the miners' shacks into early American antique exhibits, he shows them as small and sparse. The sources of light are almost all from the outside. Interiors are dark and gloomy, and the sun is blinding in its intensity. The Eastwood character himself is almost always backlit, so we have to strain to see him, and this strategy makes him more mysterious and fascinating than any dialogue could have.

There are some moments when the movie's myth-making becomes self-conscious. In one scene, for example, the marshal's gunmen enter a restaurant and empty their guns into the chair where Eastwood had been sitting moments before. He is no longer there; can't they see that? In the final shoot-out, the Preacher has a magical ability to dematerialize, confounding the bad guys, and one shot (of a hand with a gun emerging from a water trough) should have been eliminated—it spoils the logic of the scene. But *Pale Rider* is, overall, a considerable achievement, a classic Western of style and excitement. Many of the greatest Westerns grew out of a director's profound understanding of the screen presence of his actors; consider, for example, John Ford's films with John Wayne and Henry Fonda. In *Pale Rider,* Clint Eastwood is the director, and having directed himself in nine previous films, he understands so well how he works on the screen that the movie has a resonance that probably was not even there in the screenplay.

Panther ★ ★ ½
R, 124 m., 1995

Kadeem Hardison (Judge), Marcus Chong (Huey Newton), Courtney B. Vance (Bobby Seale), Don Baker (Brimmer), Anthony Griffith (Eldridge Cleaver), Tyrin Turner (Cy), Bokeem Woodbine (Tyrone), Nefertiti (Alma), Jennifer Lewis (Rita), Wesley Jonathan (Little Bobby). Directed by Mario Van Peebles and produced by Preston Homes and Mario and Melvin Van Peebles. Screenplay by Melvin Van Peebles.

Mario Van Peebles's *Panther* is the story of the rise and fall of a 1960s black radical movement that captured the imagination of its time. Memoirs by its founders and others have suggested that the Black Panthers never had the power or numbers they claimed, but they served a historic purpose, creating the image of an armed, militant "self-defense" group which was an alternative to the nonviolent philosophy of Martin Luther King, Jr.

The Panthers grew famous as the civil rights movement of the early 1960s was losing momentum after the assassination of King. Their message was clear: White America could no longer count on pacifist blacks to patiently hold nonviolent marches; what was coming, as James Baldwin warned, was "The Fire Next Time." News photos of Black Panthers, armed with rifles, patrolling the streets of Oakland or entering the California State Assembly, were among the key images of the time.

There is a fascinating study to be made of the Black Panther Party. *Panther* is not that film. Superficial and confusing, it cops out at the end with a fictitious thriller climax involving the Mafia, the FBI, drugs, chases, fires, and explosions—as if the reality of the Panthers' battles with the police weren't enough.

Panther does a good job, however, of capturing the idealism and excitement of the party's early days. A narrator named Judge (Kadeem Hardison), a fictitious composite, tells us that the Panthers were more or less dreamed up in a coffee shop by Huey P. Newton and Bobby Seale, whose press coverage acted as a nationwide recruitment and publicity machine. In the early days revolutionary rhetoric alternated with improvisation, as when the Panthers paid thirty cents for Chairman Mao's Little Red Book in Chinatown, and sold it to white Berkeley students for one dollar.

Those heady days, part of the Summer of Love, were soon ended, as the Panthers began to feel the pressure of the FBI. Its chief, J. Edgar Hoover, could not believe young blacks were capable of running such an organization, and suspected communists were behind it—as, indeed, he suspected they were behind everything. He infiltrated them with double agents such as Judge, and ordered local lawmen to set them up for phony arrests. Soon the whole enterprise became deadly and dangerous, and Huey Newton ominously quoted the Spanish Civil War leader Delores Ibarruri: "It is better to die on your feet than to live on your knees."

Newton, played by Marcus Chong, is well-read and articulate, forever informing the police of his rights. One of those officers is Brimmer (Joe Don Baker), who angers the FBI when he observes that the Panthers' rhetoric "sounds like the Constitution to me. With maybe a little bit of the Bill of Rights thrown in." Brimmer, who is alternately evil and insightful at the convenience of the plot, eventually runs the infiltration of the Panthers.

Newton and Seale (Courtney B. Vance) run the Oakland Panthers (the film's focus) more or less as equals, realizing they should not show up together at too many events lest the police realize how small the group really is. Minister of Information Eldridge Cleaver (Anthony Griffith) arrives on the scene at about the time Huey is jailed on a frame-up, and is less of a strategist, more of an instigator: "You gotta sit on Eldridge," Newton tells Seale.

The movie's first ninety minutes are a vivid period reconstruction of the way the Panthers grew both through community programs (they fed thousands of children from their storefront centers) and through a canny manipulation of the media. It makes a compelling story. But the climactic scenes of the movie are fabricated. We see teletype printouts, presumably from Hoover, ordering the "ultimate conspiracy." This is an alliance between the FBI and the Mafia to flood the ghetto with cheap drugs. It is a convenient fiction in the movies that the Mafia can do anything, but this plot point is sloppy right down to the wording: Would Hoover refer to his own plan as a "conspiracy"?

Mario Van Peebles has said there is no evidence that the FBI plotted to weaken the party by flooding Oakland with heroin. Although the "ultimate conspiracy" makes a convenient plot point, it does a disservice to young people who want to understand what really happened. The Panthers' end came through exhaustion, through the imprisonment or exile of their best leaders, through the harassment of the FBI, and because some members became disillusioned by the questionable activities of others. They weren't done in by the godfathers.

But that wouldn't have made an exciting ending. Instead, Panthers dodge behind crates as bullets whiz past, and a courageous martyr sacrifices his life to destroy the Mafia's drugs. This action ending is a cop-out, underlining the superficial way the characters have been treated.

Spike Lee's *Malcolm X*, dealing with related material at about the same time, does a much better job of making its characters three-dimensional, and getting us involved with them. Since *Panther* is told from the conveniently omniscient point of view of Judge, who is fictitious, I never got a real feeling for Seale and Newton as human beings.

At the end of the film, we are informed, "Before the Panthers were crushed, they had succeeded in establishing chapters in almost every state." There's the real story—how they did it, who they were, how they were crushed. That's the movie still to be made.

The Paper ★ ★ ★ ½
R, 112 m., 1994

Michael Keaton (Henry Hackett), Robert Duvall (Bernie White), Glenn Close (Alicia Clark), Marisa Tomei (Martha Hackett), Randy Quaid (McDougal), Jason Robards (Graham Keighley), Jason Alexander (Marion Sandusky), Spalding Gray (Paul Bladden). Directed by Ron Howard and produced by Brian Grazer and Frederick Zollo. Written by David Koepp and Stephen Koepp.

Ron Howard's *The Paper* gets a lot of things right about working on a newspaper, and one of them is how it screws up your personal life. You get cocooned in a tight little crowd of hyperactive competitors, and eventually your view of normality begins to blur. The phrase "I'm on deadline!" becomes an excuse for behavior that would otherwise lack any justification.

Michael Keaton is just about perfectly cast in the movie as an assistant managing editor who cannot, under any circumstances, let a big story wait until tomorrow. Not even if his pregnant wife has been waiting for hours in a restaurant with his parents. Not even if it's costing thousands of dollars an hour to delay a press run. Not even if he's not exactly sure the big story actually exists in a form that is printable. He gets a strange light in his eyes and switches into hyper drive, and only the other people who work with him can truly understand how he feels.

The movie takes place during about twenty-four hours in the life of a New York daily called the *Sun*, but clearly modeled on the *Post*. It's a scrappy tabloid that has teetered for years on the brink of bankruptcy, and its headlines scream sensationally in the biggest type (or "wood") the page will hold. But the Keaton character, whose name is Hackett, can truthfully say that it has never knowingly printed anything that was untrue. Until tonight, maybe.

A big story is breaking. Two men have been shot dead in a parked car. Two young black kids have been seen fleeing the scene of the crime. We know (because the movie tells us) that the kids are innocent. But there's political pressure to find the killers, and when the kids are arrested, every paper in town goes with the story, big. It's just that one of Hackett's reporters has overheard information indicating that the police themselves think the kids didn't do it.

A big story—if anyone in authority will go on record. Meanwhile, the minutes are ticking away toward the deadline, and Hackett's superior, a managing editor named Alicia Clark (Glenn Close), wants to go with the story they have on hand and then fix it tomorrow. To delay will cost thousands of dollars in pressroom overtime and drivers' wages. But going with the easy story sounds all wrong to Hackett, and also to his star columnist McDougal (Randy Quaid), and they go on a desperate odyssey through the night to try to get the quote they need. Meanwhile, of course, the wife and the in-laws get stood up.

All of which makes *The Paper* sound like a *film noir* set in a newspaper office. It is, in a way. But it's very perceptive about the relationships among its characters—how they talk, how they compete, what their values are. And Howard has cast the movie with splendid veteran actors, who are able to bring all the little quirks and idiosyncrasies of real people.

Robert Duvall, for example, plays the paper's editor with such depth that he turns an essentially supporting role into the man's life story—a story of broken marriages, estranged children, nightly drinking, and hidden desperation, all contained in a package of unbending journalistic integrity. I don't know if the Duvall character is based on an actual man in New York, but I have known three or four Chicago editors who could have inspired this guy, right down to his patience with strangers in a bar.

Because this is a story and not a documentary, Howard and his writers, David and Stephen Koepp, turn up the heat a little. In real life, editors may scream at one another, but they hardly ever get into fistfights in the pressroom. Nut cases may come looking for columnists they hate, but they rarely cause much harm. Cops may tell the truth to reporters, but not often with such exquisite dramatic timing. The movie is just a little bigger than life—although I, for one, admired the scene that justified a once-in-a-lifetime opportunity to shout, "Stop the presses!"

The Glenn Close character is one of the movie's more interesting. She is a professional newspaperwoman who is also, it would appear, wealthy and fashionable—and embittered, because the guys on the staff have frozen her out. She's also the heavy, until the somewhat too neat ending. But I liked the speech in which she tells a couple of the men on the staff how she feels, and why. Sometimes sexual harassment is almost impossible to define: For example, what do you call it when the guys go out for a beer and never, ever, invite this woman along?

Michael Keaton is a fast-talking actor, who may be the best in the business at showing you how fast he can think. He projects smartness, he sees all the angles, he sizes up a situation and acts on it while another actor might still be straightening his tie. He is wonderful here at projecting a quality of angry impatience: He knows he's right, he knows he's late, he knows what he has to do, and he'll explain everything later.

Watching *The Paper* got me in touch all over again with how good it feels to work at the top of your form, on a story you believe in, on deadline. Here on the movie beat everything is pretty neatly scheduled and we don't cover a lot of crimes. But I used to write real news on deadline, and those were some of the happiest days of my life. This movie knows how that feels.

The Paper Chase ★ ★ ★
PG, 111 m., 1973

Timothy Bottoms (Hart), Lindsay Wagner (Susan), John Houseman (Kingsfield), Graham Beckel (Ford), Edward Herrmann (Anderson), Bob Lydiard (O'Connor). Directed by James Bridges and produced by Robert C. Thompson and Rodrick Paul. Screenplay by Bridges.

The Paper Chase is about an aggressive, very bright, terribly engaging first-year student at Harvard Law School. The movie respects its hero, respects the school, and most of all respects the venerable Professor Kingsfield, tyrant of contract law.

Kingsfield is really the movie's central character, even though John Houseman gets supporting billing for the role. Everything centers around his absolute dictatorship in the classroom and his icy reserve at all other times. He's the kind of teacher who inspires total dread in his students, and at the same time a measure of hero worship; he doesn't just know contract law, he wrote the book.

Into his classroom every autumn come several dozen would-be Harvard law graduates, who fall into the categories we all remember from school: (a) the drones, who get everything right but will go forth to lead lives of impeccable mediocrity; (b) the truly intelligent, who will pass or fail entirely on the basis of whether they're able to put up with the crap; (c) those with photographic memories, who can remember everything but connect nothing; (d) the students whose dogged earnestness will somehow pull them through; and (e) the doomed.

One of each of these types is in the study group of Hart, the movie's hero, and the one who is truly intelligent. He's a graduate of the University of Minnesota and somewhat out of place among the Ivy League types, but he does well in class because he really cares about the law. He also cares about Kingsfield, to the degree that he breaks into the library archives to examine the master's very own undergraduate notes.

Hart is played by Timothy Bottoms, the star of *The Last Picture Show*. Bottoms is an awfully good actor, and so natural and unaffected that he shows up the mannerisms of actors like Dustin Hoffman or Jon Voight. Bottoms never seems to try; he's just there, complete and convincing. He falls in love, fatefully, with Susan (Lindsay Wagner), who turns out to be, even more fatefully, Kingsfield's daughter. Their relationship is a little hard to follow in the film; we aren't sure why she treats him the way she does—after all, she loves the guy—and the movie jerks abruptly in bringing them back together after a split-up.

But that isn't fatal because the fundamental relationship in the movie is between Hart and Kingsfield. The crusty old professor obviously appreciates the intelligence and independence of his prize student, but he hardly ever lets his affection show; there's a great scene in the classroom where he calls Hart forward, offers him a dime, and says: "Call your mother and tell her you will never be a lawyer." Houseman is able to project subtleties of character even while appearing stiff and unrelenting; it's a performance of Academy Award quality, and resulted in an Oscar for Best Supporting Actor.

Lindsay Wagner, as the daughter, is also a surprise; she made her movie debut in the unfortunate *Two People*, which had Peter Fonda as a conscience-stricken Army deserter. She wasn't able to make much of an impression in that one, but *The Paper Chase* establishes her as an actress with class and the saving grace of humor.

What's best about the movie is that it considers interesting adults—young and old—in an intelligent manner. After it's over we almost feel relief; there are so many movies about clods reacting moronically to romantic and/or violent situations. But we hardly ever get movies about people who seem engaging enough to spend half an hour talking with (what would you say to Charles Bronson?). Here's one that works.

Paperhouse ★ ★ ★
PG-13, 94 m., 1989

Charlotte Burke (Anna), Elliott Spiers (Marc), Glenne Headly (Kate), Ben Cross (Dad), Gemma Jones (Dr. Nichols). Directed by Bernard Rose and produced by Tim Bevan and Sarah Radclyffe. Screenplay by Matthew Jacobs, based on the novel *Marianne Dreams*, by Catherine Storr.

Paperhouse is a film in which every image has been distilled to the point of almost frightening simplicity. It's like a Bergman film, in which the clarity is almost overwhelming, and we realize how muddled and cluttered most movies are. This one has the stark landscapes and the obsessively circling story lines of a dream—which is what it is.

The movie takes place during the illness of Anna (Charlotte Burke), a thirteen-year-old with a mysterious fever. One day in class, Anna draws a lonely house on a windswept cliff and puts a sad-faced little boy in the window. She is reprimanded by the teacher, runs away from the school, falls in a culvert, and is knocked unconscious.

And then she dreams of a "real" landscape just like the one in her drawing, with the very same house, and with a sad boy's face in an upper window. She asks him to come outside. He cannot, because his legs will not move, and because she has not drawn any stairs in the house.

Found by a search party, Anna is returned home, where her behavior is explained by the fever she has developed. The film alternates between Anna's sickroom and her dream landscape, and very few other characters are allowed into her confined world. Among them, however, are her mother (Glenne Headly) and her doctor (Gemma Jones), and there are flashbacks to her absent father (Ben Cross), who is the distant and ambiguous father figure of so many frightening children's stories.

The film develops a simple rhythm. Anna draws, dreams, and then revises her drawings. She sketches in a staircase for the young boy, whose name is Marc, and fills his room with toys. She adds a fruit tree and flowers to the garden. And then one day she discovers, to her astonishment, that her doctor has another patient—a boy named Marc, who faces paralysis, and about whom she is very concerned.

Paperhouse wisely never attempts to provide any kind of a rational explanation for its story, although we might care to guess that the doctor is sort of a psychic conduit allowing Anna and Marc to enter each other's dreams. Anna rebels briefly against the notion that she is someone playing God for Marc, but then accepts the responsibility of her drawings and her dreams.

Paperhouse is not in any sense simply a children's movie, even though its subject may seem to point it in that direction. It is a thoughtfully written, meticulously directed fantasy in which the actors play their roles with great seriousness. Watching it, I was engrossed in the development of the story, and found myself accepting the film's logic on its own terms.

The movie's director is Bernard Rose, a young Briton who had some success with music videos before this first feature. He carries some of the same visual inventiveness of the best music videos over into his images here, paring them down until only the essential elements are present, making them so spare that, like the figure of Death in Bergman's *Seventh Seal*, they seem too concrete to be fantasies.

I will not discuss the end of the movie, except to say that it surprised and pleased me. I don't know what I expected—some kind of conventional plot resolution, I suppose—but *Paperhouse* ends instead with a bittersweet surprise that is unexpected and almost spiritual. This is not a movie to be measured and weighed and plumbed, but to be surrendered to.

Parenthood ★ ★ ★ ★
PG-13, 124 m., 1989

Steve Martin (Gil), Mary Steenburgen (Karen), Dianne Wiest (Helen), Jason Robards (Frank),

Rick Moranis (Nathan), Tom Hulce (Larry), Martha Plimpton (Julie), Keanu Reeves (Tod). Directed by Ron Howard and produced by Brian Glazer. Screenplay by Lowell Ganz and Babaloo Mandel.

Ron Howard's *Parenthood* is a delicate balancing act between comedy and truth, a movie that contains a lot of laughter and yet is more concerned with character than punch lines. It's the best kind of comedy, where we recognize the truth of what's happening even while we're smiling, and where we eventually acknowledge that there is a truth in comedy that serious drama can never quite reach.

The movie is about a lot of parents and children—four generations, from an ancient matriarch to a three-year-old. Because almost everyone in this movie has both parents and children, almost everyone in the movie is both a child and a parent, and a lot of the film's strength comes from the way it sees each generation in reaction to its parents' notions of parenthood. The complexity of the movie—there are a dozen or more important characters—must have seemed daunting on the writing level, and yet the film's first strength is in the smart, nimble screenplay, which is also very wise.

Parenthood stars Steve Martin and Mary Steenburgen as the parents of three children, with another on the way. Life is not easy for them, although they are surrounded by all of the artifacts of middle-class suburbia, such as a nice home and new uniforms for the Little League team. Martin is engaged in warfare at the office, where he wants to be made a partner, and yet he resists spending too much time at work because he wants to be a good father—a better father than his father (Jason Robards), who was cold and distant.

We can see this for ourselves when we meet the Robards character. Or can we? Robards himself feels little love for his surviving parent, a mother of whom he snarls, "Yeah, she's still alive" at a family gathering. Robards has had four children, and we meet them all in the movie: characters played by Martin, Dianne Wiest, Harley Kozak, and Tom Hulce.

The Hulce character, Robards's youngest child, is in his mid-twenties and is the family's black sheep (he is introduced with the line, "Whatever you do, don't lend him any money"). He is a compulsive gambler and liar, and yet Robards somehow keeps alive a

flame of hope for him, and loves him and cares, and so you can see that parenthood has not been simple for him, either.

We learn these and other things in an indirect way; the screenplay, by Lowell Ganz and Babaloo Mandel, with input from director Ron Howard, never reveals an obvious plot line, but instead cuts between several different family situations.

With Martin and Steenburgen, we see an attempt being made to create a typical, wholesome American nuclear family—with Martin driven almost to exhaustion by his determination to be a "good pop." Dianne Wiest plays a divorced mother of two, who is bitter about her former husband, and weary but courageous in her determination to do her best by a strong-willed sixteen-year-old daughter (Martha Plimpton) and a secretive, distracted thirteen-year-old son (Leaf Phoenix).

Kozak plays a sensible mother whose husband (Rick Moranis) is insanely obsessed with his theories about tapping the genius within young children; he reads Kafka at bedtime to their daughter, not yet four, and proudly demonstrates that she can look at a group of paper dots and calculate their square root (Martin and Steenburgen's child is only human and later eats the dots). The Hulce character is the only one not yet married, and indeed, in his gambling and lying and dangerous brinksmanship he seems to have flown entirely out of the orbit of parenthood. Perhaps the best scene in the movie is the one between Robards and Hulce after the old man has decided to make one more sacrifice for his no-good son, and then the son betrays the trust because what he really wants is not help, but simply the freedom to keep on losing.

Howard, Ganz, and Mandel have fifteen children among them, I understand, and that is easy to believe. Even such standard scenes as the annual school play, with the parents beaming proudly from the audience and the kids dropping their lines onstage, is handled here with a new spin. There are many moments of accurate observation, as when kids of a certain age fall in love with terms for excrement, or when kids at a party refuse to have the good time that has been so expensively prepared for them.

What I enjoyed most about the movie was the way so many scenes were thought through to an additional level. Howard and his collaborators don't simply make a point, they make the point and then take another look at it from a new angle, finding a different kind of truth. There is a wonderful moment, for example, in which the old matriarch (Helen Shaw) makes a wise and pithy observation, and then goes out to get into the car. Her dialogue provides a strong exit line, and a lot of movies would have left it at that, but not *Parenthood,* which adds a twist: "If she's so smart," Martin observes, looking out the window, "why is she sitting in the neighbor's car?"

In a movie filled with good performances, I especially admired the work by Martin, Steenburgen, Wiest, and Robards. What we are seeing in their performances, I think, is acting enriched by having lived, having actually gone through some of the doubts and long nights and second thoughts that belong to their characters. For Ron Howard, the movie is a triumph of a different sort: Having emerged from a TV sitcom determined to become a director, he paid his dues with apprentice work like *Grand Theft Auto,* went on to box-office and critical success with *Splash* and *Cocoon,* and now has made a wonderful film that shows him as a filmmaker mature and secure enough to find truth in comedy, and comedy in truth, even though each hides in the other so successfully.

Paris Is Burning ★ ★ ★
NO MPAA RATING, 78 m., 1991

A documentary on "voguing" and the drag balls of Harlem. Starring Carmen and Brooke, Andre Christian, Dorian Corey, Paris Dupree, Willi Ninja, Pepper Labeija, and Junior Labeija. Directed and produced by Jennie Livingston.

In Paris you will find the House of Dior and the House of Chanel. Harlem is the birthplace of houses, too, such as the House of Labeija, the House of Xtravaganza, the House of Ninja, and other clubs founded in a cosmic rebuke of the snobbery that is at the heart of high fashion. The Harlem houses were founded and organized by gay black and Hispanic men, to sponsor costume balls where prizes are given in such categories as "realness," "evening wear," "executive wear," and "bangee."

Once such events would have been known as drag balls, and the competitors would have been called drag queens. But now look at what they've mutated into: What are we to make of this young military school student, the spotlights glistening on his sword and scabbard, or the sleek business executive in a Brooks Brothers suit? If the drag balls of

years past demonstrated a kind of yearning among men who wanted to look like women, the balls in *Paris Is Burning* exhibit an even more poignant longing. The models compete to see who could pass in worlds that are almost completely closed to gays and blacks— and, most especially, gay blacks.

Paris Is Burning documents a world that was a secret until the dance style called "voguing" moved out of the balls and into the more daring of the mainstream clubs. Madonna recruited vogue dancers for her most recent world tour, and some of the stars of voguing, such as Willi Ninja, have had success in legitimate modeling and choreography.

But voguing is more than a dance style, and the balls are more than a competition for big bronze trophies—the same kinds of unwieldy, grandiose prizes people take home from bowling tournaments. Voguing is, first of all, a highly developed form of expression in which the dancers combine the typical poses of a *Vogue* model with dance moves and body positions inspired by Egyptian hieroglyphics to create pantomimes in which stories are told and statements are made. The models even compete with one another; Willi Ninja does a routine with a compact mirror and then turns the mirror onto his competitor and does another pantomime designed to suggest steps his competitor should take to become as beautiful as Willi is.

Paris Is Burning combines footage shot at several balls and interviews with some of the participants. From the competitions, we see the bizarre mated with the mundane, as when there are dress categories such as "the gay-basher who beat you up on the way here tonight," and the competitors are scored by a panel of judges who hold up cardboards with point scores on them—just like in the Olympic diving competitions.

The interviews make it clear that some of the competitors—who can look so affluent and "real" in their expensive costumes— lead marginal lives as hustlers and thieves. Until recently many of the balls were held secretly because, we learn, a lot of the costumes were stolen goods. Other costumes may be financed by prostitution. One slight young man, proud of his slender build and convincingly female appearance, talks about the men he dates: "In 99 percent of the cases, they don't want sex. Well . . . 95 percent." Shortly after the interview was filmed, he was found beaten to death.

Beatings, violence, and rejection are daily realities for men who want to pass as women,

and so there is a certain courage exhibited by their choice. There is also a social commentary. Some of the reviews of *Paris Is Burning* have called the movie depressing—because the dancers are pretending to be the kinds of people who would not accept them in real life ("After all," one person says, "how many gay black males are there in the business executive ranks?"). I was not depressed. What I saw was a successful attempt by the outsiders to dramatize how success and status in the world often depends on props you can buy, or steal, almost anywhere—assuming you have the style to know how to use them.

Paris, Texas ★ ★ ★ ★
R, 145 m., 1984

Harry Dean Stanton (Travis), Nastassja Kinski (Jane), Hunter Carson (Their Son), Dean Stockwell (Walt), Aurore Clement (Anne), Bernhard Wicki (Dr. Ulmer). Directed by Wim Wenders and produced by Don Guest. Screenplay by Sam Shepard.

A man walks alone in the desert. He has no memory, no past, no future. He finds an isolated settlement where the doctor, another exile, a German, makes some calls. Eventually the man's brother comes to take him back home again. Before we think about this as the beginning of a story, let's think about it very specifically as the first twenty minutes of a movie. When I was watching *Paris, Texas* for the first time, my immediate reaction to the film's opening scenes was one of intrigue: I had no good guesses about where this movie was headed, and that, in itself, was exciting, because in this most pragmatic of times, even the best movies seem to be intended as predictable consumer products. If you see a lot of movies, you can sit there watching the screen and guessing what will happen next, and be right most of the time.

That's not the case with *Paris, Texas.* This is a defiantly individual film, about loss and loneliness and eccentricity. We haven't met the characters before in a dozen other films. To some people, that can be disconcerting; I've actually read reviews of *Paris, Texas* complaining because the man in the desert is German, and that another character is French. Is it written that the people in movies have to be Middle Americans, like refugees from a sitcom?

The characters in this movie come out of the imagination of Sam Shepard, the playwright of rage and alienation, and Wim Wenders, a West German director who often makes "road movies," in which lost men look for answers in the vastness of great American cities. The lost man is played this time by Harry Dean Stanton, the most forlorn and angry of all great American character actors. We never do find out what personal cataclysm led to his walk in the desert, but as his memory begins to return, we learn how much he has lost. He was married, once, and had a little boy. The boy has been raised in the last several years by Stanton's brother (Dean Stockwell) and sister-in-law (Aurore Clement). Stanton's young wife (Nastassja Kinski) seems to have disappeared entirely in the years of his exile. The little boy is played by Hunter Carson, in one of the least affected, most convincing juvenile performances in a long time. He is more or less a typical American kid, despite the strange adults in his life. He meets Stanton and accepts him as a second father, but of course he thinks of Stockwell and Clement as his family. Stanton has a mad dream of finding his wife and putting the pieces of his past back together again. He goes looking, and finds Kinski behind the one-way mirror of one of those sad sex emporiums where men pay to talk to women on the telephone.

Paris, Texas is more concerned with exploring emotions than with telling a story. This isn't a movie about missing persons, but about missing feelings. The images in the film show people framed by the vast, impersonal forms of modern architecture; the cities seem as empty as the desert did in the opening sequence. And yet this film is not the standard attack on American alienation. It seems fascinated by America, by our music, by the size of our cities, and a land so big that a man like the Stanton character might easily get misplaced. Stanton's name in the movie is Travis, and that reminds us not only of Travis McGee, the private eye who specialized in helping lost souls, but also of lots of American Westerns in which things were simpler, and you knew who your enemy was. It is a name out of American pop culture, and the movie is a reminder that all three of the great German New Wave directors—Herzog, Fassbinder, and Wenders—have been fascinated by American rock music, American fashions, American mythology.

This is Wenders's fourth film shot at least partly in America (the others were *Alice in the Cities*, *The American Friend*, and *Hammett*). It also bears traces of *Kings of the Road*, his German road movie in which two men meet by chance and travel for a time together, united by their mutual inability to love and understand women. But it is better than those movies—it's his best work so far—because it links the unforgettable images to a spare, perfectly heard American idiom. The Sam Shepard dialogue has a way of allowing characters to tell us almost nothing about themselves, except for their most banal beliefs and their deepest fears.

Paris, Texas is a movie with the kind of passion and willingness to experiment that was more common fifteen years ago than it is now. It has more links with films like *Five Easy Pieces* and *Easy Rider* and *Midnight Cowboy*, than with the slick arcade games that are the box-office winners of the 1980s. It is true, deep, and brilliant.

Pascali's Island ★ ★ ★
PG-13, 101 m., 1988

Ben Kingsley (Basil Pascali), Charles Dance (Anthony Bowles), Kevork Malikyan (Mardosian), George Murcell (Herr Gesing), Helen Mirren (Lydia Neuman), Nadim Sawalha (Pasha). Directed and written by James Dearden. Produced by Eric Fellner.

There is a bittersweet loneliness in the life of an exile that exerts a romantic appeal to many people. They see themselves as a mysterious figure on a Mediterranean island, seen by all, known to few, living a life of intense privacy in full view. The problem with such a life is that it cannot sustain trust; the very essence of exile is the belief that one can only really count on oneself.

Basil Pascali is a man with such a belief, and at the beginning of *Pascali's Island* we see him at his window, his pen in hand, looking out over the harbor where a stranger is being brought ashore. Pascali (Ben Kingsley) is a spy. The year is 1908, and he has been living on the Greek island of Simi for twenty years or more, faithfully filing his reports to the sultan of the Ottoman Empire. He cannot even remember when one of his reports was acknowledged, but his payment still arrives regularly, and so he mails out his reports just as faithfully.

Since there is every likelihood that no one ever reads a word he writes, why does he persevere? Perhaps it is because, in his exile, he has become a voyeur, feeding off the lives of others as a substitute for the sterility of his own. In the course of this movie, his lifelong practice will have disastrous results.

The stranger he sees being brought ashore is Anthony Bowles (Charles Dance), an Englishman who claims to be an archaeologist. Like almost everyone in this forgotten corner of the world, however, he is probably lying about himself, and his motives can be assumed to be suspicious. He needs a translator for his work, and hires Pascali (who has been careful to put himself in the path of the job).

Another one of the exiles on the island is Lydia Neuman (Helen Mirren), a painter who drenches her pictures in the hot, blinding Mediterranean sun. Pascali has been in love with her for quite some time, from afar. He dares not draw closer because he is a spy (his official reason), and because he cannot abide sharing his privacy with anyone (his real reason). Yet he has cherished the notion that Lydia will someday be his own, and so it is with dismay that he realizes that the bluff, confident Bowles plans to romance her. Lydia is, however, something of a burnout case, and looks with bemusement on those who would love her.

Now we have the elements of the story: The voyeur who cannot trust, the adventurer who cannot be trusted, and the muse who cannot inspire. There are lots of others on the island, Turks, Greeks, Germans, all with more complicated motives than they admit. No one is quite as he seems on Simi. And then one day, in the midst of this, Bowles shockingly discovers something that is real, and that does mean what it seems to mean.

It is the perfect statue of a boy, a priceless, unblemished sculpture from ancient Greek times. Although Bowles is instantly transfixed by the worth and beauty of his find, what he cannot quite deal with is the fact that it is absolutely authentic. Such stark reality undercuts his personality, which is based on deception, on pretending to have more and to know more than he really does. How can such a man deal with the possession of the real thing?

Pascali's Island buries this question within a larger intrigue, as Pascali barters information to both sides and sets about an intrigue that ends in catastrophe. By the end of the film, everything has been lost, and the reason is that none of the characters knows how to deal with acceptance and success. At the heart of *Pascali's Island* is a deep irony: Its characters know how to mask failure, but not how to surrender it.

The movie was written and directed by James Dearden, who wrote *Fatal Attraction*, but it has almost nothing in common with that film. It is a mood piece, meditative, in which even the melodrama of the plot grows out of the flawed souls of the characters. Everything in a film like this depends on performance, and it is hard to imagine how it could have been better cast.

Ben Kingsley's performance is at the heart of everything, and he is a master at suggesting the passionate need and sadness that lurk just beneath a controlled, even cold, surface. Charles Dance, recently seen in *White Mischief* and *Plenty*, is cold, too, but with the easy surface charm of an Englishman who has spent most of his life trying to appear richer and more confident than he is. Helen Mirren plays a solitary woman painter at a time when such figures were rarely seen in the world, a woman who protects herself by seeming distracted, even slightly, charmingly, crazy. The conclusion of this movie, I suppose, is that all of these people get what they deserve, but that after all it is rather a shame.

A Passage to India ★ ★ ★

PG, 160 m., 1984

Judy Davis (Adela Quested), Victor Banerjee (Dr. Aziz), Peggy Ashcroft (Mrs. Moore), Alec Guinness (Godbole) James Fox (Fielding), Nigel Havers (Ronny Heaslop). Directed by David Lean and produced by John Brabourne and Richard Goodwin. Screenplay by Lean.

"Only connect!"—E.M. Forster

That is the advice he gives us in *Howards End*, and then, in *A Passage to India*, he creates a world in which there are no connections, where Indians and Englishmen speak the same language but do not understand each other, where it doesn't matter what you say in the famous Marabar Caves, since all that comes back is a hollow, mocking, echo. Forster's novel is one of the literary landmarks of this century, and now David Lean has made it into one of the greatest screen adaptations I have ever seen.

Great novels do not usually translate well to the screen. They are too filled with ambiguities, and movies have a way of making all their images seem like literal fact. *A Passage to India* is especially tricky, because the central event in the novel is something that happens offstage, or never happens at all—take your choice. On a hot, muggy day, the eager Dr. Aziz leads an expedition to the Marabar Caves. One by one, members of the party drop out, until finally only Miss Quested,

from England, is left. And so the Indian man and the British woman climb the last path alone, at a time when England's rule of India was based on an ingrained, semiofficial racism, and some British, at least, nodded approvingly at Kipling's "East is East, and West is West, and never the twain shall meet."

In Forster's novel, it is never clear exactly what it was that happened to Miss Quested after she wandered alone into one of the caves. David Lean's film leaves that question equally open. But because he is dealing with a visual medium, he cannot make it a mystery where Dr. Aziz is at the time; if you are offstage in a novel, you can be anywhere, but if you are offstage in a movie, you are definitely not where the camera is looking. So in the film version we know, or think we know, that Dr. Aziz is innocent of the charges later brought against him—of the attempted rape of Miss Quested.

The charges and the trial fill the second half of Lean's *A Passage to India*. Lean brings us to that point by a series of perfectly modulated, quietly tension-filled scenes in which Miss Quested (Judy Davis) and the kindly Mrs. Moore (Peggy Ashcroft) sail to India, where Miss Quested is engaged to marry the priggish local British magistrate in a provincial backwater. Both women want to see the "real India"—a wish that is either completely lacking among the locals, or is manfully repressed. Mrs. Moore goes walking by a temple pool by moonlight, and meets the earnest young Dr. Aziz, who is captivated by her gentle kindness. Miss Quested wanders by accident into the ruins of another temple, populated by sensuous and erotic statuary, tumbled together, overgrown by vegetation.

Miss Quested's temple visit is not in Forster, but has been added by Lean (who wrote his own screenplay). It accomplishes just what it needed, suggesting that in Miss Quested the forces of sensuality and repression run a great deal more deeply than her sexually constipated fiancé is ever likely to suspect. Meanwhile, we meet some of the other local characters, including Dr. Godbole (Alec Guinness), who meets every crisis with perfect equanimity, and who believes that what will be, will be. This philosophy sounds like recycled fortune cookies but turns out, in the end, to have been the simple truth. We also meet Fielding (James Fox), one of those tall, lonely, middle-aged Englishmen who hang about the edges of stories set in the Empire, waiting until their destiny commands them to take a firm stand.

Lean places these characters in one of the most beautiful canvases he has ever drawn (and this is the man who directed *Doctor Zhivago* and *Lawrence of Arabia*). He doesn't see the India of travel posters and lurid postcards, but the India of a Victorian watercolorist like Edward Lear, who placed enigmatic little human figures here and there in spectacular landscapes that never seemed to be quite finished. Lean makes India look like an amazing, beautiful place that an Englishman can never quite put his finger on—which is, of course, the lesson Miss Quested learns in the caves.

David Lean is a meticulous craftsman, famous for going to any lengths to make every shot look just the way he thinks it should. His actors here are encouraged to give sound, thoughtful, unflashy performances (Guinness strains at the bit), and his screenplay is a model of clarity: By the end of this movie we know these people so well, and understand them so thoroughly, that only the most reckless among us would want to go back and have a closer look at those caves.

Passenger 57 ★ ★ ★

R, 85 m., 1992

Wesley Snipes (John Cutter), Bruce Payne (Charles Rane), Alex Datcher (Marti Slayton), Tom Sizemore (Sly Delvecchio), Bruce Greenwood (Stuart Ramsey), Robert Hooks (Dwight Henderson), Elizabeth Hurley (Sabrina Ritchie). Directed by Kevin Hooks and produced by Lee Rich, Dan Paulson, and Dylan Sellers. Screenplay by David Loughery and Dan Gordon.

A lesser person might have found fault with certain aspects of *Passenger 57*, but not me. I worked myself into the right mood and had a good time. Sure, the movie has holes in it large enough to fly a DC-10 through, but what the hey: It may be implausible from beginning to end, but it has high energy and that kind of crazy intensity that makes you care in spite of yourself.

The movie stars Wesley Snipes as the best antiterrorist expert in the business. But he has fallen into a deep depression after the death of his wife, killed in a hostage situation in a grocery store. Snipes feels he is responsible for the death, and so he's dropped out of the big leagues and has a routine job as an inflight security instructor for an airline. Then an old pal talks him into taking a top airline security post.

Enter Charles Rane (Bruce Payne), the most notorious airplane hijacker of recent years, who is arrested and sent from Florida to California by air ("Why don't they send hijackers by car, or train?" someone asks, not unreasonably). Snipes finds himself on the same flight, going west to take his new job. When Payne's accomplices take over the airplane and murder crew members and innocent passengers, it's up to Snipes, Anonymous Passenger 57, to save the plane and stop the villain. He is helped out by a flight attendant named Marti (Alex Datcher), whom he'd fought with earlier, in flight school. Now, working side by side, they begin to fall in love while the evil Payne unveils his diabolical schemes.

Snipes's methods are just a shade unlikely. He's one of those guys who doesn't believe in using the doors when he gets on and off an airplane. At one point he is pushed out of a plane as it's about to land, and survives. (Before he was pushed, he was planning to jump.) What is the landing speed of a DC-10? Around 190 mph? How would the tarmac feel at that speed? Don't even ask; later in the film, he gets back on the plane as it's taking off, jumping from a speeding squad car onto the landing gear. Uh-huh.

My favorite implausibility involves a moment when Payne uses a diversion in order to sneak off the grounded plane and escape across the field to a nearby carnival. No one sees him leave the plane. The cops don't even have it surrounded. Therefore it is reasonable to assume he is still on board. But Snipes, who has been arrested by the local cops under the misapprehension that *he* is the hijacker, knocks out a couple of cops, steals a motorcycle, races it through a chain-link fence, and heads straight for the carnival grounds.

There's no way Snipes could know that Payne left the plane, or that he was hiding in the carnival crowds. So why does he head in that direction? Easy. He's seen a lot of movies, and knows that whenever it is humanly possible, an escaping villain will head straight for the nearest carnival. It's a matter of courtesy: He wants to make it easy for the film's director to shoot the obligatory scenes of the fist fight on the Ferris wheel and the shootout on the merry-go-round.

There are other howlers in *Passenger 57,* but never mind; the movie has a manic, headlong energy that steamrollers right over them. It doesn't have the slick polish of *Die Hard II* or *Under Siege,* but Snipes and Datcher have

a nice dueling chemistry, and Payne makes a satisfactory villain, arch and conceited—an American Alan Rickman. And where else are you going to find flight attendants whose immediate response to a hijacking is to pass out hot towels?

Passion Fish ★ ★ ★ ★
R, 135 m., 1993

Mary McDonnell (May-Alice), Alfre Woodard (Chantelle), David Strathairn (Rennie), Vondie Curtis-Hall (Sugar), Leo Burmeister (Max), Angela Bassett (Dawn/Rhonda), Lenore Banks (Nurse Quick), Nelle Stokes (Therapist No. 1), Brett Ardoin (Therapist No. 2). Directed by John Sayles and produced by Sarah Green and Maggie Renzi. Screenplay by Sayles.

Her life is essentially going nowhere before her accident. She's in a dead-end career, her marriage has ended, and she's filled with a deep discontent. Then she is paralyzed in an accident, and goes back home to Louisiana to recover, filled with resentment.

In a typical TV docudrama, this would be the setup for a heartwarming tale of uplift and courage. But John Sayles's *Passion Fish* cuts closer to the bone. This is a tough, muscular story about a headstrong woman who wants things to go her way.

The film stars Mary McDonnell as May-Alice, the soap opera star whose life is suddenly changed by fate. She has some money and a home down in the bayou country where her family is from, and after she is finished with rehabilitation therapy (where she is a very poor candidate), she goes back down there to sit in her chair and drink wine and harbor her bitterness.

She has enough money to hire a full-time companion, and she interviews several, all with a lot of problems of their own. A couple of them are hired for varying lengths of time, before they are fired or walk off the job. She is not easy to work for, and she has just about reached the bottom of the local employment pool when Chantelle, a black woman played by Alfre Woodard, arrives.

Woodard is a strong woman, too. She is also determined to keep the job. She needs it, for more reasons than we know. She sizes up the situation, sees that May-Alice needs less coddling and a lot less wine, and tries to take charge. May-Alice fights back. And *Passion Fish* is essentially about the struggle of their wills.

John Sayles says he has been interested in such relationships between client and com-

panion ever since he watched them develop in his own family. It is an interesting division of power: The companion is healthy and able-bodied, and has the freedom of movement. The client, like McDonnell, has power over the sources of money, and can try to control the other person through threats to her economic security. So there is a delicate balance, a struggle, sometimes unacknowledged, that goes on all day long.

Sayles writes his own movies, which range from *Eight Men Out* to *Matewan* to the powerful *City of Hope,* and he has rarely written more three-dimensional characters than this time. Although his subject is a mine field of clichés and the material cries out to be processed into a disease-of-the-week docudrama, he creates vivid, original characters for his story—characters like Uncle Max (William Mahoney), who comes to visit and reveals his entire lifetime in a few sentences, or May-Alice's childhood friends, or the actresses who worked with her on television.

Each of these meetings between May-Alice and her past requires her to play a different role, and that's also the case when Rennie (David Strathairn) turns up one day to make some repairs on the house. This was the guy she had a crush on in high school, before she left him and all the rest of her early life behind and moved to New York. Now he is married, and she is in a wheelchair, and it seems as if all possibilities of romance have disappeared. But things are not always as they seem.

At the heart of the movie is the uneasy relationship between May-Alice and Chantelle. May-Alice is used to being willful and spoiled. Chantelle does not find her behavior acceptable. But May-Alice has the money and Chantelle needs the job, for more urgent reasons than we first realize, and so it seems that Chantelle may have to put up with May-Alice's behavior. Yet in a deeper sense, one that only gradually reveals itself to May-Alice, what she needs most of all from Chantelle is the other woman's ability to stand up to her.

There are elements here of a vaguely similar relationship in *Driving Miss Daisy,* but Sayles has made his own film, direct and original, and in the struggle of wills between these two characters he creates two of the most interesting human portraits of 1993. The struggle at the heart of the movie is lightened by the comic portraits of May-Alice's many visitors (I would have liked to see a whole movie about Uncle Max, and an old friend named Precious deserves a short subject of her own). The romance is handled with a delicate, tentative touch that reflects the characters' feelings for one another. *Passion Fish* begins with a scene from May-Alice's soap opera, and by the end we see how far such canned melodrama is from the real lessons of life.

Patton ★ ★ ★ ★
PG, 171 m., 1970

George C. Scott (Patton), Karl Malden (Bradley), Stephen Young (Captain Hansen), Michael Strong (General Carver), Karl Michel Vogler (Rommel), Michael Bates (Montgomery). Directed by Franklin J. Schaffner and produced by Frank McCarthy. Screenplay by Francis Ford Coppola and Edward H. North.

We have all of these things buried inside of us, waiting for a movie like *Patton* to release them. The reflex patriotism of World War II is still there, we discover, Vietnam has soured us on war, but not on that war. There is a small corner of our being that will always be thrilled by Patton's dash across Europe after the Germans, and we are still a little bit in admiration of heroes on his arrogant scale. And that is why, make no mistake, *Patton* is not an antiwar film. If I read one, I read half a dozen tortuous liberal rationalizations for this movie, written by people who liked it but felt guilty afterward. *Patton* is really against war, they said; by taking us almost inside the soul of the most fanatically military of all America's generals, *Patton* was supposed to fill us with distaste for militarism. It does not, of course. But neither is it a very hawk-like movie. It is such an extraordinarily intelligent film, so sure of its purpose, that it makes war its medium but not its subject. It is not about war but about Patton at war, and it is one of the best screen biographies ever made.

Patton once said something to the effect that war was the supreme human activity because it forced men to operate at the ultimate limit of their abilities. This is not a very good justification for war, but it is a supreme test for men, and the action in *Patton* all takes place at the delicate balance point where the war meets the man. That was a basically brilliant idea in Francis Ford Coppola's original screenplay, but what makes it work so well in *Patton* is the performance of George C. Scott. He is absorbed into the role, and commands it. He is such a good

actor that the movie doesn't have to explain a lot of things; we feel we know Patton and so we're sure of our footing. That's good, because it frees director Franklin J. Schaffner from a lot of cluttering props and plot lines. *Patton* is almost three hours long but it is a surprisingly uncomplicated movie, telling its story with clean, simple scenes and shots. Schaffner is at home here; one of the best things about his *Planet of the Apes* was the simplicity of style he found for it. If *Planet* had gotten complicated, we would have laughed at it.

The simplicity of *Patton* does not lead to any loss of subtlety; just the reverse. Because we are freed from those semiobligatory junk scenes that clutter up most war movies (the wife at home, the "human interest" drained from ethnic character actors, the battle scenes that are allowed to run too long because they cost so much) we can concentrate on the man, and we can even begin to believe we understand a warrior like this one. Because it's no good being hypocritical, I guess. Generals should be generals, and not lovable quasi-political figures like Ike or MacArthur. Patton's life was war (and how sad that really was) but he was honest enough to admit it, and the movie takes its stand on that point. And so although we deplore war we find ourselves respecting the movie; *Patton* is written and directed with integrity.

Beyond that, it's an awfully good movie, and one of its best features is the way it gets its laughs. There aren't any cheap laughs in *Patton,* but there are a lot of earned ones, all serving to flesh in our idea of this brilliant, obsessed man. And a lot of the humor is simply there, embodied in the Scott performance. It turns out *Patton* is exactly the war movie we didn't realize how much we wanted to see.

Patty Hearst ★ ★ ★
R, 108 m., 1988

Natasha Richardson (Patricia Hearst), William Forsythe (Teko), Ving Rhames (Cinque), Frances Fisher (Yolanda), Jodi Long (Wendy), Olivia Barash (Fahizah), Dana Delany (Gelina), Marek Johnson (Zoya), Kitty Swink (Gabi), Pete Kowanko (Cujo). Directed by Paul Schrader and produced by Marvin Worth. Screenplay by Nicholas Kazan. Based on the book *Every Secret Thing* by Patricia Campbell Hearst with Alvin Moscow.

I met Patty Hearst twice in the spring of 1988 at the Cannes Film Festival, once in a

movie, and once in a restaurant. The effect was unsettling. In the movie, *Patty Hearst,* she was a quiet, desperate person, so lost in her ordeal that she had no clear idea of any of her motives. A person willing to hold up banks and brandish machine guns simply because of peer pressure from terrorists who had forced her to join their group. In person, she was a pleasant woman in her thirties, joking about how she was trying to trade *Patty Hearst* buttons for festival T-shirts.

I talked to her for a while, and then drifted over to the corner of the room, where I looked at her and tried to reconcile the two images, and finally realized that it was going to be impossible. Nothing in her previous life, and now nothing in her subsequent life, had any connection with the events that made Patty Hearst, at the age of nineteen, into the most famous fugitive in America.

Hearst was kidnapped by something called the Symbionese Liberation Army in 1974, and the case and its aftermath, including her famous legal ordeal, lasted until 1979. Even today, it is hard for people to place it—I saw an article mentioning Patty as a figure of the '60s—and I doubt if the case has gone into any American history textbooks, since what did it grow out of, where did it lead, what did it prove? It was all just a very odd footnote to history.

And yet the footnotes are sometimes where you find the human interest story. By what process could the heiress of America's most famous newspaper family, raised in a conventional upper-class Roman Catholic household and embracing most of the values of her parents, be transformed into the person we saw on TV in those days, brandishing a machine gun and shouting revolutionary slogans? Many children of privilege joined the "revolution," but Patty was kidnapped. What happened then?

That's the question director Paul Schrader wants to consider in this movie, and to answer it, he reconstructs the physical and mental ordeal that Hearst went through after her kidnapping. She is yanked out of a quiet evening at home with her boyfriend (Stephen Weed—how the names still have their resonance!), and thrown into the trunk of a car. Then she finds herself inside a darkened closet, where she is held for weeks, until the horizon of her world is limited to the moments when the door opens, and its population consists of half-heard voices.

The effect is to remove her entirely from everything she thought she could count on in life. When she is finally taken out of the closet and allowed to see her captors, she isn't angry, she's grateful to them for being allowed to look upon their faces. They have created a complete dependency, and from there it is only a matter of time until she identifies with the group and begins to share its aims. There is a powerful pressure, felt in all of us, to conform to what those around us consider to be proper behavior. Becoming a revolutionary might have been, for her, a form of good manners.

This is one of the oddest films Schrader has ever made. He is ordinarily a filmmaker of passion and kinetic energy, and this is a brooding and pale film, an introspective one that seems determined not to exploit the sensationalism of the case. Schrader is the favorite screenwriter of Martin Scorsese, for whom he wrote *Taxi Driver, Raging Bull,* and of course *The Last Temptation of Christ.* His own films are about guilt and passion, and they include *Cat People, American Gigolo,* and *Mishima.* When I heard that Schrader was going to film the Patty Hearst story, I thought I knew what to expect, but I was wrong.

The entire film centers on the remarkable performance by Natasha Richardson, as Patty. She convinces us she is Hearst, not by pressing the point, but by taking it for granted. She is quiet, a little sullen, not forthcoming. She tells people what they want to hear. During all of the tremendous excitement and passion of her ordeal, she hardly seems to be present; this is not a good time for her or a bad time, but a duty.

Schrader also avoids the temptation to make the SLA members into colorful firebrands. They come across as weak, sad people, so hidebound in ideology that they seem shellshocked. They are all passive personalities, under the will of the leader Cinque (Ving Rhames), who uses revolutionary rhetoric but has created in the SLA a community where no one is free. It's startling when Schrader re-enacts events we remember from TV (such as Patty's bank robbery), or uses actual TV news footage (of the firestorm that engulfed the SLA hideout). This whole story seemed so much more exciting from the outside.

Peggy Sue Got Married ★ ★ ★ ★
PG-13, 103 m., 1986

Kathleen Turner (Peggy Sue), Nicolas Cage (Charlie), Barry Miller (Richard), Catherine Hicks (Carol), Joan Allen (Maddie). Directed by Francis Ford Coppola and produced by Paul R. Gurian. Screenplay by Jerry Leightling and Arlene Sarner.

We walk like ghosts through the spaces of our adolescence. We've all done it. We stroll unseen across the high school football field. We go back to the drive-in restaurants where we all hung out, all those years ago. We walk into a drugstore for some aspirin, and the magazine rack brings back a memory of sneaking a peek at a Playmate in 1959.

Certain times and places can re-create, with a headstrong rush, what it felt like to be seventeen years old—and we are sometimes more in touch with ourselves at that age than we are with the way we felt a year ago. Have you ever received a telephone message from somebody you were in love with when you were seventeen? And didn't it feel, for a second, as if it came from that long-ago teenager, and not from the adult who left it?

Peggy Sue Got Married is a lot of things—a human comedy, a nostalgic memory, a love story—but there are times when it is just plain creepy, because it awakens such vivid memories in us. It's about a woman who attends her twenty-fifth high school reunion, and passes out, and when she comes to it is 1958 and she inhabits her own teen-age body.

Those few details make the movie sound like *Back to the Future,* but give it some thought and you will see that *Peggy Sue* is not a clone, but a mirror image. In *Back to the Future,* the hero traveled backwards through time to meet his own parents when they were teenagers. In *Peggy Sue* the heroine travels backwards to enter her own body as a teen-ager—and she enters it with her forty-two-year-old mind still intact.

What would you say, knowing what you know now, to the people you loved when you were seventeen? How would you feel if you picked up the telephone, and it was your grandmother's voice? Would you tell her she was going to die in another two years and three months? No, but you would know that, and wouldn't your heart leap into your throat, and wouldn't she wonder what was wrong with you, that you couldn't respond to her simple hello?

Peggy Sue Got Married provides moment after moment like that. It's like visiting a cemetery where all of the people are still alive. And yet it is a comedy. Frank Capra made comedies like this, in which the humor welled up out of a deep, even sentimental, drama of human emotions. There is a scene in the movie where the seventeen-year-old girl (with the mind of the forty-two-year-old woman) sits in the front seat of a car and necks with the teen-age boy that (she knows) she will marry and someday decide to divorce. Imagine kissing someone for the first time after you have already kissed them for the last time.

The movie stars Kathleen Turner, in a performance that must be seen to be believed. How does she play a seventeen-year-old? Not by trying to actually look seventeen, because the movie doesn't try to pull off that stunt (the convention is that the heroine looks adult to us, but like a teen-ager to the other characters). Turner, who is actually thirty-two, plays a teen-ager by making certain changes in her speech and movement: She talks more impetuously, not waiting for other people to reply, and she walks in that heedless teen-age way of those who have not yet stumbled often enough to step carefully. There is a moment when she throws herself down on her bed, and never mind what she looks like, it feels like a seventeen-year-old sprawled there. Her performance is a textbook study in body language; she knows that one of the symptoms of growing older is that you arrange your limbs more thoughtfully in repose.

The other important character in the movie is Charlie, her boyfriend and later her husband, played by Nicolas Cage. We meet him first as a local businessman in his early forties, and from the way he walks into a room you can tell he's the kind of man who inspires a lot of local gossip. He and his wife are separated and planning to divorce. When we see him again, he's the teen-age kid she's dating, and there are two delicate, wonderful scenes where she walks a tightrope, trying to relate to him as if she were a teen-ager, and as if she hadn't already shared his whole future.

That scene in the front seat of the car is a masterpiece of cross-purposes; she actually wants to go all the way, and he's shocked—shocked not so much by her desire, as by a girl having the temerity to talk and act that way in the 1950s. "Jeez," he says, after she makes her move, "that's a guy's line."

The movie was directed by Francis Coppola, who seems to have been in the right place at the right time. The *Peggy Sue* project got traded around from one actor and director to another (Turner's role was originally cast with Debra Winger, and Coppola was the third director on the project). After several years in which he has tried to make technical and production breakthroughs on his movies, experimenting with new film processes and new stylistic approaches with honorable but uneven results, this time Coppola apparently simply wanted to make a movie, and put some characters on the screen, and tell a story. He has, all right. This was one of the best movies of 1986.

The Pelican Brief ★ ★ ★
PG-13, 141 m., 1993

Julia Roberts (Darby Shaw), Denzel Washington (Gray Grantham), Sam Shepard (Thomas Callahan), John Heard (Gavin Verheek), Tony Goldwyn (Fletcher Coal), Hume Cronyn (Justice Rosenberg), John Lithgow (Smith Keen). Directed by Alan J. Pakula and produced by Pakula and Pieter Jan Brugge. Screenplay by Pakula.

Crime fiction sometimes achieves the status of serious literature: Raymond Chandler's private eye novels, for example. Elmore Leonard and Anne Rice are said to have the touch of the artist. Quite possibly true. John Grisham, the king of the bestseller lists, is also taken seriously in some quarters, but I'm not sure why. His plots are no better or worse than average, and his characters are at their service. His novels exist to be filmed.

The Pelican Brief was the 1993 Christmas Grisham, halfway round the year from *The Firm*, which was the Fourth of July Grisham. It is about as good, but in a different way. While *The Firm* was a muscular thriller with action sequences, *The Pelican Brief* takes place more quietly, in corners, shadows, and secret hotel rooms. True, it has a few bomb explosions and chases, but by Grisham standards, it's claustrophobic.

It's an old law of the movies that ordinary novels are easier to film than great ones, because the director doesn't have to worry about the writer's message and style, if any. *The Pelican Brief* is a good illustration of that principle. By casting attractive stars in the leads, by finding the right visual look, by underlining the action with brooding, ominously sad music, a good director can create the illusion of meaning even when nothing's there.

The Pelican Brief has been written for the screen and directed by Alan J. Pakula (*Sophie's Choice, All the President's Men, Presumed Innocent*), who is a skilled craftsman and has done about as much as possible with the material. Julia Roberts and Denzel

Washington do the rest, simply by embodying virtue and being likable.

The movie opens with the assassination of two Supreme Court justices. In New Orleans, a bright law student (Roberts) is intrigued because there seems to be no obvious motive; the justices are on opposite sides politically, so their deaths would cancel each other. Doing research, however, she discovers a connection, and writes a brief that, if true, would implicate one of the richest men in the country, and lead to the Oval Office.

Roberts is encouraged in her work by her law professor and lover (Sam Shepard). The movie uses shorthand for its character traits; the Shepard character is a recovering alcoholic who drinks or doesn't drink entirely according to the needs of the dialogue. No matter; soon he's gone, and Roberts has been targeted by sinister forces. She turns for help first to the FBI, and then to an investigative journalist (Washington).

The screenplay keeps its cards close to its chest. We see various scoundrels who *seem* guilty, but there's no proof until late in the film, and a lot of blind alleys. Some amusement is offered by the character of the president, played by smiling, bland Robert Culp as a man with the appearance of George Bush and the involvement of Ronald Reagan. There are some obvious villains, including the president's chief of staff (Tony Goldwyn), but the movie depends on ominous threats and sudden deaths rather than on colorful, memorable bad guys.

Because the atmosphere is skillfully drawn, because the actors are well cast, because Pakula knows how to construct a sequence to make it work, the movie delivers while it's onscreen. That it contains no substance or meaning is not its problem. It is a clever device to take your mind off your problems for 141 minutes. I enjoyed it until it was over; I will have little reason to think about it in the weeks to come; I will forget it in a year.

It is depressing to reflect that this shallow exercise in Washington conspiracy has been directed by the same man who made a great film, *All the President's Men*, on the same subject. Depressing, too, to remember that both films center on the work of investigative newspapermen—Woodward and Bernstein, who were smart, aggressive, and political in the earlier film, and Washington's character, who is smart, brave, shallow, and utterly apolitical in this one.

One thing the movie proves conclusively is the value of star power. Julia Roberts, re-

turning after two years off the screen, makes a wonderful heroine, warm, courageous, very beautiful. Denzel Washington shows again how credible he seems on the screen; like Spencer Tracy, he can make you believe in almost any character. Together they have a real chemistry, so potent that after the movie was over, I heard people complaining that they were never "allowed" to have a love affair. Any romance would have been rather tactless, of course, considering that the story takes place in the week or two immediately after her lover has been blown to pieces. Maybe with a Grisham story you tend to forget details like that.

Pelle the Conqueror ★ ★ ★ ½
NO MPAA RATING, 138 m., 1988

Max von Sydow (Lasse Karlsson), Pelle Hvenegaard (Pelle Karlsson), Erik Paaske (Manager), Kristina Tornqvists (Anna), Morten Jorgensen (Trainee), Axel Strobye (Mr. Kongstrup), Bjorn Granath (Erik). Written and directed by Bille August and produced by Per Holst. Based on the novel by Martin Anderson Nexo.

There were immigrants to American who thought the streets would be paved with gold. Lasse Karlsson, a middle-aged farmhand from Sweden, has more modest hopes as he sails with his young son to Denmark in the early years of this century. In Denmark, he says, they will drink coffee in bed on Sunday mornings, and eat roast pork with raisins for Sunday dinner. He cradles his son, Pelle, in his arms as their little passenger vessel noses into a small harbor, where disappointment sets in almost at once.

Almost everyone on the boat is a Swedish laborer, looking for work. Farmers have turned out to inspect them as if they were cattle. One by one, the men are hired, until finally only Lasse and Pelle are left. Nobody wants to hire Lasse (Max von Sydow). He is too old. He has a son. Half-drunk and defiant, he all but forces himself on the last of the farmers, a man named Kongstrup who has a shifty look about him. Lasse and Pelle sit in the farmer's cart as it passes through fields on its way to their futures.

Pelle the Conqueror uses this beginning, full of hope and dreams, in an interesting way. Through the seasons that follow during a long year on the Kongstrup farm, the vision somehow stays alive inside Pelle, even though life seems organized to disappoint him. The film begins with one hopeful immigration—

Sweden to Denmark—and ends with another, Pelle's decision to take his chances in the larger world.

Life on the Kongstrup farm is defined by the land, the seasons, and the personalities of the people who live there. The Kongstrups themselves hardly appear for long stretches of time; they live in a big house set aside from the farm buildings, and Mrs. Kongstrup spends her days drinking brandy while her husband chases wenches. He has no shame, not even about the one unfortunate woman who appears at his front door from time to time, their child in her arms.

In the quarters where the laborers live, life is defined by the sadism of the "Manager" (Erik Paaske), a bully who spots weaknesses in his men and exploits them. He is assisted in his cruelty by the "Trainee," a youth who takes particular pleasure in tormenting Pelle. The boy turns to his father for protection, but Lasse is too old and too weary to help. Eventually Pelle makes his own alliances for friendship and protection.

Pelle the Conqueror, which won the Grand Prix at the 1988 Cannes Film Festival, was directed by Bille August, whose previous film, *Twist and Shout,* was about teen-agers coming of age in the 1960s. In tone and sometimes in visuals, the movie resembles *The Emigrants* and *The New Land* (1974), Jan Troell's two-part epic about Scandinavians who settled in Minnesota. Both films star Max von Sydow, that mighty oak of Swedish cinema, who is unsurpassed at the difficult challenge of appearing not to act, of appearing to be simple and true even in scenes of great complexity.

The film is a richness of events. There are scenes of punishingly hard work in the fields, under the eye of the Manager. A challenge between the Manager and an independent-minded worker, with tragic results. The intrigue in the big house, where Mrs. Kongstrup exacts a particularly ironic revenge for her husband's philandering. The heartbreak of a beautiful local girl, who has fallen in love above her station.

The most touching sequence in the film involves a winter's romance between Lasse and a sailor's wife who lives in a cottage near the sea. Pelle is the first to meet the woman, whose husband has been missing for years and is presumed dead. He introduces his father to her, and the two people take a liking to one another that is practical as well as sentimental. There is a scene of great delicacy and sensible realism, in which they evaluate

their resources and decide they should live together, and afterwards Lasse is able to suggest with a smile to his son that they might soon be having coffee in bed on Sundays after all.

Von Sydow's work in the film was honored with an Academy Award nomination, well-deserved, particularly after a distinguished career in which he stood at the center of many of Ingmar Bergman's greatest films *(The Virgin Spring, The Seventh Seal).* But there is not a bad performance in the movie, and the newcomer Pelle Hvenegaard never steps wrong in the title role (there is poetic justice in the fact that he was actually named after the novel which inspired this movie). It is Pelle, not Lasse, who is really at the center of the movie, which begins when he follows his father's dream, and ends as he realizes he must follow his own.

The Perez Family ★ ★ ★   NEW
R, 112 m., 1995

Marisa Tomei (Dottie Perez), Alfred Molina (Juan Raul Perez), Anjelica Huston (Carmela Perez), Chazz Palminteri (Officer Pirelli), Trini Alvarado (Teresa Perez), Celia Cruz (Luz Paz), Diego Wallraff (Angel Diaz), Angela Lanza (Flavia). Directed by Mira Nair and produced by Michael Nozik and Lydia Dean Pilcher. Screenplay by Robin Swicord.

Mira Nair's *The Perez Family* opens with a Felliniesque scene of elegantly dressed people promenading by a beach. Then the music turns sad as they begin to wade into the waves, and there's a cut to a Cuban prison. For Havana's bourgeoise, the good times are over.

Cut to the early 1980s, and a boatload of prisoners released by Fidel Castro is sailing for the United States. We meet Juan Raul Perez (Alfred Molina), who still carries a flame of love in his heart for the wife he has not seen in twenty years. Also on board is Dottie Perez (Marisa Tomei), a sometime hooker, determined to get a fresh start in the new land.

These two Perezes are not related. Indeed, as Juan tells a U.S. immigration official (also named Perez), "If you want something done in this life, ask a Perez—there are so many of us!" They join thousands of other refugees in a temporary camp set up in Miami's football stadium, and when Dottie discovers that families can find American sponsors more readily than single people, she proposes to Juan that they become "married" to squeeze

through an immigration loophole. To increase their chances, they even recruit a youngster to be their son, and a dotty old man to be the grandfather.

Juan goes along with the scheme, but only because he is so eager to be reunited with his wife, Carmela Perez (Anjelica Huston), who got out of Cuba twenty years ago. They have been waiting for one another ever since, but now they may stumble just as they reach the finish line. Still on the boat, Juan frets about his appearance after years in prison: "My teeth are too poor to kiss my wife." Dottie boldly kisses him. "Don't worry," she says, "you can kiss your wife."

The Perez Family makes a romantic comedy out of these offbeat ingredients, and although we have not often seen such stories told about Cuban-Americans with political backgrounds, we have seen some of the same elements before, in screwball comedies. What happens is that just at the moment they are about to be reunited, both Juan and Carmela fall in love with others—but refuse to admit it.

The other key player in the cast is Chazz Palminteri, as Pirelli, a federal agent who is working with the Miami police and finds himself making frequent visits to Carmela's house when her alarm system keeps going off. The alarms have been installed by her jealous brother, who goes ballistic when she gets near any man. Carmela and Pirelli soon find that when the bells toll, they toll for them. It's fairly clear early in the film what will happen, more or less. The fun is in getting there.

There was controversy over the casting of so many non-Hispanic actors in Hispanic roles in *The Perez Family*—and there was certainly no shortage of talented Latino actors for *My Family,* a film released at about the same time. But maybe nontraditional casting is a two-way street; what's certain is that the actors bring real heart to their roles. Tomei in particular has undergone some sort of transformation from her performances in *My Cousin Vinnie* and *Only You,* and now emerges as earthier and juicier. Anjelica Huston brings some of the same conflicting passions to this role as she had in *Prizzi's Honor,* and Alfred Molina, a British actor, is surprisingly convincing as her husband.

The director, Mira Nair, is a New Yorker who was born in India. She has a special interest in new arrivals to America; her previous film, *Mississippi Masala* (1992), was about a family of Indians from Uganda, operating a motel in the South. Here, she shows a good eye for the details of immigration, some of them fairly bizarre, as when the Miami Dolphins practice on the field of their stadium while the stands and entrance halls are jammed with thousands of refugees.

There are other details: The fake Perez "family" is moved out of the stadium, housed in a church rectory, and makes money by selling flowers at stop signs. A U.S. immigration official, himself an immigrant from the Indian subcontinent, is as bemused by the laws as anyone, but sworn to uphold them. And Carmela, now a Miami suburbanite with a daughter (Trini Alvarado) her husband has never seen, is willing to say anything to be reunited with him. ("She may be the most beautiful liar I have ever met," Palminteri muses.)

The movie relies a little too much on contrivance sometimes. It's barely possible that Dottie dreams of making love to John Wayne soon after her arrival in America, and the scene where she finds out he is already dead is a funny one. But surely even in Cuba she would have known Elvis was also dead ("Elvis, too? So many assassinations!"). The movie sometimes bends the plausible to set up a laugh, and most of the time I didn't care, because I was enjoying the company of the characters.

A Perfect World ★ ★ ★ ★
PG-13, 136 m., 1993

Clint Eastwood (Red Garnett), Kevin Costner (Butch Haynes), Laura Dern (Sally Gerber), T.J. Lowther (Phillip Perry), Keith Szarabajka (Terry Pugh), Leo Burmester (Tom Adler), Bradley Whiteford (Bobby Lee). Directed by Clint Eastwood and produced by Mark Johnson and David Valdes. Screenplay by John Lee Hancock.

A Perfect World contains a prison break, the taking of a hostage, a chase across Texas, two murders, various robberies, and a final confrontation between a fugitive and a lawman. It is not really *about* any of those things, however. It's deeper and more interesting than that. It's about the true nature of violence, and about how the child is father of the man.

The film brings together the leading icons of two generations of strong, silent American leading men: Kevin Costner, as a fugitive who takes a boy as hostage, and Clint Eastwood, as the Texas Ranger who leads the pursuit. But the Costner character doesn't seem really focused on his escape, and the Eastwood character seems somewhat re-

moved from the chase. These two men first met long ago, and they both know this isn't about a chase; it's about old, deep wounds.

This is a movie that surprises you. The setup is such familiar material that you think the story is going to be flat and fast. But the screenplay by John Lee Hancock goes deep. And the direction by Clint Eastwood finds strange, quiet moments of perfect truth in the story. Both Costner and Eastwood are fresh from triumphs at the Academy Awards, but in neither *Dances With Wolves* nor *Unforgiven* will you find the subtlety and the sadness that they discover here. Eastwood has directed seventeen films, but his direction is sometimes taken less seriously because he's a movie star. *A Perfect World* is a film that any director alive might be proud to sign.

Costner's character, Butch Haynes, is a young man who drifted into trouble and was sentenced unfairly, to get him out of the way. The Eastwood character, Red Garnett, had something to do with that, and has never felt quite right about it. Escaping from prison, Haynes and another convict break in on a mother and her children at dawn. Soon they're on the road with a hostage, Phillip (T.J. Lowther), nine or ten years old.

Before long the other con is gone from the scene, and the man and the boy are cutting across the back roads of Texas. In pursuit is Red Garnett, riding in a newfangled Airglide trailer that's a "mobile command headquarters." Garnett is saddled with a talky criminologist (Laura Dern) and various other types, including a sinister federal agent who is an expert marksman. The general view is that Haynes is a desperate kidnapper. Both Eastwood and Dern think, for different reasons, it isn't that simple.

And it's not. The heart of the movie is the relationship that develops between the outlaw and the kid. You can look very hard, but you won't be able to guess where this relationship is going. It doesn't fall into any of the conventional movie patterns. Butch isn't a terrifically nice guy, and Phillip isn't a cute movie kid who makes and then loses a friend.

It's not that simple. Butch, we learn, was treated badly as a boy. His father was absent, his mother was a prostitute, the men in her life didn't like him much. Butch talks vaguely about going to Alaska. But as the man and boy drive through the dusty 1963 Texas landscape, it's more like they're going in circles, while the man looks hard at the boy and tries to see what it means to be a boy, what is the

right way and the wrong way to talk to one. He's trying to see himself in the kid.

There are, I said, some murders in the film. All of them are off-camera. One body is found in an auto trunk, the other in a cornfield. We don't see either killing; Eastwood makes a decision to stay away from the cliché of a gun firing, a body falling, and it's not until late in the film that someone is shot onscreen, and then in very particular circumstances.

But there is violence in the movie. In the film's key sequence, Butch and Phillip are given shelter for the night by a friendly black farmer (George Haynes). The next morning, Butch watches as the farmer treats his son roughly, slapping him when he doesn't behave. It's the wrong way to treat a kid, but Butch's reaction is so angry, we realize a nerve has been touched. And as a complex series of events unfolds, we discover the real subject of the movie: Treat kids right, and you won't have to put them in jail later on. The crucial violence, from which later violence springs, is when a child is treated with cruelty.

Eastwood tells the story in unexpected ways. The way Butch starts right out, for example, letting Phillip hold a gun. (But not to shoot someone with it; his reasons for doing this, in fact, are so deep you have to think long about them.) The way Phillip behaves—not as a kidnap victim, not as a friend, but more as a kid keeping his eyes wide open and seeing all he can. And scenes of quirky humor, involving runaway trailers, Halloween masks, barbecued steaks, and other details that break the tension with a certain craziness. (There is, for example, a scene in a roadside diner named "Dottie's Squat and Gobble," which is the best restaurant name I have ever seen in a movie.)

A Perfect World has the elements of a crime genre picture, but it has the depth of thought and the freedom of movement of an art film. Watching it, you may be reminded of *Bonnie and Clyde*, *Badlands*, or an unsung masterpiece from earlier in 1993, *Kalifornia*. Not because they all tell the same story, but because they all try to get beneath the things we see in a lot of crime movies, and find out what they really mean.

Permanent Record ★ ★ ★
PG-13, 92 m., 1988

Alan Boyce (David Sinclair), Keanu Reeves (Chris Townsend), Michelle Meyrink (J.G.),

Jennifer Rubin (Lauren), Pamela Gidley (Kim), Michael Elgart (Jake), Richard Bradford (Leo Verdell). Directed by Marisa Silver and produced by Frank Mancuso Jr. Screenplay by Jarre Fees, Alice Liddle, and Larry Ketron.

The opening shot of *Permanent Record* is ominous and disturbing, and we don't know why. In an unbroken movement, the camera tracks past a group of teen-agers who have parked their cars on a bluff overlooking the sea, and are hanging out casually, their friendship too evident to need explaining. There seems to be no "acting" in this shot, and yet it is superbly acted, because it feels so natural that we accept at once the idea that these kids have been close friends for a long time. Their afternoon on the bluff seems superficially happy, and yet there is a brooding quality to the shot, perhaps inspired by the lighting, or by the way the camera circles vertiginously above the sea below.

The following scenes unfold, it seems, almost without plan. We meet a couple of kids who play in a rock band together, and try to sneak into a recording studio, and are thrown out, and arrive at school late. We meet the high school principal, a man who is enormously intriguing because he reveals so little, and yet still succeeds in revealing goodness. We meet the crowd that these two kids hang out with, and we attend some auditions for a school production of *The Pirates of Penzance*. We are impressed by the fact that these teen-agers are intelligent, thoughtful, and articulate; they come from a different planet than most movie teen-agers.

To describe the opening scenes makes them seem routine, and yet they captured my attention with an intensity I still do not understand. The underlying mystery of many good movies is the way they absorb us in apparently unremarkable details, while bad movies can lose us even with car crashes and explosions. Marisa Silver, who directed this film, and Frederick Elmes, who photographed it, have done something very subtle and strong here, have seen these students and their school in a way that inescapably prepares us for something, without revealing what it is.

The kids all hang out together, but one begins to attract our attention more than the others. He is David (Alan Boyce), an intense, dark-eyed musician who everyone knows is gifted. He leads the rock band, gives lessons to his fellow musicians, and is arranging the music for the production of

Pirates. In a scene of inexplicable tension, he is told by the principal (Richard Bradford) that he's won a scholarship to a great music school. He tries to seem pleased, but complains that he is so busy—too busy. Bradford quietly reminds him the scholarship isn't until next year.

And then . . . but here I want to suggest that if you plan to see the film, you should read no further and permit yourself its surprises. I began watching this film knowing absolutely nothing about it, and this is the kind of film where that is an advantage. Let the movie unfold like life. Save the review until later.

I found myself impressed, most of all, by the subtlety with which Silver and her writers (Jarre Fees, Alice Liddle, and Larry Ketron) develop David's worsening crisis. This is not a young man made unhappy by the usual problems of TV docudramas. He doesn't use drugs, his girlfriend isn't pregnant, he isn't flunking out of school, and he doesn't have an unhappy home life. But it becomes clear, especially in retrospect, that there is no joy in his life, and we see that most clearly in the understated scene in the bedroom of the girl he sometimes sleeps with. Any other couple who do what they do together, she suggests, would be said to be going together. He nods.

There is something missing here. Some kind of connection with other people. Some exultation in his own gifts and talents. Giving guitar lessons to his friend Chris (Keanu Reeves), he is a little impatient; Chris does not strive hard enough for excellence. David, who is admired by everyone in his school, who is the one singled out by his friends for great success, has a deep sadness inside himself because he is not good enough. And that leads to the scene in which one moment he is on the side of that high bluff, and the next moment he is not.

The rest of the movie is about his friends—about the gulf he has left behind, and about their sorrow, and their rage at him. Again and again, Silver and her writers find authentic ways to portray emotions. We never feel manipulated, because the movie works too close to the heart. Perhaps the best scene in the whole film is the one where Chris, drunk, drives his car into David's yard and almost hits David's younger brother, and then, when David's father comes out on the lawn to shout angrily at him, Chris falls into his arms, weeping and shouting, "I should have stopped him." And the father holds him.

Life goes on. The school production is

held. There is a dramatic moment in which David is eulogized, and there is also the sense that years from now his friends will sometimes remember him, be angry with him, and wonder what would have become of him. This is one of the year's best films, and one reason for its power is that it clearly knows what it wants to do, and how to do it. It is not a film about the causes of David's death, and it does not analyze or explain. It is a film about the event, and about the memory of the event. The performances, seemingly artless, are appropriate to the material, and I was especially impressed by the way Bradford suggested so many things about the principal while seeming to reveal so little.

Permanent Record is Marisa Silver's second feature, after the wonderful *Old Enough* (1984), which told the story of a friendship between two thirteen-year-old girls who were from opposite sides of the tracks but were on the same side of adolescence. In that film and this one, she shows that she has a rare gift for empathy, and that she can see right to the bottoms of things without adding a single gratuitous note.

Personal Best ★ ★ ★ ★
R, 124 m., 1982

Mariel Hemingway (Chris Cahill), Patrice Donnelly (Tory Skinner), Scott Glenn (Coach), Kenny Moore (Denny Stites). Directed and produced by Robert Towne. Screenplay by Towne.

Robert Towne's *Personal Best* tells the story of two women who are competitors for pentathlete berths on the 1980 U.S. Olympics team—the team that did not go to Moscow. The women are attracted to one another almost at first sight, and what begins as a tentative exploration develops into a love relationship. Then the romance gets mixed up with the ferocity of top-level sports competition.

What distinguishes *Personal Best* is that it creates *specific* characters—flesh-and-blood people with interesting personalities, people I cared about. *Personal Best* also seems knowledgeable about its two subjects, which are the weather of these women's hearts, and the world of Olympic sports competition.

It is a movie containing the spontaneity of life. It's about living, breathing, changeable people and because their relationships seems to be so deeply felt, so important to them, we're fascinated by what may happen next. The movie stars Mariel Hemingway and Patrice Donnelly as the two women track stars, Scott Glenn as their coach, and Kenny Moore as the Olympic swimmer who falls in love with Hemingway late in the film. These four people are so right for the roles it's almost scary; it makes us sense the difference between performances that are technically excellent and other performances, like these, that may sometimes be technically rough but always find the correct emotional note.

Mariel Hemingway plays a young, naive natural athlete. We sense that she always has been under the coaching thumb of her father, a perfectionist, and that her physical excellence has been won at the cost of emotional maturity. She knows everything about working out, and next to nothing about her heart, her sexuality, her own identity. She loses an important race at a preliminary meet, is sharply handled by the father, gets sick to her stomach, is obviously emotionally distraught.

Patrice Donnelly, as a more experienced athlete, tries to comfort the younger girl. In a dormitory room that night, they talk. Donnelly shares whatever wisdom she has about training and running and winning. They smoke a joint. They kid around. They arm wrestle. At this point, watching the film, I had an interesting experience. I did not already know that the characters in the film were homosexual, but I found myself thinking that the scene was so erotically charged that, "if Hollywood could be honest," it would develop into a love scene. Just then, it did! "This is scary," Donnelly says, and then she kisses Hemingway, who returns the kiss.

Personal Best is not simply about their romance, however, it is about any relationship in which the trust necessary for love is made to compete with the total egotism necessary for championship sports. *Can* two people love each other, and at the same time compete for the same berth on an Olympic team? Scott Glenn, the coach, doesn't think so. He accepts the fact of his two stars' homosexuality, but what bothers him is a suspicion that Donnelly may be using emotional blackmail to undercut Hemingway's performance.

This is a very physical movie, one of the healthiest and sweatiest celebrations of physical exertion I can remember. There is a lot of nudity in the film—not only erotic nudity, although there is some of that, but also locker room and steam room nudity, and messing around nudity that has an unashamed, kidding freshness to it. One scene that shocks some viewers occurs between Mariel Hem-ingway and Kenny Moore, when he gets up to go to the bathroom and she decides to follow along; the scene is typical of the kind of unforced, natural spontaneity in the whole film. The characters in *Personal Best* seem to be free to have real feelings. It is filled with the uncertainties, risks, cares, and rewards of real life, and it considers its characters' hearts and minds, and sees their sexuality as an expression of their true feelings for each other.

Personal Services ★ ★ ★ ½
R, 97 m., 1987

Julie Walters (Christine Painter), Alec McCowen (Wing Commander Morton), Shirley Stelfox (Shirley), Danny Schiller (Dolly), Victoria Hardcastle (Rose), Tim Woodward (Timms). Directed by Terry Jones and produced by Tim Bevan. Screenplay by David Leland.

I'm writing this review in London, where the papers for the last few days have been filled with the scandal of the Conservative member of Parliament who had to resign his constituency after being convicted of spanking two male prostitutes who were younger than twenty-one, which is the age of consent for homosexual spankings in Britain. (Female prostitutes can legally be spanked once they are sixteen. There'll always be an England.)

This morning on the radio, they interviewed Cynthia Payne, who said she was shocked that this fine public servant had to have his reputation ruined: "What's wrong with wanting to slap somebody's bottom once in a while, so long as no harm is done? We all have our peculiarities, we just cover them up, that's all." She sounded just like all other housewives on the call-in show.

This was the same Cynthia Payne who has become something of a folk legend over here for operating what the tabloids called "the House of Cyn," a brothel catering to middle-age and elderly gentlemen with rather specialized tastes. Nicknamed the "Luncheon Voucher Madame" because she sometimes charged as little as you'd pay for a nice plate of sausages-and-mashed, Payne was acquitted on her latest round of charges and greeted outside the law court by a street full of her cheering supporters.

Payne has always insisted she did not engage in sex herself and did not supply sex to her clients. Instead, there were naughty fashion shows featuring lace undies, see-through nighties, and leather corsets. Also available were such specialties as charging men for the privilege of doing the housework and weeding her garden. Military men and successful businessmen were especially keen for the humiliation; it took their minds off their responsibilities.

Personal Services, by the Monty Python veteran Terry Jones, is an attempt to explore the peculiarly mercenary world of Payne. She is called "Christine Painter" in the movie but nevertheless is listed as an adviser and went to New York on a public relations tour. She began as a waitress who invested her savings in cheap flats and only got into the brothel-keeping business because hookers paid their rent on time.

As the movie tells it, Payne never really even intended to go into business; she just kept running across nice gentlemen who liked a bit of naughtiness once in a while. She preferred older gentlemen; they caused less trouble and were more grateful. And, as she told the court, an evening at the "House of Cyn" simply involved having a few old friends over for a party. It was all very innocent; they preferred their crumpets with tea.

Personal Services is not a sensational movie, nor does it want to be. It is a study of banality, with flashes of genuine comedy, as when a retired war hero (Alec McCowen) takes the press on a tour of the House while singing the praises of transvestism.

The heroine is played by Julie Walters, seen in the Oscar-nominated title role of *Educating Rita* and she has it just right: the tight lips, polite reserve, the proper manner and bearing, all designed to keep passion and sex in different departments, where they belong.

The British law, on the other hand, comes across as more obsessed by sex than anyone at the madam's parties. Plainclothesmen infiltrate the goings-on and deliver breathless accounts of whips and leather knickers. Many of the clients are only too happy to go into the dock and testify to the underlying innocence of their particular hobbies, and by the end of the film there is the suggestion that the heroine probably will keep right on doing what she does best: having friends in for little parties. Which, as it turned out, was exactly what happened.

Peter's Friends ★ ★ ★ ½
R, 102 m., 1992

Hugh Laurie (Roger), Imelda Staunton (Mary), Stephen Fry (Peter), Emma Thompson (Maggie), Kenneth Branagh (Andrew), Alphonsia Emmanuel (Sarah), Rita Rudner

(Carol), Tony Slattery (Brian). Directed and produced by Kenneth Branagh. Screenplay by Rita Rudner and Martin Bergman.

Ten years ago they were members of the same comedy troupe, but now they've scattered, some to London, some to Los Angeles, and Peter to the comfortable estate he has inherited in the British countryside. Now he summons them back for a New Year's Eve celebration, at which there will be laughter and tears, anger and reconciliation, and half-hearted attempts to reconstruct whatever special empathy brought them together in the first place.

The structure of *Peter's Friends* is not blazingly original—*The Big Chill* comes instantly to mind—but a movie like this succeeds in its particulars. If the dialogue is witty, if the characters are convincingly funny or sad, if there is the right bittersweet nostalgia and the sense that someone is likely to burst into "Those Were the Days," then it doesn't matter that we've seen the formula before. This is a new weekend with new friends.

They arrive one at a time. Andrew (Kenneth Branagh) has gone to Hollywood, married Carol (Rita Rudner), and is now writing her silly sitcom. Sarah (Alphonsia Emmanuel) is still dating unavailable men, and her latest is Brian (Tony Slattery), who claims unconvincingly he is about to leave his wife. Roger (Hugh Laurie) and Mary (Imelda Staunton) have married and are making tons of money writing advertising jingles, but after the death of one of their twins, Mary is paralyzed with fear about the other one. Maggie (Emma Thompson) is still alone, still pining for the perfect mate; lately she has come to think it might be Peter. And Peter himself (Stephen Fry) is unsure of his own next step. Should he keep the old family home?

The weekend will be a series of meetings and partings, dinners at which everyone talks at once, and chance encounters at which private thoughts are revealed. Some of those involve Vera (Phyllida Law), the housekeeper who has watched Peter grow up, and cares deeply for the way he never quite realized his potential.

The screenplay, by Rita Rudner and Martin Bergman, was originally written for mostly American characters, but this trans-Atlantic version became necessary when Kenneth Branagh signed on to direct. This project is not as ambitious as his *Henry V* and *Dead Again,* but it shows a sure feel for the material, and a stage actor's cheerful willingness

to go with scenes that work, even the bawdy and the sentimental. The audience must also be willing to go along, and I was, enjoying the bitchiness, the dramatic revelations, even the bad puns. (I have actually been at dinner parties where the host, asked for sugar substitute, explains that he has no Equal.)

I suppose the closing revelation in *Peter's Friends* is more or less predictable, but that didn't destroy its effect on me. I found Stephen Fry's Peter to be an immensely likable character, as kind as he is rudderless, and I admired the way that Emma Thompson's Maggie was able to switch gears, from being his would-be lover to becoming his real friend. There was also real truth in the scenes between Peter and Vera, to balance the potted self-help clichés of the Los Angeles couple.

If film is basically a voyeuristic medium, then one of the questions that might be asked about *Peter's Friends* is: Would we like to be one of these friends and attend such a reunion ourselves? I would. I liked this group better, in fact, than the friends in *The Big Chill,* perhaps because they seem to like each other more, or perhaps just because they're more amusing.

The Phantom of Liberty ★ ★ ★
R, 104 m., 1974

Adrianna Asti (Prefect's Sister), Jean-Claude Brialy (Mr. Faucaulte), Aldolfo Celi (Dr. Legendre), Michel Piccoli (Second Prefect), Monica Vitti (Mrs. Faucaulte). Directed by Luis Buñuel and produced by Serge Silberman. Screenplay by Buñuel and Jean-Claude Carriere.

Things first began to go wrong, Luis Buñuel teases us, in Spain in 1808, when Napoleon's troops arrived to liberate Toledo. In the opening scenes of Buñuel's savage comedy, *The Phantom of Liberty,* the soldiers execute those who would not be liberated. "Down with freedom!" cries one of the doomed. It is the cry of a defeated social order. The French and American revolutions have unleashed freedom on a defenseless world, and forevermore the population will be unable to rely on the authoritarian reassurance of church and state.

After a scene of typically Buñuelian surrealism—a drunken soldier tried to embrace a marble woman, and is banged on the head by the sculpture's husband—the film's action moves to contemporary France and stays there. But it doesn't stay in any one

place very long. The movie's a fluid, dizzying juggling act of many stories and cheerfully bizarre coincidences.

Buñuel sweeps us into each new vignette so quickly there's no time to hang around while the last one is tidied up. We meet characters, they confront a crisis involving insanity, illegality, doom, fetishism, institutional stupidity, or all of the above, and then, just as the cause of the crisis is revealed as a paradox, the characters cross paths with a new set of characters and we're off on their heels. Buñuel's camera often enters a scene with one set of characters and leaves with another, a device that was used again in *Slacker* (1991).

If I attempted to describe them, Buñuel's interlocking yet disconnected stories would sound bewildering. But his film is strangely lucid; it has the heightened reality of a dream. This material couldn't work if the director weren't supremely confident. And at the age of seventy-five, when most directors are dictating their memoirs, Luis Buñuel was still refining his style and finding new ways to humor his pet personal obsessions. *The Phantom of Liberty* uses his usual prejudices and fetishes to play variations on his favorite theme, which might be stated: In a world cast loose of its moorings by freedom, only anarchy is logical.

Buñuel has always, of course, included an aura of guilty sadomasochism in his movies. His characters are frequently adults pretending to be naughty little boys and girls (like the cardinal who wanted to be a gardener in *The Discreet Charm of the Bourgeoisie*). His fetishes are presented with such exquisite timing, with such a horselaugh in the face of propriety, that we've got to laugh. ("That was a wonderful afternoon little Luis spent on the floor of his mother's closet when he was twelve, and he's been sharing it with us ever since," Pauline Kael once said.)

In *The Phantom of Liberty,* for example, one of the most shocking yet funniest scenes takes place in a wayside inn. Four monks pray for a woman's ailing father. They join her in a poker game, only to be invited to another guest's room for port. The other guest and his female companion disappear, then leap back into sight (she dressed in leather and with a whip), primed for flagellation. As the shocked guests rush out of the room, the would-be victim says plaintively, "Can't at least the monks stay?"

In another scene, a mass killer, found guilty, is released and signs autographs. Guests are cheerfully scatological at the dinner table but sneak into the bathroom to eat their dinner. A man in a playground gives a little girl postcards ("Show them to your friends but not to adults!"). When her parents see the cards, which are views of historical landmarks, they fire the girl's nurse. Another little girl is reported missing at school, even though she is quite clearly there and accompanies her parents to the police station. And so on.

The most impressive thing about the movie is the way Buñuel leads us effortlessly from one wacky parable to the next. We ought to be breathless but we aren't because his editing makes everything seem to follow with inevitable logic. It doesn't, of course, but that's freedom's fault: If people want liberty, they shouldn't be expected to count on anything. *The Phantom of Liberty* is a tour de force, a triumph by a director confronting almost impossible complications and contradictions and mastering them. It's very funny, all right, but remember: With Buñuel, you only laugh when it hurts.

Philadelphia ★ ★ ★ ½
PG-13, 119 m., 1994

Tom Hanks (Andrew Beckett), Denzel Washington (Joe Miller), Mary Steenburgen (Belinda Conine), Jason Robards (Charles Wheeler), Charles Glenn (Kenneth Killcoyne), Antonio Banderas (Miguel Alvarez), Robert Ridgely (Walter Kenton). Directed by Jonathan Demme and produced by Edward Saxon and Demme. Screenplay by Ron Nyswaner.

More than a decade after AIDS was first identified as a disease, *Philadelphia* marks the first time Hollywood has risked a big-budget film on the subject. No points for timeliness here; made-for-TV docudramas and the independent film *Longtime Companion* have already explored the subject, and *Philadelphia* breaks no new dramatic ground. Instead, it relies on the safe formula of the courtroom drama to add suspense and resolution to a story that, by its nature, should have little suspense and only one possible outcome.

And yet *Philadelphia* is quite a good film, on its own terms. And for moviegoers with an antipathy to AIDS but an enthusiasm for stars like Tom Hanks and Denzel Washington, it may help to broaden understanding of the disease. It's a ground-breaker like *Guess Who's Coming to Dinner* (1967), the first ma-

jor film about an interracial romance; it uses the chemistry of popular stars in a reliable genre to sidestep what looks like controversy.

The story involves Hanks as Andrew Beckett, a skillful lawyer in a big, old-line Philadelphia law firm. We know, although at first the law firm doesn't, that Beckett has AIDS. Visits to the hospital are part of his routine. Charles Wheeler, the senior partner (Jason Robards), hands Beckett a case involving the firm's most important client, and then, a few days later, another lawyer notices on Beckett's forehead the telltale blemishes of the skin cancer associated with AIDS.

Beckett is yanked off the case and informed he doesn't have a future with the firm. He suspects he's being fired for being sick. He's correct. (Wheeler, feeling somehow contaminated by association, barks to an associate, "He brought AIDS into our offices—into our men's room!") Beckett determines to take a stand and sue the law firm. But his old firm is so powerful that no attorney in Philadelphia wants to take it on, until Beckett finally goes in desperation to Joe Miller (Denzel Washington), one of those lawyers who advertises on TV, promising to save your driver's license.

Miller doesn't like homosexuals, but agrees to take the case, mostly for the money and exposure. And then the story falls into the familiar patterns of a courtroom confrontation, with Mary Steenburgen playing the counsel for the old firm. (Her character has no appetite for what is obviously a fraudulent defense, and whispers "I hate this case!" to a member of her team.)

The screenplay by Ron Nyswaner works subtly to avoid the standard clichés of the courtroom. Even as the case is progressing, the film's center of gravity switches from the trial to the progress of Beckett's disease, and we briefly meet his lover (Antonio Banderas) and his family, most especially his mother (Joanne Woodward), whose role is small but supplies two of the most powerful moments in the film. By the time the trial reaches its conclusion, the predictable outcome serves mostly as counterpoint for the movie's real ending.

The film was directed by Jonathan Demme, who with Nyswaner finds original ways to deal with some of the inevitable developments of their story. For example, it's obvious that at some point the scales will fall from the eyes of the Washington character, and he'll realize that his prejudices against homosexuals are wrong; he'll be able to see

the Hanks character as a fellow human worthy of affection and respect. Such changes of heart are obligatory (see, for example, Spencer Tracy's acceptance of Sidney Poitier in *Guess Who's Coming to Dinner*).

But *Philadelphia* doesn't handle that transitional scene with lame dialogue or soppy extrusions of sincerity. Instead, in a brilliant and original scene, Hanks plays an aria from his favorite opera, one he identifies with in his dying state. Washington isn't an opera fan, but as the music plays and Hanks talks over it, passionately explaining it, Washington undergoes a conversion of the soul. What he sees, finally, is a man who loves life and does not want to leave it. And then the action cuts to Washington's home, late at night, as he stares sleeplessly into the darkness, and we understand what he is feeling.

Scenes like that are not only wonderful, but frustrating, because they suggest what the whole movie could have been like if the filmmakers had taken a leap of faith. But then the film might not have been made at all; the reassuring rhythms of the courtroom drama, I imagine, are what made this material palatable to the executives in charge of signing the checks.

Philadelphia is a good movie, and sometimes more than that, and the Hanks performance (which, after all, really exists outside the plot) won him the Oscar as best actor. Sooner or later, Hollywood had to address one of the most important subjects of our time, and with *Philadelphia* the ice was broken.

The Piano ★ ★ ★ ★
R, 121 m., 1993

Holly Hunter (Ada), Harvey Keitel (Baines), Sam Neill (Stewart), Anna Paquin (Flora), Kerry Walker (Aunt Morag), Genevieve Lemon (Nessie), Tungia Baker (Hira). Directed by Jane Campion and produced by Jan Chapman. Screenplay by Campion.

The Piano is as peculiar and haunting as any film I've seen. It tells a story of love and fierce pride, and places it on a bleak New Zealand coast where people live rudely in the rain and mud, struggling to maintain the appearance of the European society they've left behind. It is a story of shyness, repression, and loneliness; of a woman who will not speak and a man who cannot listen, and of a willful little girl who causes mischief and pretends she didn't mean to.

The film opens with the arrival of a thirtyish woman named Ada (Holly Hunter) and her young daughter Flora (Anna Paquin) on a stormy gray beach. They have been rowed ashore along with Ada's piano, to meet a local bachelor named Stewart (Sam Neill) who has arranged to marry her. "I have not spoken since I was six years old," Ada's voice tells us on the sound track. "Nobody knows why, least of all myself. This is not the sound of my voice; it is the sound of my mind."

Ada communicates with the world through her piano, and through sign language that is interpreted by her daughter. Stewart and his laborers, local Maori tribesmen, take one look at the piano crate and decide it is too much trouble to carry inland to the house, and so it stays there, on the beach, in the wind and rain. It says something that Stewart cares so little for his new bride that he does not want her to have the piano she has brought all the way from Scotland—even though it is her means of communication. He does not mind quiet women, is one way he puts it.

Ada and Flora settle in. No intimacy grows between Ada and her new husband. One day she goes down to the beach to play the piano, and the music is heard by Baines (Harvey Keitel), a rough-hewn neighbor who has affected Maori tattoos on his face. He is a former whaler who lives alone, and he likes the music of the piano—so much that he trades Stewart land for the piano.

"That is *my* piano—*mine!!*" Ada scribbles on a note she hands to Stewart. He explains that they all make sacrifices and she must learn to, as well. Baines invites her over to play, and thus begins his single-minded seduction, as he offers to trade her the piano for intimacy. There are eighty-eight keys. He'll give her one for taking off her jacket. Five for raising her skirt.

Jane Campion, who wrote and directed *The Piano*, does not handle this situation as a man might. She understands better the eroticism of slowness and restraint, and the power that Ada gains by pretending to care nothing for Baines. The outcome of her story is much more subtle and surprising than Baines's crude original offer might predict.

Campion has never made an uninteresting or unchallenging film (her credits include *Sweetie*, about a family ruled by a self-destructive sister, and *An Angel at My Table*, the autobiography of writer Janet Frame, wrongly confined for schizophrenia). Her original screenplay for *The Piano* has elements of the Gothic in it, of that sensibility

that masks eroticism with fear, mystery, and exotic places. It also gives us a heroine who is a genuine piece of work; Ada is not a victim here, but a woman who reads a situation and responds to it.

The performances are as original as the characters. Holly Hunter's Ada is pale, grim, and hatchet-faced at first, although she is capable of warming. Harvey Keitel's Baines is not what he first seems, but has unexpected reserves of tenderness and imagination. Sam Neill's taciturn husband conceals a universe of fear and sadness behind his clouded eyes. And the performance by Anna Paquin, as the daughter, is one of the most extraordinary examples of a child's acting in movie history. She probably has more lines than anyone else in the film, and is as complex, too—able to invent lies without stopping for a breath, and filled with enough anger of her own that she tattles just to see what will happen. She won an Oscar as best supporting actress.

Stuart Dryburgh's cinematography is not simply suited to the story, but enhances it. Look at his cold grays and browns as he paints the desolate coast, and then the warm interiors that glow when they are finally needed. And if you are oddly affected by a key shot just before the end (I will not reveal it), reflect on his strategy of shooting and printing it, not in real time, but by filming at quarter-time and then printing each frame four times, so that the movement takes on a fated, dreamlike quality.

The Piano is one of those rare movies that is not just about a story, or some characters, but about a whole universe of feeling—of how people can be shut off from each other, lonely and afraid, about how help can come from unexpected sources, and about how you'll never know if you never ask.

Picnic at Hanging Rock ★ ★ ★ ½
PG, 110 m., 1980

Rachel Roberts (Miss Appleyard), Dominic Guard (Fitzhubert), Helen Morse (Dianne), Jacki Weaver (Minnie). Directed by Peter Weir and produced by James and Hal McElroy. Screenplay by Cliff Green.

Peter Weir's *Picnic at Hanging Rock* has something of the same sense of mystery and buried terror as Antonioni's *L'Aventura*—another film about a sudden and disquieting disappearance. But it's more lush and seductive than Antonioni's spare black-and-white images: Weir films an Australian landscape that could

be prehistoric, that suggests that men have not come this way before . . . and that, quite possibly, they should not have come this time.

"This time" is 1900, when much of Australia remained unseen by European eyes, but when a staid and proper version of European culture had been established at such places as Appleyard College, presented here as a boarding school for proper young ladies. As is almost always the case in movies about proper boarding schools, an undercurrent of repressed sexuality runs through Appleyard, and especially through the person of its headmistress (Rachel Roberts).

We get a preliminary sense of that in the film's opening scenes, which show several of the young ladies preparing to spend the day picnicking at nearby Hanging Rock, a geological outcropping from time immemorial. And then there is the picnic itself, with the girls in their bonnets and parasols and immaculate white dresses, dappled in sunlight.

The film moves here at a deliberately lazy pace. The sun beats down, insects drone—and four of the young ladies, having climbed halfway up into the rock passages, are overcome by torpor. When they awake, three of them climb farther on, never to be seen again. The fourth, badly frightened, returns to the main group. A search is set into motion, and the local constable questions witnesses who saw the young girls later on in the day, but the mystery of their disappearance remains unsolved.

It's that very inconclusiveness, linked with later scenes in which the cruel nature of the headmistress is developed, that make *Picnic at Hanging Rock* so haunting. What's going on here, we ask, knowing there is no possible answer and half-pleased by the enigma. The film opens itself to our interpretations: Is the disappearance a punishment, real or imagined, for the girls' stirring sexuality? Is it a rebuke against the ancient landscape against the brash inroads of civilization? Or is it, as it was in the famous Antonioni film, a statement of nihilism: These people have disappeared, so might we, it all matters nothing, life goes on meaninglessly.

Picnic at Hanging Rock of course subscribes to none of those readings or to any reading. I've heard its ending described as inconclusive (it is) and frustrating (ditto). But *why not?* Do we want a rational explanation? Arrest and trial for vagabond kidnappers? An autopsy revealing broken necks? Poisonous snakes named as the culprits? If this film *had* a rational and tidy conclusion, it would be a good deal less interesting. But as a tantalizing puzzle, a tease, a suggestion of forbidden answer just out of earshot, it works hypnotically and very nicely indeed.

Picture Bride ★ ★ ★
PG-13, 110 m., 1995

Youki Kudoh (Riyo), Akira Takayama (Matsuji), Tamlyn Tomita (Kana), Cary-Hiroyuki Tagawa (Kanzaki), Toshiro Mifune (The Benshi), Yoko Sugi (Aunt Sode). Directed by Kayo Hatta and produced by Lisa Onodera and Diane Mei Lin Mark. Screenplay by Kayo Hatta and Mari Hatta.

Between 1907 and 1924, more than two thousand young women made the journey from Japan to Hawaii, promised to husbands they knew only through photographs. *Picture Bride* tells the story of one of them, Riyo (Youki Kudoh), who is forced to leave Yokohama under a cloud (both her parents have died of TB). She has learned a little English and hopes to make the best of the "paradise" her future husband has described in letters, but when she sees him she can't believe her eyes: He is old, in his forties, much older than the dated photograph he sent. And she is only sixteen.

His name is Matsuji (Akira Takayama), his hands are rough, his face is bronzed by the sun, and he works hard all day in the sugar cane fields. He has saved for years to pay for his bride's passage, and on his wedding night, he moves too quickly and roughly. She bites his finger and hides under her blanket, only peeking out at him shyly after he is asleep.

Life in Hawaii is centered on work, she quickly learns. She vows to save enough money to reimburse Matsuji and buy her passage back home, but the pay is only sixteen cents a day. He shows her the sea, visible over the tops of the young sugar cane plants, and tells her that they grow so quickly that soon they will be able to see only the sky. It is a parable: "By and by, we forget all about Japan."

Riyo makes a friend, Kana (played by Tamlyn Tomita of *The Joy Luck Club* and *Come See the Paradise*). Kana tells her she is blessed: "I thought I was lucky to get a handsome man for a husband, but he beats me. You are lucky to have a kind husband." Together, they do laundry in the evenings to make extra money. And the sugar cane hides the view of the sea.

Picture Bride was directed by Kayo Hatta and written by her with her sister, Mari.

Both of their grandmothers came to Hawaii from Japan, although not as picture brides, and many of the episodes in the film are based on stories passed down through the generations by the descendants of that first generation. Like stories of the old days in many cultures, this tale is probably not as harrowing as the reality; back-breaking labor under a hot sun in the cane fields is intercut with human interest and romance, and there is even an idyllic interlude where the husband takes his bride to a hidden waterfall to show her the "real paradise." Slowly, he hopes to win her trust and love.

There is a supernatural element to the picture; perhaps the cane fields are inhabited by ghosts, and indeed Riyo sees one, in an affecting scene near the end. There is tragedy, as fire destroys some fields, and tension between the Japanese and their Filipino co-workers, all overseen by a Portuguese field boss who in turn resents his Scottish overseer. A kindly local white lady inquires after the two young Japanese women when they bring the fresh laundry, but belongs to another world.

Picture Bride is one of several films of 1995 about how we gathered from all over the globe to call ourselves Americans. *My Family* is another, about Mexican-Americans. Of course, those early generations suffered much, but somehow the films are suffused with a certain serenity, because, after all, the stories had a happy ending: They produced the children and grandchildren who are telling the tales.

Pixote ★ ★ ★ ★
R, 127 m., 1981

Fernando Ramos da Silva (Pixote), Marilla Pera (Sueli), Jorge Juliao (Lilica), Gilberto Moura (Dito). Directed by Hector Babenco and produced by Sylvia B. Naves. Screenplay by Babenco and Jorge Duran.

Kids love to play by the rules. They're great at memorizing them. They repeat them to one another like ancient commandments. They never pause to question them. For the kids in *Pixote,* the rules apply to their lives in the streets as thieves, beggars, and child prostitutes. These kids are only ten or twelve years old, and at the beginning of *Pixote* we learn that there are hundreds of thousands of them living in the streets of Rio and Sao Paolo, Brazil, where more than half the population is younger than eighteen.

Pixote is the story of one of those children,

called Pixote because he is small and wide-eyed and solemn-faced and the name seems to fit. He is not a bad kid, but he lives in a fearsome environment, in which all crimes, even the most violent, are part of the daily routine. Some of the children who commit these crimes are too young to even fully understand the gravity of taking a human life. To them, a gun or a knife is a coveted possession, a prize captured from the adult world, and to use it is to gain in stature.

There is no attempt to reform these kids. They're rounded up from time to time, after a particularly well-publicized theft, mugging, or killing. They're thrown into corrupt reformatories that act as schools for crime. For all of them, the overwhelming fact of their society—the only *law* they finally understand—is that they are immune from the full force of the law until they are eighteen. They almost seem to interpret this as a license to steal, a license revoked on their eighteenth birthday, when real life begins.

Hector Babenco's film follows Pixote and several other street children through a crucial passage in their lives. They survive, they steal, they engage in innocent entertainments, they impassively observe the squalor around them, they pass through reformatory jails, they sit on the beach and dream of the future, and their lives lead up to a moment of unplanned, almost accidental violence.

Babenco shot his film on location, on the streets and inside the slum rooms of Brazil's big cities. He also cast it from among the street children themselves. Twenty-one homeless, parentless children play themselves, more or less, in this movie, and the leading character (Fernando Ramos da Silva) is an untrained, uneducated young orphan who succeeds, in this film, in creating a performance of utterly convincing realism. The film's other great performance is by Marilla Pera, as the prostitute who adopts him. (Pera won the National Society of Film Critics award for best actress for this performance; da Silva returned to the streets and was killed by police bullets in 1988.)

Babenco's filmmaking method, of casting actual people to play themselves, and then shooting on the locations where they live and work, has been used before, most successfully by the Italian neorealists. Such films as Vittorio De Sica's *Bicycle Thief* and *Shoeshine* were cast with non-actors and shot on location, and they captured a freshness and actuality that influenced the look and feel of subsequent mainstream films: After the neorealists, there was a movement in the studio films of the 1950s and 1960s toward performances, dialogue, and sets that reflected more of real life and less of the stylized Hollywood fantasies of the 1930s.

De Sica's story lines, however, were heavily, if simply, plotted, and his films drew clear conclusions about the social injustices suffered by his characters. *Pixote* is just as angry and committed as *Bicycle Thief*, but it has more of a documentary freedom. Even though it is loosely based on a novel, Babenco's film sometimes seems to be following characters no matter what they're inclined to do or say.

The one scene in the film that does seem planned is the last one, of a prostitute nursing a mournful child at her breast—and that scene, of course, is directly from John Steinbeck's *The Grapes of Wrath,* where even at the time it seemed contrived and too obviously symbolic.

The film otherwise moves with the very rhythms of life itself. It shows evil deeds (thefts, muggings, killings) that have no evil perpetrators; both criminal and target are victims. And it shows a society that perpetrates a class of child criminals because it is incapable of even really *seeing* them clearly, let alone helping to improve their lives. *Pixote* is one of the very best realistic dramas of modern cinema.

Places in the Heart ★ ★ ★
PG, 110 m., 1984

Sally Field (Edna Spaulding), John Malkovich (Mr. Will), Danny Glover (Mose), Lindsay Crouse (Margaret Lomax), Ed Harris (Wayne Lomax), Amy Madigan (Viola Kelsey). Directed by Robert Benton and produced by Arlene Donovan. Screenplay by Benton.

The places referred to in the title of Robert Benton's movie are, he has said, places that he holds sacred in his own heart: The small town in Texas where he grew up, various friends and relatives he remembers from those days, the little boy that he once was, and the things that happened or almost happened. His memories provide the material for a wonderful movie, and he has made it, but unfortunately he hasn't stopped at that. He has gone on to include too much. He tells a central story of great power, and then keeps leaving it to catch us up with minor characters we never care about.

The main story stars Sally Field as a sheriff's widow who learns from the banker that times are hard and she should sell her farm and maybe board her kids with somebody

else. She refuses. She will keep the farm and keep the kids, thank you, although she's not sure just how that will work. Then a black hobo comes knocking at the back door, asking for food, and he sort of insists that he is just the man to plant her acreage in cotton and farm it. He knows all there is to know about cotton. Since Field has no choice, she takes the man at his word, and he plants the cotton. Meanwhile, the banker, trying to solve a family problem and maybe help her at the same time, brings around a blind relative named Mr. Will, who will be a paying boarder. The three adults and the two kids form a little family that pulls together to make that farm work—and that is the central story of *Places in the Heart.*

Unfortunately, there are other stories. We meet Field's sister (Lindsay Crouse), and her brother-in-law (Ed Harris), and the local woman (Amy Madigan) he's having an affair with. Their stories function as counterpoint to the drama on the farm, but who cares? We learn just enough about the other characters to suspect that there might be a movie in their stories—but not this one, please, when their adulteries and betrayals have nothing to do with the main story.

Places in the Heart is the kind of movie where people tend to dismiss the parts they don't like. I've seen some reviews where the story of Field and the farm is the only part of the movie the critics refer to, as if Crouse, Harris, and Madigan had slipped their minds. That's wishful thinking. The subplot is there, and it's an unnecessary distraction, and it robs the movie of a lot of the sheer narrative power it would have had otherwise. It also robs us of a chance to learn more about the relationships among Field, the black farmer (Danny Glover), and the blind boarder (John Malkovich). What a group of unforgettable characters! What do they talk about in their evenings at home? Do they ever get into politics or philosophy? This is Texas in the Depression: How do they think the neighbors like the idea of a black man helping a white woman farm her land? The movie spends so much time watching the hanky-panky at the dances in town that when the Ku Klux Klan suddenly turns up in the movie, it's like it dropped out of a tree.

The movie's last scene has caused a lot of comment. It is a dreamy, idealistic fantasy in which all the characters in the film—friends and enemies, wives and mistresses, living and dead, black and white—take communion together at a church service. This is a

scene of great vision and power, but it's too strong for the movie it concludes. *Places in the Heart* can't support such an ending, because it hasn't led up to it with a narrative that was straight and well-aimed as an arrow. The story was on the farm and not in the town, and although the last scene tries to draw them together, you can't summarize things that have nothing in common.

Planes, Trains and Automobiles
★ ★ ★ ½
R, 93 m., 1987

Steve Martin (Neal Page), John Candy (Del Griffith). Directed and produced by John Hughes. Screenplay by Hughes.

The letters in the title of *Planes, Trains and Automobiles* roar across the screen like a streamliner, and the movie itself has the same confidence. The movie tells the story of two travelers who share a modest wish in life, to fly from LaGuardia to O'Hare on schedule, and it follows with complete logic the chain of events that leads them to share a soggy bed in a cheap motel in Wichita.

The travelers are played by Steve Martin and John Candy, Martin as the fastidious, anal-compulsive snob, and Candy as the big, unkempt shower-ring salesman with a weakness for telling long stories without punch lines. Both actors are perfectly cast, not so much because they are physically matched to their roles as because the movie is able to see past their differences to an essential sweetness they share.

The film was written and directed by John Hughes, who previously specialized in high-quality teen-age movies such as *Sixteen Candles* and *The Breakfast Club*. One hallmark of Hughes's work is his insistence that his characters have recognizable human qualities; he doesn't work with a cookie cutter, and the teen-age roles he wrote for Molly Ringwald, Emilio Estevez, Ally Sheedy, Matthew Broderick, and others helped transform Hollywood's idea of what a teen-age movie could be. Hughes's comedies always contain a serious undercurrent, attention to some sort of universal human dilemma that his screenplay helps to solve.

All of which may seem a million miles away from Steve Martin and John Candy, whom we left on that beer-soaked mattress in Kansas ("You should have known what would happen when you left a six-pack on a vibrating mattress," Martin complains). But *Planes, Trains and Automobiles* is a screwball comedy with a heart, and after the laughter is over, the film has generated a lot of good feeling.

The story opens in Manhattan a few days before Thanksgiving, when Candy grabs a taxi that Martin thought was his. The two men meet again at a departure lounge at LaGuardia, where their flight to Chicago has been delayed by bad weather. Martin immediately recognizes the other man as the SOB who got his cab, and inevitably, when they finally board the plane, he finds himself bumped out of first class and wedged into a center seat next to the ample Candy.

The flight eventually takes off, only to be diverted to Wichita, where Candy has enough connections through the shower-ring business to get them a room—one room with one bed. This is the beginning of a two-day nightmare for the fastidious Martin, who at one point screams at Candy that he snores and smokes, his socks smell, and his jokes aren't funny. How bad are Candy's jokes? Martin pulls out all the stops. He'd rather attend an insurance seminar than listen to one more of them. During Martin's long outburst, the camera holds on Candy's face, and we see that he is hurt, not offended. He only wants to please, to make friends, and, as usual, he has tried too hard.

Back at the Wichita airport the next morning, Martin tries to dump Candy, but fate has linked them together. Through a series of horrible misadventures on trains, buses, semi-trailer trucks, and automobiles, they end up on a highway somewhere in southern Illinois, trying to explain to a state trooper why they are driving a car that has not only crashed but burned.

There are a lot of big laughs in *Planes, Trains and Automobiles,* including the moment when the two men wake up cuddled together in the motel room, and immediately leap out of bed and begin to make macho talk about the latest Bears game. The movie's a terrific comedy, but it's more than that, because eventually Hughes gives the Martin and Candy characters some genuine depth. We begin to understand the dynamics of their relationship, and to see that although they may be opposites, they have more in common than they know. This is a funny movie, but also a surprisingly warm and sweet one.

Platoon ★ ★ ★ ★
R, 119 m., 1986

Tom Berenger (Barnes), Willem Dafoe (Sergeant Elias), Charlie Sheen (Chris), Forest Whitaker (Big Harold), Francesco Quinn (Raah), John C. McGinley (Sergeant O'Nill), Richard Edson (Sal), Kevin Dillon (Bunny). Directed by Oliver Stone and produced by Arnold Kopelson. Screenplay by Stone.

It was Francois Truffaut who said that it's not possible to make an anti-war movie, because all war movies, with their energy and sense of adventure, end up making combat look like fun. If Truffaut had lived to see *Platoon,* he might have wanted to modify his opinion. Here is a movie that regards combat from ground level, from the infantryman's point of view, and it does not make war look like fun.

The movie was written and directed by Oliver Stone, who fought in Vietnam and who has tried to make a movie about the war that is not fantasy, not legend, not metaphor, not message, but simply a memory of what it seemed like at the time to him.

The movie is narrated by a young soldier (Charlie Sheen) based on Stone himself; a middle-class college kid who volunteers for the war because he considers it his patriotic duty, and who is told, soon after he arrives in the combat zone, "You don't belong here." He believes it.

There are no false heroics in this movie, and no standard heroes; the narrator is quickly at the point of physical collapse, bedeviled by long marches, no sleep, ants, snakes, cuts, bruises, and constant, gnawing fear. In a scene near the beginning of the film, he is on guard duty when he clearly sees enemy troops approaching his position, and he freezes. He will only gradually, unknowingly, become an adequate soldier.

The movie is told in a style that rushes headlong into incidents. There is no carefully mapped plot to lead us from point to point, and instead, like the characters, we are usually disoriented. Anything is likely to happen, usually without warning. From the crowded canvas, large figures emerge: Barnes (Tom Berenger), the veteran sergeant with the scarred face, the survivor of so many hits that his men believe he cannot be killed; Elias (Willem Dafoe), another good fighter, but a man who tries to escape from the reality through drugs; Bunny (Kevin Dillon), the scared kid, who has become dangerous because that seems like a way to protect himself.

There is rarely a clear, unequivocal shot of an enemy soldier. They are wraiths, half-seen in the foliage, their presence scented on jungle paths, evidence of their passage unearthed in ammo dumps buried beneath villages. Instead, there is the clear sense of danger all around, and the presence of civilians who sometimes enrage the troops just by standing there and looking confused and helpless.

There is a scene in the movie that seems inspired by My Lai, although it does not develop into a massacre. As we share the suspicion that these villagers may, in fact, be harboring enemy forces, we share the fear that turns to anger, and we understand the anger that turns to violence.

Some of the men in *Platoon* have lost their bearings, are willing to kill almost anyone on the least pretext. Others still retain some measure of the morality of the situation. Since their own lives may also be at stake in their arguments, there is a great sense of danger when they disagree; we see Americans shooting other Americans, and we can understand why.

After seeing *Platoon,* I fell to wondering why Stone was able to make such an effective movie without falling into the trap Truffaut spoke about—how he made the movie riveting without making it exhilarating. Here's how I think he did it. He abandoned the choreography that is standard in almost all war movies. He abandoned any attempt to make it clear where the various forces were in relation to each other, so that we never know where "our" side stands and where "they" are. Instead of battle scenes in which lines are clearly drawn, his combat scenes involve 360 degrees. Any shot might be aimed at friend or enemy, and in the desperate rush of combat, many of his soldiers never have a clear idea of exactly who they are shooting at, or why.

Traditional movies impose a sense of order upon combat. Identifying with the soldiers, we feel that if we duck behind this tree or jump into this ditch, we will be safe from the fire that is coming from over there. In *Platoon,* there is the constant fear that any movement offers a fifty-fifty chance between a safe place or an exposed one. Stone sets up his shots to deny us the feeling that combat makes sense.

The Vietnam War is the central moral and political issue of the last quarter century for Americans. It has inspired some of the greatest recent American films: *Apocalyse Now, The Deer Hunter, Coming Home, The Killing*

Fields. Now here is the film that, in a curious way, should have been made before any of the others. A film that says—as the Vietnam Memorial in Washington says—that before you can make any vast sweeping statements about Vietnam, you have to begin by understanding the bottom line, which is that a lot of people went over there and got killed, dead, and that is what the war meant for them.

The Player ★ ★ ★ ★
R, 123 m., 1992

Tim Robbins (Griffin Mill), Greta Scacchi (June Gudmundsdottir), Fred Ward (Walter Stuckel), Whoopi Goldberg (Detective Avery), Peter Gallagher (Larry Levy), Dean Stockwell (Andy Civella), Sydney Pollack (Dick Mellen), Dina Merrill (Celia). Directed by Robert Altman and produced by David Brown, Michael Tolkin, and Nick Wechsler. Screenplay by Tolkin.

It would be hard to describe Griffin Mill's job in terms that would make sense to anyone who has had to work for a living. He's a vice president at a movie studio, which pays him enormous sums of money to listen to people describe movies to him. When he hears a pitch he likes, he passes it along. He doesn't have the authority to give a "go" signal himself, and yet for those who beseech him to approve their screenplays, he has a terrifying negative authority. He can turn them down. Griffin starts getting anonymous postcards from a writer who says he is going to kill him. Griffin's crime: He said he would call the writer back, and he never did.

Robert Altman's *The Player,* which tells Griffin's story with a cold, sardonic glee, is a movie about today's Hollywood—hilarious and heartless in about equal measure, and often at the same time. It is about an industry that is run like an exclusive rich boys' school, where all the kids are spoiled and most of them have ended up here because nobody else could stand them. Griffin is capable of humiliating a waiter who brings him the wrong mineral water. He is capable of murder. He is not capable of making a movie, but if a movie is going to be made, it has to get past him first.

This is material Altman knows from the inside and the outside. He owned Hollywood in the 1970s, when his films like *M*A*S*H, McCabe and Mrs. Miller,* and *Nashville* were the most audacious work in town. Hollywood cast him into the outer darkness in the 1980s, when his eclectic vision didn't fit with movies made by marketing studies. Now he

is back in glorious vengeance, with a movie that is not simply about Hollywood, but about the way we live now, in which the top executives of many industries are cut off from the real work of their employees and exist in a rarefied atmosphere of greedy competition with one another.

The Player opens with a very long, continuous shot that is quite a technical achievement, yes, but also works in another way, to summarize Hollywood's state of mind in the early 1990s. Many names and periods are evoked: silent pictures, foreign films, the great directors of the past. But these names are like the names of saints who no longer seem to have the power to perform miracles. The new gods are like Griffin Mill—sleek, expensively dressed, noncommittal, protecting their backsides. Their careers are a study in crisis control. If they do nothing wrong, they can hardly be fired just because they never do anything right.

The Player follows Griffin (Tim Robbins) during a period when his big paycheck, his luxury car, and his expensive lifestyle seem to be in danger. There is another shark in the pond, a younger executive (Peter Gallagher) who may be even sleeker and greedier, and who may get Griffin's job. This challenge comes at a bad time: Griffin is shedding a girlfriend (a woman whose superior intelligence he feeds on, while treating the rest of her like a shabby possession). And there are those postcards.

Who is sending the postcards? Griffin racks his memory and his secretary's appointment book. He has lied to so many writers that there is no way to narrow the field. Finally he picks one name and calls the guy for a meeting. The guy's girlfriend says he's out in Pasadena, seeing *The Bicycle Thief* at a revival house. Griffin drives out there, meets the guy, has a conversation with him, follows him back to a parking lot, and kills him. As if Griffin didn't have enough problems already.

The movie then follows Griffin's attempts to protect his position at the studio, evade arrest for murder, and conduct a romance with the dead man's fiancée (Greta Scacchi), who, if anything, is more cynical than Griffin. This story was first told in a novel by Michael Tolkin, who made it so compelling I read it in a single sitting. Now Altman has made it funny as well, without losing any of the lacerating anger and satire. Altman fills his film with dozens of cameos by recognizable stars, most of them saying exactly what's on their minds. And he surrounds

Griffin with the kind of oddball characters who seem to roll into Los Angeles, as if the continent was on a tilt: Whoopi Goldberg as a Pasadena police detective who finds Griffin hilarious, Fred Ward as a studio security chief who has seen too many old "Dragnet" episodes, Sydney Pollack as a lawyer who does for the law what Griffin does for the cinema, Lyle Lovett as a sinister figure lurking on the fringes of many gatherings.

Watching *The Player,* we want to despise Griffin Mill, but we can't quite manage that. He is not dumb. He has a certain verbal charm. As played by Tim Robbins, he is tall, with a massive forehead but a Dana Carvey smile, and he wears a suit well. Watching him in some shots, especially when the camera is below eye level and Altman uses a mock-heroic composition, we realize with a shock that Griffin looks uncannily like the young Citizen Kane. He has a similar morality, too, but not the breadth of vision.

Altman, who has always had a particular strength with unusual supporting characters, surrounds him with people who all seem to be sketches for movies of their own. The girlfriend played by Scacchi, whose name is June Gudmundsdottir, and who may or may not be Icelandic, is an example: a Southern California combination of artistic self-realization (she paints) and self-interest (for her, romances are like career stages). Peter Gallagher, as the rival young executive, is like the kid at school who could always push your buttons, who was so hateful you could never understand why God didn't strike him dead for smirking at you all the time. And Whoopi Goldberg, as the cop who is almost certain Griffin is a murderer, brings a certain moral detachment to her job: Would she rather apprehend a perpetrator, or enjoy the human comedy?

The Player is a smart movie, and a funny one. It is also absolutely of its time. After the savings and loan scandals, after Michael Milken, after junk bonds and stolen pension funds, here is a movie that uses Hollywood as a metaphor for the avarice of the 1980s. It is the movie *The Bonfire of the Vanities* wanted to be. There was a full-page photo of Robert Altman in one of the newsweeklies, looking sideways at the camera, grinning like someone who has waited a long time, and finally gotten in the last word. As someone who grew up on his great films, it gives me pleasure to see him make another one.

Play It Again, Sam ★ ★ ★
PG, 85 m., 1972

Woody Allen (Allan), Diane Keaton (Linda), Tony Roberts (Dick), Jerry Lacy (Bogart), Susan Anspach (Nancy), Jennifer Salt (Sharon), Joy Bang (Julie), Viva (Jennifer). Directed by Herbert Ross and produced by Arthur P. Jacobs. Screenplay by Woody Allen.

Allan lives in an apartment furnished with movie trivia. He sleeps beneath a poster for *Across the Pacific,* shaves with *Casablanca* reflected in the mirror, and fries his eggs across from *The Big Sleep.* There is not a place in the apartment from which the names Mary Astor and Sydney Greenstreet cannot be read. He is a Humphrey Bogart fan. He is more than that. He is a Humphrey Bogart pupil.

Allan's wife moved out some weeks ago and is suing for divorce, so now there are only the two people living in the apartment: Allan and Bogie. Whenever Allan reaches a crisis in his life, Bogie appears. His snap-brim is pulled down low over his eyes, and the collar is turned up on his trench coat, and there is a gat in his pocket and a Chesterfield in his mug.

"Tell her your life has changed since you met her," Bogie advises. Allan turns toward the lovely brunette sitting next to him on the sofa. He turns back to Bogie. "She won't fall for that!" Allan says. "Oh no?" says Bogie. "Try it and see."

This is pretty high-class advice, but Allan is a mess around girls. He's your average, ordinary movie freak, perfectly at home in the dark cave of a revival theater, watching the airport scene from *Casablanca.* But get him away from the movies and he gets . . . nervous. His friends try to take him to the beach. "I hate the beach! I hate the sun!" he cries. "I'm pale and I'm redheaded! I don't tan—I stroke!"

You can see that he has problems, even with Bogie on his side. His friends, Linda and Dick, try to fix him up with girls, but he splashes himself with too much Canoe and then destroys his furniture during a seizure of nonchalance. After a while it begins to occur to him that he's in love with Linda, and she likes him, and Dick is always on the phone making real estate deals.

All of this is slightly less mad than your usual Woody Allen comedy, maybe because *Play It Again, Sam* is based on Woody's Broadway play, and with a play it's a little hard to work in material like a Howard Cosell play-by-play of an assassination in South America. Still, as comedies go, this is a very funny one. Woody Allen is one of those rare comedians who understands that humor can be based on pathos as well as sadism. While the high-pressure comics overwhelm us with aggressive humor, Woody is off in the bathroom somewhere being attacked by a hairdryer.

The notion of using a Bogart character is surprisingly successful. The Bogie imitation by Jerry Lacy is good, if not great, and the movie begins and ends with variations on that great *Casablanca* ending. That, and the movie's rather conventional Broadway plot structure, give it more coherence than the previous Woody Allen films, *Take the Money and Run* and *Bananas.* Maybe the movie has too much coherence, and the plot is too predictable; that's a weakness of films based on well-made Broadway plays. Still, that's hardly a serious complaint about something as funny as *Play It Again, Sam.*

Play Misty for Me ★ ★ ★ ★
R, 102 m., 1971

Clint Eastwood (Disc Jockey), Jessica Walter (Strange Woman), Donna Mills (Girlfriend), Don Siegel (Bartender). Directed by Clint Eastwood and produced by Robert Daley. Screenplay by Jo Heims and Dean Reisner.

The girl calls up every night at about the same time and asks the disc jockey to play "Misty" for her. Some nights he does. He's the all-night man on a small station in Carmel who plays records, reads poems, and hopes to make it someday in the big city. After work (and before work, for that matter) he drinks free at bars around town, places he sometimes mentions on the air. He had a steady girl for a while, but he's been free-lancing recently, and one night he picks up a girl in a bar. Or maybe she picks him up. She's the girl who likes "Misty." She is also mad. She insinuates herself into his life with a passionate jealousy, and we gradually come to understand that she is capable of violence. At the same time, the disc jockey's old love turns up in town, and he wants nothing more than to allow himself, finally, to quit playing the field and marry her. But the new girl doesn't see it that way. And she has this thing for knives.

Play Misty for Me is not the artistic equal of *Psycho,* but in the business of collecting an audience into the palm of its hand and then squeezing hard, it is supreme. It doesn't depend on a lot of surprises to maintain the suspense. There ARE some surprises, sure, but mostly the film's terror comes from the fact that the strange woman is capable of anything.

The movie was Clint Eastwood's debut as a director, and it was a good beginning. He must have learned a lot during seventeen years of working for other directors. In particular, he must have learned a lot from Don Siegel, who directed his previous four movies and has a bit part (the bartender) in this one. There is no wasted energy in *Play Misty for Me.* Everything contributes to the accumulation of terror, until even the ordinary, daytime scenes seem to have unspeakable things lurking beneath them.

In this connection, Eastwood succeeds in filming the first Semi-Obligatory Lyrical Interlude that works. The Semi-OLI, you'll recall, is the scene where the boy and girl walk in the meadow and there's a hit song on the sound track. In Eastwood's movie, he walks in the meadow with the girl, but the scene has been prepared so carefully that the meadow looks ominous. The grass looks muddy, the shadows are deep, the sky is gray, and there is a chill in the air. The whole visual style of the movie is strangely threatening.

The movie revolves around a character played with an unnerving effectiveness by Jessica Walter. She is something like fly-paper; the more you struggle against her personality, the more tightly you're held. Clint Eastwood, in directing himself, shows that he understands his unique movie personality. He is strong but somehow passive, he possesses strength but keeps it coiled inside. And so the movie, by refusing to release any emotion at all until the very end, absolutely wrings us dry. There is no purpose to a suspense thriller, I suppose, except to involve us, scare us, to give us moments of vicarious terror. *Play Misty for Me* does that with an almost cruel efficiency.

Plenty ★ ★ ★ ½
R, 119 m., 1985

Meryl Streep (Susan), Charles Dance (Raymond), Tracey Ullman (Alice), John Gielgud (Darwin), Sting (Mick), Ian McKellen (Sir Andrew), Sam Neill (Lazar). Directed by Fred Schepisi and produced by Edward R. Pressman and Joseph Papp. Screenplay by David Hare.

At the end of World War II, a young woman stands on a hilltop in France and, as the sun bathes her in golden light, she says, "There will be days and days and days like this." That image provides the last shot in *Plenty*, which is the story of how very wrong she was.

The woman is Susan Traherne, a young English fighter in the French Resistance. She is not very seasoned and perhaps not very good at her job, but she stays alive behind enemy lines and she has a brief, poignant love affair with one of the men who parachuted down out of the night sky to fight the Germans.

The movie opens with her days in France. It follows her through the next fifteen or twenty years, and ends with that painful flashback to a day when she thought the future had nothing but good things for her. But nothing else in her life is ever as important, as ennobling or as much fun as the war. She is, perhaps, a little mad. She confesses at one point that she has a problem: "Sometimes I like to lose control."

The movie stars Meryl Streep as Susan and it is a performance of great subtlety; it is hard to play an unbalanced, neurotic, self-destructive woman, and do it with such gentleness and charm. Susan is often very pleasant to be around for the other characters in *Plenty*, and when she is letting herself lose control, she doesn't do it in the style of those patented movie mad scenes in which eyes roll and teeth are bared. She does it with an almost winsome urgency.

When she returns to England after the war, Susan makes friends almost at once. One of them is Alice (Tracey Ullman), a round-faced, grinning imp who seems born to the role of best pal. Another is Raymond (Charles Dance), a foreign-service officer who is at first fascinated by her free, Bohemian lifestyle, and then marries her and becomes her lifelong enabler, putting up a wall of patience and almost saintly tolerance around her outbursts.

It is hard to say exactly what it is that troubles Susan. At first, David Hare's screenplay leads us to her own interpretation: That after the glory and excitement of the war, after the heroism and romance, it is impossible for her to return to civilian life and suffer the boring conversations of polite society. Later, we begin to realize there is something a little willful, a little cruel, in the way she embarrasses her husband on important occasions, always seeking to say the wrong thing at the wrong time. Finally, we tend to agree with him when he explodes that she is cruel and brutish, and ungrateful to those who have put up with her.

But then there is an epilogue—a strange, furtive meeting with the boy, the parachutist, she made love with twenty years earlier. It is bathed in the cold, greenish-gray light of the saddest part of an autumn afternoon, and there is such desperation in the way they both realize that nothing will ever, ever touch them again the way the war did.

Plenty is finally not a statement about war, or foreign service, or the British middle class, but simply the story of this flawed woman who once lived intensely, and now feels that she is hardly living at all.

The performances in the movie supply one brilliant solo after another; most of the big moments come as characters dominate the scenes they are in. Streep creates a whole character around a woman who could have simply been a catalog of symptoms. Charles Dance has a thankless role, I suppose, as her long-suffering husband, but manages to suggest that he is decent as well as duped. Sting plays a nondescript young man who unsuccessfully attempts to father her child. John Gielgud has three brief scenes and steals them all.

The movie is written, acted, and directed (by Fred Schepisi) as a surface of literacy and brittle wit, beneath which lives the realization that life can sometimes be pointless and empty and sad—and that there can be days and days and days like that.

The Plot Against Harry ★ ★ ★ ½
NO MPAA RATING, 81 m., 1970

Martin Priest (Harry Plotnick), Ben Lang (Leo Perlmutter), Maxine Woods (Kay Plotnick), Henry Nemo (Max), Jacques Tylor (Jack Pomerance), Jean Leslie (Irene Pomerance), Ellen Herbert (Mae Klepper, Harry's sister), Sandra Kazan (Margie Skolnik, née Plotnick). Directed by Michael Roemer and produced by Michael and Robert Young. Screenplay by Roemer.

There is little joy in the life of Harry Plotnick. He is a low-level hoodlum, a banker for a numbers game in a New York neighborhood that was once Jewish but is now largely Hispanic and black—a neighborhood where he was once a big frog but is now without a pond. Is his numbers empire dissolving as part of a plot against him? Not really, but for Harry so many things are going wrong in so many different ways that life itself seems like a conspiracy aimed at him. Maybe everybody else got up earlier than he did today to attend a meeting on how they were all going to screw him.

As *The Plot Against Harry* opens, Harry (Martin Priest) has just been released after serving a short prison sentence. He is met by Max (Henry Nemo), his loyal chauffeur and bookkeeper, but as he returns to the old neighborhood he finds that he has to use a Chinese restaurant owner as an interpreter to even understand what his Spanish-speaking lieutenants are trying to say to him. Even more ominously, the mob seems ready to turn over his numbers business to a black man.

Harry regards these developments out of sad, tired eyes with large bags beneath them. He rarely smiles. Life has lost the ability to astonish him—until one day he almost has a traffic accident with a car that turns out to contain his ex-wife, his ex-brother-in-law, and a daughter he has never known. Life is amazing. He even has *another* daughter, he discovers, that he knew nothing about.

Now events begin to overtake Harry. He is plunged into a social whirl: One daughter is expecting, and the other is a lingerie model with a fiancé and wedding plans. His ex-brother-in-law (Ben Lang) owns a catering business and might want to take in a partner with some ready cash. His ex-wife is part of a respectable circle that includes an executive for the Heart Fund. Can Harry buy into this middle-class normality? Certainly he seems uncomfortable with the mob, where he is such small potatoes that when he testifies before a congressional crime commission, the members lose interest when they realize he knows almost nothing.

The Plot Against Harry is one of those comedies with a sprung rhythm, so that the jokes pay off by working against themselves. It's a film that makes its points through its observation of human nature, especially in such scenes as a charity benefit on a subway train and a wedding. The writer and director, Michael Roemer, doesn't build his payoffs by the boring formula of setup and punch line, but by gradually revealing the dilemma Harry finds himself in. Even the film's big moments (like the inspired scene where Harry passes out on camera at a telethon) get their laughs because of the deliberate steps by which Roemer paints the situation.

In a sense, this is filmmaking in the Robert Altman style: The camera plunges into the middle of a group of people who seem to carry on as if they're oblivious to it. They aren't playing to the camera, and the screenplay isn't aimed at the audience. Instead, the people seem strange, funny, and unique all on their own, and the audience is invited to share the filmmaker's delight as he discovers this.

The behind-the-scenes story of *The Plot Against Harry* is by now well-known. The movie was completed in 1970, but at the time, it was unable to find distribution—Hollywood didn't think it was funny. It waited on the shelf for twenty years, until Roemer decided to transfer it to video to show to his children. The video technician started to laugh as he watched it. A curiosity stirred within Roemer: Could the movie possibly be good, after all? He submitted it to the Toronto, New York, and Park City film festivals, where audiences were enthusiastic, and then he won commercial distribution, two decades later.

That adds a certain poignancy to the whole enterprise. If you see the film, pay particular attention to the performances by Martin Priest as Harry and Ben Lang as the forever-smiling ex-brother-in-law. They have a genuinely intrinsically amusing quality. Priest has acted only occasionally in the last twenty years, and Lang not at all (he went back to his job as an auditor for the state). Would their careers have happened differently if this movie had been seen in 1970? Would the movie have been a hit then? Was it ahead of its time? (Altman's revolutionary *M*A*S*H* came out the same year.) Who can say? What can be said is that this time capsule from 1970 feels, in 1990, like a jolt of fresh air.

Pocahontas ★ ★ ★
G, 81 m., 1995

NEW

With the voices of: Irene Bedard (Pocahontas), Mel Gibson (John Smith), David Ogden Stiers (Governor Ratcliffe), John Kassir (Meeko), Russell Means (Powhatan), Christian Bale (Thomas), Linda Hunt (Grandmother Willow). Directed by Mike Gabriel and Eric Goldberg and produced by James Pentecost. Screenplay by Carl Binder, Susannah Grant, and Philip LaZebnik.

Pocahontas is the best-looking of the modern Disney animated features, and one of the more thoughtful: It is about real issues, even if it treats them with naive idealism. In its view, Native Americans lived in peaceful harmony with nature until European settlers came, bringing guns and ecological destruction. The Europeans, puffed up with their notions of civilization, did not realize how much they had to learn from the Indians.

Midway in the film, after Captain John Smith (voice by Mel Gibson) has thoughtlessly dismissed the ideas of the young Indian woman he loves, Pocahontas asks: "If the savage one is me, how can there be so much you don't know?" Then follows a musical sequence during which Pocahontas (Irene Bedard) takes Smith on a whirlwind tour of the forest. Because this is a Disney picture, the animals are of course all friends of the Indian maiden, who snatches a cute cub away from a mother bear—something that even my own limited woodcraft suggests is not prudent.

The message of *Pocahontas* is that arriving settlers despoiled the forests and imposed their own version of civilization, whether or not it was wanted. Governor Ratcliffe (David Ogden Stiers), the blustering leader of the Virginia Co., is shown gleefully using cannons to level forests. And when the settlers open fire on the Indians, they retaliate by capturing John Smith and preparing to execute him. Only Pocahontas, who can empathize with both sides, can save the day.

Pocahontas is based on myth, not history. In real life, Pocahontas was eleven or twelve when she first met John Smith (who claimed in his journals that his life was saved no less than three times by women who loved him). The Englishman she married was John Rolfe. She did indeed get to go to England, where she was feted as a princess. She died in Europe, at about twenty-one. The son she had with Rolfe became one of the richest of early American settlers, and his ancestors still thrive.

Having led one of the most interesting lives imaginable, Pocahontas serves here more as a simplified symbol, an Indian maid who falls in love with a dashing blond hero, saves his life, and brings about a peace between her people and the European visitors. The dramatic challenge in the movie (as it is in *The Little Mermaid*) is that her father disapproves of the man she loves, because he belongs to a different race. He wants her to marry a member of the tribe, who she dislikes because "he's so . . . serious." When her intended is shot dead by a young British soldier and Smith is taken prisoner, her immediate thought is, "I'll never see John Smith again!" So much for any lingering regrets over the dead fiancé.

The movie hurries on to the big picture, which is that Pocahontas, raised in communion with nature, can help John Smith free himself of the moral constipation of European civilization. "You can't step in the same river twice," he learns, and "listen with your heart and you will understand." Since these lessons are taught by an Indian maiden with a waist-length mane of black hair, an hourglass figure, and a Playmate face, John Smith's heart finds it easy to listen, and soon he is singing a hymn to the new land. (He does not, however, sing a love duet with Pocahontas, because the romantic theme "If I Never Knew You" was cut from the movie, reportedly because the kids in test audiences found it boring. Without such a transition, their relationship emerges rather abruptly.)

What is especially good about *Pocahontas* is the artistry of the animation. The big picture—the new land of towering forests, sparkling steams, and rugged cliffs—is drawn with a freedom and energy that has real power. And, as in *The Lion King*, the landscape includes a precipice from which the characters can survey their domain—a rock jutting out into the sky, making an ideal pulpit for sweeping sentiments.

The weakness of the movie is its lack of a colorful villain. After Scar in *The Lion King* and the fearsome Beast in *Beauty and the Beast* (not to mention the jealous undersea denizens of *Mermaid* and the scheming Jafar of *Aladdin*), the bad guys in *Pocahontas* seem pretty nice, really. Ratcliffe, the leader of the expedition, is shown more as a buffoon than a villain. The soldier who kills Pocahontas' fiancé immediately regrets his error. The other British soldiers are essentially members of the chorus. And the Indians are all, of course, noble to one degree or another.

That leaves only the concept of Misunderstanding as the real villain—and after Pocahontas helps the two sides to communicate, there is no more dramatic tension. The film's ending is rather weak, too. After Smith describes the glories of London to Pocahontas and her eyes sparkle, she decides after all that her place is "here, with my people" and there is a bittersweet conclusion as she watches Smith's ship sail back to the Old World. I knew Pocahontas visited Europe in real life, and was hoping the movie would get her there, too; the ending came as an anticlimax.

All of these problems make *Pocahontas* less entertaining than it might have been, and the comic relief—the cute raccoon, the hummingbird, and the governor's dog—seem obligatory after the similar creatures in the other modern Disney cartoons. What's left is simply the grandeur of the New Land, which tends to ennoble all of the characters. Drawn with true artistry, and evoked in musical sequences like "Just Around the River Bend," this vision is the true star of the film, and its spirit is evoked by Old Grandmother Willow, a tree which gives Pocahontas a lot of sound advice.

The film looks great, the songs are wonderfully visualized, and the characters are appealing. *Pocahontas* is just fine as family entertainment. But on a list including *Mermaid, Beauty, Aladdin,* and *Lion King,* I'd rank it fifth. It has a lot of good intentions, but a severe scoundrel shortage.

Poetic Justice ★ ★ ★
R, 109 m., 1993

Janet Jackson (Justice), Tupac Shakur (Mailman), Khandi Alexander (Simone), Tyra Ferrell (Beauty Shop Owner), Maya Angelou (Aunt June), Che J. Avery (Thug No. 2), Lloyd Avery II (Thug No. 1), Kimberly Brooks (Kim), Rico Bueno (Ticket Taker), Maia Campbell (Shante). Directed by John Singleton and produced by Steve Nicolaides and Singleton. Screenplay by Singleton.

Poetic Justice is described as the second of three films John Singleton plans to make about the South Central neighborhood in Los Angeles. His first, *Boyz N the Hood,* showed a young black man growing up in an atmosphere of street violence, but encouraged by his father to stand aside from the gangs and shootings and place a higher worth on his life. At the end of the film, the hero's friend was shot dead.

Now comes a film told from the point of view of a young woman in the same neighborhood—Justice, played by Janet Jackson. At the beginning of the film she's on a date at a drive-in theater with her boyfriend. Words are exchanged at the refreshment stand, egos are wounded, and before long her boyfriend is shot dead. (One of the realities in both films is the desperation of a community where self-respect is so precarious that small insults can become capital offenses.)

Justice emerges from mourning determined to go it alone. What's the use of committing her heart to a man who will simply get himself killed in another stupid incident? She works in a beauty shop, where one day a mailman (Tupac Shakur) comes in and starts making soft talk. She leads him on and then lets him down with a mean trick. But the tables are turned when her friend Tesha

(Regina King) invites her to go along on a trip to Oakland. Her boyfriend has a friend who works for the post office and will let them ride along in a mail truck. Of course, the friend is Shakur.

Unlike *Boyz,* which was fairly strongly plotted, *Poetic Justice* unwinds like a road picture from the early 1970s, in which the characters are introduced and then set off on a trip that becomes a journey of discovery. By the end of the film, Justice will have learned to trust and love again, and Shakur will have learned how to listen to a woman. And all of the characters—who in one way or another lack families—will begin to get a feeling for the larger African-American family they belong to.

The scene where that takes place is one of the best in the film. The mail truck takes them down back roads until they stumble across the Johnson family picnic, a sprawling, populous affair where not all of the cousins even know each other. That makes an ideal opportunity for the four travelers to wander in and get a free meal. But along the way they're also embraced by one of the cousins, and hear some words of wisdom from another one (the poet Maya Angelou).

It is Angelou's poetry we hear on the sound track of the movie; Justice is a poet, and we are told it is hers. She has aspirations and sensitivities, and as played by Jackson she emerges as a sweet, smart woman who is growing up to be a good person. Her romance with Shakur is touching precisely because it doesn't take place in a world of innocence and naïveté; because they both know the risks of love, their gradual acceptance of each other is convincing.

Boyz N the Hood was one of the most powerful and influential films of its time, in 1991. *Poetic Justice* is not its equal, but does not aspire to be; it is a softer, gentler film, more of a romance than a commentary on social conditions. Janet Jackson provides a lovable center for it, and by the time it's over we can see more clearly how *Boyz* presented only part of the South Central reality. Yes, things are hard. But they aren't impossible. Sometimes they're wonderful. And sometimes you can find someone to share them with.

Point Break ★ ★ ★ ½
R, 122 m., 1991

Patrick Swayze (Bodhi), Keanu Reeves (Johnny Utah), Gary Busey (Pappas), Lori Petty (Tyler), John McGinley (Ben Harp).

Directed by Kathryn Bigelow and produced by Peter Abrams and Robert L. Levy. Screenplay by W. Peter Iliff.

The bodhi tree, according to the Buddhists, is the tree beneath which one finds enlightenment. That is not exactly how it works with Bodhi, the surfing bank robber who is the hero of *Point Break,* but he is such a persuasive character that the young FBI agent falls under his spell. Or maybe it is Southern California itself that attracts him—that land of surf and skydiving and strange karma, so seductive to a square football hero out of Ohio.

The hero, who has the thankless name Johnny Utah, is played by Keanu Reeves as a former Rose Bowl star with a bum knee, who joined the FBI and has been assigned to Los Angeles. A series of bank robberies is frustrating the bureau. Four robbers who call themselves the Ex-Presidents, and wear rubber masks of Nixon, Carter, Reagan, and LBJ, have pulled off a professional string of bank jobs and left not a single clue behind.

Except one. Johnny Utah is given a partner named Pappas (Gary Busey), who thinks the robbers may be surfers, because one has a tan line, and a strand of hair found at the crime was polluted with the same contaminants found at a popular surfer beach. So he convinces Utah to go undercover as a surfer and try to break the case.

This is some California movie, all right. The plot description I have just supplied could work just as easily for *The Naked Gun 2½* as for *Point Break,* which takes it deadly seriously, even after adding several other preposterous developments like a guy who gets so mad, he jumps out of a plane without a parachute, free-falls until he can tackle a guy who has one, and then holds a gun to his head.

The movie was directed by Kathryn Bigelow, a stylist who specializes in professionals who do violence. She made *Blue Steel,* with Jamie Lee Curtis as a rookie cop, and now here is Keanu Reeves in essentially the same role—a kid determined to prove himself, up against the twisted intelligence of a megalomaniac.

Bodhi, played by Patrick Swayze, is part mystic, part criminal, and all surfer. From clues developed by Pappas, it appears that he and his gang rob banks to support their surfing, and then move on when the seasons change. Johnny Utah does become friendly with them, and even falls in love with Bodhi's ex-girlfriend (Lori Petty), while trying to fit together the case. And then the plot grows truly ingenious, all the way down to its Zen ending on a lonely, storm-swept beach in Australia.

Point Break is not the kind of movie where we should spend a lot of time analyzing the motives of the characters. Once Johnny Utah realizes, for example, that Bodhi knows he's an FBI agent—should he really go skydiving with him, and let Bodhi pack the chute? Such questions are fruitless, because the movie has Utah trapped in Bodhi's spell, in which everything—free-falling, surfing, robbing banks—is part of catching the wave of life, looking for that endless ride.

Bigelow is an interesting director for this material. She is interested in the ways her characters live dangerously for philosophical reasons. They aren't men of action, but men of thought who choose action as a way of expressing their beliefs. That adds an intriguing element to their characters, and makes the final confrontation in this movie as meaningful as it can be, given the admittedly preposterous nature of the material.

Bigelow and her crew are also virtuoso filmmakers. There's a foot chase through the streets, yards, alleys, and living rooms of Santa Monica; two skydiving sequences with virtuoso photography; powerful chemistry between the good and evil characters; and an ominous, brooding score by Mark Isham that underlines the mood. The plot of *Point Break*, summarized, invites parody (rookie agent goes undercover as surfer to catch bank robbers). The result is surprisingly effective.

Point of No Return ★ ★ ★
R, 110 m., 1993

Bridget Fonda (Maggie), Gabriel Byrne (Bob), Dermot Mulroney (J.P.), Harvey Keitel (The Cleaner), Anne Bancroft (Amanda), Miguel Ferrer (Kaufman), Lorraine Toussaint (Beth). Directed by John Badham and produced by Art Linson. Screenplay by Robert Getchell and Alexandra Seros.

Point of No Return is a *Pygmalion* for our angry age. In both stories, an older teacher picks a girl out of the gutter and teaches her new skills. Professor Higgins taught Eliza to act like a lady, and now Bob teaches Maggie to be a lady and a cold-blooded assassin. Both women get a lot of lessons on how to hold their forks.

The movie stars Bridget Fonda as Maggie, a girl of the streets, who is high on drugs when she kills a cop during a drugstore robbery that goes wrong. She is sentenced to death, and to keep the story rolling along, the movie shows the sentence being carried out almost immediately (not likely in California).

But in fact she is not killed; the execution is a cover, and she awakens inside a secret government school for killers, where Bob (Gabriel Byrne) tells her she has two choices: go along with the program, or end up underneath the tombstone that already carries her name. Maggie is put through a quick course in weapons, explosives, martial arts, and good manners. The last is taught by Anne Bancroft, as an older woman who gives her a beauty make-over. She came into the center looking like a wolf girl; she leaves as a well-groomed beauty.

Bob gives her a new identity and sends her to live in Venice, California, where she soon falls in love with the photographer who lives downstairs (Dermot Mulroney). But soon she is assigned to murder a man in a restaurant, and eventually it becomes clear that Bob's bosses consider her expendable. Bob, of course, has fallen quietly in love with her, a feeling that business keeps him from acting on.

If this story sounds familiar, you have seen *La Femme Nikita*, a 1991 French thriller by Luc Besson, which was bought by Warner Bros. to be remade into this American version by John Badham (*WarGames, Stakeout*). The notion of pouring European films into Hollywood molds didn't work out with *The Vanishing*, but *Point of No Return* is actually a fairly effective and faithful adaptation, and Bridget Fonda manages the wild identity swings of her role with intensity and conviction, although not the same almost poetic sadness that Anne Parillaud brought to the original movie.

If I didn't feel the same degree of involvement with *Point of No Return* that I did with *La Femme Nikita*, it may be because the two movies are so similar in plot, look, and feel. I had déjà vu all through the movie. There are a few changes, mostly not for the better. By making the heroine's boyfriend a photographer this time, instead of a checkout clerk, the movie loses the poignancy of their relationship; Nikita liked her clerk precisely because he was completely lacking in aggression.

The movie does, at least, end on the correct note of suitably bleak melancholia. Hollywood sometimes feels it necessary to squeeze all films into happy endings (in the case of a violent thriller, that means the right people get killed). That would be all wrong with this story, which is about a woman coming to grips with her violent nature.

Poltergeist ★ ★ ★
PG, 114 m., 1982

Craig T. Nelson (Steve), Jo Beth Williams (Diane), Beatrice Straight (Dr. Lesh), Dominique Dunne (Dana), Oliver Robins (Robbie), Heather O'Rourke (Carol Anne). Directed by Tobe Hooper and produced by Steven Spielberg and Frank Marshall. Screenplay by Spielberg, Michael Grais, and Mark Victor.

Special effects in the movies have grown so skilled, sensational, and scary that they sometimes upstage the human actors. And they often cost a lot more. In *Poltergeist*, for example, the cast is made up of relatively unknown performers, but that's all right because the real stars are producer Steven Spielberg (*Raiders of the Lost Ark*), director Tobe Hooper (*The Texas Chainsaw Massacre*), and their reputations for special effects and realistic violence. Their names on this horror film suggest that its technology will be impeccable. And they don't disappoint us. This is the movie *The Amityville Horror* dreamed of being. It begins with the same ingredients (a happy American family, living in a big, comfortable house). It provides similar warnings of doom (household objects move by themselves, the weather seems different around the house than anywhere else). And it ends with a similar apocalypse (spirits take total possession of the house, and terrorize the family). Even some of the special effects are quite similar, as when greasy goo begins to ooze around the edges of a doorjamb.

But *Poltergeist* is an effective thriller, not so much because of the special effects, as because Hooper and Spielberg have tried to see the movie's strange events through the eyes of the family members, instead of just standing back and letting the special effects overwhelm the cast along with the audience. The movie takes place in Spielberg's favorite terrain, the American suburb (also the locale of parts of *Close Encounters, Jaws,* and *E.T.*). The haunted house doesn't have seven gables, but it does have a two-car garage. It is occupied by a fairly normal family (two parents, three kids) and the movie begins on a somewhat hopeful note with the playing of "The Star Spangled Banner" as a TV station signs off.

The opening visuals, however, are somewhat ominous. They're an extreme close-up of a TV screen, filled with the usual patriotic images (Iwo Jima, the Lincoln Memorial). Why so close? We're almost being invited to look between the dots on the screen and see something else. And indeed, the family's youngest daughter, an open-faced, long-haired, innocent little cherub, begins to talk to the screen. She's in touch with the "TV people." Before long she disappears from this plane of existence and goes to live with the TV people, wherever they are. Weird events begin to happen in the house. An old tree behaves ominously. The swimming pool seems to have a mind of its own. And the villains are the same people who were the bad guys in Spielberg's *Jaws*—the real estate developers. This time, instead of encouraging people to go back into the water, they're building a subdivision on top of an old graveyard.

This is all ridiculous, but Hooper and Spielberg hold our interest by observing the everyday rituals of this family so closely that, since the family seems real, the weird events take on a certain credibility by association. That's during the first hour of the movie. Then all hell breaks loose, and the movie begins to operate on the same plane as *Alien* or *Altered States*, as a shocking special-effects sound-and-light show. A closet seems to exist in another dimension. The swimming pool is filled with grasping, despairing forms of the undead. The search for the missing little girl involves a professional psionics expert, and a lady dwarf who specializes in "cleaning" haunted homes. Nobody ever does decide whether a poltergeist really is involved in the events in the house, or who the poltergeist may be, but if that doesn't prevent them from naming the movie *Poltergeist* I guess it shouldn't keep us from enjoying it.

The Pope of Greenwich Village
★ ★ ★
R, 122 m., 1984

Eric Roberts (Paulie), Mickey Rourke (Charlie), Daryl Hannah (Diane), Geraldine Page (Mrs. Ritter), Kenneth McMillan (Barney), Tony Musante (Pete), Burt Young (Bedbug Eddie). Directed by Stuart Rosenberg and produced by Gene Kirkwood. Screenplay by Vincent Patrick.

Everybody is very ethnic in *The Pope of Greenwich Village*. They all wave their hands a lot, and hang out on street corners, and have uncles in the Mafia. They have such bonds of blood brotherhood, a cousin to them is closer than your mother is to you. And they've always got some kind of con game going on the side. Take Paulie, for example. He knows this racehorse that's selling for $15,000, only the joke is, this is a champion horse because it was sired with sperm stolen directly from the winner of the Belmont. Paulie explains about the horse while he has his mouth full of a hero sandwich that's a yard long. His cousin, Charlie, tells him he's crazy. That is a compliment in this family.

Paulie and Charlie have just been fired from their jobs at a restaurant for stealing from the management. Charlie is hard up. He can no longer support his girlfriend, a long-limbed, blond aerobics instructor who seems attracted to his exotic ethnic charm. Paulie has the answer to their problems. He will buy the future champion racehorse with money from a juice loan and then pay off the loan by cracking a safe he has heard about. There is only one problem with this plan. The safe belongs to the Mafia godfather of Greenwich Village, and if he finds out who did it, not even Paulie's uncle in the Mafia can save them. Meanwhile, Charlie's girlfriend is pregnant, Paulie's car has been towed, a cop has killed himself falling down an elevator shaft, and on the sound track Frank Sinatra is singing "Summer Wind."

The Pope of Greenwich Village bills itself as a drama and is structured like a crime thriller, but I categorize it as basically a Behavior Movie. The real subject of the movie is the behavior of the characters, and the story is essentially an excuse for showboat performances. This movie is an actor's dream, and the actors involved are Eric Roberts, fresh from his triumph in *STAR 80*, as Paulie; Mickey Rourke, the hero of *Diner*, as Charlie; Daryl Hannah, right after her hit in *Splash*, as the aerobics instructor; and the usual supporting types like Tony Musante as the uncle, Burt Young—stuffing his face with pasta—as the godfather, and Geraldine Page as the tough-talking mother of the dead cop. Also, Kenneth McMillan has a well-acted key role as an old safecracker who gets caught in the middle of the whole deal.

There are times when *The Pope of Greenwich Village* seems to aspire to some great meaning, some insight into crime like *The Godfather* had. But the tip-off is the last shot, where the boys have a happy-go-lucky walk down the street and into a freeze-frame, while Sinatra is trotted out for his third encore. This movie is not really about anything except behavior, and the only human drama in it is the story of the safecracker and his family. That doesn't mean it's not worth seeing. The behavior is well-observed, although Eric Roberts has a tendency to go over the top in his mannered performance, and the last two scenes are highly unlikely. It's worth seeing for the acting, and it's got some good laughs in it, and New York is colorfully observed, but don't tell me this movie is about human nature, because it's not; it's about acting.

Popeye ★ ★ ★ ½
PG, 114 m., 1980

Robin Williams (Popeye), Shelley Duvall (Olive Oyl), Ray Walston (Poopdeck Pappy), Paul Dooley (Wimpy), Paul L. Smith (Bluto), Richard Libertini (Geezil). Directed by Robert Altman and produced by Robert Evans. Screenplay by Jules Feiffer.

One of Robert Altman's trademarks is the way he creates whole new worlds in his movies—worlds where we somehow don't believe that life ends at the edge of the screen, worlds in which the main characters are surrounded by other people plunging ahead at the business of living. That gift for populating new places is one of the richest treasures in *Popeye*, Altman's musical comedy. He takes one of the most artificial and limiting of art forms—the comic strip—and raises it to the level of high comedy and high spirits.

And yet *Popeye* nevertheless remains true to its origin on the comic page, and in those classic cartoons by Max Fleischer. A review of this film almost has to start with the work of Wolf Kroeger, the production designer, who created an astonishingly detailed and rich set on the movie's Malta locations. Most of the action takes place in a ramshackle fishing hamlet—"Sweethaven"—where the streets run at crazy angles up the hillsides, and the rooming houses and saloons lean together dangerously.

Sweethaven has been populated by actors who look, or are made to look, so much like their funny-page originals that it's hardly even jarring that they're *not* cartoons. Audiences immediately notice the immense forearms on Robin Williams, who plays Popeye; they're big, brawny, and completely convincing. But so is Williams's perpetual squint and his lopsided smile. Shelley Duvall, the star of so many other Altman films, is perfect here as Olive Oyl, the role she was born to play. She brings to Olive a certain . . . dignity, you might say. She's not lightly scorned, and although she may tear apart a room in an unsuccessful attempt to open the curtains, she is fearless in the face of her terrifying fiancé, Bluto. The list continues: Paul Smith (the torturer in *Midnight Express*) looks ferociously Bluto-like, and Paul Dooley (the father in *Breaking Away*) is a perfect Wimpy, forever curiously sniffing a hamburger with a connoisseur's fanatic passion. Even the little baby, Swee' Pea, played by Altman's grandson, Wesley Ivan Hurt, looks like typecasting.

But it's not enough that the characters and the locations look their parts. Altman has breathed life into this material, and he hasn't done it by pretending it's camp, either. He organizes a screenful of activity, so carefully choreographed that it's a delight, for example to watch the moves as the guests in Olive's rooming house make stabs at the plates of food on the table.

There are several set pieces. One involves Popeye's arrival at Sweethaven, another a stop on his lonely quest for his long-lost father. Another is the big wedding day for Bluto and Olive Oyl, with Olive among the missing and Bluto's temper growing until steam jets from his ears. There is the excursion to the amusement pier, and the melee at the dinner table, and the revelation of the true identity of a mysterious admiral, and the kidnapping of Swee' Pea, and then the kidnapping of Olive Oyl and her subsequent wrestling match with a savage octopus.

The movie's songs, by Harry Nillsen, fit into all of this quite effortlessly. Instead of having everything come to a halt for the musical set pieces, Altman stitches them into the fabric. Robin Williams sings Popeye's anthem, "I Yam What I Yam" with a growling old sea dog's stubbornness. Bluto's "I'm Mean" has an undeniable conviction, and so does Olive Oyl's song to Bluto, "He's Large." Shelley Duvall's performance as Olive Oyl also benefits from the amazingly ungainly walking style she brings to the movie.

Popeye, then, is lots of fun. It suggests that it *is* possible to take the broad strokes of a comic strip and turn them into sophisticated entertainment. What's needed is the right attitude toward the material. If Altman and his people had been the slightest bit condescending toward Popeye, the movie might have crash-landed. But it's clear that this movie has an affection for Popeye, and so much regard for the sailor man that it even bothers to reveal the real truth about his opinion of spinach.

Postcards from the Edge ★ ★ ★
R, 101 m., 1990

Meryl Streep (Suzanne Vale), Shirley MacLaine (Doris Mann), Dennis Quaid (Jack Falkner), Gene Hackman (Lowell), Richard Dreyfuss (Dr. Frankenthal), Rob Reiner (Joe Pierce), CCH Pounder (Julie Marsden). Directed by Mike Nichols and produced by Nichols and John Calley. Screenplay by Carrie Fisher.

The practicing alcoholic is familiar with a gnawing feeling in the pit of the stomach—the guilt at letting other people down, the remorse at letting himself down. Criticism in any form is likely to be met with anger, because nothing you can tell him will make him feel worse than the things he tells himself.

In the opening scenes of *Postcards from the Edge*, a comedy based on Carrie Fisher's journey through addiction, this feeling is evoked so well that you begin to suffer along with the film's heroine, played by Meryl Streep. Then the movie forgets its original impulse and turns into a comedy of manners.

The story involves Suzanne, a young actress who has a more famous actress for her mother. The father, also famous, has been misplaced somewhere along the way. As the film opens, Suzanne has awakened in the bed of yet another boyfriend she does not quite remember meeting. Her life has become a confusion of blackouts, memory lapses, screw-ups on the set, and behavior that baffles even her. All that keeps her going on the set of a movie are the frequent visits to her dressing room in the company of a woman who sells her cocaine.

Meryl Streep plays this character with a kind of defiant sweetness that recalls the late Irene Dunne. She is not a bad person and she doesn't want to cause trouble for anybody, but her drug usage has befuddled her to the point where she's not much use. Her mother (Shirley MacLaine) is also a basket case—a maintenance alcoholic who is never far from her glass of chilled white wine. But because wine is socially acceptable and drugs are not, the mother is able to deny her problem while lecturing her daughter to the point of distraction. Meanwhile, MacLaine's latest husband sleeps most of the time, possibly as a way of avoiding his wife's voice.

Suzanne barely gets through her latest film. She is obviously on the edge of a crack-up, and after another misadventure she ends up in a rehab center, where her mother comes to visit and basks in the applause of her re-covering fans. It's here that the movie takes the wrong turn, into a domestic show-biz comedy that plays up the mother-daughter rivalry at the cost of its original subject, drugs in show business.

That's not to say I didn't enjoy Shirley MacLaine's performance in this movie; her role has been made too important, and yet I appreciated every moment of it, even a welcome home party at which mother and daughter perform songs that turn into a competition for the love of those present. MacLaine creates a glorious caricature of the aging star who has to put down her daughter to maintain her own ego.

Streep is very funny in the movie; she does a good job of catching the knife-edged throwaway lines that have become Carrie Fisher's specialty. And Nichols captures a certain kind of difficult reality in his scenes on movie sets, where the actress is pulled this way and that by people offering helpful advice. Everyone wants a piece of a star, even a falling one.

What's disappointing about the movie is that it never really delivers on the subject of recovery from addiction. There are some incomplete, dimly seen, unrealized scenes in the rehab center, and then desultory talk about offscreen AA meetings, but the film is preoccupied with gossip; we're encouraged to wonder how many parallels there are between the Streep and MacLaine characters and their originals, Fisher and Debbie Reynolds. Suzanne, the young actress, has some bad moments and then comes through as a trouper, and the movie almost seems to think her real problem is an inability to communicate with her mother.

Half the people in Hollywood seem to have gone through recovery from drugs and alcohol by now. And yet no one seems able to make a movie that's really about the subject. Do they think it wouldn't be interesting? Any movie that cares deeply about itself—even a comedy—is interesting. It's the movies that lack the courage of their convictions, the ones that keep asking themselves what the audience wants, that go astray. *Postcards from the Edge* contains too much good writing and too many good performances to be a failure, but its heart is not in the right place.

Prancer ★ ★ ★
G, 103 m., 1989

Sam Elliott (John Riggs), Rebecca Harrell (Jessica Riggs), Cloris Leachman (Mrs.

McFarland), Rutanya Alda (Aunt Sarah), John Joseph Duda (Steve Riggs), Abe Vigoda (Orel Benton), Michael Constantine (Store's Santa), Ariana Richards (Carol Wetherby), Mark Rolston (Butcher Drier), Boo (Prancer). Directed by John Hancock and produced by Raffaella De Laurentiis. Screenplay by Greg Taylor.

Every once in a while you meet a kid like Jessica, who is tough and resilient and yet hangs onto her dreams. She's a nine-year-old who still believes in Santa Claus and uses logic to defend her position: If there isn't a Santa then maybe there isn't a God, and if there isn't a God then there isn't a heaven, and, in that case, where did Jessica's mother go when she died?

Jessica lives with her dad and brother on a small farm outside of Three Oaks, Michigan. Her dad grows apples and is struggling to make ends meet. He may have to sell the tractor. "Will we have enough to eat?" she asks him. "Sure," he says. "We'll have apple sauce, apple juice, stewed apples, apple pie, baked apples. . . ." One day while she's walking down the main street on her way home from school, Jessica witnesses a disturbing accident: One of Santa's reindeers falls down from a holiday decoration strung up across the street. It's Prancer, the third in line.

Nobody seems to care much about the injured decoration, which is cleared from the road. But not long after, walking home alone through the frosty woods on a cold night, Jessica comes across a reindeer with an injured leg. It stands unafraid in a moonlit clearing and seems to be asking for help. Not long after, her dad comes along in his pickup, and then they both see the deer in the road. Her dad sees that it has a bad leg and wants to shoot it, but then the reindeer disappears. And when it turns up again in the barn, Jessica hides it in an outbuilding and brings it Christmas cookies to eat. She wants to nurse Prancer back to health and return him to Santa.

OK, I know, this sounds like a cloying fantasy designed to paralyze anyone over the age of nine, but not the way it's told by director John Hancock and writer Greg Taylor. They give the film an unsentimental, almost realistic edge by making the father (Sam Elliott) into a tough, no-nonsense farmer who's having trouble raising his kids alone and keeps laying down the law. And what really redeems the movie, taking it out of the category of kiddie picture and giving it a

heart and gumption, is the performance by a young actress named Rebecca Harrell, as Jessica.

She's something. She has a troublemaker's look in her eye and a round pixie face that's filled with mischief. And she's smart—a plucky schemer who figures out things for herself and isn't afraid to act on her convictions. Her dialogue in the movie is fun to listen to because she talks like she thinks, and she's always working an angle. She believes ferociously that her reindeer is indeed Prancer, and to buy it a bag of oats she does housecleaning for the eccentric old lady (Cloris Leachman) who lives in the house on the hill.

Prancer is not filled with a lot of action. Only ordinary things happen, as when the local newspaper prints a letter that Jessica wrote to Santa, assuring him that Prancer would be back in good shape for Christmas duty (the headline, inevitably, is "Yes, Santa, there is a Virginia.") The reindeer is finally discovered, and Jessica's dad sells it to Mr. Drier, the local butcher. Of course Jessica is sure Prancer will end up as sausage meat, but, no, all Drier wants to do is exhibit the animal as a Christmas attraction.

The best thing about *Prancer* is that it doesn't insult anyone's intelligence. Smaller kids will identify with Jessica's fierce resolve to get Prancer back into action, and older viewers will appreciate the fact that the movie takes place in an approximation of the real world.

Predator ★ ★ ★
R, 105 m., 1987

Arnold Schwarzenegger (Dutch), Carl Weathers (Dillon), Elpidia Carrillo (Anna), Bill Duke (Mac), Jesse Ventura (Blain), Sonny Landham (Billy), Richard Chaves (Poncho), R.G. Armstrong (General Phillips), Shane Black (Hawkins), Kevin Peter Hall (Predator). Directed by John McTiernan and produced by Lawrence Gordon, Joel Silver, and John Davis. Screenplay by Jim and John Thomas.

Predator begins like *Rambo* and ends like *Alien*, and in today's Hollywood, that's creativity. Most movies are inspired by only one previous blockbuster.

The movie stars Arnold Schwarzenegger as the leader of a U.S. Army commando team that goes into the South American jungle on a political mission and ends up dueling with a killer from outer space. This is the kind of idea that is produced at the end of a

ten-second brainstorming session, but if it's done well, who cares?

Predator is filmed very well. It's a slick, high-energy action picture that takes a lot of its strength from its steamy locations in Mexico. The heroes spend most of their time surrounded by an impenetrable jungle, a green wall of majestic vistas populated by all sorts of natural predators in addition to the alien. I've rarely seen a jungle look more beautiful, or more convincing; the location effect is on a par with *Fitzcarraldo* and *The Emerald Forest*.

As the film opens, Schwarzenegger and his comrades venture into this jungle in search of South American officials who have been kidnapped by terrorists. They track and locate the fugitives, and move in for the kill. But as they find the bodies of team members skinned and hanging from trees, they begin to realize they're up against more than terrorists.

The predator of the movie's title is a visitor from space; that's established in the opening scene. What it is doing in the jungle is never explained. The creature lives in the trees, even though it seems to be a giant biped much too heavy to swing from vines. When Schwarzenegger finally grapples with it, we discover it is wearing a space suit, and that inside the suit is a disgusting creature with a mouth surrounded by little pincers to shove in the food.

Such details are important, of course. Stan Winston, who designed the creature, has created a beast that is sufficiently disgusting to justify Schwarzenegger's loathing for it. And the action moves so quickly that we overlook questions such as (1) Why would an alien species go to all the effort to send a creature to Earth, just so that it could swing from trees and skin American soldiers? Or, (2) Why would a creature so technologically advanced need to bother with hand-to-hand combat, when it could just zap Arnold with a ray gun? Maybe the alien is a hunter who sees Earth as some kind of terrific vacation spot, and Schwarzenegger as big game worth traveling hundreds of light-years for. Theorists on extraterrestrial intelligence have debated for years what motivation it would take to inspire aliens to hurl themselves across the galaxy, and now we know. At one point in the movie, the creature removes its helmet so it can battle Arnold *mano-a-mano*, and I was cynical enough to assume that its motivation was not macho pride, but the desire to display Winston's special effects.

None of these logical questions are very important to the movie. *Predator* moves at a breakneck pace, it has strong and simple characterizations, it has good location photography and terrific special effects, and it supplies what it claims to supply: an effective action movie.

Students of trivia might want to note that the actor inside the predator costume is Kevin Peter Hall, who also occupies the Bigfoot costume in *Harry and the Hendersons*. This guy must really be a good sport.

Prelude to a Kiss ★ ★ ★
PG-13, 110 m., 1992

Alec Baldwin (Peter Hoskins), Meg Ryan (Rita Boyle), Sydney Walker (Julius [Old Man]), Kathy Bates (Leah Blier), Ned Beatty (Dr. Boyle), Patty Duke (Mrs. Boyle), Richard Riehle (Jerry Blier), Stanley Tucci (Taylor). Directed by Norman Rene and produced by Michael Gruskoff and Michael I. Levy. Screenplay by Craig Lucas.

Empathy. The ability to put yourself in another person's shoes, to imagine what it would be like to look out at the world through another person's eyes. Most of us have no gift for it—although that sure doesn't keep us from believing other people should spend a lot more time thinking about how it feels to be us.

Prelude to a Kiss is a movie about two people who accidentally put themselves into each other's bodies, and although it could probably do more with its story, what it does is gentle and moving. The film is fairly hard to categorize, which is one of its strengths. If you've seen the coming-attractions trailer, it probably left you completely confused. I've heard the movie described as being about ghosts and reincarnation, but it's about neither, and in fact the supernatural gimmick in the story is there mostly as an excuse to explain the more interesting stuff.

The movie opens with love at first sight, between a guy who works at a Chicago publishing company (Alec Baldwin) and a woman who tends bar (Meg Ryan). They smile and their eyes light up, and in an astonishingly short time they know they must get married to one another. At the wedding, a strange thing happens, and don't read another word unless you want to learn an important story point. An old man appears, who nobody seems to know, and he wishes the young couple well, and kisses the bride on the lips. And then . . .

But we know who the old man is. His name is Julius (Sydney Walker), and he lives in Berwyn with his daughter and son-in-law, and since his wife died he has just sort of vegetated. On this day he got up, walked to the train station, and took the next train, which happened to be going to Lake Forest. And he walked into the wedding and kissed the bride.

On his honeymoon, the Baldwin character begins to realize something has gone wrong. His bride looks the same, but she isn't the same. There are subtle clues in her behavior. Things she wouldn't ordinarily say. Eventually Baldwin realizes that someone else is inside her. She is not the woman he married.

All of this will be familiar to people who have seen the play by Craig Lucas, who based this screenplay on it. It's a gimmick, all right, but an interesting one, because it's the setup for some unusually thoughtful movie dialogue, and a final scene of genuine emotional power. I won't reveal the scene. Of the dialogue, I'll say how unusual it is for Hollywood characters to talk longingly and thoughtfully about our search for happiness in this world where most assuredly we will die. *Prelude to a Kiss* is the kind of movie that can inspire long conversations afterward, about the only subject really worth talking about, the Meaning of It All.

Baldwin finds all the right notes in his performance, from yuppie barfly to guy in love to a man faced with a large metaphysical embarrassment on his honeymoon. Meg Ryan is subtle in the way she signals that perhaps she is occupied by another personality. There are small but splendid moments involving her parents (Ned Beatty and Patty Duke). But the emotional heart of the movie belongs to the old guy, Sydney Walker, a New York stage actor who got his first starring role at seventy-one.

He is wonderful here. He begins as a block of human wood, an old man who looks as if he has not one single thing to say, and then he develops eloquently into a person of poetry and longing. He is, in many of his scenes, literally playing a woman in her twenties. How he does it—how he gets away with it—is through not just craft, but heart. The payoff in the big final scene is enormously gratifying, although, if you see the movie, you may wonder, as I did, how the screenplay lets the old guy wander away at the end. I guess the filmmakers thought the center of the story was with Baldwin and Ryan. But when the old guy goes out the door, our thoughts go with him.

Presumed Innocent ★ ★ ★ ½
R, 128 m., 1990

Harrison Ford (Rusty Sabich), Brian Dennehy (Raymond Horgan), Raul Julia (Sandy Stern), Bonnie Bedelia (Barbara Sabich), Paul Winfield (Judge Larren Lyttle), Greta Scacchi (Carolyn Polhemus). Directed by Alan J. Pakula and produced by Sydney Pollack and Mark Rosenberg. Screenplay by Frank Pierson and Alan J. Pakula.

Presumed Innocent opens on a shot of a jury box in an empty courtroom, the shadows dark along the walls, the wood tones a deep oxblood, the whole room suggesting that they should abandon hope, those who enter here. On the sound track we hear Harrison Ford talking about his job as a prosecuting attorney, but as he speaks of the duty of the law to separate the guilty from the innocent, there is little faith in his voice that the task can be done with any degree of certainty.

Presumed Innocent has at its core one of the most fundamental fears of civilized man—the fear of being found guilty of a crime one did not commit. That fear is at the heart of more than half of Hitchcock's films, and it is one reason they work for all kinds of audiences. Everybody knows that fear. This movie is based on a best-selling novel by Scott Turow that became notorious for its explicit sexual content—for the detail in which it examined shocking gynecological evidence—and yet the sex wouldn't have sold many copies without the fear. How do you defend yourself against a charge of rape when you were having an affair with the dead woman, and your fingerprints are on a glass in her apartment, and the phone records reveal that you called her earlier in the evening, and it would appear that your semen has been found at the scene of the crime?

That is the dilemma in which Rusty Sabich finds himself midway through *Presumed Innocent*. Sabich, played by Harrison Ford as a man whose flat voice masks great passions and terrors, plays an assistant state's attorney who is assigned to the murder of a young woman lawyer in his office. Her name was Carolyn Polhemus (Greta Scacchi), and she had the ability to mesmerize men, especially those who could do her some good. Among those men, we discover, was Rusty Sabich himself—and also his boss, State's Attorney Raymond Horgan (Brian Dennehy), who has assigned him to the case.

At first the investigation goes slowly, and then suddenly incriminating evidence surfaces, and the investigator finds himself named as the accused. The situation is made trickier because Dennehy faces an election in a few days. How does it look when the law and order candidate has a rapist and murderer on his own staff? The Ford character faces the complete collapse of his life as he knew it. Standing by him, but bitter because of his infidelity, is his wife, played by Bonnie Bedelia.

I will not provide a single hint in this review as to whether Ford is actually guilty. Everyone who has read the book will, of course, have a good idea of which way the story is likely to unfold, but the producers cleverly floated the notion that the film could turn out differently than the book. Even if you think you know what the solution is, the performances are so clever and the screenplay—by Frank Pierson and director Alan J. Pakula—is so subtle that it could well turn out that your expectations are wrong.

Pakula has made film versions of difficult books before; *Sophie's Choice* and *All the President's Men* are among his credits. This time, his challenge was to avoid getting bogged down in the marshes of circumstantial and forensic evidence, which make good reading but can expand into interminable movie dialogue. The adaptation of Turow's novel does a good job of presenting the evidence as needed, and no more than is needed, while allowing time for the characters to establish themselves.

The lead performance, by Harrison Ford, must have been a delicate balancing act, since at every point he must seem plausible both as a killer and as an innocent man. Ford's taciturn and undemonstrative acting style is well-suited to the challenge. Greta Scacchi is well-cast, too, as the heartless Carolyn Polhemus, so warm and yet so cold. The Bonnie Bedelia performance as the wife is another tricky challenge, since she, too, must be ambiguous throughout. And the supporting performances include Paul Winfield as a judge with hidden motives, Raul Julia as a defense attorney who can't get his client to stop acting like a lawyer, and Dennehy, expansive and yet with a wall of flint when it comes to saving his own skin.

Presumed Innocent is a very quiet movie, brooding and secretive, about people who are good at masking their emotions. The audience I was with watched it with a hush. Part of the quiet was due to the absorbing nature of the story, I suppose, but a lot of it may have been caused by people reflecting,

as I always do during stories like this, that there—but for the grace of God—go we.

Pretty Baby ★ ★ ★
R, 109 m., 1978

Brooke Shields (Violet), Keith Carradine (Bellocq), Susan Sarandon (Hattie), Frances Faye (Nell), Antonio Fargas (Professor), Matthew Anton (Red Top), Diana Scarwid (Frieda). Directed and produced by Louis Malle. Screenplay by Polly Platt.

Louis Malle's *Pretty Baby* was a pleasant surprise: After all the controversy and scandal surrounding its production, it turned out to be a good-hearted, good-looking, quietly elegiac movie. That was a coup for Malle, who sometimes seemed to dare himself to find acceptable ways of filming unacceptable subjects.

His subject this time is a twelve-year-old girl who is raised in the New Orleans brothel where her mother works. She plays in the garden, she rides a pony, she likes ragtime music, and one day she's auctioned off to the man who will deflower her. This is, of course, tragically perverted, but *Pretty Baby* itself is not a perverted film: It looks soberly, and with a good deal of compassion, at its period of history and the people who occupied it.

The pretty baby of the title is named Violet, and is played by Brooke Shields, as an extraordinarily beautiful child. Before anyone had seen *Pretty Baby,* Malle was being accused of exploiting that fact. But he's thoughtful and almost cautious in his approach: Given the film's subject matter and its obligatory sex scenes, Malle shows taste and restraint. And Shields really creates a character here; her subtlety and depth are astonishing.

Malle places her in an extraordinarily well-realized world, the Storyville section of New Orleans, circa 1917. The movie pays infinite attention to detail, and looks and feels accurate: We get to know the brothel so well, with its curving staircases and baroque furnishings, we almost feel we live there too. And we get to know the people, too, especially the strange and cynical brothel-keeper Madame Nell (Frances Faye), who observes at one point in her gravelly voice: "I am old. And I know one thing: Life is very long." An almost opaque line, but she invests it with infinite weariness.

She also keeps a well-run establishment, populated by hookers like Violet's mother Hattie (Susan Sarandon), who dreams of escaping from the life and eventually suc-

ceeds: She marries a prosperous businessman from St. Louis, and moves north. She wants to take her daughter with her, but Violet won't go: For her, this house *is* a home. Violet has in the meantime gained a protector and confidant: Bellocq (Keith Carradine), the silent, eccentric photographer. He seems at first to feel no passion at all, as he takes his infinite pains to arrange the lights and shadows in which he poses the prostitutes. There is, we feel, the possibility that he's asexual. But he does have a special feeling for Violet. And on the night she is auctioned off, there are two long, anguished close-ups: Of Bellocq, and of the house's black piano player (Antonio Fargas). Both of them clearly feel the auction is an outrage. Neither one speaks out. They are both creatures of Storyville, and know how things are done.

After Hattie goes north, Violet stays in the house for a time, and then goes to live with Bellocq. Their relationship is, of course, a strange one, made more complicated by the fact that this experienced twelve-year-old prostitute is still just a little girl. One of the film's most heartbreaking scenes has Violet sitting under a tree, playing with her doll. She is pretending that the doll is herself and that she is her mother. There's such a curious mixture of resentment and envy in her game that we cringe.

Pretty Baby has been attacked in some quarters as child porn. It's not. It's an evocation of a time and a place and a sad chapter of Americana. The ragtime music and the blues that fill its sound track take on a deeper meaning, in the context of the story, and we are reminded that the artists who sang "Do You Know What It Means to Miss New Orleans?" knew very well, and perhaps for that reason missed it less than their listeners.

Pretty in Pink ★ ★ ★
PG-13, 96 m., 1985

Molly Ringwald (Andie Walsh), Harry Dean Stanton (Jack Walsh), Jon Cryer (Duckie Dale), Andrew McCarthy (Blane McDonoug), Annie Potts (Iona), James Spader (Steff McKee). Directed by Howard Deutch and produced by Lauren Shuler. Screenplay by John Hughes.

Although *Pretty in Pink* contains several scenes that are a great deal more dramatic, my favorite moments were the quietest ones, in which nothing was being said because a boy was trying to get up the courage to ask a girl out on a date, and she knew it, and he knew it, and still nothing was happening.

To be able to listen to such a silence is to understand the central dilemma of adolescence, which is that one's dreams are so much larger than one's confidence. *Pretty in Pink* is a movie that pays attention to such things. And although it is not a great movie, it contains some moments when the audience is likely to think, yes, being sixteen was exactly like that.

The movie stars Molly Ringwald as Andie Walsh, a poor girl from the wrong side of the tracks. Her mother bailed out of her life some years earlier, and she lives with her unemployed father (Harry Dean Stanton), whose first words after she wakes him one morning are, "Where am I?" Andie works in a record store in a downtown mall and wears fashions that seem thrown together by a collision between a Goodwill store and a 1950s revival.

Andie attends a high school where most of the kids are wealthy snobs, and she has a crush on a rich kid named Blane (Andrew McCarthy). Her best friends are Duckie (Jon Cryer), who is a case study of the kind of teen-age boy who thinks he can clown his way into a girl's heart, and Iona (Annie Potts), a thirtyish sprite who affects one radical hairstyle after another.

The movie's plot is old, old, old. It's about how the rich boy and the poor girl love each other, but the rich kid's friends are snobs, and the poor girl doesn't want anyone to know what a shabby home she lives in, and about how they do find true love after all. Since the basic truths in the movie apply to all teenagers, rich and poor, I wish the filmmakers had found a new plot to go along with them. Perhaps they could have made the lovers come from different ethnic groups, which wouldn't have been all that original, either, but at least would have avoided one more recycling of ancient Horatio Alger stories.

There is one other major problem with the movie, and that involves the character of Steff McKee (James Spader), the effete, chain-smoking rich snot who is Blane's best friend. He has been turned down several times by Andie and now pretends to be appalled that Blane would want to go out with such a "mutant." His snobbery almost shipwrecks the romance. Steff does have one great line of dialogue: "Money really means nothing to me. Do you think I'd treat my parents' house this way if it did?" But, as played by Spader, he looks much too old to be a teen-ager, and his scenes play uneasily

for that reason. He seems more like a sinister twenty-five-year-old still lurking in the high school corridors, the Ghost of Proms Past.

Those objections noted, *Pretty in Pink* is a heartwarming and mostly truthful movie, with some nice touches of humor. The movie was written by John Hughes, who repeats the basic situation of his *Sixteen Candles*, which also starred Molly Ringwald as a girl who had a crush on a senior boy, and whose best friend was the class geek. But Ringwald grows with every movie into an actress who can project poignancy and vulnerability without seeming corny or coy, and her scenes here with Cryer and Potts have one moment of small truth after another.

The nicest surprise in the movie is the character created by Potts. The first time we see her, she's dressed in leather and chains, but the next time, she wears one of those beehive hairdos from the early 1960s. She is constantly experimenting with her "look," and when she finally settles on conservative good taste, the choice seems like her most radical so far.

Pretty in Pink is evidence, I suppose, that there must be a reason why certain old stories never seem to die. We know all the clichés, we can predict half of the developments. But at the end, when this boy and this girl, who are so obviously intended for one another, finally get together, there is great satisfaction. There also is the sense that Molly Ringwald just might have that subtle magic that will allow her, like young Elizabeth Taylor, to grow into an actress who will keep on breaking and mending boys' hearts for a long time.

Pretty Woman ★ ★ ★ ½
R, 119 m., 1990

Richard Gere (Edward Lewis), Julia Roberts (Vivian Ward), Ralph Bellamy (James Morse), Jason Alexander (Philip Stuckey), Laura San Giacomo (Kit De Luca), Alex Hyde-White (David Morse), Amy Yasbeck (Elizabeth Stuckey), Elinor Donahue (Bridget). Directed by Garry Marshall and produced by Arnon Milchan and Steven Reuther. Screenplay by J.F. Lawton.

Because *Pretty Woman* stars Richard Gere, Hollywood's most successful male sex symbol, and because it's about his character falling in love with a prostitute, it is astonishing that *Pretty Woman* is such an innocent movie—that it's the sweetest and most openhearted love fable since *The Princess Bride*. Here is a

movie that could have marched us down mean streets into the sinks of iniquity, and it glows with romance.

Oh, it seems to be constructed out of the stuff of realism, all right. It stars Gere as an out-of-town millionaire visiting Los Angeles, who borrows his friend's car and gets lost on Hollywood Boulevard. He asks a hooker for directions to his hotel. She offers to tell him, for five dollars. For ten, she'll guide him there.

He agrees. It is important to understand that he is looking for directions, not sex, and that he has broken up—coldly and efficiently—with his current girlfriend only half an hour earlier in a terse telephone conversation. The girl gets into the car and it turns out that she knows a lot about cars, and this intrigues him. The result is that he invites her to join him in his hotel suite. But not for sex, of course, he says. But you still have to pay, of course, she says.

She is played by Julia Roberts (of *Mystic Pizza* and an Oscar-nominated role in *Steel Magnolias*) as a woman who is as smart as she is attractive, which makes her very smart. Like many prostitutes, she is able to perform the mental trick of standing outside of what she does, of detaching herself and believing that her real self is not involved. That's what *she* does. She overhears one of his telephone conversations and wants to know what *he* does.

He's a takeover artist. He buys companies, takes them apart, and sells the pieces for more than he paid for the whole. "But what about the people who work for those companies?" she wants to know. "People have nothing to do with it," he explains. "It's strictly business." "Oh," she says. "Then you do the same thing I do."

What is happening in these scenes is that the characters are emerging as believable, original, and sympathetic. Gere and Roberts work easily together; we sense that their characters not only like one another, but feel comfortable with one another. The catch is, neither one trusts the feeling of comfort. They've been hurt so often, they depend on a façade of cynical detachment. Everything is business. He offers her money to spend one week with him, she accepts, he buys her clothes, they have sex, and, of course (this being the movies), they fall in love.

They fall into a particularly romantic kind of love, the sort you hardly see in the movies these days—a love based on staying awake after the lights are out and confiding autobiographical secrets. This is the first Gere film containing more confession than nudity. During the day, the lovers try to recover their cold detachment, to maintain the distance between them. If the love story in *Pretty Woman* is inspired by *Cinderella*, the daytime scenes are *Pygmalion*, as the hotel manager (Hector Elizondo) takes a liking to his best customer's "niece," and tutors her on which fork to use at a formal dinner.

There is a subplot involving Gere's attempts to take over a corporation run by an aging millionaire (Ralph Bellamy)—a man whose lifework he is prepared to savage, even though he actually likes him. There are broad Freudian hints that Gere's entire career is a form of revenge against his father, and that Bellamy may be the father figure he is searching for. But he has an impulse to hurt what he loves, and there is one particularly painful scene in which Gere reveals to a friend that Roberts is a prostitute, and Roberts gains a certain insight by how hurtful that betrayal is.

I mentioned that the movie is sweet and innocent. It is; it protects its fragile love story in the midst of cynicism and compromise. The performances are critical for that purpose. Gere plays new notes here; his swagger is gone, and he's more tentative, proper, even shy. Roberts does an interesting thing; she gives her character an irrepressibly bouncy sense of humor, and then lets her spend the movie trying to repress it. Actresses who can do that *and* look great can have whatever they want in Hollywood.

The movie was directed by Garry Marshall *(The Flamingo Kid)*, whose films betray an instinctive good nature, and it is about as warmhearted as a movie about two cold realists can possibly be. I understand that earlier versions of the screenplay were more hardboiled and downbeat, and that Marshall underlined the romance when he came aboard as director. There could indeed be, I suppose, an entirely different movie made from the same material—a more realistic film, in which the cold, economic realities of the lives of both characters would make it unlikely they could stay together. And, for that matter, a final scene involving a limousine, a fire escape, and some flowers is awkward and feels tacked on. But by the end of the movie, I was happy to have it close as it does.

Prick Up Your Ears ★ ★ ★ ★
R, 111 m., 1987

Gary Oldman (Joe Orton), Alfred Molina (Kenneth Halliwell), Vanessa Redgrave (Peggy Ramsay), Wallace Shawn (John Lahr), Lindsay Duncan (Anthea Lahr), Julie Walters (Elsie Orton), James Grant (William Orton). Directed by Stephen Frears and produced by Andrew Brown. Screenplay by Alan Bennett.

For all of their years together, Joe Orton and Kenneth Halliwell lived in a cramped room in the north of London, up near the Angel tube stop where everything seems closer to hell. Even after Orton became famous, even after his plays were hits and he was winning awards and his picture was in the papers, he came home to the tiny hovel where Halliwell was waiting. One night he came home and Halliwell hammered him to death and killed himself.

Prick Up Your Ears is the story of Orton and Halliwell and the murder. They say that most murderers are known to their victims. They don't say that if you knew the victims as well as the murderer did, you might understand more about the murder, but doubtless that is sometimes the case. This movie opens with a brutal, senseless crime. By the time the movie is over, the crime is still brutal, but it is possible to comprehend.

When they met, Orton was seventeen, Halliwell was twenty-five, and they both wanted to be novelists. They were homosexuals, but sex never seemed to be at the heart of their relationship. They lived together, but Orton prowled the night streets for rough trade and Halliwell scolded him for taking too many chances. Orton was, by all accounts, a charming young man—liked by everybody, impish, rebellious, with a taste for danger. Halliwell, eight years older, was a stolid, lonely man who saw himself as Orton's teacher.

He taught him everything he could. Then Orton used what he'd learned to write plays that drew heavily on their life together. His big hits were *Loot* and *What the Butler Saw*, and both are still frequently performed. But when Orton won the *Evening Standard*'s award for the play of the year—an honor like the Pulitzer Prize—he didn't take Kenneth to the banquet, he took his agent.

Halliwell began to feel that he was receiving no recognition for what he saw as the sacrifice of his life. He dabbled in art and constructed collages out of thousands of pictures clipped from books and magazines. But his shows

were in the lobbies of the theaters presenting Joe's plays, and people were patronizing to him. That began to drive him mad.

Prick Up Your Ears is based on the biography that John Lahr wrote about Orton, a biography that has become famous for discovering a private life so different from the image seen by the public.

Homosexuality was a crime in the 1960s in England, but Orton was heedless of the dangers. In fact, he seemed to enjoy danger. Perhaps that was why he kept Halliwell around, because he sensed the older man might explode. More likely, though, he kept him out of loyalty and indifference and didn't fully realize how much he was hurting him. One of the early scenes in the film shows Halliwell skulking at home, angry because Orton is late for dinner.

The movie is good at scenes like that. It has a touch for the wound beneath the skin, the hurt that we can feel better than the person who is inflicting it. The movie is told as sort of a flashback, with the Lahr character interviewing Orton's literary agent and then the movie spinning off into memories of its own.

The movie is not about homosexuality, which it treats in a matter-of-fact manner. It is really about a marriage between unequal partners. Halliwell was, in a way, like the loyal wife who slaves at ill-paid jobs to put her husband through medical school, only to have the man divorce her after he's successful because they have so little in common—he with his degree, she with dishwater hands.

The movie was written by Alan Bennett, a successful British playwright who understands Orton's craft. He bases one of his characters on Lahr (played by Wallace Shawn), apparently as an excuse to give Orton's literary agent (Vanessa Redgrave) someone to talk to. The device is awkward, but it allows Redgrave into the movie, and her performance is superb: aloof, cynical, wise, unforgiving.

The great performances in the movie are, of course, at its center. Gary Oldman plays Orton and Alfred Molina plays Halliwell, and these are two of the best performances of 1987. Oldman you may remember as Sid Vicious, the punk rock star in *Sid & Nancy*. There is no point of similarity between the two performances; like a few gifted actors, he is able to re-invent himself for every role. On the basis of these two movies, he is the best young British actor around. Molina has a more thankless role as he stands in the background, overlooked and misunderstood. But even as he whines we can understand his feelings, and by the end we are not very surprised by what he does.

The movie was directed by Stephen Frears, whose previous movie, *My Beautiful Laundrette*, also was about a homosexual relationship between two very different men: a Pakistani laundry operator and his working-class, neofascist boyfriend. Frears makes homosexuality an everyday thing in his movies, which are not about his characters' sexual orientation but about how their underlying personalities are projected onto their sexuality and all the other areas of their lives.

In the case of Orton and Halliwell, there is the sense that their deaths had been waiting for them right from the beginning. Their relationship was never healthy and never equal, and Halliwell, who was willing to sacrifice so much, would not sacrifice one thing: recognition for his sacrifice. If only Orton had taken him to that dinner, there might have been so many more opening nights.

Priest ★
R, 97 m., 1995 | NEW |

Linus Roache (Father Greg Pilkington), Tom Wilkinson (Father Matthew Thomas), Cathy Tyson (Maria Kerrigan), Robert Carlyle (Graham), James Ellis (Father Ellerton), Lesley Sharp (Mrs. Unsworth), Robert Pugh (Mr. Unsworth), Christine Tremarco (Lisa Unsworth). Directed by Antonia Bird and produced by George Faber and Josephine Ward. Screenplay by Jimmy McGovern.

"*Priest*," one critic has written, "vigorously attack(s) the views of the Roman Catholic Church on homosexuality," which is just the way the filmmakers probably want the film to be positioned. Actually the film is an attack on the vow of celibacy, preferring sexuality of any sort to the notion that men should, could, or would live chastely.

The story takes us into a Liverpool rectory where the senior priest sleeps with the pretty black housekeeper, and the younger priest removes his Roman collar for nighttime soirees to gay bars. When he and his partner are caught in a police sweep, he is disgraced, but the older priest is pleased that the young man has finally gotten in touch with his emotions, and begs him to return to the church to celebrate Mass with him. (The bishop, who advises him to "piss off out of my diocese," is portrayed, like all the church authorities, as a dried-up old bean.)

The question of whether priests should be celibate is the subject of much debate right now. What is not in doubt is that, to be ordained, they have to *promise* to be celibate. Nobody has forced them to become priests, and rules are rules. The filmmakers seem to feel that since they wouldn't want to live that way, of course it is wicked that priests must.

I am aware that the touchy-feely movement is so well established that no commercial film could seriously argue for celibacy. What I object to is the use of the church as a spice for an otherwise lame story; take away the occupations of the two central characters, and the rest of the film's events would be laid bare as tiresome sexual politics. The most obnoxious scene in the film is the one where the young priest, tortured by the needs of the flesh and by another problem we will soon get to, lectures Christ on the cross: "If you were here, you'd . . ." Well, what? Advise him to go out and get laid?

The priest, named Father Greg and played by Linus Roache, picks up Graham (Robert Carlyle) for a night of what he hopes will be anonymous sex, but later Graham recognizes him on the street, and soon they are in love. This is all done by fiat; the two men are not allowed to get to know one another, or to have conversations of any meaning, since the movie is not really *about* their relationship, but about how backward the church is in opposing it.

Instead of taking the time to explore the sexuality of the two priests in a thoughtful way, *Priest* crams in another plot, this one based on that old chestnut, the inviolable secrecy of the confessional. Father Greg learns while hearing a confession that a young girl parishioner is being sexually abused by her father. What to do? Of course (as the filmmakers no doubt learned from Hitchcock's *I Confess*), he cannot break the seal of the confessional—a rule that, for the convenience of the plot, he takes much more seriously than the rules about sex. This dilemma also figures in his anguished monologue to Jesus.

Once again, the church is used as spice. (Can you imagine audiences getting worked up over the confidential nature of a lawyer-client or a doctor-patient relationship?) But here the movie leaves a hole wide enough to run a cathedral through. The girl's father confronts the priest in the confessional, threatens him, and tells the priest he plans to keep right on with his evil practice (we don't simply have a child-abuser here, but a spokesman for incest). What the film fails to realize is that this conversation is not protected by the sacramental seal, because the sinner makes it absolutely clear he is not asking forgiveness, does not repent, and plans to keep right on sinning as long as he can get away with it. At this point, Father Greg should pick up the phone and call the cops.

The unexamined assumptions in the *Priest* screenplay are shallow and exploitative. The movie argues that the hidebound and outdated rules of the church are responsible for some people (priests) not having sex although they should, while others (incestuous parents) can keep on having it although they shouldn't. For this movie to be described as a moral statement about anything other than the filmmaker's prejudices is beyond belief.

Prime Cut ★ ★ ★
R, 86 m., 1972

Lee Marvin (Nick Devlin), Gene Hackman ("Mary Ann"), Angel Tompkins (Clarabelle), Gregory Walcott (Weenie), Sissy Spacek (Poppy), William Morey (Shay). Directed by Michael Ritchie and produced by Joe Wizan. Screenplay by Robert Dillon.

Prime Cut is a movie about an enforcer for the Chicago mob (Lee Marvin) who goes to Kansas City to collect a debt. So we expect a seamy journey into the guts of the city, right? But it doesn't quite work out like that. *Prime Cut* is very different from the usual gangster movie; it's put together almost like a comic strip, with all of the good and bad things that implies, and the Marvin character has more in common with superheroes than with mobsters.

We're almost on the familiar terrain of "Steve Canyon." All of the characters are caricatures, with nicknames and gimmicks to help us identify them. There's "Mary Ann" himself, a Kansas City dealer in prostitutes played by Gene Hackman. There's Weenie (Gregory Walcott), so-called because of his habit of carrying wieners around in his pocket—some of them made out of the ground-up bodies of his enemies. And there's Clarabelle (Angel Tompkins), who is Mary Ann's wife and lives in a luxurious houseboat with a mirror on the bedroom ceiling. Clearly, this is not the turf of Cagney and Bogart.

Prime Cut is a fantasy in which everything is very simple and usually takes place outdoors, and in which the characters act toward each other with great directness and brutality. It may owe a little to Hitchcock, as so many thrillers do. There's a scene at a county fair, for example, where Marvin and a young girl played by Sissy Spacek are trying to escape Hackman's gunmen. They do it all out in the open, casually walking in front of a grandstand in full view of thousands, so the gunmen can't shoot.

This is followed by the great wheat-field chase, in which Marvin and the girl are pursued by a giant reaper. A telephoto lens is used to give the impression that the giant reaper is almost literally on top of them, and every so often there's a cut to the obscene sight of the reaper dropping another bundle of wheat. Marvin and friend are saved when his chauffeur rams a limousine into the reaper—which digests it.

It's interesting to note that during the fairgrounds chase and the reaper chase, Marvin never lets go of the girl's hand (even though both could run faster if they weren't holding hands—and could even split up to avoid the reaper). This is a whammo visual signal of the movie's total male chauvinist orientation, which became clear much earlier during Gene Hackman's "cattle auction." The cattle, you see, are fresh, naked young girls, held in pens filled with straw. They have been raised in a special "orphanage," are certified to be virgin, and can be bought to stock your local bordello. Far-out.

Now you begin to see why *Prime Cut* is like a comic strip. It is broken up into several large set pieces (the introduction, the trip to Kansas City, Marvin's rescue of one of the orphan girls, a couple of love scenes, the fairgrounds, the reaper, and a gunfight). This structure is a lot less complex than those in the gangster movies we're used to, and makes *Prime Cut* seem larger than ordinary movie life. The colors are clearer, and the characters act and react only to each other's giant-sized images. It's fun, in a way.

Prince of the City ★ ★ ★
R, 167 m., 1981

Treat Williams (Daniel Ciello), Jerry Orbach (Gus Levy), Richard Foronjy (Joe Marinaro), Don Billett (Bill Mayo), Jenny Marino (Dom Bando), Bob Balaban (Sentimassino), Lindsay Crouse (Carla Ciello). Directed by Sidney Lumet and produced by Burtt Harris. Screenplay by Jay Presson Allen and Lumet.

He will not rat on his partners. This is his bottom line. He will talk to investigators about all the other guys he knows things about. He will talk about how narcotics cops get involved in the narcotics traffic, how they buy information with drugs, how they

string out addicts and use them as informers, how they keep some of the money and some of the drugs after big busts. He will tell what he knows about how the other cops do these things. But he will not talk about his partners in his own unit. This is his code, and, of course, he is going to have to break it.

That is the central situation of Sidney Lumet's *Prince of the City*. While you are watching it, it's a movie about cops, drugs, and New York City, in that order. After the film starts to turn itself over in your mind, it becomes a much deeper piece, a film about how difficult it is to go straight in a crooked world without hurting people you love.

Drugs are a rotten business. They corrupt everyone they come into contact with, because they set up needs so urgent that all other considerations are forgotten. For addicts, the need is for the drug itself. For others, the needs are more complex. The members of the special police drug unit in *Prince of the City*, for example, take on an envied departmental status because of their assignment. They have no hours, no beats, no uniforms. They are elite free-lancers, modern knights riding out into the drug underworld and establishing their own rules. They do not look at it this way, but their status depends on drugs. If there were no drugs and no addicts, there would be no narcs, no princes of the city. Of course, their jobs are also cold, dirty, lonely, dangerous, thankless, and never finished. That is the other side of the deal, and that helps explain why they will sometimes keep the money they confiscate in a drug bust. It's as if they're levying their own fines. It also explains why they sometimes supply informers with drugs: They know better than anyone how horrible the addict's life can be. "A junkie can break your heart," the hero of this movie says at one point, and by the movie's end we understand what he means.

The film is based on a book by Robert Daley about Bob Leuci, a New York cop who cooperated with a 1971 investigation of police corruption. In the movie, Leuci is called Ciello, and he is played by Treat Williams in a demanding and grueling performance. Williams is almost always onscreen, and almost always in situations of extreme stress, fatigue, and emotional turmoil. We see him coming apart before our eyes. He falls to pieces not simply because of his job, or because of his decision to testify, but because he is in an inexorable trap and he *will* sooner or later have to hurt his partners.

This is a movie that literally hinges on the issue of perjury. And Sidney Lumet and his co-writer, Jay Presson Allen, have a great deal of respect for the legal questions involved. There is a sustained scene in this movie that is one of the most spellbinding I can imagine, and it consists entirely of government lawyers debating whether a given situation justifies a charge of perjury. Rarely are ethical issues discussed in such detail in a movie, and hardly ever so effectively.

Prince of the City is a very good movie and, like some of its characters, it wants to break your heart. Maybe it will. It is about the ways in which a corrupt modern city makes it almost impossible for a man to be true to the law, his ideals, and his friends, all at the same time. The movie has no answers. Only horrible alternatives.

The Prince of Tides ★ ★ ★ ½
R, 132 m., 1991

Nick Nolte (Tom Wingo), Barbra Streisand (Susan Lowenstein), Blythe Danner (Sallie Wingo), Kate Nelligan (Lila Wingo Newbury), Jeroen Krabbe (Herbert Woodruff), Melinda Dillon (Savannah Wingo), George Carlin (Eddie Detreville), Jason Gould (Bernard Woodruff). Directed by Barbra Streisand and produced by Streisand and Andrew Karsch. Screenplay by Pat Conroy and Becky Johnston.

By directing one good film, you prove that you had a movie inside of you. By directing two, you prove you are a real director, and that is what Barbra Streisand proves with *The Prince of Tides*, an assured and very serious love story that allows neither humor nor romance to get in the way of its deeper and darker subject.

The film stars Nick Nolte, in an Oscar-caliber performance, as an unemployed, aimless, and miserably married football coach from the South, who ventures north into the alien world of New York City after his twin sister, a poet, tries to commit suicide. This is not her first attempt, and as we learn more about the Nolte character, we begin to understand why he has special reason to care for her. They were both subjected to an unforgivable childhood.

In New York, Nolte meets his sister's psychiatrist (Streisand), who is also not happily married, and their conversations turn from the therapeutic to the personal, as both characters begin to sense that the other is lonely and cut off from ordinary human cheer. We are familiar with the general profile of such relationships from many other movies, but *The Prince of Tides* is not about anything so banal as the ways that opposites attract. It is about two people whose affection offers them a way to cure each other—if they have the courage.

We meet several members of both of their families. Streisand has a son (Jason Gould) who is clumsy at sports, and Nolte agrees to throw a football around with him, getting to like the kid in the process. Streisand also has a husband (Jeroen Krabbe) who is a famous violinist and cruel snob, who gets one-upped by Nolte in a scene so funny and impeccably written that it is a crime, a violent crime against the cinema, that the surprise was spoiled in the movie's trailers and publicity clips.

Nolte was once happily married to Blythe Danner, but there is no more love in their marriage, maybe because of the pains he feels deep inside. There is a distance between him and his children. He loves his sister (Melinda Dillon), but feels powerless to help her. His emotional life still centers around his mother (Kate Nelligan, playing both young and old, in her second great supporting performance of 1991, after *Frankie and Johnnie*). She was once dirt poor, married to a violent alcoholic who abused her and her children. Then she traded up to a local rich man whose cruelty was more refined. Her son hates her but cannot free himself of her.

The Prince of Tides is based on a novel by Pat Conroy, who also wrote *The Lords of Discipline*, another novel in which the lives of young men are scarred by the weaknesses of their elders. This time, though, the movie is not quite so simple. These are complicated people who have lived difficult lives, and a quick romance or some feel-good therapy is not going to heal their wounds. What Streisand establishes, with admirable patience as both a director and an actress here, is that the people can heal best by learning to build and trust relationships. And by making those relationships tentative learning experiences, she leads up to an extraordinary payoff in which Nolte does finally at last reach back to touch the demons that torture him.

The movie is not all grimness and pain, of course. The dinner party scene provides a big liberating laugh, and the chemistry between Nolte and Streisand—such different people—is exciting because their minds, as well as their bodies, touch and are soothed. In *Yentl* and again here, Streisand shows herself as a director who likes strongly emotional stories—but doesn't simplify them—and pays attention to the human quirks and strangeness of her characters.

The Princess Bride ★ ★ ★ ½
PG, 98 m., 1987

Cary Elwes (Westley), Mandy Patinkin (Inigo Montoya), Chris Sarandon (Humperdinck), Christopher Guest (Count Rugen), Wallace Shawn (Vizzini), Andre the Giant (Fezzik), Fred Savage (Grandson), Robin Wright (Princess Bride), Peter Falk (Grandfather), Peter Cook (Clergyman), Billy Crystal (Miracle Max). Directed by Rob Reiner and produced by Andrew Scheinman and Reiner. Screenplay by William Goldman.

The Princess Bride begins as a story that a grandfather is reading out of a book. But already the movie has a spin on it, because the grandfather is played by Peter Falk, and in the distinctive quality of his voice we detect a certain edge; his voice seems to contain a measure of cynicism about fairy stories, a certain awareness that there are a lot more things in heaven and earth than have been dreamed of by the Brothers Grimm.

The story he tells is about a beautiful farm girl (Robin Wright) who scornfully orders around a farm boy (Cary Elwes) until the day when she realizes, thunderstruck, that she loves him. She wants to live happily ever after with him, but then he leaves, and is feared killed by pirates, and she is kidnapped and taken far away across the lost lands.

"Is this story going to have a lot of kissing in it?" Falk's grandson asks. Well, it's definitely going to have a lot of Screaming Eels. The moment the princess is taken away by agents of the evil Prince Humperdinck (Chris Sarandon), *The Princess Bride* reveals itself as a sly parody of sword and sorcery movies, a film that somehow manages to exist on two levels at once: While younger viewers will sit spellbound at the thrilling events on the screen, adults, I think, will be laughing a lot.

In its own peculiar way, *The Princess Bride* resembles *This Is Spinal Tap*, an earlier film by the same director, Rob Reiner. Both films are funny not only because they contain comedy, but because Reiner does justice to the underlying form of his story. *Spinal Tap* looked and felt like a rock documentary—and *then* it was funny. *The Princess Bride* looks and feels like *Legend*, or any of those other quasi-heroic epic fantasies, and *then* it goes for the laughs.

Part of the secret is that Reiner never stays with the same laugh very long. There are a lot of people for his characters to meet as they make their long journey, and most of them are completely off the wall. There is, for example, a band of three brigands led by Wallace Shawn as a scheming little conniver, and including Andre the Giant as Fezzik the Giant, a crusher who may not necessarily have a heart of gold. After the princess tries to escape him by jumping out of a boat, Shawn informs her with relish that the high-pitched noises she hears are . . . the Screaming Eels.

Another funny episode involves Mandy Patinkin as Inigo Montoya, heroic swordsman with a secret. And the funniest sequence in the film stars Billy Crystal and Carol Kane, both invisible behind makeup, as an ancient wizard and crone who specialize in bringing the dead back to life. (I hope I'm not giving anything away; you didn't expect the princess's loved one to stay dead indefinitely, did you?)

The Princess Bride was adapted by William Goldman from his own novel, which he says was inspired by a book he read as a child, but which seems to have been cheerfully transformed by his wicked adult imagination. It is filled with good-hearted fun, with performances by actors who seem to be smacking their lips, and by a certain true innocence that survives all of Reiner's satire. And also, it does have kissing in it.

Private Benjamin ★ ★ ★
R, 110 m., 1980

Goldie Hawn (Judy Benjamin), Eileen Brennan (Captain Lewis), Armand Assante (Henri Tremont), Robert Webber (Colonel Thornbush), Sam Wanamaker (Teddy Benjamin), Barbara Barrie (Harriet Benjamin), Harry Dean Stanton (Sergeant Ballard), Albert Brooks (Yale Goodman). Directed by Howard Zieff and written and produced by Nancy Meyers, Charles Shyer, and Harvey Miller.

Howard Zieff's *Private Benjamin* is an appealing, infectious comedy starring Goldie Hawn as Judy Benjamin, a Jewish-American princess, breathless with joy on the day of her second marriage. She has a real catch: He's named Yale, he's a professional man, he wants his study done in mushroom colors. Alas, he dies in the throes of passion on his wedding night (something his grieving mother discovers when Judy solemnly repeats his last words). And Judy goes into mourning.

What's she to do? She calls in to an all-night talk show and is promised a solution by another caller. The next day, we meet the guy with the answer. Played by Harry Dean Stanton, that wonderful character actor who could be Robert Mitchum's sneaky cousin, the guy turns out to be an Army recruiter. And he solemnly paints a picture of Army life that has Judy signing up. Her subsequent shocks of discovery provide the great laughs of the movie's best scenes. She solemnly explains to a captain (Eileen Brennan) that she *did* sign up with the Army, yes, but with another Army. Where, she asks, are the private condo living quarters the recruiter promised her? And surely the Army could have afforded some draperies? In no time at all, she's cleaning the latrines with her electric toothbrush.

This is an inspired idea for a movie comedy, and Goldie Hawn has a lot of fun with it. She finds just the right note for her performance, poised halfway between the avaricious and the slack-jawed, the calculating and the innocent. She makes some kind of impression on everyone she runs up against (or into), especially Robert Webber as the square-jawed Colonel Thornbush, commander of the Army's elite paratroop unit, the Thornbushers.

It's at about this point that the movie seems to lose its unique comic direction and turn into a more or less predictable combination of service comedy and romantic farce. After Judy's parents try to rescue her from the Army, she suddenly decides to stay and stick it out. She turns into a passable soldier. She almost inadvertently captures the entire Red team and makes them Blue prisoners of war during war games. And she is invited to join the Thornbushers by Colonel Thornbush himself (who turns out to have an alternative in mind if Judy doesn't want to jump at 13,000 feet).

Along the way, she meets a sexy and eligible French bachelor who's a gynecologist. After she blackmails Thornbush into sending her to Allied Army headquarters in Paris, she falls in love with the Frenchman (Armand Assante), and gets involved in Gallic romantic intrigues. It turns out that her would-be third husband is more interested in Sunday morning soccer games and cute little downstairs maids than in the kind of marriage Judy Benjamin was brought up to desire.

This stuff is occasionally funny, but it's kind of predictable. It turns *Private Benjamin* into areas that are too familiar: We've all seen the comic situations that grow out of the courtship with the Frenchman, and we'd really rather have seen more stuff of Private Benjamin in the Army. The movie would have been better off sticking with Goldie Hawn as a female Beetle Bailey and forgetting about the changes that allow her to find self-respect, deal with the Frenchman, etc. Still, *Private Benjamin* is refreshing and fun. Goldie Hawn, who is a true comic actress, makes an original, appealing character out of Judy Benjamin, and so the movie feels alive—not just an exercise in gags and situations.

Prizzi's Honor ★ ★ ★ ★
R, 129 m., 1985

Jack Nicholson (Charley Partanna), Kathleen Turner (Irene Walker), Anjelica Huston (Maerose), Robert Loggia (Eduardo Prizzi), John Randolph (Pop Partanna), William Hickey (Don Corrado Prizzi), Lee Richardson (Dominic). Directed by John Huston and produced by John Foreman. Screenplay by Richard Condon and Janet Roach.

John Huston's *Prizzi's Honor* marches like weird and gloomy clockwork to its relentless conclusion, and half of the time, we're laughing. This is the most bizarre comedy in many a month; a movie so dark, so cynical, and so funny that perhaps only Jack Nicholson and Kathleen Turner could have kept straight faces during the love scenes. They do. They play two professional Mafia killers who meet, fall in love, marry, and find out that the mob may not be big enough for both of them.

Nicholson plays Charley Partanna, a soldier in the proud Prizzi family, rulers of the East Coast, enforcers of criminal order. The godfather of the Prizzis, Don Corrado, is a mean little old man who looks like he has been freeze-dried by the lifelong ordeal of draining every ounce of humanity out of his wizened body. To Don Corrado (William Hickey), nothing is more important than the Prizzis' honor—not even another Prizzi. Charley Partanna is the Don's grandson. He has been raised in this ethic, and accepts it. He kills without remorse. He follows orders. Only occasionally does he disobey the family's instructions, as when he broke his engagement with Maerose Prizzi (Anjelica Huston), his cousin. She then brought disgrace upon herself and, as the movie opens, is in the fourth year of self-imposed exile. But she is a Prizzi, and does not forget, or forgive.

The movie opens like *The Godfather*, at a wedding. Charley's eyes roam around the church. In the choir loft, he sees a beautiful blonde (Kathleen Turner). She looks like an angel. At the reception, he dances with her once, and then she disappears. Later that day, there is a mob killing. Determined to find out the name of the blond angel, Charley discovers even more—that she was the California hitman, brought in to do the job. He turns to Maerose for advice. She counsels him to go ahead: After all, it's good to have interests in common with your wife.

Charley flies to the coast, setting up a running gag as they establish a transcontinental commute. There is instant, electrifying chemistry between the two of them, and the odd thing is, it seems halfway plausible. They're opposites, but they attract. Nicholson plays his hood as a tough Brooklynite; he uses a stiff upper lip, like Bogart, and sounds simple and implacable. Turner, who is flowering as a wonderful comic actress, plays her Mafia killer like a bright, cheery hostess. She could be selling cosmetics.

What happens between them is best not explained here, since the unfolding of the plot is one of the movie's delights. The story is by Richard Condon, a novelist who delights in devious plot construction, and here he takes two absolutes—romantic love and the Prizzis' honor—and arranges a collision between them. Because all of the motivations are so direct and logical, the movie is able to make the most shocking decisions seem inevitable.

John Huston directed this film right after *Under the Volcano,* and what other director could have put those two back-to-back? It is one of his very best films, perhaps because he made it with friends; Condon is an old pal from Ireland, Anjelica Huston is, of course, his daughter, and Nicholson has long been Anjelica's lover. Together they have taken a strange plot, peopled it with carefully overwrought characters, and made *Prizzi's Honor* into a treasure.

The Professional ★ ★ ½
R, 112 m., 1994

Gary Oldman (Stansfield), Natalie Portman (Matilda), Jean Reno (Leon), Danny Aiello (Tony). Directed by Luc Besson and produced by Patrice Ledoux. Screenplay by Besson.

History repeats itself, the first time as tragedy, the second time as farce. So, apparently, do the films of Luc Besson. In 1992 he made *La Femme Nikita,* which in its cold sadness told the story of a tough street girl who became a professional killer and then a civilized woman. Now he has made *The Professional*, about a tough child who wants to become a professional killer, and civilizes the man she chooses as her teacher.

Besson seems fascinated by the Pygmalion story, by the notion of a feral street person who is transformed by education. He crosses that with what seems to be an obsession with women who kill as a profession. These are interesting themes, and if *The Professional* doesn't work with anything like the power of *La Femme Nikita*, it is because his heroine is twelve years old, and we cannot persuade ourselves to ignore that fact. It colors every scene, making some unlikely and others troubling.

The film opens with one of those virtuoso shots that zip down the streets of New York and in through a door, coming to a sudden halt at a plate of Italian food and then looking up at its owner. Besson must have been watching the opening of the old Letterman show. The man eating the food is a mob boss, played by Danny Aiello, who wants to put a contract on a guy. The man who has come whizzing through the streets is Leon (Jean Reno), a skillful but uneducated "cleaner," or professional hit man.

We see him at work, in opening scenes of startling violence and grim efficiency. In the course of the movie, Leon will, in effect, adopt his neighbor Matilda (Natalie Portman), a tough, streetwise, twelve-year-old girl. She escapes to Leon's nearby apartment after her family has been wiped out by a crooked top DEA enforcer named Stansfield (Gary Oldman), who wants to kill her too. Matilda wants to hire Leon to avenge the death of her little brother; in payment, she offers to do his laundry. Leon wants nothing to do with the girl, but she insists, and attaches herself like a leech. Eventually she develops an ambition to become a cleaner herself. And their fate plays out like those of many another couple on the lam, although with that thirty-year age difference.

Matilda is played with great resourcefulness by Portman, who is required by the role to be, in a way, stronger than Leon. She has seen so many sad and violent things in her short life, and in her dysfunctional family, that little in his life can surprise her. She's something like the Jodie Foster character in *Taxi Driver*, old for her years. Yet her references are mostly to movies: "Bonnie and Clyde didn't work alone," she tells him.

"Thelma and Louise didn't work alone. And they were the best." (To find a twelve-year-old in 1994 who knows *Bonnie and Clyde* is so extraordinary that it almost makes everything else she does plausible.) So Leon finds himself saddled with a little sidekick, just when the manic Stansfield is waging a personal vendetta against him.

Although *The Professional* bathes in grit and was shot in the scuzziest locations New York has to offer, it's a romantic fantasy, not a realistic crime picture. Besson's visual approach gives it a European look; he finds Paris in Manhattan. That air of slight displacement helps it get away with various improbabilities, as when Matilda teaches Leon to read (in a few days, apparently), or when Leon is able to foresee the movements of his enemies with almost psychic accuracy.

This gift is useful during several action sequences in *The Professional*, when Leon, alone and surrounded by dozens if not hundreds of law officers, is able to conceal himself in just such a way that when the cops enter an apartment in just such a manner, he can swing down from the ceiling, say, and blast them. Or he can set a trap for them. Or he can apparently teleport himself from one part of an apartment to another; they think they have him cornered, but he's behind them. So many of the movie's shoot-outs unfold so conveniently for him that they seem choreographed. The Oldman character sometimes seems to set himself up to be outsmarted, while trying to sneak up on Leon in any way not actually involving chewing through the scenery.

The premise of *La Femme Nikita* was that its heroine began as a thoroughly uncivilized character without a decent bone in her body, and then, after society exploited her savagery, she was slowly civilized through the love of a good, simple man. *The Professional* uses similar elements, rearranged. It is a well-directed film, because Besson has a natural gift for plunging into drama with a charged-up visual style. And it is well acted.

But always at the back of my mind was the troubled thought that there was something wrong about placing a twelve-year-old character in the middle of this action. In a more serious movie, or even in a human comedy like Cassavetes's *Gloria*, the child might not have been out of place. But in what is essentially an exercise—a slick urban thriller—it seems to exploit the youth of the girl without really dealing with it.

The Program ★ ★ ★
R, 115 m., 1993

James Caan (Coach Winters), Halle Berry (Autumn), Omar Epps (Darnell Jefferson), Craig Sheffer (Joe Kane), Kristy Swanson (Camille), Andrew Bryniarski (Lattimer), Duane Davis (Alvin Mack), Abraham Benrubi (Bud-Lite). Directed by David S. Ward and produced by Samuel Goldwyn, Jr. Screenplay by Ward and Aaron Latham.

The Program celebrates big-time college football at the same time it attacks it. The team at Eastern State, under the gun from alumni who aren't happy with two losing seasons, makes a courageous comeback while at the same time the star quarterback goes into rehab, a defensive hero ruins his leg, another player is caught in a cheating scandal, and a lineman named Bud-Lite pumps steroids into his veins. You can't make an omelet without breaking eggs, I guess.

The movie begins with what seems to be solid insider knowledge about how football is played in the big collegiate leagues. James Caan plays Coach Winters, a realist who sometimes perhaps wishes he could be more ethical than circumstances permit. It's his job to hold together a team that's under great moral, physical, romantic, and academic pressure—and the film provides one player to illustrate each one of those problems.

The quarterback (Craig Sheffer) is a self-destructive alcoholic whose father is also a drunk who once played for ESU. Under enormous pressure as a Heisman Trophy contender, he gets loaded and pulls suicidal stunts, while his girlfriend (Kristy Swanson) despairs. Meanwhile, a talented freshman named Darnell Jefferson (Omar Epps) enrolls, seduced on campus by the charms of a student beauty named Autumn (Halle Berry), who turns out to be dating Darnell's competitor for the halfback position. His grades are lousy, but he talks her into being his tutor, causing the other halfback, of course, to hate him.

Elsewhere on the team, Alvin Mack (Duane Davis) is a pro-bound lineman who specializes in psyching his opponents with imaginative sexual histories of their close relatives. And Lattimer (Andrew Bryniarski), who has spent three years on the punt return squad, returns to campus mysteriously pumped up with thirty-five pounds of new muscles, a wild man who everyone assumes is on steroids. Meanwhile, Coach Winters's daughter makes the mistake of taking an exam for the backup quarterback, and they both get thrown out of school.

It perhaps says something about the times we live in that these are the *good* guys. God only knows what the other teams are up to. The coach somehow guides the team through its accident-prone season, while the movie focuses on the two romantic relationships. Swanson, as the quarterback's girl, is a tennis player who despairs of his drunken behavior. And Berry, who really likes the freshman halfback, is afraid to tell her daddy she's broken up with the other back, a pre-med student.

The movie was directed by David S. Ward, whose credits include *Major League* (1989). He makes all the pieces fit, and the onfield action looks convincing, but there's a certain thinness in some of the characters. The coach, for example, is made by Caan into a man without much depth; his function is to move the plot along with lots of furrowed brows and lip twitches. And Lattimer, the muscle-bound animal, comes across more as a World Wrestling Federation stooge than a plausible college student (he illustrates team spirit by breaking car windows with his forehead).

Still, the movie's human scenes are appealing—especially the moment when Darnell finally believes his beautiful tutor loves him. And the movie seems expert on how a lineman could pump himself full of steroids and still pass the NCAA drug tests, although some of his methods for providing clean urine are too painful to contemplate. By the end of the film, I found myself simultaneously hoping that ESU would win its big game, and that the school would pull the plug on its football program. I guess that's how I was supposed to feel.

Note: The video version lacks a scene in which drunken players lie down in the road on a dare; the scene was blamed for the copycat deaths and injuries of some who saw it.

Proof ★ ★ ★ ½
R, 90 m., 1992

Hugo Weaving (Martin), Genevieve Picot (Celia), Russell Crowe (Andy), Heather Mitchell (Mother), Jeffrey Walker (Young Martin). Directed by Jocelyn Moorhouse and produced by Lynda House. Screenplay by Moorhouse.

Martin is a blind man who believes anyone might be lying to him. His lack of trust, which runs so deep it has defined his entire life and personality, began in childhood. It was his mother's custom to describe the garden outside his window to him. One day she told him there was a man raking leaves in the garden. Martin could hear nothing, and decided his mother was lying. He used a camera to take a photograph of the garden.

When we meet Martin, in the opening scenes of *Proof*, years have passed, but he is still a photographer. It is his way of checking up on his friends. He takes pictures, has them developed, asks people to describe them to him, labels them in Braille, and is alert to any contradictions in what people tell him. Martin lives alone, in a rigid and uncompromising lifestyle, and is fiercely independent. If he feels he is being overlooked in a restaurant, for example, he is capable of taking a bottle of wine and pouring it out on the table until a waiter takes notice.

Celia is Martin's housekeeper. Actually, she doesn't need the work to support herself. It is her way of getting into Martin's life. She is a photographer herself. Her walls are covered with photos of Martin. Their relationship is prickly and marked by anger; perhaps Celia enjoys the sharp edge of every conversation.

One day Martin, to his amazement, makes a friend, Andy, who works in the restaurant. They start hanging out together, which offends the possessive Celia. And so the long-established patterns of Martin's life begin to change, as Celia uses her sexuality as a device to control both men. The ending of the film is a release of pent-up tension, a calling-due of all the emotional bills that Martin has never been willing to pay. And everything comes back to that picture he took of the garden: Was his mother lying to him, or not?

Proof is a first film from Australia, written and directed by Jocelyn Moorhouse, who has the gift of creating characters who are interesting just because of who they are. The movie doesn't depend on a contrived plot or any manufactured surprises. It simply introduces us to Martin, Celia, and Andy, and the situation Martin has carefully made for himself, and as they develop their games of power and control, we become completely absorbed.

Martin, played by the tight-faced, rigidly controlled Hugo Weaving, is an original, a man who has protected himself so completely against the possibility of being hurt, that he has cut off the possibility of feeling. Celia's need for just this sort of man is the most interesting thing about her. Andy is an innocent compared to the other two.

Moorhouse has a way of putting all the pieces into place for a scene, so that it pays off in ways we could not anticipate. Observe, for example, the scene in the park, when Martin doesn't realize that the others are there. His camera becomes the occasion for comedy at the beginning, and for a troubling payoff later on. Or look at the way Moorhouse uses that original photo, the one of the garden that might or might not be empty.

If there is a kind of movie I like better than any other, it is this kind, the close observation of particular lives, perhaps because it exploits so completely the cinema's potential for voyeurism. There are not good or bad people here, simply characters driven by their needs and insecurities into a situation where something has to give. What could be more interesting?

Prospero's Books ★ ★ ★
R, 106 m., 1991

John Gielgud (Prospero), Michael Clark (Caliban), Michel Blanc (Alonso), Erland Josephson (Gonzalo), Isabelle Pasco (Miranda), Mark Rylance (Ferdinand). Directed by Peter Greenaway and produced by Kees Kasander. Screenplay by Greenaway.

Peter Greenaway's *Prospero's Books* is not a movie in the sense that we usually employ that word; it's an experiment in form and content. It is likely to bore most audiences, but will entrap others—especially those able to free themselves from the notion that movies must tell stories. This film should be approached like a record album or an art book. Each "page" is there to be studied in its complexity and richness, while on the sound track we hear one of the great voices in theater history, Sir John Gielgud's.

Greenaway begins with a crucial piece of information from Shakespeare's *The Tempest*, that final and most symmetrically perfect of the playwright's works. Prospero, once Duke of Milan, has been tossed by a storm onto a lost island, along with his daughter, Miranda, various crew members, and such resident sprites and monsters as Ariel and Caliban. But he has managed to save his books from the tempest—books he prizes more than his dukedom—and Greenaway wonders about that water-soaked library. What books did he have, and how did he use them?

The books, their typography, calligraphy,

and illustrations, are photographed in voluptuous detail. As Gielgud takes center screen in a narrative adapted from *The Tempest*, Greenaway overlays those basic images of Prospero with a series of transparencies. Pages of books appear over the central image or slide in from the sides, sometimes two or three deep, pausing for our consideration, and then vanishing to be replaced by still other images and words. The effect is something like those high school biology texts in which succeeding sheets of transparent plastic revealed the depths of the human body, one layer after another.

The human images in the film center around the idea of nudity. Here, as in such earlier films as *The Cook, the Thief, His Wife and Her Lover,* the form and fleshiness of the nude is Greenaway's visual obsession. There are, at various times, dozens or even hundreds of unclothed bodies on the screen, seen by the director in terms of Renaissance painting, and by the philistines at the Motion Picture Association of America as, needless to say, cause for an R rating. Gielgud presides over all of these images—printed and fleshy—as a sorcerer who alone understands their master purpose.

This is not the film to see if you want to witness a performance of *The Tempest*. It is, however, a fascinating film if you are interested in the play, in Shakespeare, or in the breathtaking era when manuscripts and the printed word began to pull Europe out of the Dark Ages and into what we congratulate ourselves is a more enlightened time. *Prospero's Books* would be an ideal film to watch on laserdisk, where with a hand-held remote you could freeze any frame and study its subtleties. It is also a wonderful film to listen to; Gielgud does a great many of the speaking roles, and, at eighty-seven, seems in full and sonorous command of his vocal instrument.

Prospero's Books really exists outside criticism. All I can do is describe it. Most of the reviews of this film have missed the point; this is not really Shakespeare, not really *The Tempest*, not a narrative; it need not make sense, is not "too difficult" because it could not have been any less so. It is simply a work of original art, which Greenaway asks us to accept or reject on his own terms.

Psycho III ★ ★ ★
R, 93 m., 1986

Anthony Perkins (Norman Bates), Diana Scarwid (Maureen), Jeff Fahey (Duane),

Roberta Maxwell (Tracy), Hugh Gillin (Sheriff Hunt), Lee Garlington (Myrna). Directed by Anthony Perkins and produced by Hilton A. Green. Screenplay by Charles Edward Pogue.

How well we remember Norman Bates. Tens of thousands of movie characters have come and gone since 1960, when he made his first appearance in *Psycho*, and yet he still remains so vivid in the memory, such a sharp image among all the others that have gone out of focus.

Most movies are disposable. *Psycho* supplied us with the furnishings for nightmares. "Dear Mr. Hitchcock," a mother wrote the master, "after seeing your movie my daughter is afraid to take a shower. What should I do?" Send her to the dry cleaners, Hitch advised her.

In *Psycho III*, there is one startling shot that completely understands Norman Bates. Up in the old gothic horror house on the hill, he has found a note from his mother, asking him to meet her in Cabin Number Twelve. We know that although his mother may have frequent conversations with him, she is in no condition to write him a note. Norman knows that, too. He stuffed her himself. As he walks down the steps and along the front of the Bates Motel toward his rendezvous, the camera tracks along with him, one unbroken shot, and his face is a twitching mask of fear.

The face belongs to Anthony Perkins, who is better than any other actor at reflecting the demons within. Although his facial expressions in the shot are not subtle, he isn't overacting; he projects such turmoil that we almost sympathize with him. And that is the real secret of Norman Bates, and one of the reasons that *Psycho III* works as a movie: Norman is not a mad-dog killer, a wholesale slasher like the amoral villains of the Dead Teen-ager Movies. He is at war with himself. He is divided. He, Norman Bates, wants to do the right thing, to be pleasant and quiet and pass without notice. But also inside of him is the voice of his mother, fiercely urging him to kill.

At the beginning of *Psycho III*, only a short time has passed since the end of *Psycho II*. In a nearby convent, a young novice (Diana Scarwid) blames herself when an older nun falls to her death. She runs out into the night, gets a ride with a sinister motorist (Jeff Fahey), and ends up at the Bates Motel. Fahey arrives there, too, and is hired as a night clerk. Other people also turn up: an investigative reporter who wants to do a story

on Norman; a local woman who gets drunk and is picked up by Fahey; and finally a crowd of rowdies back for their high school reunion.

By the end of the movie, many of these people will be dead—and because this is a tragedy, not a horror story, some of the dead ones won't deserve it, and others will survive unfairly.

The movie was directed by Perkins, in his filmmaking debut. I was surprised by what a good job he does. Any movie named *Psycho III* is going to be compared to the Hitchcock original, but Perkins isn't an imitator. He has his own agenda. He has lived with Norman Bates all these years, and he has some ideas about him, and although the movie doesn't apologize for Norman, it does pity him. For the first time, I was able to see that the true horror in the *Psycho* movies isn't what Norman does—but the fact that he is compelled to do it.

There are a couple of scenes that remind us directly of Hitchcock, especially the scene where the local sheriff dips into the ice chest on a hot day, and doesn't notice that some of the cubes he's popping into his mouth have blood on them. Perkins permits himself a certain amount of that macabre humor, as when he talks about his hobby ("stuffing things") and when he analyzes his own case for the benefit of the visiting journalist. But the movie also pays its dues as a thriller, and there is one shocking scene that is as arbitrary, unexpected, tragic, and unfair as the shower scene in *Psycho*. Only one, but then one of those scenes is enough for any movie.

The Public Eye ★ ★ ★ ★
R, 99 m., 1992

Joe Pesci (Leon Bernstein), Barbara Hershey (Kay Levitz), Stanley Tucci (Sal), Jerry Adler (Arthur Nabler), Jared Harris (Doorman). Directed by Howard Franklin and produced by Sue Baden-Powell. Screenplay by Franklin.

The Public Eye contains a couple of great, juicy movie performances. They're from Joe Pesci and Barbara Hershey, playing New York City fringe dwellers who try to make a living from the kinds of people who come out after dark. They also fall in love, I think. You may think differently. They're the kind of people who should ask themselves, am I really in love, or does it just feel so good when I stop hitting myself over the head with this pistol butt?

It's the 1940s. Pesci plays a guy named

Bernzy, who is a free-lance photographer for the tabloids. He cruises the night in a souped-up coupe with a police radio under the dash and a darkroom in the trunk. He takes pictures of mobsters, politicians, crooks, gamblers, cops, and ladies who ain't no ladies. A lot of these people are dead when they sit for their portraits. When Bernzy sells a picture to the *Daily News*, it runs a credit line that says: "Photo by the Great Bernzini."

He takes his work seriously. Someday he wants to publish a book of his photos. He thinks ordinary pictures of ordinary people can be art. Bernzy reminds me of Weegee, the great New York City street photographer, who also took pictures of the disreputable and the unlovely, and thought his work was art. They laughed at him, but check out his prices in the galleries.

Bernzy is the perpetual outsider. His relationships are all through the viewfinder. One night, Kay Levitz (Hershey) asks him for a favor. She runs a nightclub she inherited from her husband, who was old when she married him and dead shortly after. There are people who think she married him to get the club. Now they want the club, but they don't want to marry her. They want to muscle her out. Kay thinks maybe Bernzy can give her some advice, help her out.

He is willing to try. He is willing, even though his lifetime policy is—don't get involved. The writer-director, Howard Franklin, is subtle and touching in the way he modulates the key passages between Pesci and Hershey. There is a lot that goes unsaid between them. We can maybe guess from Bernzy's eyes and actions how he feels about her, but he never tells her. He keeps his distance. He can maybe hope she feels the same way. She plays it close.

The movie surrounds them with a gallery of colorful nighttime characters—vice detectives, rival photographers, mob bosses, broken-down critics who mourn the bad novels they never wrote. The photography occupies the beloved territory of *film noir:* night, wet streets, cars with running boards, dames with low necklines, guys with diamond pinky rings, empty marble newspaper lobbies, guns, highballs, furnished apartments. This was an era when the good guys smoked cigars, and the bad guys smoked cigarettes.

One of the best things about the movie is the way it shows us how seriously Bernzy takes his work. He doesn't talk about it. He does it, with that cigar stuck in his mug, leading the way with the big, ungainly Speed-Graphix with the glass flashbulbs. In the movie's big scene of a mob assassination, he stares death in the face to get a great picture. He doesn't even seem especially noble. It's what he bred himself to do. At one point he is asked to turn off the police radio in his car, and he says, "It doesn't *turn* off." This is his philosophy of life.

The plot of the movie advances the story on the surface, while the romance develops in an unacknowledged subterranean fashion. Everything leads up to a moment when Bernzy turns his head away from Kay and says, "You have no idea what I would have done for you." This is the best kind of love—unrequited. There are moments in *The Public Eye* that made me think a little about *Casablanca,* especially the earlier scenes when Bogart is still mad at Bergman. Higher praise is not necessary.

Pulp Fiction ★ ★ ★ ★
R, 154 m., 1994

NEW

(See related Essay, p. 906, and Film Clip, p. 888.)

John Travolta (Vincent Vega), Bruce Willis (Butch Coolidge), Samuel L. Jackson (Jules), Uma Thurman (Mia), Harvey Keitel (Mr. Wolf), Tim Roth (Pumpkin), Amanda Plummer (Honey Bunny), Maria de Medeiros (Fabienne), Ving Rhames (Marsellus Wallace), Eric Stoltz (Lance). Directed by Quentin Tarantino and produced by Lawrence Bender. Screenplay by Tarantino and Roger Avary.

Quentin Tarantino is the Jerry Lee Lewis of cinema, a pounding performer who doesn't care if he tears up the piano, as long as everybody is rocking. His movie *Pulp Fiction* is a comedy about blood, guts, violence, strange sex, drugs, fixed fights, dead-body disposal, leather freaks, and a wristwatch that makes a dark journey down through the generations.

Seeing this movie at the Cannes Film Festival, I knew it was either one of the year's best films, or one of the worst. Tarantino is too gifted a filmmaker to make a boring movie, but he could possibly make a bad one: Like Edward D. Wood, Jr., proclaimed the Worst Director of All Time, he's in love with every shot—intoxicated with the very act of making a movie. It's that very lack of caution and introspection that makes *Pulp Fiction* crackle like an ozone generator: Here's a director who's been let loose inside the toy store, and wants to play all night.

The screenplay, by Tarantino and Roger Avary, is so well written in a scruffy, fanzine way that you want to rub noses in it—the noses of those zombie writers who take "screenwriting" classes that teach them the formulas for "hit films." Like *Citizen Kane, Pulp Fiction* is constructed in such a nonlinear way that you could see it a dozen times and not be able to remember what comes next. It doubles back on itself, telling several interlocking stories about characters who inhabit a world of crime and intrigue, triple-crosses, and loud desperation.

The title is perfect. Like those old pulp mags named *Thrilling Wonder Stories* and *Official Detective,* the movie creates a world where there are no normal people and no ordinary days—where breathless prose clatters down fire escapes and leaps into the dumpster of doom.

The movie resurrects not only an aging genre but also a few careers. John Travolta stars as Vincent Vega, a midlevel hit man who carries out assignments for a mob boss. We see him first with his partner Jules (Samuel L. Jackson); they're on their way to a violent showdown with some wayward yuppie drug dealers, and are discussing such mysteries as why in Paris they have a French word for Quarter Pounders. They're as innocent in their way as Huck and Jim, floating down the Mississippi and speculating on how foreigners can possibly understand each other, since they don't speak English.

Travolta's career is a series of assignments he can't quite handle. Not only does he kill people inadvertently ("The car hit a bump!"), but he doesn't know how to clean up after himself. Good thing he knows people like Mr. Wolf (Harvey Keitel), who specializes in messes, and has friends like the character played by Eric Stoltz, who owns a big medical encyclopedia, and can look up emergency situations.

Travolta and Uma Thurman have a sequence that's funny and bizarre. She's the wife of the mob boss (Ving Rhames), who orders Travolta to take her out for the night. He turns up stoned, and addresses an intercom with such grave, stately courtesy Buster Keaton would have been envious. They go to Jack Rabbit Slim's, a 1950s theme restaurant where Ed Sullivan is the emcee, Buddy Holly is the waiter, and they end up in a twist contest. That's before she overdoses and Stoltz, waving a syringe filled with adrenaline, screams at Travolta, "*You* brought her here, *you* stick in the needle! When I bring an O.D. to *your* house, *I'll* stick in the needle!"

Bruce Willis and Maria de Medeiros play another couple: He's a boxer named Butch Coolidge who is supposed to throw a fight, but doesn't. She's his sweet, naive girlfriend, who doesn't understand why they have to get out of town *right away*. But first he needs to make a dangerous trip back to his apartment to pick up a priceless family heirloom—a wristwatch. The history of this watch is described in a flashback, as Vietnam veteran Christopher Walken tells young Butch about how the watch was purchased by his great-grandfather, Private Doughboy Orion Coolidge, and has come down through the generations—and through a lot more than generations, for that matter. Walken's monologue builds to the movie's biggest laugh.

The method of the movie is to involve its characters in sticky situations, and then let them escape into stickier ones, which is how the boxer and the mob boss end up together as the captives of weird leather freaks in the basement of a gun shop. Or how the characters who open the movie, a couple of stickup artists played by Tim Roth and Amanda Plummer, get in way over their heads. Most of the action in the movie comes under the heading of crisis control.

If the situations are inventive and original, so is the dialogue. A lot of movies these days use flat, functional speech: The characters say only enough to advance the plot. But the people in *Pulp Fiction* are in love with words for their own sake. The dialogue by Tarantino and Avary is off the wall sometimes, but that's the fun. It also means that the characters don't all sound the same: Travolta is laconic, Jackson is exact, Plummer and Roth are dopey lovey-doveys, Keitel uses the shorthand of the busy professional, Thurman learned how to be a moll by studying soap operas.

It is part of the folklore that Tarantino used to work as a clerk in a video store, and the inspiration for *Pulp Fiction* is old movies, not real life. The movie is like an excursion through the lurid images that lie wound up and trapped inside all those boxes on the Blockbuster shelves. Tarantino once described the old pulp mags as cheap, disposable entertainment that you could take to work with you, and roll up and stick in your back pocket. Yeah, and not be able to wait until lunch, so you could start reading them again.

The Purple Rose of Cairo ★ ★ ★ ★
PG, 87 m., 1985

Mia Farrow (Cecilia), Jeff Daniels (Tom Baxter/Gil Shepherd), Danny Aiello (Monk), Van Johnson (Larry), Alexander H. Cohen (Raoul Hirsh). Directed by Woody Allen and produced by Robert Greenhut. Screenplay by Allen.

About twenty minutes into Woody Allen's *The Purple Rose of Cairo,* an extraordinary event takes place. A young woman has been going to see the same movie over and over again, because of her infatuation with the movie's hero. From his vantage point up on the screen, the hero notices her out in the audience. He strikes up a conversation, she smiles and shyly responds, and he abruptly steps off the screen and into her life. No explanation is offered for this miraculous event, but then perhaps none is needed: Don't we spend our lives waiting for the same thing to happen to us in the movies?

Life, of course, is never as simple and dreamy as the movies, and so the hero's bold act has alarming consequences. The movie's other characters are still stranded up there on the screen, feeling angry and left out. The Hollywood studio is aghast that its characters would suddenly develop minds of their own. The actor who *played* the hero is particularly upset, because now there are two of him walking around, one wearing a pith helmet. Things are simple only in the lives of the hero and the woman, who convince themselves that they *can* simply walk into the sunset, and get away with this thing.

The Purple Rose of Cairo is audacious and witty and has a lot of good laughs in it, but the best thing about the movie is the way Woody Allen uses it to toy with the very essence of reality and fantasy. The movie is so cheerful and open that it took me a day or two, after I'd seen it, to realize how deeply Allen has reached this time. If it is true, and I think it is, that most of the time we go to the movies in order to experience brief lives that are not our own, then Allen is demonstrating what a tricky self-deception we practice. Those movie lives consist of *only* what is on the screen, and if we start thinking that real life can be the same way, we are in for a cruel awakening.

The woman in the movie is played by Mia Farrow as a sweet, rather baffled small-town waitress whose big, shiftless lug of a husband bats her around. She is a good candidate for the magic of the movies. Up on the screen, sophisticated people have cocktails and plan

trips down the Nile and are recognized by the doormen in nightclubs. The hero in the movie is played by Jeff Daniels (who was Debra Winger's husband in *Terms of Endearment*). He is a genial, open-faced smoothie with all the right moves, but he has a problem: He *only* knows what his character knows in the movie, and his experience is literally limited to what happens to his character in the plot. This can cause problems. He's great at talking sweetly to a woman, and holding hands, and kissing—but just when the crucial moment arrives, the movie fades out, and therefore, alas, so does he.

Many of Allen's best moments come from exploring the paradox that the movie character knows nothing of real life. For example, he can drive a car, because he drives one in the movie, but he can't start a car, because he doesn't turn on the ignition in the movie. Mia Farrow thinks maybe they can work this out. They can learn from each other. He can learn real life, and she can learn the romance of the movies. The problem is, both of them are now living in real life, where studio moguls and angry actors and snoopy reporters are making their life miserable.

Allen's buried subject in *The Purple Rose of Cairo* is, I think, related to the subjects of his less successful movies, *Stardust Memories* (1980) and *Zelig* (1983). He is interested in the conflicts involving who you want to be, and who other people want you to be. *Stardust* was about a celebrity whose fame prevented people from relating to anything but his image. *Zelig,* the other side of the coin, was about a man whose anonymity was so profound that he could gain an identity only by absorbing one from the people around him. In *Purple Rose,* the movie hero has the first problem, and the woman in the audience has the second, and when they get together, they still don't make one whole person, just two sad halves.

Purple Rose is delightful from beginning to end, not only because of the clarity and charm with which Daniels and Farrow explore the problems of their characters, but also because the movie is so intelligent. It's not brainy or intellectual—no one in the whole movie speaks with more complexity than your average 1930s movie hero—but the movie is filled with wit and invention, and Allen trusts us to find the ironies, relish the contradictions, and figure things out for ourselves. While we do that, he makes us laugh and he makes us think, and when you get right down to it, forget about the fantasies; those are two of the most exciting things that could happen to anybody in a movie. The more you think about *The Purple Rose of Cairo*, and about the movies, and about why you go to the movies, the deeper the damned thing gets.

A Pyromaniac's Love Story ★ ★
PG, 96 m., 1995   **NEW**

William Baldwin (Garet), John Leguizamo (Sergio), Sadie Frost (Hattie), Erika Eleniak (Stephanie), Michael Lerner (Perry), Joan Plowright (Mrs. Linzer), Armin Mueller-Stahl (Mr. Linzer), Mike Starr (Sgt. Zikowski). Directed by Joshua Brand and produced by Mark Gordon. Screenplay by Morgan Ward.

A Pyromaniac's Love Story starts out like a lighthearted charmer, and then it goes on, and on, and on—circling the same plot idea so doggedly that I began to wonder idly what it might have been like as a short subject. It doesn't have a mean bone in its body or, for that matter, a brain in its head.

The movie takes place in the Kensington district of Toronto, that charming mix of ethnic shops and open-air vegetable markets. Of course, Toronto is never mentioned by name (Americans might not be able to deal with such an exotic location, I guess), but much of the tone of the film comes from the leafy, peaceful streets upon which lovers spill out their secrets.

Much of the story involves a little neighborhood pastry shop named Linzer's, where a young and handsome pastry chef named Sergio (John Leguizamo) works behind the counter. One night a strange blonde (Erika Eleniak) walks in off the street and kisses him, but he fails to respond, because his heart belongs to a waitress named Hattie (Sadie Frost). "Cupid dances on his eyelids," the narrator tells us.

Meanwhile, old Mr. Linzer (Armin Mueller-Stahl) confesses that his store is going broke, and that he fears not being able to support the wife he loves (Joan Plowright). He asks Sergio to burn down the shop so he can collect the insurance money. The next day, the shop burns down.

I will not reveal who set the fire, although the identity of the pyromaniac is not the point of the story. The point is that nearly *everyone* in the plot confesses to the crime, sooner or later, and all of them have love as their motive.

The other key characters include Garet (William Baldwin), who is in love with Stephanie, who in turn is the mysterious blonde who kissed Sergio. There is also Garet's millionaire father who wants to protect his son from arrest as a pyromaniac, and a friendly local police sergeant who keeps refusing to accept confessions, and Hattie's father (Michael Lerner), who casts a benevolent eye from behind his deli counter.

Now that you understand the setup, understand that the movie essentially just recombines these characters and their motives. Various people confess to the crime because of their love for other people, who in turn are also likely to confess, and there are painfully contrived scenes like the one where Garet tries to commit suicide but is easily distracted.

Leguizamo makes, it must be said, a good-looking and cheerful leading man, and showed in *Carlito's Way* that he has genuine presence. Here the movie needs every trace of his charisma to shore up the sappy situation he finds himself in. William Baldwin has an even more thankless role, as a goofy misfit who treasures his limp as another man might cherish his dog. One question the movie dares not ask is how any woman could possibly endure his company, much less love him. Sadie Frost has a winning, straightforward likability, and Erika Eleniak does a nice job with her rich-girl dialogue.

But the movie has nowhere to go. The characters behave like simpletons, breaking up and getting back together again at the convenience of the plot. The director, Joshua Brand, has created some good television ("I'll Fly Away," "Northern Exposure"), and at least he has the nerve to go for the sort of cheerful whimsy of *Moonstruck, Sleepless in Seattle,* or *While You Were Sleeping.* But whimsy without wit is like an empty smile.

Q

Q & A ★ ★ ★ ½
R, 134 m., 1990

Nick Nolte (Mike Brennan), Timothy Hutton (Al Reilly), Armand Assante (Bobby Texador), Patrick O'Neal (Kevin Quinn), Lee Richardson (Leo Bloomenfeld), Luis Guzman (Luis Valentin), Charles Dutton (Sam Chapman), Jenny Lumet (Nancy Bosch), Leonard Cimino (Nick Petrone). Directed by Sidney Lumet and produced by Arnon Milchan and Burtt Harris. Screenplay by Lumet.

Sidney Lumet's *Q & A* is an excitingly well-crafted police movie, but he's a good director, and I think that was the easy part for him. What was hard—what the movie is really about—is the rough and careless way that cops and other tough guys throw around racial insults. I'm not talking about how they address their clients out in the streets; I'm talking about how they regard each other— the blacks and Irish and Jews and Hispanics and Italians and Slavics who make up their world. It is almost a badge of honor in certain circles to use, and ignore, racist verbal labels.

What does that kind of talk signify? Is it said in affection? Sometimes. Sometimes not. Is it said as a territorial thing—I'm Italian and you're not? Is it tribal, reminding everyone of loyalties that can be called on in times of trouble? At some level it's accepted— everyone in this movie uses racial and ethnic slang constantly—and yet, at another level, it is just what it sounds like, a kind of macho name-calling.

In Lumet's New York City, the streets are seen as dangerously near to spinning out of control. To the Irish-American chief of the homicide bureau (Patrick O'Neal), that means it is time to close ranks. It's a war out there, he believes, between the cops and the people who would destroy the city (by which

he instinctively means blacks and Hispanics). When a legendary Irish street cop named Brennan (Nick Nolte) shoots a Puerto Rican in a slum doorway, O'Neal calls in a young assistant D.A. (Timothy Hutton) to head the investigation. But he briefs Hutton very specifically: "This is an open-and-shut case."

It is not. Hutton begins to suspect that Brennan may have committed murder. His investigation leads him into the lives of people in many different ethnic groups—and he is shocked one day when a Hispanic drug dealer (Armand Assante) walks in with a woman (Jenny Lumet) Hutton once dated and still loves.

He meets her privately and asks her to come back to him. She will not. He assumed she was Hispanic when they dated, and she will never forget the look in his eyes, she says, when he met her father for the first time and saw that he was black. Is it always there, the movie wonders, that instinctive racial discrimination that seems to be absorbed when we're young and has to be unlearned as part of the process of growing up and growing better?

The movie is about such questions, but in a subtle way, while the central story involves a web of treachery, bribery, and deceit. This is a movie with a large cast, and one of the ways Lumet deals with that is to use fine, experienced actors who almost exude the traits of their characters. There's Charles Dutton, as a hard-boiled black detective who explains that his real color is "blue"— "and when I was in the army, it was olive drab." There's Luis Guzman as his partner, a Puerto Rican detective who knows and accepts the realities of the streets but has his limits. There's Lee Richardson as an old Jewish lawyer who has high standards and gives wise counsel to Hutton—but is also finally part of the system. And Leonard

Cimino has only a few small scenes as an ancient Mafia don, but he conveys the reality of his power with ruthless and yet wryly humorous wisdom.

These people and others give us the sense that *Q & A* isn't just about a hermetically sealed plot, that its tendrils reach out into the whole hierarchy of law enforcement in a city like New York, and that the patterns seen here in the 34th Precinct are repeated in every other precinct and every other big American city. Nick Nolte's performance is central to that feeling. He knew Hutton's late father—a hero cop—and he also knows dirt on the father that he can use if he has to. It's fascinating to see the way he works on this kid. He's been screwing the system so long, he knows just what buttons to push.

One of the most interesting characters in the movie is Bobby Texador, the drug kingpin, played by Armand Assante in one of the best character performances of the year. I didn't recognize Assante at first behind the beard and the silken, poetic speech, but what I did recognize was an original character—not simply your standard movie drug dealer, but a man whose skills and cleverness had led him to success in his business and who was smart enough to want out (it's the rare drug millionaire—or any millionaire— with the imagination to have as much fun spending money as making it).

Lumet has made a lot of other movies about tough big-city types of one kind or another *(Dog Day Afternoon, Serpico, Network, Prince of the City, The Verdict)*, but this is the one where he taps into the vibrating awareness of race which is almost always there when strangers of different races encounter each other in situations where one has authority and another doesn't. The law provides a context for how cops treat civilians, criminal or not, but does it also provide an arena where a racial contest for power in the city takes place? Can the law be color-blind when none of its instruments are? It is fascinating the way this movie works so well as a police thriller on one level, while on other levels it probes feelings we may keep secret even from ourselves.

Queen Margot ★ ★
R, 143 m., 1994

Isabelle Adjani (Margot), Daniel Auteuil (Henri de Navarre), Jean-Hugues Anglade (Charles IX), Vincent Perez (La Mole), Pascal Greggory (Duc d'Anjou), Julien Rassam (Duc d'Alencon), Virna Lisi (Catherine de Medici). Directed by Patrice Chereau and produced by Claude Berri. Screenplay by Daniele Thompson and Chereau.

When I saw *Queen Margot* for the first time in May 1994 at the Cannes Film Festival, it was like looking at the home movies of complete strangers—in this case, the French. All of the many, many characters on the screen were apparently intimately familiar to those around me, but I was at sea. Eventually a few familiar faces came swimming toward me from out of long-ago history classes: Catherine de Medici, for example. But the film didn't seem much concerned with explaining people and relationships, and devoted its energies instead to an almost unwatchable visual style, made up of endless close-ups and a restlessly roving camera.

The film was, however, a big-budget, prestigious French production, widely predicted to win a best actress award for Isabelle Adjani, who does an astonishing job of portraying the sexually insatiable Margot at many ages and stages of dress. When the jury perversely gave the award instead to Virna Lisi, for her work as Margot's mother, Catherine, it came almost as an insult: The star was passed over for the supporting actor. When the film opened in New York, the ads mentioned its Special Jury Prize but pointedly did not mention the award for Lisi.

It was clear at Cannes that *Queen Margot* was going to be slow sailing for a North American audience, and Miramax has done what it could to make the experience easier. The movie has been trimmed to a still more than adequate 143 minutes, and begins with several screens of historical background—so wordy that some audiences may be intimidated even before the first shot.

Then we plunge into the cauldron itself. The director, Patrice Chereau, sure that

his French audience knows his characters as well, say, as Americans might know the headliners at Woodstock, wants to convey the atmosphere at a court where marriage was a political weapon, Catholic and Protestant were at each other's necks, and the most useful attendant was the Royal Poisoner.

He opens on a bewildering array of characters who are not established, with motives which must be guessed. The early scenes do not allow us to easily enter the film. Eventually, we figure out who is doing what and to whom, but the film's narrative makes it hard for us to care. It is all made up of close-ups (heads, shoulders, heaving bosoms) and scurryings hither and thither, and night shots of orgies of sex and violence. "I need a man!" Margot cries at one point, and goes out window-shopping in the street, while the chorus grunts out vaguely Gregorian syllables.

The Catholic Margot has been married, early in the film, to the feckless Henri de Navarre (Daniel Auteuil), the Protestant who would become Henri IV. But they are in a hissing match before they're fairly down the aisle, and there's no question of them sleeping with one another; their union is for the purpose of ending religious war. Catherine de Medici meanwhile plays politics, and favorites, with her three sons, who mope about while Margot slips aside with la Mole (Vincent Perez), the lover she has found in the streets.

The film proceeds by way of stabbings, fits, rapes, orgies, lies, betrayals, and adulteries to its set piece, the St. Bartholomew's Day Massacre, at which some fifty thousand Protestants were murdered and dumped into mass graves. These scenes are shot with an awesome technical competence, but go on much too long (even after trims since Cannes) and lose their point since we know few of the characters being murdered.

Much more effective is a quiet subplot involving a poisoned book; its reader, licking his finger to turn the pages, will eventually kill himself. When the wrong person picks up the book, the result is the best double take in the movie, and certainly the best deathbed speech: "I've read too much. Understand?"

Isabella Adjani is one of the more remarkable actresses of her time, and throws herself into roles like this with courageous abandon. Remember, for example, *Camille Claudel* (1989), based on the life of the woman sculptor who was the mistress of Rodin, but whose talent was shrugged aside because of her sex,

and who ended in an asylum. Adjani in that film, scrabbling with her bare hands in a cold field for the clay to make her sculptures, had a passion similar to Adjani in *Queen Margot*, living in a jungle of human duplicity. The difference is, in the earlier film we cared about her, and what was happening to her. *Queen Margot* is like elaborate illustrations for a book we haven't read.

Queen of Hearts ★ ★ ★ ½
NO MPAA RATING, 115 m., 1989

Ian Hawkes (Eddie), Vittorio Duse (Nonno), Joseph Long (Danilo), Anita Zagaria (Rosa), Eileen Way (Mama Sibilla), Vittorio Amandola (Barbaraccia), Tat Whalley (Beetle). Directed by Jon Amiel and produced by John Hardy. Screenplay by Toni Grisoni.

Queen of Hearts has the same sort of magical romanticism as *Moonstruck*, but in a more gentle key. It's the story of a big, loving Italian family that moves from Italy to London, where Papa wins enough at cards to open a little café. Eddie, the young son who is the hero of the story, grows up in the café, and eventually figures out a way to save it when an old family enemy follows them from Italy and tries to drive them into bankruptcy.

The movie tells this story mostly through Eddie's eyes. He's a smart eleven-year-old who doesn't miss much, although he believes all the family legends, even the one about how his parents fell in love and eloped. The movie opens with this legend as he imagines it: The mother engaged to be married to the horrible butcher Barbaraccia, the father spiriting her out of her parents' house, the loving couple pursued to the top of the local church tower and then leaping to their death—their lives saved when they land in a passing hay wagon.

In London, Eddie's father gets a job as a waiter and then takes advice from a talking pig, bets on the right cards, and wins the money to open the café. And then, as Eddie himself arrives on the scene, the family history grows a little more realistic. The café becomes the center of family life, especially after two of his grandparents arrive from Italy—his mother's mother, and his father's father. The old people hate each other, of course, but their hate is the sort that could almost be mistaken for affection.

Then disaster strikes, when the evil Barbaraccia also arrives from Italy, sets up a gambling shop in the neighborhood, and even pays Eddie's older brother to go to work for him. Will the family lose the café? Will Barbaraccia finally win his revenge? Will Eddie lose his best friend, Beetle, whose father runs the local bookie joint?

All of these questions are settled with the most buoyant charm and good cheer in *Queen of Hearts*, which is a truly happy movie and was directed by Jon Amiel, the British director of that brilliant but truly unhappy TV miniseries, "The Singing Detective." All the despair and bitterness seem to have drained out of Amiel during that project, leaving him nothing but sunshine and a touch of supernatural playfulness for *Queen of Hearts*.

The secret of the success of *Moonstruck*, I've always thought, was that the movie had a level above the realistic—a level at which coincidences were permitted, and people had grand romantic revelations, and dogs knew when to howl at the moon. *Queen of Hearts* has the same kind of freedom. Most of it is grounded in the real world, I suppose—but the real world as seen by a kid with a hyperactive imagination, who believes every one of his father's tall tales. Part of the fun of the movie comes because we know more than the kid. We know, for example, what bad trouble his family is in, and we know it's impossible that he could help them out. But he doesn't know that—and so he saves the day.

Queen of Hearts has no stars to help sell it, and may even lose some viewers who think it's an Italian movie and don't like subtitles (it's in English). I hope it weathers those problems, though, and begins to develop an audience. It's the kind of movie that grows on you, letting you in on the family jokes and involving you in the family feuds. By the end, you feel good, in a goofy way, and then when you think back over the movie you realize that under the fantasy and the humor there was also a fairly substantial story. A story about what it means to belong to a family.

Quest for Fire ★ ★ ★ ½
R, 100 m., 1982

Everett McGill (Noah), Ron Perlman (Amoukar), Nameer El-Kadi (Gaw), Rae Dawn Chong (Ika). Directed by Jean-Jacques Annaud and produced by John Kemeny and Denis Heroux. Screenplay by Gerard Brach.

There are basically two ways to regard *Quest for Fire*. The movie is either (a) the moving story of how scattered tribes of very early men developed some of the traits that made them human, or (b) a laughable caveman picture in which a lot of lantern-jawed actors jump around in animal skins, snarling and swinging clubs at one another. During the movie's opening scenes, I found myself seeing it in the second way, as a borderline comedy. But then these characters and their quest began to grow on me, and by the time the movie was over I cared very much about how their lives would turn out.

Other viewers report some of the same confusion. The movie has been compared with such varied works of art as *2001: A Space Odyssey* and *Alley Oop*. The question, I suppose, is whether you can make your own leap of imagination into the world of the movie—whether you're willing to identify with these beetle-browed ancestors who made more important discoveries, in their way, than all of the Nobel laureates put together. I found I *was* willing, and I was a little surprised at how much affection the movie generated.

Quest for Fire was shot on rugged locations in Canada and Scotland and takes place at the dawn of man. It introduces us to a tribe of primitive men who guard their most precious possession, which is fire. They know how to tend it and how to use it, but not how to make it. And after a jealous tribe of less-advanced creatures attacks them and destroys their fire, three men set out on an odyssey to seek another tribe that possesses fire and to steal it from them. Along the way, there are terrifying adventures. A saber-toothed tiger chases the men up into a tree and keeps them there for days. On another occasion, the heroes are trapped between an unfriendly tribe of apes and a herd of mastodons. In each situation, the men realize that simply running away won't work; they can't run fast or far enough. And so they slowly and painfully figure out a solution to their dilemma. Climbing the tree, for example, is rather obvious, but their solution to the mastodon problem is a brave inspiration.

Eventually the men discover another tribe, a more advanced tribe that lives in primitive huts and knows how to make fire and has even developed arts (they decorate themselves with mud, and their clay pots have drawings of animals scratched on them). The leader of the wanderers lusts after one of the women of the new tribe, and after a strange initiation ceremony he has sex with her. Soon he will make one of his greatest discoveries: The difference between lust and love and how it leads to the difference between isolation—and loneliness.

Quest for Fire compresses prehistory quite radically, of course. It's a little much to expect that one man in one span of a few weeks could make the scientific, emotional, and tactical discoveries that take place in the movie. Our progress as a race must have been slower than that (although Loren Eiseley writes in his books of the amazing explosion of the size of the human brain in just a handful of generations). *Quest for Fire* isn't science, though, it's an imaginary re-creation of our past, and it uses history for inspiration, not as a data source. The only two technical advisers listed in the credits are, appropriately, a novelist and a scientific popularizer: Anthony Burgess created the special primitive languages in the film, and Desmond Morris choreographed the body language and gestures.

I suggested earlier that there's probably a temptation to laugh during *Quest for Fire*, especially during such touchy scenes as the one in which early woman teaches early man that it *wasn't* as good for her as it was for him. I smiled during those scenes. But, thinking over my response, I realize that I wasn't smiling at the movie, but at the behavior of the characters. Man is a comic beast. For all of our dignity, we are very simple in many of our wants and desires, and as we crawled out of the primeval sludge and started our long trek toward civilization, there must have been many more moments of comedy than of nobility.

Quest for Fire cheerfully acknowledges that, and indeed some of its best scenes involve man's discovery of laughter. When one of the primitive tribesmen is hit on the head by a small falling stone, the woman from the other tribe laughs and laughs. Our heroes are puzzled: They haven't heard such a noise before. But it strikes some sort of deep chord, I guess, because later, one of the tribesmen deliberately drops a small stone on his friend's head, and then everybody laughs: The three men together with the woman who taught them laughter. That's human. The guy who got hit on the head is, of course, a little slow to join in the laughter, but finally he goes along with the joke. That's civilization.

The Quick and the Dead ★ ★
R, 103 m., 1995

Sharon Stone (Ellen), Gene Hackman (Herod), Russell Crowe (Cort), Leonardo DiCaprio (Kid), Tobin Bell (Dog Kelly), Roberts Blossom

(Doc Wallace), Kevin Conway (Eugene Dred), Keith David (Sergeant Cantrell). Directed by Sam Raimi and produced by Joshua Donen, Allen Shapiro, and Patrick Markey. Screenplay by Simon Moore.

The Quick and the Dead takes the premise of those old Tough Man contests and moves it to the Old West, where the sadistic despot of a small town holds a shoot-off every year. The rules are simple: The last man alive wins a big cash prize. It's a movie that is intimately familiar with the conventions of Westerns, especially those rules which state (a) that when a Kid comes riding into town for a showdown with the big man, he is probably the man's unacknowledged son, and (b) when a woman rides into town, also for a showdown, she is probably seeking revenge for a terrible wrong in the past.

The movie stars Gene Hackman as a man named Herod, who lives in a dark, Dickensian house that looms at the end of Main Street. Protected by henchmen in long black leather coats, he collects a 50 percent tax on all business in the town, shoots anyone who gets out of line, and holds his bloody competition once a year.

Anyone can enter. The contestants are paired off, and at the stroke of twelve on the town clock, they stand in the middle of the street and shoot at each other. One must die in order for the other to win. Then it's on to the next round (in this town it's *High Noon* over and over again). The last man standing collects the prize money.

Herod is always the last man standing. I figured that out because he's still alive. His motives for holding this contest may seem obscure, but actually they are pretty clear: He holds it because it provides a simplistic story structure for the movie, giving it a long series of duels on Main Street as a substitute for any form of genuine dramatic conflict.

You'd think contestants would have to be pretty hard up to enter a contest where the odds are about ten-to-one in favor of their being killed. But there's no shortage of entrants, including one guy who adds an ace to his deck every time he kills someone, and another who cuts a scar into his arm after every kill. Also arriving are two strangers: the Kid (Leonardo DiCaprio), and Ellen (Sharon Stone). The Kid is cocky and self-confident: "Damn, I'm fast!" he says after polishing off one opponent, and later he asks idly, "Is it possible to improve on perfection?"

Ellen is a little harder to read. She is a lone rider who puffs on a thin black cigar and makes a bartender regret it when he assumes she's a hooker. She's sexy in leather pants and a trim outfit (and later manages to find a ballroom gown in her saddlebags). She wants to enter the contest. Hackman, who is attracted to her, doesn't want either Ellen or the Kid to shoot it out, possibly because he suspects that the Kid is his own son.

Oh, he denies it. But the Kid is adamant. "I'm his son," he declares, "and if this is the only way he's gonna admit that, so be it." In other words (I think), the theory is that if the Kid kills Hackman, by golly, *that'll* make him admit it.

The movie's story, as you have grasped, isn't much. But *The Quick and the Dead* is not without its qualities. The director is Sam Raimi (the *Evil Dead* movies, *Darkman*) and he displays once again his zest for stylistic invention. Early in the movie, a character gets shot through the hat brim, and the sun shines through the hole into the camera lens. A nice touch, but Raimi tops it later in the film by showing the sun shining through a bullet hole clean through a guy's body, and by a third shot in which we look down Main Street through a large hole in a man's head.

The cinematographer, Dante Spinotti (*Last of the Mohicans*), makes the material look terrific. The lowering skies around the isolated town make it look ripe for vengeance of biblical proportions, and there are quiet satirical touches, as when a man stands in a saloon door and his shadow seems about six miles long. It also helps the visuals that it rains all the time in this town (although when it doesn't, nothing is green).

It must also be said that Hackman somehow survives the material. I am beginning to believe he is an actor who can say anything and make it work. As preposterous as the plot was, there was never a line of Hackman dialogue that didn't sound as if he believed it. The same can't be said, alas, for Sharon Stone, who apparently believed that if she played her character as silent, still, impassive, and mysterious, we would find that interesting. More swagger might have helped. Do you suppose she took the plot *seriously?*

Quiz Show ★ ★ ★ ½
PG-13, 133 m., 1994

NEW

John Turturro (Herbie Stempel), Rob Morrow (Dick Goodwin), Ralph Fiennes (Charles Van Doren), Paul Scofield (Mark Van Doren), David Paymer (Dan Enright), Hank Azaria (Albert Freedman), Christopher McDonald (Jack Barry). Directed by Robert Redford and produced by Redford, Michael Jacobs, Julian Krainin, and Michael Nozik. Screenplay by Paul Attanasio.

Why fix them? Why not just make the questions easier? The audience doesn't want to see the contestants—they want to see the money.
—dialogue from *Quiz Show*

A milestone in the decline of American values came in the mid-1950s, when it was revealed that many of the top TV quiz shows were rigged—that contestants were being supplied with the answers. This was a milestone, not because of the scandal, which was a small storm to weather, but because of the result.

The early quiz shows rewarded knowledge, and made celebrities out of people who knew a lot of things and could remember them. The postfix quiz shows rewarded luck. On "The $64,000 Question" and "Twenty-One," you could see people getting rich because they were smart. Today people on TV make money by playing games a clever child can master. The message is that it's not necessary to know anything, because you can be ignorant and still get lucky.

The 1950s have been packaged as a time of Eisenhower and Elvis, Chevy Bel-Airs and blue jeans, crew cuts and drive-ins. *Quiz Show* remembers it was also a decade when intellectuals were respected, when a man could be famous because he was a poet and a teacher, when TV audiences actually watched shows on which experts answered questions about Shakespeare and Dickens, science and history. All of that is gone now.

The first show, CBS's "The $64,000 Question," was apparently on the level. But across the street at NBC's "Twenty-One," executives and sponsors watched the ratings, and realized that some contestants drew more viewers than others. A grating know-it-all named Herbert Stempel won for weeks on "Twenty-One," partly because he was being given the answers. The executives decided his appeal was wearing thin. So they broke the news to him: He'd had a free ride long enough, and now it was time to lose.

Stempel took that news very badly. Meanwhile, America liked his successor, an attractive, disarming intellectual named Charles Van Doren, who was a member of one of America's great literary families; his father,

Mark, and his uncle, Philip, were beloved and respected. Blinded not so much by money as by fame, Charles had agreed to cheat. And when Stempel blew the whistle on the whole setup, a congressional investigator brought the deception tumbling down.

Robert Redford has directed *Quiz Show* as entertainment, history, and challenge. It is fun as a thriller; we find ourselves sort of hoping Van Doren doesn't get caught. It works as a memory of the first decade in which a society that used to sit on the front porch went inside and stared at the tube. And then it asks us what we might have done, if someone offered us a lot of money and popularity for pretending to be smarter than we were.

The movie shows the sponsors casting the contestants as if they were regulars on a soap opera. It also reflects intriguing conflicts of race and class: Herbert Stempel (John Turturro) is portrayed as an unpolished Jew who is replaced by Van Doren (Ralph Fiennes), an urbane WASP. The congressional investigator, Richard Goodwin (Rob Morrow), is a Jew who is attracted to the genteel intellectualism of the Van Dorens (who, at a family dinner, play a Shakespeare trivia game). Goodwin attempts to bring down the quiz shows on Stempel's testimony while giving Van Doren a pass—just because he likes him. "You're the Uncle Tom of the Jews," his wife accuses him. But he cannot help himself; Charles himself has become such a friend that he cannot bear to bring him crashing down. In a way, the movie subtly argues, Goodwin arrived at the same casting decision as the sponsors.

The movie uses real names throughout, including the network (NBC) and the sponsor (Geritol, which cured "tired blood" and made you "feel stronger fast"). It depicts TV producer Dan Enright (David Paymer) and game show host Jack Barry (Christopher McDonald) and there is a certain fascination in the fact that the movie, to use a 1950s catch phrase, "names names." There is real poignancy in its portrayal of the upright, ethical Mark Van Doren (Paul Scofield) realizing what has happened to his son.

There are also little shocks along the way, as characters reveal that they have standards we no longer much adhere to. One executive says, in justifying the fix, "It isn't like we're hardened criminals here—we're in show business." His moral justification was higher ratings. Today on TV, so many sins are justified in the name of ratings that any other standard hardly exists. Then, such reasoning was new.

The screenplay, by former *Washington Post* film critic Paul Attanasio, is smart, subtle, and ruthless. And it is careful to place blame where it belongs. Oh, yes, Charles Van Doren was wrong to take the answers and play the game. But he has paid for his moment of weakness a thousand times over, year after year; to this day, millions of people remember him as "the guy who cheated on the quiz show." The network, the sponsors, and the producers set him up, and then they all stepped clear when the scandal broke.

The movie makes it clear that NBC and Geritol were able to claim they "knew nothing" about the rigged games, although they clearly did. And Dan Enright, the producer, was soon back at work making more TV shows. Only the contestants have continued to pay, and pay, and pay. There is a theological belief that it is a greater sin to tempt than to be tempted, and this movie firmly reminds us of that.

Now take stock of what we have lost in the four decades since "Twenty-One" came crashing down. We have lost a respect for intelligence; we reward people for whatever they happen to have learned, instead of feeling they might learn more. We have forgotten that the end does not justify the means—especially when the end is a high TV rating or any other kind of popular success. And we have lost a certain innocent idealism. Charles Van Doren lied on a quiz show, and then the standards that created that quiz show went on to infect ever-widening circles, until Oliver North could lie to Congress, and then run for it.

R

Racing with the Moon ★ ★ ★ ½
PG, 108 m., 1984

Sean Penn (Hopper), Elizabeth McGovern (Caddie), Nicolas Cage (Nicky), Suzanne Adkinson (Sally), Julie Phillips (Alice). Directed by Richard Benjamin and produced by Alain Bernheim and John Kohn. Screenplay by Steven Kloves.

I'd like to start with a hypothetical question: How long has it been since you went to a movie that ended with the words "I love you"? For me, it had been a very long time, and one of the simpler pleasures of *Racing with the Moon* was to observe the movie marching inevitably toward those three words. A deeper pleasure was that the movie arrived there with grace and charm.

The story takes place in California in 1943, with the United States at war and teen-agers volunteering for the service. We meet a couple of high school kids, Hopper and Nicky, who are pinspotters down at the bowling alley and otherwise spend their time cutting classes, shooting pool, hitching rides on trains, and talking about the meaning of life. We are reminded of Tom and Huck. One night Hopper goes to the movies. His eyes meet the girl who is selling him his ticket, and he is thunderstruck by her. Her name is Caddie. Nicky already has a girlfriend, a plump little blonde named Sally. Hopper starts a campaign to win Caddie's heart, by slipping her flowers anonymously and tracking her down in the high school library. It appears that Caddie is a rich kid who lives in the house on the hill. But she likes Hopper anyway, and he likes her, and *Racing with the Moon* turns into a love story.

So far, what we have here is a movie that could go in several different directions. It could be sappy, it could be great, it could be dripping with so much nostalgia that it would

feel like a memory even while we were watching it. *Racing with the Moon* doesn't fall into the *Summer of '42* nostalgia trap, but tries to be honest with its romantic characters. The performers are probably the reason that approach works so well. The three leading actors are Sean Penn and Elizabeth McGovern, as the young lovers, and Nicolas Cage, as Penn's friend. It's a pleasure to watch them work.

Penn, in particular, shows a whole side we didn't see in movies like *Bad Boys* or, needless to say, *Fast Times at Ridgemont High*. He's somehow better-looking than before, and more relaxed and confident. He doesn't come across with a lot of distracting self-importance. He plays the kind of kid who uses a rough exterior—smoking and shooting pool—as a kind of cover-up for the intelligence and sensitivity underneath, and one of the movie's best quiet moments comes when he reveals how well he can play the piano. McGovern, who had such a sweet face and such a wicked charm as the mistress in *Ragtime*, seems younger here. She has a secret she keeps from Penn, but only because she loves him. The way she plays against him is fun to watch: She's not a flirt and she's not coy, but instead she's open with this kid and has fun teasing him; there's a scene where she sets him up for a date with her girlfriend, and it's written and choreographed so carefully that it takes you back to any soda fountain you may ever have inhabited. Cage is good, too, reckless and self-destructive and dreamy, and by the end of the movie we really have a feeling for their complex relationships with each other.

Racing with the Moon is a movie like *Valley Girl* or *Baby, It's You*, a movie that is interested in teen-agers and willing to listen to how they talk and to observe, with great tenderness, the fragility and importance of their first

big loves. It's easy to end a movie with "I love you," but it's hard to get there honestly.

Radio Days ★ ★ ★ ★
PG, 88 m., 1987

Mia Farrow (Sally White), Seth Green (Joe), Michael Tucker (Father), Josh Mostel (Abe), Tito Puente (Bandleader), Danny Aiello (Rocco), Diane Keaton (New Year's Singer), Wallace Shawn (Masked Avenger), Dianne Wiest (Bea). Directed by Woody Allen and produced by Robert Greenhut. Screenplay by Allen.

I can remember what happened to the Lone Ranger in 1949 better than I can remember what happened to me. His adventures struck deeply into my imagination in a way that my own did not, and as I write these words there is almost a physical intensity to my memories of listening to the radio. Television was never the same. Television shows happened in the TV set, but radio shows happened in my head.

That is one of the truths that Woody Allen evokes in *Radio Days*, his comedy about growing up in the 1940s. Another one is that glamour and celebrity meant something in those days. And for millions of people living in ordinary homes in ordinary neighborhoods, the radio brought images of beings who lived in a shimmering world of penthouses and nightclubs, in dressing rooms and boudoirs.

The hero of *Radio Days* is an ordinary person like that: an adolescent Jewish kid who grows up in Brooklyn in a house full of relatives and listens passionately to the radio. But the movie is not simply his story. It is also the story of 1940s radio itself, and it recreates many of the legends that he remembers hearing.

For example, the story of the burglars who answered the phone in a house they were burgling and won the jackpot on "Name That Tune," and the prizes were delivered the next day to their bewildered victims. Or the embarrassing plight of the suave radio host who liked to play around and got locked on the roof of a nightclub with the cigarette girl. Or the way the macho heroes of radio adventure serials turned out, in real life, to be short little bald guys. (The one legend Allen leaves out is the scandal of the kiddie-show host who growled "That oughta hold the little bastards" into an open mike.)

Radio Days cuts back and forth between the adolescent hero's working-class neighborhood in Brooklyn and the glamorous radio world of Manhattan. And, like radio, it jumps easily from one level of reality to another. There are autobiographical memories of relatives and school, neighbors and friends, and then there are the glittering radio legends that seeped into these ordinary lives.

Allen is not concerned with creating a story with a beginning and an end, and his movie is more like a revue in which drama is followed by comedy and everything is tied together by music, by dozens of lush arrangements of the hit songs of the 1940s. He has always used popular music in his movies (remember the opening of *Manhattan?*), but never more than this time, where the muscular, romantic confidence of the big-band sound reinforces every memory with the romance of the era.

There are so many characters in *Radio Days*, and they are in so many separate vignettes, that it's hard to give a coherent description of the plot or plots. In form and even in mood, the movie it's closest to is Federico Fellini's *Amarcord,* which also was a memory of growing up—of family, religion, sex, local folk legends, scandalous developments, and intense romantic yearnings, underlined with wall-to-wall band music. In a way, both films have nostalgia itself as one of their subjects. What they evoke isn't the long-ago time itself, but the memory of it. There is something about it being past and gone and irretrievable that makes it more precious than it ever was at the time.

As part of this nostalgic feeling, Allen seems to have made a deliberate attempt to use as many of his former actors as possible. The movie is a roll call of casts from earlier films, from Mia Farrow and Diane Keaton to Tony Roberts, Danny Aiello, Dianne Wiest, Jeff Daniels, and Wallace Shawn. And viewers with good memories will notice there also are many actual radio veterans in the movie, such as Don Pardo and Kitty Carlisle, and the shadows of others, such as Bill Stern, whose inspirational parables about sports heroes are mercilessly satirized.

The one actor who is not visible is Allen. But his teen-age alter ego (Seth Green) provides a memory of young Allen in *Take the Money and Run,* and then there is Allen's own voice on the sound track, evoking those golden days of yesteryear. There also is the Allen irreverence in several moments of absolutely inspired comedy, such as a classroom show-and-tell session, or the time the young hero collects dimes for Israel and then spends them on a boxtop secret decoder ring and has to face the rabbi's wrath.

Radio Days is so ambitious and so audacious that it almost defies description. It's a kaleidoscope of dozens of characters, settings, and scenes—the most elaborate production Allen has ever made—and it's inexhaustible, spinning out one delight after another. Although there is no narrative thread from beginning to end, there is a buried emotional thread. Like music, the movie builds toward a climax we can't even guess is coming, and then Allen finds the perfect images for the last few minutes, for a bittersweet evocation of good-bye to all that.

His final moments are staged on a set representing a rooftop on Times Square, with a smoker puffing his cigarette on a Camel billboard, while in another direction a giant neon top hat is lifted and lowered. This set is so overblown and romantic, it's like the moment in *Amarcord* when all of the townspeople get into boats and go out to watch the great ocean liner go past, and we see that the liner is obviously a prop—a vast, artificial Christmas tree of shimmering lights and phony glory. Allen finds the same truth that Fellini did: What actually happens isn't nearly as important as how we remember it.

A Rage in Harlem ★ ★ ★
R, 98 m., 1991

Forest Whitaker (Jackson), Gregory Hines (Goldy), Robin Givens (Imabelle), Zakes Mokae (Big Kathy), Danny Glover (Easy Money), Badja Djola (Slim), Stack Pierce (Coffin Ed), George Wallace (Grave Digger), Screamin' Jay Hawkins (Himself). Directed by Bill Duke and produced by Stephen Woolley and Kerry Boyle. Screenplay by John Toles-Bey and Bobby Crawford.

A Rage in Harlem is a love story surrounded by a gangster movie, and the love story wins.

The lovers are Forest Whitaker, as Jackson, a big, bashful, sweet, and innocent kid, and Robin Givens, as Imabelle, a smooth operator with a trunk full, instead of a heart full, of gold. It's the mid-1950s. She's stolen the gold from her criminal partners in Mississippi, and brought it up to New York in a trunk, pursued by various low-lifes from her previous existence. In Harlem, she's broke and homeless and isn't sure how to dispose of the gold, so she needs a fall guy. Some guy so naive and dumb she can move in and use him as a cover while she plans her next move. Jackson is the obvious victim. That's before they fall in love.

They meet at the annual Undertaker's Ball, where Jackson is surprised to find himself, because as a devout, church-going young man he has nothing to do with the types who hang around there—including Goldy (Gregory Hines), his street-smart brother. He is thunderstruck by his first sight of Imabelle, who ignores him until she realizes this is her ideal patsy. Then she asks him to dance ("It's easy. Just grab me and squeeze"), and he realizes she is the most beautiful and wonderful woman in the world.

He is not quite right. She reads him for an easy mark, and plans to use him as part of her plan to keep her hands on the gold. But then something strange happens. They go to his room, where she is blindsided by his innocence and sincerity—transformed by the pure sweetness of his love. For the first time in Imabelle's life, she's met a man who idealizes her, and the experience is almost too much for her. She struggles. She tries to remain true to her criminal ideals. But big, goofy, virginal Jackson looks at her adoringly, and her heart flutters.

The relationship between Jackson and Imabelle is at the heart of *A Rage in Harlem*, which is based on a novel by Chester Himes (1909–84), who specialized in atmospheric crime novels, and has walk-ons for two of his familiar characters: Grave Digger Jones and Coffin Ed Johnson, made famous in his *Cotton Comes to Harlem.* It also has roles for a great many other characters, among them Easy Money (Danny Glover), a numbers boss; Big Kathy (Zakes Mokae), a transvestite brothel keeper; and Slim (Badja Djola), a gang leader from the South who is Imabelle's former lover, and who knows about the gold.

Himes's novel is densely plotted, and so is the movie, as Easy Money schemes to get his hands on the gold, and Slim arrives from

Mississippi with his own henchmen. Jackson is a babe in these woods, but Hines, as his con-man brother, uses his street connections to try to save them. Hines also tries to explain to his kid brother that Imabelle is a con artist, but the kid doesn't believe him, and, for once, he's right.

The movie has a nice period atmosphere, which is remarkable, since it was shot with Cincinnati doubling for Harlem, and it captures some of the texture of Himes's novel, his love of characters who use their wits to outsmart each other. What's best in the movie is the chemistry between Whitaker (who played the title role in *Bird*) and Givens, who is surprisingly effective in her first feature role. Their first love scene together—where the bashful kid awkwardly wins her heart—is sexier than any number of more explicit scenes. And their reunion at the end is just right.

Raging Bull ★ ★ ★ ★
R, 119 m., 1980

Robert De Niro (Jake La Motta), Cathy Moriarty (Vickie La Motta), Joe Pesci (Joey), Frank Vincent (Salvy), Nicholas Colasanto (Tommy Como), Theresa Saldana (Lenore), Frank Adonis (Patsy), Mario Gallo (Mario). Directed by Martin Scorsese and produced by Irwin Winkler and Robert Chartoff. Screenplay by Paul Schrader and Mardik Martin.

Martin Scorsese's *Raging Bull* is a movie about brute force, anger, and grief. It is also, like several of Scorsese's other movies, about a man's inability to understand a woman except in terms of the only two roles he knows how to assign her: virgin or whore. There is no room inside the mind of the prizefighter in this movie for the notion that a woman might be a friend, a lover, or a partner. She is only, to begin with, an inaccessible sexual fantasy. And then, after he has possessed her, she becomes tarnished by sex. Insecure in his own manhood, the man becomes obsessed by jealousy—and releases his jealousy in violence.

It is a vicious circle. Freud called it the "madonna-whore complex." Groucho Marx put it somewhat differently: "I wouldn't belong to any club that would have me as a member." It amounts to a man having such low self-esteem that he (a) cannot respect a woman who would sleep with him, and (b) is convinced that, given the choice, she would rather be sleeping with someone else. I'm making a point of the way *Raging Bull* equates

sexuality and violence because one of the criticisms of this movie is that we never really get to know the central character. I don't agree with that. I think Scorsese and Robert De Niro do a fearless job of showing us the precise feelings of their central character, the former boxing champion Jake La Motta.

It is true that the character never tells us what he's feeling, that he is not introspective, that his dialogue is mostly limited to expressions of desire, fear, hatred, and jealousy. But these very limitations—these stone walls separating the character from the world of ordinary feelings—tell us all we need to know, especially when they're reflected back at him by the other people in his life. Especially his brother and his wife, Vickie.

Raging Bull is based, we are told, on the life of La Motta, who came out of the slums of the Bronx to become middleweight champion in the 1940s, who made and squandered millions of dollars, who became a pathetic stand-up comedian, and finally spent time in a prison for corrupting the morals of an underage girl. Is this the real La Motta? We cannot know for sure, though La Motta was closely involved with the production. What's perhaps more to the point is that Scorsese and his principal collaborators, actor Robert De Niro and screenwriter Paul Schrader, were attracted to this material. All three seem fascinated by the lives of tortured, violent, guilt-ridden characters; their previous three-way collaboration was the movie *Taxi Driver*.

Scorsese's very first film, *Who's That Knocking at My Door* (1967), starred Harvey Keitel as a kid from Little Italy who fell in love with a girl but could not handle the facts of her previous sexual experience. In its sequel, *Mean Streets* (1972), the same hang-up was explored, as it was in *Taxi Driver*, where the De Niro character's madonna-whore complex tortured him in sick relationships with an inaccessible, icy blonde, and with a young prostitute. Now the filmmakers have returned to the same ground, in a film deliberately intended to strip away everything but the raw surges of guilt, jealousy, and rage coursing through La Motta's extremely limited imagination.

Raging Bull remains close to its three basic elements: a man, a woman, and prizefighting. La Motta is portrayed as a punk kid, stubborn, strong, and narrow. He gets involved in boxing, and he is good at it. He gets married, but his wife seems almost an after-

thought. Then one day he sees a girl at a municipal swimming pool and is transfixed by her. The girl is named Vickie, and she is played by Cathy Moriarty as an intriguing mixture of unstudied teen-ager, self-reliant survivor, and somewhat calculated slut.

La Motta wins and marries her. Then he becomes consumed by the conviction she is cheating on him. Scorsese finds a way to visually suggest his jealousy: From La Motta's point of view, Vickie sometimes floats in slow motion toward another man. The technique fixes the moment in our minds; we share La Motta's exaggeration of an innocent event. And we share, too, the La Motta character's limited and tragic hang-ups. This man we see is not, I think, supposed to be any more subtle than he seems. He does not have additional "qualities" to share with us. He is an engine driven by his own rage. The equation between his prizefighting and his sexuality is inescapable, and we see the trap he's in: La Motta is the victim of base needs and instincts that, in his case, are not accompanied by the insights and maturity necessary for him to cope with them. The raging bull. The poor sap.

Ragtime ★ ★ ★ ½
PG, 156 m., 1981

Howard E. Rollins, Jr. (Coalhouse Walker), James Cagney (Rhinelander Waldo), Brad Dourif (Younger Brother), Mary Steenburgen (Mother), James Olson (Father), Elizabeth McGovern (Evelyn Nesbit), Kenneth McMillan (Willie Conklin), Pat O'Brien (Delmas), Mandy Patinkin (Tateh), Moses Gunn (Booker T. Washington). Directed by Milos Forman and produced by Dino De Laurentiis. Screenplay by Michael Weller.

Milos Forman apparently made a basic decision very early in his production of E.L. Doctorow's best-selling novel, *Ragtime*. He decided to set aside the book's kaleidoscopic jumble of people, places, and things, and concentrate on just one of the several narrative threads. Instead of telling dozens of stories, his film is mostly concerned with the story of Coalhouse Walker, Jr., a black piano player who insists that justice be done after he is insulted by some yahoo volunteer firemen.

Doctorow's novel was an inspired juggling act involving both actual and fictional characters, who sometimes met in imaginary scenes of good wit and imagery. The Coalhouse story was more or less equal with several others. A film faithful to the book would have had people walking in and out of each other's lives in an astonishing series of coincidences. That might have been a good film, too. It might have looked a little like Robert Altman's *Nashville* or *Buffalo Bill,* and indeed Altman was the first filmmaker signed to direct *Ragtime.* But we will never see what Altman might have done, and Forman decided to do something different. He traces the ways in which Coalhouse Walker enters and affects the lives of an upstate New York family in the first decade of the century. The family lives in White Plains, New York, in a vast and airy old frame manor, and it consists of Father, Mother, and Younger Brother, with walk-ons by a grandfather and a young son.

For Younger Brother, the sirens of the big city call, in the form of an infatuation with the chorus girl Evelyn Nesbit (Elizabeth McGovern). That's before the saga of Coalhouse Walker alters his life. Coalhouse (in a superb performance by Howard E. Rollins, Jr.) meets the family by accident, or maybe by fate. A young black woman gives birth to Coalhouse's son, and then the family takes in both the woman and her son, hiring her as their maid. Coalhouse comes calling. He wants to marry the mother of his child. He has earned enough money. Everything's all set for the ceremony, when an event takes place that changes everything. The local volunteer firemen, enraged that a black man would own his own Model T, block the car's way in front of their station. They pile horse manure on the front seat. And Coalhouse, quite simply, cannot rest until he sees his car restored to him in its original condition.

The story develops quickly into a confrontation. Coalhouse barricades himself into New York's J. Pierpont Morgan Library, and issues a set of demands. The library is surrounded by police and guardsmen, led by Police Commissioner Rhinelander Waldo (the great James Cagney, out of retirement). Father (James Olson) gets drawn into negotiations, and Younger Brother (Brad Dourif) is actually one of Coalhouse's lieutenants, in blackface disguise. Meanwhile, Mother is running off with a bearded immigrant who started out making cutout silhouettes on the streets and is now one of the first film directors.

The story of *Ragtime,* then, is essentially the story of Coalhouse Walker, Jr. Forman, a Czechoslovakian with an unusually keen eye for American society—his credits include *One Flew Over the Cuckoo's Nest* and *Hair!*—has made a film about black pride and rage

and . . . not *only* white racism, which we sort of expect, but also white liberalism.

The great achievement of *Ragtime* is in its performances, especially Rollins and the changes he goes through in this story, from youthful romantic love to an impassioned cry "Lord, why did you fill me with such rage?" Olson, quiet and self-effacing, is subtly powerful as Father. Mary Steenburgen is clear-voiced, primly ethical Mother who springs a big surprise on everyone. Pat O'Brien has two great scenes as a corrupt, world-weary lawyer. Kenneth McMillan blusters and threatens as the racist fire chief. And when Cagney tells him "people tell me . . . you're slime," there is the resonance of movie legend in his voice.

Ragtime is a loving, beautifully mounted, graceful film that creates its characters with great clarity. We understand where everyone stands, and most of the time we even know why. Forman surrounds them with some of the other characters from the Doctorow novel (including Harry Houdini, Teddy Roosevelt, and Norman Mailer as the architect Sanford White), but in the film they're just atmosphere—window dressing. Forman's decision to stick with the story of Coalhouse is vindicated, because he tells it so well.

Raiders of the Lost Ark ★ ★ ★ ★
PG, 115 m., 1981

Harrison Ford (Indy), Ronald Lacey (Teht), John Rhys-Davies (Sallah), Karen Allen (Marion), Wolf Kahler (Dietrich). Directed by Steven Spielberg and produced by Frank Marshall. Executive producers, George Lucas and Howard Kazanjian. Screenplay by Lucas and Philip Kaufman.

Raiders of the Lost Ark is an out-of-body experience, a movie of glorious imagination and breakneck speed that grabs you in the first shot, hurtles you through a series of incredible adventures, and deposits you back in reality two hours later—breathless, dizzy, wrung-out, and with a silly grin on your face. This movie celebrates the stories we spent our adolescence searching for in the pulp adventure magazines, in the novels of Edgar Rice Burroughs, in comics—even in the movies. There used to be a magazine named *Thrilling Wonder Stories,* and every shot in *Raiders of the Lost Ark* looks like one of its covers. It's the kind of movie where the hero gets out of bed wondering what daring exploits and astonishing, cliff-hanging, death-defying threats he will have to survive in the next ten seconds.

It's actually more than a movie; it's a catalog of adventure. For locations, it ticks off the jungles of South America, the hinterlands of Tibet, the deserts of Egypt, a hidden submarine base, an isolated island, a forgotten tomb—no, make that *two* forgotten tombs—and an American anthropology classroom. For villains, it has sadistic Nazis, slimy gravediggers, drunken Sherpas, and scheming Frenchmen. For threats, it climaxes with the wrath of God, and leads up to that spectacular development by easy stages, with tarantulas, runaway boulders, hidden spears, falling rock slabs, burning airplanes, runaway trucks, sealed tombs, and snakes. Lots of snakes. For modes of conveyance, it looks like one of those old world's fair panoramas of transportation: It has horse carts, biplanes, motorcycles, submarines, ships, horse, trains, and trucks. No bicycles.

For heroes, it has Indiana Jones (Harrison Ford) and his former and future girlfriend, Marion (Karen Allen). She's the kind of girl . . . well, to make a long story short, when they first met ten years ago, Indiana deflowered her, and that made her so mad at men that she moved to the mountains of Tibet, opened a bar, and started nightly drinking contests with the Sherpas. She'll never forgive him, almost.

The time is 1936. Indy is an American anthropologist who learns that the Nazis think they've discovered the long-lost resting place of the Ark of the Covenant, the golden casket used by the ancient Hebrews to hold the Ten Commandments. Indy's mission: Beat the Nazis to the prize. He flies to Tibet, collects Marion and a priceless medallion that holds the secret of the Ark's location, and then tries to outsmart the Nazis. What is a little amazing about *Raiders of the Lost Ark* is that this plot somehow holds together and makes some sense, even though it functions primarily as a framework for the most incredible series of action and stunt set pieces I've ever seen in a movie. Indiana and Marion spend the entire film hanging by their fingernails—literally, at one point, over a pit of poisonous snakes.

They survive a series of gruesome and dreadful traps, pitfalls, double-crosses, ambushes, and fates worse than death (of which this movie suggests several). And Indiana engages in the best chase scene I've seen in a film. (I include, in second place, the chase from *The French Connection,* with *Bullitt* in third.) The chase involves a truck, three jeeps, a horse, a motorcycle, and an awesomely difficult stunt in which a character is required to make a 360-degree turn of the speeding truck. All of these spectacles are achieved with flawless movie technology brought to a combination of stunts, special visual effects, and sheer sweat. The makers of this film have covered similar ground before, if perhaps never so fluently; George Lucas, the executive producer, gave birth to the *Star Wars* movies, and Steven Spielberg, the director, made *Jaws* and *Close Encounters*. The rest of the all-star crew's work includes photography by veteran British cinematographer Douglas Slocombe, appropriately stirring and haunting music by *Star Wars* composer John Williams, sets by *Star Wars* production designer Norman Reynolds and art director Les Dilley, and countless wonderments by Richard Edlund, who supervised the visual effects.

Two things, however, make *Raiders of the Lost Ark* more than just a technological triumph: its sense of humor and the droll style of its characters. This is often a funny movie, but it doesn't get many of its laughs with dialogue and only a few with obvious gags (although the biggest laugh comes from the oldest and most obvious gag, involving a swordsman and a marksman). We find ourselves laughing in surprise, in relief, in incredulity at the movie's ability to pile one incident upon another in an inexhaustible series of inventions. And the personalities of the central characters are enormously winning. Harrison Ford, as Indy Jones, does not do a reprise of his *Star Wars* work. Instead he creates a taciturn, understated, stubborn character who might be the Humphrey Bogart of *The Treasure of the Sierra Madre* with his tongue in his cheek. He survives fires, crushings, shootings, burnings. He really hates snakes. Karen Allen plays the female lead with a resilient toughness that develops its own charm. She can handle herself in any situation. She *really* hates snakes.

Raiders of the Lost Ark is a swashbuckling adventure epic in the tradition of *Star Wars*, *Superman*, the James Bond pictures, and all the other multimillion-dollar special-effects extravaganzas. It wants only to entertain. It succeeds. Watch it with someone you know fairly well. There will be times during the film when it will be necessary to grab somebody.

The Rainbow ★ ★ ★
R, 104 m., 1989

Sammi Davis (Ursula Brangwen), Paul McGann (Anton Skrebensky), Amanda Donohoe (Winifred Inger), Christopher Gable (Will Brangwen), David Hemmings (Uncle Henry), Glenda Jackson (Anna Brangwen), Dudley Sutton (MacAllister), Glenda McKay (Gudron Brangwen). Produced and directed by Ken Russell. Screenplay by Ken and Vivian Russell. Adapted from the novel by D.H. Lawrence.

Although much of D.H. Lawrence's original notoriety in Britain came from the sexual passion in his novels, what offended convention even more, I believe, was his belief that an artistic free spirit need not be concerned with hidebound ideas of social class. When he began to write, in the years before World War I, Britain was a nation of rigid social stratification. Everything depended on who your parents were, and what your accent was. The notion that one could break loose and fly was deeply revolutionary.

In *The Rainbow* and its sequel, *Women in Love*, Lawrence created two modern heroines who refused to have their lives defined by their class and their sex. They were defiant. They were artistic. They were not ashamed to have sexual feelings, just as men did. Although neither novel is even remotely pornographic in the current sense of the word, they were censored, banned, and pilloried when they were first published—attacked by men who feared that such ideas could lead anywhere, could lead even to women demanding the vote. At the time, Lawrence's *The Rainbow* was as controversial as his *Lady Chatterley's Lover*.

Ken Russell, the iconoclastic English director of such wildly different films as *Tommy*, *The Boyfriend*, and *The Lair of the White Worm*, first made his feature-length reputation with the brilliant *Women in Love*, released in 1969. Twenty years later, he is back with a film version of the first novel. The two films are linked by Glenda Jackson, who now plays the mother of the character she played in 1969.

The movie takes place in rural England around the time of the First World War, and centers on the story of Ursula Brangwen (Sammi Davis), daughter of an old-established and respectable farming family, who has no desire to march in step with the requirements of her family tradition. She is restless and inquisitive, and in Winifred, the local school teacher (Amanda Donohoe) she finds an older woman to model herself after.

Winifred is well-read, independent of mind, healthy of body. She is not married, and has become a schoolteacher because teaching and the stage were then two of the few professions in which a single woman could support herself. Her independence makes her a daily offense to the master of the school, one of those coarse male sadists Lawrence could draw so well. But to her students, she is a breath of freedom.

It is from Winifred that Ursula first learns that a woman's life need not be rigidly bound by social convention. They go for walks together and read books together, and Ursula falls in love with the older woman—not into sexual love, although that seems like a possibility, but into idealistic love. This woman becomes a symbol of Ursula's own quest.

But then things go wrong. We have already met Uncle Henry (David Hemmings), the strong-willed, complacent local mine owner. In his own way, he, too, is sexually liberated—although for him that means passing up conventional marriage for the pleasures of the flesh. Ursula is surprised and deeply shocked when Winifred marries Henry. This seems to her like a betrayal of their friendship, but for Winifred it is a hard, realistic choice; for a woman to have power in those days, she had to marry it.

There is also a man in Ursula's life—Anton Skrebensky (Paul McGann), something of a free spirit, who is attracted by Ursula's headstrong love of opinions and ideas. They fall in love, but then Ursula discovers that Anton is not as free as she thought. He talks easily and convincingly about the "woman question," and seems to support her convictions, but in the end he wants a conventional wife, someone whose will has been broken according to society's requirements. *The Rainbow* sets this story against the pastoral beauty of the English countryside, but this is not a nostalgic costume drama, dripping with atmosphere. Russell has kept all of the hurt and anger of Lawrence's fiction. This is a movie that speaks to today, that could feel like an anthem to a young woman who feels that her spirit is not free.

Ken Russell is the most prolific of modern British directors, and the most uneven. Some of his films, like the recent *Gothic*, seem to have been composed and directed in a fit of mania. Others respect more traditional values, and in *The Rainbow* he has made a measured, thoughtful literary adaptation. He obviously believes Lawrence's message is as appropriate now as it was then, and he is right.

Raining Stones ★ ★ ★ ½
NO MPAA RATING, 90 m., 1994

Bruce Jones (Bob), Julie Brown (Anne), Gemma Phoenix (Coleen), Ricky Tomlinson (Tommy), Tom Hickey (Father Barry), Mike Fallon (Jimmy), Ronnie Ravey (Butcher), Lee Brennan (Irishman). Directed by Ken Loach and produced by Sally Hibbin. Screenplay by Jim Allen.

Raining Stones is the latest, the gentlest, and the funniest of Ken Loach's films about working-class life in modern Britain. It tells the stories of men clinging precariously to their self-respect, in a world with no jobs for them. Loach's previous film, *Riff-Raff*, was about itinerant construction workers, who lived in abandoned flats that they "liberated." Here his family still has its own home, but as the film opens the hero, Bob, is trying to steal a sheep.

Bob (Bruce Jones) and his best friend, Tommy (Ricky Tomlinson), hope to sell the sheep to a local butcher. But his price is not right, and they're reduced to making the rounds of the local pubs, with boxes filled with mutton for sale. Bad goes to worse: While they're in one pub, Bob's old van is stolen from out back.

Bob and his wife, Anne (Julie Brown), live with their daughter, Coleen (Gemma Phoenix), in a poor district in the north of England. They are short on funds, but Bob is determined to provide his daughter with a new dress for her first communion. The parish priest tries to talk him out of it (cheaper or secondhand dresses are available), but Bob wants the best for his daughter, and the movie is the story of how he tries to raise the money to buy the dress.

This outline may seem as sentimental as a Chaplin story. Nothing could be further from the truth. Bob is a desperate man in hard times, and his friend Ricky is also unmanned by the lack of a job (his daughter gives him money from her wages or perhaps from drug sales; left alone, he weeps). The two men are ready for anything: stealing green turf, for example, from the lawn of the local Conservative Association.

Loach is not obsessed with plot. We know what Bob needs, and we see him trying to raise the money to get it, but his efforts are as disorganized as his thinking. (The movie is much more realistic about poverty than a

film about the homeless like *With Honors*, with its smoothly whirling plot.) He borrows money from the wrong sorts of men, gets in trouble when he can't pay it back, and is involved by accident in a death that is not his fault, but might seem so.

The screenplay is by Jim Allen, who lives, I understand, in a district much like the one in the film. His dialogue reflects the humor and resiliency of these people living in economic uncertainty, and it's hard to remember a character whose underlying decency and pluck are more attractive than Bob's. More good feeling comes from the character of Father Barry (Tom Hickey), the local priest. Clergymen are so routinely portrayed as humbugs in the movies that it is startling to find a good one, who understands the situation exactly and gives the same advice we would give (but which a priest theoretically should not).

The dialogue is all in the dialect of the district, and is sometimes hard to understand, although I was never in doubt about what essentially was being said. I saw the movie for the first time at the 1993 Edinburgh Film Festival, where about half the British audience also seemed to have trouble with the accents—but agreed, during a Q&A with Loach, that they could understand what was necessary, and that the rest added to the atmosphere. (Stanley Kauffmann, in *The New Republic*, compares the experience to attending an opera in a foreign language: "If we've read a synopsis, we're all right. With Loach, we don't need a synopsis, because we can understand half and fill in the rest.") Loach actually did subtitle *Riff-Raff*, but here, I agree with him, it's not necessary.

The film is good-hearted and the characters are easy to identify with, but what I liked best was the underlying humor, even in this desperate situation. These are characters whose minds have not been deadened and who are naturally articulate and even poetic. Even their obscenities are musical and well-timed, not merely crude. The movies are filled with people who want to win fortunes or blow up the world. I cared more about the first communion dress.

Rain Man ★ ★ ★ ½
R, 128 m., 1988

Dustin Hoffman (Raymond Babbitt), Tom Cruise (Charlie Babbitt), Valeria Golino (Susanna), Jerry Molen (Dr. Bruner), Jack

Murdock (John Mooney), Michael D. Roberts (Vern), Ralph Seymour (Lenny), Lucinda Jenney (Iris), Bonnie Hunt (Sally Dibbs). Directed by Barry Levinson and produced by Mark Johnson. Screenplay by Ronald Bass and Barry Morrow.

Is it possible to have a relationship with an autistic person? Is it possible to have a relationship with a cat? I do not intend the comparison to be demeaning to the autistic; I am simply trying to get at something. I have useful relationships with both of my cats, and they are important to me. But I never know what the cats are thinking. That is precisely the situation that Charlie Babbitt (Tom Cruise) is faced with in *Rain Man*.

His brother, Raymond (Dustin Hoffman), is "high-level" autistic. He can carry on conversations, stick to a schedule, compile baseball statistics, memorize dinner menus, and become disturbed when anything upsets his routine. He can also count 246 spilled toothpicks in an instant, and calculate square roots in a flash. But what is he thinking?

There is a moment in *Rain Man* that crystallizes all the frustrations that Charlie feels about Raymond, a moment when he cries out, "I know there has to be somebody inside there!" But who? And where? *Rain Man* is so fascinating because it refuses to supply those questions with sentimental but unrealistic answers. This is not a movie like *Charly* in which there is a miracle cure.

Rain Man works so well within Raymond's limitations because it is a movie about limitations, particularly Charlie's own limited ability to love those in his life, or to see things from their point of view. As the film opens, we see Charlie frantically trying to juggle his way out of a crisis in his Los Angeles business, which seems to consist of selling expensive imported automobiles out of his hip pocket. He is driven, unhappy, a workaholic. One day he receives word that his father—a man with whom he has had no contact for years—has died back east. At the reading of the will, he learns that he has received a pittance (including a prized 1949 Buick Roadmaster), and that his father's $3 million fortune has gone into a trust.

Who is the trust for? Performing some amateur detective work, Charlie discovers with a shock that it goes to support an older brother he never knew he had—an autistic brother who has been institutionalized for years. Visiting Raymond at the home where he lives, Cruise finds a methodical, mechanical, flat-voiced middle-aged man who "definitely" knows things, such as that tapioca pudding is "definitely" on the menu, and that his favorite TV program is "definitely" about to come on the air.

Rain Man follows this discovery with a story line that is as old as the hills. Angry that he has been cut out of his share of the inheritance, Charlie takes Raymond out of the mental home and vows to bring him to live in California. But Raymond will not fly (he "definitely" recites the dates and fatalities of every airline's most recent crash). And so Charlie puts Raymond in the front seat of the 1949 Buick and they head out on a cross-country odyssey of discovery.

It is an old formula, but a serviceable one, using shots of the car against the sunset as punctuation. The two brothers meet genuine actual Americans on the road, of course, and have strange adventures, of course, and although we have seen this structure in dozens of other movies, it is new this time because for Raymond it is definitely not a voyage of discovery.

Everything changes in the movie except for Raymond. In a roadside diner somewhere along the way, he still stubbornly insists on the routines of the dining room in his mental institution: The maple syrup is definitely supposed to be on the table before the pancakes come. Charlie at first does not quite seem to accept the dimensions of Raymond's world, and grows frustrated at what looks like almost willful intractability. Eventually, toward the end of the journey, he finds that he loves his brother, and that love involves accepting him exactly as he is.

Rain Man is a project that Hoffman and Cruise have been determined to bring to the screen for a long time. Barry Levinson came on board after three previous directors signed off on this material. The problem, of course, was Raymond. If fiction is about change, then how can you make a movie about a man who cannot change, whose whole life is anchored and defended by routine? Few actors could get anywhere with this challenge, and fewer still could absorb and even entertain us with their performance, but Hoffman proves again that he almost seems to thrive on impossible acting challenges. "You want taller?" he says in the audition scene in *Tootsie.* "I can play taller. You want shorter? I can play shorter. You want a tomato?" And he can play autistic.

At the end of *Rain Man,* I felt a certain love for Raymond, the Hoffman character. I don't know quite how Hoffman got me to do it. He does not play cute, or lovable, or pathetic. He is matter-of-fact, straight down the middle, uninflected, unmoved, uncomprehending, in all of his scenes—except when his routine is disrupted, when he grows disturbed until it is restored. And yet I could believe that the Cruise character was beginning to love him, because that was how I felt, too. I loved him for what he was, not for what he was not, or could not be.

The changes in the movie all belong to Charlie, who begins the film as a me-first materialist, a would-be Trump without a line of credit. By the end of the film Charlie has learned how to pay attention, how to listen, and how to be at least a little patient some of the time. He does not undergo a spiritual transformation; he simply gets in touch with things that are more important than selling cars. He is aided in this process by his girlfriend Susanna (Valeria Golino), a Latina who loves him but despairs of ever getting him off autopilot.

By the end of *Rain Man,* what have we learned? I think the film is about acceptance. Charlie Babbitt's first appearance in the movie has him wheeling and dealing in the face of imminent ruin, trying to control his life and the lives of others by blind, arrogant will-power. What Raymond teaches him is that he can relax, because try as he might, he will always be powerless over other people. They will do just about what they choose to do, no matter how loud Charlie Babbitt screams. Raymond has a lot he can teach Charlie about acceptance, even if it is the solitary thing he knows.

Raise the Red Lantern ★ ★ ★ ★
PG, 126 m., 1992

Gong Li (Songlian), Ma Jingwu (Chen Zuoqian), He Caifei (Third Wife), Cao Cui (Second Wife), Jin Shuyuan (First Wife), Kong Lin (Maid). Directed by Zhang Yimou and produced by Chiu Fu-sheng. Screenplay by Su Tong.

The fourth wife of the rich old man comes to live in his house against her will. She has been educated, and thinks herself ready for the wider world, but her mother betrays her, selling her as a concubine, and soon her world is no larger than the millionaire's vast house. Its living quarters are arrayed on either side of a courtyard. There is an apartment for each of the wives. She is quietly informed of the way things work here. A red lantern is raised each night outside the quarters of the wife who will be honored by a visit from the master.

So opens *Raise the Red Lantern,* a Chinese film of voluptuous physical beauty and angry passions. It was one of 1991's Academy Award nominees in the foreign language category, directed by Zhang Yimou, whose *Ju Dou* was nominated in 1990. This film, based on the novel *Wives and Concubines* by Su Tong, can no doubt be interpreted in a number of ways—as a cry against the subjection of women in China, as an attack on feudal attitudes, as a formal exercise in storytelling—and yet it works because it is so fascinating simply on the level of melodrama.

We enter into the sealed world of the rich man's house, and see how jealousies fester in its hothouse atmosphere. Each of the four wives is treated with the greatest luxury, pampered with food and care, servants and massages, but they are like horses in a great racing stable, cared for at the whim of the master. The new wife, whose name is Songlian, is at first furious at her fate. Then she begins to learn the routine of the house, and is drawn into its intrigues and alliances. If you are given only one game to play, it is human nature to try to win it.

Songlian is played by Gong Li, an elegant woman who also starred in quite different roles in Zhang Yimou's two previous films. In *Red Sorghum,* she was a defiant young woman, sold into marriage to a wealthy vintner; she takes over his winery after his death and makes it prosperous with the help of a sturdy peasant who has earlier saved her from rape. In *Ju Dou,* she was the young bride of a wealthy old textile merchant, who enslaved both her and his poor young nephew—with the result that she and the nephew fall in love, and the merchant comes to a colorful end in a vat of his own dyes.

Zhang Yimou is obviously attracted to the theme of the rich, impotent old man and the young wife. But in *Raise the Red Lantern,* it is the system of concubinage that he focuses on. The rich man is nowhere to be seen, except in hints and shadows. He is a patriarchal, offstage presence, as his four wives and the household staff scheme among themselves for his favor.

We meet the serene first wife, who reigns over the other wives and has the wisdom of longest experience in this house. Then there are the resigned second wife and the competitive third wife, who is furious that the master has taken a bride younger and prettier than herself. The servants, including the young woman assigned to Songlian, have their own priorities. And there is Dr. Gao (Cui Zhihgang), who treats the wives, and whose medical judgments are instrumental in the politics of the house. The gossip that whirls among the wives and their servants creates the world for these people; little that happens outside ever leaks in.

Zhang Yimou's visual world here is part of the story. His master shot, which is returned to again and again, looks down the central space of the house, which is open to the sky, with the houses of the wives arrayed on either side, and the vast house of the master at the end. As the seasons pass, the courtyard is sprinkled with snow, or dripping with rain, or bathed in hot, still sunlight. The servants come and go. Up on the roof of the house is a little shed that is sometimes whispered about. It has something to do with an earlier wife who did not adjust well.

Zhang uses the bold, bright colors of *Ju Dou* again this time; his film was shot in the classic three-strip Technicolor process, now abandoned by Hollywood, which allows a richness of reds and yellows no longer possible in American films. There is a sense in which *Raise the Red Lantern* exists solely for the eyes. Entirely apart from the plot, there is the sensuous pleasure of the architecture, the fabrics, the color contrasts, the faces of the actresses. But beneath the beauty is the cruel reality of this life, just as beneath the comfort of the rich man's house is the sin of slavery.

Rambling Rose ★ ★ ★
R, 112 m., 1991

Laura Dern (Rose), Robert Duvall (Daddy), Diane Ladd (Mother), Lukas Haas (Buddy), John Heard (Willcox Hillyer). Directed by Martha Coolidge and produced by Renny Harlin. Screenplay by Calder Willingham.

Here is a movie as light as air, as delicate as a flower. Breathe on it and it will wither. It tells the story of an impossibly sweet and strange Southern family, and the troubled teen-age girl who comes to live with them and brings a sharp awareness of carnality under their roof, with only the most cheerful of results. The screenplay by Calder Willingham is based, I have heard, on autobiographical reminiscence, but nostalgia in this case has bestowed a lot of benevolence onto the past.

The year is 1935. The Hillyer family lives in a spacious old Southern manse with a big lawn and lots of trees and porches, overlooking the road that crosses the creek. There's Daddy (Robert Duvall) and Mother (Diane Ladd) and Buddy (Lukas Haas) and a couple of other kids. One day Rose (Laura Dern) comes to stay with them, walking up the path swinging her cardboard valise like a calling card. She is nineteen years old, and has gotten into unspecified troubles with unspecified men, and to Buddy, who is thirteen, this is a high recommendation.

Daddy is a lawyer who has invited Rose to come and stay with the family, not as a maid but as a guest. "Rosebud," he tells her, "I swear to God you are as graceful as a capital letter 'S.' You'll give a glow and a shine to these old walls." And so she does, bringing as well a glow and shine to Buddy's nocturnal imaginings and adolescent fantasies.

What is special about *Rambling Rose*, however, is the way love takes first place ahead of sex. Although the materials of the story are lurid—Rose is a "borderline nymphomaniac," the local doctor concludes—neither Daddy nor Mother seems shocked by her behavior or flamboyant style of dress. They understand that she has been through some hard times, they accept her as she is, they hope to give her some help in life.

For Buddy, who is at that age when a whisper of décolletage is worth a roomful of schoolbooks, Rose is a godsend. He is fascinated by her guileless sexuality, and there is a breathless scene where he essentially conducts a natural history field trip across her upper body. But Rose is not really interested in Buddy. She loves Daddy with a fierce, burning passion because she admires him so much—worships him, and is eternally grateful that he rescued her from those unspecified men. The way that Duvall handles her passionate advance is one of the treasures of this film.

Rambling Rose was directed by Martha Coolidge, and probably benefited from being made by a woman. Men, I think, are sometimes too single-minded about sex. Bring up the subject, and it's all they can think about. Coolidge takes this essentially lurid story and frames it with humor and compassion, putting sexuality in context, understanding who Rose really is and what stuff the family is really made of.

The plot in *Rambling Rose* is slight and elusive; if it were not for a framing device, it might almost have none. The movie is all

character and situation, and contains some of the best performances of the year, especially in the ensemble acting of the four main characters. Laura Dern finds all of the right notes in a performance that could have been filled with wrong ones; Diane Ladd (her real-life mother) is able to suggest an eccentric yet reasonable Southern belle who knows what is really important; Robert Duvall exudes that most difficult of screen qualities, goodness; and Lukas Haas (the boy in *Witness*) brings to his study of Rose such single-minded passion you would think she was a model airplane.

Rambo: First Blood Part II ★ ★ ★
R, 90 m., 1985

Sylvester Stallone (Rambo), Richard Crenna (Trautman), Charles Napier (Murdock), Steven Berkoff (Podovsky). Directed by George P. Cosmatos and produced by Buzz Feitshans. Screenplay by Stallone and James Cameron.

Rambo, subtitled *First Blood Part II* and continuing the adventures of Sylvester Stallone's one-man army, is two movies in one. First there's a hard-boiled, high-energy, violent action picture, which will probably find a large and enthusiastic audience. Lurking beneath the action is a political statement accusing the U.S. government of such base political motives that I was, quite simply, astonished. *Rambo* is not left wing or right wing, but belongs to the paranoid wing of American politics, in which villains left and right crawl under the covers together and conspire to annihilate John Rambo.

If you saw the original *First Blood*, which was a big hit, you remember Rambo. He is a returned Vietnam hero, a superbly trained fighting machine who is considered by his superior officers to be the finest soldier they have ever seen. But Rambo becomes unhinged by civilian life, and by the insults which he believes society is heaping on men like himself, who risked their lives to fight the war. So Rambo reverts to his military training and turns into a one-man army dedicated to destroying the establishment that does not honor him.

At the end of *First Blood*, Rambo was captured after blowing up half a town and wiping out countless civilian and military authorities. If anyone had been keeping count, he would have qualified as the nation's most prolific mass killer. In the opening scenes of *Rambo*, he is breaking rocks on a chain gang when his old superior officer (Richard Crenna) arrives with a mission: Rambo is needed to parachute into Southeast Asia and scout out a suspected POW compound holding missing Americans. Any questions, Rambo? "Only one," he tells Crenna. "This time, do we get to win?"

His question places *Rambo* squarely within the revisionist genre of Vietnam movies, in which the war is refought with a happy ending. *Uncommon Valor,* the two *Missing in Action* movies, and this film are all about missions to free American MIAs and kill countless Asian soldiers. The basic assumption is that we lost the war because "the politicians" prevented men like Rambo from doing what they were trained to do. And indeed, again this time he has his hands tied: he's only supposed to take pictures, not engage in violence. Needless to say, if they only want pictures, they've picked the wrong mass murderer for the job.

Rambo's mission is outlined by a suspicious American intelligence officer (the square-jawed, rugged Charles Napier, a favorite of Russ Meyer *and* Jonathan Demme). Only after Rambo parachutes into the night does it become clear that Napier doesn't really want the mission to succeed. In logic so impenetrable that I would love to have somebody run it past me again, the movie argues that it would be politically embarrassing for American MIAs to be found at this late date, and that therefore it would be best if Rambo's mission fails. If he *does* come back with photos, they'll be suppressed. In that case, I was wondering, why sponsor the mission in the first place—and especially with a loose cannon like Rambo? No matter; the movie turns into an efficient action picture, with Rambo wiping out legions of North Vietnamese and Russians with a variety of weapons, including explosive-tipped arrows. Back at headquarters, Napier does all he can to sabotage the mission, but it becomes clear that Rambo could have won the Vietnam war by himself, had he been unleashed, and everything leads to a big climax, a helicopter dogfight. The strange thing about *Rambo* is that it works despite its politics. Its conspiracy theory is so angry and so unlikely that we tend to ignore it, sit back, and enjoy the action.

Ran ★ ★ ★ ★
R, 160 m., 1985

Tatsuya Nakadai (Lord Hidetora), Akira Terao (Taro, Eldest Son), Jinpachi Nezu (Jiro,

Second Son), Daisuke Ryn (Sahuro, Youngest Son), Mjeko Harada (Lady Kaede, Taro's Wife), Yoshiko Miyazaki (Lady Sue, Jiro's Wife), Masayuki Yui (Tango, Hidetora's Servant), Peter (Kyoami, The Fool). Directed by Akira Kurosawa and produced by Serge Silberman and Masato Hara. Screenplay by Hideo Oquino, Masato Ide, and Kurosawa.

One of the early reviews of Akira Kurosawa's *Ran* said that he could not possibly have directed it at an earlier age. My first impression was to question that act of critical omnipotence. Who is to say Kurosawa couldn't have made this film at fifty or sixty, instead of at seventy-five, as he has? But then I thought longer about *Ran,* which is based on Shakespeare's *King Lear* and on a similar medieval samurai legend. And I thought about Laurence Olivier's Lear and about the *Lear* I recently saw starring Douglas Campbell and I realized that age is probably a prerequisite to fully understanding this character. Dustin Hoffman might be able to play Willy Loman by aging himself with makeup, but he will have to wait another twenty years to play Lear.

The character contains great paradoxes, but they are not the paradoxes of youth; they spring from long habit. Lear has the arrogance of great power, long held. He has wide knowledge of the world. Yet he is curiously innocent when it comes to his own children; he thinks they can do no wrong, can be trusted to carry out his plans. At the end, when his dreams have been broken, the character has the touching quality of a childlike innocence that can see breath on lips that are forever sealed, and can dream of an existence beyond the cruelties of man. Playing Lear is not a technical exercise. I wonder if a man can do it who has not had great disappointments and long dark nights of the soul.

Kurosawa has lived through those bad times. Here is one of the greatest directors of all time, out of fashion in his own country, suffering from depression, nearly blind. He prepared this film for ten years, drawing hundreds of sketches showing every shot, hardly expecting that the money would ever be found to allow him to make the film. But a deal was finally put together by Serge Silberman, the old French producer who backed the later films of Luis Buñuel (who could also have given us a distinctive Lear). Silberman risked his own money; this is the most expensive Japanese film ever made, and, yes, perhaps Kurosawa could not have made it until he was seventy-five.

The story is familiar. An old lord decides to retire from daily control of his kingdom, yet still keep all the trappings of his power. He will divide his kingdom in three parts among his children. In *Ran,* they are sons, not daughters. First, he requires a ritual statement of love. The youngest son cannot abide the hypocrisy, and stays silent. And so on.

The Japanese legend which Kurosawa draws from contains a famous illustration in which the old lord takes three arrows and demonstrates that when they are bundled, they cannot be broken, but taken one at a time, they are weak. He wishes his sons to remain allies, so they will be strong, but of course they begin to fight, and civil war breaks out as the old lord begins his forlorn journey from one castle to another, gradually being stripped of his soldiers, his pride, his sanity.

Nobody can film an epic battle scene like Kurosawa. He has already abundantly demonstrated that in *The Seven Samurai,* in *Yojimbo,* in *Kagemusha.* In *Ran,* the great bloody battles are counterpointed with scenes of a chamber quality, as deep hatreds and lusts are seen to grow behind the castle's walls.

King Lear is a play that centers obsessively around words expressing negatives. "Nothing? Nothing will come of nothing!" "Never, never, never." "No, no, no, no, no." They express in deep anguish the king's realization that what has been taken apart will never be put together again, that his beloved child is dead and will breathe no more, that his pride and folly have put an end to his happiness. Kurosawa's film expresses that despair perhaps more deeply than a Western film might; the samurai costumes, the makeup inspired by Noh drama, give the story a freshness that removes it from all our earlier associations.

Ran is a great, glorious achievement. Kurosawa must often have associated himself with the old lord as he tried to put this film together, but in the end he has triumphed, and the image I have of him, at seventy-five, is of three arrows bundled together.

Rapa Nui ★ ★
R, 107 m., 1994

Jason Scott Lee (Noro), Esai Morales (Make), Sandrine Holt (Ramana). Directed by Kevin Reynolds and produced by Kevin Costner and Jim Wilson. Screenplay by Tim Rose Price and Reynolds.

Rapa Nui slips through the *National Geographic* Loophole. This is the Hollywood convention that teaches us that brown breasts are not as sinful as white ones, and so while it may be evil to gaze upon a blond *Playboy* centerfold and feel lust in our hearts, it is educational to watch Polynesian maidens frolicking topless in the surf. This isn't sex; it's geography.

For years in my liberal youth I thought this loophole was racist, an evil double standard in which white women were protected from exposure while "native" women were cruelly stripped of their bras, not to mention the equal protection of the MPAA. While watching *Rapa Nui*, in which there are dozens if not hundreds of wonderful bare breasts on view, I have changed my mind. Since women's breasts are the most aesthetically pleasing part of the human anatomy, it is only a blessing if your culture celebrates them.

The movie, which is sublimely silly, takes place in the South Seas in the carefree days before missionaries and other visitors arrived to distribute brassieres, smallpox, and VD. The action takes place on Easter Island, "the navel of the world," whose inhabitants languish under a senile king. The king is of the Long Ear tribe, which has enslaved the Short Ears and impoverished the island by building dozens of giant stone faces. The purpose of the faces is to attract the great White Canoe, which the king believes will carry him off to heaven. No face can be big enough. "Build another one," he tells the slaves at one point. "Then take the rest of the day off."

This is a king, played with superb comic timing by Eru Potaka-Dewes, who has lots of good lines. "Tell me you won't make fish hooks of my thigh bones," he tearfully implores his high priest. The priest, however, has the movie's best line: "I'm busy! I've got chicken entrails to read!" Meanwhile, sweating slaves pull giant sledges and plot rebellion.

The plot stars Jason Scott Lee as Noro, a young Long Ear who has fallen in love with a Short Ear girl, the breathtakingly lovely Ramana (Sandrine Holt). He goes to the chief for permission to marry her, which is granted—but on two conditions. (1) He must win the annual competition among the young men of the island; (2) she must spend six months locked in the darkness of the Cave of the White Virgin.

This is a lot better deal for him than her. The competition, sort of a Polynesian triathlon, requires the young men to climb down a cliff to the sea, swim to an offshore peak, climb the peak, steal the first eggs of spring from birds' nests, swim back with them, climb

the cliff, and present the eggs to the chief. Break an egg, and you're an omelet. Meanwhile, the bride-to-be slowly goes blind in the Cave of the White Virgin, so called because that's what you become after you lose your tan in the dark—always assuming, of course, that you were a virgin to begin with.

Concern for my reputation prevents me from recommending this movie. I wish I had more nerve. I wish I could simply write, "Look, of course it's one of the worst movies ever made. But it has hilarious dialogue, a weirdo action climax, a bizarre explanation for the faces of Easter Island, and dozens if not hundreds of wonderful bare breasts." I am, however, a responsible film critic and must conclude that *Rapa Nui* is a bad film. If you want to see it anyway, of course, that's strictly your concern. I think I may check it out again myself.

The Rapture ★ ★ ★ ★
R, 92 m., 1991

Mimi Rogers (Sharon), David Duchovny (Randy), Patrick Bauchau (Vic), Kimberly Cullum (Mary), Will Patton (Sheriff Foster). Directed by Michael Tolkin and produced by Nick Wechsler, Nancy Tenenbaum, and Karen Koch. Screenplay by Tolkin.

As flies to wanton boys, are we to the gods; They kill us for their sport.

—Shakespeare, *King Lear*

Her life is a bleak and sinful void. She finds God and is reborn. But then, after a period during which she finds peace through her new beliefs, her life becomes a void again—this time, on God's terms. Sharon, the woman played brilliantly and courageously by Mimi Rogers in *The Rapture*, is a character like Job, tested by God to the breaking point. Unlike Job, she finally refuses to be toyed with any longer.

Her story is told in one of the most challenging and infuriating movies I've seen—a radical, uncompromising treatment of the Christian teachings about the final judgment. Almost all movies with a religious theme are made by people who are themselves religious, or who piously pretend to be. *The Rapture*, written and directed by Michael Tolkin, is seen from a more literal, skeptical point of view: All right, he seems to be saying, if this is what the end of creation is going to be like, then we should stare unblinking at its full and terrifying implications.

As the movie opens, Sharon and her lover, Vic (Patrick Bauchau), are swingers, mate-swappers who cruise the bars together, looking for likely prospects. When they find others who want to swing, they go home for sexual games that Sharon finds increasingly unrewarding. Is this all life is—partying all night and spending her days in a tiny cubicle, working as an operator for the telephone company?

Tolkin uses Sharon's daytime job as a metaphor for modern man, who communicates more easily than ever before, but more impersonally. Sharon's job requires her to talk to hundreds of people all day long, but in a mechanical way. Her nighttime sex life is almost a reaction to the sterile existence of her days.

Then she overhears some of her co-workers talking during a lunch break about "the rapture," about the imminent Second Coming of Christ, about "the boy," who is their prophet. She is curious, and is taken to one of their meetings, and finds that all over the world some people are sharing the same dream of the imminent end of the world. It is a dream she has herself. Torn between her sinful existence and the hope of these believers, she attempts to commit suicide, but instead experiences an overwhelming spiritual experience and is born again.

Ah, but the movie does not lead us where we expect it to go after her experience. She leaves Vic, she finds a partner who is spiritually healthier, she has a daughter, she leads a blameless life, and then, when the girl is about six, Sharon becomes convinced that the Second Coming is imminent. She goes out into the wilderness with her daughter to await the moment when she expects God to gather the two of them into heaven. And she waits. And waits. And a national park policeman takes pity on them, as they stand under the merciless sun.

Sharon is guilty, I believe, of the sin of pride. She thinks she knows when, and how, God will call her. God does not perform according to her timetable. And yet Tolkin does not cheat us with an ending in which Sharon is simply seen as deluded. God does exist in this film, and he does make judgments about individuals such as Sharon, and the world does end, with the fearsome horsemen of the apocalypse in the sky, and the bars falling from the doors of the prison cells.

It is simply that, by the time of the judgment, Sharon has had enough. She commits a shocking action; she tries to stand firm and unflinching in her faith, but she finally comes to believe that God has asked too much of her. Her actions in the last twenty minutes of this film send audiences boiling out of the theater engaged in fierce discussions. After decades of "religious" films that were simply sentimentalized fables, here is a film that demands its audiences make their own peace with the rules of an inflexible diety.

Watching the film, I began to realize that I would feel cheated if Tolkin did not give us some vision of heaven—did not take Sharon to another plane, in one way or another. He does not cheat us, and the closing passages of this film are stunning in their implications. It is true that on a limited budget *The Rapture* is not able to give us sensational special effects—a state-of-the-art heaven, if you will. It doesn't matter. He gives us an idea of heaven that transcends any possible special effect, and brings us face to face with the awful, and awe-full, consequences of that day when the saints go marching in.

Ready to Wear ★ ★ ½
R, 133 m., 1994

NEW

Sophia Loren (Isabella de la Fontaine), Julia Roberts (Anne Eisenhower), Tim Robbins (Joe Flynn), Kim Basinger (Kitty Potter), Danny Aiello (Major Hamilton), Marcello Mastroianni (Sergei [Sergio]), Lauren Bacall (Slim Chrysler), Sally Kellerman (Sissy Wanamaker). Directed by Robert Altman and produced by Altman. Screenplay by Altman and Barbara Shulgasser.

The truth is, there *is* a lot of doggy-do in Paris. Robert Altman has been attacked in some quarters for making a Paris movie in which people are always stepping in it and wiping it off their feet. The amazing thing is that all French movies aren't filled with it. Gérard Depardieu should be as famous for his footwork as for his dramatic range. The French take their dogs with them everywhere. I was in a French restaurant once when a guy came in with his dog and had the dog sit right at the table with him. The maitre d' rushed over and told the guy he couldn't be served unless he buttoned his shirt.

Altman's *Ready to Wear*, originally titled *Pret-a-Porter* before it was figured out that Americans speak English, uses doggie calling cards as a motif for the French fashion industry, in which people are always stepping in something, so to speak. The fashion industry is the most sublimely silly of human

enterprises, making billions by convincing most of the human race to dress interchangeably and the rest to dress like the victims of a cruel jest. Once a year the industry gathers in Paris for the annual "ready to wear" shows, at which designers trot out their new clothes and the world's fashion press has a great time. Altman has chosen this ritual as the latest target for one of his cheerfully rude human comedies, and boy, has the bleep hit the fan.

The movie is a "hate letter" to the fashion industry, sniffed *Time* magazine's Richard Corliss, adding, "when you hear the word *contempt*, you think of Robert Altman." Funny. When I hear the word *contempt* I think of Kurt Cobain. So there you are. Lots of other people are also offended by Altman's irreverent view of the fashion industry's delicate egos, but the purpose of a movie like *Ready to Wear* is not to play fair or be objective—but to entertain.

Is *Ready to Wear* entertaining? Not as much as I would have preferred. I think Altman and his writer, Barbara Shulgasser, should have gone further and been meaner; too many of his jokes are generic slapstick, instead of being aimed squarely at industry targets. If there had been a way, for example, to work in more about anorexia and bulimia, booming diseases the fashion industry shares responsibility for, that would have been fine with me.

As it is, Altman assembles a huge cast of characters (the movie is like a reunion of everyone he has ever worked with) and heaves them into a cauldron of a plot which crosses paths, lives, and swords. A running narration has been one of his favorite devices since the loudspeaker announcements in *M*A*S*H* and *Brewster McCloud*, and this time it's supplied by Kim Basinger, as a breathlessly dimwitted cable reporter who says everything just a little wrong.

Other characters include a smarmy photographer (Stephen Rea) and the three fashion magazine editors (short Linda Hunt, tall Sally Kellerman, and British Tracey Ullman) who are all trying to hire him; old lovers from Rome (Sophie Loren and Marcello Mastroianni) who meet after many years; a snotty designer (Richard E. Grant) who learns his favorite model is pregnant; a transvestite buyer for Marshall Field's (Danny Aiello); the mistress (Anouk Aimee) of a widely hated fashion czar whose death much cheers everyone; and two American reporters (Tim Robbins and Julia Roberts) who spend most of the time in bed, drinking and making love.

At least one fashion reporter has protested that the depiction of this last couple is libelously inaccurate. I dunno. Maybe things like that don't happen on the fashion beat. At a movie premiere once, I happened upon two of my colleagues having sex in the bathroom of a hospitality suite. So there you are.

The movie's many story strands are loosely woven; we glimpse people in the background of one shot and then learn more about them later, as Altman builds the sense of a community. One of the liberating things about his style, in such films as *M*A*S*H*, *McCabe and Mrs. Miller*, *Nashville* and *The Player*, is that he doesn't focus on a small group of foreground actors, but lets you see how his characters are part of a communal setting. Individual egos clash with the group's view of itself.

There are some nice moments here. Robbins and Roberts, who hardly leave their room, create the bittersweet sense of a self-contained affair that has no reference to their real lives, past or future, and will wither on exposure to reality. Loren and Mastroianni, rerunning the striptease scene from *Yesterday, Today and Tomorrow* (1964), find a kind of elegiac tone that reminded me of a magical moment from Fellini's final film, *Intervista*, where Mastroianni and Anita Ekberg remembered their great fountain scene from *La Dolce Vita*. And Basinger's tortured journalese is very funny.

There is also an undeniable pleasure simply in people-watching. In *Ready to Wear* you will see Lauren Bacall, Harry Belafonte, Teri Garr, Forest Whitaker, Naomi Campbell, Lyle Lovett, Christy Turlington, Cher, and countless others, sometimes shot in scenes that feel improvised in the midst of real events. The result is a little like a comedy crossed with a home movie.

It is also, like many home movies, somewhat rambling, and too much dependent on knowing the names of all the players. If you know nothing about the fashion industry, your enjoyment of *Ready to Wear* is likely to be limited. If you know everything about it, your reaction, judging from the early returns, is likely to be purple-faced rage. That leaves, let's see, people who know something about the long and wonderful career of Robert Altman, and who are likely to find this film, if not among his best, very nice to have, all the same.

Real Genius ★ ★ ★ ½
PG-13, 105 m., 1985

Val Kilmer (Chris Knight), William Atherton (Professor Hathaway), Gabe Jarret (Mitch), Michelle Meyrink (Jordan Cochran), Jonathan Gries (Laslo [recluse]), Robert Prescott (Kent Torokvei), Severn Darden (Dr. Meredith). Directed by Martha Coolidge and produced by Brian Grazer. Screenplay by Neal Israel, Pat Proft, and Peter Torokvei.

It is probably not true that all American college students have been lobotomized and pumped full of sex hormones, although most movies treat them that way. Some students are more like the ones we meet in *Real Genius*. They are smart but socially uncertain and relativity is easier for them to understand than what to say on a first date. This is the first movie in a long time that's set on a college campus where the students are supposed to be intelligent. The campus is apparently Cal Tech, and the students are the next generation of great physicists, the kind who will write papers proving that everything we know is wrong.

The movie involves the saga of Mitch (Gabe Jarret), a brilliant high school student whose Science Fair project has revised the theory of laser beam technology. He is personally recruited by Prof. Hathaway (William Atherton), a famous physics professor who wants the kid to work in his personal laboratory. Once on campus, the kid meets the legendary Chris Knight (Val Kilmer), who was the most brilliant freshman in history, and who is now a junior whose mind is beginning to be cluttered by mischief. The two students room together—and there seems to be a third person in the room, a strange, wraith-like bearded figure who disappears into the clothes closet, and doesn't seem to be there when the door is flung open.

The professor is running a scam. He has a Defense Department contract for a sophisticated laser device so accurate that it could incinerate a single man on earth from a base in orbit. The professor is using his students as slave labor to do most of the work on the project while ripping off the government grant to build himself a new house. The students, meanwhile, have no idea they're working on a weapons system, and are more interested in using laser beams to lead everyone to a "Tanning Invitational" they've set up by turning a lecture hall into a swimming pool.

Real Genius allows every one of its charac-ters the freedom to be complicated and quirky and individual. That's especially true of Jordan (Michelle Meyrink), a hyperactive woman student who talks all the time and never sleeps and knits things without even thinking about it, and follows Mitch into the john because she's so busy explaining something that she doesn't even notice what he's doing. I could recognize students like this from my own undergraduate days. One of the most familiar types on campus (and one of the rarest in the movies) is the self-styled eccentric, who develops a complex of weird personality traits as a way of clearing space and defining himself.

Real Genius was directed by Martha Coolidge, who made *Valley Girl*, one of the best and most perceptive recent teen-age movies. What I like best about her is that she gives her characters the freedom to be themselves. They don't have to be John Belushi clones, or fraternity jocks, or dumb coeds. They can flourish in all of their infinite variety, as young people with a world of possibilities and a lot of strange, beautiful notions. *Real Genius* contains many pleasures, but one of the best is its conviction that the American campus contains life as we know it.

Re-Animator ★ ★ ★
NO MPAA RATING, 95 m., 1985

Jeffrey Combs (Herbert West), Bruce Abbott (Dan Cain), Barbara Crampton (Megan Halsey), David Gale (Dr. Carl Hill), Robert Sampson (Dean Halsey), Gerry Glack (Mace), Carolyn Purdy-Gordon (Dr. Harrod). Directed by Stuart Gordon and produced by Brian Yuzna. Screenplay by Dennis Paoli, William J. Morris, and Gordon.

One of the most boring experiences on Earth is a trash movie without the courage of its lack of convictions. If it only wants to be cynical, it becomes lifeless in every moment—a bad dream on the screen. One of the pleasures of the movies, however, is to find a movie that chooses a disreputable genre and then tries with all its might to transcend the genre, to go over the top into some kind of artistic vision, however weird.

Stuart Gordon's *Re-Animator* is a pleasure like that, a frankly gory horror movie that finds a rhythm and a style that make it work in a cockeyed, offbeat sort of way. It's charged up by the tension between the director's desire to make a good movie and his realization that few movies about mad scientists and dead body parts are ever likely to be very good. The temptation is to take a camp approach to the material, to mock it, as Paul Morrissey did in *Andy Warhol's Frankenstein*. Gordon resists that temptation, and creates a livid, bloody, deadpan exercise in the theater of the undead.

Seeing this movie at the Cannes Film Festival, I walked in with no particular expectations, except that I hoped *Re-Animator* would be better than the festival's run-of-the-mill exploitation films. I walked out somewhat surprised and reinvigorated (if not re-animated) by a movie that had the audience emitting taxi whistles and wild goat cries. In its own way, on its own terms, in its corrupt genre, this movie worked as well as any other movie in the festival.

I was reminded of Pauline Kael's sane observation: "The movies are so rarely great art, that if we can't appreciate great trash, there is little reason for us to go."

The movie's story involves . . . but why bother? In the ads, the hero was described as having a good head on his shoulders, and another one in the laboratory dish in front of him. That more or less captures the essence of *Re-Animator*. Driven by an insane desire to vindicate himself by creating living beings out of dead body parts, a scientist uses his intelligence to burrow more and more deeply into sheer madness.

Gordon's direction, and particularly his use of special effects, will come as no surprise to anyone who saw his famous *Warp* trilogy onstage. He borrows from the traditions of comic-book art and B-grade thrillers, using his special effects not as set pieces for us to study, but as dazzling throwaways as the action hurtles ahead. By the end of the film, we are keenly aware that nothing of consequence has happened, but so what? We have been assaulted by a lurid imagination, amazed by unspeakable sights, blind-sided by the movie's curiously dry sense of humor. I guess that's our money's worth.

Red ★ ★ ★ ★
R, 95 m., 1994

Irene Jacob (Valentine), Jean-Louis Trintignant (the Judge), Frederique Feder (Karin), Jean-Pierre Lorit (Auguste), Samuel Lebihan (Photographer), Marion Stalens (Veterinarian), Teco Celio (Barman), Bernard Escalon (Record Salesman). Directed by Krzysztof Kieslowski and produced by Marin Karmitz and Gerard Ruey. Screenplay by Krzysztof Piesiewicz and Kieslowski.

At this moment, in this café, we're sitting next to strangers. Everyone will get up, leave, and go their own way. And then, they'll never meet again. And if they do, they won't realize that it's not for the first time.

—Krzysztof Kieslowski

One of the opening images in *Red* is of telephone lines, crossing. It is the same in life. We are connected with some people and never meet others, but it could easily have happened otherwise. Looking back over a lifetime, we describe what happened as if it had a plan. To fully understand how accidental and random life is—how vast the odds are against any single event taking place—would be humbling.

That is the truth that Kieslowski keeps returning to in his work. In *The Double Life of Veronique,* there is even a moment when, if the heroine had looked out of a bus window, she might have seen herself on the street; it's as if fate allowed her to continue on one lifeline after choosing another. In *Red,* none of the major characters know each other at the beginning of the movie, and there is no reason they should meet. Exactly.

The film opens in Geneva, in an apartment occupied by a model named Valentine (Irene Jacob). She makes a telephone call, and the phone rings at the same time in an apartment just across the street, occupied by Auguste (Jean-Pierre Lorit), a law student. But she is not calling him. Her call is to her boyfriend, who is in England, and who she rarely sees. As far as we know, Valentine and Auguste have never met. And may never meet. Or perhaps they will.

One day Valentine's car strikes a dog, and she takes it to the home of its owner, a retired judge (Jean-Louis Trintignant). He hardly seems to care for the dog, or for her. He spends his days in an elaborate spying scheme, using wiretaps to monitor an affair being carried on by a neighbor. There is an instant spark that strikes between the old man and the young woman—a contact, a recognition of similarity, or sympathy—but they are forty years apart in age, and strangers to one another, and have met by accident, and . . .

The story becomes completely fascinating. We have no idea where it is going, where it could possibly go. There is no plot to reassure us. No goal that the characters hope to attain. Will the young woman and the judge ever meet again? What will come of that? Does it matter? Would it be good, or bad?

Such questions, in *Red,* become infinitely more interesting than the questions in simpleminded commercial movies, about whether the hero will kill the bad guys, and drive his car fast, and blow things up, or whether his girlfriend will take off her clothes. Seeing a movie like *Red,* we are reminded that watching many commercial films is the cinematic equivalent of reading *Dick and Jane.* The mysteries of everyday life are so much deeper and more exciting than the contrivances of plots.

We learn something about Auguste, the law student who lives across the way. He has a girlfriend named Karin (Frederique Feder). She specializes in "personal weather reports" for her clients, which sounds reasonable, something like having a personal trainer or astrologer, until we reflect that the weather is more or less the same for everybody. But perhaps her clients live in such tight boxes of their own construction that each one has different weather.

Valentine talks to her boyfriend. They are rarely together. He is someone on the phone. Perhaps she "stays" with him to save herself the trouble of a lover whose life she would actually share. She goes back out to the house of the old judge, and talks to him some more. We learn more about the lives he is eavesdropping on. There are melodramatic developments, but no one seems to feel strongly about them.

And Valentine and Auguste. What a good couple they would make! Perhaps. If they ever meet. And if, in the endless reaches of cosmic time, there had been the smallest shift in the lifetimes of Valentine and the judge, they could have been the same age. Or another infinitesimal shift, and they would have lived a century apart. Or never lived at all. Or if the dog had wandered somewhere else, Valentine would not have struck him, and met the judge. Or if the judge had had a cat . . .

Think about these things, reader. Don't sigh and turn the page. Think that I have written them and you have read them, and the odds against either of us ever having existed are greater by far than one to all of the atoms in creation.

Red is the conclusion of Kieslowski's masterful trilogy, after *Blue* and *White,* named for the colors in the French flag. At the end of *Red* the major characters from all three films meet—through a coincidence, naturally. This is the kind of film that makes you feel intensely alive while you're watching it, and sends you out into the streets afterward eager to talk deeply and urgently, to the person you are with. Whoever that happens to be.

Red Heat ★ ★ ★
R, 106 m., 1988

Arnold Schwarzenegger (Ivan Danko), James Belushi (Art Ridzik), Peter Boyle (Lou Donnelly), Ed O'Ross (Viktor Rostavili), Larry Fishburne (Lt. Stobbs), Gina Gershon (Cat Manzetti), Marjorie Bransfield (Waitress). Directed by Walter Hill and produced by Hill and Gordon Carroll. Screenplay by Harry Kleiner, Hill, and Troy Kennedy Martin.

Red Heat is not the first movie about a couple of very different cops, and it will not be the last, but as the formula goes, this is a superior example. It's an action picture with a sense of humor and slyly comic performances by Arnold Schwarzenegger and James Belushi, and it's an example of slick professionalism.

Hollywood calls movies like this "high concept" pictures, because you can summarize the plot in a few words, and the words could go like this: Schwarzenegger plays a tough Russian cop who follows a criminal to Chicago and teams up with Belushi as a Chicago slob who knows more about clout than *glasnost.* Take that line and you have the movie. All you have to do is plug in a plot and some shoot-outs and chase scenes.

The man who directed and co-wrote *Red Heat* is Walter Hill, and he is a master at doing just that. Hill specializes in male buddy and action movies, and he more or less reinvented this genre with *48 Hours* and its pairing of Nick Nolte and Eddie Murphy. One of the nice things about *Red Heat* is that it doesn't rip off Hill's earlier picture (except for the basic concept, of course), and finds new things to say about an odd couple of law enforcement.

The Schwarzenegger character is a straight-arrow Russian cop, all business, muscular and tough. The Belushi character is the kind of cop who doesn't believe in busting his buns every second of every day, and who is capable of advising his Soviet comrade to lighten up. He is assigned to Schwarzenegger as sort of a guide and bodyguard, and together they stumble across the usual assortment of weirdos and conspiracies.

What actually happens in the plot is fairly unimportant in movies like this. Style is everything, and if there is a rapport between the two stars, then everything else falls into place. *Red Heat* works because Schwarzenegger and Belushi are both basically comic actors; Arnold's whole career is based on his ability to see the humor in apparently hard-boiled situations. That doesn't mean the actors stand around cracking one-liners, but that even the straight sequences are setups for later payoffs, and you get the quiet feeling that both actors are amused by the material.

The premise is that Schwarzenegger, nicknamed Iron Jaw, would rather die than bend, and that Belushi would rather bend than die. Confronted with the capitalistic excesses of Chicago, Schwarzenegger has some conventional Russian criticisms, and Belushi responds with dialogue that often sounds ad-libbed, even if it's not. The two of them both have to placate the hard-boiled captain (Peter Boyle), who issues stern warnings when they violate departmental procedure. At one point, Belushi is actually taken off the case, although that, of course, doesn't change any of his behavior. Boyle's role is the thankless one in the film; the stern chief is the oldest cliché in cop movies, with his obligatory lectures on protocol to tough cops who shift back and forth on their feet like guilty schoolboys.

The film is punctuated by violence, a great deal of violence, although most of it is exaggerated comic-book style instead of being truly gruesome. Walking that fine line is a speciality of Hill, who once simulated the sound of a fist on a chin by making tape recordings of Ping-Pong paddles slapping leather sofas.

Red Rock West ★ ★ ★ ½
R, 98 m., 1994

Nicolas Cage (Michael), J.T. Walsh (Wayne), Dennis Hopper (Lyle), Lara Flynn Boyle (Suzanne), Timothy Carhart (Deputy Greytack), Dwight Yoakam (Truck Driver). Directed by John Dahl and produced by Sigurjon Sighvatsson and Steve Golin. Screenplay by John Dahl and Rick Dahl.

Red Rock West is a diabolical movie that exists sneakily between a Western and a thriller, between a *film noir* and a black comedy. When I saw it at the Toronto Film Festival in 1992, I assumed it would be arriving in theaters in a few weeks. Instead, it almost missed theatrical release altogether, maybe because it's so hard to categorize. After playing on cable and being released on video, it was booked into the Roxie Theater in San Francisco, whose owner liked it so much he thought it deserved to be seen on the big screen. After breaking the theater's house record for any

feature, it is now going into theaters around the country.

No wonder. This is a movie like *Blood Simple* (which it somewhat resembles) or the David Lynch movies, constructed out of passion, murder, revenge, and a quirky sense of humor. The plot is incredibly complicated. It is also easy to follow and, eventually, makes perfect sense. This kind of lovingly contrived melodrama requires juicy actors, who can luxuriate in the ironies of a scene, and the movie has them: Nicolas Cage, J.T. Walsh, Dennis Hopper, and Lara Flynn Boyle. They must have had a lot of fun with this material.

The movie stars Cage as a poor but honest drifter who arrives, nearly broke, in the small Western town of Red Rock. He walks into the local saloon, and is mistaken by the owner (Walsh) as the professional killer from Texas that Walsh has hired to murder his wife (Boyle). Cage plays along with the joke, collects an advance on the hit, and goes out to Walsh's ranch to visit the wife. There is, of course, an immediate sexual attraction between them. He thinks it only fair to let her in on the secret. She then offers to pay Cage to murder her husband.

So Cage has two offers on the table when a stranger (Dennis Hopper) drives into town. This is, of course, the *real* hit man from Texas. Walsh is not amused to discover he has paid an advance to the wrong man.

Okay. So that's the setup. It's ingenious, but it doesn't even begin to suggest the pleasures of this movie, which depend less on plot than on the reactions of the characters to finding themselves in such a plot. Cage's drifter is especially interesting, because most of the time he's operating without a good idea of the whole situation; he has to keep quiet and look like he knows what the others think he knows.

At some fundamental level, all he really wants to do is get out of Red Rock and never come back again, and the movie's running gag is that he keeps leaving town and finding himself returning to it. The "Welcome to Red Rock" sign turns up in the movie like a signpost in a nightmare. And eventually it's clear that Cage, and all of the others, are going to be trapped there until they bring their deadly quadrangle to some sort of conclusion.

J.T. Walsh, whose character has secrets I will not reveal, is an interesting movie villain because he seems so superficially open and honest (one of his first big roles, significantly,

was as a Chicago alderman in *Backdraft*). Other villains snarl and bluster. He desperately tries to reason things through, to appeal to logic or to dependable strategies like threats. In a way he's the most confused by the labyrinthine situations he finds himself in, since they don't seem to respond to reasonable strategies.

Hopper plays a version of the character he has become famous for: the smiling, charming, cold-blooded killer with a screw loose. All he really wants to do is collect his money and do his job, and he only gets dangerous when he realizes how thoroughly a simple hit has been screwed up. Lara Flynn Boyle, cool under fire, diabolical in her ingenuity, has both Cage and the audience wondering how she really thinks about him; one of the pleasures the movie saves until the very end is a revelation of what she really values, and why.

Red Rock West was directed by John Dahl, who cowrote it with his brother, Rick. John was thirty-four, Rick was twenty-eight, and this was their second feature. It's the kind of movie made by people who love movies, have had some good times at them, and want to celebrate the very texture of old genres like the Western and the *film noir*. In a sense, we've been in Red Rock many times before: It's a town where plots lie in wait for unsuspecting visitors, where hatred runs deep, where love is never enough of a motive for doing anything when cash is available.

Reds ★ ★ ★ ½
PG, 200 m., 1981

Warren Beatty (John Reed), Diane Keaton (Louise Bryant), Edward Herrmann (Max Eastman), Jerzy Kosinski (Zinoviev), Jack Nicholson (Eugene O'Neill), Maureen Stapleton (Emma Goldman), Paul Sorvino (Louis Fraina), Gene Hackman (Pete Van Wherry). Directed and produced by Warren Beatty. Screenplay by Beatty and Trevor Griffiths.

The original John Reed was a dashing young man from Portland who knew a good story when he found one, and, when he found himself in the midst of the Bolshevik revolution, wrote a book called *Ten Days That Shook the World* and made himself a famous journalist. He never quite got it right again after that. He became embroiled in the American left-wing politics of the 1920s, participated in fights between factions of the Socialist Party and the new American Communist Party, and finally returned to Moscow on a series of noble fool's errands that led up, one way or another, to his death from tuberculosis and kidney failure in a Russian hospital. He is the only American buried within the Kremlin walls.

That is Reed's story in a nutshell. But if you look a little more deeply you find a man who was more than a political creature. He was also a man who wanted to be where the action was, a radical young intellectual who was in the middle of everything in the years after World War I, when Greenwich Village was in a creative ferment and American society seemed, for a brief moment, to be overturning itself. It is that personal, human John Reed that Warren Beatty's *Reds* takes as its subject, although there is a lot, and maybe too much, of the political John Reed as well. The movie never succeeds in convincing us that the feuds between the American socialist parties were much more than personality conflicts and ego-bruisings, so audiences can hardly be expected to care which faction is "the" American party of the left.

What audiences can, and possibly will, care about, however, is a traditional Hollywood romantic epic, a love story written on the canvas of history, as they used to say in the ads. And *Reds* provides that with glorious romanticism, surprising intelligence, and a consistent wit. It is the thinking man's *Doctor Zhivago*, told from the other side, of course. The love story stars Warren Beatty and Diane Keaton, who might seem just a tad unlikely as casting choices, but who are immediately engaging and then grow into solid, plausible people on the screen. Keaton is a particular surprise. I had somehow gotten into the habit of expecting her to be a touchy New Yorker, sweet, scared, and intellectual. Here, as a Portland dentist's wife who runs away with John Reed and eventually follows him halfway around the world, through blizzards and prisons and across icy steppes, she is just what she needs to be: plucky, healthy, exasperated, loyal, and funny.

Beatty, as John Reed, is also surprising. I expected him to play Reed as a serious, noble, heroic man for all seasons, and so he does, sometimes. But there is in Warren Beatty's screen persona a persistent irony, a way of kidding his own seriousness, that takes the edge off a potentially pretentious character and makes him into one of God's fools. Beatty plays Reed but does not beatify him: He permits the silliness and boyishness to coexist with the self-conscious historical mission.

The action in the movie takes Reed to

Russia and back again to Portland, and off again with Louise Bryant (Keaton), and then there is a lengthy pause in Greenwich Village and time enough for Louise to have a sad little love affair with the morosely alcoholic playwright Eugene O'Neill (Jack Nicholson). Then there are other missions to Moscow, and heated political debates in New York basements, and at one point I'm afraid I entirely lost track of exactly why Reed was running behind a horsecart in the middle of some forgotten battle in an obscure backwater of the Russian empire. The fact is, Reed's motivation from moment to moment is not the point of the picture. The point is that a revolution is happening, human societies are being swept aside, a new class is in control—or so it seems—and for an insatiably curious young man, that is exhilarating, and it is enough.

The heart of the film is in the relationship between Reed and Bryant. There is an interesting attempt to consider her problems as well as his. She leaves Portland because she is sick unto death of small talk. She wants to get involved in politics, in art, in what's happening: She is so inexorably drawn to Greenwich Village that if Reed had not taken her there, she might have gone on her own. If she was a radical in Portland, however, she is an Oregonian in the Village, and she cannot compete conversationally with such experienced fast-talkers as the anarchist Emma Goldman (Maureen Stapleton). In fact, no one seems to listen to her or pay much heed, except for sad Eugene O'Neill, who is brave enough to love her but not smart enough to keep it to himself. The ways in which she edges toward O'Neill, and then loyally returns to Reed, create an emotional density around her character that makes it really *mean* something when she and Reed embrace at last in a wonderful tear-jerking scene in the Russian train station.

The whole movie finally comes down to the fact that the characters matter to us. Beatty may be fascinated by the ins and outs of American left-wing politics sixty years ago, but he is not so idealistic as to believe an American mass audience can be inspired to care as deeply. So he gives us people. And they are seen here with such warmth and affection that we sense new dimensions not only in Beatty and Keaton, but especially in Nicholson. In *Reds*, understanding his desire, apologizing for his passion, hanging around Louise, handing her a poem, throwing her out of his life, he is quieter but much more

passionate than in the overwrought *The Postman Always Rings Twice*.

As for Beatty, *Reds* is his bravura turn. He got the idea, nurtured it for a decade, found the financing, wrote most of the script, produced, and directed and starred and still found enough artistic detachment to make his Reed into a flawed, fascinating enigma instead of a boring archetypal hero. I liked this movie. I felt a real fondness for it. It was quite a subject to spring on the capitalist Hollywood movie system, and maybe only Beatty could have raised $35 million to make a movie about a man who hated millionaires. I noticed, here at the end of the credits, a wonderful line that reads:

Copyright © MCMLXXXI Barclays Mercantile Industrial Finance Limited.
John Reed would have loved that.

The Ref ★ ★ ★
R, 97 m., 1994

Denis Leary (Gus), Judy Davis (Caroline), Kevin Spacey (Lloyd), Robert J. Steinmiller, Jr. (Jesse), Glynis Johns (Rose), Raymond J. Barry (Huff), Richard Bright (Murray), Christine Baranski (Connie). Directed by Ted Demme and produced by Ron Boxman, Richard LaGravenese, and Jeff Weiss. Screenplay by LaGravenese and Marie Weiss.

The Ref is a flip-flopped, updated version of O. Henry's "The Ransom of Red Chief," in which a kidnapper naps more than he was counting on. The movie stars sometime stand-up comic Denis Leary as Gus, a would-be jewel thief who sets off an alarm in a private house in an affluent Connecticut hamlet, and in desperation kidnaps a married couple on Christmas Eve and orders them to drive to their home.

Once there, he assumes, he will have time to plot his next move. But he doesn't get a moment's peace, because the couple he has kidnapped, Caroline and Lloyd, have been fighting for years, are constantly at each other's throats, and are both completely incapable of surrendering in an argument.

The couple, played by Judy Davis and Kevin Spacey, are smart, bitter, and articulate—and boy, can they fight. Gus is almost forgotten at times; he has a gun, but he can't get the floor. He tries to explain: "People with guns can do whatever they want. Married people without guns—for instance, you—do not get to yell! Why? No guns! No guns, no yelling! See? Simple little quiz!"

That doesn't stop them for a second. After the kidnapper demands rope to tie them up, for example, Lloyd says they don't have any, but Caroline helpfully remembers some bungee cord in the kitchen, and that sets off Lloyd, who thinks his wife is being cooperative because she's attracted to the criminal. Caroline explains that she was frightened: "Humans get frightened because they have feelings. Didn't your alien leaders teach you that before they sent you here?"

The situation at the house grows even more desperate after the couple's young son arrives home from military school. The kid is a conniver who has made piles of money by blackmailing a teacher (named Siskel) at his military academy, and now he's impressed by Gus and basically welcomes new excitement in his life. *And* all of Lloyd's hated relatives are scheduled to arrive shortly for a holiday supper.

At some point during this process, the relationship between Gus and his victims subtly shifts; he becomes not so much the kidnapper as the peacemaker. He tries to enforce silence, truces, agreements. The couple begin to cooperate with him, maybe because they're afraid of his gun, but more likely because the situation takes on a logic of its own. (It's pretty clear Gus isn't going to shoot them.) Lloyd's relatives know the couple has been seeing a marriage counselor, and so it's agreed that Gus will pretend to be the marriage counselor so that the kidnapper can continue right through the Christmas Eve gathering.

Material like this is only as good as the acting and writing. *The Ref* is skillful in both areas. Denis Leary, who has a tendency, like many stand-up comics, to start shouting and try to make points with overkill, here creates an entertaining character. And Davis and Spacey, both naturally verbal, develop a manic counterpoint in their arguments that elevates them to a sort of art form.

There are a lot of supporting characters in the story: the relatives, with their own problems; the local police chief; Gus's rummy-dummy partner; the drunken neighbor dressed as Santa Claus; and of course Siskel, the teacher from the military school, who the kid is blackmailing because he photographed him consorting with topless dancers. The director, Ted Demme, juggles all these people skillfully. Even though we know where the movie is going (the ref isn't really such a bad guy after all), it's fun to get there.

The Remains of the Day ★ ★ ★ ½
PG, 134 m., 1993

Anthony Hopkins (Stevens), Emma Thompson (Miss Kenton), James Fox (Lord Darlington), Christopher Reeve (Mr. Lewis), Peter Vaughan (Stevens's Father). Directed by James Ivory and produced by Mike Nichols, John Calley, and Ismail Merchant. Screenplay by Ruth Prawer Jhabvala.

In 1958, an old man in a big old car begins a journey across England to the sea. His name is Stevens, and for many years he has been the head butler at Darlington Hall, a famous country house. He is going to visit a woman he has not seen in a long time: Miss Kenton, who was once the housekeeper at Darlington. He thinks perhaps she can be persuaded to resume her old position under the hall's new owner, a retired American congressman.

Both Stevens and Darlington Hall are anachronisms. Stevens comes from a tradition of personal service; his goal in life is to serve his employer to the best of his ability, and as we get to know him, we realize that this was his *only* goal: He allowed it to blind him to all of the other promises of life.

The Remains of the Day tells the story of Stevens's trip to the sea, and what he finds there. Along the way, in flashback, we see his memories of the great days at the hall, when Lord Darlington played host to the world's leaders, and it seemed at times the future of Britain was being decided. And slowly we begin to realize that things were not as they seemed, that Darlington was not as wise as he thought, that Stevens was blind to the reality around him.

The Remains of the Day is based on the Booker Prize novel by Kazuo Ishiguro, which I would have thought almost unfilmable, until I saw this film. So much of it takes place within Stevens's mind, and it is up to the reader to interpret what the butler remembers: to deduce reality through the filter of a narrow, single-minded man. The reality is that Lord Darlington, in the years before World War II, had great sympathy for Germany, and hoped to bring about a separate peace between Britain and the Nazis. In this he was not precisely evil; he was deluded, shortsighted, easily persuaded by the pieties of genteel racism. He was, as a dinner guest brutally informs him, an amateur, who should have left international relations to the professionals.

The movie has been made by the team of director James Ivory, producer Ismail Merchant, and writer Ruth Prawer Jhabvala. After *A Room With a View* and *Howards End*, they are at the height of their powers, taking us inside a society where tradition is valued, even at the cost of repressing normal human feelings. The feelings, for example, that Stevens (Anthony Hopkins) might be expected to feel for Miss Kenton (Emma Thompson).

In a British country house of the period, the head butler and the housekeeper would have been equals, roughly speaking, each supervising the two major realms of service. Miss Kenton is clearly attracted to the butler, but he is terrified of intimacy, and sidesteps it through a fanatic devotion to his work. The film demonstrates this in a series of quiet, almost secretive scenes, in which she pushes, and he flees. The most painful, and brilliant, shows Miss Kenton surprising Stevens in his room, reading a book. What book? she asks. He hides the cover. She pursues him, cornering him, snatching the book away to find it is a best-selling romance. She had not imagined he read romances! He only reads, he stiffly explains, to improve his vocabulary.

Does Stevens possess any ordinary human feelings? Quite possibly, but something has led him to bury them. We meet his father (Peter Vaughn), himself a butler, who reared the son to a rigid idea of service—so rigid that when the father is actually dying upstairs, Stevens does not abandon his post at an important dinner party.

The motor journey unfolds, as incident and memory reveal one secret after another. We begin to understand the nature of Darlington's behavior. The lord (played by that most urbane and civilized actor, James Fox) is not a worldly man (he even recruits Stevens to explain "about the birds and the bees" to a godson who is obviously far beyond a zoological approach to sex). Cultivated and flattered by Nazi sympathizers and anti-Semites, he sponsors "international conferences" that will eventually lead to Darlington Hall being described as a traitor's nest. Does Stevens hear what is discussed at the meetings where he serves? What does he think about it? It is not the butler's place, he explains, to listen to his employer's conversations, or form opinions of them.

As the political disaster of Darlington Hall unfolds, a personal disaster is also in the making. Miss Kenton, discouraged in her approaches to Stevens, eventually bolts from her job. And it is only many years later that she contacts Stevens again, by letter, leading to his motor trip. Perhaps at some place buried deep in the darkness of his hopes, there is the thought that she might . . . still be interested in him?

The closing scenes paint a quiet heartbreak. The whole movie is quiet, introspective, thoughtful: a warning to those who put their emotional lives on hold, because they feel their duties are more important. Stevens has essentially thrown away his life in the name of duty. He has used his "responsibilities" as an excuse for avoiding his responsibility to his own happiness.

The Remains of the Day is a subtle, thoughtful movie. There are emotional upheavals in it, but they take place in shadows and corners, in secret. It tells a very sad story—three stories, really. Not long before the film opened I praised a somewhat similar film, Martin Scorsese's *The Age of Innocence*, also about characters who place duty and position above the needs of the heart. I got some letters from readers who complained the movie was boring, that "nothing happens in it." To which I was tempted to reply: If you had understood what happened in it, it would not have been boring.

Repo Man ★ ★ ★
R, 92 m., 1984

Harry Dean Stanton (Bud), Emilio Estevez (Otto), Tracey Walter (Miller), Olivia Barash (Leila). Directed by Alex Cox and produced by Jonathan Wacks and Peter McCarthy. Screenplay by Cox.

Repo Man is one of those movies that slips through the cracks and gives us all a little weirdo fun. It is the first movie I know about that combines (1) punk teen-agers, (2) automobile repossessors, and (3) aliens from outer space. This is the kind of movie that baffles Hollywood, because it isn't made from any known formula and doesn't follow the rules. The movie begins with a mad scientist careening down a New Mexico road in his Chevy Malibu. He is stopped by a cop, who finds some really strange things happening in the car's trunk. Then the action moves to Los Angeles, where a punk kid (Emilio Estevez) is passing the time by going to dances and banging his head against other kids' heads, to demonstrate his affection.

The kid runs into a guy named Bud (Harry Dean Stanton), who is an auto repossessor. Bud tricks the kid into driving a repo car for

him, and before long the kid is a full-time auto repossessor, learning the ropes. The ropes are pretty tough. Repo men, we learn, live their lives on the edge, operating under extreme tension that is caused partly by their working conditions and partly because as Stanton explains, "I've never known a repo man who didn't use a lot of speed." Harry Dean Stanton is one of the treasures of American movies. He has appeared in a lot of films without becoming a big star, but he has that total cynicism that brings jobs like repo into focus. In the movie, he and Estevez make a nice team; the beaten veteran and the cocky kid, and they cruise the streets looking for cars.

Meanwhile (and here I will be careful to respect some surprises in the story), the government is looking for that Chevy Malibu, because it is connected to the possibility that alien beings have visited the Earth. The feds put out a $10,000 reward for the car, which makes it the jackpot every repo man in L.A. is looking for. Hot on the trail of the car, Stanton and Estevez get into a duel with the famed Rodriguez brothers, known as the bandits of repo. All of this works very nicely, but what's best about *Repo Man* is its sly sense of humor. There are a lot of running gags in the movie, and the best of them involves generic food labels, of all things. (There is a moment involving some food in a refrigerator that gave me one of the biggest laughs I'd had at the movies in a long time.) The movie also has a special way of looking at Los Angeles, seeing it through Harry Dean Stanton's eyes as a wasteland of human ambitions where a few bucks can be made by the quick, the bitter, and the sly.

I saw *Repo Man* near the end of a busy stretch on the movie beat: Three days during which I saw more relentlessly bad movies than during any comparable period in memory. Most of those bad movies were so cynically constructed out of formula ideas and "commercial" ingredients that watching them was an ordeal. *Repo Man* comes out of left field, has no big stars, didn't cost much, takes chances, dares to be unconventional, is funny, and works. There is a lesson here.

The Rescuers Down Under ★ ★ ★
G, 76 m., 1990

With the voices of Bob Newhart (Bernard), Eva Gabor (Miss Bianca), John Candy (Wilbur), George C. Scott (McLeach), Tristan Rogers (Jake), Adam Ryen (Cody), and Wayne Robson (Frank). Directed by Hendel Butoy and

Mike Gabriel and produced by Thomas Schumacher. Screenplay by Jim Cox, Karey Kirkpatrick, Byron Simpson, and Joe Ranft.

Animation can give us the glory of sights and experiences that are impossible in the real world, and one of those sights, in *The Rescuers Down Under*, is of a little boy clinging to the back of a soaring eagle. The flight sequence and many of the other action scenes in this new Disney animated feature create an exhiliration and freedom that's liberating. And the rest of the story is fun, too.

The movie marks a return for the tiny rescue squad of brave little mice, first seen in *The Rescuers* (1977). This time they're called to Australia after receiving word that an eagle and a little boy have been kidnapped by an evil poacher, McLeach (with the rasping voice of George C. Scott). Two intrepid rescuers, Bernard and Miss Bianca, with voices by Bob Newhart and Eva Gabor, fly down under on an airline run by, and consisting of, Wilbur the Albatross, whose voice is by John Candy.

Various flight sequences make up a lot of the movie—not only the soaring grace of the eagle, but also the seagull's flopping ineptitude. The animation in these action scenes, like those on Disney's wonderful *Little Mermaid* of 1989, is fully realized, convincing, and entertaining. After a few uncertain years in the 1970s and early 1980s, the Disney animators (assisted now by computers) are back in top form.

The movie's story pits the hero, a little boy named Cody, against the evil poacher McLeach. The villain roams the outback in a gigantic land craft that seems to be a combination of army amphibious vehicle and launching pad. His goal is to capture members of endangered species and sell them for profit—and when the kid tries to protect the eagle, McLeach captures him, too.

It's customary in Disney pictures for the major characters to have minor sidekicks, and there are some delightful new characters in this movie, including Jake, a kangaroo mouse; Joanna, a slithering goanna lizard who is McLeach's sidekick; and Frank, a frill-necked lizard who helps engineer a jailbreak. The good animals conspire against the bad ones and the poacher, as everything leads up to a cliff-hanging sequence in which the next generation of eagles is at stake.

There's one reservation I have about the movie. Why does the villain have to be so noticeably dark-complexioned compared to all of the other characters? Is Disney aware of the racially coded message it is sending? When I made that point to another critic, he argued that McLeach wasn't dark-skinned—he was simply always seen in shadow. Those shadows are cast by insensitivity to negative racial stereotyping.

Reservoir Dogs ★ ★ ½
R, 99 m., 1992

Harvey Keitel (Mr. White), Tim Roth (Mr. Orange), Michael Madsen (Mr. Blond), Chris Penn (Nice Guy Eddie), Steve Buscemi (Mr. Pink), Lawrence Tierney (Joe Cabot), Quentin Tarantino (Mr. Brown). Directed by Quentin Tarantino and produced by Lawrence Bender. Screenplay by Tarantino.

Now that we know Quentin Tarantino can make a movie like *Reservoir Dogs*, it's time for him to move on and make a better one. This film, the first from an obviously talented writer-director, is like an exercise in style. He sets up his characters during a funny scene in a coffee shop, and then puts them through a stickup that goes disastrously wrong. Most of the movie deals with its bloody aftermath, as they assemble in a warehouse and bleed and drool on one another.

The movie has one of the best casts you could imagine, led by the legendary old tough guy Lawrence Tierney, who has been in and out of jail both on the screen and in real life. He is incapable of uttering a syllable that sounds inauthentic. Tierney plays Joe Cabot, an experienced criminal who has assembled a team of crooks for a big diamond heist. The key to his plan is that his associates don't know one another, and therefore can't squeal if they're caught. He names them off a color chart: Mr. White, Mr. Orange, Mr. Blond, Mr. Pink, and so on. Mr. Pink doesn't like his name. "You're lucky you ain't Mr. Yellow," Tierney rasps.

The opening scene features an endlessly circling camera, as the tough guys light cigarettes and drink coffee in one of these places where the tables are Formica and the waitresses write your order on a green-and-white Guest Check. They argue, joke, and BS each other through thick clouds of smoke; it's like *The Sportswriters on Parole*. There's a funny discussion of tipping. Then they walk out of the restaurant, and are introduced in the opening credits, as they walk menacingly toward the camera. They have great faces: the glowering Michael Madsen; the apprehensive Tim Roth; Chris Penn, ready for

anything; shifty Steve Buscemi; Tierney, with a Mack truck of a mug; Harvey Keitel, whose presence in a crime movie is like an imprimatur.

The movie feels like it's going to be terrific, but unfortunately Tarantino's script doesn't have much real curiosity about these guys. He has an idea, and trusts the idea to drive the plot, without insights or psychology. The idea is that the tough guys, except for Tierney and the deranged Madsen, are mostly bluffers, creatures of these latter days when criminals study TV to find out how to act. They have big guns but are not skilled stickup men and are not good at handling themselves in desperate situations.

We see the bungled crime in flashbacks. Tarantino has a confident, kinetic way of shooting action—guys running down the street, gun battles, blood and screams. Then the action centers in the warehouse, where Madsen sadistically toys with a character he thinks is a cop, and the movie ends on a couple of notes of horrifying poetic justice.

One of the discoveries in the movie is Madsen, who has done a lot of acting over the years (he had a good role in *The Natural*), but here emerges with the kind of really menacing screen presence only a few actors achieve; he can hold his own with the fearsome Tierney, and reminds me a little of a very mean Robert De Niro. Tarantino himself is also interesting as an actor; he could play great crazy villains.

As for the movie, I liked what I saw, but I wanted more. I know the story behind the movie—Tarantino promoted the project from scratch, on talent and nerve—and I think it's quite an achievement for a first-timer. It was made on a low budget. But the part that needs work didn't cost money. It's the screenplay. Having created the characters and fashioned the outline, Tarantino doesn't do much with his characters except to let them talk too much, especially when they should probably be unconscious from shock and loss of blood.

Return of the Jedi ★ ★ ★ ★
PG, 133 m., 1983

Mark Hamill (Luke Skywalker), Harrison Ford (Han Solo), Carrie Fisher (Princess Leia), Billy Dee Williams (Lando Calrissian), Anthony Daniels (C-3PO), David Prowse (Darth Vader), James Earl Jones (Vader's Voice), Alec Guinness (Obi-Wan Kenobi). Directed by Richard Marquand and produced by Howard Kazanjian. Screenplay by Lawrence Kasdan and George Lucas.

Here is just one small moment in *Return of the Jedi*, a moment you could miss if you looked away from the screen, but a moment that helps explain the special magic of the Star Wars movies. Luke Skywalker is engaged in a ferocious battle in the dungeons beneath the throne room of the loathsome Jabba the Hutt. His adversary is a slimy, gruesome, reptilian monster made of warts and teeth. Things are looking bad when suddenly the monster is crushed beneath a falling door. And then (here is the small moment) there's a shot of the monster's keeper, a muscle-bound jailer, who rushes forward in tears. He is brokenhearted at the destruction of his pet. Everybody loves somebody.

It is that extra level of detail that makes the Star Wars pictures much more than just space operas. Other movies might approach the special effects. Other action pictures might approximate the sense of swashbuckling adventure. But in *Return of the Jedi*, as in *Star Wars* and *The Empire Strikes Back*, there's such a wonderful density to the canvas. Things are happening all over. They're pouring forth from imaginations so fertile that, yes, we do halfway believe in this crazy Galactic Empire long ago and far, far away.

Return of the Jedi is both a familiar movie and a new one. It concludes the stories of the major human characters in the saga, particularly Skywalker, Han Solo, Princess Leia, and Darth Vader. It revisits other characters who seem either more or less than human, including Ben (Obi-Wan Kenobi), Yoda, Chewbacca, and the beloved robots C-3PO and R2-D2. If George Lucas persists in his plan to make nine Star Wars movies, this will nevertheless be the last we'll see of Luke, Han, and Leia, although the robots will be present in all the films.

The story in the Star Wars movies is, however, only part of the film—and a less crucial element as time goes by. What *Jedi* is really giving us is a picaresque journey through the imagination, and an introduction to forms of life less mundane than our own. In *Jedi*, we encounter several unforgettable characters, including the evil Jabba the Hutt, who is a cross between a toad and the Cheshire cat; the lovable, cuddly Ewoks, the furry inhabitants of the "forest moon of Endor"; a fearsome desert monster made of sand and teeth; and hateful little ratlike creatures that scurry about the corners of the frame. And there is an admiral for the Alliance who looks like the missing link between Tyrannosaurus Rex and Charles de Gaulle.

One thing the Star Wars movies never do is waste a lot of time on introductions. Unlike a lot of special-effects and monster movies, where new creatures are introduced with laborious setups, *Jedi* immediately plunges its alien beasts into the thick of the action. Maybe that's why the film has such a sense of visual richness. Jabba's throne room, for example, is populated with several weird creatures, some of them only half-glimpsed in the corner of the frame. The camera in *Jedi* slides casually past forms of life that would provide the centerpiece for lesser movies.

The movie also has, of course, more of the amazing battles in outer space—the intergalactic video games that have been a trademark since *Star Wars*. And *Jedi* finds an interesting variation on that chase sequence in *Star Wars* where the space cruisers hurtled through the narrow canyons on the surface of the Death Star. This time, there's a breakneck chase through a forest, aboard airborne motorcycles. After several of the bad guys have run into trees and gotten creamed, you pause to ask yourself why they couldn't have simply flown *above* the treetops . . . but never mind, it wouldn't have been as much fun that way.

And *Return of the Jedi* is fun, magnificent fun. The movie is a complete entertainment, a feast for the eyes and a delight for the fancy. It's a little amazing how Lucas and his associates keep topping themselves. From the point of view of simple moviemaking logistics, there is an awesome amount of work on the screen in *Jedi* (twice as many visual effects as *Star Wars* in the space battles, Lucas claims). The fact that the makers of *Jedi* are able to emerge intact from their task, having created a very special work of the imagination, is the sort of miracle that perhaps Obi-Wan would know something about.

Return of the Secaucus Seven ★ ★ ★
NO MPAA RATING, 110 m., 1981

Mark Arnott (Jeff), Gordon Clapp (Chip), Maggie Cousineau-Arndt (Frances), Adam Le Fevre (J.T.), Bruce MacDonald (Mike), Jean Passanante (Irene), John Sayles (Howie), Maggie Renzi (Katie). Directed and written by John Sayles. Produced by William Aydelott and Jeffrey Nelson.

A friend asked me what *Return of the Secaucus Seven* was about. "It's the story of your life," I said.

"*My* life?"

Well, and my life, too. Everybody's life who was younger once and demonstrated against one thing or another, and is older now and stumped for the moment by the curiosity that the most outspoken advocate of change in our society is Ronald Reagan. The movie tells the story of a group of friends who set out during the late 1960s to join the March on the Pentagon, and were arrested in Secaucus, New Jersey, on charges they still do not fully understand. So they didn't make it to the Pentagon, where their brain power might have made the difference in Abbie Hoffman's plan to levitate that building.

Those were strange times. Even Norman Mailer, in his *Armies of the Night,* reported that when the Yippies started to chant and meditate and try to levitate the Pentagon, he looked to see if it had started to rise: An unlikely event, of course, but one that a reporter would always kick himself for if he had missed it. Years have passed since those days. The original members of the Secaucus Seven have grown older now, can taste their thirtieth birthdays, and as the movie opens have gathered for a weekend reunion in the country. The film tells the story of their weekend, as they take their measure and remember the 1960s.

The Sixties. A director once told me that he had been interviewed by a group of college editors, one of whom asked him, "Was drug usage really prevalent back in the 1960s?" He didn't know whether to laugh or cry. The Secaucus Seven has the same choice. They are never again going to be as young as they were, but they still remember their days of activism so sharply that they refuse to cut loose from them. These days, people still go through their thirtieth birthday crisis, all right, but they seem to hold it on their fortieth birthday.

The Secaucus Seven has grown slightly, with the addition of spouses, lovers, and even children. They gather to play basketball, sing songs, get drunk, fight, break up, and sleep together—or apart. In mood, the film resembles Alain Tanner's wonderful *Jonah Who Will Be 25 in the Year 2000.* Some of the Seven have become fairly successful. There are a congressional aide and a medical student. There is also a kid who is still trying to make it as a folk singer, an occupation that no longer pays very well even if he had the

talent, which he does not. And another who has chosen to stay in the old hometown and pump gas.

John Sayles, who wrote and directed the movie, made it as a labor of love (and financed it by writing the screenplays for *Piranha* and *Alligator,* so he may still not quite have evened the scales). He alternates among the various couples and groupings and intrigues, and at first the movie is frankly confusing. We can't keep everybody straight, and there's too much explanation of who they all are and what they've all done. Before long, though, we have everyone sorted out. We know the relationships. And we grow quietly grateful that Sayles has chosen not to pack his weekend reunion with a series of dramatic confrontations and crises. There are no overdoses, suicides, or murders. Only the adjustments such a weekend would be expected to bring, and the inevitable bitterness when one couple has broken up, and the old and new lovers have to confront one another.

This is not a perfect film. Odds and ends stick out, and some scenes have a certain gracelessness. But it is an absorbing film that contains shrewd observations about human nature, and more than its share of humor. We leave with mixed feelings: We feel like we've ended that reunion, and at the same time we're relieved that we did not. It is easier to be young if your friends don't age on you.

Reversal of Fortune ★ ★ ★ ★
R, 110 m., 1990

Glenn Close (Sunny von Bulow), Jeremy Irons (Claus von Bulow), Ron Silver (Alan M. Dershowitz), Annabella Sciorra (Carol), Uta Hagen (Maria), Fisher Stevens (David Marriott), Christine Baranski (Andrea Reynolds). Directed by Barbet Schroeder and produced by Edward R. Pressman and Oliver Stone. Screenplay by Nicholas Kazan.

I followed the investigative accounts of the von Bulow case with that special attention I always pay to the troubles of society people. With their advantages and connections, they have a better chance of being involved in a stimulating crime. Some of them, it is true, simply stab or shoot one another, but a few go to the trouble of using classic means—poisons and deceptions, subterfuge and wit. With all the lack of subtlety in modern murder, it is heartening to find that a few people still aspire to the perfect crime.

Having seen *Reversal of Fortune*, the story of Claus von Bulow's two trials on the charge of attempting to murder his wife, I am no closer than before to a clear idea of who did what, or why. That is the charm of the movie. Something terrible happened to Sunny von Bulow on that winter day eleven years ago, and nobody knows exactly what it was. The victim still lingers in a coma. Her husband was convicted of murder, but his conviction was overturned, and there is compelling suspicion that some of the evidence used against him was fishy.

And now we have this film, based on a book by Alan J. Dershowitz, the famous Harvard professor who conducted Claus von Bulow's appeal. It is a surprisingly entertaining film—funny, wicked, sharp-tongued, and devious. It does not solve the case, nor intend to. I am afraid it only intends to entertain. Because Sunny von Bulow does indeed lie in a coma, I felt at first a little guilty that I enjoyed the film so much. But I am in attendance as a critic, not a priest or prosecutor, and, like the other witnesses, I can only testify from my own experience.

The genius of *Reversal of Fortune* is that the story is narrated by Sunny from her sickbed. We hear her voice, wondering aloud at the chain of events caused by that day when she sank into her long sleep. She guides us through the details of the case. She reminisces about the first time she met Claus, about what she felt for him, about how their marriage progressed. She confesses herself as confused as anyone about what happened on her last day of consciousness. "You tell me," she says, and somehow this gives us permission to look at the film in a more genial mood.

The opening shot, taken from a helicopter, shows the great mansions of Newport, Rhode Island. They stand like sentinels at the edge of the sea, flaunting their wealth at the waves. In one of those mansions Sunny von Bulow lived with Claus and the children they had together or previously. How could one not be entertained by living in such a place? And yet, Sunny seems to seek the escape of unconsciousness. She abuses pills and alcohol. After brief forays into the world, she retreats to her bed. She is not really present for her family; her mind is clouded, and her memory shaky. While her body goes through the motions of smoking and drinking and taking pills, her mind yawns and dozes.

One day she nearly dies, probably of an overdose, but is rescued in time. A year later, she is not so lucky, and by the time help is summoned she is in a coma. What happened? The maid says she was worried for hours before Claus would let her call for help. Claus says he thought she was sleeping; she had often slumbered deeply before. But how did she end up on the bathroom floor? And what about the insulin? Did Claus administer a fatal overdose? Whose insulin was it, anyway? And who found it?

The question of the insulin is what finally brings Alan Dershowitz into the appeal, after Claus is found guilty. The evidence was gathered by private investigators hired by Sunny's children, and then turned over to the authorities, and Dershowitz decides that the rich simply cannot be permitted to hire their own police and decide among themselves which evidence should be made available. It isn't fair. There are also questions about many other aspects of the case—so many that, if Claus is not innocent, there is at least no way to prove that he is guilty.

Reversal of Fortune is above all a triumph of tone. The director, Barbet Schroeder, and the writer, Nicholas Kazan, have not made a docudrama or a sermon, but a film about personalities. The most extraordinary personality in the film is von Bulow's, as he is played by Jeremy Irons. He appears as a man with affections and bizarre mannerisms, a man who speaks as if he lifted his words from an arch drawing-room comedy, who smokes a cigarette as if hailing a taxi. Irons is able to suggest, subtly, that some of this over-the-top behavior is the result of fear. Von Bulow cannot modulate his tone, cannot find the right note, because beneath his façade he is quaking.

And yet he keeps up a brave front. That is one of the best qualities of the film, the way it shows him trying to brazen his way out of an impossible situation. If he wins, he keeps the fortune and the lifestyle. If he loses, he ends his life in jail. The man who can save him is Dershowitz, played by Ron Silver as a hyperkinetic showboat who surrounds himself with students and acolytes, possibly as a protection against the fear of silence. The law students plunge like beavers into their research, triumphantly emerging with new strategies for their leader, who does not like von Bulow much and doubts his innocence, but believes the case raises important legal points.

Glenn Close is important too, as Sunny. She appears in some flashbacks as well as narrating the film, and we see the things we need to notice: Her beauty and personality when she's got it together, and the vague lost confusion of her alcoholic and tranquilized daydreams. Without nudging us, the film shows us two things. First, why a man might finally be tempted to allow his wife to slip into the oblivion she seems so desperately to desire. Second, how she could have accidentally overdosed in any event.

What happened? Who knows. The movie's strength is its ability to tantalize, to turn the case this way and that, so that the light of evidence falls in one way and then another. You tell me.

Rhapsody in August ★ ★ ★
PG, 98 m., 1992

Sachiko Murase (Grandmother), Richard Gere (Her Nephew), Hisashi Igawa (Her Son), Narumi Kayashima (His Wife), Tomoko Ohtakara (Their Daughter), Mitsunori Isaki (Shinjiro: Their Daughter), Toshie Negishi (Kane's Daughter). Directed by Akira Kurosawa and produced by Hisao Kurosawa. Screenplay by Akira Kurosawa.

Akira Kurosawa made this film in his early eighties, and there were those who thought he was losing his touch, that the vision that made him one of the greatest of directors was fading at last. In his seventies he gave us late masterpieces like *Ran*, but his *Dreams* (1990) was not well received, and *Rhapsody in August* was considered a disappointment when it premiered at Cannes in May 1991. It is not one of his great films, but shows him thoughtfully trying to come to peace with the central event of his times.

The movie takes place during one summer in the life of a very old woman (Sachiko Murase) whose husband was killed by the atomic bomb dropped on Nagasaki. Her children and grandchildren have come to visit her, and there are reports from the deathbed of her brother, who immigrated to Hawaii many years before, prospered, and took an American wife and American citizenship. Now he is mortally ill, and while the old woman decides whether to answer his call for a last meeting, a reconciliation, he dies.

Not long after, her nephew (Richard Gere), the man's son, comes to Japan to visit. He is half Japanese, half Caucasian, and around him the subject of her husband's death is discussed only gingerly; perhaps he would not like to be reminded that the bomb was dropped by

Americans. He speaks Japanese, is polite and interested, and eventually learns the story of his uncle's death. And there is a scene beyond all words in which the old lady and another woman friend, equally old, gather to remember their dead. There is no dialogue; they need no speech for their memories.

Kurosawa has always been a director of great images, and in his old age he has permitted himself more fanciful, less realistic ones. There is a great eye that opens in the sky in this movie, and symbolizes, I suppose, the light that flowered in the sky when the bomb dropped on Nagasaki. There is a rose engulfed by ants, which may have something to do with those who fled from the devastation of the bomb. There is the twisted jungle gym of a school playground, left the way it looked after the heat of the bomb melted it into a grotesque sculpture. And there is the image of the old woman, walking in wind and rain, her umbrella defiantly offered against the elements.

These images and the dialogue about the bomb are counterpointed by the daily lives of the grandchildren, who are rather one-dimensional, chattering creatures used to show how the younger generation does not much remember or care about the great events of the years before they were born. Gere, as the nephew, is more attentive, and eventually he offers his apologies for the death of his uncle, and the old woman forgives him.

This sequence in particular was criticized at Cannes, where one journalist cried out at a press conference, "Why was the bomb dropped in the first place?" and when the film played at the Tokyo Film Festival, critics of Japanese militarism said Kurosawa had ignored the historical facts leading up to the bomb. Kurosawa's response was simple: He wanted his film to say that war was between governments, not people. The use of a Japanese-American character was deliberate. It is as if, at this point in his life, he wants to close this particular set of books—at least as far as his art is concerned.

Another veteran Japanese director, Shohei Imamura, has made a film about the bomb that is more disciplined and pointed. His *Black Rain* (1989, not to be confused with the Michael Douglas thriller) is about the social aftermath of the bomb in Japan, where those suspected of radiation poisoning became less attractive marriage prospects. His film has edge and bite. The Kurosawa is more of a sigh, a letting-go, but interesting because of that very quality. Seeing that twisted playground artifact, I was reminded of another playground, in Kurosawa's great *Ikiru* (1952), which is the story of a dying bureaucrat who devotes all of his waning energies to getting a city playground constructed, and then dies there, sitting on a swing in the snow.

Richard Pryor Here and Now
★ ★ ★ ★
R, 94 m., 1983

A documentary written and directed by Richard Pryor and produced by Bob Parkinson and Andy Friendly.

Is there anyone else in America who could have pulled off this film? *Richard Pryor Here and Now* is a documentary of one man talking. Pryor walks onto the stage of the Saenger Theater in New Orleans, establishes an immediate rapport with the audience, and away he goes. At the end of the movie we have been wrung out with laughter—and with a few other things, too, because Pryor is more than a comedian in this film: He's a social commentator and a man talking honestly about himself.

This is Pryor's third concert film. The first one, *Richard Pryor Live in Concert,* was made before he set himself on fire while freebasing cocaine. The second, *Richard Pryor Live on the Sunset Strip* (1982), recorded his first filmed concert after the accident, and included his description of Jim Brown's attempts to talk him out of drug use, and Pryor's own now-famous dialogue with cocaine. In *Here and Now,* filmed in August 1983 with Brown as executive producer, Pryor firmly says he hasn't used drugs or alcohol for seven months. The arithmetic would seem to suggest that he hadn't stopped using everything when he made the second film, or that he had a relapse after his initial hospitalization. I mention that only because the Richard Pryor we see on screen in *Here and Now* has obviously found some kind of peace with himself that was lacking in the *Sunset Strip* film.

He can smile more easily. He doesn't have to reach for effects. He handles audience interruptions with grace and cool. He is the master of his instrument. And he takes bigger chances. Some of his material covers familiar ground—sex, booze, race, marriages. But all along he's showing his gift for populating the stage with a lot of different characters. He goes in and out of accents, body language, and characters, giving us confused drunks, defensive husbands, shrill wives, uptight WASPs, impenetrable Africans ("Everybody speaks English," one tells him in Zimbabwe, "but what language do you speak at *home?*"). And then at the end of his act, he goes into an extended characterization of a street black shooting heroin. In this character are humor and pain, self-deception and touching honesty, and the end of the sketch comes closer to tragedy than it does to comedy.

Pryor is a spokesman for our dreams and fears, the things we find funny and the things we're frightened of. He has assumed a role that has previously been filled by such comedians as Will Rogers, Lenny Bruce, Mort Sahl, and Woody Allen—all men who, as Rogers put it, talked about what they'd just seen in the papers. Pryor works off issues and subjects that are absolutely current, and he addresses them with a humor that is aimed so well, we duck. His story could have gone either way. He could have been killed in that wasteful accident. But he was not, and now, given a second chance, he is paying his dues.

Richard Pryor Live on the Sunset Strip
★ ★ ★ ★
R, 82 m., 1982

Directed by Joe Layton and produced by Richard Pryor.

At the beginning of this film, Richard Pryor is clearly nervous. He is back on a stage for the first time since he set himself on fire. That means he is working with the stand-up comedian's greatest handicap, the audience's awareness of his vulnerability. Whatever else they do, comics must project utter confidence in their material, and when Pryor had his accident, he also had his whole hip image blown out from under him. So it's a shaky start. He begins by almost defiantly using the word "fuck" as an incantation, employing it not so much for shock value (does it still have any?) as for punctuation. His timing is a little off. He is not, at first, the supremely confident, cocky Richard Pryor of his earlier films. But as he gets rolling, as he populates the stage with a whole series of characters, we watch the emergence of a Richard Pryor who is older, wiser, and funnier than before. And the last fifty or sixty minutes of this film are extraordinary.

Richard Pryor Live on the Sunset Strip was filmed at the Hollywood Palladium, down at the unfashionable east end of that legendary street of rock clubs, restaurants, hookers and heroes, hot-pillow motels, and some of the most expensive real estate in the world. The movie opens with a montage of the strip's neon signs (including the Chateau Marmont, where John Belushi died). Then it cuts inside to the Palladium auditorium, and Pryor walks onstage and lays claim to being the most talented one-man stage show in existence right now.

His gift is to be funny and painfully self-analytical at the same time. Like Bill Cosby, he gets a lot of his material out of memories of growing up black in America. But he sees deeper than Cosby, and his vignettes capture small truths and build them into an attitude. In the brilliant middle sections of this film, he uses just his own voice and body to create little one-act plays, such as the one where he recalls working in a Mafia-owned nightclub in Ohio. In that one, his Italian-American-gangster accent is perfectly heard; in another skit, about the animals in Africa, he turns into a gifted physical comedian, getting laughs out of his impressions of the movements of gazelles, water buffaloes, and lions—and ending with a hilarious observation of the body language of two whites passing each other on the street in black Africa.

The whole middle passage of the film is that good. The last twenty minutes is one of the most remarkable marriages of comedy and truth I have ever seen. He talks with great honesty about his drug addiction, his accident, and how his life has changed since he stopped using drugs. He confesses that in the three weeks before his accident, he holed up alone in his room with his cocaine pipe, which talked to him in reassuring, seductive tones uncannily like Richard Nixon's. Then a friend, the actor Jim Brown, came to see him, and asked him flat-out, "Whatcha gonna do?" There was nothing he wanted to do but hide in drugs. What he finally did was set himself on fire.

I saw the film the same day that actor Shay Duffin opened his one-man evening with Brendan Behan at the Apollo Theater Center in Chicago. The papers that day carried the news that Belushi had overdosed. Behan, of course, killed himself with alcohol. Some day, inevitably, an actor will give us an evening with John Belushi. The dramatic structure is all there, for the Behans and Belushis: The genius, the laughter, and the doomed drive to self-destruction. Watching *Richard Pryor Live on the Sunset Strip*, a breath-taking performance by a man who came within a hair of killing himself with drugs,

was like a gift, as if Pryor had come back from the dead to perform in his own one-man memory of himself. It is good we still have him. He is better than ever.

Richie Rich ★ ★ ★
PG, 103 m., 1994

NEW

Macaulay Culkin (Richie Rich), John Larroquette (Laurence Van Dough), Edward Herrmann (Mr. Rich), Jonathan Hyde (Cadbury), Christine Ebersole (Mrs. Rich), Stephi Lineburg (Gloria), Michael McShane (Professor Keenbean). Directed by Donald Petrie and produced by Joel Silver and John Davis. Screenplay by Tom S. Parker and Jim Jennewein.

The underlying story of *Richie Rich* is as old as the hills: The poor little rich boy has all the expensive toys he needs, but is lonely and neglected, and has no playmates his own age. What's sort of wonderful is the way this movie takes that old formula and makes it fresh and new, with actors who give it wit and charm.

One of those actors is Macaulay Culkin, whose recent string of bombs *(The Nutcracker, The Good Son, The Pagemaster)* almost made me forget that the kid does have an engaging screen personality, when he isn't shoehorned into the wrong projects. This is his comeback, and possibly the last film in which he will be able to play a little boy (clues: He gets his first zit, and notices that an aerobics instructor, played by Claudia Schiffer, has certain qualities far beyond those of a buddy). Time marches on, and someday we'll be able to see little Macaulay with a beard and a cigarette.

In *Richie Rich* he plays the richest kid in the world. He lives in a mansion of incalculable luxury, with his parents and his personal valet, and one of the surprises of the movie is that these characters are *not* the stuffy, distant stereotypes that we'd expect in this genre. Instead, they're warm and funny, and Richie likes them. His dad is played by Edward Herrmann (looking more than ever like a benevolent Franklin Roosevelt), his mom is Christine Ebersole, and Jonathan Hyde plays Cadbury, the valet, who looks after Master Richie with the discretion of Jeeves and the devotion of Mr. Watson.

Rich Industries is one of those movie conglomerates that manufactures lots and lots of everything. Down in the basement of the mansion, the brilliant Professor Keenbean (Michael McShane) works on prototypes for still more brilliant inventions, including a

robot bee, and Richie has fun visiting him. Yet Richie is not happy. He's a naturally gifted baseball player, but never gets to play with anybody his own age, and one day, while representing his father at a factory opening, he sees some kids playing a sandlot game across the street. He wants to join in, but they scorn him, and Cadbury ushers him back aboard the corporate helicopter.

The story of course has a villain. His name is Laurence Van Dough, and he's played by the invaluable John Larroquette as a slick, oily executive with Rich Industries, who schemes to sabotage the Rich family plane, and take control of the company for himself. For a time it appears his scheme has worked—Richie's parents disappear in the Bermuda Triangle—but Richie wasn't on the plane, and takes control of the company himself.

It goes without saying that the kid can make better decisions than the board of directors, and soon Rich Industries' profits are higher than ever. Richie invites his poor inner-city friends over to the house to play (they like the Kid-a-Pult, which hurtles them through the air). Meanwhile, Mom and Dad float around on a rubber raft, making the best of the situation. ("We're out of Perrier and caviar," Herrmann dolefully tells Ebersole, inspecting the emergency rations. "We're down to the champagne.")

Richie Rich contains no elements of startling originality, but director Donald Petrie, the writers, and the actors supply what such an enterprise needs above everything else: style. The movie is bemusing precisely because it knows exactly what it is, and never tries too hard or strays into cheap payoffs. Richie's world—his toys, his staff, his new playmates, even the danger he's in at the hands of the scheming villain—are all seen with a certain sunniness. The movie has the lightness of a 1930s fantasy, and none of the ham-handed obviousness of many modern movies about kids. I was a little amazed how much I enjoyed it.

Rich in Love ★ ★ ★
PG-13, 105 m., 1993

Albert Finney (Warren Odom), Jill Clayburgh (Helen Odom), Kathryn Erbe (Lucille Odom), Kyle MacLachlan (Billy McQueen), Piper Laurie (Vera Delmage), Ethan Hawke (Wayne Frobiness), Suzy Amis (Rae Odom). Directed by Bruce Beresford and produced by Richard D. Zanuck and Lili Fini Zanuck. Screenplay by Alfred Uhry.

Households like this exist only in the movies, which is all right, because that's one of the reasons we go to the movies: to see people who are crazier than we are. The Odom family, the subjects of Bruce Beresford's *Rich in Love,* live in an elegant old Southern mansion, surrounded by balconies and trees and easy livin'. Life is seemingly without problems, until one day Warren Odom (Albert Finney) comes home and discovers that his wife has left him.

He reads her farewell note with incredulity, little suspecting it was rewritten by his peppy teen-age daughter Lucille (Kathryn Erbe). She didn't change the content much; she just thought it could have been better phrased. Lucille, who is the narrator of the story, is a free spirit who must have come late in life to the Odoms, since Warren has retired and lives all day at home—one of the reasons his wife (Jill Clayburgh) moved out.

Life goes on. Warren and Lucille cruise the county, searching for the missing woman, but at the same time Warren finds solace in the friendly arms and delicious baked goods of a local woman (Piper Laurie) who lends a sympathetic ear. Then visitors arrive: Lucille's older sister (Suzy Amis) and her new husband (Kyle McLachlan), who have decided to move in for a while.

The tradition of Southern Gothic is ancient and well-established, and does a good deal to paper over the unlikeliness of many of the elements of *Rich in Love.* Like *Fried Green Tomatoes, Steel Magnolias,* and *Rambling Rose,* not to mention Beresford's own *Driving Miss Daisy,* these characters live to a different rhythm than people in the North (or, I suspect, the real people of the South). They're colorful and irreverent and eccentric and romantic, and they gab a lot about life and fate.

The movie is filled with small, warmly realized scenes. I enjoyed every moment of the quasi courtship between Finney and Laurie, and especially a wonderful moment by Laurie when she comes to deliver a cake and, not incidentally, inquire about the rumor that Mrs. Odom has returned home. There is another fine scene between Erbe and Clayburgh, who explains why she had to leave home. Erbe and her boyfriend (Ethan Hawke) have a quiet and matter-of-fact love scene that is freshly written. And Suzy Amis, who has had small roles in movies like *The Big Town* and *Where the Heart Is,* comes into her own here as the weary, cynical older sister, in a star-making role.

There is a comfort level established right at the top of the film with Finney's performance; like many British actors, he is comfortable with Southern accents, and he's also comfortable in blue jeans and Jeeps, and has a careful courtliness that is perfect for his soirees with the Piper Laurie character.

Beresford, who is an Australian, once again shows that he has some sort of natural affinity for the American South. Make a list of the better recent films about that region, and it will include his *Tender Mercies, Crimes of the Heart, Driving Miss Daisy,* and now this film.

I must confess I didn't much believe the story; despite being about a marriage that appears to have run its course, *Rich in Love* is essentially a fantasy, in which family problems are sort of interesting and not very tragic, and you can learn from them, and everything turns out just right. Not much believing the story, by the way, didn't diminish my enjoyment one bit.

The Right Stuff ★ ★ ★ ★
PG, 193 m., 1983

Sam Shepard (Chuck Yeager), Ed Harris (John Glenn), Fred Ward (Gus Grissom), Dennis Quaid (Gordon Cooper), Scott Glenn (Alan Shepard), Barbara Hershey (Glennis Yeager), Mary Jo Deschanel (Annie Glenn), Pamela Reed (Trudy Cooper). Directed by Philip Kaufman and produced by Irwin Winkler and Robert Chartoff. Screenplay by Kaufman.

At the beginning of *The Right Stuff,* a cowboy reins in his horse and regards a strange sight in the middle of the desert: the X-1 rocket plane, built to break the sound barrier. At the end of the film, the seven Mercury astronauts are cheered in the Houston Astrodome at a Texas barbecue thrown by Lyndon B. Johnson. The contrast between those two images contains the message of *The Right Stuff,* I think, and the message is that Americans still have the right stuff, but we've changed our idea of what it is.

The original American heroes were loners. The cowboy is the perfect example. He was silhouetted against the horizon and he rode into town by himself and if he had a sidekick, the sidekick's job was to admire him. The new American heroes are team players. No wonder Westerns aren't made much anymore; cowboys don't play on teams. The cowboy at the beginning of *The Right Stuff* is Chuck Yeager, the legendary lone-wolf test pilot who survived the horrifying death rate among early test pilots (more than sixty were killed in a single month) and did fly the X-1 faster than the speed of sound. The movie begins with that victory, and then moves on another ten years to the day when the Russians sent up Sputnik, and the Eisenhower administration hustled to get back into the space race.

The astronauts who eventually rode the first Mercury capsules into space may not have been that much different from Chuck Yeager. As they're portrayed in the movie, anyway, Gus Grissom, Scott Carpenter, and Gordon Cooper seem to have some of the same stuff as Yeager. But the astronauts were more than pilots; they were a public-relations image, and the movie shows sincere, smooth-talking John Glenn becoming their unofficial spokesman. The X-1 flew in secrecy, but the Mercury flights were telecast, and we were entering a whole new era, the selling of space. There was a lot going on, and there's a lot going on in the movie, too. *The Right Stuff* is an adventure film, a special-effects film, a social commentary, and a satire. That the writer-director, Philip Kaufman, is able to get so much into a little more than three hours is impressive. That he also has organized this material into one of the best recent American movies is astonishing. *The Right Stuff* gives itself the freedom to move around in moods and styles, from a broadly based lampoon of government functionaries to Yeager's spare, taciturn manner and Glenn's wonderment at the sights outside his capsule window.

The Right Stuff has been a landmark movie in a lot of careers. It announces Kaufman's arrival in the ranks of major directors. It contains uniformly interesting performances by a whole list of unknown or little-known actors, including Ed Harris (Glenn), Scott Glenn (Alan Shepard), Fred Ward (Grissom), and Dennis Quaid (Cooper). It confirms the strong and sometimes almost mystical screen presence of playwright Sam Shepard, who played Yeager. And it joins a short list of recent American movies that might be called experimental epics: movies that have an ambitious reach through time and subject matter, that spend freely for locations or special effects, but that consider each scene as intently as an art film. *The Right Stuff* goes on that list with *The Godfather, Nashville, Apocalypse Now,* and maybe *Patton* and *Close Encounters.* It's a great film.

Risky Business ★ ★ ★ ★
R, 96 m., 1983

Tom Cruise (Joel), Rebecca De Mornay (Lana), Curtis Armstrong (Miles), Bronson Pinchot (Barry), Joe Pantoliano (Guido). Directed by Paul Brickman and produced by Joe Avnet and Steve Tisch. Screenplay by Brickman.

Risky Business is a movie about male adolescent guilt. In other words, it's a comedy. It's funny because it deals with subjects that are so touchy, so fraught with emotional pain, that unless we laugh there's hardly any way we can deal with them—especially if we are now, or ever were, a teen-age boy. The teenager in the movie is named Joel. His family lives in a suburb on Chicago's North Shore. It's the sort of family that has three cars: the family station wagon, Mom's car, and Dad's Porsche. As the movie opens, Mom and Dad are going off on vacation to a sun-drenched consumer paradise and their only son, Joel, is being left alone at home. It's a busy time in Joel's life. He's got college board exams, an interview with a Princeton admissions officer, and finals at high school.

It gets to be an even busier time after his parents leave. Joel gets involved in an ascending pyramid of trouble. He calls a number in one of those sex-contact magazines and meets a young hooker who moves into the house. He runs afoul of the girl's pimp. His mother's expensive Steuben egg is stolen. His dad's Porsche ends up in Lake Michigan. The family home turns into a brothel. He blows two finals. And so on. This description may make *Risky Business* sound like a predictable sitcom. It is not. It is one of the smartest, funniest, most perceptive satires in a long time. It not only invites comparison with *The Graduate,* it earns it. Here is a great comedy about teen-age sex.

The very best thing about the movie is its dialogue. Paul Brickman, who wrote and directed, has an ear so good that he knows what to leave out. This is one of those movies where a few words or a single line says everything that needs to be said, implies everything that needs to be implied, *and* gets a laugh. When the hooker tells the kid, "Oh, Joel, go to school. Learn something," the precise inflection of those words defines their relationship for the next three scenes.

The next best thing about the movie is the casting. Rebecca De Mornay somehow manages to take that thankless role, the hooker with a heart of gold, and turn it into a very specific character. She isn't all good and she

isn't all clichés: she's a very complicated young woman with quirks and insecurities and a wayward ability to love. I became quietly astounded when I realized that this movie was going to create an original, *interesting* relationship involving a teen-ager and a hooker. The teen-age kid, in what will be called the Dustin Hoffman role, is played by Tom Cruise, who also knows how to imply a whole world by what he won't say, can't feel, and doesn't understand.

This is a movie of new faces and inspired insights and genuine laughs. It's hard to make a good movie and harder to make a good comedy and almost impossible to make a satire of such popular but mysterious obsessions as guilt, greed, lust, and secrecy. This movie knows what goes on behind the closed bathroom doors of the American dream.

Rita, Sue and Bob Too ★ ★ ★
R, 95 m., 1987

George Costigan (Bob), Siobhan Finneran (Rita), Michelle Holmes (Sue), Lesley Sharp (Michelle), Kulvinder Ghir (Aslam), Willie Ross (Sue's Father), Patti Nicholls (Sue's Mother), Paul Oldham (Lee). Directed by Alan Clarke and produced by Sandy Lieberson. Screenplay by Andrea Dunbar.

I've seen *Rita, Sue and Bob Too* twice, and the audiences were uneasy both times. They didn't seem sure exactly what to feel about this film. I'm not sure, either. The movie is a bleak, sardonic British comedy about the violation of a taboo: A married man in his thirties has affairs with two teen-age girls who are his baby-sitters. If this were a solemn TV docudrama with a psychiatrist to explain everything, we could relax. But it's an angry comedy, further complicated because both of the girls are so sassy and irreverent that it's hard to see them as victims.

The movie opens in a grim housing estate on the barren outskirts of a nondescript midlands city. One long shot establishes the scene: A drunk lurches into view, totters down the sidewalk, and disappears into a depressing brick building, and then a girl comes scurrying out, dressed for school, and runs down the street to meet her friend, whose front yard is occupied by a motorcycle gang.

The two girls are Rita and Sue. They are in their mid-teens but they already look worn by life, and yet they're filled with spirit. Rita (Siobhan Finneran) is more conventional, Sue (Michelle Holmes) is more likely

to say things for shock effect, but they're peas in a pod. Like a lot of adolescent best friends, they can finish each other's sentences, and sometimes when the vibes are right they can even speak in unison.

That night they go to baby-sit at Bob and Michelle's home in a nearby suburb that is cosmetically more attractive than where Rita and Sue live, although perhaps there is just as much desperation behind the picture windows. There's a great scene of the two girls sitting side by side on a sofa, bouncing in time to a music video; we can see how young they really are, something that's not always very obvious.

Late at night, Bob brings his wife home and offers to drive the two girls home. Instead, they drive into the country, park overlooking the town, and have sex. Bob proposes the idea, they giggle, and then they get right to it, right there in the car. This is the scene that's hard to read. It is sordid, and Bob's behavior is certainly immoral, and yet the sex itself has a sort of low, bawdy humor to it, and the girls seem surprisingly casual about it.

To fortunate people with middle-class opportunities, the whole episode is likely to seem shocking. But the film means to shock, and the statement it makes is a political one. Rita and Sue come from utterly deprived homes, from the culture of poverty. Nothing is happening in their lives. Bob provides variety, someone to gossip and speculate about, and his demands are no more inconvenient for them than the casual, brutal promiscuity they see at home. The movie challenges us to disapprove of the conditions that produced Rita and Sue, rather than to take a safe, superficial stand against that rascal Bob.

But here I am lecturing, and the curious thing about *Rita, Sue and Bob Too* is that it does not lecture and contains no speeches. It is a comedy, if a sometimes depressing one, and the best thing in it is the irrepressible sauciness of the two girls. If this were an American film, it would be an R-rated sex romp without a brain in its head, another soft-core baby-sitter saga. But *Rita, Sue and Bob Too* is one of those recent small-scale British films that are more interested in human nature than in selling lots of tickets with lots of sex.

This is a movie about two tough, deprived girls from the worst part of town, and an irresponsible, feather-brained adult who thinks he's taking advantage of them when in fact they're a whole lot more worldly and cynical than he is. These aren't bad girls. They're totally without standards—after all, they haven't been taught any—but they have a sense of humor and high spirits, and this is one of those movies you talk about a lot afterward, because the motives of all the characters are so complicated that you're not absolutely sure just who came out ahead.

A River Runs Through It ★ ★ ★ ½
PG, 123 m., 1992

Craig Sheffer (Norman Maclean), Brad Pitt (Paul Maclean), Tom Skerritt (Reverend Maclean), Brenda Blethyn (Mrs. Maclean), Emily Lloyd (Jessie Burns), Edie McClurg (Mrs. Burns). Directed by Robert Redford and produced by Redford and Patrick Markey. Screenplay by Richard Friedenberg.

Robert Redford's poetic, elegiac *A River Runs Through It* is about how a father attempts to pass on to his children the fundamental principles of his life. But it is more than that. It is also about how one of his sons remembers those lessons years later, as they applied to him, and to a brother who died too young. The father was a Presbyterian minister in Montana in the years before World War I. Some of his lessons were taught on Sundays, in his sermons. More of them were taught in trout streams.

Fly-fishing stands for life in this movie. If you can learn to do it correctly, to read the river and the fish and yourself, and to do what needs to be done without one wasted motion, you will have attained some of the grace and economy needed to live a good life. If you can do it and understand that the river, the fish, and the whole world are God's gifts to use wisely, you will have gone the rest of the way.

This memory of a Western childhood was first told in a book published some twenty years ago by Norman Maclean, after he retired as a professor of English at the University of Chicago. It was a story his father told him he should someday try to write. The book was published to little fanfare by the university press, and immediately found an audience. Many printings later it is one of the sacred books in the libraries of many people—one of the books that actually taught them something, like *Walden* or *Huckleberry Finn*.

Redford's film version makes the crucial decision to keep Maclean's voice in the film; his own prose is read as a narration, by Red-

ford, so that we do not simply see events as they happen; we are reminded that they are memories from long ago, and that the author has spent time and trouble to draw the lessons from them.

The movie stars Craig Sheffer as Norman, the older son, more serious, learning to write by taking his papers in to his father's study, invariably to be told, "Good. Now make it half as long." Brad Pitt is the younger brother, Paul, an impetuous, golden-haired free spirit who drinks too much and gets in card games, and wants nothing more than to stay in Montana all of his life, working for a newspaper. Norman has more serious aspirations; he wants to teach literature. But it is Paul who is the better fly fisherman, and who, at least one day, is perfect at what he does.

The movie was shot on locations that suggest the bounty of the Western states in those days. The towns uneasily straddle the divide between the modern and the frontier. As the boys grow up, they meet young ladies, and date, and consider their futures, and Redford elaborates on the book in ways that flesh out the characters of Paul and his mother, and some of the people in their lives, including a young Indian woman Paul dates in defiance of town opinion, and the high-spirited Jessie (Emily Lloyd), who eventually becomes Norman's wife.

This must have been a very difficult movie to write. It is not really about the events that happen in it. They are only illustrations for underlying principles. Leave out the principles, and all you have left are some interesting people who are born, grow up, and take various directions in life. Redford and his writer, Richard Friedenberg, understand that most of the events in any life are accidental or arbitrary, especially the crucial ones, and we can exercise little conscious control over our destinies. Instead, they understand that the Rev. Maclean's lessons were about how to behave no matter what life brings; about how to wade into the unpredictable stream and deal with whatever happens with grace, courage, and honesty. It is the film's best achievement that it communicates that message with such feeling.

River's Edge ★ ★ ★ ½
R, 100 m., 1987

Crispin Glover (Layne), Dennis Hopper (Feck), Keanu Reeves (Matt), Ione Skye (Clarissa), Daniel Roebuck (Leitch Sampson), Joshua

Miller (Tim), Roxana Zal (Maggie). Directed by Tim Hunter and produced by Sarah Pillsbury and Midge Sanford. Screenplay by Neal Jimenez.

I remember reading about the case at the time. A high school kid killed his girlfriend and left her body lying on the ground. Over the next few days, he brought some of his friends out to look at her body, and gradually word of the crime spread through his circle of friends. But for a long time, nobody called the cops.

A lot of op-ed articles were written to analyze this event, which was seen as symptomatic of a wider moral breakdown in our society. *River's Edge*, which is a horrifying fiction inspired by the case, offers no explanation and no message; it regards the crime in much the same way the kid's friends stood around looking at the body. The difference is that the film feels a horror that the teenagers apparently did not.

This is the best analytical film about a crime since *The Onion Field* and *In Cold Blood*. Like those films, it poses these questions: Why do we need to be told this story? How is it useful to see limited and brutish people doing cruel and stupid things? I suppose there are two answers. One, because such things exist in the world and some of us are curious about them as we are curious in general about human nature. Two, because an artist is never merely a reporter and by seeing the tragedy through his eyes, he helps us to see it through ours.

River's Edge was directed by Tim Hunter, who made *Tex*, about ordinary teen-agers who found themselves faced with the choice of dealing drugs. In *River's Edge*—that choice has long since been made. These teen-agers are alcoholics and drug abusers, including one whose mother is afraid he is stealing her marijuana and a twelve-year-old who blackmails the older kids for six-packs.

The central figure in the film is not the murderer, Sampson (Daniel Roebuck), a large, stolid youth who seems perpetually puzzled about why he does anything. It is Layne (Crispin Glover), a strung-out, mercurial rebel who always seems to be on speed and who takes it upon himself to help conceal the crime. When his girlfriend asks him, like, well, gee, she was our friend and all, so shouldn't we feel bad, or something, his answer is that the murderer "had his reasons." What were they? The victim was talking back.

Glover's performance is electric. He's like a young Eric Roberts, and he carries around a constant sense of danger. Eventually, we realize the danger is born of paranoia; he is reflecting it at us with his fear.

These kids form a clique that exists outside the mainstream in their high school. They hang around outside, smoking and sneering. In town, they have a friend named Feck (Dennis Hopper), a drug dealer who lives inside a locked house and once killed a woman himself, so he has something in common with the kid, you see? It is another of Hopper's possessed performances, done with sweat and the whites of his eyes.

River's Edge is not a film I will forget very soon. Its portrait of these adolescents is an exercise in despair. Not even old enough to legally order a beer, they already are destroyed by alcohol and drugs, abandoned by parents who also have lost hope. When the story of the dead girl first appeared in the papers, it seemed like a freak show, an aberration. *River's Edge* sets it in an ordinary town and makes it seem like just what the op-ed philosophers said: an emblem of breakdown. The girl's body eventually was discovered and buried. If you seek her monument, look around you.

The River Wild ★ ★
PG-13, 108 m., 1994

NEW

Meryl Streep (Gail), David Strathairn (Tom), Kevin Bacon (Wade), Joseph Mazzello (Roarke), Stephanie Sawyer (Willa), Buffy (Maggie [dog]), Elizabeth Hoffman (Gail's Mother), Victor H. Galloway (Gail's Father), Diane Delano and Thomas F. Duffy (Diane Delano and Thomas F. Duffy). Directed by Curtis Hanson and produced by David Foster and Lawrence Turman. Screenplay by Denis O'Neill.

The River Wild is one of the movies you *want* to play along with, you really do, but it gets so many details subtly wrong that finally you lose patience and turn on it. It's a replay of the *Deliverance* formula, in which city folks try their luck in nature, and find that the most dangerous predator is Man. Just because it's been done before doesn't mean it can't work again. But it requires more care at the nuts-and-bolts level than this film is able to provide.

The movie stars Meryl Streep as a former Montana river guide, who wants to take her family back home for a white-water rafting expedition. Her husband (David Strathairn)

is reluctant; he's a workaholic who has seriously alienated his young son by making it obvious he prefers his office to his home. But at the last minute Dad does join the family and its faithful dog, Maggie, for the long-awaited vacation.

As they embark, they become aware of another group of rafters—three rough-hewn men, led by Kevin Bacon. And as they float farther downstream, away from roads and civilization, they can't seem to shake the other boat. Strathairn even saves Bacon from drowning, knocking him out when he panics and threatens to pull them both under. ("You saved my life," Bacon tells him, adding the movie's best line: "You didn't have to hit me, though.")

It's obvious the strange men are bad guys; what other function could they serve in the movie? But just to be sure we don't miss the point, the screenplay supplies one of those handy movie radios—the kind where you switch it on, and it immediately supplies a news item exactly describing the suspicious characters. Then one of the three men disappears (and there are ominous fly-buzzing noises on the sound track as Maggie sniffs in the bushes). And it becomes clear that Streep will be required to guide all of these people through (ominous drum roll) the Gauntlet.

The screenplay sets up the Gauntlet in classic movie style. ("It's off the scale," Streep says. "One man was killed, and another one paralyzed for life. The rangers no longer allow anyone to try it.") We know with perfect certainty that the heroes of this movie will try it, however. And that the meek, workaholic dad, with his wire-rim glasses, will get his chance to prove how much of a man he really is.

Movies like this are so predictable in their overall stories that they win or lose with their details. Among the best elements of *The River Wild* are the performances by Bacon, as the charming but sinister bad guy, and Streep, who puts a lot of humor and intelligence into her character. Robert Elswit's cinematography is great-looking; people are going to want to know where this river is, so they can raft it.

But in the specifics of the situation, the movie is always a little wrong. There is a scene, for example, where a park ranger (a former classmate of Streep's) stops along to ask the group if everything is all right. The bad guys have guns pointed into the backs of Strathairn and Streep, they're all lined up stiffly in a row, and their answers are so forced and pained, it's clearly obvious some-

thing is very wrong. Obvious, except to the ranger. The scene could have been handled more convincingly if Bacon's sidekick had simply kept the kid in the woods, as hostage.

And what about the sequences in which Strathairn cuts cross-country, climbing mountains, fording rivers, walking faster than the river flows. Impossible, but he does it. At one point, in a scene so ludicrous I wanted to laugh aloud, he even starts a fire to send smoke signals to his wife. At another point, he clings to the side of a cliff, while we ask ourselves what earthly reason he had for climbing it. And he works wonders with his handy Swiss Army knife.

The climax is the running of the Gauntlet, which is well photographed but so much of a preordained set piece it's hardly worth the bother. By the end of the film we haven't been surprised by much of anything, and the characters have only been briefly freed from the requirements of the plot. *The River Wild* was constructed from so many ideas, characters, and situations recycled from other movies that all the way down the river I kept thinking: Been there. Done that.

The Road Warrior ★ ★ ★ ½
R, 97 m., 1982

Mel Gibson (Max), Bruce Spence (Gyro Captain), Vernon Wells (Wez), Emil Minty (Feral Kid), Virginia Hey (Warrior Woman). Directed by George Miller and produced by Byron Kennedy. Screenplay by Terry Hayes, Miller, and Brian Hannant.

The Road Warrior is a film of pure action, of kinetic energy organized around the barest possible bones of a plot. It has a vision of a violent future world, but it doesn't develop that vision with characters and dialogue. It would rather plunge headlong into one of the most relentlessly aggressive movies ever made. I walked out of *The Road Warrior* a little dizzy and with my ears still ringing from the roar of the sound track; I can't say I "enjoyed" the film, but I'll hardly forget it. The movie takes place at a point in the future when civilization has collapsed, anarchy and violence reign in the world, and roaming bands of marauders kill each other for the few remaining stores of gasoline. The vehicles of these future warriors are leftovers from the world we live in now. There are motorcycles and semi-trailer trucks and oil tankers that are familiar from the highways of 1982, but there are also bizarre customized racing cars, of which the most fearsome has two steel posts on its front to which enemies can be strapped (if the car crashes, the enemies are the first to die).

The road warriors of the title take their costumes and codes of conduct from a rummage sale of legends, myths, and genres: They look and act like Hell's Angels, samurai warriors, kamikaze pilots, street-gang members, cowboys, cops, and race drivers. They speak hardly at all; the movie's hero, Max, has perhaps two hundred words. Max is played by Mel Gibson, an Australian actor who starred in *Gallipoli*. Before that, he made *Mad Max* for the makers of *The Road Warrior*, and that film was a low-budget forerunner to this extravaganza of action and violence. Max's role in *The Road Warrior* is to behave something like a heroic cowboy might have in a classic Western. He happens upon a small band of people who are trying to protect their supplies of gasoline from the attacks of warriors who have them surrounded. Max volunteers to drive a tanker full of gasoline through the surrounding warriors and take it a few hundred miles to the coast, where they all hope to find safety. After this premise is established with a great deal of symbolism, ritual, and violence (and so few words that sometimes we have to guess what's happening), the movie arrives at its true guts. The set piece in *The Road Warrior* is an unbelievably well-sustained chase sequence that lasts for the last third of the film, as Max and his semi-trailer run a gauntlet of everything the savages can throw at them.

The director of *The Road Warrior*, George Miller, compares this chase sequence to Buster Keaton's *The General*, and I can see what he means. Although *The General* is comedic, it's also very exciting, as Keaton, playing the engineer of a speeding locomotive, runs an endless series of variations on the basic possibilities of two trains and several sets of railroad tracks. In *The Road Warrior*, there is basically a truck and a road. The pursuers and defenders have various kinds of cars and trucks to chase or defend the main truck, and the whole chase proceeds at breakneck speed as quasi-gladiators leap through the air from one racing truck to another, more often than not being crushed beneath the wheels. The special effects and stunts in this movie are spectacular; *The Road Warrior* goes on a short list with *Bullitt*, *The French Connection*, and the truck chase in *Raiders of the Lost Ark* as among the great chase films of modern years.

What is the point of the movie? Everyone

is free to interpret the action, I suppose, but I prefer to avoid thinking about the implications of gasoline shortages and the collapse of Western civilization, and to experience the movie instead as pure sensation. The filmmakers have imagined a fictional world. It operates according to its special rules and values, and we experience it. The experience is frightening, sometimes disgusting, and (if the truth be told) exhilarating. This is very skillful filmmaking, and *The Road Warrior* is a movie like no other.

Robin Hood: Prince of Thieves ★ ★
PG-13, 138 m., 1991

Kevin Costner (Robin Hood), Morgan Freeman (Azeem), Christian Slater (Will Scarlett), Alan Rickman (Sheriff of Nottingham), Mary Elizabeth Mastrantonio (Maid Marian), Nick Brimble (Little John). Directed by Kevin Reynolds and produced by John Watson, Pen Densham, and Richard Lewis. Screenplay by Densham and John Watson.

Robin Hood: Prince of Thieves is a murky, unfocused, violent, and depressing version of the classic story, with little of the lightheartedness and romance we expect from Robin Hood. It's shot mostly at night or in gloomy forests, beneath overcasts or by flickering firelight or in gloomy dungeons, which is all very well for the atmosphere, but makes the action scenes almost impossible to follow.

Among the movie's many problems: Kevin Costner plays a tortured, thoughtful Robin Hood, totally lacking in the joy of living that we associate with the character. The romance between Robin and Maid Marian (Mary Elizabeth Mastrantonio) seems inspired more by necessity than by desire, as if both of them had read the book and knew they were required to fall in love with one another. The most colorful character is the villain, the Sheriff of Nottingham (Alan Rickman), but both the character and the performance are inappropriate for this film. And the amount of gore is appalling in a film that will presumably be aimed at a family market.

To begin with the gore: The movie begins with a hand being chopped off, and continues with various amputations, gorings, stabbings, burnings, floggings, hangings (a small boy is one of the intended hanging victims), explosions, and falls from great heights, before reaching a climax of sorts as the Sheriff of Nottingham attempts to rape Maid Marian, and has just succeeded in spreading her legs (a graphic floor-level shot here) before

Robin Hood comes swinging in through the window to save her.

Then there is the general moral climate of the movie, in which all of the priests are seen as corrupt or drunken swine, and the sheriff consults an old crone in a dungeon who foretells the future by reading blood and chicken bones. The leading cleric of Nottingham is a turncoat and a liar, who marries Marian to the sheriff against her will while the castle is under siege. You know we have entered a shaky liturgical era when Friar Tuck is the most religious person in the film.

The movie casts Robin Hood as sort of a populist guerilla, a Che Guevera with bow and arrow, who lives with his followers in Sherwood Forest and intercepts the king's mail by using tunnels and camouflaged hiding-places under the forest floor, Viet Cong style. His best friend and right-hand man is a Moor (Morgan Freeman), who he has brought back from the Holy Land after saving his life in prison. His biggest disciplinary problem is a young hothead (Christian Slater), who is so obviously bursting with a secret he desires to share that it's amazing Robin is able to wait almost until the end of the movie before learning it.

Much has been said about Kevin Costner's British accent, or lack of same, in advance publicity about the movie. Neither the accent nor the lack of same bothered me in the slightest. What bothered me was that the filmmakers never found the right tone for Costner to use, no matter what his accent. He isn't joyous, or robust, or comical, or heroic, but more of a thoughtful, civilized, socially responsible Robin Hood, sort of a nonpartisan saint who wants to preserve the kingdom for the absent Richard the Lionhearted. Costner plays Robin Hood as if he were Alan Alda.

Alan Rickman, in complete contrast, plays the Sheriff as if he were David Letterman: He's a wicked, droll, sly, witty master of the put-down and one-liners, who rolls his eyes in exasperation when Robin comes bursting in to interrupt the rape. Rickman's performance has nothing to do with anything else in the movie, and indeed seems to proceed from a uniquely personal set of assumptions about what century, universe, etc., the story is set in, but at least when Rickman appears on the screen we perk up, because we know we'll be entertained, at whatever cost to the story.

The only major player who finds the right tone and voice for all of his scenes is Morgan

Freeman, as the Moor, who finds humor when it is needed, courage when it is required, and somehow even survives being given a running joke that has to be carefully nurtured from one end of the movie to the other. Mary Elizabeth Mastrantonio does what she can with Marian, but must have been confused when the screenplay gave her a thoughtful, independent woman in the earlier scenes, and then turned her into a cliched damsel in distress at the end.

The costumes look as if they have things growing in them. The treehouses in Sherwood Forest permit Robin and his men to engage in a key battle scene that looks like a cross between *Tarzan* and the savage tribesmen at the end of *Apocalypse Now*. (This battle deserves greater analysis. In it, hired Celtic mercenaries attack Robin's band and are all but destroyed, after which they only then use their fire catapults, and all but destroy Robin's side, after which, for the later assault on the castle, Robin hardly seems to have lost a man.) The music is your standard rum-dummy-dum false epic dirge kind of stuff. The editing is desperate. The most depressing thing about the movie is that children will watch it expecting to have a good time.

RoboCop ★ ★ ★
R, 103 m., 1987

Peter Weller (Murphy/RoboCop), Nancy Allen (Lewis), Daniel O'Herlihy (The Old Man), Ronny Cox (Jones), Kurtwood Smith (Clarence), Miguel Ferrer (Morton), Robert DoQui (Sergeant Reed). Directed by Paul Verhoeven and produced by Arne Schmidt. Screenplay by Edward Neumeier and Michael Miner.

There is a moment early in *RoboCop* when a robot runs amok. It has been programmed to warn a criminal to drop his gun, and then to shoot him if he does not comply. The robot, an ugly and ungainly machine, is wheeled into a board meeting of the company that hopes to make millions by retailing it. A junior executive is chosen to pull a gun on the machine. The warning is issued. The exec drops his gun. The robot repeats the warning, counts to five, and shoots the guy dead.

This is a very funny scene. (Whether it was even funnier before the MPAA Code and Ratings Administration requested trims in it is, I suppose, a moot point.) It is funny in the same way that the assembly line in Chaplin's *Modern Times* is funny—because there is something hilarious about logic applied to a situation where it is not relevant.

Because the scene surprises us in a movie that seemed to be developing into a serious thriller, it puts us off guard. We're no longer quite sure where *RoboCop* is going, and that's one of the movie's best qualities.

The film takes place at an unspecified time in the future, in Detroit, a city where gang terror rules. There has been a series of brutal cop killings. A big corporation wants to market the robot cops to stamp out crime, but the demonstrator model is obviously not up to the job.

A junior scientist thinks he knows a better way to make a policeman, by combining robotics with a human brain. And he gets his chance when a hero cop (Peter Weller) is killed in the line of duty. Well, not quite killed. Something remains, and around that human core the first "robocop" is constructed—a half-man, half-machine that operates with perfect logic except for the shreds of human spontaneity and intuition that may be lurking somewhere in the background of its memory.

Nancy Allen co-stars in the movie as a woman cop who was Weller's partner before he was shot. She recognizes something familiar about the robocop, and eventually realizes what it is: Inside that suit of steel, it's her old partner, Weller. It actually shouldn't have taken her long to figure it out, since Weller's original nose, mouth, chin, and jaw are visible. His inventor apparently agrees with Batman and Robin that if you can't see the eyes of someone you know, you'll never recognize them.

The broad outline of the plot develops along more or less standard thriller lines. But this is not a standard thriller. The director is Paul Verhoeven, the gifted Dutch filmmaker whose earlier credits include *Soldier of Orange* and *The Fourth Man*. His movies are not easily categorized. There is comedy in this movie, even slapstick comedy. There is romance. There is a certain amount of philosophy, centering on the question, What is a man? And there is pointed social satire, too, as RoboCop takes on some of the attributes and some of the popular following of a Bernard Goetz.

Oddly enough, a lot of RoboCop's personality is expressed by his voice, which is a mechanical monotone. Machines and robots have spoken like this for years in the movies, and now life is beginning to copy them; I was in the Atlanta airport, boarding the shuttle train to the terminal, and the train started talking to me just like RoboCop, in an uninflected monotone. ("Your-attention-please the-doors-are-about-to-close.")

I laughed. No one else did. Since the recorded message could obviously have been recorded in a normal human voice, the purpose of the robotic audio style was clear: to make the commands seem to emanate from a pre-programmed authority that could not be appealed to. In *RoboCop*, Verhoeven and Weller get a lot of mileage out of the conflict between that utterly assured voice and the increasingly confused being behind it.

Considering that he spends much of the movie hidden behind one kind of makeup device or another, Weller does an impressive job of creating sympathy for his character. He is more "human," indeed, when he is RoboCop than earlier in the movie, when he's an ordinary human being. His plight is appealing, and Nancy Allen is effective as the determined partner who wants to find out what really happened to him.

Most thriller and special-effects movies come right off the assembly line. You can call out every development in advance, and usually be right. *RoboCop* is a thriller with a difference.

Rob Roy ★ ★ ★ ½   [NEW]
R, 134 m., 1995

Liam Neeson (Rob Roy), Jessica Lange Mary), John Hurt (Montrose), Tim Roth (Cunningham), Eric Stoltz (McDonald), Andrew Keir (Argyll), Brian Cox (Killearn), Brian McCardie (Alasdair), Gilbert Martin (Guthrie), Vicki Masson (Betty). Directed by Michael Caton-Jones and produced by Peter Broughan and Richard Jackson. Screenplay by Alan Sharp.

Strange. I thought I had seen enough sword fights in movies to last me a lifetime, but I was wrong. The sword fight in *Rob Roy* reinvents the exercise, and the movie itself brings hot red blood to the costume genre. This is a splendid, rousing historical adventure, an example of what can happen when the best direction, acting, writing, and technical credits are brought to bear on what might look like shopworn material.

What's best about the movie is its vivid picture of the time and place (Scotland, circa 1713), and the kinds of personalities produced by a world where the simple people still believed in romantic chivalry, while the aristocracy embraced decadence and court intrigue. Rob Roy is a hero not simply because he is tall, good, and strong, but because he will sacrifice his life rather than compromise his word. And the film's villains are magnificent because they are so smart, cunning, and smarmy: Not content with merely being despicable, they work at it.

The story takes place at a time when Scots-Catholic Jacobites lived in uneasy proximity with the Protestant English landowning aristocracy. A farmer and clan leader, Rob Roy MacGregor (Liam Neeson) goes to the local Marquis of Montrose (John Hurt) for a loan of one thousand pounds. He plans to use the money to buy and fatten cattle, turn a profit, and repay the loan. The marquis grants the loan.

But the secret of the money is shared by the blubbery Killearn (Brian Cox) with the foppish Archibald Cunningham (Tim Roth), a prancing dandy whose effete exterior conceals a steel-trap mind and deadly swordsmanship. Cunningham, always broke, is in debt to the marquis and needs money desperately. He waylays Rob Roy's messenger (Eric Stoltz), kills him, steals the money, and leaves MacGregor in default of his home and lands. Rob Roy then, of course, becomes an outlaw, leading his clan in defiance of the English troops.

This story outline could have produced yet another tired historical epic with yeomen dashing around on horses, quaffing ale, and eating burnt sheep with both hands while their betters practiced the minuet. ("Don't give me any more pictures where they write with feathers!" Jack Warner once pleaded with his producers.) Instead, in the hands of director Michael Caton-Jones, it produces intense character studies. Liam Neeson, tall and grand, makes an effortless hero as Rob Roy. Jessica Lange, as his wife, Mary, has a fierce strength of character that drives her to defend her home and children, defy her husband when she finds it necessary—and keep within her the secret that she has been raped, because she fears if Rob Roy discovers it, he will lose his life while seeking vengeance.

Great villains make melodrama, and Tim Roth, as Cunningham, is crucial to the success of this film. Resplendent in frilly court costumes, pudding-faced beneath a curly wig, he makes a foppish dandy; no matter how many times you saw *Pulp Fiction*, you will never recognize him as Honey Bunny's main man. What is intriguing is the way his exterior is really a disguise: In fact, he is one of

the deadliest swordfighters in England, and a sexual outlaw with an insatiable appetite, who boasts, "Love is a dung hill, and I am but a cock that climbs upon it to crow."

The conflict in *Rob Roy* is quickly simplified: Cunningham, who stole the money, is assigned by the marquis to capture Rob Roy, who is blamed for its disappearance. The key question is, whose word will the marquis believe: that of Rob Roy, a peasant, or Cunningham, an aristocrat? What is intriguing in John Hurt's performance as the marquis is the way he nurtures suspicions about Cunningham ("You are in cash, but have no means . . .") and yet is willing to have Rob Roy die, because it is a matter of saving face. A locket reveals the key to his feelings.

Another key player in the drama is the other powerful local aristocrat, the Duke of Argyll (Andrew Keir), who supports the cause of the deposed Catholic monarchy against what he sees as the Protestant usurpers. Montrose offers Rob Roy forgiveness of his debt if he will denounce Argyll as a Jacobite, but Rob Roy refuses, and eventually it is Argyll who arranges for the whole matter to be settled in a sword fight between Rob Roy and Cunningham.

The sword-fighting sequence, staged by William Hobbs, is the best of its sort ever done. In most movie sword fights the participants leap about effortlessly, their blades shimmering and clashing. Here we get the sense of the deadly stakes, and the great physical effort involved.

Cunningham chooses a rapier, Rob Roy a broadsword (their weapons reflect their personalities), and the fight is punctuated by passages of dead silence, except for heavy breathing. They become very tired. They are both wounded. The pauses grow longer, until the duel seems like a chess match, in which thought counts for more than action. It is one of the great action sequences in movie history, and *Rob Roy* is a fabulous entertainment.

The Rocketeer ★ ★ ★
PG-13, 108 m., 1991

Bill Campbell (Cliff), Jennifer Connelly (Jenny), Alan Arkin (Peevy), Timothy Dalton (Neville Sinclair), Paul Sorvino (Eddie Valentine), Terry O'Quinn (Howard Hughes). Directed by Joe Johnston and produced by Lawrence Gordon, Charles Gordon, and Lloyd Levin. Screenplay by Danny Bilson and Paul DeMeo.

The hero of *The Rocketeer* is presented as an action hero along the lines of Indiana Jones,

but the difference between this movie and the *Indy* series is fundamental: *Raiders of the Lost Ark* took the Saturday afternoon serials of the late 1930s and 1940s as an inspiration, while *The Rocketeer* takes them as a model. Indy kidded them, *The Rocketeer* copies them. The movie lacks the wit and self-mocking irony of the *Indiana Jones* movies, and instead seems like a throwback to the simpleminded, clean-cut sensibility of a less complicated time.

That doesn't mean *The Rocketeer* is not entertaining. But adjustments are necessary to enjoy it; you have to dial down, to return to an age of innocence when an eccentric inventor and a clean-eyed hero could take on the bad guys with a new gizmo they'd stumbled on by accident.

The movie stars Bill Campbell as Cliff Secord, the young test pilot who dreams of winning a big air race but instead finds himself with the opportunity of a lifetime when he straps on a contraption dreamed up by Howard Hughes and company. It's a one-man portable rocket backpack that allows Cliff to fly around the countryside with flames shooting out behind him, while wearing a helmet that, as the screenplay accurately observes, makes him look like a hood ornament. The helmet, invented by the old codger Peevy (Alan Arkin), allows him to steer, by a mechanism wisely not very well explained.

Of what use is this contraption? Need I reveal that the man who possesses it may hold the possibility of world domination in his hands? The Nazis want it, and according to an animated German propaganda movie that has fallen into American hands ("a man died for this film"), soldiers wearing rocket backpacks could swoop down on the United States and conquer it overnight. (Slight problems are ignored, such as: What condition would the hordes of Nazis arrive in after their transatlantic one-man flights? Would they run out of fuel? Be badly sunburned? Get their heels toasted by the flames? Carry sandwiches?)

A Nazi spy ring has been deployed to capture the prototype Rocketeer outfit, but the dummkopfs mistakenly steal an Electro-Lux vacuum cleaner instead, and meanwhile Cliff straps on the contraption and goes forth to battle for truth, justice, and the American way. He is surrounded in the film by the dashing Neville Sinclair (Timothy Dalton), a Hollywood star who is a Nazi sympathizer; Eddie Valentine (Paul Sorvino), a Mafia head whose men have been hired to steal the rocket suit, and Howard Hughes (Terry O'Quinn), who is the big bucks behind the invention. And there is also, of course, his girlfriend, Jenny, played by the doe-eyed and pneumatic Jennifer Connelly.

The movie's innocence extends even to its special effects, which may be state-of-the-art but sometimes seem as charmingly direct as those rockets in the "Flash Gordon" serials—the ones with sparklers hidden inside of them, which were pulled on wires in front of papier-mâché mountains. When *The Rocketeer* straps on his gizmo and goes whizzing around the screen, he looks for all the world like some harebrained kid trying to break his neck on some new contraption.

Even when the special effects are elaborate, they seem old-fashioned. There's a sequence, for example, that involves a fight on top of a flaming Nazi zeppelin, and as the explosions rocked the frame I was having flashbacks to *The Hindenberg* and that James Bond movie that also had a fight on top of a blimp.

The virtues of the movie are in its wide-eyed credulity, its sense of wonder. Bill Campbell, an actor who in this film is largely lacking in charisma, may even be the right choice for the role; he's a white-bread, Identikit leading man who seems as bland as the B actors who wore the superhero costumes in those old serials. Jennifer Connelly is sweet and sexy as his girlfriend, and projects the same innocent sensuality of the classic B-movie sexpots—an ability to seem totally unaware, for example, that she is wearing a low-cut dress. Alan Arkin has some fun as the eccentric old codger, and Dalton makes a sly villain. And when the movie is over, it's as insubstantial as cotton candy. I suppose that's a virtue.

Rocky ★ ★ ★ ★
PG, 119 m., 1976

Sylvester Stallone (Rocky), Talia Shire (Adrian), Burt Young (Paulie), Carl Weathers (Apollo Creed), Burgess Meredith (Mickey), Frank Stallone (Timekeeper). Directed by John Avildsen and produced by Robert Chartoff and Irwin Winkler. Screenplay by Sylvester Stallone.

She sits, tearful and crumpled, in a corner of her little bedroom. Her brother has torn apart the living room with a baseball bat. Rocky, the guy she has fallen in love with, comes into the room.

"Do you want a roommate?" she asks shyly, almost whispering.

"Absolutely," says Rocky.

Which is exactly what he should say, and how he should say it, and why *Rocky* is such an immensely involving movie. Its story, about a punk club fighter from the back streets of Philly who gets a crack at the world championship, has been told a hundred times before. A description of it would sound like a cliché from beginning to end. But *Rocky* isn't about a story, it's about a hero. And it's inhabited with supreme confidence by a star.

His name is Sylvester Stallone, and, yes, in 1976 he did remind me of the young Marlon Brando. How many actors have come and gone and been forgotten who were supposed to be the "new Brando," while Brando endured? And yet in *Rocky* he provides shivers of recognition reaching back to *A Streetcar Named Desire*. He's tough, he's tender, he talks in a growl, and hides behind cruelty and is a champion at heart. "I coulda been a contender," Brando says in *On the Waterfront*. This movie takes up from there.

It inhabits a curiously deserted Philadelphia: There aren't any cars parked on the slum street where Rocky lives or the slightest sign that anyone else lives there. His world is a small one. By day, he works as an enforcer for a small-time juice man, offering to break a man's thumbs over a matter of $70 ("I'll bandage it!" cries the guy. "It'll *look* broke"). In his spare time, he works out at Mickey's gym. He coulda been good, but he smokes and drinks beer and screws around. And yet there's a secret life behind his facade. He is awkwardly in love with a painfully shy girl (Talia Shire) who works in the corner pet shop. He has a couple of turtles at home, named Cuff and Link, and a goldfish named Moby Dick. After he wins forty bucks one night for taking a terrible battering in the ring, he comes home and tells the turtles: "If you guys could sing and dance, I wouldn't have to go through this crap." When the girl asks him why he boxes, he explains: "Because I can't sing and dance."

The movie ventures into fantasy when the world heavyweight champion (Carl Weathers, as a character with a certain similarity to Muhammad Ali) decides to schedule a New Year's Eve bout with a total unknown—to prove that America is still a land of opportunity. Rocky gets picked because of his nickname, the Italian Stallion; the champ likes the racial contrast. And even *here* the

movie looks like a genre fight picture from the 1940s, right down to the plucky little gymnasium manager (Burgess Meredith) who puts Rocky through training, and right down to the lonely morning ritual of rising at four, drinking six raw eggs, and going out to do roadwork. What makes the movie extraordinary is that it doesn't try to surprise us with an original plot, with twists and complications; it wants to involve us on an elemental, a sometimes savage, level. It's about heroism and realizing your potential, about taking your best shot and sticking by your girl. It sounds not only clichéd but corny—and yet it's not, not a bit, because it really does work on those levels. It involves us emotionally, it makes us commit ourselves: We find, maybe to our surprise after remaining detached during so many movies, that this time we *care*.

The credit for that has to be passed around. A lot of it goes to Stallone when he wrote this story and then peddled it around Hollywood for years before he could sell it. He must have known it would work because he could see himself in the role, could imagine the conviction he's bringing to it, and I can't think of another actor who could quite have pulled off this performance. There's that exhilarating moment when Stallone, in training, runs up the steps of Philadelphia's art museum, leaps into the air, shakes his fist at the city, and you know he's sending a message to the whole movie industry.

The director is John Avildsen, who made *Joe* and then another movie about a loser who tried to find the resources to start again, *Save the Tiger*. Avildsen correctly isolates Rocky in his urban environment, because this movie shouldn't have a documentary feel, with people hanging out of every window: It's a legend, it's about little people, but it's bigger than life, and you have to set them apart visually so you can isolate them morally.

And then there's Talia Shire, as the girl (she was the hapless sister of the Corleone boys in *The Godfather*). When she hesitates before kissing Rocky for the first time, it's a moment so poignant it's like no other. And Burt Young as her brother—defeated and resentful, loyal and bitter, caring about people enough to hurt them just to draw attention to his grief. There's all that, and then there's the fight that ends the film. By now, everyone knows who wins, but the scenes before the fight set us up for it so completely, so emotionally, that when it's over we've had it. We're drained.

Rocky II ★ ★ ★
PG, 119 m., 1979

Sylvester Stallone (Rocky Balboa), Talia Shire (Adrian), Burt Young (Paulie), Carl Weathers (Apollo Creed), Burgess Meredith (Mickey), Tony Burton (Apollo's Trainer). Directed by Sylvester Stallone and produced by Irwin Winkler and Robert Chartoff. Screenplay by Stallone.

Rocky II isn't the movie the first *Rocky* was— what could equal that original burst of vitality?—but it's a well-crafted sequel with a lot of the same appeal, and with a climactic fight scene that's sensationally effective. 1979 was a year of sequels and prequels and remakes, and, as they go, this is one of the best.

That's because it's legitimately a sequel: It continues the story and further develops the characters, instead of just ripping off a successful formula. At the end of *Rocky* we wanted to know what came next, and now we do. That's a lot different from something like *Beyond the Poseidon Adventure*, which essentially just repeats the original movie.

Rocky II begins exactly where the first movie ended, with Rocky Balboa's once-in-a-million shot at the heavyweight title. Sylvester Stallone, who directed this time as well as writing and starring, is wise to quote from that fight footage. It's a reminder of the extraordinary impact of *Rocky,* which took a tired old Hollywood genre and brilliantly rediscovered its strength.

Stallone then gives us a scene that speaks directly to our memories of the first movie. After their mutual battering, both Rocky and heavyweight champ Apollo Creed are hospitalized. And in the middle of the night Rocky opens Apollo's door and says, "Apollo? You awake?" Yeah. "Can I ask you somethin'?" Yeah. "Did you give me your best shot?" Yeah, I did. "Thank you."

Rocky's life changes dramatically, of course, after his moral victory in the fight. He's badgered by agents who want him to endorse products and do TV commercials (and he does at least one, holding a club and wearing a leopard skin and standing in a cage to endorse a men's after-shave). One of the first things he does, of course, is to marry his girlfriend Adrian (Talia Shire). They buy a car and a house. And Rocky looks around for a job.

His problem is that he can't fight again. Doctor's orders: He suffered damage to his eyes, and another fight could lead to blindness. But Rocky Balboa can't really *do* anything but fight. After a couple of menial jobs, he goes back to the gym run by his trainer, Mickey (played by Burgess Meredith in a jolly, scenery-chewing performance). These scenes—interlaced with Adrian's pregnancy and the birth of their son, Rocky, Jr. (with an astonishing head of hair)—head up to a sustained stretch of soap opera. Adrian goes into a coma. Rocky goes into a depression. Apollo Creed, driven by the need to clear his reputation, taunts Rocky for another fight in newspaper ads.

This is all pretty obvious stuff, and if it were handled with less care we might be tempted to laugh at the clichés. But Stallone as a writer has a way of getting away with things. He tells stories that are simple, basic, and human; he doesn't apologize for them, and he plays them with a conviction that makes them work.

He is also interesting as a director. The first *Rocky* was directed by John Avildsen, who placed it in a Philadelphia landscape deliberately kept barren of people who didn't figure in the story. The streets were empty, and the result was curiously effective: The characters gained a mythic stature because they were kept in relief and not marched through crowds of extras.

Stallone uses that same approach in *Rocky II.* But he also introduces an element of highly personal humor that first surfaced in *Paradise Alley* (1978), which he also wrote and directed. He likes characters who are offbeat and cheerfully grotesque. He likes scenes that are allowed to drift from realism into comic exaggeration. He likes to view life at an angle.

Paradise Alley gave us three heroic, crazy, goofy brothers, and scenes like the one in which the organ grinder's monkey is kept captive in the bathroom. *Rocky II* has fun with the wedding scene, with the absurd TV commercials, and especially with the night of the big fight. Instead of going for conventional devices to build the tension, Stallone cuts between drama and comedy, between the mounting excitement inside the fight arena and Rocky's leisurely progress through the city. Apollo Creed is sweating it out in his dressing room, but Rocky Balboa's stopping off at a parish hall for a quick blessing from the priest.

Then comes the fight scene. I wouldn't dream, of course, of telling you who wins. But the scene itself is terrific action footage, and Stallone's occasional use of slow motion seems to work here; in *Paradise Alley*'s closing fight, it was distracting and excessive. *Rocky II* tells the story crisply and with style, and keeps us hooked even during the soap opera stuff.

But almost any sequel to an enormous hit movie has this problem: We are already familiar with the qualities that made the original extraordinary. *Rocky* introduced us to this strange, eccentric, funny-talking, big lug from Philly who had turtles named Cuff and Link and a dog named Butkus, and was in love with the shy girl who worked at the pet store. It showed us Rocky's one-time shot at the big time. It established a fictional world that was fresh.

Rocky II can't do those things. It doesn't have the advantage of novelty. If you liked *Rocky,* you'll certainly want to see *Rocky II.* But the impact just can't be quite the same. Maybe that's why it's so good to have the fight scene at the end: It has such sheer animal intensity that it's got us cheering, just like the first time around.

The Rocky Horror Picture Show
★ ★ ½
R, 105 m., 1975

Tim Curry (Dr. Frank N. Furter), Susan Sarandon (Janet), Barry Bostwick (Brad), Richard O'Brien (Riff Raff). Directed by Dick Sharman and produced by Michael White. Screenplay by Sharman and Richard O'Brien.

The Rocky Horror Picture Show is not so much a movie as more of a long-running social phenomenon. When the film was first released in 1975 it was ignored by pretty much everyone, including the future fanatics who would eventually count the hundreds of times they'd seen it. *Rocky Horror* opened, closed, and would have been forgotten had it not been for the inspiration of a low-level 20th Century-Fox executive who talked his superiors into testing it as a midnight cult movie.

The rest is history. At its peak in the early 1980s, *Rocky Horror* was playing on weekend midnights all over the world, and loyal fans were lined up for hours in advance out in front of the theater, dressed in the costumes of the major characters. There were jolly reunions of Janets and Brads, the All-American couple played in the movie by Susan Sarandon and Barry Bostwick, conspiratorial knots of Dr. Frank N. Furters, the mad transvestite scientist played by Tim Curry, and clumps of Riff Raffs—he was the hunchback butler played by Richard O'Brien, who also wrote the songs.

Inside the theater, the fans put on a better show than anything on the screen. They knew the film by heart, chanted all of the lines in unison, sang along with the songs, did dances on stage, added their own unprintable additions to the screenplay, and went through a lot of props like toilet paper and water pistols. They also formed a sort of weird extended family. They met every week, exchanged ritual greetings, celebrated each other's birthdays and other major holidays, and even dated and married and gave birth to a new generation of *Rocky Horror* cultists.

It was a strange exhibitor-audience relationship, because the regulars were essentially buying tickets so they could attend their own show.

The *Rocky Horror* midnight cult still survives, in a muted form (how long into middle age, after all, can one really continue to dress up like a Transylvanian transsexual?). But as the cult slowly fades in the moonglow, Fox has taken the long-delayed step of releasing the movie on home video. There are likely to be two results: (1) A brief epidemic of *Rocky Horror* costume parties, and (2) disillusionment with the movie itself. The whole thing about *Rocky Horror* was that the movie played as a backdrop to the stage show by the fans.

As for the movie itself, it's no better than it ever was. Viewed on video simply as a movie, without the midnight sideshow, it's cheerful and silly, and kind of sweet, and forgettable.

Roger & Me ★ ★ ★ ★
R, 100 m., 1989

A documentary directed, produced, and written by Michael Moore.

The peculiar genius of *Roger & Me* is not that it's a funny film or an angry film, or even a film with a point to make—although it is all three of those things. It connects because it's a revenge comedy, a film in which the stinkers get their comeuppance at last. It generates the same kind of laughter that Jack Nicholson inspired in that immortal scene where he told the waitress what she could do with the chicken salad. It allows the audience to share in the delicious sensation of getting even.

The movie was made by Michael Moore, a native of Flint, Michigan, the birthplace of General Motors. As GM closed eleven plants in Flint and laid off some thirty-three thousand workers, Moore got mad—and this is his response. But it's not a dreary documentary about hard times in the rust belt. It's a stinging comedy that sticks in the knife of satire and twists.

The ostensible subject of the film is the attempt by Moore to get an interview with Roger Smith, chairman of General Motors. We know right away that this is one interview that is unlikely to take place. Moore, a ramshackle man-mountain who fancies baseball caps and overflowing Hush Puppies, wanders through the film like a babe in toyland. He's the kind of guy who gets in an elevator in GM headquarters in Detroit and is surprised when the button for the top floor—Smith's office—doesn't light up when it's pressed. The closest he gets to Smith is a slick, oily GM public relations man who explains why the layoffs are regrettable but necessary. (It goes without saying that the spokesman himself is eventually laid off.)

Denied access to Smith, *Roger & Me* pokes around elsewhere in Flint. It follows a deputy sheriff on his rounds as he evicts unemployed auto workers. It covers a Flint Pride parade that marches depressingly past the boarded-up store windows of downtown. It listens to enthusiastic spokesmen for Auto World, an indoor amusement park where Flint citizens can visit a replica of their downtown as it used to look before the boards went up. It listens as a civic booster boasts that Flint's new Hyatt Hotel has escalators and "big plants" in the lobby—just like the Hyatts in Atlanta and Chicago. The hotel and amusement park are supposed to create a tourism industry for Flint, but the biggest convention booked into the hotel is the state Scrabble tournament, and when Auto World goes out of business, the rueful Chamber of Commerce–type speculates that asking people to come to Flint for Auto World "is sort of like asking them to come to Alaska for Exxon World."

Many celebrities wander through the film, brought to Flint by big fees to cheer people up. Anita Bryant sings, Pat Boone suggests that the unemployed workers might become Amway distributors, and Ronald Reagan has pizza with the jobless, but forgets to pick up the check.

Meanwhile, some resourceful victims fight back. A woman advertises "Bunnies as Pets or Rabbits as Meat." Jobless auto workers hire themselves out as living statues who stand around in costume at a *Great Gatsby* charity benefit. Some local industries even improve—there's need for a new jail, for example. And the local socialites hold a charity ball in the jail the night before it opens for business. They have a lot of fun wearing riot helmets and banging each other over the head with police batons.

Roger & Me does have a message to deliver—a message about corporate newspeak and the ways in which profits really are more important to big American corporations than the lives of their workers. The movie is a counterattack against the amoral pragmatism of modern management theory, against the sickness of the *In Search of Excellence* mentality.

Michael Moore has struck a nerve with this movie. There are many Americans, I think, who have not lost the ability to think and speak in plain English—to say what they mean. These people were driven mad by the 1980s, in which a new kind of bureaucratese was spawned by Ronald Reagan and his soulmates—a new manner of speech by which it became possible to "address the problem" while saying nothing and yet somehow conveying optimism.

Roger Smith and General Motors are good at that kind of talk. *Roger & Me* undercuts it with blunt contradictions. In the movie's single most haunting image, Smith addresses a GM Christmas television hookup, reading from *A Christmas Carol* while Moore shows deputies evicting a jobless GM worker and throwing his Christmas tree in the gutter. A spokesman for GM has attacked this scene as "manipulative." It certainly is. But Smith's treacly Christmas ceremony is manipulative, too, and so is the whole corporate doublespeak that justifies his bottom-line heartlessness. The genius of *Roger & Me* is that it understands the image-manipulating machinery of corporate public relations and fights back with the same cynicism and cleverness. The wonder is that the movie is both so angry and so funny. We knew revenge was sweet. What the movie demonstrates is that it is also hilarious—for the avenged.

Romancing the Stone ★ ★ ★
PG, 106 m., 1984

Michael Douglas (Jack Colton), Kathleen Turner (Joan Wilder), Danny DeVito (Thug), Alfonso Arau (Juan), Manuel Ojeda (Zolo). Directed by Robert Zemeckis and produced by Michael Douglas. Screenplay by Diane Thomas.

It may have an awkward title, but *Romancing the Stone* is a silly, high-spirited chase picture that takes us, as they say, from the canyons of Manhattan to the steaming jungles of South America. The movie's about a New York woman who writes romantic thrillers in which the hungry lips of lovers devour each other as the sun sinks over the dead bodies of their enemies. Then she gets involved in a real-life thriller, which is filled with cliff-hanging predicaments just like the ones she writes about. The writer, played by Kathleen Turner, uses her novels as a form of escape. Throbbing loins may melt together on her pages, but not in her life. Then she gets a desperate message from her sister in South America: Unless she flies to Cartagena with a treasure map showing the location of a priceless green jewel, her sister will be killed.

What follows is an adventure that will remind a lot of people of *Raiders of the Lost Ark*, but it will be a pleasant memory. After all the *Raiders* rip-offs, it's fun to find an adventure film that deserves the comparison, that has the same spirit and sense of humor. Turner lands in Colombia, and almost instantly becomes part of the plans of a whole lineup of desperadoes. There are the local police, the local thugs, the local mountain bandits, and the local hero, a guy named Jack Colton, who is played by Michael Douglas.

Movies like this work best if they have original inspirations about the ways in which the heroes can die. I rather liked the pit full of snarling alligators, for example. They also work well if the villains are colorful, desperate, and easy to tell apart. They are. Danny DeVito, from TV's "Taxi," plays a Peter Lorre type, complete with a white tropical suit and a hat that keeps getting trampled in the mud. He's a gangster from up north, determined to follow Turner to the jewel. There's also a suave local paramilitary hero named Zolo (Manuel Ojeda), who wears a French Foreign Legion cap and lusts after not only Turner's treasure map but all of her other treasures. And Alfonso Arau plays a rural bandito who turns out to have memorized all of Turner's thrillers.

Movies like this have a tendency to turn into a long series of scenes where the man grabs the woman by the hand and leads her away from danger at a desperate run. I always hate scenes like that. Why can't the woman run by herself? Don't they both have a better chance if the guy doesn't have to always be dragging her? What we're really seeing is leftover sexism from the days when women were portrayed as hapless victims. *Romancing the Stone* doesn't have too many

scenes like that. It begins by being entirely about the woman, and although Douglas takes charge after they meet, that's basically because he knows the local territory. Their relationship is on an equal footing, and so is their love affair. We get the feeling they really care about each other, and so the romance isn't just a distraction from the action.

Rookie of the Year ★ ★ ★
PG, 103 m., 1993

Thomas Ian Nicholas (Henry Rowengartner), Gary Busey (Chet Steadman), Albert Hall (Martinella), Amy Morton (Mary Rowengartner), Dan Hedaya (Larry [Fish] Fisher), Bruce Altman (Jack Bradfield), Eddie Bracken (Bob Carson). Directed by Daniel Stern and produced by Robert Harper. Screenplay by Sam Harper.

I was absolutely lousy in Little League. I was a sub for one season, screwing up every play I was involved in. I stood out there in the middle of right field, squinting into the sun, hoping desperately that the ball would not come my way. If it did, I didn't use my glove to catch it. I used the glove for protection.

I was, in fact, a lot like Henry Rowengartner, the twelve-year-old hero of *Rookie of the Year*. It seemed like the other kids had always known how to play baseball, and that I would never know. When I was a kid, I think I might have liked *Rookie of the Year* a lot. I am no longer a kid, but I can remember those miserable Little League games, and so, in a modest way I'm grateful for this film. It is pure wish fulfillment, forty years after I needed it.

Rookie of the Year is about how Henry is the worst Little League player in history, until he steps on a ball and breaks his shoulder and is fitted with a cast that makes it look like he's always raising his arm in class. When the cast comes off, he goes with his friends to Wrigley Field, and he catches a home run ball while he's out in the bleachers, and then he throws it back—all the way to the catcher behind the plate.

There is an immediate sensation. Who is this kid with the rifle arm and the hundred-mile-an-hour delivery? It appears that the surgery or the injury has tightened his tendons in such a way that he can throw the ball faster than anyone in history. Henry becomes an overnight celebrity, and is signed to the Cubs by the team's genial owner (Eddie Bracken). Of course, he becomes a star

pitcher and wins the big game at the end of the movie.

I don't know about anyone else, but I think it makes perfect sense for the Cubs to hire a twelve-year-old as a pitcher. After all, the real owner of the Cubs is the *Chicago Tribune*, which has hired a panel of kids to be movie critics, which is a lot harder job than major league pitching.

Apart from being a great pitcher, Henry (Thomas Ian Nicholas) is basically your average twelve-year-old. He looks kind of skinny and doesn't know what to say in social situations, and is blissful every time he walks out into Wrigley Field. (Some of the movie's scenes were shot during real games with big crowds, giving the film an authenticy that *The Babe*, for example, was lacking.) Among Henry's supporters is a veteran Cubs pitcher played by Gary Busey, who gives him advice and encouragement. (Busey is slimmed down here and looks terrific—amazingly like Nick Nolte, in fact, and if he stays in shape he may be playing the hero again before long.)

The structure of the movie is fairly predictable. We get to meet some of the other players, and a Cubs announcer who is played by John Candy—who tries, but is unable to achieve the surrealistic voice effects provided every day by Harry Carey. Everything leads up to the end of the season, with the Cubs fighting for first place, and then the movie shows some creativity by *not* having Henry pitch a no-hitter, or hit a home run. How he does try to win the game is unlikely, to say the least, but entertaining.

Look, this isn't a great movie. If you're not a kid, don't see it unless there's a kid you want to see it with. But if by some chance you are a kid, reading this review, and you have ever for a moment wondered what it would be like to play major league ball at your age, then take it from the old Little Leaguer and see this movie. I really shouldn't give it three stars, but I'm going to anyway. Call it a form of revenge for all those hours of dread I spent in right field.

A Room with a View ★ ★ ★ ★
PG-13, 110 m., 1985

Maggie Smith (Charlotte Bartlett), Helena Bonham Carter (Lucy Honeychurch), Denholm Elliott (Mr. Emerson), Julian Sands (George Emerson), Daniel Day Lewis (Cecil Vyse), Simon Callow (Reverend Beebe), Judi Dench (Miss Lavish), Rosemary Leach (Mrs. Honeychurch). Directed by James Ivory and produced by Ismail Merchant. Screenplay by Ruth Prawer Jhabvala.

My favorite character in *A Room with a View* is George Emerson, the earnest, passionate young man whose heart beats fiercely with love for Lucy Honeychurch. She is a most respectable young woman from a good family, who has been taken to Italy on the grand tour, with a lady companion, Miss Bartlett. Lucy meets George and his father in their *pensione*. A few days later, while standing in the middle of a waving field of grass, the sun bathing the landscape in a yellow joy, she is kissed by George Emerson, most unexpectedly. He does not ask her permission. He does not begin with small talk. He takes her and kisses her, and for him, something "great and important" has happened between them.

Lucy Honeychurch is not so sure. She catches her breath, and Miss Bartlett appears on top of a hill and summons her back to tea, and a few months later, in England, Lucy announces her engagement to Cecil Vyse, who is a prig. Cecil is the sort of man who would never play tennis, who wears a *pince-nez,* who oils his hair, and who thinks that girls are nice because they like to listen to him read aloud. Cecil does not have many clues as to what else girls might be nice for.

Meanwhile, George Emerson and his father—who is an idealist, a dreamer, and a follower of Thoreau—take a cottage in the neighborhood. And one day George kisses Lucy again. He then delivers himself of an astonishing speech, in which he explains that love exists between them. (Not love but Love—you can hear the capital letter in his voice.) Lucy must not marry Cecil, he explains, for Cecil does not understand women and will never understand Lucy, and wants her only for an ornament. George, on the other hand, wants her as his partner in the great adventure of life.

George does not have many big scenes, other than those two. The rest of the time, he keeps a low profile and says little. But his function is clear: He is the source of passion in a society that is otherwise tightly bound up in convention, timidity, and dryness. He is the man to break the chains, to say what he thinks, to free Lucy's spirit. And that he does, with great energy and efficiency. George is my favorite character because he is such a strange bird, so intense, so filled with conviction, so convinced of Lucy's worth.

A Room with a View is the story of George and Lucy, but it is also an attack on the British class system. In the opening scenes of the movie, Lucy and Miss Bartlett have been given a room in the Italian *pensione* that does not have a view. Dear old Mr. Emerson insists that the women take his rooms, which have a view. By the end of the film, George will have offered Lucy a view out of the room of her own life. She has been living a suffocating, proper existence—and he will open the window for her. That's what's exhilarating about the film, that it is not only about perplexing and eccentric characters, it's about how they can change their lives.

The movie has been adapted from the E.M. Forster novel by three filmmakers who have specialized recently in film adaptations of literary works: Director James Ivory, producer Ismail Merchant, and screenwriter Ruth Prawer Jhabvala. Their other recent credits include *The Bostonians, The Europeans,* and *Heat and Dust.* This is the best film they have ever made.

It is an intellectual film, but intellectual about emotions: it encourages us to think about how we feel, instead of simply acting on our feelings. It shows us a young woman, Lucy Honeychurch, who is about to marry the wrong man—not because of her passion, but because of her lack of thought. Only think about your passion, the movie argues, and you will throw over Cecil and marry George. Usually thought and passion are opposed in the movies; this time it's entertaining to find them on the same side.

The story moves at a deliberate pace, with occasionally dramatic interruptions for great passion. The dialogue is stately and abstract, except when all of a sudden it turns direct and honest. The performances are perfectly balanced between the heart and the mind. At the center of everything stands Lucy, who is played by Helena Bonham Carter, that dark-browed, stubborn little girl from *Lady Jane.* Maggie Smith is wonderfully dotty as her companion. Denholm Elliott, the most dependable of all British character actors, steals scene after scene as George's free-thinking father ("Leave me my portrait of Thoreau," he insists, as they are moving from their cottage). Julian Sands is the intense young George and Daniel Day Lewis creates a foppish masterpiece in his performance as Cecil; give him a monocle and a butterfly, and he could be on the cover of the *New Yorker.*

A Room with a View enjoys its storytelling so much that I enjoyed the very process of it; the story moved slowly, it seemed, for the same reason you try to make ice cream last—because it's so good.

Rosalie Goes Shopping ★ ★ ★
PG, 94 m., 1990

Marianne Sägebrecht (Rosalie Greenspace), Brad Davis (Ray Greenspace), Judge Reinhold (Priest), Erika Blumberger and Willy Harlander (Rosalie's parents), Alex Winter (Schatzi), Patricia Zehentmayr (Barbara), John Hawkes (Schnucki). Directed by Percy Adlon and produced by Percy and Eleonore Adlon. Screenplay by Percy and Eleonore Adlon and Christopher Doherty.

Most movies have a dominant quality, and in *Rosalie Goes Shopping* that sought-after quality is Reassurance. The movie is about a woman who reassuringly provides her family with all the best things in life, and reassuringly lies to the banks and the credit-card companies that she will be able to pay for them, and reassuringly assures herself that she is a splendid wife and a wonderful mother and an exemplary human being.

Sometimes, to be sure, she has her infinitesimal little moments of doubt, and when they spring up, she goes to confession, where her parish priest listens in wonder to her tale of scams, con games, and check kitings. He gives the best advice he can, and she leaves him trying to reassure himself that he belongs in the priesthood. How does a priest feel when a penitent seems more positive about her sins than he does about her redemption?

The whole movie takes place somewhere in rural Arkansas, where Rosalie (Marianne Sägebrecht), a plump German woman with a beatific smile, has settled down with her husband to raise a large and increasingly affluent family. The husband (Brad Davis), is a crop-dusting pilot who presumably wooed and won Rosalie during a tour of duty with the air force in Germany. Now he is confronted by a wife who is a delight and a puzzlement to him. She showers the benefits of the consumer society on their family, she walks around the house in a cocoon of serenity, and yet, and yet—the question must be asked: Where does the money come from?

The answer is that the money comes from thin air. I have a friend who was once a credit-card swindler, and the way he explains it, the credit-card companies are almost pathetically happy to send you their cards and let you use them, and not as swift as they ought to be to figure out who isn't paying. When you use one card to pay another, and combine that with the judicious use of check-floating strategies and a home equity loan on a home with no equity in it, you can live pretty well in the short run. And, of course, you should never even think in the long run.

Rosalie Goes Shopping is the third movie directed by Percy Adlon and starring Sägebrecht, whose previous collaborations include *Sugarbaby* and *Bagdad Cafe*. She is an unlikely looking movie star, plump and angelic and somewhere around forty, but it cannot be denied that she has a particular screen quality: She glows. It is an innocent, benevolent glow. She is happy with herself, pleased to make others happy, and she lets tomorrow take care of itself.

The movie doesn't tell her story as a financial thriller, with lots of dates and times and bank balances. Adlon is more concerned with the meaning of what she does. She sees comfort and plenty all around her, she wants it for her family, and she finds that people will sell it to her on credit, time, and plastic. So what's the point of saving up first? Live it up now and let your ship come in tomorrow!

The family has its doubts. At least some of the children seem to suspect uneasily that Mom may be living in a dream world, and Davis would be worried, too, if he thought about such things. Certainly Rosalie's parents grow concerned when they visit from Germany and see children being raised with lax discipline, a household being run on credit—and their own return tickets being sold to raise a little emergency cash.

Rosalie Goes Shopping records the mood of a large part of society—of those people in the TV commercials and sometimes in real life, who measure their happiness by material possessions, brand names, and the latest models of the newest gizmos. Rosalie occupies the center of the film almost in a daze; she's a juggler who can keep all her balls in the air only if she stays half-hypnotized by their rhythm. Call her attention to anything—especially her current net worth—and the whole act would come crashing to the earth.

The Rose ★ ★ ★
R, 134 m., 1979

Bette Midler (Rose), Alan Bates (Rudge), Frederic Forrest (Dyer), Harry Dean Stanton (Billy Ray), Barry Primus (Dennis), David Keith (Mal). Directed by Mark Rydell and produced by Martin Worth and Aaron Russo. Screenplay by Bill Kerby and Bo Goldman.

If *The Rose* accomplished nothing else, it would deserve praise for frustrating our national desire to turn the deaths of celebrities into entertainment events. It has gotten to the point in recent years where a popular singer can hardly hope to make it without being dead, and the hot thing for Hollywood lawyers is to put together a portfolio of superstar estates.

The Elvis Industry, balanced precariously between idolatry and necrophilia, is particularly depressing, but count our dead heroes: Jim Croce, Jimi Hendrix, Jim Morrison, Buddy Holly, Otis Redding, Janis Joplin . . . and there was that stir several years ago when yearning Beatles fans tried to bury Paul McCartney the better to praise him.

The girl rock-and-roll singer portrayed by Bette Midler in *The Rose* is officially not Janis Joplin, of course; Midler and director Mark Rydell say they drew from lots of sources, and the movie shows that they did. But the popular conception is that Bette's playing Janis, and audiences are going to *The Rose* to get the lowdown on her and Bobby McGee. The reaction after the movie is over is fascinating: It's a downer, some people complain. Too depressing. You see how fickle we are with our fads. We want movies celebrating the early deaths of our heroes—but they shouldn't be too glum. It's on record that Joplin went to her doom speeded by drugs and Southern Comfort, but maybe what the fans want now is a remake of *Heaven Can Wait*, with Warren Beatty greeting her in heaven.

The Rose is not that movie, and fans hoping to chuckle along at good ol' Rose as she self-destructs will be disappointed. This movie about the pressures of rock stardom and its road tours is told from the inside in two ways: Midler and the filmmakers know what it's like because they've been there, and the movie also concentrates on staying mostly inside the Rose character's head.

Rose, in the movie, is a junkie, a drunk, dependent on uppers, downers, and levelers (she is also, I should probably add, capable of having a good time, able to belt out some terrific performances, and not totally wasted until the end). The movie suggests some of the reasons for her shotgun addictions, but most people use drugs and booze, of course, not because of the personality and behavioral "reasons" so beloved by the social help experts but—quite simply—because they got addicted, and now can't stop. Telling someone he can beat a habit once he understands "why" he's using something is as cruel

as telling a man with a broken leg that he can walk if he understands his bone structure.

The Rose seems to understand this. It is intelligent on the subject of addictions, and its insights are reflected in an interesting stylistic strategy. People on booze or certain drugs develop a tunnel vision in dealing with their environment: They focus on what's important to them at a given moment, and screen out the distractions.

The Rose handles its locations and supporting characters in that way, from Rose's point of view, so that cast members swim in and out of focus and we're seduced into Rose's state of mind. That makes the movie's gradual descent from good times into disquiet, pity, doom, and silence an especially effective one.

But some people say they don't like it, it's depressing. One is tempted to wonder what they expected (how do you base a comedy on Janis Joplin?), but maybe it's not their fault. We've been so brainwashed by the Elvis Industry and its lesser clones that we expect dead stars to come in a nice-smelling package. Used to be fans just identified with their heroes. Now they want the final word.

'Round Midnight ★ ★ ★ ★
R, 130 m., 1986

Dexter Gordon (Dale Turner), Francois Cluzet (Francis Borier), Gabrielle Haker (Berangere), Sandra Reaves-Phillips (Buttercup), Lonette McKee (Darcey Leigh), Christine Pascal (Sylvie), Herbie Hancock (Eddie Wayne), Martin Scorsese (Goodley). Directed by Bertrand Tavernier and produced by Irwin Winkler. Screenplay by David Rayfiel and Tavernier.

In Dexter Gordon's voice in this movie there is a quality that at first sounds like a great weariness. As I listened more carefully, however, I realized that there were other notes also present.

Here is a man (I speak of the character, not the actor) who has gone too far and seen too much, and who knows that in one way or another his death is near. Yet he is not impatient with those who still have long to live; he takes what remains of his precious time to speak carefully with them. And when he speaks of the world around him, it is with a quiet amazement that he is still there to see it.

I mention Gordon's voice because it plays the same notes as the music in this film. As with all great musicians, the notes that come from within are the same as the feelings that come from within. I believe that musicians who use breath to play their instruments—those who play the various horns—arrive sooner or later at a point where they play and speak in the same voice. Dexter Gordon makes it easy to hear that; the music that comes from his saxophone is sad and tender, and so are his words.

In 'Round Midnight, he plays a man named Dale Turner, an American jazzman who goes to Paris in 1959 to play at a club called the Blue Note. Turner is about sixty, an alcoholic and drug abuser whose pattern has been to pull things together for a while, and then let them slide. Each slide is closer to death. He is on the wagon in Paris, watched over by a ferocious landlady and a vigilant club owner, who want him sober so he can get his job done. In the smoky little club every night, he plays the new music of Monk and Bird, the standards of Gershwin and Porter, and songs that come up spontaneously while they are being played.

Outside in the rain one night, a young Frenchman stands by a window, listening to the music, not caring if he gets wet. He believes Dale Turner is the greatest sax player in the world, but he doesn't have enough money to go inside to hear him. One night he follows the old man out of the club, and is able to see without very much trouble that Dale needs help. So he offers it.

Dale Turner is the most hopeless kind of alcoholic, the kind who tries to stay dry by depending on his own willpower and the enforcement of others. Sooner or later his willpower will advise him to drink, and sooner or later the others will not be there, so sooner or later he will be drunk. The young Frenchman senses this, and also senses the overwhelming loneliness of Dale's life, and invites him home for food and talk.

That seemingly very slight gesture—a fan trying to help the man he admires—is the heart of 'Round Midnight. This is not a heavily plotted movie, one of these musical biographies that are weighted down with omens and light on music. It is about a few months in a man's life, and about his music. It has more jazz in it than any other fiction film ever made, and it is probably better jazz; it makes its best points with music, not words.

Dexter Gordon plays the central role with an eerie magnetism. He is a musician, not an actor, and yet no actor could have given this performance, with its dignity, its wisdom, and its pain. He speaks slowly, carefully considering, really making his words mean something, and so even commonplace sentences ("Francois, this is a lovely town you have here") are really meant. He calls everyone "Lady" in the movie, and doesn't explain it, and doesn't need to.

The music was recorded live. The director, Bertrand Tavernier, believes that in earlier jazz films, the audience could sense that the actors were not really playing; that you could see in their eyes that they were not listening to the other musicians onstage with them. In 'Round Midnight, the music happens as we hear it, played by Gordon, Herbie Hancock on piano, and such others as Freddie Hubbard, Bobby Hutcherson, Ron Carter, and Billy Higgins, with Lonette McKee on vocals. You do not need to know a lot about jazz to appreciate what is going on, because in a certain sense this movie teaches you everything about jazz that you really need to know.

There are side-stories: Dale's old loves, new possibilities, painful memories, battle with drink, and his suicidal decision to return to New York (where he is awaited by a slick agent and a patient, fatalistic heroin dealer). They all add up to the story of the end of a life. The story needs a song, and the movie has the song, 'Round Midnight.

Roxanne ★ ★ ★ ½
PG, 107 m., 1987

Steve Martin (C.D. Bales), Daryl Hannah (Roxanne), Rick Rossovich (Chris), Shelley Duvall (Dixie), John Kapelos (Chuck), Fred Willard (Mayor Deebs), Michael J. Pollard (Andy). Directed by Fred Schepisi and produced by Michael Rachmil and Daniel Melnick. Screenplay by Steve Martin.

Roxanne is a gentle, whimsical comedy starring Steve Martin as a man who knows he has the love of the whole town, because he is such a nice guy, but fears he will never have the love of a woman, because his nose is too big. His nose is pretty big, all right; he doesn't sniff wine, he inhales it.

The movie is based on Cyrano de Bergerac, a play that was written in 1890 but still strikes some kind of universal note, maybe because for all of us there is some attribute or appendage we secretly fear people will ridicule. Inside every adult is a second-grader still terrified of being laughed at.

In Roxanne, the famous nose belongs to C.D. Bales, a small-town fire chief, who daydreams of a time when the local citizens will have enough confidence in his department to actually call it when there's a fire.

In despair at the incompetence of his firemen, he hires a firefighting expert (Rick Rossovich) to train them. The expert arrives in town almost simultaneously with a tall, beautiful blonde (Daryl Hannah), who is an astronomer in search of an elusive comet.

Both men fall instantly in love with the woman. At first she has eyes for Rossovich, who is tall, dark, and handsome. But he is totally incapable of talking to a woman about anything but her body, and after he grosses her out, who can she turn to except Martin, the gentle, intelligent, poetic fire chief?

Martin is afraid to declare his love. He thinks she'll laugh at his nose. He assumes the role of a coach, prompting Rossovich, writing love letters for him, giving him advice. In the movie's funniest scene, Martin radios dialogue to Rossovich, who wears a hat with earflaps to conceal the earphone.

What makes Roxanne so wonderful is not this fairly straightforward comedy, however, but the way the movie creates a certain ineffable spirit. Martin plays a man with a smile on his face and a broken heart inside—a man who laughs that he may not cry. He has learned to turn his handicap into comedy, and when a man insults him in a bar, he counterattacks with twenty more insults, all of them funnier than the original. He knows how to deal with his nose, but he has never learned how to feel about it.

Hannah provides a sweet, gentle foil to the romantic fantasies of Martin and Rossovich. She has come to their small town because the air is clear and she can get a good view of the comet with her telescope. She isn't really looking for romance, and although she thinks Rossovich is cute, she's turned off by lines about her body. She likes his letters, though, and when she finds out the letters are really from Martin, she is able to accept him for his heart and not for his nose, which is the whole point, so to speak, of Cyrano.

All of the corners of this movie have been filled with small, funny moments. Michael J. Pollard, the getaway driver in Bonnie and Clyde twenty years ago, is back as a weird little fireman. Fred Willard is the pompous local mayor. Shelley Duvall, as the owner of the local cafe, does double-takes at the strangeness of ordinary life. And Martin proceeds manfully ahead, rescuing cats from trees, helping strangers, fighting fires, and trying to still the beating of his heart.

Ruby in Paradise ★ ★ ★ ★
NO MPAA RATING, 115 m., 1993

Ashley Judd (Ruby Lee Gissing), Todd Field (Mike McCaslin), Bentley Mitchum (Ricky Chambers), Allison Dean (Rochelle Bridges), Dorothy Lyman (Mildred Chambers), Betsy Douds (Debrah Ann), Felicia Hernandez (Persefina). Directed by Victor Nuñez and produced by Keith Crofford. Screenplay by Nuñez.

The movies are filled with stories about people who escape from unhappy homes and discover personal freedom for themselves. But the freedom they discover is seldom very convincing—it seems made out of the fantasies of lottery winners and "Star Search" finalists. Real freedom, I think, doesn't come from overnight wealth or fame. It comes from finding out what you love to do, and being able to do it.

Ruby in Paradise is a wonderful, life-affirming movie about a young woman who has that kind of luck. It's a celebration of heart, courage, and persistence. It stars Ashley Judd, in one of the very best performances of 1993, as Ruby Lee Gissing, age about twenty, who gets in the car and drives away from her dead-end existence in Tennessee, and finds herself in Florida. We never find out much about what she left behind; she doesn't want to remember it. In Florida, what she basically seeks is a job that pays enough to meet her living expenses, so she can support herself and be independent.

She finds a job, in a beachwear shop run by a woman named Mildred Chambers (Dorothy Lyman). Mildred doesn't really need an employee. It's the slow season. But Ruby stands her ground, looks her in the eye, and gets the job, and after a while she begins to like doing it. She likes dealing with the public and doing inventory and arranging the stock; retail is exciting, and it suits her.

Other aspects of the job are not so thrilling. She has a mild little flirtation, for example, with Mildred's son Ricky (Bentley Mitchum). But he's not her type, and she tries to discourage him. He isn't easily discouraged, is angered with her, tells lies to his mother, and causes her to lose her job.

And then there is a low, bleak period of unemployment and desperation, even involving a brief visit to a topless joint where she considers, and rejects, the idea of becoming a stripper.

In that entire sequence, you can see a different mentality at work than you usually

sense behind American movies. Hollywood in general sees strippers and hookers in a curiously positive light, as if the sex business is a good one for a woman to get into. Maybe that's how a lot of men in the movie business feel. Many Hollywood female characters are prostitutes even when there's no earthly reason in the plot for them to be one. See *True Romance,* for example.

Ruby in Paradise has different values. Ruby is filled with stubbornness and pride, and perhaps the best scene in the whole movie comes when Mildred Chambers discovers the truth about Ruby and her son, and goes to visit the young woman, and offers to rehire her. Study that scene—the writing, the acting, the lighting, the direction—and you will be looking at a movie that knows exactly what it is about, and how to achieve it.

Ruby in Paradise was written, directed, and edited by Victor Nuñez, a Floridian whose previous films, *Gal Young Un* and *A Flash of Green,* showed a deep sympathy with his characters. He cares about his people— what they need, how they feel. Here he has found the perfect star in Ashley Judd, who has done some television but is in her first movie role, and brings a simplicity and honesty to the performance that is almost startling in its power.

The key thing, I think, is that Judd and Nuñez allow Ruby to have the halfway feelings of real people, when that's appropriate, instead of casting all her decisions in the black-white exaggeration of most movie plotting. Look at the subtle way the movie handles her relationship with another local man, named Mike McCaslin (Todd Field). He's a pleasant, caring, ethical soul, concerned with ecology and social causes. She likes his sensitivity and his friendship. But eventually she comes to realize that he's too laid-back for her; that she has more drive, and wants to get more places than he cares about.

This is so refreshing, to see her go through these discoveries, since in most movies the women choose their men only according to qualities that would be equally valued among primates in a zoo. What we see is Ruby growing, learning, discovering things about herself. There is an important scene where Mildred takes her to a retail convention in Tampa, and at another table Ruby sees a young woman like herself, carrying a briefcase, engaged in a business meeting. At that instant, I think, Ruby stops thinking of her job as mere employment, and realizes it is a career.

My description of *Ruby in Paradise* may make it sound like events in a boring, everyday world. Nothing could be further from the truth. The greatest adventures in life don't take place in bizarre places with fantasy people. They take place as we size up the world and take our chances with it. And here is a young woman, on her own, smart and capable but still feeling her way, who makes some discoveries about what she can achieve, and what makes her happy.

When successful people tell their stories, you never hear much enthusiasm in their voices as they describe their most recent triumph. But their voices glow when they describe their first successes: their first job, or the first time their talent was recognized, or the first time they realized what they were good at doing. That first chapter is the hard one to write. Then the rest of the book takes care of itself. *Ruby in Paradise* is a breathtaking movie about a young woman who opens the book of her life to a fresh page, and begins to write.

Rudy ★ ★ ★ ½
PG, 112 m., 1993

Sean Astin (Rudy), Jon Favreau (D-Bob), Ned Beatty (Daniel), Charles S. Dutton (Fortune), Jason Miller (Coach Parseghian), Robert Prosky (Father Cavanaugh), Lili Taylor (Sherry). Directed by David Anspaugh and produced by Robert N. Fried and Cary Woods. Screenplay by Angelo Pizzo.

"Look at you. You're five foot nuthin' and you weigh a hundred and nuthin', and with hardly a speck of athletic ability."

So says Fortune, a groundskeeper at the Notre Dame stadium, to Daniel "Rudy" Ruettiger, Jr., whose dream is to play for the Fighting Irish. Rudy is not insane. He doesn't expect to start. It would fulfill his lifetime dream simply to wear the uniform and get on the field for one play during the regular season, and get his name in the tiniest print in the school archives.

Almost everyone except Fortune thinks his dream is foolish. Rudy comes from a working-class family in Joliet, where his father (Ned Beatty) joins his family, his teachers, his neighbors, and just about everybody else in assuring him that he lacks not only the brawn but also the brains to make it into a top school like Notre Dame.

But Rudy persists. And although his story reads, in outline, like an anthology of clichés from countless old rags-to-riches sports movies, *Rudy* persists, too. It has a freshness and an earnestness that gets us involved, and by the end of the film we accept Rudy's dream as more than simply sports sentiment. It's a small but powerful illustration of the human spirit.

The movie was directed by David Anspaugh, who directed another great Indiana sports movie, *Hoosiers*, in 1986. Both films show an attention to detail, and a preference for close observation of the characters rather than sweeping sports sentiment. In *Rudy*, Anspaugh finds a serious, affecting performance by Sean Astin, the erstwhile teen idol, as a quiet, determined kid who knows he doesn't have all the brains in the world, but is determined to do the best he can with the hand he was dealt.

To start with, he can't get into Notre Dame. He doesn't have the grades. But he's accepted across the street at Holy Cross, where an understanding priest (the benevolent Robert Prosky) offers advice and encouragement. Finally Rudy is accepted by Notre Dame, one of the few remaining big football schools that still has tryouts for "walk ons"—kids without starring high school careers or athletic scholarships.

It's the mid-1970s. The Notre Dame coach is Ara Parseghian (Jason Miller). He doesn't know what to make of this squirt who is happy to play on a practice team and offer his body up week after week so that the big Irish linemen can batter and bruise him on their way to a Saturday victory. Rudy isn't really even good enough to be the lowliest sub, but he has great heart (something that is observed perhaps a little too often in the dialogue).

The movie is not cluttered up with extraneous subplots. A hometown girlfriend (Lili Taylor) is left behind, and for four years Rudy turns into a grind, studying nonstop to make his grades, and sometimes sleeping on a cot in the groundskeeper's room because he doesn't have money for rent. His father continues to think he's crazy. But he shows him.

Underdog movies are a durable genre, and never go out of style. They're fairly predictable, in the sense that few movie underdogs ever lose in the big last scene. The *notion* is enormously appealing, however, because everyone can identify in one way or another. In *Rudy*, Astin's performance is so self-effacing, so focused and low-key, that we lose sight of the underdog formula and begin to focus on this dogged kid who won't quit. And the last big scene is an emotional powerhouse, just the way it's supposed to be.

Rudyard Kipling's The Jungle Book
★ ★ ★
PG, 106 m., 1994   NEW

Jason Scott Lee (Mowgli), Cary Elwes (Boone), Lena Headey (Kitty), Sam Neill (Brydon), John Cleese (Dr. Plumford), Jason Flemyng (Wilkins), Stefan Kalipha (Buldeo), Ron Donachie (Harley). Directed by Stephen Sommers and produced by Edward S. Feldman and Raju Patel. Screenplay by Sommers, Ronald Yanover, and Mark D. Geldman.

Rudyard Kipling's The Jungle Book has an excellent title, except for the first, second, and fifth words. This movie, which in its own right is a ripping adventure yarn, has so little connection to Rudyard Kipling or his classic book that the title is beyond explanation: It must simply be a cynical attempt to rip off a well-known brand name, and lure audiences who might reasonably expect it to have some connection to the book and the animated film of the same name. It has none.

The credits say it is "based on characters" from the Kipling stories. It would be more honest to say the characters have "names from the Kipling stories," since that is the only connection. The sweet innocence of Kipling's fables about a boy who learns to live among the animals is replaced here by an *Indiana Jones* clone, an action thriller that Kipling would have viewed with astonishment. What next? *Tom Sawyer* with a car chase and a shoot-out?

And yet viewed entirely apart from Kipling and the alleged source material, *The Jungle Book* is actually quite an entertaining movie, and a splendid showcase for the talent of Jason Scott Lee, who plays Mowgli, the boy who grows up in the jungle, speaks the languages of the animals, and owes more than a little to the original story of Tarzan.

Lee is a casting problem for Hollywood—he doesn't fit in the usual molds—but when he is in a role that fits, as in *Dragon: The Bruce Lee Story* or *Map of the Human Heart*, he shows a rare range of dramatic power and physical presence. Here, in a role that might have turned silly in other hands, he brings perfect conviction; he seems at home in the jungle, in action sequences, in quiet talk, and waltzing at a formal ball.

The film begins as if it's going to be a live-action version of the Disney cartoon, with young Mowgli making friends with a British girl his age, named Kitty. After a mishap separates them and he grows up in the jun-

gle, there are cute little sequences where he rescues a cub bear that has become trapped in a log. Then there's a flash-forward to the present, and we're in Temple of Doom territory.

Mowgli stumbles upon a forgotten temple in the jungle, filled with unimaginable riches. Then fate reunites him with Kitty (Lena Headley), who with her father (Sam Neill), a British officer, is stationed nearby. He comes to live on the base, among such classic colonial types as John Cleese (in pith helmet), and learns excellent English in no time flat. And a tender feeling, the beginnings of love, grows up between Mowgli and Kitty.

A sinister young officer named Boone (Cary Elwes) considers her his territory, and he and his fellow officers take delight in humiliating the young man from the trees. At a dance, Mowgli waltzes gracefully with her, but then a cruel practical joke is played, and before long Kitty's engagement to Boone is announced, with her lukewarm consent. Mowgli is crushed, but philosophical: "I run with the wolf pack. You must run with the man pack. It is the proper thing."

Kitty breaks the engagement. But Boone has noticed Mowgli's diamond-encrusted dagger, and guesses that the jungle boy has discovered the temple of treasures. In a cruel twist, he and some ruthless friends kidnap Kitty, knowing Mowgli must come after them, and that with her as a hostage he will lead them to the hoard. And now the movie truly escalates in its violent action, with business involving giant snakes, quicksand, falls from cliffs, and an eerie scene in which a man is buried alive in an ancient trap in the temple.

These scenes are unsuitable for small children, and the "PG" rating is laughable. What's hard to understand is why the producers would want to pass off *Rudyard Kipling's The Jungle Book* as a children's movie, when it holds up perfectly well as a competent example of the *Gunga Din* and *Indiana Jones* genre. The special effects are convincing, the performances are forthright, and the direction, by Stephen Sommers, recalls his energetic, lighthearted *Adventures of Huck Finn* (1993). It's a good film, in its way, and I hope the right audience finds it.

Runaway Train ★ ★ ★ ★
R, 111 m., 1985

Jon Voight (Manny), Eric Roberts (Buck), Rebecca De Mornay (Sara), Kyle T. Heffner (Frank Barstow), John P. Ryan (Ranken),

Kenneth McMillan (Eddie). Directed by Andrei Konchalovsky and produced by Menahem Golan and Yoram Globus. Screenplay by Djordje Milicevic, Paul Zindel, and Edward Bunker.

The great adventure movies have all been stories of character, not just tales of action. One of the great losses in the movies of recent years has been that sense of real character: One-dimensional people insert themselves into chases and explosions, and the mindless spectacle on the screen is supposed to replace the presence of plausible human beings.

Runaway Train is a reminder that the great adventures are great because they happen to people we care about. That was true of *The African Queen,* and of *Stagecoach,* and of *The Seven Samurai,* three movies that would otherwise seem to have little in common. And it is also true of this tale of two desperate convicts on board a train that is hurtling through the snows of Alaska.

The movie stars Jon Voight and Eric Roberts, who were both nominated for Oscars. They are two actors with dramatically different styles. Voight is always internalized and moody; Roberts has a collection of verbal and physical tics that are usually irritating, and are sometimes meant to be. Here they are both correctly cast, as two convicts in a maximum-security prison in Alaska, who escape through a drain tunnel and then blunder onto the train that takes them on their hellbound mission.

Voight plays Manny, a convict who is so distrusted by the warden that his cell doors have been welded shut for three years. "He's not a human being—he's an animal," the warden says, and this is not just stock dialogue, but the thesis on which the whole movie will rest. Roberts is Buck, a trusty who works for the prison laundry. The warden is Ranken (John P. Ryan), and he has a personal grudge against Manny. In fact, he releases him from solitary in the wicked hope that Manny will try to escape—he's done it before—and that will give Ranken license to kill him.

The opening passages are intense, but somewhat routine; they're out of the basic kit of prison movie clichés. Then the two convicts escape, and stumble by luck into one of the back cabs of a train that consists of four locomotives linked together. The train starts, the engineer suddenly collapses with a heart attack, and the movie's epic journey has begun.

Runaway Train is based on an original screenplay by the Japanese master Akira Kurosawa, whose best movies use the actors as a means of studying character. After some rewriting, *Runaway Train* was directed by Andrei Konchalovsky, the emigré Russian who figures so memorably (under a pseudonym) as Shirley MacLaine's lover in her best-seller *Dancing in the Light.* He has given the story the kind of wildness and passion it requires; this isn't a high-tech Hollywood adventure movie, but a raw saga that works close to the floor.

Once the train has started to move, the movie follows three threads. One involves the three people on the train (the two men discover after a while that a woman crew member, played by Rebecca De Mornay, is also on board, and also powerless to stop the engines). The second thread involves the railway dispatchers, who quarrel over a computer system that may possibly have the ability to clear the tracks ahead of the runaway. The third involves the ferocious determination of Ranken, the warden, to track the train by helicopter, and kill the men inside. Those elements might be enough to make *Runaway Train* a superior action movie. What makes it more than that is the dynamic inside the cab of the train. Voight is seen as a man who is intelligent enough to realize how desperate the situation is—because he has been caught not just in a physical trap, but also in a psychological one. In an impassioned speech that may be the best single scene he has ever played, he tries to explain to Roberts how limited their choices are in life. He uses a story of a man with a broom to create a parable about the impossibility of living as a free man.

The Roberts character does not quite understand the story. He is a wild man of limited intelligence, and prison life has made him dangerous—he acts without regard for the consequences. When these two men are joined by a woman, it is not just a plot gimmick; her role as an outsider gives them an audience and a mirror.

The action sequences in the movie are stunning. Frequently, in recent movies, I've seen truly spectacular stunts and not been much excited, because I knew they were stunts. All I could appreciate was their smoothness of execution. In *Runaway Train,* as the characters try to climb along the sides of the ice-covered locomotive, as the train crashes through barriers and other trains, as men dangle from helicopters and try to kill the

convicts, there is such a raw, uncluttered desperation in the feats that they put slick Hollywood stunts to shame.

The ending of the movie is astonishing in its emotional impact. I will not describe it. All I will say is that Konchalovsky has found the perfect visual image to express the ideas in his film. Instead of a speech, we get a picture, and the picture says everything that needs to be said. Afterwards, just as the screen goes dark, there are a couple of lines from Shakespeare that may resonate more deeply the more you think about the Voight character. This was one of the year's best.

Running on Empty ★ ★ ★

PG-13, 113 m., 1988

Christine Lahti (Annie Pope), River Phoenix (Danny Pope), Judd Hirsch (Arthur Pope), Jonas Abry (Harry Pope), Martha Plimpton (Lorna Phillips), Ed Crowley (Mr. Phillips), L.M. (Kit) Carson (Gus Winant), Steven Hill (Mr. Patterson), Augusta Dabney (Mrs. Patterson), David Margulies (Dr. Jonah Reiff). Directed by Sidney Lumet. Produced by Amy Robinson and Griffin Dunne. Screenplay by Naomi Foner.

How do you explain it to your children, when you take the family dog and put it out into the street, and say that it will surely find a home—and then you drive out of town, forever? That's what happens in an early scene of *Running on Empty,* and the most chilling thing about it is that the children take it fairly well. They've abandoned family dogs before. And they've left town a lot of times.

The movie is about the Popes, a married couple who have been underground since the 1960s, and about their children—especially Danny, who is a senior in high school and has never known any other kind of lifestyle. The Popes were involved with radical politics, and they blew up a building, and there was a janitor inside who they didn't know would be there. They've been on the run ever since, changing towns, changing names, learning how to find jobs that don't attract attention, learning to keep the kids home on the day they take the school picture.

But it's a funny thing about the past. The more you run from it, the more it's in your thoughts. And now time is catching up with this family. What, for example, is Danny (River Phoenix) going to do? He is a gifted piano player, and through one of his teachers he gets a scholarship to Juilliard. But he can't claim it unless he produces his high school transcripts—which are scattered back along his trail in many towns under many different names.

Arthur Pope (Judd Hirsch) has taken a hard line for years, and he's not ready to change it now. He believes that the family must stay together, must protect itself against the world. He's built a fortress mentality, and Danny shares it. He knows that if he comes clean and enters the school, he cannot see his family again; he'll have an FBI tail every moment. His mother, Annie (Christine Lahti), feels as if her heart will break. She has been running a long time, and she doesn't regret the sacrifices she made, but she can't bear the thought that Danny will have to sacrifice his future, just as she lost hers.

Life, in the short run, goes on. Danny makes a girlfriend (Martha Plimpton), whose father is the music teacher. They share secrets, but Danny cannot share his deepest one. This is the first time he's had a girlfriend, the first time he's allowed anyone to grow this close, and he has to learn a neat trick, the trick of learning to trust without being trustworthy. Plimpton knows something is wrong, but she doesn't know what.

The family has survived every crisis that came from the outside, every close call with the FBI, every question from a pushy neighbor. But this is a threat that's unanswerable, because it comes from within: It is no longer possible for these people to avoid questioning the very foundations on which they have built their lives. And that questioning leads to the movie's emotional high point, when the Lahti character calls up her father (Steven Hill), and arranges to meet him for lunch. Long ago, she broke his heart. She disappeared from his life for years. Now she wants her parents to take Danny so that he can go to music school. She will lose her son, just as her father lost her. It's ironic, and it's very sad, and by the end of the scene we have been through a wringer.

The movie was directed by Sidney Lumet, who made a movie called *Daniel* three years ago, inspired by the children of the Rosenbergs, who were charged with spying for the Russians. That film never quite came clear on what it thought about the Rosenbergs—not about whether they were guilty or innocent, but whether they were good or bad. They were seen through so many political and historical filters that we never knew who we were looking at. *Running on Empty* doesn't

make that mistake. These are people who have made a choice and are living with the consequences, and during the course of the film they will have to re-evaluate their decisions.

The family is not really political at all. Politics, ironically, have been left far behind—that kind of involvement would blow the cover of the Pope family. The film is a painful, enormously moving drama in which a choice must be made between sticking together, or breaking up and maybe fulfilling a long-delayed potential. The parents never fulfilled whatever potential they had because of their life underground. Now are they justified in asking their son to abandon his own future? And how will they do that? Push him out of the car and drive away, and trust that he will find a home, just as the dog did?

Lumet is one of the best directors at work today, and his skill here is in the way he takes a melodramatic plot and makes it real by making it specific. All of the supporting characters are convincing, especially Plimpton and her father (Ed Crowley). There is a chilling walk-on by L.M. (Kit) Carson as a radical friend from the old days. And there are great performances in the central roles. River Phoenix essentially carries the story; it's about him. Lahti and Hill have that shattering scene together. And Lahti and Hirsch, huddled together in bed, fearfully realizing that they may have come to a crossroads, are touching; we see how they've depended on each other. This was one of the best films of 1988.

Rush ★ ★ ★
R, 120 m., 1992

Jason Patric (Raynor), Jennifer Jason Leigh (Kristen), Sam Elliott (Dodd), Max Perlich (Walker), Gregg Allman (Gaines), Tony Frank (Nettle). Directed by Lili Fini Zanuck and produced by Richard D. Zanuck. Screenplay by Pete Dexter.

I wonder if anybody starts out to use drugs with the thought that they will eventually lose control over their lives. Probably not. The extraordinary delusion persists that drugs can be used "recreationally," or that somebody with "will power" can stop or cut back at will; this in spite of the testimony of countless drug users that addiction is a two-step process: First you use drugs, then they use you.

Rush is the story of two undercover narcotics agents who get badly hooked on the drugs they are buying and illegally using.

The movie depends on two strong performances for its effects, and gets them from Jason Patric and Jennifer Jason Leigh—he as Raynor, an experienced narc, she as Kristen, the recruit he takes from civilian life into an underworld of addiction.

Raynor fancies himself the master of the drug world, a grizzled veteran who knows how to fool the big-time dealers: He actually shoots drugs himself, in their presence, so they feel he cannot possibly be a cop. He explains to Kristen that she may have to shoot drugs, too, because the penalty for being caught by these bad characters is death. Sure, he says, you might get hooked, but it's easy to kick with "a few days of sweaty sheets." By the end of the film Raynor is huddled in a corner, waving a shotgun and gibbering at hallucinations, and there are no sweaty sheets in sight.

The movie has excellent credentials. Inspired by a true story, it's based on a book by Kim Wozencraft and a screenplay by Pete *(Paris Trout)* Dexter. It is the first directing effort by Lili Zanuck, coproducer of *Driving Miss Daisy,* but feels like the work of a more experienced director, especially in the way she gives full measure to the many strong supporting performances in the film.

They include an all but speechless role by Gregg Allman, as the big local dealer, who moves silently as a wraith through the ranks of his customers; Sam Elliott, as the detective who controls the two young narcs and has his worries about them; and especially by Max Perlich, in a genuinely affecting performance as Walker, the man in the middle, frightened but loyal to his friends, who gets caught in a trap and can't think his way out of it.

Leigh, of course, is a veteran by now of grubby characters in sleazy films; she has become one of the best young actresses by accepting roles some of her contemporaries would not even consider. After her extraordinary work as a doomed prostitute in *Last Exit to Brooklyn,* here she is again, looking sweet and wholesome, and descending into a world of people who have forgotten their better natures. She and Patric work well together here, in the story of two cops who buy into the logic of the drug world and may not be able to get out again.

The psychology of undercover operatives is interesting in many different fields: There are narcotics agents, counterspies, informers, recruiting decoys, all pretending to be the very thing they are pledged to defeat. Why do they like the work? Maybe because they can sin without being sinners? *Rush* toys with the possibility that the Patric character may indeed be a drug addict, fooling himself that he is a cop, and in control. Leigh believes him, and it almost gets her killed.

Ruthless People ★ ★ ★ ½
R, 93 m., 1986

Danny DeVito (Sam Stone), Bette Midler (Barbara Stone), Judge Reinhold (Ken Kessler), Helen Slater (Sandy Kessler), Anita Morris (Carol). Directed by Jim Abrahams, David Zucker, and Jerry Zucker and produced by Michael Peyser. Screenplay by Dale Launer.

It is hard to play a lovable villain, and Danny DeVito does it so easily. His eyes narrow, his voice deepens, and he speaks with great earnestness and sincerity about his selfish schemes and vile designs. *Ruthless People* opens as DeVito is having lunch with his mistress, and we can see that this is a man filled with passion. In this case, the passion is hatred for his wife and for all that she stands for, and for all that her rich father stands for, and even for all that her poodle stands for.

DeVito is the mainspring of *Ruthless People*, the engine of murderous intensity right at the center. His passion is so palpable that it adds weight to all the other performances in the movie. If we can believe he really wants to kill his wife, then we can believe he would not pay the ransom if she were kidnapped, which is the movie's comic premise.

It is, indeed, a pleasure to watch his face as he receives the first call from the kidnappers and they threaten to kill his wife if he doesn't follow every single one of their instructions to the letter. As he agrees to their stipulations, one after another, a wondrous calm spreads over his face, and the scene builds to a perfect climax.

The wife is played by Bette Midler, who makes her first entrance kicking and screaming inside a burlap bag. She has been kidnapped by Judge Reinhold and Helen Slater, who want to get even with DeVito, a clothing manufacturer who has ripped off their designs. It's a juicy role for Midler, a first cousin to the airhead housewife she played in *Down and Out in Beverly Hills*, and she milks it for all it's worth, turning into an exercise freak while being held captive in a basement.

The movie doesn't depend on just the one inspiration—the husband who doesn't want to ransom his wife. It has lots of other ideas and characters that fit together like a clockwork mechanism. We have the mistress (Anita Morris) and her boyfriend (Bill Pullman), who is not playing with a full deck. And then there are the police chief (William G. Schilling), who backs himself into an embarrassing situation, and a mad slasher (J.E. Freeman), who picks the wrong victim when he comes after Midler.

The movie is slapstick with a deft character touch here and there. It's hard to keep all the characters and plot lines alive at once, but *Ruthless People* does it, and at the end I felt grateful for its goofiness.

The discovery in the movie is DeVito. After seeing him on television's "Taxi" and here and there in character roles, I began to notice how good he was in *Romancing the Stone*. Then came his great performance in *Wise Guys*, opposite Joe Piscopo, and now this second virtuoso performance in a row.

He is, of course, very short, but there's a funny thing about his stature: It seems to be a fact of his body, not his mind or personality. In close-ups and whenever he speaks, he has so much force that he can easily command his scenes. He never seems to be compensating; he seems to be holding back. Like British actor Bob Hoskins, who is also shorter than most of the people in most of his scenes, he has a way of making the taller people around him seem unsure of what to do with their legs.

DeVito is a great joy to watch in this movie, as the turns of the plot catch him in one dilemma and then another. First he wants the kidnappers to kill his wife. Then, when he is charged with faking her kidnapping, he wants to ransom her. All along, there's a running gag as he negotiates the ransom price, and Midler has a great moment when she learns that her husband is trying to buy her back—at a discount. *Ruthless People* is made out of good performances, a script of diabolical ingenuity, and a whole lot of silliness.

S

Safe Passage ★ ★
PG-13, 98 m., 1995

`NEW`

Susan Sarandon (Mag), Nick Stahl (Simon), Sam Shepard (Patrick), Marcia Gay Harden (Cynthia), Robert Sean Leonard (Alfred), Sean Astin (Izzy), Priscilla Reeves (Mrs. Silverman), Joe Lisi (Dog Owner). Directed by Robert Allan Ackerman and produced by Gale Anne Hurd. Screenplay by Deena Goldstone.

As *Safe Passage* begins, a dysfunctional family is beginning to come apart at the seams. The father has periodic episodes of blindness, apparently psychological in origin, and the mother is thinking of moving out for some quality time of her own: After raising seven sons, she has recently begun to enjoy meals where she isn't cutting up someone else's meat.

Then there is a bulletin on the TV news: A terrorist bomb has blown up a U.S. Marines barracks in the Sinai Desert. And one of the sons, Percival, could be a victim. The other six sons reassemble in the family home, along with their feuding parents, for a long wait filled with fear, hope, and memories.

As setups go, this one is all right, I suppose, although even from the opening scenes of *Safe Passage* I feared, correctly, that the movie was going to be a long slog down familiar lanes. You pick up right away, for example, that the Singer family isn't really dysfunctional—not in the searing, painful way that families really can be. This is the kind of family whose troubles we'd all like to have, filled with characters like Patrick (Sam Shepard), the father, whose absentminded ways and strange inventions have long bemused his sons, and Mag (Susan Sarandon), the mother, who talks about leaving home but who, we suspect, is fiercely possessive of her home and family, at a level beneath her fed-up complaints.

The sons, as they gather, are the kind of collection you find in fiction more readily than in life, each one representing a quickly grasped bundle of traits and quirks. There's Simon (Nick Stahl), the youngest, somewhat bedazzled by the houseful of verbal overachievers he was born into; Izzy (Sean Astin), next youngest, who has followed his father into science and follows him around adoringly; Alfred (Robert Sean Leonard), the oldest, wise in his own way, and engaged to a woman with children of her own; Gideon (Jason London), who blames himself for Percival's possible death—because Percival (Matt Keeslar) was the track star until Gideon beat him, and then Percival, on the rebound, joined the marines. And the twins Merle (Philip Arthur Ross) and Darren (Steven Robert Ross), whose twinness is the defining thing about them.

The Singers live in a big old house with a basement and a garage and the possessions of nine people scattered willy-nilly. We get some glimpses into the ancient differences between the parents—the Shepard and Sarandon characters—which seem based on their conflicting needs to have a lot of space of their own, while simultaneously filling it with seven sons. And of course the screenplay is carefully constructed to allow each character scenes to establish himself, reveal himself, and have a personal crisis.

Because this formula is so predictable, *Safe Passage* does not move as fast as it might. And as bulletins arrive from the Sinai, we are uncomfortably aware that they seem perfectly timed to interrupt, initiate, or resolve the series of scenes inside the Singer home. The resolution of poor Percival's fate seems to be delayed until all of the other fates can be sorted out.

The cast is first-rate, and so there are individual scenes that sparkle. Many of them involve the invaluable Susan Sarandon, who just continues to grow as an actress: She inhabits her characters as naturally as favorite old sweaters. I liked the long, tequila-swilling scene between Sarandon and Marcia Gay Hardin, as the divorced mom who lives with the oldest son. At first Sarandon is suspicious and protective; then she senses a bond.

Shepard is effective, too, although his periodic bouts of blindness come across more as comic relief than as psychological symptoms. And when the Sean Astin character comes up with ideas about the cause of the blindness, they seem phoned in from another movie altogether—or maybe a sitcom. There is also some business about a neighbor with a dog that seems awkwardly contrived.

I know how *Safe Passage* is supposed to make me feel. I know I'm supposed to care deeply about the fate of Percival, far off in the desert maybe buried under tons of rubble. I know I'm supposed to be cheered that a family crisis allows each of the members of resolve old hurts and heal old wounds. The acting is good enough that sometimes I even did feel a little of that. But most of the time, I found myself watching the plot like an elaborate wind-up mechanical device. I was not often convinced this story was really happening, or happening to real people. It was more like an exercise in dramatic construction.

Saint Jack ★ ★ ★ ★
R, 112 m., 1979

Ben Gazzara (Jack Flowers), Denholm Elliott (William Leigh), James Villiers (Frogget), Joss Ackland (Yardley), Rodney Bewes (Smale), Peter Bogdanovich (Schuman), Monika Subramaniam (Monika), George Lazenby (Senator). Directed by Peter Bogdanovich and produced by Roger Corman. Screenplay by Howard Sackler, Paul Theroux, and Bogdanovich.

Sometimes a character in a movie inhabits his world so freely, so easily, that he creates it for us as well. Ben Gazzara does that in *Saint Jack,* as an American exile in Singapore who finds himself employed at the trade of pimp. He sticks his cigar in his mouth and walks through the crowded streets in his flowered sport shirts, he knows everyone, he knows all the angles—but this isn't a smart-aleck performance, something borrowed from Damon Runyon. It's a performance that paints the character with a surprising tenderness and sadness, with a wisdom that does not blame people for what they do, and thus is cheerfully willing to charge them for doing it.

The character, Jack Flowers, is out of a book by Paul Theroux, who took a nonfiction look at this same territory in *The Great Railway Bazaar,* one of the best modern books of travel. The film is by Peter Bogdanovich, and what a revelation it is, coming after three expensive flops.

Bogdanovich, who began so surely in *The Last Picture Show,* seemed to lose feeling and tone as his projects became more bloated. But here everything is right again, even his decision to organize the narrative into an hour of atmosphere and then an hour of payoff.

Everything. Not many films are this good at taking an exotic location like Singapore and a life with the peculiarities of Jack Flowers's, and treating them with such casual familiarity that we really feel Jack lives there—knows it inside out. The movie's complex without being complicated. Its story line is a narrative as straight as *Casablanca*'s (with which it has some kinship), but its details teem with life.

We meet the scheming Chinese traders Jack sometimes works for; the forlorn and drunken British exiles who inhabit "clubs" of small hopes and old jokes; the whores who do not have hearts of gold or minds at all; the odd Ceylonese girl who is Jack's match in cynicism, but not his better.

And we meet William Leigh, another remarkable fictional creation. Leigh is a British citizen out from Hong Kong on business, who looks up Jack Flowers because Jack can arrange things. To Jack's well-concealed surprise, William Leigh doesn't want a prostitute. He wants some talk, a drink, some advice about a hotel room. Jack never really gets to know Leigh, but a bond forms between them because Leigh is *decent,* is that rare thing, a good man.

Denholm Elliott, usually seen here in third-rate British horror films, has the role, and triumphs in it. It is a subtle triumph; the movie doesn't give Leigh noble speeches or indeed much of anything revealing to say, but Elliott exudes a kind of cheery British self-pride, mixed with fears of death, that communicates as clearly as a bell.

Jack Flowers, meanwhile, runs into trouble. Singapore hoodlums are jealous of the success of his brothel, so they kidnap him and tattoo insulting names on his arms (altogether a more diabolical and satisfactory form of gangland revenge than the concrete overcoat). Jack has the tattoos redecorated into flowers, as William Leigh gets drunk with him. Then, his Singapore business opportunities at an end, he signs up with an American CIA type (Bogdanovich) to run an Army brothel near a rest and recreation center.

One of the joys of this movie is seeing how cleanly and surely Bogdanovich employs the two levels of his plot. One level is Jack's story, and leads up to an attempted blackmailing scene that's beautifully sustained. The other level is the level of William Leigh, whose life is so different from Jack's, and yet whose soul makes sense to him. The levels come together in a conclusion that is inevitable, quietly noble, wonderfully satisfactory.

All of this works so well because Bogdanovich, assisted by a superb script and art direction, shows us Jack Flowers's world so confidently—and because Ben Gazzara makes Jack so special. It's not just a surprise that Gazzara could find the notes and tones to make *Saint Jack* live. He has been a good actor for a long time. What's surprising, given the difficulties of this character, is that anyone could.

The Saint of Fort Washington ★ ★ ★
R, 103 m., 1994

Danny Glover (Jerry), Matt Dillon (Matthew), Rick Aviles (Rosario), Nina Siemaszko (Tamsen), Ving Rhames (Little Leroy), Joe Seneca (Spits). Directed by Tim Hunter and produced by David V. Picker and Nessa Hyams. Screenplay by Lyle Kessler.

Walking next to some thick shrubbery recently, I saw a foot moving behind the bushes, and became aware of a warren of cardboard and old blankets in the shadows: There was a person living there. I felt embarrassed, as if I'd walked in on somebody using the toilet. And I understood something about how we respond to the homeless.

We have a tendency to look away, to not see these people huddled in doorways or holding crude signs on which they have written their life's tragedy. They embarrass us, standing before us naked, having been stripped of home, employment, family, and proper costume. They are simply unadorned human beings, without social titles and roles, and we have no script for dealing with them.

The coining of the word "homeless" has been useful, since we are not comfortable in this society with words like "beggar"; at least a name has been given to their condition. Yet homelessness is the last in line of their problems, coming in many cases after mental illness, addiction, or the simple inability to find work. In *The Saint of Fort Washington,* for example, one of the heroes is mentally ill, and the other is a Vietnam veteran who has lost everything in his life, one piece at a time, until now all that's left is chronic pain from a war wound.

The movie seems knowledgeable about the daily realities of homelessness. If you have ever stopped your car at an intersection and been approached by men with squeegees, offering to clean your windshield, you may have wondered who these guys are, where they come from, and where they go at night. This movie knows.

The story is set in New York and involves Jerry (Danny Glover), a black Vietnam veteran who has had one bad break after another, and Matthew (Matt Dillon), whose life is uprooted when a wrecker's ball comes crashing through the walls of his SRO hotel. Matthew has mental problems; he hears voices. He receives government assistance to pay his rent. But without an address, he cannot receive checks, and without a check, he cannot obtain a new address—a catch-22 that sends him onto the streets.

Jerry, an older man with great experience of urban survival, notices Matthew and takes him under his arm. The two become buddies, and Jerry shows Matthew the ropes, including the windshield-cleaning routine. Usually they are ignored by motorists, or cursed, but sometimes they get a quarter or a dollar, which they spend on fast food or an occasional drink. At night they sleep rough, or in cold weather, in the Fort Washington Shelter, an armory where hundreds of beds are lined up, row after row.

The problem with sleeping in a city shelter, we learn, is that it's more dangerous than the streets. The strong brutalize the weak, and you are likely to awaken without shoes or other possessions. Fort Washington is ruled by a vicious giant named Little Leroy (Ving Rhames), who has intimidated the guards and acts essentially as a toll collector.

The relationship between Jerry and Matthew has echoes of the friendship in *Of Mice and Men;* Jerry sees that Matthew has a childlike innocence, and grows protective of it. The two men gradually reveal details of their life stories, and engage in rambling discussions about the nature of life itself. And there are many scenes in which the director, Tim Hunter, shows in semidocumentary detail how the homeless survive. One myth is broken: These men are not lazy, and in fact work longer and harder hours than many of the employed motorists who roll up their windows and ignore them.

The film is well acted. Glover and Dillon make characters who seem comfortable with each other; it is easier to fight the world together. Both actors resist any temptation to reach for pathos in their roles. The Glover character, angered at being cheated out of a small business, has great fury at the world, but has learned mostly to control it; he needs someone to care for, and comes to love the younger man almost as a son. And Dillon, saddled with sainthood in the film's title, plays against sentimentality most of the time.

The film's flaw, I think, is to spend too much time with the melodrama surrounding the bully of the Fort Washington Shelter. The screenplay settles into a good guy–bad guy rhythm, in which most of the developments are predictable. No doubt that is thought to be more commercial. But I was more interested in the scenes that showed, in knowledgeable detail, exactly how it is possible to stay alive in the city using nothing but your wits and the uncertain generosity of strangers. Since seeing this movie, I've found myself letting those guys at intersections wash my windshield. Big deal: I've changed exactly nothing about the underlying situation. But I feel like I know who they are.

Salaam Bombay! ★ ★ ★ ★
NO MPAA RATING. 113 m., 1988

Shafiq Syed (Krishna/Chaipau), Sarfuddin Qurrassi (Koyla), Raju Barnad (Keera), Raghubir Yadav (Chillum), Aneeta Kanwar (Rekha), Nana Patekar (Baba), Hansa Vithal (Manju), Mohanraj Babu (Salim), Chandrashekhar Naidu (Chungal). Produced and directed by Mira Nair. Screenplay by Sooni Taraporevala.

The history of the making of *Salaam Bombay!* is almost as interesting as the film itself. The filmmakers gathered a group of the street children of Bombay and talked with them about their experiences, visiting the streets and train stations, bazaars and redlight districts where many of them lived. Out of these interviews emerged a screenplay that was a composite of several lives. Then many of the children were enlisted for weeks in a daily workshop, not to teach them "acting" (for that they already knew from hundreds of overacted Indian film melodramas), but to teach them how to behave naturally in front of the camera.

Out of those workshops a cast gradually emerged, and it was clear almost from the start that the star was an eleven-year-old street child named Shafiq Syed, whose history was unknown, but who proved to be such a natural filmmaker that he sometimes reminded the directors of errors in continuity. Using Syed and shooting on actual locations in Bombay, director Mira Nair has been able to make a film that has the everyday, unforced reality of documentary, and yet the emotional power of great drama. *Salaam Bombay!* is one of the best films of 1988.

Shafiq Syed plays its hero, a boy named Chaipau who works for a traveling circus. One day he is sent on an errand—to get some cigarettes from a neighboring village—and when he returns, the circus has packed up and disappeared. He goes to a nearby village and takes a train to Bombay, following some half-formed plan to return to his native village and his mother, who perhaps sold him to the circus. But Chaipau cannot read or write, and he is not quite sure where his village is, or perhaps even what it is named, and he disappears naturally into the ranks of thousands of children who live, and die, on the streets of Bombay.

These streets are without doubt a cruel and dreadful place, but as Nair sees them, they are not entirely without hope. Her Bombay seems to have a kinship with one of the Victorian slums of Dickens, who portrayed a society in which even the lowest classes had identity and a role to play. In that respect, *Salaam Bombay!* is quite different from *Pixote,* the 1981 film about Brazilian street children. Although the two films obviously have much in common, the children of *Pixote* exist in an anarchic and savage world, while those in *Salaam Bombay!* share a community, however humble.

Chaipau is an intelligent boy, stubborn and wily, and he finds a job as a runner for a man who runs a tea stall in the street. Chaipau's job is to race up flights of tenement stairs with trays of tea, and in the tenements he finds a world of poverty, sweatshops, prostitution, and drug dealing. One of the friends he makes is a pathetic sixteen-year-old girl who was sold or kidnapped away from her native village, and is being held captive by a rapacious madam who plans to sell her virginity to the highest bidder. The other characters in the neighborhood include a hopeless drunk and addict who befriends the children as best he can.

One of the subplots of the film involves the relationship between a drug dealer and the prostitute who is his common-law wife. She lives for her child, and exists in daily fear that the child will be taken from her because of the life she leads. Nair treats this woman with such sensitivity that we feel great sympathy for her when the child is threatened, and this illustrates one of the underlying beliefs of *Salaam Bombay!*—that the street life, however hard, is preferable to what happens to people once they are identified by the law and become the victims of official institutions.

It is remarkable how well Nair creates this street world and tells us its rules without seeming to force her story. One of her secrets is location shooting; not a single scene in this movie was shot on a set or in a studio, and some of the scenes—including a funeral procession—were shot with hidden cameras to capture the unrehearsed behavior of the spectators.

It is a well-known truism of filmmaking that color photography tends to make locations look better than they are; we lose the smells and the suffering, and see the bright colors and the sunlight. That happens here, I think; the very act of photographing this society has probably tended to romanticize it somewhat. And yet there are moments that remain raw and painful, as when Chaipau drops his street-smart facade for a second and we see the lonely little boy behind it.

One of the questions asked, but not answered, by the film is what should be done about these children. At one point, Chaipau and some friends are rounded up by the police and herded into a large institution that combines the worst features of an orphanage and a prison, but that doesn't seem to be the answer, and we are left with the troubling impression that in Bombay, at any event, the children seem to fare better on the streets. There they have an identity and a measure of hope. Of course, in the best of possible worlds, something would be "done" about them, but *Salaam Bombay!* takes place far from such a world, and the movie is about children doing the best they can for themselves.

Salvador ★ ★ ★
R, 125 m., 1986

James Woods (Richard Boyle), James Belushi (Dr. Rock), Michael Murphy (Ambassador Kelly), John Savage (John Cassady), Elepedia Carrillo (Maria), Tony Plana (Major Max), Colby Chester (Jack Morgan), Cynthia Gibb (Cathy Moore). Directed by Oliver Stone and produced by Gerald Green and Stone. Screenplay by Stone and Richard Boyle.

Given the headlines, you might perhaps think *Salvador* was a controversial movie about America's role in Central America, but actually it's a throwback to a different kind of picture, to the Hunter Thompson story *Where the Buffalo Roam,* where hardliving journalists hit the road in a showdown between a scoop and an overdose. The movie has an undercurrent of seriousness, and it is not happy about the chaos which we are helping to subsidize, but basically it's a character study—a portrait of a couple of burntout free-lancers trying to keep their heads above the water.

The movie stars James Woods, that master of nervous paranoia, as a foreign correspondent who has hit bottom. He's drinking, drugging, unemployed, living off past glories. When all hell breaks loose in Central America, he figures it's a good story, since he still has some contacts down there. So he enlists his best friend, a spaced-out disc jockey (James Belushi), and they load up with beer and drive their jalopy down through Mexico to where the action is.

The heart of the movie is in their relationship, and I kept being reminded of another Hunter Thompson saga, his book *Fear and Loathing in Las Vegas,* where the journalist and his lawyer drove their car through the desert, where drug-induced dragons seemed to swoop at them out of the sky. *Salvador* is a movie about real events as seen through the

eyes of characters who have set themselves adrift from reality. That's what makes it so interesting.

Once they're at their destination, Woods and Belushi start looking up Woods's old contacts, who include a neofascist general, several bartenders, and an old girlfriend. Woods makes a stab at being a correspondent—he's always on long distance to New York, trying to get credentials from a reputable news-gathering agency—while Belushi settles into the local routine of bars and loose women.

A plot of sorts emerges, along with the usual characters we expect in a story like this—the American generals and embassy spokesmen and CIA types. Woods and Belushi hurry off recklessly in all directions, keep finding themselves surrounded by the wrong people, and escape with their lives only because Woods is such a con artist.

And he is. This is the sort of role James Woods was born to play, with his glibness, his wary eyes, and the endless cigarettes. There is an utter cynicism just beneath the surface of his character, the cynicism of a journalist who has traveled so far, seen so much, and used so many chemicals that every story is just a new version of how everybody gets screwed. That's why there is a special interest in the love affair in this movie, between Woods and Elepedia Carrillo, as the local woman Maria, the woman he truly loves but who lives by a code of Catholicism and respectability—a code that seems constantly in danger of being overwhelmed by events.

The central scene in the movie is possibly the one where Woods goes to confession. He has decided to marry the woman, in order to get her out of the country before all hell breaks loose. She insists on a church wedding. And so we get an extraordinary closeup of Woods's face as he talks with the priest, and tries to make some sort of a bargain between Catholic requirements and his own total ignorance of conventional morality.

Meanwhile, we meet some of the other people on the scene, including John Savage, as a great war photographer, and Michael Murphy, as the American ambassador, a tortured liberal who speaks of peace and freedom while the CIA goes about its usual business right under his nose. The subplot involving the Savage character is not very successful. I can see what they're doing, trying to set him up as a dedicated photojournalist who will risk his life for a great picture, but when he finally does come to his personal turning

point, it's for a photo even the audience knows isn't great: A shot of an airplane swooping out of the sky. Without context, it could be any airplane, flying out of any sky.

Salvador is long and disjointed, and tries to tell too many stories for its length. A scene where Woods debates policy with the American officials sounds tacked-on, as if the director and cowriter, Oliver Stone, was afraid of not making his point. But the heart of the movie is fascinating. And the heart consists of Woods and Belushi, two losers set adrift in a world they never made, trying to play games by everybody else's rules.

Sammy and Rosie Get Laid ★ ★ ★ ½
R, 97 m., 1987

Shashi Kapoor (Rafi), Frances Barber (Rosie), Claire Bloom (Alice), Ayub Khan Din (Sammy), Roland Gift (Danny), Wendy Gazelle (Anna), Suzette Llewellyn (Vivia), Meera Syal (Rani). Directed by Stephen Frears and produced by Tim Bevan and Sarah Radclyffe. Screenplay by Hanif Kureishi.

London is not entirely made up of Westminster Abbey, the Tower, the Zoo, and bobbies on bicycles, two by two. It is also made up of the homeless in a cardboard city, under Royal Festival Hall. And of squatters living in rows of houses that seem to belong to nobody. And of people like Sammy and Rosie, living unconventional lives that they seem to improvise day by day.

Rosie is British. Sammy is from India or Pakistan—it's deliberately never made quite clear—where his father is a controversial political leader. Sammy and Rosie live in a comfortable house on a nice street that seems to be on the edge of a war zone. Anarchic mobs seem to hover just out of view. Sammy and Rosie have conventional left-wing political views, and a circle of friends that spans several races and sexes. To some degree, they are upwardly mobile. Then one day, Sammy's father (played by the famous Indian actor Shashi Kapoor) comes to visit.

He is a large, genial man who seems to genuinely love people. But as the taxi brings him from the airport, we cannot fail to notice that the driver wears a bloody headband and has an empty eye socket. The father fails to notice, however, perhaps because in his country the unfortunate are less visible, or perhaps because the cabbie is a ghostly vision that will return to haunt him throughout the movie.

We meet other people in this strange new

London. A black, for example, who seems to move freely among several groups as a spokesman for the homeless and a prophet of doom. He helps guide the bewildered father home through the dangerous streets, and then seems to casually move in as a member of the family circle. There are other friends, sexually and politically liberated, who seem to have more freedom than they are happy with. And occasionally that bloody and bandaged figure that seems to haunt the edges of the frame.

Sammy and Rosie Get Laid tells the story of all of these people in a film that is far from hopeful about the future of London. It sees the city as a bulwark of privilege against the homeless, a city in which racism is bad, but class divisions are worse and more harmful, and in which real estate values are routinely considered more important than human lives and plans. In this world, Sammy and Rosie do get laid—by each other, by various friends, and (the movie implies) by the system itself. In one scene that many critics have not applauded, the screen splits in three, horizontally, to show the outcome of a wild party. The sex is desperately cheerless, a metaphor for their lives.

The film was directed by Stephen Frears, whose last film, *My Beautiful Laundrette*, was an international success. It told the story of outsiders who banded together in an unlikely cause: Two gays—an Asian and a white neo-Nazi—became lovers and then partners in running a launderette that was financed by the Asian's rich, property-owning uncle.

In *Sammy and Rosie Get Laid,* there is also the sense that interracial love, once considered some kind of social breakthrough, is not going to change anything fundamental when all races are oppressed by the same economic system (the movie begins with the voice of Margaret Thatcher, praising prosperity while we see people living rough in an urban wasteland).

We learn that Kapoor, the father, was a great admirer of London when he studied there, before returning home to preside over a totalitarian regime. He has fond memories of the parks, walking by the Thames, going to plays at the Royal Court, and falling in love with an elegant British woman (Claire Bloom). Now, during his visit, he tries to re-create some of the magic he remembers. While gangs roam the streets, he revisits some of his favorite places, and spends some heartbreaking time with Bloom, who has never married and who still, in some ways,

loves him. The conversations they have are the emotional heart of the film, for what Kapoor is trying to believe is that his romanticism and sentimentality can exist completely apart from his politics.

It doesn't work that way, and that seems to be Frears's argument throughout the film. *Sammy and Rosie Get Laid* is a frontal attack on the favorite fantasies of anglophiles and the British themselves, who see the magical facade of London and ignore the inequalities and social crimes that are right underneath their noses. This will be a difficult film for anyone not fairly familiar with the city and its people; it doesn't have the universal comic undertones of *My Beautiful Laundrette.* It is about specific people and the specific hell they inhabit—a hell that is probably meant to be somewhat prophetic, since not all of the horrors in this film exist (yet) in London. For people who love London and yet are thoughtful about it, this film is indispensable.

The Sandlot ★ ★ ★
PG, 101 m., 1993

Tom Guiry (Scotty Smalls), Mike Vitar (Benjamin Rodriguez), Patrick Renna (Ham Porter), Chauncey Leopardi ("Squints" Palledorous), Marty York ("Yeah-Yeah" McClennan), Brandon Adams (Kenny DeNunez). Directed by David Mickey Evans and produced by Dale de la Torre. Screenplay by Evans and Robert Gunter.

If you have ever been lucky enough to see *A Christmas Story,* you will understand what I mean when I say *The Sandlot* is a summertime version of the same vision. Both movies are about gawky young adolescents trapped in a world they never made, and doing their best to fit in while beset with the most amazing vicissitudes. Neither movie has any connection with the humdrum reality of the boring real world; both tap directly into a vein of nostalgia and memory that makes reality seem puny by comparison.

The Sandlot takes place in a small American town in the early 1960s. A new boy named Scott (Tom Guiry) arrives in the neighborhood, and desperately wants to fit in. There is a local sandlot team with eight players, and so he could be the ninth—if only he could play baseball!

He cannot. He's so out of it, he doesn't even know who Babe Ruth was. He asks his stepfather to teach him to play catch (there is a quiet poignancy in being asked to be taught such a thing), and his stepdad agrees, but

puts it off, and then one day Scotty finds himself, to his horror, on the sandlot in left center field with a fly ball descending on his head, which it bounces off of.

That would be the end of his baseball career, were it not for the understanding of Benjamin Franklin Rodriguez, the best of the players, who tactfully teaches Scotty what he needs to know, thus launching the finest summer of his young life.

It is one of those summers that are hot and dusty, and the boys play baseball every day, and sometimes go to the municipal swimming pool, where they lust after the impossible vision of the beautiful lifeguard in the red swimming suit. Lust is balanced by terrors: Behind the wall at the end of their sandlot is a backyard inhabited by The Beast, a dog so large and savage that it has become a neighborhood legend. We catch glimpses of parts of it from time to time—a massive paw, slavering jowls—and from what we can see, it's about as large as a dinosaur.

One day the boys' last ball goes over the fence into the domain of The Beast. Scotty saves the day. He runs home and borrows his stepfather's ball, which happens to have been autographed by Babe Ruth, a name that means nothing to him until this ball, too, is slammed over the fence, and then the other players explain to him why his stepfather is not going to be overjoyed to learn that his trophy has become The Beast's lunch.

All of these events are told in an original, quirky, off-center, deliberately exaggerated way. This is not your standard movie about kids and baseball. It's so unconventional, it doesn't even end with the sandlot team winning the Big Game. This movie doesn't even *have* a Big Game. (The one game they play is a pushover.) The movie isn't about winning and losing; it's about growing up and facing your fears, and as the kids try one goofy plan after another to get the ball back, the story gently leaves the realm of the possible and ventures into the exaggerations common to all childhood legends.

The movie's director is David Mickey Evans, who wrote the script with Robert Gunter. Their tone and the voice-over narration remind me of Jean Shepherd's memories of growing up in northern Indiana. Memories are sharper, colors are brighter, events are more important, and a life can be changed forever in the course of a sunny afternoon.

These days too many children's movies are infected by the virus of Winning, as if kids are nothing more than underage pro athletes, and the values of Vince Lombardi prevail: It's not how you play the game, but whether you win or lose. This is a movie that breaks with that tradition, that allows its kids to be kids, that shows them in the insular world of imagination and dreaming that children create entirely apart from adult domains and values. There was a moment in the film when Rodriguez hit a fast drive directly at the pitcher's mound, and I ducked and held up my mitt, and then I realized I didn't have a mitt, and it was then I also realized how completely this movie had seduced me with its memories of what really matters when you are twelve.

The Santa Clause ★ ★ ½

PG, 95 m., 1994

Tim Allen (Scott Calvin), Judge Reinhold (Neal), Wendy Crewson (Laura), Eric Lloyd (Charlie), David Krumholtz (Bernard), Larry Brandenburg (Detective Nunzio), Mary Gross (Ms. Daniels), Paige Tamada (Elf-Judy). Directed by John Pasquin and produced by Brian Reilly, Jeffrey Silver, and Robert Newmyer. Screenplay by Leo Benvenuti and Steve Rudnick.

The Santa Clause provides at least one valuable service: It explains exactly how Santa is able to get down chimneys that are too small for him, and how he is able to enter apartments through hot water radiators and heating vents. There is also an intriguing theory, handled in a throwaway line of dialogue, to explain how Santa is able to visit everybody's house on Christmas Eve. It may have something to do with parallel time tracks, or other concepts of advanced physics.

We also learn that being Santa is not a job for eternity, but that, instead, there are various office holders, just like for county coroner or recorder of deeds. As the movie opens, Scott Calvin (Tim Allen, of TV's "Home Improvement") is a man who does not believe in Santa Claus. But then up on the rooftop there arises such a clatter, that Scott and his son, Charlie (Eric Lloyd), run into the yard to see what is the matter. And what to their wondering eyes should appear, but a great big sleigh and eight giant reindeer, up on the house.

And then, when Scott's shout startles Santa, he loses his balance and is killed in a fall from the roof. After which Scott finds a card in his pocket notifying the bearer that *he* is the new Santa Claus. Before Scott quite realizes what has happened, the old Santa has disappeared,

and he is wearing the suit and going down the chimneys.

The premise for *The Santa Clause*, written by Leo Benvenuti and Steve Rudnick and directed by John Pasquin, is a clever one, and the movie is not without real charm. One of its innovations is to provide us with a stepfather who is not a monster: Scott and his wife, Laura (Wendy Crewson), are divorced, and Laura's new husband, Neal (Judge Reinhold), is a psychiatrist, who takes a dubious position on the subject of Santa's reality, but is otherwise a fairly nice guy.

As the movie continues, Scott finds himself learning all the tricks of the Santa trade, including how to handle unfriendly dogs in strange living rooms. Certain symptoms develop: He puts on weight, from all the milk and cookies people leave out for him, and is able to grow a flowing beard in just a few days. And there are sly contemporary references, as when he suggests to one little girl that the milk put out for him tastes a little funny, and she explains it's soy milk—because on last year's visit he complained of lactose intolerance.

At the North Pole, Scott, in his new role, finds a workshop humming along under the leadership of Bernard, the head elf (David Krumholtz), who likes to do things his way, and has a good line: "We're your worst nightmare: elves with attitude." But at home, his conviction that he is actually Santa makes him into a subject for psychiatric attention.

The Santa Clause (so named after the clause on Santa's calling card that requires Scott to take over the job) is often a clever and amusing movie, and there's a lot of fresh invention in it. If I found my attention flagging, maybe it's because I am not a member of its intended audience. For kids and many teenagers and their families, this is probably going to be a popular film. I personally found I just didn't care much. That, despite its charms, the movie didn't push over the top into true inspiration. I would have traded a lot of *The Santa Clause* for just one shot of Chico Marx explaining how there ain't no sanity clause.

Santa Sangre ★ ★ ★ ★
R, 124 m., 1990

Axel Jodorowsky (Fenix), Sabrina Dennison (Alma), Guy Stockwell (Orgo), Blanca Guerra (Concha), Thelma Tixou (Tattooed Woman), Adan Jodorowsky (Fenix, eight years), Faviola

Elenka Tapia (Alma, seven years), Jesus Juarez (Aladin). Directed by Alejandro Jodorowsky and produced by Claudio Argento. Screenplay by Jodorowsky, Robert Leoni, and Argento.

Santa Sangre is a throwback to the golden age, to the days when filmmakers had bold individual visions and were not timidly trying to duplicate the latest mass-market formulas. This is a movie like none I have seen before, a wild kaleidoscope of images and outrages, a collision between Freud and Fellini. It contains blood and glory, saints and circuses, and unspeakable secrets of the night. And it is all wrapped up in a flamboyant parade of bold, odd, striking imagery, with Alejandro Jodorowsky as the ringmaster.

Those who were going to the movies in the early 1970s will remember the name. Jodorowsky is the perennial artist in exile who made *El Topo*, that gory cult classic that has since disappeared from view, trapped in a legal battle. Then he made *The Holy Mountain*, another phantasmagoric collection of strange visions, and in recent years he has written a series of fantasy comic books which are bestsellers in France and Mexico. Now he is back with a film that grabs you with its opening frames and shakes you for two hours with the outrageous excesses of his imagination.

The film takes place in Mexico, where the hero, Fenix, travels with his father's circus. His father is a tattooed strongman, and his mother is an aerialist who hangs high above the center ring, suspended from the long locks of her hair. She is also a mystic who leads a cult of women who worship a saint without arms—a woman whose arms were severed from her body during an attack by a man. The blood of this saint is *santa sangre*, holy blood, collected in a pool in a church which the authorities want to bulldoze.

The church is pulled down in the opening moments of the movie, while horrendous events take place under the big top. While the mother is suspended from her hair high in the air, she sees her husband sneak out with the tattooed lady—and she tracks them down to their place of sin, kills her, and maims her husband with acid before he cuts off her arms and then kills himself.

Or is that what actually happened? The young son, who witnesses these deeds, is discovered years later in an insane asylum, sitting up in a tree, refusing all forms of human communication. Then he receives a visitor—his mother, come to deliver him from his madness. When he re-enters the outer world, he encounters Alma, the deaf-mute girl who was his childhood friend, and who has now grown into a grave, calm young woman. And he embarks on a journey that leads into the most impenetrable thickets of Freudian and Jungian symbology.

Fenix's mother, still without arms, makes him her psychological slave. He must always walk and sit behind her, his arms thrust through the sleeves of her dresses, so that his hands do her bidding. Together they perform in a nightclub act—she sitting at the piano, he playing. But is this really happening, or is it his delusion?

Jodorowsky hardly pauses to consider such questions, so urgent is his headlong rush to confront us with more spectacle. I will never forget one sequence in the movie, the elephant's burial, where the circus marches in mournful procession behind the grotesquely large coffin of the dead animal. It is tipped over the side into a garbage dump, where the coffin is pounced upon and ripped open by starving scavengers. Another powerful image comes in a graveyard, where the spirits of female victims rise up out of their graves to confront their tormentor. And there is the strange, gentle, almost hallucinatory passage where Fenix joins his fellow inmates in a trip into town; Jodorowsky uses mongoloid children in this sequence, his actors communicating with them with warmth and body contact in a scene that treads delicately between fiction and documentary.

If Jodorowsky has influences—in addition to the psychologists he plunders for complexes—they are Fellini and Buñuel. Federico Fellini, with his love for grotesque and special people and his circuses and parades, and Luis Buñuel, with his delight in depravity and secret perversion, his conviction that respectability was the disguise of furtive self-indulgence. *Santa Sangre* is a movie in which the inner chambers of the soul are laid bare, in which desires become visible and walk into the room and challenge the yearner to possess them.

When I go to the movies, one of my strongest desires is to be shown something new. I want to go to new places, meet new people, have new experiences. When I see Hollywood formulas mindlessly repeated, a little something dies inside of me: I have lost two hours to boors who insist on telling me stories I have heard before. Jodorowsky is not boring. The privilege of making a film is too precious to him, for him to want to make a conventional one. It has been eighteen years since his last work, and all of that time the frustration and inspiration must have been building. Now comes this release, in a rush of energy and creative joy.

Saturday Night Fever ★ ★ ★ ½
R, 118 m., 1977

John Travolta (Tony Manero), Karen Gorney (Stephanie), Barry Miller (Bobby C), Joseph Cail (Joey), Paul Paps (Double J), Donna Pescow (Annette). Directed by John Badham and produced by Robert Stigwood. Screenplay by Norman Wexler.

Each night I ask the stars up above:
Why must I be a teen-ager in love?
—Dion and the Belmonts

Saturday Night Fever is an especially hard-edged case and a very good movie. It's about a bunch of Brooklyn kids who aren't exactly delinquents but are fearsomely tough and cynical and raise a lot of hell on Saturday nights. They live for Saturday night, in fact: They hang their gold chains around their necks and put on the new shirts they bought with their Friday paychecks, and they head for a place called Disco 2001, and they take pills and drink and, as Leo Sayer put it, dance the night away. Occasionally they go out to the parking lot for a session in the back seat with a girl.

John Travolta is the center of the crowd: He's Tony Manero, the best dancer, the best looker, the guy with the most confidence. His life is just as screwed up as everyone else's, but they don't know that, and they tell him: "You know somethin', Tony? You always seem to be in control."

He is not. He works all week at a paint and hardware store and comes home to a family that worships his older brother, who is a priest. The family's sketched briefly right at the beginning in a dinner scene which, like the whole movie, is able to walk the tightrope between what's funny and what's pathetic.

We meet Tony's friends and the girls that hang around them, and we are reminded that feminism has not yet conquered Brooklyn. Some of the girls, especially a spunky little number named Annette (Donna Pescow), worship Tony. He dances with Annette because she's a good dancer, but he tries to keep her at arm's length otherwise. He's caught in a sexist vise: Because he likes her, he doesn't want to sleep with her, because then how could he respect her? The female world is divided, he explains, between nice girls and tramps. She accepts his reasoning and makes her choice.

The Brooklyn we see in *Saturday Night Fever* reminds us a lot of New York's Little Italy as Martin Scorsese saw it in *Who's That Knocking at My Door?* and *Mean Streets*. The characters are similar: They have few aims or ambitions and little hope of breaking out to the larger world of success—a world symbolized for them by Manhattan, and the Brooklyn Bridge reaching out powerfully toward it. But *Saturday Night Fever* isn't as serious as the Scorsese films. It does, after all, have almost wall-to-wall music in it (mostly by the Bee Gees, but including even "Disco Duck"). And there are the funny scenes (like the one where Travolta shouts at his father: "You hit my hair!") to balance the tragic and self-destructive ones.

There's also a hint of *Rocky*, whose poster Travolta's character has on his bedroom wall. Travolta meets a Brooklyn girl (Karen Gorney) who's made it in Manhattan, sort of, as a secretary. She comes back to Brooklyn to dance, and they team up to enter a $500 disco contest. They win it, too, but not before winning has become meaningless to Travolta. Their relationship is interesting because Travolta sees Miss Gorney not so much as a girl (although he thinks she's beautiful) but as an example of how *he* might escape Brooklyn.

The movie's musical and dancing sequences are dazzling. Travolta and Miss Gorney are great together, and Travolta does one solo (in an unbroken shot) that the audiences cheered for. The movie was directed by John Badham *(The Bingo Long Traveling All-Stars)*, and his camera occupies the dance floor so well that we really do understand the lure of the disco world, for all of the emptiness and cruelty the characters find there.

Say Amen, Somebody ★ ★ ★ ★
G, 100 m., 1983

Featuring Willie May Ford Smith, Thomas A. Dorsey, Sallie Martin, the Barrett Sisters, Edward and Edgar O'Neal, and Zella Jackson Price. Directed by George Nierenberg and produced by George and Karen Nierenberg.

Say Amen, Somebody is one of the most joyful movies I've ever seen. It is also one of the best musicals and one of the most interesting documentaries. And it's a terrific good time. The movie is about gospel music, and it's filled with gospel music. It's sung by some of the pioneers of modern gospel, who are now in their seventies and eighties, and it's sung by some of the rising younger stars, and it's sung by choirs of kids. It's sung in churches and around the dining room table; with orchestras and a capella; by an old man named Thomas A. Dorsey in front of thousands of people; and by Dorsey standing all by himself in his own backyard. The music in *Say Amen, Somebody* is as exciting and uplifting as any music I've ever heard on film.

The people in this movie are something, too. The filmmaker, a young New Yorker named George T. Nierenberg, starts by introducing us to two pioneers of modern gospel: Mother Willie May Ford Smith, who is seventy-nine, and Professor Dorsey, who is eighty-three. She was one of the first gospel soloists; he is known as the Father of Gospel Music. The film opens at tributes to the two of them—Mother Smith in a St. Louis church, Dorsey at a Houston convention—and then Nierenberg cuts back and forth between their memories, their families, their music, and the music sung in tribute to them by younger performers.

That keeps the movie from seeming too much like the wrong kind of documentary—the kind that feels like an educational film and is filled with boring lists of dates and places. *Say Amen, Somebody* never stops moving, and even the dates and places are open to controversy (there's a hilarious sequence in which Dorsey and Mother Smith disagree very pointedly over exactly which of them convened the first gospel convention).

What's amazing in all of the musical sequences is the quality of the sound. A lot of documentaries use "available sound," picked up by microphones more appropriate for the television news. This movie's concerts are miked by up to eight microphones, and the Dolby system is used to produce full stereo sound that really rocks. Run it through your stereo speakers, and play it loud.

Willie May Ford Smith comes across in this movie as an extraordinary woman, spiritual, filled with love and power. Dorsey and his longtime business manager, Sallie Martin, come across at first as a little crusty, but then there's a remarkable scene where they sing along, softly, with one of Dorsey's old records. By the end of the film, when the ailing Dorsey insists on walking under his own steam to the front of the gospel convention in Houston, and leading the delegates in a hymn, we have come to see his strength and humanity. Just in case Smith and Dorsey seem too noble, the film uses a lot of mighty

soul music as a counterpoint, particularly in the scenes shot during a tribute to Mother Smith at a St. Louis Baptist church. We see Delois Barrett Campbell and the Barrett Sisters, a Chicago-based trio who have enormous musical energy; the O'Neal Twins, Edward and Edgar, whose "Jesus Dropped the Charges" is a show-stopper; Zella Jackson Price, a younger singer who turns to Mother Smith for advice; the Interfaith Choir; and lots of other singers.

Say Amen, Somebody is the kind of movie that isn't made very often, because it takes an unusual combination of skills. The filmmaker has to be able to identify and find his subjects, win their confidence, follow them around, and then also find the technical skill to really capture what makes them special. Nierenberg's achievement here is a masterpiece of research, diligence, and direction. But his work would be meaningless if the movie didn't convey the spirit of the people in it, and *Say Amen, Somebody* does that with great and mighty joy. This is a great experience.

Say Anything ★ ★ ★ ★
PG-13, 103 m., 1989

John Cusack (Lloyd Dobler), Ione Skye (Diane Court), John Mahoney (James Court), Lili Taylor (Corey Flood), Amy Brooks (D.C.), Pamela Segall (Rebecca), Jason Gould (Mike Cameron), Loren Dean (Joe). Directed by Cameron Crowe and produced by Polly Platt. Screenplay by Crowe.

She is the class brain, and so, of course, no one can see that she is truly beautiful—no one except for the sort of weird kid who wants to devote his life to kick-boxing, and who likes her because of her brains. He calls her up and asks her out. She says no. He keeps talking. She says yes. And after their first date, she tells her father she likes him because he is utterly straightforward and dependable. He is a goofy teen-ager with absolutely no career prospects, but she senses that she can trust him as an anchor.

She discusses him so openly with her father because they have made a pact: They can say anything to one another. When her parents got divorced, she chose to live with her father because of this trust, because of the openness that he encourages. Her father's love for her is equaled by his respect. And she sees him as a good man, who works long hours running a nursing home because he wants to help people.

Honesty is at the core of *Say Anything,* but

dishonesty is there, too, and the movie is the story of how the young woman is able to weather a terrible storm and be stronger and better afterward. This was one of the best films of 1989—a film that is really about something, that cares deeply about the issues it contains—and yet it also works wonderfully as a funny, warmhearted romantic comedy.

The young woman, Diane, is played by Ione Skye as a straight-A student with a scholarship to a school in England. She is one of the class beauties, but doesn't date much because she intimidates boys. The boy who finally asks her out is Lloyd (John Cusack), and he dates her not only out of hormonal urging, but because he admires her. Her father (John Mahoney) is a caring, trusting parent who will do anything he can to encourage his daughter—but his secret is that he has done too much. They find that out when IRS agents come knocking on the door with charges of criminal tax evasion.

The movie treats Diane's two relationships with equal seriousness. This is not one of those movies where the father is a dim-witted, middle-aged buffoon with no insights into real life, and it is also not one of those movies where the young man is obviously the hero. Everyone in this film is complicated, and has problems, and is willing to work at life and try to make it better.

The romance between Diane and Lloyd is intelligent and filled with that special curiosity that happens when two young people find each other not only attractive but interesting—when they sense they might actually be able to learn something useful from the other person. Lloyd has no career plans, no educational plans, no plans except to become a champion kick-boxer, and then, after he meets Diane, to support her because she is worthy of his dedication. In the way they trust each other and learn to depend on each other, their relationship reminded me of the equally complex teen-age love story between River Phoenix and Martha Plimpton in *Running on Empty.*

What's unique to this movie is how sure-footed it is in presenting the ordinary everyday lives and rituals of kids in their late teens. The parties, the conversations, and the value systems seem real and carefully observed; these teen-agers are not simply empty-headed *Animal House* retreads; the movie pays them the compliment of seeing them as actual people with opinions and futures.

Cameron Crowe, who wrote and directed

the film, develops its underlying ideas with a precise subtlety. This is not a melodrama about two kids who fall in love and a parent who gets in trouble with the IRS. It considers the story as if it were actually happening, with all the uncertainties of real life. When Diane goes in to confront a government agent, and tells him that he is harassing her father who is a good man, Crowe allows the scene to develop so that we can see more than one possibility; he even cares enough to give the IRS agent—a minor character—three dimensions.

I was also surprised to find that the movie had a third act and a concluding scene that really concluded something. Today's standard movie script contains a setup, some development, and then some kind of violent or comic cataclysm that is intended to pass for a resolution. *Say Anything* follows all the threads of its story through to the end; we're interested in what happens to the characters, and so is the movie.

The performances are perfectly suited to the characters. Ione Skye—who was a model before she was an actress—successfully creates the kind of teen-age girl who is overlooked in high school because she doesn't have the surface glitz of the cheerleaders, but who emerges at the tenth class reunion as a world-class beauty. John Cusack, a unique, quirky actor with great individuality, turns in a fast-talking, intensely felt performance that is completely original; he is so good here that if you haven't seen him in *The Sure Thing* or *Eight Men Out*, you might imagine he is simply playing himself. But his performance is a complete and brilliant invention. And John Mahoney (Olympia Dukakis's sad-eyed would-be swain in *Moonstruck*) finds the right note for a father who cares, and loves, and deceives both himself and his daughter, and tries to rationalize his behavior *because* he cares and loves.

Say Anything is one of those rare movies that has something to teach us about life. It doesn't have a "lesson" or a "message," but it observes its moral choices so carefully that it helps us see our own. That such intelligence could be contained in a movie that is simultaneously so funny and so entertaining is some kind of a miracle.

Scandal ★ ★ ★ ★
R, 112 m., 1989

John Hurt (Stephen Ward), Joanne Whalley-Kilmer (Christine Keeler), Bridget Fonda (Mandy Rice-Davies), Ian McKellen (John Profumo), Leslie Phillips (Lord Astor), Britt Ekland (Mariella Novotny), Daniel Massey (Mervyn Griffith-Jones), Roland Gift (Johnnie Edgecombe), Jean Alexander (Mrs. Keeler). Directed by Michael Caton-Jones and produced by Stephen Woolley. Screenplay by Michael Thomas.

All Stephen Ward ever really wanted to do in life was to move in the right circles, with the right friends, and be left in peace and quiet. His strategy for gaining admission to the world of British society was unorthodox, but not unkind. He found young women with promise but no prospects, and then he groomed them, coached them, took them to the right places, and introduced them to his important friends.

He was, in a sense, the Henry Higgins of his time, and his most successful Eliza Doolittle was a poor but pretty girl he discovered in a strip show. Her name was Christine Keeler, and he lovingly transformed her into a desirable companion for cabinet members, diplomats, and the aristocracy. His only miscalculation was to allow her to sleep with the British defense minister and a Russian military attache during the same period. That was a mistake that brought down a government, and cost Ward his life.

Scandal tells the story of Stephen Ward with a great deal of sympathy for his motives, and a great deal of anger against the British establishment. Although Ward was convicted of living off the earnings of a prostitute—a decision handed down after he committed suicide in the middle of his trial—the film argues that he never accepted any meaningful sums of money from anybody, and his only real motive, a rather touching one, was to do a favor for both the girls and his famous friends. If his method for doing that—arranging illicit sexual relationships—was unconventional or unsavory, let it be noted that none of the participants on either side of the bargain made the slightest complaint until they found their faces on the front pages of the newspapers.

The facts of the Ward affair are part of modern British history. Christine Keeler and her friend, Mandy Rice-Davies, moved in circles that included some of the most famous and powerful men of their time. After one of them, Defense Minister John Profumo, admitted that he had lied to Parliament about his involvement with Keeler, he was forced to resign, and eventually the widening scandal brought down the Conser-vative government of Harold Macmillan. The movie *Scandal* argues that a scapegoat had to be found to contain the outrage—and Ward, a harmless and gentle osteopath, was the victim. So efficiently and ruthlessly did the establishment circle its wagons to defend itself that even now, twenty-five years later, attempts to make *Scandal* as a TV miniseries were blocked in England, and it has finally appeared as a movie—as a political melodrama that is also an unexpectedly touching love story between almost the only two major players in the episode who never slept with one another, Ward and Keeler.

The movie's strength is that it is surprisingly wise about the complexities of the human heart. Although the newspapers scorned Keeler's claim that she and Ward were simply "close friends," the movie argues that that was quite possible, and true: She felt gratitude for his decision to pluck her from obscurity and groom her for a kind of stardom, and she believed, if she did not fully understand, that his only reward was in seeing his creation pass, respected and unquestioned, in the highest circles. Since England is one of the most class-conscious nations on earth, this sort of transfer in social strata has a powerful hold on the national imagination (cf. the Ascot scene in *My Fair Lady*, with Eliza testing her upper-class accent).

The movie stars John Hurt in one of the best performances of his career as Ward, the chain-smoking, shabbily genteel doctor, who lives in a coach house with Keeler but spends his weekends as the guest of such friends as Lord Astor, who gave him the key to a guest cottage on his estate. In an early scene, Hurt's eyes light up as he sees a pretty girl walking down the street, and somehow Hurt is able to make us understand that he feels, not lust, but simply a deep and genuine appreciation for how wonderful a pretty girl can look on a fine spring day.

Christine Keeler is played by Joanne Whalley-Kilmer, an actress previously unknown to me, and she walks a fine line with great confidence, seeming neither innocent nor sluttish, but more of a smart, ambitious, and essentially honest young woman who finds that it is no more unpleasant to sleep with rich and important men than with her poor and obscure boyfriend. Mandy Rice-Davies (Bridget Fonda) is a different type of woman, more calculating, more cynical, and probably more intelligent, and perhaps it is no accident that Rice-Davies has gone on to a certain success in business and society during the last twenty-five years, while Keeler has returned to a form of the anonymity from which Ward tried to rescue her.

Some of the most evocative scenes in the movie involve backstage moments between the two women, when they casually discuss their lovers, plan their lives, and pay the most painstaking attention to their faces. These women apply themselves more voluptuously to their makeup than to any of the men in their lives.

The movie, written by Michael Thomas and directed by Michael Caton-Jones, has the feeling of having been made from the inside. It moves effortlessly through the mine fields of British government and society, capturing such nuances as the way in which Lord Astor summons Ward to his club to inform him, shame-facedly, that the scandal has forced him to ask for the return of the key to his cottage. Always circling outside the walls of this inner sanctum are the rabble of the British gutter press—and even as a fellow newspaperman, I am willing to describe them in that way, because there is a certain level of decency in news-gathering which they seem never to have glimpsed.

Scandal is a sad story about human nature, which understands why people sometimes sleep in the wrong beds, and takes note that this is understood privately, but not publicly. When the light of day shines on these affairs, lives are destroyed. The saddest moment in the movie comes in the final courtroom scene, when Keeler is called as a witness and is mercilessly battered by the prosecutor until finally Ward stands up in the defendant's box and cries out, "That is not fair!" That is the cry of this movie.

Scarecrow ★ ★ ★
R, 112 m., 1973

Gene Hackman (Max), Al Pacino (Lion), Dorothy Tristan (Coley), Ann Wedgeworth (Frenchy). Directed by Jerry Schatzberg and produced by Robert M. Sherman. Screenplay by Garry Michael White.

Max has been in the slammer and Lionel has been away at sea. Max has been sending his prison wages back to a savings and loan in Pittsburgh, and Lionel has been sending his to a wife in Detroit and a child he's never seen. They hitch up on the Coast and hit the road with a dream of their own car wash with real nylon brushes.

It's a trip we've taken before. We took it in

Of Mice and Men, when there was a nice little farm at the end of the rainbow; we took it in *Easy Rider,* with the drug dealers who wanted to retire in Florida; we took it, most recognizably, in *Midnight Cowboy,* where the goal was those Florida orange groves.

Movies like *Scarecrow* (which shared the 1973 grand prize at Cannes) depend upon a couple of conventions. One is that we know more about the lower-middle-class characters than they know about themselves. The other is that we accept the easy rhythm of a picaresque journey without depending too much on plot. *Scarecrow* doesn't quite make it on either count, but it is a well-acted movie and for long stretches we're hoping it will work.

The performers are Gene Hackman and Al Pacino, two of the most gifted of contemporary actors, and the dialogue and locations (on the road, in taverns, at lunch counters, on a prison farm) strike a nicely realistic low key. But then director Jerry Schatzberg and his writer, Garry Michael White, commit the first of several mistakes: They tell us what the title means. The moment we hear the philosophy behind the scarecrow (he doesn't scare the crows; he makes them laugh) we begin to suspect these characters are too conscious of their symbolic roles, and we're right.

There's another problem, too. Schatzberg, a celebrated photographer, has teamed up with Vilmos Zsigmond (*McCabe and Mrs. Miller*) to produce a movie so obsessed with its visual look that it suffers dramatically. The movie is annoyingly lighted; we constantly seem to be peering through fog at the characters. In a scene or two, this could be nice. At almost two hours, it's an affectation. So is Schatzberg's willingness to allow shots to continue at length; an opening conversation at a lunch counter runs maybe three or four minutes. It's a virtuoso piece of acting by Hackman and Pacino, but after a while the shot calls attention to itself and away from them.

Still, there are fine moments, as there would have to be with Hackman and Pacino. There's a scene in a bar when a would-be fight turns into a comic striptease by Hackman. There's a bittersweet interlude with Max's sister and her girlfriend. And there are times of just rambling, as the two friends depend on each other in a big and lonely world. It's too bad everything is brought together in a big, smashing, dramatic crisis at the end; *Scarecrow* somehow should have drifted out on a lower key.

Scarface ★ ★ ★ ★
R, 170 m., 1983

Al Pacino (Tony Montana), Steven Bauer (Manny Ray), Michelle Pfeiffer (Elvira), Mary Elizabeth Mastrantonio (Gina), Robert Loggia (Frank Lopez). Directed by Brian De Palma and produced by Martin Bregman. Screenplay by Oliver Stone.

The interesting thing is the way Tony Montana stays in the memory, taking on the dimensions of a real, tortured person. Most thrillers use interchangeable characters, and most gangster movies are more interested in action than personality, but *Scarface* is one of those special movies, like *The Godfather,* that is willing to take a flawed, evil man and allow him to be human. Maybe it's no coincidence that Montana is played by Al Pacino, the same actor who played Michael Corleone. Montana is a punk from Cuba. The opening scene of the movie informs us that when Cuban refugees were allowed to come to America in 1981, Fidel Castro had his own little private revenge and cleaned out his prison cells, sending us criminals along with his weary and huddled masses. We see Montana trying to bluff his way through an interrogation by U.S. federal agents, and that's basically what he'll do for the whole movie: bluff. He has no real character and no real courage, although for a short time cocaine gives him the illusion of both.

Scarface takes its title from the 1932 Howard Hawks movie, which was inspired by the career of Al Capone. That Hawks film was the most violent gangster film of its time, and this 1983 film by Brian De Palma also has been surrounded by a controversy over its violence, but in both movies the violence grows out of the lives of the characters; it isn't used for thrills but for a sort of harrowing lesson about self-destruction. Both movies are about the rise and fall of a gangster, and they both make much of the hero's neurotic obsession with his sister, but the 1983 *Scarface* isn't a remake, and it owes more to *The Godfather* than to Hawks.

That's because it sees its criminal so clearly as a person with a popular product to sell, working in a society that wants to buy. In the old days it was booze. For the Corleones, it was gambling and prostitution. Now it's cocaine. The message for the dealer remains the same: Only a fool gets hooked on his own goods. For Tony Montana, the choices seem simple at first. He can work hard, be honest, and make a humble wage as a dishwasher. Or he can work for organized crime, make himself more vicious than his competitors and get the big cars, the beautiful women, and the boot-licking attention from nightclub doormen. He doesn't wash many dishes.

As Montana works his way into the south Florida illegal drug trade, the movie observes him with almost anthropological detachment. This isn't one of those movies where the characters all come with labels attached ("boss," "lieutenant," "hit man") and behave exactly as we expect them to. De Palma and his writer, Oliver Stone, have created a gallery of specific individuals and one of the fascinations of the movie is that we aren't watching crime-movie clichés, we're watching people who are criminals.

Al Pacino does not make Montana into a sympathetic character, but he does make him into somebody we can identify with, in a horrified way, if only because of his perfectly understandable motivations. Wouldn't we all like to be rich and powerful, have desirable sex partners, live in a mansion, be catered to by faithful servants—and hardly have to work? Well, yeah, now that you mention it. Dealing drugs offers the possibility of such a lifestyle, but it also involves selling your soul. Montana gets it all and he loses it all. That's predictable. What is original about this movie is the attention it gives to how little Montana enjoys it while he has it. Two scenes are truly pathetic; in one of them, he sits in a nightclub with his blond mistress and his faithful sidekick, and he's so wiped out on cocaine that the only emotions he can really feel are impatience and boredom. In the other one, trying for a desperate transfusion of energy, he plunges his face into a pile of cocaine and inhales as if he were a drowning man.

Scarface understands this criminal personality, with its links between laziness and ruthlessness, grandiosity and low self-esteem, pipe dreams and a chronic inability to be happy. It's also an exciting crime picture, in the tradition of the 1932 movie. And, like the Godfather movies, it's a gallery of wonderful supporting performances: Steven Bauer as a sidekick, Michelle Pfeiffer as a woman whose need for drugs leads her from one wrong lover to another, Robert Loggia as a mob boss who isn't quite vicious enough, and Mary Elizabeth Mastrantonio, as Pacino's kid sister who wants the right to self-destruct in the manner of her own choosing. These are the people Tony Montana deserves in his life, and *Scarface* is a wonderful portrait of a real louse.

Scenes from a Marriage ★ ★ ★ ★
PG, 168 m., 1974

Liv Ullmann (Marianne), Erland Josephson (Johan), Bibi Andersson (Katarina), Jan Malmslo (Peter). Directed and written by Ingmar Bergman.

They have reached a truce which they call happiness. When we first meet them, they're being interviewed for some sort of newspaper article, and they agree that after ten years of marriage, they're a truly happy couple. The husband, Johan, is most sure: He is successful in his work, in love with his wife, the father of two daughters, liked by his friends, considered on all sides to be a decent chap. His wife, Marianne, listens more tentatively. When it is her turn, she says she is happy, too, although in her work she would like to move in the direction of—but then she's interrupted for a photograph. We are never quite sure what she might have said, had she been allowed to speak as long as her husband. And, truth to tell, he doesn't seem to care much himself. Although theirs is, of course, a perfect marriage.

And so begins one of the truest, most luminous love stories ever made, Ingmar Bergman's *Scenes from a Marriage*. The marriage of Johan and Marianne will disintegrate soon after the film begins, but their love will not. They will fight and curse each other, and it will be a wicked divorce, but in some fundamental way they have touched, really touched, and the memory of that touching will be something to hold to all of their days.

Bergman has been working for years with the theme of communication between two people. At one time, he referred to it as "the agony of the couple." And who can forget the terrible recriminations and psychic bloodshed of the couples in *Winter Light* or *The Passion of Anna*? And here he seems finally to have resolved his crisis.

The years that preceded the making of this film saw a remarkable conciliation going on within the work of this great artist. In *Cries and Whispers*, he was at last able to face the fact of death in a world where God seemed silent. And now, in this almost heartbreaking masterpiece, he has dealt with his fear that all men are, indeed, islands. The film (168 minutes, skillfully and without distraction edited down from six, fifty-minute Swedish television programs) took him four months to make, he has said, but a lifetime to experience.

His married couple are Swedish upper-middle-class. He is a professor, she is a lawyer specializing in family problems (for which, read divorce). They have two daughters, who remain offscreen. They are intelligent, independent. She truly believes their marriage is a happy one (although she doesn't much enjoy sex). One evening, he comes to their summer cottage and confesses that he has gone and fallen in love with someone else. There is nothing to be done about it. He must leave her.

The way in which his wife reacts to this information displays the almost infinite range of Liv Ullmann, who is a beautiful soul and a gifted performer. Her husband (Erland Josephson) has left her literally without an alternative ("You have shut me out. How can I help us?") and still she loves him. She fears that he will bring unhappiness upon himself.

But he does leave, and the film's form is a sometimes harsh, sometimes gentle, ultimately romantic (in an adult and realistic way) view of the stages of this relationship. At first, their sexual attraction for each other remains, even though they bitterly resent each other because of mutual hurts and recriminations. The frustrations they feel about themselves are taken out on each other. At one point, he beats her and weeps for himself, and we've never seen such despair on the screen. But the passage of time dulls the immediate hurt and the feeling of betrayal. And at last, they are able to meet as fond friends and even to make love, as if visiting an old home they'd once been cozy in.

They drift apart, they marry other people (who also remain offscreen), they meet from time to time.

Ten years after the film has opened, they find themselves in Stockholm while both their spouses are out of the country, and, as a nostalgic lark, decide to spend a weekend in their old summer cottage. But it's haunted with memories, and they go to a cottage nearby.

In the last section of the film (subtitled "In the Middle of the Night in a Dark House"), Marianne awakens screaming with a nightmare, and Johan holds her.

And this is twenty years after they were married, and ten years after they were divorced, and they are in middle age now but in the night still fond and frightened lovers holding on for reassurance.

And that is what Bergman has been able to accept, the source of his reconciliation: Beyond love, beyond marriage, beyond the selfishness that destroys love, beyond the centrifugal force that sends egos whirling away from each other and prevents enduring relationships—beyond all these things, there still remains what we know of each other, that we care about each other, that in twenty years these people have touched and known so deeply that they still remember, and still need.

Marianne and Johan are only married for the first part of this film, but the rest of it is also scenes from their marriage.

Scent of a Woman ★ ★ ★ ½
R, 149 m., 1992

Al Pacino (Lt. Col. Frank Slade), Chris O'Donnell (Charlie Simms), James Rebhorn (Mr. Trask), Gabrielle Anwar (Donna), Philip S. Hoffman (George Willis, Jr.), Richard Venture (W.R. Slade). Directed and produced by Martin Brest. Screenplay by Bo Goldman.

The colonel sits alone in his room, drinking and nursing his self-pity. He is a mean, angry, sarcastic man. We sense he has always been lonely, but never lonelier than now, when he is trapped inside blindness. He lost his sight late in life, through his own stupidity, and now he gets drunk and waits for victims. There is hope for him, however, because of two fugitive threads in his personality: He is a romantic, and he possesses a grudging sense of humor.

The colonel, whose name is Slade, and who does not like to be called "Sir," is played by Al Pacino in one of his best and riskiest performances—risky, because at first the character is so abrasive we can hardly stand him, and only gradually do we begin to understand how he works, why he isn't as miserable as he seems.

He certainly seems like a sad, sorry SOB that first day when Charlie Simms goes to house-sit for him. Charlie (Chris O'Donnell) is a student at the exclusive local prep school—a scholarship kid from out West, who doesn't have money to throw around, and is happy to have this weekend job, keeping an eye on the old guy. Charlie is in a lot of trouble at school. There's going to be a disciplinary hearing on Monday about who pulled the prank that damaged the headmaster's new Jaguar, and Charlie, who knows who did it, doesn't want to be a stoolie. He could get expelled for that.

Martin Brest's *Scent of a Woman* takes Charlie and the colonel and places them in a combination of two reliable genres. There's the coming-of-age formula, in which an older man teaches a younger one the ropes. It's crossed here with the prep school movie, which from *A Separate Peace* through *If. . . , Taps, Dead Poets Society,* and *True Colors* has always involved a misfit who learns to stand up for what he believes in. The two genres make a good fit in *Scent of a Woman,* maybe because the one thing Charlie needs in school is a role model, and the one thing the colonel has always known how to do is provide one. The screenplay is by Bo Goldman *(Melvin and Howard),* who is more interested in the people than the plot.

Charlie thinks the weekend will be spent in the colonel's grim little cottage, watching the old guy drink and listening to his insults. The colonel has other ideas—more than Charlie can even begin to guess. He buys them a couple of tickets to New York, and announces they are going to do some partying in the big city. In particular he wants to indoctrinate the younger man with his ideas about women and how they are the most wonderful beings in all of God's creation.

The colonel's ideas are not Politically Correct. On the other hand, he is not a sexist animal, either; he has an old-fashioned regard for women, mixed with yearning and fascination, and the respect of a gentleman who has lived his life in the military and never known a woman very well. He almost believes he can inhale a woman's scent and tell you all about her—what color her hair is, or her eyes, and whether she has a merry light in her eyes.

All of this is done against a backdrop of very serious drinking, which Charlie looks at with growing alarm. The movie does not make the mistake of making the colonel and the student into pals with instant camaraderie. Charlie keeps his distance. He is a little afraid of the colonel, and very afraid of what might happen to him.

They rent a limousine. They take a suite at the Waldorf. They talk. The colonel lectures. Charlie, who distrusts him, answers politely, remaining guarded. The colonel does not seem to notice. They drink. They go to a hotel ballroom, where Charlie notices a beautiful young woman (Gabrielle Anwar), and the colonel engages her in conversation and talks her into doing the tango with him. He's a pretty good dancer. He is even better as an old smoothie.

There is something so touching with him. All of his life, he confides to Charlie, he has dreamed of waking up beside a good and beautiful woman. The limo driver takes them to the address of a highly recommended call girl. Charlie waits in the car. The movie could have spoiled everything by going inside with the colonel, but it stays outside with Charlie, and when the colonel comes out again he says very little, but in it we can guess that he regards women as the undiscovered country of all good and reassurance, a country he will never live in.

They arrive at a crisis, and Pacino and O'Donnell engage in the emotional equivalent of the showdown between Jack Nicholson and Tom Cruise in *A Few Good Men.* It's quite a scene—the real conclusion of the movie, although Charlie's story still has to find its own conclusion when the two men go back to the prep school. By the end of *Scent of a Woman,* we have arrived at the usual conclusion of the coming-of-age movie, and the usual conclusion of the prep school movie. But rarely have we been taken there with so much intelligence and skill.

The Scent of Green Papaya ★ ★ ★ ★
NO MPAA RATING, 103 m., 1994

Tran Nu Yen-Khe (Mui at Twenty), Lu Man San (Mui at Ten), Truong Thi Loc (The Mother), Nguyen Anh Hoa (Thi, the Old Servant Woman), Vuong Hoa Hoi (Khuyen), Tran Ngoc Trung (The Father), Talisman Vantha (Thu). Directed by Tran Anh Hung and produced by Christophe Rossignon. Screenplay by Tran Anh Hung.

Here is a film so placid and filled with sweetness that watching it is like listening to soothing music. *The Scent of Green Papaya* takes place in Vietnam between the late 1940s and early 1960s, and is seen through the eyes of a poor young woman who is taken as a servant into the household of a merchant family. She observes everything around her in minute detail, and gradually, as she flowers into a beautiful woman, her simple goodness impresses her more hurried and cynical employers.

The woman, named Mui, is an orphan—a child, when she first comes to work for the family. She learns her tasks quickly and well, and performs them so unobtrusively that sometimes she seems almost like a spirit. But she is a very real person, uncomplaining, all-seeing, and the film watches her world through her eyes. For her, there is beauty in the smallest details: a drop of water trembling on a leaf, a line of busy ants, a self-important frog in a puddle left by the rain, the sunlight through the green leaves outside the window, the scent of green papaya.

We understand the workings of the household only through her eyes. We see that the father drinks and is unfaithful, and that the mother runs the business and the family. We see unhappiness, and we also see that the mother comes to think of Mui with a special love—she is like a daughter. As Mui grows and the family's fortunes fade, the routine in the household nevertheless continues unchanged, until a day when the father is dead and the business in disarray. Then Mui is sent to work as the servant of a young man who is a friend of the family.

She has known this young man for a long time, ever since they both were children. He was the playmate of her employer's son. Now he has grown into a sleek and sophisticated man about town, a classical pianist, French-speaking, with an expensive mistress. Mui serves him as she served her first family, quietly and perfectly. And we see through small signs that she loves him. These signs are at first not visible to the man.

The Scent of Green Papaya, which was one of 1993's Oscar nominees in the foreign language category, is first of all a film of great visual beauty; watching it is like seeing a poem for the eyes. All of the action, indoors and out, is set in Saigon in the period before the Vietnam War, but what is astonishing is that this entire film was made in Paris, on a sound stage. Everything we see is a set. There is a tradition in Asian films of sets that are obviously artificial (see *Kwaidan,* with its artificial snowfalls and forests). But the sets for *Green Papaya* are so convincing that at first we think we are occupying a small, secluded corner of a real city.

The director, Tran Anh Hung, undoubtedly found it impossible to make a film of this type in today's Vietnam, which is hardly nostalgic for the colonial era. That is one reason he re-created his period piece on a sound stage. Another reason may be that he wanted to achieve a kind of visual perfection that real life seldom approaches; every small detail of his frame is idealized in an understated but affecting way, so that Mui's physical world seduces us as much as her beauty.

Some will prefer the first two-thirds of the film to the conclusion: There is a purity to the observation of Mui's daily world that has a power of its own. Toward the end of the film, plot begins to enter, and we begin to wonder when the young pianist will notice

the beautiful woman who lives under his roof and loves him so. There is an old, old movie tradition of the scene where a man suddenly sees a woman through fresh eyes, and realizes that the love he has been looking everywhere for is standing right there in front of him. These scenes can be laughable, but they can also sometimes be moving, and when that moment arrives in *The Scent of Green Papaya,* it has been so carefully prepared that there is a true joy to it.

There is another scene of great gladness, when the man begins to teach the young woman to read. So deep is the romanticism of the film that we almost question whether this is an advancement for her: Her simplicity, her unity of self and world, is so deep that perhaps literacy will only be a distraction. It is one of the film's gifts to inspire questions like that.

I have seen *The Scent of Green Papaya* three times now—the first time in May 1993 at Cannes, where it was named the best film by a first-time director. It is a placid, interior, contemplative film—not plot-driven, but centered on the growth of the young woman. As such, you might think it would seem "slower" on later viewings, but I found that the opposite was true: As I understood better what the movie was, I appreciated it more because, like a piece of music, it was made of subtleties that only grew deeper through familiarity. This is a film to cherish.

Schindler's List ★ ★ ★ ★
R, 184 m., 1993

Liam Neeson (Oskar Schindler), Ben Kingsley (Itzhak Stern), Ralph Fiennes (Amon Goeth), Caroline Goodall (Emilie Schindler), Jonathan Sagalle (Poldek Pfefferberg), Embeth Davidtz (Helen Hirsch). Directed by Steven Spielberg and produced by Spielberg, Gerald R. Molen, and Branko Lustig. Screenplay by Steven Zaillian.

Oskar Schindler would have been an easier man to understand if he'd been a conventional hero, fighting for his beliefs. The fact that he was flawed—a drinker, a gambler, a womanizer, driven by greed and a lust for high living—makes his life an enigma. Here is a man who saw his chance at the beginning of World War II, and moved to Nazi-occupied Poland to open a factory and employ Jews at starvation wages. His goal was to become a millionaire. By the end of the war, he had risked his life and spent his fortune to save those Jews, and had defrauded the Nazis for

months with a munitions factory that never produced a single usable shell.

Why did he change? What happened to turn him from a victimizer into a humanitarian? It is to the great credit of Steven Spielberg that his film *Schindler's List* does not even attempt to answer that question. Any possible answer would be too simple, an insult to the mystery of Schindler's life. The Holocaust was a vast evil engine set whirling by racism and madness. Schindler outsmarted it, in his own little corner of the war, but he seems to have had no plan, to have improvised out of impulses that remained unclear even to himself. In this movie, the best he has ever made, Spielberg treats the fact of the Holocaust and the miracle of Schindler's feat without the easy formulas of fiction.

The movie is 184 minutes long, and like all great movies, it seems too short. It begins with Schindler (Liam Neeson), a tall, strong man with an intimidating physical presence. He dresses expensively and frequents nightclubs, buying caviar and champagne for Nazi officers and their girls, and he likes to get his picture taken with the top brass. He wears a Nazi party emblem proudly in his buttonhole. He has impeccable black market contacts, and is always able to find nylons, cigarettes, brandy: He is the right man to know. The authorities are happy to help him open a factory to build enameled cooking utensils which army kitchens can use. He is happy to hire Jews because their wages are lower, and Schindler will get richer that way.

Schindler's genius is in bribing, scheming, conning. He knows nothing about running a factory, and finds Itzhak Stern (Ben Kingsley), a Jewish accountant, to handle that side of things. Stern moves through the streets of Krakow, hiring Jews for Schindler. Because the factory is a protected war industry, a job there may be a guarantee of a longer life.

The relationship between Schindler and Stern is developed by Spielberg with enormous subtlety. At the beginning of the war, Schindler wants only to make money, and at the end he wants only to save "his" Jews. We know that Stern understands this. But there is no moment when Schindler and Stern bluntly state what is happening, perhaps because to say certain things aloud could result in death.

This subtlety is Spielberg's strength all through the film. His screenplay, by Steven Zaillian, based on the novel by Thomas Keneally, isn't based on contrived melodrama. Instead, Spielberg relies on a series of incidents, seen clearly and without artificial manipulation, and by witnessing those incidents we understand what little can be known about Schindler and his scheme.

We also see the Holocaust in a vivid and terrible way. Spielberg gives us a Nazi prison camp commandant named Goeth (Ralph Fiennes), who is a study in the stupidity of evil. From the veranda of his "villa," overlooking the prison yard, he shoots Jews for target practice. (Schindler is able to talk him out of this custom with an appeal to his vanity so obvious it is almost an insult.)

Goeth is one of those weak hypocrites who upholds an ideal but makes himself an exception to it; he preaches the death of the Jews, and then chooses a pretty one named Helen Hirsch (Embeth Davidtz) to be his maid, and falls in love with her. He does not find it monstrous that her people are being exterminated and she is spared on his affectionate whim. He sees his personal needs as more important than right or wrong, life or death. Studying him, we realize that Nazism depended on people able to think like Jeffrey Dahmer.

Shooting in black and white on many of the actual locations of the events in the story (including Schindler's original factory and even the gates of Auschwitz), Spielberg shows Schindler dealing with the madness of the Nazi system. He bribes, he wheedles, he bluffs, he escapes discovery by the skin of his teeth. In the movie's most audacious sequence, when a trainload of his employees is mistakenly routed to Auschwitz, he walks into the death camp himself and brazenly talks the authorities out of their victims, snatching them from death and putting them back on the train to his factory.

What is most amazing about this film is how completely Spielberg serves his story. The movie is brilliantly acted, written, directed, and seen. Individual scenes are masterpieces of art direction, cinematography, special effects, crowd control. Yet Spielberg, the stylist whose films have often gloried in shots we are intended to notice and remember, disappears into his work. Neeson, Kingsley, and the other actors are devoid of acting flourishes. There is a single-mindedness to the enterprise that is awesome.

At the end of the film, there is a sequence of overwhelming emotional impact, involving the actual people who were saved by Schindler. We learn then "Schindler's Jews" and their descendants today number some

six thousand, and that the Jewish population of Poland is four thousand. The obvious lesson would seem to be that Schindler did more than a whole nation to spare its Jews. That would be too simple. The film's message is that one man did *something*, while in the face of the Holocaust, others were paralyzed. Perhaps it took a Schindler, enigmatic and reckless, without a plan, heedless of risk, a con man, to do what he did. No rational man with a sensible plan would have gotten as far.

The French author Flaubert once wrote that he disliked *Uncle Tom's Cabin* because the author was constantly preaching against slavery. "Does one have to make observations about slavery?" he asked. "Depict it; that's enough." And then he added, "An author in his book must be like God in the universe, present everywhere and visible nowhere." That would describe Spielberg, the author of this film. He depicts the evil of the Holocaust, and he tells an incredible story of how it was robbed of some of its intended victims. He does so without the tricks of his trade, the directorial and dramatic contrivances that would inspire the usual melodramatic payoffs. Spielberg is not visible in this film. But his restraint and passion are present in every shot.

School Daze ★ ★ ★ ½
R, 114 m., 1988

Larry Fishburne (Dap Dunlap), Giancarlo Esposito (Julian Eaves), Tisha Campbell (Jane Toussaint), Kyme (Rachel Meadows), Joe Seneca (President McPherson), Branford Marsalis (Jordan), Spike Lee (Half-Pint). Directed, produced, and written by Spike Lee.

Spike Lee's *School Daze* is the first movie in a long time where the black characters seem to be relating to one another, instead of to a hypothetical white audience. His *She's Gotta Have It* was another, and then you have to go back to films like *Sweet Sweetback's Baadasssss Song* in 1970. Although the film has big structural problems and leaves a lot of loose ends, there was never a moment when it didn't absorb me, because I felt as if I was watching the characters talk to one another instead of to me.

Most good movies are voyeuristic—we feel as if we're getting a glimpse of other people's lives—but most movies about blacks have lacked that quality. They seem acutely aware of white audiences, white value systems, and the white Hollywood establish-

ment. They interpret rather than reveal, and even in attacking mainstream white society (as Eddie Murphy does in the *Beverly Hills Cop* movies), they pay homage to it in a backhanded way. *School Daze* couldn't care less.

What's surprising is that its revolutionary approach is found in a daffy story about undergraduates at an all-black university. The movie is basically a comedy, with some serious scenes that don't always quite seem to fit. (It begins with a demonstration against the school's investments in South Africa, but doesn't remember to resolve that subject.) It deals with divisions within the student body—between Greeks and independents, and between political activists and kids who just want to get good grades.

And with utter frankness it addresses two subjects that are taboo in most "black movies"—complexion and hair. Lee divides the women on his campus into two groups, the lighter-skinned girls of the Gamma Ray sorority, with their straightened and longer hair, and the darker-skinned independents, with shorter hair or Afros. These two groups call each other the "Wannabes" and the "Jigaboos," and in a brilliant and startling song-and-dance sequence called "Straight and Nappy," they express their feelings for each other. Lee's choice of a musical production number to consider these emotionally charged subjects is an inspiration; there is possibly no way the same feelings could be expressed in spoken dialogue without great awkwardness and pain.

The division within the movie is dramatized by two characters—Dap Dunlap (Larry Fishburne), the intellectual activist and leader of demonstrations against the conservative administration; and Half-Pint (Spike Lee), the undersized kid who dreams of being initiated into the school's most popular fraternity. The two characters play cousins, and it is a sign of the movie's subtle appreciation of campus values that Fishburne, the revolutionary who rejects fraternities, quietly goes to the president of the chapter to put in a good word for his cousin.

In its own way, *School Daze* confronts a lot of issues that aren't talked about in the movies these days, not only issues of skin color and hair, but also the emergence of a black middle class, the purpose of all-black universities in an integrated society, and the sometimes sexist treatment of black women by black men. In one of the movie's most uncompromising sequences, a black fraternity pledge-master expresses concern that Half-

Pint is still a virgin (none of the brothers in this house should be virgins), and he supplies his own girlfriend (Tisha Campbell) to initiate the freshman. She actually goes through with it, tearfully, and although the scene was so painful it was difficult to watch, I later reflected that Lee played it for the pain, not for the kind of smutty comedy we might expect in a movie about undergraduates.

Although there was a brief age of "black exploitation movies" in the 1970s, there have never been very many good American movies about the varieties of the black experience. Black superstars like Eddie Murphy and Richard Pryor are essentially playing to (and with) white audiences, and serious dramas about blacks, even strong ones like *The Color Purple*, are so loaded with nobility and message that they feel like secular sermons. Now here is Spike Lee with a slight, disorganized comedy named *School Daze*, and he just sort of assumes a completely black orientation for his film. There is not a single white person in it. All of the characters, good and bad, are black, and all of the characters' references are to each other.

In *Shoot to Kill*, a 1988 Sidney Poitier film, no mention at all is made of his race until a scene where he jumps up and down and scares away a bear. Then he says, "People here act like they've never seen a black man before." The line got a big laugh from the sneak preview audience I saw it with, but when you analyze it, it was an aside pitched straight at the audience. There are no asides in *School Daze*, and no self-conscious references to blackness. The result is an entertaining comedy, but also much more than that. There is no doubt in my mind but that *School Daze*, in its own way, is one of the most honest and revealing movies I've ever seen about modern middle-class black life in America.

School Ties ★ ★ ★
PG-13, 101 m., 1992

Brendan Fraser (David Greene), Chris O'Donnell (Reece), Andrew Lowery (McGivern), Matt Damon (Dillon), Amy Locane (Sally Wheeler), Randall Batinkoff (Van Kelt), Cole Hauser (Connors). Directed by Robert Mandel and produced by Stanley R. Jaffe and Sherry Lansing. Screenplay by Dick Wolf and Darryl Ponicsan.

I had a friend named Bob Zonka, who ran a weekly newspaper in Michigan. He refused to listen to any kind of ethnic joke. "When you diminish anyone," he said, "you diminish me, and you diminish yourself." His rule even applied to "funny" ethnic jokes that weren't intended as racist—the kinds that people think it's okay to tell. "If it's that funny," he said, "change the words 'Jewish' or 'Polish' to 'Canadian,' and see if it's still so funny."

There's this Canadian guy, see, who . . .

I got his point. And I remembered Bob when I was watching *School Ties,* a movie about a Jewish kid from Scranton who gets a scholarship to a WASP prep school in New England. He's a senior when he goes there. He's been recruited because he is a terrific quarterback, and the school alumni want a winning season so bad they'll do anything to get one.

The character's name is David Greene, and he is played by Brendan Fraser as a working-class youth who sees the prep school as his shot at an Ivy League university and a profession. It is the mid-1950s, when casual anti-Semitism is still common in some circles, and the school coach advises him on his first day to not make a big thing about his Jewishness. In fact, he decides to keep it a secret, and when Rosh Hashanah falls on a Saturday, he plays in a football game before going into the school chapel that evening to read his prayers.

At first David fits in easily at the school, and we meet some of his classmates, the sons of privilege. They're third- or fourth- or fifth-generation WASP success stories, laboring under tremendous pressure to keep up the family name. For a kid like Charlie Dillon (Matt Damon), scion of a wealthy family, it's a no-win situation. If he fails, he lets the family down, but if he succeeds, it's because of family connections.

David falls in love with Sally (Amy Locane), a girl at a nearby school. She has an obvious crush on him, and brings him to an after-game party to meet her folks. And it seems as if David will be able to get away with his deception, until a drunken alum reveals his secret, and then David's world changes. Casual remarks about Jews, which he tries not to hear, are now replaced by ugly jokes in the shower room, and he has to fight Dillon and deal with a swastika painted on the door of his room.

Of course, David was wrong to conceal his Jewishness in the first place. When the school's headmaster finds him in the chapel after hours on Rosh Hashanah, he asks, "Was winning a football game worth breaking a tradition?" David's answer is, "My tradition or yours?" but of course the headmaster was implying that religion is more important than sports. David's roommate and friend, Chris Reece (Chris O'Donnell), is angry with him for not sharing his identity; it was like a lie to a friend, he implies. David points out that they've never discussed Chris's religion, either. "That's different," Chris says, and the movie seems to agree that it is.

The movie's conclusion brings together the two threads of anti-Semitism and prep-school pressure, as one of the students cheats on a test and the students are empowered to deal with it under the school's ancient honor code. The guilty student tries to pass the blame to David, relying on anti-Semitism to help him get away with it. And for the students who have to decide, the episode is an object lesson in the poison of prejudice.

School Ties is surprisingly effective. The movie opens with a hometown scene that I found cartoonish, as David fights the leader of a motorcycle gang, but then it becomes perceptive and unforgiving. It is not simply about anti-Semitism, but also about the way that bigotry can do harm by inspiring dishonesty. One of David's friends tells him it would have been best for him to proudly proclaim his Jewishness on the first day of school, and of course that is right; to remain secretive is to grant the bigots the power of their hate.

Brendan Fraser, whose previous performance was as the thawed-out prehistoric *Encino Man*—another movie about an outsider in high school—is crucial to this movie's success. His performance has to find the way between his character's ambition and pride; he knows that this prep school is the only possible route for him between working-class Scranton and a scholarship to Harvard, and he doesn't want to lose his chance. But at the expense of tradition? Theirs or his? By the end of the movie, he knows the answer to that question.

The Scout ★ ½　　[NEW]
PG-13, 101 m., 1994

Albert Brooks (Al Percolo), Brendan Fraser (Steve Nebraska), Dianne Wiest (Doctor Aaron), Anne Twomey (Jennifer), Lane Smith (Ron Wilson), Michael Rapaport (Tommy Lacy), Barry Shabaka Henley (McDermott), John Capodice (Caruso). Directed by Michael Ritchie and produced by Albert S. Ruddy and Andre E. Morgan. Screenplay by Andrew Bergman, Albert Brooks, and Monica Johnson.

The Scout starts out as a terrific comedy, continues as a pointless drama, and ends as a cornball cliffhanger. Rarely does a movie start high and go downhill so fast. It's as if the filmmakers progressively lost their nerve with every additional scene.

The film stars Albert Brooks as Al Percolo, a scout for the New York Yankees, who as the movie opens has recruited a young phenom who can do everything. He can hit, he can throw, he can run. The only thing he can't do is walk out onto the field. After the kid locks himself in the clubhouse and throws up, he escapes from the stadium and starts walking.

As punishment, the general manager (Lane Smith) banishes Percolo to the backroads of Mexico—where, to his amazement, he finds another phenom. This one, named Steve Nebraska (Brendan Fraser), throws a fastball that clocks at 109 miles an hour, and hits a home run just about every time he swings a bat. He is idolized by the fans in his obscure corner of Mexico, and seems to have no problems at all.

Meanwhile, the Yankee GM fires Percolo. So he signs Nebraska as a free agent, brings him to New York, and stages a demonstration in Yankee Stadium. The assembled owners (including George Steinbrenner in a fairly extensive cameo) are amazed, and the Yankees sign the kid for millions and millions.

It has, however, become apparent that the problems of the earlier phenom are as nothing compared to Nebraska's. The Yankees require him to see a psychiatrist (Dianne Wiest), who finds him deeply troubled and recommends daily therapy. Percolo, who has invited Nebraska to share his apartment, ends up as a surrogate father, and the movie, which began as a comedy, turns into a cross between a psychodrama and a TV Disease of the Week movie.

Too bad. The opening scenes are brilliant. Albert Brooks can be the funniest man in the movies when he has the right material, and as the hard-charging scout, on the trail of the first recruit, he's very funny. (Learning that the boy's family is devoutly Catholic, he tells them Mickey Mantle had a sister who was a nun: "Sister Micki Elizabeth Mantle.") We anticipate the movie will continue in this direction, as a send-up of baseball, dimwitted rookies, and desperate scouts.

The director, Michael Ritchie, would have been fully capable of making such a movie (he directed the strangest and best made-for-TV movie of recent years, The Positively True Adventures of the Alleged Texas Cheerleader-Murdering Mom). The screenplay is by Andrew Bergman (The Freshman, Honeymoon in Vegas), teamed with Brooks and Monica Johnson. These are bright people with an edge; you can't imagine them making a sappy movie like The Scout, but they have. It's almost easier when a movie is bad all the way through, instead of getting up our hopes only to betray them. The Scout begins with a big windup, and ends with ball four.

Sea of Love ★ ★ ★
R, 113 m., 1989

Al Pacino (Frank Keller), Ellen Barkin (Helen Cruger), John Goodman (Sherman Touhey), Michael Rooker (Terry). Directed by Harold Becker and produced by Martin Bregman and Louis A. Stroller. Screenplay by Richard Price.

Sea of Love tells an ingeniously constructed story that depends for its suspense on the same question posed by Jagged Edge and Fatal Attraction: What happens when you fall in love with a person who may be quite prepared to murder you? The movie stars Al Pacino, looking older and a little lined, but more convincing than in most of his other recent roles, as a homicide detective who is assigned to a messy murder case. The victim is a male who has been shot in his own bed, and the killer, it appears, was a woman.

Tracking down leads, Pacino crosses paths with another detective (John Goodman) who is handling a similar case. They discover that both of their victims had placed rhyming ads in one of those singles magazines where people advertise for partners. Lacking any other clues, Pacino has a brainstorm: Why don't he and Goodman place an ad of their own and then date all the women who answer it? By getting the women's fingerprints on wine glasses, the cops may be able to discover the murderer.

This notion leads to one of the movie's better sequences, as Pacino devotes half an hour apiece to assembly-line dates with a series of lonely hearts, while Goodman plays the waiter at his table. Then something unexpected happens. There is chemistry between Pacino and one of the women (Ellen Barkin), and although it is unprofessional and possibly dangerous, he sees her again and they find themselves powerfully attracted to one another.

The movie uses this attraction to set a frankly manipulative plot into motion. Is Barkin, in fact, the killer? Various hints are dropped; various clues are planted. Pacino is meanwhile portrayed as so seriously disturbed within himself that he would almost prefer to die at this woman's hands than surrender his love. (The situation has an uncanny parallel with Glenn Close's feelings for Jeff Bridges in Jagged Edge.)

The pure plot elements in Sea of Love work well enough until the very end of the movie, I suppose, when the solution turns out to be a red herring. But what impressed me most in the film was the personal chemistry between Pacino and Barkin. There can be little doubt, at this point, that Barkin is one of the most intense and passionately convincing actresses now at work in the American movies. Her performance in The Big Easy (1987) was Oscar caliber, and again this time, she seems to cross some kind of acting threshold. When she roughly embraces Pacino and then stalks around the room like a tigress in heat before returning to her quarry, there is an energy that almost derails the movie.

For Pacino, Sea of Love is a reminder of the strong presence he established in street roles in the 1970s before he drifted away into an unfocused stardom in too many softer roles. This time he seems sharp, edgy, complicated, and authentic. Goodman (who plays Roseanne Barr's husband on TV) makes a good partner for him, especially in the scenes where he stands by helplessly while his friend apparently chooses to be in love with a murderess.

Movies like this need to work on two levels. The human elements should feel right, and the initial complications of the plot should not be shortchanged at the end. I think the ending of Sea of Love cheats by bringing in a character from left field at the last moment. Part of the fun in a movie like this is guessing the identity of the killer, and part of the problem with Sea of Love is that the audience is not really played fair with. Technically, I suppose, the plot can be justified. But I felt cheated. I had good feelings for the characters and their relationship, but I walked out feeling that the plot had played fast and loose with the rules of whodunits.

Searching for Bobby Fischer ★ ★ ★ ★
PG, 107 m., 1993

Joe Mantegna (Fred Waitzkin), Laurence Fishburne (Vinnie), Joan Allen (Bonnie Waitzkin), Max Pomeranc (Josh Waitzkin), Ben Kingsley (Bruce Pandolfini), David Paymer

(Kalev), Michael Nirenberg (Jonathan Poe). Directed by Steven Zaillian and produced by Scott Rudin and William Horberg. Screenplay by Zaillian.

There was a boy, a chess player, once, who revealed that his gift consisted partly in a clear inner vision of potential moves of each piece as objects with flashing or moving tails of coloured light: He saw a live possible pattern of potential moves and selected them according to which ones made the pattern strongest, the tensions greatest. His mistakes were made when he selected not the toughest, but the most beautiful lines of light.
—A.S. Byatt, *The Virgin in the Garden*

Child prodigies are found most often in three fields: chess, mathematics, and music. All three depend upon an intuitive grasp of complex relationships. None depend on social skills, maturity, or insights into human relationships. A child who is a genius at chess can look at a board and see a universe that is invisible to the wisest adult. This is both a blessing and a curse. There is a beauty to the gift, but it does not necessarily lead to greater happiness in life as a whole.

The wonderful film *Searching for Bobby Fischer* contains in its title a reminder of that truth. Bobby Fischer was arguably the greatest chess player of all time. As a boy he faced and defeated the greatest players of his time. In 1972, after a prelude of countless controversies, he won the world chess championship away from the Russians for the first time in years. Then he essentially disappeared into a netherworld of rented rooms, phantom sightings, paranoid outbursts, and allegiance to a religious cult. He reappeared to win a lucrative chess match in Yugoslavia, for which he was willing to lose his citizenship. His games are models of elegance and artistry. His life does not inspire envy.

Searching for Bobby Fischer, a film of remarkable sensitivity and insight, tells a story based on fact, about a "new" Bobby Fischer—a young boy named Josh Waitzkin (Max Pomeranc) who was born with a gift for chess, which he nurtured in the rough-and-tumble world of chess hustlers in New York's Washington Square Park. His parents are at first doubtful of his talent, then proud of it, then concerned about how he can develop it without stunting the other areas of his life.

The film is the first intelligent one I can remember seeing about chess. That is the case even though no knowledge of chess is necessary to understand it, and some of the filmmaking strategies—such as showing most of the moves at lightning speed—simply ignore the long periods of inaction in many games. It is intelligent because it is about the meaning of chess, a game that has been compared to war and plundered for its lurking Freudian undertones, and yet is essentially just an arrangement of logical outcomes.

In the film Josh learns the moves by watching them played in the park. At first his parents, Fred and Bonnie Waitzkin (Joe Mantegna and Joan Allen), are even unaware he can play, and there is a sweet scene in which the boy allows his father to win a game, to spare his feelings. Josh's first teacher is a black chess hustler named Vinnie (Laurence Fishburne), who uses an in-your-face approach and advises unorthodox moves to throw an opponent off. Eventually Fred becomes convinced his son needs more advanced tutelage, and hires the brilliant but prickly Bruce Pandolfini (Ben Kingsley), a difficult case—but then all good chess players are difficult cases.

The difference in strategy between Vinnie and Bruce is much simplified in the film, and comes down to whether or not you should develop your queen at an early stage in the game. For the film, the queen is just a symbol of their opposed styles; the movie is really about personalities, and how they express themselves through chess.

The screenplay by Steven Zaillian *(Schindler's List),* based on Fred Waitzkin's autobiographical book, is best when it deals with the issues surrounding competitive chess. Is winning, for example, the only thing? Is chess so important that it should absorb all the attention of a young prodigy, or is his development as a normal little boy also crucial? Why does one play serious chess in the first place? There is a cautionary moment when Fred Waitzkin sees his first professional chess tournament—an ill-fitted room filled with players, mostly men, mostly silent, bending over their boards as if in prayer—and is warned that this is the world his son will inhabit.

By the end of *Searching for Bobby Fischer* we have learned something about tournament chess, and a great deal about human nature. The film's implications are many. They center around our responsibility, if any, to our gifts. If we can operate at the genius level in a given field, does that mean we must—even if the cost is the sort of endless purgatory a Bobby Fischer has inhabited? It's an interesting question and this movie doesn't avoid it. At the end, it all comes down to that choice faced by the young player that A.S. Byatt writes about: the choice between truth, and beauty. What makes us men is that we can think logically. What makes us human is that we sometimes choose not to.

The Secret Garden ★ ★ ★ ★
G, 99 m., 1993

Kate Maberly (Mary Lennox), Heydon Prowse (Colin), Andrew Knott (Dickon), Laura Crossley (Martha), Maggie Smith (Mrs. Medlock), John Lynch (Lord Craven). Directed by Agnieszka Holland and produced by Fred Fuchs, Fred Roos, and Tom Luddy. Screenplay by Caroline Thompson.

Like all great stories for children, *The Secret Garden* contains powerful truths just beneath the surface. There is always a level at which the story is telling children about more than just events; it is telling them about the nature of life. That was the feeling I had when I read Frances Hodgson Burnett's book many years ago, and it is a feeling that comes back powerfully while watching Agnieszka Holland's new film.

Some "children's films" are only for children. Some can be watched by the whole family. Others are so good they seem hardly intended for children at all, and *The Secret Garden* falls in that category. It is a work of beauty, poetry, and deep mystery, and watching it is like entering for a time into a closed world where one's destiny may be discovered.

The film tells the story, familiar to generations, of a young girl orphaned in India in the early years of this century, and sent home to England, to live on the vast estate of an uncle. Misselthwaite Manor is a gloomy and forbidding pile in Yorkshire—a construction of stone, wood, metal, secrets, and ancient wounds. The heroine, whose name is Mary Lennox (Kate Maberly), arrives from her long sea journey to be met with a sniff and a stern look from Mrs. Medlock (Maggie Smith), who manages the place in the absence of the uncle, Lord Archibald Craven (John Lynch). Mary quickly gathers that this uncle is almost always absent, traveling in far places in an attempt to forget the heartbreaking death of his young bride some years earlier.

There is little for Mary to do in the mansion but explore, and soon she finds secret passageways and even the bedroom of her late aunt—and in the bedroom, a key to a secret garden. She makes friends with a boy named Dickon (Andrew Knott), whose sister is a maid at Misselthwaite, and together they play in the garden, and he whispers the manor's great secret: The aunt died in childbirth, but her son, now nine or ten years old, still lives in the manor, confined to his bed, unable to walk.

Mary goes exploring and finds the little boy, named Colin (Heydon Prowse). He has lived a life of great sadness, confined to his room, able to see only the sky from the windows visible from his bed. Mary determines he must see his mother's secret garden, and she and Dickon are able to wheel him there in an invalid's chair, stealing him out of the house under the very nose of Mrs. Medlock.

All of this could be told in a simple and insipid story, I am sure, with cute kids sneaking around the corridors. But Holland is alert to the buried meanings of her story, and she has encouraged her actors to act their age—to be smart, resourceful, and articulate. They are so good at their jobs that we stop being aware they are children, and enter into full identification with their quest.

More of the story I must not tell, except to mention in passing the gaunt dignity of Uncle Archibald, played by Lynch with the kind of weary, sensual sadness that Jeremy Irons used to have a corner on. By the end of the film I was surprised by how much I was moved; how much I had come to care about the lonely little boy, the orphaned girl, and the garden that a dead woman had prepared for them.

This is Holland's first American film, backed by Francis Ford Coppola and produced by his longtime associates Fred Fuchs, Fred Roos, and Tom Luddy. Holland's earlier work includes *Europa, Europa*, a story of a Jewish boy who is able to save his life by passing for a Nazi youth brigade member, and *Olivier, Olivier*, another case of mysterious identity, about a long-lost son who may or may not have been found again. I found *Europa, Europa* such an incredible story that I rejected it; what lesson can be learned from the freak survival of one potential victim, while millions died? *Olivier, Olivier* I found a more successful film, although I was mystified by the function of an unexplained supernatural element in the story.

In *The Secret Garden* Holland has again made a film about a missing child, but this time her theme and her telling of it are in complete harmony. It is a beautiful, intelligent film—a fable, a lesson, and an entrancing entertainment. And Roger Deakins's photography elevates the secret garden into a place of such harmony and beauty that we almost believe it can restore the lives of those who look on it. The summer of 1993 will be remembered as the time when every child in the world wanted to see *Jurassic Park*. The lucky ones saw this one, too.

Secret Honor ★ ★ ★ ★
NO MPAA RATING, 90 m., 1984

Philip Baker Hall (Nixon). Directed and produced by Robert Altman. Screenplay by Donald Freed and Arnold M. Stone.

The most tantalizing images in Woodward and Bernstein's *The Final Days* were those stories of a drunken Richard M. Nixon, falling to his knees in the White House, embarrassing Henry Kissinger with a display of self-pity and pathos. Was the book accurate? Even Kissinger said he had no idea who the authors' sources were (heh, heh). But as Watergate fades into history, and as revisionist historians begin to suggest that Nixon might after all have been a great president—apart from the scandals, of course—our curiosity remains. What were the real secrets of this most complex president? Robert Altman's *Secret Honor*, which is one of the most scathing, lacerating and brilliant movies of 1984, attempts to answer our questions. The film is a work of fiction. An actor is employed to impersonate Nixon. But all of the names and many of the facts are real, and the film gives us the uncanny sensation that we are watching a man in the act of exposing his soul.

The action takes place in Nixon's private office, at some point after his resignation. The shelves are lined with books, and with a four-screen video monitor for the security system. The desk top is weighted down with brass and gold. From the walls, portraits peer down. Eisenhower, Lincoln, Washington, Woodrow Wilson, Kissinger. Nixon begins by fiddling with his tape recorder; there is a little joke in the fact that he doesn't know quite how to run it. Then he begins to talk. He talks for ninety minutes. That bare description may make *Secret Honor* sound like *My Dinner with André*, but rarely have I seen ninety more compelling minutes on the screen. Nixon is portrayed by Philip Baker Hall, an actor previously unknown to me, with such savage intensity, such passion, such venom, such scandal, that we cannot turn away. Hall looks a little like the real Nixon; he could be a cousin, and he sounds a little like him. That's close enough. This is not an impersonation, it's a performance.

What Nixon the character has to say may or may not be true. He makes shocking revelations. Watergate was staged to draw attention away from more serious, even treasonous, activities. Kissinger was on the payroll of the Shah of Iran, and supplied the Shah with young boys during his visits to New York. Marilyn Monroe was indeed murdered by the CIA, and so on. These speculations are interwoven with stories we recognize as part of the official Nixon biography: the letter to his mother, signed "Your faithful dog, Richard"; the feeling about his family and his humble beginnings; his hatred for the Eastern Establishment, which he feels has scorned him.

Truth and fiction mix together into a tapestry of life. We get the sensation of a man pouring out all of his secrets after a lifetime of repression. His sentences rush out, disorganized, disconnected, under tremendous pressure, interrupted by four-letter words that serve almost as punctuation. After a while the specific details don't matter so much; what we are hearing is a scream of a brilliant, gifted man who is tortured by the notion that fate might have made him a loser.

A strange thing happened to me as I watched this film. I knew it was fiction. I didn't approach it in the spirit of learning the "truth about Nixon." But as a movie, it created a deeper truth, an artistic truth, and after *Secret Honor* was over, you know what? I had a deeper sympathy for Richard Nixon than I have ever had before.

The Secret of Roan Inish ★ ★ ★ ½ NEW
PG, 103M., 1995

Jeni Courtney (Fiona), Eileen Colgan (Grandmother Tess), Mick Lally (Grandfather Hugh), Richard Sheridan (Eamon), John Lynch (Tadhg). Directed by John Sayles. Produced by Sarah Green and Maggie Renzi. Screenplay by Sayles.

One day, many years ago, an ancestor of Fiona spied a beautiful creature sunning by the sea. She was both woman and seal. We would call her a mermaid, but on that western coast of Ireland such creatures were well known as Selkies. The ancestor trapped the creature and married her, and they had children together, and lived happily, although she seemed to long for the sea. One day she learned where her husband had hidden her sealskin, up under the roof, and she put it back on and returned to the sea.

Fiona (Jeni Courtney), who is twelve or thirteen years old, is told this story by a relative. It is not told as a "fairy tale," but as an account of family history, to be taken quite seriously. And well might Fiona believe it, because ever since there have been dark-haired children in her family who were said to throw back to the Selkie, and whose eyes turned yearningly to the sea.

The year is about 1946. Fiona's mother has died, and her father can barely be budged from his mourning in the pub. She is sent to live with her grandparents, on a seacoast across from the island of Roan Inish, where the whole family once lived. There she learns the story of her little brother, Jamie, whose cradle was carried off by the waves. And there, with her grandparents and her cousin Eamon (Richard Sheridan), she first explores Roan Inish, which means in Gaelic, "island of the seals."

The secret of John Sayles's *The Secret of Roan Inish* is that it tells of this young girl with perfect seriousness. This is not a children's movie, not a fantasy, not cute, not fanciful. It is the exhilarating account of how Fiona rediscovers her family's history and reclaims their island. If by any chance you do not believe in Selkies, please at least keep an open mind, because in this film Selkies exist in the real world, just like you and me.

On Roan Inish, the girl sees a child's footprint. Then she sees the child—Jamie!—running on the sand. She calls to him, but he gets back into his cradle, which is borne out to sea by friendly seals. Of course it is hard to convince grown-ups of what she has seen. In the meantime, her grandparents face eviction from their cottage, which is to be sold to rich folks from the city. They may have to move inland. "To move off of Roan Inish was bad enough," Fiona's grandmother says, "but to move out of sight of the sea . . ." She shakes her head, making it clear that it would kill the grandfather, who thinks of the city as "nothing but noise and dirt and people that's lost their senses!"

Can Fiona and Eamon, her young cousin, restore the family's old cottages on Roan Inish? Can she reclaim Jamie from the sea? I found myself actually caring. John Sayles and Haskell Wexler, who has photographed this movie with great beauty and precision, have ennobled the material. There is a scene where a person numbed by the cold sea is warmed between two cows, and we feel close to the earth and protected.

One can easily guess how this legend could have been simplified and jollied up in other hands—how it could have been about cute little Selkies. But legends are, after all, told by adults, not children, and usually they record something essential to the culture that produces them. What this legend says, I think, is that the people who tell it live on the land but live from the sea, so that their loyalties are forever divided.

Of course this is a wonderful "family film," if that term has not been corrupted to mean simpleminded and shallow. Children deserve, not lesser films, but greater ones, because their imaginations can take in larger truths and bigger ideas. *The Secret of Roan Inish* is a film for children and teenagers like Fiona, who can envision changing their family's fate. It is also for adults, of course, except for those who think they do not want to see a film about anything so preposterous as a seal-woman, and who will get what they deserve.

September ★ ★ ★ ½
PG, 82 m., 1987

Denholm Elliott (Howard), Dianne Wiest (Stephanie), Mia Farrow (Lane), Elaine Stritch (Diane), Sam Waterston (Peter), Jack Warden (Lloyd), Ira Wheeler (Mr. Raines), Jane Cecil (Mrs. Raines), Rosemary Murphy (Mrs. Mason). Directed by Woody Allen and produced by Robert Greenhut. Screenplay by Allen.

If you could take all of the different combinations of love won and love lost from many different periods in your life and join them all together for a weekend in the country, the weekend might turn out a little like *September*. Some of the guests at your party might be older or younger than you are, or smarter or more vulnerable, or of a different sex. But when you looked closely at their romantic strivings, you would recognize yourself, because there are, after all, only so many ways to be in love with the wrong person at the wrong time.

There are six major characters in the movie, each and every one of them hungry to be loved and taken care of. And everyone in the movie loves somebody—but usually not the person who loves him. The entire weekend comes down to a series of little emotional tangos, in which the characters move restlessly from room to room, trying to arrange to be alone with the object of their love—and away from the person obsessed with them.

The dominant person in the household is Diane, the middle-aged but still charismatic movie star. Played by Elaine Stritch, she is a woman who has lived a great deal, compromised too often, and become what is known as a "survivor," which is to say, a person you are surprised is still functioning. She has been married several times, currently to Lloyd (Jack Warden), an industrialist who is no doubt proud to have won this woman who was a sex symbol when they were both much younger. (By the same token, if Marilyn Monroe were still alive today, how many men over forty would not still feel some nostalgic erotic stirring if they found themselves alone in the room with her?)

Diane has come out to the family's country place to join her fortyish daughter, Lane (Mia Farrow), who has been living there for some time, recovering from a breakdown. For several months, Lane's close companion has been Howard (Denholm Elliott), the quiet, self-effacing neighbor. Lane has allowed Howard to grow close to her, but actually she feels passion only for Peter (Sam Waterston), the writer who has taken a place nearby for the summer. Peter has rather encouraged her. But this weekend, Lane has invited Stephanie (Dianne Wiest), her closest friend, to the country. And now Peter has conceived an enormous passion for Stephanie.

So, Howard loves Lane, who loves Peter, who loves Stephanie, who is thinking of breaking up with her husband. And Lloyd loves his memories of Diane, who looks in the mirror and still finds much to love in herself. And meanwhile there is a horrible family secret lurking beneath the pleasant conversations of the mother and the daughter—a secret that will burst out later in the film, in a moment of anger.

What is Allen up to here? The structure of his story is all too neat to make a messy, psychologically complicated modern movie. In the neat pairings of couples and non-couples, Allen almost seems to be making a modern-dress Elizabethan comedy. And that may be his point. When we fall in love, we are always so wound up in the absolute uniqueness of ourselves and our loved one, in the feeling that nothing like this has ever happened before, that we cannot see how the same old patterns repeat themselves. To turn toward one person, we must turn away from another. If the person we turn to is not interested, we are left stranded, which is the way all but the luckiest of us probably feel most of the time.

Allen has made so many comedies that it is easy to insist that he make nothing else.

Actually, he is as acute an author of serious dialogue as anyone now making movies, and in *September,* most of the real action goes on in the word choices. By the precise words that they do or don't use, his characters are able to convey exactly how much of what they say is sincere, and how much is polite. Listening to Farrow gently speak to Elliott, for example, anyone but Elliott would know instantly that she does not and never will love him. Listening to Waterston talk to Farrow, anyone but Farrow would know that he does not and never will love her.

How is it that the Farrow character is perceptive enough to know what words to say to Elliott, but not sensitive enough to hear the same words when they are being said to her? That is the whole mystery of this film. We can clearly see the people we are not in love with, but when we look at the people we love, we see only what we choose to see, and hear only what we can stand to hear. *September* is the first movie in a long time that has been able to listen that closely.

The Serpent and the Rainbow ★ ★ ★
R, 98 m., 1988

Bill Pullman (Dennis Alan), Cathy Tyson (Marielle Celine), Zakes Mokae (Dargent Peytraud), Paul Winfield (Lucien Celine), Brent Jennings (Mozart), Conrad Roberts (Christophe), Badja Djola (Gaston). Directed by Wes Craven and produced by David Ladd and Doug Claybourne. Screenplay by Richard Maxwell and A.R. Simoun.

The Serpent and the Rainbow was inspired by a book by Wade Davis, a Harvard scientist who investigated the voodoo society of Haiti and identified two of the drugs used for "zombification"—drugs that lower the metabolic rate of their victims so much that they appear dead and are buried, only to be dug up later and revived.

Resurrected zombies apparently appear somewhat lobotomized, a not unreasonable result of being turned into the living dead and buried alive. Although Davis himself did not become a zombie—at least not more so than any other doctoral candidate—his adventures inspired this thriller in which a Harvard researcher, played by Bill Pullman, ventures into the heart of voodoo and witnesses strange and gruesome realities.

In the movie, Pullman plays a cross between William Hurt and Indiana Jones: he's a tall, good-looking, sensitive intellectual who is called upon to wrestle leopards, battle corpses, confront an evil voodoo leader, and eventually be buried alive along with a deadly spider that makes itself cozy on his paralyzed eyeball.

Pullman's mission in going to Haiti is to isolate the active ingredient in secret voodoo powder, so that it can perhaps be used as an anesthetic. His contact in Haiti is the beautiful Marielle Celine, played by Cathy Tyson in her first role since *Mona Lisa.* She runs a people's clinic, as the sexy heroines in these movies always do. Other local experts include Paul Winfield, as a well-connected local leader, and Brent Jennings, as a man named Mozart who knows all of the secrets in the secret ingredients.

In most voodoo movies, voodoo itself is taken only as a backdrop, a gimmick. This movie seems to know something about voodoo (it knows more than I do, anyway), and treats it seriously as a religion, a way of life, and an occult circle that does possess secrets unexplored by modern medicine. One of the most convincing elements in the movie is the way the more "modern" Haitians nevertheless regard voodoo as something not to be taken lightly. As Pullman slowly enters the voodoo society, penetrating first one level of concealment and then another, we get the sensation—unusual in a horror film—that his discoveries are genuine.

The movie was shot on location in Haiti and the Dominican Republic, and unlike most voodoo movies, it attempts to look and sound realistic—even including TV clips of the overthrow and flight of the dictator "Baby Doc" Duvalier. The visual look of the movie is stunning; there's never the sense of sets, of costumes, of hired extras, but more of a feeling of a camera moving past real people in real places. Even the obviously contrived scenes, including some of the hallucinations and voodoo fantasies, have an air of solid plausibility to them.

The film was directed by Wes Craven, a master of horror, whose credits include *Last House on the Left, Swamp Thing,* and the original *A Nightmare on Elm Street.* Craven will never advance in the Hollywood establishment until he embraces more respectable projects, and yet he has a sure touch for horror and the macabre, and *The Serpent and the Rainbow* is uncanny in the way it takes the most lurid images and makes them plausible.

Sex, Drugs, Rock & Roll ★ ★ ★
R, 96 m., 1991

Eric Bogosian in a concert film directed by John McNaughton and produced by Frederick Zollo. Screenplay by Eric Bogosian.

Eric Bogosian speaks in an insinuating voice, like one of those wise guys who knows things you don't want to hear. At least, I think that's his real voice; it provides the undertow in all the other voices he uses in this film—the voices of the panhandler, the rock star, the paranoid 1960s refugee, the rich pig, the party animal. It's the kind of voice you might happen across on the AM band of the radio at three in the morning, your headlights cutting a hole in the darkness of a highway you've never traveled before. A voice that involves you in its weariness and cynicism, that would like to paint a prettier picture, but knows human nature too well.

It is perhaps the tragedy of Bogosian's career that it began after the collapse of radio. Today he could be a talk-show host (maybe like the one he played in *Talk Radio,* a very good 1988 film, which he also wrote). But in the days of radio drama he could have been a disembodied voice, a voice like Orson Welles on "The Shadow," a voice coming out of the darkness inside your own head, knowing your secrets, and others besides.

Watching *Sex, Drugs, Rock & Roll,* I wished I was listening to it. I closed my eyes for a time, and I was right: Bogosian's art depends on sound, not sight. This is terrific material, but it doesn't have to be a movie. Bogosian here is doing a "one-man concert film," which is another word for training a camera on a guy on a stage for as long as it takes him to do his act. There is an audience somewhere, invisible until the end, and they like him. And there is Bogosian on the stage, playing a dozen or so characters, doing them as monologues designed to reveal things about them and about the world we live in.

The movie is not very well handled. It was directed by John McNaughton, whose *Henry: Portrait of a Serial Killer* shows both that he is a good director and that he might seem like an appropriate director for Bogosian's material. But McNaughton doesn't seem sure what he wants to do. He doesn't show the audience much—he doesn't want to underline the notion of a live performance—and yet at the same time he has Bogosian looking at the audience more than he looks at the camera—at us, the *real* audience. Eye contact is the soul of film. There are times when

Bogosian shouldn't be looking at the camera (when he's looking at an invisible TV interviewer, for example). But the rest of the time, we feel he's avoiding us when his characters should be buttonholing us instead.

The material here is strong. Bogosian has an ear for the way people express themselves—for a subway panhandler who anticipates rejection and patterns his spiel to respond to it, for a rich guy who has everything in the world he can buy but doesn't know what to do with most of it. His monologues re-create some of the madness of our time. In *Talk Radio* he was the host, paid to listen and respond. Here it's like he's a cross-section of the callers to the same program: the conspiracy freak, the has-been celebrity rock star, the guy with theories about women.

Bogosian impersonates these characters only up to a point. Beyond that point, he chooses to be himself, and he does that by allowing his real voice to circle beneath the fictional ones. He's not an impressionist. He's a reporter. *Sex, Drugs, Rock & Roll* is a good film, but the material is better than the film form allows it to be. Rent the tape, make an audio cassette of it, and slap it into the car radio late one night when you're driving along. And lock the doors.

sex, lies, and videotape ★ ★ ★ ½
R, 104 m., 1989

James Spader (Graham), Andie MacDowell (Ann), Peter Gallagher (John), Laura San Giacomo (Cynthia), Ron Vawter (Therapist), Steven Brill (Barfly), Alexandra Root (Girl on Tape), Earl T. Taylor (Landlord). Directed by Steven Soderbergh and produced by Robert Newmyer and John Hardy. Screenplay by Soderbergh.

I have a friend who says golf is not only better than sex but lasts longer. The argument in *sex, lies, and videotape* is that conversation is also better than sex—more intimate, more voluptuous—and that with our minds we can do things to each other that make sex, that swapping of sweat and sentiment, seem merely troublesome. Of course this argument is all a mind game, and sex itself, sweat and all, is the prize for the winner. That's what makes the conversation so erotic.

The movie takes place in Baton Rouge, Louisiana, and it tells the story of four people in their early thirties whose sex lives are seriously confused. One is a lawyer named John (Peter Gallagher), who is married to Ann (Andie MacDowell) but no longer sleeps

with her. Early in the film, we hear her telling her psychiatrist that this is no big problem; sex is really overrated, she thinks, compared to the larger issues such as how the earth is running out of places to dispose of its garbage. Her husband does not, however, think sex is overrated, and is conducting a passionate affair with his wife's sister, Cynthia (Laura San Giacomo), who is an artist and who has always resented the goody-goody Ann.

An old friend turns up in town. His name is Graham (James Spader), and he was John's college roommate. Nobody seems quite clear what he has been doing in the years since college, but he's one of those types you don't ask questions about things like that, because you have the feeling you don't want to know the answers. He's dangerous, not in a physical way, but through his insinuating intelligence, which seems to see through people.

He moves in. Makes himself at home. One day he has lunch with Ann, and they begin to flirt with their conversation, turning each other on with words carefully chosen to occupy the treacherous ground between eroticism and a proposition. She says she doesn't think much of sex, but then he tells her something that gets her interested: He confesses that he is impotent. It is, I think, a fundamental fact of the human ego in the sexually active years that most women believe they can end a man's impotence, just as most men believe they are heaven's answer to a woman's frigidity. If this were true, impotence and frigidity would not exist, but if hope did not spring eternal, not much else would spring either.

The early stages of *sex, lies, and videotape* are a languorous, but intriguing, setup for the tumult that follows. The adultery between John and Cynthia has the usual consequences and creates the usual accusations of betrayal, but the movie (and, I think, the audience) is more interested in Graham's sexual pastimes. Unable to satisfy himself in the usual ways, he videotapes the sexual fantasies of women and then watches them. This is a form of sexual assault; he has power not over their bodies but over their minds, over their secrets, and I suspect that the most erotic sentence in his vocabulary is "She's actually telling me this stuff!"

Ann is horrified by Graham's hobby, and fascinated, and before long the two of them are in front of his camera in a scene of remarkable subtlety and power, both discovering that, for them, sex is only the beginning of their mysteries. This scene, and indeed the

whole movie, would not work unless the direction and acting were precisely right (this is the kind of movie where a slightly wrong tone could lead to a very bad laugh), but Spader and MacDowell do not step wrong. Indeed, Spader's performance throughout the film is a kind of risk-taking; can you imagine the challenge an actor faces in taking the kind of character I have described and making him not only intriguing but seductive? Spader has the kind of sexual ambiguity of the young Brando or Dean; he seems to suggest that if he bypasses the usual sexual approaches it is because he has something more interesting up, or down, his sleeve.

The story of *sex, lies, and videotape* is by now part of movie folklore: how Soderbergh, at twenty-nine, wrote the screenplay in eight days during a trip to Los Angeles, how the film was made for $1.8 million, how it won the Palme d'Or at the 1989 Cannes Film Festival, as well as the best actor prize for Spader. I am not sure it is as good as the Cannes jury apparently found it; it has more intelligence than heart, and is more clever than enlightening. But it is never boring, and there are moments when it reminds us of how sexy the movies used to be, back before they could show everything, and thus had to think about nothing.

The Shadow ★ ★ ★
PG-13, 112 m., 1994

Alec Baldwin (Lamont Cranston/The Shadow), John Lone (Shiwan Kahn), Penelope Ann Miller (Margo Lane), Peter Boyle (Moe Shrevnitz), Ian McKellen (Reinhardt Lane), Tim Curry (Farley Claymore), Jonathan Winters (Barth). Directed by Russell Mulcahy and produced by Martin Bregman, Willi Baer, and Michael S. Bregman. Screenplay by David Koepp.

The Shadow opens in Tibet, where a decadent villain with long purple fingernails lounges in an opium den where the execution of his enemies—and friends—hardly raises an eyebrow. This is Ying Ko, the first of three names The Shadow will use, and he is a worthless piece of work until he is taken in hand by an ancient wise man who forces him to reform. Thus does Ying Ko become Lamont Cranston, better known as The Shadow. And thus does he move from Tibet to "that most wretched lair of villainy we know as . . . New York City."

If you grew up on radio serials and pulp magazines, this is a familiar world. But *The*

Shadow hasn't been heard on radio in decades, the pulps have crumbled to dust, and still the tacky romanticism of *The Shadow* retains its power: "Who knows what evil lurks in the hearts of men?" A fiendish laugh, and then: "The Shadow knows."

The Shadow is the kind of movie that plays better the more baggage you bring to it. If you respond to *film noir,* if you like dark streets and women with scarlet lips and big, fast cars with running boards, the look of this movie will work some kind of magic. The story itself may not be so mesmerizing, but who really cares? Style and tone are everything with a movie like this, which wants to bring to life a dark, secret place in the lurid pulp imagination.

The movie stars Alec Baldwin as Lamont Cranston, a.k.a. The Shadow, and he is a good choice for the role. Sleekly handsome, with a glint in his dark eyes, he remains utterly solemn while delivering lines like, "The weed of crime bears bitter fruit," and "Inside you beats a heart of darkness." He wears a cape and a wide-brimmed hat, and stalks the night streets, fighting crime. The sound of his voice seems to echo from inside a large, damp room and is a counterpoint for Jerry Goldsmith's score, made out of sad brass sounds and tremulous strings.

His nemesis is the last survivor of Genghis Khan, Shiwan Kahn (John Lone), who says, "Kahn conquered half the world. My task is to finish the job." Shiwan shares most of the mystical powers the old mystic gave to The Shadow, including, of course, "the power to cloud men's minds." In a plot that inevitably involves world domination, they are surrounded by many minds to cloud, including those of the police commissioner (Jonathan Winters), a mad scientist (Tim Curry), a merely goofy scientist (Ian McKellen), and gangsters who find themselves shooting at phantoms.

One mind that remains mostly unclouded belongs to Margo Lane (Penelope Ann Miller), a slinky blonde who possesses unrealized mental powers of her own, falls in love with Cranston, and begins to pick up vibes on a wavelength he thought was private. Love affairs involving superheroes are always faintly funny, because the protagonist's first responsibility is to his legend, not his romance; *The Shadow* has a wicked exchange where Margo purringly describes a dream ("I was lying naked on the beach in the South Seas . . .") and then Cranston shares his dream ("I dreamed I tore all the skin off my face and was somebody else underneath.").

The look of the film somehow supports this foolishness. The director, Russell Mulcahy, whose earlier career was not distinguished by *Highlander* or, for that matter, *Highlander 2,* has assembled a talented technical team that re-creates New York City as an Art Deco nightmare. There are diabolical dangers, like a water tank in which Cranston is sealed to drown; hallucinatory real estate, like a hotel Kahn makes invisible by hypnotizing the entire city; and sexy props like the speedboat-size Yellow Cab driven by Cranston's faithful retainer Moe (Peter Boyle).

If the movie is finally just a little less than the sum of its parts, maybe that's appropriate. The original "Shadow" novels were pounded out by Walter Gibson at a rate of sixty thousand words a week, and consumed by magazine and radio audiences not because they were individually great, but because collectively they created a dream. The Shadow was created during the Depression, when the mean streets were dark and threatening, and it was comforting that there was a denizen of the night who fought for good, not evil. It still is.

Shadowlands ★ ★ ★ ★
PG, 133 m., 1994

Anthony Hopkins (C.S. Lewis), Debra Winger (Joy Gresham), Edward Hardwicke (Warnie Lewis), John Wood (Prof. Riley), Michael Denison (Rev. Harrington), Joseph Mazzello (Douglas Gresham), Peter Firth (Dr. Craig). Directed by Richard Attenborough and produced by Attenborough and Brian Eastman. Screenplay by William Nicholson.

For many years his life has followed the same comfortable patterns. He is a teacher and a writer, a pipe-smoking bachelor who lives in his book-lined Oxford home with his brother. From his children's books, his science fiction, and his pop theology, he has gained a following, and he gives comforting talks about man's place in God's plans. Then the most extraordinary thing takes place. He falls in love.

Shadowlands is the story, based on fact, of an autumnal romance involving the British writer C.S. Lewis and a divorced American woman named Joy Gresham. They met after she wrote him an admiring letter; their correspondence led to her first visit to England, with her young son. Lewis received her as a courtesy, and was so settled in his lifelong professorial routine that he hardly knew what to do when it became clear, even to him, that he was in love.

Shadowlands has found two perfect actors to play this unlikely couple, Anthony Hopkins and Debra Winger. He is shy sometimes to the point of being tongue-tied; he nods and hems and haws and looks away, and retreats behind formulas of courtesy. She is more direct, an outspoken woman who sometimes surprises him by saying out loud what they have both been thinking, but that he would never have said. She sees at a glance the comfortable rut he is in—the dinners at his college dining hall, the evenings in front of the fire, reading while the wireless provides classical music from the BBC. She isn't out to "catch" him. It's more that he discovers he cannot imagine her going away.

Their courtship is an odd one. He issues invitations lamely, as if sure she will not accept. He is so terrified of marriage that he has to couch his proposal in "practical" terms—if he marries her, she will not be forced to leave Britain. She has to negotiate the clouded waters of university politics, the annual dinners of the college head, the curiosity and pointed questions of his nosy colleagues. When it comes to sex, he hasn't a clue, and she talks him through it: "What do you do when you go to bed?" "I put on my pajamas and say my prayers and get under the covers." "Well, then, that's what I want you to do right now, except that when you get under the covers, I'll be there."

Lewis has been confident in his writings and lectures that he knows the purpose of suffering and pain: It is God's way of perfecting us, of carving away the wrong parts, of leaving a soul ready to enter heaven. But when Joy contracts cancer, when she finds herself in terrible pain, he finds he is not at all sure of his theory. And, facing the possibility that they will be parted, together they create an idea of human life on earth that comforts him more than his theories.

Shadowlands, directed by Richard Attenborough, based on the stage play by William Nicholson, is intelligent, moving, and beautifully acted. It understands that not everyone falls into love through the avenue of physical desire; that for some, the lust may be for another's mind, for inner beauty. Anthony Hopkins, who earlier in 1993 in *Remains of the Day* gave a brilliant performance as a closed-off English butler who was afraid to love, here provides a companion performance, of a buttoned-down English intellectual who surprises himself by finding the courage to love.

Debra Winger, not afraid to look less than her best in early scenes (although her beauty glows later on in the film), is no less extraordinary: She projects a quiet empathy in creating Joy Gresham, a woman who has fallen in love with Lewis through his writings. Her character goes through a series of delicate adjustments as she meets him and realizes he is not as contented as he thinks. She believes that making one another happier is one of their purposes on earth. His ability to share that view is a small triumph, but one few people can claim.

Shadows and Fog ★ ★
PG-13, 86 m., 1992

Woody Allen (Kleinman), Mia Farrow (Irmy), John Cusack (Student Jack), John Malkovich (Clown), Kathy Bates (Prostitute). Directed by Woody Allen and produced by Robert Greenhut. Screenplay by Allen.

Most moviegoers will never have seen a film quite like Woody Allen's *Shadows and Fog* before, because they won't have seen the work of the great German expressionists of the 1920s, who used stylized sets and moody black and white atmosphere to create brooding dream-spaces. Allen's new film, which takes place in the streets and alleys and hidden rooms of a European city in the 1920s, is shot in the style of those masterpieces, but without their urgency and precision. Like many homages, it lacks the immediate inspiration that made the originals exciting.

The film opens, as advertised, with a great many shadows and a lot of fog. Dark overcoated figures glide silently through the gloom, until one of them, a tall, strong figure, strangles another. Shortly afterward, a vigilante mob comes pounding on the door of Kleinman (Woody Allen), recruiting him for their hunt through the empty streets for the vicious criminal. Kleinman doesn't want to go. On the whole, he is happier at home. But grumbling and complaining, he ventures out into the night to join the search.

That sets up a series of scenes in which lives cross paths, and coincidences allow people to have experiences they might never have had. We meet some of the other inhabitants of this fogbound, strangler-beset city, including a clown (John Malkovich) who quarrels with his girlfriend, Irmy (Mia Farrow), a sword-swallower. She races out weeping into the night and is befriended by a

prostitute (Lily Tomlin) and given shelter in a brothel also headquarters for Jodie Foster and Kathy Bates. A young student (John Cusack) comes looking for a girl, fancies Irmy, and offers her twenty dollars. She is shocked and says she would never have sex for money. At seven hundred dollars, she changes her mind.

Kleinman and his friends meanwhile prowl the streets, looking for the strangler and more often cornering each other. The city is populated by a large number of assorted characters with familiar faces, ranging from Madonna to David Ogden Stiers. There are stretches when Allen is able to demonstrate that he can obtain an expressionist look every bit as convincing as Fritz Lang, and others when the whole elaborate apparatus of his film seems simply to be a backdrop for throwaway lines by his kvetching hero.

I am an admirer of the films that inspired *Shadows and Fog*, and a lover of black and white photography. If I had to choose between seeing only b&w or color movies for the rest of my life, I would choose b&w without a moment's hesitation, because color often just smears the screen with unnecessary information, and obscures the sophisticated lighting strategies the b&w is more suited for.

As much as I admire Allen, b&w, the expressionists, and the music of Kurt Weill, however, I was not able to work up much enthusiasm for *Shadows and Fog*. It seemed like a contrivance, an exercise with a good-looking surface but no particular purpose for existing.

The movie was released by the troubled Orion Pictures Corp., which for many years provided Allen with unquestioning support for his films. During that time he emerged as one of the best of all American directors; remember the pleasures and insights of *Annie Hall, Manhattan, Radio Days, Hannah and Her Sisters,* and *Crimes and Misdemeanors.* Remember, too, the deliberate experiments with style and content in *Interiors, A Midsummer Night's Sex Comedy,* and *Another Woman.* It is an amazing body of work.

But now that kind of financial freedom is probably coming to an end for Allen, as it already long since has for most other filmmakers whose names are not Steven Spielberg or George Lucas. It's unlikely Orion will be able to continue its support, and Woody Allen will be back to playing by the usual rules. That will cost us, I am afraid, some brilliant pictures. He may make other great pictures all the same. But the more

realistic arrangements may also put him in touch with producers who will ask, not without a certain hesitation, for him to explain what, exactly, he has in mind with a movie like *Shadows and Fog.* And that is a question that this movie does not seem to have an answer for.

Shakedown ★ ★ ★
R, 105 m., 1988

Peter Weller (Roland Dalton), Sam Elliott (Richie Marks), Patricia Charbonneau (Susan Cantrell), Antonio Fargas (Nicky Carr), Blanche Baker (Gail Feinberger), Tom Waits (Officer Kelly). Directed by James Glickenhaus and produced by J. Boyce Harman, Jr. Screenplay by Glickenhaus.

If they ever stopped to collect the dead bodies in a movie like *Shakedown,* the hero would have to play a coroner. But a movie like this never looks back, and *Shakedown* is very definitely a movie like this. It's an assembly of sensational moments, strung together by a plot that provides the excuses for amazing stunts, and not much else. But then not much else is needed.

Imagine this. A private jet airplane is taking off from LaGuardia. A public defender and a tough plainclothesman are chasing it down the runway in a Porsche. At the last moment, the cop leaps from the car and grabs one of the wheels of the plane. As the plane gains altitude, he shoots a bullet through an engine, forcing the pilot to turn back. Then, as the plane approaches the runway for an emergency landing, he slips a hand grenade into the wheel well and falls into the water below. The grenade explodes, making it look like the plane crashed, while the cop swims to safety and is hauled ashore by his buddy, the defender.

You like it? Then you'll also like the scene where they're racing to the courthouse and a construction crane accidentally snags their car and lifts it over a mob and onto the courthouse steps. Or the scene where the cop gets in a fight on the roller coaster, is thrown out, uses his bare hands to pull the car's power supply loose, and then lets go, saving himself as the powerless roller coaster rockets off the tracks.

Movies like *Shakedown* are what they are. They represent a tremendous amount of craftsmanship and skill, and a fair degree of courage on the part of the stunt people who make it look real. They also require strong, unsubtle but convincing performances by the actors; too much psychological realism in a movie like this can allow the real world to distract from the thrills. And they require a director who takes no hostages, who knows how to sustain a headlong momentum, who is compelled to make the plot hurtle ahead with no regard for logic or nuance.

Shakedown was directed by James Glickenhaus, who has produced such earlier, mostly unsung, action dramas as *The Exterminator, The Soldier,* and *The Protector* (near the beginning of the picture, his disheveled plain-clothesman snoozes through a screening of *The Soldier* in a Times Square fleapit). Those films did not gather a great deal of attention, but with *Shakedown* Glickenhaus will now be recognized as another of the manic breed of young hotshots who will do anything to stage a sensational stunt.

The stars of the movie are Peter Weller, who segues from *RoboCop* to this role as a determined public defender, and Sam Elliott, Cher's aging hippie lover in *Mask,* as the plainclothes cop. Their relationship was perhaps inspired by similar teams in *48 HRS* and *Lethal Weapon,* but the stunts and firefights in this movie are so overwhelming that something has to give, and the relationship is the first thing Glickenhaus can do without.

The plot: A crooked cop tries to stick up a drug dealer in Central Park, and is shot dead. The drug dealer is brought to trial, but Weller becomes convinced that he didn't fire first, and that the incident is the tip of an iceberg of corruption in the police department. His friend Elliott becomes convinced of the same thing, and together they work inside and outside the law to help the defendant beat a murder rap, and expose other corrupt cops. Weller has some nice moments in the courtroom, although his legal style is so informal and disorganized that it's hard to believe, and Patricia Charbonneau (from *Desert Hearts*) has a nice supporting role as the opposing assistant D.A. who is also, of course, his former and future lover.

The movie has everything. There's a subplot about Weller's rich fiancée, and another one about a secret tape recording of the murder, and even some funny moments when Weller and Elliott try to top each other in absolute cynicism. But the movie is basically action and stunts, a high-tech sideshow of explosives, hurtling automobiles, shattering glass, and impossible feats. It is what it is.

Shallow Grave ★ ★
R, 93 m., 1995

NEW

Kerry Fox (Juliet), Christopher Eccleston (David), Ewan McGregor (Alex), Ken Stott (Inspector McCall), Keith Allen (Hugo), Colin McCredie (Cameron), Victoria Nairn (Woman Visitor), Gary Lewis (Male Visitor). Directed by Danny Boyle and produced by Andrew Macdonald. Screenplay by John Hodge.

Shallow Grave is a movie that might have warmed the heart of George Orwell, who in his famous essay "The Decline of the English Murder" complained that too many modern murders were simply unmotivated acts of squalid violence. "Let me try to define," he wrote, "what it is that the readers of the Sunday papers mean when they fretfully say, 'You never seem to get a good murder nowadays.'"

In the golden age of murder, which he places between 1850 and 1925, "good murders" had several distinguishing characteristics. To begin with, the murderers were generally "little men of the professional class"—doctors, lawyers, the chairman of the local Conservatives. They lived in intense respectability in semidetached houses, so that strange noises could be overheard by the neighbors. They killed not out of passion, but for convenience—to cover up an adultery or a theft, say. Their motive was often financial gain. Their method was usually poison.

The great preoccupation in the golden age of murder was, of course, disposal of the body. The classic cases feature bathtubs full of acid, bones buried in the backyard, corpses bricked up in the wall or fed to the dogs. (The disappearance of Mrs. Brach took on a special interest because of speculations along these lines.) Much of the enjoyment, for newspaper readers, came from the notion of respectable professional people desperately hauling bodies about by moonlight.

Shallow Grave does not supply a perfect murder by Orwell's standards—the first victim kills himself with drugs before his nasty new roommates can form any designs on him. But it qualifies in many other ways. The movie takes place in Glasgow, where three roommates are interviewing for a fourth. They are particularly repulsive types of supercilious yuppie twits: a doctor, an accountant, and a journalist. They delight in humiliating and mocking applicants, until finally they find a customer tough enough to impress them: Hugo (Keith Allen), a cool wise

guy. "He's . . . interesting," says Juliet (Kerry Fox), the doctor.

Hugo moves in and is found dead of an overdose the next morning, sprawled on his red bedspread (in a shot inspired by the famous painting *The Death of Chatterton*). This quite annoys his new roommates, until they discover that his suitcase is filled with cash. Then they decide that since no one knows he has come to live with them, they should dispose of the body and keep the cash.

This involves doing unsavory and unthinkable things that are completely outside their experience: Cutting off the corpse's head, hands and feet, to prevent identification. Burying the remains. Incinerating the severed parts in the hospital where Juliet works. Alex (Ewan McGregor) and David (Christopher Eccleston) certainly don't want to perform the dismemberment. They think Juliet should ("But, Juliet—you're a doctor! You kill people every day!").

The director, Danny Boyle, wants the disposal scenes to be funny, as he backlights his fastidious characters desperately sawing away at the bones of the dead. There is a touch here of the Coen Brothers' *Blood Simple,* but if you want to see how a great director gets laughs with the contrast between gruesome deeds and the desire to avoid dry-cleaning bills, look at Scorsese's *GoodFellas.*

Back at the flat, the desperate situation becomes more unmanageable. The three grow paranoid, and David, the meek accountant, moves into the attic with the cash, drilling holes in the ceiling so he can spy on the activities below. A series of visitors arrive at the flat, and discover it is unwise to go up into the attic. The body count mounts.

All of the materials are in place here for a film that might have pleased Orwell. But somehow they never come together. One of the problems, I think, is that all three conspirators are so unpleasant. Not evil—that would be fine, in material like this—but simply obnoxious in a boring way. To some degree we need to identify with their fear of discovery, and we do not: The only character we like is the police inspector (Ken Stott), who asks insinuating questions and then exchanges significant looks with his assistant.

The bottom line in any great murder case, I believe, is the sneaky suspicion that there, but for the grace of God, go we—either as victim or, in our nightmares, murderer. Since no reasonable person can remotely hope to identify with Juliet, David, or Alex, the whole case drops through.

Sharky's Machine ★ ★ ★
R, 119 m., 1981

Burt Reynolds (Sharky), Rachel Ward (Dominoe), Vittorio Gassman (Victor), Brian Keith (Papa), Charles Durning (Frisco). Directed by Burt Reynolds and produced by Hank Moonjean. Screenplay by Gerald Di Pago.

Sharky's Machine contains all of the ingredients of a tough, violent, cynical big-city cop movie, but what makes it intriguing is the way the Burt Reynolds character plays against those conventions. His name is Sharky. As the movie opens, he's an undercover narcotics cop. He blows a big case and is demoted to the vice squad—which is a bawdy, brawling, vocal gang of misfits who act like a cross between "Hill Street Blues" and a Joseph Wambaugh nightmare.

Sharky is not happy in vice. He is, in fact, not happy anywhere, not until a young woman named Dominoe enters his life. She is a hooker. She also seems to be involved with some snaky big-money characters, and so Sharky places her under twenty-four hour surveillance. That involves moving several cops, telescopes, cameras, and bugging devices into the high-rise opposite her apartment. The cops set up housekeeping and settle down for a long wait. And it's here that the movie begins to really involve us. Reynolds, as Sharky, falls in love with the woman. It is a voyeuristic love, involving spying and eavesdropping, and Sharky is not a voyeur—so it is particularly painful for him to witness the woman's sexual involvement with others.

The central scenes of the movie, involving the call girl's private life and the probing eyes of Sharky, could easily have become tawdry—could have disintegrated into a peep show. That doesn't happen, partly because Reynolds (who also directed the film) doesn't provide cheap displays of flesh, but also because the call girl is played by British actress Rachel Ward, who brings poignancy and restraint to the role. She plays a hooker who's not a tramp. She has a husky voice and an astonishing body, but there's an innocence in her manner. Later, we discover that she has been in virtual bondage to her pimp since she was an infant. She knows no other life. This is a setup of sorts, a device in the plot to allow the female lead to be both prostitute and victim, but it clarifies the relationship between Reynolds and Ward. And when they fall in love, as they inevitably do, it provides some leftover innocence to be celebrated.

Reynolds surrounds this central relationship with a lot of cops, known as Sharky's Machine. They are played by actors who have played a lot of other cops in a lot of other movies—Brian Keith, Charles Durning—and by Bernie Casey, who is playing his first cop but does it with special grace. There's a long scene in the film, reportedly improvised, in which Casey tells Reynolds what it felt like, the first time he was shot. We are reminded that cops in the movies hardly ever talk about being shot.

Sharky's Machine has a lot of plot, most of it inspired by the original novel by William Diehl. Maybe it has too much plot for a movie that Reynolds has referred to as *Dirty Harry Goes to Atlanta*. But this is an ambitious film; it's as if something inside Reynolds was chafing at the insipid roles he was playing in one car-chase movie after another. He doesn't walk through this movie, and he doesn't allow himself the cozy little touches that break the mood while they're letting the audience know how much fun Burt is having.

The result of his ambition and restraint is a movie much more interesting than most cop thrillers. *Sharky's Machine* does have a lot of action, including an extended, exhausting, brutal shoot-out at the end. But it also has the special qualities of the relationship between Reynolds and Ward (more fully developed than the camaraderie between Reynolds and Catherine Deneuve, as another hooker in another thriller, *Hustle*, in 1974). As a director, Reynolds allows himself a few excesses (one howler is the dramatic cut from a sex scene to the phallic glory of the Peachtree Plaza Hotel). But he's put a lot of his ambition in this movie, and it reminds us that there is a fine actor within the star of *Cannonball Run*.

The Shawshank Redemption ★ ★ ★ ½
R, 144 m., 1994

Tim Robbins (Andy Dufresne), Morgan Freeman ("Red" Redding), Bob Gunton (Warden Norton), William Sadler (Heywood), Clancy Brown (Captain Hadley), Gil Bellows (Tommy), Mark Rolston (Bogs Diamond), James Whitmore (Brooks Hatlen). Directed by Frank Darabont and produced by Niki Marvin. Screenplay by Darabont.

The Shawshank Redemption is a movie about time, patience, and loyalty—not sexy qualities, perhaps, but they grow on you during the subterranean progress of this story, which

is about how two men serving life sentences in prison become friends, and find a way to fight off despair.

The story is narrated by "Red" Redding (Morgan Freeman), who has been inside the walls of Shawshank Prison for a very long time, and is its leading entrepreneur. He can get you whatever you need: cigarettes, candy, even a little rock pick like an amateur geologist might use. One day he and his fellow inmates watch the latest busload of prisoners unload, and they make bets on which will cry during their first night in prison, and which will not. Red bets on a tall, lanky guy named Andy Dufresne (Tim Robbins), who looks like a babe in the woods.

But Andy does not cry, and Red loses the cigarettes he wagered. Andy turns out to be a surprise to everyone in Shawshank, because within him is such a powerful reservoir of determination and strength that nothing seems to break him. Andy was a banker on the outside, and he's in for murder. He's apparently innocent, and there are all sorts of details involving his case, but after a while they take on a kind of unreality; all that counts inside prison is its own society—who is strong, who is not—and the measured passage of time.

Red is also a lifer. From time to time, measuring the decades, he goes up in front of his parole board, and they measure the length of his term (twenty years, thirty years) and ask him if he thinks he has been rehabilitated. Oh, most surely, yes, he replies; but the fire goes out of his assurances as the years march past, and there is the sense that he has been institutionalized—that, like another old lifer who kills himself after being paroled, he can no longer really envision life on the outside.

Red's narration of the story allows him to speak for all of the prisoners, who sense a fortitude and integrity in Andy that survives the years. Andy will not kiss butt. He will not back down. But he is not violent, just formidably sure of himself. For the warden (Bob Gunton), he is both a challenge and a resource; Andy knows all about bookkeeping and tax preparation, and before long he's been moved out of his prison job in the library and assigned to the warden's office, where he sits behind an adding machine and keeps tabs on the warden's ill-gotten gains. His fame spreads, and eventually he's doing the taxes and pension plans for most of the officials of the local prison system.

There are key moments in the film, as when Andy uses his clout to get some cold beers for his friends who are working on a roofing job. Or when he befriends the old prison librarian (James Whitmore). Or when he oversteps his boundaries, and is thrown into solitary confinement. What quietly amazes everyone in the prison—and us, too—is the way he accepts the good and the bad as all part of some larger pattern that only he can fully see.

The partnership between the characters played by Tim Robbins and Morgan Freeman is crucial to the way the story unfolds. This is not a "prison drama" in any conventional sense of the word. It is not about violence, riots, or melodrama. The word "redemption" is in the title for a reason. The movie is based on a story, "Rita Hayworth and the Shawshank Redemption," by Stephen King, which is quite unlike most of King's work. The horror here is not of the supernatural kind, but of the sort that flows from the realization that ten, twenty, thirty years of a man's life have unreeled in the same unchanging daily prison routine. The director, Frank Darabont, paints the prison in drab grays and shadows, so that when key events do occur, they seem to have a life of their own.

Andy, as played by Robbins, keeps his thoughts to himself. Red, as Freeman plays him, is therefore a crucial element in the story: His close observation of this man, down through the years, provides the way we monitor changes and track and measure his influence on those around him. And all the time there is something else happening, hidden and secret, which is revealed only at the end.

The Shawshank Redemption is not a depressing story, although I may have made it sound that way. There is a lot of life and humor in it, and warmth in the friendship that builds up between Andy and Red. There is even excitement and suspense, although not when we expect it. But mostly the film is an allegory about holding onto a sense of personal worth, despite everything. If the film is perhaps a little slow in its middle passages, maybe that is part of the idea, too, to give us a sense of the leaden passage of time, before the glory of the final redemption.

She-Devil ★ ★ ★
PG-13, 99 m., 1989

Meryl Streep (Mary Fisher), Roseanne Barr (Ruth), Ed Begley, Jr. (Bob), Linda Hunt (Hooper), Sylvia Miles (Mrs. Fisher), Elisebeth Peters (Nicolette Patchett), Robin Leach (Himself), Sally Jessy Raphael (Herself). Directed by Susan Seidelman and produced by Jonathan Brett and Seidelman. Screenplay by Barry Strugatz and Mark R. Burns.

There must have been moments on the set of *She-Devil* when Roseanne Barr went into her dressing room and locked the door and asked herself what she was doing there, costarring in a movie with the immortal Meryl Streep. We're in on the amazement, because Barr has done such a thorough job of documenting her life in comedy routines, in confessional interviews, in her book, and on talk shows. Here is a woman who only a few years ago couldn't have gotten an autograph from Meryl Streep, let alone stolen a scene from her.

There's a delicious element of sweet revenge in Roseanne Barr's entire career. Here is the woman who proves for all of us that we could be TV stars and stand-up comics, if only we got a couple of breaks—because we've sure got more on the ball than the morons who *are* making it in show biz. And that sense of realized revenge is an undercurrent throughout *She-Devil*, which works both on a fictional level and as a real-life demonstration that Barr and Streep are indeed right there in the same movie.

If Barr is correctly cast, so is Meryl Streep, who has always had a rich vein of comedy bubbling through her personal life—few people are merrier during interviews—but who has dedicated her career to playing serious or even tragic women, most of them with accents. Here she's given a juicy role to sink her teeth into: Mary Fisher, the best-selling romance novelist who seems to be what would happen if the genes of Barbara Cartland, Jackie Collins, and Danielle Steel were combined in the same trash compactor. It's a role that calls out for broad, fearless interpretation, and Streep has a lot of fun with it.

Roseanne Barr's character is named Ruth, and she's a fat, plain suburban housewife with a mole under her lower lip that looks like a surgically implanted raisin. She is married, none too securely, to an accountant named Bob (Ed Begley, Jr.), who dreams of moving up in the ranks of his profession by becoming an accountant to the stars. Fate grants his wish. He meets Mary Fisher during an incident involving a spilled drink at a charity benefit, and one thing leads to another so rapidly that he cruelly drops off his wife at home before ending up in bed with the lustful novelist.

The heart of the movie involves the revenge Ruth takes out on her husband and Mary Fisher—revenge so thorough and methodical that she even takes time to jot down the areas of her husband's life she wants to destroy: first, his home. Then his family, career, and freedom, in that order. Bob has accused her of being a she-devil, and she is more than willing to play the role. She will haunt the faithless bastard until he wishes he had never heard of accounting, much less of Mary Fisher.

She-Devil was directed by Susan Seidelman, whose credits include *Desperately Seeking Susan*, the underrated *Making Mr. Right*, and the recent *Cookie*. She has a sure touch for off-center humor, the kind that works not because of setups and punch lines, but because of the screwy logic her characters bring to their dilemmas. In the middle passages of this movie, she goes for broad comic strokes, especially in the way she portrays the gauche lifestyle of Mary Fisher, whose home looks like a Holiday Inn's wet dream. Streep, as Fisher, has erected a glamorous fictional facade around the mundane actual facts of her life, and it is with grim precision that Barr's character pulls it to pieces.

When Zsa Zsa Gabor's treacherous schoolmate added ten years to the actress's official age by producing that old school yearbook not long ago, I felt a twinge of sympathy for Zsa Zsa. If there is no honor among women lying about their ages, then what is sacred? But the Mary Fisher character in *She-Devil* is such a vain and snobbish woman that we can take a sadistic delight in Barr's most devilish scheme, which is to disguise herself as a nurse, locate the novelist's feisty mother (Sylvia Miles) in an old-folks' home, and produce her to the press along with a detailed history of Fisher's true past.

Begley, that tall, vaguely handsome, and subtly bewildered actor from "St. Elsewhere," is the fulcrum for a lot of humor. His character requires him to operate consistently from the basest motives: lust, greed, and envy. He projects these emotions so effortlessly, I hope they're grooming him for the Donald Trump story. Willing to betray his wife on a moment's notice but yet more interested in Fisher's body and fame than in the inner character she presumably possesses, he is a shallow and utterly worthless man, until the she-devil teaches him a lesson.

Debut movies are traditionally tricky for

TV stars. For every Pee-wee Herman who finds the perfect movie vehicle, there's a Henry Winkler who doesn't. Roseanne Barr could presumably have made an easy, predictable, and dumb comedy at any point in the last couple of years. Instead, she took her chances with an ambitious project—a real movie. It pays off, in that Barr demonstrates that there is a core of reality inside her TV persona, a core of identifiable human feelings like jealousy and pride, and they provide a sound foundation for her comic acting. The proof of it is that, on the basis of this movie, Meryl Streep didn't have to retire to her own dressing room to ask herself what she was doing in a movie with Roseanne Barr.

Shoah ★ ★ ★ ★

NO MPAA RATING, 563 m. on five cassettes, 1986

A documentary directed and produced by Claude Lanzmann.

For more than nine hours I sat and watched a film named *Shoah,* and when it was over, I sat for a while longer and simply stared into space, trying to understand my emotions. I had seen a memory of the most debased chapter in human history. But I had also seen a film that affirmed life so passionately that I did not know where to turn with my confused feelings. There is no proper response to this film. It is an enormous fact, a 563-minute howl of pain and anger in the face of genocide. It is one of the noblest films ever made.

The film's title is a Hebrew word for chaos or annihilation—for the Holocaust. The film is a documentary, but it does not contain images from the 1940s. There are no old newsreel shots, no interviews with the survivors of the death camps, no coverage of the war crimes trials. All of the movie was photographed in the last five or six years by a man named Claude Lanzmann, who went looking for eyewitnesses to Hitler's "Final Solution." He is surprisingly successful in finding people who were there, who saw and heard what went on. Some of them, a tiny handful, are Jewish survivors of the camps. The rest are mostly old people, German and Polish, some who worked in the camps, others who were in a position to observe what happened.

They talk and talk. *Shoah* is a torrent of words, and yet the overwhelming impression, when it is over, is one of silence. Lanzmann intercuts two kinds of images. He shows the faces of his witnesses. And then he uses quiet pastoral scenes of the places where the deaths took place. Steam engines move massively through the Polish countryside, down the same tracks where trains took countless Jews, gypsies, Poles, homosexuals, and other so-called undesirables to their deaths. Cameras pan silently across pastures, while we learn that underneath the tranquility are mass graves. Sometimes the image is of a group of people, gathered in a doorway, or in front of a church, or in a restaurant kitchen.

Lanzmann is a patient interrogator. We see him in the corners of some of his shots, a tall, lanky man, informally dressed, chain-smoking. He wants to know the details. He doesn't ask large, profound questions about the meaning of the extermination of millions of people. He asks little questions. In one of the most chilling sequences in the film, he talks to Abraham Bomba, today a barber in Tel Aviv. Bomba was one of the Jewish barbers ordered to cut off the hair of Jewish women before they were killed in Treblinka. His assignment suggests the shattering question: How can a woman's hair be worth more than her life? But Lanzmann does not ask overwhelming and unanswerable questions like this. These are the sorts of questions he asks:

You cut with what? With scissors?

There were no mirrors?

You said there were about sixteen barbers? You cut the hair of how many women in one batch?

The barber tries to answer. As he talks, he has a customer in his chair, and he snips at the customer's hair almost obsessively, making tiny movements with his scissors, as if trying to use the haircut as a way to avoid the questions. Their conversation finally arrives at this exchange, after he says he cannot talk any more:

A. I can't. It's too horrible. Please.

Q. *We have to do it. You know it.*

A. I won't be able to do it.

Q. *You have to do it. I know it's very hard. I know and I apologize.*

A. Don't make me go on, please.

Q. *Please. We must go on.*

Lanzmann is cruel, but he is correct. He must go on. It is necessary to make this record before all of those who were witnesses to the Holocaust have died.

His methods in obtaining the interviews were sometimes underhanded. He uses a concealed television camera to record the faces of some of the old Nazi officials whom he interviews, and we look over the shoulders of the TV technicians in a van parked outside the buildings where they live. We see the old men nonchalantly pulling down charts from the wall to explain the layout of a death camp, and we hear their voices, and at one point when a Nazi asks for reassurance that the conversation is private, Lanzmann provides it. He will go to any length to obtain this testimony.

He does not, however, make any attempt to arrange his material into a chronology, an objective, factual record of how the "Final Solution" began, continued, and was finally terminated by the end of the war. He uses a more poetic, mosaic approach, moving according to rhythms only he understands among the only three kinds of faces we see in this film: survivors, murderers, and bystanders. As their testimony is intercut with the scenes of train tracks, steam engines, abandoned buildings, and empty fields, we are left with enough time to think our own thoughts, to meditate, to wonder.

This is a long movie but not a slow one, and in its words it creates something of the same phenomenon I experienced while watching *My Dinner with André.* The words themselves create images in the imagination, as they might in a radio play. Consider the images summoned by these words, spoken by Filip Muller, a Czech Jew assigned to work at the doors of the gas chambers, a man who survived five waves of liquidations at Auschwitz:

A. You see, once the gas was poured in, it worked like this: It rose from the ground upwards. And in the terrible struggle that followed—because it was a struggle—the lights were switched off in the gas chambers. It was dark, no one could see, so the strongest people tried to climb higher. Because they probably realized that the higher they got, the more air there was. They could breathe better. That caused the struggle. Secondly, most people tried to push their way to the door. It was psychological; they knew where the door was; maybe they could force their way out. It was instinctive, a death struggle. Which is why children and weaker people and the aged always wound up at the bottom. The strongest were on top. Because in the death struggle, a father didn't realize his son lay beneath him.

Q. *And when the doors were opened?*

A. They fell out. People fell out like blocks of stone, like rocks falling out of a truck.

The images evoked by his words are inutterably painful. What is remarkable, on reflection, is that Muller is describing a struggle that neither he nor anyone else now alive ever saw. I realized, at the end of his words, that a fundamental change had taken place in the way I personally visualized the gas chambers. Always before, in reading about them or hearing about them, my point of view was outside, looking in. Muller put me inside.

That is what this whole movie does, and it is probably the most important thing it does. It changes our point of view about the Holocaust. After nine hours of *Shoah*, the Holocaust is no longer a subject, a chapter of history, a phenomenon. It is an environment. It is around us. Ordinary people speak in ordinary voices of days that had become ordinary to them. A railroad engineer who drove the trains to Treblinka is asked if he could hear the screams of the people in the cars behind his locomotive:

A. Obviously, since the locomotive was next to the cars. They screamed, asked for water. The screams from the cars closest to the locomotives could be heard very well.

Q. *Can one get used to that?*

A. No, it was extremely distressing. He knew the people behind him were human, like him. The Germans gave him and the other workers vodka to drink. Without drinking, they couldn't have done it.

Some of the strangest passages in the film are the interviews with the officials who were running the camps and making the "Final Solution" work smoothly and efficiently. None of them, at least by their testimony, seem to have witnessed the whole picture. They only participated in a small part of it, doing their little jobs in their little corners. If they are to be believed, they didn't personally kill anybody, they just did small portions of larger tasks, and somehow all of the tasks, when added up and completed, resulted in people dying. Here is the man who scheduled the trains that took the Jews to die:

Q. *You never saw a train?*

A. No, never. We had so much work, I never left my desk. We worked day and night.

And here is a man who lived 150 feet from a church where Jews were rounded up, held, and then marched into gas vans for the trip to the crematoriums:

Q. *Did you see the gas vans?*

A. No—yes, from the outside. They shuttled back and forth. I never looked inside; I didn't see Jews.

What is so important about *Shoah* is that the voices are heard of people who did see, who did understand, who did comprehend, who were there, who know that the Holocaust happened, who tell us with their voices and with their eyes that genocide occurred in our time, in our civilization.

There is a tendency while watching *Shoah* to try to put a distance between yourself and the events on the screen. These things happened, after all, forty or forty-five years ago. Most of those now alive have been born since the events happened. Then, while I was watching the film, came a chilling moment. A name flashed on the screen in the subtitles, the name of one of the commandants at Treblinka death camp. At first I thought the name was "Ebert"—my name. Then I realized it was "Eberl." I felt a moment of relief, and then a moment of intense introspection as I realized that it made no difference what the subtitle said. The message of this film (if we believe in the brotherhood of man) is that these crimes were committed by people like us, against people like us.

But there is an even deeper message as well, and it is contained in the testimony of Filip Muller, the Jew who stood at the door of a crematorium and watched as the victims walked in to die. One day some of the victims, Czech Jews, began to sing. They sang two songs: "The Hatikvah," and the Czech national anthem. They affirmed that they were Jews and that they were Czechs. They denied Hitler, who would have them be one but not the other. Muller speaks:

That was happening to my countrymen, and I realized that my life had become meaningless. (His eyes fill with tears.) Why go on living? For what? So I went into the gas chamber with them, resolved to die. With them. Suddenly, some who recognized me came up to me. . . . A small group of women approached. They looked at me and said, right there in the gas chamber . . .

Q. *You were inside the gas chamber?*

A. Yes. One of them said: "So you want to die. But that's senseless. Your death won't give us back our lives. That's no way. You must get out of here alive, you must bear witness to our suffering and to the injustice done to us."

And that is the final message of this extraordinary film. It is not a documentary, not journalism, not propaganda, not political. It is an act of witness. In it, Claude Lanzmann celebrates the priceless gift that sets man apart from animals and makes us human, and gives us hope: the ability for one generation to tell the next what it has learned.

A Shock to the System ★ ★ ★
R, 89 m., 1990

Michael Caine (Graham Marshall), Elizabeth McGovern (Stella Anderson), Peter Riegert (Robert Benham), Swoosie Kurtz (Leslie Marshall), Will Patton (Lieutenant Laker), Jenny Wright (Melanie O'Connor), John McMartin (George Brewster), Barbara Baxley (Lillian). Directed by Jan Egleson and produced by Patrick McCormick. Screenplay by Andrew Klavan.

It's the voice that does it. The flat Michael Caine delivery that always seems to imply there are more angles than meet the eye. Caine plays the narrator and hero of *A Shock to the System*, and as he dryly describes his progress up the corporate ladder and his steps toward a refurbished love life, we realize that this is the voice of a man who thinks he can get away with murder, and may be right.

In the movie, Caine is Graham Marshall, next in line to head the department in the big New York ad agency where he works. But then a smarmy pest of a younger man (Peter Riegert) gets the job. Meanwhile, Caine's life on the home front is an unendurable round of boredom and domestic psychological torture, engineered by his wife (Swoosie Kurtz). One day while he is down in the basement replacing a fuse, Caine gets a nasty electrical shock, and it starts him to thinking.

A Shock to the System is the story of how Caine methodically eliminates the barriers to his professional success and personal pleasure. To say more would be to spoil some of the fun. The movie toys with us as it shows Caine almost getting caught, as it plants clues we're sure somebody will find, and as it introduces the character of a genial Connecticut police detective (Will Patton) who persists in asking uncomfortable questions. Will the cop or anybody else figure out what Caine is doing? By cleverly manipulating the conventions of the crime movie, director Jan Egleson and writer Andrew Klavan lead us up one garden path and down another.

Michael Caine is a splendid movie actor, a consummate professional who is fun to watch in any film because there is always a layer of irony and fun right there below the surface. That makes him especially entertaining as a villain; his charm makes his sins seem permissible, or at least understandable. He rarely plays villains we hate. More often, we want him to get away with his sins. Since the sins he commits in *A Shock to the System* are wicked ones, that sets up a nice tension inside the movie. We see things from his point of view, we are invited to identify with him, and yet when the Connecticut detective comes calling, we think it's about time.

The movie is filled with sneaky personalities and office traitors; it's *Crimes and Misdemeanors* crossed with *Wall Street*. Riegert is especially effective as the underling who becomes an insufferable overling. Swoosie Kurtz has fun with the whining housewife who can't leave well enough—or, indeed, anything—alone. And there is a nice performance by Elizabeth McGovern as the office colleague who provides a sympathetic shoulder for Caine to cry, and breathe, upon.

They have a scene together that's a small masterpiece, one everyone can recognize from real life, where the two office workers meet at the nearby bar and find that they are in complete agreement that they are right and good and brilliant and unappreciated, and that everyone else is full of it. There's some delicate comic acting here: Caine with his fragile male ego so easily bruised, and McGovern with psychic bandages, and eyes that say "there, there."

Movies have been growing depressingly nice lately, and *A Shock to the System* is a refreshing change of pace. It isn't a nice movie. There once was a time when movies were allowed to be embittered, dark, and brooding, and when evil was occasionally allowed to have a momentary victory. Now the conventional movie ends with a cheerleading scene. But *A Shock to the System* confounds our expectations and keeps us intrigued, because there's no way to know, not even in the very last moments, exactly which way the plot is going to fall.

The Shootist ★ ★ ★ ½
PG, 100 m., 1976

John Wayne (The Shootist), Lauren Bacall (The Widow), James Stewart (The Doctor), Ron Howard (The Son), Harry Morgan (The Sheriff), John Carradine (The Undertaker), Hugh O'Brian (The Gambler), Richard Boone (The Gunman). Directed by Don Siegel and produced by M.J. Frankovich and William Seif. Screenplay by Miles Hood.

The old man was around for a long time. When he played the fresh-faced Ringo Kid in *Stagecoach,* back in 1939, he was already thirty-two years old. And I didn't believe it either until I'd counted the credits twice—but *Stagecoach* was his sixtieth film. John Wayne grew, role by role, into the most mythic presence in American movies. Some of the roles were pretty bad ones, but maybe at the time we didn't know that. Maybe at the time we were ten or twelve years old, and it was a Saturday afternoon, and what we registered was that Wayne was up there on the screen, squinting into the sun, making decisions, ready for action. For my generation, while presidents came and went, John Wayne merely grew a little more thoughtful.

He rides onscreen in *The Shootist* afraid that he is dying. Not afraid he'll be killed, but afraid he's dying, which is the last thing we anticipated a John Wayne character would do of his own accord. It is 1901: He has outlived his century. A sawbones in the next state has given him the bad news and now he wants to hear it from the lips of Doc Hostetler, who nursed him back to health after a violent afternoon twenty years ago. And so he rides, the Shootist, into a Carson City to which the Old West has become an embarrassment. The streets are still wide enough to turn a mule train in, but now an abashed little horse trolley runs down the middle of them, and electricity's going to put the horse out of business next year. The pain is way down deep in his back, and he rides on a red velvet cushion he stole out of a whorehouse. It doesn't do a damn bit of good. Hostetler hems and haws and comes out with it: cancer. Two months to live, six weeks, maybe less. In the meantime he can do what he wants. After a while he won't feel like doing much.

In his time, the Shootist shot a lot of men dead. Out at the livery stable, burnt into the leather of his saddle, they find his name: J.B. Books. His arrival in Carson City immediately becomes news. Hostetler steers him over to a boarding house run by the Widow Rogers, who shows him a two-dollar room. It'll do fine. Books settles down to die. But all these gunfighters had the same problem: People weren't content to let them die in bed, because they made too good a trophy.

So there is a tricky dilemma: To die with some measure of dignity, and to avoid being shot in the meantime. As the film opens, Books has eight days. You will be surprised with what gentleness and humanity he lives them, before the inevitable gunfire at the end. And unless you have already discovered that John Wayne is an actor as well as a movie star, you will be surprised by the dimensions he provides for J.B. Books.

The movie isn't a bit sentimental. Everybody in town wants the bastard dead, except for the Widow Rogers and her son, Gillom. Even Doc Hostetler, who knows what people can go through toward the end of these illnesses, stops Books at the door and advises him point-blank not to wait around and see how things will eventually feel. The Sheriff is almost cheerful at the prospect of Books's approaching end. The Undertaker offers a free funeral, free tombstone, free casket, free flowers, even two mourners thrown in at no extra charge. "You son of a bitch," Books says, "you aim to do to me what they did with John Wesley Hardin. Lay me out and parade every damn fool in the state past me at a dollar a head, half price for children, and then stuff me in a gunny sack and shovel me under." He is correct.

Still, eight days are enough to establish the beginnings of human contact. The Widow Rogers is appalled at first to have a killer as her paying guest, but an affection and respect grows up between them. Her kid, Gillom, contracts a case of hero worship even while trying to swindle the Shootist out of his horse. And Wayne, as Books, occupies the substantial center of the film. He vows to read a newspaper through from front to back before he dies. He sends his Sunday-go-to-meeting clothes out to the cleaners. And he challenges three old Carson City enemies to meet him in the saloon at eleven o'clock Monday morning.

It's here that the movie doesn't quite work. We hardly know the three enemies. We don't know why they'd oblige the Shootist's wish to die in a gunfight. We understand his reasoning, but not theirs. And the movie's final scene, in which Gillom Rogers symbolically steps into the Shootist's boots, is just a little too neat to be real. Westerns probably have to end along these lines with confrontations and gunfire and heroism, but *The Shootist* will be remembered for the quieter scenes that came before.

The cast is excellent because it understands the material, and sympathizes with it: James Stewart, as the doctor, and Lauren Bacall, as the widow, play scenes with Wayne that absolutely make us forget we're watching a movie. Gaunt old John Carradine has been an undertaker all his life; finally they cast him as one. Don Siegel's direction reveals a sensitivity we didn't suspect after films like *Dirty Harry.* And observe the way

John Wayne says "Good day, Mrs. Rogers" to Lauren Bacall for the last time.

Shoot the Moon ★ ★ ★ ½
R, 124 m., 1982

Albert Finney (George Dunlap), Diane Keaton (Faith Dunlap), Karen Allen (Sandy), Peter Weller (Frank), Dana Hill (Sherry). Directed by Alan Parker and produced by Alan Marshall. Screenplay by Bo Goldman.

Alan Parker's *Shoot the Moon* is a film that sometimes keeps its painful secrets even from itself. It opens with a shot of a man in agony. In another room, his wife, surrounded by four noisy daughters, dresses for a dinner that evening at which the man will be honored. The man has to pull himself together. His voice is choking with tears, he telephones the woman he loves and tells her how hard it will be to get through the evening without her. Then he puts on his rumpled tuxedo and marches out to do battle. As we watch this scene, we assume that the movie will answer several of the questions it raises, such as: What went wrong in the marriage? Why is the man in such agony? What is the nature of his love for the other woman? One of the surprises in *Shoot the Moon* is that none of these questions is ever quite answered, and we are asked to fill in the gaps ourselves.

That is not necessarily a flaw in the film. *Shoot the Moon* is not the historical record of this marriage, but the emotional history. It starts with what should be a happy marriage. A writer of books (Albert Finney) lives with his beautiful, funky wife (Diane Keaton) and their four rambunctious daughters in a converted farmhouse somewhere in Marin County, California. Their house is one of those warm battle zones filled with books, miscellaneous furniture, and the paraphernalia for vast projects half-completed. We learn that the marriage has gone disastrously wrong. That the man is determined to stalk out and be with his new woman. That the wife, after a period of anger and mourning, is prepared to react to this decision by almost deliberately having an affair with the loutish but well-meaning young man who comes to build a tennis court. That the husband and wife still harbor fugitive feelings of love and passion for another.

We never really learn how the marriage went wrong. There is the usual talk about how one partner was not given the room to grow, or the other did not have enough "space"—concepts that love would render meaningless, but that divorce makes into savagely defended positions. We also learn just a tantalizing little about the two new lovers. Albert Finney's new woman (Karen Allen) is so cynical about their relationship in one scene that we wonder if their affair will soon end (we never learn). Diane Keaton's new man (Peter Weller) is so emotionally stiff, closed-off, that we don't know for a long time whether Keaton really likes him, or simply desires him sexually and wants to use him to spite her husband.

Does it matter that the movie doesn't want to provide insights in these areas? I think it does. When Ingmar Bergman covered similar grounds in his *Scenes from a Marriage*, he provided us with enough concrete information about the issues in the marriage that it was possible for us to discuss the relationship afterward, taking sides, seeing both points of view. After *Shoot the Moon*, we don't discuss the relationship, we discuss our questions about it. And yet this is sometimes an extraordinary movie. Despite its flaws, despite its gaps, despite two key scenes that are dreadfully wrong, *Shoot the Moon* contains a raw emotional power of the sort we rarely see in domestic dramas.

The film's basic conflict is within Albert Finney's mind. He can no longer stay with his wife, he must leave and be with the other woman, and yet he still wants to own the family and possessions he has left behind. He doesn't want his ex-wife dating other men. He wants to observe the birthday of an eldest daughter (Dana Hill) who hates him and resents his behavior. He remodeled the house with his own hands, and cannot bear to see another man working on it. In one scene of heartbreaking power, he breaks into his own house and finds himself beating his daughter because he loves her so much and she will not love him.

In scenes like that (and in the quiet scenes where Hill asks, "Why did Daddy leave us?" and Keaton answers, "I don't think he left you; I think he left me"), *Shoot the Moon* is a great film. In scenes like the one where they fight in a restaurant, or argue in court, it ranges from the miscalculated to the disastrous. *Shoot the Moon* is a rare, good film, and yet, afterward, most of my thoughts were about how it might have been better. It is frustrating to feel that the filmmakers knew their characters intimately, but chose to reveal them only in part.

Shoot to Kill ★ ★ ★
R, 100 m., 1988

Sidney Poitier (Warren Stantin), Tom Berenger (Jonathan Knox), Kirstie Alley (Sarah), Clancy Brown (Steve), Richard Masur (Norman), Andrew Robinson (Harvey), Kevin Scannell (Ben). Directed by Roger Spottiswoode and produced by Ron Silverman and Daniel Petrie, Jr. Screenplay by Harv Zimmel, Michael Burton, and Petrie.

Shoot to Kill is yet another example, rather late in the day, of the buddy movie, that most dependable genre from the early 1970s. The formula still works. Two characters who have nothing in common are linked together on a dangerous mission, and after a lot of close calls they survive, prevail, and become buddies. The movie got more than the usual amount of attention because it marked Sidney Poitier's return to acting after ten years behind the camera. He didn't win any awards for this performance, but it was nice to have him back.

Poitier plays Warren Stantin, an FBI agent who holds himself personally responsible after a kidnapper kills two hostages and escapes into the Pacific Northwest. The killer (Clancy Brown) is a sneering sadist who joins up with a group of sportsmen who plan to trek into the wilderness on a fishing trip. His plan: Kill them and force their guide to lead him through the wilderness to the Canadian border.

The guide is played by Kirstie Alley from the TV show "Cheers," in a robust display of pink cheeks and deep breathing. She leads her charges into the woods. Her boyfriend (Tom Berenger, seen in *Platoon*) is at a base station, and Poitier tries to convince Berenger to lead him after the fugitive. Of course, the mountain man doesn't believe the city slicker can keep up on a tough cross-country hike that includes some rock climbing, and, of course, Poitier is determined to prove himself.

Have we seen this before? I think so. The route passes along a standard wilderness obstacle course, including a terrifying rope bridge over a chasm far below. Alley leads her group across, but then Brown sabotages the bridge, and Berenger nearly falls to his death before Poitier comes to his rescue. Later, it's Berenger's turn to save Poitier's life, and gradually the two men come to respect one another.

There are just a few teeny-weeny holes in this plot. For example: Why would the FBI let one agent go out as Poitier does, on a hunch? Why does another FBI agent spill the beans over the radio, since the quarry would likely be listening? Why walk for arduous miles across a grueling landscape when it might be easier to hitch a ride? Why put us through the whole cross-country trek when, at the end, the payoff comes not in the mountains but at sea?

Only a churl would ask such questions. *Shoot to Kill* is a genre movie in which the specifics hardly matter. Only the formula is important: Two guys team up, conquer great difficulties, and become friends. And at that level, *Shoot to Kill* works like an efficient machine. Poitier and Berenger create a nice give-and-take chemistry, and there are some funny gags, mostly involving the city slicker's uneasiness around horses. The device of cutting back and forth between Kirstie Alley's group and their pursuers keeps the buddy formula from growing too oppressive. And the action scene at the end is effective, although I question whether a gun can fire underwater. *Shoot to Kill* is fast-food moviemaking: quick, satisfying, and transient. Now let's see Poitier in something more challenging.

Short Cuts ★ ★ ★ ★
R, 189 m., 1993

Tim Robbins (Gene Shepard), Madeleine Stowe (Sherri Shepard), Andie MacDowell (Ann Finnigan), Bruce Davison (Howard Finnigan), Julianne Moore (Marian Wyman), Matthew Modine (Dr. Ralph Wyman), Jack Lemmon (Paul Finnigan), Jennifer Jason Leigh (Lois Kaiser), Christopher Penn (Jerry Kaiser), Lily Tomlin (Doreen Piggot), Peter Gallagher (Stormy Weathers). Directed by Robert Altman and produced by Cary Brokaw. Screenplay by Altman and Frank Barhydt.

Los Angeles always seems to be waiting for something. Permanence seems out of reach; some great apocalyptic event is on the horizon, and people view the future tentatively. Robert Altman's *Short Cuts* captures that uneasiness perfectly, in its interlocking stories about people who seem trapped in the present, always juggling.

The movie is based on short stories by Raymond Carver, but this is Altman's work, not Carver's, and all the film really has in common with its source is a feeling for people who are disconnected—from relatives, church, tradition—and support themselves with jobs that never seem quite real. It is hard work, no doubt, to be a pool cleaner, a

chauffeur, a phone-sex provider, a birthday cake decorator, a jazz singer, a helicopter pilot, but these are professions that find you before you find them. How many people end up in jobs they planned for? Altman is fascinated by the accidental nature of life, by the way that whole decades of our lives can be shaped by events we do not understand or even know about.

Short Cuts understands and knows, because it is filmed from an all-seeing point of view. Its characters all live at the same time in the same city, and sometimes their paths even cross, but for the most part they don't know how their lives are changed by people they meet only glancingly.

Imagine the rage of the baker (Lyle Lovett), for example, when he gets stuck with an expensive birthday cake. We could almost comprehend the cruel, anonymous telephone calls he makes to the parents (Andie MacDowell and Bruce Davison) who ordered the cake, if we didn't know their child missed his birthday because he was hit by a car. Imagine what *they* would say to the unknown driver (Lily Tomlin) who struck their child. But we know that she wanted to take him to a doctor; the boy refused because he has been forbidden to get into the cars of strangers, and besides, he seemed okay. If you knew the whole story in this world, there'd be a lot less to be angry about.

The movie's characters all seem to be from somewhere else, and without parents. Their homes are as temporary as the trailer park two of the characters inhabit, where people come and go, no one knows from where, or to where. The grandparent (Jack Lemmon) of the injured little boy has disappeared for years. Faced with a son and grandson he hardly knows, he spends most of his time talking about himself. The jazz singer would rather drink than know her daughter.

Sad, insoluble mysteries seem right under the surface. Three men go on a fishing trip and discover the drowned body of a woman. They have waited a long time and come a long way for this trip, and if they report the woman, their trip will be ruined. So, since she's already dead, what difference will a few more days make? And what would the police do, anyway? There's a motorcycle cop (Tim Robbins) in the movie, who seems to be a free-lancer, responsible to no one, using his badge simply as a way to get his will, spending a lot of time cheating on his wife (Madeleine Stowe), who finds his lies hilarious.

Almost everybody drinks all through this

movie, although only a few characters ever get exactly drunk. It's as if life is a preventable disease, and booze is the medication. Sex places a very slow second. The pool cleaner's wife (Jennifer Jason Leigh) supplements the family income by working as a phone-sex performer, spinning verbal fantasies to strangers on the phone, while sitting bored in her living room, changing her baby's diapers. Her husband (Christopher Penn) is angry: "How come you never talk that way to me?" Think about that. He's married to her. They sleep in the same bed. He can have actual physical sex with her. But he envies the strangers who will never meet her—who value her inaccessibility: She services their fantasies without imposing her own reality.

Some of these characters, if they could find each other, would find the answers to their needs. The baker, for example, has unexplored reserves of tenderness. He could help the sad young woman (Lori Singer) who plays the cello, and waits for those moments when her mother (Annie Ross), the jazz singer, is sober. The cop would probably be happier talking with the phone-sex girl than carrying on his endless affairs, which have no purpose except to anger his wife, who is past caring. He likes the deception more than the sex, and could get off by telling the stranger on the other end of the phone that he'd been cheating with *another* phone-sex girl.

Yet these people have a certain nobility to them. They keep on trying. They hope for better times. The hash-house waitress (Tomlin) loves her husband (Tom Waits), who is so good to her when he's not drinking that she forgives the dark times when he is drinking. The parents of the little boy find an unexpected consolation from the baker. The wife (Anne Archer) of one of the fly-fishermen finds a new resolve and freedom. Life goes on.

Altman has made this kind of film before, notably in *Nashville* (1976) and *The Player* (1992). He doesn't like stories that pretend that the characters control their destinies, and their actions will produce a satisfactory outcome. He likes the messiness and coincidence of real life, where you can do your best, and some days it's just not good enough. He doesn't reproduce Raymond Carver's stories so much as his attitude.

In a Carver story (and you should read one if you never have), there is typically a moment when an ordinary statement becomes crucial, or poetic, or sad. People get blinding glimpses into the real nature of their lives; the routine is peeled aside, and they can see they've been stuck in a rut for years, going through the motions. Sometimes they see with equal clarity that they are free to take charge, that no one has sentenced them to repeat the same mistakes.

Carver died in 1988, at fifty, of a brain tumor. He believed he would have died at forty, of alcoholism, if he hadn't found a way to stop drinking. When he knew the cancer would kill him, he wrote a poem about that bonus of ten years, called "Gravy." Altman, who spend most of the 1980s in a sort of exile after Hollywood declared him noncommercial, continued to make films, but they didn't have the budgets or the distribution a great filmmaker should have had. Then came the comeback of *The Player*, and now here is *Short Cuts*. Gravy.

Shy People ★ ★ ★ ★
R, 120 m., 1988

Jill Clayburgh (Diana), Barbara Hershey (Ruth), Martha Plimpton (Grace), Merritt Butrick (Mike), John Philbin (Tommy), Don Swayze (Mark), Pruitt Taylor Vince (Paul), Mare Winningham (Candy). Directed by Andrei Konchalovsky and produced by Menahem Golan and Yoram Globus. Screenplay by Gerard Brach, Konchalovsky, and Marjorie David.

Two great early shots define the two worlds of *Shy People*. The first is circular, the second straight ahead.

The film's opening shot circles at a vertiginous height above Manhattan, showing the canyons of skyscrapers with people scurrying below like ants. The camera moves through a complete circle, finally coming to rest inside a high-rise apartment where a restless teen-ager and her distracted mother have no idea what to do about each other.

The second shot, a few minutes later in the film, is also taken from a height: we are above a speedboat that drones relentlessly into the heart of the Louisiana bayou country. This shot, inexplicably thrilling, is like scenes from adventure books we read when we were kids. We feel a quickening of excitement as the boat penetrates the unknown.

The two shots define the two women who are at the heart of the film. Jill Clayburgh plays a shallow, sophisticated Manhattan magazine writer, who convinces her bosses at *Cosmopolitan* to let her write about her family roots. And Barbara Hershey plays

Clayburgh's long-lost distant cousin, who lives in isolation in a crumbling, mossy home in the heart of the bayou. The movie is essentially about the differences between these women, about family blood ties, and about the transparent membrane between life and death.

Shy People is one of the great visionary films of recent years, a film that shakes off the petty distractions of safe Hollywood entertainments and develops a large vision. It is about revenge and hatred, about mothers and sons, about loneliness. It suggests that family ties are the most important bonds in the world, and by the end of the film, Clayburgh will discover that Hershey is closer to her "dead" husband than most city-dwellers are to anybody.

Yet the film is not without a wicked streak of humor. Clayburgh invites her precocious daughter (Martha Plimpton) to accompany her into the Louisiana backwaters, where the adolescent girl meets Hershey's ill-assorted sons. One is literally locked in an outbuilding when the New Yorkers arrive, another is light in the head, and still another is disowned and never mentioned, because he dared to move out of the bayou and open a nightclub in town. As the girl flirts with her cousins, and the women warily spar with each other, the darkness of the swamp closes in.

Shy People was directed by Andrei Konchalovsky, the Russian emigre whose other English-language movies include *Runaway Train* and *Duet for One*. Because he is an outsider, he is not so self-conscious about using American images that an American director might be frightened away from. The world of *Shy People* is the world of Erskine Caldwell's *Tobacco Road*, or Faulkner's Snopes family, of Al Capp and Russ Meyer. Hershey and her family are not small, timid people, but caricatures, and it's to Hershey's credit that she is able to play the role to the hilt and yet still make it real.

There are great sequences in the film, including one extraordinary night in which Clayburgh is lost in the swamp, is up to her neck in the fetid waters, and sees, or thinks she sees, the ghost of Hershey's dead husband.

There is a barroom fight in which the wrathful Hershey wades into her son's nightclub with a gun. Most extraordinary of all, there are spooky, quiet moments in which the mosquitoes drone in the sleepy heat of midday, while the two women pore over old photograph albums.

Sid & Nancy ★ ★ ★ ★
R, 111 m., 1986

Gary Oldman (Sid Vicious), Chloe Webb (Nancy Spungen), Drew Schofield (Johnny Rotten), David Hayman (Malcolm McLaren), Debby Bishop (Phoebe), Jude Alderson (Ma Vicious). Directed by Alex Cox and produced by Eric Fellner. Screenplay by Cox and Abbe Wool.

His real name was John Simon Ritchie, and his father was a trombone player who left before he was born. His mother wore her hair long and went to all the hippie festivals with the little boy at her side. They lived in London's East End, within the culture of poverty and drugs. When he was fifteen, Ritchie dropped out of school. When he was seventeen, he was one of the most famous people in England, although by then he was known as Sid Vicious of the notorious Sex Pistols.

What did he respond to when the American girl, Nancy Spungen, came into his life? She was a groupie from New York, but she was also an authority figure who pushed him to try harder, complained when he was not given his due, and plotted to get him better deals and wider exposure. If she had not bled to death that night in New York, she might have made Vicious really amount to something, someday.

The astonishing thing about *Sid & Nancy* is the amount of subtle information it gives us about their relationship, given the fact that the surface of the movie is all tumult and violence, pain and confusion. This movie doesn't take the easy way out and cast these two lovers as Romeo and Juliet, misunderstood waifs. It sees beneath their leather and chains, their torn T-shirts and steel-toed boots, to a basically conventional relationship between an ambitious woman and a man who was still a boy.

They needed each other. Spungen needed someone to mother, and Vicious, according to his friends, needed self-esteem and was immensely proud that he had an American girlfriend. They were meant for each other, but by the end it was all just ashes and bewilderment, because they were so strung out on drugs that whole days would slip by unnoticed. In their fantasies of doomed romance, they planned to go out together in a suicide pact, but by the end they were too sick to even go out together for a pizza.

By now, everybody knows that Vicious woke up one morning in New York's Chelsea

Hotel to find Spungen's dead body. He was booked on suspicion of murder, released on bail, and two months later was dead of a drug overdose. The available evidence strongly suggests that he did not stab Spungen to death, but that she died of one of those untidy accidents that befall drug abusers. A human being is a dangerous thing to let loose in a room with itself, when it cannot think.

There were some good times earlier in their story, but on the evidence of this movie there were not many. By the time Spungen met Vicious in London in the mid-1970s, the Sex Pistols were the most infamous punk rock band in the world. But they were in the position of Gandhi in that apocryphal story where he sees the mob run past and races to get in front of his followers. The punk conceit was a total rejection of conventional society; their credo was the line by Johnny Rotten, the Pistols' lead singer: "Got a problem and the problem is you." For the Pistols to stay in front of that mob, they had to be meaner, more violent, more negative than their followers. How did it feel to stand on a bandstand and make angry music while your fans stood face to face, banging heads until unconsciousness came?

Sid & Nancy suggests that Vicious never lived long enough to really get his feet on the ground, to figure out where he stood and where his center was. He was handed great fame and a certain amount of power and money, and indirectly told that his success depended on staying fucked up. This is a big assignment for a kid who would otherwise be unemployable. Vicious did his best, fighting and vomiting and kicking his way through his brief days and long nights, until Spungen brought him a measure of relief. Some nights she was someone to hold, and other nights she was someone to hold onto. What difference did it make?

Sid & Nancy makes these observations with such complexity, such vividness, and such tenderness that at the end of the film a curious thing happens. You do not weep for Vicious, or Spungen, but maybe you weep for all of us, that we have been placed in a world where it is possible for people to make themselves so unhappy. Vicious was not a hero, just a guy who got himself into a situation he couldn't handle. But to thousands of London kids, he represented an affront to a society that offered no jobs, no training, no education, and no entry into the world of opportunity. If life offers you nothing, the least you can offer it is the finger.

Performances like the ones in this film go beyond movie acting and into some kind of evocation of real lives. Vicious is played by Gary Oldman and Spungen is played by Chloe Webb, and there isn't even a brief period at the top of the movie where we have to get used to them. They are these people, driven and relentless.

The movie was directed by Alex Cox, who made *Repo Man* a couple of years ago, and here he announces himself as a great director. He and his actors pull off the neat trick of creating a movie full of noise and fury, and telling a meticulous story right in the middle of it.

But why should anyone care about a movie about two scabrous vulgarians? Because the subject of a really good movie is sometimes not that important. It's the acting, writing, and direction that count. If a movie can illuminate the lives of other people who share this planet with us and show us not only how different they are but, how even so, they share the same dreams and hurts, then it deserves to be called great. If you have an open mind, it is possibly true that the less you care about Sid Vicious, the more you will admire this movie.

Sidewalk Stories ★ ★ ★ ½
R, 97 m., 1989

Charles Lane (Artist), Nicole Alysia (Child), Sandye Wilson (Young Woman), Darnell Williams (Father), Trula Hoosier (Mother), Michael Baskin (Doorman), George Riddick (Street Partner). Directed, produced, and written by Charles Lane.

Charles Lane's film *Sidewalk Stories* is a silent movie shot in black and white. If you are absolutely sure you wouldn't want to see a silent, black-and-white movie, read no further. There is no help for you here.

What I want to evoke is the different consciousness created by watching a silent film. Sitting in the dark, viewing *Sidewalk Stories*, I became aware that somehow my attention had been heightened and I was looking at the screen with more intensity than would usually be the case. Why was this? I think perhaps the silent format inspires us to participate more directly in the movie. A sound film comes to us, approaches us—indeed, it sometimes assaults us—from the screen. But a silent film stays up there on the glowing wall, and we rise up to meet it. We take our imagination and join it with the imagination of the filmmaker.

That's what happened to me during *Sidewalk Stories.* Another interesting thing also happened. Watching this movie photographed in New York City in 1989, I found myself being set free from a lot of my stereotypes and preconceptions about the big city by the fact that the film was silent. In a sound film, the characters usually represent themselves. In a silent film, they represent a type. They stand for others like themselves, which is one reason silent films are more universal than talkies.

In sound movies set in modern cities, for example, we are likely to assume that street people are violent, disturbed, and antisocial. *Sidewalk Stories* opens with a long, elaborate tracking shot past a row of sidewalk entertainers—jugglers, pavement artists, magicians, three-card-monte shills—and because the film is silent we do not assume they are all clones of Travis Bickle. They seem gentler, more universal characters, like people we would meet in a film by Chaplin. That's a strange assumption, since the movie is set in an area of present-day Greenwich Village where drug dealers and other vermin are always present, and yet the silent film somehow mythologizes the characters.

The shot ends on a shot of the Artist (played by Charles Lane himself). He is a small, determined black man who has set up his easel and hopes to persuade pedestrians to pay him to draw them. Right next to his spot on the pavement is another artist, a tall, broad bully who also wants this turf. He pushes the Artist to the ground. The Artist gets up. He pushes him over again. The Artist gets up again. He pushes him over a third time. The Artist begins to get up, thinks better of it, and pushes himself back down to the ground—saving the bully trouble.

This is, almost movement for movement, a comic bit of business from Charlie Chaplin. It's as if Lane is starting his film by acknowledging that debt. Then he moves on. As the story develops, the Artist befriends the mother of a small girl, and after an altercation in an alley involving the mother and the girl's father, the Artist finds to his consternation that he has been left with the little girl—and it's up to him to protect her.

In a sound movie, he would go to a social agency. In a silent movie, of course, he takes her home with him—home to the rude little room where he is a squatter in the ruins of a church marked for demolition. And he begins to figure out how to care for the little orphan. (The child is played perfectly by

Lane's own daughter, Nicole Alysia, and her naturalness is one of the strengths of the movie.) The domestic details, right down to the box of cornflakes, all provide comic possibilities. And when it turns out that the child's crayon scrawls are snapped up as "modern art," the movie takes a wicked turn.

The movie's story develops as a melodrama in which the Artist is befriended by a successful businesswoman (Sandye Wilson), threatened by thugs, and eventually is able to restore the child to her rightful mother (Trula Hoosier). Along the way there are the kinds of confrontations between rich and poor that Chaplin liked to explore, including a scene where the businesswoman invites the Artist and the child to her high-rise apartment, but the doorman doesn't want to let them in. Lane is endlessly inventive in the ways he finds to create humorous situations and tell his story through images, and the sound-track music, by Marc Marder, reinforces everything that happens. The movie, at ninety-seven minutes, seems shorter.

I have a quarrel with one thing Lane does. At the end of the film, the camera lingers in a public place where some of the homeless have congregated. They're panhandlers, asking the passing public for change, and gradually, slowly, we begin to be able to hear their voices on the sound track: "Remember the homeless!" "Can you spare a quarter?" The sound in this sequence was not necessary. Lane's whole movie has already made the points that he now reinforces with spoken dialogue. It violates the magic of silence. But up until then, *Sidewalk Stories* weaves a spell as powerful as it is entertaining.

The Silence of the Lambs ★ ★ ★ ½
R, 116 m., 1991

Jodie Foster (Clarice Starling), Anthony Hopkins (Dr. Hannibal Lecter), Scott Glenn (Jack Crawford), Anthony Heald (Dr. Frederick Chilton), Ted Levine (Jamie Gum), Kasi Lemmons (Ardelia Mapp). Directed by Jonathan Demme and produced by Edward Saxon, Kenneth Utt, and Ron Bozman. Screenplay by Ted Tally.

It has been a good long while since I have felt the presence of Evil so manifestly demonstrated as in the first appearance of Anthony Hopkins in *The Silence of the Lambs*. He stands perfectly still in the middle of his cell floor, arms at his sides, and we sense instantly that he is not standing at attention; he is standing at rest—like a savage animal confident of the brutality coiled up inside him. His speaking voice has the precision of a man so arrogant he can barely be bothered to address the sloppy intelligence of the ordinary person. The effect of this scene is so powerful that it underlies all the rest of the movie, lending terror to scenes that do not even involve him.

Like all great entrances in the movies, his is carefully prepared. We learn that his character, Dr. Hannibal Lecter, is both a brilliant psychiatrist and a mass murderer, known as "Hannibal the Cannibal" because he eats his victims. He is already behind bars (and unbreakable Plexiglas) when the movie opens, and, indeed, *The Silence of the Lambs* is about the search for another mass murderer, named "Buffalo Bill," who skins his victims. Operating on the theory that it takes one to know one, the FBI agent in charge of the case (Scott Glenn) thinks Lecter might be able to provide useful clues in the search for Buffalo Bill. But Lecter toys with most of his inquisitors, or dismisses them, and so the agent hits on the idea of sending in an untried young female trainee (Jodie Foster). Perhaps she will appeal to the monster.

The notion of the beauty and the beast is, of course, central to horror stories, but watching *The Silence of the Lambs* for the second time, I began to wonder if the author of the original novel, Thomas Harris, had started the project by jotting down a list of the great universal phobias and dreads. Here is a movie involving not only cannibalism and the skinning of people, but also kidnapping, being trapped in the bottom of a well, decomposing corpses, large insects, being lost in the dark, being tracked by someone you cannot see, not being able to get people to believe you, creatures who jump from the shadows, people who know your deepest secrets, doors that slam shut behind you, beheadings, bizarre sexual perversions, and being a short woman in an elevator full of tall men.

If the movie were not so well made, indeed, it would be ludicrous. Material like this invites filmmakers to take chances, and punishes them mercilessly when they fail. That's especially true when the movie is based on best-selling material a lot of people are familiar with (*The Silence of the Lambs* was preceded by Harris's *Red Dragon*, about Hannibal Lecter, which was also made into a film, *Manhunter*).

The director, Jonathan Demme, is no doubt aware of the hazards, but does not hesitate to take chances. His first scene with Hopkins could have gone over the top, and in the hands of a lesser actor almost certainly would have. But Hopkins is in the great British tradition of actors who internalize instead of overact, and his Hannibal Lecter has certain endearing parallels with his famous London stage performance in *Pravda*, where he played a press baron not unlike Rupert Murdoch. There are moments when Hopkins, as Lecter, goes berserk, but Demme wisely lets a little of this go a long way, so that the lasting impression is of his evil intelligence.

Jodie Foster is inevitably upstaged by Hopkins's rich and gruesome creation, but her steadiness and pluck are at the heart of the movie. Some interesting aspects have been provided for her character: She is "one generation up from white trash," as Lecter correctly guesses, she tries to disguise her hillbilly accent, and she has to muster up all of her courage to order a roomful of lascivious lawmen out of an autopsy room. The movie has an undercurrent of unwelcome male attention toward her character; rarely in a movie have I been made more aware of the subtle sexual pressures men put upon women with their eyes.

Against these qualities, the weak points of the movie are probably not very important, but there are some. The details of Foster's final showdown with Buffalo Bill are scarcely believable. Unless you look closely, you may miss the details of how Lecter deceives his pursuers in one grisly scene. The very last scene in the film is hard to follow. But against these flaws are balanced true suspense, unblinking horror, and an Anthony Hopkins performance that is likely to be referred to for many years when horror movies are discussed.

Silent Movie ★ ★ ★ ★
PG, 88 m., 1976

Mel Brooks (Mel Funn), Marty Feldman (Marty Eggs), Dom DeLuise (Dom Bell), Bernadette Peters (Vilma Kaplan), Sid Caesar (Studio Chief), Harold Gould (Engulf), Ron Carey (Devour), Henny Youngman (Fly-in-Soup Man). Directed by Mel Brooks and produced by Michael Hertzorg. Screenplay by Brooks, Ron Clark, Rudy DeLuca, and Barry Levinson.

There's a moment very early in *Silent Movie* (before the opening credits, in fact) when Mel Brooks, Marty Feldman, and Dom DeLuise are tooling through Los Angeles in a tiny sports car. They pass a pregnant lady at a bus stop. "That's a very pregnant lady!" Brooks says (on a title card, of course, since this is a silent movie). "Let's give her a lift!" The lady gets into the back of the car, which tilts back onto its rear wheels. Mel drives off with the front wheels in the air.

This is far from being the funniest scene in a very funny movie, but it helps to illustrate my point, which is that Mel Brooks will do anything for a laugh. Anything. He has no shame. He's an anarchist; his movies inhabit a universe in which everything is possible and the outrageous is probable, and *Silent Movie*, where Brooks has taken a considerably stylistic risk and pulled it off triumphantly, made me laugh a lot. On the Brooks-Laff-O-Meter, I laughed more than in *Young Frankenstein* and about as much as in *Blazing Saddles*, although not, I confess, as much as in *The Producers*.

Silent Movie is not only funny, it's fun. It's clear at almost every moment that the filmmakers had a ball making it. It's set in contemporary Hollywood, where Big Pictures Studio ("If it's a big picture, we've made it") teeters on the edge of bankruptcy and a takeover from the giant Engulf and Devour conglomerate. Enter Mel Funn (Brooks), a once-talented director whose career was cut short by drunkenness, who vows to save the studio by convincing Hollywood's biggest stars to make a silent movie. This is a situation that gives rise to a lot of inside jokes (I wonder whether executives at Gulf and Western, which took over Paramount, will notice any parallels), but the thing about Brooks's inside jokes is that their outsides are funny, too.

The intrepid gang of Mel, Dom, and Marty set out to woo the superstars, materializing in the shower of one (who counts his hands, puzzled, and finds he has eight) and plucking another out of a nightclub audience. (There are several "actual" stars in the movie, but it would be spoiling the fun to name them.) Everything's done amid an encyclopedia of sight gags, old and new, borrowed and with a fly in their soup. There are gags that don't work and stretches of up to a minute, I suppose, when we don't laugh—but even then we're smiling because of Brooks's manic desire to entertain. There's a story about the days, years ago, when Brooks was a writer for Sid Caesar and Caesar would march into the writers' office, pick up their desks, brandish them and shout "*funnier!*" I think the lesson rubbed off.

In a movie filled with great scenes, these moments are classics: The battle with the Coke machine. The behavior with the horse on the merry-go-round. The nightclub scene. The dramatic reaction of Engulf and Devour's board of directors to the photo of sexpot Vilma Kaplan. The fly in the soup. The Pong game in the intensive-care unit. The . . . but space is limited: Perhaps I should mention, though, that the movie isn't really silent. It's filled with wall-to-wall music, sound effects, explosions, whistles, and crashes and, yes, one word.

Silent Running ★ ★ ★ ★
G, 90 m., 1972

Bruce Dern (Lowell), Cliff Potts (Wolf), Ron Rivkin (Barker), Jesse Vint (Keenan), Mark Persons, Steven Brown, Cheryl Sparks, Larry Wisenhunt (Drones). Directed by Douglas Trumbull and produced by Michael Gruskoff. Screenplay by Deric Washburn, Mike Cimino, and Steve Bochco.

In the not very distant future, man has at last finished with Earth. The mountains are leveled and the valleys filled in, and there are no growing plants left to mess things up. Everything is nice and sterile, and man's global housekeeping has achieved total defoliation. Out around the rings of Saturn, a few lonely spaceships keep their vigil. They're interplanetary greenhouses, pointed always toward the sun. Inside their acres and acres of forests, protected by geodesic domes that gather the sunlight, the surviving plants and small animals of Earth grow. There are squirrels and rabbits and moonlit nights when the wind does actually seem to breathe in the trees: a ghostly reminder of the dead forests of Earth.

The keeper of one of these greenhouses, Freeman Lowell, loves the plants and animals with a not terribly acute intelligence. *Silent Running* is his story. In an earlier day, he might have been a forest ranger and happily spent the winter all alone in a tower, spotting forest fires. Now he is millions of miles from Earth, but his thoughts are filled with weedings and prunings, fertilizer and the artificial rainfall.

One day the word comes from Earth: Destroy the greenhouses and return. Lowell cannot bring himself to do this, and so he destroys his fellow crew members instead. Then he hijacks his spaceship and directs it out into the deep galactic night. All of this is told with simplicity and a quiet ecological concern, and it makes *Silent Running* a movie

out of the ordinary—especially if you like science fiction.

The director is Douglas Trumbull, a Canadian who designed many of the special effects for Stanley Kubrick's *2001*. Trumbull also did the computers and the underground laboratory for *The Andromeda Strain*, and is one of the best science-fiction special-effects men. *Silent Running*, which has deep space effects every bit the equal of those in *2001*, also introduces him as an intelligent, if not sensational, director.

The weight of the movie falls on the shoulders of Bruce Dern, who plays the only man in sight during most of the picture. His only companions are Huey, Louie, and Dewey, who are small and uncannily human robots who help with the gardening. They're OK with a trowel but no good at playing poker, as their human boss discovers during a period of boredom.

Dern is a very good, subtle actor, who was about the best thing in Jack Nicholson's directing debut, *Drive, He Said*. Dern played a basketball coach as a man obsessed with the notion of winning—and the deep-space ecologist this time is a quieter variation on the theme.

Silent Running isn't, in the last analysis, a very profound movie, nor does it try to be. (If it had, it could have been a pretentious disaster.) It is about a basically uncomplicated man faced with an awesome, but uncomplicated, situation. Given a choice between the lives of his companions and the lives of Earth's last surviving firs and pines, oaks and elms, and creepers and cantaloupes, he decides for the growing things. After all, there are plenty of men. His problem is that, after a while, he begins to miss them.

Silkwood ★ ★ ★ ★
R, 128 m., 1983

Meryl Streep (Karen Silkwood), Kurt Russell (Drew Stephens), Cher (Dolly Pelliker), Craig T. Nelson (Winston). Directed by Mike Nichols and produced by Nichols and Michael Hausman. Screenplay by Nora Ephron and Alice Arlen.

When the Karen Silkwood story was first being talked about as a movie project, I pictured it as an angry political exposé, maybe *The China Syndrome, Part 2*. There'd be the noble, young nuclear worker, the evil conglomerate, and, looming overhead, the death's-head of a mushroom cloud. That could have been a good movie, but predictable. Mike

Nichols's *Silkwood* is not predictable. That's because he's not telling the story of a conspiracy, he's telling the story of a human life. There are villains in his story, but none with motives we can't understand. After Karen is dead and the movie is over, we realize this is a lot more movie than perhaps we were expecting.

Silkwood is the story of some American workers. They happen to work in a Kerr-McGee nuclear plant in Oklahoma, making plutonium fuel rods for nuclear reactors. But they could just as easily be working in a Southern textile mill (there are echoes of *Norma Rae*), or on an assembly line, or for a metropolitan public school district. The movie isn't about plutonium, it's about the American working class. Its villains aren't monsters; they're organization men, labor union hotshots, and people afraid of losing their jobs. As the movie opens, Karen Silkwood fits naturally into this world, and the movie is the story of how she begins to stand out, how she becomes an individual, thinks for herself, and is punished for her freedom. Silkwood is played by Meryl Streep, in another of her great performances, and there's a tiny detail in the first moments of the movie that reveals how completely Streep has thought through the role. Silkwood walks into the factory, punches her own time card, automatically looks at her own wristwatch, and then shakes her wrist: It's a self-winding watch, I guess. That little shake of the wrist is an actor's choice. There are a lot of them in this movie, all almost as invisible as the first one; little by little, Streep and her coactors build characters so convincing that we become witnesses instead of merely viewers.

The nuclear plant in the film is behind on an important contract. People are working overtime and corners are being cut. A series of small incidents convinces Karen Silkwood that the compromises are dangerous, that the health of the workers is being needlessly risked, and that the company is turning its back on the falsification of safety and workmanship tests. She approaches the union. The union sees some publicity in her complaints. She gets a free trip to Washington—her first airplane ride. She meets with some union officials who are much more concerned with publicity than with working conditions, and she has a little affair with one of them. She's no angel. At home in Oklahoma, domestic life resembles a revolving door, with her boyfriend (Kurt Russell) packing up and leaving, and her friend (Cher), a

lesbian, inviting a beautician to move in. It's a little amazing that established movie stars like Streep, Russell, and Cher could disappear so completely into the everyday lives of these characters.

The real Karen Silkwood died in a mysterious automobile accident. She was on her way to deliver some documents to a *New York Times* reporter when her car left the road. Was the accident caused in some way? Was she murdered? The movie doesn't say. Nor does it point suspicion only toward the company. At the end there were a lot of people mad at Karen Silkwood. *Silkwood* is the story of an ordinary woman, hard-working and passionate, funny and screwed-up, who made those people mad simply because she told the truth as she saw it and did what she thought was right.

Silverado ★ ★ ★ ½
PG-13, 132 m., 1985

Kevin Kline (Paden), Scott Glenn (Emmett), Kevin Costner (Jake), Danny Glover (Mal), Linda Hunt (Stella), Jeff Goldblum (Slick), Brian Dennehy (Sheriff Cobb), Rosanna Arquette (Hannah), John Cleese (Sheriff Langston). Directed and produced by Lawrence Kasdan. Screenplay by Lawrence Kasdan and Mark Kasdan.

Walking home after the second Western was over at the Princess Theater, we'd play the roles we had seen on the screen. We were seven or eight years old at the time, but we didn't have the slightest difficulty in identifying with the cowboys in the movies. All of their motives were transparently clear to us—except, possibly, why anyone would want to kiss a girl when he could be practicing his lasso tricks instead.

The Westerns I remember from those days have been filtered through a golden haze of time, but the one thing I am sure I remember correctly is that they were fun. They were high-spirited, joyous, anarchic movies in which overgrown adolescents jumped on their horses and whooped and waved their hats in the air, and rode as fast as the wind to the next town and to the next adventure.

Silverado is a Western like that. I mean the comparison to be praise. This movie is more sophisticated and complicated than the Westerns of my childhood, and it is certainly better looking and better acted. But it has the same spirit; it awards itself the carefree freedom of the Western myth itself—the myth of a nation "endlessly realizing Westward,"

as Robert Frost had it, with limitless miles of prairie and desert and mountain, interrupted only occasionally enough for a dozen men to shoot at each other without all of them necessarily getting hit.

Silverado is the work of Lawrence Kasdan, the man who wrote *Raiders of the Lost Ark*, and it has some of the same reckless brilliance about it. It's the story of four cowboys who join up together, ride into town, refuse to knuckle under to the corrupt sheriff, and end up fighting for justice. This is a story, you will agree, that has been told before. What distinguishes Kasdan's telling of it is the style and energy he brings to the project.

The cowboys include a sweet-faced young man who hopes to make his fortune (Kevin Kline), a black man who vows to avenge his father's murder (Danny Glover), a taciturn loner (Scott Glenn) who gets restless when he's not a long way from civilization, and his goofy brother (Kevin Costner). They meet along the way, after Glenn saves Kline from death in the desert, and together they help Costner escape from jail. Joining up with Glover, they ride on into the next town, Silverado, which is dominated by a slick sheriff (Brian Dennehy) and a gambling saloon run by a formidably competent little woman named Stella (Linda Hunt, in a scene-stealing performance).

I will not tell you too much of what happens next, but then perhaps I do not need to. If you are familiar with the Western, you will be familiar with this one. What may seem a little strange is that, if there is any nostalgia connected to this film, it will be found in our hearts and not in the characters on the screen. Too many Westerns in the last fifteen years have been elegies to a dead past, played out by actors remembering the cowboy roles of their youth (remember, if you can, the last Westerns of Robert Mitchum, William Holden, Randolph Scott, John Wayne, Joel McCrea, Kirk Douglas). *Silverado* contains a group of talented young actors (Scott Glenn, the oldest, is in his forties), and this is not their last Western but, in many cases, their first. The movie is set at the time when the West was still being opened up, when there was still opportunity there, and when the bad guys were still so unsophisticated they could fall for a dumb trick like getting trapped in a box canyon.

What does it prove, this movie about a bunch of cowboys held together by honor, this movie about bartender philosophers, evil sheriffs, and young pioneer women with lines like "My beauty will pass someday, but the land will only grow more beautiful." What does it prove? That the Western myth is most at home in a setting of innocence, that *Silverado* understands that, and that somewhere in our hearts there may still be memories of little boys and girls who chose up sides for who got to be the good guys on the long walk home.

Sing ★ ★ ★
PG-13, 99 m., 1989

Lorraine Bracco (Miss Lombardo), Peter Dobson (Dominic), Jessica Steen (Hannah), Louise Lasser (Rosie), George DiCenzo (Mr. Marowitz), Patti LaBelle (Mrs. DeVere). Directed Richard Baskin and produced by Craig Zadan. Screenplay by Dean Pitchford.

The roots of *Sing* can be found firmly planted in the clichés of the past, in all those Rooney and Garland pictures where they rented the old barn and put on a show, or in the Beach Party movies where they held a rock 'n' roll benefit to rescue the teen center. This time, a Brooklyn high school is going to be closed, and the school board has refused permission for the students to hold their traditional spring talent show.

No reason is given for the ban on the show, but, of course, none is needed. It is necessary for the show to be prohibited in order for the students to defy the ban and put it on anyway. If there is one absolutely obligatory shot in a movie of this sort, it's the one where the evil fuddy-duddy comes bursting into the back of the auditorium and demands that the show be halted—only to be squelched by a triumphant song-and-dance number.

Since absolutely everything in *Sing* is completely predictable, I was surprised how much I enjoyed the movie. It's a victory of style over substance, and its energy owes a lot to Lorraine Bracco and Patti LaBelle, who play two of the teachers in the high school. Both of these women are absolute individuals, and the confidence with which they present themselves has a lot to do with the movie's whole tone.

Bracco is a thin, intense brunette with a Brooklyn accent and a face full of character and humor. She's wry and tough, and she has a key scene early in the movie where she stares down a tough kid who tries to assault her and offers him a choice: Go along with my program, or go to jail. The power of this scene carries over to the whole movie, really,

giving the material a weight it might not have had otherwise.

LaBelle, the rock legend from Philadelphia, is not given much of a character to play; there are times when she almost seems to be appearing as a guest star. But there's a song-and-dance sequence where she takes the stage and shows the kids how it's done, and the scene is a showstopper, like the Pee-wee Herman sequence in *Back to the Beach:* The plot goes on hold, and the movie simply has a great time for five minutes.

The plot, as I said, has been seen before. We know, of course, that there must be a romance, preferably between a good girl and a bad boy she can redeem. The girl is played by Jessica Steen, as a good-hearted senior who has nothing to do with the local hoods like Peter Dobson. Both kids have family problems. Steen's mother (Louise Lasser) is a widow who moans constantly over the ordeal of running the family diner. Dobson's brother is a small-time thief who takes the kid along on robberies—including, of course, Lasser's diner.

The plot questions are equally predictable: Will the bad kid repudiate his brother, win the respect of the girl, and dance in the big musical? Will the girl convince her mother that life is worth living? Will the teachers and their principal succeed in defying the board of education? Will the show go on? Are there stars in the sky? Sometimes it's fun watching the setups for scenes you know will follow. For example, when the girl gives her mother tickets to the show, and the mother turns them down, saying she's too busy to attend. What do you want to bet that at a key moment, the mother will turn up in the back of the auditorium and exchange a heartfelt nod of forgiveness with her daughter on the stage?

I'm of two minds about genre pictures like this one. On the one hand, I'd prefer something I hadn't seen before. On the other hand, because the plot has been phoned in, I'm free to observe the performances. And Lorraine Bracco was a particular pleasure. In this film and two others *(Someone to Watch Over Me* and *Dream Team)*, she has emerged as one of those rare actors who has obvious and tangible integrity on the screen; she can sell dialogue even as tired as the lines in this script, because she puts her own spin on them. High school talent shows always end with somebody being thrust into the spotlight of stardom. In *Sing*, it's the teacher.

Singles ★ ★ ★
PG-13, 99 m., 1992

Bridget Fonda (Janet Livermore), Campbell Scott (Steve Dunne), Kyra Sedgwick (Linda Powell), Sheila Kelley (Debbie Hunt), Jim True (David Bailey), Matt Dillon (Cliff Poncier), Bill Pullman (Dr. Jamison), James Le Gros (Andy). Directed by Cameron Crowe. Produced by Crowe and Richard Hashimoto. Screenplay by Crowe.

Singles tells the story of a loosely knit band of friends and neighbors who live in an apartment building in Seattle and dream of love. They are all in their twenties, and reasonably attractive, and not particularly desperate, but they share a plight everyone can identify with: the difficulty of finding a match between someone you like, and someone who likes you. It always seems to work out that if one half of the equation is right, the other is wrong.

One couple in the movie (Campbell Scott and Kyra Sedgwick) seem to be more or less right for one another, but they play a dangerous game of one-upmanship, based on pride. Which one will telephone the other? How long should the other wait before calling back? They're thinking about each other so incessantly, they almost lose touch, because there is always a point at which a non-returned call stops being intriguing and becomes a rejection.

Another would-be couple (Bridget Fonda and Matt Dillon) seems completely wrong. He is a singer in a rock band, and cultivates a deliberately laid-back indifference to women in general and Fonda in particular. She, of course, assumes the fault is all her own. Visiting his apartment, she finds pinups of busty women. Is that what he likes? She visits a plastic surgeon, and in the movie's funniest scene fights a duel with him over the image of her hypothetical new body on his computer screen.

Singles was written and directed by Cameron Crowe, who has explored this territory before. He wrote the screenplay for *Fast Times at Ridgemont High,* not my favorite movie, and then wrote and directed *Say Anything* (1989), which was one of the wisest and most touching movies about teen-agers I have seen. Now, moving on to the twenty-somethings, he has adopted a casual sketch style, where scenes are separated by blackouts and the point of each episode is to show some facet of human nature, usually one that makes us squirm.

The movie will challenge some audiences simply because it is not a 1-2-3 progression of character and plot. There is no problem at the beginning and no solution at the end; the film is about a life process that is, by its very nature, inconclusive—the search for happiness. Crowe's insights into the material include one particular perception: In your twenties, you tend to spend more time putting yourself on the map than worrying about anyone else's happiness. Look at the earnestness with which the Scott character promotes his idea for a Seattle rapid-transit system. Does he believe in trains? Only to a degree. What he really believes in are *his* trains.

The Bridget Fonda character, on the other hand, doesn't value herself highly enough. You can see that when she considers plastic surgery to please a guy who doesn't even like her in the first place. She wants to be an architect, but for the moment is working as a waitress. A wise man once said: "What you do instead of your real work . . . *is* your real work."

Some of Crowe's sketches are pokes at easy targets, including those videotape dating services in which people advertise for partners. Sheila Kelley plays a young woman who is consciously shopping for an eligible man; she knows where they can be found, just as a hunter knows which watering holes attract the lions. There's a funny sequence where she goes to a videographer (*Batman* director Tim Burton) who will direct her in the kind of video that would probably attract only the kind of man she should stay far away from.

Singles is not a great cutting-edge movie, and parts of it may be too whimsical and disorganized for audiences raised on cause-and-effect plots. But I found myself smiling a lot during the movie, sometimes with amusement, sometimes with recognition. It's easy to like these characters, and care about them.

Single White Female ★ ★ ★
R, 107 m., 1992

Bridget Fonda (Allison Jones), Jennifer Jason Leigh (Hedra Carlson), Steven Weber (Sam Rawson), Peter Friedman (Graham Knox), Stephen Tobolowsky (Mitchell Myerson). Directed and produced by Barbet Schroeder. Screenplay by Don Roos.

There is a certain rising tide of madness in *Single White Female* that is one of the movie's pleasures—evidence that it was made by a man who directs films instead of simply manufacturing them. This is a story which, in other hands, could have simply been an all-female slasher movie, but Barbet Schroeder, who produced and directed it, has a mordant humor that pushes the material over the top. It is a slasher movie, and a little more.

Hollywood likes movies with a "high concept," by which they mean, I think, a low concept—a plot idea that can be simply explained in one sentence that will sell. *Single White Female* has a terrific high concept: It's about a "roommate from hell." Allison, the heroine, played by Bridget Fonda, advertises for a roommate, and after carefully screening out several nut cases and victims of assorted obsessions, ends up with a candidate who looks ideal.

Her name is Hedra Carlson. She is played by Jennifer Jason Leigh as a sweet-faced, friendly little innocent. Those are the ones you have to look out for. I cannot find "hedra" in my unabridged dictionary, and yet somehow the name teases me. Surely it is the name of a mythological beast? One with a rent receipt in one hand and a kitchen knife in the other?

The progression of the movie is more or less as we expect it, beginning with Allison and Hedra as close friends and ending in bloodshed and death. What is intriguing is the way Schroeder progresses from beginning to end. There are many steps along the way, involving downstairs neighbors, boyfriends, and others who belong to Allison and soon seem to belong to Hedra, too, as do lots of Allison's clothes and eventually even her hairstyle and coloring. Hedra, it is revealed, was a twin, and apparently wants to become one again, if only a twice-orphaned one.

One of the first shots in the movie shows the building where Allison has her apartment. It is one of those vast New York buildings that make ideal settings for movies like *Rosemary's Baby*—clanging, echoing old structures that give the director an excuse for carefully planted gimmicks, like that screwdriver that makes the elevator door budge.

Schroeder, whose most recent credits include *Barfly*, the Mickey Rourke drunk movie, and *Reversal of Fortune*, with Jeremy Irons as Claus von Bulow, is clearly fascinated by characters at the extremes of the human spectrum. That is perhaps why *Single White Female* builds to a manic crescendo instead of simply delivering the required number of slashes and quitting. There is one climax after another after another here, until it seems as if the characters will drop of exhaustion, and yet they fight on. There is a kind of mad artistic zeal to their passionate duel, underlined by the fact that both Fonda and Leigh pull out all the stops in their performances, and that they do eventually look so much like one another that it's creepy.

I have long adopted a generic approach to film criticism, evaluating movies as examples of what they aspire to be. No genre is beyond redemption or beneath contempt, and here the slasher genre is given its due with strong performances and direction. Of course, you may despise movies like this, but that is another subject.

Sirens ★ ★ ★ ½
R, 96 m., 1994

Hugh Grant (Anthony Campion), Tara Fitzgerald (Estella Campion), Sam Neill (Norman Lindsay), Elle Macpherson (Sheela), Portia De Rossi (Prue), Kate Fischer (Giddy), Pamela Rabe (Rose Lindsay). Directed by John Duigan and produced by Sue Milliken. Screenplay by Duigan.

Although they are often charged with being emotionally distant, the British and their colonies have produced more than their share of sexual outlaws, from Oscar Wilde to Aleister Crowley to D.H. Lawrence to Francis Bacon, to balance the ledger. The central figure in *Sirens* seems perhaps vaguely inspired by another legendary British bohemian, Augustus John, an artist whose models and mistresses were interchangeable, and who delighted in scandal.

But in fact he is based on a less known figure, Norman Lindsay, a colorful Australian painter who lived on an estate where his art coexisted side-by-side with an experiment in living. In the film, Lindsay's freewheeling life-style has attracted not only an extraordinarily open-minded wife, but also a group of models for whom clothing is often optional. They share his permissive views on sensuality.

Since one of the models is played by Elle Macpherson, the *Sports Illustrated* centerfold, and since Ms. Macpherson is featured in the advertising above the actual stars of the movie, you might understandably have the idea that *Sirens* is an exploitation film, or at least the sort of overwrought erotic melodrama Ken Russell became known for with

Women in Love and *Listzomania*. The movie does indeed feature much footage of Macpherson and her sister sirens in the nude, but it is smarter, more thoughtful, and more good-tempered than you might expect. (As the critic Rich Elias put it, "At last! A skin flick for English majors!")

The film, set between the wars, is seen mostly through the eyes of a shy Anglican clergyman named Anthony Campion (Hugh Grant), who has been asked by his bishop to look in on Lindsay (Sam Neill) during a visit to Australia. The painter is rumored to have painted a blasphemous portrait, and the bishop hopes perhaps a word to the wise will prevent a scandal. Campion and his wife Estella (Tara Fitzgerald) arrive at the painter's sprawling estate to find a warm welcome, a guest cottage of their own, and a very gradual seduction process under way.

I can easily imagine where this premise might lead in the hands of many directors. But *Sirens* is the work of John Duigan, of *Flirting*, and he seems to be wise and relaxed about sexual matters; he sees them with both affection and amusement, and is less interested in sex itself than in his characters' shifting attitudes toward it. What we see immediately is that Lindsay is a Pan of sorts, under whose direction people are inspired to have experiences that might lessen their inhibitions. And we learn that the Campion marriage could benefit from such experiences.

The clergyman is at first quite proper and distant, and Hugh Grant is able to project his unease with great conviction. Grant *(Bitter Moon, Four Weddings and a Funeral)* is an actor who specializes in propriety under fire. He clears his throat, he stammers becomingly, he hems and haws, he apologizes in advance for almost everything he says, and yet there is an appealing puppyish quality to his personality that inspires women to reassure him in one way or certainly another. Here he looks on with alarm as his wife grows all too intrigued by the freedoms practiced by the Lindsay menage, and yet when some of the sirens grow friendly toward him, he is hard-pressed to keep his mind on his theological duty.

There is no particular plot in *Sirens* so much as a general observation of the process by which the Campions are gradually transformed into warmer and more inquisitive partners. While that is happening, Lindsay paints, and several interlocking domestic intrigues develop without any great urgency. It's interesting that the Lindsay character

doesn't seem to feel any need to personally direct the unfolding scenario; unlike, say, Crowley, who had a need to write the script and dominate the proceedings, Lindsay simply creates an atmosphere in which everyone feels free to act on their impulses.

The movie places little emphasis on the mechanics (or the necessity) of actual seduction, being more concerned with how the visitors absorb the philosophy of freedom which Lindsay and his sirens practice. They find a willing pupil in Estella, who becomes a particular challenge to Sheela, the Macpherson character. She invites the clergyman's wife to go swimming at dawn, sketches her while she sleeps, and in general provides a gentle tug in the direction of more freedom.

In the hands of another director, *Sirens* might be less subtle in its style and more concerned with some kind of definite erotic payoff. Duigan would rather nudge than push. No doubt he knows all about the coteries that grew up around many infamous painters in the earlier years of this century, and is curious about how they worked, and why. By providing his British visitors as both observers and victims, he is able to study the process of seduction without making seducing the whole point of the film. The result is a good-hearted, whimsical movie which makes no apologies for the beauty of the human body and yet never feels sexually obsessed. Strange: It's not often you smile this much during an erotic film.

Sister Act ★ ★ ½
PG, 100 m., 1992

Whoopi Goldberg (Deloris), Maggie Smith (Mother Superior), Kathy Najimy (Mary Patrick), Wendy Makkena (Mary Robert), Mary Wickes (Mary Lazarus), Harvey Keitel (Vince LaRocca), Bill Nunn (Eddie). Directed by Emile Ardolino and produced by Teri Schwartz. Screenplay by Joseph Howard.

The first time I saw the coming attractions trailer for *Sister Act*, I roared with laughter and delight. The second time, I laughed again. Even the third time I smiled. It's one of the great trailers. Unfortunately, it's better directed than the movie. The trailer has high energy and whammo punch lines. The movie is sort of low-key and contemplative and a little too thoughtful.

Now I am left with this dilemma: Would I have enjoyed the movie more if I knew nothing about it going in? That's a good question, since the trailer reveals almost every big

laugh in the movie, so that when they come along we nod in recognition instead of laughing in surprise. *Sister Act* is a release from Touchstone, which was notorious a few years ago for essentially revealing the whole movie in its trailers. The studio said it was going to reform, but seeing the trailer for *Sister Act* will significantly reduce the enjoyment of anyone seeing the film.

The movie's based on a promising idea: Whoopi Goldberg plays Reno lounge singer whose lover (Harvey Keitel) is a casino boss. When she accidentally witnesses a murder, Keitel orders her rubbed out, she flees to the police, and is hidden in a convent through a witness protection program. The mother superior (Maggie Smith) is dubious about this new "nun," but the other sisters like her a lot, and before long she's the choir leader, teaching the sisters to boogie.

There are laughs in this material, but most of them come from the dialogue. The director, Emile Ardolino, does not have a touch for comedy and his pacing is consistently too languid for this material. He has no visual style at all; every shot is the obvious textbook approach, to such a degree that the film seems directed on automatic pilot, but at least Goldberg and her fellow nuns (especially Kathy Najimy as the jolly Sister Mary Patrick) are able to create life and humor when the camera is upon them.

The rest of the movie is pretty dreary. The Reno crime scenes are played more or less straight. The crime plot—involving a stool pigeon in the police department—is handled so badly that the hero cop (Bill Nunn) busts the jaw of the traitor before he could possibly have been sure who he was. And it's strange how a lot of the dialogue is mellow when it should crackle.

There are good things in the movie, of course. Many of Goldberg's scenes are funny, and there's an older nun (Mary Wickes) who has some great one-liners, and when the swinging nuns start rocking in the choir, that's almost as funny in the movie as it was in the trailer. But mostly *Sister Act* plays like a missed opportunity.

Ardolino, whose credits include the heartwarming *Chances Are* and the dreadful *Three Men and a Little Lady,* simply doesn't seem able to direct as if he believes his material is funny. It doesn't have the zest and sparkle it needs; scenes move too slowly, dialogue settles upon itself, routine reaction shots are clicked off with deadly precision. Whoever edited the trailer has a much better idea of what's good in this material than the man who directed the movie.

Sisters ★ ★ ★
R, 93 m., 1973

Margot Kidder (Danielle Breton), Jennifer Salt (Grace Collier), Charles Durning (Joseph Larch), Bill Finley (Emil Breton), Lisle Wilson (Philip Woode). Directed by Brian De Palma and produced by Edward R. Pressman. Screenplay by De Palma and Louisa Rose.

Brian De Palma's *Sisters* was made more or less consciously as an homage to Alfred Hitchcock, but it has a life of its own and it's a neat little mystery picture. The opening is pure Hitchcock. The movie begins with events so commonplace they're almost trivial, and the horror of the situation is revealed only gradually. A lithe fashion model and a young newspaperman meet on a quiz show (it's called "Peeping Tom" and asks the question, what would *you* do if you were inadvertently made voyeur-for-a-day?). She wins a set of stainless steel cutlery, he wins dinner for two at a supper club, and they decide they like each other.

After a few brushes with a mysterious stranger who may or may not be her former husband, the young couple spend the night together and in the morning he is brutally knifed to death. And, no, I haven't given away too much of the plot. Because there are a few complications. For example, the girl is half of a famous set of Siamese twins. She's the nice one, but her sister isn't—not at all.

Then there's the crusading young girl newspaper reporter, kind of a women's lib Lois Lane, who lives across the courtyard and witnesses the crime (à la *Rear Window*). She calls the police, but they resent a recent series of exposés she's written. And when they visit the so-called murder apartment they find no blood, no body, no signs of a crime; only the sweet young fashion model.

I don't suppose I can reveal another line of the plot without spoiling some of De Palma's nice surprises. But the movie works not so much because of the twists and turns and complications as because of the performances. In a movie industry filled with young actresses who look great but can't act so well (especially when they've got to play intelligent characters), De Palma has cast two of the exceptions: Margot Kidder and Jennifer Salt.

Both of them are really fine, but Jennifer Salt is the bigger surprise because she's so convincing as the tough, stubborn, doggedly persistent outsider. It's a classic Hitchcock role. She's totally uninvolved and innocent, and in possession of information no one will believe. She can't doubt the evidence of her own eyes, but the cops mistrust her, the body's gone—and the killer knows who and where she is.

De Palma directs with a nice feeling for the incongruous. There is, for example, Ms. Salt's delightful suburban mother (Mary Davenport), who wishes sometimes her daughter would stop writing those newspaper columns and settle down in a nice, comfortable marriage. There's the mysterious stranger (Bill Finley), who looks like an extraterrestrial crossed with a Cold War spy. And there is even the other sister, the other Siamese twin, about whom perhaps the less said the better.

Sixteen Candles ★ ★ ★
PG, 93 m., 1984

Molly Ringwald (Samantha Baker), Anthony Michael Hall (The Geek), Michael Schoeffling (Jake Ryan), Gedde Watanabe (Long Duk Dong), Paul Dooley (Jim Baker). Directed by John Hughes and produced by Hilton A. Green. Screenplay by Hughes.

Sixteen Candles is a sweet and funny movie about two of the worst things that can happen to a girl on her sixteenth birthday: (1) Her grandparents shrieking "Look! She's finally got her boobies!" and (2) her entire family completely and totally forgetting that it's even her birthday. The day goes downhill from there, because of (3) her sister's wedding to a stupid lunkhead, (4) her crush on the best-looking guy in the senior class, and (5) the long, involved story about how a freshman boy named the Geek managed to get possession of a pair of her panties and sell looks at them for a dollar each to all the guys in the locker room.

If *Sixteen Candles* begins to sound a little like an adolescent raunch movie, maybe it's because I haven't suggested the style in which it's acted and directed. This is a fresh and cheerful movie with a goofy sense of humor and a good ear for how teen-agers talk. It doesn't hate its characters or condescend to them, the way a lot of teen-age movies do; instead, it goes for human comedy and finds it in the everyday lives of the kids in its story.

The movie stars Molly Ringwald as Samantha, a bright-eyed teen-ager who pulls off the difficult trick of playing a character who takes everything too seriously—without ever taking herself too seriously. The movie's told mostly from her point of view, and it's like *Valley Girl*—it's about young kids who think a lot about sex, but who are shy and inexperienced and unsure and touchingly committed to concepts like True Love. She has a crush on a senior boy named Jake (Michael Schoeffling), who looks like Matt Dillon, of course, and doesn't even know she's alive. Meanwhile, the Geek (Anthony Michael Hall) is in love with her. Also, there are complications involving Jake's stuck-up girlfriend, Samantha's impossible grandparents, various older and younger brothers and sisters, and a foreign exchange student named Long Duk Dong, who apparently has come to this country to major in partying.

Sixteen Candles contains most of the scenes that are obligatory in teen-age movies: The dance, the makeout session, the party that turns into a free-for-all. But writer and director John Hughes doesn't treat them as subjects for exploitation; he *listens* to these kids. For example, on the night of the dance, Samantha ends up in the shop room with the Geek. They're sitting in the front seat of an old car. The Geek acts as if he's sex-mad. Samantha tells him to get lost. Then, in a real departure for this kind of movie, they really start to talk, and it turns out they're both lonely, insecure, and in need of a good friend.

There are a lot of effective performances in this movie, including Paul Dooley as Samantha's harried father, Blanche Baker as the zonked-out older sister, Hall as the Geek, and Gedde Watanabe as the exchange student (he elevates his role from a potentially offensive stereotype to high comedy). Ringwald provides a perfect center for the story, and her reaction in the first scene with her grandmother is just about worth the price of admission.

Skin Deep ★ ★ ★
R, 102 m., 1989

John Ritter (Zach), Vincent Gardenia (Barney), Alyson Reed (Alex), Joel Brooks (Jake), Julianne Phillips (Molly), Chelsea Field (Amy), Peter Donat (Sparky), Don Gordon (Curt). Directed by Blake Edwards and produced by Tony Adams. Screenplay by Edwards.

Blake Edwards, who directed *Skin Deep*, is like a magician who distracts you with his rapid-fire patter and his sexy assistant while he's switching the rabbits behind his back. The movie is the ultimately serious story of a man who bottoms out on those two vices of the moment, drinking and womanizing. But this is the only serious movie I can think of that contains a ballet for glow-in-the-dark condoms.

The hero of the story is a novelist named Zach (John Ritter), whose life is coming apart at the seams. He's got writer's block. He can't stop chasing every pretty girl who comes along. His wife is leaving him. His agent is dying. He gets arrested for drunk driving about twice a week. His house has burned to the ground. The opening scene is an indication of his desperation: His mistress catches him in bed with her hairdresser, and then his wife walks in on all three of them.

Zach's fundamental problem is alcoholism. He's one of those drunks whose evenings develop in stages. Early on, he can be charming and seductive to women. A little later, he knows how to play Cole Porter on the piano. In the morning, he is likely to wake up in his bartender's guest room, having thrown up in the aquarium, stuck the dog to the ceiling with Super Glue, and wrapped himself in toilet paper because he was cold.

Although Zach's situation is desperate, Edwards approaches him with the detachment and maniacal glee of a sardonic jokester. Zach is a pathetic case, but the movie is wicked and lighthearted as it follows his misadventures with a parade of bedable women. One of them is a massive body-builder. Another likes to pour lighter fluid on his piano and set it afire. In the scene I will undoubtedly remember the longest, he goes to bed with a rock star's girlfriend, who suggests he wear one of the star's condoms—an iridescent glow-in-the-dark model that leads to two of the strangest and funniest scenes Edwards has ever filmed.

If this character seems a little familiar, that's because we've met him before in films by Blake Edwards. He has a lot in common with the Dudley Moore characters in *10* and *Micki & Maude*, the Burt Reynolds character in *The Man Who Loved Women*, and the Jack Lemmon character in *That's Life*. All of these men were in love with sensible, intelligent, dependable, responsible, beautiful women, usually their wives—and yet were driven by lust into the arms of transient conquests, and by alcoholism into the hands of understanding bartenders.

Indeed, the role of best friend and confidant is more important in all of these films than the roles of any of the women except for the one the character starts with. Who could forget Brian Dennehy as the bartender Moore poured his troubles out to in *10*? Or Richard Mulligan, the boss who helped Moore weather the pressures of bigamy in *Micki & Maude*? The John Ritter character in *Skin Deep* is so desperate, he needs two confessors: not only a bartender (Vincent Gardenia) but also a psychiatrist (Michael Kidd).

And yet what can they tell him? That he drinks too much? His alcoholism is visible to everyone in his life, but not to him, and (as Louis Armstrong once said about jazz) there's some folks that, if they don't know, you can't tell 'em. Ritter drinks and complains and suffers and moans and makes a public spectacle of himself and can't write and becomes impotent and considers suicide and thinks he has all of these problems, and finally it takes the shrink to say: "Do you know what I tell alcoholics who want me to help them? First, stop drinking."

This is sound advice, and drunks would save millions in therapy dollars if all psychiatrists were as realistic. But *Skin Deep* is not a *Clean and Sober* set in Malibu. It's a curious hybrid of the serious and the profane, of desperation and farce. The women in the movie all have something in common—they're interesting, opinionated individuals. That goes without saying; bimbos would be turned off by the Ritter character on first sighting, but these women make the mistake of staying around long enough to discover that he is complex and charming, and that gets them into a lot of trouble, since he grows steadily more complex and less charming the more he drinks.

Ritter's performance in *Skin Deep* is a transitional role; he has more depth here, more dimension, than he's shown before, and he is able to handle the trickiest part of playing a drunk in a movie, which is to understand that you are both the clown and the straight man. You're not only the fool, you're the foil that lets other people seem funny. The daring thing Edwards does in *Skin Deep* is to try to combine two entirely different tones within the same film. This is a smart, sensitive film that knows a lot about human nature, and it also has sequences that are deliberately designed to outrage. Look at the ground Edwards covers in that scene where his hero goes to dinner with his ex-wife, ex-mother-in-law, ex-stepson, and the stepson's girlfriend. There's wit, rudeness, satire, lust, and pathos, all effortlessly rolled up to-

gether. *Skin Deep* is sort of a filmmaker's triathlon, and if Edwards doesn't set any new records, at least he enters every event.

Slacker ★ ★ ★
R, 97 m., 1991

Directed, produced, and written by Richard Linklater.

Slacker is a movie with an appeal almost impossible to describe, although the method of the director, Richard Linklater, is as clear as day. He wants to show us a certain strata of campus life at the present time—a group of people he calls "slackers," although anyone who has ever lived in a campus town will also recognize them under such older names as beatniks, hippies, bohemians, longhairs, peaceniks, weirdos, or the Union Regulars (for surely every campus with a student union also has a seemingly permanent body of current and former students who hang around all day drinking free coffee refills and wondering whether life as they know it exists outside the union).

Linklater wants to watch these people and listen to them, but he does not much want to get involved in their lives or follow them through the mechanics of a plot. So he has borrowed an excellent technique from the surrealists and pushed it to its logical conclusion. Surrealist directors such as Luis Buñuel, in movies like *The Phantom of Liberty*, would follow one story for a scene or so, and then—when the characters bumped into another group of people—spin off and follow *them* for a while, and so on until the end of the movie.

Linklater does the same thing at a speeded-up pace that allows him to carom through the slacker community of Austin, Texas, like a cue ball with a camera. Example: Early in the film, a taxi driver picks up a fare (Linklater), who hangs over the back seat and expounds at length on his theory that every time you think of a possibility, that possibility becomes a separate reality on some other level of existence. The taxi driver is not much interested. He drops off his fare just as a car speeds away and some passersby find a woman hit-and-run victim in the street. As help is called, the camera moves in a leisurely circle until it regards a rooming house just as the same hit-and-run car pulls up in front of it. We join the driver of this car in his flat, until he is arrested by police and charged with running down his mother. Then, outside again, we follow some passersby until they . . .

And so on. This sounds like an annoying method, but actually it's rhythmic and soothing—and funny—as Linklater moves through an apparently unlinked assortment of people, including a thief who is buttonholed by his victim and taken for a walk; a man who "knows" that one of the moon astronauts saw an alien spacecraft, but his radio transmission was cut off by NASA; a woman who owns a vial containing the results of an intimate medical procedure carried out on Madonna; and various folk singers, strollers, diners, sleepers, paranoids, do-gooders, quarreling couples, friends, lovers, children, and conspiracy theorists.

We don't get a story, but we do get a feeling. We are listening in on a whole strata of American life that never gets paid attention to in the movies—the people who believe the things they read in magazines sold in places that smell like vitamin B. They have special knowledge, occult beliefs, revolutionary health practices. They know they are being lied to. Listen to them and you will learn how things really are. In a sense, Linklater has invented his whole style in order to listen to these people. He doesn't want to go anywhere with them. He doesn't need a car chase to wrap things up. He is simply amused.

The movie maybe runs on a little too long. Maybe you won't think so. The point is not really what is said, but the tone of voice, the word choices, the conversational strategies, the sense of life going on all the time, everywhere, all over town. In a conventional Hollywood movie, as the brain-dead characters repeat the few robotic phrases permitted them by the formulas of the screenplay, they walk down streets and sometimes I yearn to just peel away from them, cut across a lawn, walk through the wall of a house, and enter the spontaneous lives of the people living there. *Slacker* is a movie that grants itself that freedom.

Sleeper ★ ★ ★ ½
PG, 88 m., 1973

Woody Allen (Miles Monroe), Diane Keaton (Luna), John Beck (Erno), Marya Small (Dr. Nero). Directed by Woody Allen and produced by Jack Grossberg. Screenplay by Allen and Marshall Brickman.

So how would you feel if your name was Miles Monroe and you ran the Happy Carrot Health Food Store in Greenwich Village and you went into St. Vincent's Hospital for a minor operation one morning and woke up two hundred years in the future? And America had become a police state? And the underground wanted to use you because you were the only person alive without an identification number?

What Woody Allen does is scream bloody murder and claim to be a coward: "I'm even beaten up by Quakers." But life becomes a grim struggle, etc., and Woody finds himself at battle with the thought police.

If the plot sounds slightly insane, recollect that one Allen movie began with Howard Cosell doing a play-by-play of an assassination, and another had Woody slapping Listerine under his arms and squirting Right Guard into his mouth before a big date.

Sleeper establishes Woody Allen as the best comic director and actor in America, a distinction that would mean more if there were more comedies being made. Without making a count, I'd guess that a dozen action movies get made for every comedy, which says more about our taste than our comedians. Mel Brooks only seems to get geared up every three years or so, but Allen is prolific as well as funny.

He gives us moments in *Sleeper* that are as good as anything since the silent films of Buster Keaton. There is, for example, a scene where a futuristic instant pudding erupts from a mixing bowl and threatens to fill the kitchen; Woody beats it down with a broom. The scene is part of a long sequence in which he has to pretend to be a robot house servant; he lurches about and buzzes and finally tears up the robot assembly line (in a scene like something from *Modern Times*). Protesting all the way, Allen eventually penetrates into the inner circles of the underground and the government, and discovers the terrible truth about the nation's dictator, known as The Leader.

Nine months earlier, The Leader's home had burned down leaving nothing of The Leader but his nose. Through great medical innovation, the nose has been kept alive ever since, and the plan is to use genetic engineering to grow, or clone, The Leader's body back onto the nose. Inevitably, Allen is mistaken as the chief surgeon.

Whether the movie's Leader bears any relationship to the nation's current chief executive is a secret that only Woody Allen knows; he does not, however, go to many pains to keep it.

There's also a funny satirical scene in which Allen, as a genuine relic of 1973, is asked to identify such artifacts as General de Gaulle, a *Playboy* centerfold, and a Howard Cosell broadcast ("When people committed great crimes, they were forced to watch that.").

Sleeper is the closest Allen has come to classic slapstick-and-chase comedy, and he's good at it. His earlier films depended more on plot (except for *Everything You Always Wanted to Know about Sex*).

And sometimes he had a tendency to get a little sentimental as in *Take the Money and Run*, which opened with a hilarious documentary style biography of its hero, but then got bogged down in a love story that Allen apparently took seriously. (There was even a slow-motion Semi-Obligatory Lyrical Interlude in which Allen and his girl ran through the park and he didn't even seize the opportunity to satirize a Salem commercial.)

This time, though, he moves at breakneck speed and will risk anything, especially the plot, for a gag. Things move so fast we don't even get around to wondering how, in the middle of the movie, Allen got into the Miss America contest . . . and won.

Sleepless in Seattle ★ ★ ★
PG, 100 m., 1993

Tom Hanks (Sam Baldwin), Meg Ryan (Annie Reed), Ross Malinger (Jonah Baldwin), Rita Wilson (Suzy), Victor Garber (Greg), Tom Riis Farrell (Rob), Carey Lowell (Maggie Baldwin). Directed by Nora Ephron and produced by Gary Foster. Screenplay by Ephron, David S. Ward, and Jeff Arch.

If love at first sight is a reality, then in this information age there should also be the possibility of love at first "cyber contact." When people meet via computers or personal ads or phone-in radio shows—when their first sight of each other is through a communications medium—isn't it still possible that some essential chemistry is communicated? That the light in an eye can somehow be implied even over thousands of miles?

That's the hope explored in Nora Ephron's *Sleepless in Seattle*, an unapologetically romantic movie about two people who fall in love from opposite sides of the continent, through the medium of a radio program. In Baltimore, Meg Ryan plays a woman who is already safely engaged—too safely—to a man whose only fault is that he appears to be allergic to almost everything. Then one night, driving in her car, she tunes in a broadcast as a young boy is appealing to the host for help with his father.

Driving through the night, Ryan listens to

the story. The man (Tom Hanks) is called to the phone, and we learn that after his wife died he went into a deep depression before finally packing up his son and moving from Chicago to Seattle. He thought a change of scenery might help, but apparently it hasn't.

Something in the man's voice—or maybe something in his soul that is transmitted along with his voice—appeals to Ryan. She can't get this guy out of her mind. Meanwhile, in Seattle, we get to know the Hanks character, who is an awfully nice man but very sad, and his son (Ross Malinger), who hopes his dad will meet the right woman. His dad has indeed met a woman (Dana Ivey), but since she has a laugh that resembles a hyena's mating call, the son doesn't consider her a contender.

Ephron develops this story with all of the heartfelt sincerity of a 1950s tearjerker (indeed, the movie's characters spend a lot of time watching *An Affair to Remember* and using it as their romantic compass). There is no irony, no distance, no angle on the material. It is about two people who are destined for one another, and that's that. And that was fine with me.

Ephron's earlier screenplay for *When Harry Met Sally* starred Ryan and Billy Crystal, and spent a lot of time showing Harry and Sally not meeting. This film, too, keeps its lovers separate most of the time—although there is a fuzzy scene when Ryan stands in the middle of the street and Hanks gawks at her, and bells ring in his libido.

The plot mechanics, in fact, reminded me of some of those contrived 1940s and 1950s romantic melodramas where events conspired to bring the lovers close but no closer, and then the writers toyed with us by manufacturing devices to keep them apart. By the end of *Sleepless in Seattle*, we're hoping the lovers will meet atop the Empire State Building (a steal from *An Affair to Remember*), and the movie is doing everything to keep that from happening short of assigning Donald Trump to tear it down.

The actors are well suited to this material. Tom Hanks keeps a certain detached edge to his character, which keeps him from being simply a fall guy. Meg Ryan, who is one of the most likable actresses around and has a certain ineffable Doris Day innocence, is able to convince us of the magical quality of her sudden love for a radio voice, without letting the device seem like the gimmick it assuredly is. *Sleepless in Seattle* is as ephemeral as a talk show, as contrived as the late show, and yet so warm and gentle I smiled the whole way through.

Sleuth ★ ★ ★ ★
PG, 138 m., 1972

Laurence Olivier (Andrew Wyke), Michael Caine (Milo Tindle), Alec Cawthorne (Inspector Doppler), Eve Channing (Marguerite), John Matthews (Sergeant Talvant), Teddy Martin (Constable Higgs). Directed by Joseph L. Mankiewicz and produced by Morton Gottleib. Screenplay by Anthony Shaffer.

We come upon Andrew Wyke, the mystery writer, in an appropriate setting. He's in the middle of his vast garden, which is filled with shrubbery planted to form a maze. There is no way into, or out of, the maze—unless you know the secret. The better we come to know Andrew Wyke, the more this seems like the kind of garden he would have.

Wyke is a game-player. His enormous Tudor country manor is filled with games, robots, performing dolls, dart boards, and chess tables. He also plays games with people. One day poor Milo Tindle comes for a meeting with him. Milo is everything Wyke detests: only half-British, with the wrong accent, and "brand-new country gentleman clothes."

But Milo and Andrew's wife have fallen in love, and they plan to marry. So Andrew has a little scheme he wants to float. He is willing—indeed, happy—to give up his wife, but only if he can be sure she'll stay gone. He wants to be sure Milo can support her, and he suggests that Milo steal the Wyke family jewels and pawn them in Amsterdam. Then Milo will have a small fortune, and Andrew can collect the insurance.

Up to this point, everything in *Sleuth* seems so matter-of-fact that there's no hint how complicated things will get later on. But they do get complicated, and deadly, and reality begins to seem like a terribly fragile commodity. Andrew and Milo play games of such labyrinthine ferociousness that they eventually seem to forget all about Andrew's wife (and his mistress) and to be totally absorbed with stalking each other in a macabre game of cat and mouse.

Sleuth, a totally engrossing entertainment, is funny and scary by turns, and always superbly theatrical. It's the kind of mystery we keep saying they don't make anymore, but sometimes they do, and the British seem to write them better than anyone. The movie is based on the long-running play by Anthony Shaffer, who also wrote Alfred Hitchcock's *Frenzy*. Both films have in common a nice flair for dialogue and a delicate counterpoint between the ironic and the gruesome.

What really makes the movie come alive—what makes it work better than the play, really—are the lead performances by Sir Laurence Olivier, Michael Caine, and Alec Cawthorne. Olivier plays the wealthy mystery writer Andrew Wyke as a true-blue British eccentric: His head, like his house, is cluttered with ornate artifacts largely without function. The hero of his detective stories, the wonderfully named St. John Lord Merridewe, is equally dotty. Olivier is clearly having fun in the role, and he throws in all kinds of accents, asides, and nutty pieces of business. Michael Caine, who might seem an unlikely candidate to play Milo Tindle, turns out to be a very good one. He manages somehow to seem smaller and less assured than Olivier (even while he towers over Sir Laurence). And he is strangely touching as he dresses up in an absurd clown's costume to steal the jewels. Inspector Doppler, the kindly old investigator who suspects that Andrew has murdered Milo, is played by Alec Cawthorne, a veteran stage actor making his movie debut.

It's difficult to say more about *Sleuth* without giving away its plot—which in this case would be a capital offense. Let me just mention that the play makes a remarkably easy transition to the screen because of director Joseph L. Mankiewicz's willingness to respect its timing and dialogue, instead of trying to jazz it up cinematically. And, despite the fact that most of the movie takes place indoors, we never get the sense of visual limitations because Ken Adams's set designs give us such an incredible multitude of things to look at (and through) in the mansion.

Small Change ★ ★ ★ ★
PG, 104 m., 1976

Geory Desmouceaux (Patrick), Philippe Goldman (Julien), Christine Pelle (Madame), Jean-François Stevenin and Chantal Mercier (The Teachers). Directed by François Truffaut. Screenplay by Truffaut and Suzanne Schiffman.

There's a moment in François Truffaut's *Small Change* that remembers childhood so well we don't know whether to laugh or cry. It takes place in a classroom a few minutes before the bell at the end of the school day. The class cutup is called on. He doesn't have the answer (he never does), but as he stands up his eyes stray to a large clock outside the window. The hand stands at twenty-eight minutes past the hour. Click: twenty-nine minutes. He stalls, he grins, the teacher repeats the question. Click: thirty past, and the class bell rings. The kid breaks out in a triumphant grin as he joins the stampede from the room.

This moment, like so many in Truffaut's magical film, has to be seen to be appreciated. He re-creates childhood, and yet he sees it objectively, too: He remembers not only the funny moments but the painful ones. The agony of a first crush. The ordeal of being the only kid in class so poor he has to wear the same sweater every day. The painful earnestness that goes into the recitation of a dirty joke that neither the teller nor the listeners quite understand.

Truffaut has been over some of this ground before. His first feature, *The 400 Blows*, told the painful story of a Paris adolescent caught between his warring parents and his own better nature. In *Small Change* he returns to similar material in a sunnier mood. He tells the stories of several kids in a French provincial town, and of their parents and teachers. His method is episodic; only gradually do we begin to recognize faces, to pick the central characters out from the rest. He correctly remembers that childhood itself is episodic: Each day seems separate from any other, each new experience is sharply etched, and important discoveries and revelations become great events surrounded by a void. It's the accumulation of all those separate moments that create, at last, a person.

"Children exist in a state of grace," he has a character say at one point. "They pass untouched through dangers that would destroy an adult." There are several such hazards in *Small Change*. The most audacious—Truffaut at his best—involves a two-year-old child, a kitten, and an open window on the tenth floor. Truffaut milks this situation almost shamelessly before finally giving us the happiest of denouements. And he exhibits at the same time his mastery of film; the scene is timed and played to exist exactly at the border between comedy and tragedy, and from one moment to the next we don't know how we should feel. He's got the audience in his hand.

That's true, too, in a scene involving a little girl who has been made to stay at home as a punishment. She takes her father's battery-powered megaphone and announces indignantly to the neighbors around the court-

yard that she is hungry, that her parents have gone out to a restaurant without her, and that she has been abandoned. The neighbors lower her food in a basket: Chicken and fruit but not, after all, a bottle of red wine one of the neighborhood kids wanted to put in.

In the midst of these comic episodes, a more serious story is developed. It's about the kid who lives in a shack outside of town. He's abused by his parents, he lives by his wits, he steals to eat. His mistreatment is finally found out by his teachers, and leads to a concluding speech by one of them that's probably unnecessary but expresses Truffaut's thinking all the same: "If kids had the vote," the teacher declares, "the world would be a better and safer place."

Smash Palace ★ ★ ★ ★
R, 100 m., 1982

Bruno Lawrence (Al Shaw), Anna Jemison (Jacqui Shaw), Greer Robson (Georgie Shaw), Keith Aberdeen (Ray Foley), Des Kelly (Tiny). Directed and produced by Roger Donaldson. Screenplay by Donaldson, Peter Hansard, and Bruno Lawrence.

Step by step, this powerful movie takes a man from perfect happiness into a personal hell. By the end of the film, the man is behaving irrationally, but here's the frightening thing: Because we've followed him every step of the way, we have to admit he's behaving as we ourselves might, in the same circumstances. The man in *Smash Palace* is Al Shaw, a Grand Prix driver who leaves the racing circuit to take over his father's auto garage in New Zealand. Played by Bruno Lawrence, Al is a straight-talking, direct man who enjoys working with his hands and takes a vast delight in the affections of his wife and the love of his small daughter. It's a long way from the Grand Prix to repairing transmissions, but he's happy with his work and content to raise a family in peace and quiet. His wife (Anna Jemison) is not so content. She wanted him to leave the racing circuit before he was killed, but now, in the quiet backwaters of New Zealand, she is going quietly stir-crazy. She begins an affair with a local cop (Keith Aberdeen) and finally tells her husband she's leaving him. She's moving into town.

Her decision starts him on a series of wrong moves that may seem logical, one by one, but which eventually add up in the minds of others to a simple conclusion: He has lost his reason. He is jealous—of course.

He holds a great fury against his wife and the cop. But, much more important, he misses his daughter. He wants custody. But because he acts in ways that are violent and frightening to his wife (and because her lover is on the police force, which must respond to the domestic emergencies he creates), he works himself into a Catch-22: The more he does to take back his daughter, the closer he is to losing her. Finally, he kidnaps her. He takes her out into the woods where they live together for a time in isolation and happiness. It's an idyll that can't last. But *Smash Palace* doesn't lead up to the inevitable violent conclusion we might expect. All along the way, this film prefers the unexpected turns of actual human behavior to the predictable plot developments we might have expected, and, at the end, there's another turn, a fascinating one.

Smash Palace is one of 1982's best films, an examination of much the same ground as *Shoot the Moon*, but a better film, because it has the patience to explore the ways in which people can become consumed by anger (*Shoot the Moon* contented itself with the outward symptoms). One of the reasons the movie works so well is the performances, which are all the stronger because they come from actors we have not seen before. Bruno Lawrence, bald-headed, wiry, tough, and surprisingly tender, is just right as the man who loses his family. Anna Jemison has a difficult assignment as his wife: We're on his side, and yet we see the logic of her moves. Keith Aberdeen is properly tentative as the other man; he feels love and lust, and yet is not unaware of the unhappiness he is causing. And there's a guy named Des Kelly who plays Tiny, an employee at the Smash Palace who looks on, and sees all, and wishes he knew what to do.

The movie was directed by a young filmmaker named Roger Donaldson, who, in a sense, *is* the New Zealand film industry. He has produced six features for New Zealand television, and his first feature film, *Sleeping Dogs*, starred Warren Oates in a horrifying and plausible fantasy about the American occupation of New Zealand. Now comes this film, so emotionally wise and observant that we learn from it why people sometimes make the front pages with guns in their hands and try to explain that it's all because of love. Love, yes, but also the terrible frustration of trying to control events, to make people do what you want them to do, what you "know" would make them happy—no matter what they think. The hero of *Smash Palace* does not act wisely, but if we are honest, it's hard to see where we might have acted differently.

Smooth Talk ★ ★ ★ ½
PG-13, 92 m., 1986

Laura Dern (Connie), Treat Williams (Arnold Friend), Mary Kay Place (Katherine), Elizabeth Berridge (June), Levon Helm (Harry), Sarah Inglis (Jill). Directed by Joyce Chopra and produced by Martin Rosen. Music by James Taylor. Screenplay by Tom Cole.

There is a certain kind of teen-ager who always seems to be waiting for something. Others live in the moment, but these waiting ones seem to be the victims of time. It stretches before them in long, empty hours. You can look at them and almost literally see the need in their eyes. It is a need to be someone else, somewhere else.

Connie, the heroine in *Smooth Talk*, is a girl like that. She is about fifteen years old, tall, blonde, unformed. At least that is the vision of her we receive the first time we see her. Then there is a transformation scene. She leaves her house, dressed like a teen-ager on the way to a ballgame, and meets her friends at the mall. They go into the ladies' room and apply makeup and mascara and stuff their jackets into their bags, and when they emerge they look like the runners-up in the Madonna lookalike contest. Sexy beyond their own knowledge, they parade through the mall, attracting attention they do not know how to handle. There is a risky, reckless bounce in their step; they are still waiting, but now they seem to know what they are waiting for.

Appearances deceive. Emotionally, Connie is younger than she looks. At home, she suffers because her mother clearly prefers her older sister. She suffers, too, from the well-meaning idiocy of her father, who talks in vague terms of "finally having a home of our own," as if this were Connie's goal, too, and she would always be fifteen and always coming home to it. She looks at her father as if he were speaking a foreign language. He looks at her as if he were seeing someone else. Connie is played by Laura Dern, an actress who seems perfectly suited to this role; she is a chameleon who looks twelve in one shot, eighteen in the next, and is able to suggest the depth of her unhappiness by the way she tries to seem cheerful.

The first hour of *Smooth Talk* is deceptive.

Nothing much seems to happen. Connie and her friends hang out. Connie fights with her parents. Connie waits through the long, endless afternoons of summer. This is the setup for the second half of the movie, which is an astonishing denouement.

Because *Smooth Talk* depends so completely on surprise, it is hard to know how to write about it. Many will be shocked by the movie's ending, and would want to be warned. Others will see it as a modern morality tale, a Grimm story for the late twentieth century, a time when evil seems more banal and seductive than it should. I will walk lightly around the ending without revealing it.

Smooth Talk is based on a short story by Joyce Carol Oates, who so often finds the materials of classic tragedy in the lives of everyday people. Although the movie is shocking, it is not sensational in the way it might have been—if it had been handled as a horror story, say, instead of as a morality play. Oates's story, adapted by Tom Cole and directed by Joyce Chopra, is about a young girl who is surrounded by sexuality, who is curious about it, who flirts dangerously in the wrong places, and who not only learns her lesson, but grows up, all at once, into a different person than she was.

What happens is that a boy (Treat Williams) sees her at the drive-in. He says his name is Arnold Friend, and that he wants to be *her* friend. Everything about this guy is all wrong. He is nowhere near being as young as he says. There is a bad look in his eye. He pals around with another guy, who doesn't say anything, and doesn't need to, because one look at him and you realize he is missing important parts.

Connie walks around in her shorts and halter top, and Arnold Friend watches her. He makes a pass at her, and she puts him off with the kind of cute flirtation that would work with another kid, but Arnold just looks at her—looks through her—and a chill wind seems to blow. One Sunday when Connie is left at home alone and the family is all hours away, Arnold Friend comes to visit. He does not physically rape her. What he does is much worse than that. He talks to her in a way that forever brings an end to her innocence.

Smooth Talk is not a "teen-age movie." It is not, despite its plot, a horror film. It is a study in deviant psychology, and in the power that one person can have over another, especially if they push in the direction where the other person is already headed. The movie is almost uncanny in its self-assurance, in the

way it knows that the first hour, where "nothing" happens, is necessary if the payoff is to be tragic, instead of merely sensational. The movie is also uncanny in what it does with its last three shots. I watched them, and could not believe so much could be implied so simply. Leave the movie before it's over, and you miss almost everything, because what Connie does at the very end of the film is necessary. It makes *Smooth Talk* the story of the process of life, instead of just a sad episode.

The Snapper ★ ★ ★ ½
R, 95 m., 1993

Tina Kellegher (Sharon), Colm Meaney (Dessie), Ruth McCabe (Kay), Colm O'Byrne (Darren), Eanna Macliam (Craig), Ciara Duffy (Kimberley). Directed by Stephen Frears and produced by Lynda Myles. Screenplay by Roddy Doyle.

Here is a movie about some Irish people who love to talk, and take great joy from it. There are times when they have arguments simply for the sake of the art, and they don't always mind being overheard, because they love an audience. Two alone may be silent. Add a stranger at the other end of the room, and they'll start talking, putting on a subtle performance.

This trait is at the heart of the comedy in *The Snapper*, which is a very funny movie about the people packed into small houses on a small street in a tight little neighborhood in Ireland. As the film opens, Sharon Curley (Tina Kellegher), the oldest girl among six children, discovers she is pregnant. She tells her parents, Dessie (Colm Meaney) and Kay (Ruth McCabe), who do not take the news very well, but love her and instinctively stand by her. The father's reaction to the news is typical; first he is incredulous, then he shouts, then he grows philosophical and invites Sharon down to the corner pub for a drink and a bit of a chat.

The telephone is scarcely necessary in the Curley neighborhood; it works too slowly compared to gossip, which soon spreads the news to all ears. A mystery remains, however, about the identity of the father. Sharon refuses for the longest time to identify him, until his own pub gossiping does him in. It's not that she's ashamed, or protective; it's that the circumstances of the impregnation, while both were drunk, casts little credit on anyone, and besides, he's not the sort of bloke she fancies, being a ready-made figure of fun.

All of the stages of the gossip and eventual revelation have to be talked over extensively, of course. Sharon meets her girlfriends down at the pub, where they share giggles and cigarettes and disparagements and fantasies about men. Her dad meets his pals in another room of the same pub and issues dire warnings about the fate of the unknown father, without realizing in one scene that he is actually talking to him.

The Snapper has been directed with a warm, light touch by Stephen Frears, who in *My Beautiful Laundrette* and *Sammy and Rosie Get Laid* showed a similar feeling for closely knit communities in London. But the Irish feel here is distinctive, and much of it no doubt comes from the screenplay by Roddy Doyle, based on his novel. This is Doyle's second story about the same people and milieu; the first was directed by Alan Parker as *The Commitments*. What he sees, and what the films reflect, is that the Irish taste for gossip is leavened by a large amount of understanding and forgiveness. These characters understand human nature.

Look, for example, at the relationship between Sharon and her father in this film. He treats her like a good friend, does not condescend to her femininity or her pregnancy, and is less concerned with "appearances" than with fairness. He and his wife are, in fact, model parents, although that is not always evident in the chaos of their small home, in which up to eight people have to share the same bathroom. Crowded together without privacy, their strategy is to live in public; the whole family shares everything.

Look, too, at the performance by the man who is revealed as the baby's father (I will not name him, although by the time the movie does, it isn't much of a surprise). Look at his all-too-human weaknesses, look at his drinking, look at his own family, and notice how the movie judges him. Almost anyone could get drunk and make a "mistake," but only an "ejit" (the local word for idiot) would boast about it to his mates down at the pub. His sin is not so much lust as stupidity.

The Snapper sees its characters with warmth and acceptance, and earns its laughs by being wise about human nature.

Sniper ★ ★ ★
R, 97 m., 1993

Tom Berenger (Tom Beckett), Billy Zane (Richard Miller), J.T. Walsh (Chester Van Damme). Directed by Luis Llosa and produced by Robert L. Rosen. Screenplay by Michael Frost Beckner and Crash Leyland.

Sniper expresses a cool competence that is a pleasure to watch. It isn't a particularly original film, but what it does, it does well. We've seen so many bad movies about guys walking through the jungle with rifles that it's interesting the way this one grabs us through its command of the locations and its storytelling skill.

The plot could have been borrowed from a Western. Tom Berenger plays a hired gun who knows the terrain well. Billy Zane is the hotshot kid who is an expert marksman but has never killed a man. They're hired as a team to knock off some bad guys, and along the way a rivalry develops, until at the climax their very lives are threatened.

The movie gives this formula a modern political touch by making both Berenger and Zane U.S. military men, acting under secret orders from the National Security Council. Their assignment is to knock off Panamanian leaders the NSC doesn't like, in order to change the outcome of approaching elections. The film's director, Luis Llosa, is a Peruvian, and perhaps this subplot about Yankee imperialism was appealing to him, but the movie simply accepts the illegality of the assignment and gets on with it.

Berenger is a skilled veteran (he could be the character he played in *Platoon,* twenty years down the road). Zane, however, outranks him—and is determined to take command of their little mission, even after it becomes clear he could not find his way out of the jungle with a trail of jelly beans behind him. It's up to Berenger to introduce him to the dangers of the jungle—animal, insect, and human—and eventually they penetrate to the secret rendezvous where their targets will be meeting.

Any movie set in a forest or jungle has trouble convincing us the characters have actually gone anywhere, since all of the trees look the same. Llosa does a good job of making the terrain look real and keeping us oriented, so that we can halfway follow the strategy—until an ending so drenched in rain we have to take him on faith.

It is, I admit, strange that *Sniper* is so blasé about the fact that the heroes are murderers.

After all of those angry Costa-Gavras thrillers about corrupt American death squads, here is a movie that pragmatically assumes that's the way the world turns. Because the movies are such a curiously voyeuristic form, we identify with the heroes and accept their actions, at least as long as the film runs. Afterward, there are some hard questions to answer, but not about Llosa's filmmaking skill.

Soapdish ★ ★ ★ ½
PG-13, 92 m., 1991

Sally Field (Celeste Talbert), Kevin Kline (Jeffrey Anderson), Robert Downey, Jr. (David Barnes), Cathy Moriarty (Montana Moorehead), Whoopi Goldberg (Rose Schwartz), Elisabeth Shue (Lori Craven), Carrie Fisher (Betsy Faye Sharon), Garry Marshall (Edmund Edwards), Teri Hatcher (Ariel Maloney). Directed by Michael Hoffman and produced by Alan Greisman and Aaron Spelling. Screenplay by Robert Harling and Andrew Bergman.

Soapdish is *Network* crossed with *Beyond the Valley of the Dolls,* a soap opera about a soap opera, with a plot that churns together sex, scandal, jealousy, secrets from the past, television in-jokes, and the supreme sacrifice of becoming a brain donor. It's the funniest movie since *The Freshman,* and was written by the same man, Andrew Bergman, this time with the collaboration of Robert Harling and the screwball timing of director Michael Hoffman.

The movie takes place onstage and backstage at one of those long-running daytime soaps with endless plot twists and an almost acrobatic ability to combine sex with the headlines. The current plot line involves the homeless in Jamaica, neurosurgeons, lascivious nurses, and a mute girl in a bathing suit who turns out to be a long-lost daughter, and miraculously regains her power of speech, but contracts a rare condition that will cause her brain to explode within a few days unless her mother agrees to a brain transplant, to be undertaken on the bar of a Jamaican resort, as the surgeon mutters, "I've operated under worse conditions."

The plot, as I have briefly sketched it (and believe me, I've left out most of it), intertwines shocking events that are happening to the characters with equally shocking events affecting the actors in the soap. It literally defies description. And yet the actors somehow hold it together with gifted farcical acting, which involves playing everything completely seriously—especially the completely goofy parts.

Sally Field stars as "America's Sweetheart," the beloved and famous long-running heroine of the soap, who is now the victim of a conspiracy involving the predatory Montana Moorehead (Cathy Moriarty), a blond sex bomb who promises the show's callow young producer (Robert Downey, Jr.) a roll in the hay if he will write Field out of the part.

Field's interests are defended by her best friend and longtime head writer (Whoopi Goldberg), who can't believe Downey wants to resurrect a character who was beheaded in an old episode, but will now be miraculously restored to life. The character was played by Field's long-ago flame (Kevin Kline), who is now reduced to appearing in *Death of a Salesman* in a Florida dinner theater.

The movie knows a lot about television, and has fun with such characters as the network boss (Garry Marshall) and the producer, who is played by Downey as a shameless liar who will blame anything on anybody just to protect his position on the show. Then there is a surprise subplot involving a balloon messenger girl (Elisabeth Shue), who wrangles a bit part as one of the Jamaican homeless, only to suddenly find herself playing a leading role, both on camera and behind it.

This is the kind of movie that is a balancing act, really. If it doesn't work, it fails spectacularly, but it does work, and it succeeds in making its plot clear even though the basic story device is unending confusion. The bravura scenes are distributed nicely among the cast (Kline in front of a senile dinner theater audience, Goldberg and Field artificially staging a scene in a mall to inspire autograph hounds, Moriarty seducing Downey with promises of unimaginable sexual license, if only he writes Field out of the show). Even a TelePrompTer is funny for a scene.

Of the filmmakers, the one best known to me is Andrew Bergman, who wrote and directed *The Freshman* and wrote the hilarious *The In-Laws*. His inventions are like a juggling act, in which three or four plots are kept simultaneously in the air, while the connections between the characters grow increasingly bizarre. Since all of the characters in *Soapdish* are shamelessly venal and banal (the big motivations are lust, greed, jealousy, and vanity), the movie has the purity of a Marx Brothers comedy. Also some of the anarchy.

Some Kind of Wonderful ★ ★ ★
PG-13, 95 m., 1987

Eric Stoltz (Keith Nelson), Mary Stuart Masterson (Drummer Girl), Craig Sheffer (Hardy Jenns), Lea Thompson (Amanda Jones), John Ashton (Mr. Nelson), Elias Koteas (Skinhead). Directed by Howard Deutch and produced by John Hughes. Screenplay by Hughes.

Most movies are not about people. Most movies are about things, and in the category of things I include those movie stars who have become such icons that "they," rather than their characters, perform the adventures in movies.

Hardly ever do we get an American movie about adults who are attempting to know themselves better, live better lives, get along more happily with the people around them. Most American movies are about the giving and receiving of violent pain. That's why I look forward to John Hughes's films about American teen-agers. His films are almost always about the problems of growing up and becoming a more complete person.

Some Kind of Wonderful, which Hughes wrote and produced, and which Howard Deutch directed, is a movie like that. It's not a great movie. It progresses slowly at times and it uses some fairly standard characters. But it is not about whether the hero will get the girl. It is about whether the hero *should* get the girl, and when was the last time you saw a movie that even knew that could be the question?

The film stars Eric Stoltz as Keith, a pleasantly shaggy young man who is an outsider at his high school. He would rather be an artist than fit in with the crowd, and his best friend is another outsider, a tomboy (Mary Stuart Masterson). Keith has a crush on Amanda Jones (Lea Thompson), who is the school sexpot. She goes steady with a stuck-up rich kid.

Here we have all the ingredients, I suppose, for another standard John Hughes teen-ager film. But Hughes always gives his characters the right to be real, and by the end of *Some Kind of Wonderful*, I felt a lot of empathy for these kids.

The Thompson character, for example, is not just a distant, unattainable symbol, but a young woman with feelings. The tomboy doesn't just pine from afar, but helps Keith in his campaign to win a date with this girl of his dreams. And in the final sequence, in which the tomboy acts as chauffeur on the dream date, the dialogue isn't about sex; it's about learning to be true to yourself and not fall for the way people are packaged. By the movie's end, all the characters have learned something about themselves.

I guess I'm making this sound like a film they should show in sociology class. *Some Kind of Wonderful* is a worthwhile film, all right, but it's also entertaining—especially in the scenes between Stoltz and John Ashton, who plays his father. Ashton wants his kid to go to college; the kid would rather devote the energy to his artwork. This disagreement doesn't quite degenerate into a shouting match, and by the end of the film the two are able to have a surprisingly civilized fight about it.

All of the actors in this story are appealing, but my favorite was Masterson as the tomboy whose love is totally overlooked by this guy who thinks he knows all about her. There's something a little masochistic about the way she volunteers to chauffeur him on his big date, but something sweet, too, in the way she cares for him. She has a lot of tricky scenes in which she has to look one way and feel another way, and she's good at them.

Some Kind of Wonderful is yet another film in which Hughes and his team show a special ability to make an entertaining movie about teen-agers which is also about life, about insecurity, about rejection, about learning to grow. As somebody who sees almost all the new movies, I sometimes have the peculiar feeling that the kids in Hughes's movies are more grown up than the adults in most of the other ones.

Something Wild ★ ★ ★ ½
R, 106 m., 1986

Jeff Daniels (Charlie Driggs), Melanie Griffith (Lulu Hankel), Ray Liotta (Ray Sinclair), Margaret Colin (Irene), Jack Gilpin (Larry Dillman), Su Tissue (Peggy Dillman). Directed and produced by Jonathan Demme. Screenplay by E. Max Frye.

She has his number. She looks him straight in the eye and tells him he's the kind of guy who sometimes walks out on a check in a restaurant, just for the secret little sexual charge he gets out of it. He squirms and tries to deny it, but she knows. He's supposed to get right back to the office, but she suggests a little ride around town, and the next thing he knows, he's handcuffed to the bed in a sleazy motel and she's holding the phone up to his mouth so he can lie to his boss.

The opening sequence of Jonathan Demme's *Something Wild* is filled with such a headlong erotic charge that it's hard to see how he can sustain it, and, in fact, he can't. After an hour or so of exuberant sexual comedy, the movie settles down into a slightly more conventional groove, and we can begin to guess what's coming next. It's still a good movie; it's just not as inspired as those risky opening scenes where Demme closes his eyes and steps on the gas.

The movie stars Jeff Daniels as Charlie, a superficially conventional businessman whose heart is easily stirred by boldness in women, and Melanie Griffith as Lulu, an alcoholic sex machine with a very creative imagination. Daniels plays some of the same notes here that he used in *Terms of Endearment,* where he was the sound, dependable, serious husband and father who liked to fool around with cute coeds. He looks like he was born to wear a suit and a tie, but he has that naughty look in his eye. Griffith's performance is based not so much on eroticism as on recklessness: She is able to convince us (and Daniels) that she is capable of doing almost anything, especially if she thinks it might frighten him.

Even while they're standing on the sidewalk in front of that restaurant and she's pretending to accuse him of theft, there's a charge between them. The casting is crucial in a movie like this; there has to be some kind of animal compatibility between the man and the woman or it doesn't matter how good the dialogue is.

Once they've made their connection, Daniels willingly goes along for the ride. After a while she even takes his handcuffs off, although he sort of liked the idea of having lunch in a restaurant with the cuffs dangling from one of his wrists. They drive down the East Coast from New York to Tallahassee, while she steals money from cash registers and he sinks into the waking reverie of the sexually drained.

There's a wonderful scene where she takes him home to meet her mother, introducing him as her husband: "See, Mama? Just the kind of man you said I should marry." Her mother greets them, feeds them, welcomes them and then lets Daniels learn that she knows exactly what's going on: "You look out for that girl." I was reminded of Bonnie's mother in *Bonnie and Clyde,* who saw so clearly through the romance to the death that was approaching.

At Griffith's high school reunion, Daniels runs into the last person he wants to see, the accountant from his office. And Griffith runs into the last person she wants to see, her husband, who is fresh out of prison. He follows them, takes them captive, and forces them to join him on a crime spree. And Daniels realizes that he must fight, not only for the woman he has started to love, but for his life. It's here that the movie begins to feel more conventional, even though a newcomer named Ray Liotta is mesmerizing as the evil husband with vengeance on his mind. We have seen stories before that are more or less like this one, and it becomes easier to foresee the movie's ending. After the freedom and anarchy of the opening and middle scenes, the closing passages feel like a reduction of tension.

But *Something Wild* is quite a movie. Demme is a master of finding the bizarre in the ordinary. Remember his *Melvin and Howard* and the topless dancer who had a cast on her arm? If he had conceived this movie as a "madcap comedy," it probably wouldn't have worked. The accomplishment of Demme and the writer, E. Max Frye, is to think their characters through before the very first scene. They know all about Charlie and Lulu, and so what happens after the meeting outside that restaurant is almost inevitable, given who they are and how they look at each other. This is one of those rare movies where the plot seems surprised at what the characters do.

Sometimes a Great Notion ★ ★ ★
PG, 114 m., 1971

Paul Newman (Hank), Henry Fonda (Henry), Michael Sarrazin (Dan), Lee Remick (Hank's Wife). Directed by Paul Newman and produced by John Foreman. Screenplay by John Gay.

Paul Newman's *Sometimes a Great Notion* tells sort of an old-fashioned story about prideful clans carving empires out of the wilderness. The characters seem a little familiar, too. Take the three most important. Henry Fonda is the proud old patriarch, Paul Newman is the son who stays at home but makes up his own mind, and Michael Sarrazin is the kid brother who comes back to the land with all sorts of half-baked notions and scores to settle. So far, the relationships remind us of *Hud.*

But then Newman starts tunneling under the material, coming up with all sorts of things we didn't quite expect, and along the way he proves himself (as he did with *Rachel, Rachel*) as a director of sympathy and a sort of lyrical restraint. He rarely pushes scenes to their obvious conclusions, he avoids melodrama, and by the end of *Sometimes a Great Notion,* we somehow come to know the Stamper family better than we expected to.

The story takes place during a timber strike in the Northwest. The local merchants (especially the neurotic fellow who runs the movie theater and the dry cleaners) are going broke because money has dried up. The striking timber workers idly hang around the union office. But the Stamper family continues to work in defiance of the strike, and despite the fact that Fonda has broken half the bones on his left side in an accident.

Sarrazin, Newman's half-brother by Fonda's second wife, comes home to help—and also to mope, to get over a bummer of a year, and to suggest to Newman's wife (Lee Remick) that maybe she should clear out from the obsessed Stamper clan. There are a lot of things left fairly unclear, though; I'm not quite sure what was on Remick's mind during most of the movie. The character is left wavering, and we don't fully understand her relationship to her husband. Newman shortchanges what you might call the indoor scenes in order to give us the lumber business.

The best scene in the film takes place during a day of work. The Stamper men seem terribly small as they bring enormous trees crashing to the ground, wrap chains around them, and load them on trucks with big, musclebound machines. The direction of this scene is superb; the reality and the danger of the huge logs are caught in a way that defines the men and their job better than any dialogue could.

Another scene that reveals Newman's insight as a director takes place at a lumbermen's picnic. Some of the strikers invite some of the Stampers to a game of touch football. The game develops into a brawl, of course, but in an interesting way; instead of going for a hard-action approach to the scene, Newman shoots it in a sort of twilight, bittersweet style. All through the film, he avoids making the strikers into heavies and their hatred for the Stampers seem melodramatic. Instead, they're clumsy, resentful enemies, and when they try to sabotage a Stamper lumber raft, they only wind up drifting out to sea—and having to be rescued by the Stampers.

The movie doesn't seem very sure of what it thinks about the Fonda character's fierce and stubborn pride. The character himself believes all that matters is getting up for another day, and working, and eating, and sleeping, and getting on with life. Another character, a brother-in-law, played by Oscar nominee Richard Jaeckel, has been "saved" at the local fundamentalist church and has a sort of sweet simplicity that seems out of place—until the scene where he dies. He dies in a way that is truly filled with grace and humor, and the scene is one of the several things in *Sometimes a Great Notion* that make it worth seeing, even if its overall design is murky.

Songwriter ★ ★ ★ ½
R, 94 m., 1985

Willie Nelson (Doc Jenkins), Kris Kristofferson (Blackie Buck), Melinda Dillon (Honey Carder), Rip Torn (Dino McLeish), Lesley Ann Warren (Gilda), Richard Sarafian (Rocky Rodeo). Directed by Alan Rudolph and produced by Sydney Pollack. Screenplay by Matthew Leonetti.

Songwriter is one of those movies that grows on you. It doesn't have a big point to prove, and it isn't all locked into the requirements of its plot. It's about spending some time with some country musicians who are not much crazier than most country musicians, and are probably nicer than some. It also has a lot of good music.

The movie stars Willie Nelson as a country songwriter named Doc Jenkins, who has a real bad head for business. One day he gets fast-talked into selling control of his company to a slick operator named Rocky Rodeo (Richard Sarafian). Homeless and betrayed, he turns for support to his best friend, a country music star named Blackie (Kris Kristofferson). Blackie, meanwhile, is being promoted by a sleazy manager named Dino (Rip Torn) who has somewhere found a neurotic young singer named Gilda (Lesley Ann Warren). In an early scene that lets us know this movie is not going to be routine, Blackie tries to foist Gilda off on an audience that has paid to see Blackie, and when the audience rebels, Blackie grabs the mike and starts advising them to commit anatomical impossibilities upon themselves.

During the course of some days and nights on the road and back home in Austin, Doc comes up with a clever scheme. Instead of writing any more songs for the despised Dino, he'll write his songs under a pseudonym, and give them to Gilda to record. Blackie will

include Gilda on his next tour, and Dino will get screwed. This seems like a good idea to everybody, especially Gilda, who has a tricky drinking problem and thinks she might be falling in love with Doc.

The movie unwinds casually, introducing us to the other people in the lives of these characters. The most important is Doc's former wife (Melinda Dillon), and the best scene in the movie is where Doc visits her and the kids, and is shy and sweet and tremendously moving. Another good scene is one where Gilda invites Doc into her bed, and he tries to be gentle and tactful in explaining that he doesn't think that's a good idea. Willie Nelson is the key to both of those scenes, and it's interesting how subtle his acting is. Unlike a lot of concert stars whose moves tend to be too large for the intimacy of a movie, Nelson is a gifted, understated actor. Watch the expression on his face as he turns down Gilda; not many actors can say as much with their eyes.

Songwriter was directed by Alan Rudolph, who also made *Choose Me*. Rudolph's teacher was Robert Altman, and, like Altman, he specializes in offbeat rhythms of a group of characters in an unpredictable situation. We never have a clear idea of where *Songwriter* is headed; is it about Doc's love for his first wife, or Gilda's self-destruction, or Rocky Rodeo's con games? It's good that we don't know, because then we don't know what to expect next, and the movie can surprise us.

Both Rudolph and Altman also specialize in unlikely combinations of actors; Kris Kristofferson and Nelson don't, at first, seem to belong in the same movie with Warren, Torn, and Dillon, but watch them work together. One of Torn's great unsung roles was in *Payday*, the movie based on the last days of Hank Williams, Sr. This time, he's like the same character a little further down the road, a little more spaced out. Kristofferson is basically the straight man, the hero's best friend. Nelson sings less and acts more than we expected. And Lesley Ann Warren's performance is endlessly inventive: She takes the fairly standard character of a kooky would-be singer, and makes her into a touching, unforgettable creation.

Sophie's Choice ★ ★ ★ ★
R, 157 m., 1982

Meryl Streep (Sophie), Kevin Kline (Nathan), Peter MacNicol (Stingo), Greta Turken (Leslie Lapidus), Gunther Maria Halmer (Rudolf

Hoess). Directed by Alan J. Pakula and produced by Pakula and Keith Barish. Screenplay by Pakula.

Sometimes when you've read the novel, it gets in the way of the images on the screen. You keep remembering how you imagined things. That didn't happen with me during *Sophie's Choice*, because the movie is so perfectly cast and well-imagined that it just takes over and happens to you. It's quite an experience.

The movie stars Meryl Streep as Sophie, a Polish-Catholic woman, who was caught by the Nazis with a contraband ham, was sentenced to a concentration camp, lost her two children there, and then was somehow spared to immigrate to Brooklyn, U.S.A., and to the arms of an eccentric charmer named Nathan. Sophie and Nathan move into an old boardinghouse, and the rooms just below them are taken by Stingo, a jug-eared kid from the South who wants to be a great novelist. As the two lovers play out their doomed, romantic destiny, Stingo falls in love with several things: with his image of himself as a writer, with his idealized vision of Sophie and Nathan's romance, and, inevitably, with Sophie herself.

The movie, like the book, is told with two narrators. One is Stingo, who remembers these people from that summer in Brooklyn, and who also remembers himself at that much earlier age. The other narrator, contained within Stingo's story, is Sophie herself, who remembers what happened to her during World War II, and shares her memories with Stingo in a long confessional. Both the book and the movie have long central flashbacks, and neither the book nor the movie is damaged by those diversions, because Sophie's story is so indispensable to Stingo's own growth, from an adolescent dreamer to an artist who can begin to understand human suffering. The book and movie have something else in common. Despite the fact that Sophie's story, her choices, and her fate are all sad, sad stories, there is a lot of exuberance and joy in the telling of them. *Sophie's Choice* begins as a young Southerner's odyssey to the unimaginable North—to that strange land celebrated by his hero, Thomas Wolfe, who took the all-night train to New York with its riches, its women, and its romance. Stingo is absolutely entranced by this plump blond Polish woman who moves so winningly into his life, and by her intense, brilliant, mad lover.

We almost don't notice, at first, as Stingo's odyssey into adulthood is replaced, in the film, by Sophie's journey back into the painful memories of her past. The movie becomes an act of discovery, as the naive young American, his mind filled with notions of love, death, and honor, becomes the friend of a woman who has seen so much hate, death, and dishonor that the only way she can continue is by blotting out the past, and drinking and loving her way into temporary oblivion. It's basically a three-character movie, and the casting, as I suggested, is just right. Meryl Streep is a wonder as Sophie. She does not quite look or sound or feel like the Meryl Streep we have seen before in *The Deer Hunter* or *Manhattan* or *The French Lieutenant's Woman*. There is something juicier about her this time; she is merrier and sexier, more playful and cheerful in the scenes before she begins to tell Stingo the truth about her past. Streep plays the Brooklyn scenes with an enchanting Polish-American accent (she has the first accent I've ever wanted to hug), and she plays the flashbacks in subtitled German and Polish. There is hardly an emotion that Streep doesn't touch in this movie, and yet we're never aware of her straining. This is one of the most astonishing and yet one of the most unaffected and natural performances I can imagine.

Kevin Kline plays Nathan, the crazy romantic who convinces everyone he's on the brink of finding the cure for polio and who wavers uncertainly between anger and manic exhilaration. Peter MacNicol is Stingo, the kid who is left at the end to tell the story. Kline, MacNicol, and Streep make such good friends in this movie—despite all the suffering they go through—that we really do believe the kid when he refuses to act on an unhappy revelation, insisting, "These are my *friends*. I love them!"

Sophie's Choice is a fine, absorbing, wonderfully acted, heartbreaking movie. It is about three people who are faced with a series of choices, some frivolous, some tragic. As they flounder in the bewilderment of being human in an age of madness, they become our friends, and we love them.

Sounder ★ ★ ★ ★
G, 105 m., 1972

Cicely Tyson (Rebecca Morgan), Paul Winfield (Nathan Lee Morgan), Kevin Hooks (David Lee Morgan), Carmen Mathews (Mrs. Boatwright), Taj Mahal (Ike), James Best (Sheriff Young), Janet MacLachlan (Camille, the Teacher), Sylvia "Kuumba" Williams (Harriet). Directed by Martin Ritt and produced by Robert B. Radnitz. Screenplay by Lonne Elder III.

Sounder is a story simply told and universally moving. It is one of the most compassionate and truthful of movies, and there's not a level where it doesn't succeed completely. It's one of those rare films that can communicate fully to a child of nine or ten, and yet contains depths and subtleties to engross any adult. The story is so simple because it involves, not so much what people do, but how they change and grow. Not a lot happens on the action level, but there's tremendous psychological movement in *Sounder,* and hardly ever do movies create characters who are so full and real, and relationships that are so loving.

The movie is set in rural Louisiana in about 1933, and involves a black sharecropper family. The boy, David Lee, is twelve or thirteen years old, just the right age to delight in the night-time raccoon hunts he goes on with his father and their hound, Sounder. The hunts are not recreation but necessity. There is no food and no money, and at last, the father steals a ham in desperation. He's sentenced to a year at hard labor, and it's up to the mother and the children (two of them too small to be much help) to get the crop in. They do. "We'll do it, because we have to do it," the mother says.

The boy sets out to find the labor camp where his father is being held. He never does, but he comes across a black school where the teacher talks to him of some of the accomplishments of blacks in America. He decides that he would like to attend her school; by special dispensation, he had been attending a segregated school near his home as sort of a back-row, second-class student.

He returns home, the father returns home, and there is a heartbreaking moment when, for the boy, no school in the world could take him away from this family that loves him. He runs away, filled with angry tears, but his father comes after him and talks to him simply and bluntly: "You lose some of the time what you go after, but you lose all of the time what you don't go after."

The father has a totally realistic understanding of the trap that Southern society set for black sharecroppers, and he is determined to see his son break out of that trap, or else. The scene between the father (Paul Winfield) and the son (Kevin Hooks) is one of the greatest celebrations of the bond between parents and children that I have ever seen in a movie. But it is only one of the scenes like that in *Sounder.*

The mother is played by Cicely Tyson, and it is a wonder to see the subtleties in her performance. We have seen her with her family, and we know her strength and intelligence. Then we see her dealing with the white power structure, and her behavior toward it is in a style born of cynicism and necessity. She will say what they want to hear in order to get what she wants to get.

The story is about love, loss, anger, and hope. That's all, and it's enough; not many movies deal with even one of those subjects with any honesty or power. Hope is probably the emotion evoked most by *Sounder*—the hope of the parents that the school will free their bright and capable son from the dead end of sharecropping; the hope of the teacher, who is representative of the Southern growth of black pride and black studies; and, of course, the boy's hope.

The movie was attacked in a few quarters because of this orientation. It is merely "liberal," some of its critics say. It isn't realistic, it's deceiving. I don't think so. I think it has to be taken as a story about one black family and its struggle. It is, I suppose, a "liberal" film, and that has come to be a bad word in these times when liberalism is supposed to stand for compromise—for good intentions but no action. This movie stands for a lot more than that, and we live in such illiberal times that *Sounder* comes as a reminder of former dreams. It's not surprising that the boy in the movie reminded Mrs. Coretta Scott King of her husband.

This is a film for the family to see. That doesn't mean it's a children's film. The producer, Robert B. Radnitz, has specialized in authentic and serious family films *(A Dog of Flanders, The Other Side of the Mountain).* The director, Martin Ritt, is one of the best American filmmakers (his credits include *Hud, The Molly Maguires,* and *The Great White Hope*), and he has made *Sounder* as a serious and ambitious undertaking. There is no condescension in it, no simplification. The relationship between the man and wife is so completely realized on a mature level that it comes as a shock; we'd forgotten that authentic grown-ups can be portrayed in films. We'd thought, for a moment, that to be a movie adult you had to drive a fast car, be surrounded by sexy dames, and pack an arsenal. *Sounder* proves it isn't so.

South Central ★ ★ ★
R, 100 m., 1992

Glenn Plummer (Bobby), Carl Lumbly (Ali), Christian Coleman (Jimmie), Byron Keith Minns (Ray Ray), LaRita Shelby (Carole), Kevin Best (Genie Lamp). Directed by Steve Anderson and produced by Janet Yang and William B. Steakley. Screenplay by Anderson.

When Bobby gets out of jail, he is still only a kid, but a kid who has been raised on the mean streets of South Central Los Angeles. He is met outside the police station by a car filled with his fellow gang members, and they spray warm beer on a cop before roaring away, laughing. The gang is the only family he really knows, and his days of freedom are like a brief window that opens before the gang gets him back behind bars again—this time, in prison for ten years, for murder.

South Central is a movie about the cycle of crime and gangs that places a generation of young black men on a merry-go-round between violence in the streets and in prison. In some sense, Bobby (Glenn Plummer) is already a loser on his first day of freedom; his best friend, Ray Ray (Byron Keith Minns), is the leader of a gang who knows how to flatter this guy and give him "respect," and talk him into committing murder.

During his brief time on the streets, Bobby discovers that he has a son by his girlfriend, Carole (LaRita Shelby), who is already in the early stages of the drug addiction that will control her life. When he gets out of prison ten years later, Bobby finds Carole completely lost to cocaine, working as a hooker. And his son, who should be blossoming in the innocence of the fourth grade, has already been recruited by Ray Ray as a junior gang member.

But something important happened to Bobby in prison. He came into contact with members of the prison Muslim community, who gave him books to read and ideas to think about, and taught him self-respect. And they did that within a prison system that is seen very clearly in the film as an interlocking struggle between clearly defined racial groups. One of the best scenes in the film shows Muslims and members of the Ayrian Nation negotiating, within generally accepted prison rules, for a penalty Bobby will have to pay for getting out of line.

By the time he leaves prison, Bobby has at last grown enough to see clearly how the gangs have used people like him—how gang leaders are really cynical businessmen who use the dumb, the weak, and the young to commit crimes for them. Everything leads to a crucial final scene in which Bobby and Ray Ray struggle for control of Bobby's son. It is time to break the endless cycle.

One of the words you hear a lot in this movie is "dis," which is street slang for "disrespect," as in "you dissin' me." It is a sad insight on inner-city culture that a word like "disrespect" would be so common that it needed to be shortened. It is also sad that, as used, it has nothing to do with respecting someone for who he is. It is a word often synonymous with "fear," and when a character in this movie asks for respect, it is often because he has a gun and can command it. *South Central* knows about a world where people give respect because they do not want to be killed.

The movie is based on *Crips*, a novel by a South Central L.A. high school teacher named Donald Bakeer. It was written and directed by Steve Anderson, whose view of prison life has a particular authenticity. His anger is also authentic, as he shows clearly how the gangs use drugs and violence to enforce a new kind of slavery. If people are addicted to crack, they will need money to buy it. That helps the gangs two ways: (1) they sell the drugs, making money, and (2) they can encourage addicts to steal, deal, and prostitute for drug money, and then tax the proceeds of their crimes.

Some of the saddest scenes in *South Central* show Carole, who was still almost a child when Bobby's son was born, collapsed in bed in a cocaine haze, and then pulling herself together to go out and try to sell her body. The son lives in this world and knows no other, and so we grow completely involved with Bobby's determination to give his son a chance.

This movie, like *Boyz N the Hood*, is uncompromising in its view of how things work in a neighborhood like South Central. It was made before the Los Angeles riots in April 1992, but it provides a stark picture of the anger that was waiting to boil over. News reports try to tell us what happened in Los Angeles, but fail, because they are limited to the facts. Movies like this one let us feel the emotions.

Southern Comfort ★ ★ ★
R, 106 m., 1981

Keith Carradine (Spencer), Powers Boothe (Hardin), Fred Ward (Reece), Franklyn Seales (Simms), T.K. Carter (Cribbs), Lewis Smith (Stuckey). Directed by Walter Hill and produced by David Giler. Screenplay by Michael Kane, Hill, and Giler.

Southern Comfort is a well-made film, but it suffers from a certain predictability. I suspect the predictability is part of the movie's point. The film is set in the Cajun country of Louisiana, in 1973, and it follows the fortunes of a National Guard unit that gets lost in the bayous and stumbles into a metaphor for America's involvement in Vietnam.

The movie's approach is direct, and its symbolism is all right there on the surface. From the moment we discover that the guardsmen are firing blanks in their rifles, we somehow know that the movie's going to be about their impotence in a land where they do not belong. And as the weekend soldiers are relentlessly hunted down and massacred by the local Cajuns (who are intimately familiar with the bayou), we think of the uselessness of American technology against the Viet Cong.

The guardsmen are clearly strangers in a strange land, and they make fatal blunders right at the outset. They cut the nets of a Cajun fisherman, they "borrow" three Cajun boats, and they mock the Cajuns by firing blank machine-gun rounds at them. The Cajuns are not amused. By the film's end, guardsmen will have been shot dead, impaled, hung, drowned in quicksand, and attacked by savage dogs. And all the time they try to protect themselves with a parody of military discipline, while they splash in circles and rescue helicopters roar uselessly overhead. All this action is shown with great effect in *Southern Comfort*. The movie portrays the bayous as a world of dangerous beauty. Greens and yellows and browns shimmer in the sunlight, and rare birds call to one another, and the Cajuns slip noiselessly behind trees while the guardsmen wander about making fools and targets of themselves. *Southern Comfort* is a film of drum-tight professionalism.

It is also, unfortunately, so committed to its allegorical vision that it never really comes alive as a story about people. That is the major weakness of its director, the talented young Walter Hill, whose credits include *The Warriors*, *The Driver*, and *The Long Riders*. He knows how to make a movie look great, and how to fill it with energy and style. But I suspect he is uncertain about the human dimensions of his characters. And to cover that up, he makes them into larger-than-life stick figures, into symbolic units who stand for everything except themselves. That tendency was carried to its extreme in *The Driver,* a thriller in which the characters were given titles (the Driver, the Girl) rather than names. It was also Hill's approach in *The Warriors,* which translated New York gang warfare into the terms of Greek myth. His approach bothered me so much in *The Warriors* that I overlooked, I now believe, some of the real qualities of that film. It bothers me again in *Southern Comfort.*

Who *are* these men? Of the Cajuns we learn nothing: They are invisible assassins. Of the guardsmen, however, we learn little more. One is swollen with authority. One intends to look out for himself. One is weak, one is strong, and only the man played by Keith Carradine seems somewhat balanced and sane. Once we get the psychological labels straight, there are no further surprises. And once we understand the structure of the movie (guardsmen slog through bayous, get picked off one by one), the only remaining question is whether any of them will finally survive.

That's the weakness of the storytelling. The strength of the movie is in its look, in its superb use of its locations, and in Hill's mastery of action sequences that could have been repetitive. The action is also good: The actors are given little scope to play with in their characters, but they do succeed in creating plausible weekend soldiers. "We are the Guard!" they chant, and we believe them. And there is one moment of inspired irony, when they are lost, cold, wet, hungry, and in mortal fear of their lives, and one guy asks, "Why don't we call in the National Guard?"

Speechless ★ ★
PG-13, 98 m., 1994

Michael Keaton (Kevin), Geena Davis (Julia), Christopher Reeve (Freed), Bonnie Bedelia (Annette), Ernie Hudson (Ventura), Charles Martin Smith (Kratz), Gailard Sartain (Cutler), Ray Baker (Garvin). Directed by Ron Underwood and produced by Renny Harlin and Geena Davis. Screenplay by Robert King.

The romance and marriage of James Carville and Mary Matalin inspired consternation among those who could not understand how such polar opposites could stand each other's company: Why—he worked for Clinton's campaign, and she worked for Bush's! I was underwhelmed. They were complete counterparts in everything except political ideology, and anyone who thinks political

campaigns are about ideology has never been involved in one.

They are, in fact, more about photo opportunities, "sexy issues," sound bites, and image, a point the new movie *Speechless* makes early and often. Allegedly *not* inspired by Carville and Matalin (uh-huh), the film is set in New Mexico, where two consummate bozos are running against one another. The biggest story in the state involves, not politics, but a bear cub that is trapped in a drain pipe at the zoo, and so of course all political strategy boils down to which candidate can identify himself with Winnie the Pooh.

Into the Democratic side of the campaign comes an itinerant speech writer named Kevin (Michael Keaton), who is not even quite sure at first of his candidate's name. Suffering from insomnia, he wanders into an all-night store and finds himself fighting over the Nydol with a woman named Julia (Geena Davis). They fall in love at first sight, start arguing over everything (sitcoms, music on the radio), become romantic under the vast desert sky, and end up making love. The automotive sex scene is, of course, suitable for *Ebert's Little Movie Glossary:* In all such scenes, the grappling couple inevitably activates the horn, lights, radio, windshield wipers, etc.

Come the dawn, and the new friends separate. She, of course, is a strategist for the Republican candidate. Their romance continues, but they don't realize they're political enemies until they both appear at a school Career Day. And here the movie dumbs it down, by showing her anger at his "deception." Their anger inspires some cute reaction shots from the kiddies, but wouldn't these two pros (who have no respect for their candidates) find the discovery funny, rather than enraging? In the real world, once you've slept with someone under the vast desert sky and tiptoed around the awesome possibility of love, it isn't going to make much difference that the other person is a Republican, or even a Democrat.

The movie then slides into its obligatory middle passages, in which the lovers of course feud, and Julia's former fiancé turns up. He's a superstar foreign correspondent named Freed (Christopher Reeve), who bears an uncanny resemblance to Arthur (Scud Stud) Kent, and veteran moviegoers can settle back and watch the predictable moves as Julia considers rehitching with Freed while Kevin gets mad and sabotages her candidate's Tele-PrompTer. (At one point, a candidate gazes

earnestly into the camera and declaims, "Someone is in the kitchen with Dinah!")

Speechless is not without its charms. Both Keaton and Davis are smart as people and smart as actors, and that shows: They generate a nice combination of physical and intellectual chemistry. Bonnie Bedelia and Ernie Hudson have some good moments as campaign pros.

It's just too bad that the director, Ron Underwood, didn't find a way to use more of the offbeat, eccentric character mannerisms that made his earlier films (*Tremors* and *City Slickers*) so much better than their genres. Here the level of humor is dialed safely down to the sitcom setting, which limits what can happen, and how much we can care about it.

Speed ★ ★ ★ ★
R, 115 m., 1994

Keanu Reeves (Jack Traven), Dennis Hopper (Howard Payne), Sandra Bullock (Annie), Joe Morton (Captain McMahon), Jeff Daniels (Harry), Alan Ruck (Stephens), Glenn Plummer (Jaguar Owner). Directed by Jan De Bont and produced by Mark Gordon. Screenplay by Graham Yost.

Speed is like an ingenious wind-up machine. It's a smart, inventive thriller that starts with hostages trapped on an elevator and continues with two chases—one on a bus, one on a subway—so that it's wall-to-wall with action, stunts, special effects, and excitement. We've seen this done before, but seldom so well, or at such a high pitch of energy.

The movie stars Keanu Reeves as a member of the Los Angeles bomb squad. He and his veteran partner (Jeff Daniels) are called in after a mad bomber severs the cables holding an elevator in a high-rise building. Now the terrified passengers are trapped between floors, and the bomber wants three million dollars or he'll push a button and blow off the car's emergency brakes. This situation in itself might make the heart of a thriller, but it's only a curtain-raiser for *Speed,* which turns into a battle of the wills between Reeves and the madman.

The bomber is played by Dennis Hopper, the most dependable and certainly the creepiest villain in the movies right now. He's a former cop with a grudge, an intelligent man with a big bag of tricks who seems able to anticipate every one of Reeves's moves. He wants not only the ransom money but also the satisfaction of humiliating the LAPD, and when he's outsmarted on the elevator caper, his next trick is truly diabolical.

He rigs an ordinary Los Angeles rapid transit bus so that if it exceeds fifty miles an hour, a bomb will be armed—and then, if its speed falls below fifty miles an hour, the bomb will explode. This is an inspiration that will raise many questions for anyone who has ever been in L.A. traffic, but never mind: It provides the basis for an extended, suspenseful chase sequence that comes up with one ingenious crisis after another.

Reeves manages to get himself on board the bus, of course. And after the driver is shot by a passenger, another passenger (Sandra Bullock) grabs the wheel while Reeves tries to think a way out of the dilemma, and the bus cruises at fifty-five miles an hour—in the wrong lanes, in the wrong directions, sideswiping other cars, causing accidents, and eventually ending up on an empty freeway that would provide clear sailing—if it weren't for a fifty-foot gap in an overpass. Can a bus really leap a fifty-foot space? This is the kind of movie where you don't ask questions like that.

The screenplay, by Graham Yost, piles on complications until the movie's very construction is a delight. Bullock keeps her cool at the wheel while Reeves tries stunts like going under the bus to try to disarm the bomb while it continues to bounce along at high speed. Meanwhile, the story intercuts between Hopper, who is issuing ultimatums and dropping sinister hints, and Daniels, back at headquarters, who is using computers to try to figure out the identity of the blackmailer.

When the bus episode finally ends, we sit back, drained, ready for the movie to end, too. But it has another surprise in store, a chase on a subway train, with Bullock held hostage and handcuffed inside one of the cars. All of this is of course gloriously silly, a plundering of situations from the *Indiana Jones* and *Die Hard* movies all the way back to *The Perils of Pauline,* but so what? If it works, it works.

Keanu Reeves has rarely had a role like this before. In fact, in his previous film, he played the mystical Prince Siddhartha, and generally he tends toward dreamy, sensitive characters. That's why it's sort of amazing to see him so cool and focused here, a completely convincing action hero who is as centered and resourceful as a Clint Eastwood or Harrison Ford in similar situations. He and Bullock have good chemistry; they appreci-

ate the humor that is always flickering just beneath the surface of the preposterous plot. And Hopper's dialogue has been twisted into savagely ironic understatements that provide their own form of comic relief.

Films like *Speed* belong to the genre I call Bruised Forearm Movies, because you're always grabbing the arm of the person sitting next to you. Done wrong, they seem like tired replays of old chase clichés. Done well, they're fun. Done as well as *Speed,* they generate a kind of manic exhilaration. The director, Jan De Bont, has worked as a cinematographer on many action classics, including *Basic Instinct* and *Die Hard.* Here he shows his own mastery, in a great entertainment.

The Spider's Stratagem ★ ★ ★
PG, 100 m., 1973

Giulio Brogi (Athos Magnani), Alida Valli (Draifa), Tino Scotti (Costa), Pippo Campanini (Gaibazzi). Directed by Bernardo Bertolucci and produced by Giovani Bertolucci. Screenplay by Bernardo Bertolucci.

Thirty years before, Athos Magnani was a great man, a popular hero, and the leading anti-fascist in the district. But then he was killed, and time has stood still for his little town ever since. It is filled with "old men, madmen, and mad old men," and even though Athos is thirty years dead, he is still the most vital presence in the community.

One day a young man gets off the train for a visit in the village. He is Athos Magnani, Jr., and he looks exactly like his father—so much so, indeed, that his father's mistress attempts to substitute him and begin life all over again in the late 1930s. The son wants to find the killer of his father, in a way. In another way, *The Spider's Stratagem* isn't about a search for a killer, or the truth from the past, or anything else, except a question of human identity: What's more important, who we are, or who people think we are?

The movie is by Bernardo Bertolucci, who later made *Last Tango in Paris.* It's a movie with a beautiful cinematic grace, a way of establishing atmosphere and furthering plot without a lot of talking. We learn all we need to know about the relationship between the father, the son, and the town, in one group of opening shots. The boy stops on "Via Athos Magnani"—a street named for his father—and then approaches the square where his father's statue stands. Bertolucci lines up the deep-focus shot so that it begins with the son completely blocking out

the statue. Then, as he walks through the square, the statue completely obscures the son.

He's on a strange sort of quest. He doesn't seem to really care much who killed his father (if you'll forgive me for not taking the plot at quite face value). In a way, he is his own father, or his father's alter-ego. Magnani was the only vital life force in the district, and the district defined itself by his energy. Even the fascist brownshirts gained stature and dignity because Magnani opposed them, and Bertolucci demonstrates this with a great scene at an outdoor dance. The brownshirts order the band leader to play the fascist anthem. All dancing stops, and everyone looks at Magnani to see what he'll do. Coolly, elegantly, he selects the most beautiful girl and begins to dance with her.

But this is, alas, the last waltz in town, because before long Magnani is shot during a concert. The events leading up to his death, and the identity of his killers, remain very murky. Three fellow anti-fascists claim to have done it, in order to (a) punish Magnani for squealing to the police, and (b) provide the district with a genuine martyr. But did they really? It's hard to say.

The Spider's Stratagem is not, as you've probably gathered, a mass-audience movie. It will have most appeal to people sensitive to Bertolucci's audacious use of camera movements and colors; Pauline Kael said a long time ago that, of all directors influenced by Godard, Bertolucci has been the only one to extend Godard's way of looking, instead of just copying. *The Spider's Stratagem* documents that, and is better to look at than analyze.

Spike of Bensonhurst ★ ★ ★
R, 101 m., 1988

Sasha Mitchell (Spike Fumo), Ernest Borgnine (Baldo), Anne DeSalvo (Sylvia), Sylvia Miles (Congresswoman), Talisa Soto (India), Geraldine Smith (Helen Fumo), Antonia Rey (Bandana's Mother), Rick Aviles (Bandana), Maria Pitillo (Angel), Karen Shallo (Blondie), Chris Anthony Young (Carmine). Directed by Paul Morrissey and produced by David Weisman and Nelson Lyon. Screenplay by Alan Bowne and Morrissey.

Movies imitate life, life imitates movies. Travolta played Tony Manero in *Saturday Night Fever,* Stallone played Rocky Balboa in *Rocky,* and now here is Spike Fumo, a cocky kid from Brooklyn who fools around with the wrong girls, and wants to be a boxer.

Where did he come from? Out of those earlier movies, I'll bet, just like American gangsters in the 1930s learned how to dress and talk by studying Cagney and Raft.

Spike is a thoroughly irresponsible, completely likable character—a kid like everybody knows, who gets away with murder while his friends wait with fascination for a comeuppance that never comes. He lives in an Italian section of Brooklyn, where he boxes out of the local gym and has eyes for a cute blonde who happens to be the daughter of the neighborhood Mafia boss. The boss doesn't want Spike hanging around his daughter. The daughter is being saved for the snotty son of the local Congresswoman. But the problem is, she loves Spike.

That's the setup for Paul Morrissey's *Spike of Bensonhurst*, which is not the best comedy ever made but has energy and local color and a charismatic lead performance by Sasha Mitchell, as Spike. When he gets an unmistakable signal from the mob boss (Ernest Borgnine) that he should leave the neighborhood right away, he goes to live in a nearby Puerto Rican neighborhood with Bandana (Rick Aviles), a friend of his who is also a boxer. And there he falls in love with Bandana's sister, the beautiful, raven-haired India (Talisa Soto). This is the kind of guy that song was written about—the one where if he's not with the one he loves, he loves the one he's with.

The comedy in this movie is generated mostly out of broad racial stereotypes, and I know people who were offended by it; one person told me the film was nothing but an extended racist slur against Italians and Puerto Ricans. This is a hard call. I do not think the filmmakers or the actors had any racist intents. I think they were inspired more by the ethnic humor of TV sitcoms and movies like *Saturday Night Fever*. And because offense was not intended, perhaps none should be taken. When Bandana's mother says she's pleased to meet a kid with Mafia connections because it's a way to move up in the world, is this racism? Or irony? Or sarcasm on her part? The fact that we have to guess makes it funny.

For a movie about a hero who gets both of his girlfriends pregnant, this is a chaste film. Spike never even kisses the beautiful India, although she has her lips parted in expectation at one moment, while we lean forward in our seats. When we learn she's pregnant, we're thunderstruck, because we're still waiting for that first kiss. Talisa Soto, who plays

India, is a famous model who photographs, let it be said, as the most beautiful woman in the movies since Daphne Zuniga. She is gorgeous, but, alas, she cannot act.

Morrissey should have worked with her, showing her how to move more naturally, how not to always look as if she were waiting for a late train. And dialogue coaches might have helped with her speaking voice, which is uninflected and passionless, lacking energy and personality. If she wants to act, and is willing to study hard, there is little she cannot have, because she already has the one thing most movie actors never obtain, an electricity with the camera.

The second half of the movie is not as funny as the first, but there are several big scenes that pay off nicely, especially a wedding party paid for by the Congresswoman (Sylvia Miles), with Borgnine as the guest of honor. *Spike of Bensonhurst* contains Borgnine's funniest performance in a long time; the character is suited to his larger-than-life acting style, and he has a nice comic rapport with Anne DeSalvo, as his wife. The domestic arrangements of a middle-class Mafia household are examined here as hilariously as in *Married to the Mob*, and if we do not care much about the final fight by the time it comes, well, neither do the fighters.

The Spy Who Loved Me ★ ★ ★ ½
PG, 125 m., 1977

Roger Moore (James Bond), Barbara Bach (Anya Amasova), Curt Jurgens (Stromberg), Richard Kiel (Jaws), Caroline Munro (Naomi), Bernard Lee (M), Desmond Llewelyn (Q), Lois Maxwell (Miss Moneypenny). Directed by Lewis Gilbert and produced by Albert R. Broccoli. Screenplay by Christopher Wood and Richard Maibaum.

The best of the James Bond adventures have always depended on cheerfully silly violence, and *The Spy Who Loved Me* is one of the best. It's heartening to see there's life in the old series yet. The first 007 caper was released in 1962, and here's Bond back once again with his beautiful girls, his lethal gadgets, and that tuxedo that never seems to wear out no matter how many mountains he climbs or deserts he treks in it.

There have been a lot of obituaries for the 1960s recently, but, no, Virginia, the sixties will never die, not so long as there is another twenty million dollars somewhere in the world to film another James Bond thriller. Bond lives in that yesterday we can vaguely

remember: in a world of conspicuous consumption, fast cars, unliberated women, bizarre weapons, man-eating creatures of land, air, and sea, archvillains with German accents, and a British Empire upon which the sun has not yet set, although it's getting rather dusky out. The Bond universe is an anachronism, but one we've grown fond of, and *The Spy Who Loved Me* celebrates it with abundant energy. There was a time there, during some of the middle Bonds, when the series seemed to be losing its nerve, to be apologizing for its excesses. But not this time: *The Spy Who Loved Me* is gloriously ridiculous from beginning to end, and that's as it should be.

The stories in a lot of the Bond movies bear only the most tenuous relationship to the original fantasies of Ian Fleming, and that's especially true here. The plot involves a villain named Stromberg, who has a plan to capture nuclear submarines and use them to start World War III, after which he will rule the Earth from his undersea headquarters. British Agent 007 (Roger Moore) is assigned to trace the missing British sub, and Soviet Agent XXX (Barbara Bach) is after the Russian sub.

The chase leads to all sorts of places: Cairo, the pyramids, the desert, Sardinia. And it features the best would-be Bond-killer since the immortal Odd Job in *Goldfinger*; Stromberg's hired assassin, named Jaws (Richard Kiel) stands seven-feet-two-inches tall, has hands about the size of the Sears catalog, and sharp steel teeth that can chomp through wood and steel, attacking sharks and foreign agents.

It's in the showdowns with Jaws that the movie has a lot of its fun. Jaws can tear apart vans, kill a shark one-on-one, hurl Bond through the air with ease, but he keeps getting almost killed—and one of the movie's standing jokes is his incredible power of survival. Agents 007 and XXX, meanwhile, make their way through incredible difficulties to the one obligatory scene in every Bond movie—the scene involving a gigantic indoor set where the destruction of the world is being plotted and enemy troops dressed in matching jumpsuits scurry about on catwalks high up under the ceiling.

The movie is jammed with special effects. It contains, in fact, almost as many spectacular stunts and effects as *Star Wars*, although their terrestrial locale may make them seem more routine. There's a car that turns into a submarine, and a tanker that turns into a sub-snatcher, and all sorts of guided missiles and instruments of oceanic warfare and spectacular explosions, and of course the underwater headquarters of the evil Stromberg, with its hungry sharks lurking at the bottom of the elevator shaft. *The Spy Who Loved Me* is in the tradition of the best Bonds: thrilling, sexy, ridiculous, gimmicky, violent, and, what all the Bonds are supposed to be, preposterous escapist fun.

Stakeout ★ ★ ★
R, 115 m., 1987

Richard Dreyfuss (Chris Lecce), Emilio Estevez (Bill Reimers), Madeleine Stowe (Maria McGuire), Aidan Quinn (Stick), Dan Lauria (Phil Coldshank), Forest Whitaker (Jack Pismo), Ian Tracey (Caylor Reese). Directed by John Badham and produced by Jim Kouf and Cathleen Summers. Screenplay by Kouf.

Richard Dreyfuss has always had a certain cockiness about him. He carries himself like a high-school basketball guard, ready to fake you out and go for the basket. And he talks the same way, often with a little smile to let you know there's an edge to his thinking, an angle. He had that way about him in *The Apprenticeship of Duddy Kravitz,* and he has it still. It keeps me watching him even during the slow passages of his movies; there's always the feeling that what you see is not necessarily all you get.

Dreyfuss and his style are the two best things in *Stakeout,* a movie that consists of a good idea surrounded by a bad one. The good idea is the film's basic premise: Two cops stake out a good-looking woman whose ex-boyfriend is a dangerous escaped convict. During the long, weary hours while they're watching her, one of the cops falls in love. He finds a way to move into her life, leaving his partner stuck across the street with the binoculars.

That's the good idea, further fleshed out with the notion that Dreyfuss and his partner (Emilio Estevez) alternate shifts with two other cops who don't much like them. What would happen if the other cops saw Dreyfuss waking up in bed with the suspect?

The movie's bad idea is that this comic notion needs to be surrounded by a violent thriller. The opening scenes of the film are abrupt and bloody, as the dangerous convict (Aidan Quinn) escapes from prison and heads toward a showdown with Dreyfuss and Estevez. The closing scenes are another bad idea, still one more of those routine Hol-

lywood chases and shoot-outs, with a fight on a boat for good measure.

The two parts of the movie don't go together. The violence is out of keeping with the humor. The humor can't develop in a context of brutality. And yet there's a long central stretch in the movie when things do work, when the courtship between Dreyfuss and the suspect (Madeleine Stowe) gets interesting. Dreyfuss poses as a telephone repairman, bugs her phones, falls in love with her, and eventually begins conducting his investigation from her bedroom. Estevez is stuck with the essentially thankless role of the guy who has to wait across the street and react to everything, but his reactions provide a lot of the movie's humor.

I liked the relationship between Dreyfuss and Stowe, who plays a headstrong Latino, but I might have liked it more if they had cast a funnier actress in the role—maybe Maria Conchita Alonso. Since it's likely that the director, John Badham, tested Alonso for this role, I wonder why he didn't cast her. Perhaps because she has an irrepressible good humor about her, and always seems to be amused by everything; she has the same sort of extra angle that Dreyfuss delivers. Maybe Badham was afraid that good humor would work against the violence of his opening and closing scenes.

But all that's speculation. All I can say is *Stakeout* is an example of a movie that would have been a lot better if the filmmakers had been prepared to trust the human dimensions of their characters—to follow these people where their personalities led. Instead, Badham takes out an insurance policy by adding the assembly-line violence.

What is it? Has mainstream Hollywood so lost touch with simple human nature that you can't have a cop movie without everyone being blown away?

Stardust Memories ★ ★
PG, 89 m., 1980

Woody Allen (Sandy), Charlotte Rampling (Dori), Jessica Harper (Violinist), Marie-Christine Barrault (Frenchwoman). Directed by Woody Allen and produced by Robert Greenhut. Screenplay by Allen.

Woody Allen's *Stardust Memories* is a deliberate homage to *8½,* the 1963 film in which Federico Fellini chronicled several days in the life of a filmmaker who had no idea where to turn next. The major difference between the two films is that Fellini's movie

was *about* a director bankrupt of new ideas, while Allen's is a movie *by* a director with no new ideas. I know that sounds harsh, especially when applied to one of the few American directors who can be counted on for freshness and intelligence, but *Stardust Memories* is an incomplete, unsatisfying film.

The movie begins by acknowledging its sources of visual inspiration. We see a claustrophobic Allen trapped in a railroad car (that's from the opening of *8½,* with Marcello Mastroianni trapped in an auto), and the harsh black-and-white lighting and the ticking of a clock on the sound track give us a cross-reference to the nightmare that opens Ingmar Bergman's *Wild Strawberries.* Are these the exact scenes Allen had in mind? Probably, but no matter; he clearly intends *Stardust Memories* to be his *8½,* and it develops as a portrait of the artist's complaints.

Most of the action of the film centers around two subjects. The first is a weekend film seminar (obviously patterned after Judith Crist's weekends at Tarrytown, N.Y.), to which the Allen character has been invited. The second subject is a very familiar one, Allen's stormy relationships with women. The subjects blend into the basic complaint of the Woody Allen persona we have come to know and love, and can be summarized briefly: If I'm so famous and brilliant and everybody loves me, then why doesn't anybody *in particular* love me?

At the film seminar, the Allen character is constantly besieged by groupies. They come in all styles: pathetic young girls who want to sleep with him, fans who want his autograph, weekend culture vultures, and people who spend all their time at one event promoting the next one they're attending. Allen makes his point early, by shooting these unfortunate creatures in close-up with a wide-angle lens that makes them all look like Martians with big noses. They add up to a nightmare, a nonstop invasion of privacy, a shrill chorus of people whose praise for the artist is really a call for attention.

Fine, except what *else* does Allen have to say about them? Nothing. In the Fellini film, the director-hero was surrounded by sycophants, business associates, would-be collaborators, wives, mistresses, old friends, all of whom made calls on his humanity. In the Allen picture, there's no depth, no personal context: They're only making calls on his time. What's more, the Fellini character was at least trying to create something, to harass his badgered brain into some feeble act of thought. But the Allen character expresses only impotence, despair, uncertainty, discouragement. All through the film, Allen keeps talking about diseases, catastrophes, bad luck that befalls even the most successful. Yes, but that's what artists are for: to hurl their imagination, joy, and conviction into the silent maw. Sorry if I got a little carried away. *Stardust Memories* inspires that kind of frustration, though, because it's the first Woody Allen film in which impotence has become the situation rather than the problem. This is a movie about a guy who has given up. His relationships with women illustrate that; after the marvelous and complex women in *Annie Hall* and *Manhattan,* in *Stardust Memories* we get a series of enigmas and we never really feel that Allen is connecting with them. These women don't represent failed relationships, they represent walk-throughs.

Woody Allen has always loved jazz and the great mainstream American popular music. There's a lot of it in *Stardust Memories,* but it doesn't amplify or illustrate the scene this time—it steals them. There's a scene where Allen remembers a wonderful spring morning spent with a former love (Charlotte Rampling), and how he looked up in his apartment to see her there, and for a moment felt that life was perfect. As Allen shows that moment, Louis Armstrong sings "Stardust" on the sound track, and something happens that should not be allowed to happen. We find our attention almost entirely on Armstrong's wonderfully loose jazz phrasing.

Stardust Memories is a disappointment. It needs some larger idea, some sort of organizing force, to pull together all these scenes of bitching and moaning, and make them lead somewhere.

STAR 80 ★ ★ ★ ★
R, 102 m., 1983

Mariel Hemingway (Dorothy Stratten), Eric Roberts (Paul Snider), Cliff Robertson (Hugh Hefner), Carroll Baker (Dorothy's Mother), Roger Rees (Aram Nicholas). Directed by Bob Fosse and produced by Wolfgang Glattes and Kenneth Utt. Screenplay by Fosse.

Bob Fosse dresses all in black and makes films about the demonic undercurrents in our lives. Look at his credits: *Cabaret, Lenny, All That Jazz,* and now *STAR 80.* Although his Broadway musicals have been upbeat entertainment, he seems to see the movie camera as a device for peering into our shames and secrets. *STAR 80* is his most despairing

film. After the Nazi decadence of *Cabaret,* after the drug abuse and self-destruction in *Lenny,* and the death-obsessed hero of *All That Jazz,* here is a movie that begins with violent death and burrows deeper. There were times when I could hardly keep my eyes on the screen, and a moment near the end when I seriously asked myself if I wanted to continue watching.

And yet I think this is an important movie. Devastating, violent, hopeless, and important, because it holds a mirror up to a part of the world we live in, and helps us see it more clearly. In particular, it examines the connection between fame and obscurity, between those who have a moment of praise and notoriety, and those who see themselves as condemned to stand always at the edge of the spotlight. Like Martin Scorsese's *Taxi Driver,* it is a movie about being an outsider and about going crazy with the pain of rejection.

The movie tells the story of two young people from Vancouver. One of them was Dorothy Stratten, a shy, pretty blonde who thought her hands and feet were too big, who couldn't understand why anyone would value her, and who was close enough to some sort of idealized North American fantasy that she became the 1979 Playmate of the Year. The other was Paul Snider, a Vancouver small-timer who worked as a salesman, con man, and part-time pimp. When Paul saw Dorothy behind the counter of a hamburger stand, he knew she was his ticket to the big time. Dorothy resisted his compliments at first, but he was so relentless in his adoration that she surrendered to his fantasies. Paul masterminded Dorothy's rise. He arranged the photo session that attracted the eye of *Playboy*'s talent scouts. He bought her dresses and flowers. He pushed her into the limelight and then edged into it next to her. But then she went to Los Angeles and found the real stardust, the flattery of the Playboy Mansion, the attentions of young men whose sports cars were bought with their own money, while Paul's was bought with hers.

Paul had a vanity license plate made: STAR 80. But Dorothy had moved out of his world, had been given a taste of a larger world that, frankly, Paul didn't have the class to appreciate. She fell in love with a movie director. She went out of town on location. She and Paul drifted apart, and he went mad with jealousy and resentment. On August 14, 1980, Dorothy went back to the shabby little North Hollywood bungalow they had rented together, and Paul murdered her.

STAR 80 begins with the murder. Everything else is in flashback, and, therefore, the film has no really happy scenes. Dorothy's triumphs are all stained with our knowledge of what will happen. Every time she smiles, it's poignant. We know Paul will go berserk and kill her, and so we can see from the beginning that he's unbalanced. Fosse knows his material is relentlessly depressing, and so he doesn't try for moments of relief. Although we enter the world of *Playboy* and see Dorothy partying in the mansion and posing in nude modeling sessions, although the whole movie is concerned with aspects of sex, there is never an erotic moment. Fosse keeps his distance, regarding Dorothy more as a case study than as a fantasy. That makes Mariel Hemingway's performance as Dorothy all the more powerful. She has been remade into the sleek, glossy Playmate image, but she still has the adolescent directness and naiveté that she used so well in *Manhattan* and *Personal Best.* She's a big kid. Her eyes open wide when she gets to Los Angeles, and she's impressed by the attention she's receiving. The character she plays is simple, uncomplicated, shallow, and so trusting that she never does realize how dangerous Paul is.

The other performances in the movie are equally strong. Eric Roberts as Paul even succeeds in persuading us to accept him as a suffering human being rather than as a hateful killer. Like Robert De Niro as Travis Bickle in *Taxi Driver,* he fills his role with so much reality that we feel horror, but not blame. Carroll Baker, as Dorothy's mother, is heartbreakingly incapable of connecting in any meaningful way with her daughter.

What is the point of *STAR 80?* I'm not sure, just as I wasn't sure of the points of *In Cold Blood* or *Lacombe, Lucien* or "The Executioner's Song." There is no redemption in the movie, no catharsis. It unblinkingly looks at the short life of a simple, pretty girl, and the tortured man who made her into something he couldn't have, and then killed her for it. The movie seems to be saying: These things happen. After it was over, I felt bad for Dorothy Stratten. In fact, for everybody.

Stargate ★
PG-13, 119 m., 1994

Kurt Russell (Colonel Jack O'Neil), James Spader (Dr. Daniel Jackson), Jaye Davidson (Ra), Viveca Lindfors (Catherine), Alexis Cruz (Skaara), Leon Rippy (General West), John Diehl (Lieutenant Kawalsky), Carlos Lauchu

(Anubis). Directed by Roland Emmerich and produced by Joel B. Michaels, Oliver Eberle, and Dean Devlin. Screenplay by Devlin and Emmerich.

Stargate is the kind of movie where a soldier can be transported to "the other side of the known universe" in a whirlpool of bizarre special effects, step into a temple on an alien planet, and say, "What a rush!"

It is also the kind of movie where the sun god Ra, who has harnessed the ability to traverse the universe at the speed of light, still needs slaves to build his pyramids. And where the local equivalent of a Nubian princess is sent into the chamber of the Earth visitors to pleasure them. Don't tell me there aren't any coincidences. The movie *Ed Wood*, about the worst director of all time, was made to prepare us for *Stargate*.

The movie opens with the title "Egypt, 1928." (Other titles say "Present Day" and "Military Installation, Creek Mountain, Colorado"—the latter, of course, with rum-dummy-dum military music.) Scientists uncover a mysterious archeological find. Flash forward to the Present Day, where Egyptologist Daniel Jackson (James Spader), looking uncannily like John Lennon, explains his theories to a roomful of experts, who walk out after about two sentences.

Jackson, who is considered a crackpot, is obviously the man the U.S. government would choose to translate the hieroglyphics on the secret find of that 1928 expedition—a giant circle of carved stone which is a stargate, left behind by the builders of the pyramids. And of course Jackson and Col. Jack O'Neil (Kurt Russell) are the guys to walk through the gate, leading a squad of soldiers with automatic weapons.

The journey through time and space is done with the technique, but not the style, of a similar journey in *2001*. On the other side, the Earth visitors find a desert planet ruled by the god Ra, who is played by Jaye Davidson, previously known for embodying the secret of *The Crying Game*. Here, dressed like a cross between a pharaoh and a Vegas showgirl, he rules a curious society in which spaceships use pyramids as landing pads, but the citizens live like desert nomads from *Lawrence of Arabia*. His voice is distorted by a synthesizer so that it drops several octaves and sounds like an elevator recording with a cold.

Let's say a stargate *was* discovered, allowing instantaneous travel across the universe,

and opening onto a planet that could be inhabited by humans. What would the appropriate response be? Awe? Ambition? Curiosity? Not at all. Col. O'Neil's orders: "Track down signs of any possible danger. If I find any, blow up the stargate."

The movie is so lacking in any sense of wonder that it hurtles us from one end of the universe to the other, only to end in a gunfight between the good guys and the bad guys, while the colonel's bomb ticks down. (Like all movie bombs, it comes equipped with a bright red digital readout device that displays the countdown while beeping.)

Stargate is like a film school exercise. Assignment: Conceive of the weirdest plot you can think of, and reduce it as quickly as possible to action movie clichés. If possible, include sun god Ra, and make sure something gets blowed up real good.

Starman ★ ★ ★
PG, 112 m., 1984

Jeff Bridges (Starman), Karen Allen (Jenny Hayden), Charles Martin Smith (Mark Shermin), Richard Jaeckel (George Fox). Directed by John Carpenter and produced by Larry J. Franco. Screenplay by Bruce A. Evans and Raynold Gideon.

Starman begins by reminding us of Voyager, that little spacecraft that is even now speeding beyond the solar system. Remember Carl Sagan on the "Tonight" show, explaining to Johnny about all the messages that were on board, in case someday an alien race found this postcard from Earth? Voyager carried greetings in all of the tongues of man, and there is something inevitable about the scene, early in *Starman*, when we get an extraterrestrial visitor who has studied them carefully, and is able to say "hello" a hundred different ways.

The starman of the title is a ball of glowing light. He, or it, has traveled to Earth in response to the invitation from Voyager, but of course the Air Force treats the spacecraft as a possible invader and shoots missiles at it. Knocked off course, the starman lands in rural Wisconsin, where it becomes the identical clone of a dead house painter. The painter's widow (Karen Allen) is stunned when she sees this creature from beyond the grave. It is even more difficult when she realizes this is not her husband, but something infinitely different that just happens to look exactly like her husband. The visitor is very smart, but has a lot to learn, and at first it

controls its human host body with a lot of awkward lurching. Meanwhile, government officials led by Richard Jaeckel are seeking the extraterrestrial for "security" reasons, and scientist Charles Martin Smith hopes to get there first and record the historic moment of man's first meeting with a race from another world.

All of this seems like a setup for a science-fiction movie, but what's interesting is the way the director, John Carpenter, makes a U-turn and treats *Starman* as a road movie. The visitor (played by Jeff Bridges) forces Allen to start driving in the direction of the Great Meteor Crater, where he has a rendezvous with his ride home. And as the two characters spend time together as refugees from the search parties, they begin to communicate, and the woman's initial hostility turns into respect and finally into love. This is a wonderfully sweet process, especially as Allen and Bridges go about it. *Starman* contains the potential to be a very silly movie, but the two actors have so much sympathy for their characters that the movie, advertised as space fiction, turns into one of 1984's more touching love stories. Meanwhile, Carpenter provides many of the standard scenes from earlier road movies, including a stop in a roadside diner where the alien's uncertain behavior draws attention. And there's an interlude in Vegas where the extraterrestrial tries to outsmart the slots.

The most interesting thing about *Starman* is probably Bridges's approach to playing a creature from another world. The character grows gradually more human as the film moves along, but he is never completely without glitches: His head movements are birdlike, his step is a little uncertain, he speaks as if there were just a millisecond's delay between brain and tongue. Actors sometimes try to change their appearance; Bridges does something trickier, and tries to convince us that Jeff Bridges is not inhabited by himself. I think he succeeds, and that *Starman* makes Voyager seem like a good investment.

Star Trek: Generations ★ ★
PG, 106 m., 1994

Patrick Stewart (Captain Picard), William Shatner (Captain Kirk), Malcolm McDowell (Soran), Jonathan Frakes (Commander Riker), Brent Spiner (Lieutenant Commander Data), LeVar Burton (Lieutenant Commander LaForge), Whoopi Goldberg (Guinan), Michael Dorn (Lieutenant Worf), Gates McFadden (Dr.

Crusher), Marina Sirtis (Counselor Deanna Troi). Directed by David Carson and produced by Rick Berman. Screenplay by Ronald D. Moore and Brannon Braga.

The Star Trek saga has always had a weakness for getting distracted by itself, and *Star Trek: Generations,* the seventh installment, is undone by its narcissism. Here is a movie so concerned with in-jokes and updates for Trekkers that it can barely tear itself away long enough to tell a story. From the weight and attention given to the transfer of command on the *Starship Enterprise,* you'd think a millennium was ending—which is, by the end of the film, how it feels.

The movie opens during a maiden run for the newly christened *Enterprise B;* plans call for it to take a little dash around the solar system with some reporters on board. But then a call for help is received, and there's polite jockeying for position between the newly appointed Captain Harriman (Alan Ruck) and the just-retired Captain Kirk (William Shatner). Kirk is obviously better equipped to handle the crisis, but alas, the ship itself is unequipped, unmanned, and unready for an emergency.

The emergency involves a free-floating coil of space energy, which has captured two ships in what I think was called its "gravametric field." (Star Trek has never been shy of polysyllabic pseudoscientific gobbledegook, and *Generations* bathes in it; the victims' "life signs are phasing in and out of our spacetime continuum!")

One of the survivors is the intense Dr. Soran (Malcolm McDowell), of the El Aurian species, who insists he *must* get back to his ship. It explodes in the Nexus force field, however, and the story leaps forward seventy-eight years. Captain Picard (Patrick Stewart) finds himself on a rescue mission to an observatory where Dr. Soran is again rescued, and again insists he must return, and lo, here comes the Nexus again, along with an explanation by Guinan (Whoopi Goldberg), the *Enterprise*'s resident mystic, who explains that those caught in the Nexus are "bathed in joy."

We learn that Soran will do anything for that joy, including destroying stars and their planets with millions of inhabitants, just to nudge the Nexus a little out of its way. His calculations are astonishingly precise: By using solar probes to destroy an entire solar system, he can steer the Nexus so that it brushes right above a rickety steel platform he

has constructed in an alien desert, and he can sort of leap up into it and be absorbed in joy.

Meanwhile, there is a lot happening aboard the *Enterprise,* which has a way of being constantly buffeted by force fields and gravametric explosions *except* when Quietly Meaningful Dialogue is being exchanged; at such times the ship is perfectly still. I would estimate that the command deck is being buffeted, filled with smoke, and showered with electrical sparks a good third of the time, with the computers all flashing superfluous "Alert!" warnings, just when you want them to tell you something helpful.

The Star Trek series has always specialized in hilariously klutzy hardware, but outdoes itself this time; the TV cameramen in the opening scenes wear little lights on their heads that illuminate only the centers of the faces of their subjects (surely by the twenty-first century, man, even newsman, will not have forgotten how to light a whole face). And the computer controls aboard the starship now seem modeled on the multiple-choice cash registers at McDonald's, where you just push the Big Mac button instead of needing to know how much it costs.

The running joke this time involves Lieutenant Commander Data (Brent Spiner), a computerized android who tries out a tricky emotion chip and suddenly understands jokes he was told years ago. This notion could have led to some funny scenes, but does not, and the scene where Data shorts out (or his chip crashes, or something) is acted and directed so uncertainly it is positively puzzling.

The Star Trek movies and TV shows always consider at least one Big Important Human Question, and this time it has to do with the Choice Between Happiness and Reality. When you get sucked into the Nexus, see, you *think* you are living once again through the most joyous days of your life. This would be great, except you kinda know you're not, and so both Captain Kirk and Captain Picard must choose between the hazards of reality and the seductive dream world. There's a lesson here somewhere. Hell, there's a lesson here everywhere.

I will not be giving away any secrets if I reveal that Captain Kirk dies in the course of the movie. Countless Trekkers solemnly informed me of this fact in advance. Leave it to Kirk to be discontent with just one death scene, however. Kirk's first death is a very long silence, but he has dialogue for his second one. Oh, my, yes he does. And slips away so subtly I was waiting for more.

I, for one, will miss him. There is something endearing about the Star Trek world, even down to and including its curious tradition that the even-numbered Star Trek movies tend to be better than the odd-numbered ones. And it's fun to hear the obligatory dialogue one more time (my favorite, always said by someone watching the giant view screen, where an unearthly sight has appeared: "What . . . the . . . hell . . . is . . . *that?*").

Star Trek seems to cross the props of science fiction with the ideas of Westerns. Watching the fate of millions being settled by an old-fashioned fistfight on a rickety steel bridge (intercut with close-ups of the bolts popping loose and the structure sagging ominously), I was almost amused by the shabby storytelling. Why doesn't more movie science fiction have the originality and imagination of its print origins? In *Stargate,* the alien god Ra was able to travel the universe, yet still needed slaves to build his pyramids. In *Star Trek: Generations,* the starship can go boldly where no one has gone before, but the screenwriters can only go vice versa.

Star Trek: The Motion Picture ★ ★ ★
G, 132 m., 1979

William Shatner (Kirk), Leonard Nimoy (Spock), DeForest Kelley ("Bones" McCoy), James Doohan (Scotty), George Takei (Sulu), Walter Koenig (Chekov). Directed by Robert Wise and produced by Gene Roddenberry. Screenplay by Harold Livingston.

Two things occurred to me as I watched *Star Trek:*

• The producers have succeeded at great expense in creating a toy for the eyes. This movie is fun to watch.

• Epic science-fiction stories, with their cosmic themes and fast truths about the nature of mankind, somehow work best when the actors are unknown to us. The presence of the *Star Trek* characters and actors—who have become so familiar to us on television—tends in a strange way to undermine this movie. The audience walks in with a possessive, even patronizing attitude toward Kirk and Spock and Bones, and that interferes with the creation of the "sense of wonder" that science fiction is all about.

Let's begin with the toy for the eyes. The *Star Trek* movie is fairly predictable in its plot. We more or less expected that two of the frequent ingredients in the television episodes would be here, and they are: a confrontation between Starship *Enterprise* and some sort of alien entity, and a conclusion in which basic human values are affirmed in a hostile universe. In *Star Trek: The Motion Picture*, the alien entity is an unimaginably vast alien spaceship from somewhere out at the edge of the galaxy. The movie opens as it's discovered racing directly toward Earth, and it seems to be hostile. Where has it come from, and what does it want?

The Starship *Enterprise*, elaborately rebuilt, is assigned to go out to intercept it, with Admiral Kirk, of course, in charge. And scenes dealing with the *Enterprise* and the other ship will make up most of the movie—if the special effects aren't good, the movie's not going to work. But they are good, as, indeed, they should be: The first special-effects team on this movie was fired, and the film's release was delayed a year while these new effects were devised and photographed. (The effects get better, by the way, as the movie progresses. The alien ship looks great but the spaceports and futuristic cities near the film's beginning loom fairly phony.)

The *Enterprise*, perhaps deliberately, looks a lot like other spaceships we've seen in *2001*, *Silent Running*, *Star Wars*, and *Alien*. Kubrick's space odyssey set a visual style for the genre that still seems to be serviceable. But the look of the other spaceship in *Star Trek* is more awesome and original. It seems to reach indefinitely in all directions, the *Enterprise* is a mere speck inside of it, and the contents of the alien vessel include images of the stars and planets it has passed en route, as well as enormous rooms or spaces that seem to be states of a computer-mind. This is terrific stuff.

But now we get to the human level (or the half-human level, in the case of Mr. Spock). The characters in this movie are part of our cultural folklore; the "Star Trek" television episodes have been rerun time and time again. Trekkies may be unhappy with me for saying this, but there are ways in which our familiarity with the series works against the effectiveness of this movie. On the one hand, we have incomprehensible alien forces and a plot that reaches out to the edge of the galaxy. On the other hand, confronting these vast forces, we have television pop heroes. It's great to enjoy the in-jokes involving the relationships of the *Enterprise* crew members and it's great that Trekkies can pick up references meant for them, but the extreme familiarity of the Star Trek characters somehow tends to break the illusion in the big scenes involving the alien ship.

Such reservations aside, *Star Trek: The Motion Picture* is probably about as good as we could have expected. It lacks the dazzling brilliance and originality of *2001* (which was an extraordinary one-of-a-kind film). But on its own terms it's a very well-made piece of work, with an interesting premise. The alien spaceship turns out to come from a mechanical or computer civilization, one produced by artificial intelligence and yet poignantly "human" in the sense that it has come all this way to seek out the secrets of its own origins, as we might.

There is, I suspect, a sense in which you can be too sophisticated for your own good when you see a movie like this. Some of the early reviews seemed pretty blasé, as if the critics didn't allow themselves to relish the film before racing out to pigeonhole it. My inclination, as I slid down in my seat and the stereo sound surrounded me, was to relax and let the movie give me a good time. I did and it did.

Star Trek II: The Wrath of Khan
★ ★ ★
PG, 113 m., 1982

William Shatner (Kirk), Leonard Nimoy (Spock), Ricardo Montalban (Khan), DeForest Kelley ("Bones" McCoy), Kirstie Alley (Lieutenant Saavik). Directed by Nicholas Meyer and produced by Robert Sallin. Screenplay by Jack B. Sowards.

The peculiar thing about Spock is that, being half human and half Vulcan and therefore possessing about half the usual quota of human emotions, he consistently, if dispassionately, behaves as if he possessed very heroic human emotions indeed. He makes a choice in *Star Trek II* that would be made only by a hero, a fool, or a Vulcan. And when he makes his decision, the movie rises to one of its best scenes, because the *Star Trek* stories have always been best when they centered around their characters. Although I liked the special effects in the first movie, they were probably not the point; fans of the TV series wanted to see their favorite characters again, and *Trek II* understood that desire and acted on it.

Time has passed since the last episode. Kirk has retired to an administrative post. Spock is commanding the *Enterprise*, with a lot of new faces in the crew. The ship is on a mission concerning the Genesis device, a new invention which, if I understand it correctly, is capable of seeding a barren planet with luxuriant life. A sister ship, the USS

Reliant, is scouting for lifeless planets and finds one that seems to be dead, but its instruments pick up a small speck of life. Crew members investigate, and find the planet inhabited by an outlaw named Khan, who was exiled there years ago by Kirk, and has brooded of vengeance ever since.

Khan is played as a cauldron of resentment by Ricardo Montalban, and his performance is so strong that he helps illustrate a general principle involving not only *Star Trek* but *Star Wars* and all the epic serials, especially the James Bond movies: Each film is only as good as its villain. Since the heroes and the gimmicks tend to repeat from film to film, only a great villain can transform a good try into a triumph. In a curious way, Khan captures our sympathy, even though he is an evil man who introduces loathsome creatures into the ear canals of two *Enterprise* crew members. Montalban doesn't overact. He plays the character as a man of deeply wounded pride, whose bond of hatred with Admiral Kirk is stronger even than his traditional villain's desire to rule the universe.

There is a battle in outer space in this movie, a particularly inept one that owes more to "Captain Video" than to state-of-the-art special effects. I always love it when they give us spaceships capable of leaping across the universe, and then arm them with weapons so puny that a direct hit merely blows up a few control boards and knocks people off their feet. Somehow, though, I don't much care if the battles aren't that amazing, because the story doesn't depend on them. It's about a sacrifice made by Spock, and it draws on the sentiment and audience identification developed over the years by the TV series.

Perhaps because of that bond, and the sense that an episode may be over but the *Enterprise* will carry on, the movie doesn't feel that it needs an ending in a conventional sense. The film closes with the usual *Star Trek* end narration, all about the ship's mission and its quest, and we are obviously being set up for a sequel. You could almost argue that the last few minutes of *Trek II* are a trailer for *Trek III*, but, no, that wouldn't be in the spirit of the *Enterprise*, would it?

Star Trek III: The Search for Spock
★ ★ ★
PG, 105 m., 1984

William Shatner (Kirk), DeForest Kelley ("Bones" McCoy), James Doohan (Scotty),

Walter Koenig (Chekov), George Takei (Sulu), Nichell Nichols (Uhura), Mark Lenard (Sarek), Leonard Nimoy (Spock). Directed by Leonard Nimoy and produced by Harve Bennett. Screenplay by Bennett.

Read no further if you don't want to know whether Mr. Spock is alive at the end of *Star Trek III: The Search for Spock*. But, if you, like me, somehow had the notion that there was a 100 percent chance that they would find Spock (if only so he would be available for *Star Trek IV*), then you will be relieved to learn that his rediscovery and rebirth pay due homage to the complexities of the Vulcan civilization. By the end of this movie, all Mr. Spock has to do is raise one of those famous eyebrows, and the audience cheers.

This is a good but not great *Star Trek* movie, a sort of compromise between the first two. The first film was a *Star Wars* road company that depended on special effects. The second movie, the best one so far, remembered what made the "Star Trek" TV series so special: not its special effects, not its space opera gimmicks, but its use of science fiction as a platform for programs about human nature and the limitations of intelligence. *Star Trek III* looks for a balance between the first two movies. It has some of the philosophizing and some of the space opera, and there is an extended special-effects scene on the exploding planet Genesis that's the latest word in fistfights on the crumbling edges of fiery volcanoes.

There is also a great-looking enemy spaceship that resembles a predatory bird in flight (although why ships in the vacuum of space require wings is still, of course, a question *Star Trek* prefers not to answer).* The ship is commanded by the fairly slow-witted Klingon warrior Kruge (played by Christopher Lloyd of "Taxi"), who falls for a neat little double cross that is audacious in its simplicity. The movie's plot involves a loyal attempt by the *Enterprise* crew to return to the planet Genesis in an attempt to reunite Spock's body and spirit. The alien spaceship is in the same sector, attempting to steal the secret of Genesis, a weapon from the last movie that begins by bringing life to dead planets and goes on from there. The showdown between the Klingons and the *Enterprise* crew resembles, at times, one of those Westerns where first Bart had the draw on Hoppy and then Hoppy had the draw on Bart, but the struggle to the death between Kirk and Kruge

takes place against such a great apocalyptic background that we forgive all.

The best thing the *Star Trek* movies have going for them is our familiarity with the TV series. That makes for a sort of storytelling shorthand. At no point during this film, for example, is it ever explained that Vulcans are creatures of logic, not emotion—although we have to know that in order to understand most of the ending. It's not necessary. These characters are under our skins. They resonate, and a thin role in a given story is reinforced by stronger roles in a dozen others. That's sort of reassuring, as (a fanfare, please) the adventure continues.

*Leonard Nimoy sent me a helpful explanation: "The Klingon Bird of Prey has wings for the same reason that our own space shuttle does. It can land in an Earth-like atmosphere."

Star Trek IV: The Voyage Home
★ ★ ★ ½
PG, 119 m., 1986

William Shatner (Kirk), Leonard Nimoy (Spock), DeForest Kelley ("Bones" McCoy), Catherine Hicks (Gillian Taylor), Robert Ellenstein (Federation President), Brock Peters (Cartwright), John Schuck (Klingon Ambassador), Jane Wyatt (Spock's Mother). Directed by Leonard Nimoy and produced by Harve Bennett. Screenplay by Steve Meerson, Peter Krikes, Bennett, and Nicholas Meyer.

When they finished writing the script for *Star Trek IV*, they must have had a lot of silly grins on their faces. This is easily the most absurd of the *Star Trek* stories—and yet, oddly enough, it is also the best, the funniest, and the most enjoyable in simple human terms. I'm relieved that nothing like restraint or common sense stood in their way.

The movie opens with some leftover business from the previous movie, including the Klingon ambassador's protests before the Federation Council; these scenes have very little to do with what the rest of the movie is about, and yet they provide a certain reassurance (like James Bond's ritual flirtation with Miss Moneypenny) that the series remembers that it has a history.

Meanwhile, the crew of the Starship *Enterprise* is still marooned on a faraway planet with the Klingon starship* they commandeered in *Star Trek III*. They vote to return home aboard the alien vessel, but on the way they encounter a strange deep-space probe.

It is sending out signals in an unknown language which, when deciphered, turns out to be the song of the humpback whale.

It's at about this point that the script conferences must have really taken off. See if you can follow this: The *Enterprise* crew determines that the probe is zeroing in on Earth, and that if no humpback songs are picked up in response, the planet may well be destroyed. Therefore, the crew's mission becomes clear: Since humpback whales are extinct in the twenty-third century, they must journey back through time to the twentieth century, obtain some humpback whales, and return with them to the future—thus saving Earth. After they thought up this notion, I hope the writers lit up cigars.

No matter how unlikely the story is, it supplies what is probably the best of the *Star Trek* movies so far, directed with calm professionalism by Leonard Nimoy. What happens is that the *Enterprise* crew land their Klingon starship in San Francisco's Golden Gate Park, surround it with an invisibility shield, and fan out through the Bay Area looking for humpback whales and a ready source of cheap nuclear power.

What makes their search entertaining is that we already know the crew members so well. The cast's easy interaction is unique among movies, because it hasn't been learned in a few weeks of rehearsal or shooting; this is the twentieth anniversary year of "Star Trek," and most of these actors have been working together for most of their professional lives. These characters *know* one another.

An example: Admiral Kirk (William Shatner) and Mr. Spock (Leonard Nimoy) visit a Sea World-type operation, where two humpback whales are held in captivity. Catherine Hicks, as the marine biologist in charge, plans to release the whales, and the Trek crew needs to learn her plans so they can recapture the whales and transport them three centuries into the future.

Naturally, this requires the two men to ask Hicks out to dinner. She asks if they like Italian food, and Kirk and Spock do a delightful little verbal ballet based on the running gag that Spock, as a Vulcan, cannot tell a lie. Find another space opera in which verbal counterpoint creates humor.

The plots of the previous Trek movies have centered around dramatic villains, such as Khan, the dreaded genius played by Ricardo Montalban in *Star Trek II*. This time, the villains are faceless: The international whale hunters who continue to pursue and massacre whales despite clear indications that they will drive these noble mammals from the face of the earth. "To hunt a race to extinction is not logical," Spock calmly observes, but we see shocking footage of whalers who are doing just that.

Instead of providing a single human villain as counterpoint, Star Trek IV provides a heroine, in Hicks. She is obviously moved by the plight of the whales, and although at first she not unreasonably doubts Kirk's story that he comes from the twenty-third century, eventually she enlists in the cause and even insists on returning to the future with them, since of course, without humpback whales, the twenty-third century also lacks humpback whale experts.

There are some major action sequences in the movie, but they aren't the high points; the Star Trek saga has always depended more on human interaction and thoughtful, cause-oriented plots. What happens in San Francisco is much more interesting than what happens in outer space, and this movie, which might seem to have an unlikely and ungainly plot, is actually the most elegant and satisfying Star Trek film so far.

Leonard Nimoy, we've got you now.

In Star Trek III, *the Klingon starship was in the shape of a vast, evil bird of prey—inspiring me to ask, in my review of that film, why a starship needed wings to operate in interstellar space. After all, the* Enterprise *certainly didn't have wings.*

You wrote me a helpful note, explaining that the Klingon vessel needed wings because it operated in planetary atmospheres.

All right, except in Star Trek IV, *when the* Enterprise *crew commandeers the Klingon ship and uses it to travel through time, there is a scene in Golden Gate Park where the ship levitates vertically from the grass. If it can conquer gravity, then once again, I ask, why does it have wings?*

Your answer, please?

"It doesn't conquer gravity," he told me soon after the movie opened. "It uses vertical take-off technology, like the Harrier jets in the Royal Air Force."

Oh.

Star Trek V: The Final Frontier ★ ★
PG, 108 m., 1989

William Shatner (Admiral James T. Kirk), Leonard Nimoy (Mr. Spock), DeForest Kelley (Dr. Leonard McCoy), James Doohan (Montgomery Scott), Walter Koenig (Pavel Chekov), Nichell Nichols (Commander Uhura), George Takei (Sulu). Directed by William Shatner and produced by Harve Bennett. Screenplay by David Loughery.

There was a moment in Star Trek V—only one, and a brief one, but a genuine one— when I felt the promise of awe. The Starship Enterprise was indeed going where no man had gone before, through the fabled Great Barrier which represents the end, or perhaps the beginning, of the finite universe. What would lie beyond? Would it be an endless void, or a black hole, or some kind of singularity of space and time that would turn the voyagers inside out and deposit them in another universe? Or would the barrier even reveal, as one of the characters believes, the place where life began? The place called by the name of Eden and countless other words?

As the Enterprise approached the Barrier, I found my attention gathering. The movie had been slow and boring until then, with an interminable, utterly inconsequential first act, and a plot that seemed to exist in a space-time singularity all its own. But now, at last, the fifth Star Trek movie seemed to be remembering what was best about the fictional world of Star Trek : Those moments when man and his ideas are challenged by the limitless possibilities of creation.

As I've said, my awe was real. It was also brief. Once the Enterprise crew members (and the Vulcan who was holding them hostage) had landed on the world beyond the Barrier, the possibilities of God or Eden or whatever quickly disintegrated into an anti-climactic special-effects show with a touch of The Wizard of Oz thrown in for good measure. I do not want to give away important elements in the plot, but after you've seen the movie, ask yourself these questions: (1) How was it known that the voyagers would go beyond the Barrier? (2) What was the motivation behind what they found there? (3) How was it known that they would come to stand at exactly the point where the stone pillars came up from the earth? (4) In a version of a question asked by Kirk, why would any entity capable of staging such a show need its own starship? and (5) Is the Great Barrier indeed real, or simply a deceptive stage setting for what was found behind it? (What I'm really complaining about, I think, is that Star Trek V allows itself enormous latitude in the logic beneath its plot. If the Barrier is real, what exactly are we to make of the use to which it is put?)

Before we get to ask those questions, Star Trek V spends much of its time meandering through some of the goofiest scenes in the entire series. The movie opens with the taking of three hostages on a desert planet, who have been captured for the sole purpose of luring Captain Kirk and his starship to the planet, so that the ship can be commandeered for the voyage through the Barrier. I have explained these plot details in one sentence. The movie takes endless scenes, during which the key crew members of the Enterprise need to be summoned back to their ship in the middle of a shore leave. And that process, in turn, requires interminable scenes of Kirk, Spock, and Bones on a camping trip in Yosemite, during which they attempt to sing "Row, row, row your boat" and nearly succeed in sinking the entire movie. If there is a sillier and more awkwardly written scene in the entire Star Trek saga than this one, I've missed it.

After the pointless opening scenes, the movie begins to develop a plot of sorts, but it is so confused and inadequately explained that there are times when we simply give up and wait for what's next. That was particularly the case during the inexplicable closing scenes, where the humans and the Klingons seem to join sides after an off-camera speech by a former Klingon leader who had been put out to pasture. Since this leader is identified as having been badly treated by the Klingons in his retirement, how did he suddenly regain the authority to negotiate a truce? And, for that matter, do we really *want* to see the mighty Klingons reduced to the status of guests at a cocktail party?

One of the trademarks of the Star Trek saga has been the way the supporting characters are kept alive in little subplots. In Star Trek V, the Enterprise starts its voyage while the ship is suffering a series of mechanical failures, and that involves countless brief scenes in which Scotty, the chief engineer, emerges from beneath a piece of equipment, brandishes his wrench, and says he'll have things fixed in a moment. Two or three of these scenes might have been enough.

Another irritation is the way in which we meet apparently major characters, including those played by David Warner, Laurence Luckinbill, and Cynthia Gouw, who are introduced with fanfares of dialogue and then never developed or given anything to do. The entire movie seems crowded with loose ends, overlooked developments, and forgotten characters, and there are little snatches of dialogue where some of these minor characters seem to be soldiering on in their original subplots as if unaware that they've been cut from the movie.

Star Trek V is pretty much of a mess—a movie that betrays all the signs of having gone into production at a point where the script doctoring should have begun in earnest. There is no clear line from the beginning of the movie to the end, not much danger, no characters to really care about, little suspense, uninteresting or incomprehensible villains, and a great deal of small-talk and pointless dead ends. Of all of the *Star Trek* movies, this is the worst.

Star Trek VI: The Undiscovered Country
★ ★ ★
PG, 109 m., 1991

William Shatner (Kirk), Leonard Nimoy (Spock), DeForest Kelley ("Bones" McCoy), Walter Koenig (Chekov), Nichelle Nichols (Uhura), George Takai (Sulu). Directed by Nicholas Meyer and produced by Ralph Winter and Steven-Charles Jaffe. Screenplay by Meyer and Denny Martin Flinn.

At the end their signatures are written large across the screen: William Shatner, Leonard Nimoy, DeForest Kelley, and the others who have been playing the crew of the Starship *Enterprise* for the past twenty-five years. The implication is that the original voyage of *Star Trek* has come to an end—that the characters and players of the first television series and the six *Star Trek* movies will now go where no *Star Trek* actor has gone before, into retirement, and that if there is another *Star Trek* movie it will star, perhaps, the cast of TV's "Star Trek: The Next Generation."

I am not so sure, however. This sixth *Star Trek* film has so much more life and interest than the dreary *Star Trek V: The Final Frontier* that perhaps it will tempt Paramount into still another story for Captain Kirk and his crew (perhaps a training voyage for the new generation?). *Star Trek VI: The Undiscovered Country* begins, as so many *Star Trek* stories do, with a story set in the future but parallel to contemporary developments. In this case, as the Klingon empire begins to self-destruct after a Chernobyl-type explosion on one of its moons, the obvious reference is to the disintegration of the Russian empire.

As the Klingons sue for peace, the *Enterprise* is assigned to go out to the edges of Federation space and negotiate with them. Captain Kirk is bitterly reluctant; he doesn't believe the Klingons can be trusted, ever. But Mr. Spock informs him of an alleged ancient Vulcan proverb: "Only Nixon can go to China."

There are a lot of lines like that in the script by Nicholas Meyer and Denny Martin Flinn, and a lot of lines by Shakespeare, too, who supplies not only the movie's subtitle but also many references from *Hamlet* and elsewhere ("He is better in the original Klingon," one of the enemy snorts). At one point two of the supporting actors, the distinguished Shakespeareans David Warner and Christopher Plummer, seem to be trading familiar quotations instead of dialogue, but the strange thing is, it's effective; in its pop-culture way, *Star Trek* has taken on a kind of epic quality over the years, and such references help establish the notion that the story really does take place in a future that remembers the past.

If the dialogue is from Shakespeare, the plot seems borrowed more from an old British country house mystery; one or more disloyal members of the *Enterprise* crew fire on a Klingon star cruiser and then transport themselves on board to murder those who have come to ask for peace. Through plot complications that would have made Agatha Christie proud, the clues to the identity of the killers depend on bloody boots and bootprints, and figuring out who was where, and when.

Star Trek has always been more allegory than science fiction. There is a kind of integrity, indeed, in the deliberately low-tech sets; the movies have always remained true to the klutzy art direction of the TV series, and in a post-*2001* and *Star Wars* age the bridge of the Enterprise still looks as if it were made out of old Captain Video props and a 1950s housewares show.

It doesn't matter, because the movies aren't really based on sets, or even much on action; they're about ideas and relationships, and here we see the old friendships of the *Enterprise* tested, and hear new versions of the same old jokes about how Vulcans don't understand jokes. It's entertaining, and reassuring.

Why on earth (or anywhere else) would Paramount want to retire this crew, which is as familiar and comforting as old family friends, and which does its job with the effortless grace of long familiarity? In Shakespeare, the "undiscovered country" is death. And elsewhere the bard refers to one who dies as being like an actor who goes off to "study a long silence." I don't know if that will work here. I doubt frankly that the crew of the *Enterprise* can stop talking long enough to die.

Star Wars ★ ★ ★ ★
PG, 121 m., 1977*

Mark Hamill (Luke Skywalker), Carrie Fisher (Princess Leia), Harrison Ford (Han Solo), Alec Guinness (Obi-Wan Kenobi), David Prowse (Darth Vader), James Earl Jones (Vader's Voice), Kenny Baker (R2D2), Anthony Daniels (C3PO). Directed by George Lucas and produced by Gary Kurtz. Screenplay by Lucas.

Every once in a while I have what I think of as an out-of-the-body experience at a movie. When the ESP people use a phrase like that, they're referring to the sensation of the mind actually leaving the body and spiriting itself off to China or Peoria or a galaxy far, far away. When I use the phrase, I simply mean that my imagination has forgotten it is actually present in a movie theater and thinks it's up there on the screen. In a curious sense, the events in the movie seem real, and I seem to be a part of them.

Star Wars works like that. My list of other out-of-the-body films is a short and odd one, ranging from the artistry of *Bonnie and Clyde* or *Cries and Whispers* to the slick commercialism of *Jaws* and the brutal strength of *Taxi Driver*. On whatever level (sometimes I'm not at all sure) they engage me so immediately and powerfully that I lose my detachment, my analytical reserve. The movie's *happening*, and it's happening to me.

What makes the *Star Wars* experience unique, though, is that it happens on such an innocent and often funny level. It's usually violence that draws me so deeply into a movie—violence ranging from the psychological torment of a Bergman character to the mindless crunch of a shark's jaws. Maybe movies that scare us find the most direct route to our imaginations. But there's hardly any violence at all in *Star Wars* (and even then it's presented as essentially bloodless swashbuckling). Instead, there's entertainment so direct and simple that all of the complications of the modern movie seem to vaporize.

Star Wars is a fairy tale, a fantasy, a legend, finding its roots in some of our most popular fictions. The golden robot, lion-faced space pilot, and insecure little computer on wheels must have been suggested by the Tin Man, the Cowardly Lion, and the Scarecrow in *The Wizard of Oz.* The journey from one end of the galaxy to another is out of countless thousands of space operas. The hardware is from *Flash Gordon* out of *2001,* the chivalry is from *Robin Hood,* the heroes are from Westerns and the villains are a cross between Nazis and sorcerers. *Star Wars* taps the pulp fantasies buried in our memories, and because it's done so brilliantly, it reactivates old thrills, fears, and exhilarations we thought we'd abandoned when we read our last copy of *Amazing Stories.*

The movie works so well for several reasons, and they don't all have to do with the spectacular special effects. The effects *are* good, yes, but great effects have been used in such movies as *Silent Running* and *Logan's Run* without setting all-time box-office records. No, I think the key to *Star Wars* is more basic than that.

The movie relies on the strength of pure narrative, in the most basic storytelling form known to man, the Journey. All of the best tales we remember from our childhoods had to do with heroes setting out to travel down roads filled with danger, and hoping to find treasure or heroism at the journey's end. In *Star Wars,* George Lucas takes this simple and powerful framework into outer space, and that is an inspired thing to do, because we no longer have maps on Earth that warn, "Here there be dragons." We can't fall off the edge of the map, as Columbus could, and we can't hope to find new continents of prehistoric monsters or lost tribes ruled by immortal goddesses. Not on Earth, anyway, but anything is possible in space, and Lucas goes right ahead and shows us very nearly everything. We get involved quickly, because the characters in *Star Wars* are so strongly and simply drawn and have so many small foibles and large, futile hopes for us to identify with. And then Lucas does an interesting thing. As he sends his heroes off to cross the universe and do battle with the Forces of Darth Vader, the evil Empire, and the awesome Death Star, he gives us lots of special effects, yes—ships passing into hyperspace, alien planets, an infinity of stars—but we also get a wealth of strange living creatures, and Lucas correctly guesses that they'll be more interesting for us than all the intergalactic hardware.

The most fascinating single scene, for me, was the one set in the bizarre saloon on the planet Tatooine. As that incredible collection of extraterrestrial alcoholics and bug-eyed martini drinkers lined up at the bar, and as Lucas so slyly let them exhibit characteristics that were universally human, I found myself feeling a combination of admiration and delight. *Star Wars* had placed me in the presence of really magical movie invention: Here, all mixed together, were whimsy and fantasy, simple wonderment and quietly sophisticated storytelling.

When Stanley Kubrick was making *2001* in the late 1960s, he threw everything he had into the special effects depicting outer space, but he finally decided not to show any aliens at all—because they were impossible to visualize, he thought. But they weren't at all, as *Star Wars* demonstrates, and the movie's delight in the possibilities of alien life forms is at least as much fun as its conflicts between the space cruisers of the Empire and the Rebels.

And perhaps that helps to explain the movie's one weakness, which is that the final assault on the Death Star is allowed to go on too long. Maybe, having invested so much money and sweat in his special effects, Lucas couldn't bear to see them trimmed. But the magic of *Star Wars* is only dramatized by the special effects; the movie's heart is in its endearingly human (and non-human) people.

See review of The Hidden Fortress, *p. 853, which inspired Lucas.*

State of Grace ★ ★ ★ ½
R, 134 m., 1990

Sean Penn (Terry), Ed Harris (Frankie), Gary Oldman (Jackie), Robin Wright (Kathleen), John Turturro (Nick), Burgess Meredith (Finn). Directed by Phil Joanou and produced by Ned Dowd, Randy Ostrow, and Ron Rotholz. Screenplay by Dennis McIntyre.

State of Grace is not quite sure which is worse—murder, or yuppies moving into the neighborhood. That's one of its charms. The movie is so sincere and confused in its values that it mirrors the goofy loyalties and violent pathology of its characters. They're low-level Irish-American gangsters who operate in the Hell's Kitchen area of New York City, west of Times Square, and one measure of their success as gangsters is the fact that rising rents are forcing them out of the neighborhood.

The movie opens with a reunion. Terry (Sean Penn), who used to live in the neighborhood, has been on the road for a few years. Now he's back in town, and embracing his best friend Jackie (Gary Oldman) in one of the sleazy saloons where gangsters and winos seem to be the only customers.

Crime in this neighborhood is a family affair. The Irish gang is led by Jackie's older brother Frankie (Ed Harris), who has moved to the suburbs and calls the shots from his middle-class house on a tree-lined street, far from the drug deals that pay his mortgage. The two brothers have a sister named Kathleen (Robin Wright), who has also tried to get out of the neighborhood—she works as a clerk in an uptown hotel. But she and Terry used to be in love, and so, of course, Fate is going to have a hand in what happens next.

Since a great deal of what happens in *State of Grace* depends on an important secret that is not revealed until the second half of the movie, I will have to tread gingerly around some of the details. But the most interesting aspect of the movie is right up front: The confused notion by Jackie that he is, in some way, protecting the neighborhood by committing crimes there. Although the gang's main business seems to be selling drugs, Frankie is willing to pull some jobs simply as a civic service. For example, he takes Terry along one night when he burns down a construction office on a site that will soon be a yuppie apartment building.

Frankie is probably crazy, or maybe his mind has been completely addled by the drugs and booze he has channeled through it. His idea of making arson into fun is to pour the gasoline between himself and the door, and then see if he can run through it without killing himself. He also likes to hold target practice up on the roof. And he is capable of shocking, cold-blooded killing, as he shows in one of the movie's most surprising scenes, a reconciliation with the Mafia that has an unexpected ending.

Gary Oldman's performance in the movie is the best thing about it. Sean Penn is just as good an actor, but he has the lead, and there's not as much he can do with it. He has to be sane and tortured and conflicted, and battle with his opposing emotions. All standard screenplay stuff. Oldman's character is more pure. He acts only on the basis of his instincts and prejudices, or out of vengeance and fear. His character doesn't have to do the fancy footwork.

There are moments in the film that are absolutely chilling—as when Ed Harris, who wanted to be at arm's length from the crimes committed for his profit—finds that he has to personally kill someone he loves. But the movie's plot paradoxically gets less and less original, the more complicated it becomes. At the outset, when it seems concerned only with the behavior of its characters, it's original and challenging. Then it turns into a story filled with familiar elements, and by the end everything is happening by the numbers.

What's best about *State of Grace* is what's unique to it—the twisted vision of the Oldman character, who lives in a world of evil and betrayal and has somehow thought himself around to the notion that he is doing the right thing.

Stay Hungry ★ ★ ★
R, 102 m., 1976

Jeff Bridges (Craig Blake), Sally Field (Mary Tate), Arnold Schwarzenegger (Joe Santo), R.G. Armstrong (Thor Erickson), Robert Englund (Franklin), Helena Kallianiotes (Anita), Roger E. Mosley (Newton), Woodrow Parfrey (Uncle Albert), Scatman Crothers (William). Directed by Bob Rafelson and produced by Harold Schneider and Rafelson. Screenplay by Charles Gaines and Rafelson.

Bob Rafelson's *Stay Hungry* is ungainly and confused at times—it stretches its seams a little too much—but it's a breath of fresh air—a quirky, funny, oddball movie about the most unlikely characters ever to be trapped in the same plot. Jeff Bridges plays the lead, an Alabama blueblood of uncounted generations of aristocracy. He's involved in a real estate deal that involves convincing a gymnasium owner to sell his property so a high-rise can go up. Bridges visits the gym, becomes fascinated by the earnest body-builders and fierce female karate instructors and sort of forgets to do anything about the deal. And one of the body-builders (the former Mr. Universe, Arnold Schwarzenegger, who likes to work out in a rubber Batman suit) introduces him to a sweet young thing he can't help falling in love with.

The girl is played by Sally Field, and she's a simple country type who doesn't exactly fit in with Bridges's genteel cousins; she attends a family party dressed in something that looks mail-ordered from Frederick's of Hollywood. Bridges begins to get letters from his Uncle Albert, who points out that this newfound interest in muscle-building and girls without any breeding is going to qualify him as the family's first black sheep since the cousin who moved to Puerto Rico and opened a goat farm. Meanwhile, the would-be real estate investors turn out to be

mob types with a penchant for sending guys around to wreck the air conditioning.

The movie doesn't concern itself very much with plot; like Rafelson's *Five Easy Pieces* and the underrated *The King of Marvin Gardens*, it introduces us to sharply defined, rather odd characters and then lets them mix it up. The movie is episodic, and some of the episodes are brilliant. Among the best is a scene in which the aged family retainer (Scatman Crothers) announces his resignation and his intention of taking a suit of armor with him, another in which several dozen body-builders race through the startled streets of Birmingham, a harrowing fight scene in a gym in which people throw weights at each other, and a tables-turned situation in which a hooker is forcibly given a massage.

Schwarzenegger, in his first dramatic role, turns in an interesting performance as Bridges's newfound buddy. He works out incessantly, speaks in an Austrian accent, and then turns out to be the lead fiddler in a bluegrass band (people in Rafelson movies are always revealing unsuspected musical abilities).

One of the best things about *Stay Hungry* is that we have almost no idea where it's going; it's as free-form as *Nashville* and Rafelson is cheerfully willing to pause here and there for set pieces like the woman's karate class and the eventual Mr. Universe competition (in which the muscled competitors, back-lit, rise slowly onto a revolving stage in a moment reminiscent of the sunrise in *2001*). When the movie's over, we're still not sure why it was made (maybe it's a subtle comment on Southern class structure—very subtle), but we've had fun and so, it appears, has Rafelson.

Steel Magnolias ★ ★ ★
PG, 118 m., 1989

Sally Field (M'Lynn Eatenton), Dolly Parton (Truvy Jones), Shirley MacLaine (Ouiser Boudreaux), Daryl Hannah (Annelle Dupuy Desoto), Olympia Dukakis (Claree Belcher), Julia Roberts (Shelby Eatenton Latcherie), Tom Skerritt (Drum Eatenton), Sam Shepard (Spud Jones), Dylan McDermott (Jackson Latcherie), Kevin J. O'Connor (Sammy Desoto). Directed by Herbert Ross and produced by Ray Stark. Screenplay by Robert Harling.

Steel Magnolias is essentially a series of comic one-liners leading up to a teary tragedy, but

let it be said that the one-liners are mostly funny and the tragedy deserves most, but not all, of the tears. The movie takes place down in Louisiana during what is said to be the 1980s and involves a tightly knit group of women friends whose husbands (being absent, depressed, or dead) leave them lots of time to gossip at the beauty parlor.

Gossip is what they do best, and one of the characters even appropriates Alice Roosevelt Longworth's immortal line, "If you have something bad to say about somebody . . . sit down right here beside me!" What the women treasure most is anyone with a "past," and when the gawky new girl at the beauty parlor confesses that she "thinks" she is married, they draw closer and hold their breath.

The beauty shop is operated by Dolly Parton in still another reminder that she is one of the sunniest and most natural of actresses. Into her hands, at the beginning of the movie, comes a young bride-to-be (Julia Roberts), who almost faints when she sees herself in the mirror. It's not shock, it's diabetes, but a glass of orange juice brings her around. Parton has just hired a new girl (Daryl Hannah), who does her best with the mother of the bride (Sally Field). Dropping in to exchange insights are Shirley MacLaine, as the richest and meanest woman in town, and Olympia Dukakis, whose character has lost her husband but has a potbellied suitor on the horizon.

These six women are the steel magnolias of the title, Southern belles who are dippy on the outside but strong enough inside to survive any challenge, of which in this film there are many. At first we are not aware of impending tragedy, however, because the movie sticks so successfully to its comic dialogue. I doubt if any six real women could be funny and sarcastic so consistently (every line is an epigram), but I love the way these women talk, especially when Dukakis observes, "What separates us from the animals is our ability to accessorize."

The men do not amount to much in this movie. Tom Skerritt, as the father of the bride, spends much of his time trying to chase pigeons from his trees and the rest of his time grinning benevolently. Sam Shepard, as Parton's husband, lays abed in depression many days and then gets a job on an offshore oil rig that keeps him away for a week at a spell. Dylan McDermott, who is going to marry the bride, is a pleasant nonentity who gets upstaged, or lost track of entirely, at the key events in his life. And then there is the hapless Kevin J. O'Connor, whose seduction of Shirley MacLaine has progressed to the point where she will actually wink at him in church.

No, this is a woman's picture. And the women in it cook and sew and mend and drive each other around town. They fight and make up and hug each other and cry. They get their hair done. And when tragedy strikes and there is a death in their little group, they have the strength to grieve and the character to smile through their tears.

The big scene in the movie is a brief, heartbreaking monologue by Sally Field, who asks God the question that is often uppermost in all our minds: "Why?" The way she asks it, and the words she uses, are tremendously effective, and, yes, we are moved. I heard some snuffling and the blowing of noses. But then the tears are followed by a great big laugh that is very funny but is right on the brink of being a cheap dramatic trick, and we're reminded that *Steel Magnolias*, for all its pretensions, is closer to *Miss Firecracker* than to *Terms of Endearment*.

The movie was written by Robert Harling, based on his own play, and has been directed by Herbert Ross, who choreographs wonderfully entertaining performances from all the women in his cast—especially MacLaine as the town nut case who lurches around in overalls, towed by a big ugly dog. The principal pleasure of the movie is in the ensemble work of the actresses, as they trade one-liners and zingers and stick together and dish the dirt. *Steel Magnolias* is willing to sacrifice its overall impact for individual moments of humor, and while that leaves us without much to take home, you've got to hand it to them: The moments work.

Stella ★ ★ ★ ½
PG-13, 106 m., 1990

Bette Midler (Stella Claire), John Goodman (Ed Munn), Trini Alvarado (Jenny Claire), Stephen Collins (Stephen Dallas), Marsha Mason (Janice Morrison), Eileen Brennan (Mrs. Wilkerson), Linda Hart (Debbie Whitman), Ben Stiller (Jim Uptegrove). Directed by John Erman and produced by Samuel Goldwyn, Jr. Screenplay by Robert Getchell.

Stella is the kind of movie they used to call a tearjerker, and we might as well go ahead and still call it that, because all around me at the sneak preview people were blowing their noses and sort of softly catching their breath—you know, the way you do when you're having a great time. It tells a story that is predictable from beginning to end, except that who would have predicted this old story still had so much life in it, or that the actors would fill it with such warmth and sentiment? *Stella* may be corny, but it's got a great big heart.

The basic plot elements are more or less the same as the last time this story was filmed, starring Barbara Stanwyck, in 1937. A poor but plucky mother has a daughter out of wedlock, proudly refuses financial aid from the rich man who is the father, and raises the girl on her own. Mother and daughter love each other, but the day comes when the mother—a former barmaid now selling cosmetics door to door—realizes that the father and his sophisticated fiancée can give the girl (now of college age) the advantages she needs. So the mother gives away her daughter—all but drives her away—and the ending is pure melodrama.

"Audiences came to sneer and stayed to weep," film historian Leslie Halliwell said of the 1937 version. They're likely to do the same thing this time. Every charge you can make against this movie is probably true—it's cornball, manipulative, unlikely, sentimental, and shameless. But once the lights go down and the performances begin, none of those things really matter, because this *Stella* has a quality that many more sophisticated films lack: It makes us really care about its characters.

Bette Midler and Trini Alvarado play the mother and daughter as well as I can imagine them being played, with style and life. They don't put on long faces and march through the gloom. Midler must have played around with a lot of walks and a lot of accents—she must have experimented with attitudes and personal styles—before she hit on the right note for Stella. She's a tough broad who, as the movie opens in 1969, tends bar for a living and has even been known to climb up on the bar when they play "The Stripper" on the jukebox. She's not educated, but she's smart and funny, and has a determined, independent attitude toward life.

The bar is a working-class, shot-and-beer joint. One night a slick customer comes in wearing a cashmere sweater and a nice smile. He likes the way she has fun when she dances. Against her better judgment, they have an affair, she gets pregnant, he halfway offers to marry her, she says nothing doing, and the rest of the movie is about how she raises the kid, named Jenny, on her own. The father (Stephen Collins) stays in the picture, however, because he comes to love his daughter. So does his fiancée (Marsha Mason). And there is the steady guy in Stella's life, a bartender named Ed (John Goodman) who is a pal, not a lover, and sticks with her through her problems while piling up a lot of his own.

The movie, directed by John Erman and written by Robert Getchell, doesn't miss a single opportunity to generate emotion from its story. There's the girl's sixteenth birthday party, where nobody comes. The lonely Christmas Eve. The crush that Jenny gets on a sincere young preppy, and the way her mother embarrasses her by dancing with the waiter at a posh Florida resort. What *Stella* proves is that no scene is really hackneyed or predictable unless the people making the movie think of it that way. Midler and Alvarado put so much belief into their scenes, so much unforced affection and life, that only an embittered grinch could refuse to be touched.

In an odd sort of way, some of the same notes in *Stella* were played, not so well, in Midler's previous tearjerker, *Beaches* (1988). That one was more sophisticated and cool and knowledgeable, and not half as effective. There are scenes here of great difficulty which Midler plays wonderfully; the scene, for example, where she goes to Marsha Mason's office to ask if Jenny can come to live with Mason and Collins. She believes the time has come to let Jenny take advantage of her father's culture and position, even if that means she loses her daughter: "I'm not gonna let nothing stand in the way of my Jenny," she says. She learns that Mason, the chic publishing executive, comes from a poor, rural background. She asks about Mason's sisters. Are they successful? Are they happy? Mason's face shows they are not. "I knew it," Midler says. "They didn't get out."

Although the story in *Stella* is what manipulates the audience, the style is what makes the movie glow. Midler's Stella shows quiet flashes of the Midler stage persona, especially when she puts people down, and in moderation, the flashes work. So does the movie's refusal to allow Stella to live in self-pity. She sheds some tears, yes, but in her own mind she has achieved a series of victories in bearing a daughter, preserving her own self-esteem, and launching Jenny into the great world. *Stella* is the kind of movie that works you over and leaves you feeling good, unless you absolutely steel yourself against it. Rent it to sneer. Watch it to weep.

Stevie ★ ★ ★ ★
NO MPAA RATING, 102 m., 1981

Glenda Jackson (Stevie Smith), Mona Washbourne (Her Aunt), Alec McCowen (Freddie), Trevor Howard (The Man). Directed and produced by Robert Enders. Screenplay by Hugh Whitemore.

Stevie Smith came across a newspaper clipping one day that told of a man who drowned within a few hundred yards off the shore. The people on the beach saw him waving, and they waved back. The truth, as Stevie expressed it in a famous poem, was the man's problem was just like her own:

> I was much too far out all my life
> And not waving, but drowning.

In those lines, Stevie Smith made an image of her own life, and it is an image that Glenda Jackson's film *Stevie* expresses with clarity, wit, and love.

Stevie Smith was a British poet of considerable reputation, who died in 1971 at the age of sixty-nine. She spent almost all of her life living in a small home in the London suburb of Palmers Green, where she moved as a child. She worked every day in an office in the city, until her growing reputation as a poet allowed her to take an early retirement. She lived with an old maid aunt, and eventually she became an old maid herself. We watch this process as it is punctuated by a marriage proposal, by a visit to Buckingham Palace for tea with the queen, by a half-hearted suicide attempt. Every night, there was definitely a glass or two or more of sherry, or sometimes gin.

To the world, she must have appeared to be an exemplary example of a talented English eccentric. Her poems were irreverent, sharply satirical, and laconic. She was capable of writing one day:

> The Englishwoman is so refined
> She has no bosom and no behind.

And on another day, writing about death:

> I have a friend
> At the end
> of the world.
> His name is a breath
> Of fresh air.

She was not waving, but drowning. The film *Stevie* captures this laconic despair, but it also does a great deal more. It gives us a very particular portrait of a woman's life. The movie is based on a play by Hugh Whitemore, and it contains one of Glenda Jackson's greatest performances. She knows this character well. She played Stevie on the London stage and on a BBC radio production before making this film. She does what great actors can do: She takes a character who might seem uninteresting, and makes us care deeply about the uneventful days of her life.

Although *Stevie* is totally dominated by Jackson's performance, it is not a one-character film by any means. The veteran British actress Mona Washbourne provides a magnificent performance as Stevie's maiden aunt, who is a little dotty and a little giggly and very loving, who likes her glass of sherry and wears flowered print dresses that Stevie says look like a seed catalog illustration titled "They All Came Up." Alec McCowen plays Freddie, the not-so-young man who comes calling, and whose proposal Stevie rejects. And the wonderful Trevor Howard has an ambiguous part as "The Man." On one level, "The Man" is just someone she met at a literary party and conned into giving her rides to poetry readings. At another level, especially when he is seen by himself, telling us about Stevie and reading some of her lines, he is the understanding, forgiving father figure Stevie never had.

Movies like *Stevie* run the risk of looking like photographs of stage plays, but *Stevie* somehow never feels that way. Even though it uses the artifices of the stage (including remarks addressed by Glenda Jackson directly to the audience), and even though a lot of its dialogue is poetry, *Stevie* always feels as if it occupies this woman's life. She is the poet, we are her confidantes, and it is a privilege to get to know her. I have perhaps given the impression that *Stevie* is grim and depressing. It is not at all. It is very sad at times, of course, but there are other times of good humor and barbed wit, when she's not drowning, but waving.

Stop Making Sense ★ ★ ★ ½
NO MPAA RATING, 88 m., 1984

With the Talking Heads: David Byrne, Chris Frantz, Jerry Harrison, and Tina Weymouth. Guest musicians: Edna Holt, Lynn Mabry, Steve Scales, Alex Weir, and Bernie Worrell. Directed by Jonathan Demme and produced by Gary Goetzman.

The overwhelming impression throughout *Stop Making Sense* is of enormous energy, of life being lived at a joyous high. And it's not the frenetic, jangled-nerves energy of a rock band that's wired; it's the high spirits and good health we associate with artists like Bruce Springsteen. There are a lot of reasons to see concert films, but the only ones that usually get mentioned are the music and the cinematography. This time the actual physical impact of the film is just as exhilarating: Watching the Talking Heads in concert is a little like rock 'n' roll crossed with "Jane Fonda's Workout." The movie was shot during two live performances of the Talking Heads, a New York rock band that centers on the remarkable talent of its lead singer, David Byrne. Like David Bowie, his stage presence shows the influence of mime, and some of his best effects in *Stop Making Sense* are achieved with outsize costumes and hand-held lights that create shadow plays on the screen behind him.

Given all the showmanship that will develop later during the film, the opening sequences are a low-key, almost anticoncert throwaway. Byrne walks on a bare stage with a ghetto-blaster in his hand, puts it down on the stage, turns it on and sings along with "Psycho Killer." Eventually he is joined onstage by Tina Weymouth on bass. Then stagehands wander out from the wings and begin to assemble a platform for drummer Chris Frantz. Gear is moved into place. Electrical cables are attached. The backup singers, Edna Holt and Lynn Mabry, appear. And the concert inexorably picks up tempo.

The music of the Talking Heads draws from many sources, in addition to traditional rock 'n' roll. You can hear the echoes, in Byrne's voice, of one of his heroes, country singer Hank Williams. In the music itself, there are elements of reggae and of gospel, especially in the driving repetitions of single phrases that end some of the songs. What is particularly delightful is that the Talking Heads *are* musical: For people who have passed over that invisible divide into the age group when rock sounds like noise, the Heads will sound like music.

The film is good to look at. The director is Jonathan Demme (*Melvin and Howard*), making his first concert film, and essentially using the visuals of the Talking Heads rather than creating his own. Instead of the standard phony cutaways to the audience (phony because, nine times out of ten, the audience members are not actually reacting to the moment in the music that we're hearing), Demme keeps his cameras trained on the stage. And when Byrne and company use the stage-level lights to create a shadow play behind them, the result is surprisingly more effective than you might imagine: It's a live show with elements of *Metropolis*.

But the film's peak moments come through Byrne's simple physical presence. He jogs in place with his sidemen; he runs around the stage; he seems so happy to be alive and making music. Like Springsteen and Prince, he serves as a reminder of how sour and weary and strung-out many rock bands have become. Starting with Mick Jagger, rock concerts have become, for the performers, as much sporting events as musical and theatrical performances. *Stop Making Sense* understands that with great exuberance.

Stormy Monday ★ ★ ★ ½
R, 93 m., 1988

Melanie Griffith (Kate), Tommy Lee Jones (Cosmo), Sting (Finney), Sean Bean (Brendan). Directed by Mike Figgis and produced by Nigel Stafford-Clark. Screenplay by Figgis.

"Why is it," someone was asking the other day, "that you movie critics spend all of your time talking about the story, and never talk about the visual qualities of a film—which are, after all, what *make* it a film?" Good question. Maybe it's because we work in words, and stories are told in words, and it's harder to use words to paint pictures. But it might be worth a try.

Stormy Monday is about the way light falls on wet pavement stones, and about how a neon sign glows in a darkened doorway. It is about the attitudes that men strike when they feel in control of a situation, and the way their shoulders slump when someone else takes power. It is about smoking. It is about cleavage. It is about the look on a man's face when someone is about to deliberately break his arm, and he knows it. And about the look on a woman's face when she is waiting for a man she thinks she loves; he is late, and she fears it is because he is dead.

Stormy Monday is also about symbols. It takes place mostly near the seedy waterfront of Newcastle, where a crooked Texas millionaire is trying to run a nightclub owner out of business, so he can redevelop the area with laundered money. But now we're back to the story again. You see how easy it is to slip. The movie uses a lot of symbols of America: The flag, stretched large and bold behind a podium. Baton-twirlers. A curiously frightening old man with a sinister smile, who struts in front of the baton twirlers, his shoulders thrown back, tipping his hat to

the crowd. A car—big, fast, and red. Bourbon whiskey. Marlboros and cigars.

It is also about lonely furnished rooms, and rain, and standing in the window at night looking out into the street, and signaling for someone across a crowded nightclub floor, and about saxophones, which are the instrument of the night. It is about the flat, masked expressions on the faces of bodyguards, and about the face of a man who is consumed by anger. And it is about kissing, and about the look in a woman's eyes when she is about to kiss a man for the first time. And it is about high heels, and cleavage. I believe I already mentioned cleavage. Some images reoccur more naturally than others.

The movie is not all images. It is also about sounds. About the breathy, rich, and yet uncertain tone of Melanie Griffith's voice, which makes her sound as if she's been around the track too many times, and yet is still able to believe in love. And the flat, angry voice of Tommy Lee Jones, who never seems to raise his voice, or need to. And about the innocence in the voice of Sean Bean, an earnest young man who only wants a job, and gets trapped in a bloodbath. And about the voice of Sting, who looks Jones in the eye and talks as flat and angry as he does, until Jones's shoulders slump. And about saxophones, the sound of the night.

It is also about the sound of a deliberately discordant performance of "The Star Spangled Banner," and about explosions and gunfire and squealing tires, and about modern jazz from Krakow. It is about the sound of ice cubes in a glass, and smoke being exhaled, and bones being broken. It is about the sound of a marching band, and about the voice of a disc jockey who wants to sound American and doesn't know when to stop. And about how a woman tells a man, "I get off work at midnight." And how she looks when she says that. And how he looks.

So there's your review.

The Story of Qiu Ju ★ ★ ★ ½
NO MPAA RATING, 100 m., 1993

Gong Li (Qiu Ju), Lei Lao Sheng (Village Head), Liu Pei Qi (Qiu Ju's Husband), Ge Zhi Jun (Mr Li, Local Public Security Chief), Yang Liu Chun (Sister-in-Law). Directed by Zhang Yimou and produced by Ma Fung Kwok. Screenplay by Liu Heng.

The Story of Qiu Ju begins with a shot of a Chinese city scene, the streets teeming with people, most of them on foot or bicycle.

Eventually the camera isolates three of them: a man sprawled uncomfortably on a cart, and two women who are pushing him. One of the women is very pregnant. After they arrive at a doctor's office, she explains that her husband has been kicked in the groin by their village political leader.

The doctor is not the sort to inspire confidence. He advises rest. Soon the women—sisters—are making the journey back home again, pulling the cart through cold winter weather to their rural village. The husband is inclined to take his fate philosophically, and wait for his pain to subside. Not Qiu Ju, the wife. "If we can't fix your plumbing, we may be stuck with the single-child policy," she laments. She wants to see justice done.

So begins the story of two very stubborn people, Qiu Ju and the political head, played by Lei Lao Sheng. Qiu Ju is played by Gong Li, the most famous Chinese actress, and the movie is directed by Zhang Yimou, the most successful of the "fifth generation" of Chinese directors. She has starred in all of his films: *Red Sorghum, Ju Dou, Raise the Red Lantern*. Even in the gritty worlds of the first two films, she looked beautiful, and in the third she was glamorous. But here, in Zhang's first film set in present-day China, she looks worn, tired, and very pregnant.

She goes to the local police chief, demanding that the political leader apologize to her husband and make financial reparations. The policeman works out a compromise, but then the leader throws the money contemptuously at her feet. So she refuses the payment, and sets off to appeal the case to a regional leader. She will spend much of the movie on foot and in crowded trains, appealing to higher and higher authorities, as the film essentially follows her through a vertical cross-section of modern China.

At first, to be sure, we are not quite certain what the film's period is. In Qiu Ju's village, life continues as it has for many years, and it is a little shock to see the first automobile in the movie; we could almost think ourselves in an earlier century. Qiu Ju is also from an earlier time, and when she visits the regional capital she is quickly conned by a dishonest cab driver.

The movie is a departure for Zhang, whose *Raise the Red Lantern* was shot almost entirely inside an elaborate set representing a rich man's house. This time, his famous star disguised by drab clothes and a well-developed pregnancy, he shoots on city streets with a concealed camera. One of the pleasures of the film is to see everyday China, which appears on screen unrehearsed and natural. Only three of the movie's actors are professionals, and the others essentially play themselves.

The movie's style and narrative seem inspired by postwar Italian neorealism, which attempted to tell the stories of ordinary people with ordinary problems. Qiu Ju stubbornly sets off on one journey after another, appealing to district police chiefs, regional political leaders, and finally even to the courts. All the authorities agree that she has a case. They keep suggesting the same remedies: A fine for the village leader and an apology. But the leader's pride will not allow him to seem humbled before a woman (the husband and his aggrieved loins are by now reduced to bystander status).

There is a point in the film when it begins to seem repetitive: The leader will remain unbending; Qiu Ju will keep appealing. Then we begin to connect with the underlying story of the film, which is about the rhythm of village life, the relationships of friend and family, and the approaching birth of Qiu Ju's child. It is also interesting to note her style of conduct. She is angry, but she is often quite subdued in her confrontations; her strategy involves tenacity rather than pyrotechnics.

If a similar story were set in America, it would probably be made more obviously funny, and star someone famous for pluck—Sally Field, for example. Zhang's approach is more understated. Watching the film, we find the humor for ourselves, and along the way we absorb more information about the lives of ordinary people in everyday China than in any other film I've seen.

Storyville ★ ★ ★ ½
R, 110 m., 1992

James Spader (Cray Fowler), Joanne Whalley-Kilmer (Natalie Tate), Jason Robards (Clifford Fowler), Charlotte Lewis (Lee), Michael Warren (Nathan LeFleur), Michael Parks (Michael Trevallian). Directed by Mark Frost and produced by David Roe and Edward R. Pressman. Screenplay by Frost and Lee Reynolds.

If you find yourself in New Orleans on a bad day in the winter, after dark, when it is drizzling and cold, and you are on one of the back streets of the French Quarter, you are likely to have one of two reactions. You may be uncomfortable and unhappy. Or you may be wrapped in a delicious melancholy, savor-

ing the damp and the loneliness because it creates the perfect mood for melodramatic gothic excess. You are, in other words, either a pragmatist or a romantic.

Storyville is a movie for people who like New Orleans better when it is dark and mysterious. It is for romantics. It is not for pragmatists, who will complain that the characters do not behave according to perfect logic, and that there are holes in its plot. They will be right, of course—this is not an airtight movie—but they will have missed the point, and the fun.

The movie is a lurid example of the genre of Southern gothic excess, a story of feckless youths and crooked politicians and dangerously seductive women and secrets that creep down through the generations with their tails between their legs. It is altogether proper that Jason Robards is in the movie; he is never more at home than when playing a corrupt old patriarch, bourbon in hand, advising the young folks on how to sell their souls for the best dollar.

Robards represents the older generation in *Storyville,* although his exact relationship with the film's hero is left murky until the very end. The hero is played by James Spader, an actor who is unexcelled at portraying lazy-eyed, hedonistic narcissists; this time, he's a young man running for Congress, although his sense of personal immunity is so complete that he suspects nothing when a beautiful Vietnamese woman (Charlotte Lewis) invites him to visit her Jacuzzi on one of those dreary nights when all the sins are taking place indoors.

Is she really attracted to him? Or is she acting under orders from her evil father? Or is the devious Robards somehow involved? And what to do with the dead body (none of the above) that eventually emerges from Spader's midnight rendezvous? Those are questions of interest to the other two women in the candidate's life: his birdbrained wife, who has been on hold for years, and his former lover (Joanne Whalley-Kilmer), who is now the prosecuting attorney, and thinks he may be guilty of murder.

Because the story is set in New Orleans, none of these mysteries can be solved simply by examining the current generation. There are secrets of the past to rummage through, including the mysterious suicide of Spader's father, and the fate of some missing documents. And there are additional complications in the present, involving the activities of a pornographer (Charles Haid) whose

subjects are both less and more than they seem.

The movie was directed and co-written by Mark Frost, one of David Lynch's key collaborators on "Twin Peaks," who started on this screenplay a couple of years before the Lynch project. You can see something of the same sensibility—the willingness to follow a tangled labyrinth of evil and deception as it spirals down through the generations. The difference is that Frost's *Storyville* takes its story seriously, or at least pretends to, while the "Twin Peaks" projects are at pains to distance the filmmakers from the material. With Lynch's recent work, it's as if he wants you to know he's superior to the material. Frost doesn't mind being implicated—he likes this kind of stuff, and plunges into the dark waters of his plot with real joy.

So did I. There is a scene that helps illustrate my enjoyment. Spader goes to visit the beautiful Vietnamese woman, who lives on an upper floor on a deserted street in the Quarter. A crooked vice cop, lurking in the shadows, takes note of the candidate and his destination. There are two ways to read this scene. The pragmatist could scornfully point out (a) how stupid a political candidate would have to be in order to attend such a rendezvous in the middle of his campaign, and (b) how convenient that the vice cop would be stationed in the very spot to see him.

The gothic melodramatic romanticist, on the other hand, would view the scene in this way: (a) how wonderfully bold and reckless for the hero to follow his heart into danger, down mean, wet streets to a passionate rendezvous, and (b) no shot of a sinister man in a shadowy doorway is ever completely unnecessary.

Straight Out of Brooklyn ★ ★ ★
R, 91 m., 1991

George T. Odom (Ray Brown), Ann D. Sanders (Frankie Brown), Lawrence Gilliard, Jr. (Dennis Brown), Barbara Sanon (Carolyn Brown), Reana E. Drummond (Shirley), Matty Rich (Larry), Mark Malone (Kevin). Directed, produced, and written by Matty Rich.

Matty Rich was seventeen when he started to make *Straight Out of Brooklyn,* and only nineteen at the time of its release. I put those facts right at the top of this review because originally I was not going to lead with them; this is a strong, good film, and I thought if I mentioned the director's age, that would seem like condescension.

But then I thought—no, hold on, this is astonishing news, that a seventeen-year-old kid from the Brooklyn housing projects, with no backing and no money and no rich family, could actually make this film and get it released. We read all the time about "disadvantaged urban youth," but here is a firsthand report from the front lines.

The movie covers a few days in the lives of a high school kid, who lives with his sister and his parents in a project. The story begins with brutal frankness, as the father, drunk, beats his wife and throws things around the apartment while the kids cower in the next room. In the morning, surrounded by the wreckage of their few possessions, the young man determines that this cannot go on any longer—that somehow he has to change the course his life seems set on.

During the day he hangs out with a couple of friends, and they begin to talk about the possibility of committing a crime. One of the friends (played by Matty Rich himself) suggests that maybe they could get a job in a relative's gas station. But the hero is too angry and impatient for that, and when his girlfriend suggests making something of himself in college, his angry reply is that he doesn't have four or five years to spend in college. And besides (he tells her, as they look across to the Manhattan skyline), does she think the rich people who own Wall Street got there by following the rules? Not likely.

For most of the movie, the characters stand poised between two possible choices—between crime, and trying to do the right thing. But the movie finds time to develop some of their complexities as they make up their minds, in well-written scenes such as the one where the mother actually defends her husband, even though he beats her; hospitalized by his brutality, she refuses to denounce him. And there are scenes of everyday life, goofing around, small talk, passing time. It all adds up to a convincing portrait of a big-city black teen-ager who feels that if he does not take some sort of conclusive action, life will clamp him into poverty and discouragement.

Matty Rich will someday, I imagine, make slicker movies than *Straight Out of Brooklyn.* Movies with more so-called entertainment and production values. But will he ever make a movie more obviously from his heart? He financed this film in bits and pieces, asking the actors to work for free, filming on weekends over a period of two years, draining his family and friends of available cash, looking

for loans and deferrals—and the important thing is, he kept at it, and it's an honest, effective film.

I remember a conversation more than twenty years ago with Francis Ford Coppola, who was speculating about the coming technological breakthroughs in filmmaking—the cheap, portable film and video cameras, and sound and editing equipment. He felt maybe people could start going out and making their own films, instead of just going to the movies on Saturday night. And he felt the authenticity of those films might be overwhelming.

The technical advances are now mostly in place. With a nine-hundred-dollar camcorder, anyone can make a video film that would have cost the networks tens or hundreds of thousands of dollars twenty years ago. But not many people have used this technology to make films any more meaningful than "America's Funniest Home Videos." No wonder. The invention of desktop publishing has not resulted in a flood of great literature, either. But Matty Rich has put the pieces together and used them to make a film out of his own experience. The edges are rough and the ending is simply a slogan printed on the screen. But the truth is there, and echoes after the film is over.

Straight Time ★ ★ ★ ½
R, 114 m., 1978

Dustin Hoffman (Max Dembo), Theresa Russell (Jenny Mercer), Harry Dean Stanton (Jerry Schue), Gary Busey (Willy Darin), M. Emmet Walsh (Earl Frank), Sandy Baron (Manny). Directed by Ulu Grosbard and produced by Stanley Beck and Tim Zinnemann. Screenplay by Alvin Sargent, Edward Bunker, and Jeffrey Boam.

Straight Time is a great sleeper, a film good enough that we wonder why we didn't hear more about it. So does Dustin Hoffman, who sued Warner Brothers for what he considered the mishandling of the picture. He may have had a point; his performance here as Max Dembo, ex-con turned thief, is one of his very best.

Max gets out of prison determined to go straight. It's not easy. Under the conditions of his parole, for example, he can't take a job that involves the handling of money. But a girl in an employment office does find him a job, at a can company. And when he asks her out to dinner, she accepts. He also finds a room he can afford to rent, and so he's doing fairly well. He's on the road to personal reha-

bilitation, as his parole officer might put it. The parole officer (M. Emmet Walsh) is not, however, very good at the rehabilitation game. He's mean-spirited, suspicious, and sadistic, all behind a large, cynical smile. He busts Max on suspicion of drug use, causing him to lose his job—and that's enough for Max, who returns to the trade he knows best, theft.

Straight Time is based on a novel by an excon, and it feels authentic. What especially absorbs us is the way the movie projects the feeling of being a thief—the compulsion, the addiction, the rush of adrenaline, the fear. It's also good at explaining why this guy would be attractive to a girl, and especially the girl at the employment office.

She's played by Theresa Russell, who does a good job of projecting her feelings. She doesn't talk a lot, but she listens well, and she's drawn to the mysteries in Max's character. He wants to keep her out of his jobs but not out of his life, and she is eventually willing to settle for his terms.

Max pulls several jobs. He sticks up a grocery, for example, and then a pawnshop, where he gets the shotgun that will be useful in his stick-ups of a bank and a jewelry store. He enlists old buddies as his accomplices, and Harry Dean Stanton is especially good as an ex-con who almost succeeds in going straight. Stanton's got it all together: A house, a swimming pool, hamburgers grilled on the patio . . . but he can't resist the urgency of Max Dembo's sales pitch.

The robberies themselves have the same sense of manic desperation we felt in *Dog Day Afternoon.* And they have something else, as well: They project the feeling that Max Dembo, without admitting it even to himself, *wants* to get caught again. He lingers. He dawdles. His partner is calling out the number of seconds that have elapsed, as part of their plan to get out before the cops arrive. But Max Dembo isn't listening. Maybe that's part of the emotional payoff he needs, stretching a job to its last second, walking out the back door as the cops come in the front, taunting society while at the same time almost begging for punishment.

Hoffman's performance reminds me of his Ratso Rizzo in *Midnight Cowboy,* especially in his ways of telling the world to go to hell. Ratso was far gone on his own personal death trip, of course, and Max Dembo has whole moments when he rathers enjoys life. But they're similar in their moves, their choices. They belong outside society because it doesn't dare have places for them. Maybe *that's* what turns the girl on; maybe she has a sheltering instinct.

Straight Time exists so close to the drabness and desperation of its story that it might turn some people off. Hoffman must have known that; this is such a personal project that after he bought the original novel he planned to direct it himself before deciding, instead, on the Broadway and sometime movie director Ulu Grosbard. But Hoffman and Grosbard don't change details just to make their movie more palatable. Instead, they stick with Max Dembo, figuring him out, following his impulses, until those oddly disturbing final photographs—his mug shots—with the eyes suggesting that somehow this particular human being was *always* doomed.

Stranger than Paradise ★ ★ ★ ★
R, 90 m., 1984

John Lurie (Willie), Eszter Balint (Eva), Richard Edson (Eddie), Cecillia Stark (Aunt Lottie), Danny Rosen (Billy), Rammellzee (Man with Money), Tom Decillo (Airline Agent). Directed by Jim Jarmusch and produced by Sara Driver. Screenplay by Jarmusch.

Stranger than Paradise is filmed in a series of uninterrupted shots; the picture fades in, we watch the scene, and when the scene is over, there's a fade to black. Then comes the next fade-in. This is not a gimmick, but a visual equivalent of the film's deadpan characters, who take a lot to get excited.

The movie's hero is Willie (John Lurie), who arrived on these shores from Hungary about ten years ago, and has spent the intervening decade perfecting his New York accent and trying to make nothing out of himself. He lives in an apartment where the linoleum is the highlight. On a good day, he'll sleep late, hang out, play a little poker. His cousin Eva arrives from Budapest. This is the last thing he needs, a sixteen-year-old girl who needs a place to stay. She hates him, too. But she has to kill some time before she goes to Cleveland to live with her aunt Lottie. She has good taste in American music, but not according to him. Willie's friend, Eddie, comes over occasionally and eyeballs Eva. Nothing much happens. She leaves for Cleveland.

The screen is filled with large letters: ONE YEAR LATER. This in itself is funny, that we'd get such a momentous time cue in a movie where who even knows what day it is. Eddie and Willie get in some trouble over

a poker game and Eddie suddenly remembers Willie's cousin in Cleveland. They go to see her. It is cold in Cleveland. Eva has bought the American Dream and is working in a fast-food outlet. They all go to look at the lake, which is frozen. Aunt Lottie turns out to make Clara Peller look like Dame Peggy Ashcroft. The guys say to hell with it and head for Florida. Then they come back and get Eva and take her along with them. They have a postcard that makes Florida look like paradise, but they wind up living at one of those hotels where the permanent guests live in the woodwork. Everything goes sour. Eva wants to go back to Hungary. The guys lose all their money at the dog races. Creeps start hanging around. It will take a miracle to give this movie an upbeat ending. There is a miracle.

Stranger than Paradise is a treasure from one end to the other. I saw it for the first time at the 1984 Cannes Film Festival, where it was having its first public showing. Half the people in the theater probably didn't speak English, but that didn't stop them from giving the movie a standing ovation, and it eventually won the Camera d'Or prize for the best first film. It is like no other film you've seen, and yet you feel right at home in it. It seems to be going nowhere, and knows every step it wants to make. It is a constant, almost kaleidoscopic experience of discovery, and we try to figure out what the film is up to and it just keeps moving steadfastly ahead, fade in, fade out, fade in, fade out, making a mountain out of a molehill.

Strapless ★ ★ ★
R, 103 m., 1990

Blair Brown (Lillian Hempel), Bruno Ganz (Raymond Forbes), Hugh Laurie (Colin), Billy Roch (Gerry), Camille Coduri (Mrs. Clark), Gary O'Brien (Mr. Clark), Bridget Fonda (Amy Hempel), Spencer Leigh (Hus), Alan Howard (Mr. Cooper), Suzanne Burden (Romaine Salmon). Directed by David Hare and produced by Rick McCallum. Screenplay by Hare.

The most romantic passage in any relationship, I sometimes think, is just before you start beginning to know the other person. That person still remains an intriguing mystery, so you can project your desires and fantasies onto him or her: that person potentially represents everything you've been searching for. The other person, of course, is equally free to project fantasies upon your screen, and at some point in this process, the two

people agree that they were destined for each other. Then the painful and difficult process of getting to know the other person begins, and destiny takes a holiday.

The opening scenes of David Hare's *Strapless* are poised at precisely such a moment in the relationship of two strangers: Lillian, an American nurse who has worked for several years in London, and Raymond, a mysterious stranger she meets while on holiday. They encounter each other in a church. Each is clearly intrigued. Raymond is the kind of man who seems able to anticipate just what a woman wants to hear, and to say it just before she knows she needs to hear it. Lillian, an independent and lonely woman, finds herself saying things she thought she'd never say again.

Back in London, life goes on. Lillian (Blair Brown) is involved in labor activities at the hospital, where the nursing staff opposes budget cuts by the Thatcher regime. At home, her life is complicated by the arrival of Amy, a younger sister (Bridget Fonda), who sleeps with a succession of boyfriends and makes vague plans to support herself as a dress designer. One day Amy tells Lillian she is pregnant and plans to have the baby—primarily, it would seem, in order to experience the wonders of going through natural childbirth while listening to Mozart.

Lillian is appalled by the irresponsibility of Amy's life, but she is also burdened by the responsibilities of her own; as the head of the strike committee, she spends long hours nursing and then additional hours in negotiations, and as an American she sometimes feels she is an outsider no matter what she does. Then Raymond (Bruno Ganz, the sad angel in *Wings of Desire*) comes back into her life. He has a home in London, it would seem. An expensive little house that is decorated in impeccable taste and filled with the most exquisite personal possessions.

Everything about Raymond speaks of money and taste. But who is he, really, and where does he come from? How does he make his money? Can Lillian trust him? These are questions that fade in the flame of their passion, but they need to be answered, and Raymond is clearly incapable of answering them. He is, in fact, incapable of any commitment at all, and the viewer begins to suspect that he is addicted to only the early stages of a relationship. He likes the intrigue of seduction, but not the messiness of love.

Strapless was written and directed by the playwright David Hare *(Plenty, A Map of the*

World), who includes one perfect scene that explains Raymond without explaining him. I will not diminish the pleasure of the scene by describing it, except to say that it provides us with a glimpse of Raymond's past that makes us feel a particular sympathy for him, as we do for any wounded creature.

The title of the movie is referred to in a scene where the two sisters and some other women try on strapless gowns that Amy has designed, and Amy says, "They shouldn't stay up, but they do." Presumably David Hare is trying the same trick with the whole movie, suspending his characters and plot in the air without benefit of the usual structural supports. That works with the relationship between Raymond and Lillian, which must be an enigma in order to work at all. But the movie falters badly in its subplot about labor unions and industrial relations—it's as if Hare wanted to work some social commentary into a story that has no room for it.

Strawberry and Chocolate ★ ★ ★ ½   `NEW`
R, 104 m., 1995
(See related Film Clip, p. 877.)

Jorge Perrugoria (Diego), Vladimir Cruz (David), Mirta Ibarra (Nancy), Francisco Gatorno (Miguel). Directed by Tomas Gutierez Alea and produced by Miguel Mendoza. Screenplay by Senal Paz.

"I knew he was homosexual," the young man explains to his friend, "because they had chocolate ice cream, and yet he ordered strawberry." Thus does the shortage of consumer products in Castro's Cuba reveal the inner workings of the libido.

The young man's name is David (Vladimir Cruz), and he recently had a disenchanting experience with his fiancée. They went to a cheap hotel to make love for the first time, but she was dismayed by the shabbiness of the surroundings and could not understand how the man who loved her could bring her there. David was understanding, they left without making love—and the next time we see them, it is at her marriage to another man.

So David is on the rebound that day in the park when Diego (Jorge Perrugoria) sits at his table and starts to eat the strawberry ice cream. Diego is obviously gay: He's swishy, wearing his sexuality as a badge of honor. And he has eyes for the handsome young David, inviting him back to his flat for coffee, and then staging a fake scenario where the coffee spills on David's shirt, Diego in-

sists David take it off so he can wash it, and . . .

And nothing unfolds as we expect. *Strawberry and Chocolate* is not a movie about the seduction of a body, but about the seduction of a mind. It is more interested in politics than sex—unless you count sexual politics, since to be homosexual in Cuba is to make an antiauthoritarian statement whether you intend it or not.

The movie has been directed by Tomas Gutierez Alea, at seventy-two the greatest of Cuba's filmmakers and one of its most contradictory. An early supporter of Castro and the head of the revolution's underground film unit, he made *Stories of the Revolution* (1960) about the overthrow of the Batista regime. He founded the national film unit. Yet his own films have questioned life under Castro: The famous *Memories of Underdevelopment* (1968) is about an intellectual adrift in revolutionary Havana, and now here is a film in which Diego taps his brow and says, "This is a thinking head—and if you have ideas, they ostracize you."

The character of Diego is much more complex than he first appears. He is a little older than David, handsome, and well-off by Cuban standards. He lives in a small, cluttered apartment, but at least he lives there alone, and it is filled with art, books, opera recordings, and even contraband Scotch. He stages art exhibitions. He is widely read, sophisticated, and critical of the way Cuba is run today. At one point, he takes David up to a rooftop, lets his arm sweep across Havana, and says, "We live in one of the world's most beautiful cities. You're just in time to see it before it collapses in shit."

It is a little startling to hear such lines in a movie made in Havana, by Cubans; perhaps Castro's control of the arts is not as extreme as we think? It's the tension between our notions of Cuba and Diego's reckless behavior that gives *Strawberry and Chocolate* much of its fascination: Gutierez Alea is showing us a man who takes chances with both his sexuality and his politics.

At first, of course, Diego wants to seduce David, who is a naive university student and a devout Marxist. David's friend at school is the rigid Miguel (Francisco Gatorno), a future bureaucrat, who encourages David to return to Diego and spy on him—which is one of the reasons David returns to the intriguing flat of his new friend, but not the only one. Actually, he is fascinated by the photographs and books he sees at Diego's,

and the music that's always playing, and the fresh ideas that are churning in his new friend's mind.

The movie reminded me of *Educating Rita*, and, of course, of *Pygmalion*, in the way young people, hungry for knowledge, absorb it from older ones who are in love with them; the love remains suspended while the ideas sink in. And all around are semidocumentary glimpses of today's Havana: the ancient Detroit cars in the streets, the way color and life penetrate even dismal slums, the gloominess of Marxist orthodoxy, the ambiguity of characters like Nancy (Mirta Ibarra), who heads the revolutionary committee in Diego's building but is much more flexible than she seems.

Sometimes the movie, based on a short story and screenplay by Senal Paz, is a little too arch in its writing. At one point David says that the atomic bomb was dropped by Truman Capote, setting up Diego's line, "Not Capote! He was a homosexual!" My guess is that the likelihood of David even knowing Capote's name is next to zero, and that the line shows Paz peeking through with a one-liner he couldn't resist.

As with all statements from today's Cuba, *Strawberry and Chocolate* can be seen reflected in many different mirrors. My first reaction was to wonder how Gutierez Alea could get away with such pointed criticisms of his country. Yet conservative Cuban exiles in Miami called it propaganda, precisely *because* it gives the impression that Cubans can safely be critical of Castro. Have it either way: The movie has real strength and charm, especially in the way it leads us to expect a romance, and then gives us a character whose very existence is a criticism of his society.

Streamers ★ ★ ★ ★
R, 118 m., 1984

Matthew Modine (Billy), Michael Wright (Carlyle), Mitchell Lichtenstein (Richie), David Alan Grier (Roger), Guy Boyd (Rooney), George Dzundza (Cokes). Directed by Robert Altman and produced by Altman and Nick H. Mileti. Screenplay by David Rabe.

Robert Altman's *Streamers* is one of the most intense and intimate dramas I've ever seen on film. It's based on the play by David Rabe, about young soldiers waiting around a barracks for their orders to go to Vietnam. Most directors, faced with a play that takes place on one set, find ways to "open it up" and add new locations. Altman has moved in the opposite direction, taking advantage of the one-room set to tighten the play until it squeezes like a vise. Watching this film is such a demanding experience that both times I've seen it, it has been too much for some viewers, and they've left. Those who stay, who survive the difficult passages of violence, will find at the end of the film a conclusion that is so poetic and moving it succeeds in placing the tragedy in perspective.

It is the era of Vietnam. In a barracks somewhere, three young men wait for their orders. They are Billy, who is white and middle-class; Roger, who is black and middle-class; and Richie, a dreamy young man who likes to tease the others with hints that he is a homosexual. The only other occupants of the barracks are two drunken master sergeants, Rooney and Cokes, who are best friends and who are stumbling through idiotic revelry in an attempt to drown the realization that Cokes has leukemia. Into this little world comes Carlyle, an angry young black man who is gay, and whose conversations with Richie will lead the others into anger and denial before the situation finally explodes.

There are some surprises, but the developments in *Streamers* flow so naturally out of the material that its surprises should be left intact. A lot can be said, however, about the acting, Altman's direction, and Rabe's writing. I didn't see this play on stage and don't know how it worked there, but Altman is so completely the visual master of this material that we're drawn into that barracks room and into its rhythms of boredom, drunkenness, and passion.

The actors are all unknown to me, except for George Dzundza, who plays Cokes. They are all so natural that the dialogue has an eerie double quality: We know it's written dialogue because it has a poetry and a drama unlikely in life, but Rabe's ear is so accurate it sounds real, and the performers make it so convincing there's never a false note. The two key performances are by Mitchell Lichtenstein, as Richie, and Michael Wright, as Carlyle. Richie is indeed homosexual, as we realize long before his barracks mates are willing to acknowledge it. He likes to tease the others with insinuations that they may be gay, too. Billy boasts that he is straight, but he protests too much. Roger tries to be a peacekeeper. Then Carlyle wanders in from another unit. He is drunk and angry, collapses, sleeps it off, blearily looks around, figures out Richie, and tries to make a connection.

But there is a lot more going on here than sexual competition. *Streamers* uses both sex and race as foreground subjects while the movie's real subject, war, hovers in the background and in several extraordinary monologues—one about snakes, one about a battle, and one about the realities of parachuting. As the veteran master sergeants make their drunken way through the movie, they drop these hard realities into the lives of the unseasoned kids. And when anger turns to violence and a tragedy occurs, it is up to one of the fat old guys (Dzundza) to deliver a monologue that is one of the most revealing, intimate, honest, and moving speeches I've ever heard.

Street Smart ★ ★ ★
R, 97 m., 1987

Christopher Reeve (Jonathan Fisher), Mimi Rogers (Alison Parker), Morgan Freeman (Fast Black), Kathy Baker (Punchy). Directed by Jerry Schatzberg and produced by Menahem Golan and Yoram Globus. Screenplay by David Freeman.

Sometimes you run across a movie that's far from perfect and yet it contains things that are so good they take your breath away. *Street Smart* is a movie like that—a clever thriller with a lot of unbelievable scenes and a sappy ending, but two wonderful performances.

The performances are by Morgan Freeman, as a Times Square pimp, and by Kathy Baker, as one of the hookers he controls. They play their characters as well as I can imagine them being played. Freeman has the flashier role, as a smart, very tough man who can be charming or intimidating—whatever's needed. Baker is a small-town girl who has been a hooker for years, who lives by the rules of the street but still has feelings.

Surrounding their performances is a plot that would have been interesting if it had been handled more realistically. Christopher Reeve plays a magazine reporter who concocts a completely fictional story about a colorful pimp. After the story is published and creates a sensation, the district attorney becomes convinced that the subject of the story is really the Freeman character—who is on trial for murder. He subpoenas Reeve's notes, but of course there aren't any.

From this promising beginning, *Street Smart* takes its story in two different directions. On one hand, we get a satirical view of the New York publishing and television industries, with André Gregory as the cynical magazine publisher and Reeve as an overnight journalism star who is instantly hired as a TV street reporter. On the other hand, we get Reeve trying to cover his tracks by going back and doing the reporting he should have done in the first place.

This second story—which involves Freeman and Baker—is much more interesting than the first. The pimp quickly figures out Reeve's problem and offers him a deal: He'll agree that he was the subject of the fictional story if Reeve provides him with an alibi. Reeve refuses. Freeman turns dangerous and violent: He's facing a life sentence and, for him, this isn't a matter of ethics but of his life.

The second hour of *Street Smart* almost seems to be scenes from two different movies. Freeman's dialogue is particularly good, as he analyzes Reeve's motives, talks about people who condescend to him, and terrorizes Baker for becoming Reeve's friend. There is one powerful, frightening scene where he threatens her with scissors; the power on the screen reminded me of vintage De Niro or Pacino.

Many of the street scenes have the uncanny feeling of real life, closely observed. For example, look at the scene where Freeman and his sidekick take Reeve for a tour of the streets in their Cadillac. When Freeman decides to discipline one of his girls, he squeezes her into the front seat, too, so Reeve is forced to confront reality up close, and maybe get blood on his suit. The staging of this scene—four people all in the front seat—is what makes it work.

The movie's other story, the one involving the magazine and TV news, is sort of silly. It's impossible to believe Reeve would so quickly become a TV newsman, difficult to believe most of the stories he reports, and incredible that Baker somehow always knows exactly where, in all of Manhattan, Reeve is going to be doing his next remote TV report.

The end of the movie is also a disappointment. It's yet another shoot-out. Screenwriters have grown so lazy in recent years that it's almost too much to ask them to resolve a plot on human terms. The last reel of most thrillers now involves the obligatory death of the villain, as if death were a solution. Since we know that's how the movie will end, the last reel is a loss—a waste of the movie's own time. And in *Street Smart* where Freeman creates such an unforgettable villain, I really resented it when he wasn't given the chance to participate in his own fate.

As a film school exercise, would-be screenwriters should be required to rewrite thrillers like this, with real human endings instead of the out of the standard sequence: chase, shoot-out, death, fade out. When an actor like Freeman goes to the trouble of creating a great character, the film should go to the trouble of providing him with a final scene.

Streetwise ★ ★ ★
R, 92 m., 1985

Directed by Martin Bell and produced by Cheryl McCall. Reported by Mary Ellen Mark.

The mother is being frank about her daughter. She says she knows the girl is working as a prostitute, but she figures "it's just a phase she's going through." Her daughter is about fifteen years old. That is not the most harrowing moment in *Streetwise,* a heartbreaking documentary about the street children of Seattle. There are worse moments, for example the one where a street kid tries to talk to her mother about the fact that her stepfather "was fooling around . . . doing perverted things with me" when she was a baby. "Yes," says the mother philosophically, "but now he's stopped."

The subject of runaway, abducted, and abandoned children has received a lot of attention in the news, but never anything remotely like *Streetwise,* which enters into the lives of these underage survivors as they fight for life and love on the streets of Seattle. The movie was inspired by a *Life* magazine article on a group of the kids, who, at an age when other kids are in school, are learning to be hookers, thieves, con men, pushers, and junkies. Now comes this movie, which contains extraordinary everyday footage, which the filmmakers obtained by spending months hanging out with the kids, until they gained their trust and their cameras became accepted.

The street kids lead horrifying lives, but sometimes there are moments of acceptance and happiness. They cling to each other. They relate uneasily with a social worker who seems philosophically resigned to the facts of street life. They try to dodge the cops. They live in an abandoned hotel, get money by begging and prostitution, eat by raiding the dumpsters behind restaurants. They even have a system for marking garbage so they don't eat food that's too old.

What is amazing is that some of these kids are still in touch with their parents. One girl shrugs that her mother is off to the woods for a weekend: "I've always known she don't love me or shit. So OK." She hugs herself. Another girl tries to talk to her mother, who says, "Be quiet. I'm drinking." A kid named DeWayne goes to visit his father in prison and gets a long lecture about smoking, drinking, and taking drugs, and a pie-in-the-sky speech about how they're going to open a thrift shop when the old man gets out of prison. The next time we see DeWayne, it is at his funeral; he hanged himself in a jail cell.

You walk out of *Streetwise* realizing that these aren't bad kids. They are resourceful, tough, and true to their own standards. They break the law, but then how many legal ways are there for fourteen-year-olds to support themselves? They talk about their parents in a matter-of-fact way that, we suspect, covers up great wounds, as when one girl says she's never met her natural father—"unless maybe I dated him once."

Streetwise is surprising for the frankness of the material it contains. How did the filmmakers get these people to say these things, to allow the cameras into their lives? We see moments of intimacy, of violence, of pain. The answer, I suspect, is that a lot of these kids were so starving for attention and affection that by offering both, the filmmakers were able to get whatever they wanted. Some of the scenes are possibly staged, in the sense that the characters are aware they are in a movie, but none of the scenes are false or contrived. These are children living rough in an American city, and you would blame their parents if you didn't see that the parents are just as alienated and hopeless, and that before long these kids will be damaged parents, too.

Strictly Ballroom ★ ★ ★
PG, 94 m., 1993

Paul Mercurio (Scott Hastings), Tara Morice (Fran), Bill Hunter (Barry Fife), Pat Thomson (Shirley Hastings), Gia Carides (Liz Holt), Peter Whitford (Les Kendall). Directed by Baz Luhrmann and produced by Tristram Miall. Screenplay by Luhrmann and Craig Pearce.

The plot of *Strictly Ballroom* is as old as the hills, but the characters in the movie seem to come from another planet. Surely nobody in Australia dresses like this, talks like this, takes ballroom dancing as seriously as this? They do? The true weirdness of the movie comes when we begin to realize the director *didn't* make everything up; only real life could possibly have inspired a world this bizarre.

The movie, which crosses Astaire and Rodgers with Mickey and Judy and adds a dash of Spinal Tap, is a comedy posing as a docu-drama about competitive ballroom dancing in Australia. Everyone in the movie takes the sport, or art, with deadly seriousness, and their world revolves around the Pan-Pacific Grand Prix Amateur Championships (which, despite its grand name, seems to be a local event). Like synchronized swimming (the most hilarious event in Olympics history), competitive ballroom dancing is essentially lighthearted fun spoiled by lead-footed rules.

The film's hero is Scott (Paul Mercurio), a pleasant young man with a mad light in his eyes, who, according to the pseudodocumentary that opens the film, was born to win the Pan-Pacific. But then he jeopardizes his chances by recklessly ignoring the rules and forcing his partner to join him in a dance routine that was (gasp!) spontaneous and improvised.

His partner is enraged, and leaves him. His mother, a former championship dancer, is beside herself. The estimable Barry Fife (Bill Hunter), the autocratic czar of ballroom contests, is deeply offended. Only the good-hearted Fran (Tara Morice) believes in him, and offers to become his partner. This is despite her lack of experience, her general ungainliness, and her homely appearance. Familiar with the great tradition of come-from-behind movies, however, we somehow suspect that if she ever takes off those glasses, and does something with her hair . . .

Strictly Ballroom was directed and co-written by Baz Luhrmann, who, according to the movie's press materials, has been fascinated with the insular world of Australian competitive ballroom dancing since he was a youth. The story, by Luhrmann and various collaborators, was first staged as an amateur production ten years ago, and has been through many incarnations leading up to this film, which is so tightly packed with characters and situations that it seems, in its own way, as obsessed as the dancers themselves.

Luhrmann, like many first-time directors, is intoxicated with the possibilities of the camera. He uses too many wide-angle shots, in which the characters look like blowfish mugging for the lens, and too many story lines, until we worry we may have lost track of something, but what works is an exuberance that cannot be faked. As Scott and Fran prepare for the Pan-Pacifics, as Barry Fife struggles to retain his stranglehold on competitive dancing, as Scott discovers that his meek and silent father was once a Pan-Pacific contender, the movie hurtles toward a conclusion sanctified by *Saturday Night Fever* and so many other movies we could hold a trivia contest just by naming them.

What's best about the movie is the sense of madness and mania running just beneath its surface. In one sense, the characters care about nothing but ballroom dancing. They eat, drink, and sleep it, and talk of nothing else. Their costumes alone are a tip-off that they've had no contact with the real world for years. Yet in another sense, ballroom dancing is simply the strategy they use to hold the world at bay. They are profoundly frightened of change, and have created an insular little world, with rigid rules and traditions; here they can be in control, as the larger world goes haywire. Scott's attempt to introduce anarchy—and new dance steps—into their tiny enclave is all the funnier because he, too, cares about nothing but dancing. He doesn't even *want* to be a rebel. But it's in his blood.

Stripes ★ ★ ★ ½
R, 105 m., 1981

Bill Murray (John), Harold Ramis (Russell), Warren Oates (Sergeant Hulka), P.J. Soles (Stella), Sean Young (Louise), John Candy (Ox). Directed by Ivan Reitman and produced by Reitman and Dan Goldberg. Screenplay by Goldberg, Len Blum, and Harold Ramis.

Stripes is an anarchic slob movie, a celebration of all that is irreverent, reckless, foolhardy, undisciplined, and occasionally scatological. It's a lot of fun. It comes from some of the same people involved in *National Lampoon's Animal House,* and could have been titled *National Lampoon's Animal Army* with little loss of accuracy. As a comedy about a couple of misfits who find themselves in the U.S. Army's basic training program, it obviously resembles Goldie Hawn's *Private Benjamin.* But it doesn't duplicate that wonderful movie; they could play on the same double feature. *Stripes* has the added advantage of being a whole movie about the Army, rather than half a movie (*Private Benjamin* got sidetracked with Hawn's love affair).

The movie is not only a triumph for its stars (Bill Murray and Harold Ramis) and its director (Ivan Reitman), but a sort of vin-

dication. To explain: Reitman directed, and Murray starred in, the enormously successful *Meatballs,* which was an entertaining enough comedy but awfully ragged. No wonder. It was shot on a shoestring with Canadian tax-shelter money. What Murray and Reitman prove this time is that, given a decent budget, they can do superior work—certainly superior to *Meatballs,* for starters. For Harold Ramis, who plays Murray's grave-eyed, flat-voiced, terminally detached partner in *Stripes,* this is a chance, at last, to come out from behind the camera. Ramis and Murray are both former Second City actors, but in Hollywood, Ramis has been typecast as a writer *(Animal House, Meatballs, Caddyshack),* maybe because he sometimes looks too goofy for Hollywood's unimaginative tastes.

In *Stripes,* Murray and Ramis make a wonderful team. Their big strength is restraint. Given the tendency of movies like this to degenerate into undisciplined slapstick, they wisely choose to play their characters as understated, laid-back anarchists. Murray enlists in the Army in a what-the-hell mood after his girlfriend throws him out, and Ramis enlists because one stupid gesture deserves another. They're older than the usual Army recruit, less easily impressed with gung-ho propaganda, and quietly amazed at their drill instructor, Sergeant Hulka, who is played by Warren Oates with tough-as-nails insanity.

The movie has especially good writing in several scenes. My favorite comes near the beginning, during a session when recruits in the new platoon get to know one another. One obviously psycho draftee, who looks like Robert De Niro, quietly announces that if his fellow soldiers touch him, touch his stuff, or interfere in any way with his person or his privacy, he will quite simply be forced to kill them. Sergeant Hulka replies: "Lighten up!"

The movie's plot follows basic training, more or less, during its first hour. Then a romance enters. Murray and Ramis meet a couple of cute young military policewomen (P.J. Soles and Sean Young), and they happily violate every rule in the book. One funny scene: Murray and Soles sneak into the kitchen of the base commander's house and do unprecedented things with kitchen utensils.

It's an unwritten law of these movies that the last half hour has to involve some kind of spectacular development. In *Animal House,* it was the homecoming parade. In *Stripes,* the climax involves the Army's latest secret

weapon, which is a computerized, armored, nuclear weapons carrier disguised as a recreational vehicle. Murray's platoon is assigned to go to Europe and test it. Murray, Ramis, and their girls decide to test it during a weekend holiday swing through the Alps. After they cross the Iron Curtain, all hell breaks loose.

Stripes is a complete success on its intended level—it's great, irreverent entertainment—but it was successful, too, as a breakthrough for Ramis, Reitman, and Murray, on their way to *Ghostbusters.* Comedy is one of the hardest film genres to work in. Nobody knows all its secrets, not even Woody Allen and Mel Brooks. Here's a comedy from people who know some of the secrets most of the time.

Stroszek ★ ★ ★ ★
NO MPAA RATING, 108 m., 1978

Bruno S. (Stroszek), Eva Mattes (Eva), Clement Scheitz (Scheitz), Wilhelm von Homburg (Pimp), Burkhard Dreist (Pimp), Clayton Szlapinski (Scheitz's Nephew), Ely Rodriguez (Indian). Directed, produced, and written by Werner Herzog.

Werner Herzog has subtitled *Stroszek* as "a ballad," and so it is: It's like one of those bluegrass nonsense ballads in which impossible adventures are described in every verse, and the chorus reminds us that life gets teedjus, don't it? But because Herzog has one of the most original imaginations of anyone now making movies, *Stroszek* is a haunting and hilarious ballad at the same time, an almost unbelievable mixture of lunacy, comedy, tragedy, and the simply human.

Consider. He gives us three main characters who are best friends, despite the fact that they're improbable as people and impossible as friends. There's Stroszek himself, just released from prison in Germany. He's a simple soul who plays the piano and the accordion and never quite understands why people behave as they do. There's Eva, a dim but pleasant Berlin prostitute. And there's old Scheitz, a goofy soul in his seventies who has been invited to live with his nephew in upstate Wisconsin.

This mixture is further complicated by the fact that Stroszek is played by Bruno S., the same actor Herzog used in *Kaspar Hauser.* Bruno S. is a mental patient, described by Herzog as schizophrenic, and it's a good question whether he's "acting" in this movie or simply exercising a crafty survival instinct. No matter: He comes across as saintly, sensitive, and very strange.

The three friends meet when Eva's two pimps beat her up and throw her out. She comes to live with Stroszek. The pimps (evil hoods right out of a Fassbinder gangster movie) later visit Stroszek and Eva and beat them both up, leaving Stroszek kneeling on his beloved piano with a school bell balanced on his derriere.

It is clearly time to leave Berlin, and old Scheitz has the answer: Visit his relatives in America. The nephew lives on a Wisconsin farm in an incredibly barren landscape, but to the Germans it's the American Dream. They buy an enormous mobile home, seventy feet long and fully furnished, and install a color TV in it. Eva gets a job as a waitress, and turns some tricks on the side at the truck stop. Stroszek works as a mechanic, sort of. Old Scheitz wanders about testing the "animal magnetism" of fence posts.

The Wisconsin scenes are among the weirdest I've ever seen in a movie: Notice, for example, the visit Stroszek and Eva get from that supercilious little twerp from the bank, who wants to repossess their TV set and who never seems to understand that nothing he says is understood. Or notice the brisk precision with which an auctioneer disposes of the mobile home, which is then carted away, all seventy feet of it, leaving the bewildered Stroszek looking at the empty landscape it has left behind.

Stroszek gets most hypnotically bizarre as it goes along, because we understand more of the assumptions of the movie. One of them is possibly that Kaspar Hauser might have become Stroszek, had he lived for another century and studied diligently. (Hauser, you might remember, was the "wild child" kept imprisoned in the dark for nineteen years, never taught to speak, and then dumped in a village square.)

The film's closing scenes are wonderfully funny and sad, at once. Stroszek and Scheitz rob a barber shop, and then Stroszek buys a frozen turkey, and then there is an amusement park with a chicken that will not stop dancing (and a policeman reporting "The dancing chicken won't stop"), and a wrecker driving in a circle with no one at the wheel, and an Indian chief looking on impassively, and somehow Herzog has made a statement about America here that is as loony and utterly original as any ever made.

Stuart Saves His Family ★ ★ ★ [NEW]
PG-13, 98 m., 1995

Al Franken (Stuart Smalley), Laura San Giacomo (Julia), Vincent D'Onofrio (Donnie), Shirley Knight (Stuart's Mom), Harris Yulin (Stuart's Dad), Lesley Boone (Jodie). Directed by Harold Ramis and produced by Lorne Michaels and Trevor Albert. Screenplay by Al Franken.

It goes a long way toward explaining the problems of Stuart Smalley when you find out that when he was young, his father's nickname for him was "Waste of Space." Growing up in Minneapolis, Stuart's father was an alcoholic, his mother a codependent and enabler, his sister a compulsive eater, and his brother just waiting until he was old enough to do drugs. Stuart fled as soon as he could to Chicago, where he was soon a member of four twelve-step programs.

Stuart, of course, is the continuing character on "Saturday Night Live" who hosts his own cable show aimed at twelve-steppers, and shares pearls of wisdom like, "It is easier to put on slippers than to carpet the entire world." His own life is lived in a constant whirl of meetings, chats with sponsors, making amends, and wondering how to Do the Next Right Thing. He also has a big problem with Taking Other People's Inventory, especially in his job as a waiter, where he gives the customers advice about smoking, drinking, and eating that they desperately do not want to hear.

Stuart was created by the actor Al Franken. It is important to emphasize this because he seems to have an independent existence of his own, like Father Guido Sarducci. His segments were some of the funniest moments in the recent checkered history of "SNL," but I wondered, going in to see the movie, whether his sketches could be stretched out to feature length. They could be. *Stuart Saves His Family* is a genuine surprise: a movie that is as funny as the "SNL" stuff, and yet with convincing characters, a compelling story, and a sunny, sweet sincerity shining down on the humor.

As the movie opens, Stuart is in crisis. His cable show has been moved to the middle of the night and seems destined to be canceled. "I couldn't even keep a show on cable access," he sobs, "and that's supposed to be like a constitutional right, or something." His solution to this and many problems is to put on his pajamas and go to bed for six days, and the movie answers at last any specula-

tion about how Stuart shares his bed: He shares it with Twinkies and Peanut Butter Cups.

In twelve-step programs everyone is supposed to have, and eventually be, a sponsor, and Stuart has a corps of four who come knocking at his door. But what blasts him out of his bed is a call from Minneapolis, where his family is undergoing another of its periodic crises. He takes the long bus ride north to save them.

Dad (Harris Yulin) is a heavy drinker and puts down his kids ("I've fed you well—*that's* painfully obvious"). Mom (Shirley Knight) has long since bought into his bullying, and spends her time putting enormous meals on the table. Sis Jodie (Lesley Boone) is a compulsive overeater, and brother Donnie (Vincent D'Onofrio) smokes so much pot he hardly notices he hasn't redecorated his bedroom since junior high school.

Stuart loves his family and tries to explain them ("My father grew up in the Great Depression—his mother's"). But the crisis deepens: An aunt has left the family a $60,000 house that leads to legal problems, and Stuart only makes them worse. ("Let me get this straight," he says, "I need to *lie* to save my family from perjury?")

The movie uses flashbacks to establish the various family diseases. When little Stuart entered the TV contest to name the Ajax white knight, for example, he liked his entry (Sir Clean-a-Lot) until his father started calling him Sir Eat-a-Lot. Life in the Smalley household has not gotten better. And Stuart, in his oversize hand-knit sweaters, hardly seems competent to tame them with his advice and homely sayings. They only get him in trouble. When a couple of drunks get mean after Stuart won't let them buy him a beer, for example, it doesn't help when he advises them, "I think you're acting out the shame and powerlessness of that frightened child inside of you."

The beauty of *Stuart Saves His Family*, written by Franken and directed by Harold Ramis, is that it's somehow true to Stuart at the same time it sees the humor in him. You'd think he might become obnoxious at feature length, but he becomes more likable, especially because of his unforgiving self-criticism ("Listen to me! I'm should-ing all over myself!"). The movie is also unobtrusively wise about the real nature of the problems in Stuart's family, and doesn't offer easy solutions or a phony happy ending. I not only enjoyed Stuart Smalley, doggone it, I *liked* him; and that attitude of gratitude ain't just a platitude.

Sudden Impact ★ ★ ★
R, 117 m., 1983

Clint Eastwood (Harry Callahan), Sondra Locke (Jennifer Spencer), Pat Hingle (Chief Jannings), Bradford Dillman (Captain Briggs). Directed and produced by Clint Eastwood. Screenplay by Joseph C. Stinson.

Most of what you hear about pop art and pop culture is pure hype. But there comes a moment about halfway through *Sudden Impact*, a Dirty Harry movie, when you realize that Harry has achieved some kind of legitimate pop status, as the purest distillation in the movies of the spirit of vengeance. To all those cowboy movies we saw in our youth, all those TV westerns and cop dramas and war movies, Dirty Harry has brought a great simplification: A big man, a big gun, a bad guy, and instant justice.

We learned early to cheer when John Wayne shot the bad guys. We cheered when the cavalry turned up, or the Yanks, or the SWAT team. What Eastwood's Dirty Harry movies do is very simple. They reduce the screen time between those cheers to the absolute minimum. *Sudden Impact* is a Dirty Harry movie with only the good parts left in. All the slow stuff, such as character, motivation, atmosphere, and plot, has been pared to exactly the minimum necessary to hold together the violence. This movie has been edited with the economy of a thirty-second commercial. As a result, it's a great audience picture. It's not plausible, it doesn't make much sense, it has a cardboard villain and, for that matter, a hero who exists more as a set of functions (grin, fight, chase, kill) than as a human being. But none of those are valid objections. *Sudden Impact* is more like a music video; it consists only of setups and payoffs, its big scenes are self-contained, it's filled with kinetic energy, and it has a short attention span. That last is very important, because if anyone were really keeping track of what Callahan does in this movie, Harry would be removed from the streets after his third or fourth killing. Dirty Harry movies are like Roadrunner cartoons; the moment a body is dead, it is forgotten, and nobody stands around to dispose of the corpses.

The movie's basically a revenge tragedy. A young woman (Sondra Locke) and her sister are sexually attacked at a carnival by a group of quasi-human bullies. The sister goes nuts, and Locke vows vengeance. One by one, she tracks down the rapists, and murders them by shooting them in the genitals and forehead. Dirty Harry gets assigned to the case, and the rest is a series of violent confrontations. Occasionally there's comic relief, in the form of Harry's meetings with his superiors, and his grim-jawed putdowns of anyone who crosses his path. ("Suck fish heads," he helpfully advises one man.)

If the movie has a weakness, it's the plot. Because I'm not sure the plot is relevant to the success of the film, I'm not sure that's a weakness. The whole business of Locke's revenge is so mechanically established and carried out that it's automatic, and because she has a "good" motive for her murders, she doesn't make an interesting villain. If Eastwood could create a villain as single-minded, violent, economically chiseled, and unremittingly efficient as Dirty Harry Callahan, then we'd be onto something.

Sugar Hill ★ ★ ★ ★
R, 123 m., 1994

Wesley Snipes (Roemello Skuggs), Michael Wright (Raynathan Skuggs), Theresa Randle (Melissa), Clarence Williams III (A.R. Skuggs), Abe Vigoda (Gus Molino), Ernie Hudson (Lolly Jonas). Directed by Leon Ichaso and produced by Rudy Langlais and Gregory Brown. Screenplay by Barry Michael Cooper.

Sugar Hill is a dark, bloody family tragedy, told in terms so sad and poetic that it transcends its genre and becomes eloquent drama. To call this film a "drug thriller" is like describing *Macbeth* as a murder mystery, or *Long Day's Journey Into Night* as a soap opera. In its rich visual style, its powerful acting, and the unexpected grace of its dialogue, it tells a deeply affecting story.

The film stars Wesley Snipes and Michael Wright as Roemello and Raynathan Skuggs, two brothers whose childhoods were seared by drugs. They have seen their mother die of an overdose, and their father crippled by mob bullets after withholding money in a drug deal. Now, as young men in Harlem, they're drug dealers themselves—working with the same Mafia boss who ordered their father shot.

On a materialistic level, life is good for them. Roemello lives in an apartment of dark, burnished woods and deep reds and bronzes; its interiors reminded me of Don Vito's home in *The Godfather*, and indeed, Bojan Bazelli's cinematography throughout the movie creates the same kind of shadowed, luxurious world that was inhabited by the Corleones.

But Roemello is not happy with his life, and Snipes portrays him as a man who has gotten to the point where he can hardly bear to see what goes on around him. A small boy on a bicycle brandishes a handgun. Another gang wants a piece of the action in his territory, and he doesn't want to face the violence that is likely to result. And in a drab apartment, his father (Clarence Williams III) sits paralyzed from the waist down, waiting for his next fix.

Roemello wants out. Nobody wants him out. His brother believes they are on the brink of a breakthrough to the *really* big time. And Gus Molino (Abe Vigoda), the ancient Mafia boss who controls the drugs, thinks it would be a very bad idea for them to quit now—even though he's behind the division of the territory.

Some of these plot elements are not unfamiliar from many other movies, including Snipes's own *New Jack City* and 1993's *Carlito's Way*. But *Sugar Hill* exists in another dimension. Leon Ichaso's direction and Barry Michael Cooper's screenplay are deliberately aiming for the deep human tragedy in this story, and away from the formula crime elements. Sometimes we can be snobs about genres, and think that a Harlem drug story can only exist on a certain level, but as I was watching this film I was reminded of classical tragedy, and of Shakespeare and Eugene O'Neill.

The film's central pain comes from the fact that the suffering caused by drugs goes on and on and on, one generation after the next. The memory of the dead mother and the daily rebuke of the father's sad existence do not stop the Skuggs brothers from dealing the same drugs, from the same supplier, that destroyed their parents' lives. There is even a certain brooding logic to it; Roemello has won revenge by killing the man who actually shot his father. But he has not touched Gus Molino, who ordered the shooting—because at that level it was, after all, business. And Gus Molino has never looked too deeply into who killed his triggerman (of course he knows it was Roemello), because he accepts the feelings that were involved.

There is a certain conservatism here, a certain respect for continuing to do things in the old ways, that both Roemello and Gus understand. It is the entry of the new gang into the neighborhood (led by Ernie Hudson) that threatens the balance. And even more threatening is Roemello's disenchantment. "It's not that I'm scared, man," he tells his brother. "It's just that I see something you don't."

Roemello has met a woman, Melissa (Theresa Randle), and loves her, but she wants nothing to do with him because he is a drug dealer. She's serious; it isn't an act. He tells her he's leaving the business. She will believe that when she sees it. Their relationship goes deeper than romance usually does in this genre; there is quick passion, yes, but also thought for future consequences. She believes it is not enough to love someone. You must also be able to trust him, and to believe he will be alive for you.

Few movies have been this thoughtful and serious about a problem that has been cheapened by so many gun-crazy movies and TV shows. *Sugar Hill* looks unblinkingly at what drugs do—not simply to the bodies of those who use them, but to the lives and future of those touched by them, even if they don't use them. My only problem with the film is with the very last scene, which looks suspiciously tacked-on, as if the filmmakers, having taken their story to its logical conclusion, could not leave it there.

Sugar Hill is in danger of being overlooked by its intended audience, and unappreciated by the audience that will be drawn by exploitative ads. Here is a Harlem drug drama starring Wesley Snipes, one of the top action stars in the movies, and it's logical to assume it's a thriller. It's not. It is appropriate for the same audiences who saw and understood *Schindler's List*, *Philadelphia*, and *The Remains of the Day*. Of course they will hear some words and see some drug abuse and violence they may not be accustomed to, but that is because this passionate tragedy is not about a very nice world.

The Summer House ★ ★ ★
NO MPAA RATING, 82 m., 1993

Jeanne Moreau (Lili), Joan Plowright (Mrs. Monro), Julie Walters (Monica), Lena Headey (Margaret), David Threlfall (Syl), John Wood (Robert). Directed by Waris Hussein and produced by Norma Heyman. Screenplay by Martin Sherman.

It is clear the marriage is a bad idea. "I'm marrying a man nobody likes," the bride-to-be confides. "I thought it was just me." And yet it appears the marriage will go forward

nonetheless. All the players have their roles, the plans have been made, the invitations issued, the alterations made on the family wedding gown. Only a miracle can save the future bride from a mistake she will regret for the rest of her life, starting immediately.

That is the setup for *The Summer House*, an odd and amusing comedy of manners. Marriage is, of course, an institution in which men and women should take an equal role, but marriage *ceremonies* are the province of women. They take infinite delight in the detail work. The man's job is to deliver himself on the right day at the right time.

The Summer House understands this. There is a man in the picture, a hapless would-be groom named Syl (David Threlfall), who has arrived in his early forties without having mastered a single skill designed to make his presence bearable. But most of the characters are women: Margaret (Lena Headey), the quiet young girl who has no idea why she consented to marriage; her mother, Monica (Julie Walters), who at first doesn't doubt the wisdom of the match; Syl's mother, Mrs. Monro (Joan Plowright), who knows her son and is *sure* the marriage is a mistake; and—sweeping into town for the ceremony—Monica's old school chum from France, Lili (Jeanne Moreau).

The movie sees these women in unguarded, quirky moments. We're only gradually allowed to discover what they're really up to. Margaret would essentially rather be a nun in Egypt than marry anybody. Monica frets that since the invitations have been sent out and the arrangements made, it's too late to call things off. Mrs. Monro, who has lived under the same roof with her son for years, pities the poor girl. And Lili, who affects the style of an aging prima donna and likes to wave her cigarette holder around, reads the whole situation in a moment and makes a solemn promise that the marriage will never take place.

The movie, directed by Waris Hussein and based on the novel *The Clothes in the Wardrobe* by Alice Thomas Ellis, could possibly have handled this same situation with a sitcom approach, but it's too smart and original for that. It has wicked fun showing the smug pomposity of the prospective groom, and the shyness and desperation of the intended bride, who takes up smoking and drinking in her need to blot out the impending event.

Jeanne Moreau has been a treasure of the movies for thirty-five years, often playing

roles something like this one. If you stop to think about it, her famous role in Truffaut's *Jules and Jim* was a similar woman, an imperious free spirit who decides what's to be done, and makes it happen. Here, playing a flamboyant woman who nevertheless keeps her real thoughts closely guarded, she brings about a final scene of poetic justice as perfect as it is unexpected.

Sunday Bloody Sunday ★ ★ ★ ★
R, 110 m., 1971

Glenda Jackson (Alex Greville), Peter Finch (Dr. Daniel Hirsh), Murray Head (Bob Elkin), Peggy Ashcroft (Mrs. Greville), Tony Britton (Businessman), Maurice Denham (Mr. Greville). Directed by John Schlesinger and produced by Joseph Janni. Screenplay by Penelope Gilliatt.

The official East Coast line on John Schlesinger's *Sunday Bloody Sunday* was that it is civilized. That judgment was enlisted to carry the critical defense of the movie; and, indeed, how can the decent critic be against a civilized movie about civilized people? My notion, all the same, is that *Sunday Bloody Sunday* is about people who suffer from psychic amputation, not civility, and that this film is not an affirmation but a tragedy.

The story involves three people in a rather novel love triangle: A London doctor in his forties, a divorced woman in her thirties, and the young man they are both in love with. The doctor and the woman know about each other (the young man makes no attempt to keep secrets) but don't seem particularly concerned; they have both made an accommodation in order to have some love instead of none at all.

The screenplay by Penelope Gilliatt takes us through eight or nine days in their lives, while the young man prepares to leave for New York. Both of his lovers will miss him—and he will miss *them*, after his fashion—but he has decided to go, and between them, they don't have enough pull on him to make him want to stay. So the two love affairs approach their ends, while the lovers go about a melancholy daily existence in London.

Both the doctor and the woman are involved in helping people, he by a kind and intelligent approach to his patients, she through working in an employment agency. The boy, on the other hand, seems exclusively preoccupied with the commercial prospects in America for his sculpture (he does things with glass tubes, liquids, and electricity). He isn't concerned with whether his stuff is any good, but whether it will sell to Americans. He doesn't seem to feel very deeply about anything, in fact. He is kind enough and open enough, but there is no dimension to him, as there is to his lovers.

It is with the two older characters that we get to the core of the movie. In a world where everyone loses eventually, they are still survivors. They survive by accommodating themselves to life as it must be lived. The doctor, for example, is not at all personally disturbed by his homosexuality, and yet he doesn't reveal it to his close-knit Jewish family; maintaining relations-as-usual with them is another way for him to survive. The woman tells us late in the film, "Some people believe something is better than nothing, but I'm beginning to believe that nothing can be better than something." Well, maybe so, but we get to know her well enough to suspect that she will settle for something, not nothing, again the next time.

The glory of *Sunday Bloody Sunday* is supposed to be the intelligent, sophisticated— civilized!—way in which these two people gracefully accept the loss of a love they had shared. Well, they *are* graceful as hell about it, and there is a positive glut of being philosophical about the inevitable. But that didn't make me feel better for them, or about them, the way it was supposed to; I felt pity for them. I insist that they would *not* have been so bloody civilized if either one had felt really deeply about the boy. The fact that they were willing to share him is perhaps a clue: They shared him not because they were willing to settle for half, but because they were afraid to try for all. The three-sided arrangement was, in part, a guarantee that no one would get in so deep that being "civilized" wouldn't be protection enough against hurt.

The acting is flawless. Peter Finch is the doctor, Glenda Jackson the woman, and Murray Head the young man. They are good to begin with and then just right for Gilliatt's screenplay and Schlesinger's direction. They are set down in a very real and sad London (seen mostly in cold twilights), and surrounded by supporting actors who resonate in a way that fills in all the dimensions of the characters. I think *Sunday Bloody Sunday* is a masterpiece, but I don't think it's about what everybody else seems to think it's about. This is not a movie about the loss of love, but about its absence.

Superman ★ ★ ★ ★
PG, 144 m., 1978

Christopher Reeve (Superman/Clark Kent), Marlon Brando (Jor-El), Gene Hackman (Lex Luthor), Margot Kidder (Lois Lane), Ned Beatty (Otis), Jackie Cooper (Perry White), Glenn Ford (Jonathan Kent), Trevor Howard (First Elder), Valerie Perrine (Miss Teschmacher). Directed by Richard Donner and produced by Pierre Spengler. Screenplay by Mario Puzo, David Newman, Leslie Newman, and Robert Benton.

Superman is a pure delight, a wondrous combination of all the old-fashioned things we never really get tired of: adventure and romance, heroes and villains, earthshaking special effects, and—you know what else? Wit. That surprised me more than anything: That this big-budget epic, which was half a decade making its way to the screen, would turn out to have an intelligent sense of humor about itself.

The wit, to be sure, is a little slow in revealing itself. The film's opening scenes combine great intergalactic special effects with ponderous acting and dialogue—most of it from Marlon Brando, who, as Superman's father, sends the kid to Earth in a spaceship that barely survives the destruction of the planet Krypton. Brando was allegedly paid $3 million for his role, or, judging by his dialogue, $500,000 a cliché. After Superbaby survives his space flight and lands in a Midwestern wheat field, however, the movie gets down to earth, too. And it has the surprising ability to have *fun* with its special effects. That's surprising because special effects on this vast scale (falling airliners, derailing passenger trains, subterranean dungeons, cracks in the earth, volcanic eruptions, dams bursting) are so expensive and difficult that it takes a special kind of courage to kid them a little—instead of regarding them with awe, as in the witless *Earthquake*.

The audience finds itself pleasantly surprised, and taken a little off guard; the movie's tremendously exciting in a comic book sort of way (kids will go ape for it), but at the same time it has a sly sophistication, a kidding insight into the material, that makes it, amazingly, a refreshingly offbeat comedy.

Most of the humor centers, of course, around one of the central icons of American popular culture, Superman (who, and I quote from our common memory of hundreds of comic books and radio and TV shows, in his

dual identity as Clark Kent is a mild-mannered reporter for the *Daily Planet*). The producers held a worldwide talent search for an actor to play Superman, and although "talent searches" are usually 100 percent horsefeathers, this time, for once, they actually found the right guy.

He is Christopher Reeve. He *looks* like the Superman in the comic books (a fate I would not wish on anybody), but he's also an engaging actor, open and funny in his big love scene with Lois Lane, and then correctly awesome in his showdown with the archvillain Lex Luthor. Reeve sells the role; wrong casting here would have sunk everything.

And there would have been a lot to sink. *Superman* may have been expensive, all right, but the money's there on the screen. The screenplay was obviously written without the slightest concern for how much it might cost. After Clark Kent goes to work for the *Daily Planet* (and we meet old favorites Perry White, Lois Lane, and Jimmy Olsen), there's a nonstop series of disasters just for openers: Poor Lois finds herself dangling from one seatbelt after her helicopter crashes high atop the Daily Planet Building; Air Force One is struck by lightning and loses an engine; a thief climbs up a building using suction cups, and so on. Superman resolves his emergencies with, well, tact and good manners. He's modest about his abilities. Snaps a salute to the president. Says he's for "truth, justice, and the American Way." And, of course, falls in love with Lois Lane.

She's played by Margot Kidder, and their relationship is subtly, funnily wicked. She lives in a typical girl reporter's apartment (you know, a penthouse high atop a Metropolis skyscraper), and Superman zooms down to offer an exclusive interview and a free flight over Metropolis. Supposing *you're* a girl reporter, and Superman turns up. What would you ask him? So does she.

Meanwhile, the evil Lex Luthor (Gene Hackman) is planning an apocalyptic scheme to destroy the entire West Coast, plus Hackensack, New Jersey. He knows Superman's weak point: the deadly substance Kryptonite. He also knows that Superman cannot see through lead (Lois Lane, alas, forgets). Luthor lives in a subterranean pad that's a comic inspiration: A half-flooded, subterranean train station. Superman drills through the earth for a visit.

But enough of the plot. The movie works so well because of its wit and its special effects. A word more about each. The movie begins with the tremendous advantage that almost everyone in the audience knows the Superman saga from youth. There aren't a lot of explanations needed; that's brilliantly demonstrated in the first scene where Superman tries to change in a phone booth. Christopher Reeve can be allowed to smile, to permit himself a double entendre, to kid himself.

And then the special effects. They're as good in their way as any you've seen, and they come thick and fast. When the screenplay calls for Luthor to create an earthquake and for Superman to try to stop it, the movie doesn't give us a falling bridge or two, it gives us the San Andreas Fault cracking open. No half measures for Superman. The movie is, in fact, a triumph of imagination over both the difficulties of technology and the inhibitions of money. *Superman* wasn't easy to bring to the screen, but the filmmakers kept at it until they had it right.

Superman II ★ ★ ★ ★
PG, 127 m., 1981

Christopher Reeve (Superman/Clark Kent), Gene Hackman (Lex Luthor), Ned Beatty (Otis), Margot Kidder (Lois Lane), Terence Stamp (General Zod), Jackie Cooper (Perry White), Sarah Douglas (Ursa), Jack O'Halloran (Non), Valerie Perrine (Eve). Directed by Richard Lester and produced by Alexander and Ilya Salkind and Pierre Spengler. Screenplay by Mario Puzo, David Newman, and Leslie Newman.

I thought the original *Superman* was terrific entertainment—and so I was a little startled to discover that I liked *Superman II* even more. Perhaps the secret of the sequel is that it has more faith in Superman. Before the original *Superman* was released in 1978, the producers knew he could carry a speeding locomotive, all right—but could he carry a movie? They weren't sure, and since they were investing millions of dollars in the project, they didn't want to rest a whole movie on the broad shoulders of their unknown star, Christopher Reeve. So they began *Superman* ponderously, on the planet Krypton, with the presence of Marlon Brando as a sort of totem to convince audiences that this movie was big league. They told us of Superman's origins with a solemnity more befitting a god. They were very serious and very symbolic, and it wasn't until Superman came to Earth that the movie really caught fire. *Then,* half an hour or more into its length, it

started giving us what we came for: Superman flying around with his red cape, saving mankind.

Superman II begins in midstream, and never looks back (aside from a brief recap of the first movie). In many ways, it's a repeat of the last ninety minutes of the first film. It has the same key characters, including archvillain Lex Luthor. It continues the love story of Lois Lane and Superman, not to mention the strange relationship of Lois and Clark Kent. It features the return of three villains from Krypton, who when last seen were trapped in a one-dimensional plane of light and cast adrift in space. And it continues those remarkable special effects.

From his earliest days in a comic book, Superman always has been an urban hero. He lived in a universe that was defined by screaming banner headlines and vast symbolic acts, and *Superman II* catches that flavor perfectly with its use of famous landmarks like the Eiffel Tower, the Empire State Building, Niagara Falls, and the Coca-Cola sign in Times Square. He was a pop hero in a pop world, and like Mickey Mouse and the original Coke trademark, he became an instantly recognizable trademark.

That's why the special effects in both *Superman* movies are so crucial. It is a great deal simpler to show a rocket ship against the backdrop of outer space than to show Kryptonian villains hurling a city bus through the air in midtown Manhattan. But the feeling of actuality makes Superman's exploits more fun. It brings the fantastic into our everyday lives; it delights in showing us the reaction of the man on the street to Superman's latest stunt. In the movie, as in the comic book, ordinary citizens seem to spend their days glued to the sidewalk, gazing skyward, and shouting things like "Superman is dead!" or "Superman has saved the world!"

In *Superman II* he saves large portions of the world, all right, but what he preserves most of all is the element of humanity within him. The *Superman* movies made a basic decision to give Superman and his alter ego, Clark Kent, more human feelings than the character originally possessed. So *Superman II* has a lot of fun developing his odd dual relationship with Lois Lane. At long, long last, Lois and Superman make love in this movie (after champagne, but discreetly off-screen in Superman's ice palace). But Lois and Clark Kent also spend the night together in highly compromised circumstances, in a Niagara Falls honeymoon haven. And the

movie has fun with another one of those ultimate tests that Lois was always throwing at Clark to make him admit he was really Superman. Lois bets her life on it this time, hurling herself into the rapids below Niagara Falls. Either Clark can turn into Superman and save her—or she'll drown. And what then? All I can say is, Clark does *not* turn into Superman.

This scene has a lot of humor in it, and the whole film has more smiles and laughs than the first one. Maybe that's because of a change in directors. Richard Donner, who made the first *Superman* film and did a brilliant job of establishing a basic look for the series, was followed this time by Richard Lester (*A Hard Day's Night, The Three Musketeers*), and this is some of Lester's best work. He permits satire to make its way into the film more easily. He has a lot of fun with Gene Hackman, as the still-scheming, thin-skinned, egomaniacal Lex Luthor. And he draws out Christopher Reeve, whose performance in the title role is sly, knowing, and yet still appropriately square. This movie's most intriguing insight is that Superman's disguise as Clark Kent isn't a matter of looks as much as of mental attitude: Clark is disguised not by his glasses but by his ordinariness. Beneath his meek exterior, of course, is concealed a superhero. And, the movie subtly hints, isn't that the case with us all?

Superman III ★ ★ ½
PG, 125 m., 1983

Christopher Reeve (Superman/Clark Kent), Richard Pryor (Gus Gorman), Annette O'Toole (Lana Lang), Robert Vaughn (Ross Webster). Directed by Richard Lester and produced by Alexander Salkind. Screenplay by David and Leslie Newman.

Superman III is the kind of movie I feared the original *Superman* would be. It's a cinematic comic book, shallow, silly, filled with stunts and action, without much human interest. What's amazing is that the first two *Superman* movies avoided that description, creating a fantasy with a certain charm. They could have been manipulative special-effects movies, but they were a great deal more. With this third one, maybe they've finally run out of inspiration.

The big news about *Superman III* is, of course, the presence of Richard Pryor in the cast. But Pryor isn't used very well here. He never really emerges as a person we care about. His character and the whole movie seem assembled out of prefabricated pieces. The first two films were too, in a way, but real care was taken with the dialogue, and we could occasionally halfway believe that real people had gotten themselves into this world of fantasy. Not this time. *Superman III* drops most of the threads of the first two movies—including Lois Lane's increasingly complex love affair with Clark Kent and Superman—and goes for the action. There's no real sense of what Superman, or Clark, ever really feels. The running gag about the hero's double identity isn't really exploited this time. The sheer amazingness of Superman isn't explored; the movie and the people in it take this incredible creature for granted. After the bird and the plane, it's "Superman" when it should be SUPERMAN!

The plot involves the usual scheme to control the Earth. The villain this time is Robert Vaughn, as a mad billionaire who wants to use satellites to control the Earth's crops and become even richer. He directs his satellites and weapons systems by computer, and that's how he hooks up with Pryor, as a brilliant, but befuddled, computer programmer. Superman, meanwhile, has a couple of things on his mind. After Lois Lane leaves to go on vacation at the beginning of the movie (in a particularly awkward scene), Clark goes home to his Smallville High School reunion, and has a love affair with Lana Lang (Annette O'Toole). It's sweet, but it's not half as interesting as the Ice Castle footage with Lois Lane in *Superman II.* Then Superman gets zapped with some ersatz Kryptonite and turns into a meanie, which is good for some laughs (as a practical joke, he straightens the Leaning Tower of Pisa).

All of this is sort of fun, and the special effects are sometimes very good, but there's no real sense of wonder in this film—no moments like the scene in *Superman* where California threatened to fall into the sea and Superman turned back time to save humanity. After that, who cares about Robert Vaughn's satellites? Or Richard Pryor's dilemma? Pryor can be a wicked, anarchic comic actor, and that presence would have been welcome here. Instead, like the rest of *Superman III,* he's kind of innocuous.

Superstar: The Life and Times of Andy Warhol ★ ★ ★
NO MPAA RATING, 87 m., 1991

A documentary with interviews given by Andy Warhol and featuring commentary by

Holly Woodlawn, Dennis Hopper, Grace Jones, Ultra Violet, Viva, David Hockney, and Roy Lichtenstein. Directed, produced, and written by Chuck Workman.

The one thing everyone knows about Andy Warhol is that he once said that, in the future, everyone would be famous for fifteen minutes. This is the sort of news people like to hear. Warhol himself was a grand master of publicity, remaking himself into one of the most famous people in the world by always presenting the same face—an unchanging blank bored cipher—which he turned faithfully upon more people at more parties than anyone else in the history of New York City.

He was the master of the nonconversation, the nonreply, the verbal put down. Legions of journalists turned up to interview him, and, of course, he was always willing to be interviewed, but he never *said* anything. "Yes." "No." "I don't know." Those answers were his faithful servants, and when the desperate interviewer supplied an answer or a theory of his own, Warhol would nod and say, "That's right." Or maybe simply "yes." Sometimes, if it could not be avoided, "no."

His management of the media was, of course, an exercise in passive aggression. The more he seemed not to care, the more he intrigued people. The less he sought publicity, the more of it he attracted. And, of course, there was a method to his vagueness. He worked tirelessly to put himself into places where he could experience indifference; he never missed an opportunity to be bored.

The result of his lifelong image-construction is that there is precious little of Andy Warhol onscreen in Chuck Workman's *Superstar: The Life and Times of Andy Warhol.* And there is not a single moment of personal revelation; not a single frame of film in which Andy lets his guard down. He is a pale, blank, monosyllabic, unresponsive presence, and yet the strange thing is, the film succeeds despite that. And it succeeds on his terms, by making us pay attention to him without revealing any of his secrets.

Or perhaps we learn a few. There is a priceless moment when his relatives from back in Pennsylvania say they were surprised to discover how much he was like them. Put that moment beside those in which such famous people as Dennis Hopper or David Hockney talk about Warhol, and you will discover that he was like *them,* too. Perhaps he was the original inspiration for Woody Allen's *Zelig,* the man who couldn't help taking on

the coloration and characteristics of everyone he met.

If Warhol himself was a cipher, his work was a trumpet blast of aggressive self-confidence. His soup cans and Mao portraits, his wallpaper and movies and silkscreen prints, became part of the visual image of his time. He came to fame in the 1960s, but survived that decade and continued to be important after the work of many of his contemporaries had been revealed as fads and passing fancies. To view *Superstar* is to be reminded of how pervasively his view saturated our visual universe, how omnipresent he was.

"He was a pointer," Dennis Hopper says in the film. "He did what Marcel Duchamp said an artist should do. He pointed at things, and then we could see them." He pointed first at the Campbell's soup cans and the Coca-Cola trademark, and called them Pop Art, but then he started pointing at people and just by his pointing made them "superstars." What he did was reveal that there is little difference between the famous and the obscure, except that the famous are better known.

The movie has a strangely ingratiating quality to it. Workman (the man who does the compilation documentaries for the Oscar cast) is content to let his subject gradually reveal itself. He collects witnesses and bits of old films and TV interviews, clips from Warhol movies and speculations by his friends and family. And finally what we are left with is an artist whose greatest art was his attitude. Not just the blank passivity he served up to the public, but also what I would make bold to describe as his enthusiasm. He saw, he pointed, we saw. If he had been talkative, it might not have worked.

The Sure Thing ★ ★ ★ ½
PG-13, 94 m., 1985

John Cusack (Walter Gibson), Daphne Zuniga (Alison Bradbury), Anthony Edwards (Lance), Boyd Gaines (Jason), Tim Robbins (Gary Cooper), Lisa Jane Persky (Mary Ann Webster), Viveca Lindfors (Professor), Nicollette Sheridan (Sure Thing). Directed by Rob Reiner and produced by Roger Birnbaum. Screenplay by Steven Bloom and Jonathan Roberts.

The love story is one of Hollywood's missing genres. The movie industry seems better at teen-age movies like *Porky's,* with its sleazy shower scenes, than with screenplays that involve any sort of thought about the love lives of its characters. That's why *The Sure Thing* is a small miracle. Although the hero of this movie is promised by his buddy that he'll be fixed up with a "guaranteed sure thing," the film is not about the sure thing but about how this kid falls genuinely and touchingly into love.

The movie's love story begins in an Eastern college classroom. Walter Gibson (John Cusack) walks into his English class and falls immediately into love with Alison Bradbury (Daphne Zuniga), who is smart and good-looking and not one of your brainless movie broads. He asks her out, but succeeds, of course, in acting like a total nerd, and she invites him to get out of her life. End of act one. In act two, Walter plans to spend his Christmas vacation in Los Angeles, where his buddy says the Sure Thing is eagerly awaiting his arrival. Alison also plans to go to L.A., to visit her fiancé, who is studying to be a boring middle-class vegetable. They both sign up for rides, and, of course, they both wind up in the back seat of the same car. At first they don't talk. Then they start to fight. Then they are ditched at the side of the road and have to hitchhike to L.A. together.

I know this is an obvious movie ploy. I know, in fact, that what will happen next is completely predictable: They'll fight, they'll share experiences, they'll suffer together, and eventually they'll fall in love. I know all of these things, and yet I don't care. I don't care because love is always a cliché anyway, and the only thing that makes it endlessly fascinating is that the players are always changing. These two particular characters, Walter and Alison, played by these two gifted young actors, Cusack and Zuniga, make *The Sure Thing* into a special love story.

One of the unique things about the movie is that the characters show a normal shyness about sex. Most movie teen-agers seem to be valedictorians from the Masters & Johnson Institute. They're born knowing more about sex than Rhett Butler would have been able to teach Scarlett O'Hara. They are also, of course, not shy, not insecure, not modest, and occasionally not human. Walter and Alison are closer to real teen-agers, with real doubts and hesitations and uncertainties. The other surprising thing about the film is that it successfully avoids an obligatory sex scene with the Sure Thing (Nicollette Sheridan, in a thankless role). This film is so revolutionary, it believes sex should be accompanied by respect and love! By the end of the movie, when Walter and Alison finally do kiss, it means something. It means more, in fact, than any movie kiss in a long time, because it takes place between two people we've gotten to know and who have gotten to know each other.

Swamp Thing ★ ★ ★
R, 102 m., 1982

Louis Jourdan (Arcane), Adrienne Barbeau (Alice), Ray Wise (Dr. Holland), Dick Durock (Swamp Thing), David Hess (Ferret), Nicholas Worth (Brung). Directed by Wes Craven and produced by Benjamin Melniker and Michael Uslan. Screenplay by Craven.

Swamp Thing had already won my heart *before* its moment of greatness, but when that moment came, I knew I'd discovered another one of those movies that fall somewhere between buried treasures and guilty pleasures. The moment comes after Dr. Alec Holland, brilliant scientist, is attacked by thugs, is splashed with his own secret formula, catches on fire, leaps into the swamp, and turns into Swamp Thing when the formula interacts with his body and the vegetation in the swamp. Crawling back onto dry land, Swamp Thing is not recognized by his former girlfriend, the beautiful Alice Cable (Adrienne Barbeau). But after the thugs fill him with machine-gun bullets and hack off his left arm, Alice asks, "Does it hurt?" and Swamp Thing replies, "Only when I laugh."

That was the movie's moment of greatness. There are others that come close, as when Swamp Thing, dripping with moss and looking like a bug-eyed spinach soufflé, says "There is great beauty in the swamp . . . if you know where to look." And when the evil villain (Louis Jourdan) drinks the secret formula and confidently waits for it to transform him into a powerful genius, he discovers that the formula doesn't so much *change* you, as develop what is already latent within you. Therefore, once a horse's ass, *always* a horse's ass.

This is one of those movies like *Infra-Man* or *Invasion of the Bee Girls:* an off-the-wall, eccentric, peculiar movie fueled by the demented obsessions of its makers. *Swamp Thing* first saw the light of day, so to speak, as a hero in a celebrated series of DC Comics. The movie version was written and directed by Wes Craven, who made *Last House on the Left,* a movie I persist in admiring even in the face of universal repugnance. Craven also made *The Hills Have Eyes,* which even I found decadent, and the made-for-NBC movie *Stranger in Our House,* with Linda Blair. This time, with *Swamp Thing,* he betrays a certain gentleness and poetry along with the gore; in fact, this movie is a lot less violent than many others in the same genre. Craven's inspiration seems to come from James Whale's classic *Bride of Frankenstein* (1935), and he pays tribute in scenes where his swamp monster sniffs a flower, admires a young girl's beauty from afar, and looks sadly at a photograph in a locket. *Swamp Thing* doesn't stop there; it also contains an exact visual quote from Russ Meyer's *Lorna,* and a scene in which the jailer in a dungeon cheerfully quotes the title of a Werner Herzog film: "It's every man for himself, and God against all!"

Will you like this film? Yes, probably, if you like monster and horror movies. The movie occupies familiar ground, but it has a freshness and winsome humor to fit it, and Craven moves confidently through the three related genres he's stealing from (monster movies, mad scientist movies, and transformation movies—in which people turn into strange beings). There's beauty in this movie, if you know where to look for it.

Swann in Love ★ ★ ★
R, 110 m., 1984

Jeremy Irons (Charles Swann), Ornella Muti (Odette de Crecy), Alain Delon (Baron de Charlus), Fanny Ardant (Duchesse de Guermantes), Marie-Christine Barrault (Madame Verdurin). Directed by Volker Schlondorff and produced by Nicole Stephane. Written by Peter Brook, Jean-Claude Carriere, and Marie-Helene Estienne.

All of the reviews I've read of Volker Schlondorff's *Swann in Love* treat it like a classroom assignment. The movie is described as a version of one of the stories that make up *Remembrance of Things Past,* the epic novel by Marcel Proust, and then the exercise becomes almost academic: "Compare and contrast Proust and Schlondorff, with particular attention to the difference between fiction and the film." Imagine instead, that this is not a film based on a novel, but a new film from an original screenplay. It will immediately seem more lively and accessible. Because not one person in a hundred who sees the film will have read Proust, this is a sensible approach; it does away with the nagging feeling that one should really curl up with those twelve volumes before going to the theater.

Schlondorff's *Swann in Love*—as opposed to Proust's—is the story of a pale young man who goes one day to visit a prostitute, and is actually indifferent to her until she stands him up. Then he becomes obsessed. She is not the right woman for him, but her very wrongness becomes fascinating. Because she is vulgar, because she lies, because she toys with his affection, and most particularly because she lets him smell the orchid in her bodice, she becomes the most important person in the world to him, and he throws his life and reputation at her feet. Proper society, of course, disapproves of his affair—and talks of nothing else. In the elegant salons where ladies and gentlemen gather, Swann is not welcome if he brings along his Odette, but because he cannot be happy without her, this is no punishment. In the most humiliating scenes in the movie, he abjectly follows her through the night, knocks on a door he hopes is hers, and stands in her boudoir while she nonchalantly disrobes and dresses for an appointment with another man.

Casting is everything in a film like this. Jeremy Irons is perfect as Charles Swann, pale, deep-eyed, feverish with passion. This was his third movie (after *The French Lieutenant's Woman* and *Betrayal*) in which love seemed necessary to his nature. We can believe his passion. As Odette, Schlondorff has cast Ornella Muti, who has a sort of languorous bemusement that is maddening: We wonder if she is even capable of understanding that the man before her is mad with love and desire, and then we realize, of course, that her very *inability* to care is what creates her fatal attraction. *Swann in Love* is a stylish, period love story, surrounding its central characters with still other pathetic seekers of perfection (Alain Delon is wonderful as a gloomy homosexual who pursues an idealized form of misery). Yet at the film's end, we've probably learned nothing except that lovers were as silly in 1875 as they are now. Sillier, perhaps; they had more time.

The Swan Princess ★ ★ ★
G, 80 m., 1994

NEW

With the voices of: Jack Palance (Rothbart), John Cleese (Jean-Bob), Steven Wright ("Speed"), Sandy Duncan (Queen Uberta), Steve Vinovich (Puffin), Howard McGillin (Prince Derek), Michelle Nicastro (Princess Odette). Directed by Richard Rich and produced by Rich, Terry Noss, and Tom Tobin. Screenplay by Rich and Brian Nissen.

The Swan Princess reveals itself as a film of our politically correct times in an early scene, where a prince makes the mistake of telling a princess she is "beautiful." Is that all? she asks. What else am I? The prince is at a loss for words: "What else is there?" And so the princess huffily marches out of his life, and into all sorts of dire predicaments, simply because the prince—whom she has known since childhood—could not think to say that she was also clever.

This is, I think, progress; beauty has long been the only attribute of princesses in fairy tales, aside from a certain vapid wistfulness. And Princess Odette, the heroine of Richard Rich's full-length animated cartoon, is a smart young lady, although not smart enough to stay away from the magical spells of the evil Rothbart, who desires her father's kingdom and hopes to win it through fraud, by stealing her hand in marriage. His spell turns her into a swan, who can be seen as a princess only when the moon is upon the lake.

The Swan Princess, inspired in part by *Swan Lake*, is probably the best in a series of Disney wannabes—animated features combining music, advanced graphics, and more sophisticated characters, in the tradition of Disney's enormous hits *The Little Mermaid*, *Beauty and the Beast*, *Aladdin*, and *The Lion King*. It doesn't quite reach that standard (the songs aren't very memorable and the animation isn't as supple and detailed), but as holiday family entertainment, it does very nicely, and is at least as good as, say, Disney's straight-to-video best-seller *The Return of Jafar*.

Rich, who produced, directed, and wrote the film, and Steve Gordon, who did the animation, have obviously studied Disney's recent successes carefully. Their heroine, Princess Odette, is in the tradition of the Little Mermaid, and cannot make herself seen or heard by the man she loves. Her greatest assets are three jolly little supporting characters: a turtle, a frog, and a puffin, who provide comic relief like the obligatory sidekicks in Disney films. There are several big production numbers. And the climax, as in *The Little Mermaid*, involves her desperate attempts to make herself known to a prince who is about to be horribly deceived.

My favorite among the characters, if only for his perfect name, is Jean-Bob the frog, with a voice by John Cleese. He has a funny adventure involving a castle moat, protected by two hungry alligators, who snap at him during his endless attempt to get across. I

also liked Rothbart, with a voice by Jack Palance (during his "No More Mr. Nice Guy" number he even does a one-armed push-up). The prince, as is usual in such stories, has all the depth of a model in an underarm deodorant ad.

The story begins with the birth of Odette and young Prince Derek, in neighboring kingdoms, and their parents' desire to have them marry someday. All during childhood they cannot, of course, stand the sight of one another, but then they fall in love, and Derek makes the mistake of calling her merely beautiful, and Rothbart begins his evil scheme.

The Swan Princess is better-looking, faster-moving, and more interesting than the pallid *Thumbelina* and *Rock-a-Doodle*, non-Disney challengers at the animated box office that came out at about the same time. Despite the comparatively limited resources at his disposal, Richard Rich shows that he understands the recent Disney animated renaissance and can create some of the same magic. The movie isn't in the same league as Disney's big four, and it doesn't have the same crossover appeal to adults, but as family entertainment it's bright and cheerful, and it has its moments.

Sweetie ★ ★ ★ ½
R, 100 m., 1990

Genevieve Lemon (Sweetie), Karen Colston (Kay), Tom Lycos (Louis), Jon Darling (Gordon), Dorothy Barry (Flo), Michael Lake (Bob), Andre Pataczek (Clayton). Directed Jane Campion and produced by John Maynard. Screenplay by Gerard Lee and Campion.

Curious experience, this movie. The first time I saw it, at the 1989 Cannes Film Festival, I didn't know what to make of it. I doubted if I "liked" it, and yet it was certainly a work of talent. There was something there. I didn't *feel* much from it, though; the experience seemed primarily cerebral. Then six months later I saw *Sweetie* a second time, and suddenly there it all was, laid out in blood and passion on the screen, the emotional turmoil of a family's life. Maybe the second time I found the heart of the movie, and the first time I had been distracted by the substance.

The film takes place in Australia, in the present, in a world that has been carefully art-directed to make the commonplace look a little strange. It has been directed by Jane Campion, a short-film maker, and photographed by Sally Bongers, whose compositions and color sense give everything a sensation of heightened reality, or unreality. The acting style edges toward parody, the material is unforgiving of Australian middle-class life in the boondocks, and then, pow!—Sweetie waltzes onto the screen.

We have already met the rest of her family, including her sister, Kay (Karen Colston), who tries to lead a relatively normal life, and her parents, Flo and Bob, who do lead relatively normal lives by the device of denying their bizarre family reality. Then Sweetie (Genevieve Lemon) comes back into their lives—Sweetie, the spoiled daughter whose cute, childish antics have persisted right on up to the onset of middle age.

It becomes clear that Sweetie has always terrorized this family. In the early days (suggested in flashbacks), Dad spoiled Sweetie and told her what a wonderful little girl she was, and Sweetie, the monster, took his approval as an assignment to hold center stage in all family events and terrorize those who would not pay attention to her. In more recent years, grown obese, obnoxious, and more obviously unbalanced, Sweetie has drifted in and out of their lives. Her return is like a family disease that has gone out of remission.

There are scenes in this movie that are perfect set pieces. One of them is the "lunch meeting" held by Dad and Sweetie's "manager," a stoned zombie who slips beneath the table in the midst of negotiations. Another is Sweetie's refusal to come down from the tree. Still another, funny and horrifying at the same time, is Sweetie's demonstration of what a clever girl she is. Look! She can stand on a straight chair and make it tilt so that she rides it back down without falling off or breaking anything! We can guess how often this terrorized family has been forced to applaud this stunt of stultifying banality.

Sweetie is not, however, a family drama or a docu-drama of any conventional sort. It looks and feels too strange for that, and there are too many deft touches in the dialogue and sly looks out of the side of the camera's lens. It is a story with a realistic origin, told with a fresh and bold eye. "In most films," Campion says, "what people are doing is trying to pretend the shots aren't there." Campion and Bongers don't do that. All of their shots are there. Look at the way the little boy in the next yard is presented by the camera. Observe the look of the family's house and yard. And the feral way Sweetie hides under her blanket and barks at her father. How the movie is seen is part of the experience.

In my reviews, I try never to discuss whether "you," whoever you are, will enjoy a movie or not. I do not know you and would not presume to guess your tastes. I imagine most people will have a hard time with *Sweetie*, simply because I did the first time. But this movie is real, it's the genuine article, and it's there on the screen in all of its defiant strangeness. Most movies slide right through our minds without hitting anything. This one screams and shouts every step of the way.

Swimming to Cambodia ★ ★ ★
NO MPAA RATING, 87 m., 1987

Written by and starring Spalding Gray.
Directed and produced by Jonathan Demme.

Spalding Gray is an actor who had a small role in *The Killing Fields* (the assistant to the American ambassador), and in this movie he talks about that performance and other matters. He sits at a table—a glass of water and a microphone before him, a couple of maps behind him—and talks and talks. Because he is a good talker, and because he has something to say, this curious idea for a movie actually works.

Swimming to Cambodia is based on a one-man, two-evening stage performance that Gray polished and took on tour a couple of years ago. It has been edited down to less than two hours and directed by Jonathan Demme with an unobtrusive authority. There are subtle light and music cues, a few sound effects such as fluttering helicopter blades, and, for the rest, there is Gray's face and his voice.

His monologue begins with his auditions for the role in *The Killing Fields*, the film that told the story of a friendship between a *New York Times* correspondent and his Cambodian assistant. The assistant, Dith Pran, was played by Haing S. Ngor, who won an Academy Award for his performance. Gray won no awards for his work in the movie and indeed is a minor character whose few scenes are shown in the course of his monologue.

What he had, during the course of the shooting in Thailand, was a great deal of spare time. He seems to have used this time to investigate not only the fleshpots of Bangkok, but also the untold story of the genocide that was practiced by the fanatic Khmer Rouge on their Cambodian countrymen. He recounts in great and gory detail all of his findings, from the infamous "banana show" in a local nightclub to the disappearance of millions of Cambodians in the greatest mass murder of modern history.

He is a spellbinding storyteller, and as he speaks, something occurs that might be called the "radio phenomenon." This is the same effect that was created in *My Dinner with André* (1981), another movie in which the characters simply sit and talk. Although we are essentially only seeing a face on a screen, we are picturing the story's events in our minds; it's like listening to a radio play.

Gray is not afraid to be dramatic. His voice races quickly through a litany of images, his arms wave, his eyes flash. Then sometimes he is quiet, contemplative. This is a monologue that has been polished during many hundreds of hours on the stage, and although he makes it sound fresh, he is so familiar with it that he can gallop through a tricky passage with the confidence of an auctioneer. Like a good preacher, some of his power comes from the sheer virtuosity of his speech.

Gray's theater performance, and now this film, have been praised in many quarters, but in the *New Yorker* review, Pauline Kael was not amused. She admired Demme's direction and even Gray's presence, but asked aloud if it had occurred to him that he was exploiting the genocide in Cambodia for his own aggrandizement. This is a serious charge, particularly since Gray did not, of course, personally witness anything at all in Southeast Asia except some strip shows, some local scenery, and the filming of part of *The Killing Fields*. His material about the war is all hearsay.

I respect what Kael is getting at, but I ask myself this question: Would it have been more worthy for Gray to talk about the strippers and the moviemaking while ignoring the fact that *The Killing Fields* was inspired, indirectly, by the deaths of those millions of people? There is a fine line to be drawn here, and I am not sure where it falls.

Of course, *Swimming to Cambodia* is, on some level, self-aggrandizement. All actors might enjoy the thought of a feature film devoted entirely to their face and their voice, but few would have the nerve to go ahead with one. On the other hand, literally all possible subjects are exploited whenever they are turned into fiction. All war movies, for example, take the suffering and deaths of untold victims and use them as the setting for a fictional story about a few idealized characters. Is *Swimming to Cambodia* any more exploitive than *The Deer Hunter, Pla-*

toon, or for that matter, *Paths of Glory* or *All Quiet on the Western Front?*

None of us can directly experience more than we actually see and hear. Everything else is hearsay. All we really know, for sure, is what happened to us. There's that story about the actor hired to play the gravedigger in *Hamlet.* Asked what the play was about, he replied, "It's about this gravedigger, who meets a prince. . . ."

Swimming to Cambodia is about this actor, who meets a war.

Swimming With Sharks ★ ★ ★
R, 97 m., 1995

Kevin Spacey (Buddy Ackerman), Frank Whaley (Guy), Michelle Forbes (Dawn Lockard). Directed by George Huang and produced by Steve Alexander. Screenplay by Huang.

The reason Hollywood stories fascinate us, I think, is not because of the glamour and the sex appeal, but because of the greed and savage raw ambition. Which is more exciting: making love with Michelle Pfeiffer, or producing a Michelle Pfeiffer movie that will make you rich and famous? For a lot of people in Hollywood, that's a no-brainer, and *Swimming With Sharks* is about two of them.

Buddy Ackerman (Kevin Spacey) is vice president of production for a big studio. Guy (Frank Whaley) is his new personal assistant. Guy's job is basically to take all of Buddy's crap and serve him as a servile sycophant, twenty-four hours a day. That's called paying his dues. Once Buddy had to do it, too. Someday Guy may be a vice president, too. Depending on who you talk to, these kinds of relationships are called networking, or sado-masochism.

Ackerman is a first-class, gold-plated egotistical monster, the kind of man whose morning greeting is likely to be, "Shut up! Listen! Learn!" He is filled with little lessons, like, "If they can't start a meeting without you, that's the only kind of meeting worth going to." When *Time* magazine excoriates him as a purveyor of mindless violence, he orders Guy to "buy up every copy of *Time* in town, and shred it."

Guy is quiet but single-minded. He wants to be very big in this town someday, and hopes that working for Buddy will give him a head start. When we first meet him, he's having lunch with a table full of other ambitious young would-be executives at Musso and Frank's. He's telling an anecdote about

how Shelley Winters was asked to audition for a producer once, and simply pulled her Oscars out of her handbag and lined them up on his desk.

It would be a great story, if the others had heard of Shelley Winters (one of them finally remembers her from *The Poseidon Adventure*). The point is that Guy knows his movies. The point is also, maybe, that you don't need to know anything to succeed in Hollywood if you're ruthless enough. (When a hot young director named Foster Kane is being discussed, no one knows enough to observe that he has two-thirds of Citizen Kane's name.)

A beautiful woman appears in Guy's life. Her name is Dawn Lockard (Michelle Forbes). She's very successful, but asks Guy to lunch or dinner. He can't believe his good fortune. ("Her car phone bills are more than your rent," Buddy tells him). Then Dawn explains that she needs "access" to Buddy and therefore deliberately intends to get on Guy's good side (by any means necessary, we gather). Soon they're dreaming of the movies they'll make together.

It would not be fair to reveal how this triangle develops, or what it produces. Nor am I sure it leads to a plausible ending for this movie. The best parts of *Swimming With Sharks* are in the details—in how Guy develops telephone and lying skills, or how Buddy manipulates the phones. Eventually Guy learns the biggest lesson of all from Buddy, and in the dark humor of that logic the film finds its conclusion.

Swimming With Sharks was written and directed by George Huang, who was himself a personal assistant in Hollywood, and whose networking must have paid off, since he got a movie out of it. His plot may be overwritten and the ending may be less than satisfying, but his eye and ear are right. In Hollywood, where power is the ultimate aphrodisiac, it is also the ultimate excuse for almost any conceivable behavior. Powerful executives, agents and stars behave the way they do—because they can. Huang finds great humor in that situation, and, unless I am mistaken, some quiet bitterness as well.

Switching Channels ★ ★ ★
PG-13, 105 m., 1988

Kathleen Turner (Christy Colleran), Burt Reynolds (John L. Sullivan IV), Christopher Reeve (Blaine Bingham), Ned Beatty (Roy Ridnitz), Henry Gibson (Ike Roscoe), George Newbern (Siegenthaler), Al Waxman (Berger),

Ken James (Warden Terwillinger), Barry Flatman (Zaks), Ted Simonett (Tillinger). Directed by Ted Kotcheff and produced by Martin Ransohoff. Screenplay by Jonathan Reynolds.

Newspapers once had editions all day long, and reporters were forever feeding rewritemen a new angle for the replate. The front-page headlines changed from edition to edition, to make the news seem forever breathlessly new. Now that kind of continuing update is left to television; ever notice how Headline News updates the breaking stories while repeating the feature stuff over and over again?

The Front Page is, of course, a comedy about newspapers—the most famous newspaper comedy ever written. It was conceived in the hothouse of the Chicago newspaper world in the 1920s, when a dozen reporters were chasing every story, and there were new editions all day long. Those were the days when a "scoop" meant you stole a story right out from under the other guy's nose. These days, an "exclusive" is more likely to mean you outbid the opposition for the serial rights to a TV star's steamy confessions.

So maybe it's only appropriate that the latest remake of *The Front Page* involves, not newspapers, but a TV cable news operation. Ben Hecht and Charles MacArthur, who wrote the classic play, might even approve; they abandoned Chicago for Hollywood, where remakes were routine and the 1931 screen version of *The Front Page* was updated nine years later in *His Girl Friday* by simply making one of the boys in the press room into a girl.

The Front Page was filmed again by Billy Wilder in 1974, with Jack Lemmon and Walter Matthau, and now here is Ted Kotcheff's 1988 version, titled *Switching Channels* and starring Burt Reynolds, Kathleen Turner, and Christopher Reeve. It's not as good as *His Girl Friday,* but it's comparable with the others.

Turner plays a hard-driving TV news reporter who seems willing, in the opening credits, to go anywhere and do anything as long as the videotape is rolling. Reynolds is her ex-husband and current boss, the managing editor of the cable news operation. And on a long-overdue vacation, Turner falls in love with Christopher Reeve, a New York millionaire. She decides to quit TV, marry Reeve, and move to New York, but hold on a minute—a famous criminal is scheduled to be executed at midnight, and Reynolds will do anything to keep his star reporter on the story.

This is more or less the same premise as the first three versions, allowing for the adjustments that have to be made when the star reporter is a woman (as Rosalind Russell was in the 1940 edition). Christopher Reeve's role has been greatly expanded (the fiancé was mostly offstage in the earlier versions), and I'm not sure that's a good thing; too much time is wasted while Reynolds and Reeve insult each other while the news is put on hold.

But Kathleen Turner has perfect timing as the long-suffering anchor, and she and Reynolds work up a nice sweat and some good chemistry in their relationship, which seems to be based on a few good memories and a whole lot of one-liners. The Reeve character is unnecessary much of the time, but Reeve has fun with it anyway, with his floppy tailored suits, his newly blond hair, and his willingness to accommodate the obviously derailed Turner.

The details of the update don't much matter, either. This time the convicted man is hidden inside a Xerox machine instead of a roll-top desk, but the basic mechanics of the original Hecht-MacArthur story are still sound, and *Switching Channels* is true to the obsessive-compulsive hostility that is the fuel for all good reporters.

There is, however, one major lapse that should not go unreported. As everyone who has ever seen the play knows, it ends with the most famous closing line in American theatrical history: "The son of a bitch stole my watch!" The first two movie versions couldn't get away with that language, but the 1974 version did, and now here it is 1988, and *Switching Channels* has the temerity to leave the line out altogether (even though Reynolds steals Reeve's expensive pen, in what looks like a setup). If the ghosts of Hecht and MacArthur see this movie, may they haunt the filmmakers, their spectral voices complaining, "The sons of bitches didn't steal our greatest line!"

Swoon ★ ★ ★
NO MPAA RATING, 95 m., 1992

Daniel Schlachet (Richard Loeb), Craig Chester (Nathan Leopold, Jr.), Ron Vawter (State's Attorney Crowe), Michael Kirby (Detective Savage), Michael Stumm (Doctor Bowman), Valda Z. Drabla (Germaine Reinhardt). Directed by Tom Kalin and produced by Kalin and Christine Vachon. Screenplay by Kalin.

Swoon reopens once again the notorious thrill-killing of Bobby Frank, whose murder in the 1920s became an international scandal when it was revealed that two rich young Chicago homosexuals, Richard Loeb and Nathan Leopold, Jr., had committed the crime. Their motives were chilling: They wanted to do it simply to prove to themselves that they were smart enough to get away with it. Leopold and Loeb escaped the death penalty only because of an impassioned defense by Clarence Darrow, the best-known defense attorney of his time, who argued they were insane, and used their homosexuality as proof of insanity.

The case has been made into two previous movies—Alfred Hitchcock's *Rope* (1948) and Richard Fleischer's *Compulsion* (1959)—but both to one degree or another played down the topic of homosexuality. This new version by writer-director Tom Kalin plays it up, sometimes in ways that are fairly disturbing, as when he seems to linger on the ways the dominant Loeb was able to control the more submissive Leopold by using sex as a weapon.

The movie, shot in black and white, has the look of modern men's fashion photography, and Kalin deliberately allows anachronistic props into the frame (a TV channel changer and a push-button phone, for example) to make the film's reality level more ambiguous. This is a period picture that knows it is a period picture, and is also aware of later periods; there is no attempt to fix the story's attitudes in the 1920s, and there is a subtle but unmistakable level of the film that addresses the killing in terms of sadomasochistic chic. The murder of Bobby Frank is seen, not as a criminal act, but as a sexual adventure that got out of hand.

The question then becomes, how should one interpret the film? Kalin does not use the argument that society is to blame, that because homosexuality was outlawed, Leopold and Loeb were somehow forced into the lapse of sanity that led to the murder. There is every indication in the film that Loeb in particular enjoyed the whole event, not just the murder, but the way it demonstrated his power over Leopold; one imagines he would have been capable of the same crime in a more permissive era, or, for that matter, if he had not been homosexual at all. He is simply an evil person.

Leopold, on the other hand, is a weak one, whose relationship with Loeb is complex. Sex is a part of it. So is fear; he dreads losing the approval and friendship of this man he finds so attractive, and does what he does almost in a daze of need and apprehension. Later in a long life, he tried to redeem himself, in prison and on parole, and there was never the sense that he was as essentially evil as Loeb.

What is the movie trying to show us? The power of sexual control, for one thing; Loeb, who is depraved, is also highly intelligent, and everything he does seems almost like an exercise, to prove that he can do it. *Swoon* goes much deeper than the other studies of the Frank case, because it tries to show exactly how the psychosexual balance between the two killers made a murder possible, when neither Leopold nor Loeb could possibly have killed by himself. Loeb was incapable of the act, and Leopold incapable of the desire.

This is the kind of movie that inspires discussion afterward. It is being reviewed as an example of the new "queer cinema," deliberately gay films by openly gay filmmakers, but I am not sure *Swoon* would have needed to be much different if the killers had been heterosexual lovers. I don't think what they did resulted from the fact that they were gay; I believe similar acts throughout history, in tolerant times and repressive ones, have been committed by all kinds of people born without what we call the conscience (as Loeb was) or without the courage to follow it (Leopold). It is probably true that more people fall in Leopold's category than Loeb's, which is why he has always drawn more sympathy from students of the case. It is easier and more reassuring to imagine being seduced into evil, than to imagine not even knowing what evil is.

T

A Tale of Springtime ★ ★ ★ ½
PG, 107 m., 1992

Anne Teyssedre (Jeanne), Hugues Quester (Igor), Florence Darel (Natacha), Eloise Bennett (Eve), Sophie Robin (Gaelle). Directed by Eric Rohmer and produced by Margaret Menegoz. Screenplay by Rohmer.

Two women meet at a party. The more they talk, the more they realize that they enjoy each other more than the party—that they didn't really want to come to the party anyway. One is Natacha (Florence Darel), a teen-age piano student. The other is Jeanne (Anne Teyssedre), who teaches philosophy. Jeanne is between apartments, and doesn't much want to spend the night at the apartment of her lover, who is out of town; she feels strange being there when he's away. Natacha's face lights up. Her father is away on business—he's nearly always away, in fact—and so Jeanne can spend the night at her place.

Ah, but the father is not so far away on business as his daughter believes, or pretends to believe, and the next morning the teacher and the parent meet, somewhat awkwardly. The father is apologetic, gets some clean clothes, makes himself scarce. Jeanne is embarrassed. Natacha is very quiet and deep, and we realize she wants to throw this woman into her father's path. She is a matchmaker.

The father does not consider himself in need of a match because he already has a lover, Eve (Eloise Bennett). And by this point in my plot summary, if I were to give you one or two more hints, such as that the characters are French and that everyone is particularly civilized, you would be right to guess that *A Tale of Springtime* is a film by Eric Rohmer.

Rohmer has been at work for years now on his cautionary tales, from *My Night at Maud's*

(1969) through *Boyfriends and Girlfriends* (1987), with stops for *Claire's Knee, Chloe in the Afternoon,* and *Pauline at the Beach.* All of his films teach a lesson, sometimes a little one (such as that it is unwise to tell fibs), sometimes a big one (such as that it is not a kindness to tell someone you love them unless you really do).

A Tale of Springtime is the first of a series of four films on the seasons, and that is why, I think, Natacha's fancy lightly turns to thoughts of love. She does not like her father's girlfriend, wants to escort her from the scene and replace her with Jeanne, a woman she hardly knows, after all, and who may have no desire to be thrown into the path of the father. Natacha is young enough that she does not fully understand the complexities of love, and she even arranges an accidental meeting in the family's summer cottage, where Jeanne feels she has been lured under false pretenses.

Nothing very dramatic usually happens in a Rohmer film, or at least nothing loud and violent. The characters are usually too well behaved, and sometimes too distracted by their own problems to pay much attention to the plot Rohmer has thrust them into. That's one of the pleasures of a film like this; we can recognize the rhythms of real life, in which personal drama sometimes has to wait while we attend to routine duties. There's the sense in a Rohmer film that the characters are free to walk out, if they want to; they're not on assignment to stick with the plot to the bitter end, as they are in a Hollywood film.

The appeal of a Rohmer film depends on the personal charm of the actors; they are usually pleasant, bright, and bourgeois, and we want them to find happiness but are not going to lose much sleep if they fail in their quest. The real appeal may be that they lead

lives like ours, but in other bodies and with other friends. Their decisions are like test drives for trips we might take ourselves someday.

Talk Radio ★ ★ ★ ★
R, 110 m., 1988

Eric Bogosian (Barry), Ellen Greene (Ellen), Leslie Hope (Laura), John C. McGinley (Stu), Alec Baldwin (Dan), John Pankow (Dietz), Michael Wincott (Kent), Linda Atkinson (Sheila Fleming). Directed by Oliver Stone and produced by Edward R. Pressman and A. Kitman Ho. Screenplay by Eric Bogosian and Stone.

Alan Berg was a Denver talk radio host who was murdered on June 18, 1984. He was a goofy-looking bird, with a thin face and a bristly white beard that hid the ravages of teenage acne. He wore reading glasses perched far down on his nose, and he dressed in unlikely combinations of checks and stripes and garments that looked leftover from the 1950s. When the members of a lunatic rightwing group gunned him down in the driveway of his home, they could not have mistaken him for anybody else.

I met Berg three or four times. The first time I was going to be on his radio show; I listened to it as I drove from Boulder to Denver. He was chewing out some hapless housewife whose brain was a reservoir of prejudice against anyone who was the slightest bit different from her. Berg was telling her that no one in their right mind would want to be anything like her at all.

Why were you so hard on that lady? I asked him when we were on the air.

"She was asking for it. Why would she call up and feed me all those straight lines if she didn't want me to tell her how stupid she was?"

Cruel, perhaps, but quite possibly correct. Berg was the top radio personality in Denver because he told people exactly what he thought of them. It was unusual to hear somebody on the radio who was not tailoring his words to the sensibilities of his audience. Talking with Berg off the air, I found that he was a man who had been through a lot, including the loss of a law practice in Chicago because of alcoholism. Now he was sober and successful, but I had the feeling that he was grateful every morning for somehow having pulled out of his crash dive. I liked him. When I learned that he had been murdered, my first reaction was disbelief that anyone could have taken him that seriously. Jeez, didn't they know he was just another poor bastard trying to earn a living?

Oliver Stone's film *Talk Radio* is inspired by the murder of Alan Berg, but it is not based on his life. Berg was older, calmer, and more amused by life than Barry Champlain, the tortured talk radio host in the movie. Berg was also not self-destructive or suicidal, and Champlain is both. When he is mailed a suspicious box in a plain brown wrapper, he puts it next to the microphone. When he gets a call from the man who mailed the box, and the man hints that it contains a bomb, Champlain opens it on the air. When another caller rants and raves incoherently about Champlain's beliefs and calls him a coward, Champlain asks him to come over to the radio station—and invites the man, a disheveled, wild-eyed street person, to come into the studio.

Champlain works in a studio in a Texas high-rise, surrounded by other high-rises. I was aware all during the movie of the thousands of windows with a view into his studio. When the man who sent the box says, "I can see you have it," I cringed, because I imagined someone with a sniper-scope. But Barry Champlain, played with rasping, aggressive sarcasm by Eric Bogosian, simply doesn't care. He is gambling with his life in the same self-hating way as people who get drunk and point a speedboat into the blackness of a storm.

Talk Radio is directed by Stone with a claustrophobic intensity. The camera rarely leaves the radio studio—and then it's only for brief flashbacks into the hero's troubled personal life, or for a personal appearance he makes at a basketball game where some of the fans seem to have crawled out from under their rocks for the purpose of acting weirdly toward him. Most of the movie takes place during the long nights of the radio program, and the movie's beginnings as a stage play are evident when several key characters—including Champlain's former wife—turn up on the scene to bare their hearts to him.

Even so, the movie doesn't feel as boxed-in as many filmed plays do, perhaps because radio itself is such an intimate, claustrophobic medium. It's not over there in the TV set; it's inside your head. In a sense we become listeners of "The Barry Champlain Show," and as he pushes his listeners more and more insistently, egging them on, we begin to feel how some of the people out there in the night could go over the edge. *Talk Radio* is based on a play that Bogosian wrote and starred in, and it was the right decision to star him in the movie, too, instead of some famous star. He feels this material from the inside out, and makes the character convincing. That's especially true during a virtuoso, unsettling closing monologue in which we think the camera is circling Bogosian—until we realize the camera and the actor are still, and the backgrounds are circling.

Alan Berg is more famous in death than life. His memory haunts many people, even those who never heard him on the radio, because his death could be read as a message: Be cautious, be prudent, be bland, never push anybody, never say what you really think, offer yourself as a hostage to the weirdos even before they make the first move. These days, a lot of people are opposed to the newfound popularity of "trash television," and no doubt they are right and the hosts of these shows are shameless controversy-mongers. But at least they are not intimidated. Of what use is freedom of speech to those who fear to offend?

The Tall Guy ★ ★ ★ ½
R, 90 m., 1990

Jeff Goldblum (Dexter King), Emma Thompson (Kate Lemon), Rowan Atkinson (Ron Anderson), Emil Wolk (Cyprus Charlie), Geraldine James (Carmen), Kim Thomson (Cheryl). Directed by Mel Smith and produced by Paul Webster. Screenplay by Richard Curtis.

The Tall Guy is a sweet, whimsical, and surprisingly intelligent comedy about an American actor in London, who falls in love with a nurse and finds that he has to treasure the gift of romance and not take it for granted. The tall guy is played by Jeff Goldblum, whose character wanders through the movie in need of a haircut and a shot of self-confidence. The nurse is Emma Thompson, and she is trim and organized—one of those women with the disconcerting practice of telling you exactly what they think, just when you were trying to find a cowardly way to weasel it out of them.

The movie is narrated by Goldblum's character, whose name is Dexter, and who has spent five years as "the tall guy" in a two-man show starring the rude and obnoxious short comedian Ron Anderson (Rowan Atkinson). Anderson hogs the spotlight so much that the audience hardly even realizes there's a stooge in the cast. Dexter, meanwhile, bicycles home to his rented room in the flat of a nymphomaniac, whose lovers paddle nakedly through the kitchen at odd hours in search of a glass of water.

One day Dexter finds himself at the hospital, and is riven by a thunderbolt of love for the nurse, whose name is Kate Lemon, although his mind insists on remembering her as Kate Tampon. Desperate to ask her for a date, he signs up for a series of inoculations for a fictitious trip to Morocco, and eventually she does go out with him, and up to her room with him, and they roll passionately across oranges and stale Wheatabix cubes and are in love.

All of this would not in itself make *The Tall Guy* worth seeing, despite the charm of Thompson and the drollery of Goldblum, if it were not for the direction by Mel Smith and the script by Richard Curtis, who assume that their audience has a certain level of intelligence and information. That makes the movie more fun even for those viewers who do not always know what they are referring to.

For example: The typical Hollywood script assumes that its audience was born yesterday and knows nothing. There are no topical references to anyone or anything. Events occurring more than ten years previously are tacitly assumed not to have happened at all. Even the names of small cities are replaced with the names of larger ones, to avoid giving offense. References to the names of authors, poets, painters, or presidents are left out if at all possible, although sports figures are very occasionally allowed to slip in. No character is now, or ever has been, a member of any political party.

I get so weary of movies that assume I, and my fellow viewers, know nothing. Plots that involve a rudimentary introduction of good and bad guys, and the elimination of the second by the first, not without difficulty. Characters who never talk about anything real—anything, indeed, other than the plot. The last third of *The Tall Guy* turns into a hilarious send-up of the modern musical, when Dexter somehow gets cast in a musical version of *The Elephant Man*. This production, called *Elepant!*, must be the funniest deliberately bad play in a movie since Mel Brooks's "Springtime for Hitler" in *The Producers*. Thank God they didn't decide no one in the audience had ever heard of the Elephant Man (most people are assumed to have heard of Hitler).

Near the end of this movie, Kate, the girlfriend, accuses Dexter of having an affair with a young actress. How does she know this? Not because she stumbles across Polaroids they took of each other in their knickers. No, she figures it out because, at a cast party, Dexter fills the other woman's glass with champagne, which she allows him to do without acknowledgment. Taking someone for granted like that is a sure sign, Kate says, that they are lovers. She is right, of course, and this movie is right about a great many things, one of them being that there is a market for comedy among people who were not born yesterday.

Tall Tale: The Unbelievable Adventures of Pecos Bill ★ ★ ★   **NEW**
PG, 96 m., 1995

Patrick Swayze (Pecos Bill), Oliver Platt (Paul Bunyan), Roger Aaron Brown (John Henry), Nick Stahl (Daniel Hackett), Scott Glenn (J.P. Stiles), Stephen Lang (Jonas Hackett), Jared Harris (Head Thug Pug), Catherine O'Hara (Calamity Jane). Directed by Jeremiah Chechik and produced by Joe Roth and Roger Birnbaum. Screenplay by Steven L. Bloom and Robert Rodat.

Tall Tale: The Unbelievable Adventures of Pecos Bill is a warm-blooded, high-spirited family adventure film about a twelve-year-old boy who saves his family's farm from an evil villain, with the help of Pecos Bill, Paul Bunyan, and John Henry (the steel-drivin' man), plus a walk-on by Calamity Jane. The movie may strike today's kids as startling in its originality, since each of these characters is an actual individual human being, unlike such plastic-faced clones as the Ninja Turtles and the Mighty Morphin' Power Rangers.

The movie takes place in Paradise Valley, an unspoiled Western area which a scheming bad guy named Stiles wants to destroy with strip mining. (This side of the plot seems borrowed from the John Prine song, "Paradise Valley," which "Mr. Peabody's coal trains are haulin' away.") We meet the Hackett family, which turns down Stiles's offer of fifty dollars an acre because this land is their land, and there's almost a tragedy when one of Stiles's hired guns wounds the father, Jonas (Stephen Lang).

That galvanizes young Daniel Hackett (Nick Stahl), who in the early scenes doesn't much like working on the farm, which he tells his dad is "just a piece of dried-up old ground." After his dad is wounded, Daniel falls asleep in a boat on the farm lake, and is magically transported to a Texas desert, where he meets Pecos Bill (Patrick Swayze), the first of several legendary heroes his father has told him about. They will teach him the value of standing up for your beliefs.

The movie, directed by Jeremiah Chechik, enters easily into the spirit of its tall tales, as Pecos saves Daniel from a couple of varmints and then decides to help him save the family farm, too. That involves recruiting other heroes to lend a hand, and they find Paul Bunyan (Oliver Platt) living in a luxury log cabin that is literally made from a log—a giant Sequoia. During Daniel's visit to logging country, he actually finds himself trapped in a sawmill with the whirling blade inching closer by the second, a cliché so old it may be new to some kids.

Pecos, Paul, and the kid hit the road with Bunyan's blue ox, Babe, after a little run-in when Pecos declares, "I ain't apologizin' to no ox!" They come across John Henry (Roger Aaron Brown) during a spike-driving contest between himself and a steam-driven pile driver, and Calamity Jane (Catherine O'Hara) saves them all a lot of trouble during a saloon brawl, although she doesn't get equal time with the guys.

The movie is visually gorgeous, with shots like a mountain meadow afloat in orange butterflies. And the production design is imaginative; I especially liked the private train of Mr. Stiles (Scott Glenn), which features a duplex personal dining car and a towering locomotive that looks like a Nazi war memorial. The train is way too high to go through a tunnel, but why sweat the details?

I guess I wasn't kidding about the old-fashioned human element in the story. Today's children's heroes have been cleverly manufactured to have no personalities, nationalities, or human attributes, other than a taste for pizza. The Ninja Turtles, G.I. Joe, the Power Rangers, and other popular characters can be mass-produced for shipment all over the world, where they will be equally faceless for kids of all nations.

They limit the imagination. There are only so many fantasies you can project onto Power Ranger clones. Pecos Bill, John Henry, Paul Bunyan, and Calamity Jane are, on the other hand, rompin' stompin' characters that you can actually pretend to be. (Do kids pretend to be Ninja Turtles? I don't want to know.) They have real adventures involving times, places, and people—instead of technological adventures involving blowing things up. The villains in this story are people with names and agendas, not simply objects for target practice. I know it's odd to praise a film like *Pecos Bill* for its humanistic values, but these are strange days in which we live.

Tampopo ★ ★ ★ ★
NO MPAA RATING, 117 m., 1987

Tsutomu Yamazaki (Ooro), Nobuko Miyamoto (Tampopo [Dandelion]), Koji Miyamoto (Man in White Suit), Ken Watanabe (Gun), Rikiya Yasuoka (Pisken), Kinzo Sakura (Shohei). Directed by Juzo Itami and produced by Juzo Itami, Yasushi Tamaoki, and Seigo Hosogoe. Screenplay by Itami.

Tampopo is one of those utterly original movies that seems to exist in no known category. Like the French comedies of Jacques Tati, it's a bemused meditation on human nature, in which one humorous situation flows into another off-handedly, as if life were a series of smiles.

As it opens, the film looks like some sort of Japanese satire of Clint Eastwood's spaghetti Westerns. The hero is Ooro (Tsutomu Yamazaki), a lone rider with a quizzical smile on his face, who rides a semi instead of a horse. Along with some friends, he stages a search for the perfect noodle restaurant, and cannot find it. Then he meets Tampopo (Nobuko Miyamoto), a sweet young woman who has her heart in the right place, but not her noodles.

The movie then turns into the fairly free-style story of the efforts by Tampopo and her protector to research the perfect noodle and open the perfect noodle restaurant. Like most movies about single-minded obsessions, this one quickly becomes very funny. It might seem that American audiences would know little and care less about the search for the perfect Japanese noodle, but because the movie is so consumed and detailed, so completely submerged in "noodleology," it takes on a kind of weird logic of its own.

Consider, for example, the *tour de force* of a scene near the beginning of the movie, where a noodle master explains the correct ritual for eating a bowl of noodle soup. He explains every ingredient. How to cut it, how to cook it, how to address it, how to think of it, how to regard it, how to approach it, how to smell it, how to eat it, how to thank it, how to remember it. It's a kind of gastronomic religion, and director Juzo Itami languishes in creating a scene that makes noodles in this movie more interesting than sex and violence in many another.

The movie is constructed as a series of episodes along the route to the perfect noodle restaurant. Some of the scenes hardly even seem to apply, but are hilarious anyway—the treatment, for example, of a man who dies in the pursuit of the perfect bowl of noodles. *Tampopo* doesn't limit itself to satirizing one genre of Hollywood film, either; although the central image is of an Eastwood-style hero on an ultimate quest, there are all sorts of other sly little satirical asides, including one so perfectly aimed that even to describe it would take away some of the fun.

Humor, it is said, is universal. Most times it is not. The humor that travels best, I sometimes think, is not "universal" humor at all, but humor that grows so specifically out of one culture that it reaches other cultures almost by seeming to ignore them. The best British comedies were the very specifically British films like *The Lavender Hill Mob* and *School for Scoundrels*. The best Italian comedies were local products like *Seduced and Abandoned*. The funniest French films were by Tati, who seemed totally absorbed in himself. And this very, very Japanese movie, which seems to make no effort to communicate to other cultures, is universally funny almost for that reason. Who cannot identify with the search for the perfect noodle? Certainly any American can, in the land of sweet corn festivals, bake-offs, and contests for the world's best chili.

Tank Girl ★ ★
R, 104 m., 1995

NEW

Lori Petty (Tank Girl), Naomi Watts (Jet Girl), Anne Cusack (Sub Girl), Malcolm McDowell (Kesslee), Ice-T (T-Saint), Don Harvey (Sergeant Small), Brian Wimmer (Richard), Jeff Kober (Ripper), Reg E. Cathey (Ripper), Scott Coffey (Ripper). Directed by Rachel

Talalay and produced by Richard Lewis, Pen Densham, and John Watson. Screenplay by Tedi Sarafian.

Whatever the faults of *Tank Girl*, lack of ambition is not one of them. Here is a movie that dives into the bag of filmmaking tricks and chooses all of them. Trying to re-create the multimedia effect of the comic books it's based on, the film employs live action, animation, montages of still graphics, animatronic makeup, prosthetics, song and dance routines, models, fake backdrops, holography, title cards, matte drawings, and computerized special effects. All I really missed were 3-D and Smell-O-Vision.

The movie is set in the year 2033, after a meteor has struck the Earth, creating a global desert. "You gotta squeeze twelve in a bathtub," Tank Girl tells us in the opening narration, ". . . so it ain't *all* bad." The planet is mostly ruled by the evil Water & Power Co., run by a madman named Kesslee (Malcolm McDowell), who controls most of the water supply and whose name is possibly a misspelled anagram for "leaks."

Living outside the W&P sphere is a small group of self-sufficient desert rats, who pump water by hand to grow hydroponic crops. Tank Girl (Lori Petty) is one of their number, and when Keslee's troops attack the commune, she wipes out eight of them before she's hauled before the evil monster himself.

McDowell, who has specialized lately in weirdo villains, thinks she might be useful in his war on the Rippers (anagram for Sippers?—oh, never mind). They're kangaroo-men who were developed in a DNA experiment, as Ultimate Soldiers: They're smart as men, can hop like crazy, and always have a place to keep their grenades. (The actors playing them, including Ice-T, are a little easier to identify than the stars of *Planet of the Apes*.) Some Rippers remember life before their DNA got manipulated; one solemnly tells Tank Girl, "I used to be Ted Smith, assistant manager of Chief Auto Parts in Cincinnati, Ohio."

Tank Girl refuse the chance to work for Kesslee, and after making a friend of the shy Jet Girl (Naomi Watts), she wages war against Water & Power, in scenes involving lots of machine guns, tanks, planes, grenades, electrocution, and even a weapon that is plunged into the victim, draining his blood while simultaneously purifying it into water.

Under the direction of Rachel Talalay, the movie plunges headlong into technique. Some

of the locations, like the desert commune, are obviously scale models. Others are elaborate sets, including the dark satanic mills where Kesslee sets his slaves to work. Tank Girl careens through this landscape with an evil snicker and incredible good luck, dodging death and causing a lot of pain to the genital areas of her enemies. She talks back to her captors ("Hey! I have two words for you: Brush your teeth!"). She smiles at the camera in a heroically gratuitous Busby Berkeley dance routine. And of course she prevails.

Enormous energy went into this movie. I could not, however, care about it for much more than a moment at a time, and after a while its manic energy wore me down. The director Sidney Lumet has a book out about how he makes movies. In it he observes that slowly paced scenes can actually make a movie seem to go faster than a relentless pacing that never stops. Uh-huh.

Tap ★ ★ ★
PG-13, 111 m., 1989

Gregory Hines (Max Washington), Suzanne Douglas (Amy), Sammy Davis, Jr. (Little Mo), Savion Glover (Louis), Joe Morton (Nicky), Dick Anthony Williams (Francis). Characters based on themselves: Sandman Sims, Bunny Briggs, Steve Condos, Jimmy Slyde, Pat Rico, Arthur Duncan, and Harold Nicholas. Directed by Nick Castle and produced by Gary Adelson and Richard Vane. Screenplay by Castle.

Imagine how Bruce Springsteen would feel if rock 'n' roll lost its popularity overnight, and you'd know, I guess, how the great tap dancers felt in the early 1950s. One day, tap dancing was enormously popular (I can remember half the kids in my grade school class taking lessons at Thelma Lee Ritter's Dance Studio, up above the Princess Theater on Main Street in Urbana, Illinois). The next day, it was passé—blown away by rock. And there was another cruel blow for many of the tap stars, who were black: As the civil rights movement gained strength, tap dancing itself was seen as projecting the wrong image of black people.

Tap stars Gregory Hines as Max Washington, the son of one of the greatest tap dancers—a man who is a great dancer himself, but has thrown away his heritage to lead a life of crime. Now he is out of prison and on the streets again, and his old associates want him to pull a big-time jewel heist. But upstairs over Sonny's, the shabby dance club his father used to run on Times Square, people who love him have other plans for him.

The club is run by Little Mo (Sammy Davis, Jr.). His daughter, Amy (Suzanne Douglas) runs a tap academy on the second floor, and upstairs on the third floor there's a sort of retirement home for Mo and seven of his pals, old tap dancers. Little Mo dreams that there could be a fusion of tap and rock, and that Sonny's is just the place to launch it. He wants Max to lead the way.

What we have here, then, is the outline for a fairly standard musical plot. Will Max steal the jewels or return to his dancing heritage? Will Little Mo be able to teach him to dream again? And, of course, will Max and Amy fall in love? They were lovers once before, but now there is coldness between them, because Max has grown hard and cynical. And he grows even more bitter when he's insulted by the director of a Broadway show who doesn't know beans about tap dancing.

The parts of this plot seem recycled out of old musicals, all right, but the spirit of the film is fresh and the characters are convincing. Gregory Hines has been dancing professionally since he was a juvenile in the 1950s, but he's better known as an actor, and here he has a role that challenges him on both levels. He has a way of being strong, and being subtle about it. Sammy Davis, Jr., has never had a juicier role in a movie, and for once he isn't playing himself—he's playing the opposite of glitter and glitz, and his sincerity is believable. And the discovery of the movie is Suzanne Douglas, who can dance and act and looks beautiful on the screen. Her chemistry with Hines is real, and that makes his somewhat predictable role more interesting.

And then there are those old guys who live upstairs. The movie has cast the roles with legendary tap-dance veterans: Sandman Sims, Bunny Briggs, Steve Condos, Jimmy Slyde, Pat Rico, Arthur Duncan, and Harold Nicholas. There is a scene where the youngster is unwise enough to suggest that they've lost their legs, and they accept the challenge with enthusiasm, each one putting on a show of his best stuff. This scene, like the whole movie, is lighted and photographed by director Nick Castle and cinematographer David Gribble to create a kind of warm, shadowy, nostalgic feeling; we see the old times as if through a veil of good memories.

The weakness of *Tap*, as I've suggested, is that almost everything that happens in the movie is borrowed, more or less frankly, from old movie lore. In a way, that's also a

strength: This is a musical about musicals, as well as being a tap-dance movie about tap dancers. This film about the decline of tap is, itself, a form of resurrection.

Taps ★ ★ ★
PG, 126 m., 1981

George C. Scott (General Bache), Timothy Hutton (Brian Moreland), Ronny Cox (Colonel Kerby), Sean Penn (Alex), Tom Cruise (David). Directed by Harold Becker and produced by Stanley R. Jaffe and Howard B. Jaffe. Screenplay by Darryl Ponicsan and Robert Mark Kamen.

Taps is a meditation on two subjects for which some adolescents have a great capacity: idealism and authoritarianism. It takes place in a realistic setting (it was shot on location at Valley Forge Military Academy), but it is not intended as a realistic film. There are all sorts of clues, including the pointed absence of all but one of the academy's adult faculty members, to indicate that *Taps*, like the emotionally similar *Lord of the Flies*, is using its realistic texture as a setting for a fantasy about human nature.

The film begins with an emotionally stirring commencement exercise at Bunker Hill Military Academy (as the school is called in the film). Sousa marches fill the air, the cadets march around the parade ground looking gloriously proud of themselves, and the reviewing stand is dominated by the legendary old General Harlan Bache, the academy's commander. Bache is played by George C. Scott, and it is probably no accident that his performance in this movie echoes his title role in *Patton* (1970): He is an iron-willed and yet incurably romantic professional soldier.

We soon meet the leading upperclassman, Brian Moreland (Timothy Hutton). He has been selected to lead the cadet corps next year. In one of the most important evenings of his life, he is granted the great privilege of having dinner with old General Bache and sipping some of the old man's brandy. Soon after, however, this whole network of discipline, glory, and tradition is destroyed when it's revealed that the school's pigheaded trustees intend to sell the school and its land to some condominium developers (it is almost worth the price of admission to hear Scott pronounce "condominiums"). Bache is removed from the scene, in a dramatic development I will not reveal. And then Moreland, the cadet commander, takes in-

ventory of the school's supplies of weapons and decides to lead the student body in making a stand for it. They'll take over the school in a military occupation, bar the gates, mount machine guns, and guard posts, and issue a set of demands designed to save the school.

The central passages of *Taps* are devoted to this scheme. The students barricade themselves in the school grounds, the police and National Guard surround the school, and a standoff develops. Meanwhile, within the student body, tensions develop between those kids who are unstable and a little too violent, and those who would secretly rather be on the outside looking in. Hutton, as Moreland, does a lot of learning and soul-searching as he tries to hold his mad scheme together.

There are obviously various problems of plot (such as: Where are the other faculty members? Why are the outside authorities both so stupid and so uncompromising? Why would the trustees have no appreciation of the school's tradition? Why would the grade-school-age cadets be issued live ammunition?, etc.). These questions do not really matter. *Taps* is basically a character study, a portrait of the personalities engaged in the showdown. And, like *Lord of the Flies*, it observes that adolescent males can easily translate the idealistic lessons they have been taught into a rationale for acting in ways that are rigid, dogmatic, and self-justifying.

Taps works as an uncommonly engrossing story, primarily because the performances are so well done. All of the cadet roles are well acted, not only by seasoned actors like Hutton (who won an Academy Award for *Ordinary People*) but even by the very young kids who struggle with guns and realities much too large for them. By the film's end, we share their love for their school, we despair at the situation they have gotten themselves into, and we are emotionally involved in the outcome. After the film, there are some ideas to think about, involving the implications when might and right are on the same side—and when they are not.

Tatie Danielle ★ ★ ★
NO MPAA RATING, 112 m., 1991

Tsilla Chelton (Tatie Danielle), Catherine Jacob (Catherine Billard), Isabelle Nanty (Sandrine), Neige Dolsky (Odile), Eric Prat (Jean-Pierre Billard), Laurence Fevrier (Jeanne Billard). Directed by Etienne Chatiliez and produced by Charles Gassot. Screenplay by Florence Quentin.

Here is a film about an unpleasant old lady who sits up at night thinking about ways to make life difficult for those who love her. She manipulates them with guilt, she deceives them with lies, she appeals to them with piteous tears, and she walks on their flower beds. What a crone.

And yet Etienne Chatiliez's *Tatie Danielle* plays, perversely, as a comedy: as a two-edged movie about human nature. So often when we speak of movie characters as being "human," we mean that they are nice. We forget that being human can also involve being nasty, vindictive, greedy, and scheming. Tatie Danielle is a spoiled old lady who has become expert, after long years of study, at the art of imposing on other people.

She is, above all, an actress. When we first meet her she is already practicing her art. She says one thing in private and another in public. She seeks pity for herself. She makes life miserable for her overworked, exhausted, and equally elderly servant, who eventually falls off a ladder while trying to please her. The servant dies, and Tatie Danielle goes to live with a middle-aged nephew, his wife, and their family in the city. They don't really want her. But she buys her way in by giving them some of her substantial wealth, and then, once she is established in her own room, she terrorizes the household.

She can't eat the food. The noise is too much for her. She invades all of their social events, entrancing the guests with manufactured stories of her sufferings. She drives away the servants. Finally the family, desperately needing to escape, goes on vacation, and hires a sitter to look after Tatie Danielle. This girl, plump, blonde, and self-centered, will not play Tatie's games. She calls the bluff.

Tatie Danielle is played in the movie by Tsilla Chelton, a woman of boundless energy, who is able to project the guile of her character without overacting. She makes it appear that Tatie Danielle gets a certain amount of pleasure out of her meanness—that this is a lonely old woman's only form of amusement. Her nephew and his wife, played by Eric Prat and Catherine Jacob, are a pushover for her. They're simple, decent people, who only want to do the right thing—but who can never please Tatie Danielle because her only pleasure comes from stirring up their guilt.

And then there is the minder, the woman brought in to tend to Tatie. Played by Isabelle Nanty, she has her own agenda. She is

selfish, too, and has no time to suffer fools. She calls Tatie's bluffs. There is a long, elaborate sequence in which poor Tatie manages to call the police and get on the front pages as a shamefully neglected senior—but even this revenge doesn't affect the young woman, because she simply doesn't care. Everything leads to an ending of ironic poetic justice. The movie's last shot is perfect.

The most refreshing thing about *Tatie Danielle* is that it allows an old woman the same freedom as any other movie character, to be unpleasant and mean-spirited. The movies too often sentimentalize old people. They are either wise or childlike, and in either case they seem to have outgrown the weaknesses of youth. Tatie Danielle hasn't. Maybe that's what keeps her alive.

Taxi Blues ★ ★ ★
NO MPAA RATING, 110 m., 1991

Pyotr Mamonov (Liosha [Jazzman]), Piotr Zaitchenko (Schlikov [Taximan]), Vladimir Kachpour (Old Netchiporenko), Natalia Koliakanova (Christina), Hal Singer (Himself), Elena Satonova (Nina). Directed by Pavel Lounguine and produced by Marin Karmitz. Screenplay by Lounguine.

The bleak and passionate Russian film *Taxi Blues* is one of those movies that seems to exist in two ways at once: It tells a central story, while at the same time telling us another story with the elements around the edge of the frame. The first story involves an obsessive relationship between a hard-headed taxi driver and an irresponsible jazz musician. The other material provides an offhand, casual, and therefore, doubly interesting view of daily life in today's Moscow.

The film begins as a taxi driver, completely at home in the mean streets and familiar with all the angles on the black market, picks up a carload of drunken musicians for a night on the town. One by one they disappear, until finally the last one, a saxophonist named Liosha, stiffs him for a steep seventy-ruble fare. The driver, named Schlikov, does not take this passively. He haunts the jazzman's usual hangouts until he corners him, and then holds his precious saxophone hostage while forcing the man to work out the fare with manual labor.

But there is more than simply bill-collecting going on here. The musician is Jewish, and the taxi driver is casually anti-Semitic, although open-minded enough to be surprised about some of the things he learns

about Jews ("They drink like Russians!" he says admiringly of Liosha, who, in fact, drinks like an alcoholic). There is another conflict in the film, between the image of the stalwart, muscular, working-class driver and the thin, tired-eyed musician, who live in completely different worlds. The driver sees the musician as a parasite, the musician sees the driver as a drone, and yet somehow they work out an uneasy arrangement that borders on friendship.

What brings them together is mutual dependency, and it's there that the second level of the movie—the everyday life—comes into play. We see the makeshift sleeping quarters of the driver, who covers every square inch of his small room with posters extolling the women and creature comforts of the West. We see the jazz clubs and speakeasies where Moscow bohemians cluster together for mutual support. And we understand such relationships as the one between the driver and his girlfriend, who works in a meat-packing plant and is therefore invaluable as a black market connection.

The movie is an example of the kind of long-repressed truth-telling that seems to be welling up in today's unsettled Soviet Union, which in the midst of its troubles is experiencing great ferment in the arts. *Taxi Blues* has nothing to do with any official Soviet view of what a film should show, or tell, or be, and everything to do with the Western notion of the movie director as an impassioned witness to his society.

The filmmaker is a forty-one-year-old Soviet Jew named Pavel Lounguine, who was a scriptwriter for years before making a chance contact with a Paris producer who cofinanced this film. Like many films that come from passion, it has been an unexpected commercial and critical hit; it won the best director award at the Cannes Film Festival in 1990, and is a box office winner in Russia and throughout Western Europe.

It is clear from the energy in the story that Lounguine has been waiting a long time to get his hands on the camera, and his point of view swoops and soars through Moscow like a bird released from its cage. If the story is sometimes hard to take—neither one of the protagonists is very pleasant to be around—the anger and passion of the director are exhilarating. And the film is also interesting just for the objective information it displays. Without mental pictures of a place, we fall back on postcards: Red Square, the Kremlin, Lenin's tomb. Now I will also remember the taxi driver's room, and the lust in the eyes of everyone lucky enough to gaze upon a black market steak.

Taxi Driver ★ ★ ★ ★
R, 112 m., 1976

Robert De Niro (Travis Bickle), Jodie Foster (Iris), Albert Brooks (Tom), Harvey Keitel (Sport), Leonard Harris (Palantine), Peter Boyle (Wizard), Cybill Shepherd (Betsy). Directed by Martin Scorsese and produced by Michael Phillips and Julia Phillips. Screenplay by Paul Schrader.

Taxi Driver shouldn't be taken as a New York film; it's not about a city but about the weathers of a man's soul, and out of all New York he selects just those elements that feed and reinforce his obsessions. The man is Travis Bickle, ex-Marine, veteran of Vietnam, composer of dutiful anniversary notes to his parents, taxi driver, killer. The movie rarely strays very far from the personal, highly subjective way in which he sees the city and lets it wound him.

It's a place, first of all, populated with women he cannot have: Unobtainable blond women who might find him attractive for a moment, who might join him for a cup of coffee, but who eventually will have to shake their heads and sigh, "Oh, Travis!" because they find him . . . well, he's going crazy, but the word they use is "strange." And then, even more cruelly, the city seems filled with men who *can* have these women—men ranging from cloddish political hacks to street-corner pimps who, nevertheless, have in common the mysterious ability to approach a woman without getting everything wrong.

Travis could in theory look for fares anywhere in the city, but he's constantly drawn back to 42nd Street, to Times Square and the whores, street freaks, and porno houses. It's here that an ugly kind of sex comes closest to the surface—the sex of buying, selling, and using people. Travis isn't into that, he hates it, but Times Square feeds his anger. His sexual frustration is channeled into a hatred for the creeps he obsessively observes. He tries to break the cycle—or maybe he just sets himself up to fail again. He sees a beautiful blonde working in the storefront office of a presidential candidate. She goes out with him a couple of times, but the second time he takes her to a hard-core film and she walks out in disgust and won't have any more to do with him. All the same, he calls her for another date, and it's here that we get close

to the heart of the movie. The director, Martin Scorsese, gives us a shot of Travis on a pay telephone—and then, as the girl is turning him down, the camera slowly dollies to the right and looks down a long, empty hallway. Pauline Kael's review called this shot—which calls attention to itself—a lapse during which Scorsese was maybe borrowing from Antonioni. Scorsese calls this shot the most important one in the film.

Why? Because, he says, it's as if we can't bear to watch Travis feel the pain of being rejected. This is interesting, because later, when Travis goes on a killing rampage, the camera goes so far as to adopt slow motion so we can see the horror in greater detail. That Scorsese finds the rejection more painful than the murders is fascinating, because it helps to explain Travis Bickle, and perhaps it goes some way toward explaining one kind of urban violence. Travis has been shut out so systematically, so often, from a piece of the action that eventually he has to hit back somehow.

Taxi Driver is a brilliant nightmare and like all nightmares it doesn't tell us half of what we want to know. We're not told where Travis comes from, what his specific problems are, whether his ugly scar came from Vietnam—because this isn't a case study, but a portrait of some days in his life. There's a moment at a political rally when Travis, in dark glasses, smiles in a strange way that reminds us of those photos of Bremer just before he shot Wallace. The moment tells us nothing, and everything: We don't know the specifics of Travis's complaint, but in a chilling way we know what we need to know of him. The film's a masterpiece of suggestive characterization; Scorsese's style selects details that evoke emotions, and that's the effect he wants. The performances are odd and compelling: He goes for moments from his actors, rather than slowly developed characters. It's as if the required emotions were written in the margins of their scripts: Give me anger—fear—dread. Robert De Niro, as Travis Bickle, is as good as Brando at suggesting emotions even while veiling them from us (and in many of his close-ups, Scorsese uses almost subliminal slow motion to draw out the revelations). Cybill Shepherd, as the blond goddess, is correctly cast, for once, as a glacier slowly receding toward humanity. And there's Jodie Foster, chillingly cast as a twelve-year-old prostitute whom Travis wants to "save." Harvey Keitel, a veteran of all of Scorsese's films (he was the violent maniac in *Alice Doesn't Live*

Here Anymore) is the pimp who controls her, and he's got the right kind of toughness that's all bluff.

These people are seen almost in flashes, as if darkness threatens to close over them altogether. *Taxi Driver* is a hell, from the opening shot of a cab emerging from stygian clouds of steam to the climactic killing scene in which the camera finally looks straight down. Scorsese wanted to look away from Travis's rejection; we almost want to look away from his life. But he's there, all right, and he's suffering.

Tell Them Willie Boy Is Here ★ ★ ★ ½
PG, 96 m., 1970

Robert Redford (Cooper), Katharine Ross (Lola), Robert Blake (Willie Boy), Susan Clark (Liz). Directed by Abraham Polonsky and produced by Philip A. Waxman. Screenplay by Polonsky.

Abraham Polonsky's *Tell Them Willie Boy Is Here* is a simple, direct, almost stark retelling of an event that took place in 1909. It's about Willie Boy, a Paiute Indian whose personal fight for freedom was elevated by the press into an Indian uprising against President William Howard Taft. It is also about white racism and Indian pride, and it is no ordinary Western. It marked the resumption of the directorial career of Polonsky, interrupted twenty years earlier by the House Committee on Un-American Activities during the Hollywood witchhunt. Before he was blacklisted in 1950, Polonsky had written Robert Rossen's *Body and Soul* and directed John Garfield in the classic *Force of Evil*.

Polonsky, who also wrote *Willie Boy*, is at pains to tell his story without gimmicks. It's about how Willie Boy (Robert Blake) comes back to the reservation to marry the girl he loves, Lola (Katharine Ross). But her father forbids them to see each other. In a confrontation, Willie Boy kills the father in self-defense and then goes on the run with Lola. The Indians accept the event as "marriage by capture," forced upon Willie Boy because, as he tells Lola, "I've asked for you the white man's way, and I'm through asking." But Lola, it turns out, was a favorite of the reservation superintendent (Susan Clark), a proper Bostonian who wanted her to be a teacher. At the superintendent's insistence, the sheriff (Robert Redford) gets up a posse and goes after the couple.

Almost all the movie is concerned with the chase, which takes place at a time when

President Taft is visiting the area. The president's visit has drawn dozens of newspaper reporters to town, and they sensationalize Willie Boy's case. When Willie Boy accidentally kills one of the members of the posse, an instant "uprising" is born in the papers. Redford wants to forget the whole thing: "It's Indian business, and besides, this posse couldn't catch a dog in the street." But the publicity forces him to keep after Willie Boy, until a final personal confrontation.

Redford gets top billing, and is very good as the sheriff. He has a natural feel for acting in movies; he makes small gestures do the work of large ones, and he can convey a lot of meaning without spelling it out in dialogue. But the film's real star is Robert Blake, who played one of the killers in *In Cold Blood*. Blake is all gristle and nerve and pride, and gained his greatest fame as TV's Baretta.

The movie is paced more slowly than we'd expect for a Western, but then it's not really a Western at all, but a study of personality. There aren't a lot of action scenes and shoot-outs; this is essentially an essay on the stereotypes by which white men have attempted to justify their theft of the Indian lands and independence. *Tell Them Willie Boy Is Here* works powerfully on that level, and it is impossible to see it without thinking that the same sort of exploitation still goes on today.

10 ★ ★ ★ ★
R, 123 m., 1979

Dudley Moore (George), Julie Andrews (Sam), Bo Derek (Jenny), Robert Webber (Hugh), Dee Wallace (Mary Lewis), Sam Jones (David), Brian Dennehy (Bartender). Directed by Blake Edwards and produced by Edwards and Tony Adams. Screenplay by Edwards.

Blake Edwards's *10* is perhaps the first comedy about terminal yearning. Like all great comedies, it deals with emotions very close to our hearts: In this case, the unutterable poignance of a man's desire for a woman he cannot have. The woman, of course, must be unbelievably desirable (and the hero of *10*, on a scale of 1 to 10, gives this particular woman an 11). It helps, too, if the man is short, forty-two years old, and filled with inchoate longings.

You remember inchoate longings. They used to stalk the pages of novels by Thomas Wolfe, back in the years before the Me Generation and the cult of instant gratification. There used to be a time, incredibly, when you couldn't have something *just because you wanted it*—*10* remembers that time. Its hero,

Dudley Moore, begins *10* as a man who seems to have more or less what any man could desire. He is a successful composer. His girlfriend is Julie Andrews. He has a great house up in the hills, he drives a Rolls-Royce, he has cable TV with remote tuning.

But then one day, driving his Rolls down Santa Monica Boulevard, he is visited by a vision. She is a preternaturally beautiful young woman in the next car. She turns to regard him, and he is instantly, helplessly, in love. She turns away. She must be about her business. She is dressed in a bridal gown and is on her way to the church to be married.

He follows her. He is stung by a bee in the church. He has six cavities painfully filled by her father, who is a dentist. Groggy from pain pills and brandy, he finds himself aboard an airplane flying to Mexico—where, amazingly, he winds up at the same resort as his ideal woman (and, of course, her husband—one of the vacuous beach-boy types with a smile fit for a Jockey T-shirts model).

Blake Edwards's screenplay now plunges into some slightly more serious waters, where we will not follow. What we're struck with, in *10*, is the uncanny way its humor gets laughs by touching on emotions and yearnings that are very real for us. We identify with the characters in this movie: Their predicaments are funny, yes—but then ours would be, too, if they weren't our own.

The central treasure in the film is the performance by Dudley Moore. There must have been times when Moore wondered if he'd *ever* get the girl. In *10*, he does. He also brings his character such life and dimension that *10* is a lot more than a comedy: It's a study in the follies of human nature.

The girl (the one who scores 11) is played by Bo Derek. She is so desirable, such a pure and cheerful embodiment of carnal perfection, that we're in there with Dudley Moore every step of the way, even when he's slogging it out to Ravel's interminable "Bolero." Julie Andrews has a small but delightful role as the sensible mistress, and the movie also has warm performances by Robert Webber, as Moore's vulnerable gay friend, and by Brian Dennehy, as a particularly understanding bartender in Mexico.

10 is not only one of the best films Blake Edwards has ever made, but was something of a turning point in his career: The previous decade he had alternated between successful Pink Panther movies and non-Panther flops like *The Tamarind Seed, The Wild Rovers,* and *The Carey Treatment.* Did he have another

good straight movie in him? Yes, as a matter of fact, he did.

Tender Mercies ★ ★ ★
PG, 93 m., 1983

Robert Duvall (Mac Sledge), Tess Harper (Rosa Lee), Betty Buckley (Dixie), Wilford Brimley (Harry), Ellen Barkin (Sue Anne), Allan Hubbard (Sonny). Directed by Bruce Beresford and produced by Philip S. Hobel. Screenplay by Horton Foote.

Tender Mercies visits some fairly familiar movie territory, and achieves some quietly touching effects. The movie's about the rhythms of a small Texas town, and about the struggle of a has-been country singer to regain his self-respect. It might remind you of parts of *The Last Picture Show* and *Honkytonk Man,* with a little bit of *Payday* thrown in (that was the movie starring Rip Torn, based on the last days of the dying Hank Williams, Sr.). This time, the broken-down country singer is named Mac Sledge. He's at the end of his personal road. He was once a big star and a hero to young musicians around the Southwest, but as his final act opens he's sitting in a fleabag motel outside a small Texas town, drinking himself to death, and fighting for the bottle with another guy he hardly even knows.

When he wakes up on the floor the next morning, the other guy is gone and Sledge is hung over, broke, and without prospects. He throws himself on the mercy of the young widow who runs the motel: He'll work for his room and board. She agrees to that, and throws in $2 an hour, but says he can't drink while he's at the motel. He agrees, and that is the day his life turns around and he begins the rebuilding process.

Tender Mercies tells the story of the relationship between the singer and the young widow in a quiet, subtle way; this isn't one of those movies that spells everything out. The key to the movie's tone is in the performance by Robert Duvall as Sledge. Duvall plays him as a bone-weary, seedy, essentially very simple man who needs some values to hold onto. The widow can provide those, and can also provide the stability of a home and family (she has a young son, whose father was killed in Vietnam). What the Duvall character wants to do, essentially, is keep a low profile, work hard, not drink, and forget about the glories of country singing. It's hard for him to remain invisible, though, after the local paper prints a story and the members of a local band start dropping around for advice. There are more complications: Sledge's ex-wife is still touring as a country singer, and would like to turn his eighteen-year-old daughter against him.

What's interesting about *Tender Mercies* is the way it refuses to approach this material as soap opera *or* as drama. The movie's told more like one of those quiet, sly *New Yorker* stories where the big emotional moments sneak up on you, and the effects are achieved indirectly. Sometimes this movie smiles (as in a scene of a double baptism). Sometimes it simply sits there and talks straight (as in a touching speech by Sledge on the meaning of life). Sometimes its low budget allows the seams to show (as in the unconvincing concert scene involving Sledge's wife). But mostly it just lets these stories happen, lets them get to know these people, and see them dealing with life. Some of them get better, and some of them get worse. It's like a country song.

Terminal Velocity ★ ★

PG-13, 102 m., 1994

Charlie Sheen (Ditch Brodie), Nastassja Kinski (Chris Morrow), James Gandolfini (Ben Pinkwater), Christopher McDonald (Kerr), Gary Bullock (Lex), Hans R. Howes (Sam), Melvin Van Peebles (Noble), Suli McCullough (Robocam). Directed by Deran Sarafian and produced by Scott Kroopf and Tom Engelman. Screenplay by David Twohy.

You've gotta hand it to *Terminal Velocity.* This movie may be dumb as a box of shredded wheat, but it has the damnedest action sequence I've seen since Arnold Schwarzenegger blasted the bad guy with the missile in *True Lies.* Nastassja Kinski is locked in the trunk of a red Cadillac, which is taken on board a cargo plane. Charlie Sheen pursues in another plane, walks on its wing, hauls himself aboard the cargo plane, and then finds himself, Kinski, and the Cadillac all falling through the air—with a villain on the hood shooting at him. This is an assignment for Houdini.

Sheen's behavior in this and other scenes is so close to the self-parody of his work in the *Hot Shots* movies that he almost seems to be telling us something—such as, that he takes the movie with less-than-perfect seriousness. No wonder. It's based on such a goofy premise that with just a nudge here and a pun there it could easily have become *Hot Shots Part Cinq* and taken advantage of the franchise. It's not so much that Sheen can keep a straight face in any situation, as

that he always seems to be testing himself with the situations he gets himself into.

In *Terminal Velocity* he plays a skydiving instructor so reckless he's had twelve safety violations in the last month. He's the kind of guy who paints "Kiss This" on his derriere and paraglides into downtown Phoenix. One day a beautiful blonde (Kinski) turns up at his skydiving school and wants an instant lesson. That sets off a long chain of events involving mistaken identities, stolen gold, three-legged dogs, and the KGB (or, as Sheen calls it, "the KG used-to-B"). By the end of the movie, needless to say, nothing less than the survival of the free world is at stake.

I dare not reveal too much of the plot, although it's so absurd that even Kinski giggles while explaining its finer points. The purpose of the movie is essentially to provide a platform for stunts and special effects so weird that we watch goggle-eyed, wondering how in God's name they're gonna get out of each predicament. Kinski is apparently doomed in so many different situations in the movie that it becomes a running gag.

There are times when Deran Sarafian, the director, seems so enthralled by movie formulas that he uses them even in the face of common sense. Sheen, for example, is always getting jumped from behind. Fine; except how do you explain a late scene where he is jumped from behind by a guy who has no reason to do so, and starts talking to him moments later? It's like they were using a computer script-writing program that inserted JUMPED FROM BEHIND before every dialogue scene.

Sheen seems aware of the movie's comic possibilities, and must surely have had a smile on his face when he designed his character's haircut, which seems inspired by the pompadour of the hero of a little-seen but long-remembered movie named *Johnny Suede.* Kinski has a hair motif, too—it's always in her eyes—but she brings a bright, bemused air to her character, and has fun juggling various accents.

Is there a reason to see this movie? I am reminded of categories in the Michelin travel guides. *Terminal Velocity* does not deserve a Journey or even a Detour, but it is indeed a Sight.

Terminal 2: Judgment Day
★ ★ ★ ½
R, 135 m., 1991

Arnold Schwarzenegger (The Terminator), Linda Hamilton (Sarah Connor), Edward

Furlong (John Connor), Robert Patrick (T-1000), Earl Boen (Dr. Silberman), Joe Morton (Miles Dyson). Directed and produced by James Cameron. Screenplay by Cameron and William Wisher.

In *Terminator 2: Judgment Day*, the future once again comes hunting to kill John Connor. Even though the world after the nuclear holocaust of 1997 is ruled by machines, a single man can still make a difference—and that man is Connor, who is a youngster as the movie opens, but is destined to grow up into the leader of the human resistance movement against the cyborgs.

You will recall from the original *The Terminator* (1984), or perhaps you will not, that the first Terminator, played by Arnold Schwarzenegger, was sent back from the future to kill Connor's mother (Linda Hamilton). That mission failed, and the young man was born, and so, now, in *Terminator 2*, two Terminators journey back from the future: a good one, played by Schwarzenegger, who is assigned to protect young Connor, and a bad one, played by Robert Patrick, whose mission is to destroy him. (Terminators, by the way, look like humans but are made of high-tech materials and have computer brains; the bad one, named T-1000, was apparently named after his great-grandfather, a Toshiba laptop.) You'd think those machines of the future would realize their mission is futile; that since Connor is manifestly the leader of the human resistance, their mission to kill him obviously must fail. But such paradoxes are ignored by *Terminator 2*, which overlooks an even larger one: If indeed, in the last scene of the film, the computer chips necessary to invent Terminators are all destroyed, then there couldn't have been any Terminators—so how come they exist in the first place? Science fiction has had fun toying with such paradoxes for generations, but *Terminator 2* takes the prudent course of simply ignoring them and centering its action in the present, where young John Connor (Eddie Furlong) is a wild street kid, being raised in a foster home because his birth mother (Hamilton) is a prisoner in a mental hospital. They think she's crazy, of course, because she keeps trying to warn mankind about the approaching nuclear disaster.

From the opening chase scene—in which young Connor, on a fast motorcycle, outruns T-1000, at the wheel of a semi—*Terminator 2* develops a close relationship between the young boy and the good Terminator. Before long young Connor even discovers that Schwarzenegger is programmed to follow his instructions, and so he orders the awesome machine to stop killing people. The result is a neat twist on the tradition of the Schwarzenegger special effects film; this time, instead of corpses littering the screen, the Arnold character shoots to maim or frighten. It's fun for a kid, having his own pet Terminator, and that's one of the inspirations in the screenplay by director James Cameron and William Wisher—Schwarzenegger becomes a father figure for young Connor. Another intriguing screenplay idea is to develop the Terminator's lack of emotions; like Mr. Spock in *Star Trek*, he does not understand why humans cry.

Schwarzenegger's genius as a movie star is to find roles that build on, rather than undermine, his physical and vocal characteristics. Here he becomes the straight man in a human drama—and in a human comedy, too, as the kid tells him to lighten up and stop talking like a computer. After the kid's mother escapes from the mental home, the threesome works together to defeat T-1000, while at the same time creating an unlikely but effective family unit.

While that's happening on the story level, the movie surpasses itself with special effects. There are the usual car chases, explosions, and fight scenes, of course, all well done, but what people will remember is the way the movie envisions T-1000. This cyborg is made out of a newly invented liquid metal that makes him all but invincible. Shoot a hole in him, and you can see right through him, but the sides of the hole run together again, and he's repaired and ready for action. In one grotesque scene, his entire body is twisted into a bizarre sculpture, but it recombines, and in another scene, he is frozen with liquid nitrogen and shattered into a million pieces, but when the pieces melt they flow together and he's as good as new. These scenes involve ingenious creative work by Industrial Light & Magic, the George Lucas special-effects shop. The basic idea for T-1000 was first tried out by ILM in *The Abyss* (1990), where an undersea station was invaded by a creature with a body made entirely of water. The trick is to create a computer simulation of the movement desired, and then use a computer paintbox program to give it surface color and texture—in this case, the appearance of liquid mercury. The computer images are then combined with the live action; T-1000 turns from shiny liquid into a human being through

a dissolve from the effect to the actor. All of that work would simply be an exercise if the character itself were not effective, but T-1000, as played by Patrick, is a splendid villain, with compact good looks and a bland expression. His most fearsome quality is his implacability; no matter what you do to him, he doesn't get disturbed and he doesn't get discouraged. He just pulls himself together and keeps on coming.

The key element in any action picture, I think, is a good villain. *Terminator 2* has one, along with an intriguing hero, a fierce heroine, and a young boy who is played by Furlong with guts and energy. The movie responds to criticisms of excessive movie violence by tempering the Terminator's blood lust, but nobody, I think, will complain it doesn't have enough action.

Terms of Endearment ★ ★ ★ ★
PG, 129 m., 1983

Debra Winger (Emma Horton), Shirley MacLaine (Aurora Greenway), Jack Nicholson (Breedlove), Jeff Daniels (Flap Horton), Danny DeVito (Vernon), John Lithgow (Sam Burns). Directed, produced, and written by James L. Brooks.

When families get together to remember their times together, the conversation has a way of moving easily from the tragedies to the funny things. You'll mention someone who has passed away, and there'll be a moment of silence, and then somebody will grin and be reminded of some goofy story. Life always has an unhappy ending, but you can have a lot of fun along the way, and everything doesn't have to be dripping in deep significance.

The most remarkable achievement of *Terms of Endearment*, which is filled with great achievements, is its ability to find the balance between the funny and the sad, between moments of deep truth and other moments of high ridiculousness. A lesser movie would have had trouble moving between the extremes that are visited by this film, but because *Terms of Endearment* understands its characters and loves them, we never have a moment's doubt: What happens next is supposed to happen, because life's like that. *Terms of Endearment* feels as much like life as any movie I can think of. At the same time, it's a triumph of show business, with its high comic style, its flair for bittersweet melodrama, and its star turns for the actors. Maybe the best thing about this

movie is the way it combines those two different kinds of filmmaking. This is a movie with bold emotional scenes and big laughs, and at the same time it's so firmly in control of its tone that we believe we are seeing real people.

The movie's about two remarkable women, and their relationships with each other and with the men in their lives. The mother is played by Shirley MacLaine. She's a widow who lives in Houston and hasn't dated a man since her husband died. Maybe she's redirected her sexual desires into the backyard, where her garden has grown so large and elaborate that she either will have to find a man pretty quickly or move to a house with a bigger yard. Her daughter, played by Debra Winger, is one of those people who seems to have been blessed with a sense of life and joy. She marries a guy named Flap who teaches English in a series of Midwestern colleges; she rears three kids and puts up with Flap, who has an eye for coeds.

Back in Houston, her mother finally goes out on a date with the swinging bachelor (Jack Nicholson) who has lived next door for years. He's a hard-drinking, girl-chasing former astronaut with a grin that hints of unspeakable lusts. MacLaine, a lady who surrounds herself with frills and flowers, is appalled by this animalistic man and then touched by him.

There are a couple of other bittersweet relationships in the film. Both mother and daughter have timid, mild-mannered male admirers: MacLaine is followed everywhere by Vernon (Danny DeVito), who asks only to be allowed to gaze upon her, and Winger has a tender, little affair with a banker.

The years pass. Children grow up into adolescence, Flap gets a job as head of the department in Nebraska, the astronaut turns out to have genuine human possibilities of becoming quasi-civilized, and mother and daughter grow into a warmer and deeper relationship. All of this is told in a series of perfectly written, acted, and directed scenes that flow as effortlessly as a perfect day, and then something happens that is totally unexpected, and changes everything. I don't want to suggest what happens It flows so naturally that it should be allowed to take place.

This is a wonderful film. There isn't a thing that I would change, and I was exhilarated by the freedom it gives itself to move from the high comedy of Nicholson's best moments to the acting of Debra Winger in the closing scenes. She outdoes herself. It's a great performance. And yet it's not a "performance." There are scenes that have such a casual gaiety that acting seems to have nothing to do with it. She doesn't reach for effects, and neither does the film, because it's all right there.

Tess ★ ★ ★ ★
PG, 180 m., 1980

Nastassja Kinski (Tess), Peter Firth (Angel Clare), Leigh Lawson (Alec d'Urberville), Rosemary Martin (Mrs. Durbeyfield), Sylvia Coleridge (Mrs. d'Urberville), John Collin (John Durbeyfield), Tony Church (Parson), Brigid Erin Bates (Girl in Meadow). Directed by Roman Polanski and produced by Claude Berri. Screenplay by Gerard Brach, Polanski, and John Brownjohn.

Roman Polanski's *Tess* is a love song with a tragic ending—the best kind of love song of all, just so long as it's not about ourselves. He tells the story of a beautiful young girl, innocent but not without intelligence, and the way she is gradually destroyed by the exercise of the male ego. The story is all the more touching because it is not an unrelenting descent into gloom, as it might have been in other hands, but a life lived in occasional sight of love and happiness. Tess is forever just on the brink of getting the peace she deserves.

The movie is based on a novel by Thomas Hardy, but Polanski never permits his film to become a Classics Illustrated; this isn't a devout rendering of a literary masterpiece, but a film that lives and breathes and has a quick sympathy for its heroine. Nastassja Kinski is just right for the title role. She has the youth, the freshness, and the naïveté of a Tess, and none of the practiced mannerisms of an actress engaged to "interpret" the role. That's good because Tess is a character who should stick out like a sore thumb in many scenes, and Kinski's occasional shy awkwardness is just right for the story of a girl who attempts to move up in social class on sheer bravado.

The story involves a young girl who will be the victim, the prey, and sometimes the lover of many men, without ever quite understanding what it is that those men want of her. The first man in her life is her father, a drunken farmer named John Durbeyfield, who discovers from the local parson that he is related to the noble local family of d'Urbervilles. The farmer and his wife immediately send their beautiful daughter, Tess, off to confront the d'Urbervilles and perhaps win a position in their household.

Tess is almost immediately seduced by a rakish cousin. She becomes pregnant, and her child dies soon after it is born. She never tells the cousin. But later, after she falls in love with the son of a local minister and marries him, she confesses her past. This is too much for her new husband to bear; he "married down" because he was attracted to Tess's humble origins. But he is not prepared to accept the reality of her past. He leaves on a bizarre mission to South America. Tess, meanwhile, descends to rough manual labor for a few pennies an hour. She is eventually reunited with her cousin (who is not a complete bastard, and complains that he should have been informed of her pregnancy). She becomes his lover. Then the wayward husband returns, and the physical and psychic contest for Tess ends in tragedy.

As a plot, these events would be right at home in any soap opera. But what happens in Polanski's *Tess* is less important than how Tess feels about it, how we feel about it, and how successfully Polanski is able to locate those events in a specific place and time. His movie is set in England, but was actually photographed in France. It is a beautifully visualized period piece that surrounds Tess with the attitudes of her time—attitudes that explain how restricted her behavior must be, and how society views her genuine human emotions as inappropriate. This is a wonderful film; the kind of exploration of doomed young sexuality that, like *Elvira Madigan*, makes us agree that the lovers should never grow old.

Testament ★ ★ ★ ★
PG, 90 m., 1983

Jane Alexander (Carol Wetherly), William Devane (Tom Wetherly), Ross Harris (Brad), Roxana Zal (Mary Liz), Lukas Haas (Scottie), Philip Anglim (Hollis), Leon Ames (Henry Abhart), Rebecca De Mornay (Mother with Baby). Directed by Lynne Littman and produced by Jonathan Bernstein and Littman. Screenplay by John Sacret Young.

Testament may be the first movie in a long time that will make you cry. It made me cry. And seeing it again for a second time, knowing everything that would happen, anticipating each scene before it came, I was affected just as deeply. But the second time I was able to see more clearly that the movie is more than just a devastating experience, that it has a message with a certain hope.

The film is about a suburban American family, and what happens to that family after a nuclear war. It is not a science-fiction movie, and it doesn't have any special effects, and there are no big scenes of buildings blowing over or people disintegrating. We never see a mushroom cloud. We never even know who started the war. Instead, *Testament* is a tragedy about manners: It asks how we might act toward one another, how our values might stand up in the face of an overwhelming catastrophe.

The movie begins with one of those typical families right out of TV commercials. The father (William Devane) is a physical-fitness nut. The mother (Jane Alexander) is loving, funny, and a little harried. The kids include a daughter who practices the piano, a son who races his dad up hills on their ten-speed bikes, and a little boy who guards the "treasure" in the bottom drawer of his chest. The movie follows these people long enough for us to know them, to appreciate their personalities, their good and weak points, and then one sunny afternoon the war starts.

Most of the film is about what happens then. Anarchy does not break out. There is some looting, but it is limited. For the most part, the people in the small northern California town stick together and try to do the best that they can. There are meetings in the church. There are public-health measures. A beloved community leader (Leon Ames, of TV's "Life with Father" many years ago) is a ham-radio operator, and makes contact with a few other places. A decision is made to go ahead with the grade-school play. Life goes on . . . but death invades it, as radiation poisoning begins to take a toll, first on the babies, then on the children, until finally the cemetery is filled and the bodies have to be burned on a pyre.

The movie finds dozens of small details to suggest existence after the bomb. All the kids, for example, take the batteries out of their toys and computer games, and turn them in for emergency use. Gasoline is rationed, and then runs out. The survivors have no garbage collection, no electricity, and, worst of all, no word from elsewhere. The sky gradually grows darker, suggesting realistically that a nuclear war would finally kill us all by raising great clouds of dust that would choke the Earth's vegetation.

In the midst of this devastation, Jane Alexander, as the mother, tries to preserve love and decency. She stands by her children, watches as they grow in response to the challenges, cherishes them as she sees all her dreams for them disappear. It is a great performance, the heart of the film. In fact, Alexander's performance makes the film possible to watch without unbearable heartbreak, because she is brave and decent in the face of horror. And the last scene, in which she expresses such small optimism as is still possible, is one of the most powerful movie scenes I've ever seen.

Tex ★ ★ ★ ★
PG, 103 m., 1982

Matt Dillon (Tex), Jim Metzler (Mason), Meg Tilly (Jamie), Bill McKinney (Pop), Frances Lee McCain (Mrs. Johnson), Ben Johnson (Cole Collins). Directed by Tim Hunter and produced by Ron Miller. Screenplay by Charlie Haas and Hunter.

There is a shock of recognition almost from the beginning of *Tex,* because we're listening to the sound of American voices in an authentically American world, the world of teen-age boys trying to figure things out and make the right decisions. The voices sound right but may be a little unfamiliar, because adolescents on television are often made to talk in pseudo-hip sitcom nonspeak. Here in *Tex* are the clear voices of two young men who are worthy of attention. Their names are Tex and Mason. They're brothers, one about eighteen, the other fourteen and a half. They live by themselves in a rundown house on some land outside a rural suburb of Tulsa. Their father is a rodeo cowboy who hardly ever stops in at home and forgets to send money for weeks at a time. These two kids are raising themselves and doing a pretty good job of it.

The movie tells the story of a couple of weeks in their lives. These are the kinds of weeks when things can go either well or badly—and if they go badly, we sense, Tex could get his whole life off to the wrong start. The brothers are broke. Mason sells their horses to raise money to buy food and get the gas turned back on. That makes Tex angry and sad; he's a kid looking for trouble.

We meet the other people in their world. There's the rich family down the road, dominated by a stern father who makes his teenagers toe a strict line. His kids are just as unpredictable as anyone else's, but he doesn't believe that. He believes their two undisciplined friends, Tex and Mason, are leading

them into trouble and practically dragging them to late-night beer parties. There's another complication. His daughter and Tex are beginning to fall in love.

There's another friend, a local kid who got a girl pregnant, married her, and moved to Tulsa to start a family. He's dealing drugs. Mason knows this intuitively and surely, and knows the kid is heading for trouble. Tex knows it, too, but there comes a time in this story when Tex just doesn't give a damn, and when the drug dealer happens to be there, Tex accepts a ride into Tulsa with him. Tex doesn't do drugs himself, but he gets into a very scary situation with another dealer, and there's a harrowing scene in which Tex wavers just at the brink of getting into serious trouble.

There is more to this movie's story, but the important thing about it isn't what happens, but how it happens. The movie is so accurately acted, especially by Jim Metzler as Mason and Matt Dillon as Tex, that we care more about the characters than about the plot. We can see them learning and growing, and when they have a heart-to-heart talk about "going all the way," we hear authentic teen-agers speaking, not kids who seem to have been raised at Beverly Hills cocktail parties.

Tex is based on a famous novel by S.E. Hinton, who has had two of her other novels filmed by Francis Ford Coppola. She knows a great deal about adolescents, and her work is unaffected by sentimentality and easy romance. It's authentic. But the backgrounds of the two filmmakers are also interesting. Tim Hunter and Charles Haas bought the book and wrote the screenplay, and Hunter directed. Their previous collaboration was a little movie named *Over the Edge,* about teen-agers who feel cornered and persecuted by the rigid middle-class rules of a cardboard Denver suburb. That movie, a small masterpiece containing Matt Dillon's first movie appearance, never got a fair chance in theaters. Now here are Hunter and Haas again, still remembering what it's like to be young, still getting the dialogue and the attitudes, the hang-ups and the dreams, exactly right.

Texasville ★ ★ ★ ½
R, 123 m., 1990

Jeff Bridges (Duane Jackson), Cybill Shepherd (Jacy Farrow), Annie Potts (Karla Jackson), Timothy Bottoms (Sonny Crawford), Cloris Leachman (Ruth Popper), Randy Quaid

(Lester Marlow), Eileen Brennan (Genevieve). Directed by Peter Bogdanovich and produced by Barry Spikings and Bogdanovich. Screenplay by Bogdanovich.

The Royal Theater still stands on Main Street in Anarene, Texas, but it has been closed for more than thirty years now and the paint is peeling away from its weather-beaten sign. In the course of *Texasville,* Peter Bogdanovich's camera pauses for just a second to regard it, and to my surprise I remembered the name of Sam the Lion. He was the man who used to own the Royal, back before television came along and forced small-town movie theaters out of business.

Sam the Lion and the other characters in Bogdanovich's *The Last Picture Show* (1971) remain somehow fresh in the memory, even though it's been years since I saw the movie. The simple, stark black-and-white images of that great film have the poignancy of pictures from your high school days—of earlier, simpler times.

Now comes Bogdanovich's *Texasville,* an almost unprecedented reunion of many of the same people, on both sides of the camera. It is, in a sense, like a high school reunion, taking people we last saw in 1951 and continuing their histories in the early 1980s. The story is again by Larry McMurtry, who wrote a sequel to his earlier novel. The screenplay and direction are again by Bogdanovich, who in 1971 was at the dawn of his career and now needs this project as a comeback. Most of the stars are back, too, including Cybill Shepherd, Jeff Bridges, Timothy Bottoms, Randy Quaid, Cloris Leachman, and Eileen Brennan (although Ben Johnson, who was perhaps the best thing in the earlier film, and along with Leachman won an Oscar for his work, isn't here because Sam the Lion is dead).

The location is the same, too: a small Texas town where everybody knows everybody, and they all seem to be having affairs, and everybody knows all about it. In 1951, Sonny, the Bottoms character, had an affair with the coach's wife, and both Sonny and Duane (Bridges) were in love with Jacy (Shepherd), the town's cool and inaccessible beauty. Then Duane went off to fight the war in Korea, and Jacy moved to Dallas, and now, as we resume the story, it's Duane's son who is sleeping with half the women in town. Sonny is the town mayor and runs the convenience store, but he gets confused some days and doesn't seem quite sure what's going on around him. And Duane is married to Karla (Annie Potts) and has met his match.

Then Jacy comes back to town. Everybody knows the news at once, of course, and speculation flies. She wound up in Italy, apparently, and had some kind of a minor career as an actress in B-movies, but now she's divorced and has just lost a child, and has come back home to gather herself. Shepherd makes her entrance in the movie by emerging, dripping wet, from the waters of a lake and startling Duane, who is floating in his boat. And we're reminded that in the earlier film she looked great in a bathing suit, too—so perfect she inflamed the fantasies and desires of a generation of young men in Anarene.

The difference between then and now, between *The Last Picture Show* and *Texasville*, is between nostalgia and human comedy, between a film that wanted to be bittersweet and one that also wants to be raucous. Things are simply not as *serious* in Anarene as they used to be. Adulteries are not tragedies, but material for gossip. The kids of some thirty years earlier have not grown up into adults like Sam the Lion, but into middle-aged adolescents. Dreams are hardly ever spoken of at all. And yet underneath somewhere there is still the heartbeat of the old values.

The Last Picture Show was lean and hard-bitten, and Bogdanovich said he didn't want to shoot it in color because that would "prettify" it. *Texasville* is in color, probably on the studio's uncompromising insistence, and it suffers by comparison; the color makes things seem jollier and more picturesque, and takes the edge off the real suffering that's going on here. And still all the same, there are shadows and sorrows in Anarene, and one of the things that's touching is the way the town has informally and tacitly agreed to overlook some of Sonny's problems and help him out when they can.

In 1951, Jacy was content to be the center of male attention, to be a tease and a flirt. Now that three decades have passed, she sees things a little differently, and one of the unexpected developments in this film is the way she makes friends with Karla, Duane's wife, and they get to be so thick that actual rumors get started. Duane, meanwhile, has his own problems in the romantic area, not to mention trying to deal with his son's, and one of the most common attitudes in this movie is lethargy in the face of overwhelming developments. The town motto could be, "What you gonna do?"

Bogdanovich brings some of the story threads together in a long sequence built around the Anarene centennial celebration, and there is a parade in which Jacy gets to wave from a float decorated with the tactless legend, "Homecoming Queen Through the Ages." There are also some moments of heartfelt emotion, confession, and tragedy, and the oil crisis and other international events occasionally hover on the horizon, but in general the town seems to be preoccupied as ever with its own personalities and memories, as if it were sitting for its portrait.

Is *Texasville* as good as *The Last Picture Show*? No, because the previous picture was complete, and this one seems to lack a genuine reason for existence. Jacy does indeed return to town, but, once there, she seems to fall easily into the general aimlessness, and the citizens of Anarene seem so accepting of human nature that they have given up having any dreams or expectations for it. There has to be more to life than screwing around. Well, doesn't there?

And yet in a subtle way, *Texasville* is making the same point as the previous film: That the last picture show has closed, and that the dreams of the old West, the dreams in movies like *Red River* (which was the last movie that played at the Royal), have been forgotten, and now under these wide Texas skies people lower their eyes to smaller concerns and lives without vision. During the Centennial celebration, one of the living exhibits is labeled "County's Oldest Inhabitant." I wonder what Sam the Lion would have thought about that.

That Obscure Object of Desire ★ ★ ★ ★
R, 103 m., 1977

Fernando Rey (Mathieu), Carole Bouquet and Angela Molina (Conchita). Directed by Luis Buñuel. Screenplay by Buñuel and Jean-Claude Carriere.

The man is middle-aged, impeccably dressed, perfectly groomed, obviously respectable. He has just barely caught his train. A young woman comes running down the station platform, also trying to catch the train. The man's face reflects intense annoyance; he whispers something to the conductor, gives him a tip, and is allowed into the train's restroom. He emerges with a pail of water, which, as the young lady tries to climb aboard, he pours on her head.

Ah, satisfaction . . . he settles down in his seat, only to discover intense curiosity among his fellow travelers. One of them, a psychologist who is a dwarf, finally speaks: "I could not help seeing what you did. I can tell from your appearance that you are a gentleman. Therefore, you must have had an excellent reason. . . ."

"Yes," the gentleman replies pleasantly, "I had a *most* excellent reason." Seeming almost flattered by their curiosity, he tells them a story. And so, on a note both calm and sly, begins Luis Buñuel's *That Obscure Object of Desire*.

Buñuel's characters did battle with erotic desire for more than fifty years. They tended to be vain and fastidious people, middle class, concerned with maintaining their self-respect. Yet, they had a way of coming off second best to lust, jealousy, and an assortment of peculiar sexual obsessions. And as Buñuel grew older, he seemed to learn more about their weaknesses with every year, and to find their passions increasingly funny. He made this film when he was seventy-seven.

Take, for example, his hero this time, the completely respectable Mathieu (Fernando Rey). He is a widower with no interest in most women; unless he feels true passion, he says, he would just as soon leave them alone. One day a new maid comes to serve him his dinner. She is Conchita; cool, elegant, gently mocking. He is lost. He is hopelessly in love, but his advances serve only to drive Conchita further away.

He tries what he thinks is a civilized approach, arranging with her mother to provide for the family's financial needs in return for, ahem . . . but Conchita protests: "I wanted to give myself to you, but you tried to buy me!" He would by now, indeed, give her anything he has, but she disappears. Then he discovers her again, by accident, in Switzerland. Their life becomes a strange, erotic game of cat-and-mouse, in which the virginal Conchita torments him by her inaccessibility. At last Mathieu is ready to settle for anything—even sleeping with her without touching her. He is totally enthralled.

Buñuel relishes themes of erotic frustration. His most memorable heroines are those who deny themselves, and we remember the niece sleeping in her hair shirt in *Viridiana*, and Catherine Deneuve's masochistic pastimes in *Belle de Jour* and *Tristana*. This time, though, Buñuel seems to be reaching deeper, to be saying something more. Conchita is not simply denying herself to the man who loves her; she is teaching him a lesson about his own complex nature, about his need for a woman who would be always unattainable.

And Buñuel, of course, is exercising his own dry and totally original wit. His film is filled with small, droll touches, with tiny peculiarities of behavior, with moral anarchy, with a cynicism about human nature that somehow seems, in his hands, almost cheerful. His most obvious touch is perhaps his best: to dramatize Conchita's tantalizing elusiveness, he has cast two actresses to play her. So just when poor Mathieu has all but seduced this Conchita, the other emerges from the dressing room. Pour a pail of water on her head? Yes, we imagine Buñuel nodding wisely, a man could easily be driven to such an extreme.

Note: The story behind the casting could make a movie of its own. Buñuel originally cast Maria Schneider, and when they had a falling-out after a month, he cast Carole Bouquet and Angela Molina to replace her, alternating between the two obviously quite different actresses quite arbitrarily, and with no explanation. The lesson, perhaps, is that obsessions are blind, and so self-centered that the objects of desire can be interchangeable.

That's Dancing! ★ ★ ★
PG, 105 m., 1985

With hosts Mikhail Baryshnikov, Ray Bolger, Sammy Davis, Jr., Gene Kelly, and Liza Minnelli. Directed by Jack Haley, Jr., and produced by David Niven, Jr., and Haley. Screenplay by Haley.

There is a sense in which it is impossible to dislike *That's Dancing!* and another sense in which movies like this—made by splicing together all the "good parts"—are irritating and sort of unfair to the original films. Given the choice of seeing *Singin' in the Rain* again or spending the same amount of time looking at scenes from *Singin'* and maybe sixty other films, I'd rather see the real movie all the way through. But *That's Dancing!* is not setting an either-or test for us; what it basically wants to do is entertain us with a lot of good dance scenes from a lot of good, and bad, movies, and that is such a harmless ambition that I guess we can accept it.

The movie has been put together by Jack Haley, Jr., and David Niven, Jr., and it recycles Haley's formula in *That's Entertainment!* (1974), the original slice-and-dice anthology from Hollywood's golden ages. There also has been a *That's Entertainment II* (or "too," I seem to recall), and the law of diminishing returns is beginning to apply. Sooner or

later, we'll get *That's All, Folks!* In the first movie, for example, we got Gene Kelly's immortal title dance number from *Singin' in the Rain;* in the first movie, we got Donald O'Connor's equally immortal "Make 'em Laugh" sequence; and that leaves Kelly and O'Connor's only somewhat immortal "Moses Supposes" number for this film. Pretty soon we're going to be getting *That's What's Left of Entertainment!*

That's Dancing! shares with the earlier movies an irritating compulsion to masquerade as a documentary, which it isn't. The tone is set by Kelly's opening generalizations about the universality of dance, etc., while we see *National Geographic* outtakes of dancing around the world: tribes in Africa, hula skirts in Hawaii, polkas, geisha girls, and so on. Kelly is later spelled by such other dance analysts as Liza Minnelli, Ray Bolger, Mikhail Baryshnikov, and Sammy Davis, Jr., all of whom can dance with a great deal more ease than they can recite pseudo-profundities.

There is, however, a lot of good dancing in this movie, including rare silent footage of Isadora Duncan. We see Busby Berkeley's meticulously choreographed dance geometries, the infinite style of Fred Astaire, the brassy joy of Ginger Rogers, the pizazz of Cyd Charisse and Eleanor Powell, a charming duet between Bill "Bojangles" Robinson and Shirley Temple, and a dazzling display by the Nicholas Brothers, who were the inspiration for the dance team played by the Hines brothers in *Cotton Club.* The movie is up-to-date, with John Travolta from *Saturday Night Fever* and footage from break-dance movies, *Flashdance,* and Michael Jackson's *Thriller.* But perhaps its most pleasing single moment is a little soft-shoe by Jimmy Cagney, who was perhaps not the technical equal of Astaire, but was certainly on the same sublime plane when it came to communicating sheer joy.

One of the insights offered in the narration of *That's Dancing!* is that Astaire was responsible for the theory that you should see the entire body of the dancer in most of the shots in a dance scene, and that the scene should be shown in unbroken shots, as much as possible, to preserve the continuity of the dancer's relationship with space and time. That's the kind of seemingly obvious statement that contains a lot of half-baked conclusions. True, you have to see the dancer's whole body to appreciate what he's doing (look at the disastrous choreography in Travolta's *Stayin' Alive,* which inspired Ginger

Rogers to call it a dance film—"from the waist up"). But you also need the cutaways to show the faces of the dancers, and the chemistry between them, as when Astaire and Rogers have their enchanted dancing lesson in *Swing Time.* True, shooting the whole thing in one unbroken take preserves the integrity of the visual record—but what about the sensational dance sequences in *Flashdance* that were achieved by literally cutting between different dancers, all doing their own specialty? All that really matters is the end result.

What conclusions can be drawn from the movie's survey of sixty years of dancing on screen? I can think of one, sort of obvious and sort of depressing: Style has gone out of style. New dancers in recent dance movies are in superb physical shape and do amazing things on the screen, but they do not have the magical personal style of an Astaire or a Kelly. They're technicians. And there's another thing: They don't really dance together. A lot of them are soloists, or two soloists sharing the same floor. When Astaire and Rogers danced together, they danced *together.* And that is maybe what dancing is finally all about.

That's Entertainment! ★ ★ ★ ★
G, 132 m., 1974

Selected scenes from MGM musicals between 1929 and 1958, introduced by Frank Sinatra, Fred Astaire, Gene Kelly, Mickey Rooney, Liza Minnelli, Elizabeth Taylor, James Stewart, Donald O'Connor, and others. Written, produced, and directed by Jack Haley, Jr.

It used to be said that the trickiest thing about a musical was to figure out a way for the characters to break gracefully into song. Maybe that was all wrong. Maybe the hardest thing was for them to stop, once the singing had started. That's my notion after seeing *That's Entertainment!,* a magical tour through the greatest musicals produced by the king of Hollywood studios, Metro-Goldwyn-Mayer.

This isn't just a compilation film, with lots of highlights strung together. Those kinds of movies quickly repeat themselves. *That's Entertainment!* is more of a documentary and a eulogy. A documentary of a time that began in 1929 and seemed to end only yesterday, and a eulogy for an art form that will never be again.

Hollywood will continue to make musicals, of course (although, curiously enough, the form never has been very popular overseas). But there will never be musicals like this again, because there won't be the budgets, there won't be the sense of joyous abandon, there won't be so many stars in the same place all at once, and—most of all—there won't be the notion that a musical has to be "important."

The various segments of the film are introduced and narrated by MGM stars of the past (Fred Astaire, Gene Kelly), superstars like Frank Sinatra and Elizabeth Taylor, offspring like Liza Minnelli, and even a ringer like Bing Crosby (he was a Paramount star, but never mind). They seem to share a real feeling of nostalgia for MGM, which, in its heyday, was not only a studio, but also a benevolent and protective organization ruled by the paternal Louis B. Mayer. Liza Minnelli sounds at times as if she's narrating a visit to her mother's old high school. The movie avoids the trap of being too worshipful in the face of all this greatness. It's not afraid to kid; we see Clark Gable looking ill at ease as he pretends to enjoy singing and dancing, and we see a hilarious montage of Judy Garland and Mickey Rooney ringing endless changes to the theme, "I know—we'll fix up the old barn and put on a show!"

And then there are the glorious, unforgettable moments from the great musicals. My favorite musical has always been *Singin' in the Rain*, the 1952 comedy about Hollywood's traumatic switch to talkies. *That's Entertainment!* opens with a montage of musicals (neatly surveying three decades of film progress), and later returns to the two most unforgettable numbers in the film: Gene Kelly sloshing through puddles while singing the title song, and Donald O'Connor in his amazing "Make 'em Laugh," in which he leaps up walls, takes pratfalls, and dives through a set.

There are other great moments: The closing ballet from *An American in Paris;* Nelson Eddy and Jeanette MacDonald being hilariously serious in *Rose Marie;* Astaire and Ginger Rogers, so light-footed they seem to float; Gene Kelly's incredible acrobatics as he does his own stunts, swinging from rooftop to rooftop; William Warfield singing "Old Man River" in *Showboat;* Judy Garland singing "You Made Me Love You" to a montage of stills of Clark Gable; Garland, again, with "Get Happy" (and a vignette of little Liza's first movie appearance, aged about three); the acrobatic woodchopper's scene

from *Seven Brides for Seven Brothers;* and even Esther Williams rising from the deep.

The movie's fun from beginning to end. It's not camp, and it's not nostalgia: It's a celebration of a time and place in American movie history when everything came together to make a new art form.

That's Entertainment! III ★ ★ ★ ½ [NEW]
G, 113 m., 1994

Hosted by June Allyson, Cyd Charisse, Lena Horne, Howard Keel, Gene Kelly, Ann Miller, Debbie Reynolds, Mickey Rooney, and Esther Williams. Directed and produced by Bud Friedgen and Michael J. Sheridan. Screenplay by Friedgen and Sheridan.

The first two *That's Entertainment!* movies pretty well plundered the MGM vaults of classic moments from the Golden Age of Hollywood Musicals—an age that ran from the 1930s until the 1950s and was more or less synonymous with MGM's own ascendancy as the lion king of Hollywood studios. Settling down for a screening of *That's Entertainment! III,* I expected to watch the archivists scraping the bottom of the barrel. Instead, they've discarded the barrel altogether, so to speak; most of the scenes in this film never found their way into movie theaters, and have languished for years, unseen, in the studio's vaults.

The result is a genuinely fascinating film, one that may tell more about MGM musicals, and aspects of American society, than a film devoted to still more highlights from musical numbers that *did* make their way into films. The reasons why these sequences in *III* were cut from films are many, having to do with commerce, taste, race, sex, and running time. They are interesting today because, in many cases, they are brilliant; in other cases, because they are awful; in some cases, because they are revealing; and in all cases because if it were not for this film we would never have seen them. This is like permission to rummage all by ourselves in MGM's cellar.

The clips are introduced and sometimes commented on by stars who still survive from those legendary days, none more ageless and poignant than Lena Horne, who shows a scene from *Cabin in the Sky* (1943) in which she sang in a bubble bath. The scene was cut, she says quietly, because in those days it was thought too "risqué" to show a black woman in a bubble bath.

We also hear her wonderful performance

of "Can't Help Lovin' Dat Man" from *Till the Clouds Roll By* (1946), and then see a scene from *Show Boat* (1951), in which the song is performed by Ava Gardner. Horne was originally considered for the character played by Gardner, but rejected because of her race. The difference between the two song versions is a hint of what MGM lost with that decision.

On other occasions, the studio played fast and loose with musical numbers, snipping them out and recycling them later. A split-screen technique is used to show Cyd Charisse and Joan Crawford, both performing "Two-Faced Woman." Charisse's version was cut from *The Band Wagon* (1953). It's slinky and sexy. The same year, the song was reused in Crawford's *Torch Song,* where she performs it in an odd costume and "tropical" makeup. This version—the one that was used—is grotesque. (The crowning detail is that neither actress actually sang the song; it was dubbed for both movies by a singer named India Adams.)

By using earlier versions of scenes that later made it into films, the movie allows us to compare performances. Usually that means noticing the differences. With Fred Astaire, it means noting the incredible similarities. Astaire filmed the song-and-dance number "I Wanna Be a Dancin' Man" for *The Belle of New York* (1952), wearing sport clothes. The studio decided he would look better in formal clothes, and reshot the scene. Watching the two numbers side by side, we realize that Astaire was so perfectly rehearsed and so disciplined that he was able to reproduce the earlier dance routine down to the smallest detail—while seeming effortlessly improvisational, of course.

Other stuff you will see here and nowhere else: scenes shot by Judy Garland for *Annie Get Your Gun* before she was fired for personal problems and replaced by Betty Hutton. Garland singing "Mr. Monotony," later cut from *Easter Parade.* The "March of the Doagies" production number from *The Harvey Girls* (1946). A Debbie Reynolds solo of "You Are My Lucky Star," cut from *Singin' in the Rain.* A fabulous dance duet between Astaire and Charisse, cut from *Brigadoon.* And, from an MGM experiment with "novelty acts," a musical scene involving a trio of female acrobats who did double-jointed contortions while singing. (We don't need an explanation to figure out why that one was cut.)

One of the most sparkling presences in the

film is Esther Williams, the swimming champion who starred in a series of incredibly successful musicals shot on, and under, the water. She narrates documentary footage to show how she and her costars were apparently able to do choreographed swimming for entire musical numbers without ever taking a breath.

It's another cohost, Mickey Rooney, who most successfully evokes the atmosphere at MGM's Culver City lot in those days. MGM, it was said had "more stars than are in the heavens," and a talent-laden roster of producers and directors to keep them busy. What is most remarkable, watching this time, is to reflect that the studio was so rich in talent and imagination, even its outtakes are worth seeing, half a century later.

Thelma & Louise ★ ★ ★ ½
R, 128 m., 1991

Susan Sarandon (Louise), Geena Davis (Thelma), Harvey Keitel (Hal), Michael Madsen (Jimmy), Christopher McDonald (Darryl), Stephen Tobolowsky (Max), Brad Pitt (J.D.). Directed by Ridley Scott and produced by Scott and Mimi Polk. Screenplay by Callie Khouri.

Thelma & Louise is in the expansive, visionary tradition of the American road picture. It celebrates the myth of two carefree souls piling into a 1956 T-Bird and driving out of town to have some fun and raise some hell. We know the road better than that, however, and we know the toll it exacts: Before their journey is done, these characters will have undergone a rite of passage, and will have discovered themselves.

What sets *Thelma & Louise* aside from the great central tradition of the road picture—a tradition roomy enough to accommodate *Easy Rider, Bonnie and Clyde, Badlands, Midnight Run,* and *Rainman*—is that the heroes are women this time: working-class girlfriends from a small Arkansas town, one a waitress, the other a housewife, both probably ready to describe themselves as utterly ordinary, both containing unexpected resources.

We meet them on days that help to explain why they'd like to get away for the weekend. Thelma (Geena Davis) is married to a man puffed up with self-importance as the district sales manager of a rug company. He sees his wife as a lower order of life, to be tolerated so long as she keeps her household duties straight and is patient with his tantrums. Louise (Susan Sarandon) waits tables

in a coffee shop and is involved with a musician who is never ever going to be ready to settle down, no matter how much she kids herself.

So the girls hit the road for a weekend (Thelma is so frightened of her husband she leaves him a note rather than tell him). They're almost looking to get into trouble, in a way; they wind up in a saloon not too many miles down the road, and Thelma, a wild woman after a couple of margaritas, begins to get caught up in lust after a couple of dances with an urban cowboy.

That leads, as such flirtations sometimes tragically do, to an attempted rape in the parking lot. And after Louise comes to her friend's rescue, there is a sudden, violent event that ends with the man's death. And the two women hit the road for real. They are convinced that no one would ever believe their story—that the only answer for them is to run, and to hide.

Now comes what in a more ordinary picture would be the predictable stuff: the car running down lonely country roads in front of a blood-red sunset, that kind of thing, with a lot of country music on the sound track. *Thelma & Louise* does indeed contain its share of rural visual extravaganza and lost railroad blues, but it has a heart, too. Sarandon and Davis find in Callie Khouri's script the materials for two plausible, convincing, lovable characters. And as actors they work together like a high-wire team, walking across even the most hazardous scenes without putting a foot wrong.

They have adventures along the way, some sweet, some tragic, including a meeting with a shifty but sexy young man named J.D. (Brad Pitt), who is able, like the dead saloon cowboy, to exploit Thelma's sexual hungers, left untouched by the rug salesman. They also meet old men with deep lines on their faces, and harbingers of doom, and state troopers, and all the other inhabitants of the road.

Of course, they become the targets of a manhunt. Of course, every cop in a six-state area would like to bag them. But back home in Arkansas there's one cop (Harvey Keitel) who has empathy for them, who sees how they dug themselves into this hole and are now about to get buried in it. He tries to reason with them. To "keep the situation from snowballing." But it takes on a peculiar momentum of its own, especially as Thelma and Louise begin to grow intoxicated with the scent of their own freedom—and with

the discovery that they possess undreamed-of resources and capabilities.

Thelma & Louise was directed by Ridley Scott, from Britain, whose previous credits *(Blade Runner, Black Rain, Legend)* show complete technical mastery, but are sometimes not very interested in psychological questions. This film shows a great sympathy for human comedy, however, and it's intriguing the way he helps us to understand what's going on inside the hearts of these two women—why they need to do what they do.

I would have rated the movie at four stars, instead of three and a half, except for one shot: the last shot before the titles begin. This is the catharsis shot, the payoff, the moment when Thelma and Louise arrive at the truth that their whole journey has been pointed toward, and Scott and his editor, Thom Noble, botch it. It's a freeze frame that fades to white, which is fine, except it does so with unseemly haste, followed immediately by a vulgar carnival of distractions: flashbacks to the jolly faces of the two women, the roll of the end credits, an upbeat country song.

It's unsettling to get involved in a movie that takes 128 minutes to bring you to a payoff that the filmmakers seem to fear. If Scott and Noble had let the last shot run an additional seven to ten seconds, and then held the fade to white for a decent interval, they would have gotten the payoff they deserved. Can one shot make that big of a difference? This one does.

Thelonious Monk: Straight, No Chaser
★ ★ ★ ½
PG-13, 88 m., 1989

Thelonious Monk Quartet: Charlie Rouse, tenor saxophone; Larry Gales, bass; Ben Riley, drums. Thelonious Monk Octet: Charlie Rouse, tenor saxophone; Phil Woods, alto saxophone; Johnny Griffin, tenor saxophone; Ray Copeland, trumpet; Jimmy Cleveland, trombone; Larry Gales, bass; Ben Riley, drums. Duo piano performance by Tommy Flanagan and Barry Harris. Narration by Samuel E. Wright. Directed by Charlotte Zwerin and produced by Zwerin and Bruce Ricker.

Right before I sat down to write this review, I put on the 1956 album *Brilliant Corners* by Thelonious Monk. If you are not very familiar with Monk, you may not recognize the title. But if you have ever found yourself in a bar with a good jukebox, you will recognize the music. The title song is a happy one, but it is not mood that carries the stamp of Monk; it is authority. He played the piano as if he knew exactly what every note should mean and be and had known it for a long time.

That is why *Thelonious Monk: Straight, No Chaser* is vaguely disturbing right from the opening scenes. We can sense there is something wrong here, and unless we know the life history of Monk, we don't know what it is. The music is great, free-spirited, and liberating, but in the person of Monk there is a shadow of some kind, a vagueness, a disinclination to connect. The movie never does put a name to Monk's condition, but by the end of the film enough people who loved him have made enough references to it that we know what we need to know: He went gradually and rather stoically mad.

The last years of his life, we learn, were spent sitting quietly in the room of a friend. He did not play jazz anymore, but when friends would come over to play, they knew he could still listen because he would leave the door of his room open. The mental illness, whatever it was, must have begun many years earlier. There is a shot in this movie of Monk in an airport somewhere, turning around and around in the same place, engrossed in this repetition as if it were some kind of meditation. And throughout the movie, when Monk talks, it seems to be in a kind of code, and when he looks at the camera, he doesn't quite look at the camera.

This is a new movie, but the footage of Monk in it is more than twenty years old, shot for German television by Christian Blackwood in 1967 and 1968. Two decades passed before the by-now-forgotten footage was mentioned by Blackwood to Bruce Ricker, whose *Last of the Blue Devils* (1980) was a landmark documentary about Kansas City jazz. Using the Blackwood footage of Monk as their foundation, Ricker and documentarian Charlotte Zwerin began tracking down the survivors who knew Monk best: his son; his tenor sax player, Charles Rouse; his manager; his road manager; and Baroness Nica de Koenigswarter, who appeared in Monk's life at about the time his wife was near exhaustion with the effort of dealing with him, and seems to have shared both the effort and the man with her.

They all seem to remember more or less the same man; there are not a lot of different versions of Monk in this movie. He was, they agree, a musical genius, and of course history has proven them right. He could see the clear line through to the end of a composition that baffled other people, and his squiggles on a piece of paper, interpreted by Monk as if anybody should have been able to understand them, often turned out to be immortal works of jazz. He gathered other geniuses around him—John Coltrane was a member of his Blue Note band in the late 1950s—and he traveled, recorded, played, composed, jammed, inspired, and produced music that changed forever the way modern jazz sounds.

At the same time, he drifted into himself. His reveries must have become seductively comfortable to him. At some point he withdrew and wasn't there anymore for his friends. He was locked inside. The movie doesn't go into detail about this gradual process, and for that, in a way, I am grateful, because his music puts us in our own mood for reverie, not diagnosis. I had heard the music before. What the film gave me was an opportunity to see Thelonious Monk creating some of it and, just as important, an opportunity to see how those who knew him loved him.

Therese ★ ★ ★ ½
NO MPAA RATING, 90 m., 1987

Catherine Mouchet (Therese), Aurore Prieto (Celine), Silvie Habault (Pauline), Ghislane Mona (Marie), Helene Alexandridis (Lucie), Jean Pelegri (Father), Armand Meppiel (The Pope). Directed by Alain Cavalier and produced by Maurice Bernart. Screenplay by Cavalier and Camille De Casabianca.

Therese is such a strong, pure, apparently simple movie that there's a temptation to let it carry us along. We don't want to ask questions. And yet at the end of this movie there are so many unanswered questions that we realize the movie is one long question: What was the secret of Therese Martin's joy?

She was known as the "Little Flower of Jesus." As a girl, she wanted to enter the strict cloisters of the Carmelite nuns, and when she was refused permission she went all the way to the Pope to finally obtain it. Inside the walls, she struck everyone with the openness and sweetness of her disposition, and after she died in 1897 she became famous through the publication of her journal. She was canonized in 1925.

The movie centers itself around the depth of her passionate love affair with Jesus. The nuns are figuratively wed to Christ in the ceremony which admits them to the order, and in Therese's case she seems to have taken the wedding not only seriously but literally. In a way, *Therese* is the story of a girl who dies on her honeymoon.

The story is told with stark visual simplicity by Alain Cavalier, who shoots against plain backdrops and includes only those costumes or props that are needed to make sense of a scene. His real visual subject is the human face. And after Therese is admitted to the closed convent, where a vow of silence is usually enforced, the faces themselves seem to speak.

We become familiar with the other nuns. With an old, old woman of great saintliness. With a wise mother superior. With a young nun who has a crush on Therese. And with Therese herself, who is played by Catherine Mouchet with a kind of transparent, low-key ecstasy. There is a real sense of the community of the convent. In one of the movie's best scenes, a man comes from outside to bring gifts of food to the nuns, who cover their faces and flutter around him like blinded birds.

Therese is not like any other biographical film of a saint—or of anyone else. It makes a bold attempt to penetrate to the mystery of Therese's sainthood, and yet it isn't propaganda for the church and it doesn't necessarily even approve of her choice of a vocation. Perhaps the local bishop was right, in saying Therese was too young for the strenuous life of the convent. Perhaps her devotion to Jesus was indeed, as Andrew Sarris wrote in his review of the film, "displaced sexuality and transsubstantiated fetishism."

This movie is so deep and so subtle that we cannot ever be sure just what the filmmaker thinks about Therese. That's one of the reasons I found it so disturbing and provoking. What Cavalier gives us is a portrait of the externals of sainthood, and just those internals that can be glimpsed and guessed through the eyes of a gifted actress. He makes no statement about his material. After we've seen the movie, we ask ourselves what it was that motivated Therese, and whether perhaps it was good even though it violates modern notions, and we also ask ourselves why she was so happy. We would not be happy living her life. But then we are not saints.

They Shoot Horses, Don't They?
★ ★ ★ ★
PG, 123 m., 1970

Jane Fonda (Gloria), Michael Sarrazin (Robert), Susannah York (Alice), Gig Young

(Rocky), Red Buttons (Sailor), Bonnie Bedelia (Ruby), Severn Darden (Cecil). Directed by Sydney Pollack and produced by Irwin Winkler and Robert Chartoff. Screenplay by James Poe and Robert E. Thompson.

Erase the forced smiles from the desperate faces, and what the dance marathons of the 1930s came down to was fairly simple. A roomful of human beings went around and around within four walls for weeks at a time without sleep, populating a circus for others who paid to see them. At the end, those who didn't collapse or drop dead won cash prizes that were good money during the Depression. And the Depression, in an oblique sort of way, was the reason for it all. The marathons offered money to the winners and distraction to everyone else. To be sure, some of the marathons got pretty grim. Contestants tried to dance their way through illnesses and pregnancies, through lice and hallucinations, and the sight of them doing it was part of the show. Beyond the hit tunes and the crepe paper and the free pig as a door prize, there was an elementary sadism in the appeal of the marathons.

Among American spectator sports, they rank with stock-car racing. There was always that delicious possibility, you see, that somebody would die. Or freak out. Or stand helplessly while his partner collapsed and he lost the investment of thousands of hours of his life.

They Shoot Horses, Don't They? is a masterful re-creation of the marathon era for audiences that are mostly unfamiliar with it. In addition to everything else it does, *Horses* holds our attention because it tells us something we didn't know about human nature and American society. It tells us a lot more than that, of course, but because it works on this fundamental level as well it is one of the best American movies of the 1970s. It is so good as a movie, indeed, that it doesn't have to bother with explaining the things in my first two paragraphs; they are all there (and that's where I found them), but they are completely incorporated into the structure of the film.

Director Sydney Pollack has built a ballroom and filled it with characters. They come from nowhere, really; Michael Sarrazin is photographed as if he has walked into the ballroom directly from the sea. The characters seem to have no histories, no alternate lives; they exist only within the walls of the ballroom and during the ticking of the

official clock. Pollack has simplified the universe. He has got everything in life boiled down to this silly contest; and what he tells us has more to do with lives than contests.

Sarrazin meets Jane Fonda, and they became partners almost absentmindedly; he wasn't even planning on entering a marathon. There are other contestants, particularly Red Buttons and Bonnie Bedelia in splendid supporting performances, and they are whipped around the floor by the false enthusiasm of Gig Young, the master of ceremonies. "Yowzza! Yowzza!" he chants, and all the while he regards the contestants with the peculiarly disinterested curiosity of an exhausted god.

There are not a lot of laughs in *Horses*, because Pollack has directed from the point of view of the contestants. They are bitter beyond any hope of release. The movie's delicately timed pacing and Pollack's visual style work almost stealthily to involve us; we begin to feel the physical weariness and spiritual desperation of the characters.

The movie begins on a note of alienation and spirals down from there. *Horses* provides us no cheap release at the end; and the ending, precisely because it is so obvious, is all the more effective. We knew it was coming. Even the title gave it away. And when it comes, it is effective not because it is a surprise but because it is inevitable. As inevitable as death.

The performances are perfectly matched to Pollack's grim vision. Jane Fonda is hard, unbreakable, filled with hate and fear. Sarrazin can do nothing, really, but stand there and pity her; no one, not even during the Depression, should have to feel so without hope. Red Buttons, as the sailor who's a veteran of other marathons and cheerfully teaches everybody the ropes, reminds us that the great character actor from *Sayonara* still exists, and that comedians are somehow the best in certain tragic roles.

And that's what the movie comes down to, maybe. The characters are comedians trapped in tragic roles. They signed up for the three square meals a day and the crack at the $1,500 prize, and they can stop (after all) whenever they want to. But somehow they can't stop, and as the hundreds and thousands of hours of weariness and futility begin to accumulate, the great dance marathon begins to look more and more like life.

Thief ★ ★ ★ ½
R, 126 m., 1981

James Caan (Frank), Tuesday Weld (Jessie), Willie Nelson (Okla), James Belushi (Barry), Robert Prosky (Leo), Tom Signorelli (Attaglia), John Santucci (Urizzi), Tom Erhart (Judge). Directed by Michael Mann and produced by Jerry Bruckheimer and Ronnie Caan. Screenplay by Mann.

Michael Mann's *Thief* is a film of style, substance, and violently felt emotion, all wrapped up in one of the most intelligent thrillers I've seen. It's one of those films where you feel the authority right away: This movie knows its characters, knows its story, and knows exactly how it wants to tell us about them. At a time when thrillers have been devalued by the routine repetition of the same dumb chases, sex scenes, and gunfights, *Thief* is completely out of the ordinary.

The movie stars James Caan as a man who says he was "raised by the state" and spent eleven years in prison. As the movie opens, he's been free four years, and lives in Chicago. He is a highly skilled professional thief—a trade he learned behind bars from Okla (Willie Nelson), a master thief. The film's opening sequence establishes Caan's expertise as he cracks a safe with a portable drill. Caan sees himself as a completely independent loner. But we see him differently, as a lonely, unloved kid who is hiding out inside an adult body. He's a loner who desperately needs to belong to somebody. He trusts his partner (James Belushi), but that's not enough. He decides, on an almost abstract intellectual level, to fall in love with a cashier (Tuesday Weld), and in one of the movie's best scenes he tells this woman, who is essentially a stranger, all about his life in prison and his plans for the future. She takes his hand and accepts him.

But there is another person who comes into his life: Leo, the master criminal, the fence who sets up heists and hires people to pull them. Leo, in a wonderfully complex performance by the sad-faced Robert Prosky, knows how to enlist Caan: "Let me be your father," he says. "I'll take care of everything." He does. He even supplies Caan and Weld with an illegally obtained baby boy when they're turned down at the adoption agency. But once the thief goes with Leo, his life gets complicated. The cops seem to be on his case. His phone is bugged. Everybody knows his business. The movie leads up to one final caper, a $4 million diamond heist in Los Angeles, and then it ends in a series of double crosses and a rain of violence.

This movie works so well for several reasons. One is that *Thief* is able to convince us that it knows its subject, knows about the methods and criminal personalities of its characters. Another is that it's well cast: Every important performance in this movie successfully creates a plausible person, instead of the stock-company supporting characters we might have expected. And the film moves at a taut pace, creating tension and anxiety through very effective photography and a wound-up, pulsing score by Tangerine Dream.

If *Thief* has a weak point, it is probably in the handling of the Willie Nelson character. Nelson is set up well: He became Caan's father-figure in prison, Caan loves him more than anybody, and when he goes to visit him in prison they have a conversation that is subtly written to lead by an indirect route to Nelson's understated revelation that he is dying and does not want to die behind bars. This scene is so strong that it sets us up for big things: We expect Willie to get out, get involved in the plot, and be instrumental in the climax. That doesn't happen. There is a very nice courtroom scene, during which you'll have to pay close attention to catch on to the subverbal and illegal conversation conducted between the judge and the lawyer. But then the Nelson character quickly disappears from the movie, and we're surprised and a little disappointed. Willie has played the character so well that we wanted more. But, then, I suppose it is a good thing when a movie creates characters we feel that strongly about, and *Thief* is populated with them. It's a thriller with plausible people in it. How rare.

Thieves Like Us ★ ★ ★ ½
R, 123 m., 1974

Keith Carradine (Bowie), Shelley Duvall (Keechie), John Schuck (Chicamaw), Bert Remsen (T-Dub), Louise Fletcher (Mattie), Ann Latham (Luie). Directed by Robert Altman and produced by Jerry Bick. Screenplay by Calder Willingham, Joan Tewkesbury, and Altman.

Like so much of his work, Robert Altman's *Thieves Like Us* has to be approached with a certain amount of imagination. Some movies are content to offer us escapist experiences and hope we'll be satisfied. But you can't sink back and simply absorb an Altman film;

he's as concerned with style as subject, and his preoccupation isn't with story or character, but with how he's showing us his tale. That's the case with *Thieves Like Us*, which no doubt has all sorts of weaknesses in character and plot, but which manages a visual strategy so perfectly controlled that we get an uncanny feel for this time and this place. The movie is about a gang of fairly dumb bank robbers, and about how the youngest of them falls in love with a girl, and about how they stick up some banks and listen to the radio and drink Coke and eventually get shot at.

The outline suggests *Bonnie and Clyde*, but *Thieves Like Us* resembles it only in the most general terms of period and setting. The characters are totally different; Bonnie and Clyde were anti-heroes, but this gang of Altman's has no heroism at all. Just a kind of plodding simplicity, punctuated by some of them with violence, and by the boy with a kind of wondering love. They play out their sad little destinies against two backdrops: One is the pastoral feeling of the Southern countryside, and the other is an exactly observed series of interior scenes that recapture just what it was like to drowse through a slow, hot summer Sunday afternoon, with the radio in the background and the kids playing at pretending to do Daddy's job. If Daddy is a bank robber, so what?

The radio is constantly on in the background of *Thieves Like Us*, but it's not used as a source of music as it was in *American Graffiti* or *Mean Streets*. The old shows we hear are not supposed to be heard by Altman's characters; they're like theme music, to be repeated in the film when the same situations occur. "Gangbusters" plays when they rob a bank, for example, even though the bank would have been closed before "Gangbusters" came on. That's OK, because the radio isn't supposed to be realistic; it's Altman's wry, elegiac comment on the distance between radio fantasy and this dusty, slow-witted reality.

At the heart of the movie is a lovely relationship between the young couple, played by Keith Carradine and Shelley Duvall. They've both been in Altman movies before (just about everybody in view here is in his stock company), and it's easy to see why he likes them so. They don't look like movie stars. They share a kind of rangy grace, an ability to project shyness and uncertainty. There's a scene in bed that captures this; it's a two-shot with Keith in the foreground and Shel-

ley, on her back, eyes to the ceiling, slowly exhaling little plumes of smoke. Nothing is said. The radio plays. Somehow we know just how this quiet, warm moment feels.

The movie's fault is that Altman, having found the perfect means for realizing his story visually, did not spend enough thought, perhaps, on the story itself. *Thieves Like Us* is not another *Bonnie and Clyde*, and yet it does end in a similar way, with a shoot-out. And by this time, we've seen too many movies that have borrowed that structure; that have counted on the bloody conclusion to lend significance to what went before. In *Thieves Like Us*, there just wasn't that much significance, and I don't think there's meant to be. These are small people in a weary time, robbing banks because that's their occupation, getting shot because that's the law's occupation.

Altman's comment on the people and time is carried out through the way he observes them; if you try to understand his intention by analyzing the story, you won't get far. Audiences have always been so plot-oriented that it's possible they'll just go ahead and think this is a bad movie, without pausing to reflect on its scene after scene of poignant observation. Altman may not tell a story better than any one, but he sees one with great clarity and tenderness.

The Thin Blue Line ★ ★ ★ ½
NO MPAA RATING, 101 m., 1988

A film directed by Errol Morris and produced by Mark Lipson.

One dark night in 1976, a Dallas police officer named Robert Wood was shot dead by someone inside a car he had stopped for a minor traffic violation. The man who was convicted of that murder, a young drifter named Randall Adams, was, when this film was released in the summer of 1988, in the eleventh year of a life sentence. The chief witness against him, David Harris, had been sentenced to death for another murder. In the tense last moments of *The Thin Blue Line*, David Harris confesses to the murder of Officer Wood. Those moments were the result of a thirty-month investigation by Errol Morris, one of America's strangest and most brilliant documentary filmmakers, who sometimes jokes that he is not a "producer-director" but a "detective-director." Morris originally went to Texas to do a documentary on Dr. James Grigson, a Dallas psychiatrist nicknamed "Doctor Death" because in countless capital murder cases over fifteen years, he has invariably predicted that the defendants deserved the death penalty because they were sociopaths who would certainly kill again. While researching Grigson, Morris interviewed Randall Adams, a young man who had no criminal record until the Wood case.

"Adams told me he was innocent," Morris told me at the Toronto Film Festival, "but everybody in prison tells you they are innocent. It was only after I met David Harris that I began to suspect that the wrong man had been convicted of murder."

Although *The Thin Blue Line* assembles an almost unassailable case for Adams and against Harris, it is not a conventional documentary—not a feature-length version of one of those "60 Minutes" segments in which innocent men are rescued from Death Row. Although he makes documentaries, Errol Morris is much more interested in the spaces between the facts than with the facts themselves. He is fascinated by strange people, by odd word choices and manners of speech, by the way that certain symbols or beliefs can become fetishes with the power to rule human lives.

Morris's first film was *Gates of Heaven* (1978), which I believe is one of the greatest films ever made. Ostensibly a documentary about two pet cemeteries in Northern California and the people who owned them, it is in fact one of the most profound, and funniest, films ever made about such subjects as life and death, success and failure, dreams and disappointments, and the role that pet animals play in our loneliness. Although *Gates of Heaven* has never failed to fascinate and amaze the approximately fifty audiences I have seen it with, it has never reached large numbers of people because of its subject matter; people quite simply think they don't want to see a movie about pet cemeteries, and only enthusiastic word-of-mouth has kept the movie alive (it is only recently available on home video).

Morris's next film, about the strange and wonderful people he found in and around a small southern town, was called *Vernon, Florida*. It played on PBS in 1981. In the years which followed, although he has worked on several projects, there was no new Morris film until *The Thin Blue Line*. For a time in the early 1980s, he supported himself as a private detective. Then the case of Randall Adams began to obsess him, and the result is a film that takes its viewers back to the

events on the night when Robert Wood was shot dead.

Morris has assembled many of the key witnesses in the case, including Randall Adams, who seems passive and defeated about the fate that deposited him in a life sentence for murder, and David Harris, who talks wonderingly about the fact that a person's whole life can be changed because he happens to be in the wrong place at the wrong time.

"Is Randall Adams an innocent man?" Morris asks Harris.

"I'm sure he is."

"How can you be sure?"

"Because I'm the one that knows."

Morris's visual style in *The Thin Blue Line* is unlike any conventional documentary approach. Although his interviews are shot straight on, head and shoulders, there is a way his camera has of framing his subjects so that we look at them very carefully, learning as much by what we see as by what we hear.

In addition to the interviews, Morris uses staged reconstructions of the murder of Officer Wood—the car without headlights, the pursuit by the police vehicle, the approach of Wood, the behavior of his fellow officer, even the lazy, slow-motion whirl of a drive-in milkshake that flies through the air and falls to earth soon after Robert Wood's bullet-ridden body.

Morris also uses other kinds of images. There are scenes from *Swinging Cheerleaders,* the film that Adams and Harris saw together in a drive-in before the murder. (Harris said they saw the last show; Morris has discovered there was no late show on the night in question.) There are also close-ups of physical evidence, of places, of clocks visualizing the impossible chronology of some of the testimony. We see family photographs that reconstruct moments in David Harris's troubled childhood. We see guns, empty streets, newspaper headlines, all-night food stores.

The use of this footage is repetitive and rhythmic, and underlined by the cold, frightening, original music score by Philip Glass. The result is a movie that is documentary and drama, investigation and reverie, a meditation on the fact that Randall Adams was plucked from the center of his life and locked up forever for a crime that no reasonable person could seriously believe he committed.

Footnote 1989: As a result of this film, the case against Adams was reopened, his conviction set aside, and he was released from prison.

Things Change ★ ★ ★
PG, 105 m., 1988

Don Ameche (Gino), Joe Mantegna (Jerry), Robert Prosky (Joseph Vincent), J.J. Johnston (Frankie), Ricky Jay (Mr. Silver), Mike Nussbaum (Mr. Green), Jack Wallace (Repair Shop Owner), Dan Conway (Butler). Directed by David Mamet and produced by Michael Hausman. Screenplay by Mamet and Shel Silverstein.

Things Change is a neat little exercise in wit and deception in which an old Italian-American shoeshine man convinces the Mafia boss of Lake Tahoe that he is the man *behind* the man behind the man. His secret is to have no secret. He answers every question truthfully. He does most of his talking about how to get a perfect shoeshine. By the end of the film, we have witnessed a con so perfect that the people pulling it didn't even want to pull a con.

The movie was directed by David Mamet, who wrote it with Shel Silverstein. Coming after the diabolical trickery of *House of Games* (1987), it confirms Mamet's gift for leading us through truly bewildering plots. What makes his movies so entertaining is that the characters are bewildered, not the audience, which is usually the case with sloppier screenwriters. He makes us co-conspirators.

His story is based on a series of accidents, coincidences, and misunderstandings. It begins when Gino, the old Chicago shoeshine man (Don Ameche), is escorted from his shop and taken into the presence of a local crime chief (Mike Nussbaum) and asked to confess to a murder. If Gino agrees, he will be back on the street in three years and the mob will give him his dream—a fishing boat of his own in Sicily.

First he refuses. Then he changes his mind. The dialogue in this scene is pure Mamet, the repetition of ordinary phrases that take on sinister meanings. Describing the murder of a man in the street, a mobster punctuates each paragraph with the line, "This is public knowledge," before finally coming to his point: "What I am now about to tell you is not public knowledge." When I write it down, it doesn't sound funny. When you hear it, you laugh. It is Mamet's gift to know how words work aloud.

Gino is assigned to Jerry, a younger Mafioso (Joe Mantegna), whose job is to guard him over the weekend until he can confess on Monday. The two men retire to a hotel room, where Jerry grows restless, says the hell with it, and decides to take the old guy to Tahoe for the weekend. In Nevada, Jerry is spotted by a chauffeur as a guy from the Chicago mob, and Gino is immediately assumed to be very important. No one has ever seen him before—but that's just proof of how important he is. Of course, they get the suite with the sunken tub, free of charge, plus unlimited credit in the casino.

Mamet and Silverstein now unspin a labyrinthine plot in which half-truths and assumptions follow one after another until Gino is in the presence of the local Mafia boss (Robert Prosky). The don has invited Gino and Jerry to his mountain estate for two reasons: to embrace them if they are the real thing, and to kill them if they are not. In a scene involving exquisite timing and painfully drawn-out silences, the boss tries to get answers without seeming to ask questions, and Gino tries to answer without saying anything. There is not a word or a glance or a moment of body language that feels wrong in this scene—and the scene is the crux of the movie.

More complications follow, which I will leave for you to discover. The chief delight in the movie is the joining of comedy and menace: The Mantegna character is keenly aware that one wrong step will result in instant death, but the Ameche character is able to save them both by simply being himself. There is a moment when Ameche and Prosky sit against a wall in the sun, two old men with their shoes off, and we sense that the local guy would almost rather not know that his visitor is not a Mafia don, because he plays the part so well.

I've been looking at a lot of *films noir* lately—those stylish black-and-white crime movies from the 1940s in which evil was found to lurk just below the surfaces of ordinary American lives. *Things Change* is a film in which the surface is evil and goodness lurks beneath. The strangest thing about the film is the way the bond between the Ameche and Prosky characters seems to redeem the Nevada boss, to convince him if only for an afternoon that the real reason he got into crime was to demonstrate his loyalty to his friends.

If there is a flaw in the movie, it is Mamet's deliberation. A clever movie should always be quicker than its audience, and here there are moments when we have time to see ahead into the plot. Mamet has a genuine gift for movie direction—his films are not just illustrations of his dialogue, but have an energy

of their own—but timing is the area where he needs to tinker. His dialogue for the stage is written in such a way that an actor reading it is almost forced to time it the way Mamet imagined it. His characters punctuate their sentences by repeating the same words and phrases for emphasis. But in the movies, words exist in a different kind of time than on the stage, and Mamet tends to play around and find what works for his dialogue.

The performances here are all wonderful, especially Ameche's. Working in the midst of a cast that is otherwise entirely drawn from the Mamet stock company, he finds just the right note of bewilderment and cleverness. The character is never other than a confused old Italian shoeshine man, and yet time and again he saves himself by somehow finding the right thing to say. Joe Mantegna, as his keeper, walks a fine line between desperation and comedy—and isn't afraid to go broader in scenes where he pantomimes what Ameche should be saying and doing. And Robert Prosky, his face a mask of jovial cunning, is touching in the way he wants to believe in this stranger who is so apparently phony. *Things Change* is a delicate balance of things that don't easily go together: farce, wit, violence, and heart. Here they do.

35 Up ★ ★ ★ ★
NO MPAA RATING, 127 m., 1992

A documentary film directed and produced by Michael Apted.

35 Up is the latest installment in the most engrossing long-distance documentary project in the history of film. It began twenty-eight years ago, when a group of ordinary British citizens of various backgrounds were interviewed about their views of the world—at the age of seven. Ever since, at seven-year intervals, director Michael Apted has revisited the subjects for an update on their lives and views, and in this new film the children born in the mid-fifties are marching into middle age, for the most part with few regrets.

Before writing this review, I went back to look again at *28 Up* (1985), which had just been released on video. I wanted to freshen my memory of Neil, the loner who has become the most worrisome of Apted's subjects. When we first see him, at the age of seven, he is already clear on how he wants to spend his life: He wants to be a bus driver, choosing the route himself, telling all of his passengers what to look out of the windows. By fourteen, Neil was a visionary with

big hopes for his life, but something happened between then and twenty-one, when we found him angry and discontented. At twenty-eight, in an image that has haunted me, he was an outcast, living in a small house trailer on the shores of a bleak Scottish lake, and there was real doubt in my mind whether he would still be alive at thirty-five.

He is. He still lives alone, still harbors the view that people cannot quite be trusted to choose for themselves, still doubts he will find a wife to put up with him. Now he lives in subsidized housing on a Scottish island, where last year he directed the village pageant. He was not invited to direct it again this year, and he complains morosely that if people would only learn to follow instructions, the pageant might have turned out better.

Most of the other subjects of the film have turned out more happily. There is Tony, who at seven wanted to be a jockey and at fourteen had found employment as a stable boy. In an earlier film we saw him studying "the knowledge," the year-long process by which a London cabbie must learn his city before he is granted a license, and now, at thirty-five, his children growing up nicely, he is happy to own his own taxi. He realized his dreams, he says; he was a jockey, briefly, and once got to race against Lester Piggott.

We revisit the three "working-class girls" of the earlier films, who gather around a pub table to assess their lives, with which they are reasonably content. And we see the progress of an upper-class boy who came across as such a snob at twenty-one that he declined to be interviewed at twenty-eight. He is back at thirty-five, somewhat amazingly involved in a relief project for Eastern Europe, and we sense that he has grown out of his class snobbery (to a degree; he cannot resist pointing out a portrait of a royal ancestor).

In my review of *28 Up*, I quoted Wordsworth: "The child is father of the man." We can see that even more clearly in *35 Up*. The faces gather lines and maturity, the hair sometimes is beginning to turn gray, the slenderness of youth has started to sag. But the eyes are the same. The voices are the same—deeper but still expressing the thoughts of the same person who was already there, somehow formed, at the age of seven. And in almost every case the personality and hopes of the seven-year-old has predicted the reality of the adult life. (There is one exception, a woman who seemed depressed and aimless at twenty-one, but has undergone a remarkable transformation into cheerful adulthood; I would like her to talk frankly, sometime, about what happened to her between twenty-one and later.)

Some of the subjects complain ruefully that the project has violated their privacy. One of the working-class women says that she is well content with her life, except every seven years when Apted comes nosing around. Others have opted out of *35 Up* because they no longer welcome the attention. Most have remained, apparently with the thought that since they have gone this far, they might as well stay the distance.

Somewhere in the midst of the *Up* project lurks the central mystery of life. How do we become who we are? How is our view of ourselves and our world fashioned? Educators and social scientists might look at these films and despair, because the essential ingredients of future life all seem to be in place at seven, formed in the home and even in the womb before school or the greater world has had much impact. Even more touchingly, in the voices and eyes of these people at thirty-five, we see human beings confronting the fact of their own mortality.

Nearly thirty years have passed since the camera first recorded them peering out at the world around them. In another seven years, most of them will be back again. None has yet died. The project will continue as long as any of them cooperate. Eventually the time will come when only two or three are still alive, and then none. And many years in the future, viewers will be able to look at this unique record and contemplate the beauty and mystery of life. I am glad most of the subjects of this project have sacrificed their privacy to us every seven years, because in a sense they speak for us, and help us take our own measure.

36 Fillette ★ ★ ★ ½
NO MPAA RATING, 92 m., 1989

Delphine Zentout (Lili), Etienne Chicot (Maurice), Olivier Parniere (Bertrand), Jean-Pierre Leaud (Boris Golovine), Berta Dominuez D. (Anne-Marie), Jean-Francois Stevenin (The Father), Diane Bellego (Georgia). Directed by Catherine Breillat and produced by Emmanuel Schlumberger and Valerie Seydoux. Screenplay by Breillat.

36 Fillette follows a few crucial days in the life of Lili, a fourteen-year-old French girl whose body is ripe and whose soul is troubled by an unhappy home life. One night during a miserable family vacation at a tacky resort, she talks her older brother into taking her to a disco, and there she begins a series of risky flirtations with older men.

The first man she encounters fancies himself to be a playboy, but he is in fact a middle-aged salesman who is still locked into his adolescent dream of picking up girls in his convertible. After he picks up Lili, he finds he is in for more than he bargained for. She is not a victim but a tough little cookie who tantalizes him all night long, until finally he gives up, protesting that at his age he simply lacks the stamina for an extended chase. When I first saw him I was prepared to scorn him as an irresponsible adult taking advantage of an inexperienced girl, but by this point in the evening I could see the rueful humor in his situation.

Drifting on through the dreary resort where she finds herself, Lili (Delphine Zentout) encounters a man who is said to be a famous French personality of some sort—and indeed, he is played by a famous actor, Jean-Pierre Leaud, who long ago in Truffaut's *The 400 Blows* (1959) portrayed the same kind of angry, alienated adolescent who now confronts him. He listens to her intently, looks at her quizzically, and gives her some weary advice. No doubt his advice is correct, but she is too young to understand it, and must make her own mistakes.

The next day is another day of unhappiness with her parents, who mostly seem to drink, sleep, and fight. She is alienated and isolated, and she decides it is "miserable" to be a virgin, so she sets out to flirt with danger, not quite knowing what she is looking for, or if she really wants it. She dresses boldly and goes out to hitchhike into town, and again crosses paths with the tired, alcoholic playboy (Etienne Chicot). He leads an exhausted night life in gloomy discos, and decides he doesn't want to have anything to do with her because she is underage. But she taunts him with her flamboyant dress and voluptuous body, and then dances away when he begins to respond. Eventually they fall into some kind of tacit friendship, based on a mutual desperation they recognize in each other.

At first we are prepared to blame the man for taking advantage of a vulnerable teenager. But that is not the subject of this particular film, which the director, Catherine Breillat, says is somewhat autobiographical. *36 Fillette* (the title is a French bra size) is a film told from Lili's point of view, and the middle-aged man is almost a prop; at this moment in her life, any man would have done, since she is not sure what she's looking for anyway.

We have caught her at a moment when her unhappiness has coincided with her sudden discovery of her sexuality and the power she can have over men. With a boldness born of anger and naïveté, heedless of danger, she sets out to manipulate this man. Her psychological motivations are hinted at in a scene where her father is uncaring, but this is a film of observation, not analysis.

The key scene in the film is a long, meticulously observed emotional fencing match in the man's hotel room, during which they both sense, perhaps, that despite the gulf between them they share the same loneliness and unhappiness with themselves. This is a great scene, and its whole delicate existence depends on the performance by Delphine Zentout, a sixteen-year-old in her acting debut. She gives a brave and convincing performance.

The movie is controversial because of the difference in age between the two lovers, and because of the girl's blatant, if naive, sexuality. But Breillat has made a film far more complex than it might seem. This film depicts the sort of situation one should deplore, but the film is so specifically about two particular people that it slips away from convention and just quietly goes its own way.

Thirty-Two Short Films About Glenn Gould ★ ★ ★ ★
NO MPAA RATING, 94 m., 1994

Colm Feore (Glenn Gould), Derek Keurvorst (Gould's Father), Katya Lada (Gould's Mother), Devon Anderson (Young Glenn, Age Three), Joshua Greenblatt (Young Glenn, Age Eight), Sean Ryan (Young Glenn, Age Twelve), Kate Hennig (Chambermaid), Sean Doyle (Porter). Directed by François Girard and produced by Niv Fichman. Screenplay by Girard and Don McKellar.

How to suggest an actual human life on film? Most biopics shape the enigmatic events of life into the requirements of fiction, so that most lives seem the same, and only the professions and the time periods change. François Girard's *Thirty-Two Short Films About Glenn Gould* brilliantly breaks with tradition and gives us a movie that actually inspires us to *think* about what it was like to be this man.

Glenn Gould (1932–1982), born in Toronto, could play and read music before he was four years old. Taught only by his mother until he was ten, he was soon giving concerts in Canada and the United States, where Leonard Bernstein was one of his admirers. He became one of the great concert pianists of his time, and then, on April 10, 1964, without advance notice, he gave his last concert and refused to perform in public ever again.

That was not the end of his career but the beginning of an extraordinary second career, in which he channeled all of his efforts into making recordings. His choice of the recording studio over the concert stage was explained in different ways at different times; he didn't like the idea of a performer upstaging the music, he would say, or he could not abide the idea that some people in the audience had better seats than others.

He stayed at home, in Toronto recording studios and hotel rooms, cultivating a benign eccentricity, talking to his friends endlessly on the telephone but sparingly in person. And he left behind a rich recorded legacy, including his performances of Bach's Goldberg Variations (one of Gould's Bach performances has since left the solar system on board *Voyager I*).

Thirty-Two Short Films About Glenn Gould was inspired by the Goldberg Variations, and is a series of brief vignettes suggesting variations on the artist's life. Colm Feore plays the pianist, as a calm, physically economical man whose most highly developed sense, we feel, is his hearing. There is a scene midway in the film where Gould enters a roadside diner where he is apparently a familiar face. As he waits for his eggs to arrive, he listens to the conversations around him, and the sound track pieces these words of strangers together in such an intense way that we listen, too. In another scene, he asks a hotel chambermaid to listen to a recording, and then he judges its effect upon her. Again, in a recording studio, he listens to a piece of music twice, and then says, "I think we might really have something there."

The movie does not deliver, or suggest, a rounded life story. But it leaves us with a much richer idea of his life than a conventional biopic might have. We see the young Gould at his piano (from childhood, he always fancied a stool just fourteen inches off the ground, placing his eyes not far above finger-level). And we see him listening intensely to a radio broadcast of a concert. Our imagination is challenged to feel the music entering him.

There are other episodes, some as mundane as a telephone call to a friend, others as startling as that last concert in 1964, where he soaks his hands in warm water, then walks slowly through backstage corridors, hesitates before walking onstage, and signs a stagehand's program, adding the words, "the last concert."

Some of the "short films" show episodes from a life. Some show ideas inspired by the music. Some are the documentary testimony of friends, including Yehudi Menuhin, who talk with the warm recollection they might use at a memorial service. One brief sequence simply shows Gould sitting in a chair, listening. We gather he became a hermit of sorts, but a contented one, doing what he loved. The movie makes no suggestions at all about his sexual life, does not deal in gossip, and seems almost proud of its outsider's viewpoint. The filmmakers do not claim to know the secrets of Glenn Gould, but only to be fascinated by them.

The notes with the movie recall that when one of the producers, Barbara Willis-Sweete, was working in the late 1970s as a bartender at the hotel where Gould was living, she followed him late one night as he left with a large bag. He eventually dropped it in a garbage can, and she retrieved it, to find it contained only old newspapers. The point of this story, I think, is not what the bag contained, but that the bartender followed him. The film is made in something of the same spirit, as if the filmmakers admire Gould's work, are puzzled by his life, and want to follow him, unobserved. They discover no great answers or revelations, but by the end of the film they, and we, have a remarkable impression of a life lived curiously, but well.

This Boy's Life ★ ★ ★ ½
R, 114 m., 1993

Robert De Niro (Dwight), Ellen Barkin (Caroline), Leonardo DiCaprio (Toby), Jonah Blechman (Arthur Gayle), Eliza Dushku (Pearl), Chris Cooper (Roy). Directed by Michael Caton-Jones and produced by Art Linson. Screenplay by Robert Getchell.

The great idea in the 1950s, if things weren't working out, was to go West. Maybe things would be better there. After her divorce, Caroline packs her son into the old Nash sedan and drives out to Washington State, hoping for a fresh start, and hoping, too, that Toby will calm down and start doing better in school. Their journey's end is the ominously named town of Concrete, where

Caroline meets a man named Dwight who wants to marry her. She can't think of a better idea. Dwight offers security, a paycheck, and a father figure for young Toby. This time, Caroline is determined that the marriage will work.

Toby is not so sure. He sees right away that Dwight is as phony as a three-dollar bill—that beneath the posturing and the bluster is a sworn enemy. Caroline might be able to see that, too, except that she is desperate and Dwight seems like a port in a storm. After the wedding, the mother and her son move in with Dwight, and the trouble starts.

This Boy's Life is based on a memoir by Tobias Wolff, the Toby of the story, who survived Concrete and Dwight and settled his old scores in the pages of his book. It plays like fiction, and yet it has the particular details of a story burned into the memory. Dwight, for example, doesn't tell people to shut up. He tells them, "Shut your pie-hole!" The expression has a peculiar unpleasantness, and yet in a way it is funny. That would also describe Dwight.

He is played in the film by Robert De Niro, in one of his most distinctive performances. De Niro shows Dwight as a man whose low self-esteem borders on self-contempt, and who tries to cover it by finding fault in everyone around him. He is a verbal bully, a sadist, a liar, an emotional con man. Toby hates him.

Caroline, played by Ellen Barkin, perhaps sees her husband clearly enough, but has made a decision early in the marriage: She will not get in between Dwight and Toby. She wants the marriage to survive (although it will never "work" in any positive sense). She is a bystander in the war. Maybe that works out all right for Toby, who is forced as a consequence to grow up more quickly, to develop confidence in himself, to learn to take a stand.

What keeps Toby going is the conviction that there must be better places than Dwight's house, and better things to do than play a victim. Toby has a brother—separated from him and his mother by the messiness of the divorce—who is a student at Yale, and Toby doesn't envy him so much as see him as a possible salvation, a way out of Concrete.

Toby is played by Leonardo DiCaprio, a relative newcomer (he's done TV, and had the lead in *Critters III*). The movie is successful largely because he is a good enough actor to hold his own in his scenes with De Niro, so that the movie remains his story, and he isn't upstaged by the loathsome but colorful Dwight.

Watching *This Boy's Life*, I was reminded of the angers and wounds of my own childhood, which was a happy one but contained, as everyone's does, moments when the world seemed unfair and treacherous. Toby, for example, works hard at a paper route (a "long route," as we used to say), and then he finds that Dwight has essentially stolen his money. When someone does something like that to you, it doesn't matter what his "reasons" were—he's a liar and a thief, and if he doesn't know it, it's because he's sick.

Dwight is sick. He's like a child himself, actually; even while he's taking from others, he feels eternally short-changed, put-upon, misunderstood. It's more of his bad luck that he drew Toby as a stepson. He senses that Toby sees through him, and that increases the intensity of his misbehavior. At times, Dwight borders on self-parody—he overplays himself, as if somehow desperately trying to show it's all a put-on.

The movie is very involving. We identify with Toby, we understand (but do not excuse) Caroline's passivity, and in Dwight, as played by De Niro, we see a pathetic but unforgettable villain. The book, as I said, is based on a memoir from real life, and indeed the original Dwight lived on in Concrete until just a few years ago. I wish he had lived to see this movie. I picture him in the lobby afterward, complaining how he had been misunderstood.

This Is Elvis ★ ★ ★ ½
PG, 88 m., 1981

Featuring documentary footage of Elvis Presley. Voices: Elvis (Ral Donner), Joe Esposito (Himself), Linda Thompson (Herself), Priscilla Presley (Lisha Sweetnam). Directed, produced, and written by Malcolm Leo and Andrew Solt.

This Is Elvis is the extraordinary record of a man who simultaneously became a great star and was destroyed by alcohol and drug addiction. What is most striking about its documentary footage is that we can almost always see both things happening at once. There is hardly a time when Elvis doesn't appear to be under the influence of mind-altering chemicals, and never a time, not even when he is only weeks from death, when he doesn't possess his special charisma. The movie's lesson is brutal, sad, and inescapable: Elvis Presley was a man who gave joy to a great many people but felt very little of his own, because he

became addicted and stayed addicted until the day it killed him.

This movie does not, however, intend to be a documentary about Presley's drug usage. It just turns out that way, because Presley's life turned out that way. The film is a re-creation of his life and image, and uses documentary footage from a wide variety of sources, including Presley's own professionally made home movies. Not all the footage is even really of Presley. Some early childhood scenes are fiction, with a young actor playing Elvis. They don't work, but they're soon over. A few other scenes are also faked, including one shot following Presley into his home on the night he died, and another showing him rushing to his mother's sickbed (the double is an Elvis imitator named Johnny Harra). But the faked footage adds up to only about 10 percent of the movie, and is helpful in maintaining continuity.

The rest of the film's footage is extraordinary, and about half of it has never been seen anywhere. This film isn't just a compilation of old Elvis documentaries. The filmmakers got permission from Presley's manager, Colonel Tom Parker, to use Presley's own private film archives and to shoot inside Graceland, his mansion. They include footage that was not even suspected to exist, including scenes from a birthday party Elvis had in Germany when he was still in the Army (we see a very young Priscilla at the party), scenes of Elvis's parents moving into Graceland, scenes with Elvis clowning around with buddies, and shots taken inside his limousine very near the end, when he was drunk and drugged and obviously very ill. There are also sequences during which we frankly wonder if he will be able to make it onto the stage.

The documentary also includes some of Presley's key television appearances, including his first guest appearances on the old "Dorsey Brothers Bandstand" and the "Ed Sullivan Show" (with Ed assuring America that Elvis was "a real decent, fine boy . . . Elvis, you're thoroughly all right"). There is newsreel footage of Elvis getting out of the Army (and, significantly, observing "it was so cold some nights we had to take bennies to stay awake"). There is an old kinescope, long thought to be lost, of a TV special hosted by Frank Sinatra to welcome Elvis back to civilian life (and in his duet with Sinatra, Presley is confused and apparently under the influence of tranquilizers).

The young Elvis in this movie is an entertainer of incredible energy and charisma.

The charisma stays, but somewhere along the way we notice a change in his behavior, a draining away of cheerfulness, a dreadful secret scourge. And in the film's final scenes, Presley is shockingly ill: He's bloated, his skin is splotchy, he's shaking and dripping with sweat, and, in one very painful sequence shot during a concert, he cannot remember the words to his songs. But he pushes through anyway, and his final renditions of "My Way" and "Are You Lonesome Tonight?" are beautiful and absolutely heartbreaking. He may have lost his mind, but he never lost his voice or his heart.

Elvis Presley should, of course, still be alive. The film interviews his former bodyguards about his drinking and drug usage, and they argue convincingly that they could not stop him from doing what he was determined to do. But an addict, of course, has only two choices, no matter how he might deceive himself that he has many. He can either continue to use, or he can ask for help.

The irony in Presley's case is that his own doctor was apparently the source of most of his drugs. Could Elvis have stopped? Sure. Would he have been alive today? Probably. But he was never able to admit his addiction and find the will to seek help. And he was surrounded by foot-kissers and yes-men. This movie shows the disintegration and death of a talented man who backed himself into a corner. He did it his way.

This Is My Life ★ ★ ★
PG-13, 93 m., 1992

Julie Kavner (Dottie Ingels), Samantha Mathis (Erica Ingels), Caroline Aaron (Martha Ingels), Gaby Hoffman (Opal Ingels), Carrie Fisher (Claudia Curtis), Dan Aykroyd (Arnold Moss). Directed by Nora Ephron and produced by Lynda Obst. Screenplay by Nora Ephron and Delia Ephron.

The smell of the greasepaint and the roar of the crowd are narcotics that have destroyed countless families, as documented in shelves of showbiz biographies. *This Is My Life* tells the story of yet another family that has to deal with a performer's ego, but it's a kinder, gentler ego, and at times we even sympathize with it.

The title represents a tug of war between two characters who both lay claim to it. One is Dottie Ingels (Julie Kavner), smart and edgy, who works in the Macy's cosmetics department with a microphone, using comedy to harangue customers into buying skin-care preparations. The other is her daughter Erica (Samantha Mathis), who narrates the movie, and who has grave misgivings about her mother's showbiz ambitions.

Erica and her younger sister, Opal (Gaby Hoffman), live with their mother and an older relative in Queens, where they have been abandoned by a father who has disappeared into a second marriage. They're proud of their mom, and they go along with her when she rehearses imaginary appearances on the Carson program. But when Dottie gets a couple of breaks and it begins to look as if she might actually make it in showbiz, the girls are appalled. What's in it for them?

The movie, directed by Nora Ephron and based on a novel by Meg Wolitzer, unfolds along predictable lines. What makes it work is the attention to character quirks. I enjoyed, for example, the way the screenplay avoids the usual clichés about actors and managers, and supplies instead a chic, cigarette-waving talent scout (Carrie Fisher) and her boss, a famous agent (Dan Aykroyd), who is named Arnold Moss, is referred to by the girls as The Moss, and eats paper napkins for a pastime.

When Dottie goes out West to make the comedy club circuit and maybe get her big break on Carson, the girls are overseen by a series of baby-sitters recruited from local comedy clubs. They watch their mom on TV, and are appalled when everything turns into material for her act—even the death of a beloved aunt. In the movie's quietest and best scene, they find out where their father is and take the train to Albany to visit him. They're sure he will welcome them, but that isn't what happens, in a scene where a cameo performance by their father's second wife (Caroline Aaron) brings a breathtaking human dimension to the material.

Is Dottie a monster for leaving her girls behind while she seeks a showbiz career? Are the girls selfish because they don't want their mom to realize her dream? "Given a choice," Dottie wails, "between their mother depressed and suicidal in the next room, and their mother ecstatic in Hawaii, they'd choose suicide every time." We have the feeling this is a line that will eventually wind up in the act.

Ephron, making her directing debut, is possibly drawing from issues in her own life. It is hard to imagine this material being about a man. The notion dies hard that a mother's place is with her children, even if society also requires that same mother to work full-time in order to support them.

Odds are that Dottie's gamble will bring her daughters a better life, but that's not what the movie is about.

There have been showbiz movies told from the point of view of neglected children, and others told from the POV of parents who hardly have time for their children, and, of course, there was *Mommie Dearest*, about showbiz kids who would have preferred abandonment. But what's new about *This Is My Life* is that it's an argument between the two points of view—with the mother and her daughters each demanding their own rights. There is humor in this approach, and also some truth.

This Is Spinal Tap ★ ★ ★ ★
R, 87 m., 1984

Rob Reiner (Marty DiBergi), Michael McKean (David St. Hubbins), Christopher Guest (Nigel Tufnel), Harry Shearer (Derek Smalls). Directed by Rob Reiner and produced by Karen Murphy. Screenplay by Christopher Guest, Michael McKean, Harry Shearer, and Reiner.

The children born at Woodstock are preparing for the junior prom, and rock 'n' roll is still here to stay. Rock musicians never die, they just fade away, and *This Is Spinal Tap* is a movie about a British rock group that is rocketing to the bottom of the charts.

The movie looks like a documentary filmed during the death throes of a British rock band named Spinal Tap. It is, in fact, a satire. The rock group does not really exist, but the best thing about this film is that it could. The music, the staging, the special effects, the backstage feuding, and the pseudo-profound philosophizing are right out of a hundred other rock groups and a dozen other documentaries about rock.

The group is in the middle of an American tour. The tour is not going well. Spinal Tap was once able to fill giant arenas, but its audiences have grown smaller and smaller, and concert dates are evaporating as the bad news gets around. No wonder. Spinal Tap is a bad rock 'n' roll band. It is derivative, obvious, phony, and pretentious, and it surrounds itself with whatever images seem commercial at the moment (a giant death's-head on stage, for one). The movie is absolutely inspired in the subtle way it establishes Spinal Tap's badness. The satire has a deft, wicked touch. Spinal Tap is not that much worse than, not that much different from, some successful rock bands. A few breaks

here or there, a successful album, and they could be back in business. (Proof of that: A sound track album, "Smell the Glove," is getting lots of air play with cuts like "Sex Farm.")

The documentary is narrated by its director, Marty DiBergi, played by Rob Reiner, the director of the real movie. He explains that he was first attracted to the band by its unusual loudness. He follows them on tour, asking profound questions that inspire deep, meaningless answers, and his cameras watch as the group comes unglued. One of the band members brings in a girlfriend from England. She feuds with the group's manager. Bookings are canceled. The record company doesn't like the cover for the group's new album. One disastrous booking takes Spinal Tap to a dance in a hangar on a military base. The movie is brilliant at telling its story through things that happen in the background and at the edges of the picture: By the end of the film, we know as much about the personalities and conflicts of the band members as if the movie had been straightforward narrative.

There are a lot of great visual jokes, which I don't want to spoil—especially the climax of the band's Stonehenge production number, or another number that involves them being reborn from womblike stage props. There also are moments of inspired satire aimed at previous styles in rock films, as when we get glimpses of Spinal Tap in its earlier incarnations (the band started as sort of a folk group, plunged into the flower-people generation, and was a little late getting into heavy metal, satanism, and punk).

This Is Spinal Tap assumes that audiences will get most of the jokes. I think that's right. "Entertainment Tonight" and music TV and Barbara Walters specials have made showbusiness trade talk into national gossip, and one of the greatest pleasures of the movie is that it doesn't explain everything. It simply, slyly, destroys one level of rock pomposity after another.

Three Men and a Baby ★ ★ ★
PG, 99 m., 1987

Tom Selleck (Peter), Steve Guttenberg (Michael), Ted Danson (Jack), Nancy Travis (Sylvia), Margaret Colin (Rebecca). Directed by Leonard Nimoy and produced by Ted Field and Robert W. Cort. Screenplay by James Orr and Jim Cruickshank.

Three Men and a Baby begins with too many characters and too much plot, and fifteen minutes into the film, I was growing restless. It spends a lot of time describing the lifestyles of three bachelors—Tom Selleck, Steve Guttenberg, and Ted Danson—who share a luxury apartment and play host to a never-ending stream of girlfriends. We meet too many of the girlfriends and too many of their friends, and then it's the morning after Selleck's big birthday bash, and on the doorstep outside their apartment is a bassinette containing a little baby named Mary. From that point on, the movie finds its rhythm, and it works.

The baby was apparently fathered by Danson, an actor who has just left to spend ten weeks shooting a film in Turkey. Selleck and Guttenberg contemplate the little bundle with dread, and Selleck's confusion is not helped when he goes to the market to buy baby food and gets a lot of advice about babies from a helpful clerk. ("You mean you don't even know how *old* your baby is?" she asks incredulously.)

Shortly after comes one of the funniest scenes in a long time, as Selleck and Guttenberg, an architect and a cartoonist, try to change Mary's diapers. The basic situation may sound familiar and even overworked, but the way they act it and the way Leonard Nimoy directs it, it builds from one big laugh to another.

The movie never steps wrong as long as it focuses on the developing love between the two big men and the tiny baby. At first they're baffled by this little bundle that only eats, sleeps, cries, and makes poo-poo—lots and lots of poo-poo. "The book says to feed the baby every two hours," Selleck complains, "but do you count from when you start, or when you finish? It takes me two hours to get her to eat, and by the time she's done, it's time to start again, so that I'm feeding her all of the time."

Those scenes are the heart of the movie. Unfortunately, there is also a completely unnecessary subplot to distract from the good stuff. *Three Men and a Baby* is a faithful reworking of a French film from a few years ago, in which the basic plot device was that "packages" were left with the bachelors on the same day—a baby and a fortune in heroin—along with the message that "the package" would be picked up a few days later.

The plot allows them to know nothing about the heroin, so they think the "package" is the baby, and that leads to a misunderstanding with some vicious drug dealers. Learning that an American remake of the French movie was being planned, I assumed

that the drug angle would be the first thing written out of the script. To begin with, it's completely unnecessary; the fact that the baby is left on the doorstep is all the story needs to get under way, and the central story is so funny and heartwarming that drugs are a downer.

But, no, Leonard Nimoy and writers James Orr and Jim Cruickshank have remade the entire French movie, drugs and all, leading to a badly staged and distracting confrontation between the heroes and the dealers in a mid-town construction site. Why bother with all the exhausted apparatus of crime and violence, recycled out of TV crime shows, when the story of the men and the baby is so compelling?

Luckily, there's enough of the domestic comedy to make the movie work despite its crasser instincts. And one of the big surprises in the movie is Tom Selleck's wonderful performance as the bachelor architect. After playing action heroes on TV and in the movies, he now reveals himself to be a light comedian in the Cary Grant tradition—a big, handsome guy with tenderness and vulnerability. When he looks at baby Mary with love in his eyes, you can see it there, and it doesn't feel like acting.

Because of Selleck and his co-stars (including twin baby girls Lisa and Michelle Blair), the movie becomes a heartwarming entertainment. There are, however, a couple of glitches at the end. When Mary's mother turns up, the men allow her to leave with the baby without even asking the obvious question on the mind of everyone in the audience: How could she have abandoned the baby in the first place? Another problem is that Selleck isn't the only one who doesn't know how old Mary is. If you follow the various dates mentioned in the script, the filmmakers also haven't a clue. But by the time the movie reaches its predictable but comfortable ending, who cares?

Three of Hearts ★ ★ ★
R, 97 m., 1993

William Baldwin (Joe), Kelly Lynch (Connie), Sherilyn Fenn (Ellen), Joe Pantoliano (Mickey), Gail Strickland (Yvonne), Cec Verrell (Allison), Claire Callaway (Isabella). Directed by Yurek Bogayevicz and produced by Joel B. Michaels and Matthew Irmas. Screenplay by Adam Greenman and Mitch Glazer.

Three of Hearts would have made a terrific 1930s screwball comedy, except that the

subject matter would have caused apoplexy among the movie censors of the era. It's about a lesbian whose bisexual girlfriend walks out on her—and about how she hires a male escort to seduce and abandon the girlfriend, who will then presumably hate men so much she'll come back home again.

My plot summary makes the movie sound like nuts, bolts, and plumbing. Actually, it's much more human than that, and funnier and more touching. It stars William Baldwin as Joe, a genial, good-looking, and not overbright employee of a Manhattan escort service. Most of his dates are with older rich women, who want to be reassured that the plastic surgery was successful. Then he's hired by Connie (Kelly Lynch), who needs an escort to her sister's wedding.

Connie had originally planned to use the wedding to introduce her family to her lover, Ellen (Sherilyn Fenn). But Ellen walked out, saying she needed more space, wanted to think over things, etc.—all the clichés that mean an affair is over. Connie and Joe have a good time at the wedding, enjoy each other, and eventually arrive at a moment of truth-telling in which Connie explains why she's not interested in sleeping with Joe, even if she has paid for it.

Joe is sympathetic. He also considers himself an expert on the hearts and minds of the female gender. Together, they devise a strategy in which he'll "accidentally" meet Ellen, date her, dump her, and reinforce her suspicions that all men are SOBs. And then, of course, Connie will be ready to wrap the poor wronged waif back into her sympathetic arms.

It doesn't quite work out that way, of course. But it doesn't work out quite as we expect either; the screenplay by Adam Greenman and Mitch Glazer understands the old screwball formulas without being tied to them, and the characters are allowed the freedom to develop in unexpected ways.

The surprise in the film is William Baldwin, star of *Backdraft* and *Flatliners* and younger brother of Alec. He begins with a fairly unsympathetic role, and makes it into an engaging character by playing Joe as a working-class guy who hasn't been ground down by cynicism, and finds there is more to the human heart than even an expert like himself would imagine. His boast is that he can seduce any woman, any time, any place, but what he discovers is that his power has not given him immunity to being seduced himself.

The movie is shot in a New York City that seems like a comfortable background rather than a series of forced locations; the characters seem to live in the city, unlike a lot of New Yorkers in the movies, who seem to be visiting there (why else would they spend so much time at tourist attractions?). Ellen is a teacher at New York University, Connie is a nurse, and Joe has to deal with his boss, the budget-minded owner of the escort service (Joe Pantoliano).

The film is also comfortable with the sexuality of the characters. Kelly Lynch creates a lesbian whose orientation is simply part of herself, like her nursing job and her sense of humor. The Sherilyn Fenn character could have been portrayed as confused and neurotic, but instead she's simply an ordinary person who is discovering new things about herself.

The whole approach to gay life in this movie is refreshingly unaffected. Not long ago I saw an arch, self-conscious film about a group of women at a writer's workshop, where a straight woman is seduced by a lesbian during many long philosophical conversations and even longer glances fraught with yearning. The whole affair was cranked up to an almost ludicrous pitch of solemnity and significance. *Three of Hearts* is more commonsensical: Romance is important, yes, but it is also baffling, surprising, and sometimes funny. And if the earth shakes, it's probably an earthquake.

Threesome ★ ★ ★
R, 93 m., 1994

Lara Flynn Boyle (Alex), Stephen Baldwin (Stuart), Josh Charles (Eddy), Alexis Arquette (Dick), Martha Gehman (Renay), Mark Arnold (Larry), Michele Matheson (Kristen), Joanne Baron (Curt Woman). Directed by Andrew Fleming and produced by Brad Krevoy and Steve Stabler. Screenplay by Fleming.

In earlier, more naive times *Threesome* would be the most controversial film of its season, a nine-day's wonder of sexual hoopla. It says something for these latter days that the first word that comes to mind, for describing it, is "sincere." The film contrives to get two boys and a girl into the same rooms of a college dormitory, and eventually into the same bed, and yet the screen doesn't sizzle, and what happens between the sheets is best described as a learning experience.

Lara Flynn Boyle, she of the sharp intelligence and edgy brunette charm, stars as a young woman named Alex. Her name is important, because it gets her wrongly classified as male, and assigned to the same two-room dorm suite as Stuart and Eddy (Stephen Baldwin and Josh Charles). In case anyone in the audience thinks this is an easy mistake to correct, the movie supplies an unlikely scene in which a campus bureaucrat looks straight at Alex and refuses to believe she is a woman, because the paperwork says otherwise.

Stuart is a campus stud, working his way through a series of meaningless encounters. Eddy is the smart one, who does Stuart's homework. He isn't experienced sexually, and when it becomes clear that Alex is attracted to him, he doesn't know how to respond. After she tries to get physical one night, he pushes her away and eventually confides that he's not sure, but he thinks he might be gay. In fact, he might even be attracted to . . . Stuart.

This possibility sets up an ironic triangle in their close quarters: Eddy wants Stuart who wants Alex who wants Eddy. The screenplay, by Andrew Fleming, who also directed the film, handles this dilemma by adding some false starts in other directions. Alex briefly dates an appalling phony named Larry, who is driven away by the roommates. And in an attempt to help Eddy figure out his sexuality, she sets up a date for him with a nice guy in the dorm who is openly gay. But the date goes nowhere, and it becomes clear that in one way or another all of the questions of gender identity are going to have to be settled by the threesome, among themselves.

It's clear (from the title on, I'd say) that sooner or later all three of these characters are going to find themselves in bed together. But when the promised scene arrives, the film mercifully spares us some kind of orgiastic pep rally; there's very little nudity in this film, and the MPAA's stern warning of "strong sexuality" could be more properly worded "strong cuddling."

What *is* strong in the movie is the language. Like many kids their age, these three are more bold in talk than action, and the movie sounds right; it sounds like undergraduate human dialogue, intended to shock, to liberate, to amuse. The dialogue is really the film's strongest element. The three actors are all smart and able to reflect the way kids sometimes use words, even very bold words, as a mask for uncertainty and shyness.

The result is a certain liberating effect. *Threesome* is not a great movie, but in its own way it is an effective one, and more than most other movies it is accurate and honest about the sexuality of young people. The characters in movies often seem to have no doubts at all about sex (unless, as is sometimes the alternative, they have nothing *but* doubts). In the audience, people with real questions and genuine problems wonder how the people in the movies got off so easy. *Threesome* is about three characters who, in the course of a school year, solve some mysteries and begin to discover themselves. No more than that. But that's enough.

3 Women ★ ★ ★ ★
PG, 125 m., 1977

Sissy Spacek (Pinky), Shelley Duvall (Millie), Janice Rule (Willie), Robert Fortier (Edgar), Ruth Nelson (Mrs. Rose), John Cromwell (Mr. Rose), Craig Richard Nelson (Dr. Maas), Maysie Hoy (Doris). Directed, produced, and written by Robert Altman.

Robert Altman's *3 Women* is, on the one hand, a straightforward portrait of life in a godforsaken California desert community, and, on the other, a mysterious exploration of human personalities. Its specifics are so real you can almost touch them, and its conclusion so surreal we can supply our own.

The community exists somewhere in Southern California, that uncharted continent of discontent and restlessness. Some of its people have put themselves down in a place that contains, so far as we can see, a spa where old people take an arthritis cure, a Western-style bar with a shooting range out back, and a singles residential motel with a swimming pool that has the most unsettling murals on its bottom.

Into this outpost one day comes Pinky (Sissy Spacek), a child-woman so naive, so open, so willing to have enthusiasm, that in another century she might have been a saint, a strange one. She takes a job at the spa and is instructed in her duties by Millie (Shelley Duvall), who is fascinated by the incorrect belief that the men in town are hot for her. Millie recruits Pinky as a roommate in the motel.

This whole stretch of the film—the first hour—is a funny, satirical, and sometimes sad study of the community and its people, who have almost all failed at something else, somewhere else. The dominant male is Edgar (Robert Fortier), a onetime stuntman, now a boozer with a beer bottle permanently in his hand. He's married to Willie (Janice Rule), who never speaks, who is pregnant, and is painting the murals. It's all terrifically new to Pinky: Drinking a beer (which she does as if just discovering the principle of a glass), or moving into Millie's apartment (which she solemnly declares to be the most beautiful place she's ever seen).

Then the film arrives at its center point, one of masked sexual horror. Millie comes home with Edgar and throws Pinky out of their bedroom, and Pinky tries to commit suicide by jumping into the pool. She survives, but as she recovers the film moves from realism to a strange, haunted psychological landscape in which, somehow, Pinky and Millie exchange personalities. *3 Women* isn't Altman out of Freud via *Psychology Today*, and so the movie mercifully doesn't attempt to explain what's happened in logical terms (*any* explanation would be disappointing, I think, compared to the continuing mystery). Somehow we *feel* what's happened, though, even if we can't explain it in so many words.

The movie's been compared to Bergman's *Persona*, another film in which women seem to share personalities, and maybe *Persona*, also so mysterious when we first see it, helps point the way. But I believe Altman has provided his own signposts, in two important scenes, one at the beginning, one at the end, that mirror one another. Millie, teaching Pinky how to exercise the old folks' legs in the hot baths, places Pinky's feet on her stomach and moves them back and forth, just as Pinky sees the apparition of two twins on the other side of the pool.

Later, when the older woman, Willie, is in labor, Millie places her legs in the same way and moves them in the same way, trying to assist the delivery. But the baby is stillborn, and so are the male-female connections in this small society. And so the women symbolically give birth to each other, around and around in a circle, just as (Altman himself suggests) the end of the picture could be seen as the moment just before its beginning.

The movie's story came to Altman during a dream, he's said, and he provides it with a dreamlike tone. The plot connections, which sometimes make little literal sense, do seem to connect emotionally, viscerally, as all things do in dreams. To act in a story like this must be a great deal more difficult than performing straightforward narrative, but Spacek and Duvall go through their changes so well that it's eerie, and unforgettable. So is the film.

Thunderheart ★ ★ ★ ½
R, 118 m., 1992

Val Kilmer (Ray Levoi), Sam Shepard (Frank Coutelle), Graham Greene (Walter Crow Horse), Fred Ward (Jack Milton), Fred Dalton Thompson (William Dawes). Directed by Michael Apted and produced by Robert De Niro, Jane Rosenthal, and John Fusco. Screenplay by Fusco.

The opening credits began with the name "Val Kilmer," and when the movie opened, with the assignment of an FBI agent to investigate a murder on an Indian reservation in South Dakota, I waited for Kilmer's first appearance. I had admired his performance as Jim Morrison so much in *The Doors* that I was eager to see what he would do next. The FBI agent was stopped by an Indian lawman, he was given a speeding ticket, he met with a veteran FBI man already on the scene, and only then, some twenty minutes into the movie, did I recognize that I had been watching Kilmer all along—that he was the agent.

Kilmer's anonymity was not a trick of makeup or lighting. He plays the role unadorned, his hair cut short and neatly combed, his shirt buttoned, his tie in a neat knot. It is something inside Kilmer that seems to conceal him; he is this straight-arrow, conservative, by-the-numbers FBI agent, just as in *The Doors* he was the Dionysian rock druggie Morrison, and it simply happens that there is no common reference between the two characters. He is so inside the one that you cannot get a glimpse of the other.

If there is an award for the most unsung leading man of his generation, Kilmer should get it. In movies as different as *Real Genius, Top Gun, Top Secret!*, and *Billy the Kid*, he has shown a range of characters so convincing that it's likely most people, even now, don't realize they were looking at the same actor. In *Thunderheart*, he plays agent Ray Levoi, who is at first undemonstrative and even rigid in his dealings with the locals. He's like one of those cops who is blind to the human situation because he's preoccupied by running the rule book through his mind. He's assigned to the case on the reservation on the unconvincing grounds that he is one-fourth Indian. His first contact is the Native American lawman, played by Graham Greene (who won an Oscar nomination for his work in *Dances With Wolves*). Soon he encounters agent Frank Coutelle, played by Sam Shepard as a laconic cynic. And not long after he meets a schoolteacher (Sheila Tousey), who

provides a breath of romantic interest—although the movie has the originality to let it be a subtle breath, and not center the whole story around it.

The movie was directed by Michael Apted and written by John Fusco, who base their story on actual events in the Dakota reservations in the early 1970s, when a militant group called AIM (for American Indian Movement) defied the FBI. This fictionalized version of the encounter involves a conspiracy to steal lands from the Indians, and the mechanics of the murder mystery and investigation are well worked out and involving.

But that wasn't what interested me the most. What's most absorbing about *Thunderheart* is its sense of place and time. Apted makes documentaries as well as fiction films, and in such features as *Coal Miner's Daughter* and *Gorillas in the Mist* and such documentaries as *35 Up* he pays great attention to the people themselves—not just what they do, and how that pushes things along. In *Thunderheart* we get a real visual sense of the reservation, of the beauty of the rolling prairie and the way it is interrupted by deep gorges, but also of the omnipresent rusting automobiles and the subsistence level of some of the housing. We feel that we're really there, and that the people in the story really occupy land they stand on.

This sense of place helps the movie with its weakest story element, the supposition that because the Kilmer character is a quarter Indian, he will somehow summon up his roots to help him decide between good and evil. An FBI agent at the time this film was shot would probably have had little difficulty in choosing between his roots and the rule book, and the rules would have won. Still, this is a movie, after all, and at the end there is a sense of rightness in the way everything turns out. There is also the sense that we have seen superior acting, especially by Kilmer.

THX 1138 ★ ★ ★
PG, 88 m., 1971

Robert Duvall (THX 1138), Donald Pleasence (SEN 5241), Don Pedro Colley (SRT), Maggie McOmie (LUH 3417). Directed by George Lucas and produced by Lawrence Sturhahn. Screenplay by Lucas and Walter Murch.

The brave new world of the American Zoetrope studio began in the late 1960s in San Francisco. Francis Ford Coppola, a young director of promise, persuaded Warner Bros. to help finance and distribute a group of features by the bright new filmmakers he'd gathered around him. Coppola had just finished a successful mainstream production for Warners', *Finian's Rainbow*, and his proposal sounded good in that era of youth films, bike films, trip films, and other high hopes.

The youth film and the others turned out to be lost causes, however, and as the American film industry moved back to traditional narrative pictures, not many of the proposed American Zoetrope films were made, and even fewer ever opened. Warner Bros., having decided to drop the San Francisco experiment, didn't back the surviving features very enthusiastically. The greatest casualty was George Lucas's *THX 1138*, a science-fiction parable set in the twenty-fifth century and displaying remarkable visual mastery.

The movie's strength is not in its story but in its unsettling and weirdly effective visual and sound style. The story is standard sci-fi stuff: Five centuries in the future, mankind inhabits vast underground cities which are programmed by computers and policed by robots. The citizens are force-fed drugs to inhibit their passions, but THX 1138 (Robert Duvall) and his mate LUH 3417 (Maggie McOmie) cut down on their drug rations and discover that they have sexual appetites. Worse still, they are in love.

What follows is a battle against the centralized computer system, a few episodes of outsmarting the dumb robot policemen, and a chase scene. None of this is very original, and the whole business of Love versus State is out of Orwell and countless lesser writers. But Lucas doesn't seem to have been very concerned with his plot, anyway. His film was inspired by a student film he did at USC, which won the National Student Film Festival in 1968. The student work was sort of a dry run for this one, exploring ways of creating inexpensive but totally convincing special effects for a futuristic society. The experiment was a success; the subterranean laboratories, apartments, and corridors in *THX 1138* have a blinding, white porcelain sameness, and the characters seem to inhabit the future's most spectacular and sanitary bathroom fixtures.

The sound effects add to the illusion of a distant and different society. The dialogue seems half-heard, half-forgotten; people talk in a bemused way, as if the drugs had made them indifferent. Their words are suspended in a muted, echoing atmosphere in which only the computer-programmed recorded an-

nouncements seem confident. And the featureless whiteness of this universe stretches away into infinity (especially in the effective scene involving a prison with no walls—how can you escape from a prison that is simply an empty void?). *THX 1138* suffers somewhat from its simple story line, but as a work of visual imagination it's special, and as haunting as parts of *2001*, *Silent Running*, and *The Andromeda Strain*.

Ticket to Heaven ★ ★ ★ ½
R, 107 m., 1981

Nick Mancuso (David), Saul Rubinek (Larry), Meg Foster (Ingrid), Kim Cattrall (Ruthie), R.H. Thomson (Linc Strunk), Jennifer Dale (Lisa). Directed by Ralph L. Thomas and produced by Vivienne Lebosh.

Ticket to Heaven is about a young man who enters the all-encompassing world of a religious cult. What makes the movie absolutely spellbinding is that it shows us not only how he is recruited into the group, but how *anyone* could be indoctrinated into one of the many cults in America today. This is a movie that has done its research, and it is made with such artistry that we share the experience of the young man.

His name is David. He is played by Nick Mancuso, a powerful young actor, as an independent type who flies from Toronto to San Francisco to discover what has happened to a friend who joined up with the cult. He is welcomed to their communal residence, joins in a meal and some singing, and is asked if he'd like to spend the weekend at a retreat on the group's farm. He would. By the end of the weekend, he is a cult member. Can it happen that fast? I've read stories claiming that some cults need only seventy-two hours to convert almost anyone to their way. The best and the brightest make the best recruits, they say. The movie shows the three techniques used to indoctrinate new members: (1) low-calorie, low-protein diets; (2) sleep deprivation; (3) "love-bombing," which involves constant positive reinforcement, the chanting of slogans and great care *never* to allow the recruit to be alone for a moment.

Although *Ticket to Heaven* does not mention any existing cult by name, it is based on a series of newspaper articles about a former Moonie. The techniques in the film could, I suppose, be used by anybody. What makes the film so interesting is that it's not just a docudrama, not just a sensationalist exposé, but a fully realized drama that involves us on

the human level as well as with its documentary material. There are scenes that are absolutely harrowing: an overhead shot of David trying to take a walk by himself and being "joined" by jolly friends; a scene where he guiltily bolts down a forbidden hamburger; a scene where another cult member whispers one sentence that sounds to us, as much as to David, like shocking heresy. By that point in the film, we actually understand why David has become so zombie-like and unquestioning. We have shared his experience.

The final scenes in the film involve a deprogramming attempt. They are not as absorbing as what went before, if only because they involve an effort of the intellect, instead of an assault on the very personality itself. I've seen *Ticket to Heaven* three times, and at first I thought the film's ending was "weaker" than the rest. Now I wonder. What cults offer is freedom from the personality. They remove from your shoulders the burden of being you. That is a very seductive offer: why else do people also seek freedom from self through drugs, alcohol, and even jogging? As David is seduced into the cult's womb, we also submit vicariously to the experience. We understand its appeal. At the end, as David's reason is appealed to, as his intellect is reawakened, as he is asked to once again take up the burden of being himself, he resists—and maybe we do, too.

Tightrope ★ ★ ★ ½
R, 114 m., 1984

Clint Eastwood (Wes Block), Genevieve Bujold (Beryl Thibodeaux), Dan Hedaya (Detective Molinari), Alison Eastwood (Amanda Block), Jennifer Beck (Penny Block). Directed by Richard Tuggle and produced by Clint Eastwood and Fritz Manes. Screenplay by Tuggle.

Most modern police thrillers are simple-minded manipulations of chases, violence, pop psychology, and characters painted in broad stereotypes. *Tightrope* contains all four of those ingredients, to be sure, but it also contains so much more that it's a throwback to the great cop movies of the 1940s—when the hero wrestled with his conscience as much as with the killer.

The movie stars Clint Eastwood as a New Orleans homicide detective who is as different as possible from Dirty Harry Callahan. The guy's name is Wes Block. His wife has recently left him, and he lives at home with his two young daughters and several dogs.

He is a good but flawed cop, with a peculiar hang-up: He likes to make love to women while they are handcuffed. The movie suggests this is because he feels deeply threatened by women (a good guess, I'd say). Detective Block is well-known to most of the kinkier prostitutes in the French Quarter, but his superiors don't know that when they assign him to a big case: A mad strangler, apparently an ex-cop, is killing hookers in the Quarter. Block's problem is that he cannot easily enter this world as a policeman after having entered it often as a client. His other problem is that when he walks into that world, all of his old urges return.

The police work in *Tightrope* is more or less standard: The interviews of suspects, the paperwork, the scenes where his superiors chew him out for not making more progress on the case. What makes *Tightrope* better than just another police movie are the scenes between Eastwood and the women he encounters. Some of them are hookers. Some are victims. One of them, played by Genevieve Bujold, is a feminist who teaches women's self-defense classes. Block has always been attracted to flashy, gaudy women, like the Quarter's more bizarre prostitutes. We do not know why his wife left him, and we are given no notions of what she was like, but right away we figure that Bujold isn't his type. She's in her mid-thirties, uses no makeup, wears sweat shirts a lot, and isn't easily impressed by cops. But somehow a friendship does begin. And it becomes the counterpoint for the cop's investigation, as he goes deeper into the messy underworld of the crimes—and as more of the evidence seems to suggest that he should be one of the suspects. It's interesting that the movie gives Eastwood two challenges: To solve the murders, and to find a way out of his own hangups and back into an emotional state where he can trust a strong woman.

Tightrope may appeal to the Dirty Harry fans, with its sex and violence. But it's a lot more ambitious than the Harry movies, and the relationship between Eastwood and Bujold is more interesting than most recent male-female relationships in the movies, for three reasons: (1) There is something at risk in it, on both sides; (2) it's a learning process, in which Eastwood is the one who must change; (3) it pays off dramatically at the end, when their developing relationship fits into the climax of the investigation. Think how unusual it is for a major male star to appear in a commercial cop picture in which the plot hinges on his ability to accept and respect a woman. Apart from the other good things in *Tightrope*, I admire it for taking chances; Clint Eastwood can get rich making Dirty Harry movies, but he continues to change and experiment, and that makes him the most interesting of the box-office megastars.

Tim Burton's Nightmare Before Christmas ★ ★ ★ ½
PG, 76 m., 1993
(See related Film Clip, p. 849.)

With the voices of: Chris Sarandon (speaking voice of Jack Skellington), Danny Elfman (singing voice of Jack Skellington), Catherine O'Hara (Sally), Glenn Shadix (Mayor), Ken Page (Oogie Boogie), Paul Reubens (Lock), Catherine O'Hara (Shock), Danny Elfman (Barrel), William Hickey (Evil Scientist). Directed by Henry Selick and produced by Burton and Denise Di Novi. Screenplay by Caroline Thompson, based on a story and characters by Burton.

The movies can create entirely new worlds for us, but that is one of their rarest gifts. More often, directors go for realism, for worlds we can recognize. One of the many pleasures of *Tim Burton's Nightmare Before Christmas* is that there is not a single recognizable landscape within it. Everything looks strange and haunting. Even Santa Claus would be difficult to recognize without his red-and-white uniform.

The movie, which tells the story of an attempt by Halloween to annex Christmas, is shot in a process called stop-action animation. In an ordinary animated film, the characters are drawn. Here they are constructed, and then moved a little, frame by frame, so that they appear to live. This allows a three-dimensional world to be presented, instead of the flatter universe of cell animation. And it is a godsend for the animators of *Nightmare*, who seem to have built their world from scratch—every house, every stick and stone—before sending their skeletal and rather pathetic little characters in to inhabit it.

The movie begins with the information that each holiday has its own town. Halloweentown, for example, is in charge of all the preparations for Halloween, and its most prominent citizen is a bony skeleton named Jack Skellington, whose moves and wardrobe seem influenced by Fred Astaire.

One day Jack stumbles into the wrong entranceway in Halloweentown, and finds himself smack dab in the middle of preparations for Christmas. Now *this*, he realizes, is more like it! Instead of ghosts and goblins and pumpkins, there are jolly little helpers assisting Santa in his annual duty of bringing peace upon earth and good will to men.

Back in Halloweentown, Jack Skellington feels a gnawing desire to better himself, to move up to a more important holiday, one that people take more seriously and enjoy more than Halloween. And so he engineers a diabolical scheme in which Santa is kidnapped, and Jack himself plays the role of Jolly St. Nick, while *his* helpers manufacture presents. (Some of the presents, when finally distributed to little girls and boys, are so hilariously ill-advised that I will not spoil the fun by describing them here.)

Tim Burton, the director of *Beetlejuice*, *Edward Scissorhands*, and the *Batman* movies, has been creating this world in his head for about ten years, ever since his mind began to stray while he was employed as a traditional animator on an unremarkable Disney project. The story is centered on his favorite kind of character, an odd misfit who *wants* to do well, but has been gifted by fate with a quirky personality that people don't know how to take. Jack Skellington is the soul brother of Batman, Edward, and the demon in *Beetlejuice*—a man for whom normal human emotions are a conundrum.

Nightmare Before Christmas is a Tim Burton film in the sense that the story, its world, and its look first took shape in Burton's mind, and he supervised their filming. But the director of the film, a veteran stop-action master named Henry Selick, is the person who has made it all work. And his achievement is enormous. Working with gifted artists and designers, he has made a world here that is as completely new as the worlds we saw for the first time in such films as *Metropolis*, *The Cabinet of Dr. Caligari*, or *Star Wars*. What all of these films have in common is a visual richness so abundant that they deserve more than one viewing. First, go for the story. Then go back just to look in the corners of the screen and appreciate the little visual surprises and inspirations that are tucked into every nook and cranny.

The songs by Danny Elfman are fun, too, a couple of them using lyrics so clever they could be updated from Gilbert and Sullivan. And the choreography, liberated from gravity and reality, has an energy of its own, as when the furniture, the architecture, and the very landscape itself gets into the act.

The movie is rated "PG," maybe because some of the Halloween creatures might be a tad scary for smaller children, but this is the kind of movie older kids will eat up; it has the kind of offbeat, subversive energy that tells them wonderful things are likely to happen. As an adult who was not particularly scared by the abduction of Santa (somehow I knew things would turn out all right), I found the movie a feast for the eyes and the imagination.

Time Bandits ★ ★ ★
PG, 98 m., 1981

Craig Warnock (Kevin), John Cleese (Robin Hood), Sean Connery (Agamemnon), Shelley Duvall (Pansy), Ian Holm (Napoleon), Ralph Richardson (Supreme Being). The Dwarfs: David Rappaport (Randall), Kenny Baker (Fidget), Jack Purvis (Wally), Mike Edmonds (Og), Malcolm Dixon (Strutter), Tiny Ross (Vermin). Directed and produced by Terry Gilliam. Screenplay by Michael Palin and Gilliam.

First reactions while viewing *Time Bandits:* It's amazingly well-produced. The historic locations are jammed with character and detail. This is the only live-action movie I've seen that literally looks like pages out of *Heavy Metal* magazine, with kings and swordsmen and wide-eyed little boys and fearsome beasts. *But* the movie's repetitive, monotonous in the midst of all this activity. Basically, it's just a kid and six dwarfs racing breathlessly through one set piece after another, shouting at one another. I walked out of the screening in an unsettled state of mind. When the lights go up, I'm usually fairly certain whether or not I've seen a good movie. But my reaction to *Time Bandits* was ambiguous. I had great admiration for what was physically placed on the screen; this movie is worth seeing just to *watch*. But I was disappointed by the breathless way the dramatic scenes were handled and by a breakneck pace that undermined the most important element of comedy, which is timing.

Time Bandits is the expensive fantasy by Terry Gilliam, one of the resident geniuses of Monty Python's Flying Circus. It is *not* a Monty Python film. It begins with a little boy who goes up to bed one night and is astonished, as we all would be, when a horseman gallops through his bedroom wall and he is in the middle of a pitched battle. Before long, the little kid has joined up with a band of six intrepid dwarfs, and they've embarked on an odyssey through history. The dwarfs, it appears, have gained possession of a map that gives the location of several holes in time—holes they can pop through in order to drop in on the adventures of Robin Hood, Napoleon, and King Agamemnon, and to sail on the *Titanic*'s maiden voyage.

As a plot gimmick, this sets up *Time Bandits* for a series of comic set pieces as in Mel Brooks's *History of the World—Part I*. But *Time Bandits* isn't revue-style comedy. It's more of a whimsical, fantastic excursion through all those times and places, and all of its events are seen through the wondering eyes of a child. That's where the superb art direction comes in—inspired work by production designer Milly Burns and costume designer Jim Acheson. I've rarely, if ever, seen a live-action movie that looks more like an artist's conception. And yet, admiring all of these good things (and I might also mention several of the performances), I nevertheless left the screening with muted enthusiasm. The movie was somehow all on the same breathless, nonstop emotional level, like an overlong Keystone Kops chase. It didn't pause to savor its delights, except right near the end, when Sir Ralph Richardson lingered lovingly over a walk-on as the Supreme Being. I had to sort things out. And I was helped enormously in that process by the review of *Time Bandits* by Stanley Kauffmann in *The New Republic*. He describes the film, unblinkingly, as a "children's movie." Of course.

There have been so many elaborate big-budget fantasies in recent years, from *Raiders* to *Superman* to *Clash of the Titans*, that we've come to assume that elaborate costume fantasies are aimed at the average eighteen-year-old filmgoer who is trying to recapture his adolescence. These movies have a level of (limited) sophistication and wickedness that is missing in *Time Bandits*. But perhaps *Time Bandits* does work best as just simply a movie for kids. I ran it through my mind that way, wondering how a kid would respond to the costumes, the panoply, the explosions, the horses and heroic figures, and, of course, the breathless, nonstop pacing. And I decided that a kid would like it just fine. I'm not sure that's what Gilliam had in mind, but it allows me to recommend the movie—with reservations, but also with admiration.

Timecop ★ ★
R, 98 m., 1994

Jean-Claude Van Damme (Walker), Mia Sara (Melissa), Ron Silver (McComb), Bruce McGill (Matuzak), Gloria Reuben (Fielding), Scott Bellis (Ricky), Jason Schombing (Atwood), Scott Lawrence (Spota). Directed by Peter Hyams and produced by Moshe Diamant, Sam Raimi, and Robert Tapert. Screenplay by Mark Verheiden.

More than most movies about time travel, *Timecop* invites you to meditate on the logical contradictions of the genre. It begins with the organization of Time Enforcement Police to prevent the tampering with time. Their job: Stop villains from tampering with the past and producing catastrophic results in the present. But right away you have some problems: How do you know which "present" is your baseline? And how can you be sure it isn't already the result of tampering with the past? Just think: A zealous timecop could change the present by *preventing* the tampering with the past.

Well, says the movie, the present is defined as Now. That is because "you can travel back in time, but not into the future, because the future hasn't happened yet." Yes, but once you *do* travel back in time, the present becomes the future which has not yet happened. And furthermore, how can a traveling timecop *return* to the present from the past without, in effect, traveling into the future?

You see what we're up against here. *Timecop*, a low-rent *Terminator*, is the kind of movie that is best not thought about at all, for that way madness lies. Even in the last frames of the film, we are being presented with paradoxes, as when a weary timecop (Jean-Claude Van Damme), having battled through the decades to set things right, returns home and is greeted by a child he has never seen before, who cries out, "Dad!" What and where is the person, identical to Van Damme, who the child has known as Dad? Doesn't that mean there is an extra timecop around? What happens when they meet?

Ah, but the movie has already answered that question, in a scene where a time-traveling evil U.S. senator meets himself in the past. The rules are, you cannot touch "yourself" without setting up a fearsome rent in the fabric of time. When the two selves make contact, they are immediately processed by a computer morphing program, which melts them into one another with some of the same fearsome consequences that made life miserable for the poor silver guy in *Terminator II.*

Timecop throws everything into the pot. It's a cop buddy movie about a political conspiracy, ranging roughly from 1863, when gold intended for the Confederates is stolen, to 2004, when it may be used to finance a political campaign. (The belief that the amount of gold that can be carried on one horse would make a financial difference in 2004 is the most optimistic element in the movie.)

Van Damme plays the cop, named Walker, who lives with his wife, Melissa (Mia Sara), in the kind of turreted, gabled, four-story Gothic manor that, as we all know, is the typical residence of Washington, D.C., policemen. The house seems too large for their needs, until we realize the movie plans to employ the Climbing Villain Syndrome in its climactic scenes, which take place on a Dark and Stormy Night; those gables will be necessary so that people can hang from them by their fingernails.

The U.S. government is concerned about attempts to alter the past, and has decided to create its timecop force, to be run by District of Columbia policemen. How the CIA let this plum get away from them is not explained. Ron Silver plays McComb, the ambitious senator who plans to manipulate the past in order to get himself elected president, and of course that makes him a criminal, guilty of "time travel with intent to alter the future."

The time travelers launch themselves into the past by being strapped into a rocket car which hurtles down rails toward a wall. Just before it hits the wall, it disappears. Fine, except when the travelers materialize in the past, the rocket car has disappeared. If it does not go into the past with them, why is it necessary? If it stays in the present, why does it disappear? And why, oh why, if travel backward is so difficult, are the travelers able to return to the present by simply pushing a button on a little gizmo they wear strapped to their bodies?

But never mind. Van Damme ventures into the past, meets Silver and other baddies there, and zips back and forth in an increasingly desperate attempt to save his life, his wife, and the future, while not getting hopelessly entangled in paradoxes. The movie, directed by Peter *(2010)* Hyams, meanwhile has some sly fun with sex scenes that turn out to be only Virtual Reality, and a moment

in 1929 when a character utters that immortal two-word saying that Forrest Gump allegedly did not invent for a bumper sticker until the 1970s.

The movie is a harvest of entries from *Ebert's Little Movie Glossary.* Not only do we get the Climbing Villain but also the Talking Killer (Silver explains his grandiose schemes when he should just simply kill Van Damme), and all of the usual clichés involving a cop who loses his partner and is assigned a new partner he doesn't like. The Bulletproof Vest Rule is also illustrated (whenever a character wearing such a vest is shot, he always falls and seems to be dead, only to be seen alive a moment later, after which it is obligatory that he unbutton his shirt and look at the vest, so that the grateful audience can see that he was wearing it).

And yet, the more I thought about it, the more I realized that the movie's logic is sound. It's not so much that the premise of the original *Terminator* has been ripped off, as that Hollywood went traveling into the past and inalterably ripped the fabric of time, and that's why we got *Timecop* with Van Damme instead of *Terminator III* with Schwarzenegger. You see what can happen.

A Time of Destiny ★ ★ ★ ½
PG-13, 118 m., 1988

William Hurt (Martin), Timothy Hutton (Jack), Melissa Leo (Josie), Stockard Channing (Margaret), Megan Follows (Irene), Francisco Rabal (Jorge). Directed by Gregory Nava and produced by Anna Thomas. Screenplay by Nava and Thomas.

A Time of Destiny is a film of strong, pure emotions, of which the most powerful are love, hate, and jealousy. It is not a film about timid little people peeking out of their small lives, but about characters whose motives are so large they are operatic, and whose faults are so ancient they are biblical. Any criticism of this film on the basis of implausibility completely misses the point.

The movie tells the story of a proud, flawed family, and the outsider who marries into it. The sickness of the family flows from the father, a proud Basque immigrant who has found success in California in the years before World War II, but still rules his life and family by old-world paternalism. As the movie opens, one of his sons is dead, another son is all but disowned, and all of his love and possessiveness are focused on his middle

daughter. When she elopes to get married, his rage and jealousy are towering.

The old man is played by Francisco Rabal as a survivor with a fierce stubbornness. He knows he is right, and one of the things he is right about is this—few men, if any, are good enough for his daughter. She is played by Melissa Leo as a girl caught halfway between modern America and the values of her childhood. And the man she elopes with, one rainy night, is played by Timothy Hutton as the kind of straight-arrow American who seems commonplace against this convoluted family's deep passions.

If jealousy is a family disease, the old man is the carrier, but his son is the victim. He is also an enigma. Played by William Hurt as a man who seems, at first glance, confident and competent, he is actually on the edge of emotional collapse. His father has no use for him because of his history of failure—failure, we suspect, inspired by the father's inability to make room inside the family for more than one strong man. The Hurt character has grown up into a man filled with grandiose notions of family tradition and pride, and they are all a fantasy, because his father considers him worthless and has written him out of the will.

This convoluted family situation sets the stage for *A Time of Destiny,* which is a melodramatic romance in which the images all seem a little larger and clearer than life. The movie was directed by Gregory Nava and produced by Anna Thomas, who together cowrote the screenplay; they are the team who made *El Norte* five years earlier, and their gift is for passionate, headlong narrative. In this film, the opening scenes are literally explosive; there is a spectacular point-of-view shot of a shell flying through a cannon barrel and down upon a straggling line of Yankee soldiers in Italy, and then we see two of the soldiers, tired beyond exhaustion, pledge to each other to somehow survive the madness.

The soldiers are Hutton and Hurt, and in a flashback we find that this pledge is not as simple as it seems. Hutton and Leo conduct a courtship in the face of her father's disapproval, and everything leads up to a rain-swept night when they elope, are married, and then are tracked down to their hotel by the father, in a towering rage. He demands that she return with him or lose his love. She agrees, promising Hutton that they will eventually be together. The old man and his daughter drive out into the dangerous night,

Hutton pursues in his car, there is an accident, and the old man dies.

For William Hurt, this is a long-awaited moment. He is simultaneously freed of his father's persecution and given a stage on which to pretend to inherit his father's crown. Hutton (who has never met Hurt and does not know what he looks like) goes off to fight the war; Hurt arranges to join the same Army group, and he vows to murder Hutton to avenge the death of his father. But during a dark and confused night of hand-to-hand fighting, the two men instead save each other's lives. That should set the stage for a reconciliation, but instead, Hurt gradually reveals the true depths of the wound inside his soul.

You see what I mean when I call the movie operatic. It glories in brooding vengeance, fatal flaws of character, coincidence, and deep morality. Its plot is so labyrinthine that it constitutes the movie's major weakness; can we follow this convoluted emotional journey? Its passions are so large that they are a challenge to actors trained in a realistic tradition, but Hurt, who has the most difficult passages, rises to the occasion with one of the strangest and most effective performances he has given. A great deal hinges on one scene that he plays before a mirror, as various aspects of his personality fight for control, and the way he plays this scene is further evidence of his power as an actor. He does not overact, and yet he is not afraid of pulling out all the stops, of taking the risk of making himself look silly. Many actors would have protected themselves by pulling back during this scene. Not William Hurt.

Even the title of *A Time of Destiny* reflects the film's vision. It is a movie about fate in an age that does not believe in fate; its plot is nineteenth-century, without apology, and it is not timid or compromised. As I watched the film, I grew increasingly grateful for the chances it was taking. This same story could have been ground in the mill of psychological realism and come out as oatmeal. But Nava and Thomas have chosen a more difficult and risky approach, and the result is muscular and brave.

The Times of Harvey Milk ★ ★ ★ ½
NO MPAA RATING, 87 m., 1985

A documentary by Robert Epstein and Richard Schmiechen, narrated by Harvey Fierstein.

Harvey Milk must have been a great guy. You get the sense watching this documentary about his brief public career that he could appreciate the absurdities of life and enjoy a good laugh at his own expense. He was also serious enough and angry enough about the political issues in his life that he eventually ran for the San Francisco Board of Supervisors and became California's first openly homosexual public official. That victory may have cost him his life.

The Times of Harvey Milk describes the lives and deaths of Milk and Mayor George Moscone, who both were shot dead in 1978 by Dan White, one of Milk's fellow supervisors. It also describes the political and social climate in San Francisco, which during the 1960s and 1970s began to attract growing numbers of gays because of its traditionally permissive attitude. Milk was one of those gays, and in old photographs we see him in his long-haired beatnik and hippie days before he eventually shaved off the beard and opened a camera store in the Castro District. It was from the Castro that Milk ran for office and was defeated three times before finally winning in the same election that placed the first Chinese-American, the first black woman, and the first avowed feminist on the board. Milk was a master at self-promotion, and the movie includes vintage TV news footage showing him campaigning on such issues as "doggy-do," and stepping, with perfect timing, into a strategically placed pile of same at the climax of the interview.

There is a lot of footage of Milk, Moscone, and White (who disapproved of homosexuals but was naive enough to once suggest that the issue be settled by a softball game between his ward and Milk's ward). It is intercut with later interviews with many of Milk's friends, including a veteran leftist who admits that he was prejudiced against gays for a long time, until he met Milk and began to understand the political issues involved. There is a Chinese-American who parallels his own radicalization with Milk's. And there is immensely moving, emotional footage of the two demonstrations inspired by the deaths of Milk and Moscone: a silent, candlelight parade of forty-five thousand people on the night of their deaths, and an angry night of rioting when White got what was perceived as a lenient sentence.

"If Dan White had only killed George Moscone, he would have gone up for life," one person says in the film. "But he killed a gay, and so they let him off easy." This is not necessarily the case, and the weakest element in *The Times of Harvey Milk* is its willingness to let Milk's friends second-guess the jury, and impugn the jurors' motives.

Many people who observed White's trial believe that White got a light sentence, not because of antigay sentiment, but because of incompetent prosecution. Some of the jurors were presumably available to the filmmakers, and the decision not to let them speak for themselves—to depend instead on the interpretation of Milk's friends and associates—is a serious bias. That objection aside, this is an enormously absorbing film, for the light it sheds on a decade in the life of a great American city and on the lives of Milk and Moscone, who made it a better, and certainly a more interesting, place to live.

Tin Men ★ ★ ★
R, 109 m., 1987

Richard Dreyfuss (BB), Danny DeVito (Tilley), Barbara Hershey (Nora), John Mahoney (Moe), Jackie Gayle (Sam), Stanley Brock (Gil), Seymour Cassel (Cheese), Bruno Kirby (Mouse). Directed by Barry Levinson and produced by Mark Johnson. Screenplay by Levinson.

They tool up to work in those bloated '50s Cadillacs from back in the days when you knew a Cadillac was the best car on the road because it was the biggest car on the road. They park their Caddys and hang around the diner, drinking coffee and killing time, talking about the citizens they've defrauded and the TV shows they're gonna watch tonight. They're tin men. They sell aluminum siding. One day, BB (Richard Dreyfuss) takes delivery on his new Caddy, and backs it out of the showroom and into the path of a Caddy owned by Tilley (Danny DeVito). Sheet metal is crunched and words are exchanged. They become mortal enemies. They hurl insults and threats at one another, and for weeks afterward they plot and scheme to wreak vengeance for the dents in the fenders of their phallic symbols.

The feud between BB and Tilley is the centerpiece of *Tin Men,* a loosely organized series of events in the lives of some middle-aged and fairly desperate Baltimore salesmen, circa 1958. These guys are worried because the law is closing in, a commission is holding hearings on their high-pressure sales techniques, and they're afraid they'll lose their jobs.

Meanwhile, they carry on in the only ways they know. They use the "loss leader" scam ("After your house becomes the neighborhood showplace, we'll give you a cut when your neighbors sign up for siding"), the *Life* magazine scam ("We need a picture of your house for a layout on how ugly houses are before the aluminum siding is added"), and the sudden breakdown scam (My buddy didn't mean to make you that offer. He hasn't been quite right lately. But I'll tell you what I will do"). And then they meet after work to trade lies and philosophies.

BB figures out a way to really get even with Tilley. He'll seduce his wife (Barbara Hershey). Two things go wrong with this plan. First, Tilley hates his wife and is happy to get rid of her. Second, BB falls in love. That is a high price to pay for a dented fender.

Tin Men was written and directed by Barry Levinson in a style similar to his inspired 1982 comedy, *Diner*. That was a movie about a crowd of teen-age buddies who were mystified by sex, life, ambition, and especially women. They were trying to grow up at an age when they were already supposed to be grown-up. The median age of the characters in *Tin Men* is probably forty-five, but they're still growing up too, and they're still mystified by sex, life, ambition, and women—by everything but Cadillacs.

Like *Diner*, Levinson's new movie uses a series of scenes strung together with the diner as home base. There, in a window booth, pouring sugar into their coffee, the salesmen discuss the bafflements of life. "This show 'Bonanza' is about a fifty-year-old father and his three forty-seven-year-old sons," one of the guys says. "What kind of a show is that?" That line is delivered by Jackie Gayle, who has a lot of the movie's funniest moments, maybe because the Dreyfuss and DeVito characters have serious undertones.

Why do BB and Tilley hate each other so much? Because they hate themselves so much. Why's that? Because they're secretly ashamed to be con men, and their Cadillacs impart a respectability they don't really feel. So if you dent their fenders, you question the very depths of their identities.

Because *Tin Men* is based on fundamental truth, it is able to be funny even in some of its quieter moments. The good jokes always hurt a little. This movie isn't slapstick and it's not a farce; it's the kind of comedy the guy was thinking about when he wrote, "We laugh, that we may not cry."

To Be or Not To Be ★ ★ ★
R, 108 m., 1983

Mel Brooks (Bronski), Anne Bancroft (Anna Bronski), Tim Matheson (Lieutenant Sobinski), Charles Durning (Colonel Erhardt), Jose Ferrer (Professor Siletski). Directed by Alan Johnson and produced by Mel Brooks. Screenplay by Thomas Meehan and Ronny Graham.

It's an old gag, the one about the actor who is always interrupted in the middle of Hamlet's soliloquy by a guy in the third row who has to go to the john and loudly excuses himself all the way to the end of the row. But I can't think of a better Hamlet for this particular gag than Mel Brooks. "That is the QUESTION!" he bellows, as the guy screws up his timing, his delivery, his concentration. And the punch line is that the guy is actually going backstage to have a quick assignation with the actor's wife.

Mel Brooks loves show business and has worked it into a lot of his movies, most unforgettably in *The Producers*. He also loves musicals and has worked musical numbers into the most unlikely moments in his movies. (Remember Frankenstein's monster doing the soft-shoe?) In *To Be or Not To Be*, Brooks combines a backstage musical with a wartime romance and comes up with an eclectic comedy that races off into several directions, sometimes successfully.

The movie costars Brooks and his wife, Anne Bancroft, working together for the first time on screen as Frederick and (Anna) Bronski, the impresarios of a brave little theatrical troupe in Warsaw on the brink of war. (Anna) Bronski, whose name is in parentheses because her husband has such a big ego, is a femme fatale with an eye for the handsome young servicemen that worship her nightly in the theater. Bronski is an all-over-the-map guy who does Hamlet's soliloquy and stars in a revue called *Naughty Nazis* in the same night and on the same stage. Then the Nazis march into Poland. What can a humble troupe of actors do to stop them? "Nothing!" Bronski declares—but then the troupe gets involved in an elaborate masquerade, pretending to be real Nazis in order to throw Hitler's men off course and prevent the success of the German plans.

When *To Be or Not To Be* was originally made, by Ernst Lubitsch in 1942, the Nazis *were* in Poland, which gave a certain poignancy to every funny line. Lubitsch's stars were Jack Benny and Carole Lombard, both

specialists in underplaying. Brooks and Bancroft go in the opposite direction, cheerfully allowing farce, slapstick, pratfalls, and puns into the story, until the whole movie seems strung together like one of the revues in Bronski's theater.

The supporting players, given license to overact, have fun. Charles Durning plays a rigid but peculiarly confused Nazi colonel, and Tim Matheson is the young aviator who excuses himself loudly and sneaks backstage to meet Bancroft. The veteran actor Jose Ferrer plays Professor Siletski, a two-faced collaborator.

It will probably always be impossible for Brooks to remain entirely within the dramatic logic of any story, and here he gives himself a lot of freedom with lines like "Sondheim! Send in the clowns!" But *To Be or Not To Be* works as well as a story as any Brooks film since *Young Frankenstein*, and darned if there isn't a little sentiment involved as the impresario and his wife, after years of marriage, surprise each other by actually falling in love.

To Live ★ ★ ★ ½
NO MPAA RATING, 125 m., 1994

NEW

Ge You (Fugui), Gong Li (Jiazhin), Niu Ben (Townchief Niu), Guo Tao (Chunsheng), Jiang Wu (Erxi), Ni Dahong (Long Er), Liu Tianchi (Fengxia [adult]), Zhang Lu (Fengxia [teen]). Directed by Zhang Yimou and produced by Chiu Fusheng. Screenplay by Yu Hua and Lu Wei.

To Live is a simple title, but it conceals a universe. The film follows the life of one family in China, from the heady days of gambling dens in the 1940s to the austere hardship of the Cultural Revolution in the 1960s. And through all of their fierce struggles with fate, all of the political twists and turns they endure, their hope is basically one summed up by the heroine, a wife who loses wealth and position and children, and who says, "All I ask is a quiet life together."

The movie has been directed by Zhang Yimou, the leading Chinese filmmaker of his generation (although this film offended Beijing and earned him a two-year ban from filmmaking). It stars his wife, Gong Li, the leading Chinese actress (likewise banned). Together their credits include *Ju Dou, Raise the Red Lantern*, and *The Story of Qui Ju*. Like them it follows the fate of a strong woman, but also this time a strong man; somehow they stick together through incredible hardships.

At first, the troubles are the husband's own fault. Fugui (Ge You) is a degenerate gambler who loses his family, home, and fortune at dice. "Turtle spawn!" his old father cries, beating him with a stick. His wife, Jiazhen (Gong Li), wants nothing more to do with him, and from a life of indolence he finds himself selling needles and thread on the street.

The man who won his house gives him a set of beautiful shadow puppets, and he goes on the road as an entertainer, quickly swept up by the Nationalist army to amuse the troops. Then one morning, drunk, he oversleeps as the army retreats, and he hears a thundering sound on the snow, which is the Red army advancing. Ever adaptable, he joins them, and eventually finds his way back to his hometown and his wife, son, and daughter.

Life is very hard. But they survive under the new communist regime. (Ironically, the man who won his house at dice is executed as a counterrevolutionary landowner.) A childhood illness causes their daughter to become mute and hard of hearing, but in the precise arithmetic of matchmaking a likely partner is found for her: a supervisor of the Red Guards at a factory, who is lame.

The story progresses in terms of temporary advances and crushing setbacks, one caused when a starving doctor, jailed by the Red Guards, cannot assist at a crucial time because he has gorged himself on seven sweet buns. Another family loss is caused by an old friend, who vows he owes them a life, and will eventually be called upon for repayment. Years come and go; jolly murals of Mao Tse Tung appear on the courtyard walls, and then fade in the sun and rain. And somehow they live.

The best art, it is said, comes from turmoil—from hard times. In China no serious filmmaking took place for decades, and now great films are coming in a torrent from that country. The authorities are not always so happy to have the nation's past examined with such frankness, and with films like *To Live* and *Blue Kite* (also released in 1994) there is a certain inexorable pattern: They are made, shown at foreign film festivals, honored (*To Live* won acting awards at Cannes), and are successful on the art house circuit—but in China they play briefly in a few sophisticated cinemas in Beijing or Shanghai, and then they disappear.

The honesty of *To Live* earned Zhang Yimou and Gong Li not only a two-year ban on further coproductions, but a ban on even speaking about their film. But *To Live* has been made, it has played all over the world, it exists on the screen as a fascinating testament about ordinary human lives conducted under terrifying conditions, when one's fate could hinge on a chance remark or an instant political edict from a zealous teenager.

To Live is a big, strong, energetic film, made by a filmmaker whose vision takes in four decades of his nation's history, and who stands apart from all the political currents, and sees that ordinary people everywhere basically want what his heroine cries out for, a quiet life. It is exciting to see these new films as they emerge from China. They are history being written, celebrated, and mourned.

To Live and Die in L.A. ★ ★ ★ ★
R, 110 m., 1985

William L. Petersen (Richard Chance), Willem Dafoe (Eric Masters), John Pankow (John Vukovich), Debra Feuer (Bianca Torres), John Turturro (Carl Cody), Darlanne Fluegel (Ruth Lanier), Dean Stockwell (Bob Grimes), Robert Downey (Thomas Bateman). Directed by William Friedkin and produced by Irving H. Levin. Screenplay by Gerald Petievich and Friedkin.

In the hierarchy of great movie chase sequences, the recent landmarks include the chases under the Brooklyn elevated tracks in *The French Connection,* down the hills of San Francisco in *Bullitt,* and through the Paris Metro in *Diva.* Those chases were not only thrilling in their own right, but they reflected the essence of the cities where they took place. Now comes William Friedkin, director of *The French Connection,* with a movie that contains a second chase that belongs on that short list. The movie is set in Los Angeles, and so of course the chase centers around the freeway system.

To Live and Die in L.A. is a law enforcement movie, sort of. It's about Secret Service agents who are on the trail of a counterfeiter who has eluded the law for years, and who flaunts his success. At one point, when undercover agents are negotiating a deal with the counterfeiter in his expensive health club, he boasts, "I've been coming to this gym three times a week for five years. I'm an easy guy to find. People know they can trust me."

Meanwhile, he's asking for a down payment on a sale of bogus bills, and the down payment is larger than the Secret Service can authorize. So, Richard Chance (William L. Petersen), the hot-dog special agent who's the hero of the movie, sets up a dangerous plan to steal the advance money from another crook, and uses it to buy the bogus paper and bust the counterfeiter.

Neat. The whole plot is neat, revolving around a few central emotions—friendship, loyalty, arrogance, anger. By the time the great chase sequence arrives, it isn't just a novelty, tacked onto a movie where it doesn't fit. It's part of the plot. The Secret Service agents bungle *their* crime, the cops come in pursuit, and the chase unfolds in a long, dazzling ballet of timing, speed, and imagination.

The great chases are rarely just chases. They involve some kind of additional element—an unexpected vehicle, an unusual challenge, a strange setting. The car-train chase in *The French Connection* was a masterstroke. In *Diva,* the courier rode his motor scooter into one subway station and out another, bouncing up and down the stairs. Or think of John Ford's sustained stagecoach chase in *Stagecoach,* or the way Buster Keaton orchestrated *The General* so that trains chased each other through a railway system.

The masterstroke in *To Live and Die in L.A.* is that the chase isn't just on a freeway. It goes *the wrong way* down the freeway. I don't know how Friedkin choreographed this scene and I don't want to know. It probably took a lot of money and a lot of drivers. All I know is that there are high-angle shots during the chase during which you can look a long way ahead and see hundreds of cars across four lanes, all heading for the escape car which is aimed at them, full-speed. It is an amazing sequence.

The rest of the movie is also first-rate. The direction is the key. Friedkin has made some good movies (*The French Connection, The Exorcist, Sorcerer*) and some bad ones (*Cruising, Deal of the Century*). This is his comeback, showing the depth and skill of the early pictures. The central performance is by William L. Petersen, a Chicago stage actor who comes across as tough, wiry, and smart. He has some of the qualities of a Steve McQueen, with more complexity. Another strong performance in the movie is by Willem Dafoe, as the counterfeiter, cool and professional as he discusses the realities of his business.

I like movies which teach me about something, movies which have researched their subject and contain a lot of information, casually contained in between the big dramatic scenes. *To Live and Die in L.A.* seems to know a lot about counterfeiting, and also about the interior policies of the Secret Service. The film isn't just about cops and robbers, but about two systems of doing business, and how one of the systems finds a way to change itself in order to defeat the other. That's interesting. So is the chase.

Tom And Viv ★ ★ ½
PG-13, 115 m., 1995

Willem Dafoe (Tom), Miranda Richardson (Viv), Tim Dutton (Maurice), Nickolas Grace (Bertrand Russell). Directed by Brian Gilbert and produced by Peter Samuelson, Marc Samuelson, and Harvey Kass. Screenplay by Michael Hastings and Adrian Hodges.

> *And I pray that I may forget*
> *Those matters that with myself*
> *I too much discuss.*
> —T.S. Eliot, "Ash-Wednesday" (1930)

At some point in their marriage Tom went mad, and promptly certified his wife.
> —Edith Sitwell

For forty years or more, up until the mid-1960s when everything went up for grabs, T.S. Eliot represented a severe poetic theology for graduate students of English, who when sober would agonize over his bleak vision of a world without surcease, and when drunk would declaim, "I grow old . . . I grow old . . . I shall wear the bottoms of my trousers rolled. Shall I part my hair behind? Do I dare to eat a peach?" Then came the decade when no one parted their hair and everyone ate the peach, and Eliot's moment passed.

Does anyone read Eliot anymore? I took down the well-worn volume this evening, and looked again through "Prufrock" and the "Quartets," hearing that familiar voice, so measured, so sad, so dry. There was obviously something behind those mournful lines, something deeply buried in the conscience. I remembered college lectures from long-ago afternoons: ". . . unhappy first marriage . . . wife insane . . . finally found happiness in second marriage. . . ."

The official line on T.S. Eliot was that in choosing his first bride, he made a very bad mistake. The young man from St. Louis who graduated from Harvard and moved to London and tried all his life to be a proper British gentleman married a woman who would make that almost impossible. Vivienne Eliot stalks through the pages of Eliot's biographers as a hysterical, paranoid, drug-ad-

dicted cross for him to bear. Only after Eliot joined with Vivienne's family to commit her to an asylum did he find peace. Memoirs by friends such as Robert Sencourt indicate that he had the patience of a saint in waiting as long as he did before he took that action.

So that was the official line. Then, in 1984, Michael Hastings wrote a play named *Tom and Viv* that told another story. In his revisionist view, Vivienne was a passionate, high-strung woman who was never an appropriate partner for a stick like Eliot. But he wooed her and won her, and then, dismayed by such revelations as her excessive menstrual flow, he reacted with revulsion to her, driving her mad. It didn't help that she had some kind of hormonal imbalance that today could be quickly and simply treated. The alcohol, the pills, and the ether that she ingested didn't help, either.

Eliot doesn't emerge from the Hastings version looking like a very nice man. After he committed his wife to an institution he never visited her, not once. And there she lived out her days. In the version according to Brian Gilbert's film *Tom and Viv,* the first Mrs. Eliot was more sinned against than sinning, and Tom was, in the words of one character, an "egotistical little shit who would like to be a saint."

It is a good story and a fascinating mystery. Unfortunately, *Tom and Viv* skids across the surface of it, failing to show us what passion or misunderstanding brought these two people together in the first place, or why they stayed together so long, or why we should care. If you are not thoroughly familiar with Eliot's poetry you will probably wonder, while watching the movie, what all the fuss is about; poetry is sort of his vague pastime in between emotional showdowns, and there is not enough sense of the role he played, between the wars, as a moral guide—a function that makes Hastings's charges more shocking.

The film is well cast. Willem Dafoe looks a little like Eliot, and has a dry, laconic, mid-Atlantic accent that might approximate his speaking voice. He is given the thankless task of suffering in silence much of the time, and hardly ever truly speaking from his real feelings, and yet he communicates the idea of a man whose poetry is "These fragments I have shored against my ruins."

Miranda Richardson, as Vivienne, is another case altogether. Richardson is a superb actress, and gives a strong performance here—but as who? The movie seems unable to decide exactly what was the matter with Viv-

ienne, although something surely was. Her brother, Maurice, advises Tom before the marriage that she needs "careful handling . . . this-side-up sort of thing." Women at dinner parties are likely to whisper to Eliot, "You do understand what she's doing to your reputation?"

She weeps, she makes embarrassing statements in public, she is hysterical, she shoves chocolate through the mail slot at Faber and Faber, where Eliot is an editor, and finally she is put into the hands of psychiatrists, and the movie can relax: It's always easy to dramatize the excesses of mental health practitioners, and so we sympathize with Vivienne while a couple of shrinks grill her with questions about monkeys and greasy poles.

Yes, how she was treated is a scandal. She was locked away for years, until, although apparently quite sane, she was incapable of remembering how to return to ordinary life. But what was the trouble, exactly? And what were the motives for Eliot's behavior? Did he commit her and then heartlessly forget her? Or stay away because that was less painful for them both?

Tom and Viv is the kind of movie that will make slow sailing for anyone who doesn't come to it with a lot of information about Tom and Viv. And *then* the problem is, the more you know about them, the less it satisfies. But it makes an intriguing footnote.

Tommy ★ ★ ★
PG, 108 m., 1975

Ann-Margret (Nora Walker), Oliver Reed (Frank Hobbs), Roger Daltrey (Tommy), Elton John (Pinball Wizard), Eric Clapton (Preacher), Keith Moon (Uncle Ernie), Jack Nicholson (Specialist), Tina Turner (Acid Queen). The Who: Pete Townshend, John Entwhistle, Daltrey, and Moon. Directed by Ken Russell and produced by Robert Stigwood and Russell. Screenplay by Russell.

Ken Russell's *Tommy* is a case of glorious overkill—a big, brassy, vulgar overproduction that works because it never stops for a breath or a second thought. It's got confidence. It's a blast of wall-to-wall music for almost two hours, and its quietest moment is a Moog-synthesized belch from Oliver Reed that sounds like the Carlsbad Caverns throwing up. There's not the slightest hint of moderation or restraint in the movie, and there shouldn't be. This is Ken Russell giving a Bronx cheer to the most pretentious of the late 1960s rock operas, turning it into a clothesline on which he strings a series of bizarre, manic production numbers. Sit down in front, slide back in your seat, and let it assault you.

The movie's purpose and achievement would be hard to figure out on the basis of what its makers say about it. Pete Townshend, who wrote the original album for The Who, says *Tommy* is an attack on the hypocrisy of organized religion. Ken Russell, who's made a specialty of films about musicians (Tchaikovsky, Mahler, and Liszt), says *Tommy* is the greatest work of art the twentieth century has produced. He was almost certainly misquoted. What he meant to say was that it was a heaven-sent opportunity for him to exercise his gift for going too far, for creating three-ring cinematic circuses with kinky sideshows.

The message of *Tommy,* if any, is contained mostly in the last thirty minutes (of which we could have done without about fifteen). By then the hero (who started out in life as a blind deaf-mute) has become the pinball superstar of all time, even though he can't see the machine. Stardom brings him a fortune, he becomes the leader of a quasireligious cult, regains his senses, and gets his own Tommy T-shirt. But then things get out of hand. Tommy is on the level, but the people around him begin to commercialize on his fame in order to peddle T-shirts, record albums, and other artifacts. Tommy's enraged fans turn on him and what they perceive as his hypocrisy. How the makers of the film feel about this commercialization can be gauged by the prominence with which the end titles inform us that the sound-track album is available on Polydor Records. To make money on a rock opera attacking those who would make money on a rock opera: that was the brave moral stand taken by *Tommy.*

But none of this matters, because Russell correctly doesn't give a damn about the material he started with, greatest art work of the century or not, and he just goes ahead and gives us one glorious excess after another. He is aided by his performers, especially Ann-Margret, who is simply great as Tommy's mother. She has one number that begins in an all-white bedroom with her sexy red dress slit up the side to about the collarbone, and ends with her slithering through several hundred pounds of baked beans. It's that kind of movie.

Tommy's odyssey through life is punctuated by encounters with all sorts of weird folks, of whom the most seductive is Tina Turner as the Acid Queen. The scene begins with Tina as the hooker upstairs from the strip parlor operated by Tommy's wicked stepfather, and ends with a psychedelic stainless steel mummy with acid in its veins. This scene is the occasion for Tommy's first smile, as well it might be.

Then there's the great pinball tournament, which is the movie's best single scene: a pulsating, orgiastic turn-on edited with the precision of a machine gun burst. Elton John, wearing skyscraper shoes, is the defending pinball champion. Tommy is the challenger. Russell cuts between the crowds, the arena, and a dizzying series of close-ups of the games (at times, we almost seem to be inside the pinball machines), and the effect is exhilarating and exhausting.

Too Beautiful for You ★ ★ ★ ½
R, 91 m., 1990

Gerard Depardieu (Bernard), Josiane Balasko (Colette), Carole Bouquet (Florence), Roland Blanche (Marcello), Francois Cluzet (Pascal), Didier Benureau (Leonce), Philippe Loffredo (Tanguy), Sylvie Orcier (Marie-Catherine). Directed, produced, and written by Bertrand Blier.

Lust occurs between bodies. Love occurs between personalities. Because we see the outsides of others but know the thoughts of ourselves, this truth causes a great deal of unhappiness and misunderstanding. And that is the subject of *Too Beautiful for You,* the story of a man who has a beautiful wife and yet falls in love with his dumpy secretary.

She isn't much to look at—so you might say, unless you saw the dreaminess in her eyes after she has been brought to passion. She wears fuzzy sweaters that she pulls down over the skirts that cling to her generous hips. She knows little about the cosmetic arts. Her hair style is sensible—which means that after you wash it and dry it, it looks washed and dried. The moment he lays eyes on her, he is thunderstruck. Her presence speaks to something deep and elemental inside of him. He cannot tear his eyes away from her.

His name is Bernard. He is played by Gerard Depardieu, that superb French actor who always seems afraid to break something. Her name is Colette. She is played by Josiane Balasko with such an honesty that you understand why anyone would love her. The wife, the woman who fulfills all standards of modern fashionable beauty, is played by Carole Bouquet, who in other films has shown herself to be warm and comical, but in this film is just what she's supposed to be—a woman whose beauty is no match for a woman who can touch a man's heart.

In *Too Beautiful for You,* Bertrand Blier tells the story of these people in a curious way that takes a little getting used to. He opens with strong, stark images of passion, and then allows some of the characters to talk directly to the audience, and then uses fantasy scenes in which we see what it would be like if the fears of adulterers were ever made real. In the most startling of the fantasies, the wife addresses a dinner party at which Colette is present and tells her friends that she knows they have always hated her because she was too beautiful.

The opening scene of the movie takes place in Bernard's automobile dealership. Colette is the new secretary. Through the glass walls of the offices, he can see her sitting in her cubicle. Their eyes meet, and then they exchange one of those groin-wrenching moments of instantaneous passion that only the movies can do justice to (I was reminded of the way Gene Tierney stared rudely and speechlessly at a man on a train in *Leave Her to Heaven*). He turns away from the strength of it. He cannot hear her, but she talks to him: "Please turn around and look at me."

The day comes to an end. They cannot get each other out of their thoughts. All day long, she has spoken to him—but only we could hear her—in terms of such tenderness and understanding that we want to hug her. She leaves to go to the bus stop. He runs after her. He has missed her. No—here she is! They look in each other's eyes and all is known between them, and all is lost.

This is grown-up love, not the silly adolescent posturing of Hollywood sex symbols. It is love beyond sex, beyond attraction, beyond lust. It is the love of need, the love that says, I am a puzzle and you are the solution. The rest of the movie's story circles around the great fact of this love.

Depardieu is one of the most endlessly fascinating actors of our time. He works constantly, in roles of such variety that to list them is astonishing: He was the hunchbacked farmer in *Jean de Florette,* and the sculptor Rodin in *Camille Claudel,* and the imposter in *The Return of Martin Guerre.* Here he plays just an ordinary man—one of the most difficult roles in the movies. He makes his passion believable because he never overacts it, and because the movie conveys it mostly through the eyes of the actress, Balasko. She sees that she is loved. Bouquet, in the movie's most difficult role, has to accept defeat of a sort: She is beautiful, but that has not been enough. People envy her and she knows she is not to be envied.

Somebody was asking the other day what the difference was between French and American films. American films are about plots, I said, and French films are about people. You can usually tell where a plot is heading, but a person, now—a person will fool you.

Tootsie ★ ★ ★ ★
PG, 116 m., 1982

Dustin Hoffman (Michael), Jessica Lange (Julie), Charles Durning (Les Nichols), Teri Garr (Sandy), Bill Murray (Roommate), Dabney Coleman (Ron), Doris Belack (Rita), Sydney Pollack (Agent). Directed by Sydney Pollack and produced by Dick Richards. Screenplay by Larry Gelbart.

One of the most endearing things about *Tootsie*, a movie in which Dustin Hoffman plays a middle-aged actress, is that the actress is able to carry most of her own scenes as herself—even if she weren't being played by Hoffman. *Tootsie* works as a story, not as a gimmick. It also works as a lot of other things. *Tootsie* is the kind of Movie with a capital M that they used to make in the 1940s, when they weren't afraid to mix up absurdity with seriousness, social comment with farce, and a little heartfelt tenderness right in there with the laughs. This movie gets you coming and going.

Hoffman stars as Michael Dorsey, a character maybe not unlike Hoffman himself in his younger days. Michael is a New York actor: bright, aggressive, talented—and unemployable. "You mean *nobody* in New York wants to hire me?" he asks his agent, incredulously. "I'd go farther than that, Michael," his agent says. "Nobody in Hollywood wants to hire you, either." Michael has a bad reputation for taking stands, throwing tantrums, and interpreting roles differently than the director. How to get work? He goes with a friend (Teri Garr) to an audition for a soap opera. The character is a middle-aged woman hospital administrator. When his friend doesn't get the job, Michael goes home, thinks, decides to dare, and dresses himself as a woman. And, improvising brilliantly, he gets the role.

That leads to *Tootsie*'s central question:

Can a fortyish New York actor find health, happiness, and romance as a fortyish New York actress? Dustin Hoffman is actually fairly plausible as "Dorothy," the actress. If his voice isn't quite right, a Southern accent allows it to squeak by. The wig and the glasses are a little too much, true, but in an uncanny way the woman played by Hoffman looks like certain actual women who look like drag queens. Dorothy might have trouble passing in Evanston, but in Manhattan, nobody gives her a second look.

Tootsie might have been content to limit itself to the complications of New York life in drag; it could have been *Victor/Victoria Visits Elaine's*. But the movie's a little more ambitious than that. Michael Dorsey finds to his interest and amusement that Dorothy begins to take on a life of her own. She's a liberated eccentric, a woman who seems sort of odd and funny at first, but grows on you and wins your admiration by standing up for what's right. One of the things that bothers Dorothy is the way the soap opera's chauvinist director (Dabney Coleman) mistreats and insults the attractive young actress (Jessica Lange) who plays Julie, a nurse on the show. Dorothy and Julie become friends and finally close confidantes. Dorothy's problem, however, is that the man inside her is gradually growing uncontrollably in love with Julie. There are other complications. Julie's father (Charles Durning), a gruff, friendly, no-nonsense sort, lonely but sweet, falls in love with Dorothy. Michael hardly knows how to deal with all of this, and his roommate (Bill Murray) isn't much help. Surveying Dorothy in one of her new outfits, he observes dryly, "Don't play hard to get."

Tootsie has a lot of fun with its plot complications; we get almost every possible variation on the theme of mistaken sexual identities. The movie also manages to make some lighthearted but well-aimed observations about sexism. It *also* pokes satirical fun at soap operas, New York show-business agents, and the Manhattan social pecking-order. *And* it turns out to be a touching love story, after all—so touching that you may be surprised how moved you are at the conclusion of this comedy.

Topaz ★ ★ ★ ½
PG, 124 m., 1970

Frederick Stafford (Andre Deveraux), Dany Robin (Nicole, His Wife), John Vernon (Rico Parra), Karin Dor (Juanita), Michel Piccoli

(Jacques Granville), Philippe Noiret (Henri Jarre), John Forsythe (Nordstrom). Directed by Alfred Hitchcock. Screenplay by Samuel Taylor.

In some ways *Topaz* is a perfectly typical Alfred Hitchcock movie, but in other ways it's something new and rather unexpected from the master. The Hitchcock style is still there, all right: The action in incongruous places, the montages showing cause and effect, the sinister qualities of everyday objects, the tightly programmed editing style. That's all there and, even if you don't notice it, it works the old Hitchcock tricks on you and you're scared when he wants you to be. But what's new in *Topaz* is Hitchcock's choice of a field of action. He goes much wider this time, using three groups of protagonists instead of one or two central characters, and his subject is nothing less than the spy systems of the Cold War.

Hitchcock claimed, and he was probably telling the truth, that he really didn't care what his movies were about. He approached them scientifically, manipulating his actors to produce the desired effects in the audience. He liked to get suspense when he wanted it; he liked to play an audience like a piano. In most of his movies, then, he ignored the "real" world and made no attempt to show things as they might really happen. He shut everybody into a Hitchcock universe and tried to trap you in it, too.

So his basic theme was usually the same: An innocent man, wrongly accused, is placed in a position where he must clear himself before he is overtaken by either the bad guys or the law. This theme is terribly useful for getting viewers involved and perhaps (psychology aside) that's why Hitchcock likes it. But in *Topaz*, he made one of his occasional excursions into other areas, and this time he went farther afield than he ever did in *Foreign Correspondent* or *The 39 Steps* or *The Birds*.

Properly speaking, *Topaz* doesn't have a hero, although it has two or three characters who function that way occasionally. It doesn't have a hero because it doesn't have a moral point of view; Hitchcock deals with an American-French-Cuban spy network at the time of the Cuban missile crisis, and yet his focus is so firmly on the spies as professionals that we hardly get the feeling we should be for the French or against the Cubans. The plot is complex, with a lot of characters left over from the mediocre Leon Uris novel. The action moves from Washington to New York to

Havana to Paris as two spy networks conspire to get information on the missile crisis to either Washington or Moscow. The movie begins with a good chase scene in Denmark, where a high-ranking Russian has defected. It's not a *Bullitt*-type chase with lots of speed and fast cutting, but one of those Hitchcock chases where everyone's forced to walk slowly and act naturally and smile a lot, nervously. The Americans finally get the Russian back to Washington where he reveals information about the Cuban missiles and also about a security leak in Paris.

Hitchcock does a good job of re-creating that far-off time, 1963. There is a fascinating sequence in Harlem where the Cuban UN delegation (remember?) had taken over the Theresa Hotel. The idea is to get some papers to photograph them. Hitchcock uses a remarkable actor, Roscoe Lee Browne, as a black journalist who saunters in and breezes out again with the secrets. Browne's scenes are the most delightful in the movie; for the most part, Hitchcock allowed his actors to remain so wooden they all look alike.

There is then some hanky-panky in Cuba, including the most protracted tearful-death scene in years (the beautiful Karin Dor done in by blue-eyed, sinister John Vernon). And then the action switches to Paris for the complicated conclusion. The interesting thing about that conclusion, by the way, is that Hitchcock goes out on a downbeat. There's no climax, no chase; just the sordid working-out of a messy game of spying. It's a nice, quiet ending, very much in keeping with the film, and *Topaz* is good Hitchcock. When you see it, wait for that scene where Michel Piccoli urges Philippe Noiret to hurry up and drink his cognac, and you tell me if you believe Piccoli expects a visitor.

Top Gun ★ ★ ½
PG, 109 m., 1986

Tom Cruise (Maverick), Kelly McGillis (Charlie), Val Kilmer (Iceman), Tom Skerritt (Viper), Anthony Edwards (Goose). Directed by Tony Scott and produced by Don Simpson and Jerry Bruckheimer. Screenplay by Jim Cash and Jack Epps, Jr.

In the opening moments of *Top Gun*, a skilled Navy pilot flies upside down about four feet above a Soviet-built jet fighter and snaps a Polaroid picture of the enemy pilot. Then he flips him the finger and peels off.

It's a hot-dog stunt, but it makes the pilot (Tom Cruise) famous within the small circle of Navy personnel who are cleared to receive information about close encounters with enemy aircraft. And the pilot, whose code name is Maverick, is selected for the Navy's elite flying school, which is dedicated to the dying art of aerial dogfights. The best graduate from each class at the school is known as "Top Gun."

And there, I think, you have the basic materials of this movie, except, of course, for three more obligatory ingredients in all movies about brave young pilots: (1) the girl, (2) the mystery of the heroic father, and (3) the rivalry with another pilot. It turns out that Maverick's dad was a brilliant Navy jet pilot during the Vietnam era, until he and his plane disappeared in unexplained circumstances. And it also turns out that one of the instructors at the flying school is a pretty young blonde (Kelly McGillis) who wants to know a lot more about how Maverick snapped that other pilot's picture.

Top Gun settles fairly quickly into alternating ground and air scenes, and the simplest way to sum it up is to declare the air scenes brilliant and the earthbound scenes grimly predictable. This movie comes in two parts: It knows exactly what to do with special effects, but doesn't have a clue as to how two people in love might act and talk and think.

Aerial scenes always present a special challenge in a movie. There's the danger that the audience will become spatially disoriented. We're used to seeing things within a frame that respects left and right, up and down, but the fighter pilot lives in a world of 360-degree turns. The remarkable achievement in *Top Gun* is that it presents seven or eight aerial encounters that are so well choreographed that we can actually follow them most of the time, and the movie gives us a good secondhand sense of what it might be like to be in a dogfight.

The movie's first and last sequences involve encounters with enemy planes. Although the planes are Soviet, the movie provides no nationalities for their pilots. We're told the battles take place over the Indian Ocean, and that's it. All of the sequences in between take place at Top Gun school, where Maverick quickly gets locked into a personal duel with another brilliant pilot, Iceman (Val Kilmer). In one sequence after another, the sound track trembles as the sleek planes pursue each other through the clouds, and, yeah, it's exciting. But the love story between Cruise and McGillis is a washout.

It's pale and unconvincing compared with the chemistry between Cruise and Rebecca De Mornay in *Risky Business*, and between McGillis and Harrison Ford in *Witness*—not to mention between Richard Gere and Debra Winger in *An Officer and a Gentleman,* which obviously inspired *Top Gun.* Cruise and McGillis spend a lot of time squinting uneasily at each other and exchanging words as if they were weapons, and when they finally get physical, they look like the stars of one of those sexy perfume ads. There's no flesh and blood here, which is remarkable, given the almost palpable physical presence McGillis had in *Witness.*

In its other ground scenes, the movie seems content to recycle clichés and conventions out of countless other war movies. Wouldn't you know, for example, that Maverick's commanding officer is the only man who knows what happened to the kid's father in Vietnam? And are we surprised when Maverick's best friend dies in his arms? Is there any suspense as Maverick undergoes his obligatory crisis of conscience, wondering whether he can ever fly again?

Movies like *Top Gun* are hard to review because the good parts are so good and the bad parts are so relentless. The dogfights are absolutely the best since Clint Eastwood's electrifying aerial scenes in *Firefox.* But look out for the scenes where the people talk to one another.

Top Secret! ★ ★ ★ ½
R, 90 m., 1984

Val Kilmer (Nick Rivers), Lucy Gutteridge (Hillary), Omar Sharif (Cedric), Peter Cushing (Bookseller). Directed by Jim Abrahams, David Zucker, and Jerry Zucker and produced by Jon Davison and Hunt Lowry. Written by Abrahams, Zucker and Zucker, with Martyn Burke.

I have a friend who claims he only laughed real loud on five occasions during *Top Secret!* I laughed that much in the first ten minutes. It all depends on your sense of humor. My friend claims that I have a cornpone sense of humor, because of my origins deep in central Illinois. I admit that is true. As a Gemini, however, I contain multitudes, and I also have a highly sophisticated, sharply intellectual sense of humor. Get me in the right mood, and I can laugh all over the map. That's why I liked *Top Secret!* This movie will cheerfully go for a laugh wherever one is even remotely likely to be found. It has political jokes and boob jokes, dog poop jokes, and ballet jokes. It makes fun of two completely different Hollywood genres: the spy movie and the Elvis Presley musical. It contains a political refugee who fled America by balloon during the Carter administration, a member of the French underground named Escargot, and Omar Sharif inside a compacted automobile.

To describe the plot would be an exercise in futility. This movie has no plot. It does not need a plot. One does not attend movies like *Top Secret!* in order to follow the story line. I think you can figure that out right away, in the opening sequence, which is devoted to the sport of "skeet surfin" and has beach boys on surfboards firing at clay targets. Instead of a plot, it has a funny young actor named Val Kilmer as the hero, a 1950s-style American rock 'n' roller who is sent on a concert tour behind the Iron Curtain, and manages to reduce East Germany to a shambles while never missing a word of "Tutti Frutti" (he never even stumbles during *a wop-bop-a-loo-bop, a lop-bam-boom*).

The movie is physical humor, sight gags, puns, double meanings, satire, weird choreography, scatalogical outrages, and inanity. One particular sequence, however, is such an original example of specifically cinematic humor that I'd like to discuss it at length. (Do not read further if you don't like to understand jokes before laughing at them.) The sequence involves a visit by the hero to a Swedish bookshop. Never mind why he goes there. The scene depends for its inspiration on this observation: People who run tape recorders backward often say that English, played backward, sounds like Swedish (especially, of course, to people who do not speak Swedish). What *Top Secret!* does is to film an entire scene and play it backward, so that the dialogue sounds Swedish, and then translate it into English subtitles. This is funny enough at the beginning, but it becomes inspired at the end, when the scene finally gives itself away.

There are other wonderful moments. The dance sequence in the East Berlin nightclub develops into something Groucho Marx would have been proud of. The malt shop musical number demolishes a whole tradition of Elvis Presley numbers. And how the ballerina makes her exit in *Swan Lake* will, I feel confident, be discussed for years wherever codpieces are sold.

Torch Song Trilogy ★ ★ ★ ½
R, 120 m., 1988

Harvey Fierstein (Arnold), Anne Bancroft (Ma), Matthew Broderick (Alan), Brian Kerwin (Ed), Karen Young (Laurel), Eddie Castrodad (David), Ken Page (Murray), Charles Pierce (Bertha Venation), Axel Vera (Marina Del Rey). Directed by Paul Bogart and produced by Howard Gottfried. Screenplay by Harvey Fierstein.

Torch Song Trilogy opens with a close-up of Arnold, the hero, looking his very worst. He's backstage at the drag club where he works as a female impersonator, and he's halfway into his makeup. You can see every facial flaw—of the male face underneath and the female face he's applying to the surface. Cigarette smoke drifts through the shot. You can almost smell the cold cream. He's talking about his life as a homosexual, and there are moments when his voice catches with emotion. We're touched that he's revealing himself so honestly. But then, of course, he breaks the spell with a throwaway oneliner.

He breaks a lot of spells that way. This is a man who has used sarcasm and self-satire to build a wall around himself. One of the earliest scenes in the movie is a flashback to childhood, when his mother surprises him on the floor of her closet playing dress-up with her high heels and her makeup. It is obvious that dressing like a woman is important to him, but later he turns that part of himself into a parody, as a drag queen who laughs first so that the joke is never on him.

Torch Song Trilogy is basically a movie about a man who slowly becomes more comfortable with himself. As written and performed by Harvey Fierstein as a long-running stage hit, it was seen as a sort of nostalgic visit to the problems gays had in the years before the horror of AIDS. The movie has more or less the same focus, but because it's a movie, it becomes more intimate and intense. It's about a man who was born gay, and has known about himself from an early age, and has accepted his homosexuality more easily than certain other facets of himself—such as his fear of loneliness, his painful insecurity about his appearance, and his almost paralyzing shyness. Homosexuality is not his problem—it is the arena for his problems.

I'm glad they let Fierstein star in the movie himself. There might have been a temptation to go out and hire some established,

bankable star who could win points for his courage in playing a gay (compare Richard Burton and Rex Harrison in *Staircase*). That would have been phony from the outset, but it would also have denied us a look at this extraordinary individual with the deep, raspy voice, and the exaggerated double takes, and the face that looks handsome from some angles, goofy from others, and ravaged when he has a hangover. I have not seen anyone quite like Harvey Fierstein in the movies before, and the fact that he is a specific individual gives this material a charm and weight it might have lacked if an interchangeable actor had played the role.

The movie is told in three major parts, with some moments in between. Arnold falls in love with Ed, a bisexual man (Brian Kerwin) who is not sure of his sexuality and certainly not sure of Arnold. Arnold loses Ed. Arnold falls in love with Alan (Matthew Broderick), and they love each other and try to build a life together. Alan is killed by gaybashers. Devastated, Arnold falls into a deep depression, which is mostly offscreen; in the last part of the film, he is friends again with Ed, and he has adopted a gay teen-ager and sounds exactly like his mother when he talks to the kid.

Written down starkly like that, the movie almost sounds like a formula of love and loss. But *Torch Song Trilogy* is seen in a lot of specific scenes, in moments like the one where Arnold wakes up before Ed in the morning, dashes into the bathroom to make himself look as good as possible, and then jumps back into bed a second before the alarm goes off. Or the moments in the alley outside the nightclub, where Arnold's friend Bertha (Charles Pierce), also a drag queen, provides a few words of advice that come from a lifetime of experience. Or the painful scene in a gay bar where Arnold is so shy he can hardly bring himself to respond to Ed. A person emerges from these moments.

There are some passages that don't work very well. The whole business of the adopted son feels unconvincing and tacked-on, and Eddie Castrodad plays the teen-ager like the precocious host of his own party. Another awkward scene involves a weekend in the country, with Arnold and Alan visiting Ed and his bride (Karen Young). Ed and Alan wind up in the hayloft (of all places), but I was never sure what the point of their infidelity was supposed to be.

The movie's ending is a powerful, painful confrontation between Arnold and his mother

(Anne Bancroft). I've had reservations about Bancroft in some of her recent performances because she tends to go over the top, but here there is no reason to hold back. She is the demonstrative, emotional mother of a son who shares many of the same mannerisms, and I believed her in the role. I also believed Arnold when he finally told her exactly what he thought about his sexuality and her attitude toward it, and when he said, "There are two things I demand from the people in my life: love and respect." He could have been speaking for anybody.

Total Recall ★ ★ ★ ½
R, 110 m., 1990

Arnold Schwarzenegger (Quaid), Rachel Ticotin (Melina), Sharon Stone (Lori), Ronny Cox (Cohaagen), Michael Ironside (Richter), Marshall Bell (George/Kuato), Michael Champion (Helm), Mel Johnson, Jr. (Benny), Roy Brocksmith (Dr. Edgemar). Directed by Paul Verhoeven and produced by Buzz Feitshans and Ronald Shusett. Screenplay by Shusett, Dan O'Bannon, and Gary Goldman.

There may be people who overlook the Arnold Schwarzenegger performance in *Total Recall*—who think he isn't really acting. But the performance is one of the reasons the movie works so well. He isn't a superman this time, although he fights like one. He's a confused and frightened innocent, a man betrayed by the structure of reality itself. And in his vulnerability, he opens the way for *Total Recall* to be more than simply an action, violence, and special-effects extravaganza.

There is a lot of action and violence in the movie, and almost every shot seems to embody some sort of special effect. This is one of the most complex and visually interesting science-fiction movies in a long time. But the plot, based on a story by the great sci-fi writer Philip K. Dick, centers on an intriguing idea: What would happen if you could be supplied with memories? If your entire "past," right up until this moment, could be plugged into your brain, replacing the experiences you had really lived through?

That's what seems to happen to Quaid, the Schwarzenegger character in *Total Recall*, although at times neither he nor we can be quite sure. We meet him in a future world where he lives in a comfortable apartment with his loving blonde wife and goes off to work every day at a construction job. His life seems idyllic, but he keeps having these dreams about Mars—dreams that finally inspire him to sign up with a strange kind of travel agency that provides you with the memory of a vacation instead of a real one.

What they do is strap you into a machine and beam the memories into your mind, so that it seems utterly convincing to you that you've been to Mars and done some dangerous spying there and fallen in love with the brunette of your specifications (Quaid specifies she be "athletic, sleazy, and demure"). Before long, sure enough, Quaid seems to be on Mars, involved in some secret-spy stuff, and in the arms of his custom-ordered brunette (Rachel Ticotin).

But is this a packaged memory or a real experience? The movie toys tantalizingly with the possibilities, especially in a scene where a convincing doctor and Quaid's own wife (Sharon Stone) "appear" in his dream to try to talk him down from it. Meanwhile, the plot—dream or not—unfolds. Mars is in the midst of a revolutionary war between the forces of Cohaagen, a mercenary captain of industry (Ronny Cox), and a small band of rebels. There is a mystery involving a gigantic reactor that was apparently built by aliens on Mars a million years ago and has been uncovered during mining operations. And can the brunette trust Quaid—even though he doesn't remember that they were once lovers?

Total Recall moves back and forth between various versions and levels of reality, while at the same time filling its screen with a future world rich with details. The red planet Mars is created in glorious visual splendor, and the inside of the Mars station looks like a cross between Times Square and a submarine. Strange creatures pop up, including mutants, weird three-breasted strippers, and a team of hit men led by Richter (Michael Ironside), Cohaagen's most vicious lieutenant.

The movie is wall-to-wall with violence, much of it augmented by special effects. Even in this future world, people haven't been able to improve on the machine gun as a weapon of murder, even though you'd imagine that firearms of all kinds would be outlawed inside an airtight dome. There are indeed several sequences in which characters are sucked outside when the air seal is broken, but that doesn't stop the movie's villains from demonstrating the one inevitable fact of movie marksmanship: Bad guys never hit their target, and good guys never miss.

Not that it makes the slightest difference, but the science in this movie is laughable throughout. Much is made, for example, of a scene where characters find themselves outside on Mars and immediately begin to expand, their eyes popping and their faces swelling. As Arthur C. Clarke has written in an essay about his *2001*, a man would not explode even in the total vacuum of deep space. (What's even more unlikely is that after the alien reactors are started and quickly provide Mars with an atmosphere, the endangered characters are spared from explosion.)

Such quibbles—and pages could be filled with them—are largely irrelevant to *Total Recall*, which is a marriage between swashbuckling space opera and the ideas of the original Philip Dick story. The movie was directed by Paul Verhoeven, whose credits range from *The Fourth Man* to *RoboCop*, and he is skilled at creating sympathy for characters even within the overwhelming hardware of a story like this. That's where Schwarzenegger is such a help. He could have stalked and glowered through this movie and become a figure of fun, but instead, by allowing himself to seem confused and vulnerable, he provides a sympathetic center for all the high-tech spectacle.

Track 29 ★ ★ ★
R, 90 m., 1988

Theresa Russell (Linda Henry), Gary Oldman (Martin), Christopher Lloyd (Henry), Colleen Camp (Arlanda), Sandra Bernhard (Nurse Stein), Seymour Cassel (Dr. Bernard Fairmont). Directed by Nicolas Roeg and produced by Rick McCallum. Screenplay by Dennis Potter.

Somebody asked me if I liked this movie, and I had to answer that I did not, but then I realized once again what an inadequate word "like" is. The reason I didn't like *Track 29* is that the film is unlikable—perhaps deliberately so. But that doesn't make it a bad film, and it probably makes it a more interesting one. Like many of the strange, convoluted works of Nicolas Roeg *(Don't Look Now, Bad Timing, Eureka, Insignificance)* it is bad-tempered, kinky, and misogynistic. But not every film is required to massage us with pleasure. Some are allowed to be abrasive and frustrating, and make us think.

The title of *Track 29* comes from the lyrics of "Chattanooga Choo-Choo," and the film's heroine is a madwoman married to a surgeon (Christopher Lloyd) who collects model trains. He has a great layout down in the basement—lots of track and a terrific collection of rolling stock—and when he's not playing with his trains, he's attending fanatic conventions of model railroaders, or being spanked in his office by a helpful nurse who wears rubber gloves (Sandra Bernhard). Although much is made of this man's obsessions, and he attends a model railroad convention which is a piece of social satire in the spirit of *Dr. Strangelove*, this character is essentially unimportant—he's window dressing. All of his pastimes are used to keep him elsewhere while the film's main event unfolds in the mind of his wife.

Her name is Linda (Theresa Russell), and she lives in a nice house that seems to have been slammed down at random in the middle of an industrial park. She drinks a lot, and has daydreams about sex, and hangs out at the hamburger shop with her best pal. One day a strange young man materializes in the town—literally. We see him appear out of thin air. This man is named Martin, and he is played by Gary Oldman as an emotional monster who amuses himself by pulling her strings. Linda meets Martin down at the hamburger stand, and before long he's back at the house, slyly insinuating himself into her delusions.

There are flashbacks to help explain this person. Linda was raped, it appears, during a visit to a carnival when she was sixteen. As we look at a memory of this event, we can vaguely see that the rapist appears to be Martin—but Martin unchanged, looking the same as he does today. And then there is talk that Linda had a child after that event, but gave the child up for adoption, and now bitterly regrets losing it. Martin now tries to present himself as that child, rediscovered after all these years. Also as lover, father-figure, baby, and tormentor.

Although Martin usually seems real enough in *Track 29* (he occupies a volume of space and casts a shadow, just like Roger Rabbit), we eventually realize that he exists entirely inside Linda's imagination. He is the star player in her madness, and when he grows destructive around the house, there is the possibility that she created him to mask her own desire to destroy her husband's obsessions. There is much craziness in this movie, many emotional outbursts, a few puzzled moments of disoriented peace, and, digging away at everything, the taunts and teasings of young Martin.

This performance by Gary Oldman is another strong example of acting to put beside his work in *Sid & Nancy* and *Prick Up*

Your Ears. He makes Martin into an insinuating, dirty-minded little bugger who accuses Linda of the most shocking things, and then smirks at her reactions. Theresa Russell, who has survived the convoluted terrain of many of Nicolas Roeg's movies (he is her husband), seems at home in this twisted landscape, and the two actors work their characters up into an orgy of mutual laceration. Meanwhile, the other stuff—the model railroading and the rubber gloves—provides the sideshow. The movie was written by Dennis Potter, the author of *Pennies from Heaven* and *The Singing Detective*, and reflects his jaundiced view of the possibility of happiness.

Look at it this way. Most of the time we go to the movies hoping to be amused, and often we are disappointed. *Track 29* does not offer amusement, but it promises confusion, frustration, weirdness, and the bizarre. You probably won't like it. But it won't disappoint you.

Trading Places ★ ★ ★ ½
R, 106 m., 1983

Dan Aykroyd (Louis Winthorpe III), Eddie Murphy (Billy Ray Valentine), Ralph Bellamy (Randolph Duke), Don Ameche (Mortimer Duke), Denholm Elliott (Coleman), Jamie Lee Curtis (Ophelia), Jim Belushi (King Kong). Directed by John Landis and produced by Aaron Russo. Screenplay by Timothy Harris and Herschel Weingrod.

Trading Places resembles *Tootsie* and, for that matter, some of the classic Frank Capra and Preston Sturges comedies: It wants to be funny, but it also wants to tell us something about human nature and there are whole stretches when we forget it's a comedy and get involved in the story. And it's a great idea for a story: A white preppy snot and a black street hustler trade places, and learn new skills they never dreamed existed.

This isn't exactly a new idea for a story (Mark Twain's *The Prince and the Pauper* comes to mind). But like a lot of stories, it depends less on plot than on character, and the characters in *Trading Places* are wonderful comic inventions. Eddie Murphy plays Billy Ray Valentine, the con man who makes his first appearance as a blind, legless veteran. Dan Aykroyd is Louis Winthorpe III, the stuck-up commodities broker. And, in a masterstroke of casting, those aging veterans Ralph Bellamy and Don Ameche are cast as the Duke brothers, incalculably rich men

who compete by making little wagers involving human lives.

One day a particularly tempting wager occurs to them. Aykroyd has had Murphy arrested for stealing his briefcase. It's an unfair charge and Murphy is innocent, but Murphy is black and had the misfortune to bump into Aykroyd in front of a snobby club. To Mortimer Duke (Ameche), a believer that environment counts for more than heredity, this is a golden opportunity to test his theory. He bets his brother that if Aykroyd and Murphy were to change places, the black street kid would soon be just as good at calling the shots in the commodity markets as the white Ivy Leaguer ever was. Because the Dukes are rich, they can make almost anything happen. They strip Aykroyd of everything—his job, his home, his butler, his fiancée, his limousine, his self-respect. They give Murphy what they've taken from Aykroyd. And the rest of the movie follows the fortunes of the two changelings as they painfully adjust to their new lives, and get involved in a commodities scam the Duke brothers are trying to pull off.

This is good comedy. It's especially good because it doesn't stop with sitcom manipulations of its idea, and it doesn't go only for the obvious points about racial prejudice in America. Instead, it develops the quirks and peculiarities of its characters, so that they're funny because of who they are. This takes a whole additional level of writing on top of the plot-manipulation we usually get in popular comedies, and it takes good direction, too.

But what's most visible in the movie is the engaging acting. Murphy and Aykroyd are perfect foils for each other in *Trading Places*, because they're both capable of being so specifically eccentric that we're never just looking at a "black" and a "white" (that would make the comedy unworkable). They both play characters with a lot of native intelligence to go along with their prejudices, peculiarities, and personal styles. It's fun to watch them thinking. The supporting cast has also been given detailed attention, instead of being assigned to stand around as stereotypes. Jamie Lee Curtis plays a hooker with a heart of gold and a lot of T-bills; Ameche and Bellamy have a lot of fun with the Duke brothers; and Denholm Elliott successfully plays butler to both Aykroyd and Murphy, which is a stretch. The movie's invention extends all the way to the climactic scenes, which involve, not the usual manic chase, but a commodities scam, a New Year's Eve party on a train, and a gay gorilla.

The Trial ★ ★ ½
NO MPAA RATING, 120 m., 1994

Kyle MacLachlan (Josef K.), Anthony Hopkins (The Priest), Jason Robards (Huld), Polly Walker (Leni), Juliet Stevenson (Fraulein Burstner), Alfred Molina (Titorelli). Directed by David Jones and produced by Louis Marks. Screenplay by Harold Pinter.

Hitchcock said that most of his films were really about the same thing, the Innocent Man Wrongly Accused. These days audiences do not have the patience to follow a man as he fights against persecution; the films of our time are about the Innocent Man Wrongly Blown Away and Immediately Forgotten. When the theme does find new life, in something like *The Fugitive*, it is translated into action, and the hero spends the movie being clever about how he eludes capture, instead of wrestling with the world's unfairness to him.

Too bad (although *The Fugitive* is a splendid film), because we all have deep wells of guilt within, and often in our dreams are framed for crimes we did not commit. In these nightmares we try to defend ourselves, try to *explain*, but the authorities ignore us. Such situations are so frightening and frustrating that I wonder how Hollywood ever got the idea that it was scarier to shoot people, or blow them up—which simply releases the tension.

Franz Kafka's novel *The Trial* is one of the best stories ever written about the Innocent Man, and all the better because there is a sense that Josef K., its hero, secretly suspects that he must have done *something* wrong to deserve such cruel treatment from the authorities.

Josef is awakened one morning by his landlady, who reports there are men to see him. She reveals by her manner that she's already found him guilty; anyone who draws unconventional visitors so early in the day is probably unreliable in many other ways. The police have come to inform Josef about the charges against him—charges that are never spelled out, although Josef spends the rest of the story trying to find out what he has allegedly done.

Do people read Kafka any longer? I am thinking of real readers, people who love the smell and feel and privacy of a book, not students working their way through an as-

signment. It is ironic that this new film of *The Trial* will probably play, for most of its viewers, as an entirely new experience. They will not have read the book, nor will most of them have seen Orson Welles's great 1963 version, also called *The Trial*.

Too bad, because this film, directed by David Jones and written by Harold Pinter, is lacking in the anger and fear which inhabited both the Kafka and Welles stories. Josef K., in the earlier versions, was outraged to his very core that he could be treated in such a way. True, he might secretly be guilty of something—who is not?—but if the state can't put a name to it, then it should stay the hell out of his life.

Kafka wrote in the early years of the century. Welles was shaped by them. Today we have been tamed by the notion of a powerful state; most of us are frightened even to be pulled over by a traffic cop. Yet we believe, naively, that if we follow the rules everything will be set straight in the end. That seems to be Josef's belief in this version of *The Trial;* he is played by Kyle MacLachlan as an upright, reserved, logical man who continues patiently to try to defend himself.

The star of Orson Welles's film was Anthony Perkins. Much better. Perkins projected the kind of man who, told he is guilty, would look in the mirror and see that they were probably right. He was jumpy, nervous, filled with squirms and ticks. Welles put him in one of the most extraordinary landscapes in movie history: a city of vast blasted empty spaces and towering lifeless apartment buildings that looked like cell blocks. When he went to visit an archive, it looked filled with the dusty records of all recorded time. When he went to appeal to a famous lawyer (played by Welles), the advocate's flat was lit by candles, and not half a dozen candles, but hundreds or thousands, blazing away on every horizontal space.

In the Welles film there always seemed to be someone in the next room, snickering, and then disappearing from view just a second before Josef could get a good look. The whole feel of the film was paranoid. This new *Trial* seems more clean and well lit. It still provides opportunities for great walk-on performances (Anthony Hopkins has a brief scene as a priest who tries to make it easier for Josef toward the end, and steals, not just the scene, but almost the last half of the movie). It is a solid, respectable screen adaptation, but it lacks the madness.

A movie need not be "faithful" to a book

(adaptations are not marriages and remakes are not adultery). But if it is based on a book at all, the filmmakers must have seen something worth preserving. In the case of Kafka's masterpiece, it is the uneasy feeling that if the state ever gets its lunch hooks into us, we're guilty until proven innocent. This queasiness is as appropriate today as in Kafka's lifetime; the trials of Josef K. foreshadow the fate of anyone unlucky enough to attract the attention of the IRS, or Rush Limbaugh.

Assignment: Buy a paperback of *The Trial* and read it. It is written in a tightly controlled, flat, factual tone that is echoed (without the intensity) in the narration of those true-crime TV infotainments. Then rent the Welles film. Then rent the Jones version of *The Trial*. Meditate on the differences among the three versions, and you will discover insights into the difference between artistry and craftsmanship, between inspired madness and mere indignation.

Tribute ★ ★ ★
PG, 123 m., 1981

Jack Lemmon (Scottie Templeton), Robby Benson (Jud Templeton), Lee Remick (Maggie Stratton), Colleen Dewhurst (Gladys Petrelli), John Marley (Lou Daniels), Kim Cattrall (Sally Haines). Directed by Bob Clark and produced by Joel B. Michaels and Garth H. Drabinski. Screenplay by Bernard Slade.

I am aware that *Tribute* hauls out some of the oldest Broadway clichés in the book, that it shamelessly exploits its melodramatic elements, and that it is not a movie so much as a filmed stage play. And yet if I were to review it just on those grounds, I would be less than honest. In the abstract, *Tribute* may not be a very good film at all. But in its particulars, and in the way they affected me, it is a touching experience.

It's supposed to be cheating to make an admission like that. I myself believe that it is a film's form, more than its message, that makes it great. And yet *Tribute* is not a visually distinguished film. It has been directed, by Bob Clark, as a straightforward job of work. There are long sequences that are obviously just filmed scenes from Bernard Slade's original stage play. Yet the characters transcend these limitations and become people that we care about.

The film is mostly Jack Lemmon's, and he deserved his seventh Academy Award nomination for his performance as Scottie Templeton, the movie's hero. We all know somebody like Scottie—if we are not, God forbid, a little like Scottie ourselves. He's a wisecracking, popular guy with hundreds of deeply intimate passing acquaintances. He also has a few friends. One of them is his business partner (John Marley) and another is his ex-wife (Lee Remick). They love him and stand by him, but he can't allow himself to reveal how much that means to him. He is also hurt by his relationship with his son (Robby Benson), who has the usual collection of post-adolescent grudges against his father. All of these relationships suddenly become much more important when Scottie discovers he is dying. The movie begins at about that point in Scottie's life, and examines how the fact of approaching death changes all of Scottie's ways of dealing with the living.

His son comes home to visit for a few weeks. His ex-wife returns to New York for a college reunion and stays to become involved in the crisis. The friend, Marley, acts as counsel and adjudicator. Other characters pass through, including a young woman (Kim Cattrall) who Scottie thinks would be ideal for his son (after all, she'd previously been ideal for Scottie himself). Veteran playgoers can already predict the obligatory scenes growing out of this situation. Scottie will be brave at first, then angry, then depressed, then willing to reach out to his son, and finally reconciled to his fate. Scottie's friends will rally around. His son will learn to love the old man. Everybody will become more human and sensitive, and the possibility of death will provide an occasion for a celebration of life. Et cetera.

What's amazing is that when these predictable situations appear, the movie makes them work. A great deal of the credit for that belongs to Lemmon and Benson. They are both actors with a familiar schtick by now: Benson trembling with emotions, Lemmon fast-talking his way into sincerity. In *Tribute*, though, the movie's characters are so close to the basic strengths of Lemmon and Benson that everything seems to work.

Take Lemmon, for example. Another actor, playing Scottie Templeton, might simply seem to be saying funny lines, alternating with bittersweet insights. Lemmon makes us believe that they're not lines; they're the way this guy talks. The big emotional changes take place underneath the surface wisecracks, making them all the more poignant. Robby Benson sometimes comes across as too vulnerable, almost affected in his sensitivity.

Here, he's good, too: Examine the early scene where his father asks what the hell's going on, and Benson begins, "Let me try to explain about that . . ." with touching formality.

Maybe your reaction to *Tribute* will depend on your state of mind. I know people who say they "saw through it," dismissing it as merely a well-made play. I know others, myself included, who were really touched by it. Perhaps the film works better because it's *willing* to be a bittersweet soap opera. Life itself, after all, is rarely a great directorial achievement, but almost always seems to work on the melodramatic level.

The Trip to Bountiful ★ ★ ★ ½
PG, 106 m., 1985

Geraldine Page (Mrs. Watts), John Heard (Ludie Watts), Carlin Glynn (Jessie Mae), Richard Bradford (Sheriff), Rebecca De Mornay (Thelma). Directed by Peter Masterson and produced by Sterling Van Wagenen and Horton Foote. Screenplay by Foote.

The thing that saves this movie from sentimentality is that the heroine is a little ornery. She's not just a sweet and gentle little old lady. She's a big old lady, with a streak of stubbornness. And just because she's right doesn't mean she's always all that nice. When *The Trip to Bountiful* tells us that she wants to leave her miserable life in the city and pay one last visit to her childhood country home, somehow we know that the movie won't be over when she hears the birds singing in the trees.

The movie stars the redoubtable Geraldine Page in her Academy Award-winning role as Mrs. Watts, a country woman who has come to live in a cramped city apartment with her son and daughter-in-law. The apartment isn't big enough for two women. They're always on each other's nerves.

The wife, Jessie Mae (Carlin Glynn), doesn't like Mrs. Watts singing her hymns around the house. Mrs. Watts's strategy is more subtle: She tries to appear long-suffering, a martyr, and she is much given to throwing herself on the couch and pulling a comforter over her head to muffle her sobs.

Both of these women have a pretty good case against each other, but it's Mrs. Watts we sympathize with. She hates life in the city, she knows it's choking her to death, and she wants to pay one final visit to Bountiful, the little town where she was born. So she goes to the train station, but the milk train doesn't stop in Bountiful anymore. So she goes to

the bus station and buys a ticket to the nearest large town. This is in Texas in 1947. Because her son and daughter-in-law have gone to the train station to head her off (she's tried to escape before), she makes her getaway.

The whole middle section of the movie is the best, as she meets another traveler on the bus, a young woman named Thelma (Rebecca De Mornay). They sit next to each other during the long, drowsy trip, and they exchange memories and confidences. Thelma is, in a way, only an excuse to give Mrs. Watts someone to talk to, so that we can eavesdrop. Yet De Mornay makes the character so interesting, so young and open-faced, that the relationship between these two women becomes the heart of the movie. Even the ending itself doesn't quite live up to it.

The Trip to Bountiful has a quiet, understated feel for the small towns of its time. The little rural bus station, with its clerk drowsing under a lonely lamp bulb, looks just right, and so do the midnight streets outside. And when the sheriff arrives, alerted to look for a runaway old lady, it's perfect the way he and the ticket agent size up the situation and let Mrs. Watts have her last look at her childhood home.

Then her family arrives: her son Ludie (John Heard) and his wife Jessie Mae. Ludie really has his work cut out with these two women. Both of them live at a time when many women lived their lives through their men, and there is not enough room inside Ludie's simple, desperate soul for both of these women. Yet there is a moment of poetry as she sits on the porch of the old farmhouse and talks about how she almost expected to see her own parents come walking through the door, just as if all those years had never passed, just as if her own lifetime was a dream, and she was still a young girl again.

The Trip to Bountiful was written by Horton Foote, who based it on his own stage play. This is Foote's second recent slice of life from Texas: *Tender Mercies*, the wonderful movie starring Robert Duvall as an alcoholic country singer, was also written by him. You can see that *Bountiful* was based on a play—it falls fairly obviously into three acts—but the rhythms and dialogue come out of unstudied real life. And Geraldine Page inhabits the central role with authority and vinegar. The movie surprises us: It's not really about conflict between the generations, but about the impossibility of really understanding that you are even a member of an older generation, that decades have gone by.

Geraldine Page, who somehow always manages to have a hint of girlishness in her performances, who always seems to be up to something roguish and not ever quite ready to cave in to age, finds just the right notes in the final scenes to tell her son something he might never be able to understand: Someday he will be old, too, and he won't be able to believe it either.

Tron ★ ★ ★ ★
PG, 96 m., 1982

Jeff Bridges (Flynn/Clu), Bruce Boxleitner (Alan/Tron), David Warner (Dillinger/Sark), Cindy Morgan (Lora/Yori), Barnard Hughes (Gibbs/Dumont), Dan Shor (Ram). Directed by Steven Lisberger and produced by Donald Kushner. Screenplay by Lisberger.

The interior of a computer is a fine and private place, but none, I fear, do there embrace, except in *Tron*, a dazzling movie from Walt Disney in which computers have been used to make themselves romantic and glamorous. Here's a technological sound-and-light show that is sensational and brainy, stylish, and fun.

The movie addresses itself without apology to the computer generation, embracing the imagery of those arcade video games that parents fear are rotting the minds of their children. If you've never played Pac-Man or Space Invaders or the Tron game itself, you probably are not quite ready to see this movie, which begins with an evil bureaucrat stealing computer programs to make himself look good, and then enters the very mind of a computer itself to engage the villain, the hero, and several highly programmable bystanders in a war of the wills that is governed by the rules of both video games and computer programs.

The villain is a man named Dillinger (David Warner). The hero is a bright kid named Flynn (Jeff Bridges) who created the original programs for five great new video games, including the wonderfully named "Space Paranoid." Dillinger stole Flynn's plans and covered his tracks in the computer. Flynn believes that if he can track down the original program, he can prove Dillinger is a thief. To prevent that, Dillinger uses the very latest computer technology to break Flynn down into a matrix of logical points and insert him *into* the computer, and at that point *Tron* leaves any narrative or visual universe we have ever seen before in a movie and charts its own rather wonderful path.

In an age of amazing special effects, *Tron* is a state-of-the-art movie. It generates not just one imaginary computer universe, but a multitude of them. Using computers as their tools, the Disney filmmakers literally have been able to imagine any fictional landscape, and then have it, through an animated computer program. And they integrate their human actors and the wholly imaginary worlds of Tron so cleverly that I never, ever, got the sensation that I was watching some actor standing in front of, or in the middle of, special effects. The characters *inhabit* this world. And what a world it is! Video gamesmen race each other at blinding speed, hurtling up and down computer grids while the movie shakes with the overkill of Dolby stereo (justified, for once). The characters sneak around the computer's logic guardian terminals, clamber up the sides of memory displays, talk their way past the guardians of forbidden programs, hitch a ride on a power beam, and succeed in entering the mind of the very Master Control Program itself, disabling it with an electronic Frisbee. This is all a whole lot of fun. *Tron* has been conceived and written with a knowledge of computers that it mercifully assumes the audience shares. That doesn't mean we *do* share it, but that we're bright enough to pick it up, and don't have to sit through long, boring explanations of it.

There is one additional observation I have to make about *Tron*, and I don't really want it to sound like a criticism: This is an almost wholly technological movie. Although it's populated by actors who are engaging (Bridges, Cindy Morgan) or sinister (Warner), it is not really a movie about human nature. Like *Star Wars* or *The Empire Strikes Back*, but much more so, this movie is a machine to dazzle and delight us. It is not a human-interest adventure in any generally accepted way. That's all right, of course. It's brilliant at what it does, and in a technical way maybe it's breaking ground for a generation of movies in which computer-generated universes will be the background for mind-generated stories about emotion-generated personalities. All things are possible.

Trouble in Mind ★ ★ ★
R, 111 m., 1985

Kris Kristofferson (Hawk), Keith Carradine (Coop), Lori Singer (Georgia), Genevieve Bujold (Wanda), Joe Morton (Solo), Divine (Hilly Blue), George Kirby (Detective). Directed by Alan Rudolph and produced by Carolyn Pfeiffer and David Blocker. Screenplay by Rudolph.

Here is a movie that takes place within our memories of the movies. The characters and the mysteries and especially the doomed romances are all generated by old films, by remembered worlds of lurid neon signs and deserted areas down by the docks, of sad cafes where losers linger over a cup of coffee, and lonely rooms where the light bulb is a man's only friend. This is a world for which the saxophone was invented, a world in which the American Motors Javelin was a popular car.

The movie begins with a man being released from prison, of course, and he is dressed in black and has a beard and wears a hat, of course, and is named Hawk, of course, and the first place he goes when he arrives in town is Wanda's Café, where Wanda keeps a few rooms upstairs for her old lovers to mend their broken dreams.

The café is on a worn-out old brick street down at the wrong end of Rain City. It's the kind of place that doesn't need to advertise, because its customers are drawn there by their fates. One day a young couple turn up in a broken-down camper. The kid is named Coop, and he knows he always gets into trouble when he comes to the city, but he needs to make some money to support his little family. His girlfriend is named Georgia, and she looks way young to have a baby, but there it is, bawling in her arms. She's a blonde with a look in her eyes that makes the Hawk's heart soar.

Coop falls into partnership with the wrong man, a black man named Solo who sits in a back booth at Wanda's Café and recites poems about anger and hopelessness. Before long, Coop and Solo are involved in a life of crime, and Hawk is telling Georgia she's living with a loser.

Wanda stands behind the counter and watches all this happen with eyes that have seen a thousand plans go wrong. She hires Georgia as a waitress. That turns Hawk into a regular customer. Wanda knows Hawk is in love with Georgia, because Wanda and Hawk used to be in love with each other, and once you learn to hear that note in a man's voice, you hear it even when he's not singing to you.

Coop and Solo are trying to sell some hot wristwatches. Hilly Blue doesn't like that.

Hilly is the boss of the local rackets, and lives in a house that is furnished like the Museum of Modern Art. The best way to describe Hilly Blue is to say that if Sydney Greenstreet could have reproduced by parthenogenesis after radioactive damage to his chromosomes, Hilly would have been the issue.

Trouble in Mind is not a comedy, but it knows that it is funny. It is not a fantasy, and yet strange troops patrol the streets of Rain City, and as many people speak Korean as English. It does not take place in the 1940s, but its characters dress and talk and live as if it did. Could this movie have been made if there had never been any movies starring Richard Widmark, Jack Palance, or Robert Mitchum? Yes, but it wouldn't have had any style.

To really get inside the spirit of *Trouble in Mind*, it would probably help to see *Choose Me* first. Both films are the work of Alan Rudolph, who is creating a visual world as distinctive as Fellini's and as cheerful as Edward Hopper's. He does an interesting thing. He combines his stylistic excesses with a lot of emotional sincerity, so that we believe these characters are really serious about their hopes, and dreams, even if they do seem to inhabit a world of imagination. Look at it this way. In Woody Allen's *The Purple Rose of Cairo*, a character stepped out of a movie and off the screen and into the life of a woman in the audience. If that had happened in *Trouble in Mind*, the woman would have asked the character why he even bothered.

Sometimes the names of movie actors evoke so many associations that further description is not necessary. Let's see. Hawk is played by Kris Kristofferson. Coop is Keith Carradine. Wanda is Genevieve Bujold. Hilly Blue is the transvestite Divine, but he is not in drag this time, allegedly. Mix them together, light them with neon reds and greens, and add a blond child-woman (Lori Singer) and a black gangster (Joe Morton) whose shades are his warmest feature, and perhaps you can begin to understand why they call it Rain City.

True Believer ★ ★ ★
R, 103 m., 1989

James Woods (Eddie Dodd), Robert Downey, Jr. (Roger Baron), Margaret Colin (Kitty Greer), Yuji Okumoto (Shu Kai Kim), Kurtwood Smith (Robert Reynard), Tom Bower (Cecil Skell), Miguel Fernandes (Art Esparza), John Snyder (Chucky Loeder), Misan Kim (Mrs. Kim).

Directed by Joseph Ruben and produced by Walter F. Parkes and Lawrence Lasker. Screenplay by Wesley Strick.

Let us now consider the case of James Woods, a name on that brief list of actors whose presence more or less guarantees that a film will be interesting. Woods works a lot. In the 1988-89 season he made *Cop*, about a dangerously out of control homicide detective, *The Boost*, about a salesman who gets swept away in the Los Angeles fast lane, and now *True Believer*, about a radical lawyer from the 1960s who has recently specialized in defending drug dealers.

The characters in these movies are not all the same man, although they all share some of Woods's high-energy restlessness. The high-flier in *The Boost*, for example, is not nearly as intelligent as Eddie Dodd, the fast-talking lawyer in *True Believer*. And yet both characters are hypnotically watchable because Woods talks fast and is always thinking, and his performances assume that the audience can listen and think as quickly as he can.

Does Woods tinker with the scripts he gets, or are they written with him in mind? In *True Believer*, he bursts into his walk-up office in Greenwich Village, says hello to his secretary, asks "What is this thing?" about a weird piece of sculpture standing in a corner, and disappears before he can get the answer. The moment has no purpose in the larger context of the movie, and yet it establishes the character, and it implies that this lawyer leads a larger life, with other concerns, that began before the movie and will continue after it's over.

Woods loves to pepper his roles with throwaways like that. It lends tension and texture even to plots that might seem standard in other hands. And the story in *True Believer* is a fairly routine version of the urban paranoia thriller, in which killers walk the streets because of corruption and compromise in high places. As the movie begins, Eddie Dodd is a burned-out pothead who represents drug dealers because they pay well, and usually in cash. He defends his practice by describing himself as being on the cutting edge of civil liberties law, no matter that all his clients are guilty.

Then a young man walks into his life: Roger Baron (Robert Downey, Jr.), an idealistic lawyer who has read all about Eddie's great cases in the sixties and wants to sit at his feet and learn. Baron soon learns he's the unpaid assistant of a cynic. But then a Korean woman walks into the office with a plea to Eddie: Her son has been in prison for eight years for a murder he did not commit. Eddie's instincts cry out to avoid the case, but the kid acts as his conscience, and before long both men are up to their necks in a dangerous investigation.

The case involves lots of flaws in the original trial: unreliable eyewitnesses, time discrepancies, conflicts of interest. In other hands, this material might seem familiar, but Woods puts a spin on it, an intensity that makes it feel important—to him, and therefore to us. And in the obligatory courtroom showdown that ends the film, Woods is able to find new ways to handle all of those old clichés about the surprise witnesses and the dramatic last-minute revelations.

Watching the film, I was not particularly impressed by Robert Downey, Jr., as the idealistic young law graduate. He seemed sort of indistinct, and I wondered why. Downey gave one of the best performances of recent years in *Less Than Zero*, as a self-destructing drug abuser. What was missing here? A few days after seeing *True Believer*, I saw Downey again in *Chances Are*, where he carries the movie effortlessly and with grace. Seeing that second fine performance, I began to get an angle on Woods: He's the kind of actor who has such high voltage, who's so wound up, that maybe a younger actor tends to defer. We've all had that feeling of being in a conversation with someone else who has seized the advantage and is keeping it. Maybe working with Woods gives you the same feeling; it takes an improvisational veteran like James Belushi, Woods's costar in *Salvador*, to match his pace.

If you run James Woods's best performances through your memory—the ones I've mentioned and *The Onion Field*, *Against All Odds*, and *Once Upon a Time in America*—you see a certain pattern emerging. Woods doesn't like dumb movies, and he doesn't like to play dumb characters. In the season of the Idiot Plot (the plot that doesn't work unless everyone in it is an idiot), Woods makes movies in which the audience has to be on its toes to keep up with him. It's quite an act, and when I see Woods on the screen in the first shot of a movie, I sort of smile to myself because I know that something strange and offbeat and maybe even inspired is about to happen.

True Confessions ★ ★ ★
R, 110 m., 1981

Robert De Niro (Des Spellacy), Robert Duvall (Tom Spellacy), Charles Durning (Jack Amsterdam), Ed Flanders (Dan T. Campion), Burgess Meredith (Seamus Fargo). Directed by Ulu Grosbard and produced by Irwin Winkler and Robert Chartoff. Screenplay by John Gregory Dunne and Joan Didion.

True Confessions contains scenes that are just about as good as scenes can be. Then why does the movie leave us disoriented and disappointed, and why does the ending fail dismally? Perhaps because the attentions of the filmmakers were concentrated so fiercely on individual moments that nobody ever stood back to ask what the story was about. It's frustrating to sit through a movie filled with clues and leads and motivations, only to discover at the end that the filmmakers can't be bothered with finishing the story.

The film is about two brothers, one a priest, the other a cop. In a nice insight in casting, Robert De Niro plays the priest and Robert Duvall plays the cop; offhand, we'd expect it to be the other way around, but Duvall is just right, seedy and wall-faced, as the cop, and after a scene or two we begin to accept De Niro as a priest (although he seems too young for a monsignor).

The brothers live in Los Angeles in 1948. It is a Los Angeles more or less familiar from dozens of other movies, especially *Chinatown* and the Robert Mitchum *Farewell, My Lovely*—a small town, really, where the grafters and the power brokers know each other (and in some cases are each other). The movie's plot is complicated on the surface but simple underneath. It centers around a creep named Amsterdam (Charles Durning), a construction tycoon who got his start as a pimp. Both brothers have had dealings with the man. When Duvall was a vice cop, he helped handle the protection for Amsterdam's whorehouses. Now De Niro, the cardinal's right-hand man, oversees the building projects of the Los Angeles archdiocese. And Amsterdam gets most of the contracts for new schools and hospitals, even though his operation is tainted with scandal.

It's tainted with more than that after the dead body of a young woman is found in a field, cut in two. Duvall's investigation leads to a madam who once took a rap for him, long ago, and to a sleazy L.A. porno filmmaker. Eventually, certain clues point all the way back to Amsterdam. Try to follow this closely: Amsterdam met the girl through a business associate, who met her as a hitchhiker. When he first gave her a lift in his car, De Niro was another passenger. The movie makes a great deal of the fact that the monsignor once shared a car with the "virgin tramp," as the newspapers label the victim. But so what? One of the maddening things about *True Confessions* is that it's shot through with such paranoia that innocent coincidences take on the same weight as evil conspiracies.

The movie's emotional center is in the cop character. He's painted as a man who's not above taking a bribe. But at the same time he has a moral code that's stiffer than his brother's. (The monsignor, for example, isn't above rigging a church raffle so that a city councilman's daughter will win the new car.) What begins to eat away at Duvall is that this Amsterdam, honored as the Catholic Layman of the Year, is a grafter and former pimp. Did he also murder the girl? Duvall frankly doesn't care: The guy is such slime he should be arrested for the crime just on general principles.

True Confessions spends a lot of effort in laying the groundwork for its complex plot, but then it refuses to ever settle things. Instead, there are inane prologues and epilogues showing the two brothers years later, their hair gray, as they sigh philosophically over impending death and shake their heads at the irony and tragedy of it all—whatever it all was.

Since this isn't a thriller, we are invited, I guess, to take it as a cynical meditation on the corruptibility of man. Joan Didion and John Gregory Dunne, who based the screenplay on his novel, see the social institutions in their story as just hiding places for hypocrites and weary, defeated men. But they never follow through on their insights. The movie has, for example, a major subplot involving an old priest (Burgess Meredith) who is being put out to pasture. The priest is evidently a symbol of something, especially since the young De Niro gets the dirty job of firing him. But the movie never comes to terms with this story; it just leaves it sitting there.

At the end of *True Confessions*, we're just sitting there, too. We have been introduced to clearly drawn and well-acted characters, we've entered a period in time that is carefully reconstructed, we've seen moments between men and women that are wonderfully well-observed. But we haven't seen a film that cares to be about anything in particular, to state its case or draw its lines, or be much more than a skilled exercise in style.

True Lies ★ ★ ★
R, 135 m., 1994

Arnold Schwarzenegger (Harry), Jamie Lee Curtis (Helen), Tom Arnold (Gib), Bill Paxton (Simon), Tia Carrere (Juno), Art Malik (Aziz), Eliza Dushku (Dana), Grant Heslov (Faisil). Directed by James Cameron and produced by Cameron and Stephanie Austin. Screenplay by Cameron.

There is a sequence near the end of *True Lies* in which Arnold Schwarzenegger is piloting a Harrier vertical-takeoff fighter plane, which hovers near a Miami high-rise while his teenage daughter clings precariously to the cockpit cover and a villain dangles by his gunbelt from one of the wing-mounted missiles. Arnold arms the missile and fires it, terrorist attached, straight through the high-rise, and it shoots down a helicopter carrying other terrorists. This takes place, I might add, shortly after a nuclear bomb has vaporized one of the Florida Keys.

It's stuff like that we go to Arnold Schwarzenegger movies for, and *True Lies* has a lot of it: laugh-out-loud moments when the violence is so cartoonish we don't take it seriously, and yet are amazed at its inventiveness and audacity. Schwarzenegger has found himself in a lot of unlikely situations in his action-packed career, and *True Lies* seems determined to raise the ante—to go over the top with outlandish and extravagant special effects scenes.

Consider, for example, a chase sequence near the beginning of the movie, in which a bad guy on a motorcycle is chased by Arnold, on a horse, through a hotel lobby. Most movies would be content with that. Not *True Lies*, which continues the chase on high-rise elevators and ends up on the hotel roof, with Arnold urging the horse to attempt a free fall into a swimming pool.

The plot is, of course, little more than a clothesline upon which to hang such set pieces. It involves Schwarzenegger as Harry, an ace U.S. spy, who has been married for fifteen years to a sweet-tempered wife named Helen (Jamie Lee Curtis), who thinks he is a computer salesman. (He works for something called the Omega Force, which describes itself in its seal as "The Last Line of Defense.") How he has successfully managed this deception is one of the many questions the film does not pause to answer.

As the film opens, Schwarzenegger and his partner Gib (Tom Arnold) are involved in a James Bondian attempt to infiltrate a rich arms dealer's black-tie party in a Swiss chateau. To say security is tight would be an understatement; the guards have machine guns and attack dogs. At the party, Schwarzenegger meets the beautiful Juno Skinner (Tia Carrere, looking much more elegant than in *Wayne's World*) and tangos with her before accomplishing his mission and surviving a bloody getaway. (Schwarzenegger's tangoing ability is reflected by the decision to film most of the dance as head-and-shoulders shots.)

Cut back to Washington, D.C., and Schwarzenegger's life of uneventful domestic tranquillity (his wife thinks he was out of town at a sales convention). But then, when it appears the dealer has sold four atomic weapons to a terrorist gang, it's up to Schwarzenegger and the surprisingly engaging Tom Arnold to stop them.

In between the action-packed first and third acts, however, is a curious second act in which Schwarzenegger becomes convinced that his wife is fooling around with a car salesman (Bill Paxton). This leads to an elaborate charade in a hotel room, where, for reasons that are much too complicated to summarize here, Jamie Lee Curtis impersonates a hooker and Schwarzenegger impersonates her client. (We are supposed to believe she doesn't recognize her husband because he has a light behind him.)

Curtis earns some laughs here, doing a quasi striptease. The physical humor is effective, and she's charmingly sexy and klutzy. But the whole scene smells fishy. If you take a step back from the movie and really think about the trick the spy is playing on his wife, it's cruel and not funny. And it sidetracks the plot. The movie is 135 minutes long, and at 120, without some of the hotel room escapade, it would be a lot better.

The director, James Cameron, is a master of action (he worked with Schwarzenegger on *Terminator 2*), and when he's doing his thing, no one does it better. That includes the third act of the movie, in which a breathless Miami newscaster reports on a high-rise terrorist drama, and barely has time to squeeze in the information that an A-bomb has just blown up one of the Keys.

Cameron is credited with the screenplay (which is "based on" a French screenplay by three others), and keeps a nice undertone of humor going. When we're learning about one of the evil terrorists, for example, here's the exchange:

"They call him the Sand Spider."

"Why?"

"Probably because it sounds scary."

One nice surprise is Tom Arnold, who has a major role—the equal of Curtis's—and fills it nicely. He has an everyman quality about him, and an ability to deliver an irreverent aside that make him a good foil for Schwarzenegger. And when he gives advice on divorce and marriage, which he does frequently, he sounds as if he speaks from experience.

True Lies doesn't rank as high as *Terminator 2* and *Total Recall* among Schwarzenegger's action epics for a couple of reasons: the unconvincing interlude where the hero suspects adultery, and the perfunctory nature of the plot. Both earlier titles had tighter, more absorbing stories. But on the basis of stunts, special effects, and pure action, it delivers sensationally.

True Love ★ ★ ★
R, 104 m., 1989

Annabella Sciorra (Donna), Ron Eldard (Michael), Aida Turturro (Grace), Roger Rignack (Dom), Star Jasper (J.C.), Michael J. Wolfe (Brian), Kelly Cinnante (Yvonne), Rick Shapiro (Kevin). Directed by Nancy Savoca and produced by Richard Guay and Shelly Houis. Screenplay by Savoca and Guay.

True Love plunges into the middle of the preparations for a marriage, and shows us a man and woman being swept toward matrimony by a tide of relatives, friends, traditions, and plans—even though they probably shouldn't get married at all. It's a comedy about uneasiness; nearly everyone in the film knows, in one way or another, that the marriage is a bad idea, but once events are set into motion, nothing can stop them. Even as the bride is on her way to the church, her father is assuring her it's not too late to back out—but to hell with your life, how can you disappoint your friends?

The movie is a fiction film that looks and sometimes feels like a documentary. The director, Nancy Savoca, who cowrote the screenplay with Richard Guay, uses a mobile camera to give us the impression we're in the middle of one of those cinema verité documentaries where life goes on regardless of the filmmakers. We're there at the family conference, and at the heartfelt confessions over kitchen tables, and in the saloons where the groom-to-be hangs out with his buddies. Although the movie has been carefully constructed, it creates the feeling of improvisation and spontaneity—a lot of scenes unfold like a movie by John Cassavetes, where the events seem to be happening while we watch them, and the camera seems to be present by a lucky chance.

The film stars Annabella Sciorra as Donna, bride-to-be at the center of a large Italian-American family in New York, and Ron Eldard as Michael, her fiancé. They've been engaged for a long time, their friends see them as a couple, and on every side there are pressures urging them toward the altar. There seems to be something about matrimony that brings out a profoundly conservative side in all of the friends and family members of a would-be couple; marriage is held up as an inevitable goal, and there is so much institutional pressure in favor of it that a couple can hold out only so long.

There is a sense in *True Love* that the marriage preparations lead to the marriage almost through the sheer force of momentum. A hall has to be hired. A menu has to be selected (with mashed potatoes dyed to match the color of the bridesmaids' dresses). Family and friends swarm about the two stars of the event until they hardly have time to communicate with each other.

But then they do talk. And gradually, as we listen, we begin to realize that *True Love* is deeper than it first seemed. The movie begins as a comedy of wedding preparations and lifestyles, but as it goes along and we get to know Donna and Michael better, we begin to suspect that these people should never get married. That Michael is an immature alcoholic, and that in some ways Donna knows it, but lacks the determination to call off the ceremony.

The key moment in the movie comes at the banquet after the wedding, and it takes place in the women's room, where Donna has fled, weeping, after Michael has informed her that he plans to go out drinking with his buddies instead of spending the wedding night with her. The chilling thing about his decision is that he doesn't seem to fully realize just how bizarre it is. He justifies it as "just one last night out with the guys," not realizing that he should already have had that night—that this, of all nights, should be his first with his wife.

Michael is a little dense in these matters, anyway. As played by Ron Eldard, he's one of those good-looking, superficially nice young men who has gotten a free ride from friends and family despite the handicap of never having had an interesting thought in his life. All of his opinions are secondhand, most of his remarks are clichés. Marriage is something he sees in terms of something he "ought" to do, rather than as a personal commitment. Even the movie's love scenes seem learned out of movies.

Donna, as played by Sciorra in the movie's central and best performance, is a wiser woman, and one who probably doesn't want to get married at all. But the institution sweeps her along. The idea of marriage and the urging of her friends are so overwhelming to her that she chooses to disregard the clear evidence of Michael's immaturity. Because all of the other wedding arrangements have been made, she is able to overlook the most important one: the choice of a suitable husband.

At the end of *True Love*, I was left with the clear impression that this marriage wouldn't last long. But it is the genius of the movie that it almost sweeps the audience along with everyone else in cheering the couple toward the altar. This is a subtle movie that invites us to read between the lines. It suggests that a lot of couples may be married to marriage rather than to each other.

True Romance ★ ★ ★
R, 120 m., 1993

Christian Slater (Clarence Worley), Patricia Arquette (Alabama Whitman), Dennis Hopper (Clifford Worley), Val Kilmer (Mentor), Gary Oldman (Drexl Spivey), Brad Pitt (Floyd, Dick's Roommate), Christopher Walken (Vincenzo Coccotti). Directed by Tony Scott and produced by Bill Unger, Steve Perry, and Samuel Hadida. Screenplay by Quentin Tarantino.

There are few objections to *True Romance* that I haven't thought of, and I dismiss them all with a wave of the hand. This is the kind of movie that creates its own universe, and glories in it. The universe in question could best be located inside the inflamed fantasies of an adolescent male mind—and not any adolescent, but the kind of teen-age boy who goes to martial arts movies and fantasizes about guns and girls with great big garbanzos. It is the kind of film that will make the best-ten lists of such supporters of the decline of civilization as Joe Bob Briggs.

And yet that doesn't make it bad. I've always tried to adopt a generic approach to the movies, judging each film in terms of its type and the expectations we have for it. And *True Romance*, which feels at times like a fire sale down at the cliché factory, is made with such energy, such high spirits, such an enchanting goofiness, that it's impossible to resist. Check your brains at the door.

The movie's hero, named Clarence, played by Christian Slater, is perhaps something like the target audience member for the movie. He works in a comic book store, spends his free time watching kung fu triple-features, and can hardly believe it when a blonde in a low-cut garbanzo-flaunter walks into his life.

Her name is Alabama (uh-huh) and she's played by Patricia Arquette. I guess it goes without saying that she's a hooker; that's the only profession available to the women in a movie like this, and is sort of convenient, because it means she doesn't have any regular hours, no parents, and is available, at least for a price. Of course, such hookers, in such movies, never charge the hero anything; Clarence exudes a magnetic appeal that transcends commerce, I guess, like when Billy Idol dropped in over at Heidi's house.

Alabama is actually a bit of an innocent. She's only been a hooker for four days (or four clients, I forget), but that has been long enough for her to pick up a vicious pimp (Gary Oldman), whom Clarence has to deal with. Clarence is courageous and stupid, two invaluable assets in this situation, and eliminates the pimp in a prelude to a cross-country odyssey, after, in a series of tortured plot manipulations, he and Alabama have come into possession of five million dollars of the mob's cocaine, which they plan to sell at a discount, before flying to Rio.

True Romance was directed by Tony Scott, whose movies like *Top Gun* and *Days of Thunder* show an affection for boys and their toys. But the film's real author, his stamp on every line of every scene, is Quentin Tarantino. As in *Reservoir Dogs*, his 1992 directorial debut, Tarantino creates a world of tough guys, bravado, wild exaggeration, lurid melodrama, easy women, betrayal, guns, and drugs. In his world, "low cut" is to "neckline" as "fast" is to "car."

The movie hurtles from scene to scene, aiming for a climax that will strike *Reservoir Dogs* fans as curiously familiar. In both films, the plot ingeniously arrives at a moment where all of the warring parties are in the same room at the same time, simultaneously shooting at each other.

There isn't a moment of *True Romance* that stands up under much thought, and yet the energy and style of the movie are exhilarating. Christian Slater has the kind of cocky recklessness the movie needs, and Patricia Arquette portrays a fetching combination of bimbo and best pal. The supporting cast is superb, a roll call of actors at home in these violent waters: Christopher Walken, Dennis Hopper, and Brad Pitt, for example.

And then there is Val Kilmer, fresh from *The Doors*, playing yet another dead rock hero. He lurks in the background of several scenes, as a muse who visits Christian Slater from time to time, dispensing heartfelt advice. Would you be surprised if I revealed that this figure is, in fact, the ghost of Elvis Presley? You would not? You will find yourself right at home here.

True Stories ★ ★ ★ ½
PG-13, 88 m., 1986

John Goodman (Louis Fyne), Swoosie Kurtz (Laziest Woman), Spalding Gray (Earl Culver), Alix Elias (Cute Woman), Annie McEnroe (Kay Culver), Pops Staples (Mr. Tucker), Jo Harvey Allen (Lying Woman), David Byrne (Narrator). Directed by David Byrne and produced by Gary Kurfirst. Screenplay by Stephen Tobolowsky, Beth Henley, and Byrne.

There are more than fifty sets of twins in David Byrne's *True Stories*, I learned by studying the press notes, and perhaps we should pause here for a moment to meditate upon that fact. A hundred twins are not going to make or break a movie, and the average audience is not going to notice more than a fraction of them.

But, consider the state of mind of the person who decided the film should *have* fifty sets of twins.

That person undoubtedly is Byrne. What was he thinking of? My hunch is that he was thinking about the movie's voodoo: the magical things that go on beneath the surface of the work of art, lending it an aura that seeps up into the visible parts. Any movie made by actors and technicians who know that the director has hired fifty sets of twins is going to be a movie made by people who think the director is a very strange man. And that will affect their work. Even the ordinary moments in *True Stories* seem a little odd, as if the actors are trying to humor the weirdo they're working for.

Byrne says the movie was influenced by true stories he read in the papers, and he has published a book of some of those stories he has collected. They range from the mundane (the happily married couple who have not spoken to one another for fifteen years) to the cosmic (the Universal Product Code on grocery items is the advance sign of the coming of the Antichrist).

In *True Stories*, Byrne visits a mythical Texas town named Virgil in which everyone is a little strange and some people are downright unique. Try to imagine Virgil as being populated by everyone who went stir-crazy in Lake Wobegon.

Byrne narrates his film and is the host for the tour of Virgil. He is a thin, quiet, withdrawn figure with a voice so flat that you have to listen to the pauses to figure out when the sentences end. He drives a new red convertible and wears Saturday night cowboy clothes. He takes us to Virgil just as it's about to celebrate "150 Years of Specialness."

There is no real plot here, just wonderment. We meet a woman too lazy to get out of bed, and a man who advertises for a wife but says she must be prepared to accept his teddy-bear figure. We meet the lying woman, who confides shocking inside scandal on many of the most important events of the last twenty-five years. She knows because she was there. We meet civic leaders and marching bands, we visit an old man who casts spells and foretells the future, and we meet a preacher who in one unbroken sentence leaps from the death of Elvis Presley to the fact that we always run out of Kleenex and toilet paper at the same time. The studio went nuts trying to figure out how to sell this film. They came down hard on the angle that it had a lot of music by the Talking Heads, the avant-garde rock group that Byrne founded and leads. It does have a lot of music in it, and that will appeal to the viewers who have made *Stop Making Sense*, the Talking Heads concert film, a hit.

But this is not a musical. It's a bold attempt to paint a bizarre American landscape. This movie does what some painters try to do: It recasts ordinary images into strange new shapes. There is hardly a moment in *True Stories* that doesn't seem everyday to anyone who has grown up in Middle America, and not a moment that doesn't seem haunted with secrets, evasions, loneliness, depravity, or hidden joy—sometimes all at once. This is almost like a science-fiction movie: Everyone on screen looks so normal and behaves so oddly, they could be pod people.

The photography is an important element of the film. The movie was shot by Ed Lachman, who has become a brand name for people interested in offbeat directors. He was the guy who followed Werner Herzog to the slopes of a volcano that was about to erupt to film *La Soufriere*, and he has worked for Wim Wenders, Shirley Clarke, Bernardo Bertolucci, Jean-Luc Godard, and Tina Turner.

This time, he finds a new look: His landscapes and city scenes are like those old postcards in which everything seems slightly skewed. His buildings look like parodies of buildings. His people are seen against indoor landscapes of the objects they own—so many objects they seem about to be buried.

And then Byrne orchestrates all of this in the most deadpan way. If you walk in looking for payoffs, you're going to be disappointed. This movie doesn't start here and go there, and the closest thing it has to a story is the quest of the shy bachelor (John Goodman) for a wife. Will he marry the woman who never leaves her bed? If he does, where will the ceremony take place? It's the kind of courtship where, when you know the woman well enough, you ask her if she'd like to get *out* of bed. You see how one thing leads to another?

Truly, Madly, Deeply ★ ★ ★
NO MPAA RATING, 89 m., 1991

Juliet Stevenson (Nina), Alan Rickman (Jamie), Bill Paterson (Sandy), Michael Maloney (Mark), Jenny Howe (Burge). Directed by Anthony Minghella and produced by Robert Cooper. Screenplay by Minghella.

For some time now I have been complaining about movies in which people return from the afterlife. My complaint is always the same: If the afterlife is as miraculous as we expect it to be, why would anyone want to return? I have my answer. They come back to watch movies on video. This is a relief. I would not want to contemplate going through eternity without occasionally being able to put *Five Easy Pieces* on the VCR.

My information about the afterlife comes from Anthony Minghella's *Truly, Madly, Deeply*, a truly odd film, maddening, occasionally deeply moving. It opens as the story of a woman consumed by grief. Her man has died and she misses him, and his absence is like an open wound. Then he returns. He steps back into her life from beyond the grave and folds her in his arms, and the passion with which she greets him is joyous to

behold. He is back, he explains, because he did not die "properly." He got caught in some kind of reality warp, I guess, between life and death, and the upshot of it is, he's back. Oh, he's dead. But he's here.

The woman is played by Juliet Stevenson, as one of those intelligent but vulnerable women like Nathalie Baye plays in French films. The man is Alan Rickman, who you will look at on the screen and know you have seen somewhere, and rattle your memory all during the movie without making the connection that he was the villain in *Die Hard*.

He was a cello player in life, and now he is one in death, and he and Stevenson hang around the house all day, making ga-ga eyes. For various reasons she has to keep his return secret from her friends, who cannot understand why she has bounced back from profound depression into a state of giddy happiness.

All of these passages of the movie are convincing, in a strange way: This is sort of a *Ghost* for grown-ups. Then the movie takes a turn toward the really odd, as various new pals of the man return from the next world to join him. This eventually leads Juliet Stevenson to deliver one of the most memorable lines of dialogue of this or any year: "I can't believe I have a bunch of dead people watching videos in my living room."

I do not want to reveal the turns the plot takes then. I will mention, however, the character played by Michael Maloney, who ventures into Stevenson's life and falls in love with her and makes her choose between this world and the next. His character is truly goofy, and charming, and in his own indirect way he leads the movie toward some truths that are, the more you think about them, really pretty profound.

Truth or Dare ★ ★ ★ ½
R, 118 m., 1991

A documentary featuring Madonna on her 1990 Blond Ambition tour. Directed by Alek Keshishian and produced by Sigurjon Sighvatsson, Steve Golin, and Madonna.

Lawsuits have been filed over moments considerably less shocking than the ones Madonna cheerfully allows to be included in *Truth or Dare*, the new documentary about her 1990 Blond Ambition tour of Japan, the United States, and Europe. This is a backstage documentary with a vengeance, an authorized invasion of privacy in which the camera follows Madonna even during intimate moments with her family and childish sex games with her backup dancers.

Although the movie seems happiest when it is retailing potential scandal, its heart is not in sex but in business, and the central value in the film is the work ethic. Madonna schedules herself for a punishing international tour of one-night stands and then delivers with a clockwork determination, explaining to a family member in Detroit that she can't go out to party because she has to conserve her strength.

Night after night the exhausting show goes on, taking on aspects of a crusade for the cast members. Ironically—given Madonna's onstage use of sacrilege as a prop—every show is preceded by a prayer session, everyone holding hands while Madonna asks God's help and recites a daily list of problems. And when her dancers have personal problems, they come to her as a counselor and mother figure.

She seems to like it that way, and halfway through the film I was even wondering if she deliberately chose insecure dancers with dependent personalities because she enjoyed playing mother to them. Madonna has kept her act fresh by adopting a long series of public star personas, yet backstage, people don't relate to her as a star, but as the boss. Her charisma comes not through glitter but through power, and there is never any doubt exactly who is in charge. We get the feeling that if show biz ever loses its appeal for her, she could be successful in business or even politics: She's a hard-headed organizer, a taskmaster, disciplined and clear-headed.

The movie follows the Blond Ambition tour from its soggy beginnings in Japan's rainy season, through a series of one-night stands across the world. There are the Los Angeles concerts with all of the celebrities backstage (Kevin Costner tells her the concert was "neat," and she sticks a finger down her throat). Detroit, her hometown, where she assures her father that she can indeed get him tickets for the show. Toronto, where the police threaten to arrest her for public masturbation ("What do they mean, masturbation?" "When you grab your crotch"). Then she tours Italy and Spain, inviting guys she has crushes on to parties, only to discover they're married or gay.

At one point in the film, talking about how lonely it is at the top, she's asked if she ever knew true love, and she answers sadly, "Sean. Sean." But she never says another word about her former husband Sean Penn. In the opening scenes she is glimpsed briefly with boyfriend Warren Beatty, but then he disappears, unmentioned, after making what sounded to me like fairly sensible observations (he complains that, for Madonna, if it doesn't happen on camera it hardly happens at all).

The organizing subject of the whole film is work. We learn a lot about how hard Madonna works, about her methods for working with her dancers and her backstage support team, about how brutally hard it is to do a world concert tour. Unlike most rock documentaries, the real heart of this film is backstage, and the onstage musical segments, while effectively produced, seem obligatory—they're not the reason she wanted to make this film. Why is work so important to her? Maybe there's a hint in the many scenes where she takes a motherly interest in the personal lives of her dancers, and even joins them between the sheets for innocent, bored, adolescent sex games. Madonna, who has had such success portraying a series of sexual roles and personalities, seems asexual on a personal level. A voyeur rather than a participant. Control and power are more interesting to her than intimacy. When she manipulates the minds of a stadium full of fans, that's exciting. It's not the same working with one person at a time.

The Turning Point ★ ★ ★ ½
PG, 119 m., 1977

Anne Bancroft (Emma), Shirley MacLaine (Deedee), Mikhail Baryshnikov (Yuri), Leslie Browne (Emilia), Tom Skerritt (Wayne), Martha Scott (Adelaide). Directed by Herbert Ross and produced by Ross and Arthur Laurents. Screenplay by Laurents.

Perfect movies are very rare, and very easy to write about. Imperfect movies are harder to write about, and the hardest reviews of all are of movies like *The Turning Point* that are touched with greatness and yet keep losing their way. The good things in it are *so* good that you cherish them, and there's the temptation to forgive the lapses.

So let's start with the good. The movie's the story of an old friendship between a great ballerina (Anne Bancroft) and a ballerina (Shirley MacLaine) who might have been great but will never really know for sure. Twenty years have passed since they were both young dancers, and now Miss Bancroft performs in Miss MacLaine's home-

town and their friendship reasserts itself. Miss MacLaine's daughter is a promising young ballerina—she already has professional experience—and Miss Bancroft arranges for her to join her company.

As Miss MacLaine accompanies her daughter to New York, three themes assert themselves: Miss MacLaine's jealousy, smoldering for twenty years; Miss Bancroft's fear of approaching age and yet her desire to see the young girl succeed; the self-doubt both women have about the choices they made of careers or marriage. These are adult themes, and *The Turning Point* handles them thoughtfully.

It also gives us a love story or two. Miss MacLaine's daughter falls in love with the ballet company's superstar (Mikhail Baryshnikov, typecast). And during the long summer of the movie's action, Miss MacLaine has to deal not only with her own feelings but with her daughter's. We're dealing here with soap opera stuff, but never in a soap opera way. *The Turning Point* confronts its big emotional moments directly and simply, and maybe that's why they affect us so much.

The straightforward dramatic sections of the movie, then, are very well written and acted; Miss Bancroft and Miss MacLaine are particularly good, and then there are sensitive supporting performances by Tom Skerritt, as Miss MacLaine's husband, and by Leslie Browne, the talented young dancer who plays their daughter. When people say they loved *The Turning Point*, they're probably thinking about moments like the one when Miss Bancroft pushes the reluctant and sick young girl back onto the stage, or when the two older women go aside at a party and finally say all the things they've bottled up, or when Miss MacLaine is so touchingly mystified by how she should react to the news of her daughter's first affair.

Those moments are good enough to make the movie. And, of course, there's also a lot of dancing in the film; Baryshnikov is a wonder, and the film's director, Herbert Ross, is a choreographer who knows how to see dance through his camera. But it's during the ballet sequences that the film breaks down, because Ross can photograph the dances so much better than he can work them into his film.

This has been a juicy, realistic, achingly human movie for most of its length, dealing with age and jealousy, love and the cruel demands of great art. So we feel real disappointment when Ross breaks the mood and the flow. He does that most unforgivingly in a sequence where Miss Browne has a triumph onstage, and Ross cuts away to close-ups of Miss MacLaine and Miss Bancroft watching her—while prophetic dialogue from earlier in the film is repeated in flashback on the sound track. Unforgivable. And the movie's climactic dance scenes—the evening at ballet, punctuated by the hoary old gimmick of a hand turning the pages of a program—are fun for ballet fans, yes, but they land with a thud in the middle of the movie's emotional drama.

To sort out my feelings: *The Turning Point*'s story is handled with real care and touches us. The movie's dance sequences are virtuoso in themselves. But the pieces don't match, and Ross doesn't help by encumbering the dance material with ungainly story devices from the 1930s. You watch this film about a woman wondering if she could have been a great dancer, and you find yourself wondering if it could have been a great film.

Turtle Diary ★ ★ ★ ½
PG-13, 97 m., 1985

Ben Kingsley (William Snow), Glenda Jackson (Neaera Duncan), Michael Gambon (George Fairbairn), Eleanor Bron (Miss Neap), Harriet Walter (Harriet). Directed by John Irvin and produced by Peter Snell. Screenplay by Harold Pinter.

I saw this scene once in the London Zoo. It happened in the gloom of an insect house. Two men stood stooped over, side by side, their hands clasped behind their backs, peering through a glass into the chamber where a rare spider lived. Their faces were bathed in the low red light coming from the enclosure.

As they watched the spider, I watched them, until at last the spider did whatever it was they had been waiting for it to do. Then they stood up, looked briefly at each other, exchanged a matter-of-fact nod, and went their separate ways. London has always seemed to me to be a city of hobbyists and fanatics, experts in obscure specialities. But this moment stands out in particular, as a spider and two voyeurs shared one of the spider's most intimate moments.

Turtle Diary, the quiet, sly, and immensely amusing film from a screenplay by Harold Pinter, begins with two more such devotees. They are obsessed by giant sea turtles. They peek through the glass as the turtles lazily wheel around and around their cramped space in a tank at the London Zoo. They meet again, by chance, in a bookshop way over on the other side of the city, where the man (Ben Kingsley) is a clerk, and the woman (Glenda Jackson) has come to buy a book on turtles. They gradually become aware that they are seeing each other frequently at the turtle house, and then they discover that each has approached the turtles' keeper with the same question: What would it take to steal those giant turtles and set them free in the sea?

Turtle Diary is about a scheme by Kingsley, Jackson, and the zoo curator to do just that. But it is about a great many other things, as well. It is about the strange boarding house where Kingsley lives in company with a jolly landlady, a moody spinster, and a Turk who never cleans up the kitchen after himself. It is about the flat where Jackson lives, alone with her pet water beetle and about the man across the landing who knows a great deal about snails. And it is about the young woman who works with Kingsley in the bookshop, and lusts after him.

In a movie filled with wonderful, small sequences, I think my favorite begins when Kingsley suddenly turns to the young woman and says, out of the clear sky, "That's a pretty dress." In the next scene they are in a pub, in the next scene a restaurant. And if you want to observe the mastery of screen acting, watch the way Kingsley keeps a poker face while discussing his sex life with the woman, and then watch the way he allows himself to smile.

Ben Kingsley's smile, so warm and mysterious, is the sun that shines all through *Turtle Diary*. This is not a predictable movie, and it does not have a predictable structure (it does not even begin to end with the climax of the turtle caper). It is about peculiar people who somewhere find the impulses to do things that make them very happy.

If this movie had been made in America, I fear, it would have turned into a burlesque, with highway cops chasing turtles down the Santa Monica Freeway. *Turtle Diary* could only have been written, directed, and acted in the country where I saw those two strangers wait with such infinite patience for the spider to do its thing.

Twenty Bucks ★ ★ ★
R, 91 m., 1994

Linda Hunt (Angeline), Christopher Lloyd (Jimmy), Steve Buscemi (Frank), Elisabeth Shue (Emily Adams), Brendan Fraser (Sam), Gladys Knight (Mrs. McCormac), Melora Walters (Stripper), Spalding Gray (Priest). Directed by Keva Rosenfeld and produced by Karen Murphy. Screenplay by Leslie Boehm and Endre Boehm.

Most movies begin at their beginnings and march sternly toward their ends, convinced that the universe makes sense, and that effect follows cause. Once in a long while a film will try to subvert that certainty. Buñuel's *The Phantom of Liberty* (1974) told one story for a while, and then peeled off to follow another set of characters, and then another. Richard Linklater's *Slacker* (1991) did the same thing, bouncing from one person to the next on a kind of guided tour of Austin, Texas.

And now here is the beguiling *Twenty Bucks*, which follows a twenty-dollar bill as it slips from one hand to another. There's no deep point to be made; the device is simply an excuse to tell half a dozen short stories. But the very lightness of the premise gives the film a kind of freedom We glimpse revealing moments in lives, instead of following them to one of those manufactured movie conclusions that pretends everything has been settled.

The bill originally finds its way into the hands of a street person (Linda Hunt), who is sure it will win her the lottery. Along the way it becomes a wedding gift, given to the groom (Brendan Fraser) by his wealthy future father-in-law (George Morfogen), as a warning that riches will not fall from trees. Then it finds its way into the garter belt of a stripper (Melora Walters) at the groom's bachelor party, and from there it indirectly leads to the best of the film's vignettes.

That's the one involving Christopher Lloyd (the mad inventor in the *Back to the Future* movies) and Steve Buscemi, who run into each other by chance. Lloyd asks Buscemi if he'll help him out with a few jobs he had in mind. He wants to pull some stickups. Buscemi thinks he's crazy, but isn't reluctant to go along, and then the caper takes on a crazy logic of its own.

Sometimes an actor will walk into a movie for fifteen minutes or so, and show you such strength that you look at him altogether differently. That's what Lloyd does here (Buscemi has done it too, in movies like *Reservoir Dogs* and *Mystery Train*). He doesn't play the holdup man as a bad guy, but as a well-spoken, intelligent, logical, firm-minded character who has a chilling reserve. By the time his segment arrives at its unexpected conclusion, I was so absorbed, I'd basically forgotten about the twenty bucks and the rest of the movie.

But the rest is good, too, including a vignette starring Elisabeth Shue as a would-be writer who keeps getting put down. The story of Endre Boehm's original screenplay is almost as problematic as the fate of the twenty-dollar bill. He wrote this story in 1935. It gathered dust for more than half a century before he handed it to his son, Leslie, who read it, liked it, did a rewrite, and saw it into production. Some of the language and situations (like the stripper at the bachelor party) were no doubt not in the original version, but the spirit seems to come through unchanged: A wonderment at the unpredictable world we live in, and the way chance plays a role in our lives, even when we'd like to think we're calling the shots.

28 Up ★ ★ ★ ★
NO MPAA RATING, 136 m., 1985

Featuring Tony Walker, Bruce Balden, Suzanne Dewey, Nicholas Hitchon, Peter Davies, Paul Kligerman, John Brisby, Andrew Brackfield, Charles Furneaux, Neil Hughes, Jackie Bassett, Lynn Johnson, Susan Sullivan, and Simon Basterfield. Directed by Michael Apted and produced by Margaret Bottomley and Apted.

The child is father of the man.
—William Wordsworth

Somewhere at home are photographs taken when I was a child. A solemn, round-faced little boy gazes out at the camera, and as I look at him I know in my mind that he is me and I am him, but the idea has no reality. I cannot understand the connection, and as I think more deeply about the mystery of the passage of time, I feel a sense of awe.

Watching Michael Apted's documentary *28 Up,* I had that feeling again and again, the awe that time does pass, and that the same individual does pass through it, grows from a child to an adult, becoming someone new over the passage of years, but still containing some of the same atoms and molecules and fears and gifts that were stored in the child.

This film began in 1964 as a documentary for British television. The assignment for Michael Apted was to interview several seven-year-olds from different British social classes, races, backgrounds, and parts of the country, simply talking with them about what they found important or interesting about their lives. Seven years later, when the sub-

jects were fourteen, Apted tracked them down and interviewed them again. He repeated the process when they were twenty-one, and again when they were twenty-eight, and this film moves back and forth within that material, looking at the same people when they were children, teen-agers, young adults, and now warily approaching their thirties.

We have always known that the motion picture is a time machine. John Wayne is dead, but the angle of his smile and the squint in his eye will be as familiar to our children as it is to us. Orson Welles is dead, but a hundred years from now the moment will still live when the cat rubs against his shoe in *The Third Man,* and then the light from the window catches his sardonic grin. What is remarkable about *28 Up* is not, however, that the same individuals have been captured at four different moments in their lives. We quickly grow accustomed to that. What is awesome is that we can see so clearly how the seven-year-old became the adolescent, how the teen-ager became the young man or woman, how the adult still contains the seeds of the child.

One sequence follows the lives of three upper-class boys who come from the right families and go to all the right schools. One of the boys is a snot, right from the beginning, and by the time he is twenty-one he is a bit of a reactionary prig. We are not surprised when he declines to be interviewed at twenty-eight; we could see it coming. We are curious, though, about whether he will check back in at thirty-five, perhaps having outlived some of his self-importance.

Another little boy is a winsome loner at seven. At fourteen, he is a dreamy idealist, at twenty-one he is defiant but discontented, and at twenty-eight—in the most unforgettable passage in the film—he is an outcast, a drifter who moves around Great Britain from place to place, sometimes living in a shabby house trailer, still a little puzzled by how he seems to have missed the boat, to never have connected with his society.

There is another little boy who dreams of growing up to be a jockey, and who is a stable boy at fourteen, and does get to be a jockey, briefly, and now drives a cab and finds in his job some of the same personal independence and freedom of movement that he once thought jockeys had. There is a determined young Cockney who is found, years later, happily married and living in Australia and doing well in the building trades. There is a

young woman who at twenty-one was clearly an emotional mess, a vague, defiant, bitter, and unhappy person. At twenty-eight, married and with a family, she is a happy and self-assured young woman; the transformation is almost unbelievable.

As the film follows its subjects through the first halves of their lives, our thoughts are divided. We are fascinated by the personal progressions we see on the screen. We are distracted by wonderment about the mystery of the human personality. If we can see so clearly how these children become these adults—was it just as obvious in our own cases? Do we, even now, contain within us our own personal destinies for the next seven years? Is change possible? Is the scenario already written?

I was intending to write that certain groups would be particularly interested in this movie. Teachers, for example, would hardly be able to see *28 Up* without looking at their students in a different, more curious light. Poets and playwrights would learn from this film. So would psychiatrists. But then I realized that *28 Up* is not a film by or for experts. It is superb journalism, showing us these people passing through stages of their lives in such a way that we are challenged to look at our own lives. It is as thought-provoking as any documentary I've ever seen.

I look forward to the next edition of this film, when its subjects are thirty-five. I have hope for some, fear for others. It is almost scary to realize this film has given me a fair chance of predicting what lies ahead for these strangers. I almost understand the motives of those who chose to drop out of the experiment.

29th Street ★ ★ ★
R, 101 m., 1991

Danny Aiello (Frank Pesce, Sr.), Anthony LaPaglia (Frank Pesce, Jr.), Lainie Kazan (Mrs. Pesce), Frank Pesce (Vito Pesce), Robert Forster (Sgt. Tartaglia), Rick Aiello (Jimmy Vitello). Directed by George Gallo and produced by David Permut. Screenplay by Gallo.

One of my favorite things on television is the news coverage of lucky lottery winners. There they are, sitting in their living rooms, holding the winning ticket and expounding on their plans. They get a mike shoved in their faces and suddenly they're benevolent investors and financiers, announcing good deeds such as buying their mother a home or paying off their in-laws' pickup truck.

I always have the sense that there's more than meets the eye in those stories, and George Gallo's *29th Street* has the same conviction. This is more or less the true story of a man named Frank Pesce, Jr., who was born with good luck and tormented by it all of his life, right up until the time the worst possible thing happened to him, which was that he won the 1976 New York State Lottery. Why would that be a terrible thing? I can't say without revealing too many of the movie's surprises, but trust me. To paraphrase a famous line from *Raging Bull*, if he loses, he loses, and if he wins, he loses.

The movie stars the feckless Anthony LaPaglia as Frank Junior, and Danny Aiello as his father, whose luck is as bad as his son's is good. The family lives together in a crowded row house, in riotous good will, held more or less in line by Mrs. Pesce (Lainie Kazan), who sings operatic arias in the kitchen while the men sit in the next room and look at her in sheer love and wonderment. Frank Senior's great dream in life is to move his family to Queens, and his great passion is for his lawn (he chases away cats because of a belief that their body heat can burn holes in the grass).

The Pesces in this movie have their origins in real people (indeed, the real Frank Junior is a character actor who appears as his own older brother, Vito), but in *29th Street* they seem to emerge mostly from the long tradition of Italian-Americans in the movies. They are loosely related to the characters in *GoodFellas, Married to the Mob, True Love,* and *Spike of Bensonhurst*, and Aiello, as the head of the family, has all the necessary warmth and passion to lead them.

The great cross of his life is his son's good luck. Even Frank Junior's bad luck is good luck, as when he's stabbed in a fight with a girl, but then the surgeons discover a tumor in its earliest stages and are able to remove it. If he hadn't been stabbed, who knows what mischief that tumor might have caused? His good luck almost seems to exhibit a sense of humor, as when he keeps trying to lose his car, so he can report it stolen, but it keeps being found and returned to him.

Then he enters the first New York State Lottery. And, of course, he is among the finalists for the big prize. His problem is, by then he no longer possesses the ticket because of some urgent dealings with mobsters who are on his father's case. And so, when he wins . . .

Well, I have a slight problem with what happens then. The explanation at the end of the movie is so neat and tidy that I couldn't really believe it, especially not after the movie showed me two different explanations for what happened. The ending is so unlikely, indeed, that I suspect it is the literal truth, and that such a thing did happen, exactly like that, to the real Frank Pesce, Jr. No screenwriter could have dreamed it up.

Still, Anthony LaPaglia struggles manfully with it, and makes it about as convincing as it can be. If you saw a little-noticed 1990 Alan Alda movie named *Betsy's Wedding,* you will remember LaPaglia, who stole the show as a mafioso who fell hopelessly in love with Ally Sheedy, as a cop. Again this time, he shows a genuine comic gift. The ending aside, *29th Street* is a movie of considerable energy and good humor, with the expansive Aiello, the uninhibited Kazan, and the screwy LaPaglia having a lot of fun with the material.

Twice in a Lifetime ★ ★ ★ ½
R, 117 m., 1985

Gene Hackman (Harry), Ann-Margret (Audrey), Ellen Burstyn (Kate), Amy Madigan (Sonny), Ally Sheedy (Helen), Stephen Lang (Keith), Darrell Larson (Jerry), Brian Dennehy (Nick). Directed and produced by Bud Yorkin. Screenplay by Colin Welland.

Everyday American life is so rare in the movies these days that some of the pleasures of *Twice in a Lifetime* are very simple ones, like seeing a family around a dinner table, or watching a kid sister prepare for her wedding day. The rhythms of life and the normal patterns of speech seemed almost unfamiliar, after all the high-tech thrillers and teen-age idiot films I've seen. This film was so sensible, perceptive, and grown-up that I almost looked for the subtitles.

The film stars Gene Hackman as a working man whose marriage is happy in all the official ways, and dead in the personal ways. His wife (Ellen Burstyn) has centered her life entirely around her home and her family to such an extent that on Hackman's birthday she doesn't even want to go out with him. She tells him to go down to the corner tavern and enjoy himself. And she means it. There is a lot missing in this marriage.

At the saloon, Hackman meets the new barmaid (Ann-Margret) and begins a wary process of falling in love with her. He eventually decides to leave his wife and move in with this woman, and this decision causes upheaval throughout his family. His wife is devastated. But the angriest family member is his oldest daughter (Amy Madigan), who bitterly resents the way he's dumping them—especially when her kid sister (Ally Sheedy) is about to get married.

Twice in a Lifetime stacks its cards very carefully. One of the strengths of the movie is that it allows us to see so many points of view. Hackman has not simply dumped his wife for a sex bomb: the Ann-Margret character has been around the block a few times and operates from a center of quiet realism. It is possibly true that the life and growth has gone out of his marriage. Perhaps he deserves another chance—although the movie is too hasty to assume that his wife does, too, if only she knew it.

The most complicated and interesting character in the movie is Amy Madigan's angry daughter. She's mad about more than the broken marriage. Her husband is out of work, and in her late twenties she feels somewhat trapped by her marriage and children. A lot of her hopes have gone into her kid sister. She wants her to go to college and make a future for herself, but Ally Sheedy is rushing into her own early marriage, blinded by young love.

Madigan acts as the contact point between the various parts of the story: loving her sister, exasperated by her, standing by her mom, resentfully excluding her father. It's quite an assignment, and as she tries to balance all those demands we see one of the most complex movie characters in a long time (have you noticed how many recent movies assign their characters one mood and think that's enough?).

The Gene Hackman and Ann-Margret characters are complex, too. They are attracted not by lust but by the promise of a new life. They both feel that when they get up in the morning there's nothing to look forward to all day. This movie knows one of the differences between young love and middle-aged love: Kids often are motivated by romance, but people in their forties and fifties sometimes are inspired by the most romantic notion of all—idealism, and the notion that they have found a mate for their minds.

The least-defined character in *Twice in a Lifetime* is the wife, played by Burstyn. Her husband has made his decision and left her to make hers. At first she is simply lost. Eventually she starts picking up the pieces, and she gets a job in the local beauty parlor.

She even gets a new hairdo (in one of the movies' most durable clichés). By the end of the film she has started to realize that she, too, was trapped by the marriage. But there is the slightest feeling that her realization owes more to the convenience of the screenplay than to her own growth.

The movie does not have a conventional happy ending. Life will go on, and people will strive, and new routines will replace old ones. The movie has no villains and few heroes. But it has given us several remarkable scenes, especially two confrontations between Madigan and Hackman, one in a bar, the other at a wedding rehearsal, in which the movie shows how much children expect from their parents, and how little the parents often have to give. Growing up is learning that parents are fallible. The people who find that hardest to learn are parents.

Twilight Zone—the Movie

Prologue and Segment One Written and directed by John Landis. Starring Dan Aykroyd, Albert Brooks, Vic Morrow, and Doug McGrath. ★ ★

Segment Two Directed by Steven Spielberg. Written by George Johnson. Starring Scatman Crothers. ★ ½

Segment Three Directed by Joe Dante. Written by Richard Matheson. Starring Kathleen Quinlan, Jeremy Light, and Kevin McCarthy. ★ ★ ★ ½

Segment Four Directed by George Miller. Written by Richard Matheson. Starring John Lithgow and Abbe Lane. ★ ★ ★ ½

PG, 101 m., 1983

Produced by Steven Spielberg and inspired by the television series created by Rod Serling.

Every year at Oscar time, somebody comes up with the bright idea of making the Academy Awards into a fair fight. Instead of making the voters choose among five widely different performances, they say, they ought to have five actors playing the same scene. That way you'd really be able to see who was best. It's an impractical idea, but *Twilight Zone— the Movie* does almost the same thing. It takes four stories that are typical of the basic approach of the great "Twilight Zone" TV series, and has four different directors try their hand at recapturing Rod Serling's "wondrous land whose boundaries are that of imagination." And the surprising thing is, the two superstar directors are thoroughly

routed by two less-known directors whose previous credits have been horror and action pictures.

The superstars are John *(Blues Brothers)* Landis and Steven *(E.T.)* Spielberg. The relative newcomers are Joe Dante, whose *The Howling* was not my favorite werewolf movie, and George Miller, whose *The Road Warrior* is some kind of a manic classic. Spielberg, who produced the whole project, perhaps sensed that he and Landis had the weakest results, since he assembled the stories in an ascending order of excitement. *Twilight Zone* starts slow, almost grinds to a halt, and then has a fast comeback.

Landis directed the first episode, which stars Vic Morrow in the story of a bigot who is transported back in time to Nazi Germany and Vietnam and forced to swallow his own racist medicine. This segment is predictable, once we know the premise, and Landis does nothing to surprise us. Because we know that Morrow was killed in a helicopter accident during the filming of the segment, an additional pall hangs over the whole story.

Spielberg's segment is next. It stars Scatman Crothers as a mysterious old man who turns up at an old folks' home one day and literally gives the residents what they think they want; to be young again. The easily anticipated lesson is that one lifetime is enough. Spielberg's visual style in this segment is so convoluted and shadowy that the action is hard to follow; the master of clear-cut, sharp-edged visuals is trying something that doesn't work.

But then comes Joe Dante's weird, offbeat segment about a traveler (Kathleen Quinlan) who strays off the beaten path and accepts an offer of hospitality from a fresh-faced young kid who looks healthy and harmless. Once Quinlan is inside the roadside farmhouse where the kid lives, however, she's in another dimension—a bizarre world telepathically projected by the boy's imagination. The kid loves video games and TV cartoons, and he's trapped a whole group of adults in his private fantasies. The art direction in this segment is especially good at giving the house interior a wonderland quality.

George Miller's fourth segment stars John Lithgow in a remake of a famous "Twilight Zone" TV story in which a nervous air traveler sees (or imagines that he sees) a little green man hacking away at the engine of his airplane. But there *couldn't* be a little green man out there—could there? The beauty of *Twilight Zone—the Movie* is the same as the

secret of the TV series: It takes ordinary people in ordinary situations and then zaps them with "next stop—the Twilight Zone!"

Twins ★ ★ ★
PG, 107 m., 1988

Arnold Schwarzenegger (Julius Benedict), Danny DeVito (Vincent Benedict), Kelly Preston (Marnie Mason), Chloe Webb (Linda Mason), Bonnie Bartlett (Mary Ann Benedict), Hugh O'Brian (Granger). Directed and produced by Ivan Reitman. Screenplay by William Davies, William Osborne, Timothy Harris, and Herschel Weingrod.

When he is shown into the orphanage where his twin brother spent his childhood, Julius Benedict is able to point out the very bed where his brother must have slept. "That's amazing," a nun says. "How did you know?" Julius smiles. "Hit vas seem-pull," he says. "Hit is zah bed by zah fire eggstinguisher. The zame one I would haf chozun. In zah event of fire, he could grab zah eggstinguisher and zave all of zah roar-phans."

The accent belongs to Arnold Schwarzenegger, who has long had a gift of comedy, but has seldom had a comedy to exercise it in. In *Twins*, teamed up in several different ways with Danny DeVito, he gets the movie off to a funny start. The movie begins with Schwarzenegger as the unpaid assistant of a scientist who lives on an island somewhere between Bora Bora and Australia. Discovering that he has a twin brother he has never known about, Arnold commandeers an inflatable dinghy and starts rowing for the nearest airport.

Meanwhile, back in the States, DeVito is in trouble. He's a professional con man who also does amateur cons in his spare time. His sideline is stealing luxury cars at the airport and selling them to chop shops, and about the time Arnold is arriving in America, DeVito is thrown into jail with hundreds of dollars of unpaid parking tickets. Arnold tracks him down in a jail cell, and tells him of their secret past. The diminutive DeVito, of course, does not believe this muscular Teuton is his twin. Few would. But if Schwarzenegger has bail money, DeVito is prepared to play along with him.

Good comedies often have central ideals that are transparently simple. *Twins* is an example. When the movie opened, there were giant billboards all over the United States showing DeVito's picture with the block letters "Schwarzenegger" underneath, and vice versa. It's a brilliant sell, and a clever idea—but the reason it works so well in the movie is that both Schwarzenegger and DeVito have genuinely tender sides to their natures. You know the movie is a running gag, but somehow there's a sweetness in their relationship that makes the plot seem less manipulated.

The explanation for their twinship is that both men were the result of a eugenics experiment in which the sperm from six different fathers was combined into a kind of natal milkshake and administered to their mother. The men represented brains, brawn, and other attributes, and the woman was as nearly perfect as possible. But the experiment misfired and produced, not one perfect baby, but twins.

"Your brother got all of the good stuff," DeVito is told years afterward, when he finally confronts the mastermind behind the bizarre experiment. "You got the leftovers." That's why Schwarzenegger is an awesome physical specimen who speaks six languages and is a brilliant scientist, and why DeVito is a small-time hustler who manages to steal the wrong cars. For example, a late-model Cadillac that just happens to have a trunk containing industrial contraband worth millions.

When I saw the plot turning toward the contraband, I began to grow apprehensive. And when the movie introduced a murderous industrial spy, my heart sank. I thought I could foresee yet another Hollywood movie in which the third act was jettisoned in favor of a shoot-out and a chase. In the event, however, director Ivan Reitman soft-pedals the subplot involving the stolen goods, and actually manages to supply the movie with a real ending involving thought, dialogue, and other elements that recently have tended to disappear in the last twenty-five minutes of Hollywood entertainments.

The movie supplies both men with love interests—DeVito with a long-suffering girlfriend (Chloe Webb, from Sid & Nancy), and Schwarzenegger with Kelly Preston, who plays a hilarious love scene with him on the floor of a motel room. Why the floor? Because that's where Arnold prefers to sleep. The movie claims that the Schwarzenegger character is a virgin, and there is a certain justification for that; the filmmakers claim that this is actually Arnold's first love scene, in fourteen years of stardom.

Schwarzenegger's gift for comedy was apparent in his very first film, the documentary Pumping Iron (1974), and in his first feature, Bob Rafelson's Stay Hungry, two years later. But it has had precious little use since then in a series of high-voltage action pictures, even though Schwarzenegger always finds a way to introduce comic dialogue or some sort of self-deprecating humor even in the most violent films. This time, given comedy from beginning to end, he handles it with ease. DeVito's performance is equally assured, but less surprisingly, since we already knew he could cover this ground. Twins is not a great comedy—it's not up there with Reitman's Ghostbusters, and DeVito is not as funny as he was in Ruthless People and Wise Guys—but it is an engaging entertainment with some big laughs and a sort of warm goofiness.

Two English Girls ★ ★ ★ ★
R, 108 m., 1972

Jean-Pierre Leaud (Claude), Kika Markham (Anne Brown), Stacey Tendeter (Muriel Brown), Sylvia Marriott (Mrs. Brown), Marie Mansart (Madame Roc), Phillipe Leotard (Diurka), Mark Peterson (Mr. Flint), Irene Tunc (Ruta). Directed by François Truffaut and produced by Claude Miler. Screenplay by Truffaut and Jean Gruault.

It's wonderful how offhand François Truffaut's best films feel. There doesn't seem to be any great effort being made; he doesn't push for his effects, but lets them flower naturally from the simplicities of his stories. His film, Two English Girls, is very much like that. Because he doesn't strain for an emotional tone, he can cover a larger range than the one-note movies. Here he is discreet, even while filming the most explicit scenes he's ever done; he handles sadness gently; he is charming and funny even while he tells us a story that is finally tragic.

The story is from the second novel by Henri-Pierre Roche, who began writing at the age of seventy-four and whose first novel, Jules and Jim, provided the inspiration for nearly everyone's favorite Truffaut film. The two novels (and the two films) are variations on the same theme: What a terrible complex emotional experience it is to have to share love.

We would say that both stories involve romantic triangles, but Roche seems to see them more simply (and poignantly) as the shared dilemmas of people caught helplessly in their situations. Nobody sets out deliberately to involve himself in a triangular relationship—not when the love involved is real. It hurts too much.

Truffaut introduces us to Claude, a young French art critic, and then introduces him to Anne Brown, an English girl visiting in Paris. They form a friendship, and the girl invites him to come and visit her mother and sister in Wales. During the visit, he falls in love (or thinks he does) with the sister, Muriel. They want to marry, but they both have poor health, and it is decided to put off the marriage for a year. Claude returns to Paris, where Anne follows after a while, and then they fall into a sexual relationship that passes for a time as love. The virgin Muriel, meanwhile, remains passionately in love with Claude and nearly has an emotional breakdown when she learns that he no longer plans to marry her.

The story, as it unfolds, is involved but never untrue. Love itself is an elusive prize that passes among them; it is their doom that whenever two of them are together, it is the third who possesses love. The film relates love and loss so closely that we almost forgive Claude for his infidelities and stubbornness. Perversely, he wants to be apart from Muriel (and later Anne) so that he can desire all the more.

If Two English Girls resembles Jules and Jim in theme, it has an unmistakable stylistic relationship to Truffaut's little-seen masterpiece of 1970, The Wild Child. Both films used diaries, journals, and a spoken narration in order to separate us from the immediate experience of the stories. Truffaut wants us to feel that we're being told a fable, a sad winter's tale, that is all the more touching because these events happened long ago and love is trapped irretrievably in the past.

His visual strategy for creating this feeling is another favorite device from The Wild Child: the iris shot. (Put simply, this is the use of a slowly contracting circle to bring a shot to an end, instead of a fade or a cut). The iris isolates one element in the picture, somehow making it feel alone and vulnerable—and past. The film is photographed in a low-keyed color, and the sound recording is also a little muted; this isn't a film for emotional highs, we sense, because it's far and away too late for these lost love opportunities to be regained.

The one scene that violates this tone is as necessary as it is effective; when Muriel finally makes love with Claude we feel the terrible force of her passion, pent up for so many years, and then the camera pans to the blood-stained sheet and goes out of focus. Put in so many words, this probably sounds crude and obvious; in fact, this is almost the only red in the film, and is Truffaut's perfect visual metaphor for the fact that these three people have created a lot of their own unhappiness by avoiding or deflecting the consequences of their emotional feelings.

Jules and Jim was a young man's film (Truffaut was twenty-eight when he made it). *Two English Girls* is the film of a man some ten or twelve years down the road; it is still playful and winsome, but it realizes more fully the consequences of an opportunity lost. The final scene shows Claude, fifteen years later, wandering in the garden where he used to walk with Anne and Muriel. There are English children playing there, and he thinks to ask one of them, "Are you Muriel Brown's daughter?" But he doesn't, because . . . well, because.

The Two Jakes ★ ★ ★ ½
R, 128 m., 1990
(See also *Chinatown*)

Jack Nicholson (Jake Gittes), Harvey Keitel (Jake Berman), Meg Tilly (Kitty Berman), Madeleine Stowe (Lillian Bodine), Eli Wallach (Cotton Weingerger), Ruben Blades (Mickey Nice), Frederic Forrest (Chuck Newty), David Keith (Loach, Jr.), Richard Farnsworth (Earl Rawley), Tracey Walter (Tyrone Otley). Directed by Jack Nicholson and produced by Robert Evans and Harold Schneider. Screenplay by Robert Towne.

Here at long last is Jack Nicholson's *The Two Jakes*, seven years in the trade papers, center of prolonged teeth-gnashing at Paramount Pictures, and it turns out to be such a focused and concentrated film that every scene falls into place like clockwork; there's no feeling that it was a problem picture. It's not a thriller and it's not a whodunit, although it contains thriller elements and at the end we do find out whodunit. It's an exquisite short story about a mood, and a time, and a couple of guys who are blind-sided by love.

The movie takes place in postwar Los Angeles—the 1940s of the baby boom and housing subdivisions—instead of the 1930s city where *Chinatown* was set. It's not such a romantic city anymore. And private eyes like J.J. Gittes (Jack Nicholson) are a little more worn by time and care. The Gittes of *Chinatown* was the spiritual brother of Philip Marlowe. But now it is after the war, and Gittes has moved out of the two-room suite into a

building of his own. He heads a staff of investigators. He belongs to a country club and has a fiancée and has put on some weight. One of these days he's going to stop calling himself an investigator altogether, and become a security consultant.

But he still handles some of the old kinds of cases. The cases where the outraged husband bursts into the motel room and finds his wife locked in the arms of a priapic adulterer, and then the investigator leaps in with a camera and takes photos that will look bad in divorce court. He knows, Gittes tells us in the film's opening narration, that he shouldn't get involved in messy situations like that anymore. He's outgrown them. They're beneath him. But sometimes he still takes the jobs.

That's how he meets the other Jake—Jake Berman (Harvey Keitel), a property developer who thinks his wife (Meg Tilly) is fooling around with his partner. So Gittes tutors Berman on how to act when he bursts in through the door, and what to say, and then they stake out a motel where the evil act is confidently expected to take place. But Berman doesn't follow the script. A gun appears from somewhere, and the partner is shot, and the partner's wife (Madeleine Stowe) thinks that maybe it wasn't a case of adultery at all. Maybe it was cold-blooded murder, and Berman intended to kill his partner so that he and his wife could collect the partner's share of the property development. That might make Gittes accessory to murder.

So far, what we have here is the kind of plot that any private eye movie might have been proud of. But *The Two Jakes* uses the plot only as an occasion for the deeper and more brooding things it has to say. Everyone connected with this movie seems to have gone through the private eye genre and come out on the other side. The screenplay is by Robert Towne, who at one stage in the project's troubled history was going to direct it. He has not simply assembled some characters from his *Chinatown*, added some new ones, and thrown them into a plot. This movie is written with meticulous care, to show how good and evil are never as simple as they seem, and to demonstrate that even the motives of a villain may emerge from a goodness of heart.

Jack Nicholson has directed the film, and Vilmos Zsigmond has photographed it, in the same spirit. This isn't a film where we ricochet from one startling revelation to another. Instead, the progress of the story is

into the deeper recesses of the motives of the characters. We learn that Gittes, fiancée and all, is still deeply hurt by the murder of the Faye Dunaway character in *Chinatown;* he will never be over her. We learn that the property being developed by Berman has been visited before by Gittes, in that long-ago time. We learn that love, pure love, is a motive sufficient to justify horrifying actions. And we learn that when the past has been important enough to us, it will never quite leave us alone.

The movie is very dark, filled with shadows and secrets and half-heard voices, and scratchy revelations on a clandestine tape recording. Out in the valley where the development is being built, the sunshine is harsh and casts black shadows, and the land is cruel—the characters are shaken by earthquakes which reveal that the land rests uneasily on a dangerous pool of natural gas.

The performances are dark and gloomy, too, especially Nicholson's. He tones down his characteristic ebullience and makes Gittes older and wiser and more easily disillusioned. And he never even talks about the loss which hangs heavily on his heart; we have to infer it from the way his friends and employees tiptoe around it. Right from his first meeting with the Keitel character, when he notices they are wearing the same two-tone shoes, he feels a curious kinship with him, and that leads to a key final confrontation which I will not reveal. And he feels something, too, for the Meg Tilly character, who has been deeply hurt in her past and is afraid to express herself. She is like a bird with a broken wing.

The point of *The Two Jakes* is that love and loss are more important than the mechanical distribution of guilt and justice. When Nicholson and Keitel, as the two Jakes, have their final exchange of revelations, it is such a good scene because the normal considerations of a crime movie are placed on hold. The movie is really about the values which people have, and about the things that mean more to them than life and freedom. It's a deep movie, and a thoughtful one, and when it's over you can't easily put it out of your mind.

2010 ★ ★ ★
PG, 157 m., 1984

Roy Scheider (Heywood Floyd), John Lithgow (Curnow), Helen Mirren (Kirbuk), Bob Balaban (Chandra), Keir Dullea (Bowman), Douglas Rain (HAL 9000). Directed and produced by

Peter Hyams. Screenplay by Hyams. Based on a novel by Arthur C. Clarke.

All those years ago, when *2001: A Space Odyssey* was first released, I began my review with a few lines from a poem by e.e. cummings:

> *I'd rather learn from one bird how to sing*
> *than teach ten thousand stars how not*
> *to dance.*

That was my response to the people who said they couldn't understand *2001*, that it made no sense and that it was one long exercise in self-indulgence by Stanley Kubrick, who had sent a man to the stars, only to abandon him inside some sort of extraterrestrial hotel room. I felt that the poetry of *2001* was precisely in its mystery, and that to explain everything was to ruin everything— like the little boy who cut open his drum to see what made it bang.

2001 came out in the late 1960s, that legendary time when yuppies were still hippies, and they went to see the movie a dozen times and slipped up to the front of the theater and lay flat on their backs on the floor, so that the sound-and-light trip in the second half of the movie could wash over them and they could stagger to the exits and whisper "far out" to one another in quiet ecstasy. Now comes *2010*, a continuation of the Kubrick film, directed by Peter Hyams, whose background is in more pragmatic projects such as *Outland,* the Sean Connery space station thriller. The story is by Arthur C. Clarke (who, truth to tell, I always have suspected was a little bewildered by what Kubrick did to his original ideas). *2010* is very much a 1980s movie. It doesn't match the poetry and the mystery of the original film, but it does continue the story, and it offers sound, pragmatic explanations for many of the strange and visionary things in *2001* that had us arguing endlessly through the nights of 1968.

This is, in short, a movie that tries to teach ten thousand stars how not to dance. There were times when I almost wanted to cover my ears. Did I really want to know (a) why HAL 9000 disobeyed Dave's orders? or (b) the real reason for the Discovery's original mission? or (c) what the monoliths were trying to tell us? Not exactly. And yet we live in a most practical time, and they say every decade gets the movies it deserves. What we get in *2010* is not an artistic triumph, but it is a triumph of hardware, of special effects, of slick, exciting filmmaking. This is a movie that owes more to George Lucas than to Stanley Kubrick, more to *Star Wars* than to *Also Sprach Zarathustra*. It has an ending that is infuriating, not only in its simplicity, but in its inadequacy to fulfill the sense of anticipation, the sense of wonder we felt at the end of *2001*.

And yet the truth must be told: This is a good movie. Once we've drawn our lines, once we've made it absolutely clear that *2001* continues to stand absolutely alone as one of the greatest movies ever made, once we have freed *2010* of the comparisons with Kubrick's masterpiece, what we are left with is a good-looking, sharp-edged, entertaining, exciting space opera—a superior film of the *Star Trek* genre.

Because *2010* depends so much upon its story, it would be unfair to describe more than the essentials: A joint Soviet-American expedition sets out for the moons of Jupiter to investigate the fate of the Discovery, its crew, and its on-board computer HAL 9000. There is tension on board between the American leader (Roy Scheider) and the Soviet captain (Helen Mirren), and it's made worse because back on Earth, the superpowers are on the brink of nuclear war over Central America. If Kubrick sometimes seemed to be making a bloodless movie with faceless characters, Hyams pays a great deal of attention to story

and personality. But only one of the best moments in his movie grows out of character (the touching scene where a Soviet and an American hold onto each other for dear life during a terrifying crisis). The other great moments are special-effects achievements: a space walk threatened by vertigo, the awesome presence of Jupiter, and a spectacular flight through the planet's upper atmosphere.

It is possible that *no* conclusion to *2010* could be altogether satisfying, especially to anyone who still remembers the puzzling, awesome simplicity of the Star Child turning to regard us at the end of *2001*. This sequel has its work cut out for it. And the screenplay compounds the difficulty by repeatedly informing us that "something wonderful" is about to happen. After we've been told several times about that wonderful prospect, we're ready for something *really* wonderful, and we don't get it. We get a disappointingly mundane conclusion worthy of a 1950s sci-fi movie, not a sequel to *2001*. I, for one, was disappointed that the monoliths would deign to communicate with men at all—let alone that they would use English, or send their messages via a video screen, like the latest generation of cable news.

So. You have to make some distinctions in your mind. In one category, *2001: A Space Odyssey* remains inviolate, one of the handful of true film masterpieces. In a more temporal sphere, *2010* qualifies as superior entertainment, a movie more at home with technique than poetry, with character than with mystery, a movie that explains too much and leaves too little to our sense of wonderment, but a good movie all the same. If I nevertheless sound less than ecstatic, maybe it's because the grave eyes of the *2001* Star Child still haunt me, with their promise that perhaps someday man would learn to teach ten thousand stars how to sing.

U

Uforia ★ ★ ★ ★
PG, 100 m., 1985

Cindy Williams (Arlene), Harry Dean Stanton (Brother Bud), Fred Ward (Sheldon), Alan Beckwith (Brother Roy), Beverly Hope Atkinson (Naomi), Harry Carey, Jr. (George Martin), Diane Diefendorf (Delores), Robert Gray (Emile). Directed by John Binder and produced by Gordon Wolf. Screenplay by Binder.

I've always wanted to know one of those women you read about in the *National Enquirer,* those intense Midwestern housewives who are sucked up into flying saucers and flown to Mars, where they have their measurements taken, and are told they will be contacted again real soon. It's not that I want to hear about the trip to Mars. I'd just enjoy having her around the house, all filled with a sense of mystery and purpose.

Uforia is a great and goofy comedy about a woman just like that. Her name is Arlene, and she works as a supermarket checker in a backwater town in the Southwest. She reads all the UFO publications and believes every word, and knows in her heart that They are coming. But the movie is not really about whether They come or not. It's about how waiting for Them can give you something wonderful to think about, to pass the time of those dreary, dusty days.

The movie has two other characters who get involved in Arlene's dream. One of them is named Sheldon, and he is the kind of good ol' boy who drives through the desert in a big ol' convertible, with the car on cruise control and his feet propped up on the dashboard and a can of beer in his hand.

The other one is named Brother Bud, a phony faith-healer who conducts revival services in a tent outside of town. When Sheldon sees Arlene at the supermarket, he falls in love, and before long he has settled down, sort of, in her mobile home. Sheldon and Brother Bud are brothers, and Sheldon hires on with Bud to portray a guy whose sick leg gets healed every night. Meanwhile, Arlene's faith grows that the UFO will arrive at any moment.

This is one of those movies where you walk in not expecting much, and then something great happens, and you laugh, and you start paying more attention, and then you realize that a lot of great things are happening, that this is one of those rare movies that really has it. *Uforia* is not just another witless Hollywood laugh machine, but a movie with intelligence and a sly, sardonic style of humor. You don't have to shut down half of your brain in order to endure it.

The casting is just perfect. Cindy Williams is the cornerstone, as Arlene, a woman whose hopes and dreams are too big for the small corner of the Earth she has been given to occupy. She doesn't know what to do when she meets Sheldon (played by Fred Ward, from *Remo Williams* and *The Right Stuff*). She likes this guy and she hasn't had a man in a long time. But, then again, she always gets her heart "broke" when she falls for a guy, and so she prays for guidance and starts on the tequila.

Ward gives a wicked performance as the good ol' boy Sheldon. He's Smokey and the Bandit with brains. He has a couple of double takes in this movie that are worth the price of a ticket. And he's not a male chauvinist pig, although everything in his background probably points him in that direction. He doesn't see Arlene as a conquest, but as just the lady he's been looking for. He gets a little tired of the flying-saucer stuff, however.

Harry Dean Stanton plays Brother Bud. This is exactly the kind of role Stanton has been complaining that he's tired of: the weary, alcoholic con man with the jolly cynicism. Yet they keep casting him in these roles, and in *Uforia* you can see why: Nobody does a better job. He has an assistant in the movie, a junior evangelist named Brother Roy (Alan Beckwith), whose face shines with conviction and who is always bathed in wonderment and glory. The quiet, offhand way Stanton deals with him is one of the movie's many treasures.

Uforia didn't have a lot of money and a big ad campaign behind it. It doesn't have big stars, unless you are the kind of movie lover for whom the names Cindy Williams, Harry Dean Stanton, and Fred Ward guarantee a movie will at least be interesting.

Like *Repo Man* and *Turtle Diary* and *Hannah and Her Sisters,* it is willing to go for originality in a world that prizes the entertainment assembly line. I was hugging myself during this movie, because it had so many moments that were just right.

The Unbearable Lightness of Being
★ ★ ★ ★
R, 172 m., 1988

Daniel Day-Lewis (Tomas), Juliette Binoche (Tereza), Lena Olin (Sabina), Derek de Lint (Franz), Erland Josephson (The Ambassador), Pavel Landovsky (Pavel), Donald Moffat (Chief Surgeon), Daniel Olbrychski (Interior Ministry Official), Stellan Skarsgard (The Engineer), Tomek Bork (Jiri). Directed by Philip Kaufman and produced by Saul Zaentz. Screenplay by Jean-Claude Carriere.

In the title of Philip Kaufman's *The Unbearable Lightness of Being,* the crucial word is "unbearable." The film tells the story of a young surgeon who attempts to float above the mundane world of personal responsibility and commitment, to practice a sex life that has no traffic with the heart, to escape untouched from the world of sensual pleasure while retaining his privacy and his loneliness. By the end of the story, this freedom has become too great a load for him to bear.

The surgeon's name is Tomas, and he lives in Prague; we meet him in the blessed days before the Russian invasion of 1968. He has an understanding with a woman named Sabina, a painter whose goal is the same as his own—to have a physical relationship without an emotional one. The two lovers believe they have much in common, since they share the same attitude toward their couplings, but actually their genitals have more in common than they do. That is not to say they don't enjoy great sex; they do, and in great detail, in this most erotic serious film since *Last Tango in Paris.*

One day the doctor goes to the country, and while waiting in a provincial train station, his eyes fall upon the young waitress Tereza. He orders a brandy. Their eyes meet. They go for a little walk after she gets off of work, and it is clear there is something special between them. He returns to Prague. One day she appears in the city and knocks at his door. She has come to be with him. Against all of his principles, he allows her to spend the night, and then to move in. He has betrayed his own code of lightness, or freedom.

The film tells the love story of Tomas and Tereza in the context of the events of 1968, and there are shots that place the characters in the middle of the riots against the Russian invaders. Tereza becomes a photographer, and tries to smuggle pictures of the uprising out of the country. Finally, the two lovers leave Prague for Geneva, where Sabina has already gone—and then Tomas resumes his sexual relationship with Sabina because his philosophy, of course, is that sex has nothing to do with love.

Crushed by his decision, Tereza attempts her own experiment with free love, but it does not work because her heart is not built that way. Sabina, meanwhile, meets a professor named Franz who falls in love with her so urgently that he decides to leave his wife. Can she accept this love? Or is she even more committed to "lightness of being" than Tomas, who tutored her in the philosophy? In the middle of Sabina's indecision, Tereza appears at her door with a camera. She has been asked to take some shots for a fashion magazine and needs someone to pose nude. Sabina agrees, and the two women photograph each other in a scene so carefully choreographed that it becomes a ballet of eroticism.

By this point in the movie, a curious thing had happened to me as a viewer. I had begun to appreciate some of the life rhythms of the characters. Most films move so quickly and are so dependent on plot that they are about events, not lives. *The Unbearable Lightness of Being* carries the feeling of deep nostalgia, of a time no longer present, when these people did these things and hoped for happiness, and were caught up in events beyond their control.

Kaufman achieves this effect almost without seeming to try. At first his film seems to be almost exclusively about sex, but then we notice in countless individual shots and camera decisions that he does not allow his camera to become a voyeur. There is a lot of nudity in the film, but no pornographic documentary quality; the camera does not linger, or move for the best view, or relish the spectacle of nudity. The result is some of the most poignant, almost sad, sex scenes I have ever seen—sensuous, yes, but bittersweet.

The casting has a lot to do with this haunting quality. Daniel Day-Lewis plays Tomas with a sort of detachment that is supposed to come from the character's distaste for commitment. He has a lean, intellectual look, and is not a voluptuary. For him, sex seems like a form of physical meditation, rather than an activity with another person. Lena Olin, as Sabina, has a lush, voluptuous body, big-breasted and tactile, but she inhabits it so comfortably that the movie never seems to dwell on it or exploit it. It is a fact of nature. Juliette Binoche, as Tereza, is almost ethereal in her beauty and innocence, and her attempt to reconcile her love with her lover's detachment is probably the heart of the movie.

The film is based on the novel by the Czech novelist Milan Kundera, whose works all seem to consider eroticism with a certain wistfulness, as if to say that while his characters were making love, they were sometimes distracted from the essentially tragic nature of their existence. That is the case here. Kaufman, whose previous films have included *The Right Stuff* and a remake of *Invasion of the Body Snatchers,* has never done anything remotely like this before, but his experiment is a success in tone; he has made a movie in which reality is asked to coexist with a world of pure sensuality, and almost, for a moment, seems to agree.

The film will be noticed primarily for its eroticism. Although major films and filmmakers considered sex with great frankness and freedom in the early and mid-seventies, films in the last decade have been more adolescent, more plot- and action-oriented. Catering to audiences of adolescents, who are comfortable with sex only when it is seen in cartoon form, Hollywood has also not been comfortable with the complications of adult sexuality—the good and the bad. What is remarkable about *The Unbearable Lightness of Being,* however, is not the sexual content itself, but the way Kaufman has been able to use it as an avenue for a complex story, one of nostalgia, loss, idealism, and romance.

Un Coeur en Hiver ★ ★ ★ ½
NO MPAA RATING, 102 m., 1993

Daniel Auteuil (Stephane), Emmanuelle Beart (Camille), Andre Dussollier (Maxime), Elisabeth Bourgine (Helene), Brigitte Catillon (Regine), Maurice Garrel (Lachaume). Directed by Claude Sautet and produced by Jean-Louis Livi and Philippe Carcassonne. Screenplay by Yves Ulmann, Jacques Fieschi, and Jerome Tonnerre.

Un Coeur en Hiver. A heart in winter. There are those who somehow cannot love, who were born or made without that gift in their personality. In all other ways they may be complete, but something is broken inside, and love, which can heal so many things, cannot repair it. *Un Coeur en Hiver* is the story of such a man.

His name is Stephane. He is an expert builder and repairer of violins—so good that the greatest violinists from all over the world come to his studio in Paris. He is not the owner, however, but an employee, and happy to be employed. Relations with the public he leaves with Maxime, who has been his boss and coworker for many years.

It is a crucial point, I think, that *Un Coeur en Hiver* begins with a narration by Stephane describing the relationship of these two men. They are not homosexual—indeed, by the end of the film they will have come to blows over the same woman—but Stephane's life is defined by the fact that he works for Maxime, admires him, envies his social skills, and depends on him as a shield against the world. Maxime has those gifts which Stephane lacks, and so by staying close to him, Stephane can make use of them. It is a symbiotic relationship.

One day a beautiful young woman, Camille, a gifted violinist, comes into the workshop. She needs advice on her violin, which the two men are able to give her. Soon she is dating Maxime, as Stephane looks on from a distance. Then Camille and Stephane have a conversation about her playing, and two things become evident: Stephane hears a great deal when he listens to music, and Camille has fallen in love with him.

She tells Maxime. It is regrettable, and messy, but there it is: She loves his partner and must leave him. She goes to Stephane. He is flattered, and overwhelmed; he finds her beautiful, and desires her. That would be the end of the story, except that it gradually develops that Stephane is in no mood to commit himself to their relationship. He is not physically incapable, but it's as if his personality is impotent. Or almost as if Stephane is more comfortable when Maxime takes care of those kinds of details.

Un Coeur en Hiver, directed by Claude Sautet, has the intensity and delicacy of a great short story. It reveals how superficial most movie romances are—because they make love too simple, and too easy a solution. The heart has needs that love does not understand, and for Stephane, perhaps the comfort of his routine and the consolations of his craft are more valuable than the risks of intimacy.

Daniel Auteuil plays Stephane. He has an inward-looking face, a repose; he tells us more about himself in the narration than he tells anyone in the film. Camille is Emmanuelle Beart, beautiful, yes, but required here to be a convincing violinist and a theorist about music. She is given a difficult role, and avoids its hazards brilliantly. She must throw over one man and be rejected by another (many of the crucial scenes are in public), and yet seem not foolish but simply unlucky. She must maintain her dignity, or the film will become the story of a woman scorned, which it is not. It is the story of a man not scorned—of how Stephane psychologically cannot take the woman from Maxime.

As a general rule, the characters in French films seem more grown-up than those in American films. They do not consider love and sex as a teen-ager might, as the prizes in life. Instead, they are challenges and responsibilities, and not always to be embraced. Most movie romances begin with two people who should be in love, and end, after great difficulties, with those two people in love. Here is a movie about two people who should not be in love, and how they deal with that discovery.

Under Fire ★ ★ ★ ½
R, 128 m., 1983

Nick Nolte (Russell Price), Gene Hackman (Alex Grazier), Joanna Cassidy (Claire), Ed Harris (Oates). Directed by Roger Spottiswoode and produced by Jonathan Taplin. Screenplay by Ron Shelton and Clayton Frohman.

This is the kind of movie that almost always feels phony, but *Under Fire* feels real. It's about American journalists covering guerrilla warfare in Central America, and so right away we expect to see Hollywood stars transplanted to the phony jungles of one of those movie nations with made-up names. Instead, we see Hollywood stars who create characters so convincing we forget they're stars. And the movie names names: It's set in Nicaragua, in 1979, during the fall of the Somoza regime, period.

We meet three journalists who are there to get the story. This is not the first small war they've covered, and indeed we've already seen them packing up and leaving Africa. Now they've got a new story. Nick Nolte is Price, a photographer. Gene Hackman is Grazier, a TV reporter who dreams of becoming an anchorman. Joanna Cassidy is a radio reporter. During the course of the story, Cassidy will fall out of love with Hackman and into love with Nolte. These things happen under deadline pressure. Hackman cares, but not enough to affect his friendship with both of them.

The story is simply told, since *Under Fire* depends more upon moments and atmosphere than on a manufactured plot. During a lull in the action, Hackman heads back for New York and Nolte determines to get an interview with the elusive leader of the guerrillas. He doesn't get an interview, but he begins to develop a sympathy for the rebel cause. He commits the journalistic sin of taking sides, and it leads him, eventually, to a much greater sin: faking a photograph to help the guerrilla forces. That is, of course, wrong. But *Under Fire* shows us a war in which morality is hard to define and harder to practice. One of the key supporting characters in the movie is a mysterious American named Oates (played by Ed Harris). Is he CIA? Apparently. He's always in the thick of the dirty work, however, and if his conscience doesn't bother him, Nolte excuses himself for not taking an ethical stand. There are, in fact, a lot of ethical stands not taken in this movie. It could almost have been written by

Graham Greene; it exists in that half-world between exhaustion and exhilaration, between love and cynicism, between covering the war and getting yourself killed. This is tricky ground, and the wrong performances could have made it ridiculous (cf. Richard Gere's sleek sexual athlete in *Beyond the Limit*). The actors in *Under Fire* never step wrong.

Nolte is great to watch as the seedy photographer with the beer gut. Hackman never really convinced me that he could be an anchorman, but he did a better thing. He convinced me that he thought he could be one. Joanna Cassidy takes a role that could have been dismissed as "the girl" and fills it out as a fascinating, textured adult. *Under Fire* surrounds these performances with a vivid sense of place and becomes, somewhat surprisingly, a serious and moving film.

Under Siege ★ ★ ★
R, 120 m., 1992

Steven Seagal (Casey Ryback), Tommy Lee Jones (Strannix), Gary Busey (Commander Krill), Erika Eleniak (Jordan Tate), Patrick O'Neal (Capt. Adams), Nick Mancuso (Tom Breaker). Directed by Andrew Davis and produced by Arnon Milchan, Steven Seagal, and Steven Reuther.

When I saw the coming-attractions trailer for *Under Siege*, I had the feeling I'd already seen the movie: Terrorists land on the USS *Missouri* and occupy the great battleship. The crew is caught off guard and neutralized. But the bad guys overlook one man—the cook—who turns into a one-man army and fights back. The formula is obvious: "Die Hard Goes to Sea." I walked into the screening in a cynical frame of mind, but then a funny thing happened. The movie started working for me.

One reason for that is obvious: the overwhelming and convincing presence of the battleship itself. I learn, by reading the production notes, that director Andrew Davis and his team did not shoot on the real *Missouri*, but instead used the decommissioned USS *Alabama*. In many shots the ship appears to be at sea when it's actually docked in Mobile, Alabama. They could have fooled me. This movie does a terrific job of making every scene play like a real event on a ship at sea, and that's part of its charm. There's even a walk-on by George Bush, visiting the ship before its fateful final voyage.

The cast is also effective. The star is Steven

Seagal, who has cut off his pony tail to play a former navy hero who is now serving out his last tour as a cook. The reasons for that assignment are complicated (he was a hero who got in trouble, but the skipper is his friend), but Seagal makes a convincing cook; he can hit a target with a carving knife at twenty paces, and he even looks like he's put on a few pounds on the job, sipping the bouillabaisse.

The villains are superb, vile and deliriously insane. They're played by Tommy Lee Jones, as a former undercover operative for the CIA, and Gary Busey, as a disillusioned officer on board the ship. Jones has developed into one of the most effective and interesting villains in the movies, maybe because he's not afraid to go over the top—as he does here, masquerading as a heavy-metal rocker and later spieling political slogans into the radio like a deranged dictator. Busey, as the turncoat officer, plays his big murder scene in drag, gnashing the scenery as if he's enjoying every bite.

The plot of the movie is, of course, absurd, involving a half-explained scheme to steal the ship's nuclear warheads, off-load them to a stolen North Korean submarine, and sell them in the Middle East. Never mind. The details of the cat-and-mouse chase around the ship are exciting and well directed. And director Davis is not above the put-on, as when he introduces *Playboy*'s Miss July 1989 (Erika Eleniak) into the plot, and has her follow Seagal on his dangerous rounds for no better reason than because she seems utterly incongruous in every scene.

Andrew Davis is not a director whose name is known to many moviegoers, I suppose, but he has built up an impressive body of action work: His *Code of Silence* was the best Chuck Norris movie, his *The Package* was a terrific Gene Hackman thriller, and he directed Seagal's movie debut in *Above the Law* (1988). Here he uses some of his trademarks: effective fight scenes, electronic gimmicks, quirky casting of the supporting roles, bigger-than-life heroes and villains.

Under the Volcano ★ ★ ★ ★
R, 109 m., 1984

Albert Finney (Geoffrey Firmin), Jacqueline Bisset (Yvonne Firmin), Anthony Andrews (Hugh Firmin), Ignacio Lopez Tarso (Dr. Vigil), Katy Jurado (Senora Gregoria). Directed by John Huston and produced by Michael Fitzgerald. Screenplay by Guy Gallo.

The consul drinks. He has been drinking for so many years that he has arrived at that peculiar stage in alcoholism where he no longer drinks to get high or to get drunk. He drinks simply to hold himself together and continue to function. He has a muddled theory that he can even "drink himself sober," by which he means that he can sometimes find a lucid window through the fog of his life. *Under the Volcano* is the story of the last day in his drinking.

He lives in Cuernavaca, Mexico, in the years just before World War II. He is not really the British consul anymore: he was only a vice consul, anyway, and now that has been stripped from him, and he simply drinks. He has a few friends and a few acquaintances, and his long days are spent in a drunk's never-ending occupation, monitoring his own condition. On this morning, for example, he had a bit too much and passed out in the road. One of those things. Earlier, or later, sometime in there, he had stumbled into a church and prayed for the return of his wife, who had left him. Now he sits on his veranda talking with his half-brother. He turns his head. His wife is standing in the doorway. He turns back. It cannot be her. He looks again. She is still there. Turns away. It cannot be. Looks again. A hallucination. But it persists, and eventually he is forced to admit that his wife has indeed returned, in answer to his prayers.

He drinks. He passes out. He wakes. The three of them set off on a bus journey. A peasant is found dead on a roadside. Later, in a bar, there is an unpleasantness with a whore. Still later, the day ends in a ditch. The consul's day is seen largely through his point of view, and the remarkable thing about *Under the Volcano* is that it doesn't resort to any of the usual tricks that movies use when they portray drunks. There are no trick shots to show hallucinations. No spinning cameras. No games with focus. Instead, the drunkenness in this film is supplied by the remarkably controlled performance of Albert Finney as the consul. He gives the best drunk performance I've ever seen in a film. He doesn't overact, or go for pathos, or pretend to be a character. His focus is on communication. He wants, he desperately desires, to penetrate the alcoholic fog and speak clearly from his heart to those around him. His words come out with a peculiar intensity of focus, as if every one had to be pulled out of the small hidden core of sobriety deep inside his confusion.

The movie is based on the great novel by Malcolm Lowry, who used this day in the life of a drunk as a clothesline on which to hang several themes, including the political disintegration of Mexico in the face of the rising tide of Nazism. John Huston, the sure-footed old veteran who directed the film, wisely leaves out the symbols and implications and subtexts and just gives us the man. Lowry's novel was really about alcoholism, anyway; the other materials were not so much subjects as they were attempts by the hero to focus on something between his ears.

The movie belongs to Finney, but mention must be made of Jacqueline Bisset as his wife and Anthony Andrews as his half-brother. Their treatment of the consul is interesting. They understand him well. They love him (and, we gather, each other). They realize nothing can be done for him. Why do they stay with him? For love, maybe, or loyalty, but also perhaps because they respect the great effort he makes to continue to function, to "carry on," in the face of his disabling illness. Huston, I think, is interested in the same aspect of the story, that within every drunk is a man with self-respect trying to get free.

Unforgiven ★ ★ ★ ★
R, 130 m., 1992

Clint Eastwood (William Munny), Gene Hackman (Little Bill Daggett), Morgan Freeman (Ned Logan), Richard Harris (English Bob), Jaimz Woolvett (Schofield Kid), Saul Rubinek (W.W. Beauchamp), Frances Fisher (Strawberry Alice), Anna Thompson (Delilah Fitzgerald). Directed and produced by Clint Eastwood. Screenplay by David Webb Peoples.

Clint Eastwood's *Unforgiven* opens with a shot of the hero, William Munny, standing at the graveside of his wife. The shot is similar to one with John Wayne in John Ford's *She Wore a Yellow Ribbon*. Given Eastwood's familiarity with classic Westerns, it may be a deliberate echo. Women in Westerns have always been a civilizing influence on the violence of the frontier, bringing schools, churches, white picket fences, and apple pies. Men in the West, left to their own devices, imagine and create such a violent world that they can hardly leave the house unarmed.

William Munny was once, we learn, a gunfighter, and not a very nice one. He killed not simply bad guys, but also women and children, and he doesn't feel very good about that. Now he is trying to support his mother-less family by working as a hog farmer, and when the word comes of a $1,000 bounty on the heads of two cowboys who have carved up a prostitute, he accepts the challenge. He needs the money, and perhaps he is attracted to his old ways.

The prostitute was attacked in Big Whiskey, Wyoming, a town ruled by Little Bill Daggett (Gene Hackman), a sheriff who mirrors Munny's own ambiguity about violence and domesticity. Daggett does not permit firearms in his town, and tries to settle disputes peaceably. In adjudicating the brawl at the brothel, for example, he orders the two cowboys to give the saloon owner a couple of horses, in lieu of damages. This is justice of a sort, although not, of course, for the scarred young prostitute, who is treated like so much property. An older hooker (Frances Fisher) is enraged, and raises the money for the bounty on the cowboys.

Like the traditional Western it is, *Unforgiven* sets up this situation in detail and at leisure. We sense in the first few minutes that the plot will lead up to a final violent test of William Munny and his partners. And in a Western like this, that means their personalities and characters will be tested; unlike the new violent urban adventures, Westerns place greater weight on the meaning of gunfights and deaths. They aren't simply stunts, providing a moment of activity before being quickly forgotten.

Munny is told about the bounty in the first place by a kid (all Westerns seem to have a kid) named, inevitably, the Schofield Kid and played by Jaimz Woolvett. He's too nearsighted to shoot straight, and knows he needs help. Munny in turn recruits an old partner, Ned Logan (Morgan Freeman), and they ride into Big Whiskey, only to discover that another famous gunfighter, English Bob (Richard Harris), has also arrived on the scene.

English Bob is trailed by a writer for pulp Western magazines (Saul Rubinek), who interviews the sheriff on his theories about killing, and does research for his report on the impending showdown. His presence essentially signals the death of the Old West, which is in its last days as a reality and its first days as the stuff of legend and entertainment. The movie is filled, in a low-key way, with other inventions and developments signaling the intrusion of the modern.

Unforgiven is not simply about its plot—about whether William Munny collects the bounty, and about who gets killed in the

process—but also about what it means to kill somebody, and how a society is affected when people get killed. Hackman's sheriff is a key element in developing this theme. He is capable of being likable, sensible, friendly, and even funny, but he also harbors a streak of violent sadism, and uses his badge as an excuse to beat his victims. He looks so peaceable up there on the roof of his house, nailing shingles, but like the "peaceful" town he takes such pride in, he harbors a vicious streak.

Eastwood's direction of the film, with cinematography by Jack Green, doesn't make the West seem particularly scenic. A lot of the shots are from the inside looking out, so that the figures seem dark and obscure and the brightness that pours through the window is almost blinding. The effect is to diminish the stature of the characters; these aren't heroes, but simply the occupants of a simple, rude society in which death is an everyday fact.

Eastwood bought the story for this movie years ago, and sat on it, he says, until he was old enough to play it. Indeed, all four of the major actors in the film (Eastwood, Hackman, Freeman, and Harris) are on the shady side of sixty, and the enormous success of *Unforgiven*—both at the box office and in the Academy Awards—indicates that somehow this theme, of older men still trapped in a dance of death, rang a bell. The only way to criticize a movie, Jean-Luc Godard once wrote, is to make another movie. For Clint Eastwood, one of the most intelligent and self-aware of filmmakers, *Unforgiven* may have been a reaction to the rising tide of meaningless violence in films and on television. In a way, this is a movie about how, when you kill someone, they're really dead.

Unlawful Entry ★ ★ ★
R, 109 m., 1992

Kurt Russell (Michael Carr), Ray Liotta (Officer Pete Davis), Madeleine Stowe (Karen Carr), Roger E. Mosley (Officer Roy Cole), Ken Lerner (Roger Graham), Deborah Offner (Penny), Carmen Argenziano (Jerome Lurie), Andy Romano (Captain Hayes). Directed by Jonathan Kaplan and produced by Charles Gordon. Screenplay by Lewis Colick.

I believe it is quite possible to get trapped by a nightmare in which the forces of authority are arrayed against you and there is no plausible way to prove your innocence. Sometimes I mentally draw up reading lists for my

long incarceration for a crime I did not commit. The fear of that fate is at the heart of *Unlawful Entry*, which also plays on another fairly common fear, that your spouse is so gullible that he or she will be deceived by the forces that are destroying your life.

The movie opens with a home invasion. Nightclub developer Michael Carr (Kurt Russell) and his wife, Karen (Madeleine Stowe), are spending a quiet night at home when a man breaks in through a skylight and holds a knife to Karen's neck. The man escapes, and the Carrs call the cops. That's their first mistake. One of the cops who answers the call is a bright-eyed, tense street veteran named Pete Davis (Ray Liotta), who seems like a nice kid until he starts insinuating himself into the Carrs' lives.

Davis grows obsessed with the conviction that Karen Carr needs him to protect her—that Michael, her husband, isn't up to the job. The cop is clever enough that the full dimensions of his obsession aren't apparent for a while, especially not to Karen, who is nice to him and even has a drink with him after he does his Officer Friendly act for the kids at the grade school where she teaches.

If Karen is deceived at first by the cop's polite facade, so is her husband, who goes along for a ride one night in a squad car with Davis and his partner (Roger E. Mosley), and is first fascinated by the experience, and then disgusted when Davis puts him to a test by producing the man who broke into their house and inviting Michael to beat him.

Michael's disinclination to beat a helpless man confirms Davis's suspicion that this is not the right man to protect Karen from the dangers of the world. He begins to drop around at strange times: for example, when Karen is in the pool or when the Carrs are making love. Michael sees clearly that the cop is nuts, but Davis is subtle and clever, and others aren't so quick to agree. Eventually Michael is behind bars and Davis is out there in the night with Karen Carr on his mind.

The movie is a thriller, with all the usual trappings of a thriller, but the director, Jonathan Kaplan, is able to place the story in a plausible world. The performances go for unstrained realism, the settings are slice-of-life, and until the final scenes even the sicko cop seems somewhere within the realm of possibility. Unlike *Basic Instinct*, which turned the wattage up so high that it was clearly only a thriller, *Unlawful Entry* has undertones of a serious social drama; we see how defenseless ordinary citizens can be against someone with a delusion.

It's curious, at times during the movie, how much Kurt Russell and Ray Liotta resemble one another. I never noticed that before. Maybe it's their hair, or the way they're photographed, but there's the sense that they are twins—one snug inside a comfortable middle-class haven, the other wandering the night in rage and discontent. The way the actors play against one another, in a scene at a party for potential investors, for example, is intriguing because it suggests that each character knows exactly how to push the other's buttons.

For Liotta, Pete Davis is a dream role—the psychopath who can turn in a plausible imitation of a straight arrow. Russell has the more thankless role of the threatened husband, and does what needs to be done with it. And it's interesting how Madeleine Stowe is friendly to Davis; she doesn't lead him on, but she makes the mistake of not instantly nipping his fantasies in the bud.

One of the movie's subtexts involves ways to feel safe in a big city. The Carrs discuss a high-tech alarm system, a gun, and a big, savage attack dog. They try the first two. On the basis of this movie, the big dog might not have been a bad idea.

An Unmarried Woman ★ ★ ★ ★
R, 124 m., 1978

Jill Clayburgh (Erica), Alan Bates (Saul), Michael Murphy (Martin), Lisa Lucas (Patti), Cliff Gorman (Charlie), Pat Quinn (Sue), Kelly Bishop (Elaine), Linda Miller (Jeannette), Andrew Duncan (Bob), Penelope Russianoff (Tanya). Directed by Paul Mazursky and produced by Mazursky and Tony Ray. Screenplay by Mazursky.

It is, Erica thinks, a happy marriage, although perhaps she doesn't think about it much. It's *there*. Her husband is a stockbroker, she works in an art gallery, their daughter is in a private high school, they live in a high-rise and jog along the East River. In the morning there is "Swan Lake" on the FM radio, and the last sight at night is of the closing stock prices on the TV screen. Had she bargained for more?

One day, though, swiftly and cruelly, it all comes to an end: Her husband breaks down in phony tears on the street and confesses he's in love with another woman. A younger woman. And so her happy marriage is over. At home, consumed by anger, grief, and

uncertainty, she studies her face in the mirror. It is a good face in its middle thirties, and right now it looks plain scared.

So end the first, crucial passages of Paul Mazursky's *An Unmarried Woman*. They are crucial because we have to understand how *completely* Erica was a married woman if we're to join her on the journey back to being single again. It's a journey that Mazursky makes into one of the funniest, truest, sometimes most heartbreaking movies I've ever seen. And so much of what's best is because of Jill Clayburgh, whose performance is, quite simply, luminous.

We know that almost from the beginning. There's a moment of silence in the morning, right after Erica's husband and daughter have left the house. "Swan Lake" is playing. She's still in bed. She's just made love. She speaks from her imagination: "The ballet world was thrilled last night. . . ." And then she slips out of bed and dances around the living room in her T-shirt and panties, because she's so happy, so alive . . . and at that moment the movie's got us. We're in this thing with Erica to the end.

The going is sometimes pretty rough, especially when she's trying to make sense out of things after her husband (Michael Murphy) leaves her. She gets a lot of support and encouragement from her three best girl friends, and some of the movie's very best scenes take place when they meet for long lunches with lots of white wine, or lie around on long Sunday mornings paging through the *Times* and idly wondering why *their* lives don't seem to contain the style of a Bette Davis or a Katharine Hepburn. And then there are the scenes when she talks things over with her daughter (Lisa Lucas), who's one of those bright, precocious teenagers who uses understatement and cynicism to conceal how easily she can still be hurt.

After Erica gets over the period where she drinks too much and cries too much and screams at her daughter when she doesn't mean to, she goes to a woman psychiatrist, who explains that men are the problem, yes, but they are not quite yet the enemy. And so Erica, who hasn't slept with any man but her husband for seventeen years, finds herself having lunch in Chinese restaurants with boors who shout orders at waiters and try to kiss her in the back seat of a cab. There's also the self-styled stud (Cliff Gorman) who's been hanging around the art gallery, and she finally does go up to his place—warily, gin-

gerly, but she has to find a way sometime of beginning her life again.

And then one day a British artist is hanging a show at the gallery, and he asks her if she doesn't think one side of the painting is a little low, and she says she thinks the *whole* painting is too low, and he doesn't even seem to have noticed her as he says, "Let's discuss it over lunch." They fall in love. Oh, yes, gloriously, in that kind of love that involves not only great sex but walking down empty streets at dawn, and talking about each other's childhood. The painter is played by Alan Bates, who is cast, well and true, as a man who is perfectly right for her and perfectly wrong for her, both at the same time.

An Unmarried Woman plays true with all three of its major movements: The marriage, the being single, the falling in love. Mazursky's films have considered the grave and funny business of sex before (most memorably in *Bob & Carol & Ted & Alice* and *Blume in Love*). But he's never before been this successful at really dealing with the complexities and following them through. I wouldn't want to tell you too much about the movie's conclusion, but believe this much: It's honest and it's *right*, because Mazursky and Jill Clayburgh care too much about Erica to dismiss her with a conventional happy ending.

Clayburgh takes chances in this movie. She's out on an emotional limb. She's letting us see and experience things that many actresses simply couldn't reveal. Mazursky takes chances, too. He wants *An Unmarried Woman* to be true, for starters: We have to believe at every moment that life itself is being considered here. But the movie has to be funny, too. He won't settle for less than the truth *and* the humor, and the wonder of *An Unmarried Woman* is that he gets it. I've been reviewing movies for a long time now without ever feeling the need to use dumb lines like "You'll laugh—you'll cry." But I did cry, and I did laugh.

Untamed Heart ★ ★ ★
PG-13, 102 m., 1993

Christian Slater (Adam), Marisa Tomei (Caroline), Rosie Perez (Cindy), Kyle Secor (Howard), Willie Garson (Patsy), James Cada (Bill No. 1), Gary Groomes (Bill No. 2). Directed by Tony Bill and produced by Bill and Helen Buck Bartlett. Screenplay by Tom Sierchio.

Untamed Heart is an unabashed romance, wrapped up in a working-class story about a waitress and a dishwasher and their worlds.

It's a fairy tale with dishwater hands, starring Marisa Tomei as a waitress on the all-night shift at a Minneapolis diner, and Christian Slater as the silent, mysterious kid in the kitchen who never seems to have anything to say.

Because of the film's prologue, we know something about the Slater character. He was raised by nuns in an orphanage, and had a weak heart—so weak he sometimes lost consciousness on the playground. An operation left a scar running across his chest, but as the film moves up to the present he needs a heart transplant, urgently.

The problem is, he doesn't want the transplant, because he was told some strange story by the nuns about being raised in the jungle and being given the heart of a great ape, which makes him ferocious and strong. So he lives by himself, reads a lot, washes dishes, and doesn't talk—except to Tomei, who breaks through his reserve when she bandages a cut on his hand.

Tony Bill's direction walks a thin line between the fable of the underlying story and the realism of the world the characters live in. When Tomei walks home late one night through the park (read: forest), she is attacked by would-be rapists (read: wolves), and rescued by the dishwasher, who has been following her (read: handsome prince). She discovers his story, and their romance blossoms, tenderly and tentatively.

The movie is kind of sweet and kind of goofy, and works because its heart is in the right place. Marisa Tomei is winning and warm, and deserved her Oscar for this role, and Slater, who doesn't have much to say, projects the right note of mystery and doomed romance.

There are a lot of salt-of-the-earth supporting characters, of whom my favorite is Rosie Perez, as Tomei's fellow waitress and best friend. Perez essentially plays the same character she did so well in *White Men Can't Jump*, and because I liked her there, I liked her here, although she has less to do. She smokes a lot, but then so does Tomei and almost everyone else in sight. Maybe that's because this story should somehow really be about people in their forties, and so the young actors think they'll look older if they smoke. Or maybe smoking is now seen as a sign of working-class status.

The issue of age was lurking right under the surface for me all through this film. Somehow the actors, in their early twenties, seemed to have found themselves into a Saroyan story about middle-aged losers having one last fling at idealism. Did it ever occur to the filmmakers to cast the film older? Or is the box office youth cult so well-established that older roles are transposed into younger ones? I liked Tomei and Slater here; I'll bet they'd be dynamite in these roles in twenty years.

Up the Sandbox ★ ★ ★
R, 98 m., 1973

Barbra Streisand (Marjorie), David Selby (Paul), Ariana Heller (Elizabeth), Jacobo Morales (Fidel Castro), Carol White (Miss Spittlemeister). Directed by Irvin Kershner and produced by Robert Chartoff and Irwin Winkler. Screenplay by Paul Zindel.

It's a little hard to make a movie about a woman's liberation when the woman in question is happy with her life, in love with her husband, and looking forward to having her third child. Such a woman somehow doesn't seem to be your typical *MS* subscriber.

I'm dealing in stereotypes, of course, but so does *Up the Sandbox*—sometimes. This is a Barbra Streisand movie, and so we know the central character won't (can't) be stereotyped; nothing even remotely like Streisand has existed in movies before. But the movie's other characters stray dangerously close to becoming case histories for Gloria Steinem.

Streisand plays Marjorie, a woman who once wrote a term paper so brilliant that her old professor still remembers it. She doesn't; she's set aside plans for an academic career and devotes herself to loving her husband, raising her children, and maintaining a New York apartment that even Erma Bombeck would describe as a mess.

Marjorie's husband is a professor at Columbia, and of course he's brilliant and engaged in "important" work and is fascinating to young women at cocktail parties—particularly, Marjorie observes, young women with low-cut dresses. This causes her some concern, and so do the erratic guerrilla raids staged on her apartment by her mother. Marjorie's mother is a spokesman for all that women's lib is against: She wants Marjorie to move to the suburbs, play cards, engage in housekeeping competition with the other women in the block, and, in general, degenerate gracefully into the zombie-like state of housewives who are attracted to detergents (but nothing else) by sex appeal.

Marjorie retaliates with a series of fantasies which sometimes work, in terms of the movie, and sometimes fail terribly. The best ones are inspired. Director Irvin Kershner (who directed the best party scene of 1971 in his comedy masterpiece *Loving*), gives us another party that is horrifying in its realism.

It's the thirty-third anniversary for Marjorie's mom and dad, and Mom seizes on her after-dinner speech as the proper occasion to (1) urge Marjorie to surrender to the suburbs and (2) announce that Marjorie is preggers. Marjorie's fantasy is to the point. She mashes her mother's face into the anniversary cake and then they wrestle under the table while a tipsy cousin shoots the action for a home movie.

Scenes like this work as fierce, funny satire; but some of the other fantasies (particularly a visit to an African tribe where the women carry the spears and the men wash the dishes) are a waste of effort. Considerable effort; the cast went to Africa to film them, and perhaps they cost so much money Kershner was reluctant to cut them out.

No matter; Streisand herself is really fine in *Up the Sandbox*, which was more or less her first straight role (depending on how you took *On a Clear Day You Can See Forever*). She does not give us a liberated woman, or even a woman working in some organized way toward liberation. Instead, she gives us a woman who feels free to be herself, no matter what anyone thinks. This is a kind of woman, come to think of it, who is rare in American movies; female intelligence on the screen still actually seems quietly revolutionary, which is a sad truth but one *Up the Sandbox* does nothing to further.

V

Vagabond ★ ★ ★ ★
NO MPAA RATING, 105 m., 1986

Sandrine Bonnaire (Mona), Macha Meril (Madame Lanier), Stephane Friess (Jean-Pierre), Laurence Cortadellas (Elaine), Marthe Jarnias (Tante Lydie), Yolande Moreau (Yolande), Joel Fosse (Paulo). Directed by Agnes Varda. Screenplay by Varda.

The opening shot moves in ever so slowly across the bleak fields of a French winter landscape. Two trees stand starkly outlined at the top of a hill. There is no joy here. As the camera moves closer, we see in the bottom of a ditch the blue and frozen body of a young woman. A field hand discovers her and sets up a cry. Soon the authorities are there with their clipboards, recording those things which can be known, such as the height and weight and eye color of the corpse, and wondering about all the things which cannot be known, such as her name and why she came to be dead in the bottom of a ditch.

Then we hear Agnes Varda's voice on the sound track, telling us that she became absorbed by the mystery of this young stranger's last months on earth and sought the testimony of those people who had known her. *Vagabond*, however, is the story of a woman who could not be known. And although there are many people who can step forward and say they spoke with the young woman, sheltered her, gave her food and drink, shared cigarettes and even sex with her, there is no one to say that they knew her.

Vagabond tries to feel like a documentary, a series of flashbacks to certain days in the last months of the girl's life. Actually, it is all fiction. And, like all good fiction, it is able to imply much more than it knows. From bits and pieces of information that the girl spreads out among the people that she meets, we learn that she was born of middle-class par-

ents, that she took secretarial training, that she worked in an office but hated it, that eventually she went on the road, carrying her possessions and a tent in a knapsack on her back, begging food and shelter, sometimes doing a little work for a little money.

She looks ordinary enough, with her wide, pleasant face and her quiet smile. People talk about how bad she smells, but we cannot know about that. She rolls her own cigarettes and sometimes prefers them to food. Sometimes in a cafe, when she is given a few francs, she spends them on the jukebox instead of on bread.

Only gradually do we realize that she contains a great passivity. When a goat herder and his wife take her in, feed her and give her a small trailer to spend the winter in, she does not embrace the opportunity to help them in their work. She sits inside the trailer, staring blankly ahead. She is utterly devoid of ambition. She has gone on the road, not to make her fortune, but to drop out completely from all striving.

It is hard to read her signals. Sometimes she seems to be content, opening the flap of her tent and staring out, half-blinded, at the brightness of the morning sun. She stops for a few days in a chateau and laughs with the old countess who lives there as they get drunk on the countess's brandy and the old lady complains that her son is only waiting for her to die. She seems to respond briefly to a woman professor, an agronomist who takes her along in the car as she inspects a plague among the plane trees. But is she really warming up to these people, or only providing them with a mirror that reflects their own need to touch somebody?

One of the most painful subtleties of this film is the way we see the girl's defenses finally fall. One day after another, almost without seeming to, she sinks lower and

lower. The life of the vagabond becomes the life of the outcast, and then the outcast becomes the abandoned. Finally, the abandoned becomes an animal, muddy and unkempt, disoriented, at the bottom, no longer bewildered, frightened, amazed at how low she has fallen. Finally she cries, and we remember how young and defenseless she is, under that tough skin.

What a film this is. Like so many of the greatest films, it tells us a very specific story, strong and unadorned, about a very particular person. Because it is so much her own story and does not seem to symbolize anything—because the director has no parables, only information—it is only many days after the end of the film that we reflect that the story of the vagabond could also be the story of our lives. For how many have truly known us, although many have shared our time?

Valley Girl ★ ★ ★
R, 95 m., 1983

Nicolas Cage (Randy), Deborah Foreman (Julie), Elizabeth Dailey (Loryn), Michael Bowen (Tommy), Colleen Camp (Mom), Frederic Forrest (Dad). Directed by Martha Coolidge and produced by Wayne Crawford and Andrew Lane. Screenplay by Crawford and Lane.

Disgruntled and weary after slogging through Sex-Mad Teen-ager Movies, I came upon *Valley Girl* with low expectations. What can you expect from a genre inspired by *Porky's*? But this movie is a little treasure, a funny, sexy, appealing story of a Valley Girl's heartbreaking decision: Should she stick with her boring jock boyfriend, or take a chance on a punk from Hollywood? Having seen many Sex-Mad Teen-ager Movies in which a typical slice of teen-ager life consisted of seducing your teacher, being seduced by your best friend's mom, or driving off to Tijuana in search of hookers, I found *Valley Girl* to be surprisingly convincing in its portrait of kids in love. These *are* kids. They're uncertain about sex, their hearts send out confusing signals, and they're slaves to peer pressure.

The movie stars Deborah Foreman as Julie, a bright, cute high school girl who is in the process of breaking up with her blond jock boyfriend (Michael Bowen). He's gorgeous to look at, but he's boring and conceited and he does the one thing that drives all teen-age girls mad: He sits down next to them in a burger joint and casually helps himself to their lunch. One night at a party, Julie meets Randy (Nicolas Cage). He's a lanky, kind of goofy-looking kid with an appealing, crooked smile. He's also a punk from across the hills in Hollywood. Julie likes him. He makes her laugh. He's tender. It's awesome. She falls in love. And then her friends start working her over with all sorts of dire predictions, such as that she'll be "totally dropped" if she goes out with this grotty punk. Caving in to peer pressure, Julie agrees to go to the prom with the jock. And then there's the big climax where the punk gets his girl.

One of the nicest things about this movie is that it allows its kids to be intelligent, thoughtful, and self-analytical. Another thing is that it allows the *parents* to be modern parents. Have you ever stopped to think how *dated* all the parents in teen-ager movies are? They seem to have been caught in a time warp with Dagwood and Blondie. In *Valley Girl*, the parents (Frederic Forrest and Colleen Camp) are former hippies from the Woodstock generation, now running a health food restaurant and a little puzzled by their daughter's preppy friends. It's a perfect touch.

And here's one more nice thing about *Valley Girl*. Maybe because it was directed by a woman, Martha Coolidge, this is one of the rare teen-ager movies that doesn't try to get laughs by insulting and embarrassing teenage girls. Everybody's in the same boat in this movie—boys and girls—and they're all trying to do the right thing and still have a good time. It may be the last thing you'd expect from a movie named *Valley Girl*, but the kids in this movie are human.

Valmont ★ ★ ★ ½
R, 140 m., 1989

Colin Firth (Valmont), Annette Bening (Merteuil), Meg Tilly (Tourvel), Fairuza Balk (Cecile), Sian Phillips (Madame De Volanges), Jeffrey Jones (Gercourt), Henry Thomas (Danceny), Fabia Drake (Madame De Rosemonde). Directed by Milos Forman and produced by Paul Rassam and Michael Hausman. Screenplay by Jean-Claude Carriere.

Valmont was the second film within twelve months based on the same story about sexual intrigue in eighteenth-century France. It was directed by Milos Forman, a Czech now living in America. The earlier version, *Dangerous Liaisons*, was directed by Stephen Frears, who is British. What we are given here is a delicious opportunity to compare the same material as filtered through two different national temperaments, and on the basis of this film, each lives up to its reputation: The British director's film is more cool and cerebral, while the Czech director's film is more sensuous and voluptuous.

The bare events in the two films are more or less the same. The Marquise de Merteuil, a widow of a certain age, amuses herself by setting up sexual intrigues among her acquaintances. She has a lover, Gercourt, who rejects her because he plans to marry Cecile, a young virgin. The widow enlists a close friend, Valmont, who is a complete cad, to seduce Cecile—thus depriving Gercourt of the girl's innocence. The friend goes to a country home to seduce the virgin, but immediately falls under the spell of Madame de Tourvel, a breathtaking young married woman who is visiting there at the same time. Events play themselves out with utter depravity until the evil plans of the schemers are undermined by the one thing they had not anticipated: the appearance of true love.

There are no doubt countless tones and shadings with which to tell this story, but Forman and Frears have found such different approaches that their two films could be seen on the same double bill with little redundancy except in the names of the characters. It is possible that Frears is more faithful to the spirit of the scandalous classic by Choderlos de Laclos, whose book has been banned and praised for two hundred years. The story is about an age when love was less prized than status or money, when families routinely married their innocent young daughters off to decrepit leeches with a title or a fortune. In that society, one of the great pleasures for the wicked was manipulating the lives of the naive—and the Marquise de Merteuil is shown as an intellectual sadist whose greatest sexual pleasures came from preventing other people from attaining theirs.

The Frears version, which was released late in 1988, contained a great deal of talk and an occasional homage to a magnificently powdered bosom. Now here is *Valmont*, the Forman version, in which—it cannot be denied—many of the characters would actually rather make love than talk about it.

The casting of the two movies betrays the sentiments of their directors. For the elegant Glenn Close, who played the Marquise in 1988, we now get the saucy Annette Bening. For the detached and ironical John Malkovich, as Valmont, we get the sometimes charming Colin Firth, whose feelings seem closer to the surface. For the almost ethereal Uma Thurman, who played the young virgin, there is the delightful Fairuza Balk, who seems closer to Shakespeare's Juliet than to de Laclos's innocent little Cecile. Only the character of Madame de Tourvel, the dreamy married woman, is cast in a similar fashion in the two films; Michelle Pfeiffer (1988) and Meg Tilly (1989) may differ in many ways, but they are alike in their ability to project a sexual curiosity that gnaws at their marriage vows.

Milos Forman is one of the most successful directors of our time (his credits include two Academy Award winners, *One Flew Over the Cuckoo's Nest* and *Amadeus*). In *Valmont*, he has mounted a beautiful period production that uses locations, sets, settings, and costumes to create a world so seductive that sexual intrigue seems to drip from the ceilings and collect in the corners in little pools of psychic lust. His characters not only think of little but sex, they do little except sleep with one another or talk about it. If there is a flaw in Colin Firth's Valmont, it's that the character seems to enjoy sex so much that it is difficult to imagine him possessing the discipline to use it as a weapon.

The most affecting passages in the film involve two sets of lovers: Valmont and Madame de Tourvel, of course, and then the innocent Cecile and Danceny (Henry Thomas), her young harp teacher. Although Cecile has been promised to the loathsome Gercourt (Jeffrey Jones), it is in the clear young eyes of Danceny that she sees her love reflected, and they leave each other romantic notes hidden in the wrappings of the harp. He is her Romeo.

De Tourvel, as played by Tilly, is less naive. She is a married woman, she understands her depraved society, and she knows full well that Valmont is a sexual brigand who will love her and leave her. He even tells her so himself. Her problem is, the more she thinks about it, the more she would like to be loved, even to be left. She enters into a liaison in that spirit, but then finds to her own surprise that she actually cares for him—and there is an affecting scene in which she waits in the rain outside his house, humiliating herself because she will not be sent away until she sees him.

If *Dangerous Liaisons* was a movie to stimulate the mind, *Valmont* is more compelling for the emotions. I admired the earlier movie, but I watched it as if I were watching creatures in a human zoo, observing their behavior with my own detached amusement. In *Valmont,* I found myself falling into the same trap that de Laclos set for his characters—I found myself beginning to care about these people. I even wanted them to be happy, which was more than they wanted for each other. The frightening thing about the film is that at the end, after all the hearts have been broken and all the cynical compromises have been made, I could see how many of these characters would be able to make their adjustments and be happy, even surrounded by the wreckage of their ideals. It is always a little disturbing to see people sell out at a profit. Maybe that's what the film wants us to discover.

The Vanishing ★ ★ ★ ½
NO MPAA RATING, 100 m., 1991

Johanna Ter Steege (Saskia), Gene Bervoets (Rex), Bernard-Pierre Donnadieu (Raymond Lemorne). Directed by George Sluizer and produced by Sluizer and Anne Lordon. Screenplay by Tim Krabbé and Sluizer.

One of the most intriguing things about *The Vanishing* is the film's unusual structure, which builds suspense even while it seems to be telling us almost everything we want to know. The movie is a thriller based on a domestic tragedy—on a wife who inexplicably vanishes into thin air, and of her husband's three-year search for information about what happened to her. Almost from the beginning of the film, we know more than the husband does, and yet the more we know, the more we wonder and fear.

The film opens on a clear bright summer's day, as a Dutch couple drives down the expressway for a cycling holiday in France. They've had a little domestic quarrel, nothing important, but now they are happy again as they stop at a roadside gas station for gas

and refreshments. They throw around a Frisbee. They bury a couple of coins to mark the spot forever. The wife goes back to the station to buy beer and soft drinks, and she never returns. She disappears.

At first the husband cannot believe what has happened. He leaves a note on their car and goes looking for her. He can even see, in the background, the bright dot of her red hair in an idle Polaroid he snapped while waiting for her. Where did she go? The question becomes an obsession with him, even years later after he has lost hope of finding her alive. He simply needs to know.

Now at this point I must be cautious about what I write, because I don't want to spoil the film. Let it be said that we know from fairly early on who is responsible for the disappearance. He is a pleasant family man with a round, open face, and he seems mostly pleased with himself. We do not know how he abducted her, or what happened to her then, although there are clues. On the surface, he does not seem to be an evil man. He certainly doesn't fit the profile of a killer. But there is something twisted there, and we learn more about it as we learn more about his life story.

The husband has advertised all over France and Holland for his wife. He can think of nothing else—even though he is in a new relationship with a woman who tries to understand the obsession. The abductor, of course, has seen the advertisements. He is not without sympathy for this man. And so the final scenes unfold.

The Vanishing is a thriller, but in a different way than most thrillers. It is a thriller about knowledge—about what the characters know about the disappearance, and what they know about themselves. The movie was directed by George Sluizer, based on a screenplay he did with Tim Krabbé, which in turn was based on Krabbé's novel *The Golden Egg.* Together they have constructed a psychological jigsaw puzzle, a plot that makes you realize how simplistic many suspense films really are. The movie advances in a tantalizing fashion, supplying information obliquely, suggesting as much as it tells, and everything leads up to a climax that is as horrifying as it is probably inevitable.

Vanya on 42nd Street ★ ★ ★ ½   [NEW]
PG, 119 m., 1994

Wallace Shawn (Vanya), Julianne Moore (Yelena), Brooke Smith (Sonya), Larry Pine

(Dr. Astrov), George Gaynes (Serybryakov), Lynn Cohen (Maman), Phoebe Brand (Marina), Jerry Mayer (Waffles), Madhur Jaffrey (Mrs. Chao), André Gregory (Himself). Directed by Louis Malle and produced by Fred Berner. Screenplay by David Mamet.

A table, some chairs, many shadows reaching out into the unseen depths of an abandoned theater, and a long night of truthtelling. These are the elements of *Vanya on 42nd Street,* a film which reduces Chekhov's *Uncle Vanya* to its bare elements: loneliness, wasted lives, romantic hope, and despair. To add elaborate sets, costumes, and locations to this material would only dilute it.

The movie is the result of a five-year theatrical experiment. The stage director André Gregory and the actor Wallace Shawn, who collaborated on *My Dinner with André* (1981), gathered other actors and began to perform *Vanya* here and there around New York, in small theaters or even in the apartments of friends. Any room would do. They were more interested in the words, using a translation by David Mamet that makes the dialogue both conversational and somehow more formal, more thoughtful, than ordinary conversation.

One night Louis Malle, the French filmmaker who made *My Dinner with André,* came to see the work in progress, and suggested that he film it. So the old friends were reunited after a decade, and the opening scenes of *Vanya on 42nd Street* suggest the earlier film, as the principals make their way through the streets of Manhattan for a rendezvous. We see the actors arriving for work, carrying paper cups of coffee, making their way into the New Amsterdam Theater, where faded glory waits under a layer of dust and cast-about furniture.

The play starts before we realize it. One moment we are settling in with Gregory and a few other observers for a rehearsal, and the next the lighting has been subtly altered, and the big old table on the stage has become a sitting room on a rural estate in Russia.

The characters are among the most familiar in literature. Uncle Vanya (Shawn), now in his forties, has for many years managed the estate for Serybryakov (George Gaynes), the husband of his late sister. This man has now returned to the estate with his young wife, Yelena (Julianne Moore). Vanya hates Serybryakov—feels he has wasted his life making money for him—and feels a secret passion for Yelena. He is enraged that Sery-bryakov has returned with plans to sell the estate and make its residents homeless.

Also in the household are Sonya (Brooke Smith), who is Vanya's niece; Maman (Lynn Cohen), their old mother; Marina (Phoebe Brand), a family retainer; and the sad, haunted figure of Dr. Astrov (Larry Pine), a neighbor who comes many nights to sit and drink himself into oblivion. The emotional connections are these: Serybryakov feels himself too old for the young Yelena; Vanya feels himself the right age for her, but cut off by poverty; and poor quiet Sonya has nursed a quiet love for Dr. Astrov for years.

The subject of the play is, What use should we make of our lives? The deeper subject is the fear of the characters that they have wasted theirs. Serybryakov is a gambler and a wast-rel, who has tossed away the fortune he obtained from Vanya's dead sister. Yelena has become the wife of this hollow man. Vanya has spent his life in an obscure corner of the world, managing an estate whose owner can hardly be bothered to visit it. Astrov is lost in alcohol, Sonya dares not even speak of her love for him, and all of them go around and around, repeating the same patterns, nursing the same resentments, until something must break.

Something does, in the famous scene where Vanya picks up a revolver and threatens to end the charade with bloodshed. But there are quieter moments in the play that are even more violent, as, in the middle of the night, the characters finally tell each other what they truly dream, love, and fear.

Malle, whose films are usually much larger (*Atlantic City, Pretty Baby, Au Revoir, les Enfants*) shows again, as he did with *My Dinner with André*, that he is the master of a visual style suited to tightly encompassed material. There is not a shot that calls attention to itself, and yet not a shot that is without thought. From time to time, he draws back from the drama to remind us of the watchers in the theater, and has André Gregory, the director of the stage version, murmur a few quiet words of comment or explanation to his guests. Gregory's attitude—absorbed, fascinated, unobtrusive—sets the tone for how to watch the play, and Malle's camera goes for exactly the same tone.

The title *Vanya on 42nd Street* suggests some kind of jazzy updating of Chekhov, a modern-dress revisionism. The film is just the opposite. Although the actors' clothing and their cardboard cups of coffee are ad-missions that the production is taking place right now, the drama seems to take place outside time. It is not about characters in nineteenth-century Russia, but about anyone who feels their lives have been placed on hold—that some "necessity," such as a family responsibility or a financial need, has required them to spend years going through motions that are irrelevant to what they really feel and need.

All of the characters have thrown away their lives, but none is more agonized about it than Vanya. Wallace Shawn's performance in this role has been criticized in some quarters because the actor is, well, too comic, or too much of a tortured nebbish, to be a Chekhovian hero. I felt the opposite. Shawn is so specific, so entirely himself, that he brings Vanya right down to the bottom line: He is not great, not brilliant, not smooth, not lucky with women, but by God he has feelings, too! And among them is the conviction that he has been dealt a rotten hand.

At the end of the film, there is a long monologue by Sonya, the quiet one whose family role has been as a passive background presence. At last she says what she thinks. The scene is wonderfully handled by Brooke Smith, who gives expression to what Sonya hopes: That if there is nothing to be done in this life, at least we may find a perfect mercy beyond the grave. The film ends with not much conviction that this will happen—but at least the characters can, once again, dream.

The Verdict ★ ★ ★ ★
R, 122 m., 1982

Paul Newman (Frank Galvin), Charlotte Rampling (Laura Fischer), Jack Warden (Mickey Morrissey), James Mason (Ed Concannon), Milo O'Shea (Judge Hoyle), Edward Binns (Bishop Brophy), Julie Bovasso (Maureen Rooney), Lindsay Crouse (Kaitlin Costello). Directed by Sidney Lumet and produced by Richard Zanuck and David Brown. Screenplay by David Mamet.

There is a moment in *The Verdict* when Paul Newman walks into a room and shuts the door and trembles with anxiety and with the inner scream that people should *get off his back*. No one who has ever been seriously hung over or needed a drink will fail to recognize the moment. It is the key to his character in *The Verdict*, a movie about a drinking alcoholic who tries to pull himself together for one last step at salvaging his self-esteem.

Newman plays Frank Galvin, a Boston lawyer who has had his problems over the years—a lost job, a messy divorce, a disbarment hearing, all of them traceable in one way or another to his alcoholism. He has a "drinking problem," as an attorney for the archdiocese delicately phrases it. That means that he makes an occasional guest appearance at his office and spends the rest of his day playing pinball and drinking beer, and his evening drinking Irish whiskey and looking to see if there isn't at least one last lonely woman in the world who will buy his version of himself in preference to the facts. Galvin's pal, a lawyer named Mickey Morrissey (Jack Warden) has drummed up a little work for him: An open-and-shut malpractice suit against a Catholic hospital in Boston where a young woman was carelessly turned into a vegetable because of a medical oversight. The deal is pretty simple. Galvin can expect to settle out-of-court and pocket a third of the settlement—enough to drink on for what little future he is likely to enjoy.

But Galvin makes the mistake of going to see the young victim in a hospital, where she is alive but in a coma. And something snaps inside of him. He determines to try this case, by God, and to prove that the doctors who took her mind away from her were guilty of incompetence and dishonesty. In Galvin's mind, bringing this case to court is one and the same thing with regaining his self-respect—with emerging from his own alcoholic coma. Galvin's redemption takes place within the framework of a courtroom thriller. The screenplay by David Mamet is a wonder of good dialogue, strongly seen characters, and a structure that pays off in the big courtroom scene—as the genre requires. As a courtroom drama, *The Verdict* is superior work. But the director and the star of this film, Sidney Lumet and Paul Newman, seem to be going for something more; *The Verdict* is more a character study than a thriller, and the buried suspense in this movie is more about Galvin's own life than about his latest case.

Frank Galvin provides Newman with the occasion for one of his great performances. This is the first movie in which Newman has looked a little old, a little tired. There are moments when his face sags and his eyes seem terribly weary, and we can look ahead clearly to the old men he will be playing in ten years' time. Newman always has been an interesting actor, but sometimes his resiliency, his youthful vitality, have obscured his performances; he has a tendency to always look great, and that is not always what the role calls for. This time, he gives us old, bonetired, hung over, trembling (and heroic) Frank Galvin, and we buy it lock, stock, and shot glass.

The movie is populated with finely tuned supporting performances (many of them by British or Irish actors, playing Bostonians not at all badly). Jack Warden is the old law partner; Charlotte Rampling is the woman, also an alcoholic, with whom Galvin unwisely falls in love; James Mason is the ace lawyer for the archdiocese; Milo O'Shea is the politically connected judge; Wesley Addy provides just the right presence as one of the accused doctors. The performances, the dialogue, and the plot all work together like a rare machine.

But it's that Newman performance that stays in the mind. Some reviewers have found *The Verdict* a little slow-moving, maybe because it doesn't always hum along on the thriller level. But if you bring empathy to the movie, if you allow yourself to think about what Frank Galvin is going through, there's not a moment of this movie that's not absorbing. *The Verdict* has a lot of truth in it, right down to a great final scene in which Newman, still drinking, finds that if you wash it down with booze, victory tastes just like defeat.

Vice Versa ★ ★ ★ ½
PG, 97 m., 1988

Judge Reinhold (Marshall), Fred Savage (Charlie), Corinne Bohrer (Sam), Swoosie Kurtz (Tina), Jane Kaczmarek (Robyn), David Proval (Turk), William Prince (Avery), Gloria Gifford (Marcie), Beverly Archer (Mrs. Luttrell), Harry Murphy (Larry). Directed by Brian Gilbert and produced by Dick Clement and Ian La Frenais. Screenplay by Clement and La Frenais.

Who would have guessed it? Who would have been able to predict that the plot of one of 1987's worst movies could produce one of 1988's most endearing comedies? Here at last is proof that the right actors can make anything funny, or perhaps it is proof that the wrong actors cannot. The name of the movie is *Vice Versa,* and when they made it in 1987 it was called *Like Father, Like Son.* The screenplays for the two movies are amazingly similar, through a rare Hollywood coincidence. But what a difference there is in the movies.

It was, I must admit, with lagging step and a heavy heart that I made my way to see *Vice Versa.* I had sincerely disliked *Like Father, Like Son,* which starred Dudley Moore and Kirk Cameron in the story of a father and son whose minds magically enter each other's bodies, forcing them to trade identities. Now here was *Vice Versa,* which stars Judge Reinhold and Fred Savage in the story of a father and son whose minds magically enter each other's bodies, forcing them to trade identities. If the material was bad when it was fresh, how could it be good when it was familiar?

My state of mind lasted for perhaps the first five minutes of the movie. Then I was laughing too hard to care. I suppose film students of the future will want to analyze the differences between the two treatments of similar material, to see how Reinhold and Savage and director Brian Gilbert and writers Dick Clement and Ian La Frenais got it right when the 1987 team got it all wrong. I would prefer to think maybe it was a matter of style.

Reinhold plays a Chicago department store executive, divorced, hard-working, upward-bound in his organization. Savage plays his eleven-year-old son, who comes to stay for a few weeks while his mother is on vacation. At one point, while they are both touching an ancient gold-trimmed Tibetan skull, they are unwise enough to wish that they could be each other. Through a mysterious, magical process that need not concern us, Reinhold and Savage are suddenly consumed in a searing bolt of light, and their personalities are transferred. That puts a little boy into a man's body and, as the title suggests, vice versa.

The movie's plot situations are fairly predictable. The kid goes to the department store in his dad's body, plays with the drums in the musical instrument section, acts like a kid with his secretary, and behaves strangely at a board meeting. Meanwhile, his dad, in a kid's body, goes to school in a limousine, barks orders into the phone, finishes exams in three minutes, and talks back to the teachers. In a couple of the best scenes, the kid (as his dad) visits his grade school teacher, and gets even with the bullies who have been tormenting him. And the dad (as his son) tells his girlfriend things he lacked the courage to say when he was an adult.

All of this is fun and well-done, but it is simply plotting. What makes *Vice Versa* so wonderful is the way Reinhold and Savage are able to convince us that each body is

inhabited by the other character. They are masters of body language. Notice, for example, the scene where Reinhold demolishes the fifth-grade bullies and then, when he thinks no one is watching him, swings his arm through the air in a joyous boilermaker. Look, too, at the restless and immature way he suggests that a child would inhabit an adult body; children haven't yet had their spirits broken to make them sit still all the time.

Savage, as the adult inside the kid, is equally good at moving with quiet confidence, even impatience, and ordering people around, and expecting to be obeyed. After he calls a limousine and it lets him out in front of the department store, he strides inside and a doorman asks the chauffeur, "Is he famous?" "He's about to be," the chauffeur says, "because I'm gonna kill him."

Vice Versa is a treasure of a movie, in which the performances hold the key. It's a movie that finds its humor in many small moments of truth and accurate observation, and if there is even a certain gentle knowledge of human nature in this film, you know what? That is not necessarily wrong for a comedy, not even in the cynical weathers that surround us.

Victor/Victoria ★ ★ ★
R, 133 m., 1982

Julie Andrews (Victor/Victoria), James Garner (King), Robert Preston (Toddy), Lesley Ann Warren (Norma), Alex Karras (Squash), John Rhys-Davies (Cassell). Directed by Blake Edwards and produced by Edwards and Tony Adams.

I've always felt this way about female impersonators: They may not be as pretty as women, or sing as well, or wear a dress as well, but you've got to hand it to them; they sure look great and sing pretty—for men. There are no doubt, of course, female impersonators who practice their art so skillfully that they cannot be told apart from real women—but that, of course, misses the point. A drag queen should be maybe 90 percent convincing as a woman, tops, so you can applaud while still knowing it's an act.

Insights like these are crucial to Blake Edwards's *Victor/Victoria,* in which Julie Andrews plays a woman playing a man playing a woman. It's a complicated challenge. If she just comes out as Julie Andrews, then of course she looks just like a woman, because she is one. So when she comes onstage as

"Victoria," said to be "Victor" but really (we know) actually Victoria, she has to be an ever-so-slightly imperfect woman, to sell the premise that she's a man. Whether she succeeds is the source of a lot of comedy in this movie, which is a lighthearted meditation on how ridiculous we can sometimes become when we take sex too seriously.

The movie is made in the spirit of classic movie sex farces, and is in fact based on one (a 1933 German film named *Viktor und Viktoria*, which I haven't seen). Its more recent inspiration is probably *La Cage Aux Folles*, an enormous success that gave Hollywood courage to try this offbeat material. In the movie, Andrews is a starving singer, out of work, down to her last franc, when she meets a charming old fraud named Toddy, who is gay, and who is played by Robert Preston in the spirit of Ethel Mertz on "I Love Lucy." Preston is kind, friendly, plucky, and comes up with the most outrageous schemes to solve problems that wouldn't be half so complicated if he weren't on the case. In this case, he has a brainstorm: Since there's no market for girl singers, but a constant demand for female impersonators, why shouldn't Andrews assume a false identity and pretend to be a drag queen? "But they'll *know* I'm not a man!" she wails. "Of course!" Preston says triumphantly.

The plot thickens when James Garner, as a Chicago nightclub operator, wanders into Victor/Victoria's nightclub act and falls in love with him/her. Garner refuses to believe that lovely creature is a man. He's right, but if Andrews admits it, she's out of work. Meanwhile, Garner's blond girlfriend (Lesley Ann Warren) is consumed by jealousy, and intrigue grows between Preston and Alex Karras, who plays Garner's bodyguard. Edwards develops this situation as farce, with lots of gags depending on split-second timing and characters being in the wrong hotel rooms at the right time. He also throws in several nightclub brawls, which aren't very funny, but which don't much matter. What makes the material work is not only the fact that it is funny (which it is), but that it's about likable people.

The three most difficult roles belong to Preston, Garner, and Karras, who must walk a tightrope of uncertain sexual identity without even appearing to condescend to their material. They never do. Because they all seem to be people first and genders second, they see the humor in their bewildering situation as quickly as anyone, and their cheer-ful ability to rise to a series of implausible occasions makes *Victor/Victoria* not only a funny movie, but, unexpectedly, a warm and friendly one.

Vincent ★ ★ ★ ★
NO MPAA RATING, 99 m., 1989

A documentary written and directed by Paul Cox and produced by Tony Llewellyn-Jones. Words by Vincent van Gogh, read by John Hurt.

"How rich art is! If only one can remember what one has seen."—Vincent van Gogh, in a letter to his brother.

"Dear Theo," the letters always began, and there were more than 750 of them, written by Vincent van Gogh to his brother, Theo. The painter spoke of his life, his finances, his health, his prospects, his opinions of the art world—but most of all he spoke about his paintings, and about the discoveries he was making. To read the letters while looking at the paintings (as you can do if you have the book *Vincent by Himself*) is like having van Gogh take you by the hand and lead you through an exhibit of his work. Few other painters have left such a moving and honest personal correspondence.

If you only read the letters and look at the works, however, you will miss something—the look of the everyday world that van Gogh was transforming into his paintings. What Paul Cox has done in *Vincent*—which is the best film about a painter I have ever seen—is to take his camera to some of the places van Gogh painted, and to re-create some of the others in his imagination. This is not, however, one of those idiotic "art appreciation" films in which we see the windmill and then we see the painting of the windmill; Cox knows too much about art to be that simplistic. Instead, he adopts the role of a disciple of the painter, a man who wants to stand in the same places and see the same things as a simple act of love toward van Gogh's work.

All of the words on the sound track are from Vincent's letters to Theo, read by the British actor John Hurt. On the screen, we see landscapes such as van Gogh might have seen, and we visit some of the places where he painted. But there are fictionalized, created sequences as well: scenes of farmers in their fields, or peasants walking down country lanes, or shadows sweeping across fields of sunflowers. And there is a magical sequence in which the people in a room go about their daily business until they arrange themselves, seemingly by accident, into a reproduction of a painting.

Sometimes Cox makes no effort to photograph specific things that van Gogh might have seen or been influenced by. Instead, his camera visits woods and fields, and watches birds and flowers, and meanders down alleyways populated with people who seem to harbor some of the weariness and fear of so many of van Gogh's models. The words continue over these images as well, creating the illusion that the painter is narrating the film himself.

The best parts of the film are the most specific. Cox uses close-ups to show the smallest details of some of the paintings, while the narration describes the painter's technical discoveries and experiments. There are times when we almost seem to be looking at the very brushstroke that van Gogh is describing in a letter. These moments create a sense of the specific. We aren't looking at stars in the sky, or fields of flowers, or a portrait of the artist; we're looking at frozen moments in time when van Gogh's brush moved just such a way in response to his feeling and his craft. The strokes seem enormous, on the big movie screen, and they call our attention to the detail, to the way that van Gogh's paintings were not about their subjects but about the way he saw his subjects.

So much of the popular image of van Gogh is crude and inaccurate, fed by the notion that he was "mad," fueled by the fact that he cut off his ear. There is an entirely different Vincent here, a poetic, thoughtful man who confides everything to his brother, who is not mad so much as completely open to the full range of his experience, including those parts that most of us prudently suppress. *Vincent* is the most romantic and yet the most sensible documentary about a painter I can imagine.

Vincent & Theo ★ ★ ★ ½
PG-13, 138 m., 1990

Tim Roth (Vincent van Gogh), Paul Rhys (Theo van Gogh), Johanna Ter Steege (Jo Bonger), Wladimir Yordanoff (Paul Gauguin), Jean-Pierre Cassel (Dr. Paul Gachet). Directed by Robert Altman and produced by Ludi Boeken. Screenplay by Julian Mitchell.

How to portray the artist at work? Directors through the years have shown them sporadically applying paint to canvas, but for the most part the artist's task in the movies is to drink wine, argue by candlelight, and spend a good deal of time in unheated studios with undressed models. The big dramatic scenes involve confrontations with those who do not understand his genius: His dealers, his lovers, his public, and his creditors.

Only occasionally does a film come along where we get the sensation that actual creation is taking place before our eyes. That happens when the filmmakers are also in the art of creating, and transfer their inspiration to the characters in a sort of artistic ventriloquism. *Camille Claudel* (1989) had that feeling, as Isabella Adjani grubbed about in a ditch, digging up clay for her sculptures. And now here is Robert Altman's *Vincent & Theo*, another film that generates the feeling that we are in the presence of a man in the act of creation.

True art is made as if God were a lot of little cottage industries. Artists take up shapeless raw material—paint or clay, or a blank sheet of paper—and transform it into something wonderful that never existed before. This is such a joyous activity that I am at a loss to understand how an artist could ever be unhappy, and yet so many are. Perhaps, like God, they grieve when man ignores their handiwork.

Vincent van Gogh was one of the unhappiest of artists. Some medical experts now believe it was because he suffered from a maddening ear disease. *Vincent & Theo* does not attempt a diagnosis. It simply regards the fact that van Gogh, whose paintings most people today instinctively love from the first moment they see them, suffered all of his life from overwhelming rejection. He did not paint because he wanted to; he painted because he had to. He did not develop a style; he painted in the only way he could. During his lifetime he sold only one painting. How would you feel, if you worked a lifetime to create beautiful things for people to look at, and they turned their backs and chose to look at ugly things instead? And if you saw your brother sacrifice himself to support your lonely work?

Altman's approach in *Vincent & Theo* is a very immediate, intimate one. He would rather show us things happening than provide themes and explanations. He is most concerned with the relationship that made the art possible, the way in which Theo, the younger brother, essentially became Vincent's parent and patron. We meet van Gogh (Tim Roth) and his brother (Paul Rhys) in the middle of their relationship, we hear them fight and see them through the thickets

of exasperation, and at the end we realize that it took two obsessives to create the work of Vincent van Gogh: The brother who painted it, and the brother who believed that to support the painting was the most important thing he could possibly do with his lifetime.

The movie takes place inside and outside the claustrophobic art world of Paris in the late nineteenth century, where the two Dutch brothers try to make their mark. Theo is a passable art dealer, skilled at selling safe paintings to cautious people, and he is lucky in finding employers who sympathize with his more radical tastes and eventually give him the opportunity to strike out on his own. Even then, given free rein, he is unable to sell his brother's work. And Vincent lives in a series of barren rooms and small houses, writing continuously to his brother (the apparent subject is art, but the buried subject is usually money).

There is the sense that Vincent had no knowledge of the way people normally behave toward one another. At some point in his childhood, he failed to decipher that code. Consider the scene where the prostitute (Jip Wijngaarden) comes to pose for him. She is cold and hungry, and the only support of her daughter. Vincent asks her to come and live with him. She explains her needs. He agrees to them. His need is to have someone to paint, and everything else—the expense, the distraction, the responsibility, and certainly the subject of sex—never occurs to him.

His painting is such a direct expression of his mood, indeed, that ordinary human speech often seems unnecessary. He is the rare artist who truly does speak through his work, and Altman dramatizes that in a remarkable scene in a field of sunflowers, where, as van Gogh paints, Altman's camera darts restlessly, aggressively, at the flowers, turning them from passive subjects into an alien hostile environment. The film is able to see the sunflowers as Altman believed van Gogh saw them. To make a sunflower stand for anything other than itself is a neat trick, and Altman accomplishes it in his own way, as van Gogh did in his.

The details of van Gogh's life are here. The infamous ear episode. The fights with Theo. The death. *Vincent & Theo* follows the trajectory of a biopic more faithfully than we might have expected, given Altman as the director. This is a more classically constructed film than much of his work, and although Altman says it's that way because

he had to follow the chronology of a man's life, I think the reason is more complex: That van Gogh's personality was so fractured and tortured that the movie needed to be stable and secure, as a frame for it.

Vision Quest ★ ★ ★ ½
R, 108 m., 1985

Matthew Modine (Louden Swain), Linda Fiorentino (Carla), Michael Schoeffling (Kuch), Ronny Cox (Louden's Dad), Harold Sylvester (Tanneran), Charles Hallahan (Coach), R.H. Thomson (Kevin), J.C. Quinn (Elmo), Frank Jasper (Shute). Directed by Harold Becker and produced by Jon Peters and Peter Guber. Screenplay by Darryl Ponicsan.

We think we know the story pretty well already: Young wrestler has two dreams, (a) to win the state championship, and (b) to win the love of a girl. The defending state champion is a man-mountain who carries telephone poles to the top of stadiums. The girl is an independent drifter who is twenty years old and doesn't take the hero seriously. By the end of the movie, the only suspense is whether it will end with a victory in bed or in the ring. Although *Vision Quest* sticks pretty close to that outline, it is nevertheless a movie with some nice surprises, mostly because it takes the time to create some interesting characters. The movie's hero, Louden Swain, is probably the closest thing to a standard movie character, but Matthew Modine plays him with such an ingratiating freshness that he makes the character quirky and interesting, almost in spite of the script.

The other people in the movie are all real originals. They include Louden's father (Ronny Cox), who has lost the family farm and his wife, but still retains the respect of his son; Louden's best pal (Michael Schoeffling), who bills himself as a "half-Indian spiritual adviser"; a black history teacher (Harold Sylvester) who cares about Louden and listens to him; an alcoholic short-order cook (J.C. Quinn) who works in the kitchen of the hotel where Louden's a bellboy, and a wrestling coach (Charles Hallahan) who has mixed feelings about Louden's drive to get down to the 168-pound class so he can wrestle the toughest wrestler in the state. All of those characters are written, directed, and acted just a little differently than we might expect; they have small roles, but they don't think small thoughts.

And then there is the movie's most original creation, the twenty-year-old drifter,

Carla (Linda Fiorentino). Without having met the actress, it's impossible for me to speculate on how much of Carla is original work and how much is Fiorentino's personality. What comes across, though, is a woman who is enigmatic without being egotistical, detached without being cold, self-reliant without being suspicious. She has a way of talking—kind of deliberately objective— that makes you listen to everything she says.

All of these people live in Spokane, which looks sort of wet and dark in many scenes, and feels like a place that prizes individuality. Instead of silhouetting the Modine character against the city and a lot of humble supporting roles, and turning him into a Rocky of wrestlers, the movie takes time to place the character in the city and in the lives of the other people. We begin to value his relationships, and it really means something when the short-order cook puts on a clean shirt and goes to the big wrestling meet.

The movie's plot doesn't really equal its characters. After the Rocky movies and *Breaking Away* and *The Karate Kid* and a dozen other movies with essentially the same last scene, it's hard to care about the outcome of the big fight, or race, or match, because, let's face it, we know the hero's going to win. Just once, why couldn't they give us characters as interesting as the ones in *Vision Quest*, in a movie where they'd be set free from the same tired old plot and allowed to live?

Visions of Eight ★ ★ ★
NO MPAA RATING, 110 m., 1973

Segments directed by Milos Forman, Arthur Penn, Kon Ichikawa, Claude Lelouch, John Schlesinger, Mai Zetterling, Juri Ozerov, and Michael Pfleghar. Produced by Stan Marguiles.

The idea sounded like a great one at the time: Eight important directors would be given their own budgets and camera crews and dispatched to Munich to record their personal visions of the 1972 Olympics. What nobody could have anticipated, perhaps, is how similar many of those visions would be. Too often during *Visions of Eight* the Olympic events are reduced to slow-motion ballets that finally just repeat themselves.

There is, I suppose, some interest in Kon Ichikawa's slow-motion replay of the 100-meter dash; the world's fastest men are slowed down to grotesque life-sized robots with pumping cheeks and contorted faces, and we get a feeling for the event's special agony.

But the sequence is held too long; and so is Arthur Penn's segment on pole vaulting. We get jump after jump in slow motion, but all of that footage doesn't tell us as much about the vaulters as one single shot, near the end, where Penn shows us a competitor meticulously removing an invisible piece of lint from his hand grip.

There are other small touches that make the film worth seeing. In Claude Lelouch's segment on the losers, for example, there's an astonishing display of bad sportsmanship from a defeated boxer who refuses to leave the ring. For three or four minutes caught in a single take, he expresses his contempt for the decision and his outrage at the crowd (which generously boos him).

There's another kind of losing, too. In Mai Zetterling's segment, we see a massive weightlifter as he nervously circles the weights, and we can almost taste his apprehension. We've seen other competitors lift this bar (which takes five men to carry from the stage), and we know how heavy it is. So does he. He circles the stage, breathing deeply, trying to psych himself into the lift. He approaches the bar, grabs it, backs away. Circles some more. Just looking at him, we sense he can't lift it. He approaches the bar again, heaves, gets it a foot off the ground, then throws it back down again with disgust and walks off the stage. In a moment like that, we begin to understand something of the difficulties of the weightlifter.

The movie's still, beautiful center is occupied by the fawnlike Soviet gymnast Ludmilla Tourischeva. She's in Michael Pfleghar's segment on the women in the Olympics, and he shows us her entire routine on the uneven parallel bars. It is an exercise of grace made possible through superb athletic skill, and he wisely refuses to gimmick it up with cuts or slow motion. (Surely, as a general rule, the beauty of the Olympic events is that they take place in real time; slowing down Tourischeva's gymnastics would have missed the point.)

The most successful segment was directed by John Schlesinger, who considers the twenty-six-mile marathon race from the point of view of one of the British competitors. We see the runner in his home in the north of England, getting up every morning to run ten miles to and from work. Some days he runs home for lunch. On Saturdays he does a complete marathon course. We get a real feel for the loneliness of the long-distance runner as we see him running on dreary country roads during an overcast morning.

Then Schlesinger shows the runner at the Olympics, and in a stunning use of imagination, he gives us dream-like sequences designed to suggest what goes through the mind of the marathon runner: Memories of the long morning runs, thoughts of his family, wordless awareness of his surroundings. Schlesinger intercuts this footage with rather superficial coverage of the murdered Israelis.

His is the only segment to refer to the tragedy, and at first he doesn't really seem to have anything coherent to say. But then he pulls his images together in his last few minutes; as Avery Brundage is making his closing speech as if the whole Olympic pageantry hadn't already turned to ashes with the murders, a final dogged marathon runner, hours behind the rest, stubbornly runs into the stadium and crosses the finish line. That's it, Schlesinger seems to be saying: The dignity of this loser, still loyal to his sport, eclipses the electric scoreboards and the official blazers.

Visions of Light: The Art of Cinematography ★ ★ ★ ½
NO MPAA RATING, 90 m., 1993

A documentary directed by Arnold Glassman, Todd McCarthy, and Stuart Samuels and produced by Samuels. Screenplay by McCarthy.

It is commonplace to observe that a film has good cinematography, but far less common to discuss what is meant by that. Sometimes all it means is that the pictures are pretty, and for many people, I think, "cinematography" somehow connects with vast outdoor vistas—the sand dunes in *Lawrence of Arabia*, or the Texas plains in *Days of Heaven*. But great cinematography can also consist of the look in an eye, the tense space between two people, or the shadows in the corner of a cramped room.

Visions of Light is a documentary that will likely cause everyone who sees it to look at movies a little differently in the future. It is a film about cinematography, consisting of a great many great shots and sequences, commented on by the men (and a few women) who photographed them.

The only way to criticize a movie, Jean-Luc Godard famously said, is to make another movie. Certainly the best way to criticize cinematography is to show it. Here we begin with some of the earliest shots in which the artistry of motion picture photography began to pull away from the mere fact that it could record light and movement on film. At the very first, of course, filmmakers simply pointed their cameras at things, and then audiences gasped when they could see them. But then the lure of style began to seduce them. Cinematographers such as Billy Bitzer, working with D.W. Griffith, began to move the camera in for close-ups, and intercut shots to create an emotional rhythm, and move the camera itself, and soon cinematography was born.

In Britain, the cinematographer was originally known as the "lighting cameraman," and indeed light—the way it falls on the subject, the way it is present or absent—is at the heart of the craft. I remember the late James Wong Howe telling an audience at the Chicago Film Festival how he battled with the technical advisers from Technicolor when he was shooting *The Adventures of Tom Sawyer,* which was only the third or fourth film made in the process. They advised him to pour on light, lots of it, even in the scene where Tom and Becky are lost in the cave. He cut the light by three-quarters, and made the scene feel real. They complained that you couldn't even see most of the cave. Exactly.

In *Visions of Light,* many great cinematographers talk about their relationships with directors, with shots, and with the light. It is always hard to say exactly where a director's contribution ends and the cinematographer's begins, but it is always true that it's the cinematographer's responsibility to realize the director's vision—and sometimes, they hint here, to supply it.

Sometimes their skill consists merely of taking advantage of a happy chance. One of the most beautiful and effective shots shown in this film is from Richard Brooks's *In Cold Blood,* photographed by Conrad Hall in 1967. On the night he is to be hanged from the gallows, the murderer played by Robert Blake looks out through a window peppered with rain. Looking through his viewfinder, Hall discovered that the light through the window caught the shadows of raindrops as they trickled down the glass, and projected them against Blake's face, creating the illusion of ghostly tears. "He told me not to move, and not to cry," Blake remembered. The shot cries for him.

There are many other shots here, from Gregg Toland's deep focus work in *Citizen Kane* through to Haskell Wexler's work on *Who's Afraid of Virginia Woolf?* which might have been retitled by Richard Burton and Elizabeth Taylor, *Who's Afraid of Haskell Wexler?,* since they let him photograph them

with a distinctly unflattering realism, and the shots so suited the mood of the piece that it became one of their great collaborations.

Faithful readers will not be surprised to learn that the black and white cinematography, of course, is more beautiful than the color. Black and white, I believe, contains the naked soul of the cinema. Color photography merely supplies its clothes. In a segment devoted to Stanley Cortez's great cinematography on Charles Laughton's *Night of the Hunter* (1955), the young cinematographer Allen Daviau talks about the reluctance with which the great cameramen left b&w, with its greater poetry and mystery, for the prosaic reality of color. Certainly the shot shown from the film—Lillian Gish sitting grimly on a porch with a rifle, while Robert Mitchum loiters on a sidewalk—recalls the film's almost surrealistic sense of horror. There is another shot in the film where Mitchum's shadow from a street lamp is cast, stark and terrifying, on a child's bedroom ceiling. The whole style bespeaks b&w.

The cinematographers quoted here all speak of the greater difficulty of lighting black and white, but of its greater rewards. Of all of the crimes television has committed against the movies, its lame-brained enforcement of the color rule is the worst. It came about because in the late 1960s, when most people began to have color sets, it was naively believed that they wanted to see only color movies in television. As anyone who has ever watched *It's a Wonderful Life* or *Casablanca* on TV can testify, b&w actually looks better on TV than color does. (The first network to return to b&w footage in a newscast will be surprised to find that its ratings jump.)

Visions of Light is the kind of movie that will affect the way you look at movies. It calls your attention to what is being shown on the screen, when you are perhaps more used to following what is happening in the story. Look, here, at a scene from *Rosemary's Baby.* The character played by Ruth Gordon is seen at the end of a corridor, on the telephone. Cinematographer William Fraker remembers that the director, Roman Polanski, asked him to move the camera so that audiences could see only Gordon's back; the rest of her body was concealed by a door. So sinister was the call and so great the audience's curiosity, Fraker remembers, that when the shot played, everyone in the theater unconsciously shifted to one side, trying to see around that door.

Vixen ★ ★ ★
x, 68 m., 1969

Erica Gavin (Vixen), Harrison Page (Niles), Garth Pillsbury (Tom), Michael O'Donnell (O'Banlon), Vincent Wallace (Janet), Robert Aiken (Dave), Jon Evans (Jud). Directed and produced by Russ Meyer. Screenplay by Robert Rudelson.

Some time ago it might have been necessary to devise all sorts of defenses for Russ Meyer's *Vixen,* finding hidden symbolism and all that. But I see no reason why we can't be honest: *Vixen* was the best film of its day in that uniquely American genre, the skin-flick.

It is also a celebration of zestful direction and photography, and a lot of the time it's very funny. In a field filled with cheap, dreary productions, Meyer is the best craftsman and the only artist. He has developed a directing style so open, direct, and good-humored that it dominates his material; what a relief it was to hear laughter during a skin-flick, instead of the dead silence that usually envelops their cheerless audiences.

Vixen is not only a good skin-flick, but a merciless put-on of the whole genre. As Terry Southern demonstrated with his novel *Candy,* you can't satirize pornography without writing it. The movie version of *Candy* failed because it lacked the courage to find itself ridiculous; how can a put-on take itself seriously? *Vixen,* on the other hand, catalogs the basic variations in skin-flick plots and ticks them off one after another.

It's done with such droll dialogue and high humor that even the most torrid scenes somehow manage to get outside themselves; instead of placing his hero and heroine in the shower and grinding away in the panting style of his imitators, Meyer takes the basic shower scene, writes it with hilariously malaprop dialogue ("We decided to stop doing this when we were twelve," Vixen's brother protests), and intercuts it with a scene outside in which a red-bearded Irish Communist makes a speech to a black draft dodger.

Meyer is also heavy on the redeeming social value department. His characters debate communism, Cuban Marxism, Vietnam, draft-dodging, civil rights, and airplane hijacking, deciding in favor of civil rights and against the others.

The story line is barely strong enough to hold the scenes together; it involves a bush pilot and his wife (Vixen, portrayed admirably by Erica Gavin) who take another couple on a fishing weekend in Canada. Also present are

Vixen's brother and his black friend, a draft evader protesting what he believes is a racist war. The Irish Marxist wanders in later from somewhere. There is also a Royal Canadian Mounted Policeman who wanders off somewhere.

At the time the movie was released, "redeeming social value" was a key line of defense against charges that a movie was pornographic. Meyer's inspiration was to put all of the redeeming speeches at the end. "The audience will know," he once said, "that when the characters get on the airplane, the good parts are over." Sound advice.

W

Walkabout ★ ★ ★ ★
PG, 95 m., 1971

Jenny Agutter (The Girl), Lucien John (Brother), David Gumpilil (Aborigine), John Mellon (Father). Directed by Nicolas Roeg and produced by Si Litvinoff. Screenplay by Edward Bond.

It is possible to consider *Walkabout* entirely as the story it seems to be: The story of a fourteen-year-old girl and her little brother, who are abandoned in the Australian outback and then saved through the natural skills of a young aborigine boy. It is simpler and easier to consider it on that level, too, because *Walkabout* is a superb work of storytelling and its material is effortlessly fascinating. There's also a tendency (unfortunate, probably) to read *Walkabout* as a catch-all of symbols and metaphors, in which the Noble Savage and his natural life are tested and found superior to civilization and cities. The movie does, indeed, make this comparison several times. Hundreds of miles from help, the girl turns on her portable radio to hear a philosopher observe: "It is now possible to state that 'that is' is." Well, this isn't exactly helpful, and so we laugh. And more adolescent viewers may have to stifle a sigh and a tear when the girl is seen, at the movie's end, married to a cloddish office clerk and nostalgically remembering her idyllic days in the desert.

The contrast between civilization and man's more natural states is well-drawn in the movie, and will interest serious-minded younger people (just as, at the level of pure story, *Walkabout* will probably fascinate kids). But I don't think it's fruitful to draw all the parallels and then piously conclude that we would all be better off far from the city, sipping water from the ground, and spearing kangaroos for lunch. That sort of comparison doesn't really get you anywhere and leaves you with a movie that doesn't tell you more than you already knew. I think there's more than that to *Walkabout*. And I'm going to have a hard time expressing that additional dimension for you, because it doesn't quite exist in the universe of words. Even in these days of film experiments, most movies have their centers in the worlds of plots and characters. But *Walkabout* . . .

Well, to begin with, the film was directed and photographed by Nicolas Roeg, the cinematographer of *Petulia* and many other British films. Roeg's first stab at direction was as co-director of *Performance*. This was his first work as an individual. I persisted in seeing *Performance* on the level of its perfectly silly plot, and on that level it was a wretched movie indeed. People told me I should forget the plot and simply enjoy the movie itself, but I have a built-in resistance to that notion, usually. Perhaps I should have listened. Because Roeg's *Walkabout* is a rare example of that kind of movie, in which the "civilized" characters and the aborigine exist in a wilderness that isn't really a wilderness but more of an indefinite place for the story to be told. Roeg's desert in *Walkabout* is like Beckett's stage for *Waiting for Godot*. That is, it's nowhere in particular, and everywhere.

Roeg's photography reinforces this notion. He is careful to keep us at a distance from the physical sufferings of his characters. To be sure, they have blisters and parched lips, but he pulls up well short of the usual clichés of suffering in the desert. And his cinematography (and John Barry's otherworldly music) make the desert seem a mystical place, a place for visions. So that the whole film becomes mystical, a dream, and the suicides which frame it set the boundaries of reality. Within them, what happens between the boy and the girl, and the boy and the little brother, is not merely "communication" or "survival" or "cooperation," but the same kind of life-enhancement that you imagine people feel when they go into the woods and eat berries and bring the full focus of their intelligence to bear on the problem of coexisting with nature.

Wall Street ★ ★ ★ ½
R, 125 m., 1987

Charlie Sheen (Bud Fox), Michael Douglas (Gordon Gekko), Daryl Hannah (Darien Taylor), Martin Sheen (Carl Fox), Terence Stamp (Sir Larry), Hal Holbrook (Lou Mannheim), Sean Young (Kate Gekko), James Spader (Roger Barnes), Saul Rubinek (Harold Salt), Sylvia Miles (Realtor). Directed by Oliver Stone and produced by Edward R. Pressman. Screenplay by Stanley Weiser and Stone.

How much is enough? the kid keeps asking the millionaire stock trader. How much money do you want? How much would you be satisfied with? The trader seems to be thinking hard, but the answer is, he just doesn't know. He's not even sure how to think about the question. He spends all day trying to make as much money as he possibly can, and he cheerfully bends and breaks the law to make even more millions, but somehow the concept of "enough" eludes him. Like all gamblers, he is perhaps not even really interested in money, but in the action. Money is just the way to keep score.

The millionaire is a predator, a corporate raider, a Wall Street shark. His name is Gordon Gekko, the name no doubt inspired by the lizard that feeds on insects and sheds its tail when trapped. Played by Michael Douglas in Oliver Stone's *Wall Street*, he paces relentlessly behind the desk in his skyscraper office, lighting cigarettes, stabbing them out, checking stock prices on a bank of computers, barking buy and sell orders into a speaker phone. In his personal life, he has everything he could possibly want—wife, family, estate, pool, limousine, priceless art objects—and they are all just additional entries on the scoreboard. He likes to win.

The kid is a broker for a big Wall Street firm. He works the phones, soliciting new clients, offering secondhand advice, buying and selling and dreaming. "Just once I'd like to be on *that* side," he says, fiercely looking at the telephone a client has just used to stick him with a $7,000 loss. Gekko is his hero. He wants to sell him stock, get into his circle, be like he is. Every day for thirty-nine days, he calls Gekko's office for an appointment. On the fortieth day, Gekko's birthday, he appears with a box of Havana cigars from Davidoff's in London, and Gekko grants him an audience.

Maybe Gekko sees something he recognizes. The kid, named Bud Fox (Charlie Sheen), comes from a working-class family. His father (Martin Sheen) is an aircraft mechanic and union leader. Gekko went to a cheap university himself. Desperate to impress Gekko, young Fox passes along some inside information he got from his father. Gekko makes some money on the deal and opens an account with Fox. He also asks him to obtain more insider information, and to spy on a competitor. Fox protests that he is being asked to do something illegal. Perhaps "protests" is too strong a word—he "observes."

Gekko knows his man. Fox is so hungry to make a killing, he will do anything. Gekko promises him perks—*big* perks—and they arrive on schedule. One of them is a tall blond interior designer (Daryl Hannah), who decorates Fox's expensive new high-rise apartment. The movie's stylistic approach is rigorous: We are never allowed to luxuriate in the splendor of these new surroundings. The apartment is never quite seen, never relaxed in. When the girl comes to share Fox's bed, they are seen momentarily, in silhouette. Sex and possessions are secondary to trading, to the action. Ask any gambler.

Stone's *Wall Street* is a radical critique of the capitalist trading mentality, and it obviously comes at a time when the financial community is especially vulnerable. The movie argues that most small investors are dupes, and that the big market killings are made by men like Gekko, who swoop in and snap whole companies out from under the noses of their stockholders. What the Gekkos do is immoral and illegal, but they use a little

litany to excuse themselves: "Nobody gets hurt." "Everybody's doing it." "There's something in this deal for everybody." "Who knows except us?"

The movie has a traditional plot structure: The hungry kid is impressed by the successful older man, seduced by him, betrayed by him, and then tries to turn the tables. The actual details of the plot are not so important as the changes we see in the characters. Few men in recent movies have been colder and more ruthless than Gekko, or more convincing. Charlie Sheen is, by comparison, a babe in the woods; I would have preferred a young actor who seemed more rapacious, like James Spader, who has a supporting role in the movie. If the film has a flaw, it is that Sheen never seems quite relentless enough to move in Gekko's circle.

Stone's most impressive achievement in this film is to allow all the financial wheeling and dealing to seem complicated and convincing, and yet always have it all make sense. The movie can be followed by anybody, because the details of stock manipulation are all filtered through transparent layers of greed. Most of the time we know what's going on. All of the time, we know why.

Although Gekko's law-breaking would of course be opposed by most people on Wall Street, his larger value system would be applauded. The trick is to make his kind of money without breaking the law. Financiers who can do that, like Donald Trump, are mentioned as possible presidential candidates, and in his autobiography Trump states, quite simply, that money no longer interests him very much. He is more motivated by the challenge of a deal, and by the desire to win. His frankness is refreshing, but the key to reading that statement is to see that it considers only money, on the one hand, and winning, on the other. No mention is made about creating goods and services, or manufacturing things, or investing in a physical plant, or contributing to the infrastructure.

What's intriguing about *Wall Street*—what may cause the most discussion—is that the movie's real target isn't Wall Street criminals who break the law. Stone's target is the value system that places profits and wealth and the Deal above any other consideration. His film is an attack on an atmosphere of financial competitiveness so ferocious that ethics are simply irrelevant, and the laws are sort of like the referee in pro wrestling, part of the show.

WarGames ★ ★ ★ ★
PG, 110 m., 1983

Matthew Broderick (David), Dabney Coleman (McKittrick), John Wood (Falken), Ally Sheedy (Jennifer), Barry Corbin (General Beringer). Directed by John Badham and produced by Harold Schneider. Screenplay by Lawrence Lasker and Walter F. Parkes.

Sooner or later, a self-satisfied, sublimely confident computer is going to blow us all off the face of the planet. That is the message of *WarGames*, a scary and intelligent thriller that is one of the best films of 1983. The movie stars Matthew Broderick as a bright high school senior who spends a lot of time locked in his bedroom with his home computer. He speaks computerese well enough to dial by telephone into the computer at his school and change grades. But he's ready for bigger game. He reads about a toy company that's introducing a new computer game. He programs his computer for a random search of telephone numbers in the company's area code, looking for a number that answers with a computer tone. Eventually, he connects with a computer. Unfortunately, the computer he connects with does not belong to a toy company. It belongs to the Defense Department, and its mission is to coordinate early warning systems and nuclear deterrents in the case of World War III. The kid challenges the computer to play a game called "Global Thermonuclear Warfare," and it cheerfully agrees.

As a premise for a thriller, this is a masterstroke. The movie, however, could easily go wrong by bogging us down in impenetrable computerese, or by ignoring the technical details altogether and giving us a *Fail Safe* retread. *WarGames* makes neither mistake. It convinces us that it knows computers, and it makes its knowledge into an amazingly entertaining thriller. (Note: I do not claim the movie is *accurate* about computers—only convincing.) I've described only the opening gambits of the plot, and I will reveal no more. It's too much fun watching the story unwind. Another one of the pleasures of the movie is the way it takes cardboard characters and fleshes them out. Two in particular: the civilian chief of the U.S. computer operation, played by Dabney Coleman as a man who has his own little weakness for simple logic, and the Air Force general in charge of the war room, played by Barry Corbin as a military man who argues that men, not computers, should make the final nuclear decisions.

WarGames was directed by John Badham, best known for *Saturday Night Fever* and *Blue Thunder,* a thriller that I found considerably less convincing on the technical level. There's not a scene here where Badham doesn't seem to know what he's doing, weaving a complex web of computerese, personalities, and puzzles; the movie absorbs us on emotional and intellectual levels at the same time. And the ending, a moment of blinding and yet utterly elementary insight, is wonderful.

The War of the Roses ★ ★ ★
R, 117 m., 1989

Michael Douglas (Oliver Rose), Kathleen Turner (Barbara Rose), Danny DeVito (Gavin D'Amato), Marianne Sägebrecht (Susan), Sean Astin (Josh at Seventeen), Heather Fairfield (Carolyn at Seventeen), G.D. Spradlin (Harry Thurmont). Directed by Danny DeVito and produced by James L. Brooks. Screenplay by Michael Leeson.

The first and last shots of *The War of the Roses* show us a divorce attorney with a tragic tale to tell. He informs a client that there will be no charge. "I get paid $425 an hour to talk to people," he says, "and so when I offer to tell you something for free, I advise you to listen carefully." He wants to tell the story of a couple of clients of his, Oliver and Barbara Rose, who were happy, and then got involved in a divorce and were never happy again.

The attorney is played by Danny DeVito, who also directed *The War of the Roses,* and although I usually dislike devices in which a narrator thinks back over the progress of a long, cautionary tale, this time I think it works. It works because we must never be allowed to believe, even for a moment, that Oliver and Barbara are going to get away with their happiness. The lawyer's lesson is that happiness has nothing to do with it, anyway. He doubts that any marriage is destined to be happy (of course, as a divorce lawyer, he has a particular slant on the subject). His lesson is more brutal: Divorce is survivable. If only the Roses had listened.

The movie stars Michael Douglas and Kathleen Turner as the doomed Roses, and although both actors also teamed with DeVito in *Romancing the Stone,* no two movies could be more dissimilar. *The War of the Roses* is a black, angry, bitter, unrelenting comedy, a war between the sexes that makes James Thurber's work on the same subject look almost resigned by comparison.

And yet the Roses fell so naturally and eas-ily into love in those first sunny days so long ago. They met at an auction, bidding on the same cheap figurine, and by evening they were in each other's arms. ("If this relationship lasts," Barbara muses, "this will have been the most romantic moment of my life. If it doesn't, I'm a complete slut.")

He went into law. She went into housekeeping. They were both great at their work. Oliver made a lot of money, and Barbara spent a lot of money, buying, furnishing, and decorating a house that looks like just about the best home money can buy. Meanwhile, a couple of children, one of each sex, grow up and leave home, and then Barbara decides she wants something more in life than the curatorship of her own domestic museum. One day she sells a pound of her famous liver pâté to a friend and realizes that she holds in her hand the first money she has actually earned for herself in seventeen years. It feels good. She asks for a divorce. She wants to keep the house.

That is the beginning of the war. There have been battles of the sexes before in the movies—between Spencer Tracy and Katharine Hepburn, between George C. Scott and Faye Dunaway, between Mickey and Minnie—but never one this vicious. I wonder if the movie doesn't go over the top. The war between the Roses begins in the lawyer's office and escalates into a violent, bloody conflict that finally finds them both barricaded inside their house beautiful, doing battle with the very symbols of their marriage—the figurines, the gourmet kitchen range, the chandelier.

There are a great many funny moments in *The War of the Roses,* including one in which Turner (playing an ex-gymnast) springs to her feet from a prone position on her lawyer's floor in one lithe movement, and another in which Douglas makes absolutely certain that the fish she is serving for dinner will have that fishy smell. But the movie treads a dangerous line. There are times when its ferocity threatens to break through the boundaries of comedy—to become so unremitting we find we cannot laugh.

It's to the credit of DeVito and his costars that they were willing to go that far, but maybe it shows more courage than wisdom. This is an odd, strange movie, and the only one I can remember in which the moral is, "Rather than see a divorce lawyer, be generous—generous to the point of night sweats."

The War Room ★ ★ ★ ½
NO MPAA RATING, 100 m., 1994

A behind-the-scenes documentary of Bill Clinton's presidential campaign, featuring James Carville, George Stephanopoulos, Mary Matalin, and Mickey Kantor. Directed by D.A. Pennebaker and Chris Hegedus and produced by R.J. Cutler, Wendy Ettinger, and Frazer Pennebaker.

Professional campaign managers have had a bad image as long as they've had an image at all, which is roughly since the publication of Joe McGinniss's *The Selling of the President: 1968.* The occupation did not gain any luster in November 1993 when Ed Rollins shot himself in the foot with his tales of bribing New Jersey preachers. The typical campaign manager is seen as a Machiavellian spin doctor, and that's on a good day.

Perhaps the documentary *The War Room* will bring a deeper dimension to the profession's image. At the least, it may dispel the notion that campaign managers pervert the course of democracy with behind-the-scenes omniscience; the surprise in the film is that they're often as confused as their candidates sometimes seem to be.

Filmed by the veteran documentarian D.A. Pennebaker and his wife, Chris Hegedus, the movie follows key members of Bill Clinton's campaign team from the snows of New Hampshire in January 1992 to the victory celebration in Little Rock in November of that year. The movie's stars are James ("The Ragin' Cajun") Carville, the impish chief strategist for the Clinton campaign, and George Stephanopoulos, the young, polished former Rhodes scholar who was the campaign's media director.

The two are seen working together in an inside-outside combination. Stephanopoulos, often in a suit and tie, handsome in a Kennedyesque way, is the relaxed, usually calm press spokesman. Carville, a tense and driven man who seems to shop for his clothes at the LSU sports store, works behind the scenes, often in the campaign's "war room" in a converted newspaper office in Little Rock.

Strategists would no doubt like to see themselves like modern Napoleons, moving pawns on the maps of continents. More often, this film shows, they get involved in screwy debates about the color, typography, and size of their campaign posters. Their dedication to "the Candidate" is easily matched by the intensity with which they despise their opponents—and especially their opponents' troops, suspected in New Hampshire of tearing down Clinton signs (something Carville's volunteers would never, ever do . . . except, of course, in retaliation).

Most of the opening footage in the film was gathered by Pennebaker and Hegedus from TV and documentary crews who were on the scene in the early primaries; their own footage begins at about the time of the Democratic Convention, which nominated Clinton, and follows Carville and Stephanopoulos down the increasingly rocky road to the election victory. They allow the cameras access to surprisingly unguarded moments, as when they brief their squad of spin doctors after one of the Clinton-Bush debates ("Just keep on repeating that Bush was on the defensive all night"), and when the press reports on Clinton's draft history, Carville complains, "Every time somebody even farts the word 'draft,' it makes the paper."

Given the various scandals and would-be scandals that pursued the Clinton campaign, it seems almost incredible that he survived, and won. There is footage from grim early days in New England, right after the supermarket tabloids broke the first charges of Clinton's adultery, and footage months later, two days before the election, of Stephanopoulos calmly talking on the phone with a man who had still more hearsay he wanted to ventilate.

What you realize, watching Carville and Stephanopoulos move between grand strategy and damage control, is that they are good at their jobs, and probably as honest as was possible under the circumstances. Certainly their decision to allow access by documentarians shows a willingness to be seen warts and all. Carville is moving in a speech to his troops on the eve of the election. Exhausted, strung out, on the brink of tears, he tells them that politics has been his life, and that it is a life worth living.

Of course, during the course of the campaign his own personal life changed dramatically when he became engaged to Mary Matalin, the strategist for the Bush campaign. How did they meet, how did they start dating, and what did they talk about? Now *that* would have made a movie.

The Waterdance ★ ★ ★ ½
R, 107 m., 1992

Eric Stoltz (Joel Garcia), Wesley Snipes (Raymond Hill), William Forsythe (Bloss), Helen Hunt (Anna), Elizabeth Pena (Rosa).

Directed by Neal Jimenez and Michael Steinberg. Produced by Gale Anne Hurd and Marie Cantin. Screenplay by Jimenez.

I have a friend with a spinal injury who told me one day that he intensely disliked being praised for his "courage." He said courage was something you voluntarily chose to exercise; he had not chosen to be paralyzed, and after his injury, he had no choice except to learn to cope as best he could. I argued that it took courage to *choose* to cope—that some people simply gave up. He had heard that argument before. He said that for many of his friends in the rehabilitation process, there was no realistic choice. You either retreated into a shell, or you did what was necessary to become as independent as possible. "A better word than courage," he said, "is curiosity. Either I can sit around in self-pity, or I can see what life has in store for me now."

That kind of matter-of-fact realism is behind every frame of *The Waterdance*, a film about a writer who is injured in a climbing accident, and loses the use of his legs. The movie is not sentimental, not a tearjerker, does not want our pity, asks only for our attention. It is about the sorts of experiences one is likely to go through in the months after such an accident. The film was written and codirected by Neal Jimenez, who is a gifted writer (*The River's Edge* was his screenplay), and who has lived through most of the experiences in the film.

The Waterdance stars Eric Stoltz as Joel Garcia, the central character, and follows him in great detail from the moment when he wakes up after his accident. He is in a brace to prevent further injury to his spine, and eventually the brace comes off, physical therapy begins, and he becomes involved in the lives of his fellow residents in the rehabilitation ward—especially Raymond (Wesley Snipes), who considers himself a Romeo but has been abandoned by his woman, and Bloss (William Forsythe), a biker whose prejudices are easily aroused by Raymond, who is black, and Joel, who is Hispanic.

The process of rehabilitation is slow and frustrating. It begins with denial and depression, and leads through difficult steps into an acceptance that is necessary if anything else is to be done. Joel's physical learning process is joined by an emotional one, involving his relationship with Anna (Helen Hunt), the woman he loves. Jimenez doesn't give us some soppy romance here, but a

complex relationship: Anna is married to another man, has discussed leaving him for Joel, but now has to reevaluate everything in terms of Joel's new reality. The film deals frankly with their new relationship, including its sexual aspects, and also painfully considers the adjustments the other men are going through.

Jimenez is a good reporter, and *The Waterdance* has its foundation in specific details. It isn't about "heart" and "courage," but about exactly and precisely what such an experience looks and feels like. It is impossible not to identify, especially when the patients develop an overpowering resentment for the hospital's telephone operators, who leave them hanging on "hold" almost as a game.

Some of the sequences—such as an outing to a strip club with a young Korean kid from the ward—reminded me a little of similar scenes in *One Flew Over the Cuckoo's Nest*. But the dramatic purpose was sound: It was time for the characters to stop being patients, and start being actors in the real world once again.

Eric Stoltz makes interesting choices as Joel. He is quiet, intellectual, given to statements of oblique irony. He doesn't go for big, canned speeches. He observes. He grows very angry at times, but always in terms of precisely what is happening to him. His friendships with Raymond and Bloss are seen realistically. These are not people he would choose to associate with under ordinary circumstances. Thrown in with them, he becomes their friend, cares about them, and yet observes what they're going through with a certain writer's attentiveness. Maybe he is making notes for this movie.

Films are so often about big, dumb conflicts and predictable conclusions. *The Waterdance* is about the everyday process of continuing one's life under a tragically altered set of circumstances. It considers what life is, and under what conditions it is worth living. After all the cheap sentiment that's been brought to this subject over the years, it is exhilarating and challenging to see a movie that knows exactly what it's talking about, and looks you straight in the eye.

Waterworld ★ ★ ½   **NEW**
PG-13 120 m., 1995

Kevin Costner (Mariner), Dennis Hopper (Deacon), Jeanne Tripplehorn (Helen), Tina Majornio (Enola), Michael Jeter (Gregor), Gerard Murphy (Nord), R.D. Call (Enforcer).

Directed by Kevin Reynolds and produced by Charles Gordon, John Davis, and Kevin Costner. Written by Peter Rader and David Twohy.

So here it is at last, *Waterworld*, two years and $200 million in the making. In the old days in Hollywood, they used to brag about how much a movie cost. Now they apologize. There's been so much publicity about this movie's budget that a review of the story seems beside the point; I should just print the spreadsheets.

The cost controversy aside, *Waterworld* is a decent futuristic action picture with some great sets, some intriguing ideas, and a few images that will stay with me. It could have been more, it could have been better, and it could have made me care about the characters. It's one of those marginal pictures you're not unhappy to have seen, but can't quite recommend.

The movie begins with the trademark Universal globe spinning in space, and then we see the polar ice cap melting while a deep voice (not James Earl Jones for a change) sets the story in "the future," when all of the Earth is covered in water. Cut to Mariner (Kevin Costner), aboard his trimaran, a sailing vessel that looks made out of spare parts from *Mad Max*.

The first shot of an action hero is supposed to set the tone for a movie; remember your initial glimpses of James Bond or Batman, and compare them with *Waterworld*, which shows Mariner peeing into a bottle, pouring the fluid into a homemade chemistry set, cranking a handle to process it, and then drinking in. Then he gargles, and spits on his little lime tree, so we know how he gets fresh water and vitamin C.

I would have welcomed more of those details about the global floating culture that Mariner is a part of. But like so many science fiction movies, this one bypasses the best possibilities of the genre: Instead of science and speculation, we get a lot of violent action scenes.

Mariner is a loner, a "mutie," or mutant, with gills behind his ears and webbed feet. He goes to trade at a big floating "atoll," which is like a seagoing version of the post-apocalyptic city in *Mad Max Beyond Thunderdome*. He has something they want. "Mmmm!" says a trader. "Pure dirt! 3.2 kilos!" He trades it for cash, spends some of it at the bar, and meets Helen (Jeanne Tripplehorn), the bartender. Then he offends the locals by refus-

ing to contribute to their gene pool, and is locked in a cage when the fortress comes under attack from Smokers—renegade outlaws who prowl the seas in souped-up Jetskis.

The leader of the Smokers is Deacon (a chain-smoker, of course), played by Dennis Hopper as another of his violent cackling looneys. Hopper is the standard-issue villain of the 1990s, and his appearances would grow tiresome if he weren't so good at them, adding weird verbal twists that make his characters seem smarter and more twisted.

The Smokers' attack on the atoll is a virtuoso action sequence, including stunts where guys on Jetskis speed up a ramp and fly over the atoll walls, landing in the lagoon inside. (It's a little strange to see Hells Angels types doing the same basic water-ski stunts perfected forty years ago in all those Esther Williams pictures set at Cypress Gardens.)

Mariner is freed by Helen, whose price is that he must help her and a young girl named Enola (Tina Majorino) escape. He's forced to agree, and soon they're sailing the high seas and squabbling ("This is my boat, and I got it the way I like it"). Mariner would just as soon throw Helen and the girl overboard, but we know the obligatory outcome: He'll get to like them. He does, grudgingly, and then discovers the Smokers want the girl because she has a map tattooed in her back that shows the way to land. The relationship scenes are pretty grim, apart from a long-delayed kiss, and a breathtaking visit beneath the waves to visit a drowned city.

There are a lot of amazing props in the movie, including various flying and sailing machines and medieval/futuristic weapons. And a few smiles, as when Deacon's ship turns out to be the Exxon Valdez (with a portrait of Capt. Joe Hazelwood still on display). I am not quite sure, however, that I believed the scene where Deacon fired up his men with promises of dry land, and they all trooped down into the hold of the Valdez and started rowing it like a Roman galley.

Kevin Costner obviously decided to play his character as a poker-faced outsider, not entirely human, and although that's a logical choice it isn't a very entertaining one; Mel Gibson, in a similar role as Mad Max, went for energy and good humor, and was more fun. There is also a certain lack of imagination in the story. These floating people have the whole globe to explore, but they seem to hang out in the same small patch of sea with the same characters. Are there different cul-

tures elsewhere? Different adaptations to the flood? The movie doesn't care.

It's said *Waterworld* 's first cut was a good deal longer than its final 120-minute running time, and you can sense that occasionally, as when Mariner fights off an attack by the Smokers and then immediately takes Helen on the trip beneath the sea, when it seems the Smokers must still be in sight. But basically the movie plays smoothly as a combination of chases, fights, bizarre locations, special effects, and the cold, distant, slowly thawing behavior of Mariner toward his passengers. I'll remember some of the sights in *Waterworld* for a long time. But I won't necessarily want to see them again.

Wayne's World ★ ★ ★
PG-13, 95 m., 1992

Mike Myers (Wayne Campbell), Dana Carvey (Garth Algar), Rob Lowe (Benjamin Oliver), Tia Carrere (Cassandra), Brian Doyle-Murray (Noah Vanderhoff), Lara Flynn Boyle (Stacy). Directed by Penelope Spheeris and produced by Lorne Michaels. Screenplay by Mike Myers, Bonnie Turner, and Terry Turner.

I walked into *Wayne's World* expecting a lot of dumb, vulgar comedy, and I got plenty, but I also found what I didn't expect: a genuinely amusing, sometimes even intelligent, undercurrent. Like the *Bill and Ted* movies, this one works on its intended level and then sneaks in excursions to some other levels, too.

The movie is inspired by "Saturday Night Live" 's long-running parody of local access cable TV. *Wayne's World* originates from the paneled basement room of its host, Wayne Campbell (Mike Myers), who looks to be in his late twenties but still lives at home with his parents in Aurora, Illinois. Wayne's sidekick is Garth Algar (Dana Carvey), looking uncannily like Artie Johnson and operating with the brain power of a clever seven-year-old. The two of them interview strange guests, drool over posters of their favorite models, and use the word "excellent" a whole lot.

Onto this basic situation, director Penelope Spheeris and writers Myers, Bonnie Turner, and Terry Turner have grafted a plot of overwhelming predictability: An ad executive (Rob Lowe) spots their show and sees it as the ideal vehicle for a client (Brian Doyle-Murray) who owns a chain of video arcades. Wayne and Garth don't want to sell out for the big bucks (individual cashier's checks for $5,000), but get outsmarted.

Meanwhile Wayne falls in love with a foxy Chinese chick (Tia Carrere) who's the lead singer in a heavy metal band. Of course, Lowe tries to win her away from him, which leads up to the final emotional showdown, etc., etc.

The plot is not exactly the point here. It's only a clothesline. What is funny about *Wayne's World*—sometimes really funny—are the dialogue and sight gags. The movie wants to be a laffaminit extravaganza like the Zucker and Abrahams productions, but with slyer humor, more inside jokes, throwaway references, and just plain goofiness, as when the characters occasionally break into their own language. Some of the biggest laughs in the film could not possibility be described, because their humor depends entirely on the fact that the filmmakers were weird enough to go for them in the first place.

One quality that grew on me during the film was Myers's conversations with the camera. In a sense, this whole movie is a cable access documentary on his life, and particularly on his great and helpless crush on Tia Carrere. The Dana Carvey character doesn't wear as well; the fact that his personality has a severely limited range of notes doesn't prevent him from playing them over and over. But the movie is so good-spirited we forgive him.

A few days before *Wayne's World* was screened, I got a letter from my local cable access people, advising me of some of the real shows they run and asking me to have a look. I have already been looking, but my reactions may not please them very much. In a way, their best programs are their worst ones—because in aspiring to professionalism, they aspire also to the canned predictability of routine TV. The access shows I like the best are the ones on which I can never be sure what is going to happen next. *Wayne's World* gets that right.

Wayne's World 2 ★ ★ ★
PG-13, 90 m., 1993

Mike Myers (Wayne Campbell), Dana Carvey (Garth Algar), Christopher Walken (Bobby Cahn), Tia Carrere (Cassandra), Kim Basinger (Honey Hornee). Directed by Stephen Surjik and produced by Lorne Michaels. Screenplay by Mike Myers, Bonnie Turner, and Terry Turner.

The secret to the comedy of the *Wayne's World* movies is their good will. They're vulgar, offensive, raunchy, and even, in the precise diction of the MPAA Code and Ratings Administration, "ribald," but they are never mean-spirited, and in Wayne Campbell and Garth Algar the series has created two characters it is impossible to dislike.

Wayne and Garth, played by Mike Myers and Dana Carvey, are of course the cohosts of their own cable access TV program in Aurora, Illinois. In the first film they broadcast out of the basement of Wayne's house, but now they have moved up—all the way to quarters in an abandoned warehouse, where they're sandwiched in between cooking classes, providing a daily report on lives of benign and elated stupidity.

It would be a mistake to describe them as nerds. They *meet* a couple of nerds during the course of *Wayne's World 2*, and the two species are nothing alike. One clear clue that they're not nerds is that they have the inexplicable ability to attract babes. As the sequel opens, Wayne is still dating a beautiful Chinese-American rock singer named Cassandra (Tia Carrere), and before long Garth goes to the laundry and meets a lithe blonde named Honey Hornee ("Hor-NAY"), played by Kim Basinger.

The combined sexual activities of these two couples would probably not occupy three column inches altogether in the *Penthouse* letters column, but a lot of heat is generated, as in the scene where Ms. Hornee kisses Garth for the first time, and he levitates. Wayne's idyll develops problems, however, when a rival for Cassandra appears in the person of the sleek, slick record producer Bobby Cahn (Christopher Walken), who wants to spirit Cassandra away to Los Angeles and out of Wayne's life.

Cassandra, to give her credit, never for a moment takes Bobby seriously. A greater barrier to their happiness is the arrival of her father from Hong Kong, which leads to the movie's funniest sequence, in which the newly arrived dad is revealed as a martial arts expert. Wayne faces him in a deadly karate match, complete with badly dubbed dialogue and loud whooshing noises every time they swing their arms.

The plot is set in motion by a dream, in which Jim Morrison appears to Wayne in a desert, and advises him to hold a rock concert in Aurora ("If you book them, they will come"). The preparations for Waynestock occupy most of the picture, as the boys travel to London to recruit the world's greatest stage manager (Ralph Brown), now retired to a life of retailing the same boring and false rock anecdotes over and over again.

One of the charms of Wayne and Garth is their vocabulary, which in the first film relied extensively on variations of the verb "hurl," but in this one has been expanded to include a name for a substance that had previously gone nameless, "lung butter." They also get a lot of mileage out of "Schwinnnggg!," which they pronounce every time a babe walks by.

If Wayne and Garth ever grow confident of their success, the series will be over. Everything depends on the delighted disbelief with which they greet every new victory. Backstage at a rock concert, they flaunt their press passes with childlike pride, and when a security man slams a gate in their face, Wayne protests, "Hey, my girlfriend's in there!" The guard replies, "A lot of people's girlfriends are in there." Wayne and Garth peer forlornly through the steel mesh, our brothers under the skin.

The Weavers: Wasn't That a Time!
★ ★ ★ ★
PG, 78 m., 1982

Featuring Lee Hays, Ronnie Gilbert, Fred Hellerman, and Pete Seeger. Directed by Jim Brown and produced by Brown, George Stoney, and Harold Leventhal.

Here is one of the most joyous musical documentaries in a long time, a celebration of the music and the singers that made up the Weavers. There are, I suppose, a lot of people who don't know who the Weavers were, but for a time in the fifties they were the top pop quartet in America, and for twenty years their recordings were a key influence on modern American folk music.

The owners of old Weavers record albums treasure them. I have four or five, and when things get depressing and the sky turns overcast and grim, I like to play one of them. There's just something magical about the joy with which the Weavers sing "Goodnight, Irene" or "Kisses Sweeter than Wine" or "The Sloop John B." or "This Land is Your Land."

The Weavers reached their popular peak in the fifties, with a string of Top Ten hits, which also included "On Top of Old Smokey," "Tzena, Tzena," and "If I Had a Hammer" (which was written by the Weavers, and not, as many people believe, by Bob Dylan). The height of their popularity unfortunately coincided with the height of McCarthyism, and the Weavers, all of them longtime left-wing activists, were blacklisted. They couldn't get jobs on television or in nightclubs, and their records were banned.

For several years in the late fifties, the group existed primarily on records. And the artists went their separate ways: Ronnie Gilbert into theater, Fred Hellerman into San Franciso-area media projects, Pete Seeger into a successful solo concert career, and Lee Hays into semi-retirement on his New England farm.

There were many calls for a Weavers reunion (in some circles, an event more fervently desired than the Beatles reunion). And in May of 1980, Lee Hays himself convened such a reunion, inviting the other Weavers and their families and friends to a picnic on his farm. As they sat around and sang and played, the idea of a public reunion began to take shape, and on November 28 and 29 of 1980, they held one last historic concert at Carnegie Hall.

The Weavers: Wasn't That a Time! is not simply a concert film, however, but a documentary about the Weavers. The director, Jim Brown, was a neighbor of Hays, and grew to admire the old man who kept on singing after his legs were amputated for diabetes and his heart needed a pacemaker.

Brown's film begins with the picnic at Hays's farm, flashes back to newsreel and archive footage of the Weavers in their prime, and then concludes with the concert in Carnegie Hall. It is impossible not to feel a lump in your throat as the Weavers gather once again on stage, and it's hard not to tap your feet when they start to sing.

Seeing this film is a wonderful experience. I'd recommend it wholeheartedly to those who don't know about the Weavers. I imagine that Weavers fans won't need any encouragement.

A Wedding ★ ★ ★ ½
PG, 125 m., 1978

Desi Arnaz, Jr. (Dino Corelli), Carol Burnett (Tulip Brenner), Geraldine Chaplin (Rita Billingsley), Howard Duff (Dr. Meecham), Mia Farrow (Buffy Brenner), Vittorio Gassman (Luigi Corelli), Lillian Gish (Nettie Sloan), Lauren Hutton (Photographer), Viveca Lindfors (Ingrid Hellstrom), Pat McCormick (MacKenzie Goddard), Dina Merrill (Antoinette Goddard), Nina Van Pallandt (Regina Corelli). Directed and produced by Robert Altman. Screenplay by John Considine, Patricia Resnick, Allan Nicholls, and Altman.

The two families in Robert Altman's *A Wedding* live right there in the closets with their skeletons. They present a cheerful facade to the outer world, of old Lake Forest money on the one hand and new Southern money on the other. But just beneath the surface there are jealousies and greeds and hates, and the random dirty tricks of fate.

Altman plunges gleefully into this wealth of material; there are forty-eight characters in his movie, give or take a few, and by the film's end we know them all. We may not know them *well*—at weddings there are always unidentified cousins over in the corner—but we can place them, and chart the lines of power and passion that run among them. And some of them are drawn as well as Altman has drawn anyone.

That's because *A Wedding* is a lot deeper and more ambitious than we might at first expect. It begins in comedy, it moves into realms of social observation, it descends into personal revelations that are sometimes tragic, sometimes comic . . . and then it ends in a way that turns everything back upon itself. The more you think about what Altman's done, the more impressive his accomplishment becomes.

A Wedding aims to upset our expectations. It takes our society's most fertile source of clichés and stereotypes—a society wedding—and then chisels away at it with maniacal and sometimes savage satire. Nobody gets away: not the bride and groom, so seemingly "ideal;" not the loving parents on either side; not the relatives, with their little dramas that are no doubt played out on every family occasion; and not even the staff of wedding coordinators, chefs, photographers, musicians, and other accomplices.

Altman begins in solemnity and ceremony, with the high Episcopalian wedding. Desi Arnaz, Jr., and Amy Stryker, as the wedding couple, are all but lost in the chaos: The bishop fumbles his lines, a camera crew maneuvers awkwardly behind the palms, and, meanwhile, back at the mansion, the groom's grandmother (Lillian Gish) drops dead of anticipated mortification.

Her death is concealed when the wedding party returns to the mansion: Concealed from the family and from the single guest who turns up for the magnificently catered affair. Altman introduces us almost effortlessly to the house jammed with people; his compositions allow characters to be established in the backgrounds while the plot is being pushed ahead in the foreground, so it's as if we're wandering around the house like everyone else.

There are any number of subplots. The parents of the groom are Nina Van Pallandt, whose drug habit is ministered to by the family doctor, and Vittorio Gassman, an Italian who seems to have sinister associations in his past. The bride's parents are Carol Burnett, all sweetness and convention until—gasp!—she's wooed by one of the guests, and Paul Dooley, vulgar, hard-drinking, with a tad too much affection for his youngest daughter (Mia Farrow).

Farrow, it develops, is pregnant—by her sister's new husband, perhaps, or (it develops) by any other member of his class at military school. Other characters reveal themselves as drunks, unreconstructed Communists, secret weepers, fountains of jealousy, reservoirs of lust, or advocates of diverse sexual proclivities.

This is the sort of material that easily lends itself to farce, and, when it does, Altman cheerfully follows. But he leads in other directions, as well. He moves so slyly from one note to another that when Pat McCormick attempts a clumsy seduction of Carol Burnett, we're moved simultaneously by comedy and pathos. And there are scenes of extraordinary emotional complexity, as when a singalong is organized in the basement dining room, or when Nina Van Pallandt tearfully and defiantly reviews the terms under which she's lived her marriage.

Like Altman's other movies with lots of characters (*M*A*S*H*, *McCabe and Mrs. Miller*, the incomparable *Nashville*), *A Wedding* doesn't fit easily into established feature film categories. For some viewers, it won't satisfy; it doesn't set up situations and then resolve them in standard ways. It's got all the disorganization and contradictions of life—and then Altman almost mystically gives everything a deeper meaning by the catastrophic surprise he springs on us near the end.

The Wedding Banquet ★ ★ ★
NO MPAA RATING, 112 m., 1993

Winston Chao (Wai Tung), May Chin (Wei Wei), Mitchell Lichtenstein (Simon), Sihung Lung (Mr. Gao), Ah-Leh Gua (Mrs. Gao). Directed by Ang Lee and produced by Lee, Ted Hope, and James Schamus. Screenplay by Lee, Neil Peng, and Schamus.

To the degree that one can fashion a life that is completely satisfying, Wai Tung believes he has done so. A young Chinese man from

Taiwan, gay, in his late twenties, he lives with his American companion, Simon, in a comfortable brownstone in New York, and manages some loft buildings he has purchased. All is well. Except for the letters and phone calls from his parents, who wonder, with increasing urgency, when he is going to marry a nice Chinese girl and present them with a grandchild.

They do not guess he is homosexual. Nor can he bring himself to tell them. One day his friend Simon devises an ingenious plan to make everyone happy. In one of Wai Tung's lofts there lives a young Chinese woman, Wei Wei, an artist who cannot pay her rent. In despair she plans to return to China. She likes Wai Tung very much. Why, asks Simon, shouldn't Wai Tung marry Wei Wei—providing her with a green card to allow her to stay in America, while at the same time placating his faraway parents?

Wai Tung, in desperation and optimism, seizes upon this scheme. Wei Wei is convinced to go along. And then all of their neatly made plans go astray when Wai Tung's parents announce they will travel from Taiwan for the wedding. We are now, we sense, entering *La Cage aux Folles* country, and *The Wedding Banquet* does take some of the same delight in constructing a comedy of misunderstandings and deceptions. But the movie also has a warm heart, and by the end somehow manages to become very moving.

The director, Ang Lee, approaches his material in a low-key way, not punching up the big dramatic or comic moments. And the actors, especially Winston Chao as Wai Tung, have a curious fatalism about them, as if their characters are resigned to the worst. There are moments of obvious comedy: for example, when the parents subscribe to a matchmaking service for their son, who specifies he requires a very tall opera singer, only to find that the service can supply one. But there are more moments when the film deals simply and directly with the feelings and fears of its characters.

For Wei Wei (May Chin), the pretend marriage with Wai Tung makes good sense, but is also painful, because she has a crush on him and would like to be married to him for real. For Wai Tung, the whole charade is uncomfortable, because it is dishonest. And for Simon (Mitchell Lichtenstein), his American boyfriend, what starts as a lark ends painfully, as he hangs around the outskirts of the wedding, his omnipresence never quite explained.

The father and mother (Sihung Lung and Ah-Leh Gua) arrive with shining eyes, but cannot fail to sense a certain lack of sincerity between the loving couple. A wedding by a justice of the peace does not match their vision of a suitable ceremony. And then an old friend of the father's materializes, now a successful restaurant owner, and offers to stage a proper Chinese wedding banquet. The banquet is the movie's great set piece, as booze and tradition and deception and expectation all come together, and lead, in an unlikely way, to happiness.

The Wedding Banquet is not a particularly slick film; the plot construction feels contrived, and the acting of the two younger men is somewhat self-conscious, although the parents are magnificent. What makes the film work is the underlying validity of the story, the way the filmmakers don't simply go for melodrama and laughs, but pay these characters their due. At the end of the film, I was a little surprised how much I cared for them.

Weeds ★ ★ ★
R, 115 m., 1987

Nick Nolte (Lee Umstetter), Lane Smith (Claude), William Forsythe (Burt), John Toles-Bey (Navarro), Joe Mantegna (Carmine), Ernie Hudson (Bagdad), Mark Rolston (Dave), J.J. Johnson (Lazarus), Rita Taggart (Lillian). Directed by John Hancock and produced by Bill Badalato. Screenplay by Dorothy Tristan and Hancock.

Weeds tells a story as old as the movies—the rags-to-riches saga of a troupe of theatrical amateurs who bring their show to Broadway—but it tells it with such a distinctive style, such a curious mixture of pathos and offhand wit, that it works for one more time. There's never a moment when there's much doubt about the outcome, but the movie gets there by a series of small delights and surprises.

The movie opens with the hero trying to kill himself in prison. He throws himself over a railing, but breaks only his arms. Then he tries to hang himself. No luck. He's in for life, with no possibility of parole, and so in desperation he does something that's even harder for him than suicide: He checks a book out of the prison library.

The prisoner's name is Lee Umstetter, played by Nick Nolte with a certain weathered weariness and a way of hanging his head to one side and walking crooked. He's a lifer

with a broken spirit, until the books put ideas in his head and he writes a play in prison. He decides to produce it, and the auditions provide a scene that's a small masterpiece, as one convict sings "The Impossible Dream" and another one recites "Eeny Meeny Miney Moe," which is the only poem he knows, and not a good one for prison recitals.

The play is a success, and a warmhearted middle-aged drama critic (Rita Taggart) falls in love with Nolte and tries to convince the governor to commute his sentence. The rest of the movie involves Nolte's attempts to round up his old prison friends, reassemble the troupe on the outside, and take the show on the road. First stop, San Francisco. Then Iowa, Illinois, and Broadway. The opening night off-Broadway supplies an example how the movie finds surprises in familiar themes. We see a famed drama critic, drenched by a rainstorm, arriving late and trying to compose himself for the opening curtain. Will he be able to be objective? The movie gets such a big laugh with his arrival that we hardly care. The opening night party at Sardi's has more surprises, and the scene is stolen by Anne Ramsey, as Nolte's ramshackle but lovable mother. And there's another great moment, done with body language and a perfect double-take, when Nolte is so overjoyed he tries to kiss Ernie Hudson, one of his fellow actors, on the lips.

The troupe develops into a tight-knit band, played by Nolte, Hudson, Lane Smith, William Forsythe, John Toles-Bey, Mark Rolston, and J.J. Johnson, with Joe Mantegna as a professional New York actor who joins them midstream and seems baffled by what kind of situation he's walked into. There is a real sense of community in their little group, which communicates itself even if the play they are performing does not. It's usually the case with plays-within-movies that the plays seem less than convincing, although in this movie there's a reason for that.

Unfortunately, the whole prison sequence at the end of the film is also less than convincing, and so are the recycled '60s leftist panaceas that pass, in that sequence, as electrifying truth-telling. It's all a little too pat. *Weeds* is a movie that is best when it observes small moments of human truth, and at its worst when it tries to inflate them into large moments.

A Week's Vacation ★ ★ ★ ½
NO MPAA RATING, 102 m., 1980

Nathalie Baye (Laurence Cuers), Gerard Lanvin (Pierre). Directed by Bertrand Tavernier. Screenplay by Tavernier, Colo Tavernier, and Marie-Francoise Hans.

It's nothing special, just an overcast day in Lyons when everybody's going to work just as usual. A car pulls out of the stream of traffic, and a young woman gets out. Her name is Laurence, she is a schoolteacher, and this day she does not feel like teaching school. It is more than that: She cannot. There is no particular crisis. A great tragedy has not descended on her life. In fact, things are going fairly well. She is thirty-one years old, she lives with her boyfriend, she has been teaching at the same school for ten years. It is simply that large and inarticulate emotions are welling up inside her, and she is desperately unhappy. She goes to see her doctor, and he prescribes a week's vacation.

A Week's Vacation is as simple, and as complicated, as that. It was directed by Bertrand Tavernier, the gifted French filmmaker who has made his hometown of Lyons the locale for some of his best work, including The Clockmaker (1974). That movie was based on a novel by Georges Simenon, and A Week's Vacation could well have been; it has the same matter-of-fact fascination with the great depths and unexpected secrets in the lives of people who outwardly seem ordinary. A Week's Vacation follows the schoolteacher, played by Nathalie Baye, as she spends her week of freedom wandering without a plan through her city, her past, and her sexuality. She meets a friendly café owner and talks to him. She goes out to the country to visit her father, who is so old he has surely discovered the answer to the puzzle of life, but it has made him speechless. Returning to the city, she has an embarrassing encounter. The café owner, mistaking her friendliness for sexual interest, tries to kiss her. She was not thinking along those lines. As they both try to free themselves from the awkward situation, as he damns himself for being such a fool, there comes a turning point in her week's vacation: It seems to me that this foolish encounter, this mundane sexual pass based on mistaken assumptions, is the catalyst she needs to get back into life again.

What is best about Tavernier is his feeling for the ordinary currents of everyday life. He creates such empathy between his audiences and his characters that when they fall into a reverie, we have no difficulty imagining their thoughts. In A Week's Vacation, he has taken the occasional feeling we all have that we just can't go on any longer, not because of sadness or illness or tragedy, but simply because we have forgotten why we set out in the first place on this journey of life. And he has shown us the answer. The key is in that funny, embarrassing, fumbling little attempt at a kiss: We keep on plugging away because we never know when someone might decide to kiss us, and, better still, because it's so interesting to see how we'll react.

Weird Science ★ ★ ★ ½
PG-13, 94 m., 1985

Anthony Michael Hall (Gary), Kelly LeBrock (Lisa), Ilan Mitchell-Smith (Wyatt), Bill Paxton (Chet), Suzanne Snyder (Deb), Judie Aronson (Hilly). Directed by John Hughes and produced by Joel Silver. Screenplay by Hughes.

Weird Science combines two great traditions in popular entertainment: Inflamed male teen-age fantasies and Frankenstein's monster. Then it crosses them with a new myth, of the teen-age computer geniuses who lock themselves in their bedrooms, hunch over their computer keyboards, and write programs that can change the universe.

In the movie's opening scenes, a couple of bright kids write a program with their specifications for a perfect woman. They feed in centerfolds and magazine covers, measurements and parameters. Then, for additional brain power, they tap into a giant government computer. And at exactly that instant, lightning strikes (just as it did in The Bride of Frankenstein), and out of the mix of bytes and kilowatts steps . . . a perfect woman.

She is played by Kelly LeBrock in the movie, and she has full, sensuous lips, and a throaty English accent, and a lot of style. She is a little more than the kids had bargained on. For one thing, she isn't an idealized Playmate, all staples and no brains, but an intelligent, sensitive woman who sees right through these teen-age boys and tries to do them some good.

That's why Weird Science is funnier, and a little deeper, than the predictable story it might have been. The movie is the third success in a row for John Hughes, a director who specializes in films about how teen-agers really talk and think. His two earlier films were Sixteen Candles and The Breakfast Club, and they both featured a young actor named Anthony Michael Hall, who is the costar of Weird Science.

Hall was the geek in Sixteen Candles and the intellectual in Breakfast Club, and I like John Hughes's definition of a geek: "A geek is a guy who has everything going for him, but he's just too young. By contrast, a nerd will be a nerd all of his life." Hall talks fast, with a sprung rhythm that lets you feel you can hear him thinking. He has the ordinary lusts of a teen-age boy, but once he invents this perfect woman, he is quick to catch on to the advantages: For example, your status in high school is sure to change dramatically if a gorgeous model thinks you're the max.

Hughes's earlier teen-age films depended mostly on character and dialogue (which was fine). This one has a lot of special effects, including some reverse photography that plays tricks with time. But the center of the film is the simple, almost elementary insight that fantasies can be hazardous: You've got to be careful what you ask for, because you might get it. Kelly LeBrock is wonderful as the fantasy woman, because she plays the character, not for sex, but for warmth and an almost motherly affection for these two kids. "All you have to do is command me," she says at one point. "You created me. You are my master." It could be soft porn, but the way she says it, her voice has a wink.

We're No Angels ★ ★ ★
PG-13, 101 m., 1990

Robert De Niro (Ned/Father Reilly), Sean Penn (Jim/Father Brown), Demi Moore (Molly), Hoyt Axton (Father Levesque), Bruno Kirby (Deputy), Ray McAnally (The Warden), James Russo (Bobby), Wallace Shawn (The Translator). Directed by Neil Jordan and produced by Art Linson. Screenplay by David Mamet.

Robert De Niro and Sean Penn have two of the best faces in the movies—screwed up, sideways faces with a lot of mischief in the eyes. We're No Angels is a movie made for those faces, and one of the pleasures of watching the film is to see them looking sidelong at each other as they try to figure a way out of the complicated mess they're in. The movie has a lot of other good stuff to look at (including dramatic period locations in a small Canadian town) and to listen to (dialogue by David Mamet), but I can think of no other recent movie in which so much of the pleasure lies in watching the expressions on the faces of the actors—especially when they're reacting, not talking.

The movie is set in the 1930s and stars De Niro and Penn as a couple of convicts who are doing hard time in a prison that looks like it was hammered together out of Sing Sing, the Bastille, and the underworld in *Mad Max Beyond Thunderdome.* This is a great, evil, venal prison, populated by vindictive killers and sadistic guards, and when De Niro and Penn escape from it, freedom is like a splash of cold air in their faces: They go tumbling down snowy slopes in a desolate forest wilderness, until they get a lift from an old lady and end up in a small border town.

Their objective: To cross the bridge that spans the river between the U.S. and Canada. Their problem: They have been mistaken for two priests and have been given shelter in the local monastery. Their solution: To go along with the gag and pretend to be priests, even though anyone in his right mind could plainly see they're fugitives from a 1930s prison movie.

Mamet and Neil Jordan, who directed the movie, wisely remember the most important thing about any mistaken-identity comedy: The fact that someone's identity is mistaken is not always funny even the first time and rarely thereafter. Movies that depend on mistaken identities for their laughs are among the slowest, dreariest slogs through cinema. What's important is that the heroes be funny no matter who people think they are—and that the other characters be funny even despite the mistakes they're making.

Most of the characters in *We're No Angels* pass that test, especially the crew at the local monastery (Hoyt Axton as the prior, Ken Buhay as a foreign bishop who insists on saying grace, and Wallace Shawn as the bishop's translator). Demi Moore has an important supporting role as a local woman with a child who is attracted to De Niro, but because no comic spin was put on her character, her scenes don't add much. They provide, in fact, a serious undercurrent that the movie doesn't necessarily need.

These days a lot of movies are shot on location, but I've rarely seen a location used more effectively than in *We're No Angels,* where the small town of Mission, in British Columbia, has been dressed to match the Depression era. The town, the surrounding peaks, the river, and the waterfall provide a genuine sense of place. De Niro and Penn are both essentially serious dramatic actors, and maybe the reality of the location gave

them such a solid grounding that they felt they had permission for the necessary goofiness.

Wes Craven's New Nightmare ★ ★ ★

R, 112 m., 1994

Robert Englund (Krueger/Englund), Heather Langenkamp (Herself), Wes Craven (Himself), Jeffrey John Davis (Freddy's Hand Double), Miko Hughes (Dylan), Matt Winston (Chuck), Rob LaBelle (Terry), David Newsome (Chase Porter), Marianne Maddalena (Herself). Directed by Wes Craven and produced by Marianne Maddalena. Screenplay by Craven.

Every kid knows who Freddy is. He's like Santa Claus, or King Kong.
—dialogue from *Wes Craven's New Nightmare*

Wes Craven's New Nightmare is a horror film within a horror film. The director, who plays himself, explains at one point, "The only way to stop Freddy is to make another movie." Freddy, of course, is Freddy Krueger, the most durable of modern horror monsters—a hideously scarred man in a felt fedora, who has knives for fingers.

He apparently died once and for all in *Freddy's Dead: The Final Nightmare* (1991), the sixth film in the series, but that was exactly the problem: The *Nightmare* movies had generated an evil force which, once liberated by Freddy's death, was set free to haunt the nightmares of the people involved in making the movies.

They would include Craven, who directed the original *Nightmare on Elm Street* in 1984 and now returns to the series for the first time; Heather Langenkamp, who was a teenager in the first movie and is now a young mother; Robert Englund, who plays Freddy; John Saxon, who appeared in the first and third films; and even Robert Shaye, founder and president of New Line Pictures, which has produced the series.

Considering that Craven's original nightmare movie was famously inspired by a series of *Los Angeles Times* articles about people who told relatives of their fears of killer nightmares—and then died the next night— it would seem as if Craven and his cast were asking for trouble here. That's part of the fascination, as *Wes Craven's New Nightmare* dances back and forth across the line separating fantasy from reality. This is the first horror movie that is actually *about* the question, "Don't you people ever think about the

effect your movies have on the people who watch them?"

As the movie opens, Langenkamp is happily married to a movie special effects guy (David Newsom), and dotes on their young son Dylan (Miko Hughes). Then a series of tragedies and alarming omens takes place— including the real Los Angeles earthquake, which is seamlessly inserted into the plot. She's terrified. At the same time, other members of the *Nightmare* movies have had their sleep haunted by dreams suggesting, well, that the nightmare is not over.

Craven, a bearded, scholarly man who was once a humanities professor, is effective in the scenes where he discusses this phenomenon with Langenkamp and others: "We should never have killed Freddy," he admits, because Freddy was not simply a fictional character played by the normal and friendly Robert Englund, but also a manifestation of ancient demonic forces which, enraged by his death, have returned.

Craven's screenplay explores the possibilities of this situation in a way that loops back on itself, as New Line's Shaye and other professionals play themselves. The answer is obviously to make another movie in order to exorcise the evil for once and all, but meanwhile there are psychiatrists, talk show hosts, and others to consider, and questions that stray close to the creepy ("Would you trust Robert Englund alone with little Dylan?")

The climax of the film is one of those patented descents into the underworld that the *Nightmare* series has specialized in. The sets and special effects are by some of the same people who worked on *The Fugitive,* and there are truly amazing sequences, as when the little boy wanders across an eight-lane freeway, or when the characters find themselves wandering in Freddy's subterranean lair.

Serious fans of horror movies relate only in a secondary way to the chills themselves; they're connoisseurs of the genre, the special effects, the makeup, the in-jokes. They're going to love this movie, which seems to have been made not only for but by Fangoria fans. But it also works for general audiences. I haven't been exactly a fan of the *Nightmare* series, but I found this movie, with its unsettling questions about the effect of horror on those who create it, strangely intriguing.

Wetherby ★ ★ ★ ★
R, 118 m., 1985

Vanessa Redgrave (Jean Travers), Ian Holm (Stanley Pilborough), Judi Dench (Marcia Pilborough), Marjorie Yates (Verity Braithwaite), Tim McInnerny (John Morgan), Suzanna Hamilton (Karen Creasy), Joely Richardson (Young Jean). Directed by David Hare and produced by Simon Relph. Screenplay by Hare.

A man kills himself among strangers. They never knew who he was, and they do not know why he chose to die. A man dying among strangers is like a tree falling unobserved in the forest. Death, especially suicide, requires resonance from those who knew the living person before it can be assigned its proper meaning. That is why *Wetherby* is such a haunting film, because it dares to suggest that the death of the stranger is important to everyone it touches—because it forces them to decide how alive they really are.

The movie begins with a woman who is living a sort of dead life. Her name is Jean Travers (played by Vanessa Redgrave); she was once in love with a young man who went off to fight the war and was killed. He was not killed gloriously, but stupidly, while getting involved in someone else's drunken quarrel, but he was dead all the same. As the movie opens, Jean has been teaching school in the small town of Wetherby, where her life is on hold. She doesn't walk around in a state of depression, she does have friends, she is a good teacher, but she is not engaged in life because she put all of her passion into the boy who died so many years ago.

One night she throws a small dinner party. Everyone drinks wine and sits around late, talking. One of the men at the table, John Morgan, sits mute all evening and finally makes a short speech about pain and love and honesty that sounds as if every word were written with his own bitter tears. The next day, John Morgan comes back to Jean's house, sits down for a cup of tea, and kills himself. A funny thing comes out in the investigation: John Morgan was not known to any of the people at the dinner party. Apparently he invited himself.

The film moves from this beginning into an examination of the people who were touched by the death. In addition to Jean, there are the Pilboroughs (Ian Holm and Judi Dench), the local constable (Tom Wilkinson), and a young woman (Suzanna Hamilton) who knew the dead man. Some small suspense develops

for a while when it appears that Jean spent some time upstairs with John Morgan during the evening of her party—but that, and many other things, seem to be dead ends.

The movie flashes back into events in Jean's youth, and she is played as a young girl by Joely Richardson, Redgrave's daughter. There is an innocence and tenderness in those early scenes, as young Jean and her boyfriend kiss and neck and make promises, and as Jean gradually realizes that she is looking forward to marriage but he is much more excited by the prospect of putting on a uniform and going overseas. He goes overseas, and in some ways this movie is about the fact that Jean has become a middle-aged woman still waiting for him to come back.

Wetherby was written and directed by David Hare, who also wrote the film *Plenty*. Both films are about women who were never able to fully live their lives after what happened to them during the War. I admire both films, but I found *Wetherby* more moving, because the heroine of *Plenty* was essentially a disturbed woman using her war memories as a crutch, and Jean Travers is a whole and healthy woman who only needs to give herself the permission to live. I left the movie thinking that was the lesson she learned from John Morgan. Hoping so, anyway.

We Think the World of You ★ ★ ★
PG, 91 m., 1989

Alan Bates (Frank), Gary Oldman (Johnny), Frances Barber (Megan), Liz Smith (Millie), Max Wall (Tom), Kerry Wise (Rita). Directed by Colin Gregg and produced by Tomasso Jandelli. Screenplay by Hugh Stoddart.

Here is a movie about one love that dares not speak its name, and another that can only bark. It and *Le Chat* are the only films I can think of about the common human practice of projecting emotions onto animals—of making a dog or a cat stand for another person, and treating the animal the way one would like to treat the human.

We Think the World of You stars Alan Bates as Frank, a lonely middle-aged man who has been in love for a long time with Johnny, a younger married man (Gary Oldman). This love has brought him nothing but frustration and loneliness. The time is the early 1950s in Britain, where homosexuality was a crime and arrest would have instantly destroyed Frank's modest civil-service career. But homosexuality was also not widely perceived or understood in those days, and so Frank

occupies a strange, undefined position in Johnny's life, as a "friend" who gives financial support to Johnny's wife and child, and also to Johnny's mother, who used to be Frank's maid.

The implication is that Frank was first attracted to Johnny years earlier, that their relationship has never been very honest on either side, and that Johnny has tried to have it both ways—marrying and having a child, while still stringing Frank along for his financial support. But there are complicating factors, such as Johnny's choice of a particularly unpleasant and overbearing wife (Frances Barber), and his penchant for committing crimes and getting sent to prison, where he is free of both his lover and his wife.

Soon after the film opens, Johnny is in prison and Frank is desperate for visiting privileges. But neither Johnny's wife nor his mother will carry a message into the prison for him. Frank's life turns into a humiliating round of self-abasing visits to these monstrous people, who know well enough why he cares about Johnny, but will not admit it.

They lie to themselves, but then this entire film is about lies. The central lie involves the fact of homosexuality. Frank is gay but cannot admit it. Johnny is at least bisexual, but uninterested in confronting that fact. His wife and mother are happy to have Frank's money while snickering behind his back. But there is one completely honest creature in the movie, and that is Evie, Johnny's German shepherd.

When Johnny goes to prison, the dog is kept locked up inside the house or in a small pen. Frank begins to fret about its well-being. It is a fine animal, healthy and high-spirited, and it needs to run in the fresh air to keep its sanity. Locked up, it begins to grow mean, morose, and sick, and when it snarls, it is beaten. There is a parallel here, of course, with Johnny, who like his dog is being kept locked up.

Frank begins to obsess about the dog. He wants to take it for walks. He worries that it will die of imprisonment. He tries to send messages into jail to Johnny, begging for custody of the dog, but of course the stupid people who have the dog do not deliver the messages, and eventually the whole story comes down to the way Frank projects his love onto the dog, and all the others conspire to keep the dog away from him.

We Think the World of You requires us to pay attention, since the characters are usually not talking about the things they really care for, or saying what they really mean. It is not a particularly "entertaining" film in the usual sense, because so much of Frank's life is sad, boring, or frustrating. But this is a film that rewards attention. It is wise and perceptive about human nature, and it sees how all of us long for love and freedom, and how the undeserved, unrequited love of an animal is sometimes so much more meaningful than the crabbed, grudging, selfish terms that are often laid down by human beings.

The Whales of August ★ ★ ★
NO MPAA RATING, 90 m., 1987

Bette Davis (Libby Strong), Lillian Gish (Sarah Webber), Vincent Price (Mr. Maranov), Ann Sothern (Tisha Doughty), Harry Carey, Jr. (Joshua), Frank Grimes (Mr. Beckwith), Mary Steenburgen (Young Sarah). Directed by Lindsay Anderson and produced by Carolyn Pfeiffer and Mike Kaplan. Screenplay by David Berry.

The two old women have been at war for years, until they have become beloved enemies. Now death is near for both of them—not today or tomorrow or perhaps even this year, but before long. For decades, since they were children, they have returned to this old cottage on an island off the coast of Maine, where in August it has been their custom to watch at twilight as the whales pass on their journeys to wherever it is that whales go. Although they make plans for the future and argue over whether they should install a new picture window, there is the sense that this will be their last summer in the cottage.

That is the story. As stories go, it is conventional enough, but in *The Whales of August*, as in grand opera, the story is only the occasion for the performances. This film stars Lillian Gish and Bette Davis, and to cast those two actresses as the leads of the same movie is to make their very presences more important than anything else. This is not their fault, nor do they use it as the occasion for self-conscious acting, for any inappropriate drawing of attention to themselves. It is just a fact.

Lillian Gish, who was born in 1896, was the star of D.W. Griffith's *The Birth of a Nation* (1915), the first great narrative film. She appeared in some 150 movies before and since. Bette Davis, who was born in 1908, was one of the great movie queens of Hollywood's golden age. Together they make this movie into the kind of project that filmmakers dream about

but are rarely about to arrange. They are supported in the film by two other actors who bring a lot of memories onscreen with them: Vincent Price and Ann Sothern.

The film mostly takes place during the course of one day, which ends in a birthday dinner party and a good deal of truth. It begins with Gish and Davis gingerly talking around many of the issues that have divided them for years—and some of the issues, we feel, are not nearly so important to them as the simple satisfaction of being right, of prevailing in a personality struggle that has continued since childhood. Gish is the older sister, but in slightly better health. Davis, whose character is blind, has the blind person's love of order and continuity, as a way of finding her way around not only a familiar house but a familiar life.

Nothing of great moment happens during the day, but many small moments occur. One of them, the most touching, is Gish's quiet "private time" with the memory of her late husband. She speaks to him in a monologue that is not only moving but surprisingly passionate. Another special moment occurs when the two sisters walk out on the lawn to look for the whales, which only Gish can see. And I liked the subtle verbal gamesmanship that was the real subject of most of their conversations.

Many of the crucial moments in the movie play mostly in close-up, and I could not help meditating on these famous faces as I watched them. At her great age, Gish still sometimes looks girlish, capable of teasing and practical jokes, but the moment when she lets her hair down in front of the portrait of her dead husband is a revelation, because it contains a genuine erotic content, a sense of memory of her character's romance with this man. Davis contains surprises, too. In so many of the roles in the third act of her career, her face was a painted mask of makeup—not out of vanity, but because she was often cast as a painted madwoman or harpy. Here, devoid of much makeup, her features emerge with strength and a kind of peace that is no longer denying age. Both women, in other words, are beautiful.

Against such competition, supporting actors have their work cut out. Ann Sothern is sensible and cheery as a neighbor woman, who has shared the lives of these sisters for many years and accepts them. She is sort of a peacemaker, whose life lacks the complexity that the sisters' long struggle has created. The other major character in the film is the

old aristocrat, down on his luck, played by Vincent Price with a self-deprecating humor that creates dignity out of thin air. Mr. Maranov, his character, was once a "real" member of European nobility, but now has no money and no prospects, and depends on the kindness of strangers. His previous sponsor has died, and now he is searching for someone else to support him. He knows this, and everyone else knows it, and yet he still retains a certain nobility, even as a beggar. It is an interesting character.

The movie was directed by Lindsay Anderson, whose previous films have been nothing at all like this one, to put it mildly. After *This Sporting Life*, *If*, *O Lucky Man*, and *Britannia Hospital*, here is a quiet film of a conventional story, a star vehicle designed to show everyone to advantage. This is not one of Anderson's great films, but he succeeds at the assignment he has set himself. There is a story that during the filming of *The Whales of August*, Anderson told Miss Gish one day that she had just performed wonderfully in a close-up. "She should," Miss Davis declared. "She invented them."

What's Eating Gilbert Grape? ★ ★ ★ ★
PG-13, 117 m., 1994

Johnny Depp (Gilbert Grape), Juliette Lewis (Becky), Mary Steenburgen (Betty Carver), Leonardo DiCaprio (Arnie Grape), John C. Reilly (Tucker Van Dyke), Darlene Cates (Momma), Laura Harrington (Amy Grape), Mary Kate Schellhardt (Ellen Grape), Crispin Glover (Bobby McBurney), Kevin Tighe (Mr. Carver). Directed by Lasse Hallstrom and produced by Meir Teper, Bertil Ohlsson, and David Matalon. Screenplay by Peter Hedges.

In the small but eventful world of Gilbert Grape, emergencies are a natural state. His younger brother, Arnie, has a way of climbing the town water tower and refusing to come back down. His mother, who weighs five hundred pounds, spends days at a time just sitting on the sofa. His best friend, Bobby, is an apprentice at his dad's funeral parlor and loves to talk about the tricks of the trade. His boss, who runs the local grocery store, is under threat from the big new supermarket on the edge of town, which has live lobsters in a tank—something the folks in Endora, Iowa (pop. 1,091), can't stop talking about.

Gilbert Grape is more or less equal to these challenges, but life is not easy for him. What helps is the small town itself. In a big city, we sense, the Grape family would be isolated and dysfunctional, but in Endora, where everybody knows everybody and Gilbert fits right in, life is more possible, and the family is at least quasi-functional.

What's Eating Gilbert Grape? makes of these materials an enchanting story of people who aren't misfits only because they don't see themselves that way. Nor does the film take them with tragic seriousness; it is a problem, yes, to have a retarded younger brother. And it is a problem to have a mother so fat she never leaves the house. But when kids from the neighborhood sneak around to peek at the fat lady in the living room, Gilbert sometimes gives them a boost up to the window. What the hell.

The movie, written by Peter Hedges and based on his novel, has been directed by a Scandinavian, Lasse Hallstrom, for whom families seem to exert a special pull. His credits include *My Life as a Dog* (1985), about a young boy's coming of age amid eccentric Swedish rural people and first love; and the underrated 1991 film *Once Around*, in which Richard Dreyfuss married into a family that was appalled by his abrasiveness.

The special quality of *What's Eating Gilbert Grape?* is not its oddness, however, but its warmth. Johnny Depp, as Gilbert, has specialized in playing outsiders (*Edward Scissorhands, Benny and Joon*), and here he brings a quiet, gentle sweetness that suffuses the whole film. Leonardo DiCaprio, who plays Arnie, the retarded kid brother, was nominated for an Academy Award, and deserved it. His performance succeeds in being both convincing and likable. We can see both why he's almost impossible to live with, and why Gilbert and the rest of the Grapes choose to, with love.

For all of their resiliency, however, the Grapes seem stuck in a rut in Endora. Gilbert, who appears to be around twenty-one years old, hangs out with other guys his age, drinking coffee and making small talk and quizzing Bobby about the undertaking business. On his delivery rounds for the grocery store, he makes frequent stops at the home of Mrs. Carver (Mary Steenburgen), a lonely housewife who is always much less lonely after Gilbert's visits. At home, Gilbert oversees his two younger sisters; the household runs according to rituals, and for some time the kitchen table, with dinner on it, has been brought to Momma (Darlene Cates) so that she won't have to go to it.

Then a young woman named Becky (Juliette Lewis) arrives in town, in an RV

driven by her grandmother (Penelope Branning). They're on vacation, traveling from nowhere to nowhere, and they pause in Endora long enough for Becky and Gilbert to begin a romance. And love, as it often does, acts as a catalyst for the Grapes, breaking the patterns that might have held them for a lifetime. When Gilbert brings Becky to meet Momma, we sense a tension and an excitement that is breaking the pattern of years.

One of the movie's best qualities is its way of looking at the fat mother and the retarded brother with sympathy, but not pity. Darlene Cates, making her movie debut, has an extraordinary presence on the screen. We see that she is fat, but we see many other things, too, including the losses and disappointments in her life, and the ability she finds to take a grip and make a new start. And DiCaprio, as Arnie, somehow finds a way to be difficult and invaluable at the same time.

Movies like *What's Eating Gilbert Grape?* are not easily summarized; they don't have that slick "high concept" one-sentence peg that makes them easy to sell. Maybe all I've said still leaves you wondering what the movie is about. But some of the best movies are like this: They show everyday life, carefully observed, and as we grow to know the people in the film, maybe we find out something about ourselves. The fact that Hallstrom is able to combine these qualities with comedy, romance, and even melodrama makes the movie very rare.

What's Love Got to Do With It ★ ★ ★ ½
R, 120 m., 1993

Angela Bassett (Tina Turner), Laurence Fishburne (Ike Turner), Cora Lee Day (Grandma Georgiana), Jenifer Lewis (Zelma Bullock), Phyllis Yvonne Stickney (Alline), Sherman Augustus (Reggie), Chi (Fross). Directed by Brian Gibson and produced by Doug Chapin and Barry Krost. Screenplay by Kate Lanier.

When it came right down to it, in the divorce court, Ike Turner didn't even want Tina Turner to keep her name. Born as Anna Mae Bullock in Nutbush, Tennessee, she was given her stage name by Ike early in their relationship. At the end, she was so eager to get away from him that she surrendered any claim to record royalties, publishing rights, and anything else, except "Tina Turner," which she told the judge she had worked

very hard for. "That name's got my daddy's blood written all over it," Ike protested. But it would be more accurate to say it was written in Tina's own blood.

What's Love Got to Do With It ranks as one of the most harrowing, uncompromising show biz biographies I've ever seen. It is a tradition in the genre that performers must go through hard times in order to eventually arrive at fame, but few went through harder times than Tina Turner. The movie shows Ike, jealous of her talent and popularity, turning into a violent wife-beater, and it shows her putting up with a lot more than she should have, for a lot longer.

The movie begins with a prologue in which little Anna Mae can sing louder than anyone else in the Nutbush church choir. A few years later, in St. Louis, she sees Ike Turner onstage and is intoxicated by his slick charm. Part of his act consists of inviting women from the audience to sing with his band. A few notes, and he shoos them away. But when Anna Mae Bullock got up on that stage, she came to stay. And soon, an innocent who hardly understands the world she is entering, she's on tour with Ike and his band.

The movie stars Angela Bassett and Laurence Fishburne as Tina and Ike. They played the parents of the hero in *Boyz N the Hood*, but here they are in another universe—Bassett fiery and convincing as Tina, Fishburne, in a powerful performance, able to show us both Ike's charm and his violent side. The singing on the movie's sound track is by Tina Turner, but Bassett's performances of the songs are so much in synch—not just lip-synch, but physically, and with personality and soul— that it always seems as if we're watching Tina at work.

As the two of them reach the heights of show business, with platinum records and big Vegas bookings and lots of money, their personal life turns into a nightmare. The movie shows Ike strung out on cocaine, flaunting his endless string of girlfriends, and subjecting Tina to verbal and physical abuse. A few friends advise her to walk away. Most of the people around them, intimidated by Ike or grateful for a generous drug supply, are enablers.

The most harrowing scene in the movie comes one night as Ike beats Tina yet once again, and bleeding and battered she walks out of their hotel and down a highway and into a Ramada Inn, where she says, "My name is Tina Turner, and my husband and I have had an argument. I have thirty-two cents in my pocket. If you give me a room I promise you I will pay you back as soon as I can." The manager gives her a room. The Ramada Inn roadside sign is prominent in the scene because, as Tina wrote in her autobiography, *I, Tina*, she will forever be grateful to the motel for taking her in.

But what is amazing is that the scene isn't the end of Tina and Ike's relationship. The movie is unflinching in its willingness to show that Tina, like many battered wives, made excuses for her violent husband and believed his apologies and gave him more chances, long after she should have walked away. Finally she finds the strength to resist through Buddhist meditation techniques, and there is an unforgettable scene late in the film where she is about to open a big engagement and Ike slips past security and into her dressing room with a gun, and she finds the inner strength to face him down and not cave in, and go onstage like a professional.

What's Love Got to Do With It has a lot of terrific music in it (including a closing glimpse of the real Tina Turner), but this is not the typical show biz musical. It's a story of pain and courage, uncommonly honest and unflinching, and the next time I hear Tina Turner singing I will listen to the song in a whole new way.

When a Man Loves a Woman ★ ★ ★ ★
R, 126 m., 1994

Andy Garcia (Michael Green), Meg Ryan (Alice Green), Lauren Tom (Amy), Tina Majorino (Jess Green), Mae Whitman (Casey Green), Ellen Burstyn (Emily). Directed by Luis Mandoki and produced by Jordan Kerner and Jon Avnet. Screenplay by Ronald Bass and Al Franken.

Here is a wise and ambitious film about the way alcoholism affects the fabric of a marriage. So many movies about the disease simplify it into a three-step process: gradual onset, spectacular bottom, eventual recovery. It isn't that simple; most alcoholics never even give themselves a chance to recover. And recovery is a beginning, not an end. *When a Man Loves a Woman* is about an alcoholic who recovers—and about her husband, who in some ways dealt with her better when she was drunk.

The movie stars Meg Ryan as Alice, a San Francisco junior high school counselor who drinks all day, every day. Her husband, Michael, an airline pilot played by Andy Garcia, knows she gets loaded on occasion, but has no idea of the extent of her drinking. "It

starts at four in the morning," she finally confesses, telling him some of her secrets ("You know how we'll be in the car and then I have to run back in the house because I forgot something?"). The movie opens as she begins a steep dive toward her bottom. One day after school she goes out drinking with a friend, and forgets to come home until after midnight. Another day, drunk, she slaps her older daughter and then passes out in the shower, landing on the bathroom floor in a crash of glass, water, and blood.

It's a relief for her to admit her addiction. She's been hiding it too long. Her husband is warm and understanding, arranging for her to check into a treatment facility. It's after Alice sobers up that Michael's unhappiness begins. Early in the film we have seen how much in love he is, how attentive, how accepting. To some degree, he is giving himself points for being a nice guy. Sure, she hid a lot of her drinking (a practiced alcoholic can easily drink three or four times more booze than others might be aware of). But the drinking she couldn't hide (the episode with the eggs, the scene in Mexico, the night she locks herself out of the house) would be unacceptable to many spouses. Not goodhearted, accepting Michael, who is, in recovery jargon, a born enabler.

At the treatment facility, Alice begins learning to live with the disease. She makes close friendships with other recovering alcoholics. On visiting day, when a fairly fearsome-looking fellow patient offers to play with their daughter, she reassures her husband: "He's not a child molester. He's an armed robber." Back home, Alice attends a lot of AA meetings, and confides in friends she meets there. Michael is not sure he likes this so much. One evening he comes home to find Alice deep in a tête-à-tête with a man she met in the treatment center. "I can't remember how long it's been since *we* sat and talked that way," Michael says.

They have fights, mostly because Michael still has the habit of handling everything, settling problems with the children, making decisions. Now that Alice is ready to participate more fully in the family, he feels threatened. And she is emotionally fragile, too. One day she's in a foul mood and he wants to know why, so he can help, and she explains that she is simply having a very bad day and there is nothing either one of them can do about it, and he can't accept that. He needs to know the reason, so he can fix it. They fight.

What makes that scene so good is that it ends inconclusively. The movie doesn't pretend to be able to fix things, either. The strength of the screenplay by Ronald Bass and Al Franken is that it pays close attention to the feelings of both characters. It isn't just about Alice's recovery. It's about Michael's recovery *from* Alice's recovery. The writers make an unusual team: Bass won an Oscar for writing *Rain Man;* Franken writes and plays the twelve-step guru Stuart Smalley on "Saturday Night Live." In the SNL bits, the jargon of twelve-step groups is kidded ("I'm good enough, I'm smart enough, and doggone it, people like me"). In the screenplay, the movie understands how AA helps alcoholics create a language to describe their feelings and deal with them.

Yet *When a Man Loves a Woman* is not simply a docu-drama about the disease of the month. It's fresh and original in the way it sees its characters. The director, Luis Mandoki *(White Palace),* is evenhanded in seeing events through the eyes of both Michael and Alice—and of their young daughters, who see and hear more than the grown-ups realize, and ask hard questions ("Are you getting divorced?"). I couldn't find a false note in Ryan's performance—and only one in Garcia's, a smarmy Hollywood speech at the end of the movie that must, I think, be blamed on the filmmakers. (The movie's obvious close was one speech earlier.)

Then there is the character of the couple's pregnant nanny and housekeeper, Amy, played by Lauren Tom. Amy is onscreen only briefly, but is written and acted with such a perfect feel for tone and dialogue that she seems immediately real. She knows all about not enabling. One night as the kids are screaming and Michael is going berserk, she roots herself in the kitchen, preparing her own dinner. She knows what is her problem and what is not her problem. She has a line of dialogue ("It worked") that, in context, is both unexpected and perfect.

Alcoholism has been called a disease of denial. What *When a Man Loves a Woman* understands is that those around the alcoholic often deny it, too, and grow accustomed to their relationship with a drunk. When the drunk gets sober, he or she becomes a fuller and more competent person, and that can threaten the old relationship. That's why professionals call alcoholism a "family disease." It's a hard concept to understand, but here is a movie that understands it.

When Harry Met Sally . . . ★ ★ ★
R, 95 m., 1989

Billy Crystal (Harry Burns), Meg Ryan (Sally Albright), Carrie Fisher (Marie), Bruno Kirby (Jess), Steven Ford (Joe), Lisa Jane Persky (Alice), Michelle Nicastro (Amanda). Directed by Rob Reiner and produced by Reiner and Andrew Scheinman. Screenplay by Nora Ephron.

When Harry Met Sally . . . is a love story with a form as old as the movies and dialogue as new as this month's issue of *Vanity Fair*. It's about two people who could be characters in a Woody Allen movie if they weren't so sunny, and about how it takes them thirteen years to fall in love. We're with them, or maybe a little ahead of them, every step of the way.

Harry meets Sally for the first time at the University of Chicago in the spring of 1977, when they team up to share the driving for a trip to New York. Both plan to start their careers in the city—she as a journalist, he as a labor organizer. Presumably they are both successful, since they live in those apartments that only people in the movies can afford, but their professional lives are entirely offscreen. We see them only at those intervals when they see each other.

They meet, for example, three years later, at LaGuardia. She's with a new boyfriend. They meet a few years after that, when they're both in relationships, and a few years after that, when her boyfriend has left and his wife wants a divorce. They keep on meeting until they realize that they like one another and they become friends, even though on their very first cross-country trip Harry warned Sally that true friendship is impossible between a man and a woman because the issue of sex always gets in the way.

The movie apparently believes that—and it also suggests that the best way to get rid of sex as an issue is to get married, since married people always seem too tired for sex. That and other theories about sex and relationships are tested as if Harry and Sally were a proving grounds for *Cosmopolitan*, until finally, tired of fighting, they admit that they do love one another after all.

The movie was written by Nora Ephron, and could be a prequel to her novel and screenplay *Heartburn*, which starred Jack Nicholson and Meryl Streep in the story of a marriage and divorce. But this marriage seems headed for happier times, maybe because most of the big fights are out of the way before love is even declared. Harry is played by Billy Crystal and Sally is Meg Ryan, and they make a good movie couple because both actors are able to suggest genuine warmth and tenderness. This isn't a romance of passion, although passion is present, but one that becomes possible only because the two people have grown up together, have matured until they can finally see clearly what they really want in a partner.

Ephron's dialogue represents the way people would like to be able to talk. It's witty and epigrammatic, and there are lots of lines to quote when you're telling friends about the movie. The dialogue would defeat many actors, but Crystal and Ryan help it to work; their characters seem smart and quick enough to almost be this witty. It's only occasionally that the humor is paid for at the expense of credibility—as in a hilarious but unconvincing scene where Sally sits in a crowded restaurant and demonstrates how to fake an orgasm. I laughed, but somehow I didn't think Sally, or any woman, would really do that.

When Harry Met Sally . . . was directed by Rob Reiner, the onetime Meathead of "All in the Family," whose credits now qualify him as one of Hollywood's very best directors of comedy (his films include *The Sure Thing, Stand by Me, This is Spinal Tap,* and *The Princess Bride*—each film completely different from the others, each one successful on its own terms). This film is probably his most conventional, in terms of structure and the way it fulfills our expectations, but what makes it special, apart from the Ephron screenplay, is the chemistry between Crystal and Ryan.

She is an open-faced, bright-eyed blonde; he's a gentle, skinny man with a lot of smart one-liners. What they both have (to repeat) is warmth. Crystal demonstrated that quality in his previous film, the underrated *Memories of Me*, and it's here again this time, in scenes where he visibly softens when he sees that he has hurt her. He is one of the rare actors who can make an apology on the screen and convince us he means it. Ryan (from *Innerspace* and *D.O.A.*) has a difficult assignment—she spends most of the movie convincing Harry, and herself, that there's nothing between them—and she has to let us see that there is something, after all.

Harry and Sally are aided, and sometimes hindered, in their romance by the efforts of their two best friends (Carrie Fisher and Bruno Kirby), who meet on a blind date arranged by Harry and Sally to provide possible partners for Sally and Harry. They're the kind of people who don't make it hard for themselves, who realize they like each other, accept that fact, and act on it. Harry and Sally are tougher customers. They fight happiness every step of the way, until it finally wears them down.

Where the Day Takes You ★ ★ ★
R, 105 m., 1992

Sean Astin (Greg), Lara Flynn Boyle (Heather), Peter Dobson (Tommy Ray), Balthazar Getty (Little J), Ricki Lake (Brenda), James Le Gros (Crasher), Dermot Mulroney (King). Directed by Marc Rocco and produced by Paul Hertzberg. Screenplay by Michael Hitchcock, Kurt Voss, and Rocco.

"I'll bet you can never guess why I ran away from home," says a runaway teen-ager to her new boyfriend in *Where the Day Takes You*. "Sure I can," he says. "You were raped by either your father or your stepfather. Everybody runs away for the same reason."

He isn't far off. And the movie, which was shot on and around Hollywood Boulevard, shows a side of runaway kids we haven't seen before: How they form surrogate families in the streets, seeking reassurance and security that they never felt at home.

The movie is effective, well-acted, and convincing. And that was a surprise for me, since a look at the cast (Dermot Mulroney, Sean Astin, Lara Flynn Boyle, Balthazar Getty, and Ricki Lake among them) led me, walking into the theater, to anticipate some sort of junior Brat Pack caper. Maybe the director, Marc Rocco, is good with actors. Or maybe these actors haven't had this kind of strong material to work with before.

Mulroney carries the movie, as the King, leader of a group of runaways who live in a hollowed-out cave under the Hollywood Freeway and support themselves by begging, stealing, and prostitution. He is not what could be described as a good influence on the kids who join up with him, but he is a steadying presence, and feels genuine responsibility for his "family." Just as they band together for security, he perhaps feels a need to exercise responsibility, to look out for those who are obviously not able to survive by themselves.

Many of the other characters are sharply drawn, including Greg, played by Sean Astin, who is powerless over drugs and places himself in one desperate situation after another, finally popping his last balloon in a pathetic exit scene. Balthazar Getty is very effective in a scene where he tries to be a male prostitute but hates himself for it. And Boyle is good in the somewhat stereotyped role of the pretty newcomer to the group.

The screenplay, by Michael Hitchcock, Kurt Voss, and Rocco, contains a lot of documentary information about where runaways hang out, why they hate the police, and how they try to survive in a system that seems set up specifically to crush them. It is not a poetic or pseudoromantic view of runaway life (which seems like a hell interrupted by occasional laughs), but on the other hand it isn't hysterical, either. It shows how young people need families and will form their own if they are failed by those they were born into.

The story is convincing up until the end, which feels manufactured for movie purposes. One of the things it illustrates is that trouble has a way of attracting more trouble; the nature of the law and society are such that these characters cannot exist without breaking laws, whether they intend to or not, and that automatically sets in motion a chain of additional broken laws, including evasion of arrest. An insignificant initial crime can mushroom into a situation of true desperation.

Watching *Where the Day Takes You*, I was reminded of the 1985 Oscar-nominated documentary *Streetwise*, shot among homeless runaways in Seattle. Both films have many of the same qualities, although the documentary pays more attention to the efforts, successful and otherwise, made by social agencies working with street kids. The bottom line is the same: Kids run away, they band with other kids, and society seems organized to destroy them whether or not they're asking for it.

While You Were Sleeping ★ ★ ★   [NEW]
PG, 100 m., 1995

Sandra Bullock (Lucy), Bill Pullman (Jack), Peter Gallagher (Peter), Peter Boyle (Ox), Jack Warden (Saul), Glynis Johns (Elsie), Micole Mercurio (Midge), Jason Bernard (Jerry). Directed by Jon Turteltaub and produced by Joe Roth and Roger Birnbaum. Screenplay by Daniel G. Sullivan and Fredric Lebow.

While You Were Sleeping is one of those movies that blindside you with their charm. It starts out seeming sappy, and your expectations sink: Is everybody in this movie going to be cuddly and sort of dumb? Is every emotion

and plot development going to be given a long windup before the pitch? Seems like it, but then a funny thing happens. While you're making up your mind that the movie's going nowhere, it starts to go somewhere.

The movie stars Sandra Bullock, who became a star in *Speed* by surviving high-speed chases on a bus and a subway train, and she is back in the subway again, playing Lucy, who "sits in a booth like a veal," selling tickets. She has a crush on Peter (Peter Gallagher), a daily customer who looks to her like the perfect man. One day Peter is mugged and thrown onto the tracks, and she races out of her booth and saves his life, although not without a dumb scene where she bends over his unconscious body and tells him, "Mister, there's a train coming, and it's fast!"

Hearing that line, I wondered what kind of person would say it. Was Lucy going to be a simpleminded innocent? Would anyone in real life be capable, under the circumstances, of thinking of such a goofy line? I doubted it, and I was beginning to develop an intense dislike for the movie, especially after Peter is hospitalized with a Movie Coma (a medical condition that requires him to remain unconscious for precisely as long as is convenient for the plot). Through a silly misunderstanding, the members of Peter's family become convinced that Lucy is his fiancée. Why does she allow them to persist in their misunderstanding? Because the plot depends on it, that's why.

Peter's family is one of those human groups that move as a unit. You hardly ever see just one of them. They move into the frame as a block of four or five, as if they're strapped together or posing for a photo. His dad is Peter Boyle, his grandmother is Glynis Johns, and his godfather is Saul (Jack Warden), who is a lovable old cuss who figures out Lucy's secret right away, but keeps it, because he knows that Lucy is the nicest person who has drifted into the family's life in years.

Enter now the character of Jack (Bill Pullman), who is Peter's brother. He appreciates the fact that Lucy has saved his brother's life, and soon he is walking her home through the snow, and, of course, they are falling in love with each other, although, again for purposes of the plot, they have to pretend to be unaware of this. By this point, in a lesser movie, I would have been squirming in my seat. But a strange thing had happened. Somehow, without my noticing, I had grown to like Lucy very much, and now Jack was growing on me, too. In fact, amazingly, I

was beginning to *care* about the movie, even though it was clearly hammered together out of completely predictable elements.

There aren't many movie actors we simply *like*. Marilyn Monroe was one, and that quality, not sex appeal, is why she has remained such a durable memory. On the basis of *Speed* and *While You Were Sleeping*, Sandra Bullock may be another. She plays Lucy in a low key, as a shy, unassertive young woman, and so, of course, late in the film when she has to stand up for herself, we're proud of her. She makes us feel protective. And Bill Pullman has real charisma, too: He's got the right chemistry for this love story in which sweetness is more important than passion.

As for the plot, there is a point at which it seems predictable, and then we get beyond that point, and start *enjoying* its predictability, because once we see where it's headed there is a pleasure in watching it delay and prolong the inevitable—toying with clichés as if they were new playthings. It has a lot of fun, for example, with the Other Man in Lucy's life, an unwanted downstairs neighbor who knows he isn't loved and has lines like, "I seen the way you looked at him—like you just saw your first Trans-Am."

Light romantic comedy is one of the trickiest of all movie genres. Usually it doesn't work. Sometimes it does, as in *When Harry Met Sally*, *Sleepless in Seattle*, and *Four Weddings and a Funeral*. The characters in *While You Were Sleeping* aren't as smart or quirky as the people in those three movies, and the dialogue doesn't crackle in the same way, but the movie works all the same: It's a feel-good film, warm and good-hearted, and as it was heading for its happy ending, I was still a little astonished how much I was enjoying it.

The Whistle Blower ★ ★ ★ ½
PG, 100 m., 1987

Michael Caine (Frank Jones), James Fox (Lord), Nigel Havers (Bob Jones), Felicity Dean (Cynthia Goodburn), John Gielgud (Sir Adrian Chappel), Kenneth Colley (Bill Pickett), Gordon Jackson (Bruce). Directed by Simon Langton and produced by Geoffrey Reeve. Screenplay by Julian Bond.

The Whistle Blower is about the British spy establishment, but at first it doesn't feel at all like a spy movie. It begins as the quiet account of the daily life of a middle-aged man who has set up in the office equipment business and who almost welcomes his anonymity. He was once in intelligence, he was once at the center of important matters, but now he has put all that behind him.

The man is played by Michael Caine, with a quiet self-effacement that is very convincing. He is mild and soft-spoken, and it is clear that to some extent he is living his life through the life of his son, whom he loves very much. The son is a likable, disorganized, untidy, very serious young man who is in love with an older woman with children.

Caine is not sure this is the right relationship, but in his performance there are a few quiet, crucial moments when he seems to do nothing—he just sort of stands there in a shot, regarding those around him—and you can feel his hope that his son will be happy.

Caine is such a good actor that he doesn't overplay those moments or indeed seem to play them at all. Yet they underlie the whole film. We begin by understanding that Caine has placed action behind him, we identify with his new emotional calm, we sense his love for his son and that prepares us for everything that follows.

It is important that I not reveal, however, too much of what follows. *The Whistle Blower* is not a conventional spy thriller, but it does depend upon surprises and unexpected revelations of character, and they grow naturally out of the story. In general terms, I can say that Caine's son becomes a pawn in an intelligence game with much higher stakes and that what Caine eventually comes to understand is that little people such as himself and his son are expendable in the view of the entrenched establishment that rules the country.

Like another British thriller, *Defence of the Realm,* this movie uses the British spy apparatus as a way of dramatizing the class distinctions that still exist in Britain. The Caine character is in reaction against the feeling that nothing—not God, not the throne, not patriotism, certainly not security considerations—is as important as defending a network of privilege. The crucial moment in the film comes when Caine accuses a traitor of letting innocent people die, just so that he can continue to have tea with the queen. The steps by which Caine arrives at this speech are what the movie is about.

The Whistle Blower was hardly ahead of the headlines in Britain. The Spycatcher controversy had the country in an uproar against the action of five bewigged Law Lords, solemnly forbidding the press from printing details from a book that was a world-wide bestseller. The book alleges, of course, that a head of British intelligence was a Soviet mole from the start, the same assumption *The Whistle Blower* is founded on.

Despite a few obligatory scenes of threats and violence, most of the action in the movie takes place within the mind of the Caine character. Having taken his leave of Hollywood with the truly dreadful *Jaws the Revenge,* Caine returned to England in three quite different performances: this one, the slimy Soho mob boss in *Mona Lisa,* and the maverick spy who tries to prevent a nuclear explosion in *The Fourth Protocol.* The three performances are completely different, and yet it is hard to see what Caine does differently in them. He has the same dry, flat inflection, the sometimes masked face, the way of seeming to stand completely impassively until action is called for, the sense of enormous reserves of strength and anger banked inside. Yet in *Mona Lisa* he is a villain, in this film he is a decent, angry man, and in *The Fourth Protocol* he is more of an action hero.

It all seems to come from inside. The one thing you will rarely catch Caine doing in a movie is seeming to go for an effect. Maybe that's why he achieves them so consistently; the screen is a magnifying glass that rarely forgives excess.

What's especially nice about *The Whistle Blower* is that it never quite lets plot become more important than character. Like a novel by Graham Greene, it isn't really about what happens, but about how the events feel to the characters and how they change them. There is a scene in this movie, a quiet walk and talk between father and son, that is as touching a portrait of parenthood as any I can remember.

White ★ ★ ★ ½
R, 92 m., 1994

Zbigniew Zamachowski (Karol Karol), Julie Delpy (Dominique), Janusz Gajos (Mikolaj), Jerzy Stuhr (Jurek), Grzegorz Warchol (Elegant Man), Jerzy Nowak (Peasant), Aleksander Bardini (Notary), Cezary Harasimowicz (Inspector). Directed by Krzysztof Kieslowski and produced by Marin Karmitz. Screenplay by Krzysztof Piesiewicz and Kieslowski.

The hero of *White* tries to make money by performing in the Paris Metro. But he is not a musician, and his instrument—a pocket comb with a sheet of paper folded over it—doesn't inspire many donations. He's reached the bottom of the barrel, this sad-sack migrant from Poland whose beautiful wife has divorced him. And he is homesick. At last inspiration strikes. A friend is flying to Poland. Karol (Zbigniew Zamachowski) will ship himself home curled up inside the man's suitcase.

Is this possible? Better not to ask. The movie creates a great droll comic moment when the friend lingers at the baggage claim carousel in the Warsaw airport until it becomes unmistakable that the luggage . . . has been lost. And then there is a scene showing that the missing suitcase, with Karol still inside, has been stolen. Thieves open it, are bitterly disappointed to find only a man inside, and beat him. Then they cast him aside onto a rubbish heap. It is bitterly cold. Bloody but optimistic, he surveys the grim landscape and says, "Home at last."

Depending on your state of mind, these events may sound funnier, or more painful, than they really are. Krzysztof Kieslowski directs *White* in a deadpan, matter-of-fact style that treats his strange subject matter as if it were merely factual. *White* is the middle film in his trilogy based on the colors of the French flag, coming between *Blue,* which was about a woman coming to grips with the death of her husband, and *Red,* about a woman whose accidental friendship with a judge leads to profound changes in her life. All of these films approach their subjects with such irony that we cannot take them at face value; *White* is the anticomedy, in between the antitragedy and the antiromance.

Kieslowski is Polish, now working in France, and in *White* he considers the new, post-Communist Poland. His hero (whose name, Karol, is Polish for Charlie, not a coincidence) was a hairdresser before leaving for Paris, and he discovers that his brother is still operating the family salon. He agrees to do a few heads every day, and meanwhile looks around for opportunities. One quickly comes: The friend who shipped him to Poland now knows a man who wants to pay someone to kill him. A job's a job, although this one eventually provides the most poignant moment in the movie.

A capitalist Poland provides opportunities for someone like Karol, who has soon schemed and maneuvered himself into a position of relative wealth, and begins a complicated plan to lure his former wife (Julie Delpy) back to Poland. His relationship to her is complicated; he has not been able to make love with her since their wedding day, but exactly how he feels about this and what his plans are after her return remain mysteries that the movie only gradually unveils.

Kieslowski allows a great deal of apparent chance in his stories. They do not move from A to B, but wander dazedly through the lives of their characters. That lends a certain suspense; since we do not know the plot, there is no way for us to anticipate what will happen next. He takes a quiet delight in producing one rabbit after another from his hat, hinting much, but revealing facts about his characters only when they must be known.

In all of his films, there are sequences that are interesting simply for their documentary content: We're not sure what they have to do with the story, if anything, but we are interested to see them unfolding for their own sake. In *Blue,* the heroine's pragmatic reaction to her husband's death gave hints of greater secrets still to come. In *Red,* there are two lives that never quite seem to interlock, but always seem about to. In *White,* there is the marvelous indirection of Karol's comeback in Poland, the way in which he becomes successful almost by intuition.

The colors blue, white, and red in the French flag stand for liberty, equality, and fraternity, and one of the small puzzles Kieslowski sets us is how these concepts apply to his plot. As Karol deviously sets a snare for the wife he loves and hates—as he gains control of the relationship, in a way—it is hard to see how "equality" could be involved in such a struggle for supremacy. Afterward, thinking about the film, beginning to see what Kieslowski might have been thinking, we see even richer ironies in his story.

White Fang ★ ★ ★
PG, 104 m., 1991

Klaus Maria Brandauer (Alex), Ethan Hawke (Jack), Seymour Cassel (Skunker), Susan Hogan (Belinda), James Remar (Beauty), Bill Mosely (Luke). Directed by Randal Kleiser and produced by Marykay Powell. Screenplay by Jeanne Rosenberg, Nick Thiel, and David Fallon.

Jack London's great novel *White Fang,* which held me in its spell when I was ten and again thirty years later, is the story of a dog, and the dog's journey through many kinds of human habitations, under many kinds of masters. Much of that story can be glimpsed in this new film of *White Fang,* although not so distinctly, because the movie is the story of a boy and not a dog.

The boy's name is Jack (Ethan Hawke), and he has come out to the Yukon in 1898 to prospect his dad's claim in the great Gold Rush. He meets up with a couple of prospectors (Klaus Maria Brandauer and Seymour Cassel), and they travel by dogsled into the wilderness of the Arctic winter. Their adventures are intercut with the early days of White Fang, a wolf with some dog blood, whose mother is killed when he is a pup. White Fang is captured by Indians, then traded to men who train him for dog fights, and then finally comes into the possession of Jack, who takes him along when he goes to live at the claim.

The London novel was intended as a comparison of dogs and men, in which most men came up short. In the book, the dog eventually becomes the property of a mining engineer, who takes it back to a sunny retirement in California. The Disney version, of course, transmutes the adult into Jack the teen-ager, and ends with a joyous reunion of man and beast after the human decides not to go to California after all, but heed the call of the wild. Jack has good reason to stick with White Fang, who by the end of the film has saved him from being eaten by a bear and killed by thieving claim jumpers.

We are agreed then, that the movie makes no serious claim to be a version of the Jack London novel. (That project would be mostly about dogs, and require patience on the order of the 1989 film, *The Bear,* which took a year to film because each of the animal movements had to be separately photographed. Fans of *The Bear* will be pleased that its star, Bart, makes a guest appearance here.) *White Fang* is, however, a superior entertainment on its own terms, a story of pluck and survival at a time when men poured into the Yukon dreaming of riches, and found mostly disease and death.

The movie is magnificently photographed on location. The performances are authentic and understated, and Brandauer makes a convincing veteran prospector, part hard-bitten, part dreamer. As the boy, Ethan Hawke is properly callow at the beginning and properly matured at the end, although it's all he can do to carry off the final joyous reunion with the dog. And the dog itself (played by Jed) is a fine-looking, intelligent animal so good at displaying its fangs that I actually believed it could scare off a bear.

Movies like this are an antidote to the vio-lent and defeatist thrillers a lot of younger moviegoers seem to be hooked on. It's an adventure, it's exciting, it stirs the imagination, and there are scenes of terrific suspense—as when Jack ventures out on that thin ice, or gets cornered by the bear. Like *The Black Stallion, Never Cry Wolf,* and *Crusoe,* it's a film that holds the natural world in wonder and awe. And it might even inspire someone to read the novels of Jack London, who was such a good writer he could tell a story that I fell in love with when I was ten years old and much harder to please than I am now.

White Fang 2: Myth of the White Wolf
★ ★ ★
PG, 106 m., 1994

Scott Bairstow (Henry Casey), Charmaine Craig (Lily Joseph), Al Harrington (Moses Joseph), Anthony Michael Ruivivar (Peter), Victoria Racimo (Katrin), Alfred Molina (Rev. Leland Drury), Paul Coeur (Adam John Hale), Geoffrey Lewis (Heath). Directed by Ken Olin and produced by Preston Fischer. Screenplay by David Fallon.

White Fang 2: Myth of the White Wolf is a rousing adventure about a boy and his dog and their girlfriends. The movie tells the story of Henry (Scott Bairstow), a teenage gold prospector in the Yukon, who gets involved in the cause of a nearby Indian tribe that's being threatened by an evil mining company. Henry is much helped by his dog, White Fang, but while they are separated in the middle parts of the film he falls in love with an Indian girl, and White Fang falls in love with a she-wolf. These romances lead to an ending that is positively awash with joyous reunions, and I cannot think what restraint led the filmmakers to leave out a double wedding ceremony.

Neither this film nor the earlier *White Fang* (1991) owes much to the classic Jack London novel, beyond a title and a location. London told the story of a dog. These films tell the stories of people and their canine friends. If the movie inspires any viewers to read the book, they'll discover a more hard-bitten, realistic view of the north. But the movie tells a high-spirited, romantic tale that at times plays like an outdoorsy Indiana Jones adventure.

A prologue explains why Jack, the hero of the previous film, is no longer around: He has moved to California and left White Fang with his friend Henry. (Jack was well played by Ethan Hawke, later seen slumped on a sofa and bitterly chain-smoking his way through *Reality Bites*, his days in the Yukon a distant memory.) Henry has lots of bags of gold nuggets hidden under the floorboards of his cabin, and decides to take them to town by raft. Apparently he is unaware that the river leads to rapids and a waterfall, which separate Henry from the gold and White Fang, and nearly kill them both.

Henry is taken in by a tribe of Haida Indians, whose civilized and gentle life-style is under threat by some shady characters from the nearby town. A man who says he is a minister (Alfred Molina) keeps trying to talk them off of their land. But Henry and a beautiful young Haida girl (Charmaine Craig) literally stumble on their secret when they fall down the air shaft of a gold mine. (This scene, and several others, seem directly inspired by Nancy Drew and the Hardy Boys; nothing like stumbling across the Secret of the Old Mine Shaft.)

The movie has been skillfully directed by Ken Olin, who provides lots of excitement and adventure without ever lingering for long on bloodshed or graphic violence. The PG rating is appropriate, and younger children will probably respond to the sense of freedom and exhilaration generated by these characters in their rugged Colorado and Canadian settings.

One thing I rather missed, however, was the earlier film's extensive plotting involving the dog. This time White Fang is offscreen and missing for long periods of time, perhaps because it is easier to train actors than dogs. The filmmakers are also a little too willing to hint that White Fang understands English; early in the film, after Henry fails to bag a caribou that White Fang has rounded up for him, Henry says, "Sorry, White Fang; looks like it's potatoes for supper again tonight," and the dog droops its ears and whines sadly. Soon it will be picking out simple tunes on the piano.

What's best about the film is a kind of fresh-air exuberance, an innocence. The adventures in this movie are *fun*—not frightening, violent, or depressing. The villains are bad, but not subhuman, and at the end I was positively grateful for a scene where the bad guy tries to get away in a wagon full of gold, with the heroine tied up behind him, and Henry and the dog trying to save her. This was so old-fashioned it was almost daring.

White Hunter, Black Heart ★ ★ ★
PG, 112 m., 1990

Clint Eastwood (John Wilson), Jeff Fahey (Pete Verrill), Charlotte Cornwell (Miss Wilding), Norman Lumsden (Butler George), George Dzundza (Paul Landers), Edward Tudor Pole (Reissar), Marisa Berenson (Kay Gibson). Directed and produced by Clint Eastwood. Screenplay by Peter Viertel, James Bridges, and Burt Kennedy.

Film directors have to be a little like God, convinced that they have the correct answer to every question, and the responsibility to impose their opinion on everyone around them. Nice-guy directors—those praised for listening to their colleagues, keeping an open mind, and encouraging their actors to improvise—rarely make great movies. Great directors are routinely described as mean sons of bitches, but there is awe in the voices describing them.

John Huston was not, by most accounts, a nice guy. He ran roughshod over marriages, friendships, and responsibilities, he had a habit of losing interest in a project halfway through, and he indulged his passions for horses, drink, gambling, and women as if he had the divine right to be supplied endlessly with same. In his last years, crippled by emphysema, he nevertheless did present his daughter Anjelica with the role of her career in *Prizzi's Honor*, and he grew closer to his other children, helping their careers while he somehow struggled through the making of *The Dead*—a brave film he correctly predicted would be his last.

Huston was a legend, larger than life, and his best films were about men something like himself. The actor who mirrored Huston the best was Humphrey Bogart, in *The Maltese Falcon*, *Treasure of the Sierra Madre*, and *The African Queen*, and it is Huston's making of the *Queen* that supplied Clint Eastwood with the subject for *White Hunter, Black Heart*.

The original screenplay for *The African Queen* was adapted from C.S. Forester's novel by James Agee, a hard-drinking, hard-smoking writer, who Huston expected to drink all night with him, be his tennis partner in the morning, and his collaborator in the afternoon. This regimen probably hastened the heart attack that brought an end to Agee's work on the *Queen*, and when Huston went to Africa with Bogart and Katharine Hepburn to film the movie, he took along a young writer named Peter Viertel, who did the final version of the screenplay.

Viertel was a privileged observer to what has become one of the legendary location shoots of Hollywood history, and his novel from the mid-1950s, *White Hunter, Black Heart*, was obviously based on the experience. It did not paint a flattering portrait of "John Wilson," the Huston character, who was more concerned with shooting an elephant than shooting a movie. After he finished the novel, Viertel told me, he sent it to Huston, who—to give him his due—said he enjoyed it and did nothing to prevent its publication. Huston was not a hypocrite and did not pretend to be other than he was.

Now comes Clint Eastwood to produce and direct the long-delayed film of Viertel's book, and to star as John Huston, familiar accent and all. It must have taken some nerve for Eastwood to tackle this project. It is hard enough for a famous movie actor to disappear into a character who is not himself—but almost impossible for him to disappear into another famous character, into someone equally legendary and familiar.

In the early scenes of *White Hunter, Black Heart*, Eastwood fans are likely to be distracted to hear Huston's words and vocal mannerisms in Eastwood's mouth, and to see Huston's swagger and physical bravado. Then the performance takes over, and the movie turns into a thoughtful film about the conflicts inside an artist. Huston emerges as a strong-willed, intelligent man who, nevertheless, places his own desires above his ideals, who rails at Hollywood's dishonesty and yet is not above keeping an expensive film on hold while he abandons his location to go elephant shooting.

Why does he want so badly to shoot an elephant? Perhaps because he has not shot one before. Perhaps to prove he is brave. Perhaps to give the elephant the privilege of being shot by John Huston. The obsession wraps itself around his evasions and self-justifications until the character's motive is hardly important; he is selfish enough that he will do it simply because he wants to.

There is a lot more to *White Hunter, Black Heart* than this description suggests. I especially enjoyed the verbal fencing matches between Eastwood and George Dzundza, as his producer, and his confidences and confessions to Jeff Fahey, in the Viertel role. But what it comes down to is a man who puts his career on hold and keeps his colleagues waiting while he indulges in his own determined ego-gratification.

Why did Eastwood make this movie? At

one time I thought it was an attack on the Hollywood where he has functioned as a particularly successful outsider. Now I wonder if it isn't also intended as a contrast to some of the action heroes he's played in other movies. The Eastwood hero almost always does what he damn well pleases. Here is a movie about a man who does what he pleases, but it doesn't make him a hero.

White Men Can't Jump ★ ★ ★ ½
R, 115 m., 1992

Wesley Snipes (Sidney Deane), Woody Harrelson (Billy Hoyle), Rosie Perez (Gloria Clemente), Tyra Ferrell (Rhonda Deane), Cylk Cozart (Robert). Directed by Ron Shelton and produced by Don Miller and David Lester. Screenplay by Shelton.

White Men Can't Jump is a movie about black basketball hustlers and a white guy who cons some of them and is conned by the others. But that plot description doesn't begin to do justice to this movie, which is all about language and timing and loyalty and betrayal, and is very smart and very funny.

The movie takes place on the asphalt outdoor basketball courts of Los Angeles—on Venice Beach, in the Crenshaw neighborhood, in Watts, and wherever else money is wagered on the outcome of the game. It stars Wesley Snipes as a black basketball hustler whose other jobs are suffering because of the downturn in the economy, and Woody Harrelson as a white guy from out of town who uses his goofy look (floppy shorts, backwards cap, and a distracted grin) to lure victims into betting on his game. Neither one of these guys hustles basketball purely for the enjoyment of the game. Snipes does it to make money (his wife is on his case), and Harrelson does it at least partly because he's a compulsive gambler.

What the movie knows is how the game is played in the tough urban circles where these guys operate. The director, Ron Shelton, who also wrote the screenplay, knows how his characters talk and sound, and how they get into each other's minds with nonstop taunting and boasting. The language is one of the great joys of this film, not just because of its energy and spirit (most of the characters are gifted verbal improvisers) but because of its originality. The usual four-letter words and their derivatives are upstaged by some of the most creative and bizarre insults I have ever heard in a movie.

It's interesting that this is not simply a

basketball movie. Shelton, whose first film as a director was the great baseball comedy *Bull Durham* (1988), knows all about sports that are played by adults for adult reasons; about how the appearance of boys at play can obscure the reality of men at work. And in *White Men Can't Jump*, he has given both Harrelson and Snipes women who want their men to be more responsible than they know how to be.

Harrelson's Puerto Rican girlfriend is played by Rosie Perez, who all but steals the movie with one of the funniest performances since Susan Sarandon's in *Bull Durham*. You may remember Perez from *Do the Right Thing*, where she played the Spike Lee character's girlfriend, but here she unleashes an entirely new side to her character, as a brassy Brooklynite who spends her days laying down the law to Harrelson and studying the almanac. She dreams of being a contestant on "Jeopardy," and when she gets her chance, her appearance works in terms of the movie—it's funny, but it's not a stunt. This is Oscar-caliber supporting work.

The Perez and Harrelson characters have an enthusiastic physical relationship, which is treated with refreshing directness. There are no "sex scenes" as we have come to expect them, but instead an easy, friendly warmth that is expressed, in her case, through comfort with nudity. Often in the movies you have the sensation that actors in love scenes have rehearsed to the point of choreography, so that every shot can be calculated down to the most subtle, teasing, backlit nuance. Here Perez and Harrelson create characters who know each other and enjoy one another.

Snipes's home life is more complicated; he's married (to Tyra Ferrell, who played Doughboy's mom in *Boyz N the Hood*), has kids, and is hustling basketball because his daytime jobs aren't paying the bills. He needs the money. He and Harrelson team up, fight, team up again, and the movie supplies the predictable sports formulas leading up to the big game. But even here it has surprises—and the payoff isn't exactly what we suspected. Here is a comedy of great high spirits, with an undercurrent of sadness and sweetness that makes it a lot better than the plot itself could possibly suggest.

White Mischief ★ ★ ★
R, 100 m., 1988

Sarah Miles (Alice), Joss Ackland (Broughton), John Hurt (Colville), Greta Scacchi (Diana),

Charles Dance (Erroll), Susan Fleetwood (Gwladys), Alan Dobie (Harragin), Hugh Grant (Hugh), Jacqueline Pearce (Idina), Catherine Neilson (June), Trevor Howard (Soames). Directed by Michael Radford. Produced by Simon Perry. Screenplay by Radford and Jonathan Gems, based on the book by James Fox.

In the years between the first and second world wars, the more affluent British settlers in Kenya developed a lifestyle that became famous for its luxury and scandalous for its decadence. In their so-called Happy Valley, on the slopes of the Aberdare mountains, where the climate was close to home, they built their ranches and villages, made a lot of money, and tried to ignore the war clouds gathering over Europe. Some of them worked hard and most of them partied hard, and as war grew closer their detachment seemed more and more of a scandal.

Then, on the eve of war, the settlement was rocked by a murder that is still one of the most famous crimes of the British Empire, the crime at the center of *White Mischief*. An older rancher, Sir Henry Jock Broughton (Joss Ackland) had returned from a trip to England with a wild young bride named Diana (Greta Scacchi). She had married for money, a fact Jock had few illusions about, but what he did not expect was that she would so quickly flaunt her cynicism in the colony. She fell under the power of the handsome young Earl of Erroll (Charles Dance), a shameless womanizer, and their affair scandalized the colony until the day of January 24, 1941, when the Earl was found shot dead in his car, not far from an exclusive club where he had last been seen with Diana.

Jock Broughton was charged with the murder, but eventually was acquitted, and the case remains officially unsolved to this day. The one survivor who might have been sure about the identity of the killer, Diana Broughton, died a few years ago. But the case lives on in British memory, partly because it occurred in a colony that was living in luxury while the homeland itself was enduring the Battle of Britain and the terrors of World War II.

White Mischief is an elegant, almost luxurious, retelling of the story of Jock, Diana, and the earl, filmed on location in Kenya at great expense, and forming a sort of companion piece to *Out of Africa*, which takes place in East Africa at the beginning of the same era but among much different sorts of people. In the movie, the period is lovingly restored—the clothes, the cars, the rambling architecture, the lifestyle that could not conceive that Kenya would ever be independent, and was scarcely able to even see racism, much less decry it. Happy Valley is seen as a society of narcissists, in love with their own beauty and idle charm, and existing primarily to drink and to gossip.

In this society, Jock is a figure of some dignity at first. Erect and proud in middle age, he is Establishment through and through. But he makes the mistake of falling in love with the beautiful young Diana, and he makes another mistake, too—he goes broke. Diana is carefree as the wind, and hardly even wants to hurt Jock's feelings. She is simply too selfish and irresponsible to think much about them. When the Earl of Erroll sees the opportunity for an entertaining affair, both he and Diana make the mistake of underestimating Jock—of pushing him too far, too publicly.

The film was directed by Michael Radford (who also made the recent version of *1984*), and he goes for atmosphere rather than plot. I think that is the right decision. A languorous scene at a party gradually trails down into a lazy, low-key orgy, and the tone is just right: These people are almost too comfortable to be perverted. Radford is especially good at finding the tensions in a party scene, where various couples are changing partners and not everybody likes it, but nobody misses it.

One of the keys to the movie's re-creation of Happy Valley is in the large supporting cast, including John Hurt as a rough-hewn local farmer who is also in love with Diana; Sarah Miles as a promiscuous local woman whose affairs feed the gossip mills; and the late Trevor Howard, in his last performance, as a local landowner who tries to give Jock some good advice. All of these people come together to create a genuinely interesting period piece, in which nobody is quite sure who shot the Earl of Erroll, but most people would agree he had it coming to him.

White Palace ★ ★ ★ ½
R, 103 m., 1990

Susan Sarandon (Nora Baker), James Spader (Max Baron), Jason Alexander (Neil), Kathy Bates (Rosemary), Eileen Brennan (Judy), Spiros Focas (George), Jeremy Piven (Kahn). Directed by Luis Mandoki and produced by Mark Rosenberg, Amy Robinson, and Griffin Dunne. Screenplay by Ted Tally and Alvin Sargent.

"I'm forty-three years old," she tells him. "On my next birthday I'm going to be forty-four."

"I'm twenty-seven," he says.

They look at each other, and then they fall into each other's arms, in a spontaneous expression of sexual passion. The moment gets a laugh, because we like it when movie characters allow their emotions to overcome them. But the underlying issue is more serious. This couple isn't "appropriate" for each other. A lot of people are made uncomfortable by May-December romances, especially when it's the woman who's the older party.

White Palace was billed as a Cinderella story like *Pretty Woman*. But there are some differences. This time, it's not a rich executive falling in love with a gorgeous hooker, but a young ad executive falling for an older woman who's a waitress down at the local hamburger joint. Also, there's some doubt about who stands to benefit most from the relationship: The young man, who is uptight and distant, or the older woman, who knows how to be honest and is also (as a song on the sound track reminds us) at her sexual prime.

The executive, played by James Spader, is told several times by women in the movie that he has beautiful eyes and is really good-looking. Neither the compliments nor much of anything else seem to reach him. He's shut down emotionally since his young wife was killed in an auto accident. The woman, played by Susan Sarandon, lives in a dump and hangs out in smoky bars after work, but she can reach him—first with sex, and then with an overall attraction that he finds mesmerizing.

But the movie isn't really about that attraction. It's a film on the subject of appropriateness. Spader is fascinated by this woman and wants to be with her, but he also feels it necessary to hide her from his upper-middle-class Jewish circle of family and friends. They would disapprove, he guesses, because of her background, her age, and her religion. So he lies and evades and avoids taking her to a friend's wedding, and when he finally does break down and take her to a family dinner, it's a disaster. That's partly because a few of the women at the party resent her—they see Spader as a prime catch to be matched with an appropriate single woman, not thrown away on a short-order waitress. But part of the blame is Sarandon's, too: She drinks too much and causes an unnecessary confrontation at the dinner table.

Why? Because she found out Spader was lying to her—that he didn't really want to invite her to the dinner, until she forced him into it. From that point the movie follows time-honored lines; she flees, he follows, etc. But before it falls into formula, *White Palace* has raised interesting questions about those romances that fall outside of socially approved formulas.

It is the easiest thing in the world to slide comfortably into an "appropriate" relationship with a partner who conforms with the tastes and prejudices of your social circle. Yet many people, nevertheless, find themselves in nonconformist relationships, and my guess is that the depth of feeling in those relationships is often greater. If your partner does not match society's definition of the sort of person you should be in love with, then presumably he or she fills some deeper need—in the words of a famous British beer ad, refreshes the parts others cannot reach.

That's the dilemma faced by Spader in *White Palace*. He has never met a woman who reaches him more deeply than Sarandon does. Not even his wife. Is it love? He doesn't know. It's need. It's compulsion. Yet she exists so far outside his social circle he doesn't want to let her in. He lives in an expensive apartment. She lives in a ramshackle house where, one day, her electricity is shut off. ("Isn't it a hoot being poor?" she asks.) The strength of the movie is when it deals with the subject of a nonconforming relationship. The best moments involve verbal bolts of lightning—comic insights that blindside us.

But the weakness of the film is when it falls into the same sappy romantic clichés as countless other love stories. The final scene in the movie, for example, is such a loathsome version of such an idiotic cliché that I couldn't believe my eyes. And yet there's a lot that's good in *White Palace*, involving the heart as well as the mind.

Who Framed Roger Rabbit ★ ★ ★ ★
PG, 103 m., 1988

Bob Hoskins (Eddie Valiant), Christopher Lloyd (Judge Doom), Joanna Cassidy (Dolores), Charles Fleischer (Roger's voice), Stubby Kaye (Marvin Acme). Directed by Robert Zemeckis and produced by Robert Watts and Frank Marshall. Screenplay by Jeffrey Price and Peter S. Seaman.

I stopped off at a hot dog stand before the screening of *Who Framed Roger Rabbit*, and ran into a couple of the other local movie critics. They said they were going to the same screening. I asked them what they'd heard about the film. They said they were going to see it for the second time in two days. That's the kind of word of mouth that money can't buy.

And *Who Framed Roger Rabbit* is the kind of movie that gets made once in a blue moon, because it represents an immense challenge to the filmmakers: They have to make a good movie while inventing new technology at the same time. Like *2001, Close Encounters,* and *E.T.,* this movie is not only a great entertainment, but a breakthrough in craftsmanship—the first film to convincingly combine real actors and animated cartoon characters in the same space in the same time and make it look real.

I've never seen anything like it before. Roger Rabbit and his cartoon comrades cast real shadows. They shake the hands and grab the coats and rattle the teeth of real actors. They change size and dimension and perspective as they move through a scene, and the camera isn't locked down in one place to make it easy, either—the camera in this movie moves around like it's in a 1940s thriller, and the cartoon characters look three-dimensional and seem to be occupying real space.

In a way, what you feel when you see a movie like this is more than appreciation. It's gratitude. You know how easy it is to make dumb, no-brainer action movies, and how incredibly hard it is to make a movie like this, where every minute of screen time can take days or weeks of work by the animators. You're glad they went to the trouble. The movie is a collaboration between the Disney studio and Steven Spielberg, the direction is by Robert *(Back to the Future)* Zemeckis, and the animation is by Raymond Williams. They made this a labor of love.

How did they do it? First they plotted every scene, shot by shot, so they knew where the live actors would be, and where the animated characters would be. Then they shot the live action, forcing actors like Bob Hoskins, the star, to imagine himself in a world also inhabited by cartoons (or "Toons," as the movie calls them). Then they laboriously went through the movie frame by frame, drawing in the cartoon characters. This is not a computer job. Real, living animators did this by hand, and the effort shows in moments like the zowie zoom shots where the camera hurtles at Roger Rabbit and then careens away, with the rabbit changing size and perspective in every frame.

But I'm making the movie sound like homework for a movie class. *Who Framed Roger Rabbit* is sheer, enchanted entertainment from the first frame to the last—a joyous, giddy, goofy celebration of the kind of fun you can have with a movie camera. The film takes place in Hollywood in 1947, in a world where humans and Toons exist side by side. The Toons in the movie include not only new characters like Roger Rabbit and his wife, the improbably pneumatic Jessica, but also established cartoon stars like Bugs Bunny, Betty Boop, Dumbo, Mickey Mouse, and both of the great ducks, Donald and Daffy (they do an act together as a piano duo).

The Toons live in Toontown, a completely animated world where the climax of the movie takes place, but most of the time they hang out in a version of Hollywood that looks like it was borrowed from a 1940s private-eye movie. The plot revolves around the murder of a movie tycoon, and when Roger Rabbit is framed for the murder, private eye Hoskins gets caught in the middle of the action. As plots go, this one will be familiar to anyone who has ever seen a hard-boiled '40s crime movie—except, of course, for the Toons.

The movie is funny, but it's more than funny, it's exhilarating. It opens with what looks like a standard studio cartoon (Mother goes shopping and leaves Roger Rabbit to baby-sit her little brat, who immediately starts causing trouble). This cartoon itself, seen apart from the movie, is a masterpiece; I can't remember the last time I laughed so hard at an animated short. But then, when a stunt goes wrong and the cartoon "baby" stalks off the set and lights a cigar and tells the human director to go to hell, we know we're in a new and special universe.

The movie is filled with throwaway gags, inside jokes, one-liners, and little pokes at the screen images of its cartoon characters. It is also oddly convincing, not only because of the craft of the filmmakers, but also because Hoskins and the other live actors have found the right note for their interaction with the Toons. Instead of overreacting or playing up their emotions cartoon-style, Hoskins and the others adopt a flat, realistic, matter-of-fact posture toward the Toons. They act as if they've been talking to animated rabbits for years.

One tricky question is raised by a movie like this: Is it for kids, or adults, or both? I think it's intended as a universal entertainment, like *E.T.* or *The Wizard of Oz,* aimed at all audiences. But I have a sneaky hunch that adults will appreciate it even more than kids, because they'll have a better appreciation of how difficult it was to make, and how effortlessly it succeeds. Kids will love it too—but instead of being amazed at how they got the rabbits in with the humans, they'll be wondering what adults are doing walking around inside a cartoon.

Whore ★ ★ ★
NC-17, 85 m., 1991

Theresa Russell (Liz), Benjamin Mouton (Blake), Antonio Fargas (Rasta), Sanjay (Indian), Michael Crabtree (First Man), John Diehl (Derelict), Ginger-Lynn Allen (Wounded Girl). Directed by Ken Russell and produced by Dan Ireland and Ronaldo Vasconcellos. Screenplay by Russell and Deborah Dalton.

"I'm a prostitute. That's what I do," quoth a woman in a story in the newspaper, reporting that televangelist Jimmy Swaggart was stopped by police while driving down the wrong side of the road, and was found to have a hooker in his car. The directness of the quote seemed refreshingly honest to me, and reminded me of Liz, the heroine of this movie.

She is a prostitute, too. That's what she does. *Whore* is the story of her professional life, told without adornment or sentimentalism or any of the phony romantic myths that Hollywood likes to bring to the oldest profession. This is the real stuff. Now that millions of people have sniffled and applauded for *Pretty Woman,* perhaps some of them would find it interesting to see what life might *really* be like for a character like the one played by Julia Roberts.

I enjoyed *Pretty Woman* enormously, but I didn't for a moment imagine it reflected anything real about the life of a prostitute. I was amused to learn that the movie has recently been edited into a cleaned-up version for the airlines, in which Richard Gere and Roberts are basically just good friends who happen to meet when she gives him directions. If they try to edit *Whore* for the airlines, they'll be left with a short subject.

The movie is based on a play called *Bondage,* written by a London taxi driver named David Hines, who based it on the stories told to him by hookers who hailed his cab late at night. It has been moved from London to Los Angeles, and the screenplay has been written by director Ken Russell and Deborah

Dalton, who produced a radio series on prostitution. They are at pains to show the life of their title character as dangerous, lonely, and violent. Even so, they give Liz, their heroine, one break: She isn't completely strung out on drugs.

Liz is played by Theresa Russell, the actress you call when you need great skill combined with great courage. Liz works the streets of L.A. with a knowledge won through hard experience, and often she talks directly into the camera, providing her rules of the road, which include: never kiss anybody, get the money first, use protection, and never get into a van unless you know what's in the back.

She knows the streets she works. She knows how to run through high-rise lobbies and downtown plazas to get away from people, she knows how to spot weirdos (some of the time), and she knows that the life is killing her. She originally got into prostitution as a way to escape from an abusive husband and support herself and her child. Now the child is in a foster home. The streets were dangerous and so she got involved with a pimp, and now the pimp is dangerous. She is essentially in bondage.

Her street knowledge is sad and wise. She used to like sex, until she realized most men bought her services, not for pleasure, but in anger. She sees the hate in their eyes. She understands prostitution sometimes isn't about sex at all, but about power. A man who feels powerless over women can spend some money and have power over her.

Russell plays Liz as a plucky woman, smart, not deceived, but terribly sad. Ken Russell (no relation) has made *Whore* as the other side of his 1984 film, *Crimes of Passion*. That film has its moments, but was essentially very silly, starring Kathleen Turner in a better performance than the screenplay deserved, as a woman who was a fashion designer by day and a call girl in the evening. *Whore* is not about a world where the heroine can do anything with her days except try to pull herself together after the night before.

Whore has been given the NC-17 rating. *Pretty Woman*, of course, got an R. Russell has complained that the ratings system is penalizing his movie because it tells the truth, after rewarding *Pretty Woman* for glamorizing prostitution. He may have a point, but then again *Pretty Woman* was about a character who lived in an R-rated world, and *Whore* is about a woman who lives in the real one.

Who's the Man ★ ★ ★
R, 90 m., 1993

Doctor Dre (Doctor Dre), Ed Lover (Ed Lover), Badja Djola (Lionel), Cheryl "Salt" James (Teesha Braxton), Jim Moody (Nick Crawford), Andre Blake (Lamar), Rozwill Young (Griles), Colin Quinn (Frankie Flynn). Directed by Ted Demme and produced by Charles Stettler and Maynell Thomas. Screenplay by Seth Greenland.

Who's the Man is a fresh, funny update of movies like *Cotton Comes to Harlem*—a comedy about a couple of very bad barbers who pass the police exam by accident, and turn out to be good at solving crimes. The movie stars long, tall Ed Lover and short, round Doctor Dre as characters with the same names, although to their friends they are "Before and After," and to crooks they look more like Abbott and Costello.

As the movie opens, they're partners on the last chair of a Harlem barbershop owned by Nick (Jim Moody), a neighborhood leader who has seen the block gradually taken over by dope dealers, who are themselves being replaced by real estate speculators. To Lover and Dre, these are not pressing concerns; they're more interested in inventing bizarre new hairstyles, which they claim to have seen on famous former clients.

Nick finally has to fire them; they're getting so many complaints that none of the customers will let them anywhere near their hair. Nick's better idea: They should take the police exam. It's a multiple choice, which they both take by spelling "abacadaba" in the a-b-c-d spaces. They pass, to their amazement, and become the two most inept recruits in the history of the force.

The movie was directed by Ted Demme (nephew of Jonathan), and has a sharp look and feel; there's a good ear for dialogue, a nice comic rhythm, and performances by Lover and Dre that could quite possibly make them into a movie comedy team. The film seems ripe for sequels.

Most of the humor grows out of human nature. There's a funny running gag involving a duty sergeant's determination to keep Doctor Dre from ever eating another doughnut, and another feud involving the sergeant's refusal to call anyone "Doctor" unless he has a medical degree. I also enjoyed the gags after the cops take their beaten-up squad car into a storefront customizing shop, where it's turned into a street rod, with surprising results for the next cops who drive it.

Beneath the humor, though, is an undercurrent of seriousness, mostly represented by the character of Nick, whose barber shop represents continuity and responsibility on a street where drugs are taking over. In one scene, he threatens a drug dealer while reminding him that he gave him haircuts when he was a little boy. In another, he warns local residents that gentrification can be a danger, as neighborhoods grow too expensive for the present inhabitants. The movie's bad guy is a developer who is trying to run Nick out and buy up the entire neighborhood—although perhaps not in order to build the condos he keeps talking about.

Seth Greenland's screenplay includes a running commentary on countless television shows (did Redd Foxx actually fake his own death to outsmart the IRS?), and there's a payoff at the end inspired by "The Beverly Hillbillies." A lot of the humor, though, seems to spring from the personalities and relationships of Doctor Dre and Ed Lover themselves, who, like Cheech and Chong and Laurel and Hardy and the teams mentioned in the movie, have an easy chemistry. My notion is that *Who's the Man* could turn out to be a star-maker.

Wide Sargasso Sea ★ ★ ★ ½
NC-17, 100 m., 1993

Karina Lombard (Antoinette Cosway), Nathaniel Parker (Rochester), Rachel Ward (Annette Cosway), Michael York (Paul Mason), Martine Beswicke (Aunt Cora), Claudia Robinson (Christophene). Directed by John Duigan and produced by Jan Sharp. Screenplay by Sharp, Carole Angier, and Duigan.

She is a beautiful woman who lives caught in a web of superstition and fear, on an island in the sun. He is a rakish, handsome young man from England, out to visit his friends and perhaps make his fortune. A marriage is arranged between them—a marriage no less attractive because she is the mistress of a great estate. At first, love is the only thing that matters. Then shadows begin to fall, caused by their own weaknesses, and also by the black magic of voodoo.

This is the sort of story outline you might expect to find on the back of a paperback romance novel, one of those books with a heaving bosom on the cover, and a dark tower with a light in one window. But the Gothic tradition has inspired all sorts of writers, perhaps because it provides a shortcut to our deepest yearnings and fears, and this is in fact the plot of *Wide Sargasso Sea*, a novel by Jean Rhys, the British novelist whose reputation continues to hold strong among those lonely few who actually read good fiction, instead of simply buying it.

Rhys got the idea for her novel from *Jane Eyre*, the novel by Charlotte Brontë—or perhaps she got it from the classic 1943 movie with Joan Fontaine and Orson Welles (intoning, from a great height in a very deep voice, "You are a strange girl, Jane Eyre"). Both novel and movie contain the same mystery, although not much is made of it: Who was the first Mrs. Rochester?

Rochester is, of course, the brooding, possibly evil, undeniably attractive man who finally marries Jane Eyre, after sending her into fits of trepidation by his very presence. True to the Gothic tradition, he first appears menacing and dangerous, towering over her in fact and especially in her imagination. Only in the end does he consent to fulfill her romantic longings. And all the time, lurking beneath the surface of the story, is the offstage presence of the first wife, the woman he married in the Caribbean, the woman nobody ever speaks about.

Wide Sargasso Sea tells her story. The movie ends some time before the events in *Jane Eyre* begin. The first Mrs. Rochester, we learn, is named Antoinette Cosway (Katrina Lombard). She is a beautiful, sultry, high-spirited young mulatto woman of the islands, living on a plantation she has inherited, running it with slaves and ancient family retainers, including the sinister Christophene (Claudia Robinson), whose visions and warnings are inspired by voodoo.

When Rochester (Nathaniel Parker) arrives from Europe, he is ignorant of the island ways, but he has a certain charm and she finds him funny. One of the film's best scenes has her laughing merrily, after he literally passes out while meeting her for the first time. He seems innocent, and harmless enough. She likes him.

At first their romance is simple and ideal, based on physical attraction and the exuberance of being young. Later, after they marry, things begin to change. He is not so nice, and not so simple. And although she is strong, the laws and customs of the time give all the power to men, so that he owns her as effectively as if she, too, were a slave. Gradually, worn down by his betrayal and the sly mind games he plays (and perhaps the victim of voodoo), she goes subtly mad.

Wide Sargasso Sea was directed by John Duigan, an Australian director not familiar to me until I saw *Flirting*, one of the best films of 1992. That was a film about a romance between two kids at boarding schools. This film, so different, shows him once again able to find the right tone for his material, so that scenes work not simply because they are technically right, but because they feel right. He is particularly forthright about the eroticism in his story; the film has been rated NC-17, which will hurt its box-office chances, but it needs its frankness to deal with the powerful erotic drives that are just beneath the surface of its mannered society.

I have rarely seen a film that more effectively conveyed the climate it takes place in; the island is sunny and humid, the nights warm and damp, and sweat is allowed to glisten on the skins of the actors, instead of being mopped up and dusted down by the makeup artists. The hothouse atmosphere permeates every scene, creating an unhealthy climate in which young love is perverted, promises become lies, and jealousy is the strongest emotion.

There have been a lot of books and movies continuing or extending popular stories; I even saw a book the other day claiming to tell what happened to Huck Finn after Mark Twain's book left off. The Rhys novel and this film, however, hardly need *Jane Eyre* in order to exist. The story is complete in itself—sad, haunted, inevitable.

Widows' Peak ★ ★ ★ ½
PG, 101 m., 1994

Mia Farrow (Miss O'Hare), Joan Plowright (Mrs. Doyle Counihan), Natasha Richardson (Edwina), Adrian Dunbar (Godfrey), Jim Broadbent (Clancy), Anne Kent (Miss Grubb), John Kavanagh (Canon). Directed by John Irvin and produced by Jo Manuel. Screenplay by Hugh Leonard.

Widows' Peak is another one of those sly, witty, quietly ribald comedies that started coming out of Ireland in the early 1990s. Set in the 1920s in a village named Kilshannon, it tells the story of a tightly knit group of widows and a stranger who shakes things up. The movie does, it turns out, have a plot, and even a surprise twist ending. But they're not really the point: *Widows' Peak* is more about sharp-edged humor and barbed tongues and women who maintain a façade of perfect respectability while getting up to all sorts of mischief.

The widows of the title live in comfy cottages all clustered together on a hill outside of town. And in these years right after World War I, which took a toll of a generation of young men, there are a lot of widows. They are ruled over by a dowager named Mrs. Doyle Counihan (Joan Plowright), who is the arbiter of manners and the social queen bee. She has taken under her special protection the one spinster in the area, Miss O'Hare (Mia Farrow), who seems perfectly harmless until she is aroused—which, one day, she most certainly is.

When a new widow named Edwina Broome (Natasha Richardson) moves into the area, Miss O'Hare is immediately hostile. (At a tea party to welcome the newcomer, when Mrs. Broome is unwise enough to say that her late British husband had once liked to shoot in Ireland, Miss O'Hare snaps, "What did he shoot? Irishmen?")

Mrs. Doyle Counihan cannot understand why her protégé is so unfriendly to the newcomer. Mrs. Counihan sees Mrs. Broome in an entirely different light, as a possible bride for her forty-ish, hapless son Godfrey (Adrian Dunbar). And Godfrey is intrigued, too, although on a picnic he is shocked by Mrs. Broome's language and her startlingly open-minded ideas about courtship.

We get to meet the others in the village, especially a likable local dentist named Clancy (Jim Broadbent). And as days add up into weeks, the battle lines are drawn between the sophisticated Mrs. Broome and the intense, spiteful Miss O'Hare.

If *Widows' Peak* existed only on the levels I have described, and ended simply by resolving this plot, that would be enough. Like such other Irish films as *The Snapper*, *Hear My Song*, *Into the West*, and *The Crying Game*, it uses understated humor and fluent, witty speech; it's a delight to listen to, as it gradually reveals how eccentric these apparently respectable people really are. But there is more to it, a good deal more, which I will not reveal, even to hint at, because that would be spoiling the fun.

The screenplay for the movie was originally written by the playwright Hugh Leonard after a conversation with the actress Maureen O'Sullivan, who said she regretted never having appeared in a movie with her daughter, Farrow. That was some fifteen years ago; this production casts Farrow in the part originally intended for her mother, and Richardson in what was once the Farrow part.

The casting works; sparks fly the moment

the two women first see each other on the screen, and one of the most entertaining elements in the film is the way Farrow's Miss O'Hare is fearlessly willing to cause scenes—to insult this newcomer in public. There is always something funny about rudeness (it breaks laws and tension at the same time), and here Leonard's dialogue brings it to a fine pitch. This is a movie, like many of the classic British comedies of the 1950s, in which everyone on the screen is essentially nutty as a fruitcake, but we enjoy them so much we hope they never catch on.

Wild at Heart ★ ★ ½
R, 126 m., 1990

Nicolas Cage (Sailor Ripley), Laura Dern (Lula Pace Fortune), Diane Ladd (Mariette Fortune), Willem Dafoe (Bobby Peru), Isabella Rossellini (Perdita Durango), Harry Dean Stanton (Johnnie Farragut), Crispin Glover (Dell), Grace Zabriskie (Juana). Directed by David Lynch and produced by Monty Montgomery, Steve Golin, and Joni Sighvatsson. Screenplay by Lynch.

There is something inside of me that resists the films of David Lynch. I am aware of it, I admit to it, but I cannot think my way around it. I sit and watch his films and am aware of his energy, his visual flair, his flashes of wit. But as the movie rolls along, something grows inside of me—an indignation, an unwillingness, a resistance. At the end of both *Blue Velvet* and *Wild at Heart*, I felt angry, as if a clever con man had tried to put one over on me.

My taste is in the minority. *Blue Velvet* (1986) was hailed as one of the best films of the decade. Lynch's "Twin Peaks" was a cult hit on television. Now comes *Wild at Heart*, which won the Palme d'Or at the 1990 Cannes Film Festival, to great cheers and many boos, some of the latter from me. I do not think this is the best film that played at Cannes that year (what about Depardieu in *Cyrano?*) and I do not even, in fact, think it is a very good film. There is something repulsive and manipulative about it, and even its best scenes have the flavor of a kid in the school yard, trying to show you pictures you don't feel like looking at.

The movie is lurid melodrama, soap opera, exploitation, put-on, and self-satire. It deals in several scenes of particularly offensive violence, and tries to excuse them by juvenile humor: It's all a joke, you see, and so if the violence offends you, you didn't get the joke. Well, violence in itself doesn't offend me. But *Wild at Heart* doesn't have the nerve to just be violent, it has to build in its excuses.

Take, for example, an opening scene where the hero (Nicolas Cage) is attacked by a black man on a staircase at a party. The man is a killer hired by the evil mother (Diane Ladd) of Cage's girlfriend (Laura Dern). He pulls a knife on Cage, whose character is the local version of Elvis Presley crossed with James Dean and Tab Hunter. Cage disarms him, and then smashes him to a pulp, viciously and with great thoroughness, taking the man's hair in his hand and pounding his skull violently against the marble floor until the bones crack and blood spatters and the man is dead. Then Cage staggers to his feet, steadies himself on the handrail, lights a cigarette, and glares up from beneath lowered brows, gasping for breath, the cigarette dangling from his lip.

Some people laugh when they see this scene. They like the way the look is overplayed—Cage looks like a villain in a silent movie. I didn't laugh. I saw the payoff as Lynch's attempt to defuse the violence—to excuse a racially charged scene of unapologetic malevolence. There are other such scenes in the movie. The scene, for example, when the clerk gets his hand blown off with a shotgun, and crawls around on the floor looking for it, talking about how they can sew hands back on these days. Lynch cuts to a dog running from the building with the bloody hand in its mouth. This shot is lifted from Kurosawa's *Yojimbo*, but not many people in the audience will read it as an homage.

And then there's the scene where the villain (Willem Dafoe) blows off his own head with a shotgun, and the head flies through the air and bounces along on the ground. This was the scene that got to the MPAA's film rating board, which threatened *Wild at Heart* with an X. But the movie qualifies for an R rating by adding a little gunsmoke to the shot, so that you can't see the head coming off quite so clearly.

The violence aside, *Wild at Heart* also exercises the consistent streak of misogyny in Lynch's work. He has a particular knack for humiliating women in his films, and this time the primary target is Diane Ladd, as Mariette Fortune, the town seductress and vamp. The way this woman is photographed, the things she is given to do, and the dialogue she has to pronounce are equally painful to witness. Not even Hitchcock was ever this cruel to an actress. Laura Dern is Ladd's real-life daughter, and in the movie she, too, is subjected to the usual humiliations. Ever since I witnessed the humiliation of Isabella Rossellini in *Blue Velvet*, I've wondered if there is an element in Lynch's art that goes beyond filmmaking; a personal factor in which he uses his power as a director to portray women in a particularly hurtful and offensive light.

All of these wounds and maimings are told within the framework of a parody, in which Dern and Cage are young lovers on the run from unspeakable secrets in the past, and the vengeance of Dern's mother and her hired goons. It's a road picture with a 1950s T-Bird convertible as the chariot, and lots of throwaway gags about Cage's snakeskin jacket, his "personal symbol of individuality." Cage does a conscious imitation of Presley in all of his dialogue, and even bursts into song a couple of times, delivering "Love Me Tender" from the hood of the car in the big climax.

I've seen the movie twice now. I liked it less the second time. Take away the surprises and you can see the method more clearly. Like *Blue Velvet*, this is a film without the courage to declare its own darkest fantasies. Lynch wraps his violence in humor, not as a style, but as a strategy. Luis Buñuel, the late and gifted Spanish surrealist, made films as cheerfully perverted and decadent as anything Lynch has ever dreamed of, but he had the courage to declare himself. Lynch seems to be doing a Bunuel script with a Jerry Lewis rewrite. He is a good director, yes. If he ever goes ahead and makes a film about what's really on his mind, instead of hiding behind sophomoric humor and the cop-out of "parody," he may realize the early promise of his *Eraserhead*. But he likes the box office prizes that go along with his pop satires, and so he makes dishonest movies like this one. Understand that it's not the violence I mind. It's the sneaky excuses.

Willie and Phil ★ ★ ★
R, 116 m., 1980

Michael Ontkean (Willie), Margot Kidder (Jeannette), Ray Sharkey (Phil), Jan Miner (Mrs. Kaufman), Tom Brennan (Mr. Kaufman), Julie Bovasso (Mrs. D'Amico), Louis Guss (Mr. D'Amico), Kathleen Maguire (Mrs. Sutherland). Directed and written by Paul Mazursky and produced by Mazursky and Tony Ray.

Willie and Phil meet after a screening of Truffaut's *Jules and Jim*, which is a movie about two good friends and how they both fall in love with the same woman, who becomes the third good friend. Shortly after they see the movie, in Greenwich Village in 1970, Willie and Phil meet Jeannette, and then the three of them spend the 1970s working out their own version of a triangle.

If Paul Mazursky's *Willie and Phil* is supposed to be a psychologically plausible telling of this story, then it doesn't work. The movie gives away its own game right at the beginning, with the reference to *Jules and Jim*. These aren't real people in this movie; they're characters. They don't inhabit life, they inhabit Mazursky's screenplay—which takes them on a guided tour of the cults, fads, human potential movements, and alternative lifestyles of the decade during which zucchini replaced Faulkner as the most popular subject on campus.

But I don't think *Willie and Phil* was intended to work on a realistic level, or that we're intended to believe that Willie, Phil, and Jeannette are making free choices throughout the movie. In a subtle, understated sort of way, Mazursky is giving us a movie that hovers between a satirical revue and a series of lifestyle vignettes. The characters in his movie are almost exhausted by the end of the decade (weren't we all?). Not only have they experimented with various combinations of commitments to one another, but they've also tried out most of the popular 1970s belief systems.

Willie (Michael Ontkean) is a high school teacher as the movie opens, but he wants to be more, to feel deeply, to think on more exalted levels, and his journey through the decade takes him into radicalism, back to the earth, and all the way to India for lessons in meditation. Phil (Ray Sharkey) says he wants love and security, but he holds himself at arm's length from Jeannette and other possible sources of love. Unable to communicate, he channels all of his energy into making it in the communications industries. Jeannette (Margot Kidder) . . . well, what does she want? To love, to be loved, not to be possessed, to be free, to commit, but not to be trapped, to . . . have kids? A career? Willie? Phil?

I think Mazursky's suggesting something interesting about the 1970s. It was a decade without a consuming passion, without an overall subject or tone. Every decade from the 1920s to the 1960s had an overriding theme, at least in our collective national imagination, but in the 1970s we went on life-style shopping trips, searching for an impossible combination of life choices that would be morally good, politically correct, personally entertaining, and outperform the market—all at once.

And what were we left with in the 1980s? Confusion, vague apprehension, lack of faith in belief systems, EPA mileage estimates, megavitamins as the last blameless conspicuous consumption, and, echoing somewhere in the back of our minds, Peggy Lee singing "Is That All There Is?" How'd we get stuck? Why'd we wind up with a sense of impending doom when we tried every possible superficial substitute for profound change? Mazursky finds this note and strikes it in *Willie and Phil*, and that's what's best about his movie.

But like the decade itself, *Willie and Phil* is not completely substantial or satisfying. What redeems it, curiously, are the scenes involving Willie's Jewish parents, Phil's Italian parents, and Jeannette's Southern mother. Their scenes are reactions to what's happening to their kids in the 1970s, and they work like field trips from other decades. The parents observe, try to understand, are baffled, react with resentment, anger, love, confusion. I loved it when the Italian mother, trying to figure out how Jeannette was going to sleep with her boyfriend in the house of her ex-husband while the ex-husband bunked downstairs and the parents took the guest room, got up, said it was all just too complicated for her, and left for the airport. That's sort of the motif for this movie.

Willie Wonka and the Chocolate Factory
★ ★ ★ ★
G, 98 m., 1971

Gene Wilder (Willie Wonka), Jack Albertson (Grandpa Joe), Peter Ostrum (Charlie), Michael Bollner (Augustus Gloop), Aubrey Wood (Mr. Bill), Gunter Meissner (Mr. Slugwork). Directed by Mel Stuart and produced by Stan Margulies and David L. Wolper. Screenplay by Roald Dahl.

Kids are not stupid. They are among the sharpest, cleverest, most eagle-eyed creatures on God's Earth, and very little escapes their notice. You may not have observed that your neighbor is still using his snow tires in mid-July, but every four-year-old on the block has, and kids pay the same attention to detail when they go to the movies. They don't miss a thing, and they have an instinctive contempt for shoddy and shabby work. I make this observation because nine out of ten children's movies are stupid, witless, and display contempt for their audiences, and that's why kids hate them. Is that all parents want from kids' movies? That they not have anything bad in them? Shouldn't they have something good in them—some life, imagination, fantasy, inventiveness, something to tickle the imagination? If a movie isn't going to do your kids any good, why let them watch it? Just to kill a Saturday afternoon? That shows a subtle kind of contempt for a child's mind, I think.

All of this is preface to a simple statement: *Willie Wonka and the Chocolate Factory* is probably the best film of its sort since *The Wizard of Oz*. It is everything that family movies usually claim to be, but aren't: Delightful, funny, scary, exciting, and, most of all, a genuine work of imagination. *Willie Wonka* is such a surely and wonderfully spun fantasy that it works on all kinds of minds, and it is fascinating because, like all classic fantasy, it is fascinated with itself.

It's based on the well-known Roald Dahl children's book, and it was financed by the Quaker Oats Company as an experiment in providing high-quality family entertainment. It succeeds. It doesn't cut corners and go for cheap shortcuts like Disney. It provides a first-rate cast (Gene Wilder as the compulsively distrustful chocolate manufacturer, Jack Albertson as the game old grandfather), a first-rate production, and—I keep coming back to this—genuine imagination.

The story, like all good fantasies, is about a picaresque journey. Willie Wonka is the world's greatest chocolate manufacturer, and he distributes five golden passes good for a trip through his factory and a lifetime supply of chocolate. Each pass goes to a kid, who may bring an adult along, and our hero Charlie (a poor but honest newsboy who supports four grandparents and his mother) wins the last one.

The other four kids are hateful in one way or another, and come to dreadful ends. One falls into the chocolate lake and is whisked into the bowels of the factory. He shouldn't have been a pig. Another is vain enough to try Wonka's new teleportation invention, and winds up six inches tall—but the taffy-pulling machine will soon have him back to size, right? If these fates seem a little gruesome to you, reflect that all great children's tales are a little gruesome, from the Brothers Grimm to Alice to Snow White, and certainly not excluding Mother Goose. Kids are not sugar and spice, not very often, and they appreciate the poetic justice when a bad kid gets what's coming to him.

Wind ★ ★ ★
PG-13, 126 m., 1992

Matthew Modine (Will Parker), Jennifer Grey (Kate Bass), Cliff Robertson (Morgan Weld), Jack Thompson (Jack Neville), Stellan Skargsard (Joe Heiser), Rebecca Miller (Abigail Weld), Ned Vaughn (Charley Moore). Directed by Carroll Ballard and produced by Mata Yamamoto and Tom Luddy. Screenplay by Rudy Wurlitzer and Mac Gudgeon.

I have always thought of the America's Cup as an event where rich people in blue blazers sit around getting drunk and eating chowder, while weird-looking sailboats are manned by beach bums trying to make their aging millionaire skippers look good. *Wind,* a new movie about the America's Cup races, does not altogether dispel my notion, but it places the focus out on the water instead of ashore, and it contains some of the most exciting sailing footage I can imagine.

The movie spans two races, as seen through the eyes of tanned, rugged Will Parker (Matthew Modine), a good helmsman who has been hired by a self-made millionaire (Cliff Robertson) to lead his crew. Parker's girlfriend Kate (Jennifer Grey) is an equally skilled sailor, but after Will and Kate smooch too much during practice sessions, she's thrown off the crew. Will grouches but goes along, and Kate leaves him in anger, only to team up with an eccentric designer who believes boats would go faster if they were designed using airplane principles.

This is not your average sports movie-type romance, especially since Will teams up with the millionaire's daughter (Rebecca Miller), and eventually all four of them—Will, Kate, the designer, and the daughter—settle in the middle of the Nevada desert and decide to build their own boat from scratch.

The sports rivalry in the movie isn't standard, either. The first race is won by an Australian (Jack Thompson), who then becomes the guy to beat in the next race—but Thompson isn't depicted as a villain; he's simply a good sportsman. That means *Wind* is really about racing, instead of being about personalities. It simply abandons most of the clichés associated with movies like this.

The movie was directed by Carroll Ballard, who has made a specialty out of stories about men and nature. His credits include two great films, *The Black Stallion* and *Never Cry Wolf,* and here again he shows a man using his intelligence and his love of nature to try to prove something. The movie has three sensational race sequences, so well photographed by John Toll that we have the sensation we're able to float effortlessly a few feet away from the competing boats and see everything. There are shots and camera angles here so spectacular they amazed me; knowing what I know about cameras and photography, I wasn't able to figure out how the cinematographer got the shot.

Ballard knows a lot of people may not understand the mechanics of sail races, and so he does a clever thing. He supplies an Australian sportscaster who narrates some of the action, and he also uses computer simulations to explain things: how a boat can tack into the wind, for example, or what a "wind shadow" is. This information is communicated painlessly, so that by the final race we know enough strategy to understand what's at stake, and why.

I also like the character of Heiser (Stellan Skargsard), an obsessed European airplane designer who lives as a recluse in the desert and talks the others into accepting his yacht design. As the four of them team up, the millionaire's daughter raises the money while Kate and Heiser go through the motions of romance, and we realize Kate and Will are still in love. This situation is presented by Ballard without being belabored, and that's what's intriguing about it: The tensions are left hanging, so they continue to interest us, instead of being resolved in a lot of standard dialogue.

The real reason to see this movie, though, is because it makes a big yacht race seem so glorious, such grand adventure. Ballard is a former cinematographer with a knack for visualizing the outdoors. Seeing *Wind,* I was reminded of the black stallion approaching the boy in the surf, or the amazing scene in *Never Cry Wolf* where a man found himself surrounded by a vast sea of buffalo. The experience here is just as exhilarating.

Wings of Desire ★ ★ ★ ★
NO MPAA RATING, 130 m., 1988

Bruno Ganz (Damiel), Solveig Dommartin (Marion), Otto Sander (Cassiel), Curt Bois (Homer), Peter Falk (Himself). Directed by Wim Wenders and written by Wenders and Peter Handke.

In notes that he wrote after directing *Wings of Desire,* Wim Wenders reflected that it would be terrible to be an angel: "To live for an eternity and to be present all the time. To live with the essence of things—not to be able to raise a cup of coffee and drink it, or really touch somebody." In his film, this dilemma becomes the everyday reality of two angels, who move through Berlin observing people, listening, reflecting, caring. They can see and hear, but are cut off from the senses of touch, taste, and smell. Human life appears to them as if it were a movie.

The angels look like two ordinary men, with weary and kind faces. They can move through the air free of gravity, but in all other respects they appear to the camera to be just as present as the human characters in a scene. Their role is a little unclear. They watch. They listen. Sometimes, when they are moved by the plight of a human they care about, they are able to stand close to that person and somehow exude a sense of caring or love, which seems to be vaguely perceived by the human, to whom it can provide a moment of hope or release.

The angel we are most concerned with in the film is Damiel, played by Bruno Ganz, that everyman of German actors whose face is expressive because it is so lived-in, so tired. He moves slowly through the city, hearing snatches of conversation, seeing moments of lives, keenly aware of his existence as a perpetual outsider. One day he comes across Marion (Solveig Dommartin), a trapeze artist, and is moved by her sadness. He helps her in the ways that he can, but eventually he realizes that he does not want to end her suffering so much as to share it.

That is the problem with being an angel. He can live forever, but in a sense, he can never live. To an angel, a being who exists in eternity, human lives must seem to be over in a brief flash of time, in a wink of history, and yet during our brief span, at least humans are really alive—to grow, to learn, to love, to suffer, to drink a cup of coffee, while an angel can only imagine the warmth of the cup, the aroma of the coffee, the taste, the feel.

Damiel determines to renounce immortality and accept human life with all its transience and pain. And in that act of renunciation, he makes one of the most poignant and romantic of gestures. He is accepting the limitations not only of his loved one, but of life itself.

Wings of Desire was directed by Wenders (whose credits include *Paris, Texas* and *The American Friend*), and cowritten by Wenders and Peter Handke, the German novelist who also wrote and directed *The Left-Handed Woman.* They are not interested in making some kind of soft-hearted, sentimental Hollywood story in which harps play and everybody feels good afterward.

Their film is set in divided Berlin, most insubstantial of cities because its future always seems deferred. Most of the film is shot in black and white, the correct medium for this story, because color would be too realistic to reflect the tone of their fable. Many of the best moments in the film have no particular dramatic purpose, but are concerned only with showing us what it is like to be forever an observer. Ganz walks quietly across empty bridges. He looks into vacant windows. He sits in a library and watches people as they read. He is there, and he is not there. The sterility of his existence almost makes us understand the choice of Lucifer in renouncing heaven in order to be plunged into hell, where at least he could suffer, and therefore, feel.

This is the kind of film that needs to be seen in a meditative frame of mind. It doesn't much matter what happens in the story, but it does matter how well we are able to empathize with it, how successfully we are able to enter into the state of mind of an angel. Leaving the movie, I reflected that sometimes we are bored by life, and feel as if nothing exciting is happening. But if we had spent eternity as an angel, observing life without feeling it, and then were plunged into a human body with its physical senses, think what a roar and flood of sensations would overwhelm us! It would be almost too much to bear. It would be everyday life.

Winter of Our Dreams ★ ★ ★
R, 89 m., 1983

Judy Davis (Lou), Bryan Brown (Rob), Cathy Downes (Gretel), Baz Luhrmann (Pete). Directed by John Duigan and produced by Richard Mason. Screenplay by Duigan.

Rob runs a bookstore and lives in one of those houses where the bedrooms hang under the eaves; one false move and you dash your brains out onto the living room floor below. Lou is a prostitute who lives on the streets. They both once had a friend named Lisa, back in the late 1960s when they were all part of the Australian protest movement. Now Lisa has been murdered, and Lou, searching for a meaning in her life or death, runs into Rob again. She thinks he's a trick. He thinks she's an interesting, complicated person who deserves his attention. I think she's closer to the mark.

This is the setup for *Winter of Our Dreams,* an Australian film starring two popular Aus-

tralian new wave actors, Judy Davis (of *My Brilliant Career*) and Bryan Brown (of *Breaker Morant* and TV's "A Town Like Alice"). Davis brought a kind of wiry, feisty intelligence to *My Brilliant Career,* playing an Australian farm woman who rather felt she would do things her own way. She's wonderful this time, in a completely different role as an insecure, distrustful, skinny street waif. It's Brown who is the trouble. Maybe it's the performance, maybe it's the character, or maybe it's Brown, but I've rarely seen a more closed-off person on the screen. When the story calls for him to reach out to Davis, we feel he's holding his nose. Sometimes there are movies where the leading actors cannot stand one another (Ken Wahl said he was only able to kiss Bette Midler in *Jinxed!* by thinking of his dog), and maybe Brown just couldn't express the feelings that were in the script. But I was never really convinced that he cared for Davis.

That's less of a handicap later in the movie, however, when the Brown character is *required* to draw back from any involvement with this pathetic street kid. The relationships in *Winter of Our Dreams* are very tangled—maybe too tangled. Brown's character has been married for six years to Gretel (Cathy Downes), a handsome, smart woman who has a lover. They have an open marriage, and there's no objection when Brown brings Davis home for the night. Davis, taking this all in, can't understand it. Trying to learn how to feel again, she can't understand why anyone would deliberately trivialize his feelings. The key passages in the film involve Brown's discovery that Davis is a heroin junkie, and then her tortured period of drug withdrawal. They are both pretending to care for one another, and after Davis gets straight maybe Brown will become her lover, while his wife disappears into the woodwork. That is not, however, even remotely in the cards, and there's a painful scene during a party at Brown's house, where Davis realizes that Brown is *very* married, open marriage or not.

There seem to be two movements in *Winter of Our Dreams.* One is Davis's movement away from the cynicism and despair of prostitution, and back toward an ability to care for another person. The other is Brown's initial concern for this girl, and then his retreat back into his shell. Davis performs her movement magnificently. Brown didn't win my sympathy for a moment. What just barely saves this film is the fact that we're not *supposed* to like the Brown character. As for Davis, she's a wonder.

Wise Guys ★ ★ ★ ½
R, 92 m., 1986

Danny DeVito (Harry Valentini), Joe Piscopo (Moe Dickstein), Harvey Keitel (Bobby DiLea), Ray Sharkey (Marco), Dan Hedaya (Tony Castelo), Captain Lou Albano (Fixer), Julie Bovasso (Lil Dickstein), Patti LuPone (Wanda Valentini). Directed by Brian DePalma and produced by Aaron Russo. Screenplay by George Gallo.

Wise Guys tells the story of Harry and Moe, two low-level hoodlums who become the toys of the Mafia gods. They're just ordinary guys, working stiffs who live next door to each other in houses tucked under a New Jersey expressway. They dream of the day when they'll be assigned to really important jobs, like shaking down widows. But when the godfather holds his morning staff meetings in the back booth of his favorite restaurant, these guys get humiliated: Their job is to pick up the boss's laundry.

The two friends are played by Joe Piscopo, as Moe Dickstein, and Danny DeVito, as Harry Valentini. They move with easy familiarity through the world of the mob; sometimes the little guys get the best view. They all know so much, in fact, that when they screw up, when they do something that is very, very bad, they don't even have to be told they're dead. It goes without saying.

Here's what they do. They go to the track with Fixer, the mob's chief enforcer (played by Captain Lou Albano, the gigantic professional wrestler). Their assignment is to place a bet for Tony, the boss (Dan Hedaya). DeVito gets to thinking, which is always dangerous. The boss has been betting on the wrong horses for weeks. They could be heroes by placing the money on the nose of the horse that DeVito knows will win. Better still, they could get rich by betting on the winning horse and then letting Fixer and the boss believe the money was lost.

This is a great plan, except unfortunately, this is the one day that the boss's horse comes in first, and so DeVito and Piscopo have lost the boss hundreds of thousands of dollars. This is bad. It is so bad that DeVito is plunged into a lobster tank at the restaurant, and Piscopo is suspended over a pit full of attack dogs. Then the boss thinks up their *real* punishment: He will secretly assign each one of them to kill the other one. It's here that the movie really gets rolling. The two wise guys hit the road, looking for safety, looking for a mob elder statesman who can bargain for their safety. And we begin to realize that the movie is filled with an inexhaustible supply of great character actors, that we are going to meet a lot of people in this story, and they are all going to be memorable.

In New Jersey, there was Hedaya as the boss, clean-shaven and slick, and Albano as Fixer, in one of the year's great supporting roles. Then, in Atlantic City, we meet the casino manager Bobby DiLea, played by the great Harvey Keitel. He doesn't want anyone to get killed in his casino, and once Harry and Moe check into the penthouse suite (using Fixer's stolen credit card), he knows he is going to have to be very lucky to keep that from happening. Very lucky, or very weird.

Wise Guys is an abundant movie, filled with ideas and gags and great characters. It never runs dry. It never has the desperation of so many gangster comedies, which seem to be marching over the same tired ground. This movie was made with joy, and you can feel it in the sense of all the actors working at the top of their form.

The movie was directed by Brian DePalma, who specializes in movies about crime and whose credits include *Scarface, Body Double,* and *Dressed to Kill.* I admired all those movies—indeed, I think DePalma is one of the best stylists at work right now—but I wouldn't have suspected that he had this comedy in him. His early credits include such problematic comedies as *Hi, Mom!* (which was one of Robert De Niro's first movie jobs), but here's this polished, confident comedy that never seems to step wrong.

A lot of the credit goes to Piscopo and De-Vito, who develop an instant, easy camaraderie. I really did feel that they care for each other. I liked the way DeVito waved his arms and demanded attention, and the way Piscopo played his slightly slower, sweeter, dumber pal. DeVito has been good in other recent movies (such as *Romancing the Stone*), but this is the first time he's been at the top of the cast, and really free to show his stuff. He is inspired: This could be a new beginning for his career. Piscopo, from "Saturday Night Live," has worked less in the movies, and has always seemed in search of a character. Here he finds one.

And then there's that gallery of supporting performances. Albano is so fearsome as Fixer that I found myself laughing at a time I don't think was supposed to be funny: There's a reference to "Mrs. Fixer." Keitel is suave and sinister as the casino boss, always staying within character, playing it straight, not going for laughs, and so getting more of them.

Laughter doesn't come out of formula, or stupidity, or the manipulation of things that worked before in other films. It comes out of characters and performances, out of people who have some measure of reality, and whose dilemmas we can share. *Wise Guys* is broad and farcical, but there's not a moment when Moe and Harry stop being lovable, and even sort of believable.

Wish You Were Here ★ ★ ★ ½
R, 92 m., 1987

Emily Lloyd (Lynda), Tom Bell (Eric), Jesse Birdsall (Dave), Geoffrey Durham (Harry Figgis), Pat Heywood (Aunt Millie), Geoffrey Hutchings (Hubert). Directed by David Leland and produced by Sarah Radclyffe. Screenplay by Leland.

Her mother's dead, her father's a drunk, and inside of her beats a spirit that is free and true. But this is a working-class neighborhood of an English provincial town in 1951, when a girl such as Lynda was expected to know her place, to apologize by her very manner for having come from humble origins, and done little to distinguish herself. Lynda isn't made that way. The boys like to look at Betty Grable's legs in the cinema, so Lynda flashes her knickers on the beach. What's to lose?

Wish You Were Here tells the story of an adolescent girl with a spirit that refuses to be crushed, but who has few ways to express herself. Her father absolutely fails to comprehend her. An aunt sees her as a bad girl, a problem girl. The lads of the town see her as a tramp and a possible good time. There is no one in the town to understand her high spirits and good nature, except, perhaps, for the little old lady who plays piano in the tea room and applauds her the day she tells a customer to shove it.

Wish You Were Here is a comedy with an angry undertone, a story of a free-spirited girl who holds a grudge against a time when such girls were a threat to society, to the interlocking forces of sexism and convention that conspired to break their spirits. Because the film sometimes doesn't know whether to laugh or cry, it's always interesting: We see a girl whistling on her way to possible tragedy.

The movie was written and directed by David Leland. You may have seen or heard about *Personal Services,* an earlier movie he wrote. It was based on the story of a notorious British madam named Cynthia Payne, who ran a house of ill repute for old-age pensioners and retired military men with kinky tastes.

Although *Wish You Were Here* never makes the connection, it is based on stories that Payne told Leland about her childhood, when sex was something nobody talked about and sexual initiation was accompanied by ignorance, fear, and psychic trauma. Payne could never quite see what the fuss was about—still can't, if the latest headlines about her are correct. Her approach was completely amoral: If sex is something they want and you can supply, and you can benefit as much as, or more than, they can, then where's the problem?

The answer is, of course, that there can be endless problems, especially to a girl so essentially innocent and vulnerable as Lynda in this movie. After she gets a job at the bus station, her boss walks in to catch her flashing her legs for the appreciative bus drivers. A young local lad fancies himself a Don Juan, and gets her into bed, only to appear in the bedroom door in a silk dressing gown, smoking a cigarette in a holder, and doing his Ronald Colman imitation (which is, as it turns out, his idea of sex).

"Do you fancy me?" he asks. "Not half as much as you fancy yourself," she says, and the night ends with her still largely ignorant about the facts of life. But her schooling resumes at the hands of a middle-aged projectionist at the local theater, who understands the mechanics of sex and totally lacks any understanding of human nature—hers, or his own.

Under the circumstances, it is hard for Lynda to keep smiling, to think positive in the face of a general conspiracy to treat sex as filthy and herself as worthless. The last shot of the movie will strike some people as hopeless and misleading romanticism; I prefer to see it as optimism in the face of despair.

The key to this movie is the performance by sixteen-year-old Emily Lloyd as Lynda. The screenplay could have gone a dozen different ways, depending on who was cast in the role. Lloyd is so fresh, so filled with fun and rebellion, that she carries us past the tricky parts on the strength of personality alone. It's one of the great debut roles for a young actress. I was reminded of a cross between Julie Christie in *Darling* and Rita Tushingham in *A Taste of Honey.* It'll be interesting to see what the future holds for her. More than it did for Lynda, I imagine, and for Cynthia Payne.

The Witches ★ ★ ★
PG, 92 m., 1990

Anjelica Huston (Miss Ernst/Grand High Witch), Mai Zetterling (Helga), Jasen Fisher (Luke), Rowan Atkinson (Mr. Stringer), Bill Paterson (Mr. Jenkins), Brenda Blethyn (Mrs. Jenkins), Charles Potter (Bruno Jenkins), Anne Lambton (Woman in Black). Directed by Nicolas Roeg and produced by Mark Shivas. Screenplay by Allan Scott.

The best children's stories are the scariest ones, because to kids they seem most likely to contain the truth. A lot of stories end with everybody living happily ever after, but they're boring stories unless there seems to be a good chance that unspeakable dangers must be survived on the way to the ending. Roald Dahl's children's stories always seem to know that truth, and the best thing about Nicolas Roeg's film of Dahl's book *The Witches* is its dark vision—this is not only a movie about kids who are changed into mice, it's a movie where one of the mice gets its tail chopped off.

The film opens on an ominous note in Norway, with Luke (Jasen Fisher) being told stories about witches by his old grandmother (Mai Zetterling). They're real, she says, and they walk among us. But you can spot them if you get a good look at them, because they have square feet. They're also bald and have pointy noses, but the important thing is they're not imaginary. The grandmother has even heard tell of a Grand High Witch, who rules all of the others, and is the most terrible of all.

Tragedy strikes. Luke's parents are killed in a car crash. He travels with his grandmother to England on family business, and they end up in a seaside hotel which is hosting a convention of the Society for the Prevention of Cruelty to Children. Somehow when you see the head of the society, Miss Ernst (Anjelica Huston), you don't feel good about your chances of having cruelty prevented to you if you're a child.

Huston, whose energy dominates the film, dresses like a vampire vamp with stiletto heels, a tight black dress, a severe hairstyle, and blazing red lipstick. Roeg often photographs her using lenses which make her leer into the camera, and she's always towering over everybody, especially little boys like Luke. Wandering through the labyrinthine hallways of the old hotel, Luke stumbles upon a private meeting one day, and discovers to his horror that the Society is actually a convention of witches—and that Huston, the fabled Grand High Witch, has plans to turn all of the children in England into mice.

Luke is, of course, discovered while eavesdropping, and becomes the first child forced to drink a secret potion and become a mouse. And it's here that the genius of the late Jim Henson comes into play, as his special effects team creates a world in which gigantic pieces of furniture tower over the little boy-mouse and some of his friends, as they try to survive cats and extermination and save the children of England.

Some of the sequences are predictable from other movies about people who shrink to microscopic size. Others are fresh, including the way Luke is finally able to convince his grandmother he is her grandson and not a mouse. Lucky for him she believes in witches already. The movie turns into a race against time, good against evil, and Roeg doesn't spare his young audiences the sinister implications of the plot.

This is the first so-called children's movie from Nicolas Roeg, that most unorthodox of directors, whose credits include *Don't Look Now, Track 29, Eureka,* and *Insignificance.* He almost always expresses a twisted, sinister sensuality in his films, and in this one that sensibility expresses itself in his willingness to let the child-mice face some of the real dangers of their predicament. The result is that the movie might be too intense for smaller viewers (although some of them these days seem hardened to anything). But *The Witches* is an intriguing movie, ambitious and inventive, and almost worth seeing just for Anjelica Huston's obvious delight in playing a completely uncompromised villainess.

The Witches of Eastwick ★ ★ ★ ½
R, 125 m., 1987

Jack Nicholson (Daryl), Cher (Alexandra), Susan Sarandon (Jane), Michelle Pfeiffer (Sukie), Veronica Cartwright (Felicia), Richard Jenkins (Clyde), Keith Jochim (Walter). Directed by George Miller and produced by Neil Canton, Peter Guber, and Jon Peters. Screenplay by Michael Christofer.

It's all done with the ambidextrous eyebrows. Jack Nicholson can elevate either brow singly to express his intention of getting away with murder, and he can elevate them in unison to reflect his delight when he has done so. In the annals of body language, his may be a small skill, but it's a crucial one, because it makes us conspirators with Nicholson; he's sharing his raffish delight with us.

He does that a lot in *The Witches of Eastwick,* in which he plays the devil: a role he was born to fill. He finds himself in Eastwick, a sedate New England village, after being invoked by three bored housewives who have not found what they are looking for in the local male population. Nicholson is exactly what they are looking for, by definition, because he can be all things to all people.

He buys the big mansion on the edge of town, moves in, and starts cooking. Nobody knows where he came from or what his story is, and he's certainly an oddball: Look at those floppy, ungainly clothes, or remember the time he began to snore, deafeningly, at the village concert. But the three women who summoned him aren't complaining, because he's giving each one of them just what she wants.

The women are played in the movie by Cher, Michelle Pfeiffer, and Susan Sarandon, and they have a delicious good time with their roles. These women need to be good at double takes, because they're always getting into situations that require them. When they're together, talking up a storm, they have the kind of unconscious verbal timing that makes comedy out of ordinary speech. We laugh not only because they say funny things but because they give everyday things just a slight twist of irony.

But it's Nicholson's show. There is a scene where he dresses in satin pajamas and sprawls full length on a bed, twisting and stretching sinuously in full enjoyment of his sensuality. It is one of the funniest moments of physical humor he has ever committed. There is another sequence in which he presides over a diabolical celebration in his mansion, orchestrating unspeakable acts and realizing unconscious fantasies. In the hands of another actor it might look ridiculous, but Nicholson seems perfectly at home with the bizarre.

The Witches of Eastwick is based on the John Updike novel, which must have presented a mine field for George Miller, the director. Fantasies usually play better on the page than on the screen, because in the imagination they don't seem as ridiculous as they sometimes do when they've been reduced to actual images. There are moments in *The Witches of Eastwick* that stretch uncomfortably for effects—the movie's climax is overdone, for example—and yet a lot of the time this movie plays like a plausible story about implausible people. The performances sell it. And the eyebrows.

Withnail & I ★ ★ ★ ★
R, 104 m., 1987

Richard E. Grant (Withnail), Paul McGann (Marwood), Richard Griffiths (Monty), Ralph Brown (Danny), Michael Elphick (Jake), Daragh O'Malley (Irishman), Michael Wardle (Isaac Parkin), Una Brandon-Jones (Mrs. Parkin). Directed by Bruce Robinson and produced by Paul M. Heller. Screenplay by Robinson.

Withnail & I takes place in England at the end of the Swinging Sixties. Two would-be actors live in squalor and poverty in a mean little flat in a wretched section of London. They are cold, desperate, broke, and hung over. They dream of glory but lurk about in the corners of pubs to keep warm.

One of them is Withnail, who is tall, craggy, and utterly cynical. He affects a kind of weary bitterness. The other is Marwood, younger, more optimistic, more impressionable. Their situation is desperate. "Something has to happen," Withnail says, "or I'm going to crack."

Then he has an inspiration: His rich and eccentric Uncle Monty has some sort of a place in the country. They'll talk him into lending it to them, and perhaps the change of scenery will give them the courage to carry on. The scene that begins when they appear at the door of Monty's London mansion is sly and droll, filled with hazardous currents and undertows as Monty takes a fancy to young Marwood. He agrees to lend them his country place.

The country is bitter, cold, angry, and hostile. Neighbors will not talk to them. Farmers will not sell them firewood. Their wives will not part with eggs or milk. Huddled over a wretched blaze made of Uncle Monty's furniture, Withnail and Marwood contemplate a bleak prospect: They have no food, fuel, money, or (worst of all) drink. Outside the door, the idyllic countryside is roamed by randy bulls.

Then Uncle Monty arrives unexpectedly and sets himself on a determined romantic pursuit of young Marwood, who wants nothing to do with him. Withnail confesses that he told his uncle that Marwood was gay, "because otherwise how would we have gotten the cottage?" Uncle Monty is, however, not only gay but also rich and fat, and the erotic tension in the cottage is interrupted by large and leisurely meals.

The performances make the movie, and Richard Griffiths is wonderful as Uncle Monty: overfed, burbling with second-hand eloquence, yet with a cold intelligence lurking behind his bloodshot eyes. It's the best supporting performance in a British movie since Denholm Elliott in *A Room with a View.* Withnail and Marwood, played by Richard E. Grant and Paul McGann, are like Rosencrantz and Gildenstern: They know all their lines but are uncertain about which direction the play is taking.

Withnail & I is a comedy, but a grimly serious one. Nothing is played for laughs. The humor arises from poverty, desperation, and bone-numbing cold. It is not the portrait of two colorful, lovable characters, but of two comrades in emotional shipwreck. The movie is rigorously dyspeptic, and that's why I liked it: It doesn't go for the easy laughs or sentimentalized poverty, but finds its humor in the unforgiving study of selfish human nature.

Without a Trace ★ ★ ★ ½
PG, 119 m., 1983

Kate Nelligan (Susan Selky), Judd Hirsch (Menetti), David Dukes (Graham Selky), Stockard Channing (Jocelyn). Directed and produced by Stanley Jaffe. Screenplay by Beth Gutcheon.

"A woman's bravery and a police detective's relentless search for her missing son provide the elements of suspenseful human drama in Without a Trace.*"*

—Press release

They have it exactly wrong. The press release describes what might have happened to this story if it had been turned into one of those TV docudramas where every emotion is predictably computed. What makes *Without a Trace* interesting is that it's *not* predictable, because it goes with the ebbs and flows of imperfect human beings. It's not about a woman's bravery but about her intelligence and vulnerability. It's not about a detective's relentless search, but about routine police work, made up of realism and hunches.

Without a Trace opens with a sequence that is very painful, since we know from the movie's title what's about to happen. A young mother (Kate Nelligan), who lives alone with her first-grader, gets him up, gets him his breakfast, scolds him for feeding his breakfast to the dog, tells him he's a good boy, and sends him off to school. He's almost seven—sort of young to walk alone to school, but it's only two blocks and there's a crossing guard. Nelligan goes off to school herself. She's an English professor at Columbia University. She comes home and waits for her child. He's late. She makes a call. He never arrived at the school. She calls the police and a search begins at once, but her son has apparently disappeared into thin air. There are door-to-door canvasses, helicopter searches, anonymous phone calls, predictions by psychics, and a neighborhood campaign to put "missing" posters in store windows. But there is no little boy.

One of the unexpected things about *Without a Trace* is that it's not really about the police search for the child. Instead, it's about what happens to people when tragedy turns into open-ended frustration. The mother waits and waits. The detective in charge of the case (Judd Hirsch) follows up leads and does all the things a competent cop is supposed to do. The city lends its resources and pays for an expensive investigation. But everything leads to nothing.

The central passages of the film are the best, as Nelligan plays an intelligent, civilized woman fighting to keep control. She feels rage, yes, but she is a rational person and she tries to behave reasonably. Underneath, she is deeply grieving. It takes her best friend (Stockard Channing) to suggest, after several months, that perhaps it is time to give up and admit that the little boy must be dead. It's time to let go of the past and rebuild her own life. Nelligan rejects that reasoning. And the movie remains neutral. What *is* the right answer: Should she accept what looks like the inevitable, or should she continue to hope? Nelligan's performance grows immensely subtle at this point. We can almost read her mind, and what we are reading is a battle between instinct and intelligence, between common sense and a mother's love.

Then a "suspect" is arrested—a gay sadomasochist. The circumstantial evidence against him is overwhelming. But Nelligan refuses to be bullied into agreement by a police department eager to close its books on the case. She becomes convinced that the man is innocent. And *Without a Trace*, which could so easily have been just another police drama, grows into a thought-provoking movie about how we behave, and why. It asks hard questions. It also has its moments of joy, but it earns every one of them.

Without You I'm Nothing ★ ★ ★
R, 89 m., 1990

Sandra Bernhard (Herself), John Doe (Himself), Steve Antin (Himself), Lu Leonard

(Sandra's Manager), Ken Foree (Emcee), Cynthia Bailey (Roxanne); Female backup singers: Grace Broughton, Kimberli Williams, Axel Vera, Estuardo M. Volty; Male backup singers: Kevin Dorsey, Arnold McCuller, Oren Waters. Directed by John Boskovich and produced by Jonathan D. Krane. Screenplay by Sandra Bernhard and Boskovich.

You're a very special audience tonight. No, really!

Rock stars rarely talk to their audiences except in throwaway lines. There is a godlike detachment about them. In nightclubs, Vegas lounges, and the "entertainment rooms" of resort hotels, however, performers are talking all the time. They're relating to their audience with a mixture of confession, autobiography, and facile sincerity. The typical act in such a place is the same night after night and year after year, and interchangeable with other acts. It's canned; it's been fixed. Remember the Fabulous Baker Boys. And yet there is a great emphasis on insisting that *tonight* is different. That *this* audience is really very special. No, really!

Sandra Bernhard's *Without You I'm Nothing* seems to be set in lounge act hell. She plays a series of cabaret artists doomed to appear night after night before a completely indifferent audience. In this version of hell, time runs together, and so do the acts—so that at times she's doing Nina Simone, or borscht belt, or Burt Bacharach, or a set designed for a gay bar.

Some reviews of the film have suggested she "imitates" Simone or Streisand or Diana Ross. Nothing could be further from the truth. Bernhard is actually working in the ancient nightclub tradition of "emulation," in which obscure performers try to wrap the mantle of greatness around themselves. Having no hits of their own, they draw applause by singing the greatest hits of other people. The deep irony is that when applause comes, it is usually for the original, not the copy; the Vegas lounge singer does "Strangers in the Night," and the audience applauds for Sinatra.

All of this takes its toll in self-esteem, and although some lounge singers are happy people who enjoy entertaining, many are wrapped in bitterness and boredom as they sing to rooms full of indifferent strangers. They tell the audience it's "really special" tonight because it isn't special—it's the same as last night. They say "I love ya" but they mean "If you loved me but I know you don't." Their patter is based on wishes, not realities. And that is the essential

insight of *Without You I'm Nothing.* It is a heart-rending, merciless assault on the phoniness of entertainment rhetoric.

Early in the film, there is a scene in Sandra Bernhard's dressing room. She prepares herself for the performance and addresses the camera directly, telling us how beautiful she is, how desirous. Although I have found Bernhard intriguing ever since I first saw her as one of Jerry Lewis's kidnappers in *The King of Comedy*, she is not, in fact, beautiful in the conventional sense. Her features are too angular and her mouth too angry for the current norm (although, for my taste, her face would wear better in the long run than a conventional cover girl's, because it would be more interesting). The point of the movie is, however, that she believes herself beautiful and seductive and irresistible, and she insists that we feel the same way. There is naked aggression here, the resentment that is usually buried in lounge act patter.

She goes onstage and her strange show begins. It is not really an act but a fantasy about a series of acts, in which she adopts wigs, makeup, and disguises to show that she can "be" anybody—or that there is no real person there. Her patter and songs are intercut with mysterious appearances by a beautiful black woman (Cynthia Bailey), who wanders through the film and leaves a rude message at the end. This woman is explained as her "alter ego," which is really no explanation at all. Bernhard is joined onstage by backup singers—some of them transvestites, according to the movie's credits, so maybe they prove the point that anybody can be anything. Nightclub announcements are made in extreme close-up, showing only a woman's beautiful lipsticked lips—perhaps in contrast to Bernhard's own less lovely mouth.

Bernhard sings. She does standup. She does autobiographical material about her childhood. She is angry, she is sad, she defies us to like her. And occasionally she unleashes her stage ego—telling us the things many performers probably yearn to say, which is that they are beautiful, they are gifted, they can do anything and be anybody. The audience looks on in boredom and begins to drift away, and in response her act grows more and more insistent, until in a shocking finale she drapes herself in the American flag and then removes it to reveal herself almost nude. It's as if she's saying she will do anything to hold our attention. That no secret is too private, no revelation too shaming.

It's an uneasy experience, sitting through this film. Parts of it are funny, parts of it are moving, and parts of it are uncomfortable and off-putting. It's not a jolly night out at the movies. My first reaction, frankly, was that I wasn't enjoying myself. Then I analyzed that feeling. This is not, after all, a "concert film" that wants only to entertain. It is about concert films, and about show business. It is about vanity and narcissism, performers and audiences, self-love and self-hate. And it may be about the only lounge act in history that you'll be able to remember a month later.

Witness ★ ★ ★ ★
R, 120 m., 1985

Harrison Ford (John Book), Kelly McGillis (Rachel), Josef Sommer (Schaeffer), Lukas Haas (Samuel), Alexander Godunov (Daniel Hochleitner). Directed by Peter Weir and produced by Edward S. Feldman. Screenplay by Earl Wallace.

Witness comes billed as a thriller, but it's so much more than a thriller that I wish they hadn't even used the word "murder" in the ads. This is, first of all, an electrifying and poignant love story. Then it is a movie about the choices we make in life and the choices that other people make for us. Only then is it a thriller—one that Alfred Hitchcock would have been proud to make.

The movie's first act sets up the plot, leaving it a lot of time to deal with the characters and learn about them. The film begins on an Amish settlement in Pennsylvania, where for two hundred years a self-sufficient religious community has proudly held onto the ways of their ancestors. The Amish are deeply suspicious of outsiders and stubbornly dedicated to their rural lifestyle, with its horses and carriages, its communal barn-raisings, its gas lanterns instead of electricity, hooks instead of buttons.

An Amish man dies. His widow and young son leave on a train journey. In the train station in Philadelphia, the little boy witnesses a murder. Harrison Ford plays the tough big-city detective who gets assigned to the case. He stages lineups, hoping the kid can spot the murderer. He shows the kid mug shots. Then it turns out that the police department itself is implicated in the killing. Ford is nearly murdered in an ambush. His life, and the lives of the widow and her son, are in immediate danger. He manages to drive them all back to the Amish lands of Pennsylvania before collapsing from loss of blood.

And it's at this point, really, that the movie begins. Up until the return to Amish country, *Witness* has been a slick, superior thriller. Now it turns into an intelligent and perceptive love story. It's not one of those romances where the man and woman fall into each other's arms because their hormones are programmed that way. It's about two independent, complicated people who begin to love each other because they have shared danger, they work well together, they respect each other—*and* because their physical attraction for each other is so strong it almost becomes another character in the movie.

Witness was directed by Peter Weir, the gifted Australian director of *The Year of Living Dangerously*. He has a strong and sure feeling for places, for the land, for the way that people build their self-regard by the way they do their work.

In the whole middle section of this movie, he shows the man from the city and the simple Amish woman within the context of the Amish community. It is masterful filmmaking. The thriller elements alone would command our attention. The love story by itself would be exciting. The ways of life in the Amish community are so well-observed that they have a documentary feel. But all three elements work together so well that something organic is happening here; we're *inside* this story.

Harrison Ford has never given a better performance in a movie. Kelly McGillis, the young actress who plays the Amish widow, has a kind of luminous simplicity about her; it is refreshing and even subtly erotic to see a woman who doesn't subscribe to all the standard man-woman programmed responses of modern society.

The love that begins to grow between them is not made out of clichés; the cultural gulf that separates them is at least as important to both of them as the feelings they have. When they finally kiss, it is a glorious, sensuous moment, because this kiss is a sharing of trust and passion, not just another plug-in element from your standard kit of movie images.

We have been getting so many pallid, bloodless little movies—mostly recycled teen-age exploitation films made by ambitious young stylists without a thought in their heads—that *Witness* is like a fresh new day. It is a movie about adults, whose lives have dignity and whose choices matter to them. And it is also one hell of a thriller.

The Wiz ★ ★ ★
G, 133 m., 1978

Diana Ross (Dorothy), Michael Jackson (Scarecrow), Nipsey Russell (Tinman), Ted Ross (Lion), Mabel King (Evillene), Theresa Merritt (Aunt Em), Thelma Carpenter (Miss One), Lena Horne (Glinda the Good), Richard Pryor (The Wiz). Directed by Sidney Lumet and produced by Rob Cohen. Screenplay by Joel Schumacher.

Magical tornadoes can strike down anywhere, I guess, and spin you off to the land of Oz. On that wonderfully logical premise, the classic *Wizard of Oz* was transformed into a Broadway musical named *The Wiz*, and then the most expensive movie musical ever made. Is the movie a match for the 1939 Judy Garland version? Well, no, it's not—what movie could be?—but as a new approach to the same material, it's slick and energetic and fun.

The Wiz is set in present-day New York City, and finds its locations in fanciful sets suggesting Harlem, Coney Island, school playgrounds, the subway system, and a sweatshop. Our heroine, Dorothy, has been transformed from a Kansas teen-ager to a twenty-four-year-old black schoolteacher. And Diana Ross wears the same simple white frock for the entire film and projects a wide-eyed innocence that kind of grows on you.

Some churlish souls suggested, however, that *The Wiz* strains our credibility too much. That a twenty-four-year-old schoolteacher should be too sophisticated to consort with cowardly lions and scarecrows and men made out of tin. Pay no attention: Critics like that wouldn't know a yellow brick road if they saw one.

The Wiz asks for our suspension of disbelief and earns it (after a slow start) in that great shot of Dorothy and the Scarecrow dancing across a yellow brick bridge toward the towers of Manhattan. Up until then the going has been a little awkward. We don't really understand why Dorothy's such a mope at her aunt's dinner party—and, after she and her dog Toto are whirled away by a snowstorm, the scene in the playground really drags. Lots of graffiti people, drawn on the walls, come to life and dance about like a Broadway chorus line (which, of course, they are), and then Dorothy finally finds her first yellow brick.

It's good that the Scarecrow is the first traveling companion she meets; Michael Jackson fills the role with humor and warmth.

Nipsey Russell is fine as the Tinman, too, but Ted Ross sort of disappears into his lion's costume, done in by the makeup man. We can't see enough of him to get to know him.

There are lots of good scenes in the Emerald City. A dance sequence, for example, where The Wiz calls the shots and everybody instantly changes their clothes to stay in fashion. A run-in with a roller coaster. The scenes in the subway, where Dorothy and her friends are chased by enormous, menacing trash bins that snap their jaws ferociously. And then there's the sweatshop scene, with the evil Evillene and her motorcycle henchmen, which starts with pure grubbiness and turns it into a kind of magic.

Finally, at the very end of the journey, there's Richard Pryor as The Wiz, coward at heart, filled with doubts, hiding behind the electronic gadgets he uses to enslave the Emerald City and keep Evillene at bay. The songs get a little sticky about here—all sorts of unthrilling messages about how you can achieve anything if only you believe—but Diana Ross knows how to sell them, and she has a virtuoso solo in a totally darkened frame that reminds us of Barbra Streisand's closing number in *Funny Lady*.

The movie has great moments and a lot of life, sensational special effects and costumes—and Ross, Jackson, and Russell. Why *doesn't* it involve us as deeply as *The Wizard of Oz*? Maybe because it hedges its bets by wanting to be sophisticated *and* universal, childlike *and* knowing, appealing to both a mass audience and to media insiders. *The Wizard of Oz* went flat-out for the heart of its story; there are times when *The Wiz* has just a touch too much calculation.

Wolf ★ ★ ★
R, 121 m., 1994

Jack Nicholson (Will Randall), Michelle Pfeiffer (Laura Alden), James Spader (Stewart Swinton), Kate Nelligan (Charlotte Randall), Richard Jenkins (Detective Bridger), Christopher Plummer (Raymond Alden), Eileen Atkins (Mary). Directed by Mike Nichols and produced by Douglas Wick. Screenplay by Jim Harrison and Wesley Strict.

Wolf stars Jack Nicholson as a top editor for a New York publishing house, who is bitten by a wolf and begins to turn into a werewolf, just as a billionaire tycoon buys the company and replaces Nicholson with a back-stabbing yuppie. Nicholson, snarling with rage, bites the yuppie, who also begins to grow hair and fangs. The result is a canny portrait of the emotional climate in the New York publishing industry.

The movie contains most of the materials of traditional werewolf movies. Much significance is attached to the full moon, and horses shy away when Nicholson comes near, and his sense of smell develops to the point where he can tell that a man had tequila for his breakfast. There is of course the obligatory eccentric old scientist with the foreign accent, who explains werewolves to Nicholson. And beautiful women to be his lovers and/or victims.

But *Wolf* is both more and less than a traditional werewolf movie. Less, because it doesn't provide the frankly vulgar thrills and excesses some audience members are going to be hoping for. And more, because Nicholson and his director, Mike Nichols, are halfway serious about exploring what might happen if a New York book editor *did* become a werewolf.

Nicholson looks tired and aging in the opening scenes. He's playing Will Randall, a soft-spoken, pipe-smoking literary man of the old school, whose authors are loyal to him. Then a rich investor (Christopher Plummer) buys the firm and throws a party, during which he takes Nicholson out on the lawn to tell him he is being fired. His replacement, a traitor Nicholson thought was his friend, is the polished young hypocrite Stewart Swinton (James Spader, playing what can only be called the James Spader role, and playing it very nicely, too).

This scenario doesn't develop as office politics as usual, however, because of the strange experience Nicholson had a few nights earlier in Vermont, where he was bitten by a wolf. Soon hair begins to flourish around the wound, and Nicholson sleeps all day but is awake all night, and his wife (Kate Nelligan) is caught in an adulterous affair because Nicholson is able to smell his rival on his wife's clothing. Meanwhile, Laura, the millionaire's daughter (Michelle Pfeiffer), becomes Nicholson's confidant. Any enemy of her father's is a friend of hers.

The tone of the movie is steadfastly smart and literate; even in the midst of his transformation, the Nicholson character is capable of sardonic asides and a certain ironic detachment. He does, however, grow more predatory. "I'm going to get you," he promises Spader. And after he urinates on the younger man's shoes, he explains: "I'm marking my territory."

All of this is not quite as poignant as it might have been. A similar movie, David Cronenberg's *The Fly*, starred Jeff Goldblum as a scientist who realizes he is gradually becoming a fly, and Geena Davis as the woman who tries to love him in spite of . . . well, in spite of the fact that he's a fly. There was true emotion there, and dread. Nicholson's character, on the other hand, seems to enjoy becoming a wolf. He begins to look younger and stronger, and although he fears what he may do and sometimes demands to be locked up, there is the sense that being a wolf is not completely unacceptable to him. Of course (this is strictly my personal opinion), it is better to be a wolf than a fly.

The Pfeiffer character is described fairly accurately in one of Nicholson's speeches as the kind of person who puts up a hostile exterior, but when you get past that, you find a hostile interior. Not much of an effort is made to convince us of their romantic chemistry; they are partners mostly because they share the same enemies.

Like many Nichols movies, *Wolf* gains by surrounding the story with sharply seen places and details. The publishing house inhabits a classic old architectural landmark with an open atrium (ideal for a wolf who wants to eavesdrop), and other action takes place at the millionaire's estate, with its vast lawns and forests, its Gothic main house, and its rambling outbuildings and guest cottages. The atmosphere adds to the effect; it would be difficult to stage a werewolf story in a condo.

What is a little amazing is that this movie allegedly cost $70 million. It is impossible to figure where the money all went, even given the no doubt substantial above-the-line salaries. The special effects are efficient but not sensational, the makeup by Rick Baker is convincing but wisely limited, and the movie looks great, but that doesn't cost a lot of money. What emerges is an effective attempt to place a werewolf story in an incongruous setting, with the closely observed details of that setting used to make the story seem more believable. Nicholson is very good with the material (some of his line readings are balancing acts of the savage and the sublime), but this material can only take him, and us, so far.

A Woman's Tale ★ ★ ★
PG-13, 94 m., 1992

Sheila Florance (Martha), Gosia Dobrowolska (Anna), Norman Kaye (Billy), Chris Haywood (Jonathan), Ernest Gray (Peter), Myrtle Woods (Miss Inchley). Directed by Paul Cox and produced by Cox and Santhana Naidu. Screenplay by Cox.

Paul Cox's *A Woman's Tale* is a portrait of an old lady of great wit and courage, who faces death as she has faced everything else, on her own terms. *A Woman's Tale* does not sentimentalize its heroine, does not make her cute or lovable or pull any of those other tricks we use to deny the realities of old age. It allows her strong opinions and a skeptical irony, and makes her into one of the great characters of recent movies.

The old woman's name is Martha. She is played by Sheila Florance, who won the Australian Academy Award for her performance. She is about eighty years old, and lives in a flat with a cat, a parakeet, and a few prized possessions, and she gets around well enough to look after Billy, the disintegrating old man who lives next door.

Her other important relationships include an unpleasant one, with her son, who wants to shelve her in a nursing home; a loving one, with Anna (Gosia Dobrowolska), the visiting nurse; an amused one, with Miss Inchly, who is nearly ten years older; and a fighting one, with her landlord, who wants her to move.

Martha's secret is that she is dying. She knows it, Anna knows it, and the others will not be given the satisfaction of being told. She wants to die as she has lived, in her own way, in her own apartment, and the zest with which she defends herself is one of the movie's great joys.

The film has been written by Cox as several days in Martha's life, during which she does as much living as some of us would be lucky to manage in a year. She is a coconspirator in Anna's affair with a married man, and lets the lovers use her bed ("I am going to die in it; you had might as well love in it"). She sees Billy through his usual crises, chats with her pets, goes for walks to check out the neighborhood, and at night, when the pain keeps her awake, she listens to the radio talk shows and calls in with pointed advice.

The movie is not just about her activities, however. It is also about her continued occupation of a body that has served her for eight decades and is now failing her. The movie is quite frank about Martha's physicality. Her face is a mass of wrinkles, her body is too thin, and when we see her in her bath, we are moved with compassion that such a great spirit should inhabit such a frail vessel.

She has her memories, including some erotic ones, and she takes a frank interest in the life of a neighborhood prostitute. At eighty, it is not so much that she approves or disapproves as that she has lived a long time and knows what goes on in this world. Her greatest threat comes through an alliance between her landlord, who battles to get rid of her, and her well-meaning son, who thinks he is helping her by his efforts to rid her of independence.

Paul Cox, born in Holland, long a resident of Australia, is one of the best directors of our time. His films often deal with loneliness; his credits include *Man of Flowers*, starring Norman Kaye (the Billy of this film) as a gentle recluse, *Lonely Hearts*, about a disastrous dating service match, and *Cactus*, about the possibility of blindness. *A Woman's Tale* is one of his best works—one of the best films of the year.

Sheila Florance, who spent most of her life as an actress in Australia, was dying when she made this film about a woman who is dying. She knew it, Cox knew it, and although she was sometimes in pain she focused on the performance and made it her message to the rest of us, about a process we will all face in one way or another. She died some months after finishing the film; here she still lives, in humor, dignity, and a fine proud anger.

A Woman Under the Influence
★ ★ ★ ★

R, 155 m., 1974

Peter Falk (Nick Longhetti), Gena Rowlands (Mabel Longhetti), Katherine Cassavetes (Mama Longhetti), Lady Rowlands (Martha Mortensen), Fred Draper (George Mortensen). Directed by John Cassavetes and produced by Sam Shaw. Screenplay by Cassavetes.

John Cassavetes's *A Woman Under the Influence* gives us a woman whose influences only gradually reveal themselves. And as they do, they give us insight not only into one specific, brilliantly created, woman, but into some of the problems of surviving in a society where very few people are free to be themselves. The woman is Mabel Longhetti, wife and mother and (in some very small, shy, and faraway corner) herself. Her husband, Nick, is the head of a construction

gang and a gregarious type with an expansive nature; he's likely to bring his whole crew home at 7 A.M. for a spaghetti dinner.

Mabel isn't gregarious, but she tries. She tries too hard, and that's her problem. She desperately wants to please her husband, and when they're alone, she does. They get along, and they do love one another. But when people are around, she gets a little wacky. The mannerisms, the strange personal little ways she has of expressing herself, get out of scale. She's not sure how to act, because she's not sure who she is. "I'll be whatever you want me to be," she tells Nick, and he tells her to be herself. But who is that?

The film takes place before and after six months she spends in a mental institution. Her husband has her committed, reluctantly, after she begins to crack up. There have been some indications that she's in trouble. She behaves strangely when some neighbor children are brought over to stay for a while with her own, and the neighbor is afraid to leave his kids because of the way she's acting. But what, exactly, is "strange"? Well she's insecure, hyper, manic. She laughs too much and pushes too hard. She's not good with other people around. So her husband does what he thinks he has to do and commits her. But what about him? What kind of a guy is he? It's here that *A Woman Under the Influence* gets to be complicated, involved, and fascinating—a revelation. Because if Mabel is disturbed, then so is he. He's as crazy as she is, maybe more so. But because he's a man and has channels for his craziness, he stays at home and she gets sent away.

Their ways with kids, for example, are revealing. She feels insecure around them. She's not confident enough to be a mother, and almost wants to be another kid. But the father, when he takes over the responsibility of raising them, yanks them out of school in the middle of the day and drags them, bewildered, to the seashore for the most depressing, compulsory day at the beach we can imagine. And then on the way home, he lets them share a six-pack with him. If Mabel wants to be one of the kids, Nick wants them to be three of the boys.

I don't suppose (although I'm not sure) that real families like this exist, and I don't think Cassavetes wants us to take the film as a literal record. The characters are larger than life (although not less convincing because of that), and their loves and rages, their fights and moments of tenderness, exist at exhausting levels of emotion.

Nick, as played by Peter Falk, shouts and storms and is always on. Mabel (Gena Rowlands, who won an Oscar nomination), seems so touchingly vulnerable to every kind of influence around her that we don't want to tap her, because she might fall apart. Because their personalities are so open, so visible, we see what might be hidden in a quieter, tidier film: that Nick no less than Mabel is trapped in a society where people are assigned roles, duties, and even personalities that have little to do with what they really think and who they really are. This is where Cassavetes is strongest as a writer and filmmaker: at creating specific characters and then sticking with them through long, painful, uncompromising scenes until we know them well enough to read them, to predict what they'll do next, and even to begin to understand why.

Mabel and Nick and their relatives and friends are fully realized, convincing, fictional creations, even though Cassavetes does sometimes deliberately push them into extreme situations. There's a scene, for example, where Nick goes almost berserk in throwing a party for Mabel, who's due home from the institution, then tells all the nonfamily guests to leave immediately and then berates the family, and Mabel, and himself, in a painful confrontation around the dining room table. The scene's just too extreme to take literally. But as psychodrama, or whatever you want to call it, it abandons any niceties or evasions and deals directly with what the characters are really thinking.

There's also the scenes of great quiet comedy, as when one of Nick's coworkers somehow dumps his entire plate of spaghetti into his lap and the others battle between decorous table manners and their desire to laugh. There's Gena Rowlands's incredible command of her physical acting resources to communicate what Mabel feels at times when she's too unsure or intimidated to say. There's Falk, in a performance totally unlike his Columbo, creating this character who's so tender, so much in love, and so screwed up. I have a friend who said, after seeing *A Woman Under the Influence*, that she was so affected, she didn't know whether to cry or throw up. Well, sometimes that's the choice life presents you with—along with the laughs.

The Wonderful Horrible Life of Leni Riefenstahl ★ ★ ★ ½ [NEW]

NO MPAA RATING, 183 m., 1994

Directed by Ray Muller and produced by Hans-Jurgen Panitz, Jacques and Dimitri de Clercq, Waldemar Janusczak, and Hans-Peter Kochenrath. Screenplay by Muller.

If Leni Riefenstahl had done nothing notable before the age of sixty, what a wonderful life we would say she has lived since then. Now in her early nineties, she is not only the world's oldest active scuba diver, but is directing an undersea documentary. In her sixties, she went by herself to live with the Nuba, an African tribe, and recorded their lives in a book of photographs. *The Wonderful Horrible Life of Leni Riefenstahl* shows her at the end of a day of scuba diving. The boat has docked, and she walks down the pier with two men— the captain, and Horst, her younger companion and cinematographer.

The body language says everything. The two men walk ahead, carrying gear, engaged in conversation. She walks behind them, alone, carrying her own gear and oxygen tank. They don't lend her a hand, or offer to carry the tank for her, and what this says is that, at ninety-one, they do not think she needs special consideration. She's one of the guys.

If Riefenstahl were anyone else, this footage alone would justify a documentary. The images of her exploring the ocean bottom are extraordinary, holding out the promise that old age can be held indefinitely at bay. But Riefenstahl has not, of course, lived a normal life, and the actions which will forever define her reputation took place not in her sixties but in her thirties, when she directed two documentaries that will always be linked with Adolf Hitler and his Nazi party.

Triumph of the Will (1934) was a film about the Nazi Party Congress in Nuremberg, an event largely staged for the benefit of her camera, which showed a confident Hitler nodding approvingly as massed ranks of Nazi troops march in review. Three years later, she directed *Olympia*, a documentary on the Berlin Olympiad.

These are by general consent two of the best documentaries ever made. But because they reflect the ideology of a monstrous movement, they pose a classic question of the contest between art and morality: Is there such a thing as pure art, or does all art make a political statement?

This documentary by Ray Muller was made with Riefenstahl's agreement, if not always with her happy cooperation. He reconstructs her career, beginning with her emergence as a star and director of German "mountain films," a late-1920s genre that glorified a cult of idealized heroism with stories of adventures in the German Alps. Hitler saw her mountain films and apparently became a fan (there were persistent rumors, but never any evidence, that he became her lover). He hired her to make a short film about the 1933 Nazi rally, and then her great documentary about the Nuremberg event.

Riefenstahl is at pains to insist she was never a member of the Nazi party. Her position has always been that she was an artist, working in a vacuum. The tragedy of her career, from her view, is that *Triumph of the Will* and *Olympia* gained such fame, and were so closely identified with Nazism, that she was never able to finish another film. There were other documentaries about the Nazi rallies, but nobody remembers the others; only hers, because it was so good.

The Wonderful Horrible Life of Leni Riefenstahl is not convinced by her lifelong self-justification, and subjects her to strenuous on-camera questioning. She is unyielding. More than able at the age of ninety-one to defend herself, she has rehearsed over the years an elaborate explanation and justification for her behavior. There is no mention in her films of anti-Semitism, she points out. She did not know until after the war about Hitler's genocidal policies against the Jews. She was a naive artist, unsophisticated about politics, detached from Nazi party officials with the exception of Hitler, her friend—but not a close friend. She was concerned only with images, not ideas.

And so on. But it has been pointed out that the very absence of anti-Semitism in *Triumph of the Will* looks like a calculation; excluding the central motif of almost all of Hitler's public speeches must have been a deliberate decision to make the film more efficient as propaganda. Nor could it have been easy for a film professional working in Berlin to remain unaware of the disappearance of all of the Jews in the movie industry.

In the film, Riefenstahl engages in onscreen debates with Muller, and then is seen visiting the site of the 1938 Olympiad with the surviving members of her film crew. They talk about some of their famous shots—from aerial techniques to the idea of digging a hole for the camera, so that athletes could loom over the audience. Shots from the film are a reminder of how beautiful and effective it was. And we sense Riefenstahl's true passion for filmmaking. But there are candid moments, when she is not aware of the camera, when she shares quiet little asides with her old comrades, which, while not damning, subtly suggest a dimension she is not willing to have seen.

The impression remains, after the film is over, that if Hitler had won, Leni Riefenstahl would not have been so quick to distance herself from him. Her postwar moral defense is based on technicalities. Undoubtedly in the atmosphere of the Nuremberg Trials she was not eager to face conviction or punishment as a war criminal. But, ironically, if she had confessed and renounced her youthful ideas, she might have had a more active career. It is her unconvincing, elusive self-defense that continues to damn her.

This movie is fascinating in so many different ways: As the story of an extraordinary life, as the reconstruction of the career of one of the greatest of film artists, as the record of an ideological debate, as a portrait of an amazing old woman. At its heart is the question of the soul and purpose of art. Can art be detached from its context? The pyramids were constructed at the cost of the lives of uncounted thousands of slaves. Do we remember them today? Do their deaths diminish the monuments they built? One dilemma of Leni Riefenstahl's wonderful, horrible life is that it has been so long. It would be so much easier to simply study the films without still having to deal with the unrepentant woman.

Working Girl ★ ★ ★ ★

R, 116 m., 1988

Melanie Griffith (Tess McGill), Harrison Ford (Jack Trainer), Sigourney Weaver (Katharine Parker), Alec Baldwin (Mick Dugan), Joan Cusack (Cyn), Philip Bosco (Oren Trask), Nora Dunn (Ginny), Olympia Dukakis (Personnel Director). Directed by Mike Nichols and produced by Douglas Wick. Screenplay by Kevin Wade.

The problem with working your way up the ladder of life is that sometimes you can't get there from here. People look at you and make a judgment call, and then, try as you might, you're only spinning your wheels. That's how Tess McGill feels in the opening scenes of *Working Girl*. She is intelligent and aggressive, and she has a lot of good ideas about how to make money in the big leagues of high finance. But she is a secretary. A secretary with too much hair. A secretary who rides the Staten Island ferry to work. A secretary who started talking like a little girl because it was cute when she was eleven and is still talking the same way, except now she is thirty. There is no way anybody is ever going to take her seriously.

One day, Tess (Melanie Griffith) gets a new boss at the mergers and acquisitions firm where she works. The boss (Sigourney Weaver) is a woman of almost exactly Tess's age, but with a different set of accessories. For example, she talks in a low, modulated voice, and wears more businesslike clothes, and has serious hair. "If you want to get ahead in business," Tess muses, "you've got to have serious hair." She gets along fine with her boss until the boss goes on a skiing holiday and breaks her leg and ends up in traction for six weeks. Then Tess goes into her boss's computer, and finds that the boss was about to steal one of Tess's brilliant suggestions and claim it as her own.

This makes her fighting mad, and so she begins an elaborate deception in which she masquerades as an executive at the firm, and figures out a way to meet a guy named Jack Trainer (Harrison Ford), who is the right guy at another firm to make the deal happen. She meets Trainer at a party and gets drunk and ends up in bed with him, even though she *explained* to him, "I have a head for business and a bod for sin." Will he ever take her seriously now? Yes, it turns out he will, because he likes her, and because he thinks her idea really is pretty brilliant.

That's the setup for *Working Girl*, which is one of those entertainments where you laugh a lot along the way, and then you end up on the edge of your seat. Structurally, the film has some parallels with *The Graduate*, Nichols's 1967 classic—including a climactic scene where an important ceremony is interrupted by the wrong person bursting in through the door. But this movie is the other side of the coin. *The Graduate* was about a young man who did not want to make money in plastics. *Working Girl* is about a young woman who very definitely wants to make money in mergers.

This is Melanie Griffith's movie in the same way that *The Graduate* belonged to Dustin Hoffman. She was not an obvious casting choice, but she is the right one, and in an odd way her two most famous previous roles, in *Body Double* and *Something Wild*, work for her. Because we may remember her

from those sex-drenched roles, there is a way in which both Griffith and her character are both trying to get respectable—to assimilate everything that goes along with "serious hair."

Supporting roles are crucial in movies like this. The Sigourney Weaver role is a thankless one—she plays the pill who gets humiliated at the end—and yet it is an interesting assignment for an actor with Weaver's imagination. From her first frame on the screen, she has to say all the right things while subtly suggesting that she may not mean any of them. If she is subtle, so is Harrison Ford, an actor whose steadiness goes along with a sort of ruminating passion; when he's in love with a woman, he doesn't grab her, he just seems to ponder her a lot. Weaver and Ford provide the indispensable frame within which the Griffith character can be seen to change.

The plot of *Working Girl* is put together like clockwork. It carries you along while you're watching it, but reconstruct it later and you'll see the craftsmanship. The Kevin Wade screenplay is sort of underhanded, the way it diverts us with laughs and with a melodramatic subplot involving Griffith's former boyfriend, while all the time it's winding up for the suspenseful climax. By the time we get to the last scenes, the movie plays like a thriller, and that's all the more effective because we weren't exactly bracing for that. *Working Girl* is Mike Nichols returning to the top of his form, and Melanie Griffith finding hers.

Working Girls ★ ★ ★
NO MPAA RATING, 90 m., 1987

Louise Smith (Molly), Ellen McElduff (Lucy), Amanda Goodwin (Dawn), Marusia Zach (Gina), Janne Peters (April), Helen Nicholas (Mary). Directed by Lizzie Borden and produced by Borden and Andi Gladstone. Screenplay by Borden and Sandra Kay.

There is, I imagine, somewhere in the mind of every man who goes to a prostitute the fantasy that he is somehow unique; that the woman has never met anyone quite like him before, and that, although her other clients may be "johns," he is an individual.

Working Girls both supports and destroys that illusion. The prostitutes in this movie may, indeed, never have met anyone quite like certain clients before, but that is not necessarily a compliment. What makes each man different is the nature of his fantasy life, the specific scenario he is seeking from a prostitute. What makes each man the same

is that there are only so many fantasies, and so many ways to fulfill them, and, for the working girls, only so many hours in a day.

Working Girls takes place during one day in a Manhattan bordello. The routine is well-established. The guys call in, the "phone girl" makes an appointment or a sales pitch, the women pass the time with idle small talk and gossip, and occasionally something truly exciting happens—such as when the phones are put on hold and the madam has a temper tantrum.

One by one, the guys come in through the door, each one burdened with the weight of his uniqueness. "How's everything?" one of the hookers asks a client. "Terrific," he says. "We have a new secretary at the office." "Yeah, it's been pretty busy around here," the girl says. "I can imagine," the guy says.

Some of the johns have really wild scenarios going on in their heads. One of them, for example, wants a hooker to enact a situation in which she is blind and only sexual intercourse with the guy can make her see again.

Others are into more kinky situations, but the bottom line is always the same: What goes on in bed between the hooker and the john is simply the occasion for the man to replay old and deep needs that have been in place for years. The woman is relatively unimportant, because she is not the fantasy but more like the supporting cast.

Working Girls has a lot of fascinating stuff in it, but most of it has to do with management and capitalism, not sex. We learn a great deal about clean towels, birth control, disease prevention, and never putting the phones on hold. We also learn a lot of euphemisms: For example, "Make sure the client is completely comfortable before you take any money." In other words, make sure the guy is naked, because then you know he's not a cop.

The movie is told largely through the eyes of Molly (Louise Smith), a lesbian whose lover doesn't know what she does for a living. After Molly arrives at work (on her ten-speed bike), we meet the other girls, some of them naive, some of them middle-age and weary, all of them bereft of illusions about men.

Sometimes, however, something touching happens in the sessions behind the closed doors. There are fugitive moments of tenderness, quiet passages of communication. It is a cliché that prostitutes are really selling companionship, not sex, and *Working Girls* seems to support that notion. What is remarkable is not that the girls are cynical and hardened, but that they have retained as much gentleness and empathy as they have. Like workers in more respectable professions such as psychiatry, medicine, and the ministry, they seem to have the ability to care, if only for a short time, about some of their clients, and to be nice to them. By the end of this movie, you wonder where they find not only the patience, but also the strength.

Working Girls is not a slick and dramatic movie. There are moments that seem forced and amateurish, and the overall structure of the story is fairly predictable. What the movie does have, though, is the feeling of real life being observed accurately. I was moved less by the movie's conscious attempts at artistry than by its unadorned honesty: The director, Lizzie Borden, has created characters who seem close to life, and her movie helps explain why the world's oldest profession is, despite everything, a profession.

The World According to Garp ★ ★ ★
R, 126 m., 1982

Robin Williams (Garp), Mary Beth Hurt (Helen Holm), Glenn Close (Jenny Fields), John Lithgow (Roberta), Hume Cronyn (Mr. Fields), Jessica Tandy (Mrs. Fields), Swoosie Kurtz (Hooker), Amanda Plummer (Ellen James). Directed by George Roy Hill and produced by Hill and Robert L. Crawford. Screenplay by Steve Tesich.

John Irving's best-selling novel, *The World According to Garp*, was cruel, annoying, and smug. I kept wanting to give it to my cats. But it was wonderfully well-written and was probably intended to inspire some of those negative reactions in the reader. The movie version of *Garp*, however, left me entertained but unmoved, and perhaps the movie's basic failing is that it did not inspire me to walk out on it. Something has to be wrong with a film that can take material as intractable as *Garp* and make it palatable.

Like a lot of movie versions of novels, the film of *Garp* has not reinterpreted the material in its own terms. Indeed, it doesn't interpret it at all. It simply reproduces many of the characters and events in the novel, as if the point in bringing *Garp* to the screen was to provide a visual aid for the novel's readers. With the book we at least know how we feel during the saga of Garp's unlikely life; the movie lives entirely within its moments,

keeping us entirely inside a series of self-contained scenes.

The story of Garp is by now part of best-selling folklore. We know that Garp's mother was an eccentric nurse, a cross between a saint and a nuisance, and that Garp was fathered in a military hospital atop the unconscious body of a brain-damaged technical sergeant. That's how much use Garp's mother, Jenny Fields, had for men. The movie, like the book, follows Garp from this anticlimactic beginning through a lifetime during which he is constantly overshadowed by his mother, surrounded by other strange women and women-surrogates, and asks for himself, his wife and children only uneventful peace and a small measure of happiness.

A great deal happens, however, to disturb the peace and prevent the happiness. Garp is accident-prone, and sadness and disaster surround him. Assassinations, bizarre airplane crashes, and auto mishaps are part of his daily routine. His universe seems to have been wound backward.

The movie's method in regarding the nihilism of his life is a simple one. It alternates two kinds of scenes: those in which very strange people do very strange things while pretending to be sane, and those in which all of the dreams of those people, and Garp, are shattered in instants of violence and tragedy.

What are we to think of these people and the events in their lives? The novel *The World According to Garp* was (I *think*) a tragicomic counterpoint between the collapse of middle-class family values and the rise of random violence in our society. A protest against that violence provides the most memorable image in the book, the creation of the Ellen James Society, a group of women who cut out their tongues in protest against what happened to Ellen James, who had her tongue cut out by a man. The bizarre behavior of the people in the novel, particularly Garp's mother and the members of the Ellen Jamesians, is a cross between activism and insanity, and there is the clear suggestion that without such behavior to hold them together, all of these people would be unable to cope at all and would sign themselves into the nearest institution. As a vision of modern American life, *Garp* is bleak, but it has something to say.

The movie, however, seems to believe that the book's characters and events are somehow real, or, to put it another way, that the *point* of the book is to describe these colorful characters and their unlikely behavior, just

as Melville described the cannibals in *Typee*. Although Robin Williams plays Garp as a relatively plausible, sometimes ordinary person, the movie never seems bothered by the jarring contrast between his cheerful pluckiness and the anarchy around him.

That created the following dilemma for me. While I watched *Garp*, I enjoyed it. I thought the acting was unconventional and absorbing (especially by Williams, by Glenn Close as his mother, and by John Lithgow as a transsexual). I thought the visualization of the events, by director George Roy Hill, was fresh and consistently interesting. But when the movie was over, my immediate response was not at all what it should have been. All I could find to ask myself was: What the hell was *that* all about?

A World Apart ★ ★ ★ ★
PG, 112 m., 1988

Barbara Hershey (Diana Roth), Jodhi May (Molly Roth), Jeroen Krabbe (Gus Roth), Carolyn Clayton-Cragg (Miriam Roth), Linda Mvusi (Elsie). Directed by Chris Menges and produced by Sarah Radclyffe. Screenplay by Shawn Slovo.

A World Apart was written by a woman who grew up in South Africa in the 1960s, while her parents were involved in the anti-apartheid movement, and it is very much a daughter's story; even though her parents were brave and dedicated, their child still nurses a sense of resentment because she did not get all of the attention she felt she deserved. *A World Apart* is both political and personal—a view of a revolutionary as the middle-class mother of a normal thirteen-year-old girl.

The girl's name is Molly (Jodhi May), and the film opens with episodes from her typical childhood in an affluent white South African community. She takes ballet lessons, she is picked up after class in a big American convertible piloted by her friend's mother, she attends the usual birthday parties, and splashes in a neighbor's swimming pool. The only thing unusual about her life is that some of her parents' friends are black—and in white South Africa in 1963, that is very unusual indeed.

Her parents are the Roths, Diana and Gus, and they are involved in a lot of activities she knows nothing about. One night her father comes to say goodbye to her, and the next day he is gone, having fled the country one step ahead of arrest on charges of communist subversion. Her mother stays behind, works for an anti-government newspaper, and moves in left-wing circles. A law is passed authorizing the government to detain anyone for up to ninety days on suspicion of subversive activities, and Diana Roth (Barbara Hershey) is one of the first to be detained.

We see this detention in two ways. Through the eyes of the mother, it is a terrifying form of torture, in which she is separated from her family and given no certain future to look forward to. She is interrogated daily by a government official who tries to ingratiate himself with her as kind of a good guy—he falls a little in love with her—but she adopts a stoic mask of determined resistance.

Hershey's own mother steps in to take care of the family during the period. For Molly, everything in her life turns out to have changed. Her best friend, for example, is suddenly cold toward her. She isn't invited to any more birthday or pool parties. Her parents are criminals and so she is somehow a criminal and a pariah, too. Meanwhile, on another front, the brother of the family's maid dies in the hands of the police, and political turmoil begins to simmer.

From a certain point of view, there is an irony here. Why should we care that a thirteen-year-old is not invited to swimming parties, when millions of black South Africans are denied elementary civil rights? From another point of view, A World Apart is stronger because it chooses to deal with the smaller details of specific lives. Unlike Cry Freedom, which was painted on such a large canvas that subtlety was lost, A World Apart is about the specific ways in which individual lives are affected by a legal system in which one's rights depend on one's race.

I spent a year in South Africa, in 1965, at the University of Cape Town, and I have often been disturbed by the ways in which so many fictional depictions of the country seem unable to communicate what it is like to live there. For most people of all races in South Africa, most days are fairly routine, devoted to the various activities of family and work, getting and spending and caring, that are the bedrock of lives everywhere. The country is not some sort of permanent political passion play. It is possible to fall into a workable, even comfortable, routine. It is by showing the placid surface of everyday life that A World Apart is able to dramatize how close beneath that surface the police state resides. For those who do not rock the boat, South Africa can be a very pleasant place to live.

Diana Roth rocks the boat, and through her daughter's eyes we see the result of that action. As played by Barbara Hershey, Roth is not an ideal mother, although she is a dutiful one; there is a certain hardness in her, an edge of anger that focuses on injustice and sometimes overlooks the needs of her family in what seem to be the more urgent needs of society. This is another fine, strong performance by Hershey, who has emerged in recent years as one of our best actresses.

Jodhi May, as young Molly, is equally impressive, and in many ways this is her movie. The screenplay (by Shawn Slovo, based on her own memories) gives May much to work with, but the ways in which her eyes express hurt and rejection are all her own. (Hershey, May, and Linda Mvusi, who plays the family's maid, shared the best actress award at the 1988 Cannes Film Festival.)

A World Apart has moments of almost unbearable hurt. One of them is at the moment when Hershey thinks her imprisonment is over, and is wrong. Another is when young Molly discovers the truth of a friend's rejection. Another, very powerful, is at the funeral of the murdered black man—a scene smaller, but more powerful, than the similar scene in Cry Freedom. The film is the first directorial work by Chris Menges, the cinematographer of The Killing Fields and The Mission. It is strong, angry, and troubling.

Wrestling Ernest Hemingway ★ ★ ★
PG-13, 122 m., 1994

Robert Duvall (Walt), Richard Harris (Frank), Shirley MacLaine (Helen), Sandra Bullock (Elaine), Piper Laurie (Georgia). Directed by Randa Haines and produced by Todd Black and Joe Wizan. Screenplay by Steve Conrad.

Two old men meet in the Florida sunshine. They could not be more different. They could not be more alike. One of them once wrestled with Ernest Hemingway, or so he says. The other spent most of his life as a barber in Cuba. In one way or another, both men are still wrestling with Ernest Hemingway: wrestling with the macho code he buried in most of his fiction, and wrestling also with the dark, fearsome places he wrote about, where our deaths await us.

These are not subjects the two old men talk about, of course. They talk about other things. About the available women in their small corner of the world, and about their families, which seem buried in the past. And they talk about the weather, about the news

in the papers, about the movies. Although they would seem to have nothing in common, they find themselves spending more and more time together, because—well, bluntly, because they are lonely and afraid to say so.

Wrestling Ernest Hemingway is based on a screenplay by Steve Conrad that could also have been a short novel, told mostly in dialogue. It has been directed by Randa Haines with an affection for the sunny, slightly shabby Florida locations where the population includes a lot of older people with time on their hands. The old guys are played by Robert Duvall, who is Walt, the Cuban; and Richard Harris, who is Frank, an Irishman and former Caribbean skipper.

Duvall is almost unrecognizable in the early scenes, behind clever makeup and a quiet accent. He plays a very gentle man, who cherishes a great passion for Elaine (Sandra Bullock), a cheerful waitress at the corner diner. It is his daily ritual to order two fried bacon sandwiches from her, one for breakfast, one for lunch. He flirts with her, shyly, and she lets him.

Harris hides behind no makeup and very few clothes; he likes to do push-ups without his clothes on. He's got a couple of women in his sights: Georgia (Piper Laurie), who he sees at the movie matinee several times a week, and who always eludes his requests for a date, and Helen (Shirley MacLaine), his landlady, who will occasionally drink his Irish whiskey, but draws the line there; her former husband was a no-good bum, and she doesn't need another one.

The Harris character sometimes says he is seventy, sometimes that he is seventy-five. He is much more worldly than Duvall's old barber, but no more successful with women. Duvall, in fact, seems incredibly innocent about women, and is crushed when he goes to ask Elaine to a dance, and discovers she is engaged. We never find out why he learned so little about women in Cuba, especially in a barbershop, where little else must have been discussed.

But never mind. The movie is essentially about the close observation of behavior. Like some of Hemingway's stories, the real action is all implied. The characters trade small talk, and we sense that larger issues are lurking beneath their cheerfulness.

Wrestling Ernest Hemingway was released a few weeks after Grumpy Old Men, another movie about two old guys (Jack Lemmon and Walter Matthau), but the approaches couldn't be more different. *Grumpy* is about comic characters, and about stars who embody them with their own famous personas. *Wrestling* is about quieter, more thoughtfully seen characters, and the actors are willing to dial down emotionally.

Audiences did not embrace this approach. Most of the successful movies about old guys are about the defiance of age. Consider, for example, the great success of *Cocoon*, in which the older characters were seen bursting with life and energy. Here we have a more sobering view. Walt and Frank have no great, urgent concerns, and their health at least seems to be okay, but they don't have much to do. Even more important, they don't have anyone who much cares what they do. Still, they keep on plugging, nursing their dreams of romance and happiness. Even when there is no longer an audience for it, a man must still behave according to his code. Hemingway wouldn't have had to wrestle with that.

Y,Z

The Year of Living Dangerously ★ ★ ★ ★
PG, 114 m., 1983

Mel Gibson (Guy Hamilton), Linda Hunt (Billy Kwan), Sigourney Weaver (Jill Bryant), Michael Murphy (Pete Curtis), Noel Ferrier (Wally O'Sullivan), Bill Kerr (Colonel Henderson). Directed by Peter Weir and produced by Jim McElroy. Screenplay by David Williamson, Weir, and C.J. Koch.

The Year of Living Dangerously achieves one of the best re-creations of an exotic locale I've ever seen in a movie. It takes us to Indonesia in the middle 1960s, a time when the Sukarno regime was shaky and the war in Vietnam was just heating up. It moves us into the life of a foreign correspondent, a radio reporter from Australia who has just arrived in Jakarta, and who thrives in an atmosphere heady with danger. How is this atmosphere created by Peter Weir, the director? He plunges into it headfirst. He doesn't pause for travelogue shots. He thrusts us immediately into the middle of the action—into a community of expatriates, journalists, and embassy people who hang out in the same bars, restaurants, and clubs, and speculate hungrily on the possibility that Sukarno might be deposed. That would be a really big story, a corrective for their vague feelings of being stuck in a backwater.

Guy Hamilton, the journalist (Mel Gibson), is a lanky, Kennedyesque, chain-smoking young man who has a fix on excitement. He doesn't know the ropes in Indonesia, but he learns them quickly enough, from a dwarfish character named Billy Kwan. Billy is half-Oriental and half-European, and knows everybody and can tell you where all the bodies are buried. He has a warm smile and a way of encouraging you to do your best, and if you sometimes suspect he has unorthodox political connections—well, he hasn't

crossed you yet. In all the diplomatic receptions he's a familiar sight in his gaudy tropical shirts. *The Year of Living Dangerously* follows Guy and Billy as they become friends, and something more than friends; they begin to share a common humanity and respect. Billy gets Guy a good interview with the local Communist Party chief. He even introduces Guy to Jill Bryant (Sigourney Weaver), a British attaché with two weeks left on her tour. As the revolution creeps closer, as the stories get bigger, Guy and Jill become lovers and Billy, who once proposed to Jill, begins to feel pushed aside.

This sounds, no doubt, like a foreign correspondent plot from the 1940s. It is not. *The Year of Living Dangerously* is a wonderfully complex film about personalities more than events, and we really share the feeling of living in that place, at that time. It does for Indonesia what Bogdanovich's *Saint Jack* did for Singapore. The direction is masterful; Weir (whose credits include *Picnic at Hanging Rock*) is as good with quiet little scenes (like Billy's visit to a dying child) as big, violent ones (like a thrilling attempt by Guy and Billy to film a riot).

The performances of the movie are a good fit with Weir's direction, and his casting of the Billy Kwan character is a key to how the film works. Billy, so small and mercurial, likable and complicated and exotic, makes Indonesia seem more foreign and intriguing than any number of standard travelogue shots possibly could. That means that when the travelogue shots *do* come (and they do, breathtakingly, when Gibson makes a trip into the countryside), they're not just scenery; they do their work for the film because Weir has so convincingly placed us in Indonesia. Billy Kwan is played, astonishingly, by a woman—Linda Hunt, a New York stage actress who enters the role so fully that

it never occurs to us that she is not a man. This is what great acting is, a magical transformation of one person into another. Mel Gibson (of *The Road Warrior*) is just right as a basically conventional guy with an obsessive streak of risk-taking. Sigourney Weaver has a less interesting role but is always an interesting actress. This is a wonderfully absorbing film.

Year of the Gun ★ ★ ★
R, 111 m., 1991

Andrew McCarthy (David Raybourne), Valeria Golino (Lia Spinelli), Sharon Stone (Alison King), John Pankow (Italo Bianchi), Mattia Sbragia (Giovanni), George Murcell (Pierre Bernier). Directed by John Frankenheimer and produced by Edward R. Pressman. Screenplay by David Ambrose.

The hero of John Frankenheimer's *Year of the Gun* is trapped in the same situation that Alfred Hitchcock found so useful: He is an innocent man, wrongly accused. This is the stuff of nightmares. He has lived blamelessly, but a combination of circumstances have conspired to make him look blatantly guilty. And nobody can see more clearly how guilty he seems than the innocent man himself.

In *Year of the Gun*, his name is David Raybourne, played by Andrew McCarthy. It is the mid-1970s, and Raybourne is an American free-lance writer, living in Rome, writing a novel. It is the time of the Red Brigades, of underground terrorist groups with fierce and unbending codes to enforce their secrecy. It is also the time of extraordinary police tactics to combat them—including secret assassination squads. Raybourne is a typical innocent American, uninvolved, living in what looks like a dreamworld to the European practitioners of realpolitik. Danger is all around him, but it can't touch him;

after all, he's an American citizen—here's his passport.

Raybourne begins writing a thriller based on a Red Brigade plot to kidnap a major Italian political leader. What he does not know is that the real Red Brigade is preparing to kidnap the famous politician Aldo Mori. If his novel were to fall into the wrong hands, it would look very much as if he had inside information. He must have been talking to someone.

Frankenheimer's Rome is off-season, not filled with lots of tourists, looking wet and gray. Raybourne is living the life of an exile in a rented room. He meets some people, including Alison King (Sharon Stone), a freelance photographer with a reputation for being in dangerous places at the right time. She's sold a lot of high-profile pictures. He also meets a Roman woman (Valeria Golino), and falls in love.

Among the characters in his exile's world are the editors and journalists of Rome's English-language daily newspaper, who are essentially outsiders like himself. Maybe some of them have connections it would be best not to examine too deeply. Then there are other people, apparently strangers, who swim into his view and seem to take an interest in him. Raybourne is such an innocent that it never occurs to him he could seriously be suspected of anything by anybody—certainly not of anything important. He is almost bemused by his own insignificance.

The novel falls into the wrong eyes. It appears to one side that Raybourne must be involved with the Red Brigades, and to the other that he may be prepared to betray them. Everything leads to a chilling scene on a hilltop outside of town, at which Raybourne discovers that ordinary innocent visiting Americans might indeed get shot dead for their naivete, and that just because someone likes you doesn't mean they can help you.

Frankenheimer's palate is perfectly suited to this material. The grays and browns of his autumn Rome, and the wet skies above it, cast a kind of weary Le Carréian gloom over the landscape. Andrew McCarthy, an open-faced, clean-cut actor, is a good choice for the lead; he looks like an innocent abroad. One of the things Frankenheimer is able to do is place this character in Rome, bury him in it, instead of simply using the city for location backdrops. There is a long foot chase of a kind we have seen before, but Frankenheimer makes it fresh by using architectural and street details as elements of the chase; it's like one of those chases in *The Third Man* that seem to be defined by the cityscape.

Will the Italian politics in *Year of the Gun* interest American audiences? In recent years moviegoers have seemed to develop a stubborn indifference to thriller plots that make them think. They prefer action and special effects. Frankenheimer's approach to this dilemma is to make Raybourne as much of an outsider as anyone in the audience. He's just a guy trying to make a buck writing a book. Too bad it's the wrong book.

Yentl ★ ★ ★ ½
PG, 134 m., 1983

Barbra Streisand (Yentl), Mandy Patinkin (Avigdor), Amy Irving (Hadass), Nehemiah Persoff (Papa). Directed and produced by Barbra Streisand. Screenplay by Jack Rosenthal and Streisand.

To give you a notion of the special magic of *Yentl*, I'd like to start with the following complicated situation:

Yentl, a young Jewish girl, wants to be a scholar. But girls are not permitted to study books. So she disguises herself as a boy, and is accepted by a community of scholars. She falls in love with one of them. He thinks she is a boy. He is in love with a local girl. The girl's father will not let him marry her. So he convinces Yentl to marry his girlfriend, so that at least he can visit the two people he cares for most deeply. (The girlfriend, remember this, thinks Yentl is a boy.) Yentl and the girl are wed. At first Yentl manages to disguise her true sex. But eventually she realizes that she must reveal the truth. That is the central situation in *Yentl*. And when the critical moment came when Yentl had to decide what to do, I was quietly astonished to realize that I did not have the slightest idea how this situation was going to turn out, and that I really cared about it.

I was astonished because, quite frankly, I expected *Yentl* to be some kind of schmaltzy formula romance in which Yentl's "secret identity" was sort of a running gag. You know, like one of those plot points they use for Broadway musicals where the audience is really there to hear the songs and see the costumes. But *Yentl* takes its masquerade seriously, it treats its romances with the respect due to genuine emotion, and its performances are so good that, yes, I really did care.

Yentl is Barbra Streisand's dream movie. She had been trying to make it for ten years, ever since she bought the rights to the Isaac Bashevis Singer story it's based on. Hollywood told her she was crazy. Hollywood was right—on the irrefutable logical ground that a woman in her forties can hardly be expected to be convincing as a seventeen-year-old boy. Streisand persisted. She worked on this movie four years, as producer, director, cowriter, and star. And she has pulled it off with great style and heart. She doesn't really look like a seventeen-year-old boy in this movie, that's true. We have to sort of suspend our disbelief a little. But she *does* look seventeen, and that's without a lot of trick lighting and funny filters on the lens, too. And she sings like an angel.

Yentl is a movie with a great middle. The beginning is too heavy-handed in establishing the customs against women scholars (an itinerant book salesman actually shouts, "Serious books for men . . . picture books for women"). And the ending, with Yentl sailing off for America, seemed like a cheat; I missed the final scene between Yentl and her "bride." But the middle 100 minutes of the movie are charming and moving and surprisingly interesting. A lot of the charm comes from the cheerful high energy of the actors, not only Streisand (who gives her best performance) but also Mandy Patinkin, as her long-suffering roommate, and Amy Irving, as the girl Patinkin loves and Streisand marries.

There are, obviously, a lot of tricky scenes involving this triangle, but the movie handles them all with taste, tact, and humor. It's pretty obvious what strategy Streisand and her collaborators used in approaching the scenes where Yentl pretends to be a boy. They began by asking what the scene would mean if she *were* a male, and then they simply played it that way, allowing the ironic emotional commentaries to make themselves.

There was speculation from Hollywood that *Yentl* would be "too Jewish" for middle-American audiences. I don't think so. Like all great fables, it grows out of a particular time and place, but it takes its strength from universal sorts of feelings. At one time or another, almost everyone has wanted to do something and been told they couldn't, and almost everyone has loved the wrong person for the right reason. That's the emotional ground that *Yentl* covers, and it always has its heart in the right place.

Young Frankenstein ★ ★ ★ ★
PG, 108 m., 1974

Gene Wilder (Dr. Frankenstein), Peter Boyle (His Monster), Madeline Kahn (Elizabeth), Cloris Leachman (Frau Blucher), Gene Hackman (Blind Man), Teri Garr (Inga). Directed by Mel Brooks and produced by Michael Gruskoff. Screenplay by Gene Wilder and Brooks.

The moment, when it comes, has the inevitability of comic genius. Young Victor Frankenstein, grandson of the count who started it all, returns by rail to his ancestral home. As the train pulls into the station, he spots a kid on the platform, lowers the window, and asks: "Pardon me, boy; is this the Transylvania station?" It is, and director Mel Brooks is home with *Young Frankenstein*, his most disciplined and visually inventive film (it also happens to be very funny). Victor is a professor in a New York medical school, trying to live down the family name and giving hilarious demonstrations of the difference between voluntary and involuntary reflexes. He stabs himself in the process, dismisses the class, and is visited by an ancient family retainer with his grandfather's will.

Frankenstein quickly returns to Transylvania and the old ancestral castle, where he is awaited by the faithful houseboy Igor, the voluptuous lab assistant Inga, and the mysterious housekeeper Frau Blucher, whose very name causes horses to rear in fright. The young man had always rejected his grandfather's medical experiments as impossible, but he changes his mind after he discovers a book entitled *How I Did It* by Victor Frankenstein. Now all that's involved is a little grave-robbing and a trip to the handy local Brain Depository, and the Frankenstein family is back in business.

In his two best comedies, before this, *The Producers* and *Blazing Saddles*, Brooks revealed a rare comic anarchy. His movies weren't just funny, they were aggressive and subversive, making us laugh even when we really should have been offended. (Explaining this process, Brooks once loftily declared, "My movies rise below vulgarity.") *Young Frankenstein* is as funny as we expect a Mel Brooks comedy to be, but it's more than that: It shows artistic growth and a more sure-handed control of the material by a director who once seemed willing to do literally anything for a laugh. It's more confident and less breathless.

That's partly because the very genre he's satirizing gives him a strong narrative he can play against. Brooks's targets are James Whale's *Frankenstein* (1931) and *Bride of Frankenstein* (1935), the first the most influential and the second probably the best of the 1930s Hollywood horror movies. Brooks uses carefully controlled black-and-white photography that catches the feel of the earlier films. He uses old-fashioned visual devices and obvious special effects (the train ride is a study in manufactured studio scenes). He adjusts the music to the right degree of squeakiness. And he even rented the original *Frankenstein* laboratory, with its zaps of electricity, high-voltage special effects, and elevator platform to intercept lightning bolts.

So the movie is a send-up of a style and not just of the material (as Paul Morrissey's dreadful *Andy Warhol's Frankenstein*). It looks right, which makes it funnier. And then, paradoxically, it works on a couple of levels: first as comedy, and then as a weirdly touching story in its own right. A lot of the credit for that goes to the performances of Gene Wilder, as young Frankenstein, and Peter Boyle as the monster. They act broadly when it's required, but they also contribute tremendous subtlety and control. Boyle somehow manages to be hilarious and pathetic at the same time.

There are set pieces in the movie that deserve comparison with the most famous scenes in *The Producers*. Demonstrating that he has civilized his monster, for example, Frankenstein and the creature do a soft-shoe number in black tie and tails. Wandering in the woods, the monster comes across a poor, blind monk (Gene Hackman, very good) who offers hospitality and winds up scalding, burning, and frightening the poor creature half to death.

There are also the obligatory town meetings, lynch mobs, police investigations, laboratory experiments, love scenes, and a cheerfully ribald preoccupation with a key area of the monster's stitched-together anatomy. From its opening title (which manages to satirize *Frankenstein* and *Citizen Kane* at the same time) to its closing, uh, refrain, *Young Frankenstein* is not only a Mel Brooks movie but also a loving commentary on our love-hate affairs with monsters. This time, the monster even gets to have a little love-hate affair of his own.

Young Sherlock Holmes ★ ★ ★
PG-13, 109 m., 1985

Nicholas Rowe (Holmes), Alan Cox (Watson), Sophie Ward (Elizabeth), Anthony Higgins (Rathe), Susan Fleetwood (Mrs. Dribb), Freddie Jones (Cragwitch), Nigel Stock (Waxflatter). Directed by Barry Levinson and produced by Mark Johnson. Executive producer, Steven Spielberg. Screenplay by Chris Columbus.

It really does make sense, once you've overcome the novelty of the idea, that Sherlock Holmes and John H. Watson originally met while at school. Their friendship is the sort of immature bond that can best be forged between adolescents, based on Watson's hero worship and Holmes's need for an admiring audience. There has always been something of the eternal teen-ager about Holmes and Watson, especially in their love of gadgets and mysteries and technical intricacies, and their complete bafflement when faced with such complex subjects as human nature, for example, or women.

Young Sherlock Holmes suggests that Holmes and Watson met in their middle teens, at an English public school, and that Holmes solved his first case at about the same time. This theory involves a rewriting of their historic first meeting, but the movie suggests that it set a pattern for many more meetings to come: Watson blunders into the orbit of the supercilious Holmes, who casually inspects him and uses a few elementary clues to tell him everything about himself.

The school they attend is one of those havens of eccentricity that have been celebrated in English fiction since time immemorial. It is run by Rathe (Anthony Higgins), a bright young man, but it is also inhabited by old professor Waxflatter (Nigel Stock), a retired don who hopes to invent the first airplane, and who regularly launches unsuccessful flights from the tops of the school buildings.

Holmes and Watson look, as schoolboys, like younger versions of the men they would someday become. Holmes (Nicholas Rowe) is tall, slender, and taciturn, and Watson (Alan Cox) is short and round and near-sighted. Watson is in every sense the new boy, always available to run an errand for the adored Holmes, to provide a cheering section, and to chronicle the great man's adventures.

The plot of *Young Sherlock Holmes* seems constructed out of odds and ends of several stories by Arthur Conan Doyle. For unknown reasons, several men with no apparent connection to one another die under mysterious circumstances. To Watson's amazement, Holmes finds the missing connection, determines that they have died while hallucinating, identifies the hallucinatory drug and its means of attack, and arrives at a likely suspect.

If these story elements seem typical of Conan Doyle, there is also a lot in this movie that can be traced directly to the work of Steven Spielberg, the executive producer. The teen-age heroes, for example, are not only inspired by Holmes and Watson, but are cousins of the young characters in *The Goonies*. The fascination with lighter-than-air flight leads to a closing scene that reminded me of *E.T.* And the villain's secret temple, with its ritual of human sacrifice, was not unlike scenes in both Indiana Jones movies.

It also doesn't take a Sherlock Holmes to identify the one element of *Young Sherlock Holmes* that definitely doesn't fit; that's the character of Elizabeth, a fetching young girl played by Sophie Ward. She is the granddaughter of the mad inventor, and also lives at the school, and we are asked to believe that young Holmes has had a schoolboy crush on her. I personally do not believe that Sherlock Holmes, the great investigator, ever even began to penetrate the mystery of women, but the movie just barely gets away with the character of Elizabeth by having Holmes swear there will never be another woman for him, for the rest of his life.

The elaborate special effects also seem a little out of place in a Sherlock Holmes movie, although I'm willing to forgive them because they were fun. The traditional world of Holmes (in the movies, anyway) has been limited to fogbound streets, speeding carriages, smoky sitting rooms, and the homes and laboratories of suspects. In this film, we get a series of hallucinations that are represented by fancy special effects, and then there's the pseudo-Egyptian temple of doom at the end.

The effects were supplied by Industrial Light & Magic, the George Lucas brain trust, and the best one is a computer-animated stained-glass window that fights a duel with a priest. I liked the effect, but I would have liked it more if, at the end of the movie, Holmes had drawn Watson aside, and, using a few elementary observations on the apparent movement of the stained glass, had deduced the eventual invention of computers.

Zelig ★ ★ ★
PG, 79 m., 1983

Woody Allen (Leonard Zelig), Mia Farrow (Dr. Fletcher). Interviews: Susan Sontag, Irving Howe, Saul Bellow, Bricktop, Bruno Bettelheim, Professor John Morton Blum. Directed by Woody Allen. Produced by Robert Greenhut. Screenplay by Allen.

Woody Allen's *Zelig* represents an intriguing idea for a movie, and it has been made with great ingenuity and technical brilliance. That's almost enough. In fact, if *Zelig* were only about an hour long, it would be enough, but the unwritten code of feature films requires that it be longer, and finally there is just so much Zelig that we say enough, already.

The movie is a fake documentary, a film that claims to tell the story of Leonard Zelig, a once-famous American who suffered from a most curious disease: He was a human chameleon. He was so eager to please, so loath to give offense, so willing to blend right in, that perhaps some change took place at a cellular level, and Zelig began to take on the social, intellectual, and even physical characteristics of people that he spent time with. Put him with a psychiatrist, and he began to discuss complexes. Put him next to a Chinese man, and he began to look Oriental. This ability to fit right in propelled Zelig, we are told, to the heights of fame in the earlier decades of this century. He hobnobbed with presidents, was honored by ticker-tape parades, and his case was debated by learned societies. *Zelig* at first seems to be simply the documentary record of Zelig's case, but then another level begins to sneak in.

We are introduced (always through the documentary means of newsreel film, still photos, old radio broadcasts, and narration) to one Dr. Eudora Fletcher, who is a psychiatrist. She takes Zelig as a patient, and eventually they fall in love (we can see it happening, by implication, in documentary footage that apparently concerns other matters). The best thing about *Zelig*, apart from its technical accomplishment, is the way Woody Allen develops the human story of his hero; we get a portrait of a life and a poignant dilemma, peeking out from behind the documentary façade. The technical approach of *Zelig* has been experimented with before, most memorably in the fictional *March of Time* newsreel that introduced *Citizen Kane*. In that movie, we saw Charles Foster Kane apparently standing on balconies with Hitler and talking with Mussolini. In *Zelig*, the

actors (Woody Allen, Mia Farrow, and dozens more) are so successfully integrated into old footage that we give up trying to tell the real from the fictional.

Zelig is a technical success, and it is also a success as a statement: Allen has a lot to say here about the nature of celebrity, science, and the American melting pot. He has also made an essay about film itself; the way that *Zelig*'s documentary material goes at right angles to its human story makes us think about the line between documentary and poetic "truth."

But the problem is, all of those achievements are easily accomplished at less length than the movie takes. The basic visual approach is clear from the first frames, and although it continues to impress us, it ceases after a while to amaze us. The emerging of Zelig's personality is intriguing, but the documentary framework allows it to emerge only so far, and no farther. We're left wanting more of Zelig and less of the movie's method; the movie is a technical masterpiece, but in artistic and comic terms, only pretty good.

Zentropa ★ ★ ★
R, 107 m., 1992

Jean-Marc Barr (Leopold Kessler), Barbara Sukowa (Katharina Hartmann), Udo Kier (Lawrence Hartmann), Ernst-Hugo Jaregard (Uncle Kessler), Erik Mork (Pater), Jorgen Reenberg (Max Hartmann), Henning Jensen (Siggy), Max von Sydow (Narrator). Special appearance: Eddie Constantine (Colonel Harris). Directed by Lars Von Trier and produced by Peter Aalbaek Jensen. Screenplay by Von Trier and Niels Vorsel.

Zentropa is a strange, haunting, labyrinthine film about a naive American in Germany just after the end of World War II. The American, named Leo, doesn't quite know what he's doing there; he has come to take a role in rebuilding the country because, he explains, it's about time Germany was shown some kindness. No matter how that sounds, he is not a Nazi sympathizer or even particularly pro-German—just confused. His uncle, who has a job on the railroad, gets Leo a job as a conductor on a Pullman car, and he is gradually drawn into a whirlpool of Germany's shames and secrets.

This process begins when Leo (Jean-Marc Barr) meets a sexy heiress (Barbara Sukowa) on the train. She seduces him and then takes him home to meet her family, which owns the company—named Zentropa—which manufactures the trains. These were the very trains that took Jews to their deaths during the war, but now they run a humdrum daily schedule, and the woman's Uncle Kessler (Ernst-Hugo Jaregard) poses as another one of those good Germans who were only doing their jobs.

Another guest at the house is a shadowy American intelligence man (Eddie Constantine, who has played the gravel-voiced Yankee in countless European productions). He has the goods on Uncle Kessler and can prove he was a war criminal, but it is all just confusing to Leo. Americans have been portrayed as naive innocents abroad for generations, but rarely has an American been more feckless than Leo, who goes back to his job on what increasingly looks like his own personal death train.

The narrative is told in a deliberately disjointed style by the film's Danish director, Lars Von Trier, whose strength is in the film's astonishing visuals. He shoots in black-and-white and color, he uses double exposures, optical effects, and trick photography, he places his characters inside a many-layered visual universe so that they sometimes seem like insects, caught between glass for our closer examination.

The movie is symbolic, although perhaps in a different way for every viewer. I read it as a film about the death throes of Naziism, which is represented by the train, and the moral culpability of Americans and others who turned up too late to save the victims of these trains and the camps where they delivered their doomed human cargo. The train, and the Nazi state, are dead, but like cartoon figures they continue to jerk through their motions; the message from the brain has not reached the body.

The best moments in the movie are the purely visual ones. Two trains shunting back and forth, Barr on one and Sukowa on another. An underwater shot of blood spreading. An incredibly evocative sequence on what it must be like to drown. And a hypnotic shot of train tracks, while Max von Sydow's voice invites us to return to Europe with him, and surrender our wills.

Zentropa, originally titled *Europa*, won both the directing award and a technical prize at the 1991 Cannes Film Festival, although both together did not satisfy Von Trier. Clearly thinking his film deserved the Palme d'Or (which went to *Barton Fink*, a film with certain similarities), he gave the jury the finger and stalked off. His anger is reflected in *Zentropa*, but so is the technical mastery the jury was honoring. The film is too confusing to be successful, but too striking and visually beautiful to be ignored.

Revivals and Restorations

An American in Paris ★ ★ ★ ½
G, 115 m., 1952

Gene Kelly (Jerry Mulligan), Leslie Caron (Lisa), Oscar Levant (Adam), Nina Foch (Milo), Georges Guetary (Henri). Directed by Vincente Minnelli and produced by Arthur Freed.

An American in Paris swept the Academy Awards for 1951, with Oscars for best picture and the major technical categories: screenplay, score, cinematography, art direction, set design, and even a special Oscar for the choreography of its eighteen-minute closing ballet extravaganza.

Singin' in the Rain, released in 1952 and continuing the remarkable golden age of MGM musicals, didn't do nearly as well on its initial release. But by the 1960s, *Singin'* was routinely considered the greatest of all Hollywood musicals, and *An American in Paris* was remembered with more respect than enthusiasm.

Now that the film has been restored for a national theatrical release and an eventual relaunch on tapes and laserdiscs, it's easy to see why *Singin'* passed it in the popularity sweepstakes. Its story of two Americans in Montparnasse—a struggling painter (Gene Kelly) and a perennial piano student (Oscar Levant)—is essentially a clothesline on which to hang recycled Gershwin songs ("I Got Rhythm," "S'Wonderful") and a corny story of love won, lost, and won again. Compared to *Singin'*'s tart satire of Hollywood at the birth of the talkies, it's pretty tame stuff.

And yet *American* has many qualities of its own, not least its famous ballet production number, with Kelly and Leslie Caron symbolizing the entire story of their courtship in dance. And there are other production numbers, set in everyday Parisian settings, that are endlessly inventive in their use of props and locations.

The stories of the two movies are curiously similar. In both of them, Kelly must break his romance of convenience with a predatory older blonde (Nina Foch in *American,* Jean Hagen in *Singin'*) in order to follow his heart to a younger, more innocent brunette (Leslie Caron and Debbie Reynolds). In both, he is counseled by a best friend (Oscar Levant and Donald O'Connor). And in both there is a dramatic moment when all seems lost, just when it is about to be gained.

Singin' is the more realistic picture, which is perhaps why it holds up better today. *American* has scenes that are inexplicable, including the one where Levant joins Kelly and their French friend Henri (Georges Guetary) at a café. When he realizes they are both in love with the same woman, Levant starts lighting a handful of cigarettes while simultaneously trying to drink coffee. Maybe it seemed funny at the time.

There's also a contrast between the Nina Foch character—a possessive rich woman who hopes to buy Kelly's affections—and Jean Hagen's brassy blonde, a silent star whose shrieking voice is not suited to the sound era. Foch's blonde is just plain sour and unpleasant. Hagen's blonde is funny and fun. And, for that matter, there's no comparing the ingenues, either: Caron, still unformed, a great dancer but a so-so actress, and Reynolds, already a pro in her film debut, perky and bright-eyed.

The version now being released is a "true" restoration, according to the experts at Turner Entertainment, who say the job they did on *American* compares to the salvage work in *Gone With the Wind* and *Lawrence of Arabia.* Because two reels of the original negative were destroyed by fire, painstaking lab work was necessary to match those reels to the rest of the film. The result is a bright and fresh-looking print, in which the colors are (probably deliberately) not as saturated or bold as in the classic Technicolor process.

The ads say the movie is now in stereo. This is not quite true. Only the eighteen-minute ballet has been reprocessed into a sort of reconstructed stereo, and if a theater plays the whole film in stereo, the result may be the kind of raw-edged sound I heard at a press screening, before the projectionist gave up and switched to mono. The best choice would probably be to start in mono and physically switch to stereo when the ballet starts—although why so much labor is expended on quasi-stereo effects is beyond me. The real reasons to see *An American in Paris* are for the Kelly dance sequences, the closing ballet, the Gershwin songs, the bright locations, and a few moments of the ineffable, always curiously sad charm of Oscar Levant.

Bambi ★ ★ ★ ½
G, 69 m., 1942

In the annals of the great heartbreaking moments in the movies, the death of Bambi's mother ranks right up there with the chaining of Mrs. Jumbo and the moment when E.T. seems certainly dead. These are movie moments that provide a rite of passage for children of a certain age: You send them in as kids, and they come out as sadder and wiser preteen-agers.

Seeing *Bambi* again, I was reminded of the strength of the movie's most famous scene. I was sitting behind a four-year-old who asked his mother, "Where's Bambi's mom?" during that long, sad passage before Bambi's father comes along to explain the facts of death. How do you answer a question like that? For some kids, *Bambi* probably represents their first exposure to the existence of death.

And there are other moments in the movie almost as momentous. *Bambi* exists alone in the Disney canon. It is not an adventure and not a "cartoon," but an animated feature that describes, with surprising seriousness the birth and growth of a young deer. Everybody remembers the cute early moments when Bambi can't find his footing and keeps tripping over his own shadow. Those scenes are among the most charming the Disney animators ever drew.

But in the course of little more than an hour, those funny moments are followed by Bambi's exposure to man, his first experience with guns and killing, the death of his mother, and the destruction of the forest by fire. By then the deer has grown to young adulthood, and finds that he must battle another stag for the favors of the female deer he fancies.

The movie ends after Bambi has become a father. Do you remember the last shot? It shows Bambi and his own father, two proud stags silhouetted against the sky. Meanwhile, Bambi's mate takes care of raising his child. This is as it should be in the world of Bambi; the hero is raised by his own mother, while his father poses on the mountaintop.

Bambi is essentially a fable about how children are born, raised, and come of age in a hard, cruel world. Its messages are many. Young viewers learn that fathers are absent and mysterious authority figures, worshiped and never blamed by mothers, who do all the work of child-raising. They learn that you have to be quick and clever to avoid being killed deliberately—and that even then, you might easily be killed accidentally. They learn that courtship is a matter of "first love" and instant romance with no communication, and that the way to win the physical favors of the desired mate is to beat up all the other guys who want to be with her. And they learn that after you've grown to manhood and fathered a child, your role is to leave home and let your mate take care of the domestic details.

Hey, I don't want to sound like an alarmist here, but if you really stop to think about it, *Bambi* is a parable of sexism, nihilism, and despair, portraying absentee fathers and passive mothers in a world of death and violence. I know the movie's a perennial classic, seen by every generation, remembered long after other movies have been forgotten. But I am not sure it's a good experience for children—especially very young and impressionable ones.

We forget how real animated cartoons seem to small children. Think back. When you were very young, didn't you always consider the cartoons to be more real than the live-action features, because the colors were brighter, the edges were sharper, and the motives and behavior were easier to understand? That's how I felt, and for me, *Snow White* and *Pinocchio* and *Dumbo* were not fantasies but realities. There's a tradition in our society of exposing kids to the Disney classics at an early age, and for most kids and most of the Disney movies, that's just fine. But *Bambi* is pretty

serious stuff. I don't know if some little kids are going to be ready for it.

Beyond the Valley of the Dolls
NC-17, 109 m., 1970 | NEW

With Dolly Read, Cynthia Myers, Marcia McBroom, David Gurian, John LaZar, Michael Blodgett, Edy Williams, Erica Gavin, Phyllis Davis, Charles Napier and the Strawberry Alarm Clock. Directed and produced by Russ Meyer. Screenplay by Roger Ebert.

Beyond the Valley of the Dolls, *a movie for which I wrote the screenplay in 1969, has over the years become a cult film. Although it would not be appropriate for me to review it, I offer the following observations written for* Film Comment *magazine on the occasion of the movie's tenth anniversary, in 1980.*

Remembered after ten years, *Beyond the Valley of the Dolls* seems more and more like a movie that got made by accident when the lunatics took over the asylum. At the time Russ Meyer and I were working on *BVD* I didn't really understand how unusual the project was. But in hindsight I can recognize that the conditions of its making were almost miraculous. An independent X-rated filmmaker and an inexperienced screenwriter were brought into a major studio and given carte blanche to turn out a satire of one of the studio's own hits. And *BVD* was made at a time when the studio's own fortunes were so low that the movie was seen almost fatalistically, as a gamble that none of the studio executives really wanted to think about, so that there was a minimum of supervision (or even cognizance) from the Front Office.

We wrote the screenplay in six weeks flat, laughing maniacally from time to time, and then the movie was made. Whatever its faults or virtues, *Beyond the Valley of the Dolls* is an original—a satire of Hollywood conventions, genres, situations, dialogue, characters, and success formulas, heavily overlaid with such shocking violence that some critics didn't know whether the movie "knew" it was a comedy.

Although Russ Meyer had been signed to a three-picture deal by 20th Century-Fox, I wonder whether at some level he didn't suspect that *BVD* would be his best shot at employing all the resources of a big studio at the service of his own highly personal vision, his world of libidinous, simplistic creatures who inhabit a pop universe. Meyer wanted everything in the screenplay except

the kitchen sink. The movie, he theorized, should simultaneously be a satire, a serious melodrama, a rock musical, a comedy, a violent exploitation picture, a skin flick, and a moralistic exposé (so soon after the Sharon Tate murders) of what the opening crawl called "the oft-times nightmarish world of Show Business."

What was the correct acting style for such a hybrid? Meyer directed his actors with a poker face, solemnly, discussing the motivations behind each scene. Some of the actors asked me whether their dialogue wasn't supposed to be humorous, but Meyer discussed it so seriously with them that they hesitated to risk offending him by voicing such a suggestion. The result is that *BVD* has a curious tone all of its own. There have been movies in which the actors played straight knowing they were in satires, and movies which were unintentionally funny because they were so bad or camp. But the tone of *BVD* comes from actors directed at right angles to the material. "If the actors perform as if they know they have funny lines, it won't work," Meyer said, and he was right.

The movie was inspired only incidentally by *Valley of the Dolls.* Neither Meyer nor I ever read Jacqueline Susann's book, but we did screen the Mark Robson film, and we took the same formula: Three young girls come to Hollywood, find fame and fortune, are threatened by sex, violence, and drugs, and either do or do not win redemption. The original book was a *roman a clef,* and so was *BVD,* with an important difference: We wanted the movie to seem like a fictionalized exposé of real people, but we personally possessed no real information to use as inspiration for the characters. The character of teenage rock tycoon Ronnie "Z-Man" Barzell, for example, was supposed to be "inspired" by Phil Spector—but neither Meyer nor I had ever met Spector.

The movie's story was made up as we went along, which makes subsequent analysis a little tricky. Not long ago, for example, I was invited up to Syracuse University to discuss Russ Meyer's work, and the subject of Z-Man came up. (Readers who have seen *BVD* will know that Z-Man is a rock Svengali who seems to be a gay man for most of the movie, but is finally revealed to be a woman in drag.) Some of the questions at Syracuse dealt with the "meaning" of Z-Man's earlier scenes, in light of what is later discovered about the character. But in fact those earlier scenes were written before either Meyer or I knew Z-Man was a transvestite: that plot development came on the spur of the moment. So, too, did such inspirations as quoting a *Citizen Kane* camera movement from a stage below to a catwalk above, or the use of the Fox musical fanfare during the beheading sequence. They asked at Syracuse if Meyer's use of the Fox trademark music was a put-down of the studio system. Meyer's motive was much more basic: By using the music, he hoped to establish a satiric tone to the scene that would moderate the effect of the beheading and help protect against an X rating.

In the event, of course, *Beyond the Valley of the Dolls* was rated X anyway. There is a story about that. If the movie were to be rated today, it would probably get an R rating with a few small cuts. It was a very mild X. That was because Meyer and the studio were aiming for the R rating. When they didn't get it, Meyer believed the ratings board had felt obligated to give the "King of the Nudies" an X rating, lest it seem to endorse his movie to the Majors.

Because the movie was stuck with the X, Meyer wanted to re-edit certain scenes in order to include more nudity (he shot many scenes in both X and R versions). But the studio, still in the middle of a cash-flow crisis, wanted to rush the film into release. Meyer still waxes nostalgic for the "real" X version of *BVD*, which exists only in his memory but includes many much steamier scenes starring the movie's many astonishingly beautiful heroines and villianesses.

The visit to Syracuse was a chance for me to see *BVD* again for the first time in a few years. The movie still seems to play for audiences; it hasn't dated, apart from the rather old-fashioned narrative quality it had even at the time of its release. It begins rather slowly, because so many characters have to be established and such an ungainly plot has to be set in motion. (The story is such a labyrinthine juggling act that resolving it took a quadruple murder, a narrative summary, a triple wedding, and an epilogue.) But the last hour has a real kinetic energy, and the scenes beginning with Z-Man's psychedelic orgy and ending with his death are, I must say on Meyer's behalf, as exciting, terrifying, and dynamic as any such sequence I can remember. That stretch of *BVD* is pure cinema, combining shameless melodrama, highly charged images of violence, sledgehammer editing, and musical overkill. It works.

And the movie as a whole? I think of it as an essay on our generic expectations. It's an anthology of stock situations, characters, dialogue, clichés, and stereotypes, set to music and manipulated to work as exposition and satire at the same time; it's cause and effect, a wind-up machine to generate emotions, pure movie without message. The strange thing about the movie is that it continues to play successfully to completely different audiences for different reasons. When Meyer and I were hired a few years later to work on an ill-fated Sex Pistols movie called *Who Killed Bambi?* we were both a little nonplussed, I think, to hear Johnny Rotten explain that he liked *Beyond the Valley of the Dolls* because it was so true to life.

Note: Because of the obvious conflict of interest, I am not providing Beyond the Valley of the Dolls *with a star rating.*

Blade Runner: The Director's Cut ★ ★ ★
R, 115 m., 1992

Harrison Ford (Rick Deckard), Rutger Hauer (Roy Batty), Sean Young (Rachael), Edward James Olmos (Gaff), M. Emmet Walsh (Bryant), Joe Turkel (Tyrell), Daryl Hannah (Pris). Directed by Ridley Scott and produced by Michael Deeley. Screenplay by Hampton Fancher and David Peoples.

One of the benefits of home video is that it sometimes allows the director to have the last word—if not sooner, then later. Ever since Steven Speilberg released the "Special Edition" of his *Close Encounters of the Third Kind*, directors have been reediting their movies and releasing versions that are longer, or sexier, or more profound, or in any event different from the versions that were originally released to theaters.

Sometimes the changes are minor—a few more nude scenes or some longer dialogue. Sometimes they are substantial, as in the new director's version of Ridley Scott's *Blade Runner* (1982). Scott has abandoned the Harrison Ford narration of the original version, added some moments to the love affair between Ford and Sean Young, fleshed out a few other scenes, and, most notably, provided what he describes as a "somewhat bleaker ending."

This is, he says, the version he would have released in 1982 if he could have. The Ford narration was added because the studio feared audiences would not understand his story of a futuristic Los Angeles. The new ending, which is ironic and inconclusive and gives Ford an existentialist exit line, was of course dropped by studio executives for a more standard violent outcome.

I watched the original *Blade Runner* on video a few years ago, and now, watching the director's cut, I am left with the same overall opinion of the movie: It looks fabulous, it uses special effects to create a new world of its own, but it is thin in its human story. The movie creates a vision of Los Angeles, circa 2020, which is as original and memorable as such other future worlds as Fritz Lang's *Metropolis* or George Lucas's *Star Wars* planets. Unimaginable skyscrapers tower over streets that are clotted with humanity; around the skirts of the billion-dollar towers, the city at ground level looks like a Third World bazaar.

The Ford character inhabits this city as a "blade runner"—a cop assigned to track down and kill "replicants," who are artificial humans, built through genetic engineering. After an uprising on an outworld, six replicants have returned secretly to Earth, where their deaths have been ordered by the slimy leader of an evil megacorporation (Joe Turkel). Ford, on their trail, encounters Rachael (Sean Young, in an early role) and falls in love with her, as the screenplay toys with the nature of humanity.

I have always been moved by the special cruelty done to the replicants, who are supplied with phony memories (they have a life span of four years, yet think they remember their childhoods). One of the film's poignant scenes has Ford coldly telling Young what she remembers from when she was a little girl—because she has the same memories as all other replicants.

Seeing the movie again, even in this revised version, I still felt the human story did not measure up to the special effects. Ford is always good when surrounded by amazing visuals, perhaps because he keeps cool and does not seem to notice them. Sean Young and, more briefly, Rutger Hauer, are effective as replicants who want only to live the lives they seem to have been given. But the character of Tyrell, the evil billionaire, has never been convincing, and the way he is murdered doesn't say much for his security measures. And the love affair between Ford and Young, though properly bittersweet, seems to exist more for the plot than for them.

And yet the world of *Blade Runner* has undeniably become one of the visual touchstones of modern movies. The movie's Los Angeles, with its permanent dark cloud of smog, its billboards hundreds of feet high, its street poverty living side by side with incredible wealth, may or may not come true—but there aren't many ten-year-old movies that look more prophetic now than they did at the time.

Carnival of Souls ★ ★ ★
NO MPAA RATING, 80 m., 1962

Candace Hilligoss (Mary Henry), Sidney Berger (John Linden), Frances Feist (Landlady), Herk Harvey ("The Man"), Stanley Leavitt (Doctor), Art Ellison (Minister), Tom McGinnis (Boss). Directed and produced by Harold "Herk" Harvey. Screenplay by John Clifford.

Carnival of Souls is an odd, obscure horror film that was made on a low budget in 1962 in Lawrence, Kansas, and still has an intriguing power. Like a lost episode from "The Twilight Zone," it places the supernatural right in the middle of everyday life and surrounds it with ordinary people. In 1989, the movie was revived in art houses around the country, and it's possible that it plays better today than when it was released. It ventures to the edge of camp, but never strays across the line, taking itself with an eerie seriousness.

The movie stars Candace Hilligoss, one of those worried blondes like Janet Leigh in *Psycho,* as a young woman who goes along for the ride when two hot-rodders hold a drag race. On a narrow wooden bridge, one of the cars crashes through a railing and plunges into the flooded river below. Police and volunteers search for the wreckage in vain— and then Hilligoss appears on a sandbar, dazed and covered with mud.

What happened to the others? How did she escape? She doesn't know. Indeed, she doesn't care. She's a brittle, cynical woman who works as a church organist but doesn't take religion seriously. That's despite the fact that the organ seems to be trying to tell her something. There is a sensational overhead shot in an organ factory, looking down past the steep, angled pipes to her diminutive figure far below, and another effective moment when she's in a car on a deserted highway and the radio picks up only organ music.

A few days after she crawls out of the river, the woman leaves town for a job playing the organ in Utah, and in one of the movie's best shots, a cadaverous face appears in the car window. It's the face of a ghostly figure who will follow her to Utah (the figure is played by the film's director, Harold "Herk" Harvey). In Utah, she checks into one of those B-movie boardinghouses, presided over by the cherubic Frances Feist.

There's one other boarder, a Mr. Linden (Sidney Berger), who is a definitive study of a nerd in lust.

Unlike most of today's horror movies, *Carnival of Souls* has few special effects— some wavy lines as we pass through various levels of existence and that's it. Instead, it depends on crisp black-and-white photography, atmosphere, and surprisingly effective acting. It's impossible to know whether this movie was seen by such directors as David Lynch or George Romero, but in the way it shows the horror beneath the surface of placid small-town life, it suggests *Blue Velvet,* and a shot of dead souls at an abandoned amusement park reminded me of the lurching undead in *Night of the Living Dead.*

Casablanca ★ ★ ★ ★
NO MPAA RATING, 102 m., 1942

Humphrey Bogart (Rick Blaine), Ingrid Bergman (Ilsa Lund), Paul Henreid (Victor Laszlo), Claude Rains (Captain Louis Renault), Sydney Greenstreet (Ferrari), Peter Lorre (Ugarte), S.Z. Sakall (Carl), Conrad Veidt (Major Strasser), Dooley Wilson (Sam). Directed by Michael Curtiz and produced by Hal B. Wallis. Screenplay by Julius J. Epstein, Phillip G. Epstein, and Howard Koch.

Casablanca is The Movie.

There are greater movies. More profound movies. Movies of greater artistic vision or artistic originality or political significance. There are other titles we would put above it on our lists of the best films of all time. But when it comes right down to the movies we treasure the most, when we are—let us imagine—confiding the secrets of our heart to someone we think we may be able to trust, the conversation sooner or later comes around to the same seven words:

"I really love *Casablanca.*"

"I do too."

This is a movie that has transcended the ordinary categories. It has outlived the Bogart cult, survived the revival circuit, shrugged off those who would deface it with colorization, leaped across time to win audiences who were born decades after it was made. Sooner or later, usually before they are twenty-one, everyone sees *Casablanca.* And then it becomes one of their favorite movies.

It is The Movie.

In 1992, *Casablanca* was fifty years old. That is a long time in movie history, since the movies themselves are only about a hundred. But it is an instant in the span of time, and

some of the people who made it, including two of its writers, are still alive. The stars are all dead, but Curt Bois, who played the little pickpocket who warned visitors to Casablanca against the pickpockets, died only in 1992. The story of how it was made, of how quickly and inevitably this wonderful film seemed to flow through the studio system, is part of Hollywood legend. It is told again in the book, *Casablanca: The Script and the Legend, 50th Anniversary Edition* (Overlook Press, $16.95), which includes the screenplay, a memoir by cowriter Howard Koch, and essays by various people who love the film, myself included.

Movies are, in a sense, immortal. It is likely that people will be watching *Casablanca* centuries from now (and how wonderful it would be if we could see movies from centuries ago). In another sense, however, movies are fragile. They live on long flexible strips of celluloid, which fade, and tear, and collect scratches every time they travel through a movie projector. And sometimes films burn or disintegrate into dust.

For the fiftieth anniversary of *Casablanca,* the Turner movie division, which now owns the film, brought out a restored black-and-white 35mm theatrical print. The chances are it looks better than any version of *Casablanca* you have ever seen. This new print was also the basis for a new videotape release of the film, and prints of comparable quality have been made into laserdiscs by Warner Bros. and the Criterion Collection. I admire the tape and both of the discs, but I will offer one urgent piece of advice: If there is any way you can see this movie in 35mm in a theater, with an audience, do it.

And as for The Movie itself . . .

The key passages in *Casablanca,* of course, are the ones that immediately follow the unexpected entrance of Ingrid Bergman, as Ilsa, into Rick's place. These are unusual among classic movie scenes in being more emotionally affecting on subsequent viewings than they are the first time, and indeed, *Casablanca* is one of those rare films that actually improves with repeated viewings.

The first time we see the film we know nothing of the great love affair between Rick and Ilsa in Paris, and so we are simply following along, and the byplay between Ilsa and Rick has still to be decoded. We know it means something, but as yet we don't fully understand it. Then the film continues, and we experience the memories of Paris, we understand the depth of Ilsa's feelings, and the movie sweeps on to its magnificent conclusion. The *next* time we see it, every word between Ilsa and Rick, every nuance, every look or averted glance, has a poignant meaning. It is a good enough scene the first time we see it, but a great scene the second time.

In a sense the whole movie demands the same kind of repeated viewings. Find, if you can, someone who has never seen it, and sit next to your friend during the film. You will almost certainly find yourself more involved than your companion. Your friend is not an insensitive boor; he or she simply does not understand, as you do, the infinite gradations of poignancy to be found behind every look, and overheard in every line. And a first viewing may not even pick up on some of the film's quieter asides, such as the subplot involving the young woman who will do anything to help her husband get out of Casablanca.

If familiarity makes the movie more effective, it also exposes some weaknesses that are not at first apparent. There came a time, in my history with *Casablanca*, when I realized that I did not like Victor Laszlo, the Paul Henreid character, very much. He is a heroic leader of the resistance, but he has no humor and no resilience. If in peacetime he finds himself in political office, I believe he will be most comfortable in a totalitarian regime. When at the end of the film Rick tells a lie about what happened between himself and Ilsa, in order to preserve Ilsa's image in Laszlo's eyes, Laszlo hardly seems to care. In fact, I think he hardly deserves Ilsa. Rick tells her that her place is at Victor's side, but does Victor notice her there, or need her there? In the long run he is married to his career and his heroism, and there will be more nights when she hears "As Time Goes By" and realizes she made a mistake when she got on that airplane.

Of course, *Casablanca* is not about love anyway, but about nobility. Set at a time when it seemed possible that the Nazis would overrun civilization, it seriously argues that the problems of a few little people don't amount to a hill of beans. The great break between *Casablanca* and almost all Hollywood love stories—even wartime romances— is that it does not believe love can, or should, conquer all. As I analyze my own feelings about the small handful of movies that affect me emotionally, I find that I am hardly ever moved by love, but often moved by self-sacrifice.

Like everyone who deeply cares for movies,

I identify with some characters more than I might want to admit. In *Casablanca*, I identify with Rick, and what moves me is not his love for Ilsa but his ability to put a higher good above that love. The Henreid character is a pig because he wants to have his cake and eat it too. What kind of a serious resistance fighter would drag a woman around with him, placing her and his work in unnecessary danger, unless his ego required her adoration? A true hero would have insisted on leaving Casablanca alone, both for the good of his work and for the happiness of the woman he loves. Laszlo is so blind he does not even understand what exists between Rick and Ilsa. The movie makes a half-hearted attempt to show that Ilsa loves both men, but we can read her heart.

Bogart has never been more touching than as he sits alone with his bottle and his cigarette, drenched in self-pity. The cruelty with which he assaults Ilsa after she walks back into the empty club is all the more painful because it is masochistic; talking that way hurts Rick himself much more than it hurts her. He is tearing at an open wound. She is a little slow to understand, but then one of the screenplay's subtle qualities is that Ilsa is always a beat behind what is really happening.

If it were true, as legend has it, that the ending of the movie was not written until the last day, and that Bergman never knew which of the two men Ilsa would end up with, that would explain her air of being slightly dazed. Alas, this wonderful legend is almost certainly not true, because the Hollywood Production Code of the day would not have allowed her to abandon the man she was legally married to, and stay behind with the man she loves. No matter how often we hear that the ending was not delivered until the last day of shooting, *Casablanca* could only have ended as it does. And not simply because of the code, but also because the whole moral undercurrent of the movie requires Rick to sacrifice Ilsa.

Yet Bergman is utterly convincing as she turns from one man to the other on the tarmac of the airport. She is torn. And emotional confusion in the presence of a man she loves was always one of Bergman's strongest qualities as an actress. We can see that in Hitchcock's *Notorious*, a film with a buried theme remarkably similar to *Casablanca*, in which Cary Grant plays the man who loves her—but must pretend not to because of the higher goal of fighting the enemy.

Michael Curtiz's direction of *Casablanca*

is remarkable for being completely economical. He creates a picture we would be hardpressed to improve, and does it without calling attention to the fact that it has been directed at all. Mostly he uses the basic repertory of cinematic storytelling, as encoded by Griffith and rehearsed in thousands of earlier films: establishing shot, movement, medium shots, alternating close-ups, point-of-view shots, reactions. Is there a single shot that calls attention to itself for its own sake? I cannot think of one (there are dozens in *Citizen Kane*). Curtiz is at the service of the characters and the story. Nobody ever asks, "Remember that great shot in *Casablanca*?" because there are no great shots in *Casablanca*. Anyone who thinks there are was misinformed.

Howard Hawks, asked for his definition of a great movie, said: "Three great scenes, no bad scenes." *Casablanca* multiplies his formula by four.

Cinderella ★ ★ ★
G, 74 m., 1950

Voices by Ilene Woods, Eleanor Audley, Verna Felton, Claire Dubrey, Helene Stanley, Luis Van Rooten, Don Barclay, Rhoda Williams, and James MacDonald. Directed by Wilfred Jackson, Hamilton Luske, and Clyde Geronimi. Directing animators: Eric Larson, Milt Kahl, Frank Thomas, John Lounsbery, Wolfgang Reitherman, Ward Kimball, Ollie Johnston, Marc Davis, Les Clark, and Norm Ferguson.

Walt Disney's *Cinderella* is considered by the studio to be a perennial that blooms every seven years or so, just in time for a new generation of kids. It has been several generations since I saw it as a kid, although when I saw it again recently, it was clear that it hadn't changed that much, and neither, in certain ways, had I.

This time around I was more aware of the power of the full-animation techniques, and I appreciated Disney's policy of using unfamiliar voices for the dubbing, instead of the studio's guess-that-voice derbies of recent years. But in other ways the movie still worked for me just as it had the first time. When those little mice bust a gut trying to drag that key up hundreds of stairs in order to free Cinderella, I don't care how many Kubrick pictures you've seen, it's still exciting.

You doubtless remember the original story. You may not—as I did not—remember how much the Disney studio expanded and supplemented it. Disney's most valuable and original contribution to the *Cinderella* tale was the addition of dozens of animals to the story. The screen fairly bursts with little birds helping Cinderella to dress, little mice helping her to plot, a dog to leap to the rescue, and an evil cat named Lucifer to chase the birds, pounce on the mice, spit at the dog, and do its best to come between Cinderella and Prince Charming.

These animals serve much the same function as the Seven Dwarfs (and assorted birds and forest animals) did in *Snow White*. They provide a chorus, moral support, additional characters to flesh out a thin story, and a kaleidoscope of movement on the screen. When one of the little birds creeps under Cinderella's pillow to awaken her in the morning, it doesn't matter that I was aware of the shameless manipulation of the animators; I grinned anyway.

Using the traditional techniques of full animation, the Disney artists provided each animal with a unique flavor and personality. What they also did (as Richard Schickel observed in *The Disney Version*) was shamelessly wag the buttocks of all of the animals as a way of making them seem even livelier; a Disney quadruped has its center of gravity somewhere below its navel and its pivot point right beneath the wallet. With all that action going on, no wonder they never wore pants.

If there is an obvious difference between *Cinderella* and such predecessors as *Pinocchio* and *Snow White*, it's in the general smoothing-out of the central characters' appearances. Snow White herself looked fairly bland, but the other characters in the first decade of Disney animation had a lot of personality in their faces. They were allowed to look odd. *Cinderella* seems to come right out of its time, the bland postwar 1950s. Cinderella looks like the Draw Me girl, Prince Charming has all of the charm of a department-store dummy, and even the wicked stepsisters seem petulant rather than evil. Only the old king, his aide, and a few of the mice look bright enough to split a ticket.

Yet the movie works. There are dozens of little dramas played out for a minute or two by the mice, who must outsmart the cat and alert the dog. There are touching moments involving the king, who wants an heir more than anything, and looks on glumly as his son rejects all the women in the kingdom— except for one. And then there is that thrilling montage at the end, while the stepsisters desperately try to get the glass slipper to fit,

while the mice sneak the key to Cinderella. You've got to hand it to her: The kid still has life. Another seven years, anyway.

Citizen Kane ★ ★ ★ ★
NO MPAA RATING, 119 m., 1941

Orson Welles (Kane), Joseph Cotten (Jedediah Leland), Dorothy Comingore (Susan Alexander), Ray Collins (Jim Geddes), George Coulouris (Walter Parks Thatcher), Agnes Moorehead (Mrs. Kane), Ruth Warrick (Emily Norton). Directed and produced by Orson Welles. Screenplay by Herman J. Mankiewicz and Welles.

In 1941, Orson Welles had finished what would eventually become known as the greatest movie of all time. But he was having trouble getting it released.

Citizen Kane told the story of an aging press tycoon whose arrogance had alienated him from everyone who loved him, and who had died alone inside the vast Gothic pile of his lonely castle in Florida. To many observers, Charles Foster Kane bore an uncanny resemblance to William Randolph Hearst, the aging press tycoon who lived in San Simeon, his famous California castle. And to Hearst's underlings, *Citizen Kane* was so unflattering to their boss that they banned all mention of it from the Hearst papers, radio stations, and wire services. For good measure, they also banned all mention of every other movie from the same studio, RKO Radio Pictures.

During one extraordinary moment in the negotiations leading up to the release of *Citizen Kane,* the very existence of the film itself was in doubt. Terrified by the possibility of an anti-Hollywood campaign by the Hearst press, a group of industry leaders, led by MGM's Louis B. Mayer, offered RKO a cash settlement to simply destroy the film. It would have covered RKO's costs and added a small profit. But by then Welles had already sneak-previewed the movie to so many powerful opinion-makers that it was too late to sweep it under the rug.

Citizen Kane never did get a proper national release, however. It could not play in the major theaters in many cities, because they were block-booked by the big studios, which boycotted it. It could not be advertised in the influential Hearst papers (the ads referred only to a mysterious "New Screen Attraction"). And although the film was instantly hailed by many critics, John O'Hara in *Newsweek* and Bosley Crowther in the *New*

York Times among them, it won only one Academy Award—which Welles shared with Herman Mankiewicz, for the screenplay.

The legends of *Citizen Kane* and Orson Welles were, in the next half century, to become one of the central myths of Hollywood: How a boy genius in his mid-twenties was given a completely free rein to make exactly the movie he wanted to make, and how in response he made the greatest movie of all time, only to see both the film and his own career chewed up and spat out by the venal, small-minded Hollywood establishment. Welles became the great outsider hero of cinema, central to the French auteur critics, championed by independent filmmakers, cited by anyone who wants to make an argument for film art over film commerce.

And now Welles is dead and so are many of the other bright-eyed young people in his Mercury Theater troupe who went West to make a movie. But the legend of *Citizen Kane* lives on. It is routinely voted the greatest film of all time, most notably in the international polls by the British film magazine *Sight & Sound* in 1962, 1972, and 1982. And in 1991, on the film's fiftieth anniversary, a bright, sparkling new restored print of *Citizen Kane* played over the country.

There is a certain irony in the national release of this revival, since *Citizen Kane* is now owned by Ted Turner, an international media baron with certain similarities to both Hearst and Kane. All three men came from humble origins, got their first broken-down media property cheap, had a vision of a new mass audience, and became famous millionaires who settled down with actresses.

Turner says he has the time to watch only three or four movies a year, but I'll bet *Citizen Kane* is among them. And perhaps he notices parallels with his own career: how his undoubted achievements and great successes are sometimes undermined by a failure of taste. Kane's great downfall came because he fell in love with a humble shopgirl and became determined to turn her into a great opera singer, despite her lack of talent. The Achilles' heel in Turner's career came when he fell in love with a sleazy technical innovation named colorization, and became determined to turn black-and-white movies into ersatz color movies, despite the outraged protests of film lovers everywhere. Yes, the Ted Turner who has made the beautiful, lovingly restored new print of *Citizen Kane* is the very same man who also wanted to colorize Welles's masterpiece.

"Make me one promise," Welles told his friend Henry Jaglom a few weeks before his death. "Keep Ted Turner and his goddamned Crayolas away from my movie." In the event, it was a document fifty years old that kept Turner's crayons away from *Kane*. Welles's original contract with RKO, hailed at the time as the most extraordinary contract any studio had ever given any filmmaker, guaranteed Welles's absolute control over every aspect of the production—including its color, or lack of same.

And so the new print that went into release around the country looks substantially the same as when the movie had its premiere in 1941. For many filmgoers, that will be a revelation. More than most films, *Citizen Kane* must be seen in a 35mm theatrical print to be appreciated.

I've seen *Kane* at least fifty times on 16mm, videotape, and laserdisc. I have gone through it a scene at a time, using a stop-frame film analyzer, at least twenty-five times in various film classes and at festivals. Yet I've seen it in 35mm only twice: In 1956, when it had its first major re-release and I was in junior high school, and in 1978, when a new print was shown at the Chicago Film Festival.

From my 1956 viewing, I remember only the overwhelming total impression of the film, which in its visual sweep and the sheer audacity of its imagination outclassed all the small-minded entertainments I was used to seeing at the movies. From the 1978 viewing, I remember how the brightness and detail of the 35mm print opened up the corners and revealed the shadows of the great film.

Citizen Kane makes great use of darkness and shadow. Welles, working with the gifted cinematographer Gregg Toland, wanted to show a man's life that was filled to bursting with possessions, power, associates, wealth, and mystery. He created a gloomy, dark visual style for the picture, which in 35mm reveals every nook and cranny to contain a treasure or a hint. And because of Toland's famous deep-focus photography, the frame is filled from front to back as well as from left to right.

The first apartment of Kane's mistress, for example, contains the paperweight he drops much later when he dies. It's on a table with other odds and ends. The famous warehouse shot at the end of the film includes a portrait of young Charlie Kane with his parents. You can see those details easily in 35mm, but not so easily in the 16mm prints of the movie, or even in the superb laserdisc issued

by the Criterion Collection. If you've only seen the movie on broadcast television or in a beaten-up 16mm classroom print, you may be amazed at the additional details visible in 35mm.

The story of the making of *Citizen Kane* is by now one of the central legends of movie lore. Many books have been written about the film, most notably *The Citizen Kane Book* (Little, Brown) by Pauline Kael, with her famous essay "Raising Kane," which argues that the contribution of writer Herman Mankiewicz to the production has been underappreciated. Robert Carringer, a Welles expert at the University of Illinois, has published *The Making of Citizen Kane* (University of California Press), with much analysis of visual strategies and production details. And Harlan Lebo's *Citizen Kane: The Fiftieth Anniversary Album* (Doubleday) includes many inside details from interviews with the participants. (Example: Welles gashed his left hand in the scene where he tears apart Susan's apartment, and pulls it out of camera view in the close-up where he picks up the paperweight.)

Recently, at the University of Colorado, I went through *Citizen Kane* once again, with a 16mm film analyzer, joined by several hundred students, faculty, and townspeople. We sat in the dark, and audience members called out "Stop!" when there was something they wanted to discuss. Scene by scene and sometimes shot by shot we looked at the performances, the photography, the special effects.

For the fiftieth-anniversary salute to *Kane*, I reread all of the books once again. There is much disagreement about many of the facts. You can read that Hearst did personally see *Citizen Kane*, or that he did not. That Hearst, if he did see the film, was offended by it, or actually rather enjoyed it. That Welles took credit for the work of his associates, or that he inspired them to surpass all their earlier achievements.

Reading the many accounts of *Citizen Kane* is a little like seeing the movie: The witnesses all have opinions, but often they disagree, and sometimes they simply throw up their hands in exasperation. And the movie stands there before them, a towering achievement that cannot be explained yet cannot be ignored. Fifty years later, it is as fresh, as provoking, as entertaining, as funny, as sad, as brilliant, as it ever was. Many agree it is the greatest film of all time. Those who differ cannot seem to agree on their candidate.

A Viewer's Guide to *Citizen Kane*

"Rosebud." The most famous word in the history of cinema. It explains everything, and nothing. Who, for that matter, actually *heard* Charles Foster Kane say it before he died? The butler says, late in the film, that he did. But Kane seems to be alone when he dies, and the reflection on the shard of glass from the broken paperweight shows the nurse entering the room.

Gossip has it that the screenwriter, Herman Mankiewicz, used "rosebud" as an inside joke, because as a friend of Hearst's mistress, Marion Davies, he knew "rosebud" was the old man's pet name for the most intimate part of her anatomy.

Deep Focus. Everyone knows that Orson Welles and his cinematographer, Gregg Toland, used deep focus in *Kane*. But what is deep focus, and were they using it for the first time? The term refers to a strategy of lighting, composition, and lens choice that allows everything in the frame, from the front to the back, to be in focus at the same time. With the lighting and lenses available in 1941, this was just becoming possible, and Toland had experimented with the technique in John Ford's *The Long Voyage Home* a few years earlier.

In most movies, the key elements in the frame are in focus, and those closer or further away may not be. When everything is in focus, the filmmakers must give a lot more thought to how they direct the viewer's attention, first here and then there. What the French call *mise-en-scène*—the movement within the frame—becomes more important.

Optical Illusions. Deep focus is especially tricky because movies are two-dimensional, and so you need visual guideposts to determine the true scale of a scene. Toland used this fact as a way to fool the audience's eye on two delightful occasions in the film.

One comes when Kane is signing away control of his empire in Thatcher's office. Behind him on the wall are windows that look of normal size and height. Then Kane starts to walk into the background of the shot, and we realize with surprise that the windows are huge, and their lower sills are more than six feet above the floor. As Kane stands under them, he is dwarfed—which is the intent, since he has just lost great power. Later in the film, Kane walks over to stand in front of the great fireplace in Xanadu, and we realize it, too, is much larger than it first seemed.

Visible Ceilings. In almost all movies before *Citizen Kane*, you couldn't see the ceilings in rooms because there weren't any. That's where you'd see the lights and microphones. Welles wanted to use a lot of low-angle shots that would look up toward ceilings, and so Toland devised a strategy of cloth ceilings that looked real but were not. The microphones were hidden immediately above the ceilings, which in many shots are noticeably low.

Matte Drawings. These are drawings by artists that are used to create elements that aren't really there. Often they are combined with "real" foregrounds. The opening and closing shots of Kane's great castle, Xanadu, are examples. No exterior set was ever built for the structure. Instead, artists drew it, and used lights behind it to suggest Kane's bedroom window. "Real" foreground details such as Kane's lagoon and private zoo were added.

Invisible Wipes. A "wipe" is a visual effect that wipes one image off the screen while wiping another into view. Invisible wipes disguise themselves as something else on the screen that seems to be moving, so you aren't aware of the effect. They are useful in "wiping" from full-scale sets to miniature sets.

For example: One of the most famous shots in *Kane* shows Susan Alexander's opera debut, when, as she starts to sing, the camera moves straight up to a catwalk high above the stage, and one stagehand turns to another by holding his nose. Only the stage and the stagehands on the catwalk are real. The middle portion of this seemingly unbroken shot is a miniature, built in the RKO model workshop. The model is invisibly wiped in by the stage curtains, as we move up past them, and wiped out by a wooden beam right below the catwalk. Another example: In Walter Thatcher's library, the statue of Thatcher is a drawing, and as the camera pans down it wipes out the drawing as it wipes in the set of the library.

Invisible Furniture Moving. In the early scene in the Kanes' cabin in Colorado, the camera tracks back from a window to a table where Kane's mother is being asked to sign a paper. The camera tracks right through where the table would be, after which it is slipped into place before we can see it. But a hat on the table is still trembling from the move. After she signs the paper, the camera pulls up and follows her as she walks back

toward the window. If you look sharply, you can see that she's walking right through where the table was a moment before.

The Neatest Flash-Forward in *Kane*. Between Thatcher's words "Merry Christmas" and ". . . a very Happy New Year," two decades pass.

From Model to Reality. As the camera swoops above the nightclub and through the skylight to discover Susan Alexander Kane sitting forlornly at a table, it goes from a model of the nightclub roof to a real set. The switch is concealed, the first time, by a lightning flash. The second time we go to the nightclub, it's done with a dissolve.

Crowd Scenes. There aren't any in *Citizen Kane*. It only looks like there are. In the opening newsreel, stock footage of a political rally is intercut with a low-angle shot showing one man speaking on behalf of Kane. Sound effects make it sound like he's at a big outdoor rally. Later, Kane himself addresses a gigantic indoor rally. Kane and the other actors on the stage are real. The audience is a miniature, with flickering lights to suggest movement.

Slight Factual Discrepancies. In the opening newsreel, Xanadu is described as being "on the desert coast of Florida." But Florida does not have a desert coast, as you can plainly see during the picnic scene, where footage from an earlier RKO prehistoric adventure was back-projected behind the actors, and if you look closely, that seems to be a pterodactyl flapping its wings.

The Luce Connection. Although *Citizen Kane* was widely seen as an attack on William Randolph Hearst, it was also aimed at Henry R. Luce and his concept of faceless group journalism, as then practiced at his *Time* magazine and *March of Time* newsreels. The opening "News on the March" segment is a deliberate parody of the Luce newsreel, and the reason you can never see the faces of any of the journalists is that Welles and Mankiewicz were kidding the anonymity of Luce's writers and editors.

An Extra with a Future. Alan Ladd can be glimpsed in the opening newsreel sequence, and again in the closing warehouse scene.

The Most Thankless Job on the Movie. It went to William Alland, who plays Mr. Thompson, the journalist assigned to track down the meaning of "Rosebud." He is always seen from behind, or in backlit profile. You can never see his face. At the movie's world premiere, Alland told the audience he would turn his back so they could recognize him more easily.

The Brothel Scene. It couldn't be filmed. In the original screenplay, after Kane hires away the staff of the *Chronicle*, he takes them to a brothel. The Production Code office wouldn't allow that. So the scene, slightly changed, takes place in the *Inquirer* newsroom, still with the dancing girls.

The Eyeless Cockatoo. Yes, you can see right through the eyeball of the shrieking cockatoo, in the scene before the big fight between Kane and Susan. It's a mistake.

The Most Evocative Shot in the Movie. There are many candidates. My choice is the shot showing an infinity of Kanes reflected in mirrors as he walks past.

The Best Speech in *Kane*. My favorite is delivered by Mr. Bernstein (Everett Sloane), when he is talking about the magic of memory with the inquiring reporter:

"A fellow will remember a lot of things you wouldn't think he'd remember. You take me. One day, back in 1896, I was crossing over to Jersey on the ferry, and as we pulled out, there was another ferry pulling in, and on it there was a girl waiting to get off. A white dress she had on. She was carrying a white parasol. I only saw her for one second. She didn't see me at all, but I'll bet a month hasn't gone by since, that I haven't thought of that girl."

Genuine Modesty. In the movie's credits, Welles allowed his director's credit and Toland's cinematography credit to appear on the same card—an unprecedented gesture that indicated how grateful Welles was.

False Modesty. In the unique end credits, the members of the Mercury Company are introduced and seen in brief moments from the movie. Then smaller parts are handled with a single card containing many names. The final credit down at the bottom, in small type, says simply:

Kane . . . . Orson Welles

Diabolique ★ ★ ★ ½

NO MPAA RATING, 116 m., 1955

NEW

Simone Signoret (Nicole Horner), Vera Clouzot (Christina Delasalle), Paul Meurisse (Michel Delasalle), Charles Vanel (Inspector Fichet), Noel Roquevert (M. Herboux), Therese Dorny (Mme. Herboux), Pierre Larquey (M. Drain), Michel Serrault (M. Raymond). Directed and produced by Henri-Georges Clouzot. Screenplay by Clouzot, Jerome Geronimi, Frederic Grendel, and Rene Masson.

If it had accomplished nothing else, *Diabolique* would deserve our affection for two reasons: It contains the original of Peter Falk's TV character Columbo, and it inspired one of the funniest stories in screen history. (See below.) Henri-Georges Clouzot's 1955 thriller, now rereleased in a restored print, however, accomplishes much more, creating a diabolical double-reverse plot that keeps the audience guessing right up to the thoroughly implausible final scene.

The movie takes place in a French boys' boarding school run by a headmaster who makes life there as unpleasant for the teachers as for the boys. Michel Delasalle (Paul Meurisse) is a sadist and a pinchpenny, who serves the students rotten fish and slaps around his wife Christina (Vera Clouzot), even though the school really belongs to her.

The boys hate him and the teachers seem to despise him, especially the strapping Nicole (Simone Signoret), who has until recently been his mistress. As the movie opens, Nicole is pressing ahead with a plan she has already explained to Christina. It's an elaborate scheme in which they will visit Nicole's home in a distant village, lure Michel there, drown him in a bathtub, and secretly return to the school to dump the swine in the swimming pool, where he will seem to be a suicide or accident victim.

This is not the plot. It is merely the setup, and the plot proper begins after the body apparently disappears from the pool and Michel's suit is returned from the cleaners. Are the women going mad? Can they trust the evidence of their eyes and ears—or believe their clear memory of Michel's dead body staring up goggle-eyed at them from beneath the water in the bathtub?

"Please do not reveal the ending to those who have not yet seen the film!" Clouzot pleads with his final frame. I would not dream of it. But I will observe that the ending would not have happened quite the way it does without the passive cooperation of Inspector Fichet (Charles Vanel), who has apparently figured everything out and is well placed to prevent the final outcome, but waits too long.

Of course he isn't exactly swift on his feet. He shuffles onto the scene in a rumpled old raincoat, chewing on a cigar and asking apparently aimless questions. His favorite technique is to repeat a question, pretending that he hasn't heard the answer, although it's quite clear that what he hopes to do is trap a suspect in a contradiction. In appearance, mannerism and strategy, Fichet is Columbo; Falk added a squint, a dirtier raincoat, and more humor.

The famous plot of the movie usually deceives first-time viewers, at least up to a point. The final revelations are somewhat disappointing, but Clouzot doesn't linger over them. The most disturbing elements of the movie are implied, not seen, in the seedy air of the teachers, all of whom have seen better days and at least one of whom should probably be in jail.

The movie was made by Signoret in her heyday as a fleshier, blowsier French version of Marilyn Monroe. She makes a dramatic contrast to the petite Vera Clouzot, the director's wife; he often frames little Christina with Nicole and Michel looming over her. There is the possibility, just hinted at, that Nicole may have lesbian designs on Christina. And there is a shabby depravity in the way Christina is so defeated by her husband that she lets him continue to run her school (and abuse her) even after he starts an open affair with the Signoret character.

The movie has fun with the usual whodunit details: the split-second timetables, and the sleepy old guard who must open the gates to let anyone in or out of the school grounds. The inspector also amuses himself reconstructing timetables and quizzing a small student who seems to see and hear impossible things. Then comes the ending, inspired by *Gaslight*, in which a woman is either going mad, or nothing is as it seems. *Diabolique* is so well constructed that even today it works on its intended level—up until, say, the last thirty seconds.

THE FAMOUS STORY: A man wrote to Alfred Hitchcock: "Sir, After seeing Diabolique, *my daughter was afraid to take a bath. Now she has seen your* Psycho *and is afraid to take a shower. What should I do with her?" Hitchcock replied: "Send her to the dry cleaners."*

Dr. Strangelove: or, How I Learned to Stop Worrying and Love the Bomb [NEW]
★ ★ ★ ★
PG, 93 m., 1964

Peter Sellers (President Merkin Muffley, Dr. Strangelove, Captain Lionel Mandrake), George C. Scott (General Buck Turgidson), Sterling Hayden (General Jack D. Ripper), Keenan Wynn (Colonel Bat Guano), Slim Pickens (Major T.J. "King" Kong), Peter Bull (Ambassador), Tracy Reed (Miss Scott). Directed and produced by Stanley Kubrick. Screenplay by Kubrick, Terry Southern, and Peter George.

In the days after it first opened in early 1964, Stanley Kubrick's *Dr. Strangelove* took on the enchanted aura of a film that had gotten away with something. Johnson was in the White House, the Republicans were grooming Goldwater, both sides took the Cold War with grim solemnity, and the world was learning to be comfortable with the term "nuclear deterrent," which meant that if you blow me up, I'm gonna blow you up, and then we'll all be dead. "Better dead than Red," some said. Others said the opposite. The choice was not appealing.

The Bomb overshadowed global politics. It was a kind of ultimate hole card in a game where the stakes were life on earth. Then Kubrick's film opened with the force of a bucketful of cold water, right in the face. What Kubrick's Cold War satire showed was not men at the mercy of machines, but machines at the mercy of men—especially the loony Gen. Jack D. Ripper (Sterling Hayden).

Commanding a wing of the Strategic Air Command, he orders the B-52 bombers under his command to attack the Soviet Union. When an aghast British military attaché (Peter Sellers) tries to stop him, Ripper sucks on a huge phallic cigar while explaining the Commie plot to taint our water supply and deplete our "precious bodily fluids." He refuses to reveal the code that could recall the nuclear-armed planes, and eventually shoots himself while the world careens toward doom.

Events on Ripper's army base are intercut with scenes on board one of the B-52s, and with an emergency meeting in the Pentagon's War Room—still one of the most memorable sets ever constructed for a movie, with its vast global maps looming over a huge round table with an unblinking circle of light above it. Here U.S. president Merkin Muffley (Sellers again) learns with horror from his strategic adviser. Dr. Strangelove (Sellers in his third role) that the Russians have a Doomsday Machine, set to launch a counterattack if the Soviet Union is bombed. It appears that neither the Doomsday Machine nor one of the U.S. bombers can be dissuaded from their missions.

The movie's screenplay, by Terry Southern with help from Kubrick and Peter George, fashions this scenario into a dark comedy of errors, illuminated by flashes of brilliant satire. Some of the dialogue has entered the language—"precious bodily fluids," of course, and also the way the dim-witted Col. Bat Guano (Keenan Wynn) hints darkly of Commie "pre-verts." The scene at the telephone booth between Guano and the British attaché, who does not have the correct small change to call the White House and save the world, is one of the movie's best-constructed gags.

If Sterling Hayden makes a glowering, paranoiac General Ripper, George C. Scott is brilliant as his counterpoint, Gen. Buck Turgidson, head of the Joint Chiefs of Staff, who chews gum, makes faces, and breaks one piece of bad news after another to the president. And Sellers, as president, has a series of painfully labored hotline conversations with the Soviet premiere ("He went and did a funny thing, Dimitri . . .") that reduce nuclear annihilation to the level of a very serious social gaffe.

At about the same time Joseph Heller's *Catch-22* was showing the way language can be tortured into new shapes and meanings, *Dr. Strangelove* had the same kind of verbal wit: "The auto-destruct mechanism destroyed itself," we learn, and "You can't fight in the War Room!" And in contrast to the abstract debates in the Pentagon, there's the simple patriotism of the B-52 pilot, Maj. "King" Kong (Slim Pickens), who promises his crew there's going to be promotions and decorations all around. His exit from the movie, riding a bomb like a bronco, remains one of the most famous moments in modern film.

The only part of the film that doesn't really work is the War Room sequence that comes between Pickens's wild ride and the closing nuclear montage. Sellers, as Strangelove, battles hilariously with his misbehaving bionic hand, but the dialogue doesn't seem to lead anywhere, and the sequence seems oddly inconclusive. In an earlier shot in the War Room, we've seen a long table covered with cakes and pies, and it's said Kubrick intended to end the scene with a pie fight. I'm happy that he didn't, but maybe he could have moved the whole scene earlier; after Pickens rides that bomb to the ground, the only possible segue is to all those mushroom clouds.

Seen after thirty years, *Dr. Strangelove* seems remarkably fresh and undated—a clear-eyed, irreverent, *dangerous* satire. And its willingness to follow the situation to its logical conclusion—nuclear annihilation—has a purity that today's lily-livered happy-ending technicians would probably find a way around. Its black-and-white photography helps, too, putting an unadorned face on its deadly political paradoxes. If movies of this irreverence, intelligence, and savagery were still being made, the world would seem a younger place.

Doctor Zhivago ★ ★ ★
PG-13, 200 m., 1965   **NEW**

Omar Sharif (Yuri), Julie Christie (Lara), Geraldine Chaplin (Tonya), Rod Steiger (Komarovsky), Alec Guinness (Yevgraf), Tom Courtenay (Pasha), Siobhan McKenna (Anna), Ralph Richardson (Alexander). Directed by David Lean and produced by Carlo Ponti. Screenplay by Robert Bolt.

When David Lean's *Doctor Zhivago* was released in 1965, it was pounced upon by the critics, who found it a picture-postcard view of revolution, a love story balanced uneasily atop a painstaking reconstruction of Russia. Lean was known for his elaborate sets, his infinite patience with nature and climates, and his meticulous art direction, but for Pauline Kael, his "method is basically primitive, admired by the same sort of people who are delighted when a stage set has running water or a painted horse looks real enough to ride."

Sometimes one must admit one is precisely that sort of person. I agree that the plot of *Doctor Zhivago* lumbers noisily from nowhere to nowhere. That the characters undergo inexplicable changes of heart and personality. That it is not easy to care much about Zhivago himself, in Omar Sharif's soulful but bewildered performance. That the life of the movie is in its corners (the wickedness of Rod Steiger's voluptuary, the solemn pomposity of Tom Courtenay's revolutionary). That "Lara's Theme," by Maurice Jarre, goes on the same shelf as "Waltzing Matilda" as tunes that threaten to drive me mad.

And yet the stage has running water, and the horses look real enough to ride. *Doctor Zhivago,* restored and revived for its thirtieth anniversary, is an example of superb oldstyle craftsmanship at the service of a soppy romantic vision, and although its portentous historical drama evaporates once you return to the fresh air, watching it can be seductive. Consider, for example, the early shot of the red star glowing above the dark tunnel opening where the workers march in and out. The shot of a child peering through a frosted pane with the claws of branches tapping against it. The cavalry charge on the Bolshevik marchers. Or the way snow crystals dissolve into flowers, and a flower dissolves into Lara's face.

Lean did nothing less than re-create Moscow and its countryside at the time of the Russian revolution, using locations in Spain and Canada (which supplied the vast landscape with the tiny train making its way across it). He accepted the challenge of setting most of the key scenes in winter, with all the attendant difficulties of photographing snow (both artificial and real). There is a moment when Zhivago and Lara enter the abandoned dacha, and the snow and frost have preceded them, turning everything into a winter fairyland. It is a scene where you simultaneously think about the skilled set decoration, and catch your breath at the beauty.

The story is based on Boris Pasternak's novel, much praised on its publication in 1958 as a daring defiance of Russian censorship. So it was, but today the story, especially as it has been simplified by Lean and his screenwriter, Robert Bolt, seems political in the same sense *Gone With the Wind* is political, as spectacle and backdrop, without ideology.

The specific political content of *Doctor Zhivago* is seen mostly as sideshow: charges by the czar's troops on demonstrating students; the caution of Alec Guinness's Soviet official; the unyielding way in which Tom Courtenay's general, once a poet, now says "history has no room for personal feelings." *Doctor Zhivago* believes that history should have a lot of room for personal feelings—that the problems of its little people *do* amount to more than a hill of beans—and that's perhaps why the Russians didn't like Pasternak: He argued for the individual over the state, the heart over the mind.

The first two hours of the two hundred–minute movie are the best, and the most personal. Rod Steiger gives one of the performances of his career as Victor Komarovsky, the investor and scoundrel who victimizes first a woman and then her daughter, Lara (Julie Christie). Zhivago (Omar Sharif) first meets Lara at this time; he attends at the mother's deathbed, and later looks on as she enters a wedding party and shoots at Komarovsky, gaining a vision which he will carry with him through his marriage to the loyal and steadfast Tonya (Geraldine Chaplin).

Zhivago is cold to Komarovsky: "What happens to a girl like that when a man like you is finished with her?" The response is colder: "Interested? I give her to you—as a wedding present." This sets up Zhivago's romantic obsession, which finds its moral justification when the doctor meets Lara, now a nurse, behaving heroically on a battlefield. There is the temptation to get so swept up in their idealism that we forget (come on!) that the old doctor-and-nurse routine is a venerable building block of soap opera.

Watching the film again, I found it hard to believe that the Chaplin character could be so understanding. Later, when Komarovsky offers Lara an opportunity to save the life of herself and her child, call me a realist, but I thought she should have taken it. And the final pathetic scene, with Zhivago staggering after the woman on the Moscow street, is unforgivable. So, yes, it's soppy and manipulative and mushy. But that train looks real enough to ride.

Easy Rider ★ ★ ★

R, 94 m., 1969

Peter Fonda (Wyatt), Dennis Hopper (Billy), Jack Nicholson (George Hanson), Karen Black (Karen). Directed by Dennis Hopper and produced by Peter Fonda. Screenplay by Fonda, Hopper, and Terry Southern.

Nobody went to see *Easy Rider* only once. It became one of the rallying points of the late sixties, a road picture and a buddy picture, crossed with sex, drugs, rock and roll, and the heady freedom of the open road. And it did a lot of repeat business, young audiences celebrating their nihilistic narcissism while the sweet smell of pot drifted through theaters. Seeing the movie twenty-five years later, as I just have, is like entering a time machine. It provides all sorts of little shocks of recognition, as when you realize they aren't playing "Don't Bogart that Joint" for laughs.

Peter Fonda and Dennis Hopper played Captain America and Billy, journeying cross-country on their motorcycles, using a drug deal in Los Angeles to finance a trip to Mardi Gras in New Orleans. The drug they sold (to a dealer played by rock producer Phil Spector) was cocaine, but their drug of choice was marijuana. They were both hippies, wearing their long hair and fringed jackets like a badge, but the grass only seemed to zonk Billy, who got the giggles around the campfire at night. Captain America, who could handle it better, was cool, quiet, remote, a Christ figure who flew the American flag on his gas tank, his helmet, and the back of his leather jacket. (It would be a year later, after

the release of *Joe,* that flag decals were co-opted by the Right.)

The making of the movie became a Hollywood legend. Fonda and Hopper took their screenplay (cowritten with Terry Southern) to the traditional home of motorcycle movies, American-International. But Sam Arkoff turned them down, and they shopped it around before finding funding at Columbia. The movie was made on such a limited budget that there was no money for an original musical score, so Hopper, the director, slapped on a scratch track of rock-and-roll standards for the first studio screening. The executives loved the sound and insisted the songs be left in, and *Easy Rider* begat countless later movies, from *American Graffiti* on, that were scored with oldies.

Motorcycle movies were not chic in 1969, but *Hell's Angels on Wheels* had made an attempt in 1967 to break free of the booze-and-violence clichés. Directed by Richard Rush *(The Stunt Man),* it was a largely overlooked precursor to *Easy Rider,* sharing the same cinematographer, Laszlo Kovacs, and even the same little-known actor in a colorful supporting role: Jack Nicholson, who played a gas station attendant named Poet. *Hell's Angels on Wheels* was a great-looking movie, but it was still trapped in the ghetto of bike-movie clichés. It took *Easy Rider* to link two symbols of rebellion—motorcycles and the hippie counterculture—and catch the spirit of the time.

Easy Rider was playing in theaters at about the time Woodstock Nation was gathering in upstate New York, and for its twenty-fifth anniversary Columbia has restored the film for a fresh release on tape and laserdisc. Looking at it again, I find it more of a period piece than living cinema, but a period piece of special value, because it captures so surely the tone and look of a particular moment in time. Like the movie of *Woodstock,* it evokes the idealism and the utopian social vision of a brief moment when the "youth generation" did indeed seem on the ascendancy, and drugs still seemed to work.

Seen today, by a viewer free of mind-altering substances, *Easy Rider* is both touchingly naive and rather slow-opening. There's heavy symbolism as Fonda throws away his wristwatch before setting off on the journey, and the establishing scenes, as Captain America and Billy stash their loot in a gas tank and set off down the backroads of the Southwest, are slowly paced—heavy on scenery, light on dialogue, pregnant with symbolism and foreboding.

One of their bikes needs work, and they borrow tools at a ranch, leading to a labored visual juxtaposition of wheel changing and horse shoeing. Then they have dinner with the weathered rancher and his Mexican-American brood, and Fonda delivers the first of many quasi-profound lines he will dole out during the movie: "It's not every man who can live off the land, you know. You can be proud." (The rancher, who might justifiably have replied, "Who the fuck asked you?" nods gratefully.)

Tooling on down the road, Captain America uses the high and wide handlebars that this movie made famous; experienced bikers tell me they were mostly for show, along with the teardrop gas tank that was only good for a run of one hundred miles. A hitchhiker leads them to a hippie commune that I *think* seemed inspiring in 1969, but today looks stultifyingly banal. A "performance troupe" sings "Does Your Hair Hang Low?" on a makeshift stage, while stoned would-be hippie farmers wander across the parched earth, scattering seed. "Uh, get any rain here?" Billy asks. "Thank you for a place to make a stand," Captain America says, while fending off the attentions of a hippie chick (ah, yes, how the old terms return!), and then a group leader gives the Captain and Billy a tab of acid and the solemn advice, "When you get to the right place, with the right people—quarter this." (They eventually use it in a New Orleans cemetery, sharing with two hookers; it's a bad trip, but then again, maybe that was the wrong place with the wrong people.)

If *Easy Rider* had continued in the vein of these opening scenes, it's a good question whether anyone would remember it today. But the film comes alive with the electrifying entry of the Jack Nicholson character, a lawyer named George Hanson who they meet in a jail cell. (Significantly, they have been jailed for "parading without a permit" after wheeling their bikes into a small-town Fourth of July parade.)

Historic moments in the cinema are not always so easy to identify: Nicholson's jailhouse dialogue in *Easy Rider* made him a star. "You boys don't look like you're from this part of the country," he says. He's a drunk, and apparently a great disappointment to his rich father. He's also a lawyer, on familiar terms with the local cops, and after he arranges their release he supplies the name of a reputedly top-notch whorehouse in New Orleans, and recalls that he has set out for

Mardi Gras on several occasions without ever getting past the state line. That sets up the film's most famous shot, of George on the back of Billy's motorcycle, wearing a football helmet.

Nicholson's work in *Easy Rider* created a sensation among audiences, who picked up on his sardonic, irreverent personality and were primed for his next film, *Five Easy Pieces* (1970), with its immortal chicken salad sandwich dialogue. And even after twenty-five years, *Easy Rider* comes alive while the Nicholson character is in the movie. That night around the campfire, he samples grass for the first time ("Lord have mercy, is that what that is?") and then explains his theory that extraterrestrials walk among us. There is a way he has of talking in this scene that he would return to many times during his career, a sort of confiding tone in which he shares outrageous information as if anyone should be proud to receive it.

George is killed shortly after, by rednecks who have seen them in a roadside café and decide they look "like refugees from a gorilla love-in." The impact of his death seems foreshortened in the movie, which deals with it briefly before racing on to New Orleans. They find the legendary whorehouse (curiously empty for the Mardi Gras season), and go on the cemetery outing with the two hookers (one of them played by Karen Black in her film debut, and both of them surprisingly willing to spend hours without pay during what should be their busiest season).

The last act of the movie is preordained. There have been many omens along the way (and even a brief flash-forward of Captain America's flaming death). Rednecks in a pickup truck use a shotgun to blast both men from their bikes. The camera climbs high into the sky on a crane, pulling back to show us the inevitable fate, I guess, of anyone who dares to be different. The symbolic deaths of heroes became common in movies after *Bonnie and Clyde* (1967), and Pauline Kael noted in her *Easy Rider* review that "the movie's sentimental paranoia obviously rang true to a large young audience's vision. In the late sixties, it was cool to feel that you couldn't win, that everything was rigged and hopeless." Flower Children, meet Generation X.

One of the reasons America inspires so many road pictures is, obviously, that we have so many roads. One of the reasons we have so many buddy pictures is that Hollywood doesn't understand female characters and doesn't know what to do with them

(there are so many hookers in the movies because, as characters, they share the convenience of their real-life counterparts: They're easy to find and easy to get rid of).

The motorcycle picture was a special kind of road/buddy movie that first came clearly into view with Marlon Brando in *The Wild One* (1954), flourished in the late 1960s, and more or less disappeared a few years later. Many of them featured Hell's Angels (Sonny Barger was the resident "technical adviser" and costar), but *Easy Rider* used a more pure form of the lure of the open road. The movie grew out of the AIP pictures like *The Wild Angels* (1966, also starring Fonda), but it also expressed a vision that the counterculture believed in at the time: The notion that you could leave the city and return to more natural roots. That kind of authenticity seems to be what Captain America and Billy are looking for, and they find it on the ranch and at the hippie commune, but the message is that right-wing, repressive America won't let them have it—is afraid to let them be different.

Of course, the drugs may play a role, too. Billy is paranoid in early scenes, possibly because of all the pot he smokes, and in later scenes they're all too oblivious to the dangers they court with their strange appearance, in hostile small towns. (There's a significant scene where they excite the teenage girls in a restaurant with their aura of sexual danger, and the local good old boys feel threatened and plot revenge.) In scenes like one where Hopper and Fonda teach Nicholson how to inhale, there's a quietly approving air, as if life is a treatable disease, and pot is the cure.

Many deep thoughts were written in 1969 about Fonda's dialogue in a scene set the night before his death. Hopper has just detonated with glee because they've made it to their destination with their drug money still intact. "We blew it," Fonda tells him. "We blew it, man." Heavy. But doesn't the movie play differently today than its makers intended? Cocaine in 1969 carried different connotations than it does today, and it is possible to see that Captain America and Billy died not only for our sins, but also for their own.

Fantasia ★ ★ ★ ★
G, 117 m., 1940

With Leopold Stokowski and the Philadelphia Orchestra. Narrative Introductions: Deems Taylor. Production Supervision: Ben Sharpsteen. Story Direction: Joe Grant and Dick

Huemer. Musical Direction: Edward H. Plumb. Musical Film Editor: Stephen Csillag. Recording: William E. Garity, C.O. Slyfield, J.N.A. Hawkins.

Cartoon figures had hard edges before *Fantasia* was made in 1940, and many of them moved to rinky-tink music. Walt Disney did not invent animation, but he nurtured it into an art form that could hold its own against any "realistic" movie, and when he gathered his artists to create *Fantasia* he felt a restlessness, a desire to try something new.

The basic idea of the film had already been decided upon: take some of the most familiar compositions of classical music and illustrate them with animated drawings. Simply said. And some of the passages in the film would be in forms that were long familiar to the Disney artists. Mickey Mouse's adventures in "The Sorcerer's Apprentice" section, for example, placed him in a visual universe that was familiar to anyone who had ever seen Mickey in a cartoon.

But for other sections of the film, Disney wanted to try some new approaches. In their definitive 1981 book *Disney Animation,* studio artists Frank Thomas and Ollie Johnston remember the way Walt insisted on something new in the sequence where a fairy flies around the wood scattering fairy dust everywhere. Disney walked into a meeting, they recall, and saw a pastel drawing of a fairy. He liked it, especially its soft, luminescent quality. That's what he wanted in his film.

If there's one thing the book makes clear, it's that there's a lot more to animation than just drawing little animals and cartoon characters and having them hop around. The artists experimented for weeks with the fairy sequence, and eventually used a whole arsenal of techniques to get the desired effects: not only straightforward drawing and traditional animation, but also foreground and background matte paintings, gels, trick dissolves, multilayered paintings, and other special effects. The effortless magic of the sequence hardly suggests the painstaking work that went into it.

Throughout *Fantasia,* Disney pushes the edges of the envelope. And what makes this fiftieth anniversary re-release of the film special is the effort the studio has gone to in restoring the movie as it originally looked. *Fantasia* was the first movie released in stereophonic sound. Disney called his process "Fantasound," and used three speakers: one behind the screen and one on either side.

The original sound track, featuring Leopold Stokowski and the Philadelphia Orchestra, has been remastered, scrubbed, cleaned of hisses and pops, and now glows with its original warmth. "Fantasound" has also been restored in the version I saw, and is demonstrated in an opening sequence where Stokowski leads first one side of his orchestra, then the other, then the center, then all together, so that the audience can clearly hear the sources of the sound.

The picture looks better, too—cleaner and brighter. One surprising item of trivia about *Fantasia* is that the fiftieth anniversary release of the film in 1990 was actually its first true national release. It was originally "roadshowed" in theaters equipped with special sound, and in later years was released piecemeal, here and there, always showing somewhere, never everywhere.

Purists will be pleased that the Disney people have also made the momentous decision to release the film in its original aspect ratio of 1:1.33—in other words, in a format about four feet wide for every three feet high. This is the format in which *Fantasia* and almost every other film made before 1953 was originally filmed in.

In several other rereleases of its classics, including such works as *Pinocchio* and *Snow White*, Disney cropped the top and bottom of the original artists' work in order to create the spurious illusion that the film was "widescreen." This proved nothing and was a form of desecration committed against drawings where everything had been carefully framed in the first place. It may seem like a small point to some people, but we're talking about film masterpieces here. Would anybody think it was all right to crop the side off a great painting just to make it match a newly fashioned shape? At last, with *Fantasia*, Disney has done the right thing.

Faster, Pussycat! Kill! Kill! ★ ★ ★   NEW
NO MPAA RATING, 83 m., 1965

Tura Satana (Varla), Haji (Rosie), Lori Williams (Billie), Susan Bernard (Linda), Stuart Lancaster (Old Man), Dennis Busch (Vegetable), Paul Trinka (Kirk), Ray Barlow (Victim). Directed by Russ Meyer and produced by Meyer and Eve Meyer. Screenplay by Jack Moran.

I last reviewed a Russ Meyer movie *(Vixen)* in 1968. In 1969, I wrote the screenplay for Meyer's *Beyond the Valley of the Dolls* ("simultaneously the best and worst movie ever

made"—Michael Dare, *Film Threat* magazine). In the years since, I have passed on reviewing other Meyer films; there was an obvious conflict of interest.

But now, with the rerelease of Meyer's 1965 film *Faster, Pussycat! Kill! Kill!* perhaps the statute of limitations has expired. Besides, why not a review from someone who *has* a conflict of interest? Meyer's fans are vociferously partisan, and here is the movie that director John Waters *(Polyester, Hair Spray)* called "beyond a doubt, the best movie ever made. It is possibly better than any film that will be made in the future." Completing the circle, Stephen Holden, in his recent review of the film in the *New York Times*, credited Meyer with having invented John Waters, not to mention Madonna. What *is* it about Meyer that spurs critics to this hyperbole?

I think it is an intensely personal reaction to the visceral power of Meyer's unusual images. Take away all the jokes, all the elaborate camera angles, all the violence, all the action, and all the sex, and what remains is the quintessential Russ Meyer image: A towering woman with enormous breasts, who dominates all of the men around her, demands sexual satisfaction, and casts off men in the same way that, in mainstream sexual fantasies, men cast aside women.

Meyer's extraordinary women are, of course, fascinating to those with breast fetishes, but look a little longer and you will notice that the breasts are not always presented as centers of desire. Instead, they're weapons used to intimidate men. Tura Satana, who plays the lead in *Faster, Pussycat*, is extraordinary in appearance: Her makeup, with its slashes of kabuki-style eyebrows, looks terrifying. Her black costume seems suited to a motorcycle gang. She never smiles. And her abundant cleavage seems as firmly locked in place as a Ninja Turtle's breastplate. One cannot think of her as fondleable.

What deep recesses of the psyche do these images address? The feminist and lesbian film critic B. Ruby Rich, writing at length on *Pussycat* in the *Village Voice*, said she dismissed *Pussycat* twenty years earlier as just a skin flick. Seeing it again during its revival at New York's Film Forum, she had a different reaction, viewing it now as female fantasy, its images of "empowerment" fascinating to her. Meyer, from the beginning of his career and almost without exception, has filmed only situations in which women wreak their will upon men.

He does so within a frenetic style of quick-cutting, exuberant action, pop and comic-book imagery, and dialogue that seems phoned in from another universe. Consider, for example, the dinner table scene in *Faster, Pussycat! Kill! Kill!*—the most bizarre meal I have ever seen on film, with the single exception of *The Cook, the Thief, His Wife and Her Lover.*

The events leading up to the meal: Tura Satana, as the black-clad dominatrix, is racing her Porsche in the desert against cars driven by her female lover (Haji) and another go-go dancer (Lori Williams). They kidnap a young girl (Susan Bernard), after Satana breaks the back of her boyfriend with one swift karate move.

They stop for gas. The talkative attendant (Mickey Foxx) chatters away about "seeing America first," his eyes glued to Satana's cleavage. "You won't find it down there, Columbus!" she sneers. He tells them that an old man, who lives in the desert with his two sons, has a hoard of money hidden on his property. One of the sons, named Vegetable (Dennis Busch), is muscle-bound but dim-witted, and they see him carrying his father to their pickup truck.

Following the truck to an isolated desert shack, they concoct a story to explain their prisoner, and the lustful old coot (Stuart Lancaster) orders lots of fried chicken prepared. The coot and his sons sit down at dinner with the women (all dressed in bulging bikinis, halter-tops, etc.), and when the go-go dancer says something Satana doesn't like, the dominatrix simply stands up and belts her. How does the father respond? With a tolerant chuckle: "Women! They let 'em vote, smoke, and drive—even put 'em in pants! And what happens? A Democrat for president!"

Later, the coot orders his muscular son to assault Satana, who discourages him with her karate skills, and then tries to crush him against a wall with her Porsche. The victim uses his strength to hold off the car. Meyer uses quick cuts between the victim, the spinning wheels, and a stiletto heel jamming down on the gas. For him, Satana digging her car's rear wheels into the sand is the female equivalent of impotence.

I remember seeing *Pussycat* in 1967. I was amazed. I had simply never seen characters like this before, in the movies or (needless to say) anywhere else. After inventing the skin flick with *The Immoral Mr. Teas* (1959), Meyer had, by the mid-1960s, moved beyond the nudie market, and in films including *Lorna, Mud-*

honey, Faster Pussycat, Common Law Cabin, and *Good Morning and Goodbye* branched out into the wider exploitation market dominated by American International.

Of all his early films, *Faster, Pussycat* has found the widest audience. It has had huge grosses in the 1990s in Germany and France, has had a punk rock band named after it, and went into general rerelease around America. What attracts audiences is not sex and not really violence, either, but a pop art fantasy image of powerful women, filmed with high energy and exaggerated in a way that seems bizarre and unnatural, until you realize Arnold Schwarzenegger, Sylvester Stallone, Jean Claude Van Damme, and Steven Seagal play more or less the same characters. Without the bras, of course.

Fellini's 8½ ★ ★ ★
NO MPAA RATING, 138 m., 1963

Marcello Mastroianni (Guido Anselmi), Claudia Cardinale (Claudia, the Dream Girl), Anouk Aimee (Luisa Anselmi), Sandra Milo (Carla), Rossella Falk (Rossella), Barbara Steele (Gloria Morin), Mario Pisu (Mezzabotta). Directed by Federico Fellini and produced by Angelo Rizzoli. Screenplay by Fellini, Tullio Pinelli, Ennio Flaiano, and Brunello Rondi.

If you were watching the 1993 Academy Awards telecast, you saw Federico Fellini at his effortless best, taking center stage and handling the crowd with more poise, humor, and authority than any of the high-priced stars who surrounded him. He invited the audience to relax. He professed surprise at being honored—and then confessed he was not surprised at all. He commanded his wife, Giulietta Masina, to stop crying—at once! Watching him, you received an overwhelming impression of a man who felt thoroughly comfortable with himself.

That is the impression Fellini always gives, like an orchestra conductor who knows the music and trusts his players. And that is one of the reasons his 1963 masterpiece, *Fellini's 8½,* is such an unlikely film, since it pretends to be autobiographical and yet shows us a movie director who is emotionally frayed and artistically bankrupt.

The movie is currently being revived around the country with a new 35mm print in glorious black and white. It's on video, but it's so big and rich it deserves to be seen on the big screen, and this thirtieth anniversary revival may be your last chance for a long time. *8½* routinely places high on those polls that ask critics and directors to list the ten greatest films of all time.

Fellini directed it on the rebound from the enormous international success of *La Dolce Vita* (1961), which made both him and Marcello Mastroianni famous. *La Dolce Vita* remains, for my money, the best of Fellini's films; it's a sad, shocking, exuberant portrait of a Roman gossip columnist having a crisis of the spirit. But *8½* is a great film in its own way, and despite the efforts of several other filmmakers to make their own versions of the same story, it remains the definitive film about director's block.

The movie stars Mastroianni, always Fellini's alter ego, as Guido, a director who has had a big hit and now seeks to recover from it at a health spa. But he is hounded there and everywhere by those who depend on him— his producer, his writer, his mistress, his would-be stars. The producer has spent a fortune to build a gigantic set of a rocket ship, but Guido has a secret: He doesn't have a clue what his next movie will be about.

The movie proceeds as a series of encounters between Guido and his conscience. He remembers his childhood, his strict parents, his youthful fascination with a tawdry woman who lived down by the beach. His mistress (Sandra Milo) follows him to the spa, and then his chain-smoking, intellectual wife (Anouk Aimee) follows, and is enraged at him—as much for his bad taste in women as for his infidelity.

Then follows one of the most famous sequences in all of modern films: In his daydreams, Guido occupies a house with all of the women in his life, past and present, and they all love him and forgive him, and love one another. But then there is a revolt, and he cracks a whip, trying to tame them. Of course he cannot.

The movie is the portrait of a man desperately trying to weld together the carnal and spiritual sides of his nature; the mistress and the wife, the artistic and the commercial. From time to time a muse appears to him: a seductive, calm, smiling dream woman (Claudia Cardinale). She offers him the tantalizing possibility that all will be forgiven, and all will be well. But she is elusive and ethereal, and meanwhile the producer is growing desperate.

All of Fellini's movies contain his trademarks, such as constructions that stand between the earth and the sky, and parades in which the characters proceed like circus performers. This film gives us the rocket set, a tower to nowhere, and ends at dusk with a sad circus parade, the clowns leading all of the people in Guido's life around and around in circles.

Thirty years after Fellini made *8½,* films like this have grown rare. Audiences demand that their movies, like fast food, be served up hot and now. The self-indulgence and utter self-absorption of Fellini, two of the film's charms, would be vetoed by modern financial backers. They'd demand a more commercial genre piece. These days, directors don't worry about how to repeat their last hit, because they know exactly how to do it: Remake the same commercial formulas. A movie like this is like a splash of cold water in the face, a reminder that the movies really can shake us up, if they want to. Ironic that Fellini's film about artistic bankruptcy seems richer in invention than almost anything else around.

Gone With the Wind ★ ★ ★ ★
NO MPAA RATING, 231 m., 1939

Clark Gable (Rhett Butler), Vivien Leigh (Scarlett O'Hara), Leslie Howard (Ashley Wilkes), Olivia de Havilland (Melanie Hamilton), Hattie McDaniel (Mammy), Butterfly McQueen (Prissy). Directed by Victor Fleming and produced by David O. Selznick. Screenplay by Selznick and Sidney Howard.

How did *Gone With the Wind* look when it was first released? How green were the fields, how red was the soil? I was not there and cannot say. I saw the film in each of its three major theatrical revivals—in 1954, 1961, and 1967—and I have seen it on video. But when I looked at the new version produced by Turner Entertainment, I found that memory is a treacherous thing. This version looks terrific, but is it faithful to the original?

Gone With the Wind was fifty years old in 1988, and in preparation for its golden anniversary, a team of technicians worked more than two years to restore it to its original quality. The challenge facing them was daunting. Simply to obtain a theatrical-quality print of *Gone With the Wind,* much work needed to be done. Prints of the film have gone through so many generations of copies since its 1939 premiere that the versions often seen by modern audiences are a pale shadow of the original glory. Colors have become washed out, the sound track has collected pops and hisses, and the contrast is sometimes so high that many small details are lost.

Yet earlier attempts to "modernize" the film over the years have often ended in catastrophe. The most misguided work on the film was done in 1967, when MGM decided to release it as a "wide-screen" movie. Simple mathematics will show why this was a tragic error. The original film was shot in the classic 1:1.33 ratio, which means that the picture was about four feet wide for every three feet in height. By converting it into a wide-screen image, MGM was forced to chop at the top and bottom, and about a quarter of the original image was lost.

This loss was most apparent in spectacular scenes like the street-of-dying-men sequence in Atlanta, where Scarlett O'Hara wanders into the devastation of Sherman's siege of Atlanta and finds a street filled with the wounded. The camera pulls back and back, finally revealing hundreds of thousands of casualties, framed by a Confederate flag. But not in the 1967 version, where much of the original image was invisible.

When Ted Turner, the Atlanta cable king, bought MGM in 1986, the crown jewel in the package was Gone With the Wind. He ordered yet another "restored version" for the film's fiftieth anniversary, and this new version was shown on his TNT cable station before its release on video. Turner has become notorious in recent years for his colorized versions of many classic films—he savaged Casablanca with the vulgar treatment—but with Gone With the Wind his technicians faced a different challenge. Their assignment was to restore the color quality of a Technicolor film that had aged badly during five decades of wear and tear.

Gone With the Wind was filmed in three-strip Technicolor, a complex process that involved shooting three different negatives of the same scene, each recording one primary color. The three negatives were combined to produce the bright Technicolor look of many of the best color films of the 1940s and 1950s. But it was not a subtle process, and it was not used subtly; many Technicolor films were awash in bright, even gaudy, primary colors, and the process seemed most appropriate for musicals and costume pictures. More realistic films tended to be shot in black and white, and it was not until the 1960s—when black and white was denied to them—that many directors began to consciously exclude bright colors from color films, controlling the color palette instead of

trying to get as much color as possible on the screen.

The ill-starred 1967 re-release version of Gone With the Wind was transferred by MGM to a new one-strip color process that has turned out, over the past twenty years, to age very badly. Films originally shot in the process, such as The Graduate, have faded quickly; bad prints have taken on the washed-out colors of old newspaper rotogravure sections. For their fiftieth anniversary re-release of the film, Turner technicians went back to the original three-strip master negatives of Gone With the Wind, which were stored at Eastman House in Rochester, New York. And there they found some problems. Although much of the film had survived intact, some sections had suffered shrinkage, so that the three strips were no longer perfectly aligned. Other scenes had gone out of focus in the middle or around the edges. Repair work was necessary, sometimes on a frame-by-frame basis.

But enough about technicalities. How does Gone With the Wind play after fifty years? It is still a great film, above all because it tells a great story. Scarlett O'Hara, willful, spoiled, scarred by poverty, remains an unforgettable screen heroine, and I was struck again this time by how strong Vivien Leigh's performance is—by how stubbornly she maintains her petulance in the face of common sense, and by how even her heroism is undermined by her character flaws.

The ending of the film still plays like a psychological test for the audience. What do you think we should really conclude? The next-to-last speech in the movie, Rhett Butler's "Frankly, my dear, I don't give a damn," is one many audience members have been waiting for; Scarlett gets her comeuppance at last. Then comes her speech about Tara, about how, after all, tomorrow is another day. Some members of the audience will read this as an affirmation of strength, others as a renewed self-delusion. (The most cynical will observe that Scarlett, like many another divorcée disappointed in love, has turned to real estate as a career.)

As I was watching the film, I was struck by the subtlety of the color in the restored version. I was not sure I altogether approved of it. My memories of Gone With the Wind are of a movie in bold, bright colors—the flames of the burning of Atlanta were bright red, as were the lips of the heroines. This fiftieth anniversary version has a more modern look to the color, with the brights somewhat muted

and the flesh tones more true. Have the Turner technicians changed the look of the original or restored it? After all, I am not remembering the 1939 version, but later releases that were already suffering from the ravages of time.

An article by Richard May, who headed the restoration effort, addresses this issue obliquely: "(We) had to take into consideration how people 'thought' GWTW looked originally, together with how today's audience, used to contemporary color styles in film and television, would react to any unusual color choices." He seems to be coming within a hairbreadth here of admitting that his team "modernized" the color by toning down the brightness of the original three-strip Technicolor. I sensed a little of that—the flames of Atlanta, for example, now look more orange than red. But perhaps my memory deceives me. Twenty-two years after I last saw the movie on a large screen, I cannot be sure.

Turner supplied critics with video clips comparing several scenes in three versions—1954, 1967, and the new version—and in them the principal visible difference is that the new version has clearer, truer colors, and the print is not banged-up, faded, or scratched. Gone With the Wind looks like a new movie again, not a battered veteran of the revival wars. The restoration brings out visual details that have been lost through the generations—the shadowy backgrounds of candle-lit rooms, for example—and makes the film effortlessly watchable by removing all the years of decay.

The film's sound track has been cleaned up considerably, thanks to the almost magical things that modern sound technicians can do. A lot of the surface noise—the quiet hissing on the video version—has been eliminated, and there are moments so clean that you can actually hear the squeaking of Clark Gable's shoes.

The bottom line is that this is a praiseworthy restoration, removing generations of grime and noise from one of the greatest of all Hollywood productions, and presenting it, crisp and clean, in its original aspect ratio. I would not have expected such a conscientious job from Ted Turner, who has expressed such zeal for the vandalism of black-and-white movies. But I must give credit where due.

The Hidden Fortress ★ ★ ★ ★
NO MPAA RATING, 139 m., 1958

Toshiro Mifune (General Rokurota Makabe), Misa Uehara (Princess Yukihime), Takashi Shimura (General Nagakura), Susumu Fujita (General Tadokoro). Directed by Akira Kurosawa and produced by Kurosawa and Masumi Rumimoro. Screenplay by Kurosawa and Rumimoro.

Hidden Fortress is grand, bold movie-making—a Japanese adventure classic that combines elements of samurai films, Westerns, and myths of heroes and commoners. It does something else, too. It reveals many of the sources of the *Star Wars* movies so clearly that you can almost see R2D2, C3PO, and Princess Leia there on the screen. Now that we've had two sequels to *Star Wars,* how about this as a prologue?

The movie was made in 1958 by Akira Kurosawa, the greatest of Japanese directors, and it attracted a lot of attention at the time. It was the first Japanese movie in Cinemascope, it was one of the most expensive Japanese movies ever made, and it confirmed Kurosawa's role as a master of adventure epics. His *Seven Samurai* (1954) inspired Hollywood's *Magnificent Seven,* but it took George Lucas to use *The Hidden Fortress* as the starting point for the most popular American movies ever made.

The irony is that *The Hidden Fortress* has hardly been seen in this country. A much-shortened version had brief engagements in the early 1960s, but then it went out of release and the rights were allowed to lapse until late in 1983, when, for the first time, this uncut 139-minute version was brought to America. The best video version is the Criterion Collection's laserdisc, with a letterboxed format so Kurosawa's entire widescreen compositions are visible.

The debt of the *Star Wars* pictures to Kurosawa is obvious almost from the opening shots, when two hapless Army underlings, one short, one tall, stagger through an empty landscape bemoaning their fates. Then the other story elements fall into place: a brave, outcast warrior general; a proud and fierce princess who is forced to disguise herself as a commoner; a feared military leader who first opposes the princess's cause but then supports it; a mysterious hidden fortress that must be captured, defended, or destroyed; and, of course, chases and swordfights and appeals to tradition and history.

Does all of this sound more than vaguely familiar? Lucas gives full credit: He told Kurosawa he saw the movie in film school, never forgot it, and used the characters of the two foot soldiers as an inspiration for his two inseparable androids.

Kurosawa has made better movies, but never one more filled with humor and energy. His story isn't made into a dirge about honor and violence, but into a celebration of high spirits. The two foot soldiers enlist in the service of the general (Toshiro Mifune) without knowing who he is or that the woman accompanying him is their princess. They all conspire to move a wagonload of gold from one kingdom to another, concealing the gold inside sticks of firewood and hiding themselves in a procession to a firewood festival. There are close scrapes, double-crosses, cases of mistaken identity, and a thrilling lance-fight between Mifune and that other great Japanese star, Susumu Fujita. An overnight stop in a rowdy frontier town will remind you of the saloon planet in *Star Wars.*

There are also several breathtakingly great individual shots. One comes early in the film, when thousands of prisoners riot and run crazily down a long, sweeping flight of steps, overwhelming their captors. Another comes during the duel with lances, when the troops in the background are choreographed to mirror every move of the fight with their own body movements. And there's the firewood festival, with waves of celebrants dancing around the flames in a pagan dream. Seeing *The Hidden Fortress* is like visiting the wellspring of the Force.

It's All True ★ ★ ★
G, 85 m., 1993

A documentary directed by Richard Wilson, Myron Meisel, and Bill Krohn, based on an unfinished film by Orson Welles. Produced by Regine Konckier, Richard Wilson, Bill Krohn, Myron Meisel, and Jean-Luc Ormieres. Screenplay by Krohn, Wilson, and Meisel.

It is sometimes forgotten that Orson Welles was famous and successful even before he made his first film, *Citizen Kane,* in 1941. He was the most controversial radio star in the nation and a leading light on Broadway, all before his directing debut at twenty-four. One evening in Chicago when most of his lecture audience was kept away by a blizzard, he introduced himself to the sparse crowd: "I am an actor, a director, a writer, a producer . . . and a magician. Why are there so many of me and so few of you?"

Citizen Kane made him Hollywood's wonder kid, and then he made *The Magnificent Ambersons,* which was famously taken out of his hands so that a botched ending could be tacked on by the studio. Welles was not in Los Angeles to defend his film because he was on location in Brazil, directing an anthology film named *It's All True,* which Nelson Rockefeller thought would cement wartime relationships between the United States and Latin America, and which almost everyone else, possibly except for Welles and his team, thought was a cockamamie project from the beginning.

"The Nelson Project," as Welles was later sardonically to call it, would include a Mexican bullfighting sequence, a documentary about "carnival" in Rio, a lot of samba dancing in Technicolor, and a black-and-white sequence telling the story of four poor peasants who sailed their raft more than a thousand miles to ask the president of Brazil for help for their people.

Much of the footage for *It's All True* had already been shot when the studio, RKO, pulled the plug on Welles's budget and ordered him home. The movie was never released, *Ambersons* was butchered badly in his absence, and his career, which began with what many believe is the greatest film ever made, never ever quite recovered. Welles spent the rest of his life fighting a reputation as a dilettante who didn't finish things, but the *It's All True* fiasco was not his fault.

Now here is a documentary named *It's All True* that brings together much of the surviving footage from the South American adventure, and adds interviews with Welles, cinematographer Joseph Biroc, his associate Richard Wilson, and others who worked on the project. Because Welles is arguably the most magnetic and mercurial of all American directors, the film would be interesting on any grounds, but it is also impressive because of the long raft sequence, shown here in an essentially complete state.

The story of the four fishermen and their 1,650-mile journey along the coast of Brazil was already famous before Welles filmed it. But the filming began on a note of tragedy. While Welles was shooting the men on the raft in Rio's Guanabara Bay, the tiny craft overturned and one the men—their leader, known as Jacare—was lost. The same day, RKO pulled the plug, but Welles struggled on with a skeleton crew, and eventually did shoot a silent, black-and-white documentary-style story, which he planned to score and narrate back in Los Angeles.

The narration was never recorded. The footage was thought lost for years, until it surfaced in a Paramount vault. Now you can see it, like a ghost film from the past. In its unusual camera angles it resembles some of the compositions Welles would use in his Shakespeare films *Macbeth* and *Othello*, and in its more heroic moments it looks like something by Sergei Eisenstein. The fishermen never really emerge as individuals, but their feat—sailing 1,650 miles in the open sea, without navigational aids, in a craft smaller than a bed—remains incredible.

Welles appears both young and old in the film. In a sequence shot years ago, he leans toward the camera in a conspiratorial pose, deliberately acting; in later footage he simply tells the old story once again. Both Welles and the filmmakers who compiled this documentary after his death insist it was Rockefeller and his friend John Hay Whitney who encouraged the South American project, although the controversial Charles Higham biography of Welles says the Brazilian minister of propaganda first dreamed up the scheme. Rockefeller embraced it, Higham says, for shady motives; it may have fit into his plans to channel money to pro-Nazi groups under the cover of anti-Nazi activities. (It must be said that Higham's lurid view of Rockefeller's secret motives does not find much support elsewhere.)

What is clear is that Welles, still in his mid-twenties, and heady with the success of *Kane* and the apparent success of *Ambersons*, got swept up in a wave of patriotic fervor and embarked on the South American project without really asking himself if this trip was necessary. In Brazil, with no definite script or game plan, and with input from countless American and Brazilian functionaries, he seemed to improvise his way through the film. Maybe, given the money, he would have finished it. Maybe not. What remains is some dramatic quasi-documentary footage by Welles, surrounded by the poignant story of a project that went so far wrong that Welles spent four decades under its shadow.

It's a Wonderful Life ★ ★ ★ ★
NO MPAA RATING, 129 m., 1946

James Stewart (George Bailey), Donna Reed (Mary Hatch), Lionel Barrymore (Mr. Potter), Thomas Mitchell (Uncle Billy), Henry Travers (Clarence). Directed and produced by Frank Capra. Screenplay by Frances Goodrich, Albert Hackett, and Capra.

The best and worst things that ever happened to *It's a Wonderful Life* are that it fell out of copyright protection and into the shadowy no-man's-land of the public domain. Because the movie is no longer under copyright, any home video outfit that can get its hands on a print of the movie can release it, at no cost, as often as it wants to. That led to the rediscovery, starting in the early 1970s, of Frank Capra's once-forgotten film, and its elevation into a Christmas tradition. PBS stations were the first to jump on the bandwagon, using the saga of small-town hero George Bailey as counterprogramming against expensive network holiday specials. To the general amazement of TV program directors, the audience for the film grew and grew over the years; many families made the movie an annual ritual.

That was the best thing that happened to *It's a Wonderful Life*, bringing cheer into the lives of director Frank Capra and star James Stewart, who both considered it their favorite film. The worst thing—which inspired Stewart to testify before a Congressional committee and Capra to issue a deathbed plea—was that the movie was colorized. Movies in the public domain are so defenseless that you could cut one up to make ukulele picks, and who could legally prevent you? And so a garish colorized version, destroying the purity of the original black-and-white images, has been seen on cable, is available for local syndication, and is sold and rented on videocassette.

It is a great irony that the colorized version *has* been copyrighted, and so many stations are paying a great deal for the rights to an inferior version of a movie that they could show for free in black and white. If I were a local television program director with taste and a love of movies, I would find out when my competitor was going to air his colorized version and counterprogram with the original black and white movie, patting myself on the back for a public service. Maybe I could promote my screening with a clip of Jimmy Stewart telling Congress, in that famous voice of perfect drawling sincerity, "I tried to look at the colorized version, but I had to switch it off—it made me feel sick."

What is remarkable about *It's a Wonderful Life* is how well it holds up over the years; it's one of those ageless movies, like *Casablanca* or *The Third Man,* that improves with age.

Some movies, even good ones, should only be seen once. When we know how they turn out, they've surrendered their mystery and appeal. Other movies can be viewed an indefinite number of times. Like great music, they improve with familiarity. *It's a Wonderful Life* falls in the second category.

I looked at the movie once again, on the splendid new laserdisc edition from the Criterion Collection, which has been transferred from the best available materials. I'd seen it four or five times before and was planning to view perhaps an hour, just to check out the transfer. I couldn't stop watching. The movie works like a very strong and fundamental fable, sort of a *Christmas Carol* in reverse: Instead of a mean old man being shown scenes of happiness, we have a hero who plunges into despair.

The hero, of course, is George Bailey (Stewart), a man who never ever quite makes it out of his quiet birthplace of Bedford Falls. As a young man he dreams of shaking the dust from his shoes and traveling to far-off lands, but one thing and then another keeps him at home—especially his responsibility to the family savings and loan association, which is the only thing standing between Bedford Falls and the greed of Mr. Potter (Lionel Barrymore), the avaracious local banker.

George marries his high school sweetheart (Donna Reed, in her first starring role), settles down to raise a family, and helps half the poor folks in town buy homes where they can raise their own. Then, when George's absent-minded uncle (Thomas Mitchell) misplaces some bank funds during the Christmas season, it looks as if the evil Potter will have his way after all. George loses hope and turns mean (even his face seems to darken, although it's still nice and pink in the colorized version). He despairs, and is standing on a bridge contemplating suicide when an Angel Second Class named Clarence (Henry Travers) saves him and shows him what life in Bedford Falls would have been like without him.

Frank Capra never intended *It's a Wonderful Life* to be pigeonholed as a "Christmas picture." This was the first movie he made after returning from service in World War II, and he wanted it to be special—a celebration of the lives and dreams of America's ordinary citizens, who tried the best they could to do the right thing by themselves and their neighbors. After becoming Hollywood's poet of the common man in the 1930s with an extraordinary series of populist parables (*It Happened One Night, Mr. Deeds Goes to*

Town, Mr. Smith Goes to Washington, You Can't Take It With You), Capra found the idea for *It's a Wonderful Life* in a story by Philip Van Doren Stern that had been gathering dust on studio shelves.

For Stewart, also recently back in civilian clothes, the movie was a chance to work again with Capra, for whom he had played Mr. Smith. The original trailer for the movie (included on the Criterion disc) played up the love angle between Stewart and Donna Reed and played down the message—but the movie was not a box-office hit, and was all but forgotten before the public domain prints began to make their rounds.

It's a Wonderful Life is not merely a heart-warming "message picture." The conclusion of the film makes such an impact that some of the earlier scenes may be overlooked—such as the slapstick comedy of the high school hop, where the dance floor opens over a swimming pool, and Stewart and Reed accidentally jitterbug right into the water (this covered pool was not a set but actually existed at Hollywood High School). There's also the drama of George rescuing his younger brother from a fall through the ice, and the scene where Donna Reed loses her bathrobe and Stewart ends up talking to the shrubbery. The telephone scene—where an angry Stewart and Reed find themselves helplessly drawn toward each other—is wonderfully romantically charged. And the darker later passages have an elemental power, as the drunken George Bailey staggers through a town he wants to hate, and then revisits it through the help of a gentle angel. Even the corniest scenes in the movie—those galaxies that wink while the heavens consult on George's fate—work because they are so disarmingly simple. A more sophisticated approach might have seemed labored.

It's a Wonderful Life did little for Frank Capra's postwar career, and indeed he never regained the box-office magic that he had during the 1930s. Such later films as *State of the Union* (1948) and *Pocketful of Miracles* (1961) have the Capra touch but not the magic, and the director did not make another feature after 1961. But he remained hale and hearty until a stroke slowed him in the late 1980s, and at a seminar with some film students (shown on the Criterion disc) he was asked if there were still a way to make movies about the kinds of values and ideals found in the Capra films.

"Well, if there isn't," he said, "we might as well give up."

La Strada ★ ★ ★ ½
NO MPAA RATING 107 m., 1954

Giulietta Masina (Gelsomina), Anthony Quinn (Zampano), Richard Basehart (The Fool), Aldo Silvani (Circus Owner), Marcella Rovere (Widow), Livia Venturini (Nun). Directed by Federico Fellini and produced by Dino De Laurentiis and Carlo Ponti. Screenplay by Fellini and Tullio Pinelli.

Federico Fellini's *La Strada* tells a fable that is simple by his later standards, but contains many of the obsessive visual trademarks that he would return to again and again: the circus, and parades, and a figure suspended between earth and sky, and one woman who is a waif and another who is a carnal monster, and, of course, the seashore. Like a painter with a few favorite themes, Fellini would rework these images until the end of his life.

The movie is the bridge between the postwar Italian neorealism which shaped Fellini, and the fanciful autobiographical extravaganzas which followed. It is fashionable to call it his best work—to see the rest of his career as a long slide into self-indulgence. I don't see it that way. I think *La Strada* is part of a process of discovery that led to the masterpieces *La Dolce Vita* (1960), *8½* (1963), and *Amarcord* (1974), and to the bewitching films he made in between, like *Juliet of the Spirits* (1965) and *Fellini's Roma* (1972).

La Strada is the first film that can be called entirely "Felliniesque." It was rereleased, in a restored print presented by Martin Scorsese, at a poignant moment: Fellini received an honorary Oscar at the 1993 Academy Awards, with his wife Giulietta Masina applauding tearfully in the front row. Between then and the 1994 rerelease, both died.

The story is one of the most familiar in cinema. A brutish strongman named Zampano (Anthony Quinn) tours Italy, living in a ramshackle caravan pulled by a motorcycle. He needs an assistant for his act, and from a poor widow at the seaside he purchases her slow-witted daughter Gelsomina (Giulietta Masina). He is cruel to the young woman, but she has a Chaplinesque innocence that somehow shields her from the worst of life, and she is proud of her accomplishments, such as learning to play his signature tune on a trumpet.

In a provincial town, Gelsomina is struck breathless by the Fool, a high-wire artist who works high above the city street. Zampano signs up with an itinerant circus, where the Fool (Richard Basehart) is employed. He mocks Zampano, who attacks him in a rage and is jailed. The Fool is attracted to Gelsomina, but sees that she has formed an enduring bond with the strongman, and leaves so they can be together. But Zampano's jealousy and rage return; he kills the Fool, Gelsomina goes mad, and all is in place for one of Fellini's favorite endings, in which a defeated man turns to the sea, which has no answers.

Seeing the film again after several years, I found myself struck first of all by new ideas about the Fool. The film intends us to take him as a free and cheerful spirit (the embodiment of Mind, Pauline Kael tells us, with Zampano as Body and Gelsomina as Soul). But he has a mean, sarcastic streak I had not really registered before, and his taunting of the dim Zampano is sadistic. To some degree he is responsible for his own end.

Masina's character is perfectly suited to her round clown's face and wide, innocent eyes; in one way or another, in *Juliet of the Spirits*, *Ginger and Fred*, and most of her other films, she was always playing Gelsomina. Her performance is inspired by the silent clowns (I was reminded of Harry Langdon in *The Strong Man*), and is probably a shade too conscious and knowing to be consistent with Gelsomina's retardation. The character should never be aware of the effect she has, but we sometimes feel Gelsomina's innocence is calculated.

It is Quinn's performance that holds up best, because it is the simplest. Zampano is not much more intelligent than Gelsomina. Life has made him a brute and an outcast, with one dumb trick (breaking a chain by expanding his chest muscles), and a memorized line of patter that was perhaps supplied to him by a circus owner years before. His tragedy is that he loves Gelsomina and does not know it, and that is the central tragedy for many of Fellini's characters: They are always turning away from the warmth and safety of those who understand them, to seek restlessly in the barren world.

In almost all of Fellini's films, you will find the figure of a man caught between earth and sky. (*La Dolce Vita* opens with a statue of Jesus suspended from a helicopter; Marcello Mastroianni opens *8½* floating in the sky, tethered to earth.) They are torn between the carnal and the spiritual. You will also find the waifs and virgins and good wives, contrasted with prostitutes and temptresses (Fellini in his childhood encountered a vast, buxom woman who lived in a shack at the beach, and made her a character again and again). You will find journeys, processions, parades, clowns, freaks, and the shabby melancholy of an empty field at dawn, after the circus has left. (Fellini's very last film seen in this country, *Intervista* [1987] ends with such an image.)

And you will hear it all tied together with the music of Nino Rota, who, starting with *I Vitelloni* in 1953, faithfully composed for Fellini some of the most distinctive film scores ever written, merging circus music and pop songs with the sadly lyrical sounds of accordions and saxophones and lonely trumpets (the tune ending in a rude trumpet squawk, which Zampano teaches to Gelsomina, is mirrored in the nightclub scene in *La Dolce Vita*).

When Fellini died, the critic Stanley Kauffmann wrote an appreciation in *The New Republic* that ended with the words: "During his lifetime, many fine filmmakers blessed us with their art, but he was the only one who made us feel that each of his films, whatever its merits, was a present from a friend." In the words of a film about him, "Ciao, Federico."

Lawrence of Arabia ★ ★ ★ ★

PG, 216 m., 1962 (re-released 1989)

Peter O'Toole (Lawrence), Alec Guinness (Prince Feisel), Anthony Quinn (Auda Abu Tayi), Jack Hawkins (General Allenby), Jose Ferrer (Turkish Bey), Omar Sharif (Sherif Ali), Anthony Quayle (Colonel Brighton), Claude Rains (Mr. Dryden), Arthur Kennedy (Jackson Bentley), Donald Wolfit (General Murray). Directed by David Lean and produced by Sam Spiegel. Screenplay by Robert Bolt. Restored director's cut produced and reconstructed by Robert A. Harris and Jim Painten.

What a bold, mad act of genius it was, to make *Lawrence of Arabia*, or even think that it could be made. In the words twenty-seven years later of one of its stars, Omar Sharif: "If you are the man with the money and somebody comes to you and says he wants to make a film that's four hours long, with no stars, and no women, and no love story, and not much action either, and he wants to spend a huge amount of money to go film it in the desert—what would you say?"

The impulse to make this movie was based, above all, on imagination. The story of Lawrence is not founded on violent battle scenes or cheap melodrama, but on David Lean's ability to imagine what it would look like to see a speck appear on the horizon of the desert, and slowly grow into a human being. He had to know how that would feel before he could convince himself that the project had a chance of being successful.

There is a moment in the film when the hero, a British eccentric named T.E. Lawrence, has survived a suicidal trek across the desert and is within reach of shelter and water—and he turns around and goes back to find a friend who has fallen behind. This sequence builds up to the shot in which the shimmering heat of the desert reluctantly yields the speck that becomes a man—a shot that is held for a long time before we can even begin to see the tiny figure. On television, this shot doesn't work at all—nothing can be seen. In a movie theater, looking at the stark clarity of a 70mm print, we lean forward and strain to bring a detail out of the waves of heat, and for a moment we experience some of the actual vastness of the desert and its unforgiving harshness.

By being able to imagine the sequence, the filmmakers were able to see why the movie would work. *Lawrence of Arabia* is not a simple biography or an adventure movie—although it contains both elements—but a movie that uses the desert as a stage for the flamboyance of a driven, quirky man. Although it is true that Lawrence was instrumental in enlisting the desert tribes on the British side in the 1914–17 campaign against the Turks, the movie suggests that he acted less out of patriotism than out of a need to reject conventional British society and identify with the wildness and theatricality of the Arabs.

T.E. Lawrence must be the strangest hero to ever stand at the center of an epic. To play him, Lean cast one of the strangest actors in recent movie history, Peter O'Toole, a lanky, almost clumsy man with a sculptured face and a speaking manner that hesitates between amusement and insolence. O'Toole's assignment was a delicate one. Although it was widely believed that Lawrence was a homosexual, a multimillion-dollar epic filmed in 1962 could not possibly be frank about that. And yet Lean and his writer, Robert Bolt, didn't simply cave in and rewrite Lawrence into a routine action hero.

Using O'Toole's peculiar speech and manner as their instrument, they created a character who combined charisma and craziness, who was so different from conventional military heroes that he could inspire the Arabs to follow him in that mad march across the desert. There is a moment in the movie when O'Toole, dressed in the flowing white robes of a desert sheik, does a victory dance on top of a captured Turkish train, and almost seems to be posing for fashion photos. This is a curious scene because it seems to flaunt gay stereotypes, and yet none of the other characters in the movie seem to notice—nor do they take much notice of the two young desert urchins that Lawrence takes under his protection.

What Lean, Bolt, and O'Toole create is a sexually and socially unconventional man who is simply presented as what he is, without labels or comment. Could such a man rally the splintered desert tribes and win a war against the Turks? Lawrence did. But he did it partially with mirrors, the movie suggests; one of the key characters is an American journalist (Arthur Kennedy), obviously inspired by Lowell Thomas, who single-handedly retailed the Lawrence myth to the English-language press. The journalist admits he is looking for a hero to write about. Lawrence is happy to play the role. And only role-playing would have done the job; an ordinary military hero would have been too small-scale for this canvas.

For a movie that runs 216 minutes, plus intermission, *Lawrence of Arabia* is not dense with plot details. It is a spare movie with clean, uncluttered lines, and there is never a moment when we're in doubt about the logistical details of the various campaigns. Lawrence is able to unite various desert factions, the movie argues, because (1) he is so obviously an outsider that he cannot even understand, let alone take sides with, the various ancient rivalries; and (2) because he is able to show the Arabs that it is in their self-interest to join the war against the Turks. Along the way he makes allies of such desert leaders as Sherif Ali (Omar Sharif), Prince Feisel (Alec Guinness), and Auda Abu Tayi (Anthony Quinn) both by winning their respect and by appealing to their logic. The dialogue in these scenes is not complex, and sometimes Bolt makes it so spare it sounds like poetry.

I've noticed that when people remember *Lawrence of Arabia*, they don't talk about the details of the plot. They get a certain look in their eyes, as if they are remembering the whole experience, and have never quite been able to put it into words. Although it seems to be a traditional narrative film—like *The Bridge on the River Kwai*, which Lean made just before it, or *Doctor Zhivago*, which he made just after—it actually has more in common with essentially visual epics such as Kubrick's *2001* or Eisenstein's *Alexander Nevsky*. It is spectacle and experience, and its ideas are about things you can see or feel, not things you can say. Much of its appeal is based on the fact that it does not contain a complex story with a lot of dialogue; we remember the quiet, empty passage, the sun rising across the desert, the intricate lines traced by the wind in the sand.

Although it won the Academy Award as the year's best picture in 1962, *Lawrence of Arabia* would have soon been a lost memory if it had not been for two film restorers named Robert A. Harris and Jim Painten. They discovered the original negative in Columbia's vault, inside crushed and rusting film cans, and they also discovered about 35 minutes of footage that had been trimmed by distributors from Lean's final cut. To see it is to appreciate the subtlety of F.A. Young's desert cinematography—achieved despite blinding heat and the blowing sand, which worked its way into every camera. *Lawrence of Arabia* was one of the last films to be photographed in 70mm (as opposed to being blown up to 70mm from a 35mm negative). It is a great experience to see it as Lean intended it in 1962—and also a humbling one, to realize how the motion picture industry is losing the vision to make epic films like this, and settling for safe narrative formulas instead.

The Manchurian Candidate ★ ★ ★ ★
PG-13, 126 m., 1962

Frank Sinatra (Bennett Marco), Laurence Harvey (Raymond Shaw), Janet Leigh (Rosie), Angela Lansbury (Raymond's Mother), Henry Silva (Chunjin), James Gregory (Senator John Iselin), Leslie Parrish (Jocie), John McGiver (Senator Thomas Jordan), Khigh Dhiegh (Yen Lo), James Edwards (Corporal Melvin). Directed by John Frankenheimer and produced by George Axelrod and Frankenheimer. Screenplay by Axelrod.

Here is a movie that was made in 1962, and it feels as if it were made yesterday. Not a moment of *The Manchurian Candidate* lacks edge and tension and a cynical spin—and what's even more surprising is how the film now plays as a political comedy, as well as a thriller. After being suppressed for a quarter of a century, after becoming an unseen legend that never turned up on TV or on home video, John Frankenheimer's 1962 master-

piece now re-emerges as one of the best and brightest of modern American films.

The story is a matter of many levels, some of them frightening, some pointed with satirical barbs. In a riveting opening sequence, a group of American combat infantrymen are shown being brainwashed by a confident Chinese communist hypnotist, who has them so surely under his control that one man is ordered to strangle one of his buddies and shoot another in the head, and cheerfully complies.

Two members of the group get our special attention: the characters played by Frank Sinatra and Laurence Harvey. Harvey seems to be the main target of the Chinese scheme, which is to return him to American society as a war hero, and then allow him to lead a normal life until he is triggered by a buried hypnotic suggestion, and turned into an assassin completely brainwashed. to take orders from his enemy controller. Harvey does indeed re-enter society, where he is the son of a Republican dowager (Angela Lansbury), and the stepson of her husband (James Gregory). Gregory is a leading candidate for his party's presidential nomination, and more than that I choose not to reveal. Meanwhile, Sinatra also returns to civilian life, but he is haunted by nightmares in which he dimly recalls the terrifying details of the brainwashing. He contacts Harvey (who is not, we must remember, a conscious assassin, but merely a brainwashed victim). Sinatra also becomes central to a Pentagon investigation of a possible plot that affected all the members of his platoon—which disappeared on patrol and returned telling the same fabricated story.

Midway in his investigation, Sinatra meets and falls in love with a woman played by Janet Leigh, and their relationship provides the movie with what looks to me like a subtle, tantalizing suggestion of an additional level of intrigue. They meet in the parlor car of a train, where Sinatra, shaking, cannot light a cigarette and knocks over the table with his drink on it. Leigh follows him to the space between cars, lights a cigarette for him, and engages him in a very weird conversation, after which they fall in love and she quickly ditches her fiancé. What's going on here? My notion is that Sinatra's character is a Manchurian killer, too—one allowed to remember details of Harvey's brainwashing because that would make him seem more credible. And Leigh? She is Sinatra's controller.

This possible scenario simply adds another level to a movie already rich in intrigue. The

depths to which the Lansbury character will sink in this movie must be seen to be believed, and the actress generates a smothering "momism" that defines the type. By the end of the film, so many different people have used so many different strategies on Harvey's overtaxed brain that he is almost literally a zombie, unable to know what to believe, incapable of telling who can be trusted.

The Manchurian Candidate got glowing reviews when it was first released in 1962. (Pauline Kael wrote: "It may be the most sophisticated political satire ever made in Hollywood.") But then it was shelved in a dispute between United Artists and Sinatra. For more than twenty-five years, memories of *The Manchurian Candidate* have tantalized those who saw it at the time. Was it really as good as it seemed? It was.

Metropolis ★ ★ ★ ★
NO MPAA RATING, 120 m., 1926, 1984 (sound version)

Alfred Abel (Leader), Gustay Frohlich (His Son), Brigitte Helm (Maria), Rudolf Klein-Rogge (Rotwang), Heinrich George (Foreman). Directed by Fritz Lang. Screenplay by Lang and Thea Von Harbou. New sound track by Giorgio Moroder.

Fritz Lang's 1926 film *Metropolis* is one of the great achievements in the silent era, a work so audacious in its vision and so angry in its message that it is, if anything, more powerful today than when it was made. But it is rarely seen today; even in the era of insatiable home TV watching, silent films are condemned to the hinterlands of film societies and classrooms.

That is a great loss. Lang's movie is one of the great overwrought fantasies of German Expressionism, a story of a monstrous twenty-first-century city in which the workers labor like robots in their subterranean factories, while the privileged classes dance the night away, far above. The plot is broad melodrama: The son of the ruler of Metropolis visits the underground city and falls in love with a revolutionary named Maria, who makes impassioned speeches against the tyrants above. But the ruler orders a mad scientist to provide his new robot with Maria's face, creating a false Maria who will mislead the workers. Some of the individual scenes are amazing in their visual power, especially our first sight of the workers marching to their jobs, and a bizarre Art Deco factory wall where the humans are treated as parts of the machines. The movie was widely influential: The scene where the robot is turned into the false Maria was the inspiration for all the 1930s transformations of Frankenstein's monsters. Yet the original *Metropolis* is hardly known to today's filmgoers.

But now Giorgio Moroder, the composer of "Flashdance—What a Feeling" and the sound tracks for such movies as *Cat People*, has resurrected *Metropolis*, discovered or reconstructed some of its missing scenes, added some color tinting, and released it with a sound track of 1984 pop music. When this version of the movie was premiered at the 1984 Cannes Film Festival, it was sold primarily for its possibilities as a midnight cult film. In some sort of weird cultural inversion, Pat Benatar and Adam Ant would be used to sell Fritz Lang.

After you've seen the film with its new sound track, however, the notion seems almost sane. Silent films have always been accompanied by some sort of musical accompaniment—everything from orchestras to solo pianos. And in recent years such silent classics as *Napoleon* and *Peter Pan* have been resurrected with new scores. This is even the second time around for *Metropolis*, which was given a track of electronic music by the BBC in the 1970s. Moroder, however, has gone all the way and tarted up *Metropolis* with the same kinds of songs you'd expect to hear on MTV—he treats *Metropolis* like a music video. The film is too strong and original to be reduced to a formula, however; it absorbs the sound track, instead of being dominated by it, and the result is a film that works and a sound track that is an addition.

Some purists will not approve of Moroder's choice in music. Kevin Thomas of the *Los Angeles Times* was especially offended by the use of songs with words ("which sound especially silly because they're so painfully redundant"), but the words didn't bother me because, frankly, I didn't find myself listening to them. They are part of the background, and Fritz Lang's great film, so lovingly reconstructed, is the magnificent foreground.

Midnight Cowboy ★ ★ ★
R, 113 m., 1969

Dustin Hoffman (Ratso Rizzo), Jon Voight (Joe Buck), Sylvia Miles (Cass), John McGiver Mr. O'Daniel), Brenda Vaccaro (Shirley), Barnard Hughes (Towny). Directed by John Schlesinger and produced by Jerome Hellman. Screenplay by Waldo Salt.

Long after it was first released, *Midnight Cowboy* remains one of a handful of films that stay in our memory after the others have evaporated. Its love story between two drifters, the naive Joe Buck and the street-savvy Ratso Rizzo, is a reference point for other films. Some of its moments, like the one where Ratso pounds on a nudging taxi and shouts, "I'm walking here!" have entered into the folklore.

And yet, and yet . . . a 1994 viewing of the film confirms my original opinion, expressed in 1969, that the movie as a whole doesn't live up to its parts. And that Joe and Ratso rise above the material, taking on a reality of their own while the screenplay detours into the fashionable New York demimonde. *Midnight Cowboy* is a good movie with a masterpiece inside, struggling to break free.

The best thing in the movie is the acting, by Jon Voight and Dustin Hoffman as a simple-minded Texas drifter and a cynical Broadway street operator. This was the movie that established Voight's career, and proved that Hoffman, after the triumph of *The Graduate*, had many more notes inside of him—and was destined to become one of the great character actors of his time. Voight and Hoffman both won Oscar nominations as best actor. Over their shoulders, we could see a real world, the world of Times Square in the 1960s, which at the time seemed bleak and dangerous—but in the less innocent 1990s seems positioned halfway between our current despair and the lingering myths of Damon Runyon.

The characters and their immediate world are absolutely right, then. But the director, John Schlesinger, was not willing to tell their story with the simplicity I think it required. He took those two magnificent performances and dropped them into a trendy, gimmick-ridden exercise in fashionable cinema. The ghost of the Swinging Sixties haunts *Midnight Cowboy*, and robs it of the timelessness it should possess.

I wrote at the time: "Joe Buck and Ratso are castaways in *Midnight Cowboy*. They go their own ways, cold and wet, thrown out with the garbage, sharing their dreams of Florida or the ultimate rich broad. They live their own lives, become two of the permanent inhabitants of our imagination, like Bonnie and Clyde. They exist apart from the movie, outside of it. Their lives have nothing to do with Andy Warhol parties, or escort services, or hard Park Avenue dames. And who can really believe they would ever find themselves on that bus to Florida? It is cruel

to take the reality of Times Square—the existence of the real people like Ratso and Joe—and tell their story as if it were a soap opera. The form that has been imposed on this story simply will not fit."

I still feel that is the case. What has happened to *Midnight Cowboy* is that we've done our own editing job on it. We've forgotten the excesses and the detours, and remembered the purity of the central characters and the Voight and Hoffman performances. Seeing the movie again was a reminder of what else, unfortunately, it contains.

The heart of the movie is that Joe Buck, who thinks he will become the lover of a rich woman and be supported by her in a life of luxury, finds his small-town dreams destroyed. Although he briefly makes some money as a hustler, he finds he is expendable, disposable—and lacking the skills to survive in the city. Then he meets Ratso Rizzo, a person entirely outside his experience. Ratso is well-named. He makes his own way in the city, hated, asking no favors. When Joe finds himself used and discarded, Ratso shows him how to survive. *Midnight Cowboy* should have been about their self-discovery, about the process that took place as they learned to know each other.

Instead, it reaches outside the relationship for a string of melodramatic scenes that will not do. The most offensive is a psychedelic Andy Warhol party scene. Although the scene now provides a certain historical record (and it is fun to spot Warhol "superstars" in cameos), this basic party scene had already, in 1969, been staged many times. In the world they inhabited, there would have been almost no chance of Joe and Ratso being invited to such a party.

Another unnecessary episode involves a religious fanatic with his electric Christ. It might just barely have been pulled off, if only Jesus hadn't started blinking like a car-lot Santa Claus. Another difficult scene involves Joe's sexual encounter with a shy, middle-aged homosexual from Chicago. It goes wrong, Joe reacts violently, and slams the man in the mouth with a telephone, sending false teeth flying. The violence here was particularly shocking in 1969, less so today; but both now and then I wondered if Joe would actually have behaved that way. The action was praised as bravely realistic at the time—but doesn't it reflect a reality that Joe Buck himself might not inhabit? Is he really capable of such violence? Wouldn't he more likely simply have left suddenly?

One of the subtexts of the movie is Joe's own homosexuality, which he has never faced or understood. One scene that does work, in developing that theme, is the awkward encounter in the dark movie theater with the kid with horn-rims. But this scene is damaged by flashbacks to Joe's earlier life in Texas, that only offer the appearance of an explanation. The sexual fiasco with the young girl in Texas, and the smothering sexuality of his unattractive grandmother, provide ready-made Freudian shorthand: These experiences, the movie says, led to today's Joe Buck. Does it matter?

In my 1969 review of the film, I complained about the many songs on the sound track. "How long," I asked, "will it be before we recover from *The Graduate* and can make a movie without half a dozen soul-searching pseudo-significant ballads? When we dump the songs, we'll also be able to get rid of all those scenes of riding on buses, walking the rainy streets, hanging around, etc., that are necessary while the songs are being sung."

The answer, we now know, is that it will be a very long time indeed. The Semi-Obligatory Lyrical Interlude (which I defined at about the time *Midnight Cowboy* was released) is now a standard element in movie storytelling. A song is performed, a montage is provided, and time passes. Sometimes the songs are very good (it is a genuine pleasure to hear "Everybody's Talkin' at Me") but the fact remains, the lyrics *tell* us about the characters when the film should be *showing* us instead.

All of these doubts about *Midnight Cowboy* exist entirely apart from the performances of Dustin Hoffman and Jon Voight. It is a tribute to them, and to the core of honesty in Waldo Salt's screenplay and Schlesinger's direction (which both won Oscars), that Ratso and Joe Buck emerge so unforgettably drawn. But if films could be revised, or rewritten, it is possible to see now how this one could be made more pure.

Note: Midnight Cowboy was rated "X" by the MPAA when it was first released, and became the first (and last) X-rated film to win an Academy Award as best picture. At the time, the nudity and the frank portrait of prostitution and homosexuality was shocking. Later, the movie was re-rated "R," and in a sense it is responsible for its own new rating. Midnight Cowboy introduced a grimy realism to films about street life in American cities. The subject matter that it opened up was endlessly revisited by other films, from Panic in Needle Park *to* Drugstore Cowboy. *Eventually, this film came to seem mild compared to its descendants.*

My Fair Lady ★ ★ ★ ★
G, 171 m., 1964   NEW

Audrey Hepburn (Eliza Doolittle), Rex Harrison (Henry Higgins), Stanley Holloway (Doolittle), Wilfrid Hyde-White (Pickering), Gladys Cooper (Mrs. Higgins), Jeremy Brett (Freddie), Theodore Bikel (Zoltan Karpathy), Mona Washbourne (Mrs. Pearce), Elsom (Mrs. Eynsford-Hill). Directed by George Cukor and produced by Jack L. Warner. Screenplay by Alan Jay Lerner.

In *My Fair Lady*, which is the best stage musical of all time and one of the most loved romances, no one ever gets kissed. The most the leading man can concede about the heroine is that he has grown accustomed to her face. His rival is invited into her house, but would rather just stand outside on the street where she lives. And both her father and the man she loves consider marriage to be an abomination which they have been fortunate to escape.

There is, furthermore, no false sentimentality about the rags-to-riches rise of Eliza Doolittle, an unwashed Cockney who is plucked from Covent Garden and transformed into a "lady" by Professor Henry Higgins. "I may have sold flowers but I never sold myself," she tells him. "Now that I'm a lady, that's all I have to sell." Eliza returns to Higgins in the end not because he has reformed his attitudes, but because he has defended them. ("The question is not whether I have treated you rudely, but whether I have treated anyone else any better.") The play's famous last line ("Eliza? Where the devil are my slippers?") is a demonstration of his perversity.

And yet *My Fair Lady* is one of the most joyous musicals ever written. Most of the songs are simply about being happy. What the story celebrates is not romance but intelligence—about being liberated from ignorance and set free to realize your potential. This story is so powerful that every age has embraced it; it began as a Greek legend and was retold in Elizabethan and Victorian times and reached its present form as George Bernard Shaw's *Pygmalion* (1912), with its clear-eyed dissection of the British class system.

When Alan Jay Lerner and Frederick Loewe chose Shaw's play as the story for *My Fair Lady*, it must have seemed unlikely material. Certainly today no one would invest a dime in it. But by wisely keeping much of Shaw's barbed and articulate dialogue and marrying it with wonderful songs, they created a masterpiece. George Cukor filmed it in 1964, with Audrey Hepburn and Rex Harrison in the leads, and for the film's thirtieth anniversary it was restored by Robert A. Harris and James C. Katz, the same men who rescued *Lawrence of Arabia*.

I saw the restoration as it was meant to be seen, in wide screen and stereo sound, and although it is being rereleased primarily for the home video market, if you can get anywhere near a theatrical presentation, try to see it. Not only don't they make movies like this anymore—they can't. The movie industry is no longer interested in musicals about adults, let alone adults with ideas.

The story is well known. Eliza (Hepburn) is first insulted for her accent by the famous linguist Higgins (Harrison), and then offers him a shilling a lesson to teach her to speak like a lady. Higgins and his friend Colonel Pickering (Wilfrid Hyde-White) make a bet on the outcome, and Higgins transforms Eliza in six months. The supporting characters, who are all given major screen time and spirited Shavian speeches, include Eliza's father (Stanley Holloway) and Henry's mother (Gladys Cooper). Only poor lovestruck Freddie (Jeremy Brett) doesn't have a brain in his head: Shaw, impatient with romantic plotting, sticks him in when he needs him and then drops him without another word.

The story expresses boundless optimism. You can see it reflected in the decor of Henry Higgins's home, which is packed with the latest mechanical gadgets for teaching people how to speak better. (Including an ingenious gas flame that leaps up when Eliza pronounces her *h*s correctly.) You can see it, too, in Shaw's notion that if accent is the marker of class, then change your accent, and you can change your class. This was a revolutionary (if dubious) message in England in 1912, and is still thought-provoking.

As Higgins and Pickering train Eliza, a subterranean love story develops, and explodes with "The Rain in Spain," a song in which all three celebrate their success: Eliza at last can speak properly! Her solo, which follows, is "I Could Have Danced All Night," and it begins by referring to their dance of joy, and then subtly makes it clear that it is Henry Higgins in particular that she could have danced with. (It is one of the best-known bits of movie trivia that Hepburn's songs were dubbed by Marnie Nixon.)

Higgins seems hardly to notice the girl,

except as the object of his experiment. Even at the end of the film, after Eliza has stalked out and he has tracked her to his mother's house, their long conversation together is not one of sweet talk, confession, and reconciliation—but of Shavian analysis of the situation. If these people are ever to fall in love, it will be with their heads, instead of the usual parts.

Cukor's film is a pleasure to behold. Harrison, suave and distant and somehow reptilian around the eyes, makes a Higgins who never ever seems a pushover for Eliza. Hepburn, so touchingly waiflike, brings a poignancy to her coming-out scenes that is magical; she never seems quite confident that anyone will like her. The story needs its third wheel, Pickering, to give Higgins someone to bet against and argue with, and Wilfrid Hyde-White is plummy, apple-cheeked, and confiding. And Stanley Holloway's Mr. Doolittle (who would probably have been written out by modern Hollywood) gets some of Shaw's most pointed lines. "Have you no morals?" Higgins asks him. "No. I can't afford them."

Cecil Beaton designed the production, the sets and costumes, from a remarkably realistic Covent Garden to the famous scene at Ascot, in which all of the many extras are dressed in whites, blacks, and grays—a backdrop for Henry, in his sensible brown tweed suit, and Eliza, who has a touch of red in her dress. This is one of the best-looking movies ever made.

As I watched it, I wondered what had happened to the tradition that produced it. Warner Bros. filmed it with a sumptuous budget, and wasn't afraid of its wit, its literacy, its ideas. Audiences loved the intricacies of Lerner's lyrics. And no one thought, even for an instant, that Henry Higgins and Eliza Doolittle should do anything obvious like actually touch one another.

Nothing But a Man ★ ★ ★ ½
NO MPAA RATING, 92 m., 1964

Ivan Dixon (Duff), Abbey Lincoln (Josie), Julius Harris (Will), Gloria Foster (Lee), Martin Priest (Mill Worker), Leonard Parker (Frankie). Directed by Michael Roemer and produced by Robert Young, Roemer, and Robert Rubin. Screenplay by Roemer and Young.

Nothing But a Man is a film more famous than familiar. Since its release in 1964, it has been cited as one of the first and best of a new era of films about African-Americans,

but even at the time, its release was spotty, and today there are few people who have seen it. Now the national rerelease of a restored print reveals that the movie is even better than I remembered it; the basic drama remains strong, but what's also surprising is how well the more subtle moments hold up, and how gifted the actors are.

The movie stars Ivan Dixon as Duff, a section hand on a southern railroad. His life is hard and lonely. He and his fellow workers live in a railroad car that is parked near the current job, and hard manual labor all day is followed in the evening by drinking, cards, and small talk. There is not much resembling a social life, until one day Duff goes to a church social and meets the preacher's daughter, a schoolteacher named Josie (Abbey Lincoln).

He asks her out. After some hesitation, she agrees. She isn't accustomed to dating railroad workers, and her parents are certainly opposed to the match: They didn't educate her so she could marry a roughhewn laborer who (it becomes known) already has a son. But Duff and Josie find themselves drawn to one another, and then the movie asks its central question: Can Duff overcome his feelings of hopelessness and inadequacy in order to accept the happiness that is his, if he'll take it?

We meet some of the people in his life. There's Jocko (Yaphet Kotto), a fellow worker, hard-drinker, patronizer of prostitutes, scoffer at ambition. He assures Duff that he's aiming too high, that he should be looking for girls in bars instead of at church socials. We also meet Duff's father, Will, in a powerful performance by Julius Harris. He is a macho but deeply flawed man, who lives with a long-suffering woman (Gloria Foster) who understands him, sometimes to her regret. He has not been much of a father to Duff, and is not about to start now. And for Duff, his painful relationship with his father is a reminder of his poor record with his own son.

The movie asks a simple question: Will Duff be able to accept the love that Josie offers, and extend love in turn to his son? The answer is not simple, however, and the movie develops a genuine emotional payoff as Duff struggles with himself.

Nothing But a Man was directed by Michael Roemer, and cowritten by Roemer and Robert Young, who is also the cinematographer. They were documentarians at the time, determined to make a serious film about black Americans. Young has gone on to an

important career as the director of films with a social conscience (*The Ballad of Gregorio Cortez, Dominick and Eugene*), but Roemer has only recently been rediscovered with the rerelease of this film and the darkly comic *The Plot Against Harry* (1970).

For the actors, *Nothing But a Man* might have been a launching pad for many other roles, had it been more widely seen. Abbey Lincoln did appear in some other films, including *For Love of Ivy* (1966), before concentrating, probably rightly, on her career as a jazz singer. Ivan Dixon was also in *A Patch of Blue* and *Car Wash*. Julius Harris, whose performance here as the angry, defeated father is so effective, participated in the early-1970s blaxploitation period, with supporting roles in *Black Caesar* and *Superfly*.

Nothing But a Man is remarkable for not employing the easy liberal pieties of its period in an attempt to reassure white audiences that all stories have happy endings. Perhaps as a result, it didn't "cross over" and find a wider audience, and as a $300,000 production it didn't find many promotional resources. Now it is back, coinciding with the resurgence of Abbey Lincoln's own singing career—a film that was good then, and is still good now.

Othello ★ ★ ★
NO MPAA RATING, 91 m., 1952

Orson Welles (Othello), Michael Mac Liammoir (Iago), Robert Coote (Roderigo), Suzanne Cloutier (Desdemona), Fay Compton (Emilia), Doris Dowling (Bianca), Michael Laurence (Cassio). Directed and produced by Orson Welles. Screenplay by Welles.

Orson Welles's *Othello* is one of his least-seen films, but it inspired one of the best-known anecdotes about the master's impoverished work conditions. The movie was shot in bits and pieces between 1948 and 1951, with the actors sometimes languishing on locations while Welles flew off to raise more money. Improvisation concealed a multitude of shortcomings. On the day when Welles was prepared to film the murder of Cassio, for example, the costumes had not arrived, or not been paid for (the stories differ), and so he simply moved the scene to an old Turkish bath and dressed his actors in towels.

The result probably looks better than it would have otherwise, which is often the case with a Welles improvisation (he keeps the camera close to a flurry of blades and swordplay). But *Othello*'s compromises were not all so happy, and the resulting film, made only a decade after the boy wonder had conquered Hollywood with *Citizen Kane,* was a ragged production with a sound track that was badly out of synch. Even after winning the Palme d'Or at the 1952 Cannes Film Festival, it failed to open in America until 1955, and since then has been seen only rarely, in shabby 16mm prints.

Yet there was a film there. From its opening shots, where the camera looks down on a solemn funeral procession, *Othello* exhibits Welles's flair for dramatic compositions. Instead of the tame eye-level visuals of many films of Shakespeare plays, where the camera is content to watch great actors saying great words, Welles approaches *Othello* as a work intended at least equally for the eye.

Part of his approach was born of necessity: He could not afford to record sound on many of his locations, and so he placed the camera to make the actor's lips invisible, shooting over shoulders or at oblique angles. He planned to dub the dialogue in later. He was also handicapped by a revolving-door cast; his final Desdemona, Suzanne Cloutier, was the third actress in the role. Continuity was made even more difficult because some scenes were shot on locations in two or even three different countries, a doorway in Morocco leading to a piazza in Venice.

Welles finally pulled the whole project together, dubbing many of the voices himself. But watching the film was distracting; the dubbing was so careless that there was often no correlation between the words and the lip movements. And so the film remained, intriguing but imperfect, until Welles's daughter, Beatrice Welles-Smith, teamed with Chicago producers Michael Dawson and Arnie Saks and they went looking for the materials to restore the film to its vanished glory.

The tattered 16mm prints were obviously unusable, but in a New Jersey warehouse they found a long-mislaid 35mm master negative of the movie, along with the sound track. (There is poetry in that New Jersey warehouse; remember that Charles Foster Kane was headed for just such a place in search of his own childhood the night he met Susan Alexander.)

The visual print was in good condition, apart from some messy splices. But the sound track was a mess. Everything—dialogue, music, sound effects—was recorded on one track, and although modern digital technology allowed the restorers to isolate the dia-

logue, how could they recombine it with the rest? Eventually they commissioned composer and arranger Michael Pendowski to start all over again, rerecording the score with members of the Chicago Symphony Orchestra and Chorus and the Lyric Opera Chorus.

Then the words were dropped back in again by audio expert Ed Golya and sound engineer John Fogelson, who re-created the sound effects. They filtered out the noise on the original track, and the movie's audio is now in digital surround stereo, with the dialogue and the lip movements in much better synch.

The entire restoration cost more than $1 million. There is irony in the fact that if Welles had had that kind of money, no restoration would have been necessary. The restorers now claim that *Othello* looks and sounds better than it ever did before in its checkered history, even on the night when it won the Cannes festival. I'm sure they're correct.

The film itself is a strange experience, always visually interesting but sometimes difficult to follow. A close familiarity with Shakespeare will help, even though Welles, as usual, takes great liberties with the original play. *Othello* is essentially a tragedy based on words that lead to misunderstandings; Welles films it more as classical tragedy, with processions, poses, ceremonies, and dramatic visual compositions. The movie opens and closes with an event unknown in Shakespeare, the funeral procession of the bodies of Othello and Desdemona, and proceeds with interplay between Welles, as the Moor, and Dublin actor Michael Mac Liammoir, founder of the Gate Theater, as a curiously engaging Iago in his only filmed dramatic role.

This restoration, a labor of love, came preceded by *The Filming of Othello,* a 1978 German TV documentary (in English) that was unreleased in the United States until 1987. It featured the now aged Mac Liammoir sharing drinks and memories with fellow cast member Hilton Edwards in a Dublin pub. Welles himself hosted the film, sitting at a moviola, smoking an outsize cigar, and holding forth with memories and recollections. Even in the documentary, Welles cannot seem to focus on *Othello,* and his anecdotes wander here and there while we see only tantalizing glimpses of the film. Now his *Othello* is available as he presumably intended it— almost in spite of himself.

Peeping Tom ★ ★ ★ ½
NO MPAA RATING, 109 m., 1960

Carl Boehm (Mark Lewis), Moira Shearer (Vivian), Anna Massey (Helen Stephens), Maxine Audley (Mrs. Stephens), Edmond Knight (Arthur Baden), Bartlet Mullins (Mr. Peters). Directed and produced by Michael Powell. Screenplay by Leo Marks.

In 1960, the year in which the psychic violence of Hitchcock's *Psycho* aroused such a storm, a film named *Peeping Tom* was premiered in London, was savaged by all the major British critics, brought the career of its director nearly to an end, and was then all but forgotten. The director was Michael Powell, whose credits included *The Thief of Bagdad* and *The Red Shoes,* and who was to make only four more very low-budget films after this one. He had worked with Hitchcock in the 1920s but apparently had not learned the master's gift of disguising abnormal criminal behavior as entertainment.

Peeping Tom has remained a legendary but unseen film ever since its release and burial (Susan Sontag uses it as a reference point in *On Photography*), and now it's in the process of rediscovery. It was first seen in America at 1978's Telluride Film Festival and then was purchased for U.S. release by a group backed by Martin (*Taxi Driver*) Scorsese. Now it's on video.

Perhaps the delay of more than twenty years works in the film's favor. Its story of a lonely voyeur's sadistic killings was horrifying in 1960, and Powell's visual strategy was to cloak the story in lurid rotogravure colors and deliberately banal settings—but now the film's dated clothing, mannerisms, and locations give it an additionally creepy flavor. We're given a man whose crimes are committed through, by, and because of cameras— and it's as if those crimes have been developing in the lab all these years.

The film stars the open-faced, blond actor Carl Boehm, whose regular Teutonic features and neatly combed-back hair give him the curious look of being too straight, too regular. And of course he's the opposite. He works as an assistant movie cameraman and then comes home to the boardinghouse that used to be his father's home. Upstairs, in seclusion, his sick obsession is to run films of his murder victims—women he has photographed as he killed them.

One day, by chance, he meets the girl who lives downstairs (Anna Massey). And here we have a classic Hitchcock situation, in which a possible victim is in constant danger, we know it, and she doesn't. The girl becomes his confidant, to a degree, and he spares her ("I never want to photograph *you!*") while committing another murder and hiding the body on the set of a movie.

Massey learns from him that his father had been a perverted psychologist who wanted to record Boehm's entire childhood on film—and who filmed and tape-recorded his childish screams of fright. As a man, the killer's crimes are often elaborate re-enactments of his childhood terrors.

Is the film as disgusting as the British critics found it? Yes, but it is also very moving, a case study that could have been simply sadistic but emerges (especially because of the Boehm performance) as a tragic record of a destroyed life. Perhaps that's why *Peeping Tom* was so disturbing to its first viewers: It is *not* distanced into "entertainment" like *Psycho*, but remains unforgivingly as the story of horrible crimes seen straight-on.

Pinocchio ★ ★ ★ ★
G, 88 m., 1940

With the voices of: Dick Jones (Pinocchio), Christian Rub (Geppetto), Cliff Edwards (Jiminy Cricket), Evelyn Venable (The Blue Fairy), Walter Catlett (Honest John), Charles Judels (Stromboli), Charles Judels (Coachman), Frankie Darro (Lampwick). Supervising directors: Ben Sharpsteen and Hamilton Luske. Animation direction: Fred Moore, Milton Kahl, Ward Kimball, Eric Larson, Franklin Thomas, Vladimir Tytla, Arthur Babbitt, Woolie Reitherman. Story adaptation by Ted Sears, Webb Smith, Joseph Sabo, Otto Englander, William Cottrell, Erdman Penner, and Aurelius Battaglia.

Was there ever a scarier, more exciting animated feature than *Pinocchio*? I doubt it—at least not if you're somewhere between the ages of five and ten, and can identify with its blockheaded little hero. Pinocchio, who is not the brightest character in the history of cartoons, wants only to be a good little boy, but he's trapped by scoundrels who want to use him as a sideshow attraction, and then he's kidnapped and sent to an island where he will be turned into a donkey and put to work in the salt mines all day long.

I remembering seeing *Pinocchio* for the first time when I was just about the right age, and identifying with every single moment of the movie. Seeing it again the other day, for

the third or fourth time, I was struck again by what a great animated film it is. Many people choose *Snow White* as their favorite feature cartoon from Disney's golden age. My choice is *Pinocchio*.

The movie, made in 1940 and carefully restored for the 1992 re-release, comes from the era of full animation, before Disney and all the other animators started cutting corners. New films like *The Little Mermaid* and *Beauty and the Beast* have returned to this tradition, thanks to labor-saving help from computers, but in 1940 real human artists lovingly illustrated every frame of this movie, and weren't afraid to take pains with the details, like the waves on the ocean that curl back in horror at the approach of Monstro the Whale.

The movie looks great, it contains terrific songs (including the immortal "When You Wish Upon a Star"), and the story is scary in a way kids can identify with. Pinocchio is without a doubt the most passive and simpleminded of the Disney cartoon heroes, but he's surrounded by a colorful gallery of villains and connivers, including the evil Stromboli, who thinks there is money to be made from a wooden puppet who can walk and talk. And on the good side, of course, there are Jiminy Cricket, whose high-wire act on a violin string is one of the greatest moments in the history of animation, and the kindly old Geppetto, who wants a son and is overjoyed when his puppet comes to life.

The scenes that haunted my childhood dreams mostly took place on Pleasure Island, that isle of lost boys where the carnival pleasures of shooting pool and smoking cigars were only a lure to trap the kids before they could be turned into donkeys. And then, of course, there is the thrilling adventure with Monstro the Whale, whose cavernous belly swallows up Geppetto when he goes to sea in search of his missing son.

The beauty of *Pinocchio* is that what happens to Pinocchio seems plausible to the average kid—unlike what happens, say, to the Little Mermaid. Kids may not understand falling in love with a prince, but they understand not listening to your father, and being a bad boy, and running away and getting into real trouble. The movie is genuinely exciting and romantic, and great to look at in this wonderfully restored version, its colors fresh and sparkling, the story timeless.

Singin' in the Rain ★ ★ ★ ★
G, 102 m., 1952

Gene Kelly (Don Lockwood), Donald O'Connor, (Cosmo Brown), Debbie Reynolds (Kathy Seldon), Jean Hagen (Lina Lamont), Millard Mitchell (Producer). Directed by Gene Kelly and Stanley Donen and produced by Arthur Freed. Screenplay by Adolph Green and Betty Comden.

The image that everyone remembers from *Singin' in the Rain* has Gene Kelly hanging from a lamppost and swinging his umbrella in the wild joy of new love. The scene builds to a gloriously saturated ecstasy as Kelly stomps through the puddles of water in the gutters, making big wet splashes.

The entire sequence, from the moment Kelly begins to dance until the moment the cop looks at him strangely, is probably the most joyous musical sequence ever filmed. It celebrates a man who has just fallen in love and has given himself over to heedless celebration. And the rainwater provides the dancer with a tactile medium that reflects his joy in its own noisy way.

Singin' in the Rain has been voted one of the greatest films of all time in international critics' polls, and is routinely called the greatest of all the Hollywood musicals. I don't think there's any doubt about that. There are other contenders—*Top Hat, Swing Time, An American in Paris, The Band Wagon, Oklahoma, West Side Story*—but *Singin' in the Rain* comes first because it is not only from Hollywood, it is about Hollywood. It is set at the moment in the late 1920s when the movies first started to talk, and many of its best gags involve technical details.

A restored print of the movie, made from the original three-strip Technicolor process with its brilliant reds and yellows, went into national release to celebrate *Rain*'s fortieth anniversary in 1992. It is also available in video, including high-quality laserdiscs from MGM and Criterion. Looking at it again proves that the movie still has every ounce of its original charm, but then that didn't come as a surprise to me, since I've seen it at least once a year since the first time I saw it at Chicago's late, lamented repertory house, the Clark Theatre.

Unlike most of the movie musicals of recent years, *Singin' in the Rain* was not based on a Broadway stage production; it worked the other way around, with a London and Broadway musical in the 1980s being based on the movie. The original screenplay held up so well that the Tommy Steele stage version in London followed the film even in small details.

The movie was cobbled together fairly quickly in 1952 to capitalize on the success of *An American in Paris*—which won the Academy Award as the best picture of 1951 and also starred Gene Kelly. The new movie had an original screenplay by Adolph Green and Betty Comden, and new songs by Nacio Herb Brown and Arthur Freed. But some of the songs, including the famous title tune, were anything but new. The Criterion Collection laserdisc includes old film clips of a version of "Singin' in the Rain" from *Hollywood Review of 1929*, "You Were Meant for Me" from *Broadway Melody of 1929*, and "Beautiful Girl" from the Bing Crosby musical *Going Hollywood* (1933).

Film historian Ron Haver, who does the scene-by-scene commentary on an alternate sound track of the laserdisc, points out that *Singin' in the Rain* was not immediately hailed for its greatness. It did well at the box office, but won no Academy Awards and was on no critics' year-end lists of best films. Only after it went into repertory in 1958, as part of a package of MGM classics, did audiences begin to realize how special it was.

The influential critic Pauline Kael was managing a repertory theater in Berkeley then, and her program notes, calling the movie "just about the best Hollywood musical of all time," helped establish the movie's eventual reputation.

Maybe because the movie was made quickly and with a certain freedom (and because it was not based on an expensive stage property), it has a wonderfully free and improvisational feeling. We know that sequences like Donald O'Connor's neck-breaking "Make 'Em Laugh" number had to be painstakingly rehearsed, but it feels like it was made up on the spot. So does "Moses Supposes," with O'Connor and Kelly dancing on tabletops.

Debbie Reynolds was still a teen-ager when she starred in the movie, and there is a light in her eyes to mirror the delight of her character, who is discovered leaping out of a cake at a party and soon becomes the on-screen voice of Lena Lamont (Jean Hagen), a silent star whose voice is not suited to talkies, to say the least. The movie's climax, as Reynolds flees from a theater while Kelly shouts out "Stop that girl!" and tells everyone who she is, and that he loves her, is one of those bravura romantic scenes that make you tingle no matter how often you see it.

There's great humor in *Singin' in the Rain*, too, especially in the scenes that deal with the technical difficulties of the early days of talkies. Lena Lamont can never seem to remember which flower arrangement holds the concealed microphone, and so her voice booms and whispers as she turns her head back and forth. This was not an imaginary problem for early actors in the talkies; Chicago bandleader Stanley Paul collects early sound movies with scenes that reflect that very problem.

Although *Singin' in the Rain* has been on video in various versions for a decade and is often seen on TV, a big-screen viewing will reveal a richness of color that your tube may not suggest. The film was photographed in bold basic colors—the yellow raincoats are an emblem—and director Stanley Donen and his cast have an energy level that's also bold, basic, and playful. But is this really the greatest Hollywood musical ever made? In a word, yes.

Spartacus ★ ★ ★
PG-13, 187 m., 1960

Kirk Douglas (Spartacus), Laurence Olivier (Crassus), Jean Simmons (Varinia), Charles Laughton (Gracchus), Peter Ustinov (Batiatus), John Gavin (Julius Caesar), Tony Curtis (Antoninus), Woody Strode (Black Gladiator). Directed by Stanley Kubrick and produced by Edward Lewis. Screenplay by Dalton Trumbo.

At the time of its first release in 1960, *Spartacus* was hailed as the first intellectual epic since the silent days—the first Roman or biblical saga to deal with ideas as well as spectacle. Even the ending was daring. The crucified hero is denied a conventional victory, and has to be consoled with the hope that his ideas will survive.

Seen three decades later in a lovingly restored version, *Spartacus* still plays like an extraordinary epic, and its intellectual strength is still there. But other elements of the film are dated. The most courageous thing about it, from today's standards, is that it closes without an obligatory happy ending, and an audience that has watched for 187 minutes doesn't get a tidy, mindless conclusion.

The film tells the story of the Roman slave Spartacus (Kirk Douglas), who toils for the Roman Empire while dreaming, the narrator assures us, "of the death of slavery—which would not come until 2,000 years later." He is sentenced to death after biting a Roman guard, but spared by Peter Ustinov, as Batiatus, a broker of gladiators. Spartacus is trained in the arts of combat at Batiatus's gladiatorial academy, where one day two powerful men arrive from Rome, one with his wife, the other with his fiancée. The spoiled women ask to be entertained by the sight of two fights to the death, and Spartacus is matched with a skilled black gladiator (Woody Strode), who spares him and is killed.

The notion of being forced to fight for the entertainment of spoiled women enrages Spartacus, who leads a slave revolt that eventually spreads over half of Italy. Leading his men into battle against weak and badly led Roman legions, Spartacus stands on the brink of victory, before his troops are finally caught between two armies and outnumbered.

All of this takes place against a backdrop of Roman decadence, and we become familiar with the backstage power plays of the Senate, where Crassus (Laurence Olivier) hopes to become a dictator at the expense of the more permissive and gentler old man Gracchus (Charles Laughton). There are also sexual intrigues; Gracchus is a womanizer, and Crassus a bisexual, who is attracted to a handsome young slave (Tony Curtis), but is also driven by the desire to win the love of the slave woman Varinia (Jean Simmons), who is the wife of Spartacus.

The movie was inspired by a bestseller by Howard Fast, and adapted to the screen by the blacklisted writer Dalton Trumbo. Kirk Douglas, executive producer of the film, effectively broke the blacklist by giving Trumbo screen credit instead of making him hide behind a pseudonym. The direction is by the thirty-one-year-old Stanley Kubrick, who realizes the ideas of Douglas, Fast, and Trumbo, but cannot be said to add much of his own distinctive style to the film.

I've seen *Spartacus* three times now—in 1960, 1967, and 1991. Two things stand up best over the years: the power of the battle spectacles, and the strength of certain of the performances, especially Olivier's fire, Douglas's strength, and Laughton's mild amusement at the foibles of humankind. The most entertaining performance in the movie, consistently funny, is by Ustinov, who upstages everybody when he is onscreen (he won an Oscar). Some of the supporting performances now seem dated and the line readings stilted; dialogue like "How will I ever be able to thank you?" delivered by a senator placed in charge of a legion, gets a bad laugh.

All historical films share the danger that their costumes and hairstyles will age badly.

Spartacus stands at a divide between earlier epics, where the female characters tended to look like models for hairdressing salons, and later epics that placed more emphasis on historical accuracy. But the hairstyles of the visiting Roman women at the gladiatorial school are laughable, and even Jean Simmons looks too made up and coiffed at times.

Balancing against those dated elements are some that were ahead of their time, including a muted but sophisticated understanding of sexual motivation. Olivier's character becomes more complex in this revival than it was at the time, because of the restoration of a key scene, cut by censors, in which he and Tony Curtis share a bath together, and he confesses, "I like both oysters and snails," leaving little doubt where either is to be found, as far as he is concerned. That brings his desire for Jean Simmons into focus: He wants her not merely to possess her, but as a form of victory over Spartacus.

The film has been restored by Robert A. Harris, the same man who brought *Lawrence of Arabia* back to its original glory, and Harris has done a good job. The full 187 minutes of screen time has been pieced back together from various shorter release versions; the color has been renewed by going back to the original materials and restoring them; the sound track is in six-track Dolby, and the 70mm, wide-screen picture reminds us of when movies filled our entire field of vision.

One aspect of the sound track is distracting: In the early days of stereo, movies such as *Spartacus* used the left track for characters on the left side of the screen, and the right track for those on the right, and then switched for the reverse shot—a disorienting auditory experience for the audience. Today's approach in surround sound puts the voices on the center channel and the effects on the side, a better approach.

Perhaps the most interesting element of *Spartacus* is its buried political assumptions. The movie is about revolution, and clearly reflects the decadence of the parasitical upper classes and the superior moral fiber of the slaves. But at the end, Spartacus, like Jesus, dies on the cross. In the final scene, his wife stands beneath him and holds up their child, saying "He will live as a free man, Spartacus." Yes, but the baby's freedom was granted him not as its right, but because of the benevolence of the soft-hearted old Gracchus. Today, that wouldn't be good enough.

Stairway To Heaven (A Matter of Life and Death) ★ ★ ★ ★   NEW
PG, 104 m., 1946

David Niven (Peter Carter), Kim Hunter (June), Roger Livesey (Dr. Reeves), Raymond Massey (Abraham Farlan), Marius Goring (Conductor 71), Abraham Sofaer (Judge), Richard Attenborough (Pilot), Robert Coote (Bob Tropshaw). Directed and produced by Michael Powell and Emeric Pressburger. Screenplay by Powell and Pressburger.

Stairway to Heaven (1946) is one of the most audacious films ever made—in its grandiose vision, and in the cozy English way it's expressed. The movie, which has been restored in a Technicolor print of dazzling beauty, is by Michael Powell and Emeric Pressburger (*The Red Shoes, The Life and Death of Colonel Blimp*), the most talented British filmmakers of the 1940s and 1950s.

"This is the universe," a voice says at the beginning of *Stairway to Heaven*. "Big, isn't it?" The camera pans across the skies—but the story, as it develops, is both awesome and intimate, suggesting that a single tear shed for love might stop heaven in its tracks.

The story opens inside the cockpit of a British bomber going down in flames over England in the last days of World War II. The pilot, Peter (David Niven), establishes radio contact with a ground controller, an American named June (Kim Hunter). Peter is unflappable in the face of death, and an instant rapport springs up between the two disembodied voices ("I love you, June. You're life, and I'm leaving it"). Then Peter jumps out of the plane before it crashes.

What follows is a breathtaking pastoral moment, as the pilot, somehow alive, washes ashore and sees a young woman, far away, riding her bicycle home. It is, of course, June, and soon they are deeply in love. But there is a problem. Peter was not intended to live. Heaven has made an error, and an emissary, Heavenly Conductor 71 (Maurice Goring), is sent to fetch him back. Peter refuses to go, and a heavenly tribunal is convened to settle the case. This fantasy is grounded in reality by a brain operation the pilot must undergo; perhaps his heavenly trial is only a by-product of the anesthetic.

The British title of this film was *A Matter of Life and Death,* and when the Americans retitled it *Stairway to Heaven,* Powell wrote in his autobiography, he felt they had missed the point. But *Stairway to Heaven* may be a more expressive title, and certainly there *is* a

stairway in the film, part of the incredible contribution of production designer Alfred Junge, who also provides one of the most spectacular shots in movie history, a view of Heaven's underside: vast holes in the sky with tiny people peering down over the edges. The heavenly scenes are shot in black and white, and the movie is filled with technical tricks, as when "real life" freezes while spirits leave their bodies.

The film's most audacious leap is to the trial in heaven to decide whether Peter will be allowed to stay on earth. Junge creates a heavenly amphitheater that fills the sky, and fills it with infinite ranks of heaven's population. Standing on one precipice, the prosecutor, an American played by Raymond Massey, argues against the British pilot. In one of the comic touches that deflates any excess profundity, he argues that Peter and June could never be happy together because they come from different cultures. First, we hear a radio broadcast of a cricket match; then an American big band broadcast. He asks the jury: "Should the swift current of her life be slowed to the crawl of a match of cricket?"

But of course the question is not whether Peter and June will be happily married, but whether they will be married at all, and here the tear of love, captured on a rose petal by the Heavenly Conductor, becomes crucial evidence.

Stairway to Heaven has as its subtext the jockeying for power between Britain and America that took place after World War II. British critics, at the time, sniffed that the film was too pro-American. What today's audiences will find amazing is the sheer energy of its invention. Powell and Pressburger (who always shared the writing, directing, and producing credits, and whose production company was known as "The Archers"), were not timid in reaching for new visual effects, and among the many startling sights in *Stairway to Heaven* is an eyeball's point-of-view of its eyelid closing, before the brain operation.

There's also sly humor. Heaven has a Coke machine for the arriving Yanks; newly appointed angels are seen carrying their wings under their arms in plastic dry-cleaner bags; the dialogue at the trial includes complaints like, "Would you repeat the question? It has 'enamored' in it."

Today's movies are infatuated with special effects, but often they're used to create the sight of things we can easily imagine:

crashes, explosions, battles in space. The special effects in *Stairway to Heaven* show a universe that never existed until this movie was made, and the vision is breathtaking in its originality.

As a kid, Martin Scorsese discovered The Archers on TV, watching "Million Dollar Movie" on a New York station that would show the same film seven days in a row. He says that's how he did his homework. It's appropriate that the restoration of *Stairway to Heaven* is "presented by Martin Scorsese."

A Star Is Born ★ ★ ★
PG, 175 m., 1954 (1983)

Judy Garland, James Mason, Jack Carson, Tommy Noonan, Charles Bickford. Directed by George Cukor.

A Star Is Born hasn't merely been restored. It has been rediscovered. George Cukor's 1954 movie, which starred James Mason and Judy Garland in the story of Hollywood lives destroyed by alcoholism, always has been considered one of the great tear-jerking Hollywood melodramas, populated with bravura performances. But has it ever been praised for its purely cinematic qualities? I don't think so, and yet it showed Cukor's mastery not only of the big effects, but also of subtle lighting and exquisite compositions. It's an irony, but if Warner Bros. hadn't chopped twenty-seven minutes out of the movie in 1954 and tried to throw them away, the whole movie never would have been rereleased in its current form. It is very good to have the missing footage back, of course, but it's even better to have the whole movie back again, a landmark of Hollywood melodrama.

Although this version is exactly as long as Cukor's final cut in 1954, it doesn't have quite all the footage. Two major production numbers and a charming little scene in a drive-in restaurant were rediscovered by film historian Ron Haver (after months of detective work). Haver also found the movie's complete stereo sound track, but about seven minutes of the visual footage seem to be gone forever—and so this restoration uses an effective montage of music, dialogue, and production stills to bridge the gaps. Seeing this version of the movie makes it clear what major surgery was performed by Warner Bros. The studio chopped out an entire Judy Garland musical number, "Here's What I'm Here For," filled with fire and energy. That's wonderful to have back again, but the other

major restored sequence is almost indispensable to the film.

It's a scene from fairly early in the film. The alcoholic movie star (Mason) has convinced the young band vocalist (Garland) to risk everything and try for a movie career. With his support, she's on the brink of stardom. She's recording a song with a studio orchestra, and afterward she rests on a staircase with Mason. He proposes marriage. She says he drinks too much. He promises to reform. Neither one realizes that their whole conversation is being recorded by an eavesdropping overhead mike. Then, as a joke by the director, the proposal is played back for all the musicians to hear—and Garland accepts. By taking out that proposal scene, Warner Bros. had a movie that skipped unconvincingly from Garland's movie debut to her elopement with Mason. The earlier missing footage—the scenes represented by the still photos—also represented important bridging material, covering an uncertain period during which Garland thinks Mason has forgotten about her. Without those scenes, the movie skips directly from Garland's early hopes to her first day at the studio, with no period of uncertainty.

The missing scenes are good to have back again. But the movie's central scenes are even better to see again. There is an absolutely brilliantly lit and directed scene in a darkened nightclub, with Garland singing while the camera prowls silently among the musicians' instruments; it's one of the best examples of composition I've ever seen. And near the end of the movie, there's Garland's big, bravura scene, in which she interrupts a big production number for a heart-rending dressing-room conversation with her studio chief (Charles Bickford). And then, of course, there is Mason's sad, lonely walk into the sea, and the movie's unforgettable closing line: "Good evening, everyone. This is Mrs. Norman Maine."

A Star Is Born is one of the rare films that successfully integrate music with drama; it's not exactly a musical, but it has more music than most musicals. It's also not exactly a serious drama—it's too broad and predictable for that—but it's the sort of exaggerated, wide-gauge melodrama that Rainer Werner Fassbinder would experiment with twenty years later; a movie in which larger-than-life characters are used to help us see the melodramatic clichés that we do, indeed, sometimes pattern our own lives after.

I was lucky enough to visit George Cukor

at his Hollywood home in December of 1981. He said he had never seen the butchered version of *A Star Is Born* and never would. "If they wanted it shorter," he said, "I could have sweated out twenty-five minutes here and there, and nobody would have missed them. Instead, they took an ax to the movie." George Cukor died on the evening before he was to see a rough version of this restored print. That is sad, but then Cukor, of course, knew what his original movie looked like. Now the rest of us can know, too.

A Streetcar Named Desire ★ ★ ★
PG, 126 m., 1951

Vivien Leigh (Blanche DuBois), Kim Hunter (Stella), Marlon Brando (Stanley Kowalski), Karl Malden (Mitch). Directed by Elia Kazan and produced by Charles K. Feldman. Screenplay by Tennessee Williams.

Marlon Brando didn't win the Academy Award in 1951 for his acting in *A Streetcar Named Desire*. The Oscar went to Humphrey Bogart for *The African Queen*. But you could make a good case that no performance had more influence on modern film acting styles than Brando's work as Stanley Kowalski, Tennessee Williams's rough, smelly, sexually charged hero.

Before this role, there was usually a certain restraint in American movie performances. Actors would portray violent emotions, but you could always sense to some degree a certain modesty that prevented them from displaying their feelings in raw nakedness. Brando held nothing back, and within a few years his was the style that dominated Hollywood movie acting. This movie led directly to work by Brando's heirs, such as Montgomery Cliff, James Dean, Jack Nicholson, and Sean Penn.

The film itself, hailed as realistic in 1951, now seems claustrophobic and mannered—and all the more effective for that. The Method actors, Brando foremost, always claimed their style as a way to reach realism in a performance, but the Method led to superrealism, to a heightened emotional content that few "real" people would be able to sustain for long, or convincingly.

Look at the way Brando, as Kowalski, stalks through his little apartment in the French Quarter. He is, the dialogue often reminds us, an animal. He wears a torn T-shirt that reveals muscles and sweat. He smokes and drinks in a greedy way; he doesn't have the good manners that 1951 performances often assumed. (As a contrast, look at Bogart's grimy riverboat captain in *The African Queen*. He's also meant to be rude and crude, but beneath the oil and sweat you can glimpse Bogart's own natural elegance.) At the same time, there is a feline grace in Brando's movements; he's a man, but not a clod, and in one scene, while he's sweet-talking his wife, Stella (Kim Hunter), he absentmindedly picks a tiny piece of lint from her sweater. If you can take that moment and hold it in your mind with the famous scene where he assaults Stella's sister, Blanche DuBois (Vivien Leigh), you can see the freedom Brando is giving to Stanley Kowalski—and the range.

When *A Streetcar Named Desire* was first released, it created a firestorm of controversy. It was immoral, decadent, vulgar, and sinful, its critics cried. And that was *after* substantial cuts had already been made in the picture, at the insistence of Warner Bros., driven on by the industry's own censors. Elia Kazan, who directed the film, fought the cuts and lost. For years the missing footage—only about five minutes in length, but crucial—was thought lost. But this 1993 restoration splices together Kazan's original cut, and we can see how daring the film really was.

The 1951 cuts took out dialogue that suggested Blanche DuBois was promiscuous, perhaps a nymphomaniac attracted to young boys. It also cut much of the intensity from Stanley's final assault of Blanche. Other cuts were more subtle. Look at the early scene, for example, where Stanley plants himself on the street outside his apartment and screams, "Stella!" In the censored version, she stands up inside, pauses, starts down the stairs, looks at him, continues down the stairs, and they embrace. In the uncut version, only a couple of shots are different—but what a difference they make! Stella's whole demeanor seems different, seems charged with sexual lust. In the apartment, she responds more visibly to his voice. On the stairs, there are closeups as he descends, showing her face almost blank with desire. And the closing embrace, which looks in the cut version as if she is consoling him, looks in the uncut version as if she has abandoned herself to him.

Another scene lost crucial dialogue. Stella tells her sister, "Stanley's always smashed things. Why, on our wedding night, as soon as we came in here, he snatched off one of my slippers and rushed about the place

smashing the light bulbs with it." After Blanche is suitably shocked, Stella, leaning back with a funny smile, says, "I was sort of thrilled by it." All that dialogue was trimmed, perhaps because it provided a glimpse into psychic realms the censors were not prepared to acknowledge.

The restored version of the film extends the conversation that Blanche has with a visiting newspaper boy, making it clear she is strongly attracted to him. It also adds details from Blanche's description of the suicide of her young husband; it is now more clear, although still somewhat oblique, that he was a homosexual, and she killed him with her taunts.

Despite the overwhelming power of Brando's performance, *Streetcar* is one of the great ensemble pieces in the movies. Kim Hunter's Stella can be seen in this version as less of an enigma; we can see more easily why she was attracted to Stanley. Vivien Leigh's Blanche is a sexually hungry woman posing as a sad, wilting flower; the earlier version covered up some of the hunger. And Karl Malden's Mitch—Blanche's hapless gentleman caller—is more of a sap, now that we understand more fully who he is really courting, and why.

The movie was shot, of course, in black and white. Dramas made in 1951 nearly always were. Color would have been fatal to the special tone. It would have made the characters seem too real, when we need them exactly like this, black and gray and silver, shadows projected on the screens of their own dreams and needs. Watching the film is like watching a Shakespeare tragedy. Of course the outcome is predestined, but everything is in the style by which the characters arrive there. Watch Brando absently scratching himself on his first entrance. Look at the way he occupies the little apartment as if it were a pair of dirty shorts. Then watch him flick that piece of lint.

Tokyo Story ★ ★ ★ ★
G, 139 m., 1953

Chishu Ryu (Old Father), Chiyoko Higashiyama (Old Mother), So Yamamura (Married Son), Haruko Sugimura (Married Daughter), Setsuko Hara (Widowed Daughter-in-law), (Younger Daughter), Kyoko Kagawa Shiro Osaka (Younger Son). Directed by Yasujiro Ozu and produced by Takeshi Yamamoto. Screenplay by Kogo Noda and Ozu.

Yasujiro Ozu's *Tokyo Story* tells a tale as simple and universal as life itself. It is about a few ordinary days in the lives of some ordinary people, and then about the unanticipated death of one of them. What it tells us about the nature of life or death is not new or original—what could be?—but it is true.

Ozu's story can be summarized in a few words. An old couple make the long train trip to Tokyo to visit their children. During their stay of a week or so, they're treated politely but with a certain distraction; life moves quickly in the big city, and there is not always time for the parents and their courtly provincial ways. On the train journey home, the mother falls ill. The children are summoned, and all but one are at the bedside when she dies.

There is a great sadness, of course, and sympathy for the old father. But life must go on. The children were casually indifferent to their parents in life. Now that the mother is dead, they speak of their regrets that they didn't do more for her; but they also maneuver quietly for some of her possessions, and within a day after the funeral they have all returned to the city, leaving the father alone.

Of all the relatives, the one who is most considerate of the father is not even a blood relative; a daughter-in-law, the widow of a son who died, was the warmest toward the old couple when they were in Tokyo, and now she is the kindest to the old man. He tells her, after his wife's funeral, that she should remarry as soon as possible. "My son is dead," he says, "and it is not right for you not to marry." He says he would feel better if she forgot his son; he does not see any irony in this attitude, so soon after his wife's funeral, and perhaps there really isn't any.

Tokyo Story was made in 1953, or at about the same period that a group of great Japanese films was beginning to make a first impression on Western audiences. The best-known are *Rashomon, Ugetsu Monogatari,* and *Gates of Hell.* But *Tokyo Story* was not imported at that time, and not until 1972 was it introduced to the West, by the legendary Japanese film scholar Donald Ritchie, who brought it to the Venice Film Festival over the protests of many Japanese who said Ozu was "too Japanese" to be understood by outsiders. Actually, the film is an illustration of an interesting principle: Those movies which are most local and specific often travel better than more "popular" entertainments from the same country.

Ozu is perhaps the greatest of Japanese directors, and one of the most unique. He is not interested in vast sweeping plots, but in the nuances of human behavior, and look here at how silences, quiet acknowledgments, subtle shifts of position, tell the whole story. Notice, too, his great tact in not milking the story for a cheap emotional payoff. The quiet way in which the old father (Chishu Ryu) deals with his loss, and expresses his gratitude to his kind daughter-in-law (Setsuko Hara) could have been handled as soap opera. Ozu gives it the depth of true feeling.

Tokyo Story is a good example of Ozu's famous visual style, in which he uses his camera as an impassive, honest observer. Most of his shots are from the eye-level of a Japanese person seated on a floor mat, and he tends to begin a shot before people enter a room, and hold it for a moment after they leave, so that the transience of their lives can sink in. His movies are not all hectic behavior. Notice the "pillow shots" he uses to suggest the passage of time. He will provide a shot of some nearby exterior for a moment or two, just to provide an almost musical pause instead of hurrying to the next scene.

This objectivity creates an interesting effect. Because we are not being manipulated by devices of editing and camera movement, we do not at first have any very strong reaction to *Tokyo Story*. We miss the visual cues and shorthand used by Western directors to lead us by the nose. With Ozu, it's as if the characters are living their lives unaware that a movie is being shot. And so we get to know them gradually, begin to look for personal characteristics and to understand the implications of little gestures and quiet remarks.

Tokyo Story moves slowly by our Western standards and requires more patience at first than some moviegoers may be willing to supply. Its effect is cumulative, however; the pace comes to seem perfectly suited to the material. And there are scenes that will be hard to forget: The mother and father separately thanking the daughter-in-law for her kindness; the father's laborious drunken odyssey through a night of barroom nostalgia; and his reaction when he learns that his wife will probably die.

2001: A Space Odyssey ★ ★ ★ ★
G, 141 m., 1968

Keir Dullea (Bowman), Gary Lockwood (Poole), William Sylvester (Dr. Heywood Floyd), Daniel Richter (Moonwatcher), Douglas Rain (HAL 9000 [Voice]), Leonard Rossiter (Smyslov), Margaret Tyzack (Elena), Robert Beatty (Halvorsen), Sean Sullivan (Michaels), Frank Miller (Mission Controller). Directed and produced by Stanley Kubrick. Screenplay by Kubrick and Arthur C. Clarke.

It was e e cummings, the poet, who said he'd rather learn from one bird how to sing than teach ten thousand stars how not to dance. I imagine cummings would not have enjoyed Stanley Kubrick's *2001: A Space Odyssey,* in which stars dance but birds do not sing. The fascinating thing about this film is that it fails on the human level but succeeds magnificently on a cosmic scale.

Kubrick's universe, and the spaceships he constructed to explore it, are simply out of scale with human concerns. The ships are perfect, impersonal machines which venture from one planet to another, and if men are tucked away somewhere inside them, then they get there, too. But the achievement belongs to the machine. And Kubrick's actors seem to sense this; they are lifelike but without emotion, like figures in a wax museum. Yet the machines are necessary because man himself is so helpless in the face of the universe.

Kubrick begins his film with a sequence in which one tribe of apes discovers how splendid it is to be able to hit the members of another tribe over the head. Thus do man's ancestors become tool-using animals. At the same time, a strange monolith appears on Earth. Until this moment in the film, we have seen only natural shapes: earth and sky and arms and legs. The shock of the monolith's straight edges and square corners among the weathered rocks is one of the most effective moments in the film. Here, you see, is perfection. The apes circle it warily, reaching out to touch, then jerking away. In a million years, man will reach for the stars with the same tentative motion.

Who put the monolith there? Kubrick never answers, for which I suppose we must be thankful. The action advances to the year 2001, when explorers on the moon find another of the monoliths. This one beams signals toward Jupiter. And man, confident of his machines, brashly follows the trail.

Only at this point does a plot develop. The ship is manned by two pilots, Keir Dullea and Gary Lockwood. Three scientists are put on board in suspended animation to conserve supplies. The pilots grow suspi-cious of the computer, "HAL," which runs the ship. But they behave so strangely—talking in monotones like characters from "Dragnet"—that we're hardly interested.

There is hardly any character development in the plot, then, and as a result little suspense. What remains fascinating is the fanatic care with which Kubrick has built his machines and achieved his special effects. There is not a single moment, in this long film, when the audience can see through the props. The stars look like stars and outer space is bold and bleak.

Some of Kubrick's effects have been criticized as tedious. Perhaps they are, but I can understand his motives. If his space vehicles move with agonizing precision, wouldn't we have laughed if they'd zipped around like props on *Captain Video?* This is how it would really be, you find yourself believing.

In any event, all the machines and computers are forgotten in the astonishing last half-hour of this film, and man somehow comes back into his own. Another monolith is found beyond Jupiter, pointing to the stars. It apparently draws the spaceship into a universe where time and space are twisted.

What Kubrick is saying, in the final sequence, apparently, is that man will eventually outgrow his machines, or be drawn beyond them by some cosmic awareness. He will then become a child again, but a child of an infinitely more advanced, more ancient race, just as apes once became, to their own dismay, the infant stage of man.

And the monoliths? Just road markers, I suppose, each one pointing to a destination so awesome that the traveler cannot imagine it without being transfigured. Or as cummings wrote on another occasion, "Listen—there's a hell of a good universe next door; let's go."

Note: This movie is best viewed in the letter-boxed version, which preserves the wide-screen compositions.

The Wages of Fear ★ ★ ★ ★
NO MPAA RATING, 148 m., 1953

Yves Montand (Mario), Charles Vanel (Jo), Vera Clouzot (Linda), Folco Lulli (Luigi), Peter Van Eyck (Bimba). Directed by Henri-Georges Clouzot and produced by Louis Wipf. Written by Clouzot and Jerome Geronimi.

When the great French thriller *The Wages of Fear* was first released in America, it was missing parts of several early scenes—because it was too long, the U.S. distributors said, and because they were anti-American, according to the Parisian critics. Now that the movie is available for the first time in the original cut of director Henri-Georges Clouzot, it is possible to see that both sides have a point.

The film's extended suspense sequences deserve a place among the great stretches of cinema. Four desperate men, broke and stranded in a backwater of Latin America, sign up on a suicidal mission to drive two truckloads of nitroglycerin three hundred miles down a hazardous road. They could be blown to pieces at any instant, and in the film's most famous scene Clouzot requires them to turn their trucks around on a rickety, half-finished timber platform high above a mountain gorge.

Their journey also requires them to use some of the nitroglycerin to blow up a massive boulder in the road, and at the end, after a pipeline ruptures, a truck has to pass through a pool of oil that seems to tar them with the ignomy of their task. For these are not heroes, Clouzot seems to argue, but men who have valued themselves at the two thousand dollars a head that the oil company will pay them if they get the nitro to the wellhead where it is needed.

The company, which significantly has the same initials as Standard Oil, is an American firm that exploits workers in the unnamed nation where the film is set. The screenplay is specific about the motives of the American boss who hires the truck drivers: "They don't belong to a union, and they don't have any relatives, so if anything happens, no one will come around causing trouble." There are other moments when the Yankee capitalists are made out as the villians, and reportedly these were among the scenes that were trimmed before the film opened in the United States.

The irony is that the trims have been restored at a time when they have lost much of their relevance, revealing that the movie works better as a thriller than as a political tract, anyway. The opening sequence, set in the dismal village where unemployed men fight for jobs, is similar to the opening of John Huston's *Treasure of the Sierra Madre* (1948), even down to the detail of visiting the local barber, but while Huston used his opening to establish his characters and work in some wry humor, Clouzot creates mostly aimless ennui.

Although eager to establish his anti-American subtext, he reveals himself as a reactionary in sexual politics, with the inexplicable character of Linda (Vera Clouzot), who does menial jobs in the saloon. She is in love with one of the local layabouts (Yves Montand, in his first dramatic role), who slaps her around and tells her to get lost, and she spends most of her time sprawled on the ground, although always impeccably made up. There is no apparent purpose for this character, apart from the way she functions to set up such lines as, "Women are no good."

If the opening sequences, now restored, have a tendency to drag, the movie is heart-stopping once the two trucks begin their tortuous three-hundred-mile journey to a blazing oil well. The cinematographer, Armand Thirard, pins each team of men into its claustrophobic truck cab, where every jolt and bump in the road causes them to wince, waiting for a death that, if it comes, will happen so suddenly they will never know it.

Clouzot does an especially effective job of setting up the best sequence, where first one and then the other truck has to back up on the unstable wooden platform in order to get around a hairpin bend in the trail. The first truck is used to establish the situation, so we know exactly what Montand is up against when he arrives at the scene: Rotten timbers break, the truck begins to slide sideways, a steel support cable gets caught on the side of the truck, and we are watching great technical work as it creates great fiction.

When William Friedkin remade *The Wages of Fear* as *Sorcerer* in 1977, he combined this scene with a later one, in a jungle setting, to create a sequence where a truck wavers on a vast, unstable suspension bridge. Friedkin had greater technical resources, and his sequence looks more impressive, but Clouzot's editing selects each moment so correctly that you can see where Friedkin, and a lot of other directors, got their inspiration.

One thing that establishes *The Wages of Fear* as a film from the early 1950s, and not from today, is its attitude toward happy endings. Modern Hollywood thrillers cannot end in tragedy for their heroes, because the studios won't allow it. *The Wages of Fear* is completely free to let anything happen to any of its characters, and if all four are not dead when the nitro reaches the blazing oil well, it may be because Clouzot is even more deeply ironic than we expect. The last scene, where a homebound truck is intercut with a celebration while a Strauss waltz plays on the radio, is a reminder of how much Hollywood has traded away by insisting on the childishness of the obligatory happy ending.

The Wild Bunch: The Director's Cut ★ ★ ★ ★   NEW
R, 144 m., 1969

William Holden (Pike), Ernest Borgnine (Dutch), Robert Ryan (Thornton), Edmond O'Brien (Sykes), Warren Oates (Lyle Gorch), Jaime Sanchez (Angel), Ben Johnson (Tector Gorch), Emilio Fernandez (Mapache). Directed by Sam Peckinpah and produced by Phil Feldman. Screenplay by Walon Green and Peckinpah.

In an early scene of *The Wild Bunch*, the bunch rides into town past a crowd of children who are gathered with excitement around their game. They have trapped some scorpions and are watching them being tortured by ants. The eyes of Pike (William Holden), leader of the bunch, briefly meet the eyes of one of the children. Later in the film, a member of the bunch named Angel is captured by Mexican rebels, and dragged around the town square behind one of the first automobiles anyone there has seen. Children run after the car, laughing. Near the end of the film, Pike is shot by a little boy who gets his hands on a gun.

The message here is not subtle, but then Sam Peckinpah was not a subtle director, preferring sweeping gestures to small points. It is that the mantle of violence is passing from the old professionals like Pike and his bunch, who operate according to a code, into the hands of a new generation that learns to kill more impersonally, as a game, or with machines.

The movie takes place in 1913, on the eve of World War I. "We gotta start thinking beyond our guns," one of the bunch observes. "Those days are closing fast." And another, looking at the newfangled auto, says, "They're gonna use them in the war, they say." It is not a war that would have meaning within his intensely individual frame of reference; he knows loyalty to his bunch, and senses it is the end of his era.

This new version of *The Wild Bunch*, carefully restored to its original running time of 144 minutes, includes several scenes not widely seen since the movie had its world premiere in 1969. Most of them fill in details from the earlier life of Pike, including his guilt over betraying Thornton (Robert Ryan), who was once a member of the bunch but is now leading the posse of bounty hunters on their trail. Without these scenes, the movie seems more empty and existential, as if Pike and his men seek death after reaching the end of the trail. With them, Pike's actions are more motivated: He feels unsure of himself and the role he plays.

I saw the original version at the world premiere in 1969, as part of a week-long boondoggle during which Warner Bros. screened five of its new films in the Bahamas for 450 critics and reporters. It was party time, not the right venue for what became one of the most controversial films of its time—praised and condemned with equal vehemence, like *Pulp Fiction*. At a press conference the following morning, Holden and Peckinpah hid behind dark glasses and deep scowls. After a reporter from *Reader's Digest* got up to attack them for making the film, I stood up in defense; I felt, then and now, that *The Wild Bunch* is one of the great defining moments of modern movies.

But no one saw the 144-minute version for many years. It was cut, not because of violence (only quiet scenes were removed), but because it was too long to be shown three times in an evening. It was successful, but it was read as a celebration of compulsive, mindless violence; see the uncut version, and you get a better idea of what Peckinpah was driving at.

The movie is, first of all, about old and worn men. Holden and his fellow actors (Ernest Borgnine, Warren Oates, Edmund O'Brien, Ben Johnson, and the wonderful Robert Ryan) look lined and bone-tired. They have been making a living by crime for many years, and although Ryan is now hired by the law, it is only under threat that he will return to jail if he doesn't capture the bunch. The men provided to him by a railroad mogul are shifty and unreliable; they don't understand the code of the bunch.

And what is that code? It's not very pleasant. It says that you stand by your friends and against the world, that you wrest a criminal living from the banks, the railroads, and the other places where the money is, and that while you don't shoot at civilians unnecessarily, it is best if they don't get in the way.

The two great violent set pieces in the movie involve a lot of civilians. One comes through a botched bank robbery at the beginning of the film, and the other comes at the end, where Pike looks at Angel's body being dragged through the square, and says "God, I hate to see that," and then later walks into a bordello and says "Let's go," and everybody knows what he means, and they walk out and begin the suicidal showdown with the heavily armed rebels. Lots of

bystanders are killed in both sequences (one of the bunch picks a scrap from a woman's dress off of his boot), but there is also cheap sentimentality, as when Pike gives gold to a prostitute with a child, before walking out to die.

In between the action sequences (which also include the famous scene where a bridge is bombed out from beneath mounted soldiers), there is a lot of time for the male bonding that Peckinpah celebrated in most of his films. His men shoot, screw, drink, and ride horses. The quiet moments, with the firelight and the sad songs on the guitar and the sweet tender prostitutes, are like daydreams, with no standing in the bunch's real world. This is not the kind of film that would likely be made today, but it represents its set of sad, empty values with real poetry.

The undercurrent of the action in *The Wild Bunch* is the sheer meaninglessness of it all. The first bank robbery nets only a bag of iron washers—"a dollar's worth of steel holes." The train robbery is well planned, but the bunch cannot hold onto their takings. And at the end, after the bloodshed, when the Robert Ryan character sits for hours outside the gate of the compound, just thinking, there is the payoff: A new gang is getting together, to see what jobs might be left to do. With a wry smile he gets up to join them. There is nothing else to do, not for a man with his background.

The movie was photographed by Lucien Ballard, in dusty reds and golds and browns and shadows. The editing, by Lou Lombardo, uses slow motion to draw the violent scenes out into meditations on themselves. Every actor was perfectly cast to play exactly what he could play; even the small roles need no explanation. Peckinpah possibly identified with the wild bunch. Like them, he was an obsolete, violent, hard-drinking misfit with his own code, and did not fit easily into the new world of automobiles and Hollywood studios.

Seeing this restored version is like understanding the film at last. It is all there: why Pike limps, what passed between Pike and Thornton in the old days, why Pike seems tortured by his thoughts and memories. Now, when we watch Ryan, as Thornton, sitting outside the gate and thinking, we know what he is remembering. It makes all the difference in the world.

Woodstock ★ ★ ★ ★
R, 225 m., 1969

Directed by Michael Wadleigh and produced by Bob Maurice.

The movies are, of course, a time capsule, and I have rarely felt that more sharply than while watching the twenty-fifth anniversary edition of *Woodstock*. What other generation has so completely captured its youth on film, for better and worse, than the Woodstock Nation? Watching the film today, for someone like me who also saw it on the day it was premiered, inspires meditation as well as joy, dark thoughts as well as hopeful ones.

The making of the film was a happy accident. I remember meeting the director, Michael Wadleigh, in an editing room up in a loft in New York City, months before the movie was released. He talked about how he and his partner, producer Bob Maurice, threw together a production team at the last moment, and descended on the Woodstock site because they had a hunch it might be more than just another rock concert.

What they came away with was 120 miles of footage, which an editing team headed by Thelma Schoonmaker and Martin Scorsese assembled into a three-hour film. The balance was perhaps 60 percent about the music and 40 percent about the event itself—about how 400,000 people were drawn to a farm in upstate New York, where the facilities could not remotely sustain or feed them, and where a thunderstorm soaked them, but where somehow they celebrated, as the film's subtitle has it, "three days of peace and music."

This new "director's cut," available on tape and laserdisc, adds an additional forty-five minutes, including sets by Janis Joplin and Jefferson Airplane that were not in the original film. It also expands the film's final performance, by Jimi Hendrix, which includes his pyrotechnic version of "The Star-Spangled Banner."

That performance was attacked by some at the time as a desecration of the national anthem. Hearing it again the other day, I found it the most stirring version of the song I have ever heard. Hendrix tortured his electric guitar to create the sound of bombs bursting in air, as they were at that moment in Vietnam, and like a jazzman he improvised, working in bits of other songs (I've heard this version many times, but only on this hearing did I pick up fifteen notes of "Taps"). As Hendrix plays, the camera shows the last act of Woodstock. Most of the 400,000 have gone home. A few forlorn wanderers walk barefoot across the muddy fields, trying to find shoes that will fit. Trash crews pick up the debris. The event is over. And then the editors slowly reverse the time flow, so that the field fills again, horizon to horizon, with a mass of humanity. It was then and probably still is the largest crowd ever gathered.

It is probable that Woodstock would not have been possible without Vietnam. They are two sides of the same coin: the grinning nun flashing a peace sign to the camera at the concert, and the war. One of the heroes of the film is the Port-a-San man, in charge of servicing the portable toilets. After swabbing out a few units, he confides to the camera that he has a son out there in the crowd somewhere—"and another one in the DMZ, flying helicopters."

The concert, with its pot smoking, its skinny-dipping, its warnings about "bad acid," its famous shot of a couple disrobing and making love in a meadow, and Country Joe leading a sing-along of "Feel Like I'm Fixin' to Die Rag," was in its own way a peace rally. Without the war to polarize American society, these 400,000 people might not have felt so much in common. I remembered that time when strangers flashed the peace sign

to each other, when costume and attitude created a feeling of camaraderie, when it was believed that music made a difference and could affect society. All of that is gone, gone, gone.

So are some of the performers, dead of drugs. Hendrix, of course, and Janis Joplin, who has always seemed weathered in my memory, but here seems touchingly young, because she did not grow older with the rest of us. Others were survivors: Roger Daltry, Joan Baez, Grace Slick, who in the Airplane set looks like a fresh-faced college girl. Even Country Joe McDonald looks young here. It was all so long ago.

The structure of the documentary is roughly chronological. We see the fields being prepared, the stage being built, the massive traffic jams forming. We see crowds trampling over the fences, and there is the moment when the event, conceived as a profit-making enterprise, is officially declared a "free concert." (There is an amusing moment when the late Bill Graham, a concert promoter who always kept his eye on the gate, advises the organizers, facetiously I think, to fill ditches with flaming oil to keep the gate-crashers out.)

Woodstock was made at a time before rock concerts were routinely filmed (although earlier documentaries about the Stones, Bob

Dylan, and the Newport Jazz Festival pointed the way). The stars were not performing for the camera. Richie Havens casually stops in the middle of a set to tune his guitar. Sha-Na-Na does a cornball double-time version of "At the Hop" and doesn't care how it looks. Joan Baez puts down her guitar and sings "Swing Low, Sweet Chariot," and nobody worries that it will slow down the show. Night follows day, day follows night, Hugh Romney of the Hog Farm announces, "What we have in mind is breakfast in bed for 400,000 people." Army helicopters drop food, blankets, medical supplies—and flowers. Babies are born and no one is killed, and for a moment it seems that the spirit of Woodstock Nation could prevail.

Looking up my old review of the movie, I find that I began it with a quote from the Chicago Seven trial. Accused conspirator Abbie Hoffman is asked where he resides, and he replies, "Woodstock Nation." His attorney asks him to explain to the judge and jury where that is. "It is a nation of alienated young people," Hoffman says. "We carry it around with us as a state of mind, in the same way the Sioux Indians carry the Sioux nation with them. . . ."

Yes, I thought, looking at the old clipping. And look what happened to the Sioux.

Film Clips

Woody Allen

New York, October 12, 1994—Woody Allen's new comedy, *Bullets Over Broadway,* is about a man who takes his art so seriously he is willing to kill for it. The man is a gangster, circa 1930, who gets involved in the rewrite of a play, and doesn't want anybody screwing it up.

We're discussing this as a concept. We're drinking coffee in Allen's editing room, in midtown Manhattan. He's on the ratty old couch, I'm in a chair, and there are shadows all around. I'm asking: If you had to choose between saving the works of Shakespeare or the life of a drowning person, such as your mother, which would you choose?

"Well," he said, "usually the example is not your mother, because there are a lot of people who would save their mother. Usually, the way they phrase the question, it's just a nameless derelict." He paused to consider. "I think you have to go with saving the person, right? I mean, you have to. Because I'm not that committed a Shakespeare fan. The question would be harder for me if I was saving the work of certain other people. Louis Armstrong, for example."

What about if you had to choose between the nameless derelict, and your own life work?

"Oh, I don't care about my life work for a second. When I die, I don't care what they do with it. They can flush it down the toilet. There's that delusion that it's going to have some meaning to you when, in fact, you'll be a nonexistent thing; there'll be not a trace of consciousness. So it becomes completely irrelevant, what happens after your death. Totally. It doesn't mean a thing."

To you, but . . .

"To me, yeah, and so I don't care."

He didn't, either. I could tell it from his voice. And in a sense he was speaking from experience, because the recent events in his life made it seem possible that he would lose his life's work, or the freedom to go on making more of it. Two years ago Allen was an American artistic hero, a legend, a good guy. Then came all the charges and countercharges, all the headlines, and the astonishing sight of Allen giving press conferences to deny child molestation.

Investigators have not turned up any evidence of Allen's guilt, and now the charges seem to have quietly disappeared. But did the tumult in his life bring his artistic work to a halt? Not for a second.

"I've done a lot," he said. "I finished *Husbands and Wives,* I wrote and directed *Manhattan Murder Mystery.* I wrote and directed *Don't Drink the Water* for television. I played with my jazz band without missing a session. I wrote a play that's going to be done this season, and I wrote and directed *Bullets Over Broadway.* Because, you know, for me one thing had nothing to do with the other. The legal battles I've been in were basically fought by my lawyers. There was nothing I could do about it."

Many times when we've talked, I said, you've said that you consider suicide every day.

He nodded.

And so now, I said, comes probably the worst possible thing that could happen to you. And you don't kill yourself. You continue to work. My belief is, if you were guilty, you would have killed yourself. Or been paralyzed in some way. Your work is all about guilt. I don't think you could have survived as a guilty person.

"You're exactly right. I thought the whole business was foolish. I thought it was going to blow over in two days; I never even took it seriously when it first happened. Apart from the horribleness of not being able to see my children, those of us on the inner circle—myself, my sister, my close friends—found it almost amusing.

"But from a total nonevent, a multi-million dollar industry grew. I mean, magazines all over the world, newspapers, television . . . lawyers were hired, private detectives were hired, more lawyers were brought in, psychiatrists were brought in. It was incredible. And *nothing had happened.* I certainly wasn't going to participate in the craziness. I worked, I never missed an evening with my jazz band, and I conducted my life normally."

I was afraid at the beginning, I said, that maybe it would turn out like the Fatty Arbuckle case—where here was a great Hollywood comedian and whether he was guilty or not, people simply couldn't find him funny anymore. I wondered if after all the controversy people would never be able to laugh at a Woody Allen picture again.

"Yes, people said to me, 'Are you worried about this having an impact in your career?' But from where I sat, it *couldn't* have an impact. Am I going to be less popular? I was not popular when people *thought* I was popular. I never had a big audience to begin with. And it never mattered to me. If people said to me tomorrow that I couldn't make a movie again because no one would come, it wouldn't bother me in the slightest."

He was looking into the middle distance, seeing possibilities that had perhaps occurred to him more than once.

"I almost had a secret hope that maybe this would change my life in a way I didn't have the nerve to do. They'd say I could never make a film again. And I could wake up in the morning and think, 'Oh, great, that option is closed to me. I don't have to think about it. I don't have to feel guilty that I'm not making films.' And I could write for the theater, which is something I like, or even stay home and write a novel.

"But I never thought I was in the position of Fatty Arbuckle. I mean, he was a tremendous star. When you're a writer, you have control over your own fate. I mean, it would not bother me in the slightest if I'd awakened this morning and stayed in my apartment and was working on my typewriter or lying on the bed writing a book."

It was strange, listening to this detachment, this declaration of self-sufficiency, and then thinking about *Bullets Over Broadway*. Because the movie expresses the belief that art is worth fighting for, even killing for, and there are moments that I thought might be autobiographical—reflecting not Woody's life, but his feelings.

The film is very funny. It is also relentlessly logical, like many great comedies, and follows its reasoning no matter what the consequences. It stars John Cusack as a young playwright whose latest work is being produced on Broadway. The catch: The financing comes from a mobster, who insists that his girl friend (Jennifer Tilly) star in the play. The girl friend attends rehearsals with a mob bodyguard (Chazz Palminteri), who sits in the dark and watches the play and then begins to make suggestions. Before long, the thuggish bodyguard is rewriting the entire play, and it's clear he's much more of an artist than the Cusack character. The waters grow murky when he realizes that his boss's girl friend is so untalented she is going to destroy his work.

"He has the commitment of a genuine artist," Allen said. "He can't compromise; he can't do less than he's able to do. It's irrelevant to him that the play is a hit and it's going to be fine and they'll replace the bad actress with someone, later on down the line. The thought that his work isn't all that it could be is driving him crazy."

Is that autobiographical in a way?

"Not so much for me."

But you fight for your work. . . .

"Yes, I fight for it but I'm not a dedicated artist, really. I would fight with producers if I had to. But I'm not an artist in the way this guy was. That is, a perfectionist. If I'm shooting, and it's five o'clock at night and there's a basketball game on at seven, I'm not going to do the extra takes and miss the first quarter. Or, if it's freezing cold and I wanna get a shot, I'll say, Okay, we'll move it inside and put the conversation in a restaurant instead of the street. I compromise for my own comfort.

"When I first started making films, nothing was more important for me than the film. Like the first two films. But now I've made like twenty-five or something. I started to keep filmmaking in its perspective. I recently did *Don't Drink the Water* for television, and they pointed out to me that if I went to Budapest, I could have shots of great scope and it would be tremendous and it would cost us very little money. But I wouldn't go. And then they said, 'Look, if we just go up to Canada for a week, you could do a week up there of the exteriors, in Montreal, and it would look great.' I ended up shooting the entire thing within like six blocks of my house and it all takes place behind the Iron Curtain or some Middle Eastern country. And it's just fine."

Most directors would instantly want to go to Budapest, I said.

"But would it really make the picture any better? There are artists who kill for their work in nonlethal ways, you know what I mean? They don't actually kill but they're so ruthless and selfish their whole lives that they kill you in so many ways. Is it worth it?"

Will what you've gone through in the last couple of years ever find its way into a film?

"It isn't all played out yet, but when it is, it's possible that I would want to make a certain kind of film about it. It would have to be a real-life film, not a fiction film."

A documentary?

"I have an idea for a film that's half documentary and half not documentary and it would be a gift to my children. I would want them to know who behaved well in this and who did not behave well. I'm not talking about any controversy with Mia because that's not what's on my mind at all.

"In this whole situation, apart from the two protagonists, there were a number of other major participants. There was the psychiatric system, the legal system, the press . . . and there were a number of heroes who were really terrific and a number of people who were just awful. Just unconscionably awful. In any phenomenon, whether it's McCarthyism or Nazism or whatever, there are people who rise to the top and do the right thing and people who don't. And, you know, I think that when the kids grow up they should know who behaved in their best interests, and who failed them.

"So I have a real interesting film but I want to do it when all the dust settles; when the whole thing is well over and is all clear. I want to make sure everyone had their full time to behave well—to either, you know, suddenly show up as a villain or redeem themselves if they had done something unscrupulous. I think it would make an interesting piece one day and something that I would like to leave for the children."

A silence fell. He had spoken so quietly, so softly, and with so much anger.

"But, apart from that," he said, "I just go along making the films that I can think of at the time. It isn't that there is a vast storehouse of billions of great ideas. It's when a picture's over, I go into a room and start to think of a new idea. And whatever comes is what I do."

Atom Egoyan

March 8, 1995—Pieces of time. That's what the movies have been called. Usually they begin with the first piece and continue with the second piece, onward to the inevitable conclusion. But currently there's a small group of filmmakers who don't think that way. They shuffle the deck. You can't put all the pieces together until the movie is over. It's challenging, and it can be fun.

Atom Egoyan is a director like that. Some directors make movies like onions, peeling off one layer after another. He works in the opposite way. His new movie, *Exotica,* reconstructs the onion, one layer at a time. It starts with small pearls of a story that seem mysterious and unconnected, and gradually the whole form becomes clear. It's a curiously satisfying experience.

Egoyan is a filmmaker from Toronto, in his thirties, whose work *(Next of Kin, Speaking Parts, Calendar, The Adjuster)* is familiar on the festival and art house circuits. With *Exotica,* he is finding a wider audience. It won the Cesar as the year's best foreign film in France, has set box office records in Canada, and arrives here with ads and trailers that make it look like a sex-soaked thriller.

"They made a great commercial for the film," he was telling me the other day. "They cut from one character with a gun to another one with something strapped around his waist." So maybe the viewers figure the guy has a bomb strapped to himself, right? Are they in for a surprise when they find out it's birds' eggs!

Exotica begins with disconnected pieces. A scene in airport customs. A scene in a sex club, where a table dancer and her client have a strange rapport. A scene in a pet shop. A weird conversation between the sweet woman who runs the sex club and its satanic disc jockey. How are these people connected?

Egoyan's *Exotica* goes on the list with other recent films, including Tarantino's *Pulp Fiction,* Kieslowski's *Red,* and Manchevski's Oscar-nominated *Before the Rain.* All four burrow into labyrinths of time. They double back on themselves. They present scenes that seem to say one thing and actually say another. They bait and switch.

"There's a sense of predetermination with most movies," Egoyan was telling me. This was during a recent Chicago visit. "The movie begins. You know it's going to end in ninety minutes. No matter where it may go, its course is set. So there's something fatalistic. To try and reorient that, to create a sense of play, is such a natural challenge."

That's what he does in *Exotica,* and it's breathtaking the way the plot reveals itself, and we see how the characters are related, in the present and the past.

The most enigmatic relationship is between the dancer in the sex club (Mia Kirshner) and her client (Bruce Greenwood). They meet in a place that drips with sex, but finally sex has nothing to do with the bond between them. We sense tenderness and sympathy on her part, a wounded need on his. Two other characters also seem related through sex—a gay man picks up a partner at the ballet—but they, too, are revealed to have a different kind of connection.

The club advertises, "Look, but don't touch." In *The Adjuster,* Egoyan's 1991 film, a film censor secretly videotapes X-rated movies, so she can show them to her sister. "I'm voyeuristic myself," Egoyan said, "and I think anyone who's making films would be lying if they said they weren't. That's what films are all about: watching people behave. Directing is about orchestrating things you would like to see happen."

And, he might have added, in the *way* you would like to see them happen. In a sense, *Pulp Fiction* jarred the movie audience awake, telling them, hey, movies don't just start and grind away; they're free to leap around in time. With *Exotica,* Egoyan is pushing the same envelope. As the plot reveals itself, as surprise dovetails into surprise, we are required to be so alert, so observant, that it's like we're making the film, too. Watching at his side.

Jodie Foster

December 21, 1994—Over a period of five days I interviewed Jodie Foster twice about her new film *Nell.* The first time, in New York, was for television, and she supplied the smooth sound bites she'd been performing all morning for dozens of visiting interviewers. The second time, in Chicago, was for print, and we talked for more than two hours.

It's kind of unusual these days for a star to hit the road. In the old days you'd have an actor or a director coming through town every week. These days, most interviews are on an assembly line. The studios enthrone their stars in a hotel on one of the coasts, and lob journalists at them like human sacrifices.

Going on the road was her own idea, Foster said. *Nell* was not only a movie she starred in, but the first film from her own production company. So she wanted careful attention paid to it. "I didn't want it to be stuck on a publicity production line where the press goes on a junket and someone hands them the stupid hat and the T-shirt and the blower or whatever it is and it just feels like another hundred movies. I just feel like a different thing happens when you have the time to really talk to people about what you think the movie is about. Because you get into this six-minute sound-bite thing and it becomes shameless promotion. It's really about buying prime-time TV. It's not about the film."

Yeah, I said, when you do twenty interviews, and each one is five minutes long, it's a little like a nightmare where you're trapped inside "Entertainment Tonight."

"I grapple with that all the time," she said. "I ask myself, am I an insincere person because I can do these little sound-bite things, condensing the pitch into thirty seconds? You have to make peace with the process and so I only promote movies I care about. If I did it for a movie I hated or had no connection with, then I would really feel like an impostor."

I look at her, and listen to her, and I remember. Twenty years ago, when she was twelve, I interviewed Jodie Foster for the first time, about a Martin Scorsese movie named *Taxi Driver*. The deal was, we would meet for lunch at a health-food hangout on Sunset Boulevard. I expected her to turn up with her mother and her manager and a publicist and a makeup person, but she turned up all by herself, and ate a spinach salad, and talked about the movie.

There was some controversy over her role in *Taxi Driver* because she played a street waif who had become a prostitute. Would the role damage someone so young? Five minutes of talking with Foster (who had started in toothpaste commercials at three and starred in movies since she was eight), and I knew I didn't have to worry, not about her, anyway. She was telling me about her discussions of directing with Scorsese and her observation of Robert De Niro's acting style. And a few months later, when the film played at the Cannes Film Festival, she sat calmly at a press conference in front of five hundred people and translated everything into and out of French.

So she's smart. That we know. What we know now, twenty years later, is that she has survived: She seems to know how to guide her career through the shoals of Hollywood, where there aren't often great roles for women, but she makes them happen for herself.

Her Academy Awards have come for *The Accused* (1988), where she played a rape victim, and *The Silence of the Lambs* (1991), where she was an FBI agent up against a brilliant serial killer. The same year she made *Silence*, she also directed her first film, *Little Man Tate*, and played a working-class mother trying to deal with the fact that her son may be a genius. The project may have indirectly reflected her own relationship with her mother, who has been both manager and friend.

Now comes her work in *Nell*. She plays a wild child, the surviving member of a set of twins, who has been isolated all her life in a North Carolina wilderness with her dysfunctional mother. Nell can take care of herself, and she can speak, but her language sounds like a strange singsong of nonsense, with the haunting pattern of familiar syntax buried somewhere deep inside. And her body language is that of someone who has not seen a person her own age for a long time, except in a mirror.

Foster bought the rights to the Mark Handley play *Idioglossia*, which inspired the screenplay. She changed the sex of its subject from male to female. She found the director, Michael Apted, who had explored the rural South for *Coal Miner's Daughter*. She was able to hire Liam Neeson for his first role since his milestone performance in *Schindler's List*. And for the other lead she wanted Natasha Richardson, not so much because she was Neeson's wife as because Natasha and Jodie had become friends years earlier when Foster starred in *Hotel New Hampshire*, directed by Richardson's father, Tony. You look at the parts

that went into *Nell* and you're not surprised that you're impressed by the whole.

"Liam first came to us and really wanted to play the role," she said. "For me, the only reason to have somebody in a film is if they love it. And he's not afraid to be sensitive, which was crucial. Natasha's so intelligent, and you can't hide that on the screen. She doesn't have to wear spectacles to be smart. She just is, so she can play the vulnerability underneath."

In the film, Neeson is a doctor who is led to the newly discovered "wild woman" living in the wilderness. Richardson is a psychologist. Only gradually do they crack the code of Nell's language and see that she is not retarded, merely very different. And that she may have lessons to teach them.

"'Otherness' is a big thing for me," Foster said. "I'm always drawn to characters that live lives that I couldn't lead. People who survive and don't allow the world to change them. Maybe this movie will give someone the idea that if Nell can be herself, maybe it's okay for them to be brave, too, about their idiosyncratic natures and their otherness."

You're so verbal, I said, that I don't know how you found a way to play this woman who can hardly communicate at all, and speaks no known language for much of the movie.

"I was petrified. I didn't know what I was going to do. I did the research thing; but it didn't pan out. How can you research Nell? Finally I realized all I really had to do was just be emotionally available. And that meant no hair, no makeup, no costumes, no props, no other person to talk to. You're on your own and you just have to find an emotional connection to everything. You drink a cappuccino, hang out with the guys. Then someone says 'action!' and you just do it. I don't think there's any more preparation than that."

In the film, she talks to herself, repeating what sound like empty syllables until Neeson and Richardson make a breakthrough. And she moves with an eerie choreography.

"Everything depends in Nell's situation. If Liam moves his hand up, then that changes my performance. If he starts talking or something comes out his face, that is going to change my performance. It's not like I'm *supposed* to do this or that. But underneath there is a very complicated script with very complicated language and everything Nell says makes sense and I could tell you what it all means. By the end of the film, the audience understands everything."

Working with Michael Apted, she said, was fairly simple, because he doesn't theorize about a movie. The director of the famous British *7–14–21–28–35 Up* series, which has been visiting the same group of people every seven years since they were seven, he goes from such documentaries to thrillers like *Blink* and epics like *Gorillas in the Mist*.

"The only question that he will ever ask is, 'Is it real or is it not?' If he was making a movie about boring people who only watched TV, it would be the most boring film you've ever seen. He wants the story to tell itself and he wants the characters to tell their own story. What makes him right for a movie like this is that he will never kind of, like, typecast the movie and say, 'The head of the clinic is the bad guy so I'm going to cast some bad guy, J.T. Walsh or whoever.' The only thing he asks is, what are these people like, who are they, what do they believe?"

The reviews on the picture, I said, seem to be basically good.

She grinned. "You know what I hate? This is the only thing that will make me write a letter to a critic. I don't like it when reviews aren't about the movie. When they're about how much money somebody made, or who they're sleeping with, or if they got the job via some connection, or about how Fox is putting X amount of dollars into it. The review just turns into this whole corporate thing."

If you were a critic, what would you have praised this year?

"Well, *Pulp Fiction.* I actually sort of enjoyed it. I mean, I'm not wild about it. But with *Natural Born Killers . . .* you look and you go, my God! The mixing! My God! The direction! The photography! But then you ask yourself, what end does it serve? It's like Oliver Stone was saying, 'I'm an incredible drummer and I can go like this for an hour and a half and do stuff that no one else can do!' But who cares? It felt to me like a betrayal to the talent of the people that were involved to have it go to such an incredibly inhuman end. I didn't get it."

When are you going to direct again?

"Right now. A film with Holly Hunter called *Home for the Holidays,* which is sort of a comedy that turns into a drama, about a woman who, on the worst day of her life, with all this terrible stuff happening to her, has to get on a plane and go to her parents' house for Thanksgiving. Basically, the entire second act of the movie is around a table with a turkey and all these secrets unfolding and everybody hating each other."

You've had some moments like this in your life?

"It was a great thing for my mom the day we all just said, like, 'You don't ever have to have Christmas again—because one of us will, and then you can just come and bring wine and you can feel like you're a guest.' It was liberating for her, and for us too. I realized I could have my own Christmas. I could invite my mom and say, 'If you want to come, that's great. But you can't complain about my linen, because it's my house!'"

You've had a good relationship with your mother?

"Oh, yeah! It's great. And now it's better, because she's a friend."

That's a true family statement: "It's great, and now it's better."

She smiled. "It's better because you don't have the same

old issues. You've gone through the hard times and you've figured out how to turn it into something more healthy for both of you. I get along with her so much better now that she knows I'm not going to go out there and stub my toe twenty-four times a day."

She still worries about you?

"She has so much fun worrying about my siblings now that I'm off the hook for a while. I went to my sister's and they had like this big soap opera because my sister decided to cook with her ex-husband, for her husband and everyone else."

With her ex-husband, for her current husband?

"Yeah, because her ex-husband is a really good cook. And they love to cook together and his wife just left him so he didn't have anybody to be with for the holidays and she had the kids for Thanksgiving and he was going to be alone so she said, 'Well, maybe he should come.' And my mom is just sitting in the middle there going, 'Ummmm,' and saying things like, 'That's my favorite son-in-law.' Wreaking havoc. I'm like watching her and I went up to my sister and I just said, 'I'm so glad that you're having the drama this year because I get to, like, leave completely unmolested.'"

And you were thinking while you were sitting there that you were directing *Home for the Holidays.*

"I was. And it's funny. I'm not sure my mom really likes this movie very much. She hasn't talked about it yet—which has to mean that she is somehow offended and doesn't want to get into it. Finally I said, 'Obviously, you don't like it because you haven't had some kind of opinion about it.' And she said, 'It's very cute.' So, I'm waiting. You know, I steal from people constantly. It's true I stole a lot of things that she said, but it doesn't mean that the character has *anything* to do with her. I can tell she's definitely miffed, but. . . ."

She shrugged. "It'll all be all right if it's a good movie."

Mel Gibson

May 10, 1995—Outside the Paramount hotel suite in Chicago last weekend, there was a big poster of Mel Gibson, starring in *Braveheart.* Someone had added a mustache and goatee to Gibson's face, and drawn an arrow going through his head.

"He's gonna be p.o.'ed when he sees that," I said.

"He drew it himself," a press agent said.

There is a certain playful quality to Gibson, even when he is staring a fifty-three million-dollar bill straight in the eye. His epic of *Braveheart* cost at least that much, and opens May 24 amid curiosity about whether the public will be attracted to the saga of a Scots patriot named William Wallace, who lived approximately from 1270 to 1305 and led his countrymen in battle against England.

Inspired by a screenplay by Randy Wallace ("no relation, except spiritual"), Gibson spent months on location in Scotland and Ireland, not only starring in *Braveheart* but also directing it—including its battle scenes, which are many, fearsome, and expert. Some scenes were so bloody that mechanical horses were used to take falls that might have injured real animals.

But—who was William Wallace?

He was, according to *Braveheart*, a charismatic leader of his people, who led Scots troops to victory at Stirling and elsewhere, declaring Edward I of England ("Longshanks") his enemy, and taking "freedom!" as his rallying cry. His innovations on the battlefield, ranging from new weapons to devious strategy, would rank him with Caesar, Grant, and Rommel, if true.

He was, according to history, a man more celebrated in myth than in fact (Robert Bruce, who followed Wallace as leader of the Scots, is better documented, because of a higher caste). *The Wallace,* an epic poem in twelve thousand stanzas, was written about Wallace by Blind Harry the Minstrel, and was responsible for much of the legend, even though Blind Harry himself is of dubious provenance.

Wallace was, according to Mel Gibson, someone he first encountered "when I was a youngster of twenty-odd and I used to go out with my buddies and we'd have a few beers and play pool and tell lies. The place we used to frequent was called the William Wallace Hotel and it had a painting of a hairy guy over the bar. I thought he was just the dead former piano player. So that was what I knew of William Wallace before this."

Gibson cheerfully acknowledges that screenwriter Wallace made up most of the story of *Braveheart,* and he made up the rest. Setting the story just before the dawn of accurate history, he had a lot of license.

"Tons," Gibson said. "I'll give you an example. You know the scene where they saturate the battlefield with flammable stuff and they lure the English onto it and set it on fire?" He grinned. "We didn't even know what that burning stuff was. Had they discovered petroleum then? We didn't know what to call it; it was just black gook. It was introduced into the picture when it was dumped on them by the enemy, and I guess they said, like, 'Hey, this is good stuff!' and took it with them.

"All those battles, we cooked them. We just made up strategies and went for it. One battle was known as the battle of Stirling Bridge, but I left out the bridge, because I wanted a horse charge. When it comes to facts about Wallace, he's a footnote. There are some facts known about him, but there's a lot of empty spots and a lot of these legends grew up about him. That he was seven feet tall and all that. The screenplay pinched a lot of the story from Blind Harry and made up the rest."

Yet the movie, at more than three hours, has a stirring epic tone, as Wallace refuses to compromise even though he is offered bribes of lands, gold, and a title by Longshanks. And there are romantic sequences, too, including

a youthful marriage to a childhood sweetheart, and, later in his life, an affair with no less than the Princess of Wales, a French woman played by Sophie Marceau, who traitorously informs him of the plans of her English husband and father-in-law "because . . . of the way you are looking at me now."

What will impress most audiences is the awesome energy of the battle scenes, which would distinguish a director much more experienced than Gibson. (This is his second directorial effort, after 1993's *The Man Without a Face.*) Many medieval battle sequences need a traffic cop, and seem to consist of men and horses frantically milling. Gibson's battles are clearly choreographed, and involve not only strategy but surprises—including one especially devious trap laid for the British cavalry by the ingenious Scots.

That's one scene where real horses couldn't be used, for fear of injury. "We never did anything unsafe for the animals," Gibson said. "Things like a tip-over; you can't do that. It's too hard on a horse. So that's why you bring the dummies in. We said, 'Hey, we want some mechanical horses that look pretty good, that we can do tricks with.' And they all scratched their heads and invented these things and they're pretty simple, really. It's just air cylinders, and they have a steel skeleton and it's a life-sized horse. Except they only weigh 150 pounds, instead of a ton, so you can actually drop them on people.

"Using them, I was able to have battle scenes of incredible chaos going on. You'll see this guy in slow motion ducking, and you won't know why, but then a horse will go flying right over the top of his head. Stuff like that."

The battle scenes involved thousands of Irish soldiers ("much better trained than extras") and, of course, a lot of real horses, too. "They've got push-button ponies that sit down and roll over and talk almost," Gibson said. "They're so well trained that they just walk up and then you say, 'Okay.' And the horses go, 'Did he say "Okay"? I'd better fall over now.' And they fall over, and you give them a candy bar. It looks awful but it's nothing for the horse."

People are going to be saying there's a lot of violence in this movie, I said. And this kind of violence is incredibly immediate because it's two guys standing there, hacking away at each other. It's personal, intimate violence, not just shooting somebody one hundred yards away.

"I designed it so that it wasn't gratuitous," Gibson told me. "I wanted the audience to feel like they were in the middle of it and to experience the full hell, you know, the taste of hell. It was kind of a realism of battle that I wanted, that I hadn't seen before. I wanted to make it shocking, hard, and brutal, and juxtapose that against what I think is, really, a romantic picture.

"When we first cut the picture, of course, it was worse. Not for me but for some guy who just came in to a test screening from eating an ice cream cone and he was, like, he couldn't believe it, because there were brains flying everywhere. It was too much. The object is to keep the audience in the theater, in the seats, so we had to kind of bring it down a level."

In advance coverage of the summer movie season, Gibson's *Braveheart* has taken some of the shrapnel that missed Kevin Costner's two hundred-million-dollar *Waterworld*, with both movies described as multimillion-dollar epics fueled by the ambitions of their stars. Gibson is at pains to emphasize that his film cost fifty-three million dollars, not the seventy million dollars sometimes reported. And, indeed, given today's prices, he did not overspend: What's on the screen is awesome—the medieval castles and fortresses, the authentic villages, the landscape, the weather, the costumes, and those battle scenes.

Gibson's strategy for getting the movie financed was the same one that has served Clint Eastwood so well: As a director, he is sure of getting a top star for his movie—himself. Gibson won the clout for a production like *Braveheart* with such box office hits as *The Road Warrior* and the three *Lethal Weapon* movies. Today, he says, he could collect a twenty-million-dollar salary for making *Lethal Weapon 4*. But he doesn't much want to.

"I know they've written a script," he said, "and it's sort of waiting on a desk someplace, but I just—I've done it already. I don't want to bore anyone. It might be so wonderful, but I don't see how; I really don't."

The payday isn't a factor?

"Money's never bothered me. When I had two cents I felt just as good as I do now. And I've never, for a minute, ever worried about it, so that happens to be one of my things where I was fortunate. I never gave a damn. I always had a dime. And as long as I had a dime, I was okay."

Tomas Gutierez Alea

Park City, Utah, February 8, 1995—Here is a Cuban film about a flamboyant homosexual who is freely critical of his government and society. It was shot on location in Havana. It is now in release around the world. How, I asked myself—*how* was it possible that this film was financed and produced in Cuba, and actually shown there, and the filmmaker was not disciplined by the government?

If I really want to know, I can ask him. Tomas Gutierez Alea is sitting across from me on the sofa in a little house in Utah, where his film *Strawberry and Chocolate* has just played in the Sundance Film Festival. His wife is curled up over there on a cushion. Neither one looks as if they have come from stretches in Castro's dungeons.

Before I ask him, I roll my mental clock back a couple of decades, to a meeting of the National Society of Film Critics. It is the early 1970s, and we are gathered at the Algonquin Hotel in New York for our annual meeting, and Andrew Sarris, our chairman, is proposing a special

resolution in support of Gutierez Alea, whose *Memories of Underdevelopment,* we learn, is in danger of being suppressed by the Cuban government. I get the impression that Gutierez Alea himself may end up marking off the months and years on mossy dungeon stones with his fingernails.

Twenty years roll past, however, and Gutierez Alea still lives in Cuba, still makes films, is still critical—and I can see with my own eyes that, at seventy-two, he is healthy and in good humor. Can it be that the plight of the arts in Cuba has been overdramatized? That there is more freedom than we imagine?

"I've been making films more than thirty years," he says, in quick, accented English, "and I've been making films very critical, always. How is it possible? I should say that the image that you have here about Cuba, here in the States, is a stereotyped image: black and white. It is a Stalinist regime, or hell, or something like that." He shrugged. "Others, in Cuba, say it is paradise. Not many, but some. And it should be neither one thing or the other. It's a place where you fight to live in, for there are many problems; it is very complex and you cannot reduce that image to say it is hell, or dictatorship, or something like that. It is a place where you fight for things."

That is what his hero does in *Strawberry and Chocolate.* The film is about two young men, one straight and very Marxist, one gay and very dubious about his country. The film opens when the gay character, Diego, tries to pick up the straight character, David, at a café. ("I knew he was homosexual," David remembers, "because they had chocolate ice cream, and yet he ordered strawberry.") David accepts Diego's invitation to have coffee at his home, but eludes a seduction attempt. And Diego, who stages art and photography exhibitions, whose small flat is filled with paintings, books, recordings, and sculpture, begins to take a different kind of interest in David: as a mental conquest, not a physical one.

The movie, which began as a sexual dance, continues as a cerebral one. David returns (telling himself he is "gathering evidence" of Diego's anti-Marxist tendencies), and Diego shares his enthusiasms. I was reminded of Michael Caine, revealing his love of literature in *Educating Rita.* Eventually Diego makes some fairly pointed criticisms about the way things are going. Taking David up to a rooftop and sweeping his arm across Havana, he says, "We live in one of the world's most beautiful cities. You're just in time to see it before it collapses in shit."

Not the kind of dialogue one associates with films produced by the Havana Film Institute. In fact, ah . . . I almost hesitate to ask . . . have Fidel Castro and his ministers *seen* the film?

"Well, I'm sure they saw it. I don't know what they say about it."

And the general reception in Cuba?

"Fantastic . . . from the audience. It got very cold reviews from the newspapers, very poor, short and cold because many people didn't like the film on a certain level, you know. But for the audience it was a record, something like a million. It was, how do you say . . . it was the film that had the most audience, the most successful film."

A blockbuster.

"Blockbuster, yes." He beamed.

And it also opened in Spain?

"In Spain, also, and that was a surprise to me because in Spain they don't know the Latin America cinema. They don't care about us, and yet it became in the first place of box office, so it was really important. And for me, it was great pleasure because for the first time one of my films is exposed everywhere in the world."

Gutierez Alea is a filmmaker who literally grew up with the Cuban revolution. Like many Cuban artists and intellectuals of the 1950s he supported Castro's uprising against the Batista regime. In 1955, fresh back from studies in Italy and filled with the theology of neorealism, he made a short film that was seized by Batista's police. After Castro came to power, he founded the Film Institute, and his first feature, *After the Revolution* (1960), told three short stories about the uprising. But his films since then have either avoided politics (like the comedy *The Twelve Chairs* in 1962) or taken a critical perspective, like *Memories of Underdevelopment* (1968), which portrayed the unease of Havana intellectuals in a newly revolutionary society.

We have a picture in this country, I told him, of Cuba as a country that is rigid ideologically. When I saw this film, I said to myself: This film is shot in Havana, these people live in Havana, so my ideas are too simple.

Gutierez Alea raised his eyebrows. I felt like a dog worrying the wrong bone.

"But it has always been like that. There exist characters like Miguel (a humorless Marxist in the film), who is dogmatic, narrow, and fanatic. You can find that character in Cuba. And also the opposite, people who are very aggressive against that attitude. Who believe it is tolerant to try to understand those who are different. Not only because they are gay but also because they think different than you. You have to admit that people can think differently and coexist with you. That is what the film tries to tell."

There is a theory, I said, that in countries where there is repression, art flowers—even if forced underground—because the artist thrives in resistance. You've heard about this theory, I'm sure.

"I've heard about those kinds of things," he said. "I don't think so. I think the best should be to have the opportunity for everyone to say everything he wants to say. To develop your imagination."

It's my impression that homosexuality is more controversial in Latin cultures than in the United States. Is that true? Is it more shocking to bourgeois society to be gay in Havana than in Europe or America?

He nodded. "You also have discrimination. But the difference is that here you fight openly, the gays finally proclaim their condition openly, and that is a very big step against discrimination. In Cuba, or in Latin America, it is not so easy. But even in Cuba, now, I heard about a festival of transvestites that was held. Some years ago it would be impossible to imagine such a thing. I believe that people grow and become more mature. That is happening in our society and we can understand things better now than fifteen years before."

So much in your film depends on the casting, on the tension between the straight character played by Vladimir Cruz and the homosexual, played by Jorge Perrugoria. The gay is frankly swish: He flaunts his sexuality. Where did you find the actor?

"I saw Perrugoria in an amateur film; he's a theater actor. He and the other one were not the types that I was looking for. I wanted a more mature man for this gay character; not necessarily handsome, but beautiful in his interior—a man that could fascinate this young student because of his culture, his world, his humanity. But not because he was handsome. And I wanted them very different in age, one about twenty, the other about forty.

"But I couldn't find them, and I am glad. The hand of God came to help me, because I found these two actors better than those that I imagined. And they have the same age. We had to make one of them look older and the other one look younger."

When I was watching the film, at first I thought the gay character seemed too flamboyant. Then as the film went on I got used to him; it seemed like a brave statement that he was making, to go out in public and behave like that.

"That's why, in the beginning, when he's trying to conquer the attention of this young man, he shows himself as how he is; he tries to be very aggressive. But there is also dramatic reason. If this gay character acts like a straight man, then there is no problem for the Communist militant to go into the street and to be seen openly with him—because nobody will think that he's gay, you see?"

You've been making films in Cuba for forty years. How is it now compared to the past?

He took a sip from a cup of tea.

"When I look backwards," he said, "I find that I have been very lucky because I had no money. The only money I earned is my official salary as a filmmaker. My salary, in Cuba, is the same as any other filmmaker. And it is in Cuban pesos, which is nothing. But I had the opportunity to make the films that I wanted to make during all my career, and making films is my life, so I've been lucky."

This film is making a lot of money, I said. Where will that money go to you?

"To the distributor (Miramax). They bought it from the Havana Film Institute, so it will be part for the Film Institute and part for the distributor, and nothing for us."

He seemed to accept that prospect with equanimity. How do you feel, I asked, about the fact that if you were from some other country you could make one hundred thousand or half a million or whatever, to have in your pocket, and you cannot have that money because you are Cuban? Do you ever think about that, or do you agree with the theory that the money should go back to the Film Institute?

Gutierez Alea smiled, and opened his arms. "Look, I am human. I know the value of money. But for me it is more important to have been making the films that I have made, than to have money and not being able to make these films."

He smiled. "But I would like also to have that money, of course."

There are a lot of filmmakers in this country, I said, who would rather have the money, and so they make the films that will pay it to them.

"But look," he said. "I am an old man already. And I know, for me, it would be very sad to look at myself in the mirror after all these years and say, I have all the money I wanted to have—but where's my life?"

Tommy Lee Jones

Los Angeles, June 29, 1994—Winning an Oscar, it is said, means an actor gets a pass for a year or two. For a brief moment he seems to be the master of his destiny. Tommy Lee Jones won the Oscar in March for his work in *The Fugitive,* but by then his Oscar surge was already well under way, as if Hollywood had anticipated the award. He is one of the busiest actors of 1994.

Consider. He plays a mad Irish bomber in *Blown Away,* which is now in theaters. He will open soon as a publicity-seeking state's attorney in *The Client,* based on the John Grisham best-seller. Then he stars as a prison warden in Oliver Stone's *Natural Born Killers,* opening in August. Then comes his work in the title role of a biopic about the complex and unhappy baseball legend Ty Cobb. After that comes *Good Old Boys,* the movie he is currently starring in and directing, for a Turner cable network.

At one point while we were talking recently, I asked Jones where he lived, and he replied, without the shadow of a smile, "Most of the time, I live on location." He is a busy actor, and success has so surrounded him that he even agrees to do the occasional press interview. Yet I sense he does not enjoy it, not at all. It's not that he's rude or hostile or impatient. It's that he's so controlled and polite you sense he's acutely uncomfortable, talking about acting and about himself. Nor is he exactly wordy.

Maybe, I found myself wondering, that's why he plays such great villains, such flamboyant and bitterly self-mocking bad guys in movies like *Under Siege* or *Blown Away,* or good guys with an edge, like his federal marshal in *The Fugitive.* Maybe he's so controlled in real life that he likes to go over the top in the movies. It's a release.

I tested my theory cautiously.

A lot of actors say it's more fun to play the bad guy, I said.

"I don't say that," he said.

You often play the bad guy, I said.

"Yeah," he said, "but it's not for fun."

O . . . kay.

Uh, in *Blown Away* and *The Client,* and also in *Under Siege,* there are various levels of flamboyance in the characters that you play. Yet as an individual, you seem rather quiet and self-contained. . . .

"Yes."

. . . and I imagine in your private life, you're pretty much on that same level. These characters allow you to strut, to give speeches and depart on wild flights of fancy. Is that a release for you, a recreation? Is it a reach?

Jones considered. "Well," he said, "it's a profession. I play characters and I try to play them in a manner that's appropriate to the script. Physical movement and vitality of language is part of character. I don't need much of a character in my life. I've already got one; my family knows who I am and I don't have a reason to make an impression on the world around me unless it's in a professional context. Acting is not a personal experience; it's a job."

That struck me as an immensely sane statement for an actor to make, considering how many actors I've interviewed who talk about getting lost in their roles—how characters take them over, moving into their psyches and setting up housekeeping.

It seems like there's a wider range in your roles recently, I said. Is that a bonus of getting to be more widely recognized?

"I think so."

A pause. Jones shifted in his chair, and began to stroke the beard he grew for *Good Old Boys.*

"I saw an interview with Mr. Mitchum a long time ago," he said at last. "Mr. Mitchum said that back in the 1940s, in the studio system, if you did well, you didn't get to do better; you only got to do more. Nowadays I think it's possible that if you do well, you'll get a chance to do better. I think maybe the business and the art form have both changed for the better in that regard."

In your case, what you were doing well was playing villains in action thrillers. But some of these forthcoming movies look like a change of pace.

"I liked *Under Siege.* I thought it was a lot of fun. I thought it was pretty, too. I liked all that blue and red. I liked the boat. I just liked it. I thought it was cool. And I didn't take it very seriously at all. It was just good entertainment. I suppose *The Fugitive* is also a thriller or an action thing. But there was something about it that made you think that it was happening now and that it was real and it was new. It exuded spontaneity somehow."

He stroked his beard again.

"There's another action film coming up. It's called *Blown*

Away and I haven't seen it all. We worked as hard as we could to please the people we were working for. What it feels like to sit through it from beginning to end, I don't know."

Your character is Irish.

"Yes, sir."

You have a very authentic accent.

"Oh, good! I got away with it." The ghost of a smile.

How did you prepare for that? Did you meet any Irish people; listen to them, talk to them?

"First, you read a lot of books. Then you work with a dialectician, which is a person who's hired to teach accents to actors. And you listen to hours of tapes of people from Belfast. And then you follow your Irish friends around and watch what they do with their hands."

What do they do with their hands?

"Use them in different ways. Put it all together and you might be lucky enough to fake it."

Would you be able to go into a bar in Belfast and pass?

"No."

Again, this is a little startling, and refreshing, after all the actors I've interviewed who promised me they were mistaken for foreign cab drivers, nurses, diplomats, surgeons, and chefs.

"I don't think I could convince them that I was from Ireland. Maybe I could for a little while if I didn't say much, depending on how hard I had to fool them. I could fool part of the people part of the time."

The reason this interview is not exactly whizzing along, I thought to myself, is that Tommy Lee Jones is only speaking the simple truth, in as few words as necessary. People in general, and actors in particular, tend to grease the conversational skids with a little genial nonsense from time to time, but Tommy Lee seems allergic to chitchat.

"Natural Born Killers," I said. He nodded. It is an Oliver Stone film about the way the public makes heroes out of killers, perhaps because they're dazzled by their celebrity. The movie was finished long before O.J. Simpson got into the backseat of the white Bronco, but the message seems timeless.

"I think it's a good movie," Jones said. "It's a lot of fun. It's a satire. There'll be a temptation to say the movie is appealing to the worst in the audience, that it's another hatchet movie. But I think the movie goes far, far above that. It's a work of art."

Some movies are violent, I said, and some movies are about violence.

Jones nodded. "Violence is not that good a standard by which to judge quality. The legend of *Three Little Pigs* is a violent story. Look at the poor wolf. He falls down the chimney and gets scalded. He never gets anything to eat. Look at 'Rock-a-bye Baby in the Treetop.' What's gonna happen when the wind blows?"

Ty Cobb, I said. When Jones accepted his Oscar last March, he made a very short speech. "This is the greatest award an actor can receive," he said. "The only thing a man can say at a time like this is, 'I am not really bald.'" That was because he was bald at the time, to play the role of the gifted and unhappy baseball legend.

"Very complicated," Jones said. "Cobb is a complicated man. I think that's a fair statement."

So the movie is not going to be about just another baseball hero.

"Not just another baseball hero, no. It's an elegant movie about a rather elegant man. Mr. Cobb is thought of essentially as a rattlesnake, but you have to conclude that he was a pretty tough guy. After he left baseball, he had a lot of problems. He was a real racist. An anti-Semite. None of his family members would attend his funeral. They didn't like him personally. Does a guy like that have any redeeming qualities? Well, yes. No one's entirely beyond redemption. Otherwise they wouldn't call it 'redemption,' would they?"

I guess not. Did baseball give him happiness?

"Oh, hell, no! Nothing gave him happiness. He set ninety-three batting records; but they weren't enough. He didn't bat a thousand."

What attracted you to the character?

"I have an enormous respect for American athletic desire."

And that's what he had.

"Plenty of."

He stroked his beard.

Jennifer Jason Leigh

November 22, 1994—The table has long since been cleared for the last time, and the wits who surrounded it rest in their graves, but the *idea* of the Algonquin Round Table lives on. For a decade, from the 1920s through the 1930s, the brightest and the funniest writers in New York gathered every day for lunch around a huge round table at the Algonquin Hotel, and then they went back to their typewriters and made each other famous by quoting what they said there.

Today the names may not be famous any longer. A remarkable new movie, *Mrs. Parker and the Vicious Circle*, celebrates the wits of the Round Table, but how many people in the audience will have heard of them? I know who Heywood Broun, Alexander Woolcott, George S. Kaufman, "F.P.A.," and Harold Ross were, because that's my job. Robert Benchley was the most famous humorist of his time, author of best-sellers, the star of a series of Hollywood short subjects. Do people under forty know his name? And what about Dorothy Parker, the wittiest person at the table, the only woman in a closed circle of men? They still teach her short story "Big Blonde" in English classes, but do undergraduates still quote "Candy is dandy,/But liquor is quicker"?

And do people still practice what was once called the Art of Conversation—consciously trying to sound smart, witty, informed? One-upping one another? I have a vision of the republic as a nation of glassy-eyed TV watchers, their senses of humor hammered into oblivion by the stupidities of sitcoms. Does an audience still exist that can listen *fast enough* to appreciate the dance of words around the Algonquin table?

I hope so. Seeing *Mrs. Parker and the Vicious Circle* at its world premiere last May at the Cannes Film Festival was an awakening experience because it brought words to the front of the screen: You had to listen as intently as you watched. And at the center of the circle, her cynicism a barrier against the terror of silence, was Dorothy Parker.

Alan Rudolph's movie is, oddly enough, a love story, of the devotion that endured for years between Parker and Robert Benchley, who were married to various other people, who had many affairs, but who never slept with one another—because that would have spoiled the one perfect thing in their flawed and destructive lives.

The characters are played in the film by Jennifer Jason Leigh and Campbell Scott. Although no people could be less alike, they reminded me somehow of the characters of C.S. Lewis and his American wife in *Shadowlands*—because there, too, was a meeting of the spirits that did not depend on the physical level of a relationship.

Jennifer Jason Leigh has played many characters in her career: a high school beauty queen in *Fast Times at Ridgemont High*, a tragic prostitute in *Last Exit to Brooklyn*, a criminal's girlfriend in *Miami Blues*, a housewife who works in the phone sex business in *Short Cuts*. Dorothy Parker is her best work so far, as a small, dark, intense, very bright, very lonely woman who used words to keep the world at bay, and alcohol to speed the passage.

The movie begins in the early 1920s, with Parker, Benchley, and others on strike against their low wages at *Vanity Fair*. It follows them through the birth of the *New Yorker*, where Parker was the drama critic, and then to Hollywood, where Benchley became a movie and radio star, and Parker was a screenwriter whose credits included the first *A Star in Born*. Then Benchley dies of liver failure in New York (the movie provides the unforgettable verbal report of a friend "racing around the Stork Club trying to find blood donors"), and Parker, still famous, descends by slow stages to death by alcoholism.

"My mother helped me prepare for the role," Leigh told me one afternoon last May at Cannes. "We'd go every night and sit in bars. I'd drink port and she'd drink wine and we would read Parker's poems to one another. I did all the research—any member of the cast of this movie could write a doctorate on the Round Table—but finally I just had to sort of leap into Dorothy Parker's skin. For me, the key was that she was incredibly myopic. But she never wore her glasses. And I think her nearsightedness did the same thing for her as the alcohol. It softened the edges of the world that she saw so painfully. She sipped whiskey all day long. Her line was that she was 'seldom drunk but rarely sober.'"

She comes across as so brave in her sadness, I said.

"She loved to cry. She'd see a horse pulling a cart in the street, and start crying. She said, 'Three drinks and I become St. Francis of Assisi.' She could annihilate someone with a single sentence, but the first feeling everybody had about Dorothy Parker was that they needed to take care of her. This gentle soul."

Benchley was another gentle soul. "He was her rock. Her catcher in the rye. She could call him at four A.M. and he would take the next train to be with her. Everybody needs a Benchley. If they'd ever made love, perhaps that wouldn't have been the case anymore. They were keeping something sacred. He really was her soul mate. She referred to him as a saint. No one didn't love Benchley.

"But they drifted apart after they went to Hollywood. She got very political, and he didn't. And she never forgave him for one night when she was trying to get him to take a stand on something, and he said, 'Don't bat those ingenue eyes at me; you're not an ingenue anymore.'"

There is a scene in the movie where Benchley visits Parker in the hospital after a suicide attempt. "Rudolph set the scene up and just let the camera roll," Leigh remembered, "and we did it, Campbell and I, and after the take we looked at one another and said, 'Were we acting?' Rudolph created an environment, boundaryless, blurring the lines, until it was almost like living this person's life."

Toward the end of the film's New York scenes, Parker goes to a psychiatrist, who questions the need of the Algonquin circle to remain always in one another's company. They'd meet for lunch, then to go a salon, then to the theater, then to dinner, then to a speakeasy. Never alone. When Benchley and Parker vowed to get serious about their writing, they rented a private office—together. The psychiatrist questions their unwillingness to ever leave their charmed circle.

"It was so painful for her to write," Leigh said. "For all of them. She said it was the loneliest life there is, to be a writer. With a painter, you had the world. With an actor, you were surrounded with people. But with a writer, it was just you and your paper. You were always faced with your inadequacies. Dorothy said, 'I write five words and erase seven.' It took her six months to write a short story.

"When amongst her friends, she didn't have to encounter herself. She was reflected through their eyes as a person who was alive and could make everyone laugh. So she didn't want to face that room and that typewriter—that 'dreadful machine' she called it—and she actually threw away a typewriter once, because she couldn't figure out how to change the ribbon."

The usual Hollywood biopic arranges the facts of the life in a grid supplied by the countless clichés of earlier filmed biographies. They plant clues in Act One that pay off at the end. They "explain" everything. What I appreciated about *Mrs. Parker* was that it explains nothing. It simply observes with sympathy, as a lonely woman with a verbal gift drinks away her happiness while making others laugh.

The performance by Leigh doesn't analyze or explain, or underline points so we won't miss them. It simply exists: the best kind of acting. At the end of the film you still may not know who Broun or Woolcott or F.P.A. or the others were, but you might be curious to find out. (The place to start would be *The Portable Dorothy Parker*, still in print after forty years.) What you will understand, just from the film, is how words connect with feelings, even when they don't seem to, and how Dorothy Parker's gift kept her going long after the booze and the depression should have killed her. Later, thinking back over the film, you realize that she got most of her biggest laughs, not for being funny, but simply for telling the truth.

Milcho Manchevski

March 1, 1995—A kid in Macedonia wants to be a movie director, but there are no openings in the official film school in Belgrade. One day a professor from Southern Illinois University comes to lecture in his hometown, and the kid gives the professor a pitch about how he wants to go to film school, and the professor says, "Fine, send me some of your work," and the kid mails his writings and some of his short films off to Carbondale, and they give him a scholarship.

So Milcho Manchevski arrives in Illinois, thinking he speaks English. "I had learned it in school, but they don't teach you all the words. For example, I didn't what they meant by . . ." He mentions a noun. I agree that if you want to speak English it is essential to know that noun. "Steve James taught me that word," Manchevski says proudly. "He was a few years ahead of me."

Steve James went on to direct *Hoop Dreams,* and Milcho Manchevski went on to direct *Before the Rain,* and now it is 1995 and Manchevski's film has been nominated for an Academy Award in the best foreign film section. Let's not get started on the subject of *Hoop Dreams* and the Oscars.

Before the Rain is quite a film. The winner of the Golden Lion at the 1994 Venice Film Festival, it has been compared to Tarantino's *Pulp Fiction,* Kieslowski's *Red,* and Egoyan's *Exotica,* and like those influential films it has a plot that winds back upon itself, so that, in the words of T.S. Eliot, "In my beginning is my end." It is not often that a single film, a first film, announces that a major director has arrived, but on the basis of *Before the Rain,* Manchevski must be taken seriously.

His film's style is not directly influenced by Tarantino and the others; the screenplay was written in 1991. It's as if they all simultaneously grew tired of A-to-Z narrative, and decided to exploit the ability of film to circulate freely in time. The result makes the film seem more alive, more spontaneous.

The story takes place in Macedonia and London, and is told in Macedonian, Albanian, and English, although not very much of any one of them (one of the characters is a monk who has taken the vow of silence). Manchevski, who was born in Macedonia, is resigned that not very many Americans know exactly what that country is.

All of it used to be Yugoslavia? I asked him during a recent visit to Chicago.

"It was Macedonia, which was part of Yugoslavia."

There's a disagreement, isn't there, about the use of the word "Macedonia"?

"Yes. The Greeks think they own the copyright."

But it's been called Macedonia for a long time.

"Well, the geographic region has been called Macedonia since Philip, in 5 B.C. He came up with it; he has the copyright."

He grinned. Manchevski is a youthful, thirtyish man with an easy smile and easy English that now includes all the necessary nouns. After graduating from SIU, he tried to get several features off the ground, but found himself working instead on TV commercials, experimental films, and MTV music videos. (Proving that it's a small world, his video of "Tennessee" for Arrested Development won the MTV and Billboard awards for best rap video of 1992.)

He called in some favors and commitments from his video and commercial contacts, he said, to put together the financing for *Before the Rain.* And he somehow convinced the film insurance companies to underwrite a risky production in a potential war zone. ("The political-risk companies gave us five different scenarios of how war could start as we're shooting there.")

Macedonia is just on the edge of the current bloody struggles between Serbs and Croats, and has its own long history of bloodshed between Christians and Muslims. It stands to one side of the current fighting, but the atmosphere there, Manchevski says, "is like waiting for something to happen and you're not quite sure what it's going to be. It could be tragic. It could be the end of something and by the same token, it could be cleansing and the beginning of something new; just as the rain washes you and now you're new."

The movie has three sections. In the first, the young Macedonian monk finds, hiding in his cell, an Albanian girl accused of a murder. In the second, Alexander, a famous photographer, born in Macedonia but now a world citizen and a Pulitzer winner, is reunited in London with the married woman he has long been involved with. In the third, the photographer returns to Macedonia to discover his homeland tense and unhappy. He wants to visit the first woman he ever loved, but since he is Christian and she is Muslim, no one else on either side very much wants that to happen.

It would not be right, or wrong, to say the action in each section takes place after the one before. Manchevski plays a little trick of time on us, so that we cannot be sure. The point is to show the action moving in a circle. And in his story, people today hate each other because their parents and grandparents hated each other, and so time repeats itself, around and around.

"There are two moments in the film," Manchevski told me, "where the circle is sort of broken. Ann [the woman in London] sees some photographs. If the story were a perfect circle, those photographs couldn't be there. And there's a phone call that shouldn't be possible. Those two things are bits of Zen; bits of time paradox. Also, they could be a sign that the circle is not round, and maybe in the next round it can open—perhaps with an act of self-sacrifice like what Alexander does."

So the message is in the structure of the film?

He shrugged. "Maybe what it takes, to break the circle, is for someone to say, 'Well, I don't agree with this endless bitterness. If I'm going to be paying you back for the fact that your grandfather killed my grandfather's sheep, it's going to go on forever.'"

The purpose of the London section is to show that regional wars are no longer content to stay in their regions. There is a virtuoso sequence in a restaurant, where as two important characters hold a conversation in the foreground, a seemingly unrelated discussion begins in the background, and then explodes unpredictably.

"What I'm saying is, at some point you won't be able to change the channel," Manchevski said. "These troubles don't stay in some far corner of the world. They come into your living room. As we were editing the film, it actually happened in London, when some local violence in Georgia spilled over into London, where the ambassador of ex-Soviet Georgia was killed. Some innocent bystanders were taken for the sisters-in-law of one of the guys involved there. All of a sudden you have a couple of English women who don't know where Soviet Georgia is, but who get killed as part of this."

I asked Manchevski if he had another project in the works.

"Nothing. Not a thing. I liked making this film. I liked the storytelling part of it; I liked the work. I liked getting sucked into it. At the same time, there's just a lot of crap in the movie business, spending so much time with people you don't like. If I had the balls to retire now, it would be brilliant."

Are you serious?

"If I had the balls and the money, I would do it. There are a lot of books I would like to read."

You don't feel that work is necessary?

"It's not so much the working or not working. It's having the choice of who you work with and how you do it."

What kind of stories do you want to tell? What kind of a filmmaker do you want to be?

"Stories about people that surprise you; that like, take you on unexpected turns. A journey where when the first part ends and the second part begins, you ask, 'Where the hell are we? Where is this?' Stories that play with your mind a little bit."

They must be proud of you in Macedonia.

He nodded happily. "It's a country where, even in volleyball, the national team cannot be called the Macedonian National Team. Suddenly a Macedonian film does well. People respond to that. The theaters were almost dead because of pirate video and TV, so this was the first time there was a hit movie in about, like, twelve years."

I heard it outgrossed *The Fugitive* in Macedonia.

He smiled. "Yes, although I'm sure *The Fugitive* will outgross it in the United States."

Gregory Nava

April 25, 1995—Why don't we ever see Latino families in the movies? All the other American ethnic groups have given us movies about their march through the generations, but Latinos, until now, have been represented mostly by crime movies and comedies, neither presenting their culture in an especially positive light. A Chicano I know went to see *American Me,* a film by Edward James Olmos, that is brave and powerful but unremitting in its portrait of a man destroyed by prison, and came out saying, "If I wasn't Chicano, this movie wouldn't have made me want to know any."

But now comes Gregory Nava's *My Family,* opening soon, a joyful film that reaches out its arms and embraces three generations of a Mexican-American family in all of its dreams and sorrows. It's an epic, the kind of big-hearted, ambitious film that is rarely made these days—a film like *Gone With the Wind* or *The Godfather,* with a big canvas and lots of characters and a sense of destiny tracing itself down through the generations.

Will it succeed at the box office? At a time when other minorities—blacks, Asians—are box-office gold, there has never been a big hit about American Latinos. Only the personal clout of Francis Ford Coppola, the executive producer, who made a call to New Line's president Robert Shaye, got a green light for *My Family,* despite its commercial mix of romance, joy, violence, and redemption.

The movie was directed by Nava, who co-wrote it with his wife and producer, Anna Thomas. They were Oscar nominees for the screenplay for Nava's *El Norte* (1983), the story of an epic journey by a brother and sister who trek from Guatemala to Los Angeles. For *My Family,* which is set in a vibrant neighborhood tucked in under a bridge in East Los Angeles, they put together a cast that reads like a roll call of Hispanic stars: Jimmy Smits, Edward James Olmos, and Esai Morales play three of the sons of the Sanchez family, and other roles are filled by faces newer to American audiences, such as Eduardo Lopez Rojas, Mexico's most famous actor, who plays the family patriarch, and the beautiful Constance Marie, from *Salsa* and TV's "Santa Barbara," as a nun who turns into a political activist.

Most films about Hispanic-Americans have been crime-oriented. *My Family* is not. It is a family portrait that includes all kinds of heartwarming moments, family moments, involving food, birth, sex, religion, arguments, dreams, humor.

"That's what life is really like," Nava told me the day after his movie's world premiere at the Sundance Film Festival last January. He is a tall, demonstrative man whose presence seems to express the exuberance in his films. "In Latino family life, you can go from comedy to tragedy in the course of a day; it's a real roller-coaster ride. That's one of the things I think is exciting about our culture. I wanted to deal with the serious things, yes, but there are so many other things. I couldn't imagine making a film about Latino life without a lot of dancing in it, for example, because that's such an important part of our life."

And so there is a passage in the film where a young man and a young woman who have both had a very hard time of it, who have closed into themselves, begin dancing in the street one day, and that is their redemption. And there are other passages of children who grow up and make their choices for right or wrong, so that the family produces a lawyer, a writer, and a convict. There is the joy of a daughter who becomes a nun, and the shock when she turns "political." And a scene of incredible, quiet power, where the two old parents of these generations share a cup of coffee and decide that, all in all, God has been good to them.

The movie was shot largely on location in East Los Angeles, in a real house on a real street in a real neighborhood—a street, Nava says, which "was incredible, because it had the backdrop of the bridge and there was this dirt street and when you arrived, there were all these chickens running around. I said, 'This is it! What an incredible place!' Ten or fifteen years ago, they would have thought the street should be paved over, but now, since it's lasted so long, I think it should be preserved forever as the last remaining dirt street in East Los Angeles."

As the film begins, a young man from Mexico (Jacob Vargas) gets in trouble in his village and walks north to Los Angeles, in the early 1920s, to live with an elderly relative. He marries and moves into the house, which grows and changes through the decades with the family, until it becomes almost a character in itself. As the years go past, we see his wife (Jennifer Lopez) rounded up with thousands of other Mexican-Americans (most of them American citizens) and shipped by train far south into Mexico, as part of a brutal anti-"foreigner" movement under the Hoover administration. But she finds her way back, in a scene of incredible courage and persistence.

We see the family serve in the war, and we trace the rise of the postwar street gangs (described on the sound track as "macho bullshit" by the narrator, a writer played by Olmos). The gangs recruit a son played by Esai Morales. And in more modern times we see a daughter (Constance Marie) grow active in politics, a son (Enrique Castillo) become a lawyer, and another son (Jimmy Smits) search for direction in his life. The grandparents (now played by Rojas and Jenny Gago) stay where they have lived their lives, tending the garden in the backyard. It is an American saga, all told by Edward James Olmos as the son who became a writer.

"I think Latinos have always had an innate understanding of the importance of family," Nava told me. "All the great novels from Latin America, *One Hundred Years of Solitude, House of Spirits,* they're always family stories that take place over generations. I wanted to make a movie in which the family itself is the protagonist."

He also wanted, he said, to show that family issues get handed down through the generations: "All too often we see things get resolved very quickly in the movies. In reality, things are passed from the one generation to the next, so by the time the Jimmy Smits character grows up, he's already inherited all this stuff that's happened to the family before. It's told with many different characters over three generations but finally it's all one story, of this family and how they grow and change over the years."

It is also, like many ambitious films, a project that almost did not get made. Although *El Norte* was a substantial box office success, it was seen as an "art film," and Nava and Thomas were determined that *My Family* would be a popular, mass-audience film; although their focus was not on crime, Coppola's *The Godfather* was one of their inspirations, in the way it showed the generations of a family unfolding one after another.

One problem, Nava said, is that the Hispanic movie audience in America has never been as cohesive as, say, African-American filmgoers. "We expect this film to appeal to everybody, but if it's going to open strong on the first weekend—which is what the studios go by—it needs to appeal first of all to the Latino market. Because Hollywood wasn't sure that would happen, we were turned down by one studio after another."

Then Tom Luddy, who produces in association with Coppola and is a founder of the Telluride Film Festival, saved the project. Luddy, a fan of *El Norte* since he premiered it at Telluride, brought Coppola's Zeotrope in as coproducer with New Line, which is opening the movie on six hundred screens for the May 5 weekend—the Latinos' Cinco de Mayo holiday.

One of the things he wanted to do in the film, Nava said, was celebrate an artistic sense that makes even the poorest Chicano neighborhood bright and cheerful: "So often in the movies poverty looks grim and depressing. But in a Chicano neighborhood, even with a little money, the people make it look happy. We are a very house-proud people. The lawns are neat, and inside every little knick-knack is in its exact place."

"Chicanos haven't had a lot of chance to work in the film industry," Nava said, "so you don't have a lot of production designers and people you can work with. The visual genius of the community has gone into painting, and the most exciting painters in Los Angeles today are the Chicano painters. My favorite is named Patssi Valdez, and she does all these beautiful house interiors; they're gorgeous paintings. So we actually hired her—she'd never worked on a movie before—to work with us to design the interior of the house. So there are all these reds and purples and blues and all the vibrant colors, and they all come from her painting and reflect the vibrant reality of the way people decorate their houses in East Los Angeles.

"I wanted in the film to have this poverty reflect the beauty the people have and the pride they have in their homes. There's a false dichotomy in the movies: If it's rich it can be beautiful, but if it's poor, it must be horrible and bleak. The reverse can also be true. I think Orson Welles had an interesting angle on wealth in *Citizen Kane,* where it's oppressive and horrible. In *My Family,* it's poor but it is very beautiful and I wanted to capture that in the film. I feel that there's no reason why a plaster flamingo against a pink wall can't be just as beautiful as anything in *The Age of Innocence.*"

Paul Newman

New York, December 27, 1994—I really liked this movie, I told Paul Newman.

"Thank you," he said.

There was one reaction shot you had, when she lifted up her sweater, teasing you—an old friend, but still a possible lover. The audience really loved you at that moment. You seemed kind of embarrassed and delighted and . . .

"That's what it is," he said, "Adult embarrassment."

It was a scene midway in *Nobody's Fool,* between New-man and Melanie Griffith, as the restless wife of his employer. Newman plays an alcoholic sixty-year-old construction worker named Sully, liked by everyone except those who counted on him, like his family. He has been flirting for years, maybe, with the Griffith character, whose husband (Bruce Willis) cheats on her with local floozies. There is the possibility that maybe Sully could restore happiness to her life, and so, in a moment of play, she pulls up her sweater to let him see that her appurtenances are all in the right place. The key element of the scene is not her action, but his reaction, which is done in just such a way that the audience laughs with warmth, instead of humor.

How do you do something like that? I asked him. Can you even say how you do it?

"I wouldn't know. The funny thing is, if you're cookin',

you don't have any memory of that. There can be no single emotion that could be identified with something like that. I mean, it just has to be a splash of colors and that's all it is. It's appreciation, a surprise, embarrassment, delight, a desperate attempt to keep his cool . . . all those things."

We were talking in his hotel suite, one afternoon last September, right after *Nobody's Fool* had its press premiere. It was originally scheduled to open in early October, but then the studio took another look at it and moved it back to December openings in New York and Los Angeles, and January in the rest of the country, because they figured Newman had a shot at an Academy Award nomination.

Watching the movie, I wrote down the word "humility." Newman never seemed to be reaching for an effect, never conscious of his appearance on the screen. He seemed content to be within the character, to be Sully and to participate in Sully's life and problems. There was no movie star edge showing outside the character.

When I told Newman that, he answered indirectly: "Maybe he's a lot closer to me than I'd care to admit, so that there really wasn't a lot of digging; you know, you just have to be available. And if you just have the patience and the security of knowing that's really all you have to do, you don't *have* to push for anything."

I never heard a line, I never saw a gesture, that indicated you were reaching for anything.

"I think the only way that that can happen is if you have a director who is patient to wait, and an actor who is patient to allow. If either one insists upon some other formula, then I don't think it's likely to happen. Benton really likes actors. He trusts the process and so I guess it gave me the security to know that I didn't have to push something for expediency; that I could simply wait for it."

Benton. Robert Benton. He's known for collaborating with actors on some of their best work, like Art Carney in *The Late Show* (1977) and Dustin Hoffman in *Kramer Vs. Kramer* (1979), and Sally Field in *Places in the Heart* (1984). *Nobody's Fool* is, more than usual, an actor's picture. There is no particular plot to drive it: No economic, criminal, or romantic necessity that must be served. We sense it is not crucial that Newman and Griffith connect by the end of the picture, nor are we much exercised by Newman's pending court cases for reckless driving. We know his eighth-grade teacher (Jessica Tandy) is not well, but we doubt the final scene will be at her deathbed, either.

The crucial element in the film is the arrival in Sully's small upstate town of his son (Dylan Walsh) and grandson (Alex Goodwin). Walsh has separated from his wife, they've each taken custody of one of their children, and now he returns to the father he never knew very well. He is suspicious. Over a period of time, he will see if his suspicions are justified. And Sully will discover that if it is too late to be a good father, it may not be too late to be a good grandfather.

How did the project get started?

"Benton sent it to me."

You read it, and . . .

"And had a choice of doing a picture that was a block-buster or to explore this vehicle."

What was the title of the blockbuster?

"Aw . . . I couldn't say."

And you took the vehicle.

"Well, I'm old enough and smart enough to do that now. And the allure of that gamble is much more attractive."

He is old enough, at sixty-nine, and for some time he has been smart enough to do what seems to be the right, rather than the opportunist, thing. He goes for years now, sometimes, between pictures, and his recent ones have all been decisions based on the apparent worth of the project: He did a continuation of the *Hustler* character Eddie Felson in Martin Scorsese's *The Color of Money* (1986), and then an inspired impersonation of the rascally Louisi-ana governor Huey Long in *Blaze* (1989). He was a sane general at the dawn of the Cold War in *Fat Man and Little Boy* (1989), which was not a successful movie, and a too-sane Kansas City lawyer who drove his wife mad with his probity in James Ivory's *Mr. and Mrs. Bridge* (1990), which was a very good movie. He makes news regularly with his multi-million-dollar popcorn and salad dressing empire, which gives its profits to charity, and it is worth asking how many major movie stars would have the self-confidence to put their picture on a jar of oil and vinegar and not give a damn what people thought.

One interesting aspect of the film is that there aren't a lot of people visible in it, except for the actual cast members. There are a few extras meandering in the back-ground of some shots—driving down the street, sitting in the back booths of the bar—but not many, and not very visible. When characters walk down the street, there aren't forty extras on the sidewalk, being choreographed by an assistant director.

"It gave it a containment, didn't it?" Newman said. "It's such a personal story; it's all takes place within the circle of the characters. We were all pretty close when we made the movie."

Jessica Tandy was ill when she was shooting the film, wasn't she?

"She was okay but she was a bit fragile. You got a lot to learn from that lady; graceful and determined."

And filled with a fierce, focused energy that you sensed was pure craft, allowing the performance to happen no matter how the actress felt that day, or what she thought about her health.

I asked Newman about his earlier hint that the movie might be somewhat autobiographical.

"Not so much in specific events," he said, "as in the trajectory of the character. He was aloof and distant and

mistook that for independence. He became . . . available. He wasn't so stuck in cement that he couldn't be alert to the potential that exists in change. That's the real miracle of that character; some primordal instinct in him that says, when his son and grandson appear, 'Hold it, this could be worth something.' That's the part of that charac-ter that touched me."

Do you feel you've learned to be more available over the years?

"Yes . . . but, see, everything in this business demands that you keep your distance—because if you don't, you get eaten alive. That's the only way you can protect your privacy and your identity. At least that's the way it af-fected me. There are people who are comfortable being public figures. They bathe in it. The second the light gets turned on, suddenly they blossom like a bed of spring flowers. They've got a much easier time of it than some-one who is private by nature. And I envy that."

It is well known that the Newman's son, Scott, died in a drug-related incident. I wondered if the movie character was perhaps able to say things that the actor, in life, did not get the chance to say. I didn't have the courage to bring up the subject directly, but . . .

There's a nice line in the movie, I said. The son says, "You never were a father. Why did you decide to be a grandfather?" Your character says, "Well, you have to start sometime."

"Yeah," Newman said. "What was it that Oscar Wilde said, about never apologizing and never explaining?" He reached for a glass of mineral water and seemed ready to change the subject. "How are the Bears going to do?" In September, it was a good question. "The Bears won the championship the year that we shot *Color of Money* in Chicago, and I can remember with such clarity . . . we were in the Whitehall Hotel, and I remember looking out the window . . . we had shot late that night, and an assis-tant cooked dinner, and Mary Elizabeth Mastrantonio and Tom Cruise and a bunch of actors came over for hamhocks and beans. And we looked out the window at midnight and could hear all the distant cheering and noise and stuff and coming down that street—was it Chestnut?—there was a guy splayed out on the hood of a car, leaning back against the windscreen, the car was going conser-vatively fifty miles an hour, this guy had nothing to hold on to, and you knew if that driver tapped his brakes, that guy would simply propel himself off into the future with little or no means of support or protection. I always won-dered what happened to that guy; whether he survived that."

When the Bears won, it was the first time Chicago had won anything in ages.

"Yeah. Do you often go on these publicity things? It's kind of an . . . well, not an ordeal, exactly, but doing so many interviews is like double-parking in front of a whore house; scant satisfaction to both parties."

But it's worth it when the film is good, I said. It's nice how it ends; I like the last shot, the repose, as the camera rests on your face, and you're asleep. . . .

"Fade to black."

Oliver Stone

August 17, 1994—Oliver Stone said he was standing in a post office in Bali, talking on the pay phone. He'd gotten up early so he didn't have to stand in a long line for the phone.

What's it like there? I asked.

"It's a strange island. There are a lot of demons here— Balinese devils. You don't sleep very much. I almost drowned two days ago."

You what?

"There are very strong tides in the ocean. I was swimming with my kid and I guess we got too far out and we got swept out about three or four hundred yards. The waves were pounding and it was very, very scary. It took an hour and a half to get back in."

That's what it's like with Oliver Stone. You pick up the phone and thirty seconds later he's fighting for his life.

"We basically kept our heads above water until they could get some boards out to us," he said. "It's really wild out here."

How old is your son?

"Sean is only nine years old. He's not the greatest swimmer in the world."

Were you facing the possibility that you might die?

"Absolutely."

I love talking with Oliver Stone because his life is such a drama, such a striving against man and nature. Maybe that's why his films are always so charged up; they partake of his personality. Another reason his films fascinate me is that they're like the weather report: updates on the psychic climate of the nation.

The new one, *Natural Born Killers,* is about a media circus surrounding a couple of gleeful mass murderers who go on a killing rampage and become celebrities. Stone was still editing it when the O.J. Simpson case broke. In his movie, crowds were cheering the killers. In real life, crowds were lining the L.A. freeways to wave at O.J. driving past in the white Bronco.

Mahatma Gandhi once joked about running fast to keep in front of his followers. Oliver Stone must feel the same way about real life. His movie *Wall Street,* with its famous speech about greed, came out about the time they arrested Michael Milkin. And now, perfectly timed, here is this crazy, brilliant, chaotic movie *Natural Born Killers,* a satire about the way we have turned violence into a TV spectator sport.

Not many people make movies like this because not many people get this angry and still retain their sense of

humor. It is being compared to Kubrick's *A Clockwork Orange* in some quarters, but I think his *Dr. Strangelove* is a better match, because it's funnier.

The movie stars Woody Harrelson and Juliette Lewis as Mickey and Mallory, a loving couple who go on a killing spree across America, making sure they get credit for every death. They kill fifty-two people, utterly without remorse—except for the Indian, of course. It was a shame the Indian had to die.

The early stages of their odyssey are like a hallucinatory nightmare, but then, after they're arrested, the movie turns into more of a circus. There's Tommy Lee Jones as the ringmaster, a crazed prison warden who seems to feed on the rage of his prisoners, and Robert Downey Jr. as the clown, the host of a tabloid TV show who will do anything to get Mickey and Mallory on the air.

"Satire," Stone was telling me, "is exaggeration and distortion. You have to take reality and warp it. What's happened in the last couple of years is that the reality quotient has caught up with the satire. I mean, this stuff was happening on television while we were still making the movie. By the time the Bobbitt thing happened, I kind of had to wonder, you know. Mickey and Mallory are not so outrageous. They'd be in *TV Guide* for a couple of weeks and get a big play and then people would be bored and want to move on to the next one."

And look at the O.J. Simpson thing. They're talking about not holding the trial on election day in California, for fear people would rather watch TV than vote.

"Worse things are going to happen. The movie's not just about the media, I hope. It's about a three-headed monster. There's the police force, which is corrupt in the picture. There's a huge prison system led by Tommy Lee Jones. And there's the media."

Do you think we're using violence in order to entertain ourselves, in the news, in a way that wasn't true fifty years ago?

"Even five years ago, in the L.A. basin, it used to be you'd see real news. Now, all you basically see are clips from murders—local murders preferably. The accent is on ambulances and police and the concept of fear.

"You could say it goes back to Nixon. Because he got votes by telling us criminals were everywhere. He made it a political issue in the country. It culminated with the Willy Horton ads being used to beat Dukakis. Now the news is selling Fear, with a capital F. It's not good for the country because it's a false issue. Actual violent crime has stayed pretty much the same, or gone down, since the late 1960s."

But you wouldn't guess that by watching TV, especially the popular tabloid news shows that mix actors in with actual witnesses and participants to make "reconstructions" of terrible crimes, so that every day you can vicariously participate in a fresh tragedy. *Natural Born Killers* takes that to its ultimate entertainment value in a sequence where Downey, as the TV reporter, actually joins Mickey and Mallory in a prison riot. Later, threatened with death himself, he reasons that his killers will have to leave somebody as a witness, so they can get "credit." But . . . there *is* a witness. He has forgotten his TV camera.

Stone's visual style in the movie is an ultimate expression of an approach he was working toward in *The Doors* and *JFK*. It combines intricate editing with a lot of special effects that put more than one kind of image on the screen at a time. You see similar things done on MTV. He'll have his characters in front of a horizon, and the sky will be replaced by an image of something else.

Working with his longtime collaborator, the cinematographer Robert Richardson, he uses just about every conceivable kind of film. The movie contains 35mm, 16mm, Super 8, video, newsreel footage, still photos, and animation. And this is not simply a stunt. They know that our minds react differently to various kinds of moving images; that's why some TV shows are made on film, not tape, and why most commercials are. We can sense the difference, and when we're watching *Natural Born Killers* it's important that some moments feel like the news, some feel like archival footage, and some feel like commercials or MTV videos.

Stone also uses a wide range of styles in the movie. The most outrageous example is a flashback to the childhood of the Juliette Lewis character. It's shot in the form of a sitcom, and stars Rodney Dangerfield as her father. But this is a cruel sitcom on which the laugh track continues to chuckle while Rodney assaults his daughter.

The overall impression I had, watching the movie, was of a manic channel-surfing experience, in which, no matter how quickly I switched from one channel to another, I couldn't stay ahead of the nightmare which was enveloping all the media.

The film's vision was so stark that it was originally slapped with the dreaded NC-17 by the MPAA's ratings board. Stone made several trips back to the MPAA before finally getting the R rating, which is essential for the film to get wide distribution. Even so, the MPAA's warning about the film's contents is more dire than usual. Although I can't say what the movie looked like in its NC-17 version, I am reminded that when I talked to Stone about it last December, he said that viewers would imagine they were seeing more violence than they really were; that a second viewing might surprise them with what was actually there on the screen.

"This film is very cartoonlike," Stone said this week, on the phone from Bali. "I know what real violence is. I've done it with *JFK* and *Born on the Fourth of July*, and *Platoon*. When I show a bullet that's tumbling through the air, or a knife that goes through a plate-glass window and sticks in somebody's back, you can't for one second assume that it's realistic. We're taking a tongue-in-cheek approach to it, and some people don't understand that. They take things pretty literally. There's no gore in there.

It's not like the chain saw scene in *Scarface*, or the tongue-biting scene in *Midnight Express*. The MPAA didn't understand and they were very tough. I had to go back five times to get this through."

What specifically were they objecting to?

"I think it was just an overwhelming abundance of violence and chaos. I think the chaos upset them more. It scared 'em."

Stone based his film on a screenplay by Quentin Tarantino, rewriting it extensively. What it turned into, he said, was a combination of two of his favorite genres, the road movie and the prison picture.

"If you stay inside a genre," he said, "they're less apt to rip you up for trying something. They're familiar with the genre. So, once I had the genres, I decided to go all out and show their interior states, try to show that the two killers are not just stick figures. They have an interior life, created not only by their abusive parents, but also because they are the children of this genocidal century. We have shots of Armenia in there; we have shots of Russia, Germany, Vietnam; we have animals being killed, pollution occurring, the world being economically eaten, all of which kick into this cycle of violence.

"I can't tell you there's always a consistent logic to what we did; we'd go from black and white to color as we felt it. We often shot in different formats as we were shooting and then we decided in the editing room what to do. But it was always set out to be as chaotic as possible."

And it succeeded, I said.

"I hope so," he said.

And then he had to go. I think somebody else wanted to use the phone.

Quentin Tarantino

October 5, 1994—So thank God for tape recorders, because in the old pen-and-paper days this would be the act of a desperate man, trying to keep up with Quentin Tarantino, who talks like he's being paid by the word and starts every sentence in the middle of the previous one.

We're sitting in the corner of this cavernous ballroom on the top floor of the Carlton Hotel at the Cannes Film Festival. Way cool. Tarantino's got the biggest hit at the festival, *Pulp Fiction*, and in a couple of days they're going to give it the Palme d'Or, which is the Grand Prize in any language.

"Five years ago about now, yeah, was the last year in the video store," he is remembering. It is part of the folklore that Tarantino worked in a video store, devouring movies by the thousands, by the pound, by the yard, letting them churn in his imagination and then writing lurid, violent, macho screenplays that were *born* to be called *Pulp Fiction* or *Reservoir Dogs* or *True Romance*, titles like that.

He's thirty-one. I met him the first time when he was

twenty-nine. Two years ago, when he brought *Reservoir Dogs* to Cannes, he was happy to sit at a table on the beach and eat spaghetti. Now the whole top floor of the Carlton has been roped off for him.

Bruce Willis and John Travolta, two of the stars of *Pulp Fiction,* are also at the festival, angling to get a word in edgewise, because Tarantino is a joyous, arm-waving, head-shaking, table-pounding cascade of cinematic theory and big plans. This is the only man I know who makes Jay Leno look like he has an ordinary chin. Tarantino's jaw juts out like a figurehead, parting the waves in advance of his opinions. And he has all these . . . theories.

If you ever get a chance to see a movie named *Sleep With Me,* you'll understand what I mean. This is a low-budget film made by a friend of Tarantino's, and in the middle of the film Tarantino plays a party guest. He plants himself in the middle of the floor and loudly explains why *Top Gun* is actually a homosexual love story. How the navy pilots love one another, and their jet planes are phalluses, and when one flies upside-down right above another one, well, how plain can it get? "Come over to the *gay side!*" he shouts. "That's the message!"

Tarantino's theory actually makes a certain amount of sense. I wonder if he talked it over with Tony Scott, who directed not only *Top Gun* but also *True Romance,* last summer's crimefest, which was written by Tarantino. Doesn't matter. The point is, Tarantino is *always* loudly explaining a theory. He talks so much, he'd be a bore if he weren't so interesting.

I ask him whether he thinks there is any correlation between violence on the screen and violence in society. Not an original question, but a conversation-opener when a guy has just directed a movie with some of the more unique forms of mayhem ever seen on the screens of Cannes. Here is every word of his answer, because I want you to understand how he talks:

"Okay! My answer is the easiest answer in the world, to me: 'It's just a movie and that's the way I feel!' However, while I do not believe there is absolutely any correlation of people seeing a movie and going out and acting it out in real life, and as an example, people go, 'Well, what about the Borgias? There were no movies back then.' Well, even more important, what about Tokyo? It's the safest city I've ever been in and they have the most violent cinema I've ever seen. However, how much society and the image we see go hand-in-hand, I don't know the answer to that. However, I do know that I'm a good person, yet I grew up watching *The Wild Bunch* and *Deliverance* on a double-feature when I was eleven years old. All right, you know?

"So the bottom line is, my No. 1 responsibility is not to society at large; it's to my characters. And to be true to them. If you had to stop and think what some idiot might do after seeing the movie, you'd never do anything."

All right. You begin to sense how a video store clerk turned himself into a movie director. How he talked an

established actor like Harvey Keitel into appearing in a $24,000 movie like *Reservoir Dogs,* and then jumped the budget to $400,000—still peanuts—on the strength of Keitel's participation. How before he even finished that film, he had already sold the screenplays to *True Romance* and Oliver Stone's *Natural Born Killers.* How *Pulp Fiction* was the most eagerly awaited film at Cannes last May simply because Tarantino made it.

The movie tells several interlocking stories—three main ones, and then a framing story starring Tim Roth and Amanda Plummer as a couple of lovey-doveys (he calls her "Honey Bunny") who sit in a restaurant and talk themselves into holding it up. Then there's a story involving John Travolta and Samuel L. Jackson as enforcers for a mobster. And then Travolta is ordered to take the mobster's wife (Uma Thurman) out to a nightclub. And then that leads to a scene that will feel like a needle straight through your heart.

Meanwhile Bruce Willis is a boxer who does not throw a fight he was supposed to throw, which means the mob wants to kill him so he has to get out of town, fast, with his girlfriend. But meanwhile he and the mob boss, the last man he wants to see, run into each other and end up in the basement of a gun shop, where some very weird stuff is going on. While also Travolta and a buddy end up with a body accidentally on their hands, and Harvey Keitel is a Mr. Fix-It who specializes in cleaning up other people's messes. And in the middle is a speech delivered by Christopher Walken to a little boy, that starts slow and builds into the biggest laugh of the year.

None of this even touches the genius of the movie, which resides in its humor, its invention, its crazy energy, its peculiar dialogue, and its headlong rush through a loop-the-loop plot. It's got interlocking stories that seem to double back on themselves, like a Mobius strip, so that in the final scene of the movie the characters walk in on what was earlier the first scene in the movie. It might seem that the movie has contradicted itself somehow, ending before it began—that characters are now alive who were earlier dead.

"Okay," I told Tarantino, "I was just talking to your agent and he explained the timeline to me and then he found out he was wrong. And then two of us started in and we both got confused. So, is there a time paradox in the plot? Does the chronology involve an impossibility?"

"No, there's not an impossibility," he said. "I know that for a fact. I'm very careful about that. I mean, it'd be kinda silly, and the worst kind of sloppy, if you did a movie the way I did it and then tripped it up."

He was drinking coffee, and he spilled some, and began to mop it up with a napkin.

"It's all carefully written. It's like when Buñuel cast two different actors to play the same part. But if you're going to do that, you've got to be totally clear. The worst thing you can do is confuse an audience. With *Pulp* you might momentarily be confused but you've been given enough hints as you've been watching the movie that you can catch up with it."

One thing I was waiting for, I said, was the scene where everybody is standing in a circle with their guns pointing at one another. And if they all pull their triggers, then everybody dies. That was how you ended *Reservoir Dogs* and *True Romance,* and sure enough, it's *sort* of how you end *Pulp Fiction.*

Tarantino's head was pumping up and down. "I loved it when *True Romance* came out and people were saying they couldn't believe I ended it the same way I did *Dogs.* To me, the Mexican standoff is the modern-day equivalent of the Western showdown. I never felt gypped when Sergio Leone ended every Western he did with a showdown; that's just the way they ended. But every single one of them was different.

"And every single one of my stories is different. One of the things I kinda like is my stuff leads to a volatile conclusion. Everything's been building and building and building and then, it's like, how can I stretch this out the most? I want to send you out the door like you've seen a movie. So often these days movies have bad endings. I almost don't expect a movie to have a good ending anymore.

"I remember when I watched John Woo's *A Better Tomorrow II,*" he said, mentioning the legendary Hong Kong action director whose films were obviously an influence back when he was carrying home armloads from the video store. "I was watching it with a buddy of mine, and it's all building to this big climax. We hadn't seen this movie before, so we didn't know they were going to have the biggest shoot-out in the history of film. My friend turns to me and goes, 'If they don't get naked and boogie at the end of this movie, this has been for nothing.' *He was right!* Doesn't matter that we enjoyed everything leading up to the end, it had to end in like a big way or it was all nothing!"

You really love movies, don't you?

"I'll walk outside and if it's raining, if I just fell in love with a girl, I might go do the Gene Kelly dance in the rain. When I was a little kid, I'd see a Charles Bronson movie and I'd stand in the mirror and, like, pretend I was Charles Bronson talking down the bully. If I see an action movie and the guy's wearing a cool jacket or something in it, I want to buy that jacket."

He can buy a lot of jackets. You're represented by the William Morris Agency, I said. You're king of the festival, big stars are working with you, and it's all happened so quickly. Will you still have this anarchic energy in your films after you get embraced by the Hollywood mainstream?

"My integrity will always be the same. I mean, I might fail. But I find it almost impossible to believe that I'll ever do a movie for the wrong reasons because—it's just too *hard* to make a movie! It takes too long! It's a year of your life! And I can't believe I'll ever do something completely

for money because I'm making enough money now. I never want my overhead to get so big that I gotta do stuff I don't care about.

"In a way, doing a movie you didn't care about would be worse than working behind a counter. It would be a death! When I was working behind a counter, I was going forward. Making a bad movie would be going backwards."

Talking like this, he had hardly noticed the storm gathering around him. A publicist was tugging at his chair, trying to angle Tarantino in front of some TV cameras. Fans had somehow infiltrated as far as a glass door, and were pounding on it. Bruce Willis was edging in on the other side, suggesting they go get some lunch.

"When I'm writing a movie," he said, "I hear the laughter. People talk about the violence. What about the comedy? *Pulp Fiction* has such an obviously comic spirit, even with all the weird things that are happening. To me, the most torturous thing in the world, and this counts for *Dogs* just as much as *Pulp,* is to watch it with an audience that doesn't know they're supposed to laugh. Because that's a death. Because I'm hearing the laughs in my mind and there's this dead silence of crickets sounding in the audience, you know?"

Sigourney Weaver

New York, January 10, 1995—There was an article not long ago in *Variety,* the showbiz bible, saying that Sigourney Weaver was third on the list of stars who could "open" a movie, worldwide. That placed her right up there with Arnold Schwarzenegger and the other male action heroes, mostly on the basis of her work in the *Alien* series. But the article didn't make much of it.

"It went on and on," Weaver was recalling, "about Arnold and the other top box-office men, and what that meant about their careers. But it didn't even say, isn't it interesting that there's a woman in the top three? They sort of went, like, it was a fluke."

The article *could* have gone on to say that Sigourney Weaver is the only Hollywood star who is among the top three action stars *and* also makes serious art films, like her latest work, Roman Polanski's *Death and the Maiden.* That would have made her unique, too. Or it could have pointed out what uncanny taste she has in choosing projects, so that in the years since she first came into view in *Alien* (1979), she has had essentially one box office success after another. There have been disappointments, but look at *The Year of Living Dangerously* (1983), *Ghostbusters* (1984), *Half Moon Street* (1986), *Gorillas in the Mist* (1988), and *Working Girl* (1988), not to mention the *Ghostbusters* and *Alien* sequels.

That the same woman could appear as a science fiction icon and the star of Polanski's visceral new drama about political torture is remarkable. That she could be completely credible in both—battling a slimy alien spider and then engaging in a struggle of words with a charming, elusive torturer in a serious art film—is also remarkable. If the same could be said about Schwarzenegger, Stallone, Willis, or Van Damme, you can be sure you wouldn't have had to wait until this article to read about it.

"It's funny," she said. "I seem to fall between the cracks. I'm not considered a legitimate action hero because I'm a woman. But I'm not considered in the same category with high-toned actresses like Glenn Close and Meryl Streep because I'm an action figure. See what I mean?"

I told her I effortlessly thought of her in both categories, and that in fact her "serious" work in movies like *Year of Living Dangerously* or *Gorillas in the Mist*—where she was a smart woman living in a dangerous environment—made her more credible in the action movies.

"Well, that's lovely," she said. "But people don't see me that way. I've been in so many different kinds of movies, some people think of me with gorillas, and others, the little ones, know *Ghostbusters,* you know, and the sci-fi fans analyze the *Alien* movies. So I have this sort of spotty support group; it looks like I almost can't win. I'm amazed that overseas my movies are very much seen. I would not have been asked to do *Death and the Maiden* if that weren't so."

We were talking in New York after the first American screenings of the film, last December. It opened on the coasts to qualify for academy consideration (Weaver is considered a very possible Oscar nominee), and now opens more widely around North America.

In *Death and the Maiden* she plays Paulina, a woman who was a political prisoner in an unnamed country (for which we should probably read Chile). She was imprisoned, tortured, and raped by a man whose face she never saw, but whose verbal style and physical presence she could never forget: even his smell is indelible for her. Time passes. She is released. A new regime takes over the country.

In prison, she held out because she was loyal to her husband, a political dissident. After she was freed, she discovered he'd been unfaithful. A deep bitterness takes hold, and she resists sex with him. They live in a lonely house on a deserted landscape. One night her husband's car blows a tire and he is given a lift home by a charming stranger. Feigning sleep, hiding behind the bedroom door, she realizes the stranger is her former torturer. That sets up the main body of the film, in which she surprises the man, ties him to a chair, and puts him through an inquisition—while he uses his considerable intelligence in an attempt to convince her, and her husband, he is the wrong man.

The movie was based by Polanski on Ariel Dorfman's play, a success on Broadway and elsewhere, and also stars Ben Kingsley as the possible torturer, and Stuart Wilson as her husband. They are the only three characters onscreen: A woman and two men who each, in his way, has made her a victim.

Why did Polanski cast Weaver in this role? Possibly because he saw both her intelligence and her strength. She has always played smart women—particularly in the *Alien* series—and yet she is identified in our minds as a tall, sinewy woman who probably could tie a man to a chair and contemplate killing him. (Can we easily see Glenn Close or Meryl Streep doing that? It is an interesting question.)

"In the beginning," Weaver said, "I was very afraid of physically hurting Ben Kingsley by accident, and Roman would have to take me aside and say, 'When you tie those knots, it's all right if you give them a little tug; it's all right to hurt him just a little bit. He'll be fine.' And I knew Ben was in some pain because of the tape I put across his mouth. I had such a horror of actually hurting him. Then, as we got to know each other better it was sort of like a wonderful high-wire act. I always knew that as far out as I went, he would be out there to catch me.

"Of course, the thing that may be hard for people to accept is that the relationship between torturer and victim is very complicated. There have even been incidences where the victim has married the torturer after prison. It's a very complicated thing. I really felt, and Roman let me go with this, that there've been two bad men in this woman's life. One of them is her husband who, in many ways, has been a torturer because he doesn't want to talk about what happened to her. The only thing that kept her going through this terrible experience was the feeling she was saving this man and when she got out, he'd be there for her. So when she discovers him in bed with another woman, nothing in her life has hurt more than that. That is the biggest crime in the film. He wants to make love anyway even though she's terribly upset. There are many different kinds of rapes going on. She also tortures him with recriminations and guilt.

"And in the case of Ben's character . . . the few moments of tenderness she experienced in prison were also with this man. He'd been kind to her, he'd cleaned her, he played music to her. In other words, it was very complicated and we wanted to make sure that it was not black and white. That they shared an intimate animal memory. Not that any part of it was good or pleasurable for her, but that she responded as a helpless child would to the few instances of tenderness during that experience."

Seeing the film for the first time, Weaver said, she was surprised by some of the editing choices Polanski made. There were painful scenes, for example, exploring her sex life with her husband: "There were takes that went much further, where she really struggled against him. Roman didn't think the audience could take it. But I think that's the truth of their relationship and, in fact, I've always felt it was hard to believe that they end up together. Most relationships don't survive the experience of someone being tortured and imprisoned.

"Then the scene we did of her behind the door, when she first hears the doctor's voice, was some of my best work and he's included about half a second of it. If he'd included more of it maybe it would be clearer to the audience. I was astonished by how little of my emotional work in the beginning he did use, and I can't see it objectively."

There was a distant quality to her voice, as if she was remembering a somewhat different film from the one she had seen, a film assembled from her memories of shots that had been filmed but not used. Yet she seemed more contemplative than unhappy. I asked her if she'd like to have an "actor's cut" of the film.

"Not really. You know, I feel so fortunate that it was Roman's. Another director might have made this more Paulina's picture, because that's the way it was written. He resolutely makes it like *Rashomon*, where you're with each of the three characters, trying to decide whose point of view is the most valid. At one point I said to him, 'You know, the camera's often at my back when I'm saying something that I think is important for the audience to know about what happened to me.' He laughed and said, 'You only think it's interesting when it's on you.' I said, 'No, I want to make sure that they're following what I'm saying about this man and what I feel about it because they're all thinking, is she crazy or is she sane?' Seeing the film, I'm surprised by how little it was on Paulina for key moments. I know he has the material because I saw all the rushes and he chose not to because he doesn't want her to dominate this story. He wants you to have your sympathies tugged from one to another all the time—which I respect enormously. It's not the conventional way of doing it."

She seemed to be holding back a little. I asked her if she *missed* the shots that weren't there.

She shrugged very slightly. "Well, I do feel that at several points. But at least I know that I *did* it, so if he doesn't want to use it . . . it's one thing if I wasn't able to do it, then I would feel funny about it. But the fact that he had it all and chose to do it this way, I guess, he feels that she gets there in the end . . . which is fine, you know. . . ."

The film was shot in Paris, she said, which created an odd experience for her. "If you're from a theoretically healthy democracy and you read in detail one first-hand account after another of what happened to another long-standing democracy overnight, you can never see the world the same again. In fact, working in Paris, what was strange, when I walked around, I always felt the Nazi presence. I was so conscious that there had been a time in Paris where this very thing was going on. I found it so chilling to walk down those streets. I would notice people of a certain age, and I would wonder, what they were doing?"

If you looked back over your career, I asked, would you see anything revealed that you didn't know at the time, about the characters you've played?

"I think I do my work for women mostly. I want to feel that a woman looks at the screen and says to herself, 'I know what that is and I'm glad that that's expressed.' I'm drawn to women who, for some reason, are cut off from other women because of their experience or their passion. Like Dian Fossey's great passion for the gorillas. They isolate themselves from other people for a certain purpose. There're so many people within each of us and to be able to play with that in a story . . . I remember with *Alien*, since I'd never done a film before, telling myself, gosh, now I have a choice; do I try to play the character consistently from beginning to end? And I went, gosh, well, I'm not very consistent as a person so why should I think that this person is? So, then you learn to play each scene for all it's worth and if you string them all together, then you have sort of a recognizable human being."

You always play competent women. In so many movies, women are so weak. They never seem able to run, for example, without being dragged by the hand by the male hero. Have you ever noticed that?

"Yes, yes; with the tight skirt. Inevitably. When I was at Yale, they did a production of *The Tempest*, and I went to the director, and I said, 'Miranda grew up on an island. She wears buckskins, she knows how to hunt and fish, she hasn't had the benefits of a courtly upbringing.' I thought he was going to fall over with a heart attack. It was so alien to his concept of Miranda as this lovely little creature with long hair and a long dress reading her book."

Definitely not Sigourney Weaver.

Terry Zwigoff

Park City, Utah, May 16, 1995—"I don't ski," Terry Zwigoff was moaning. "I don't have a cellular phone. I don't have a bottle of Evian water. I don't belong here."

This was last January at the Sundance Film Festival. He looked unhappily around the bar of the Stein-Erickson Lodge, a vast hotel in the mountains above the ski resort of Park City. Cheerful skiers in Thinsulate parkas were sipping decaf cappuccinos. Zwigoff, who was wearing a beard and a sweater with animals knitted on it, shook his head.

"My movie is about a guy who was the most unpopular kid in high school. I could identify with him because I was, too. Now I come here and I feel like I'm back in high school."

We had met at the lodge to discuss *Crumb*, Zwigoff's great and astonishing new documentary about R. (for Robert) Crumb, the San Francisco underground comic artist whose style straddled the 1960s like his famous "Keep on Truckin'" panel. The movie, now going into national release, is *not* about underground comics. It is about the way Crumb has hung on by his fingernails to life and sanity, using art as his lifeline. *Crumb* is one of those defining experiences, like *Hoop Dreams*, like *Gates of Heaven*, that shows you how documentary films can reach parts of the human condition that fiction films don't even know about.

Zwigoff looks like vast stretches of his own human condition need first-aid even as we speak. He is small, intense, with worry lines chiseled between his eyes, and although *Crumb* is an enormous hit (and would win the Sundance prize as best documentary), he almost seems to wonder if it was worth the sacrifices he made to film it.

He spent nine years on his film while averaging an income of "about two hundred dollars a month," and "living with back pain so intense that I spent three years with a loaded gun on the pillow next to my bed, trying to get up the nerve to kill myself."

The two of you must have made a great pair, I said. You were making a film about Crumb's misery while you were in greater misery.

"I think that helped. It was very hard to talk him into doing it. I had to call in every favor he owed me. We'd been friends for a while. He just wasn't interested; he doesn't like publicity."

In the film, we meet R. Crumb, his mother, his brothers Charles and Max, his wife, and various friends. We do not meet his two sisters, who wanted nothing to do with the film (one of them, Zwigoff said, has demanded "reparations" of four hundred dollars a month from Crumb for his "crimes against women"). There is a great deal about Crumb's art: his in-your-face caricatures of greedy, lustful, violent, scatological characters, flaunting their needs, perversions, and desires. There is much more about the conditions that produced it, and as we watch *Crumb* the portrait of an bizarre, dysfunctional family emerges.

There is great unease about Crumb's father, who looks terrifyingly normal in family photographs but severely punished his sons. There is a visit to the family home, occupied by Crumb's mother and by his brother, Charles—who was the first cartoonist in the family, but withdrew to permanent seclusion in an upstairs bedroom, never drawing again, or leaving the house. We also meet Max, a San Francisco monk who sits on a bed of nails, drawing a long linen cloth through his intestinal tract to cleanse it, and who is also an artist.

Crumb was obviously deeply wounded not only by his family, but by high school, where, deeply unpopular, he developed his fixation on women with hefty haunches. One of the few sources of pleasure for his male cartoon characters is riding piggyback on callipygian girlfriends; after Crumb does the same thing at a gallery opening of his work, we understand that the practice is literally, and sincerely, autobiographical.

We also learn that many of the characters who occur frequently in his drawings and comic strips are based quite closely on people he hated or lusted after in high school, and that much of his work is an elaborate process of revenge. As we get to know him and meet his family, it becomes clear that this artistic process has somehow held him together, and perhaps spared him the sorts of existence that trapped his brothers.

"When I started," Zwigoff told me, "I was doing a more conventional biography of what I thought was one of the great artists of our time. But things that led in different directions ultimately shaped the film. I just kept going back to his family; maybe because I was going through this intense psychotherapy at the time. The reason I hit it off with Charles—or Robert himself, for that matter—was because I was just like those guys in high school."

It seems as if Robert's art became a way for him to deal directly with the issues in his life.

"I think the larger part of what kept Robert the saner member of the family was the *success* from his artwork, not the art itself. Just getting it on paper alone in a room obviously didn't help Max or Charles too much."

Robert is always smiling, I said. It's like everything is a wry joke: "Boy, my family is crazy and weird and isn't this funny. . . ."

"He's laughing to keep from crying," Zwigoff said.

There's one moment when he's talking about his father, and he lapses into silence, and we see this infinite sadness in his face.

"Yeah, it's where he says his father never spoke to him again after seeing one of his comics. It's a rare, off-guard moment. He's very media savvy and knows enough to keep a front on."

There are several times in the film, I said, where Robert becomes the interviewer, questioning his mother or brothers for your sake.

"He was very helpful to me in that way. But there were other times he was completely uncooperative and seemed to be trying to sabotage the film. I had known him for a long time, and we had played in this same crummy band together. After he agreed to the film, I said the only way I really wanted to do it was by including Charles and Max and his mother.

"I'd met them in the early 1970s. I was traveling with him to New York and he said, 'Why don't we just pull over and stay at my parents' house? I haven't seen them in a couple of years. Would you mind spending a night there?' I spent this incredibly memorable night at their house talking to Charles and his mother, and really liked them a lot, and I always thought it would be no film without them. Of course I had no idea at that point how *much* they would figure into the film.

"So when we started the film, Robert called them on the phone. They remembered me, they liked me, so yeah, okay, they'd do the film, you know, whatever. So a couple of months later I hired a crew and we got to the motel and his mother said no, she wouldn't film. He went over there and couldn't get a real answer out of her. We were in this motel room for four days. Finally I talked to her all day and she sort of warmed up and said, 'okay, okay—but you can only do Charles upstairs in his room.' So we filmed him and we're coming down the stairs and my cinematographer,

Maryse Alberti, a French woman, says, 'Terry, we must film the mother.' I said I asked her like a hundred times; she doesn't want to be filmed. 'Let me place the light. We will just start filming her.' She throws up this light and his mother is really angry and cursing us and screaming.

"I said, 'Take the light down and let's just go; leave her alone.' 'No, no, we just do it.' So as soon as she turns the camera on his mother, she says, 'Oh, well, it's too late now; I'm in the movie.' And she really got into it."

The scenes upstairs in Charles's bedroom are among the most haunting in the film. Literate, intelligent, and even amused by his own predicament, he has a stack of battered paperbacks, which he reads and rereads, and in a closet there is artwork from his brief productive period in his teens. He talks about his lifelong obsession with the 1950 version of the film *Treasure Island* and its young hero, played by Bobby Driscoll, who in a sense represents all of the daring that the agoraphobic Charles was never able to muster.

"The one night we spent at his house," Zwigoff said, "two blocks away, the local movie theater, which had been there since they were kids, was playing *Treasure Island* on a rerelease. Robert was trying to talk Charles into going and Charles was going through this unbelievable dilemma. He didn't want to leave the house but he was dying to see this movie again. Robert said, 'Look, me and Terry will walk you over there. We'll sit with you; we'll bring you back.' He couldn't leave the house."

The film was "technically" shot between 1985 to 1991, Zwigoff said, "but there's a period there, about 1986 through 1988, where my back was so bad I was in bed most of the time, suicidal." While filming was going on Crumb's reputation was continuing to grow, nourished by the current popularity of comics and graphic novels about Generation X, and the boom in 1960s art among collectors. Shortly after principal photography was finished, Crumb, his wife, and their daughter, Sophie, moved permanently to the south of France.

"Sophie's eleven now," Zwigoff said. "She's directed her first film; a ninety-minute film, feature length. She wrote it, she cast it, she shot it. I asked Robert if it's any good and he said, 'I don't speak a word of French. I can't tell if it's any good.' But he said that technically it's amazing. There are these long, sophisticated tracking shots. He said she studies *Touch of Evil* on videotape, and is a very happy, well-adjusted kid. "

Are they happier over there?

"He seems to be happier than I've ever known him. He's coming to the States in May. For some bizarre reason he agreed to go on the Garrison Keillor show. We have this pretty terrible band that we've had for years, called the Cheap Suit Serenaders, and agreed to go on this show, you know. Turned down the Letterman show and all these other things but radio was okay."

He doesn't seem too concerned about making a lot of money or becoming famous with his art.

"He was offered, like, millions to license the 'Keep on Truckin'" drawing for Toyota, but they only wanted that one drawing. He wanted to sell them a lot of other stuff. He tells them, 'How about I have this girl with her head cut off being stuffed into the trunk of the Toyota?' When they didn't go for that, he turned them down."

    ★★   ★★   ★★

Footnote: What happened to R. Crumb's brothers, Charles and Max, after the filming of the documentary? The following is a spoiler; read no further until you've seen the film, where some developments come as dramatic revelations.

For Charles, life in the upstairs bedroom grew increasingly pointless, and eventually he took his own life.

"He saved up an overdose of his medication to kill himself," Zwigoff told me. *"Robert called me up to tell me that Charles had killed himself. I was very upset, but Robert just sorta said, 'Well, he was good as dead anyway.' Real callous about it. But later I talked to somebody who happened to be staying at his house when his mother called him and told him. And I asked, 'How did he react when that phone call came in?' And he said, 'He acted like he didn't care, but then I heard him all night long. He went up to his studio and he was pacing all night.'*

"Charles was the guy he was closest to in the entire world; the one who really shaped his whole sense of humor and his art. It was a big, devastating blow to him. And yet, he was right: Charles was sort of dead already."

After Charles died, his mother destroyed all of his artwork and the elaborate journals that are seen in the film before Robert could rescue them.

What's the follow-through story on Max?

"Max isn't doing too well. He called me from the hospital a couple of months ago. He'd lost about forty pounds and he had weird nervous damage to his legs."

Probably from sitting on that bed of nails.

"No, it's actually a vitamin deficiency. The doctors theorize he had this severe deficiency of vitamin B_{12}. He has these crazy theories of diet and nutrition so they got him all screwed up, but they were getting him better by giving him vitamin injections and he eventually left the hospital. You know, in the film . . . I didn't even touch the surface on Max."

Essays

Hanks and Gump

Summer 1994—On a Saturday afternoon in August, six weeks into the run of *Forrest Gump*, every seat in the movie theater was filled— filled with the ordinary people of Michigan City, Indiana, who were like the movie audiences of my youth: Not loud, not restless, not talking to the screen, not filled with bloodlust, but quite happily absorbed in the picture. At times some of them were crying. Looking around, I saw that many of those crying were men. I did not know what to make of this.

I had come to see *Forrest Gump* again because people would not stop talking to me about it. As a professional movie critic, I am like a lightning rod for anyone who has just seen a movie: They tell me if they liked it or not, as if I'd made it myself. Not in twenty-seven years on the job has a movie created more conversation among ordinary people, among the folks who only go to two or three movies a year. They just plain love it. More, they are moved by it, and they get a funny smile on their face when they talk about it, because they do not know why they are moved. The film doesn't deliver in any conventional way, and they are not quite sure what it's about. But it gets to them.

And then they mention Tom Hanks, who plays Forrest Gump, and they ask me if I thought it was a good performance, because, well, they add, "it really wasn't a performance, was it?" They don't think Hanks *is* Forrest Gump, not exactly, but they can't catch him acting in the movie. They know how he got to them somehow, but they couldn't capture him in the act of doing it, and so now, thinking back, they wonder if what he did should qualify as "acting," or whether it was (they finish with a relieved nod) "just good casting."

Tom Hanks, who in the minds of some of these people might as well be Forrest Gump, is certain to get an Academy Award nomination for his performance in the movie. He may even win the Oscar for best actor, which would make it two in a row, after his award in April 1994 for *Philadelphia,* the 1993 film where he played a man dying of AIDS. In the summer of 1993, he had another big audience success with *Sleepless in Seattle,* as a lonely widower who meets a woman through a talk show, and is almost prevented from finding his future with her, while the audience, which knows everything, desperately wants him to be happy. The summer before that, in 1992, Hanks played the manager of an all-girl baseball team in *A League of Their Own,* and there, too, the audience was on his side, hoping his character would overcome his alcoholism and make a new start to his career.

For an actor, the odds against making a truly good movie are discouraging in Hollywood, which uses formulas and deals and habit patterns to push even the most original projects into narrow channels. The odds against making four in a row, four movies where the audience truly and deeply cares about your character, are so awesome that even a Spencer Tracy or a James Stewart would have thought himself blessed at the end of such a run. Hanks has done it.[*]

Tom Hanks right now is in the unique position of being the best-loved movie actor in America, and the strange thing is, America hardly knows what to make of that, because Hanks is so hard to pin down. In some of my conversations about *Forrest Gump,* I ask people what they like the most about Tom Hanks in the movie, and they come to a dead stop. There is nothing they *particularly* like about Hanks in the movie because there was nothing they particularly noticed about him. It is the ultimate tribute to an actor, when an audience leaves the theater remembering only the character he played.

Is there even, for that matter, a character that can be described as a "Tom Hanks type"? Hanks has rarely in his career played ordinary, realistic, three-dimensional human beings. There is usually an edge of fantasy, magic, winsome humor, or otherworldly detachment about his most successful roles. The major exception, his full-hearted excursion into straight realism, is in *Philadelphia,* where AIDS is fighting his character for possession of his body, and where, in scenes like the luminous sickbed conversation with his mother (Joanne Woodward), he touches notes that everyone can identify with. He's also living in the real world in *Nothing in Common* (1987), as a cynical, fast-talking ad man who's too busy for family values, until he learns his dad (Jackie Gleason) is sick; then he discovers what's really important in life. In his upcoming film *Apollo 13,* he plays James Lovell, the astronaut whose moon mission was aborted when an oxygen tank exploded, and whose emergency return to earth was a global nail-biter. The movie is being directed by Ron Howard, who likes to go for an everyday-life feel, and is likely to be pretty realistic.

Still, despite such performances, you can't easily imagine Hanks playing the kinds of slice-of-life roles that Pacino, Hoffman, or De Niro specialize in. Tom Hanks is not and never could be Travis Bickle. More often, the Hanks character in a movie is like the characters played by Buster Keaton or Jacques Tati—universal figures in which some attributes are so exaggerated that the ordinary repertory of human tics and impulses is overlooked. In a silent film, many of the characters played by Hanks would be introduced with a card reading simply, "The Young Man." To
[*]In the summer of 1995, *Apollo 13* made five.

a surprising extent, most of his successful movie roles are in fantasies.

In *Splash* (1984), his first big role, he costars with a mermaid. He is a bachelor who runs a business in Manhattan, and might be mistaken for an ordinary guy, if it weren't for the mermaid, and for a certain dreamy quality that the producers must have seen when they cast him: He's the kind of guy you can somehow imagine in love with a mermaid.

In *Dragnet* (1987), he is Sgt. Joe Friday's partner, whose great responsibility is to pretend that Friday's robotic PoliceSpeak makes sense. Like Jack Webb and Harry Morgan in the original TV series, Dan Aykroyd and Hanks, in the movie, are too weird, too stylized, to ever be mistaken for *real* cops. Webb's TV series was a satire of itself, with every scene ending in a punchline and the "Dragnet" theme, and in the movie you can sense Hanks subtly stiffening himself into a parody.

Big (1988) has one of his best performances, as a child who is granted his wish of inhabiting an adult's body. In *The Burbs* (1989), he's a goofy suburbanite who skips his vacation to stay home and spy on his bizarre neighbors. In the magical and overlooked *Joe Vs. the Volcano* (1990), he is the central figure in a fable: a victim of overwork in a factory dungeon, told he has six months to live because of a "Brain Cloud," who sails to the South Seas to offer himself as a human sacrifice to be hurled into a volcano.

It might appear that Hanks plays a more realistic character in *Sleepless in Seattle,* but consider: His widower in that movie quits his Chicago job and takes his young son and moves to a houseboat in Seattle, where he spends most of the movie trapped in a plot only the audience understands—a plot that manipulates him so that he becomes the hostage of fate. His real role in the movie is to represent all us on our blind quest for the happiness we sense is just beyond our grasp. His character's philosophy in that movie could be borrowed from Forrest Gump's mother: "Life is like a box of chocolates; you never know what you're gonna get."

Tom Hanks in his key roles plays a sort of Everyman, a put-upon, misunderstood, overworked, middle-class guy, basically nice, who means well, tries hard, wants to please and be pleased, and is tossed about by the winds of chance. "I don't know if we each have a destiny," Forrest Gump says, "or if we're floating and accidental, like on a breeze, but I think like maybe it's both—both happening at the same time." And the film's famous opening and closing shots of a feather, at the mercy of the wind, is the right image to go with that thought.

If there is a common theme to a Hanks character, an element that draws him to certain roles, it may be the element of fable. Fables teach a lesson in mythical terms, and there is something of the moral and the myth lurking beneath the surfaces of his key films: *Splash, Big, Nothing in Common, Joe vs. the Volcano, Sleepless in Seattle,* and of course *Forrest Gump.* It is even there in *The Bonfire of the Vanities,* which is among other things a sermon against greed.

Traditional movie stars are larger than life. Robert Mitchum once told me that he asked his wife: "Dorothy, why do they think I'm such a big deal? You know me as well as anyone, and you don't give a shit. So why do they care?" And his wife replied, "Mitch, it's because they're smaller than your nostril." The big screen makes some actors into gods, into personalities so large and overwhelming that they enter our dreams and fashion our ideas about what men and women should be. Not everyone can model for that role, and the great stars do have something magical, but the screen itself plays an important role in the process. (That is why we never care as deeply about TV stars as about movie stars.)

There is a smaller category, however, of actors who are not "bigger than life," but somehow just like life—people we feel we know and understand, and are comfortable with. We sense that these actors embody not our fantasies, but our lives. Watching them we feel congratulated, because we are watching ourselves. They reassure us that in our ordinariness we also have a kind of importance. The actors who can do that—Buster Keaton, Spencer Tracy, James Stewart, Henry Fonda, Robert Duvall, Gene Hackman, and Tom Hanks—occupy a special category. We do not value them as highly as such performers as James Cagney, Mitchum, James Dean, Robert De Niro, Al Pacino, Tom Cruise, or Sean Penn, because it seems to us they aren't "acting," but embodying qualities which must not be very special to possess, since, after all, we possess them ourselves.

The central triumph of Tom Hanks as a movie actor is that, most of the time, we believe he thinks a lot like us, and does more or less what we would do, but that he somehow does it on a larger or more ennobling scale. It is the James Stewart quality. But few actors can obtain it; with most, you see their egos peeking through, or you catch them trying too hard. The camera is a lie detector, and Hanks must be a fundamentally good person to play such roles—either that, or he is an even better actor than we think.

I've met Hanks several times, in interview situations and on sets. I don't have any idea what he's really like. These are artificial situations, where he gets to choose how he presents himself, and what he chooses is to be very levelheaded and smart, with a strong element of the wry. He's much the same in one of his favorite extracurricular roles, as a talk show guest. On Letterman and Leno, he's quick and articulate, a natural comedian, comfortable inside his body. He never seems to search for a word or strive for a laugh; in that he's like Cary Grant. Letterman is the best bullshit detector among the TV talk hosts, but Hanks, who as a big movie star should be a ripe target, finesses him with understatement, directness, and irony.

It is all done so well that we realize only later we learned nothing at all about "Tom."

The real Tom Hanks was born thirty-eight years ago in Oakland, California, and attended California State College in Sacramento, where he took drama classes, acted in Ibsen, and met a man named Vincent Dowling, who was director of the Great Lakes Shakespeare Festival in Cleveland. Dowling invited Hanks to Cleveland, where he appeared in a lot of Shakespeare (even winning a local critics' award for his work in *Two Gentlemen of Verona*). The great British actors often begin their careers at Stratford; it is somehow just like the man who would play Forrest Gump that he began in Shakespeare, too, but in Cleveland.

After time on the stage in New York, Hanks moved to Los Angeles, and was cast in "Bosom Buddies" on ABC during the 1981–82 season. He already seemed like a seasoned comedy pro, comfortable in his persona, as a Catholic school-bus driver who gets engaged in the underrated *Bachelor Party* (1984), his first role of any consequence. And later the same year he played the lead in *Splash*. There was no long period of bit roles and starvation; he was a star at twenty-eight.

I still feel he was cast incorrectly in *Splash,* the comedy where he fell in love with a mermaid played by Daryl Hannah. His brother in the film was the fat and genial John Candy, who spent his days composing inflamed letters to sex magazines, and I thought it would have been funnier if the mermaid (who had never seen a human male before) chose Candy instead of Hanks. That would have been a better use of Candy, and a better use of Hanks, too, whose best roles have him as an island of curiosity in a sea of mystery. He is never at his best in movies where he's the one who has the answers.

Look at him instead in *Big,* where he convinces us that his adult body is inhabited by a gawky, hyperactive adolescent. The plot has given us a thirteen-year-old boy who is just at that age when the girls in the class shoot up into Amazons, while the boys remain short and squeaky-voiced. The film's hero has been humiliated in front of the girl of his dreams (he's too short to ride with her on an amusement ride), and he wishes desperately to be transformed into an adult. He gets his wish—and Hanks takes over the character, as a thirteen-year-old mind is magically transported into a thirty-year-old body, and the kid finds his true calling—working for a toy company. His secret is, he's the only one at the company who really loves to play with the toys, and Hanks finds a childlike body language for shots such as one where he skips through the company's lobby.

Joe Vs. the Volcano, which was written and directed by John Patrick Shanley (the author of *Moonstruck*) has been written off as a critical and commercial flop. I think it is one of the most original comedies of recent years, and it contains a performance by Hanks that works as an island of calm and sanity in the middle of the plot's madness.

From the film's opening shots of the loathsome factory—a vast block of ugliness set down in a sea of mud—the film's art design and special effects place Hanks in a world as imaginary as Oz. The notion that he will ever really sacrifice himself to the volcano is absurd, but he seems determined to go ahead with it.

The role in the hands of another actor would have been impossible, because there is never a moment when the character can find an anchor to reality. Hanks does not need one. The key to his performance here is acceptance: Without fuss, without blinking, he accepts the film's bizarre reality, and because he never fights it we can relax and accept it too.

It is that same matter-of-fact quality, of making himself at home in a world not his own, that underlies Hanks's work in *A League of their Own* and, especially, *Forrest Gump.* In the baseball picture, he is a man who has always played in a man's game, and when he finds himself coaching a team of women, his strategy is to simply keep on doing what he knows. He doesn't try to fight it, he doesn't figure it out, he simply coaches.

In *Philadelphia,* as a dying man determined to be treated correctly by the law firm which has fired him, the Hanks character has two major characteristics: pride, and anger. Either of these is an easy excuse for overacting, but Hanks understands here, as he did in the very different *A League of Their Own,* that the audience understands the situation and doesn't need to be told about it through "acting." It is always better if a film can make you understand how a character feels without the character having to do very much, externally, to explain his emotions.

Hanks's most memorable scene in *Philadelphia* is the one where he plays a recording of an aria from the opera *Andrea Chenier* for his lawyer (Denzel Washington), and while it's playing, provides a heartbreaking running commentary. The aria is sung to her lover by a French noblewoman at the time of the Revolution, and describes the death of her mother at the hands of a mob. It is an interesting choice of aria because it does *not* exactly parallel the condition of Hanks's own character. Instead, by explaining it to his lawyer, what the dying man is saying is: If you can understand the feelings of this woman, who exists in a world unfamiliar to you, you can understand the feelings of anyone—even my own, in the gay world which you are also so apart from. It is the kind of virtuoso scene that pleads to be overacted (the character, after all, is talking *over* Maria Callas). Hanks does not compete with Callas, however. He adopts the note of a teacher; he wants to share something that he knows. That is the feeling I sense beneath a lot of his performances; he chooses characters who can teach us something, often in the form of a fable.

Much was made of Hanks's decision to star in *Philadelphia* because he thus became, in a phrase that became much-used, the first major box office star to portray a homosexual. More daring, in my opinion, was his willingness to portray himself as so desperately sick: The character is sympathetic enough that many straight actors might have happily played him, but would they have been willing to reduce themselves, through weight loss and makeup, to the stark specter of skin and bones and Kaposi's sarcoma which Hanks occupied in the final scenes?

In accepting the Academy Award for *Philadelphia*, Hanks made a speech which will rank among Oscar's odder moments. Some, listening to it at the time, were moved by his tribute to those who had died from AIDS, and who the movie sought to remember. Others, including those who read it in transcript, were frankly unable to make much sense of it. I was reminded of Laurence Oliver's famous acceptance speech after they gave him an honorary Oscar. The audience greeted it with a standing ovation, but the next day, when Oliver called Michael Caine and asked him what *he* thought of it, Caine told him that, frankly, he hadn't understood a word. "Quite so," Oliver said, confessing that his mind had gone blank and, as a seasoned stage veteran, he had fallen back on pseudo-Shakespearean folderol.

Hanks was filming *Forrest Gump* at the time he made his speech, and perhaps that fact makes it a little more understandable. Like *Gump*, the speech contained the right sentiments if not always complete lucidity, and it placed feeling above sense. His ability to do that convincingly is one of the reasons Hanks is able to make Forrest a human being and not a case study.

Still, *Forrest Gump* is one of the most mysterious acting jobs I have ever seen. Looking at the movie again on that summer afternoon in Indiana, surrounded by the snuffling audience, I began with the hypothesis that Hanks's secret was to do, as nearly as possible, nothing. The secret of the performance, I told myself, is that he does what Dustin Hoffman did in *Rainman:* He finds precisely the right note, and holds it. Playing a man with an IQ of seventy-five and a limited vocal range, he sits or stands impassively, usually wearing that uniform of a blue shirt buttoned at the collar, and speaks dispassionately, unaware that he has somehow been placed at the center of all of the key events of recent American history.

Looking at the film, I found that my theory would not hold. What on a first viewing looked like a one-note performance was revealed, during this later viewing, as wide-ranging but so enormously subtle that the range is there almost without our realizing it. One of the reasons the movie has such an emotional impact may be that Hanks, by not seeming to reach for an effect, catches our hearts unprotected.

His physical performance is minimalist. He is usually sitting or standing impassively, and even in the scenes where he runs and runs (from bullies, on the football field, in Vietnam, and then across America), his face seems set. The closest Hanks comes to physical acting is in the

miraculous special effects scenes, where director Robert Zemeckis and his technicians place Hanks in the same video frames with JFK, John Lennon, LBJ, and George Wallace. Here he does a perfect job of affecting the slight stiffness and formality that people adopt in the presence of the famous, as if standing at attention.

To understanding the soul of Hanks's performance in the movie, what you have to do is listen to his voice. There are a lot of lines people remember from the film; his momma's sayings, of course, and his own philosophical insights ("You do the best with what God gave you"). But listen to the line he uses on the night he proposes marriage to Jenny (Robin Wright): "I'm not a smart man, but I know what love is." It seems at first to be delivered in a monotone, but listen carefully, and you hear that he subtly but firmly emphasizes the beats of both "love" and "is," making them absolutely equal, and a little more stressed that the rest of the sentence. Not "what *love* is," and not "what love *is*," which are the ways an ordinary actor would try to sell the sentence, but "what *love is*." The delivery prevents the line from sounding like pleading. It is a statement of fact, and by the quiet emphasis he puts on it, we sense how very strongly he feels.

Or listen to what he says on his wedding day, when Lieutenant Dan (Gary Sinese) arrives, walking on artificial legs, and introduces Forrest to his fiancée. The line is simply, "Lieutenant Dan!" Two words, but invested with affection, a teasing quality, and relief that Lieutenant Dan has escaped his demons. After the movie I tried to imitate the way Hanks said the name, and I failed. I could never get more than one note in at a time.

Forrest's voice is what carries the movie. He narrates it, he speaks in it, he quotes others. Some of the dialogue would tempt another actor to go for the punch line. When Forrest "invents" the bumper sticker "Shit Happens," for example, that's obviously a laugh line, but Hanks knows the laugh is there anyway, and so he doesn't go for it. To punch the line would imply that Forrest knows it is funny, and of course that would be a mistake—a mistake Hanks is too good to make.

Any successful movie invites nay-saying, and I've read criticism of the film as an insult to the mentally retarded, as a right-wing vision of America disguised in liberal clothing, and as a free ride on the coattails of our nostalgia. One critic thought it was all too significant that the microphone malfunctions during the peace rally, and we never hear what Forrest says to the crowd. But of course the point was not what he said, it was that he was there. Forrest is a Witness, careening from one historical milestone to another, just as all of us are. If he has no control over the events in his society, neither do we. It isn't true, as some critics say, that the movie simplifies our time by providing Forrest's simple homilies ("Death is just a part of life") and self-forgiving formulas ("Stupid is as stupid does"), thereby congratulating the audience on its own supposed ignorance. What the movie does is show how touching, how human, it is to carry on in the face of war, assassination, disaster, and disease, clinging to these lifelines that make us human.

Tom Hanks is at the top of his game right now, with four films in a row that have gone straight into the hearts of the audience, making him (dare I say of a man still young?) beloved. That is partly because he has had good luck in his choice of roles, and partly because he was ready to play them. It is also because there is something within Tom Hanks that audiences respond to positively. The movies are kind of a truth machine, allowing us to sit in the dark and stare as closely as we like at every nuance of an actor's manner and personality. (When, in real life, do we ever get to look at anyone that closely?)

Bad guys can become stars, and good guys can come across as jerks, but when a star is sensed to have the rare qualities of the characters he plays, and when those characters strike a chord in the audience's imagination, then there is the possibility that a myth will be born, that a Stewart, a Bogart, a Monroe, will be created.

Tom Hanks right now seems to be in the process of such a myth-creation. Actors are always at the mercy of their material, their directors, their costars, and even the social atmosphere at the time a movie is released. (Certainly the twenty-fifth anniversary summer of *Woodstock* was the perfect time for *Forrest Gump* to be playing.) My notion is that when an actor does something good, he probably deserves praise, but when he does something bad, he may not deserve blame—because in the movies, nobody can fake the genuine, but everybody can screw it up. Maybe Hanks has simply been lucky, with these four films. Maybe he has developed some kind of gift for being able to look at such unlikely material as *Forrest Gump* (or even *Joe Vs. the Volcano*) and seeing through the goofiness to the promise. Whatever it is, he has found a way to play a certain kind of character on the screen, in such a way that when the audience leaves the theater, they do not think of Tom Hanks or even of Forrest Gump so much as they think of themselves, as if they have just been through something mysterious and important.

A Tribute to Burt Lancaster

October 24, 1994—With the rugged features of a matinee idol and the physique of a trapeze artist, Burt Lancaster might easily have been typecast by Hollywood. Although he celebrated his physical grace and was not shy about appearing in action pictures, there was another side to his acting, right from the first: An angry, intellectual, introspective side that led him to give some of the best performances of his generation.

From the earliest days of his career, while other stars were letting agents and studios guide their careers, Lancaster directed his own destiny; you could put together

two film festivals, one of Lancaster as Hollywood star, the other of Lancaster as serious actor, and hardly believe you were looking at the same man. In some films, you'd see the laughing bravado. In others, you'd be reminded of Norman Mailer's comment: "I've never looked in eyes as chilling as Lancaster's."

Lancaster died in his Los Angeles home Thursday, at eighty, of a heart attack. He had been ill for some time, following a stroke. "It's the passing of a giant," said Kirk Douglas, his costar in six pictures. "But Burt will never die. We'll always be able to see him swinging from a yardarm in *The Crimson Pirate,* and shooting with me in *Gunfight at the O.K. Corral.*"

Yes, and we'll also always be able to see him saying "Don't touch the suit," in *Atlantic City;* and coldly wrecking the lives of those around him in *The Sweet Smell of Success;* and finding freedom deep within himself in *The Birdman of Alcatraz;* and spending a long, sorrowful day of farewells in *The Swimmer;* and bringing a snakelike attractiveness to an Italian nobleman in *The Leopard.*

Few major stars of the last half century compiled such a distinguished and varied filmography. And when his career seemed on the wane in a Hollywood infatuated with young action heroes, he reinvented himself in Europe, working for directors like Luchino Visconti and Louis Malle.

Lancaster was born in New York in 1913, and was a college graduate who also trained and worked as a circus trapeze artist before making his first film, *The Killers,* in 1946. He became a star in a series of Hollywood crime pictures, some of them very good, like *Criss Cross* and *Sorry, Wrong Number,* both in 1948. And he became a box office force in *The Flame and the Arrow* (1950) and *The Crimson Pirate* (1952). He won an Academy Award for best actor in *Elmer Gantry* (1960).

I interviewed him in 1986, when he and Douglas were costarring in the comedy *Tough Guys.* He was a man who said exactly what he thought, and when I mentioned that he'd been going in some new directions in the previous ten years—meaning that as a compliment about such films as *Executive Action, Conversation Piece, Atlantic City,* and *Local Hero,* his eyes narrowed.

"I started going in new directions back in 1953," he told me. "That was when I went from *From Here to Eternity* to *Come Back, Little Sheba.* I always tried to do things that would expand me as an actor. You find out people don't want you to do that. 'Make another *Vera Cruz,*' they say. 'Make another picture like *Trapeze.* Don't do *The Leopard,* for God's sake!'"

The Leopard (1963), set one hundred years earlier, had Lancaster as an aging nobleman alarmed by rapid changes in Italian society, and the rise of the Mafia. I asked him if his decision to go to Italy and work with Visconti, so soon after winning the Oscar, didn't violate all conventional wisdom: Didn't people advise him to stay at home and make big hits?

He looked pained at my question. "I'm sorry, my friend, but you're talking through your hat. I bought eleven copies of *The Leopard* because I thought it was a great novel. I gave it to everyone. But when I was asked to play in it, I said no, that part's for a real Italian. But, lo, the wheels of fortune turned. They wanted a Russian, but he was too old. They wanted Olivier, but he was too busy. When I was suggested, Visconti said, 'Oh, no! A cowboy!' But I had just finished *Judgment at Nuremberg*, which he saw, and he needed three million dollars, which Twentieth Century-Fox would give them if they used an American star, and so the inevitable occurred. And it turned out to be a wonderful marriage. My best work."

He paused. "But you see, nobody told me not to do it. I was the one who said I couldn't do it."

I got the point. At a time when few Hollywood stars could or would march to a different drummer, Burt Lancaster did it his way.

Death of a Dream Palace

November 22, 1994—One day it was winter. The next day there was a wet restlessness in the wind, and it was March. We knew it was March because Dan-Dan the Yo-Yo Man always came to town, right around St. Patrick's Day. He visited all the grade school playgrounds, driving up in his fat maroon Hudson and jumping out with the yo-yo already in the air. He passed out fliers for the annual yo-yo contest at the Princess Theater.

The yo-yo was the first of many things I failed to master in life. Oh, I could Walk the Dog and Loop the Loop. But I was never able to Rock the Baby, and so I was always disqualified on the first Saturday, the day when every kid in Urbana was up on the stage of the Princess with his yo-yo. Two weeks later, when Dan-Dan presided over the finals, a kid would win a new Schwinn bike. The kid was never me.

The Princess closed forever two weeks ago. Friends and relatives sent me clippings in the mail from the *Champaign-Urbana News-Gazette*. "The Last Picture Show in Urbana," the headline said. It was also the only picture show in Urbana. Old clippings show it was in business as early as 1915. It was the place where I learned to love the movies.

In 1950 television was still a rumor in Champaign-Urbana. Some jerk down the street might put up a big antenna and be able to drag in a test pattern from Peoria, but for everybody else, mass media meant the radio and the movies. Over in Champaign they had the Rialto, the Orpheum, the Virginia, the Park, and the Illini, which was down by the railroad station and specialized in movies about nudist camps and the Mademoiselles of Gay Paree. On campus, there was the Co-Ed. In Urbana, there was the Princess, where the program changed twice a week, and there was a Kiddie Matinee on Saturdays.

The Kiddie Matinee was the biggest bargain in town. For exactly nine cents, you got a double feature, five color cartoons, a newsreel, the coming attractions, and a chapter of a serial starring Batman or Sheena, Queen of the Jungle. In March, you got Dan-Dan the Yo-Yo Man.

Your parents dropped you off at noon. You waited in the alley that ran down the side of the theater. Some of the older kids had just finished their Saturday morning dance classes at Thelma Lee Rose's dance studio, which was upstairs over the theater. When the Princess doors opened there was a mad rush for tickets and seats: Front row was the best. Usually your parents gave you twenty cents, which was enough for Jujubes and popcorn, with a penny left over for the jawbreaker machine.

First came the color cartoons, five of them, each exactly six minutes long. After "Th-th-th-that's All, Folks!" came the first half of the double feature, which was always a Western: Hopalong Cassidy, Rex Allen, Roy Rogers, Gene Autry, or those two slightly kinky, sinister figures, Lash LaRue and Whip Wilson, who are due to be rediscovered any day now in camp circles. Then came the serial, the newsreel ("In sunny Cypress Gardens, mermaids learn that what goes up, comes down!") And the ads for Urbana Pure Milk Co. and Reliable Furniture. Then came the second feature, which in my memory is always a cartoon starring the Bowery Boys with Huntz Hall and Leo Gorcey.

For a kid in grade school, going to the movies was one of the few acts in life you could undertake entirely on your own. You chose your own seat. You ate your own popcorn. You lived out the adventures on the screen with an intensity that no later masterpiece by Spielberg or Lucas would ever equal. You laughed, you shrieked, and when the hero even *looked* like he was going to kiss the girl, you groaned.

The Princess in those days was not without its ominous side. Every show started with a notice offering a five-dollar reward "for the apprehension and conviction of vandals." Then came a dire warning: "Ladies! Hang Onto Your Bags! Do Not Leave Them On The Seat Next To You!" In the boys' room, which was downstairs off the lobby, junior high school kids clustered in corners and smoked cigarettes. There was running warfare between the ushers and kids who tried to sneak in through the exit door. And if you bumped against the back of the seat in front of you, some junior thug was likely to turn around and threaten you with a knuckle sandwich.

Eventually I grew too old for the Kiddie Matinees. I became one of the students at Thelma Lee Rose's, learning the fox-trot and the box step. One Friday night Miss Rose held a dance for her students, and I asked a girl from my grade at school, and when we got to the doorway that led up a steep flight of stairs to her studios, I discovered to my humiliation that I had made a mistake and the dance was not until the following week.

My date and I pooled our funds and bought tickets to

The Bridge Over the River Kwai, which was the current feature at the Princess, and it was the best movie I had ever seen in my life. And my date let me put my arm around her, and that was even better.

In the Princess Theater I saw Lawrence of Arabia and The Long, Long Trailer and Pat Boone in April Love and Doris Day in Young at Heart and hundreds of other movies. Eventually I made my way across town for Citizen Kane and Bergman and Fellini at the Park (which had become the Art) and The Immoral Mr. Teas at the Illini (still under the same management).

One day, after I left Champaign-Urbana for the big city to the north, I learned that the Princess had been renamed the Cinema. And it seemed to me that in the very change of name, an era had passed and a crucial mistake had been made, because who would ever rather go to the Cinema than to the Princess?

Eventually they divided the old theater into two smaller auditoriums. They experimented with cheaper ticket prices. Business fell off. The students at the nearby University of Illinois were presumably looking at videos, or logged onto the Internet. A giant multiscreen megaplex opened south of town, on Route 45. You could walk to the Princess, but the new extravaganza wasn't even in Champaign or Urbana.

In the movie The Last Picture Show, the last movie shown in the local theater was Red River, with John Wayne. At the Cinema, the final double bill was Ed Wood, a comedy about a 1950s exploitation film director, and Red Rock West, a triple-cross film noir. The night before they closed, they took in fifty dollars. Admission was three dollars until six P.M., and five dollars afterward. Still the biggest bargain in town.

Better Than Hoop Dreams?

The committee found five better pictures is the glib explanation.

—Bruce Davis, executive director,
Motion Picture Academy

February 22, 1995—Like most everyone who was stunned last week when Hoop Dreams failed to be nominated for an Academy Award as best documentary, I was stumped by one obvious comeback: "Have you seen the five films that *were* nominated?" I had not.

"The nominating committee simply found five films it thought were better," its chairman, Walter Shenson, told me. "We see all the films. Our critics do not." Shenson added that he personally had given Hopp Dreams his highest rating.

He had a point. I had not seen the five nominated films—so how could I be so sure Hoop Dreams was better than them, and deserved to be nominated?

Now I have the answer. I have seen the five films. I was able to view them in the last few days. And I am afraid my answer is: Yes, Hoop Dreams is better than all five of the nominated films, and a lot better than three of them.

There are basically two kinds of documentaries: Those about events that have already happened, and those about events that happen as the film is being made.

In the first category fall traditional documentaries like Ken Burns's Civil War. The second category includes films from the cinema verité movement, in which the camera follows people as they lead their lives, and the filmmakers cannot predict the outcome. This category would include Hoop Dreams, which followed two Chicago youths for five years, from grade school to college, as they followed the dream of becoming professional basketball players.

Some films, of course, straddle these categories; an example would be Michael Moore's Roger & Me, which combines documentary footage of Flint, Michigan, with present-day confrontations between Moore and his targets. Other documentaries, like Errol Morris's The Thin Blue Line, fall outside of both categories: They're basically reconstructions of events.

Great films can be made in all of these styles. What is obvious is that the committee that chose this year's Oscar nominees was fond of documentaries about things that have already happened. They do not seem receptive to cinema verité.

"They're old-fashioned and they go for documentaries made up of talking heads and stock footage," Barbara Kopple told me. The winner of two documentary Oscars (for Harlan County, U.S.A. and American Dream), she makes movies that unfold as they are being photographed; at one point in the earlier film, about a miners' strike, a company guard actually fires a shot at a camera.

—"Talking heads and stock footage." It is important to understand what she means. The filmmaker gathers archival, newsreel, and television footage from as many sources as possible, and ties it together with new footage of people who are interviewed talking about the events we see. Sometimes there is a narrator.

—"Cinema verité." It is helpful to understand this term, too. There is usually not a narrator, and the camera tries to be a fly on the wall, unobserved, as real events unfold. In Hoop Dreams, there are moments we can barely believe—like the one where fifteen-year-old Arthur Agee, recruited by a suburban high school to play basketball, then dropped from the squad and from his paid scholarship, is coolly told his transcript cannot be released until he pays his tuition. In that scene is the kind of truth you do not find any other way.

The volunteers on the academy's documentary nominating committee attend movies four hours a night, two nights a week, for nearly three months. It is a hard job, and one would be grateful for their effort—if only they did a better job. They must like talking heads and stock footage, because all five of their 1995 nominees fall in that category.

Of the five films they nominated, two are not feature-length. One *(Complaints of a Dutiful Daughter)* is forty-four minutes long, and another *(D-Day Remembered)* clocks in at fifty-four minutes. The committee likes brevity; committee confidante and former member Mitchell W. Block, whose company, Direct Cinema, distributes *D-Day Remembered*, was quoted as saying, "If *Hoop Dreams* had come in at a tight two hours, it might have sailed right through." (The film's 165 minutes did not seem too long, however, to the most severe critics of running time, the film editors, who nominated it for an Oscar in their category.)

Viewing the five nominees was, for me, an enjoyable experience. I will be giving four of them favorable reviews.

—Frieda Lee Mock's *Maya Lin: A Strong Clean Vision*, is a film about the young Chinese-American woman who designed the Vietnam Veterans' Memorial in 1982, and about the extraodinary decade in her life that followed. We learn how she entered the competition, and learned she had won it. Then there is the extraordinary bitterness her design aroused. Today, when the memorial is hailed as a triumph of public sculpture, it is easy to forget the vicious attacks by such as Pat Buchanan and Rep. Henry Hyde (who thought it should be white, be above ground, and have a flagpole at the apex). There is an unforgettable shot of Lin's face, her eyes solemn and sad, as her design is attacked at a hearing.

Then we see how well the memorial works today, and the familiar rituals of those visiting it. The film moves on to show Maya Lin's designs for the Civil Rights Memorial in Montgomery, Alabama, and other works, including a sculpture made from tons of broken glass. There is not much about Maya Lin herself in the film—the personal details are limited to memories of childhood—but there is a strong sense of her personality and work, and we wonder that one so young could not only have survived the tempest surrounding the construction of the Vietnam Memorial, but continue to grow without letting fame affect her.

—*A Great Day in Harlem*, by Jean Bach, Matthew Selig, and Susan Peehl, has great imagination in its choice of subject matter. Its inspiration is a historic photograph taken for *Esquire* in 1958, showing all of the jazz greats who could be assembled on one front stoop in Harlem. It interviews as many of the people involved as could be found, including the photographer, Art Kane: the art director, Robert Benton; surviving jazz musicians (Dizzy Gillespie, Art Blakey, Bud Freeman, Buck Clayton, and others). There is also inspired footage of jazz performances from the period, and the movie is introduced by the great 1944 jazz short *Jammin' the Blues*.

What we are left with is a memory of a time gone by, when there really was a jazz community, when the key figures knew one another, when commercialism had not replaced invention. We hear about who came early and who came late, who made them laugh and who made

them worry, who dressed to be noticed and who blended in, and how all the kids from the street got into the shot. It is not only a wonderful film, but a wonderful idea: Starting with an old photograph, a day and an age are brought back to life.

—*Freedom on My Mind* is a film about the flowering of the civil rights movement in the 1950s and 1960s. Produced and directed by Connie Field and Marilyn Mulford, it uses archival footage of freedom riders, sit-ins, marches, voter registration drives, and Klan rallies to evoke the reality of those days, and then talks to some of the surviving participants.

The historic footage, gathered from newsreels and TV broadcasts, is stark and moving, if largely familiar. The present-day witnesses recall those years as the watersheds in their lives, but the film is not always clear about who it is talking to, or why: Bob Moses, who organized voting rights drives, is well established, but unless you already knew that Endesta Ida Mae Holland grew up to be a playwright, you would not learn it here. What is most deeply impressive is the courage of the people of all races who put their lives on the line to end segregation. The movie does well what has been done before; it would be at home in a classroom.

—*Complaints of a Dutiful Daughter,* by Deborah Hoffman, proves the principle that a compelling film can be made without regard for cost or equipment. Seemingly photographed by the director's friend on a home video camera, it tells the story of the gradual descent into Alzheimer's Disease of her mother, Doris. The director tells the story while sitting at her desk, talking into the camera: The early signs of memory loss, the "periods" when her mother grew fixated on note taking, or packing her bags, or stocking up on Lorna Doones.

The film is a little vague on one crucial point. Although it shows Mrs. Hoffman living independently in an apartment and then moving into a residence for Alzheimer's patients, it is unclear about just when the move was made, leaving the impression that the mother was living on her own after the time when that was really safe for her. Of course one of the points of the film is Deborah Hoffman's reluctance to take her proud mother's independence away.

D-Day Remembered, directed by Charles Guggenheim, is the one film of the five I cannot review favorably. It held my attention, yes, but it is limited in its ambition and technique. Here we don't have talking heads, only stock footage: newsreel and Signal Corps film showing the preparations for the landing at Normandy, its terrible toll, and the ultimate Allied success. Much of this footage is very familiar; I have seen certain shots many times before.

The film's narrator tells us things while the film illustrates them, but the pictures and words may not really match. "It was no secret to the Germans that an Allied invasion was imminent," the narrator intones, while we see old Nazi footage of two officers talking, then looking out a window. Who are they? When and where was the shot taken? Were they really discussing the imminent invasion? You don't ask such questions about a film like this.

Along with the narrator (David McCullough), there are many other voices on the sound track—"character voices," including Southerners, British, African-Americans, Irish, and Germans, with bits of comment ("They were first class, the Airborne! They were spot-on!"). The film is vague about these voices; the end credits list many names under "those who were there," but are these the voices of actual participants? Some sound too young.

Now to the bottom line: Are these "five better films" than *Hoop Dreams*? I would say they are not. *Hoop Dreams* was a film that cut to the bone, that gave us the sensation of watching lives unfold. It told more about the lives of young black men in American cities than any other film I have seen. It showed their families, their neighborhoods, their dreams. The filmmakers spent years following William Gates and Arthur Agee, along the way discovering moments I will not soon forget.

The five nominated films are all moving and worthy, and *Maya Lin* and *A Great Day in Harlem* are more than that: They deserve theatrical release, and will get a warm reception from me when they open. *Freedom on My Mind* will provide context and history for those who do not know about the watershed of the civil rights struggle. Anyone who has seen a loved one fight Alzheimer's will be moved by Deborah Hoffman's testimony. And the D-Day film, much as it resembles countless other entries in the "Victory at Sea" genre, records a crucial chapter of history.

Still, none of them is anywhere near the film that *Hoop Dreams* is.

But . . . it's all a matter of opinion, right? I think one thing and you may think another.

True, criticism is all opinion. Well, almost all. Once, a long time ago, a former colleague of mine said in a review that *The Valachi Papers* was better than *The Godfather*. The next time I saw him, I told him: "Every once in a while, matters of opinion stray over into errors of fact."

Ginger Rogers: In Memoriam

April 25, 1995—"Everything Fred did, I did backwards."

That is the most famous line attributed to Ginger Rogers, quoted in every article about her. Whether she ever really said it or not, it was true: She was the partner for the best dancer in the movies, in his best films, and she not only mirrored his every step, she did it in high heels.

Miss Rogers, who died Tuesday at eighty-three, was, in her heyday, one of the best-loved of the great Hollywood stars, not only by the public, but by her co-workers, who found her refreshingly down-to-earth in comparison to the prima donnas of the studio system. Her earthiness may have been just what the Astaire-Rogers team needed; Astaire was so polished and suave he hardly seemed mortal, and the wisecrack at the time was, "She gives him sex appeal, and he gives her class."

Together, they made ten 1930s musicals for RKO that are generally agreed to be the high point of screen dancing. Their two best films were probably *Top Hat* (1935) and *Swing Time* (1936), and other titles included their first partnership in *Flying Down to Rio* (1933), *Shall We Dance?* (1937), and *The Story of Vernon and Irene Castle* (1939). Then they didn't work together until *The Barkleys of Broadway* (1949), their last film together.

Their films were mostly in black and white, which emphasized the elegant lines of their costumes and movements, and Astaire insisted that their dance numbers be filmed in extended full-length shots, so that you could see that they were really dancing. He didn't believe in cutaways to smiling close-ups, and his approach made long, arduous rehearsals necessary: They couldn't do a few steps at a time, but had to perform the whole number perfectly.

"We weren't born Siamese twins," Rogers told *Variety*, "but sometimes you'd think we were. Everywhere I went, people would ask, 'Where's Fred?'" Yet she was a movie star long before she teamed with Astaire. Coached by her mother, Lela, who raised her as a disciplined, clean-living Christian Scientist, she headlined on Broadway in the 1920s and made nineteen movies before her first with Astaire. After their partnership ended in 1939, she won the Academy Award for best actress in 1940 for *Kitty Foyle*, and by 1945 was Hollywood's highest-paid actress.

Rogers was a trouper who kept on working even after the starring roles were no longer being offered. She made seventy-three movies in all, appeared on countless TV shows, and in the 1960s starred in *Hello, Dolly!* on Broadway and toured her own stage show. She was showered with countless awards, although a 1992 tribute to her at the Kennedy Center was marred when Astaire's widow, Robin, refused to grant permission for any of her scenes with Fred to be shown. "I've got lots of others," she said.

Miss Rogers was raised and trained in the golden age of Hollywood studios, and played her starring role to the end. I remember meeting her at the 1983 Montreal Film Festival, where her arrival was delayed after she sent back a limousine because it didn't match her costume and luggage.

The big movie dance star that year was John Travolta, who had followed his hit *Saturday Night Fever* with a sequel, *Staying Alive*, that had just been released. In the movie, one dance scene is done with smoke from dry ice covering the floor, concealing the dancing feet. "Huh!" said Miss Rogers. "The kids today, they think they can dance with their faces."

New Jersey Safari with David Letterman

November 15, 1994—One day last summer, David Letterman, Gene Siskel, and I spent an afternoon wandering up and down a street in East Orange, New Jersey, knocking on people's doors.

"Hi, I'm Dave Letterman," Dave would say. "I have Siskel and Ebert right here. Do you have any questions about the movies?"

Usually they didn't. One man said he hadn't seen a movie since *The Last of the Mohicans,* and I had the strangest feeling he was talking about the 1936 Randolph Scott version. A woman said she was on her way to a funeral. Letterman asked if we could do any yard chores or clean out her gutters while she was gone.

A crew from the Letterman program was taping this door-to-door visit for later use on "The Late Show." As a TV viewer, I'd always been half-convinced that such epics were setups; that the residents of the street were not selected entirely at random, and might even in some cases be actors.

I was surprised to discover that Letterman was indeed winging it. The New Jersey street was chosen so much at random that Letterman almost didn't find it. We set out in a caravan from the Ed Sullivan Theater in mid-Manhattan, and by the time we were in New Jersey the parade had gotten separated and the drivers were calling each other on their cellular phones.

David Letterman is one of the more endearing enigmas on television today. He seems to live his life in public; we see him sitting at home, fretting over a cable TV installer who's late. But it's "Dave" we're looking at—a TV character in a nightly sitcom that also stars his friend, the bandleader Paul Shaffer, and his producer, Robert Morton, forever bobbing and smiling from the shadows, a telephone glued to his ear. The real Letterman is not so easy to see, and although I have appeared on his program perhaps two dozen times over the years, I don't have any clues about his reality.

The origins of the Letterman program can be found, I think, in the old Jack Benny program—which, both on radio and TV, was a program about the making of a program. The cast was made up of Benny, his wife Mary Livingstone, his valet Rochester, and his employees. A typical show involved Jack in meetings with his announcer, Don Wilson, or his sponsor, Lucky Strike. Or he might get involved in the problems of the members of his band. Sometimes guest stars would be misfits in his band, especially the drummer, Frankie Remley, who was said to have a drinking problem.

Letterman (and to various degrees Jay Leno and Johnny Carson) ported the same formula over to TV and applied it to a talk show. On "The Late Show," Don Wilson is played by Paul Shaffer, Robert Morton is the authority figure who the puckish star has to pretend to obey, and the eternally at-sea Calvert DeForest is like all of those annoying characters played on Benny by Mel Blanc. The real subject of the Letterman show *is* the Letterman show, and "Dave" is a character on it just like the others.

That's why it was fascinating to be able to spend a whole afternoon in East Orange with Letterman. It was a rare opportunity to meet him offscreen. I've had a few dressing-room chats with him before TV appearances, but they were cursory goodwill exchanges. Letterman, I suspect, doesn't believe in leaving his performance backstage. He finds the show plays better when his *entire* relationship with a guest is in front of the cameras. I doubt if he knows his perennial favorite guests, like Teri Garr or Charles Grodin, any better than he knows Gene Siskel or me. (In fact, the last time I had lunch with Teri Garr, she asked me what I thought Letterman was really like—although, with Garr, that in *itself* might have been a put-on. You see what tangled webs we weave.)

So there we were, on a lovely summer day in New Jersey, on a street that climbed up a hill so we could look over the river at the towers of Manhattan. The cars were unloaded, the crew began to prepare their gear, and Letterman and Siskel and I stood in the sun and chatted.

What did we talk about? Michael Jordan, mostly. Why he retired from basketball. Why he was playing baseball. Whether he would ever return to basketball. What did male adults do for conversation before the invention of professional sports? Michael Jordan provided an instant frame of reference, shared expertise and knowledge, and a reassuring protection against conversational intimacy. By talking about him, we did not have to talk about anything else.

We knocked on a door, and taped an exchange with the man and wife who lived in the house. I was quietly surprised at how calmly the couple accepted the presence of these strange creatures on their front porch. Decades of watching television has made us all into "personalities." We walked across the street. Knocked on another door.

What I began to pick up on, as we went from door to door like a trio of sitcom salesmen, is how quick Letterman's mind is. How he can find a comic angle in a situation by viewing it slightly askew. He had a writer along with him, and a segment producer, and they had ideas, too (so did Gene and I), but some of the best moments, the ones that made it into the final piece (four hours condensed to four minutes), were David's.

"I have to go to a funeral," that woman said. Another performer might have expressed his sympathy, and withdrawn. Not Letterman. "Can we come along?" he asked. And then he offered our services for yard chores. After the woman had agreed that the gutters could use some cleaning, she drove away in her car. We found ladders and baskets and climbed up to the gutters and filmed ourselves cleaning out the dead leaves. A great comic moment on TV, if I say so myself. But Letterman was not finished. Later, on our way back to Manhattan, we borrowed a funeral home, and shot low-angle footage of ourselves ostensibly filing past a coffin.

Some of the residents of the street did not know who we

were—not Siskel and myself, which was quite plausible, but also not Letterman. One woman worked nights in an emergency room, and so never saw "The Late Show." She was cool to us, and we repaired to the sidewalk to plan our next move. Then her mother-in-law explained who Letterman was, and she hurried out to offer him a gift: an original railway sign from her husband's collection. Then we talked to her about the movies. She hardly ever went.

At another house, a middle-aged man and his adult son appeared at the door. Both were drivers for a local bakery. Their routes were run before dawn; they were home in the afternoons. No, they never went to the movies, because they were always in bed too early. "Then can we offer you one hundred dollars to shave off your mustaches?" Letterman asked. Gee, said the older man; he'd had his mustache since Vietnam. Letterman produced two crisp new hundred-dollar bills. Both men agreed.

Walking into their house to help them shave off their mustaches, I had thoughts of my own. Was this a proper role for me to play? I take my film criticism seriously. I doubted that Pauline Kael, my heroine, would spend an afternoon like this in New Jersey and find herself shaving off any mustaches. And was the show somehow, in a subtle way, *using* these two men? Letterman could spare the two hundred dollars. So did that mean he was buying them—buying their mustaches, even one that had been growing since Vietnam?

By now, we were in the spotless kitchen of the home, and the men had bath towels around their necks and were applying shaving cream, while the cameras rolled. My eyes caught Gene's, and I guessed that he was having some of the same thoughts. But a few minutes later, as we were leaving, the man and his son were breaking up with laughter over the whole episode: You're sitting at home and David Letterman knocks on your door and gives you one hundred dollars to shave off your mustache! How are the guys at the bakery ever going to believe it? When is this gonna play on TV?

And then I thought that I had taken the situation too seriously. It belonged to that genre of Letterman programming that could be described as High Goofy. It has absolutely no purpose other than the one it obviously achieved: to take the routine of an ordinary day, and inject a grin into it.

Later on, Letterman gathered his cast and crew, and several of the neighbors, and we sat along a low stone wall and took off our socks and looked for ticks. After all, a visit to the countryside in wild East Orange can be dangerous, and who in Manhattan has not heard of Lyme disease? And then we headed back to Manhattan.

There was one revealing moment. Inside one house (I will not reveal the details) we saw something that put us all in mind of mortality and the inexorable passage of time. Back out on the sidewalk, Letterman was quiet, thinking

about it, and then he said, "That's exactly how it goes. You're young and the whole world is ahead of you, and then one day you're not young anymore, and the whole world is behind you, and it's all over."

Then we talked some more about the National Basketball Association.

Did I get any other insights into the "real" David Letterman? Yes, I did. I got a few when the two of us exchanged minutely detailed arcania about the Steak 'n' Shake, a restaurant chain that is popular in his hometown, Indianapolis, and in mine, Urbana-Champaign. We knew the slogans by heart: "Four Ways to Enjoy: Car, Table, Counter, and TakHomaSak!" We knew that the chain "uses only government-inspected choice cuts of meat, ground in our own commissaries." That the motto was "In Sight, It Must Be Right!" And that the founder of the chain was named A.H. (Gus) Belt, whose signature on the menu used to be preceded by the words, "Thanks For Your Liberal Patronage!"

Talking with Letterman about the Steak 'n' Shake, I suddenly felt a connection over the years to his adolescence, in which he had sat with his buddies in those restaurants, and read the menus, and realized that they were very funny. Others saw them as merely menus, and ordered their Double Steakburgers and Tru-Flavor Shakes, and were satisfied. But I can visualize young Dave Letterman, his gap tooth revealed in a goofy grin, as he reads the menu aloud to his friends: "*Man, oh man!* Specializing In Selected Foods With a Desire to Please the Most Discriminating!" And in that moment, I foresee his entire career, and I know all about the "real" David Letterman that I really need to know.

A Nighttime Talk Show Mystery

November 15, 1994—It is an open secret that the "spontaneous exchanges" on talk shows are somewhat planned in advance. What has surprised me is how often the hosts depart entirely from the script. In many appearances on the Leno, Carson, and Letterman programs, I would estimate that less than half of what happened was foreseen, and in some cases entire appearances were ad-libbed. The "pre-interview" is more like a safety net.

The routine for a guest on one of the nighttime talk shows is that, a day before the planned appearance, you have a telephone conversation with the segment producer. He or she wants to know what's on your mind, what has happened lately in your life, what's funny or amusing. You try to think of interesting stuff.

In the case of Gene Siskel and myself, the producers hold separate interviews, because we don't want to know what the other guy may be thinking of discussing. We find we work better together when it's spontaneous.

That once led to an episode on the Letterman show that

is still so cloaked in mystery that neither Gene nor I quite understand what happened.

As nearly as I can reconstruct it, Gene suggested to a segment producer that it might be fun to tell David a story that Gene and I call "The Buddy Hackett Story." (See below.) When the producer broached this idea to me, in a separate call, I was annoyed: "That's *my* story!" I said. "Gene shouldn't tell it. Also, I tell it faster and funnier than he does. He always gets bogged down in boring minutiae about where everybody was sitting when the episode took place."

The next day, we arrived at the Ed Sullivan Theater to tape the show. The segment producer came to me privately and said, "Gene is going to try to tell the story. But you should interrupt him and insist on telling it yourself. He knows you are going to interrupt."

The producer then went to Gene and told him that when he started to tell the story, I would interrupt him.

On the air, Letterman set us up with a straight line. Gene started telling the story. I interrupted him. He attempted to continue telling the story. I insisted that it was *my* story, and I should tell it. Gene was getting annoyed, I could tell, and said something like, "We're wasting a lot of valuable network time here." I pushed ahead, insisting that I should tell the story. Gene wouldn't let me. In my mind, I was fully prepared to do whatever was necessary to either (a) tell the story, or (b) prevent Gene from doing so.

The situation at this point was off the map, and to the viewers might have seemed like genuine anger. And then Letterman broke in: "Boys, boys, boys! *I'll* tell the story."

And he did—perfectly.

During the commercial break, Siskel was unhappy with me. The situation had gotten completely out of hand, he said. I had been bullheaded in my insistence on telling the story. I should have let him tell the story. But it was *my* story, I said!

After the show, Siskel, thinking it over, grew more objective. "If I truly thought the situation was out of control, then I should have just let you tell the story."

"I thought I was doing the right thing," I said. "I thought I was *supposed* to keep interrupting you."

"No," said Gene, "I was supposed to finish the story."

Our eyes met. We realized that in our separate briefings we had *both* been told to tell the story. Neither one of us had been prepared to cave in to the other. Given our mutual stubbornness, it was inevitable that we would both insist on pressing ahead.

So . . . had we been set up? Was Letterman planning all along to tell the story? Had the segment producer deliberately given us instructions that would lead to a fight?

Letterman had seemed so spontaneous as he told the story. It seemed like he had brilliantly defused a potentially unpleasant situation. Was this an example of skillful improvisation? Perhaps, but then again, he *had* been com-

pletely prepared. He knew the story by heart. Had he intended to tell it? Or was this just an example of his ability to think quickly?

I don't know for sure. Neither does Siskel.

"That was great TV," the producer, Robert Morton, told us after the show. I still don't know who deserved the compliment, or exactly why.

**   **   **

THE BUDDY HACKETT STORY

Jack Lemmon, Gene Siskel, and I were sitting at a table in the Gaslight Club in Chicago, in the mid-1970s. At a nearby table, four women were celebrating a birthday. One of them headed our way with a menu.

"She wants an autograph," Lemmon said.

He was right. The woman looked straight at Siskel and said, "Aren't you Gene Siskel? It's my friend's birthday, and she'd love to have your autograph."

"Why, sure," said Gene, with a big grin, signing the menu.

"You've made my day!" the woman said.

"Your day is far from over," Gene said. "Did you notice who is sitting right here next to me?"

"Jack Lemmon!" cried the woman, "Oh, my God! Mr. Lemmon—I'm so sorry I didn't notice you! We see Mr. Siskel on our local TV, and I never thought I'd see you in Chicago!"

"Think nothing of it," Lemmon said graciously, signing the menu.

"This has *really* made my day!" the woman said.

"And," said Siskel, "your day *still* isn't over! Look who's sitting right here!"

He pointed to me.

The woman's face broke into a delighted smile. "Why," she said, "if it isn't Buddy Hackett!"

Secrets of *Pulp Fiction*

Charlottesville, Va., May 2, 1995—For four days we sat in the dark, tiptoeing through *Pulp Fiction* one scene at a time, using a laserdisc machine so you could freeze a frame or slowly creep through the movie. There were about three hundred of us, and democracy ruled: Anybody could make an observation, and we'd stop and discuss it. Our mission: to take a *very* close look at this labyrinthine film.

Of course there are people who intensely dislike *Pulp Fiction*. It is possibly the most unpopular movie ever to gross one hundred million dollars at the American box office. I've received mail from those who hate the movie. They say it is too violent, too graphic, too obscene, or "makes no sense." Many say they walked out after twenty, thirty, or sixty minutes. (Given its circular time line, of course it made no sense to them; this is literally a movie where you have to wait until you can say, "This is where we came in.")

Among those who admire it, however, Quentin Tarantino's film is the most passionately loved and obsessed-about film of recent years; the discussions about its smallest details have reached the same pitch as the furor over Kubrick's *2001,* which inspired a book that transcribed even the directions for the Zero Gravity Toilet. On campuses and among younger viewers, there is no other recent film approaching its appeal.

We were analyzing *The Fiction,* as it is sometimes called, at the University of Virginia, where I was spending a week as the first Kluge Film Fellow. Patricia Kluge, founder of the Virginia Festival of American Film, sponsors the fellowship on Thomas Jefferson's beautiful campus (although what Jefferson would have thought about Vincent Vega and Honey Bunny is hard to imagine).

I've done shot-by-shot analyses of dozens of films, from *Citizen Kane* to *The Silence of the Lambs,* and I find that when you gather a lot of serious film people in the dark and invite them to talk during the movie, somebody will have the answer to every question.

At Virginia, for example, one of the voices in the dark was unmistakably that of a young boy; he sounded about eleven. I wondered if he should be watching this R-rated film. That was before he started citing specific line references from the screenplay, which he had downloaded from the Internet. It was his twelfth viewing (and, yes, he was accompanied by a parent).

At the end of the four days, my own admiration for the movie had only deepened. It is more subtle and complex than at first it seems; the Oscar-winning screenplay, by Tarantino and Roger Avary, turns out to contain the answers to mysteries that baffle viewers in a first viewing, and it makes connections that only occur to you after time.

The film tells interlocking stories, which unfold out of chronological order, so that the movie's ending hooks up with the beginning, most of its middle happens after the ending, and a major character is onscreen after he has been shot dead. Why is the movie told in this way? For three reasons, perhaps: (1) Because Q.T., as his fans call him, is tired of linear plots that slog wearily from A to Z; (2) to make the script reveal itself like "hypertext," in which "buttons" like the gold watch or "foot massage" lead to payoffs like Butch's story or Vincent's date from hell; and (3) because each of the main stories ends with some form of redemption. The key redemption—the decision by Jules (Samuel L. Jackson) to retire from crime after his life is saved by a "miracle"—is properly placed at the end of the film even though it doesn't happen at the end of the story.

The first time I saw the movie, in May 1994 at the Cannes Film Festival, I thought it was very violent. As I saw it a second and third time, I realized it wasn't as violent as I thought—certainly not by the standards of modern action movies. It *seems* more violent because it often delays a payoff with humorous dialogue, toying with us. Our body count at Virginia turned up only seven major deaths. (Read no further if you do not want to know major plot details.) The dead:

—Three guys in the apartment—one in the chair, one on the couch, and one in the bathroom—are killed by Vincent (John Travolta) and Jules (Jackson).

—Marvin, the fourth guy from the apartment, is accidentally killed while sitting in the backseat of Jules and Vincent's car.

—Vincent Vega is killed by Butch (Bruce Willis).

—Two men are killed at the pawnshop: Maynard, the store owner, and his friend Zed.

—In addition, there are two unseen or implied deaths, of the boxer killed in the ring by Butch, and of "the Gimp," dressed in leather in the pawnshop basement.

Against this body count, there are several people who are saved in the movie. Mia (Uma Thurman) is brought back from the dead after an overdose; Marcellus Wallace (Ving Rhames) is saved by Butch in the basement; and many potential victims in the coffee shop are saved after Jules talks Honey Bunny (Amanda Plummer) and Pumpkin (Tim Roth) into calling off their stickup. And, of course, the lives of Jules and Vincent are saved, when a volley of shots in the apartment misses them. Jules chooses to call this a miracle, a sign from God, and retires from crime. Vincent shrugs it off, and pays the price. There is also an important, hilarious, subplot about the saving of Butch's gold watch.

One thing we kept noticing during our shot-by-shot odyssey was that much of the violence is off-screen. When the guys in the apartment are shot, the camera is on Jules or Vincent, not on the victims. When the hypodermic needle goes into Mia's chest, the camera cuts away at the last instant to a reaction shot (instant comic relief from Rosanna Arquette, who is into body-piercing, and is delighted to have witnessed the ultimate piercing). The gunshot in the backseat of the car is offscreen. The violence in the pawnshop basement is graphic, but within the boundaries of standard movie fights.

The more you watch the movie, the more you're convinced that there is a hidden spiritual level in the plot. Much has to do with the famous briefcase which belongs to Marcellus Wallace, and which Jules and Vincent capture in the apartment. We never see its contents, which emit a golden glow. There have been countless theories about what's in it ("an Egg MacGuffin," said somebody at Virginia), but of course we will never know. What we can notice is that the combination to its lock is "666"—the sign of Satan. That has led to speculation that the Band-Aid on the back of Marcellus's neck conceals the number "666." Is Marcellus the devil? That's unknowable, but reflect that Jules, who believes he has been saved by God, lives—while Vincent, the scoffer, dies.

He's shot by Butch as he comes out of the bathroom

(lots of things happen in this movie while people are in the john). A detail that escaped me the first time, however, is that Butch uses a gun belonging to Marcellus, who left it on the counter of Butch's apartment while going to get coffee and doughnuts. (Marcellus has joined Vincent in the stakeout for Butch because, of course, Jules has already resigned.) "The guys who wrote this screenplay weren't lazy," someone said at Virginia; "it's interesting how they worked all this detail in even though most people will miss it."

A theme running through the movie is that many of the weapons do not work or are not used as they are intended (the gun that misses Jules, the gun that kills Vincent, the gun that accidentally kills the guy in the backseat, the guns in the coffee shop robbery, the guns belonging to the pawnshop guys). After Jules is converted, his own gun *prevents* violence in the coffee shop.

On the film's less significant side, there are also many secrets to discover. In Jack Rabbit Slim's, for example, the waiter playing Buddy Holly (Steve Buscemi) was Mr. Pink in Q.T.'s *Reservoir Dogs*. Three other cast members from *RD* (Tim Roth, Harvey Keitel, and Tarantino) are also in *PF*. There is a Vic Vega in *RD,* perhaps related to Vincent Vega.

As Butch sneaks up on his own apartment, the words "Jack Rabbit Slim's" emerge from an open window he walks past. One particularly neat bit of continuity happens in the pawnshop, where there is a neon sign for Killian's Red beer. Some of the letters are burnt out, so the sign says only "Kill Ed." Later, when Butch escapes on Zed's motorcycle, he looks at the key ring, which has a big metal "Z." Add the Z to the sign and you get "Kill Zed," which is what happened. The motorcycle has the word "Grace" painted on its gas tank, and as Butch escapes—well, there, but for the grace of God . . .

There were two visual touches we discussed a lot. One is the golden glow which mysteriously suffuses the screen as Jules and Vincent open fire in the apartment; is it connected somehow with the briefcase? Does it link the devil's case with the devil's work? Another is a curious head-on shot of Bruce Willis, who looks straight at the camera while Marcellus Wallace instructs him to fix a fight. The lighting is used to shadow exactly half of Willis's face; a line runs down his forehead, nose, and chin. Or . . . is it lighting? The line of demarcation between light and shadow is so sharply defined that we wondered if makeup was used to augment the effect. We looked at the scene repeatedly using freeze frames, but were unable to decide.

One element I've barely touched on is the film's humor. The dialogue is very funny, and some of it echoes great literature in a modern, profane form: The opening exchange between Jules and Vincent about what the French call Quarter Pounders, for example, is a reminder of the conversation between Jim and Huckleberry Finn about why the French don't speak English. Jules is constantly quoting what he identifies as Ezekiel 25:17 from the Bible, and although some of the words are the same, he has embroidered a lot. (See below.)

A basic strategy in the film is to use humorous dialogue to delay the payoff of a moment of violence. While the Uma Thurman character is dying on the floor, for example, Travolta and Eric Stoltz have a hysterical debate over how to use the hypodermic needle.

This strategy is set up in the opening shot, where Jules and Vincent have a long, funny discussion about foot massage while walking down a long hotel corridor. The shot is done in one unbroken take. They arrive in front of the door to the fatal apartment, decide it is not yet time to enter, and walk further down the hall to continue their discussion. But now the camera no longer joins them; it stays planted in front of the door, and pans to look at them, walking away. The visual language says that the apartment is the first priority; the camera seems almost impatient as the discussion continues, and that builds tension.

Pulp Fiction delights some audience members and disturbs others, I think, for the same reason: because it toys with their expectations. It does not seem willing to play by the rules. It imposes its own order on the material. Just at a time when American action films have seemed bogged down in a morass of formulaic plots, here is one which throws out everything they teach in the Hollywood screenwriting workshops and reinvents a genre from scratch. *Pulp Fiction* is likely to be the most influential film of the next five years, and for that we can be thankful, because it may have freed us from uncounted predictable formula films.

★★   ★★   ★★

WHAT JULES SAYS

The hitman Jules (Samuel L. Jackson) frequently quotes "Ezekiel 25:17" in *Pulp Fiction,* but in fact he has greatly altered the Bible passage. The actual passage says:

"And I will execute great vengeance upon them with furious rebukes; and they shall know that I am the Lord, when I shall lay my vengeance upon them."

Here's what Jules says, adding bits from the twenty-third Psalm and his own rhetoric:

"The path of the righteous man is beset on all sides by the iniquities of the selfish and the tyranny of evil men. Blessed is he who, in the name of charity and good will, shepherds the weak through the valley of darkness, for he is truly his brother's keeper and the finder of lost children. And I will strike down upon thee with great vengeance and with furious anger those who attempt to poison and destroy my brothers. And you will know my name is the Lord when I lay my vengeance upon thee."

How to Attend a Film Festival

Yes, you can attend a film festival. Not just the one in your hometown, but even the glittering events in Venice, Berlin, and Toronto. Almost all film festivals are open to the public, a fact the public does not always realize. For movie fans, the combination of a film festival and a holiday destination makes an attractive package—going to the movies gets you in off the slopes or the beaches, and allows you to meet fellow movie buffs instead of boring ordinary people.

The Cannes Festival, held in the middle of May every year, is of course the largest and most famous in the world, but also one of the most difficult to get credentials for. It's essentially a trade fair, and it's best if you have connections. However, some tickets are made available to the public on a daily basis, and other tickets, especially to the trade screenings, are to be found if you are enterprising. Most other festivals, however, actively encourage people who aren't in the business. Of the big ones I've attended, my favorites are Montreal in August and Toronto in September, which are the two big "destination" festivals in North America. Both are particularly eager to accomodate visitors, and offer ticket and hotel packages.

The two major independent American festivals are Telluride, over the Labor Day weekend, which combines premieres with tributes and revivals, and Sundance (Park City, Utah), which is the top showcase for American independent work. Two of my other favorites are the Virginia Festival of American Film, in Charlottesville in late October, which specializes in U.S. films; and the Hawaii festival in November, concentrating on films from the Pacific rim. Hawaii, which recently added a sidebar event dedicated to the giant-screen IMAX and Omnimax films, has an aloha spirit all its own.

Most of the big-city festivals in the United States cater mostly to people who live in the cities themselves, and attract fewer out-of-town visitors than the Canadian festivals. The big five are New York, Chicago, Los Angeles, San Francisco, and Seattle. The smaller U.S. festivals, like Denver, Cleveland, Dallas, Houston, Philadelphia, and Miami, likewise are mostly aimed at locals.

Overseas, the Edinburgh Film Festival is part of the amazing explosion of festivals that takes over the town for most of the month of August. The movies have to compete with theater, classical music, dance, books, and a fringe theater festival that attracts more than five hundred companies. The Venice Film Festival, in late summer, is an opportunity to visit the beautiful city and sample the Bellinis at the Hotel Excelsior and the gossip at the Lion Bar. And here's a nice pairing: The Deauville Festival, in France, specializes in American films. The Sarasota festival, in Florida, specializes in French films.

After Cannes, the most important European festival is either Venice or Berlin, but many smaller festivals, such as San Sebastian, Cambridge, and Deauville, have created niches for themselves. Most of the countries of Eastern Europe have festivals which actively recruit Western visitors.

There are also smaller regional film festivals in many American cities, and specialist festivals devoted to science fiction and fantasy, animation, and documentaries. Dusty and Joan Cohl, founders of the Toronto festival, even launched a Floating Film Festival in 1991, and plan to cruise the Caribbean in February 1996 while presenting films every day.

Here's where to write for information on some of the key festivals, arranged alphabetically, as compiled with the research assistance of Monica Eng and with information from *Variety,* the showbiz bible:

Austin, Texas. "Heart of Film" festival, celebrating screenwriters. October.
707 Rio Grande, #101, Austin, TX 78701.

Asian-American Film Festival. July.
Asian Cinevision, 32 E. Broadway, 4th floor, New York, NY 10002.

Baltimore. March.
C/o Museum of Art, Art Museum Drive, Baltimore, MD 21218.

Berlin. Early February.
Budapester Str. 50, D-1000, Berlin 30, Germany.

Brussels. Late January.
Place Madou 8, Bte. 5, Brussels, Belgium.

Cambridge. July.
Arts Cinema, 8 Market Passage, Cambridge CB2 3PF England.

Cannes. Mid-May.
71 rue du Faubourg St. Honore, 75008 Paris, France.

Chicago. October.
415 N. Dearborn, Chicago, IL 60610.

Cleveland. April.
1621 Euclid Ave., Ste. 428, Cleveland, OH 44115.

Cork. October.
C/o Triskel Arts Center, Tobin Street, Cork, Ireland.

Dallas. April.
USA Film Festival, 2917 Swiss Ave., Dallas, TX 75204.

Deauville (American Cinema).
Early September.
33 Ave. MacMahon, 75017, Paris,
France.

Denver. Mid-October.
1430 Larimer Sq., #201, Denver,
CO 80202.

Edinburgh. August.
Film House, 88 Lothian Rd.,
Edinburgh, EH3 9BZ, Scotland.

Gdansk (Polish Film Festival).
September.
Piwna 22, P.O. Box Nr. 192, 80–831
Gdansk, Poland.

Hawaii (Films of Asia-Pacific).
Early November.
700 Bishop St., Ste. 400,
Honolulu, HI 96813.

Houston. Late April.
Box 56566, Houston, TX 77256.

Indianapolis (Heartland Film
Festival). October.
613 N. East St., Indianapolis,
IN 46202.

Jerusalem. July.
P.O. Box 8561, Jerusalem 91083,
Israel.

London. November.
National Film Theater, South Bank,
London SE1, England.

Los Angeles. June.
AFI Festivals, 2021 N. Western
Ave., Los Angeles, CA 90027.

Melbourne. Mid-June.
G.P.O. Box 296, Fitzroy, Victoria
3065, Australia.

Miami. Early February.
444 Brickell Ave., Ste 229,
Miami, FL 33131.

Mill Valley. Early October.
38 Miller Ave., Ste. 6, Mill Valley,
CA 94941.

Minneapolis/St. Paul. Rivertown
Film Festival. Late April, early
May.
University Film Society, 425
Ontario Street SE. Minneapolis,
MN 55414.

Montreal. Late August, early
September.
1455 rue de Maisonneuve Ouest,
Montreal, Quebec H3G 1M8,
Canada.

Moscow. July.
10 Khokhlovsky Pereulok, 109028
Moscow, Russia.

Munich. Late June, early July.
Kaiserstrasse 39, D-8000 Munich
40, Germany.

Newark Black Film Festival.
Wednesdays, late June through July.
Newark Museum, 49 Washington
St., Newark, NJ 07101.

New York. Mid-September.
Film Society of Lincoln Center, 140
W. 65th St., New York, NY 10023.

Palm Springs (Comedy).
Mid-January.
Box 2230, Palm Springs, CA
92263–2230.

Philadelphia (Philafilm). July.
P.O. Box 43039, Philadelphia, PA
19129.

St. Petersburg, Russia. Late
June.
10 Kamennoostrovsky Ave., St.
Petersburg, Russia 197101.

San Francisco. Early May.
San Francisco Film Society, 1521
Eddy St., San Francisco, CA 94115.

San Sebastian. September.
Apartado Correos 397, Box 397,
20080 San Sebastian, Spain.

Sarasota. November.
Cine-World Film Festival P.O. Box
3378, Sarasota, FL 34230

Seattle. May.
801 E. Pine St., Seattle, WA 98122.

**Spoleto Festival of Two
Worlds.** Late June.
Via Cesare Beccaria, 18, Rome
00196, Italy.

Sundance (Park City, Utah). Third
week in January.
C/o Sundance Institute, P. O. Box
16450, Salt Lake City, UT 84116

Sydney. Mid-June.
P.O. Box 25, Glebe, N.S.W. 2037,
Australia.

Taormina. Late July.
Taormima Arte, Via Pirandello 31,
Taormina 98039, Italy.

Telluride, Colorado. Labor Day
Weekend.
C/o National Film Preserve, Box
B1156, Hanover, NH 03755.

Tokyo. September.
No. 3, Asano Daisan Bldg., 2-4-19
Ginza Chou-ku, Tokyo 104, Japan.

**Toronto International Film
Festival.** Second week in
September.
2 Carlton Street, Suite 1600,
Toronto, Ontario M5B 1J3, Canada.

Vancouver. Mid- to late
September.
303–788 Beatty St., Vancouver, BC
V6B 2M1, Canada.

Venice. Early September.
Ca. Giustinian, San Marco, 30124
Venice, Italy.

**Vevey, Switzerland, Comedy Film
Festival.** Late July,
Place de la Gare 5, CH-1800, Vevey,
Switzerland.

**Virginia Festival of American
Film.** Charlottesville, last weekend in
October.
Box 3697, 104 Midmont Lane,
University of Virginia,
Charlottesville, VA 22903.

Wine Country. Mid-July.
Box 303, Glen Ellen, CA 95442.

A Movie Lover's Source List

Where can I find this movie?

Every year I receive letters from readers of the *Companion* who complain they can't find many titles in their local video stores. Although many communities have stores that take pride in the range of their stock, other video stores practice a hit-oriented philosophy, and stock multiple copies of the latest hits instead of extending their range a little.

It is possible, however, to rent or buy virtually every one of the thousands of movies on tape and laserdisc. Updated and expanded for 1996, here is a list of companies that rent or sell videos by mail. Many of them have toll-free 800 numbers and accept credit cards over the phone. Most of them issue catalogs, and a few of the catalogs are particularly informative. Four of the most useful and comprehensive are Movies Unlimited, for almost all mainstream videos; Facets Video, for art, foreign, classic, documentary, silent, experimental, and underground videos; Loonic Video, for animation; and Sight & Sound, for imported laserdiscs.

Captain Bijou. P. O. Box 87, Toney, AL 35773-0087. Publishes fat bulletins filled with rare videos, original movie posters, still photos, movie mags, tin signs, comics, sci-fi, autographs, collectibles, etc. 1-205-852-0198.

Complete Guide to Special Interest Videos. The new 1995–96 edition lists ten thousand videos you'll probably not find in the local stores, including how-to, language, cooking, travel, and more. A unique resource, $19.95 from James-Robert Publishing, 15838 N. 62nd St., Scottsdale, AZ 85254-1988. (1-800-383-8811). Also available on CD-ROM and PC versions.

Facets Video. 1517 W. Fullerton, Chicago, IL 60614. The nation's leading specialists in subtitled, classic, documentary, and independent films, plus a wide range of American films, and the best stock of foreign films in the nation. Quality is a criteria; Facets does not stock potboilers. Their yearly catalog ($9.95 including shipping) has the page size of a tabloid newspaper, runs 288 pages, and lists thousands of VHS and laserdisc titles including even obscure underground films. They also publish a bimonthly catalog of new releases, special promotions, etc., for $12 a year. Best deal is $14.95 a year for both catalogs. They rent-by-mail most tapes in the catalog. 1-800-331-6197, or in Illinois, 1-312-281-9075.

Home Film Festival. P.O. Box 2032, Scranton, PA 18501-9952. The original rent-by-mail people, with a large selection of titles that rent at $6 for one, $11 for two, $16 for three (plus shipping), and can be kept for three days. They ship to you via UPS; you mail tapes back by U.S. mail, in return packaging that is included. HFF gives a member's discount on purchases over $50. For the 192-page catalog, call 1-800-258-3456, or, in Philadelphia, 1-800-633-3456.

Ken Crane's LaserDisk. 15251 Beach Blvd., Westminster, CA 92683. Claims to stock all available laserdiscs, gives a 10 percent discount, ships free via UPS. Issues periodic sixty-page catalogs, sometimes has special sale titles. 1-800-624-3078.

Laser Craze. 329 Newbury St., Boston, MA 02115. Stocks and discounts thousands of discs, publishes *Picture This*, a bimonthly magazine and catalog. 1-617-267-3311.

Laser Disk Newsletter is a monthly for fanatics about sound and picture quality, edited and published by Douglas Pratt, author of the authoritative *Laser Video Disc Companion*, who seems to inspect every new disc a frame at a time. Comprehensive reviews, heavy on the technical specs, of most new laserdiscs. No other publication provides such minute detail. Pratt only reviews and does not sell. Sample copy free; subscription $35 a year, from P.O. Box 420, East Rockaway, NY 11518. 1-800-551-4914.

Laser Video File. This is a glossy paperback biannual, a cooperative effort of the laser industry, that attempts to list every single laserdisc available—some 6,400 titles—including karaoke discs. Subscription $9.95 from Box 828, Westwood, NJ 07675.

Laser Video Library rents high-priced laserdiscs by mail. Rentals range from $15 to $25 on discs retailing in the $89 to $200 range. Primarily a rental service, although discs can be purchased at a 10 percent discount. Tim Mullen rents only the expensive ones. Box 663, Loveland, OH 45140; 1-800-765-8397.

Laserviews, published ten times a year, a slick magazine devoted to news, interviews, reviews, and technical articles about laserdiscs. $2.50 for a sample from 3-A Oak Road, Fairfield, NJ 07004.

Loonic Video. 2022 Taraval St., Suite 6427, San Francisco, CA 94116. The founder, Lory-Michael Ringuette, is a B-movie actor *(The Video Dead)* who searches out lost, unusual, and cult films and cartoons. Among the titles in Loonic's latest mailing: *Mars Needs Women*, 1930s Tom & Jerry cartoons, Jayne Mansfield's unknown last film, old Bob & Ray television shows, cartoons, vintage Late Late Shows. Most tapes are $15.95. Catalog is $1. New number: 1-510-526-681.

Metro Golden Memories. 5425 W. Addison St., Chicago, IL 60641. Specialists in rare movies from 1912 through about 1965, and tapes of classic television shows. They publish a free catalog of old radio shows from 1932–55. 1-312-736-133.

Movies Unlimited. 6736 Castor Avenue, Philadelphia, PA 19149. Their catalog is enormous and doubles as a reference work on movies available on video. The 1994 edition was telephone-book-sized at 736 pages, cost $7.95 plus $3 shipping, and lists over 30,000 titles, including VHS, Beta, and laserdiscs. Regular updates are issued during the year. Sales only. Orders at 1-800-523-0823, or to order a catalog call 1-800-466-8437.

Picture Start, Inc./Kid Start Entertainment. 1725 W. Catalpa Avenue, 3rd Floor, Chicago, IL 60640. Independently produced award-winning short and feature films in video, for sale or rental, and 16mm films for rental. Hard-to-find experimental, animated, documentary, and underground films, plus traveling programs of festival winners. Useful as a source of short subjects for a film society. The 120-page catalog is descriptive and illustrated. 1-312-769-2489, fax: 1-312-769-4467.

Proud To Be . . . is a mail order company specializing in black-oriented videos. They publish a catalog and *The Collector's Corner* newsletter and have movies by and about blacks in such categories as children's films, sports, opera, theater, dance, comedy, gospel, reggae, and educational documentaries, as well as many features. One Kendall Square, Building 600, Suite 125, Cambridge, MA 02139; 1-800-441-4588.

Quality Comics and Video Store specializes in offbeat, cult, and B-grade materials, and describes itself as "a full-service cultural cesspool." They rent and sell by mail, and the catalog is seventy-five cents from 20 Division St., Somerville, NJ 08876.

Sight & Sound Laser Disks. 27 Jones Rd., Waltham, MA 02154. In Japan, more people watch laserdiscs than tapes, and the quality of some Japanese discs is legendary. In addition to discounting virtually all new U.S. discs, this company imports Japanese pressings (in the original language plus Japanese subtitles). "The owners are dedicated in a way that true artists are dedicated," writes *Companion* reader Charles Thomas of Cambridge, MA. Catalogs issued monthly. A new specialized catalog of Japanese and Hong Kong imports, at 420 pages the only one of its kind, is $39.95. 1-617-894-8633, or fax 1-617-894-9329. They also have an on-line bulletin board; call for info.

Perfect Vision. This is a unique quarerly magazine, written by and for video and audio fanatics. No other publication has more exacting standards, and it's a must for operators of high-end home entertainment systems. Each issue contains some 150 tightly packed pages of articles about movies and video, technical and artistic controversies, and reviews of new equipment. $7.50 an issue, $26 a year. Box 360, Sea Cliff, NY 11579, or order by credit card at 1-800-222-3201.

TLA Video. 1520 Locust, Philadelphia, PA 19102. Prides itself on a wide-ranging selection including many foreign films and independent features. Their catalog includes helpful, knowledgeable thumbnail descriptions indicating that the TLA folks have viewed most of the videos themselves. Yearly catalog (338 pages) is $5.95 plus shipping and handling. 1-800-333-8521, 1-215-922-3838, or 1-215-790-1513.

Video Learning Library. Specializes in nontheatrical videos, special-interest, instructional and how-to films. More than ten thousand titles. If you want to learn how to do something— plant a garden, speak a language— this is the place. Their 705-page catalog is $19.95. They rent by mail and

sell. 15838 N. 62nd St., Scottsdale, AZ 85254. 1-800-345-1441.

Viewfinders. P.O. Box 1665, Evanston, IL 60204. Publishes a seventy-two-page *Catalog of Uncommon Video* including animation, art, ballet, classical music, documentaries, jazz, nature, and opera, and Beta is represented on many titles. 1-800-342-3342; in Illinois, 1-708-869-0600.

Whole Toon Catalog. Box 369, Issaquah, WA 98027-0369. They boast "the most comprehensive selection of animation on earth," and showcase it in an illustrated ninety-four-page catalog that doubles as a reference book. Included: The fifty greatest cartoons of all time, and where to find them. 1-206-391-8747; fax 1-206-391-9064.

One Hundred Scenes in One Hundred Years

For the centennial of cinema, one hundred great moments from the movies:

• Clark Gable in *Gone With the Wind:* "Frankly, my dear, I don't give a damn."

• Buster Keaton standing perfectly still while the wall of a house falls over upon him; he is saved by being exactly placed for an open window.

• Charlie Chaplin being recognized by the little blind girl in *City Lights.*

• The computer Hal 9000 reading lips in *2001: A Space Odyssey.*

• The singing of the "Marseillaise" in *Casablanca.*

• Snow White patting Bashful on the head.

• John Wayne putting the reins in his mouth in *True Grit* and galloping across the mountain meadow, weapons in both hands.

• Jimmy Stewart in *Vertigo,* approaching Kim Novak across the room, realizing she embodies all of his obsessions—better than he knows.

• The early film experiment proving that horses do sometimes have all four hooves off the ground.

• Gene Kelly singin' in the rain.

• Samuel L. Jackson and John Travolta discussing what they call Quarter Pounders in France, in *Pulp Fiction.*

• The Man in the Moon getting a cannon shell in his eye, in the Melies film *A Voyage to the Moon.*

• Pauline in peril, tied to the railroad tracks.

• A boy running joyously to greet his returning father, in *Sounder.*

• Harold Lloyd hanging from a clock face.

• Orson Welles smiling enigmatically in the doorway in *The Third Man.*

• An angel looking down sadly over Berlin, in Wim Wender's *Wings of Desire.*

• The Zapruder film of the Kennedy assassination: over and over again, a moment frozen in time.

• A homesick North African, sadly telling a hooker that what he really wants is not sex but couscous, in Rainer Werner Fassbinder's *Ali: Fear Eats the Soul.*

• The Road Runner, suspended in midair.

• Zero Mostel throwing a cup of cold coffee at the hysterical Gene Wilder in Mel Brooks's *The Producers,* and Wilder screaming: "I'm still hysterical! Plus, now I'm wet!"

• An old man all alone in his home, faced with the death of his wife and the indifference of his children, in Yasujiro Ozu's *Tokyo Story.*

• "Smoking." Robert Mitchum's response, holding up his cigarette, when Kirk Douglas offers him a smoke in *Out of the Past.*

• Marcello Mastroianni and Anita Ekberg wading in the fountain in *La Dolce Vita.*

• The moment in Akira Kurosawa's *High and Low* when a millionaire discovers that it was not his son who was kidnapped, but his chauffeur's son—and then the eyes of the two fathers meet.

• The distant sight of people appearing over the horizon at the end of *Schindler's List.*

• R2D2 and C3PO in *Star Wars.*

• E.T. and friend riding their bicycle across the face of the moon.

• Marlon Brando's screaming "Stella!" in *A Streetcar Named Desire.*

• Hannibal Lecter smiling at Clarice in *The Silence of the Lambs.*

• "Wait a minute! Wait a minute! You ain't heard nothin' yet!" The first words heard in the first talkie, *The Jazz Singer* (1927), said by Al Jolson.

• Jack Nicholson trying to order a chicken salad sandwich in *Five Easy Pieces.*

• "Nobody's perfect." Joe E. Brown's last line in *Some Like It Hot,* explaining to Tony Curtis why he plans to marry Jack Lemmon even though he is a man.

• "Rosebud."

• The shooting party in Renoir's *Rules of the Game.*

• The haunted eyes of Antoine Doinel, Truffaut's autobiographical hero, in the freeze-frame that ends *The 400 Blows.*

• Jean-Paul Belmondo flipping a cigarette into his mouth in Godard's *Breathless.*

• The casting of the great iron bell in Andrei Tarkovsky's *Andrei Rublev.*

• "What have you done to its *eyes?*" Dialogue by Mia Farrow in *Rosemary's Baby.*

• Moses parting the Red Sea in *The Ten Commandments.*

• An old man found dead in a child's swing, his mission completed, at the end of Kurosawa's *Ikiru.*

• The haunted eyes of the actress Renee Falconetti in Dreyer's *The Passion of Joan of Arc.*

• The children watching the train pass by in Ray's *Pather Panchali.*

• The baby carriage bouncing down the steps in Eisenstein's *The Battleship Potemkin.*

• "Are you lookin' at me?" Robert De Niro in *Taxi Driver.*

• "My father made them an offer they couldn't refuse." Al Pacino in *The Godfather.*

• The mysterious body in the photographs in Antonioni's *Blowup.*

• "One word, Benjamin: Plastics." From *The Graduate.*

• A man dying in the desert in von Stroheim's *Greed.*

• Eva Marie Saint clinging to Cary Grant's hand on Mount Rushmore in *North by Northwest.*

- Astaire and Rogers dancing.
- "There ain't no sanity clause!" Chico to Groucho in *A Night at the Opera*.
- "They call me Mr. Tibbs." Sidney Poitier in Norman Jewison's *In the Heat of the Night*.
- The sadness of the separated lovers in Jean Vigo's *L'Atalante*.
- The vast expanse of desert, and then tiny figures appearing, in *Lawrence of Arabia*.
- Jack Nicholson on the back of the motorcycle, wearing a football helmet, in *Easy Rider*.
- The geometrical choreography of the Busby Berkeley girls.
- Robert Mitchum in *The Night of the Hunter*, with "love" tattooed on the knuckles of one hand, and "hate" on the other.
- The peacock spreading its tail feathers in the snow, in Fellini's *Amarcord*.
- Joan Baez singing "Joe Hill" in *Woodstock*.
- Robert De Niro's transformation from sleek boxer to paunchy nightclub owner in *Raging Bull*.
- Bette Davis: "Fasten your seat belts; it's gonna be a bumpy night!" in *All About Eve*.
- "That spider is as big as a Buick!" Woody Allen in *Annie Hall*.
- The chariot race in *Ben-Hur*.
- Barbara Harris singing "It Don't Worry Me" to calm a panicked crowd in Robert Altman's *Nashville*.
- The game of Russian roulette in *The Deer Hunter*.
- Chase scenes: *The French Connection, Bullitt, Raiders of the Lost Ark, Diva*.
- The shadow of the bottle hidden in the light fixture, in *The Lost Weekend*.
- "I coulda been a contender." Brando in *On the Waterfront*.
- George C. Scott's speech about the enemy in *Patton*: "We're going to go through him like crap through a goose."
- Rocky Balboa running up the steps and throwing his hands into the air, with all of Philadelphia at his feet.
- Debra Winger saying good-bye to her children in *Terms of Endearment*.
- The montage of the kissing scenes in *Cinema Paradiso*.
- The dinner guests who find they somehow cannot leave, in Buñuel's *The Exterminating Angel*.
- A knight plays chess with Death, in Bergman's *The Seventh Seal*.
- The savage zeal of the Klansmen in Griffith's *Birth of a Nation*.
- The problem of the door that won't stay closed, in Jacques Tati's *Mr. Hulot's Holiday*.
- "I'm still big! It's the pictures that got small!" Gloria Swanson in *Sunset Boulevard*.

- "We're not in Kansas anymore!" Judy Garland in *The Wizard of Oz*.
- An overhead shot beginning with a entrance hall, and ending with a close-up of a key in Ingrid Bergman's hand, in Hitchcock's *Notorious*.
- "There ain't much meat on her, but what's there is choice." Spencer Tracy about Katharine Hepburn in *Pat and Mike*.
- The day's outing of the mental patients in *One Flew Over the Cuckoo's Nest*.
- "I always look well when I'm near death." Greta Garbo to Robert Taylor in *Camille*.
- "It took more than one night to change my name to Shanghai Lily." Marlene Dietrich in *Shanghai Express*.
- "I'm walkin' here!" Dustin Hoffman in *Midnight Cowboy*.
- W.C. Fields flinching as a prop man hurls handfuls of fake snow into his face in *The Fatal Glass of Beer*.
- "The next time you got nothin' to do, and lots of time to do it, come up and see me." Mae West in *My Little Chickadee*.
- "Top o' the world, Ma!" James Cagney in *White Heat*.
- Richard Burton exploding when Elizabeth Taylor reveals their "secret" in *Who's Afraid of Virginia Woolf?*
- Henry Fonda getting his hair cut in *My Darling Clementine*.
- "Badges? We ain't got no badges. We don't need no badges. I don't have to show you any stinkin' badges!" Alfonso Bedoya to Humphrey Bogart in *The Treasure of the Sierra Madre*.
- "There's your dog. Your dog's dead. But there had to be something that made it move. Doesn't there?" Line from Errol Morris's *Gates of Heaven*.
- "Don't touch the suit!" Burt Lancaster in *Atlantic City*.
- Gena Rowlands arriving at John Cassavetes's house with a taxicab full of adopted animals, in *Love Streams*.
- "I want to live again. I want to live again. I want to live again. Please God, let me live again." Jimmy Stewart to the angel in *It's a Wonderful Life*.
- Burt Lancaster and Deborah Kerr embracing on the beach in *From Here to Eternity*.
- Mookie throwing the trash can through the window of Sal's Pizzeria, in *Do the Right Thing*.
- "I love the smell of napalm in the morning." Dialogue by Robert Duvall, in *Apocalypse Now*.
- "Nature, Mr. Allnut, is what we are put in this world to rise above." Katharine Hepburn to Humphrey Bogart in *The African Queen*.
- "Mother of mercy. Is this the end of Rico?" Edward G. Robinson in *Little Caesar*.

Questions for the Movie Answer Man

Here are some of the best Q's and A's from the past year's run of "The Movie Answer Man," a weekly column I write for the *Sun-Times*. It's also run by some of my syndication clients, and is posted weekly in the Ebert section of CompuServe.

Q. *For the past few weeks I've been dating a woman who is smart, kind, attractive, and genuinely fun to be with . . .* but *who talks loudly in movie theaters. Must I throw away this fine, fine woman because of her one (albeit serious) social shortcoming? I have, unfortunately, determined that she's beyond rehabilitation. Quiet "sshhh!"s lead only to her talking just as loudly, but right into my ear. (Andy Ihnatko, Westwood, Mass.)*

A. Obtain a joy buzzer. Hold her hand loosely. Every time she talks during a movie, squeeze it. Let me know how it works.

Q. *I read that whenever Quentin Tarantino is getting interested in some woman, he shows her* Rio Bravo *and "she better like it." My own particular litmus tests for prospective Significant Others isn't a film, but a format. If she tells me she prefers colorization to the original black and white, I tell her to close the door from the outside. (Michael Zey, Austin, Tex.)*

A. An excellent early-warning strategy, because anyone who prefers colorization to the original black and white is eventually going to reveal serious character flaws in a number of other areas.

Q. *My wife and I were watching* The Grifters *on laserdisc last night and about ten minutes into it she remarked that it would have been much better had it been filmed in black and white. No problem, I said, and promptly turned the color off. She was right! Suddenly the atmosphere of the Jim Thompson book seemed to pop out more. We both found it greatly more enjoyable. We started rattling off a list of recent movies that would benefit from this goofy trick. (Chris Yaryan)*

A. In theory I am against tampering with the original color format of a film (see above). But it's strange how adding color to a b&w movie destroys it, while viewing a color movie in b&w often seems to enhance it. This fits into my general theory that b&w is more dreamlike and mysterious, and color is more realistic.

Q. *We went to see* Junior *and got into a big argument afterward. In the movie, Arnold Schwarzenegger is artificially implanted with a human egg, and becomes pregnant. Is this possible? (Joe Rogers, Chicago)*

A. Strangely enough, it might be. According to Victoria Weisenberg, an instructor at the St. Francis Hospital School of Nursing, in Evanston, such an event would be known as an ectopic pregnancy: "The zygote, or egg, has little extensions named trophoblasts that implant on the womb wall. In one well-known case involving an Austrian woman with a hysterectomy, the attachment was to her abdominal wall, and the embryo was able to develop. It has not happened *yet* with a man, but is theoretically possible."

And after all, Arnold is Austrian.

Q. *Who would win in a fight to the finish, Batman or Superman? (Steve Kass, Chicago)*

A. Superman, of course, since Batman is only human and the Man of Steel has superhuman qualities. If Batman used Kryptonite, however, that would of course tilt the balance. But the Answer Man began wondering about *other* superheroes, and when your question was presented to famed science fiction creator George Alec Effinger, he responded: "I was a Marvel comics writer back in the early seventies, and there was (and may still be) a definite hierarchy of who could beat up whom. Thor was tops, being a god, and then it went (if my memory is right) Hulk, Spiderman, Thing (and so on; Hulk and Spiderman may have been reversed). I used to match up the Marvel and DC versions of similar characters: Batman vs. Daredevil, Submariner vs. Aquaman (oh boy, spot Aquaman two touchdowns and a field goal), Hawkeye vs. Green Arrow, etc. Then I became much too literary to care about such things. Sure, you bet."

Q. *My wife and I are often disappointed when viewing a movie on TV because we can not understand much of what the actors are saying. It seems they make a minimum effort to enunciate. When we watch an old movie, vintage 1930s and '40s, it is a joy to listen to the actors speak and be understood. In addition to the mumbling there is often background noise that drowns out much of what is being said. Have you noticed this yourself? (E. John Berger, Mission Viejo, Calif.)*

A. I have indeed. So has David J. Bondelevitch of the CompuServe ShowBiz Forum, who writes: "One reason that dialogue intelligibility was so high in the thirties and forties was that virtually everything was shot on a soundstage. Now, for realism, virtually everything is shot on location, so you get a lot more background noise."

And here is a response from an actor, Ed Hooks: "I have appeared a lot in front of the camera. The sound you hear on the final print is actually built, layer by layer. Take, for instance, a scene in a night club. If I have dialogue with another actor at a table and, in the background, there are people dancing and music playing etc., they will actually have everybody mime their actions and move silently, so the dialogue at the table can be recorded. Then they will separately record the music and the crowd noises and then, in the mixing room, put it all together. Coupled with all of the technical wizardry there is the added element of actors who do not enunciate clearly. Anyway, your perception is correct. The sound on your VCR is only semi-okay."

Q. *Is it possible that Disney took* The Lion King *into the shop for a little retooling between its first and second release? I thought the best sight gag in the movie was when Timon and Pumbaa staged their mini-luau to lure away the hyenas. There's a hilarious contrast between carefree Timon, doing his manic little hula, and poor, pragmatic Pumbaa, stuck motionless on a plate, agony in his eyes and sweat literally spouting out of every pore. So, a few weeks back, I take the kids to the re-release and wait patiently for my favorite scene and . . . lo and behold! No sweat! No agony! Pumbaa's lying on the plate, big smile on his face, apparently having the time of his life! At first, I think I'm suffering from MAMLS (Middle-age Memory Loss Syndrome), but my eleven-year old daughter, who remembers* everything, *backs me up on it. (Chuck Mathias, Tacoma, Wash.)*

A. But Don Hahn, who produced *The Lion King* for Disney, does not. "There are very definitely *not* two versions out there," he told me. "Before we animated, we had contemplated Pumbaa being really nervous. But finally we settled on just two of them having a great time doing the hula. The movie has not changed. Pumbaa is enjoying himself, an apple in his mouth, not sweaty or nervous."

After I talked with Hahn, I got e-mail from no less than David Pruiksma, the artist who animated all the Pumbaas in the luau sequence, who wrote: "I can assure you that only one version of the scene exists. The sequence was done in about three weeks and there was no time for monkeying around with alternate 'takes' of any scenes."

Q. *Why do the photos of Samuel L. Jackson in the* Pulp Fiction *ads show him with short hair, instead of the giant, curly 'do he wears in the movie? (Joanna Brandon, Chicago)*

A. I wish my answer was more intriguing, involving marketing decisions about whether a conservative haircut sells more tickets than a Jheri-Curl, but the truth is: When they were shooting the publicity stills, they couldn't find the wig that Jackson wore in the movie.

Q. *Why is the type font for the credits of movie posters and ads so hard to read? The font is very narrow and tall. Is this some kind of standard that the industry has adopted? If so, I think it should be changed. (Don Black)*

A. Those spindly, microscopic letters are the result of Hollywood contract language, according to Sherman Wolf, whose Chicago firm handles ads for many studios. "On newspaper ads that are 7.5 inches deep or more," he told me, "the rule is that the credits have to be there. If more than one actor is listed, that triggers a requirement that a lot of other names be included, like director, writer, cinematographer, and so on. Space is expensive, and they want the credits to take up as little space as possible. Contracts specify that the credits must run in a type size that is a certain percentage of the height of the title. They cannot make the words shorter, but they can make them narrower—squeezing more into a smaller space."

Q. *You rate a movie with stars. The way I rate a movie is as follows. If, after the movie is half-over, I am conscious of the fact that my rear is sore for sitting for an hour, it is a bad film. Otherwise, the movie was worth the money! (Mark Dub, Warren, Mich.)*

A. In other words, your rear has feelings which are separate from physical reality, and exist entirely on a subjective mental plane. I have heard of holy men who meditated for years to attain this state, although not necessarily in the place where you have developed it.

Q. *Why is there a double standard regarding male vs. female nudity in the movies? Why are women seen naked so much more often than men? Do you suppose, as directors keep pushing at the taboo envelope, we'll have more full frontals in our future? Is the small-but-growing number of female directors changing this equation at all? (Martha Barnette, Louisville, Ky.)*

A. Genitals, of either sex, reduce any scene to a documentary. Nudity below the waist is fatal to the dramatic impact of any scene, drawing attention away from the characters, dialogue, and situation. W.C. Fields felt uneasy sharing the screen with a baby or an animal, because he felt attention would be drawn away from him. If he had lived a little longer, I feel sure he would have added genitals to his list.

Q. *I might just be imagining this, but in* Pulp Fiction, *during the scene in which Bruce Willis is in the cab, is the background, as seen through the cab's back window, black and white? If so, this is the most ridiculous thing that I have ever seen, although the movie was fantastic. (David N. Bernick, Media, Pa.)*

A. Yes, in a color movie, the world seen through the back window of that cab is black and white. Why did director Quentin Tarantino do this? Probably as a movie in-joke, since in the B movies that *Pulp Fiction* is inspired by, the "back projection" process was sometimes noticeably shoddy. In his movie *Family Plot,* Alfred Hitchcock likewise used an obviously phony back projection process through a car's rear window, perhaps enjoying the sense of artifice.

Q. *I recently saw* The Client *on a United Airlines flight and noticed that the soundtrack had been dubbed to replace profanities with substitute words. I would assume that a bit of violence may also have been removed, for example during the suicide episode. My guess is that the resulting movie would be given a PG rating. There are many popular movies that I would love to rent for viewing with my family if only they were rated G or (maybe) PG. Cleaning up the language, removing the sex, and toning down any graphic violence would make very little difference to the entertainment value for many people of the movies I'm talking about. Are "airline edits" available anywhere for rental? Have studios ever considered issuing "family" and "mature" versions of the same movie? (Jon Bale, San Jose, Calif.)*

A. Such versions are not available through ordinary rental and sale channels. Some directors are so disturbed by the "airline edits" of their films that they have their names removed (Robert Mulligan, for example, took his name off of *The Man in the Moon*). Their contracts usually include the studio's right to edit for in-flight and broadcast use, however. Most directors would violently oppose a similar edited version for commercial video channels. I am sure you are correct that a market for such films exists; I doubt that an R movie could easily be transformed into a PG, but it would be easier to tone down a PG-13. I believe, however, that films are works of art, not commodities, and that every film should be seen as the director intended.

Q. *I just got back from seeing* Dumb and Dumber. *To say that this is the worst movie I have ever seen would be a gross understatement. The four people who saw it with me were all ready to walk out, but I kept them there by saying, "Roger Ebert said he laughed so loud, he embarrassed himself—so it must get better." I was wrong. This movie gets a "worse-than-*Darkman*" rating in my book, and having just lost a parakeet that my wife and I have had ever since we first met three years ago, I wasn't thrilled with the parakeet joke either. (Robert S. Fish, Columbus, Ohio)*

A. I did indeed write "I laughed so loudly I embarrassed myself." Then I added: "*But* because I know that the first sentence of this review is likely to be lifted out and reprinted in an ad, I hasten to add that I did not laugh as loudly again, or very often."

Q. *Regarding* Pulp Fiction, *the character Jules played by Samuel L. Jackson recites a bible passage twice in the movie. It's bogus, but no reviews have remarked on this. Have I missed something or do film critics regard this sort of thing as detail-mongering? (Ken Nichols, Grand Terrace, Calif.)*

A. Tarantino-watcher Paul Chapman of London, England, noted in the CompuServe Showbiz Forum: "Jules says he's quoting from Ezekiel, 25:17. But he isn't. The second half of his speech corresponds closely to the biblical text, but the rest seems to be a mishmash of invention, expansion, and interpretation. The text of this speech was transmitted on a BBC radio program, which I recorded. Here is what he says:

The path of the righteous man is beset on all sides by the iniquities of the selfish and the tyranny of evil men. Blessed is he who, in the name of charity and good will, shepherds the weak through the valley of darkness, for he is truly his brother's keeper and the finder of lost children. And I will strike down upon thee with great vengeance and furious anger those who attempt to poison and destroy my brothers. And you will know my name is the Lord when I lay my vengeance upon thee.

"My theory is that Jules did once know the passage verbatim, but it has become corrupted in his mind and infected with black political sound bites (two mentions of the word *brother*, for example) and the need to justify his profession to his conscience."

Q. *Continuing the discussion of what's inside the mystery briefcase in* Pulp Fiction. *When I saw the movie, I took the glow coming from the briefcase as a reference to Robert Aldrich's* Kiss Me Deadly *(1955). Mike Hammer chased around after that briefcase, which glowed when opened (and exploded if opened for too long) because it contained a nuclear bomb. Also there is a reminder of the glowing briefcase in* Repo Man *(1984) if I'm not mistaken. (B.F. Helman, Chicago)*

A. The movie's co-author, Roger Avary, replies: "Originally the briefcase contained diamonds. But that just seemed too boring and predictable. So it was decided that the contents of the briefcase were never to be seen. This way each audience member would fill in the 'blank' with their own ultimate contents. All you were supposed to know was that it was 'so beautiful.' No prop master can come up with something better than each individual's imagination. At least that was the original idea. Then somebody had the bright idea (which I think is a mistake) of putting an orange light bulb in there. Suddenly what could have been anything became anything supernatural. Didn't need to push the effect. People would have debated it for years anyway, and it would have been much more subtle. I can't believe I'm actually talking about being subtle."

Q. *I watched the colorized version of* Miracle on 34th Street. *What bothered me the most were the color combinations that were used. The maker of the tape replied to my inquiries by stating that the colors were the exact colors used on the sets. The colors were written down and the "colorizers" just followed the script. My problem is with some of the color combinations. The kid in the court room wore green pants and blue socks. In one of the last scenes, where the X-ray machine was presented, there was a green couch on a blue rug. My question is, were blue and green popular color combinations when this film was made? (Eugene Kellick, Morton Grove, Ill.)*

A. Colorization is always a mistake, because the colors must be laid on top of the original black and white. Therefore, brighter colors are necessary, leading to all those men in 1930s and 1940s movies who seem to be dressed for golf. It's not relevant when they say the "original colors" were used, since the colors used for a black and white movie were not selected for how they looked on the set—but for how they photographed in black and white.

Q. *My wife and I just watched* Speed *for the second time on home video, and want to know if you caught the same edit snafu as we did. Early in the movie, Keanu Reeves shoots Jeff Daniels in the* left *leg to free him from Dennis Hopper in the parking lot. The next scene shows Daniels and Reeves getting accolades from the city and Daniels has his cane in his* right *hand and a bandage on his* right *leg. At the end of the following scene (in the bar celebrating), Daniels leaves with the cane back in his* left *hand while he favors his* left *leg. (Forget that both legs seem just perfect as he enters the window to Hopper's home the next morning in full SWAT gear). Also, why does Hopper's holding the phone with his right hand against his left ear seem so unnatural? I know his left thumb was blown off, but I've yet to find anyone who will put a phone in their right hand and raise it crossover style to their left ear to talk. Believe me, I've trying this on people for a few weeks! Does it strike you as odd? (Gary G. Naeyaert, Lansing, Mich.)*

A. Not as odd as it probably does to the people you've been trying it on.

Q. *I recall a rumor that* The Exorcist *used subliminal messaging to affect the audience. When I saw it on its initial theatrical release, I passed out at one point—and I don't faint easily. It was early in the film when she was having her brain X-rayed: The scene showed Regan with a needle on the end of a tube stuck in her neck, and there's a gyrating X-ray machine and the machine-gun-like sound of sheets of film rapidly advancing. I recoil at the thought that a movie could have such an impact on me without some kind of unfair advantage. Maybe the hype surrounding the film and the crowded theater set me up for it. When I came to, I noticed that I'd slumped down and jammed my shins against the metal edge of the seat in front of me. They were cut and bleeding. Probably one of the few times that watching a movie led to physical injury. (Tom Norris, Braintree, Mass.)*

A. A couple of years ago at the Hawaii Film Festival I did a frame-by-frame analysis of *The Exorcist* with Owen Roizman, its cinematographer. Using freeze-frame on a laserdisc, he revealed two single frames in which a satanic face is superimposed over the face of Linda Blair, who played Regan. The audience was pretty impressed, but there were no injuries.

Q. *During the credits of every movie, we see the "Foley Editor." Exactly what are these? And are there movies in which*

viewers can "really notice" them at work? (Randy Johnson, Newport Beach, Calif.)

A. According to Ephraim Katz's magnificent new *Film Encyclopedia,* Foley artists work on the sound track after production, specializing in sounds made by people (kisses, footsteps, etc.). If they do their jobs well, you do not notice them at all.

Q. *I teach marketing at Concordia College. I understand that Viacom plans to use the fifty-million-customer base of Blockbuster Video, where two million transactions are recorded every day, to "reverse engineer" movies. In other words, scripts and stars will be determined by data gathered from marketing surveys. What do you think about this? (Craig C. Lien, St. Paul, Minn.)*

A. If it were not absolute goofiness, I would be alarmed. Viacom is likely to lose millions on "reverse engineered" movies, because one of the problems in entertainment marketing is that people don't know what they want until they see it. *Star Wars* tested so horribly that Fox considered recycling the footage into a Saturday morning kiddie show. It doesn't take a genius (or a marketing survey) to know Tom Cruise or Whoopi Goldberg sells tickets, or that a Schwarzenegger science fiction film will probably do well. Beyond that, though, the marketers are likely to find people "want" movies similar to those they just enjoyed. This is the wisdom that gave us *Honey, I Blew Up the Kid.* Marketing works for soap and fast food. But in a volatile area like popular entertainment, it provides obvious answers at great cost, while counseling against original proposals because the survey audience cannot relate to them. How well do you think *Pulp Fiction, Silence of the Lambs, Forrest Gump, Schindler's List,* or *Quiz Show* would have tested, as compared to such sure-fire backward-engineered projects as: *Wagons East, On Deadly Ground, City Slickers II,* or *Highlander III*? Viacom and Blockbuster specialize in selling what others have created, and they are good at that. They will discover it is much trickier to create what others will sell.

Q. *When I walked out of* Hoop Dreams, *I said to my date it was the best movie I had seen in years. After talking endlessly about it to anyone who would listen to me, I have convinced myself that it was one of the top three movies I have ever seen. The fact that it was not nominated for an Oscar tells me the Academy is a political backscratching organization that doesn't have a clue. I cannot express how disappointed I am. (Kevin Brouillette, Kansas City, Mo.)*

A. The bizarre oversights of the Academy's documentary committee have been a scandal for years. One good thing may result from their egregious snub of *Hoop Dreams:* The resulting stink has been too big for the Academy to overlook, and its president, Arthur Hiller, has promised an investigation. The Academy has been able to ignore protests in past years from critics, documentary filmmakers, and other "outsiders," but this year, I understand, there was an outraged outcry from many Academy members themselves, including some members of its board of directors.

Q. *How is it that music companies can sell movie soundtracks that don't include all of the music selections from the movie? I purchased the soundtrack for* When a Man Loves a Woman *for a particular song. I didn't know the title, so couldn't check the list of contents. Nowhere on the CD did it say "some of" the soundtrack, but my song wasn't there. I wrote to Buena Vista Productions and told them of my disappointment, but received no answer. I'm fed up! (Mary Carrino, Berwyn, Ill.)*

A. "In some cases copyright permission for certain songs is granted only for use in the movie and not on the soundtrack album," according to Buena Vista's Chicago spokesman, Jeff Marden. "In the case of *When a Man Loves a Woman*, both the Rickie Lee Jones song and an REM song ('Everybody Hurts') were not available on the soundtrack for this reason." To be on the safe side, he says, check out the end titles, when all songs are listed. ("I know this is difficult at best," he adds.)

Q. *While in Puerto Rico recently I went to see* The Shawshank Redemption. *It featured subtitles in Spanish, and I know enough Spanish to tell that the profanity spoken in English was muted to the point of nonexistence in the subtitles. In fact, while the movie was rated R in English, it could easily have been downgraded to PG-13 in Spanish. Does this kind of language-cleansing happen commonly? (Dave Blanchard, Kent, Ohio).*

A. "The common industry practice on subtitling," according to a source at Castle Rock Foreign Distribution, "is to use what is called 'neutral language,' intended to impart a 'sense' of the original dialogue while avoiding certain phrases that could prove more shocking when read than heard." And in answer to what would probably be your next question—is the same process used when foreign films are subtitled in English?—the answer is "no," possibly because in America these days there are no phrases that prove more shocking when read than heard.

Q. *Why is it in the movies that whenever the radio plays "Moonlight Serenade" by Glenn Miller, the next thing that happens is the Japanese attack Pearl Harbor? (Dana L. Marek, Pasadena, Texas)*

A. What goes around, comes around. Every time you hear The Doors, we attack Vietnam.

Q. *For the past twenty years, my husband and I have been trying to identify the female off-screen narrator in* To Kill a Mockingbird. *Do you know who she is? (Julia Van Buskirk, Geneva, Ill.)*

A. The great Kim Stanley. And check out her work in *The Goddess*, a 1958 film loosely inspired by the career of Marilyn Monroe. Bonus answer: The voice on the telephone in *Rosemary's Baby* is Tony Curtis.

Q. *Heard a delicious rumor that* The Madness of King George *was originally named* The Madness of George III, *but they changed the title for the American release because they were afraid everyone would think this was a sequel! Is this true? (Molly Ivins, Austin, Tex.)*

A. Absolutely true. And then there was the Hollywood producer who asked his partner, "Have you seen *Henry the Fifth*?" And the partner replied, "Hell, I haven't even see the first four."

Q. *Every film I've seen by director John Landis, from* Animal House *to* Blues Brothers *to* Coming to America, *and including even Michael Jackson's "Thriller" video, uses the phrase, "See you next Wednesday." This is obviously an inside joke, but what does it mean? (Kris Gallimore, Thunder Bay, Ontario)*

A. The line was used in the telephone call from orbit in Stanley Kubrick's *2001: A Space Odyssey*, and has become a Landis calling card. Not to be outdone, Kubrick has set a scene in a bathroom in every one of *his* movies.

Q. *Who is your favorite American director currently working and why? Also, who is an up-and-coming to look out for? (Kenneth Alan Goldman, Medford, Mass.)*

A. The best American director is Martin Scorsese, whose work is filled with such energy, passion, and love of film that every frame seems alive. His *Raging Bull* was voted in three different polls the best film of the 1980s, and a case can be made for *Taxi Driver* in the 1970s and *GoodFellas* in the 1990s. Among the up-and-coming directors, I like Quentin Tarantino *(Pulp Fiction)*, John Dahl *(The Last Seduction)*, Carl Franklin *(One False Move)*, Atom Egoyan *(Exotica)*, and Gregory Nava *(My Family)*.

Q. *Why do some actresses insist on keeping it secret when they use a double for a nude scene? If they are too modest to do their own scenes, wouldn't they want to credit the double so the public would know they hadn't seen the star's body? (Francis T. Kennedy, Oakville, Conn.)*

A. This assumes that modesty is the motivation for using a double. More frequently, it is vanity. The actress uses the best-looking double in town and wants you to think it's her. Some actors do the same thing, although Mel Gibson and Michael Douglas are so proud of doing their own work that they seem to include a bare-bums scene in almost every one of their movies.

Q. *It's five years until the start of the 21st century. What does 20th Century-Fox do then? (Harris Allsworth, Chicago)*

A. The name stays the same, according to Nancy Meyer of Fox's Chicago office. My own hunch, however, is that the word "Fox" will be emphasized—just as it currently is on the TV network—and "20th Century" will appear mainly on letterheads and contracts.

Q. *I'm a photographer, and have been wondering—who started the Orange and Blue Movement? All those movies where each scene has to have something blue and something orange in it? A good example would be* Trading Moms, *with Sissy Spacek. There are lots of others in the last two years. I think it began with night city scenes mimicking neon reflections on faces. The actor usually has an warm (orange) main light on his/her face from a forty-five degree angle, and has a cold (blue) kicker light skimming the shadow side of his face. Warm colors appear to move forward and cold colors recede, so it adds depth to an object. Someone grabbed this theme of color and a movement began. (Jim Langley, Phoenix, Ariz.)*

A. Frankly, Jim, I thought you might be hallucinating. But I referred your question to the great cinematographer Owen Roizman, a five-time Oscar nominee. He responds: "I don't think he is hallucinating. When we are shooting at night we have a tendency to look for reasonable sources of light to justify or enhance what we are shooting. When we are in areas that don't have many sources, we tend to turn to 'moonlight' as one of them. Some people fantasize that moonlight is blue whereas others envision it as a cold white light. Neither is correct, but that is a long story. The 'blue' believers generally use the 'moonlight' as a backlight or edge light, otherwise known as a kicker. What sets off the blue very nicely is a warm tone, such as orange. Hence the orange and blue.

"The other approach is that generally a warmer tone of front or side light is very pleasing at night, like fire or candle light, or for that matter a dimmed lamp light. If everything is lit with just the warm tones it has a tendency to get 'muddy' looking, but if some blue light is introduced somewhere, either in the shadows or backlight, etc., it gives the subject a much more pleasing quality.

"I used this approach on *Wyatt Earp* on almost all of my night work and I was very pleased with it. I must have done something right because I received a nomination for it. I know you hated the picture but I didn't write it so I'm off the hook."

Q. *Columbia Pictures has changed their logo within the past year. It's still a lady with a torch, but as the camera pulls back from the torch bearer, I notice she looks uncannily like Annette Bening. Was she the model for the new logo? (Daniel E. Tienes, St. Louis, Mo.)*

A. "It's not her," according to John Moore, a Columbia spokesman in Chicago. "The figure is a computer-gener-ated image. But many people have asked the same question."

Q. *Help me settle something. If Writer A and Writer B both wrote their opinions on a film—both with diligence and pride in their work—what difference in the two pieces would identify Writer A as a Film Critic and Writer B as someone just offering an opinion? Take the weekly feature you see in some papers, where kids review films. At what point do they cross the line, and can be called Critics as opposed to Reviewers? Is there some sort of certification program, like taking the Sally Struthers correspondence course in gun repair? (Andy Ihnatko, Westwood, Mass.)*

A. This is a fascinating question, not unrelated to, "at what point do we know Swift doesn't really intend for the starving Irish to eat their babies?" The noncritic Reviewer will often betray himself by these mistakes: (1) Pretense of objectivity; (2) reluctance to introduce extraneous knowledge; (3) predictions of which audiences will or will not enjoy the film; (4) bashfulness about writing in the first person; (5) distancing self from actual experience of viewing the film; (6) an overwritten first paragraph. The genuine Critic will write in such a way as to acknowledge that he had a subjective personal experience which he wants to share with you, and which reminded him of other films or other subjects. He will wear his knowledge lightly and never presume to speak for other than himself.

Q. *I notice that the advance ads for* Tank Girl *quote Jeff Craig of Sixty Second Preview as saying, "This movie kicks major butt!" As a critic, what is your reaction to his review? (Susan Lake, Urbana, Ill.)*

A. Jeff Craig's name in a movie ad is a one-second tip-off that the distributors are desperate. They would not use him if they had more legitimate critics to quote. According to *People* magazine, Craig provides rave quotes for virtually every movie he considers—even though he doesn't see most of the movies he "reviews," depending on eight staff members. (Funny: I actually find time to see all the movies myself.) Craig's payoff is seeing his name in print in a movie ad. In the case of *Tank Girl,* it's a good question whether *anyone* from Craig's staff even saw the movie, since United Artists strictly embargoed all preview screenings until the Tuesday before it opened—several days after Craig's "major butt" quote first appeared.

Q. *What's the story on the refusal of the actor's branch of the Motion Picture Academy to admit Rodney Dangerfield to membership? (Charlene Smith, Dubuque, Iowa)*

A. He still don't get no respect. Dangerfield has been top-billed in five features, two of them grossing more than one hundred million dollars, and last year had an acclaimed supporting role in *Natural Born Killers.* But his bid for

Academy membership was turned down. "I got a letter from Roddy McDowell, the head of the actor's branch," Dangerfield told me. "He wrote that I should 'improve my craft,' and apply again later. Hey, I'm seventy-three years old. What am I gonna do? Apply again when I'm 104?"

Q. *We saw* Red *and were so deeply impressed by this great film that we rented* Blue *and* White *on video. Can it really be true that Krzysztof Kieslowski is actually retiring and will make no more films? (Emerson Thorne, Evanston, Ill.)*

A. I asked Kieslowski, fifty-three, about that at the Academy Awards, and he insisted it was true, although "nothing is forever." But two days earlier, at the Independent Spirit Awards, Julie Delpy, the star of *White*, smiled and said, "Krzysztof loves to kid. It may just be for publicity."

Q. *Over the past few years I've seen stories on the future form that cinema will take, such as HDTV via satellite to theater. Most of these stories seem to think that filmgoing as we know it—a group experience in a large theater with actual celluloid—will die out. Nevertheless, seeing a beautiful reissue of* The Wild Bunch *recently gave me hope that forty years from now I'll still be able to walk into a cinema and be able to catch a restored print of the great films I grew up with. What do you think will happen to the film experience in the future? (Chris Giardino, Toronto)*

A. There is no substitute for celluloid. Even the best video has a sharp drop-off at either end of the visible spectrum, diluting the bright whites and dark shadows that are essential to film. Also, according to video theorist Jerry Mander, in his book *Four Arguments for the Abolition of Television*, video and film work on the human mind differently. Film creates a dreamlike reverie state, while TV creates a form of mild hypnosis. This helps explain why we remember old movies better than old TV shows. The subject came up at this year's pre-Oscar dinner for the cinematography nominees, where George Fisher, chairman and CEO of Eastman Kodak, told me flatly: "If video ever replaces film in theaters, it will not be in the foreseeable future. If I didn't believe that, I would not have left Motorola to come to work at Eastman."

Q. *I'm writing from Taipei again where there's a movie playing called* Fart King. *This is the actual title as it appears in the newspapers here. That's* not *the unusual part. The unusual part is the banner across the bottom of the newspaper ad that promises the movie has:* ACTION WITH UNNECESSARY SPECIAL EFFECTS. *Question: How unnecessary does a special effect have to be before the director determines that it should be kept? (Bob Zix-Kong, Taipei)*

A. Thanks for your continuing updates on cinematic developments in Taipei.

Q. *How gracious of you to show my letter about* Forrest Gump *to Tom Hanks. He wrote me a letter of thanks and sent me fifteen dollars to take a friend with me to the movies and buy some popcorn. Thank God for people like you and Tom Hanks to take time out of your busy days to make an eighty-four-year-old feel important. (Marie Hangel, Chicago)*

A. Your letter of praise for Hanks's performance struck me as so heartfelt that I really wanted Tom to see it. By the way, Mrs. Hangel, I received a separate letter, that you may not know about, from your friend Mindie Bright. She wrote: "Mr. Hanks sent her fifteen dollars for *one* movie with a friend and popcorn. Are you kidding? Marie will go to the senior citizen's ladies' showings for fifty cents or one dollar. She'll be at the movies all year around now!"

Q. *More and more films have night scenes with steam coming from all over to emphasize the drama. Today I just got suckered and saw the film* Bad Boys, *which takes place in Miami. In the opening scene, there was steam everywhere: In the buildings, in the stairways, on the streets. I'm from Florida, but I've been gone a few years. Have they started installing underground steam-heating lines in Miami? When I lived there most buildings had air-conditioning instead of steam heat. Or, as I suspect, have the "production designers" finally lost their marbles? Come on guys, let's try to make an action movie that doesn't look like a bad MTV clip. (Richard Hubbell, Arlington, Va.)*

A. That's not steam. It's smoke from the dry ice used to cool the fresh stone crabs.

Q. *Ever notice that when characters in costume dramas use a term modern audiences aren't likely to understand, they immediately follow it with the definition? In* Rob Roy, *for example: "He's a vile Jacobite! A supporter of the exiled King James!" (Rich Elias, Delaware, Ohio)*

A. This is just a precaution. Hollywood learned its lesson with titles like *Wrestling Ernest Hemingway* and *Searching for Bobby Fischer*, which bombed because nobody knew who Ernest Hemingway or Bobby Fischer was. On the other hand, *Beethoven's 2nd* was a hit because everyone knew Beethoven was a dog.

Q. *Does it strike you that some movie sound effects are overdone? I've noticed in recent years that when a movie couple gets passionate, their kisses sound like they're sucking a peach. If I kissed my wife that sloppily, she'd wipe off her face and send me to the guest room for the night. And what about movie punches? Movies have been overdoing fight sound effects for years. My most vivid memory of* Rocky III *was of Sylvester Stallone and Mr. T beginning their fight with punches that would kill the average person. Do you feel that sound effects are as clichéd as some of the other areas you cover in your* Little Glossary? *(Steven Bailey, Jacksonville Beach, Fla.)*

A. I don't know if they use peaches, but I remember visiting the sound effects session of a Charles Bronson movie named *Hard Times* and watching them tape-record themselves beating the hell out of a Naugahyde sofa with Ping-Pong paddles.

Q. *If you go back and watch any Jeff Goldblum movie, you'll invariably notice at least one scene in which Jeff is both eating and talking at the same time, or drinking and talking at the same time. It drives me nuts. Sure, we all do it on occasion. But Jeff seems to think that it's great acting. Maybe way back when, some Hollywood director said, "This kid's got talent! Look at him eat and talk at the same time. Wow, he looks so natural." Jeff should realize there are other ways to appear natural on film. Don't get me wrong, I think he's a good actor, I'm just tired of his shtick. Michael J. Fox is another great eater/talker/actor, but then again, so's my dad—no big deal there. (Steve Glasberg, Agoura Hills, Calif.)*

A. I say if you can't do it as well as John Belushi did it in *National Lampoon's Animal House*, you shouldn't even try it.

Q. *Last night in a bar someone made the ridiculous claim that Humphrey Bogart and Ed Sullivan were brothers. Naturally, I jumped at the chance to make back the money I had just spent on beer and pool by making a twenty-dollar bet with this sadly deluded individual. He insists he's right, but doesn't claim a source, calling it "common knowledge." And you better not come back and tell me that they were brothers, or I'll have to question the whole concept of reality and meaning in my life. (Charles Faubert, Montreal)*

A. Collect the twenty dollars. Bogart had two sisters, Frances and Catherine. Sounds like you have a sure thing with this sucker. Now bet him that Charlie Sheen and Emilio Estevez are brothers.

Q. *I've been thinking about this for years, but a recent revival of* Dr. Zhivago *made me write. Zhivago takes place in Russia. The characters are Russian. But we hear English, of course, since this is an English-speaking movie. Now that we've settled that point, I ask: If we're hearing English, why aren't we seeing English? Why are all the signs and newspapers written in Russian? Shouldn't the sight be consistent with the sound? (Richard Covello, WNIB radio, Chicago)*

A. Two reasons. (1) I think we're supposed to forget we're hearing English, and assume the characters are talking Russian, so of course they would read Russian. If

that seems shaky, try (2), which is that since the movie will be dubbed or subtitled into dozens of other languages, you'd have indignant French or Japanese audiences looking at English signs in Russia and complaining of cultural imperialism. Better to leave the signs in Russian, so they'll play convincingly in every market.

Q. *We saw* The Madness of King George *the other night. Pretty good. However, the first scene showed some heavy wooden doors. As the camera panned in you could read the graffiti carved on the doors. The most prominent was the date "1867." It bothered the heck out of me to start the movie with this obvious continuity issue. Was this a director's idea of a joke or an IQ test? (John T. Bear, Atlanta, Ga.)*

A. The scene was shot at Eton College, which is about five hundred years old, and students have been carving graffiti on that door for all of that time, according to Nicholas Hytner, director of the film: "We didn't notice the date until we were editing the film. We couldn't go back and reshoot because the actors were unavailable and college was in full session. We were confident that the credit roll at the beginning of the film would obscure some of what couldn't be hidden by editing and filters."

Q. *A credit is given to Elizabeth Stone in many of Oliver Stone's movies. She is called the "Naijo No Ko." What does that title refer to? (John L. Santoianni III)*

A. The credit for Stone's former wife is a Japanese term that loosely translates as "spiritual adviser," according to Stone's assistant, Annie Mei-Ling.

Q. *What mystifies me is why the Academy of Motion Picture Arts and Sciences, of all organizations, still insists on using Panned and Scanned film clips on their awards programs. The Academy should be in the forefront of organizations educating the public on the benefits of letterboxing. (Gordon Meyer, North Hollywood, Calif.)*

A. Excellent point. Clips on the Oscarcast which fill up the entire TV screen do so by eliminating the parts of the widescreen image that do not fit inside the narrower TV ratio. Directors should insist that their nominated films be shown in the letterbox format, displaying the full width of their original compositions. While they're at it, they might provide the Academy with *new* scenes from their films, instead of using the same tired old overexposed scenes that have been telecast repeatedly for months.

The Best Films of the Year

1. *Hoop Dreams*

This wonderful film follows a couple of Chicago eighth-graders named William Gates and Arthur Agee through six years of their lives, as they pursue the elusive dream of someday playing professional basketball. But the film is not just about basketball. It's about life as it is lived in a big American city, and like all great films it makes us think in new ways about the world around us.

Gates and Agee, genuinely talented, are recruited to play for a suburban high school with a high-powered sports program. But as fate and injury affect their careers, we grow involved in their lives—meeting their parents, neighbors, relatives, coaches. And one myth after another about the "inner city" is demolished, as we see how their extended families pull together to help the kids.

The movie works on many levels. It is an exciting sports picture, with breathtaking game sequences. It is a thriller. It is heavy drama. And there is comedy. Yes, it's a documentary, but no fiction film in 1994 was more entertaining or more memorable. The incredible persistence of the fimmmakers—Steve James, Frederick Marx, and Peter Gilbert—over six years has resulted in a film where we can actually see people growing up on the screen. Those who take the trouble to see this film will recognize its greatness.

2. *Red, White, and Blue*

Three films, named for the colors in the French flag, and written around the concepts of liberty, equality, and fraternity. They were directed by Krzysztof Kieslowski, a Polish filmmaker now living in France, and I link them together because he considers them a trilogy, and because they all opened here in 1994. I admire *Red* the most, but all share in Kieslowski's refusal to be nailed down to dumb formulas. They exist in a world of discovery and surprises, where the characters react to unexpected events in unconventional ways.

In *Blue*, for example, Juliette Binoche stars as the widow of a symphony conductor, who goes to live on an obscure street in Paris, and tries to lose herself in the big city. In *White*, a Polish hairdresser (Zgigniew Zamachowski), divorced, homeless, jobless, ekes out a living in the Paris Metro by performing on a pocket comb. Then he convinces a friend to take him back to Warsaw—by concealing him in airline luggage. And he plots revenge on his beautiful ex-wife (Julie Delpy). In *Red*, Irene Jacob stars as a young woman living in Geneva whose car strikes a dog belonging to a retired judge—leading to a relationship that owes everything to its accidental nature.

Kieslowski is one of the most gifted filmmakers at work today, which makes it all the more inexplicable that, at fifty-three, he has announced his retirement. These films can be seen separately or together, in any order; they make a resounding statement against the lockstep mentality that produces so many formula films. Life contains random chance and great surprise; why can't the movies?

3. *Pulp Fiction*

Quentin Tarantino began with three interlocking stories about crime and lowlife sleaze, and then twisted his time line like a Mobius strip, so that it seemed to end before it began. The stories all involved crime, deception, violence, and depravity, but the treatment is ironic and often comic, and the dialogue is so fresh and original that even the seamiest scenes generate a certain charm.

More than any other movie this year, *Pulp Fiction* got people talking. The film's many deliberate and accidental puzzles (what was in the briefcase? what happened to the guy in the leather suit?) caused endless debate on campuses, and the sheer invention of such sequences as the macabre "date" between John Travolta and Uma Thurman was dazzling, in a year of limp-brained "thrillers."

On the other hand, the movie was also widely attacked as a violent, unsavory portrait of worthless people. The notion that a movie is bad if it is about bad people, or good if it is about good people, is one of the most common delusions of those who have not given the question much thought.

4. *Forrest Gump*

This was the year's *other* most talked-about movie, although I wonder how many people liked both *Forrest Gump* and *Pulp Fiction* as much as I did. If *Pulp* was embraced by the dread counterculture, *Gump* was given a bear hug by Rush Limbaugh, who found it espoused the virtues he most values. I found the film more apolitical, a delicate, witty meander down memory lane, especially evocative for those who were born around the time Forrest was, about forty-five years ago.

The title performance by Tom Hanks was a balancing act: Forrest is slow, but not dumb, and although we like him, he doesn't seem to much care about things ("thayngs") like that. In his accidental way he takes note of many of the events that shaped recent American history: the killing of Kennedy, the Vietnam war, the rise of a sports culture, the counterculture, the peace movement, the sexual revolution, drugs, entreprenurial experimentation, jogging, AIDS, bumper stickers, and so on.

He doesn't know what to make of much of what he sees. But he clings to old values and universal truths taught to him by his mother (Sally Field), and he bumbles through, creating along the way a reminder to the audience that they have muddled through, too. Few movies have created a more powerful sense in their audiences of a shared experience.

5. *The Last Seduction*

This is the kind of tight brassy, tough, smart movie that Hollywood used to make in the 1940s when it would have masqueraded as a B-grade *film noir*. Now it hits like a blast of fresh air. The movie stars Linda Fiorentino in what is surely the best female performance of the year (although she was ineligible for an Oscar nomination because the movie played on HBO before going out to a theatrical run). She plays a woman who likes money very much, and who knows what buttons to push on the men who will help her get some.

The film's obvious antecedent is Billy Wilder's *Double Indemnity*, although the hard-boiled performance by Ann Savage in the less-known *noir Detour* is also probably an influence. What Fiorentino gives us is a dangerous dame who is not afraid of men, does not compromise, and is not locked into a formula that requires her to cave in during the last act.

The movie was directed by John Dahl, who *twice* has had films rescued from cable hell by the admiration of critics and smart audiences. His *Red Rock West* played on Showtime before growing into a sleeper hit, and *Last Seduction* received some of the year's best reviews from London critics before American distributors could see its quality.

6. *Fresh*

This was one of the year's best-acted and best-written films, the story of a twelve-year-old Brooklyn boy (Sean Nelson) who works as a runner for drug dealers. He's very smart, he's liked and respected by the men he works for, but he is wise beyond his years and sees more than anyone realizes. One day his father (Samuel L. Jackson, in another perfectly modulated performance) gives him a lesson in chess. And then, using the pieces on a board in his bedroom, Fresh plots a way to settle all of his scores.

The movie was directed and written by Boaz Yakin, whose plotting is so subtle that for the first half of the movie we're hardly aware there is a plot: It all seems like just observation and behavior. Then Yakin lets the other shoe drop, in a climax of mounting ingenuity and logic. The way *Fresh*'s scheme unfolds was one of the great pleasures of moviegoing in 1994.

7. *The Blue Kite*

The most exciting film industry outside America right now is in China, where a "fifth generation" of filmmakers is rushing into production with passionate examinations of their nation's recent history. Tian Zhuangzhuang, who made *The Blue Kite*, tells his story through the eyes of a young man named Tietou ("Iron Head"), who is born in

the early 1950s. Times are hard and food is scarce, but there is a neighborly spirit in the small courtyard where his family lives. Then his father, a librarian, is swept away by chance in the first of many waves of political reform, and Tietou and his mother bounce from her second to her third husbands—both good men—while trying to survive the sometimes insane political currents. The film is a true epic, which gives us the sense of what it was like to be Chinese during a time of hope, turmoil, and suffering.

8. *Natural Born Killers*

Much praised but equally loudly attacked, sometimes by those who had previously championed the work of director Oliver Stone. I found it, like most of his work, essential viewing even if you hated it (which I did not), because he aimed so clearly at our national condition.

We live in a time when most people are more interested in scandals than news. When mastering the details of the Simpson case is an entertaining alternative to taking any interest in serious events. When tabloid TV shows have the form of news but the content of sensationalist gossip. When a person's fame inspires many to forgive him his other crimes. That is what *Natural Born Killers* is about: our national hunger for scandal and sensation, the way the media indulge it in a feeding frenzy, and the way our standards of taste and morality are disintegrating in the process. Those who hated this film may have been attacking the messenger rather than hearing the message.

9. *The New Age*

This film opened and closed in the wink of an eye, but it was the year's sharpest, most observant critique of the way we live now. Written and directed by Michael Tolkin (who wrote *The Player* and directed *The Rapture*), it starred Judy Davis and Peter Weller as an affluent Los Angeles couple who unexpectedly find themselves unemployed and unable to maintain their expensive lifestyle.

At first they treat this predicament as a bad joke. Then they try to fight back by opening a trendy boutique. Eventually they face ruin. They take inventory of their skills ("we're good at shopping and talking") and their fears ("having to work to make money"), and descend into the quick-fix New Age wonderland of gurus and psychics, looking for deliverance. My hunch is this movie was doomed before it ever got out of L.A., by executives who could not bear to look at their own problematic present lives and possible futures.

10. *Quiz Show*

No, no, no, America did *not* "lose its innocence" in 1954, when the quiz show scandal broke. We have been losing, and regaining, our innocence on a regular basis with every generation. It's just that a certain kind of trust—that TV was what it seemed, and would keep faith with us—was lost when it was revealed that the highest-rated quiz shows, with contestants who became national celebrities, were phony.

Robert Redford's film, with a subtle script by Paul Attanasio, did a wonderful job of showing how seductive the fix was: how bright, principled young men like Charles Van Doren were persuaded by the deady payoffs of cash and fame. Ralph Fiennes, from *Schindler's List*, was splendid as Van Doren, and Rob Morrow was well cast as the congressional investigator who wanted to bring down the shows but was dazzled by Van Doren's personal charm. The movie named names, including sponsors and networks, and pointedly observed that only the contestants ever really suffered from the quiz show scandals; the guilty pros kept right on working, shaping the television of tomorrow.

**   **   **

At film festivals, the juries sometimes award a "Special Jury Prize," which goes to films that are not quite in first place, but too good for second place. This year, five films deserve that honor. All of them contain interesting performances. Listed alphabetically, they are:

Bullets over Broadway, Woody Allen's fiendishly funny examination of the lengths some people will go to in defense of their art—people, for example, like a mob hitman (played with sublime unself-consciousness by Chazz Palminteri) who finds himself involved in the rewrite of a Broadway play.

Four Weddings and a Funeral, directed by Mike Newell, made British newcomer Hugh Grant into an overnight star, and was a fresh reminder of Andie MacDowell's fresh wit. It followed the uncertain development of a romance as it developed during a series of ceremonies for other people.

Imaginary Crimes, directed by Anthony Drazan, contained one of the year's best performances, by Harvey Keitel, as a con man who usually stays just this side of the law with his get-rich-quick schemes, while trying to be a good father to his two exasperated daughters.

The Madness of King George, directed by Nicholas Hytner, contained another great performance, by Nigel Hawthorne, as the dotty British monarch who lost both the American colonies and his mind. His eccentric behavior delivers him into the hands of an implacable early psychologist (Ian Holm). As the court wheels and deals for rights to the throne, he confounds them all, and becomes one of the year's most lovable characters.

The Shawshank Redemption contained two remarkable performances, by Tim Robbins and Morgan Freeman, as convicts who survive decades behind bars without losing their spirit. Written and directed by Frank Darabont, based on a Stephen King novella, the film won the hearts of those who saw it—but many stayed away because of the ungainly title.

**   **   **

If those five film's are all tied somewhere between tenth place and eleventh place, here is my list of the next ten alphabetically:

Blue Sky, directed some three years ago by the late Tony Richardson and shelved as a victim of hte Orion bankruptcy, told an uneven story, but its performances were superb: Jessica Lange as a troubled air force wife, and Tommy Lee Jones as the husband with the love and patience to put up with moods that shaded into madness.

Was I the only person who thougth Abel Ferrara's *Body Snatchers* was terrific? The third remake of the Jack Finney classic was set on an army base in the south, and starred Gabriel Anwar as the teenage girl who begins to realize that her parents have become pod people. Meg Tilly is creepy and effective as the stepmother, and the movie is very scary, but Warner Bros. hardly opended it theatrically before shipping it off to video.

Tim Burton's *Ed Wood* was a movie for movie-lovers, a loving black-and-white examination of the career of "the worst director of all time," whose *Plan 9 from Outer Space* and *Glen or Glenda?* are treasured wherever bad movies are seen. Johnny Depp was lovable in the title role, and Martin Landau deserved his Oscar for his work as fading horror star Bela Lugosi.

The Senegalese filmmaker Ousmane Sembene is Africa's most distiguished director, and his *Guelwaar* was a colorful, sometimes hilarious, insightful look into modern life in a village where two factions—Christian and Islamic—almost come to blows over a funeral. Sembene creates a real feeling of community, of tensions between tradition and the modern, of the way far-off politics affect the way longtime neighbors view each other.

Bigas Luna's *Jamon Jamon* was the funniest sexy movie, or the sexiest comedy, since *Like Water for Chocolate*. The movie was an outrageous throwback to the days when directors took crazy chances, counting on their audience to keep up with them. Set in a small town where everybody sooner or later seems to sleep with the wrong person, it evokes the anarchic spirit of Buñuel and Almodovar in a story involving underwear models, bordellos, prize pigs, lurid melodrama, vast improbabilities, sexy soap opera, heartfelt romance, and heedless raunch.

Jodie Foster created a completely original character and a new style to play her, in Michael Apted's *Nell,* the story of a wild child isolated in a backwoods cabin, and the two professionals (Liam Neeson and Natasha Richardson) who come to deal with her case, and find her dealing with them, as well.

The Scent of Green Papaya, directed by Tran Anh Hung, was one of the year's most beautiful and romantic films. Set in Saigon between the 1940s and the early 1960s, it was shot entirely on sets on a Paris soundstage—a meticulous recreation of the house on a small, green-leafed street where a poor young woman (Tran Nu Yen-Khe) comes to work as a servant. She falls in love with the young man who is good friend of the family, but it is many years before her love breathtakingly blossoms.

Speed was the year's cleverest, slickest thriller, a non-stop extravaganza of action starring Keanu Reeves, Sandra Bullock, and a preposterous plot involving a bus that dares not to slow below fifty miles per hour. As a bonus, the movie added scenes set on an elevator and a subway train, and director Jan De Bont avoided some clichés and milked others to keep the action fresh.

Thirty-Two Short Films About Glenn Gould, directed by François Girard. This was an experiment in documentary, based on the life of the great, reclusive Canadian pianist. Using an actor, Colm Feore, to play Gould, Girard created a series of vignettes—some realistic, some impressionistic, some experimental—to suggest aspects of his life.

When a Man Loves a Woman, starring Meg Ryan and Andy Garcia, was a wise and ambitious film about the way alcoholism affects the fabric of a marriage. Ryan plays a schoolteacher whose alcoholism is usually so well timed and hidden that her husband, an airline pilot, doesn't suspect it. The film really gets interesting after Ryan begins the process of recovery, and Garcia discovers that perhaps he preferred a dependent, insecure wife to the new woman she is becoming.

★★   ★★   ★★

So. Twenty-five great films. And here are thirty more, any one of which I'd be happy to see again:

Barcelona, Belle Époque, Blink, China Moon, Clerks, Crooklyn, The Crow, Guarding Tess, Heavenly Creatures, Immortal Beloved, It Could Happen to You, I.Q., Junior, Lion King, Little Big League, Mrs. Parker and the Vicious Circle, Only You, The Paper, Raining Stones, Ready to Wear (Pret-à-Porter), Red Rock West, Sirens, Sugar Hill, Sunday's Children, To Live, Vanya on 42nd Street, War Room, Widow's Peak, and *The Wonderful, Horrible Life of Leni Riefenstahl.*

During 1994 I reviewed 206 films—a record, as studios pumped more and more titles into their pipelines. These fifty-five titles mean, let's see, that I had a good or great experience at the movies about 26 percent of the time. And I had some pretty fair times, too.

The *Sight and Sound* Lists

Although no list of the "greatest movies of all time" can be anything but arbitrary, the lists which follow come the closest to having some kind of international authority. Every ten years, starting in 1952, the respected British film magazine *Sight and Sound* conducts a worldwide poll to determine the names of the greatest films of all time. The first four surveys polled film critics. The most recent survey, in 1992, also polled directors, producing two lists that are interesting in their differences.

What the lists show first of all is the changing currency of cinematic greatness. Chaplin's stock goes down, Keaton's goes up, Chaplin bounces back. Hitchcock appears on the list, and Bergman disappears. The two names which remain constant over the decades are Orson Welles and Jean Renoir, although in 1952 *Citizen Kane* was still not widely enough seen to make the list.

What is the use of such a list? I can think of one use: I often get letters from film lovers who want to know where to start in their survey of the great films of the past.

Start here.

The 1992 List:

Critics' Choices

1. *Citizen Kane*, Orson Welles
2. *La Regle du Jeu (Rules of the Game)*, Jean Renoir
3. *Tokyo Story*, Yasijuro Ozu
4. *Vertigo*, Alfred Hitchcock
5. *The Searchers*, John Ford
6. (tie). *L'Atalante*, Jean Vigo; *The Passion of Joan of Arc*, Carl Theodore Dreyer; *Pather Panchali*, Satyajit Ray; *Battleship Potemkin*, Sergei Eisenstein
10. *2001: A Space Odyssey*, Stanley Kubrick

Directors' Choices

1. *Citizen Kane*
2. (tie) *Raging Bull*, Martin Scorsese; *8½*, Frederico Fellini
4. *La Strada*, Fellini
5. *L'Atalante*
6. (tie) *Modern Times*, Charlie Chaplin; *The Godfather*, Francis Ford Coppola; *Vertigo*
9. (tie) *The Seven Samurai*, Akira Kurosawa; *The Passion of Joan of Arc*; *The Godfather Part II*, Coppola; *Rashomon*, Kurosawa.

The 1982 List

1. *Citizen Kane*
2. *La Regle du Jeu*
3. (tie) *The Seven Samurai; Singin' in the Rain*, Stanley Donen and Gene Kelly
5. *8½*
6. *Battleship Potemkin*
7. (tie) *L'Avventura*, Michelangelo Antonioni; *The Magnificent Ambersons*, Welles; *Vertigo*
10. (tie) *The General*, Buster Keaton and Clyde Bruckman; *The Searchers*
12. (tie) *2001: A Space Odyssey; Andrei Roublev*, Andrei Tarkovsky
14. (tie) *Greed*, Erich von Stroheim; *Jules et Jim*, François Truffaut; *The Third Man*, Carol Reed

The 1972 List

1. *Citizen Kane*
2. *La Regle du Jeu*
3. *Battleship Potemkin*
4. *8½*
5. (tie) *L'Avventura; Persona*, Ingmar Bergman
7. *The Passion of Joan of Arc*
8. (tie) *The General; The Magnificent Ambersons*
10. (tie) *Ugetsu Monogatari*, Kenji Mizoguchi; *Wild Strawberries*, Bergman

The 1962 List

1. *Citizen Kane*
2. *L'Avventura*
3. *La Regle du Jeu*
4. (tie) *Greed; Ugetsu Monogatari*
6. (tie) *Battleship Potemkin; The Bicycle Thief*, Vittorio De Sica; *Ivan the Terrible*, Eisenstein
9. *La Terra Trema*, Luchino Visconti
10. *L'Atalante*

The 1952 List

1. *The Bicycle Thief*
2. (tie) *City Lights*, Chaplin; *The Gold Rush*, Chaplin
4. *Battleship Potemkin*
5. (tie) *Louisiana Story*, Robert Flaherty; *Intolerance*, D.W. Griffith
7. (tie) *Greed; Le Jour Se Lève*, Marcel Carne; *The Passion of Joan of Arc*
10. (tie) *Brief Encounter*, David Lean; *Le Million*, Rene Clair; *Le Regle du Jeu*

Four-Star Reviews

About Last Night . . .
Accidental Tourist, The
After Hours
After the Rehearsal
Age of Innocence, The
Alex in Wonderland
Alice Doesn't Live Here Anymore
Amadeus
Amarcord
American Dream
American Graffiti
Angel at My Table, An
Another Woman
Apocalypse Now
Apollo 13
At the Max
Au Revoir les Enfants
Autumn Sonata
Awakenings

Badlands
Bad Lieutenant
Bang the Drum Slowly
Barfly
Beauty and the Beast
Before the Rain
Being There
Best Boy
Betrayal
Big Easy, The
Birdy
Black Stallion, The
Blood Simple
Blow Out
Blue Collar
Blume in Love
Body Snatchers
Born on the Fourth of July
Bounty, The
Boyz N the Hood
Breaking Away
Bring Me the Head of Alfredo Garcia
Broadcast News
Bronx Tale, A
Brothers' Keeper
Bugsy
Burden of Dreams
Bye Bye Brazil

California Split
Carmen (ballet)

Carmen (opera)
Casablanca
Chariots of Fire
China Syndrome
Chinatown
Chocolat
Chuck Berry Hail! Hail! Rock 'n' Roll
Citizen Kane
City of Hope
Claire's Knee
Close Encounters of the Third Kind:
    The Special Edition
Color Purple, The
Coming Home
Conversation, The
Cook, the Thief, His Wife and Her
    Lover, The
Cotton Club, The
Cries and Whispers
Crimes and Misdemeanors
Crumb
Crying Game, The

Damage
Dances With Wolves
Dance With a Stranger
Dawn of the Dead
Day After Trinity, The
Day for Night
Day of the Jackal, The
Days of Heaven
Dead Again
Dear America: Letters Home From
    Vietnam
Deer Hunter, The
Dick Tracy
Discreet Charm of the Bourgeoisie,
    The
Diva
Do the Right Thing
Down and Out in Beverly Hills
Draughtsman's Contract, The
Dresser, The
Driving Miss Daisy
Drugstore Cowboy
Dry White Season, A

El Norte
E.T.—The Extra-Terrestrial
Exorcist, The
Exotica

Falcon and the Snowman, The
Falling From Grace
Fanny and Alexander
Fantasia
Farewell My Concubine
Farewell, My Lovely
Fellini's 8 ½
Fellini's Roma
Field of Dreams
Fish Called Wanda, A
Fitzcarraldo
Five Easy Pieces
Flirting
Forrest Gump
Four Friends
Frenzy
Fresh
Friends of Eddie Coyle, The
Fugitive, The

Gambler, The
Gandhi
Garden of the Finzi-Continis, The
Gates of Heaven
Getting It Right
Godfather, The
Godspell
Gone With the Wind
GoodFellas
Good Morning, Vietnam
Grand Canyon
Great Santini, The
Grifters, The
Guelwaar

Hair
Halloween
Hannah and Her Sisters
Hardcore
Harlan County, U.S.A.
Harry and Tonto
Heartland
Hidden Fortress, The
High Hopes
Homicide
Hoop Dreams
Hoosiers
Household Saints
Housekeeping
House of Games
Howards End

Iceman
Il Ladro di Bambini
Indiana Jones and the Temple of Doom
I Never Sang for My Father
Interiors
It's a Wonderful Life

Jaws
JFK
Johnny Got His Gun
Joy Luck Club, The

Kagemusha
Kalifornia
Karate Kid, The
Killing Fields, The
King of the Hill

La Belle Noiseuse
La Cage aux Folles
Ladybird, Ladybird
La Lectrice
Last Detail, The
Last Emperor, The
L.A. Story
Last Picture Show, The
Last Seduction, The
Last Tango in Paris
Last Temptation of Christ, The
Late Show, The
Lawrence of Arabia
Léolo
Less Than Zero
Lethal Weapon
Life Is Sweet
Light Sleeper
Like Water for Chocolate
Little Big Man
Little Dorrit
Little Mermaid, The
Local Hero
Long Good Friday, The
Lorenzo's Oil
Lost in America
Love Story
Love Streams
Lucas

Macbeth
Madame Sousatzka
Mad Max Beyond Thunderdome
Madness of King George, The
Malcolm X
Manchurian Candidate, The
Manhattan Project, The

Man in the Moon, The
Man of Iron
Manon of the Spring
Man Who Would Be King, The
Map of the Human Heart
Marriage of Maria Braun, The
M*A*S*H
McCabe and Mrs. Miller
Mean Streets
Menace II Society
Mephisto
Metropolis
Micki & Maude
Mighty Quinn, The
Mishima
Mississippi Burning
Mr. and Mrs. Bridge
Mona Lisa
Monsieur Hire
Moonlighting
Moonstruck
Moscow on the Hudson
My Dinner with André
My Family
My Father's Glory
My Left Foot
My Mother's Castle

Naked
Nashville
National Lampoon's Animal House
Natural Born Killers
Network
Nosferatu
No Way Out

Officer and a Gentleman, An
Once Upon a Time in America
One False Move
On Golden Pond
Onion Field, The
Ordinary People
Out of Africa

Paper Chase, The
Paperhouse
Parenthood
Paris, Texas
Passage to India, A
Passion Fish
Patton
Peggy Sue Got Married
Perfect World, A
Permanent Record
Personal Best

Phantom of Liberty, The
Piano, The
Pixote
Platoon
Player, The
Play Misty for Me
Prick Up Your Ears
Prince of the City
Prizzi's Honor
Public Eye, The
Pulp Fiction
Purple Rose of Cairo, The

Radio Days
Raging Bull
Raiders of the Lost Ark
Raise the Red Lantern
Ran
Rapture, The
Red
Return of the Jedi
Reversal of Fortune
Richard Pryor Here and Now
Richard Pryor Live on the Sunset
  Strip
Right Stuff, The
Risky Business
Rocky
Roger & Me
Room with a View, A
'Round Midnight
Ruby in Paradise
Runaway Train
Running on Empty

Saint Jack
Salaam Bombay!
Santa Sangre
Say Amen, Somebody
Say Anything
Scandal
Scarface
Scenes from a Marriage
Scent of Green Papaya, The
Schindler's List
Searching for Bobby Fischer
Secret Garden, The
Secret Honor
Shadowlands
Shoah
Short Cuts
Shy People
Sid & Nancy
Silent Movie
Silent Running

Silkwood
Singin' in the Rain
Sleuth
Small Change
Smash Palace
Sophie's Choice
Sounder
Speed
STAR 80
Star Is Born, A
Star Wars
Stevie
Stranger than Paradise
Streamers
Streetcar Named Desire, A
Streetwise
Stroszek
Sugar Hill
Sunday Bloody Sunday
Superman
Superman II

Talk Radio
Tampopo
Taxi Driver
10

Terms of Endearment
Tess
Testament
Tex
That Obscure Object of Desire
That's Entertainment!
They Shoot Horses, Don't They?
35 Up
Thirty-Two Short Films About
    Glenn Gould
This Is Spinal Tap
3 Women
Tokyo Story
To Live and Die in L.A.
Tootsie
Tron
Trouble in Mind
28 Up
Two English Girls
2001: A Space Odyssey

Uforia
Unbearable Lightness of Being, The
Under the Volcano
Unforgiven
Unmarried Woman, An

Vagabond
Verdict, The
Vincent

Wages of Fear, The
Walkabout
WarGames
Weavers, The: Wasn't That a Time!
Wetherby
What's Eating Gilbert Grape?
When a Man Loves a Woman
Who Framed Roger Rabbit
Willie Wonka and the Chocolate
    Factory
Wings of Desire
Withnail & I
Witness
Woman Under the Influence, A
Woman's Tale, A
Woodstock
Working Girl
World Apart, A

Year of Living Dangerously, The
Young Frankenstein

Index

Titles with asterisks are on Roger Ebert's ten-best list for the year in which they opened.

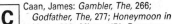

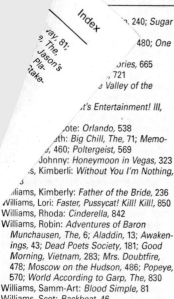